ST. JAMES GUIDE TO

BIOGRAPHY

ST. JAMES GUIDE TO

BIOGRAPHY

EDITOR
PAUL E. SCHELLINGER

ST. JAMES PRESS
CHICAGO AND LONDON

© 1991 by St. James Press Inc.

For information, write:
ST. JAMES PRESS
233 East Ontario Street
Chicago 60611, USA

or

2-6 Boundary Row
London SE1 8HP, England

British Library Cataloguing in Publication Data

St. James Guide to Biography
   1. Biography
   I. Schellinger, Paul E., *1962 –*
016.92

ISBN 1-55862-146-6

Library of Congress Catalog Card Number 90-63663

First edition.

Typeset at BookMasters, Ashland, Ohio

CONTENTS

EDITOR'S NOTE

Each entry in this book surveys biographies that have been written on an individual. We do not supply biographical data on the entrants, but rather bibliographical and critical analysis of biographies already available.

Entrants have been selected on the basis of: 1) their contribution to their respective art or profession; 2) the fame and/or notoriety they have achieved in world history; and 3) the number of biographies that have been written on them. Someone who is the subject of only one biographical work, regardless of his or her importance, has not been included since our purpose is to provide expert discrimination between and among the various biographies available to the reader. We have included individuals of both general and scholarly interest, from all fields of human endeavor.

Each entry contains a bibliographical listing of biographies written on the subject, along with a signed, critical essay reviewing the biographies listed. The bibliography lists only those biographies available in English and provides details of original U.S. and U.K publications; subsequent editions are noted whenever a reviewer makes reference to them in the essay. No attempt has been made to list all editions or reprints of an individual biography.

For a work that has been translated into English, we provide, in addition to English-language publication data, details of its original publication, including foreign title, place and date of publication, and translator, whenever these items could be determined. The exception is when the English title is the same as its foreign original, as is often the case with biographies whose titles consist of a single proper noun. In such instances the translator and place and date of foreign publication are provided. Foreign-language works unavailable in English have been excluded from the bibliographies, though we have provided abbreviated citations within the essays themselves whenever a reviewer makes reference to untranslated works. (As a rule, reviewers have refrained from treating untranslated foreign-language books at length.) Likewise, works that bear tangentially on the biography of an individual, such as critical studies, general histories, magazine or journal articles—i.e., all works that do not qualify as book-length *biographies*—are as a rule cited within the text and not included in the bibliography. Exceptions have been made in those cases in which a critical work, for example, has proven to be an important source of biographical information on the subject. Autobiographies, memoirs, and diaries by the subject are often briefly mentioned in the essays, where they receive abbreviated citations.

To aid the reader, we have given the biographer's last name in capital letters at the beginning of the section in the essay in which his or her biography receives its most sustained review. If the biographer's last name is the same as that of the subject, or where two biographers have the same last name, the first name is also set in capital letters. The word "AND" has been capped to indicate joint authors (". . . the biography by MILLER AND ADAMS. . ."), as a way of distinguishing such instances from those where two separate works are grouped and discussed together (". . . the biographies by WARD and DAVIES. . . "). When an essay reviews more than one biography by the same author, the biographer's last name is set in capital letters at the beginning of the paragraph wherein each work is reviewed *if these occur in separate sections of the essay.* If more than one work by the same author is reviewed in a single paragraph, the biographer's name is capped only once. In either case, dates are provided in parentheses to distinguish between the biographies.

The bibliographies do not in every case represent exhaustive listings of the biographies available for an entrant. In fact, many of the essayists have chosen to discuss only the most important or current works from among the many available, or have selected as many biographies as could be reasonably reviewed in the allotted space. We have attempted to provide as comprehensive an overview as possible of the biographical writing on each entrant, while at the same time giving in-depth critical treatment of the important biographies for both scholarly and general use.

CONTRIBUTORS

Courtney S. Adams
Steven A. Agoratus
Gary L. Aho
Isabel Aitken
John T. Alexander
M. J. Alexander
Sharon G. Almquist
Stuart Andrews
Andrew J. Angyal
Martine Natat Antle
William W. Austin
Liahna Babener
Christopher J. Barnes
Mary-Rose Barral
Milly S. Barranger
Mark T. Bassett
B. W. Bateman
Rosemarie A. Battaglia
Roger B. Beck
Alice H. R. H. Beckwith
Robyn Bell
Jean V. Berlin
Caroline Bingham
Daniel W. Bjork
Stephen A. Black
Robert G. Blake
Lynn Z. Bloom
Catherine C. Bock
Garry Boulard
Larry G. Bowman
James C. Bradford
John Braeman
Juliane Brand
Mary Jo Bratton
Patricia Brauch
Mary Elizabeth Brown
Maria F. Bruno
Hallman B. Bryant
Martin Bucco
Robert E. Burkhart
Edward Burns
David H. Burton
Camilla Cai
John J. Carbon
Paul Carlton
Geoffrey Carnall
Gisela Casines
Faya Causey
Petra ten-Doesschate Chu
Hamilton E. Cochrane
A. O. J. Cockshut
Marilyn Shevin Coetzee
Michael Cogswell
Anne Compliment
David R. Contosta
Stanley Corkin
Craig Cotter
Don M. Cregier
Lynda Lasswell Crist

Robert Rhodes Crout
John Cruickshank
Judith M. Curran
Thomas J. Curran
Eugene Current-Garcia
Marcia A. Dalbey
John A. Day
Dennis R. Dean
David C. Dennard
James I. Deutsch
Michael J. Devine
Richard C. Dickey
John Ditsky
Justus D. Doenecke
Susan M. Doll
Colleen P. Donagher
Reade W. Dornan
Linda Downs
Sina Dubovoj
Richard J. Dunn
John J. Dwyer
Anthony O. Edmonds
Harry Edwin Eiss
Robert Richmond Ellis
Martin Ennis
Lawrence M. Enoch
Betsy Fahlman
Joseph Flibbert
Phylis Floyd
Maurice G. Fortin
Mike F. Foster
Mortimer H. Frank
Stephen G. Fritz
Phyllis Frus
Elizabeth Lane Furdell
William M. Gargan
Robert A. Gates
Nadine F. George
Brian Gilliam
C. Herbert Gilliland, Jr.
Erlis Glass
Lionel K. J. Glassey
Gerhard Glière
Charlotte Goddard
Justin Goddard
Steven Goldleaf
Douglas Gomery
A. C. Goodson
Frederic Goossen
Ian A. Gordon
Susette Ryan Graham
Patricia Grassi
Floyd K. Grave
Martin Gray
Nan Hackett
Mindy Friddle Hagebak
Christopher Hailey
Colin R. Hall
Charles Hallisey

Craig L. Hanson
Robin Grollmus Hanson
James Harding
Maurice Harmon
Richard P. Harmond
Robert James Havlik
Paul Hawkshaw
Barbara Hayley
Donald E. Heidenreich, Jr.
Peter Heidtmann
Michael Herbert
Marlene A. Hess
Roger S. Hewett
Michael Hicks
Erna Hilfstein
James L. Hill
W. Kenneth Holditch
Gary Hoppenstand
Jeffrey Hopper
David L. Howard
Patricia Howard
Kenneth A. Howe
Diana Emery Hulick
Richard A. Hutch
Jane Campbell Hutchison
Anthony P. Inguanzo
Donald C. Irving
Glen Jeansonne
Alan Jefferson
Douglas M. Jesseph
Meri Jiménez
Douglas Johnson
Marnie Jones
Steven E. Jones
Jacob Judd
William K. Kearns
Newton E. Key
Helen Killoran
Joshua Kind
Keneth Kinnamon
David Kirby
Robert S. La Forte
Mary Lago
Jacqueline Lauby
Donald A. Lawniczak
Bryan F. Le Beau
Judith Lee
John L. Leland
Alison Leslie
Van Michael Leslie
A. H. T. Levi
Honor Levi
Maria R. Lichtmann
Stephen D. Lindeman
Maurice Lindsay
Elizabeth Dominique Lloyd-Kimbrel
Barbara A. Looncy
Alfred D. Low
Roger Lowman

C. Grant Luckhardt
Maxine N. Lurie
Sally MacGregor
Louis K. MacKendrick
Robert James Maddox
Lois N. Magner
Jane Nash Maller
Phillip Mallett
David B. Mattern
L. J. Maxwell-Stewart
Robert McBride
Joseph M. McCarthy
Ian McGowan
Alister E. McGrath
Colin Meir
Thomas F. Merrill
Sheryl L. Meyering
E. H. Mikhail
Julia I. Miller
Marcia J. Miller
Amy B. Millstone
F. C. Molloy
David Morgan
John Morrill
Doris B. Morton
Charles A. Moser
Michael A. Mullett
Whitney R. Mundt
Alan Murphy
Bruce J. Murray
Nicolas H. Nelson
Robert E. O'Connor
D. H. O'Leary
Joseph T. Orchard
Robert M. Otten
Ritchie Ovendale
Janet Overmyer
Victor N. Paananen
Jacqueline K. Parker
Jeffrey D. Parker
Joseph F. Patrouch
Donna Price Paul
William A. Pelz
Jason R. Peters
Barbara Bennett Peterson
Donald K. Pickens
Martin Picker
Rebecca C. Pilcher
Nicholas Christopher Polos
Betty Frances Pope
George Thomas Potter
Cecilia Powell
John Powell
Alan Pratt
James J. Preston
Ryan Prout
Fred D. Ragan
Brian Abel Ragen
A. W. Raitt

Honora Raphael Weinstein
David Reid
Kelvin J. Richardson
John Ridland
Paula R. Riggs
Marvin Rintala
Patricia Roberts
James E. Rocks
Michael Rodriguez
Kay Rogers
Pat Rogers
Daniel Dean Roland
Daniel Rosenberg
Joseph Rosenblum
Mary Rossabi
Morris Rossabi
Matt Rowe
A. J. R. Russell-Wood
Robert A. Ryan
Thomas W. Ryba
Christine A. Rydel
Mendel Sachs
Murray Sachs
James Sambrook
Todd H. Sammons
Frederick H. Schapsmeier
Carolyn Poling Schriber
Richard Sears
Kenneth E. Shewmaker
Francis Shor
Narasingha P. Sil
Brooks D. Simpson
Clyde Curry Smith
John Snarey
Julie Robin Solomon
Lydia M. Soo
Paul H. Stacy
S. J. Stearns
Suzanne Stratton
Susan A. Stussy
Jacob Susskind
Daniel E. Sutherland
Richard C. Taylor
Thomas J. Taylor
Martin Thies
Philip Thody
R. Larry Todd
John Tolan
Simon Trussler
Bernard Tucker
Rosalyn Tureck
Howard N. Tuttle
Nancy C. Unger
Lucilia M. C. Valério
Hans J. van Miegroet
Linda K. Varkonda
Richard A. Voeltz
Phyllis E. Wachter
Linda Wagner-Martin

William T. Walker
Edward Wasiolek
Noelle A. Watson
Harold H. Watts
Steven Weiland
Leigh Ann Whaley
Nick Whistler
John Wickersham
Peter Wild
John R. Williams
Robert F. Willson, Jr.
George Woodcock
James Woodress
Leigh Woods
Esmond Wright
Carolyn Yalkut
Bruce W. Young
Harry Zohn

ST. JAMES GUIDE TO
BIOGRAPHY

Abigail Adams
Henry Adams
John Adams
John Quincy Adams
Joseph Addison
James Agee
Edward Albee
Louisa May Alcott
Alexander the Great
Alexander I of Russia
Horatio Alger
Sherwood Anderson
Anne of England
Susan B. Anthony
Saint Thomas Aquinas
Corazon Aquino
Louis Armstrong
Benedict Arnold
Matthew Arnold
Herbert Henry Asquith
Fred Astaire
Attila the Hun
W. H. Auden
Saint Augustine of Hippo
Augustus Caesar
Marcus Aurelius
Jane Austen

Johann Sebastian Bach
Francis Bacon
George Balanchine
James Baldwin
Arthur James Balfour
Honoré de Balzac
Béla Bartók
Count Basie
Charles Baudelaire
Aubrey Beardsley
Francis Beaumont and John Fletcher
Samuel Beckett
The Venerable Bede
Ludwig van Beethoven
Menachem Begin
Aphra Behn
Alexander Graham Bell
Giovanni Bellini
Saul Bellow
Ruth Benedict
David Ben-Gurion
Arnold Bennett
Alban Berg
Ingmar Bergman
Henri Bergson
George Berkeley
Hector Berlioz
Sarah Bernhardt
Leonard Bernstein
Ambrose Bierce
Otto von Bismarck
Georges Bizet
William Blake
Alexander Blok
Giovanni Boccaccio
Humphrey Bogart
Niels Bohr
Anne Boleyn

Jorge Luis Borges
Lucrezia Borgia
James Boswell
Sandro Botticelli
Margaret Bourke-White
Elizabeth Bowen
Johannes Brahms
Marlon Brando
Bertolt Brecht
André Breton
Benjamin Britten
Charlotte and Emily Brontë
Charles Brockden Brown
John Brown
Elizabeth Barrett Browning
Robert Browning
Anton Bruckner
William Jennings Bryan
William Cullen Bryant
Martin Buber
Pearl S. Buck
Buddha
Mikhail Bulgakov
John Bunyan
Edmund Burke
Fanny Burney
Robert Burns
Aaron Burr
Sir Richard Francis Burton
Richard Burton
George Gordon, Lord Byron

Mother Frances Cabrini
James Cagney
Pedro Calderón de la Barca
Maria Callas
John Calvin
Albert Camus
Truman Capote
Thomas Carlyle
Andrew Carnegie
Lewis Carroll
Jimmy Carter
Enrico Caruso
George Washington Carver
Mary Cassatt
Fidel Castro
Willa Cather
Saint Catherine of Siena
Catherine of Aragon
Catherine de' Medici
Catherine II of Russia
Catullus
Miguel de Cervantes
Paul Cézanne
Marc Chagall
Neville Chamberlain
Charlie Chaplin
Charlemagne
Charles I of England
Charles II of England
Charles V, Holy Roman emperor
Geoffrey Chaucer
Anton Chekhov
G. K. Chesterton
Frédéric Chopin

Kate Chopin
Winston Churchill
Marcus Tullius Cicero
Cleopatra
William Cobbett
Samuel Taylor Coleridge
Colette
John Coltrane
Christopher Columbus
Sir Arthur Conan Doyle
Confucius
Joseph Conrad
John Constable
Constantine the Great
James Cook
James Fenimore Cooper
Nicholas Copernicus
Hernando Cortès
Noël Coward
Hart Crane
Stephen Crane
Joan Crawford
Crazy Horse
Davy Crockett
Oliver Cromwell
Bing Crosby
E. E. Cummings
Marie Curie
George Armstrong Custer

Salvador Dali
Dante
Georges Danton
Clarence Darrow
Charles Darwin
Jacques-Louis David
Bette Davis
Jefferson Davis
James Dean
Simone de Beauvoir
Eugene Debs
Claude Debussy
Daniel Defoe
Edgar Degas
Charles de Gaulle
Eugène Delacroix
Frederick Delius
Thomas De Quincey
René Descartes
John Dewey
Sergei Diaghilev
Charles Dickens
Emily Dickinson
Denis Diderot
Marlene Dietrich
Isak Dinesen
Walt Disney
Benjamin Disraeli
Saint Dominic
John Donne
Hilda Doolittle
John Dos Passos
Fyodor Dostoevsky
William O. Douglas
Frederick Douglass
Sir Francis Drake

Theodore Dreiser
John Dryden
W. E. B. DuBois
Alexandre Dumas (*père*)
Isadora Duncan
Albrecht Dürer
Bob Dylan

Amelia Earhart
Thomas Alva Edison
Edward I of England
Edward II of England
Edward III of England
Edward VII of England
Jonathan Edwards
Albert Einstein
Dwight D. Eisenhower
Sergei Eisenstein
Eleanor of Aquitaine
Sir Edward Elgar
George Eliot
T. S. Eliot
Elizabeth I of England
Elizabeth II of England
Duke Ellington
Ralph Waldo Emerson
Desiderius Erasmus
Erik Erikson

William Faulkner
Federico Fellini
Henry Fielding
W. C. Fields
Edward Fitzgerald
F. Scott Fitzgerald
Gustave Flaubert
Ford Madox Ford
Henry Ford
John Ford
E. M. Forster
Anatole France
Saint Francis of Assisi
Francisco Franco
François I of France
Benjamin Franklin
Franz Joseph I of Austria
Frederick the Great of Prussia
Sigmund Freud
Robert Frost
Margaret Fuller

Thomas Gainsborough
Galileo Galilei
John Galsworthy
John Galt
Vasco da Gama
Indira Gandhi
Mahatma Gandhi
Federico García Lorca
Giuseppe Garibaldi
Judy Garland
David Garrick
Marcus Garvey
Elizabeth Gaskell
Paul Gauguin
Genghis Khan

George III of England
George V of England
George VI of England
George Gershwin
Edward Gibbon
André Gide
Allen Ginsberg
George Gissing
William Gladstone
William Godwin
Johann Wolfgang von Goethe
Nikolai Gogol
Emma Goldman
Oliver Goldsmith
Samuel Goldwyn
Benny Goodman
Mikhail Gorbachev
Maxim Gorky
Glenn Gould
Francisco Goya
Cary Grant
Ulysses S. Grant
Robert Graves
El Greco
Graham Greene
Pope Gregory the Great
Johannes Gutenberg

Hadrian
Alexander Hamilton
Dashiell Hammett
George Frideric Handel
Hannibal
Thomas Hardy
Nathaniel Hawthorne
Franz Joseph Haydn
William Hazlitt
William Randolph Hearst
Georg Wilhelm Friedrich Hegel
Martin Heidegger
Heinrich Heine
Lillian Hellman
Ernest Hemingway
Henri IV of France
Henry IV of England
Henry V of England
Henry VIII of England
O. Henry
Patrick Henry
Katharine Hepburn
George Herbert
Theodor Herzl
Hermann Hesse
Alfred Hitchcock
Adolf Hitler
Thomas Hobbes
William Hogarth
Friedrich Hölderlin
Billie Holliday
Oliver Wendell Holmes, Jr.
Herbert Hoover
Gerard Manley Hopkins
Horace
A. E. Housman
William Dean Howells
Langston Hughes

Victor Hugo
David Hume
Aldous Huxley
Thomas Henry Huxley

Henrik Ibsen
Saint Ignatius of Loyola
Washington Irving
Christopher Isherwood
Ivan IV of Russia
Charles Ives

Andrew Jackson
Stonewall Jackson
James I of England
James II of England
Henry James
William James
Robinson Jeffers
Thomas Jefferson
Saint Jerome
Jesus Christ
Saint Joan of Arc
Saint John of the Cross
Pope John Paul II
Lyndon Johnson
Samuel Johnson
Al Jolson
John Paul Jones
Ben Jonson
Joseph II, Holy Roman emperor
James Joyce
Julius Caesar
Carl Gustav Jung
Justinian I

Franz Kafka
Wassily Kandinsky
Immanuel Kant
Edmund Kean
John Keats
John F. Kennedy
Johannes Kepler
Jerome Kern
Jack Kerouac
John Maynard Keynes
Nikita Khrushchev
Søren Kierkegaard
Martin Luther King, Jr.
Rudyard Kipling
Paul Klee

Marquis de Lafayette
Charles Lamb
Sir Allen Lane
D. H. Lawrence
Robert E. Lee
Vivien Leigh
Vladimir Lenin
John Lennon
Leonardo da Vinci
Doris Lessing
Gotthold Ephraim Lessing
C. S. Lewis
Sinclair Lewis
Abraham Lincoln

Mary Todd Lincoln
Charles Lindbergh
Franz Liszt
David Livingstone
David Lloyd George
John Locke
Jack London
Henry Wadsworth Longfellow
Louis IX of France
Louis XI of France
Louis XIV of France
Amy Lowell
James Russell Lowell
Robert Lowell
Clare Boothe Luce
Martin Luther
Rosa Luxemburg
Sir Charles Lyell

Douglas MacArthur
Hugh MacDiarmid
Niccolò Machiavelli
James Madison
Ferdinand Magellan
Gustav Mahler
Norman Mailer
Maimonides
Malcolm X
Stéphane Mallarmé
Thomas Malthus
Édouard Manet
Thomas Mann
Katherine Mansfield
Mao Tse-tung
Marie Antoinette
Christopher Marlowe
Andrew Marvell
Karl Marx
Mary I of England
Mary Queen of Scots
Henri Matisse
Somerset Maugham
Guy de Maupassant
Giuseppe Mazzini
Joseph McCarthy
Carson McCullers
Margaret Mead
Lorenzo de' Medici
Golda Meir
Herman Melville
H. L. Mencken
Gregor Mendel
Felix Mendelssohn-Bartholdy
Thomas Merton
Klemens Metternich
Michelangelo
Ludwig Mies van der Rohe
John Stuart Mill
Arthur Miller
Henry Miller
John Milton
Honoré Mirabeau
Mohammed
Jean-Baptiste Molière
Claude Monet
James Monroe

Marilyn Monroe
Michel de Montaigne
Baron de Montesquieu
Bernard Law Montgomery
George Moore
Henry Moore
Sir Thomas More
John Pierpont Morgan
Berthe Morisot
William Morris
Samuel Morse
Mother Teresa
Louis Mountbatten
Wolfgang Amadeus Mozart
John Muir
Edvard Munch
Edward R. Murrow
Benito Mussolini

Vladimir Nabokov
Napoleon Bonaparte
Napoleon III
Carrie Nation
Jawaharlal Nehru
Horatio Nelson
Nero
Pablo Neruda
John Henry (Cardinal) Newman
Sir Isaac Newton
Nicholas II of Russia
Friedrich Nietzsche
Florence Nightingale
Vaslav Nijinsky
Richard Nixon

Sean O'Casey
Flannery O'Connor
Frank O'Connor
John O'Hara
Georgia O'Keeffe
Laurence Olivier
Eugene O'Neill
J. Robert Oppenheimer
George Orwell
Wilfred Owen

Thomas Paine
Charlie Parker
Dorothy Parker
Francis Parkman
Charles Parnell
Blaise Pascal
Boris Pasternak
Louis Pasteur
Saint Patrick
George Patton
Saint Paul
Anna Pavlova
William Penn
Samuel Pepys
Eva and Juan Perón
Saint Peter
Peter I of Russia
Francesco Petrarch
Philip II of Macedon
Philip II of Spain

Edith Piaf
Pablo Picasso
Piero della Francesca
Harold Pinter
William Pitt (the younger)
Sylvia Plath
Edgar Allan Poe
Marco Polo
Pompey
Alexander Pope
Cole Porter
Katherine Anne Porter
Ezra Pound
Elvis Presley
Sergey Prokofiev
Pierre-Joseph Proudhon
Marcel Proust
Giacomo Puccini
Henry Purcell

François Rabelais
Sergei Rachmaninov
Jean Racine
Sir Walter Raleigh
Raphael
Maurice Ravel
Ronald Reagan
Wilhelm Reich
Rembrandt
Pierre-Auguste Renoir
Cecil Rhodes
Richard I of England
Richard II of England
Richard III of England
Samuel Richardson
Armand (Cardinal) Richelieu
Rainer Maria Rilke
Arthur Rimbaud
Diego Rivera
Paul Robeson
Maximilien Robespierre
John D. Rockefeller
Auguste Rodin
Theodore Roethke
Eleanor Roosevelt
Franklin Delano Roosevelt
Theodore Roosevelt
Christina Rossetti
Dante Gabriel Rossetti
Gioacchino Rossini
Henri Rousseau
Jean-Jacques Rousseau
Peter Paul Rubens
John Ruskin
Bertrand Russell

Anwar Sadat
J. D. Salinger
George Sand
Carl Sandburg
Margaret Sanger
Jean-Paul Sartre
Erik Satie
Girolamo Savonarola
Dorothy Sayers
Johann Friedrich von Schiller

Arnold Schoenberg
Arthur Schopenhauer
Franz Schubert
Robert Schumann
Albert Schweitzer
Sir Walter Scott
Alexander Scriabin
Elizabeth Seton
Madame de Sévigné
William Shakespeare
George Bernard Shaw
Mary Wollstonecraft Shelley
Percy Bysshe Shelley
Richard Brinsley Sheridan
Dmitri Shostakovich
Jean Sibelius
Sir Philip Sidney
Frank Sinatra
Upton Sinclair
Edith Sitwell
Adam Smith
John Smith
Joseph Smith
Tobias Smollett
Alexander Solzhenitsyn
Benedict de Spinoza
Madame de Staël
Joseph Stalin
Sir Henry Morton Stanley
Sir Richard Steele
Gertrude Stein
John Steinbeck
Stendhal
Laurence Sterne
Wallace Stevens
Robert Louis Stevenson
James Stewart
Alfred Stieglitz
Harriet Beecher Stowe
Lytton Strachey
Richard Strauss
Igor Stravinsky
August Strindberg
Louis Sullivan
Sun Yat-sen
Jonathan Swift
Algernon Charles Swinburne
John Millington Synge

Rabindranath Tagore
Elizabeth Taylor
Peter Ilyich Tchaikovsky
Pierre Teilhard de Chardin
Alfred, Lord Tennyson
Saint Teresa of Avila
William Makepeace Thackeray
Margaret Thatcher
Saint Thomas à Becket
Dylan Thomas
Henry David Thoreau
Tintoretto
Titian
Marshall Tito
Alexis de Tocqueville
Leo Tolstoy
Arturo Toscanini

Henri de Toulouse-Lautrec
Anthony Trollope
Leon Trotsky
Harry S. Truman
Ivan Turgenev
Joseph Mallord William Turner
Mark Twain

Paul Valéry
Sir Anthony Van Dyck
Vincent van Gogh
Lope Félix de Vega Carpio
Diego Velázquez
Giusseppe Verdi
Paul Verlaine
Jan Vermeer
Paolo Veronese
Victoria of England
François Villon
Voltaire

Richard Wagner
Andy Warhol
Booker T. Washington
George Washington
Evelyn Waugh
John Wayne
Max Weber
Daniel Webster
Simone Weil
Orson Welles
Duke of Wellington (Arthur Wellesley)

H. G. Wells
John Wesley
Edith Wharton
James Abbott McNeill Whistler
Stanford White
Walt Whitman
John Greenleaf Whittier
Oscar Wilde
Laura Ingalls Wilder
Thornton Wilder
Wilhelm II of Prussia
William I of England
Tennessee Williams
William Carlos Williams
Woodrow Wilson
Ludwig Wittgenstein
Thomas Wolfe
Mary Wollstonecraft
Thomas (Cardinal) Wolsey
Virginia Woolf
William Wordsworth
Christopher Wren
Wright Brothers
Frank Lloyd Wright
Richard Wright
John Wycliffe

William Butler Yeats

Émile Zola
Huldreich Zwingli

ADAMS, Abigail, 1744–1818; American letter-writer and chronicler of the American Revolution; wife of John Adams, mother of John Quincy Adams.

Akers, Charles W., *Abigail Adams: An American Woman*. Boston, Little Brown, 1980.

Bobbé, Dorothie, *Abigail Adams: The Second First Lady*. New York, Minton Balch, 1929.

Levin, Phyllis L., *Abigail Adams: A Biography*. New York, St. Martin's, 1987.

Richards, Laura E., *Abigail Adams and Her Times*. New York and London, Appleton, 1917.

Whitney, Janet, *Abigail Adams*. Boston, Little Brown, 1947; London, Harrap, 1949.

Withey, Lynne, *Dearest Friend: A Life of Abigail Adams*. New York, Free Press, and London, Collier/Macmillan, 1981.

*

The wife of one United States president and the mother of another, as well as a prolific letter-writer who unwittingly chronicled the American Revolution through a woman's eyes, Abigail Adams has been the subject of surprisingly little commentary until this century. Beginning in the 1920s with Bobbé's biography, Adams' correspondence with family and important figures such as Thomas Jefferson and author Mercy Otis Warren have been rediscovered, resulting in three biographies in the last decade.

Unfortunately, the early biographies by BOBBÉ and RICHARDS share some common weaknesses. Both are often steeped in overdramatic, sentimental rhetoric. Bobbé, for example, loses credibility by including dialogue that smacks of fiction, with very few notes to document the conversations. Even the author's comments are peppered with exclamation marks, adding to the melodrama. The same is true of Richards' dialogue. Richards, moreover, often quotes Adams' letters at length when summarization would be more appropriate. Further, both biographies suffer by avoiding the troubled side of the Adams family, such as Abigail's anguish over an alcoholic, debt-ridden son, her belief that none of her children married well, and her tendency to be a domineering mother. On the other hand, Richards provides a solid historical background to such early New England customs as courtship and meal etiquette. Similarly, Bobbé provides some interesting details about fashion (including descriptions of the garb worn by Adams and other family members) and the houses in which Adams and her family lived.

While the sources of Bobbé and Richards are mostly limited to Abigail Adams' letters to her husband, WHITNEY draws additionally on conversations with two direct descendants of Adams. The result is a biography steeped in history, since much of the account is organized around American Revolution occurrences. Unfortunately, a great deal of the dialogue sounds forced and is frequently undocumented. Further, Whitney indicates that Adams' stance on feminism was much stronger than her mixed feelings about the role of women in America, as examined by other biographers, actually suggest.

Fortunately, AKERS provides a closer inspection of Adams' letters, revealing her paradoxical views concerning feminism. This sensitive and scholarly account of Adams' life provides enlightening commentary, especially regarding her famous letter to her husband, requesting him to "remember the ladies," and her "separate but equal" contention that women deserved better education and more legal rights so that they could become better wives and mothers.

Akers begins early with Adams' parents' background, basing much of the biography on the letters of Adams and her family. Other sources include a variety of journals and books, including the journal of John Adams. The result is carefully documented dialogue lifted directly from letters and journals, and revelations about Adams that previous biographies do not provide.

Unlike Richards, Bobbé, and Whitney, Akers keeps a comfortable distance from his subject and is not against disclosing Adams' bitterness at being separated from her husband for years at a time, or mentioning her disappointment over her son's irresponsibility and her daughter's ill-fated marriage. Moreover, Akers provides an excellent discussion of how Abigail's political beliefs often mirrored her husband's, including her elitist distrust of the masses in America. Many of these views are revealed by Akers through Adams' correspondence with Thomas Jefferson, which was often lively yet stormy, since, like her husband, she was opposed to Jefferson's liberal political stance.

LEVIN offers an excellent account of Adams' life, complete with an impressive list of sources and detailed notes. Levin's lengthy book provides much more information about Adams' relationships with family and friends alike. She includes, for example, in-depth accounts of the courtships of Adams' children, including author Royall Tyler's romance with Adams' daughter, as well as accounts of Adams' rather flirtatious correspondence with James Lovell and her admiration for and communication with Mercy Otis Warren. Levin also provides an impressive description of Adams' visit to Europe, which includes the places and people she visited as well as her reactions to European culture.

Although familial relationships in WITHEY are not treated with the depth found in Levin, Withey provides a more historical scope, beginning with the history of Adams' hometown. The description of the courtship of John and Abigail Adams, for example, includes wedding preparations as well as the ordeal of smallpox vaccinations, and what such a risky medical procedure meant to New Englanders in the 18th century. Furthermore, the author's discussions of such concepts as child-rearing (for instance, the Puritan-based belief that children were inherently sinful) provides a welcome background to much of Adams' successes and failures.

—Mindy Friddle Hagebak

ADAMS, Henry, 1838–1918; American historian and writer.

Adams, James Truslow, *Henry Adams*. New York, A. and C. Boni, and London, Routledge, 1933.

Baym, Max, *The French Education of Henry Adams*. New York, Columbia University Press, 1951.

Cater, Harold Dean, *Henry Adams and His Friends*. Boston, Houghton Mifflin, 1947.

Chalfant, Edward, *Both Sides of the Ocean: A Biography of Henry Adams: His First Life*. Hamden, Connecticut, Archon Books, 1982.

Contosta, David R., *Henry Adams and the American Experiment*. Boston, Little Brown, 1980.

Donovan, Timothy Paul, *Henry Adams and Brooks Adams*. Norman, University of Oklahoma Press, 1961.

Harbert, Earl N., *The Force So Much Closer Home: Henry Adams and His Family*. New York, New York University Press, 1977.

Homans, Abigail Adams, *Education by Uncles*. Boston, Houghton Mifflin, 1966.

Levenson, J. C., *The Mind and Art of Henry Adams*. Stanford, California, Stanford University Press, 1957.

Russell, Francis, *Adams, An American Dynasty*. New York, American Heritage Publications, 1976.

Samuels, Ernest, *Henry Adams* (3 vols.). Cambridge, Massachusetts, Harvard University Press, 1948–64. (Vol. I, *The Young Henry Adams*; vol. II, *The Middle Years*; vol. III, *The Major Phase*.)

Samuels, Ernest, *Henry Adams*. Cambridge, Massachusetts, Harvard University Press, 1989.

Scheyer, Ernest, *Circle of Henry Adams*. Detroit, Wayne State University Press, 1970.

Shepard, Jack, *The Adams Chronicles: Four Generations of the Adams Family*. Boston, Little Brown, 1975.

Stevenson, Elizabeth, *Henry Adams: A Biography*. New York, Macmillan, 1955.

*

The first biographical study of Henry Adams was composed by Adams himself. This autobiographical work, written in the third person and published shortly after his death as *The Education of Henry Adams* (1918), was enthusiastically received and has since become a classic in American letters. But *The Education* is cast as a confession of Adams' repeated failures to learn what he needed to know in order to understand life in the modern world. In the process, Adams engages in biographical distortion and unwarranted self-deprecation. He is also completely silent about the 20-year period covering his marriage to Marian Hooper and the years just after her tragic suicide. Further detracting from the work are several final chapters that attempt to make tortured analogies between early 20th-century society and several laws from the physical sciences. Despite its flaws, *The Education* remains the best source of information on Adams' childhood and youth. Anyone wishing to go beyond the many distortions of *The Education* should consult J. C. Levenson et al, *The Letters of Henry Adams* (Cambridge, Massachusetts, Harvard University Press, 6 vols., 1982–88). An earlier volume of letters edited by Harold D. Cater, *Henry Adams and His Friends* (Boston, Houghton Mifflin, 1947), includes a lengthy introduction that gives much information, unavailable elsewhere, on Adams' rich private life.

The first genuine biography of Adams is a brief work by James Truslow ADAMS, who, although sharing the same last name, was not a member of Henry's family. Intended as an introduction to a multi-volume edition of Adams' collected works (which was not published because of the Great Depression), this biography relies too heavily on *The Education*, and on an early

edition of selected letters edited by Worthington Chauncey Ford, to provide many fresh insights into its subject.

By far the most comprehensive of Adams' biographies is the three-volume work by SAMUELS, with a one-volume condensation and revision that appeared a quarter century after the trilogy itself was completed. Samuels seeks to separate Adams from the persona of failure that he contrived for himself in *The Education* and to present his subject as accurately as other sources would allow. As a student of American literature, Samuels is most interested in detailing the literary and creative sources of Adams' writings. The historian may find this ambitious biography too narrative in places, and thereby lacking in close analysis of historical forces and events.

A second three-volume biography has been projected by CHALFANT. Only the first volume has appeared, covering Adams' life to 1862. Like Samuels, Chalfant rejects the myth of failure conveyed in *The Education*. Concentrating on what he considers Adams' early political maturity, Chalfant asserts, with some exaggeration, that Henry exerted considerable influence on councils of state in his early and middle twenties.

In her one-volume biography, STEVENSON chooses to view Adams' life even more thematically, as a lifelong struggle to find ways of controlling power in a democratic society that could see no danger in its unbridled energies. Although Adams' warnings were largely unappreciated in his own time, Stevenson believes that post-World War II America is ready to recognize some of the nation's faults and to reflect on Adams' more thoughtful criticisms of waste and exploitation. CONTOSTA's brief biography likewise organizes Adams' life around a specific theme. For Contosta, nearly all Adams' works focused on the unfolding American experiment that aimed to create a higher humanity on the western shores of the Atlantic. Although Adams wished the experiment to succeed, Contosta proposes, he ended his life with grave doubts that his countrymen ever could escape from the common failings of humanity. BAYM explores the many French influences on Adams' life and thought, particularly during the last three decades of his live. LEVENSON's work is a cultural and intellectual biography by a distinguished literary critic.

Other works deal with Adams' famous family and its powerful influences on him. Chief among these is HARBERT, who asserts that "the Adams heritage largely made Henry the man that he became." RUSSELL and SHEPHERD each provide a history of the Adams family, both of which offer insights into the debt Henry owed to his famous forebears. DONOVAN explores the influences that Henry and his brother Brooks exerted on each other as historians. HOMANS, one of Adams' nieces, offers a charming portrait of a favorite uncle. The influence of Adams' many illustrious friends is explored by SCHEYER.

—David R. Contosta

ADAMS, John, 1735–1826; American political leader, second president of the United States.

Adams, James Truslow, *The Adams Family*. Boston, Little Brown, 1930.

Adams, John Quincy and Charles Francis Adams, *John Adams.* Philadelphia, Lippincott, 1871.

Akers, Charles W., *Abigail Adams: An American Woman.* Boston, Little Brown, 1980.

Allison, John M., *Adams and Jefferson: The Story of a Friendship.* Norman, University of Oklahoma Press, 1966.

Bowen, Catherine Drinker, *John Adams and the American Revolution.* Boston, Little Brown, 1950.

Brown, Ralph Adams, *The Presidency of John Adams.* Lawrence, University of Kansas Press, 1975.

Burleigh, Anne Justen, *John Adams.* New Rochelle, New York, Arlington House, 1969.

Chinard, Gilbert, *Honest John Adams.* Boston, Little Brown, 1933.

Falkner, Leonard John, *John Adams, Reluctant Patriot of the Revolution.* Englewood Cliffs, New Jersey, Prentice-Hall, 1969.

Peterson, Merrill D., *Adams and Jefferson: A Revolutionary Dialogue.* Athens, University of Georgia Press, 1976; Oxford, Oxford University Press, 1978.

Russell, Francis, *Adams, An American Dynasty.* New York, American Heritage Publications, 1976.

Shaw, Peter, *The Character of John Adams.* Chapel Hill, University of North Carolina Press, 1975.

Shepherd, Jack, *The Adams Chronicles.* Boston, Little Brown, 1975.

Smith, Page, *John Adams* (2 vols.). New York, Doubleday, 1962.

*

Compared to the other founders of the American republic, John Adams has received relatively little attention until recent years. This situation resulted from the fact that Adams was not associated with any one great event, from his reputation as a dour and difficult man, and from the fact that his conservative outlook did not appeal to American historians, who have generally subscribed to a more liberal interpretation of the nation's past. However, the American bicentennial in 1976 and the increasing interest in conservative thought have resulted in a series of studies on John Adams over the past two or three decades.

The earliest full-scale biography of Adams was written jointly by his son and grandson, John Quincy and Charles Francis ADAMS. The authors make good use of family papers in order to focus on what they consider the four crises of John Adams' public life: his legal defense of Captain Preston; his early call for independence in 1775; his resistance to French demands during peace negotiations with Great Britain in 1783; and his refusal to go to war with France in 1798. Unfortunately, the authors fail to make use of much personal knowledge of their forebear, which may have made him appear much more likable and human. Charles Francis Adams also edited a ten-volume edition of his grandfather's works (1850–56). A more complete edition of John Adams' papers is being published by Harvard University Press under the direction of Lyman Butterfield.

Following the biography of his son and grandson, nothing of any substance was published on Adams until CHINARD's life in 1933. Chinard does much to rescue Adams' character by portraying him in a generally warm and human light. He also examines Adams' political ideas very sympathetically. Two decades

later BOWEN's equally sympathetic study focused on the first half of her subject's life and career, giving Adams much of the credit that he deserves as a leader of the American Revolution. By far the most thorough of the more recent Adams biographies is by SMITH, who was among the first to research Adams' extensive papers, then just released by the family for scholarly use. Smith strives to examine all sides of Adams' complex character, viewing his life and thought as part of the times in which he lived.

BURLEIGH's work on Adams concentrates on his role as a political philosopher during the revolution and early republic. SHAW also focuses on Adams' political thoughts and actions, attempting to explain their seeming contradictions within the social and cultural milieu that helped to shape them. Both ALLISON and PETERSON analyze the revealing correspondence and friendship between Adams and Thomas Jefferson. BROWN explores Adams' presidency and is generally favorable toward the second president. AKERS' excellent biography of Adams' capable wife Abigail also aids in understanding Adams, as well as in illuminating the foundations of their highly successful family.

The work by James Truslow ADAMS, who was not a member of the John Adams family, is the earliest of the family histories. The nation's bicentennial spawned two other family histories, those by RUSSELL and SHEPHERD. The latter was a companion to a well-received series broadcast in 1975 on National Public Television, entitled *The Adams Chronicles.* Among the best biographies for children is the one by FALKNER.

—David R. Contosta

ADAMS, John Quincy, 1767–1848; American political leader, 6th president of the United States.

Bemis, Samuel Flagg, *John Quincy Adams and the Foundations of American Foreign Policy.* New York, Knopf, 1949.

Bemis, Samuel Flagg, *John Quincy Adams and the Union.* New York, Knopf, 1956.

East, Robert A., *John Quincy Adams: The Critical Years, 1785–94.* New York, Bookman Associates, 1962.

Hargreaves, Mary W. M., *The Presidency of John Quincy Adams.* Lawrence, University Press of Kansas, 1985.

Hecht, Marie B., *John Quincy Adams: A Personal History of an Independent Man.* New York, Macmillan, 1972.

Lipsky, George A., *John Quincy Adams: His Theory and Ideas.* New York, T. Y. Crowell, 1950.

Nagel, Paul C., *Descent From Glory: Four Generations of the John Adams Family.* New York and Oxford, Oxford University Press, 1983.

Richards, Leonard L., *The Life and Times of Congressman John Quincy Adams.* New York and Oxford, Oxford University Press, 1986.

Shepherd, Jack, *Cannibals of the Heart: A Personal Biography of Louisa Catherine and John Quincy Adams.* New York, McGraw-Hill, 1980.

*

For decades following his death in 1848, John Quincy Adams was neglected by biographers. Political associate William Henry Seward issued a short memorial in 1849, emphasizing Adams' advocacy of antislavery; Josiah Quincy followed nine years later with a forgettable effort. John T. Morse, editor of the American Statesman Series, contributed a short and serviceable summary in 1882, five years after grandson Henry Adams had offered a family defense disguised as a documentary history of New England Federalism. Henry's brother Brooks added some more biographical information in *The Degradation of the Democratic Dogma* (1920), a book which makes all too clear some of the themes of the Adams family heritage. Finally, Bennett Champ Clark's 1933 biography, *John Quincy Adams, Old Man Eloquent,* is a lively if superficial life. None of these volumes served as a satisfactory biography.

Most scholars agree that the most complete study remains the two-volume biography by BEMIS. The first volume, concentrating on Adams' diplomatic career, did much to establish Adams' reputation as a great secretary of state. It is a rich and absorbing account, essential to an understanding of American diplomacy during the early 19th century, although subsequent scholarship by Walter LaFeber and others has added to our understanding of Adams' concept of American empire. The second volume, devoted primarily to Adams' years in Congress, is disappointingly thin on his presidency. Grounded in impressive archival research, Bemis' biography, although dated in some particulars, and without much insight into Adams' personal life, remains unchallenged as the best account of Adams' public career.

RICHARDS' examination of Adams' post-presidential career serves as a useful corrective to celebrations of Old Man Eloquent's battles against southern advocates of slavery on the floor of the House of Representatives, while placing Adams' activities in their political context. Richards takes advantage of recent scholarship on antimasonry, antislavery, and American political economy, although he overlooks the irony of how Adams as secretary of state had laid the foundation for the very territorial expansion and spirit of manifest destiny he was to oppose so vehemently as a congressman.

Several historians have concentrated on aspects of Adams' life in detail. EAST chooses to examine young man Adams, taking him from his return from Europe to enter Harvard in 1785 to his selection as a diplomatic envoy to Holland in 1794, in a study of adolescence and maturation under the pressure of great expectations. LIPSKY prefers to explore the life of the mind in what remains the only extended explication of Adams' ideas about government, slavery and abolition, and social order in a republic. Absent, however, is any clear understanding of Adams' changing conception of the nature and purpose of an American empire. HARGREAVES, remedying the major flaw in Bemis' work, presents a more positive portrayal of Adams' administration, emphasizing its accomplishments and explaining how Adams' conception of an independent executive presiding over a republic of virtue and intelligence fostered by a plan of economic development collapsed under the emergence of sectional tensions, popular politics, and political organizations. Some critics have observed that this reexamination is at times extremely partial to its subject (a flaw not limited to this volume in the American Presidency Series) and suspect in its uncertain handling of the electoral crisis of 1824–25.

Most recent biographies have explored the private side of Adams' life, with particular attention to the burdens and benefits of the Adams' family heritage. HECHT's effort leaves the reader unsatisfied, for the author relied too much on Adams' papers, and treated her subject not only sympathetically but also somewhat uncritically. NAGEL's effort at a family history is a signal triumph, skillfully weaving together the family legacy, personal inclination, and public life to present Adams as a son, husband, and father. Most absorbing is SHEPHERD's account of Adams' troubled marriage to Louisa Catherine Johnson and of the pressures he placed on his sons to succeed.

Adams' writings are being edited as a part of the massively ambitious Adams Family Papers Project. When complete, such revealing documents as Adams' diary, previously edited in expurgated form by Charles Francis Adams and available in a single-volume condensation created by Allan Nevins, will be available to the interested reader. However, the excruciatingly slow pace at which volumes appear renders this at best a long-term hope.

—Brooks D. Simpson

ADDISON, Joseph, 1672–1719; English writer.

Aikin, Lucy, *The Life of Joseph Addison* (2 vols.). London, Longman, 1843.

Dobree, Bonamy, "The First Victorian," in *Essays in Biography: 1680–1726.* Oxford, Oxford University Press, 1925.

Johnson, Samuel, "Addison," in *The Lives of the English Poets.* London, 1781.

Macaulay, Thomas Babington, *Essay on the Life of Addison.* New York, E. Maynard, 1892; originally published in *Edinburgh Review*, 1843.

Smithers, Peter, *The Life of Joseph Addison.* Oxford, Clarendon Press, 1954; revised 1968.

*

JOHNSON established the method and the issues that would dominate biographies of Addison until the mid-20th century. He approaches his subject primarily as a writer who happened to have a somewhat significant political career. Johnson's account is a literary biography that interweaves a life story with substantial textual criticism. His account combines narrative about Addison's personal and professional life with evaluations of the aesthetic virtues of a poem, play, or essay. For biographical information Johnson relied upon the comments (contained in letters, memoirs, and recorded remarks) of Addison's contemporaries: Richard Steele, Thomas Tickell, Alexander Pope, as well as numerous Whig and Tory politicians. While these sources provide vivid firsthand observations, they also create a focus upon a few problematic or controversial incidents: Addison's abandonment of a clerical career, the dispute with Pope over Tickell's *Iliad*, the 1719 pamphlet war with Steele, and the death-bed drama staged for young Lord Warwick. Johnson concludes his account by asserting that Addison's writings display a moral character in which "nothing will be found but purity and excellence" and that no testimony by either Addison's friends or enemies disputes this conclusion. Johnson remains the first source on Addison a reader should consult. His chronology is sound and thorough; his conclusions about the man and the works are objective; and the expression of his literary judgments classic: "Whoever wishes to attain an English style, familiar but not coarse, and elegant but not ostentatious, must give his days and nights to Addison."

Sixty years later AIKIN had access to more printed material than Johnson did, especially to Addison's letters. In addition to the 26 letters by Addison already in print (*Addisoniana*, 1803) Aikin reprinted the correspondence and letter book bequeathed to Addison's executor. Like Johnson, Aikin writes a book that interweaves biography with literary criticism. Generously quoting letters to and from Addison (87 in all) as well as from his writings, Aikin's biography becomes hagiography when she refuses to permit any blemishes, personal or poetic, to cloud her idealization of the man and author. Aikin's book, essentially the typical Victorian "beauties of" tome, is a tedious read.

MACAULAY's reading of Aikin's book prompted his own long biographical account of Addison to rectify what he perceived as Aikin's errors. These are not so much errors of particular fact as conceptual errors that oversimplify both the historical age and the individual personality. First, Macaulay presents Addison's character and works in the context of Augustan politics, history, and literature to determine where his ideas are commonplaces and where they are original insights. Second, Macaulay stresses unflattering personal traits such as excessive modesty; for example, he accepts Pope's depiction of Addison as the hypocritical "Atticus" presiding over a fawning circle of younger poets. Addison is not the bloodless saint Aikin presents, nor are his works disembodied tomes of eternal wisdom. Third, Macaulay argues that Addison is important as a satirist who reformed rather than scorned; his literary method, not the specific cultural values he espoused, make him worth reading. Macaulay clearly knows Addison's times better than Aikin. Though as smugly sure of his own opinion as Aikin, Macaulay is easier to read because he is at least open to contradictory evidence and to the idea that a human being is more a paradox than a formula.

DOBREE's biography is a revisionist book. Working with virtually the same resources that Aikin and Macaulay used 80 years before but tempted by insights from modern psychology, Dobree depicts a very different Addison. Both Addison's personal and literary qualities are interpreted by Dobree as attempts to compensate for a lack of social status, money, and strong character. Addison lives—and recommends others live—along the straight and narrow because it is safe. Addison is indeed what Aikin and Macaulay say he is, the first Victorian, but to Dobree it is a term of opprobrium, not praise. The controversies of Addison's life were mere tempests in teapots, notable because they are the only disturbances in a placid life. Dobree freely interprets Addison's motivations and decisions with little reference to sources. His principle of interpretation is a reductionist's consistency: Addison's youthful search for acceptance, status, and income is the key to understanding all his subsequent behavior, both literary and personal. Dobree, the first professional literary scholar to write a life of Addison, knows the political and literary history of Augustan London better than did Macaulay. Even those who

object to his reading of Addison's character should appreciate the cultural backdrop Dobree vividly if subjectively provides.

SMITHERS wrote the first non-literary biography of Addison. Though attentive to the circumstances of composition, the history of publication, and contemporary response to all of Addison's major writings, Smithers avoids the kind of literary evaluation that Johnson, Aikin, Macaulay, and Dobree perform. His primary focus is Addison's political career. Taking seriously Addison's dreams of public service "that fired him from his earliest days at Oxford," Smithers depicts this Roman concept of citizenship as shaping Addison's ambition: "An upright character and conduct, good service to the state, with embellishments of learning, culture, and urbanity, reveal themselves as parts in a single pattern of life." Smithers employs sources previously unavailable to biographers. To flesh out the sketchy details of Addison's youth, he uses county and parish histories. For Addison's parliamentary and secretarial work Smithers employs varied materials from the Public Record Offices: the State papers, Colonial Office records, Privy Council minutes. Smithers also incorporates the extensive correspondence of Addison and his contemporaries, finally complete and readily available in modern editions by Walter Graham (all 702 extant letters by Addison), Rae Blanchard (Steele), Harold Williams (Swift), and George Sherburn (Alexander Pope). Smithers thus presents rounded views of puzzling or controversial episodes that allow modern readers to realize the source of tensions without the necessity to assign blame. Smithers' book is the definitive life.

—Robert M. Otten

AGEE, James, 1909–1955; American writer.

Bergreen, Laurence, *James Agee: A Life*. New York, Dutton, 1984.

Doty, Mark A., *Tell Me Who I Am: James Agee's Search for Selfhood*. Baton Rouge, Louisiana State University Press, 1981.

Kramer, Victor A., *James Agee*. Boston, Twayne, 1975.

Larsen, Erling, *James Agee*. Minneapolis, University of Minnesota Press, 1971.

Madden, David, editor, *Remembering James Agee*. Baton Rouge, Louisiana State University Press, 1974.

Moreau, Geneviève, *The Restless Journey of James Agee*. New York, Morrow, 1977.

Spears, Ross and Jude Cassidy, editors, with Robert Coles, *Agee: His Life Remembered*. New York, Holt, 1985.

*

For one whose life was so brief, James Agee has stimulated exceptional attention from scholars and adulation from others. BERGREEN's book, described by its publisher as the "first full-scale biography" of James Agee, is also the latest to be published. The author was able to locate unpublished sources of material, and he notes that in many instances he was the first biographer to use some of Agee's letters and papers. Bergreen chose not to use superscript numbers within the text, but the book is well documented by endnotes that refer to pages in the text. There is also an extensive bibliography. *James Agee: A Life* is a thorough, engagingly written study of the writer's life.

Whereas Bergreen concentrates on Agee's life rather than on his works, MOREAU attempts to explore the "complex relationship" between them. She finds Agee's life and his work to be inseparable, and therefore warns that the reader "must not look for actual biography" in her book. Instead, she writes, her goal was "to reconstruct his inner adventure, to rediscover his conscious personality and the dynamism of his unconscious mind." By treating Agee "not as an object but as a subject," Moreau suggests, she enables the reader to become "aware of the currents of his inner life, its oscillations between exaltation and apathy, faith and doubt, rebellion and resignation, joy and despair." But despite her disclaimer that *Restless Journey* is not biography, it depicts in convincing fashion Agee's growth from unconfident youthfulness to literary maturity. Its fault lies in Moreau's insistent psychologizing: "Every image of joy had its twin image of anguish; every happiness seemed strangely fragile and transitory; sadness marred the most perfect joy; a vague foreboding of unknown tragedy permeated everything."

KRAMER has published a number of articles about Agee in addition to his bio-critical study in the Twayne series. However meritorious his study may be, it cannot be called satisfactory biography or definitive scholarship. It serves its modest purpose as a general introduction to James Agee and his work.

LARSEN's *James Agee* is also an introductory work, but aimed at a more youthful audience. Like other pamphlets in the University of Minnesota series on American writers, Larsen's monograph on Agee disdains scholarly documentation. But its 45 pages are well written, and it may be recommended for the lay person who wishes to know a little bit about the romantic figure of James Agee.

Each of the remaining biographies is specialized—each in its own way. MADDEN offers a collection of essays by persons who, in most cases, knew Agee personally. The essays are valuable as first-person reminiscences—vignettes, really. Though the book is not comprehensive biography, if offers some wonderful insights. Madden's introduction is unexpectedly ambivalent, but it provides an appreciative frame of reference for the collection.

DOTY's book is an attempt "to determine the extent to which James Agee used autobiographical writing as a means to sort out his own life," and is as much literary analysis as it is biography. Doty's thesis is that Agee's art was an expression of his life, and his book is therefore centered on Agee's life. Doty was able to obtain interviews with several persons who knew Agee intimately, including his three wives, and this primary source material enhances the value of the book. Doty's biography is fully footnoted and includes an extensive bibliography.

Finally, the volume edited by SPEARS AND CASSIDY might be termed a print version of a filmed literary biography. The editors completed their film, "Agee," in 1979, and it received an Academy Award nomination. Their book is based on interviews conducted during the filming, and it is, accordingly, generously illustrated. Robert Coles, who has written perceptively about James Agee in *Irony in the Mind's Life* (1974), provides a narrative to bind together the many brief interviews. *Agee: His Life Remembered* might be called a pictorial biography, but it is

more than that; it is an appreciation of James Agee and the ways in which he touched many other lives.

—Whitney R. Mundt

ALBEE, Edward, 1928–   ; American playwright.

Amacher, Richard E., *Edward Albee*. Boston, Twayne, 1968; revised 1982.

Bigsby, C. W. E., *Albee*. Edinburgh, Oliver and Boyd, 1969.

Hirsch, Foster, *Who's Afraid of Edward Albee?* Berkeley, California, Creative Arts, 1978.

Kolin, Philip C., editor, *Conversations with Edward Albee*. Jackson, University Press of Mississippi, 1988.

McCarthy, Gerry, *Edward Albee*. New York, St. Martin's, and London, Macmillan, 1987.

Roudané, Matthew C., *Understanding Edward Albee*. Columbia, University of South Carolina Press, 1987.

Rutenberg, Michael E., *Edward Albee: Playwright in Protest*. New York, DBS Publications, 1969.

Wasserman, Julian N., editor, *Edward Albee: An Interview and Essays*. Houston, Texas, University of St. Thomas, 1983.

*

Biographical material is sparse and opaque for Edward Albee, whose early *Zoo Story* (1958) is, with Arthur Kopit's *Oh Dad, Poor Dad, Momma's Hung You in the Closet and I'm feeling So Sad* (1960), still considered the American entry into the Theatre of the Absurd, despite Albee's insistence that it is not absurd at all. Some personal information can be found occasionally in interviews and play reviews in major periodicals such as the *New Yorker* (specifically 25 March 1961 and 19 December 1964), and in introductions to book-length critical works. At the center of biographical analysis of Albee is his own statement, in answer to a question about the importance of his biography to an understanding of his work, in an interview in WASSERMAN's collection of essays: "Biography and me? Oh, I think totally unimportant. It seems to infuriate some scholars that they can't pin everything down because I tend to be a fairly private person."

BIGSBY provides a "Life and Early Plays" chapter to his otherwise literary critical analysis, describing in broad strokes Albee's "life of a spoilt rich boy, with servants, private tutors, and winter visits to Florida and, less exotically, Arizona." Orphaned and raised by adoptive parents (his father was owner of a chain of theatres), Albee ambled his way through a series of grade school failures, the pattern of which continued into his college years; by the age of 19 he was done with anything that might be called a formal education. From that point, his biography is echoed in his plays (his own denials notwithstanding): a domineering mother (*The American Dream*), a loving grandmother (*Sandbox*), his New York "pudding days" from age 20 to 30 (*Zoo Story*), and a life of destructive sexuality and madness (*Who's Afraid of Virginia Woolf?*).

AMACHER also provides the basic biographical facts—

schooling, salad days, first successes—and thoroughly discusses Albee's continental reputation (especially in Germany), which began with his first work and continues through *The Lady from Dubuque* (1980). He also summarizes the playwright's present writing routine, aesthetic predilections, and life-style, "between an elegant loft in . . . Manhattan and a house overlooking the Atlantic in Montauk, Long Island." Amacher's attempts to give Albee a "dark and suspenseful shadow" to his otherwise innocuous bachelorhood is not always convincing, because it tries to guess at Albee's "future creations."

McCARTHY points out that "Albee has always shared his thoughts on theatre with his public," but those thoughts are rarely about his personal life. McCarthy only touches on Albee's involvement with the Playwrights Unit, a production venture that placed "non-Broadway" plays on Broadway from 1963 to 1972, including some work by Sam Shepard, Terrence McNally, and LeRoi Jones; its remnants are found in Albee's own art center, a summer retreat for writers and other artists. This Modern Dramatists study hurries to a critical analysis of the plays and offers only a disappointingly short bibliography.

KOLIN contains 20 of the more than 80 interviews Albee has granted, but even in his copious interviews (RUTENBERG includes two), Albee stays close to his plays, free with comments regarding structure and character, but more reserved concerning the details of his personal life, or how his plays might be informed by reference to the playwright's experiences. Albee himself is loquacious in the formal interview, his preferred journalistic communication. An early play, *Fam and Yam* (1963), was in the interview format, between "a famous American playwright who resembled William Inge, and a young American playwright who resembled Mr. Albee." Readers can glean biographical material from it at their own risk.

HIRSCH makes much of a thin argument that Albee's homosexuality is integral to his writing, a view generally shared by other critics but treated at length here. Hirsch takes a biographical approach to interpreting the Albee canon, concentrating on character study in the light or shadow of Albee's homosexuality, and finding "coded gay drama" in Albee's enigmatic and not entirely successful play, *Tiny Alice* (1965).

ROUDANÉ's strength is a long bibliography pointing to major critical work on Albee. Despite the intent of the series (understanding contemporary American literature), Roudané still avoids direct biographical discourse, leaping to play analysis from the shaky platform of undocumented assumptions regarding Albee's personal predilections.

—Thomas J. Taylor

ALCOTT, Louisa May, 1832–1888; American writer.

Anthony, Katharine, *Louisa May Alcott*. New York, Knopf, 1938; London, Cresset, 1939.

Bedell, Madelon, *The Alcotts: Biography of a Family*. New York, C. N. Potter, 1980.

Cheney, Ednah D., *Louisa May Alcott: Her Life, Letters, and Journals*. Boston, Roberts, 1889.

Elbert, Sarah, *A Hunger for Home: Louisa May Alcott and Little Women*. Philadelphia, Temple University Press, 1984; revised and enlarged, with subtitle *Louisa May Alcott's Place in American Culture*, New Brunswick, New Jersey, Rutgers University Press, 1987.

Meigs, Cornelia L., *The Story of the Author of Little Women: Invincible Louisa*. Boston, Little Brown, 1933.

Moses, Belle, *Louisa May Alcott, Dreamer and Worker: A Story of Achievement*. New York, Appleton, and London, Sampson Low, 1909.

Saxton, Martha, *Louisa May: A Modern Biography of Louisa May Alcott*. Boston, Houghton Mifflin, 1977; London, Deutsch, 1978.

Stern, Madeleine B., *Louisa May Alcott*. Norman, University of Oklahoma Press, 1950.

Worthington, Marjorie, *Miss Alcott of Concord: A Biography*. New York, Doubleday, 1958.

*

Because of her versatile career as a writer of children's classics and adult fiction, as well as her linkage to 19th-century New England's influential Transcendental circle, Louisa May Alcott has been the subject of numerous book-length biographies in the 100 years since her death. Chronicles of her life written for mature readers have ranged from adoring reminiscences to probing psychoanalytical treatments. Early biographers, on the whole, confuse the idealized girlhood of Jo March in *Little Women* with Alcott's own, presenting a romantic account of her upbringing and later life, while subsequent scholars have looked beneath such domestic mythology to discover darker, more complex patterns of personal experience.

Readers seeking a relatively straightforward record of Alcott's life will turn first to STERN's amply detailed work, which recounts Alcott's youth in an eccentric family, traces her unremitting struggle to provide financial support for her high-minded but penniless parents, and examines her evolution as a professional writer. Stern, who has also edited and published several of Alcott's forgotten or pseudonymous fictional works, does particular justice to the diverse achievements of Alcott's literary career, broadening our understanding of her importance beyond the scope of her enduring popularity as the author of *Little Women*, and examining the imaginative genesis of her art. The biography, however, is marred by its overly affectionate tone and inadequate scrutiny of the Alcott family dynamics. Bronson Alcott, an improvident, self-absorbed husband who spurned wage-earning as immoral, thus forcing his family into poverty and sacrificial labor on his behalf, is portrayed uncritically, even reverentially, a consequence in part of Stern's decision to tell the story from Louisa's youthful point of view.

The same shortcomings, more emphatically present, compromise most of the earlier life histories of Alcott. CHENEY, herself a protégé of the father and an acquaintance of Louisa, provides the first important biography, interweaving a chronology of the subject's life with extensive excerpts from her letters and journals. While the primary sources are illuminating, the narrative is fragmented as a result of this interruptive technique, and the worshipful attitude and Victorian pieties of the biographer are cloying. Cheney's vision of Alcott as "duty's faithful child'' (Bronson's phrase) establishes a conceptual prototype that dominates Alcott biography well into the 1970s. Cheney, like many of her successors, also neglects to provide more than a cursory glimpse at the rich New England cultural milieu that gave rise to the humanitarian, abolitionist, and proto-feminist views of Louisa May Alcott, views undelineated in this work.

MOSES, writing for older children, provides a fuller and more cohesive chronology but falls into veneration at the expense of analysis, as does MEIGS, whose Newberry Medal-winning biography for young adults is nonetheless artfully written and introduces much new material. Both biographies reduplicate Cheney's undiscerning equation of the March family in *Little Women* with the Alcotts, producing a misleading picture of childhood contentment. However, Meigs' report of the notorious Fruitlands venture, a failed Utopian community founded by Bronson Alcott—a formative experience in Louisa's life—remains the most thorough account on record. WORTHINGTON reworks the Cheney material with minor additions, intending to dramatize the heroic dimensions of Alcott's life but disclosing, perhaps unwittingly, its drabness.

ANTHONY's 1938 biography is cooler in tone and offers a more penetrating look at the emotional pathologies in the Alcott domestic circle. Anthony is the first to diagnose the stresses on the family brought about by the father's impractical idealism and the mother's invalidism. She presents an unsentimental, even unamiable view of Alcott from the outset, characterizing her as a precocious child who, recognizing the ruinous effects of her parents' quixotic schemes and sensing their unarticulated conjugal unhappiness, took upon herself at a young age the burden of sustaining the family through distress and financial exigency.

As Anthony argues, that burden weighed Alcott down for life, shortening her girlhood, driving her prematurely—with disastrous effects on her health—toward wage-earning and a permanent obsession with money, squelching her own marital opportunities, and robbing her of the personal gratifications that might otherwise have accompanied her success and celebrity. Though Anthony offers a convincing portrait of the penalties exacted by filial duty, she places disproportionate blame for Louisa's self-sacrifice on her ineffectual mother. Readers will also be annoyed by Anthony's habit of evading direct assertions in favor of vague intimations and rhetorical questions, leaving crucial issues coyly unresolved.

In a more sympathetic treatment, SAXTON affirms Anthony's basic conception of Alcott, expanding upon her predecessor's psychological method, but arguing her case more directly and documenting it more persuasively. She corrects Anthony's imbalanced judgment about Alcott's parents, demonstrating sharply the damaging impact of Bronson Alcott's ''saintly parasitism'' and gentle tyranny over his female family, and she provides a cogent feminist analysis of forces, personal and social, that pushed Louisa into a life of self-abnegation and thwarted sexuality. Saxton's is the best and most incisive biography available.

BEDELL's family history, which traces the clan through Louisa's youth and early adulthood, provides the fullest context yet for an understanding of her formative life. Bedell reinforces Saxton's portrayal and offers revealing insights into the motivations and compulsions of all the Alcotts, particularly Bronson, whose role as the egocentric patriarch is underscored here, but whose contributions to philosophy and educational theory are more

charitably represented. Mrs. Alcott emerges as a more admirable figure than previously presented, and her personal sufferings are more sharply drawn.

The two versions of ELBERT's biography augment the feminist analysis of Saxton and Bedell, emphasizing Alcott's contributions to the political debates of her day, including the antislavery movement, suffragism, and reformist causes. Elbert offers a deft fusion of literary criticism and biography, showing better than prior scholars the ways in which Alcott's personal and professional lives intersected, and exploring the cultural climate that shaped and in turn was shaped by her.

While no single Alcott biography might be viewed as definitive, the recent treatments by Saxton, Bedell, and Elbert provide the most pointed and provocative analyses of their subject. These contemporary scholars, delivered from the uncritical idolatry of prior authors, afford readers a complex understanding of Louisa May Alcott's accomplished but mirthless life.

—Liahna Babener

ALEXANDER THE GREAT [Alexander III], 356 B.C.– 323 B.C.; king of Macedon.

Arrian, *The Campaigns of Alexander*, translated by Aubrey de Selincourt. London, Penguin, 1958.

Curtius Rufus, Quintus, *History of Alexander*, translated by John C. Rolfe. Cambridge, Massachusetts, Harvard University Press/Loeb Classics, and London, Heinemann, 1946.

Diodorus Siculus, *Bibliotecha Historica*, translated by C. Bradford Welles (12 vols.). Cambridge, Massachusetts, Harvard University Press/Loeb Classics, and London, Heinemann, 1963–71.

Fox, Robin Lane, *Alexander the Great*. London, A. Lane, and New York, Dial Press, 1973.

Green, Peter, *Alexander the Great*. London, Weidenfeld and Nicolson, and New York, Praeger, 1970.

Plutarch, *Plutarch's Lives*, translated by Bernadotte Perrin (11 vols.; Alexander contained in volume VII). Cambridge, Massachusetts, Harvard University Press/Loeb Classics, and London, Heinemann, 1914–26.

Tarn, William, *Alexander the Great* (2 vols.). Cambridge, Cambridge University Press, 1948.

*

The magnitude of Alexander's achievement has necessarily generated an enormous body of biographical writing both ancient and modern. Modern biographies are largely based on the four principal extant Classical biographies whose very different interpretations explain the diversity of the modern readings. The ancient biographers themselves drew upon a mass of sources, some accurate, some not, some dating from Alexander's own day and some the product of later generations.

ARRIAN, a Bithynian Greek writing in the mid to later part of the 2nd century A.D., begins his biography with an acknowledgement of the mass of Alexander material already extant and declares his intention of trying to separate the legendary from attested historical fact. He identifies his sources as Ptolemy and Aristobulus—consequently displaying a good grasp of the military aspects of Alexander's campaign and of its geographical dimensions. His declared aim is to follow the movements and delineate the actions of Alexander, and he believed, with a good deal of justification, that his biography would compare favourably with those of his predecessors. However, Arrian's work is unsatisfactory in three respects. It is limited by the nature of its two principal sources; the work contains no account of Alexander's youth or of Philip's establishment of Macedonian hegemony over the mainland Greek states, both of which are essential to a proper understanding of Alexander and his own subsequent campaigns in Greece and Asia. Nor does Arrian conceal his Stoic inclinations—we find frequent moral censure of what Arrian considers Alexander's "excessive ambition"—or his political bias against autocratic government. Nor, importantly, does Arrian seem to have shared Alexander's unusual (for a Greek) tolerance of Barbarian customs. As a result he is quite unable to analyse objectively Alexander's attempted synthesis of Greek and Persian culture. Nevertheless, Arrian's account stands out among the ancient biographies for its general accuracy of detail and overall trustworthiness. The overriding impression one takes from it is of Alexander's essential "areté" (virtus).

PLUTARCH, a native of Boeotia, whose biography preceded that of Arrian by perhaps 50 years, used a variety of sources without a great deal of critical discrimination, something hardly excused by his opening statement that he is writing biography rather than history. In addition to the more usual sources Plutarch certainly had before him some sort of "Alexander collection" of letters, of unknown authenticity, quotations from which appear in his narrative.

Even by the none too exacting standards of the ancient world Plutarch's biography is decidedly unsatisfactory when dealing with the military campaign against Persia. Notorious is the gross exaggeration of the size of Darius' armies and of the casualties they allegedly suffered at Alexander's hands. Plutarch is also conspicuous for his inclusion of a number of episodes that have been identified as belonging to a vulgate sub-tradition of Alexander biography and that are almost certainly fraudulent; and for his habit of making statements that are directly opposed by others in the text. In biographical terms the chief value of Plutarch's account lies in its demonstration to the modern reader of the several differing interpretations of the Alexander story—and of the anecdotes that had emerged to support them—which confronted the ancient writers and to greater or lesser extent determined the nature of their biographies.

DIODORUS, a Sicilian Greek who wrote about 40 B.C., provides his account of Alexander in the 17th Book of his "Universal History." This lengthy work has traditionally suffered at the hands of critics, and the Alexander section is no exception. Tarn (see below) notes Diodorus' propensity for "filling his available space with matter quite immaterial, while he leaves out important things like the pursuit of Darius and the crossing of the Hydaspes."

Much scholarly ink has been spilled on the subject of Diodorus' sources. Certainly he does not appear to have used Ptolemy, but whatever may be the origin of his material the net effect is that Diodorus' account gives a more Greek (as opposed to Macedonian) and Persian view of events than do those of Ar-

rian or Plutarch. A well-known instance is his recounting of the fate of the large body of Greek mercenaries that fought for Darius under the able leadership of their leader Memnon.

Diodorus also possessed a highly moral and utilitarian view of the role of history—he thought it should edify and instruct the reader—and consequently his interest lay in pointing to the moral elements of mens' actions. Naturally such an approach tended to the inclusion of episodes and anecdotes that a better historian or biographer would either have avoided or at least prefaced with a careful statement of doubt as to authenticity.

QUINTUS CURTIUS RUFUS, a shadowy figure about whom virtually nothing is known, wrote his history of Alexander during the 1st century A.D.—precisely when is not clear. Of the ten Books of which it was composed, the first two are missing and gaps exist in three others. Curtius was a considerable rhetorician but not, as he himself admits, a scrupulous historian. These two characteristics are brought out in the number of speeches in his narrative, most of them anything but accurate approximations of what might have been said and nearly all highly coloured; and in Curtius' all too common fault of failing to knit up his facts (a word that has to be used with care with regard to Curtius) into a coherent whole.

Curtius' principal source seems to have been Cleitarchus, although the weight of current scholarly opinion holds that he used a corrupted intermediary now lost to us. J. C. Rolfe notes Curtius' stylistic similarity to Livy and, in view of his pronounced rhetorical inclination, to Seneca, his pointed and studied word-order, pithy sentences and poetic colouring.

As in Diodorus the influence of Fortune over the destiny of Alexander is everywhere apparent, as is its gradual transformation of Alexander into a tyrant. Tarn sees this as evidence of Curtius' closeness to the Peripatetic interpretation of Alexander's life, but also finds in Curtius' account evidence of the parallel Stoic doctrine of Alexander's corruption ab initio. In any event the resulting portrait is not at all flattering.

What then is the reader to make of the summary of Alexander's qualities that Curtius gives in the 10th Book? This, surprisingly, is very largely favourable and cannot be reconciled with the picture Curtius has built up in the preceding Books. While this contradiction vitiates Curtius' work, we have to acknowledge Curtius as a vital source for our knowledge of both Macedonian and Persian custom and of the usually neglected role of Antigonus in securing Alexander's position in the debatable lands of Cappadocia and Paphlagonia.

TARN's two-volume work is massive in the range and penetration of its scholarship. Tarn writes with an authority, command, and persuasiveness rarely matched. His separation of his work into two volumes—the first the narrative biography, the second its supporting scholarship—enables Tarn to maintain the pace of his narrative without burdening the text with lengthy digressions and longer footnotes. While the second volume is accessible to the reasonably well informed reader, it is unquestionably written for the serious Alexander scholar; Tarn uses this volume as a forum in which to do scholarly battle with previous generations of Alexander historians.

In his preface to the narrative, Tarn writes that the history of Alexander "depends chiefly on the examination of literary texts," and he therefore produces a lengthy and thorough evaluation of the ancient biographies and their sources. In the course of this examination he demolishes many cherished theories and not a few Alexander myths, searching out the dubious source, fraudulent anecdote, or merely confused and confusing statement. Alexander himself Tarn describes as "one of the greatest of mankind" and this view informs the biography throughout.

Tarn's Alexander, although initially fired by the Panhellenic vision of Isocrates, rises above its narrow nationalism to attempt the first cultural synthesis of East and West, something that baffles his bigotted and fearful followers. Tarn singles out Alexander's residence at Ecbatana as the beginning of Alexander's tragedy: "the tragedy of increasing loneliness, of a growing impatience with those who could not understand, a failure which nevertheless bore greater fruit than most men's successes."

Tarn also argues that Alexander did not seek to dominate the known world but instead conceived of himself as a "reconciler" of it. Tarn's Alexander is an idealist and a romantic but also a superb soldier and strategist, a dreamer endowed, as dreamers rarely are, with enormous practical ability and common sense. "It is this combination" writes Tarn, "which gives Alexander his place in history."

Such is the extent and depth of Tarn's scholarship (he cites Hindu and Chinese as well as the more usual Classical sources and calls upon archaeology to support his literary conclusions) that his reading of Alexander and of his achievement is extremely persuasive. One caveat is that, partly as a result of the very density of his scholastic achievement and partly because he wrote at a time when many wished to find it, he attributes to Alexander a benevolent cosmopolitan humanitarianism that more detached observers have failed to find.

GREEN may be said to represent the reaction against such enthusiastic biographical interpretations. Green's principal source for his detailed account of Alexander's military campaigns is, naturally enough, Arrian, and his book is equipped with numerous useful battle-plans, maps, and photographs to provide greater clarity. However, Green discards Arrian (whom he terms "a master of artful omission") when dealing with Alexander himself. Green's Alexander is inherently vengeful and violent by nature. Thus Green's biography stands much closer to those of Curtius and Diodorus, even Plutarch, although he dismisses the more ludicrous stories of the vulgate tradition.

According to Green, Alexander's capacity for political intrigue, not to mention murder, had been well developed in his successful struggle for recognition as Philip's heir. Green chooses to emphasise the insecurity of Alexander's position—a young man surrounded by a body of older, ambitious, and ruthless generals, menaced by the bitter hostility of the major Greek states whose armies had been smashed at Chaeronea but whose political aspirations remained intact. Out of this came, inevitably, the judicial murders of Parmenio, Philotas Cleitus, and Callisthenes and wontonly barbaric acts such as Alexander's allegedly deliberate burning of Xerxes' palace.

Like Curtius and Tarn, Green identifies Ecbatana as a moral turning-point: after this Alexander becomes increasingly prey to illusions of despotic grandeur, exemplified by his arrogant attempt to impose proskynesis on his Macedonian followers.

Unsurprisingly Green dismisses any attempt to attribute an ideological basis to Alexander's policy of Orientalisation—it is mere opportunism—and regards the Panhellenic crusade as a cynical smokescreen for his ruthless subjugation of the Greek city-states. Green is equally dismissive of Alexander's political

settlement in Asia: "For Alexander conquest and areté were all—the dull but essential business of administration held no charms for him."

Naturally enough such a reading rejects the very notion of an Alexandrian "conquest through righteousness" as being "an idea which still casts its spell over some modern historians." However, not even Green can doubt the energy and skill that especially characterised Alexander's leadership. Although Green's biography is a salutary corrective to those modern writers who would make of Alexander an exponent of universal brotherhood it is for all too cynical and pessimistic a reading—it exaggerates what was certainly deleterious but minimises that which was as certainly worthwhile.

FOX deliberately eschews a moralistic interpretation of Alexander's career and equally refuses to confine his achievement within the parameters of impersonal historical forces. Instead Fox refocuses our attention on the man himself, explaining Alexander's ambitions, behaviour, and achievements by relating these to Alexander's absorption in Homeric legend, more particularly in his identification with Achilles, quintessential Homeric hero, an identification that produced in Alexander the perennially fascinating combination of the noble and the ruthless.

Fox brings forward an impressive array of evidence in support of this contention, basing his case on the premise that the dullest accounts do not necessarily provide the most accurate versions of the man or of his career. According to Fox his interpretation enables us to see Alexander as he probably saw himself, freeing the modern student from the accumulated burden of 23 intervening centuries of misdirected criticism. It also enables us to reconcile apparently contradictory aspects of Alexander's behaviour by referring us back to an heroic standard that could embrace both cruelty and pity, murderous rage and noble self-restraint. Fox's position rarely requires him to explain away inconvenient facts to bolster a preconceived moral view of Alexander as either tyrant or just ruler. This is a romantic, possibly romanticised version of Alexander's life, but it nevertheless displays a pleasing internal coherency lacking in those biographies that strenuously try to force Alexander into alien political and ethical frameworks. Fox's background historical knowledge—especially of Philipine Macedonia and Achaemenid Persia—is everywhere apparent, and a judiciously balanced amount of detail adds both colour and weight to a narrative that is both well placed and well written.

Unfortunately the 1975 edition is somewhat lacking in explanatory maps and diagrams (for example, of the major battles), and the relatively few photographs have not been so placed as to complement the text. The chief virtue of this biography lies in its eloquent and closely argued analysis of the mainspring to Alexander's character and in its sturdy refusal either to excuse or blacken its subject's actions.

—D. H. O'Leary

ALEXANDER I of Russia, 1777–1825; Russian czar.

Almedingen, E. M., *The Emperor Alexander*. New York, Vanguard, and London, Bodley Head, 1964.

Cate, Curtis, *The War of Two Emperors*. New York, Random House, 1985.

Gribble, Francis H., *Emperor and Mystic: The Life of Alexander I of Russia*. Kent, Nash and Grayson, and New York, Dutton, 1931.

McConnell, Alan, *Tsar Alexander I: Paternalistic Reformer*. New York, Crowell, 1970.

Paleologue, Maurice, *The Enigmatic Czar: The Life of Alexander I*, translated by Edwin and Willa Muir. New York, Harper, and London, Hamilton, 1938.

Palmer, Alan W., *Alexander I: Tsar of War and Peace*. New York, Harper, and London, Weidenfeld and Nicolson, 1974.

Strakhovsky, Leonid I., *Alexander I of Russia: The Man Who Defeated Napoleon*. New York, Norton, 1947; London, Williams and Norgate, 1949.

Troyat, Henri, *Alexander of Russia: Napoleon's Conquerer*, translated by Joan Pinkham. New York, Dutton, 1982; London, New English Library, 1984 (originally published as *Alexandre Ier: le Sphinx du Nord*, Paris, Flammarion, 1980).

*

Lacking translations of Nicholas Schilder's *Imperator Alekandr Pervy* (4 vols., St. Petersburg, 1890–1904) and Grand Duke Nicolas Mikhailovich's *Le Tsar Alexandre Ier* (St. Petersburg, 1900), which are still considered the most important sources since they are based on state papers and family documents in archives that remain closed to Westerners, English-language readers still have a vast number of biographies of Alexander I to choose from. Alan McConnell (see below) notes that K. Waliszewski's *La Russie il y a cent ans: le règne d'Alexandre Ier* (3 vols., Paris, 1925) contains a bibliography of 44 pages, with 4000 works devoted to the War of 1812 alone. Scores upon scores of important works and interesting and insightful memoirs remain untranslated, including Constantine de Grunwald's *Alexandre Ier: le Tsar Mystique* (Paris, 1955) and the Russian memoirs by Derzhavin, I. I. Dmitriev, Shishkov, F. F. Vigel, Ermolov, F. Glinka, Grech, Iakushkin, and others. While most of the English-language works fall far short of the major Russian and French sources, readers and researchers in English can still make their way reliably into the character and the milieu of "The Crowned Sphinx."

GRIBBLE's 1931 treatment, which draws chiefly on Grand Duke Nicolas' biography, examines the human as opposed to the military Alexander, excluding military or political events and failing to make any new discoveries. But the biography serves as a mildly entertaining introduction; as one reviewer noted, "it is useful enough in its way as an invitation to more solid reading."

PALEOLOGUE, whose book is also intended for a popular audience, represents an advance over Gribble in readability, although his attempt to spin out the mystery implied in the work's title often leads him to questionable conclusions, both historically and pyschologically. Paleologue overemphasizes the tsar's romances and relies too strictly on a formulaic approach to understanding his character. While his dramatic and lively style will be attractive to readers looking for scandal, as an introduction to Alexander and his history Paleologue's book is often misleading. This work contains no bibliography or index.

STRAKHOVSKY's biography was the first written in English to set out the circumstantial evidence that Alexander had arranged his own death in 1825. Strakhovsky believes that Alexander did not die in Taganroq in 1825 but lived under the name of Fyodor Kuzmich in Siberia until 1864. Much of the book focuses on evidence in support of this thesis, including a 15-page appendix that collects corroborating statements from various sources: newspaper, memoirs, private remarks from historians. Strahkovsky also presents all possible contradictions to his theory. Some readers will be convinced that Alexander could live incognito for another 39 years; others will treat the notion as mere historical fiction. Stravkhovsky skims over much of Alexander's life, and the book is weak on Alexander's personal relationships. It has an adequate bibliography and index, but there are no page references for the numerous quotations.

ALMEDINGEN's biography, solidly based on previously published materials, is yet another treatment intended for a popular audience. It is devoted primarily to exploring Alexander's complex personality, though it presents no new information and shows little real insight. Almedingen is at her best when discussing the relationship between Alexander and his wife. However, she unwittingly suggests her own inability to arrive at any coherent or even very challenging conclusions about her subject when she writes, "to the end, we are left with the sense of being able to do no more than study separately each feature of the 'crowned sphinx.'"

PALMER is the first English-language biographer to demonstrate a solid understanding of Alexander's historical period. While maintaining Alexander as the center of focus, Palmer's well-written study explores foreign affairs and military strategies, as well as domestic affairs and Alexander's personal life, in greater detail than any previous biography available in English. To Palmer's portrait of Alexander is added another dimension through the author's extensive use of the letters of the Empress Elizabeth, thus allowing the reader to view Alexander—with all his imperfections—through the eyes of his wife. Palmer also refutes briefly and effectively the mystery and conjecture surrounding Alexander's staged "death." Based on a very wide range of published sources, Palmer's book fulfills the scholar's demand for thorough documentation and also serves as an excellent introduction to both the man and his period for the general reader.

TROYAT's book, while weaker both in its portrayal of Alexander and in the historical perspective it demonstrates, is equipped with a fair index and an epilogue containing a convincing argument that dismisses the legends of Alexander's survival. This, like most of Troyat's biographies of Russian figures, makes for entertaining reading, largely reliable and always easy to follow, though also largely neglectful of recent scholarship. For some readers, Troyat's vignette-oriented approach and talent for creating a tangible mood will outweigh the work's shortcomings as scholarship and make it the biography of preference.

For readers interested in Alexander's involvement in the Russian campaign of 1812, CATE's recent study is a useful and readable introduction that ought to serve most readers' needs better than the earlier works. But, as suggested by any reasonable bibliography of the available material, the reader has several thousand choices here, ranging from Caulaincourt's firsthand account (a memoir by the man who was closest to Napoleon during the Russian campaign), to Carl von Clausewitz's *The Campaign in Russia of 1812* (London, 1843), to General Sir Robert Wilson's *Narrative of the Events During the*

Invasion of Russia (London, 1860). Of more recent vintage are works by Eugene V. Tarle, *Napoleon's Invasion of Russia* (New York, 1942) and Alan Palmer, *Napoleon in Russia* (New York, 1967). Cate excels in most respects over nearly all these works, especially in his recreation of the physical and emotional turmoil experienced by the soldiers and in his insights into the complex political situations and moods surrounding this war. His book also contains a thorough, scholarly bibliography. McCONNELL's work, mentioned above, is a modest but very solid biography of Alexander. What it may sometimes lack in historical narrative or psychological acuity is more than compensated by its extremely valuable "Bibliographic Note," a necessarily abbreviated but judicious guide through the important secondary sources published prior to 1970.

—Noelle A. Watson

ALGER, Horatio, 1832–1899; American writer.

Gardner, Ralph, *Horatio Alger; or, the American.* Mendota, Illinois, Wayside Press, 1964.

Hoyt, Edwin P., *Horatio's Boys: The Life and Works of Horatio Alger, Jr.* Radnor, Pennsylvania, Chilton, 1975.

Mayes, Herbert, *Alger: A Biography without a Hero.* New York, Macy-Masius, 1928.

Russell, Roy, *Holy Horatio.* Santa Barbara, California, Capri Press, 1976.

Scharnhorst, Gary, *Horatio Alger, Jr.* Boston, Twayne, 1980.

Scharnhorst, Gary, *The Lost Life of Horatio Alger, Jr.* Bloomington, Indiana University Press, 1985.

Tebbel, John, *From Rags to Riches: Horatio Alger, Jr. and the American Dream.* New York, Macmillan, 1963.

*

MAYES' early biography of Horatio Alger is provocative and amusing even as it presents a good deal of misinformation. Many scholars have noted Mayes' absurd fabrications: he gives Alger a stammer he did not have, paints Alger as a rake frolicking with a prostitute in Paris when in fact he was attending divinity school in Massachusetts, and even went so far as to invent an Alger Diary. Somewhat surprisingly, given his penchant for fancy, Mayes (unlike John Tebbel, see below) does not find suggestions of homosexuality in both Alger's work and his life, a point of speculation that, while tempting to some biographers, remains unsupported by the available evidence on Alger's private life.

TEBBEL provides one of the best sources on Alger's life. Serving in part as a corrective to such early writers as Mayes, Tebbel's work is both comprehensive in its research and reliable in the accuracy of its detail. Tebbel picks up the "Rags to Riches" theme underlying Alger's work and suggests that Alger engaged in a kind of "moral journalism" that reflected the most characteristic social trends of 19th-century America. Though he does not say so directly, Tebbel sees Alger's work as a product of a unique period of Social Darwinism in American history.

GARDNER's book is an easy to read composite picture of Alger's life and personal background. Though his analysis lacks depth, especially in the historical background that was the basis for Alger's themes, and though Gardner has neglected many of the sources that were available to him, his work is clearly written and well organized, focusing narrowly on Alger's life and providing sharp insights that could prove useful for further analysis.

HOYT furnishes one of the finest descriptive treatments of Alger's background. Focusing on the "Alger Boys," the basis for most of Alger's stories, Hoyt expands his scope to include a fairly comprehensive analysis of Alger's life and work. Hoyt is unique in his examination of the "lumber materials" out of which Alger created the framework for his stories. Hoyt's sources are reliable, and his work will prove valuable to researchers.

RUSSELL provides a fair but limited analysis of Alger's life. While his book displays a sense of humor that makes reading it enjoyable, Russell offers little new material. He does speculate on some darker aspects of Alger's life, work, and character, and his insights often prove interesting even if unsubstantiated.

SCHARNHORST's 1980 Twayne book on Alger takes advantage of much recent scholarship. A focused treatment of Alger's life, with some background of his times, this book, like many in the Twayne series, provides excellent primary and secondary bibliographies and would therefore be a good starting place for both the student and the scholar. Scharnhorst avoids conjecture when treating the hazy areas of Alger's life, supplying instead a well-organized presentation of the various theories already forwarded. Scharnhorst's 1985 *Lost Life* again draws on the most recent sources (many of which had been admirably compiled by Bob Bennett, *Horatio Alger, Jr.: A Comprehensive Bibliography*, 1980). In this second work, Scharnhorst offers his own views on the troublesome areas of Alger's life, often straying from the straight biographical path. While neither of Scharnhorst's books can be called definitive, Scharnhorst remains an essential source on Alger for his up-to-date research, his clear presentation, and his careful, detailed analysis.

—Nicholas Christopher Polos

ANDERSON, Sherwood, 1876–1941; American writer.

Burbank, Rex, *Sherwood Anderson.* New York, Twayne, 1964.

Howe, Irving, *Sherwood Anderson.* New York, W. Sloane, 1951.

Schevill, James, *Sherwood Anderson: His Life and Work.* Denver, University of Denver Press, 1951.

Sutton, William A., *The Road to Winesburg: A Mosaic of the Imaginative Life of Sherwood Anderson.* Metuchen, New Jersey, Scarecrow Press, 1972.

Townsend, Kim, *Sherwood Anderson.* Boston, Houghton Mifflin, 1987.

Weber, Brom, *Sherwood Anderson.* Minneapolis, University of Minnesota Press, 1964.

*

TOWNSEND's biography is clearly superior to others written of Sherwood Anderson. Aside from being able to draw on the scholarship of other biographers, Townsend has benefitted from the resources of a major publisher. For example, the book's design is simple but attractive, and it includes 16 pages of photographs. Townsend does not use internal citation, preferring endnotes that refer by page number to passages within the text. This method of attribution aids readability—at the expense, perhaps, of some precision. In content, Townsend's biography demonstrates better balance than either of the other major biographies. Townsend concentrates on telling the story of Anderson's life, avoiding the mistake of reading Anderson's work as if it were always autobiographical.

SUTTON's biography looks like a computer-generated typescript, with ragged right margins, underlining rather than italics, a typewriter-style typeface, and so on. It is unfortunate that the immense amount of research Sutton has done could not have been more aesthetically presented. Sutton's book also suffers by comparison with the literary merit of Townsend's biography. While Sutton's *Road to Winesburg* is a storehouse of information about Anderson, it is injudiciously inclusive. For example, Sutton finds it necessary to tell the reader that during Anderson's nine months of high school, he "attended a total of 144 days out of a possible 176." Such details as this are found throughout the book, and, lacking any real indication of their significance, they might have been excluded without loss of interest. Sutton also includes "mosaics"—interchapters consisting of quotations culled from Anderson's writings—whose relevance is not immediately self-evident. Sutton, of course, did not regard this inclusiveness as a fault; he considered himself to be a "careful curator of the facts of [Anderson's] life," and he hoped thereby "to make a significant contribution to the understanding of his art."

HOWE's biography is well written, but it contains much less biographical data than Townsend's book, and much more literary analysis. Howe does not include any photographs, and his documentation is lacking. He simply declines to use citation of any kind, although he includes a bibliographical note at the end of the book. While Howe's biography remains a major contribution to the literature about Sherwood Anderson, his focus on Anderson's work rather than on his life renders this book less than satisfactory as biography.

Of the remaining biographies, SCHEVILL's is the most thorough. But it is not entirely reliable because Schevill attempts to impose his interpretation of Anderson's work on Anderson's life story. As Schevill writes in his introduction, "the conflict between reality and imagination [is] the backbone of Anderson's work." For Schevill, that conflict is also the "clue to his life." This forced reading leads Schevill to make some uncritical judgments about Anderson. And it is difficult to take seriously the judgments of a man who seems to say that without Anderson's example, the achievement of Hemingway and Faulkner would not have been possible.

BURBANK's biography is somewhat more scholarly than Schevill's. Burbank offers a fairly thorough bibliography of secondary sources (Schevill's bibliography is nearly non-existent), and his sources are footnoted (Schevill provides no documentation). But Burbank's biography follows the usual pattern of other books in the Twayne series: the biographical chapter is brief, and most of the book is devoted to literary interpretation and

criticism. For this reason, Burbank's book must be termed less than satisfactory as biography, although it remains a good introduction to Sherwood Anderson and his work. WEBER's book—properly speaking, a monograph—is also an introductory work that, like other pamphlets in the University of Minnesota Series on American Writers, is aimed primarily at students.

—Whitney R. Mundt

ANNE BOLEYN. See **BOLEYN, Anne.**

ANNE [Anne Stuart], 1665–1714; English monarch.

Brown, Beatrice C., *Anne Stuart, Queen of England.* London, G. Bles, 1929.
Connell, Neville, *Anne, the Last Stuart Monarch.* London, T. Butterworth, 1937.
Curtis, Gila, *The Life and Times of Queen Anne.* London, Weidenfeld and Nicolson, 1972.
Green, David, *Queen Anne.* London, Collins, and New York, Scribner, 1970.
Gregg, Edward, *Queen Anne.* London, Routledge, 1980.
Hopkinson, Marie R., *Anne of England: The Biography of a Great Queen.* London, Constable, and New York, Macmillan, 1934.

*

For more than 200 years after her death, Queen Anne was generally represented as a woman of mediocre intellect unexpectedly elevated to a position beyond her abilities by the Revolution of 1688 and by the circumstance that her elder sister Mary died childless. She occupied her throne, it was said, without glamour or distinction. In the course of the 12 years of her reign, England and Scotland were united in 1707 into Great Britain; the duke of Marlborough's victories in the War of the Spanish Succession brought Britain to the front rank of European powers; and there was a great flowering of literary talent. The view of such 19th-century writers as the influential Agnes Strickland was that Queen Anne presided over the exciting events of the period with little understanding of their significance and with even less appreciation of the genius of those of her subjects who possessed it. In the last two volumes of her *Lives of the Queens of England* (12 vols., 1840–48), Strickland presented a full-length biography of Anne, based on a limited range of original materials, of which the themes are that Anne was conscientious but dull and irresolute, and that she was dominated throughout her reign by the more formidable personalities of Sarah, Duchess of Marlborough, and Abigail, Lady Masham. This interpretation was followed by Herbert Paul in *Queen Anne* (1906), which is less a biography than a lavishly illustrated collection of essays on aspects of the queen's reign, and survived to 1929 in BROWN's unhistorical reconstruction of episodes in Anne's life for which little evidence remains. Brown's book has no table of contents, bibliography, or index and contains verbatim reports of wholly imaginery "conversations"; it is only worthy of notice at all because its author later produced a respectable though incomplete edition of *The Letters of Queen Anne* (1935).

HOPKINSON, in a lively if somewhat amateurish study, foreshadowed a change in the traditional portrayal by emphasising Anne's stubbornness and strength of character: "[she] was no weakling, no pawn in the hands of others as has so often been erroneously stated. Nor yet was she a fool . . . . " This more positive view of Anne's character and qualities was sustained by CONNELL in a book that incorporated to some degree the then up-to-date scholarship of G. M. Trevelyan's *England Under Queen Anne* (1930–34) on the political and military history of the reign. Connell stressed Anne's resistance to the arrogance of Sarah and her reluctance to relinquish the prerogative power of choosing, and dismissing, her ministers. He also rejected the idea that Anne secretly favoured a Jacobite restoration to follow her death. Connell's was the standard work for some 30 years.

The publication of G. S. Holmes' magisterial *British Politics in the Age of Anne* (1967) transformed historians' understanding of the political background to Anne's reign. GREEN exploited Holmes' work, and his own access to the Marlborough papers—hitherto only available to Sir Winston Churchill among 20th-century scholars for his *Marlborough: His Life and Times* (1933–38)—to refine earlier interpretations of Anne's life. Green portrays a good-natured, essentially commonplace woman who was yet motivated by a remarkably tough sense of patriotism and duty. This devotion enabled her to withstand the pressures put upon her, not only by vehement women friends like Sarah and Abigail, but also by hard-bitten politicians like Rochester, Harley, St. John, and the lords of the Whig junto. Green investigated particularly carefully the surviving descriptions of Anne's infirm health, undermined by frequent pregnancies and by the psychological anguish occasioned by the fact that none of her children survived beyond the age of 11. CURTIS added little to Green in a straightforward popular biography in a "Kings and Queens of England" series.

The outstanding modern analysis of Anne's life and reign is that by the American scholar GREGG. In his closely reasoned study the reaction against the 19th-century view of Anne receives its clearest statement. Anne was, according to Gregg, a skilful and ambitious politician who knew the value of power and was at least a match for those who sought to wrest it from her. She stuck to the ill-defined rules of constitutional monarchy as they were understood in what Gregg calls "the great watershed between the violence of the 17th century and the stability and prosperity of the 18th century." She tried to be moderate and tolerant, and she did not permit her own devotion to the Church of England to interfere with a pragmatic approach to the political difficulties posed by religious dissent. She had an Elizabethan recognition of the necessity of stability within a unified nation. In one respect, Gregg argues, Anne was a true Stuart; she thought of her ministers as royal servants rather than as spokesmen of parties or as leaders of parliamentary majorities. This had the effect of temporarily perpetuating political disharmony, and also of preserving royal prerogatives and royal influence over policy into the Hanoverian period. At the same time, the opinions and attitudes of the queen gave a clear shape and direction to her reign, the main events of which owed much to her personality and her determination. Gregg succeeds well in blending the queen's life into the complexities of international and domestic politics, and he is particularly informative on the tensions of the last four years of her reign. One weakness common to every biography of Anne remains, however: though Gregg does not overlook the role of Anne in politics before her accession to the throne, his treatment of this formative period in Anne's life is less confident, accurate, and complete than the description of her reign as queen. Nevertheless, Gregg's book will not readily be superseded as the most authoritative life of its subject currently available.

—Lionel K. J. Glassey

ANTHONY, Susan B(rownell), 1820–1906; American suffragist.

Anthony, Katharine S., *Susan B. Anthony: Her Personal History and Her Era.* New York, Doubleday, 1954.
Barry, Kathleen, *Susan B. Anthony: A Biography of a Singular Feminist.* New York, New York University Press, 1988.
Dorr, Rheta C., *Susan B. Anthony: The Woman Who Changed the Mind of a Nation.* New York, F. Stokes, 1928.
Harper, Ida Husted, *Life and Work of Susan B. Anthony* (3 vols.). Indianapolis, Hollenbeck Press, 1898–1908.
Lutz, Alma, *Susan B. Anthony: Rebel, Crusader, Humanitarian.* Boston, Beacon Press, 1959.

*

To make sure that she would go down in history "correctly represented," Anthony worked with HARPER in her Rochester attic, assembling a public record of her struggles for equal justice for women. The result is a meticulous chronological collection of activities, speeches, letters, party planks, hearings, diary entries, and travels in three volumes (the third was published after Anthony's death). Harper's work, along with the six-volume *History of Woman Suffrage*, compiled by Elizabeth Cady Stanton, Anthony, Matilda Joslyn Gage, and Ida Husted Harper, have shaped most subsequent biographical accounts. The name and place indexes at the end of volumes two and three of the Harper biography are useful for the scavenging student wishing to establish a personal connection to the mythic 19th-century heroine's rollcall of acquaintances and stormy night stopovers on the crossroads of America.

Subsequent biographers recast Anthony to fit into the ethos of their times. DORR, the new-woman-as-professional-journalist, attempts to humanize and feminize the "towering figure" of the once radical wing of the suffrage movement. Thus when Anthony attempts to speak out at the New York State Teachers convention in 1852, it is with trembling knees and shaking hands, standing as "straight and slim as a young pine tree, in her fine broché shawl and close fitting bonnet," while men vote on permitting a female to address them. Vivid, homey descriptions of "Aunt Susan's girls" suggest rather than analyze the generational, ideological, tactical, and class-based shifts in the suffrage movement in 1890. Anna Howard Shaw is, for instance, "the roly-poly little Methodist preacher, rather narrowly educated, rather inexperienced in life, brimming with harmless egotism, loving applause, yet as unselfish as a saint" and Anthony's favorite; whereas Carrie Chapman Catt is "of the same intellectual, unemotional type as Susan herself," with a "genius for organization . . . executive ability and . . . [the] power of raising money." Here the student should supplement Dorr's account with the books and journal articles of Ellen Carol DuBois, or with Steven M. Buechler's *The Transformation of the Woman Suffrage Movement: The Case of Illinois, 1850–1920* (New Brunswick, New Jersey, Rutgers University Press, 1986).

Katharine ANTHONY'S biography yields a more complex personal and psychological picture of Susan B. Anthony. (Despite the common surname, the biographer is unrelated to her subject.) Like Dorr a journalist, Katharine Anthony's education at Chicago, Heidelberg, and Freiburg is broader, as is her use of sources, including interviews with contemporaries, and of papers on deposit with the Library of Congress. Tensions in relationships and social content, and the private side of Susan B., add a fuller dimension to this biography.

A popular writer of biographies of women, LUTZ delved into Anthony's life at the behest of the latter's niece, Lucy Anthony. The 19th-century social movement context is effortlessly recreated, aided by earlier research for a biography of Anthony's mentor and partner, Elizabeth Cady Stanton. Feminist friendships and communities underlie Lutz's story (herself a Vassar graduate). She uses newly available letters and papers (subsequently donated to the Schlesinger Library, Radcliffe College) to demythologize the "towering heroine" of earlier works. In this context, the Bostonians' critique of Anthony's "lust for power and autocratic control" in the 1860s is balanced by Isabella Beecher Hooker's comments: "Sometimes she fails in judgment according to the standards of others, but in right intentions never, nor in faithfulness to her friends . . ." The second generation leaders (Aunt Susan's girls) also are brought to life by Lutz.

In the last of the biographies of Anthony, all written by women, BARRY is the first scholar to recast the documentary template assembled by Anthony and Harper, and the first to develop a coherent feminist interpretation. Written by a sociologist turned historian, Barry's biography is most likely to appeal to the imaginations of contemporary students. Her focus is on reconstructing Anthony's transforming choices—those that moved her from a self-denigrating, rigid personal piety to a radical egalitarianism that viewed women as a class, oppressed by male-defined institutions. Except for new information on the Kansas campaign and the Train controversy, the story is not new. Its excitement lies in Barry's theory of interpretation. Anthony's mother for the first time looms as more important than her father in Susan's self-definition. Anthony's resentment of marriage as a "self-annihilating" loss of freedom of action to male primacy, and her refusal to be so bound, is reinterpreted as a role-transforming choice, one that contributes to her growing political consciousness as the "new true woman," not the "hybrid species" or "old main" of pop-culture disdain. Anthony found her emotional center with other women and in the organization of single-gendered social spaces, according to Barry, like the Woman's Rights movement, the Woman's State (New York) Temperance Society, the National Woman's Suffrage Association.

Work by Lee Virginia Chambers-Schiller, *Liberty, A Better Husband: Single Women in America, the Generations of 1780–1840* (New Haven, Connecticut, Yale University Press, 1984) and Martha Vicinus, *Independent Women, 1850–1920* (University of Chicago Press, 1985) add support to the new woman per-

spective. Barry's account is less keenly drawn as the second generation of feminists enters the scene after the 1890 National American Woman Suffrage Association merger. Conceptual clarification, balance, and further analysis can be found in Joan Hoff-Wilson's *Signs* article (Autumn 1987), in William L. O'Neill, *Everyone Was Brave: the Rise and Fall of Feminism in America* (Chicago, Quadrangle, 1969), Jill K. Conway, *The Female Experience in Eighteenth and Nineteenth Century America: A Guide to the History of American Women* (Princeton University Press, 1985), and Zillah R. Eisenstein, *The Radical Future of Liberal Feminism* (Boston, Northeastern University Press, 1986).

—Jacqueline K. Parker

ANTONINUS, Marcus Aurelius. See **AURELIUS, Marcus.**

AQUINAS, Saint Thomas, *ca.* 1225–1274; Italian philosopher and theologian.

Bourke, Vernon J., *Aquinas' Search for Wisdom.* Milwaukee, Wisconsin, Bruce Publishing, 1965.

Chesterton, G. K., *St. Thomas Aquinas.* London, Hodder and Stoughton, and New York, Sheed and Ward, 1933.

Foster, Kenelm, editor and translator, *The Life of St. Thomas Aquinas: Biographical Documents.* London, Longman, and Baltimore, Maryland, Helicon Press, 1959.

Petitot, Hyacinthe, *The Life and the Spirit of Thomas Aquinas,* translated by Cyprian Burke. Chicago, Priory Press, 1966.

Pieper, Josef, *Guide to Thomas Aquinas,* translated by Richard and Clara Winston. New York, Pantheon, 1962; London, Faber, 1963.

Vaughan, Roger W. B., *The Life and Labours of Saint Thomas Aquin* (2 vols.). London, Longman, 1872; edited by Dom Jerome Vaughan, London, Burns and Oates, and New York, Catholic Publication Society, 1890.

Weisheipl, James A., *Friar Thomas D'Aquino: His Life, Thought, and Work.* New York, Doubleday, 1974; London, Blackwell, 1975.

*

Owing to his consummate intellectualism, the personal details of Thomas Aquinas' life have been swallowed up by his theological achievement. Thus, most modern biographies of Thomas can be distinguished not by their treatment of the facts of his life—which, in comparison to what is known about modern historical figures, are few and far between—but either by the way they describe the significance of his intellectual achievement or the way they relate the facts of his life to this achievement.

Any biographical study of Thomas necessarily depends on the earliest historical sources. In FOSTER, some of the most important have been collected, translated, and edited "to confront the readers as directly as possible with the personality of St. Thomas." Unfortunately, this collection is hardly comprehensive. Although three lives of Thomas were written between

1318–1330, Foster draws on the life of Bernard Gui instead of William of Tocco's or Peter Calo's because Gui's is more biographically modern: it avoids the incredible legends, rhetorical flourishes and extraneous detail of the others. Well intentioned as they may be, Foster's criteria of selection are questionable. Not only do they betray a (perhaps warranted) anti-supernatural bias, but they so sanitize the extant biographies that one gets little flavor of the period's hagiographic style. Shortcomings notwithstanding, Foster serves as an interesting supplement to the modern treatments of Thomas' intellectual development. Useful also are the excerpts of the canonization inquiry, sections on Thomas from Tolomeo of Lucca's *Ecclesiastical History* and from Gerard de Franchet's *Lives of the Brothers* and *Short Chronicle*. Foster paints a biographical picture in which intellectual pursuits and contemplation merge, and Thomas' work is revealed as that in which "contemplation stupendously fertilized reason."

Though dated, VAUGHAN represents a serviceable (but often credulous) biography of Thomas that weaves together in a text of some 544 pages most of the well-known biographical details contained in the earliest sources. (The American edition is a pared version of the two-volume, 1,859-page English edition.) One might expect that such a lengthy treatment of Thomas would greatly enlarge knowledge of his achievement and personality, but, compared to some of the shorter, more recent biographies, Vaughan's work stands as interpolative, bloated and—according to 20th-century historiographic standards—quite naive. In its narrative inventiveness, it sometimes reads like Louis De Wohl's historical novel of Thomas, *The Quiet Light* (1950). Nevertheless, Vaughan's contextualizations of Thomas' works are quite accessible to those with little philosophical or theological sophistication.

Published in French in 1926, PETITOT's book is one of the first biographical attempts to blend objectivity with piety, to analyze Thomas' thought not as a sequence of unchanging verities but as a response to intellectual debates, to bring together the ascetical and mystical dimensions of Thomas' thought, and to analyze the development of Thomas' theology against the background of prevailing historical and sociological conditions. All of this was to be accomplished via a philosophical approach (known as "integralism") that Petitot borrowed from the Catholic modernist Blondel, mediated through Petitot's friend Père de Poulpiquet. Petitot's goal was to capture the principle that integrated and interanimated the contradictory features of Thomas' thought. The result is a book much too brief for Petitot's vaulting ambition but useful, nonetheless, because it interestingly conveys how Thomas' intellectualism was governed by profound spirituality and fidelity to the Roman Catholic tradition. Also perceptive is Petitot's grasp of the importance of salvation and sanctification in Thomas' writings and how these issued from personal devotion, a point often missed by philosophical biographers. Ultimately, however, Petitot's quest for an animating principle finds its rest in the trite observation that Thomas subordinated his senses, emotions, and his formidable literary, artistic, and administrative talents to a single monothematic intention: the achievement of his theological vocation.

Of all the 20th-century biographies of Thomas, CHESTERTON's has enjoyed the most success and popularity. Ralph McInerny, Anton Pegis, and Étienne Gilson have all judged it something of an unparalleled artistic achievement. Chesterton

succeeds where Petitot failed; with great wit and a profound sense of paradox, he captures both the spirit of Thomas the man and Thomism the philosophy in less than 200 pages. This is not to say that the somewhat stodgy criticisms of Pieper are without teeth. True, Chesterton's work is not perfect in emphasis, balance, or the marshalling and narration of facts, and it is written in a journalistic style that caused Masie Ward sore anxiety before publication. Even so, its author has a deft way of relating history and theology, so that the former becomes a parable on the latter. (Particularly good is Chesterton's explanation of Thomas' philosophy as an appreciation of particularity and *esse*.) It is a happy compliment that the most canny treatment of Thomas is by a journalist, since Thomas' writings are journalistic in their simplicity and clarity.

PIEPER's book is the most difficult biography mentioned here, save those of Bourke and Weisheipl. Under 200 pages—like the works of Petitot and Chesterton—it also covers similar historical ground with similar intent. Pieper, too, hopes to capture what is unique, characteristic or essential about Thomism as manifested in the life and writings of its founder. Pieper's work is different, however, in that it has neither its predecessor's readability nor Petitot's philosophical straightjacket. The emergent picture of Thomas is that of a synthesizer who because of his originality, thoroughness, and precision deserves the title "paradigm of the scholastic movement." Pieper's point is that Thomas was a *both/and* not an *either/or* thinker; that he combined the eclectic thinking of the Church Fathers, Platonism, Neoplatonism, and Aristotelianism in a new synthesis subordinated to the principles of Christian dogma. This emphasis upon many origins is a useful antidote to those thinkers—Chesterton may be included—who tend to exaggerate the Aristotelian influence on Thomas. Pieper also offers an illuminating discussion of the relationship between the simplicity of Thomas' theological writings and his brilliance as a teacher.

BOURKE provides one of the most ambitious attempts to relate Thomas' personal biography and intellectual development. Bourke's approach is eccentric in that he spurns usual techniques of narration (in which intellectual development is treated simultaneously with personal development) in favor of the distracting technique of separating personal biography (odd numbered chapters) and the intellectual achievements (even numbered chapters). This does, however, allow the reader to choose between Thomas' biography or his intellectual development, though Bourke's dry, pedantic style makes the latter preferable to the former. Bourke, like Weisheipl, carefully considers the original historical sources and often corrects mistakes about Aquinas' lineage, whereabouts, and experiences. Of all of Thomas' biographers, Bourke is one of the least credulous about miracle stories and one of the most careful to avoid asserting any dubious fact. Bourke shuns psychological reconstruction, a device employed freely by De Wohl, Vaughan, Chesterton, and Petitot. Bourke's strength lies in his able treatment of Thomas' thought and educational experiences, and his meticulous descriptions of the curricula at Montecassino, Naples, Cologne, and Paris in relation to the development of Thomas' theology and his growth in wisdom. This book is obviously intended for only the most serious student of intellectual biography.

Of recent biographies of Thomas, WEISHEIPL's ranks highest in total achievement. It is the most detailed, scholarly, and historiographically sound biography available in English. Weisheipl's intention in writing this book identifies his audience: "I thought of writing the kind of book that I should have liked to have read when I began my own Thomistic studies over 30 years ago." One must realize that this is the retrospective intention of a mature Thomist, an intention that far exceeds the needs of most first-year philosophy students. Foremost in Weisheipl is the care with which he attempts the historical study of Thomas. He intends a direct comparison between his historical method and the critical study of the Bible. Weisheipl intends to "demythologize" the original biographical sources and make Thomas' thought relevant for the late 20th century. This, he thinks, might ease the philosophical impasse between creative Thomists and historians of Thomism. The result is a portrayal of Thomas' intellectual development that recognizes the open-endedness of Thomism identified by Pieper. Weisheipl is in top form when describing the environment in which Thomas' thought took root, an environment characterized by rivalry between papal and secular power, the rise of the Mendicants, the emergence of popular, apocalyptic mysticism, and the maturation of scholasticism. The result is a picture of Thomas that shows him to be a man of his period, a "modern" for his time. Although a bit drier in style than the other biographies, save that of Bourke, Weisheipl's work contains many useful features: definitions and Latin etymologies, copious endnotes, a catalogue of authentic works of Thomas, and a multilingual bibliography of primary and secondary sources.

For the reader interested in a balanced view of Thomas' life and achievement, the best course would be to read Chesterton for the spirit of Thomism, Foster for the biographical sources, Bourke for intellectual development, and Weisheipl for sound history.

—Thomas Ryba

AQUINO, Corazon, 1933–   ; president of the Philippines.

Burton, Sandra, *Impossible Dream: Marcos, Aquino, the Unfinished Revolution.* New York, Warner Books, 1988.
Crisostomo, Isabelo T., *Cory: Profile of a President.* Quezon City, Philippines, J. Kriz, 1986; Brookline, Massachusetts, Branden, 1987.
Komisar, Lucy, *Corazon Aquino: The Story of a Revolution.* New York, Braziller, 1987.
Yap, Miguela, *The Making of Cory.* Quezon City, Philippines, New Day, 1987.

*

Corazon Aquino's distinction lies not only in her becoming the Philippines' first woman president, but also in that, before her husband Benigno Aquino's assassination in 1983, no one had ever heard of her. Her astonishing emergence, after having been a self-effacing housewife for nearly 30 years, fired the imaginations of four writers in different parts of the globe. None of the four published biographies is official, although Sandra Burton's

most recent account, less a biography than a narrative of events, contains personal interviews with Corazon Aquino that must have had her approval. Lucy Komisar, who was refused interviews with Aquino and her family, informs us that Aquino is writing her own memoirs. If that is so, this forthcoming autobiography will captivate not only the general reader but doubtless her biographers.

Time journalist BURTON has published the most recent book on Corazon Aquino, although the author was less concerned about Aquino's personal life history than in relating the web of events and complex personalities surrounding Corazon Aquino's rise to power. Nonetheless, Burton's book is indispensable to the scholar, since it is based on innumerable, carefully documented eyewitness accounts, while the general reader would find in this fast-paced and vivid depiction of events a wealth of information about the person of Corazon Aquino, whose deliberate self-effacement was rooted less in her limited abilities than in her strict and highly religious upbringing. Burton alone of Corazon Aquino's biographers interviewed her on more than one occasion, and the reader is given to understand that the interviews were informal and spontaneous, as between meetings of friends.

Less vivid and readable is KOMISAR's biography. This feminist freelance writer was inspired to write a life of Corazon Aquino because of her commitment to non-violence in a world dominated by men, and because of Corazon Aquino's remarkable transformation from meek housewife to powerful president. Like Burton, Komisar draws on interviews with highly placed individuals—with the exception of the subject herself, who refused to be interviewed—who knew Aquino personally. Much of Komisar's book is a critique of the United States' role in the Philippines from earliest days to President Reagan's staunch support of the Marcoses, while her analysis of Philippine history rests on her perception of the Philippines as a feudal country exploited throughout its history by a wealthy landed minority. Therein lies the author's discomfort with Corazon Aquino, scion of a very rich Philippine family, a contradiction she does not attempt to resolve. In her exhaustive recounting of Corazon Aquino's first year in power, Komisar does little more than relate events, although her admiration for the president's non-violent strategy and for her refusal to be a mere stand-in for her assassinated husband are apparent. If one overlooks the book's dryness and repetition, it is a solid, factual account of Corazon Aquino's life from her birth through the first year of her presidency, the most complete of the four biographies of Corazon Aquino.

Two Filipino have written biographies; published in the same year, they present widely different perspectives. CRISOSTOMO, a political journalist, equates history with fate, which, he says, determined Ninoy's assassination and Corazon Aquino's rise to her extraordinary role as the Philippines' first woman president. Although Crisostomo claims that his book is not a biography, he delves in detail into both Corazon and her husband Ninoy's early lives and influences, stressing that Corazon was not as unprepared to assume the presidency as has been widely held. Not only did she come from a highly political family, but from the time of her marriage to Ninoy at 21, she participated in his political life and was a major link between him and the opposition when he was incarcerated for seven and a half years. Crisostomo alone of her biographers criticizes Aquino the president:

for appointing only men of wealth to positions of power, for discouraging a multi-party system, and for suspending the constitution and assuming legislative power. Verbose and at times repetitive, Crisostomo nonetheless offers an exhaustive account of Corazon Aquino's presidential campaign that is lacking in other biographies.

More hagiography than biography is YAP's (lawyer turned housewife) first book. Basing her work not on any interviews but on newspaper accounts and secondary sources, Yap portrays Corazon Aquino as a Joan of Arc who rescued her country after the death of her martyr husband, depicted as an imitator of Christ's sufferings. Corazon Aquino is guided by God in her trials and is larger than life. This book offers little that is new or original for the general reader or scholar, but might be useful as a starting point for a biography of the celebrated president.

—Sina Dubovoj

* * *

ARMSTRONG, Louis, 1901–1971; American jazz musician.

Collier, James L., *Louis Armstrong: An American Genius.* New York, Oxford University Press, 1983; as *Louis Armstrong: A Biography,* London, M. Joseph, 1984.

Collier, James L., *Louis Armstrong: An American Success Story.* New York, Macmillan, 1985.

Giddins, Gary, *Satchmo.* New York, Doubleday, 1988.

Goffin, Robert, *Horn of Plenty: The Story of Louis Armstrong,* translated by James F. Bezou. New York, Allen Towne, 1947 (originally published as *Louis Armstrong, le Roi du Jazz,* Paris, P. Seghers, 1947).

Hoskins, Robert, *Louis Armstrong: Biography of a Musician.* Los Angeles, Holloway House, 1979.

Jones, Max and John Chilton, *Louis: The Louis Armstrong Story 1900–71.* Boston, Little Brown, and London, Studio Vista, 1971; revised edition, with new introduction by Dan Morgenstern, New York and London, Da Capo, 1988.

Panassié, Hugues, *Louis Armstrong.* New York, Scribner, 1971 (originally published by Éditions du Belvédère, Paris, 1947).

Pinfold, Mike, *Louis Armstrong: His Life and Times.* Tunbridge Wells, Kent, Spellmount, and New York, Universe Books, 1987.

*

Armstrong wrote well, with pleasure and with care. Two fine scholars, Morgenstern and Giddins, recently studying his typescripts in the context of his whole life and all the literature about him, have shown that his book, *Satchmo: My Life in New Orleans* (1954), deserves more trust than some of his interviews and far more than *Satchmo* is granted by COLLIER, indefatigable biographer of Armstrong, Ellington, and—his favorite—Benny Goodman. Collier's big book of 1983 requires study by specialists, but his article on Armstrong in the *New Grove Dictionary of Jazz* (1988) suffices for many purposes; his 265-page book of 1985, classified by the Library of Congress as "juvenile," presents his judgments most clearly. Morgenstern's testimony in favor of *Satchmo* (1986) accounts explicitly for some of Collier's bias and deserves consideration by any reader of Collier. HOSKINS' biography frequently invites readers to compare variant sources of information, without getting bogged down by rival claims. His book is distinguished also by a 10-page "filmography," a descriptive listing of the extremely various films in which Armstrong made an appearance.

The English team of writers, JONES AND CHILTON, as practicing jazz musicians and responsible journalist-critics, knew and admired Armstrong through the years. Their book of 1971 includes many vivid excerpts from their own interviews and a splendid array of pictures, integrated with their text. The economical 1975 version adds a few new bits of information. It is now superseded by the 1988 reprint. Another English writer, PINFOLD, produced a short "life and times" of Armstrong in 1987 with a point of view rather anti-American, perhaps useful as an antidote to some popular patriotic accounts.

Two French writers, PANASSIÉ and GOFFIN, each wrote a pioneering study in 1947, with some collaboration from Armstrong, who had begun to know them in 1932. Goffin's ample book was immediately translated and widely read. Panassié's slighter, narrower volume waited until 1971 to appear in English. Both are sifted by experts, including all the American and English authors listed here. Each has a French perspective, however, that may warrant sustained attention from some non-expert admirers of Armstrong's work in its global values. Yet another French writer (composer too), André Hodeir, justly attracts students who read music notation: Hodeir's book of 1954, *Hommes et problemes du jazz,* translated in 1956 as *Jazz, its Evolution and Essence,* features technical accounts of Armstrong's achievement not yet superseded by any writer, and Hodeir's technical focus does not neglect historical or biographical facts relevant to the music.

Readers who want a concise, non-technical study of Armstrong's life, character, and work may well prefer above all competition GIDDINS' *Satchmo.* Giddins loved the music as a boy in the 1960s, and he was lucky to know Armstrong's personal strengths in his last years. He advanced to more and more scholarly writing about many kinds of jazz, and his biography of Armstrong is an exciting culmination so far, making use of many unpublished narratives, reflections, and letters. It differs from Armstrong's own *Satchmo* in many ways—most obviously in following the career beyond New Orleans on through the long life—but it is faithful to the tone of "Satchmo" himself. The pictures almost overwhelm this fine text, but need not do so if readers slow down to notice the distinctive organization into two big parts, each with seven subdivisions. Together the two parts constitute a convincing interpretation of the career as a whole and of its lasting significance.

—William W. Austin

* * *

ARNOLD, Benedict, 1741–1801; American Revolutionary general and traitor.

Arnold, Isaac N., *The Life of Benedict Arnold: His Patriotism and his Treason.* Chicago, Jansen McClurg, 1880.

Boylan, Brian R., *Benedict Arnold: The Dark Eagle*. New York, Norton, 1973.

Decker, Malcolm, *Benedict Arnold: Son of the Havens*. Tarrytown, New York, W. Abbatt, 1932.

Flexner, James T., *The Traitor and the Spy: Benedict Arnold and John André*. New York, Harcourt, 1953.

Paine, Lauran, *Benedict Arnold: Hero and Traitor*. London, Hale, 1965; New York, Roy Publishers, 1967.

Sellers, Charles C., *Benedict Arnold: The Proud Warrior*. New York, Minton Balch, 1930.

Sherwin, Oscar, *Benedict Arnold: Patriot and Traitor*. New York, Century, 1931.

Sparks, Jared, *The Life and Treason of Benedict Arnold*. Boston, Hilliard Gray, 1835.

Sullivan, Edward D., *Benedict Arnold: Military Racketeer*. New York, Vanguard, 1932.

Todd, Charles B., *The Real Benedict Arnold*. New York, A. S. Barnes, 1903.

Wallace, Willard M., *Traitorous Hero: The Life and Fortunes of Benedict Arnold*. New York, Harper, 1954.

*

Before Isaac N. Arnold (no relation to his subject) tried to balance the account, biographers of Benedict Arnold explained his treasonous behavior as the result of the general's inherently evil nature. This approach was best characterized by SPARKS' harsh assessment that Arnold, as a child, was no more than a cruel bully and that his career went downhill ever afterwards. Sparks interpreted all of Arnold's life through the distorting lense of his one despicable act. In the iconography of the American Revolution, Arnold took the place of Satan, the fallen angel, and like him, it was difficult to remember that he had ever graced the celestial realm.

Isaac ARNOLD attempted to retrieve Benedict Arnold's reputation by carefully examining his military record and extolling his patriotic service without condoning his treason. Coldly received at the time—one reviewer wrote that it would only result in showing "that Arnold was a villain of a deeper dye than is commonly supposed"—this well-researched effort to show that Arnold was "not so black as he was painted" set the tone and pattern for most subsequent biographies. It was the first of many attempts to explain the paradox of Arnold's patriotism and treason and is valuable for the numerous letters it includes as well as for printing Arnold's "Thoughts on the American War" (1782).

A spate of biographies—by DECKER, SELLERS, SHERWIN, and SULLIVAN—appeared in the 1930s, all exploring Arnold's motivation and concluding that he acted primarily from greed. All were written as variations of the theme best put by Decker: Arnold "was first and always a Connecticut trader." Over-written and one-sided, they are a step backward from Arnold's attempt to capture the whole man. TODD is equally one-dimensional, though for different reasons. He blames Peggy Shippen Arnold, the general's second wife, for leading the great man astray. All of these biographies are unreliable. Decker's is most useful, however, for the letters it prints.

The next decades brought new and more sophisticated attempts to come to grips with Arnold and his treachery, this time through a psychological approach. PAINE's short and attractive treatment found both Arnold's courage and treason rooted in his restless and intense ambition. FLEXNER, though not strictly a biography of Arnold, is the most accessible of the books discussed and thus makes a good introduction to the subject. His story focuses on the treason episode and includes a good deal of material on John André, but Arnold's wartime career is well summarized, though Flexner does not hesitate to speculate where evidence is lacking. The account is engagingly written, but without source notes.

Surprisingly, the best study of Arnold so far written, by WALLACE, is also the most scholarly. The impetus for this work was the "nature and motivations of treason," but the Cold War elements of the book do not impinge heavily on this very fine character study of Arnold. The author eschews the simplistic, materialist explanations of his predecessors, finding in Arnold "a brilliant and daring soldier" who was so hungry for "power and glory and high social standing," that he ruthlessly pursued his objectives with a furious energy that rode roughshod over the mores of his society. Wallace's writing is lively, his judgments are careful, and his portrait of Arnold is convincing. The extensive bibliography is an added bonus.

An attempt was made in the Vietnam-era to revaluate Arnold's career in the light of that morally foggy war. But BOYLAN's thesis, that Arnold was "one of Revolutionary America's greatest heroes" because "what was treason to one man was patriotism and loyalty to his neighbor" does not work. Boylan has managed to turn Sparks on his head, finding in Arnold's every move sincere motives and beneficial effects. The author accepts Arnold's own contention at face value—that he betrayed his country for its own good, that the French alliance betrayed the Revolution, that the war was unwinnable, and that his defection would hasten its end. It is an intriguing but simplistic solution to an enigma. Arnold's life was a mystery, his motives complex, his end tragic. Wallace seems to have been the only one to appreciate that.

—David B. Mattern

ARNOLD, Matthew, 1822–1888; English poet and critic.

Chambers, Sir Edmund Kerchever, *Matthew Arnold: A Study*. Oxford, Clarendon Press, 1947.

Honan, Park, *Matthew Arnold: A Life*. London, Weidenfeld and Nicolson, and New York, McGraw-Hill, 1981.

Kingsmill, Hugh (pseudonym of Hugh Kingsmill Lunn), *Matthew Arnold*. New York, Dial Press, and London, Duckworth, 1928.

Neiman, Fraser, *Matthew Arnold*. New York, Twayne, 1968.

Paul, Herbert, *Matthew Arnold*. New York and London, Macmillan, 1902.

Rowse, A. L., *Matthew Arnold: Poet and Prophet*. London, Thames and Hudson, 1976; Lanham, Maryland, University Press of America, 1986.

Russell, G. W. E., editor, *Letters of Matthew Arnold 1848-88*. London and New York, Macmillan, 1895.

Russell, G. W. E., *Matthew Arnold*. London, Hodder and Stoughton, and New York, Scribner, 1904.

Saintsbury, George, *Matthew Arnold*. Edinburgh, Blackwood, and New York, Dodd Mead, 1899.

Trilling, Lionel, *Matthew Arnold*. New York, New York University Press, and London, Allen and Unwin, 1939.

*

In a prefatory note to the 1895 edition of Arnold's *Letters*, G. W. E. Russell noted that his friend Matthew Arnold desired not to be the subject of a biography, saying that Arnold's correspondence provided the nearest approach to a narrative of his life. Since that time and a great many volumes on Arnold later, the two representative works of Arnold biographical scholarship to date are those written by Honan and Trilling. Yet other eminent scholars have paid tribute to Arnold the man while criticizing his poetry and prose. Though they provide an on-going record of Arnold biographical scholarship, such books tend to lack the focus and continuity of a more conventional biography such as Honan's. Unlike Trilling, they fail to create a holistic portrait of the man behind the works, but rather seem more interested in assessing the writings as separate entities unto themselves.

Although SAINTSBURY claims that one can better know a man through a critical examination of his writings, his partiality for Arnold ends with the poetry since he is often hostile to some of the speculative ideas in the prose. This book, written 11 years after Arnold's death, may reflect a certain degree of rivalry on the part of the author. PAUL, a friend of Arnold's who states in a prefatory note to his book that he sometimes owed the most to Saintsbury when he had been "least able to agree with him," thematically reviews Arnold's life and achievements, but in a chronological fashion.

Even more noteworthy than RUSSELL's contribution on Arnold to the "Literary Lives Series" is his two-volume collection of Arnold's *Letters*, one of the first authentic records of Arnold's life. According to Richard Garnett in the *Dictionary of National Biography*, even though most of these letters are addressed to members of Arnold's family and are therefore "wanting the stimulus arising from the collision of dissimilar minds," they do depict Arnold's moral character just as his writings reveal aspects of his intellectual character.

Some regard KINGSMILL's biography as anti-Victorian because it reflects the age of Stracheyian criticism in which it was written. Interestingly enough, Kingsmill himself recognizes the existence of biographical bias although he says that such bias may be attributed to his own background. In a tongue-in-cheek manner, he suggests that perhaps the reader needs to have a sketch of the biographer's life in order to better see where the biographer was shortsighted in his views on his subject or why he emphasized some ideas over others. CHAMBERS' short volume, consisting of only 134 pages, may seem like a bare bones study, but by taking no particular critical approach and veering away from the interpretive in favor of the strictly informative, his is perhaps one of the few purely biographical books written about Arnold before Honan wrote his more extensively researched work.

NEIMAN's work is a bit more modern and lively in its tone than Chambers' book. Neiman provides a chronology of Arnold's life as well as a fairly good annotated bibliography of Arnold scholarship. Initially, Neiman traces Arnold's diverse activities as an inspector of schools and then briefly surveys the poetry that ultimately led to his election to the post of Professor of Poetry at Oxford. When the discussion turns to Arnold's main intellectual concerns as they are contained within his written essays and lectures, the factual data are subordinated to the critic's interpretive commentary. It were as if the complexity and controversial nature of Arnold's thought almost compels the literary biographer to engage in a certain degree of critical speculation.

ROWSE justifies the writing of yet another Arnold biography by stating that it is just as important to approach Arnold from the vantage point of his Celtic mother as from the perspective of his famous father, Dr. Arnold. Rowse observes that because we are living in a post-Freudian age, we should take a more psychological view of this father-son relationship. He also sees a need to review Arnold's often overlooked contributions to educational reform, especially since, according to Rowse, the scope of Matthew's work affected a far greater number of people than did his father's more limited involvement with the British public schools.

TRILLING's is one of the most notable books on Arnold and, judging from the numerous reprintings of the original 1939 text, is also one of the most popular "intellectual" biographies of any literary figure. Trilling wrote during a time when the Victorians were generally well regarded. Although his is not a biography in the traditional sense, since he consulted no unpublished material, Trilling does write a "biography of Arnold's mind." Unlike those books concerned primarily with interpretation that seem to lack any overall developmental context within which to place the critical analysis, Trilling treats Arnold's ideas through their development. By presenting what he calls the "logic and architecture" of Arnold's thought as it is organically developed, Trilling believes he can help clarify what Arnold actually said and meant so that his ideas will not be misrepresented or misunderstood. Trilling admits that though he could have paid more attention to the aesthetics of Arnold's poetry, he would be the first to admit the importance of the poetry since the "poet's vision gave the prose writer his goal." There are those who criticize Arnold's vision for being "too simple, genteel, incomplete," but the way he saw the world was greatly influenced by the historical time and place in which he lived. Trilling concentrates more on public issues of political and cultural import and on the psychological ramifications of Arnold's attitudes than does his so-called biographical rival Honan.

HONAN, as he states in his preface, "decided in 1970 to write a definitive biography—or as Painter said he attempted for Proust a book close, full, and scholarly, accurate in every detail—for the Arnold specialist and general reader alike." Using many unpublished letters, journals, and diaries and getting the complete cooperation of family members, Honan can claim that "three-quarters of the biographical data in this book" has not appeared in any previous study of Arnold. His aim was to give "an authentic sense of Arnold's own historical present" in order to come as close to the "livingness" or sense of the real life of Arnold as possible. Although the broad outline of Arnold's life was already well-established, Honan documents in greater detail the influence of Arnold's mother, provides added information about Arnold's schooling, explores his early insecurities as a young dandy, and discusses the ways in which Arnold settled down, a process that certainly helped to win him the approval of his future father-in-law. Honan describes Arnold's courtship and marriage to Frances Wightman. He also takes great pains to convince the reader that he has uncovered the identity of "Marguerite" of Arnold's love poems, an issue that is the source of considerable but far less conclusive speculation on the part of Trilling as well. For Honan, Marguerite can be none other than Mary Claude, a friend in the Arnold-Clough set. Whereas Trilling apologizes in his preface for not making his discussion of Clough clearer and more solid, it is quite possible that in the case of Mary Claude, Honan has overstated the importance of that circle in the intimate life of the young poet.

According to reviewer Denis Donoghue, the real strength of Honan's biography is its portrait of Arnold as family man, especially his relationship with his six children, three of whom died during Arnold's lifetime. Although Honan has been criticized for not being emphatic enough as to what points he wants to highlight over others, Honan's discussion of Arnold as European and his presentation of some of the continental thinkers who helped shape his ideas, such as Goethe and Spinoza, as well as British intellectuals including Carlyle and Newman, is of particular interest. One possible criticism is that if Honan is indeed writing a "definitive" biography, he should have looked more closely at Arnold's poetry, attempting to show a more direct connection between the prose and the poetry, although many of the biographers already mentioned also seem weak in their assessment of how the positive ideas of the prose pieces relate to the darker-toned poetry. But a decided strength of the biography, according to Tennyson scholar Christopher Ricks, is the way in which Arnold's "greatness and goodness" emerges as an important byproduct of his personal development. Despite the fact that Arnold's ideas are not always agreed upon by admirers and detractors alike, the host of Arnold biographers generally depict a gentle, genteel genius, and few perform this task with more devotion and care than Honan and Trilling.

—Phyllis E. Wachter

ASQUITH, Herbert Henry [1st Earl of Oxford and Asquith], 1852–1928; English statesman.

Asquith, Lady Cynthia, *Diaries 1915–18*. London, Hutchinson, 1968; New York, Knopf, 1969.

Asquith, Margot, *An Autobiography* (2 vols.). New York, G. H. Doran, and London, T. Butterworth, 1920.

Jenkins, Roy, *Asquith: Portrait of a Man and an Era*. London, Collins, 1964; New York, Dutton, 1966.

Koss, Stephen, *Asquith*. London, A. Lane, and New York, St. Martin's, 1976.

*

Biographies of Asquith are, given his significance in British politics, surprisingly few in number. Learning about Asquith is not easy; he was an uncooperative subject for biographers. Detesting journalists and perhaps even the electorate, he avoided inspiring campaign biographies during his political career. No substantial biography, either adulatory or critical, appeared during his lifetime. For all practical purposes, he kept no diary. His autobiographical books, *Fifty Years of British Parliament* (2 vols., 1926) and *Memories and Reflections 1852–1927* (2 vols., 1928), hastily composed in old age in the disappointed hope of making money, are not much help. These four autobiographical volumes are factually imprecise, disorganized, and quite unrevealing of their author. They deserve the disuse into which they have fallen.

Asquith did write, almost entirely to women other than his two wives, almost endless personal letters that are precise, elegant, and exceedingly revealing of their author. Those letters are the most important single source for biographical insight into Asquith. Indeed, what is of value in his autobiographical books is largely drawn from heavily expurgated versions of his letters, which he borrowed back for this purpose from his female correspondents. Some of those expurgated letters appeared not long after their author's death as *H.H.A.: Letters of the Earl of Oxford and Asquith to a Friend* (2 vols., 1933–34). The most important letters are the 300,000 words written during 1912–15 to Venetia Stanley. About half of these letters appear, most for the first time, in the volume recently edited by Michal and Eleanor Brock, *Letters to Venetia Stanley* (1982). The Brocks argue that Asquith's letters to Stanley are the most remarkable self-revelation by a British prime minister. This may well be so. Certainly the self they reveal is unattractive: intellectually vain, socially ambitious, contemptuous of his less powerful but sometimes more gifted cabinet colleagues, Asquith was far from being lovable or even likable. His lack of judgment in writing, even during cabinet meetings, so copiously to a woman 35 years his junior may prove his biographical undoing. In those letters the prime minister reveals not only himself but almost all of the major British military and naval secrets of the first year of World War I, including some not known to at least some of his cabinet colleagues. Many of Asquith's letters were quite probably in violation of the Official Secrets Act, which had been pushed through Parliament by his own cabinet. Except for their unsupported suggestion that Asquith's lust for Stanley may have caused him to drink less, the extensive commentary by the Brocks is judicious, helping make their edition of his letters the most important biographical study of Asquith. Since their chronological coverage is so necessarily narrow, the burden of explaining the rest of Asquith's long life is left to two earlier, broader biographies, those of Jenkins and Koss.

In spite of his subtitle, JENKINS is not seriously concerned with describing "an Era." His focus is on Asquith as a senior member of the British political elite. This Asquith surely was, but there was no "Asquith era," not even during his prime ministership, and Jenkins is, despite his enthusiasm for Asquith, unable to construct such. Asquith as politician Jenkins explains as the best example of the classical tradition in British politics. Jenkins' book is a superior example of a recognizable genre: one British politician writing about an earlier master of politics, with more than a suggestion that the author is following in, and filling, the master's footsteps. Jenkins' is the most widely read biography of Asquith, partly at least because of its author, who in admiring Asquith's ambition and liberalism revealed that he, too, was both ambitious and (in spite of being then a member of the Labour Party's front bench) a liberal at heart. Jenkins downplays Asquith's lechery and alcoholism, perhaps not viewing them as weaknesses. More probably, Jenkins wanted to see no flaws in his hero, forgetting that tragedy is the result of the hero's tragic flaw. Even if Jenkins had possessed clearer vision, there was, as his preface makes explicit, the onmipresent shadow of Asquith's elder daughter, who not only controlled access to much of the documentary evidence, but was ever vigilant, until her death in 1969, that no unfavorable word be published about her beloved father. Lady Violet Bonham Carter (after 1964 Lady Asquith of Yarnbury) never wrote extensively about her father, but she did succeed in long preventing any informed critical evaluation being written.

By the time KOSS was writing his biography, his subject's most (and perhaps only) faithful child was dead. Koss therefore had much more open access to archival materials, and he made excellent scholarly use of those materials. His is a solid, objective, and thoughtful account of Asquith's political career. Koss sees Asquith as neither hero nor villain. Even Koss, however, does not describe Asquith in fully human terms. Koss candidly admits that his book is political biography, not a full-scale biography. He therefore intentionally avoids emphasizing Asquith's personal life, since he sees no real connection between his subject's personal and political lives. This dichotomy creates a large gap in Koss' book, especially concerning the first four decades of Asquith's life.

The first half of that life has never been fully described. There are at least some valuable sources into the second half of Asquith's personal life, in books by and about other members of his family. His second wife, MARGOT ASQUITH, published almost endless memoirs, full of astonishing and sometimes accurate accounts of her husband, the most valuable version of which may be that published in 1920, when the memory of her husband's fall from power in 1916 was still painfully fresh. Equally fascinating, and much more reliable, is Daphne Bennett's biography of the second Mrs. Asquith, *Margot: A Life of the Countess of Oxford and Asquith* (1984). A daughter-in-law, Lady CYNTHIA ASQUITH, provides in her diaries detached and detailed descriptions of Asquith in domestic circumstances. John Jolliffe, in memorializing Asquith's eldest son (*Raymond Asquith: Life and Letters*, 1980), perhaps unintentionally reveals the contempt of a son for his father. Raymond Asquith never forgave his father for having taken up with Margot Tennant even before the first Mrs. Asquith died young. It is therefore no surprise that the prime minister, so energetic a letter writer, never wrote to his son on the Western Front before that son was killed in the Battle of the Somme, ordered by the father.

—Marvin Rintala

ASTAIRE, Fred, 1899–1987; American dancer, actor, and singer.

Adler, Bill, *Fred Astaire: A Wonderful Life: A Biography.* New York, Carroll and Graf, 1987; London, Robson, 1988.
Croce, Arlene, *The Fred Astaire and Ginger Rogers Book.* New York, Outerbridge and Lazard, and London, W. H. Allen, 1972.
Delamater, Jerome, *Dance in the Hollywood Musicals.* Ann Arbor, Michigan, UMI Research Press, 1981.
Green, Stanley and Bert Goldblatt, *Starring Fred Astaire.* New York, Dodd Mead, 1973; London, W. H. Allen, 1974.
Mueller, John, *Astaire Dancing: The Musical Films.* New York, Knopf, 1985; London, Hamilton, 1986.
Pickard, Roy, *Fred Astaire.* New York, Crescent Books, 1985.
Thomas, Bob, *Astaire, The Man, the Dancer.* New York, St. Martin's, 1984; London, Weidenfeld and Nicolson, 1985.

*

ADLER's short, lively, and well-written biography touches on several familiar themes. Adler insists that Astaire was a consummate artist and entertainer whose unsurpassed achievement on stage, television, and screen created an American legend. Yet he does not write with blind adulation, but tells the story of an eminently decent man whose smile, charm, and fine manners, besides his great talent, made him a most beloved figure. Adler's extensive research includes interviews with such people as George Balanchine, who called Astaire "the greatest dancer in the world." Adler insists on two aspects of Astaire's career that have often been neglected: his singing and his dramatic roles. He quotes Irving Berlin saying that Astaire was "a great singer, as good as any of them, as good as Jolson, Crosby, and Sinatra." Adler also covers Astaire's later life, including his marriage to Robyn Smith, his attempt to found a dancing school, and the writing of his autobiography, *Steps in Time* (1959), a delightful book full of anecdotes as only Astaire could tell them. Adler's book includes 16 excellent photographs, an Epilogue listing Astaire's stage musicals, movies, television appearances, recordings, as well as musical numbers Astaire choreographed and songs he wrote. It also contains a useful bibliography, something other books fail to supply. Any study of Fred Astaire should begin with Adler's book.

CROCE's book on Astaire and Ginger Rogers reveals much about Astaire as a taskmaster and a perfectionist in the art of modern dance. Though somewhat narrow in scope, this book is useful in describing what Percy Hammond of the New York *Herald Tribune* called "Astaire's winged dogs." While concentrating on Astaire at work on the dance floor, Croce also shows us something of Astaire's ability to work well with many different people. This work will be useful to those more interested in the art of dance than in the personal life of Fred Astaire. DELAMATER devotes a chapter to Astaire and Ginger Rogers that helps complete the picture of Astaire as a trained musician and highlights his eclectic style of choreography. Delamater's book also includes interesting views by Astaire's fellow entertainers.

GREEN AND GOLDBLATT focus on Astaire as a film star. Their well-executed book offers excellent coverage of Astaire's many performances but makes little reference to his private life or his complex personality. While useful for its keen insight into the details of Astaire's dancing style, the book says little of Astaire's dramatic roles later in his career.

MUELLER features Fred Astaire in his solo roles in musical films. His book is equipped with a fair index, but its real value lies in its reproduction of first-rate photographs of the best Astaire productions. A four-page bibliography of material on Astaire includes such valuable sources as the BBC feature, "The Fred Astaire Story" (1975). Also included are many interviews with entertainment personalities. Mueller makes no attempt to examine the many myths that surround Astaire's life, and while his book is a gold mine of sources, it says very little about Astaire as an actor or singer.

PICKARD provides, with the exception of Adler, the most comprehensive biography of Astaire. Written in a lively and enjoyable style, his work also has the advantage of covering much of Astaire's later life. Though not the definitive work, Pickard's volume is well worth reading. THOMAS also covers the bulk of Astaire's life and career. Unlike Pickard, Thomas devotes a large section of his book to Astaire's character, his many foibles, and his rapid development into one of the world's most accomplished dancers. He succeeds in capturing the "Fred Flair" on the dance floor and gives some insight into what Astaire was trying to portray in his dance patterns, based on his philosophy of entertainment. Thompson's work provides some useful, relatively recent sources.

—Nicholas Christopher Polos

———————

ATTILA, *ca.* 406–453; king of the Huns.

Brion, Marcel, *Attila: The Scourge of God*, translated by Harold Ward. New York, R. M. McBride, and London, Cassell, 1929 (originally published as *La Vie d'Attila*, Paris, Gillimard, 1928).

Gordon, Colin, *The Age of Attila: Fifth-Century Byzantium and the Barbarians*. Ann Arbor, University of Michigan Press, 1960.

Grousset, René, *The Empire of the Steppes: A History of Central Asia*, translated by Naomi Walford. New Brunswick, New Jersey, Rutgers University Press, 1970 (originally published by Payot, Paris, 1939).

Mänchen-Helfen, Otto J., *The World of the Huns*. Berkeley, University of California Press, 1973.

Thompson, E. A., *A History of Attila and the Huns*. Oxford, Clarendon Press, 1948.

*

Since the Huns never developed a written language, all biographies of Attila are dependent on primary sources that are generally hostile to the invader from the East. Such Greek and Roman historical accounts as the works of Ammianus Marcellinus have been, until recently, the only records available on the Huns and their leaders who swept through the Roman Empire in the fourth and fifth centuries. Archeological evidence, which was relatively immune to the biases of the written sources, began to be uncovered after World War II, and scholars started to use this material a decade or so later.

MÄNCHEN-HELFEN consulted the widest variety of sources of any historian in his book on Attila and the Huns. Sifting through records, histories, and accounts in languages ranging from Greek to Russian to Chinese, Mänchen-Helfen produced a comprehensive study of Hunnic civilization. This staggering display of erudition may overwhelm the general reader. In addition, Mänchen-Helfen devotes considerable effort and space to disputing other scholars. He writes, for example, "Ammianus' de-

scription is distorted by hatred and fear. Thompson, who believes almost every word of it, accordingly places the Huns of the later half of the fourth century in the 'lower stage of pastoralism.'" Many of his quarrels could profitably have been relegated to footnotes because they interrupt the flow of the narrative and entangle the reader in highly specialized scholarly controversies. Yet Mänchen-Helfen's observations on Attila's society, military technology and tactics, and religious views are authoritative, and the breadth of topics about Hunnic society that he considers is impressive. He frequently cites the archeological discoveries made in the U.S.S.R., Hungary, Germany, and other lands through which the Huns traversed, and students of art history will need to consult his work for the most convenient summary of Hunnic art. The heavy emphasis on philology will deter some readers, but if they omit those sections they will find much of value on Attila and the society from which he emerged. In addition, no student can afford to ignore Mänchen-Helfen's extensive bibliography.

THOMPSON does not draw from the same astonishing breadth and number of sources as Mänchen-Helfen, and his work is not as well documented. He scarcely uses non-literary sources because he doubts the value of the archeological evidence. He writes that "even an expert archaeologist, if he were to undertake to write of the Huns, could scarcely make any profitable use of the finds." Having scant training in art history, Thompson cannot interpret the material evidence as well as Mänchen-Helfen. Moreover, as a classicist, he is not well versed in Central Asian studies, and his discussion of Hunnic society is thus not always convincing. Yet Thompson's work has the virtue of being a narrative, chronological biography of Attila. It is not as choppy in its organization as Mänchen-Helfen's book, and its focus is truly on Attila, while Mänchen-Helfen encompasses the Hunnic impact on history and places less emphasis on Attila himself. As a narrative study free of the philological concerns and the elaborate bibliographic apparatus of Mänchen-Helfen, Thompson is better suited to the general reader, though scholars will first need to consult the more comprehensive and detailed work of Mänchen-Helfen.

The other biographical works are disappointing. BRION does not cite a single source he consulted for his rather sensationalized life-and-times of the Hunnic invader. He invents dialogue and reads the minds of the leading figures. Typical for the writing of which the reader should be wary is the following: "Vigilas glanced at Chrysaphius as though to say, 'What did I tell you?' And both smiled at the puerile delight which Edecon, forgetting all his suspicions, took in this banquet." In short, Brion's is an unreliable book, a work of fiction masquerading as a biography.

GROUSSET's much more accurate and well-regarded general history of Central Asia yet disappoints because of the relatively brief space accorded to Attila. The original subtitle, "Attila, Genghis-Khan, Tamerlan" is belied by the lack of specifics on the life and times of Attila, who is covered in one section of a chapter. Moreover, Grousset could not take into account the archeological discoveries and the published works of the post-World War II period. GORDON translates fragments from the works of the Byzantine writer Priscus of Panium and from the Greek writings of the Theban Olympiodorus. Since Gordon limits himself to the fifth century, he does not translate the important fourth-century account of Ammianus Marcellinus. Nonetheless, the translation is valuable, though Gordon does not critically interpret the accounts.

—Morris Rossabi

* * *

AUDEN, W(ystan) H(ugh), 1907–1973; English-American poet.

Carpenter, Humphrey, *W. H. Auden: A Biography.* Boston, Houghton Mifflin, and London, Allen and Unwin, 1981.
Farnan, Dorothy J., *Auden in Love.* New York, Simon and Schuster, 1984; London, Faber, 1985.
Miller, Charles H., *Auden: An American Friendship.* New York, Scribner, 1983.
Osborne, Charles, *W. H. Auden: The Life of a Poet.* New York, Harcourt, 1979; London, Eyre Methuen, 1980.
Rowse, A. L., *The Poet Auden: A Personal Memoir.* London, Methuen, 1987.

*

W. H. Auden disapproved of biographies of authors, and relished reading them. He often announced that he wanted no biography of himself written, and asked that his friends destroy his letters after his death. Few of them took this request seriously, and since his death Auden has been the subject of several memoirs and biographies. These works present a fascinating man who united many disparate qualities, and some of them illuminate parts of Auden's works, but thus far none seems to do justice to Auden as both an interesting character and a great writer.

OSBORNE's was the first full biography to appear after Auden's death. Osborne, a friend of Auden's, can directly describe parts of Auden's later life. His book is very readable, perhaps because it tells many gossipy anecdotes and quotes many of Auden's *bon mots.* Auden moved in several circles: musical, homosexual, theological, and literary. Osborne tends to make the musical and bohemian Auden central. Where he is out of sympathy with one of Auden's interests, whether it is his conversion to Christianity or his enthusiasm for the works of J. R. R. Tolkien, Osborne seems unable to believe that the interest was in fact important to Auden himself. But Osborne does not hide his biases, and he provides what seems a rounded portrait of the poet.

CARPENTER had access to many of Auden's letters and papers that were unavailable to Osborne, and his work is the fullest available biography of Auden. Carpenter gives a much more detailed description of all parts of Auden's life, especially the earlier years, than does Osborne. His work is balanced and unjudgmental, but perhaps for that reason it seems unfocused. Carpenter devotes a good deal of attention to Auden's eccentric behavior and his at times unusual sex life. Some of this is interesting, and the description of the relationship with Chester Kallman is vital to an understanding of Auden, but too often the great poet is lost in anecdotes about the dotty man in dirty clothes and carpet slippers. Carpenter sometimes makes interesting connections between Auden's life and his works. (For in-

stance, he shows how "The Temptation of St. Joseph" section of *For the Times Being* springs not just from Auden's recent conversion, but also from his reaction to Kallman's infidelity.) But too often he does little more than tell where Auden was when writing this or that poem.

FARNAN's primary subject is Auden's relationship with Chester Kallman. (Farnan was a friend of Kallman's at the University of Michigan and later married his father.) Farnan is not entirely sympathetic to Auden (she claims he put a curse on her while dabbling in sympathetic magic in the early 40s), and her writing is pedestrian, but her work is a revealing portrait of the most important relationship in Auden's life. Farnan's memoir is in fact as much a memoir of Chester Kallman as of W. H. Auden. She quotes from many fascinating letters between Auden and Kallman, most notably a 1941 Christmas letter in which Auden expresses his love for Kallman, and his pain at Kallman's infidelity, in terms of Christian mysteries.

Like Farnan, MILLER met Auden during his stay at the University of Michigan in the early 40s. Miller worked for Auden as a cook in Ann Arbor and remained his friend for the rest of his life. Miller's Boswellian portrait of Auden, which is based on journals Miller kept throughout his life, sometimes has a fascinating specificity. Miller sets forth the domestic details of Auden's households in Michigan and New York with great vividness, and he manages to describe Auden's eccentricities—his compulsive punctuality, his extreme untidiness—without treating these and other quirks as the poet's central characteristics. He also records a great deal of Auden's conversation. Miller's more general reflections sometimes seem unnecessary, but the book is well written and engaging. It is, however, the story of one writer's friendship with Auden, rather than a full biography.

ROWSE's book on Auden is also the record of one man's reaction to the poet, rather than a full account of his life. Rowse knew Auden when the poet was an undergraduate at Oxford and saw him occasionally throughout his life. But their relationship was never particularly close, and Rowse seems to have little sympathy for either the man or his work. His brief memoir is an unpleasant book that tells us more about Rowse's various hobbyhorses than about Auden and his work.

Both Osborne and Carpenter draw on Stephen Spender's collection *W. H. Auden: A Tribute* (1975), and the contributors to that volume present fascinating accounts of many parts of Auden's life. For the interrelation of Auden's life and work, the best resource is Edward Mendelson's *Early Auden* (1981), which covers the years up to Auden's move to America in 1939.

—Brian Abel Ragen

* * *

AUGUSTINE OF HIPPO, Saint, 354–430; theologian, philosopher, church father.

Bentley-Taylor, D., *Augustine: Wayward Genius.* London, Hodder and Stoughton, 1980; Grand Rapids, Michigan, Baker Book House, 1981.
Bonner, Gerald, *St. Augustine of Hippo: Life and Controversies.* London, SCM Press, 1963.

Bourke, Vernon, *Augustine's Quest for Wisdom*. Milwaukee, Bruce Publishing, 1945.

Brown, Peter, *Augustine of Hippo: A Biography*. Berkeley, University of California Press, and London, Faber, 1967.

Chabannes, Jacques, *St. Augustine*, translated by Julie Kernan. New York, Doubleday, 1962.

Greenwood, David, *St. Augustine*. New York, Vantage Press, 1957.

Guardini, Romano, *The Conversion of Augustine*, translated by Elinor Briefs. Westminster, Maryland, The Newman Press, and London, Sands, 1960 (originally published as *Die Bekehrung des heiligen Aurelius Augustinus*, Leipzig, J. Hegner, 1935).

McCabe, Joseph, *St. Augustine and His Age*. New York, Putnam, and London, Duckworth, 1902.

McDougal, Eleanor, *St. Augustine: A Study of His Personal Religion*. London, SCM Press, and New York, R. R. Smith, 1930.

Meer, Frederick van der, *Augustine the Bishop: Life and Work of a Father of the Church*, translated by Brian Battershaw and G. R. Lamb. London, Sheed and Ward, 1961.

O'Meara, John J., *The Young Augustine: The Growth of St. Augustine's Mind up to His Conversion*. London, Longman, 1954.

Papini, Giovanni, *Saint Augustine*, translated by Mary Prichard Agnetti. New York, Harcourt, and London, Hodder and Stoughton, 1930.

Smith, Warren T., *Augustine: His Life and Thought*. Atlanta, Georgia, John Knox Press, 1980.

West, Rebecca, *St. Augustine*. Edinburgh, P. Davies, and New York, Appleton, 1933.

*

According to F. van der Meer (see below), one of the reasons for the proliferation of biographies on Augustine is that "we have a more intimate knowledge of St. Augustine than that of any other individual in the whole world of Antiquity." Intimate knowledge may imply accuracy, but proliferation in itself does not. Any novice venturing into the mine field of Augustine biography risks being tripped up by a crank interpretation.

All biographies of the Bishop of Hippo depend, in varying degrees, on Augustine's *Confessions* (*ca.* 400; for a good modern edition, with excellent notes, see John K. Ryan, *The Confessions of Augustine*, Garden City, New York, Image Books, 1960). The problem with this work is that it is not historiography in the modern sense; it is a confession of sin, faith, and glorification anchored in autobiographical meditation. Any history it contains is a rhetorical reconstruction of Augustine's early life in the light of his conversion. Nevertheless, except for Possidius, (Augustine's contemporary, who wrote the first biography of him), *The Confessions* represent the most direct *entrée* into the life of Augustine. Subsequent biographies depend heavily upon it, Augustine's letters, and his theological works for their historical grounding.

Of those secondary works that treat the entire personal life of Augustine against the backdrop of his intellectual development, BROWN's is unsurpassed. Magisterial in scope, it achieves a near perfect balance between personal and intellectual biography because of Brown's successes in historical contextualization. Of all Augustine biographies, this is the most elegantly written; it moves critically between original sources and secondary literature and—for a work originally published in 1967—remains a model of modern scholarship. Though it deals incisively with the early Augustine—his Manichaean involvement, his contemplative orientation, his unnatural affection for his mother—as well as his work as a bishop, its expositions of his difficult theology (particularly his works on the Trinity, grace, and predestination) are not very precise. Without pretense of plumbing its depths, Brown reads Augustine's theology as a guide to the complex personality of its author, and does so with common sense and good humor. The multilingual bibliography is still useful; it crowns Brown's book as the best English biography written to date.

In comparison to Brown, other attempts to deal with the entire personal life of Augustine fare poorly. CHABANNES represents an extreme. Too brief, condescending, novelistic, maudlin, and unctuous, Chabannes represents a style—unfortunately not yet dead—of Roman Catholic writing for lay audiences. The scholarly value of this meditation on the life of Augustine is marginal. Equally useless is the early work by McCABE, "an attempt to interpret the life of [Augustine] . . . by the light of psychology rather than by that of theology." Despite his claim, McCabe fails to evidence any recognizable theory of psychology behind his work's biographical intentions. One suspects that "psychology" here is merely a convenient instrument for the criticism of those aspects of Augustine's life and teachings that McCabe finds personally repugnant. Behind much of this work is the tacit assumption that Augustine's theological notions (predestination in particular) are rooted in a twisted conception of sexuality, the product of his conversion.

The works of Greenwood and Smith, though brief and uninspired, are not as offensive as those by McCabe or Chabannes. GREENWOOD's book is devotional in nature, very short, with a highly selective narrative couched in simple English. Its last chapter is useful for the reader ignorant of Augustine's general relevance to Western civilization. There Augustine is tritely painted as the greatest father of the church and a literary genius. SMITH, in contrast, is more detailed but shares Greenwood's simple devotional intent. Singling out a lay audience, Smith explicitly states his intention to use the biography of Augustine to "make witness to the grace of God as seen in Jesus Christ." But, for the most part, this intention does not compromise Smith's biographical narrative. The major defect of this work is that it is entirely derived from the biographies by Brown and others, as well as from other secondary sources. Read with care, however, it is the most accessible short life of Augustine.

Worth mentioning only as a curiosity is the work by WEST. Intending it as a "simple account of Augustine's personal life and background," Dame West has no aspirations to present Augustine's philosophy or theology. The result is a biographical essay on the manners of the ancients, one in which the reader is served up more of Dame West's opinions than facts about Augustine. Her deepest insight into Augustine's person is that he was torn by a perceived dualism between purity and filth, virtue and sin, renunciation and sexuality, spirit and matter—a dualism which, she asserts, is a necessity to the creative processes of the artistic temperament.

Bonner, Bourke, and Bentley-Taylor each focus in detail on the development of Augustine's theology across his entire career.

The oldest of these, BOURKE is the companion volume to a work on Thomas Aquinas but is theologically much weaker than the later work. Bourke's primary concern is to unfold Augustine's career as a theologian and churchman, in addition to describing his contemplative vocation and trinitarian formulations. Oddly absent, however, is a systematic description of Augustine's doctrine of predestination. Bourke is properly read as a guide to the way in which the events of Augustine's life led to his theology and not as a guide to the internal logic of his theology.

Better for theological content is BONNER, who provides a capable discussion of the theology behind the Manichaean, Donatist, and Pelagian controversies. Bonner is very good on original sin and the Augustinian doctrine of predestination. This is probably because fresh winds had begun to blow through Roman Catholic scholarship by the time his work was written. Bonner's biography is addressed to the intelligent layperson and to students of theology and history who are generally in need of references to original texts and modern studies.

More accessible than either Bourke or Bonner is the small work of BENTLEY-TAYLOR. Its virtue is that it covers the same theological ground in much simpler language. Even so, it does not shirk Augustine's theology but explains it with great facility. Defects, given its intention, are few. Its slightly evangelical character means that Augustine's contemplative vocation is given short shrift since it would only complicate the case for Augustine's evangelical Christianity. Unfortunately, Bentley-Taylor relies almost entirely upon primary sources, thus effectively sealing himself off from the balance provided by scholarly consensus. Together, these defects conspire to make the author's interpretation of Augustine quirky and anachronistic. But the errors thus committed are not sufficient to eliminate the work's usefulness as a simple introduction.

McDOUGAL employs a peculiarly "new age" analogy designed to open a dialogue with the Hindu tradition. She argues that, according to the categories of Hindu thought, Augustine's life and spiritual development may be best construed as that of a *bhakti* yogi, a practitioner of the path of loving devotion to God. She also admits that there are aspects of the *karma* (activist) and *jnana* (intellectualist) yogi about him, as well. Augustine is thus viewed as a sort of Westernized Hindu, the tacit agendum being to convince the reader that every dimension of the Hindu tradition finds integration in this great Western saint. Although marred by the imposition of alien categories, this biography will be of particular interest to students of comparative religion or missiology. Augustine emerges as a religious figure whose spirituality is more important than his theology, a spiritual adept whose devotion blazes a trail to the transcendent reality that is "alike in the West and the East."

Of those works that treat only a portion of Augustine's life, MEER's is the most scholarly and competent. A large work, it is entirely concerned with Augustine's 43-year episcopacy of Hippo Regius. Foremost here is van der Meer's wish to describe Augustine's daily existence against the cultural and religious climate of the area. Included are descriptions of Augustine's catechetical and homiletical writings, the region's paganism, popular piety and feast days, his relations with the Jews, Donatists, and Pelagians, and, of course, his pastoral work. As a very detailed guide to the post-conversion Augustine, this book is unri-

valed because of its critical concern with both original sources and modern scholarship. If it has any significant defect, it is that van der Meer's own pastoral interests lead him to deny that Augustine was a contemplative—an opinion reckoned idiosyncratic by a majority of scholars.

Finally, three works pay particular attention to the conversion of Augustine against the background of his intellectual life and personal development. Best of these by far is O'MEARA's because of its control of speculation and its unbiased presentation of historical fact. O'Meara portrays the spiritual transformation of Augustine not as a sudden epiphany but as a gradual process of personal development consonant with the Roman Catholic notion of conversion. He draws his comparison between Augustine and Newman and not between Augustine and St. Paul because Augustine's conversion was a gradual sequence in which conversion of the intellect preceded conversion of the will. This is demonstrated by O'Meara in a carefully crafted argument that stays close to *The Confessions* and Possidius' *Life of Augustine*. Augustine emerges as an individual who, after his conversion, viewed Christianity and Neoplatonism—in grand Patristic style—as two approaches to the same Truth. Although much research has been done on the Manichaean and Neoplatonic origins of Augustine's thought since it was written, O'Meara's work is still the best biographical guide to these influences.

GUARDINI is concerned with the same span of biographical time as O'Meara but with a different agendum and without the rigorous scholarly apparatus. Guardini attempts a reconstruction of how Augustine's spiritual development must have seemed to Augustine from moment to moment. The result is a moving description of a genius groping toward fulfillment, a history of an intellectual and spiritual struggle whose final moment is the result of a divine intervention. Because of the role Guardini assigns grace in the transformation of Augustine, his approach is the opposite of O'Meara's, which keeps the importation of supernatural explanations to a minimum. Also interesting is the way in which Guardini moves diachronically between contemporary ideas and the thought of Augustine in order to give the latter fresh meaning today.

A much less distinguished work in the spirit of Guardini and O'Meara is that of PAPINI. Despite his protestations to the contrary, Papini spends two-thirds of his work retelling the autobiographical details of *The Confessions*. Papini is not up to the challenge of describing the intellectual content of Augustine's work. Instead, he opts for novelistic effects such as imaginative reconstruction to present personal spiritual biography. A fitting epitaph for this book is provided by Papini himself: "I am as much like Augustine as a winged ant is like a condor." Still, for those needing an ant's-eye view of a great genius, this work has value.

For the reader interested in a balanced survey of Augustine's life and thought, the best course of readings would be Brown for general biography, O'Meara for the conversion of Augustine, Meer for Bishop Augustine and Bonner for Augustine's theological development.

—Thomas Ryba

AUGUSTUS [Gaius Octavius; Gaius Julius Caesar Octavi-anus], 63 B.C.-A.D. 14; Roman statesman and emperor, founder of the imperial Roman government.

Allen, Bernard M., *Augustus Caesar.* London and New York, Macmillan, 1937.
Baker, George P., *Augustus: The Golden Age of Rome.* New York, Dodd Mead, and London, Grayson, 1937.
Birkenfeld, Günther, *Augustus*, translated by Winifred Ray. New York, Liveright, and London, Constable, 1935.
Buchan, John, *Augustus.* Boston, Houghton Mifflin, and London, Hodder and Stoughton, 1937.
Holmes, Thomas R. E., *Architect of the Roman Empire* (2 vols.). Oxford, Clarendon Press, 1928-31.
Massie, Allan, *The Caesars.* London, Secker and Warburg, 1983; New York, F. Watts, 1984.
Millar, Fergus and Erich Segal, editors, *Caesar Augustus: Seven Aspects.* Oxford, Clarendon Press, and New York, Oxford University Press, 1984.
Walworth, Nancy Z., *Augustus Caesar.* New York, Chelsea House, 1989.
Williams, John, *Augustus.* New York, Viking, 1972; London, A. Lane, 1973.

*

While no less important to Roman history, Augustus Caesar does not enjoy the same amount of literary effort that marks his predecessor, Julius Caesar. Like most ancient Roman figures, the bulk of our knowledge about Augustus is derived from contemporary works by a few prolific critics and devotees. And again like most ancient Roman figures, modern works on Augustus tend to take either a severely negative viewpoint or are outright hagiography. HOLMES' early work is a simple but well-done historical portrayal that makes little attempt to interpret or comment. It is mostly concerned with Augustus' efforts to reconstruct the Roman political structure.

1937 saw three major works on Augustus published. That by BUCHAN is not subtle in its adoration of the emperor, and the style in which the book was written at times approaches drama. However, it is masterfully done and easy to read. Buchan's portrayal of the Emperor's character is open to question, but his work is no less well documented than any other account. BAKER's work is similar in scope to Buchan's, but it is less well done. Baker has infused much personal emotion into his work, which is ill prepared and contains numerous misprints and errors. ALLEN's book is intended for a younger or generalist audience; it serves well as a simple account of the life of Augustus. However, Allen is not an expert in Roman history, a shortcoming reflected in the superficial treatment of most aspects of Roman civilization. Nor does the book provoke one to further thought, since most concepts have been simplified to the point where the reader is not left to wonder about alternatives.

Also from this period is a work of biographical fiction by BIRKENFELD. While much of the work is conjecture or outright fantasy, Birkenfeld did his homework well and presents an interesting and accurate portrayal of the times. The work is included here mainly due to Birkenfeld's excellent job of portraying the mindset of the emperor. The much later fiction from WILLIAMS is less successful and less accurate.

The work edited by MILLAR AND SEGAL is actually a collection of unrelated articles and essays with Augustus and his times as a central theme. As a whole, the work does not serve as an adequate biography of Augustus, but taken individually the essays offer some excellent glimpses into the emperor's life and milieu. Most of them deal with Augustus' relationship to a certain element of Roman society, such as "Augustus and the Poets." The work, intended for the serious scholar, requires considerable background knowledge.

MASSIE's book is intended to serve as an introduction to and popular history of the first of the Roman emperors, including Augustus. Its best features include its brevity and its treatment of some of the popular misconceptions regarding Rome's first emperors. WALWORTH's recent effort, intended for a grade-school audience, is accurate and very readable.

In sum, there is no outstanding work on Augustus. Though dated, Buchan's is probably the best overall work, while Walworth or Massie will serve for quick, reliable reading.

—Lawrence M. Enoch

AURELIUS, Marcus [Marcus Aurelius Antoninus], 121–180; Roman emperor and philosopher.

Birley, Anthony, *Marcus Aurelius: A Biography.* Boston, Little Brown, and London, Eyre and Spottiswoode, 1966; revised edition, New Haven, Connecticut, Yale University Press, and London, Batsford, 1987.
Farquharson, A. S. L., *Marcus Aurelius: His Life and World*, edited by D. H. Rees. Oxford, Blackwell, and New York, W. Salloch, 1951.
Grant, Michael, *The Roman Emperors: A Biographical Guide to the Rulers of Imperial Rome 31 B.C.–A.D. 476.* New York, Scribner, and London, Weidenfeld and Nicolson, 1985.
Sedgwick, Henry D., *Marcus Aurelius.* New Haven, Connecticut, Yale University Press, 1921.

*

SEDGWICK's study is based on letters to and from Marcus Aurelius. Several of the chapters are composed of these letters along with brief commentaries. This work was written for modern devotees of the *Meditations* of Marcus Aurelius. (An excellent translation of this work, containing commentary by the translator, was done by A. S. L. Farquharson in 1944.) Sedgwick is very partial to his subject, defending him from both ancient and modern criticisms.

The first two chapters of Sedgwick's work discuss Stoicism and several Stoic philosophers. Sedgwick considers Stoicism to be a religion; the Stoic philosophers to be prophets of that religion; and Marcus Aurelius as its sincerest practitioner. Sedgwick also believes that Marcus Aurelius did not persecute the early Christians but that he and other Roman magistrates merely enforced the laws that the Christians broke by refusing to sacrifice to the state gods. Only seven of the book's 20 chapters directly cover the life of Marcus Aurelius, though several of the other chapters indirectly supply the reader with information about him. Such is the case with the fourth chapter, which examines Roman literary circles during the life of Marcus Aurelius. The extensive use of letters to and from Marcus Aurelius allows the emperor and his associates to speak for themselves, and thus the reader receives an insider's view of events. However, the lack of commentary by the author hurts the work.

FARQUHARSON's work is a series of essays, collected and published after his death, that examine various aspects of Marcus Aurelius' life. Farquharson, as noted above, had previously published a translation of the *Meditations* of Marcus Aurelius (2 vols., Oxford, 1944), the best translation available of the emperor's reflections. The work also contains an introduction and commentaries on the text. Two other translations of the *Meditations* will be of use to anyone interested in the emperor since the introductions contain short but useful biographies. The first is *Meditations of Marcus Aurelius*, translated by Marc Casaubon with an introduction by W. H. D. Rouse (London, Dent, 1948). It contains a standard biography, but Rouse faults Marcus Aurelius for not making sure that Christians received "a fair hearing." *The Meditations of Marcus Aurelius Antoninus*, translated by G. M. A. Gruber (Indianapolis, Bobbs-Merrill, 1963), gives a fine summary of the emperor's life, discussing his education and his abandonment of rhetoric for philosophy. Gruber describes Marcus as a good family man who was modest and humble and disliked being emperor because it took him away from his studies.

GRANT's work contains short biographies of every emperor from Augustus to Romulus Augustulus. The section on Marcus Aurelius breaks no new ground and makes no controversial statements. However, anyone looking for a brief biography of the philosopher-emperor should turn to Grant.

BIRLEY's study was first published in 1966. The 1987 edition is larger than the earlier work, the author having made use of new scholarship, which mostly appeared in journals. While Birley discusses many of the social and cultural trends of Marcus Aurelius' reign, this is primarily a biography of the emperor. Birley has tried to write a biography of his subject "as accurately as possible, and allowing him to speak for himself." Thus, the text has passages and extended quotations from the writings of the emperor, but unlike Sedgwick Birley provides ample commentary.

The study begins with a discussion of the imperial system in the second century A.D. The second chapter discusses the ancestors of Marcus Aurelius, following the rise of his clan—the gens Annia—from its obscure beginnings in the centuries before Christ to its rise to high social position just before Marcus Aurelius' birth in 121 A.D. For the early years of Aurelius' life there is little hard information. In dealing with this period, Birley describes the Roman customs and traditions concerning the education and raising of a child of Marcus Aurelius' status. For the immediate post-teen years to the emperor's death in 180 A.D, Birley has more primary sources to consult. He depicts Marcus Aurelius as studious by nature and attentive to the duties of whatever post his adoptive father, the Emperor Antoninus Pius, assigned him to. Birley discusses Stoicism, and Marcus Aurelius' studies of it, as well as the *Meditations* of Marcus Aurelius, in detail. The emperor's campaigns are discussed in some detail as well.

Birley has placed at appropriate points in the text chronological charts so that the reader can keep track of events important

to the life of Marcus Aurelius. The book contains several appendices, the first discussing ancient and modern sources Birley has consulted. The second appendix contains detailed genealogical charts for the Emperors Trajan, Hadrian, and Antoninus Pius, Marcus Aurelius' three predecessors, a chart for Marcus Aurelius' family in general, and one dealing specifically with his mother. Two of the other appendices examine Christianity and the Macromannic Wars. The final appendix provides additional information on the illustrations that appear in the study.

—Anthony P. Inguanzo

AUSTEN, Jane, 1775–1817; English writer.

Austen-Leigh, J. E., *A Memoir of Jane Austen*. London, Bentley, 1869.

Cecil, David, *A Portrait of Jane Austen*. London, Constable, 1978; New York, Hill and Wang, 1979.

Chapman, R. W., *Jane Austen: Facts and Problems*. Oxford, Clarendon Press, 1948.

Halperin, John, *The Life of Jane Austen*. Baltimore, Maryland, Johns Hopkins University Press, and Brighton, Sussex, Harvester Press, 1984.

Hill, Constance, *Jane Austen: Her Home and Her Friends*. London and New York, J. Cape, 1902.

Honan, Park, *Jane Austen: Her Life*. London, Weidenfeld and Nicolson, 1987; New York, St. Martin's, 1988.

Jenkins, Elizabeth, *Jane Austen: A Biography*. London, Gollancz, 1938; New York, Pellegrini and Cudahy, 1949.

*

It is not at first sight obvious why biographical work on Jane Austen should be, in the main, so inferior to that written about any other author of comparable status. With two or three exceptions, such as the work of Austen-Leigh, Chapman, and Cecil, she has only attracted unscholarly, gossipy writers with a weak sense of reality. The reasons, so far as they may be discerned, seem to be mainly as follows: her life was uneventful; Jane Austen lived in the midst of a large family that would not have excited posterity had a great genius not appeared in it; some of the documents that might have been most interesting were destroyed by her sister; her genius is demonstrated in her works but not very much in her life, letters, or conversation; she was the contemporary of other great writers such as Scott and Coleridge, whose genius, though certainly not more wonderful, made an altogether greater stir in the world. But the chief reason for some extraordinarily persistent errors (as late as 1984 a professor was still attempting to find biographical material in the novels) has been the inevitably fruitless attempt to apply romantic canons to a classical writer, to seek in her letters the kind of useful secondary materials for judging the works—materials that may legitimately be sought in the letters of Shelley and Keats—coupled perhaps with a subconscious disappointment that this great writer was unlike so many others in having no hidden scandals, no perverse impulses, nothing to appeal to readers of lurid confessions in the popular press.

The searchers for romance and scandal have the less excuse because the first biographer, the novelist's nephew, AUSTEN-LEIGH, who had been the youngest mourner at the funeral more than 50 years before he wrote, showed a truer line. His book remains indispensable. He catches the essential point, which so many have perversely chosen to miss, that Jane Austen was very like any other good woman of her time, class, and circumstances—except for her genius. He records her devotion to her sister, her strong royalism in early years, her thoughtful and precocious reading, her troubles with publishers, and her high-spirited love of extempore nonsense. Very telling, because so unself-conscious, is Austen-Leigh's memory that her nephews and nieces had no idea she was a great genius—they only mourned a dear aunt and friend. His account of her death is simple and memorable, and he records her last words in reply to the question, did she want anything: "Nothing but death."

HILL's book, written in the form of a literary pilgrimage to the places where Jane Austen lived, is illustrated with agreeable sketches. Hill accepts Miss Befroy's account of a disappointed love in 1799 and attributes to this Austen's later refusal of marriage. But the grasp of character is weak, and there is too much about "undefinable charm," and too many sentences begin with phrases like: "How often must she have looked . . . "

JENKINS' book is a sensible, workmanlike production free of unnecessary speculation. She stresses, as a corrective to over-idyllic views of a peaceful family in a quiet England, the shock of the execution of a relative in the French Revolution, to which she attributes Jane Austen's lifelong dislike of France. Jenkins' view of the love disappointment is balanced: "One cannot doubt that she suffered very much" but "she was not the woman to be prostrated." Pointing to the earthiness of the letters, Jenkins asserts the folly of searching for personal revelations and idiosyncrasies in the polished art of the novels.

CHAPMAN writes with the authority of the best editor of Austen's novels and is extremely well informed and accurate. He is thorough on her ancestry and assiduous, though not over-speculative, in his pursuit of the "unnamed gentleman" of Austen-Leigh's memoir. His view of Jane Austen's religion is substantially the same as Austen-Leigh's, that she simply records the "opinions and practices then prevalent." But Chapman is oddly evasive in his discussion of the important passage in the letters where she regrets the lack of religious content in Sir John Moore's words before death. It was left to later writers like Cecil to point to the obvious truth that she meant exactly what she said, and that, given the strength and persistence of her faith, it should surprise nobody that she said it. Chapman steers, however, a sensible middle course between the two images of her social manner left by eye-witnesses, "the husband-hunting butterfly" and "the poker of whom everybody was afraid," dismissing the first as anachronistic and the second as coming from a "poisoned source."

CECIL's volume is slight but judicious and useful. It is beautifully illustrated with family, architectural, and topographical materials. It is more an exact and subtle study of milieu and character than a full biography. Cecil thinks that probably not much real information was lost by the burning of letters, since the engrained reticence would have inhibited revelations of deep feelings. Jane Austen, he thinks, was romantic only about the navy. He sees her fundamental beliefs and attitudes as more similar to Johnson's than to those of any of her own contemporaries.

He gives perhaps the most convincing of all accounts of her religious beliefs and feelings, showing their strength while rejecting attempts to assimilate her too much to the newer Evangelical views of her time. "Stern rather than sweet" is his final summary of her religion.

Of HALPERIN's volume it is unnecessary to say much. The mental and emotional level of the author is well seen when he says in the introduction that "having to stop for a footnote . . . is like having to answer the doorbell while making love." He heads one chapter, for no particular reason, "The Treacherous Years"—perhaps because one volume of Leon Edel's life of Henry James has this title? Completely missing the tone of some light-hearted remarks in Austen's letters, Halperin professes to find in them a "note of sexual desperation." Nor has HONAN provided us with anything substantially new about Jane Austen's life. Despite the fact that Honan was the first to make use of family papers that have come to light in this century, his biography does nothing to clarify our picture of the writer. Good sense remains, as it has always been, the one indispensable requirement for the writing of biography, and it is a little sad that so few of Jane Austen's biographers have possessed it.

—A. O. J. Cockshut

BACH, Johann Sebastian, 1685–1750; German composer.

David, Hans T. and Arthur Mendel, editors, *The Bach Reader: A Life of Johann Sebastian Bach in Letters and Documents.* New York, Norton, 1945; revised edition, 1972.

Forkel, Johann Nikolaus, *Johann Sebastian Bach: His Life, Art, and Work*, translated by Charles Sanford Terry. London, Constable, and New York, Harcourt, 1920 (originally published by Hoffmeister and Kühnel, Leipzig, 1802).

Geiringer, Karl, with Irene Geiringer, *Johann Sebastian Bach: The Culmination of an Era.* New York, Oxford University Press, 1966; London, Allen and Unwin, 1967.

Schweitzer, Albert, *J. S. Bach* (2 vols.), translated by Ernest Newman. London, Breitkopf and Härtel, 1911 (originally published, in French, by Breitkopf and Härtel, Leipzig, 1905; enlarged German edition, Breitkopf and Härtel, 1908).

Spitta, Philipp, *Johann Sebastian Bach* (3 vols.), translated by Clara Bell and J. Fuller Maitland. London, Novello, 1884–85 (originally published by Breitkopf and Härtel, 2 vols., 1873–80).

Terry, Charles Sanford, *Bach: A Biography.* London, Oxford University Press, 1928.

Wolff, Christoph, et al, editors, *The New Grove Bach Family.* New York, Norton, and London, Macmillan, 1983.

*

This survey focuses on biographies of Johann Sebastian Bach that are based on the writings of his own time and on data that has been appraised as the most authoritative since Bach's death in 1750.

The first overall account of the life of J. S. Bach was published in 1754, in the last installment of the periodical *Lorenz*

Mizlers Musikalische Bibliothek, a publication associated with Mizler's Society of the Musical Sciences. The authors of this article were Bach's son, Carl Philipp Emanuel, and Johann Friederich Agricola, another pupil of Johann Sebastian. This is the only biographical report of any substantial length to emerge from primary sources. Translated into English in *The Bach Reader*, edited by Hans T. David and Arthur Mendel (see below), the article spans nine pages and has provided seminal material for later research, including a list of Bach's then published works, an "approximate" list of works still unpublished, a brief critique of his composition, his performance, his knowledge of church organs, and of his "moral character."

This first full-length biography appeared in 1802, 52 years after Bach's death. FORKEL was a friend of Bach's eldest son, Wilhelm Friedemann, and his more illustrious son, Carl Philipp Emanuel. He received biographical information from them, most substantially from Emanuel. Although written half a century after Bach's death, a period in which musical and societal conditions had changed radically, Forkel's information and evaluations stand as the first carefully researched account of the work and activities of Johann Sebastian. However, his view of Bach's place in history is colored by an intense and all-embracing German nationalism. Forkel pronounces, in the last paragraph of the book: "And this man, the greatest musical poet and the greatest musical orator that ever existed, and probably ever will exist, was a German. Let his country be proud of him; let it be proud, but, at the same time, worthy of him."

Inevitably, Forkel's treatment of the materials received from Sebastian's sons is at times colored by his own views. Inaccuracies also were bound to occur. (See the excellent footnotes to the Forkel biography in *The Bach Reader*.) Still, Forkel preserves pertinent data that may otherwise have disappeared, and, as the first conscientiously researched biography, it retains significant historical interest.

A later classic in Bach biography is by SPITTA. This work embodies a vast compendium of data on Bach's ancestry, his life, his musical development, and the history of the musical forms he employed. In addition, Spitta includes analyses of compositions by Johann Sebastian, his predecessors, and his contemporaries, with occasional musical illustrations. Spitta's own reflections on all this material are interwoven throughout. This is a work on the grand scale, unequalled by anything written since, although a fair amount of data has been revised by modern scholarship.

SCHWEITZER's work is similar but not equal in scope to Spitta's. It stimulated great interest on the part of both professionals and the lay public due particularly to Schweitzer's emphasis on the relationship between text and music. Schweitzer focuses on Bach's "tone-painting," matching the pictorial aspect of a word to its musical configuration and identifying for the reader the particular musical figures in the instrumental music that he says represent "grief," "tumult," "terror," "sighing," etc.—historically, a valid approach. But he carries this method to extremes, for he fashions a blanket theory that applies musical designs in Bach's instrumental music to a formula whereby specific abstract musical figures are said to represent, consistently, the character and mood attached to specific words in his vocal music. This categorical approach not only reflects Wagner's leitmotif ideas, but, even more importantly, illustrates Schweitzer's tie to the deterministic thought of the mid and late 19th century,

a mode of thought quite inapplicable to Bach's own age. Schweitzer's work has, of course, a place in the history of Bach scholarship, but the expansion of musicological research in the 20th century has produced results well beyond much of the material here.

TERRY's work was long regarded as a basic, reliable chronicle of the life of Johann Sebastian. Terry describes his book in the opening of his preface as "a record of Bach's career, not a critical appreciation of his music." His meticulous care as a scholar brought valuable clarification to the subject of Bach's life and his family. In his conclusion, he reproduces a list of Bach's possessions at the time of his death. Appendix I sets out an ancestral tree showing Bach's lineage, and Appendix II lists his descendants. The book is enriched with 76 photographic illustrations of places and people pertinent to Bach's life and career.

The volume edited by DAVID AND MENDEL is devoted to original source material, except for a biographical overview by the editors. The original obituary by Carl Philipp Emanuel and Johann Friederich Agricola and the entire Forkel biography are included. Vignettes by Bach's contemporaries on diverse aspects of his life, work, and personality supply strong supplementary interest.

Although the major part of GEIRINGER's book is devoted to considerations of the works of Bach's major collections, some 100 pages are devoted to his life and career. The Geiringers' material is based on reliable data, up-to-date in 1966. The brief conclusion, dealing with the fate of Bach's widow, Anna Magdalena, and the children is written with an admirable sympathy for the human side of the story.

The most recent biography of Johann Sebastian Bach, by WOLFF, ET AL, represents the results of the latest and most reliable biographical findings and the thought of contemporary scholars in the field. This volume also includes essays about the lives of other members of the Bach family, all derived from the *New Grove Dictionary of Music and Musicians* (London, 1980, Vol. I). It presents, however, an advance on this material. Here, "the text has been re-read and modified by the original authors and corrections and changes have been made," according to the preface by Stanley Sadie, the editor of the *Dictionary*. The article in this volume on Johann Sebastian is a joint effort. The Contents lists the authors as follows: Walter Emery (I-VI), Christoph Wolff (VII-XXI), Nicholas Temperley (XXII). This biography is mandatory reading for anyone seeking basic, authoritative information on the events and activities in the life of Johann Sebastian.

—Rosalyn Tureck

BACON, Francis, 1561–1626; English philosopher, essayist, and statesman.

Abbott, Edwin A., *Francis Bacon: An Account of His Life and Works*. London, Macmillan, 1885.
Anderson, Fulton, *Francis Bacon: His Career and His Thought*. Los Angeles, University of Southern California Press, 1962.

Bevan, Bryan, *The Real Francis Bacon, a Biography*. London, Centaur Press, 1960.

Bowen, Catherine Drinker, *Francis Bacon: The Temper of a Man*. Boston, Little Brown, and London, Hamilton, 1963.

Campbell, John, *The Life of Lord Bacon*. London, J. Murray, 1853.

Church, Richard W., *Bacon*. London, Macmillan, and New York, Harper, 1884.

Crowther, James G., *Francis Bacon: The First Statesman of Science*. London, Cresset Press, 1960.

Dixon, William H., *Personal History of Lord Bacon*. Boston, Ticknor and Fields, and London, J. Murray, 1861.

Du Maurier, Daphne, *Golden Lads: Sir Francis Bacon, Anthony Bacon, and Their Friends*. London, Gollancz, and New York, Doubleday, 1975.

Du Maurier, Daphne, *The Winding Stair: Francis Bacon, His Rise and Fall*. London, Gollancz, 1976; New York, Doubleday, 1977.

Epstein, Joel J., *Francis Bacon: A Political Biography*. Athens, Ohio University Press, 1977.

Fuller, Jean Overton, *Francis Bacon*. London, East-West Publishers, 1981.

Levine, Israel, *Francis Bacon*. London, L. Parsons, and Boston, Small Maynard, 1925.

Macaulay, Thomas Babington, *Lord Bacon*. London, Longman, 1852.

Mallett, David, *The Life of Francis Bacon*. London, A. Miller, 1740.

Marwil, Jonathan, *The Trials of Counsel: Francis Bacon in 1621*. Detroit, Wayne State University Press, 1976.

Montagu, Basil, *The Life of Francis Bacon*. London, W. Pickering, 1834.

Nichol, John, *Francis Bacon: His Life and Philosophy* (2 vols.). Edinburgh, Blackwood, and Philadelphia, Lippincott, 1888.

Rawley, William, *The Life of the Right Honorable Francis Bacon*. London, 1657.

Skemp, A. R., *Francis Bacon*. London, T. C. and E. C. Jack, and New York, Dodge, 1912.

Spedding, James, *An Account of the Life and Times of Francis Bacon* (2 vols.). Boston, Houghton Osgood, and London, Trübner, 1878.

Sturt, Mary, *Francis Bacon*. London, Kegan Paul, and New York, Morrow, 1932.

Williams, Charles, *Bacon*. London, A. Barker, and New York, Harper, 1933.

*

In 1657 Francis Bacon's chaplain and posthumous editor, RAWLEY, produced the first English account of Bacon's life. Anecdotal, celebratory, and at times oblique (he alludes to but does not spell out Robert Cecil's efforts to hinder Bacon's career), Rawley's text avoids all those difficult subjects—Bacon's prosecution of Essex, his coddling of royal favorites, his acquiescence in the torturing of defendants, and his impeachment for taking bribes—that were to become the focus of so many later examinations of Bacon's moral character. Rawley prefers to take the high road and reflect upon "the Issues of his Brain; in which he was ever happy and admir'd, as *Jupiter* was in the production of *Pallas*."

It is not until MALLET's 1740 treatment of Bacon's life that we meet with a biographer with claims to a "scrupulous attachment to truth" and a desire to use biography as a tribunal before which Bacon's character can be arraigned. Mallet's is the first full-blown English biography to draw heavily on Bacon's own letters, but is perhaps more useful to the modern scholar as an indicator of 18th-century attitudes toward Jacobean Absolutism than as a chronicle of Bacon's life. For Mallet reads Bacon's sanctioning of oppressive patents and taking of bribes as a sign of Bacon's failure to protect "Liberty," in aligning himself with the tyrannical James I, who saw "his subjects as slaves . . . his parliaments as usurpers."

But indeed the art of Baconian biography reaches maturity in the 19th century with a slew of studies whose intensity and comprehensiveness perhaps owe something to this era's contested cultural absorption of science and technology. These 19th-century accounts have yet to be matched, let alone surpassed, by 20th-century biographers. MONTAGU's hefty tome, with its complex and often cumbersome notes and its copious extracts from Bacon's letters, represents the first scholarly biography of its subject. Keyed to his edition of the works of Bacon, Montagu's biography hails Bacon as a philosophical, pedagogical, and scientific reformer, whose reforms, if carried out, would have improved, so our author tells us, the socio-economic conditions of the 19th century itself. He particularly praises Bacon's promotion of scientific objectivity, through his analysis of the "Idols of the Mind." Using quotations from his works and letters to create an almost novelistic sense of Bacon's inner life, Montagu is intent on justifying Bacon's actions against those who would deem him morally defective. Montagu defends his subject at every turn, from his prosecution of Essex, to his presence at Peacham's torture, to his taking of bribes, that latter charge being merely a "matter of custom." Montagu argues that Bacon was put in a "false position" by a "mean king and a base court favorite" and relies heavily on the dubious testimony of Bacon's servant, Thomas Bushel, that James used Bacon as a scapegoat for Buckingham's misdemeanors.

Montagu's over-enthusiastic defense of Bacon prompted MACAULAY's scathing biography in the form of a book review of Montagu's text. While lauding Montagu as a collector of materials, Macaulay dissents from his opinion as a biographer, going so far as to raise the Baconian spector of the "idola tribus" against a Montagu whom Macaulay suspects of being mesmerized by Bacon's "genius," thus concluding that Montagu's "mode of defending Bacon seems to us by no means Baconian." In contrast, Macaulay prefers to see Bacon as a "man whose principles were not strict," and attacks him for his self-interested "betrayal" of Essex, his condoning of torture, his flattering of Buckingham, and his support for James' policies, which allowed for the defeat of James' son-in-law in Bohemia. Though he admits that the phrase sounds like "a contradiction in terms," Macaulay sees Bacon's conduct as "withstanding the progress of improvement."

The dispute between Montagu and Macaulay, which hinged upon a reading of Bacon's ethical behavior, laid the conceptual groundwork for a host of subsequent major and minor biographies throughout the rest of the 19th century and on into the 20th. Lord CAMPBELL writes as one familiar with the law, and his book, part of his series on the lives of the Lord Chancellors, is useful to the modern scholar insofar as it provides detailed explanations of Bacon's legal work. Otherwise, Campbell takes Montagu's tack, arguing that Bacon suffered from the "stings of vulgar ambition" and descended to "servile adulation" of James I. DIXON, in contrast, defends Bacon's moral character, making use of new letters provided by Spedding's edition of Bacon's complete works. He argues that Bacon's failure to advance quickly in government service proves he was not servile and corrupt. Dixon's prose is torn between reverie and melodrama (the first chapter is entitled "Purity of His Youth") and flawed by what 20th-century scholars would now deem metaphorical excess in a biographer. Dixon, however, spends more time on Bacon's early parliamentary years than Montagu had, and he provides more intimate details of Bacon's daily life—illnesses, debts, and relations with friends, etc. Dixon's panegyric was however too much for the anonymous writer of *The Life and Correspondence of Francis Bacon* (1861), who produced an obsessive book-length biography *cum* attack on Dixon's book.

For comprehensiveness and considered opinion, SPEDDING's two-volume biography, culled from his seven-volume edition of the *Letters and Life of Francis Bacon* (7 vols., 1861–74), remains the most important biography of Bacon to date. Sympathetic, stately, well-documented, and eminently readable, Spedding's work provides a thoroughgoing treatment of the political and religious controversies that shaped Bacon's career and thought at every stage. The biography is particularly good at explaining Bacon's efforts to ameliorate the Non-conformist wing of the Anglican Church in hopes of reincorporating it within the Church hierarchy. Spedding sees Bacon as a peacemaker, taking a moderate position in both Church and secular politics. As the editor of the definitive complete works of Francis Bacon (14 vols., 1857–74), Spedding also does well in placing Bacon's political and occasional writings in context: Bacon's editor regally dismisses attacks on Bacon's ethics in his prosecution of Essex, arguing that although execrable, fee-taking was a regular feature of judicial life during the period. But unlike Montagu he rejects as spurious the testimony of Thomas Bushel that James intentionally sacrificed his Lord Chancellor to save his favorite. Spedding sees Bacon's life as motivated by three forces: his mother's Puritan zeal, his father's government service, and his own sense of the possibilities of science. And he eulogizes the scientific Bacon as heroic, seeing his ideas "as immortal as the human race." Circumspect in his speculations, Spedding judiciously refuses to make claims for Bacon's thoughts on issues for which we have insufficient evidence. Where Spedding falls short is in his failure to read Bacon's scientific program in the contexts of other intellectual movements, notably in navigation, mathematics, and medicine. Further, Spedding, like previous biographers, fails to discuss the significance of Bacon's contacts outside of the court.

In contrast to Spedding, ABBOT's biography of Bacon has been seen as another trenchant attack on Bacon's ethics. Abbot reads Bacon's political career pragmatically, against what he sees as the Machiavellianism of Elizabeth's court, one based on falsehood and deceit and rivalries between competing factions. For Abbot, Bacon suffered from a "monstrous self-confidence" as well as a penchant for obsequiousness. While Abbot's approach is perhaps harsh at times, his examination of Bacon's behavior against the context of *Realpolitik* is valuable. Abbot pursues the hypothesis that Bacon's political advice to the king coupled with his inability to dissuade the king from applying impositions accelerated the collision between king and Parliament that ultimately led to civil war at mid-century. While this hypothesis, as posed, is suspect historiography, Abbot's willingness to highlight Bacon's role in the controversy between king and Parliament over the Royal Prerogative is valuable, though this aspect of Bacon's career still needs more study. CHURCH's fluent volume views Bacon as an obsequious, cringing place-server. Instead of seeing Bacon's politics as the context through which to read the scientific writings, Church curiously does the reverse, arguing that Bacon's yielding to royal authority is akin to Bacon's caveat that we must obey nature in order to master her.

The last major 19th-century biographer is NICHOL, who, in his very readable volume, poses as an objective moderator of the ethical debates over Bacon's life, ultimately seeing Bacon as a divided consciousness: on the one hand dedicated to doing good through the advancement of learning, and on the other, set on advancing himself servilely at court. And it is perhaps to this unfortunate division, so aptly articulated by Nichol, that we owe the dearth of initiative in reading Bacon's science in light of his political interests.

Biographies through the first third of the 20th century tend to be minor affairs, recapitulating the ethical debates of the earlier biographies, and only occasionally contributing new information or insights. The biographies by SKEMP and LEVINE are of little use to the serious scholar. STURT's volume opens as a belated defense of Bacon against Macaulay. Her popular biography draws an engaging picture of Bacon's life at Gray's Inn and his tenure in the royal bureaucracies of Elizabeth and James. In addition to documenting Bacon's political career, Sturt reserves pages for considering Bacon's profligacy and his domestic affairs, including his life at York House and his care of his estates and gardens. WILLIAMS' sometimes elliptical prose provides a sense of Bacon's life against the intellectual and socio-political currents of his time. Though the times often overshadow the life, Williams' prose narrative of the events leading up to Bacon's impeachment is clear.

A host of popular biographies appeared in the early 1960s, coinciding with the 400th anniversary of Bacon's birth, but none of these can lay claim to definitive 20th-century treatments of their subject. BEVAN's popular biography focuses attention on Bacon's relationships with his family, friends, and rivals, much of it gleaned from the Lambeth Palace Library holdings of the papers of Anthony Bacon. There is also a useful chapter on Francis' residence in France. Though not scholarly, Bevan's book is notable for being perhaps the first modern biography to allude to the possibility of Bacon's homosexuality, examining the documents concerning Bacon's relation with his servant Henry Percy. CROWTHER attempts to trace the threads of "science and politics in the complex skein of [Bacon's] extraordinary life." Interested in Bacon as a "statesman of science," Crowther sees Bacon's interest in politics, often naively, as a way of promoting science, and not the other way around. While Crowther traces the political career, he also considers the significance of scientific references in Bacon's diary, as well as the influence on Bacon's thinking of the voyages of discovery. In addition to examining Bacon's friendship with Tobie Matthew, Crowther cursorily considers, only to dismiss, reports of Bacon's homosexuality. ANDERSON examines the intellectual background of Bacon's life and thought. Clear and informative, the

study suffers from lack of critical documentation. Anderson takes on the "character studies" of Bacon's life as well as those commentators who apply anachronistic political norms to the evaluation of Bacon's political practices. Ultimately, Anderson sees Bacon's downfall as a symbolic attack by the Commons on the King's Prerogative. BOWEN's well-written account captures Bacon's multifaceted personality, seeing Bacon, à la Nichol, as plagued by two "conficting ambitions"—one intellectual, the other political. Lacking scholarly critical apparatus, Bowen is nonetheless thorough in explicating the Coke/Bacon controversy.

The biographical output of the 1970s was eclectic. DU MAURIER's two-volume study of Anthony and Francis Bacon, is written in a lively prose style, with no notes, but with a concise bibliography of sources. In her first volume Du Maurier examines in some detail the early married life of Bacon's mother and father under the reigns of earlier Tudors. This first volume focuses on Antony Bacon's career abroad, including a charge of sodomy brought against him in France. She looks at Bacon's prosecution of Essex in light of Antony's involvements with the Earl. Her second book focuses on Francis's life after the death of his brother in 1601. Du Maurier makes ample use of the contemporary letters of Chamberlain and Tobie Matthews, along with extended discussions of private and cultural life at James' court. In sum, Du Maurier's work examines Bacon's life through his involvement with family, friends, and colleagues, rather than through assessing his public record.

MARWEIL's is an unwieldy, sometimes unfocused, and unnecessarily convoluted examination of Bacon's public career, though the author starts off with the interesting intent of explaining Bacon's motives for writing the *History of Henry VII* after his impeachment. Working backwards, the book begins with the impeachment and then goes on to consider Bacon as courtly suitor, royal counselor, and finally as historian. EPSTEIN offers a clear though perhaps too concise scholarly study of Bacon's political career. After an opening chapter that examines the work of previous biographers, Epstein reviews Bacon's speeches and activities in Parliament in support of Crown policy. In his conclusion, Epstein systematizes Bacon's political thought in terms of his views on empire and the Prerogative debates between Crown and Parliament. He also cogently combats the idea that Bacon's involvement in politics was detrimental to his philosophy.

—Julie Robin Solomon

BAEDA. See **BEDE.**

BALANCHINE, George, 1904–1983; Russian-born American choreographer and ballet dancer.

Buckle, Richard and John Taras, *George Balanchine, Ballet Master: A Biography.* London, Hamilton, and New York, Random House, 1988.

Danilova, Alexandra, *Choura: The Memoirs of Alexandre Danilova.* New York, Knopf, 1986; London, Dance Books, 1987.
Geva, Tamara, *Split Seconds: A Remembrance.* New York, Harper, 1972; London, Cape, 1986.
Kirstein, Lincoln, *The New York City Ballet.* New York, Knopf, 1973; London, A. and C. Black, 1979.
Taper, Bernard, *Balanchine: A Biography.* New York, Macmillan, and London, Collier, 1974.

*

Geva and Danilova, Balanchine's first wife and mistress respectively, offer complementary information because both were with him in the small group of Russian ex-patriate dancers when they were absorbed into Diaghilev's company in 1924. One has to plough through 53 chapters of GEVA's sordid past life before Balanchine arrives, but what she says about him is revealing in those years around the Russian Revolution. Her descriptions of pettiness and jealousy in the Maryinsky, and of how Balanchine was ostracised by its management for being "too advanced" after the Revolution, is well told.

DANILOVA was also subsequently abandoned, though, like all Balanchine's past loves, she remained in touch with him and was often sought for particular roles. She has some vital comments on his methods of working: "*Apollon Musagete* . . . is now regarded as a landmark in dance history, a ballet that gave birth to a new era . . . revolutionary for the simple reason that at times we had to dance on flat feet—that was astonishing." She also remembers: "George trained me—he trained all of us to pay attention to the music. We had to count—it was all very precise . . . how exciting it could be to see someone dance right on top of the music."

During his time with Diaghilev, Balanchine became principal choreographer to the Ballets Russes; he was the only favoured man in the Grande Entourage without emotional connection; he was jealously regarded by both Massine and Lifar; and he established a lifelong artistic relationship with Stravinsky. The many books of correspondence and memoirs that principally concern Stravinsky should not be overlooked in deep research of Balanchine. They give flashes of insight into his steadfastness and manner of working from the composer's point of view, although they are not biographical in the true sense.

Balanchine's Complete Stories of the Great Ballets, edited by Francis Mason (1954) is by now rather out of date. Its use still holds for Balanchine's own words: a chronology of the Ballet between 1469–1953 scrupulously revised from several sources; 11 pages of autobiographical material—terse, frank, and professionally intact so far as it goes; notes and comments on children and Ballet; on dancers, dancing and choreography. In addition there is a reprint (from *Dance News* of 1949) of Balanchine's important article on Diaghilev 20 years after his death. All this is invaluable.

KIRSTEIN contains hundreds of pictures and charts the progress of the New York City Ballet, which he and Balanchine established in New York in 1934 (as Ballet Society). It is laid out like a diary, with its informative text as adjunct to and guide through the pictures. Balanchine becomes its main theme, an episodic biography through his choreography, until 1973.

The volume by BUCKLE AND TARAS is scrupulously researched. There are details of Balanchine's many romances,

marriages, and associations which all tend to show him to advantage. Balanchine passes on from one to another and the partings become inevitable rather than painful. Speaking of Balanchine's working methods, the authors write, "He always made a dance with one person in mind, and if another person were to dance it, he changed the steps. He never tried to make you look like someone else." And regarding his self-confidence and assertiveness they quote him saying to Diaghilev, who wanted to cut a variation of *Apollo*, "The choreography is fine. It's the dancer who is no good." Few would dare to do this, but Balanchine got his way.

TAPER's work has often been regarded as *the* biography, but he tends always to side with Balanchine at moments of doubt in behaviour. By contrast, Buckle and Taras' book is always evenhanded and generally more scholarly, though the two books together will give a sound reading of the very talented man who welded classical tradition on to modern Ballet by means of his own complete knowledge of the Dance and a trained musical background.

—Alan Jefferson

BALDWIN, James (Arthur), 1924–1987; American writer.

Eckman, Fern Marja, *The Furious Passage of James Baldwin.* London, M. Joseph, and New York, M. Evans, 1966.

Rosset, Lisa, *James Baldwin.* New York, Chelsea House, 1989.

Troupe, Quincy, editor, *James Baldwin: The Legacy.* New York, Simon and Schuster, 1989.

Weatherby, W. J., *Squaring Off: Mailer vs. Baldwin.* New York, Mason/Charter, and London, Robson Books, 1977.

Weatherby, W. J., *James Baldwin: Artist on Fire.* New York, D. I. Fine, 1989; London, M. Joseph, 1990.

*

Baldwin's 1961 *Nobody Knows My Name* signaled the writer's official entry into the civil rights movement as one of its most eloquent voices, and *The New Yorker*'s publication the following year of "Letter from a Region in My Mind" established him as a literary celebrity. Baldwin also had three bestsellers to his name by the time ECKMAN's biography was published; he was, nonetheless, at the relative midpoint of a long and frenetic career that would end 21 years after her profile of him appeared. Now out of print, Eckman's work is thus circumscribed by its early publication and by the fact that, inevitably, a good portion of its information—about Baldwin's troubled relationship with his stepfather, for example; his struggle with his first novel; the Greenwich Village days; his evolution as an impassioned spokesman for civil rights; and much else—is recounted and often amplified in Weatherby's *Artist on Fire.*

Despite these limitations, Eckman provides a worthy and readable introduction to Baldwin, and is worth a trip to a library to locate. She is an impressive writer who renders her subject and his energetic lifestyle in vivid and telling detail. Baldwin is

"jagged as a sliver," "salt rubbed in the wounds of the nation's conscience," "the shriek of the lynched." He resembles a "wood carving in a Gothic cathedral" and is "economically built, even stingily, tiny and narrow, so thin it is hard to believe he casts a shadow." Her detailed, lyrical descriptions of Baldwin's appearance and mannerisms capture him with an immediacy further heightened by her practice of transcribing interviews with the author with his repetitions, pauses, and emphases intact. She thus captures Baldwin's distinctively vigorous diction, lending to the pages a pleasing vitality apparent in lines such as these from his discussion of the Selma voter-registration drive: "And those *faces.* My God. You know? The face of the poor white in the South is a—a real *blasphemy.* A *real blasphemy.* Anyway, we started trying to feed the people. But the sheriff was not allowing anybody to talk to anyone on the line. You couldn't *talk* to them. You were not allowed to *talk* to them."

Additional attractions of Eckman's book are her lengthy treatment of Baldwin's high school years and his first hard-core encounter with racism at a job in New Jersey, as well as her inclusion of several essays and vignettes he composed for high school publications. Sometimes sentimental and limited in scope, articles such a "Harlem Then and Now" written for *The Douglass Pilot* nonetheless reveal an impressive young talent and are poignant pieces of Baldwin history. Much of the book is based on interviews with the author staged over roughly two and a half years, and Eckman also draws on the writer's works, newspaper and magazine articles by or about him, and interviews with acquaintances. A brief section of source notes appears at the conclusion, but the book is not indexed, nor are there appendices.

WEATHERBY's *Artist on Fire* is also based on numerous personal interviews—Weatherby knew Baldwin for 28 years—as well as interviews with friends and acquaintances, Baldwin's works, and a generous range of secondary sources. This new work essentially subsumes the Baldwin profile that appeared in Weatherby's *Squaring Off* (1977); thus the earlier book is valuable only to readers specifically interested in both Norman Mailer *and* Baldwin or their uneasy, sporadically friendly relationship. Like Eckman, Weatherby treats Baldwin's early years as a self-conscious boy who was teased about his protruding eyes and was simultaneously intimidated and enthralled by his brutal and melancholy stepfather David. But Weatherby surpasses Eckman to follow Baldwin's life through his publishing career and civic activism to his death from cancer of the esophagus at age 63.

Weatherby lacks the vivacious immediacy and poetic detail of Eckman, and the book suffers at times from a lack of transitions and occasionally has a jarring pastiche effect. Regardless, Weatherby provides a detailed and lengthy account of Baldwin's life, and the book's broader scope and its amplification of many aspects of the author's works, lifestyle, civil rights activities, and professional and personal relationships recommend it. While Eckman, for example, discusses Richard Wright's early mentorship of Baldwin, she does not, as Weatherby does, delve into Baldwin's marked uneasiness with his literary predecessor or the likelihood that the younger writer's seeming hostility stemmed from his sense of having failed Wright after both Harper and Doubleday rejected a manuscript of what would later be published as *Go Tell It on the Mountain.* Like Eckman, Weatherby

explores incidents such as Baldwin's abortive attempt to find some common ground with Robert Kennedy or the tempestuous staging of *Blues for Mister Charlie*, but goes into new territory as well to explore, for example, Baldwin's 20-year relationship with Dial Press and Dial editors such as E. L. Doctorow, his fascination with Henry James and that writer's influence on him, friendships with artist Beauford Delaney, writer William Styron, and many others. Weatherby occasionally succumbs to intrusive commentary on Baldwin's need to "knock literary father figures off their pedestals"—Wright and Faulkner apparently among them—a need allegedly born of Baldwin's own ambiguous attitude toward his stepfather. Weatherby does not attempt extensive literary analysis or interpretation but does chart critical and public reactions to Baldwin's various works through to the apparent waning of the writer's force.

Neither Eckman nor Weatherby deifies Baldwin, who emerges with the vagaries of his personality intact. He is portrayed as an impassioned, anguished artist and a generous, courageous activity committed to serving as witness to the plight of the black American. He also emerges as a prickly, volatile character, lax about repaying borrowed money and inclined to arrive extremely late or not at all for many commitments. Baldwin did maintain a breathless pace that could have undone a far less fragile individual, and yet he remained unrelenting in his civil rights activism, his commitment to his writing, and his immersion in a frenetic social life he largely orchestrated himself. Both books capture that energetic pace well.

To their credit, Eckman and Weatherby do not delve into Baldwin's love life in search of "kiss and tell" revelations, although it is clear he was regularly surrounded by an entourage not only of genuine friends but of hangers-on and would-be intimates—a fact he apparently took into stride with a certain resigned pride. Baldwin's ambiguity over his sexuality and his sense of being dispossessed by both race and possible illegitimacy are not skirted either. Aside from his brother David and his sister Gloria, the Baldwin family remains largely in the shadows, as do friends of long standing such as Lucien Happersberger. Perhaps the authorized biography now underway by close Baldwin associate David Adams Leeming will reveal more of them and their relationships with Baldwin. Weatherby provides a lengthy source notes section and a thorough index.

Two additional books released in 1989 may be helpful to readers interested in the details of Baldwin's life: ROSSET's *Black Americans of Achievement* biography targeted for junior high and high school audiences and TROUPE's collection of reminiscences, profiles, and literary analyses from Amiri Baraka, Toni Morrison, Henry Louis Gates, Jr., William Styron, Chinua Achebe, Mary McCarthy, and others. Rosset's volume is not footnoted but does provide an index and boasts dozens of interesting photographs of Baldwin, the Harlem of his childhood, and classic shots from the civil rights movement. The book focuses a good deal on the civil rights era and offers readers a Baldwin chronology, a list of his works, and a brief list of secondary sources. Troupe's collection also includes numerous photographs, many of them previously unpublished, and he has compiled an extensive bibliography of secondary sources on Baldwin's life and works. While not straight biography, Troupe contains relevant and honest recollections of Baldwin from many

who knew him well and also includes several Baldwin pieces—among them "Notes of a Native Son"—and interviews with the author. Like many anthologies, the book is not indexed.

—Anne Compliment

BALFOUR, Arthur James, 1848–1930; English statesman.

Dugdale, Blanche E. C., *Arthur James Balfour, First Earl of Balfour* (2 vols.). London, Hutchinson, 1936; New York, Putnam, 1937.

Egremont, Max, *Balfour: A Life of Arthur James Balfour*. London, Collins, 1980.

Mackay, Ruddock F., *Balfour: Intellectual Statesman*. Oxford and New York, Oxford University Press, 1985.

Young, Kenneth, *Arthur James Balfour: The Happy Life of the Politician, Prime Minister, Statesman, and Philosopher, 1848–1930*. London, G. Bell, 1953.

Zebel, Sydney H., *Balfour: A Political Biography*. London, Cambridge University Press, 1973.

*

In 1882, when asked about the future prospects of the young nephew of Lord Salisbury, the great Liberal Party leader Gladstone remarked that Balfour represented "the high and best type of English gentleman" who would someday be the leader of the Conservative party. Beatrice Webb, however, observed that Balfour never regarded politics very seriously but "as only part of a somewhat amusing game." These two statements illustrate the complexity and fascination of Balfour the man and politician.

Near the end of his life Balfour began to write his autobiography, but failing health forced him to give up the project; he instead cooperated with his niece Blanche DUGDALE in writing an authorized biography. The result of this collaboration is a well-written and sympathetic two-volume treatment of Balfour's life and political career. Volume one covers the period of Balfour's youth and political career up to his fall from power in 1906, while the second picks up with the Liberal victory and ends with Balfour's death in 1930.

Dugdale paints her uncle as a man of great talent who was often misunderstood because of his air of detachment and indolence. She argues that this style was largely dictated by Balfour's weak physical constitution and his philosophic nature. Furthermore, Balfour was deeply affected when at the age of 27 the woman he might have married died. Dugdale recounts the telling incident of Balfour's breakdown at her funeral. This image certainly is in contrast to the generally held notion of Balfour as the cool, unemotional intellectual. Dugdale rightfully acknowledges Balfour's many accomplishments, yet she also examines his failures. Dugdale's book still stands on its own merits as the starting point for any study of Balfour for either the beginning student or serious scholar.

Since the publication of Dugdale's work, the private and public records for the period have become available. Nevertheless, the subsequent biographies of Balfour have done little to alter the main lines of Dugdale's earlier work. Though written decades after Dugdale, YOUNG adds little to what is already known about Balfour. The writing style and documentation are at best indifferent, and the work is thus not very useful to either the general reader or scholar. Of some value is EGREMONT. Claiming access to previously unavailable papers (those of Balfour's secretary J. S. Sandars), Egremont offers an entertaining and informative look at Balfour. The chief value of the book is in it's readability and evocative portrait of the age Balfour lived in.

Two relatively short but good biographies by Zebel and Mackay round out the studies of Balfour. ZEBEL concentrates on Balfour's political career. He handles with authority the complexities of party politics of the period and gives solid coverage to Balfour's achievements after his tenure as prime minister. Never completely comfortable with speaking from the platform, Balfour's political style was intellectual and patrician. Since Balfour's most important contributions were in administration and defense, two areas not highly visible to the public, Zebel argues that he failed to receive the general recognition that he deserved. Zebel's writing style is clear and concise. His balanced study of Balfour's political career serves the needs of the general reader and student. Scholars will find little new in Zebel and will be disturbed by his tendency to rely at times on the published sources rather than the available primary documents.

MACKAY examines areas previously neglected by biographers. While his book skips over some of the more familiar aspects of Balfour's life and career, it should not be overlooked by anyone wishing to gain a better understanding of the subject. Mackay brings attention to Balfour's achievements in education, national defense, and foreign relations. Important new insights are provided into Balfour's intellectual life as a published philosopher and a Fellow of the Royal Society. Mackay also addresses some of the more delicate questions about Balfour's life by refuting the charges that he was either a hermaphrodite or homosexual.

But, above all, "born and bred" a Tory, Balfour put his considerable intellectual and political talents to work defending the establishment against the advancing forces of change. Mackay argues that Balfour's career in politics was a remarkable one of achievement, demise, and recovery. While he never enjoyed the public popularity of Gladstone or Joseph Chamberlain, Mackay concludes that Balfour's "courage, integrity, charm, and wit command much admiration and a good deal of affection."

—Van Michael Leslie

BALZAC, Honoré de, 1799–1850; French writer.

Bertault, Philippe, *Balzac and the Human Comedy*, translated by Richard Monges. New York, New York University Press, 1963.

Festa-McCormack, Diana, *Honoré de Balzac*. Boston, Twayne, 1979.

Gribble, Francis, *Balzac: The Man and the Lover*. London, Nash and Grayson, 1929; New York, Dutton, 1930.

Hunt, Herbert J., *Honoré de Balzac: A Biography*. London, Athlone Press, 1957.

Lawton, Frederick, *Balzac*. London, G. Richards, and New York, Wessels and Bissell, 1910.

Maurois, André, *Prometheus: The Life of Balzac*. New York, Harper, and London, Bodley Head, 1966 (originally published by Hachette, Paris, 1965).

Pritchett, V. S., *Balzac*. London, Chatto and Windus, and New York, Knopf, 1973.

Sandars, Mary F., *Honoré de Balzac: His Life and Writings*. London, J. Murray, 1904; New York, Dodd Mead, 1905.

Zweig, Stefan, *Balzac*, translated by William and Dorothy Rose. New York, Viking, 1946; London, Cassell, 1947.

*

The very early biographies of Balzac available in English are by now, as might be expected, from a purely scholarly point of view long out of date. SANDARS includes all the colourful elements of Balzac's life: the dreadful cash crises, the lunatic schemes for acquiring money, the 50,000 cups of coffee off which he lived and from which he died, the relationships with the Marquise de Castries and Mme Hanska, and the enormous intensity of the literary activity crammed into the period between *Les Chouans* of 1829 and Balzac's death in 1850. In a charming, competent, if unscholarly way, she makes the best of her subject's tempestuous life, almost ideal material for a biographer, offering plentiful amounts of such key ingredients as romantic and financial successes, with political ambition and literary fame, peaks of hope and chasms of failure thrown in for good measure. Even today it is impossible not to enjoy this biography. The period flavour adds to the fascination, as does the reasonably strict adherence to the known facts.

LAWTON wrote his life in order better to foster an appreciation of the *Comédie humaine*. He plods through the life, filling in the background with great sweeps of his brush and so obliterates any detailed sketching to appraise, for instance, what he calls the "Romantic School of fiction with its egoistic lyricism." Of Balzac's father we read that he was said to have "united in himself the Roman, the Gaul, and the Goth, and possessed the attributes of these three races in boldness, patience and health." The literary register of the biography is accurately indicated by the flatulence of its prose. It has out-served its purposes.

GRIBBLE, as his title suggests, makes no pretence to anything other than sensationalism. "Detailed criticism of Balzac's writings," we are told, "may be left to the Professors of Literature." As for the biographers, "[Balzac's] earlier biographers either did not know the facts or had reasons for distorting some of them and suppressing others." Gribble's attempts to put right these failings are not entirely successful. With the publication of the letters to Mme Hanska, Gribble tells us, we now know about one of the "world's famous love stories." That will surprise anyone who has read them. Also to be revealed, says the preface, is "the gruesome skeleton in the Balzac cupboard": an uncle of Balzac's "suffered the supreme penalty of the law for murder." This then is the equivalent of tabloid biography, together with the regulation feigning of shock and surprise.

FESTA-McCORMACK's monograph is invaluable for its chronology and annotated bibliography, the well-made index, and the excellent, succinct notes. However, the critical comments are controversial, and there is a very similar French volume now available in English, by BERTAULT, which does the same job in the same way but marginally better, and with greater critical skill.

PRITCHETT's book is intended to be a lavishly illustrated coffee-table introduction to Balzac, but it is nonetheless accurate and helpful. The text is naturally anecdotal, with wry smiles on every page. The material is presented factually, the illustrations are well chosen, and the book includes a good index and select bibliography.

For ten years after its appearance, ZWEIG's biography was undoubtedly the best introduction to Balzac available in English. Given its flamboyant subject, however, this is a somewhat dull book, smoothly written, but without scruple with regard to the occasional embellishment of historical fact. Zweig had the advantage of being able to draw on André Billy's fine two-volume *Vie de Balzac* (1944), ignored for instance by Festa-McCormack, but Zweig's rather heavy treatment of so colourful a character is almost astonishingly pedestrian, and the book has not been served well by its translators.

The greatest English authority on Balzac of recent years has been HUNT, whose critical work has been supplemented by an outstanding, if relatively brief, biography (whereas Bertault puts his biographical material together with his critical and historical account of the novels into a single book). The chief quality of Hunt's biography remains the balance born of long acquaintance. He deplores equally, for instance, indignation against Mme Hanska, who finally consented to marry Balzac in the year of his death, and sentimentality in her favour. Hunt shows considerable psychological perceptivity in tracing Balzac's changes of mood throughout his packed adult life, as well as the vicissitudes in his relationships with those closest to him. Hunt's only discernible shortcoming as a biographer is to wish that history had been other than it was. Such remarks as "One cannot but regret" and "It is permissible to regret" are warning signs when they slip from an historian's pen that he is finding it difficult to tell the truth, a duty however that in the end Hunt does not fail to perform.

MAUROIS quotes 25 Balzac specialists in the introduction to his biography and another score in the notes, but he "has sought to fill a gap" on the grounds that Billy and Zweig wrote "before the recent great flowering of Balzac scholarship." Maurois' style is vivid: "Balzac was by turns a saint, a criminal, an honest judge, a corrupt judge, a minister, a fop, a harlot, a duchess, and always a genius." If his re-creation of the life is vivid, his interpretations, lurking everywhere, are on the whole convincing. This is now the best non-scholarly introduction to the work of Balzac, and among the best biographies in English. It is quite lengthy, with a rather perfunctory bibliography, an index, and a chronology of works. Though the style is lively, there are exaggerations and distortions of the truth. The more scholarly biography by Hunt is to be preferred.

—A. H. T. Levi

BARTÓK, Béla, 1881–1945; Hungarian composer.

Antokoletz, Elliott, *Béla Bartók: A Guide to Research.* New York and London, Garland, 1988.

Bónis, Ferenc, editor, *Béla Bartók: His Life in Pictures and Documents,* translated by Sára Karig and Lili Halápy. New York and London, Boosey and Hawkins, 1964; translation revised by Kenneth McRobbie, New York, Belwin Mills, 1972 (originally published by Corvina, Budapest, 1964).

Demény, János, editor, *Béla Bartók Letters,* translated by Péter Balabán and István Farkas. New York, St. Martin's, and London, Faber, 1971 (originally published by Corvina, Budapest, 1971).

Fassett, Agatha, *Béla Bartók's Last Years: The Naked Face of Genius.* Boston, Houghton Mifflin, and London, Gollancz, 1958; as *Béla Bartók: The American Years,* New York, Dover, 1970.

Griffiths, Paul, *Bartók.* London, Dent, 1984.

Haraszti, Emil, *Béla Bartók: His Life and Works,* translated by Dorothy Swainson. Paris, Lyrebird Press, 1938.

Helm, Everett, *Bartók.* London, Faber, 1971; New York, Crowell, 1972.

Juhász, Vilmos, *Bartók's Years in America.* Washington, D.C., Occidental Press, 1981.

Lesznai, Lajos, *Bartók,* translated by Percy M. Young. New York, Octagon, and London, Dent, 1973.

Milne, Hamish, *Bartók: His Life and Times.* Tunbridge Wells, Midas Books, and New York, Hippocrene Books, 1982.

Moreux, Serge, *Béla Bartók,* translated by G. S. Fraser and Erik de Mauny. London, Harvill Press, 1953; New York, Vienna House, 1974 (originally published as *Béla Bartók: Sa Vie, son Oeuvre, son Langage,* Paris, R. Masse, 1949).

Stevens, Halsey, *The Life and Music of Béla Bartók.* New York, Oxford University Press, 1953.

Tallián, Tibor, *Béla Bartók: The Man and His Work.* Budapest, Gondolat, 1981.

Ujfalussy, József, *Béla Bartók,* translated by Ruth Pataki. Boston, Crescendo Publishing, 1972 (originally published by Corvina, Budapest, 1971).

*

The full biographies of Béla Bartók divide naturally into "major" and "minor" categories. The major works are those by Stevens, still the most important single work on the composer in English, Ujfalussy, Tallián, and Griffiths. The others, though each has its virtues, must be viewed as supplementary.

STEVENS' biography, remarkable in that it appeared so soon after the composer's death, combines a concentrated, thorough overview of the life in its first half, carefully laid out chronologically, with penetrating discussion of the music constituting its second half. Stevens treats Bartók's life and his music equally well, and in an equally clear fashion, something most of the other biographers handle less successfully. That Stevens was himself a distinguished composer lends weight to his comments on Bartók's music.

UJFALUSSY is especially good at tracing political complications in Hungary, and their effect on Bartók's life and work, during the early years of this century. Writing, so to speak, from the inside, Ujfalussy is also perceptive in his discussion of Bartók's folksong collecting and research. The same can be said of TALLIÁN, who is at least equal to Ujfalussy in his understanding of the political influences on Bartók, and who exploits Bartók's letters to a greater extent. Tallián's critical treatment of the music is highly intelligent though often somewhat romantic in tone. GRIFFITHS concentrates much more heavily on the music than any of the others, employing purely biographical data largely as a series of pegs upon which to hang musical discussion. Griffiths provides abundant musical illustrations.

Of the remaining biographers, all treating Bartók's life to a lesser extent, LESZNAI spends two-thirds of his space on the composer's life and work up to the early 1920s, with correspondingly less emphasis on the significant years of his maturity. MOREUX, writing at a time when Bartók's name was not yet the household word it was to become, is dated, though his volume is interesting for its concentration on the folksong influence in Bartók and its preface by Arthur Honegger. HELM's book is scarcely more than a monograph and, like those by Lesznai and Griffiths, is one in a composers series. It is notable for its large number of illustrations.

MILNE's volume, though brief, is concentrated and contains some illustrations not duplicated elsewhere. A recent work, it expresses a more contemporary view of the composer's stature. HARASZTI is fascinating in his presentation of a composer whose reputation at the time of publication had just begun to spread through the musical world. It is a precious document from Bartók's lifetime, indicating that at least within the intellectual circles of music Bartók already was a figure of importance, though his worldwide significance would have to wait another two decades for full recognition. Sándor Veress' introduction is noteworthy.

A number of other works add considerably to the body of material on Bartók. ANTOKOLETZ's exploration of documents by and about the composer is encyclopedic, with almost 900 entries in a variety of languages, carefully and thoughtfully annotated. It is indispensable to serious Bartók research. DEMÉNY's collection of nearly 300 letters, with extensive notes by the author, provides insight into the mind of one of musical history's most reclusive geniuses. It forms part of Demény's decades-long study of the composer, much of which remains untranslated.

BÓNIS' book brings together the richest collection of photographs of Bartók and his milieu now available. It is especially valuable in depicting sites and persons connected with the composer's youth and formative years, and also contains programs, early manuscript excerpts, and many other documents. Its preface is an excellent short biography. The FASSETT and JUHÁSZ volumes are curiosities, concentrating as they do on Bartók's American years, though in different ways. Fassett's little book is personal, sentimental, open to the charge of inaccuracy but compelling and moving all the same. Juhász records oral comments by a number of unnamed friends and associates of Bartók during his exile. Its tone combines the hagiographical with the political, one of its admitted purposes being to counteract the co-optation of Bartók by the Communist regime in Hungary. Nevertheless, Juhász provides another and broader glimpse of Bartók's final years.

—Frederic Goossen

BASIE, Count [William], 1904–1984; American jazz composer, bandleader, and pianist.

Dance, Stanley, *The World of Count Basie*. New York, Scribner, and London, Sidgwick and Jackson, 1980.

Hodie, Andre, *Toward Jazz*. New York, Grove, 1962.

Horricks, Raymond, *Count Basie and His Orchestra: Its Music and Musicians*. London, Citadel Press, 1957.

Morgan, Alum, *Count Basie*. New York, Hippocrene, and Tunbridge Wells, Spellmount, 1984.

Schuller, Gunther, *The History of Jazz* (vol. I: *Early Jazz*, and vol. II: *The Swing Era*). New York, Oxford University Press, 1968, 1989.

Shapiro, Nat and Nat Hentoff, editors, *The Jazzmakers*. New York, Rinehart, 1957.

Sheridan, Chris, *Count Basie: A Bio-Discography*. New York, Greenwood Press, and London Greenwood/Eurospan, 1986.

*

At the time of publication, HORRICKS purported to be a full-scale study of Basie's roles as a pianist and bandleader as well as a discussion of his influence on jazz generally. Written approximately two-thirds of the way through Basie's career, it is not a complete survey of the life, nor does it have much critical rigor. Its most enduring feature is the large section given over to biographical sketches of Basie's numerous sidemen.

MORGAN, who had done a highly-acclaimed Basie discography for Horrick's book, later produced a short biography (70 pp.) for the *Jazz Masters Series* that was published at the time of Basie's death and thus covers the entire career. It is organized chronologically, contains much quoted material from Basie's contemporaries, and is quite laudatory. It does not probe deeply into the basic issues of Basie's distinctive musical style, his achievement as a long-lasting bandleader, or his relationship to other Big Bands and performers of the time. The book is graced by a number of excellent photographs and a short but useful discography.

A few essays are discerning in their discussion of Basie and his role in American popular music. SHAPIRO's chapter "William 'Count' Basie," in an anthology of articles about significant jazz artists, provides a balanced, favorable view of Basie which, although it was written in the late 1950s, emphasizes points that have endured as the legacy. Basie's role as a leader who exercised a persuasive but not oppressive control over his men both on and off the stand is stressed. Discussions of his pianistic style and his ability to convey musical leadership through his control of the rhythm section are also excellent.

HODIE's two essays on Basie from a collection of his articles on jazz are most probing, although neither essay deals with the bandleader's most celebrated achievement: the refinement of the swing beat. "The Count Basie Riddle" (1954, pp. 97–108) is an analysis of Basie's ability to achieve such sophistication in his piano performances with seemingly so few notes and minimal effort. "Basie's Way" (1957, pp. 109–16) is a discussion of the relentless drive of the band to swing as a unit and the price that such precision exacted on the band members' abilities to swing as individual soloists.

In both of SCHULLER's extensive volumes, Basie's contributions to the stylistic evolution of jazz are treated. His role as pianist in the Kansas City bands, the Blue Devils and Benny Moten, is discussed briefly in *Early Jazz*. His work with his own bands is analyzed more extensively in *The Swing Era*, some 40 pages under "The Quintessence of Swing." Although Basie's important role in the development of swing rhythm is acknowledged, Schuller criticizes the bandleader as relying too much on melodic clichés.

As yet no definitive biography of Basie has been written; however, two Basie scholars have published works that will contribute significantly toward such a study. DANCE's collection of 34 interviews with Basie's musical associates throughout his career can serve as very useful source material. SHERIDAN's bio-discography is a massive 1,350-page typescript with extensive sections of text containing biographical information inserted among various parts of the discography. Sheridan calls his work a chronicle of Basie's life rather than a biography. He does not attempt to develop any themes that span the biographical detail; however, he does provide a four-page Prologue that is an outstanding summary of Basie's achievement.

Basie's autobiography, *Good Morning Blues: The Autobiography of Count Basie as Told to Albert Murray* (New York, Random House, 1985), published a year after his death, is the best source for the present about the unfolding of the bandleader's life and his reactions to the numerous people with whom he was associated. It is more authoritative than the usual "as told to" autobiography of a celebrity. Writer Albert Murray had Basie's full cooperation with interviews as well as notes and tapes that the bandleader had kept over the years. Basie's high level of professionalism and his dedication to the perfection of his own style throughout one of the longest careers in jazz make impressive leitmotifs, although the reader may find tedious Murray's dutiful accounting of one engagement, tour, or band after another spanning this half-century career.

—William K. Kearns

BAUDELAIRE, Charles, 1821–1867; French poet.

Burton, Richard D. E., *Baudelaire in 1859: A Study in the Sources of Poetic Creativity*. Cambridge and New York, Cambridge University Press, 1988.

Carter, A. E., *Charles Baudelaire*. Boston, Twayne, 1977.

De Jonge, Alex, *Baudelaire, Prince of Clouds: A Biography*. New York, Paddington Press, 1976.

Hemmings, F. W. J., *Baudelaire the Damned*. London, Hamilton, and New York, Scribner, 1982.

Hyslop, Lois Boe and Francis E. Hyslop, Jr., editors, *Baudelaire: A Self-Portrait: Selected Letters*. London and New York, Oxford University Press, 1957.

Hyslop, Lois Boe, *Baudelaire: Man of His Time*. New Haven, Connecticut, and London, Yale University Press, 1980.

Jones, Percy Mansell, *Baudelaire*. London, Bowes, and New Haven, Connecticut, Yale University Press, 1952.

Pichois, Claude, with additional research by Jean Ziegler, *Baudelaire*, translated by Graham Robb. London, Hamilton, 1989.

Ruff, Marcel A., *Baudelaire*, translated by Agnes Kertesz. New York, New York University Press, and London, University of London Press, 1966 (originally published by Hatier-Boivin, Paris, 1957).

Sartre, Jean-Paul, *Baudelaire*, translated by Martin Turnell. London, Horizon Press, 1949; New York, New Directions, 1950 (originally published by Gallimard, Paris, 1947).

Shanks, Lewis P., *Baudelaire: Flesh and Spirit*. London, Noel Douglas, and Boston, Little Brown, 1930.

Starkie, Enid, *Baudelaire*. London, Gollancz, and New York, Putnam, 1933; revised edition, London, Faber, 1957.

Symons, Arthur, *Charles Baudelaire: A Study*. London, E. Matthews, and New York, Dutton, 1920.

Williams, Roger L., *The Horror of Life: Charles Baudelaire, Jules de Goncourt, Gustave Flaubert, Guy de Maupassant, Alphonse Daudet*. London, Weidenfeld and Nicolson, and Chicago, University of Chicago Press, 1980.

*

The problems inherent in writing the life of any French poet (in what language to quote his poetry? how to convey the quality of his literary achievement?) are exacerbated in the case of Baudelaire by the fact that, were it not for his relatively sparse writings, his life would form a singularly dispiriting catalogue of failures, frustrations, and complaints, added to which are the constantly querulous tone of his letters, the lack of direct information about some of the key figures in his existence, notably his mulatto mistress Jeanne Duval and the still unidentified J. G. F., and, above all, the aura of perversion and satanism that clung to his name for so long after the trial and condemnation of *Les Fleurs du Mal* (1857).

It is no doubt because of the latter condition that English-speaking readers had to wait so long for any attempt to present these problems with an account of Baudelaire's life. This eventually came in the 1920 study by SYMONS, the poet and critic whose *The Symbolist Movement in Literature* in 1899 had made him into the leading exponent of modern French poetry in the English-speaking world. Only a relatively small part of the book is devoted to Baudelaire's life, since Symons' main aim is to persuade his readers to take Baudelaire seriously as a great poet by means of an enthusiastic appreciation of his works, linking them to the poetic glories of the past.

It was not until ten years later that the first real biography of Baudelaire appeared in English. Still apparently preoccupied with the poet's scandalous reputation, SHANKS sets out to prove that Baudelaire was a "sensitive and sentimental poet." The result is a recital of the then known facts of Baudelaire's life, couched in a somewhat effusive style, with no bibliography, no references, and with the poetry rendered into rather stilted English verse.

Soon thereafter, in 1933, appeared the first version of STARKIE's biography, rewritten and revised in 1957. This is a far more scholarly work, with a great deal of detail and based on much original research. Its style is however undistinguished and the chapters of literary criticism may strike one nowadays as old-fashioned, but in its time it was extremely influential in establishing Baudelaire outside France as a poet of genius and a reputable subject for academic study. As Joanna Richardson has rightly said, in her book about Enid Starkie, "It was left to her to suggest the causes of [Baudelaire's] emotional problems, to indicate his depth and his significance, to present him as an idealist and a moralist, a man who had profoundly studied society and himself. It was left to her to place Baudelaire in his literary context: to show, at a time when he was excluded from every university syllabus, that he was among the pre-eminent French poets." The thoroughness of the 1957 edition of this massive work was such that there seemed little need for another English life of Baudelaire for some considerable time, though in 1957, the year of the centenary of *Les Fleurs du Mal*, there was also published a book exemplifying a different approach to biography: this is the volume by the HYSLOPs, which, as its subtitle indicates, is a portrait of the poet that emerges from a selection of his letters, translated and edited with a running commentary.

1957 had also seen the publication in French of RUFF's book on the man and his works, in a series primarily aimed at French students. A slightly abridged English translation appeared in 1966. The biographical part is necessarily restricted in scope, but the book as a whole gives a penetrating account of Baudelaire's personality and his writings. Similar in intention is CARTER's volume in Twayne's World Authors series. Like Ruff, Carter was an established Baudelaire scholar, and both books can be recommended as judicious introductions to Baudelaire, though the account they give of his life is inevitably perfunctory.

The next full-scale life of Baudelaire in English after Starkie's was that written by DE JONGE. As its title implies, it concentrates more on the outwardly picturesque side of the poet's existence: it contains little in the way of scholarly apparatus and it is not of any great psychological or critical profundity. But it is written in a lively style, disfigured by occasional bouts of petulance when contemporaries of Baudelaire are castigated for having behaved badly toward him (Maxime Du Camp is a "vile little man," the "foolishness" of the "ignoble" Sainte-Beuve is alleged to elicit "tears of impotent rage" from the biographer). Much more profound, serious, and sober is the book by HEMMINGS, which goes beyond the outward peculiarities of Baudelaire's behaviour to the religious torments that are at the heart of his experience, and which recognizes that it is impossible to present a wholly unproblematical narration of the facts of his existence. Also from the beginning of the 1980s dates the second HYSLOP book about Baudelaire, which complements the earlier self-portrait by a series of brief essays on his dealings with his contemporaries—artists, sculptors, musicians, thinkers, and politicians, as well as men of letters.

Mention should be made of four other books containing information on Baudelaire's life. JONES' little volume contains only the briefest of biographical sketches. Two other works deal with particular aspects of the poet's life, but their quality is such that no biographer could afford to ignore them. WILLIAMS provides a scrupulous examination of the whole of Baudelaire's medical history in his study of the effects of syphilis on five 19th-century French authors. BURTON focuses on the year 1859, argued to be vital in the poet's career, a three-month stay with his mother in Honfleur having led to an unexampled if short period of literary creativity. SARTRE's famous and controversial essay on Baudelaire is rather short on facts and sometimes cavalier in its assessment of them; in addition to which it appears implacably hostile to the poet in its dissection of his psyche. As Sartre's

first attempt at existential psychoanalysis, it is nevertheless an approach to a kind of life-story that retains at least some of its methodological interest.

In recent years, knowledge of Baudelaire's life has been transformed by the discovery of hitherto unknown letters and documents, by studies of his friends and associates, and by revision of the dating of old material. This means that the only biography of Baudelaire that takes account of all the facts unearthed up to now is that by PICHOIS; originally published in French in 1987, it has been expertly translated and somewhat adapted by Graham Robb, a British Baudelaire scholar. Because it is so full and based on such massively complete erudition, it is an unequalled and authoritative source of information, even though some readers may find its sheer weight of detail slightly oppressive.

—A. W. Raitt

BEARDSLEY, Aubrey, 1872–1898; English illustrator.

Benkovitz, Miriam J., *Aubrey Beardsley, an Account of His Life*. New York, Putnam, and London, Hamilton, 1981.

Brophy, Brigid, *Black and White: A Portrait of Aubrey Beardsley*. London, Cape, 1968; New York, Stein and Day, 1969.

Brophy, Brigid, *Beardsley and His World*. London, Thames and Hudson, and New York, Harmony, 1976.

Easton, Malcolm, *Aubrey and the Dying Lady: A Beardsley Riddle*. London, Secker and Warburg, and Boston, Godine, 1972.

Heyd, Milly, *Aubrey Beardsley: Symbol, Mask, and Self-Irony*. New York, P. Lang, 1986.

Langenfeld, Robert, editor, *Reconsidering Aubrey Beardsley*. Ann Arbor, Michigan, and London, UMI Research Press, 1989.

Reade, Brian and Frank Dickinson, *Aubrey Beardsley: Exhibition at the Victoria and Albert Museum*. London, Her Majesty's Stationary Office, 1966.

Reade, Brian, *Beardsley*. London, Studio Vista, 1967; as *Aubrey Beardsley*, New York, Viking, 1967.

Weintraub, Stanley, *Beardsley: A Biography*. London, W. H. Allen, and New York, G. Brazillier, 1967.

Weintraub, Stanley, *Aubrey Beardsley: Imp of the Perverse*. University Park, Pennsylvania State University Press, 1976.

*

LANGENFELD's volume offers a century-long listing of works on Beardsley, collected by Nicholas Salerno, which of course includes all the items offered here. This "Annotated Secondary Bibliography" presents 1566 works, in alphabetical order by author, and thus becomes the indispensible instrument for the study of the man and his work. Part one of the text, "Beardsley in Time" contains nine essays that consider the artist's life and art through his relation to and understanding of the art, social life, and psychological and critical currents of the 1890s.

READE (1967), a leading Beardsley researcher, produced here what is considered the best collection of image and annotation; his longer essay offers interpretation of some of Beardsley's motifs in terms of his sexuality and his presumed homosexuality. Such speculation, including incest with his sister, prevalent in many writers—Brophy and Benkovitz avoid the territory for the most part—angers and exasperates Salerno, who claims that "the evidence is simply not there, or has yet to be revealed . . . Beardsley the man comes through as asexual, as an artist given to cerebral debauchery only." Reade was also the organizer of the major Beardsley exhibition, and his 1966 catalog is filled with various essays, including Reade's biographical sketch, all pertaining to Beardsley's life, art, and influence.

The first contemporary biography of Beardsley is that of WEINTRAUB (1967), still regarded as the most synthetic life study. Weintraub presents a straightforward marshalling of details of Beardsley's family and social life, and his extensive knowledge of other writers' memoirs from Beardsley's era is used to present an objective picture of various key moments in the artist's career. Weintraub's achievement is held all the more interesting because he had not had access to Beardsley's unexpurgated letters. These became available in Henry Maas, J. L. Duncan, and W. G. Wood, *The Letters of Aubrey Beardsley* (London, 1970). This volume presents the correspondence chronologically, with many annotations and concise biographical introductions to various periods in Beardsley's life. Although the collection has been judged meticulous in its editing, dissent has focused on the moralizing attitude of the editors. Moreover, most of the letters come from the period 1896–98, when the artist had to leave London. And so a dark and mysterious figure emerges—removed from his larger personality—under the strain of mortal illness and the necessary self-banishment.

WEINTRAUB (1976) wanted only to revise his earlier, well-received work; but reacting to the changed climate of the 1970s, which permitted certain tales to be told, and newly available documents—both Beardsley's and those of his contemporaries—he decided upon a totally new work. Here as well he was able to react to the criticism that his first book had treated visual analysis without confidence.

BENKOVITZ, like Weintraub, is loathe to speculate about either psychological or aesthetic problems. A thoroughly researched work, it attempts a literal re-telling of Beardsley's life, with few illustrations. While his focus is on Beardsley's most productive period, 1894–98, Benkovitz concentrates on his character and his relationships to family and often celebrated friends.

In a different approach, HEYD offers a psychological study in which she affirms the closeness of Beardsley's best known artistic motifs to his life—a life and an art without sentiment, ironic and aesthetically aloof. The work presents a detailed study of the 19th-century background and examines the personal meaning and possible psychological significance for the artist in his use of Wagner, the Pierrot, embryos, dwarfs, hermaphrodites, Pan, and the *femme fatale*.

EASTON, who apparently views the artist as a transvestite with transsexual fantasies, focuses on Beardsley's sexuality. Easton offers an extended picture, with allusions to secret documents, of Beardsley's homosexual friends and also of his sister Mabel, who is felt to hold the secret of Beardsley's life, if not his art. General agreement holds that Easton's heated assertions are all inconclusive.

BROPHY (1976) provides a psychological study of Beardsley's life and personality. She gives careful attention to his relationship with his mother and his early life and their continuing

influence on his art and life. Brophy also focuses on Beardsley's sister. Photographs of the artist and his friends, as well as his places of residence, produce a more intimate view. This work was the culmination of Brophy's interest in Beardsley that had begun with her attraction to his response to Victorian philistinism. Brophy's earlier focus (1968) had been primarily analytical, and biographical information had been related to artworks, their themes and attitudes.

—Joshua Kind

BEAUMONT, Francis, 1584–1616; FLETCHER, John, 1579–1625; English playwrights and collaborators.

Bliss, Lee, *Francis Beaumont*. Boston, Twayne, 1987.
Gayley, Charles M., *Beaumont, the Dramatist*. New York, Century, 1914; as *Francis Beaumont, Dramatist*, London, Duckworth, 1914.
Squier, Charles L., *John Fletcher*. Boston, Twayne, 1986.
Wallis, Lawrence B., *Fletcher, Beaumont, and Company: Entertainers to the Jacobean Gentry*. New York, King's Crown Press, 1947.

*

Any biography of Francis Beaumont, Elizabethan-Jacobean dramatist, must inevitably devote considerable space to his collaboration with John Fletcher, Shakespeare's heir as lead dramatist of the King's Men. Recognizing this responsibility, GAYLEY explores the playwrights' collaboration in detail, attempting to identify the signature stylistic traits of each man. One of Gayley's chief goals is to carve out a canon for Beaumont while acknowledging that any effort to sunder these twins is impossible.

Gayley begins by impressing on the minds of his readers that the family roots of the two playwrights differ significantly. Beaumont was the son of Sir Francis Beaumont, a justice of the Common Pleas court and descendant of a respected Anglo-Norman household. The baronial estate of Grace-Dieu, located near Nottingham, was renowned for its architectural magnificence and its breathtaking setting in Charnwood Forest. The biographer makes a good deal of Beaumont's childhood experiences roaming freely in the woods and on the greenswards of this pastoral estate. (In this he seems to be following Wordsworth's idealized account of the boy's natural education.) Yet Francis and his brother John also "breathed an atmosphere of literature and national life," which led them to compose verse of great promise at an early age.

Francis and his brothers John and Henry were admitted to Oxford in 1597. Beaumont did not take a degree but instead entered the Inner Temple, one of the Inns of Court, to seek a law degree. This enterprise led to another dead end, and the next we hear of Francis is as author of *Salmacis and Hermaphroditus,* a lengthy erotic poem in the Ovidian tradition. Gayley believes that this poem won Beaumont recognition from other Elizabethan poets, most notably Ben Jonson. Both Beaumont and Fletcher contributed commendatory verses to the 1607 edition of

Volpone, suggesting that the young men met when they entered the "circle of Ben." Using evidence of Jonson's influence on his style—humor characters, a disdain for popular taste, a satiric manner—Gayley argues strongly for Beaumont's sole authorship of *The Woman-Hater* (1607).

Although the collaboration between Beaumont and Fletcher began in 1608, with the production of their first tragicomedy *Philaster*, Beaumont, according to Gayley, probably followed his first humor comedy with another satire, this time of apprentice-knight romances, *The Knight of the Burning Pestle* (1608?). Gayley uses tests of "diction and manner of thought" to support his claim of single authorship. He also believes that Beaumont was capable of selecting material and prose forms to suit the variety of characters and scenes required by this entertaining burlesque.

Of special interest in Gayley's study is his painstaking effort to piece out the individual contributions of Beaumont and Fletcher to the 50 or more plays on which they reportedly labored. His identification of Beaumont's stylistic signature—his affinity for burlesque and satire, his gift for writing heroic verse, his "critical" faculty—represents a significant contribution to early 20th-century scholarship. He traces Beaumont's controlling hand in several of the major tragicomedies and the playwrights' chief tragedy, *The Maid's Tragedy*. Recent studies have concluded, however, that verse tests and stylistic analyses, lacking any external supporting evidence, are suspect tools for determining contributions to collaborative literary products. Gayley's book may be fairly reliable as a description of the facts of Beaumont's life and times, but it is not as useful as a critical study of the plays or as an analysis of the role of each playwright in the received canon.

BLISS' critical biography follows the prescriptive Twayne formula, although the book also attempts to describe Beaumont's unique contribution to the collaboration and to Elizabethan-Jacobean drama. The biographer examines the literary friendship of Beaumont and Jonson, citing the "warm, even jocular, tone" of Beaumont's commendatory verses to several of Jonson's plays as evidence of a close relationship. These verse epistles are written in heroic couplets that approach the grace and sophistication of those composed by the master. Worth particular notice, according to Bliss, is Dryden's remark that Jonson submitted his compositions to Beaumont's censure, even seeking the aid of his friend in "contriving" plots. This claim appears extravagant and revisionist, but it does lend support to the widely held belief among contemporaries that Beaumont's "sterner muse" controlled the extravagance of Fletcher's imagination.

Bliss' survey of the playwright's life and work incorporates an impressive amount of recent scholarship. The book proffers the somewhat bold claim tht Beaumont the gentleman may have taken special pains to avoid identification with plays commonly attributed to him. He either turned "quasi-professional" out of a temporary need for money or remained financially secure while he undertook playwrighting out of interest or to follow the path beaten by friends. His marriage to Ursula Isely and sudden departure from London seem to suggest that he grew disillusioned with the theatrical and/or political scene. The retirement could as well have been a decision prompted by "a gentleman's sense that marriage and the prospect of heirs necessitated a change of life-style."

This interesting thesis makes Bliss' biography worth reading. She agrees with Gayley (and other critics) that Beaumont's is the major contribution to *A King and No King* and *The Maid's Tragedy*. She also praises *The Knight of the Burning Pestle* as a comedy of "rare originality." Bliss concludes that Beaumont rcmains an elusive figure whose early work showed a distinctive ironic cast. The body of drama traceable to his hand is too small to justify useful generalizations about his dramatic achievement. But Bliss observes that time has been kinder to Beaumont than Fletcher, primarily because of the critical respect for the satiric wit and metadramatic dimensions of *The Knight of the Burning Pestle*.

SQUIER's first chapter, "Master John Fletcher, Playwright: The Life," is an excellent, factual, and concise survey of the little that is known about the playwright's life and career. Squier likewise includes a short biographical account of Francis Beaumont's life in the same chapter. His description of their collaboration employs the latest and most reliable scholarship on the subject. The book offers a useful chronology that contains information about Fletcher's life and dates of publication and performance of his plays.

WALLIS' fifth chapter, "The Time, The Place, The Men," provides a readable, though sometimes openly conjectural, account of the playwrights' careers in the Jacobean theater. Fletcher's association with the King's Men and his collaboration with Shakespeare are subjects treated with care and insight here. Wallis also attempts to define the exact nature of Ben Jonson's influence—as political and aesthetic mentor—on both Beaumont and Fletcher.

—Robert F. Willson, Jr.

BEAUVOIR, Simone de. See **DE BEAUVOIR, Simone.**

BECKET, Saint Thomas. See **THOMAS À BECKET.**

BECKETT, Samuel, 1906–1989; Irish writer.

Bair, Dierdre, *Samuel Beckett: A Biography*. New York, Harcourt, and London, Cape, 1978.

Cohn, Ruby, *Back to Beckett*. Princeton, New Jersey, Princeton University Press, 1973.

Cooke, Virginia, *Beckett on File*. London and New York, Methuen, 1985.

Federman, Raymond and John Fletcher, *Samuel Beckett: His Works and His Critics*. Berkeley, University of California Press, 1970.

Gontarski, S. E., editor, *On Beckett: Essays and Criticism*. New York, Grove, 1986.

Kenner, Hugh, *Samuel Beckett: A Critical Study.* New York, Grove, 1961; London, Calder, 1962; revised and expanded edition, Berkeley, University of California Press, 1968.

O'Brein, Eoin, *The Beckett Country: Samuel Beckett's Ireland.* Dublin, Black Cat Press, in association with London, Faber, 1986.

*

Once asked why he declined requests for interviews, Samuel Beckett replied, "No views to inter." This anecdote sums up the justifications for Beckett's request not to have a biography written about him during his lifetime. When a man spends his life "trying to eff the ineffable," it is painful for him to imagine his own brief existence perpetuated in print. He actually requested that scholars not deal with his personal life, a request respectfully honored by every scholar who ever dealt with his work.

Except one. BAIR worked from a graduate student's perspective, despite every cordial request on the part of Beckett not to do so, including his more than gracious remark that he would neither help nor hinder her work. The result is critical analysis largely uninformed, questionable scholarship, and rhetoric with a bias. With very limited resources, mostly letters to Thomas McGreevy, Bair puts together something that satisfied her Ph.D. requirement but little else. Even acknowledging Beckett's "desperate attempts to guard his privacy against the encroachments of celebrity," Bair's underlying tone, one of crassness if not downright disrespect, has removed her study from serious consideration.

Scholars dealing with Beckett's work from a more enlightened point of view have had occasion to briefly note some biographical facts, such as Beckett's dialogues with George Duithuit, in which he states his now famous *raison d'être* for art: "nothing to express . . . but the obligation to express." COHN briefly discusses Beckett's early life and inserts a biographical paragraph in front of each chapter, placing the work to be discussed in Beckett's chronology, and adds photos of Beckett's birthplace and Paris apartment building. Several essays in GONTARSKI discusses Beckett's inaccessability to the casually curious but generosity and candor to friends.

In KENNER's critical study, some of Beckett's biography is inserted discreetly to form a basis for Beckett's approach to his work, but the real thrust is a study of the philosophical basis for the bleak view Beckett presents in all his work. His association with James Joyce, especially during the writing of *Finnegan's Wake,* puts Beckett in any Joyce biography as well. A strong bibliographical document by FEDERMAN AND FLETCHER does everything to order Beckett's writing chronologically; his Irish heritage and early Paris years are not a secret. This definitive (to 1970) bibliography, annotated with marvelous detail concerning Beckett's publishing career, is indispensable for all subsequent scholarship. It contains a considerable amount of biographical information, especially regarding Beckett's associations with Joyce.

COOKE's work, part of the series of "Writers On File" information sources from Metheun, contains chronologies and brief critical comments on each work. O'BRIEN offers a wonderful coffee-table book, as much about Dublin and Ireland as about Beckett. The views come not only from Beckett's own life but from the literary references throughout his work. By photo-

graphing Beckett's homeland, and inserting quotations from the work, the book becomes both an album of remembrances and a sketchbook for ideas. O'Brien finds information on Beckett's old motorcycle, for example, and supplies a catalog photo of it.

Any number of Beckett's close friends could have written his biography from a scholarly and personal perspective. A. J. (Con) Levanthal, Calvin Israel, John Kobler, his editors and publishers, all adhered to Beckett's request to refrain during his lifetime. Now very promising on the horizon is the authorized biography by James Knowlson, Director of the Beckett Archives at Reading University. This will be a major literary event (Knowlson has set aside five years of his life to complete the task), making use of every resource to finally capture the life of a man whose views on the ontological void, however bleak, included full-length portraits of humor and love among the frescoes of the skull.

—Thomas J. Taylor

BEDE (Baeda; The Venerable Bede), *ca.* 673–735; English (Anglo-Saxon) scholar, historian, and saint.

Chambers, R. W., *Bede.* London, Oxford University Press/British Academy, 1937.

Colgrave, Bertram and R. A. B. Mynors, editors, *Bede's Ecclesiastical History of the English People* (containing a Life of Bede by Colgrave in the Preface). Oxford, Clarendon Press, 1969.

Plummer, Charles P., editor, *Venerabilis Baedae Historiam Ecclesiasticam* (containing an English Life of Bede in the Preface). Oxford, Clarendon Press, 1896.

Thomson, A. H., *Bede, His Life, Times, and Writings.* Oxford, Clarendon Press, 1935.

*

Bede, the author of the *Ecclesiastical History of the English People,* lived and worked, from the age of seven until his death, in the monastery of Wearmouth and Jarrow in the north of England in what was then the Kingdom of Northumbria. He was familiar with the poetry of his native tongue (the Northumbrian dialect of Anglo-Saxon) and became a fluent writer in Latin, in which all his works are composed.

Very little is known of Bede's life, and any attempt to write a full biography must fall back on illustrating the monastic life of the seventh century rather than recounting specifically Bede's actual life. The closest approach, by THOMSON, is entitled significantly *Bede, His Life, Times, and Writings.*

Only two primary documents exist for the life of Bede. The first is a short 200-word autobiographical note appended to the manuscript copies of his *History,* which is followed by a list of his works—schoolbooks for the novices, lives of the saints, histories, works of theology. The second document is a moving account of Bede's last few days, written by a young pupil named Cuthbert, who was later to become Abbot of the monastery. On this slight basis—and a knowledge of the life and manners of the time—any fuller account must be based. A study of some of the standard works on the period will provide the necessary background. Among these are F. M. Stenton, *Anglo-Saxon England* (Oxford, 1947); E. S. Duckett, *Anglo-Saxon Saints and Scholars* (New York, 1947); D. Whitelock, *The Beginnings of English Society* (London, 1952); and P. H. Blair, *Introduction to Anglo-Saxon England* (1956).

Since no book-length biography is possible, the best sources are those shorter biographical studies prefaced to the numerous editions of Bede's *History of the English People*. The most scholarly are by PLUMMER (1896) and COLGRAVE/MYNORS (1969). Plummer's Life was part of the preface to his edition of the Latin text of the *History*. The Colgrave/Mynors edition is equally scholarly; it has the advantage for English-language readers of providing an English translation facing each page of the Latin text.

The best short life of Bede, which combines the known facts with a brilliant appreciation of Bede and his works, is by CHAMBERS. This work was first delivered as one of the annual "lectures on a master mind" before the British Academy and subsequently printed in their Proceedings.

—Ian A. Gordon

* * *

BEETHOVEN, Ludwig van, 1770–1827; German composer.

Bory, Robert, *Ludwig van Beethoven: His Life and Work in Pictures*. London, Thames and Hudson, and New York, Atlantis Books, 1960.

Cooper, Martin, *Beethoven: The Last Decade 1817–27*. London and New York, Oxford University Press, 1970.

Herriot, Edouard, *The Life and Times of Beethoven*, translated by Adelheid I. and William J. Mitchell. New York and London, Macmillan, 1935 (originally published as *La Vie de Beethoven*, Paris, Gallimard, 1929).

Kendall, Alan, *The Life of Beethoven*. London, Hamlyn, 1978.

Knight, Frida, *Beethoven and the Age of Revolution*. London, Lawrence and Wishart, 1973; New York, International Publishers, 1974.

Landon, H. C. Robbins, *Beethoven: A Documentary Study*. New York, Macmillan, and London, Thames and Hudson, 1970.

Matthews, Denis, *Beethoven*. London, Dent, 1985.

Newman, Ernest, *The Unconscious Beethoven: A Study in Musical Psychology*. London and New York, Knopf, 1927.

Rolland, Romain, *Beethoven the Creator: the Great Creative Epochs: From the Eroica to the Appassionata*, translated by Ernest Newman. London, Gollancz, and New York, Harper, 1929 (originally published as *Beethoven: les Grandes Époques créatrices*, Paris, Éditions du Sablier, 1928).

Schindler, Anton, *Beethoven as I Knew Him: A Biography*, edited by Donald MacArdle, translated by Constance Jolly. London, Faber, and Chapel Hill, University of North Carolina Press, 1966 (originally published as *Biographie von Ludwig van Beethoven*, Münster, Aschendorff, 1840).

Scott, Marion, *Beethoven*. London, Dent, and New York, Dutton, 1934.

Solomon, Maynard, *Beethoven*. New York, Macmillan/Schirmer, 1977; London, Cassell, 1978.

Sonneck, Oscar George, *Beethoven: Impressions by His Contemporaries*. New York, Schirmer, 1926.

Sterba, Edith and Richard, *Beethoven and His Nephew*, translated by Willard Trask. New York, Pantheon, 1954; London, Dobson, 1957.

Sullivan, John William Navin, *Beethoven, His Spiritual Development*. London, Cape, and New York, Knopf, 1927.

Thayer, Alexander W., *Thayer's Life of Beethoven*, edited and revised by Elliot Forbes. Princeton, New Jersey, Princeton University Press, 1964 (originally published as *Ludwig van Beethovens Leben*, Berlin, F. Schneider, 1866–79).

Tyson, Alan and Joseph Kerman, *The New Grove Beethoven*. London, Macmillan, and New York, Norton, 1983.

Wegeler, Franz and Ferdinand Ries, *Remembering Beethoven*, translated by Frederick Noonan. Arlington, Virginia, Great Ocean Publishers, 1987; London, Deutsch, 1988 (originally published as *Biographische Notizen über Ludwig van Beethoven*, Coblenz, Hirsch, 1838).

*

Since Schlosser's reminiscence of Beethoven (Prague, 1828) appeared within a year of the composer's death, biographies have followed at a steady rate. The most valuable studies draw on the wealth of surviving public and private documents. In addition to the letters, diaries and memoirs, two important sources have been available to Beethoven's biographers: music journalism, which saw a considerable gain in popularity at about the time Beethoven began his career, and the Conversation Books, through which Beethoven's visitors communicated with the composer after he became deaf.

Several unreliable biographies, however, ignore or even manipulate some of these sources in order to cast Beethoven as a Romantic hero, without confronting some of the less attractive aspects of his character. SCHINDLER, for example, though providing an indispensable first-hand record of Beethoven's later years, should be read with caution. For a time Beethoven's factotum, Schindler aspired to be the composer's most trusted friend, and his book is frequently distorted by hero worship. He tried to create discord between Beethoven and his family and friends, and attempted to mislead posterity by destroying some two-thirds of the Conversation Books and forging many entries (some relating to the behaviour of Beethoven's nephew) in those which remained. While his book contains much, particularly concerning the performance of Beethoven's music, that is available nowhere else, Schindler was among the first to advance the Beethoven myth to which all subsequent biographies have had to respond, and which has itself been the subject of an entire study (Allesandra Comini, *The Changing Image of Beethoven: A Study in Mythmaking*, New York, Rizzoli, 1987).

WEGELER AND RIES, long time friends of the composer, give a more disinterested account. They offer a series of vivid episodes which illuminate Beethoven's character in authentic detail. Both writers knew the composer long before Schindler did. Ries, for example, knew Beethoven's teachers in Vienna and gives unrivalled insights into his student years there. Ries is also informative on the genesis and performance of the *Eroica* symphony. Wegeler is our most reliable witness to the more personal areas of Beethoven's life: we are indebted to him for the significant revelation that the composer "was never out of love."

THAYER's monumental work, owing much to the mid-19th century movement toward scientific historiography, remains a principal source and the starting point for all later biographers. Thayer originally set out to reconcile differences between Schindler's book and the Wegeler/Ries volume, but his research involved the amassing of such a quantity of source materials—from official court records to reminiscences by anyone who had known the composer—that his study soon grew into the two weighty volumes we have today. Thayer also aimed to provide his American readers with a full historical background to the changing European political situation. He has produced a slow-moving book, admirably clear in style, but continuously discursive. The depth of field is illustrated by Thayer's beginning his study, not with the composer's birth, but with a history of Electoral Court at Bonn (40 pages) and in tracing Beethoven's ancestry from the 17th century (11 pages). He does not venture into musical analysis, but tries to build a comprehensive portrait of Beethoven the busy professional musician, pursuing his career in early 19th-century Vienna. But the myth exerted its power even on this scrupulous American scholar, and after assembling a vast quantity of documents, Thayer abandoned his study at the year 1816, at which period evidence of Beethoven's less attractive qualities became impossible to ignore. His work was completed by later scholars, and Elliot Forbes' edition is still the backbone of modern Beethoven scholarship. However, readers should check the publication dates of Beethoven's works against a modern dictionary, such as the New Grove.

Several worthwhile studies appeared in the early 20th century (e.g., SCOTT's much-revised and often sensitive study in the "Master Musicians" series, updated by MATTHEWS in the more impersonal style of 1980s scholarship), but they have been eclipsed by modern biographies reflecting the latest research. TYSON AND KERMAN, expanded from their entry in the New Grove, is the most accurate study to date, impressive in its dense factual content. This short book is necessarily a condensed account of Beethoven's life; the rich texture of quotations that gives Thayer's work its special quality is absent, and of course it lacks the immediacy of the first-hand accounts by Schindler, Wegeler and Ries. But although its primary function is to supply exact information (dates wrongly given in Thayer are here corrected, and this book supplies the only reliable worklist, as well as the most up-to-date bibliography), Tyson and Kerman do not altogether avoid discussing more subjective areas such as Beethoven's personality and the spiritual development in his music. The book is clear to read and straightforward to use; the well sub-divided organisation allows for easy retrieval of specific items of information—the ideal companion to a more discursive volume.

Perhaps the finest of such discursive accounts is SOLOMON's widely read Beethoven. Full of insights, openly interpretive, Solomon combines sound historical investigation with a mixture of more speculative techniques. He probes the documentary sources more critically than does Thayer and delves boldly into the mystery of Beethoven's character. Solomon selects enigmas from Beethoven's life and subjects them to psychoanalytical probing. It has long been known, for instance, that Beethoven thought he was up to two years younger than his real age; many writers

have claimed that the error was his father's, a deliberate attempt to enhance Beethoven's precocity. Solomon discovers that the confusion lay with the composer, links this with Beethoven's reluctance to quash a rumour of his royal and illegitimate descent, and explains both by reference to Freud's "family romance fantasy." Solomon's deductive masterpiece is his investigation of the identity of the "Immortal Beloved"—a piece of detective work occupying almost 10% of the narrative section of the book. He also writes descriptively about the music, pointing the reader toward analytical possibilities (motivic compression in the Eroica, myth-resonances in Fidelio) while remaining accessible to the non-specialist. Solomon challenges the Beethoven myth but leaves the composer's stature undiminished, and his deeply probing study is written up in lively prose. Readers looking for just one biography should consider choosing Solomon. Serious students will need to have Thayer and Tyson/Kerman on hand as well.

Among biographies with an historical emphasis, COOPER's specialized study, which tackles Beethoven in his most difficult period both personally and professionally, merits attention. Cooper describes the changing society of early 19th-century Vienna during the last decade of Beethoven's life, and shows how the Missa Solemnis can be seen as a response to the religious and philosophical attitudes of the time. Cooper is not afraid to draw bold connections between life and works, and his book includes valuable musical analyses. An appendix by Larkin gives the most recent diagnosis of Beethoven's poor health, a topic that has fascinated medically-minded musicians since NEWMAN's controversial interpretation of Beethoven's symptoms. The most elegant of Beethoven's biographers, Newman relied on facts some of which are now questioned, but his inspired amateur incursion into physiology and psychoanalysis (surely a source for Solomon) is still well worth reading.

KNIGHT's investigation, broader in scope than Cooper's, deals with Beethoven's response to the revolutionary times in which he lived. HERRIOT shows the importance of the heroic ideal for Beethoven, and traces the influence on him of figures such as Schiller, Goethe and, of course, Napoleon. He goes on to show Beethoven's influence on succeeding generations of creative artists as diverse as Berlioz, Delacroix and Zola. Neither Knight nor Herriot attempts to deal directly with the music.

ROLLAND, whose remarkable study links man and music inextricably, focuses on Beethoven in the first decade of the 19th century and incorporates much descriptive analysis of the music. Writing under the spell of the Beethoven myth, Rolland is subjective and intuitive; but his insights are valuable despite his dated approach.

Two further studies, those by Sullivan and Sterba, illustrate both the strengths and limitations of interpretive biographies. SULLIVAN's enormously influential little book traces the composer's spiritual development as it is manifest in the music. Although his approach is wholly subjective, his deductions often contribute more to our experience of Beethoven's music than do more factual accounts of the composer's external life. The STERBAs, by contrast, do not attempt to illuminate the music in any way, but they have altered all our ideas about Beethoven the man. They apply Freudian psychoanalysis to Beethoven's family relationships in a consciously demythologising account, which is only slightly marred by its reliance on sources now thought to be partly suspect, including the Conversation Books.

Among documentary and pictorial biographies, Sonneck, Landon, Bory and Kendall each stands out. Both SONNECK and LANDON offer compilations of contemporary testimony with brief commentaries, while BORY presents a genuine biography in pictures, with locations, portraits and documents cogently ordered and superbly reproduced. A biographical sketch accompanies the illustrations. KENDALL offers a more complete account; probably the most balanced of the illustrated biographies, its text is thoughtful and makes few concessions to the coffee table.

—Patricia Howard

BEGIN, Menachem, 1913–   ; Israeli statesman.

Haber, Eithan, *Menachem Begin: The Legend and the Man*, translated by Louis Williams. New York, Delacorte, 1978.
Hirschler, Gertrude and Lester S. Eckman, *Menachem Begin, From Freedom Fighter to Statesman*. New York, Shengold, 1979.
Silver, Eric, *Begin: A Biography*. London, Weidenfeld and Nicolson, 1984; as *Begin: The Haunted Prophet*. New York, Random House, 1984.
Sofer, Sasson, *Begin: An Anatomy of Leadership*. Oxford and New York, Blackwell, 1988.

*

HABER, a military correspondent of Israel's largest circulation evening newspaper, published this account of the "hero" of his work around the time Begin assumed the premiership. The approach is journalistic and even conversations are imaginatively reconstructed. Its principal strength lies in the first-hand records Haber has collated from Begin's family, including his sister and daughter, as well as his political colleagues and members of the Irgun Z'vai Leumi and what in some ways was its Polish predecessor, the Betar. Haber concentrates on the period leading up to the *Altalena* incident in June 1948, and in particular provides an important account of Begin's relationship with the Lohamei Herut Yisrael, or "as it would be more familiarly known, *LEHI* to its friends and the Stern Gang to its British enemies." Begin's terrorist activities, particularly the blowing up of the King David Hotel, the flogging of the British officers, and the "execution" of the two sergeants are viewed sympathetically and cited as having precipitated the British withdrawal from Palestine.

HIRSCHLER AND ECKMAN have been described as having written a history of Israel from the perspective of those who were considered for years as dissidents by the Israeli establishment. The first part of the book concentrates on the background to Begin's terrorist activities, and the authors offer a penetrating account of how the British suspension of the use of corporal punishment in the mandate after the flogging incident won the Irgun new recruits and led to "positive action." Particular attention is paid to Begin's significance as a domestic politician in Israel, his adversarial relationship with Ben-Gurion, his visits overseas to Britain, South Africa, and the United States, as well as his handling of world statesmen such as Kissinger. After

Camp David, Begin is viewed as attempting to achieve two goals for Israel: permanent peace and the elimination of poverty.

The biographies published after the war in Lebanon offer rather a different perspective. SILVER, who has been Jerusalem correspondent for both *The Guardian* and *The Observer* and witnessed many of the events he describes at first hand, offers a more ambivalent impression of Begin. Writing from the standpoint that "it is hard to understand the degree of British blindness to Jewish suffering" in the 1940s, Silver views Begin's terrorist activities as being largely responsible for the British withdrawal from Palestine, and places them in the long-term perspective of Mrs. Thatcher's receiving Begin at 10 Downing Street as Prime Minister of Israel after having said previously that she could never shake the hand of the man responsible for the hanging of the two British sergeants. Silver, however, is highly critical of Begin's premiership, of his relations with Syria, of his bombing of the Iraqi nuclear reactor, and of his apparent view that "he alone knew how to deal with the Arabs." Begin, however, is exonerated from responsibility for the Sabra and Shatilla massacres: "he was not told until after the event, and he was not advised of the risks beforehand." His "reign" is seen as having "suffered from his autocratic style of leadership" and, in the end, Silver describes him as "an unrepentant terrorist who won the Nobel Peace Prize, then launched another war." The Israel Begin created "in his own image was more nervously Jewish, more aggressive and more isolated."

SOFER, a lecturer in International Relations at the Hebrew University of Jerusalem, rather than writing a political biography of Begin, has compiled a series of essays analysing the Israeli leader's world view, political methods, and ideological teachings. Sofer cites the observation in *The Times*, when Begin was elected Prime Minister, that his victory was proof that in the end terrorism pays, but this series of essays does not concentrate on those incidents that Begin himself believed "accomplished two things: the emergence of the Palestine question as an international problem, and the acquisition of political support that made the establishment of the state possible." Instead Sofer offers perceptive insights into Begin's political credo, and in particular his writings on "the revolt," explaining its ideological origins and historical laws: Begin had "a deep, almost mystical recognition of the sovereign right conferred upon every nation to achieve independence, a right to be exercised even by violent means." A great deal of this work concentrates on what Sofer sees as Begin's failure as a Prime Minister and as a national leader, deriving from his faulty conception of reality and his failure as a decision maker. The overall conclusion offered is that Israel in 1977 was ripe for wide-ranging internal reform, but despite favourable international and strategic circumstances "Begin failed to meet his challenge and left a society in a state of economic bankruptcy, moral decline, without political stability, riven and divided."

—Ritchie Ovendale

BEHN, Aphra, 1640–1689; English writer.

Duffy, Maureen, *The Passionate Shepherdess*. London, Cape, and New York, Avon, 1977.

Hahn, Emily, *Aphra Behn*. London, Cape, 1951.
Sackville-West, Vita, *Aphra Behn: The Incomparable Astrea*.
  London, G. Howe, 1927.
Woodcock, George, *The Incomparable Aphra*. London and New
  York, T. V. Boardman, 1948.

*

Aphra Behn lived in a time of moral liberation to which she
responded by writing in the spirit of the Restoration period,
matching the eroticism the male writers of the time, like
Etherege and Vanbrugh, Farquhar and Wycherley, evoked in
their plays, which competed with her on the London stage of the
1670s and 1680s. Her writings shocked the Richardsonian senti-
mentalists of the 18th century, and almost all Victorians, who
tended to equate the writer with her works, so that she also
acquired the reputation of being a woman of intensely loose
morals.

The results of this situation were that Aphra Behn's works fell
out of print, and nobody for a long time had any interest in writing her biography, so that no Life of Aphra Behn was published
from the scanty accounts written shortly after her death in 1689
until the early 20th century.

The immediately posthumous notices, attributed to "One of
the Fair Sex," are now generally recognized as the work of the
Grub Street writer Charles Gildon, who was one of Aphra
Behn's friends in the last few years of her life. Gildon's first
brief notice, an *Account of the Life of the Incomparable Mrs.
Behn*, served as a preface to her play, *The Younger Brother, or,
The Amorous Jilt*, which was published in 1696. A longer version, *The History of the Life and Memoirs of Mrs. Behn*, introduced Behn's collected *Histories and Novels* published later in
the same year.

Charles Gildon was well known as a capable literary hoaxer,
and his account of Behn is highly unreliable, filled with inaccuracies and with tales so grossly improbable that they seem unlikely in any circumstances. Whole passages read so much in the
style of Mrs. Behn's own novels that one suspects Gildon collected fragments of her incomplete or abandoned works and
adapted them for incorporation into her life. Judgment of this
early account is complicated by the fact that Aphra Behn *did*
have an unusual life; she *did* spend part of her youth in the colony of Surinam, and she *did* act as a spy for the English government in the Low Countries.

Nobody considered it worth examining Gildon's accounts critically until in 1913 an American scholar, Ernest Bernbaum,
sought to prove in two essays, *Mrs. Behn's Oroonoko* and *Mrs.
Behn's Biography, a Fiction*, that Gildon was wrong about
Aphra Behn's ancestry and also about her journey to Surinam.
Later scholarship has proved Bernbaum wrong on these points,
and though Gildon is shown to be right here and there, the
latter's account can be taken as unreliable unless otherwise
confirmed.

Interest in Aphra Behn began to rise rather broadly in the
early Georgian era, first among literary people. In 1913 E. A.
Baker collected and published her novels and stories, and in
1915 the eccentric Montague Summers, scholar, occultist, and
eroticist, published what is still the definitive six-volume edition
of her works with a biographical introduction that revealed little
not yet known about her. After World War I interest in Aphra
Behn was intensified by the recognition that she had been the
first professional woman writer. The intellectual feminists, particularly of the Bloomsbury circle, began to take her up, and
one of that group, Vita SACKVILLE-WEST, published in 1927
the first actual book concerned entirely with the life of Aphra
Behn. It is a short volume, less than 100 pages long, and disappointingly flippant and condescending. Sackville-West had
been clearly affected by her acquaintance with Lytton Strachey.
She did no more than finally place on the shelf a book about
Behn; it added no new facts of biographical interest, no profound
new insights.

After World War II, WOODCOCK undertook to write a full-
length study of Behn, which is partly biographical, but also, because so little serious commentary had been written on Aphra
Behn's writings, inevitably critical as well, with lengthy assessments of the works. Woodcock researched extensively, and very
little in the way of new facts about Aphra Behn has been added
to the record since his book appeared. It is in some ways a ten-
dencious biography, for Woodcock stresses the libertarian aspects of Aphra Behn's attitudes (perhaps not paying sufficient
attention to her strong monarchist loyalties) and also presents her
as a feminist predecessor.

In more recent years the growth of feminism has provided a
reverent public for writings about Aphra Behn, but in biographical terms the harvest has been slight, and few of the writers
who have noticed her recently have added greatly to our knowledge of her life. Some, such as HAHN, have tended to sensationalize and romanticize that life in a reversal of the 19th-
century ostracism of Behn as a loose woman. Aphra emerges as
the glorious female libertine. Others have used her life to prove
feminist points without attempting to study the relationship between her work and her personality, which is the real task of the
literary biographer.

One book stands out among the recent publications on Aphra
Behn as a true and original biography. This is *The Passionate
Shepherdess* by DUFFY. Maureen Duffy is a novelist who feels
her professional debt to Aphra Behn as a courageous predecessor, and she has researched so thoroughly that one feels there is
little room left to find new facts about the shadowy sides of
Aphra Behn's life. She has definitely established her subject's
ancestry and her early life as no previous writers had done, and
she deals capably with the more open years of her adult life.
Duffy also discusses Behn's works with much sensitivity, and,
apart from the improbabable event of a cache of new material
being discovered in the attics of some English country homes, it
is unlikely that we shall need a new biography of Aphra Behn
for years ahead.

—George Woodcock

––––––––––––

BELL, Alexander Graham, 1847–1922; Scottish-born American scientist and inventor.

Bruce, Robert V., *Bell: Alexander Graham Bell and the Conquest of Solitude*. Boston, Little Brown, and London, Gollancz, 1973.
Burlingame, Roger, *Out of Silence into Sound: The Life of Alexander Graham Bell*. New York, Macmillan, 1964.

Costain, Thomas B., *The Chord of Steel: The Story of the Invention of the Telephone*. New York, Doubleday, 1960.

Mackenzie, Catharine D., *Alexander Graham Bell, the Man who Contracted Space*. Boston, Houghton Mifflin, 1928.

Osborne, Harold S., *Biographical Memoir of Alexander Graham Bell 1847–1922*. Washington, D.C., National Academy of Sciences, 1943.

Parkin, J. H., *Bell and Baldwin: Their Development of Aerodromes and Hydrodromes at Baddeck, Nova Scotia*. Toronto, University of Toronto Press, 1964.

Rhodes, Frederick L., *Beginnings of Telephony*. New York, Harper, 1929.

Winefield, Richard, *Never the Twain Shall Meet: Bell, Gallaudet, and the Communications Debate*. Washington, D.C., Gallaudet University Press, 1987.

*

While Alexander Graham Bell is best known for his invention of the telephone, few are aware of his broad interests and other activities, such as his contributions to the teaching of the deaf, his development of the disc phonograph, and his early experiments in aerodynamics. Much of this imbalance in public awareness was Bell's own fault, for he was extremely reticent to discuss his career during his lifetime and wanted no part of biography. Until he became involved in patent litigations over the invention of the telephone, he was very lax in his record keeping. After that period, however, he saved everything: patents, notes, correspondence, etc. Most of the Bell Family papers are now housed in the Manuscript Division of the Library of Congress, and it is on these materials biographers must rely for data about his early life.

The first biography of Bell was by MACKENZIE. While not a satisfactory biography, it is of some interest because Mackenzie served Bell as secretary for so many years. The work by BURLINGAME is also unsatisfactory as biography since it is mostly about the history of the telephone. BRUCE was the first to gain access to the complete Bell records, and to this day his biography stands as the definitive work on Bell.

Because of his diverse interests, early invention of the telephone, and long life, many details of Bell's activities are scattered in works on the history of the telephone, the history of aeronautics, and the history of the education of the deaf. COSTAIN's book, while not a true biography, gives much of the flavor of Bell's early family life in Canada and of the events that led to his early experiments on the telephone. RHODES gives a technical account of Bell's early telephone models and their subsequent improvement by other inventors. The book by PARKIN is an excellent contribution to the history of aeronautics, describing Bell's experiments on kites and his developments and patents on flying machines and hydrofoil crafts. The book by WINEFIELD is the best to help understand the reasons for Bell's long fight to promote "oralism" as the ideal method to teach the deaf. A complete bibliography of Bells' works can be found in the OSBORNE "Memoir." The best balanced view of this interesting and complex man, however, continues to be the work by Bruce.

—Robert James Havlik

BELLINI, Giovanni, *ca.* 1430–1516; Italian painter.

Fry, Roger E., *Giovanni Bellini*. London, At the Sign of the Unicorn, 1899; New York, Longman, 1901.

Goffen, Rona, *Giovanni Bellini*. New Haven, Connecticut, Yale University Press, 1989.

Hendy, Philip and Ludwig Goldscheider, *Giovanni Bellini*. Oxford and London, Phaidon Press, and New York, Oxford University Press, 1945.

Pallucchini, Rodolfo, *Giovanni Bellini*, translated by R. H. Boothroyd. Milan, Martello, and London, Heinemann, 1962 (originally published by Del Turco, Florence, 1949).

Robertson, Giles, *Giovanni Bellini*. Oxford, Clarendon Press, 1968.

*

Bellini, universally acknowledged by modern art historians to be the most important early Renaissance painter in Venice, remains an elusive and ill-defined personality. While a reasonable amount of contemporary documentation for his career survives, such as signed and dated paintings and some contracts and letters about commissioned works, Venice, unlike Florence, lacked a tradition of artists' biographies, and when Giorgio Vasari profiled Bellini condescendingly in his *Lives* (1550 and 1568), his view was distorted by his own Florentine bias. Meanwhile, though mid-16th century Venetian authors such as Ludovico Dolce were spurred to write art criticism as a response to Vasari, by that time Bellini tended to be judged only in relation to his pupils Giorgione and Titian, by whom he had been overshadowed.

The modern "rediscovery" of Bellini, as for many early Renaissance artists, was effected through the naive yet enthusiastic appreciations of Victorian English critics, especially John Ruskin, who called two of Bellini's works, the *Frari Triptych* and the *San Zaccaria Altarpeice*, "the two best pictures in the world" (Oxford lecture, 1870). Nearly 30 years later, FRY's book was the first monograph to focus on Bellini's art, though it amounts to little more than a short critical essay. Fry was perhaps the leading exponent of turn-of-the-century formalist criticism, based on the "aesthete's" appreciation of art. Thus while his book does contain some brief, and mostly valid historical judgments on such issues as the nature of classical revival in Quattrocento Venice, the focus is on the visual form of Bellini's works and the stylistic changes that took place over the artist's prolific career spanning six decades. Fry's book contains nuggets of acute visual analysis, but there are few references to historical and biographical source material.

Well-illustrated with many black-and-white plates, the book by HENDY AND GOLDSCHEIDER attempts to cover the life and work of the artist with greater thoroughness, though the bulk of the writing concentrates, as did Fry's, on questions of stylistic development. The authors more clearly define the three major stages in Bellini's career: the early phase, up to about 1470, reflecting the influence of Giovanni's father Jacopo Bellini and his brother-in-law Andrea Mantegna; a second period, from the 1470s to 1490s, marked by paintings displaying greater luminosity and richer color, made possible, in part, by a shift in medium from tempera to oil; and a late style in which questions arise about the interaction between Bellini and his young pupils,

Giorgione and Titian. Despite the emphasis on style in the book, there is a vagueness in connoisseurship judgments, or the criteria used to distinguish Bellini's autograph paintings from those produced by his workshop. In addition, little attention is paid to historical questions other than the circumstances of Bellini's birth (date? legitimacy?), and there is virtually no analysis of iconography in Bellini's paintings, notwithstanding a recognition of the singular treatment of subject matter in certain religious and allegorical works.

PALLUCCHINI's monograph includes a catalogue that covers the artist's entire oeuvre, but the entries are not exhaustive, lacking bibliographic information specific to each work, and rarely identifying condition or medium. Many of Pallucchini's attributions are also questionable, since the author failed to discriminate clearly between master and workshop. Once again, the survey of Bellini's life focuses almost exclusively on artistic influences and the stylistic developments over the painter's career.

ROBERTSON has produced perhaps the single most useful introduction to Giovanni Bellini, although it cannot be termed definitive. Robertson presents more factual and historical information than had earlier writers, summarizing or briefly excerpting the documentary evidence, although most of the author's attention is still addressed to issues of style with little discussion of iconography or content. While Robertson's attributions to Bellini's hand are more restrictive than Pallucchini's, implying the use of more selective criteria, these distinctions are not articulated clearly. Further, the monograph lacks a comprehensive catalogue of Bellini's paintings.

GOFFEN's book takes a radically different approach from those discussed thus far, representative of an important current in recent art historical writing. Goffen's methodology is stated at the outset, when she suggests that the questions previously considered foremost in Bellini studies, especially connoisseurship, are "coincidental to the central issue, which is to understand Bellini's creative processes and appreciate his art in its cultural and historical context." The latter phrase is the key to understanding Goffen's books, since it is unquestionably the "context" that dominates. Although there are some passages addressing stylistic development, these are fragmented due to the organization of the book, which is divided into chapters covering the thematic content of the paintings (religious works, portraits, allegories, and mythologies) rather than following the artist's career chronologically. The strengths of Goffen's book include its many fine color illustrations, an appendix that summarizes and excerpts all of the surviving documents on Bellini's life and career, an excellent bibliography, and "checklists" of both the paintings Goffen judges to be autograph as well as those produced by the workshop (although again few criteria are presented to support these attributions). As opposed to earlier studies, Goffen includes extended discussions on iconography and much valuable information on the nature of art patronage in Venice and on aspects of the city's society and culture as reflected in its art. Nonetheless, Bellini as a creative individual tends to get somewhat lost in the emphasis on the historical milieu, and one still awaits a definitive monograph that would balance historicism and iconographic analysis with a more sensitive approach to the artist himself.

—Julia I. Miller

BELLOW, Saul, 1915–   ; Canadian-born American writer.

Dutton, Robert R., *Saul Bellow*. Boston, Twayne, 1971; revised edition, 1982.
Harris, Mark, *Saul Bellow: Drumlin Woodchuck*. Athens, University of Georgia Press, 1980.
Kiernan, Robert F., *Saul Bellow*. New York, Centinuum, 1989.
Scheer-Schazler, Brigitte, *Saul Bellow*. New York, Ungar, 1972.
Tanner, Tony, *Saul Bellow*. Edinburgh and London, Oliver and Boyd, 1965; New York, Barnes and Noble, 1967.

*

There is no proper biography of Bellow to date, perhaps because the novelist has been averse to self-disclosure and uncooperative with interviewers questioning him about anything but his ideas and his writing. Readers seeking information about his life beyond the standard reference guides must make do with critical introductions to his life and works such as those by TANNER, DUTTON, SCHEER-SCHAZLER, and KIERNAN, each of which includes a brief (sometimes very brief) biographical essay.

The best of these guides is by KIERNAN, if only because it is the most substantial and the most complete, analyzing Bellow's fiction through *More Die of Heartbreak* (1987). Faced with a paucity of biographical information, Kiernan resorts to locating real-life counterparts of some of Bellow's characters and noting that to some degree his fiction is "a mirror of his domestic life." He does concede that "fiction is not a reliable guide to its author's life," but he believes that Bellow is as autobiographical as any other author, weaving "details of his experience into the warp of his novels." Such speculation as he and other critics have indulged in about the experiences that show up in novels like *Humboldt's Gift* (Bellow's friendship with Delmore Schwartz and his contested divorce settlement with his third wife) and *Mr. Sammler's Planet* (his coverage of the Six-Day War in Israel for *Newsday* and his conflicts with campus radicals in the 1960s) doubtless spurs Bellow's readers to read back from the works to the life, but this exercise is no substitute for the revelations and pleasures of biographical narrative. What is needed is a critical biography that examines the way those sources are transformed from Bellow's life and experience, which on their own are the worthy subjects of a coherent narrative.

HARRIS' memoir, although highly idiosyncratic, can serve as an object lesson in the general difficulty of undertaking the biography of a living subject, and it may have influenced potential Bellow biographers to postpone their pursuit because of his demonstrated reluctance to sit for a portrait. Harris relates the history of his 20-year relationship with Bellow, first as fellow novelist and teacher and then as would-be biographer. The friendship was unequal from the beginning, with Harris playing the fool and flatterer much like Boswell, whom he regarded as his model, and becoming frustrated by Bellow's subtle avoidance and obviously increasing annoyance. The memoir reads like a novel because Harris was forced to adjust his plan for a full-scale, definitive life when Bellow started to avoid him, acting like the Drumlin Woodchuck of Frost's poem. Bellow's wily resistance then became the subject and theme of the memoir, and the method became ironic, with Harris flaunting his failed attempts to trail his subject around for two to three weeks a year.

In nearly 17 years he spent no more than 12 days in Bellow's company, but he fills in the space between meetings by inserting appropriate scenes from Bellow's novels, quotations from his prose, mentions of their telephone conversations, and worried references to potential rival biographers, proving himself adept at showing his subject in action and capturing his conversation.

Reflecting on his biographical project four years after it was published, Harris wrote, "I had hoped in my Bellow book to introduce reforms in the way we write biography and manage our public literary life" (*New York Times Book Review*, 4 November 1984). He admits that in this endeavor he failed miserably, but what about the more traditional goal of capturing a life in words? Critics are seriously divided over the question of Harris' success, with some calling the result a highly readable narrative, of interest for its novelistic qualities, especially its high comedy. Others found it unreliable and gossipy, guilty of catering to the contemporary thirst for information about the private lives of celebrities.

It is possible to admire the book without considering it satisfactory biography. In the *Times Literary Supplement* (6 February 1981) Julian Symons (himself a fictional biographer) called it "a work of ingenious and intelligent artifice. At no point does it bear any resemblance to a biography of Saul Bellow. . . . Certainly, however, this wary woodchuck and the clumsy hunter who is never going to catch him are splendid comic characters." And James Atlas (the biographer of Delmore Schwartz) concludes that "this odd biographer has managed to capture Bellow despite his preoccupation with himself. . . . The table talk recorded here sounds just like Bellow—or just like Bellow ought to sound, anyway" (*New York Times Book Review*, 16 November 1980). The *Times Book Review* also chose it as one of the Notable Books of 1980.

On the other hand, critics who prefer biography in its pure form were aghast that Harris could not get Bellow's birthday right or catch the names of various women in his life. Earl Rovit in the *Library Journal* called the biography a "mean-spirited, self-serving, and inconsequential effort" (15 September 1980). Harris admits in his book that Bellow refused further cooperation after reading an excerpt from the work in progress in *Georgia Review* in 1978. He resented the way he came off: "Bad-tempered. Nasty, snappish. I don't see myself that way." He also dismissed the whole genre in a sentence: "Biography is a specter viewed by a specter." Although Harris included Bellow's disgust at his biographical attempts in the memoir itself, other critics did not find this self-deprecatory strategy disarming. Writing in the *New York Review of Books* (22 January 1981), James Wolcott found the study "an attempt to do Saul Bellow dirt, to take him down a few notches."

Bellow's reaction to Harris' attempt makes one wonder how cooperative he would be with any biographer. Calling *Drumlin Woodchuck* an "unbiography" that nonetheless tells us much about Bellow, David Kirby says that "it convinces the reader that Bellow's tenacious opposition to monumentalization is no pose" (*America*, 21 February 1981). Perhaps we are destined to have only critical studies for the time being.

Ruth Miller's *Saul Bellow: A Biography of the Imagination* (forthcoming from St. Martin's Press, New York) was unavailable for review at the time of this writing.

—Phyllis Frus

BENEDICT, Ruth, 1887–1948; American anthropologist.

Caffrey, Margaret M., *Ruth Benedict: Stranger in This Land*. Austin, University of Texas Press, 1989.
Mead, Margaret, *Ruth Benedict*. New York, Columbia University Press, 1974.
Modell, Judith, *Ruth Benedict: Patterns of a Life*. Philadelphia, University of Pennsylvania Press, 1983; London, Chatto and Windus, 1984.

*

Even though only three biographies have been written about Ruth Benedict, they are all superb contributions both to the anthropological literature and to the genre of biography itself. All three were written by women who place this complex and sometimes enigmatic figure within the context of her discipline, seeking to reveal something of the poet/scientist that Ruth Benedict embodied during the early years when anthropology blossomed under the scrutiny of one of its most powerful founders, Franz Boas.

MEAD's brief essay on Benedict is a loving tribute to her teacher and friend. The last half of the book contains a number of important essays written by Benedict on a variety of topics. The first portion contains Mead's assessment of her former colleague. Mead sets out to explore the motivating factors behind one of the first women to attain major status as a social scientist. While at one level Benedict was a part of upper-middle-class American society, at another she remained an outsider all of her life. This marginality was somewhat remedied by her discovery of anthropology, a discipline anchored in the study of the "other," one that could help her to become an integrated person. At the late age of 34, Benedict went to Columbia University to study under Boas and to act as his teaching assistant. Mead's biography touches on several critical transitions in Benedict's life; her unhappy marriage, the problem of being a barren woman, her partial deafness, difficulty in conducting field work, and especially her contribution to the general subfield known at that time as "culture and personality."

MODELL's work is the first full-fledged biography of Benedict. It includes an outstanding bibliography, family photographs, original interviews with anthropologists who knew Benedict, and a good index. This volume sweeps the reader through powerful moments of discovery, inspiration and defeat characteristic of Benedict's extraordinary life, capturing something of the personality and temperament of its subject by using a variety of good sources, particularly diaries and letters. Modell includes an excellent section on how she wrote the biography, noting a considerable ambivalence among informants: Benedict was deeply admired by some as a sensitive and charismatic figure who radiated an almost mystical power, while others thought she was vague, too poetic and aloof. Modell notes deep religious questions at the root of Benedict's anthropology. During a lengthy friendship with Edward Sapir, the great linguist/anthropologist/poet, Benedict struggled between anthropology and poetry. In the long run she took a definite stand against the pursuit of poetry as a career. Modell's volume includes excellent sections on Benedict's work during the war years, her particular penchant for "national character" studies, and her eventual role as a popularizer of anthropology.

The most recent biography of Ruth Benedict, CAFFREY's is

an excellent and thorough exploration of Benedict as an anthropologist, humanist and feminist. Caffrey sees Benedict's life as a "... case history in cultural feminism, a feminism derived from other than political sources, focused on changing the values and beliefs that make up the framework of a culture rather than working through laws or the courts, with an emphasis on covert rather than overt change." Here Caffrey differs from the two previous biographers, who did not see Benedict as a feminist. Caffrey pursues this feminist theme throughout the volume in the context of a number of painful as well as humiliating circumstances of Benedict's life—her difficult marriage, the reluctance of a male-dominated academic world to either promote or to pay her on an equal basis, and her inner loneliness as a woman. Especially valuable here is the discussion of the controversy surrounding Benedict's work. In various ways Benedict raised questions about the identity of anthropology: was it a science or a branch of the humanities? how "subjective" can a social scientist become? She was never threatened by "subjectivity," which in her work was always part of the overall process of understanding another culture, alongside the equally necessary "objectivity" striven for through systematic observation.

In all three of these biographies Benedict is treated with great respect. Increasingly the field of anthropology is discovering the validity of Benedict's final address as President of the American Anthropological Association, where she argued that anthropology must always be both a science and part of the humanities.

—James J. Preston

BEN-GURION, David, 1886–1973; Polish-born Israeli statesman.

Avi-hai, Avraham, *Ben-Gurion, State-Builder: Principles and Pragmatism 1948–63.* New York, Wiley, 1974.
Bar-Zohar, Michael, *Ben-Gurion: The Armed Prophet*, translated by Len Ortzen. Englewood Cliffs, New Jersey, Prentice-Hall, 1966 (originally published by Fayard, Paris, 1966).
Kurzman, Dan, *Ben-Gurion: Prophet of Fire.* New York, Simon and Schuster, 1983.
St. John, Robert, *Ben-Gurion.* New York, Doubleday, and London, Jarrolds, 1959.
Teveth, Shabtai, *Ben-Gurion: The Burning Ground 1886–1948.* Boston, Houghton Mifflin, and London, R. Hale, 1987.

*

AVI-HAI's study rests on English and Hebrew sources, the writings of Ben-Gurion, and the works of leading Israeli and other Jewish public figures. He concedes that an authoritative and carefully researched biography has yet to be written. Avi-hai is thoroughly acquainted with the varied political, socio-economic, and cultural problems of Palestine and the conditions of the Arab minority and those of neighboring Arab states. Though focussing on the years 1948–63, Ben-Gurion's years of ministry at the head of Israel's cabinet, Avi-hai does not neglect the preceding 13 years of Ben-Gurion's leadership of the quasi-governmental Jewish Agency for Palestine.

Avi-hai is primarily concerned with the relationship between

Ben-Gurion's principles and pragmatic action, and he applies this thesis consistently throughout the study. Thus the author claims that Ben-Gurion favored consenting to the partition of Palestine and to the creation of the Jewish state in only part of cis-Jordanian Palestine, since this would lead to a speedy strengthening of the Jewish position. Avi-hai is unduly concerned with fitting his subject into a preconceived frame. In regard to sources, he combed Ben-Gurion's collected speeches and articles as well as the proceedings of the Knesset (Parliament) and of Zionist Congresses.

BAR-ZOHAR does not claim to be fully impartial. His book is divided into three parts: "The Visionary," "The Leader," and "The Wounded Lion." Bar-Zohar sees Ben-Gurion as having changed his tactics according to circumstances both in domestic and foreign affairs, but never swerving from his basic principles. Relying on earlier biographies of Ben-Gurion such as those by Barnett Litvinov, *Ben-Gurion of Israel* (1954), Robert St. John (see below), and a Hebrew biography by Bracha Habas, who focusses on Ben-Gurion's youth (1886–1915), Bar-Zohar's book also draws on Ben-Gurion's personal diary, notebooks, private and official correspondence and files, various published collections of his articles, and the 19 volumes of his complete works. A shortcoming of Bar-Zohar's book is the absence of detailed footnotes and references. On the whole this is a journalistic account rather than a scholarly contribution.

KURZMAN is a veteran foreign correspondent for the *Washington Post* and recipient of several awards. His *Ben-Gurion* rests on an impressive bibliography in English and Hebrew, including periodicals. He has also used English and Hebrew transcripts of taped oral histories obtained from friends and associates of Ben-Gurion, and other important collections such as the Negev desert kibbutz of Sde Boker as well as correspondence with such leading contemporaries as Yitzchak Ben-Zvi, Vladimir Jabotinsky, and Chaim Weizmann. Additionally, Kurzman has drawn upon interviews with a virtually endless number of Israelis and Jews abroad over many years. While he admires Ben-Gurion, Kurzman's is not a hagiographic study. He often points to Ben-Gurion's foibles and vulnerabilities, noting that Ben-Gurion long blinded himself to the full meaning of the Holocaust until World War II was over, and that he risked a new genocide in a war of liberation. His diaries show his bitter feuds with Chaim Weizmann and Menachem Begin but a strange affection for his most implacable enemy Vladimir Jabotinsky, the leader of the Zionist Revisionists.

ST. JOHN's book, which has an index but not footnotes or references, is useful, though it is no scholarly work. The author holds the view that Ben-Gurion was a man both of action and of thought, whose life was dedicated to the preservation of the Jews as a people, who established Israel as a state, and who supported the rights of man everywhere. St. John recounts the sequence of events but does not offer any analysis of them or attempt to explain Ben-Gurion's complex character.

TEVETH provides a very readable book that contains notes, a glossary, and an index, and is altogether an impressive achievement. The author has worked extensively in both American and Israeli archives. Teveth points out that though Ben-Gurion warned already in 1933 against the Hitler threat and the likely "destruction" of Europe's Jews, he was during World War II more concerned for the fate of the Yishuv. Even as late as June 1944, Ben-Gurion refused to believe that an actual genocide had occurred and was still in progress. He shared this attitude with most Zionist leaders and Jewish writers. Teveth does not cover, however, the antecedents of the struggle for independence, nor does he treat in detail the 1948 declaration of the establishment of Israel or the following war. The Epilogue shows the arrival of Ben-Gurion, the "king of the Jews," in the death and DP camps in Europe. Still, Teveth offers an indispensable work for the serious student.

—Alfred D. Low

BENNETT, (Enoch) Arnold, 1867–1931; English writer.

Barker, Dudley, *Writer by Trade: A View of Arnold Bennett.* London, Allen and Unwin, and New York, Atheneum, 1966.

Beardmore, George and Jean Beardmore, editors and translators, *Arnold Bennett in Love: Arnold Bennett and His Wife Marguerite Soulié, a Correspondence.* London, D. Bruce and Watson, 1972.

Drabble, Margaret, *Arnold Bennett, A Biography.* London, Weidenfeld and Nicolson, and New York, Knopf, 1974.

Pound, Reginald, *Arnold Bennett: A Biography.* London, Heinemann, 1952; New York, Harcourt, 1953.

Swinnerton, Frank, *Arnold Bennett: A Last Word.* London, Hamilton, and New York, Doubleday, 1978.

*

The BEARDMORES' selection of letters between Bennett and his first wife from 1907 to his death in 1931, linked together by their commentary, is more than a mere collection; the letters are well connected and well documented, fulfilling their aim of producing "the distillation of over a quarter of a million words into a comprehensive narrative." They see Marguerite Soulié as a sympathetic character, with Bennett somewhat at fault toward the end of the marriage. The opposite view is taken by BARKER, who provides further details about Marguerite, with information about Dorothy Cheston, the mother of Bennett's daughter. The two works taken together give an intriguing, two-sided picture of the domestic Bennett.

Whereas he is principally interested in the mature Bennett, POUND, using Bennett's journal, his diaries, letters, and oral communication with his friends, is particularly illuminating about Bennett's background in the Potteries, his family, and his first work in a solicitor's office. The influence of his father, and his likeness to him, are stressed. Pound charts Bennett's beginnings as a journalist on the *Staffordshire Sentinel* and *Tit-Bits* magazine. Using hitherto unpublished sources, with subsidiary journals and notebooks to complement Bennett's principal journal, 1896–1931, Pound dwells on the less "domestic" Bennett, his foreign travels and his yachting, as well as his grander life as a successful writer. The work and the life are well integrated in this biography, which elucidates Bennett's approach to his novels, and quotes extensively from his own commentaries on and criticism of his work. He uses letters from Joseph Conrad and H. G. Wells to confirm "word of mouth" from friends and family.

DRABBLE acknowledges the work of Pound ("I owe [him] a great debt, though I've tried not to rely on it too much"). Some of the same anecdotes appear in both biographies. Drabble is more evenhanded about Marguerite and Dorothy Cheston: the latter emerges as a woman of strength and character, and Drabble points out Bennett's "impatience with Dorothy's theatrical ventures." Her biography is written as an act of homage to a writer who comes from the same part of England as she does, and her local knowledge and affinity with Bennett lie happily with her literary criticism.

Unlike the above biographers, and not entirely successfully, SWINNERTON desires to separate Bennett from his amorous difficulties, and to present him as he was known to his circle of friends. He analyses Bennett's temperament, the rows with his wife and Dorothy Cheston, and the latter's "wilfulness." He uses the evidence of Winifred Nerney, Bennett's servant. Swinnerton offers a book of personal memories, sometimes resentful on Bennett's behalf of the way of he has been treated by other biographers.

—Barbara Hayley

BERG, Alban, 1885–1935; Austrian composer.

Adorno, Theodor, *Alban Berg: The Master of the Smallest Link,* translated by Juliane Brand and Christopher Hailey. Cambridge, Cambridge University Press, 1991 (originally published by E. Lafite, Vienna, 1968).

Carner, Mosco, *Alban Berg: The Man and the Work.* London, Duckworth, and New York, Holmes and Meyer, 1975; revised edition, 1983.

Monson, Karen, *Alban Berg.* Boston, Houghton Mifflin, and London, Macdonald, 1979.

Perle, George, "Berg," in *The New Grove Second Viennese School.* London, Macmillan, and New York, Norton, 1980; revised edition, 1983.

Redlich, Hans F., *Alban Berg: The Man and His Music.* London, J. Calder, and New York, Abelard-Schuman, 1957 (condensed from *Alban Berg: Versuch einer Würdigung,* Vienna, Universal Edition, 1957).

Reich, Willi, *The Life and Work of Alban Berg,* translated by Cornelius Cardew. London, Thames and Hudson, 1965 (originally published as *Alban Berg,* Zurich, Atlantis Verlag, 1963).

*

There is a disconcerting discrepancy between the abundant source material surrounding Alban Berg and the deficiencies of the published biographical studies. This situation has resulted in part from the fact that the composer's widow, who died in 1976 at the age of 91, took great care to preserve her husband's papers but limited scholarly access and discouraged any truly candid exploration of Berg's complex and singularly opaque personality. For example, the German and especially the English-language editions of Berg's letters to his wife (*Alban Berg: Briefe an seine Frau,* Munich, A. Langen- G. Müller Verlag, 1965; *Alban Berg: Letters to his Wife,* edited, translated, and annotated by Bernard Grun, London, Faber, 1971) are heavily cut and edited, rendering a rich source at once misleading and unreliable. A broader problem concerns the difficulty of balancing a differentiated assessment of Berg's complicated artistic personality against the intricate strategems of his private life and profound loyalties to the other members of that triumvirate known as the "Second Viennese School," Arnold Schoenberg and Anton Webern. A balanced assessment would require a sensitive investigation of Berg's psychological make-up, as well as mastery and a critical reading of the voluminous and often contradictory sources. Recent scholarship has begun to address such issues, but there is as yet nothing even remotely resembling a definitive biography of Berg (in either English *or* German). Thus the present literature must be judged by the more modest standards of the introductory "life-and-work" essay.

The works by Reich, Redlich, and Adorno are valuable as documents by men who knew or had studied with Berg. REICH's "authorized biography" is a translation and condensation of a book that was itself based on an earlier study compiled shortly after Berg's death (Willi Reich, *Alban Berg*, 1937). With the stated purpose of presenting Berg's "human aspect" and "high spirituality," Reich weaves a largely uncritical narrative around a compilation of important sources, including reviews, letters, Berg essays, and passages from an unpublished biographical study by Berg's boyhood friend Hermann Watznauer. While occasionally enlivened by personal anecdotes, Reich's work lacks broader perspective (shedding little light, for instance, on Berg's relationship to Schoenberg and Webern) and is wooden in its organization. The musical analyses, which rely heavily upon Berg's own written descriptions, are weak. Altogether, Reich is a disappointing work for someone who had been so close to Berg and had such ready access to the sources; it is however, a valuable sourcebook and is illustrated by a number of rare photographs.

REDLICH's "transcription and condensation" of a German-language biography contains some historical and contextual passages added for the English-language edition. Redlich's research was hampered by limited access to sources and restrictions imposed by Berg's widow, but he writes with intelligence, perspective, and critical insight. It is by far the most professional of the available biographies, and while somewhat less detailed than Reich (though fuller in its account of Berg's relationship to Schoenberg and Webern), the biographical narrative is well told and the musical analyses present a perceptive and integrated analytic point of view.

ADORNO's book, which expands upon the author's contribution to Reich's 1937 volume, is not a traditional biography, but the wealth of anecdotal detail and psychological insight demand its inclusion as a major biographical source. While written as a corrective to Redlich, Adorno is an ideal *subjective* complement to that more *objective* work, and it is profitable to read the two books in tandem. Adorno places Berg and his music in a broader cultural and philosophical context than had any other writer, making this an essential *second* book for anyone interested in the composer and his time.

PERLE's expanded entry for the *New Grove* is informed by original research for two highly recommended books on Berg's operas (George Perle, *The Operas of Alban Berg*, 2 vols., Berkeley, University of California Press, 1980–85) as well as his 1977 revelation regarding Berg's affair with Hanna Fuchs-

Robettin and the existence of a secret program for the *Lyric Suite*. Though scrupulous and insightful, the biographical account is disappointingly cursory, especially regarding the earlier years. The musical discussion, however, presents a particularly lucid specialist's account of the evolution of Berg's stylistic individuality. Perle provides the only works list, catalogue of writings, and bibliography (through 1983, though far from comprehensive) that is entirely reliable.

MONSON's volume, proclaiming itself the "fullest and most readable life to date," is a popular biography that exploits the sensational biographical discoveries by Perle and others. The author embroiders the familiar narrative of her predecessors with a few gossipy anecdotes and uneven insights; the book is, moreover, poorly documented, plagued by errors, and lacking in balance, particularly in its treatment of Berg's personal life. The musical discussion, aimed at a lay audience, is barely serviceable and lacks musical examples.

CARNER, like Monson, is built upon foundations laid by others, and is thus largely derivative. Beyond that the book is badly written, poorly organized, repetitious, frustratingly simple-minded, and peppered with irrelevant footnotes. Berg's early years and works are given perfunctory treatment (there is, for instance, no mention of Watznauer) and the analyses (likewise largely derivative) lack the imaginative sophistication of Adorno or the cogency of Redlich or Perle. New information regarding Berg's relationship to certain French and Italian composers (including personal communications by Malipiero and Milhaud) is given inordinate prominence, while the author's access to the then published correspondence between Berg and Schoenberg (now available in *The Berg-Schoenberg Correspondence: Selected Letters*, translated and edited by Juliane Brand, Christopher Hailey, and Donald Harris, New York and London, Norton, 1987) is not balanced by a knowledge of other relevant sources such as the Berg-Webern correspondence. The revised and expanded edition of Carner's book incorporates most—though not all—of the major biographical discoveries to that date, making it the most comprehensive English-language biographical narrative, but one that can be recommended only by default.

—Christopher Hailey

BERGMAN, Ingmar, 1918–   ; Swedish film director.

Cowie, Peter, *Ingmar Bergman: A Critical Biography*. New York, Scribner, and London, Secker and Warburg, 1982.
Gado, Frank, *The Passion of Ingmar Bergman*. Durham, North Carolina, Duke University Press, 1986.
Gibson, Arthur, *The Silence of God: Creative Response to the Films of Ingmar Bergman*. New York, Harper, 1969.
Steene, Birgitta, *Ingmar Bergman*. New York, Twayne, 1968.
Young, Vernon, *Cinema Borealis: Ingmar Bergman and the Swedish Ethos*. New York, D. Lewis, 1971.

*

Almost every critic who has written about Ingmar Bergman finds his films to be, to some degree, autobiographical. Consequently, these critics—and there must be 30 of them—pick around in his life for details to bolster their critical insights. Some of them do it brilliantly, casting beams of light on Bergman's childhood, his associates, his reading, his sex life, or his theology. On this last topic, GIBSON is best, but in addition there are David R. Nelson, *Ingmar Bergman: The Search for God*, 1966, and Richard Blake, *The Lutheran Milieu of the Films of Ingmar Bergman*, 1978. Treating Bergman's dreams are Vlada Pertic, editor, *Films and Dreams: An Approach to Bergman*, 1981, and John Donner, *The Personal Vision of Ingmar Bergman*, 1962, which, despite its title, is not essentially biographical.

The best of these is a large study (544 pages) by GADO, who spells out exactly what he is up to: he finds recurring themes in Bergman to be "surrogates for conflicts deep in Bergman's personal history. The relationship of that inner drama to the artistic creation agitated by it is my central subject." Gado's initial chapters, "The Depths of Childhood" and "A Foothold in Theater," detailed and intense, present new information, frequently appalling; for example, Bergman's saying, "It doesn't matter what government is in power, so long as it is possible to go on performing theater."

A similar kind of biographical treatment deserves comment: the book-length critical study that begins, routinely and competently, but briefly, with an introductory chapter or two of biography; for example, Chapter I of STEENE, "A Biographical Note"—six pages. Yet another approach is less personal than ethnographic—that is, Bergman as a part of his context or landscape, variously defined. YOUNG—note his subtitle about the Swedish Ethos—sounds like some of his biographical entries, such as Paul Bitten Austin, *On Being Swedish*, 1968, or Robert Hendlin, *Suicide and Scandinavia*, 1964.

All of these approaches, however useful to the film historian or aesthetician, never add up to a satisfying biography. All alone, as a full biography, is COWIE. Cowie presents the chronological story of Bergman's life, stopping at appropriate dates to fulfill the promise of his subtitle: *A Critical Biography*. Moments of trauma in Bergman's life—fear, sadism, anger, frustration, punishment, humiliation—are used to illustrate themes in his movies. This leads to a few lapses. For example, "Bergman's immersion in Nazi life and culture at an impressionable age" is not explored; it is merely mentioned to account for a touch of the Gothic or supernatural in *The Serpent's Egg*. If he feels a concept illuminates a movie, Cowie becomes completely engaged. For example, "Bergman's childhood was clouded by a terrible fear of punishment and humiliation." The most thorough of all Bergman biographers, Cowie takes the reader back to the 16th century for family "piety, diligence, and an innate conservatism"; he also frequently includes details that may not influence Bergman's art (early bed-wetting, stammering, ulcers, formal education, his wives and children, administrative jobs).

One final book must be mentioned—indeed recommended—for filling in gaps (tax problems, spankings, working methods, money, masturbation, suicide attempts, dreams, divorces), many personal opinions (about Olivier, for example, and Garbo), and passions (jealousy, lying, depression, friendships, loneliness, and tedium—"tedium hung like a damp dishcloth round my soul"): Bergman's own *The Magic Lantern* (1988). No biographer would dare sum up Bergman's life as painfully as Bergman

himself (quoting Strindberg): "Life is short but it can be long while it lasts."

—Paul H. Stacy

BERGSON, Henri, 1859–1941; French philosopher.

Chevalier, Jacques, *Henri Bergson*, translated by Lilian A. Clare. New York, Macmillan, and London, Ryder, 1928.

Hanna, Thomas, editor, *The Bergsonian Heritage*. New York, Columbia University Press, 1962.

Ruhe, Algot and Nancy Margaret Paul, *Henri Bergson: An Account of His Life and Philosophy*. London, Macmillan, 1914.

Slosson, Edwin E., *Major Prophets of Today*. Boston, Little Brown, 1914.

*

HANNA's *The Bergsonian Heritage* is a collection of papers presented as a tribute to Bergson on the centenary of the philosopher's birth. Hanna attempts to situate Bergson in the historical-academic atmosphere of his time. His references to Bergson are only incidentally biographical, as he deals not so much with "the man" as with "his works." Yet several of the contributions treat Bergson's personal life and his relations with students and colleagues. Jean Hyppolite gives us an insight into Bergson, the student among students, his love of learning, his interest in various disciplines, his friendships at the Sorbonne and the College de France. He is eloquent in describing the enthusiasms and the frustrations of Bergson. All these, Hyppolite claims, are important in the construction of an intellectual biography. Maurice Merleau-Ponty points out the difficulties Bergson encountered—"a philosopher under a curse"—and looks at him retired and almost silent, yet aware of a great following for the many years of his active teaching and his firmness in the pursuit of truth. Merleau-Ponty gives us an insight into Bergson the mystic, and he dwells on the honors bestowed on Bergson after the years of difficulties and contrasts, all the while tracing the philosopher's thought as it develops. Vladimir Jankelevitch sees Bergson against the background of the Greek philosophers—an innovator, but one who practiced simplicity to the end of his life, and called for a return to this virtue as a prerequisite for philosophical reflection. Marcel Bataillon looks at Bergson's teaching career, including his public lectures; gives details of the public's attendance; speaks of Bergson's eloquence, his seriousness and zeal. He tells of Bergson's contacts with the Spanish in his good-will mission to that country and of the simple tenor of Bergson's life. His biographical note stresses the active side of Bergson. Jean Wahl acquaints the reader with the vicissitudes of Bergson at the Sorbonne because of his *new* philosophy. Gabriel Marcel also tells of life at the Sorbonne and at the College de France with Bergson. Contrary to the judgment of Bataillon, he sees Bergson as militating against the spirit of seriousness.

CHEVALIER's book bears witness to the intellectual activity of Bergson, for the author attended Bergson's lectures in Paris and wrote from personal experience. After a general discussion of the milieu and the historical period in which Bergson lived,

Chevalier dedicates a long chapter to "the man and the work." Herein he tells of Bergson's life, his intellectual training and achievements, often quoting the words of Bergson himself. He goes into specific details of Bergson's development first as student and then as teacher, focusing on the specific characteristics of his personality in his relations with his fellow students and, later, his colleagues. He takes note of his excellent and vast education and the evident superiority of his intellect, open to multiple aspects of learning. Chevalier's book is rich in anecdotes, sometimes humorous, always revealing the man and the reaction of his fellows. Upon reading this work one gains a clear perspective on Bergson's influence and reputation inside and outside of France.

The volume by RUHE AND PAUL aims to serve as a guide to Bergson's works; the biographical material is subsidiary to an account of Bergson's thought and teaching. While viewing Bergson's as a typical French professor's life, Ruhe and Paul do offer some interesting details of his early years, marked by indecision about the choice between science and philosophy. Most often writers use Bergson's own words to bring out a trait of character or reveal the beginning of the thought that was to develop. They also cover an interesting and seldom noted period of Bergson's life, his "spiritual retreat" during which his thought matured. Their descriptions of place and of Bergson's diverse activities at that time further highlight the story of his life, just before his philosophical debut.

Besides including quotations from Bergson's lectures and writings, this book traces his movements from one teaching position to another, from one habitation to another, from one honor to another while books, articles, and pamphlets about this philosophy multiply. Ruhe and Paul provide a useful source of information about this philosopher whose life is intimately related to his thought. Other works for which the briefest biography serves as introduction to the thought that defines the man include Leszek Kolakowski, *Bergson* (1985), A. E. Pilkington, *Bergson and His Influence* (1976), and R. R. Lacey, *Bergson* (1989).

SLOSSON's volume deals with the lives and works of several philosophers, among them Henri Bergson. Slosson's purpose is to present each as clearly as possible and "to convince [himself] that these men are real flesh and blood, not paper and ink." Accordingly, although the 64 pages devoted to Bergson are not pure biography, they contain many interesting facts, anecdotes, and personal events of Bergson's life to make his character and personality come alive. Slosson rehearses the details of Bergson as student, teacher, lecturer, educator, diplomat, "mystic" even, conveying to the reader a lively picture of the man whose life, according to Slosson, is that of a prophet in his chosen field. Speaking about the great following Bergson acquired among all sorts of people, Slosson relieves his "prophet" of responsibility for the misuse or misintrepetation of his philosophy or the rash, spontaneous actions inspired by his enthusiasm. Slosson takes note of Bergson's encounters with other philosophers, particularly in America, and his reaction to them and their culture. Slosson closes his section on Bergson with a note on "How to Read Bergson," and an annotated bibliography of writings by and about Bergson—a good listing up to 1914, but not comparable to P. A. Y. Gunter's *Henri Bergson: A Bibliography of Bergson* (1974; revised edition, 1986). Despite its relative brev-

ity, Slosson's presentation of Bergson's life in relation to his works is well worth reading.

—Mary-Rose Barral

BERKELEY, George, 1685–1753; Irish philosopher and bishop.

Fraser, Alexander Campbell, *The Life and Letters of George Berkeley, D. D.* Oxford, Clarendon Press, 1871.

Gaustad, Edwin S., *George Berkeley in America.* New Haven, Connecticut, Yale University Press, 1979.

Hicks, George Dawes, *Berkeley.* London, E. Benn, 1932.

Luce, Arthur A., *The Life of George Berkeley Bishop of Cloyne.* London and New York, T. Nelson, 1949.

Stock, Joseph, *An Account of the Life of George Berkeley, D. D., Late Bishop of Cloyne in Ireland.* London, J. Murray, 1776; reprinted in Berman, David, editor, *George Berkeley: 18th-Century Responses* (2 vols.), New York, Garland, 1988.

Wisdom, John O., *The Unconscious Origins of Berkeley's Philosophy.* London, Hogarth Press, 1953.

*

Given Berkeley's place in the history of philosophy and his remarkably varied career, it is surprising that he has been the object of so little attention from biographers. Nearly every study of Berkeley's philosophy contains a perfunctory chapter that repeats the salient particulars of his life, but to date only six works attempt serious biography.

LUCE has written unquestionably the standard work in the field. Published as a companion to the nine-volume edition of Berkeley's works, it incorporates material unavailable to previous biographers and is a very readable presentation. It is not, however, above criticism. Luce lacked the requisite critical detachment from his subject and thus his work tends toward hagiography. Moreover, his account moves quite quickly over episodes of interest. For example, Luce devotes only two pages to a summary of the mathematical controversy provoked by Berkeley's *Analyst*, and the treatment of Berkeley's life in London literary circles is too superficial to be of much use.

FRASER's work is an excellent complement to Luce, despite the fact that it was first published well over a century ago. At over 700 pages, it contains a wealth of useful information. Luce himself described it as "a mine for biographers and a quarry of rough-hewn material," and the judgment stands. Fraser interleaves narrative passages, letters, and other writings, which makes for a surprisingly vibrant portrait of Berkeley in his milieux. On points where Luce and Fraser disagree, one at least has recourse to Fraser's voluminous footnotes, which may lead to new research.

GAUSTAD's volume, much more limited in scope, is an admirably executed work. Dealing only with Berkeley's journey to Newport as part of his project to found a college in America, Gaustad covers all of the relevant ground and gives an excellent treatment of this five-year period in Berkeley's life as well as the background to the failed enterprise. Philosophers may find it short on an account of Berkeley's thought, but this is hardly a serious drawback.

HICKS provides essentially a commentary on Berkeley's philosophy, but it contains sufficient biographical material to be mentioned here. Hicks presents Berkeleyan metaphysics and epistemology in relation to Berkeley's philosophical predecessors and successors, but also includes an extended chapter on Berkeley's "Life and Times." It breaks no new biographical ground, but is a source for someone principally interested in Berkeley's philosophy with a secondary interest in the biography.

STOCK is of strictly antiquarian interest, his work having been published more than two centuries ago and now reprinted as part of a series that explores 18th-century responses to Berkeley. It is unreliable on certain points and has been wholly superseded by Fraser and Luce, but can be read profitably by historians interested in how Berkeley was seen by his contemporaries.

WISDOM should be read only for amusement. An attempt at the discredited genre of "psychobiography," his work is useless for serious purposes. Wisdom presents his study in the orthodox Freudian idiom, and the text is replete with talk of sublimation, oral stages, unresolved oedipal conflict, good and bad feces, etc. Read for amusement, it can reach comic heights but must be avoided at all costs by anyone seriously interested in Berkeley's life.

—Douglas M. Jesseph

BERLIOZ, Hector, 1803–1869; French composer.

Barzun, Jacques, *Berlioz and the Romantic Century* (2 vols.). Boston, Little Brown, 1950; London, Gollancz, 1951; as *Berlioz and His Century: An Introduction to the Age of Romanticism*, Cleveland, World Publishing, 1956.
Cairns, David, *Berlioz 1803-32: The Making of an Artist*. London, Deutsch, 1989.
Clarson-Leach, Robert, *Berlioz: His Life and Times*. London, Midas, and New York, Hippocrene, 1983.
Crabbe, John, *Hector Berlioz, Rational Romantic*. New York, Taplinger, and London, Kahn and Averhill, 1980.
Elliott, John H., *Berlioz*. London, Dent, 1938.
Macdonald, Hugh, *Berlioz*. London, Dent, 1982.
Turner, W. J., *Berlioz: The Man and His Work*. London, Dent, 1934.
Wotton, Tom S., *Hector Berlioz*. London, Oxford University Press, 1935.

*

When asked what was the best edition of a book, Dr. Johnson replied: "The latest." This is particularly the case with biographies of Berlioz, whose music has taken so long to establish itself since his death in 1869 that research into his life and work is still going on. No man is a prophet in his own country, and, except for a few discerning musicians, France promptly forgot about him as soon as he died. If mentioned at all, he was dismissed as an eccentric and a *poseur*. The first extended French biography, by Adolphe Boschot (three volumes, 1906-13), did little to change this impression. As late as 1939 another French biographer, Guy de Pourtalès, reported sadly that Berlioz's music still attracted little interest in France, and that, when featured in concert programmes, it was badly played. The situation was different in Germany, where, even during Berlioz's lifetime, conductors enthused about the music and included it in their repertory. It was Germany, too, that initiated the first complete edition of his orchestral scores. In England, as well, Berlioz had many supporters, and by the 1930s his music was regularly heard there. To this period belongs TURNER's book, the first full-length study in English. For years Turner had championed Berlioz, and his pioneering book, though overtaken by later research, is still worth reading. So also is WOTTON's, which appeared in the following year. As the leading Berlioz scholar of the time, Wotton wrote with the benefit of 50 years' study of his subject. His criticism is informed and his judgments are authoritative. ELLIOTT is straightforward, though not particularly informative. MACDONALD, in any case, supersedes him in the "Master Musicians" series. The biographical sketch is crammed within 75 pages, and the greater part of the book is devoted to technical consideration of the music.

None of the earlier biographers had access to the mass of documentation that had become available by 1950, the year of BARZUN's imposing two-volume biography. Wotton had been a personal friend of Barzun and had given him the valuable archives he had built up over the years. To these Barzun was able to add the results of his own wide-ranging research, including many unpublished letters, manuscripts and documents of every description. The bibliography alone covers 75 pages and includes details of every picture, bust, caricature, photograph and print ever made of the composer. Barzun is so intent on getting the record straight that he adds an appendix listing errors and omissions in the German edition of the music and in earlier biographies. He does not give music examples in the text, although he discusses the music at length and with authority. Barzun's remains a monumental study.

CRABBE's book, a novel and stimulating presentation of Berlioz as an intellectual, examines the literary influences that formed Berlioz's taste and shows how his acquaintance with art and history coloured the music and the brilliant journalism he wrote. This might be described as an intellectual and artistic biography. CLARSON-LEACH offers no original research in his popular biography, but the work is enriched by illustrations that, among others, show many of the places still standing where Berlioz lived.

The latest major biography is, like Barzun's, in two volumes, of which the first appeared in 1989. CAIRNS was especially qualified to write it since, unlike many music critics, he had actually played in the orchestra (percussion) at performances of *La Damnation de Faust*. His book appears at a time when Berlioz has become a subject of academic research and a respectable target for scholarly enquiry. Much new material has become available since Barzun wrote, including several hundred unpublished letters, and this enables Cairns to give a fuller picture. The first volume takes us up to 1832 and the sensational "grand concert dramatique" Berlioz organized to launch his *Symphonie Fantastique* and *Lélio* on an astonished Paris audience, which included Liszt, Chopin, Paganini, Hugo and Dumas. Like Barzun, Cairns does not feature musical examples and avoids technical appraisal, although the works, as he rightly says, are a "dominant presence" and analyses of them are smoothly blended in with the narrative of the life. Typical of his penetrating approach to Berlioz is the comment: "His is not consoling music. Its nerves are exposed. With all its ardours and exaltations, it is disturbingly alive to the torments of man's existence, outside and within. Its passionate sense of beauty carries with it an acute awareness of how frail and ephemeral beauty is." At the same time Cairns draws a vivid picture of the intense, witty young genius who was to compose music that is like no other. Cairns writes with a journalist's eye for colourful detail (he is music critic of the London *Sunday Times*) and the scholar's regard for precision. Despite the vast amount of material he handles he never loses sight of the wood for the trees. The narrative flows easily, is highly readable and is unimpeded by the footnotes, which are discreetly tucked away at the back, each important statement or quotation buttressed by impeccable references to the exact source. There is no doubt that Cairns is the first choice for anyone who wants a full-length portrait supported by the latest research. The second and final volume will be well worth waiting for.

—James Harding

BERNHARDT, Sarah [*born* Henriette-Rosine Bernard], 1844–1923; French actress.

Arthur, Sir George, *Sarah Bernhardt*. London, Heinemann, and New York, Doubleday, 1923.

Baring, Maurice, *Sarah Bernhardt*. London, Davies, 1933; New York, Appleton-Century, 1934.

Emboden, William, *Sarah Bernhardt*. London, Studio Vista, 1974; New York, Macmillan, 1975.

Richardson, Joanna, *Sarah Bernhardt*. London, Reinhardt, 1959.

Row, Arthur William, *Sarah the Divine*. New York, Comet Press, 1957.

Skinner, Cornelia Otis, *Madame Sarah*. Boston, Houghton Mifflin, 1966; Bath, Chivers, 1973.

Verneuil, Louis, *The Fabulous Life of Sarah Bernhardt*, translated by Ernest Boyd. New York and London, Harper, 1942 (originally published as *La Vie Merveilleuse de Sarah Bernhardt*, Montréal, Éditions Variétés, 1942).

*

Any biographer of Sarah Bernhardt faces two formidable tasks. The first of these involves sifting through the mass of materials that testifies to the length and breadth of her career as the most famous international star of the 19th century. The second task involves the exercise of judgment in using these materials, for Bernhardt was herself instrumental in generating publicity of all kinds—not all of it consistent with fact.

The earliest biographers came under the strong spell of Bernhardt's personality and the idealized version of her life she had set down in her own memoirs, *Ma Double Vie* (1907). ARTHUR's book, for example, offers a brief and nearly mythic account of her childhood which might as well have been drawn directly from Bernhardt's memoirs, and he recapitulates Bernhardt's emphases on her patriotic exploits at the expense of other key events, such as the conception of her son and only child, Maurice. The problem Arthur's book offers to the general reader lies in the extremely narrow range of incidents it treats. It seems to have been guided in this partly by Arthur's primness, partly by Bernhardt's highly selective view of her own life, and partly by Arthur's manifest grief at Bernhardt's recent death and his consequent desire to memorialize her in the most flattering way.

BARING is, like Arthur, British, and his impressions of Bernhardt are similarly shaped by his first having seen her act and then, later, meeting her. He is also typical of her earliest biographers in his gentlemanly skirting of her failures on the stage, and in his reluctance to deal with the more sensational elements of her private life. He is especially informative on those roles he himself had seen Bernhardt play, and on her collaborations with the French playwright and director, Victorien Sardou. Baring repeats at some length Bernhardt's opinions of other actors whose work she had seen, particularly British ones, suggesting something of the actress' own tastes and techniques. On the other hand, Baring regards Bernhardt's acting as "unconscious," and so renders her skill the function of inspiration or of accident.

VERNEUIL is the first—and so far the only—French biographer to have his work translated into English. Verneuil's testimony is particularly valuable, not only because he married Bernhardt's granddaughter and wrote two of the final plays in which the actress appeared, but also because as a Frenchman he captures the nationalistic strains in Bernhardt's roles, aided that way by his familiarity with the French stage and its history over several decades.

Because he was close to the actress in her declining years, Verneuil is able to recreate very fully a period when Bernhardt had partly receded from the glare of publicity. Verneuil is good, too, in suggesting the shrewd commercial instincts that animated Bernhardt's long career as a manager and producer. He is not flattering to Sarah's efforts as a playwright, but himself falls victim to the playwright's impulse to render her life in dialogue during episodes where he cannot himself have been present; and in so doing he undercuts some of his other claims to reliability.

ROW's biography comes from a sometime press agent for Bernhardt. This biographer's own youthful experience as an actor manifests itself in a fascination in the overlap between the actress' work onstage and her private life which, although speculative and tortured at times, does suggest the nature of her commitment to her roles—and particularly as it informed her choices in stage vehicles. As a whole, this short book offers glimpses of Bernhardt rather than a continuous picture of her life, and at its best yields sharp images in its selectivity that ameliorate in part its tendencies toward idolatry and mythification.

RICHARDSON is the first of the biographers treated so far who never saw Bernhardt on the stage. By naming and conceding Bernhardt's mythic quality, Richardson succeeds in moderating the worshipful tones of the earlier biographers. She deals frankly as well with Bernhardt's fall from critical favor beginning in the 1890s, which came as a sort of penalty for her huge popular success. Richardson's short and numerous chapters disclose Bernhardt's life in many of its facets, and so reduce the mingling between public and personal concerns that tends to blur the actress' work in earlier biographies.

SKINNER's book is notable for bringing the sensibility of an important actress to bear on Bernhardt's life. Skinner does particularly well in treating the early and middle phases of Bernhardt's career, suggesting that the actress' technique froze together with her reputation in her later years on the stage. She calls a number of sources into question that had been credited by all previous biographers except Richardson; and she, more than the other biographers who had seen Bernhardt act, seems able to distance herself from her girlish impressions in evoking qualities that typified Bernhardt's style.

EMBODEN's book represents the most recent of Bernhardt biographies. It might properly be called "an illustrated life," containing the best and largest collection of photographs of the actress in any biography. At times Emboden's terseness and taste for the dramatic lead him to oversimplify facets of Bernhardt's career—as he does when belittling the acting of her husband, Jacques Damala, who, in fact, attracted a good deal of favorable attention at the time of his earliest appearances opposite Sarah.

Emboden's chapters on Bernhardt's recording and film careers oppose the tendency of Skinner and others to dismiss Bernhardt's later acting as merely repetitive and desperate. They capture instead an actress who saw the future clearly and who sought to make herself part of it. Emboden also evokes the gambling spirit that enlivened Bernhardt's career as an actress from its first years until its end, within days of her death.

—Leigh Woods

BERNSTEIN, Leonard, 1918–1990; American conductor and composer.

Gradenwitz, Peter, *Leonard Bernstein: The Infinite Variety of a Musician.* London, Berg Publishers, 1987.
Peyser, Joan, *Bernstein: A Biography.* New York, Beach Tree Books, 1987.
Robinson, Paul, *Bernstein.* New York, Vanguard, and London, Macdonald, 1982.

*

ROBINSON states in his Preface that his book "was developed from radio programs broadcast over CJRT-FM in Toronto." The rather slim volume comprises 111 pages of text and devotes three chapters to straightforward biographical data. Chapters four, five, and six consider Bernstein as an interpreter of music, while chapter seven, "A Summing Up," is largely devoted to his conducting career. A discography of some 36 pages and a selected bibliography of peripheral material swells the book to 149 pages.

One of Robinson's stated goals is "to offer a balanced overview of Bernstein the Conductor." To this end he devotes chapter four to "Music before 1800," with chapters five and six focused on Beethoven and Mahler, respectively. These deal

/briefly with the standard works of each composer. Robinson does not attempt a deep analysis of Bernstein's thought, and his comments are couched in terms understandable to the layman.

GRADENWITZ's format is similar to that of Robinson: a straightforward biography of four chapters followed by a consideration, not of Bernstein's performance, but of his compositions. In chapter four, "From Juvenile Songs to Broadway," Gradenwitz traces the gradual development of Bernstein's early creativity, covering various abstract early compositions. Chapters five and six deal with his symphonic works, his theatre music, and his ballet music. Chapter seven is entirely given over to "West Side Story," and chapter eight moves on to his later compositions. Chapter nine departs from Bernstein's music to relate his activities as a musical pedagogue, and chapter ten, the last chapter, is devoted chiefly to laudatory descriptions by professional colleagues in relating their experiences with him. Bibliographical materials in Gradenwitz's volume include a list of Bernstein's writings, "Bibliographical Literature," "Analytical Theses and Essays," and general literature that refers to Bernstein. Films and Video Tapes and a selected bibliography complete the Appendices.

On an entirely different level, PEYSER has written a biography incorporating the positive aspects of Bernstein as a musician with analyses of the negative aspects of his character and interpersonal behavior. Peyser states in her Preface: "The purpose of this book is to try to find out why Bernstein is the way he is, why he made the choices he did, and why, with his fame and wealth, his later years have been characterized by frustration and despair." Peyser's text includes fair and generous laudatory evaluations. Shedding light on his immense gift, she also does not hesitate to reveal specific destructive aspects of his behavior, both toward himself and toward others. As a result, Peyser's biography stands as the most detailed and multi-faceted source of information available about Bernstein.

However, this biography is greatly enriched by reaching well beyond the central character to deal with the complex tapestry of musical life in the mid and late 20th century, woven by composers and performers who contributed to its history, particularly in the United States. Via Bernstein's life, Peyser has written a carefully researched account of a significant area of the musical activity of our century. The text, with its introduction and acknowledgments, covers 465 pages. No appendices of discography or bibliography are included, but her exhaustive coverage in interviews and research produces a long index replete with varied references and names of people in wide-ranging disciplines and personal relationships.

—Rosalyn Tureck

BEYLE, Marie-Henri. See **STENDHAL.**

BIERCE, Ambrose, 1842–1914; American writer.

De Castro, Adolphe, *Portrait of Ambrose Bierce.* New York, Century, 1929.

Fatout, Paul, *Ambrose Bierce: The Devil's Lexicographer.* Norman, University of Oklahoma Press, 1951.

Fatout, Paul, *Ambrose Bierce and the Black Hills.* Norman, University of Oklahoma Press, 1956.

Grattan, C. Hartley, *Bitter Bierce: A Mystery of American Letters.* New York, Doubleday, 1929.

Grenander, M. E., *Ambrose Bierce.* New York, Twayne, 1971.

McWilliams, Carey, *Ambrose Bierce: A Biography.* New York, A. and C. Boni, 1929.

Neale, Walter, *Life of Ambrose Bierce.* New York, Neale, 1929.

O'Connor, Richard, *Ambrose Bierce: A Biography.* Boston, Little Brown, 1967; London, Gollancz, 1968.

Saunders, Richard, *Ambrose Bierce: The Making of a Misanthrope.* San Francisco, Chronicle, 1985.

Starrett, Vincent, *Ambrose Bierce.* Chicago, W. M. Hill, 1920; as *Buried Caesars*, Chicago, Covici McGee, 1923.

Walker, Franklin, *Ambrose Bierce: The Wickedest Man in San Francisco.* San Francisco, Colt Press, 1941.

Wiggins, Robert A., *Ambrose Bierce.* Minneapolis, University of Minnesota Press, 1964.

*

Many biographies have been written about Ambrose Bierce, but no modern work can be termed both definitive and scholarly. Bierce is a likely subject for re-examination. He was a gifted writer: the 12 volumes of his collected works include devastatingly witty epigrams, satire, journalism, poetry, and fiction, among other pieces. He was fearless, commended for bravery during the Civil War. He was handsome, attracting many female admirers. He was adventurous, willing to undertake a trek westward through untamed country, to mine for gold in the Dakota Territory, or to seek combat in Mexico. And there may be renewed popular interest in Bierce resulting from the 1989 film "Old Gringo," which was based upon the novel by the noted Mexican writer, Carlos Fuentes, who in turn is said to have taken his inspiration from accounts of Bierce's final days in Mexico.

FATOUT's 1951 biography deals inconclusively with the mystery surrounding Bierce's Mexican adventure and his death there, but it is the most comprehensive and scholarly book on the life of Ambrose Bierce. Fatout was a member of the English Department at Purdue University in Indiana when he conducted his research, and he was given access to family papers by members of the Bierce family still living in that state. His book is readable and fully documented.

It must be read in conjunction with Fatout's 1956 book on Bierce's experiences in the Black Hills. Bierce spent several months there in 1880 as general agent of a mining company organized to extract gold from the land near Deadwood. He finally left in disgust over niggardly financing. *Ambrose Bierce and the Black Hills* is a full-length treatment of this period in Bierce's life—a period that Fatout's earlier biography deals with only in passing.

GRENANDER's biography, like both of Fatout's books, is scholarly and fully attributed. As biography it is too brief to be satisfactory—in 75 pages little can be said about a life so complex and varied as that of Ambrose Bierce. The remaining 100 pages of text in Grenander's book are devoted to evaluation of his works, as is customary for books in the Twayne series. The volume is a quick and reliable introduction to the man and his works. But it falls short as biography.

O'CONNOR's biography is a highly readable, popular work, but casual in its citation and heavily dependent on published secondary sources, whereas both Fatout and Grenander appear to have made special efforts to locate original materials. But O'Connor—a facile writer and experienced biographer—has nevertheless produced an entertaining account of Bierce's life, and it probably is the biography of choice for the casual reader rather than the researcher.

In 1929, just 15 years after the death of Ambrose Bierce, four biographies were published. Of these, GRATTAN's can be dismissed most easily—by the author's own admission. He apologizes for the paucity of information on which his book is based, noting that most of the persons who claimed to have known Bierce intimately turned out to be less than authoritative. Grattan also acknowledges that Bierce's daughter refused to allow him access to her father's letters. He apologizes for using footnotes (which are, in fact, quite infrequent), saying that he wishes future students to quarrel with his authorities rather than with him. Only about 25,000 words of his text are biographical (about 35 percent of the book). The remainder is based upon Bierce's published works.

DE CASTRO's biography, also published in 1929, is important for its original source material. Adolphe Danziger, as Adolphe de Castro was then known, met Bierce in 1886, and over the next several years the two men experienced a love-hate relationship—disputing over matters of collaboration, copyright, and finances, among other things. Bierce did not hold Danziger's reliability and credibility in high regard, and the reader will share the same doubts. The biography is self-serving in its account of the relationship between Danziger and Bierce, and at the same time it is almost sycophantic.

NEALE's book is, like de Castro's work, important for its original source material. Neale was the publisher of Bierce's collected works, published in 1909. They had met in 1901, and Neale regarded himself as Bierce's close friend. He writes in the preface that Bierce had asked Neale to become his biographer. Most of the book might be called a reminiscence, as it deals with the period of their relationship. That it is an account of Bierce's life as Neale knew him is both its value and its flaw, as there is no corroboration offered—no citations of any kind. There are many lengthy direct quotations that Neale must have reconstructed years later, suggesting either a photographic mind or a degree of creativity. And there is a good deal of peripheral material, such as a chapter on plagiarism that involves Bierce only tangentially. But Neale's book, for all its discursiveness, is nonetheless valuable.

McWILLIAMS' book is a rather remarkable work for a 24-year-old writer—as thorough and as well written as the work of an experienced scholar. Unfortunately, McWilliams does not consider citations to be of much importance; his bibliography, however, is extensive. One notes with interest that while McWilliams thanks Bierce's daughter Helen for her patience and generosity with information, Grattan was forced to consult a lawyer about her intransigence, Neale minimizes her knowledge of her father, and de Castro merely mentions her in passing.

Besides the full-length works cited above, there are several short biographies that should be mentioned. STARRETT's 1920 volume was the first to be devoted exclusively to Bierce, according to Starrett. A critical and biographical monograph, it was limited to 250 copies. WALKER's slim volume of 46 pages, printed on fine paper in an edition of 550 copies, relies on the biographies of McWilliams and Neale for details of Bierce's life. WIGGINS' 48-page introduction to Bierce in the "University of Minnesota Pamphlets on American Writers Series" is chiefly of interest to young students. SAUNDERS' 110-page book concentrates on Bierce's California years and contains a number of photographs not available in earlier biographies.

—Whitney R. Mundt

BISMARCK, Otto Eduard Leopold von, 1815–1898; German statesman, first Chancellor of German Empire.

Crankshaw, Edward, *Bismarck*. New York, Viking, and London, Macmillan, 1981.

Eyck, Erich, *Bismarck and the German Empire*. London, Allen and Unwin, 1950.

Gall, Lothar, *Bismarck: The White Revolutionary* (2 vols.), translated by J. A. Underwood. London, Allen and Unwin, 1986 (originally published by Propyläen, Frankfurt am Main, 1980).

Headlam, James W., *Bismarck and the Foundation of the German Empire*. New York, Putnam, 1899.

Kent, George O., *Bismarck and His Times*. Carbondale, Southern Illinois University Press, 1978.

Lowe, Charles, *Prince Bismarck: An Historical Biography* (2 vols.). London and New York, Cassell, 1885.

Medlicott, W. N., *Bismarck and Modern Germany*. London, Hodder and Stoughton, and New York, Harper, 1965.

Palmer, Alan, *Bismarck*. London, Weidenfeld and Nicolson, and New York, Scribner, 1976.

Pflanze, Otto, *Bismarck and the Development of Germany* (3 vols.). Princeton, New Jersey, Princeton University Press, 1963-90.

Robertson, Charles G., *Bismarck*. London, Constable, 1918; New York, Holt, 1919.

Stern, Fritz, *Gold and Iron: Bismarck, Bleichroder, and the Building of the German Empire*. New York, Knopf, and London, Allen and Unwin, 1977.

Taylor, A. J. P., *Bismarck: The Man and the Statesman*. New York, Knopf, and London, Hamilton, 1955.

*

Otto von Bismarck, the "Iron Chancellor," architect of German unification, has been the focus of thousands of scholarly and amateur studies since his dismissal as chancellor by Kaiser Wilhelm II in 1890. The first account of Bismarck in English, a two-volume study written in 1885 by LOWE, the *Times of London* correspondent in Berlin, offers an interesting journalistic as opposed to academic perspective on the statesman. Lowe's first volume covers the period from Waterloo to the founding of the

German nation in 1871, while volume two explores in exhaustive detail Bismarck's chancellorship.

HEADLAM, like Lowe, gives a contemporary's insight into the Chancellor's personality and achievements, paying particular attention to the years 1847-71 (from his marriage to Johanna v. Puttkamer and his service in the Diet through the Constitutional Crisis and Wars of Unification). Only three sparse chapters are devoted to Bismarck's post-unification policies. Unlike Lowe, however, Headlam, a historical advisor to the British Foreign Office, relies more on scholarly works, including M. Busch's three-volume *Some Secret Pages of his History* (London, 1898) and Charles Lowe's *Bismarck's Table Talk* (London, 1900; an abridged translation of H. von Poschinger's three-volume *Fürst Bismarck und die Parlamentarier*), as the basis for his book. Headlam's is a readable account that portrays the Iron Chancellor in a very favorable light, as "bold and decisive" and "cautious and prudent." This work, however, has a detectable Francophobic bias, as in Headlam's ascription of the Franco-Prusian War to the French people's "sleeping jealousy of Prussia."

ROBERTSON's 1919 biography, *Bismarck*, is a surprisingly favorable, even fawning, portrayal of Germany's first chancellor. His first chapter, "Germany and the German Problem," examines the deeper intellectual currents of the early 19th century that helped shape Bismarck's own character.

Originally published in a three-volume German edition in 1941, EYCK's *Bismarck and the German Empire* is a one-volume English condensation that appeared in 1950. In the same vein as the earlier biographies, Eyck devotes roughly two-thirds of his study to Bismarck's nation-building and only one-third to his duties as chancellor of the new Reich. Writing as a survivor of Nazi Germany, Dr. Eyck offers a different perspective than did his predecessors. While the author admits that he considers Bismarck to have been the "most important personality in the history and development not only of Germany, but of the whole of Europe, in the second half of the 19th century," he is more skeptical about the legacy of Bismarck's actions. "It is quite another question," Eyck writes, "whether his deeds and achievements helped the genuine progress of Germany and Europe, whether he belongs to the forces of Good or of Evil." Bismarck's reliance on militarism, on the "doctrine of 'blood and iron' and its brilliant and triumphant realization remained overwhelmingly strong," even after Bismarck had departed the historical stage. Eyck, a liberal, does not attempt to conceal his political sympathies, and this makes for interesting reading. Perhaps Eyck is at his best in the final chapter when describing domestic politics after 1871.

The controversial historian A. J. P. TAYLOR is the first biographer in the English language to devote more than half of his study to the chancellor after German unification. This biography is filled with flowery prose and entertaining tidbits about Bismarck's likes and dislikes, his love of food, women and drink, his proclivity "to tears at any public or private crisis," his fierce distaste for opposing viewpoints. While Taylor is quite good at recounting stories about the Iron Chancellor's private and public behavior, he is best at making provocative statements. To take but one example, Taylor claims: "Far from using the [Franco-Prussian] war in order to promote unification, [Bismarck] sought unification in order to continue the war," but offers no proof to support his assessment. Taylor also suggests, in contrast to other accounts, that Bismarck had "no real devotion to the monarchy" and "no faith in the strength of traditional beliefs and institutions." His Bismarck is not a titan or god, but rather a fallible human being, who could not "create the current of events," but "only float with it and steer." Like Eyck, Taylor portrays Bismarck as a great statesman, even a constitutionalist, who cannot be held responsible for the events of the Third Reich. "All he had in common with Hitler," Taylor writes, "was a determination to make his will prevail." If not entirely convincing, Taylor's work is certainly stimulating, and his biography provides a valuable corrective to those books that take for granted Bismarck's ability to foresee and master without difficulty the course of events.

PFLANZE promised in 1963 a second volume of his *Bismarck and the Development of Germany;* in fact, two further volumes appeared in late 1990. Volume I, which has been revised and expanded for the new three-volume set, is the only volume to be considered here. It provides us with a sensitive and scholarly portrayal of Bismarck's career through 1871 and is based upon impressive research. Pflanze assesses Bismarck's actions not solely in terms of his successful foreign policy but also, and equally importantly, in view of German domestic affairs. In taking a different tack from previous historians, Pflanze maintains that the chancellor's obsession with the "expediency of power" promoted the darker side of the German character with its emphasis on militarism, nationalism, and authoritarianism. So too does he place the blame on Bismarck for Germany's weak parliamentary democracy and for establishing "an unfortunate precedent in German history upon which men of other aims and other conscience were eventually to capitalize." Pflanze also attempts to debunk the view commonly held by German historians that German nationalism had widespread support prior to unification by suggesting that the German nationalist movement became a force only under the skillful management of Bismarck. Pflanze's book is well worth reading not only for its point of view but also for its clarity of presentation and the breadth of scholarship upon which it is based.

MEDLICOTT offers a concise and even-handed survey of Bismarck's career from roughly 1862 until his death in 1898. While he agrees with Taylor and Eyck that Bismarck was not "the sole architect and mechanic of German fortunes or misfortunes," and that he "did not come into politics with ready-made plans or unswerving principles," Medlicott concurs with Pflanze that Bismarck did not create Prussian militarism. It had its roots in Prussian history; Bismarck was simply the agent and exploiter of this preexistent force. This small book, which covers both domestic and foreign policy before and after 1871, is an indispensable starting point.

PALMER's book, while a quite detailed synthesis of previous scholarship, does not offer a fresh perspective from which to view Bismarck. The same is generally true of KENT, whose pedestrian narrative is redeemed only by incisive footnotes, which provide a valuable introduction to the research of the 1960s and early 1970s. Less reliable, however, is CRANKSHAW's *Bismarck.* Completed in 1980 before the publication of Gall's massive biography, this work, based on Bismarck's collected letters and memoirs and some secondary sources, does little more than rehash previous scholarship. More distressing, however, are such errors as Crankshaw referring to Leo X instead of Leo XIII (p. 309), Gründungszeit instead of Gründerzeit (p. 315), and Itzen-platz instead of Itzenplitz—Bismarck's minister of commerce (p. 317). An interesting angle on Bismarck is provided by STERN's provocative exploration of the relationship between the chancellor and his Jewish banker, Gerson Bleichröder. This work is intended to complement rather than supersede existing biographies of Bismarck.

By far the most comprehensive and impressive biography of the Iron Chancellor, recently translated from the German and now available in paperback, is that by GALL. His work, less a narrative than an analytical piece on Bismarck himself, is a study about personality rather than about the socio-political forces that shaped him. Gall's Bismarck is a "lone wolf" who "stood for no one but himself," a "conservative revolutionary who paid tribute to the past without becoming a slave to it." Bismarck, in Gall's view, belongs to Hegel's "world-historical individuals." Gall's ability to guide the reader through the labyrinth of Bismarck's foreign and domestic policy with precision must be admired. For Gall, Bismarck's success in foreign policy lay in his flexibility, his failures in domestic affairs in his inability to comprehend the impact of urbanization and to respect parliamentary government. Gall's biography is required reading for all serious students of Bismarck.

—Marilyn Shevin Coetzee

BIZET, Georges, 1838–1875; French composer.

Curtiss, Mina S., *Bizet and His World.* New York, Knopf, 1958; London, Secker and Warburg, 1959.
Dean, Winton, *Bizet.* London, Dent, 1948; revised as *Georges Bizet: His Life and Work,* London, Dent, 1965.
Parker, Douglas, *Georges Bizet: His Life and Works.* London, Kegan Paul, and New York, Harper, 1926.

*

It is ironic that the best biographies of one of France's greatest composers should have been written by Anglo-Saxons. True, there are a number of books about Bizet in French, but none of them can equal, for documentation, accuracy, or depth of insight, those by Curtiss and Dean, an American and Englishman, respectively. PARKER's book, the first full-length English biography, has been outdated by the discovery of important new material, but it remains interesting as an early attempt to gain Bizet the recognition he deserved. Dean's biography appeared in 1947 and was reprinted, much enlarged, in 1964, thanks to the pioneering scholarship of Curtiss (see below), whose book had been published in 1958.

DEAN's book was originally a "Master Musicians" volume in which, as usual with this series, half the space was devoted to the subject's life and the remaining half to a strictly musical analysis. The format went quite a long way to solving the old problem of how to link the man with his work and vice-versa. Even in the earlier edition of the book Dean had shown flair in his appreciation of Bizet as a composer. In the second edition, through study of scores and other items not available when he first wrote, he was able to reinforce his claim for Bizet as a master of opera. Dean looks afresh at the music of *Carmen*—so familiar as to be taken for granted—and reveals the composer's harmonic originality, his mastery of orchestration and tone colour, and his skill at dramatic psychology. At the same time, while benefiting from Curtiss' researches, though not always reaching the same conclusions, Dean found that Bizet's unhappy marriage, up to then represented as an idyll, explained many hitherto baffling aspects of his character. The result was that Dean virtually rewrote his book, which now gives an invaluable picture of Bizet as man and musician. In addition, it includes a useful calendar of events during Bizet's lifetime, a detailed catalogue of works both published and unpublished, a who's who of important characters, and a translation of a rare newspaper article by the composer.

CURTISS was not a musician, and, indeed, her book only came about through a chance event that occurred while she was researching the novelist Marcel Proust. Her book is a perfect example of one type of biography, that in which the writer attempts to portray the subject as seen through the latter's own eyes and those of his contemporaries, rather than through the biographer's. Complete objectivity is, of course, impossible, though Curtiss' book triumphantly exemplifies the method. "The method I have used," she wrote, "seems to me comparable to the weaving of a tapestry designed by a pointillist or perhaps more accurately to a historical painting carried out in *montage*. To a large extent I have abjured the author's right to interpolation . . . although I know that the average reader prefers to accept an author's opinion rather than to formulate his own."

Most of her sources were, and are, unpublished. Each statement is scrupulously documented and every quotation duly and ably footnoted. This can only be done when the biographer is in full control of a wealth of material, which Curtiss certainly was. The title of her book, *Bizet and His World*, expresses exactly her intention, for she sets Bizet precisely in the world of the Second Empire he inhabited—its opera houses, its musical intrigues, its flushed and feverish society and, eventually, its destruction at the hands of Bismarck, who, incidentally, admired *Carmen* so much that he saw it 27 times. The Appendixes contain full translations of significant unpublished letters and a fascinating analysis of Bizet's own music library.

Between them, Dean and Curtiss tell us the most about Bizet, as man and musician, that we shall ever need to know. It is also pleasant to relate that, far from being rivals, they collaborated on terms of great friendship and profited from each other's research in the most graceful fashion.

—James Harding

BLAKE, William, 1757–1827; English poet, painter, and engraver.

Bentley, G. E., Jr., *Blake Records*. Oxford, Clarendon Press, 1969.

Bentley, G. E., Jr., *Blake Records Supplement*. Oxford, Clarendon Press, 1988.

Bruce, Harold, *William Blake in This World*. London, Cape, and New York, Harcourt, 1925.

Davis, Michael, *William Blake: A New Kind of Man*. Berkeley, University of California Press, and London, Elek, 1977.

Ellis, Edwin J., *The Real Blake: A Portrait Biography*. London, Chatto and Windus, and New York, McClure Phillips, 1907.

Gilchrist, Alexander, *Life of William Blake* (2 vols.). London, Macmillan, 1863; edited by Ruthven Todd, 1942.

Lindsay, Jack, *William Blake: His Life and Work*. London, Constable, 1978; New York, G. Braziller, 1979.

Lister, Raymond, *William Blake: An Introduction to the Man and to His Work*. London, G. Bell, and New York, F. Unger, 1968.

Margoliouth, Herschel M., *William Blake*. London and New York, Oxford University Press, 1951.

Swinburne, Algernon Charles, *William Blake: A Critical Essay*. London, Hotten, 1868; revised edition, London, Chatto and Windus, 1906.

Symons, Arthur, *William Blake*. London, Constable, and New York, Dutton, 1907.

Wilson, Mona, *The Life of William Blake*. London, Nonesuch Press, 1927; 3rd edition, edited by Geoffrey Keynes, London and New York, Oxford University Press, 1971.

Wright, Thomas, *The Life of William Blake* (2 vols.). Olney, Buckinghamshire, T. Wright, 1929.

*

In 1828 John Thomas Smith published a 35-page memoir of Blake in volume 2 of his *Nollekens and his Times*. This essay is still valuable today for its firsthand account of Blake, and together with Allan Cunningham's 37-page essay on Blake in volume 2 of *Lives of the Most Eminent British Painters, Sculptors, and Architects* (1829), brings to the forefront issues of major importance for all subsequent biographers. Although Cunningham's essay was more widely read despite its extensive borrowing from Smith, it served as the prime source for biographical information until the publication of Alexander Gilchrist's *Life of William Blake* in 1863.

GILCHRIST's is the first full-length biography and the product of extensive research that began around 1855 and continued until his death in 1861. Gilchrist personally interviewed Blake's former friends and associates, including John Linnell, Samuel Palmer, George Richmond, and Crabb Robinson. After Gilchrist's death in 1861, his wife Anne, with the help of the brothers William Michael and Dante Gabriel Rossetti, completed the volume, which was published in 1863. G. E. Bentley, Jr., points out that, "never has an important literary reputation been posthumously established so instantaneously and effectively." Gilchrist's biography received favorable reviews in every major journal, including a 46-page article published in the *London Quarterly Review* in 1869 that was reprinted for inclusion in the second edition of 1880.

For the 1880 edition, William Michael Rossetti provided a catalogue raisonné of Blake's writings and paintings, many of which have been lost or have yet to come to light. Dante Gabriel Rossetti edited selections from all of Blake's poetry that had been published to date, but because of his "revisions," the text bears little resemblance to the actual poetry as Blake originally intended. The 1942 edition, with annotations by Ruthven Todd, is generally considered to be the standard biography.

SWINBURNE's account is still useful for its insightful commentaries on Blake's early poetry and for a few firsthand accounts of Blake from Seymor Kirkup. In the 1906 edition Swinburne attributes Blake's defects to his Celtic blood and his greatness to his English upbringing. For the most part, Swinburne's book is an enthusiastic exercise in praise of Blake as a fellow practitioner of "art for art's sake." He describes Blake's "Marriage of Heaven and Hell" as the greatest product of the 18th century in the line of high poetry and spiritual speculation.

Swinburne's commentary marks the beginning of enthusiastic, well-meaning, but frequently inaccurate appreciations of Blake, including the biographical section in *The Works of William Blake*, edited by Edwin J. Ellis and William Butler Yeats (3 vols., 1893). For this volume, Ellis and Yeats offered a symbolic system that would explain Blake's work by linking it to the Kabbala and to the myths and legends of the Irish peasantry. Included in this volume, and again in ELLIS' *The Real Blake* (1907), is the notion that Blake was actually the son of an Irish bastard named John O'Neil, who was forced to leave Ireland for financial and political reasons. In England he married Ellen Blake and appropriated her last name. To date no factual information supporting Ellis' argument has surfaced.

SYMONS' volume contains previously unpublished factual information drawn from parish registers and contemporary accounts of Blake. Symons includes every account of Blake that was printed during his lifetime, and between his death and the publication of Gilchrist's *Life of William Blake*. Symons' publication of these items has now been superseded by the photographic facsimile edition of *Nineteenth Century Accounts of William Blake*, by Joseph Wittreich, (Gainesville, Florida, Scholars Facsimiles and Reprints, 1970).

WILSON's book was the most important full-length biographical treatment of Blake to appear since Gilchrist's and is often cited as the standard, authoritative biography. Wilson's study makes generous use of previously unpublished material; it contains 24 plates and six appendices, including the "Rossetti MS." Of interest is Wilson's defense of Blake against charges of insanity by those who seek excuses from having to account for Blake's "Prophetic Books." Wilson also refuses to retreat, as Gilchrist does, from discussions of Blake's radical social, religious, and political views, and yet she maintains a balanced, thorough treatment of her subject. Of the six editions of Wilson's biography, that dating from 1971 is the preferred edition since Keynes has verified quotations, checked references, and added a substantial number of footnotes.

Wilson is sometimes cited as the first to make use of the diary of James Farington (edited by James Greig, New York, 1923), although BRUCE, two years earlier, also cites the diary as a source. Bruce's biography relies heavily on reminiscences by those who knew Blake and as such offers nothing new. Still of interest here are conversations recorded with or about Blake by such literary figures as Charles Lamb, Robert Southey, and William Wordsworth. Included in this unpretentious biography are 11 illustrations and a chart depicting the life and publications in chronological order, along with a list of Blake's acquaintances. Much of the information here is dated and in some instances inaccurate. A major weakness is the surprising lack of footnotes.

After Wilson's biography with Keynes' annotations, very little new biographical information has surfaced, and consequently most subsequent biographies reprint previously published material. WRIGHT's book is factually inaccurate but contains several interesting photographs of places associated with Blake that are now altered in appearance and includes contemporary references to Blake from the correspondence of John Johnson and William Haley. Although this information appears in Wright for the first time, it has since been corrected and republished elsewhere. Volume 2 of this work contains appendices of "Decorations in Blake's Works" and "Blake's Painting, Color Prints, Sketches and Engravings."

MARGOLIOUTH provides a detailed account of Blake's early years and discusses the development of myth in Blake's poetry. The major weakness here is Margoliouth's tendency to oversimplify the complex issues brought out in his study. Similar in scope is DAVIS' study whose major weaknesses are its lack of footnotes and its extensive borrowing from Bentley, Gilchrist, and Wilson. LINDSAY displays familiarity with the subject matter but adds no new insights. Again, a major weakness here is that his footnotes are far more confusing than they are informative. Perhaps the best recent study for the general reader is by LISTER. Lister, himself an artist, provides a sound treatment of the life and includes 31 plates and a secondary bibliography. Lister argues that Blake's apparent confusion and contradictions were due to the complexity of the ideas with which he grappled.

Blake Records, compiled by BENTLEY, is the most detailed and factually accurate collection of biographical information, and as such it is indispensable as a scholarly resource. Bentley attempts to locate, verify, and reprint every account of Blake. Material included begins with the apprenticeship of Blake's father in 1737 and continues until the death of Blake's wife Katherine in 1831. Also included are appendices on Blake's residences, his financial accounts, and a list of engravings with 67 illustrations, including Blake's plates for Blair's *Grave*. Bentley makes generous use of footnotes that provide the reader with references to facts as they are presented in previous biographies. Bentley published a supplement to the *Blake Records* in 1988 that contains new material relating to Blake's life discovered since the publication of the 1969 volume. The research and documentation in these two volumes provide all of the information needed for future biographers.

—Jeffrey D. Parker

BLOK, Alexander, 1880–1921; Russian poet and playwright.

Chukovsky, Kornei, *Alexander Blok as Man and Poet*, translated and edited by Diana Burgin and Katherine O'Connor. Ann Arbor, Michigan, Ardis, 1982 (originally published, Petrograd, 1924).

Orlov, V. N., *Hamayun: The Life of Aleksandr Blok*, translated by Olga Shartse. Moscow, Progress, 1980 (originally published, Moscow, 1978).

Pyman, Avril, *The Life of Aleksandr Blok* (2 vols.). Oxford and New York, Oxford University Press, 1979–80.

*

A prominent literary critic and children's author, Kornei CHUKOVSKY was a near contemporary and colleague of Blok, and his several writings on the poet combined close knowledge of literary text and context with a perceptive understanding and recollection of him in human terms. This, the second of Chukovsky's two book-length treatises on Blok, is divided into two sections. The first, subtitled "Blok as Man" (part two is a survey of his poetic development), is not a biography proper so much as a chronologically based essay on Blok as a personality and child of his times; but its quality and the relative paucity of other material in English make it worthy of attention. In Chukovsky's view (which was taken over and elaborated by many subsequent Russian commentators) Blok emerges as the scion of a civilized gentry family with a natural love of order in his life. But behind the schizoid mask, his "composure was an illusion." In his writings he is revealed as the terrified prophet of chaos, frenzy, and doom; during the revolution and shortly before his death, Blok seemed physically fit, with "the strength to carry cabbages on his back from far-off cooperatives," yet he identified himself as a dying man.

Chukovsky was a political liberal before the 1917 revolution, and although writing in 1924 before any hard ideological clampdown, he was still under censorship constraint, and Blok had already been semi-canonized as one of the few erstwhile literary Decadents who supposedly effected an internal *perestroika* and embraced the Bolshevik order. In fact, though, Blok's political stance was a highly ambivalent and unstable one, which partly caused, and itself collapsed under the weight of, his cosmic despair. Chukovsky never quite tells us this. While talking initially of Blok's "immense, optimistic faith in the life-saving role of the revolution," he only implicitly makes it apparent that Blok's revolution was not to be confused with the Bolshevik putsch of 1917. The causes of his spiritual collapse after 1918 are hinted at rather that spelt out. For instance, there is a pointedly complete quotation of the late poem in which Blok invoked the spirit of Pushkin and his message of "secret freedom." This nebulous treatment of Blok's post-revolutionary biography is common to most Soviet monographs. Despite this drawback, however, Chukovsky's booklet is an excellent introduction to Blok's life and personality.

ORLOV was for many decades the doyen of Soviet scholars of Alexander Blok. His biography of Blok appeared in Russian in Moscow in 1978. The English translation, by a non-native, is awkward in places, poised uneasily between stilted literary and colloquial registers, as also is the rendering of some proper nouns and of the jargon used, for instance, to describe the Scythian group's belief in a "petty-bourgeois, anarchal-maximalist utopia." Orlov provides an accepted Bolshevik interpretation of historical events and allows them to assume, "by default," that Blok viewed them in these terms; Blok's romantic, elemental, revolutionary idealism is thus taken as embracing also a series of correct Leninist political conclusions (and the Christ figure in his poem *The Twelve* is therefore interpreted as a purely moral emblem). Only gradually does it emerge that "his faith in the future was at odds with his trust in the present." The collapse of Blok's idealism coincided with his gradual physical breakdown. But there is no mention by Orlov of the syphilis that also undermined his constitution. This may partly be characteristic Soviet coyness (we are given no details, either, of Blok's

frequent surrender to debauchery), but the effect is to suggest that Blok was physically destroyed by the failure of his hopes for the revolution as he understood it—i.e., by Bolshevik betrayal of his ideals. In fact, Orlov implicitly offers more than a narrowly doctrinaire view, and if one learns to read the implications of his ideological statements and omissions, his account emerges as an enlightened and intriguing one.

Several English monographs and essays deal with separate aspects of Blok's literary output and involve some biographical commentary. The best of them are: Victor Erlich, *The Double Image* (1964), Sergei Hackel, *The Poet and the Revolution* (1975), and F. D. Reeve, *Aleksandr Blok: Between Image and Idea* (1962). However, the most trustworthy and complete life of Blok in any language is the two-volume study by PYMAN. Blok died early enough and politically in good enough odour to benefit posthumously from a record number of appreciations and memoirs by almost everyone that had significant contacts with him. Pyman makes her way discerningly through this mass of information, including notebook and other archival material. She seldom forces her own opinion, and her digressions are well motivated by a need to provide literary, historical, or cultural commentary and background. As Blok noted in 1914, "My life is a series of incredibly confused human relationships; my life is a series of broken hopes," and Pyman accurately charts the progression of agony, orgy, optimism, frustration, and remorse. From the ideological standpoint, a portrait emerges differing sharply from sentimental or other, condescending Soviet views, like that of Gorky who wrote that Blok reminded him of "a child in a fairy tale, lost in the forest." Ultimately, perhaps, Blok was more politically astute than Gorky, but he was tormented and tossed back and forth in history's arena, as he was in his art and personal relations. His tragedy was in recognizing too clearly the artist's doomed role in a doom-ridden age. Unlike some contemporaries, and poets of the earlier century, the role of teacher or preacher was denied to him: "The only way Blok could hope to command the attention of his audience was the way of the pelican," as Pyman nicely puts it—by offering people his inner truth and living experience.

Strangely, the medical causes of Blok's death in Pyman's presentation seems to efface the spiritual asphyxia he also suffered in Bolshevik Russia. The truth probably lies in a combination of her evidence with that of Orlov. Pyman's biography also contains what Orlov's altogether lacks: a scholarly apparatus of bibliographical sources, reference notes, index, etc.

—Christopher J. Barnes

BOCCACCIO, Giovanni, 1313–1375; Italian writer and diplomat.

Bergin, Thomas G., *Boccaccio*. New York, Viking, 1981.
Branca, Vittore, *Boccaccio: The Man and His Works*, translated by Richard Monges. New York, New York University Press, 1976.

Carswell, Catherine, *The Tranquil Heart: Portrait of Giovanni Boccaccio*. London, Lawrence and Wishart, and New York, Harcourt, 1937.

Chubb, Thomas C., *The Life of Giovanni Boccaccio*. London, Cassell, and New York, A. and C. Boni, 1930.

Hutton, Edward, *Giovanni Boccaccio: A Biographical Study*. London and New York, J. Lane, 1910.

MacManus, Francis, *Boccaccio*. London and New York, Sheed and Ward, 1947.

Serafini-Sauli, Judith P., *Giovanni Boccaccio*. Boston, Twayne, 1982.

Symonds, J. A., *Giovanni Boccaccio as Man and Author*. London, J. C. Nimmo, and New York, Scribner, 1895.

*

Only a few years after Walter Pater had rekindled interest in the Northern Renaissance, in which he saw embodied his aesthetic and human ideal of "burning with a bright gem-like flame," SYMONDS, clearly influenced by Pater and also teaching at Oxford, linked in 1895 Dante, Petrarch, and Boccaccio as "the three founders of Modern Literature." Perhaps wrongly, he regards Boccaccio's influence on subsequent Italian literature as greater than that of the other two. The *Decameron*, he writes, "elevates the legends of a hundred generations . . . to the rank of clear, self-conscious art." Symonds has written a brief but powerful book, still well worth reading, sweeping in its vision of Boccaccio's achievement and place in the history of literature, revealing about the values of his own society, scholarly in its attempts to solve such biographical riddles as that of Boccaccio's legitimacy, and erudite in tracing the mind behind the huge literary effort in Latin and Italian.

HUTTON's book, with footnotes, an index, a bibliography, a series of appendices, and a synopsis of the *Decameron*, also begins with a consideration of the trio Dante, Petrarch, and Boccaccio. But unlike Symonds, Hutton does not find Boccaccio fundamentally out of sympathy with Dante. Unusually, but gratifyingly, Hutton pays more attention than most biographers to Boccaccio's work outside the *Decameron*, however much it may lack unity and consist for the most part of "vast compilations" like the *De genealogia deorum*. Hutton's book remains excellent, although it makes demands on the reader's knowledge of Latin and Italian. Considerations of Boccaccio's influence on Chaucer and of his astrological interests have laid foundations on which subsequent scholars have erected important structures. His treatment of Boccaccio's attitude toward female characters is of special interest.

CHUBB's approach 20 years later reflects the taste of his period for informal biography. There are chattily reconstituted conversations. Conjecture in the implied interpretations of personalities and events seeps everywhere into the narrative. There are, it is true, Latin quotations, a bibliography, and an index, but this is a biography to be read quickly, enjoyed, and left behind. The register is too light for the ambitiousness of the task, to re-create "the complex personality of an extremely interesting and extremely human man of letters." That needs a more sober approach than Chubb's, which is studded with "terrific outcries," exclamation marks, "sensations of horror," and "great draughty halls of stern castles."

CARSWELL points out that no writer before Boccaccio "dreamed of writing avowedly for women readers, and not many great writers have done so since." This is an exaggeration, as is the statement that Boccaccio, with Dante and Petrarch, "form . . . the remarkable trio which divides the medieval world from our own." Although the book contains notes, a "select list of authorities," and a helpful index, it is still clearly intended to be read, not consulted, and the reader will get no help from the chapter headings. Sources are not attributed, and there are some technical weaknesses (as over the meaning of the sin of *acedia*, a temptation to abandon the spiritual life and spiritual effort altogether), but the biography is a pleasantly informative introduction to the literature of the Renaissance in Italy.

MacMANUS' volume is overwritten, and the writer's strain communicates itself to the reader. Is Naples "like any beautiful slut," and are mosaics and monuments "sacramental of human faith"? MacManus is too aware of World War II and of his own lack of the scholar's pretentions. His account of Boccaccio's life, while accurate, is narrated in too arch a style.

The two outstanding biographies after Hutton are undoubtedly those of Branca and Bergin. BRANCA, the discoverer of the autograph of the *Decameron* and the acknowledged world authority on Boccaccio, is an eminent academic. His biography precedes a much shorter critical second book on the *Decameron*. Branca draws on the best of modern scholarship, scrupulously giving references to his sources for all assertions, and he has a magisterial command of the literary and historical background of his subject. Indeed Branca makes what was ultimately a fairly uneventful life interesting precisely by bringing alive the society and the culture in which Boccaccio was nourished. The scholarly difficulties about dates and attributions have now been resolved (Boccaccio's illegitimacy, too, is now taken for granted), and Branca presents a fascinating account of the growth of Boccaccio's mind, finding "new and thoughtful human, moralistic and historical interests," for instance, in the *Zibaldone Magliabechiano*, the *De casibus*, and the *De mulieribus*. Branca's reading of Boccaccio's mind carries conviction throughout. For a somewhat dry but scholarly account of the demonstrable facts about Boccaccio's life, Branca's book is indispensable reading. It contains quotations in Latin together with notes and an index.

BERGIN, who has also written lives of Dante and Petrarch and translated works of each, as well as of Vico and Machiavelli, is a major Italian Renaissance literary scholar, writing here for a less professional readership than that which Branca had in mind. There are here two biographical-historical chapters followed by a chronological presentation of Boccaccio's works, their sources, genesis, and influence. The authorities used are mostly American or English, although some are too lightweight to fit into a book drawing so heavily on Branca. As Bergin rightly points out, Branca has summarised virtually all the available information, while Hutton, Chubb, and MacManus are all now out of date. Bergin's historical background material suffers from too much compression, with seven popes to one paragraph, and the book does supremely well only what it sets out to do, which is to present Boccaccio's achievement to the modern reader in plain English, giving reasons for the importance and interest of the individual works.

The final work to be considered is the excellent monograph by SERAFINI-SAULI. As is usual for the Twayne series, the book is relatively brief, contains an excellent "chronology" of the life together with an introduction, notes, and bibliography. Unhappily, Serafini-Sauli and Bergin appear not to have known of each other's existence, although both depend heavily on Branca. For anyone in search of information or distilled critical assessment in a hurry, Serafini-Sauli's is the best available book on Boccaccio. Bergin's pace is more leisurely after the introductory chapters. Branca is detailed, but not forbidding, and his is the volume to choose for full and reliable information.

—A. H. T. Levi

BOGART, Humphrey, 1899–1957; American film actor.

Barbour, Alan G., *Humphrey Bogart*. New York, Pyramid Books, 1973; London, Star Books, 1974.

Benchley, Nathaniel, *Humphrey Bogart*. Boston, Little Brown, and London, Hutchinson, 1975.

Cooke, Alistair, *Six Men*. New York, Knopf, and London, Bodley Head, 1977.

Eyles, Allan, *Bogart*. New York, Doubleday, and London, Macmillan, 1975.

Gehman, Richard, *Bogart*. Greenwich, Connecticut, Fawcett, 1965.

Goodman, Ezra, *Bogey: The Good Bad Guy*. New York, L. Stuart, 1965.

Greenberger, Howard, *Bogey's Baby*. New York, D. McKay, 1978.

Hyams, Joseph, *Bogie: The Biography of Humphrey Bogart*. New York, New American Library, 1966.

Hyams, Joseph, *Bogart and Bacall: A Love Story*. New York, D. McKay, and London, M. Joseph, 1975.

McCarty, Clifford, *Bogey: The Films of Humphrey Bogart*. New York, Citadel Press, 1965.

Michael, Paul, *Humphrey Bogart: The Man and His Films*. Indianapolis, Bobbs-Merrill, 1965.

Ruddy, Jonah and Jonathon Hill, *The Bogey Man: Portrait of a Legend*. London, Souvenir Press, 1965.

Thompson, Verita and Donald Shepherd, *Bogie and Me: A Love Story*. New York, St. Martin's, 1982; London, W. H. Allen, 1983.

*

A renewal of interest in Humphrey Bogart's films during the mid-1960s spawned the first book-length biographies and filmographies of the actor. The gossipy and entertaining books by GEHMAN and RUDDY AND HILL serve as examples of the adoration and legend spawned by the star worship that became inextricable from the actor's life and career. Produced for the film and Bogart buff, the McCARTY and MICHAEL filmographies are liberally splashed with photos and movie stills. Plot sketches, cast lists, and other credits for each of Bogart's films fill out these nostalgic volumes. Michael's 17-page biography concisely summarizes the actor's life and career.

Composed mainly of interview material gathered from Bogart and his associates for a magazine article, with commentary by the author, GOODMAN's book is almost unique among adoring eulogies of Bogart in its strident anti-Bogart tone. Despite its lack of documentation, the book is interesting as an illustration of the intensity of emotions aroused in observers by Bogart's fame and notoriety.

HYAMS (1966), a journalist and friend of Bogart, offers the most balanced biography of Bogart to date. Well-researched and with the cooperation of Bogart's wife, Lauren Bacall, Hyams' entertainingly written book examines Bogart's development as an actor and pokes through legend with appropriate skepticism to search out the man himself.

The early 1970s wave of nostalgia for Hollywood's golden years brought about a number of Bogart biographies. Chiefly a film review, BARBOUR's work sketches Bogart's career as iconoclast anti-hero. Well illustrated with film stills, though somewhat hamstrung by the need to fit into a series format, the book leaves detailed biography to others, making brief occasional forays into events or influences on Bogart to trace his development as an actor. The work includes a list of unbilled short films, or shorts as well as a filmography and a bibliography. In an appreciation of Bogart the actor, EYLES, a British film author and critic, includes a brief biographical sketch but concentrates on the legend of Bogart the anti-hero. The book includes color pictures.

Among the large body of reminiscences by Bogart's acquaintances, mostly appearing as anecdotes in larger works, are a few of book or chapter length. BENCHLEY, a good friend of the actor, offers a warm collection of anecdotes, with a wealth of quotations by contemporaries, much childhood details, and many previously unpublished photographs. Written by another friend, COOKE's chapter on Bogart is a witty, understated, entertaining portrait by a contemporary. Generalized, deliberately lighthearted discussions devoted to uncritical remembrances, these works best serve the researcher as a source of quotations and views.

In the course of relating the story of Bogart's romance of and marriage to Bacall, some works successfully expose Bogart's personality and private side. The entertaining HYAMS (1975) essentially expands the section of the 1966 work covering Bogart's life with Lauren Bacall. It is valuable mainly for the first-hand reminiscences of the author, who knew his subjects well enough to be able to puncture the balloon of legend with day-to-day reality. GREENBERGER's sympathetically composed book, appearing some years later, adds perspective to Hyams. Both are best read in company with chapters dealing with Bogart in Lauren Bacall's memoirs (*By Myself*, 1978), by far the most effective portrayal yet of Bogart the man. Bacall's touching, emotive narrative of her life with Bogart exposes his personality, emotions, and life in a manner that strikingly separates the legend from Bogart's inner life.

Written by Bogart's studio assistant, supposedly to reveal her affair with the star, the chatty THOMPSON will appeal mostly to those interested in tell-all Hollywood gossip. Nonetheless, the book's descriptions of the behind-the-camera technical details of movie-making provide a few interesting moments.

—Steven A. Agoratus

BOHR, Niels, 1885–1962; Danish physicist.

Blaedel, Niels, *Harmony and Unity: The Life of Niels Bohr*, translated by Geoffrey French. New York and Berlin, Springer-Verlag, and Madison, Wisconsin, Science Tech, 1988 (originally published by Rhodos, Copenhagen, 1985).

Moore, Ruth, *Niels Bohr: The Man, His Science, and the World They Changed*. New York, Knopf, 1966.

Rozenthal, S., editor, *Niels Bohr: His Life and Work as Seen by His Friends and Colleagues*. Amsterdam, North-Holland, and New York, Wiley, 1967 (originally published by J. H. Schultz, Copenhagen, 1964).

Silverberg, Robert, *Niels Bohr, the Man Who Mapped the Atom*. Philadelphia, Macrae-Smith, 1965.

*

Biography of scientists tends toward the hagiographical and is further tainted by faulty assumptions; e.g., that the real purpose of the biography is to explain and popularize the science, but with the caveat that any "popularization" is necessarily marred because the science will be incorrect. This is particularly true of biographies of 20th-century physicists, since any effort to put what is essentially mathematical in expression into words may be considered inadequate. As a result, neither Moore nor Blaedel can pass muster with the scientific community, although either is rather more readable than Rozenthal's collection. SILVERBERG was written for young people and disappeared quickly; the author is best known for his science fiction, once considered glib and superficial but currently in some vogue.

Both Moore and Blaedel had access to the volume edited by Rozenthal; MOORE acknowledges use of a prepublication copy, and uses a number of anecdotes. Since she does not footnote, specific identification of sources is impossible. This is a cause for concern because there are some oddities; in one photograph the wife of M. L. E. Oliphant is identified as "Lady Rutherford" and Rutherford's death is attributed to injuries received when he fell from a tree he was pruning, an incident lacking from standard biographical sources for Rutherford. Nevertheless, Moore is by far the most coherent and interesting account, and should serve for any reader not dedicated to precise scientific explication or scholarly apparatus.

BLAEDEL has the advantage of a command of Danish, and has documented sources, albeit in a somewhat cursory fashion. His work is therefore considerably more detailed than Moore's. It is, however, marred by long sentences and absurdly short chapters, a function perhaps of the difficulty of following the most complex scientific development of the early 20th century in and out of an international community of scientists fragmented by two world wars. Moore was closer in time to the excitement of Bohr's failed attempt to set science free from political censorship, and perhaps as a result makes this episode especially vivid; Blaedel seems more interested in establishing Bohr as a specifically Danish hero. Blaedel's translator appears competent, but has committed one standard fault: in the notes, there are references to a source as *Mindebog*, but the bibliography gives this title only in its English translation as *Memorial Book*. In this case the confusion is crucial, since the English-language version of the work appears to be *Niels Bohr*. The variant titles of the Danish original are thus mystified further. In general, Blaedel is an adequate biography, perhaps more accurate overall than Moore, if considerably less exciting to read.

Scientists—or at least physicists—will no doubt continue to prefer ROZENTHAL's volume, which features articles by Bohr's colleagues and family members. Some of the memoirs are truly moving; others read like a scientist's version of a gossip column, filled with names that will often be unfamiliar to the nonscientist (or even to the scientist, if he or she is much under the age of 60.) Anyone who has read this work and Moore or Blaedel may be sure of knowing most of the relevant facts of Bohr's life and scientific achievement.

—Nadine F. George

BOLEYN, Anne, *ca.* 1507–1536; second wife of Henry VIII of England and mother of Elizabeth I.

Bruce, Marie Louise, *Anne Boleyn*. London, Collins, and New York, McCann, 1972.

Chapman, Hester, *Anne Boleyn*. London, Cape, 1974.

Erickson, Carolly, *Mistress Anne*. New York, Summit Books, 1984; as *Anne Boleyn*, London, Macmillan, 1984.

Friedmann, Paul, *Anne Boleyn: A Chapter of English History 1527–36* (2 vols.). London, Macmillan, 1884.

Ives, E. W., *Anne Boleyn*. Oxford and New York, Blackwell, 1986.

Warnicke, Retha M., *The Rise and Fall of Anne Boleyn: Family Politics at the Court of Henry VIII*. Cambridge and New York, Cambridge University Press, 1989.

*

FRIEDMANN provided the scholarly foundation for Boleyn research for 90 years, particularly through his access to the Hapsburg archives. Alerting the reader to the pitfalls of Tudor correspondence, he also places much emphasis on diaries, foreign observations, and public papers in assembling Anne's life. The result is a balanced, thoroughly documented, two-volume portrait of Anne and others at the Henrician court. Friedmann argues for an earlier birthdate than the usually accepted 1507, and he places Mary Boleyn's marriage in 1521 rather than 1520. While acknowledging that Anne's attraction for Henry may have accelerated the divorce from Catherine of Aragon and subsequent break with Rome, Friedmann argues that the king, "a thoroughly immoral man," was intent on ridding himself of his Spanish wife in order to get a male heir even before Anne entered the picture. Anne's appearance is described in comparatively generous terms in this pioneering work.

Two popular books on Anne that draw heavily on Friedmann appeared in the 1970s. The better, more imaginative life is by BRUCE, who lets the reader judge the Boleyn character in a well-written, illustrated book. Her Anne is no pawn; Boleyn takes a more active role in persuading the king to secure a crown for her by interesting him in "Lutheran arguments for schism with the Pope." Though exculpating Anne for adultery and incest, Bruce notes that Anne's political carelessness aided her enemies in destroying her. An extensive bibliography and anno-ated list of sources is helpful. CHAPMAN's footnoted, generally sympathetic life of the queen attributes Anne's charac-ter and actions to the often immoral environment of the court. She includes some rather ominous descriptions of Anne's ap-pearance, noting prominent neck moles, protruberant eyes, and an extra fingernail. Otherwise this is a traditional biography that covers little new ground for the serious reader.

ERICKSON's tome is very readable and moderately sympa-thetic to Anne. Erickson argues that Anne bore no responsibility for the fall of Cardinal Wolsey, though the king may have un-consciously blamed her. Anticlericalism, arrogance, and his fail-ure to procure the desired results in the legatine trial brought an end to Wolsey's chancellorship. Though she writes for a general audience, Erickson provides some occasional documentation for her interpretation of a woman caught up in a maelstrom of change over which she had little control. But Erickson's Anne comes across as shrewish and abrasive, pushy and slatternly, particularly when compared to the saintly Catherine of Aragon. Given her personality, Anne's fall was just as inevitable as Wol-sey's. Unfortunately, Erickson fails to persuade the reader that Anne was aware of how fragile her position was in this danger-ous setting that she helped to create through her own vindictive-ness.

The most authoritative work on Anne for many years will be IVES' thorough account, which unabashedly acknowledges a debt to Friedmann's scholarship and Bruce's imagination. Bene-fitting from previously untapped primary sources in scattered manuscript collections and from the wealth of recent scholarship done on the politics and society of the 16th century, Ives can better investigate not only Anne's youth and training in France, but the lives of her early suitors as well. His use of the king's love letters is very effective, though he does regret not having better access to the French diplomatic archive of the period. Ives is brilliant in placing Anne against the Tudor era background, and he finds that she played a much larger, more responsible role than earlier historians had thought. While Erickson suggests that Henry tired of Anne's nastiness almost immediately upon mar-rying her, Ives insists that as late as the fall of 1535 Anne was still loved and powerful. Then Henry met Jane Seymour, a blonde and docile contrast to the intelligent and spirited Anne. The Boleyn faction, including Cromwell, was thrown into a tizzy as the queen's enemies went on the offensive. Abandoning Anne to those enemies, Cromwell saved himself by engineering a coup against her, using spies planted in her circle. Ives calls Anne's execution judicial murder in this sympathetic life of a self-made queen, and marks the accession of her daughter, Eliz-abeth I, as the ultimate historical vindication. Conveying a healthy skepticism for his sources, Ives exhaustively explores ju-dicial records, estate records, private expense accounts, and state papers. The footnotes are detailed, and Ives includes gene-alogies, lists of titles, and an explanation of his bibliographic abbreviations. Ives' magisterial book is the one to read.

WARNICKE should not be ignored, however, for her analysis of Tudor beliefs concerning witchcraft and curses is fascinating. Evil spirits could be blamed for Catherine's failure to produce a son, for Anne's seduction of Henry, for Anne's miscarriage. Witches were decried for their excessive lust and their aphrodi-siacs, all of this fitting with the general belief that Anne had bewitched the king. Her miscarriage of a deformed fetus, be-lieved to be the result of incest and adultery, provided Cromwell with the evidence to fortify his case against Anne. Warnicke takes issue with Ives' conclusion that factional maneuvering brought Anne down, and suggests Ives' reliance on the com-ments of Imperial Ambassador Eustace Chapuys is shortsighted. Rather it was society's ignorance about conception and preg-nancy that undermined her, and by her contemporaries she must be judged. Warnicke's perspective is fresh, and her readable book is scholarly and well documented with over 50 pages of endnotes and bibliography. She includes appendices about Nicholas Sander, an early Catholic critic of Anne, Anne's choir-book, and two poems of Sir Thomas Wyatt. This should be read as a companion-piece to Ives.

—Elizabeth Lane Furdell

BORGES, Jorge Luis, 1899–1986; Argentine writer.

Bell-Villada, Gene H., *Borges and His Fiction: A guide to His Mind and Art.* Chapel Hill, University of North Carolina Press, 1981.

Cohen, John M., *Jorge Luis Borges.* Edinburgh, Oliver and Boyd, and New York, Barnes and Noble, 1973.

Di Giovanni, Norman T., editor, *In Memory of Borges.* London, Constable/Anglo-Argentine Society, 1988.

Rodriguez Monegal, Emir, *Jorge Luis Borges: A Literary Biog-raphy.* New York, Dutton, 1978.

Stabb, Martin S., *Jorge Luis Borges.* New York, Twayne, 1970.

Yates, Donald, *Jorge Luis Borges: Life, Work, and Criticism.* Frederickton, New Brunswick, York Press, 1985.

*

To undertake a biography of Borges would seem at first sight to be a difficult and unrewarding task. The details of the great Argentinian writer's life appear unremarkable, even humdrum. Moreover, Borges (with his characteristic mix of irony and play-fulness) was given to distorting and even falsifying his life story. He was above all a bookish man, and while he adored discussing literature, and would do so almost endlessly, he was reticent about personal matters. The only exception to this in his own writings is the "Autobiographical Essay" published in *Aleph and Other Stories* (1970). This is in itself an elliptical document, more notable for what it omits than for what it reveals. Never-theless, it provides a valid basis for consideration of his life, a life lived primarily through the medium of literary texts. The best of the more recent studies of Borges take his point and dis-cuss his life and work as a textual phenomenon.

Brief biographies preface many of the works of criticism de-voted to Borges. Of these, that contained in the first two chap-ters of BELL-VILLADA's book is most comprehensive and illuminating. Bell-Villada concentrates on Borges' position as both a cosmopolitan and a deeply patriotic Argentinian. The dy-namic tension between these two poles of identity forms, in Bell-Villada's view, the principal axis of his development as a writer. He reminds us that the Borges who learned first to speak and read in English, and who travelled extensively throughout

Europe in his youth, was also the poet who wrote that "The years I had lived in Europe are illusory, I have always lived (and will) in Buenos Aires." YATES, STABB, and COHEN all cover similar ground, each summarizing the known details of Borges' life; as literary critiques, however, none is primarily concerned with researching their subject's life in depth. Cohen's synopsis is most interesting in this respect, for he looks at Borges' early career as a member of, and proselyte for, the Spanish *Ultraismo* group. Highly critical of both the aims and literary talent of certain members of the group, Cohen charts his subject's move away from their dogmatic and near-sighted iconoclasm with approval.

Despite Borges' enormous popularity in the English-speaking world, only one full-length biography (as opposed to literary study) has been published in English, that by RODRIGUEZ MONEGAL. A Uruguayan, Rodriguez Monegal had a great deal of contact with Borges, and it is clear to see why this long involvement was necessary. Borges was an elusive quarry whose manner in interview, though always courteous, could be infuriatingly oblique. Rodriguez Monegal has done an excellent job of both conveying his subject's charm to the reader and at the same time refusing to be charmed into credulity himself. As a result, this book is recognized internationally as the standard biography of Borges. Only Alicia Jurado's *Genio y figura de Jorge Luis Borges* (Buenos Aires, 1966), unfortunately unavailable in English translation, has the same scope and stature as Rodriguez Monegal's book. Jurado, too, was a close acquaintance of Borges, allowing her to penetrate the veils of ironic concealment laid in her path by the writer and his family.

Some critics have reacted with anger to Rodriguez Monegal's study, many no doubt disappointed by the ordinariness of Borges' life as compared to his soaring and imaginative fictions. John Sturrock, for example, writing in a *New York Times* review, accused Rodriguez Monegal of doing a "terrible thing" by "grubbing around for the roots of Borges' fiction in the dull details" of his life. But if Borges' work means anything, it surely proves that the human imagination is limitless, and not bound by the prosaic circumstances of any one life. Rodriguez Monegal seeks to show the strange alchemy by which such "dull details" are transformed into dazzling *tours de force* of fantasy.

Rodriguez Monegal comments that he conceived of this biography as "a commentary on and an extension of his 'Autobiographical Essay,'" and the idea of commentary and explication is central to the book. In this work, the life of the subject is conceived of as text; as text it is examined, minutely and with all the techniques of textual criticism at Rodriguez Monegal's disposal. The disadvantages of this approach are twofold: first, it gives the subject's life the shape of a literary text, whereas an individual life is an altogether messier affair. Second, and perhaps more important, the agenda for the biography is set out for Rodriguez Monegal by the primary text, Borges' essay. Thus we find both writers skirting circumspectly around several topics, not least of which is the enigma of Borges' late and short-lived experiment in marriage. Though emphatically not an "authorized biography," it bears the marks of "authorization" in this sense. Much of what he describes will be familiar to students and initiates, but much more is new and provoking. With certain discreet gaps in the established story, Rodriguez Monegal is daring enough to speculate, and honest enough to admit his speculation. Not a biography but a volume of tribute to the deceased

writer, the work edited by DI GIOVANNI, nevertheless contains some fascinating memoirs and biographical fragments. Of particular interest are the essays by Graham Greene and Norman Thomas di Giovanni, the latter a longtime friend, translator, and collaborator who worked closely with Borges over a number of years. As we have seen, the most penetrating studies of Borges' life and work tend to come from close personal acquaintances of his, and di Giovanni would be ideally placed to continue and complement the work of Emir Rodriguez Monegal and Alica Jurado. Such a full-length work, with a consideration of the author's entire *oeuvre* in the context of his life, would be much appreciated by serious scholars and students.

—Alan Murphy

BORGIA, Lucrezia, 1480–1519; duchess of Ferrara.

Bellonci, Maria, *The Life and Times of Lucrezia Borgia*, translated by Bernard Wall. London, Weidenfeld and Nicolson, and New York, Harcourt, 1953 (originally published by A. Mondadori, Milan, 1939).

Erlanger, Rachel, *Lucrezia Borgia, a Biography*. New York, Hawthorn Books, 1978; London, M. Joseph, 1979.

Gilbert, William, *Lucrezia Borgia, Duchess of Ferrara: A Biography* (2 vols.). London, Hurst and Blackett, 1869.

Gregorovius, Ferdinand, *Lucrezia Borgia: A Chapter from the Morals of the Italian Renaissance*, translated by J. L. Garner. London, Phaidon Press, 1948.

Harcourt-Smith, Simon, *The Marriage at Ferrara*. London, J. Murray, 1952.

Haslip, Joan, *Lucrezia Borgia: A Study*. London, Cassell, and Indianapolis, Bobbs-Merrill, 1953.

*

Lucrezia completes the Borgias: without her they are just a pair of Machiavellian supermen. She gives the story its most intriguing questions: what could Cesare have told her after killing her second (and best loved) husband? How could she continue to suffer such unending catastrophe smilingly?

We should start with GREGOROVIUS, whose small, dense study begins serious research on Lucrezia with an operatic flourish. It is dedicated to the great Roman dynasties, such as still survived in 1874—the year the book first appeared—and has the advantages of being alert to the political habits of a near-feudal society. Overtly Romantic in setting, with breathtaking landscapes overlooking the action, it is nevertheless an acute book. Its errors of overstatement might be attributed to the excited air of discovery it exudes. For it is a pioneer work of biography as we know it today: diligent primary research combined with novelistic, "historically reconstructed" narrative. Gregorovius, a poet and historian, was naturally sympathetic to Lucrezia Borgia. As Duchess of Ferrara Lucrezia was a gracious and generous patron to learned men; by falling in love with the great court poet Pietro Bembo, she captured Gregorovius' heart. His descriptions evoke an atmosphere of melancholy magnificence.

This study, by comparison with his masterwork, The History of the City of Rome in the Middle Ages (8 vols. London, 1894–1902), is lightweight, but it contains a vast amount of scholarship. Though it projects a world that to us seems unreal—the splendid settings, the pageantry of grand opera—it brings a clarity of psychological insight borrowed from the form of the novel.

Gregorovius' biography has been superseded as a work of purely historical interest, but such an excellent book need never be obsolete. It remains a standard by which those that follow can be measured.

BELLONCI's biography of Lucrezia provides a more cheery portrait of the time: the style is pleasant and readable throughout, and the narrative demonstrates the influence of Gregorovius. The book is a complete conjectural reconstruction, but it is worth noting that none of the reconstructed episodes is inconsistent with available evidence. It is the clearest and most entertaining of the biographies to date. Similar to this in intention, but far inferior in execution, is HASLIP's "study." This is a book in which facts are not so much adduced to complete an argument as stuck on to decorate it. The glutinous prose presumably aids the process of adhesion.

Gregorovius spoke of "the dignity of woman" and showed how it was a perilously small thing in the hands of the Renaissance dynasts; he presented Lucrezia as a supplicant, and maintained her true quality in the nobility of her suffering. ERLANGER's commendable book emphasises, in order perhaps to restore the balance, Lucrezia's experience in the political arena. Gregorovius' work was a reaction to the perceived notion of Lucrezia as a Borgia, that is, a political manipulator with no scruples: poison, incest, and treachery are the conventional trappings of the tale. Erlanger has absolutely no dealings with moody atmosphere or novelistic licence. This is not to say the book is bloodless, for it knows its own area of competence and is a thorough and detailed account of known evidence. The detail is as magnificent in its way as the peaks and ruined castles of Gregorovius, though it appears at first excessive. A modest note at the front of the book provides the key to Erlanger's preoccupation with catalogues of finery and pomp. When we read that a single ducat was a working-man's wages for a month, we appreciate the fantastic investment in appearance that a wedding outfit costing 45,000 ducats (for Cesare) represented. With the wealth of whole cities on their backs, members of Lucrezia's caste were walking emodiments of formidable political power. Erlanger reminds us that Lucrezia exercised some of that power, though of course her sphere was always limited.

GILBERT's was among the first biographies to be favourable to Lucrezia, and though it is adequately researched, the book has not weathered as well as Gregorovius'. It is an exhaustive study (running into two volumes), and though the dynastic feuds are painstakingly enumerated, the action appears to take place in a political vacuum. HARCOURT-SMITH's volume is, by contrast, a fine work, and though it chooses to take the familiar novelistic approach to the story, it convincingly portrays Lucrezia as a much tougher and more assertive individual. There are many books dedicated to the Borgias as a family; some are sensational, others academic, like those already discussed. But only a handful of authors have chosen to write on Lucrezia alone.

Fortunately, they are among the most intriguing and enchanting works on this most notorious of families.

—Alan Murphy

BOSWELL, James, 1740–1795; Scottish writer.

Brady, Frank, *James Boswell: The Later Years 1769–95*. New York, McGraw-Hill, and London, Heinemann, 1984.

Daiches, David, *James Boswell and His World*. New York, Scribner, and London, Thames and Hudson, 1976.

Finlayson, Iain, *The Moth and the Candle*. New York, St. Martin's and London, Constable, 1984.

Fitzgerald, Percy, *The Life of James Boswell* (2 vols.). London, Chatto and Windus, and New York, D. Appleton, 1891.

Hyde, Mary, *The Impossible Friendship: Boswell and Mrs. Thrale*. Cambridge, Massachusetts, Harvard University Press, 1972; London, Chatto and Windus, 1973.

Lewis, D. B. Wyndham, *The Hooded Hawk; or, the Case of Mr. Boswell*. London, Eyre and Spottiswoode, 1946; New York, Longman, 1947.

McLaren, Moray, *The Highland Jaunt: A Study of James Boswell and Samuel Johnson upon Their Highland and Hebridean Tour of 1773*. London, Jarrolds, 1954; New York, W. Sloane, 1955.

McLaren, Moray, *Corsica Boswell: Paoli, Johnson, and Freedom*. London, Secker and Warburg, 1966.

Pearson, Hesketh, *Johnson and Boswell: The Story of Their Lives*. London, Heinemann, and New York, Harper, 1958.

Pottle, Frederick A., *James Boswell: The Earlier Years 1740–69*. New York, McGraw-Hill, and London, Heinemann, 1966.

Tinker, Chauncey B., *Young Boswell*. London, Putnam, and Boston, Atlantic Monthly Press, 1922.

Vulliamy, C. E., *James Boswell*. London, G. Bles, 1932; New York, Scribner, 1933.

*

The author of one of the very greatest of all biographies, Boswell himself has not been the subject of much distinguished work until recent times. Our sense of Boswell has been revolutionized by a single dramatic event, or series of events. This was the discovery in the 1920s and 1930s of large caches of his private papers, notably his ongoing journal and much of his correspondence. The first limited edition of these papers appeared between 1928 and 1934, but fresh discoveries soon made a fuller edition necessary. In various forms these have been published since 1950 in the Yale Edition; our knowledge of Boswell's day-to-day existence has thereby been transformed, leaving earlier studies more or less redundant for working purposes.

None of the 19th-century treatments matters very much. Unquestionably, the most significant document was the essay Macaulay wrote in 1831, followed a year later by Carlyle's parallel study. Both are nominally reviews of a version of Boswell's *Life of Johnson*: in the case of Macaulay especially, the judgment of Boswell (as a divine fool who stumbled on the secret of creating an immortal book) exercised a profound influence on subsequent discussion. Nobody completely escaped the influence, though G. B. Hill sought to correct the view in a number of works chiefly focused on Johnson, while FITZGERALD's two-volume life of Boswell is garrulous, lively, and woozy on details.

Boswell figures briefly in one classic of the biographer's art, *The Portrait of Zelide* (1925) by Geoffrey Scott, an intensely poetic account of the life of Isabella de Charriere, who was an early girlfriend of the young Scotsman at the time of his Grand Tour on the European Continent. Otherwise, the story is largely a blank until TINKER's *Young Boswell* (1922), a well-organized and thoughtful work whose fate it was to fall instantly in value once the new manuscripts had been discovered. Nonetheless, Tinker made good sense of the materials then known to exist, and he added to his contribution by editing Boswell's letters in 1924, the first attempt at a collected edition. The Yale series now supplements the correspondence very fully, but Tinker's work provides a bedrock for any student of the subject.

The next few years were dominated by the unraveling of the story as it emerged in the newly found material, and until this was fully assimilated, no substantial new biography could be attempted. It should be stressed that the first book to be written by the greatest Boswellian student of our century, F. A. Pottle (see below), has a slightly misleading title: *The Literary Career of James Boswell, Esq* (1929) is in fact a fully annotated bibliography, not a sustained narrative. The best-known life of this period is VULLIAMY's book of 1933, always dismissed by Boswellian scholars as hopelessly misguided and hostile. Vulliamy was a lively enough writer but intemperate and unreliable on factual matters. Later popular biographies have been stronger: the work of D. B. Wyndham LEWIS (1947) still has its admirers. McLAREN's studies of Boswell's travels (in the Hebrides and Corsica) made some contemporary impact and are still readable. PEARSON's study is the work of a practiced biographer who can tell a story, though his approach lacks analytic rigor. A more subtle though briefer narrative is that of DAICHES, which is especially shrewd on Boswell's Scottish background. Rather more lightweight is FINLAYSON's volume, although it avoids glaring error or total shallowness. There is still room for a good popular life of Boswell that will incorporate the vast wealth of new material still in the process of publication in the Yale series.

There is at length a truly standard life of Boswell, though it came out in two stages and from two different hands. POTTLE wrote the first part, dealing with the earlier years (1740–69). It was followed at an interval of 18 years by BRADY's companion volume on the later years, 1769–95. (Brady had earlier been responsible for a pioneering study entitled *Boswell's Political Career*, 1965). Together the two volumes make a satisfactory whole, as each author was more concerned with setting the record straight than with speculative psychobiography. Pottle is perhaps the more assured in tone, but Brady is equally dependable and deft in organization. For the first time readers have at their fingertips a sound chronological life-history of Boswell that takes full account of amazing hoards now preserved chiefly at Yale University. It is certain that subsequent writers will wish to vary the picture, and there is abundant scope in the huge variety

of Boswellian personalia now before us. But Pottle and Brady collectively make up a reliable and thoughtful treatment of Boswell as he now appears to us.

Mention should be made of one distinguished work in a specialized area, that of HYDE. This charts the difficult relations of Boswell and Hester Thrale (later Piozzi), rivals not just in Johnson's friendship but also (after the great man's death) as his biographer. Hyde performs an exemplary task in following out this story, a bleak one occasionally irradiated by comedy and showing Boswell in some of his most characteristic form.

—Pat Rogers

BOTTICELLI, Sandro, *ca.* 1445–1510; Italian painter.

Bertram, Anthony, *Sandro Botticelli*. London and New York, Studio Publications, 1948.

Bode, Wilhelm von, *Sandro Botticelli*, translated by F. Renfield. London, Methuen, and New York, Scribner, 1925 (originally published by Propyläen-Verlag, 1921).

Cartwright, Julia, *The Life and Art of Sandro Botticelli*. London, Duckworth, and New York, Dutton, 1904.

Ettlinger, L. D. and Helen Ettlinger, *Botticelli*. London, Thames and Hudson, 1976; New York, Oxford University Press, 1977.

Horne, Herbert, *Alessandro Filipepi, Commonly Called Sandro Botticelli*. London, G. Bell, 1908; as *Botticelli, Painter of Florence*, Princeton, New Jersey, Princeton University Press, 1980.

Levey, Michael, *Botticelli*. London, National Gallery, 1974.

Lightbown, Ronald, *Sandro Botticelli* (2 vols.). Berkeley, University of California Press, and London, Elek, 1978; revised with subtitle *Life and Work*, New York, Abbeville Press, and London, Thames and Hudson, 1989.

Mandel, Gabriele, *The Complete Paintings of Botticelli*. London, Weidenfeld and Nicolson, and New York, Abrams, 1970.

Salvini, Roberto, *All the Paintings of Botticelli*, translated by John Grillenzoni. London, Oldbourne, and New York, Hawthorne Books, 1965.

Steinmann, Ernst, *Botticelli*, translated by Campbell Dodgson. London, H. Grevel, 1901 (also published, in English, by Velhagen and Kalsing, Bielefeld and Leipzig, 1901).

Yashiro, Yukio, *Sandro Botticelli and the Florentine Renaissance*. London and Boston, Medici Society, 1925.

*

To a greater extent than for most Renaissance artists, Botticelli has been the victim of his *fortuna critica*. Although still praised by Giorgio Vasari, who included a biography of the artist in his *Lives* (1550 and 1568), Botticelli fell into obscurity over the next three centuries. It was not until the 1870s that some English artists and critics, including Dante Gabriel Rossetti, Walter Pater, and above all John Ruskin, "rediscovered" Botticelli. In 1873, Pater's appreciative essay on Botticelli could refer to him as "a comparatively unknown artist" (in *Studies in the History of the Renaissance*, 1873), but within a few decades Botticelli had become a household word, and works like his *Birth of Venus* were world famous. Botticelli's paintings not only influenced the style of Pre-Raphaelite artists such as Rossetti and Burne-Jones, but the wistful melancholy of his figures, the mysterious complexity of his allegorical works, and the romantic appeal of events associated with Botticelli in 15th-century Florence—from the murder of Giuliano de' Medici to the rise and fall of Savonarola—struck a powerful chord in the late-Victorian imagination. Therein lies the problem in Botticelli biography and criticism over the last century. The modern view of the artist, filtered through a later 19th-century sensibility, ascribes to Botticelli a febrile, possibly neurotic, even morbid personality, though this reflects more on the *fin-de-siècle* in which it developed than on the Quattrocento. It was Ruskin, for example (in the essay "Ariadne Florentina," 1873), who first linked Botticelli's mythological paintings with the story of Giuliano de' Medici and his ideal lady, Simonetta Vespucci, and further hypothesized Botticelli's unrequited passion for the doomed Simonetta. This legend was then accepted by a host of biographers, especially early 20th-century writers such as CARTWRIGHT and BODE, to name the best, but was still repeated as fact for decades, as in BERTRAM. Serious scholars have had to exert much effort to disprove the story; part of the difficulty is that very little evidence about Botticelli himself survives beyond archival records for some of his commissions and their patrons. Yet the underlying romantic view of Botticelli that generated the Simonetta myth has dominated critical and historical literature on the artist. Thus STEINMANN, while acknowledging that much writing on the artist was little more than interpretive speculation, happily noted "we are very willing to let him remain in a romantic twilight," and so, too, have many other critics, even as late as LEVEY in 1974.

This persistent view, however, led the first serious archivist to examine Botticelli's life to go to the opposite extreme. HORNE's biographical study was the earliest to rely exclusively on the surviving documentary record, and included transcriptions of the documents themselves. Horne approached the artist and his works according to the known facts and presented, among other reasoned judgments, a thorough rejection of the Simonetta legend. Published originally in a limited edition, Horne's book reprinted in 1980, and John Pope-Hennessy, in his introduction to the reprint, went so far as to call Horne's book "the best monograph in English on an Italian painter." Yet even Roger Fry, an early defender of Horne (in *Burlington Magazine*, 1926), admitted that Horne's was "dry as dust," and few modern readers would disagree. It remains of great use for scholars, but Horne endeavored to dissociate himself so thoroughly from the prevailing sentimental opinion that he eliminated virtually all aesthetic or formal response to Botticelli as an artist. Indeed, Horne's pedanticism led to a backlash that prompted ever more subjective critical biographies, culminating in the curiosity by YASHIRO, an author who, constantly alluding to his exotic position as a Japanese writing about a European artist, found Botticelli's "poetic" use of line and conceptual approach to nature thoroughly Japanese in spirit.

One turns with gratitude to two recent studies that unite solid art historical scholarship with sensitive, but not sentimental, appreciation of the artist's work. The definitive text is the two-volume monograph of LIGHTBOWN. The first volume of the 1978 edition is a well-written account of the artist's life and work, offering convincing assessments on a variety of style and attribution questions, yet adhering with scrupulous accuracy to the documented facts. Lightbown gives balanced and pragmatic judgments on certain art historical issues that have occupied much modern scholarship, such as the extent of the influence of Neoplatonism on the style and content of Botticelli's mythological works, and the evidence for Botticelli as a follower of Savonarola. The first volume also prints transcriptions of the documents, and has a selective, annotated bibliography. The second volume is a compete catalogue, furnishing for every autograph or attributed work a thorough consideration of condition and provenance, along with bibliography. While SALVINI and MANDEL are also useful for such catalogue information, neither matches Lightbown in exhaustiveness or breadth. The 1989 edition of Lightbown is a reprint of the original first volume, though lacking the appendix of transcribed documents. Without the documents or the second catalogue volume, the 1989 edition is geared more to general readers than to scholars, but it has the benefit of being exceptionally well-illustrated, almost entirely by excellent color plates (the original edition has mostly black-and-white illustrations). In its thoroughness and scholarly high standards, Lightbown's monograph is, and no doubt will remain, unsurpassed.

The monograph by ETTLINGER makes no claim to being comprehensive, but like Lightbown it is readable, carefully researched, and attains a fine balance between pedanticism and subjective appreciation of the artist. Though perhaps too gruffly dismissive of some of the more subtle iconographic interpretations of Botticelli's allegories, it is surely the best of the shorter introductions to the artist and his work.

—Julia I. Miller

BOURKE-WHITE, Margaret, 1904–1971; American photojournalist.

Brown, Theodore, *Margaret Bourke-White: Photojournalist*. Ithaca, New York, Cornell University Press, 1972.
Goldberg, Vicki, *Margaret Bourke-White: A Biography*. New York, Harper, 1986; London, Heinemann, 1987.
Silverman, Jonathan, *For the World to See: The Life of Margaret Bourke-White*. New York, Viking, and London, Secker and Warburg, 1983.

*

GOLDBERG's biography is the most complete of the three works and focuses most specifically on the photographer's life. The author's method is to use factual criteria to reconstruct the character of her subject with particular attention to Bourke-White's family background as well as to early parental influence. In this regard, her father's work with machines (especially presses), his status as an amateur photographer, and her ethical culture schooling are described as primary influences in the development of a gifted and driven artist. Having set the stage in this manner, the author proceeds to give a history of the photographer's first work as well as an assessment of its quality. At this point, she also emphasizes Margaret Bourke-White's ability to be in tune with the times, while constructing a psychological profile of this career woman by making reference to Bourke-White's psychological records and using references from notes and diaries.

This modeling emphasizes the quality of the photographer's relations to men and her sex life while some context is provided by a description of the sex role expectations of the period. Here the vernacular quality of Goldberg's prose becomes evident, for she introduces brief quotes from Bourke-White's various admirerers and colleagues to depict an attractive yet almost compulsively ambitious photographer. In support of this thesis, Goldberg is constantly pointing out how Bourke-White was the first to be at a given location.

She couples this information with substantial and useful background on the major picture magazines of the 1930s, such as *Life, Look,* and *P.M.,* and provides data on their photographic reproduction methods and their content in order to explain Bourke-White's successful or unsuccessful alliance with each of them. *Fortune* magazine, the periodical that first brought Bourke-White to prominence, is treated even more closely by describing its layout and contributors, as well as information about the quality of the photographer's negatives and prints in relation to the final printed product. The artist's approaches to her subject matter are discussed by providing a cultural and artistic context and by incorporating data on what is involved in the making of these photographs. The emphasis is on timing in this regard. Assignments crucial to the photographer's professional ascent are carefully described as are the specific times when she did a particularly good job under the usually adverse conditions in which she chose to work.

In essence, this first extensive biography integrates Bourke-White's work and her life while contextualizing both within the framework of the period's photojournalism, a structure that is expanded by including contemporary assessments of her work by critics and fellow photographers. The dramatic quality of this life and work approach apparently influenced Goldberg's chapter headings, which have titles such as ''First Loves and Secrets'' and ''Machinery is the New Messiah.'' This last is a quotation from Bourke-White, who was herself a prolific writer and speaker. Indeed, she wrote an autobiography in 1963 titled *Portrait of Myself.* Goldberg refers to this work but bases much of her book on interviews, family letters, and notes typed by the artist. Her research shows good attention to fact and detail, and her biography is based on more intimate sources than Silverman's volume.

As a whole, SILVERMAN's work emphasizes Bourke-White's work over her life. Chapters are internally connected through the use of overall themes and emerge in the form of somewhat disconnected expository anecdotes, which in turn are organized around the places Bourke-White visited. Using a hyperbolic vocabulary, Silverman has the photographer move from one adventurous assignment to the next, highlighting the sheer physical difficulty of taking the pictures she did. This approach does provide useful information about the actual shooting techniques that Bourke-White used and how she saw and visualized when she took pictures. In particular, Silverman takes us through a visual description of how she understood lighting and used it for composition and modeling.

Silverman bases much of his information on Bourke-White's autobiography as well as letters and transcripts of her speeches. Little of this quoted information is private and Silverman appears to take it at face value, offering little interpretation. The extensive quotations do, however, provide a glimpse into the flavor of Bourke-White's prose and give a sense of first person narrative. Silverman's book, lavishly illustrated with images that echo the brown tonality of the original prints, provides a good interpolation of pictures and writing, demonstrating exactly how important her written work was. These writings are also used to explain the pictures by furnishing background on the subject matter and how it was approached.

Two interesting aspects of the Silverman biography are discussions of the photographer's alleged communist affiliation during the McCarthy era and her relationship to news magazines and their editors. As does Goldberg, he describes contemporary reactions to Bourke-White's work, while the book's illustrations make this as much a book about her as a paean to industry and social progress.

BROWN uses a similar blend of information about Bourke-White's professional life coupled with her imagery, and this exhibition catalog may have been a model for Silverman's later work. The catalog does contain some brief biographical material in the first section of the text, the rest being devoted to her work and its contextualization within the framework of 20th-century art.

—Diana Emery Hulick

BOWEN, Elizabeth, 1899–1973; Irish writer.

Austin, Allan E., *Elizabeth Bowen.* New York, Twayne, 1971.
Craig, Patricia, *Elizabeth Bowen.* London and New York, Penguin, 1986.
Glendinning, Victoria, *Elizabeth Bowen: Portrait of a Writer.* London, Weidenfeld and Nicolson, 1977; with subtitle, *A Biography,* New York, Knopf, 1978.
Kenney, Edwin J., *Elizabeth Bowen.* Lewisburg, Pennsylvania, Bucknell University Press, 1975.

*

GLENDINNING has written an admirably perceptive and interesting life of Elizabeth Bowen. She accepts her subject as she finds her, understanding her somewhat amoral temperament. Glendinning knows where Bowen's habit of emotional containment comes from—the losses through death and illness of those close to her. She safe-guarded herself from further trauma, her stammer the only visible sign of the effect of her father's mental breakdown. Glendinning is refreshingly clear about human motivation and temperament. From the psychological point of view her approach is both complex and precise; she writes in an analytical, cooly rational way. Her judgments rise persuasively from the assembled detail.

At the same time the brief critical synopses of the novels and short stories are acute and revealing. There is none of the flat paraphrasing that spoils so many literary biographies. Glendinning is capable of concise, decisive views and shows good sense in her observations on human nature and on human relationships.

CRAIG writes in a refreshing, lively, and summarising manner. Hers is a short work that provides interesting vignettes of Elizabeth Bowen's life and less interesting critical judgments on the novels and short stories. Because her book came out later than Glendinning's, it has a few additional facts, but essentially it relies for its biographical information on Glendinning and is not forthcoming about personal details.

Bowen's autobiographical writings are also useful. *Seven Winters* (1942), which she called "a fragment of autobiography" and is only 60 pages in length, describes Bowen's life in Dublin up to the age of seven. *Bowen's Court* (1942) is a long account of the family since the 18th century. It provides considerable insight into the life of the aristocracy. Further insight into the lives of Bowen's class is found in her history of the Dublin hotel in which they liked to gather, *The Shelbourne: A Centre in Dublin Life for More than a Century* (1951). It gives an entirely different sense of Irish life from that encountered in realistic novels of the postrevolutionary period.

Because Elizabeth Bowen tended to be secretive about her own private life, not many critics have attempted to read her novels in the light of the known biographical material. Even so, the volumes by KENNEY and AUSTIN make good use of her life in discussing her fiction. Both of the major works, by Glendinning and Craig, suffer from having been written so soon after Bowen's death. A full-scale biography still needs to be written.

—Maurice Harmon

BRAHMS, Johannes, 1833–1897; German composer.

Chissell, Joan, *Brahms*. London, Faber, 1977.

Colles, Henry C., *Brahms*. London, J. Lane, and New York, Brentano, 1908.

Dale, Kathleen, *Brahms: A Biography with a Survey of Books, Editions and Recordings*. Hamden, Connecticut, Archon Books, and London, Bingley, 1970.

Deiters, Hermann, *Johannes Brahms: A Biographical Sketch*, translated by Rosa Newmarch. London, T. F. Unwin, 1888 (originally published by Breitkopf and Härtel, Leipzig, 1880).

Erb, John L., *Brahms*. London, Dent, and New York, Dutton, 1905.

Fuller Maitland, J. A., *Brahms*. London, Methuen, 1911.

Gál, Hans., *Johannes Brahms: His Work and Personality*, translated by Joseph Stein. London, Weidenfeld and Nicolson, and New York, Knopf, 1963 (originally published by Fischer Bücherei, Frankfurt am Main, 1961).

Geiringer, Karl, *Brahms: His Life and Work*, translated by H. B. Weiner and Bernard Miall. Second enlarged edition, London, Oxford University Press, 1947 (originally published as *Johannes Brahms: Leben und Schaffen*, Vienna, R. M. Rohrer, 1935).

Hill, Ralph, *Brahms: A Study in Musical Biography*. London, D. Archer, 1933.

Holmes, Paul, *Brahms: His Life and Times*. Southborough, Kent, Baton Press, 1984.

James, Burnett, *Brahms: A Critical Study*. London, Dent, and New York, Praeger, 1972.

Keys, Ivor, *Johannes Brahms*. London, C. Helm, and Portland, Oregon, Amadeus, 1989.

Latham, Peter, *Brahms*. London, Dent, 1948.

May, Florence, *The Life of Johannes Brahms* (2 vols.). London, E. Arnold, 1905.

Murdoch, William, *Brahms: With an Analytical Study of the Complete Pianoforte Works*. London, Rich and Cowan, 1933.

Niemann, Walter, *Brahms*, translated by C. A. Phillips. New York, Knopf, 1929 (originally published by Schuster and Loeffler, Berlin, 1920).

Pulver, Jeffrey, *Johannes Brahms*. London, Kegan Paul, and New York, Harper, 1926.

Schauffler, Robert H., *The Unknown Brahms; His Life, Character, and Works, Based on New Material*. New York, Crown Publishers, 1933.

Specht, Richard, *Johannes Brahms*, translated by E. Blom. London, Dent, and New York, Dutton, 1930 (originally published, Dresden, 1928).

*

As befits a composer who won early recognition in England, Brahms has been well served by biographies in English. None of the works cited above matches the scale of the standard work, Max Kalbeck's monumental *Johannes Brahms* (4 vols., Berlin, 1904–14), but the fruits of Kalbeck's research have been drawn upon by almost all later authors, with a greater or lesser degree of acknowledgment.

The earliest biographical study has considerable historical interest, as its author, DEITERS, first met Brahms in the 1850s, Originally published some 20 years before the composer's death, it was brought up to date by Newmarch in 1888 but remains incomplete. Deiters' own complete and revised edition of 1898 was never translated into English.

MAY also knew Brahms, having studied piano with him in the 1870s, and her biography is preceded by an invaluable introduction about Brahms as player and pedagogue. Although later biographers had the advantage of greater historical perspective, few rival May's immediacy. Some may find the frequent references to the "beloved master" wearing, but May is not blind to the weaknesses of Brahms's character, and she produces a remarkably balanced study. 1905 also saw the publication of ERB's monograph for the "Master Musicians" series. The accompanying appendices will undoubtedly have been useful to the contemporary reader, but the prose is heavy and the narrative overlarded with dates and opus numbers.

Colles and Fuller Maitland both worked for *The Times* of London where they helped champion Brahms' music. COLLES concentrates on analysis of the music, but FULLER MAITLAND takes a wider angle. His work is an interesting testament to an age in which Brahms' reputation was not yet assured: it is prefaced by an "introductory note of enthusiasm" in which the author sees fit to justify his advocacy of Brahms. The biographical section is relatively short but it is followed by a useful account of the controversy surrounding Brahms and the Wagner-Liszt axis.

NIEMANN claims to have written the "first critical biography" of Brahms. The book is divided into two parts. Part I, couched in a fanciful literary style, deals with the life and includes chapters on Brahms the man and Brahms as pianist, conductor, and teacher. Neimann's discussion of works stresses the composer's reliance on his classical forbears.

SPECHT was an intimate of Brahms' circle in Vienna, and as a result he is able to give an authoritative account of Brahms' last years. In general, however, the biography is highly subjective, and the speculative approach adopted, for instance, in the opening chapter's description of Brahms' progress along the Rhine, can no longer be justified. Here, as elsewhere in the book, invention and detailed research prove to be awkward bedfellows.

The centenary of Brahms' birth in 1933 saw a spate of new biographies. HILL concentrates on a "study of the composer *in broad outline*, showing the several conflicting sides of his character as displayed in his intercourse with his friends and acquaintances." Both MURDOCH and PULVER adopt the same plan as Niemann—the biography followed by a discussion of Brahms the man and an account of his works. In the case of Murdoch the latter is arbitrarily restricted to those works in which a piano is used. Pulver's biography is well researched, but his literary style is precious: "moiety" is used instead of "half," and epithets such as "the high priest of the classic cult, the noble singer" abound.

By far the most interesting study of the 1933 crop is by the American writer, SCHAUFFLER. In the 30 years leading up to publication Schauffler made several trips to Europe in order to interview surviving members of Brahms' circle. The result is a rich fund of anecdote. Although Schauffler claims to offer the first detailed analysis of Brahms' repressed love life, the book is not salacious in tone; rather it represents an honest attempt to cut through prevailing orthodoxies.

A custodian of the *Gesellschaft der Musikfreunde* in Vienna, GEIRINGER had unrivalled access to Brahms' papers. His biography broke new ground by bringing to light unknown letters between Brahms, his family, and his friends. This contributed to a fuller and more intimate picture of Brahms' personal relationships than had previously been possible. The prose style is somewhat severe, but Geiringer's commitment to his subject is never in doubt.

LATHAM's study replaced the work by Erb in the "Master Musicians" series. It is a stylish, elegantly written account that offers no new insights but presents its material clearly and concisely. As ever with this series the appendices are extremely thorough and informative.

GÁL studied with Brahms' amanuensis, Eusebius Mandyczewski, and later collaborated with him for 20 years on the complete edition of the composer's works. With this pedigree he claims to be the "last surviving bearer of a direct Brahms tradition." Gál's is one of the strongest Brahms studies, and although it is very much weighted to a discussion of the works, this is done with a lightness of touch that maintains the interest of the non-specialist reader. Sadly, the bibliographical apparatus is weak. DALE's volume includes a biography, but its value lies principally in the survey of books, editions, and recordings.

JAMES has adopted a deliberately controversial angle in his study. Claiming (with some justification) that scholars are unlikely to unearth much new material about Brahms' life, James argues that the only *raison d'être* of a new biography is its relevance to the present day. The result is a book rich in unusual insights but idiosyncratic in character, better suited to the specialist than the general reader.

It is hard to determine the exact purpose of CHISSELL's volume. It is slender in substance and popular in tone, yet the text is interspersed with large sections of music that often have little relevance to the matter at hand. HOLMES, too, aims at the wider public. His text flows easily and the book is copiously illustrated, but the pictures are given irritating captions that merely serve to trivialise the narrative.

The latest addition to the Brahms bibliography is by KEYS. The biographical section concentrates on Brahms' relationship with Clara Schumann, but in the absence of any new material Keys is unable to come up with any significantly new interpretations. In general the biography is well written, though a serious student of the works will look elsewhere for enlightenment.

—Martin Ennis

BRANDO, Marlon, 1924–   ; American stage and film actor.

Brando, Anna Kashfi and E. P. Stein, *Brando for Breakfast*. New York, Crown Publishers, 1979.

Carey, Gary, *Brando!* New York, Pocket Books, 1973.

Fiore, Carlo, *Bud: The Brando I Knew*. New York, Delacorte Press, 1974; London, Hart-Davis MacGibbon, 1975.

Frank, Alan, *Marlon Brando*. New York, Exeter Books, 1982.

Higham, Charles, *Brando: The Unauthorized Biography*. New York, New American Library, 1987; London, Grafton, 1989.

Jordan, René, *Marlon Brando*. New York, Galahad Books, 1973; London, Star Books, 1975.

Shipman, David, *Brando*. New York, Doubleday, and London, Macmillan, 1974.

Thomas, Bob, *Marlon: Portrait of the Rebel as an Artist*. New York, Random House, 1973; London, W. H. Allen, 1974.

*

The biographies of Marlon Brando form a pyramid, the tiers arising in a geometric progression. The base is formed by a number of superficial surveys that spend all their energy on his movie career; only the first 15 or 20% of each is truly biographical— "Beginnings" and "Broadway Fame"; "The Making of a Rebel" and "The Method Conquers the Theatre"; "A Myth is Born" and "Budding into Brando" are the particular approaches of, respectively, SHIPMAN, FRANK, and JORDAN.

The next tier up from these half-pictorial books, and twice as informative, is occupied by a friend who knew Brando intermittently and a wife who knew him no longer and no better—Carlo Fiore and Anna Kashfi Brando. FIORE, a drug addict, vulgar, self-serving and petty, compiles unattractive "facts" (trusting Fiore is difficult): Brando snores, never reads newspapers, had crabs twice, "was in a state of perpetual erection," has "the hands of a syphilitic dwarf," sits while urinating, takes sleeping pills, "objects to pot," and found Fiore an all but indispensable adviser and friend. Typical of this friend's blunt conclusions is that Brando is "the ultimate Male Chauvinist Pig." Anna KASHFI BRANDO, once a wife and eternally vicious and vindictive, reports her own "years of thorns and vinegar": Brando is a clumsy seducer, a slob (his car is "a mobile garbage can"), arrogant, narcissistic, masochistic, etc. One of her blunt conclusions is that Brando is "modern gothic: grotesque, contradictory, impossible." Though both authors rant and rave, a vivid image of Brando (and of themselves) emerges.

The third tier of books, by CAREY and THOMAS, is twice as good as the second. Interestingly, both belabor the point that Brando is a rebel. The consequence of this approach is—in Carey—a long list of Brando's pranks, insults, eccentricities, feuds, insensitivites, extravagances, and mistakes. Thomas, less vicious, has an even longer list of judgments, one that admits some praise, even hyperbole: "Brando acted with a wit, intensity and animal energy that had never been seen in films before"; "He made the most complete and unchallengeable comeback in the history of film" (in *The Godfather*); "Marlon [was] obsessed by sex, in all its aspects"; "As an exercise in human folly, the second *Mutiny on the Bounty* is unsurpassed in film history." In 1957 Truman Capote published an intensely researched half-biography, half-interview coyly mocking the sensitivity, intellectual superiority, and paranoia of Brando (reprinted as "The Duke in His Domain," in *Selected Writings*, 1963. Though its tone is nasty—Brando frequently brings out the worst in people, and Capote's worst is legendary—the essay is both a beautiful piece of writing and an extraordinary document.

HIGHAM's full biography, twice as good as Carey or Thomas, occupies the pinnacle of the pyramid. A fuller, more accurate biographer of Brando is not one of civilization's greater needs; this will do for the time being. Brando arrives in Hollywood on page 100 of Higham. This allows an unprecedented and leisurely attention to the early Brando—parents, childhood homes, accidents, games, relatives, schools, sports, jobs. The result is not only the best biography, but in a profound and balanced sense, the only one. He gracefully and generously assimilates the work of Kashfi and Fiore, which he sadly calls "much the best books available to date." Though he, too, includes some of the gossip, corrected and muted, he is not satisfied to leave us with the image of a man urinating in a sink, but a man of thoughtful talent, rash politics, sincere family connections (no one else glances at his sons and daughters the same way), professional disagreements that have two considered sides, and an intelligent and tormented and human complexity. Higham seems to take seriously something Brando said of himself in an interview: "All men, when they reach my age, unless they are absolute idiots, must feel a sort of emptiness inside, a sense of anguish, of uselessness. And consider my generation. It is horribly hybrid, torn by painful contradictions." This complex concept eludes all biographers of Brando except Higham, who alone stands at the apex.

—Paul H. Stacy

BRECHT, Bertolt, 1898–1956; German playwright.

Bentley, Eric, *The Brecht Memoir*. New York, PAJ Publications, 1985.

Bunge, Hans, editor, *Living for Brecht: The Memoirs of Ruth Berlau*, translated by Geoffrey Skelton. New York, Fromm International, 1987 (originally published as *Brechts Lai-Tu*, Darmstadt, Luchterhand, 1985).

Cook, Bruce, *Brecht in Exile*. New York, Holt Rinehart, 1982.

Esslin, Martin, *Brecht: A Choice of Evils*. London, Eyre Methuen, 1959; as *Brecht: The Man and His Work*, New York, Doubleday, 1960.

Ewen, Frederic, *Bertolt Brecht: His Life, His Art, and His Times*. New York, Citadel Press, and London, Calder and Boyars, 1967.

Fuegi, John, *Bertolt Brecht: Chaos, According to Plan*. Cambridge and New York, Cambridge University Press, 1987.

Hayman, Ronald, *Brecht: A Biography*. London, Weidenfeld and Nicolson, and New York, Oxford University Press, 1983.

Lyon, James K., *Bertolt Brecht in America*. Princeton, New Jersey, Princeton University Press, 1980; London, Methuen, 1982.

Needle, Jan and Peter Thomson, *Brecht*. Oxford, Blackwell, 1980.

Völker, Klaus, *Brecht: A Biography*, translated by John Nowell. New York, Seabury Press, 1978; London, Boyars, 1979 (originally published as *Bertolt Brecht: Eine Biographie*, Munich and Vienna, C. Hanser, 1976).

Willett, John, *Brecht in Context: Comparative Approaches*. London and New York, Methuen, 1984.

Witt, Hubert, editor, *Brecht as They Knew Him*, translated by John Peet. Berlin, Seven Seas, and New York, International Publishers, 1974; London, Lawrence and Wishart, 1975 (originally published as *Erinnerungen an Brecht*, Leipzig, Reclam, 1964).

*

James K. Lyon wrote in *Bertolt Brecht in America* (see below), "there were almost as many Brechts as there were people who know him." That observation holds true for his biographers as well, whose treatments seem to revolve around four issues: his personality, his treatment of women, his adherence to the tenets of communism, the success and originality of his works.

Appearing in 1959, ESSLIN's biography set the controversies in motion by questioning the depth of Brecht's political commitment. For Esslin, Brecht is a rebellious adolescent who never grew up, a Schweikian character who "defeats the powers that be, the whole universe in all its absurdity, not by opposing but by complying with them." Brecht is an opportunist who uses the iniquities of capitalism to work out his own contradictory nature, particularly the anarchism of his youth, his attraction to didacticism, and feelings of nihilism and despair. Brecht is a ruthless individualist who leans on the hospitality of the East German communists while maintaining his Austrian passport, his West German publisher, and his Swiss bank account. Esslin's book has gone into its fourth edition, evidence of its appeal to Esslin's anti-communist readers, its moments of brilliance, and its highly readable format. Only one third of it rehearses the bare facts and dates of Brecht's life; the rest comprises Esslin's contentious analysis of Brechtian theater and ideology. Esslin's style is fluid, and he avoids cheap shots about Brecht's sexual encounters, which could have been drawn on to support his theses.

VÖLKER has answered Esslin with a careful and comprehensive discussion about the social elements that lie at the heart of Brecht's plays and the suffering of a German expatriot robbed of his homeland. Völker portrays Brecht as an honest socialist who understood that capitalism distorts people and their relationships, rendering them incapable of living by a moral code. Brecht had differences with the American and East German communists not because he advocated too little communism, but because he demanded too much; consequently, he parted company with the others on aesthetic issues. Völker, the only biographer who seems to understand the Lukacs/Brecht debate at its most technical level, grapples with all the controversies in a clear narrative that makes sense of the data. Missing, however, is any real appreciation of what made Brecht a difficult personality and an unconventional lover. Völker is also sketchy on Brecht's years in America.

Two other comprehensive biographies pale next to Völker's. EWEN's early narrative sets the context for Brecht's life with extensive detail about the politics, philosophy, literature, and economics of the times. Only now and again, however, does he demonstrate a direct connection between these events and Brecht. He portrays Brecht as more absorbed with his art than with external events, thus naive about political matters. Ewen explains away the themes of Brecht's plays with full descriptions of this century's demogogues and world wars when violence and terror are taken for granted. Additionally, he all but ignores Brecht's cynicism, referring instead to his "humaneness in time of upheaval," and he slides over Brecht's mistreatment of women.

HAYMAN's comprehensive biography is much bolder about Brecht's intriguing appetites for pleasure, but Hayman sometimes resorts to titilation when dealing with Brecht's exploits. Generally evenhanded in his treatment, Hayman regards Brecht as the "wise man who found it necessary from boyhood onwards to be devious." Hayman is best when explaining Brecht's contributions to experimental theater, since he shows genuine understanding of Brechtian technique. The weakness in this biography lies in the juxtaposition of weighty and incidental detail that is meant for color but intrudes on the narrative and detracts from a coherent interpretation of fact.

A superb complement to Völker's biography is LYON's *Brecht in America* for its integrity and detail. Lyon arranged more than 100 interviews and sifted through telephone wire taps, letters, newspaper and magazine clippings, and records from the Immigration and Naturalization Service to shape and reveal the complexity of Brecht's inner conflict. He combines the humanity and kindness of a man also destitute of real tenderness, the extreme individualist and extreme collectivist, the hard-line Stalinist who refuses control. Lyon believes that the only passion that Brecht took more seriously than his writing was his ideology. A useless version of Brecht's American exile is COOK's journalistic biography that plays fast and loose with its sources and seems to be written solely to debunk Brecht's reputation.

Two poignant (because the authors were mistreated by Brecht) memoirs are those by BENTLEY, translator and critic, and the volume by BUNGE/BERLAU; the latter was Brecht's collaborator and mistress. Berlau openly talks about her lifelong obsession with Brecht and communism. More obscure, indeed concealed, is any significant revelation about her relationship to Brecht's wife, Helene Weigel, and his other mistresses. Editor Eric Bunge discreetly leaves Berlau's text, sometimes erroneous in fact, unamended and unfootnoted. Bentley's tiny memoir is more openhanded as he explores his dealings with Brecht's female protectors and his own inability to say why he admired Brecht even though the men differed radically on the merits of communism and the women around him. Despite the confessional tone, Bentley too appears to be withholding some information.

Four works that deserve brief mention weave Brecht's biography into a discussion of his plays and theories. WILLETT's work should be consulted for its understanding of Brecht's importance to English-language literature; especially noteworthy are Willett's chapters on Piscator and Auden. NEEDLE AND THOMSON attempt to set right those biographers who have underrated Brecht and misunderstood his dramaturgy. They address those critics like Hayman and (later) John Fuegi who believe that as a director Brecht willingly betrayed his own theories when he needed dramatic effect. FUEGI includes an interesting discussion of the evolution of the *Verfremdungs Theorie*. The result is superficial, however, because Fuegi unexplainably eschews a scholarly approach and too preemptively dismisses Brecht's ideological foundations. WITT's collection of 34 brief selections combines personal anecdote with theoretical commentary by many Germans who worked with Brecht.

—Reade W. Dornan

BRETON, André, 1896-1966; French writer.

Balakian, Anna, *André Breton: Magus of Surrealism.* New York, Oxford University Press, 1971.
Browder, Clifford, *André Breton: Arbiter of Surrealism.* Geneva, Droz, 1967.
Caws, Mary Ann, *André Breton.* Boston, Twayne, 1971.
Matthews, J.H., *André Breton: Sketch for an Early Portrait.* Amsterdam and Philadelphia, J. Benjamin, 1986.

*

In the preface to her study, which is primarily devoted to Breton's works, CAWS states with good reason that no book can entirely encompass the life or activities of André Breton. Actually, Breton's *Entretiens* (1952) and the short biographical notes included in *André Breton, Poésie et Autre* (1960) consitute our principal sources of biographical documentation about Breton. As Caws remarks, Breton insisted on remaining "transparent" and "demanded that his works be left *open*." It is true that we know little of Breton's childhood and upbringing. His writings, unlike those of hiis contemporaries Proust, Mauriac, or Gide, do not offer information about his family, though they reveal a great deal about his adult life. They describe his activities beginning in 1915 and continuing through his productive collaboration with other artists and writers. Still, even today many of his trips or "pilgrimages" remain poorly documented.

Although Breton became the most active and central figure of the surrealist movement, one should keep in mind that surrealism was mostly a collaborative movement, therefore it is essential to examine Breton in relation to other writers and poets. Surrealsim was an interdisciplinary venture born from the visual arts and it is, therefore, not surprising to find Breton in the company of painters and photographers throughout his life.

MATTHEWS, like Caws, begins his study with Breton's early interest in poetry, his experience in a psychiatric hospital where he served in 1917, and his participation in the Dada movement in Paris, Matthews carefullly follows Breton's literary and artistic exchanges with the artist Picabia, whom he considered a pioneer int he area of linguistic and pictorial representation. Breton's dominant personality is depicted through his numerous exclusions or even "excommunications" and reconciliations with members of the surrealist movement. Matthews' sophisticated study gives English readers some valuable insights into how Breton is portrayed in French criticism. The sixth chapter focuses on Sigmund Freud and demonstrates how Breton was not interested so much in therapy as in poetic experimentation—i.e. he was more fascinated by Freudian theories than by their application. Although his meeting with Freud in 1921 was disappointing, Matthews points out that it marked a crucial moment in Breton's life since Freud had "recommended free association in the treatment of mental disorders" and Breton had "advised writers to apply it to themselves." This subject has been a focus of conflicting interpretations and is well documented in Matthews' study, which refers to the critical works by Marguerite Bonnet and Michel Sanouillet, two eminent French critics on Breton.

BALAKIAN and BROWDER, whose works will be discussed below by turns, are the only critics who give us some insights into Breton's early years. Anna Balakian's study is also based on conversations with Breton's daughter, Aube, and some of Breton's friends. Her first chapter, entitled "The Man and his Background," informs us that Breton was an only child who identified more closely with his father and his grandfather than with his mother. She argues that "other women could be so much more attractive, radiant, warm than the mother whom he shunned and who did not live into his maturity," Balakian also determines that Breton's bourgeois background was a dominant factor in the development of his life. Clifford Browder gives us additional informatin as he follows Breton from 1906 to 1912 at the Collége Chaptal, where he was introduced to some of the literature that would later influence his writing. Neither work clarifies the enigma surrounding Breton's birthdate. Although in the *Manifeste du surréalisme*, (1924) Breton insisted he was a Pisces, he might have been born on the 18th rather than on the 19th of February and therefore might be either a Pisces or an Aquaris. This detail is of th utmost importance for a writer who identified himself through astrology and who explored occultism.

It was as a medical assitant at the hospital of Nantes and at the psychiartic hospital of Saint Didier that Breton first developed his idea of "automatic writing." Breton's terminology, as Anna Balakian demonstrates, came from Dr. Pierre Janet, who "called the ecstasy of his hysteric young women patients 'amour fou,' their vision 'convulsive'; Breton was to appropriate these expressions and transform their medical sense into poetic ones." Balakian's second chapter, entitled "The Young Poet in Paris," traces Breton's frienships with Jean Vaché, Apollinaire, Pierre Réverdy, and Louis Aragon, In 1916 Breton made his literary contacts with the Dadaists of the Café Voltaire in Zurich. Clifford Browder gives an account of the meetings of the Rue Fontaine, where Breton lived with his wife Simone Kahn, and of the *Bureau de Recherches Surréalistes*, which opened in 1924. He also traces Breton's rather precarious financial situation: "During the worst period, the intervention of a friend permitted him to open a small gallery which he christened Gradiva."

Balakian's 11th chapter highlights Breton's political involvement: his protest against the war in Morocco in 1925, the Nazi Putsch in 1934, his attacks of the "Moscow trials" and of the Stalinist regime, and his strong interest in Hegel, Marx, and Engels. This chapter constitutes an excellent source of documentation on Breton's visit to the United States; his divorce from his wife Jacqueline Lamba in Reno, and his famous speech at Yale University in 1942, where he addressed "a generation of youths preparing to go into the army in the darkest moment of the war." Browder on the other hand takes a close look at Breton's plitical career and more particularly at how his disillusionment with Communism led to his admiration of Charles Fourier, a socialist thinker. He concludes that Breton was "more a man of ideas than a man of action." Balakian's 14th chapter traces Breton's return to France in 1946 after the war, "a phantom, a stranger in his own country," at a time when "the old manifestoes frothing with promises to change the world [seemed] painfully out of step with the times."

Browder offers the reader a succint examination of Breton's production in his 11th chapter, citing his automatic texts, his poetry and his declarations on surrealism. This work serves as a good overall introduction to Breton's works. Browder considers rebellion to have been the main factor in Breton's life: "All forms of social conservation were to be subverted, above all the 'abject trinity' of Family, Country and Religion." Breton emerges form Browder's study as a figure who, at the end of his life, remained "the arch rebel, the eternal adventureer, and the idealist with an unshakable faith in human potentialites."

—Martine Natat Antle

BRITTEN, Benjamin, 1913–1976; English composer.

Blyth, Alan, *Remembering Britten*. London, Hutchinson, 1981.
Britten, Beth, *My Brother Benjamin*. Bourne End, Buckinghamshire, Kensal Press, 1986.
Holst, Imogen, *Britten*. London, Faber, 1966; 3rd edition, Faber, 1980.
Kennedy, Michael, *Britten*. London, Dent, 1981.
Mitchell, Donald and John Evans, editors, *Benjamin Britten 1913–76: Pictures From a Life*. London, Faber, 1978; with subtitle *A Pictorial Biography*, New York, Scribner, 1978.
Mitchell, Donald, *Britten and Auden in the 30s: The Year 1936*. London, Faber, and Seattle, University of Washington Press, 1981.
White, Eric W., *Benjamin Britten: A Sketch of His Life and Works*. London, Boosey and Hawkins, 1948; revised by John

Evans as *Benjamin Britten: His Life and Operas*, London, Faber, and Berkeley, University of California Press, 1983.

*

Fame came so early to Britten that biographical studies began to appear from his 35th year. Many, like WHITE's, were regularly revised during Britten's life, and completed after his death. All the problems involved in writing the biography of a contemporary are shown in White's book. There is an abundance of verifiable fact: there is also a stifling inhibition of truth. White says in the first edition that he accepted the commission to write it "as soon as [he] could be assured of the approval of Britten himself." A biography that is dependent on the approval of the subject is indeed limited. White draws a warmly sympathetic portrait of the composer. But while he is knowledgeable on Britten's professional career and a particularly useful source on the founding and early development of the Aldeburgh Festival, he fails to probe the difficult area of Britten's relationship with colleagues; White writes of "jealousy" and "misunderstandings" but the failings are always on the part of others, and this diminishes the value of his personal testimony.

KENNEDY successfully overcomes this obstacle. His is at present the only biography that attempts a disinterested assessment of Britten. Writing out a deep love of the music, Kennedy had access to a rich cache of source material, and he hints at more to be released some day. This well-founded supply of information sets the tone for a book that has constant recourse to quotation from letters, diaries, recorded interviews, and private reminiscences: the authentic voice of the composer speaks on every page. However, in this concise study, divided between biography and critical analysis, Kennedy often seems cramped by the constraints of the Master Musicians Series format, and could clearly have given a fuller account of the genesis and performance history of major works had space allowed. Personal issues are not avoided, however: in a chapter called "Pride and Prejudice," Kennedy sifts the evidence available to him and draws an eminently balanced portrait of a sometimes difficult and demanding colleague who also inspired an almost fanatical loyalty in his friends. His analysis of the problematic reception of the Coronation opera, *Gloriana*, demonstrates his ability to understand complex responses to contemporary music. Kennedy's is the essential biography, which other books embellish but do not replace.

Personal reminiscences form the basis of two other books. BLYTH builds a series of interviews with friends and colleagues into an invaluable record of "how a great composer lived, worked and behaved." Blyth's book illustrates the many-sidedness of Britten's character, and the picture that finally emerges is of a superbly gifted professional with an obsession for making every detail of his performances perfect. Blyth brings out both the ruthlessness (in interviews with Keller, Del Mar and Reiss) and (with Tippett and Holst) the composer's very great charm.

Charming on its own terms, BETH BRITTEN's memoir focuses on the early period, up to *Peter Grimes*. She includes intimate domestic details—pet names, nursery routines, family dramatics—in an artless but totally authentic record. Much of the book is devoted to family letters, published here for the first time. They vividly illuminate the student years, and are especially valuable as a record of Britten's American period. (Her accounts of both the attitudes and the practical details of life on either side of the Atlantic could interest an historian of this period, not just the student of Britten's music.) The work offers a wealth of insights that only this author could give: the similarity, for example, between Peter Pears' voice and that of Britten's mother.

Two books from MITCHELL can be seen as preliminaries to the official biography that has yet to be written. *Britten and Auden in the Thirties* (1981) is a study of a developing composer, focusing on working methods and on the music itself. Writing perceptively about the artistic relationship between Britten and Auden, Mitchell has much to reveal about the processes by which the music took shape. He also relates the music to the decade, making a useful contribution to cultural history. MITCHELL AND EVANS' pictorial biography (1978) is an important study and a model of its kind. Some of the success of the book is undoubtedly due to the compilers' skill in selecting images that interest as photographs, not just as documents of the subject. Informal shots, both of rehearsals and relaxation, predominate over posed portraits. This rich resource will enhance the reading of any of the cited biographies.

Finally, HOLST, who tells a simple success story, offers a straightforward biography in a series designed for young people—a division of society for which Britten had great interest and sympathy. It is a feature of the Great Composers series that short music examples that young people could play or sing are included in the text, and Holst has been ingenious in finding the less obvious candidates for inclusion. She tells a plain and factual tale, without interpretation or critical assessment. Her narrative is brought to life by personal details arising from her close friendship with the composer. The chapter on amateur music-making has a special immediacy. The appeal of this short book is by no means restricted to the young audience for whom it is intended.

—Patricia Howard

BRONTË, Charlotte, 1816–1855; English writer.
BRONTË, Emily, 1818–1848; English writer.

Chitham, Edward, *A Life of Emily Brontë*. Oxford and New York, Blackwell, 1987.
Fraser, Rebecca, *Charlotte Brontë*. London, Methuen, 1988.
Gaskell, Elizabeth, *The Life of Charlotte Brontë*. London, Smith Elder, and New York, Appleton, 1857.
Gérin, Winifred, *Anne Brontë*. London, Nelson, 1959.
Gérin, Winifred, *Branwell Brontë*. London, Nelson, 1961.
Gérin, Winifred, *Charlotte Brontë: The Evolution of Genius*. Oxford, Clarendon Press, 1967; New York, Oxford University Press, 1987.
Gérin, Winifred, *Emily Brontë: A Biography*. Oxford, Clarendon Press, 1971.
Robinson, A. Mary, *Emily Brontë*. London, W. H. Allen, 1883.
Winnifrith, Tom, *The Brontës and Their Background: Romance and Reality*. London, Macmillan, and New York, Barnes and Noble, 1973.

Winnifrith, Tom, *A New Life of Charlotte Brontë*. London, Macmillan, and New York, St. Martin's, 1988.

*

The separability of Brontë art from Brontë biography has been the question facing every Brontë biographer and most readers of the Brontë novels. The life story of the Brontë sisters (three who lived to become well-known novelists, two who died as school-girls), and of the brother who was an aspiring poet and painter, would fascinate readers even if these lives were not reflected in two of England's classic novels, *Jane Eyre* and *Wuthering Heights*. But wherever readers turn in the works of the Brontës, they sense the particular force of unique experience, the border-land tension between fact and fiction. Thus Brontë biography often must deal with the Brontë fictions as much as with available facts about the Brontë lives. With many writers and artists there is but a fine line between autobiography and fiction, and Charlotte Brontë did much to develop the form of the fictional auto-biography, giving her first novel the full title of *Jane Eyre: An Autobiography*. That the title page claimed this was a work "Ed-ited by Currer Bell," and that Emily Brontë and Anne Brontë chose the pseudonyms of Ellis and Acton Bell, led early readers and reviewers to wrongful assumptions about the Brontës, some claiming them to be male writers, some insisting that all the works were by one writer using different pen names.

Brontë biography began with the "Biographical Notice of El-lis and Acton Bell," which Charlotte wrote for the 1850 edition of *Wuthering Heights*. This novel, along with Anne Brontë's *Agnes Grey*, had been published as a three-volume work in 1848, nearly coincident with the appearance of *Jane Eyre* from another publisher. With much confusion about the authorship of these works and with both of her sisters dead by May 1848, Charlotte found it essential to reveal that these had been books by three sisters using pseudonyms. Her brief biographical state-ment centers on the origin and authorship of the novels and on the illnesses and early deaths of her sisters. In both this bio-graphical comment and her preface to Emily's novel, Charlotte established a view of Emily that profoundly influenced genera-tions of readers. To Charlotte, Emily was someone in whom "the extremes of vigor and simplicity seemed to meet"; she could be "magnanimous, but warm and sudden; her spirit alto-gether unbending"; and perhaps Charlotte's most pertinent com-ment is her insistence that "an interpreter ought always to have stood between [Emily] and the world."

Charlotte's call for an interpreter is the call her father made to her friend and fellow novelist, Elizabeth GASKELL, soon after Charlotte's death, and Gaskell's *The Life of Charlotte Brontë* be-came one of the monuments of 19th-century literary biography. Like most of the Brontë biographies that would follow, Gaskell's is the story of the Brontë family, of whom, apart from her father, Charlotte was the last survivor. Gaskell, like Brontë enthusiasts today, visited Brontë sites and was affected by the rugged beauty of Yorkshire. Because she had known Charlotte for only five years, Gaskell drew heavily upon available letters and accounts by people who had known Charlotte and her brothers and sisters.

The Gaskell life was encumbered by lack of information, by the need to respect the sensitivities of the yet living Brontë fa-ther and husband, and by reticences conventional in Victorian writing. Even so, Gaskell's book so infuriated the schoolmaster

who had been the model for *Jane Eyre*'s Mr. Brocklehurst, and so troubled the family for whom Branwell Brontë had been a tutor, that Mrs. Gaskell made substantial revisions in her second edition. Gaskell's major reticence concerned the extent and last-ing effect of Charlotte's emotional attachment to M. Heger, the teacher with whom she had studied during two years in Brussels. In downplaying this important relationship, Gaskell necessarily had to emphasize the strain Branwell Brontë's debilitation caused his sister in order to account for the intensity of Char-lotte's emotions during the last decade of her life. Thus, al-though a most readable work, and a model life of a novelist by a novelist, Mrs. Gaskell's biography has been superseded in accu-racy by later biographies, but it has never been rendered obso-lete for Brontë readers. Gaskell's Charlotte Brontë and the struggling Jane Eyre often merge, but the immediacy of such descriptions as she gives of Haworth and the Brontë Parsonage, and such vignettes as she presents of the sisters reading and working together are hard even for more objective later biogra-phers to ignore, and thus Gaskell's *Life* becomes a necessary subject in later lives of the Brontës.

No biography of Emily Brontë appeared for more than 30 years after her death. Although ROBINSON's early volume marked the start of renewed interest in Emily and her work, no adequate, separate biography of her appeared until well into the 20th century, as Brontë biography slowly proceeded in two ma-jor directions that can be termed the fictional and the founda-tional. The fictional line would lead to a sensationalizing of episodes and sometimes of the whole Brontë story, and included the 20th century's efforts to provide sequels to or spinoffs from Brontë novels. Library shelves often commingle more reliable biographies and such titles as *The Secret of Charlotte Brontë*, *The Bewitched Parsonage* with *Return to Wuthering Heights* and other popularized accounts. The more foundational materials that became available included the many little volumes of Brontë childhood writing; compilations (though often erroneous) of Charlotte's letters, including the important letters to M. Heger; and, even into the 1980s, contractual documents and a likely photograph of Charlotte.

Biographical commentary concerning Charlotte remains more extensive even as Emily's literary stature has equaled if not eclipsed her sister's, and this is a consequence of the relative abundance of material concerning Charlotte. Very few letters, some school exercises, birthday diary entries, and poetry manu-scripts survive of Emily's unpublished writing. Thus, the life of Charlotte remains the principal resource for information about Emily.

Biographers and critics have often been frustrated and misled by earlier mismanagement, including forgery, of Brontë letters and manuscripts. As WINNIFRITH points out in his 1973 study, we must understand that "biographical certainty about the Brontës is necessarily impossible," and the claim of any biogra-pher to authority must depend upon that writer's forthrightness in acknowledging if not avoiding speculation where information is lacking or misleading.

There have been two efforts to collect Brontë correspon-dence—Clement K. Shorter's *The Brontës: Life and Letters* (2 vols., London and New York, 1908), and T. J. Wise and J. A. Symington's *The Brontës: Their Lives, Friendships and Corre-spondence* (4 vols., Oxford, 1932). More recently Christine Alexander has greatly clarified biographers' understanding of the Brontës' childhood writing in her *The Early Writings of Charlotte Brontë* (Oxford, Blackwell, 1983).

Until recently the most authoritative Brontë biographies have been GÉRIN's separate lives of Charlotte, Emily, Anne, and Branwell, with the Charlotte Brontë volume remaining the keystone work. Over the past quarter of a century many more interpretive biographies surround the Gérin works, and the pages of the *Brontë Society Transactions* continue to contribute biographical information. The late 1980s brought FRASER's *Charlotte Brontë*, in which Fraser views Charlotte as a "phenomenon," both in the ordinariness of much of her domestic existence and in the extraordinariness of her achievements. Attempting a balanced view of her subject and mindful of the unevenness of earlier biographies, Fraser nonetheless makes occasional claims that beg substantiation. If, for example, Charlotte was in 1847 "the most celebrated author in England," how did that celebrity differ from the celebrity of such writers as Scott and Thackeray, to whom Charlotte so frequently referred? Reviewers have pointed to Fraser's numerous small errors in fact or documentation, and hers must remain a more popular than authoritative biography. In 1990 the best biographies remain Gérin's, supplemented and occasionally qualified by Winnifrith's two books and Edward Chitham's *A Life of Emily Brontë*.

WINNIFRITH's 1988 biography of Charlotte is concise and avoids speculation. Winnifrith, augmenting Gérin, centers on those parts of Charlotte's life that bear most on her literary career. Winnifrith downplays such staples of Brontë biography as the eccentricity of Charlotte's father, and presents him as both the typical Victorian *paterfamilias* and as an exceptional survivor of many misfortunes. This biography attends to topical issues—Charlotte Brontë as "pupil," "writer," "teacher," "wife"—and in chapters on each of her major novels examines the relationship of the life to the fiction. General readers may find that this biography demands too much familiarity with Brontë works and with earlier biographies, but Brontë scholars must turn to Winnifrith for the best informed current biographical perspective.

CHITHAM's more expansive biography of Emily sets for itself many of the tasks that distinguish Winnifrith's life of Charlotte—self-awareness of the biographer's responsibilities, especially toward earlier biographies; the hazards of even the most seemingly autobiographical writings by the subject; the attractiveness to readers and biographers of speculation about Emily's powers of vision, religious beliefs, and passions. Chitham's introduction explains how we can come to understand anything at all about Emily Brontë and states his intention of tracking and evaluating every piece of information, terming his an "investigative" biography. (With Winnifrith, Chitham had earlier covered much of this ground in *Brontë Facts and Brontë Problems* [London, Macmillan, 1983]. Much of Chitham's biographical investigation concerns the chronology of Emily's life and the places she knew. While he looks very closely at her poetry as a major source for understanding the growth of her mind and understanding, he is cautious about using the poetry to suggest the life history, insisting instead on the insights it provides into her emotional life. Some readers may find him practicing the speculation about the writing that he finds indefensible in biography, but Chitham generally specifies the terms of his speculation, scrupulously separating fact from opinion. In the midst

of several chapters about *Wuthering Heights* he reminds readers that no biographer can explain that book, but he shows us ways in which it is "consistent with Emily's life as we know it and in particular with her inner life, as that emerges before us in her rare oracular statements, and especially in her poetry."

Brontë biography and Brontë fiction may as much mutually puzzle as mutually inform, and the most reliable biographies keep readers aware of this difficulty even as they assess and reassess the available facts and interpret or investigate Brontë writing.

—Richard J. Dunn

BROWN, Charles Brockden, 1771–1810; American writer.

Allen, Paul, *The Life of Charles Brockden Brown*. Delmar, New York, Scholars' Facsimiles and Reprints, 1975 (erroneously attributed to William Dunlap and published by J. P. Parke, Philadelphia, 1815).

Axelrod, Alan, *Charles Brockden Brown, an American Tale*. Austin, University of Texas Press, 1983.

Clark, David Lee, *Charles Brockden Brown: Pioneer Voice of America*. Durham, North Carolina, Duke University Press, 1952.

Grabo, Norman S., *The Coincidental Art of Charles Brockden Brown*. Chapel Hill, University of North Carolina Press, 1981.

Ringe, Donald A., *Charles Brockden Brown*. New York, Twayne, 1966.

Rosenthal, Bernard, editor, *Critical Essays on Charles Brockden Brown*. Boston, G. K. Hall, 1981.

Vilas, Martin S., *Charles Brockden Brown: A Study of Early American Fiction*. Burlington, Vermont, Free Press Association, 1904.

Warfel, Harry R., *Charles Brockden Brown: American Gothic Novelist*. Gainesville, University of Florida Press, 1949.

Wiley, Lulu Rumsey, *The Sources and Influence of the Novels of Charles Brockden Brown*. New York, Vantage Press, 1950.

*

The story behind ALLEN's biography of Brown is as important as the book itself. Charles E. Bennett relates in the "Introduction" to the Allen reprint that when Brown died, his wife and family needed money to make ends meet. Elizabeth Brown decided that two books, the fragments entitled "System of General Geography" and the "Life" of Brown, might earn the much needed income. Allen, a journalist from Philadelphia, was selected to complete both fragments. Allen did not meet contractual deadlines, and the "General Geography" was never published. Allen had written a volume of Brown's biography, but it was a hurried, overly critical, incomplete, and unsatisfactory effort. The Browns decided to replace Allen with William Dunlap, with the stipulation that Dunlap revise as little of the already typeset Allen as possible. When finished with his revisions, Dunlap was given credit for the biography.

Both the advantages and disadvantages of Allen arise from his close proximity to his subject. Allen had access to firsthand information about Brown, and his views of Brown's world are those of an on-the-spot observer. Allen did not have to rely solely upon secondary sources to construct Brown's social and political environment; Allen himself was very much part of that environment. In addition, as Bennett suggests in his Introduction, Allen attempted an honest, critical appraisal of Brown, and this, in part, is what alienated Allen from Brown's family: they expected a tribute. Contemporary readers may find Allen's writing style, with its archaic language, difficult to read. Also, Allen's use of Brown's own writings (various letters and prose extracts) is very extensive and at times burdensome. Nevertheless, any serious examination of Brown should begin with Allen.

WARFEL is a more contemporary academic study of Brown. It follows Brown's life chronologically from his Quaker background, early childhood years and career as a law student, through his introduction to literature, his role as one of America's first professional novelists, and finally ending with Brown's work as editor and political writer. Warfel's style is a bit heavy-handed, making this somewhat difficult reading. Warfel is also dated, his efforts lacking the information provided by the benefits of contemporary scholarship. Yet Warfel gives the reader not only a detailed look at Brown's life, but an evenhanded and fairly objective analysis of Brown's work as well.

CLARK's study is also academic in tone. It divides Brown's life into eight major areas, including his childhood years and early apprenticeship in literature, his career as a journalist, his successes and failures as a novelist, his attempts at literary criticism and his efforts as historian and political pamphleteer. A noteworthy feature of Clark's book is his chapter based on the correspondence between a young Brown and a woman known only as Henrietta G. (who was three years his senior). These letters reveal a great deal about Brown's personal philosophy of life. Clark's treatment of Brown is fair, and at times insightful, but his use of language is awkward and jargonistic, making this study, like Warfel's, fairly difficult to read. Clark's academic mindset, again like Warfel's, is firmly rooted in the early 1950s, so that some of his comments may seem dated to the contemporary scholar. All in all, though, Clark provides a solid examination of the many facets of Brown's personal and public career in letters.

AXELROD offers the most recent evaluation of Brown, and one of the best to date. Axelrod blends the facts of Brown's life with a superior analysis of his era. He effectively traces and relates the influences on Brown's work and life within a well diagnosed frame of Brown's American cultural worldview. Axelrod's emphasis is not so much on the facts of Brown's life (though Axelrod is substantially documented) as on Brown's place in the larger social and literary American culture. Axelrod's perceptions of Brown and his America are as astute as they are comprehensive.

RINGE has chapters on both Brown's life (with a summary of critical appraisals of his place in American letters) and his novels, *Wieland, Ormond, Arthur Mervyn* and *Edgar Huntly*, as well as on his lesser novels and his final literary efforts. WILEY also provides a chapter on Brown's life, but concentrates more on the specific influences on his literary career, his novels, his writing methods, and on the influence that Brown exerted on others. GRABO, primarily a literary study focusing on the use

and function of coincidence in Brown's writings, provides historical background to Brown's fiction. ROSENTHAL is a collection of critical essays on Brown, though the Introduction to the collection provides historical and biographic information about Brown. Of particular interest is the anonymous review, originally published in 1819, of Dunlap's *The Life of Charles Brockden Brown* (the biography first begun by Allen). VILAS is an early literary study of Brown, and it offers a brief look at Brown's life, as well as outlines and critical material on the author's major literary efforts. Finally, the book-length bibliography prepared by Patricia Parker, *Charles Brockden Brown: A Reference Guide* (Boston, G. K. Hall, 1980), provides the most complete listing of works both by and about Brown.

—Gary Hoppenstand

BROWN, John, 1800–1859; American abolitionist.

Abels, Jules, *Man on Fire: John Brown and the Cause of Liberty.* New York, Macmillan, 1971.

Boyer, Richard O., *The Legend of John Brown: A Biography and a History.* New York, Knopf, 1973.

Du Bois, W. E. B., *John Brown.* Philadelphia, G. W. Jacobs, 1909.

Furnas, J. C., *The Road to Harper's Ferry.* New York, Sloane, 1959; with subtitle, *Facts and Follies of the War on Slavery,* London, Faber, 1961.

Malin, James C., *John Brown and the Legend of Fifty-Six.* Philadelphia, American Philosophical Society, 1942.

Oates, Stephen B., *To Purge this Land with Blood.* New York, Harper, 1970.

Redpath, James, *The Public Life of Captain John Brown.* Boston, Thayer and Eldridge, 1860.

Sanborn, Franklin B., *Life and Letters of John Brown.* Boston, Roberts, and London, Low Marston, 1885.

Stavis, Barrie, *John Brown: The Sword and the Word.* New York, A. S. Barnes, 1970.

Villard, Oswald Garrison, *John Brown 1800-59: A Biography 50 Years After.* Boston, Houghton Mifflin, 1910.

Warren, Robert Penn, *John Brown: The Making of a Martyr.* New York, Payson and Clarke, 1929.

Webb, Richard D., *The Life and Letters of Captain John Brown.* London, Smith Elder, 1861.

Wilson, Hill Peebles, *John Brown: Soldier of Fortune.* Lawrence, Kansas, H. P. Wilson, 1913.

*

Brown's body had hardly begun to moulder in the grave before REDPATH's salute appeared. Holding strong abolitionist sentiments, which were shared by a growing body of public opinion, Redpath mixes biographical data (drawn from diaries and letters that would be employed by later biographers) with romantic eulogy. Important as a period piece, the book is essentially a work of hagiography, notwithstanding its usefulness; WEBB also falls into this category.

SANBORN was the first of the major biographers of Brown. His workmanlike, if worshipful, product benefits from continuing contact with Brown well before and his family long after the Civil War. He employs previously unavailable evidence, reports, correspondence, discussions, and recollections. As one of the nation's foremost abolitionists and one of Brown's closest collaborators—a member of the "Secret Six"—Sanborn could offer both abundant documentation and unique insight. He assesses the famous "Pottawatomie massacre" at length, concluding that it constituted "the opening scenes of a war": Brown's violence, Sanborn claims, was an inevitable development, dwarfed however by the greater evil of slavery and the violence its abolition required. Consequently, he denies Brown's "insanity." Sanborn's remained the best work in the field until the early 20th century.

Drawing heavily on the data collected by Sanborn, DU BOIS presents a striking biography on the occasion of the 50th anniversary of the Harper's Ferry Raid. Considered by the author (known even then as one of the nation's outstanding scholars) as "one of the best written" of his books, it stresses the relationship between Brown and the African-American people: their interactions developed on a basis of mutual respect and shared abhorrence of slavery and white supremacy. Brown is placed in an evolving context over time—a perspective many of his biographers lack—joining with Blacks in a militant commitment to abolition and progressing to increasingly direct confrontation with slaveholders, a development which helped shape national viewpoints. Premising his biography upon the criminality of slavery and the invalidity of white supremacy (by no means a consensus view among Brown's biographers), Du Bois considers Brown a model for those who would challenge injustice no matter the sacrifice, a point well amplified in the final chapter.

VILLARD's weighty opus became the standard in the field upon its publication. A pioneer, with Du Bois, of the NAACP, Villard had in fact published a not altogether objective review of Du Bois' book in *The Nation*, without printing Du Bois' reply (the two were occasionally at odds during that period). Villard was the grandson of William Lloyd Garrison, outstanding abolitionist and reformer. His work is the most exhaustively detailed of all, covering every facet of Brown's life: family, religious life, business, philosophy, activities, trial, execution. Villard, assisted by Katherine Mayo, energetic collector of material, including interviews with Brown's surviving kin (the accuracy of whose recollections is questioned in Robert E. McGlone, "Rescripting a Troubled Past: John Brown's Family and the Harper's Ferry Conspiracy," *Journal of American History*, March, 1989). Villard differs with Sanborn's approach to the Pottawatomie incident. Though sympathetic to Brown, Villard is critical of what he considers his subject's irresponsible actions in Kansas. He also occasionally questions the practicality of Brown's plans to free the slaves. Still, one can find no biographer who worked more painstakingly to assess the meaning of Brown's life: the volume is indispensable to an understanding of Brown.

Over a period of 30 years, there appeared a number of direct attacks on the character of Brown and on the veracity of his sympathetic biographers. Wilson, Warren, and, finally, Malin, were generally hostile to any notion of Brown's heroism. WILSON finds in Brown a character devoid of positive features. Though WARREN's more substantial and better-written effort makes a move toward a balanced assessment, quoting Villard here and Wilson there, his Brown is a pretentious and egotistical seeker of headlines, with a bloodthirsty streak. Writing with wit and sarcasm, Warren does not take Brown's abolitionist and religious convictions seriously. Plainly, the "Old Man" portrayed here is cruel, intolerant, and vain. Warren makes inconsiderable reference to slavery or to the evolution of a more militant abolitionist trend in the nation, thus supplying little context.

MALIN was the most scholarly of the negative biographers. His book dwells on Brown's Kansas experiences: the Pottawatamie incident becomes the focus. For its abundant data the book retains value, though it is weakened by key inaccuracies and misrepresentations. A significant portion of the work is given over to a sharp critique of the sympathetic biographers, which is of certain use in assessing Malin's own approach and method. That Brown had anything to do with slavery, or that slavery was in any way bound up with the crisis enveloping the United States, goes virtually unmentioned. Interestingly, Malin's use of the lower case "n" in "Negro" was no longer a universal practice at the time he wrote. Malin devotes the bulk of his 750 pages to expose the "hoax" or "legend" of Brown's greatness. John Brown emerges here as little more than a wayfarer with extreme ideas, whose reputation has been glorified and exaggerated. The book stands as the most significant and challenging of the anti-Brown works.

FURNAS—an anti-Brown biographer of lesser stature—defines in sardonic tones the actions of Brown and his supporters as the result of a childish, romantic adventurousness derived from having taken tales of gallant knights literally and too seriously. Furnas claims they imbibed and internal- ized these stories and fantasized about them through adulthood, clearly an expression of deviant behavior. As for the context and dynamics of the slavery question, Furnas presents little of either, choosing instead a psychological basis for evaluating Brown's life.

OATES' sympathetic volume is perhaps the most accessible biography of Brown. Utilizing an unprecedented range of sources, it is compellingly presented (as are the author's works on Lincoln, Nat Turner, and M. L. King, Jr). Oates makes a strong case for Brown's lifelong anti-racism, citing his support for Black education, his role in the Underground Railroad, his relationships with Frederick Douglass, Harriet Tubman, Martin Delany, and Henry Highland Garnet. Brown and his men, writes Oates, "regarded the black man as a human being who had a right to be free and were prepared to spill Southern blood to break his chains if that's what it took." That Brown's anticipation of a slave uprising in response to his Raid was mistaken, Oates does not deny. He finds Brown somewhat arrogant, often excitable, occasionally cruel, though he does not make light of the Pottawatomie affair, observing that it came in retaliation for murders by pro-slavery men. Oates takes issue with the "insanity" thesis, noting the contemporary vagueness of "insanity" and the desperation of the kinsmen who testified to Brown's madness to save the "Old Man" from execution. Indeed, it is the prevalent racist attitudes among contemporary whites—from which Brown deviated—that the author finds unhealthy: "It was not Brown's angry, messianic mind, but the racist, slave society in which he lived—one that professed 'under God' to provide liberty and justice for all—that helped bring John Brown to Harper's Ferry." Oates' blending of subject and context makes this one of the leading books in the field.

STAVIS can be placed squarely in the sympathetic camp: his concise, sensitive work reads easily. ABELS apparently takes no side. He finds that Brown's achievements—he shook "the national will"—out-weighed his "warts." The narrative is smooth and readable. The reader is not spared the details of the Pottawatomie massacre, and is frequently invited to compare Brown with Oliver Cromwell. Though Abels' description of those around Brown (the "Secret Six" and others) shows that a movement (whose mass character is not fully conveyed in the book) of likeminded people operated during the 1850s, his analysis questions the sincerity of its adherents. He avers that Brown's supporters were guilty liberals of a sort, who used John Brown. Likewise does Abels portray abolitionists (and Black abolitionists as a whole are not assessed) as self-serving, without sincere anti-slavery commitment: "Abolitionism *needed* martyrs." Still, the author generally dissents from the view that his subject was insane.

But for BOYER's untimely death, his work would have been the first of a two-volume set, the second volume to have dealt exclusively with the Raid. As it is, his study is the most meticulous examination of Brown's pre-1859 life available. Boyer establishes a broad context in which many Americans began to conclude, with Brown, "that the crimes of this *guilty land* will never be purged *away*, but with Blood." Boyer maintains that Brown reflected broader developments and thought processes, and he does not question Brown's sanity. The author consults a particularly wide range of source materials. His asides on Theodore Parker, Henry Ward Beecher, Frederick Douglass, and others are well-connected to the main subject, buttressing the thesis that militant abolitionism was an articulate and growing current, of which Brown was an exponent. Boyer appends a lengthy description of the manuscript collections containing Brown materials, of use to researchers in the field.

—Daniel Rosenberg

BROWNING, Elizabeth Barrett, 1806–1861; English poet.

Boas, Louise Schutz, *Elizabeth Barrett Browning*. Oxford, Clarendon Press, 1929; New York, Longman, 1930.

Forster, Margaret, *Elizabeth Barrett Browning: A Biography*. London, Chatto and Windus, 1988; New York, Doubleday, 1989.

Hewlett, Dorothy, *Elizabeth Barrett Browning: A Life*. New York, Knopf, 1952; London, Cassell, 1953.

Ingram, John H., *Elizabeth Barrett Browning*. Boston, Roberts, and London, W. H. Allen, 1888.

Mander, Rosalie, *Mrs. Browning: The Story of Elizabeth Barrett*. London, Weidenfeld and Nicolson, 1980.

Taplin, Gardner B., *The Life of Elizabeth Barrett Browning*. London, J. Murray, and New Haven, Connecticut, Yale University Press, 1957.

Whiting, Lilian, *The Brownings: Their Life and Art*. Boston, Little Brown, and London, Hodder and Stoughton, 1911.

*

INGRAM's book, written for the Famous Women series, was the first full-length biography of Elizabeth Barrett Browning (henceforth EBB, the form she used to sign most of her letters). Ingram acted more as compiler than author, assembling the comments of EBB's friends and contemporaries. For this feature it is useful to the researcher, despite its occasional factual inaccuracies. The book also illustrates the high reputation EBB's poetry enjoyed at the end of the 19th century. Ingram, unlike many of EBB's later biographers, discusses her poetry, and he does so in the most glowing terms: "Her poetic inspiration was of the highest," he writes, and he speaks of her "magnificent aspirations, . . . glowing thoughts, . . . brilliant scintillations of genius, . . .innumerable gem-like passages of pathos, . . . passionate rushes of language, and . . . daring assaults upon time-honored customs."

More reliable, though equally gossipy, is WHITING's account. A friend of EBB's son, Robert Wiedeman ("Pen") Browning, Whiting learned from him about the Brownings' domestic life, though Pen was only 12 when his mother died. Whiting also had access to previously unpublished letters in painting her well-illustrated portrait of the two poets and their age.

For many readers and biographers, the most fascinating aspect of EBB's life is her romance with Robert. Frances Winner (Francesca Vinciguena) called her joint biography *The Immortal Lovers: Elizabeth Barrett and Robert Browning* (1950), thus showing where her interest lay, and one thinks as well of the fictional depiction in Rudolf Besier's *The Barretts of Wimpole Street* (1930). BOAS, too, focuses on Robert's pursuit of Elizabeth; one-third of the book's 216 pages is devoted to the year and a half of courtship. Primarily a love story, Boas' study does provide entertaining and informative material on EBB's friends such as Richard Hengist Horne and Mary Russell Mitford, so the reader recognizes that EBB did have a life of her own before Robert fell in love with her.

For the general reader the best place to begin is HEWLETT. As late as 1980 the *Times Literary Supplement* praised the book for its "sensitive and thorough understanding of Mrs. Browning's genius and personality" (5 September 1980). Like Boas, Hewlett dwells on the romance, devoting 60 pages to Robert's wooing. Though not averse to sentimentalizing, Hewlett doesn't shrink from discussing the difficulties in the marriage. She points out the four miscarriages that EBB suffered and notes that EBB and Robert had problems adjusting to each other after they moved to Italy in 1846.

Drawing heavily on the letters then available, Hewlett allows the reader to hear her subject's voice; hence, as William C. De Vane observed in his review, "the reader gets the impression of knowing the poet intimately and closely" (*Saturday Review of Literature*, 18 October 1952). Hewlett also spoke to descendants of the Brownings and Barretts and used unpublished material in private as well as public collections. The work provides little psychological or literary analysis but maintains that the drowning of Edward Barrett, Elizabeth's favorite brother, in 1840 provides a key to understanding EBB's behavior. More than earlier biographers, Hewlett discusses EBB's early life—a third of the book covers the period before 1845—and Hewlett was an early champion of EBB's father, usually presented as a domestic tyrant. She also sought to rehabilitate the reputation of EBB's poetry, claiming, without much evidence, that the Victorians were right to assess it better than Robert's.

To EBB's biographers, only slightly less fascinating than her romance is her dog, Flush (about whom Virginia Woolf wrote a book-length account). Hewlett includes a previously unpublished letter on the death of Flush and a water-color by EBB's brother Alfred of EBB and her dog. Other, more useful inclusions are an early draft of sonnet 16 and an anecdote about EBB by the Florentine G. G. Giannini.

More scholarly, and, unhappily, more dull, is TAPLIN's work, hailed at its appearance as the definitive biography. Taplin, who read all the letters and visited every place in England and Italy associated with the Brownings, provides a wealth of detail about the life and the composition of the poems. He adds information about EBB's early life at Hope End, and though he paints EBB's father in traditionally dark tones, he acknowledges that the man fascinated his family. Taplin also observes that financial concerns played a role in his opposition to EBB's marriage, for she had a private income useful in maintaining the large Barrett family.

Taplin is not impressed with EBB's poetry, reflecting the contemporary attitude. In "A Century of Criticism" he shows how opinion changed from the time that John Ruskin linked EBB's name with Shakespeare to the far lower estimation of her work 100 years later. This chapter also shows that even during her lifetime not everyone shared Ruskin's enthusiasm. Taplin summarizes the themes of the major poems and provides a valuable bibliography.

Five years after Taplin's book appeared, Philip Kelley began turning up a treasury of EBB manuscripts. Thus, Taplin's book, still a good place for the scholar to start, is now authoritative rather than definitive. MANDER's book is neither, running through the life in 162 pages, ten of these a summary of *Aurora Leigh*. The *Times Literary Supplement*'s assessment of "cursory" (5 September 1980) accurately characterizes the work, though it does include good illustrations, a chronology of the Brownings' travels, and EBB's "A Night Watch by the Sea," a poem about a drowning that was published in April 1840, three months before Edward Barrett's death, and never reprinted in EBB's lifetime. Mander's lack of citations and occasional inaccuracies will not trouble the casual reader seeking a short, unanalytical account of the life, but the scholar will find little here.

Far better, though still not definitive, is FORSTER, who draws on the manuscripts discovered since Taplin's biography appeared. Much of this new material relates to EBB's early life, such as the diaries for 1831–32, and Forster devotes half her book to the pre-Robert years, thereby presenting a more balanced account than her predecessors. The EBB who emerges from this work is complex but not especially likeable. One sees a woman who was selfless toward Robert but also selfish about sharing his time with others. One sees how EBB preached republicanism but practiced domestic tyranny over her servants. Forster seeks to dispel various long-held beliefs about EBB, such as her supposed tuberculosis and her rumored fall from a horse. EBB's illnesses appear to have been largely psychosomatic; they were also useful for securing attention and leisure. According to Forster, EBB was as much responsible as her father for her "imprisonment" in Wimpole Street. Forster also notes the various disagreements between EBB and Robert. Though she concludes that the marriage was happy, she does not gloss over the couple's conflicts concerning spiritualism, politics, and the rearing of their son. The volume is well-illustrated with 35 pictures and includes a helpful list of EBB's published writings—letters, diaries, and poetry. For a work seeking to heighten interest in EBB as a writer, and considering that Forster edited the *Selected Poems of Elizabeth Barrett Browning* (1988), the book is strangely silent about this subject. Many readers may also object to the wealth of detail, which includes much about Flush's various abductions and ransomings, even what the Brownings ate for breakfast in Florence.

Forster called her study "A Biography"; in a sense *the* biography is yet to be written that will analyze EBB's poetry and prose and attempt to understand this very human woman. In another sense, EBB left her own biography in her letters and diaries. Anyone seeking a full portrait must first or last turn to these, where the real EBB lives.

—Joseph Rosenblum

BROWNING, Robert, 1812–1889; English poet.

Griffin, William H. and Harry C. Minchin, *The Life of Robert Browning, with Notices of His Writing, His Family and His Friends.* New York, Macmillan, and London, Methuen, 1910; revised and enlarged, London, Methuen, 1938.

Irvine, William and Park Honan, *The Book, the Ring, and the Poet: A Biography of Robert Browning.* New York, McGraw-Hill, 1974; London, Bodley Head, 1975.

Miller, Betty Bergson, *Robert Browning: A Portrait.* London, J. Murray, 1952; New York, Scribner, 1953.

Orr, Alexandra ("Mrs Sutherland Orr"), *Life and Letters of Robert Browning* (2 vols.). London, Smith Elder, and Boston, Houghton Mifflin, 1891.

Ward, Maisie, *Robert Browning and His World* (2 vols.). New York, Holt, 1967–69; London, Cassell, 1968–69.

*

ORR's two-volume work is the nearest we have to an "official" biography. Mrs. Orr knew Browning well during the last part of his life and had access to many important letters (from which she quotes extensively) from Browning's circle of friends. Since she did not know Browning in his youth, much of her information about his early years was provided by family members. The main weakness of Mrs. Orr's life is her treatment of Browning's courtship. She did not have at her disposal the letters exchanged between Robert and Elizabeth, which supply a detailed history of that famous love affair, and thus her chronology of the events of that important period is sometimes in error. Although no actual thesis is developed, Orr voices certain strong opinions regarding Browning's religious views and his attitude toward his wife's interest in spiritualism. Her sympathy is clearly with Browning in his suspicion of mediums, and she commends him for his sure and steady, if unorthodox, Christian faith. Her biography is more a "loving remembrance," as she says, than a full scale life study. Ironically, Pen and Sarianna Browning disliked Orr's book, especially her analysis of Browning's declining poetic powers in old age.

GRIFFIN AND MINCHIN's collaboration, though written nearly a century ago, is still regarded as the "standard life" of Browning. The material for this biography was amassed in notes by Professor Griffin, a friend of Browning's son and sister, from whom came much of the information about Browning's early history. He also drew upon the recollections of many of the poet's surviving friends. Upon the death of Griffin the project was completed by Professor Minchin, whose intention was "to be more complete and exact" than previous biographers, such as Mrs. Orr, who did not have access to many important letters and diaries. Though they do not attempt a systematic interpretation of the facts of Browning's life and work and provide no detailed criticism of the poetry, Griffin and Minchin include a great deal about the origins, sources, and reception of the verse.

The main weakness of this study lies in its treatment of Browning's later years; here the biography is extremely bland and typically Victorian in its reticence, omitting mention of Browning's relationships with Julia Wedgwood and Isabella Blagden. In the revised edition of 1938, some enlargements on the record were made based on updated research, such as the study of Browning's debt to Shelley by F. A. Pottle (Chicago, 1923) and William Clyde De Vane's indispensable study, *A Browning Handbook* (New York, 1935). Also incorporated were fresh biographical materials drawn from *The Last Days, Letters, and Conversations of Walter Savage Landor* (1934) and *The Letters of Owen Meredith to R. and R. B. Browning* (1936). Certain facts and inferences are drawn from *Correspondence of Robert Browning With Isa Blagden* (1923), but scant use is made of this source and the friendship with Julia Wedgwood is still unmentioned. The result is a biography that is both judicious and restrained: more a "sympathetic review and interpretation of the accepted facts," as Minchin claimed in the preface, than an attempt to see the life of Browning "through a temperament."

MILLER investigates Browning's life in light of Freudian theory. Although she draws on no new sources of letters or journals, she drafts a new portrait of Browning from an examination of his relationships with his mother and later his wife. Miller points out that Browning was so close to his mother that he even suffered sympathetic illnesses; shared pains and headaches were common. She also states that Browning was always attracted to women who were older than he was (Elizabeth Barrett was six years his senior). In their marriage Elizabeth became the maternal figure who directed and controlled not only Browning but their child as well, never giving him a chance to perform as a father in any real sense. Browning also acquiesced in the matter of Elizabeth's spiritualism, though he believed it to be totally bogus. Browning's relationships with other women—Isa Blagden, Julia Wedgwood, Lady Ashburton, and Miss Egerton Smith—all show the same psychological need for female companions whom he felt were wiser, morally superior, and more commanding than himself. As the subtitle of this study indicates, the book is a "portrait" rather than a full-length biography. Miller's technique of highlighting some episodes in Browning's life and discounting others assumes a reader who is already familiar with the basic details of Browning's life. Furthermore, she neglects aspects of the poet's life and work that do not fit her thesis; thus the book must be used with some caution. However, it remains as one of the first and best interpretive accounts of Browning to date.

WARD's two volumes provide a more sustained reading of Browning's life than previous modern biographers had achieved. She treats Browning as a man of anomalous character who had almost a dual personality. Picking up on a trait Henry James noticed about Browning in his novelette entitled *The Private Life* (1893), Ward asserts that Browning was two people—a bourgeois social climber and at the same time a complex poet of genius. In her second volume Ward tries to reconcile the simple public image Browning projected with the hidden intellectual character he reveals as a writer. As her subtitle indicates, Ward's concern is with Browning's "world" as well as his personality. She puts a great deal of emphasis on the poet's association with his contemporaries—Henry James, Carlyle, Tennyson, Mill, Thackeray, Hawthorne and others. Perhaps the most controversial note struck in this biography is Ward's thesis that Browning was a Catholic *manqué* for whom the church of Rome had a powerful attraction. She takes particular pains to "deconstruct" some of the current biographical misconceptions that surround Browning such as the notion that the senior Browning was a passive man, that the poet avoided relationships with people of his own age group as a young man, and that Browning did not manage the practical or parental affairs, leaving both tasks to Elizabeth. In short, Ward rejects Miller's conception of a neurotic Browning whose personality was twisted by a mother-fixation. Thus, Ward offers not so much a new picture as a return to the older image of Browning the Christian poet-prophet, perhaps because her study draws so heavily on bibliographic sources prior to World War I.

IRVINE AND HONAN use the techniques of modern biographical scholarship in an attempt to produce the "definitive" life of Browning. They give a meticulous, detailed account, superseding the earlier biographies whose mythifying prevented us from seeing the human side of Browning. The authors give a good deal of attention to examining the poetry, which is put against the events of Browning's life to help document and explain the story. Picking up on Miller's psychological arguments, Irvine takes Browning's life-long obsession with white gloves, which he never went outdoors without, as indicative of his need "to conceal the unresolved conflicts of his own personality from the world's eye." Thus, in his poems Browning adopted the point of view of characters unlike himself as a camouflage. The authors maintain that Browning's natural reticence and the Victorian tendency toward autobiographical discretion make him a figure who blocks all efforts at analysis of his innermost self. Although he had a wide circle of friends, none was intimate, and therefore little is revealed even in his private correspondence (much of which, deemed inappropriate for publication, was burned after his death). Irvine and Honan present what is known in a clearly written, well-documented narrative that presents the data in a detached, objective manner. They indulge in neither adulation nor admonishment and offer little speculation about those areas of Browning's life where the facts are inaccessible. The authors provide the fullest account to date, however, of his relationship with his mother, his marriage, his development as a poet (including Shelley's influence on him), his contributions to impressionism, and the techniques of the dramatic monologue.

—Hallman B. Bryant

BROZ, Josip. See **TITO, Marshal.**

———————

BRUCKNER, Anton, 1824–1896; Austrian composer.

Doernberg, Erwin, *The Life and Symphonies of Anton Bruckner.*
London, Barrie and Rockliff, 1960; New York, Dover, 1968.
Engel, Gabriel, *The Life of Anton Bruckner.* New York, Roerich
Museum, 1931.
Redlich, Hans F., *Bruckner and Mahler.* London, Dent, and
New York, Farrar Straus, 1955.
Schönzeler, Hans-Hubert, *Bruckner.* New York, Grossman, and
London, Calder and Boyers, 1970.
Watson, Derek, *Bruckner.* London, Dent, 1975.
Wolff, Werner, *Anton Bruckner, Rustic Genius.* New York, Dutton, 1942.

*

There is little room for disagreement among Bruckner's biographers about the principal chronological facts of his life. We know when and where he was born, when and where he died, when he moved from place to place, and when and where he composed his major works. Apart from matters of length and style, when his biographers differ, it is in their treatment of issues arising from his enigmatic personality. His inveterate revising, his students' tampering with his scores, his relationships with Brahms, Hanslick, and Wagner, his religiosity, his propensity for courting younger women, his preoccupation with death, his countrified mannerisms, etc., have all provided plenty of grist for the biographer's mill.

Because access to Bruckner's primary sources has been limited for most of this century, English-language biographies have relied very much on their Austro/German counterparts. The two most important of these are August Göllerich's and Max Auer's mammoth, if somewhat rambling, *Anton Bruckner: ein Lebens und Schaffensbild* (Regensburg, 1922–37) and Max Auer's, *Anton Bruckner: sein Leben und Werk* (6th edition Vienna, 1966). Both are in sorry need of revision. Because the English-language biographies are far more cursory and very much concerned with introducing Bruckner and his music to what has been, in large part, a skeptical public, Auer's and Göllerich's inaccuracies in detail seldom find their way into the English works, Their assumptions on larger issues sometimes do. For example, most English biographers accept Göllerich's and Auer's incorrect speculation that the *Nullte* Symphony was composed in 1863–64 rather than 1869.

With the exception of the Engel and Schönzeler volumes, the English-language biographies are of the "Life and Works" type. The following remarks are confined to the biographical portions of these studies. No attention has been given the analyses that are sometimes suspect.

Credit for the first, albeit short, book-length English-language Bruckner biography goes to ENGEL, who acknowledges Auer at the outset. The work remains useful as an illustration of the fervor with which the early "Brucknerites" approached their subject. Some acerbic remarks about the music of Engel's own time

and some sweeping aesthetic judgements are difficult to justify, but such comments are confined for the most part to the final chapter.

Along the same lines, although far broader in scope, is the work of lifelong Bruckner campaigner WOLFF. This book suffers from occasional lapses in syntax because the author is writing in a second language. It also contains numerous personal interpolations that can be distracting. Wolff is too kind to the composer's students—the Schalk brothers and Ferdinand Löwe—on the issue of tampering with Bruckner's scores. Nevertheless it is a labor of love from an ardent and knowledgeable Bruckner admirer. It also contains some useful information on socio-economic conditions in 19th century Austria.

The chronological portion of REDLICH's *Bruckner and Mahler* is also brief (25 pages). The remainder of the Bruckner section of the work is devoted to character studies, musical analyses, and an excellent discussion of the "original versions" question. This is a more scholarly and detached, though no less sympathetic view of the composer. Readers searching only for biographical facts will be frustrated by the amount of psychoanalytic musing in which the author indulges.

DOERNBERG's book is intended, by the author's admission, "for all the wide circle of music lovers." It has been criticized correctly for placing too much emphasis on the symphonies and downplaying the significance of the composer's sacred music. It contains translations of numerous excerpts from Bruckner's correspondence as well as from the memoirs of his pupils, Friederich Eckstein and Friederich Klose. This is the only access in English to these materials. Doernberg also provides an interesting essay on the dissemination of Bruckner's music in this century—itself a fascinating subject.

The 1970s saw the production of two English-language biographies—by WATSON and SCHÖNZELER. Again the chronological portion of Watson's book is brief. It provides some valuable information on the material Bruckner studied in his early years. Schönzeler, on the other hand, offers a brief but insightful essay on the music and devotes the remainder of the volume to the most extensive English-language biography of the composer. It is richly illustrated with photographs and facsimiles and concludes with an annotated bibliography and discography. It is a good place to start for biographical information in English on Anton Bruckner.

—Paul Hawkshaw

———————

BRYAN, William Jennings, 1860–1925; American lawyer and politician.

Anderson, David D., *William Jennings Bryan.* Boston, Twayne,
1981.
Ashby, LeRoy, *William Jennings Bryan: Champion of Democracy.* Boston, Twayne, 1987.
Cherny, Robert, *A Righteous Cause: The Life of William Jennings Bryan.* Boston, Little Brown, 1985.
Coletta, Paolo E., *William Jennings Bryan* (3 vols.). Lincoln,
University of Nebraska Press, 1964–69.

Herrick, Genevieve F. and John O. Herrick, *The Life of William Jennings Bryan*. Chicago, J. R. Stanton, 1925.

Hibben, Paxton, *The Peerless Leader: William Jennings Bryan*, completed by C. Hartley Grattan. New York, Farrar and Rinehart, 1929.

Koenig, Louis W., *Bryan: A Political Biography of William Jennings Bryan*. New York, Putnam, 1971.

Long, John C., *Bryan: The Great Commoner*. New York, Appleton, 1928.

Newbranch, Harvey E., *William Jennings Bryan: A Concise but Complete Story of His Life and Services*. Lincoln, Nebraska, University Publishing Company, 1900.

Werner, Morris R., *Bryan*. New York, Harcourt, and London, Cape, 1929.

Williams, Wayne C., *William Jennings Bryan: A Study in Political Vindication*. New York and Chicago, F. H. Revell, 1923.

Williams, Wayne C., *William Jennings Bryan*. New York, Putnam, 1936.

*

A vast quantity of information documents the life of William Jennings Bryan. We have his own perspective in the rich record his letters, speeches, memoirs, and accounts of his travels provide. A whole host of biographies exist, many of which look to only one part of his life, centering on, for example, his presidential elections or the Scopes trial or his interest in questions of foreign policy and imperialism. There are also a number of biographies written before the entire story could be told. The two biographies by WILLIAMS are representative of this type. Both attempt to vindicate Bryan's career, as the title of the first biography (1923) suggests. Williams' deep admiration for Bryan damages his efforts. Similarly, NEWBRANCH's biography, despite its claim to be "complete," cannot adequately assess the politician's importance. The HERRICKS, cashing in on the news value, produced a biography of Bryan within the month of his death. Their work simply collated information that was already known.

The biographies published shortly after Bryan's death, such as LONG's in 1928 and WERNER's in 1929, were intended for popular consumption. Long's biography is generally positive while Werner's is critical. Werner ironically casts the story in Darwinian terms, titling the chapter that accounts for Bryan's birth as "The Origin of the Species" and the next chapter, which chronicles his growing to manhood, as "The Struggle for Existence." He foregoes irony in later chapters, finding "all the abysmal ignorance of Bryan's mind exhibited" in his discussions of evolution.

The first scholarly biography, written by HIBBEN, is highly critical as well. This, the first biography fully to document its sources, looks for every evidence of Bryan as a sharp politician rather than a crusader. Hibben's Bryan is naive: "Had he set out to destroy the solar system he could not have taken on a bigger job" than his plan in 1896. Hibben finds Bryan to be a failure: he was "a beaten man before the electoral canvass began. Victory was not in him or of him. The very speech that won him the nomination in Chicago was a speech not of triumph but of failure." This Bryan was predestined for defeat: he was "imprisoned" by a circle of women in his childhood who "suppressed" him; he was born into a heritage of Scotch-Irish immigrants who

represented a "tradition of defeat"; even his religion argues the "faith of submission." "William Jennings Bryan was of those meek who may inherit but will never conquer the earth."

Of course, a biographer cannot record the life of a man who lost the presidency three times, who resigned the position of Secretary of State while Europe was at war, and who was humiliated by Clarence Darrow, without discussing failure. More recent biographies tend to be more circumspect than Hibben, however. Bryan had tremendous impact on his own age and upon ours. His life is fascinating precisely because he had such impact while suffering repeated failures.

Recent biographies consider Bryan's contribution to our own world. CHERNY takes the metaphor Bryan used in his famous Chicago speech as an organizing principle to make sense of his life. He casts Bryan's entire life as a crusader, a crusader for Free Silver or Peace, a crusader against Imperialism or Evolution. This strategy, in a brief biography, necessarily simplifies Bryan's complex personality and his political role.

ASHBY opens by juxtaposing Bryan with the Farm Aide Concert in Champaign-Urbana in 1985 to identify the connections and distinctions between Bryan's populism and the populism of our own culture. Ashby sees Bryan as the person who defined the great issues of his period—the nature of industrialized democracy, morality in farm policy. In contrast, Cherny emphasizes his last years with his futile interest in fundamentalism and prohibition. ANDERSON looks beyond stereotypes of "the Boy Orator" or Darrow's victim at the Scopes trial to see the man whose eloquent ideas laid the foundation for 20th-century American liberalism. Anderson's assertion that Bryan's significance lies in the fact that he single-handedly made the transition from pre-Civil War idealism to the 20th century's Great Society is hyperbolic, but his discussion of that transition and Bryan's role in it is solid. For Anderson, Bryan's strength was his use of language rather than his political ideology: consequently, he focuses on Bryan the writer.

Perhaps the best single-volume life is KOENIG's political biography. Koenig is a gifted narrator of factual stories. Readers who seek compelling narrative should read this well-written, solid, detailed account. He puts to rest, finally, the myth that the "Cross of Gold" speech was the single act by which Bryan won the 1896 presidential nomination. He does so, analyzing Bryan's "intricate strategy," in a compelling account that animates the events of the Chicago convention. Koenig has the gift of bringing the man and his times to life. He gives a gripping, poignant account of the Scopes trial; Koenig's strategies heighten the drama. His insight into the issues is clear, nevertheless. For Koenig, Bryan failed to make the case for the relevance of Fundamentalist religious thinking to modern problems: "ironically, there was no one better qualified than Bryan" to explain those connections.

Serious students of Bryan's career must read COLLETTA's definitive biography in three volumes. In terms of scope and detail it is the best Bryan biography. For every facet of Bryan's long, various, and complex career, Coletta places the man in his intellectual, political, and cultural context. Volume I takes Bryan through 1908. Volume II, which covers four years, focuses on Bryan's advocacy of world peace and neutrality against the background of America's growing interest in Imperialism and the outbreak of war in Europe. Volume III covers the last ten years of Bryan's life. It provides a complete discussion of the complex intellectual history behind the Scopes trial. Coletta sets Bryan's position into the context of Protestant thought on evolution as no other biographer has done. This approach necessarily limits the biographer's options for narrative drama. Readers interested in compelling narrative placed in the context of social history who do not need the depth of detail that Coletta provides should turn to Koenig.

Ultimately, no biography can retrieve from the past for us today what it was to have been captivated by this man. William Jennings Bryan will always remain an enigma. He was such an electrifying orator that many who disagreed with him about everything were swayed by the power of his words—for the duration of his speech. That said, within the limitations of the genre, Bryan has been well served.

—Marnie Jones

BRYANT, William Cullen, 1794–1878; American poet and editor.

Bigelow, John, *William Cullen Bryant*. Boston, Houghton Mifflin, 1890.

Bradley, William A., *William Cullen Bryant*. New York and London, Macmillan, 1905.

Brown, Charles H., *William Cullen Bryant*. New York, Scribner, 1971.

Godwin, Parke, *A Biography of William Cullen Bryant, with Extracts from His Private Correspondence* (2 vols.). New York, Appleton, 1883.

Johnson, Curtiss, *Politics and Belly-full: The Journalistic Career of William Cullen Bryant*. New York, Vantage Press, 1962.

Peckham, Harry H., *Gotham Yankee: A Biography of William Cullen Bryant*. New York, Vantage Press, 1950.

*

The biography by GODWIN, Bryant's son-in-law and associate on the *New York Evening Post*, was included as the first two volumes of a complete life and edition of Bryant's writings. This biography is a formal, uncritical and soberly adulatory narrative, scrupulous in detail (as Godwin knew it), which on occasion reveals a shrewd understanding of his father-in-law; it is particularly rich in previously unpublished poems and letters, which are often misquoted, however. The first chapter is Bryant's own autobiographical sketch, written in 1874–75 and treating his life only up to his departure for Williams College. Godwin focuses on the public Bryant, primarily because the private Bryant did not discuss office matters at home and considered his leisure time for his books, his family, and the poetic muse. Also, even though Godwin does discuss Bryant's poetry, there is little critical examination of his works and some misdating of poems. Godwin is particularly valuable in his treatment of Bryant's work as an editor and his trips to Europe (which more recent biographers have never emphasized adequately), but he slights the important American travels. This is a slow-paced work, chock full of extracts from Bryant's letters, but valuable for the personal connection between the biographer and his subject.

A considerable number of commemorations and lives of Bryant were written soon after his death, but Bigelow's and Bradley's studies stand out as the most important of those memorials. BIGELOW's appeared in the prestigious American Men of Letters Series; he was also an associate on the *Evening Post* and so filled his biography with many personal recollections of Bryant as editor and public figure. Bigelow does not use a chronological structure but organized his work by subject—Bryant as journalist, poet, tourist, orator, and the life. Bigelow's chapter on Bryant as poet discusses the practical problems of balancing his journalistic with his poetic career. He also argues that Bryant's isolation from people was not a reflection of his personal coldness but rather his unwillingness to compromise his political and editorial opinion; this question of Bryant's aloofness has always been a major issue among biographers. Bigelow's biography was reprinted in 1980 with a short introduction by John Hollander.

BRADLEY's biography, in the important English Men of Letters Series, examines the poetry with more attention and tends to overemphasize the influence of Puritanism on Bryant. Nonetheless, this is a judicious biography that covers well the principal events of Bryant's life and offers short but astute and fair judgments along the way; objectivity and respect for his subject define the biographer's interpretation in this work.

PECKHAM's was among the first modern biographies of Bryant, the first lengthy work on his life in 60 years, but it does not use any of the scholarly research during the previous several decades that had set some of the record straight. Peckham's work is effusive and excessive, overblown in style, and draws invalid conclusions from the material. It is clearly to be avoided. On the other hand, JOHNSON's study of Bryant's journalistic career, while factually derived from earlier sources, is a worthy examination of Bryant's liberal politics, open-mindedness and, as Johnson describes it, his good judgment. Because so much of Bryant's time was spent editing the New York newspaper, it is important to recognize the contribution he made to the political journalism of the time and the extent to which this work took away from his poetry. Johnson read all 52 years of the *Evening Post* that Bryant edited and has assessed the importance of that work in a readable book.

The major modern biography of Bryant is by BROWN. He has made good use of the earlier scholarly research and the extensive collections of Bryant papers in American libraries, as well as of the letters, which began publication, under the editorship of Thomas G. Voss and William Cullen Bryant II, four years after Brown's biography appeared. Even though Brown did not have the Voss-Bryant edition of letters, he quotes Bryant as a letter and an editorial writer to portray the complexity of Bryant's character. The strength of Brown's work is in the balance he brings to the picture of Bryant's life: he describes the New York literary and political scene in good detail, Bryant's attitudes toward Lincoln, and his extensive travels. What is less satisfactory about this biography is its assessment of Bryant as a poet and as a critic of literature. Brown established the early literary career and talks about the growth of Bryant's poetic talent and commitment, but he is less interested in placing Bryant among his literary peers than in the New York scene. But that deficiency in no way compromises an otherwise thorough biography of this important 19th-century American literary figure.

—James E. Rocks

BUBER, Martin, 1878–1965; Austrian-born Jewish philosopher.

Friedman, Maurice, *Martin Buber's Life and Work* (3 vols.). New York, Dutton, 1981–83.
Hodes, Aubrey, *Encounter with Martin Buber.* London, A. Lane, 1972.
Vermes, Pamela, *Buber.* London, P. Halban, and New York, Grove, 1988.

*

FRIEDMAN's three-volume *Life and Work* is the major biographical study of Martin Buber to date. It is an immense work of scholarship by an academic deeply immersed in Buber's philosophy. Friedman describes it as "an attempt to show Buber's thought and work as his active response to the events and meetings of his life." Through the heavy weight of detail and philosophical discussion, a portrait of Buber as a man of integrated thought and action does indeed emerge. The importance to Buber of dialogue with others is illustrated by copious quotations from the three volumes of his correspondence so far published (edited by Grete Shaeder, an abridged version of which is planned for publication in English). For Buber's early life, Friedman draws on Buber's own "Autobiographical Fragments" (translated by the author in *The Philosophy of Martin Buber*, edited by Schilpp and Friedman, 1963). Friedman's own relationship with Buber figures prominently in the last volume of his work, but, as he points out in his preface, his access to the vast unpublished correspondence held in the Buber Archive was very limited and did not allow him to gain much insight into Buber's relationships with those closest to him. Full notes and sources for each chapter are included at the end of each volume.

In contrast to Friedman's lengthy work, VERMES' study is a slim volume in Peter Halban's series, "Jewish Thinkers." A concise account of Buber's life provides a framework for a full and clear discussion of his thought. The book contains a good bibliography.

HODES' work is not a chronological biography. Its starting point is the author's own relationship with Buber. The two met in 1953, when Buber became mentor as well as friend to the young Hodes. The bias of the book is toward Buber's last years in Israel, when Hodes knew him, but political events or remembered conversations are used to introduce aspects of Buber's philosophical or political thought, which are then traced back to their origins. Eichmann's trial in Jerusalem, for example, opens a discussion of Buber's German heritage. His relations with other thinkers, such as Bertrand Russell and Dag Hammarskjold, are discussed, as is his interest in contemporary Eastern think-

ers, Gandhi and Tagore. This is a personal portrait, a lively contrast to Vermes' factual clarity and Friedman's erudition.

—Isabel Aitken

BUCK, Pearl S., 1892–1973; American writer.

Harris, Theodore F., *Pearl S. Buck: A Biography* (2 vols.). New York, J. Day, and London, Eyre Methuen, 1969–71.
Doyle, Paul A., *Pearl S. Buck.* New York, Twayne, 1965.
Spencer, Cornelia, *The Exile's Daughter, A Biography of Pearl S. Buck.* New York, Coward-McCann, 1944.
Stirling, Nora B., *Pearl Buck, A Woman In Conflict.* Piscataway, New Jersey, New Century Publishers, 1983.

*

The first complete biography of Pearl S. Buck was written by HARRIS, who used a tape recorder and introduced lengthy quotes directly from Pearl Buck that were scrupulously checked and edited for accuracy. Buck wrote of Harris, "he knows me better than anyone," and indeed they had a close friendship. Harris reveals very personal details about Buck (for example, why her mother had called her Pearl), and he provides snapshots of Chinese friends, houses, meals, birth of babies, festivals—in short the tastes, sights, and smells of China as seen by Buck at the turn of the 20th Century. Of all the biographies of Pearl Buck, Harris' contains the richest detail, the largest number of anecdotes, the most intimate personal revelations, and the most vivid local color. But Harris is never gossipy or prurient, and he reveals also Buck's vulnerable side in a way subsequent biographers would not. These utilize the Harris volumes as their standard and starting point, and would become inceasingly analytical, for critical analysis is something Harris' biography lacks. In fact, reviewers of the first volume, while for the most part very positive, were skeptical of his "overly admiring hero-worship" and complained of his "embarrassingly adulatory" tone. But this did not phase Harris, who in his second volume raised Buck's stature from a novelist to world leader in fostering cross-cultural understanding and working for peace. Volume two contains significant correspondence between Buck and national and international leaders such as Eleanor Roosevelt and Senators Estes Kefauver, Richard L. Newberger, and James Eastland over the immigration legislation to allow Korean orphans to enter America.

SPENCER's biography shows Buck to be a much stronger woman, in the sense of more ambitious and calculating, than the Harris volumes, but is not as colorfully written nor as detailed. One of Spencer's opening quotes from Buck's work illustrates Buck's unabashed desire for fame and glory: "I want to be the best wife in the world, the best mother. I want to make a lot of lovely things in stone and bronze, perpetual things. I want to see the world and people . . . there isn't anything I don't want to do." Spencer for the first time traced Buck's ancestry, and her book reproduces numerous excellent photographs of Pearl Buck at all stages of her life. Spencer treats Buck's early writings in greater detail, mentioning various essay contests she won with her mother's encouragement. Buck appears much more as a role model for women in this biography, with Spencer developing the woman-to-woman relationships and networks that Buck created or joined. A harder, yet still refined, Pearl S. Buck emerges from these pages, tempered by discipline and hard work.

DOYLE's volume places Buck in the proper historical context while at the same time examining her work. It was the first critical study of her writings and contains a mention of nearly every review of her works. Useful as a literary guide to Buck's work, this biography clearly broke new ground in analysis, and illustrates why Pearl Buck ''is the most widely translated American author'' abroad, with only Mark Twain coming close. Doyle correctly explains her historical significance and that of her writings on developing China, and interprets the intellectual themes that marked her greatness. He places some of her obscure works, such as *Kinfolk* and *Command The Morning*, into the context of her life, and he does an excellent job of showing how her humanitarian achievements had a close affiliation with her writings. The biography also shows how Bolshevism or socialism became attractive to the Chinese during the 1920s and laid the groundwork for the future revolutions in China of Sun Yat-sen and Mao Tse-tung. Doyle's excellent book may remain as the standard analytical work on the writings of Pearl S. Buck.

STIRLING's work is more analytical than the Harris or Spencer volumes about the personality and character of Buck, but it does not emphasize literary criticism as much as the Doyle volume. Stirling's book uses reminiscences and information gathered from people who had known Pearl Buck, and hers is also the most dramatically written of all the biographies, opening with the Nanking Incident of 1927 and then flashing back to Buck's early life. Stirling also provides vivid historical backdrops for the events in Buck's life. The first biography completed since Buck's death in 1973, it honored Buck on the 10th anniversary of her death.

—Barbara Bennett Peterson

BUDDHA [Siddhartha Gautama], *ca.* 563 B.C.-*ca.* 483 B.C.; Indian philosopher and founder of Buddhism.

Alabaster, Henry, *The Wheel of the Law*. London, Trübner, 1871.

Arnold, Sir Edwin, *The Light of Asia*. London, Trübner, and Boston, Roberts, 1889.

Beal, Samuel, *The Fo-sho-hing-tsan-king: A Life of Buddha by Asvaghosa Bodisattva*. Oxford, Clarendon Press, 1883; New York, Scribner, 1900.

Beck, L. Adams, *The Life of the Buddha*. London, Collins, 1939.

Bigandet, Paul, *The Life or Legend of Gaudama the Buddha of the Burmese* (2 vols.). London, Trübner, 1880.

Brewster, Earl H., *The Life of Gotama the Buddha*. London, Kegan Paul, and New York, Dutton, 1926.

Carrithers, Michael, *The Buddha*. Oxford and New York, Oxford University Press, 1983.

Carus, Paul *The Gospel of Buddha*. Chicago, Open Court, 1984.

Davids, Caroline A. F. Rhys, *Gotama the Man*. London, Luzac, 1928.

Davids, T. W. Rhys, *Buddhism: Being a Sketch of the Life and Teachings of Gautama, the Buddha*. London, Society for Promoting Christian Knowledge, and New York, Pott Young, 1877.

Edwardes, Michael, editor, *A Life of the Buddha from a Burmese Manuscript*. London, The Folio Society, 1959.

Foucher, Alfred, *The Life of the Buddha According to the Ancient Texts and Monuments of India*, translated by Simone Brangier Boas. Middletown, Connecticut, Wesleyan University Press, 1963 (originally published by Payot, Paris, 1949).

Herold, A. Ferdinand, *The Life of the Buddha*, translated by Paul Blum. New York, Boni, 1927; London, T. Butterworth, 1929 (originally published by H. Piazza, Paris, 1922).

Ikeda, Daisaku, *The Living Buddha: An Interpretive Biography*, translated by Burton Watson. New York, J. Weatherhill, 1976.

Johnston, Edward, translator, *The Buddhacarita; or, Acts of the Buddha* (2 vols.). Calcutta, Baptist Mission Press, 1935; Delhi, Motilal Banarsidass, 1972.

Kalupahana, David J. and Indrani, *The Way of Siddhartha: A Life of the Buddha*. Boulder, Colorado, Shambhala, 1982.

Kelen, Betty, *Gautama Buddha in Life and Legend*. New York, Lothrop Lee, 1967; Singapore, G. Brash, 1989.

Ling, Trevor, *The Buddha: Buddhist Civilization in India and Ceylon*. London, Temple Smith, and New York, Scribner, 1973.

Mizuno, Kogan, *The Beginnings of Buddhism*, translated by Richard L. Gage. Tokyo, Kosei Publishing, 1980.

Nanamoli, Bhikkhu, *The Life of the Buddha*. Kandy, Sri Lanka, Buddhist Publication Society, 1978.

Narada, Thera, *The Buddha and His Teachings*. Saigon, Vietnam, 1964.

Oldenberg, Hermann, *Buddha: His Life, His Doctrine, His Order*, translated by William Hoey. London, Williams and Norgate, 1882 (originally published by W. Hertz, Berlin, 1881).

Pye, Michael, *The Buddha*. London, Duckworth, 1979.

Rockhill, W. Woodville, *The Life of the Buddha, and the Early History of His Order*. London, Trübner, 1884; Boston, J. R. Osgood, 1885.

Saddhatissa, H., *The Life of the Buddha*. London, Allen and Unwin, and New York, Harper, 1976.

Snellgrove, David, editor, *The Image of the Buddha*. London, Serindia, 1978.

Thomas, Edward J., *The Life of Buddha as Legend and History*. London, Kegan Paul, and New York, Knopf, 1927.

*

Buddha, a title meaning ''the enlightened one,'' is a common epithet for the Indian religious teacher who founded and continues to inspire various Buddhist traditions around the world. Western scholars, ''correcting'' traditional chronologies, usually date his lifetime to the sixth century B.C., although there is no absolute certainty to this, and at least some likelihood that he lived a century or so later.

All modern biographies of the Buddha depend on and draw from traditional accounts of his life produced at different times and places by Buddhists. These accounts, not surprisingly, are not critical biographies. Didactic in nature, they are rich in symbolism and mythic patterning, as well as miracles and wonders. Scholars once commonly spoke of "the legend" of the Buddha, rather than of his biography, and up until the 20th century some doubt persisted among Western scholars whether these accounts had any historical basis at all. But aside from being grist for the modern biographer's mill, these traditional accounts are valuable in their own right. They allow us to see the concerns and assumptions that Buddhists themselves brought to the biography of the Buddha, concerns which have their own validity even if they are often at odds with the interests of a modern biographer. Many of these accounts have been translated, and readers interested in Buddhist biographies of the Buddha may turn to those by ALABASTER, BEAL, BIGANDET, EDWARDES, or ROCKHILL; a particularly authoritative translation of a classic account of the Buddha's life—classic both for Buddhists and for modern scholars—is provided by JOHNSTON.

Some modern biographies are little more than uncritical retellings of traditional accounts with an eye for drama or the religious values of the story. A kind of veneration for the Buddha permeates many of these biographies, as is evident in ARNOLD's classic. BECK, BREWSTER, CARUS, and HEROLD have written biographies of this sort, and they indicate how popular such works were earlier in this century. Although this venerative style of biography has generally been discredited by scholarly research into the history of the Buddha's biography, some, like KELEN's, continue to be written. For all their faults from an uncritical use of sources, these biographies often read better than more scholarly accounts.

The consensus among scholars now is that the Buddha was in fact a historical figure, but the traditional accounts of his life are products of a long and complex process of composition. Thus a major problem for any critical biographer is dealing with the composite nature of the available sources. The most satisfactory solution to this problem is to acknowledge the process of composition within the modern biography. PYE, for example, provides three versions—historical, legendary, and mythological—of the Buddha's life, and thus effectively abandons the more conventional structure of a biography.

The most discerning and sophisticated treatment of the various literary sources is by THOMAS, who saw that there is no simple recovery of a historical core in the traditional accounts. If we reject parts of the traditional accounts merely because they are "unpalatable to modern tastes," Thomas writes, then we risk "suppressing valuable evidence as to the character of our witnesses." Thomas also saw that "normal circumstances are quite as likely to be invented as miracles," and that rejecting the obviously mythological was no sure route to historical facts.

The earliest narrative accounts of the Buddha's life were not literary only, but were sculpted in friezes on various Buddhist monuments. There has been a great deal of research on the connections between the development of the Buddha's biography, Buddhist art, and ritual practice. FOUCHER was a pioneer in the exploration of these connections, and although his biography is now 40 years old, it remains one of the best academic accounts of the Buddha's life available. Early artistic representations of the Buddha's life should not be ignored by anyone interested in biographies of the Buddha. As SNELLGROVE

says, they "often vibrate with life and are graced by a charming naiveté." Snellgrove provides convenient access to a wide range of art depicting the life of the Buddha.

Another popular approach to the composite nature of the traditional accounts is "the subtraction method"—subtracting from the sources whatever is judged to be a later addition and reconstructing a biographical narrative from what remains. In the light of research by such scholars as Thomas, the criteria for selecting material with the subtraction method often seem arbitrary. Two older works, by T. W. Rhys DAVIDS and OLDENBERG, are good examples of the results of this method. Both are classics in the academic literature about Buddhism, and although their use of sources may seem naive today, they continue to exert considerable influence on general ideas about the character of Buddhism.

A difficulty that faces those who use the subtraction method is that very little remains for the modern biographer to use when it is practiced rigorously. But while we may know for certain very little about the Buddha's life, quite a lot more is known about his teaching; in this our knowledge of the Buddha is little different from our knowledge of Socrates. Given this situation, some modern biographers have adopted the basic structure of the Buddha's life from traditional accounts, and have used this biographical framework to introduce Buddhist thought more generally. For example, CARRITHERS, to take one of the most elegant biographies in this mode, discusses various kinds of meditation within the rubric of the Buddha's quest for enlightenment. This combination of "life and teachings" has been particularly attractive to modern Buddhist authors, such as MIZUNO, NARADA, NANAMOLI, and SADDHATISSA, and it is easy to see why. As Saddhatissa says, "Expressed in the formal terms in which it has been recorded by the Scriptures, the Buddha's teaching appears dry and forbidding. It comes to life in the stories we have of the Buddha's day-to-day activities as a teacher."

Almost all critical biographies of the Buddha interpret his life by placing it in historical context. The benefit of such efforts is that we see the historical figure more clearly, even though we only know about him as an individual through more legendary accounts. The most sustained, and also the most imaginative exploration of historical context is LING. He uses the idea of context for understanding the Buddha in two ways: first, he looks at the historical conditions "out of which the Buddha emerged" and second, at "the distinctively new phenomenon which resulted in due course from the Buddha's life and work." Even though we grasp the Buddha's historicity better through an exploration of his cultural context, such a "life and times" approach raises a critical dilemma for his biographers. Can a biographer focus narrowly on the life of the Buddha or does the biographer have to explore much Buddhist thought and history in order to understand the Buddha?

The paucity of hard facts about the Buddha's life has always demanded some imagination on the part of his biographers. Some modern biographers, such as IKEDA and the KALUPAHANAs—all Buddhists—have been creative in their imaginative reconstructions of the Buddha's life, even as they have restricted themselves with cues taken from the traditional accounts. Sometimes, however, imagination departs almost completely from the traditional biographies. C.A.F. Rhys DAVIDS wrote her own biography as if it were the Buddha's autobiography, putting into the Buddha's mouth what she would have had him say. Her biography tells us more about Mrs. Rhys Davids, who was a great scholar of Buddhism, than about the Buddha. When imagination becomes so central in any reconstruction of the Buddha's life, biography shades into fiction. Thus, ironically, the traditional accounts of the Buddha's life, the same ones which struck Western scholars as no more trustworthy than fiction, remain essential elements in any critical biography of the Buddha.

—Charles Hallisey

BULGAKOV, Mikhail, 1891–1940; Russian writer.

Curtis, J.A.E., *Bulgakov's Last Decade: The Writer as Hero.* Cambridge and New York, Cambridge University Press, 1987.
Natov, Nadine, *Mikhail Bulgakov.* Boston, Twayne, 1985.
Proffer, Ellendea, *Bulgakov: Life and Work.* Ann Arbor, Michigan, Ardis, 1984.
Wright, A. Colin, *Mikhail Bulgakov: Life and Interpretations.* Toronto, Ontario, University of Toronto Press, 1978.

*

The format of the three full-length studies of Bulgakov prohibits classifying them as pure biographies; rather, they are investigations into his life and works. The proportions devoted to both aspects vary according to each author's stated purpose. That they tend to concentrate in various degrees more on the literature than the life results from the fact that until very recently the Bulgakov archives were closed to scholars. In spite of this obvious hardship, all three books are quite accurate in the major details. For sources the authors depend mainly on memoirs and reminiscences of Bulgakov's contemporaries, the published descriptions of archival material by the leading Soviet Bulgakov scholar, Marietta Chudakova, and, in two cases, interviews with Bulgakov's family and friends. They also rely on Bulgakov's own writing: his stories, novels, and plays; his most autobiographical works "Notes on the Cuff" and "To a Secret Friend"; as well as his semi-autobiographical fiction.

Scholarly in scope and intent, WRIGHT's book was the first major full-length study of Bulgakov published in English. This highly detailed analysis, academic in tone and manner, concentrates primarily on interpreting "every major work or group of works," with only about 20% of the text directly concerning Bulgakov's biography. Since he admits that he has "taken an unashamedly ideological approach," Wright chooses instead to explore Bulgakov's principal themes, for which he does find parallels in his subject's life.

One of Wright's chief sources for the background material was Bulgakov's second wife, Lyubov Evgenievna Belozerskaya-Bulgakova, with whom Wright conversed and whose then unpublished memoirs he read. (These have since come out as *My Life With Mikhail Bulgakov* [Ann Arbor, Michigan, Ardis, 1983], an impressionistic, sometimes disjointed and rambling, though fairly accurate account of the events of 1924–32.) Wright's extensive selected bibliography (535 items) also attests

to his careful research. In general, his objective portrayal of Bulgakov's life is competent but lackluster. Though he does supply the basic story, Wright obviously prefers analyzing the literature to discussing the personality—in spite of his assertion that he hopes his book will "be of interest to those trying to form a picture of Bulgakov the man." He is more successful in his assessment of Bulgakov the writer.

PROFFER accomplishes what Wright set out to do: she makes Bulgakov come alive as writer and man. Her well-illustrated investigation, published almost simultaneously with her *A Pictorial Biography of Mikhail Bulgakov*, contains as much—if not more—scholarly apparatus as Wright's study, but Proffer tells the tale in an engaging manner and in a highly narrative style. She also manages to evoke the atmosphere of the early days of the Soviet Union and the milieu in which Bulgakov lived and wrote. Her analysis of the literature also offers insights into the mind and personality of her subject. In addition, Proffer's concluding chapter, "The World According to Bulgakov," brings together the two foci of her study: literary analysis and biography, the latter comprising nearly one-half of this lengthy book. Prior to this final chapter, she separates the biographical chapters from the literary analysis, acknowledging that while there might be "methodological objections to this" format, she does so in order "that the reader who is mainly concerned with the general biography can easily find his way through the relevant chapters." This structure makes the book easy to use for both the specialist and the general reader.

Perhaps Proffer's biography offers a more complete and intimate account of Bulgakov because she knew not only Belozerskaya, as did Wright, but also his third wife, Elena Sergeevna, who was with Bulgakov during the writing of *Master and Margarita*. Elena kept a diary of Bulgakov's final years (at his insistence) and preserved his archives with great devotion. Proffer also had the advantage of knowing intimately the memoirist, Nadezhda Mandelstam (wife of the poet Osip Mandelstam) who made available to Proffer details of the life of the Bulgakovs, with whom she was close in the 1930s.

NATOV sets out to provide "a convenient survey of Bulgakov's life and works"; in essence, she succeeds. Hers is the most general of the studies, not at all meant for specialists. The first, biographical, chapter is superficial, but adequate for the purpose. She supplements this with a section on the semi-autobiographical works and with references throughout the text to incidents from Bulgakov's life as they are needed to elucidate points about the literature. With some critical interpretation, Natov summarizes the main characters, themes, and plots of the works in a rather mechanical style. She does provide a chronology and a selected bibliography, with brief annotations of the secondary sources.

A recent study by CURTIS, who had access to the archives, for the most part concerns itself with a detailed study of Bulgakov's literary activity during the final years of his life. Curtis corrects minor errors in both Wright and Proffer without diminishing the value of the two books. Proffer still remains the definitive work on Bulgakov in English.

—Christine A. Rydel

BUNYAN, John, 1628–1688; English writer and preacher.

Bacon, Ernest, *Pilgrim and Dreamer: John Bunyan, His Life and Work.* Exeter, Paternoster Press, 1983.

Brittain, Vera, *Valiant Pilgrim: The Story of John Bunyan and Puritan England.* New York, Macmillan, 1950; as *In the Steps of John Bunyan: An Excursion into Puritan England,* London and New York, Rich and Cowan, 1950.

Brown, John, *John Bunyan: His Life, Times, and Work.* London, W. Isbister, and Boston, Houghton Mifflin, 1885; tercentenary edition, revised by F. M. Harrison, London, Hulbert, 1928.

Froude, James A., *Bunyan.* New York, Harper, and London, Macmillan, 1880.

Griffith, Gwilym O., *John Bunyan.* London, Hodder and Stoughton, 1927; New York, Doubleday, 1928.

Gunn, Judith, *Bunyan of Elstow.* London, Hodder and Stoughton, 1985.

Harrison, Frank M., *John Bunyan: A Story of His Life.* London Hulbert, 1928.

Hill, Christopher, *A Turbulent, Seditious, and Factious People: John Bunyan and His Church 1628–1688.* Oxford, Clarendon Press, 1988; as *A Tinker and a Poor Man: John Bunyan and His Church,* New York, Knopf, 1989.

Sharrock, Roger, *John Bunyan.* London, Hutchinson University Library, 1954; revised edition, London, Macmillan, and New York, St. Martin's, 1984.

Talon, Henri, *John Bunyan: The Man and His Works,* translated by Barbara Wall. Cambridge, Massachusetts, Harvard University Press, and London, Rockliffe, 1951 (originally published by Éditions "Je Sers," Paris, 1948).

Winslow, Ola E., *John Bunyan.* New York, Macmillan, 1961.

*

As part of the English Men of Letters Series, FROUDE's work represents the 19th century's growing interest in Bunyan's literary art rather than his religious experiences. Since Froude is unsympathetic to Calvinism and the Evangelical view, he writes with theological distance. He focuses on the Romantic view of Bunyan as a man of "natural genius," who captured human life with remarkable accuracy. Although seven of the ten chapters are largely biographical, critical attention is given to Bunyan's major works. The modern scholar will find that documents discovered after the first printing of Froude's book have made it unreliable on some facts, such as the early dispute over which side of the Civil War Bunyan served on. While Froude says Bunyan probably served on the Royalist side, we now have proof that he served in the Parliamentary army (a view that Thomas Babington Macaulay had deduced earlier). Despite its being dated, this work is readable and useful for its stress on Bunyan's literary value.

BROWN's thoroughly researched and massive work corrects Froude's and has become the standard biography for the last century. For 39 years the minister of Bunyan Meeting, Brown was the first to make use of the documents opened by the Royal Commission on Historical Manuscripts and other original sources in the Bedfordshire area. In fact, he begins the biography with early church life in Bedfordshire and continues to keep the focus on Bunyan in relation to the church in Bedford. The first edition includes chapters on *The Pilgrim's Progress, The*

Holy War, Bunyan's posthumous works, and a thorough listing of the editions, versions, illustrations, and imitations of *The Pilgrim's Progress.* It also discusses Bunyan's portraits, traces his descendants and ministerial successors, and explains the problem of when and where Bunyan wrote *The Pilgrim's Progress.* The revised edition by Harrison relegates marginal notes, editorial comments, and addenda to the ends of chapters and to appendices so as to leave Brown's text intact. While this 500-page volume contains facts, illustrations, lists, and data concerning the life and times of Bunyan, making it a vast "repository of research and antiquarian lore" (Sharrock, *The English Novel*), it lacks a sustained narrative. For that the reader should turn to HARRISON's own biography, an imaginative and highly readable account of Bunyan's life. Although the author confesses a "clear and unashamed case of hero-worship," Harrison's slim volume is considered one of the better tercentenary biographies commemorating Bunyan's birth. It follows Brown's work closely, except Harrison admittedly tries to correct "a deficiency" in Brown by devoting more attention to Bunyan's first wife and to John Gifford's influence. Brown and Harrison serve as complements whereby one is voluminous in detail for the scholar, while the other is short and concise for the general reader.

GRIFFITH's biography, coming after Brown's, offers the defense for yet another life story on the basis of presenting the "human story" of Bunyan, which "must almost inevitably be somewhat obscured" in the massive scholarly detail of Brown's work. Griffith presents an engaging narrative, well researched and well written. While essentially following Brown, he does depart on the origin and date of *The Pilgrim's Progress,* placing it in the period 1666–72, rather than 1675–76 as Brown does. He also suggests that *The Heavenly Footman* provided the inspiration for the famous allegory, a probability that Brown admitted in his 4th edition. Griffith also devotes chapters to Bunyan's views of women in the church, family roles, the poor, and Bunyan's verse. Although tending somewhat toward the romantic, this work moves forward with a steady pace, not lingering too long over knotty problems of Bunyan scholarship. As the *Spectator* asserted, "A more satisfying or better balanced biography we have seldom read" (25 February 1928). For a solidly based understanding of the man Bunyan, the reader should not overlook this work.

BRITTAIN combines thorough research with a highly imaginative style to produce a fascinating biography. As its English title, *In the Steps of John Bunyan,* suggests, Brittain follows the topography of the villages and countryside to recreate Bunyan's life and times. In so doing, her work reflects much more than the local traditions about landmarks and events to supplement the facts. The introduction admirably summarizes the major problems of Bunyan biography and explains how the discovery of recent documents changes such important facts as the date and place of Bunyan's imprisonment when he wrote the *Pilgrim's Progress.* Thus in her narrative she incorporates the important new material of Joyce Godber, the Bedfordshire Archivist. Also useful are an extensive bibliography and 56 photographs, drawings, and maps. While critics acknowledge her thorough research and careful documentation, they have reservations about the extent of her imaginative style. Chad Walsh suggests the work "hovers somewhat between a straight biography and a historical novel, but is closer to the former" (*New York*

Times, 10 December 1950). The book will appeal to a wide range of readers but especially college students.

Although the volumes by TALON, SHARROCK, and HILL are not purely biographical, they are important recent works that contain the latest findings and interpret Bunyan for late 20th-century students and scholars. For a literary perspective, Sharrock's concise treatment of the man, his milieu, and major works is attractive to younger students and the reader looking for a good, solid introduction to Bunyan. Talon, a Frenchman and Roman Catholic, brings a fresh perspective while remaining objective and fair to the Puritan tradition and Bunyan's faith. Thorough in scholarship, Talon's study gives "as brilliant a picture of the social and the theological background as of Bunyan's religious experience and his artistry" (*Spectator,* 31 August 1951). In a major reinterpretation of Bunyan, the Marxist historian Hill emphasizes the 17th-century political, economic and social backdrop and attempts to put Bunyan back into the revolutionary age in which he lived. While extremely thorough and solid in scholarship, the work overstates the case for the thinker-preacher's radicalism.

WINSLOW, the winner of a Pulitzer Prize for her biography of Jonathan Edwards, presents a lucid life of Bunyan based on sound scholarship. Although she brings no new discoveries and no major reinterpretation to her study, she succeeds in relating a warm, sensitive account of her subject. In her prologue she expresses the difficulty of all biographers in constructing a life with only a scant factual record; and because of the recent studies of Brittain, Talon, and Sharrock, she explains the necessity of restricting the scope of her work. Yet what makes this volume outstanding, from the opening pages on Bunyan's boyhood to the closing paragraphs about his swift death, is Winslow's eloquent style. This readability is what makes this work the best biography for the general reader. If one were to read only a single life of Bunyan it should be this one. Sharrock has suggested that Winslow's work surpasses Brown's. The author attaches her scholarly apparatus to the end of the book and includes a list of Bunyan's published works and a bibliography.

Popular Bunyan biographies for all ages continue to pour out, and the juvenile market remains strong. GUNN's is a compact volume emphasizing the inner struggle and conflict of a man attempting to understand Christianity and his fight to overcome depression and terror in his jail years. Gunn narrates Bunyan's story in a clear, straightforward style, with no discussion of the individual works but some explanation of such concepts as the conflict between the king and Parliament. No evidence of her sources appears except in a brief bibliography at the end.

The evangelical popular market also remains a fertile area for Bunyan readership today. BACON has written a good representative work. He makes no apology for his evangelical sympathies, stating it is time for a biography by one sympathetic to Bunyan's Puritanism. He presents Bunyan as one who can still speak to a scientific and technological age because of the need to know God. Bacon draws on a number of general background works and earlier biographies, which he incorporates within the text, and his work reflects the changes in facts made by the latest discoveries.

—Marlene A. Hess

BURKE, Edmund, 1729–1797; English statesman, orator, and political philosopher.

Ayling, Stanley, *Edmund Burke: His Life and Opinions.* London, J. Murray, and New York, St. Martin's, 1988.

Bissett, Robert, *The Life of Edmund Burke* (2 vols.). London, G. Cawthorn, 1798.

Cone, Carl B., *Burke and the Nature of Politics* (2 vols.). Lexington, University of Kentucky Press, 1957–64.

Kirk, Russell, *Edmund Burke: A Genius Reconsidered.* New Rochelle, New York, Arlington House, 1967.

Kramnick, Isaac, *The Rage of Edmund Burke: Portrait of an Ambivalent Conservative.* New York, Basic Books, 1977.

MacCormick, Charles, *Memoirs of the Rt. Hon. Edmund Burke.* London, Lee and Hurst, 1787.

Magnus, Philip, *Edmund Burke, a Life.* London, J. Murray, 1939; New York, Russell, 1973.

Morley, John, *Burke.* London and New York, Macmillan, 1888.

Prior, James, *Memoir of the Life and Character of the Right Hon. Edmund Burke.* London, Baldwin Craddock, 1824.

*

PRIOR's biography was the best of the 19th-century works on Burke, and it became the standard work on Burke for Victorian writers. It continued the idealistic picture of Burke that had first been developed by BISSET in his 1798 biography. Like Bisset, Prior was sympathetic to Burke. Prior rejected the critical portrayal of Burke by MacCORMICK, Burke's first biographer, who attacked Burke for having deserted the Whig party over the debate on the French Revolution. His negative attitude toward Burke is the result of contemporary party politics and is polemical rather than empirical.

Prior made extensive use of Burke's works published from 1808–13, and of his speeches published in 1816. He emphasized Burke's role in the impeachment trial of Hastings and his conflict with Fox. In a fifth edition published in 1854, Prior argued that the publication of Burke's correspondence in 1844 (4 vols.) provided further evidence to support his positive view of Burke.

MORLEY's work, part of the English Men of Letters Series, together with the various editions of Prior's biography, determined the portrait of Burke taken into the 20th century by literary and political historians. Morley investigates Burke from the conflicting perspectives of "how far he was a splendid pamphleteer of a faction, and how far he was a contributor to the universal stock of enduring wisdom." He considers Burke's early life and education to be important influences on his later thinking and career. His involvement in Irish affairs and his career in politics, especially his attachment to the Rockingham Whigs, are considered significant in the formation of Burke's political philosophy.

Morley's biography contains good analysis of some of Burke's early writings, particularly *A Vindication of Natural Society,* as well as the later works such as *Reflections on the Revolution in France.* It is in the main a political biography, but at the same time Morley does not overlook Burke's character and philosophical ideas. He contends that it was Burke's attitude toward and response to the French Revolution that made him an internationally renowned figure.

MAGNUS was the first biographer of Burke to make use of the Burke papers at Wentworth House, and this is the main significance of his work. It is a shame that Magnus did not utilize the manuscript source in a more representative fashion. As Cone states in the preface to his biography (see below), Magnus applied the manuscripts "sparingly." Magnus includes much quotation, which is however corrupt. He is very critical of "the Burkes," and he includes Edmund Burke in the financial relations of his brother Richard and his "kinsman" William.

CONE's first volume is the first biography to make use of the Burke manuscripts in the Fitzwilliam papers at the Sheffield Central Library. Cone also delved into such sources as unpublished dissertations, articles, and books dealing with specific aspects of Burke's life and career. What emerges from this wealth of material is a narrative from the birth of Burke until 1782 and the fall of the North ministry.

Cone's main thesis is that Burke was a "party politician rather than a political philosopher." He continues by arguing that "had Burke died before the French Revolution began, I doubt that we should think of him as a practical philosopher." Burke, by 1782, had attained the zenith of his career as a party politician, and it was only later that he became "the seer, the prophet, the sage, the philosopher."

In terms of information, Cone's work is superior to that of Prior's. At the time of publication it was also the most thorough and fairest political biography to have appeared. It is more accurate than previous works and places Burke in his historical context through a comprehensive discussion of contemporary party politics.

Cone was praised for his handling in volume two of Burke and the politics of India, which previous scholars had dealt with in a cursory fashion. Cone was also lauded for his thorough use of the East India Company's archives. What he failed to do in this second volume is to discuss the private life of Burke. The second half of the book deals with Burke's attack on the French Revolution.

KIRK's is a terse biography both of Burke's personal and political life. Kirk made use of new manuscripts and scholarly publications that have appeared since 1950. He believes Burke to be the archetype for both conservatives and radicals: "If conservatives would know what they defend, Burke is their touchstone; and if radicals wish to test the temper of their opposition, they should turn to Burke." Kirk deals with the four major involvements of Burke's life: the American colonies; constitutional issues and party politics; the impeachment of the Governor General of India, Warren Hastings; his attack of the French Revolution.

As KRAMNICK stated in his preface, he wished to present a "new" Burke to his readers in his psychobiography. He claims that it was his reading of the nine volumes of Burke's correspondence that led him to his method of psychohistory and his conclusions about Burke. Kramnick sought to destroy the traditional image of Burke as the "prophet of conservatism" and the "assumed legendary status" he had acquired. His approach has permitted Kramnick to examine aspects of Burke's life left untouched by previous biographers. No other biographer before or since has penetrated into the mind and emotions of Burke.

The main argument presented here is that Burke was a man filled with "rage," that this rage was the outcome of complex psychological problems rooted in his childhood. Kramnick stresses Burke's separation from his father from age six to eleven, which resulted in Burke's alleged homosexuality: "His unresolved oedipal conflict becomes the intrapsychic, psychoanalytic issue which colors his entire life; it would be aspects of this irresolution which would recur in later neuroses." From this analysis of Burke's psychological condition, Kramnick argues that Burke's politics were ambivalent, often more radical than conservative. Often assumptions drawn from psychological speculations are made without enough empirical evidence to support them.

The most recent biography of Burke is that of AYLING, the first work to be published since the completion of the full modern edition of Burke's correspondence completed in 1978. This is a well-written and very easy to read summary of Burke's personal life and political activities and thought. Ayling has provided a well-balanced portrait of Burke without any particular axe to grind. "If he is 'the father of English conservatism' he is also the man (of course no Tory but a Whig) who espoused such liberal reforms as relief for Dissenters and Catholics; mitigation of the laws permitting life imprisonment for debt . . . and most persistently and passionately of all, if sometimes misguidedly, reform of the government and administration of British India in what he understood to be the interests of the Indians themselves."

Ayling questions the orthodoxy that holds Burke to be the most important of British writers who distanced themselves from the Enlightenment. This is conceded as true during the decade, of the *Reflections*, but Burke held Montesquieu in great esteem, calling him "the greatest genius who has enlightened this age."

Ayling contends that Burke's thought is only understandable against the "variable and transient background of either contemporary public events or his personal and family circumstances." This approach of giving equal attention to Burke's family life and the context of the times makes the biography useful to those interested not simply in Burke per se, but also in the England in which he lived. As one reviewer put it: "This is biography at its best and every student of the 18th century will want to read it" (*Library Journal*, Fall 1989).

—Leigh Ann Whaley

BURNEY, Fanny (Frances; Madame d'Arblay), 1752–1840; English writer.

Adelstein, Michael, *Fanny Burney*. New York, Twayne, 1968.

Dobson, Austin, *Fanny Burney*. London and New York, Macmillan, 1903.

Doody, Margaret, *Frances Burney: The Life in the Works*. Cambridge, Cambridge University Press, and New Brunswick, New Jersey, Rutgers University Press, 1988.

Edwards, Averyl, *Fanny Burney 1752–1840: A Biography*. London, Staples Press, 1948.

Gérin, Winifred, *The Young Fanny Burney*. London and New York, T. Nelson, 1961.

Hahn, Emily, *A Degree of Prudery: A Biography of Fanny Burney*. New York, Doubleday, 1950; London, A. Barker, 1951.

Hemlow, Joyce, *History of Fanny Burney*. Oxford, Clarendon Press, 1958.

Kilpatrick, Sarah, *Fanny Burney: A Biography*. Newton Abbot, David and Charles, 1980; New York, Stein and Day, 1981.

Lloyd, Christopher, *Fanny Burney*. London and New York, Longman, 1936.

Masefield, Muriel, *The Story of Fanny Burney*. Cambridge, Cambridge University Press, 1927.

Simons, Judy, *Fanny Burney*. London, Macmillan, and New York, Barnes and Noble, 1987.

*

For much of the time since her death in 1840, the main source of biographic information on Frances (or Fanny) Burney has been her own diary and letters. These appeared in editions published between 1842 and 1846, and again 1889, when her earlier diary appeared. A modern edition of her journals came out between 1972 and 1984, providing a far more complete and accurate version (*The Journal and Letters of Fanny Burney*, edited by Joyce Hemlow *et al*, 12 vols., 1972–84). But independent biography was slow to catch up, with the result that her private jottings have perhaps loomed too large in our sense of Burney, relegating her outstanding creative achievement—especially in the novel—to a subsidiary position.

The first serious attempt at a life was the volume by DOBSON in the English Men of Letters Series in 1903 (Burney was one of the few women admitted to this eminent company). Inevitably this work is now critically outdated, and its knowledge of Burney's life was limited by the gaps in the diaries, as then available. Worst of all, Dobson devotes just one chapter, "Half a Lifetime," to the last 50 years of Burney's long life. However, it is a sane, positive, and readable survey, which still has a number of pertinent things to say.

There is less to be said for the next few works to appear, although Constance Hill's books on the Burney family, especially *The House in St Martin's Street* (1907), provided valuable new information. The studies by MASEFIELD, LLOYD, and EDWARDS are now supplanted, and indeed all previous work was rendered largely obsolete by HEMLOW's compendious and pioneering work. This is the standard life of Burney, weighty, exhaustive, and comprehensive. Hemlow had carried out lengthy research into the scattered family papers and brought a new level of scholarship and thoroughness to the task. Hemlow reveals the chequered story of the Burney lineage, brings skeletons out of the family closet, and gives new attention to Burney's career as wife and mother. It could be said that Hemlow does not supply a very deep reading of the literature as literature, but she does probe the novels and plays for personal clues to Burney's intellectual and personal development. Hemlow's work remains a key item in Burney scholarship.

Other biographies since World War II have added little. HAHN, unsympathetic though occasionally shrewd, is very thin on the later years; GÉRIN's is a slight book compared to her important later work on the Brontë circle. KILPATRICK is workmanlike and serviceable. However, outside Hemlow, the most interesting contributions of the period include two lives of Fanny's father, Dr. Charles Burney, by Percy A. Scholes (*The Great Dr. Burney*, 2 vols., 1948) and Roger Lonsdale (*Dr. Charles Burney*, 1965). The latter work especially affords many insights into the milieu of the daughter. Most recent books on Burney have shifted toward criticism rather than biography, though some, such as ADELSTEIN's, contain brief and reliable details on the life. SIMONS provides a short but sensible survey of Burney with a largely literary-critical emphasis.

The most important and adventurous of recent works is DOODY's book. As the subtitle suggests, Doody approaches Burney's personality through her works. She does not set out to rival Hemlow in detailing every facet of Burney's day-to-day existence, but proceeds instead to subject Burney's writings to extensive and often brilliant critical exploration. A new degree of attention is given, for example, to the plays, mostly unperformed and unpublished. Doody attempts a radical reappraisal of Burney's character and output, claiming that her novels are "violent": Burney is "a student of aggression and obsession." Deft and sophisticated readings of the novels are buttressed by a clear sense of the writer's troubled family life, and a thoroughgoing psychological case is made for the negative influence of her father on her creative output.

Denying that she has made Charles Burney "the villain of the piece," Doody nonetheless argues convincingly that the father crushed many of the daughter's impulses toward creation and was partly responsible for prolonging her dreary life at court under Queen Charlotte. There is considerable documentation of the crushing effect of her "daddies" (her father and the tutelary figure of Samuel Crisp), and on the need Frances acquired to get permission from others (usually male) before she could write anything. In addition Doody is good on the tangled dealings with Hester Thrale (later Piozzi), and more willing than some to concede Burney's faults as manifested in this relationship. All around, Doody makes more sense of Burney's existence, in particular her emotional history, than any previous biographer, and has written the first account of Burney's life that gives an adequate sense of her burning urge to write. While Hemlow remains the fullest source of biographical data, Doody has probed further into the personal origins of Burney's art.

—Pat Rogers

BURNS, Robert, 1759–1796; Scottish poet.

Carswell, Catherine, *The Life of Robert Burns*. London, Chatto and Windus, 1930; New York, Harcourt, 1931; revised edition, Edinburgh, Canongate, 1990.

Crawford, Thomas, *Burns: A Study of the Songs and Poems*. Edinburgh, Oliver and Boyd, and Stanford, California, Stanford University Press, 1960.

Currie, James, editor, *The Works of Robert Burns with an Account of His Life* (4 vols.). London, T. Cadell and W. Davies, 1800–04.

Daiches, David, *Robert Burns*. New York, Rinehart, 1950; London, G. Bell, 1952.

Ferguson, J. de Lancey, *Pride and Passion: Robert Burns 1759–96*. New York, Oxford University Press, 1939.

Fowler, Richard H., *Robert Burns*. London, Routledge, 1988.

Hecht, Hans, *Robert Burns: The Man and His Work*, translated by Jane Lymburn. London and Edinburgh, Hodge, 1936; revised edition, with preface by Sir Patrick Dollan, Hodge, 1950.

Lindsay, Maurice, *Robert Burns: The Man, His Work, the Legend*. London, MacGibbon and Kee, 1954.

Lockhart, John G., *Life of Robert Burns*. Edinburgh, Constable, and London, Hutchinson, 1828; New York, W. Stodart, 1831.

Snyder, Franklyn B., *The Life of Robert Burns*. New York, Macmillan, 1932.

*

Glasgow's Mitchell Library contains probably the most comprehensive Burns Collection in Europe. Much of it is based on misinformation or is otherwise inaccurate and out of date. Much of it, possibly the majority, is, in the Scots proverbial phrase, simply "cauld kail re-het"(cold cabbage reheated). I have therefore selected ten key biographies, either because they were thought significant—and therefore influential—in their day, or because they are useful now. Little prior to the publication of Auguste Angelliers' *Robert Burns: La Vie, les Oeuvres* (Paris, 1893) is of much certain factual value. Angellier, whose book only appeared in French, went back to primary sources and did not accept the sweepings of rumour; but much new material has come to light in the ensuing century.

CURRIE, the first official biographer, was a convinced teetotaler, and from his own no doubt sincere viewpoint painted Burns' decline as being due to alcoholism (which we now know it was not), and other related but unspecified depravities. Though he was doubtless well intentioned, Currie, a medical man, had neither the training nor, indeed, access to enough material for his account to have much real value. Nevertheless, his priggish moral verdicts on Burns' drinking and sexual habits coloured the views of virtually every writer on Burns prior to Angellier.

The first widely popular biography of Burns was that by LOCKHART. It was reprinted several times throughout the 19th century, and eventually turned up in the well-known Everyman series of popular classics. Lockhart's volume does not, of course, have the benefit of the author's personal knowledge of his subject, which makes his life of his father-in-law, Sir Walter Scott, such a valuable source-book, despite its tidyings-up and trimmings. Because of Lockhart's graceful style and reputation as a figure in the second order of the Scottish literary hierarchy, the book achieved an authority it did not deserve.

Lockhart disapproved of Burns' radical leanings and sexual proclivities. Franklyn Bliss Snyder described the book as "inexcusably inaccurate from beginning to end, at times demonstrably mendacious." For all its celebrity, therefore, Lockhart's *Burns* can only be regarded as a period-piece today, though it inspired some interesting thoughts on the poet from Thomas Carlyle when he reviewed it. He, too, accepted Lockhart's perpetuation of the Currie drunkenness legend, and was suitably patronising from a great moral height.

SNYDER's was the first book in English to apply scholarly biographical methods, separating rumour from fact and being suitably sceptical where the evidence is lacking. Snyder uncovered many new points and throughout displays a sympathetic understanding of social conditions in Burns' Scotland. His book, of which there was only an American printing, remains rewarding and readable. All its sources are noted at the end of each chapter.

One of the most generally acceptable of Burns biographies remains HECHT's *Robert Burns*, in Jane Lymburn's excellent English translation. His book is consistently accurate and full of information. There is, however, perhaps a slight sense of "outside looking in," a distancing of the author from his subject and a detachment that perhaps shows itself most noticeably in a lack of sociological background detail.

By the time Hecht's book first appeared in English in 1936, a biography had appeared that was most certainly not distanced from its subject. It is difficult now to understand the furore caused by CARSWELL's book when it came out in 1931. Its sexual frankness no doubt played some part in arousing the "Holy Willies" who then dominated the Burns Federation, which threatened to ensure the book's "death." Letters of abuse filled newspaper columns for days, and the author even received a symbolic bullet through the post. Nevertheless, the book scored a considerable success, and now, 60 years later, appears in a new edition with an Introduction by Thomas Crawford (for whose own book, see below).

Carswell made up her own mind on the solutions to the unresolved ambiguities and problems in Burns' life-story, adapted unsubstantiated gossip and rumour as fact when it suited her purpose, and went flat out to create a warm-blooded character in whom her readers could immediately believe. As a kind of impressionistic depiction, Carswell's book is brilliantly successful; but obviously, none of the facts so skilfully woven into her easy narrative can be proven beyond reasonable doubt on her say alone. It must be said, however, that despite the emotional sweep of her tale-telling, she does not stoop to the vulgar pruriency and slap-dash style of writing that characterises the five fictional volumes through which James Baker later exploited Burns' life-story.

One of the most enjoyable accounts of Burns' life is that of De Lancey FERGUSON, whose method is to consider Burns from such different angles as Scotland, Education, Men, Women, Livelihood, Song and The Scot, thus filling in a wealth of informative background detail not otherwise brought together. Unfortunately, his book appeared on the eve of World War II and therefore did not immediately win the plaudits it deserved. De Lancey Ferguson was, of course, the first systematic editor of Burns' letters (*Letters of Robert Burns*, 1931), an edition only recently superseded by the corrected and enlarged new edition edited by Ross Roy for the Oxford University Press.

Although David Daiches and Thomas Crawford both state that their main business is with Burnsian literary criticism rather than with biography, both academics are worth attention. CRAWFORD addresses a scholarly audience rather than the general reader, providing very full references. DAICHES, one of the most level-headed and lucid academic critics 20th-century Scotland has produced, is particularly good on Burns' education and early influences. Although much of his attention is also devoted to the poetry itself, he is careful always to relate it to the circumstances in which it was written. His study has been reprinted often.

LINDSAY, the present writer, presents for the general reader an integrated account of Burns' life and work in the context of the latest information, and sets that life in the context of a late 18th-century Scotland threatened with governmental conversion to North Britain. Lindsay examines the growth of the cult of Burns as the National Bard. Because of the popularity of his poems with all classes of society, Burns in all probability saved the Scots tongue from extinction; and so, together with Scott, whose Waverley Novels awakened popular interest in Scottish history, rescued Scotland's threatened sense of nationhood. The appreciation of Burns and his work is thus set firmly in the context of the changing attitudes of late 20th-century Scotland. Lindsay has also published a *Burns Encyclopaedia* (4th edition, London, Hale, 1988), which carries the full texts of the only two accounts of the poet's life by his contemporaries, Robert Heron and Maria Riddell.

FOWLER's book is a clear and well-written account by an Australian. It's main importance is perhaps that it focuses technical geological knowledge and speaks authoritatively on the soil conditions of the farm Burns and his father worked. Fowler reaches the conclusion that Burns was a bad farmer.

—Maurice Lindsay

BURR, Aaron, 1756–1836; American lawyer and statesman.

Lomask, Milton, *Aaron Burr* (2 vols.). New York, Farrar Straus, 1979; revised edition, 1982.
Parmet, Herbert and Marie B. Hecht, *Aaron Burr: Portrait of an Ambitious Man*. New York, Macmillan, 1967.
Parton, James, *The Life and Times of Aaron Burr*. New York, Mason, 1857; in 2 vols., Boston, Osgood, 1877.
Schachner, Nathan, *Aaron Burr, a Biography*. New York, F. A. Stokes, 1937.
Wandell, Samuel H. and Meade Minnigerode, *Aaron Burr: A Biography Written, in Large Part, from Original and Hitherto Unused Sources*. New York, Putnam, 1927.

*

PARTON's two-volume work first appeared in 1857 and was enlarged in 1877. This allowed Parton to make use of several scholarly pieces that had been published as well as a variety of documents that had come to light. However, the new material did not cause Parton to change any of his views of Burr, and thus the second edition was criticized, as the first had been, for being too favorable to Burr—a criticism one comes across as late as 1927.

Parton was the first scholar to make use of the few published papers of Burr, the papers of friends and enemies, and contemporary newspapers. He interviewed those acquaintances of Burr who were still alive when he was researching the work. He thus made use of the *Memoirs of Aaron Burr: With Miscellaneous Selections From His Correspondence* (New York, Harper, 1837) and *The Private Journal of Aaron Burr During His Residence of Four Years in Europe: With Selections from His Correspondence* (New York, Harper, 1838), both of which were edited by his friend M. L. Davis, whom Burr entrusted with some papers.

Parton's work was the standard study of Burr until the publication of WANDELL AND MINNIGERODE's two-volume study in 1925. This work is based on a variety of primary sources, including material written by Burr, by his wives and parents, as well as the papers of friends and enemies. The authors also made use of *The Aaron Burr Conspiracy* (1903) by W. F. McCaleb and *The Life of John Marshall* (1916) by A. J. Beveridge. In the preface the authors state that they had tried to give Burr's view of events without being too favorable to him. They seem to have satisfied contemporaries on this point since McCaleb, in the introduction to this study, writes that Wandell and Minnigerode's work was a "dispassionate study of the man." The work contains a large bibliography of primary and secondary materials.

SCHACHNER's work, which appeared in 1937 and did not break any new ground, is a large single-volume study that has made extensive use of such primary sources as Burr's own writings, the writings of friends and enemies, and contemporary newspaper accounts. Schachner also used Spanish and French archives to provide more insight into the complicated political situation in the West. To support the statements he makes about Burr, he has placed throughout the text excerpts from the primary and secondary sources that he has consulted. The volume contains a large bibliography and is a well-written, comprehensive study that is still quite useful today.

Thirty years passed by until another major biography of Burr appeared. PARMET AND HECHT's work is an extremely well-written biography of the man. The authors have made extensive use of primary and secondary materials to provide us with what has been described as a "well-rounded biography of Burr."

LOMASK's two-volume study of Burr has eclipsed all others. Lomask was the first to make extensive use of the definitive collection of Burr documents that was first issued on microfilm in 1978 as *Papers of Aaron Burr*, edited by Mary Jo Kline, and later published as *The Political Correspondence and Legal Papers of Aaron Burr* (Princeton, New Jersey, Princeton University Press, 1983). Besides making use of Dr. Kline's work, Lomask has made use of the papers of Burr's contemporaries and secondary sources in an attempt to discover who the real Aaron Burr was. Lomask feels that Burr was essentially a good man who was not guilty of treason. He describes Burr as a devoted family man who looked upon politics as a game, a "form of entertainment." Each volume of Lomask's work contains a full bibliography. Lomask's is the finest biography of Burr to date.

—Anthony P. Inguanzo

BURTON, Sir Richard Francis, 1821–1890; English explorer and writer.

Bercovici, Alfred, *That Blackguard Burton!* Indianapolis, Bobbs-Merrill, 1962.
Brodie, Fawn M., *The Devil Drives: A Life of Sir Richard Burton*. London, Eyre and Spottiswoode, and New York, Norton, 1967.
Burne, Glen S., *Richard F. Burton*. Boston, Twayne, 1985.

Burton, Lady Isabel, *The Life of Captain Sir Richard F. Burton* (2 vols.). London, Chapman and Hall, 1893.

Dearden, Seton, *The Arabian Knight: A Study of Sir Richard Burton.* London, Barker, 1936; as *Burton of Arabia*, New York, McBride, 1937; revised edition, Barker, 1953.

Dodge, Walter Phelps, *The Real Sir Richard Burton.* London, Unwin, 1907.

Downey, Fairfax Davis, *Burton: Arabian Nights Adventurer.* New York and London, Scribner, 1931.

Edwardes, Allen (D. A. Kingsley), *Death Rides a Camel: A Biography of Sir Richard Burton.* New York, Julian Press, 1963.

Farwell, Byron, *Burton: A Biography of Sir Richard Francis Burton.* London, Longman, and New York, Holt, 1963.

Hastings, Michael, *Sir Richard Burton: A Biography.* London, Hodder and Stoughton, and New York, Coward McCann, 1978.

Hitchman, Francis, *Richard F. Burton, K.C.M.G.: His Early, Private and Public Life* (2 vols.). London, Sampson Low, 1887.

Rice, Edward, *Captain Sir Richard Francis Burton: The Secret Agent Who Made the Pilgrimage to Mecca, Discovered the "Kama Sutra," and Brought the "Arabian Nights" to the West.* New York, Scribner, 1990.

Richards, Alfred Bates ("An Old Oxonian"), *A Short Sketch of the Career of Captain Richard F. Burton.* London, W. Mullan, 1880.

Schonfield, Hugh J., *Richard Burton, Explorer.* London, H. Joseph, 1936.

Stisted, Georgiana M., *The True Life of Captain Sir Richard F. Burton.* London, H. S. Nicols, 1896; New York, Appleton, 1897.

Wright, Thomas, *The Life of Sir Richard Burton* (2 vols.). London, Everett, and New York, Putnam, 1906.

*

Two major biographies of Sir Richard Burton were published during their subject's lifetime. RICHARDS, writing as "An Old Oxonian," was a friend from college days who had become editor of the London *Morning Advertiser.* His brief, laudatory account is illuminating on Burton's personality and early life but contains much unreliable hearsay about later events. HITCHMAN was privileged to have access to an unpublished memoir by Burton himself, but he infuriated Burton by plagiarizing heavily not only from this work but from Burton's published writings. Hitchman's unacknowledged fidelity to the extremely outspoken memoir resulted in much embarrassment for Burton and his wife, with attacks on Burton in the press following publication of Hitchman's book.

Three years after Burton died, his widow, herself dying of cancer wrote a two-volume 1,200 page biography. LADY BURTON's idealized, romanticized portrait of her Rabelaisian spouse was intended—as she had once admitted—to "hide his faults from everyone," especially his attraction to eastern eroticism. Nevertheless, Lady Burton's bowdlerized life remains a major source, is quite readable, and happily contains many extracts from her husband's diaries and journals, which she later burned. Lady Burton's biography was soon followed by that of Georgi-

ana STISTED, Burton's niece, whose effusive biography is both a panegyrical defense of her uncle's more outrageous behavior and a diatribe against his "vain and bigoted wife."

The first decade of the 20th century brought two further biographies of Burton, by WRIGHT and DODGE, the latter intended as a rejoinder to the former's hostility. Wright was a friend and biographer of John Payne, whose translation of the *Arabian Nights* he accused Burton of plagiarizing. Norman Penzer, a folklorist who in the 1920s edited several of Burton's works and compiled an annotated bibliography, discounted Wright's charge and corrected numerous factual errors in his biography. The best that can be said for Wright is that he is equally rude to Richard and Isabel Burton, is gossipy and entertaining, and industriously collected a great number of apocryphal Burton anecdotes. In contrast, Dodge's admiring and much shorter sketch is factually accurate but pedestrian.

Almost a generation passed before three new lives of Burton appeared in the 1930s. DOWNEY and SCHONFIELD are largely derivative from previous biographies but sympathetic, lively, and free of Victorian prolixity and circumlocution. Less popularized and more scholarly is DEARDEN, although he too conducted little new research. These books are impressionistic portraits rather than comprehensive biographies. While good enough brief introductions to Burton in their time, they have been entirely superseded by later, more detailed studies.

In the 1960s yet another generation of writers discovered the Victorian daredevil. Although the books by BERCOVICI, EDWARDES, and FARWELL were marketed within a few months of each other, they have little in common. The first is a fictionalized potboiler, the second a volume in the pornographic "Julian Press Library of Sex Research," while the third is the first attempt to rewrite Burton's life using documentary sources other than the subject's own writings. Unfortunately Farwell, who claimed to have spent seven years researching his book (as well as retracing most of Burton's peregrinations), chose not to use footnotes, so that some of his conclusions—e.g., about the controversial relationship between Burton and fellow-explorer John Hanning Speke—lack authority. But despite this weakness and a rather dry style, Farwell's remains the most balanced of all the Burton biographies.

If Farwell is judicious, BRODIE is tendentious. The thesis of this professional biographer (who wrote of such diverse personalities as Mormon prophet Joseph Smith and Reconstruction politician Thaddeus Stevens) is that Burton was demon-driven by bizarre sexual fantasies to pursue the exotic and the erotic in a search for identity. This theme is hardly new with Brodie, and she underpins it here with an elaborate Freudian psycho-sexual analysis. Like Allen Edwardes before her (although she gives him no credit), Brodie argues that Burton was a satyr, that he was probably bisexual, and that much of his bedevilment was attributable to his mother's overpossessiveness and his prudish wife's frigidity. Brodie overstrains her questionable thesis but her book represents an industrious job of research into archival sources—and all her sources are cited. The narration is lucid and sprightly—although clarity would be improved by more maps and a chronology—and there is an excellent index and a good choice of illustrations.

After Farwell and Brodie, HASTINGS is anticlimactic. Novelist and playwright rather than scholar, in writing of Burton Hastings made his first venture into nonfiction (except for a short essay about Rupert Brooke). The result is indifferent. Although Hastings claims to have searched archives and conducted interviews, his book has no source notes and only sketchy acknowledgments. A modified stream-of-consciousness writing style and "recreated" dialogues do not strengthen credibility, any more than the numerous factual errors and other instances of hasty writing and poor editing. Hastings' peevish complaints about Brodie's methods and about the unwillingness of certain persons to reveal information in their possession suggest weaknesses in his own research techniques. The most useful feature of Hastings' biography is a partially annotated list of Burton's writing, more complete and detailed than the good one in Brodie.

Like other bio-bibliographical studies in the Twayne series, BURNE's work combines a sketch of the subject's life with criticism of his literary output. Burne adds nothing to the biographical details of Burton's life, and little to their interpretation. RICE, a journalist who previously wrote lives of Thomas Merton and Margaret Mead, reworks the familiar material entertainingly but does not advance scholarship about Burton. Rice notes that "many of Burton's letters (and much other material) are sequestered in private or government collections and much remains unread and unexamined," but he neglected to correct this deficiency.

—Don M. Cregier

BURTON, Richard, 1925–1984; Welsh stage and film actor.

Alpert, Hollis, *Burton.* New York, Putnam, 1986.
Bragg, Melvyn, *Richard Burton: A Life.* Boston, Little Brown, 1988; as *Rich: The Life of Richard Burton*, London, Hodder and Stoughton, 1988.
Cottrell, John and Fergus Cashin, *Richard Burton: A Biography.* London, Barker, 1971; as *Richard Burton, Very Close Up*, Englewood Cliffs, New Jersey, Prentice-Hall, 1972.
David, Lester and Jhan Robbins, *Richard and Elizabeth.* New York, Funk and Wagnalls, and London, Barker, 1977.
Ferris, Paul, *Richard Burton.* New York, Coward McCann, and London, Weidenfeld and Nicolson, 1981.
Jenkins, Graham, with Barry Turner, *Richard Burton, My Brother.* New York, Harper, and London, M. Joseph, 1988.

*

BRAGG's biography, the longest of those listed here, in cadenced, at times almost poetic prose, presents a psychological view of Burton. It includes what none of the others do: excerpts from the unpublished memoir of Philip Burton (Richard's "adoptive father," from whom the actor took his new last name) as well as entries from Richard Burton's unpublished notebooks, which Bragg estimates total about 350,000 words. These notes, taking up about half of Bragg's biography, are absolutely fascinating; they show Burton practicing to be a writer and are presumably truthful. Bragg writes intimately, sometimes too much so, as when the reader receives medical details of Elizabeth Taylor's illnesses.

Bragg paints vivid scenes in detail, causing the reader to sympathize with Burton's poor Welsh mining background, his drinking, his womanizing, his complex and ambiguous relationship with Elizabeth Taylor. He also discusses all of Burton's movies, both the failures and successes, as well as his plays and even his radio programs. While Bragg attempts to be evenhanded, his sympathy for Burton is clear. He feels that Burton "can too easily seem merely macho, boorish, boozy and short of sensitivity." He dwells on Burton's immense talent, his honesty, and his physical pain, seeing him as "the stuff of heroes" for returning to the stage after the Taylor divorce when his health was very bad. He also sees *Cleopatra* as a major cause of change in Burton: afterward he was "poisoned by guilt" and by "one woman who brought out the finest and the most destructive forces in him."

JENKINS, the actor's brother, in his turn snipes, understandably from his perspective, at Philip Burton: "The teacher was in need of a favourite, a young hopeful who could fulfil, by proxy, the dreams of a frustrated actor." The two had a "curious, close relationship." He states that the family as a whole, not just their father, made Philip Burton Richard's guardian: "For Philip Burton, as much as for Rich, it was a first claim to fame." The family did not go to Richard's Oxford performances since "we acknowledged, more readily than Phil Burton, I believe, that like every youngster Rich needed the chance to find his own way."

Whereas Bragg nearly canonizes Sybil Burton, Jenkins sees the marriage as "a quick dash for security" for Richard. Jenkins relates inside stories of family tensions and pride and cites examples of his brother's generosity. His account of the Burton-Taylor relationship seems fair, and while excusing Burton's "indiscretions as a game," he does admit to his brother's drinking and quotes from interviews to show "that my brother was capable of making a fool of himself."

COTTRELL AND CASHIN give a great deal of credit for Burton's success to his grammar school teacher Meredith Jones, as they say Burton himself did. Philip Burton comes off better than in Jenkins' account. The authors interviewed Burton's Welsh neighbors, relatives, Elizabeth Taylor, and Richard Burton himself, to paint a fairly rosy picture. They feel that Burton's womanizing was greatly exaggerated. The book's anecdotal style reads easily, just a step and a half up from fan magazine prose, using numerous clichés: "reaped a wild wind of scandal," and "the agony and ecstasy of living in Rome," for example.

DAVID AND ROBBINS also write almost fan magazine prose, presenting, unsurprisingly, many of the same anecdotes as Cottrell and Cashin in almost the same words. This is an adoring look at the famous couple, Burton and Taylor: "They were . . . our fantasies played out before us." David and Robbins spend several pages defending the pair, pointing out that today their relationship would not be scandalous. The divorce is blamed on Burton's drinking and womanizing.

ALPERT writes a straightforward, no-nonsense, intelligent, seemingly objective rendering of anecdotes and facts, focusing on Burton's life. He says his book is meant "to preserve an accurate image of Burton before he fades into time's distance." This clear-headed account would seem to do just that.

Welsh-born FERRIS did not interview Elizabeth Taylor, and Richard Burton would not help, although Ferris did reach some of Burton's relatives. He focuses on the life, frankly placing himself in many of the interview scenes. The style is not verbose, but straightforward and seemingly factual. He oozes less over the star than some of the other biographers. This nonpartisan account nevertheless does include negative comments by Anthony Quayle as to Burton's "gamesmanship," which one-upped Quayle on stage.

—Janet Overmyer

BYRON, George Gordon, Lord, 1788–1824; English poet.

Bellamy, R. L., *Byron the Man*. London, K. Paul, 1924.

Blessington, Marguerite, *Conversations of Lord Byron with the Countess of Blessington*. London, H. Colburn, 1834; revised as *Journal of the Conversations of Lord Byron*, New York, Scribner, 1893; London, Bentley, 1894.

Brent, Peter, *Lord Byron*. London, Weidenfeld and Nicolson, 1974.

Buxton, John, *Byron and Shelley: A Friendship Renewed.* Middletown, Connecticut, Wesleyan University Press, 1967; with subtitle, *History of a Friendship*, London, Macmillan, and New York, Harcourt, 1968.

Crompton, Louis, *Byron and Greek Love*. London, Faber, and Berkeley, University of California Press, 1985.

Drinkwater, John, *The Pilgrim of Eternity: Byron, a Conflict.* London, Hodder and Stoughton, and New York, G. Doran, 1925.

Galt, John, *Life of Lord Byron*. London, Colburn and Bentley, and New York, Harper, 1830.

Grebanier, Bernard, *The Uninhibited Byron*. New York, Crown, 1970; London, P. Owen, 1971.

Knight, G. Wilson, *Lord Byron: Christian Virtues*. London, Routledge, 1952; New York, Oxford University Press, 1953.

Knight, G. Wilson, *Lord Byron's Marriage*. London, Routledge, and New York, Macmillan, 1957.

Marchand, Leslie A., *Byron: A Biography* (3 vols.). New York, Knopf, and London, J. Murray, 1957.

Mayne, Ethel C., *Byron*. London, Methuen, and New York, Scribner, 1912.

Moore, Thomas, *Letters and Journals of Lord Byron: With Notices of His Life* (2 vols.). London, J. Murray, 1830 (also published as *Life of Lord Byron*).

Origo, Iris, *The Last Attachment*. London, Cape and Murray, 1949.

Quennell, Peter, *Byron: The Years of Fame*. London, Collins, and New York, Viking, 1935.

Quennell, Peter, *Byron in Italy*. London, Collins, and New York, Viking, 1941.

Raphael, Frederick, *Byron*. London, Thames and Hudson, 1982.

*

Byron's first biographer, MOORE, had known the poet well. Moore was a truthful and a kindly man, and these characteristics were likely to be in conflict when he was writing of someone whose reputation was so lurid, so contradictory, and so fascinat-

ing as Byron's. One feature, which later biographers were to find of the greatest importance, Byron's homosexuality, is omitted, perhaps more from incomprehension than from reticence. Moore is perhaps a little sentimental in his presentation of the last attachment to Teresa Guiccoli, writing as if the two were married to each other, rather than each to another person. He sees Byron as a born Romantic, and thus plays down such significant features as his strongly Augustan taste in literature, and his dislike of the work of his Romantic contemporaries. In the main, though, Moore achieved a friendly portrait, free from gross idealization of blatant scandal-mongering, which is more than can be said for many of his successors.

GALT, writing immediately after Moore, and in part against what he took to be Moore's amiable disposition to paint only the sunny side, presented Byron as one whose "dwelling was amidst the murk and the mist, and the home of his spirit in the abysm of the storm, and the hiding-places of guilt." Galt is terse about Teresa Guiccoli, whom he describes as a "buxom parlour-boarder." He saw himself, probably, as correcting, for the benefit of a serious British public, the over-lax tone of Moore.

Lady BLESSINGTON writes only about the last year of Byron's life, but as Byron was much given to reminiscence, regret and self-analysis, her account really includes a good deal from all periods of the life. She stresses Byron's detestation of cant and his claim to know his own faults better than anyone else could. She thought his professed bad opinion of mankind partly a pose. Blessington combines a sense, shared with Byron himself, of cosmopolitan superiority to English insular respectability with a determination not to be under the spell of a man who had fascinated so many women. Thus she says that his voice was "agreeable but effeminate"—a comment Byron would not have relished. She often conceals names with dashes, though often the identity is obvious enough. She regards Byron's love for Guiccoli as genuine and likely to be permanent, and presents him as utterly puzzled by his wife's motives for leaving him. He is shown as genuinely affectionate to his half-sister, Augusta, to the memory of his daughter, by Claire Claremont, Allegra, and to his daughter, Ada, about whom Byron said: "I am told she is clever . . . I hope not . . . above all I hope she is not poetical." In general, a more mellow, less outrageous, more normal man emerges in Lady Blessington's portrait.

In 1869–70, Harriet Beecher Stowe, an American with an immense reputation in mid-Victorian England, published articles based on conversations with Lady Byron, which aimed to vindicate the latter in her marital separation by maintaining that the reason was Byron's incest with his half-sister, Augusta Leigh. Interest and controversy were thus revived, but the next notable contribution was delayed until 1912, when MAYNE produced a full, well-documented account. This work contains a stinging rebuke to Mrs. Stowe in an appendix, where Mayne alludes to the suppressed poem *Don Leon* and the supposed "marriage secret," which were later to assume much greater importance in the work of Knight (see below). Mayne stresses the strength and lasting importance of Byron's early Harrow School friendships. Her Byron is, moreover, a consistent character, not so very different, except in genius, from the common run of humanity. Only his weaknesses were better documented and more discussed than those of most people. The author makes full use of the public's new disposition to accept greater frankness on intimate matters. BELLAMY's work is largely dependent on

Mayne's. Though not an important contribution, it is readable and elegant. The following quotation will give the flavour: "Men seek perfection in the object of their love; women imperfection, but in this case each found rather too much of the usual desideratum."

DRINKWATER, too, is anxious to remove the "full Mephistophelean panoply" from his subject. He attributes much of the scandal surrounding Byron to wild, unsubstantiated gossip. After a lengthy discussion of the incest issue, Drinkwater concludes that he would not give a verdict against him if put on a jury, but hints that it may have been true all the same. Claire Claremont, and some others are said to have "thrown themselves" at Byron, whose character becomes more weak-willed and well-meaning than the general tradition had allowed.

QUENNELL's two books have the smooth expertise of the practised biographer, turning to a new subject, about which he is not obsessed. His Byron, "far from shunning disaster," had a "sense of guilt that enjoined that he should go in search of it." Quoting extravagant statements of love and constancy, he comments that "the element of truth is strictly relative." His Byron is endlessly puzzled by his own character and destiny.

ORIGO's book is a useful specialized study of Byron's relation with Teresa Guiccoli, making use of abundant documentation. Origo confirms the view of other writers that Byron had a chameleon nature by showing him behaving entirely according to Italian conventions. She shows both partners as trampling ruthlessly on whatever stood in their way, but of the two it was Byron who sometimes played the moralist. Byron did not want women to understand him (as his wife disastrously had) but to amuse him. Teresa is shown as exceedingly strong-willed, silly but not stupid. Origo quotes Disraeli, who spoke of Byron's "strong common-sense," but shows him also as yearning for rehabilitation in England.

KNIGHT's two books are deeply-felt, and may perhaps disappoint admirers of his Shakespeare criticism by their special pleading. Byron's hatred of cant, intolerance of lies, his detestation of cruelty are set against sexual errors, largely venial, and often exaggerated by report. Knight's second book (1957) is speculative and hardly convincing in its use of literary evidence. But its presentation of Byron as constitutionally bisexual, and of his flaunting other vices, real and imaginary, to cover a genuine shame about this, may well carry conviction. Knight regards the incest story as probably untrue, but in any case a blind offered by Lady Byron to cover the "marriage secret," her experience of an unnatural form of intercourse, in which she was treated as a boy. He sees a recurring pattern of "idealized and passionate love of youth, both sexual and maternal, accompanied by instincts of protection and education, and widening out to human service in general. . . . " He prophecies that his praise of Byron's moral worth will appear obviously right in future times.

MARCHAND's biography is the best-documented, the fullest, and on the whole the best in existence. He refuses to state a thesis, thus implicitly criticizing many of his predecessors. He does not think Byron much more inconsistent than most people, only more honest in admitting inconsistency. Byron did not try to suppress the facts of his life, and many of the remaining mysteries are due to the fact that after his death his friends did. He accepts the evidence for the initiation into sexual play by a servant when Byron was nine or ten: hence much of the precocity and premature world-weariness. Byron was "too idealistic to refrain from blowing bubbles, and too realistic to refrain from pricking them." Marchand's handling of sources and of the work of earlier writers is exemplary.

BUXTON offers a very useful specialized study of Byron and Shelley, whom he sees as on the whole more important in each other's lives than anyone else, especially in the stimulus each gave to the other's poetic gift. He regards Byron's early Calvinist training as a persistent and underrated influence. Agreeing with this, GREBANIER sees Byron engaged in the search for the unpardonable sin, in order to confirm his reprobation. Grebanier, disagreeing with Knight, makes the incest theme central. Early titillation in Byron's experience, he claims, was responsible for a lifelong separation in his mind between the ideas of love and sex, and also for his extreme comtempt of hypocrisy. The book claims for itself more originality than it achieves.

BRENT's book, which has an introduction by Lady Longford, is a picture book derived from secondary sources, but sensible in its judgments. More than most writers on Byron, Brent stresses Byron's religious impulses. He interprets the last journey to Greece as a courting of death, since "if he did not feel, he did not feel that he lived." RAPHAEL's book is a vulgar and unnecessary picture book, whose low quality is well-instanced in its first sentence: "Byron's was a life which, as the movie trailers used to say, had everything."

The only contribution of importance since Marchand and Buxton is CROMPTON's work, expanded from a chapter in a proposed history of homosexuality. Crompton acknowledges his debt to Wilson Knight, but is more analytical and circumstantial than previous writers in his account of the part played by Byron's bisexual temperament in the formation of his whole character and life.

Also worth mentioning is Doris Langley Moore's *The Late Lord Byron* (1961), a capable discussion of the events affecting future biographical writing in the immediate aftermath of Byron's death.

—A. O. J. Cockshut

CABRINI, Mother Frances Xavier, 1850–1917; Italian-born American nun and saint.

A Benedictine of Stanbrook Abbey, *Saint Frances Xavier Cabrini.* London, Burns and Oates, 1948.

Borden, Lucille Papin, *Francesca Cabrini: Without Staff or Script.* New York, Macmillan, 1945.

Di Donato, Pietro, *Immigrant Saint: The Life of Mother Cabrini.* New York, McGraw-Hill, 1960.

Farnum, Mabel, *The Life of Mother Cabrini, American Saint: A Story for Youth.* New York, Didier, 1947.

Joan Mary, Sister, *Mother Cabrini.* Staten Island, New York, Apostolate of the Press, 1952; as *Mother Cabrini, by a Daughter of St. Paul,* Boston, St. Paul Editions, 1977.

Keyes, Frances Parkinson, *Mother Cabrini: Missionary to the World.* New York, Farrar Straus, 1959.

Lorit, Sergio C., *Frances Cabrini.* New York, New City Press, 1970.

Martignoni, Angela, "*My Mission is the World*": *The Life of Mother Cabrini*, translated by Clarence Tschippert. New York, Vatican City Religious Book Company (Catholic Action Library), 1949.

Martindale, C. C., S. J., *Mother Francesca Saverio Cabrini: Foundress of the Missionary Sisters of the Sacred Heart*. London, Burns and Oates, 1931.

Maynard, Theodore, *Too Small A World: The Life of Francesca Cabrini*. Milwaukee, Bruce Publishing, 1945.

Saverio de Maria, M.S.C., *Mother Frances Xavier Cabrini*, translated by Rose Basile Green. Chicago, Missionaries of the Sacred Heart, 1984 (originally published as *La Madre Francesca Saverio Cabrini*, Turin, Societa Editrice Internazionale, 1927).

Windeatt, Mary Fabayan, *St. Frances Cabrini*. Rockford, Illinois, Tan Books and Publishers, 1989.

*

English-language readers may now start where Cabrini's biographers usually do, with Mother SAVERIO. Saverio joined the Missionaries of the Sacred Heart in 1894 and witnessed much of Cabrini's later life. She provides a good narrative and first accounts of anecdotes that later biographers use. Translator Rose Basile Green adds an index and bibliography, rarities in Cabrini literature.

Saverio's theoretical framework has two elements. One is Divine Providence. Providence seems to have worked directly to cause Cabrini's successes: there is little attention to Cabrini's personal gifts. Obstacles are also due to Providence and are tests rather than limitations of personality or conflicts between people or institutions. This approach allows Saverio to examine in detail both the difficulties Mother Cabrini surmounted and the work she accomplished. The second element is the centrality of Cabrini's community. Saverio's focus on the Missionaries results in a smooth narrative. Cabrini's personal faith leads naturally to the spirituality integral to the Missionaries' community and to this biography.

Cabrini's progress to canonization inspired several authors. MARTINDALE feared not doing justice to events so recent that many participants were still alive; his book is primarily a commentary on Saverio. A BENEDICTINE OF STANBROOK ABBEY is more adventurous, putting names and faces to the obstacles Saverio had attributed to Providence. His most original contribution is using Cahenslyism to explain opposition to Cabrini's work.

MAYNARD's strength is his attention to historical context. Although his book lacks scholarly apparatus, the preface mentions use of Saverio, Cabrini's *Letters*, canonization material, and oral history. Maynard includes information on Cabrini's Missionary community, but he also sees Cabrini as a figure in the Italian diaspora. In discussing the supposed Italian neglect of their faith, Maynard describes both the economic pressures and the political and cultural background influencing the immigrants. He contributes the thesis that Cabrini provided a figure around whom Italian Catholics could rally, rather than clinging to provincial loyalties or abandoning Catholicism for nationalism. Maynard's attention to context permits him to explain Cabrini's anti-Protestant sentiments as congruent to the times in which she lived.

Rather than Cahenslyism, Maynard concentrates on the men whose "help" proved unhelpful: New York Archbishop Michael Augustine Corrigan, caught between pastoral and fiscal responsibility; and the Scalabrinian fathers, whose financial ineptitude and insistence that the Missionaries be subordinate to them nearly wrecked Cabrini's New York work. Such a concentration allows Maynard to elaborate on Cabrini's personality, notably her business acumen. However, Maynard neglects the possibility that personality quirks were exacerbated by the systemic favoring of men and clergy, at the expense of women and laity.

BORDEN emphasizes Cabrini's sanctity. This approach leads her to dramatize the many mysterious coincidences throughout Cabrini's life, beginning with the flock of doves that heralded her birth. It also leads her to highlight official recognition of Cabrini's saintliness, which creates problems when the Church seemingly fails to recognize Cabrini's religious precocity. For example, to explain why Cabrini was not permitted to receive Communion until her early teens, it is not enough for Borden to explain that that was the custom then; she has to discuss Pius X's advocacy of childhood communion. These digressions can interfere with a smooth narrative.

Borden marks a transition to biographies suitable for pious rather than scholarly or popular reading. MARTIGNONI is a case study of such pious works. Martignoni skips over the complications in Cabrini's life, such as her years in Antonia Tondini's religious community. Inaccuracies render her narrative dramatic, but suspect. Martignoni, though, has a useful chronology of Cabrini's activities. Similarly, Sister JOAN MARY neglects the Missionaries' tending the sick in a New Orleans yellow fever epidemic to concentrate on the sisters' making scapulars to protect the endangered. Sister Joan's immigrants do not neglect their faith; they are hampered by a language barrier. The 1977 edition uses Cabrini to espouse modern causes, holding up Cabrini's large family as an example to birth control and abortion advocates.

Novelist DI DONATO's biography introduces a new sort of hagiography. In Di Donato, Cabrini is a saint because she performs works of mercy and elicits the love of the people. Di Donato revives an aspect first treated in Maynard, and gives himself reason to write warm-hearted vignettes of Italian life, especially in New York City. LORIT also focuses on Cabrini's service. He goes beyond her service to the Italians and suggests that by 1895 Cabrini was concerned to internationalize her Missionaries, who were increasingly engaged in international service. His work contains little inaccuracies (only Lorit claims no one met Cabrini at the dock on her first New York voyage), but it is sober, complete, and readable.

Cabrini has inspired several juvenile biographies. WINDEATT is a read-aloud or beginning book. Windeatt's story is accurate, though incomplete and pitched at a child's level of understanding. FARNUM is for children able to read for themselves; it omits detail, ignores Cabrini's historical situation, and portrays the Italians as helpless people in need of leadership. KEYES is a good example of the burdens juvenile biographies about Italian-American saints have to bear. The book must be set up so a child can read a chapter at a sitting; Keyes accordingly invents a character to deliver monologues on Cabrini for the benefit of two parochial school girls. The book tries to explain the finer points of Catholicism, and to inculcate American as well as religious values, a role for which Cabrini is not always suitable.

Only Keyes criticizes Cabrini's prejudice against Nicaragua's "local customs" of not providing sufficient clothing for female servants, casual acceptance of irregular sexual liaisons, and illegitimacy.

Sister Mary Louise Sullivan, M.S.C., is finishing a work which is more carefully documented than previous biographies, and which promises to provide more information on Cabrini's life before 1889 and on her advocacy of Italian immigrants in the United States.

—Mary Elizabeth Brown

CAGNEY, James, 1899–1986; American film actor.

Bergman, Andrew, *James Cagney.* New York, Pyramid Books, 1973.

Dickens, Homer, *The Films of James Cagney.* New York, Citadel, 1972.

Freedland, Michael, *Cagney: A Biography.* New York, Stein and Day, 1974; as *James Cagney,* London, W. H. Allen, 1974.

McGilligan, Patrick, *Cagney: The Actor as Auteur.* Cranbury, New Jersey, A. S. Barnes, 1975; revised edition, 1982.

Offen, Ron, *Cagney.* Chicago, H. Regnery, 1972.

Schickel, Richard, *James Cagney: A Celebration.* Boston, Little Brown, and London, Pavillion, 1985.

Warren, Doug, with James Cagney, *James Cagney: The Authorized Biography.* New York, St. Martin's and London, Robson Books, 1983.

*

One of the first full-length treatments of Cagney, by film critic SCHICKEL, reverses the usual trend among star biographers by delivering a well-considered analysis of Cagney's career centering on his anti-hero character, the economics, power, and maneuvers of film-making in the 1930s, and film reviews and criticism. Interviews with Cagney are a prime source of Schickel's readable book.

Two film biographies from the 1970s briefly but effectively cover Cagney's life and film persona. At 249 pages, DICKENS' book is more than a fan-oriented photo collection. A 31-page life-and-career sketch, discussing Cagney's role as an anti-hero, leads into the meat of this book, an encyclopedia compilation of data not only on Cagney's films but also his Broadway plays, including plot synopses, credits, critical reviews, notes, and photographic stills, making Dickens an excellent source book for Cagney films and plays. BERGMAN, a film historian, is not afraid to discuss failures or critical mistakes. His book, a critical film-by-film review, effectively ties Cagney's life and development as an actor into his career. Based mostly on contemporary articles, the book is a bit eulogistic concerning Cagney himself, perhaps due to the need to fit a series format. It contains a filmography.

Offen and Freedland provide the first detailed, book-length accounts of Cagney's rise to stardom. Aimed mainly at Cagney buffs, the lengthy volume by OFFEN covers Cagney's life

and times in an interesting, anecdote-filled narrative, to which Cagney did not, as the book notes, add his own voice. Although lack of the subject's participation is not necessarily a problem, some self-admittedly dramatized conversations and thoughts make the book more valuable as a fictionalized biography portraying the mood of a time and place than as a source on Cagney's life. Writing with the cooperation of Cagney and his close friends, FREEDLAND is one of the first to illumine the modest, honest man behind Cagney's screen image. Rather than detracting from the book, occasional Hollywood publicity-type passages set a tone in placing Cagney in the proper context of his time, the Depression-era Hollywood of escapist image and fantasy. Covering Cagney's life in detail, Freedland's work is very useful as a reference on Cagney and as a history of Hollywood's golden years, with Cagney at its center.

McGILLIGAN refreshingly concentrates on a well-researched, readable analysis of Cagney's career, studio politics, and development as an actor throughout his career at the expense of Hollywood gossip. The book's thesis of the actor's contribution to his film character and roles engenders a discussion of Cagney's films more balanced than the usual eulogisms of film biographies. Revised in 1982 to take advantage of the appearance of Cagney's autobiography, the book includes a filmography and bibliography.

Written with the extensive cooperation of Cagney and his close friends in the last years of their lives, WARREN's book is a warm account of Cagney that makes the reader feel familiar with its subject, particularly in descriptions of Cagney and his old friends in their latter years. It covers particularly well such controversies as Cagney's battles with his studio, though it steers clear of others. In places it is thus more of a life and times, as authorized biographies tend to become, than an analysis. Nonetheless, the work's extensive interviews at times are almost a collective memoir. There is the usual filmography and an index, although no bibliography.

In addition to the book-length works on Cagney, there is a large body of studio and entertainment industry material, most of it designed to promote a film. This material is topical and detailed, but must be carefully sifted for reliability. Cagney awaits a perceptive, substantially impartial biography assigning studio legend and publicity its place in his life, rather than becoming a part of the text. Almost any biography of Cagney should be read with his own life story, *Cagney by Cagney* (1976), an unassuming, self-effacing, entertaining collection of stories and spoonfuls of philosophy, well-grounded in the economic and social reality of movie-making, that meld to show Cagney's battle to the top in the hard-bitten, money-grabbing entertainment industry of the 1920s and 30s.

—Steven A. Agoratus

CALDERÓN DE LA BARCA, Pedro, 1600–1681; Spanish playwright and poet.

Lund, Harry, *Pedro Calderón de la Barca: A Biography.* Edinburg, Texas, Andres Noriega Press, 1963.

Parker, Alexander A., *The Mind and Art of Calderón: Essays on the "Comedias"*, edited by Deborah Kong. Cambridge and New York, Cambridge University Press, 1988.

Trench, Richard C., *An Essay on the Life and Genius of Calderón*. 2nd edition, London, Macmillan, 1880.

*

Unfortunately, Calderón has not been the subject of a scholarly biography, quite a loss considering that he is one of the most important figures in Spanish drama. Lund (see below) is the only full-scale biographical work available in English; however, other works, not available in translation, contribute to our knowledge of Calderón's life. Two of them, Cristóbal Pérez Pastor's *Documentos para la biografía de Don Pedro Calderón de la Barca* (Madrid, 1905) and Emilio Cotarelo y Mori's *Ensayo sobre la vida y obras de Calderón* (Madrid, 1924), form the foundation for the study of Calderón's life. The former is particularly useful because of its collection of legal documents pertaining to Calderón. Another work, though not exclusively a biography, José I. Tejidor's *Calderón de la Barca* (Madrid, 1967), has a lengthy biographical section in which the author takes every year in the playwright's life and highlights what was happening not only in Spain but elsewhere around the world that might be of significance to the Spaniards; this yeoman approach has the advantage of providing a quick reference guide. And, finally, Ciriaco Morón Arroyo, in *Calderón: pensamiento y teatro* (Santander, 1982), devotes a few pages in his first chapter to Calderón's biography, noting how tragic events in the dramatist's life are reflected in his works, but does not provide any new information on the writer's life.

TRENCH devotes a chapter to Calderón's life; however, because this work is an introduction to the dramatist, he spends a substantial portion of the chapter discussing the intellectual milieu and Spanish Golden Age dramatic practices. What he does say about Calderón is culled from Calderón's first biographer, Juan de Vera Tassis, in his preface to *Primera Parte de Comedias* (Madrid, 1685). While Trench did correct Vera Tassis throughout, he did not have available to him many of the documents uncovered by Pérez Pastor. Although the essay is full of factual information about events in Calderón's life, it provides little insight into his personality.

While one might forgive Trench's scholarship and style because of the date of his book, one cannot be as kind to LUND, except to say that, mercifully, according to the publisher only 300 copies were printed. As Lund says in the Preface, this essay is to be an introduction to the English-speaking public to this Spanish dramatist, yet, whenever he quotes from Calderón's plays, Lund fails to provide the necessary translations. Because not much is known about Calderón's personality, Lund speculates on how several of his plays may be used to understand the dramatist. Although Lund says that he conducted research on Calderón's life in Spain, the only piece of "valuable" information he "uncovers" is that Calderón had an illegitimate son— not much of a discovery. This biography is poorly organized, inelegantly written, and of little if any use to those interested in learning about Calderón.

PARKER, one of the greatest authorities on Calderón, spends a few pages in his latest work discussing the playwright's life. However, he does not really give a detailed account of the events in Calderón's life, but rather focuses on certain key incidents and the impact they had on his work. Although throughout the rest of the book Parker frequently refers back to Calderón's life, he does so as part of his critical evaluation and commentary on the plays, rather than as a means of shedding new light on the details of this great playwright's life.

—Gisela Casines

CALLAS, Maria, 1923–1977; Greek-American operatic soprano.

Ardoin, John, *The Callas Legacy*. London, Duckworth, and New York, Scribner, 1977.

Ardoin, John, *Callas at Julliard: The Master Classes*. London, Robson Books, and New York, Knopf, 1987.

Callas, Evangelia, with Lawrence G. Blochman, *My Daughter, Maria Callas*. New York, Fleet Publishing, 1960; London, L. Frewin, 1967.

Linakis, Steven, *Diva: The Life and Death of Maria Callas*. Englewood Cliffs, New Jersey, Prentice-Hall, 1980; London, P. Owen, 1981.

Lowe, David A., editor, *Callas, as They Saw Her*. New York, Ungar, 1986; London, Robson Books, 1987.

Meneghini, G. B., with R. Allegri, *My Wife Maria Callas*, translated by Henry Wisneski. New York, Farrar Strauss, 1982; London, Bodley Head, 1983.

Segalini, Sergio, *Callas, Portrait of a Diva*, translated by Sonia Sabel. London, Hutchinson, 1981.

Stancioff, Nadia, *Maria: Callas Remembered*. New York, Dutton, 1987; London, Sidgwick and Jackson, 1988.

Stassinopoulos, Arianna, *Maria: Beyond the Callas Legend*. London, Weidenfeld and Nicolson, 1980; as *Maria Callas: The Woman Behind the Legend*, London, Hamlyn, and New York, Simon and Schuster, 1981.

Wisneski, Henry, *Maria Callas: The Art Behind the Legend*. New York, Doubleday, 1975; London, R. Hale, 1976.

*

The circumstances in which Maria Callas often found herself invited so much attention from the media that her career was over-covered, and many thousand words and pictures existed before the more popular biographers produced snap judgments between covers. Later, a number of pictorial histories emerged (vital to understanding such a charismatic character as Callas), and then the serious chronologies of performances and recordings. Eventually appeared the impartial and more scholarly biographies.

Evangelia CALLAS, the singer's mother, had the closest blood-tie, but the book about her daughter is no work of art. It is back-biting, petty and goes no further than 1966. It does contain a few items of unique information and family pictures unavailable elsewhere, but these are only of marginal interest.

LINAKIS, a so-called cousin whom Callas scarcely knew, seized the opportunity to write a "candid biography," which is neither, but it also contains interesting pictures. LOWE's book is a patchwork affair, interesting in some details, but no complete biography. Other peoples' views on Callas and a survey of her performances (done better elsewhere) comprise part of this volume; fellow artists contribute compliments and Callas is allowed to include a few of her own views.

STANCIOFF, for some time Callas' secretary, offers the coolest and, at the same time, a very close account from one who had no need to cower, and received Callas' friendship, respect and confidence. The firsthand coverage of *Medea*, the Pasolini film, is valuable—as are accounts of Callas' whims and childish fancies. Stancioff gives the best account of Onassis' behaviour and life on his yacht.

STASSINOPOULOS offers the best all-around biography, emphasising the cruelty of the public and of opera house managements (Covent Garden honourably excepted) which alternated with adoration and heroine-worship. She expresses as well the Diva's own moods and behaviour, especially toward her family: "New York, the perfect haven for *monstres sacrés*, had decided that Maria had overstepped the limit. It was one thing to be eccentric, extravagant, temperamental, tempestuous and quite another to be mean and ungrateful to your mother." The three persons who did Callas most enduring harm were her mother, Elsa Maxwell and Aristotle Onassis, as Stassinopoulos explains candidly. She also details—as far as is possible—the sinister mystery of Callas' death and immediate cremation. "In the hushed luxury" of her Paris house she was "suffocating, too despairing and too resigned even to cry for help."

MENEGHINI has written his own account of 12 years as Callas' husband. It comes over well in translation as a humble, eventually pathetic story from a somewhat crude provincial, out of his depth in Society and the principal centres of music. Meneghini cites numerous, credible examples of Callas' love for him in the early days and leaves no doubt that he successfully launched her career. But he fails to understand that the 28 years which separated their ages could never remain bridged; and when Onassis arrived on the scene, Meneghini admits he was beaten.

WISNESKI's large-format book provides photographs for 34 of the mature opera performances as well as three from the Greek years; for the film of *Medea*; and for her master classes. He provides very detailed performance statistics and a discography of all recordings. ARDOIN, who probably possesses more personal information on Callas than any other individual, has extracted and sifted valuable statistics for his 1982 volume. He alludes to many of Callas' foibles and tantrums in the studio that were all symptomatic of the insecure, fragile workaholic. Many of her colleagues (and rivals) play their part in this book.

ARDOIN's 1987 book displays Callas toward the end of her life accomplishing a triumph as teacher. This volume contains a self-revealing, thumb-nail autobiography (taken down from life), which is often self-critical. It is followed by 74 musical items, widely selected, mostly arias and not all for sopranos. They give an unusual indication of Callas' musical perception, knowledge and technical accomplishment. On every page, among the pertinent musical examples, is a pearl of wisdom: "This aria is a killer. It is difficult at the beginning and more difficult at the end. Before you try to sing it, plan it out carefully, cold-bloodedly . . . " (from *Medea*).

One has to go back to Stassinopoulos every time for the real clues to Callas' character: her inability to come to terms with life in an adult manner; her attachments to far older men (her Greek-American godfather, Eddie Bagarozy, Meneghini, Serafin, Visconti and Onassis); and her rages at those who were satisfied with the less than perfect. There is, however, much left to be written: a psychological study is needed.

—Alan Jefferson

CALVIN, John [*born* Jean Chauvin], 1509–1564; French theologian and reformer.

Bouwsma, William J., *John Calvin: A 16th-Century Portrait*. London and New York, Oxford University Press, 1987.
Ganoczy, Alexandre, *The Young Calvin*, translated by David Foxgrover and Wade Provo. Philadelphia, Westminster, 1987; Edinburgh, T. Clark, 1988 (originally published as *Le Jeune Calvin: Genèse et Évolution de sa Vocation Réformatrice*, Wiesbaden, F. Steiner, 1966).
Hunt, Robert N. C., *Calvin*. London, Centenary Press, 1933.
MacKinnon, James, *Calvin and the Reformation*. London and New York, Longman, 1936.
McGrath, Alister E., *A Life of John Calvin: A Study in the Shaping of Western Culture*. Oxford, UK, and Cambridge, Massachusetts, Blackwell, 1990.
Parker, Thomas H. L., *John Calvin*. London, Dent, and Philadelphia, Westminster, 1975.
Reyburn, Hugh Y., *John Calvin, his Life, Letters and Work*. London and New York, Hodder and Stoughton, 1914.
Walker, Williston, *John Calvin, the Organizer of Reformed Protestantism 1509–64*. New York and London, Putnam, 1906.
Wendel, François, *Calvin, The Origins and Development of His Religious Thought*, translated by Philip Mairet. London, Collins, and New York, Harper, 1963 (originally published as *Calvin, Sources et Évolution de sa Pensée Religieuse*, Paris, Presses Universitaires, 1950).

*

Four full-length biographies of Calvin appeared in English during the period 1906–36. WALKER's biography set new standards for English-language Calvin studies in the 20th century. Although the study by REYBURN drew liberally on original sources, its importance has since diminished. MacKINNON and HUNT draw substantially on the same source materials as the earlier biographers. It is generally agreed that there is little to distinguish these four biographies, each of which is now superceded. Inevitably, they are significantly dependent, to a greater or lesser extent, on the 16th-century biographies of Théodore de Bèze (Beza) and Nicolas Colladon, and the work of French writers, especially A. Lefranc's *Jeunesse de Calvin* (1888) and the seven-volume study by E. Doumergue, *Jean Calvin, les hommes et les choses de son temps* (1899–1927). Since there is no way of verifying much of the material included in the 16th-century biographies, an element of uncertainty will invariably continue to attend the reconstruction of Calvin's career, especially its earlier period prior to 1536.

The post-war period has seen an explosion in Calvin studies, with a corresponding increase in the historical and theological competence of more recent biographies. New standards were set by WENDEL, whose command of the existing primary and secondary source materials was then unrivaled. Wendel's work is partly biography and partly a superb exposition of Calvin's religious ideas, with the latter illuminating aspects of the former. Biographically, Wendel is dependent for his knowledge of Calvin's earlier period on Doumergue and Lefranc, and he tends merely to summarize, rather than critically evaluate, their findings. Although Wendel has subsequently been corrected on points of detail, his study is still widely regarded as perhaps the most reliable biography of Calvin available.

GANOCZY's major study of the young Calvin provides a detailed examination of Calvin's career up to his exile in Strasbourg (1538). It is easily the best study available of Calvin's early period, and includes detailed analysis of two major questions concerning this part of his career: at what point, and for what reasons, did Calvin cease to be a moderate Fabrisian reformer and move over to the more radical views of the Protestant Reformation? Ganoczy is generally regarded as having provided his readers with a reliable and perceptive account of Calvin's actions and motives on both counts. Calvin himself speaks of a 'sudden conversion' (*subita conversio*); Ganoczy argues that this is a theological interpretation of history, rather than a description of what happened to Calvin. In other words, Calvin has interpreted a series of events, perhaps spaced out considerably over time, as pointing to the intervention of God in his life. In discussing the sources upon which Calvin drew in constructing the first edition of his *Institutes of the Christian Religion* (Basle, Switzerland, 1536), Ganoczy is able to demonstrate Calvin's dependence on earlier works of Luther, as well as illuminate other possible sources. Of especial importance at this point is his discussion of the thesis, attributed to the German scholar Karl Reuter, that Calvin was decisively influenced during his Parisian period by the Scottish theologian John Mair (or Major), who was active at the Collège de Montaigu around the period when Calvin is thought to have been in residence. This theory has had considerable influence within modern Calvin scholarship, and in dismissing it Ganoczy demonstrates that at no point during his formative period does Calvin refer to, quote, or otherwise engage with Mair. One of the deficiencies of Ganoczy's study is its strict chronological delimitation. Calvin's career after 1538 is virtually unexamined, except insofar as individual aspects of it (especially Calvin's writings of the 1550s) cast light upon his earlier period.

PARKER's study, written at a popular level, and strongly hagiographical at points, spans Calvin's entire career. Parker's account of events is generally reliable, although his interpretation of events is rarely critical of either Calvin's actions or intentions. The 200-page biography is notable chiefly for its questioning of the conventional dating of Calvin's Paris period, traditionally held to have begun in the fall of 1523. Arguing that a 17th-century source (Desmay's *Remarques sur la vie de Jean Calvin*) misunderstands an entry in the Noyon register of 1523, and basing himself upon a study of the procedures and conventions of the University of Paris in the late Middle Ages, Parker suggests that Calvin may have begun his training at Paris as early as 1520 or 1521, with the move to the university of Orléans taking place two or three years earlier than the conventional date. Although Parker's account of Calvin's movements during the period 1520–30 has yet to win general acceptance, it has served to highlight the potential unreliability of at least some of the traditional sources on which the confident statements of the earlier biographers were based.

BOUWSMA deliberately eschews the term "biography," preferring the more nuanced "portrait." Nevertheless, his recent volume is unquestionably biographical. Although short on new facts concerning Calvin's career (the conventional account is merely restated, without significant modifications or additions), Bouwsma's major contribution to Calvin scholarship has been to elucidate the intellectual and cultural world against which the drama of Calvin's career was played out. In particular, Bouwsma highlights the importance of the notion of 'anxiety' in understanding Calvin's actions and outlooks on a number of central points. The Calvin to emerge from Bouwsma's account is considerably more subtle than the conventional biographies allow. Calvin is shown to be a complex character, steeped in a knowledge of the humanistic scholarship of his period. Bouwsma argues that most of what is genuinely creative in Calvin's thought is to be ascribed to his humanism, rather than to his allegiance to the specific ideas and methods of the Reformation. Rich in quotations from Calvin, this biography illuminates, better than any other, aspects of the complex intellectual world that Calvin inhabited and changed. Bouwsma explores the manner in which Calvin is at the same time medieval and modern and he discusses the implications of this for the historical evaluation of Calvin. Bouwsma also identifies certain strands of Calvin's thought which, in his view, account for the successes of Calvinism, not least his willingness to ground his ideas in the political realities of the 16th century.

McGRATH's 350-page biography places Calvin more firmly in the social and political world of the 16th century. Concentrating on historical events, he argues for a revision of the traditional understanding of Calvin's Paris period (suggesting, for example, that he did not attend the Collège de La Marche), and for an increased awareness of the influence of existing Genevan practices and conventions on Calvin's thought. McGrath also traces Calvin's growing impact on his native France during his lifetime, and clarifies the relation between Calvin's religious thought and the emergence of capitalism, engaging in critical dialogue with Max Weber and his followers. Unlike the other biographers discussed, McGrath does not end his account with Calvin's death, but traces his impact on the shaping of modern western culture, initially through Calvinism, and subsequently through a cluster of social, political, religious, and economic attitudes that have had considerable influence on the formation of modern North American culture.

—Alister E. McGrath

CAMUS, Albert, 1913–1960; French writer.

Brée, Germaine, *Camus*. New Brunswick, New Jersey, Rutgers University Press, 1959.

Lottman, Herbert R., *Albert Camus: A Biography*. London, Weidenfeld and Nicolson, and New York, Doubleday, 1979.

McCarthy, Patrick, *Camus: A Critical Study of His Life and Work*. New York, Random House, and London, Hamilton, 1982.

Parker, Emmett, *Albert Camus: The Artist in the Arena*. Madison, University of Wisconsin Press, 1965.

Thody, Philip, *Albert Camus 1913–60: A Biographical Study*. London, Hamilton, 1961; New York, Macmillan, 1962.

*

The earliest English-language studies of Camus paid relatively little attention to the details of his biography, emphasizing instead his ideas and literary art. After Camus' death, however, the second editions of two of these books, by BRÉE and THODY respectively, focused more on the details of his life. They derived some of these details from an earlier study in French by Quilliot (1956), but Brée in particular also had the benefit of direct contact with Camus and some wartime knowledge of his native Algeria.

The first quarter of Brée's book is biographical; the remainder analyses Camus' essays, novels and plays. Brée is valuable for her description of Camus' Algerian background and emphasizes its importance in his literary work. Thody has more to say about the specifically political element in Camus' life both in North Africa and in France. He provides more detail than Brée, and pays attention to the autobiographical element in Camus' writings. Thody's book, subtitled "a biographical study," analyses Camus' literary works while moving chronologically through the phases of Camus' career. Certainly the most detailed and most balanced general biography to appear prior to 1979, Thody combines detachment and common sense with clear expository gifts.

Despite Thody's objectivity, PARKER considers that Thody probably undervalues Camus' political pronouncements by tending to regard them as too idealistic and lacking in practical efficacy. Parker defends Camus' political positions strongly but sensibly. In what is essentially an account of Camus' journalistic writings, Parker includes a good deal of biographical information from 1934 to 1960. Although Camus' earlier years are necessarily ignored, particular light is thrown on his life in the Algeria of the 1930s and the France of the 1950s. Parker offers useful biographical detail on such topics as Camus' attitude toward the U.S.S.R., his feelings about the Spanish Civil War, the Moslem population of Algeria, the Algerian War, the Hungarian revolt of 1956, etc., all of which helps to fill out our sense of Camus' character and of his highly moral view of politics.

LOTTMAN's massive book (750 pages) is strictly biographical, towering above all others in the amount of new and detailed information it contains. Lottman corrects many errors of fact contained in earlier works and even shows Camus' own belief about his family origins to be mistaken. He reports everything produced by what he terms his "field investigation"—the tracking down of a vast number of individual witnesses and the uncovering of a mountain of documentary evidence. His energy and persistence enable him not only to correct the previously accepted genealogy of the Camus family but to produce many new facts concerning Camus' schooling, his reading and general intellectual development, his enthusiasm for sport, the first onset of tuberculosis, his considerable debt to the Acault family (relatives on his mother's side), the oddly paradoxical role of Jean Grenier in his relatively brief membership in the Communist Party, his travels with his wife and Yves Bourgeois through Germany, Austria, Czechoslovakia and northern Italy in 1936, and the tragic collapse of his first marriage because of his young wife's drug addiction.

Like Brée, but in much more detail, Lottman describes many of the contexts within which Camus lived and worked. For example, in his account of Camus' early experience in Paris, working on *Paris-Soir*, Lottman offers considerable background information concerning the *Paris-Soir* organization. He also provides an illuminating account of the Gallimard dynasty and its role in French publishing. Lottman is the first biographer to provide details of Camus' stay in Oran between January 1941 and August 1942, as well as new references to the account Camus received from the Algerian writer, Emmanuel Roblès, of a typhus epidemic near Tlemcen in the spring of 1941. This has obvious significance for the writing of *The Plague*.

Whereas previous American and British authors are vague in their accounts of Camus' activities in occupied France, Lottman went to great lengths in tracing contacts in order to provide a detailed picture of Camus' role. While he was obviously obliged to take some information on trust, Lottman appears to have cross-checked evidence where this proved possible. He is also careful to avoid romantic exaggeration, and Camus emerges the more convincingly as a result. The reader is also helped by a description of the "Combat" organization with which Camus was associated, and by valuable general comments on some of the moral and intellectual dilemmas to which the experience of occupation and resistance gave rise.

Some aspects of Camus' post-war activities are less satisfactorily treated by Lottman than by Parker (e.g., the controversy with Mauriac over the punishment of wartime collaborators), and Lottman is also rather reserved in his account of the Sartre/Camus debate over *The Rebel*. Nevertheless, Lottman's predominant attitude is one of general approval, though one could, of course, criticize him on the grounds that his appetite for facts too often distorts his sense of discrimination. That Lottman should describe the precise route taken daily by the young Camus to his primary school, and later to the *lycée*, appears superfluous. Similarly, we hardly need to know that Camus' first wife, Simone Hié, had a trousseau which included "sixteen bedsheets, four bolsters, six pillow cases, a set of tableware, and for her personal use two pairs of pyjamas, a dishabille, a bed jacket, six slips, six nightgowns." Nevertheless, Lottman's remains an outstanding biography and a unique source of knowledge concerning Camus' life.

In a concluding note Lottman writes, "I am certain that I corrected errors, but I must have committed new errors. Let the reader with pertinent information contribute to later biographies or a revision of this one by calling attention to them." McCARTHY, whose biography appeared three years after Lottman's, partly responds to the latter's remark by interviewing a number of individuals who were also interviewed by Lottman, some of whom gave rather different replies in the two instances. In general, however, McCarthy depends heavily on Lottman's research, differing from him in two main ways: by adding an analysis of Camus' philosophical and political ideas, and by adopting a much more critical and dismissive attitude to his subject. Thus McCarthy asserts that Camus "was a bad philosopher and . . . has little to tell us about politics." This is part of a general intention to "cut through the myths" surrounding Camus. He describes the tributes paid by most earlier critics as "ridiculous" and wishes to replace them with the image of "the unsaintly, anguished and curiously indifferent Camus."

McCarthy uses the same term "ridiculous" to characterize Camus' political position between the outbreak of World War II and the fall of France in 1940. He agrees that this position was held by many European left-wingers, but upbraids Camus in particular for sticking to absolute moral principles in the sphere of politics and also presents him as an appeaser who "placed much hope in Neville Chamberlain." Later, of course, despite his fragile health, Camus took some part in the underground movement in occupied France (though not until 1943 or early 1944). McCarthy is not slow to claim—no doubt with some justification—that after 1945 Camus allowed his role as a resister to be exaggerated just as he allowed his earlier membership in the Communist Party of Algeria to be underplayed.

While it is no doubt healthy that a distinctly iconoclastic biography of Camus should exist, it is a pity that so many of McCarthy's statements should fly in the face of the facts (e.g., his claim that young Frenchmen have "almost ignored" Camus since his death). McCarthy remains informative and very readable concerning the facts of Camus' life, though many readers familiar with Camus' thought and literary achievement will find him inadequate and unsatisfactory on the subject of Camus' contribution to 20th-century intellectual life.

—John Cruickshank

CAPOTE, Truman, 1924–1984; American writer.

Brinnin, John, *Truman Capote: Dear Heart, Old Buddy*. New York, Delacorte, 1986; as *Truman Capote: A Memoir*, London, Sidgwick and Jackson, 1987.

Clarke, Gerald, *Capote*. New York, Simon and Schuster, and London, Hamilton, 1988.

Garson, Helen, *Truman Capote*. New York, Ungar, 1980.

Inge, Thomas, editor, *Truman Capote: Conversations*. Jackson, University Press of Mississippi, 1987.

Reid, Kenneth, *Truman Capote*. Boston, Twayne, 1981.

Rudisill, Marie and James Simmons, *Truman Capote: The Story of His Bizarre and Exotic Boyhood by an Aunt Who Helped Raise Him*. New York, Morrow, 1983.

*

The number of full-scale Capote biographies is limited, in part because his status as a "media celebrity," often eclipsing his literary fame, produced numerous biographical articles and interviews. CLARK's work provides the definitive text on Capote. Although Clarke devotes little attention to Capote's early years in Alabama, his depiction of Capote's life from the time he moved to New York in 1932 is exhaustive—the result of eight years' work. Clark details the many famous friends and lovers Capote had, with a necessary emphasis on Capote's homosexual relations. The publication of *In Cold Blood* (1965) signaled the high point of Capote's literary career, while he reached his social apes with "the party of the decade," the 1966 event Clarke de-

scribes as Capote's self-coronation. Clarke then shows how Capote's life degenerated into a dependency on alcohol, drugs and short-lived affairs until his death in 1984. Clark's biography reads like that of a Hollywood star since Capote was always surrounded by the glitterati. In 547 pages the reader becomes fully acquainted with Capote the writer, wit, celebrity, homosexual.

Although not in the form of a traditional biography, INGE's book also provides informative insights into Capote and his life. This book contains 29 interviews with Capote, ranging from his first in 1949 to a "self-interview" in 1980. Conducted by prominent figures such as David Frost, Gloria Steinem, and Andy Warhol, the interviews highlight how information about Capote's background/biography changed throughout the years as Capote manipulated this information to create his public persona. Inge's book is also resourceful since it contains biographical commentary by the individual writers to augment the interviews. This addition makes the discrepancies in Capote's account more pronounced and interesting.

BRINNIN's book derives from his personal journals covering the lengthy friendship and "intimate association" he had with Capote. In a gossipy, fragmented presentation Brinnin cites Capote's various and fleeting relationships with other men, his disdain for academics, his celebrity status, and some of Capote's more famous homosexual friends, such as Tennessee Williams and Montgomery Clift. This "memoir" does not deal with Capote's youth or family at all.

GARSON's treatment, written before Capote's death, contains a brief section on Capote's childhood before moving into a depiction of his later years, with an emphasis on his 23 year affair with Jack Dunphy (Capote dedicated *In Cold Blood* to Dunphy and Harper Lee, his childhood friend). Garson concentrates on the 1950s and 60s and examines the period of Capote's "nonfiction" novel writing, noting very well Capote's mercurial behavior, his extensive travels, and how his increased drinking and sexual meanderings signaled his deterioration.

REID's text delves more extensively into Capote's childhood and the elderly cousins and uncle he lived with. The breakup of his mother's marriage and Capote's being shipped to Alabama are chronicled, along with how Capote's early teachers at first thought he was retarded because of his poor school work (his IQ was later found to be far into the "genius" range). Reid depicts the early New York years, which marked his movement away from being the somber, "southern" writer into the wittier, more sophisticated author. Reid also examines the elements that constituted Capote's public persona versus Capote as literary figure and is incisive, almost painfully so, in his depiction of the grueling efforts Capote directed toward the writing of *In Cold Blood*.

RUDISILL AND SIMMONS' treatment details, in individual chapters, those people who made Capote's "family" in Alabama. More than half of this book discusses these figures, their background, and their eccentricities, rather than Capote himself. The authors declare this to be an accounting of Capote's "bizarre" boyhood, and their recounting of his early family and experiences supports the claim. Rudisill was Capote's aunt, who took him to New York in 1931 for delivery to his mother. (Rudisill indicates September 1931; Clarke cites September 1932.) Rudisill then shuttled back and forth between New York and Alabama as family matters dictated. Her permanent return to the

South signaled the end of Capote's relations with his family in Alabama. Rudisill's book ends with a lament about how Capote refused to visit them, would not return calls, or answer their letters.

—Kenneth A. Howe

CARLYLE, Thomas, 1795–1881; Scottish essayist and historian.

Burdett, Osbert, *The Two Carlyles.* London, Faber, 1930; Boston, Houghton Mifflin, 1931.

Campbell, Ian, *Thomas Carlyle.* London, Hamilton, and New York, Scribner, 1974.

Froude, J. A., *Thomas Carlyle: A History of the First 40 Years of His Life, 1795–1835* (2 vols.). London, Longman, and New York, Harper, 1882.

Froude, J. A., *Thomas Carlyle, 1834–81: A History of His Life in London* (2 vols.). London, Longman, and New York, Harper, 1884.

Froude, J. A., *My Relations with Carlyle.* London, Longman, and New York, Scribner, 1903.

Hanson, Lawrence and Elizabeth Hanson, *Necessary Evil: The Life of Jane Welsh Carlyle.* London, Constable, and New York, Macmillan, 1952.

Holme, Thea, *The Carlyles at Home.* London and New York, Oxford University Press, 1965.

Kaplan, Fred, *Thomas Carlyle: A Biography.* Cambridge, Cambridge University Press, and Ithaca, New York, Cornell University Press, 1983.

Symington, A. J., *Some Personal Reminiscences of Carlyle.* London, A. Gardner, 1886.

Symons, Julian, *Thomas Carlyle: The Life and Ideas of a Prophet.* London, Gollancz, and New York, Oxford University Press, 1952.

Wilson, David A., *The Truth About Carlyle.* London, Alston Rivers, 1913.

Wilson, David A., *Life of Carlyle* (6 vols.). London, K. Paul, 1923–34.

Wylie, W. H., *Thomas Carlyle: The Man and His Books.* London, M. Japp, 1881.

*

WYLIE's book was written before Carlyle's death and published very soon after it. It is somewhat humourless, crediting the ever-voluble and many-volumed Carlyle with having learnt in the cradle that ''Silence is golden.'' But, though it shows a failure to connect theory and practice, or preaching and conduct, in Carlyle's life, it is not uncritical, initiating a complaint that we may wish more successors had followed about the violence and brutality of Carlyle's reaction to the draconian policies of Governor Eyre, for example.

Far and away the most important of all works on Carlyle remains that of J. A. FROUDE. Froude's work is central for two separate reasons: it is easily more distinguished than any other writings on Carlyle, and it became the focus of most of the suc-

ceeding controversies, and the starting-point for later writers. Controversy began when Froude published Carlyle's own *Reminiscences* and his wife's *Letters and Memorials*, annotated after her death, in a spirit of severe self-criticism, by her sorrowing husband. Family opinion was divided; Froude was supported by surviving siblings but bitterly attacked by Carlyle's niece Mary. Soon after, when the four-volume biography appeared, the controversy intensified. Froude, remembering how Carlyle had despised the reticence and false adulation of many of the biographies of his time, and sincerely anxious to present a truthful portrait of a man he revered as a prophet, and had known intimately for many years, startled the public with his revelations of Carlyle's selfish ill-temper, railing contempt for most of humanity, and impossible character as a husband. His aim was to show a contrast between the greatness of the man's mind and prophetic imagination and the pettiness of much of his everyday life, though even here Carlyle is portrayed as always honest and truthful, in his own way loyal to wife and friends.

No doubt, Froude made too absolute a distinction between the life and work. He is reluctant to admit that the emotional violence, the self-centred rhetoric, the hasty, prejudiced judgment that marred Carlyle's everyday behaviour were also found in works like *The Nigger Question* and *Shooting Niagara*, where Carlyle so patently misjudged the long-term consequences of the Reform Bill of 1867. Strange, too, is the way Froude, the son of a High Church cleric and the early friend and associate of the leaders of the Oxford Movement, allows to pass unchallenged Carlyle's strange conviction that the Calvinism of his parents was historic Christianity, instead of an aberrant and rapidly passing sectarian extremism. But these blemishes by no means prevent the book from being a great one. With abundant and detailed evidence Froude offers one of the most moving portraits of the grandeur and littleness of human nature ever composed.

On Carlyle's marriage, Froude had a specially difficult problem. He had become convinced, upon what seems now to be sound evidence, that Carlyle was impotent. It seemed impossible, in the 1880s, to say this. What he did say, about Carlyle's unreasonable ill-temper, proved startling enough. But he wrote a justificatory piece, published posthumously, under the title *My Relations With Carlyle*, which gives his reasons for his view about Carlyle's impotence. An acrimonious controversy, begun with the biography, was exacerbated by this volume. Crichton-Browne and Alexander Carlyle launched a bitter attack, and WILSON, who proclaimed Carlyle, with more fervour than intelligibility, ''the Confucius of the English-speaking races,'' devoted many volumes and most of the rest of his life to the refutation of what he regarded as vile calumny. The work was unfinished when he died in 1933, and the final volume was written by his nephew. The two delusions, that Carlyle was the wisest of all God-given guides to human life, and that, being so, he must have been as saintly as he was wise, rob this painstaking work of much of its value. As argument it is weak, and though it contains some new material, the fulness of Froude's treatment, and the latter's intimate knowledge of the man, mean that Wilson's additions have only a limited interest. The intimate connection between the work of Froude and Wilson may be summed up with a characteristic quotation from the latter: ''The impartial critic is reluctantly (!) driven to use very strong language indeed, and declare that in historical fidelity Mr. Froude's account . . . is inferior even to Froude's other writings.'' This about perhaps the most eminent writer, with the single exception of Johnson, to devote himself seriously to biography in the English language.

SYMINGTON's work, which is only a brief sketch, is interesting for its attempt to maintain two incredible propositions, that Carlyle was a lifelong believer in the religion taught by his parents, and that he was not really a difficult husband, but only appeared to be so, out of false modesty, when he commented after her death on his wife's journals. He implied absurdly that Froude's High Church background prevented true insight on the first point.

BURDETT's book is a shrewd character sketch, which tends to correct previous exaggerations. He shows convincingly how Carlyle's "teaching" was marred by his personal egoism. He has a deep respect for Froude, and shows that the outcry against him had been partly due to the public's sentimental adulation for an aged seer to whom people no longer listened very attentively. Burdett regards marital discord as inevitable in a marriage between a wife who craved constant attention and a husband who desired to be left alone. His most damning judgment is not easy to dissent from: the hero worship to which Carlyle summoned mankind blinded mankind to his worship of success and selfishness.

The HANSONs offer the most detailed study of the marriage, which confirms, in the main, Froude's conclusions. SYMONS' book is little more than an abbreviated summary of Froude. HOLME's book is a useful monograph on the Chelsea house, of which she was curator, and on the daily lives of the Carlyles and their various suffering servants, who were prevented from going to bed by Carlyle's selfish preference for smoking his pipe in their quarters at midnight. CAMPBELL fails to make good his claim to a new view, and his defence of some of Carlyle's uglier characteristics is lame. For instance, he suggests that if Carlyle had seen the West Indian "niggers" at close quarters, he would no doubt have been much more sympathetic than he was in *The Nigger Question*. This is little more than wishful thinking; Campbell is, perhaps, yet another Scottish writer who appears to suppose that the honour of Scotland is somehow involved in Carlyle's moral rectitude. Much the fullest and best recent study is that of KAPLAN, which is well-written and well-balanced. Its judgments are inclined to be a little bland, but at least the reader is provided with a sound basis for judgments of his own. Though it does not rival Froude in literary power, it is based on wider sources, and can be recommended to anyone for whom Froude's work may be dauntingly long.

—A. O. J. Cockshut

CARNEGIE, Andrew (Morrison), 1835–1919; Scottish-born American industrialist and philanthropist.

Alderson, Bernard, *Andrew Carnegie: From Telegraph Boy to Millionaire.* London, C. A. Pearson, 1902; as *Andrew Carnegie: The Man and His Work,* New York, Doubleday, 1902.
Farrah, Margaret Ann, *Andrew Carnegie: A Psychohistorical Sketch* (dissertation). Ann Arbor, Michigan, University Microfilms International, 1982.

Hacker, Louis, *The World of Andrew Carnegie.* Philadelphia, Lippincott, 1968.
Hendrick, Burton J., *The Life of Andrew Carnegie* (2 vols.). New York, Doubleday, 1932; London, Heinemann, 1933.
Livesay, Harold C., *Andrew Carnegie and the Rise of Big Business.* Boston, Little Brown, 1975.
Swetnam, George, *Andrew Carnegie.* Boston, Twayne, 1980.
Wall, Joseph Frazier, *Andrew Carnegie.* New York, Oxford University Press, 1970.
Winkler, John K., *Incredible Carnegie.* New York, Vanguard Press, 1931.

*

Carnegie's first biographer of note, the eulogistic ALDERSON, concentrates on Carnegie's rise to power and riches in industry and finance. Appearing at the beginning of Carnegie's long philanthropic career, the work is best read as part of the body of commentary on Carnegie during his lifetime. An exposé intended for the leisure reading of a general audience, WINKLER's account of Carnegie's career is entertaining and lively, with informative descriptions of steel-making and industrial processes. The work is more a chronicle of such key events in Carnegie's career as the Homestead strike than an integrated portrait of the man. Winkler occasionally stresses minor matters or stretches evidence to maintain his narrative's dramatic continuity. Nonetheless the work contains some sharp insights into Carnegie's character. Read as a companion to both Alderson and Hendrick, Winkler's work presents an important counterpoint to the otherwise eulogistic theme of early Carnegie biography and reminds us of the polarity of opinion Carnegie aroused during and after his life.

The first well-researched, serious biography, the two volume HENDRICK, depends heavily upon papers and interviews supplied by Carnegie's wife and business associates. A life-and-times concentrating on chronology and detail rather than analysis and controversy, Hendrick's text is well-organized, easy to read, and entertaining, with reproductions of source materials illustrating textual points. Interviews with family and contemporaries lend the text a lively tone, successfully capturing the spirit of Carnegie's vibrant personality. With an index and a bibliography, Hendrick's biography is useful for a detailed familiarization with Carnegie's life and career and was long considered the standard work.

HACKER gives the purest and fullest exposition of a theme running through almost every biography of Carnegie, the Industrial Revolution's remaking of America. Hacker surveys the political, social, and intellectual climate of the 19th century to conclude (in a reaction to revisionist histories) that the large-scale industrialization built the U.S. into a powerful, wealthy nation in a short period of time. The last quarter of the book focuses on Carnegie and his career as representative of the 19th-century businessman made rich and powerful by the Industrial Revolution. Hacker's book is characterized by balanced and careful research and methodology. The book's economic theory and history will perhaps most benefit the advanced reader.

Examining Carnegie's reputation as an author, SWETNAM summarizes, by subject, writings and speeches attributed to Carnegie and illustrates their place in his life in a biographical sketch. Part of the ongoing scholarly debate as to the attribution, value, and motivations of Carnegie's utterances and philosophies, the book concentrates on concise recapitulations and evaluations rather than historical analysis or literary criticism. The work best serves as a bibliography of Carnegie's writings and does a good job of indicating his role as a spokesman of business and the Industrial Revolution.

One of the first full-length biographies to present a balanced, analytical view of Carnegie, WALL's is an extensively documented, well-organized, very readable work. Wall masterfully brings together, with perspective and humor, the social, economic, and technological circumstances of the Industrial Revolution in a rich narrative of Carnegie's rise. Concentrating on the public life of Carnegie, using papers unavailable to other researchers, the work delicately traces the machinations and often unabashed about-faces Carnegie performed in reconciling his role as an owner and capitalist with that of preacher of peace and friend of labor. Wall's is the standard work on Carnegie, and the source for in-depth treatment of such specific subjects as the Homestead strike.

LIVESAY concentrates on Carnegie's leading role in the growth of the steel business to mammoth proportions during the 19th century. This work traces the evolution from early in Carnegie's career of several managerial, financial, and manufacturing innovations. Tailored to the size standards of the *Library of American Biography* series, the book leaves prolonged discussions and documentation to lengthier biographies. A concise, readable, well-researched survey with a bibliography, the work is a good starting point for familiarization with Carnegie.

FARRAH gives full and formal treatment to the private Andrew Carnegie. Her well-documented analysis, based on psychoanalytic theory but not burdened with psychological jargon or pedantry, brings the lesser-known aspects of Carnegie's personality and emotions to the forefront in a lively, appealing style. Farrah weaves together Carnegie's thoughts and feelings as a thinker and writer as well as industrialist and philanthropist to arrive at solidly reasoned motivations for his accomplishments. Direct textual references to the greater body of Carnegie scholarship bring continuity and perspective to the overall portrait of the man. The work defines technical and psychological terms, and contains a bibliography. It is best read after familiarization with Carnegie's life and exploits in Hendrick, Wall, and Livesay.

—Steven Agoratus

CARROLL, Lewis [*born* Charles Lutwidge Dodgson], 1832–1898; English writer and mathematician.

Clark, Anne (Anne Clark Amor), *Lewis Carroll: A Biography.* New York, Schocken, and London, Dent, 1979.

Collingwood, Stuart Dodgson, *The Life and Letters of Lewis Carroll.* London, Unwin, and New York and London, T. Nelson, 1898.

Green, Roger L., *Lewis Carroll.* London, Bodley Head, 1960; New York, H. Z. Walck, 1962.

Hudson, Derek, *Lewis Carroll.* London, Constable, 1954; revised as *Lewis Carroll: An Illustrated Biography,* Constable, 1976.

Kelly, Richard, *Lewis Carroll.* Boston, Twayne, 1977; revised edition, 1990.

Lennon, Florence Becker, *Victoria Through the Looking-Glass: The Life of Lewis Carroll.* New York, Simon and Schuster, 1945; London, Cassell, 1947; revised as *The Life of Lewis Carroll,* New York, Collier, 1962.

Moses, Belle, *Lewis Carroll in Wonderland and at Home: The Story of His Life.* New York and London, D. Appleton, 1910.

Pudney, John, *Lewis Carroll and His World.* New York, Scribner, and London, Thames and Hudson, 1976.

Reed, Langford, *Life of Lewis Carroll.* London, W. and G. Foyle, 1932.

Wood, James P., *The Snark was a Boojum: A Life of Lewis Carroll.* New York, Pantheon, 1966.

*

Immediately upon Carroll's death, his nephew, COLLINGWOOD, put together and published the "official" life of Carroll, a 400-page volume that both Hudson and Kelly (see below) consider more a pious memorial than a critical, evenhanded view. It is nevertheless a valuable source compiled by a man who knew Carroll and his world firsthand. Rev. T. B. Strong, a man who also knew Carroll intimately, wrote a much shorter essay about him for the *Cornhill* in March 1898, that provides a more rational view.

Isa Bowman's recollections of her relationship with Carroll, *The Story of Lewis Carroll, Told for Young People by the Real Alice in Wonderland, Miss Isa Bowman* (London, 1899; as *Lewis Carroll as I Knew Him,* with introduction by Morton N. Cohen, New York, 1972), though not biography proper, nevertheless contains interesting insights into what was probably Carroll's most important relationship with a girl/woman. In 1902, Florence Milner wrote a short biography, "Lewis Carroll: A Biographical Sketch," for *Alice's Adventures in Wonderland and Through the Looking-Glass* (Chicago, 1902), which includes early drawings and excerpts from nonfictional works, as well as a consideration of Carroll's general artistic ability.

MOSES' biography, written for children, contains some critical evaluation, a few materials not in the previous biographies (mainly discussions of Carroll's various word games), and the famous photograph of Carroll as a young man seated pensively in a chair.

REED's biography appeared on the 100th anniversary of Carroll's birth. More a collection of fond recollections by those who knew Carroll, the work nevertheless offers some critical evaluation of the works. Apparently, Reed was also able to see some correspondence between Carroll and Ellen Terry that has since disappeared (though Terry's autobiography also contains references to it).

LENNON's biography, first published in 1945, is an extensive study (387 pages) of both Carroll's psychology and the times he lived in. Lennon is not afraid to draw possible inferences, and she has provided future scholars with possibilities for debate. Unfortunately, the work is not well organized. B. J. Thompson (*Catholic World,* May 1945) states: "It is a book for psychiatrists and historians, but not for simple-minded lovers of Alice. Such readers will be inclined to think the whole thing outjabberwocks 'Jabberwocky.'" The work includes an index and illustrations. It was revised in 1962 and reprinted with a new introduction by Lennon in 1972.

In 1954, Roger Lancelyn Green published "The Real Lewis Carroll" (*Quarterly Review,* January 1954), an important discussion of Carroll's life that evaluates previous biographies and attempts to dispel many of the myths. In the same year, HUDSON gained access to the letters Carroll wrote to his family and to Macmillan, several documents that Duncan Black discovered at Christ Church, Oxford, concerning Carroll's period as Curator of the Common Room, and prior-to-publication viewing of *The Diaries of Lewis Carroll* (edited by Roger Lancelyn Green, London and New York, 1954; reprinted with supplements, 1971). These new sources allowed Hudson to write what remains the best biography of Carroll. It includes three appendices: "Last Memories of Lewis Carroll by the Late Viscount Simon, Mrs. A. T. Waterhouse, Miss H. L. Rowell and Mrs. Arthur Davies"; "Introduction to 'The Guildford Gazette Extraordinary' by Lewis Carroll"; and "Der Jammerwoch" (the German translation of "Jabberwocky"); as well as an index, notes and references, and a few black-and-white photographs and samples of Carroll's writing. Hudson avoids, even disparages, psychoanalytic interpretation, yet in a seemingly contradictory move he includes analysis of Carroll's handwriting at several points and even delves into phrenology.

Hudson is at his best when discussing Carroll at the height of his life and career; the book is little more than an annoying patchwork of correspondence when dealing with the early and later years. There is a good discussion of the possible origins of various portions of the two Alice books, and of Carroll's picky concerns over the actual publishing of the books. Hudson takes up other elements of the Carroll mystique, such as his relationships with young girls and apparent lack of interest in mature women, but not in great depth; Hudson tends to view Carroll in a positive, innocent light in these matters.

But Hudson is not just exonerating Carroll of all his faults. He reveals the less attractive side of Carroll and discusses his eccentricities, leaving an impression of a man to be admired for a certain kind of genius, a man who was very generous (more willing to give away money than to loan it), though extremely shy (possibly because of his stuttering), who was able to understand and relate to children but not adults, who could be extremely stubborn, and who really did have some psychological problems. Even so, a final analysis of Hudson must admit his protective attitude toward Carroll.

GREEN's biography briefly discusses Carroll's early life, beginning years at Oxford, and his writing up through the Alice books. It contains a good photograph of Carroll, and a list of Carroll's publications. This, along with Green's many other publications on Carroll (often containing biographical information), are all worthwhile studies. However, Green's above-mentioned essay is still perhaps his most important contribution.

WOOD's biography is an amusing book for young readers that attempts nevertheless to deal with some serious concerns, such as Carroll's sexual oddities. David Levine's drawings make a good complement to the writing. Wood's book has a vitality about it that older children should find enjoyable. It contains no index.

PUDNEY's brief biography, though well written and presenting thoughtful discussions of Carroll's failures (e.g., his attempts to further mathematical education), his nonsexuality, the many problems with "Sylvie and Bruno," as well as his successes, is mainly of value for its many illustrations, including many of Carroll's own photographs and drawings. Also included are such interesting illustrations as Quinten Massys' *Ugly Duchess* (the

inspiration for Tenniel's Duchess), a picture of Mary Badcock (the model for Tenniel's Alice), and some caricatures of Carroll by Harry Furniss.

CLARK's biography includes 40 illustrations, extensive references, a selected bibliography, and an index. It is a thorough, well-researched biography by the former secretary of the Lewis Carroll Society and editor of its journal, "Jabberwocky." Clark is thus in a good position to know about recent studies on Carroll. She presents Carroll as a typical Victorian, moral and upright—perhaps a correct response to the less kind interpretations in light of Carroll's correspondence, which at times demonstrates a conscientiousness pushed to absurdity. Clark discusses Carroll's artistic development beginning with his childhood attempts to amuse his siblings, and she offers some criticism on his adult works. While her biography is basically sound, her obvious determination to avoid conjecture leaves it a bit dry. It is a good companion volume to Hudson's earlier biography.

KELLY's study aims principally to show Carroll's mastery of the art of nonsense and need to bring order to chaos. It incorporates materials by Morton N. Cohen, Edward Guiliano, and others that have appeared since Clark's biography. Included is a brief chronology, notes and references, a far from complete annotated bibliography, and an index. The first chapter, appropriately titled "Life and Time," is a brief, straightforward biography, while the rest of the work is literary criticism.

—Harry Edwin Eiss

CARTER, Jimmy, 1924–   ; American political leader, 39th president of the United States.

Glad, Betty, *Jimmy Carter: In Search of the Great White House*. New York, Norton, 1980.

Kucharsky, David, *The Man from Plains: The Mind and Spirit of Jimmy Carter*. New York, Harper, 1976; Condon Collins, 1977.

Lasky, Victor, *Jimmy Carter: The Man and the Myth*. New York, R. Marek, 1979.

Mazlish, Bruce, and Edwin Diamond, *Jimmy Carter: A Character Portrait*. New York, Simon and Schuster, 1979.

Meyer, Peter, *James Earl Carter: The Man and the Myth*. Kansas City, Kansas, Sheed Andrews, 1978.

Miller, William L., *Yankee from Georgia: The Emergence of Jimmy Carter*. New York, Times Books, 1978.

Wooten, James T., *Dasher: The Roots and the Rising of Jimmy Carter*. New York, Summit Books, and London, Weidenfeld and Nicolson, 1978.

*

All of the Carter biographies appeared during a five-year period beginning in 1976, the year of Jimmy Carter's rise from obscurity to defeat incumbent Gerald R. Ford and capture the presidency. Although there have been books focusing on different aspects of Carter's presidency, there has been no new biography in a decade.

Each of the seven biographies follows one of four biographical types: religious, psychoanalytic, narrative, and the slam. The first Carter biography, which came out during the 1976 presidential campaign, is one of two that interprets Carter primarily through his religious beliefs. KUCHARSKY, a writer for *Christianity Today,* identifies Carter's evangelical ethos, along with his born-again experience, as the keys to understanding the former president. Using secondary sources, Kucharsky accounts for Carter's attitudes and behavior as logical applications of his religious principles.

A problem with the book is that Kucharsky ignores other important factors, such as Carter's southern heritage, his rural roots, and his military years, that help to explain Jimmy Carter. Another problem is that Kucharsky, obviously thrilled at the prospect of an evangelical running for president, is too eager to find only truth and beauty in Jimmy Carter. His book is rife with statements such as "Carter has always tried to answer even the toughest questions in easy terms and plain language." Kucharsky concludes that the time is right for a leader like Jimmy Carter, but he provides no careful argument that would convince readers to reach the same conclusion.

The other biography that focuses on the importance of Carter's religious views is the work by MILLER. Instead of emphasizing Carter's evangelical roots, Miller, who teaches ethics at Indiana University, argues that Carter fundamentally represents a continuation of traditional New England Puritanism with its emphasis on diligence, thoroughness, and ceaseless efforts at self-improvement. In addition, Miller views Carter's spoken affinity for the teachings of the great Protestant theologian Reinhold Niebuhr to be authentic. He suggest that Carter's frequent statement of his intention to make government as moral as the people was not a cynical campaign appeal, but an effort to apply a part of Niebuhr's notion of the link of Christianity to politics. Miller argues that Carter has a Niebuhrian view of politics as a self-critical struggle for social justice. Politics as struggle fits well with the understanding that Carter is essentially a Yankee Puritan.

Miller's book is similar to Kucharsky's in that both lack citations, are favorable to Jimmy Carter, and depend greatly on Carter's own words for their characterizations. Miller's book is distinguished by more extensive research, interviews with many significant Carter associates, at least a somewhat critical perspective, and a persuasive case for Carter as Puritan Niebuhrian. Nevertheless, it is perceptive commentary, not a definitive biography. Miller's argument is imaginative, but not tied directly to Carter's religious actions. The reader needs to learn more of how Carter's religious beliefs have manifested themselves in his behavior. As with the Kucharsky book, Miller's work is too one-dimensional to convey a full portrait of the man.

The biography that does focus on Carter's actions is WOOTEN's narrative following Carter's life through the 1977 resignation of budget director Bert Lance. A *New York Times* reporter, Wooten uses a you-are-there style in an unsystematic yet sympathetic story of Carter's life. Lacking citations, an index, and even a table of contents, Wooten rambles through his impressionistic tale. Strangely, in light of his background as a Presbyterian minister, Wooten pays little attention to the role of religion. While some biographies are so analytical and so in search of meaning that they neglect to convey the events of the

subject's life, Wooten tells us what happened in great detail, with many anecdotes. With no framework for understanding, however, the anecdotes often seem irrelevant.

Both slam biographies are subtitled *The Man and the Myth,* and both authors find a gap between the popular image of Jimmy Carter and their perception of him.

MEYER compares Carter's campaign statements with the results of his first two years in office, and he is right that President Carter did not deliver on a good number of the promises made by candidate Carter. A problem with the book is that Meyer does not account for this discrepancy in any reasonable manner. A strong case can be made that Carter's management style and outsider image, so useful in capturing the presidency, inhibited his ability to govern. This type of analysis is absent. Much of Meyer's book is unsubstantiated charges and simple name-calling. One 50-page chapter, labelled "The Weirdo Factor," explains that Carter is a Southern Baptist and proceeds to misrepresent Carter's religious views and those of mainstream Southern Baptist congregations. This book is unfair to Carter, not careful scholarship, and uninteresting.

The LASKY slam is nastier than Meyer's. Lasky's Carter is driven entirely by ambitions with no regard for decency, morality, and truth. To support this view Lasky has seemingly compiled every charge made by anyone about Carter. The problem is that Lasky makes no effort to corroborate charges, but simply lists them with the implication that they are valid. Perhaps the ultimate problem with Lasky's book is that, despite the title, the author fails to dispel any myths about Carter. There is nothing new in this book regarding either Carter's political life as governor and president or his private life. What the reader does learn is that Victor Lasky's disdain for Carter is so extreme that the author ignores the basic standards of biographers to calumniate Jimmy Carter.

The psychobiographies of Carter, by Mazlish and Diamond, and by Betty Glad, are both good books. MAZLISH AND DIAMOND, a collaboration between a political historian and a journalist, state their intention to write an "interpretive biography: an account relating the major themes of Jimmy Carter's life one to the other." After studying Carter's behavior and his words, they concluded that his actions and policies emerged from six traits: a strong sense of belonging, a drive to excel, self-confidence, self-control, a Tolstoyian understanding of leadership as appealing to the goodness of the people, and his comfort with personal contradictions and ambiguities (e.g., both a liberal and a conservative). The book explains Carter's life as manifestation of these six traits.

The authors interviewed Carter's personal and political associates and made extensive use of written sources, especially his autobiography. Their biography is an accurate description of Carter's life and an interesting analysis of the man. The book's weakness is the common problem of psychobiographies: the circularity in analysis. The authors decide that certain traits can account for Carter's behavior, then find those traits in his words and actions. Nevertheless, Mazlish and Diamond have written a balanced and intriguing account of a complex individual. Their case for what makes Jimmy Carter tick is convincing.

GLAD's biography is a well-documented narrative that explains how Carter reached his peculiar understanding of what the country needed as president. The president would have to be a Washington outsider, his own person, and hold an idealized view of the American people as moral and compassionate. She is effective in explaining the development of these views, particularly the impact of his years as governor of Georgia.

For readers who want a relatively brief (247 pages), well-written description of Carter's life that also provides a sense of the man, the Mazlish and Diamond book is the choice. For readers who want a more detailed (546 pages), yet still readable account of both the events of Carter's life and the evolution of his thinking, Glad's book will be a satisfying choice. Readers who want a full account of his presidency and his remarkably productive work as ex-president must wait for a biography not yet written.

—Robert E. O'Connor

———————

CARUSO, Enrico, 1873–1921; Italian operatic tenor.

Caruso, Dorothy, *Enrico Caruso, His Life and Death*. New York, Simon and Schuster, 1945; London, W. Laurie, 1946.

Freestone, John and Harold J. Drummond, *Enrico Caruso: His Recorded Legacy*. London, Sidgwick and Jackson, 1960; Minneapolis, T. S. Dennison, 1961.

Fucito, Salvatore and Barnet J. Beyer, *Caruso and the Art of Singing*. London, T. F. Unwin, and New York, F. A. Stokes, 1922.

Gaisberg, Fred W., *The Music Goes Around*. New York, Macmillan, 1942; as *Music on Record*, London, R. Hale, 1946.

Jackson, Stanley, *Caruso*. London, W. H. Allen, and New York, Stein and Day, 1972.

Kolodin, Irving, *The Metropolitan Opera*. New York, Knopf, 1966 (first published 1936).

Ybarra, T. R., *Caruso*. New York, Harcourt, 1953; London, Cresset Press, 1954.

*

DOROTHY CARUSO's sentimental book is nevertheless enlivened by some 20 photographs of her husband on and off stage, and shows 14 of his inimitable caricatures. A list of revealing facts includes: "He weighed 3 lbs. less after each performance"; "he loved children and dogs." There are useful appendices: his operatic repertoire, a discography, and the high points of his life. Although disorganised in her presentation, Mrs. Caruso writes with sincerity and discloses many aspects of Caruso's character and manner not found elsewhere. There are some very amusing incidents as well as verbatim reproductions of his letters in an hilariously fractured English. His (unexpected) toughness in negotiation is also reported, and there is a harrowing account of his death.

JACKSON's chatty, gossipy account of Caruso's life, well-researched and crammed with facts, is easily approached from a good index. But he frequently assumes too much, even stating confidentially what Caruso was *thinking*, and embroiders events when no witnesses existed.

YBARRA romances even more, including reconstructed conversations in the first person; yet he has a wealth of information to impart in an old-fashioned prose. There are such questionable statements as: "There can be no doubt that, deep down, Enrico Caruso asked little of life but the sun, sociability, and the spaghetti of Naples." Perhaps what Ybarra intended was that, given the simple life, Caruso would not have become a highly-strung, over-emotional hypochondriac; but this quality is exactly the reason for his ability to give performances of vocal and histrionic eminence, without which there would be no biography. The "Monkey House Incident" (or Scandal), when Caruso was briefly arrested and fined for assaulting a woman at the New York Zoo in 1906, is told in a slightly different manner from Jackson's, with Ybarra's personal view of the matter—valuable or not—to sum up.

FUCITO is thoroughly fulsome, but gives details not found elsewhere. Here, the value lies in Fucito's proximity as accompanist and coach in New York between 1915–21, together with a unique presentation of all Caruso's daily exercises to warm up his voice and keep it in trim, whether he was singing that day or not.

The absence of a scholarly biography leads one to the only practical method of judging his vocal abilities: his records. GAISBERG is useful only for his firsthand account of how he recorded Caruso's first ten arias one afternoon in 1902 against orders from his masters. Thus began the gramophone industry as a serious concern, with fortunes for the later HMV/Victor companies and for the tenor. Although this event is retailed by others, they have all got certain details wrong—according to the source.

FREESTONE AND DRUMMOND concentrate entirely upon Caruso's 78s, offering interesting and valuable sidelights on his life. Soon after he began finding regular time to record, it was Caruso himself who determined the choice of songs or arias, so that his preferences, contemporary abilities, and a discernible darkening of the voice all contribute to a kind of biography in sound. The whole of his output, available on CD, further amplify these points. Each 78 side is briefly discussed, and the book includes a comprehensive index.

KOLODIN's encyclopedic account of the Metropolitan Opera, its singers, characters and performance history, emphasises Caruso's enormous contribution to that institution. His activities are related in detail from début in 1903 to the finale (and 607th performance in a total of 37 different roles) on Christmas Eve 1920. Although Caruso occupies only a small part of Kolodin, and is encountered *passim*, his singing career in the U.S.A. is not covered in such detail elsewhere. Kolodin writes fluently and well: "Abbreviated though it was by his death at 48, Caruso's was not only one of the longest careers in Metropolitan history, but also one of the most influential. . . . The difficulty of getting tickets for Caruso performances vastly stimulated the general habit of subscription. His effect on the repertory, in the establishment of the Puccini literature, in popularizing such works as *Pagliacci* and *Aida*, was equally basic. . . . In sincerity, in fervor, in devotion to his art, he was the peer of any opera singer in history."

—Alan Jefferson

———————

CARVER, George Washington, *ca.* 1864–1943; American botanist.

Bontemps, Arna W., *The Story of George Washington Carver.* New York, Grossett and Dunlap, 1954.

Edwards, Ethel, Jim Hardwick, and Willis D. Weatherford, *Carver of Tuskegee.* Cincinnati, Ohio, Psyche Press, 1971.

Elliott, Lawrence, *George Washington Carver: The Man Who Overcame.* Englewood Cliffs, New Jersey, Prentice-Hall, 1966.

Graham, Shirley and George D. Lipscomb, *Dr. George Washington Carver: Scientist.* New York, J. Messner, 1944.

Guzman, Jessie P., *George Washington Carver: A Classified Bibliography.* Tuskegee, Alabama, Tuskegee Institute, 1954.

Holt, Rackham, *George Washington Carver: An American Biography.* New York, Doubleday, 1963.

Imes, George L., *I Knew Carver.* Harrisburg, Pennsylvania, J. H. McFarland, 1943.

Manber, David, *Wizard of Tuskegee: The Life of George Washington Carver.* New York, Crowell-Collier, 1967.

McMurry, Linda O., *George Washington Carver, Scientist and Symbol.* New York, Oxford University Press, 1981; Oxford, 1982.

Miller, Basil W., *George Washington Carver, God's Ebony Scientist.* Grand Rapids, Michigan, Zondervan, 1943.

*

BONTEMPS furnishes an amusing version of the life of George Washington Carver intended primarily for a juvenile audience. It is written with some restraint and sensitivity to portray the role model of an American Negro who has risen from humble depths to become a world-famous scientist. Bontemps' research is fairly solid and most of his materials come from the Library of Congress, the Booker T. Washington Papers, the George Washington Carver Papers, and the Robert Russa Moton Papers from the Tuskegee Institute of Alabama. Bontemps concentrates on the early life of Carver from 1896 to 1915, the period of Carver's life that lacks documentary evidence. Because of this emphasis the book has some merit and is worth consulting.

EDWARDS drew most of her resource materials from the files and documents in the Tuskegee Collection and from personal interviews. Though difficult to find, her book has some merit because it describes in accurate detail Carver's life while at Tuskegee and his accomplishments there both as a scientist and a man of academic affairs.

ELLIOTT has written a short biography (256 pages, with a good bibliography at the end) whose central theme is how Carver succeeded against the odds. This should delight those interested in the Negro in American History who are looking for models of success in the racism of early 20th-century America. Most of Elliott's research is solid since he obtained many personal interviews from substantial people who knew Carver, such as Dr. Luther H. Foster, the President of Tuskegee, the people of the Carver Foundation at Tuskegee Institute, including Austin W. Curtis, who was Carver's trusted assistant, and Robert W. Fuller at the George Washington Carver National Monument, at Diamond, Missouri. The Foreward is written by Frederick D. Patterson, who had worked with Carver for almost 14 years.

While Elliott spends much time relating Carver's personal philosophy to that of Booker T. Washington (especially to Washington's Atlanta concept of "the hand," and the Negro's position in American society), the book nonetheless lacks depth. Its strength lies in the detailed explanation of Carver's scientific accomplishments. Elliott's conclusion is that Carver "helped to revolutionize the economy of the South," which is a fair assay of Carver's achievements.

GRAHAM AND LIPSCOMB have written a unique book, published the year after Carver died, whose main theme concentrates on Carver's life as a scientist and only peripherally treats Carver as the man in history. It does make a unique contribution in this respect, but for the main events of Carver's life the reader needs to look elsewhere.

GUZMAN's work is not really a biography, but belongs in this category because it offers useful materials otherwise difficult to find, in the form of a "bibliography-in-depth." The major sources are taken from the rich collection at the Tuskegee Institute.

HOLT's is the oldest of the biographies, written the year Carver died though not published until 20 years after Carver's death. Naturally there is no bibliography included in this short book (350 pp.), but the 23 photographs are good, as is the index. Holt's research is based on interviews with Carver, and the supreme merit of the book is that although it is an older publication Holt tried to correct some of the "fairy tales" that circulated about Carver. Holt also used the Carver Papers at the Tuskegee Institute. While the book is somewhat laudatory and inaccurate in some minor details, it includes some good anecdotes not found in some newer biographies. Holt pictures Carver as a humble, misunderstood, brilliant scientist, an able educator, and an inspiration to all who knew him. He paints a clear picture of Carver the man—a man who answered every letter he ever received, and who returned the many checks in the mail with a note saying: "The best things could not be bought or sold." Holt has a good sense of humor, which many recent authors seem to lack. Anyone who wants to know Carver should start with Holt's work.

IMES offers a small book filled with personal observations of Carver. Its only salient merit is that it gives one an inside view of Carver the man. While not a comprehensive work regarding Carver's life, and though difficult to find, it may be worth searching for.

MANBER's short book is easy to read, but it offers little that is new. There are some good photographs, and the basic theme is on Carver's work at Tuskegee. Manber calls Carver "the Black Leonardo," and extravagantly claims that Carver single-handedly brought agriculture reform to the South. He even quotes Christy Barth (in his *Pioneers of Plenty*), who claimed that Carver was the "first and greatest chemurgist." Much of Manber's material, however, can easily be found in other works.

McMURRY provides the definitive biography (even though she called Carver "The Peanut Man"). This is a well-documentedwork that attempts valiantly to dispose of the myths surrounding Carver. It describes Carver's significant accomplishments while objectively examining his contributions to agriculture, science, race relations, and education. Her research is solid, ranging all the way from the Tuskegee Archives to resources available at the Carver National Monument, to the Michigan History Collection (mostly private letters) and the Library of Congress. She also uses taped interviews, the B. T. Washington Papers, the *Negro History Bulletin*, the Iowa State Document Collection, Simpson College, the J. P. Guzman Collection of Carver materials, and materials from the *Journal of Southern History*. While it is true that McMurry sometimes paints Carver as a "folk hero," and that mythology and reality often become blurred, she is quick to admit that it was difficult to pin down some of the exact facts. She has an engaging style, paints an intimate picture based on wide-ranging research, and concludes that Carver was a "Black Horatio Alger who story offered hope to those who tried." To her Carver is a gentle spirit, a gifted teacher, an almost forgotten figure who deserves a scholarly but critical study. John Blassingame of Yale wrote of McMurry's book: "Carver the promoter, showman, master teacher, idealistic dreamer, painter, devotee of the Southern inter-racial co-operation, captivating orator, myth, symbol, and flirter with the radical left emerges in all his complexity."

MILLER's book examines Carver at work in his laboratory. For those interested in the scientific method this book has some value, but for general information about Carver look elsewhere.

Dorothy Porter's *The Negro in the United States: A Selected Bibliography* (Washington, D.C., Library of Congress, 1970) indicates the research path to be taken by anyone interested in Carver's life. She cites two general works that offer valuable additions to Carver's biography: Edwin R. Embree, *Thirteen Against the Odds* (1944), and Mary W. Ovington, *Portraits in Color* (1927). Both works contain excellent essays on Carver that shed some light on him as a significant man in American Negro history.

—Nicholas Christopher Polos

———————

CASSATT, Mary, 1845–1926; American painter.

Carson, Julia M. H., *Mary Cassatt*. New York, D. McKay, 1966.
Hale, Nancy, *Mary Cassatt*. New York, Doubleday, 1975.
McKown, Robin, *The World of Mary Cassatt*. New York, T. Y. Crowell, 1972.
Sweet, Frederick A., *Miss Mary Cassatt, Impressionist from Pennsylvania*. Norman, University of Oklahoma Press.
Wilson, Ellen, *American Painter in Paris: A Life of Mary Cassatt*. New York, Farrar Straus, 1971.

*

SWEET correctly observes that much of the literature that precedes his publication on Mary Cassatt suffers from factual errors and misrepresentations. Prior to Sweet's book, the only extensive Cassatt biography was published in French in 1913 by Archille Segard (*Un Peintre des Enfants et des Mères, Mary Cassatt*), which was based upon information provided by the artist when she was in her late 60s. A museum professional, Sweet has the benefit of years of firsthand contact with Cassatt's art, which he made one of the focuses of his professional career. His major goal is to chart Cassatt's development as an artist, but within the full context of her personality and environment, thus

intertwining her life and her art. What allowed Sweet to achieve his goal so admirably was the full cooperation of Cassatt's surviving relatives and friends who provided significant interviews and made available their personal records plus a large number of previously unpublished letters written by the artist between 1890 and 1926. This primary material provides a rich source of new information about Cassatt's life. To these invaluable resources, Sweet brings solid research skills and a sincerity that assures his book the status of a standard on Cassatt. He not only corrects the record on many errors presented in earlier works, but he provides a valuable starting point for subsequent researchers. Sweet's book, well written and readable, carries a sense of authority born of directness and freedom from speculation. At the same time, Sweet has been criticized for dwelling too much upon his sources and passing too lightly over the artistic and psychological discussion of his subject. This book is an excellent resource for scholars and makes enjoyable reading for the general public.

If Sweet is too tied to his documentation, HALE brings to Cassatt's biography the touch and perspective of the novelist. Hale profits greatly from Sweet's research: Sweet shared his files with her, a gift that she enhanced by several years of personal research, including additional contacts with Cassatt's family and friends. Hale's research is solid and augments the contributions of Sweet. Scholars will appreciate her excellent index and her annotated bibliography, but they may be frustrated by her lack of textual citations. As the daughter of practicing painters, Hale prides herself on taking the artist's perspective and expresses her belief "that an artist's work is not merely like his life; it is his life." She professes herself to be interested in personal and artistic character rather than strict biography. This approach compelements Hale's experience as a novelist, but it produces a book with a decidedly romantic tone and a tendency toward supposition about moods, feelings, and motivations. On the other hand, the book benefits from the perspective of a woman author who relates to Cassatt's complex personality and rejects the easy material cliches that characterize the commentaries of many male writers. In particular, Hale does an excellent job of reflecting upon the events of Cassatt's later life, a period left virtually untouched by other writers. Hale, like Sweet, has been criticized for an uncritical attitude toward Cassatt's art stemming from strong personal and indiscriminate admiration for the artist. This book has much to offer the scholar and should be read in tandem with Sweet's to develop a fully humanized portrait of Mary Cassatt.

CARSON published her biography of Cassatt in the same year as Sweet, a fact which invites comparison in terms of sources and scope. Like Sweet and Hale, Carson enjoyed the assistance of Cassatt's surviving family and friends and consequently had access to new information through interviews and unpublished correspondence. The result is a well-researched and pertinent biography with some new information and significant quotes. At 176 pages, the text is relatively brief and selective but is adequately documented. The book is written for the general public rather than scholars and raises no major critical or historical issues. It is, however, an appropriate introductory biography that effectively communicates the importance of Mary Cassatt as an artist and captures the spirit of her life and times.

McKOWN's book is part of the Women of America series, a context that has been questioned by some reviewers given Cassatt's expatriot status. Journalistic in style, the text focuses as much on 19th-century France and other Impressionists as it does on Cassatt. McKown does an excellent job of weaving together Cassatt's life and time but makes little effort to fathom the psychological or aesthetic dimensions of his subject. McKown's sources are dependable (he makes good use of authors such as Sweet), but there is no evidence of original research nor any concern for scholarly citation.

WILSON's biography has little to recommend it when compared to the books cited above. While based on many of the same sources as Sweet and Hale, this book is careless about detail and prone to speculation, or even invention, concerning mood and motivation. It is interesting that Hale characterizes Wilson as "full of life and feeling" and "excellent at setting a scene, sketching a character, establishing a milieu." Hale teeters on the brink of receiving harsh criticism for taking too much liberty in these very areas; Wilson plunges in head first. Romantic in tone and journalistic in style, Wilson's book is speculative and misleading and of little use to any reader.

The above books all feature small selections of illustrations of Cassatt paintings and historical drawings and photographs from her life. These are in small format and mainly reproduced in black and white with a few presented in full color. In all cases, the illustrations add to the impact of the text but contribute little to an appreciation for Cassatt's art. Given the plethora of excellent catalogues and monographs on Cassatt's work, the reader would be well advised to augment the above biographies with more art-historically oriented books in order to gain a full sense of Cassatt's life as expressed in her art.

—John A. Day

CASTRO (RUZ), Fidel, 1926–   ; Cuban revolutionary and political leader.

Bourne, Peter G., *Fidel: A Biography of Fidel Castro*. New York, Dodd Mead, 1986.

Dubois, Jules, *Fidel Castro: Rebel-Liberator or Dictator?* Indianapolis, Bobbs-Merrill, 1959.

Franqui, Carlos, *Family Portrait with Fidel: A Memoir*. London, Cape, 1983; New York, Random House, 1984.

Martin, Lionel, *The Early Fidel: Roots of Castro's Communism*. Secaucus, New Jersey, L. Stuart, 1978.

Matthews, Herbert L., *Fidel Castro*. New York, Simon and Schuster, 1969.

Stein, Edwin C., *Cuba, Castro, and Communism*. New York, McFadden-Bartell, 1962.

Szulc, Tad, *Fidel: A Critical Portrait*. New York, Morrow, 1986; London, Hutchinson, 1987.

*

The first biography appeared shortly after Castro took power in 1959. DUBOIS, a journalist sympathetic to the revolution, wrote his account in 20 days early in 1959. Concentrating on Castro's armed struggle against Batista, Dubois writes an exciting account of audacious attacks, narrow escapes, courage, and comaraderie. Based largely on interviews with both sides during the war, the book portrays a heroic struggle to eliminate a cruel dictator.

Dubois' discussion of Castro's childhood is sketchy at best, and his book on the whole is not very well documented. In addition, Dubois consistently makes excuses for his subject's bad behavior. Although Dubois' Castro is not a saint, the Cuban leader's limitations are minimized. Dubois answers the question of the subtitle, "Rebel Liberator or Dictator?" by predicting the former, although he is not entirely sure. In the final chapter, Dubois seems to be trying to convince himself that Castro could not become a tyrant because of his respect for constitutional governments and his hatred for the Batista dictatorship. Reading the book now brings contrary feelings: a joy at the victory of the brave revolutionaries and a great sadness at knowing that the hero is about to betray the goals of the revolution.

In contrast, nobody could ever accuse STEIN of excessive generosity toward Castro. His book portrays Castro as a filthy, deranged Communist who intends to help the Soviet Union control the world. According to Stein, Castro's problem began with his illegitimate birth, which caused his character to develop its "violent, unstable, and schizophrenic" nature. Referring throughout the book to Castro as the "Beatnik Dictator," Stein's Castro is so venomous that it is difficult to understand why anyone ever followed him.

Stein's primary intention is to alert readers to the threat Castro poses to democracies, including the United States, rather than to present a careful, documented biography of an important figure. He provides no citations, nor even an index. The book's lack of documentation, Stein's Cold War obsession, and a pervasively negative depiction of every aspect of Castro's life combine to produce a portrayal of Fidel Castro that is cartoonish and unbelievable. The reason to read this book is neither to learn about Castro nor about Cuba, but to understand the intensity of feeling toward the perceived reality of a powerful international Communist conspiracy.

MATTHEWS first interviewed Fidel Castro in the Sierra Maestra mountains in 1957, and he interviewed him many more times before his biography appeared in 1969. Matthews admires Castro's ideals and goals, yet he is troubled by much of what happened after Castro took over in 1959. Much of the book is devoted to tortured efforts at explaining away the dark side of the revolution. Matthews does not ignore unpleasantries, but usually accounts for them as necessary reactions to crises or as passing phases. Often Matthews lets Castro himself express his justifications. Despite the many hours Matthews spent with Fidel, the book is disappointing. It offers few insights into Castro's character, as Matthews seems reluctant to make an analysis of the man. What emerges is a sense of Matthews' own anguish and confusion toward his subject and the Cuban revolution.

After the 1969 publication of Matthews' biography, several years passed without a fresh biography. MARTIN's book is only a limited effort. Martin did not set out to write a biography of Fidel Castro, but to explore the roots of Castro's Communism. A popular question among individuals concerned with understanding Fidel and the Cuban revolution has been the origin of his communism and the timing of his conversion to that ideology. Did Castro adopt Marxism-Leninism as a convenient rationale for retaining power after defeating Batista in 1959? Or had Castro become a Marxist-Leninist much earlier and hidden his beliefs for strategic reasons? Martin carefully explores Castro's activities as a student leader to conclude that Castro accepted Marxism as early as 1948.

On its own terms, the book's main argument is not convincing. Martin demonstrates that Castro held radical views at an early age, but these radical views were not necessarily Maxist. A more serious problem is that the focus on the development of Castro's Marxism seems too limiting. Similarly, the focus on Castro's ideology does not contribute to building a complete portrait of a complex man. If Castro has been motivated by a single obsession, Martin's own evidence suggests that that obsession has not been Marxism-Leninism.

Despite its limitations, Martin's book is a well-documented study by an author who has lived in Cuba since 1961. Martin knows Cuba thoroughly and provides fascinating explanations of several events by placing them in the Cuban cultural context. Although he at times may be overly generous toward President Castro's own explanations, the book is a balanced, reasoned account. It covers little of Castro's life since 1959, so does not describe the repression of the regime. For this reason, Martin's Castro emerges as a heroic figure. Indeed, if Castro had been killed in 1959, almost all of his biographers likely would view him most favorably.

The biographies of the 1980s are more successful in providing a sense of the man, although they differ in approach and perspective. FRANQUI, a disillusioned Cuban revolutionary, wrote a highly personal account of his experiences with Castro during the struggle to overthrow Batista and the early years of the regime. Franqui's book is an entertaining memoir of his years with Castro, first as a journalist working underground in the revolution, then as the editor of a newspaper during the early years of the regime. The book reads like a series of letters written daily by an idealistic friend. Franqui wants the regime to be different from what it was becoming, but slowly his commitment to truth forces him to recognize the unpleasant reality and to flee Cuba. He makes no effort to provide systematic analysis and includes no citations. Nevertheless, by vividly describing the world around his subject, Franqui provides a unique insight into the character of Fidel Castro.

BOURNE, a psychiatrist, used a psychoanalytic approach to try to explain Castro, citing secondary sources to provide the facts for his psychoanalytic analysis. Focusing on Castro's life through 1965, Bourne argues that Castro craves power because he is seeking to overcome the indignity of his illegitimate birth. Communism serves Castro as the means through which he can retain power in the traditional strong Iberian mode of the dominant "caudillo."

Most readers who like psychoanalytic biographies will look favorably on Bourne's book. Although there are a good number of factual errors and Bourne downplays the repression of the regime, the essential arguments are psychoanalytically plausible. Readers who dismiss psychoanalytic biographies by authors who have never met their subjects will find the Bourne book absolutely silly.

Closest to a definitive biography of Fidel Castro is SZULC's exhaustive study. Szulc, a journalist, depended on interviews, many with Castro himself, who sat for long interviews in 1984 and 1985 and encouraged other leaders of his government to speak with Szulc. Combined with extensive interviewing in the United States and an exhaustive review of secondary sources,

Szulc amassed an impressive quantity of information that he reduced to a book of slightly under 800 pages. With an emphasis on the early years through the Bay of Pigs, the book is readable, well-written, balanced, and thoroughly documented.

Despite the quality of the book, reading it is not totally satisfying. Castro remains secretive about his private life, so Szulc never adequately describes the interface of the private man and the public figure. Also, the work contains so many seemingly pointless details that it lacks vitality. Szulc is a liberal anti-Communist who admires Castro's bravery, yet is distressed at his rigidity and repression of dissent. How did the fighter for freedom come to put so many of his critics in jail? Szulc seems to believe that the answer must be somewhere in the details, but nothing emerges.

Despite its limitations, Szulc's book remains an outstanding work. Although the author had unusual access to Castro, he did not produce a glowing report of the dictator and his revolution. When the evidence suggests that Castro is lying, Szulc makes this interpretation. By any standard, the book is a fine biography. In comparison with the other Castro biographies, it is superior.

—Robert E. O'Connor

————————

CATHER, Willa, 1873–1947; American writer.

Bennett, Mildred R., *World of Willa Cather*. New York, Dodd Mead, 1951; revised edition, Lincoln, University of Nebraska Press, 1961.

Bonham, Barbara, *Willa Cather*. Philadelphia, Chilton, 1970.

Brown, E. K., *Willa Cather: A Critical Biography* (completed by Leon Edel). New York, Knopf, 1953.

Brown, Marion M. and Ruth Crone, *Willa Cather: The Woman and Her Works*. New York, Scribner, 1970.

Brown, Marion M. and Ruth Crone, *Only One Point of the Compass: Willa Cather in the Northeast*. Danbury, Connecticut, Archer, 1980.

Byrne, Kathleen and Richard Snyder, *Chrysalis: Willa Cather in Pittsburgh 1896–1906*. Pittsburgh, Historical Society of Western Pennsylvania, 1980.

Lee, Hermione, *Willa Cather: Double Lives*. New York, Pantheon, 1989; with subtitle *A Life Saved Up*, London, Virago, 1989.

Lewis, Edith, *Willa Cather Living: A Personal Record*. New York, Knopf, 1953.

O'Brien, Sharon, *Willa Cather: The Emerging Voice*. New York and Oxford, Oxford University Press, 1987.

Robinson, Phyllis, *Willa: The Life of Willa Cather*. New York, Doubleday, 1983.

Sergeant, Elizabeth S., *Willa Cather: A Memoir*. Philadelphia, Lippincott, 1953.

Woodress, James, *Willa Cather: Her Life and Art*. New York, Pegasus, 1970.

Woodress, James, *Willa Cather: A Literary Life*. Lincoln, University of Nebraska Press, 1987.

*

Two early biographies of Cather were sentimental memoirs by friends. SERGEANT, who met Cather at *McClure's* magazine in New York, recalls the writer's most prolific years, particularly from 1910 to 1930. Though she and Cather often disagreed on social issues, they maintained their friendship through their literary discussions. These Sergeant shares, along with Cather's comments on her works in progress. Cather's long-standing personal companion, LEWIS writes a self-effacing memoir, portraying Cather as fearless and high-spirited, though she does acknowledge Cather's occasional melancholy. Originally intending simply to document material for biographer E. K. Brown, Lewis later published her recollections, without an index or notes. She recounts Cather's life, organizing chronologically by geographic location—a method followed by nearly all of the biographers after her. Interesting segments include explanations for the genesis of Cather's work, descriptions of the two women's living quarters and Cather's writing habits, and identification of the actual people from whom Cather drew her fictional characters. Lewis emphasizes most heavily Cather's years at *McClure's*.

As Lewis intended, E. K. BROWN relied extensively on her memoir. Historically important as the first authorized biography of Cather, by someone who did not personally know her, Brown's work is now outdated by Cather material that has since become available. More than 1,200 letters and three volumes of Cather's newspaper columns were added to the Cather corpus after Brown's book, along with collections of her speeches, interviews, and short stories. However, many of Brown's critical assessments have endured, and his 12-page epilogue remains a succinct, overall assessment of Cather's nature, style, and contribution.

With his second text on Cather (1987), WOODRESS supplants Brown's biography as well as his own earlier biography (1970), which he intended as an interim work, anyway. This is the seminal treatment of Cather's life, leaving no gaps and conveying a vivid sense of the pace of the writer's life, including her friendships, moves, illnesses, social interests, and her travels, especially to research for novels. Documenting Cather's attitudes and impressions with letters, Woodress is a cautious and judicious interpreter; he seeks proof and does not speculate, surmise or guess. For example, factual evidence being absent, Woodress rejects Cather's purported lesbianism and, instead, believes she led a celibate life. For Woodress, the pivotal time in Cather's life came in 1912, when she left *McClure's* and her "apprentice" period and began drawing on her own past experiences. Woodress summarizes all of Cather's short stories and novels and offers critical commentary. Infrequently the critical views of others are shared. His thorough analyses assist readers who may not be intimately familiar with all of Cather's works.

Applying a feminist and psychoanalytic approach, O'BRIEN's provocative text combines biography and critical analysis as it delineates Cather's lesbianism and analyzes her early rejection and then later acceptance of female artistry. O'Brien shows how the writer vascillated between sexual models, rejecting her mother and adopting a male persona. Her study concludes with the 1913 novel *O Pioneers!* in which Cather unveils her own fictional voice and, for the first time, portrays female creativity. O'Brien focuses on the emotional side of Cather's life: her personality, behavior, family, friends, and writing. She jettisons the organizing device of most of Cather's biographers, that of creating chapters based on the writer's geographical location. Also unique to O'Brien's biography are a thoughtful assessment of Cather's fondness for music, an explanation for Cather's attraction to Stephen Crane as her first mentor, an examination of one of Cather's major images, that of an enclosed space, and a chapter-length consideration of the impact of Sarah Orne Jewett on the writer. O'Brien interprets Cather's fictional characters in terms of how they reflect the writer's own psychological state; therefore knowledge of Cather's early short stories makes O'Brien's text more meaningful. Though the index is very accessible, the absence of a bibliography is regrettable, especially since O'Brien obviously relied upon a fascinating array of family documents, letters, and diaries for her analyses of Cather's mother, grandmothers, and great-aunt.

LEE makes some sensitive and insightful comments about Cather's early life, but once she establishes Cather as a novelist, she concentrates on a textual analysis of Cather's artistic accomplishments rather than on her personal life. Lee reads *The Song of the Lark* (1915) as an autobiography and a dramatization of Cather's credo. ROBINSON provides a fairly short, readable, and adoring biography concentrating on Cather's years before her novels. Robinson documents her text with academic-style notes, though she subordinates Cather's fiction in favor of more personal and popular issues. For example, unlike the Woodress index, with its literary divisions, Robinson's index includes personal characteristics such as Cather's cigarette smoking and her subtraction of years from her age. Based on her reading of Cather's surviving letters, Robinson reconstructs events. She assumes Cather was a lesbian because the facts Robinson shares make lesbianism very possible. BYRNE AND SNYDER document Cather's developmental years in Pittsburgh when she made several key, lifelong friendships. The authors provide several amusing interviews with some of Cather's former students and colleagues that are not available elsewhere.

Several non-scholarly biographies by fellow Nebraskans are available. In their first book (1970), BROWN AND CRONE review Cather's novels set in Nebraska and discuss the writer's rootedness to past ideals and poetic forms, her dislike of the machine age, and her carefully cultivated literary persona. In their second book (1980), Brown and Crone revisit the three northeastern locations where Cather spent her summers writing: Jaffrey Center, New Hampshire; Grand Manan Island, New Brunswick; and Northeast Harbor, Maine. Along with comments on Cather's writing habits and her preference for a garret room are some unflattering, gossipy recollections by those who knew the writer. BENNETT surveys the history, people, and places around Red Cloud, Nebraska, Cather's family home, which the writer incorporated into her work. Bennett updates the whereabouts of those individuals Cather used in her fiction, and she discusses Cather's passion toward the prairie. The addition of notes and an index to the revised edition helps to overcome the sometimes disorganized arrangement of topics keyed to quotes by Cather. A farm wife who grew up near Red Cloud, BONHAM summarizes Cather's life and provides no more than a line or small paragraph about the writer's works. Her perfunctory style might be appropriate for younger readers.

—Barbara A. Looney

CATHERINE OF SIENA [Caterina Benincasa], 1347–1380;
Italian mystic, diplomat, and saint.

Drane, Mrs. Augusta Theodosia, *The History of Saint Catherine of Siena and Her Companions* (2 vols.). London, Burnes and Oates, 1880.

Gardner, Edmund G., *Saint Catherine of Siena: A Study in the Religion, Literature, and History of the 14th Century in Italy.* London, Dent, and New York, Dutton, 1907.

"Mademoiselle Mori," ("M.R."), *St. Catherine of Siena and Her Times.* London, Methuen, 1906.

Richardson, Jerusha Davidson, *The Mystic Bride: A Study of the Life-Story of Catherine of Siena.* London, T. W. Laurie, 1911.

Scudder, Vida D., *Saint Catherine of Siena as Seen in Her Letters.* London, Dent, and New York, Dutton, 1905.

*

There are five sources for the life of Catherine of Siena. First comes the *Life*, finished in 1395, also known as the *Legenda*, by her third confessor Fra Raimundo della Vigne, published in 1553. There are also French, English, German, and Spanish versions. Second, there is the *Processus*, a collection of letters and other documents testifying to Catherine's sanctity, gathered together between 1411 and 1413 to promote her canonical cult. Third comes the *Supplementum* to the *Life* by Fra Tommaso Caffarini of about 1414, never published in its entirety. Fourth, there is the *Legenda abbreviata* (or "minore"), an abridgement by Caffarini of the *Life* partly published in 1479. Fifth come the letters, edited in six volumes of which the *editio princeps* is by Aldo Manuzio, the famous humanist printer (Venice, 1500). The letters were dictated, as Catherine did not learn to write until three years before her death. The foundation for all modern biographies is the edition of the sources by the Bollandists in the April 1675 volumes of *Acta Sanctorum* (63 vols., 1643–1902).

The SCUDDER translation and edition of a selection of the letters offers important insights not only into Catherine's spirituality but also into her political activity and pastoral advice. The letters are accompanied by a commentary whose slightly condescending tone is warranted by the letters' excessively mannered, non-literary style. The letters will presumably require de-coding for most modern readers unaccustomed to the devotional clichés of medieval saints, or to their formal modes of address, even when they write in trance or to popes: "In the Name of Jesus Christ crucified and of sweet Mary: Most holy and dear father in Christ sweet Jesus: I Catherine, servant and slave of the slaves of Jesus Christ, write to you in his precious Blood . . . " The commentary is clearly written for the devout rather than the historically or theologically initiated, and says little about what is of real interest, which is the extraordinary intensity of Catherine's language and the inconsistent violence of the imagery: "I impose upon you nothing save to see yourselves drowned in the blood and flame poured from the side of the Son of God".

The translation imports false archaisms into the text that are not accurately calculated to make the same impression as the original was meant to convey. It is for instance impossible to disentangle Catherine's technical doctrine of "discretio" from this translation, which wrongly translates the absence of that quality as "indiscretion." The occasional "dost" strikes a false rhetorical note, and the allusions implicit in "slave of slaves"

(popes sign themselves "slaves of the slaves of God," *servus servorum dei*), or "grafted on the substance of one Tree, Jesus" (John XV), go unexplained. In spite of helpful points made in the introduction and a useful background chronology, this is essentially an attempt to demonstrate that saints on whom the highest mystical gifts are bestowed are nonetheless able to be practical and sensible. The attitude toward the spiritual and physical events narrated is totally uncritical. Even the most unlikely, such as "miraculously" learning to write, are accepted at their face value. The commentary draws on Burlamacchi's in the 1707 edition of the *Works* edited by Gigli.

Burlamacchi and Gigli are also referred to in the rare footnotes of *Saint Catherine of Siena and Her Times*, by "MORI," but we are not told who they are and, although there is an index, they are not in it. The author presupposes some knowledge of mystical writings, even outside the Christian tradition, treating Catherine's life as "woven of three distinct threads, namely contemplation, active charity and self-immolation," and readers are expected to know their Dante, and a very little elementary Italian. The author is curiously expert in the social history of medieval Tuscany. The possibility that the miraculous cures might be due to "faith healing" is not discounted, although the biography does romanticize the life, as do the stylized medieval paintings of her ecstasies and visions added as illustrations. This is a conventionally pious hagiography, informed with more than usual background knowledge for its date, but characteristically mixing legend and fact, so providing neither proper history nor what could have been the fascinating account of the growth of a legend. The paintings, for instance, clearly show the stigmata with which we are told God had consented at Catherine's request not to mark her body. The *Legenda* reports her as saying on Laetare Sunday 1375 that she thought the pain would kill her, although it was relieved on the following Sunday.

RICHARDSON intends to present Catherine as a "representative for all time of womanhood and saintship." Her work is something of a curiosity in that it is openly critical of Catherine's political, peace-making role, claiming that "woman is faithful to her nature and her destiny only when she remains a saint and a mother," presumably an attack on the paucity of married female saints and the breviary rubric's double negative in describing them as "neither a virgin nor a martyr," but still to modern ears anti-feminist. The mystery of inaccurate quotations from scripture and the reminiscences of Dante by someone who had never read him are satisfactorily resolved with reference to the historical circumstances, a Biblical florilegium, and a secretary who was a devotee of Dante, but this is clearly not a scholarly book. It has a moral, which it makes forcefully and unconvincingly.

The best biography is clearly that by GARDNER, scholarly for the date although not critical of the sources, and using the 19th-century biographies as appropriate, notably that in two volumes by DRANE published in 1880. Gardner, who has an index and a bibliography, prints unpublished letters in Italian and is meticulously accurate on everything to do with date and sources. He is also expert in the political and general historical background of *trecento* Tuscany. There is only a short but penetrating final section on the letters, and if there is the occasional moral judgment, there is no conjecture beyond what the historical sources allow, or even invite, and the psychological observations are invariably sensible. This is not only the best available biography of Catherine, but a thoroughly workmanlike biography of a medieval saint.

—A. H. T. Levi

CATHERINE OF ARAGON, 1485–1536; queen consort of Henry VIII.

Claremont, Francesca, *Catherine of Aragon*. London, R. Hale, 1939.

Dixon, William H., *History of Two Queens: Catherine of Aragon, Anne Boleyn* (4 vols.). London, Hurst and Blackett, 1873–74.

Du Boys, Albert, *Catherine of Aragon and the Sources of the English Reformation*, translated and edited by Charlotte M. Yonge. London, Hurst and Blackett, 1881.

Froude, J. A., *The Divorce of Catherine of Aragon: The Story as Told by the Imperial Ambassadors Resident at the Court of Henry VIII*. New York, Scribner, and London, Longman, 1891.

Harpsfield, Nicholas, *A Treatise on the Pretended Divorce Between Henry VIII and Catherine of Aragon*. Printed for the Camden Society, 1878.

Kelly, Henry, *The Matrimonial Trials of Henry VIII*. Stanford, California, Stanford University Press, 1976.

Luke, Mary M., *Catherine the Queen*. New York, Coward McCann, 1967; London, F. Muller, 1968.

Mattingly, Garrett, *Catherine of Aragon*. Boston, Little Brown, 1941; London, Cape, 1942.

Parmiter, Geoffrey de C., *The King's Great Matter: A Study of Anglo-Papal Relations 1527–34*. New York, Barnes and Noble, and London, Longman, 1967.

Paul, John E., *Catherine of Aragon*. New York, Fordham University Press, and London, Burns and Oates, 1966.

Strickland, Agnes, *Lives of the Queens of England from the Norman Conquest* (6 vols.). London, G. Bell, 1893-99.

*

The list of biographical sources for Catherine of Aragon can be divided into two types of treatment. The first type includes standard biographical treatments by Claremont, Dixon, Du Boys, Luke, Mattingly, Paul, and Strickland. The second type includes considerations of Catherine's divorce from Henry VIII from a political and religious viewpoint, and it includes the works by Froude, Harpsfield, Kelly, and Parmiter. These works treat Catherine's story only in the light of her repudiation by her husband because of her inability to bear him a living male heir.

MATTINGLY's 1942 monograph is still the most useful biography. The author concludes by noting the limitations on Catherine's willingness to oppose Henry VIII and the significance of these limitations on the eventual religious settlement in England. For Mattingly, Catherine of Aragon is a reactionary, if admirable, figure in English history who deserves praise for not throwing England into a civil war in defense of her marriage. Though somewhat dated in his outlook, Mattingly's scholarship deserves commendation. CLAREMONT is the only 20th-century biographer other than Mattingly to cover this tragic queen's life in full. Unabashedly sympathetic to Catherine, Claremont sees Anne Boleyn as a cold, calculating upstart. Claremont's book is also notable because more than one fourth of the text is devoted to Catherine's Spanish origins as the daughter of Ferdinand of Aragon and Isabella of Castile, the rulers who unified Spain.

DIXON focuses more on Anne Boleyn than on Catherine of Aragon. For Dixon, Henry VIII is a tyrant who was brutal to both Catherine of Aragon and Anne Boleyn,, although the author reflects a traditional English Protestant bias in favor of Anne Boleyn. DU BOYS writes as a strong admirer of Catherine of Aragon. He concludes his treatment of her by quoting her deathbed scene from Shakespeare's *Henry VIII* to praise her, and he stresses that the memory of Catherine of Aragon retained the respect of the people even in Protestant England. Du Boys views her as a woman of outstanding courage and blameless good character, who valiantly bore her matrimonial ill fortune with fortitude. LUKE provides a fiction writer's simplistic view of Catherine of Aragon. Although her work is well illustrated, it lacks documentation and is fit for popular and public library consumption, not for the use of anyone interested in a scholarly treatment. Interestingly, Luke, like Du Boys, quotes Shakespeare's *Henry VIII* to honor Catherine of Aragon.

PAUL's work is a collective biography of Catherine of Aragon and the political and religious figures who supported her in the divorce crisis. It is particularly valuable for the portraits it contains of little known women supporters of Catherine of Aragon such as Gertrude Mountjoy, Marchioness of Exeter; Margaret Pole, Countess of Salisbury; Maria de Salinas; Lady Willoughby d'Eresby; and Elizabeth Stafford, Duchess of Norfolk. Paul also provides skillful brief portraits of humanists such as St. Thomas More and St. John Fisher and many Catholic martyrs.

STRICKLAND provides a Victorian woman's view of Catherine of Aragon's life. Strickland writes, ''Sustained by her infinite grandeur of soul, her piety, and lofty rectitude, she passed through her bitter trials without calumny succeeding in fixing a spot on her name. . . . In fact, Shakespeare alone has properly appreciated and vividly portrayed the great talents, as well as the moral worth, of the right royal Katherine of Aragon.''

Of the works focusing more on Catherine of Aragon's divorce than on her life, HARPSFIELD's has particular value as a contemporary Catholic account, written in defense of Catherine of Aragon. KELLY's volume is also worthy of special note, since the author is a canon law scholar who clearly believes that Henry VIII had a valid case, claiming that he was invalidly married to his brother's widow despite biblical traditions of the levirate and Julius II's brief in support of Catherine of Aragon's marriage.

FROUDE provides a Victorian Protestant account that sees the divorce as a struggle between progress and reaction. He concludes by stating, ''those who continue to believe that the victory won in the 16th century was a victory of right over wrong, have no need to blush for the actions of the brave men who, in the pulpit or in the Council Chamber, on the scaffold or at the stake, won for mankind the spiritual liberty which is now the law of the world.''

PARMITER overlaps with Kelly's work, although his focus is more clearly on the diplomatic story of England's break with

Rome. Little in this work makes Catherine of Aragon visible as an individual other than as the target of a process of marriage dissolution.

No modern biography adequately treats the life of Catherine of Aragon from a feminist perspective. Existing biographies only consider the impact of nationality and religion—not that of gender—on her life. Intellect and character did not save Catherine of Aragon from the disgrace caused by her inability to bear a male heir to Henry VIII, and her biography could provide significant insight into 16th-century gender roles if treated from a feminist perspective.

—Susan A. Stussy

CATHERINE DE' MEDICI, 1519–1589; queen consort of Henry II of France.

Heritier, Jean, *Catherine de' Medici*, translated by Charlotte Haldane. New York, St. Martin's, 1959 (originally published by Fayard, Paris, 1940).

Mahoney, Irene, *Madame Catherine*. New York, Coward McCann, and London, Gollancz, 1975.

Neale, J. E., *The Age of Catherine de' Medici*. London, Cape, 1943.

Roeder, Ralph, *Catherine de' Medici and the Lost Revolution*. New York, Viking, and London, Harrap, 1937.

Ross Williamson, Hugh, *Catherine de' Medici*. New York, Viking, and London, M. Joseph, 1973.

Sichel, Edith, *Catherine de' Medici and the French Reformation*. London, Constable, and New York, Dutton, 1905.

Sichel, Edith, *The Later Years of Catherine de' Medici*. London, Constable, and New York, Dutton, 1908.

Strage, Mark, *Women of Power: The Life and Times of Catherine de' Medici*. New York, Harcourt, 1976.

Van Dyke, Paul, *Catherine de' Medici* (2 vols.). London, J. Murray, and New York, Scribner, 1922.

Waldman, Milton, *Biography of a Family: Catherine de' Medici and Her Children*. Boston, Houghton Mifflin, 1936; London, Longman, 1937.

*

Readers unfamiliar with the 16th century in France will find NEALE's brief volume useful as a preface to the more detailed biographies of Catherine de' Medici discussed here. Neale's work, a series of lectures, gives the reader a concise overview of the social, religious, and political events of Catherine's time. Despite an offensive reference to Catherine's "unscrupulous Italianate mind" and Neale's ominous comparisons between the state of the world in 1943 and the 16th century, this book continues to be a fine introduction to Catherine's milieu.

Biographers of Catherine de' Medici must evaluate an enormous number of pertinent sources. Included among these are the reports of various ambassadors to the French court, personal diaries, official court records, and Catherine's letters. Many of these observations were highly prejudiced by religious belief and national loyalty and must be used with great care. Catherine's

own correspondence did not become readily available to scholars until the end of the 19th century with the publication, between 1880–1909, of a ten-volume edition by Hector de la Ferriere and Baguenault de Puchesse.

Studies of Catherine' life written prior to this time are of limited value and are often marred by uncritical acceptance of biased sources. Writers frequently depicted her as duplicitous, jealous, vengeful, a poisoner who dabbled in the black arts and, of course, the "monster of St. Bartholomew." Modern scholars, while not holding Catherine blameless, see her as a somewhat shortsighted politician whose goal was to maintain the power of the throne for her sons and to keep France from civil war. It was her lack of vision, rather than an evil nature, that resulted in disaster. Unfortunately, many biographers of Catherine de' Medici, including the later ones, are somewhat careless about documenting statements attributed to her.

The reader who has time for only one biography should choose either Van Dyke's or Mahoney's. Of the modern books about Catherine, these are the only two that adequately document their sources with extensive footnotes. Even though VAN DYKE's two-volume study was written in 1922, its meticulous scholarship makes it more worthwhile than many later biographies. Van Dyke used new evidence from archives in England, France, Italy, and Switzerland to write the first English-language biography of Catherine de' Medici based entirely on original sources. The author spends some time explaining the background so the reader can view Catherine's actions in the context of her times. The author cautions, however, that he tries to show things as Catherine saw them; events she perceived as unimportant are not given much attention. There are extensive notes and evaluations of sources at the end of the second volume, along with a detailed bibliography.

MAHONEY's more recent, single-volume work uses Van Dyke as a secondary source. Mahoney has done extensive research in primary materials. She is less interested in explaining the 16th century to her reader than in delving into Catherine's somewhat enigmatic character, which, Mahoney admits in the epilogue, will always remain something of a mystery.

SICHEL's volumes are "a study of persons, not an ordered narration of events." These books are a series of essays exploring various aspects of Catherine's life and times. The reader seeking a precise chronological narrative of Catherine's life should look elsewhere. The earlier volume (1905) is noteworthy for its discussion of Catherine's role in fostering the arts—something many other biographers neglect in their zeal to describe Catherine's political machinations. The author consulted sources contemporary with Catherine de' Medici and later studies, as well as Catherine's own letters. A chronology at the end of the volumes is very helpful, but there are some careless errors in the text—incorrect dates, for example.

The strength of ROEDER's book lies in its analysis of the social and political complexities of 16th century France. It contains some very good chapters on the decline of feudalism and the rise of capitalism in France that help the reader understand the problems Catherine faced. However, Roeder sometimes devotes so much attention to impersonal economic and social forces that Catherine seems to be no more alive than a cardboard cut-out placed against a moving background. Roeder has included some very useful chronologies, genealogical tables, and an extensive bibliography. The major problem with both Sichel's and Roeder's work is inadequate documentation of sources within the text. The reader is often left to wonder about the origin of many of the quotations used.

HERITIER, whose book covers Catherine's entire life in chronological order, is erratic in his treatment of sources. There are times when the author is vague, as shown when he cites "reliable sources," whom he declines to name or footnote, for the approximate date when Henri II and Diane de Poitiers became lovers. At other times, Heritier's analysis of documents is careful and highly illuminating, as in his discussion of sources for stories of the carnage on St. Bartholomew's Day. Though Heritier spends some time explaining the background of the religious conflict in France, some knowledge of the period would be helpful to the reader of this book.

STRAGE's book belongs strictly in the realm of popular literature. This is not a conventional biography but a selection of dramatic incidents in the lives of Catherine de' Medici, Diane De Poitiers, and Marguerite of Navarre, showing their relationships with each other and how each woman exerted influence at a time when it was believed proper for women to be powerless. There is an extensive bibliography at the end of this book but no notation of sources. This study adds nothing new to the existing literature about Catherine de' Medici.

The biographies by ROSS WILLIAMSON and WALDMAN are more appropriately considered docudrama than serious scholarship. These writers are rather cavalier in the treatment of their sources. Both books have sections that imply the author has an intimate knowledge of Catherine's innermost thoughts. Williams even manages to psychoanalyze the dead when he asserts that Catherine's "maternal dominance" was responsible for her son's homosexuality. As for Waldman, one can only wonder if he knows the difference between history and fiction when he lists a "cast of characters" at the beginning of his book and later asserts that Catherine was so distraught at one point that she walked around for months "staring into every face out of her short-sighted pop eyes."

—Paula R. Riggs

CATHERINE II [the Great], 1729–1796; empress of Russia.

Alexander, John T., *Catherine the Great: Life and Legend.* New York and Oxford, Oxford University Press, 1989.

Almedingen, Marthe Edith von, *Catherine: Empress of Russia.* New York, Dodd Mead, 1961; as *Catherine the Great, a Portrait,* London, Hutchinson, 1963.

Altenhoff, Herbert T., *Catherine the Great: Art, Sex, Politics.* New York, Vantage Press, 1975.

Anthony, Katherine S., *Catherine the Great.* New York, Garden City Publishing, 1925; London, Cape, 1926.

Aretz, Gertrude *The Empress Catherine.* London, Godfrey and Stephens, 1947.

Castera, Jean-Henri, *The Life of Catherine II, Empress of Russia,* revised and translated by William Tooke. London, Longman, 1799.

Cronin, Vincent, *Catherine: Empress of All the Russias.* New York, Morrow, and London, Collins, 1978.

De Madariaga, Isabel, *Russia in the Age of Catherine the Great.* New Haven, Connecticut, Yale University Press, and London, Weidenfeld and Nicolson, 1981.

Gooch, George P., *Catherine the Great and Other Studies.* London and New York, Longman, 1954.

Grey, Ian, *Catherine the Great: Autocrat and Empress of All Russia.* London, Hodder and Stoughton, 1961; Philadelphia, Lippincott, 1962.

Haslip, Joan, *Catherine the Great: A Biography.* New York, Putnam, and London, Weidenfeld and Nicolson, 1977.

Kaus, Gina, *Catherine: The Portrait of an Empress,* translated by June Head. New York, Halcyon House, 1935; as *Catherine the Great,* London, Cassell, 1935.

Oldenbourg, Zoë, *Catherine the Great,* translated by Anne Carter. New York, Pantheon, and London, Heinemann, 1965.

Oliva, L. Jay, editor, *Catherine the Great.* Englewood Cliffs, New Jersey, Prentice-Hall, 1971.

Raeff, Marc, editor, *Catherine the Great: A Profile.* New York, Hill and Wang, 1972.

Thomson, Gladys S., *Catherine the Great and the Expansion of Russia.* London, English Universities Press, 1941.

Troyat, Henri, *Catherine the Great,* translated by Joan Pinkham. Henley-on-Thames, A. Ellis, 1978; New York, Dutton, 1980 (originally published by Flammarion, Paris, 1977).

Waliszewski, Kasimir, *The Romance of an Empress: Catherine II of Russia.* New York, Appleton, and London, Heinemann, 1894 (originally published by Plon Nourrit, Paris, 1893).

*

Until recently the biographical literature in English about Catherine the Great comprised only popularizations of diverse quality. Now the books by de Madariaga and Alexander have revolutionized such writing, the former as a huge life-and-times survey, the first broad gauged and carefully researched study of her long reign (1762–1796), the latter as the first authoritative popular biography squarely based on modern international scholarship. Both are quite favorable in their treatment of Catherine as a sovereign and deflate such widespread myths as the notion of "Potemkin villages" and huge numbers of lovers.

The distinctive features of ALEXANDER's biography include its emphasis on the reign, with only a long background chapter on Catherine's youth and career before seizing the throne, much attention to questions of health, and a general concept of her life as involving a series of crises and conquests. Perhaps most striking to the popular audience is Alexander's explication of the horse story, the most outrageous of the many legends about Catherine's sex life. The epilogue, "The Legend of Catherine the Great," points out her markedly dualistic reputation and surveys popular images purveyed on stage and screen. Vigorously written (with a fondness for alliteration), Alexander's biography draws on a wide range of primary sources, especially Catherine's writings and her love notes to Peter Zavadovsky (which are translated in the appendix), and makes much use of the court registers, the Russian and foreign press and cartoons, as well as published and unpublished scholarship in English, Russian, French, and German. Its broad appeal is indicated by its adoption by several book clubs and selection for the Byron Caldwell

Smith award for the best book by a Kansas author published in 1987–88. Its only significant weakness concerns Catherine's broader cultural role, but as a primarily political biography that is a focus it shares with de Madariaga's much longer book.

Although DE MADARIAGA's book is not mainly a biography, Catherine is quite central: her diplomacy and reform policies in matters such as education, finances, and the western borderlands receive more attention than in Alexander's more compact book. De Madariaga's study may be too long and detailed for some readers, but she plans soon to publish a shortened version aimed at the college market. Some may be irritated at her British practice of not translating French quotations. There are some mistakes in dates, but in general this big book is well researched, soundly reasoned, and wittily written. It lacks illustrations, however, and is rather traditional in concept, with little attention to matters of medical and social history, for example. It is especially significant in historiographical terms as the first comprehensive scholarly survey to appear in almost 100 years.

All the other biographies appear distinctly inferior to the two foregoing works mainly because they rest on shallow research and more narrow concepts of Catherine's life and times. A few, such as ALTENHOFF's pornographic travesty, are simply silly and inept. Nearly all the others are now seriously out of date, such as Castera, Tooke, Cronin, Aretz, Thomson, Troyat, and Waliszewski. The anthologies edited by RAEFF and OLIVA provide varied materials, and the former is especially good on cultural politics although many of the translated excerpts are rather dated. Neither gives a connected life-study.

GOOCH's collection of essays is concise and written with verve, and places Catherine solidly in a European context, but it too draws on few sources, especially writings in Russian. The same is true of CRONIN's popularization, which tries to conceal its author's ignorance of Russian and prudishly avoids sexual issues. HASLIP's volume adds nothing because of its author's ignorance of Russian and Russian history. ANTHONY's biography may have been popular in the 1920s but it looks hopelessly old-fashioned today, although Anthony deserves praise for her fine edition of Catherine's memoirs (1927), an edition far superior to that of Maroger and Budberg. Knowledge of the different versions of these memoirs is one of the qualities that sets off some biographers from others. Castera and Tooke could not use Catherine's memoirs, of course, because none had been published when they wrote, but Haslip, Troyat and Waliszewski have no such excuse.

The book first written by CASTERA and then rewritten several times to include fresh material from TOOKE is important now only in historiographical terms and for the wide influence it has had over three centuries. It is a hodgepodge of fact and fancy; Tooke tried manfully to save Castera from some of his wrongheadedness and ignorance. But later popularizers such as WALISZEWSKI and TROYAT have shown little discrimination in their rewritings of Castera/Tooke. Troyat in particular had remained terribly out of date because of his ignorance of works in English and his generally slapdash methods of research.

The popular biography by ALMEDINGEN is weakly researched with a bibliography of only nine items. It is very favorable to its subject and sees her as showing signs of genius within a year of arrival in Russia. But unlike nearly all other biogra-

phers, Almedingen believes Paul was Peter III's son. About Catherine's lovers, Almedingen says there were 15-20 but that nobody can be sure of the exact number. Catherine is lauded as "truly great because she succeeded in creating a perfect fusion between her personality and her work, because she was wholly whole in all she did." In short, she was "possibly the greatest woman ruler of all ages." Almedinger also portrays her as not religious at all but a daughter of the German Enlightenment (which could be quite religious as a matter of fact) and cites her "genius for salesmanship and passion for publicity." About Catherine's sexuality Almedingen admits "a great many black patches, but nearly all of them had politics rather than sex at their matrix."

Similarly weak in research is KAUS' biography, but it is quite good in analyzing Catherine's memoirs and depicting court politics before her seizure of the throne. Kaus sees Catherine as marked for life by her mother's neglect of her in childhood. Her youth is portrayed as quite chaste, in contrast to Alexander's pointing to her early interest in sexuality and the significance of her dalliance with her uncle. Moreover, Kaus neglects Catherine's reign and her policies as empress; hers is one of several treatments that rely too heavily on the memoirs, which have little to say about her reign directly.

Unbalanced in the above sense and in others as well is GREY's biography, which devotes only slightly more than half its pages to the reign and gives only a two-page bibliography. Grey criticizes Catherine as neither creative nor selfless nor original; she allegedly ruled only in her own interests, not for her country or people. Her domestic policy saw no victories and she ruled as a reactionary, as the French Revolution supposedly revealed. Under Catherine privilege was entrenched and serfdom reached its apogee, says Grey, and she made no effort to reform serfdom or to arrest its growth—assertions that de Madariaga has challenged. Her triumphs in foreign affairs Grey also censures for lack of vision and statesmanship. Catherine herself was "almost devoid of artistic talents"; even her letters Grey disdains as "never more than the work of an ungifted amateur." Grey concludes that Catherine deserves her title only as a "brilliant adventurer," and that by the time of her death Russia had stagnated too long for reform to be effective; revolution was already inevitable.

Even less balanced is OLDENBOURG's biography, which gives Catherine's pre-1762 life almost twice as much space as her long reign. Her main interest is in Catherine as a person. Oldenbourg relies heavily on Catherine's memoirs and sees her life as "first and foremost a court tragedy" in which she acted out the role assigned her with resolute focus on survival at all costs. Her treatment of Peter III and Paul is strongly criticized. Thus her preference for young lovers is labeled "her own Oedipus, or rather Jocasta, complex," i.e., she loved them as she did not love Paul. Yet Oldenbourg defends her against salacious stories: "the quasi-official manner in which her favorites were appointed appealed to people's imaginations and earned Catherine a reputation she never thought she deserved." After Potemkin's death "all that was left to her now was the fierce call of a sensuality the more tyrannical in that out of an ineradicable habit of prudishness she persisted in disguising it as mere affection." Oldenbourg's conclusion is strongly negative and moralistic: "She claimed to govern alone, but in fact she was guided entirely by the interests of the ruling class. She claimed to be liberal and was in fact reactionary. She was wildly generous, but in giving she never deprived herself of anything. She patronized art and letters so that artists and writers would glorify her, but she did not really like them, for her taste, like her intelligence, was superficial.'' Catherine is contrasted with her dead husband: ''she emerged from the trial which shattered the heart and spirit of her partner hardened, battle-scarred, debased and depersonalized. She survived, thanks to her powerful, almost animal vitality'' and her adroitness at ''the profession of kingship.''

—John T. Alexander

CATULLUS, Gaius Valerius, *ca.* 84 B.C.–*ca.* 54 B.C.; Roman poet.

Frank, Tenney, *Catullus and Horace: Two Poets in Their Environment.* Oxford, Blackwell, and New York, Holt, 1928.
Harrington, Karl P., *Catullus and His Influence.* New York, Longman, 1923.
Macnaghten, Hugh, *The Story of Catullus.* London, Duckworth, 1899.
Small, Stuart P., *Catullus: A Reader's Guide to the Poems.* Lanham, Maryland, University Press of America, 1983.
Wiseman, T. P., *Catullus and His World: A Reappraisal.* Cambridge and New York, Cambridge University Press, 1985.
Wright, Frederick A., *Three Roman Poets: Plautus, Catullus, Ovid: Their Lives, Times and Works.* London, Routledge, and New York, Dutton, 1938.

*

A famous love poet and notorious adulterer is bound to attract the biographer's interest. Especially so when the poet's mistress, commonly identified as the wife of a prominent Roman politician, is herself an important personality in Roman political and social life, and whose name is tainted with suspicion after Cicero implied that she murdered her husband. However, biography of Classical writers is not a popular genre. This is partly because of the lack of sources—for Catullus we only have the account of Suetonius and a note by Apuleius in the first century—and partly because a ''biographical'' approach to Classical literature—i.e., the idea that to understand a writer's work it is first necessary to understand his life—is now largely unfashionable. Catullus has perhaps had more than his fair share of biographies, but it is not surprising to find that a common fault in many of them is a romantic speculation on the part of biographers fascinated by the story of a childhood in Verona and the curious paradox of a scandalous love affair and a wealth of poetry celebrating marriage and chastity.

An example of this fascination is to be found in HARRINGTON's book. Though not strictly speaking a biography, the early chapters are entirely biographical. The reader is treated to a vivid, speculative account, which spares none of the intrigue surrounding Catullus' life, but which clarifies none of the details. MACNAGHTEN's book suffers in the same way. It is a lively account, but indulges too freely in imagination, and de-

parts too abruptly from the few sources we have of Catullus' life, to be of any use to the serious scholar. While it is true that much of Catullus' life must be reconstructed through the poetry, Macnaghten places too much confidence in the biographical details given in the poems and fails to distinguish adequately between Catullus-in-the-poems and Catullus the poet. Another result of this approach is that the biography reads rather like a running commentary on the poems.

From Macnaghten, the reader may turn gratefully to WISEMAN, who begins his work with a warning against reading the poetry of Catullus with modern eyes. Wiseman directs the reader to a deeper understanding of Catullus—the man and his poetry—by exploring the personalities and political and social events surrounding Catullus' life, and literary commonplaces of his day. It is a successful approach. Although Wiseman is as much concerned with Catullus' world as with Catullus, he derives from his survey of the poet's world a detailed portrait of the poet, and he demonstrates that we cannot begin to understand Catullus without understanding the context in which he lived. Wiseman makes extensive use of sources contemporary with Catullus, for example Cicero, and leaves little room for imaginative speculation. Here he compares favourably with WRIGHT, for whom the ''Catullus and his world'' approach is too often an excuse for imaginative digression. A book devoted to the study of three poets rather than one is naturally limited, and in Wright's work this results in overgeneralisations and the absence of such detailed references so abundant in Wiseman's volume.

FRANK supplements the biographical sources with much information concerning the political and social events of Catullus' day. But he is not meticulous in acknowledging sources, with the result that one cannot always make a distinction between documented fact and speculation. Frank appeals to the poems as evidence of what Catullus did and how he felt without attempting to analyse the man who wrote them.

SMALL, on the other hand, gives a brief and perhaps rather too superficial analysis of most of the poems, from which he attempts to extract a consistent picture of the poet—his emotions, attitudes and beliefs. His treatment of the poems by theme helps this approach. Although Small's book is not primarily intended as a biography, it deserves discussion here because, through the survey of Catullus' poetry, the reader is invited to study the poet.

Small does not confuse biography with poetry and rashly assume that Catullus-in-the-poems is identical with Catullus the poet, as Macnaghten and perhaps also Wright and Frank have done. But he recognises that ''we are obliged to reconstruct [Catullus'] life from the poems.'' In his first chapter, Small sets out in a concise, deliberately pithy style the few established or accepted details concerning Catullus' life. It is the clearest and most straightforward account of Catullus' life in any of the biographies considered here. Although for a biography of Catullus, the reader of any level would be strongly advised to read Wiseman, Small's work—which understands so well the relevance of a biography—should not be overlooked.

—Charlotte Goddard

CERVANTES, Miguel de, 1547–1616; Spanish writer.

Bell, Aubrey F. G., *Cervantes.* Norman, University of Oklahoma Press, 1947.

Byron, William, *Cervantes: A Biography.* New York, Doubleday, 1978; London, Cassell, 1979.

Canavaggio, Jean, *Cervantes,* translated by J. R. Jones. New York, Norton, 1990 (originally published by Mazarine, Paris, 1986).

Duran, Manuel, *Cervantes.* Boston, Twayne, 1974.

Juan Arbo, Sebastian, *Cervantes: The Man and His Time,* translated by Ilsa Barea. New York, Vanguard, 1955; as *Cervantes: Adventurer, Idealist, and Destiny's Fool,* London and New York, Thames and Hudson, 1955 (originally published by Planeta, Barcelona, 1945).

MacEoin, Gary, *Cervantes.* Milwaukee, Wisconsin, Bruce Publishing, 1950.

Schevill, Rudolph, *Cervantes.* New York, Duffield, and London, J. Murray, 1919.

*

One difficulty all of Cervantes' biographers have confronted is the paucity of primary sources, forcing them to speculate on their subject from what they know about his writings and the period in which he lived. JUAN ARBO, for example, combines historical facts about Spain in the 16th century with material from Cervantes' writings, especially *Don Quixote,* and uses this information to speculate about his subject's family, his later life, and his motives as an author. Although Juan Arbo's style is straightforward, he treats Cervantes as if he were a character in a novel. His work will be of most interest to the general reader.

BELL has likewise tried to reconstruct Cervantes' life from his writings, but he has succeeded better than most biographers because of his exhaustive and careful reading of all Cervantes' works. Bell also places great emphasis on the major historical forces at the time of Cervantes' birth. In so doing, Bell compares Cervantes to other artists and writers of the Renaissance and reveals many facets of his personality that are not mentioned in other biographies. It is a welcome relief from the typical step-by-step accounts by other authors. Bell's work is clear and compelling, and should have particular appeal to those who want to understand the man in the context of his age. BYRON's approach is very similar to Bell's, though his biography is much longer and places more emphasis upon Cervantes' family. MACEOIN's work is essentially an historical novel about Cervantes. Like the others, it uses Cervantes' own works extensively. Its greatest appeal should be to non-scholarly readers.

SCHEVILL differs from the other biographers by examining whether or not Cervantes was attempting to reveal himself through his literary works. He also pays particular attention to the short stories contained in *Don Quixote.* Schevill's language is probably too sophisticated for a general audience. DURAN's work, primarily a literary criticism, is also intended for a scholarly audience. It does, however, contain a brief biography and account of Cervantes' times.

Like many other biographers of Cervantes, CANAVAGGIO analyzes Cervantes' works in search of his subject's true identity. In addition, Canavaggio criticizes the opinions of other biographers by scrutinizing their conclusions in light of what is now known about Cervantes' place and time. The result is that Canavaggio is highly skeptical about many of the judgments made by earlier biographers. Canavaggio's greatest contribution is his willingness to admit that certain aspects of Cervantes' life will forever remain obscure or subject to conjecture. Canavaggio's language is clear and colorful. This is a well-written and well-documented biography that will be an asset to the general public as well as to educators and scholars in the field of Spanish literature.

—Meri E. Jiménez

CÉZANNE, Paul, 1839–1906; French painter.

Fry, Roger, *Cézanne: A Study of His Development.* London, L. and V. Woolf (Hogarth Press), and New York, Macmillan, 1927.

Hanson, Lawrence, *Mountain of Victory: A Biography of Paul Cézanne.* London, Secker and Warburg, 1960; as *Mortal Victory,* New York, Holt Rinehart, 1960.

Lindsay, Jack, *Cézanne: His Life and Art.* London, Evelyn Adams, and New York, New York Graphic Society, 1969.

Mack, Gerstle, *Paul Cézanne.* London, Cape, and New York, Knopf, 1935.

Rewald, John, *Cézanne: A Biography.* London, Thames and Hudson, and New York, Abrams, 1986.

Venturi, Lionella, *Cézanne.* Geneva, Skira; New York, Rizzoli; and London, Macmillan, 1978.

Vollard, Ambroise, *Paul Cézanne: His Life and Art,* translated by Harold L. Van Doren. New York, N. L. Brown, 1923 (originally published by Galerie A. Vollard, Paris, 1914).

*

In the first English study of Cézanne, FRY sets out to detail the "rhythm of [Cézanne's] spiritual life." Since it was from Fry that the main impetus came for the introduction into Britain of the paintings of Cézanne and the other post-impressionists, his study, while not strictly a biography, is not only fascinating for any admirer of the paintings, but also highly informative on the growth and life of the cult of the painter's work after his death. It was Fry's championing of Cézanne and the post-impressionists that led to the early major exhibitions of their work at the Grafton Galleries in 1910 and 1912.

In his *Cézanne,* Fry attempts to bring the painter's personality alive by delving into his background and studying not only the works themselves but the development of Cézanne's style. In view of Fry's preoccupation with plastic form, it is not surprising that the principal value of this relatively slight work lies in the psychological analysis of the artist's use of form, and his understanding of volume, structure, and design.

The first comprehensive biography of Cézanne in English is by MACK, who uses previously unavailable material from family and other sources, notably the letters to Zola (the fruit of a friendship Cézanne formed at school and which lasted a lifetime), to his son, to Pissarro, and to Solari. As far as possible Mack's biography is compiled from documentary sources and includes hitherto unpublished verse from letters to Zola, written when Cézanne was about 20. But it is an excellent work on other counts as well; it details, for instance, the 19 colours Cezanne kept on his palette from about 1880 in order to achieve his characteristic, if harmoniously graded, "patchwork effect" to break up his planes and surfaces, while the impressionists themselves were using only six colours and had eliminated black.

Mack writes well and is as informative as the evidence permits about Cézanne's liaison from 1871 with the penniless Hortense Fiquet, of whose existence his father had to be kept ignorant. Mack refuses however to speculate beyond the tantalisingly slight evidence in the letters about what precisely happened in the summer of 1885 unsettling enough to stop Cézanne from painting. Cézanne's relationship with and final reliance on his son is well brought out, and Mack can be amusing, as on the first sitting for Cézanne of his dealer, Ambroise Vollard. Welcome attention is paid to financial detail and to the closed world round Tanguy's tiny colour shop where Cézanne would exchange a canvas he might well later have destroyed in a fit of rage for a few tubes of colour, and which was frequented, too, by Seurat, Gauguin, Sisley, and van Gogh. Monet, whose paintings were already fetching a respectable sum, Pissarro, and Renoir were among his customers. Mack's account contains good black-and-white photographs of Cézanne, his family, studio, and paintings.

VOLLARD's reminiscences of Cézanne derive their interest from Vollard's position as Cézanne's dealer. He had first seen Cézanne's pictures at Tanguy's shop in 1892 and, with considerable difficulty, since Cézanne proved almost impossible to find, organised a one-man exhibition of Cézanne at his small gallery in November 1895. Vollard mentions just over a score of the paintings exhibited by name. He is extremely entertaining when recounting his visit to Cézanne at Aix-en-Provence and the manner in which Cézanne's paintings were retrieved from the most unlikely of resting places. Vollard also reports the often adverse critical reaction to the 1895 exhibition, which in fact made Cézanne's name known, at least among the artistic elite. Pissarro, who had offered to lend his own paintings by Cézanne, talked of the "charm of this refined savage," and mentioned how Renoir, Degas, and Monet were all much taken by the quality of the paintings. Vollard's personal reminiscences are precious, and he is delightfully and irrepressibly anecdotal. Obviously, later research has produced more scholarly accounts of the life.

Of those in English HANSON claimed in 1960 that he wanted to correct the reputation of Cézanne the man, which seemed to him to be that of "a misogynist who lived and died ungraciously." This was not Cézanne's reputation in 1960, and even if it had been not only the reputation but the truth, Hanson's claim that "such a man could not have painted the works now famed throughout the civilized world" would still be untrue. Hanson mistakes courageous adherence to a personal vision, whatever lapses of what the biographer regards as proper behaviour this entails, for moral failings, assuming that moral turpitude is inconsistent with creative achievement, trusting too much to a personal reaction to the paintings, and writing "famed throughout the civilized world" when he means "well known."

Hanson's intention is clearly biographical, not critical. His text is speculative and conjectural, seeing "a visionary led astray by sexual frustration" in what sounds like perfectly normal reactions, and badly underestimating the extent to which the inhabitants of Aix were aware of what sort of canvases Cézanne was painting. Childhood summer excursions undertaken with Zola and Baille, both close friends, entailed reciting the "sonorous verses" of Homer, the "pompous rhetoric" of Victor Hugo, or the "softer passion" of Musset's poetry. Writing of this sort is difficult to take seriously in what purports to be a serious biography even if the reader does not understand the ineptitude of the characterisations of the work of the three poets. There is an index and a bibliography, but speculation about Cézanne's meeting and relationship with his future wife is given as fact, and the picture of Cézanne we are given in 1869 is frankly that of the misogynist for which there is little enough warrant in the context of the meeting with Hortense, and which Hanson set out to remove from the admittedly enormous accretion of legend surrounding the painter.

LINDSAY's biography, with its notes, index, and bibliography, is rather ponderously written and not as scholarly as it looks although it does contain a complete translation of Cézanne's verse. There is, for instance, simply no evidence that Cézanne met Hortense because she came to model for him and, given the state in which he kept his studio, it is inherently unlikely that he ever used a casual female model in 1869. There is a good deal of speculation smuggled in as fact, too, in Lindsay's account of the events of 1885. Lindsay adopts an initial, blusteringly aggressive attitude toward earlier biographers, particularly for their lack of care in the interpretation of dates, and toward the various legends and misinterpretations of behaviour that arose in Cézanne's later life; but Lindsay is more gracious toward the work of previous writers in the notes. In fact Lindsay had simply padded out what can be ascertained from his predecessors, particularly Vollard, whom he mercilessly pillages and patronizes, with a great deal of interesting although not strictly relevant material taken from the artistic and literary history of the second half of the 19th century. Much derives from the earlier work of John Rewald, the most internationally renowned of all Cézanne scholars.

VENTURI's account differs from other studies in its concentration in part on the history of Cézanne criticism and his development as a painter. Venturi discusses the artists who influenced Cézanne, the romantic tradition, impressionism, the effect of Pissarro's teaching, and Cézanne's concentration on volume and form, as well as Cézanne's artistic theories. The biographical outline of Cézanne's life and works which runs parallel to contemporary artistic events, is helpful. The work provides a very full bibliography, including correspondence, monographs, articles and reviews, special issues of periodicals, and a list of exhibitions. The bibliography is up to date to the time of publication, although the author himself died in 1961. Venturi's book contains copious and well-reproduced illustrations.

REWALD's contribution to Cézanne studies has been enormous. Apart from writing various monographs, he has edited the correspondence, increasing the total number of items from 207 in 1937 to 233 in the revised 1984 edition (*Letters*, translated by Seymour Hacker, New York, 1984). The revised edition also contains photographs together with sketches by the artist and others. A greater depth of character is revealed in these letters than was originally perceived by the public. There is more affection and less diffidence (e.g., asking Zola for help) than had been supposed. The notes at the end of the entries for each year and the commentaries are informed, assured and perceptive, while the biographical flow is helped by the inclusion of all available letters to or about Cézanne, giving an even clearer picture of Cézanne's relationships with painters in his own circle.

REWALD's most recent study, however, is a superbly written and illustrated biography of the artist, relying heavily on all the original documents and letters so far discovered. There is a wide-ranging discussion of Cézanne's artistic circle, his friends, and their attitudes to one another's works. The illustrations have been carefully chosen to supplement the text, with references set apart from the more famous of the paintings, so that interrelated themes and motives have been underlined as they recur in different contexts. This English version of Rewald's monograph, whose coffee-table format should deceive nobody about its scholarly excellence, refers students back to the French edition, especially that of 1936, entitled *Cézanne et Zola*, for complete references.

—Honor Levi

CHAGALL, Marc, 1887–1985; Russian painter in France.

Alexander, Sidney, *Marc Chagall, a Biography*. New York, Putnam, 1978; London, Cassell, 1979.

Bidermanas, Izis and Roy McMullen, *The World of Marc Chagall*. New York, Doubleday, and London, Aldus, 1968.

Chagall, Bella, *Burning Lights*. New York, Schocken Books, 1946; as *First Encounter*, translated by Barbara Bray, Schocken, 1983.

Compton, Susan, *Chagall*. London, Royal Academy of Arts/ Weidenfeld and Nicolson, and New York, Abrams, 1985.

Crespelle, Jean-Paul, *Chagall*, translated by B. Eisler. New York, Coward-McCann, 1970 (originally published as *Chagall, l'amour, le rêve, et la vie*, Paris, Presses de la Cité, 1969).

Haggard, Virginia, *My Life with Chagall*. New York, D. I. Fine, 1986; London, R. Hale, 1987.

Kagan, Andrew, *Marc Chagall*. New York, Abbeville Press, 1989.

Kamensky, Aleksandr, *Chagall: The Russian Years 1907–22*. New York, Rizzoli, and London, Thames and Hudson, 1989.

Meyer, Franz, *Marc Chagall*, translated by Robert Allen. New York, Abrams, and London, Thames and Hudson, 1964 (originally published by Dumont Schauberg, Cologne, 1961).

*

With that hypnotic naivete characteristic surely of his life and of his art at its best, Chagall produced his autobiography before he was 40. *My Life* (1960), first issued in French in 1931, contains some 20 etchings (several almost signature works of the artist) originally conceived in the 1920s. The work, with its breathless, single-line paragraphs, was begun in 1911 and continued during Chagall's enforced stay in Russia because of World War I and the Revolution. With Chagall's return to the West in 1922 (to Berlin and then Paris), he felt all the more strongly the need to record his childhood, early maturity and

first years in Paris, and his marriage, and so he brought the work to conclusion.

Chagall's first wife, BELLA CHAGALL, died in 1944 whispering "my notes." Since the 1930s and her deepening understanding of the impending destruction of the world of Eastern European Jewry, Bella had been compiling notes of her early well-to-do family life and of the lives of the Jews of Vitebsk, including her meeting with the impoverished Chagall. Filled with a floating, dream-like atmosphere inspired by her life with Chagall, Bella's work may be more readily available under its earliest title in English, *Burning Lights*. The work of KAMENSKY was made possible through eased access in recent years to both private collections and archives within the Soviet Union. This work prints documents previously unavailable. Unknown articles by Chagall and others are provided, along with photographs of Chagall, with his friends, during his work for the Jewish theatre of Moscow.

The standard monograph is by MEYER, at that time Chagall's son-in-law, and a well-known European art writer and museum director. Naturally, then, the well-researched and highly detailed text is the result of many interviews with the artist as well as the continuing aid of the artist's daughter Ida. The work is arranged chronologically and offers biographical events in a context primarily oriented to an interpretive skein for the work of that period. There is a valuable classified catalog that includes small black-and-white reproductions of 1000 works and augments the 600 other works reproduced in the text.

HAGGARD's memoir appeared after Sidney Alexander asked for her assistance during the 1970s when he was preparing his biography of Chagall (see below). After the death of Bella, Haggard became the artist's companion and the mother of his son David. Her text provides an account of what may have been the most harried years of Chagall's life (1945–52) and thus presents, aside from a general sense of his character, his reaction to his American exile, his return to Europe and Israel, and the creative problems of the aging artist resuming a search for subject matter and his place in the art world.

ALEXANDER based his biography on interviews personally conducted throughout the world hoping to come as objectively near to the living artist as possible. He also wished to avoid the control exerted by Chagall's family and friends, a control he felt permeated several of the previous works on Chagall. Thus he draws heavily on Chagall's writings and letters. The conversations he held with many people are often recounted verbatim and add to a genial and impressionist-like tone. No attempt is made to illustrate Chagall's art, and the photographic section is quite short. A selected bibliography is given for each of the important periods in the artist's life, following the nine sections of the text.

In the preparation of his concise work, CRESPELLE also spoke to Chagall and to many of the fascinating members of the Parisian art world who had known the artist. Crespelle's European orientation is reflected in his bibliography, where none of the works are given their English translations. The work has a warm, anecdotal, personal tone, typical of Crespelle's many works on art and artists, and no doubt well-suited to convey the quality of Chagall's temperament.

BIDERMANAS provides a visual biography. As a friend of the artist, he was able to take informal photographs of Chagall's world for several years, beginning in 1956; Roy McMullen provides biographical and analytical remarks in accompanying essays. Similarly, KAGAN offers a biographical sketch as he details the evolution of Chagall's career; appended are a detailed chronology, list of exhibitions, and a selected but extensive bibliography.

In the introduction to a catalog of a major Chagall exhibition held in London and Philadelphia, COMPTON provides a general biographical sketch as well as essays discussing Chagall's themes, emphasizing the pervasiveness of his Russian background. Especially valuable is Compton's own individual catalog entries, each of which is both a critical statement and a minute biographical vignette. Important paintings were available for this international retrospective exhibition, from every period of Chagall's evolution, and so an incisive picture of his life emerges in these entries. In addition, Chagall's works from the theatre, his stained glass, and his printmaking are also treated.

—Joshua Kind

CHAMBERLAIN, (Arthur) Neville, 1869–1940; English statesman.

Dilks, David, *Neville Chamberlain*. Cambridge and New York, Cambridge University Press, 1984.
Feiling, Keith, *The Life of Neville Chamberlain*. London, Macmillan, 1946.
Hyde, H. Montgomery, *Neville Chamberlain*. London, Weidenfeld and Nicolson, 1976.
Macleod, Iain, *Neville Chamberlain*. London, F. Muller, 1961; New York, Atheneum, 1962.
Rock, William R., *Neville Chamberlain*. New York, Twayne, 1969.

*

Winston Churchill before the House of Commons paid the following tribute to Neville Chamberlain: "Whatever else history may or may not say about these terrible, tremendous years, we can be sure that Neville Chamberlain acted with perfect sincerity according to his lights and strove to the utmost of his capacity and authority . . . to save the world from the awful, devastating struggle in which we are now engaged" (quoted in Macleod, see below). As the chief architect of Britain's policy of appeasement and the man who brought home from Munich "peace with honor," Chamberlain has been a figure of intense historical debate. Fortunately for his biographers, Chamberlain's private papers, consisting of diaries, journals, and weekly letters written alternately to his sisters Hilda and Ida, provide an invaluable source of information for any study of his controversial life.

Published just after the end of World War II, FEILING's book offers a sympathetic but not uncritical look at Chamberlain. Feiling was the first historian to have access to Chamberlain's private papers. Writing at the request of the Chamberlain family, Feiling lets Chamberlain speak of himself by furnishing frequent and sometimes lengthy quotes from his private papers.

He presents Chamberlain as a competent, hardworking political leader whose chief interests were the preservation of peace and the advancement of the lot of his fellow man.

Until the recent opening of the Chamberlain papers held at the University of Birmingham in England, Feiling provided the most detailed and reliable source available for extracts from the papers. For the beginning student or experienced scholar, Feiling remains the best single volume on Chamberlain's life. His insights into Chamberlain's character are penetrating and perceptive.

Following nearly two decades later, MACLEOD covers much the same ground as Feiling. Nevertheless, some readers might prefer Macleod's lighter writing style to Feiling's more labored efforts. Essentially an apologia, Macleod argues in defense of Chamberlain that appeasement was a policy of necessity forced on him by circumstances beyond his control. This defense, however, lacks adequate depth to be convincing. But Macleod suggests that above all Chamberlain was "a radical social reformer." Inevitably, Macleod concludes, while Chamberlain will always be linked with Munich and appeasement, this distorted image fails to do justice to the sum total of his life.

Two shorter interpretive biographies by Rock and Hyde build on the work of Feiling and Macleod. Serving as a good introduction to Chamberlain, ROCK's book gives a balanced but unoriginal account of Chamberlain's life that many will find dated by the outpouring of recent scholarship on appeasement. While Chamberlain achieved many positive objectives over the course of his public life, Rock sees him as a man of limited vision whose serious misjudgment of Hitler ended in "a sorry episode in history." Acknowledging Chamberlain's commitment to humanity and the cause of peace, Rock, argues that the shortcomings of Chamberlain's personality blinded him to the true nature of fascism and deluded him into believing that he could do business with Hitler. According to Rock, Chamberlain's chief failure was not the initial pursuit of appeasement but its continuance after the evidence indicated it was an unworkable policy.

The biography by HYDE is well written but disappointing. With access to newly opened Cabinet records and other official papers from the Public Records Office, Hyde constructs a spirited and well-reasoned defense of Chamberlain. The first 77 pages give an excellent summary of Chamberlain's early life. The chapters on Chamberlain and appeasement are less satisfying. Readers without prior background in the history of interwar Britain will find themselves somewhat confused by Hyde's failure to explain adequately the personalities and politics of the period. Furthermore, the book's lack of documentation makes it of little use for scholars.

DILKS has written what promises to be the definitive work on Chamberlain. Composed in a lively but scholarly style, this first volume covers only the first 60 years of Chamberlain's life. (A second volume on the crucial period of appeasement and the slide to war is promised.) Dilks justifies his publication of another Chamberlain biography by pointing to the fact that almost all the official documents and private papers are now available. No new or startling revelations come to light, but the meticulous detail in which the volume is written serves to illuminate Chamberlain's character and life to a degree never before achieved. The story of Chamberlain's five years as a sisal planter in the Bahamas at the turn of the century is especially fascinating.

Dilks does a first-rate job of explaining the close relationship between Chamberlain and his family, noting that it was only within the inner circle of his family, that Chamberlain felt fully comfortable. Good coverage is also given of Chamberlain's political career in the 1920s. For readers willing to tackle the 645 pages of this work, the rewards are great as new insights and a better understanding of Chamberlain can be gained.

—Van Michael Leslie

CHAPLIN, Charlie [Charles Spencer Chaplin], 1889–1977; English-American film actor, writer, producer.

Chaplin, Charles, Jr., *My Father: Charlie Chaplin.* New York, Random House, and London, Longman, 1960.

Geduld, Harry M., editor, *Charlie Chaplin's Own Story.* Bloomington, Indiana University Press, 1985.

Gehring, Wes D., editor, *Charlie Chaplin: a Bio-Bibliography.* Westport, Connecticut, Greenwood Press, 1983.

Huff, Theodore, *Charlie Chaplin.* New York, H. Schuman, 1951; London, Cassell, 1952.

Lyons, Timothy J., editor, *Charlie Chaplin: A Guide to References and Resources.* Boston, G. K. Hall, and London, Prior, 1979.

Maland, Charles J., *Chaplin and American Culture: the Evolution of a Star Image.* Princeton, New Jersey, Princeton University Press, 1989.

Manvell, Roger, *Chaplin.* Boston, Little Brown, 1974; London, Hutchinson, 1975.

McCabe, John, *Charlie Chaplin.* New York, Doubleday, and London, Robson, 1978.

McCaffrey, Donald W., editor, *Focus on Chaplin.* Englewood Cliffs, New Jersey, Prentice-Hall, 1971.

Robinson, David, *Chaplin: The Mirror of Opinion.* Bloomington, Indiana University Press, and London, Secker and Warburg, 1983.

Robinson, David, *Chaplin: His Life and Art.* New York, McGraw-Hill, and London, Collins, 1985.

*

Even though GEDULD claims that Charlie Chaplin was a "peculiarly unreliable autobiographer," he proudly provides us with the "lost autobiography" of Mr. Chaplin (originally written in 1916), if for no other reason than to allow readers an opportunity to witness a man's self-conception of his life at the pinnacle of his career. According to Geduld, Chaplin only allowed people to know what he wanted them to know about his life, and nothing else. Soon after Chaplin's first autobiography was published, he became concerned about possible misinformation presented in its text and had the book withdrawn from the market and, in addition, requested all available copies to be destroyed. (For this reason, Manvell, see below, considers this work to be a collector's item.) Geduld must be commended for restoring the original book and having it reprinted for researchers to compare with other sources on Chaplin's life. This early work is definitely written more as promotional information than true bio-

graphical data. Geduld includes a substantial "notes" section in this reprinted version, which aids the researcher with the discrepancies that exist between the 1916 book and Chaplin's 1964 autobiography.

The second attempt by Chaplin to document his life (*My Autobiography*, 1964) was written at the end of his film career. He had the advantage of hindsight and the disadvantage of faded memories when putting together this memoir. The information spans Chaplin's entire lifetime and is essential reading for any researcher. One realizes when reading through this book that Charlie Chaplin was the best in his field and that worldwide recognition provided him with many notable friends.

CHARLES CHAPLIN JR. (first son of Charlie and Lita Grey) wrote a very enlightening biography that gives important insight to his father's personal and private life (something missing in the two autobiographies). The book, as expected, tends toward sentimentality, but it provides essential information on Chaplin's home life and also contains a unique perspective on the famous "Joan Barry affair," which was over-dramatized and played an important role in his eventual downfall as an idol. Charles Chaplin Jr.'s biography is well written and allows the film researcher a wonderful glimpse at "behind-the-scenes" activity in the motion picture career of his father.

The first really well done biography on Chaplin is HUFF's. This one covers the star's career up to 1950 and is known as the "definitive" early biography of Chaplin. The book is well-documented, well-illustrated, and contains a very nice "index to films" (with plot descriptions for the Keystone and Essanay productions). Also included in this work is the "Biographical Sketches of the People Professionally Associated with Chaplin" section. These individual paragraphs prove to be very useful to the researcher. Manvell (see below) states that Huff's book was the "most authoritative account of Chaplin's life and the most thorough analysis of his films" to that time.

MANVELL's 1974 book is a rather condensed, though precise, biography with only 225 pages of text. The chapters are divided up into 10-15 year time periods and contain a great deal of information for such a short book. It is the "selected bibliography" at the end of the work that sets it apart from any previous source. Manvell's annotations for each item listed present a helpful guide for the novice researcher on Chaplin.

McCABE also provides a fairly brief biography that takes a more concentrated look at the major films of Chaplin and parallels them with his personal life during the same time periods. McCabe includes an excellent bibliography of books and journal/newspaper articles that is much more extensive than Manvell's. The filmography sections in both contain the same information written in slightly different formats.

ROBINSON has contributed two very different sources, both of which provide relevant material for study. The first and shorter of the two (1983) is arranged with vignettes in place of chapters. Robinson states that "the object of this book has been to trace Chaplin's career as it has appeared in *the mirror of opinion*." Robinson studied numerous existing biographies, articles, and manuscripts in preparation of this work, which presents a well-defined picture of Chaplin. Robinson gives credit where credit is due and merely acts as editor for much of the book. This work includes an easy-to-read graph as part of the filmography that demonstrates which individuals worked alongside Chaplin in each of his Keystone, Essanay, and Mutual films. The remaining portion of the filmography lists full cast and crew credits for Chaplin's feature-length films from 1923 to 1952.

ROBINSON went even further in his research for the second book (1985) by using the public archives in the Greater London Record Office. This book provides a great deal of new material, though it is also padded with quotes from the several earlier major works on Chaplin. All in all, the results are very rewarding to the reader and researcher. *Chaplin: His Life and Art* contains an excellent "Chaplin Chronology" section that covers over 700 notable dates in the life and career of Mr. Chaplin. Also included for the first time is a Chaplin family tree chart covering the years 1786 to 1962. Robinson's second book is interspersed with many unique photographs, reproductions of letters and manuscripts, and even Charlie Chaplin cartoons from around the world. It also includes Chaplin's tour schedules for his early British troupe tours, three complete Keystone scenarios (with the screen text included), and a filmography far superior to the ones in Huff and McCabe. Of particular interest is Robinson's section of "The FBI and Chaplin," which discusses highlights from the 1900-page file on Charlie Chaplin. One last important appendix is the "Chaplin Who's Who." This is a thorough annotated list of all the important people in Chaplin's life. It includes details on family members, co-stars, directors, and associates and is twice the size of the similar section in Huff. Overall, Robinson's second book features some welcome additional data to help direct the reader into new avenues of research. It should be considered as an essential companion to HUFF.

MALAND's work analyzes the relationship between Charlie Chaplin and the United States. He studies Chaplin much as Edmund Wilson analyzes Charles Dickens, in a work that "shows the artist as a human being grounded in a particular time and place, struggling to understand self and society and to embody that understanding in the work of art." Maland discusses the American press, government, and interest groups who all contributed to the full development of Chaplin's image. He shows how Chaplin was treated as a god-like genius of the silent screen early in his career by the same people who eventually stripped him of all dignity and caused the end of his career. Cold War politics is presented here in its most destructive light. Maland's work is exceptional and well worth the reading. The bibliography is indispensable for any serious Chaplin researcher.

McCAFFREY's short volume is beneficial for its collection of essays and reviews on Chaplin's early career. Many of the major authors on Chaplin come together here: Geduld is given credit as supervising editor, and Manvell and Lyons both supply essays. Much of the material can be found as chapters in other biographies, but the most important contributions are worth an inspection of the book. Winston Churchill provides an essay that mentions the "universality" of Charlie's film character, the little tramp. Chaplin himself is author of several essays. One of particular interest is entitled "What People Laugh At." Here, the reader is given the opportunity to catch a short glimpse of the philosophy of Charlie Chaplin.

The last two remaining essential works on Chaplin are book-length bibliographies written only four years apart. LYONS has compiled a very forceful list of writings about Chaplin that is more comprehensive than any other source available. He also includes synopses for each title in the filmography that no other major biography provides. Another strong point for Lyons is the

"Note on Archival Sources and Distributors" section, which gives the researcher much needed information on locating primary sources on Chaplin.

GEHRING's installment of the Greenwood Bio-Bibliography Series contains very little new information when compared to Lyon's work. The bibliography is less impressive and its list of musical compositions is identical. It does, however, contain a pleasant chapter entitled "Chaplin on Chaplin: an interview and an article," as well as a short discography (not easily found elsewhere).

—Richard C. Dickey

CHARLEMAGNE [Charles the Great], *ca.* 742–814; Frankish king, emperor of the West.

Almedingen, E. M., *Charlemagne: A Study.* London, Bodley Head, 1968.

Davis, H. W. Carless, *Charlemagne (Charles the Great): The Hero of Two Nations.* New York and London, Putnam, 1899.

Grant, A. J., editor and translator, *Early Lives of Charlemagne.* London, A. Moring, 1905; London, Chatto and Windus, and Boston, J. W. Luce, 1907.

Hodgkin, Thomas, *Charles the Great.* London and New York, Macmillan, 1899.

James, G. P. R., *The History of Charlemagne.* London, Longman, 1832; New York, Harper, 1833.

Lamb, Harold, *Charlemagne: The Legend and the Man.* New York, Doubleday, 1954; London, R. Hale, 1955.

Loyn, H. R., and J. Percival, editors, *The Reign of Charlemagne.* London, E. Arnold, 1975; New York, St. Martin's, 1976.

Thorpe, Lewis, editor and translator, *Two Lives of Charlemagne.* London, Penguin, and New York, Viking, 1969.

*

It has been said by one of Charlemagne's biographers, E. M. Almedingen (see below), that the normal course of a biography is not possible in his case. A biographer should follow his subject from cradle to grave, but so little is known about Charlemagne's birth and childhood, and so overwhelming are his public activities and so important the circumstances of his reign, that the normal pattern cannot be followed. It is for this reason that "The Age of Charlemagne" is a more frequent topic than "The Life of Charlemagne."

This is strange because Charlemagne was the subject of two biographies—by Einhard and Notker—both written within a century of his death, both by ecclesiastics who were filled with admiration for him, although the two works do not resemble each other in any other way. They have been edited and translated many times, and all writers on Charlemagne have used them as sources. The volumes edited and translated by GRANT and THORPE contain the texts of these two early lives.

Einhard, who is sometimes called Eginhard, was born about A.D. 775 and was present at the royal (later imperial) court of Charlemagne and his son Louis until about 828. He probably began to write his life sometime after 830, that is to say a relatively short time after the death of his master in 814, but long enough for him to have seen the ruin of his empire. He had been very close to Charlemagne and was able to write confidently about his appearance, his character, and his behaviour. He tells us that his body was large and strong, that his eyes were large and piercing, that he constantly took exercise by riding, hunting, and swimming. He praises him for his abstemiousness, his love of family (although he hints at scandals), his concern for justice and learning, and his steadfastness of purpose.

But there are problems. Einhard is reticent about his master's early life, and since he must have known about it this has suggested to many either that Charlemagne was born before the Church had sanctioned the marriage of his parents or that he had had a particularly unhappy childhood. He writes of Charlemagne having married the daughter of the King of the Lombards (whom he does not name) at his mother's bidding and then divorcing her "for some unknown reason a year later." To a later wife, Fastrada, Einhard attributes much of the cruelty of Charlemagne in his campaigns. Although he describes him as speaking Latin fluently and understanding Greek, he suggests that he had little skill in writing, "this strange task which was begun too late in life." He passes briefly, even disdainfully, over Charlemagne's assumption of the imperial title on Christmas Day, 800, and he suggests that the king was both surprised by and regretful over what happened.

A general explanation, which subsequent biographers have followed, is that Einhard took as his model the Latin Suetonius and his accounts of Roman emperors. This meant that he wrote a secular biography that was based on secular values. Charlemagne was not depicted as a warrior of God, someone serving the Christian faith by force of arms and living under the protection of holy saints and angels. He was a war leader, one who could reasonably be compared to Godfrid, the king of the Danes, a bold and successful man, who was pagan.

The other ecclesiastical biographer was a monk of Saint Gall, usually called Notker the Stammerer, who wrote in 883 or 884. Not all of the manuscript has been preserved, and the author is very ready to admit that when old men told him stories about the great king, he did not always listen. It is undoubtedly an account of the reputation of Charlemagne and of how he was remembered rather than an historical account of his life. Although Notker repeats the story of Charlemagne's being surprised, and in some ways dismayed, when he was crowned emperor, he nevertheless appears as "the most glorious," "the unconquered and the unconquerable," "God-fearing, just and devout," "the bishop of bishops." The legend has begun, although cautiously, within half a century of his death. If he does not yet work miracles, miracles are conducted in his presence. If he does not yet lead the armies of Christendom to Jerusalem, he is already seen as the protector of the Holy City.

Biographers writing in the 19th century had to take account of the deliberate brevity and conciseness of Einhard's writings and the fact that he did not seek to magnify either his subject or his office. They also had to be wary of the atmosphere of deliberate and sustained romance that surrounded the legend of Charlemagne, which became easier to study in its literary forms from the 1830s onwards. Entertainers and chroniclers of many sorts had recounted stories that were within a popular and semi-historical tradition or that were derived from the tales that

monks told to pilgrims. Charlemagne's crossing of the Pyrenees and the Saracens destroying the rearguard of his army at the battle of Roncevaux is the historical starting-point for many of these animated mythical accounts involving his nephew Roland and Bishop Turpin. The epics of "the snow-haired emperor" are told. Later legends produced new episodes in the life of Charlemagne: that he had risen from the dead in order to lead the first Crusade; that he had visited Jerusalem and Constantinople; that he had fought a great war against the king of the Africans. Sometimes the person of the king is degraded in favour of rebellious but justified lords. As the stories are transported into German, Spanish, Icelandic, and Italian literature, so the character of the king changes; he can be depicted as a bandit, or as a dotard, or as a vaguely perceived centre of power.

JAMES' biography is filled with unmitigated praise for Charlemagne. He dismisses the rumours concerning the mysteries of his birth as so many "pleasant fables," and he gets rid of the problem of not knowing what sort of education he had by saying that the world was a sufficient school, and the events by which he was surrounded sufficient instructors, to cultivate his mind and strengthen his character. The key to the man, for James, was war, which was a necessity for the time and for the country. The Franks could not have been governed without war. Charlemagne, amongst all his other qualities, had all the talents and disposition to make a great war leader.

HODGKIN stresses other factors. He pays particular attention to the fact that the pope had gone through the unusual ceremony of anointing both Pippin and his son Charlemagne, so that the latter always felt a particular responsibility to the papacy and an apprehension of divine judgement (it might have been for this reason, Hodgkin suggests, that Charlemagne rapidly rejected his mother's choice of bride, the Lombard princess, since he knew that the Pope disapproved of this union). Hodgkin does not believe many of the stories told by the early biographers: that Fastrada, his fourth wife, was responsible for Charlemagne's cruel savagery against the Saxons, or that Charlemagne was so sufficiently acute to have early perceived the future threat that would come from the Norsemen, to name two instances. However, he does accept that Charlemagne was reluctant to be made Emperor, suggesting that it was because the pope had granted him this title that he became disturbed. He accepts too that Charlemagne could put family loyalties before affairs of state, suggesting a reason to believe that apart from including the title of Emperor, there was little resemblance between the city-built Roman state and the Carolingian kingdom that was "cradled in the forest and which depended upon the loyalty of henchmen to their chief."

Other biographers, DAVIS at the end of the 19th century, and ALMEDINGEN in 1968, see all the public activities of Charlemagne as stemming from one root: his faith in God and his allegiance to the Christian Church. But LAMB, who emphasises in his narrative the drama of the life of Charlemagne, claims that when the barbarian Frank was crowned by the pope, he could not understand what an Augustus Caesar was. He had been tricked. He laughed at himself. He hastened away from Rome and never wore his coronation regalia again. He was not the servant of the Christian Church.

Thus biographers work over the original lives of Charlemagne again and again. When Einhard suggested that Charles could not write, did he mean this literally, or did he mean that Charles could not write a fine ecclesiastical script? Biographers are attracted to the mystery of a man whose reign briefly lit up the confusions of an age.

—Douglas Johnson

_____

CHARLES I, 1600–1649; English monarch.

Carlton, Charles, *Charles I: The Personal Monarch*. London and Boston, Routledge, 1983.
Gregg, Pauline, *King Charles I*. London, Dent, 1981.
Higham, Florence M. G. E., *Charles I: A Study*. London, Hamilton, 1932.
Strong, Sir Roy, *Van Dyck: Charles I on Horseback*. London, Lane, 1972.

*

Charles I was the most private of kings. He wrote little, retreated into himself readily, and presented an icy and closed visage to the world. He has proved an exceptionally elusive subject for his biographers. Most historians have blamed him for the civil wars of the mid-17th century, seeing him as determined on the pursuit of policies hated by most of his subjects and as utterly lacking in the political skills needed to manage an early modern state. Many biographers have seized on a comment Charles made in 1623 (before he even became king) and recorded at the time by William Laud (later his archbishop), seeing it as the essence of his unfitness to be king. Charles said he could never become a lawyer because "I cannot defend a bad, nor yield a good cause."

HIGHAM's biography is probably the best of the cluster of six or seven published between the two World Wars and which constitute the first serious attempts at biography of this king since his own century. Higham had a thorough grounding in the governmental records of the period (her doctoral thesis was on the office of secretary of state in the 17th century). Her other great passion was the Church of England, and she wrote a distinguished series of studies of Elizabethan and early Stuart Churchmen. Thus, although her study recognizes Charles' weaknesses as a statesman and acknowledges his pursuit of unpopular policies, it is also rooted in an admiration for his willingness to die for the Anglican Church. Her final sentences evoked his "steadfast death," which caused his subjects "in the fulness of time . . . of their own free will [to] restore the Church and Crown for which Charles and the Cavaliers had died." Her book is as moderate a statement as can be found of the case for Charles the Martyr, whose death is still recalled annually by many Anglo-Catholics. Higham solved the problem of telling the story of a King who tells us so little of himself by creating a series of tableaux in which Charles is seen in relationship to one other person in each succeeding part of his life. For the early years of the reign, for example, his story is told successively through the eyes of the duke of Buckingham, Henrietta Maria, and Sir John Eliot; and the years 1640–45 through the eyes of Strafford, Pym, and Rupert. It is a very effective device. It leads to value judgments less fashionable nowadays than in 1932, but

is at times quite moving. Thus at the end of the chapter on Laud, Higham concludes that "in the sin of Strafford's betrayal, in the loyalty of the Cavaliers, in his own deepening love of the Church for which he died, Charles was to learn the meaning of passion and sacrifice, and despising his own weakness, was to win salvation." Higham, writing of Charles' dilemmas in 1641–42, says "Charles, who loved to live by maxim, had none to guide him in his extremity. He was like a blind man at the crossroads and he had neither the imagination to realize the pass in which he stood, nor power of decision to nerve him to walk with constancy down any path." The pivotal event in her biography is the trial and betrayal of Strafford, and the account of Charles' loss of nerve as the mob screamed for Strafford's blood. Her account of how fear for the safety of his wife and children caused Charles to betray his promise to save his loyal minister is brilliantly handled. Here, if not elsewhere, Higham has the imaginative power and insight of a great novelist.

GREGG turned to Charles I after writing the biography of a very different hero of the English Revolution, the Leveller leader "Freeborn John" Lilburne. Her study is admirably clear and cool. It offers a narrative account of the reign that is balanced in its judgments and interpretations without ever startling the reader or demonstrating special insights. It sets Charles against an interpretation of the 17th century that was becoming rather outdated by 1981, and Charles himself remains rather two-dimensional. But it is a very accurate, clear, and readable account, probably the safest recommendation for those who have a limited knowledge of the period in question. It contains an exceptionally full and helpfully laid out bibliography. For example there is a section listing the 41 biographies of Charles that had been published before hers, and another section listing the best biographies of other members of his family and of those close to him.

CARLTON's biography is more ambitious. It is, in part, an attempt at psychobiography, although Carlton is aware that one cannot "recall the subject to Clio's couch." In the years of preparation for this biography, Carlton had published articles in which psychoanalytic theory was quite crudely applied to the facts of Charles' life; and reviewers had given these articles short shrift. To his credit, Carlton learnt from his critics, and the resulting full biography is perhaps the best early modern British historical biography to deploy such theories. They allow Carlton to ask questions rather than provide him with answers. Carlton has researched his subject more extensively than any of his predecessors, and he delayed publication long enough to be able to draw on the extensive "revisionist" writings on early Stuart history. He is especially good at drawing out the significance of small detail. No one has better caught the importance of the stages of Charles' relationship with his wife. If for Higham the key to the reign can be found in the betrayal of Strafford, for Carlton the key is to be found in the way the insecure Charles cocooned himself in the fantasy worlds of the Masque and the Garter ceremony, and in the "beauty of holiness" that lay at the heart of his and Laud's religious reforms. Charles believed that external order would bring about inner order and peace, and his attempts to make all his subjects behave like so many million actors in a Court Masque are the essence of his tragedy. Carlton's final chapters of a king reconciled to death and martyrdom are as moving in their way as are Higham's account of Charles' mental anguish and despair in 1641.

If, as many have argued, Charles is best understood not through his words but through the pictures he had painted, then STRONG's study of the greatest of all Van Dyck's English portraits—the painting of *Charles I on Horseback*—may get us closer to the heart of Charles' self-image than any other study. Strong offers a powerful analysis of many aspects of the painting and the cultural values it enshrines. His conclusion is that beyond the precise classical, Renaissance, and chivalric resonances of the painting, there is a "mood of calm spiritual contemplation [which] was undoubtedly Van Dyck's master stroke for that most pious of kings."

—John Morrill

CHARLES II, 1630–1685; English monarch.

Airy, Osmund, *Charles II*. London and New York, Goupil, 1901.
Ashley, Maurice, *Charles II: The Man and the Statesman*. London, Weidenfeld and Nicolson, and New York, Praeger, 1971.
Bryant, Sir Arthur, *King Charles II*. London and New York, Longman, 1931.
Hutton, Ronald, *Charles II: King of England, Scotland, and Ireland*. Oxford, Clarendon Press, and New York, Oxford University Press, 1989.
Jones, James R., *Charles II: Royal Politician*. London, Allen and Unwin, 1987.
Ollard, Richard, *The Image of the King*. London, Hodder and Stoughton, and New York, Atheneum, 1979.

*

BRYANT's is the classic biography of Charles II. Bryant was a gentleman-amateur, a man of belles lettres, the kind of author who clearly wrote not in his shirtsleeves but in his tuxedo. He wrote prolifically and patriotically about all eras of English history, but especially about the 17th century. His three-volume biography of Pepys and his edition of Charles II's letters, speeches, and declarations are companions to this life of Charles, a life which, the new impression of 1949 proudly boasted, had already sold more than 53,000 copies. It is beautifully crafted, telling the story of Charles' reign in a seamless web of narrative (though the history of his boyhood and exile during the Interregnum is very sketchy). There is never any doubt that Bryant prefers the easy-going pragmatic Stuart to the zeal of Cromwell and the Puritans; and Charles' squalid politicking and whoring are handled with delicate indulgence. Charles is seen as the founder of the British Empire and restorer of the Navy, who consistently outwitted the self-interested plutocrats who were the heirs of puritan and parliamentarian traditions. It is an effective celebration of a venal patriarchialism. The writing has a dated feel to it; the evocative writing often comes across as quaint (as in the opening of chapter one—"as the last streaks of daylight, September 3rd, 1651, fell on the Worcestershire landscape, a tall, dark fugitive drew in his horse on a lonely heath"); but it is vividly realized and Bryant has an en-

viable eye for the apt quotation from a good range of printed sources. The illustrations are anything but quaint. Not (principally) the overused Kneller and Lely portraits, but unusual engravings and a fine bust of Charles carved by Grinling Gibbons. Bryant also includes a most useful plan of the layout of Whitehall Palace, which speaks volumes about the conduct of politics in Restoration England.

AIRY's earlier biography is the product of a certain Victorian primness, against which Bryant was reacting. But it is a classic of its type. Airy had spent many years immersed in the archives of the period, editing, amongst other things, Bishop Gilbert Burnet's *History of My Own Times*, still the most essential of all personal memoirs of Charles' reign. Airy's moralizing was thus based on secure knowledge, and the book is not without sympathy for a man whose personality was warped by childhood disasters and adolescent traumas (his puberty did coincide after all with the public execution of his father). The arrested moral development is thus recognized, and the final conclusion is not quite as heartless as it seems: "His guide was not duty; it was not even ambition; it was ease, amusement and lust. The cup of pleasure was filled deep for him, and he grasped it with both hands. But pleasure is not happiness. There is no happiness for him who lives and dies without beliefs, without enthusiasm, and without love." With writing as attractive as this, one can put up with the prurience. It has a zest and an energy that make it, for this reviewer, much more of a classic biography than that of Bryant.

ASHLEY is another full-time writer who has produced more than 30 well-researched and attractively written books, mainly on the 17th century. His volume on Charles II, though one of his less probing studies, is nonetheless a cooler, more balanced, more nuanced picture than Bryant's; Charles is praised more as a political tactician than as a strategist, and his mendacity is seen both as a political strength and a moral weakness. It is especially strong as a study of Charles' relations with foreign states. Like Bryant, Ashley made effective use of all the obvious printed materials, but only scratched the surface of the manuscript collections pertinent to the reign.

OLLARD set out to write a "double biography" of Charles I and Charles II; but while the ghost of Charles I stalks the whole of the book, not least in the mind of his son, the book is really about Charles II and his determination to regain the throne after the public execution of his father and the abolition of monarchy, and his equal determination, once he had regained it, "not to go on his travels again." In other words, Charles II was determined not to repeat his father's errors. He therefore fell habitually into the opposite ones. Ollard writes well, with an easy fluency of style and an ability to move gently through a topic with minimum scaffolding. His is very much a psychological portrait of the two kings, not a study of their time. Its frame is not narrative. Ollard offers a series of discursive essays that ultimately offer a rounded picture of Charles. Amongst other things, this study offers what is probably the most convincing account of Charles II's religion, examining and holding in creative tension both the tug of Catholicism and the sceptical, deist dimensions. Charles' style of government has also never been better caught. The final 40 pages offer an engaging account of 18th- and 19th-century writings about the two kings.

JONES offers a short, pithy study of Charles' part in the politics and government of his reign. Jones has devoted a lifetime of study to the period 1658–1714 and is the author of several major monographs on subjects within that period. He therefore brought to this book a lifetime of immersion in the archives. On the other hand, the book itself is quite lightly annotated. It is more of a reflective essay than a considered piece of research. Jones' aim is both to demonstrate the extent of Charles' personal responsibility for policy and its implementation, and to measure the effectiveness of the policies he espoused. Jones traces the changing pressures of external and internal forces upon the restored monarch, and sees Charles as endlessly adapting and adjusting, winning one pyrrhic victory after another.

HUTTON has produced the best-researched and best-written biography of any Stuart monarch. It is distinctive and distinguished in several ways. First, it benefits from the sheer scale and richness of the archival research that lies behind it, which Hutton expertly shapes and controls. Second, it offers a very thorough and revealing account of Charles' exile on the Continent in the 1650s, during which many of his basic drives and prejudices were formed or nourished. Previous biographies offer thinly researched preambles to studies of the reign; Hutton offers instead a penetrating account that constantly makes possible an explanation of later events. Third, Hutton does give full coverage to Charles' policies in Scotland and Ireland as well as in England. This is the only biography yet written of the *British* monarchy in the early modern period. Despite these great strengths, however, it must be said that Hutton's book is a penetrating study of the reign more than of the monarch. Hutton confesses in an uncharacteristically diffident conclusion ("monarch in a masquerade") that "[Charles] remains . . . a set of strongly marked characteristics with a cold void at the centre of them. He was a monarch who loved masks . . . [and] behind these coverings, something was always missing." Hutton certainly identifies the king's cruelty, amorality, cynicism, *ennui*. Perhaps he misses the residue of divine right belief that his father, through his genes or through his martyrdom, had bequeathed him.

—John Morrill

CHARLES V, 1500–1558; Holy Roman emperor, king of Spain as Charles I.

Armstrong, Edward, *The Emperor Charles V* (2 vols.). London and New York, Macmillan, 1902.
Brandi, Karl, *The Emperor Charles V: The Growth and Destiny of a Man and of a World Empire*. New York, Knopf, and London, Cape, 1939.
Fernandez Alvarez, Manuel, *Charles V: Elected Emperor and Hereditary Ruler*, translated by J. A. Lalagunal. London, Thames and Hudson, 1975.
Habsburg, Otto von (Otto, Archduke of Austria), *Charles V*, translated by Michael Ross. New York, Praeger, and London, Weidenfeld and Nicolson, 1970 (originally published by Hachette, Paris, 1967).
Lewis, D. B. Wyndham, *Emperor of the West: A Study of Emperor Charles V*. London, Eyre and Spottiswoode, 1932.

Rady, Martyn, *Emperor Charles V*. London and New York, Longman, 1988.
Sandoval, Prudencio de, *The History of Charles V*, translated by Captain John Stevens. London, R. Smith, 1703 (originally published, Madrid, 1675).
Schwarzenfeld, Gertrude von, *Charles V: Father of Europe*. London, Hollis and Carter, and Chicago, H. Regnery, 1957.
Tyler, Royall, *The Emperor Charles V*. London, Allen and Unwin, and Fair Lawn, New Jersey, Essential Books, 1956.

*

There seems to have been little interest in studying Charles V at length in English before the 20th century, but the publication of his *Autobiography* (translated by Francis Simpson, London, 1862) caused him renewed attention. This work is difficult to get hold of but fascinating for the personal insight it affords. The narrative reveals a very human figure of the private man as well as the public ruler. This work in turn sparked off a review of the image of Charles V which is reflected in ARMSTRONG's book, characterised by Armstrong's estimation of Charles as "not quite a great man, nor quite a good man." A new realism is evident in the approach of the more modern biographers.

Martyn Rady (see below) is one of the many who regard BRANDI to be Charles V's greatest biographer. Brandi's work is kind in its evaluation of its subject. Brandi pursues the theme of Charles V as belonging to a bygone era of high moral and religious values. This view was first adopted by Philip III's court historian, SANDOVAL (London, 1703), who argued the anachronism of Charles V in relation to the final years of his life while maintaining Charles' more worldly ambition for success as a ruler during his political career. It is interesting to note the significance of Brandi's book during the Nazi era of German history. Otto von Habsburg (see below) points out that it went through four editions between 1937 and 1942 and suggests that this, along with its discernable latent criticisms of the Nazi regime and of Hitler in particular, can be argued to indicate that it filled an important place in the literature of the time. However, this may be going a little far as the number of editions through which it has subsequently passed shows that it is a great work in its own right.

The works of Lewis and Schwarzenfeld both have an ideological mission. LEWIS sees the hopes and aspirations of Charles V in purely religious terms and is notable for putting the reign in a wider context, looking to northern Europe: France and England. In seeking to make the problem relevant to his contemporary British readers, Lewis is anxious to draw lessons he feels should be learnt. He finishes with the words, "From Rome, Ancient and Christian, Europe derives all that makes her worth defence. By the return to Rome these things may still be preserved and the unity and safety of Europe regained."

Similarly with SCHWARZENFELD. This work began as a volume to be entitled "Pictures from Spain," and is divided into short, titled sections, although often on unusual and not wholly important events. It is well seasoned with illustrations, contains an index and potted biography of persons included, and concentrates primarily on Charles in his Spanish context. The bias is anticapitalist and, while establishing Charles V as the father of "the modern view of the world," Schwarzenfeld's work represents a departure from the traditional anachronistic view, calling its readers to revise this world.

TYLER's book is credited with much the same understanding of its subject as Brandi's. This is a well thought of attempt to get at the personality of the man and is based on the personal correspondence of the emperor with his ministers and ambassadors. The work is praised for its understanding of the emperor as a man by Charles V's descendent, Otto von Habsburg (see below).

HABSBURG writes as one would when attempting to defend a relative. He paints a highly sympathetic and emotional view of his ancestor, writing as though Charles V were on trial and he his defence lawyer, and speaking with the understated authority of one who feels he understands as few are able the psychology and position of his subject. This is an interesting though subjective book because it attempts to put Charles in his Habsburg context, and within this framework to examine the intellect and personality of the man. It is readable and presumes little former knowledge of the period.

FERNANDEZ ALVAREZ's work is also safe for the student who knows little of the man or his times. This is a well-researched and well-constructed book that includes illustration, maps, and a genealogical table. This biography, which unusually traces the life of Charles V from childhood to death, emphasises the loneliness of Charles' position as head of his many disparate dominions. It also seeks to extract the true Charles as the politician from the picture generated by many other historians, who have tended to confuse his policies with those of his councillors. This is a detailed and chronologically comprehensive study of the reign that is both helpful for the novice student and useful to the scholar who wants a fresh and lucid appraisal of the man.

RADY's book serves as an excellent introduction to the study of Charles V. With excellent opening chapters on the broader context of Charles' times, the student is guided carefully and intelligibly through the major problems encountered during the reign to emerge with a balanced overall view. This is backed up with a short document section designed to give an informed insight into various aspects of Charles' reign, both into his persona and into the political events with which he was faced. Rady also provides an illuminating appraisal of the biographies of Charles V.

—Rebecca C. Pilcher

CHAUCER, Geoffrey, *ca.* 1342–1400; English poet.

Brewer, Derek, *Chaucer and His World*. New York, Dodd Mead, and London, Eyre Methuen, 1978.

Chute, Marchette G., *Geoffrey Chaucer of England*. New York, Dutton, 1946; London, R. Hale, 1951.

Coulton, G. G., *Chaucer and His England*. London, Methuen, and New York, Putnam, 1908; revised edition, with new bibliography, London, Methuen, and New York, Barnes and Noble, 1963.

Gardner, John, *The Life and Times of Chaucer*. New York, Knopf, 1976; London, Cape, 1977.

Godwin, William, *Life of Geoffrey Chaucer* (4 vols.). London, T. Davison, 1803.

Howard, Donald R., *Chaucer: His Life, His Works, His World*. New York, Dutton, and London, Weidenfeld and Nicolson, 1987.

Jenks, Tudor, *In the Days of Chaucer*. New York, Barnes, 1904.

Lounsbury, Thomas R., *Studies in Chaucer: His Life and Writings* (3 vols.). New York, Harper, 1891–92.

Wagenknecht, Edward, *The Personality of Chaucer*. Norman, University of Oklahoma Press, 1968.

*

Over a period of 25 years, from 1875–1900, the Chaucer Society gathered together every known document relating to Geoffrey Chaucer's life into four volumes called the *Life-Records*. Much of this information has been available disparately for quite some time, but no systematic sorting, organizing, or compiling had been attempted. (This invaluable resource was re-edited and updated sporadically from 1927 to 1966 when the *Chaucer Life-Records*, edited by M. M. Crow and C. C. Olson, was published.) This abundant official evidence from the 14th century forms the authentic basis for any biography of Chaucer. These public documents provide information on his governmental positions, his family, his residences, his legal affairs and actions, his military experience, his travels, his finances, and his acquaintances and associates. However, the psychological insight, so necessary to modern biography, that might have been gleaned from contemporary diaries, journals, and personal correspondence is not to be found in the *Life-Records*; the preservation of such materials, if they ever existed, was not common practice 600 years ago.

This simultaneous wealth and dearth of information is part of what makes writing a life of Chaucer so problematic. The other difficulty is that Chaucer was a brilliant writer. Donald Howard noted in his biography (see below) that Chaucer "would be a good subject for a biography had he never written a line of poetry." But Chaucer not only wrote poetry and lived an interesting life apart from his literary endeavours; he also created a poetic *persona*, and thereby set a seductive trap for his future biographers. Literary critics make a distinction between Chaucer the author and Chaucer the Pilgrim when they discuss *The Canterbury Tales*; and in all his poetry he takes care to create a character, "Chaucer." This is a fairly common literary game of the period, particularly for writers such as Chaucer and John Langland, so much of whose poetry is ironic and therefore unreliable in establishing personal histories. The biographer's problem is to separate the person from the *persona*, and to be more than usually cautious about reading autobiographical truth into the writer's words while doing so.

Biographies of Chaucer written before the compilation of the *Life-Records* expound the Chaucer legend, and those written after the *Life-Records* appeal to facts. Short, laudatory biographies about Chaucer began to be written in the mid-1500s. The first ones were written in Latin, but in 1598 Speght wrote a short biography in English as the introduction to his edition of Chaucer's works (not all of which were really Chaucer's, but Speght did not know that). Speght used official records, literary references to Chaucer by Chaucer's contemporaries, and interpretations of references in Chaucer's alleged works to create a picture of the man. This practice of short, introductory biographical essays continued through the centuries as Chaucer scholarship became a more serious pursuit, with the biographies tending to draw on one another and perpetuate misinformation, mistakes, and myths along with actual facts.

The last of the "legend" biographies was also the first full-length biography of Chaucer. Published in 1803, GODWIN's biography met with immediate critical contempt and condemnation. It would be nice to say that this reception was the result of political prejudice, but unfortunately such is not the case. Chaucer is basically a straw man for Godwin's interest in himself. Essentially, Godwin puts himself in the place of Chaucer and then presumes that Chaucer would have naturally acted as he, Godwin, would have done in similar circumstances. Chaucer's motivations are therefore Godwin's. To be fair to Godwin, he did genuinely appreciate Chaucer's literary skill and did make some astute discoveries and interpretations concerning Chaucer's works. But he also insults previous editors of Chaucer (particularly Tyrwhitt) and indulges in pompous self-congratulation. He includes in an appendix several original documents referring to Chaucer, but these are not sufficient to sustain his bulking narrative. Godwin's biography is a digression to the outer limits: for example, in considering whether or not Chaucer read romances as a schoolboy, Godwin presents a tortuous disquisiton on popular medieval romances. In describing a judicial trial, Godwin "supposes" Chaucer into court (Chaucer, after all, probably was a member of one of the Inns of Court, possibly the Temple) and proceeds through *perhapses* to demonstrate how Chaucer (that is, Godwin) would have conducted himself.

Historical background and cultural context should not be anathema to biography; Godwin, however, uses them to overwhelm and submerge his subject. Oddly, though, this irritating compendium—"a history of every thing that existed upon the earth at the same time with Chaucer," as one frustrated reviewer noted—can sometimes be entertaining to read. Not for what it tells about Chaucer or his times—Godwin succumbs to a paternalistic attitude regarding the middle ages—but for Godwin's pompous presentation of his audacious self. Chaucer's self, whether audacious or otherwise, is not to be found here.

At the time of Godwin's biography, scholars were already sifting through Chaucerian materials in order to determine what was verifiably true, both about life and about the works that could be justly attributed to him. Sometime around 1844, Sir Nicholas Harris Nicolas wrote a life of Chaucer that became part of the first volume of the Aldine edition of Chaucer's works (1845). Nicolas' biography was a serious piece of scholarship, debunking several myths and drawing on original documents discovered by Godwin as well as many more never before printed or seriously examined, thereby contributing to what would become the *Life-Records*. Though this work is difficult to find, anyone curious about the transition from Chaucer legends to biographical truth should try tracking it down.

Meant principally as a critical and historical approach to the literature, LOUNSBURY's work in its first volume provides a succinct, reasonable, and readable account of Chaucer's life based on documented facts and cautious conjecture. As Lounsbury points out in his Introduction, "If . . . certainty cannot be attained in any given case, it is of importance that all the evidence on both sides of disputed questions shall be fully and fairly presented, so that the reader can be put in a position to come to a decision satisfactory to himself." Lounsbury denounces "the folly of speculative biography" while still understanding its appeal and the need for *educated* guesses. His two chapters, comprising 224 pages, give a thorough and fascinating survey of the progress of Chaucer life-writing. And his critical awareness makes him a valuable guide in the forest of Chaucer life-stories; for, while his first chapter is on the life of Chaucer as it can be garnered from public record, his second chapter tackles the Chaucer legend and its perpetrators. Lounsbury is unrelenting in his efforts to correct the transgressions of past so-called biographies, observing that the "transition from probability to fact is . . . a journey that is [too] speedily made," particularly in Chaucer's case. He carefully examines all the lives of Chaucer written from the 16th century through to Nicolas in the 19th, giving background on the biographers and the state of scholarship at the time. One gets from Lounsbury a clear picture of the public Chaucer and qualified observations on the private Chaucer. But one also gets an understanding of how Chaucer has been looked at through the course of centuries and of how a legend can develop. Lounsbury is an acerbic scholar, but he is also entertaining, precise, and respectful of the intelligence of his subject and his readers.

With the completion of the *Life-Records* at the turn of the century, biographers had Chaucer factually in hand. Because those facts were definite but limited, Chaucer biography of necessity adopted the "life and times" approach. JENKS' study of 1904 is a small and simple but pleasant representation of this type of biography, though its scholarship in now out of date. Jenks has a kindly, headmasterly approach to the middle ages, referring to the period and people as childlike or unsophisticated. This slight prejudice, however, does not seriously flaw what is basically a personal rumination of the wonderfulness of Chaucer's works and on what his life may have been like. Jenks does not try to make great critical leaps, but he clearly summarizes Lounsbury's points about the Chaucer legend and explains the significance of certain Chaucer facts within the context of 14th-century life. Jenks is aware that having facts available does not in itself give shape to a subjects's life, remarking that "we must be patient with the useful little dates, even if they do not interest us intensely." Jenks' purpose is to create an appreciation of Chaucer's writings, and he uses the life-story as an introduction.

COULTON's biography follows a similar format, with the first part focused on the life and the remaining parts concerned with the works and the times. Coulton, however, is a livelier and more opinionated writer than Jenks. He also takes an independent approach to interpreting the material in the *Life-Records*, an approach that, while often insightful, also leads to some unsupportable conjectures. Coulton is fully in control of his narrative, however, and his strength is his vigorous and knowledgeable depiction of the social history of the period, from children's games to the privations of the poor. Coulton, too, considers medieval society as primitive and simplistic, but his condescensions do not detract from his descriptions of actual events and activities. His is also the first biography to include illustrations and photographs to enhance the narrative, and he employs numerous contemporary quotations to give the flavour of the times. He also skillfully interweaves themes from Chaucer's poetry into his explications of historical events and social situations. While much of Coulton's material has become out-of-date because of reinterpretation and new information, he is still worth reading as an interesting early view of Chaucer and his world.

In 1912 James Root Hulbert published *Chaucer's Official Life* (reprinted in 1970 by Phaeton Press). This is not a biography of Chaucer so much as a clarification of the settings and situations with which the Chaucer documentary facts were connected. Hulbert's concern was that biographers were using the facts out of context, thereby creating new myths about Chaucer. His thin book is about the people Chaucer was known to associate with and how important or unimportant those associations were. The book is an analysis of facts contained in the *Life-Records* rather than a narrative of Chaucer's life.

With the publication of CHUTE's biography in 1946, the story of Chaucer's life becomes the focal point and frame of the biographical narrative. Chute's biography is a breath of fresh air amid the scholarly expositions that had dominated the study of Chaucer's life. (In the earlier biographies and essays, the scholar-authors tended to take center-stage over their subject.) Chute is as learned and as critical as her predecessors; but her prose style is deceptively informal, allowing her to be witty and observant while remaining unobtrusive. Rather than merely state that Chaucer was humorous and insightful, she deftly demonstrates these qualities and lets the story seemingly tell itself, to flow naturally and engagingly with a minimum of artificial aid. Chute clearly enjoys Chaucer and history. This pleasure manifests itself throughout the biography in fully realized scenes in which the reader can both observe and participate. One small example is her description of young King Edward's inauspicious Scottish campaign of 1327, which was such a pathetic and hilarious comedy of errors that it is justifiably left out of most history books. There is no condescension in Chute's approach; she takes the medieval world on its own terms and trusts her own sensibilities: " . . . we know so little about 14th-century personalities and events and Chaucer knew so much about them that it is unsafe to make assumptions . . . of this kind unless Chaucer himself gives the lead.'' She does not strain the facts of Chaucer's life; her conjectures are carefully considered and mixed with other established facts of the period. Her readings of his poetry are clever and reasonable, but they are not separated out from the rest of the narrative. With Chute, Chaucer has become human: ''Setting himself against the weight of medieval authority, Chaucer wrote of English men and women and wrote in the English tongue. He did not do it for approval or for money or for fame. He did it for love, and there is the evidence of six centuries to show that a love like that is not betrayed.''

The temptation to use the poetry to define the man has always shadowed Chaucer's biographers. Some have allowed themselves significant flights of fancy; others, held somewhat in check by the *Life-Records*, have made more cautious speculations. The frustration is palpable because the public record is by its nature limited and limiting, while the poetry is rich with allusion and with Chaucer's humanity. In 1968, WAGENKNECHT published his ''psychography'' of Chaucer, declaring his refusal to separate the person from the *persona*. Wagenknecht admits that the lack of personal correspondence or diaries hampers biographical investigation into Chaucer, but points out that personal correspondence is no guarantee of autobiographical truth, that letter-writers put on different *personas* depending on their correspondents. Wagenknecht, therefore, uses Chaucer's poetry, in a combination of psychology and literary criticism, to recreate

Chaucer's personality. He does not eschew the documentary facts; nor does he try to create facts from obscure references in the poetry. Wagenknecht is intent on showing Chaucer's sensibilities and attitudes and in doing so offers well-written analysis and some original and thoughtful readings of the poetry. This book is not a life-story, however. Since Wagenknecht's source material is the poetry, the narrative becomes more of an interpretive study of the poems, with numerous (and valid) references to other critics, both of psychology and literature. Wagenknecht's Chaucer is thoughtful, balanced, and sympathetic, but he does not come to life on Wagenknecht's pages.

Biographical speculation takes a new turn with GARDNER's 1977 biography. Gardner, a medieval scholar as well as a popular novelist, brought welcome novelistic writing skills to his biographical study. Unfortunately he also brought along his fictional skills. Gardner admits in his Introduction that he has ''attempted no more here than to convey a more or less accurate impression'' of Chaucer and his times. This is a danger signal. Gardner also acknowledges that his biography may suffer from a failing common to other biographies, ''wherein the portrait of the poet comes out oddly like a picture of the biographer.'' This, however, is an honest observation. What makes Gardner's work so appealing and yet so subversive is that the story is what is important, not ultimately Chaucer; if the facts are lacking, then through grammatical maneuverings speculation becomes fact.

Gardner is clever and has a winning way with a phrase, all of which makes his charm dangerous if the reader surrenders his skepticism. And this biography must be read with skepticism. Gardner did not do original research for the biography, and though this is not a sin, Gardner does present materials from his secondary sources in misleading ways. He often will not give the full context of an argument or theory. Gardner also indulges in historical misinterpretation, as when he states that Chaucer and John of Gaunt were intimate friends, for which there is no evidence in either the poetry or the public documents. Gardner is good at painting scenes and depicting exciting and telling historical details, and many of his conjectures are appealing, if not verifiable. Had he written an historical novel about Chaucer, he would have had a better book and the scholarly disapprobation that accompanied this biography would not have resounded as it did. (And possibly, if Gardner had been only a novelist or only a medieval scholar, some of the criticism might not have been so fierce.) The book can be a joy to read; despite some choppy organization and Gardner's indecision about how ''scholarly'' to be, the language is often exuberant and sometimes cheerfully uncouth. There are frequent instances of beautiful prose and sympathetic analysis, and Gardner clearly empathizes with his subject. But this life of Chaucer is imaginative; the transmigrations from fact into fiction are not always easy to catch, and for someone unfamiliar with Chaucer there is no safety net. Sadly, then, Gardner's book is unreliable biography though his man Chaucer is intriguing.

One year after Gardner published his biography, BREWER came out with his abundantly illustrated volume. Brewer intends to place Chaucer in the medieval world and to describe the immediacy of that world. This he does winningly, weaving the threads of the known facts of Chaucer's life both with the social and cultural concerns of the time and with insightful and personable analyses of Chaucer's poetry. In general, Brewer does not make great leaps of creative faith the way Gardner does—although he does make some suggestions regarding Chaucer's familial relationships that rely solely on a singular interpretation of some of the poetry. Accordingly, Brewer's narrative style is more formal and less inclined to flourishes than Gardner's; but Brewer's enthusiasm is not curbed by his seemingly calm conversational voice. His biography does not allow the times and the works to be separate from the life. The book flows smoothly; its historical and literary digressions do not appear to digress; and the end of the book is the end of Chaucer's life—no divisions where just the poetry is discussed. This adherence to the integrity of the life is also what makes the Chute and Gardner biographies "lives" rather than "studies."

Brewer, like Gardner, did not attempt to search out new factual information on Chaucer, relying on the 1967 revised *Life-Records*. Nor does Brewer make any really radical conclusions. He is comfortable and thoroughly familiar with his subject and his period, and that familiarity allows him to present complicated and varied ideas and events in near-seamless whole. More so than any previous biography, Brewer uses illustration as an integral part of his narrative. Pictures are scattered throughout the book, not just grouped in a signature in the middle. This arrangement subtly supports the interconnection of the verbal and the visual aspects of Chaucer's world and Chaucer's writing. And it also lets the general reader get a better sense and appreciation of a distant world rich in detail. This is wholly appropriate, for Chaucer was very much in and of his world.

In 1968 Donald Howard declared that "no real biography of Chaucer has ever been written or can be written. We do not know enough." But the appearance of the Gardner and Brewer biographies in 1977 and 1978 changed his mind; indeed, he had supported Gardner's biography, although acknowledging that Gardner made things up when there were no facts to be found. Howard, then, devoted himself to writing the life of the man Chaucer and the poet Chaucer, determining to look anew at the established records and writings rather than go hunting for new facts. He also slyly points out that, depending on the decade, some facts are more popular than other facts.

HOWARD's 1987 biography is a large book, just over 600 pages. It is a testament to Howard's skill as a writer and a scholar that much of this huge volume is eminently readable. Howard has a bit of his poet's soul, an affinity that comes through in Howard's descriptive passages and his compassionate assessments of people and poetry. This is a comprehensive work, covering all possible approaches to the age and Chaucer. Some of this material, unfortunately, is padding. Because the facts are limited, Howard (like other biographers) resorts to "probably" and "must have" in order to cover a gap in the record; but he also (like other biographers) slides from there down to "did," thereby creating a fiction that looks like a fact. Some of his suppositions about what Chaucer probably saw or whom he probably met are wishful guesswork, occurring nowhere in the official record and not really supported by internal evidence from the poetry.

These are the weakest parts of the book, the sections where lack of information gives imagination too much free rein. They are also the parts where the organization becomes confusing; where Howard hopscotches from Chaucer's life to literary criticism to historical events and disrupts his narrative flow. But the strong parts of the book—the descriptions and recreations of battles and plagues, of court intrigues and personalities—are

vivid and engrossing. Similarly strong is Howard's love of Chaucer, which perhaps explains his desire to provide answers where none can truly be given.

Had Howard lived to follow through on the final edit of his biography many of the mentioned problems probably would have disappeared and some of the length cut back. The infelicity of the last chapter, for example—which starts with Chaucer dead and then jumps backward to describe his last years—is a case in point: the emotional impact is lost. The book also provides very few illustrations, which seem to be included almost as an afterthought. Even with these concerns, though, Howard's biography is a phenomenal achievement.

Despite Howard's accomplishment, however, his biography cannot stand as the sole work to be consulted when reaching for Chaucer's life. This is perhaps appropriate. Chaucer was the master of many voices and many points of view, and to find him a reader will need to consider several voices and viewpoints. The clearer and more evocative voices belong to Chute (though somewhat out of date critically), Brewer, and Howard, with Gardner worth listening to later. Most importantly, these biographers allow Chaucer's voice to come alive on their pages, letting readers appreciate his world's "sondry folk" and "subtil compassinges."

—Elizabeth Dominique Lloyd-Kimbrel

CHEKHOV, Anton, 1860–1904; Russian writer.

Bruford, Walter Horace, *Anton Chekhov.* London, Bowes, and New Haven, Connecticut, Yale University Press, 1957.

Gillès, Daniel, *Chekhov: Observer without Illusion,* translated by Charles Lam Markmann. New York, Funk and Wagnalls, 1968 (originally published by Julliard, Paris, 1967).

Hingley, Ronald, *Chekhov: A Biographical and Critical Study.* London, Allen and Unwin, 1950; New York, Barnes and Noble, 1956.

Hingley, Ronald, *A New Life of Anton Chekhov.* New York, Knopf, and London, Oxford University Press, 1976.

Laffitte, Sophie, *Chekhov 1860–1904,* translated by Moura Budberg and Gordon Latta. New York, Scribner, 1973; London, Angus and Robertson, 1974 (originally published by Hachette, Paris, 1963).

Magarshack, David, *Chekhov: A Life.* London, Faber, 1952; New York, Grove, 1953.

Priestley, J. B., *Anton Chekhov.* London, International Textbook, 1970.

Pritchett, V. S., *Chekhov: A Spirit Set Free.* New York, Random House, and London, Hodder and Stoughton, 1988; as *Chekhov: A Biography,* London, Penguin, 1990.

Rayfield, Donald, *Chekhov: The Evolution of His Art.* New York, Barnes and Noble, and London, Elek, 1975.

Saunders, Beatrice, *Tchekov, the Man.* London, Centaur Press, 1960; Philadelphia, Dufour, 1961.

Simmons, Ernest J., *Chekhov: A Biography,* New York, Little Brown, and London, Cape, 1962.

Toumanova, Nina Andronikova, Princess, *Anton Chekhov: The Voice of Twilight Russia.* New York, Columbia University Press, and London, Cape, 1937.

Troyat, Henri, *Chekhov,* translated by Michael Henry Heim. New York, Dutton, 1986; London, Macmillan, 1987 (originally published by Flammarion, Paris, 1984).

Yermilov, Vladimir, *Anton Pavlovich Chekhov, 1860–1904,* translated by Ivy Litvinov. Moscow, Foreign Language Publishing House, 1957.

*

The massive archival material on Anton Chekhov in three major and several minor Moscow collections made up the bulk of SIMMON's research, resulting in a truly scholarly but still readable biography that has not been adumbrated by subsequent efforts, regardless of the loosening Soviet grip on Chekhov matters. Clear-headed, neutral, and scholarly, a thorough taxonomy of Chekhov's life and work, Simmons' biography still stands as the single most valuable, unbiased vision of the man. Major and comprehensive, attempting to present all the facts, drawing on "all the accessible data . . .that would contribute to an understanding of the man," Simmon's "faithful and living portrait" notes that at the 100th anniversary of Chekhov's birth (celebrated in 1960) many new documents were made available; some passages, however, have been removed from the letters "for ideological reasons" by the Soviet government, in whose hands the Chekhov papers reside. Memoir literature on Chekhov is extensive; Simmons consulted it all. With a well-annotated bibliography, a survey of the works, and a 17-page index, this remains the definitive study.

TOUMANOVA's study is cosmopolitan, a European view by someone familiar with Russian culture. Consequently, Toumanova is in a good position to interpret Chekhov's life and letters in their real setting: "Here and there I have given a brief exposition of Russian history which may help the Western reader to understand better the epoch in which Chekhov lived and wrote." The largely Russian-language bibliography also points to her special perspective on the task. Though this is her first book in English, her style is above reproach; she seems to think, however, that some of Chekhov's aloofness and apparent indifference came from his own diagnosis of his terminal illness: as a doctor he knew the truth; as a writer he chose to ignore it. Toumanova sees Chekhov's world as gone forever, writing after the revolution and looking back on her country before its upheavals. An interesting, graceful, and somehow touching view of Chekhov's world and literature, hers is the most valuable pre-World II study.

TROYAT's translator, Michael Henry Heim, takes advantage of his own work on Chekhov's letters (*Letters of Anton Chekhov,* New York, Harper, 1973)—which is selective in the letters it translates, but admirable in that it gives each letter in its entirety, instead of snippets here and there—to reintroduce Troyat's study to Western readers. Extremely novelistic in form, turning Chekhov's life into "scenes" with "dialogue" at almost every turn, Troyat demonstrates his familiarity with the Russian *mise-en-scène* (he was born in Russia and has written on Tolstoy, Pushkin, Dostoevsky and several Czars). He sees Chekhov as "bored as a sturgeon . . . understating his own life and his importance to the peasantry." Readable but subtly slanted toward

his thesis ("the engaging pessimist"), Troyat relies so heavily on the letters that his notes are exclusively dates of correspondence, with only a few acknowledgments of previous scholarship, all in footnotes. He transforms his letters into stories of their own, and while Chekhov did "compose" his letters in a way that others have seen as stylized, Troyat seems never to acknowledge that the audience of the letters was not the world but his own friends and family. The easiest kind of biography to read, but dangerously seductive in its point of view, Troyat's work is informed but not scholarly—and not thorough, tossing off biographical facts in footnotes and rushing to make Troyat's personal points.

HINGLEY's *A New Life* (1976), a "pure biography," with no claims to literary analysis or criticism, follows his earlier *Biographical and Critical Study* (1950), which protested the "Chekhov legend" of a suffering soul with an overwhelming philosophical despair that permeates everything he wrote. Hingley claims Chekhov "has something more valuable to give us than an impression of pervasive dreariness," and examines the evidence for "a more balanced view." The later study makes extensive use of newly available documentation, including Chekhov's eight volumes of letters, Olga Knipper's letters to Chekhov published in 1972, and other Russian studies. He continues to support the view that Chekhov was outwardly unemotional, reserved, and controlled, that his short stories are more important than his drama, and that he had many affairs but did not discuss them in his correspondence. Negative toward the Stanislavsky-Chekhov relationship, and not insightfully informative about Chekhov's stage work, Hingley spends a great deal of time with the earlier "comic-book" stage of Chekhov's career, during which Chekhov used the pen-name Antosha Chekhonte.

GILLÈS agrees with Hingley on the secretive, private nature of Chekhov's personality, and stresses childhood beatings and his constant fear of a father who was tyrant to the family. Gillès' writing style allows opinion to color the interpretation; almost romantic in its compassion, its sensitivity, its sense of the moment, but without being fiction, it novelizes Chekhov's life, turning events into little stories and anecdotes. While lacking the neutrality and the intellectuality of more scholarly work, it clearly touches at the heart of Chekhov the man. Antithetical to Hingley's views are those of LAFFITTE, who praises Chekov as a philosopher and seeker of truth and plays down his financial motives, taking a slightly skewed view of the importance medicine played for him. Claiming he was dedicated to the welfare of those about him, Laffitte chooses to stress Chekhov's compassion. She approaches the man as a great playwright, giving only about ten pages to his "early writings," another 15 to "Chekhov and Women" before hurrying on to his theatrical career. Her observations are not always insightful: "In September and October, 1887, Chekov wrote his play *Ivanov.* It contained some personal reminiscences."

MAGARSHACK deals with the comic/tragedy genre problem in Chekhov's plays by placing emphasis on Chekhov's belief that every work of art must have a serious purpose. Magarshack gives less importance to the stories, but cites the prolific outpourings as a sign of Chekhov's involvement with the world: "His innate scepticism and cool judgment kept him aloof from the more starry-eyed reformers of mankind." In smooth style, both scholarly and readable, implying a knowledgeability and familiarity with the subject lacking in other biographers, Magarshack says that Chekhov took his writing seriously, even using vodka to keep the mind alert during travel. Having no political point of view, Chekhov writes descriptively, that is, neutrally, a trait that has been misconstrued by other biographers as coldness and reserve; however, Magarshack notes Chekhov's disdain for the aristocracy in his later life. Chekhov admired Tolstoy's political astuteness and his belief in immortality, both essential ingredients in the novel form, and admitted that Tolstoy reproached him for writing about trifles. Magarshack provides a bibliographical index of all work, with Russian and English publication dates, including as yet (1953) untranslated work. His is an indispensable source for all subsequent biographers.

PRIESTLEY offers a brief "profile" that urges the reader "to explore further the breadth and depth of this fascinating character." Priestley treats Chekhov's early writing apprenticeship as ideal: "His search for material for short tales and articles took him everywhere in Moscow, and enabled him to study an enormous variety of men and women." He also points out that "it was Dr. Chekhov who went into the country and Anton Chekhov the writer who came back." He discusses his love life by citing what he sees as "a certain detachment, belonging to both the doctor and the writer in him, that prevented him from falling headlong in love," and, although "he could bring understanding and compassion to his account of women, in his ordinary talk he was apt to speak lightly and rather cynically about them." Priestley's work is conversational and appreciative throughout, with no hint of negative traits or mention of personal problems with Olga (their disputes are reduced to quarrels). The book includes 50 illustrations.

PRITCHETT, himself a writer of note, treats his "biographical and critical study" with considerable style. He addresses the stories and plays subjectively but feelingly, finding the man in the work rather than through letters, memoirs, etc. Relying on previous, more sedulous scholars, he credits Simmons, Magarshack, and Rayfield (among others) for details, which he then sifts through his own imagination. Thus, while erring in certain details (Chekhov's last words, for example), he touches on the essence of the man as reflected in his work. He shares Hingley's view that the stories are "nowadays overshadowed" by the plays. He provides an index but no notes or support for his statements.

RAYFIELD's study of the interrelation of Chekhov's life to his writing is much more a literary discussion than a pure biography. It nevertheless begins with his childhood and moves through *Cherry Orchard* to his death, making more of the parallels between life and details of work than most biographers. An annotated bibliography helps identify the trends of critical studies on Chekhov. SAUNDERS is in awe of the man without a clear view of his weaknesses, and takes a too-respectful approach to his life, sacrificing original scholarship (she gets his birth date wrong, for example) for an appreciative overview. BRUFORD's work is not a true biography; its few pages (59) can be described as a biographical essay, an introduction to further study. YERMILOV offers largely an analysis of plays and stories from the point of view of Soviet ideology, and consequently is unreliable as biography.

—Thomas J. Taylor

CHESTERTON, G(ilbert) K(eith), 1874–1936; English writer.

Barker, Dudley, *G. K. Chesterton*. London, Constable, and New York, Stein and Day, 1973.

Chesterton, Ada (Mrs. Cecil Chesterton), *The Chestertons*. London, Chapman and Hall, 1941.

Coren, Michael, *Gilbert, the Man Who Was G. K. Chesterton*. London, Cape, 1989; New York, Paragon House, 1990.

Dale, Alzina Stone, *The Outline of Sanity: A Biography of G. K. Chesterton*. Grand Rapids, Michigan, Eerdman, 1982.

O'Connor, John, *Father Brown on Chesterton*. London, F. Muller, 1937.

Titterton, W. R., *G. K. Chesterton: A Portrait*. London, A. Ouseley, 1936.

Ward, Maisie, *Gilbert Keith Chesterton*. New York, Sheed and Ward, 1943; London, 1944.

Ward, Maisie, *Return to Chesterton*. London and New York, Sheed and Ward, 1952.

*

There was a rush to publish in the immediate aftermath of Chesterton's death in 1936 (also the year of his *Autobiography*). The first three books were sketchy, anecdotal, and of more use as sources than as considered biographical work. First in the field, TITTERTON was a fellow journalist, and something of a hero-worshipper, whose Catholic conversion and Distributist convictions owed much to Chesterton's example. Titterton gives a lively sketch of Chesterton's life as a journalist, stresses his lifelong intellectual duel with Shaw, and has useful material on the history of *G.K.'s Weekly*. His most interesting point is that Chesterton was tempted to the heresy of total optimism and the denial of evil and sin; though he shows that it could only have been by ruthlessly suppressing a strong part of himself that he could have denied his youthful experience of evil described in the *Autobiography*.

O'CONNOR introduced the theme of conversion, one of the two issues that in later writings would be most controversial. He describes a conversation in 1912, in which Chesterton revealed that he was already at heart a Catholic, and hesitating only for fear of the possible effect on his wife, to whom he felt gratitude for his original conversion to Christianity. This led O'Connor, at the time of Chesterton's very serious illness in 1914, to visit the house, in case he should be needed to receive a dying man. In his view, the further delay of eight years was due solely to Chesterton's fear of distressing his wife and, to a lesser extent, his parents.

ADA CHESTERTON, G.K.'s sister-in-law, introduced, with a certain tactless gusto, the other controversial theme, marriage. Her account of the wedding day, and especially the wedding night, was based on one given by G.K. to Ada's husband Cecil, who had died in 1918. Ada's account reveals a strong dislike of Frances, which is her own rather than Cecil's. According to Ada, Frances had an unconquerable distaste for sex, which horrified and humiliated Gilbert; she asserted that the marriage was never consummated, a view strongly disputed, as we shall see. Though Ada liked Gilbert, she tended to see him as a weak, hen-pecked innocent, dragged unwillingly to Beaconsfield from his natural habitat, London, and somewhat cowardly in his refusal to face illness and death. His Catholicism, which she was eventually to share, she viewed rather as a following of the dead Cecil; but she was perhaps conscious of paradox when she called Gilbert "the lesser Chesterton."

These early writers prepared the way for what undoubtedly remains the best of all books on Chesterton, that of WARD (1944). It is both a work of thorough scholarship and a tribute to friendship. She was fortunate in having the example of her father, the great biographer of Newman. This memory may be partly responsible for her presentation of the life as a gradual, stately, and inevitable movement toward Rome. Ward is skillful in balancing the wayward, sloppy, ill-organized side of her subject's personality against the sharpness of his logic and the seriousness of his thought. She deals temperately, but dismissively, with Ada's account of the marriage, which she had many opportunities to view at close quarters. She stresses particularly Chesterton's love of children. The sequel (1952) adds no new interpretation but collects further anecdotes and impressions of contemporaries. One judgment quoted, that of Lytton Strachey, is striking: "I like Chesterton, when he isn't trying to be Belloc."

BARKER, who gives no references or scholarly apparatus, stresses the theme of friendship. He sees Chesterton as easily influenced, and Belloc's influence as an especially bad one. Somewhat implausibly, he presents Gilbert as dominated by his younger brother; and he sees a lasting importance in the early contact with diabolism described in the autobiography. Barker is inclined to play down the conversion to Rome, and he sharply rejects Ada's view of the marriage.

DALE, in a well-marshalled and annotated work, asserts that Chesterton was sexist: "He knew the two sexes were different, and he insisted that the superior sex was the female one." She takes Frances to be one of Gilbert's despised "Puritans," and she sees the successive Catholic conversions of Cecil, Gilbert, and Frances as a "psychological chain reaction" in which each came to feel that "by refusing to sign up under the most explicitly 'anti-pagan' banner in the modern world" they would be demonstrating pride. Dale sees Chesterton as a wise teacher strongly relevant to the 1980s.

COREN gives a sketch without scholarly apparatus that adds little to Ward in terms of facts but is sensible and balanced in dealing with controversial points. These, however, seem minor when set against an unusually strong consensus. All these accounts find the man lovable, childish, scatter-brained, and highly intelligent; and they credit him with an understanding of the deeper currents of the 20th century. The more recent works indicate that earlier attempts to write him off as dated were distinctly premature.

—A. O. J. Cockshut

CHOPIN, Frédéric, 1810–1849; Polish composer and pianist.

Atwood, William G., *Fryderyk Chopin: Pianist from Warsaw.* New York and Guilford, England, Columbia University Press, 1987.

Bidou, Henri, *Chopin,* translated by C. A. Phillips. New York, Knopf, 1927 (originally published by F. Alcan, Paris, 1925).

Boucourechliev, André, *Chopin: A Pictorial Biography,* translated by E. Hyams. London, Thames and Hudson, and New York, Viking, 1963.

Bourniquel, Camille, *Chopin,* translated by Sinclair Reed. New York, Grove, 1960 (originally published by Éditions du Seuil, Paris, 1957).

Gavoty, Benard, *Frédéric Chopin.* New York, Scribner, 1974 (originally published by Grasset, Paris, 1974).

Harasowski, Adam, *The Skeins of Legend around Chopin.* Glasgow, MacLellan, and Boston, Branden Press, 1967; expanded edition, containing recent articles from *Music and Musicians,* New York, Da Capo, 1980.

Hedley, Arthur, *Chopin.* London, Dent, 1947; New York, Pellegrini and Cudahy, 1949; third edition, revised by M. J. E. Brown, Dent, 1974.

Huneker, James, *Chopin: The Man and His Music.* New York, Scribner, 1900; revised by Herbert Weinstock, New York, Dover, 1966.

Karasowski, Moritz, *Frédéric Chopin: His Life and Letters* (2 vols.), translated by Emily Hill. London, Reeves, 1879; revised second edition, containing additional letters, New York, Scribner, and London, Reeves, 1906; abridged one-volume edition, Reeves, 1938 (originally published by Ries, Dresden, 1877).

Kobylańska, Krystyna, *Chopin in His Own Land: Documents and Souvenirs,* translated by Claire Grece-Dobrowska and Mary Filippi. Kracow, Polish Music Publications, 1955.

Liszt, Franz, *Life of Chopin,* translated by Martha Walker Cook. Philadelphia, F. Leypoldt, and New York, F. W. Christern, 1863; London, Reeves, 1877 (originally published as *F. Chopin.* Paris, M. Escudier, 1852).

Maine, Basil, *Chopin.* London, Duckworth, and New York, Macmillan, 1933.

Melville, Derek, *Chopin: A Biography, with a Survey of Books, Editions, and Recordings.* London, C. Bingley, and Hamden, Connecticut, Linnet, 1977.

Murdoch, William, *Chopin: His Life.* London, J. Murray, 1934; New York, Macmillan, 1935.

Pourtalès, Guy de, *Frederick Chopin: A Man of Solitude,* translated by Charles Bayly. London, Butterworth, 1927 (originally published as *Chopin, ou le Poète,* Paris, Gallimard, 1926).

Tarnowski, Count Stanislas, *Chopin: As Revealed by Extracts from His Diary,* translated by Natalie Janotha, edited by J. T. Tanqueray. London, Reeves, 1905.

Temperley, Nicholas, "Chopin," in *Early Romantic Masters I* (from *The New Grove Dictionary of Music and Musicians*). New York, Norton, and London, Macmillan, 1985.

Weinstock, Herbert, *Chopin: The Man and His Music.* New York, Knopf, 1949; second edition, 1959.

Wierzyński, Kazimierz, *The Life and Death of Chopin,* translated by Norbert Guterman, foreword by Artur Rubenstein. New York, Simon and Schuster, 1949; London, Cassell, 1951.

Zamoyski, Adam, *Chopin: A Biography.* London, Cassell, 1979; as *Chopin: A New Biography,* New York, Doubleday, 1980.

*

As of this writing more than 20 biographies of Chopin have been published in English. The earliest of these reveal a Victorian prejudice, with their respective authors attempting to force the composer into a preconceived image of a frail, melancholy, tortured, and, in some accounts, effeminate soul. The majority of these accounts, as well as some of the more recent ones, perpetuate a distorted picture of the composer. Many reiterate verbatim a series of groundless, mostly apocryphal "romantic" myths about Chopin's life that have little, if any, basis. Although the subject of some negative commentary, HARASOWSKI's volume contains a discussion of these myths as well as critical evaluations of all the major biographies of Chopin. Those interested in further details regarding the titles discussed in this essay should see Harasowski, as well as MELVILLE's book, which contains a more succinct evaluation of all the important Chopin literature in English.

Two weeks following Chopin's funeral in 1849, Franz LISZT sent 12 questions to Chopin's sister, concerning such things as Fryderyk's childhood, first indications of musical talent, education, departure from Poland, relations with his family as well as with George Sand, and stated his intention to write a biography of him. Chopin's sister sent the inquiry to a pupil of her brother's, who answered most of the questions and returned it to Liszt. The result of his efforts first appeared serially in a French periodical and was collected and slightly enlarged in book form under the title *F. Chopin* in 1852. There is some debate over just how much of it Liszt wrote; scholars have suggested that Liszt's mistress Princess Carolyne von Sayn-Wittgenstein wrote most of the text. The prose is very romantic, rambling, and high-blown. Liszt's biography also spawned a number of the well-known anecdotes concerning Chopin; scholar's opinions of the veracity of these tales generally range from mildly dubious to incredulous. Nevertheless, Liszt's work, a firsthand portrait of the composer by a friend and sincere admirer, with all its flaws, is not without a certain charm.

In contrast to the legends and half-truths surrounding Chopin's life, the composer's letters reveal him to be a frequently witty and down-to-earth person, a hard bargainer with his publishers, and overall a rather well-adjusted person. Unfortunately, these aspects of Chopin's character rarely emerge in the first serious biography of him, by KARASOWSKI. The texts of Chopin's letters are significantly altered in Karasowski's account, which is, like Liszt's, responsible for a great number of the apocryphal legends surrounding Chopin's life.

Henryk Opieński's edition of Chopin's correspondence, entitled *Chopin's Letters* (translated by E. L. Voynich), appeared in 1931. Although recent research has modified some of Opieński's chronology, his edition, consisting of 294 items as well as some of Chopin's diary entries, has been praised for its breadth as well as its readable translation. It has subsequently been used by most biographers as a primary source.

Chopin's complete correspondence, totaling some 8000 items, has been edited by Bronislaw Edouard Sydow and published in French and Polish. From this collection, British Chopin Scholar Arthur Hedley (see below) culled his *Selected Correspondence of Fryderyk Chopin* (1962), comprising 348 letters. Hedley omitted sections of many letters, such as any reference to Chopin's "unequivocal expressions of homosexual feeling," as described by Nicholas Temperley (see below) in his biography of Chopin.

Considerable controversy has surrounded Chopin's correspondence with Countess Delphina Potocka, which involves some possibly spurious erotic material. Some scholars regard these letters as forgeries. Mateusz Gliński's book, *Chopin's Letters to Delphina Potocka* (1960), is an unconvincing attempt to establish their authenticity. An examination of both sides of the controversy is presented in Harasowski, who suggests that a nucleus of authentic letters exists, from which others were forged. Extracts from these letters are also found in Sydow's article in the Chopin symposium edited by Stephen P. Mizwa, *Frederic Chopin: 1810–1849* (1949). *Chopin: A Self-Portrait in His Own Words*, compiled by David Whitwell (1986), consists of extracts from Voynich's edition of *Chopin's Letters* organized according to subject.

Chopin scholars hold widely divergent opinions concerning the merits of HUNEKER's biography. Described by Hedley as "an example of American journalistic quaintness," Huneker's account has also been called the work of a "charlatan" by Gerald Abraham. Other's have expressed irritation at Huneker's pervasively witty prose while praising his acute and stimulating analysis. Huneker's errors of fact are noted in the 1966 edition, which offers the corrections, added footnotes, index, and bibliography of editor Herbert Weinstock (see below).

Readers should generally avoid the biography by Count TARNOWSKI, which is largely devoid of any substantive material. Tarnowski reiterates many of the half-truths and apocryphal anecdotes, and he merely summarizes details extracted from earlier biographies. He does, however, provide a helpful synopsis of George Sand's novel *Lucrezia Floriani*, supposedly based on the novelist's relationship with Chopin in 1846, which is not available in an English translation.

Two important French accounts date from the mid-1920s. POURTALÈS, as his subtitle indicates, attempts to depict Chopin as a melancholy poet. Pourtalès is more concerned with the romantic personality than with factual details of Chopin's life, and his writing style, described as a "surfeit of poetry" by Harasowski, may be too figurative and ornate for present-day tastes. His integrity of purpose, however, ultimately deserves to be recognized. The biography by BIDOU is more down to earth than Pourtalès' but reveals little that is new. Also from this period is English critic MAINE's biography in the Great Lives Series; it is a concise and readable account.

Although much research has been done since it first appeared, MURDOCH's 1934 account is thought to be one of the best of all the Chopin biographies in English. Seen as the first advance since Frederick Niecks' work of 1888 (*Frederick Chopin as Man and Musician*), Murdoch made excellent use of Chopin's correspondence, from which he inserted long quotations into his narrative. Murdoch was influenced by the Polish writer Ferdynand Hoesick, from whose three books concerned with Chopin, dating from the turn of the century and unavailable in English, Murdoch occasionally borrowed entire passages. However, Murdoch was much more critical than Hoesick in his evaluation of the fiction surrounding Chopin. After quoting a number of these legends as told by Karasowski and others, Murdoch punctures each myth in a well-reasoned and closely-argued narrative.

The current Chopin title in the *Master Musician* Series is by HEDLEY, editor of the *Selected Correspondence*. His account, which first appeared in 1947, was revised by Hedley in 1963, and again, following his death, by Maurice J. E. Brown in 1973.

Hedley, regarded as one of the greatest Chopin authorities, and Brown, considered the leading Schubert scholar of his generation, who is also the compiler of the standard thematic index of Chopin's works, are also the authors of the biographical sections of the article on "Chopin" in *The New Grove Dictionary of Music and Musicians*, first published in 1979. Hedley's approach to the life of Chopin is different from previous biographers' in that it is not based on either Niecks' 1888 account or Opieński's collection of Chopin's letters; rather, it stems from the fruits of his own research into more recently discovered Polish and French sources. Hedley takes pains to dispel a number of the myths surrounding Chopin's life. Of particular interest is his account of Chopin's relationship with George Sand. Countering the tendency to portray Sand as Chopin's "evil genius," Hedley attempts to depict her in a more equitable manner and emphasizes the composer's debt to the novelist. (Those particularly interested in Chopin's ill-fated holiday on the island of Majorca will find an engaging perspective on his relationship with Sand in the novelist's *Winter in Majorca* [English translation, 1956], which is a vivid description of their life during that sojourn.)

The "Chopin" article in *The New Grove Dictionary* (1979) by Hedley and Brown offers a concise and relatively current account, culled in large part from the 1974 edition of Hedley's *Chopin*. It is in most particulars an updating of Hedley's article for the fifth edition of the *Grove's Dictionary*, published in 1955. The Hedley/Brown article, which also features discussion of Chopin's works by Nicholas Tempereley (see below) and an extensive bibliography compiled by the Polish music bibliographer Kornel Michalowski, is accurate, informative, and succinct.

Superseding the Hedley/Brown article is TEMPERLEY's article contained in *Early Romantic Masters I*, part of a series of articles extracted from *The New Grove Dictionary* and published in book form in 1985. Temperley's account largely follows the form of that by Hedley/Brown; however, he contributes some engaging original material, such as his discussion of Chopin's sexual orientation. Temperley's portrayal, which incorporates the latest findings in Chopin research, is concise and accurate, with information regarding almost any aspect of Chopin's life or compositions easily at hand. Both the work-list and the bibliography from *The New Grove* "Chopin" article have been substantially revised.

WEINSTOCK gives almost equal weight in his book to biography, which is first-rate, and analysis, which has been criticized as rather old-fashioned. The book was touted by its publisher as "the standard and definitive work on Chopin." Scholars, however, are somewhat less enthusiastic in their assessments. While noting Weinstock's objectivity as well as the usefulness of the book, a number of them have faulted, for example, Weinstock's transliteration of Polish names.

The Polish poet WIERZYŃSKI's book on Chopin has been praised for its sensitive writing. On the other hand, the book has also been negatively described by Melville as "tinged and embroidered with his poetic ideas so that it cannot be taken at face value."

GAVOTY in his preface characterizes previous accounts as reflecting either a French or a Polish bias, with none of them presenting an accurate portrayal of Chopin. Gavoty attempts a middle road, with adequate coverage of Chopin's early years in Poland as well as his life after leaving Warsaw. The author's style is very poetic and lively, full of polished language and paradox, though often overly self-conscious. Quotations from Chopin's letters are frequently woven into Gavoty's narrative.

ZAMOYSKI's biography of Chopin is an impressive effort. Like Gavoty, Zamoyski frequently quotes from Chopin's correspondence. The book includes a complete list of the major sources of Chopin research.

ATWOOD's recent study approaches Chopin's biography from a different angle. Focusing in the main on Chopin's career as a concert pianist, Atwood details, year by year, the concerts at which Chopin performed, from the child prodigy's first appearances to his final performance. Included in the Appendices are a complete list of all of Chopin's known concerts, as well as a number of contemporary reviews.

The best of the books dealing with Chopin iconography is KOBYLAŃSKA's 1955 compilation, which contains 602 illustrations, including facsimiles of documents, paintings, prints, and manuscripts, as well as a number of photographs of items lost or destroyed during World War II. Other pictorial accounts include those by BOUCOURECHLIEV, with a fine selection of pictures and documents, and BOURNIQUEL; both contain some misstatements of fact.

Although somewhat beyond the scope of this essay, several books dealing with Chopin's works should be mentioned. The famous quote from 21-year-old Robert Schumann's 1830 review of Chopin's op. 2 "La ci darem" Variations ("Hats off, gentlemen! A genius!") is contained, among others, in *On Music and Musicians* (edited by Konrad Wolff, 1946). Gerald Abraham's *Chopin's Musical Style* (1939) is the standard discussion of the composer's works. Although the subject of some criticism, Alfred Cortot's *In Search of Chopin* (English translation, 1951) reveals the thoughts of this great interpreter of Chopin's music. *Chopin: Profiles of the Man and the Musician*, edited by Alan Walker (1966; enlarged edition, 1978), is a symposium by 11 writers, with discussions that are substantial but "of unequal merit," as Melville notes. The Chopin Society's *Studies in Chopin*, edited by Dariusz Zebrowski (translated by Eugenie Taska, 1973), consists of seven essays discussing various aspects of Chopin's life and works. Of particular interest is Krystyna Kobylańska's classification of the different types of Chopin biographies, and her discussion of the difficulties in uncovering the "facts" of his life. David Branson's *John Field and Chopin* (1972) has received some negative criticism for overplaying Field's influence on Chopin but is revealing of Field's importance nonetheless. Jean-Jacques Eigeldinger's *Chopin: Pianist and Teacher as Seen By His Pupils* (1986) has been highly praised for its description of Chopin's piano technique and musical style as well as for its lengthy discussion concerning the interpretation of his works. The recent *Chopin Studies* (1988), edited by Jim Samson, features engaging essays by such scholars as Jeffrey Kallberg, William Kinderman, Eugene Narmour, Jean-Jacques Eigeldinger, and Carl Schacter. Their writings represent the current state of research in Chopin studies.

—Stephan D. Lindeman

CHOPIN, Kate, 1851–1904; American writer.

Rankin, Daniel S., *Kate Chopin and Her Creole Stories.* Philadelphia, University of Pennsylvania Press, 1932.

Seyersted, Per, *Kate Chopin: A Critical Biography.* Baton Rouge, Louisiana State University Press, 1969.

Toth, Emily, *Kate Chopin.* New York, Morrow, 1990; as *Kate Chopin: A Life*, London, Century, 1991.

*

RANKIN's 1932 biography, long out of print and difficult to find, is the first book-length treatment of Kate Chopin's life and work. It includes, besides the biography, eleven of her previously uncollected stories. Rankin is generally credited with having gathered together most of Chopin's papers, and his biography, though sparsely annotated, quotes liberally from interviews with family and friends, from letters of contemporaries, and from her own writings. If at times such quotation seems excessive, one must remember that not all of Chopin's writing, particularly journals and diaries, was in print when Rankin wrote; the complete edition of Chopin's works was not to become available for more than 30 years after the publication of this biography.

One can hardly fault Rankin's industry. Most of the source material currently available is the result of his research, and later scholarship has resulted in few additional discoveries and only relatively minor corrections of fact. In his assessment of Chopin as a writer, however, Rankin is less reliable. He portrays her primarily as an upper-middle-class matron, not particularly interested in literary renown, whose great passions in life were her husband and her family. While he admires Chopin's writing, he regards her most highly as a local colorist, commenting at length on her powers of description and her sympathetic portrayal of Creole life. Occasionally he attaches unnecessary or inappropriate biographical importance to a piece of fiction. Most significantly, however, he fails to appreciate Chopin's most important themes and concerns. Criticizing the "erotic morbidity" of *The Awakening*, he can ask only "was the theme deserving of the exquisite care given it?"

The standard critical biography of Chopin is that of SEYERSTED, who has also edited her *Complete Works*. This exhaustively annotated text contains a checklist of her writings and a bibliography of secondary studies through 1968—though, since Seyersted's book was published before the explosion of Chopin scholarship, this bibliography is now of minimal value. While he adds little that is factually new to Rankin's account—and indeed acknowledges his heavy debt to Rankin, particularly in his chapters on Chopin's early life—Seyersted's portrait of Chopin reveals a far more determined, self-conscious professional writer whose literary ambitions were occasionally at odds with her aristocratic upbringing. Drawing in part on a diary and letters unknown to Rankin, Seyersted sees in Chopin's early life the seeds of a pre-feminist independence that was later to reach its culmination in *The Awakening*.

Seyersted's book is, as its title indicates, a *critical* biography. While he represents as fully as Rankin the events of Chopin's life, he is most concerned with studying her development as a writer and assessing her place in American literature. He studies in considerable detail the literary and philosophical influences on Chopin's work of such writers as William Dean Howells, Mary E. Wilkins Freeman (whom she called a "great genius"), Walt Whitman and Guy De Maupassant. Chopin valued Whitman for his preoccupation with the erotic, and Maupassant, who, Seyersted maintains, probably had the strongest literary influence on her work, for his economy of style and his treatment of women's sexual lives. He repeatedly illustrates the objectivity and amorality of her fictional stance and her refusal to write thesis-dominated, reformist literature. He traces her "open, amoral treatment of women's sexual self-assertion" and her insistence on the legitimacy of sexual passion as a subject for literary treatment. As he analyzes the development of Chopin's primary theme of women's growth into self-awareness, Seyersted sees in her work an early existentialism, an emphasis on the loneliness of freedom and the suffering it brings, which anticipates Simone de Beauvoir. It was finally her "unheard of illustrations of woman's spiritual and sensuous self-assertion," which found its culmination in *The Awakening*, that both distinguished Chopin from her contemporaries and led to the storm of critical disapproval that largely silenced her several years before her death.

Liberating her from the straitjacket of regionalism into which Rankin had placed her, Seyersted distinguishes Kate Chopin from such local colorists as George Cable and Grace King and locates her instead in the broader world of naturalism and realism inhabited by such writers as Zola, Flaubert, Norris, Garland, and Dreiser. He assesses her as a daring pioneer who, though she had little influence on her contemporaries, broke new ground in American literature, and that assessment has proved sound. Despite the explosion of Chopin scholarship during the last 20 years (limiting the usefulness of his bibliographical materials), Seyersted's critical biography remains a valuable tool for scholars.

TOTH's biography became available very shortly before this essay went to press; hence, discussion of it is more cursory than the book deserves. A meticulously researched and well-paced narrative, Toth's biography nevertheless offers few new facts about Chopin's life or insights into the personality of this remarkable woman. Nor does she offer a major new critical assessment of Chopin's place in the development of American literature and ideas. Unlike the other biographers, Toth attempts, with mixed success, to delineate pervasive autobiographical elements in Chopin's fiction. In the process she discusses in some detail Chopin's affair with Albert Sampite, a Louisiana plantation owner who, according to Toth, becomes the "Alcee" in several of Chopin's pieces. Other attempts at autobiographical interpretation are less successful; often, Toth has to admit that no evidence supports her sometimes lengthy speculations. Toth successfully contradicts the assertions of Chopin's earlier biographers, particularly Rankin, that the negative reception of *The Awakening* caused Chopin to retreat into literary silence, though it is true that she published little of significance after that novel. While one might hope for more from this long-awaited biography, its eminently readable prose, its detailed notes, and a carefully selected bibliography, mostly of biographical materials, make it a worthwhile addition to the body of Chopin materials.

—Marcia A. Dalbey

CHRIST, Jesus. See **JESUS CHRIST.**

CHURCHILL, Winston Spencer, 1874–1965; British statesman and writer.

Bonham Carter, Violet, *Winston Churchill as I Knew Him.*
London, Eyre and Spottiswoode, 1965; as *Winston Churchill:
An Intimate Portrait*, New York, Harcourt, 1965.

Chaplin, E. D. W., editor, *Winston Churchill and Harrow:
Memories of the Prime Minister's Schooldays 1888–92.*
London, Harrow School Bookshop, 1941.

Churchill, Randolph S., *Winston S. Churchill* (2 vols., with
companion volumes). London, Heinemann, and Boston,
Houghton Mifflin, 1966–69.

Colville, John, *Winston Churchill and His Inner Circle.*
London, Weidenfeld and Nicolson, and New York, Wyndham
Books, 1981.

Gardner, Brian, *Churchill in His Time: A Study in a Reputation
1939–45.* London, Methuen, 1968; as *Churchill in Power,*
Boston, Houghton Mifflin, 1970.

Gilbert, Martin, *Winston S. Churchill* (8 vols., with companion
volumes). Boston, Houghton Mifflin, and London, Heinemann, 1966–88.

Higgins, Trumbull, *Winston Churchill and the Dardanelles: A
Dialogue in Ends and Means.* New York, Macmillan, and
London, Heinemann, 1963.

Howells, Roy, *Churchill's Last Years.* New York, D. McKay,
1966.

Kersaudy, Francois, *Churchill and De Gaulle.* London, Collins,
1981; New York, Atheneum, 1982.

Moran, Lord Charles, *Churchill: The Struggle for Survival
1940–65.* London, Constable, and Boston, Houghton Mifflin, 1966.

Morgan, Ted, *Churchill: Young Man in a Hurry 1874–1915.*
New York, Simon and Schuster, 1982; London, Cape, 1983.

Pelling, Henry, *Winston Churchill.* London, Macmillan, and
New York, Dutton, 1974.

Scott, A. MacCallum, *Winston Spencer Churchill.* London,
Methuen, 1905.

Taylor, A. J. P., et al, *Churchill: Four Faces and the Man.*
London, A. Lane, 1969.

Trukhanovsky, V. G., *Winston Churchill,* translated by K. Russell, A. Miller, and C. English. Moscow, Progress Publishers, 1978.

Wheeler-Bennett, Sir John, editor, *Action This Day: Working
with Churchill.* London, Macmillan, and New York, St. Martin's, 1968.

*

Beginning with SCOTT's still-valuable 1905 biography, more
books have been published about Winston Churchill than about
any other British politician. Many of those books are by
Churchill. His fondness for authorship can be explained on several levels. Especially while out of ministerial office he needed
the income that writing books could provide to sustain his expensive tastes. Writing was his preferred medium of communi-

cating with other people. In writing, neither his lisp nor his
stammer would be heard. Since writing was a solitary activity,
there was less risk of interruption by contradictory questions or
facts than in conversation. As a minister, Churchill gave his orders in writing. It was in the act of writing that his policy preferences became clear to himself as well as others. Even his
speeches were carefully written out (and privately rehearsed) in
advance, with the result that they still read well, especially in
the reliable, if not entirely complete edition by Robert Rhodes
James (*Winston S. Churchill: His Complete Speeches 1897–
1963*, 8 vols, 1974).

Writing was Churchill's way of expressing himself. It is therefore not surprising that his books are heavily autobiographical.
His longest written work, *The Second World War* (6 vols., 1948–
54), explicitly structures the events of World War II upon the
thread of his personal experiences in that war, which to Churchill
was his war. He freely uses secret British official documents in a
highly selective manner to prove that his war had been the real
war. He makes himself the hero of his story, creating his own
legend. With Franklin Roosevelt dead and Josef Stalin mute,
The Second World War became for a time a largely unquestioned
cultural heritage, possessed if not always mastered. That there
were other wars besides Churchill's is suggested by such authors
as KERSAUDY and TRUKHANOVSKY. That Churchill did not
always appear heroic to Britishers during World War II is
demonstated by GARDNER in his persuasive book.

Churchill sees *The Second World War* as a continuation of the
story of *The World Crisis 1911–18* (2 vols., 1930), his book on
World War I. That earlier book is also essentially autobiographical. A. J. Balfour described it as "Winston's brilliant Autobiography, disguised as a history of the universe." The disguise is
thin. *The World Crisis* also uses Churchill's personal experiences
as its structural thread, and the central experience in this case is
the crisis in his political career caused by the catastrophic British defeat at Gallipoli in 1915. Churchill was blamed personally
for that defeat by most of the British political elite (and soon the
British public), and sacked (to use his own term) as First Lord
of the Admiralty by Prime Minister H. H. Asquith, who wanted
to save his own skin. *The World Crisis* is Churchill's eloquent
and incisive defense of his actions concerning Gallipoli. The
most intellectually impressive of his books, it succeeds in demonstrating that he was not the villain of Gallipoli, but not in
demonstrating, as it also tries to do, that he was the hero of
Gallipoli. The only British heroes of Gallipoli did not leave it.
None were in the British Cabinet, as HIGGINS demonstrates in
his balanced study.

Missing in Churchill's autobiographical books is any sense of
self doubt. He is always proved correct. He never pauses to consider that some other politicians might have been more nearly
correct than him on some matter. He may not have even understood what others wanted to do. Churchill, as Lord Moran (see
below) told him, lacked antennae in human relationships. He had
no real grasp of other people and disliked psychology. This ignorance of others is apparent in *Great Contemporaries* (1937),
Churchill's least impressive book. In describing several other senior members of the British political elite, he fails almost completely to understand persons with whom he had spent much of
his working life. This lack of psychological insight is even more
apparent in his monumental defense of the political career of his
father, *Lord Randolph Churchill* (2 vols., 1906). In this case, he

wanted desperately to understand as well as defend his aloof and distant father, but the result is a book that could have been written by someone who had never met Lord Randolph. Much later, *My Early Life* (1958), which ends with his marriage in 1908 to Clementine Hozier, romanticizes both of Churchill's parents. It is, nevertheless (or perhaps therefore), his most charming book, helpful for anyone seeking to understand Churchill. That seeker frequently will have to read between the lines, however, for even here the author gives little evidence that he understood himself. Much less enjoyable reading is *Savrola* (1900), Churchill's autobiographical novel, written in 1897. The novel's plot is heavily affairs-of-state, its style is graceless, and its characters are wooden. The only human touch, significanty, is the moving characterization of an old nanny, one of Churchill's many tributes to his own nanny, Elizabeth Everest, the only beacon of love in his otherwise unhappy childhood.

If Churchill's autobiographical books do not reveal much of their subject, the cause is not intentional silence, let alone deceit. Churchill was an honest as well as uninhibited author, but he was also seldom introspective. He kept no diary. Since he did not understand himself, he could not explain himself in his books. This task is left to his other biographers, four of whom—Anthony Storr (writing in the important volume by Taylor and others), Moran, Bonham Carter, and Pelling—make especially significant contributions to understanding Churchill. Although none provides the definitive biography (an impossible goal, at least in Churchill's case), each makes a distinctive contribution to understanding Churchill.

Storr, a distinguished British psychiatrist whose work appears in the TAYLOR volume, apparently never met Churchill, but clearly observed him at a distance before mastering much of the Churchill literature. Storr explains Churchill's inordinate love of power (separately well described in MORGAN's book), so openly expressed and aggressively pursued, as the result of the denial of love (by all but Elizabeth Everest) to Churchill in childhood. That childhood was pathetically lonely. Churchill's school experiences were less happy than those reported in the volume edited by CHAPLIN. The adult Churchill suffered, Storr emphasizes, prolonged, recurrent periods of deep depression, which he compensated for by seeking the governing power of ministerial office. When such office was denied him, writing books and painting were alternative therapeutic weapons for Churchill. The helpfulness of Storr's analysis is suggested by his argument for the signficance of Churchill's painting. That significance is not the resulting paintings (reproduced in David Coombs' volume entitled *Churchill: His Paintings,* 1967), but lies rather in Churchill's reasons for starting to paint in 1915, immediately after Gallipoli, and persistently continuing to do so. That he found the act of painting therapeutic is acknowledged by Churchill in *Painting as a Pastime* (1948), which is as close to introspection as its author ever came. The incompleteness of Storr's analysis is evident in his failure adequately to relate Churchill's heavy drinking (which Storr minimizes) to his depression.

If Storr is brief and suggestive, MORAN is lengthy and explicit. Charles Wilson (who was ennobled as Lord Moran in 1943 by his most demanding patient) became Churchill's doctor in 1940, when Churchill was already of retirement age, and kept him alive for another quarter-century. Moran was no ordinary doctor. His medical skill and bravery brought him much honor as a young battalion medical officer during World War I, and *The*

Anatomy of Courage (1945), his eventual book on the psychology of men in battle, is impressive in both intellectual and ethical terms. As a medical school dean, he became a pillar of the British medical establishment, also serving for many years as president of the Royal College of Physicians. As Churchill's doctor he regularly kept a diary. Much of this diary, except for the sad last five years of Churchill's life (covered by HOWELLS, Churchill's nurse) was published shortly after Churchill's death, occasioning some vigorous criticism of the diarist. Some of the criticism came from doctors who felt every patient's privacy should be maintained, although no persuasive medical case was made against Moran's diagnoses or treatment of his patient. Moran's medical evidence stands, and his book remains a matchless source of reliable biographical data about, and a valuable source of insights into, Churchill.

Other criticism came from Churchill's former staff subordinates during World War II, incited by Clementine Churchill, fiercely protective of her husband's reputation. These critics were particularly stung by Moran's evidence of Churchill's failing health from 1940 on. The volume edited (perhaps too strong a word) by WHEELER-BENNETT, depicting a hyperactive war leader, was an initial response by these former subordinates. In that volume John Colville, one of Churchill's former secretaries, is especially unpleasant about Moran, and COLVILLE later returned to the attack on Moran's credibility in his 1981 book. Colville's own diary, *The Fringes of Power* (1985), containing, surprisingly, many hostile statements about Churchill, was eventually published.

Less precise about data, but equally valuable for understanding Churchill, is BONHAM CARTER's beautifully written portrait. As Violet Asquith, daughter of H. H. Asquith, Bonham Carter met Churchill at a dinner party in 1906. Among his first words to a 19-year-old girl were: "We are all worms. But I do believe that I am a glowworm." For six decades the recipient of this unusual confidence believed it to be true. When Churchill died, she published her full-length but not full-scale appreciation, which had been previewed in the volume edited by Sir James Marchant entitled *Winston Spencer Churchill: Servant of the Crown and Commonwealth* (1954). Bonham Carter's book is based on far more than the personal memories of an aged friend. The footnotes are entirely respectable. The treatment of Churchill's childhood, schooling, military service in Africa and India, and early years in Parliament, all before the author knew him, is solid. Churchill's ministerial career in the Liberal Cabinets of 1905–15 is relatively accurately described, except for repeated denigrations of David Lloyd George, whose influence on Churchill Violet Asquith resented. Because she was her father's daughter in more than hatred of Lloyd George, Bonham Carter suggests Churchill dropped her after Gallipoli, when Prime Minister Asquith sacked his First Lord of the Admiralty. Her book ends there. The implication that Churchill was her friend only so long as she could be helpful to his political career is both clear and probably justified. Every year on Churchill's birthday Bonham Carter nevertheless continued to send him a posy as a symbol of her chaste love, and her book is a final flower on his newly-filled grave. No author has painted both Churchill's arrogance and vulnerability with greater understanding and charity than Bonham Carter.

Bonham Carter's was the first book on Churchill by an untrained scholar. PELLING's book is one of many by a distinguished British historian. Drawing masterfully on a wide variety of archival and published materials, but not on personal input from Churchill's relatives or former subordinates, Pelling's chronological account is comprehensive, detailed, and objective. Churchill's political career is explained, not merely described, clearly and concisely. Pelling is brief on Churchill's childhood and generally avoids psychological interpretations, but his book is especially sophisticated in its grasp of Churchill's changing political situations. Pelling's style is lean and understated, but that may be welcome to readers tired of Churchill's ornate prose. If a reader were to read only one book about Churchill, Pelling's would doubtless be the most sensible choice.

Readers wishing to fill the gap in family perspectives in Pelling's book can choose among books by several members of Churchill's family. The book by Churchill's mother, however, is not among them: *The Reminiscences of Lady Randolph Churchill* (1908), published when her elder son was reaching ministerial office, makes no mention of his birth, and includes no photograph of him, although Churchill's only sibling does appear. Winston Churchill the father was not much more successful than Winston Churchill the son. Sarah Churchill's published recollections, *A Thread in the Tapestry* (1967), include sensitive and thoughtful impressions of her father, however. Randolph Churchill's insensitive and thoughtless impressions published in *Twenty-One Years* (1965) only hint at the grief he caused his father. The book by Mary Soames (*Clementine Churchill: Biography of a Marriage*, 1979), most conventional of Churchill's children, is a serious, substantial attempt to understand both of her parents, and she is far more revealing about her father than Winston Churchill was of his father.

Late in Churchill's life his only son, whose credentials were minimal, was chosen to write the authorized biography of his father. This RANDOLPH CHURCHILL, buttressed by a substantial research staff, planned to do in five volumes. The first two volumes, all Randolph Churchill was able to complete before his own death, take the story down to 1914. They include much valuable archival data, especially from Churchill's letters. The companion volumes contain the complete text of many documents and are a useful source in themselves. Unfortunately the cream of the companion volumes also appears, often quoted at some length, in the main volumes, so that reading both sets of volumes is heavily repetitive. Since Randolph Churchill's prose is even more affected than his father's, and displays much less intelligence, scholars may safely choose to use only the companion volumes and make their own interpretations of the documentary evidence.

The same duplication of material occurs with GILBERT's continuation of his *Winston S. Churchill*. Gilbert, an historian who served on Randolph Churchill's research staff, was chosen to complete the authorized biography after his death. Under Gilbert's stewardship the main volumes are more important reading than are the companion volumes, whose documents are probably more widely known than those included by Randolph Churchill. Gilbert's prose is ponderous, but his style is less objectionable, and his judgments are more intelligent, than his predecessor's. Gilbert uncovers many valuable nuggets, especially about Churchill's finances. The enormous length of his biography is, however, unnecessary. Following literally in Churchill's footsteps, sometimes hour by hour, is wearisome and, worse, often uninstructive. Since Gilbert is much less expert about British politics than is Pelling, the significance of those footsteps is frequently missed. An official biography can hardly be expected to be heavily critical of its subject, but Gilbert comes perilously close to hagiography. Endless appreciation is not necessarily understanding. Winston S. Churchill made his own case far more effectively than does Gilbert's *Winston S. Churchill*.

—Marvin Rintala

CICERO, Marcus Tullius, 106 B.C.–43 B.C.; Roman statesman and orator.

Bailey, D. R. Shackleton, *Cicero*. London, Duckworth, 1971; New York, Scribner, 1972.
Lacey, W. K., *Cicero and the End of the Roman Republic*. London, Hodder and Stoughton, and New York, Barnes and Noble, 1978.
Rawson, Elizabeth, *Cicero: A Portrait*. London, A. Lane, 1975; Ithaca, New York, Cornell University Press, 1983.
Stockton, David, *Cicero: A Political Biography*. London, Oxford University Press, 1971.

*

In the introduction to his book, Shackleton BAILEY explains that his biography is aimed at letting Cicero speak for himself. Cicero is known better than any other figure from Republican Rome because of the wealth of his personal letters that have come down to us. Bailey uses these to create a more intimate picture of Cicero's character than would be possible using only the politically-inspired speeches or the philosophy.

Bailey follows Cicero's life chronologically, as do all the biographers. Extracts from the letters make up a large part of the text, frequently interspersed with short contextual comments. Bailey's knowledge of the letters is unrivalled, and the style of his translations reflects Cicero's own mastery of the language. And away from the political arena, he presents images of Cicero's family life drawn from the private letters, thereby creating a book that is both scholarly and very readable.

With its single-minded use of the letters, however, Bailey lacks some of the essential ingredients offered by the other writers: he makes little use of the speeches or philosophical treatises, and this creates a rather one-sided impression of Cicero's life. Oratory was essential to his success as a new politician, and philosophical study a frequent solace during his leaner years. Of more serious concern to the reader, the letters give an unequal impression of Cicero's career; only 30 out of the 900+ surviving come from the first 40 years of his life, and some years, such as that of his consulship in 63 B.C., are totally without epistolary remains. Bailey's book tends to reflect this imbalance, and the reader may find himself wishing to know more about these unrepresented periods. In addition to this, the author might have provided more of the social and political background to the period, as well as to the man, even where Cicero is not present.

By contrast, STOCKTON aims very much at undergraduates reading Roman History at Oxford, and confines himself to the political side of Cicero's life. As a scholar of late Republican politics, Stockton is among the best, and this shows very clearly in his book. He grasps difficult problems with clarity and conciseness, unpacking individuals' motives and allegiances and offering reasonable conjecture where certainty is impossible. His wide knowledge of the subject is evident in the very detailed references to Latin literature and contemporary scholarship.

Stockton uses one chapter to introduce the legal and political background to the period which, although of great use as part of a text book for the student, does not make for exciting reading. Non-British readers may also be confused by the parallels Stockton draws between the Roman constitution and that of Great Britain. Stockton also assumes a fairly considerable prior knowledge of the subject; references are made to figures without explanation, and reference to periodicals is made in abbreviated form without a key. There are also several, though not extensive, quotations in Latin.

The reader misses in Stockton an appreciation of Cicero's personality, which a broader examination of the philosophy and personal letters might have provided. For although the book ends with a consideration of his life and character as a whole, it is all too brief and comes to the inevitable political conclusion that the last 20 years of Cicero's life were a failure. For the student of Roman Republican politics, this book will be essential reading; for the general reader interested in Cicero's life, I do not recommend it so completely.

LACEY's biography is aimed far more at the general reader: he does not take the same amount of knowledge for granted, avoids quoting in Latin and making footnotes, and his book is compact and very readable. The book covers the whole of Cicero's life concisely but fully, and concludes with an interesting look at Cicero's reputation after his death. Lacey is also fond both of the Roman Republic and of Cicero, whom Lacey regards as vital to an understanding of the period. Lacey uses Cicero's life and work to look at the period as a whole, relying on his writings for a truthful, if not completely accurate, account of the events in which he was involved. This is problematic, as it tends to place too much emphasis on Cicero's words without considering their political context.

More frustrating are the generalizations to which Lacey is prone: these concern individual characters and political affairs. Too often Lacey's own opinion is presented as fact, as when he states, ''[Cicero] lacked the charm (and tact) to obtain [entry to the nobles' circles] by social graces.'' His presentation of the Roman political situation, though generally clear, shows the same tendency, suggesting, for example, that the shifting alliances of Roman nobles were something akin to modern-day parties.

I can recommend more completely RAWSON's biography. Rawson does not confine her study to politics or social life, but presents a portrait of the whole man, setting Cicero's own writings alongside those of his contemporaries. Rawson is comfortable addressing both the general reader and the scholar; for the former, there is a generous appendix on the Roman political system, which avoids complicated details crowding the text; there is also an invaluable index of persons that will be of great use to anyone confused by the Roman practice of calling fathers and sons by the same name.

Rawson is sympathetic to her subject, and admires his character without over-estimating his role in Roman politics, as Lacey tends to do. As an historian, she appreciates the distinction be-

tween conjecture and fact, and between Cicero's impression of events and reality. Where modern scholarship is undecided, she suggests her own solutions without deceiving the reader into thinking that they are certain. Above all I admire the style with which the biography is written: the prose has, at times, the appeal of a novel or a travelogue, and scholarly detail seldom stifles the flow of the narrative.

—Justin Goddard

CLEMENS, Samuel Langhorne. See **TWAIN, Mark.**

CLEOPATRA, 69 B.C.–30 B.C.; queen of Egypt.

Bradford, Ernle, *Cleopatra*. New York, Harcourt, and London, Hodder and Stoughton, 1971.

Ferval, Claude (Aimery de Pierrebourg), *The Life and Death of Cleopatra*, translated by M. E. Poindexter. New York, Doubleday, 1924; as *The Private Life of Cleopatra*, London, Heinemann, 1930 (originally published by A. Fayard, Paris, 1922).

Franzero, Charles Marie, *The Life and Times of Cleopatra*. London, A. Redman, and New York, Philosophical Library, 1957.

Grant, Michael, *Cleopatra*. London, Weidenfeld and Nicolson, and New York, Simon and Schuster, 1972.

Hughes-Hallet, Lucy, *Cleopatra: Histories, Dreams, and Distortions*. London, Bloomsbury, and New York, Harper, 1990.

Lindsay, Jack, *Cleopatra*. London, Constable, and New York, Coward-McCann, 1971.

Volkmann, Hans, *Cleopatra: A Study in Politics and Propaganda*, translated by T. J. Cadoux. London, Elek, and New York, Sagamore Press, 1958.

Weigall, Arthur, *The Life and Times of Cleopatra*. Edinburgh and London, Blackwood, and New York, Putnam, 1914.

Wertheimer, Oskar von, *Cleopatra: A Royal Voluptuary*, translated by Huntley Patterson. Philadelphia and London, Lippincott, 1931 (originally published by Amalthea, Zürich, 1930).

*

Cleopatra belongs to that unfortunate group of historical figures whose story has been preserved almost entirely in the hands of enemies. When she died, a month after Mark Antony, their grand strategy for the unification of East and West, Hellenic and Roman peoples, died with her. From this moment Octavian, in his new guise as Augustus Caesar, achieved supreme hegemony in the Mediterranean. His success in the war was completed by the deaths of his enemies, and in the propaganda war that mirrored it his version of events was preserved and transmitted as historical fact. Augustan sources, hiding the true nature of Antony and Cleopatra's enterprise, established the story we all remember: Antony was ensnared by the sexual wiles and fabulous wealth of a foreign queen, induced to betray his family and homeland, and perished in the pursuit of personal ambition. Subsequent accounts tended to embellish the story, and whether sympathetic to Antony and Cleopatra or not, the result has been that Cleopatra's rule over the most precarious of states in the most turbulent of times becomes buried under successive accretions of myth and fantasy.

It is only in relatively recent times that biographers have felt any obligation to pierce these layers and arrive at some kind of understanding of the complex political, military, and dynastic situation. Many works published in the early part of this century are more or less elaborate and fictionalised accounts of the story handed down through Plutarch and other pro-Roman sources. In this group we could include those of WERTHEIMER (whose subtitle, "A Royal Voluptuary," indicates its contents sufficiently), FERVAL, and WEIGALL. FRANZERO's 1957 work is a throwback to this era, crude in conception and execution. These books, though entertaining in their own way, have very little claim to be considered as serious biography and could more properly be considered alongside other (more imaginative) texts like those of Shakespeare and Shaw.

For the full range of these fictions based on the life of Cleopatra, the reader could do no better than to consult HUGHES-HALLET's remarkable survey of the Cleopatra legend. The bipartite structure of this book commences with a concise biography, followed by a biography of Cleopatra as myth. Subtitled "Histories, Dreams and Distortions," it works by stripping away the reader's conditioned responses to that legend and prepares us for a more prosaic, though no less intriguing, story. Above all, it opens the way to a reconstruction of Cleopatra's political motives in choosing an apparently suicidal war against Rome. Rarely has such a sceptical eye been cast over a grander, or more tenacious, myth to such constructive effect.

VOLKMANN's masterly study of Cleopatra's life and reign is a milestone in historical attitudes to the subject. Having firsthand experience of expansionist propaganda while a professor of history in Nazi Germany, Volkmann chose to approach the matter as an historical reconstruction of the events behind Octavian's account. Although it abandons the histrionic excesses of previous biographies in favour of a calmer and more lucid style, this work always remains absorbing, more in the manner of the detective story than a poetic tale of grand passion. Volkmann takes nothing in the established story at face value; rather, he explores the reasons why Cleopatra's actions are portrayed as they are in this version. The tragic story of inevitably doomed lovers, prompted by passion to self-destruction, conceals the fact that Antony and Cleopatra's project to defeat Octavian and Rome was by no means destined to fail.

BRADFORD and LINDSAY's biographies merit consideration together, for not only were they published within a year of each other, but they set out to achieve similar objectives. Both present the known facts in the case, Bradford leaning more heavily towards the Plutarchian version, and both create accounts readily comprehensible to the general reader. Bradford is surely guilty of some overstatement in ascribing to Cleopatra (in her earlier alliance with Julius Caesar) the ambition to rule in Rome as Caesar's acknowledged empress. Both she and her father Ptolemy Auletes had cause to remember the fundamental xenophobia of Roman society. Caesar, no matter how powerful, would simply never be permitted to have a foreign queen as empress. For this reason, he never acknowledged his son by Cleo-

patra, Caesarion. Cleopatra knew this; and for Bradford to repeat the anecdote from Plutarch that she bragged of dispensing justice in the Capitol is simply to perpetuate the Augustan propaganda without inquiry. Lindsay makes no such claims. Though scrupulously balanced in his approach, the result is vivid and enthralling, a fine general introduction to the life of this great figure.

GRANT's *Cleopatra* is an exemplary work both of research and presentation. In keeping with his other biographies of ancient figures, this study is never dull, despite containing a vast array of detail. Grant's thesis, which is endorsed by Hughes-Hallet and foreshadowed by Volkmann, is that Cleopatra was attempting with Antony (and Caesar before him) a grand synthesis of Greek Hellenic and Imperial Roman civilisation. Grant occupies much time in analysing the religious-political symbolism of the great set-pieces of her reign. For example, the famed Donations of Alexandria, which in Augustan terms are promoted as another act of grand folly and hubris, is here interpreted as a political agenda made manifest. The apparently grandiose pretentions of the couple to be incarnations of the gods Dionysus and Aphrodite is likewise seen as a symbolic statement of cultural unity. The relationship between the two was an amalgam of the whole Mediterranean world, spanning Greek, Roman, and Egyptian mythology. Their war with Octavian/Augustus can therefore be presented not only as a personal power struggle, but also the last and best hope of the whole Hellenic world against the encroaching imperialism of Rome. In this they failed, and in this the importance of suppressing their version of events becomes clear. After them, there was to be no Eastern independence until Byzantium, and the peoples of the East had to be convinced of the absurdity of revolt. Grant combs through the most obscure sources (anonymous poems, ballads, coins, and monuments) in order to establish his case, and he succeeds brilliantly in reclaiming the lost Cleopatra.

—Alan Murphy

COBBETT, William, 1763–1835; English political writer.

Bowen, Marjorie (M. G. Long), *Peter Porcupine: A Study of William Cobbett.* London and New York, Longman, 1935.

Carlyle, Edward I., *William Cobbett: A Study of His Life as Shown in His Writings.* London, A. Constable, 1904.

Chesterton, G. K., *William Cobbett.* London, Hodder and Stoughton, 1925; New York, Dodd Mead, 1926.

Clark, Mary E., *Peter Porcupine in America: The Career of William Cobbett.* Philadelphia, Times and News Publishing, 1939.

Cole, G. D. H., *The Life of William Cobbett.* London, Collins, and New York, Harcourt, 1924; 3rd edition, 1947.

Green, Daniel, *Great Cobbett: The Noblest Agitator.* London, Hodder and Stoughton, 1983.

Huish, Robert, *Memoirs of the Late William Cobbett* (2 vols.). London, 1836.

Melville, Lewis (Lewis Benjamin), *The Life and Letters of William Cobbett in England and America* (2 vols.). London and New York, J. Lane, 1913.

Pemberton, William Baring, *William Cobbett*. London, Penguin, 1949.

Reitzel, W., editor, *The Progress of a Plough-Boy to a Seat in Parliament*. London, Faber, 1933; as *The Autobiography of William Cobbett*, Faber, 1967.

Sambrook, James, *William Cobbett*. London and Boston, Routledge, 1973.

Smith, Edward, *William Cobbett: A Biography* (2 vols.). London, S. Low, 1878.

Spater, George, *William Cobbett: The Poor Man's Friend* (2 vols.). Cambridge and New York, Cambridge University Press, 1982.

*

The best way to capture the essential spirit of Cobbett is to read his own accounts of his life, even though these accounts are almost wholly works of self-justification, and, as a consequence of Cobbett's great shifts in political opinion, they sometimes contradict one another. The most connected and complete of these autobiographical writings, *The Life and Adventures of Peter Porcupine* (1796), covers only its author's early life, but autobiographical references from the writings of his whole lifetime are collected and arranged chronologically (with a few linking editorial passages) in REITZEL's extremely skilful compilation. With its full source references and valuable annotations, Reitzel's work is essential reading; it is usefully supplemented by G. D. H. Coles' collection of *The Opinions of William Cobbett* (1944).

There were many 19th-century brief lives of Cobbett, including the personal attacks made upon him in his lifetime by political enemies. The most substantial of the serious lives are that by HUISH, which is inaccurate and largely hostile, but useful as a collection of contemporary critical notices, and that by SMITH, which is much fuller than Huish and sounder as to facts, but is somewhat too uncritically laudatory.

Twentieth-century biography of Cobbett begins with CARLYLE's scholarly work: though now quite superseded, this was the first biography to establish many facts that Cobbett himself concealed or misrepresented, including the year of his birth. MELVILLE's book is, like other biographies by that author, copious and slapdash; it is useful only for its long quotations from previously unpublished Cobbett family papers.

COLE (1924) writes from a socialist viewpoint, strongly influenced by J. L. and Barbara Hammonds' studies of the oppressive treatment of the poor in Cobbett's period. Though he readily concedes that Cobbett was no socialist, Cole rather too dramatically identifies early 19th-century industrial workers as "peasants unclassed, torn from the land and flung into the factory" to serve the great transition "between the aristocratic feudalism of the 18th century and the plutocratic absolutism of the new industrial system." Despite such simplifications, this is a full, graphic, and absorbing account of Cobbett's life and times, written with passionate engagement. The third edition in 1947 adds a preface with some details of a family quarrel in Cobbett's last years. Though Spater (see below) has added much factual detail concerning Cobbett's life, Cole's biography remains essential reading.

CHESTERTON and BOWEN both provide stylish, impressionistic portraits without new facts: for all the skill of these two considerable literary artists, their biographies are less lively than PEMBERTON's brief but well-finished character sketch. Two works contribute significantly to our knowledge of the beginning of Cobbett's literary career in the U.S.A. G. D. H. Cole's fully annotated edition of the letters to Thornton (1937) supplements his edition of *The Life and Adventures of Peter Porcupine*. Cole's work is further supplemented by CLARK's, which is based on an impressive variety of local documents. SAMBROOK adds a little detail from hitherto unused manuscript sources, but is chiefly useful for relating Cobbett's thought to his 18th-century literary masters and his "Romantic" contemporaries. Gerald Duff's annotated collection of letters (1974) includes only the 33 at the University of Illinois: there is still no adequate collection of Cobbett's letters.

SPATER provides the fullest and most accurate biography of Cobbett yet to appear. His work draws more widely and deeply than any of his predecessors had done upon a wealth of archive material scattered through many public and private collections on both sides of the Atlantic. A new source of particular value is the previously unknown notebook of over 100 pages compiled by James Paul Cobbett for a projected biography of his father. Spater tells for the first time the full story of the Cobbett family quarrels darkly hinted at in Cole's 1947 Preface. Spater's narrative is consistently clear, a clarity achieved in part by tucking away a vast amount of information in over 2,000 endnotes, many of considerable length, and two appendices. It would seem that every available scrap of biographical evidence has been sifted, judged, and placed. In particular, the millions of words in *Cobbett's Political Register* have been carefully scanned in order to retrieve all the stray paragraphs and sentences where Cobbett momentarily abandons the discussion of topical political issues and recalls some incident in his own life. More than once, especially often in the case of Cobbett's financial transactions, Spater has to admit that the pieces of information provided by Cobbett are utterly self-contradictory and cannot be checked externally, so that the biographer can only guess what occurred, but all the available evidence is offered fairly to the reader.

GREEN's biography is "unacademic" in a very good sense. It is a straightforward, leisurely, generous, expansive, and, above all, unaffected narrative, in which Green assumes that the humanity, common experience, and understanding of ordinary human motivation shared by the biographer and the "average reader" is sufficient for the interpretation of character. Although not heavily documented, it is thoroughly sound: no doubt all the more accurate because Spater's biography was published just in time for Green to refer to it, as he freely acknowledges. Green's does not displace Spater's as the standard life, but it makes a very good read.

—James Sambrook

COLERIDGE, Samuel Taylor, 1772–1834; English poet.

Bate, Walter Jackson, *Coleridge*. New York, Macmillan, 1968; London, Weidenfeld and Nicolson, 1969.

Campbell, James Dykes, *Samuel Taylor Coleridge: A Narrative of the Events of His Life*. London and New York, Macmillan, 1894.

Chambers, E. K., *Samuel Taylor Coleridge: A Biographical Study*. Oxford, Clarendon Press, 1938.

Charpentier, John, *Coleridge: The Sublime Somnambulist*, translated by M. V. Nugent. New York, Dodd Mead, and London, Cape, 1929 (originally published by Perrin, Paris, 1928).

Cornwell, John, *Coleridge: Poet and Revolutionary 1772–1804*. London, A. Lane, 1973.

Cottle, Joseph, *Early Recollections, Chiefly Relating to the Late Samuel Taylor Coleridge, during His Long Residence at Bristol* (2 vols.). London, Longman Rees/Hamilton Adams, 1837; revised as *Reminiscences of Samuel Taylor Coleridge and Robert Southey*, London, Houlston and Stoneman, 1847; New York, Wiley and Putnam, 1848.

De Quincey, Thomas, "Samuel Taylor Coleridge," in *Tait's Magazine*, 1834; revised version published in Volume II of *The Collected Writings of Thomas De Quincey*, Edinburgh, A. and C. Black, 1889; reprinted in *Recollections of the Lakes and the Lake Poets*, edited by David Wright, London, Penguin, 1970.

Doughty, Oswald, *Perturbed Spirit: The Life and Personality of Samuel Taylor Coleridge*. Rutherford, New Jersey, Farleigh Dickinson University Press, and London, Associated University Presses, 1981.

Fausset, Hugh I'Anson, *Samuel Taylor Coleridge*. New York, Harcourt, and London, Cape, 1926.

Gillman, James, *The Life of Samuel Taylor Coleridge* (volume one only). London, W. Pickering, 1838.

Hanson, Lawrence, *The Life of Samuel Taylor Coleridge: The Early Years*. London, Allen and Unwin, 1938; New York, Oxford University Press, 1939.

Holmes, Richard, *Coleridge: Early Visions*. London, Hodder and Stoughton, and New York, Viking, 1989.

Traill, H. D., *Coleridge*. London, Macmillan, and New York, Harper, 1884.

*

HOLMES' attractive study (the first volume of two, projected) raises timely questions about the shape of Coleridge's erratic career. Does he make sense as a poet turned critic, as a dissenting preacher turned metaphysician, or as a radical journalist turned Tory? As in his earlier work, *Shelley: The Pursuit* (1974) and the romantic biographical essays of *Footsteps* (1985), Holmes has followed his subject in person and not only in the library, turning up odds and ends of the living past in the process. The sandy cave on the river Otter with the initials "STC" renewed, as he supposes, by generations of visitors in Coleridge's wake, is a detail of slight significance to the story. Yet Holmes' evocation of it is indicative of the personality and tact of his approach. Inspired by his subject's oversized figure, he is attentive to facts while open to imaginative possibility. His first volume traces the personal sources of the poet's career as Christian radical and moral philosopher. Holmes' account of Coleridge's life to 1804 gives a stronger impression of the living character than anything since De Quincey. Its concise intelligence makes it a first choice for modern readers.

Like all modern biographers, Holmes relies on the early reminiscences of GILLMAN and COTTLE, which include documents (mainly letters) as well as firsthand reports and hearsay. Cottle was Coleridge's Bristol publisher in the heyday of Pantisocracy, Gillman his physician and host in Highgate from 1816 to the end of his life. Cottle's volume is an episodic collation mainly relating to Coleridge's early career, especially his connection with Robert Southey. It is vivid but partial, providing intimate glimpses of the poet in his social setting. Gillman sees his subject from the other end of the career. His account (Chapter IV) of the circumstances of Coleridge's removal to Highgate, and of the publication of *Christabel* and the *Biographia Literaria* at the same time, is full of incidental detail. Unfortunately, Gillman did not publish his projected second volume, which might have provided invaluable information on Coleridge's later life.

Holmes' sublation of these materials represents a distinct improvement on Campbell, Chambers (for both, see below), and others, in part because of his effective use of Coleridge's notebooks, which were largely unavailable to prior biographers. Coleridge's inner life is a story of its own, though associated, as Holmes shows, with every moment of his public life. Holmes' attention to the confessional impulse in Coleridge's character is original; his observation of the self-dramatizing turn less so, yet still remarkable as he pictures it in the notebooks, where Coleridge acted things out for his own consumption. The intense companionships of the Bristol and Stowey period come under psychoanalytic scrutiny here for the first time. This is perhaps the least satisfactory aspect of the study; Holmes seems determined to raise the psychosexual stakes, even as he insists that the conventions of romantic friendship are the proper basis for understanding Coleridge's volatile relations with Southey, Charles Lloyd, and especially Wordsworth.

Among the earlier accounts, DE QUINCEY's memoir remains particularly interesting for its candor, which scandalized Coleridge's family. De Quincey alone among his contemporaries managed to balance the books on the friend who provided the model of his own life and career. He is forthright on the matter of Coleridge's "plagiarisms," introducing it in the voice of Thomas Poole, Coleridge's early patron and champion. This is balanced by large claims for Coleridge's superiority to his unacknowledged sources. De Quincey's recollections of his first sighting of Coleridge in Bridgwater; of the character of Sara Fricker, the poet's wife; of his meeting with Klopstock in Germany; of his metaphysical maundering, balanced by notice (seldom repeated) of the quality of his topical journalism; of Coleridge in the Lakes and among the Lake poets; of the ambience of his lectures at the Royal Institution; of his opium-eating, from a sympathetic point of view; of his reforming instincts, against the grain of those who (like Hazlitt) would condemn him as a recreant Tory—all are of permanent value for considering the character of the man within the reputation. Of the chaos of Coleridge's life after leaving the Lake district in 1810, De Quincey has little to tell. His concluding comparison of Coleridge with Goethe is affectingly apt to his story of the genius who rose above personal failure.

TRAILL's compact study in the landmark "English Men of Letters" series established the conventional division of Coleridge's career into periods "poetical," "critical," and "metaphysical and theological." This Victorian anatomy persists in BATE's foreshortened treatment of a century later, which lays stress on the relation of the parts to the whole career in ways which Traill's more limited rehearsal of the facts does not. Bate's work is deeply informed in the literary culture of Georgian English; attentive to the major lyrics as they participate in Coleridge's life and thinking; and unembarrassed by the theological drift of the career. There is little here on Coleridge'ssustained attention to the life of his time, a shortcoming that reflects the limited modern understanding of Coleridge's place in English culture at large. Bate's volume may be said to represent a development of Traill's in this respect as well. Both cast him as Victorian sage in a world he aspired to transcend. Bate's work can still be recommended as the best shorter life, and the only authoritative critical biography comprehending the whole life, currently available. The concluding emphasis on Coleridge's thinking among his Victorian inheritors is of permanent value.

CAMPBELL's was the first successful effort to write a complete biography of Coleridge and though out of date remains worth consulting for details, as a reprint edition of 1970 attests. As "a narrative of the events of his life" it is superseded by Chambers, Bate, and Holmes. All provide a more commanding sense of the shape of the career as well. Coleridge's life is the stuff of a morality play as Campbell sees it through late Victorian spectacles. Failure of will is the real story here, though Campbell little recognizes the redeeming social value in the protagonist's tragic fall from large purpose. The treatment is of a piece with A. C. Bradley's Shakespeare lectures of the same period, absorbed as it is in character study. Reading it gives some idea of the background of the modern turn to a thoroughly transcendentalized Coleridge.

CHAMBERS has been standard for half a century, yet his "biographical study" does not pretend to be a critical biography, and it suffers accordingly from emphases of limited biographical interest. Based largely upon letters, some previously unpublished, it concentrates on the illustrious friendships that Coleridge struck up with men who outgrew him. Chambers' account of these is factual rather than psychological; he should be consulted as a supplement to Holmes in this connection. His research in the sources, primary and secondary, constitutes his enduring claim to attention. The depth of coverage varies. He is perfunctory on the important year Coleridge passed in Germany (the anti-German sentiment of the period after the Great War may be involved) while devoting real energy to Coleridge's journalism. Of Coleridge's life after 1804 this must still be considered the authoritative treatment.

A spate of lesser biographical studies dates to the same period, which witnessed a momentous rebirth of interest in Coleridge's work, at Cambridge and elsewhere. FAUSSET's rather breathless tour of the life and times is unashamedly romantic in feeling, novelistic in style. It is the work of a professional biographer writing for a conventionally literary audience. Much the same may be said of CHARPENTIER, the translation of whose French original is dedicated to Edith Wharton, the novelist and friend of Henry James. It is too schematic to be taken seriously as biography.

HANSON's study of Coleridge's early years is another matter. Contemporaneous with Chambers, and perhaps overlooked by later biographers in part for that reason, it is carefully researched and documented, provided with a useful analytical index, and ably composed. Hanson motors us into Ottery St. Mary

in the first sentence, but concentrates on Cambridge, Bristol, Stowey, and Germany. His book represents a comprehensive treatment of these early scenes derived from original sources and should be consulted for details of Coleridge's formative years. Yet it concludes abruptly, as though the life ended with the century.

The more recent efforts of Cornwell and Doughty have attracted little attention. CORNWELL's volume covers the same early ground as Hanson and Holmes. It is less detailed than the one, less literary-latitudinarian than the other. The interest here is mainly political; it makes the effort to reconsider Coleridge's social bearings and public aspirations through careful attention to the poetry and letters. This is a 1960s version of the poet as public speaker. It deserves to find an audience among romantic revisionists.

DOUGHTY's sprawling character study, posthumously published without notes, is a chronicle more than a shaped narrative. It lacks focus, direction, point, and any noticeable interest in Coleridge's verse.

—A. C. Goodson

COLETTE (Sidonie-Gabrielle), 1873-1954; French writer.

Crosland, Margaret, *Madame Colette: A Provincial in Paris.* London, P. Owen, 1953.
Davies, Margaret, *Colette.* Edinburgh, Oliver and Boyd, and New York, Grove, 1961.
Le Hardouin, Maria, *Colette: A Biographical Study,* translated by Erik de Mauny. London, Staples, 1958 (orginally published by Éditions Universitaires, 1956).
Marks, Elaine, *Colette.* New Brunswick, New Jersey, Rutgers University Press, 1960; London, Secker and Warburg, 1961.
Phelps, Robert, *Earthly Paradise: An Autobiography (by Colette).* London, Secker and Warburg, and New York, Farrar Straus, 1966.
Richardson, Joanna, *Colette.* London, Methuen, and New York, Dell, 1983.

*

An instructive account of Colette in her own words can be found in PHELPS. The work traces her life from her provincial childhood, through her experience of being exploited by the journalist/adventurer Willy, to the point where she became the *grand dame* of French literature. DAVIES provides a good, straightforward account of Colette's work as well as of her life and loves. The same year saw the publication of MARKS' competent account based on secondary as well as primary sources.

The most detailed and best book in English is by RICHARDSON, a very full and instructive description of an unusual personality that combined a fascination for animals and a great interest in the natural world with a not oversavoury concern with adolescent sexuality. Richardson's account also contains some very interesting photographs, reminding one of how very bearded men tended to be in the late 19th century and depicting Captain Colette, the man to whose name the writer remained faithful, playing dominoes with his wife. Miss Richardson's book is particularly good on Colette's links with the political world of her time and provides a valuable account of the general development of French life in the 20th century. It supersedes LE HARDOUIN's work and is useful to read in combination with CROSLAND's *Madame Colette*.

—Philip Thody

COLTRANE, John, 1926–1967; American jazz musician.

Cole, Bill, *John Coltrane*. New York, Schirmer Books, 1976.
Simpkins, Ormond Cuthbert, *Coltrane*. New York, Herndon House, 1975.
Thomas, J. C., *Chasin' the Trane: The Music and Mystique of John Coltrane*. New York, Doubleday, 1975; London, Elm Tree Books, 1976.

*

Each of the Coltrane biographies presents a different, although partial, perspective on the life of the musician. COLE's, which is illustrated and contains a useful bibliography, treats Coltrane with, to say the least, admiration. Cole seeks to make understandable the relationship that existed between Coltrane the musician and Coltrane the religious mystic, to find the key to unlock the mystery of this most enigmatic musician.

Cole emphasizes the influence of Coltrane's religious ideas on his music, but he has no convincing explanation of how those ideas influenced either his music or his musical development. Cole spends long sections of his biography discussing the notions of Fela Sowande, a Nigerian folklorist and composer, who was Cole's mentor but whom Coltrane knew nothing about. At the same time, he merely mentions the fact that both of Coltrane's grandfathers were ministers. Cole makes the general point that only religion has the power to rescue art from becoming mere mechanical contrivance; yet he has no methodology for showing how in Coltrane's case this works, even though it is evident that religious beliefs and music were, especially during the latter part of his life, mixed together as one in Coltrane's music. Cole also presents the reader with Coltrane as the African-American (Cole's term) who rejects the excessive intellectualization of Western Civilization for the more intuitive creative processes of India, China, and especially West Africa.

Cole's is not a comprehensive biography: the first 28 years of Coltrane's life are covered in five pages. But he does discuss the important episodes in that life, and he provides much useful information when he specifically analyzes Coltrane's saxophone solos. Using an article that Coltrane wrote with Don DiMichael for *Downbeat* and the transcriptions of his solos by Andrew White, Cole's discussion of the music is both enlightening and valuable. Even so, the book is finally unsuccessful, mainly because there is no convincing, coherent vision to render Coltrane's life comprehensible to the reader, no synthesis that adds up to a successful biography. It ends up telling us more about Cole than about Coltrane.

SIMPKINS' biography also presents a partial perspective on Coltrane. Here we are given a Coltrane who is the verbally inarticulate but musically seething voice of black anger, black rage, and black revolutionary enthusiasm; Coltrane as the man and artist who represents black anger, black pride, and black accomplishment.

THOMAS' book, which is illustrated and contains a complete Coltrane discography, is the best biography of Coltrane yet to appear. However, it is intended for the general reader and contains no scholarly apparatus at all. Thomas uses long quotations from a variety of people who knew Coltrane in one capacity or another, but the reader never knows how Thomas got those quotations or the source for them. Emphasizing Coltrane's mysticism throughout, Thomas himself takes the mystical approach in writing his book; he speculates, for example, that Coltrane's melancholic personality may have derived from the fact that he was born in Hamlet, North Carolina. Much is made of the several meetings Coltrane had with Charlie Parker, and Thomas traces Coltrane's career from the bop musician of the 1940s to the crucial switch to tenor saxophone when Coltrane became "his own man at last," and finally to 1955 when Coltrane became "Trane."

Thomas shows the range of opinion concerning the quality of Coltrane's playing, from those who thought he was simply incompetent to those who, like Thomas, considered him the greatest musician of all. The biography also provides cultural background of Coltrane's time, reviews of Coltrane's recordings, discussions of the music business, and short biographies of other musicians who played with Coltrane. Yet Thomas' major interest remains on Coltrane the mystic. He compares Coltrane to Einstein in that they both saw into the mysteries of the universe, Einstein with math, Coltrane with music, which Thomas reminds us is mathematical. He also emphasizes Coltrane's response when someone asked him, in 1966, what he wanted to be in ten years: "I'd like to be a saint."

Coltrane still awaits the biography that will do justice to his life and his work, to Coltrane the whole man.

—Donald A. Lawniczak

COLUMBUS, Christopher, 1451–1506; Italian sailor, navigator, and explorer.

Collis, John S., *Christopher Columbus*. London, Macdonald and Jane's, 1976; New York, Stein and Day, 1977.
Granzotto, Gianni, *Christopher Columbus*, translated by Stephen Sartarelli. New York, Doubleday, 1985.
Irving, Washington, *A History of the Life and Voyages of Christopher Columbus*. London, J. Murray (4 vols.), and New York, Carvill (3 vols.), 1828; as *Life and Voyages of Christopher Columbus* (3 vols.), New York, Putnam, 1848; London, J. Murray, 1849.
Madariaga, Salvador de, *Christopher Columbus*. London, Hodder and Stoughton, 1939; New York, Macmillian, 1940.
Morison, Samuel E., *Admiral of the Ocean Sea: A Life of Christopher Columbus* (2 vols.). Boston, Little Brown, 1942.

Morison, Samuel E., *Christopher Columbus, Mariner*. Boston, Little Brown, 1955.

Thacher, John B., *Christopher Columbus: His Life, His Work, His Remains as Revealed by Original Printed and Manuscript Records* (3 vols.). Cleveland, A. H. Clark, 1903.

Winsor, Justin, *Christopher Columbus and How He Received and Imparted the Spirit of Discovery*. Boston, Houghton Mifflin, 1891.

*

In 1826 IRVING, suffering from financial investments that had gone sour, went to Spain to work on the Spanish translation of a collection of Columbus documents. He was looking for a steady income and a way to enhance his literary reputation. Instead of translating the book, however, Irving spent the next three and a half years reading it, other works on Columbus, and manuscript materials in various public and private collections. When he was done, Irving produced the first English biography of Columbus that was both scholarly and popular; one that sold well and enhanced Irving's reputation. The work was originally published virtually simultaneously in 4 volumes in London and in 3 volumes in New York. Irving added information to his work in two later editions, 1831 and 1848. The last was the most complete; it relegated "illustrations" (extended comments on scholarly issues as well as maps and pictures) to a separate volume. The various versions have been collated and published in a modern edition of Irving's works, edited by John H. McElroy (1981).

Irving sees the purpose of history as furnishing "examples of what human genius and laudable enterprise may accomplish." His Columbus is a hero—divinely inspired, brave, constant, courageous—who "brought the ends of the earth into communication with each other." Columbus' treatment of the Indians was, according to Irving, "gentle and sage." He was a visionary ultimately brought down by his "intemperate enemies."

In his scholarly biography of Columbus, WINSOR criticizes Irving for his hero worship, his style, and his lack of up-to-date "canons of historical criticism." Winsor begins with a discussion of the sources on Columbus and an evaluation of previous biographies (in many different languages). He includes numerous maps, pictures, portraits, and pages from manuscripts, as well as an extensive appendix on the geographical results of the discovery.

Although Winsor tries "scientifically" to weigh the evidence while fairly evaluating Columbus and his contemporaries, his biases come through clearly. His Isabella is "deceitful," Ferdinand is a "bigot," and Columbus a "failure," a "blunderer," and a "despoiler." The discovery of America resulted from an "error in geography," Columbus' policies in dealing with and enslaving the Indians showed a lack of morals, while the voyages themselves resulted in "miseries" for his family and were a "reproach upon Spain." Columbus was subject to "rampant hallucinations," and toward the end of his life was both "mad" and "pitiable." While not alone is subscribing to the "black legend" of Spanish colonization, Winsor yet presents a rather one-sided view of the topic and of Columbus.

More favorable though less purely biographical is THACHER's three-volume work. Much in these oversized volumes consists of official documents, letters, and journals, given in both their original language and in translation. The entire third volume consists of such items as a classification of all portraits of Columbus (with illustrations), a discussion of his handwriting and of the resting place of his remains.

Thacher sees Columbus as a hero who should be forgiven much because of his "high purpose." But he spends more time analyzing the documents that are reproduced and/or translated than evaluating Columbus and what he did. As a result, this work is more valuable as an historical resource than for its treatment of Columbus' life.

The strangest biography of Columbus is by MADARIAGA. This is a long, scholarly, and argumentative work whose sole purpose is to prove that Columbus was a Jew. There are extensive footnotes, many of them in Spanish, a bibliography, and maps. But the book begins and ends with the argument that "the Colombo family were Spanish Jews settled in Genoa," and that all the mysteries about Columbus stemmed from his being a converted Jew. Much of the reasoning is far-fetched: Columbus' map-making skills, sense of mission, and desire to find gold were "peculiarly Jewish." Madariaga's conclusions have been rejected by subsequent biographers as a lot of nonsense.

MORISON, a Harvard historian and sailor, has taken a different approach to Columbus. Morison helped organize the Harvard Columbus Expedition of 1939–40, which followed parts of the routes of the four voyages. He also made other trips to places that Columbus had visited. His biographies were designed to show what Columbus "did, where he went, and what sort of seaman he was." His Columbus is more than anything else a sailor and navigator par excellence; the only one ever to come close to him was Captain Cook.

Morison's efforts resulted in three biographies. The first two were published in 1942: a two-volume version containing footnotes and an appendix on the "Remains of Columbus," and a one-volume version that eliminated the scholarly apparatus as well as some of the argumentation, condensed sections on ships, sailing, and syphilis, and added a three-page conclusion evaluating Columbus. In addition, in 1955 Morison published a brief, popular, biography of Columbus. Written in a different style (containing for example a fictional modernized newspaper account of the first discoveries), this book clearly draws on the enormous amount of information on Columbus that Morison had absorbed in his earlier work. All three versions contain detailed charts showing where the explorer "probably" went.

While attempting to present a balanced view of Columbus, Morison clearly admires his persistence and his sailing abilities. The author shares his subject's "amazement, wonder, [and] delight" at what he found. He is more concerned with and better at identifying exactly where Columbus went than imagining where he went. At times, however, this interest makes it difficult to follow the course of Columbus' life. Morison's Columbus is a great explorer and bad colonizer; he ignored the significance of his own discoveries while advancing "geographical hypotheses that made him a laughingstock for fools." He was a fascinating "man of genius" and a "marvelous" seaman. Although this Columbus was flawed, he was a success and died a wealthy man. He opened Central and South America for Spanish colonization, for the expansion of Christianity, and "did more to direct the course of history than any individual since Augustus Caesar."

COLLIS, who become fascinated by Columbus' "Cinderella story" with a "tragic ending," made two trips on cargo ships to the West Indies before preparing his brief biography. His book is written in a breezy popular style. Previous authors are evaluated, even though footnotes are spare, and there is a brief bibliography. The book is peppered with frequent literary allusions. Unfortunately, Collis relies on and quotes from authors whom he himself notes as being unreliable.

For Collis, Columbus was a "missionary," a "genius," but also a man of action who could not "lead and rule men." Columbus is compared to Don Quixote, pursuing unreal ideas, looking for gold that was always "round the corner, over the hill, a little further on," but unlike the Don at times "mean" and "treacherous." This Columbus never knew where he was or what he was doing, and while he should be given sympathy for his troubles, clearly by the end of the Fourth voyage he was no longer sane.

GRANZOTTO's biography is similar. It, too, despite the inclusion of maps and a bibliography, is a well-written popular rather than scholarly book; and Granzotto also sailed part of Columbus' route. However, his work is more even-handed in its evaluations both of previous authors and of the evidence. He effectively quotes from fictional works on Columbus—plays and literary pieces—as well as documents. His Columbus was an "unusual man," a dreamer who sometimes "hallucinated" and suffered from a "touch of madness." By the Third voyage his "imagination turned more and more into a vehicle for mad ravings." The book ends with an interesting discussion of the history of Columbus' reputation, and speculates on where his remains are buried.

While Granzotto's biography is gracefully written and fun to read, the best work on Columbus is Morison's. For most students the brief biography is sufficient; it makes the course of Columbus' life clear. For a scholarly treatment the two-volume *Admiral of the Ocean Sea* has not been surpassed.

—Maxine N. Lurie

CONAN DOYLE, (Sir) Arthur, 1859–1930; English writer and physician.

Carr, John Dickson, *The Life of Arthur Conan Doyle*. London, J. Murray, and New York, Harper, 1949.

Doyle, Adrian M. Conan, *The True Conan Doyle*. London, J. Murray, 1945; New York, Coward McCann, 1946.

Edwards, Owen D., *The Quest for Sherlock Holmes: A Biographical Study of Arthur Conan Doyle*. Edinburgh, Mainstream, and New York, Barnes and Noble, 1983; London, Penguin, 1984.

Higham, Charles, *The Adventures of Conan Doyle: The Life of the Creator of Sherlock Holmes*. London, Hamilton, and New York, Norton, 1976.

Lamond, John, *Arthur Conan Doyle: A Memoir*. London, J. Murray, and Port Washington, New York, Kennikat Press, 1972.

Norden, Pierre, *Conan Doyle: A Biography*, translated by Frances Partridge. London, J. Murray, 1966; New York, Holt, 1967 (originally published as *Sir Arthur Conan Doyle: L'Homme et l'Oeuvre*, Paris, Didier, 1964).

Pearsall, Ronald, *Conan Doyle: A Biographical Solution*. London, Weidenfeld and Nicolson, and New York, St. Martin's, 1977.

Pearson, Hesketh, *Conan Doyle: His Life and Art*. London, Methuen, 1943; revised edition, with Introduction by Graham Greene, London, Unwin, 1987.

*

Few if any writers not of the first order have encouraged so much comment as Sir Arthur Conan Doyle. The reason, of course, is that in Sherlock Holmes he created almost the archetypal detective and one of the most compelling fictional characters to be found in English literature. No account is taken here of the countless imaginary "biographical" studies or other inquiries into the supposed life of the famous detective.

His creator, Conan Doyle, left an account of his own life up to 1924: *Memories and Adventures* (London, 1924) is especially revealing in what its author has to say about his parents and his early years. By the early post-war years, following the loss of his brother in World War I, Doyle had become obsessed with Spiritualism, and the latter part of his narrative is therefore highly subjective. His friend John LAMOND's study is almost exclusively concerned with Doyle's Spiritualist interests.

The first more or less objective biography of Doyle was written by PEARSON, in the breezy popular manner that was the hallmark of his style. It was reissued with an Introduction by Graham Greene, who observes: "Mr. Pearson as a biographer has some of the qualities of Dr. Johnson—a plainness, an honesty, a sense of ordinary life going on all the time. . . . It is one of Mr. Pearson's virtues that he drives us to champion the subject against the biographer." Graham Greene remarks, however, on Pearson's overlooking "the poetic quality" in Doyle; by which he does not mean the author's dreadful sub-Kipling verses but the atmosphere with which he can invest a story.

The fact that Pearson's biography has been reissued with an Introduction by one of the 20th century's most distinguished novelists says much for its quality. It roused Doyle's son, ADRIAN CONAN DOYLE, however, to begin his slim pamphlet of protest: "In its portrayal of my father and his opinions, the book is a travesty and the personal values therein ascribed to him are, in effect, the very antithesis of everything that he represented, believed in and held dear." Unfortunately, Adrian Conan Doyle does not substantiate his charges, and by the second page of his biographical sketch he is embarked on filial observations. He objects to the emphasis put by Pearson on Dr. Joseph Bell of Edinburgh University being the main prototype of Sherlock Holmes, on the basis of Doyle's statement that "a man cannot spin a character out of his own inner consciousness and make it really lifelike unless he has the possibilities of that character within himself." Defending his father's interest in Spiritualism he protests: "My father began his investigations as a bitter opponent of any belief in a life after death and—this is of paramount importance—he refused to pronounce any final judgment before he had devoted *thirty-three* years to his researches." Unfortunately, the length of time a man takes to reach his conclusions on a subject is irrelevant if the conclusions are manifestly absurd.

Adrian, with his brother Denis and his half-sister Mary, collaborated with the writer of detective stories, John Dickson

CARR, in the production of what was no doubt meant to be the "official" biography. Unfortunately, Carr invents dialogue that was never actually spoken, writes in the gung-ho style of a boy's paper of the period, makes no reference whatsoever to the existence of Pearson's book, and hopelessly over-assesses the survivability of nearly all Doyle's work except the Sherlock Holmes novels and stories. Carr could proclaim with confidence, about Professor Challenger, a character in Doyle's late novel *The Lost World*: "If any chronicler can even write that name without a glow of pleasure, he must have the soul of a dried grape. Challenger! Professor Summerlie! Let the exclamation prints stand: these names are linked, like the Musketeers; and, like the Musketeers, they all capture our affections. They are immortal in our boyhood, nor any whit undimmed to middle age."

PEARSALL provides a very full background to Doyle's life, sometimes to the point of distracting the reader's attention. Nevertheless, the book is well researched, lucidly written, and reaches a balanced conclusion about its subject. NORDEN's book has been described as "plodding and easily misted" by Own Dudley Edwards. HIGHAM's book adds little to the sum of knowledge of Doyle's life and makes several factual mistakes, though it puts a higher value on some of Doyle's non-Holmesian works than most.

The most recent study, that by EDWARDS, concentrates on Doyle's Jesuit upbringing, on his ancestors, and on other background matters. Edwards dismisses Pearsall's book for "wanting its readers to know its author is more worthy of admiration than its subject," a charge that could much more properly be laid against Edwards' own self-consciously virtuosic account. As Trevor Royle, reviewing the book in a Scottish newspaper in the manner of a Holmes-Watson conversation, put it: " 'But how does Mr. Edwards know so much about the saintly Doyle? Elementary, my dear Watson. He has scorned the work done by other lesser mortals, and, like me, he has gone back to first principles to discover almost all there is to know about us,' Holmes chuckled. 'He even says my accent should be Scotch. What will the shade of Basil Rathbone think? And that stricture applies to you, too Watson.' I shook my head. 'Surely, this is all a little far-fetched?' Holmes took no notice of my comment."

Because of a legal action, the Doyle papers, available to Carr and others, are no longer so. The fully satisfactory biography of the creator of Sherlock Holmes has thus still to be written. Meanwhile, a combination of Pearson and Pearsall will have to do.

—Maurice Lindsay

CONFUCIUS, 551 B.C.–479 B.C.; Chinese philosopher.

Creel, H. G., *Confucius: The Man and the Myth*. New York, J. Day, 1949; London, Routledge, 1951.
Do-Dinh, Pierre, *Confucius and Chinese Humanism*, translated by Charles Lam Markmann. New York, Funk and Wagnalls, 1969 (originally published by Éditions du Seuil, Paris, 1958).
Lin, Yutang, editor and translator, *The Wisdom of Confucius*. London, Hamilton, and New York, Modern Library, 1938.
Liu, Wu-Chi, *Confucius, His Life and Time*. New York, Philosophical Library, 1955.
Smith, D. Howard, *Confucius*. London, Temple Smith, and New York, Scribner, 1973.
Wilhelm, Richard, *Confucius and Confucianism*, translated by George and Annina Danton. New York, Harcourt, and London, Kegan Paul, 1931 (originally published as *K'ungtse und der Konfuzianismus*, Berlin, de Gruyter, 1928).

*

No one doubts that Confucius (K'ung-tze) actually existed, and there are only minor disagreements as to the dates of his birth and death. Beyond that, however, biographers differ widely in their acceptance and interpretation of traditional materials. The oldest major source still identifiable, a poorly organized collection of the "Conversations of Confucius," was evidently compiled a century or so after the sage's death by descendants of his disciples. Some version of the "Conversations" now lost was known to the Han dynasty historian Ssu-ma Ch'ien, who quoted from it in his life of Confucius (*ca.* 100 B.C.), the first and only such ancient biography that we have. Written almost four centuries after Confucius' death, it is aphoristic, cryptic, and in several instances clearly mythological. Yet every subsequent biographer of Confucius, including the modern scholar, has necessarily confronted Ssu-ma Ch'ien's account to decide for himself how much of it may be authentic and what the seemingly authentic parts of it may mean. Because of the style in which it was written, a faithful translation of the "life" is almost unintelligible to Western readers, whereas a freer and smoother one may be less reliable.

Given these often insuperable difficulties, almost all recent scholarship on the life of Confucius combines biographical data from Ssu-ma Ch'ien with quotations from the *Analects*, a version of the earlier *Conversations* dating from about 170 A.D. Unfortunately, the *Analects* does not contain everything that must have been in *Conversations* because Ssu-ma Ch'ien quotes seemingly authentic passages from the latter that are not now in the *Analects*. In dealing with the *Analects*, it is best to compare two or more translations, preferring those that, like James Legge (*The Chinese Classics*, 1861–72) and Arthur Waley (*The Analects of Confucius*, 1938), include extensive notes. One should also consult more than one modern version of the life.

As translated by the Dantons, WILHELM provided the first English version of Ssu-ma Ch'ien's life of Confucius. His redaction is now valuable as a reading text only, its notes in particular being obsolete. But the chapter following the notes comments usefully on sources and themes. A major point of contention for all biographers of Confucius is the extent to which he was in any way responsible for the so-called Confucian classics. In Wilhelm's opinion, Confucius wrote nothing, but probably edited the works attributed to him. He was, nonetheless, the founder of Chinese humanism and the most important thinker in the history of his accomplished country.

LIN also translates Ssu-ma Ch'ien's life of Confucius in full, but directly from the Chinese, adding interpretations and explanations that are often extremely helpful. His handy book likewise includes one of the major translations of the *Analects* (to be compared with those of Legge and Waley) and some other well-chosen sources. In attempting to distinguish fact from fiction, however, CREEL is much more critical. His biographical chapter (IV) explains with admirable clarity what parts of the tradition we may reasonably accept. Though Creel doubts a good deal, he nonetheless constructs a detailed and surprisingly plausible Confucius as man, teacher, philosopher, and (more controversially) reformer.

LIU soon demonstrated, however, that Creel's brilliant reassessment of Confucius as a forward-looking, rather subversive revolutionary was not entirely to be accepted. For him, Confucius remained a champion of feudal ideals. With this as his theme, Liu's first seven chapters gracefully expand Ssu-ma Ch'ien's crabbed account into a consistent narrative of Confucius' life and times. In his opinion Confucius himself compiled the *Spring and Autumn Annals* but only edited the other classic works—*Changes, Poetry, History*, and *Rites*.

In a similar but less demanding book, probably suitable for high school students, DO-DINH utilizes post-Confucian commentaries (especially that called *The Golden Mean*) in a lucid, plausible biography of some 90 pages. Skillfully written and nicely illustrated, it again combines narrative elements from Ssu-ma Ch'ien with quotations from the *Analects* (here called *Conversations*). Those parts of the book dealing with other Chinese philosophical schools, however, are greatly oversimplified and might well be tempered with the complications and depth of W. T. Chan's *A Source Book in Chinese Philosophy* (1963).

Finally, it is to be noted that SMITH's volume, despite its title, is not a biography, though chapter two includes a brief sketch and a short chronology of Confucius' life appears at the end. Like Creel, Smith does not believe that Confucius wrote or edited anything. He also defends him against the charge of irreligion, and he protests, with Liu, that the great sage was no revolutionary.

—Dennis R. Dean

CONRAD, Joseph, 1857–1924; Polish-born English writer.

Allen, Jerry, *The Thunder and the Sunshine: A Biography of Joseph Conrad.* New York, Putnam, 1958.

Baines, Jocelyn, *Joseph Conrad: A Critical Biography.* New York, McGraw-Hill, and London, Weidenfeld and Nicolson, 1959.

Conrad, Jessie, *Joseph Conrad and His Circle.* London, Jarrolds, and New York, Dutton, 1935.

Curle, Richard, *The Last Twelve Years of Joseph Conrad.* New York, Doubleday, and London, Low Marston, 1928.

Jean-Aubrey, Georges, *The Sea Dreamer: A Definitive Biography of Joseph Conrad.* New York, Doubleday, and London, Allen and Unwin, 1957.

*

Some writers emerge from biographies of them as creatures in contrast to their works. With Joseph Conrad, the author of *Lord Jim*, "The Heart of Darkness," and other exotic narratives, the case is otherwise. The course of Conrad's early life is hardly less strange than the narratives he created after he gave up his wanderings on the sea and in Africa. So the Conrad biographer is faced with situations that require the sort of scrutiny that Conrad himself offers Heyst in *Victory* and the hero of *Nostromo*. What lies behind certain choices Conrad himself made?

Three works treating Conrad's life tackle less complicated issues. JESSIE CONRAD's volume is a simply presented and quite indispensable record of the author's years as Conrad's wife. CURLE, under fewer constraints than Jessie Conrad when it came to recording his observations, offers his recollections of a happy, unbroken friendship. Curle lets his mind move back and forth over his experiences with Conrad, telling what he knows and no more. Joseph Conrad's own *A Personal Record* (1912) sets out many of the important facts of his life, though as later students of that life point out this work disguises as much as it reveals.

JEAN-AUBRY offers as straightforward a narrative as possible, reconstructing the course of events that moved Conrad as a child to Russia where his father was for a time a political exile, and then to other locations in Russia, Poland, and Austria. (Conrad was early deprived of both parents and was watched over by a kind uncle.) The narrative follows Conrad to Marseilles and his chosen life on the sea. With perfect clarity Jean-Aubry narrates the uncertainty that, in his thirties, led Conrad to waver between French and English citizenship. He also traces Conrad's move, even before his retirement from the sea, from the forecastle of a ship to the writer's desk, and he includes quotations from Henry James, H. G. Wells, and others who respected Conrad's mastery of the English language. As he did for Conrad's youth and early adulthood, Jean-Aubry provides too a straightforward, readable account of Conrad's life as a writer.

Thus does Jean-Aubry establish the outlines that the two other major biographers handle in their own ways. And he deals as well as he can certain gaps in information. Most of Conrad's early correspondence no longer exists, and Jean-Aubry has to understand Conrad's early career decisions from guardian uncle's long and tender letters. Years that were formative for Conrad still remain obscure for us. Jean-Aubry gives his readers modest analyses of what may have lay behind Conrad's early detachment from the Polish cause and what specific events troubled his youthful days in Marseilles and elsewhere. But good taste (Jean-Aubry was a personal friend of Conrad's), as well as his demand for exact information, limit Jean Aubry's account. It should be added that Jean-Aubry sometimes assumes a knowledge of 19th- and early 20th-century events that the present-day reader lacks. That knowledge is provided in the other two biographies, along with other provocative materials.

Provocative is perhaps an apt word for much of ALLEN's comparatively brief book. In particular, an early love affair in France and a supposed duel related to the affair is reconstructed. Some of this, Allen suggests, becomes the substance of Conrad's late novel, *The Arrow of Gold*. Though Baines later questions the possibility of certainty about these matters, Allen nevertheless offers events and motives that excite. What also makes Allen's work interesting for some readers is its novelistic style.

BAINES' book on Conrad usually turns aside from what cannot be definitely known. When she deals with matters where certainty is not possible, such as Conrad's detachment from the Polish cause (a cause sacred to his father), she gives us clear indication that she only speculates. Baines would rather walk over solid terrain, such as that provided by Conrad's exchange of letters with his literary friends. But Baines indicates that she knows there are risks a biographer must soberly take. Her credo, to which many another biographer would give resigned agreement, runs as follows: "When a biographer has not known his subject personally, he must inevitably remain at one remove from him; a truism that is nonetheless forgotten, or deliberately disguised; for the rest such a biographer must depend on what his subject has said about himself or on the unsatisfactory, because incomplete and in the most important respects unverifiable evidence of others." Baines adds, "It is therefore impossible for the present biographer to reproduce a personality whose exceptional magnetism Conrad's friends have stressed." Or, one might add, to reconstruct the moments in Conrad's life that were the equivalents of Lord Jim's abandonment of the Patna or Kurtz's outcry in "The Heart of Darkness."

But despite this caution, Baines takes her readers a considerable distance into the heart of Conrad's own darkness: his scepticism that directed itself against both religious certainty and facile democratic hope. From Baines' book Conrad emerges as a solitary and modestly heroic man: a man to whom the crucial issue was neither religious faith nor democratic action, since neither would alter the essential reality each person faces. What counted for the man Conrad and for the writer Conrad as well was the dignity and poise with which a human being went forward in the face of odds that are likely to remain insurmountable.

This is an insight about Conrad that Baines works out with care. But one might in justice remark that it is an insight that is in various ways perceived and served in the other studies of Conrad commented on here. Jessie Conrad and Richard Curle make the suggestion modestly and casually; with them such evidence of a sad nobility simply accumulates rather than is specifically sought out. Jean-Aubry is somewhat more systematic in his portrait of a man who was, for him, both master and friend. Allen, in her account of what might be called the hidden years of Conrad's youth, gives satisfaction to those who want to see Conrad more clearly. Baines, in effect, draws back a step. Faithful to her firm biographical program, Baines sets before us a portrait of Conrad that is as full as may be. But what is put before the reader is still marked by reserves and caution, as if to say, "This is as far as biographical effort can take us." And then, perhaps, a kind of silence that points to the novels themselves, where a reader's interest in Conrad began and must indeed end.

—Harold H. Watts

CONSTABLE, John, 1776–1837; English painter.

Constable, Freda, *John Constable: A Biography*. Lavenham, Suffolk, Dalton, 1975.

Fraser, John Lloyd, *John Constable 1776–1837: The Man and His Mistress*. London, Hutchinson, 1976.

Gadney, Reg, *Constable and His World*. New York, Norton, and London, Thames and Hudson, 1976.

Leslie, Charles R., *Memoirs of the Life of John Constable, Esq., R.A., Composed Chiefly of His Letters*. London, J. Carpenter, 1843; 2nd, expanded edition, London, Longman, 1845; revised and updated by Jonathan Mayne, London, Phaidon, 1951.

Reynolds, Graham, *Constable, The Natural Painter*. New York, McGraw-Hill, and London, C. Adams, 1965.

Shirley, Andrew, *The Rainbow, a Portrait of John Constable*. London, M. Joseph, 1949.

Windsor, Robert G.W.C., *John Constable*. London, W. Scott, and New York, Scribner, 1903.

*

The first biography of Constable, by the American painter LESLIE, was published in 1843, six years after Constable's death. Leslie had been a close friend for 25 years, especially after the death of Constable's wife and his friend and confidant, Archdeacon Fisher. Leslie's biography is based upon Constable's collected letters and lecture notes (selected and edited by Leslie), and connected with commentary of his own. In the preface to the first edition, which was illustrated with mezzotints by Lucas, Leslie says that these letters have almost the form of an autobiography. He produced another, much expanded edition two years later, which has been the basis for most subsequent biographies. This is a great biography, and many people consider it the best. However, it must be remembered that the selection by Leslie was colored by friendship, and his editing reflects this.

The Mayne edition of Leslie's memoirs, published in 1951, was based on the 1845 edition. However, Mayne consulted the original manuscripts of the letters quoted in the course of the book and has drawn attention in footnotes to differences between the original and the printed texts. He notes that documentary details on Constable's early formative period, 1800–12, are lacking, and recommends that some of these gaps be filled by Farington's diaries in The Royal Library at Windsor Castle. Mayne also notes discrepancies and says that Leslie abbreviated Constable's success in Paris to emphasize his difficulties.

WINDSOR, in addition to using Leslie's memoirs, adds some letters that "fell into his hands" from friends and relatives of Constable. He also uses newspaper and review articles and notices that were published during Constable's lifetime, and reports on Constable's success in Paris exhibitions. He cautions that Leslie "is inclined to round off the edges and corners of his friend's character, and to colour it with the rosy tint of his personal regard. We must listen to what others have to say about him and form our own conclusions." In leisurely and delightful prose, Windsor quotes from others and tells of Constable's sarcasms, uttered in "soft and amiable speech, which cut you to the bone." Windsor provides good illustrations, bibliography and index, but no notes.

Art historian SHIRLEY calls Leslie's biographical account immortal, but still thinks there is something to be added. He feels that the perspective of time has shown some of Constable's foibles as a man. Shirley has used, in addition to Leslie's work, the council minutes of the Royal Academy and has inspected the Farington diaries. Joseph Farington was an advisor, helper, and friend of Constable from 1798 until his death in 1821. In his detailed diary, he reports on Constable's observations, states of mind and discouragements. Shirley's pleasurable, descriptive account quotes from the letters of Constable's mother and notes that Leslie did not think it worthwhile to preserve those of Constable's wife, Maria. He relates amusing anecdotes and discusses Constable's lectures given to further the cause of landscape painting. This is a scholarly yet informal biography, with no footnotes.

REYNOLDS, one of the leading authorities on English painting, was keeper of the Constable collection in the Victoria and Albert Museum. Reynolds writes that Constable's correspondence with friends, his comments, criticism, and personal anecdotes have been preserved to a remarkable degree, and Reynolds attempts to survey and compress this range of knowledge. He notes that Leslie depicts Constable as all amiability and goodness, and omits his bland yet intense sarcasm. The text is uninterrupted by footnotes and provides only a minimum of references. The black-and-white illustrations are well-chosen and stress the six great paintings of the Stour. There is an index and a select bibliography. Critics have variously described this book as well-written, critical and scholarly, clear and well-documented. Money (*Times Literary Supplement*, 27 February 1976) calls it the best short study available.

Reynolds acknowledges his indebtedness to Leslie and Shirley, and to R. B. Beckett's monumental *Correspondence*. Only a portion of this had been printed, but the typescript was available to him in the Victoria and Albert Museum. Beckett edited and annotated Constable's correspondence in six volumes, with a seventh volume on his discourses. These were published by the Suffolk Records Society between the years 1962–70. A further volume of documents and correspondence was added by Parris, Shields, and Fleming-Williams in 1975 (Beckett having died in 1970, soon after his last volume). Norman Scarfe, one of the founders of the Suffolk Records Society, writes a moving tribute to Beckett in the Parris volume. He praises Beckett's patience and scholarship, and his technical achievement at deciphering Constable's handwriting, "unravelling the spattered squiggles and cossings-out." He notes Leslie's omissions and "improvements," which sometimes change the meaning. Kenneth Clark, in his address at the meeting to launch the "Maria" volume, said, "Everyone interested in English art needs this new edition. It is a masterpiece of editing."

As Constable's bicentenary approached in 1976, a number of books appeared, all leaning heavily on Leslie and on the published correspondence. FREDA CONSTABLE, a member of the artist's family, has written a readable and popular account. She describes her work as an attempt to give the story of Constable's life against the background of his work. In addition to using Beckett, she uses material and illustrations from the Constable family collection, which are not the familiar ones. She is obviously familiar with the documents and digests, and compresses them well. The work is indexed but provides no footnotes.

GADNEY's work is scholarly, with quotations acknowledged in the text. It provides a good, general framework for Constable's relationships with the Royal Academy and with other artists. Illustrations, not all by Constable, could be clearer, but some are charming, especially the ones of Constable's children. Some illustrate people and places discussed and all are annotated and linked with the text.

FRASER has produced a good, solid biography. It is more substantial than Gadney's and includes more documentation. Fraser uses Beckett, Farington, and Leslie, and lists notes and

sources chapter by chapter. The work offers a bibliography, an index, and some black-and-white illustrations, including photographs and portraits of the family. Although it contains no new material, it is a scholarly, thorough, and readable biography, and gives a balanced portrait of Constable.

The Gadney and Fraser books overlap to some extent, and relate the same anecdotes. Conrad (*Spectator*, 21 February 1976) complains that they are both anecdotal rather than critical rejuvenations, but says that the selections from contemporary reviews are valuable. He feels that none of these later books replaces Reynolds.

—Patricia Brauch

CONSTANTINE I [the Great], *ca.* 280–337; Roman emperor.

Alföldi, András, *The Conversion of Constantine and Pagan Rome*, translated by Harold Mattingly. Oxford, Clarendon Press, 1948.

Baker, George P., *Constantine the Great and the Christian Revolution*. New York, Dodd Mead, 1930; London, Eveleigh Nash, 1931.

Burckhardt, Jacob C., *The Age of Constantine the Great*, translated by Moses Hadas. New York, Doubleday, and London, Routledge, 1949 (originally published in Basel, 1853).

Dörries, Hermann, *Constantine the Great*, translated by Roland Bainton. New York, Harper, 1972 (originally published by W. Kohlhammer, Stuttgart, 1958).

Firth, John B., *Constantine the Great: The Reorganization of the Empire and the Triumph of the Church*. New York, Putnam, 1905.

Gibbon, Edward, *The History of the Decline and Fall of the Roman Empire* (6 vols.). London, W. Strahan and T. Cadell, 1776–88; edited by John Bury, 7 vols., London, Methuen, and New York, Macmillan, 1909–14.

Jones, Arnold H., *Constantine and the Conversion of Europe*. London, Hodder and Stoughton, and New York, Macmillan, 1948.

MacMullen, Ramsay, *Constantine*. New York, Dial Press, 1969.

Smith, John H., *Constantine the Great*. New York, Scribner, and London, Hamilton, 1971.

*

Few figures in Western civilization have aroused as much interest and controversy as Constantine. His reign clearly marked a turning point in the history of the Roman Empire and in the growth and development of Christianity. However one views his personal "conversion" and the attendant motives, Constantine's ultimate adherence to and active imperial support for the Christian religion is unquestionable. As the first Christian emperor of a state that had traditionally viewed this religion with suspicion, Constantine represented a radical departure from the norm, a point noted and emphasized by his contemporaries. The ancient literary sources for his life and reign are fairly extensive, but they are often partisan. Although modern researchers have attempted to make sense of the resulting portraits of Constantine, supplementing and correcting the literary material with epigraphic, numismatic, and archeological evidence, we still do not have an entirely satisfactory picture of this man. Indeed, Norman Baynes' observation in his Raleigh Lecture on History, entitled "Constantine the Great and the Christian Church" (12 March 1930), is still applicable: "The representations attempted by modern scholars of the convictions and aims of Constantine have been so diverse that at times it is hard to believe that it is one and the same emperor that they are seeking to portray." Such is both the continuing lure and frustration of the field of Constantinian studies.

One of the earliest modern treatments of Constantine is that by GIBBON, who devotes the better part of five chapters (14, 17–18, 20–21) to an examination of the emperor's life and times. Despite Gibbon's anti-Christian perspective, his reconstruction of key events and his brilliant narrative style mark this work as a classic. To his credit, Gibbon draws extensively on the meticulous researches of the 17th century French historian Tillemont for much of his material.

BURCKHARDT's important essay on the age of Constantine, intended for a general readership, focuses on the late third and early fourth centuries as a period of fundamental change and transition between the ancient and medieval worlds. Burckhardt views Constantine as a man dominated by political ambition, not religion, who in his later years was attracted more to paganism than to Christianity: "In a genius driven without surcease by ambition and lust for power there can be no question of Christianity and paganism, of conscious religiosity or irreligiosity; such a man is essentially unreligious, even if he pictures himself standing in the midst of a churchly community."

The first full-length biography of Constantine written in English was that by the Oxford classicist FIRTH. Although the book appeared in the popular "Heroes of the Nations" series, it is a work of considerable erudition. Firth's intimate knowledge of the primary and secondary literature is obvious, and his careful, detailed analysis of the religious tensions and controversies of the Constantinian era is especially noteworthy. It is the author's goal to assess the man under whose auspices "one of the most momentous changes in the history of the world was accomplished, . . . the first conversion of a Roman Emperor to Christianity, with all that such conversion entailed." Firth's style of writing is somewhat formal but does not detract from the book's readability.

BAKER's study, like Firth's, is intended for the general reading public, but is much less scholarly in approach and presentation. As the book's title implies, the major emphasis here is upon the role Constantine played in the "Christian revolution" of the early fourth century, a time when "in self-defence the Christians resorted to the only possible means of avoiding their fate. That is to say, they brought about a revolution and themselves seized power." Less attention is paid to Constantine's foundation of the New Rome, his furthering of an absolutist ideology, and his administrative policies. Baker depends on earlier secondary works for most of his information. The narrative is fast-moving and vivid, and the style is decidedly popular. The author's personal familiarity with the regions and sites discussed adds to the book's appeal.

ALFÖLDI provides a penetrating study of the emperor's vision for the Roman Empire and the policies and legislative programs he adopted as a result. The author argues that Constantine, a sincere convert to Christianity since the Milvian bridge incident of 312, anticipated the need for cooperation and alliance between the Church and the Roman state if the Empire was to survive. The growth of Church influence in Roman society and government receives considerable attention. Alföldi's discussions of the numismatic evidence and the writings of the rhetorician Lactantius are thoughtful and persuasive, and his overall thesis is well argued. The translation by Mattingly from the original German is excellent. This is a substantial piece of scholarship, readily accessible to specialists and general readers alike.

The English classical historian JONES offers a more general, wide-ranging approach to the life and times of Constantine. His introduction and preliminary chapters address the nature of the source material, the relationship between Christianity and paganism in the second and third centuries A.D., the political and military crises of the same period, and the decisive impact of the emperor Diocletian. The rest of the book, some 200 pages, is devoted to an assessment of Constantine. Jones' last chapter, "Constantine's Place in History," sums up his evaluation of this key figure in Western history: "Constantine hardly deserves the title of 'Great' which posterity has given him, either by his character or by his abilities. He lacked firmness of purpose to pursue steadily his long-term objectives. . . . He was highly susceptible to flattery. . . . He shows up best as a general. . . . In the more humdrum task of administration he was weak. . . . In finance he was ruinously extravagant. . . . His ecclesiastical policy exhibits the same defects. He had a noble objective, the unity of the Church, but in pursuing it he oscillated helplessly between the various parties." This book remains an excellent introduction to the field of Constantinian studies.

DÖRRIES' provocative biography of Constantine poses the central question: Why and how did Constantine ally his own fortunes and those of the Roman Empire with Christianity? Of course, this is a major focus in most modern accounts, but Dörries' use of imperial documents attributed to the emperor himself lends a new vitality to the search for historical explanations. The author strenuously objects to some of the criticism Constantine has taken over the centuries, particularly by modern, "scientific" historians. As he notes, "To assess Constantine and his period we must see what contemporaries said about him and even more what he said about himself. . . . To be sure, the historian is not a searcher of hearts, but it is indisputable that Constantine thought of himself as a Christian. We have no right to call his own utterances into question." Dörries, to his credit, does not stop there: "Yet we must ask what kind of a Christian he was. How much of earlier Christianity did he retain? What meaning did it have for him and for his work? Only after answering these questions are we in a position to evaluate the man." In the final analysis, Constantine represents for Dörries a sincere and committed Christian, but one strongly influenced by the traditions of Roman imperial religion and piety, a man who "thought of Christ as the god of battle, of the Cross as the sign and giver of victory."

MacMULLEN's *Constantine* is a very different sort of book. Although the author does take up the question of Constantine's religious beliefs at some length, he is more inclined to offer the reader a broadly-based portrait of the emperor in the context of palace, church, and battlefield. In the introductory chapter he cautions that despite the relative abundance of sources for the period, such sources cannot be accepted uncritically. Indeed, "historians must piece out a picture of the times from sources obviously and deliberately false." The contrast here with Dörries' approach to the sources is striking. MacMullen's assessment of Constantine as a cautious innovator, whose actions were often dictated by the nature of his circumstances, is persuasive. So too is his depiction of the emperor as one who, like many of his contemporaries, was more interested in the ability of divinity to guarantee power and success than in the moral implications of religious belief. But Constantine's own description of himself as "bishop of those outside the Church" suggests a strong sense of mission, and MacMullen notes that "Constantine promoted the spread of Christianity beyond the frontiers, still more within them. . . . His motive, however, was not to save souls but, one may almost say, bodies. He aimed at the prosperity of his reign and realm through ensuring to God acceptable worship." Several well-chosen illustrations enhance the volume. Unfortunately, MacMullen offers no accompanying notes, but a brief bibliographic essay does provide some guidance for further inquiry.

The most recent authoritative account to appear is that of SMITH. By far the fullest biographical treatment, this book presents a balanced overview of most aspects of the emperor's life. Smith stresses the complex character of his subject, a man known to his contemporaries for his quick temper, aloofness, cruelty, and venality, but also for his sponsorship of charitable institutions, legal and administrative reforms along humanitarian lines, and support for the Christian Church. As such, Constantine was both saint and sinner. But while the former aspect was duly celebrated during his lifetime and more notably after his death, "all those characteristics . . . for which he might have been condemned, have been forgotten. So too has the chief charge which might have been brought against him, that he interfered in ecclesiastical affairs and in doing so diverted Christian attention from spiritual concerns by offering opportunities of acquiring political influence to the bishops." Nevertheless, in Smith's opinion Constantine remains deserving of his title "the Great," for "by successfully translating Diocletian's concepts of the roots of power, jurisdiction and stability into terms acceptable to the Christians," he was able at once to change and preserve the world he cherished. Smith is at his best in his discussion of religious issues, though his treatment of the emperor's military and financial reforms is a model of conciseness and clarity. His analyses are considerably weaker in the area of Constantinian art and architecture, where his own tastes seem to come into play. The final chapter, "The Constantine Legends," a survey of the myths and quasi-historical claims that became attached to this figure, is one of the most interesting and valuable sections in the book. Smith offers primary source documentation for his conclusions as well as access to the specialized secondary literature in notes following the text. A short bibliography, illustrations, and a genealogical chart are also provided.

—Craig L. Hanson

COOK, James, 1728–1779; English navigator and explorer.

Beaglehole, John C., *The Life of Captain James Cook*. London, A. and C. Black, and Stanford, California, Stanford University Press, 1974.

Besant, Walter, *Captain Cook*. London and New York, Macmillan, 1890.

Hoobler, Dorothy and Thomas Hoobler, *The Voyages of Captain Cook*. New York, Putnam, 1983.

Kippis, Andrew, *The Life of Captain James Cook*. London, Nicol and Robinson, 1788.

Kitson, Arthur, *Captain James Cook*. New York, Dutton, and London, J. Murray, 1907.

Villiers, Alan J., *Captain James Cook*. New York, Scribner, 1967.

Withey, Lynne, *Voyages of Discovery: Captain Cook and the Exploration of the Pacific*. New York, Morrow, and London, Hutchinson, 1987.

*

Employing various literary styles but a disagreeable sameness of approach, the biographers of James Cook have praised his intelligence, resourcefulness, determination, and courage. But all these authors have found irresistible the theme of a poor nobody rising to world fame; thus they have succeeded in surrounding Cook with an awe that has blunted more probing insights. After 200 years the analysis of Cook has barely gone beneath the surface, while the abundant attention accorded him bespeaks humanity's continuing need for heroes.

The Royal Society got the ball rolling by commissioning the first life, by KIPPIS. The Society took an interest in all scientific aspects of Cook's voyages, elevated him to membership after his second voyage, and awarded him its Copley gold medal for his paper on preventing scurvy. So the Society was promoting one of its own, through the efforts of another insider, since Kippis, who had earned a minor literary reputation by contributions to *Gentleman's Magazine* and the *Monthly Review*, but chiefly as editor of the first edition of *Biographia Britannica*, was also a fellow of the Society. Obviously much more interested in his own work as a Presbyterian divine and tutor, Kippis took few pains with his study, but he gave the Royal Society the panegyric it desired. He interviewed Cook's widow, and a few leading members of the Admiralty, to whose papers he had access, but he read none of Cook's original journals, preferring instead to rely on the official history already published by Dr. John Hawkesworth, *An Account of the Voyages Undertaken by the Order of His Present Majesty for Making Discoveries in the Southern Hemisphere* (London, 1773). Hawkesworth, a journalist in the circle of Samuel Johnson, combined material from Cook's first voyage and three other recent explorers to produce a work designed to amuse the denizens of coffee houses and literary salons. Its inaccuracies enraged Cook; some of these Kippis corrected, though he preserved Hawkesworth's stilted, overblown style. For the second and third voyages Kippis used the edition of Cook's journals prepared by Canon John Douglas, rather than the originals themselves, though Douglas was truer to Cook than Hawkesworth. Kippis took a condescending view of the Pacific's natives, and he failed to appreciate the Captain's versatile talents, though he erected a cardboard figure who embodied common sense and leadership, which played admirably to the public's expectations, making Kippis' book the standard life for over a century.

BESANT, the distinguished Victorian novelist, perpetuated some old errors and created a few new ones, but his book makes effective use of George Gilbert's journal, and a valuable history of the second voyage by George Forster (1777), both of which portrayed a more human Cook—often aloof, capable of temper, even bad judgment. Besant revealed for the first time how the Hawaiians viewed the circumstances of Cook's death. Because he could evoke settings and events with imagination, and select material intelligently, Besant created the first thoroughly interesting book on Cook, which is still worth reading, brief as it is.

KITSON was a businessman whose no-nonsense approach emphasized Cook's contributions to geographical discovery. Subtleties of character were beyond him, and an interest in the natives beneath him, but his book was the first to exploit the extensive manuscript materials in the Public Record Office and the British Museum, which led to a proper understanding of Cook's career before his first voyage around the world. Kitson also utilized Rev. George Young's researches (1836) to correct errors about Cook's boyhood, apprenticeship, and early service in the colliers. Because of its grounding in primary sources and its readability, Kitson's book succeeded Kippis' as the standard life, though its uncritical view of Cook completed the secular apotheosis of this son of a Scottish peasant.

BEAGLEHOLE was a New Zealander and the first professional historian to confront Cook, from which he never recovered. During nearly 40 years he first produced scholarly editions of Cook's journals, Joseph Banks' journals, various studies of Pacific history, then finally this ponderous book, which explains everything but Cook. He brought to light manuscripts in New Zealand and Australia without neglecting anything in Britain, and he understood geography, natural history, and anthropology, but in the end his book is less a biography than an erudite chronicle. By portraying Cook as the superbly talented navigator, surveyor, and seaman, the determined but humane leader whose only passion was for exactness, Beaglehole applied the final layer of varnish to the public figure, larger than life, but lacking visceral reality.

Because he had sailed in ships much like Cook's, Australian naval captain VILLIERS could testify vividly on many points that escaped other writers, in particular the daily horrors of life at sea, and the effects on Cook of having to deal with them over a prolonged period. All admirers of Cook find his naturalists (Joseph Banks and J. R. Forster) to be capital nuisances, and deplore how they stole the show from Cook, but Villiers also makes use of Banks to illustrate the realities of the English class system, which indirectly contributed so much to Cook's successes, frustrations, and even his death.

Another professional historian and the first American biographer of importance, WITHEY shows Cook's genuine interest in the native peoples he met, and, for the first time, gives a sympathetic account of those natives, showing how Cook's men often misunderstood them. Remarkably, the only previous author to attempt a balanced view of native cultures was Hugh Carrington (1939). Withey also provides a more objective view of J. R. Forster, based on the work of Michael E. Hoare, whose scholarship suggests he may be Cook's next interpreter. Readers seeking only a summary of Cook's career, and in popular language, should begin with HOOBLER, which succeeds an earlier equivalent in the Great Lives Series, by Rupert T. Gould (1935).

Now that the public career of James Cook has been solidly documented, and the strengths of his character well outlined, the time would seem ripe for a perceptive writer to read between the lines of the several journals, contemporary accounts, and private letters in order to portray the inner man. No one has yet plumbed Cook's emotional depths or plotted his professional development against a convincing appraisal of his deepest personal needs.

—Mike F. Foster

COOPER, James Fenimore, 1789–1851; American writer.

Boynton, Henry Walcott, *James Fenimore Cooper*. New York, Century, 1931.

Bryant, William Cullen, *Memorial of James Fenimore Cooper*. New York, Putnam, 1852.

Clymer, William B. S., *James Fenimore Cooper*. Boston, Small Maynard, 1900.

Cooper, Susan Fenimore, editor, *Pages and Pictures from the Writings of James Fenimore Cooper*. New York, Townsend, 1861.

Grossman, James, *James Fenimore Cooper*. New York, Sloan, 1949; London, Methuen, 1950.

Lounsbury, Thomas R., *James Fenimore Cooper*. Boston, Houghton Mifflin, 1882.

Phillips, Mary E., *James Fenimore Cooper*. New York, J. Lane, 1912.

Railton, Stephen, *Fenimore Cooper: A Study of His Life and Imagination*. Princeton, New Jersey, Princeton University Press, 1978.

Spiller, Robert E., *Fenimore Cooper: Critic of His Times*. New York, Minton Balch, 1931.

Walker, Warren S., *James Fenimore Cooper: An Introduction and Interpretation*. New York, Barnes and Noble, 1962.

*

GROSSMAN avoids both the condescension and hero-worship that have polarized Cooper biography. This well-researched and reliable study, the second book on Cooper in The American Men of Letters Series, examines Cooper's life in detail, assesses his character, evaluates the works, and judges his historical significance. Grossman is a practicing lawyer, and he tends to interpret the good and bad elements in Cooper's character and art in a style of syntactically balanced antitheses. Cooper emerges as an honest but gloomy misanthrope, alienated from his countrymen, whose career was erratic and whose fiction was of the second rank because "limited by the conventions of his age."

Grossman writes most incisively about the public Cooper—the European traveler, social critic, successful plantiff in numerous lawsuits, and impartial historian of American naval history. Cooper never retreated from these realities, Grossman maintains, but in his fiction, he withdrew into escapist adventure and romance. Little detail is known about the private Cooper, and

Grossman can only repeat what tradition and Susan Cooper have provided about the domestic life of the country squire. Otherwise, this book remains the fullest account—astute and sometimes unflattering—of Cooper's life and works.

Of all the biographers who preceded him, Grossman singles out BRYANT for praise. Because Cooper enjoined any family member from writing or contributing to an authorized biography, Bryant's eulogy was the only comprehensive review of Cooper's life and works for 30 years after his death. Bryant praises Cooper's genius and his honesty, and he genteely describes his public quarrels. Although Bryant and Cooper were friends, fellow authors, and politically like-minded, Bryant candidly admits Cooper was too brusque to be universally liked, but he still presents the most balanced portrayal of Cooper until Spiller. Bryant's own career as a newspaperman makes his comments about Cooper's wars with the press still pertinent today.

SUSAN COOPER, the writer's eldest daughter and longtime amanuensis, respected her father's prohibition against a full-length biography. However, her anecdotes provide glimpses of the private, domestic man that reveal a warmer, more human side than the idealized and abstracted representation of subsequent biographies.

LOUNSBURY, a Chaucerian at Yale, was asked to write the Cooper biography for the first American Men of Letters Series. He produced an admirably thorough and scholarly examination of Cooper without access to any family documents, but he could muster little sympathy for his subject. He thought Cooper unduly sensitive to criticism, possessed a character both defiant and parochial, and wrote popular fiction that did not meet the standards of either good taste or good art. Had Cooper not been dismissed from Yale, Lounsbury asserts, he might have learned enough discipline to give form to his novels and decorum to his conduct. Treating Cooper's fiction, Lounsbury praises his descriptions more than his characters (unlike almost every other critic of Cooper's fiction) though like other biographers he praises Cooper's patriotism and respects his principles. Finally, however, his condescension undercuts his judgments.

In contrast, both CLYMER and PHILLIPS engage in hero-worship to illustrate Washington Irving's encomium that Cooper was "not only a great, but a good man." Clymer quotes from unpublished letters that were unavailable to Lounsbury, but he is otherwise derivative in his critical assessments. Phillips must be warned against for her inaccuracies and can only be recommended for the profuse reproductions of engravings and photographs that appear on nearly every page.

BOYNTON was the first to have full access to the family papers and to the first published correspondence edited by Cooper's grandson in 1922, though he does not probe deeply into these resources. Boynton deliberately counters Lounsbury's assassination of Cooper's character. His method is to quote liberally from letters and documents that depict Cooper as a robust, outgoing personality who was sometimes gruff and bluntly honest, but on the whole sincere and not overly sensitive to criticism. Boynton devotes a chapter to Cooper's friendships to demonstrate he was no misanthrope. His style is exuberant and informal and given to frequent exclamations. He is more descriptive than analytical, livelier but less scholarly than Grossman. Boynton asserts rather than demonstrates that "Cooper's genius was instinct."

SPILLER is the first modern biographer to use sources objectively. He does not analyze Cooper's character but explains his development as an observer, then analyst, and finally critic of society. He includes as much quotation as interpretation, but he keeps to the narrower focus of social concern throughout. He argues that Cooper's development as a social critic was both natural and necessary for a writer in the early republic, an approach that has been influential in Cooper biography and criticism since Spiller's work.

On the one hand, RAILTON's psychological study provides an entirely new approach to Cooper biography. He moves beyond the now repetitive argument about Cooper's character to explore, through Freudian analysis, his "emotional" life as it relates to the works. On the other hand, Railton's explanation of Cooper's Oedipal complex adds to the number of documented conflicts that characterize Cooper's life, although Railton discovers their source in the psyche rather than in the times. Thus, Cooper's rebellion against his father explains his dismissal from Yale, his quarrels with the press, his creation of fictional heroes who escape civilization, and the themes of rebellion in his Revolutionary War novels. There is less of the public career examined here than in Grossman; Railton is less comprehensive by design. But he provides more connection between Cooper's inner life and his works than anyone so far. He also is the first biographer to use Beard's excellent scholarly edition of Cooper's *Letters and Journals* (6 vols., 1960–68). Beard's thorough documentation provides some new material for Cooper biography of which Railton's is the first example.

For a good, short interpretation of the life and works, WALKER provides an excellent introduction, but until James Franklin Beard's long-awaited biography appears, Grossman's book remains the definitive life of Cooper.

—Donald C. Irving

COPERNICUS, Nicholas, 1473–1543; Polish astronomer.

Birkenmajer, Ludwik A., *Nicolas Copernicus*, translated by Owen Gingerich and Jerzy Dobrzycki. Ann Arbor, Michigan, UMI Research Press, 1975 (originally published as *Mikołoj Kopernik*, Krakow, 1900).

Hoyle, Fred, *Nicolaus Copernicus: An Essay on His Life and Work*. London, Heinemann, and New York, Harper, 1973.

Koestler, Arthur, *The Sleepwalkers: A History of Man's Changing Vision of the Universe*. New York, Macmillan, and London, Hutchinson, 1959.

Rosen, Edward, *Copernicus and the Scientific Revolution*. Malabar, Florida, Krieger Publishing, 1984.

*

As historians of science were preparing to commemorate the 500th birthday of Copernicus in 1973, some of them began to scour the libraries and archives in the hope of finding some previously overlooked manuscripts and incunabula capable of shedding new light on the unresolved problems concerning Copernicus' life and work. Others pored over the known facts, trying to interpret them in a more plausible manner. These efforts resulted in a slew of publications that cleared several gray areas in Copernicus' biography and rendered most previous efforts, such as Angus Armitage's *Sun, Stand Thou Still* (1947), obsolete. However, the upcoming anniversary induced also several pseudo-experts into climbing on the Copernican bandwagon and publish biographies, or translations of biographies, full of ridiculous misinformation.

One of these is the slim work by HOYLE, otherwise a reputable astronomer, but far from being a Copernican scholar. His principal concern was to point out the main differences between the planetary theories of Ptolemy, Copernicus, and Kepler in modern mathematical notation. But while he admirably managed to obtain this aim, he failed to produce a reliable biographical sketch of Copernicus. Hoyle relied mainly on the dated biography by Leopold Prowe (*Nicolaus Coppernicus* [Berlin, 1883–84]), unaware that several conclusions drawn by Prowe have been invalidated by a variety of newly discovered documents. In particular, Hoyle stated that "Copernicus returned to Varmia in 1501, to be inducted into . . . canonry." Yet from a notarial document found in Bologna we learn that Copernicus took possession of his canonry by proxy in 1497. Similarly, Hoyle gives the year 1533 "as a likely approximation to the date of *Commentariolus*," Copernicus' "extended abstract . . . of his heliocentric theory." Hoyle's dating shows his ignorance of the pertinent literature, for it has been known since 1924 (L. A. Birkenmajer, *Stromata Copernicana*) that a manuscript of *Commentariolus* was already in 1514 present in a library of a professor at the University of Cracow. To Hoyle's numerous blunders belongs the statement that Copernicus translated a collection of Greek letters into Polish; this translation, published in 1509 and reproduced by Prowe, shows Copernicus' translation to be Latin, not Polish.

According to KOESTLER, his attempt at an inquiry into the obscure workings of the creative mind resulted in finding that "the intellectual giants of the scientific revolution [Copernicus, Kepler, Galileo] were moral dwarfs." Thus in the section entitled "The Timid Canon," Koestler twists the extant facts in his attempt to fit Copernicus into his mold for a "moral dwarf," and presents him as a coward, a niggard, and an ingrate. Koestler's best seller was severely criticized by serious historians of science, notably Stillman Drake and Edward Rosen. Among others, the latter in various articles demonstrated Koestler's unjust belittling of the great astronomer, as well as his woeful ignorance of Polish political history and geography of the region where Copernicus lived and worked. For example, Koestler states that Frauenburg (Frombork, in Polish) was situated in East Prussia, while in actuality it belonged to West Prussia. Likewise, "Ermland [Warmia, in Polish] lay wedged in between the lands of the Polish King and the Order of Teutonic Knights," while Warmia, a part of the Polish kingdom lay wholly within its borders. Speaking about the war between Warmia and the Teutonic Knights, Koestler says that "Copernicus preferred to remain . . . in his tower behind the safe walls of Frauenburg," on the northern coast, whereas Copernicus was the commander in charge of Allenstein (Olsztyn, in Polish), on the southern front.

Koestler labels Copernicus' masterpiece *De revolutionibus orbium coelestium* "the book that nobody read." If this statement is correct, then why the first edition of 1543 was followed by a second in 1566, third in 1617, fourth in 1854, and fifth in 1873, not to mention the numerous editions in various languages in our own century, remains a mystery. One thing is certain: Mr. Koestler himself did not read *De revolutionibus*, for had he done so, he would not call the star Spica, in the constellation Virgin, Copernicus' "basic star . . . used as a landmark," since in actuality Copernicus' basic star is in the constellation Ram, described by him as "of the two [stars] in the horn, the one to the west, and the first of all [stars]" (*Nicholas Copernicus Complete Works* [hereafter *NCCW*], vol. II, Warsaw and Baltimore, Johns Hopkins University Press, 1978).

In contrast with Koestler, ROSEN's book recounts Copernicus' life by examining it with a view to supplement and correct it. His short but substantial and completely objective biography is illustrated with documents translated into English, many for the first time. Rosen's biography of Copernicus is the only one in English that may be recommended both to the Copernican scholar and the general reader. The only misstatement (later on corrected in *NCCW*, vol. III, Warsaw and London, Macmillan, 1985) is the ascription of advowson—that is, the right to present a nominee for an ecclesiastical vacancy—in the Church of Holy Cross in Wrocław to the bishop of Warmia, whereas this right belonged only to the bishop of Wrocław. The question of advowson came in connection with Copernicus' position of scholaster in that Wrocław Church.

Rosen's command of Latin is truly superb, and his translation of documents, while close to the original Latin, is transformed into clear and correct English, which, unfortunately, cannot be said about the translation of BIRKENMAJER's monumental work. That large volume, containing all the biographical materials available at the time of its publication, coupled with detailed and reliable studies of Copernicus' works, is recognized as an indispensable source of information for Copernican scholars. And while some of Birkenmajer's conjectures became obsolete with the subsequent discoveries of new documents, the main core of his work is still most valuable, since it reproduces transcriptions of documents that are very hard to obtain. Thus a translation of that work into English, combined with the reproduction of the Latin texts, was greeted with great enthusiasm. Moreover, the co-investigators promised to bring the work up to date. Surprisingly, many valuable sections and chapters were not translated, while some of the obsolete ones were left intact; what emerged is of such poor quality that it cannot be recommended.

First, the Latin texts and the numerical data contain *hundreds* of typographical errors, rendering them almost totally worthless. Second, most of the English rendering of the Polish text is a long string of mistranslations, possibly because the various translators were unfamiliar not only with the subject matter but with English syntax, spelling, and idioms. It is quite puzzling why the two co-investigators failed to notice the exorbitant number of the most flagrant errors, too great in number to list here.

—Erna Hilfstein

CORTÉS, Hernán or **Hernando**, 1485–1547; Spanish conqueror of Mexico.

Diaz del Castillo, Bernal, *The True History of the Conquest of Mexico*, translated by Maurice Keatinge. London, J. Wright, 1800 (originally published, Madrid, 1632).

Gomara, Francisco Lopez de, *Cortés: The Life of the Conqueror by His Secretary*, translated and edited by Lesley Byrd Simpson. Berkeley, University of California Press, 1964.

Madariaga, Salvador de, *Hernán Cortés, Conqueror of Mexico*. New York, Macmillan, 1941; London, Hodder and Stoughton, 1942.

Prescott, William H., *History of the Conquest of Mexico*. New York, Harper, 1843.

White, Jon E. M., *Cortés and the Downfall of the Aztec Empire*. New York, St. Martin's and London, Hamilton, 1971.

*

DIAZ DEL CASTILLO and GOMARA were both eyewitnesses to Cortés' conquest of Mexico and are valuable if only for this reason. Diaz is highly critical of Cortés' behavior in Mexico, particularly his treatment of the Indians. The author's language and style will appear stilted to modern readers, although much can be learned from his accounts. He bases his narrative on Cortés' personal letters, public documents, and his own observations. Gomara, who was Cortés' private secretary, is generally laudatory, presenting Cortés as a respected, good-natured hero. His style and language mark him as a writer of the 16th century. Although awkward and repetitive at times, this account of Cortés' life is elegant, ironic, humorous, and full of dramatic tension. It can thus be read and appreciated by the educated reader today.

Writing in the mid 19th century, PRESCOTT presents an epic in prose, a romantic portrait of Cortés and his conquest of the Aztec empire. His history reads much like a novel of the period, and his syntax, diction, use of alliteration, and metaphor appear outdated in the late 20th century. Nevertheless, his historical research was exhaustive and his account remains one of the most insightful we have. Because he wrote before the emergence of modern anthropology and archeology, Prescott's work lacks a complete understanding of Aztec civilization.

WHITE, working more than a century later, was able to use discoveries about Aztec life that were unavailable to earlier biographers. He therefore gave a more balanced view of both the Aztecs and their Spanish conquerors. Instead of giving a fictitious description of Cortés' youth, about which little is known, White delves into particulars of Spanish life, including foreign influences, that may explain some of Cortés' subsequent actions. White's writing style is clear and can be understood by a general audience.

MADARIAGA's most important contribution to the literature of Cortés is his detailed description and analysis of Aztec culture at the time of the Spanish conquest. The author, one of Spain's most accomplished modern historians, has produced a well-researched and clearly written book that has appealed to scholars and general readers alike.

—Meri E. Jiménez

COWARD, (Sir) Noël, 1899–1973; English playwright, director, and actor.

Braybrooke, Patrick, *The Amazing Mr. Noël Coward*. London, D. Archer, 1933.

Briers, Richard, *Coward and Company*. London, Robson, 1987.

Greacen, Robert, *The Art of Noël Coward*. Aldington, Kent, Hand and Flower Press, 1953.

Lesley, Cole, *The Life of Noël Coward*. London, Cape, and New York, Knopf, 1976.

Marchant, William, *The Privilege of His Company: Noël Coward Remembered*. London, Weidenfeld and Nicolson, and Indianapolis, Bobbs-Merrill, 1975.

Morley, Sheridan, *A Talent to Amuse: A Biography of Coward*. New York, Doubleday, and London, Heinemann, 1969; revised edition, London, Heinemann, 1974.

*

Although Coward spent the whole of his career in a dazzling glare of publicity, he was extremely reticent about his personal life. The two volumes of autobiography (*Present Indicative*, 1937; *Future Indefinite*, 1954), which took him up to 1954 and the age of 55, are witty and interesting. Famous names bespangle the pages, brilliant triumphs punctuate the narrative, and a glittering picture emerges of the British theatre's most versatile personality. The same applies to *The Noël Coward Diaries* (edited by Graham Payn and Sheridan Morley, 1982), which cover the years from 1941 to 1969, a short while before his death. These reveal much about the surface brilliance but little about the inner life. The author does not even take us much behind the scenes in the theatre. For that we must read his fiction, especially the short stories, where he very effectively re-creates the atmosphere backstage and draws convincing portraits of actors and actresses from the life.

Neither shall we find the real Coward in BRAYBROOKE, whose book came out early in the dramatist's career when he was still something of an *enfant prodigue*. It is a straightforward piece of hagiography which, at the time, embarrassed its subject and is often inaccurate. GREACEN's monograph is a sympathetic critical study rather than a biography. The American playwright MARCHANT became acquainted with Coward during the latter's visits to the United States from the 1950s onward. His book, though not a formal biography, and lacking an index or bibliography, contains some useful sidelights on Coward. It is especially illuminating for its technical comments Coward is reported as making on Marchant's own plays, and it offers some very telling insights into the art of acting and writing for the theatre. Marchant also puts some delightful anecdotes in print for the first time. Quite a few of these are repeated by BRIERS, the London actor who put together a loose sketch of Coward's life. Briers knew Coward briefly in his public persona and has nothing to add about the man behind the public image. He gives no analysis of the work or of the man and provides no index or bibliography.

LESLEY, much more authoritative, was engaged by Coward in 1935 as a cook-valet. So eager was Lesley to give satisfaction that, behind his back, his new employer nicknamed him "Jesus Christ." Soon he became a personal friend, a member of the small and intimate circle around Coward, and a trusted companion and secretary. So he was to remain until Coward's death. In writing the biography Lesley had access to a large collection of family letters, documents, and press cuttings, for Coward's mother had scrupulously preserved every little bit of paper referring to her son's boyhood and youth. Thus he was often able to correct misstatements Coward himself had made in his published writings. For the later years he used Coward's diaries and journals. His book is therefore based on substantial documentation. What, however, gives it unique value is the author's close association with Coward, which lasted for nearly 50 years. The style is brisk and eminently readable. The picture given is one of Coward *en pantoufles*, relaxed and humorous, the home-loving man behind the public image of the ultra-sophisticate. Lesley offers, for example, an unforgettable cameo of Coward tucked up in bed early one evening, drinking Bournvita (a popular night-time drink) and studying the Bible, a course of reading suggested by Coward's friend, the writer Clemence Dane, who had inspired him with admiration for its splendid language. Episodes like this abound and help to round out the portrait with charm and warmth.

MORLEY made his acquaintance with Coward in the mid-1960s, a time when, after a period of neglect, Coward was about to enjoy a renewal of his popularity and to become something of a grand old man of the English theatre. Morley was given free access to Coward's archives of letters, diaries, and private papers. He was also able to gather information from over 100 people still alive who had known Coward well. His book fills in important gaps not covered by the autobiographical writings, notably during the 1930s and the years between 1945 and Coward's death in 1973. Coward's one proviso in authorising the biography was that there should be no investigation of his private life except where it directly involved his work. This is understandable since his public still contained many admirers from an earlier generation who did not approve of homosexuality. In the later editions of his book Morley quotes the drama critic Ken Tynan's remark—"We must all envy the talented homosexual his freedom from family ties"—and adduces this as a reason for Coward's single-minded industry and his tremendous will to succeed. Morley sets Coward's works in the context of his life and gives quick, valid, stimulating critical judgments on them. He admits that had he waited longer he might have been able to view the career in deeper perspective. Had he done so, however, he would have lost the benefit of many unique personal and eyewitness accounts. He includes a helpful chronological chart, a bibliography of Coward's works, and a lengthy list of sources consulted. The best available picture of Coward as man and artist is to be obtained from Morley and Lesley in conjunction, both of them offering instructive and enjoyable reading.

—James Harding

CRANE, Hart, 1899–1932; American poet.

Horton, Philip, *Hart Crane: The Life of an American Poet*. New York, Norton, 1937.
Unterecker, John, *Voyager: A Life of Hart Crane*. New York, Farrar Straus, 1969; London, A. Blond, 1970.
Weber, Brom, *Hart Crane: A Biographical and Critical Study*. New York, Bodley Press, 1948.

*

HORTON's work, published just five years after Crane's suicide, is a sympathetic and penetrating study of the poet's life. Combining psychological and historical approaches, Horton examines Crane as a difficult and often inscrutable personality within the literary milieu of early 20th-century America. We see Crane reading the new poetry magazines, reacting to Imagism, rubbing shoulders with other aspiring and established writers who made their way to New York, and setting himself apart from what Crane saw as the "pessimism" of T. S. Eliot's early poetry. While Horton openly addresses Crane's excesses and eccentricities without trying to excuse them, he does not belabor the more salacious elements of the poet's short, turbulent life. His brief discussion of Crane's homosexuality, for example, though marked by the attitudes of the 1930s, is honest and insightful.

Writing so soon after Crane's death, Horton could not take advantage of much revealing material that has since come to light, and his conclusions about Crane's place in the canon are at best premature, as he himself admits in the closing chapter. Written under the surveillance of Grace Hart Crane, the poet's mother, who was very interested in her son's reputation, Horton's is more or less an "official" biography, and thus at times perhaps unscrupulous. Horton also gets caught up in his own Crane-like poetic ecstacies, which tend to blur or even replace his subject's activities. As he recounts Crane's devouring the *Dialogues* of Plato, Horton writes, "he read of that clear and radiant progression from the beauties of earth upwards to that other beauty, from all fair notions to the notion of absolute beauty and the final revelation of the very essence of beauty." Here, Horton seems as much the "natural Platonist" as his subject. While Horton offers only cursory remarks on the poet's work, what critical commentary he does provide fits well into the flow of his graceful, extremely readable narrative.

WEBER, upon publication of his study, was criticized for including too much critical commentary and too little biography. But as Weber explains in his preface, "The book is, . . . neither orthodox criticism nor orthodox biography, but rather a fusion, a genetic study." In other words, Weber's is a biography of Hart Crane *as poet*. Weber believes Crane to be "unquestionably the major poetic talent of 20th-century America," and consequently seeks to establish this by means of thorough literary commentary. Using Crane's correspondence, much of which was unavailable to Horton, Weber sets out to chart the poet's intellectual development: his family's involvement with Christian Science, his voracious reading, the intellectual circles in which he moved, etc. For the rest, Weber is useful primarily for his critical analysis, which is placed together with great skill and insight, offering ways of understanding Crane's idiosyncratic style and mythos. Even so, Weber excludes many important details he considers only indirectly related to the poet *qua* poet. Weber forgoes any discussion, for example, of Crane's difficult childhood, which for Horton and Unterecker was a crucial period in the poet's life.

UNTERECKER is the reigning storehouse of information about the man Hart Crane. Acknowledging his debt to the "pioneering efforts'' of both Horton and Weber, from whose work he quotes liberally, Unterecker goes on to present a much more thorough picture of Crane than either of his predecessors had given. Drawing on the wealth of emerging documents and correspondence of which Weber had made only limited use, Unterecker corrects some imbalances in the earlier records. Where Weber had been silent on the subject of Crane's childhood, and Horton had underplayed Crane's suffering over his parents' constant squabbles, Unterecker supplies, with the aid of Crane's letters, a more thoroughly researched and elaborate account of the poet's early life.

Weber, reviewing *Voyager*, complained that Unterecker had been too undiscriminating; that he had merely accumulated and presented material without selecting or offering judgment. This is a valid criticism of the work. Unterecker provides little analysis of the poetry, and very little understanding of the intellectual and literary milieu in which Crane lived and worked. We are given, instead, nearly 800 pages of detail without a clear vision of the man and the poet.

—Martin Thies

CRANE, Stephen, 1871–1900; American writer.

Beer, Thomas, *Stephen Crane: A Study in American Letters*. New York, Knopf, 1923.

Berryman, John, *Stephen Crane*. New York, W. Sloane, and London, Methuen, 1950; revised edition, 1962.

Cady, Edwin H., *Stephen Crane*. Boston, Twayne, 1962.

Cazemajou, Jean, *Stephen Crane*. Minneapolis, University of Minnesota Press, 1969.

Colvert, James B., *Stephen Crane*. New York, Harcourt, 1984.

Knapp, Bettina L., *Stephen Crane*. New York, F. Ungar, 1987.

Linson, Corwin K., *My Stephen Crane*, edited by Edwin H., Cady. Syracuse, New York, Syracuse University Press, 1958.

Solomon, Eric, *Stephen Crane in England: A Portrait of the Artist*. Columbus, Ohio State University Press, 1964.

Stallman, R. W., *Stephen Crane: A Biography*. New York, G. Braziller, 1968.

*

In 1923, the same year Thomas L. Raymond's biographical essay on Crane was published by the Carteret Book Club, BEER's book-length biography of Crane was published. It was the first such book and remains indispensable to a serious study of Crane's life. Beer was in an excellent position to write the biography. He claimed to have received copies of letters and a shorthand report of an interview with Crane from Willis Clarke, who had collected them for his own planned biography of Crane in the early 1900s. He hired a detective agency to seek out the facts of Crane's life, and he even sailed to England to interview such contemporaries and friends of Crane as Edward Garnett and Joseph Conrad. (Conrad subsequently wrote an introduction to Beer's biography.) And in addition to having the facts firsthand, Beer wrote with an anecdotel quality that made his biography easily readable.

However, some of the strengths of the biography are also its weaknesses. The materials from Willis Clarke have never been substantiated. Nor have many of the anecdotes Beer claimed to have come from Crane's contemporaries. Also, while Beer correctly refuted several false rumors about Crane, he also purposely suppressed several important true happenings, notably Crane's romances with Cora Taylor, Amy Leslie, Nellie Crouse, and Mrs. Lily Brandon Munroe. In other words, Beer, as he admitted he would be accused of doing, whitewashed Crane. Partially on the basis of this ''cleaning-up'' attitude and partially on the basis of sloppy scholarship, Beer then jumped to some intriguing but capricious judgments about Crane's personality. For example, Beer claimed that Crane was innocent in his knowledge of women, and that he was driven by fear. Subsequent scholarship has shown such claims to be at best wild speculation. Nevertheless, Beer remains the major source of our knowledge of Crane's life.

BERRYMAN's is a curious biography that, in truth, adds little new material to Beer's biography, and though Berryman complained about Beer's ''grand inaccuracy, expurgation, and distortion,'' Berryman's biography suffers some of the same faults. For example, as R. W. Stallman pointed out in his biography of Crane, Berryman misplaced Crane's burial site, placing it in Evergreen Cemetary in Elizabeth when in fact Crane was buried in Hillside. Berryman's work, nevertheless, did correct some of Beer's faults, partially, though he was not permitted to reveal his sources, because Berryman was able to get some information from Corwin K. Linson's manuscript and to read some letters from Crane to Nellie Crouse.

Perhaps in an attempt to offer something new, Berryman extended his work beyond biography proper to a psychological study of Crane. The theories Berryman presented, drawing on Beer's statements about Crane being driven by fear and the hatred of his father, are interesting. However, critics have attacked them as based on conjecture and misinformation. For example, Stallman pointed out that Berryman's claims that Crane's ''general war upon Authority'' was rooted in jealousy and hatred of his father have no basis at all, that in fact Crane's father was a kindly man who died when Stephen was eight years old.

Several important materials on Crane came into public use after Berryman's book, notably: 100 letters by Crane, 50 by Cora Crane, 200 letters about Crane, the Cora Crane papers, the Nellie Crouse letters, and the Corwin Linson manuscript.

The LINSON manuscript, edited by Cady, was first published in 1958 under the title *My Stephen Crane*. Linson was an important American painter who became a friend of Crane during the early 1890s; some 30 years later Linson produced a manuscript of recollections of this friendship that he was unable to get published, and the manuscript was forgotten. As Cady points out, Linson, though he had an artist's sensibility, was not a trained writer, and the manuscript suffered from a lack of narrative structure and, at times, from more concern for revealing its author than its subject. In preparing the manuscript for publication, Cady reorganized it, checked out the discrepancies, omitted some material considered not essential to Crane, and changed a few obvious errors. This partial biography offers an intimate view of Crane during an important and obscure time in his life. Some black-and-white photographs are included. CADY subsequently published his own biography of Crane, which gives a solid overview of Crane's life and summarizes the principal directions of Crane criticism.

Few would argue STALLMAN's position as the foremost authority on Crane, and his book is probably as close as possible to a definitive biography on the subject. Everything is thoroughly researched, and the facts are presented in a straightforward and clear manner. It is a book filled with details, many of little importance except to the most serious scholar of Crane, to whom the biography is principally aimed. Those looking for a biography meant to bring to life the character of Crane will be disappointed, as Stallman has rigorously avoided any temptation to deal with Crane's psychology. His careful objectivity and detailed research does, however, counterbalance the earlier biographies by Beer and Berryman, who were more willing to play with the facts in order to capture the essence of Crane's personality.

Four other biographies or partial biographies have appeared in the 1980s. SOLOMON tells why Crane went to England in 1897, discusses the critical reception he received, and reveals his literary friendships. His claim that Garland and Howells did not understand Crane as well as his British friends did is not supported. COLVERT provides a decent introduction to Crane, especially to his earlier years, along with many good illustrations. KNAPP begins with a brief overview of Crane's life before moving on to other matters. CAZEMAJOU also offers a brief biography of Crane.

Lillian Gilkes' biography of Cora Crane (*Cora Crane: A Biography of Mrs. Stephen Crane*, 1960), though not on Stephen Crane proper, offers insights into his relationships with women. Unfortunately, Gilkes' massive scholarship has been undermined somewhat by some arbitrary decisions about dates and the meanings of some of her documents. It might also be said that she gets caught up in defending Cora to the unfair denigration of Crane.

—Harry Edwin Eiss

CRAWFORD, Joan, 1908–1977; American film actress.

Castle, Charles, *Joan Crawford: The Raging Star*. London, New English Library, 1977.

Considine, Shaun, *Bette and Joan: The Divine Feud*. New York, Dutton, and London, F. Muller, 1989.

Crawford, Christina, *Mommie Dearest*. New York, Morrow, 1978; London, Hart-Davis MacGibbon, 1979.

Harvey, Stephen, *Joan Crawford*. New York, Pyramid Communications, 1974.

Houston, David, *Jazz Baby*. New York, St. Martin's, 1983; London, Robson, 1984.

Newquist, Roy, *Conversations with Joan Crawford*. Secaucus, New Jersey, Citadel Press, 1980.

Thomas, Bob, *Joan Crawford: A Biography*. New York, Simon and Schuster, 1978; London, Weidenfeld and Nicolson, 1979.

Walker, Alexander, *Joan Crawford: The Ultimate Star*. London, Weidenfeld and Nicolson, and New York, Harper and Row, 1983.

Wayne, Jane Ellen, *Crawford's Men*. New York, Prentice-Hall, and London, Robson, 1988.

*

Biographies of Crawford are easily categorized according to whether they were written before or after the shocking and highly publicized stories of child abuse described by the actress' adopted daughter, Christina, in *Mommie Dearest*. Those that came before are relatively straightforward, emphasizing Crawford's rags-to-riches rise from obscurity to stardom. Those that came afterwards must try to account for the unsavory aspects of Crawford's personality that were carefully hidden from public view until her death.

HARVEY's focus is on Crawford's films and her emerging screen personality. Biographical details are kept to a minimum and are in some cases inaccurate (e.g., Crawford's other adopted daughters, Cathy and Cynthia, were not really twins, although she always referred to them as such). But Harvey's chronological analysis of the films is both thorough and thoughtful, providing a balanced assessment of Crawford's successes and failures as an actress.

NEWQUIST's collection of conversations, though published after Crawford's death, is part of the pre-*Mommie Dearest* group because it consists primarily of Crawford's own words on her early years, her film career, and her private life. After assuring the reader that "nothing . . . in this book would have offended her," Newquist makes good on his promise with a generally flattering portrait of the actress, even if he does misspell her pre-Hollywood name. Answering Newquist's queries at great length and without mincing her words, Crawford appears to be speaking quite candidly here, though her dismissal of the rumors that she mistreated her children raises some doubt as to the veracity of her other claims.

CASTLE claims to be Crawford's "authorized biographer"; but if so, he does not appear to have received any special consideration from the actress. Instead, he relies heavily on the testimony of Crawford's friends, co-workers, publicity agents, and loyal retainers, hardly any of whom have a critical word to say about her. Published shortly after Crawford's death, Castle's paean reverently concludes that she was "remarkable and magnificent . . . the stuff that moviegoers' dreams were made of."

Appearing several months later, and just before Christina was to drop her bombshell, THOMAS' biography is the most comprehensive of any that have been published to date, though the competition admittedly is meager. A veteran journalist who has chronicled the lives of more than a dozen other celebrities, Thomas provides a readable and straightforward account, seeking a balance between many of the uncritical Hollywood legends and some of the more unpleasant facts about Crawford's private life. For instance, after citing several examples of Crawford's "unthinking and sometimes horrid treatment of her children," Thomas' sympathetic interpretation is that this was "an instinctive, unreasoning reaction to the injustice that had been inflicted on her" during "her own Dickensian childhood."

After reading Thomas, many of Crawford's fans could still adore her. But with *Mommie Dearest*, those same fans were hit with stories almost too bizarre and monstrous to believe at first, but which now have been generally accepted and confirmed as true. CHRISTINA CRAWFORD's first-person account of her mother's systematic abuse of both her and her adopted brother Christopher, is quietly told, in contrast to the astonishing and occasionally sickening details described. This one book (and the 1981 motion picture with the same ironic title) instantly and irrevocably altered the public's image of Joan Crawford.

Some of the damage is undone by WALKER, whose biography is not only the best-looking of any that have been published (with more than 250 superb black-and-white photographs), but also the most carefully researched (thanks to the access the author was given to the archives at Metro-Goldwyn-Mayer). Consequently, Walker's account of Crawford's tenure at MGM (1925–43) is unsurpassed in authority and completeness, though his footing is less certain not only for the final three decades of her life, which he quickly summarizes in only 22 pages, but also for the years preceding, which are omitted almost entirely.

Those first 20 years of Crawford's life serve as the focus for HOUSTON's treatment, based in part on interviews with people who claim to have known the star-to-be during her residencies in Oklahoma, Missouri, Chicago, and New York. By assiduously retracing Crawford's steps, Houston is able to uncover many hitherto unknown details of her lonely and peripatetic childhood and adolescence. Nevertheless, his verbatim re-creation of conversations from the 1910s and 1920s, and his reliance on sources whose testimony seems based on hearsay, leaves the reader wondering how much of this evidence can be trusted.

Even less reliable is WAYNE's superficial saga, a pastiche of gossipy anecdotes spliced together under an alluring, though misleading, title. This is a biography of Crawford, not "Crawford's men," for which the author aims to expose all aspects of the actress' libido. Some of the same (and similar) stories find their way into CONSIDINE's dual biography, which chronicles along parallel lines—matching, for instance, a section on "Joan's Sex Life" with a comparable one for Bette Davis—the lives of these two screen actresses. Based largely on interviews with an assortment of Hollywood celebrities and observers, Considine builds the rivalry between Crawford and Davis into a long lasting feud of epic proportions. The book's constant cutting back and forth from Crawford to Davis seems belabored, but the behind-the-scenes story of their only film together, *What Ever Happened to Baby Jane?* (1962), yields one of the more revealing chapters in Crawford's complex life.

—James I. Deutsch

CRAZY HORSE, *ca.* 1841–1877; Oglala Sioux Indian chief.

Ambrose, Stephen E., *Crazy Horse and Custer: The Parallel Lives of Two American Warriors.* New York, Doubleday, 1975; London, MacDonald and Jane's, 1976.

Brininstool, E. A., *Crazy Horse: The Invincible Ogalalla Sioux Chief: The "Inside Stories," by Actual Observers, of a Most Treacherous Deed Against a Great Indian Leader.* Los Angeles, Wetzel Publishing, 1949.

Brown, Vinson, *Great Upon the Mountain: The Story of Crazy Horse, Legendary Mystic and Warrior.* New York, Macmillan, 1971.

Kadlecek, Edward, *To Kill an Eagle: Indian Views on the Death of Crazy Horse.* Boulder, Colorado, Johnson Books, 1981.

Sandoz, Mari, *Crazy Horse: The Strange Man of the Oglalas: A Biography.* New York, Hastings House, 1942.

*

SANDOZ wrote the first comprehensive biography of Crazy Horse, and it has remained the most important. Although there were no written accounts or documents from Crazy Horse upon which one could base an analysis of the man, from 1930–31 Sandoz and Eleanor Hinman conducted numerous interviews with the surviving friends and relatives of Crazy Horse. These interviews included one with He Dog, who was a lifelong friend of Crazy Horse. Sandoz also made use of the many extensive interviews conducted by Judge E. J. Ricker from 1906–07 with surviving Native Americans, military personnel, and settlers concerning the Plains Indians. In addition to these sets of interviews, Sandoz also employed documents, letters, and manuscripts from the period in question, though she does not cite any secondary sources in her biography.

Although Sandoz's work lacks the traditional trappings of a scholarly biography (footnotes and an index), reviewers of her work commended her ability to relate Crazy Horse's story from the Indian's point of view. Her use of speech and idioms and her insight into the culture greatly aid the understanding of the man, his people, and the times. (See reviews by Everett Dick in *American Historical Review*, July 1943, and Elaine Goodale in *The Springfield Republican* as reprinted in *Nebraska History*, April–June 1942). Sandoz will remain a standard source for both scholar and general reader.

AMBROSE describes the parallels in the lives of two of the most prominent protagonists at the Little Big Horn. As Robert Trennert, Jr. notes in his review (*Journal of American History*, September 1976), Ambrose's work largely employs secondary sources. Ambrose also makes use of the same interview collections (Hinman and Ricker) that Sandoz used as the basis for her biography.

As a biography of Custer and Crazy Horse, Ambrose accomplishes the task of relating the parallel events in both lives that led to the confrontation at the Little Big Horn. Ambrose is less successful in proving motivations behind feelings and actions in both individuals. As Jack Davis points out (*American Indian Quarterly*, Fall 1978), Ambrose attributes too much similarity between customs and culture of the Oglala's and the Plains Indians in general.

Ambrose's work is richly illustrated and provides appropriate maps. It will be easily read by general readers and of particular importance to the scholar because of its synthesis of the numerous secondary sources consulted for this work. However, as Davis also indicates, "this work does not supplant Mari Sandoz's."

BROWN offers a shorter and less scholarly treatment. His work suffers from the same deficiencies as Sandoz's: a lack of footnotes, index, and comprehensive listing of sources consulted. The author does indicate in his "Acknowledgements" that interviews were conducted with Native Americans who had received and preserved the oral traditions concerning Crazy Horse. Brown also acknowledges Sandoz and remarks on "the inspiration and helpful details of her book, which are sometimes paraphrased in this book, though without any intent to copy." This work will be of greater use to the general reader than to the scholar. Both will want to read the chapters dealing with the "Great Vision" that guided the life of Crazy Horse.

BRININSTOOL provides a compilation of both official reports and those by eye-witnesses to the death of Crazy Horse, including military and civilian observers and participants in Crazy Horse's final struggle. KADLECEK's work balances that of Brininstool with information from the Native American perspective.

—Maurice G. Fortin

***

CROCKETT, Davy, 1786–1836; American frontiersman and politician.

Dorson, Richard M., editor, *Davy Crockett: American Comic Legend*. New York, Spiral Press, 1939.

Kelly, James C. and Frederick S. Voss, *Davy Crockett, Gentleman from the Cave: An Exhibition Commemorating Crockett's Life and Legend*. Washington, D.C., National Portrait Gallery/Smithsonian Institution, 1986.

Lofaro, Michael A., editor, *Davy Crockett: The Man, the Legend, the Legacy*. Knoxville, University of Tennessee Press, 1985.

Paulding, James K., *The Lion of the West*, edited by James N. Tidwell (first performed, 1830). Stanford, California, Stanford University Press, 1954.

Schackford, James A., *David Crockett: The Man and the Legend*, edited by John B. Schackford. Chapel Hill, University of North Carolina Press, 1956.

*

SCHACKFORD presents a thoroughly researched, well-documented biography of Crockett, taking great care to separate the frontier scout, Indian fighter, and Tennessee politician from the popular mythological folk hero that emerged even before his death at the defense of the Alamo. With a scholar's meticulous precision Schackford uses manuscript collections and government documents, including court records, the *Congressional Record*, and the records of the Creek Indian War, to detail the facts of Crockett's personal life and political career. He also critically examines the literature, largely inaccurate and completely unsubstantiated, that built Crockett into a larger-than-life character. Among those 20th-century works critiqued are Shapiro's *Yankee Thunder: The Legendary Life of Davy Crockett* (New York, 1944) and "All-American Hero," *Saturday Review of Literature* (1944); Walter Blair's "Six Davy Crocketts," *Southwest Review* (1940); and Constance Rourke's fictionalized and unreliable *Davy Crockett* (1934). Schackford likewise examines the various works of "autobiography" of Crockett that appeared during the lifetime of the frontier politician. His work remains the most reliable interpretation of Crockett, placing him in the context of frontier America and describing the political environment in which he emerged to national prominence.

James Schackford and Stanley Falmsbee's annotated *Narrative of the Life of David Crockett* (1973) clarifies Crockett's own autobiography, originally published in 1834 and ghost-written by a Whig congressional colleague, Thomas Chilton of Kentucky. In a useful introduction, the editors differentiated the *Narrative* from contemporary fictional accounts of Crockett's life. Originally written for the advancement of Crockett's political career and in response to the recognition that considerable public interest existed in the handsome and likable Tennessee politician, the *Narrative* contains a number of intentional deviations from the truth. Therefore, Shackford and Falmsbee's carefully annotated *Narrative* is exceptionally useful and provides a context for understanding the original document.

LOFARO's collection of essays is essential for understanding Crockett's rise from obscurity to folk legend. The essays describe the theatrics of Frank Mayo, who successfully played Crockett in popular plays for 20 years and the remarkable commercial success of the Walt Disney television production of the 1950s. KELLY AND VOSS present an exhibition catalog that graphically depicts the material culture that developed around Crockett's life/legend. Their work relies heavily on the research of Schackford and Lofaro.

DORSON examines the *Davy Crockett Almanacs* of 1835–1856, which appeared soon after the Tennessean became a national celebrity and gained even wider appeal after the fall of the Alamo. The *Almanacs*, now extremely rare and found only in museum collections, were written by anonymous authors and have no basis in fact. These exaggerated tales of frontier life, featuring a rough, rowdy, and crude Crockett spinning incredible yarns, were published first in Nashville and later in Boston and New York.

Dorson's own work offers little scholarly analysis, nor does the introduction by Howard Mumford Jones. Rather, the volume presents, with full flavor, facsimiles of more than 40 of the grotesque woodcuts that illustrated the original pamphlets.

PAULDING's *Lion of the West*, of special note in considering Crockett biographies, is the popular stage play written in 1830 that seems to have initiated the Crockett legend. Paulding's rough frontier hero, Colonel Nimrod Wildfire, was immediately associated in the popular mind with Crockett, who actually took a bow when this play appeared in Washington. The long-forgotten play, with solid annotation and commentary, is available in Tidwell's edited version. Three years after the publication of *Lion*, *The Life and Adventures of Colonel David Crockett* (1833) by Matthew St. Clair Clarke, clerk of the United States House of Representatives, was published with information most probably provided by the subject himself. Apparently Crockett was not pleased with the final product and sought to disassociate himself from the publication. In an effort to tone down the more bombastic and boisterous storytelling in *Life and Adventures* and to assist in his effort to regain his congressional seat, Crockett collaborated with Chilton to produce the *Narrative*.

—Michael J. Devine

CROMWELL, Oliver, 1599–1658; English general and statesman, lord protector of England.

Ashley, Maurice P., *The Greatness of Oliver Cromwell*. London, Hodder and Stoughton, 1957; New York, Macmillan, 1958.

Ashley, Maurice P., *Charles I and Oliver Cromwell: A Study in Contrasts*. London, Methuen, 1987.

Fraser, Antonia, *Cromwell: Our Chief of Men*. London, Weidenfeld and Nicolson, 1973; as *Cromwell: The Lord Protector*, New York, Knopf, 1973.

Gardiner, Samuel R., *Oliver Cromwell*. London and New York, Goupil, 1899.

Gregg, Pauline, *Oliver Cromwell*. London, Dent, 1988.

Hill, Christopher, *God's Englishman: Oliver Cromwell and the English Revolution*. London, Weidenfeld and Nicolson, and New York, Dial Press, 1970.

Wedgwood, C. V., *Oliver Cromwell*. London, Duckworth, and New York, Macmillan, 1939; revised edition, 1973.

*

Regarded as a late-Victorian classic and a seminal work in what has become a vast field, GARDINER's short biography first appeared in 1899 and has been reprinted and made available from time to time in paperback. Adhering to a strict chronological approach and lacking in depth of character portrayal, his is a straightforward narrative in which Cromwell appears in Gardiner's much quoted phrase as "the greatest because the most typical Englishman of his times." For Gardiner, still in the good old Whig Liberal historical tradition, Cromwell is the leader of the Parliamentary side in the struggle for political and religious freedom that was the Puritan Revolution—a term first used by him. In that context King Charles I's execution is deemed necessary to establish a new order of things. Cromwell is seen as a man greater than his work, who subordinated himself to moral and spiritual goals too high for his people. One unfortunate drawback of the biography and a major irritation to the reader who wishes to check the author's version of specific events is the lack of an index.

ASHLEY's 1957 work was the first major biography to appear in the post-World War II era and was thus free of the unfortunate comparisons with dictators that had often seemed obligatory during the inter-war years. It was also the first since Gardiner to present Cromwell as a great patriotic Englishman. Modern objective scholarship owes much to Ashley. Nonetheless, eyebrows might be raised when he seems to explain Cromwell's massacre of the Drogheda garrison—always judged a supreme atrocity—as a successful military measure in an overall Irish policy that, while perhaps wrong, was surely in a direct continuity with that of Elizabeth I and the early Stuarts. Though he finds Cromwell an imperialist who raised his country to greatness, he sees him as a George Washington rather than a Napoleon, a builder and a fighter for freedom of conscience who led the way to religious toleration. Thus Ashley becomes a kind of disciple of Gardiner without the latter's Victorian mind-set.

One of the best biographies of Cromwell in recent times is that by HILL. That it is so eminently popular is attributable to its simplicity, its manageable proportions, and its freshness, which are all the more striking in light of the author's prodigious scholarly output so all encompassing of Puritanism and the revolution of the 17th century. Hill, the great master of socioeconomic data, long ago shed his earlier aggressive and at times abrasive Marxism and presents a very humanistic study of Cromwell the man, especially as he came to personify this revolution. More than half of the book consists of sections on Cromwell's roles as lord general, lord protector and would-be-king. These are followed by particularly incisive and reflective chapters on "The People of England and the People of God," and on "Providence and Oliver Cromwell," in which Hill examines the Calvinist contribution to the revolution in terms of modernism, a familiar theme of his. A chapter on Oliver Cromwell and English history is a remarkable historiographic essay that is informative without being pedantic. Particularly noteworthy also is a masterful analysis of Cromwell's foreign policy. His government in the 1650s, as Hill sees it, was the first to have a world strategy, a master-plan. Despite the ease and clarity of Hill's work, the general reader might be cautioned first to become familiar with the chronological framework for this intensely busy and dynamic period. In short, this is not the best biography to find out the "facts" of Cromwell's life even though it is perhaps the most thought-provoking study.

In contrast to Hill's analytical approach, WEDGWOOD, an equally gifted and prolific historian, follows in the rich narrative tradition of Macaulay and Trevelyan. Admittedly, she is a great narrator rather than a great explainer, and she is more interested in the behavior of individuals than of groups. The enchantment and absolute lucidity of her earlier studies, such as *King's Peace 1637–1641* (1955), show up as well in this short volume, which appeared first in 1939 and was completely revised in 1973. To Wedgwood, Cromwell was a good military leader—perhaps not among the greatest—who was a pragmatic politician rather than an intellectual, and who was utterly sincere in his belief that he was an instrument of God's will. Though the issue of his statesmanship will always be controversial, for his work died with him, his foreign policy, Wedgwood claims, was astoundingly successful. But most of all she finds his greatest achievement in stopping civil strife and in fostering a spirit of religious individualism. In a postscript to the later edition, Wedgwood finds him a "sad and heavily burdened" man.

Appearing in the same year as the revision of Wedgwood's brief biography was the massive work (over 700 pages) by FRASER, entitled in Britain *Cromwell Our Chief of Men*, after the poem by Milton. A highly successful author from a distinguished family of writers, Fraser, like Wedgwood, belongs in the tradition of narrative historians. Her task is to rescue Cromwell the man from obscurity, perhaps indeed from the plethora of socio-economic studies that in recent decades have tended to dehumanize him, and to make him accessible and explicable to the general reader. Not surprisingly, therefore, she eschews economic forces for politics and the interplay of events and personalities. Unfortunately there are times when she presumes general knowledge of names and places beyond the familiarity of the general reader. More daunting perhaps is the sheer mass of detail—even toward the end, where she includes an informative but gruesome chapter on what happened to Cromwell's corpse.

All in all, in spite of what might have been assumed Stuart sympathies on her part, Fraser's work is eminently objective. While not denying a darkly maniacal side in Cromwell's treatment of the Irish and in his having King Charles killed, she nonetheless sees in him a great leader who truly cared for the welfare of his people.

Those who believe that every great historical figure needs a fresh biography every so often will appreciate the courage and *élan* with which GREGG offers us yet another life of Cromwell. Having already established her scholarly credentials with biographies of John Lilburne, Charles I, and Charles II, she appears undaunted by the large corpus of Cromwelliana. This work too is addressed to the general reader but does not presume a knowledge of personalities and issues, and though lacking in the neat turns of phrase that make Wedgwood's and Fraser's works so charming, it is perhaps the most agreeable and manageable of recent biographies. Considering how sketchy is much of Cromwell's life until the age of 30, Gregg manages to flesh this early period out in a credible fashion. Particularly interesting, because they do not appear elsewhere, are Cromwell's letters to his wife and family, which reflect a strange and yet deeply felt tenderness.

In charting a course through Cromwell's public career, Gregg hits upon a most convincing explanation of his motivation and ambition—that is, since at age 40, without military training, he had become the best soldier in Europe, why could he not at age 54 guide his country out of chaos to compromise. She sympathetically presents Cromwell's dilemma of government, his loneliness in power, as a practical man, not an intellectual, in a world of imponderables.

A recent contribution to scholarly biography, in the vein of Plutarch's *Parallel Lives,* is ASHLEY's 1987 *Charles I and Oliver Cromwell.* As a work written for one familiar with both figures, it is a trenchant examination of the careers of each in terms of, for example, "soldiering," "diplomacy and war," "handling parliaments." It represents an interesting approach and, as one would expect, is balanced and objective.

—Robert A. Ryan

CROSBY, Bing, 1904–1977; American singer and film actor.

Barnes, Ken, *The Crosby Years.* New York, St. Martin's, and London, Elm Tree Books, 1980.
Bauer, Barbara, *Bing Crosby.* New York, Pyramid, 1977.
Bookbinder, Robert, *The Films of Bing Crosby.* Secaucus, New Jersey, Citadel, 1977.
Carpozi, George, Jr., *The Fabulous Life of Bing Crosby.* New York, Manor Books, 1977.
Crosby, Kathryn, *Bing and Other Times.* New York, Meredith Press, 1967; London, H. Jenkins, 1968.
Shepherd, Donald and Robert F. Slatzer, *Bing Crosby: The Hollow Man.* New York, St. Martin's, 1981; London, W. H. Allen, 1982.

Thompson, Charles, *Bing: The Authorized Biography.* London, W. H. Allen, 1975; New York, D. McKay, 1976.

*

Bing Crosby provided the official "Saturday Evening Post" version of his life in the early 1950s, when he was still a major movie star (*Call Me Lucky*, New York, Simon and Schuster, 1953). Its approach can be summed up from the dust jacket promotion: "Have fun with Bing! Probably no living celebrity has had such a good time in life as Bing Crosby." The book, penned by Pete Martin (famous for his profiles in *Saturday Evening Post*), is filled with wonderful anecdotes about the great and near great with whom Crosby dealt in the first 50 years of his life, and is important not so much for what it contains, but what it tells us Crosby thought were the positive attributes of his life. Kathryn CROSBY's book is the second wife's version. As one might expect it is heavy on the latter half of Bing's career, sweeping away all possible controversy. Here we have "the crooner" in old age, a wonderful man who sponsors golf tournaments and loves his (second set of) children.

THOMPSON, writing near the end of Crosby's life, can be seen as the official extension of these previous two volumes. As of 1990 it must stand as the authorized biography. It contains a set of most interesting photographs from the family archives and is crammed with information used by all who have written since. Thompson's selection of details, however, paints a wholly favorable portrait. For example, family relationships, not the crooner's strong point (particularly in his first family), are glossed over at best. The book does not supply a filmography, discography, or record of Crosby's vast output. (For that see Timothy A. Morgereth, *Bing Crosby: A Discography, Radio Program List and Filmography*, Jefferson, North Carolina, McFarland, 1987.) Thompson does contain innumerable errors of fact, and his book should be seen simply as good public relations, not a serious biography of a major cultural persona in 20th century mass entertainment.

BAUER offers a specialized look at the often neglected movie career of Bing Crosby. Since this is a standardized entry in the Pyramid series of quick overviews of the lives of major stars of the movies, all the basic information is there. But the series limits coverage, offers little documentation, and poorly reproduces its photographs. BARNES is not so much a biography as a personal tale told by a former producer of Crosby's records. As such it balances the film book noted above. Barnes provides a limited discography and filmography, but in the end this is a sketchy, laudatory book of little value. CARPOZI provides a rehash of Thompson, but at least deals with the first marriage and the famous sons of that sad union. BOOKBINDER is yet another version of the fawning standard Crosby biography, based on Thompson, Kathryn Crosby, and Bing Crosby. The crooner again is held in awe; no analysis is provided.

SHEPHERD AND SLATZER is the only serious Crosby biography, even with its lack of documentation. It alone at least tries to penetrate the mythic image of the relaxed, gentle crooner. In what the writers herald as the unauthorized version of the great entertainer's life, Crosby emerges as an enormously talented, though flawed, man, as indolent and irresponsible as he was intelligent and cunning: "When the cameras weren't rolling, when the mikes were turned off and the curtains were down, Bing was irresponsible and lazy, cunning and cold . . . a man who double-crossed his way to the top, riding roughshod over friends and family alike." Bing Crosby spent considerable effort creating the "image" that has been repeated in the various biographies noted above. While Shepherd and Slatzer's book may be a negative working over, the authors do offer a great deal of information. Until a thorough scholarly study comes along (and one should), this tome will have to stand as the work that at least calls the bluff of the others.

—Douglas Gomery

CUMMINGS, E(dward) E(stlin), 1894–1962; American poet.

Kennedy, Richard, *Dreams in the Mirror: A Biography of E. E. Cummings.* New York, Liveright, 1980.
Norman, Charles, *The Magic-Maker: E. E. Cummings.* New York, Macmillan, 1958; revised as *E. E. Cummings: The Magic-Maker*, New York, Duell Sloane, 1964.

*

The first biography, by NORMAN, presents a positive and reasonably accurate view of E.E. Cummings. Carefully impressionistic, the biography is limited in its coverage, partly because Norman did not make use of the full range of sources available, partly because both Cummings and Marion Morehouse, Cummings' third wife, oversaw the project. With the appearance of Richard S. Kennedy's much more complete *Dreams in the Mirror* (see below), the paucity of detail in the Norman work has become more obvious.

Norman's biography is to be praised because it presents the Cummings persona in vivid anecdote and image. Its messianic tone continued into the 1964 revision, which includes a chapter on the poet's death in 1962 and discusses the posthumously published collection, *73 Poems*. The fact remains, however, that Norman—a newspaperman, biographer, and friend of Cummings—chose to write the book because of his admiration for the poet and his work.

The Magic Maker gives the reader a portrait of the poet in his 60s, living and working his quiet days in Patchin Place and at Joy Farm, New Hampshire. It relies heavily on Cummings' recollections as they were presented in his *i: six nonlectures* (1953). In fact, nearly all Norman's material about Cummings' early life and his relationship with his parents comes from that source.

There is a troublesome disproportion in Norman's book. More information is given about the publication of the 1917 *Eight Harvard Poets* than about Cummings' years at Harvard or his subsequent disagreements with his father. Norman also discussed Cummings' play *Him* and its 1928 production in great detail, while *Santa Claus* (1946), a play equally important to Cummings, receives only slight comment. More serious are the inexplicable omissions in such areas as Cummings' mature friendships, his love affairs, his somewhat unorthodox mar-

riages, and the existence of his daughter, Nancy. Some of Norman's reticence about Cummings' first two marriages may have stemmed from the fact that Morehouse and Cummings were reading the manuscript, but there seems to be little reason for devoting five pages to Joe Gould while dismissing Cummings' first wife, Elaine Orr Thayer, with a single line. The Norman study does reprint some useful items that were then (in the late 1950s) not accessible, as well as some otherwise unrecorded comments by Cummings in conversation.

KENNEDY's biography is the fully formed body of Norman's earlier skeletal treatment. Designed to be a two-volume book, the study draws on extensive resources—friends, family, many library collections, and countless unpublished manuscripts and letters. As the title suggests, Kennedy's emphasis is on revealing the character of that most private of people, Cummings the poet and painter. Much attention is given to Cummings' childhood and early artistic efforts; even more space is devoted to his early relationships, his two unsuccessful marriages, and what was to be the tormenting relationship with his child Nancy throughout his life. As Kennedy suggests, it seems impossible that Cummings' work from his college days through the early 1930s could be studied accurately without some knowledge of the emotional turmoil that resulted from his unsettled professionalstatus, his chaotic and disappointing romances, and his ambi- valence toward his parents and the stable Cambridge society they represented.

By 1932, when Cummings began living with Marion Morehouse, he had been graduated from Harvard with the M.A. since 1916 and had worked for salary only three months of those 16 years. His financial dependence on family and friends was an unusual character manifestation, which deepened throughout his life into a kind of paranoia; as Kennedy points out, Cummings' relationship with his parents must be viewed in the context of his "professional" status as a poet and painter or, less charitably phrased, as a financial dependent.

The Kennedy biography does an excellent job of providing new information about Cummings' life. Before its publication, the most frequently used source of material about Cummings' life was his own *i: six nonlectures*, a highly selective description of his development as an artist. Although the *nonlectures* include much reminiscence about his childhood and his parents, they create a biased, if picturesque, view of Cummings. For example, Cummings stresses the centrality of the play, *Him*, but he does not explain that it is the working through of his fears after his divorce from Elaine Thayer. Again, his separateness from the Cambridge world is presented as positive, as a choice made with little conflict or regret. Kennedy supplies the necessary balance to that perspective. As he points out, Cummings "developed an increasing sense of himself as alone and at odds with almost everyone around him." Kennedy's wealth of material, always germane to his portrait of Cummings as "a vulnerable, sensitive antihero, wide-eyed with wonder before the world and readily assertive of his natural feelings," makes this a convincing study.

—Linda Wagner-Martin

CURIE, Marie [*born* Marja Sklodowska], 1867–1934; Polish-born French chemist and physicist.

Bigland, Eileen, *Madame Curie*. New York, Criterion Books, 1957.

Curie, Eve, *Madame Curie: A Biography*, translated by Vincent Sheean. New York, Doubleday, and London, Heinemann, 1938 (originally published by Gallimard, Paris, 1938).

Giroud, Françoise, *Marie Curie, a Life*, translated by Lydia Davis. New York, Holmes and Meier, 1986 (originally published by Fayard, Paris, 1981).

Reid, Robert, *Marie Curie*. New York, Saturday Review Press, and London, Collins, 1974.

*

Madame Curie, the great comprehensive biography by EVE CURIE, Marie Curie's younger daughter, was published simultaneously in France, the United States, England, Italy, and Spain. It is well illustrated with moving portraits of Marie Curie, her family, husband, children, and famous colleagues. An appendix lists prizes, medals, decorations, and honorary titles awarded to Marie Curie. Certainly Eve Curie was able to portray aspects of the life and personality of her mother which she had witnessed for herself with remarkable artistry, sincerity, and honesty, but she was also able to breathe life into episodes she recreated from documentary evidence and her intimate knowledge of her mother's character. Especially moving are the accounts of Marie Curie's childhood in Poland, the hardships of student life for a poor and lonely young woman in Paris, the excitement over the discovery of radium, and the tragic death of Pierre Curie.

By education and temperament, as well as heredity, Eve Curie was well qualified to become Marie Curie's biographer. Unlike her older sister, Nobel Laureate Irene Joliot-Curie, Eve Curie pursued a career as concert artist, music critic, and writer. After her mother's death she collected and classified Marie Curie's papers, manuscripts, and the personal documents used in writing the biography.

Despite the obvious temptation to idealize a subject to whom the biographer is so close, this remarkable portrait of Curie's life, work, and family was written with great sincerity, clarity, and honesty. Even in translation the writing is elegant, often poetic. This biography enjoyed immediate success because of the popular appeal of the story of the triumphs and tragedies that marked the life of a celebrated woman scientist. It has remained popular as a source of inspiration for young women considering a career in science. In this book, unlike those by Giroud and Reid (see below), Paul Langevin appears only as one of many colleagues. For the story of the "scandal" one must consult more recent biographies.

In preparing his comprehensive and eminently readable biography, REID gained the cooperation of many of Curie's relatives, colleagues and co-workers, and others who had participated in the exciting period of chemistry and physics that followed the discovery of radioactivity. Reid was also allowed free access to documents in the archives of the Laboratoire Curie and other relevant institutions and libraries. He has succeeded in providing a well-researched biography that makes the life and work of one of the great scientists of her era accessible to the general reader. The book also critically assesses public policy issues that were not raised in Eve Curie's biography. Perhaps the emphasis on the scandal raised by the theft and publication of incriminating letters sent by Marie Curie to Paul Langevin helps explain the popularity of Reid's biography, which served as the basis of a dramatic television series exploring the life of Marie Curie produced by BBC and Time-Life Television Productions.

Reid's biography is a work of exhaustive and comprehensive research, made possible when personal and scientific papers testifying to the life and work of Curie became accessible to scholars. Reid portrays Marie Curie as strong, tenacious, and indomitable where her scientific work was concerned. Reid sees Curie even in her private life as a complex woman, sometimes naive, apparently timid and fragile, but also tough and resolute.

GIROUD forthrightly admits that she has not written an "academic book." Perhaps the general reader will forgive the absence of footnotes, but the book also lacks a bibliography, an index, and even a table of contents. Even the section headings—such as "Humiliation," "Genius," "Fame," and "Scandal"—are more depressing than informative. The book is largely based on letters and published sources, including standard biographies of Marie Curie, Albert Einstein, and Paul Langevin. It begins with Einstein's tribute to Marie Curie as "the only person to be uncorrupted by fame" and ends with the sentence "And this was the end of the story of an honorable woman." This comment reflects on the original French title, but it lacks any special resonance in the English translation. Giroud notes that the impression she finally gained in her study of Marie Curie was of a woman quite different from the one she learned about in school. She presents her own interpretation of Curie as an irritating, captivating, passionate, and hard-working woman who played an important role in the science that led to atomic energy.

The story of Marie Curie, scientist, Nobel Laureate, and mother has inspired many biographies intended as inspirational reading for young girls. Unfortunately, many of them perpetuate the "Marie Curie Syndrome," which suggests that woman's work in science is sheer drudgery of a distinctly unglamorous and unattractive, even uncreative, nature. BIGLAND's *Madam Curie*, however, is written in a simple, direct narrative style, suitable for grades 6 to 12, and offers a good account of Curie's life and work that does not insult the intelligence of young readers.

Readers might also wish to consult Marie Curie's biography of her husband, *Pierre Curie* (1923). The English translation contains autobiographical notes. Marie Curie's thesis *Radioactive substances* is also available in an English translation (1961). For a comparison of the life and work of Marie Curie and her daughter Irene Joliot-Curie with those of other female Nobel Laureates, readers should consult Olga Opfell's work, *The Lady Laureates* (1978).

Biographies written for elementary school students include: Beverly Birch, *Marie Curie: The Polish Scientist Who Discovered Radium and Its Life-Saving Properties* (1988); Keith Brandt, *Marie Curie: Brave Scientist* (1983); Angela Bull, *Marie Curie* (1986); Edwina Conner, *Marie Curie* (1987); Naunerle C. Farr, *Madame Curie* and *Albert Einstein* (1979); Carol Greene, *Marie Curie: Pioneer Physicist* (1984); Ann D. Johnson, *The Value of Learning: The Story of Marie Curie* (1978); Mollie Keller, *Marie Curie* (1982); Louis Sabin, *Marie Curie* (1985); Ann Steinke, *Marie Curie* (1987).

Grand Obsession: Madame Curie and Her World, by Rosalynd Pfaum (1989) was unavailable for review at the time of this writing.

—Lois N. Magner

CUSTER, George Armstrong, 1839–1876; American general.

Ambrose, Stephen E., *Crazy Horse and Custer: The Parallel Lives of Two American Warriors*. New York, Doubleday, 1975; London, Macdonald and Jane's, 1976.

Connell, Evan S., *Son of Morning Star: Custer and the Little Big Horn*. San Francisco, North Point, 1984; with subtitle *General Custer and the Battle of Little Bighorn*, London, Picador, 1986.

Hofling, Charles K., *Custer and the Little Big Horn: A Psychobiographical Inquiry*. Detroit, Wayne State University Press, 1981.

Monaghan, Jay, *Custer: The Life of General George Armstrong Custer*. Boston, Little Brown, 1959.

Utley, Robert M., *Cavalier in Buckskin: George Armstrong Custer and the Western Military Frontier*. Norman, University of Oklahoma Press, 1988.

Van de Water, Frederick F., *Glory Hunter: A Life of General Custer*. Indianapolis, Bobbs-Merrill, 1934.

Whittaker, Frederick, *A Complete Life of General George Armstrong Custer*. New York, Sheldon, 1876.

*

MONAGHAN published the first truly full-scale, useful biography of Custer. His work was a major milestone since it examined the General's life from his boyhood days in Ohio and Michigan to his death on the Little Big Horn in 1876. A number of specialized studies focusing mainly on the Battle of the Little Big Horn had been published between 1876 and 1959, along with a few inferior attempts at biographies of General Custer, which were often marred by inadequate research, severe bias, and a narrow focus on Custer's frontier days with his regiment. Monaghan takes a comprehensive look at his subject and maintains a balanced perspective. He avoids making amateur psychological judgments, though he is the first author to place Custer in an understandable framework that permits a glance into the General's complex personality. Monaghan also makes skillful use of the material found in *The Custer Story: The Life and Intimate Letters of General Custer and His Wife Elizabeth* (edited by Marguerite Merington, 1950), and he integrates into his narrative the information in Elizabeth B. Custer's three books (*"Boots and Saddles"; or, Life in Dakota with General Custer* (1885), *Tenting on the Plains; or, General Custer in Kansas* (1887), and *Following the Guidon* (1890), as well as Custer's own *My Life on the Plains; or, Personal Experiences with Indians* (New York, Sheldon, 1874).

Monaghan is also the first to present readers with a systematic account of Custer's feats in the Civil War, for which he relies heavily on the official records of the war, the personal papers of a wide assortment of people who were directly or indirectly associated with Custer during the conflict, and a number of mem-

oirs by people whose thoughts throw some light on Custer's service. That section of Monaghan's work has since been eclipsed by a fine study of the General's Civil War years in Gregory J. W. Urwin's *Custer Victorious: The Civil War Battles of General George Armstrong Custer* (1983). Readers, however, should not ignore Monaghan's account of Custer's service in the Civil War, for Monaghan offers some fine insights into Custer's habits as a soldier. Overall, no one has surpassed Monaghan's effort to provide readers with a comprehensive, well-researched account of the complicated activities of a complex man who regularly sought attention and finally won undying fame by dying in a bizarre military debacle. Readers should begin their study of Custer and his times with Monaghan's biography.

UTLEY, a well-known scholar of the military phase of the closing of the American frontier, has produced the best short account of Custer's life. In the note on the sources to his book, Utley, with characteristic generosity, claims that Monaghan's biography is still the best available to readers interested in a complete understanding of Custer. Nevertheless, Utley believes there are several reasons for writing another biography. Most of Utley's readers know that he has spent the greater part of his scholarly life examining the raucous events of the post-Civil War frontier, and he modestly declares that writing a biography of Custer would at last force him to reach some conclusions about the General and his career as a soldier. His *Cavalier in Buckskin* is a superb account of Custer's post-Civil War activities. Early on in his account of Custer's life, Utley points out that his subject graduated from the United States Military Academy on June 24, 1861, and died 15 years and one day later on the Little Big Horn. In that short time, Custer went from the status of an obscure lieutenant to that of a legend. Utley devotes little space to Custer's childhood, development, or Civil War career, yet he frequently looks back on those times as he carefully expresses his opinions of the General.

Utley's book has three obvious virtues. First of all, it reflects his many years of study of the heroic, and often tragic, events of the American frontier in the 1860s and 70s. Few American scholars equal Utley's understanding of those turbulent years. Second, his work is meticulously researched. Utley had access to all the sources Monaghan employed plus the benefit of a number of seminal monographs published in the years since Monaghan's work appeared. Third, Utley is an engaging writer who captures and maintains his reader's interest early in his narrative. Though not as comprehensive as Monaghan's biography, (it was never intended to be so) Utley's is a superb piece of scholarship, and readers who wish to consult the best of the biographies on Custer will read both Monaghan and Utley.

CONNELL's *Son of Morning Star* is one of the many studies of Custer's life that is not a biography in the truest sense of the term, yet it deals with a great many facets of the soldier's life and his sometimes exasperating personality. Readers of Connell's book will develop a genuine respect for his writing style; he is adept at creating a feeling for the world in which Custer lived. Readers simultaneously will be made uneasy by the author's broad and unsubstantiated statements. To take one example, Connell observes that "Custer lost more men during the Civil War than almost any other commandant." He offers no proof other than his own assumption that Custer was a rash commander who had little regard for his men. Because Connell uses no footnotes whatsoever, readers are left to their own devices to determine the credibility of the author's claims.

VAN de WATER's title aptly summarizes his point of view. *Glory Hunter* was published the year after Elizabeth Bacon Custer died, and it did not treat the General any too favorably. Van de Water portrays Custer as a man driven to win "glory" for himself with little regard for the danger or misery his ambition brought upon others. Fairly broad in scope, Van de Water begins his account with a glance at Custer's boyhood and formative years prior to his entry into the United States Military Academy. The work is divided into three parts. Part One, entitled "Soldier" deals with Custer's exploits in the Civil War; Part Two, "Indian Fighter," concentrates on Custer's frontier service during the years 1866–73; and the final section of the book, which Van de Water entitles "Hero," details the final years leading to the Little Big Horn. Van de Water's book is lively reading. In comparison to Monaghan's full-scale work, however, it is thinly researched and replete with unsubstantiated conjecture. Once familiar with the basic facts concerning Custer's life, however, readers may well wish to read *Glory Hunter*. Van de Water did a good deal to influence a generation or two of Americans who came to accept as fact that Custer had a self-destructive character that affected nearly everyone who came near him. Readers may also wish to examine WHITTAKER's book, the first to attempt to chronicle Custer's life. Though it has numerous shortcomings, it is useful for gaining a perspective on the historiography of Custer and his biographers.

HOFLING's short study of Custer's personality leaves his readers fascinated though unconvinced. Hofling never pretends to develop a complete biographical examination of Custer's life, but he does a workman-like analysis of the General's dominant personality traits. Many readers will differ with one or more of Hofling's choices of Custer's activities or responses to particular situations as significant keys to understanding his sometimes vexing personality, but all readers will applaud the author's straightforward approach to his subject. Two related studies that readers may find intriguing are Brian Dippie, *Custer's Last Stand: The Anatomy of an American Myth* (1976), and Robert M. Utley, *Custer and the Great Controversey: Origin and Development of a Legend* (1962). Dippie and Utley examine the entire debate surrounding the Custer debacle on the Little Big Horn and attempt to explain how and why the battle has loomed so large in the American imagination. They differ somewhat from Hofling's approach, but both men provide a good deal of analysis of Custer's traits and habits on the battlefield.

AMBROSE offers another of those studies of Custer that is not quite a biography but ought be included in any account of the attempts to understand the General. His work is a remarkable comparison of two men made everlastingly famous by the Battle of the Little Big Horn. Both men were famous for their feats in warfare and notorious for their nonconformist conduct within their respective warrior societies. Ambrose offers some fascinating assessments of both men while providing his readers with a wealth of insight into the warrior cultures of both the Indian and American nations that partly explains the emergence of Crazy Horse and Custer as unforgettable military figures.

—Larry G. Bowman

DALI, Salvador, 1904–1989; Spanish painter.

Ades, Dawn, *Dali and Surrealism.* New York, Harper, 1982.

Cowles, Fleur, *The Case of Salvador Dali.* London, Heinemann, 1959; Boston, Little Brown, 1960.

Descharnes, Robert, *Salvador Dali, the Work, the Man,* translated by E. R. Morse. New York, Abrams, 1984.

Lake, Carlton, *In Quest of Dali.* New York, Putnam, 1969.

Lear, Amanda, *Persistence of Memory: A Personal Biography of Salvador Dali.* Bethesda, Maryland, National Press, 1987.

Gómez de Liaño, Ignacio, *Dali.* New York, Rizzoli, 1984 (originally published by Polígrafa, Barcelona, 1982).

Maddox, Conroy, *Dali.* New York, Crown, and London, Hamlyn, 1979.

Rogerson, Mark, *The Dali Scandal: An Investigation.* London, Gollancz, 1987.

Secrest, Meryle, *Salvador Dali.* New York, Dutton, 1986; with subtitle, *Surrealist Jester,* London, Weidenfeld and Nicolson, 1986.

Soby, James T., *Salvador Dali.* New York, Museum of Modern Art, 1941.

*

Dali's autobiographical work, *The Unspeakable Confessions of Salvador Dali* (1976), is perhaps more readily available than his earlier publications. The *Confessions* are generally felt to have added little to what Dali had already expressed in *The Secret Life of Salvador Dali* (1942) and *Diary of a Genius* (1965). These works offer few insights into Dali's creative process, and in addition to some moments of sheer mystification, they demonstrate Dali's pervasive infantile exhibitionism, focus on onanism, and scatalogical obsessions. In the display of pornographic imagery and sado-masochistic revelations, Dali may nonetheless convey his deviant and eccentric temperament better than do most biographers. Dali's writings, especially shorter pieces, are numerous: while a partial listing can be found in the volume by Ades (see below), the most complete bibliography, both of works by and on Dali, is available in *Salvador Dali: Retrospective 1920–80* (Centre Georges Pompidou, Paris, 1979–80).

DESCHARNES' enormous book, like many other more modest texts (for instance those by LEAR and GÓMEZ; the latter offers a fine, detailed chronology) suffers from its author's friendship and business involvement with Dali. Descharnes is unable to be objective about the relationship, and his generally pompous prose is supported by a bibliography containing only Dali's own writings, works illustrated by him, and his films and theatrical works.

SECREST, in sharp contrast to Descharnes, attempts a formal biography that is clearly non-partisan and exhaustively researched. She intends an analytical exploration of the emotional basis of Dali's art and behavior, pointing for instance to the extraordinary circumstance of his birth and his lifelong thematic return to his childhood in his art. But at times even Secrest has been drawn into the Dali myth. She appears best as chronicler of his behavior, leaving the reader to draw his own conclusion. One chapter, entitled "Masked Faces," discusses the still proliferating problem of Dali's prints and printed works and the many alleged forgeries of the past two decades. ROGERSON has devoted an entire book to the labyrinthine problems of publishers, public ignorance, and Dali's clearly understood desire to make money.

LAKE presents little analysis but offers (with Dali often quoted at great length) an account of Dali's appearance in Paris and New York over the course of 18 months in the late 1960s. Their association ended, with dire threats by Dali against Lake should he not show him the manuscript before publication: Dali had become horrified by Françoise Gilot's book on Picasso (on which Lake collaborated), with its many negative revelations of his fellow Spaniard.

COWLES' earlier work, on the contrary, offers an example of Dali's involvement with a close friend who was deeply influenced by Surrealism. Her work can be considered authorized since Dali himself initialized every manuscript page. Cowles presents Dali as she best knew him, in his many public aspects—as designer, literary figure, painter, jeweler, and "exhibitionist." But although Cowles understood Dali's high professionalism in these various endeavors, she could not sense that his bizarre moods and fantasies were anything other than actual mental derangement. It appears that this view satisfied Dali.

In contrast to such recent frenzied views, SOBY's pioneer work presents the young Dali in a refreshing 25-page essay that serves as a catalog introduction. Although ADES did have several conversations with the artist, her text is cooly critical in its analysis of his earlier works, presented in the context of his life events. As implied by the title, prime attention is given to Dali's relationship to the personalities and theoretical standpoint of the Surrealist movement he came to know in the late 1920s. Ade's work also offers a brief review of Dali's work in film and his activities in Hollywood. MADDOX furnishes a short yet precise review of Dali's life, with emphasis on the experiences that brought about his subject matter. The text is well illustrated, with fine critical captions.

—Joshua Kind

DANTE [Dante Alighieri], 1265–1321; Italian poet.

Anderson, William, *Dante the Maker*. London, Routledge, 1980.

Barbi, Michele, *Life of Dante*, translated and edited by Paul Ruggiers. Berkeley, University of California Press, 1954 (originally published as *Dante: vita, opere e fortuna*, 1933).

Bergin, Thomas G., *Dante*. Boston, Houghton Mifflin, 1965.

Chubb, Thomas C., *Dante and His World*. Boston, Little Brown, 1967.

Cosmo, Umberto, *A Handbook to Dante Studies*, translated by David Moore. New York, Barnes and Noble, 1947; Oxford, Blackwell, 1950.

Dinsmore, Charles Allen, *Life of Dante Alighieri*. Boston, Houghton Mifflin, and London, Constable, 1919.

Federn, Karl, *Dante and His Time*. London, Heinemann, and New York, McClure Phillips, 1902.

Fergusson, Francis, *Dante*. New York, Macmillan, and London, Weidenfeld and Nicolson, 1966.

Gardner, Edmund G., *Dante*. London, Dent, 1900.

Grandgent, Charles H., *Dante*. New York, Duffield, 1916.

Leigh, Gertrude, *New Light on the Youth of Dante*. London, Faber, 1929; Boston, Houghton Mifflin, 1930.

Page, Thomas N., *Dante and His Influence*. London, Chapman and Hall, and New York, Scribner, 1922.

Quinones, Ricardo J., *Dante Alighieri*. Boston, Twayne, 1979.

Toynbee, Paget J., *Dante Alighieri: His Life and Work*. London, Methuen, and New York, Macmillan, 1910; 4th edition, edited by Charles Singleton, New York, Harper, 1965.

*

Dante's life and work are so thoroughly enmeshed that a pure biography, at least in the modern sense, seems impossible. Little new factual information has turned up in recent times, and much of the original primary information—letters, documents, records—has disappeared. Within a decade of Dante's death in 1321, contemporaries such as Giovanni Boccaccio (1313–1375) and Leonardo Bruni (1369–1444) were already at work on biographies. The best English survey of these early studies can be found in Edward Moore's *Dante and his Early Biographers* (London, Rivingtons, 1890).

The Anglo-American revival of Dante studies at the turn of the 20th century brought forth a number of critical studies of Dante's life and work. FEDERN presents a detailed study of the political, social, and historical context of Dante's age. Federn called for more rigorous standards in Dante scholarship, noting that "most of the so-called biographies of Dante are," in the words of G. A. Scartazzini, " 'romances founded on improbable traditions and arbitrary suppositions.' "

The best of the standard biographical studies is by TOYNBEE. He was one of the first biographers to include a genealogical table of Dante's family. A notable quality of Toynbee's work is its extensive use of quotations from contemporary chronicles, giving the reader a vivid sense of Dante's world. Toynbee incorporates his own translations of narrative excerpts from early biographies by Boccaccio, Giovanni Villani, and others. In making use of this anecdotal material, Toynbee observes, "the legends and traditions which hang around the name of a great personality are not an unimportant part in his biography, and may sometimes serve to place him as well as, if not better than, the sober estimates of the serious historian." A renowned Dante scholar, Toynbee was also the author of the *Dictionary of Proper Names and Notable Matters in the Works of Dante* (1898), a standard reference work. References to autobiographical citations in Dante's works may easily be found in Toynbee's *Dictionary*.

DINSMORE's book claims to be the first comprehensive life written by an American. Dinsmore uses a conventional approach that balances the "gentle dreamer" of the *Vita Nuova* with the "stern prophet" of the *Divina Commedia*. His biography traces Dante's pilgrimage of life through exile, humiliation, disillusionment and disaster to the final wisdom and peace of the *Paradiso*.

More intellectually rigorous is GRANDGENT's *Dante*. A leading American Dantist, Grandgent presents an historical biography through which he "attempted to trace a portrait of the middle ages with Dante's features showing through." His first chapter offers a perceptive discussion of the problems confronting the Dante biographer and highlights the essential paradox of the figure of Dante remaining such a living presence despite the meager knowledge of his life. T. S. Eliot's influential critical essay on Dante (1929) established Dante's work as central to the Modernist imagination. Eliot argued that although the *Comme-*

dia ought to be read in its entirety first, studying the *Vita Nuova* was crucial to understanding Dante's medieval sensibility.

Other biographical studies from this period include those by PAGE and GARDNER—the latter is still "a convenient short compendium of the main facts." LEIGH argues that the *Commedia* and other works provide a cryptic biography of Dante's life. Leigh identifies him with the anti-papal party of the Spiritualists, followers of the mystic theologican Joachim de Flore.

BARBI's study, the most authoritative modern Italian biography of Dante, is also perhaps the most compact and accessible. Cautious and austere in his judgments, Barbi refused to include any information not verifiable from documents. As Ruggiers, who translated Barbi's work into English, notes, "Dante's works themselves form a kind of biography. The *Vita Nuova*, the *Convivio*, the *De Vulgari Eloquentia*, the *Canzoniere*, the *Epistles*, the *Ecologues*, and the *Commedia* are all memorable in one way or another for poignant passages in which Dante records his anxieties, his frustrations, and his hopes, together with the names of places and persons he has known." Unfortunately, Barbi took for granted much of the historical background of Dante's age that needs to be explained to the modern English reader. Yet Barbi and Toynbee agree on much of the basic information about Dante's life. There are relatively few extant documents relating to Dante's life, and modern archival research has turned up little that would challenge the familiar outline of that life. Nevertheless, as Ruggiers notes, "It is especially valuable that English-speaking readers should have made available to them a life of Dante by a writer who is himself an Italian and whose point of view is so entirely sympathetic with the greatest of Italian poets."

Another invaluable work of recent Italian scholarship is COSMO's, which includes a thorough biographic treatment of the various periods of Dante's life and detailed bibliographic citations at the end of each chapter. Cosmo indicates that the major "sources for the study of Dante's life are (a) the information about himself which the poet left in his works; (b) the information emerging from extant public instruments and deeds which refer to him and his family; (c) a few items of information supplied by the ancient commentators; and (d) the oldest biographies." Yet in extrapolating Dante's life from his work, Cosmo cautions, "we must not confuse Dante's artistic representation of himself with the historical reality, nor the ideal man with the real."

The 700th anniversary of Dante's birth in 1965 brought forth a series of new biographic studies of Dante. The most concise and informative guide for the general reader is by BERGIN. In his intellectual biography, Bergin presents a thorough and detailed background to the 13th century: on the power struggle between pope and emperor; the political intrigues between Guelph and Ghibelline; and the rise of Italian vernacular literature. Without idealizing medieval life, he presents a clear and lucid description of Dante's Florence. His chapter on Dante's life is exemplary, but especially useful is his discussion of Dante's reading and learning that went into the formation of the *Commedia* and other works. Less comprehensive is FERGUSSON's *Dante*, an introductory critical biography prepared for the Masters of World Literature Series. Fergusson combines straightforward critical commentary with occasional biographical details.

CHUBB provides a lengthy but conventional modern critical biography. Though Chubb breaks no new ground in Dante schol-

arship, he presents an erudite but accessible full-length biographical study that incorporates contemporary Dante scholarship without intrusive footnotes or scholarly apparatus. Chubb justifies his undertaking by quoting Barbi's observation that " 'Dante is so universal and so full of matter that he must be restudied constantly. There is no age, he indicated—and by implication—no serious student—that cannot add something new.' "

More innovative is ANDERSON's critical study of Dante's creative imagination that attempts to trace the sources of Dante's creativity and genius, making use of "recent psychological and neuro-physiological studies of creativity." His first section, "the Making of a Poet," incorporates biographic details in its study of the growth of Dante's creative imagination. Anderson focuses on "the ways in which Dante wrote, the ways in which he received his inspiration, and how he makes use of them." He speculates on how Dante selected impressions from the world and transformed them into art, which Anderson calls "storehouses of psychic energy." He also examines the sources and uses of Dante's remarkable visual or eidetic imagination. He finds in the structure of the *Commedia* a mental biography that corresponds with the growth of Dante's mind.

Perhaps the most concise of the recent critical biographies is QUINONES' *Dante Alighieri*. Following the conventional Twayne format, Quinones summarizes the salient details of Dante's life within a chronological discussion of the major works. Despite the immense volume of Dante scholarship, the lack of a definitive Dante biography in English suggests how few documented details are available about his life and how difficult it is to separate his life from his work.

—Andrew J. Angyal

DANTON, Georges-Jacques, 1759–1794; French revolutionary leader.

Beesly, Augustus H., *Life of Danton*. London and New York, Longman, 1899.

Belloc, Hilaire, *Danton: A Study*. London, J. Nisbet, and New York, Scribner, 1899.

Christophe, Robert, *Danton: A Biography*, translated by Peter Green. London, A. Barker, and New York, Doubleday, 1967 (originally published by Librairie académique Perrin, Paris, 1964).

Hampson, Norman, *Danton*. London, Duckworth, and New York, Holmes and Meier, 1978.

Madelin, Louis, *Danton*, translated by Lady Mary Boyd. London, Heinemann, and New York, Knopf, 1921 (originally published by Hachette, Paris, 1911).

Wendel, Herman, *Danton*. New Haven, Connecticut, Yale University Press, 1935; London, Constable, 1936 (originally published by E. Rowohlt, Berlin, 1930).

*

"Danton obscures and confuses everything he touches," wrote the historian Guérin. Carlyle agreed: "Few such remarkable men have been left so obscure to us as this Titan of the Revolution." Biographers of Danton have been fortunate to have in their subject a source of abiding mystery and speculation; unfortunately, few have chosen to explore the ambiguities and many have instead opted to cast Danton in their preferred image. The problem of historical sources is formidable: very few of his public pronouncements were preserved accurately, there were no private diaries, and almost no surviving letters. The evidence in the case of Danton, as at his trial in 1794, is fragmentary and circumstantial. Most biographers present the anecdotal evidence and judge its veracity according to their prejudices. Even Hampson, the most scrupulous as to the authentication of data, tellingly comments that "as soon as one tries to . . . eliminate conjecture and start from the basis of verified fact, the whole structure disintegrates." Was Danton a double agent, working for the Royalists or for the British? No definitive answer has emerged; and it is this area of uncertainty, along with the sheer verve of his personality and the audacity of his actions, that provides the enduring fascination in the matter of Georges-Jacques Danton.

Most of the earlier biographies do not repay the effort of retrieving them from obscurity. In the 19th century, authors were prone to portraying great figures of the revolution as either corrupt and venal monsters or naive patriots caught in a process beyond their control, and this trend died slowly. An interesting contrast might be made between BEESLY and BELLOC, two British authors who published their biographies in 1899, if there were anything of substance to contrast. Both present Danton in his official guise of moderate, the banner under which he flew when he went to the guillotine, turning him into something of a proto-Parliamentarian, a statesman in the liberal democratic tradition. In order to achieve this, they endeavour to gloss over his more radical proclamations, especially those made in 1789 in the Cordeliers club. Beesly goes as far as to conclude that Danton had "no personal ambition to gratify, craving only for himself a quiet country life in his old home in Arcis." This version of Danton, pale and insipid, is difficult to square with those other versions in which he is either the driving force of the Terror or the wily double- or triple-agent. In attempting to prove Danton a loyal adherent to a particular faction, these biographers miss one of the most fascinating aspects of Danton the politician: the way in which he could appear to belong to many parties at once, belonging in reality to no party but himself. Belloc, though basing his account very much in the same camp, provides a much more impressive portrait of the individual, and his biography is both fluent and attractively written. His preface on "The Revolution" at least makes explicit his assumptions about the bourgeois nature of the great event and about Danton's place in it. On the accusations of double-dealing, Belloc refuses to judge absolutely but leans toward an interpretation of innocence.

Both MADELIN and WENDEL provide extremely readable accounts, never straying from the recognised sources, but both succumb to the temptation to portray Danton in the way he would have liked to be remembered. At his trial he promised that he would "sleep in glory," and it is this tone that comes to dominate both works. Wendel's style is forceful, conveying something of the demonic side of Danton's personality; but Madelin is overblown and given to bombastic asides that add nothing to our understanding of the subject.

CHRISTOPHE's bulky biography falls into many of the same traps as its predecessors. Meant as a popular biography rather than a work of scholarship, it is at times hugely entertaining, and the most accessible of all the works on Danton. It provides a great deal of background for the general reader, and for this reason remains the best starting point for a study of Danton's life and times. But its faults loom large: it does not give any details for many of its sources, and so the distinction between documentary and anecdotal evidence is largely blurred. Christophe's melodramatic setting and portentous style can become irritating and bathetic, especially when he devotes a great deal of detailed description to scenes of complete conjecture. We might compare here Christophe's account to Hampson's (see below) of Danton's reaction to his first wife's death just days after the vote to condemn the king. Hampson briefly comments that "we know so little about Danton as a private individual that there is no means of telling what Gabrielle's death meant to him." Christophe, however, is more confident; he describes the scene fulsomely, with Danton burying his head in her closet and "breathing her well-remembered perfume." The histrionic quality of this biography only really justifies itself in the two great moments of Danton's life: his call to arms in August 1792 and his trial and death in 1794. There is no disputing the fact that Danton's life was spectacular and dramatic, but for the most part it was a drama played behind the scenes. Christophe's "fictionalised documentary" approach is the latest in a tradition of Danton biography that does its subject a disservice by overstating the moments of high drama, and by accepting much of the stuff of legend at face value.

The contrast with HAMPSON's *Danton* could hardly be greater. A detailed, scholarly work, this book is not for the reader unacquainted with the political background of the revolution. It makes few excursions into the background and "local colour" much favoured by the more descriptive biographers. Consequently it is a succinct, rich, and speculative biography that explores fully the crucial questions of double-agency, long term strategy, and Danton's true loyalties through all his many changes of side, though Hampson is honest enough not to reach any definite conclusions on these matters. In a very few pages he gives the reader a vivid impression of the dizzying complexities of the political world Danton inhabited. The final conclusion the reader is drawn to is that Danton was preoccupied above all with simple political survival, which as the Terror grew in force became a struggle for literal survival. Hampson's account begins with a welcome overview of "Danton and the Historians," which clearly delineates the various images of the revolutionary hero as seen through the distorting lenses of political prejudice. This section serves, moreover, as an antidote to the Romantic manifestation of Danton the martyr that first began in Georg Büchner's play *Dantons Tod* (1835) and which still holds a powerful grip on the popular imagination. To read Hampson's admirable work is to lose something of this florid, attractive figure; but in reading it we gain a much more satisfying sense of Danton the politician, swimming in the turbulent and turgid political waters of the revolution.

—Alan Murphy

DARROW, Clarence Seward, 1857–1938, American lawyer.

Stone, Irving, *Clarence Darrow for the Defense: A Biography.* New York, Doubleday, 1941.
Tierney, Kevin, *Darrow: A Biography.* New York, Crowell, 1979.
Weinberg, Arthur and Lila Weinberg, *Clarence Darrow: A Sentimental Rebel.* New York, Putnam, 1980.

*

An appropriate starting point for research into Clarence Darrow is Willard D. Hunsberger's exhaustive 1981 *Clarence Darrow: A Bibliography*, which lists 1627 sources, including books, articles, special collections, etc. Full-length biographies, however, are disappointingly few. Fortunately, the two currently in print, by Stone and Weinberg, are both thorough, solid works that appeal to general and academic audiences respectively.

Both books grapple with the lack of available primary source materials. Although a prolific author of both fiction and nonfiction, Darrow kept no journal and saved few letters. Material on his early formative years, so crucial in the understanding of the total man, are scant indeed. Darrow's own *The Story of My Life* (1932), written at age 74, focuses primarily on his legal career and philosophy of life. His fictionalized autobiographical account of his childhood, *Farmington*, does express many of his views on the repressive but binding prejudices and conventions of mid-19th-century small-town America, but for the most part is nostalgic and personally unrevealing.

Despite this frustrating limitation, the fact that biographical novelist STONE's bestseller, first copyrighted just three years after Darrow's death, is still in print demonstrates its enormous popularity. Stone makes Darrow three dimensional by capturing his genius and vitality without resorting to sensationalism or distortion. In addition to the text's appeal to a general audience, Stone's exhaustive research is well documented. The endnotes include secondary and primary sources, notably Darrow's private correspondence, family documents, manuscripts, legal briefs, notebooks, unpublished memoirs, and extensive personal interviews with Darrow's contemporaries.

Stone's recreated dialogue is, for many readers, what makes Darrow come alive. The more scholarly reader, however, may find it distracting due to its frequently unnatural, forced tone. Stone does, however, make excellent use of transcripts of Darrow's courtroom performance and weaves the attorney's actual words skillfully into the narrative.

Stone's work does have its shortcomings. Written so close to Darrow's death, it clearly lacks the perspective of time. Its tone is adulatory, at times even fawning. Moreover, although Stone asserts that no restrictions were imposed upon him by the Darrow family concerning what he might write or publish, Arthur and Lila Weinberg reveal that Stone gave in to the entreaties of Darrow's widow to exclude all mention of Darrow's affair and subsequent long-term platonic but close relationship with Hull House social worker Mary Field. Stone acknowledges only that Darrow ''might have'' committed adultery. Certainly the significance of Darrow's sexual relationships need not be exaggerated or sensationalized, but Stone's sanitized version of Darrow remains incomplete.

For a less popular and more scholarly view of Darrow, see the award-winning study by Arthur and Lila WEINBERG, a Chicago attorney and University of Chicago Press editor respectively. Although they too are clearly among Darrow's most fervent admirers, this portrait by these longtime scholars of Darrow is less sanitized, more critical than Stone's. While indebted to Stone's research, the Weinbergs use the added resource of Darrow's letters to Mary Field, in addition to her diary, in their successful efforts to give a complete portrait of Darrow. Less sweeping in their scope, the Weinbergs' main focus is Darrow's own 1912 trial in Los Angeles for alleged jury bribing. Darrow's motivations and unparalleled legal skills are showcased throughout.

It is unfortunate indeed that TIERNEY's superlative biography is no longer in print, but it is still available in libraries and many stores. A reader desiring only one book on the life of Darrow will find this an excellent compromise between Stone and the Weinbergs, as it contains the best qualities of each. More scholarly and critical than Stone and more comprehensive than the Weinbergs, Tierney provides a painstakingly researched and well-written study appropriate for both academic and general readers, although it does contain at least one minor error. Tierney quotes Darrow client Nathan Leopold with words actually uttered by co-defendant Richard Loeb, then compounds the mistake by attributing a crucial error of Leopold's to Loeb. This mix-up is more than compensated for, however, by the book's readability, two sections of very fine and revealing photographs, and overall excellence. Tierney's impressive research is well documented in the endnotes and his extensive bibliography will also be of use to the Darrow scholar or enthusiast.

Some readers may prefer to bypass the interpretations of others and allow Darrow to speak directly for himself. Many of his works are still in print, including *Crime, Its Causes and Treatments* (1922). Thirteen of Darrow's speeches, including nine courtroom addresses from his most famous trials, have been collected into a single volume still in print, *Attorney for the Damned: Clarence Darrow in His Own Words* (1957, edited by Arthur Weinberg, with a forward by William O. Douglas). Weinberg provides excellent background notes. Also in print is *Clarence Darrow: Verdicts out of Court* (1963), introduced by both Weinbergs, a collection of 33 of Darrow's essays, lectures, and articles from outside the courtroom. Again, the Weinberg's background notes enhance the material.

—Nancy C. Unger

DARWIN, Charles (Robert), 1809–1882; English naturalist.

Brackman, Arnold C., *A Delicate Arrangement: The Strange Case of Charles Darwin and Alfred Russel Wallace.* New York, Times Books, 1980.
Clark, Ronald W., *The Survival of Charles Darwin: A Biography of a Man and an Idea.* New York, Random House, 1984; London, Weidenfeld and Nicolson, 1985.
Colp, Ralph, Jr., *To Be an Invalid: The Illness of Charles Darwin.* Chicago, University of Chicago Press, 1977.

Darwin, Francis, *The Life and Letters of Charles Darwin* (3 vols.). London, J. Murray, 1887; New York, Appleton, 1888.

Dibner, Bern, *Darwin of the Beagle*. Norwalk, Connecticut, Burndy Library, 1960.

Gruber, Howard E., *Darwin on Man: A Psychological Study of Scientific Creativity, Together with Darwin's Early and Unpublished Notebooks*, transcribed and annotated by Paul H. Barrett. New York, Dutton, and London, Wildwood House, 1974; revised edition, Chicago, University of Chicago Press, 1981.

Himmelfarb, Gertrude, *Darwin and Darwinian Revolution*. New York, Doubleday, and London, Chatto and Windus, 1959.

Huxley, Julian, assisted by James Fisher, *The Living Thoughts of Darwin*. New York, Longman, and London, Cassell, 1939.

Huxley, Julian and H. B. D. Kettlewell, *Charles Darwin and His World*. New York, Viking, and London, Thames and Hudson, 1965.

Huxley, Leonard, *Charles Darwin*. New York, Greenberg, 1927.

Irvine, William, *Apes, Angels, and Victorians: The Story of Darwin, Huxley, and Evolution*. New York, McGraw-Hill, 1955; with subtitle, *A Joint Biography of Darwin and Huxley*, London, Weidenfeld and Nicolson, 1955.

Karp, Walter, *Charles Darwin and the Origin of Species*. New York, Harper, 1968; London, Cassell, 1969.

Keith, Sir Arthur, *Darwin Revalued*. London, Watts, 1955.

Miall, L. C., *The Life and Work of Charles Darwin: A Lecture*. Leeds, R. Jackson, 1883.

Moore, Ruth, *Charles Darwin: A Great Life in Brief*. New York, Knopf, 1954.

Moorehead, Alan, *Darwin and the Beagle*. New York, Harper, and London, Hamilton, 1969.

Ospovat, Dov, *The Development of Darwin's Theory: Natural History, Natural Theology, and Natural Selection 1838–59*. Cambridge and New York, Cambridge University Press, 1981.

Poulton, Edward B., *Charles Darwin and the Theory of Natural Selection*. New York, Macmillan, and London, Cassell, 1896.

Ruse, Michael, *Darwinism Defended: A Guide to the Evolution Controversies*. Reading, Massachusetts, Addison-Wesley, 1982.

Sears, Paul B., *Charles Darwin: The Naturalist as a Cultural Force*. New York, Scribner, 1950.

Stone, Irving, *The Origin: A Biographical Novel of Charles Darwin*. New York, Doubleday, 1980; London, Corgi, 1982.

Vorzimmer, Peter J., *Charles Darwin: The Years of Controversy: The Origin of Species and Its Critics 1859–82*. Philadelphia, Temple University Press, 1970; London, University of London Press, 1972.

Ward, Henshaw, *Charles Darwin: The Man and His Warfare*. Indianapolis, Bobbs-Merrill, and London, J. Murray, 1927.

West, Geoffrey (Geoffrey Harry Wells), *Charles Darwin: A Portrait*. New Haven, Connecticut, Yale University Press, 1938.

*

All the biographies of Darwin published since his death in 1882 have depended heavily on the great standard three-volume *Life and Letters* edited by his son, FRANCIS DARWIN. In his selection of materials for publication, Francis Darwin attempted to illustrate his father's "personal character," but the *Life and Letters* is largely an account of Darwin's career. Indeed, most of the chapters take their titles from his books.

One of the most entertaining studies of Darwin's place in history is IRVINE's sympathetic, scholarly, well-written, and witty biography of Darwin and Huxley. The remarkable contrast between Huxley's love of controversy and Darwin's retreat into the privacy of his country home, with his protective, loving family makes this book a delight to read. Another excellent biography for the general reader is provided by the well-known biographer CLARK. Almost half the book is devoted to an examination of the evolution of Darwinism, genetics, the Neo-Darwinian synthesis, and an examination of how molecular biology has taken over both evolution and genetics. An interesting account of Darwin's chronic and perplexing illnesses is presented by COLP. This detailed and scholarly "medical biography" is based on extensive research into Victorian medications, treatments, and doctors. Despite the rather limited scope of this study, it should be of interest to general readers as well as historians of science and medicine for the insights it offers into the nature of the creative process.

MOORE offers a brief, readable biography suitable for general readers. The "Note on Sources" provides a useful chronological list of Darwin's writings, letters and reminiscences by family members and friends, biographies, and books about the history of evolution. In addition to the major emphasis on *Origin of Species*, Moore also provides a good account of how Darwin came to write the *Descent of Man*, and his concept of how sexual selection helped explain problems that apparently were not explained by natural selection.

HIMMELFARB argues that the story of how Darwin's life might account for his "scientific disposition" is actually all the more confused by the wealth of information he left behind—autobiographical memoirs, letters, diaries, journals, notebooks, notes and transcriptions of his readings, annotated copies of succeeding editions of his and others writings, etc. Himmelfarb cites research showing that what seems to be plain, obvious, and straightforward in these sources is actually devious, obscure, and elusive. Himmelfarb presents a close "reconstruction of the facts" concerning the origin and development of Darwin's views, the way he was influenced by predecessors and contemporaries, what Darwin meant, what others assumed he meant, and what his theory actually implies.

The Origin is another fine addition to the long list of biographical novels by Irving STONE. Although this book is presented as a novel, with the novelist's relative freedom, it is based on the great body of Darwin scholarship and the cooperation of Darwin's descendants. In his Foreword, Allan Nevins, Professor of American History at Columbia University, characterizes *The Origin* as a work of biography "which admits imaginative detail," but does not "alter the spirit of historic truth." Those familiar with the scholarly literature will enjoy finding their favorite quotations and anecdotes—including the pot of worms kept on Emma's piano in the drawing room—gently slipped into place in this novel.

GRUBER's work is much more than a study of the thoughts of Charles Darwin. It is a stimulating investigation of the general problem of "the psychology of thinking" and the complex processes involved in the creation of new ideas and the construction of new theories. In part one, Gruber analyzes Darwin's intellectual setting, family and teachers, the development of his evolutionary thinking, and Darwin's concepts of man, mind, and materialism. Part two contains some of Darwin's early writings and a commentary on the M and N Notebooks. The book also provides a chronology of selected dates in Darwin's life, a biographical sketch of Darwin's father, and the suppressed minutes of the Plinian Society Meeting of 27 March 1927. In the second edition of this book, Gruber includes some new ideas about Darwin's two published versions of his journal of the voyage of the *Beagle*.

DIBNER provides an illustrated companion to Darwin's voyage on the *Beagle* and a brief biographical sketch of his life. The work features the controversy that followed the publication of the *Origin of Species* and the debate between Thomas Henry Huxley and Bishop Wilberforce. The book also includes facsimiles of the Darwin-Wallace Papers of 1858. MOOREHEAD, a journalist and author, developed his book from his original film script focusing on the years Darwin spent on the *Beagle*. A compelling contrast to Darwin is provided by an examination of the character and fixed biblical beliefs of Captain Robert FitzRoy. The book is wonderfully enriched by illustrations of contemporary or near-contemporary sources, including paintings and watercolors by Augustus Earle and Conrad Martens, the artists who accompanied Darwin on the voyage.

KARP's volume is also beautifully illustrated and written in a clear, straightforward style suitable for general readers and students. Although its emphasis is on Darwin as author of *Origin of Species*, this book provides a general and complete account of his life from birth to death. The text examines Darwin's search for a career, his voyage on the *Beagle*, his development as a naturalist, reflections on natural selection, his home and family, the writing of *Origin*, the controversy and final triumph of his theory. Some of Darwin's other books are alluded to but not analyzed. Suggestions for further reading are included.

The Huxleys have contributed to several books whose objective is to make Darwin's work and life accessible to the general reader. The work written jointly by HUXLEY AND KETTLE-WELL is an exciting, beautifully written, and beautifully illustrated book. The illustrations include sketches from Darwin's papers and notebooks, contemporary cartoons, and portaits of those who did battle over the theory of evolution. Unlike most brief accounts of Darwin, this book does not confine itself to the *Origin*, but presents a balanced and thorough assessment of Darwin's other works, incorporating them gracefully into the narrative. As to be expected from a Huxley, LEONARD HUXLEY's *Charles Darwin* is a beautifully written life. Ancestry, childhood and education, the voyage, and the species question are emphasized. Because of the relationship between the Huxleys and the Darwins, the book provides personal insights into Darwin's friendships, health, methods of work, and personal characteristics. JULIAN HUXLEY's *Living Thoughts*, a selection from Darwin's writings held together by commentary and analysis, provides a good introduction to Darwin's life and work. Huxley, assisted by James Fisher, uses this arrangement to give the layman a guided tour of the development of Darwin's theories and a lucid explanation of the theory of evolution. Thomas H. Huxley's *Darwiniana* (1893) is also of interest.

KEITH examines the Darwin family at The Mount, Shrewsbury, the Wedgwood family at Maer Hall, Staffordshire, and the Darwin family at Down House, Kent. Keith notes that he lived under the shadow of Down House for more than 20 years; this gave him "a mental picture of the day-to-day life led by the great naturalist," which he tries to convey to the reader in this laudatory, uncritical biography. The book is divided into two parts: the first is a thorough and balanced account of Darwin's life and work; the second examines Darwin's health, "racial heritage," business, attitude toward religion, incentives and motives, Emma Darwin, and the later history of Down House.

When MIALL prepared his lecture on Darwin's life in 1883, little information about Darwin's personal life was available. This brief biographical sketch is based on only a few published memorials, but it is of interest to read these assessments of Darwin written shortly after his death and to compare them with the products of modern critical scholarship. POULTON's book is part of the "Century Science Series," which provides popular editions of biographies of many eminent scientists. It is interesting as an evaluation of Darwin's work, especially his ideas about pangenesis, written before modern genetics was established and the Neo-Darwinian synthesis had been formulated.

OSPOVAT's book grew out of the author's study of pre-Darwinian natural history and his interest in seeing how Darwin reacted to changes in the sciences during the long years in which he gestated the *Origin*. Ospovat suggests that Darwin's theory of natural selection evolved in previously unsuspected ways during this period. Significant chunks of this book represent revised versions of previously published articles. This book, a scholarly history of ideas, contains many important insights into the development of Darwin's ideas and his interaction with his contemporaries.

RUSE offers an excellent source for those who want to trace the influence of Darwin on modern biology and the contemporary Creationist movement. Ruse has provided brilliant studies of the Darwinian Revolution and a lucid analysis of the anti-Darwinian arguments past and present. SEARS begins his book with the confrontation between Bishop Wilberforce and Thomas Huxley. Sears uses Darwin as the personification of "a great cooperative social and intellectual movement." This book is primarily concerned with moral history, moral philosophy, religion, and politics.

VORZIMMER provides a Chronological Table of the publication dates of all editions of *Origin of Species* published during Darwin's life, and the dates on which he began and completed various editions of that work, *Variation of Animals and Plants under Domestication*, and *The Descent of Man*. More a biography of these texts than of Darwin, Vorzimmer nevertheless provides incisive analytic methods to help readers understand the evolution of Darwin's thoughts and doubts as he wrote and rewrote the *Origin*. Chapter 8, "Darwin and Wallace," is a valuable examination and comparison of the co-discoverers of natural selection.

WARD's is a comprehensive biography that begins with an analysis of "Why Dr. Grant Liked Young Darwin." The Appendix contains six sections on Buffon, Erasmus Darwin, Lamark, Lyell, witnesses for natural selection, and why Darwin did not become a Lamarckian. The illustrations include many portraits of Darwin, his family, the voyage, and his fellow scientists. Although rather old-fashioned, the book is quite readable and adopts an interesting, questioning perspective. Many of the less well-known aspects of Darwin's work are examined.

WEST complains that some English reviewers assumed that his purpose in writing his *Portrait* of Darwin was to attack its subject, but West claims that his only target was dogmatism. Although the text is based only on published material, West contends that he "cannot believe that any secrets remain to be revealed"—not a good attitude for a serious biographer.

A recent attack on Darwin appears in BRACKMAN's book, which has been described as "a good idea that has run amok." Brackman, a prolific writer and journalist, argues that Darwin stole part of the theory of evolution by natural selection from Wallace and that Darwin's friends entered into a conspiracy to cover up this crime. Brackman is certainly not the first to make this charge, but his book does demonstrate the need for a fuller appreciation of Wallace as a scientist in his own right.

Finally, those who are interested in Darwin's life and work will want to read his *Autobiography*. This fascinating document has been edited by his granddaughter Nora Barlow, who restored materials originally deleted by his family and provided valuable notes and annotations. Darwin's autobiography is also available, along with Thomas Henry Huxley's autobiography and a scholarly introduction, in a volume edited by Gavin de Beer (*Autobiographies*, Oxford and New York, 1974). De Beer provides a valuable analysis of significant discrepancies between Darwin's memory, as expressed in the *Autobiography*, and the actual records of the development of his ideas and thought. De Beer has also provided a close examination of Darwin's best known scientific ideas in his book *Charles Darwin: Evolution by Natural Selection* (1963). Asa Gray's *Darwiniana. Essays and Reviews Pertaining to Darwinism* (1876) is not properly speaking a biography of Darwin, but it illuminates the impact of Darwin's theory on a remarkable American contemporary. Gray, an eminent American botanist, attempted to reconcile Darwinism and theology.

Of the many books dealing with specialized areas of Darwin's work and influence, the following are noteworthy: Alexander Alland, *Human Nature: Darwin's View* (1985); James M. Baldwin, *Darwin and the Humanities* (1909); R. F. Baum, *Doctors of Modernity: Darwin, Marx, and Freud* (1986); Gillian Beer, *Darwin's Plots: Evolutionary Narrative in Darwin, George Eliot, and 19th-Century Fiction* (1983); Arthur L. Caplan and Bruce Jennings, editors, *Darwin, Marx, and Freud: Their Influence on Moral Theory* (1984); Paul Ekman, *Darwin and Facial Expression: A Century of Research in Review* (1973); Archibald Geikie, *Charles Darwin As Geologist* (1909); Neal C. Gillespie, *Charles Darwin and the Problem of Creation* (1979); Phyllis Greenacre, *Quest for the Father: A Study of the Darwin-Butler Controversy* (1963); David L. Hull, *Darwin and His Critics: The Reception of Darwin's Theory of Evolution by the Scientific Community* (1973); George Levine, *Darwin and the Novelists: Patterns of Science in Victorian Fiction* (1988); David N. Livingston, *Darwin's Forgotten Defenders: The Encounter Between Evangelical Theology and Evolutionary Thought* (1987); Edward Manier, *The Young Darwin and His Cultural Circle* (1978); Ashley Montagu, *Darwin: Competition and Cooperation* (1973); Rudolph C. Norhausberber, *The Historical-Philosophical Significance of Comte, Darwin, Marx and Freud* (1983); Margot Norris, *Beasts of the Modern Imagination: Darwin, Nietzsche, Kafka, and Lawrence* (1985); Robert J. Richards, *Darwin and the Emergence of Evolutionary Theories of Mind and Behavior* (1987);

Jess A. Stoff and Charles R. Pellegrino, *Darwin's Universe: Origins and Crises in the History of Life* (1983); and Robert M. Young, *Darwin's Metaphor: Nature's Place in Victorian Culture* (1985).

There is also a growing body of literature on Darwin's influence in various countries, such as Patrick Armstrong, *Charles Darwin in Western Australia* (1986); Alfred Kelly, *The Descent of Darwin: The Popularization of Darwinism in Germany, 1860–1914* (1981); A. J. Marshall, *Darwin and Huxley in Australia* (1970); R. W. Nicholas and J. M. Nicholas, *Charles Darwin in Australia* (1989); James R. Pusey, *China and Charles Darwin* (1983); Alexander Vucinich, *Darwin in Russian Thought* (1988); Adel A. Ziadat, *Western Science in the Arab World: The Impact of Darwinism* (1989).

Many brief accounts of the life of Darwin have been written for young readers, including Felicia Law, *Darwin and the Voyage of the Beagle* (1985); Renee Skelton, *Charles Darwin* (1987); and Peter Ward, *The Adventures of Charles Darwin: A Story of the Beagle Voyage* (1982).

—Lois N. Magner

DAVID, Jacques-Louis, 1748–1825; French painter.

Brookner, Anita, *Jacques-Louis David*. London, Chatto and Windus, and New York, Harper, 1980.

Nanteuil, Luc de, *Jacques-Louis David*. New York, Abrams, 1985.

Schnapper, Antoine, *David*, translated by Helga Harrison. Fribourg, Switzerland, Office du Livre, 1980; New York, Alpine Fine Arts, 1982.

*

Until Brookner published her work in 1980, comprehensive biographies of David were available only to the French reader. Since that time two other studies have appeared, while a retrospective exhibition of David's career (with extensive catalogue) and a major symposium were held at the Louvre in 1989–90. These events yielded and will continue to provide new material for future reassessments of David's life.

BROOKNER meshes biography with a critical analysis of David's artistic evolution. Historical in emphasis, this investigation explores the 18th-century background for David's emergence as an artist as well as the cultural and theoretical milieu in which his art evolved. In a relatively short, prosaic text, Brookner clarifies David's beginnings, extracting from conflicting accounts and primary documents the date of his birth and his early education. She amplifies his years of study in the studio of Joseph-Marie Vien, from 1766 until 1780; his five-year Italian journey following the award of the Prix de Rome; and his marriage to Charlotte Pécoul in 1782. The core of this life is the period of the French Revolution, during which David fought for his political ideals and produced his greatest masterpieces. (Brookner here relies on David Dowd's important work, *J. L. David: Pageant-Master of the Republic*, Lincoln, University of Nebraska Press, 1948.) David's imprisonment in 1794, his divorce and later remarriage to Charlotte Pécoul are covered briefly, and we follow in more detail his roles as court painter to Napoleon and portrait painter to the new bourgeoisie. Brookner closes her work against the backdrop of the Restoration with David's exile and death in Brussels.

Scholarly in approach, Brookner draws on numerous primary documents, including Daniel and Guy Wildenstein, *Louis David, Documents complémentaires au catalogue complet de l'oeuvre* (Paris, Foundation Wildenstein, 1973), and David's own, sometimes inaccurate, journal published in 1800. This material is enhanced by contemporaneous French memoirs and lives: M. P. A. Coupin, *Essai sur J. L. David* (Paris, 1827); A. Thomé de Gamond, *Vie de David* (Paris, 1826); the eye-witness accounts of Etienne Delécluze, *Louis David, son école et son temps* (Paris, 1855); and several important 20th-century French studies including Leon Rosenthal, *Louis David* (Paris, 1904), and Louis Hautecoeur, *Louis David* (Paris, 1954). While the general reader might wish for more depth and texture in the treatment of David's personality and family life than Brookner offers, the specialist will find invaluable her extensive research on stylistic evolution and the extracts from letters, writings, and speeches. Overall, Brookner offers the English reader the only comprehensive, scholarly life of David available to date.

SCHNAPPER too interweaves biography with critical analysis of David's *oeuvre*, although here the balance shifts even more heavily to the latter. Comparable to Brookner's text in outline, Schnapper's lavishly illustrated and fluidly written volume amplifies the historical context and provides a more detailed account of David's years as court painter to Napoleon. Schnapper quotes freely from contemporaneous sources, offering greater texture than Brookner to the social climate and culture of France during David's lifetime. Although based on extensive research, this text is not footnoted, as it was intended for the general reader rather than the specialist. Nevertheless, this is an excellent source for those seeking an overview of David's life and career.

NANTEUIL wrote his life of David for Abrams' Library of Great Painters. Consonant with the series' format, this work includes a short biographical sketch (58 pages), annotations on individual paintings, which include valuable biographical details, and a summary chronology. Nanteuil compiled material from numerous publications—French and English books and articles—for his readable and reliable outline of David's life and artistic evolution. Writing for a general audience, he often paraphrases or quotes loosely from David's writings, and his text is not footnoted, limiting its value to the scholar. The student, however, will find here a useful summary of David's life and career.

—Phylis Floyd

DAVIS, Bette, 1908–1989; American stage and film actress.

Consadine, Shaun, *Bette and Joan: The Divine Feud*. New York, Dutton, and London, Muller, 1989.

Higham, Charles, *Bette: The Life of Bette Davis*. New York, Macmillan, 1981; with subtitle *A Biography of Bette Davis*, London, New English Library, 1981.

Hyman, B. D., *My Mother's Keeper*. New York, Morrow, and London, M. Joseph, 1985.

Hyman, B. D. and Jeremy Hyman, *Narrow Is the Way*. New York, Morrow, 1987.

Moseley, Roy, *Bette Davis: An Intimate Memoir*. New York, D. I. Fine, 1990.

Quirk, Lawrence J., *Fasten Your Seat Belts: The Passionate Life of Bette Davis*. New York, Morrow, 1990.

Stine, Whitney, *Mother Goddam: The Story of the Career of Bette Davis*. New York, Hawthorn Books, 1974; London, W. H. Allen, 1975.

Vermilye, Jerry, *Bette Davis*. New York, Pyramid Publications, 1973; London, Star Books, 1974.

*

VERMILYE's book, part of "The Pyramid Illustrated History of the Movies"—short (159 pages), idolatrous, half taken up with pictures, and very early (1973)—surveys the movies of Bette Davis, with no critical insights and little biographical substance. The following year STINE did a better job in every aspect—423 pages, the inclusion of much material on Davis' pre-movie theater life, and details about costumes, make-up, squabbles and friendships with writers, studios, actors, directors, and relatives. Stine's critical yardstick of Davis' career is unique: "Eighty-four films lay in the background of a career that had survived forty-three years of changing mores—690,570 feet of film, 7,673 minutes if shown continuously, 128 hours of entertainment. It would take five days and eight hours to view her creative output. Film had truly been her life." The joy of this book is that on every page, Bette Davis herself jumps in with four or five sentences of commentary (italicized, in brackets). Her comments establish once and for all two aspects of Davis biography: (1) facts are overshadowed by opinion, (2) strong personal likes and dislikes shape the drive, the feuds, the drama of both her personal and professional lives, which all biographers rightly assume cannot be separated.

Fortunately, idolatries, confessions, and attacks find a rational more objective and exact balance in HIGHAM's volume. If one book is standard, this is it. Higham is excellent on Davis' childhood, her early health (including an abortion), her start in Hollywood, her husbands and adopted children. This is the book that claims that "Crawford had for years nourished a secret desire for Bette." Higham makes generous use of Davis' own *The Lonely Life: An Autobiography* (1962), in which she gives, lopsidedly but vigorously, her side of the story. Davis mixes more philosophy and confession about her work, her friends, and her family, than any earlier book offers. On friends: "I do not regret one professional enemy I have made. Any actor who doesn't dare to make an enemy should get out of the business." On her mother and father: "In a supreme effort to make up for Daddy's boredom with us, Ruthie showered us with love. Mother was sunlit—Daddy the dark cloud. I cannot recall one moment of affection between my parents in our home." She writes of her sister and daughter with affection. Of husbands (four) and other men: "Most men came to me with muscles flexed. It is a role as popular as Hamlet and just as rarely well played." It is in this book she declares sex to be "God's joke on humanity."

Higham's book appeared too early to make use of *This 'n That* (1987), constituting volume two of her autobiography, in which Davis writes of her illnesses, accidents, cancer, broken hip, and stroke. She again confirms that "Bette Davis and her career are one and the same thing. Acting had been my life. I wouldn't want to live if I could never act again." By this time she had read, or at least heard of, her daughter's book: "I will never recover as completely from B. D.'s book as I have from the stroke. They were both shattering experiences."

Two corners of the life of Bette Davis have been explored in lurid detail. CONSADINE claims to have worked years and years and years to expose every link between Davis and Joan Crawford. Much of the book glitters like gossip, gossip of a bitchy, campy, delicious sort. However, 14 pages of "Source Notes," five pages of bibliography, two pages of acknowledgements, and an index give an aura of scholarship. No other book is so good on Bette Davis' contracts, roles she didn't get, studio arguments, Canteen work, social and sex life. Even though half of the 451-page book is about Crawford (the book's organization is a nervous ping pong back and forth), this is a rich source of information about Davis.

The other corner illuminated—too brightly—is Bette-as-mother. Probably taking emotional and financial courage from *Mommie Dearest*, daughter B. D. HYMAN writes a hate-filled account, *My Mother's Keeper*. B. D.'s perfect memory recalls everything her mother said back to the age of eight, and sometimes to five. First she reveals what her mother said about each person she worked with. Robert Stack is "the dullest actor who ever lived"; Charlton Heston is "such a pompous ass." Second, she reveals what others said of her mother ("Your mother is an obnoxious pain in the ass") or what she said to her mother ("Your fans don't want to read that Bette Davis is now a sad old drunk, rotting away in Connecticut"). Her thesis is that mother is a creature of "tension, shouting, tears, hysteria, and general unpleasantness." Its bewildered malice must have boomeranged—or paid off—for two years later her husband joins her in a fulsome, sanctimonious, Bible-quoting justification, *Narrow Is The Way* ("the revealing story of the controversy, the aftermath, and of faith") adding something to the biography of B. D. and Jeremy, but little to that of Bette Davis.

Early 1990 saw two new biographies of Bette Davis, one more irritating than dreary, one quite excellent except for an obsessive interest in male sexual defects.

That MOSELEY has written a biography, there is no doubt; whether of himself, exploiting "a Beautiful Friendship," or of Bette Davis is uncertain. Take his own word for it: "I have written the story of Bette and Roy." It is not Moseley's self-glorification that is so irritating, but the parasitical rationalizing and magnifying of how fond Bette was of him. ("Why did she choose me?") Even when Bette Davis yells, "Shut up!" he sees this as "actually a compliment." Anyway, see Roy and Bette. See Roy and Bette laugh. See Roy and Bette dance. ("Bette kept begging me to dance with her.") See Roy and Bette eat. ("She liked going out with me.") See Roy and Bette celebrate Christ-

mas. See Roy and Bette do everything but have sex ("She was willing to 'unzip' sexually for me but I didn't take advantage") and get married (though she would have been "a great deal happier").

"The research of 43 years" and 464 pages long, QUIRK's book is a *real* biography, detailed and up-to-date. More than anyone else he gives background information about each of Davis' roles, critical responses to them, about other people she worked with—actors, authors, directors—about friends and enemies in her private life (Moseley is not mentioned once), her work for war bonds, the Hollywood canteen, contract problems, her health, her abortions, her death, her will.

Quirk has one preoccupation bound to strike some readers as cheap, cruel, or tasteless: he cannot refrain from being vivid about men's sexual peculiarities. Yet his book shows a side of Bette Davis one cannot help but admire. Quirk relates an incident at a party, when Charles Laughton was being raked over the coals by vicious gossips. Davis wheeled about and said, "The man is a great artist, and you people demean yourselves, not him, by relaying such unkind stories."

—Paul H. Stacy

DAVIS, Jefferson, 1808–1889; American statesman, president of the Confederate States of America.

Cutting, Elisabeth B., *Jefferson Davis, Political Soldier*. New York, Dodd Mead, 1930.

Davis, Varina H., *Jefferson Davis, Ex-President of the Confederate States of America: A Memoir by His Wife* (2 vols.). New York, Belford, 1890.

Dodd, William E., *Jefferson Davis*. Philadelphia, G. W. Jacobs, 1907.

Eaton, Clement, *Jefferson Davis*. New York, Free Press, 1977.

Jones, J. William, *The Davis Memorial Volume*. Richmond, Virginia, B. F. Johnson, 1889.

McElroy, Robert M., *Jefferson Davis: The Unreal and the Real* (2 vols.). New York, Harper, 1937.

Pollard, Edward A., *Life of Jefferson Davis, with a Secret History of the Southern Confederacy*. Philadelphia, National, 1869.

Strode, Hudson, *Jefferson Davis* (3 vols.). New York, Harcourt, 1955–64.

*

Written by Davis' contemporaries, the biographies by Varina DAVIS and POLLARD serve as necessary but extreme correctives of each other. Pollard's journalistic, overlong, and vitriolic portrait was limned in the bitter postwar years and tagged Davis with an image that was popular North and South: scapegoat for Confederate defeat. While blaming the president for every defect of the Lost Cause, Pollard also labeled Davis an arch-conspirator for treason in the years before secession. Like Pollard, Varina Davis was an eyewitness to the short life of the Confederacy, but her advantage was in knowing her subject longest and best. Skillfully weaving his autobiography as dictated to her, the events from 1845 (when they married), and a chronicle of people and events in Mississippi, Washington, and Richmond, she produced a key primary source for anyone interested in the history of the heart of the 19th century. Varina Davis was a keen observer and analyst, wrote with verve, expressed opinions freely, and quoted a considerable body of personal correspondence. In fact, her memoir of her husband contains more biographical detail than his own ponderous and heavily legalistic apologia, *The Rise and Fall of the Confederate Government* (1881).

JONES' *Memorial Volume*, published the same year as Mrs. Davis' memoir, was approved by her and was conceived as a full biography. The narrative is secondary to the book's most valuable aspect, a stream of reminiscences and contemporary accounts of Davis that supply valuable insights into his life and career. Like another contemporary collection of personal sketches, *Life and Reminiscences of Jefferson Davis* (1890), Jones' contribution was his compilation of primary source material not to be found elsewhere. Both books also include unusual and especially clear illustrations.

A well-respected journalist, CUTTING approached her subject as an objective biographer, not a political opponent, as Pollard was, nor as a hagiographer. Written for a general audience, her work reads easily, uses a wide variety of primary and secondary sources, including some new ones from European repositories, but still leans heavily on Davis' personality and fixes the president with blame for virtually every Confederate military blunder. About half her book, in fact, covers the four years of the Confederacy, including new material on diplomacy.

Dated but reliable, the biography by DODD, himself later a public figure, is favorable but limited in scope. Balanced and lucid, this short account gives considerable space to Davis' pre-Civil War achievements and his nationalistic bent. Dodd also seeks reasons for the failure of the Confederate experience and finds that Congress, the vice-president, and most of the state governors should share that responsibility. Dodd's is a solid work that, like most Davis biographies, exaggerates the four years of the Civil War and hurries over the last 25 years of Davis' life.

Also sharing the blame for this imbalance is EATON, an eminent historian of the Old South. Profiting from publication of the early volumes of a modern edition of Davis' papers, currently in preparation, Eaton carefully describes his subject's formative years and early political accomplishments, correcting many dates and facts repeated frequently in earlier biographical accounts, wisely gives due attention to the family and Davis' friends, and generally applauds his leadership as president. But Eaton does not gloss over flaws in Davis' character and administrative skill. In nicknaming Davis the "sphinx of the Confederacy," Eaton freely admits the difficulty he had in understanding and presenting his subject, leaving room for further study by others.

Another biographer not particularly infected with emotions of the postwar South was McELROY, whose two-volume work clearly delineates Davis' lifelong devotion to the Constitution and state rights, the guiding watchwords of his political career. McElroy worked mainly from printed sources, failing to go much beyond for insights into personal and political relationships. Laden with unattributed quotations, McElroy's books rely heavily on the 1923 compilation of Davis' papers, *Jefferson Davis, Constitutionalist*, edited by Dunbar Rowland, and on

the solid scholarship of Walter L. Fleming's several insightful articles on Davis. McElroy also quotes from and analyzes Davis' speeches from his 20-year career in politics, a boon to readers. McElroy's account is proportionally accurate, and his is the best overall treatment of Davis' postwar life, particularly the indictment for treason and the preparation of Davis' memoirs in the 1870s. McElroy provides an excellent annotated bibliography that includes articles and pamphlets not cited in other biographies.

The most detailed and most frequently recommended biography is that by STRODE, an English professor who steeped himself in southern lore and won the support of the Davis family as he wrote his three-volume biography and later edited some private correspondence. Specifically intent on countering the image of Davis as aloof and cold, Strode's remedy is far from objective. Lacking a background of historical scholarship, Strode frequently fails to understand or even note the "times" that colored Davis' actions and beliefs, making his biography skewed and often mistaken. To his credit, Strode utilizes hundreds of family letters and interviews, which lace his story with useful anecdotes and colorful descriptions. His treatment of Davis' postwar career is much better than most of the other biographers' and he is sensitive to family dynamics.

—Lynda Lasswell Crist

DEAN, James, 1931–1955; American film actor.

Bast, William, *James Dean: A Biography*. New York, Ballantine, 1956.

Beath, Warren N., *The Death of James Dean*. New York, Grove, and London, Sidgwick and Jackson, 1986.

Dalton, David, *James Dean: The Mutant King: A Biography*. San Francisco, Straight Arrow, 1974; as *James Dean: A Biography*, London, W. H. Allen, 1975; revised edition, 1983.

Dalton, David and Ron Cayen, *James Dean: American Icon*. London, Sidgwick and Jackson, and New York, St. Martin's, 1984.

Howlett, John, *James Dean, a Biography*. New York, Simon and Schuster, 1975.

Schatt, Roy, *James Dean: A Portrait*. New York, Delilah, and London, Sidgwick and Jackson, 1982.

*

For the most part, biographies of James Dean lack all sense of perspective. Dean's short life (24 years), extremely brief career (a couple of Broadway plays, a few TV performances, three major films) and the monumental cult that sprang up after his death are examined, re-examined, scrutinized, combed for new details, for irrelevant details, for anything, any scrap of information or gossip, any potential scandal, any smallest word or thought connected with James Dean. The man himself is simply lost in some of the overplayed, underthought treatments of his life. Dean has been the subject of biographical comic books (literally), of a biographical documentary film, of a biographical video, and of at least two sordid semi-biographical fictions (Walter Ross, *The*

Immortal, 1958, and Edwin Corley, *Farewell My Slightly Tarnished Hero*, 1971). In addition, he is the subject of hundreds of "biographical" stories in movie magazines, exploitation newspapers, and gay-interest publications.

Many book-length studies of Dean's life focus on his supposed sexual promiscuity or his death-wish psychology, expressed in speed, recklessness, and unconventionality. Royston Ellis (*Rebel*, 1962) presents him as a "bisexual psychopath," and other works, too negligible to read, assign Dean hundreds of lovers and sexual partners, male and female. Bill Bast, a friend of Dean's, estimated that the young man would have had to live over a hundred years to fulfill all the claims made by those who said they had slept with him. Apparently, Dean was more active sexually after his death than he was while alive. At any rate, anyone's claim to intimacy with James Dean has been highly marketable for decades.

Some works distort his life by presenting it as if it began on the day he died. BEATH, by turns ghoulish and dryly circumstantial, is a prime example, focusing narrowly on Dean's death in a minute-by-minute account that typifies the irrelevant detailing James Dean inspired.

Adding to the sense of disproportion in the published lives of James Dean is the astonishing number of photographs of him. Whole books are devoted to images of James Dean. SCHATT's volume contains a brief memoir by the photographer who shot the "famous torn sweater" pictures of Dean, but the book is basically a collection of photographs of and by the young actor, many of them with no more intrinsic interest than the memorabilia in anyone's family album. Both books by Dalton contain an unusual number of photographs, but *James Dean: An American Icon* especially has hundreds. Even the best of the biographies, Howlett, has Dean's image on virtually every page. Beath, the most morbid of treatments, even includes the purported final photo of Dean, dying on a stretcher after his fatal car crash. The total impression is of a life spent in front of a succession of cameras. Certainly Dean was photogenic, but the subtext of virtually all Dean biographies becomes his narcissism and the willingness of others to record it, their eager response to it. The female equivalent is Marilyn Monroe; as with Monroe, when new images of James Dean are uncovered they immediately become the subject of a new publication. The best of the picture books, appropriately enough, is DALTON AND CAYEN's *James Dean: An American Icon* (1988), although the book is marred by Dalton's unbalanced (written) view of the subject.

DALTON's *James Dean: The Mutant King* (1974), looks like a standard biography (it even has a bibliography and an index, a feature that Dean biographies usually omit). But Dean is treated as if he were actually a member of a different species, a divinity formed by Narcissism, "Osiris Rising"; Dalton worships at the feet of a morbid cult figure, applying overlays of Jungian and Freudian psychology, Eastern mysticism, and New Age religiosity until the figure of James Dean himself disappears in such purple prose as this: "Unlike the masks of Cooper or Garbo, Jimmy's face is iridescent and multifaceted. His star is both a beacon and symbol of transition, a mysterious emanation that persists long after its source has been destroyed." Truly the source is destroyed by the time Dalton finishes his work.

A relatively calm treatment of Dean's life appears in the memoir by BAST, Dean's former roommate, written soon after the star's death. This work has the advantage of the writer's personal knowledge of his subject and of having been written long before the full James Dean mania had developed. HOWLETT's book is the best general account, although its softcover format probably prevents its inclusion in most libraries. At least Howlett treats James Dean as a human being—a neurotic, talented, unformed "adolescent" man who died tragically—not as the shaper of a new world vision. This work also recommends itself by it refusal to use every detail about James Dean exhumed in the past 35 years.

—Richard Sears

DE BEAUVOIR, Simone, 1908–1986; French writer.

Appignanesi, Lisa, *Simone de Beauvoir*. London and New York, Penguin, 1988.

Ascher, Carol, *Simone de Beauvoir: A Life of Freedom*. Boston, Beacon Press, and Brighton, Harvester, 1981.

Bair, Deirdre, *Simone de Beauvoir, a Biography*. New York, Summit Books, and London, Cape, 1990.

Francis, Claude and Fernande Gontier, *Simone de Beauvoir: A Life, a Love Story*, translated by Lisa Nesselson. New York, St. Martin's, and London, Sidgwick and Jackson, 1987 (originally published by Librairie Académique Perrin, Paris, 1985).

*

Simone de Beauvoir recounts her life in four of her books. In *Mémoirs d'une jeune fille rangée* (Paris, 1958; as *Memoirs of a Dutiful Daughter*, New York, 1959), and *La Force de L'Age* (Paris, 1960; as *The Prime of Life*, New York, 1962), she examines the period 1929–43, including her childhood, her successful classical studies, and her career as a professor. *La Force des Choses* (Paris, 1960; as *The Force of Circumstance*, New York, 1964) describes her experiences during the existentialist period as well as her association with Jean-Paul Sartre. In *Tout compte fait* (Paris, 1972; as *All Said and Done*, New York and London, 1974), the fourth volume of her memoirs, de Beauvoir "drew up the balance sheet of her life and her life's work," as Francis and Gontier note. Lisa Appignanesi comments that "to create a brief portrait of the life and work of a woman who dedicated 2000 pages to creating her own is something of an intractable proposition." One needs to keep in mind that de Beauvoir addressed her memoirs to future generations who would examine them as the model of her own generation.

BAIR's recent biography compiles an impressive and extensive amount of documentation. It draws on correspondence between Nelson Algren and Sartre, scholarly sources, a textual analysis of de Beauvoir's autobiographical writings, and on numerous interviews. Bair traces thoroughly the development of de Beauvoir's literary career, but her study is somewhat too romanticized and repetitive. It depends too often on personal comments and useless details that are cumbersome for the serious reader ("She ate a BLT club sandwich, a large glass of orange juice, . . . "). The sixth chapter particularly illustrates this weakness in terms of de Beauvoir's relationship with her classmates. Her relationship with Sartre remains the focal point of Bair's study, which often paraphrases de Beauvoir's memoirs. The 37th chapter, entitled "The Friendship of Women," presents de Beauvoir's friendships with Sylvie le Bon, Madeleine Gobeil, and Arlette, "a catalyst for many changes in de Beauvoir's life." The last chapters are the most interesting, tracing de Beauvoir's political and literary activities in the 1960s and 70s and her commitment to women's rights, such as the legalization of abortion. Bair argues that even though de Beauvoir actively participated in the women's movement, she "offered no concrete answers, no specific model or plan for action, no coherent theory upon which to build new forms of feminist behavior."

Ascher's and Appignanesi's studies are mainly designed for readers not familiar with de Beauvoir's life and works. Generally speaking, they give little space to her intellectual, political, and literary development. APPIGNANESI's work is poorly documented and at times too personal. For example, the author interprets de Beauvoir's affair with Bost as an assertion of "her own sexuality" and states that this affair "bore the traces of a revenge, an attempt on Simone's part to re-establish an equilibrium which Sartre's infatuation with Olga had savagely disrupted."

ASCHER's first chapter looks closely at de Beauvoir's memoirs and gives a succinct account of her upbringing and heritage, with special emphasis on the evolution of her intimate relationship with Sartre. This chapter is, however, descriptive rather than analytical, and it relies mostly on quotes drawn from de Beauvoir's own memoirs, which constitute Ascher's major source of reference. For a book written in the 1980s, it disappointingly ignores the current theoretical inquiry into "autobiography" and "autofiction." The chapter entitled "Clearing the Air—A Personal World" proves to be even more questionable as the author, in a letter addressed to de Beauvoir, relates her own life experiences to those of de Beauvoir. Needless to say, this study is not addressed to the serious biographer or scholar. (The same could be said of Appignanesi, who while pregnant reported her own ambivalence with respect to writing about "a woman who had studiously excised children from her world.") Ascher's study may serve, however, as a general guide for the reader who would like to be referred and "guided" to specific parts of the memoirs. She writes, for example, that "the second part of *The Prime of Life* covers the war years. For anyone interested in those years in France, this section, done partly through extracts from her journal, offers some wonderful scenes of Paris."

Ascher calls *The Prime of Life* "the joy of an individual pressing against the limits of freedom," and *Force of Circumstance* de Beauvoir's "sorrow and rage at understanding how political and social horrors hem people in." The fifth chapter successfully analyzes de Beauvoir's role in the women's movement and her ideas on feminism as they are presented in *The Second Sex* (1953).

FRANCIS AND GONTIER's biography on the other hand is extremely well documented and offers valuable sources of reference: unpublished correspondence between de Beauvoir and Nelson Algren, newspaper articles from the Lorraine region that reveal how de Beauvoir's grandfather's "financial ruin transformed the destiny of this 'dutiful' daughter," and finally a se-

ries of interviews with de Beauvoir. In spite of its lyrical overtones, Francis and Gontier's study provides the reader with valuable information, insights, and analyses of de Beauvoir's life and works. It is interesting to follow the development of de Beauvoir's relationship and differences with her father Georges de Beauvoir: "To Georges and Françoise de Beauvoir, the theatre was everything. Conversation revolved around theatrical gossip and the theatrical magazine *Comoedia* was read regularly." Francis and Gontier emphasize particularly the education de Beauvoir received at the École Normale in Neuilly, her preparation for the "agrégation," as well as the authors who played an important role in her intellectual development, especially Plato, Schopenhauer, Leibnitz, Bergson, and Hegel. Francis and Gontier claim that de Beauvoir's sense of revolt was in part due to her friendship with two surrealists, Michel Leiris and Raymond Queneau, who enabled her "to take her own position of opposition." The seventh chapter focuses on the war years and more specifically on de Beauvoir's rejection of the Vichy regime. For de Beauvoir, literature became her way to assume a part in the French resistance. "Sartre and de Beauvoir set out to contact all the writers who had relocated in the Free Zone and to secure their backing for Socialism and Liberty." Finally, we can examine in detail through Francis and Gontier Sartre and de Beauvoir's involvement with the newspaper *Combat*, whose slogan was "From Resistance to Revolution."

Undoubtedly, de Beauvoir's relationship with Sartre played a major role in her life and her works. Francis and Gontier review the multiple activities in which Sartre and de Beauvoir were actively engaged, claiming that "Jean-Paul Sartre was crowned the pope of existentialism, and de Beauvoir received the title Notre-Dame-de-Sartre." Their presentation of the spread of existentialist philosophy in the European and American press and of her philosophical essay *The Ethics of Ambiguity* (1948), in which she responded to the detractors of existentialism, prove to be informative. In the same manner, the descriptions of de Beauvoir's numerous lectures in the United States, her trips to Cuba, the Soviet Union, Brazil, Japan, Egypt and Czechoslovakia, where she was invited by the Writer's Union, contribute to our understanding of de Beauvoir's social role as a writer. Francis and Gontier's detailed study leads us to a better understanding of Simone de Beauvoir's influential role in the world.

—Martine Natat Antle

DEBS, Eugene Victor, 1855–1926; American socialist leader.

Brommel, Bernard, *Eugene V. Debs: Spokesman for Labor and Socialism.* Chicago, C. H. Kerr, 1978.
Coleman, McAlister, *Eugene V. Debs: A Man Unafraid.* New York, Greenberg, 1930.
Currie, Harold W., *Eugene V. Debs.* Boston, Twayne, 1976.
Ginger, Ray, *The Bending Cross: A Biography of Eugene Victor Debs.* New Brunswick, New Jersey, Rutgers University Press, 1949; as *Eugene V. Debs: A Biography,* New York, Collier, 1949.
Karsner, David, *Debs: His Authorized Life and Letters from Woodstock Prison to Atlanta.* New York, Boni and Liveright, 1919.

Morgan, Howard Wayne, *Eugene V. Debs: Socialist for President*. Syracuse, New York, Syracuse University Press, 1962.

Reynolds, Stephen M., *Debs: His Life, Writings, and Speeches*. Chicago, C. H. Kerr, 1908.

Salvatore, Nick, *Eugene V. Debs: Citizen and Socialist*. Urbana, University of Illinois Press, 1982.

Schnittkind, Henry T. (Henry Thomas), *The Story of Eugene Debs*. Boston, Educational Committee, 1929.

Selvin, David F., *Eugene Debs, Rebel, Labor Leader, Prophet: A Biography*. New York, Lothrop Lee, 1966.

*

SALVATORE has written the best biography of Debs: it reveals the full complexity of his character and his importance within the context of the political and cultural struggles from the Civil War to World War I. This Bancroft Prize-winning biography far outranks earlier efforts in its use of original documents, its analysis of Debs' transformation to socialism, and its insights into the failures of socialism. Salvatore disproves the view taken by many biographers that Debs was a "born radical." He traces Debs' gradual transformation from the Democratic party and capitalism to Socialism and "the spirit of fraternity." He places Debs' heritage in the complex American political tradition and demonstrates his understanding of the forces at work in his world. Thus, this biography provides a rich account of the forces for reform in 19th-century America.

Readers will find Salvatore's biography a compelling analysis of Debs' psychology. He is the first biographer to demonstrate Mabel Curry's crucial role in Debs' life. Debs' lover and fellow socialist, the wife of a Terre Haute professor, Mabel Curry's story adds much to our knowledge of Debs. Through Debs' relations with Mabel, Salvatore explores "the deep insecurity in Debs' sense of self" that other biographers miss. Mabel had an intense impact on Debs' final imprisonment. No biographer other than Salvatore explores the depths of that prison experience. Citing "a lifelong need for public affirmation," Salvatore argues that Debs experienced "an equally intense inability to recognize his own inner self or to share it with others." For the first time we get a psychologically compelling portrait of the man.

While the psychological portrait fascinates, Salvatore convincingly demonstrates that Debs' historical significance lies in his thoughts and actions. Many biographers dismiss Debs on this score: they find him a failure, a curiosity, a crank, with little connection to American thought. Salvatore proves that Debs helped drive "Big Bill" Haywood out of the party and argues persuasively that the failure of turn-of-the-century socialism cannot be attributed to Debs' unwillingness to lead.

Any biographer's attitude toward socialism, implicit or explicit, necessarily informs his or her account of Debs' life. For Salvatore, "the story is not complete and the final conclusion has not been written." Those biographers who see the movement itself as a failure, who cast it only in the past, present Debs to us as a curiosity. True, Debs himself, at the end of his life, would have shared this vision; for as Salvatore observes, Debs saw "nothing left but ashes." This image comes from a dream during his final imprisonment. Salvatore sees Debs as a "phoenix" among the ashes, "a symbol of regeneration and rebirth even in the midst of tragedy—a constant reminder of the profound potential that yet lives in our society and our culture."

Such language invites the question: is Salvatore too emotionally attached? The answer is, no. The work is compelling scholarly biography. Other biographers, in addition to Salvatore, note that his contemporaries saw in Debs a comparison to Christ. One Ohio minister, for example, saw his life as "a continual crucifixion." Such comparisons to Christ were also made to other contemporary reformers such as William Jennings Bryan and "Golden Rule" Jones. Salvatore is the only biographer who analyzes these allusions to Christ in terms of the culture that saw him as such. Analogies to Christ were not simply rhetorical devices, but a reflection of the "profound religious revival in turn-of-the-century America." After all, a picture of Jesus, not Marx, hung on Debs' Atlanta prison wall. If Salvatore at times looks for symbols in Debs' life it is only appropriate, for he demonstrates that Debs' life symbolizes the nationwide protest in reaction to the social revolution brought about by the industrial revolution. He shows that Debs' ideas and his actions were "firmly rooted in the American experience."

Earlier biographers distort both the man and the times that shaped him. The first biographers idealize him. REYNOLDS' life of Debs, written more than ten years before Debs' death, is an unapologetic psalm to the already converted: "His life is of yours; ye toilers, his brain, his body, his soul are aflame with truth in your cause." This biography is only of interest to those who want to analyze Debs' effect on his followers. KARSNER, who several years later helped Debs write his last articles on the prison system, had access to the man and his closest friends, and shared in the cause. Had he been able to find the distance essential to tell the full story, he would have been the ideal biographer. But Karsner is no Boswell: he was too close to the man to tell the truth. SCHNITTKIND's biography, despite its indebtedness to the help of Debs' brother and to Upton Sinclair, remains an external portrait. Schnittkind, a prolific biographer (who later published under the name Henry Thomas) elsewhere did not hesitate to take on "the biographical history of the world." He published this book under the auspices of the Independent Workmen's circle, the first in their series "Heroes of Peace and Liberty."

COLEMAN's biography, swift in its defense of Debs' faults, is casual in both methodology and approach. Coleman takes the stand of an omniscient narrator, slipping into Debs' psyche or the colloquial speech of the people: we are given a Debs "with a leaden heart and a brooding premonition"; elsewhere he assumes the point of view of those listening to Henry Demarest Lloyd: "This feller Lloyd might look like a dude but he talked like a man." SELVIN's slight, generalized, and novelistic treatment depends upon the work of Karsner, Coleman, and Ginger; it merely sketches out the story. Similarly, CURRIE adds nothing new.

MORGAN considers manuscripts of "secondary importance," which calls into question his qualifications as a biographer. His analysis of Debs' world is simplistic: as Morgan puts it, Debs "seemed to possess from birth the traces of radicalism that spring so often from that great watershed [frontier Indiana] of discontent." His attitude toward socialism as a movement ("If the Socialist Party seems to have no future, it at least has a past.") undercuts Debs as a quixotic character.

Neither Ginger nor Brommel shares Morgan's cavalier attitude toward primary sources. GINGER, while able to speak with Debs' contemporaries, was forced to maintain their anonymity. Throughout the early chapters he repeatedly cites "confidential sources" for his information. As the reader can never know and the biographer never judges the perspective and motives of these people, this account of Debs' crucial early years is seriously undercut. Unfortunately, Ginger's biography is further undercut because he "reluctantly omitted footnotes" at his publisher's request. He is eloquent in his defense of Debs' wife, but Brommel and Salvatore prove Ginger's account to be inaccurate. While defending Debs' wife Kate from the charge that she was unsupportive, Ginger devotes one sentence to Mabel Curry.

In 1978 BROMMEL wrote the first satisfactory scholarly biography. He discovered a number of Debs' speeches and essays that had been lost and made use of newly available collections of writings by prominent socialists. Brommel was the first to reveal the love between Debs and Curry, but he remains distant from it. He relied on the Curry collection, but he paraphrases her views. Thus, he provides a solid account, but lacks the depth and greater insight of Salvatore's work.

—Marnie Jones

DEBUSSY, (Achille) Claude, 1862–1918; French composer.

Dietschy, Marcel, *A Portrait of Claude Debussy*, edited and translated by William Ashbrook and Margaret G. Cobb. Oxford, Clarendon Press, 1990 (originally published as *Passion de Claude Debussy*, Neuchâtel, À la Baconnière, 1962).

Dumesnil, Maurice, *Claude Debussy, Master of Dreams*. New York, Washburn, 1940.

Harvey, Harry B., *Claude of France: The Story of Debussy*. New York, Allen Towne, 1948.

Lesure, François, *Debussy*. Geneva, Minkoff and Lattès, and New York, Congdon/Lattès, 1980 (English and French text).

Lockspeiser, Edward, *Debussy*. London, Dent, and New York, Dutton, 1936; 5th edition, revised by Richard Langham Smith, London, Dent, 1980.

Lockspeiser, Edward, *Debussy: His Life and Mind* (2 vols.). London, Cassell, and New York, Macmillan, 1962–65.

Serof, Victor, *Debussy: Musician of France*. New York, Putnam, 1956; London, Calder, 1957.

Vallas, Léon, *Claude Debussy: His Life and Works*, translated by Maire and Grace O'Brien. London, Oxford University Press, 1933 (originally published as *Claude Debussy et son Temps*, Paris, F. Alcan, 1932).

Young, Percy M., *Debussy*. London, E. Benn, and New York, D. White, 1968.

*

When music lovers everywhere celebrated the centennial of Debussy's birth in 1962, an exciting new biography appeared in Switzerland—Dietschy's *Passion de Claude Debussy*—and two books, by Lockspeiser, appeared in England—the fourth, revised edition of his concise study and the first volume of his far-ranging, deep-probing two-volume work. In Paris the composer Jean Barraqué's new study of Debussy's music was read at once by Lockspeiser and colleagues from all over the globe who gathered to exchange information and ideas and to form a society for coordinating further exchanges. They looked toward eventually providing material for a worthy biography, alongside scholarly editions of all Debussy's music, his letters, critical writings, and interviews. The worthy biography is still a distant goal in 1990. DIETSCHY's work, at last in English, with some up-dating to accommodate discoveries by Dietschy himself and others, is the most comprehensive account of the boy's family and his growth away from it, into the complex, elusive personality he was when he won fame in the first decade of the 20th century.

LOCKSPEISER's fifth edition, in its 115 pages of biography, presents essential findings of Dietschy and others up to 1980. Along with 128 pages about the work and 52 pages of useful appendices and index, this biography is the most reliable and balanced available.

LOCKSPEISER's big work (1962–65) assembles a wealth of evidence about Debussy's associations with poets, painters, dancers, musicians, and the "deep-seated movements" of ideas in his time. For all sorts of study of his techniques and purposes, this compilation is indispensable—a fine supplement to either Dietschy or Lockspeiser's concise book.

No ability to read music is prerequisite for using Lockspeiser's books. His few examples in notation on a staff can be skipped, for his interest in techniques is subordinate to his interest in purposes. The best authors of more technical studies acknowledge their debt to Lockspeiser's broad perspectives.

Earlier biographies of Debussy may appeal to readers for various reasons. While all these assume some acquaintance with compositions like "Clair de Lune" (Moonlight) for piano, and "La Mer" (The sea) for orchestra, some of them offer easier reading than Lockspeiser for readers who lack time to delve into opera or chamber music and who appreciate smooth narrative with emphasis on "human interest." SEROFF and DUMESNIL, brilliant musicians with life-long concern for Debussy's work, each supplied a bit of fresh evidence about his life. Seroff, author of a dozen other books on famous composers, was not scrupulous about facts (as Lockspeiser protested in a review). But Seroff still appears in print, uncorrected, in 1989. As for Dumesnil, his tone might fit a composer like MacDowell or Delius better than Debussy, but the interpretation of a master "dreamer" may help some aspiring pianists. HARVEY's book, intended for young people beginning to take an interest, relies on Lockspeiser's first edition (1936) for information; readers will not be misled.

More up-to-date is the booklet by YOUNG, whose musicianship and long experience as a writer enabled him to provide an introduction valuable for young and old alike; reading him carefully, adults who know Debussy fairly well might yet deepen their understanding.

The French scholar VALLAS devoted much of his life to studying Debussy's life and writings, though he showed more spontaneous sympathy with the music of Franck and d'Indy. While his patriotic bias exaggerates Debussy's patriotism, Vallas continues to be cited both in and outside of France. In 1962 Lockspeiser and other scholars referred to Vallas gratefully, but in 1990 there is no good reason for the translation to be kept in print.

LESURE's book includes a very brief biography to explain the 165 plates, which are well chosen and very well reproduced. The text, in both French and English, is not a perfunctory set of legends, but a genuine contribution to the long slow process of disseminating the most useful truth about Debussy. Lesure will help any biographer who eventually supersedes Dietschy, Lockspeiser, and Lesure himself.

—William W. Austin

DEFOE, Daniel, 1660–1731; English writer.

Backscheider, Paula R., *Daniel Defoe: His Life.* Baltimore, Maryland, John Hopkins University Press, 1989.

Bastian, F., *Defoe's Early Life.* London, Macmillan, and New York, Barnes and Noble, 1981.

Chadwick, William, *The Life and Times of Daniel Defoe.* London, J. R. Smith, 1859.

Dottin, Paul, *The Life and Strange and Surprising Adventures of Daniel Defoe,* translated by Louise Ragan. London, Paul, 1928 (translation of volume I of *Daniel Defoe et ses Romans,* 3 vols., 1924).

Fitzgerald, Brian, *Daniel Defoe: A Study in Conflict.* London, Secker and Warburg, and New York, Somerset, 1954.

Lee, William, *Daniel Defoe: His Life and Recently Discovered Writings* (3 vols.). London, J. C. Hotten, 1869.

Minto, William, *Daniel Defoe.* London, Macmillan, and New York, Harper, 1879.

Moore, John R., *Daniel Defoe: Citizen of the Modern World.* Chicago, University of Chicago Press, 1958.

Sutherland, James, *Defoe.* London, Methuen, 1937; Philadelphia, Lippincott, 1938.

Sutherland, James, *Daniel Defoe: A Critical Study.* Boston, Houghton Mifflin, 1971.

Watson, Francis, *Daniel Defoe.* London, Longman, 1952.

Wilson, Walter, *Memoirs of the Life and Times of Daniel De Foe* (3 vols.). London, Hurst Chance, 1830.

Wright, Thomas, *The Life of Daniel Defoe.* London, C. J. Farncombe, 1931.

*

Our meagre knowledge of Defoe's life has to depend to a large extent on his own statements, though these are often imprecise and sometimes open to question. None of the early biographies derives from sources at all close to Defoe, but all of them attempt to create a consistent character out of the slender evidence. For WILSON and CHADWICK Defoe is a political liberal: so he is for LEE to some extent, though Lee (*contra* Wilson) also stresses Defoe's conservatism in matters of religious doctrine. MINTO's conclusion is the desperate one that Defoe was habitual liar, but Minto's short sketch links Defoe to the political history of his time more capably than does any other 19th-century biography.

The earliest notable 20th-century biography is the first volume of a comprehensive three-volume critical study of Defoe by DOTTIN. Though the title of this volume is the same as that of

Charles Gildon's very hostile satirical biography of 1724, Dottin's life is highly laudatory. It is accurate and detailed, but does not read at all easily in its unidiomatic English translation; it has been effectively superseded by Sutherland in point of art and information. WRIGHT is superseded also; his volume is weak on historical background and is somewhat vitiated by a failure to reveal sources, but it is written in a graphic style.

The efforts of scholars over two centuries have failed to unearth many facts about Defoe's life: of no 18th-century writer of comparable standing is so little known. Consequently all biographers have been obliged to depend to a greater or lesser extent upon conjectures based on what are hopefully judged to be autobiographical passages in Defoe's enormous body of writings. The first life to make scrupulous and really scholarly distinctions between fact and speculation is SUTHERLAND's 1937 work, which sheds more light than any earlier or later biography on Defoe's elusive personality. Sutherland's research significantly increased our knowledge of Defoe's early career as a merchant as well as his last years; it also added much to our understanding of his attitude toward the Dissenters; but for all the biographer's efforts much of Defoe's life remains in the shadows. Sutherland makes the most fair-minded attempt yet to interpret his subject's mind and motives, treading a middle path between Defoe's own repeated claims to consistency and high principles on the one hand and the charge that he was politically corrupt on the other. This graceful and erudite work is much the best-written and most readable of all biographies of Defoe. Sutherland's later study (1972) has far more criticism than biography, but in a biographical prologue and conclusion Sutherland argues that, contrary to general belief, Defoe's political convictions were remarkably consistent.

Two short lives, by Fitzgerald and by Watson, are derivative from earlier biographies in matters of fact. FITZGERALD's is a "study in conflict," the conflicts being between Defoe's Puritan upbringing and certain non-Puritan inclinations over sexual matters, and the conflict in politics between Defoe as a representative and as a critic of his times. Such a scheme is altogether too simple and its argument requires too much unsupported speculation. WATSON's brief biography is lively but often inaccurate. The fully annotated collection edited by G. H. Healey (*The Letters of Daniel Defoe,* Oxford, 1955) of over 250 letters, reports, and memoranda to and from Defoe is far more important.

MOORE gathers some relevant material not found in Sutherland, from documents, letters, wills, and other manuscripts, and from contemporary pamphlets and periodicals; he is thus able to add significant new detail, particularly in the matters of Defoe's bankruptcy and his condemnation to the pillory. Moore's is not the ordinary kind of narrative biography. A summary "Chronological Outline" occupies only a dozen pages at the end of his book, the body of which combines the chronological and the topical: some chapters narrate episodes in Defoe's life (e.g., Boyhood, Marriage, Young Patriot, Friend of William, Bankrupt, Pillory); others discuss important topics with reference to the life as a whole (e.g., Pamphleteer and Public Servant, Poet and Wit, Traveler, Projector, Economist). This method does not prove as cumbrous as it sounds: there is no redundancy; Moore successfully weaves together the strands of Defoe's life and thought. Moore claims that Defoe is important for anyone who wishes to understand the modern world; he makes the case for

Defoe as "a pioneer in literature and journalism and history, one of the germinal minds in political and economic thought, a defender of religious toleration and an opponent of the evils of human slavery, an advocate of most of the effective reforms of the past two and a half centuries." Though modern historians are sceptical of such efforts to recognize the essentially secular modern world in the thought of a man born over three centuries ago, Moore argues his case well. Moore and Sutherland (1937) are the essential Defoe biographies.

BASTIAN, whose help was acknowledged by Moore, eventually produced his own study of the first 40 years or so of Defoe's life. Bastian's method of treating this very thinly documented period is "to scrutinise the available material more thoroughly, and to squeeze it a good deal harder than before, to extract biographical information from it." Much of the material, yet again, consists of possible stray autobiographical references in Defoe's writings. This biography is highly speculative: it must be used with cautious and constant reference to its commendably full and honest endnotes in order to evaluate the probability of Bastian's inferences. Written out of a very full knowledge of Defoe's writings and of the historical background, the work reads well.

In the longest of all the biographies, BACKSCHEIDER has managed to disinter a little more information about Defoe's commercial dealings, particularly in bricks and tiles, about his mission to Scotland, and about his relations with booksellers. Like Bastian, Backscheider suspends judgement on Defoe's moral character, but, in extreme reaction against the usual portrait of Defoe as something of an adventurer, she offers a characterisation that is almost bland. Her biography is heavily overburdened with detailed, repetitive, and at times confusing descriptions of Defoe's minor pamphlets; her literary criticism is banal.

Despite more recent researches, Sutherland (1937) remains the most readable, intelligent, and insightful of all the Defoe biographies.

—James Sambrook

DEGAS, Edgar, 1834–1917; French painter and sculptor.

Dunlop, Ian, *Degas*. New York, Harper, and London, Thames and Hudson, 1979.
Gordon, Robert and Andrew Forge, *Degas*. New York, Abrams, 1988.
McMullen, Roy, *Degas: His Life, Times, and Work*. Boston, Houghton Mifflin, 1984; London, Secker and Warburg, 1985.
Sutton, Denys, *Edgar Degas, Life and Work*. New York, Rizzoli, 1986.

*

McMULLEN's "impressively researched and immensely enjoyable" work (*The New Criterion*, November 1985) was the first real biography of Degas. A professional writer on art for magazines with a broad constituency, McMullen has produced a life-and-works volume for the general reader that has been critically acclaimed by Degas scholars.

When he began the project, McMullen set out to clear up the

"wonder" and "bafflement" Degas had been provoking for over a century. It seemed strange to him that with so much information about the artist and the period, his friends and his art, Degas remained elusive. McMullen has gone beyond the concerns of art scholarship and produced a coherent telling of Degas' life, art, and times by staying as close as possible to primary sources in Degas' own hand and to the testimonials of those who knew him. McMullen leans heavily on the letters and on the 37 extant notebooks (annotated and published by the much respected Degas expert T. Reff), volumes of capital importance, perhaps the most important key to knowing Degas. Throughout his chronological treatment, McMullen's aim was verification and the amassing of pertinent details in order to provide the most complete picture of the artist in all his peculiarities.

It is unfortunate that the publishers did not complement McMullen's organization with more and better illustrations. Works are often discussed in some detail without an accompanying illustration. In his otherwise positive review of the biography, Richard Thomas noted the author's imprecision with artistic terminology and connoisseurship.

DUNLOP and GORDON/FORGE have written valuable texts, emphasizing Degas the artist, accompanied by an excellent selection of illustrations, many of those in facsimile. Dunlop, an expert at Sotheby's, gives the reader a close reading of the artist's style—a connoisseur's look. Despite the coffee-table air of Gordon/Forge's volume, it includes many new insights into the relationship of Degas to his contemporary world. Either of these works would be a useful companion to McMullen.

In 1986, SUTTON's work on Degas appeared, much to the delight of both the author's and the artist's audience. It is a combination of an art historical survey, a critique of Degas' art, and a biography, containing many new contributions to the literature. Sutton, longtime editor for *Apollo*, writes well, in the tradition of Baudelaire, the Goncourts, and Sutton's old friend Roger Fry. Some readers may find the author's attitudes old-fashioned in light of current critical and historical trends. Post-Freudians and Marxists are thrown out with the bath water: "It is important, too, to remember that Degas' art and character are frequently interpreted in terms of our own age, not of his, and therefore motives are imputed to him that are not sustainable if the customs of his period are recalled." Some may also criticize Sutton's treatment of pictures by themes rather than by chronology, an example of the author's personal view of the artist. While the general student of Degas would probably benefit more from McMullen's overview, Sutton offers an alternative: the insightful results of a lifetime study of Degas, a manual written by a much-read, much-praised connoisseur.

—Faya Causey

DE GAULLE, Charles (-André-Marie-Joseph), 1890–1970; French general and statesman.

Barrès, Philippe, *Charles de Gaulle*. London, Hutchinson, and New York Doubleday, 1941.
Cook, Don, *Charles De Gaulle: A Biography*. New York, Putnam, 1983; London, Secker and Warburg, 1984.

Crozier, Brian, *De Gaulle* (2 vols.). London, Eyre Methuen, and New York, Scribner, 1973.

Grinnell-Milne, Duncan, *The Triumph of Integrity: A Portrait of Charles de Gaulle*. London, Bodley Head, 1961; New York, Macmillan, 1962.

Ledwidge, Sir Bernard, *De Gaulle*. London, Weidenfeld and Nicolson, and New York, St. Martin's, 1982.

Mauriac, François, *De Gaulle*, translated by Richard Howard. London, Bodley Head, and New York, Doubleday, 1966 (originally published by Grasset, Paris, 1964).

Werth, Alexander, *De Gaulle: A Political Biography*. London, Penguin, 1965; New York, Simon and Schuster, 1966.

*

When Charles de Gaulle arrived in England and made his famous broadcast from the BBC on 18 June 1940, he was totally unknown in this country. We know from Sir Edward Spears (whose plan brought de Gaulle to England) that the British government set aside a comparatively large sum of money in order to create publicity for him. But de Gaulle would not accept this, and he did not allow anyone to write a biography of him. This independence and desire for privacy posed a number of problems for biographers, both then and since. Another problem has been the length and variety of his career, so that biographers have tended to divide it into different aspects and periods. Much depended upon the moment when a particular biography was written: during the war years no one could be certain that it would be he who would direct the government of liberated France in 1944. After his resignation in 1947 no one could be sure that he would return to power in 1958, or that he would remain in power for more than two years.

All biographers have to take account of de Gaulle's own writings, and his War Memoirs particularly have assumed a dominating position, although they are not always accurate or adequate. De Gaulle features in the memoirs of almost everyone of any political importance who was active in the half-century since 1940. Possibly for this reason, some biographers have coupled an account of de Gaulle with that of some other leader, notably Winston Churchill.

The first biographer was BARRÈS (the son of the writer Maurice Barrès). He joined de Gaulle in London before going to the United States. The essence of his book is to recall a visit to Nazi Germany in 1934 when a number of high-placed officials referred respectfully to a certain Colonel de Gaulle, of whom Barrès had never heard. Back in France the politician Paul Reynard told him that this de Gaulle was the man who could save France, it was he who was the expert and the protagonist of mechanised warfare, much admired by the leaders of motorised units in the German army but ignored in France. Barrès also writes of de Gaulle's success in action during the 1940 campaign. He quotes at length from de Gaulle's speeches after June and from the conversations he had with him.

Although GRINNELL-MILNE had worked closely with de Gaulle for several months in 1940, he agrees that there is little to learn from him as a private individual. He describes him as simple, realistic, constant, a man of character. He does not accept that he was proud or arrogant. His pride was impersonal and necessarily dedicated to France, based on an inner humility.

Even more eulogistic is MAURIAC, the Catholic novelist, who was some five years older than de Gaulle and who had met him a number of times. For Mauriac there was an enormous gap between de Gaulle and the ordinary political world. Other politicians were stuck with their ideas and prejudices, while de Gaulle was free. Mauriac regrets however that de Gaulle was not more effective in changing the French people, claiming that he was too liberal and tolerant.

Like others writing in the 1960s, WERTH is less concerned with de Gaulle's activities as a soldier in the 1930s. He views de Gaulle as the most controversial figure on the contemporary world scene, and he tries to unify his argument by suggesting that de Gaulle was always a rebel: against the military establishment of pre-war France, against the armistice of 1940, against the Fourth Republic, against the Atlantic order. Werth depicts de Gaulle's character as always changing—sometimes friendly, sometimes moody (although invariably calculating); sometimes proud of his achievements, sometimes pessimistic about the future. Werth asked such questions as, did the French like de Gaulle? what will be thought of him when he dies?

While Werth's answers were usually favourable toward de Gaulle, the same cannot be said of CROZIER, who wrote the first full biography in English that followed de Gaulle from cradle to grave. Crozier acquired new documents from a variety of sources, and he consulted many who had known de Gaulle, not all of whom wished their names to be revealed. Apart from the establishment of the constitution of the Fifth Republic, and the ending of the war in Algeria, Crozier considers de Gaulle's presidency as a failure. He played the great game of politics, playing it for its own sake, not knowing when to stop, not recognising that he was failing to achieve his ends. Crozier believes that he should have retired earlier.

Ten years later LEDWIDGE made use of the official archives available in Paris, London, and Washington to write a full biography. He also called on his own experience as a diplomat who had served in Paris. Although he regards de Gaulle as an extraordinary human being, Ledwidge's account is judicious. Essential to his interpretation is the fact that de Gaulle acquired heroic stature early in his career in the 1940s. He then became a legend, that of the great man who always appeared at moments of crisis in French history.

COOK, a distinguished American journalist, using many sources (but not archives) returns to the adventure of de Gaulle's career. Cook shows a man with enormous willpower, determination, and purposefulness. Frequently, however, de Gaulle is shown as wishing to pay off old scores by riding hobbyhorses and purveying misleading ideas. This was particularly the case with regard to Franco-American relations, which revealed de Gaulle's desire to create tensions. It is not always a flattering portrait. Cook seems to agree with Winston Churchill's judgement on de Gaulle: "A great man? Why he's selfish, he's arrogant, he thinks he's the centre of the universe. Yes, he's a great man."

De Gaulle the Rebel 1890–1944, by Jean La Coutre, translated by Patrick O'Brian (1990), was unavailable for review at the time of this writing.

—Douglas Johnson

DELACROIX, Eugène, 1798–1863; French painter.

Huyghe, René, *Delacroix,* translated by J. Griffin. New York, Abrams, 1963.

Johnson, Lee, *Delacroix.* New York, Norton, and London, Weidenfeld and Nicolson, 1963.

Johnson, Lee, *The Paintings of Eugène Delacroix: A Critical Catalog* (6 vols.). Oxford, Clarendon Press, 1981–89.

Prideaux, Tom, *The World of Delacroix.* New York, Time-Life, 1966.

Spector, Jack, *Delacroix: The Death of Sardanapalus.* New York, Viking, and London, A. Lane, 1974.

Trapp, Frank A., *The Attainment of Delacroix.* Baltimore, Maryland, Johns Hopkins University Press, 1970.

*

A life-long student of Delacroix, HUYGHE offers a detailed critical examination of Delacroix's art in the larger context of his life in the first half of the French 19th century. By design, this book appeared in the centenary year of the artist's death, when the largest retrospective exhibition of his art was held at the Louvre, with smaller exhibitions held elsewhere. Much of the literature on Delacroix clusters about that year, including a fully documented catalog (in French) by Maurice Sérullaz.

JOHNSON's *Delacroix* also appeared in 1963, a kind of preparation for his later multi-volume work. Although the ostensible focus in this early book is on Delacroix's use of light and his painting techniques, a sense of his personality also emerges. Johnson's masterpiece (1981–1989) has been established as the definitive reference work for some time to come. The extended essays with which individual pictorial entries are accompanied flesh out many elements of Delacroix's life. (No such catalog had been attempted since 1885, when Alfred Robaut's work appeared—reprinted, without revision and without photographic illustration, in 1969).

That this major work on Delacroix should have been written in English is something of a paradox, for aside from two editions of Delacroix's journal (*The Journal of Eugène Delacroix,* edited and translated by Walter Pach, 1937; *The Journal of Eugène Delacroix,* edited by Hubert Wellington and translated by Lucy Norton, 1951), and one edition of his letters (*Selected Letters, 1813–63, of Eugène Delacroix,* edited and translated by Jean Stewart, 1971), none of Delacroix's very large body of literary work is available in English translation. As well, there is a dearth of formal biography of Delacroix in English. The lengthy introduction to Stewart's volume of letters, by John Russell, becomes then all the more valuable. Of the some 1600 surviving letters by Delacroix, those offered here were chosen to reveal the character of the artist. They feature his reaction to French life, arts, and establishment. Here as in the well-known journal, Delacroix appears as an urbane and sophisticated observer, a dedicated professional who was intensely involved with the problems of artistic creativity. There are no analytical introductions to the letters and only brief annotations.

SPECTOR concludes his short text on one of Delacroix's masterworks, *The Death of Sardanapalus,* with a chapter entitled ''The Psychological Background'' in which Spector summarizes our understanding of the artist's attitude toward women, his balance of sensuality and calculation, and his guilt at sensual impulse, with a tendency to equate eroticism with violence and death. Since Delacroix's Journal does not touch upon this painting, Spector combed his correspondence and contemporary memoirs for information.

PRIDEAUX's book, like others in the Time-Life series, offers a well-illustrated chronological survey of Delacroix's life. Prideaux sets forth the events and personalities that shaped Delacroix's attitude toward self and art. This work may be the best short introduction to Delacroix. TRAPP's work remains, however, the finest detailed and scholarly approach, though still fairly concise, to an understanding of the artist in English. Its 25 chapters, each focused on major artworks, provide biographical details in connection with the paintings. Through Trapp's elaborate apparatus of marginal footnotes, often with secondary illustrations, a personality emerges that extends beyond Delacroix's creative activities.

—Joshua Kind

DELIUS, Frederick, 1862–1934; English composer.

Beecham, Sir Thomas, *Frederick Delius.* London, Hutchinson, and New York, Knopf, 1959.

Carley, Lionel and Robert Threlfall, *Delius: A Life in Pictures.* Oxford, Oxford University Press, 1977; New York, Universe, and London, Thames and Hudson, 1983.

Delius, Clare, *Frederick Delius: Memories of My Brother.* London, Nicholas and Watson, 1935.

Fenby, Eric, *Delius as I Knew Him.* London, G. Bell, 1936,

Hutchings, Arthur, *Delius.* London, Macmillan, 1949.

Jahoda, Gloria, *Road to Samarkand: Frederick Delius and His Music.* New York, Scribner, 1969.

Jefferson, Alan, *Delius.* London, Dent, and New York, Octagon Books, 1972.

Palmer, Christopher, *Delius, Portrait of a Cosmopolitan.* London, Duckworth, and New York, Holmes and Meier, 1976.

Warlock, Peter (Philip Haseltine), *Delius.* London, J. Lane, 1923; revised edition, New York, Oxford University Press, and London, Bodley Head, 1952.

*

Although CLARE DELIUS was approached by other biographers (unnamed) not to write about her brother's life, she persisted, stating that her purpose was to picture Frederick as a normal boy growing up and not the musical genius he was discovered to be in later years. In spite of her intent, some of the incidents she describes clearly reveal Frederick's innate musical abilities. She makes no attempt to pose as a critic of his music compositions.

Clare Delius' anecdotes give authentic insights into the Julius Delius household. After Frederick leaves home, she was the only family member who kept in touch with him. The book contains a few pictures of the family, their homes, and two portraits of Frederick. Foss draws from this source in his addition to Warlock's book (see below).

Delius became a father figure to two young men: Peter Warlock, who at age 16 was drawn to Delius' music; and Eric Fenby, at age 21 drawn to his need for someone to write down his music after he became blind and paralyzed.

Through his years of apprenticeship, WARLOCK adored Delius, but much of the biographical content of his book is impersonal. Warlock shares the facts his subject remembers of his early life. The book is largely criticism of selected compositions, with no musical illustrations. Warlock's volume is enhanced by Hubert Foss' comments in the introduction and additions at the end.

FENBY reflects a more personal and warm relationship between the younger man and his older mentor. The "interlude," which covers several chapters, is written almost like a diary of the last six years of Delius' life. In the second section of his book, Fenby gives an enlightening account of the dictation process. He describes in detail the methods used and expresses some of his difficulties in writing the music down fast enough for Delius. Part three, entitled "The Man and the Composer," focuses on Delius' personality. In conversations with Fenby, a Christian, Delius discloses his intense devotion to Nietzsche. The conflicting beliefs never marred the strong friendship between the two. While Warlock turns against Delius after he leaves Grez, Fenby remains loyal to the end. In the last chapter Fenby gives details of the composer's death and burial. None of the other biographers can give an authentic firsthand account.

Although the biographical material in HUTCHINGS comprises a third of the book's contents, the information gives rare insights into the complexities of Delius' personality. He focuses his attention primarily on the composer's works, with musical illustrations included. Among the few photographs are scenes of Delius at Grez during his last days.

JAHODA has the captivating writing style of an historical novelist, yet the facts are substantiated by the list of sources. She packs emotion into her sentences, allowing the reader to see, feel, and experience the episodes she describes. One chapter depicts the development of Delius' opera, *Koanga*. The illustrations include portraits of Delius' family and his mentor, Edward Grieg, and lists of his music.

BEECHAM's most important contribution to Delius' career was the presentation of a full concert of his compositions in London, 1899, thereby bringing Delius to the attention of the English people. The resulting friendship gave Delius' wife Jelka courage to approach Beecham to write Frederick's biography. Beecham cites as his main sources of information Jelka's memory and some 600 letters in her possession. One gets the impression that Beecham tells what Jelka wants people to know. However, one of the most beneficial aspects of Beecham's account is his ability to describe the circumstances in which certain compositions were created. Notable among the illustrations are photographs of Grez, where Delius composed most of his works.

PALMER provides one of the most detailed and interesting biographies. For chapter titles, he uses the names of countries in which Delius lived throughout his adult life. Palmer intertwines biographical information with circumstances in each country that influenced the creation of particular works. This unique approach portrays Delius as an international, rather than merely national, figure. Photographs are scattered throughout the book, and examples of music scores are used to illustrate the analysis.

JEFFERSON had the help of the archivists of the Delius Trust, where memorabilia pertinent to Delius' life and his compositions are housed. The first five chapters are divided by dates, in which the events of Delius' life are presented consecutively. Jefferson's writing style is clear and concise. Chapter VI, entitled "Delius' craft," is an analysis of selected works. The book contains seven appendices, with one, entitled "Why Grez?" that provides a history of the little French village where Frederick and Jelka lived most of their married life.

CARLEY AND THRELFALL compiled pictures combined with excerpts from newspaper clippings, letters, diaries and scores, to cover the chronological events of Delius' life. This results in a fascinating account of an intriguing personality. The pictures come from various sources, listed at the end of the book. Lionel Carley has also compiled Delius' letters (*Delius, A Life in Letters*, 2 vols., 1983–88). Christopher Redwood has edited a volume of revealing articles published in musical journals through the years (*A Delius Companion: A 70th Birthday Tribute to Eric Fenby*, 1976).

—Betty Frances Pope

DE QUINCEY, Thomas, 1785–1859; English writer.

Eaton, Horace A., *Thomas De Quincey: A Biography*. London and New York, Oxford University Press, 1936.

Jordan, John E., *De Quincey to Wordsworth: A Biography of a Relationship*. Berkeley, University of California Press, 1962.

Lindop, Grevel, *The Opium Eater: A Life of Thomas De Quincey*. London, Dent, and New York, Taplinger, 1981.

Masson, David, *De Quincey*. London, Macmillan, and New York, Harper, 1881.

Page, H. A. (pseudonym of Alexander H. Japp), *Thomas De Quincey: His Life and Writings, with Unpublished Correspondence*. London, J. Hogg, and New York, Scribner, 1877; revised and expanded edition, London, J. Hogg, 1890.

Sackville-West, Edward, *A Flame in Sunlight: The Life and Work of Thomas De Quincey*. London, Cassell, 1936.

*

The first biography of Thomas De Quincey was published pseudonymously in 1877, 18 years after De Quincey's death. This study, by H. A. PAGE (Alexander Japp), takes De Quincey at his own estimation; indeed it consists chiefly of extracts from De Quincey's voluminous autobiographical writings, which not only occupy the first three volumes of his *Collected Works*, but are also scattered in the form of comments throughout his critical and miscellaneous writings. The elaborate construction of the persona of the Opium-Eater, in the pages of the various journals in which his work first appeared, with his wandering style and his progression by association and digression, allowed De Quincey to scatter autobiographical commentary throughout his works, whether it was relevant to the topic or not. Page reorganises these fragments into chronological order, and adds other materials to amplify De Quincey's account. Many letters, mostly from the collections of De Quincey's two daughters, are quoted at length, along with memoirs by De Quincey's relatives and friends and quotations from published memoirs. Page also writes from personal knowledge: "Considering the footing on which I stood with Mr. de Quincey during the last ten years of his life,— being admitted to him at all hours and in all moods, 'grave and gay,' I believe I had opportunities of knowing more about his affairs than any one, excepting his own family." Page tries to repudiate rumours that De Quincey constantly moved lodgings in order to avoid paying rent. Page makes little attempt to analyze or criticise his subject's writings or way of life, and sometimes in his approach he even seems to have caught some of De Quincey's rambling self-indulgence. In 1890 the book was republished in extended form, with twenty or so more letters. This later version, more commonly available, is identical in approach to the first edition. Page's biography leans toward the later years of De Quincey's life, the time that he was an established writer; only the first third describing the events prior to the publishing of the *Confessions of an English Opium Eater*.

MASSON's volume for the English Men of Letters series is worthy of note because of its writer's scholarly acquaintance with the minutiae of De Quincey's literary career, gained from his preparation of the 16 volumes of the *Collected Writing*. Masson was also acquainted with De Quincey in Edinburgh during the writer's last years. His account, more concise than those of Page or of De Quincey himself, relies heavily on the first edition of Page's study and on information imparted by De Quincey for biographical facts. Masson considers and estimates De Quincey by his qualities as a writer of a peculiarly intellectual kind, and he demonstrates his knowledge and understanding of these writings to the fore. Yet De Quincey's personality is left mysterious: as Masson notes, "with all his startling outside eccentricities, and even the glaring candours of his opium confessions, he remained an impenetrable being."

The two biographies published in 1936 differ markedly in style and approach from previous efforts, not least because they regard the early, formative years, and De Quincey's friendship with the Lake poets, as more worthy of examination than his later, settled life in Edinburgh. SACKVILLE-WEST provides a lively and readable interpretation of De Quincey's life and works, offering conjectural explanation of some of the impenetrability that daunted Masson. Aspects of De Quincey's life glossed over by former works are discovered and examined with sympathy. Such as the circumstances of De Quincey's marriage (the coolness between De Quincey and the Wordsworths was due to the fact that the former's first child was born three months before his wedding). Sackville-West emphasises De Quincey's sense of apprehension and desolation in the face of a hostile world, pointing to several episodes in De Quincey's life from his childhood onwards and various passages of his prose to illustrate this sense. Where his theories are most tentative, such as in his suggestions that De Quincey's youthful wanderings in

Wales were prolonged because he feared being accused of stealing a letter containing a draught for forty guineas, Sackville-West spells out reasons for his assumptions with vigorous exactitude. Sackville-West seeks to weave a coherent psychological pattern out of De Quincey's literary preoccupations and life story, attempting to go beyond the stated facts to reveal a coherent relationship between the fascinating mind as revealed in the prose, the eccentric personality, the opium addiction, and the artistic vision, an approach that has since become a commonplace of De Quincey interpretation.

EATON's biography is based on the voluminous collections of letters and De Quinceyan documents that had come to light since Page's first assay in this direction. "I have endeavoured, as far as it has been humanly possible, to be exhaustive in my research," Eaton remarks in his preface. The result is a detailed factual account of De Quincey's life that has stood as the standard scholarly biographical study for nearly half a century. In style and length it tends to the monumental.

A specialised study of an episode in De Quincey's life is offered by JORDAN's collection of letters, linked by biographical narrative, depicting the youthful De Quincey's infatuation with the poetry of Wordsworth, his mode of life as a neighbour of the poet and his family, and the eventual estrangement between them. Jordan offers background information and supplementary evidence to De Quincey's own *Lives of the Lake Poets*.

LINDOP's recent biography makes use of the wealth of contemporary academic studies concerning all aspects of De Quincey's life, including his writings, literary career, and opium addiction, as well as similar work done on his many famous friends and acquaintances, much of which is germane to the understanding of De Quincey. Lindop perforce tells much the same story as his forerunners, but in a clear, sympathetic, and scholarly prose narrative.

—Martin Gray

DESCARTES, René, 1596–1650; French philosopher and mathematician.

Cottingham, John, *Descartes*. Oxford and New York, Blackwell, 1986.

Grene, Marjorie, *Descartes*. Minneapolis, University of Minnesota Press, and London, Harvester Press, 1985.

Mahaffy, John Pentland, *Descartes*. Edinburgh, Blackwell, 1870.

Pearl, Leon, *Descartes*. Boston, Twayne, 1977.

Reith, Herman R., *René Descartes: The Story of a Soul*. Lanham, Maryland, and London, University Press of America, 1986.

Sorell, Tom, *Descartes*. Oxford and New York, Oxford University Press, 1987.

Vrooman, Jack R., *René Descartes: A Biography*. New York, Putnam, 1970.

*

Compared to work being done on other philososphers, the Descartes industry seems healthy and flourishing. While biography is not normally a preferred undertaking among scholars of philosophy, Descartes has attracted an unusual amount of biographical interest in the past two decades, even in the wake of Vrooman's "standard" study, published in 1970. While some of this work is formulaic and derivative, much of it builds on the tradition begun by Adrien Baillet in his *La Vie de Monsieur Descartes* (1691) and further advanced by Charles Adam in his *Vie et oeuvres de Descartes* (1910).

The best recent work is undoubtedly by VROOMAN, who relies on Adam and on the definitive edition of letters (*Correspondance*, 1936–63). Vrooman's biography is organized around a "series of portraits, each of which displays a different aspect of this many-faceted genius." This study celebrates Descartes' diversity, portraying him as a man of action, a well-bred gentleman, an impetuous traveler—certainly not an "ivory-tower philosopher"—who struggles throughout his life to overcome ill health. As the central figure in the *Discourse*, Descartes is the "hero of his own autobiography," but he is also a symbol of humanity. His words, Vrooman writes, narrate his own career, but they mirror the search for scientific, rational "truth" that was the center of Western thought in its movement from medievalism to modernity. Vrooman also devotes considerable attention to Descartes' six-year "romantic adventure" with Helen, a Dutch servant, and to the correspondence between the philosopher and Queen Christina of Sweden (the "Snow Queen"), as Descartes planned to write for the Swedish Court and establish an academy of learned men. Vrooman sees as Descartes' principal achievement—and the area of his most powerful, continuing influence—the creation of his philosophic method. He notes that Galileo and other contemporaries surpassed him as a scientist, but Descartes taught even his rivals to argue systematically: "The men of his time learned from him how to use his weapons against him." This method and its contribution to the "Cartesian spirit" Vrooman cites as Descartes' most crucial part in the intellectual revolution of the age.

Vrooman's biography replaces MAHAFFY's rhapsodic paean to Descartes. Mahaffy's Descartes is a revolutionary prodigy, wiping away the prejudices of previous generations and building a new intellectual foundation. The work includes much of the available correspondence and is still interesting for its discussion of Descartes' writing process in composing his essays. Mahaffy carefully details the planning of *The Principles of Philosophy*, and he follows Descartes through his various "mental crises."

PEARL's Twayne biography of Descartes dispenses more rapidly than others in its series with strict biography and devotes most of its pages to an examination of the *Meditations*. Clearly, biography is not Pearl's principal interest; he presents a concatenation of the facts of Descartes' life and some introductory context for understanding the term *philosophy* in the early 17th century. Pearl sees as the pivotal point in Descartes' life—his intellectual awakening—his famous three consecutive dreams, presumably divinely inspired, in 1619.

GRENE's book is part of Minnesota Press' "Philosophers in Context" series, and it is primarily a series of critical essays. But Part Two, "Descartes and his Contemporaries," adds valuable contextual knowledge to our understanding of Descartes' life. Grene identifies the philosopher's scholastic critics and

evaluates a variety of professional contexts, including the debate between Gassendi and Descartes and the "Gassendist alternative to Cartesianism." The book is at its strongest in its methodical critique of the "common sense school" and its opposition to Descartes.

REITH attributes late 20th-century interest in Descartes to a spirit of skepticism analogous to the one that "accompanied the scientific revolution just before and during the lifetime of Descartes." Reith is himself rather quirkily philosophical in his discussions and is particularly interested in Descartes' affirmation of faith in the Roman Catholic Church. His Descartes is one who, in spite of everything, is "basically loyal to the Church." This study is fresh and engaging, though perhaps overly subjective. It is a sort of spiritual biography, tracing the development of Descartes' theological thinking.

COTTINGHAM presents a critical introduction to Cartesian method and to applications of Cartesian philosohy, but he begins with a chapter on "Life and Times," which provides helpful background material for students of 17th-century science and philosophy. He warns, for example, that the "concept of science as we know it today did not exist in the 17th-century." Descartes broke new ground in his "attempt to give a systematic and comprehensive account of the universe."

SORELL's study, part of the Past Masters series from Oxford University Press, is brief and unscholarly. As it adds little to our understanding of Descartes, one wonders, indeed, about the need for such a book, even though the series as a whole may be filling some gaps in our knowledge. As an introduction, Sorell's book is at least lucid on the subject of Descartes' search for vocation, his hopes for discovering a "master science," and his changing relationship with the Jesuits.

Although one might wish for a more scrupulously footnoted biography than Vrooman's, Descartes is in far less need of a new scholarly biography than many other philosophers. Indeed, the spate of short series biographies has left us with a superfluity of general studies, although a highly focused critical study of one aspect of the life might be a welcome addition.

—Richard C. Taylor

DEWEY, John, 1859–1952; American philosopher and educational theorist.

Boydston, Jo Ann, editor, *Guide to the Works of John Dewey*. Carbondale, Southern Illinois University Press, 1970; London, Feffer and Simons, 1972.

Campbell, Harry M., *John Dewey*. New York, Twayne, 1971.

Coughlan, Neil, *Young John Dewey: An Essay in American Intellectual History*. Chicago, University of Chicago Press, 1975.

Dykhuizen, George, *The Life and Mind of John Dewey*. Carbondale, Southern Illinois University Press, 1973.

Edman, Irwin M., editor, *John Dewey: His Contribution to the American Tradition*. Indianapolis, Bobbs-Merrill, 1955.

Nathanson, Jerome, *John Dewey: The Reconstruction of the Democratic Life*. New York, Scribner, 1951.

White, Morton G., *The Origin of Dewey's Instrumentalism.* New York, Columbia University Press, 1943.

*

Until the publication of DYKHUIZEN's *Life and Mind*, the standard biographical account was the brief sketch by his daughters, edited by Jane Dewey and published in Paul A. Schilpp, *The Philosophy of John Dewey* (1939). Dykhuizen's work remains the only attempt at a comprehensive biography. A long-time philosophy professor at Dewey's undergraduate *alma mater*, the University of Vermont, Dykhuizen strove to track down the manuscript and archival sources that were available at the time he was working on the study. As a result, his book provides the foundation from which future accounts will proceed. But he appears not to have had access to the large body of Dewey's personal papers now in the archives of the Center for Dewey Studies at Southern Illinois University, Carbondale.

Dykhuizen's most important new contribution lies in his fleshing out the story of Dewey's formative years—his boyhood and undergraduate years in Vermont, his three years as a high school teacher, his graduate work at Johns Hopkins University, and his teaching at the University of Michigan before moving to the University of Chicago in 1894. From the Chicago years on, the focus is on Dewey the public man. Although the book constitutes a handy guide to the external details of Dewey's life, its treatment of Dewey's ideas and influence is typically limited to brief summaries of his books and articles. Thus, students wishing fuller analysis of Dewey as philosopher, educational theorist, and politically committed intellectual should consult the more specialized studies that have been published.

WHITE's slender but formidable study is the pioneering examination of the evolution of Dewey's thinking up to about 1894, when he was appointed head of the philosophy department at the University of Chicago—years during which he left behind Christianity and Hegelianism to formulate what became known as instrumentalism (or what Dewey himself preferred to call experimental empiricism). White supersedes Dewey's own brief memoir, "From Absolutism to Experimentalism," published in volume two of George P. Adams and William P. Montague, editors, *Contemporary American Philosophy* (2 vols., 1930). Although still must reading for students of Dewey, the work rests exclusively on Dewey's published writings of the period. This limitation is aggravated by White's tendency, as an academic philosopher, to treat ideas as abstractions having an independent life and influence of their own. Accordingly, White should be supplemented by two articles by Lewis Feuer, "H. A. P. Torrey and John Dewey: Teacher and Pupil," *American Quarterly* 10 (1958), and "John Dewey and the Back to the People Movement in American Thought," *Journal of the History of Ideas* 20 (1959).

COUGHLAN's is the most thoroughly researched and definitive account of Dewey's shift from Christianity and Hegelianism to instrumentalism. His most important new contribution lies in his exploitation of materials in the papers of George Herbert Mead at the University of Chicago Library to show the crucial importance for both men's intellectual development of the Dewey-Mead relationship. The work covers roughly the same time period as White's study, and Coughlan neatly describes the

difference in their respective approaches when he explains that White's treatment "is a philosopher's inquiry while mine is more an intellectual historian's, since it asks more insistently *why* Dewey thought what he thought and often goes outside philosophy to find the answer."

NATHANSON's book is a brief survey of Dewey's ideas designed for undergraduates and the general reader. Nathanson gives no more than the barest outline of Dewey's activities; he is even largely indifferent to the sources and evolution of Dewey's thinking. The work is an explication of what a devoted admirer sees as Dewey's most important contributions. Although uncritical and at times even superficial, the work remains the most accessible introduction to Dewey's thought for the layman. More extended sympathetic exegeses of Dewey's ideas by similarly loyal disciples are Sidney Hook, *John Dewey: An Intellectual Portrait* (1939), and George R. Geiger, *John Dewey in Perspective* (1958). The philosophical controversies in which Dewey was involved can be tracked in Sidney Morgenbesser, editor, *Dewey and His Critics: Essays from the Journal of Philosophy* (1977). John E. Smith presents balanced and lucid analyses of Dewey in his *The Spirit of American Philosophy* (1963) and *Purpose and Thought: The Meaning of Pragmatism* (1978). Similarly insightful is Richard J. Bernstein, *John Dewey* (1966).

EDMAN's introduction to his volume in the *Makers of the American Tradition Series* is thin—under 15 pages in length. The bulk of the text consists of lengthy extracts taken from the more important of Dewey's published writings. Since Dewey's prose style ranges from the turgid to the benumbing, this edited and abridged selection offers a relatively palatable introduction for the beginning student.

The volume edited by BOYDSTON is intended as a complement to the Collected Works being published under the auspices of the Center for Dewey Studies at Southern Illinois University. This collection of specially commissioned articles is a hand guide to the full range of Dewey's thought. Each article is followed by a checklist of Dewey's writings (including unpublished materials) on that topic. Topics range from Dewey's psychology, his philosophy and philosophical method, and his ethics, to his theory of art, ideas on education and schooling, and his lectures and influence in China. The volume is thus an indispensable starting point for any serious student of Dewey.

CAMPBELL's contribution suffers from pedestrian writing and a mechanical approach to the explication of Dewey's ideas. But the work is the most satisfactory attempt at a brief comprehensive survey of Dewey's thought over time. The first two chapters track Dewey's shift from his attempt to combine Christianity with Hegelianism to his formulation of instrumentalism, culminating in the publication of his *Democracy and Education* (1916). Chapters three through seven sketch the transformation of Dewey's "experimental naturalism" into a romantically inspired vision of "a scientific-esthetic millennium when the panacea of the scientific would be universally and spontaneously effective." The work closes with a chapter comparing Dewey with his more important contemporaries, followed by a brief appraisal of Dewey's place in the history of American thought, "with which," as Campbell euphemistically puts the matter, "his devoted followers will disagree."

Gail Kennedy, editor, *Pragmatism and American Culture* (1950) provides a handy introduction to the literature on Dewey's place in American intellectual life. The most complete bibliography of Dewey's writings is Milton H. Thomas, editor, *John Dewey: A Centennial Bibliography* (1962). The fullest listing of the vast secondary literature on Dewey is to be found in Jo Ann Boydston and Kathleen Poulos, editors, *Checklist of Writings about John Dewey* (1974).

—John Braeman

DIAGHILEV, Sergei, 1872–1929; Russian ballet impresario and art critic.

Beaumont, Cyril W., *The Diaghilev Ballet in London*. London, Putnam, 1940.

Benois, Alexander, *Reminiscences of the Russian Ballet*, translated by Mary Britnieva. London, Putnam, 1941.

Buckle, Richard, *Diaghilev*. London, Weidenfeld and Nicolson, and New York, Atheneum, 1979.

Calvocoressi, Michael D., *Musicians Gallery: Music and Ballet in Paris and London*. London, Faber, 1933.

Grigoriev, Serge L., *The Diaghilev Ballet 1909–29*, translated and edited by Vera Bowen. London, Constable, 1953.

Haskell, Arnold L. and Walter Nouvel, *Diaghileff: His Artistic and Private Life*. London, Gollancz, and New York, Simon and Schuster, 1935.

Haskell, Arnold L., *Ballet Russe: The Age of Diaghilev*. London, Weidenfeld and Nicolson, 1968.

Kochno, Boris, *Diaghilev and the Ballets Russes*, translated by Adrienne Foulke. New York, Harper, 1970; London, Lane, 1971.

Lambert, Constant, *Music Ho! A Study of Music in Decline*. London, Faber, and New York, Scribner, 1934.

Lieven, Prince Peter, *The Birth of Ballets-Russes*, translated by L. Zarine. London, Allen and Unwin, 1936.

Lifar, Serge, *Serge Diaghilev: His Life, His Work, His Legend*. London and New York, Putnam, 1940.

Macdonald, Nesta, *Diaghilev Observed by Critics in England and the United States 1911–29*. New York, Dance Horizons, 1975.

Massine, Leonide, *My Life in Ballet*. London, Macmillan, and New York, St. Martin's, 1968.

Nijinsky, Romola, *Nijinsky*. London, Gollancz, 1933; New York, Grossett and Dunlap, 1934.

*

BENOIS charts with personal knowledge the scarcely-known early years of Diaghilev in St. Petersburg, where he had come as a provincial law-student from Perm in 1890, to be received into the "clan" of artistic youth: Benois, Bakst, and Walter Nouvel. Benois had enormous influence on Diaghilev and describes the "Tartar's" manner gradually being softened. Right up to the creation of *Petrouchka* (for which Benois takes credit) they were close.

NOUVEL collaborates with HASKELL for their 1935 volume. Diaghilev's personal life, they show, cannot remain outside artistic considerations of his work. Diaghilev needed a principal dancer who was a "draw," but he also desired his love. Nouvel

writes "[Diaghilev] can be seen as the victim of a drama of human relationships with no hero and no villain." Haskell's writing is irritating when it switches from past to present tense and back again, but Nouvel's early memories are rewarding.

GRIGORIEV was Diaghilev's *régisseur* from 1909–29 (World War I excepted when there was no Company). As a graduate of the Imperial Ballet School and member of the Maryinsky Company in St. Petersburg, Grigoriev's knowledge and sense of discipline were in no doubt. Diaghilev once said "No one is indispensable; Grigoriev almost." Recounting his first meeting with Diaghilev Grigoriev writes, "He gave me a curious smile: his mouth alone smiled, the rest of his face remaining entirely serious . . . polite but cold." But at the news of Diaghilev's death, Grigoriev's dependence on him was such that he "could not take it in. . . . I grew dizzy and for the first time in my life I fainted." Grigoriev is loyal to his master and remains silent about the parade of Diaghilev's lovers who passed by singly (Nijinsky, Massine, Kochno, Lifar, Dolin, Markevich) while Diaghilev efficiently managed the Company; but he gives vital details of the 68 ballets created between 1909–29.

HASKELL notes in his 1968 volume that in Spring 1906, Diaghilev visited Greece, Italy, Germany and France. "His whole career showed a remarkable sense of timing. This was exactly the right time for him to establish himself in France with the Russian Exhibition." Thereafter, Haskell's treatment is a rehash of Grigoriev.

BEAUMONT's memoir starts in June 1912 and focuses on Diaghilev in London. As businessman and bookseller, he knew Diaghilev well and was privileged to attend rehearsals, noting, watching, and assessing the master's influence, and general irritation with the female *corps de ballet*.

CALVOCORESSI was Diaghilev's second-in-command in Paris between 1908–10 and deals amusingly with his experiences there. He was one of the few who stood up to Diaghilev, spoke his mind, and often got his way, particularly over finance. For once we see Diaghilev on the defensive! The account of Diaghilev watching Calvocoressi being taught *grands sauts* by Nijinsky is very funny.

The dancer's wife, Romola NIJINSKY (not to be confused with his sister Nijinska, the choreographer) writes piercingly about Diaghilev, blaming him for her husband's disintegration. Her views and descriptions of Diaghilev are often distorted and should be read cautiously. Nevertheless, she provides much that is new.

KOCHNO, Diaghilev's mysterious, aristocratic Russian secretary and scenario-writer, has compiled a photographic insight with previously unpublished essay, autobiographical note, and opinions on the classical dance all by Diaghilev. MASSINE's book is self-centred but he gives a precise account of his first meeting with Diaghilev and his grooming for the role of Joseph, left vacant by the newly-wed Nijinsky. His assumption as favourite and his artistic education as prescribed by Diaghilev serve as the model for other favourites who have not described them as fully, or at all. LIFAR gives a good personal account, but his book is too long, too self-important, and papers over too many cracks. He is bitchy about Massine and detests Boris Kochno.

LAMBERT devotes relatively few pages to Diaghilev, but what he has to say is important: "Diaghilev was far more than a mere impresario. . . . he had very much more genius than many of the artists who worked for him. His personality concentrated in a probably unparalleled way the spirit of a whole generation of artistic thought.'' Lambert analyses Diaghilev's methods and policies with great distinction.

BUCKLE provides the whole life, in depth, culled from all the above sources (in less detail) and from a multiplicity of others. His style is elegant, his knowledge profound. Buckle seldom offers a personal conclusion but works from established facts with authority. Seven of the few existing photographs of Diaghilev are included, except for the most famous one that shows his huge head, badger-streaked hair, and eyes staring straight at the camera. This is found on page 13 of MACDONALD, who devotes a whole chapter to Diaghilev, his appearance, manner, his effect on people, his attributes, and his *charm*.

LIEVEN, ''a figure often seen in St. Petersburg ballet circles,'' was particularly friendly with Benois and was ''in'' at the earliest days of Diaghilev's arrival in the capital and thereafter in the West. Apart from confirming much that is written elsewhere and giving events a different slant in an attractively pungent style, Lieven writes a perceptive chapter on Diaghilev, including a unique essay on his ''unisexuality'' and psychological makeup. He also has a chapter on the Company's finances, which concludes: ''The last six years of Diaghilev's life were more secure financially. He was no longer young. . . . he was tired, too, of the search for 'sensation' and of 'modernism'. . . . In short Diaghilev's career was already virtually finished. He could go no farther. His death was timely.''

—Alan Jefferson

DICKENS, Charles, 1812–1870; English novelist.

Adrian, Arthur A., *Dickens and the Parent-Child Relationship*. Athens, Ohio University Press, 1984.

Collins, Philip, editor, *Charles Dickens: The Public Readings*. Oxford, Clarendon Press, 1975.

Forster, John, *The Life of Charles Dickens* (3 vols.). Boston, Estes and Lauriat, and London, Chapman and Hall, 1872–74; edited and annotated by J. W. T. Ley, New York, Doubleday, and London, C. Palmer, 1928.

Johnson, Edgar, *Charles Dickens: His Tragedy and Triumph* (2 vols.). New York, Simon and Schuster, 1952; London, Gollancz, 1953.

Kaplan, Fred, *Dickens and Mesmerism: The Hidden Springs of Fiction*. Princeton, New Jersey, Princeton University Press, 1975.

Kaplan, Fred, *Dickens: A Biography*. New York, Morrow, and London, Hodder and Stoughton, 1988.

MacKenzie, Norman and Jeanne, *Dickens: A Life*. Oxford and New York, Oxford University Press, 1979.

Patten, Robert L., *Charles Dickens and His Publishers*. Oxford, Clarendon Press, and New York, Oxford University Press, 1978.

Slater, Michael, *Dickens and Women*. London, Dent, and Stanford, California, Stanford University Press, 1983.

Wilson, Edmund, ''Charles Dickens: The Two Scrooges,'' in *The Wound and the Bow*. Boston, Houghton Mifflin, 1941.

*

During a professional life of more than 30 years, Dickens maintained a particularly close author-reader relationship because all his novels appeared serially and because he was active also as magazine editor, public reader of his fiction, and frequent public speaker. Although his friend and first biographer, John Forster (see below), would claim that Dickens' private conversation seldom touched the world of his fiction, today's readers interested in Dickens' life have access to considerable primary biographical information contained in the collected letters and speeches. Just as so many Dickens characters seem to have lives that extend beyond the pages in which they appear, so do readers often find a recurrent authorial presence in the cumulative, recognizable personality called ''Dickens.'' When the biographical facts of his life-long interest in theatricals, his fascination with conjuring and mesmerism, and his love of various forms of entertainment all come to our attention, we begin to face the central biographical issue of whether the Dickens of the books more conceals or reveals the person whose private life so many biographers have chronicled and interpreted.

With the publication of the popular and monumental biography soon after his death by Dickens' longtime friend John FORSTER, contemporary readers and even family learned much about the Dickens they thought they knew from Forster's treatment of his many activities and his private life, especially his younger life, about which Dickens had been silent. Forster for the first time revealed that the hardships hinted at in the boyhood of David Copperfield had been Dickens' lot as the blacking-house working son of an imprisoned debtor; that the energies of the rapidly ascendent writer were those of one determined to have his way with the public and the publishers; and that the increasing restlessness of later years underscored the increasing sombreness of his final six or seven novels. Necessarily indirect about Dickens' relationships with the estranged wife and numerous children who survived him, Forster's book is most useful in its account of Dickens' rise to fame and of the many areas of his professional life in which Forster participated. Owner of many of Dickens' manuscripts, directly involved as correspondent and sometime proofreader as Dickens wrote, Forster had unique opportunity to pursue his ''first care''—the story of Dickens' books ''at all stages of their progress, and of the hopes or designs connected with them.'' But because Dickens in the late 1850s burned much of his correspondence, Forster, like all Dickens biographers, must acknowledge gaps in the record. The Forster biography has been reprinted numerous times, and modern readers should take advantage of such annotated editions as J. W. T. Ley's 1928 edition of Forster.

Through the later 19th and early 20th centuries, a number of less reliable lives and several biographical fictions of Dickens appeared as new information became available and as new interpretations of his writing were advanced. Biographers affected and were affected by debates about the lasting stature of Dickens, the nature of his popularity, the relationship of his life and art. WILSON's famous essay of 1941, ''Dickens: The Two Scrooges,'' presents Dickens as a complex writer in need of serious attention. Wilson did not think any authoritative book about Dickens had been published since Forster's *Life*, and that the typical Dickens expert was ''an old duffer . . . primarily interested in proving that Mr. Pickwick stopped at a certain inn.'' In arguing for a manic-depressive Dickens, Wilson sets the stage for a generation of biographers and critics who centered on the complexities of his character and the darkness of much of his life and work.

Thus it is not surprising that the best known and long-authoritative biography by JOHNSON bears the title *Charles Dickens: His Triumph and Tragedy*. Far exceeding Forster because of his access to much new information and because of his freedom from many constraints Forster faced in writing about a recently deceased author, Johnson set the standard for subsequent biographical study of Dickens. His well-illustrated, two-volume work is at once scholarly and highly readable, conveniently separating commentary on each of the major works from the biographical narrative. Johnson's Dickens is the exuberant entertainer in early writings, the increasingly militant anatomist of society in the 1840s and 1850s, and the desperately driven public performer and journalist of his final years. Johnson is also the first biographer to give due and balanced attention to Dickens' relations with Ellen Ternan, an "autumnal love" who had a clear impact on the writing of his final 12 years.

Since Johnson's work many more letters have been collected by Madeline House and Graham Storey for the continuing volumes of the Pilgrim Edition (Oxford, Clarendon Press, 1965–). These have been of great value to more recent biographers, many of whom have centered on specific aspects of Dickens' life. PATTEN examines Dickens the business man, clarifying many of the details of his relationships with his many publishers. COLLINS provides much information in his study of Dickens the public reader, and both the readings and Collins' story of Dickens' preparation and presentations of them are informative.

Details of Dickens' social and political interests, as well as his family life, have been discovered and assessed in the 20th century, and amid many biographical as well as fictionalized accounts, several prove reliable. SLATER's *Dickens and Women* is a comprehensive biographical record of Dickens' early loves, marriage, friendships, and liaisons, as well as his relationships with his daughters. ADRIAN further explores the record of Dickens as parent, noting also his attitudes toward his own parents. Both Adrian and Slater examine in detail the biographical information and consider the many representations of women and parents and children in Dickens' writing. Dickens' longstanding interest in and occasional practice of mesmerism is the subject of KAPLAN's stimulating 1975 study, *Dickens and Mesmerism*.

Between Johnson's 1952 life and Kaplan's later biography of 1988, only Norman and Jeanne MacKENZIE's single-volume *Dickens* is a reliable, readable, and generally sensible work. Like Johnson, however, the MacKenzies dramatize the Dickens story, building upon an epigraph from Henry James, "Genius always pays for the gift."

KAPLAN's larger study (1988) is the most complete biography since Johnson's, ranking with it and Forster's as the most comprehensive Dickens biographies. Kaplan's focus is more on the life than on the works, although he offers numerous incisive comments about Dickens' writing. Able to capitalize upon the many discussions of Dickens' life and work in recent years and with access to many yet unpublished letters, Kaplan provides more information more objectively than any of the previous Dickens biographers. He brings his learning to bear in a straightforward manner, and is particularly able to explain multiple

pressures at various points in Dickens' career. As an example of his informed perspective, his summation of Dickens' "first visible signs of middle age" is representative: as he worked on *David Copperfield*, his most autobiographical novel, Dickens seemed to find fatherhood and marriage troublesome, especially as childhood memories haunted him; "he had a future whose patterns promised to be similar to those he already knew, his opportunities for adventure limited by his personal and professional obligations, by the restraints of success, and by the pressure to keep earning at a high level." This is the Dickens Kaplan finds behind the character of David Copperfield, and it is such understanding of the manifold complications Dickens felt throughout his life that distinguishes this biography. Kaplan's is thus a more complicated, sometimes evasive, subject than was Forster's or Johnson's Dickens, and as Kaplan rightly devotes the majority of his attention to Dickens' adult years, he regards both the public readings and the novels as "intensely autobiographical, the disguised self-revelation that he was attracted to and with which he felt comfortable." Avoiding generally the histrionic sense of "triumph" or "tragedy," Kaplan finds Dickens' life full but, like the novel Dickens did not at age 58 live to complete, he suggests that for all its activity and flame, Dickens' life was perplexingly incomplete.

Dickens (1990), by Peter Ackroyd, was unavailable for review at the time of this writing. The most recent biography of Dickens, it has been reviewed widely (see Peter DaValle's review in *The Times Saturday Review*, London, 1 September 1990, and James R. Kincaid's in *The New York Times Book Review*, 13 January 1991).

—Richard J. Dunn

DICKINSON, Emily, 1830–1886; American poet.

Benfey, Christopher E. G., *Emily Dickinson: Lives of a Poet*. New York, G. Braziller, 1986.

Bianchi, Martha Dickinson, *The Life and Letters of Emily Dickinson*. Boston, Houghton Mifflin, and London, Cape, 1924.

Bianchi, Martha Dickinson, *Emily Dickinson Face to Face: Unpublished Letters with Notes and Reminiscences*. Boston, Houghton Mifflin, 1932.

Bingham, Millicent Todd, *Emily Dickinson, a Revelation*. New York, Harper, 1954.

Bingham, Millicent Todd, *Emily Dickinson's Home: Letters of Edward Dickinson and His Family with Documentation and Comment*. New York, Harper, 1955.

Cody, John, *After Great Pain: The Inner Life of Emily Dickinson*. Cambridge, Massachusetts, Belknap Press, 1971.

Ferlazzo, Paul J., *Emily Dickinson*. Boston, Twayne, 1976.

Griffith, Clark, *The Long Shadow: Emily Dickinson's Tragic Poetry*. Princeton, New Jersey, Princeton University Press, 1964.

Higgins, David, *Portrait of Emily Dickinson: The Poet and Her Prose*. New Brunswick, New Jersey, Rutgers University Press, 1967.

Jenkins, MacGregor, *Emily Dickinson: Friend and Neighbor*. Boston, Little Brown, 1930.

Johnson, Thomas H., *Emily Dickinson: An Interpretive Biography*. Cambridge, Massachusetts, Harvard University Press, 1955.

Mossberg, Barbara Antonia Clarke, *Emily Dickinson: When a Writer is a Daughter*. Bloomington, Indiana University Press, 1982.

Pollitt, Josephine, *Emily Dickinson: The Human Background of Her Poetry*. New York, Harper, 1930.

Sewall, Richard B., *The Life of Emily Dickinson* (2 vols.). New York, Farrar Strauss, 1974; London, Faber, 1976.

Taggard, Genevieve, *The Life and Mind of Emily Dickinson*. New York, Knopf, 1930.

Ward, Theodora, *The Capsule of the Mind: Chapters in the Life of Emily Dickinson*. Cambridge, Massachusetts, Belknap Press, 1961.

Whicher, George Frisbie, *This Was a Poet: A Critical Biography of Emily Dickinson*. New York, Scribner, 1938.

Wolff, Cynthia Griffin, *Emily Dickinson*. New York, Knopf, 1986.

*

A bewildering array of sources confronts the reader interested in Dickinson's life. One begins with primary sources: the variorum *Poems of Emily Dickinson* (1955), edited by Thomas H. Johnson; *The Letters of Emily Dickinson* (1958), edited by Johnson and Theodora Ward; and Jay Leyda's *The Years and Hours of Emily Dickinson* (1960), a compilation of historical documents arranged chronologically. These texts all contain useful explanatory comment.

To survey Dickinson lives is to proceed selectively. Although categories overlap, in navigating among biographies one recognizes certain distinctions. Biographies published prior to Johnson's editing of the poems and co-editing of the letters rely on imprecise versions of Dickinson's work; these biographies (e.g., Pollitt, Taggard, Whicher) naturally exclude discoveries made in recent decades. Biographies also separate according to aim. Portraits by people directly or indirectly involved with the poet (Bianchi, Bingham, Jenkins) differ from critical studies emphasizing Dickinson's writing (Higgins, Wolff). Some accounts specialize in treating aspects of the poet's experience: her role as a daughter (Mossberg), possible elements of her psychology (Cody, Griffith), her inner development and important friendships (Ward). The biographies further divide into introductory texts (Benfey, Ferlazzo) and full-scale accounts of Dickinson's history (Sewall's is the fullest, complemented by the studies of Johnson, Whicher, and Wolff). While recent biographies are generally more exact than their ancestors, one needs to understand how Dickinson biography originates and develops.

BIANCHI, the poet's niece, wrote the first life of Dickinson. Bianchi's impressions and memories seem distinctly hagiographical (and advance a since-disproved picture of Bianchi's mother and Dickinson as enthusiastic lifelong confidantes), but have the appeal of having been composed by a flesh-and-blood relative. In 1930, POLLITT and TAGGARD each brought out a biography; each attempts to resolve the question of whether or not Dickinson as a comparatively young woman felt a profound romantic attachment to an unidentified man. They select different candidates for Dickinson's affection, and both have failed to convince subsequent scholars. JENKINS, born in 1869 (when the poet was 38), played with Dickinson's niece and one of her nephews as a child; his memoir preserves recollections and perceptions of Dickinson and her family. Jenkins's prose is sentimental but holds insights about the poet's affection for children.

WHICHER wrote the earliest thorough biography, which maps out directions later scholars would explore. Whicher sets Dickinson against the background of New England culture and surveys her education and habit of seeking guidance, notably literary guidance, from older and supposedly wiser men. He discusses Dickinson's wit, her reading, her retreat from socializing, and identifies characteristics of her writing. Whicher also argues that her ostensible unidentified beloved was the Reverend Charles Wadswoth (a notion originating with Bianchi). Although in certain ways outdated (recent scholarship seems to prefer newspaper editor Samuel Bowles as the candidate for unidentified lover), Whicher's volume constitutes the original from which later biographies proceed.

BINGHAM, daughter of Dickinson's early editor Mabel Loomis Todd, contributes in two ways to our comprehension of the poet's experience. In her 1954 study of Dickinson's later years, Bingham reveals the one indisputable romantic attachment Dickinson felt, for Judge Otis P. Lord, who returned the poet's love. In her 1955 account of Dickinson's home, Bingham illuminates ordinary life in the poet's town and household, with the support of letters and other documentation.

WARD considers Dickinson's inner life by examining significant friendships and interpreting a group of poems. Ward's strongest contribution is her account of Dickinson's reliance on Josiah and Elizabeth Holland, Ward's grandparents. According to Ward (and later scholars agree), Dickinson particularly depended on the steady friendship of Mrs. Holland, whom the poet addressed as "Sister." Remarking on Dickinson's interior life, Ward maintains that certain poems reveal Dickinson's passage through a severe emotional crisis.

HIGGINS, however, contends that the poems "are doubtful sources of fact" and portrays Dickinson through a close reading of her letters. In evaluating the correspondence, Higgins builds a detailed case for Samuel Bowles as the unidentified man Dickinson may have loved. The care with which Higgins reads makes his study of the prose useful.

GRIFFITH combines critical explication and psychoanalytic theory to present Dickinson's father as an oppressive figure who had a disturbing influence on the poet. CODY, on the other hand, diagnoses Dickinson as afflicted by a deeply unsatisfying relationship with her mother. MOSSBERG feels that the essential qualities of Dickinson's poetry were informed by her childhood and that neither parent provided Dickinson with an example of how to proceed as an adult, much less as a woman poet; Mossberg's perspective is feminist. The accounts by Griffith, Cody, and Mossberg inevitably omit aspects of Dickinson's life irrelevant to their theses.

To date, the most influential biographies are those by Johnson, Wolff, and Sewall. (For more compact modern life histories, one can read the study by FERLAZZO, or the brief but thoughtful assessment by BENFEY.)

JOHNSON's interpretive portrait may be the best known. Like Whicher, Johnson locates Dickinson within the traditions of New England, specifically within the context of the Puritan heritage, which Johnson explains very well. Johnson portrays Dickinson as dwelling in three worlds—natural, human, and intellectual or spiritual. He populates the atmosphere Dickinson inhabited with crisp depictions of her family and companions. As Johnson presents him, the poet's father provided Dickinson with a trustworthy example of personal integrity. Two friends of Dickinson's maturity receive particular attention: Thomas Wentworth Higginson, the literary man with whom she corresponded from 1862 until her death, and who helped usher her poetry into print; and the writer Helen Hunt Jackson, who offered Dickinson respect and warm encouragement. (Johnson was the first biographer sufficiently to detail the significance of Higginson and Jackson.) Johnson illuminates subjects as diverse as the force of Dickinson's emotional attachments and the innovative achievements of her prosody. Some scholars would dispute Johnson's claim that Dickinson's feelings for Charles Wadsworth initiated her burst of greatest poetic productivity. While this claim seems reductive, Johnson's study holds much that is valuable, and modern studies of the poet's life begin with Johnson.

WOLFF's study, the most recent extended biography, devotes its early chapters to narrating Dickinson's experiences late into the 1850s (when she was in her late twenties). Wolff theorizes that as an infant Dickinson was unable to achieve satisfactory visual communication with her mother, which, Wolff suggests, caused Dickinson to cherish language as a secondary way of seeing. Noting Dickinson's refusal to declare her faith as a Christian in her ultimate salvation, Wolff reads Dickinson's poetry as in large part a prolonged argument with and movement toward God. Much of Wolff's study advances the thesis that Dickinson's poetry journeys toward faith, and a related thesis concerning the development of Dickinson's voice or literary personae. She does discuss Dickinson's multiple obligations as a daughter, woman, and writer. Especially helpful are Wolff's accounts of "Love in the Real World" and "The Possibilities for Publication." Yet events from about 1860 to 1886 tend to occupy this biography's background.

Although he remarks that "a 'definitive' biography is an academic illusion," SEWALL's life of Dickinson makes the illusion convincing. Sewall amasses virtually all the facts, myths, and theories about Dickinson, her intimates, and her environment. Because Sewall's account is less narrative than compendious, one struggles to absorb its wealth of information. The struggle's reward comes with the realization that Sewall avoids simplifying Dickinson's complex life into a convenient pattern.

Sewall's first volume scrutinizes externals: Dickinson's ancestry and culture; the intricate relations among her family members and their companions; the initial printing of Dickinson's poems and the attendant disputes among rival editors; and the "Dickinson Rhetoric" or skill in expression notable among the poet, her brother, and her sister. One becomes steeped not only in Dickinson's history but in the lives that touched hers. Among Sewall's many additions to our knowledge is fresh information about the poet's brother's marriage. Volume Two inspects Dickinson's upbringing, education, friendships, attitudes toward religious faith, enthusiasm for botany, independence, emotional tenacity, literary resources, withdrawal from the community—in short, the growth of her character. Sewall is consistent and evenhanded in evaluating all available evidence that may cast light on the poet's development. He aptly concludes with chapters on "Books and Reading" and "The Poet."

Appendices to both of Sewall's volumes hold historically important documents, some of which appear for the first time in this biography. Additionally, Sewall interweaves his account and notes with lucid synopses of many books about Dickinson, thereby providing a good introduction to the scholarship in general. Because of its scope and its scrupulousness, the Sewall biography is essential to people deeply interested in Dickinson's life.

—Robyn Bell

DIDEROT, Denis, 1713–1784; French writer, philosopher, and encyclopedist.

Blum, Carol, *Diderot: The Virtue of a Philosopher.* New York, Viking, 1974.

Crocker, Lester G., *The Embattled Philosopher: A Biography of Denis Diderot.* East Lansing, Michigan State College Press, 1954; revised edition, New York, Free Press, 1966.

Fellows, Otis E., *Diderot.* Boston, Twayne, 1977; revised edition, 1989.

Fontenay, Elisabeth de, *Diderot, Reason and Resonance,* translated by Jeffrey Mehlman. New York, G. Braziller, 1982 (originally published as *Diderot ou le matérialisme enchanté,* Paris, Grasset, 1981).

France, Peter, *Diderot.* Oxford and New York, Oxford University Press, 1983.

Mehlman, Jeffrey, *Cataract: A Study in Diderot.* Middletown, Connecticut, Wesleyan University Press, 1979.

Morley, John, *Diderot and the Encyclopedists* (2 vols.). London, Macmillan, 1878; New York, Scribner, 1879.

Wilson, Arthur M., *Diderot* (2 vols.). New York, Oxford University Press, 1957–72.

*

Most of the works about Diderot not surprisingly select some aspect of his extremely varied activity or output for attention. Most critical writing has appeared in French, and most of it has been analytical rather than biographical, but there is some straightforward biography in English. MORLEY's two-volume work of 1878, although limited by its liberal Victorian outlook and its dated literary techniques, indicated Diderot's importance as the central figure in the French Enlightenment.

The next attempt at a full-scale biography was by CROCKER, the author of further works on Diderot, including *Diderot's Chaotic Order: Approach to Synthesis* (1974), and of a controversial two-volume account of the thought of the whole of the French Enlightenment (1959 and 1963). Crocker's later work confers a retrospective value on *The Embattled Philosopher,* which it would otherwise have been possible to overlook as a novelistic approach to the writing of biography, with re-created conversations, trite or coy chapter headings ("Love Finds a Way," "Wherein Some Changes Occur"), and a good deal of atmospheric reconstruction: "On a fall day of 1729, the creaking, dust-covered stage from Langres passed through the gates of Paris. The nose of a 16-year-old provincial boy pressed against the thin window pane. . . ." There follows a somewhat fanciful evocation of what Diderot saw and experienced, from a literary point of view inexpertly contrived, with the narrator shifting un-easily between vantage points, sometimes employing the tech-niques of a novelist and sometimes those of an historian. There is however much solidly informed comment. All quotations are translated, even book titles, which is rather misleading, and there is an index.

WILSON's two volumes constitute a classic biography, al-though the later volume draws heavily on a French work by Jacques Proust (1962; revised 1967). Wilson gives his reader a formal index, bibliography, and notes as well as considerable psychological insight into his complicated subject. He shows us a Diderot uninhibitedly in search of fame and, in lieu of a heav-enly reward he didn't believe in, posthumous celebrity. Diderot in fact felt insufficiently appreciated and at least a generation ahead of his contemporaries. Wilson is particularly good on Di-derot's politics, economic circumstances, passion for Sophie Volland, and his accounts of the Louvre *salons*. He is less inter-ested in literary criticism than most writers on Diderot, and what there is of literary criticism sometimes lacks penetration to the point of inadequacy. But this is a good, readable, and accu-rate account of Diderot's life, and it is likely to remain the stan-dard full English biography for some time, although we can expect more detailed studies on some aspects of the life.

BLUM's much shorter volume draws on Morley, Crocker, and Wilson as well as on the major French sources. It gives a sharp, incisive, and clear account of Diderot's intellectual problems and the changes his thinking underwent, highlighting his interest in the possibility of virtuous atheism, his obsession with key words that recur in ever-shifting attempts to define the self ("nature," "society," "virtue"), and his messianic view of the artist's task to "lead men to virtue." The works are sensibly discussed in a biographical setting, and Diderot's own doubts and hesitancies are convincingly assessed, with the major change of outlook sit-uated somewhere between 1761 and, at the latest, 1774.

The biography by FELLOWS, first published in 1977, fits into the formula of Twayne's World Authors series, although the 1989 edition gives no open indication of that fact. Fellows en-dorses Taine's view of the preeminence of Diderot over Voltaire and Rousseau, writes engagingly, and notes how late the 20th century started fully to appreciate Diderot's achievements. He is fully aware of the hostility between the secularising academic and the traditional Catholic worlds in France during the late 19th and early 20th centuries. Fellows writes what is essentially intel-lectual history, and therefore sensibly takes account of the Soviet glorification of Diderot as the precursor of dialectical material-ism, but he is not a stylist, and the fastidious will tire of "fierce" loyalties, "bastions," "yokes," and "a severity which borders on the ruthless." However, Fellows gives a well-presented account of previous studies on Diderot and of Di-derot's own works. He is particularly good on the way in which Diderot's claustrophobia shows through in *La Religieuse*, Di-derot's indifferently written novel from which Fellows convinc-ingly disinters the important themes of madness and sexual deprivation. There is a chronology, an index, a bibliography, and notes.

Three further works should be mentioned, none of them for-mal biographies, but each containing important biographical ma-terial. MEHLMAN's 1979 work gives a very general account of its subject's career, with notes but an index only of Diderot's works. The same author published in 1982 a translation of de

FONTENAY's work which is partisan in its anti-religious ex-ploitation of Diderot's lesson in "simplicity, seriousness and in-difference." This is another light, general study without serious scholarly pretensions. Its best feature is the perceptive introduc-tion. FRANCE's book contains an expert selection of 47 of the famous letters in which Diderot always wrote at his most per-sonal. These letters, from the 189 surviving out of a total of 553, undoubtedly include the most fascinating, with examples from all the periods in Diderot's life. The book contains an introduc-tion and an index.

A series of *Diderot Studies* has been appearing sporadically since 1949, and there now seems no doubt that Diderot is in the end intellectually the key figure in the French Enlightenment as well as its leader by virtue of his editorship of the *Encyclopédie*. There is a serious need for a properly researched and psycholog-ically perceptive biography, but its author would have to com-bine an improbable degree of expertise in intellectual history with equally developed talents in literary analysis.

—A. H. T. Levi

DIETRICH, Marlene, 1901–   ; German-American film ac-tress and singer.

Dickens, Homer, *The Films of Marlene Dietrich*. New York, Cadillac Publishing/Citadel Press, 1968.
Frewin, Leslie, *Dietrich: The Story of a Star*. New York, Stein and Day, 1967.
Higham, Charles, *Marlene: The Life of Marlene Dietrich*. New York, Norton, 1977; London, Hart-Davis MacGibbon, 1978.
Kobal, John, *Marlene Dietrich*. London, Studio Vista, 1968.
Morley, Sheridan, *Marlene Dietrich*. New York, McGraw-Hill, 1976.
Walker, Alexander, *Dietrich*. London, Thames and Hudson, and New York, Harper, 1984.

*

Most biographers of Marlene Dietrich emphasize the problem of analyzing both her personal life and her image, since no one believes the two actually coincide. Those who write of Diet-rich's life, therefore, have a wide range of choices in approach-ing her: some have opted for ascertainable facts, others have examined both life and legend, while still others have traced the manifestations of cult figure and film image only.

The best brief presentation of Dietrich's life in terms of ascer-tainable facts is by DICKENS. In fact, this book seems to have been the first to publish news of the discovery of Dietrich's birth certificate after years of controversies concerning the subject's true age. As one of Cadillac Publishing Company's "films of" series, Dickens' work deals primarily with Dietrich's film ca-reer, giving by far the best account of the performer's German movies before *The Blue Angel*.

HIGHAM's biography, based on research that included over 160 interviews with Dietrich's friends, colleagues, and directors, is a well-written narrative. Higham spends a great deal of time speculating on Dietrich's masks, magic, her romanticism and her uniqueness as an image, while at the same time he treats her personal life as a series of romantic and sexual encounters with the great and near great. The possibilities of Dietrich's love life are thoroughly explored; it is enlightening to note, in this connection, that James Stewart and Marlene Dietrich are lovers in most biographies of her, but they are not in biographies of him. This trivial fact illustrates the traditional journalistic biographer's approach to female subjects. Nevertheless, Higham offers an entertaining and probably reliable version of Dietrich's career.

FREWIN's book looks even more like a novel since it lacks an index and almost all other paraphernalia of scholarly biography. It is mercifully brief, concluding with a chapter that is very typical among cult-figure biographies: entitled "What is Marlene?" The chapter presents a series of paradoxes about the subject (goddess/saloon queen; beautiful/lonely; realist/clown; artist/woman), which eventuate in the passage: "What is Marlene? I do not know." At the end of this work, we do not know either, and many readers could not care less. The puzzle of personality receives more attention here than usual, but the common pattern of biographies about such celebrities as James Dean, Judy Garland, Marlene Dietrich, and so on, is to present them as if they belonged to some other species. Romantic biographers flock to these figures, frequently obscuring them like moths around a candle.

MORLEY approaches Dietrich as legend in order to scrutinize the production and shaping of her mystique. His book is a valuable study, especially in its sections on Dietrich the cabaret singer. KOBAL's brief, copiously illustrated tribute (although with badly reproduced photographs) also traces the growth of the legend with only cursory references to the legend's life. This book's primary contribution is probably the discography in the appendix.

For the very best of Dietrich biographies, read WALKER, a film scholar whose careful analysis and balanced treatment are refreshing. He approaches Dietrich's life by dividing it into three segments: Berlin, Hollywood, and On the World Stage; each receives detailed scrutiny. In this biography both legend and life become clear. Walker finds patterns that tie various aspects of Dietrich's personality and career together; for example, he offers a compelling and convincing theory of Dietrich's relationship with the military as a formative aspect of her character. In fact, he is one of the few biographers who seems to think Marlene Dietrich might be an explicable human being. The illustrations in Walker's volume are beautifully selected and handsomely reproduced; it contains the most visual evidence that Marlene Dietrich was a true icon of film.

In her autobiography, called simply *Marlene* (1989), Dietrich repudiates all the biographies, claiming that none of her "so-called biographers ever had the courtesy to consult" her. In the course of her account she makes some extraordinary claims, including such statements as "I never went to the wild parties in Hollywood, never experienced those aspects which make it famous." Literally hundreds of photographs exist that show Marlene Dietrich—always surrounded by the rich, famous and/or beautiful, herself usually outrageously coiffed and gowned—caught up in the whirl of Hollywood nightlife. She seems less than candid in her memoir; in fact, she seems less than candid in most biographies as well. Much of the misleading information about her apparently came from the star herself. It is interesting

to note that her own life story includes relatively little "romance," but a great deal of highly knowledgeable technical information about filming, lighting, and costuming.

Another fascinating source of Dietrich biography is not a book, but a film (now available on video), called *Marlene*, directed by her friend and co-star, Maximilian Schell. In it, the actual Marlene Dietrich does not appear, only past images of her, while she (in the present tense of the film) comments in her aging but still inimitable voice. She essentially dismisses her own legend, more aware than anyone else of how her mystique was produced and what it cost her as a human being. The bitterness in her virtual dismissal of her own beautiful images is doubly ironic because she hides from the camera—in order not to reveal how little she resembles herself—even as she scorns what is revealed. She withholds a final image and thus retains her power to mystify.

—Richard Sears

DINESEN, Isak [*born* **Karen Christentze Dinesen;** *later* **Baroness Blixen-Finecke**], 1885–1962; Danish writer.

Migel, Parmenia, *Titania*. New York, Random House, and London, M. Joseph, 1968.
Thurman, Judith, *Isak Dinesen: The Life of a Storyteller*. New York, St. Martin's, 1982; with subtitle *The Life of Karen Blixen*, London, Weidenfeld and Nicolson, 1982.

*

MIGEL presents an uncritical portrait of the romantic persona that Dinesen often portrayed herself to be. Although Migel's claim that she wrote in response to Dinesen's request is technically correct, Migel herself offered to write a biography that would follow Dinesen's own instructions, and Dinesen agreed only after another writer said he could not write her biography. In a style at once anecdotal and reverent, Migel begins with a history of the Dinesen family home at Rungstedlund, drawing a direct line of descent from the poet Johannes Ewald, who once lived there, to Wilhelm Dinesen, Karen Dinesen's father; her framework is thus Dinesen's lineage as a romantic artist rather than as the member of the Danish bourgeoisie. Over half the book considers the 1950s and early 1960s, when Migel herself knew Dinesen best, and its sources are notes based on conversations with Dinesen and a few acquaintances; her account of Africa concentrates on Dinesen's relationships with Bror and Denis, and it depends on her recollections and fictionalized accounts in *Out of Africa* (1937) and *Shadows in the Grass* (1960). Migel's discussion of a few tales plays a minor part in the book and illustrates how different characters express Dinesen's personal reflections. Calling Dinesen "Tanne," the name used only by her family and intimate friends, Migel describes events and relationships from the perspective of an artist who is benevolent, sensitive, charismatic, and often misunderstood. Partly because the book often reads like a romantic novel, it seems to give an intimate view of Dinesen's friends and of her daily life. It includes useful anecdotes and valuable photographs.

THURMAN portrays Dinesen to be a complex and contradictory character. Her framework is the antithesis between the bourgeois values Dinesen associated with her mother and the romanticized aristocratic values that she associated with her father; like Migel, Thurman shows that Dinesen's tendency to idealize her father shapes her attitudes and writings, but she uses a Freudian interpretation to analyze that relationship's various implications. She begins by describing Dinesen's great-grandparents in order to present the social and cultural dynamics that governed Dinesen's family relationships. After a detailed account of Dinesen's childhood and youth, Thurman gives a year-by-year account that includes both historical and social detail and draws upon archival material—letters, unpublished manuscripts, and family documents. Thurman was the first to discuss at length the diagnosis of Dinesen's syphilis and its importance to her, and in describing Dinesen's most complicated relationships she presents and weighs varying and conflicting perspectives. Her account of Dinesen's life in Africa resists ideological judgments and provides a valuable gloss to Dinesen's own memoirs, and she provides useful biographical contexts for the major tales. The book is reliable and comprehensive, and it never gets bogged down in its own detail and analysis.

Readers will find useful perspectives on different aspects of Dinesen's life in several other books, none of which pretend to offer a complete account of her life and works. Her two memoirs, *Out of Africa* and *Shadows on the Grass*, describe actual events and persons, but they idealize Dinesen's own position and experiences. In her *Letters from Africa, 1914–1931* (edited by Frans Lasson, translated by Anne Born, Chicago, 1981) readers will find fascinating accounts of her daily life in Africa and important insights into her attitudes. Erol Trzebinski's biography of Denys Finch Hatton, *Silence Will Speak* (Chicago, 1977) provides a detailed though somewhat romanticized view of the relationship between Dinesen and Finch Hatton and complements the view of Africa in Dinesen's letters and memoirs. Thomas Dinesen's personal memoir, *My Sister, Isak Dinesen* (translated by Joan Tate, London, 1975), presents a positive view of Dinesen's relationship to her family and includes his own perspective on the African farm. *The Pact: My Friendship with Isak Dinesen* (translated by Ingvar Schousboe and William Jay Smith, Baton Rouge, 1983), Thorkild Bjornvig's description of his personal relationship with Dinesen in the early 1950s, provides insight into the intensity of her personal and familial relationships and includes biographical information not found elsewhere. In *The Power of Ares* (translated by Lise Kure-Jensen, Baton Rouge, 1987), Anders Westenholz includes previously unavailable correspondence between Dinesen's uncle, Aage Westenholz, regarding the financial conditions of the African farm. Each of these books has an explicit bias and claims authoritative insight into Dinesen's character and personal life; together, they provide a valuable composite view that complements Thurman's more objective and comprehensive biography.

—Judith Lee

DISNEY, Walt, 1901–1966; American film producer.

Feild, Robert D., *The Art of Walt Disney*. New York, Macmillan, and London, Collins, 1942.

Miller, Diane Disney (as told to Peter Martin), *The Story of Walt Disney*. New York, Holt, 1957.

Mosley, Leonard, *Disney's World: A Biography*. New York, Stein and Day, 1985; London, Grafton, 1986.

Schickel, Richard, *The Disney Version: The Life, Times, Art and Commerce of Walt Disney*. New York, Simon and Schuster, and London, Weidenfeld and Nicolson, 1968.

Shows, Charles, *Walt: Backstage Adventures with Walt Disney*. La Jolla, California, Windsong Books, 1979.

Thomas, Bob, *Walt Disney: An American Original*. New York, Simon and Schuster, 1976.

*

That famous personages often go to Herculean lengths in generating favorable public images of themselves presents a particularly formidable stumbling block for the Disney biographer. During the filmmaker's life, as well as after his death, his huge organization, in the business of creating images to begin with, controlled access to Disney archives while painstakingly projecting a Disney of sunny disposition and lighthearted good will toward all. That Disney, indeed, possessed such qualities in some measure only complicates the issue, for many of his actual traits would seem to confirm the idealized portrait, and once the biographer probes beyond the public mask he may well feel, at least initially, that he has found a personality overlapping the one manufactured by the propagandists of Disney's publicity machine. Added to that, the public has dearly yearned to believe in a eupeptic "Uncle Walt," thus encouraging what it wants to see in print. For such reasons, many sources need to be eyed with considerable circumspection.

Somewhat typically, SHOWS offers an *opéra bouffe* of backstage Disney antics: Walt hamming it up, playing practical jokes, at times turning surly but usually returning to his sunny self. THOMAS appropriately assigns far more variety to the personality, but with a view that, for all its delightful writing and many details, bears the *official stamp* of Walt Disney Productions and the lack of depth required for such certification. Though MILLER writes about Disney from the perspective of an admiring daughter—and with a style "youthfully simple," as N. E. Taylor has it—nonetheless hers is the most intimate account of the man we have. Of the many books exploring Disney's technical methods and innovations, FEILD's especially gives an insider's view reflecting the man's inventive acuity and insistent perfectionism that made the former farm boy a leader in a highly competitive industry.

Both bent on finding the truth behind the created mystique, yet both to a degree hampered in their efforts by the official guardians of the Disney image, Schickel and Mosley have produced two essential studies with differing emphases. SCHICKEL is at once the more comprehensive, complex, and speculative of the two. Though at the outset the author claims his "is a study of a public man," not a revelation of "Disney's personal life," by way of pursuing the corporate organizer, entrepreneur, and well-known figure of popular culture, Schickel also fills in many of the brush strokes in Disney's private life. On this score, Schickel finds in Disney a Midwestern loner of no great intellectual depth and little interest in cinematic art, but for all that a man highly ambitious, technically bright, and so gifted at managing business and people that he turned a one-man studio into a cluster of successful corporations. Multi-disciplined, Schickel proves particularly adept at analyzing Disney in terms of public taste, politics, religion, and psychology. In doing this, he sometimes runs the risk of ranging too far in his analyses. He doesn't hesitate to bring Freud to bear on his subject, and his comparison of the moviemaker to Ernest Hemingway (both of whom lived in Kansas City at approximately the same time), though intriguing, strikes one as strained, given the vast differences between the two men. Schickel seems torn throughout, pained on the one hand by Disney's "sickly blend of cheap formulas packaged to sell," as novelist Julian Halevy observed, yet on the other mesmerized by Disney's nationwide influence. In contrast to Schickel and not nearly so complex, MOSLEY shows himself more accepting. He sees Disney not as endlessly driven toward success by psychological weaknesses but as an exceptionally, if narrowly, talented figure with the flaws that beset many men.

Walt Disney: A Guide to References and Resources, by Gartley and Leebron (Boston, G. K. Hall, 1979) compiles the films, archives, and writings of Disney. Together with a critical survey, its annotated list of books and articles about Disney will prove a special helpmate to the biographer.

—Peter Wild

DISRAELI, Benjamin [1st Earl of Beaconsfield], 1804–1881; English statesman and writer.

Blake, Robert, *Disraeli*. London, Eyre and Spottiswoode, 1966; New York, St. Martin's, 1967.

Bradford, Sarah, *Disraeli*. London, Weidenfeld and Nicolson, 1982; New York, Stein and Day, 1983.

Clarke, Sir Edward, *Benjamin Disraeli: The Romance of a Great Career*. London, J. Murray, and New York, Macmillan, 1926.

Cromer, Evelyn Baring, 1st Earl, *Disraeli*. London, Macmillan, 1912; New York, 1913.

Froude, J. A., *Lord Beaconsfield*. London, Low Marston, and New York, Harper, 1890.

Jerman, B. R., *The Young Disraeli*. Princeton, New Jersey, Princeton University Press, 1960.

Kebbel, Thomas E., *Life of Lord Beaconsfield*. London, W. H. Allen, and Philadelphia, Lippincott, 1888.

Meynell, Wilfrid, *Benjamin Disraeli: An Unconventional Biography*. London, Hutchinson, and New York, Appleton, 1903; revised as *The Man Disraeli*, Hutchinson, 1927.

Monypenny, William F. and G. E. Buckle, *Life of Benjamin Disraeli, Earl of Beaconsfield* (6 vols.). London, J. Murray, and New York, Macmillan, 1910–20.

Pearson, Hesketh, *Dizzy: The Life and Personality of Benjamin Disraeli*. London, Methuen, and New York, Harper, 1951.

Walford, Edward, *Life and Political Career of Earl of Beaconsfield*. London, F. Warne, 1881.

*

When Disraeli died in 1881, it was generally known that his private secretary, Lord Rowton, would write the official life; so it was natural that others should attempt sketches, political appreciations, and personal evaluations. WALFORD was first off the mark, with a work somewhat flimsy in fact and evidence, which stressed Disraeli's pride of Jewish race, his foppery, the influence of his wife's money, and his intellectual brilliance. KEBBEL's work, seven years later, was more adulatory; for Kebbel the romantic glow of "Young England" had not been dimmed by nearly half a century. He endorses and admires the anti-bourgeois tone of Disraeli's aristocratic associates. Realizing perhaps that he was touching on an issue that would prove endlessly debatable, Kebbel is a strong defender of his hero's consistency. Stout denial is his preferred formula for episodes in Disraeli's career that might be considered dubious, such as his appeal for office to Sir Robert Peel, and his subsequent denial of the fact. In the aftermath of the Protectionist split of 1846, Disraeli is credited with having "raised the Conservative Party from the dust," and Kebbel hardly tries to meet the obvious objection that the result was many long years out of office.

FROUDE, the author of the standard biography of Carlyle, also wrote a short book on Disraeli. Though the points where his life impinged on Disraeli's were few and fairly unimportant, Carlyle was a persistent presence in the book, just because he was always in the author's mind. A partisan Tory work, it plays down issues like the Armenian massacre, where Disraeli's great opponent, Gladstone, might have seemed to get the better of him. Froude strongly defends Disraeli's character and honest purpose. "If he was ambitious," he says, "his ambition was a noble one." In a curious passage, Froude offers a secularist defence of the sincerity of Disraeli's religious position, especially his idea of Christianity as completed Judaism. Here he stresses an Asiatic mind as the source of Disraeli's convictions, his eloquence, and his literary and oratorical style. Interesting, and perhaps strange, is Froude's refusal, after more than two decades of social peace and increasing prosperity, to admit that the bold increase in the franchise in Derby's and Disraeli's Reform Bill of 1867 had now been justified by results. He could not forget that Carlyle had prophesied doom, or conceal a slight disappointment that Carlyle had been shown to be utterly wrong.

For MEYNELL, Disraeli's mind and character were more interesting than his political life. He sees his affection for his sister, Sarah, as the guiding star of his life, far stronger than his feeling for his wife, or the loves of his old age. He was the first to emphasize the importance for Disraeli of persistent financial troubles. Meynell sees the contest between Disraeli and Peel as essentially one between romance and dullness, so that the political merits receive little attention. He admits, in contrast to Kebbel, that Disraeli told a lie when denying that he had asked Peel for office, but is resolute in justifying the untruth. He is aware of the volte-face over Catholicism in the years between the publication of *Tancred* (1847) and the markedly hostile *Lothair* (1870); but he softens it down in such a way as to make it seem a fairly natural development rather than a cynical concession to prejudice. In general, Meynell's aim seems to be to humanize the legend for a new generation that had not known Disraeli in the flesh.

Meanwhile, in 1903, Morley had produced his voluminous life of Gladstone; and since Gladstone had lived no less than 17 years after Disraeli's death, the dilatoriness of Lord Rowton in so long producing nothing was becoming both a joke and a scandal. *The Times*, with whom the power of selection lay, appointed one of their journalists, the Ulsterman W. F. MONYPENNY, to replace Rowton. He completed with fair speed more than a third of the work, but his death at the age of 46 led to the appointment of the editor, G. E. BUCKLE. Both men were highly intelligent, keen students of politics, and expert handlers of documents. Buckle had perhaps the greater insight and distinction of style. In its reticence about sex and money, their book belongs rather to the generation before its own. But in every other respect it is a magnificent monument, one of the greatest of all political biographies, which fully justifies its immense length (over 3000 pages). Of its many qualities, we may single out here especially its ability to place the reader in the world of the year with which it is dealing, and to confront him with the information, views, hopes, and fears that affected decisions and decided success or failure.

Lord CROMER, in a brief but telling sketch, which began as a review of Monypenny's first volume, presents Disraeli as a man of undaunted courage, but with no firm principles. He emphasizes Disraeli's "oriental" love of intrigue and finery. Disraeli's greatest distinction, for Cromer, is his far-sighted understanding of the measures needed to alleviate the condition of the poor; but oddly, writing 45 years after the event, Cromer seems to take a short view of the long-term conservative effect of the franchise settlement of 1867, in which Disraeli seems to have been much more nearly right than almost all his critics.

CLARKE was one of those who applied to be entrusted with the completion of Monypenny's work at the time of his death; we cannot regret that his application was unsuccessful. He is inclined to sentimental adulation, and if he finds Disraeli on any point indefensible, he uses a phrase like "for once he was less noble than himself." His political judgment is not very coherent: he praises Disraeli's record in social reform and yet has the gravest doubts about the wisdom of the settlement of 1867. He anachronistically quotes a speech of 1859, in which Disraeli showed that he, in common with almost every leading politician at that time, had reservations about the growth of popular power, presenting it as if the experience of two generations had in no way altered perspectives. He is unfair to Peel, whom he calls "unstable," and he is vague on the subject of Disraeli's religion. On one point alone is he severe; he calls Disraeli's philandering in old age absurd.

PEARSON represents an intermediate stage between the reticence of earlier and the frankness of later biographers concerning Disraeli's private life. He sketches Disraeli's relations with Henrietta Sykes and with Lady Bradford, but also pays tribute to the sincerity of Disraeli's devotion to his wife. He over-interprets the novels in an autobiographical sense, and is apt to be incurious or superficial in his political judgments. He sees Disraeli's flattery of the Queen and others as an instinctive part of his nature, rather than the fruit of calculation.

JERMAN sees that the political story had been thoroughly told while much was still unrevealed about Disraeli's private life. His sources are good; indeed, in much of the work, he is using papers that Rowton knew, and Monypenny saw, but decided not to use. He shows Disraeli exploiting Austen for money and political advancement, and he gives a full account of Disraeli's affairs with Mrs. Bolton and Lady Sykes, a lurid tale of shared mistresses and complaisant husbands. At the same time Jerman shows Disraeli keeping a cool head, guided always more by ambition than by passion. He quotes as thoroughly representative of his subject the words: "I may commit many follies, but I shall not marry for love."

BLAKE succeeds on the whole in forming a synthesis of all previous work, and his combination of full information, wise political reflection, and sturdy common sense is attractive. While he by no means supersedes Monypenny and Buckle, his book remains the most reliable and accessible for those who want a full, but still much less detailed, account. Blake is not bemused by his subject, does not idealize him or denigrate him, but sees him, more than most writers have done, as a remarkable but not unique part of the ordinary political process. He stresses the solidity of Disraeli's family background, and the harm he did to his early career by his dandyism and outrageous writings, and by financial irresponsibility. He sees "Young England" as the reaction of a defeated aristocratic class, which Disraeli never took too seriously. In wrecking Peel's career, Blake maintains, Disraeli came near to wrecking his own and the prospects of his party. Blake sees in Disraeli's career as minister, and eventually as Prime Minister, more a brilliant Parliamentarian, a resourceful improviser, than a far-sighted statesman, and his final judgment is that while Disraeli sometimes had great and prescient ideas, he was also guilty of a good deal of nonsense. At the same time he has a natural sympathy with a man whose statesmanship was practical and tactically astute, and is somewhat impatient with Disraeli's more moralizing critics.

Since Blake, the only contribution of importance has been from BRADFORD. She was able to use new material from the Dufferin papers, which throws new light on Disraeli's early romance with Helen Blackwood and his friendship with Lady Bradford. She stresses the complicated relationship of feeling between Disraeli's wife and his sister, Sarah. The general interpretation is that he was a man of "passionate temper controlled by iron reserve." The interpretation of the novels is much too biographical, an elementary but extraordinarily common fault in literary criticism.

—A. O. J. Cockshut

DODGSON, Charles Lutwidge. See CARROLL, Lewis.

DOMINIC, Saint, *ca.* 1170–1221; Castilian churchman, founder of the Dominican order of friars.

Bedouelle, Guy, *St. Dominic: The Grace of the Word*, translated by Mary Thomas Noble. San Francisco, Ignatius Press, 1987.

Drane, Augusta T., *The History of St. Dominic, Founder of the Friars Preachers*. London and New York, Longman, 1891.

Matt, Leonard von and Marie-Humbert Vicaire, *St. Dominic: A Pictorial Biography*, translated by Gerard Meath. Chicago, H. Regnery, and London, Longman, 1957.

Tugwell, Simon, editor, *Early Dominicans: Selected Writings*. London, SPCK, and New York, Paulist Press, 1982.

Vicaire, Marie-Humbert, *Saint Dominic and His Times*, translated by Kathleen Pond. New York, McGraw-Hill, and London, Longman, 1964 (originally published as *Histoire de Saint Dominique*, 2 vols., Paris, Éditions du Cerf, 1957.

*

In France, where there is a national fascination with St. Dominic, a new biography of this saint is published approximately every ten years. Unfortunately, neither American biographers nor American translators have been able to keep pace with the French biographers, so that when one wishes to read a life of the founder of the Order of Preachers written in English, one finds little variety.

TUGWELL provides the most recent collection of early writings bearing on the biography of Dominic and the formation of his order. Contained in this translation are the *Life of St. Dominic* by Jean de Mailly, the testimonies used in the canonization process, a sermon on St. Dominic by Thomas Agni of Lentini, and biographical selections from Jordan of Saxony, Pierre de Vaux Cernai, Stephen of Bourbon, Gerard de Frachet, Fulk of Toulouse, Stephen of Salagnac, and Bernard Gui. Tugwell's selections overlap somewhat with the earlier collection of Lehner (*St. Dominic: Biographical Documents*, Washington D.C., 1964), but the two may be used in conjunction by the reader interested in assembling a composite picture of Dominic from the earliest sources.

DRANE represents an older, long work that may still be read with benefit. It follows the sensitive critical apparatus of Echard and the Bollandists. What lends the work its lasting value is the way Drane carefully reviewed the extant sources to exclude incredible legendary materials. Written with great sympathy for the Dominican order, this is no work of credulous piety but a work of sound early biography. What emerges is a vivid portrait of St. Dominic as an enemy of heresy and a champion of Truth and Charity—the latter interpreted as zeal for God. Drane trades heavily upon the Acts of Bologna, which the author believes to be the most perfect description of the saint, as well as the original works of Vincent of Beauvais, Stephen of Salagnac, Jordan of Saxony, and the Acts of Toulouse. Every believable episode in the life of Dominic is covered in detail. Like many authors of 19th-century biography, however, Drane tends to quote original sources when summaries would do.

MATT, in contrast, does not attempt to present an extensive biography of Dominic, but to convey something of the flavor of Dominic's time and travels through the media of written text and black-and-white photographs, usually alternating on odd and even pages. The narrative is very simple but enables the reader imaginatively to reconstruct what life with Dominic may have been like. This book could be used as an introduction to Dominic, except that many of the exhibits require substantially more historical background than is provided in the text. Also, the lack of a critical apparatus prevents the reader from discovering the original sources, and at points the narrative assumes a pious tone that some readers may find maudlin. Nevertheless, it does contain some very accessible history, particularly in its presentation of the Cathar heresy and its possible influence on Dominic's evangelical ideal.

VICAIRE's long work is masterly, representing the single best example of Dominican biography in English translation. Its critical apparatus is excellent, and its narrative is based on the best original sources as well as the works of the *Analecta* and *Monumenta*. Dominic emerges from its pages as an audacious organizational and spiritual genius who wished to produce a new order of man—the *vir evangelicus* or man of the gospel—and a new way of life—the *vita apostolica* based on a unique evangelical mission paralleling that of the apostles and popes. An interesting by-product of this portrayal is Vicaire's argument that the Dominican notion of the apostolic life did not come full-blown from the Cathar heresy, but was equally influenced by the Gregorian reforms and the revival of the rule of Augustine. Vicaire is unrivaled in his presentation of the social, political, and religious climate in Dominic's time, and his work contains useful appendices on archaeology and the European political scene, maps, and an extensive multilingual bibliography.

The short biography of BEDOUELLE was recently translated from the French and now fills the gap in scholarly but accessible biographies available in English. Written in a clear, popular style, this is a work of evident scholarly competence. Despite his disclaimer to having written a biography—Bedouelle would prefer to call it "a spiritual portrait"—this work covers the essential episodes mentioned in longer works. With clarity and great economy of language, Bedouelle describes the significance of Dominic in two parts. The first portion of the book is devoted to a brief biography of Dominic based on the original, credible lives, while the second portion consists of a discussion of the sources and originality of Dominican spirituality, poverty, and its evangelical mission. Stressed is the continuity between Dominican and other forms of medieval spirituality. The Dominic that emerges is not a religious innovator but a daring synthesizer who put Christology at the heart of his way of life. This is the best short introduction to the life and thought of Dominic available in English.

—Thomas Ryba

DONNE, John, 1572–1631; English poet and clergyman.

Bald, R. C., *John Donne: A Life*. Oxford, Clarendon Press, and New York, Oxford University Press, 1970.

Carey, John, *John Donne: Life, Mind, and Art*. London, Faber, and New York, Oxford University Press, 1981.

Gosse, Edmund, *The Life and Letters of John Donne, Dean of St. Paul's* (2 vols.). London, Heinemann, 1899.

Jessop, Augustus, *John Donne, Sometime Dean of St. Paul's*. London, Methuen, and Boston, Houghton Mifflin, 1897.

Walton, Izaak, *The Life of John Donne*. London, 1640; revised edition, 1658.

*

Biographies of Donne begin with WALTON's. Walton was in touch with Donne's world, knew him in his later years and knew some of his friends, and in consequence Donne was alive to him as he has not been to later biographers. Others have corrected Walton's facts and his judgment of Donne's character, but what they add to the facts they can only flesh out as life by conjecture, however shrewd; the same is true of revising Donne's character as Walton gives it. With Walton, however, there are no "Donne must haves" or "Donne would possiblys." What he tells he tells with a lively impression of the man, even if that man was something of a legend, and a legend partly created in Walton's mind by his own churchmanship and attunement to the friendship of the great and the good. His main interest is in Donne the churchman, and the story he tells is of an English Augustine, the sinner who became a saint. But for him "the remarkable error" of Donne's youth is his imprudent marriage. About the young man who wrote libertine and satirical verse we are left to guess. Walton's life is hagiography, but with a charming flavour. The eulogies pronounced by him and others on Donne's character are finely turned in their stateliness. And the account of Donne's dying is as bizarre as it is exemplary.

Some corrections of Walton's narrative and some additional facts were incorporated in Thomas Birch's article on Donne in *A General Dictionary, Historical and Critical* (vol. 4, 1734). The work of revision was carried on in the 19th century by JESSOP, who gathered much material for his article on Donne for the *Dictionary of National Biography*. Plans were discussed with Gosse for joint authorship of a full-scale biography, but Jessop accepted an invitation to contribute a life of Donne to the Leaders of Religion series and withdrew, remarking that he had "never been able to feel much enthusiasm for Donne as a poet." His life of Donne as a man of religion is dull; as a portrait, it offers no more than a dim copy of Walton's.

GOSSE did feel enthusiasm for Donne as a poet, and his life is certainly not dull. His style has some of the belles-lettristic mannerisms and cadences of the time, delicate even in its indelicacies, but it conveys a refined and vivid response to its subject. Unfortunately the fineness is not exactly "fineness of truth." Of Donne as a young man about town, he writes, "His mental and moral condition in these years of his youth were turbulent and confused. His soul, still unsteadied and unrefined, poured forth a volume of muddy waters." The inexactness of that remark shows up against Carey's comment on Donne's Elegies: "They are the record of a soul trying to coarsen itself." In spite of Gosse's enthusiasm for Donne's poetry, his taste is not very searching, and he is content to detect in Donne an affinity with late-19th-century naturalism. Notoriously, he reads the love poems as autobiography. From his reading of them he cannot doubt that Donne was having an affair with a married woman at court, whose deformed husband sat all day in a bath chair. Though he is not to be trusted on matters of fact, Gosse nevertheless made a start in determining when Donne's letters were written.

Following T. S. Eliot's "discovery" of Donne and his doctrine of the impersonality of the artist, critical fashion drew a line between Donne's life and the well-wrought urns of his verse. Gosse's blundering must have encouraged this New Critical asceticism. But meanwhile a great deal of precise detail was being recovered, especially where Donne's life fell into official records. Among the recoverers was R. C. BALD, whose biography of Donne is a monument of academic research. Bald makes a drab virtue of resisting all but the most wary conjectures about Donne's inner life and has little to say about Donne as artist in verse or prose. The whole style of his undertaking is reluctant to interpret the man or summarize him in a vivid impression of his personality. Instead he prefers to let dense accumulations of fact

speak. The result is impressive within its chosen limits. Bald makes the most of every scrap of evidence to connect Donne with his contemporaries and the history of his time. The scrupulous sifting of the evidence and close weave of the narrative arouse admiration. Even apparently unimportant details eventually assume importance. The narrative of Essex's rebellion and his subsequent detention in Egerton's house recounts events that Donne lived through. And they come to life not just as background but as part of his experience. Again the level account of the desperate way in which Donne employed all his courtier's arts to gain secular employment before resigning himself to ordination brings out with painful clarity the shifty motives of one who was constant only in inconstancy.

CAREY's book is not properly a life at all. He looks at Donne's trouble with Catholicism, at his libertinism, and at his marriage, with the aim more to interpret than inform. His intention here is the opposite of Gosse's: to shed light on the writing by means of the life, not on the life by means of the writing. He does so with the necessary sophistication and power of generalising. Brassy and brilliant, Carey has given great offence to those who think that art and life should be kept apart, and he has written incomparably the most interesting criticism of Donne since Empson's. He can be recommended to those interested in the uses of biography. But those who want to find out about Donne's life and times and anybody he might be connected with should go to Bald.

—David Reid

DOOLITTLE, Hilda [H. D.], 1886–1961; American poet and novelist.

Du Plessis, Rachel Blau, *H. D., the Career of that Struggle.* Bloomington, Indiana University Press, and Brighton, Harvester, 1986.
Guest, Barbara, *Herself Defined: The Poet H. D. and Her World.* New York, Doubleday, and London, Collins, 1984.
Robinson, Janice S., *H. D.: The Life and Work of an American Poet.* Boston, Houghton Mifflin, 1982.

*

The two biographies of H. D. that appeared in 1982 (Robinson) and 1984 (Guest) are each important works. Published several years in advance of H. D.'s centenary, the books anticipated the flood of excellent criticism published during 1986 in the special H. D. issues of *Agenda, Iowa Review, Contemporary Literature,* and the National Poetry Center collection. The biographies, both commercially published, also helped to create a wider audience for several works of H. D.'s fiction that had never been published during her lifetime (*HERmione, Nights, The Gift*). Rather than being considered only the classic Imagiste poet, H. D. during the 1980s has been recognized as a catalyst for several important currents of modernist writing, prose as well as poetry, the long sequence poem as well as the lyric.

ROBINSON intends the reader to know and understand H. D.'s writing as well as her life. She frequently quotes from the poetry and fiction to buttress not only her recounting of

H. D.'s life experiences but also that of her mental states at the time she was writing the work. For example, Robinson sees H. D.'s repetition in "Red Roses for Bronze" in the late 1920s as a manifestation of a "hysterical attack. . . . This chattering repetition gets on our nerves . . . the poetry is strained, high-pitched, high-strung." This tendency to find a single explanation for a shift in poetic technique mars Robinson's otherwise impressive account. She is given to digressions into psychoanalysis that "explain" much of H. D.'s art as well as her behavior. Robinson's authoritative tone in these instances becomes so aggressive that the reader is forced to question the need for what sometimes becomes a single explanation. Biography can play the ultimately sane role of providing numerous reasons for the subject's behavior.

Robinson gives great attention to H. D.'s long involvements with Ezra Pound, Richard Aldington, D. H. Lawrence, and Kenneth MacPherson, as well as to her relationships with the women in her life. She tries to avoid suggesting that H. D. was—psychically and aesthetically—at the mercy of these romantic relationships, but the amount of space she devotes to these situations belies her own insistence that H. D. as *writer* was leading a life separate from H. D. as *beloved*. Robinson also does much less with H. D.'s place within the Doolittle family matrix than would have been possible. If H. D. was the unpredictable combination of dependency and imperiousness that Robinson draws, surely much of her personality resulted from growing up in the household in which her Moravian mother and scientifically dedicated father and brothers were so strangely assorted. From this childhood, H. D.'s problematic passions, her tendency to succumb to an authoritative male and then later subvert that passivity, become more understandable.

Robinson has done a remarkably thorough job of showing the H. D.-D. H. Lawrence impact (although several Lawrence scholars have questioned her account). She also is very believable in showing the importance of H. D.'s later writing, and life, of her analysis with Freud.

Although the GUEST biography does not differ a great deal in substance, it does differ in tone. Guest, herself a poet, draws H. D.'s life with compassionate understanding. The anomalies of her behavior—her demands for privacy, her insistence on being loved, her absorption in her child Perdita—are neither mysterious nor inexplicable in Guest's view: they are the small price one pays for womanhood and for genius. Guest gives the reader a greater sense of H. D.'s relentless glamour, as in episodes with Harold P. Collins in London, or recovering from an abortion in Berlin in 1928. Her biography provides more context, more sense of the milieu in this floating expatriate community. Guest also works more suggestively, letting H. D.'s words and the social circumstances she creates lead the reader. While psychoanalysis must be important in any biography of H. D., and while understanding the mythic overlay to her work is crucial, Guest does not remind the reader at every turn that these motifs must remain central. Her own prose is consistently effective, and her biography leaves the reader with the sense of H. D., in death, having survived the pain of her living, largely through her art.

Both Robinson and Guest rely heavily on H. D.'s own writing (much of which, in the early 1980s, remained unpublished). One might wish, in both books, for more supplemental material (from others' memoirs, correspondence, factual records of time and place), since H. D. was a comparatively visible American writer on the Continent and in England for much of her adult life.

As both these biographies show clearly, H. D.'s own writing reveals many elements of her life and thought. Not only the poetry, but her novels *Palimpsest*, *Bid Me to Live (A Madrigal)*, *HERmione*, *The Gift*, and *Nights* have confirmed readings of her experience that her memoirs *Tribute to Freud* and *End to Torment* (about Ezra Pound) suggested. The DU PLESSIS study is more a textual and critical reading than it is formal biography, but because of H. D.'s tendency to evolve her writing through her experience, it is relevant to readers interested in H. D.'s biography.

—Linda Wagner-Martin

DOS PASSOS, John, 1896–1970; American writer.

Carr, Virginia Spencer, *Dos Passos: A Life*. New York, Doubleday, 1984.
Ludington, Townsend, *John Dos Passos: A Twentieth Century Odyssey*. New York, Dutton, 1980.

*

As influential as Faulkner, Hemingway, and Fitzgerald in shaping 20th-century American fiction, John Dos Passos was the last of these writers to be treated in a comprehensive biography. We now have two, of similar quality and approach. Both Carr and Ludington are very thorough as they take on the job of documenting the incessant globetrotting and political activism that best characterized Dos Passos' life, and the ideological alignments that always affected the shape and substance of his fiction. Furthermore, both biographers seem to view Dos Passos' life and career in terms of the same stages of personal, political, and literary development, and both understandably emphasize his earlier years of greatest political activism and literary power.

Both biographies, then, are responsible and thorough. What sets them apart, however, are the slightly divergent roles adopted by each biographer. CARR's particular forte is meticulous detail. She seems to have gone to great lengths to obtain all possible information about her subject, which often makes for exceptionally informative reading. For example, when Dos Passos was in France as an ambulance driver during World War I, he wrote a friend about suffering through a lengthy German gas attack. Having interviewed others who were at that very scene, Carr reconstructs this nightmarish event in detail, bringing to life for the reader this "strange new horror" of which Dos Passos wrote in his diaries.

Being so scrupulous, Carr does indeed provide a thorough account of Dos Passos' life. She seems particularly interested in the personal vignette, focusing greatest attention on the details of his closest relationships. Her treatment of the death of his father, for example, is certainly more complete than Ludington's. She records the obituary announcements, the oration delivered to the New York County Lawyer's Association of which the elder Dos Passos was a member, and the content of his will.

She then goes on to explore the strained family relationships John Dos Passos faced when he returned from Europe for the funeral and how the spectre of Dos Passos' illegitimacy haunted the gathering of family members.

She lingers over other interesting, private moments throughout the biography: how the young Dos Passos used distant family connections to finagle his way into the army, much to the chagrin of his Aunt Mary; Cape Cod life in the early 1930s when he and his wife Katy worked and played there; the circumstances and fallout of Katy's tragic death in the late 1940s; and his remarriage and final years at his father's farm at Spence's Point, Virginia. Carr is best with these glances at the private man. But before launching into her account of Dos Passos' life, readers should ask themselves whether or not they do indeed wish to know such things.

This is not to say that she slights her coverage of Dos Passos the radical activist and acclaimed novelist. She doesn't, but her role as compiler seems to inhibit somewhat her ability to define and interpret the larger contexts in which this public man functioned. For example, Carr does not offer much analysis of the questions surrounding Dos Passos' heightened political activity in the late 1920s: What did it mean to him? How did it change his relationship to the radical left? Why did he choose the particular causes he did? Although she certainly reports that this public activity took place, her treatment of such crucial and exciting moments in his life at times resembles a long, annotated list: thorough and readable, but ultimately unsatisfying.

By contrast, LUDINGTON is much more ready than Carr to interpret and synthesize the cultural and literary history in which Dos Passos' life was immersed. To see this difference, one can compare the respective treatments of a single moment from his radical period in the late 1920s. Just after the execution of Sacco and Vanzetti, on whose behalf Dos Passos had labored for months, he defended a young writer who had been imprisoned for publishing an "obscene" poem. Carr introduces this episode with the transition, "Dos Passos was ripe now for other protests." Though this may be true, such a general statement makes Dos Passos appear much too indiscriminant, as though he were eager to protest whatever came along. Ludington, on the other hand, attempts to make sense out of this specific act to help out a fellow writer: "Still bitter about the Sacco and Vanzetti episode, Dos Passos lamented American writers' and artists' 'indifference to politics,' which he considered 'sinister'. . . . Intent on avoiding indifference, he worked to defend a young poet," who, Ludington also makes clear, was in prison partially because he, too, had taken a political stand by publishing in a communist periodical. Here and elsewhere, Ludington has greater success in placing the details of his biographical narrative in the broader contexts of history and seeing them in terms of Dos Passos' own intellectual and political development.

Although a compiler himself, Ludington, then, also assumes the roles of interpreter and story teller. He provides the synthesis and perspective from which Carr seems to shy away. Rather than a chronological account, say, of Dos Passos' four years at Harvard, Ludington feels freer to sculpt them into a more appealing shape that allows for easier, more digestible reading. He does so without becoming himself an obtrusive presence in the narrative, nor does he allow this freedom to tempt him into liberal conjecture; the insights he offers are enlightened and conservative, ever

consistent with the details of Dos Passos' life and career as both Carr and Ludington have presented them.

Clearly, this approach has particular benefits. Ludington delivers the facts, and he presents the reader with ways of understanding them. He is able, for instance, to present the Spanish Civil War as a thoroughly traumatic and critical moment in Dos Passos' life, which, by other accounts, it certainly was. Carr dutifully reports the Dos Passos-Hemingway feud over the meaning of the War, but only Ludington moderates the battle by weighing the validity of their respective arguments in the light of history. His perspective helps to make sense of the moment. He also briefly comments on the meaning and relevance of each of Dos Passos' literary works as they are published—again, in order to integrate and synthesize the material into a more understandable, more readable whole.

—Martin Thies

DOSTOEVSKY, Fyodor, 1821–1881; Russian writer.

Abraham, Gerald, *Dostoevsky*. London, Duckworth, 1936; revised edition, 1971.

Berdyaev, Nicholas, *Dostoevsky,* translated by Donald Attwater. New York, World Publishing, and London, Sheed and Ward, 1934.

Carr, Edward H., *Dostoevsky*. Boston, Houghton Mifflin, and London, Allen and Unwin, 1931.

De Jonge, Alex, *Doestoevsky and the Age of Intensity*. London, Secker and Warburg, and New York, St. Martin's, 1975.

Dostoevsky, Aimee, *Fyodor Dostoevsky*. New York, Haskell, 1972.

Dostoevsky, Anna, *Dostoevsky, Reminiscences,* translated and edited by Beatrice Stilman. New York, Liveright, 1975.

Frank, Joseph, *Dostoevsky* (3 vols. published). Princeton, New Jersey, Princeton University Press, 1976–86; London, Robson Books, 1977–87.

Grossman, Leonid, *Dostoevsky: A Biography,* translated by Mary Mackler. London, A. Lane, 1974; New York, Bobbs-Merrill, 1975 (originally published, Moscow, 1962).

Ivanov, Vyacheslav, *Dostoevsky, Freedom and the Tragic Life,* translated by Norman Cameron. New York, Noonday Press, 1957.

Jackson, Robert L., *The Art of Dostoevsky*. Princeton, New Jersey, Princeton University Pess, 1981.

Kjetsaa, Geir, *Fyodor Dostoevsky: A Writer's Life,* translated by Siri Hustvedt and David McDuff. New York, Viking, 1987; London, Macmillan, 1988.

Lord, Robert, *Dostoevsky: Essays and Perspectives*. Berkeley, University of California Press, and London, Chatto and Windus, 1970.

Magarschack, David, *Dostoevsky*. New York, Harcourt, 1961; London, Secker and Warburg, 1962.

Meier-Graefe, Julius, *Dostoevsky, the Man and His Work,* translated by Herbert Marks. New York, Harcourt, and London, Routledge, 1928.

Murry, John Middleton, *Fyodor Dostoevsky: A Critical Study*. New York, Dodd Mead, and London, M. Secker, 1916.

Rice, James L., *Dostoevsky and the Healing Art*. Ann Arbor, Michigan, Ardis, 1985.

Simmons, Ernest, *Dostoevski: The Making of a Novelist*. London and New York, Oxford University Press, 1940.

Slonim, Marc, *The Three Loves of Dostoyevsky*. New York, Chekhov Publishing House, 1953; London, A. Redman, 1957.

Troyat, Henri, *Firebrand: The Life of Dostoevsky*, translated by Norbert Guterma. New York, Roy Publishers, and London, Heinemann, 1946.

Wasiolik, Edward, *Dostoevsky: The Major Fiction*. Boston, MIT Press, 1964.

Yarmolinsky, Avrahm, *Dostoevsky: A Life*. New York, Harcourt, 1934; revised as *Dostoevsky: Works and Days*, New York, Funk and Wagnalls, 1971.

*

Despite the enormous stature of Dostoevsky in world literature and the immense interest his life holds for us, there was no definitive biography of Dostoevsky before the appearance of FRANK's multi-volume work. Three volumes of the projected five have now appeared. Because of its length and specialized material, it is not the kind of work that someone new to Dostoevsky will want to take up. Indeed, its greatest value is to those who have an intimate acquaintanceship with Dostoevsky's work. Still, if one wishes to learn something in a detailed fashion about specific years of Dostoevsky's life, this is the work to consult. The special importance of Frank's monumental biography is the historical and political context that he brings to known facts about Dostoevsky's life. He has researched exhaustively the contemporary social and political context in which the man thought and worked. Indeed, the work is more thorough and complete than any biography we have in the Soviet Union, where clearly accessibility to primary material is easier. Volume three is particularly rich in new material. In this volume Frank explores Dostoevsky's life and thinking in the years 1859–64, that is, those years between his return from imprisonment and exile, and the advent of the mature novelist beginning with the publication of *Notes from the Underground* in 1864. Frank's biography is an impressive achievement and easily the best biography we have of Dostoevsky.

Frank's detached and documentary style is doing much to change the wild and ecstatic view that has been portrayed in some biographies, especially those of Murry, Berdyaev, and Ivanov. MURRY's early work on Dostoevsky portrayed him as a mystic and prophet, and the work is written in an exalted and ecstatic style. It is not without merit, if one keeps in mind the times and the context in which it was written. One gets from it an almost visceral sense of the explosive impact that Dostoevsky had on English readers in the early years of the 20th century. BERDYAEV, a distinguished Christian philosopher, is less ecstatic in style than Murry but as broad in his claims for Dostoevsky's vision of mankind's destiny. Berdyaev is must reading for those who want an informed and deeply penetrating study of Dostoevsky's religious vision. IVANOV was writing from the context of the Russian symbolist period, in which art, and especially the art of Dostoevsky, was seen as a conduit to "other worlds." This biography tells us as much about the Russian symbolists as it does about Dostoevsky.

Troyat and Simmons provide good overviews of Dostoevsky's life. TROYAT is lively and interesting reading, and although his judgments and creative interpretations of what Dostoevsky and others felt and thought are roughly based on available evidence, one must be attentive to what is hard evidence and what is creative interpretation. Still he makes Dostoevsky come alive in a way that Simmons does not. SIMMONS gives us the hard evidence of Dostoevsky's life, systematically put forth and documented in an exhaustive way. GROSSMAN's work is very thorough and the best of biographies by the Soviets. Dostoevsky was taboo during the Stalinist period, and Grossman's work is evidence that serious interest and scholarship on Dostoevsky continued during that time. Grossman is particularly good on Dostoevsky's work on various journals during the period between his return from Siberia and the publication of *Notes from the Underground*.

Several other works serve quite well by way of introduction and overview. CARR's work has worn well: it reads easily and is reliable. ABRAHAM's 1936 biography is a reasonable all-around introduction. It has some of the virtues of Carr's work and was updated in 1971. YARMOLINSKY's lively and informative work from 1943 was also revised and updated in 1971. MAGARSCHACK's book is mostly on the pre-1867 Dostoevsky, that is, the Dostoevsky prior to his marriage to his second wife, and with that limitation it is competent and readable. The recent translation of KJETSAA's work from the Norwegian is perhaps the best of introductions. It reads somewhat like a shortened version of Frank's masterful biography, but despite its excellence it is not a substitute for Frank.

Dostoevsky's life, at least until his marriage to his second wife in 1867 at the age of 46, was complicated, neurotic, and troubled. The special problems of Dostoevsky's life are the following: his arrest and imprisonment for conspiracy against the government; his epilepsy; his gambling; his love affair with Paulina Suslova; and his marriages to Maria Issaeva and Anna Grigorievna Snitkina. His conservative politics are also an issue of paradox and interest. Most of the biographies touch on all of these, but some of the works give special attention to one or more of the topics. RICE provides a detailed study of Dostoevsky's epilepsy, certainly the most exhaustive study we have of Dostoevsky's affliction. Freud's *Dostoevsky and Parricide* (New York, 1971) is the benchmark analysis of Dostoevsky's epilepsy, an interpretation that has been challenged by many. Rice's work is light on interpretation and heavy on documentation. Unless the reader has a special interest in this aspect of Dostoevsky's life, the volume may not be useful. Freud's work, on the other hand, is a must for any serious student of Dostoevsky. In this work Freud with his characteristic genius touches on the deepest reaches of Dostoevsky's psyche, and he has much to say about the criminal propensities that, according to him, Dostoevsky fought all of his life.

Other works of interest that treat special aspects of Dostoevsky's life are those by Lord, de Jonge, and Meier-Graefe. LORD's work treats Dostoevsky's relationship to the Petrashevsky circle and Dostoevsky's subsequent arrest and imprisonment, his epilepsy, his relationships with Solovyov, Kierkegaard, and the quality of his domestic life with his second wife Anna. DE JONGE's study is concerned largely with the thinking man. It is an intellectual biography that attempts to encompass the way Dostoevsky saw the world. It is intelligent and sophisticated, but also special in treatment. MEIER-GRAEFE, like de Jonge, is interested in Dostoevsky the poet and psychologist. His focus is on the inner man. Finally, much valuable biographical material can be found in works treating that borderline where the man's inner life—philosophical and psychological—touches on his creative works. Among the best are those by WASIOLEK and JACKSON.

Dostoevsky's love life was particularly turbulent in his early years, with a neurotic and largely unsatisfying first marriage while in exile in Siberia to the tubercular and neurotic Maria Issaeva, by whom he had no children; the self-destructive affair with a student and admirer, Paulina Suslova, while he was still married to his first wife; and then marriage to a woman 28 years his junior, Anna Grigorievna Snitkina. Something of the richness of this amatory life is caught in Pozner's *Dostoevsky's Three Loves*, although the treatment does not match the richness of the material and today seems quite outdated. The version we get of Dostoevsky's amatory life in the biography written by his daughter AIMEE DOSTOEVSKY is similarly inadequate. Indeed, much is clearly distorted, but the volume retains some value for the intimate portrait it gives us of Dostoevsky and especially of his domestic habits. SLONIM's work on Dostoevsky's loves is better than either of these two, but the best biographical source for his relations with his second wife—a marriage that was happy and fulfilling—is to be found in ANNA DOSTOEVSKY's own diary. Anna details in an objective and documentary way her life with Dostoevsky, especially the strained and difficult life they had in the first years of the marriage, with particular attention to Dostoevsky's furious gambling during these years. This diary was first published in the Soviet Union in 1925, and a selective version of the diary was published by S. S. Koteliansky in 1926. An expanded and re-edited version of the diary was published in 1971 by the Soviets and a translation by Beatrice Stilman was made available in 1975.

—Edward Wasiolek

DOUGLAS, William O., 1898–1980; American lawyer and educator, associate justice of the United States Supreme Court.

Countryman, Vern, *The Judicial Record of Justice William O. Douglas*. Cambridge, Massachusetts, Harvard University Press, 1974.

Countryman, Vern, editor, *The Douglas Opinions*. New York, Random House, 1977.

Duram, James C., *Justice William O. Douglas*. Boston, Twayne, 1981.

Simon, James F., *Independent Journey: The Life of William O. Douglas*. New York, Harper, 1980; London, Penguin, 1981.

Urofsky, Melvin I. and Philip E. Urofsky, editors, *The Douglas Letters: Selections from the Private Papers of Justice William O. Douglas*. Bethesda, Maryland, Adler, 1987.

*

Throughout his life, William O. Douglas was highly successful at personal advertisement and self-promotion. The two vol-

umes of his autobiography were consciously written so as to portray himself as he wanted to be remembered by posterity. The first volume, *Go East, Young Man* (1974), tells the story of a poor and fatherless boy from a small town in Washington state who, through sheer grit and native brilliance, made his name as one of the country's foremost legal scholars first at Columbia University and then at Yale University. Called to Washington by President Franklin D. Roosevelt, he tamed the wolves of Wall Street as chairman of the Securities and Exchange Commission. His reward came when he was tapped—without lifting a finger in his own behalf—to become an associate justice of the United States Supreme Court. In the follow-up volume, *The Court Years, 1939–75* (1980), Douglas portrays himself from his first days on the bench as the valiant champion of the maximum freedom of speech and press, the rights of the poor and downtrodden, and an expansive welfare state. If those achievements were not sufficient, he takes pride in his role in saving the wilderness, protecting the environment, and promoting world peace.

Douglas' writing is so lively and engaging that the unwary reader will readily take his self-image at face value. And Douglas has been seconded in his reputation-building efforts by a phalanx of admirers. One example is the admiring biographical sketch by John P. Frank focusing on his positions on the cases coming before the Court (in *The Justices of the United States Supreme Court 1789–1969: Their Lives and Major Opinions*, edited by Leon Friedman and Fred L. Israel, 4 vols., 1969). COUNTRYMAN presents a fuller, even more adulatory, account of Douglas as Supreme Court justice. His *Judicial Record* (1974) details Douglas' positions broken down topically under the three broad rubrics of "Democratic Government" (including "Political and Religious Freedom"); "Fair Governmental Procedures" (principally the criminal procedure guarantees of the Bill of Rights and their extension to the states); and "The Economy." Countryman's *Douglas Opinions* (1977) reprints extracts from Douglas' judicial opinions accompanied by brief introductions to supply context.

SIMON presents at least a partial corrective to these flattering portrayals in what is the first attempt at a comprehensive biography. While Simon is sympathetic to many, perhaps most, of Douglas' substantive positions on issues before the Court, he shows the other side of the man—his all-consuming ambition and egotism, his occasional deviousness, and his callousness, even cruelty, to his wives, children, and those who worked for him. Simon takes pains to correct the Douglas version on points where Douglas falsified the record to enhance his image. Joining the talents of a journalist with an expertise in constitutional law, Simon has based his account on formidable research—extensive interviews (including with Douglas himself), archival records of Columbia, Yale, and the Securities and Exchange Commission, and the papers of such Douglas Supreme Court brethren as Harlan Fiske Stone, Felix Frankfurter, and Harold H. Burton. The major limitation was Simon's lack of access to Douglas' own personal papers, which are now at the Manuscript Division, Library of Congress, Washington, D.C.

UROFSKY was the first scholar to utilize this material. Accordingly, his selection of Douglas letters is an important supplement to the published writings by and about Douglas. Urofsky has kept his accompanying notes to the minimum required to supply context to allow Douglas to speak for himself through his letters. The letters are arranged by subject matter.

Part I is comprised of letters from his years at Yale and with the Securities and Exchange Commission. Part II consists of correspondence and memoranda from the Court years, focusing on his relations with his fellow justices, his positions on freedom of speech and press, racial equality, and the "Rights of the Accused." Part III deals with such off-the-bench activities as his environmentalist involvements and foreign travels. Part IV reveals Douglas as husband, father, and friend.

DURAM's work is of mixed significance. The chapters dealing with Douglas' position on the cases before the Court arising out of World War II and on civil liberties issues in the years after retrace ground covered more fully in other accounts. More valuable is Duram's examination of Douglas' nonlegal writings—his travel accounts, his commentaries on world affairs, and his promotion of what he termed the conservation ethic.

The more important of the law review-type commentaries on Douglas as a Supreme Court justice are: Leon D. Epstein, "Economic Predilections of Justice Douglas," *Wisconsin Law Review* (1949); L. A. Powe, Jr., "Evolution to Absolutism: Justice Douglas and the First Amendment," *Columbia Law Review* 74 (1974); Hans A. Linde, "Constitutional Rights in the Public Sector: Justice Douglas on Liberty in the Welfare State," *Washington Law Review* 10 (1974); Bernard Wolfman, *et al.*, *Dissent without Opinion: The Behavior of Justice William O. Douglas in Federal Tax Cases* (1975); and Wallace Mendelson, "Mr. Justice Douglas and Government by the Judiciary," *Journal of Politics* 38 (1976).

—John Braeman

*

DOUGLASS, Frederick, 1817–1895; American abolitionist.

Bontemps, Arna, *Free at Last: The Life of Frederick Douglass*. New York, Dodd Mead, 1971.

Chesnutt, Charles W., *Frederick Douglass*. Boston, Small Maynard, and London, K. Paul, 1899.

Foner, Philip S., *Frederick Douglass: A Biography*. New York, Citadel Press, 1964.

Graham, Shirley, *There Was Once a Slave*. New York, J. Messner, 1947.

Gregory, James M., *Frederick Douglass, the Orator*. Springfield, Massachusetts, Wiley, 1893.

Holland, Frederick M., *Frederick Douglass: The Colored Orator*. New York, Funk and Wagnall, 1891.

Huggins, Nathan I., *Slave and Citizen: The Life of Frederick Douglass*. Glenview, Illinois, Scott Foresman, 1980.

Martin, Waldo E., Jr., *The Mind of Frederick Douglass*. Chapel Hill, University of North Carolina Press, 1984.

Preston, Dickson J., *Young Frederick Douglass: The Maryland Years*. Baltimore, Maryland, Johns Hopkins University Press, 1980.

Quarles, Benjamin, *Frederick Douglass*. Washington, D.C., Associated Publishers, 1948.

Washington, Booker T., *Frederick Douglass*. Philadelphia, G. W. Jacobs, 1906.

*

Readers must begin with the Douglass autobiographies, three major works reflecting different stages of a life. These are *Narrative of the Life of Douglass, an American Slave* (1845); *My Bondage and My Freedom* (1855), an expanded and revised version of the earlier work; and *Life and Times of Douglass* (1881).

A former abolitionist, HOLLAND deeply admired Douglass and enjoyed his cooperation in interviews and obtaining documents. Drawing on many then-unpublished manuscripts and making good use of newspaper files, the author intersperses his own narrative with lengthy extracts from speeches. A list of Douglass' published works is appended. Mention is made of the abolitionist milieu: conventions, personalities, controversies. Holland sides with Douglass against Garrison. In passing, the author indicates other activities, including Douglass' support for women's rights and suffrage. Though the book fails to give a broader social context, its conclusion offers a good contemporary assessment of the man.

Substantial excerpts from writings and speeches constitute approximately half of GREGORY's book. The author paints a glorified picture of a great person, blunting the book's effectiveness in presenting the human Douglass.

CHESNUTT is more professional while retaining the positive estimate that all Douglass biographies share and that their subject earned. This work was one in a series of handbook biographies of great Americans: size alone limited the extent of the information included, a fact mentioned by the author. Chesnutt, a major African-American writer, presents a moving description of slavery, shares Douglass' contempt for its contemporary rationalizers, and generally identifies with Douglass' viewpoint without portraying him as holy. The first to follow Douglass' death, Chesnutt's book sought openly to keep alive the subject's passionate commitment, acknowledging its continuing relevance at a time when others endeavored to quell its flame.

Into the latter category falls the biography by WASHINGTON, also part of a series. (Ironically, the publisher originally asked W. E. B. Du Bois to contribute the volume on Douglass.) Washington makes clear that his subject lived and worked in an age characterized by "revolution and liberation." That period, however, was "now over. We are at present in the period of construction and readjustment." The narrative is straightforward, utilizing Douglass' autobiographies and Washington's reading of other contemporary sources. He shows that Douglass and others represented a substantial constituency before the Civil War; he feels, however, that Douglass' flexibility in broadening out the abolitionist movement showed him as "more or less of an opportunist." The author briefly touches on other concerns of his subject, including women's equality and his defense of the rights of Chinese immigrants. When discussing Reconstruction, Washington expresses many of the positions for which he is reknowned. Written during the nadir in American race relations, the book's chief value lies not so much in the life story as in its interpretation and application.

On the basis of her reading of the autobiographies and of key historical works by Du Bois, Logan, and others, GRAHAM creates a popularly written work that focuses on the pre-Civil War years. She presents novelistic dialogue and character portraits loosely based on fact, while making the point that Black abolitionists were a force in the anti-slavery movement. Though she provides glimpses of the era (for example of the Lincoln-Stephen Douglas debates) and certain insights into Douglass, her book is intended as a popular introduction to the subject, not as definitive biography. It should be approached judiciously; still, the moving Epilogue, in which an overall assessment appears, may be read with profit.

QUARLES originally wrote his work as a dissertation; it remains authoritative. Making skillful use of abundant research materials—Douglass manuscripts, the contemporary press, pamphlets, diaries, and proceedings—Quarles discusses his subject against an expansive historical landscape (with reference notes posited helpfully at the foot of each page). In opening, he freely concedes little original work on his part for the early years, crediting the autobiographies as the best sources in that regard. A sensitive chapter is devoted to an honest sketch of the subject's family life. The atmosphere of abolitionism is well-epitomized: the give and take of meetings, the free-wheeling character of debate, the popular nature of anti-slavery festivals and conventions. Quarles describes the oratorical style through which Douglass got his message across in "pre-microphone America," including a masterful use of gesture and mimic. He highlights the Black component of abolitionism, the organizations of free men and women, and the famous Negro Convention movement. Consequently, both Douglass and the abolitionists acquire flesh, bone, and meaning, with which previous biographers did not sufficiently equip them. Though sympathetic to Douglass, the book contains certain criticisms: that Douglass pushed Andrew Jackson too hard for Black suffrage in the nation's capital, that he lost "his sense of balance" in joining the anti-Johnson wave, that he engaged in apparent campaign histrionics against the Democrats in the period before the 1868 elections. The book does not include an overview or conclusion; still, it renders Douglass more comprehensible than did the previous literature.

As editor of the first major compilation of Douglass' writings, FONER had greater access to the relevant source materials. The author places Douglass squarely in the center of abolitionist, anti-segregationist, feminist, peace, and other reform endeavors and concerns. Douglass emerges as a deep believer in both the humanity of all peoples and the unity of Black Americans; he withstood attacks from many quarters, including paternalistic and sectarian white abolitionists. Like Quarles, Foner has critical things to say of the postbellum Douglass: that he failed to fight adequately for economic and labor rights; that he overcommitted himself to the Republicans, even as they retreated from beneficial policies; that, despite his sensitivity to Haitian nationalism, he closed his eyes to American imperialist aims. But he "unflinchingly raised the cry for equality," reviving the old fire in his final years. Foner finds Du Bois, more than Washington, to be in the Douglass tradition. A final estimate places Douglass with Lincoln and Jefferson in the foremost ranks of democratic thinkers.

BONTEMPS' biography is written for a wider audience. Though there are no reference notes, a Note on Sources indicates usage of the autobiographies, newspaper files, and other documents. In an effective presentation, Bontemps opens up with the escape from slavery, then briefly flashes back to the subject's childhood. The author pays insufficient attention to both the breadth of anti-slavery and the wider social context, as well as to Douglass' support for other reforms. Nevertheless, he synthesizes the autobiographical data clearly and accurately.

HUGGINS too, in a contribution to a series, tells the story plainly and cogently, but gives greater attention to Douglass'

support for broader democratization. Though sympathetic, Huggins takes Douglass to task along much the same lines suggested by Quarles and Foner. A major historian, Huggins also notes that Douglass in the 1890's regained much of his early fervor, and speculates that he would not have supported the path taken by Washington.

PRESTON's work, particularly its early chapters, can be considered a breakthrough. A retired newspaperman, Preston went to the Talbot County (Maryland) records and to the private papers of Douglass' owners to trace back his subject's family tree to the early 18th century. This research also enabled Preston to pin down the birth year and the origins of Douglass' full slave name. He uncovers data on five generations of the subject's family and provides a most comprehensive picture of the setting in Douglass' youth.

MARTIN's quite original study focuses on the development of Douglass' thought in the context of contemporary humanist and egalitarian concepts. It is an "intellectual biography." While better read in conjunction with Quarles or Foner, this work points to the impact of experiences on Douglass' growth as a thinker, marking the battle with slavebreaker Covey as instrumental in "the development of his own identity." Martin holds that Douglass was a consistent humanist, a believer in a "composite nation" founded on the common humanity of all who lived in the country. The author maintains that his subject's outlook was also reflective of 19th-century "bourgeois values," complete with belief in the "self-made man" and suspicion of unions. Though capitalism was inextricably tied to racism, and notwithstanding his own humanism, Douglass accepted the free enterprise system. Still, while clearly noting the limitations or contradictions in Douglass' thought, Martin presents most clearly his subject's essential devotion to humanitarianism: this is the book's main point. Thus, to Douglass, sexism was a violation of "the principle of human identity." His backing of other measures exalting human worth (land reform, temperance, an end to capital punishment and to corporal punishment) again expressed his "universal and egalitarian humanism." Pioneering and provocative, Martin develops angles occasionally hinted at by others, but generally never before considered. The portrait is rounded, critical, and ultimately positive, crediting the subject's life with a "timeless quintessence."

Frederick Douglass, by William S. McFeely (1990), was unavailable for review at the time of this writing.

—Daniel Rosenberg

———

DOYLE, Sir Arthur Conan. See **CONAN DOYLE, Sir Arthur.**

———

DRAKE, Sir Francis, *ca.* 1540–1596; English navigator and admiral.

Barrow, John, *The Life, Voyages, and Exploits of Admiral Sir Francis Drake*. London, J. Murray, 1843.

Bradford, Ernle, *Drake*. London, Hodder and Stoughton, 1965; as *The Wind Commands Me: A Life of Sir Francis Drake*, New York, Harcourt, 1965.

Corbett, Sir Julian, *Sir Francis Drake*. London and New York, Macmillan, 1890.

Lloyd, Christopher, *Sir Francis Drake*. London, Faber, 1957; revised edition, 1979.

Thomson, George M., *Sir Francis Drake*. London, Secker and Warburg, and New York, Morrow, 1972.

Williamson, James A., *Sir Francis Drake*. London, Collins, 1951.

*

When BARROW began his biography of Sir Francis Drake, the only works available to him were Johnson's *Life of Drake*, which only went up to the circumnavigation voyage, and part of Southey's three-volume *Lives of the British Admirals* (1833–40), which dealt only briefly with Drake. Barrow examined original documents in both public and private collections, and then quoted extensively from the sources. The resulting biography is patriotic (the English are always brave and the Spanish always treacherous), and laudatory (Drake is an unblemished hero). The book contains much information that is both interesting and useful, but which is presented in its original form, undigested by the author.

Barrow's Drake was "born of humble parents," rose to power and honor through his "honest industry," perseverance, and courage. He was a plain, humane, beloved man; also religious, fair, and merciful. Along with Sir John Hawkins and Sir Martin Frobisher, Drake was "the principal founder of our naval celebrity," who introduced practical navigation and discipline to the British navy. The biographers who have followed Barrow, all English, have also emphasized his heroic qualities and actions, but have generally been less inclined to paint a one-sided picture.

CORBETT's biography, which appeared before his *Drake and the Tudor Navy* (1898), is a more substantial work. Written for a popular audience, its style is romantic, even florid at times. Drake is a "legend," his life a "fairy tale"—but true. When he first looked out at the Pacific Ocean, Corbett tells us, "His heart was overflowing—so Moses gazed upon the promised land." Then Drake, like his biblical predecessor, prayed. The fight with the Spanish Armada was the "hour [for which] Drake's whole life had been lived—the life he had lived for vengeance on the idolaters and England's enemy."

For Corbett, Drake's significance is in being among the first to see the importance of naval warfare, "to see the tremendous weapon a powerful fleet would be in the hands of the power that first used it against an enemy's trade." Drake's great accomplishment was to "stem the tide of Spanish Empire." Corbett defends Drake's reputation by maintaining that his "greed" only extended to "vengeance and renown"; all he wanted was to be the "saviour of his country." This book is easier to read than Barrow's, but like the earlier book is primarily an exercise in hero worship.

WILLIAMSON was an expert on the Elizabethan explorers. He wrote *The Age of Drake* (1938), and *Hawkins of Plymouth* (1949), before producing a biography of Drake in a series of "brief lives" on English figures. His volume is short and clearly written, in a style meant for a patriotic popular audience. It con-

tains several line maps that help the reader follow the action. While defending Drake and his reputation, Williamson does make an effort to separate fact from legend (e.g., the story of his continuing to bowl when the approach of the Armada was reported). He is careful when speculating on just where Drake actually went and what he intended to do.

The Drake that emerges from this volume has a few shades of gray, and not all of his actions receive uncritical approval. Although Williamson defends Drake's execution of Thomas Doughty, he uneasily notes "it is a queer story," and that the man could be autocratic. At no time, however, was Drake a pirate. The high point of his career was reached in 1587, after which "things ceased to go well with him, and failure took the place of success." Rather than seeing this as the result of any internal flaws in his character, Williamson sees it was part of the "inevitable" process of aging. In the end he concludes that while Drake did not create English sea power (Hawkins "built the Navy" while Drake "led it"), he did make it "great and feared."

LLOYD argues that a new work on Drake needed to incorporate the materials that had been discovered about him and published over the years by the Hakluyt Society, as well as the documents that appeared in J. Hampden, editor, *Francis Drake, Privateer* (1972) and K. R. Andrews, *Drake's Voyages* (1967). He also notes that "not everything [Drake] did was morally right, nor even successful" so that it was time for a work "not written in the spirit of hero worship." Lloyd sets Drake in the context of his times, describes the types of ships he used, the structure of the Elizabethan navy, as well as the availability of navigational instruments and maps. While briefly describing Drake's various voyages, Lloyd acknowledges, as others do but not as directly, that there are gaps in the story.

For Lloyd, Drake's career was a "curve" that started with obscurity and failure, reached its height in the brilliant actions of 1586, and then ended in "failure and disgrace." This Drake is not always right. His execution of Doughty resulted from "nervous strain"; he could be impatient and arbitrary. The case of Borough shows him "at his worst—implacable, vindictive, even dishonest." While Drake was "preeminent [as a] fighting seaman," he also clearly had his "shortcomings." Although Drake's achievements were important and his adventures exciting (the circumnavigation "is the monumental feat of Elizabethan seamanship"), in the fight with the Armada England was not outmatched—she even had the odds in her favor—and Drake was past his prime. Drake was unequaled as a commander of a squadron and as a fighter, but not as the head of a fleet. He had trouble cooperating with others and never understood the larger political implications of his actions. This Drake, though admired, is not worshiped.

Quite different is BRADFORD's work, which begins and ends with Drake's last campaign in 1595 that resulted in his death from a fever off the coast of America. Bradford sailed to many places that Drake visited, and he is familiar with some of the terrain. The book contains a bibliography and maps, both of which are helpful. Bradford tries to get beyond the "shadowy figure" found in most biographies by dealing with some of Drake's personal life, but he succeeds only in the section that discusses Drake's activities during his "retirement" years of 1589–94; too little material exists for an extended discussion of his personal life.

On the whole this is a popular history that almost always puts Drake in a favorable light. There is no pirate here, just a resolute and courageous man, "an extraordinary example of a self-made man," a "navigator of outstanding brilliance, a genius of naval warfare," and "an astonishingly able partisan-leader." Drake was a puritan, forbidding gambling or cursing on his ships, yet he was popular and charming. He had a temper and could be overbearing, but he fought "against intolerance, oppression and evil." Bradford defends the trial of Doughty as being close "to a trial by jury in England at that time." He finds the trial of Borough "comprehensible" because Drake "suffered all his life from his humble birth" and had a " 'chip on his shoulder' towards his superiors." And he mitigates Drake's failures at the end of his career as being the consequence of "unfortunate circumstances" beyond his control. In addition, Bradford speculates on Drake's actions and feelings, and he accepts legends and stories about him that others have questioned (including the authenticity of the brass plate, reputed to have been left behind by Drake, that was found in San Francisco in 1937). This book reads well, but some of its conclusions need to be treated with care.

The longest and best-illustrated book on Drake is by THOMSON. It contains pictures of Drake and other Elizabethan figures, maps to help follow his voyages, a bibliography, and brief footnotes giving references to background information and citations for some quotes. However, despite all this paraphernalia, Thomson's is not a scholarly book, and while the bibliography shows considerable research into the times, it cites few of the previous biographies of Drake.

In a number of ways this is a strange book. Its earliest chapters spend more time on John Hawkins than on Drake. Most of it is written in the form of a romantic tale, a swashbuckling action story centered on descriptions of naval and military encounters. At one point Thomson describes how in Panama with "the English running and the Cimarrons capering, the raiders drove the Spaniards before them." Drake is engaged in a "holy war"; he was not a pirate but "a man ahead of his times," a "great folk hero" like Robin Hood or Billy the Kid. Criticisms of Drake from "the graver sort of naval historians" are invariably dismissed and Drake is consistently defended. A brief evaluation at the end of the book concludes that Drake was "special," and had a "magic personality." He was both good-natured and ruthless, but most of all he was "a born explorer with a touch of the missionary thrown in."

Several of these books are recommended, each for a different reason. Barrow contains numerous quotes from original letters, useful for someone unable or unwilling to read through the extensive collections of documents from the Elizabethan voyages. Williamson and Lloyd present the most serious and balanced views of Drake and his career. Finally, Thomson has the most up-to-date material and is fun to read. None is truly a scholarly biography, and none spends more than a few lines on Drake's personal life.

—Maxine N. Lurie

DREISER, Theodore, 1871–1945; American writer and editor.

Dreiser, Helen, *My Life With Dreiser.* Cleveland, World Publishing, 1951.

Dreiser, Vera, *My Uncle Theodore.* New York, Nash Publishing, 1976.

Elias, Robert, *Theodore Dreiser: Apostle of Nature.* New York, Knopf, 1948.

Gerber, Philip, *Theodore Dreiser.* New York, Twayne, 1964.

Hakutani, Yoshinobu, *Young Dreiser.* Rutherford, New Jersey, Fairleigh Dickinson University Press, 1980.

Hussman, Lawrence, Jr., *Dreiser and His Fiction.* Philadelphia, University of Pennsylvania Press, 1983.

Kennell, Ruth, *Theodore Dreiser and The Soviet Union 1927–45: A First-Hand Chronicle.* New York, International Publishers, 1969.

Lingeman, Richard, *Theodore Dreiser* (vol. 1, *At the Gates of the City 1871–1907*). New York, Putnam, 1986.

Matthiessen, F. O., *Theodore Dreiser.* New York, W. Sloane, and London, Methuen, 1951.

McAleer, John, *Theodore Dreiser.* New York, Barnes and Noble, 1968.

Moers, Ellen, *Two Dreisers.* New York, Viking, 1969; London, Thames and Hudson, 1970.

Swanberg, W. A., *Dreiser.* New York, Scribner, 1965.

*

ELIAS' work is the first complete biography of Dreiser, an "authorized" treatment because it was begun before Dreiser's death and because Elias had access to Dreiser's files, correspondence, and to the novelist himself. Elias begins by citing the legend that unearthly spirits appeared in the Dreiser Indiana home *before* Theodore was born, thereby establishing two important aspects of Dreiser's life: the Catholic orthodoxy and stringency of his father (who had the house sprinkled with holy water to expel the spirits), and how the theme of outside forces and their impact became part of Dreiser's ideology at an early age. He examines how the family's various bouts with poverty prompted repeated moves in Indiana and to Chicago. This poverty and uprootedness caused Theodore to turn to his imagination for escape, the beginnings of his fiction. A full one-third of Elias' treatment deals with these formative conditions before even considering Dreiser's writings.

Elias details Dreiser's newspaper days fully, indicating how this background helped Dreiser develop the discursive, objective style essential to his later fiction. Elias deals extensively with *Sister Carrie* and *Jennie Gerhardt* to show the great contrast between the two in terms of critical and public reception, lows and highs in Dreiser's career. An especially interesting aspect of Dreiser's career, which Elias explores here is the indignation that resulted from his novels, the attempts at suppression that spread throughout the nation, and the way Dreiser combatted this. After An *American Tragedy*, in which Dreiser depicted the individual more as contender than victim, Elias shows how Dreiser's movement into social reform became paramount. This move culminated in his trip to the Soviet Union and in his leaving part of his estate to orphaned negroes, an act Elias interprets as the resolution of Dreiser's conflicts between his beliefs in the forces of naturalism and the individual's ability to influence the course of events.

MOERS' volume examines Dreiser as both a product of 19th-century traditions and "modern" in his approach to the human condition. Moer emphasizes two themes that give her text a unique quality: the great impact the major urban settings had on Dreiser and his literature, and Dreiser's relationships with other literary figures of his time. Moer cites events in Chicago, (e.g., the Columbian Exposition, local embezzlement scandals) to show how they provided Dreiser with a framework for *Sister Carrie*. The same holds true for New York City, where the Bowery provided Dreiser with his indigent characters. Moer also cites how New York City and Dreiser's brother Paul provided the musical background for *Sister Carrie* at a time when Tchaikovsky, Herbert, Dvorak, and Sousa were all visiting the city.

Moer's discussion of Dreiser's relationship with his colleagues emphasizes the integral role Howells played in Dreiser's career, how Dreiser perceived Howells as his ideal audience, and how the latter rejected *Sister Carrie*. Another item Moer goes into that other biographers overlook is the accusation that Dreiser plagiarized the first chapter of *Sister Carrie*. Moer shows that this is partially correct by comparing Dreiser's work with that of George Ade, a Chicago writer at that time. Moer ends her text with an examination of *An American Tragedy* as one of the 20th century's first insightful *psychological* novels, made so because the main figure mirrors Dreiser in the former's urban orientation, mythical qualities, and oppressive religious experiences.

SWANBERG offers the most comprehensive biography of Dreiser. In 502 pages, Swanberg chronicles Dreiser's life all the way from those apparitions at birth to Dreiser's declaration just before dying that he was "the loneliest man in the world." A unique and helpful aspect of Swanberg's treatment is its format. He divides the work into six books, then breaks those in 45 titled subdivisions. This allows the reader an overall sense of the book's progression; it also provides quick reference to individual aspects or events in Dreiser's life. One section details the inaccuracies that surrounded the publishing of *Sister Carrie*, misinformation which Swanberg shows was due in great part to the false stories Dreiser himself spread about the events. Another section, "The White Ghost," delves into Dreiser's early exultation at the German World War II victories and how he felt the American and British press were exaggerating their stories of German atrocities. Because of its detailed information, provocative insights, and systematic presentation, Swanberg's text offers a rich examination of Dreiser's life.

Several shorter biographies of Dreiser are also available. MATTHIESSEN's book, less polished than others because Matthiessen died before the manuscript was revised, is especially good in its depiction of the women who were influential in Dreiser's life: his mother, his public school English teacher who introduced him to novels, and the charitable Miss Fielding, one of his high school teachers, who saved money to finance what turned out to be Dreiser's one, disastrous year of college. Matthiessen also provides an explanation of Dreiser's relationships with some of his contemporary writers, such as Howells, Wharton, and Crane, and how Dreiser was influenced by the realism in Norris, Hawthorne, and James.

GERBER's account also emphasizes the early forces that shaped Dreiser. The family discord, financial problems, frequent moves, and poor schooling are detailed, supporting Gerber's thesis that Dreiser's early environment constituted a barrier to his success, as reflected in his stories. This also establishes the main theme in Gerber's Book, the examination of Dreiser's works as the fictionalizing of his own experiences. Another element that makes Gerber's book interesting is his examination of Dreiser's artistry. Gerber examines the label of Dreiser as "the world's worst great writer" and the question of whether Dreiser had a writing style at all.

In contrast to Gerber's treatment, McALEER's does not emphasize the early years. Instead McAleer moves quickly into Dreiser's newspaper days and examines how they helped Dreiser's writing and his sense of social injustice. McAleer also goes extensively into the questions of Dreiser's anti-Semitism and how that appeared in his stories. This biography is also good in its depiction of the depths Dreiser sank to after the *Sister Carrie* rejections, and the heights he reached with *An American Tragedy*, both critically and financially.

HUSSMAN's treatment cites the early influences in Dreiser's life: poverty, schooling, and religion, with an emphasis on the latter. Hussman shows how the negative aspects in Dreiser's early Catholic upbringing caused him to develop an intense relationship with his mother and siblings. He also shows some of the positive influences religion had on Dreiser in the later years, when Judaism and Unitarianism affected him. This, along with Hussman's treatment of Dreiser's womanizing, offers a two-sided look at the author.

Among the works representing a more specialized look at Dreiser's life, HAKUTANI examines the pre-fiction period, concentrating on Dreiser's education, his newspaper work, and his editorial positions. Unique in Hakutani's depiction is his analysis of what influence the French naturalists might have had on Dreiser, and his pursuit of the thesis that Dreiser's experiences made him "a romantic, realist, and mystic" all in one.

LINGEMAN offers a more comprehensive look at Dreiser's early years. His "Boyhood" section cites the poverty and deficient schooling standard in a Dreiser biography. Lingeman provides further insights, though, into the prominent role Dreiser's brother Paul played in the family and especially Theodore's life. Lingeman also goes extensively into Dreiser's early sexual activities. The main portion of Lingeman's biography explores Dreiser's "apprenticeship" years, citing his various jobs at the different newspapers and analyzing the types of articles Dreiser wrote for those papers. Lingeman concludes with the second publication of *Sister Carrie* in 1907. En route he offers an incisive look at the lengthy musings Dreiser went through to arrive at the proper psychological development for his characters.

Several books about Dreiser derive from the personal experiences of their authors. HELEN DREISER was Theodore's companion for many years; the two were married the year before his death. As a result, her book provides a more intimate look at Dreiser, especially at his various love affairs while he was involved with her and at how Dreiser used travel to escape from his problems. One unique aspect of this biography is the inclusion of letters Theodore wrote to Helen over the years. These reveal an inner side to the man not present in most other treatments.

VERA DREISER's recounting of life with her uncle is more a recalling of the various Dreiser family members, their backgrounds and relationships with Theodore. The format of this text is unusual in that Vera begins with Dreiser's funeral and how she, as the only family member present at his death, oversaw the sculptor's activity in the embalming room as he made a death-mask and mold of Dreiser's right hand for posterity.

KENNELL was Dreiser's secretary on his Russian trip; her book details his determination to make the trip despite a serious illness, and recounts his various meetings with cultural and political leaders such as Eisenstein and Mayakovsky. The inclusion of Dreiser's lengthy statements on workers' lives in Leningrad, and on his departure from the USSR, provides an historical quality not seen in most other biographies. Dreiser has written two autobiographies, *Dawn* (1931) and *Newspaper Days* (1931; originally as *A Book About Myself*, 1922). These have obviously provided much information for later biographers, and they would be of interest to anyone wanting a first-hand recounting of Dreiser's life, so long as they are willing to wade through the 500,000 words included in these volumes.

—Kenneth A. Howe

DRYDEN, John, 1631–1700; English poet and playwright.

Bredvold, Louis J., *The Intellectual Milieu of John Dryden*. Ann Arbor, University of Michigan Press, 1934.

Hollis, Christopher, *Dryden*. London, Duckworth, 1933.

Johnson, Samuel, "Dryden," in *Lives of the English Poets*. London, Whitestone Williams, 1779–81; C. Bathurst, 1781.

Myers, William, *Dryden*. London, Hutchinson, 1973.

Osborn, James M., *John Dryden: Some Biographical Facts and Problems*. New York, Columbia University Press, 1940; revised edition, Gainesville, University of Florida Press, 1965.

Saintsbury, George, *Dryden*. New York, Harper, and London, Macmillan, 1881.

Ward, Charles E., *The Life of John Dryden*. Chapel Hill, University of North Carolina Press, 1961.

Wasserman, George, *John Dryden*. New York, Twayne, 1964.

Winn, James A., *John Dryden and His World*. New Haven, Connecticut, and London, Yale University Press, 1987.

Young, Kenneth, *John Dryden: A Critical Biography*. London, Sylvan Press, 1954; New York, Russell, 1969.

*

John Dryden was less than enthusiastic about disclosing the details of his life to future biographers. "What I desire the reader should know concerning me, he will find in the body of the poem," he declared in his "Address to the Reader," prefacing "The Hind and the Panther." His friend and literary executor Congreve observed (in his dedication to Dryden's *Dramatic Works*, 1717) that he "had something in his nature, that abhorred intrusion into any society whatsoever." Perhaps as a result of this frequently expressed reticence, the 18th-century view of Dryden was light on biographical facts.

The first writer to assert the merits of John Dryden as a poet was Dr. JOHNSON, who finally set Dryden in the literary hierarchy. Johnson was much less confident about the lasting value of the plays, in any case showing himself more concerned with the versification than with their dramatic viability. Inevitably he disapproved of Dryden's "license," but was even more disap-

proving of the poet's inherent dislike of clergymen. While praising his critical acumen, Johnson took the view that, great as was the range of Dryden's ideas, and wide the scope of his learning, the poet, unlike his contemporaries Milton and Cowley, could not have lived by his learning alone.

While Dryden was not a poet whose work was greatly influenced by his personal life—he himself declared of his plays that his purpose was to please the public—Dr. Johnson was not conversant with all the details. The first fairly full investigation was undertaken by "that clumsy scholar" (as Scott's biographer Edgar Johnson calls him), Edmond Malone, in his edition of *The Critical and Miscellaneous Prose Works of John Dryden* (London, 1800).

Sir Walter Scott did not greatly add to Malone's biographical facts, but his great edition of *The Works of John Dryden* (18 vols., London, 1808), to which his biographical and critical study was an introduction, did much to restore Dryden's by then already diminished reputation. Edgar Johnson described Scott's elaborate apparatus of historical notes as "thoroughly trustworthy," adding that Scott's entire work is "a mine of information about the age." Scott's text was to be corrected in the edition brought out between 1882–93 by George Saintsbury, and again further corrected in the edition of Bernard Kreissman, *Life of John Dryden* (Lincoln, University of Nebraska Press, 1963).

Throughout the latter part of the 19th century, Dryden's "lewd and licentious expressions" were self-righteously deplored by a variety of writers, notably, and most viciously, by Lord Macaulay. Thus SAINTSBURY's study, for all its sagatious appreciation of Dryden's poetry, is of only limited value today because Saintsbury was so conditioned by the Victorian age as to be unable even to consider sexual imagery seriously. Dryden's plays, particularly those written in the 1670s, abound in it. Saintsbury simply tut-tuts and passes quickly on. Commenting on the lyric "Beneath the myrtle shade" from the play *The Conquest of Granada*, Saintsbury writes, after quoting two exquisite stanzas, "It is a thousand pities that the quotation cannot be continued; but it cannot, though the verse is more artfully beautiful even than here." For Saintsbury, this is simply another of "Dryden's delightful, but, alas, scarcely ever wholly quotable lyrics." Saintsbury, however, took the view that Dryden's plays were no more inferior to his poetry than Scott's poems were to his novels. Saintsbury thus sums up Dryden's ultimate achievement: "Considering what he started with, what he accomplished and what he left to his successors, he must be pronounced, without exception, the greatest craftsman in English letters, and as such he ought to be regarded with peculiar veneration by all . . . who are connected with the craft."

An important study of the background of "sceptical thought and Anglo-Catholic apologetics" relevant to Dryden's religious and political writings is that of BREDVOLD, who possessed a mind steeped in 17th-century thought-processes and was thus well equipped to examine the origin and development of Dryden's ideas. Hugh Macdonald's *John Dryden: A Bibliography of Early Editions and of Drydeniana* (New York, 1950) was another indication that by the end of the 1930s interest in Dryden studies was reviving. This was confirmed in the immediate post-war years both by James Osborn's book (see below) and by S. H. Monk's *A List of Critical Studies Published from 1895 to 1948* (Minneapolis, University of Minnesota Press, 1952).

The first modern popular study, aimed at the general reader rather than the specialist scholar, is that by YOUNG. Dryden and the many others who played a part in his life are vigorously filled out, and the background is colourfully depicted. Unfortunately, words are put into their mouths without any indication as to whether the words are actual quotations or merely the author's interpretation of what they might have said. Young's book, however, forms an approachable introduction to Dryden and the varied nature of his achievement. Twenty years later, HOLLIS completes the task (begun by Saintsbury) of demolishing the calumnies and correcting further errors of fact about Dryden perpetrated by that sometimes less than accurate historian, Macaulay. As a Catholic biographer, Hollis has much to say on Dryden's "religious development," leading to his conversion in later life to the Roman Catholic faith.

MYERS' short study set out to demonstrate how completely and confidently Dryden learned to "deploy a limited and perhaps debased poetic idiom in an examination of the human problems created by the pressures of history." Myers is good on the development of Dryden's thinking, dividing it into three periods: up to about 1670, with Dryden concentrating on developing a theory of poetry; the late 1670s and his confronting the obvious inadequacies of the royalist theories on which Charles II returned to the throne in the context of real power politics; finally, after the accession of James II and the poet's conversion to Catholicism, Dryden's concern with the real basis of political power. Myers concludes that Dryden was at last able "to grasp exactly what made history secular" and why "events were rarely related to virtue in a Christian rather than a Machiavellian sense." Dryden then had the task of "integrating his faith in divine love and human goodness with a steady, thoroughly modern awareness of history's infinite capacity to violate every conceivable kind of value."

Dryden scholarship took a great leap forward with the *Life of Dryden* by WARD (the editor of *The Letters of John Dryden*, Durham, North Carolina, Duke University Press, 1942). For the first time, Dryden's work is considered for what it is in an uncensorious way. For the first time too, the characters in the Dryden story are fleshed out with well-researched detail, a process complemented by OSBORN's further investigation into what have hitherto been regarded as biographical obscurities, albeit minutiae in the poet's life. Both books are indispensible to the Dryden scholar. Mention should perhaps also be made of WASSERMAN's brief study of Dryden's life and work in the Twayne series, a balanced general introduction, though virtually unobtainable in the United Kingdom.

Correcting some of the opinions, or errors, of both Ward and Osborn, and superseding all previous studies of Dryden and his work is WINN's *John Dryden and his World*. Winn declares his intention of following Dr. Johnson in transporting himself to the time of his subject and examining "what were the wants of his contemporaries, and what were his means of supplying them," rather than judging the subject by the standards of the biographer's own times. It is difficult to imagine a more fully researched, fair-minded, and lucidly written account of its subject than Winn's. Every factual statement is supported by detailed source notes for the scholar, yet the style of the narrative is such as to carry the general reader effortlessly along. Dryden's antecedents, puritan upbringing, education at Westminster School, involvement with the theatre and the Court, great material suc-

cess and subsequent fight back against his reverses are examined in detail. The background is illuminated by copious quotations from Dryden's friends, rivals, and enemies, information not otherwise readily available. There are also more than 50 illustrations and useful genealogical tables. An appendix traces the monies paid to Dryden and his wife, Lady Elizabeth Howard, and another collates all the known references to Dryden's mistress, the actress Ann Reeves.

The overwhelming quality of this biography is the effective three-dimensional detail against which Winn draws the portrait of his subject. Winn himself sums up the aim he has realised so successfully: "I like to think Dryden would share my fondest hope for this book; that it will send readers back to his works with an improved relish for the subtlety, nuance, and power of one of our finest English writers." The novelist Anthony Burgess, something of a modern counterpart to Dryden in wide-ranging professionalism, declared, on reading Winn's book, that "it undoubtedly will, as he hopes, send lovers of fine craft and high art back to Dryden."

—Maurice Lindsay

DUBOIS, W(illiam) E(dward) B(urghardt), 1868–1963; American writer, historian, and civil rights leader.

Broderick, Francis L., *W. E. B. DuBois: Negro Leader in a Time of Crisis.* Stanford, California, Stanford University Press, 1959.

DuBois, Shirley Graham, *His Day Is Marching On: A Memoir of W. E. B. DuBois.* Philadelphia, Lippincott, 1971.

Horne, Gerald, *Black and Red: W. E. B. DuBois and the Afro-American Response to the Cold War.* Albany, State University of New York Press, 1986.

Lacy, Leslie A., *Cheer the Lonesome Traveller: The Life of W. E. B. DuBois.* New York, Dial Press, 1970.

Logan, Rayford W., editor, *W. E. B. DuBois: A Profile.* New York, Hill and Wang, 1971.

Marable, Manning, *W. E. B. DuBois: Black Radical Democrat.* Boston, Twayne, 1986.

Moore, Jack B., *W. E. B. DuBois.* Boston, Twayne, 1981.

Rudwick, Elliott, *W. E. B. DuBois, a Study in Minority Group Leadership.* Philadelphia, University of Pennsylvania Press, 1960; as *W. E. B. DuBois: Propagandist of the Negro Protest*, New York, Atheneum, 1968.

*

RUDWICK, a sociologist and historian of American race relations, presents a well-documented and judiciously balanced appraisal of DuBois. Originally published in 1960, his book was re-issued in 1986 as a volume in the series Studies in American Negro Life, edited by August Meier. The 1968 publication, which contains a "Preface" by Louis Harlan, and an "Epilogue" by the author discussing DuBois' final years, has been reprinted several times. Rudwick skillfully traces DuBois' often ambivalent responses to various crises in American race relations during the first three and a half decades of the 20th century. Following DuBois' break with the leadership of the NAACP in 1934, Rudwick claims, DuBois became increasingly ineffectual, a "Prophet in Limbo." He argues that in the late 1940s, the "old but very proud man became a Communist ornament." Rudwick maintains that by promoting Pan-Africa and a segregated economy for blacks, both controversial projects that lacked NAACP approval, DuBois, a scholar and propagandist who avoided executive roles, alienated himself from the organization's leadership and brought about his downfall.

BRODERICK's work, based on solid research, stands with Rudwick's as a standard treatment of its subject. An admirer and student of DuBois who had limited access to his subject's personal papers, Broderick is yet highly critical of DuBois. He notes that DuBois' own arrogance and self righteousness often diminished his ability to provide leadership. He also finds DuBois' literary skills mediocre. Still, Broderick credits DuBois with providing the nation's loudest and strongest voice advocating nothing less than full equality for blacks and inspiring several generations of young blacks to seek higher education and intellectual pursuits.

LOGAN's collected essays comprise a fairly complete biography, one that reveals the nature and genius of DuBois' leadership. Logan's introduction notes that an exploration of the paradoxical nature of DuBois "is the most common theme, implicit or explicit, in all of the selections." The contributors, including Meier, Broderick, Rudwick and Apthecker, explore in this superb volume the numerous contradictions in DuBois's tactics and goals, his commitment to Communism during his final years, and his voluntary expatriation and renunciation of his American citizenship.

MOORE's brief biography elaborates on a theme advanced by August Meier in "The Paradox of W. E. B. DuBois," published in *Negro Thought in America, 1880–1915* (1963). Finding remarkable inconsistencies throughout his subject's life and career, the author states that his "goal amid this jumble of paradoxes . . . is to present the basic facts and configurations of [DuBois'] life. . . ." Moore provides a critical examination of DuBois' principal published works and his controversial career as an advocate for various causes. He concludes that DuBois "will always be a hard man to grasp and retain." Within his limited framework, Moore presents a solid sketch, outlining the major aspects of DuBois' life.

MARABLE's analysis of DuBois' career is a thorough, scholarly introduction to DuBois' life from a self-proclaimed "general revisionist" perspective. Based on extensive research, Marable makes use of DuBois' private papers, which were made available to the author by Herbert Apthecker, DuBois' protégé and executor of his papers. Marable's book is well written and provides information not available in earlier biographies. However, readers may remain unconvinced of the author's central theme. Marable states that there existed "a basic coherence and unity to DuBois' entire public career," but more than anything else, the author insists that DuBois remained a "radical democrat." Although in his final pages he notes that DuBois made "serious errors in judgment," Marable is generally admiring of his subject. He makes uncritical use of DuBois' own self-serving rhetoric. Broderick charges that Marable's work is "understandable as apologia but unacceptable as history."

Marable disputes the contentions of earlier writers and colleagues of DuBois, principally, in addition to Logan, Henry Lee Moon, editor of *The Emerging Thought of W. E. B. DuBois*, (1972). Both saw DuBois' fascination with Communism in the final two decades of his long life as the combined result of senility, disillusionment, and the abandonment of hope, which led a great titan to fall after betraying his ideals. Marable also challenges August Meier's view, expressed in "From Conservative to Radical: The Ideological Development of W. E. B. DuBois, 1885–1905," in *Crisis* (1959), that in his radicalism a "paradox" existed in DuBois' desire for blacks to achieve their full democratic rights while advancing at the same time the cause of racial separation. Marable views Meier as underestimating the "theoretical coherence of DuBois' general outlook." He argues that throughout his stands on varied public issues and in the vast body of public works DuBois remained essentially a "radical democrat." Marable also boldly states that DuBois deserves to be seen as the father of Pan Africanism and the "central theoritician of African independence." Marable's biography contains a bibliographical essay highly critical of DuBois' earlier biographers, particularly Broderick.

Special note must be made of DuBois' three revealing autobiographies, which are essential to understanding his intellectual development. DuBois' *Autobiography* (1963) appeared five years after his death and was edited extensively by Herbert Apthecker. The *Autobiography* should be read with DuBois' elegantly written earlier versions of his life, *Darkwater: Voices from Within the Veil* (1920), and *Dusk of Dawn: An Essay Toward an Autobiography of Race Concept* (1940).

SHIRLEY GRAHAM DuBOIS, an accomplished writer who married the black leader when he was in his 80s, after having known and admired him for many years, provides an engaging and touching account of their years together. She writes in a highly familiar manner and includes many items of personal correspondence. Her work reveals the warm, charming side of DuBois' personality, who often appeared austere in public.

HORNE attempts to refute the contention that after World War II DuBois was ineffective and no longer a force in the struggle for black rights, noting that DuBois was a major target of anti-communism in the United States. He seeks, with only limited success, to refute Rudwick's charge that DuBois was a "Prophet in Limbo" in the 1940s and 50s. LACY's book for young adult audiences explains DuBois' significance as an inspiration to young blacks.

—Michael J. Devine

DUMAS, Alexandre (*père*), 1802–1870; French writer.

Bell, Craig A., *Alexandre Dumas: A Biography and Study.* London, Cassell, 1950.

Davidson, Arthur F., *Alexandre Dumas (père): His Life and Works.* Philadelphia and London, Lippincott, 1902.

Fitzgerald, Percy, *The Life and Adventures of Alexandre Dumas.* London, Tinsley Brothers, 1873.

Gribble, Francis, *Dumas, Father and Son.* London, Nash and Grayson, and New York, Dutton, 1930.

Hemmings, F. W. J., *King of Romance: A Portrait of Alexandre Dumas*. London, Hamilton, 1979.

Maurois, André, *The Titans: A Three-Generation Biography of the Dumas*, translated by Gerard Hopkins. New York, Harper, 1957; as *Three Musketeers: A Study of the Dumas Family*, London, Cape, 1957 (originally published as *Les Trois Dumas*, Paris, Hachette, 1957).

Miltoun, Francis, *Dumas' Paris*. London, Sisley's, and Boston, L. C. Page, 1904.

Pearce, G. R., *Dumas Père*. London, Duckworth, 1934.

Ross, Michael, *Alexandre Dumas*. Newton Abbot, Devon, and North Pomfret, Vermont, David and Charles, 1981.

Spurr, Harry A., *The Life and Writings of Alexandre Dumas*. New York, F. A. Stokes, 1902; revised edition, London, Dent, and New York, Dutton, 1929.

Stowe, Richard S., *Alexandre Dumas Père*. Boston, Twayne, 1976.

*

As a subsequent biographer, Michael Ross (see below), has pointed out, FITZGERALD's life of Dumas is "more of a Victorian curiosity than a reliable account," and also "extremely biased." It is certainly a non-scholarly biography that exploits Dumas' colourful career, which had ended only three years previously. Fitzgerald attempts to defend Dumas against the accusation of dishonest charlatanism while admitting several other counts, including "vulgarity, bombast and conceit." In fact, says Ross, Dumas was "a man of infinite charm who would never intentionally hurt a fellow writer."

The "comprehensive" edition of 350 works is by no means complete, and no one can claim to have read all of them. A truly scholarly biography seems to be an impossibility. Those we have concentrate on the sheer vitality of the career that took Dumas to the extremes of riches and poverty, forced him to produce his prodigious literary effort for money rather than even attempt to live within his means, to plagiarise, to employ others to write for him, and led him to enter Naples red-shirted with Garibaldi in 1860.

Most of the early biographies are period pieces, bewitched by the exotic figure of such immense energy, but some deserve to survive. MILTOUN's *Dumas' Paris* is one. It is highly colourful, inaccurate fiction with a good seasoning of historical scandal, romance, heroes, and villains. The idiom is archaic but charming, and Miltoun tells the potential reader all he really needs to know. To complain that the vivid portrait of Paris is distorted because the idiom in which the book is written demands standards of inaccuracy that are no longer admissible is rather like complaining that a Van Gogh chair should not be able to stand up. It misses the point.

SPURR's biography is an attempt "to tell the general reader, the man in the public library," who Dumas was, what he did and did not write, and what his colleagues and the "great critics" have said about him. This is longer, calmer, and more pretentious than Miltoun and, if less entertaining, is sufficiently serious still to be useful for an account of critical reactions to Dumas in the centenary year of his birth. The other biography celebrating the anniversary is that of DAVIDSON, a conscious attempt at an old-fashioned academic work but based more on wit than on proper research. Untranslated aphorisms in even

simple Greek tend these days to deter more than to impress. There is a properly chronological division of chapters, a good index, and a table giving data on the major stage presentations. It is still useful for much of this information, for its undoubted learning, and for the clear, rapid chronology of Dumas' life.

GRIBBLE dramatizes the lives of both *père* and *fils*, without giving very much hard information. His book is anecdotal, lightweight reading, not the product of any research effort, and it does not appear with the trappings of scholarship. The short PEARCE biography is little more than an outline introduction to the major personal events, like the bankruptcy, and the emergency arrangements for a private dinner party that are said to have ensured the success of the drama *Henri III et sa cour*.

With BELL's book we approach at least the threshold of serious modern biography. This work contains an index, a list of authentic and nonauthentic works, a bibliography, and some footnotes. The book is, however, intended for the general reader and gives an intelligent, sympathetic account of its subject's career, although it does not avoid the patronising tone that the career, and the personality behind it, almost invite. The whole flamboyance and bombast of Dumas make it impossible for even his most serious admirers to avoid the frequent wry smile, although this feat is very nearly managed by STOWE, whose volume offers a chronology, index, notes, bibliography, and succinct but scholarly approach. Stowe almost completely avoids the anecdotal and the picturesque without being unduly solemn, but he achieves this result by paring the biographical content of the volume to the barest minimum. He rightly regrets the nonavailability in English of the study by Henri Clouard, *Alexandre Dumas* (Paris, A. Michel, 1955).

MAUROIS' biography derives from his 1957 book, *The Titans: A Three-Generation Biography of the Dumas Family*, itself a fascinating account of "successive manifestations of a temperament so fantastic as to have become legendary, originating in the union of a Frenchman of gentle birth and a black slave-girl of San Domingo." Indeed, the feats of the young Dumas *père* as recounted are fantastic to the point of incredibility, and Maurois for good measure laces his narrative with a totally irrelevant account of the even for those days shocking "Adam and Eve nights" at Villers-Cotterêts, where Dumas *père* was born, when it was owned by Philippe d'Orléans. Maurois has assiduously studied material from private collections and newly discovered letters not available to his predecessors. He is often right where others have been wrong, but he still allows the journalist in him to suppress the scholar, and he is not totally reliable. He emphasizes the more lurid exploits and background of Dumas *grand-père* and writes with a touch of vulgarity, unnecessarily, for example, dragging in a proud paternal boast about the height to which the young Dumas *père* could urinate. There is a touch of the conniving snigger at the expense of his subjects about Maurois' biographies which it seems possible without prudery to find distasteful.

ROSS owes Maurois a considerable debt for the new material that he borrows for his excellent, if for so colourful a figure slightly pedestrian, attempt at a standard biography by an expert on the romantic period in France. Ross, too, has an index of authentic works but includes virtually no notes, and the bibliography is rather over-selective, even perfunctory. The book is still well-written, conventional literary biography, and Ross has an eye for telling facts, notably about his subject's chaotic finances. It is the best, if not the most entertaining, biography available in English.

The biography by HEMMINGS is frankly disappointing after the author's scholarly work on Zola and Stendhal. Those books were informed but dull and here, as if to compensate, Hemmings makes a point of repeating intimate repartee between *père* and *fils* about the relative sizes of their sexual organs, which it becomes indecent as well as unnecessary solemnly to set down in a book. The biography is, however, professional and detailed and especially good on the theatrical side of Dumas' life and on his friends.

—A. H. T. Levi

———————

DUNCAN, Isadora, 1878–1927; American dancer.

Blair, Frederika, *Isadora: Portrait of the Artist as a Woman.* New York, McGraw-Hill, 1986; Wellingborough, Equation, 1987.

Desti, Mary, *The Untold Story: The Life of Isadora Duncan 1921–27.* New York, Liveright, 1929.

Dillon, Millicent, *After Egypt: Isadora Duncan and Mary Cassat.* New York, Dutton, 1990.

Dumesnil, Maurice. *Amazing Journey: Isadora Duncan in South America.* New York, Washburn, and London, Jarrolds, 1932.

Duncan, Irma and Allan Ross MacDougall, *Isadora Duncan's Russian Days and Her Last Years in France.* New York, Covici-Friede, and London, Gollancz, 1929.

Kozodoy, Ruth, *Isadora Duncan.* New York, Chelsea House, 1988.

MacDougall, Alan Ross, *Isadora: A Revolutionary in Art and Love.* Edinburgh and New York, T. Nelson, 1960.

McVay, Gordon, *Isadora and Esenin.* Ann Arbor, Michigan, Ardis, and London, Macmillan, 1980.

Schneider, Ilya Ilyich, *Isadora Duncan: The Russian Years,* translated by David Magarshack. New York, Harcourt, 1968.

Seroff, Victor, *The Real Isadora.* New York, Dial Press, 1971; London, Hutchinson, 1972.

Terry, Walter, *Isadora Duncan: Her Life, Her Art, Her Legacy.* New York, Dodd Mead, 1963.

*

The voice and personality of Isadora Duncan are, of course, best captured in her often bizarre but unaffected autobiography, *My Life* (1927). This work, however, while it reveals Duncan as an extraordinary artist and human being, and while it makes for entertaining reading, is either unreliable or sketchy on many of the facts of her life.

DESTI's *Untold Story* was the first of many memoirs written by Duncan's friends to appear after her death. Desti, Duncan's companion during her last years, begins her biography where Duncan's narrative trails off, just before her years spent in Russia. Appearing in the same year as Desti's book, DUNCAN AND MacDOUGALL's volume again focuses on the last years of the dancer's life. Irma Duncan was one of Isadora Duncan's first pupils, and MacDougall was the dancer's secretary and friend. Their work is another attempt to provide an eye-witness account, yet it also relies, to its advantage, on Isadora's personal documents and her letters to Irma. Both books offer informative and moving details of the many episodes Duncan glossed over or embellished in *My Life*, but both are finally subjective portrayals of a woman whom the authors cherished.

DUMESNIL, another friend who was charmed by his subject, focuses on Duncan's trip to South America, a six-month adventure covered in only three pages of Duncan's autobiography. Dumesnil was during this period Duncan's musical director and associate manager, and his book offers a warm and vivid firsthand portrait of the dancer. Dumesnil also gives colorful accounts of Duncan's personal life, which seems at times to have strained their professional relationship.

MacDOUGALL published another account of Duncan's life and career 31 years after his collaboration with Irma Duncan. This work is more serious and comprehensive, with perhaps the most exhaustive collection of facts relating to Isadora Duncan's dancing career we have. While it serves to balance the often sensationalistic tone of earlier accounts, MacDougall's book is nevertheless fairly lifeless in its depiction of Duncan's growth as an artist, and it tends to avoid any discussion of her emotional life. The book is well researched and contains an index along with numerous comments by Duncan's contemporaries.

SCHNEIDER, who knew Duncan in Russia, writes of her years there during the early 1920s. Though somewhat poorly organized, and evasive on the topic of Duncan's often stormy marriage to the poet Esenin, Schneider gives a lively and one feels mostly truthful account of the dancer's Russian years.

SEROFF's work, an effort to correct some of the misinformation in previous biographies, covers Duncan's entire life. Seroff too is strongest when covering her period in Russia (during which he was her intimate friend). One of the most important contributions of this extremely readable and well-researched biography, however, is the insight Seroff—a musician—provides into the peculiar musical gifts of his subject.

TERRY's biography is very brief; only the first section of the book, less than 100 pages, recounts Duncan's life. Within this space, however, Terry manages to bring Duncan's remarkable personality to life through well-chosen and carefully constructed episodes. The middle chapters, entitled "Comments," and the last section, devoted to her "legacy," discuss Duncan's philosophy of dance. Terry, a dance editor for the *New York Herald Tribune* who did not know Duncan and never saw her dance, quotes the opinions of her contemporaries and other dance professionals in order to evaluate her effect on the field of dance. The book includes both photographs and drawings by contemporary artists.

McVAY retells the story of Duncan's marriage to Esenin in a biography that is little more than an expansion of his earlier work on Esenin (1976), which is the one to read for an understanding of the poet. BLAIR offers little new material on Duncan's life, though her work contains some valuable commentary on Duncan's methods as a dancer. Blair's book is well researched and well documented, and it contains many new photographs of Duncan on stage and off.

DILLON's double biography of two women who never met intertwines the lives of Duncan and Mary Cassat, beginning with their separate journeys to Egypt. Chapters on Duncan follow those on Casset, with lyrical discussions of their arts; the technique is interesting, at times effective, but ultimately it yields unsatisfactory portrayals of both women. KOZODOY has written a biography for young adult readers that captures the spirit of her subject in an agreeable manner.

—Noelle A. Watson

DÜRER, Albrecht, 1471–1528; German painter and engraver.

Anzelewsky, Fedja, *Dürer: His Art and Life*, translated by Heidi Grieve. New York, Alpine Fine Arts Collection, 1980; London, G. Fraser, 1981 (originally published by Electa-Klett-Cotta, Stuttgart, 1980).

Conway, William M., *The Literary Remains of Albrecht Dürer*. London, C. J. Clay, 1889; as *The Writings of Albrecht Dürer*, New York, Philosophical Library, and London, P. Owen, 1958.

Grote, Ludwig, *Dürer: Biographical and Critical Study*, translated by Helga Harrison. Geneva, Skira, 1965.

Heaton, Mary M. K. (Mrs. Charles Heaton), *The Life of Albrecht Dürer of Nürnberg, with a Translation of His Letters and Journal and an Account of His Works*. London, Seeley Jackson, 1881.

Hutchison, Jane C., *Albrecht Dürer: A Biography*. Princeton, New Jersey, Princeton University Press, 1990.

Moore, T. Sturge, *Albert Dürer*. London, Duckworth, and New York, Scribner, 1905.

Panofsky, Erwin, *Albrecht Dürer* (2 vols.). Princeton, New Jersey, Princeton University Press, 1943; as *Life and Art of Albrecht Dürer* (1 vol.), Princeton University Press, 1955.

Strieder, Peter, *Albrecht Dürer: Paintings, Prints, Drawings*, translated by Nancy M. Gordon and Walter L. Strauss. New York, Abaris Books, and London, F. Muller, 1982 (originally published as *Dürer*, Milan, A. Mondadori, 1976).

Thausing, Moritz, *Albrecht Dürer: His Life and Works*, translated by F. A. Eaton. London, J. Murray, 1882 (originally published as *Dürer*, Leipzig, Seeman, 1876).

Waetzoldt, Wilhelm, *Dürer and His Times*, translated by R. H. Boothroyd. London, Phaidon, 1950 (originally published by Phaidon-Verlag, Vienna, 1935).

Wölfflin, Heinrich, *The Art of Albrecht Dürer*, translated by Alastair and Heidi Grieve. New York and London, Phaidon, 1971 (originally published by F. Bruckmann, Munich, 1905).

*

Queen Victoria's consort, Prince Albert of Saxe-Coburg, provided the initial stimulus for the study of German art and literature in late-19th-century England, when biographies of Dürer for the general reader were written by the artist and collector William Bell Scott (*Life of Dürer*, 1869), and by Mrs. Charles HEATON, both of whom still harbored the Romantic image of Dürer as the epitome of medieval piety. Heaton's volume, reprinted in 1977, offers a selection of Dürer's autobiographical writings in translation.

The first exhaustive and critical biography to be published in English was that of THAUSING. Thausing was Professor at the University of Vienna and Keeper of the Albertina Museum, rich in Dürer's prints and drawings, and the premier collection of his rare watercolors. Thausing had examined every other available painting and drawing as well, studied the known Dürer documents in the original, and had access to the notes of G. F. Waagen of the Berlin Museum. His very detailed reconstruction of the artist's life and oeuvre is still useful, although the subsequent discovery of additional works and documents has made parts of it obsolete. Thausing brought his connoisseurship to bear on the chronology and artistic value of Dürer's work, collated all of the documents then known, and destroyed several popular misconceptions about the artist, including both his supposed poverty and the alleged shrewishness of his wife, Agnes. Shortcomings of Thausing's book, however, include its reproductions, which are line copies after Dürer by a variety of 19th-century artists, and his confusion of the Dürer copyist, Wenzel von Olmütz—who signed his prints simply "W"—with Dürer's teacher, Michael Wolgemuth. This case of mistaken identity causes him to overestimate Wolgemuth's influence on his most famous pupil.

Thausing's thorough and positivistic "Vienna School" biography inspired his student, CONWAY, to translate Dürer's family chronicle, travel diary, letters, and portions of his theoretical work into plummy Cantabrigian English. These essential documents provided raw material for Lionel Cust (1897) and for the much more subjective biography by MOORE, with its emphasis on Dürer's theory of human proportion, a topic later explored more fully by Panofsky.

The outbreak of World War I brought an end to publications on Dürer in English. They resumed only in 1950 with the translation of WAETZOLDT. (The classic study of Dürer's stylistic development, by WÖLFFLIN, was only translated into English in 1971, in time for the 500th anniversary of the artist's birth.) Waetzoldt's biography is undocumented, but sets Dürer in the general context of Nuremberg society and of pre-Reformation popular piety in Germany at the close of the 15th century. It suffers, however, from the rhetoric of the Third Reich ("In the Apocalypse we feel that Dürer's St. Michael, a figure after the style of Siegfried, . . ." "Dürer's urge to self-expression is a product of that German national emotion—a tendency to self-absorption"). The book opens, too, with an apologia for Dürer's Hungarian ancestry in which it is alleged—citing only facial structure as evidence—that Dürer's father must actually have been descended from German settlers who came to Hungary in the 13th century. (It is now known that the area of Hungary from which Albrecht Dürer the Elder came was settled exclusively by Hungarians.)

The first to explore in depth Dürer's very considerable knowledge of classical Greek and Roman thought—and to view his interest in the Italian Renaissance as something other than an unfortunate lapse of taste—was PANOFSKY, who investigated Dürer's theoretical writings and their sources. Formerly a member of the Warburg Institute, he applied its iconographic method to the study of Dürer's subject matter. His book, translated into German in 1977, remains the standard English introduction to Dürer's art and theory.

Hans Rupprich's definitive, annotated edition of Dürer's complete writings (*Dürer: Schriftlicher Nachlass*, Berlin, 1956) has set the standard for postwar scholarship. Biographies by three prominent German museum men have been translated into English: Grote and Strieder, both of the Germanisches Nationalmuseum in Nuremberg, and Anzelewsky, emeritus director of the Berlin print room and author of the most recent and authoritative catalogue of Dürer's paintings (1971). GROTE's brief but useful volume for the general reader centers on Dürer's career as painter, while STRIEDER's offers a selection of Dürer's best works in all media, and brief examples of his writing in a section edited by Matthias Mende, Director of the Dürerhaus. ANZELEWSKY's sumptuously illustrated volume, the most completely documented of the three, gives the fullest account of Dürer's life and circumstances.

A new biography of Dürer by the present writer, HUTCHISON, like Anzelewsky's, takes into account Rupprich's work and the major discoveries of the Dürer 500th anniversary symposia (1971). It also incorporates material brought to light by the scholarship of the Martin Luther year (1983) and the symposia honoring Caritas Pirckheimer (1982), the Franciscan abbess to whom Dürer dedicated his Life of the Virgin series.

—Jane Campbell Hutchison

DYLAN, Bob [born Bob Zimmerman], 1941–   ; American musician and songwriter.

Scaduto, Anthony, *Bob Dylan: An Intimate Biography.* New York, Grossett and Dunlap, 1971; London, W. H. Allen, 1972; revised edition, New York, New American Library, 1979.

Shelton, Robert, *No Direction Home: The Life and Music of Bob Dylan.* New York, Beech Tree Books, 1986; Sevenoaks, New English Library, 1987.

Spitz, Bob, *Dylan: A Biography.* New York, McGraw-Hill, and London, M. Joseph, 1989.

*

SCADUTO, who wrote the first full-length biography of Bob Dylan, dispelled once and for all a great deal of the misinformation, legend, and myth surrounding Dylan—the stuff of early interviews, liner notes, and magazine pieces—that he was an orphan, a runaway, a sideman for various blues greats. In his highly readable and anecdotal narrative, Scaduto traces the transformation of Bobby Zimmerman, a middle-class Jewish boy from Hibbing, Minnesota, into Bob Dylan, protest singer, prolific songwriter, bratty rock idol, self-destructive sixties prophet, and, finally, reclusive family man.

Scaduto is especially strong in recreating the popular music scene of the early 1960s through interviews with Dylan's friends and fellow musicians. His work remains the best account of Dylan's life in New York from 1961–64, mainly because several of Scaduto's most important sources—Phil Ochs, who died in 1976, and Joan Baez, who declines now to speak with other biographers—are no longer available. Scaduto begins the practice, followed by subsequent biographers, of including a discography, both of albums and of unreleased recordings.

Scaduto ends, however, in 1972, and a new afterward and the updating in the 1979 edition do not do justice to the important more recent events in Dylan's life—his comeback tour with The Band, his divorce, his Rolling Thunder Review, the recording of some of his best work, his return to Judaism, his conversion to fundamentalist Christianity.

SHELTON likewise begins Dylan's story in Hibbing and draws on extensive interviews with Dylan and those who knew him—his mother, high school pals, former girlfriends, musicians. The focus of the book, however, is Dylan as an important creative artist. Shelton, whose review of a Dylan performance in 1961 led to his "discovery," traces Dylan's influences and musical and lyrical development with scholarly thoroughness; he provides at least a one-paragraph analysis of each of Dylan's songs recorded between 1961 and 1975. His commentary is knowledgeable and literate, his text studded with allusions and quotations from Freud and Jung, Dante and Blake, Ionesco and Eliot.

Shelton, an unabashed admirer of Dylan's work, is decidedly well-disposed toward his subject: Dylan's album *Self Portrait,* for example, acknowledged by most critics to be an artistic disaster, Shelton praises with faint damning—it is among his "least favorite Dylan albums."

Shelton furnishes a substantial, respectful artist's life, informed by the author's encyclopedic knowledge of folk and rock music in general and Dylan's work in particular (including unreleased, bootlegged recordings) by his correspondence with a host of academic critics and amateur Dylanologists, and by the sort of tireless research that turned up young Bobby's first poetic efforts—verses to his parents in honor of Mother's and Father's Days. He includes not only a discography, but an elaborate song index and bibliography.

As long as Dylan is living, performing, writing, and recording, any biography must be provisional; between the time galleys are corrected and a new biography appears in the stores, Dylan may have undergone several philosophical transformations, recorded a new album, embraced a new style, and assumed yet another persona. For now, though, serious students of Dylan and popular music will probably be best served by Shelton's intelligent and well-written account which, in a hurried last chapter, brings Dylan's story through the 1980s to the release of *Biograph,* a 5-LP retrospective released in 1985.

Readers who seek personal detail rather than poetic explication should consult the volume by SPITZ, a journalist less interested in Dylan's art than his drug consumption and sex life. While Shelton, for example, attempts a dignified treatment of Dylan's divorce ("Do we really want to know . . . who slapped whom?") and instead studies themes of loss and grief in the music, Spitz draws on court documents to provide a blow-by-blow account of marital infidelity, arguments, and custody battles. Spitz is decidedly hostile to his subject: Dylan's political and social protest is portrayed as a commercial stratagem, his surreal poetry the product of LSD, his religious and spiritual explorations neurotic symptoms.

Spitz did not secure permission to quote Dylan's lyrics, nor did he, like Scaduto and Shelton, interview Dylan himself, preferring instead to maintain his independence, to complete his avowed task of "demythifying" Dylan's life without "whitewashing."

Exhuastive research, including hundreds of interviews, nevertheless, yields a great deal of new information—from Dylan's I.Q. and high school grade point average, to his composition of "Idiot Wind" on the back of pink message slips, to his occasional snorting of cocaine before a concert; some trivia, a few significant glimpses into the creative process, lots of gossip. Spitz's style is sometimes annoyingly hip and destined to sound dated—he alludes frequently to television sit-coms and his vocabulary includes words like "wuss"—and his psychologizing is a bit naive, but his candid if unsympathetic account is generally quite readable and contains raw material that future biographers of Dylan will no doubt draw upon.

—Hamilton E. Cochrane

EARHART, Amelia, 1897–1937; American aviator.

Backus, Jean L., *Letters from Amelia: 1901–37.* Boston, Beacon, 1982.

Briand, Paul, Jr., *Daughter of the Sky: The Story of Amelia Earhart.* New York, Duell Sloan, 1960.

Goerner, Fred, *The Search for Amelia Earhart.* New York, Doubleday, and London, Bodley Head, 1966.

Klaas, Joe, *Amelia Earhart Lives: A Trip through Intrigue to Find America's First Lady of Mystery.* New York, McGraw-Hill, 1970.

Loomis, Vincent V., with Jeffrey L. Ethell, *Amelia Earhart: The Final Story.* New York, Random House, 1985.

Morrissey, Muriel, *Courage is the Price: The Biography of Amelia Earhart.* Wichita, Kansas, McCormick-Armstrong, 1963.

Pellegrano, Ann Holtgren, *World Flight: The Earhart Trail.* Ames, Iowa State University Press, 1971.

Putnam, George Palmer, *Soaring Wings: A Biography of Amelia Earhart.* New York, Harcourt, 1939; London, Harrap, 1940.

*

PUTNAM, Earhart's husband, publicity manager, and scion of the publishing family, largely created Earhart's romantic image, as his book testifies. He purports to show how a "tow-haired child" from the Midwest grew up to stand in a "blindingly bright" public light, her exploits accompanied by "snowdrifts of telegrams and letters." The breezy treatment undermines the work's value as biography. As to the continuing controversy surrounding Earhart's disappearance on her round-the-world flight in 1937, the book offers few insights, concluding that Earhart's plane crashed "somewhere near" Howland Island in the South Pacific, quite likely an erroneous assumption in the light of more recent studies.

Publicist Putnam kept a record of Earhart's cables and telephone calls made while on her world-girdling attempt. These he weaves together with logbooks and an Earhart manuscript in progress for the autobiography, *Last Flight* (1937). In the introduction to this volume, Putnam histrionically confesses that "I asked if she could not give up the project. Life held so much else"—a plea belied by his entrepreneurial efforts. (These included promotion of Amelia Earhart luggage, Earhart endorsements of automobiles, and the sale of a host of gewgaws bearing the aviator's label.) Concentrating mostly on travel description, the book acknowledges few of the complexities dogging Earhart. One can say the same in passing for the flyer's other autobiographical works, *The Fun of It* (1932) and *20 Hrs. 40 Min* (1928). Their superficial style and lack of intellectual weight mark them as publicity fodder applauded by the promoter behind the writer. Of little more help is MORRISSEY, Earhart's sister. Her title reflects the following hero worship, and her comments on Earhart's disappearance, as with Putnam's, fall short of studied thought.

The serious student will begin to take heart with Backus's collection of Earhart letters. Though occasionally flawed by hagiographic language, Backus sets the letters in the context of her own researches. Taking us from Earhart's childhood through her maturity, along the way Backus discusses the alcoholism of Earhart's father, shows Earhart as a loving family member, and a little hesitantly hints at quarrels between a driving publicity hustler and an ambitious wife scrambling to keep pace with her created image. Backus warns, however, that hers is not a rich resource on the pilot's demise.

Some studies can be too rich. In a book reminiscent of a detective thriller, KLAAS argues that Earhart and navigator Fred Noonan were agents of the United States government. Sometime during their world trip they slyly switched to a more powerful aircraft. They now had the speed and range to spy on the Japanese, illegally fortifying Pacific islands in preparation for World War II. Exploring "a nether world of subterranean adventure," we learn that Earhart might have been Tokyo Rose, that she might have escaped Japan disguised as a nun, etc. But there's more. One of the author's fellow investigators breaks a secret code and, grippingly, bumps into Earhart, very much alive nearly three decades after her "death." Unfortunately, she suspects detection and loses her pursuer. Though Klaas raises a number of valid questions, his approach will be especially appealing to conspiracy buffs.

The uncertainty surrounding Earhart's last flight also attracts less easily dazzled researchers. Yet without a touch of irony, BRIAND notes that feminist Earhart "realized that she needed a man to protect her" and married wealthy Putnam. After reviewing Earhart's personal life and including a valuable section on Putnam, Briand concentrates on Earhart's flying career. Much of this serves as background for his investigation of Earhart's disappearance. Based largely on the testimony of Pacific islander Josephine Blanco, whose statement he deems "most probably true," Briand accepts that Earhart and Noonan innocently wandered off course and belly-landed on the water off Saipan, Japan's military headquarters in the Pacific. Japanese soldiers took the two into custody and executed them the same day as the crash. The author places the spy theory in the category of "rumors." Following a similar organization, but at greater length, GOERNER reaches a somewhat different conclusion: the two aviators indeed were spies; they crash-landed in the lagoon of the Mili Atoll in the southeastern Marshalls, and the Japanese military took them by ship to Saipan. Goerner assumes the two Americans died, quite likely after harsh treatment.

On a different but related note, 30 years after the famous last flight, PELLEGRENO follows Earhart's route in a Lockheed Electra, an aircraft similar to the one used by the earlier adventurer. Pellegreno brings little new to the Earhart story generally, but her account will prove valuable to students pursuing the technical aspects of such a trip.

Completing his volume, Klaas observes with a certain chagrin that "There may be as many books about what happened to Amelia Earhart as there are about Custer's Last Stand." Among the plethora, LOOMIS rewards with his revisionist but even-handed study. Without a tinge of naysaying, he penetrates the aura Putnam projected around his wife. Behind it Loomis finds a woman beyond her depth, ill-equipped to fulfill ambitions, pegged to a marriage of convenience to her promoter. Ill health, particularly sinusitis—an affliction as debilitating to an aviator as seasickness can be to a sailor—plagued Earhart during her frequent periods of stress and emotional upset. Perhaps as a partial consequence, Earhart was not an exceptional pilot, as her several crashes previous to her final one attest. In emergency situations she became rattled and was prone to the wrong responses. Worse, she could be overconfident, even offhanded, about the essential details of taking a craft into the air. Significantly as regards her last flight, she was particularly unsure in navigation and the intricacies of radio communication. Perhaps due to her father's alcoholism, she tended to associate with alcoholics during her aviation career. Due to all-night carousing, navigator Noonan had to be "poured" into Earhart's Electra on the morning of the last takeoff. None of this bodes well for an ocean flight difficult enough in those days for an expert pilot assisted by a sober navigator.

Loomis builds a solid case in maintaining that without Noonan functioning, Earhart became confused. Along the lines of Goerner, Loomis concludes that Earhart ditched in the Mili Atoll and was imprisoned in Saipan. However, drawing on a number of sources, Loomis goes beyond Goerner in giving the details of the flyers' end. Following many weeks of confinement, Noonan was executed after he lost his temper with his captors. Sometime later, in mid-1938, Earhart died of dysentery. Loomis disagrees with the spy theory, pointing out that the night flight over the Japanese possessions would not have yielded much military information. He also notes that Earhart was a pacifist and "would never have undertaken a spy mission." Finally, he reproduces documents indicating a Japanese cover-up of an international incident still waiting to be fully aired.

Two biographies of Amelia Earhart appeared at the end of 1989, too late to be considered in this survey: Mary S. Lovell, *Sound of Wings: The Life of Amelia Earhart* (New York, St. Martin's, and London, Hutchinson, 1989); and Doris L. Rich, *Amelia Earhart: A Biography* (Washington, D.C., Smithsonian, 1989).

—Peter Wild

EDISON, Thomas Alva, 1847–1931; American inventor.

Bryan, George S., *Edison: The Man and His Work*. New York, Garden City Publishers, and London, Knopf, 1926.
Clark, Ronald W., *Edison, the Man Who Made the Future*. New York, Putnam, and London, MacDonald and Jane's, 1977.
Conot, Robert, *A Streak of Luck*. New York, Seaview, 1978.

Dyer, Frank L. and Thomas C. Martin, *Edison, His Life and Inventions* (2 vols.). New York and London, Harper, 1910; expanded version, with the collaboration of William Meadowcroft, New York and London, Harper, 1929.
Friedel, Robert D., *Edison's Electric Light: Biography of an Invention*. New Brunswick, New Jersey, Rutgers University Press, 1986.
Jehl, Francis, *Menlo Park: Reminiscences* (3 vols.). Dearborn, Michigan, Edison Institute, 1937–41.
Josephson, Matthew, *Edison*. New York, McGraw-Hill, 1959; London, Eyre and Spottiswoode, 1961.
McClure, James B., editor, *Edison and His Invention, Including the Many Incidents, Anecdotes, and Interesting Particulars Connected with the Life of the Great Inventor*. Chicago, Rhodes and McClure, 1879.
Nerney, Mary C., *Thomas A. Edison: A Modern Olympian*. New York, Smith and Hass, 1934.
Nye, David E., *The Invented Self: An Anti-Biography, from Documents of Thomas A. Edison*. Odense, Denmark, Odense University Press, 1983.
Simonds, William A., *Edison: His Life, His Work, His Genius*. Indianapolis, Bobbs-Merrill, 1934; London, Allen and Unwin, 1935.
Wachhorst, Wyn, *Thomas Alva Edison: An American Myth*. Cambridge, Massachusetts, MIT Press, 1981.

*

Edison was a more complex individual than the Mid-West American "Wizard" he became in the public mind. Readers must be able to differentiate between his public image and his true contribution to American technology and society. This task will be much easier in the future with the complete publication of Edison's papers (edited by Reese V. Jenkins, et al., 1989–). While only the first volume has been published at this writing, the complete unedited collection of nearly 3.5 million pages of his papers, which are in the Edison National Museum collection, has been issued in microfilm for the use of scholars. The Jenkins volumes are well edited, with photographs, illustrations, and comments that will be of tremendous value to anyone wishing to reinterpret the man and his contributions.

The Edison "myth" is so pervasive in American culture that two books, by WACHHORST and NYE, have been written on this topic alone. While neither is a biography, they are necessary reading for all future biographers. Wachhorst is particularly notable for his painstaking analysis of the published literature on Edison.

Early biographies of Edison suffer from several inherent flaws. Horatio Alger-type heros were popular in his time, and the basic story of Edison's life, from his midwest beginnings, to becoming a wandering telegrapher, to his penniless arrival in New York to take on the business world, fit the pattern. In addition, Edison had access to his early biographers, and his personality and penchant for anecdotes, which he frequently altered to fit the situation, only tended to perpetuate the myth. McCLURE's work, the first full-length biography, set this pattern for many later biographies. Edison's personal control is most evident in the work produced jointly by DYER, MEADOWCROFT, and MARTIN, which was considered the "official" version of his life. Dyer was Edison's attorney and Martin was editor of *Electrical World*, but the majority of the work was done by Meadowcroft, Edison's secretary. Meadowcroft expanded the book into two massive volumes in 1929. The work suffers from distortions and superficialities, based upon many of Edison's anecdotes, which reenforce the myths of his inventive genius, and downplay his personal life and business failures. It is, however, one of the best treatments of Edison's early technical work.

JEHL was an assistant in Edison's laboratory during the period of the invention of the electric light. While his book has also been found to contain many inaccuracies, and is somewhat disorganized, it is still a firsthand source for Edison's activities during the Menlo Park days.

There was renewed interest in Edison around the time of the Golden Jubilee of the invention of the electric light. Several new biographies appeared, written by a new generation of biographers. Not all of them are notable, but they all follow the pattern set years ago by McClure. The SIMONDS and BRYAN volumes fall in this category. NERNEY's work is based on some new personal interviews that are still referred to by current biographers.

The turning point in Edison biography, however, is the volume by JOSEPHSON. It is one of the first to objectively analyze Edison as a man and delve into the details of his background, training, family life, inventiveness, business acumen, successes, and failures. What emerges is a dedicated, intense inventor with an immense drive, who was a bridge between the tinker inventors of the past and modern-day industrial research organizations. Josephson is also important for his analysis of the cultural environment in which Edison's inventions took place, examining their acceptance and their eventual effects on American society. This book is the favorite of the editors of the papers of Thomas Edison.

CLARK offers a straightforward, lucid, and even-handed biography. CONOT's very readable volume shows a rougher, cruder Edison than the other books portray. Conot was one of the first biographers to have access to the Edison papers, which had been locked up for years and are now beginning to appear in printed form.

FRIEDEL provides a better indication of the type of research the Edison papers will generate in the future. While his is not a biography of the man, it is a biography of the man's ideas, particularly the invention and development of the electric light. Its analysis strips away much of the myth, publicity, and pure bravado of this unusual man who underneath still emerges as an American inventive genius.

—Robert James Havlik

EDWARD I, 1239–1307; English monarch.

Powicke, F. M., *King Henry III and the Lord Edward* (2 vols.). Oxford, Clarendon Press, 1947.
Prestwich, Michael, *Edward I*. London, Methuen, and Berkeley, University of California Press, 1988.
Salzman, L. F., *Edward I*. London, Constable, and New York, Praeger, 1968.
Seeley, R. B., *The Greatest of All th. lantagenets: An Historical Sketch*. London, R. Bentley, 1860.
Tout, Thomas F., *Edward the First*. London and New York, Macmillan, 1893.

*

Edward I has always been recognized as a great king of England, "the English Justinian," but in the eyes of the Welsh and the Scots he has an evil reputation as a ruthless imperialist. In the second half of the 19th century a new emphasis on the king's imperialist note led SEELEY to defend the older view of him as an English hero. "For 300 years 'the greatest of all the Plantagenets' had been held, by most Englishmen, in the utmost veneration," Seeley wrote, citing the judgments of Hemingford (1320): "the most excellent, wise, and sagacious king"; of Froissart (1400): "the good King Edward"; of Fabian (1494): "Slow to all manners of strife; discreet and wise, and true to his word: in arms a giant"; of Foxe (1563): "Valiant and courageous; pious and gentle"; of Holinshed (1557): "Wise and virtuous; gentle and courteous." Seeley continued, "Yet by modern writers— such as Hume and Henry, Mackintosh, Scott, and others— a very different portraiture is given. In these pages Edward is represented as ambitious, unscrupulous, artful, and vindictive. Whence arose this remarkable change in the current and tenor of our English histories?" Seeley claimed that the majority of the modern historians he cited were of Scottish birth, and that "this great perversion of history" resulted from their animus against a king whose epitaph proclaimed him *Scotorum Malleus* ("the hammer of the Scots"). In his desire to vindicate the king's character Seeley produced a hagiographical volume, and in exonerating him from all his faults and evil actions, drew an unconvincing portrait.

TOUT also considered Edward I the greatest of the Plantagenets, basing his admiration on profound knowledge of the 13th century. In his view "the great men of the 13th century embody the best ideals of the Middle Ages, but there is also something modern in their character and ambitions. Edward himself partakes of this twofold nature. As a man he seems almost purely mediaeval. Yet as an English statesman he could conceive the idea of a national state ruled by a strong king, but controlled by a popular parliament. As a diplomatist he could grasp the conception of a European equilibrium, to be maintained by a judicious policy of mediation on the part of his island kingdom. As a British patriot he longed for the time when England, Scotland, Wales and Ireland were all parts of the same kingdom." None of these views may be at present defended or commended, but Tout presented them skillfully, in a narrative of admirable clarity. His admiration for Edward I led him to play down the "wanton and brutal violence" of his extreme youth, though Edward's savage temper was never entirely overcome. In his desire to exclude no detail that might contribute to a description of Edward, Tout wrote "His complexion was dark, clear and pale"—an impossible combination! However, his statement that "Edward hated his enemies quite as heartily as he loved his friends, and liked power so well that he grew quite mad at the least opposition or contradiction" is a clear enough thumbnail sketch of a passionate autocrat.

POWICKE's great work covers the history of England in the later years of Henry III's reign. While not strictly speaking a biography of Edward I, it is essential reading for the student of Edward I's reign. This two-volume work covers the immensely important years preceding Edward's accession; his relations with his father, as an heir of mature years; and his relations with the opposition led by Simon de Montfort. The second volume concludes with an important epilogue, which comprises a sketch of Edward I's reign, and a shrewd summing-up of his character. Powicke stresses how un-English was Edward and identifies the immediate influences upon him: "He had little northern blood in him. His father was more than half a Poitevin, his mother came of Aragonese and Savoyard stock. His young wife was the child of a Castilian father. . . . " Yet, Powicke points out, the king and his magnates formed one large family: "They could all be arranged in one genealogical table, which would include also the princes of Wales and the king and great families of Scotland. . . . These people lived in a social system of land management, wardship and marriage, according to rules—feudal rules—which they observed, with delight or exasperation as the case might be, like serious children playing an intricate parlour game. It was their world. . . . " Powicke's picture of this world is compellingly presented, in a beautiful style, and Edward I takes his place in it, with his faults and virtues objectively described.

SALZMAN attempted a popular biography of Edward I, not an easy subject for a book of this type. The enormous amount of compression required to include the political, legal, ecclesiastical, military, and social aspects of the reign in a coherent narrative almost defeated the author. The fact that the narrative remained readable is a compliment to Salzman's style. The last chapter on the character of Edward, and the Appendix on the legal, constitutional, and financial background are clear summaries for the general reader.

For the serious student of the reign, PRESTWICH's recent biography is the most important book, but his style is so clear that the general reader can follow the intricate questions of the reign without difficulty. Prestwich explained that "in order to provide a clearer view of the problems that faced Edward, a thematic approach has been adopted for much of the book." This approach has produced readily comprehensible sections on several complex themes.

On the king's character Prestwich makes the point that "there are no simple judgements to be made on Edward I" because of the difficulties that arise from the very different way in which his contemporaries thought about personality: "Their minds were not cluttered with psychological concepts, and it did not even occur to them to ask if the king was clever or stupid, original or derivative, or even whether he had powers of leadership, in the sense that they would be understood today." Of all Edward I's biographers, Prestwich comes nearest to answering these questions. The extensive bibliography of his admirable book lists many works on related subjects and also a wide range of publications in periodicals.

—Caroline Bingham

EDWARD II, 1284–1327; English monarch.

Bingham, Caroline, *The Life and Times of Edward II*. London, Weidenfeld and Nicolson, 1973.
Fryde, Natalie, *The Tyranny and Fall of Edward II 1321–26*. Cambridge and New York, Cambridge University Press, 1979.
Hutchison, Harold, *Edward II: The Pliant King*. London, Eyre and Spottiswoode, 1971; New York, Stein and Day, 1972.
Johnstone, Hilda, *Edward of Carnarvon 1284–1307*. Manchester, Manchester University Press, 1946.
Tout, Thomas F., *The Place of the Reign of Edward II in English History*. Manchester, Manchester University Press, 1914.

*

Edward II has attracted few biographers, a fact that is initially surprising since his life and reign were crowded with dramatic events. Possibly these were best treated in dramatic form, in *The Troublesome Raigne and Lamentable Death of Edward the Second* (1593), by Christopher Marlowe, who did not need to be troubled by accuracy in chronology or detail.

TOUT's great work of scholarship, as its title implies, is not a biography; his major contribution is his exploration of administrative history during Edward's reign. Defining his own viewpoint in this book, he wrote, "I was impressed with the exceptional importance of the reign of Edward II in the history of administrative development in England, and notably as the point in which the marked differentiation of what may roughly be called 'court administration' and 'national administration' first became accentuated." This may seem an arid approach to the reader seeking biographical details of Edward II, but for the minutiae of the reign Tout's work is essential reading. However, Tout does not neglect biographical sources. He includes a section on the contemporary and near-contemporary chroniclers and their attitudes to the king. This is followed by a section entitled "The Personal Aspects of the Reign," in which Tout explains the chroniclers' disapproval of the king chiefly in terms of Edward's idleness and incompetence, which deeply shocked the "austerity and grim earnestness of the mediaeval mind." Tout, never devoid of humour, amusingly illustrates how differently Edward's notorious attachment to sports and "mechanic arts" might have appeared from a 20th-century viewpoint: "Had the mediaeval point of view allowed a lay prince to study at Oxford, and had 14th-century Oxford pursued modern sports and pastimes, Edward would perhaps have distinguished himself as a driver of four-in-hands and as an athlete. He would have shown his skill in 'mechanic arts' by his knowledge of motor cars and perhaps even have rowed in the University eight. Unluckily his ignorance of Latin would have made it impossible for him ever to have passed Responsions." (In Tout's day a "crammer" or later a Tutorial College could have solved this problem.)

In "The Captivity and Death of Edward of Carnarvon" (reprint from the Bulletin of the John Rylands Library, Manchester University Press, 1920), Tout concluded that the traditional account of the murder of Edward II was correct and that an account of his escape and subsequent wanderings (addressed by an ecclesiastic, Manuel de Fieschi, to Edward III) was perhaps "an intelligent attempt to exact hush money from a famous King whose beginnings had been based upon his father's murder and his mother's adultery." All Tout's works are essential reading for the student of the life of Edward II.

The same must be said of the works of Tout's student JOHNSTONE, whose *Edward of Carnarvon* is a study of the prince's life from birth to accession, and the best account of his early years. Besides covering Edward's military initiation in Scottish campaigns and his feud with his father over his friendship with Gaveston, Johnstone provides evidence of his interest in hunting and horsebreeding, his patronage of minstrels and musicians, and his liking for the Welsh prototype of the violin, the "crwth." Johnstone also wrote of Edward's enthusiasm for non-regal pursuits in "The Eccentricities of Edward II" (*English Historical Review*, XLVIII, 1933).

HUTCHISON's work, the first full-length biography of Edward II, is both well researched and readable. The subtitle, "The Pliant King," is taken from a speech by Gaveston in Marlowe's play: "I must have wanton poets, pleasant wits, / Musicians, that with touching of a string / May draw the pliant king which way I please." It seems oddly inept as a subtitle, for if the king was pliant to Gaveston's wishes, he was pliant in no other respect. "The Obstinate King" would describe him better, and go further to explain why he provoked opposition throughout his reign.

Hutchison's work is based on printed editions of medieval chronicles and on the work of modern scholars. He gives a lucid narrative of the events of the reign and a sympathetic portrait of the king. Hutchison found a credible interpretation of Edward's character in Marlowe: "Marlowe I think understood Edward of Caernarvon much better than most subsequent historians and researchers. He was more alive to the poetry and tragedy of homosexuality . . . " Hutchison faced the issue of Edward's homosexuality more forthrightly than had earlier historians, who had shown the reticence characteristic of the earlier years of the 20th century. Hutchison concludes, "The truth would seem to be that, in the choice of his ministers Edward of Caernarvon was far from incompetent, and if, in the choice of one intimate friend, there is strong evidence of homosexuality, there is no evidence that that homosexuality impaired his competence as head of state." Edward is credited with having chosen a very able minister in Hugh Despenser the younger in the later years of the reign. But, finally, Hutchison admits the "sad and incontravertable fact" that Edward II was a failure.

BINGHAM (the present writer) has written a biography of Edward II for Weidenfeld's "Life and Times" series on English monarchs. Addressed to general readers, the text provides the "Life" and copious illustrations present various aspects of the "Times," such as architecture, arts and crafts, court life, rural life, religion, and warfare. Bingham portrays Edward II sympathetically and seeks to provide a clear narrative of the reign without oversimplifying its complex events and issues.

FRYDE's work concentrates on the last years of the reign, covering the rule of Edward and the Despensers, which she describes as a "tyranny," and concluding with an account of Edward's deposition and imprisonment. Fryde offers an important introductory chapter on "Problems and Sources," and an interesting epilogue on the overthrow of Queen Isabella and Roger Mortimer by the young Edward III. Fryde's book is an impressive work of scholarship based on record sources, and her style is admirably clear; the reader is never in danger of being lost in a labyrinth of detail.

Fryde disagrees with earlier historians and presents her arguments convincingly. In particular she seeks to refute Tout's belief that the Despensers were "intelligent champions of strong monarchy." Fryde writes "There is not the slightest evidence to show that the Despensers themselves were interested in or involved with administrative reform. . . . Tout's appreciative judgment of the character of the Despenser régime and its 'achievements' on the basis of its administrative performance and innovation has distorted our understanding of the true nature of their corrupt dictatorship." Edward II himself is unattractively presented as excessively rapacious, and guilty of a reign of terror after his victory at Boroughbridge in 1322. Especially interesting from the biographical viewpoint is the seriousness with which Fryde treats the possibility that Edward II, having escaped from Berkeley Castle, was not recaptured, and therefore was not murdered. Her argument, that the letter of Manuel de Fieschi to Edward III could be true, is plausible.

While general readers may select the biographies of Hutchison or Bingham, the serious student of the reign or the future biographer of Edward II must turn to Tout, Johnstone, and Fryde, and must also bear in mind that a very great deal of work on Edward II, his reign and his contemporaries, has been published in learned periodicals. For these publications, up to 1979, Fryde's bibliography is an excellent guide.

—Caroline Bingham

EDWARD III, 1312–1377; English monarch.

Barnes, Joshua, *The History of That Most Victorious Monarch Edward III*. Cambridge, J. Hayes, 1688.

Costain, Thomas B., *The Three Edwards*. New York, Doubleday, 1958.

Johnson, Paul, *The Life and Times of Edward III*, London, Weidenfeld and Nicolson, 1973.

Longman, William, *The History of the Life and Times of Edward III* (2 vols.). London, Longman, 1869.

MacKinnon, James, *The History of Edward the Third (1327–77)*. London and New York, Longman, 1900.

Packe, Michael St. John, *King Edward III*, edited by L. C. B. Seaman. London, Routledge, 1983.

Prestwich, Michael, *The Three Edwards*. London, Weidenfeld and Nicolson, and New York, St. Martin's, 1980.

Warburton, William P., *Edward III*. Boston, Estes and Lauriet; Chicago, Jansen McClurg; and London, Longman, 1875.

*

Though many readers may wish to study Edward in the colorful pages of Froissart, a sometime member of King Edward's court whose chronicle is the most vivid, if not the most accurate, source for the reign, the earliest actual history of King Edward still cited by recent historians is that of BARNES. His history of the "most victorious king," as its name suggests, is largely laudatory. Based on a conflation of the available chronicles, it criticizes these only when they are unfavorable to Edward (as in his alleged rape of the countess of Salisbury). Barnes does also take into account the opinions of some earlier antiquaries, and prints full English translations of several important documents, notably statutes.

Packe's reference to Barnes as the only full life of Edward constitutes a serious injustice to LONGMAN, whose massive work (over 700 pages) is easily the most detailed study of the reign. Primarily a traditional narrative of political and military events, with some coverage of socio-economic matters (from a laissez-faire viewpoint), the book may go for entire chapters without mentioning any personal action by the king. While based chiefly on the chronicles, it handles them more judiciously than did Barnes, though perhaps less sceptically than some later historians.

Although beginning with some patriotic praise for King Edward's reign as "brilliant in arms" and "fruitful in social progress," Longman (unlike most other writers in English) plods grimly through the whole catalogue of English defeats in France in the latter part of Edward's reign, and ends by commenting that though the king had all the qualities to inspire unthinking hero worship, he had little claim to the commendation of the wise and thoughtful. Aside from this remark, and a rather unusual comparison of Edward Balliol's attack on Scotland with the Confederate raider *Alabama*, Longman's personal opinions are not obtrusive.

This cannot be said of MacKINNON, whose first sentence declares that Edward II was a "complete ninny," and who very evidently held a similar view of Edward III. MacKinnon was apparently a devotee of "peace, retrenchment and reform" and indulges in much sarcastic comment on Edward's chivalric excesses. As a patriotic Scot, he also gives a detailed account of Edward's early Scottish campaigns based largely on Scottish sources, which may be no more reliable than English ones but at least offer an unusual perspective. MacKinnon's sympathy for England's enemies extends to Charles V the Wise of France, in which he is followed by most later writers, though Longman had called that king "Charles the Crafty." MacKinnon claims to base his views on the (then recent) great editions of Froissart and many other chronicles edited in the later 19th century (after Longman wrote); nonetheless, much of his material turns out to be taken directly from Longman, though ornamented with MacKinnon's own scornful witticisms.

A briefer and less idiosyncratic condensation of Longman may be found in WARBURTON, whose work was apparently intended for English schoolboys, but may now be useful to those who wish to gain an impression of 19th-century scholarship on Edward without reading the longer works of Longman and MacKinnon.

A more patriotic alternative to these unenthusiastic 19th-century views of Edward III can be found in PACKE. Though his book was published posthumously in 1983 (being completed by Seaman) most of its research seems to date from the 1950s and 60s and its attitudes to the 1940s: memories of D-Day are repeatedly invoked to parallel Edward's French invasions, and in general the approach is more sympathetic to the warrior king. Packe's military analysis appears indebted to Burne's study (*The Crecy War*). Naturally, given his sympathy, Packe's last section on Edward's late defeats is much less detailed than Longman's, though this may be due to the fact that this portion was left incomplete at Packe's death. The same cause may account for a number of small errors of fact, some of which may have originated in misreadings of Packe's notes.

One of Packe's most interesting contributions is his identification of the lady in the famous Salisbury scandal as Alice, wife of Edward Montagu; this neglected suggestion is at least more plausible than Galway's theory that she was Joan of Kent. Unfortunately, in this and a few other instances, Packe's text does not clearly differentiate between an interesting hypothesis and historical fact; there are statements about the king's emotions that are in the nature of the case unverifiable.

This very occasional weakness in Packe is the frequent practice of COSTAIN, whose widely accessible book (part of his "History of the Plantagenets") should be classed with his other historical fiction. His vividly visualized work gives a series of wonderful word-pictures of the entire era of the three Edwards, but the historical basis of these creations is often slender and sometimes slanted. His romantic insistence on the beauty of Queen Philippa, for instance, prefers a fairytale formula to the known facts. The general reader may find Costain very enjoyable, but he cannot be recommended to those reading for knowledge rather than pleasure.

PRESTWICH, on the other hand, using the same title as Costain, has done a worthwhile piece of synthetic scholarship that is essentially the "times" without the "lives" for the period of the three Edwards, though there are occasional personal vignettes— a chapter on domestic policy, for instance, is enlivened by a page on Edward III's personal expenditures for gambling, buying horses, etc. Prestwich usually does well in synthesizing a wide range of recent research, though in a few cases (such as the economic effects of the Black Death) where the secondary authorities are in severe conflict, he is unable to reach a clear-cut conclusion.

The best brief balance of vividness and accuracy, life and times, may be JOHNSON. The numerous handsome illustrations suggest this is a "coffee-table" book, but Johnson actually does very well in linking the details of Edward's personal life to those of the lives of all Englishmen of his day. Though published before Packe, Johnson may be considered, for the moment, the most up-to-date short life of the king (since Packe's research, for reasons explained above, stops well short of his publication date). Like Packe, Johnson ultimately gives a favorable verdict on the old king, though his earlier chapters recognize the horrors of war and the suffering of many of the peasantry during the period.

—John L. Leland

EDWARD VII, 1841–1910; English monarch, son of Queen Victoria.

Adams, William S., *Edwardian Portraits*. London, Secker and Warburg, 1956.

Dangerfield, George, *Victoria's Heir: The Education of a Prince*. New York, Harcourt, 1941; London, Constable, 1942.

Hearnshaw, F. J. C., "King Edward VII" in Arthur Bryant, *The Man and the Hour: Studies of Six Great Men of Our Time*. London, P. Allan, 1934.

Hibbert, Christopher, *Edward VII: A Portrait*. London, A. Lane, 1976; as *The Royal Victorians: King Edward VII, His Family and Friends*, Philadelphia, Lippincott, 1976.

Lee, Sir Sidney, *King Edward VII: A Biography* (2 vols.). London and New York, Macmillan, 1925–27.

Magnus, Philip, *King Edward the Seventh*. New York, Dutton, and London, J. Murray, 1964.

Maurois, André, *King Edward and His Times*, translated by Hamish Miles. London, Cassell, 1933; as *The Edwardian Era*, New York, Appleton-Century, 1933 (originally published as *Édouard VII et son Temps*, Paris, Grasset, 1933).

St. Aubyn, Giles, *Edward VII: Prince and King*. New York, Atheneum, and London, Collins, 1979.

*

The expansive, privileged, and seemingly idle life of Edward VII, son of Victoria, long waiting as the Prince of Wales before reigning in his own right from 1901–1910, has attracted over the years historians and biographers who are just as interested in sexual peccadilloes, personality defects, psychic turmoil, private prejudices, and self-indulgences, as in politics and diplomacy. Modern biographies of Edward VII are particularly inclined in that direction.

The old, standard two-volume biography based on the Royal Archives by LEE, who literally put his life into this work, dying before the actual completion of the second volume, still invites comparison with later biographies. But it does have the feel of a biography written in a different generation. The great length and detail of Lee's work, which devotes one entire volume to Edward VII's very brief reign, does allow him to give full coverage to political and diplomatic history. But many of these events had little connection with Edward. Lee also tends to give very lengthy quotations from letters. He does not neglect the personal side of Edward, but coming from a more modest, circumspect generation, he makes no mention of Liile Langtry, Lady Brooke, or Mrs. James, all lovers of Edward. Future biographers will not be so dainty, but Lee does place Edward in the political milieu of the era, revealing a man who, particularly as Prince, had absolutely nothing of real substance to do, who oversaw and attended ceremonial functions, garden parties, operas, and plays.

MAGNUS makes Edward the man the center of study rather than dwelling endlessly on the politics and diplomacy of the age, doing so in far fewer pages than Lee. Magnus portrays Edward as a person constantly fighting off terminal boredom with more and more extravagance, whether in eating, hunting, traveling, or love affairs, which Magnus now openly acknowledges as fact. For his study Magnus consulted the Royal Archives as well as the Esher, Salisbury, and Asquith papers.

Both Lee and Magnus intended their books for a scholarly audience. But HIBBERT, taking advantage of an Edwardian craze initiated by public television, produced a popular but still soundly researched portrayal of Edward VII. Lavishly illustrated with photographs from the period, Hibbert's book delivers a plethora of entertaining anecdotal material about Edward, showing both his childishness and his sophistication. Hibbert reveals that Edward VII was not just stout, funny, and bored, but also a very complicated man. Most reviewers praised Hibbert for his colorful prose while conceding that Magnus may still be best for scholars, perhaps because Magnus' writing style is flat while

Hibbert takes the readers breathlessly from race courses to casinos, from hunting parties to operas, from picnics at Biarritz to the Pope's private quarters, as we follow Edward on his merry way. So Hibbert moves Edward the man even more to the center of the historical stage.

ST. AUBYN, head of the History Department at Eton, decided to write a biography of Edward VII after he came into possession of the papers of Francis Knollys, Edward's private secretary, his eyes and ears for almost 50 years. These papers enable St. Aubyn to throw some fresh light on some aspects of the social and sexual life of the time. St. Aubyn has written a long, detailed, and entertaining study that any Edwardian scholar cannot ignore because of Knollys' papers, if taken with the caveat that what we are reading comes from an unctuous courtier and sycophant to Edward.

Other studies related to the life of Edward VII deserve brief mention. DANGERFIELD's cursory study of the Prince of Wales has now been superseded, but not in its prose, which still bears the Dangerfield charm and style. ADAMS' portrait is still useful, providing insights into Edward's peculiarities, such as his constant gambling. The French writer MAUROIS offers an appropriately terse, and very gallic, sketch of Edward, who from the wit of beautiful women learned how to deal with men. Although not a biography of Edward, Battiscombe's chatty study of Edward's wife (*Queen Alexandra*, 1969) provides glimpses into a relationship in which Alexandra showed a remarkable sense of tolerance, even humor, on the subject, for example, of Edward's many mistresses. And finally there is a short character sketch of Edward VII by HEARNSHAW. It is of little value to scholars, yet there exists an element of irony here because Hearnshaw, along with Lee's assistant, S. F. Markham, played a central role in the eventual completion of Lee's second volume of his life of Edward VII, for which both received credit only in a "Publishers' Note" at the beginning of the book.

—Richard A. Voeltz

EDWARDS, Jonathan, 1703–1758; American pastor, theologian, and philosopher.

Allen, Alexander V. G., *Jonathan Edwards*. Boston, Houghton Mifflin, 1889.

Dwight, Sereno Edwards, *The Life of President Edwards*. New York, Converse, 1829.

Hopkins, Samuel, *The Life and Character of the Late Reverend, Learned and Pious Mr. Jonathan Edwards*. Boston, S. Kneeland, 1765.

Miller, Perry, *Jonathan Edwards*. New York, W. Sloane, 1949.

Murray, Iain H., *Jonathan Edwards: A New Biography*. Edinburgh, Banner of Truth Trust, 1987.

Parkes, Henry B., *Jonathan Edwards: The Fiery Puritan*. New York, Minton Balch, 1930.

Winslow, Ola E., *Jonathan Edwards 1703–58: A Biography*. New York, Macmillan, 1940.

*

In addition to information from his personal journals and letters, Edwards' main autobiographical writing is his *Personal Narrative* (first published in Hopkins, see below) describing the period of his youth and his collegiate career. Although the narrative is fascinating in its vivid portrayal of a young man's conversion through his response to God in nature and experience, many, such as William Scheick, suggest that it cannot be taken at "face value" since it evinces "artifice" (*Early American Literature*, 24 [1989]).

As a close friend of Edwards, who had lived and visited with the Edwards family, HOPKINS wrote his short, panegyrical biography from the perspective of an admiring eyewitness, so that a more objective account was still needed. Besides being an essential sourcebook, Hopkins' work, Perry Miller asserts, stands on its own as a "neglected classic of American biography" because of its mixture of anecdotes and personal insights into Edwards' life, which no other eyewitness account provides in such detail. DWIGHT, the great grandson of Edwards, explains that he spent "many years" researching and collecting various manuscripts and letters of Edwards to compile his detailed and ponderous work, containing long, unabridged letters and documents, which overwhelm the biographical discussion. Subsequent scholars are nevertheless dependent on this biography because it contains important primary materials, some of which have since been lost in manuscript form. Samuel Miller's *Life of Jonathan Edwards* (1839), an attempt to create a popular version of Edwards' life, is basically an abridgement of Dwight's work and long out of print.

ALLEN considered Dwight's work as inadequate since "much that would throw light upon Edwards' history is withheld from publication." The basis for this intriguing statement is only apparent in chapter six, where Allen discusses a "missing manuscript" on the trinity, that men like Oliver Wendell Holmes considered "suppressed" and "withheld," because it supposedly departed from previously published works, tending in the direction of "Arianism" or "Sabellianism." One trinity manuscript, subsequently published, contained no such deviations and proved these concerns to be unfounded; yet Allen speculates on what another missing manuscript on the trinity might have contained. The rest of his work merely approaches Edwards and his writings from a more intellectual and humanistic view than Dwight, with more in-depth analysis of Edwards' ideas.

Not until the 1930s did renewed interest in Edwards evidence itself in new biographies, which at times are tainted with 20th-century prejudices. PARKES' lively, debunking, but misinformed biography is a prime example of an inaccurate labelling of Edwards as a "Puritan"—a catch-all term of H. L. Mencken and his contemporaries, to be associated with anything supposedly religious, repressive, and out-of-date. Many might agree that Edwards was one of the last great Puritans, but few would accept Parkes' description of him as "the father of American Puritanism: before him religion meant the propitiation of a jealous God in order to secure worldly prosperity; after him it meant disinterested obedience to the law, because the law was lovely . . ." His stretching of the facts is apparent in another comment: "After [Edwards'] death, his writings transformed half the people of New England from healthy human beings to would be saints." Parkes excuses his "generalizations" by explaining that he wrote "for the general reader." While certainly

amusing and entertaining, Parkes' book is so riddled with unreliable, exaggerated, and biased assertions that it should be read as fiction. Both Parkes' book and Albert C. McGiffert's psychological biography, *Jonathan Edwards* (1932), were largely replaced by Winslow in 1940.

WINSLOW's is the most reliable and readable biography. She was the first to expand significantly upon Edwards' known history by carefully searching in the largely unexplored Yale collection, the libraries of Princeton and Forbes (at Northampton), as well as further researching in the Andover collection, which had been the basis for Dwight's study. From these collections, she added important new information, including previously unpublished letters and documents. Evidence of her painstaking research is her discovery of shopping lists and personal notes on scraps of paper and on the backs or in the margins of sermons, which provide insight into the more practical and human side of Edwards. Winslow's wider knowledge of the New England context also provides an important backdrop to understanding Edwards. Yet, when Winslow develops her thesis that Edwards' significance as a theologian was "his emphasis on religion as a transforming individual experience," she tends to translate his theology into a modern idiom that suits her own tastes. One reviewer of Winslow, C. H. Faust, considers that she follows other biographers like Allen, Parkes, and McGiffert, who have "found parts of his system admirable, when these parts have been properly translated in terms of some more or less fully elaborated contemporary system of ideas" and therefore have not presented Edwards' view of life in his own terms (*New England Quarterly*, 13 [1940]).

MILLER approaches Edwards from a new angle both in format and content. He chronologically intersperses "essential" sections of interpretive biography with sections discussing the works of Edwards, believing that "the real life of Jonathan Edwards was the life of his mind." Downplaying the importance of theology, Miller makes bold claims that Edwards was an artist of ideas, an unrecognized precursor of modern thought, and an astute disciple of Locke. In the introduction, his focus is apparent: " . . . [Edwards] speaks from a primitive religious conception which often seems hopelessly out of touch with even his own day, yet at the same time he speaks from an insight into science and psychology so much ahead of his time that our own can hardly be said to have caught up with him." Miller's book proved to be a seminal study, stirring up renewed scholarly interest in Edwards and instigating the modern edition of Edwards' writings (as yet incomplete) by Yale University Press. While many have challenged Miller's ideas, especially the overstated claims about Edwards' modernity and Locke's influence on Edwards, this work still remains a point of departure for any critical analysis of Edwards' thought. Unfortunately, since Miller had to comply with an editorial policy of a text unburdened with footnotes, the annotated copy of his text is only available in the Harvard College Library.

Questionably basing his main research of an American colonial in Scotland, MURRAY explains in his introduction that he writes primarily for a Christian audience to re-instigate interest in Edwards' life and religious ideas. So his biography is new in the sense of incorporating Edwards' theological views with his life in a sympathetic manner to reassert the primary importance of his orthodox Christian vision above any philosophical novelties. Certainly, this area of Edwards' biography is lacking, but not to the distorting degree that Murray claims. Murray interacts with other biographers like Winslow, Miller, Allen, and Parkes, both accepting and rejecting some of their interpretations, especially in the theological arena. However, at times his reassessments are inaccurate, as when he bases his claim that Edwards was not remote and aloof solely on the testimony of Edwards' close friends while excusing the historical testimony of other individuals as myth, or when he ignores the metaphysical intricacies and innovations of Edwards' thought and places him strictly within the Calvinist tradition.

More in-depth details of portions of Edwards' career, such as his Northampton years, his correspondence with Scottish friends, his journeys to different towns, and his relations with various individuals, still have proved largely elusive to scholars. Recent publications of excavated manuscripts and the ongoing work of the Yale edition have provided more biographical insights into Edwards' life. For instance, Wallace E. Anderson, the editor of Volume VI, challenges the assumption of Edwards' childhood precocity in his discovery that Edwards' "Spider Letter" was written when he was 20, not 12. Examining Edwards' editing of David Brainerd's journal in Volume VII of the Yale series, Norman Pettit rightly but astonishingly comments that Edwards "altered what he did not like and omitted what he found unacceptable." Other recent articles, like Harold P. Simonson's "Jonathan Edwards and His Scottish Connections" (*Journal of American Studies*, 21) or Charles Edwin Jones' "The Impolitic Mr. Edwards: The Personal Dimension of the Robert Breck Affair" (*New England Quarterly*, 51) are beginning to fill in the biographical gaps bit by bit. In the meantime, Winslow's remains the best strict biography.

—Marcia Miller

EINSTEIN, Albert, 1879–1955; German-born American physicist.

Clark, Ronald W., *Einstein: The Life and Times*. New York, World Publishing, 1971; London, Hodder and Stoughton, 1973.

Frank, Philipp, *Einstein: His Life and Times*. New York, Knopf, 1947; London, Cape, 1948.

Hoffmann, Banesh, *Albert Einstein: Creator and Rebel*. New York, Viking, 1972; London, Hart-Davis MacGibbon, 1973.

Infeld, Leopold, *Albert Einstein: His Work and Its Influence on Our World*. New York, Scribner, 1950.

Lanczos, Cornelius, *Albert Einstein and the Cosmic World Order*. New York, Interscience, 1965.

Pais, Abraham, *Subtle Is the Lord: The Science and Life of Albert Einstein*. Oxford and New York, Oxford University Press, 1982.

Schlipp, Paul A., *Albert Einstein: Philosopher-Scientist*. Evanston, Illinois, Library of Living Philosophers, 1949.

Whitrow, G. J., *Einstein: The Man and His Achievement*. London, British Broadcasting Corporation, 1967; New York, Dover, 1973.

*

Many biographies of Albert Einstein exist, some focusing more on the man—his personality and his experiences—and others on the development of his ideas in theoretical physics. The biographies by Frank and Hoffmann each present a balance of these two aspects. Both men were physicists who had a keen awareness of Einstein's physics as well as a personal acquaintance with him.

FRANK describes his interaction with Einstein in Prague, where he succeeded his Chair when Einstein accepted the Berlin Chair at the Kaiser Wilhelm Institute, where he had no formal teaching duties. He relates Einstein's skill as a teacher in Prague, his humility toward faculty and students alike, and his relaxed attitude in the classroom. He then describes some of the anti-semitic attitudes against Einstein in Berlin, until his (pressured) departure in 1933, when Hitler took power—"just in time to avoid arrest (and probably early execution!)". Frank tells of Einstein's great appreciation of his newly found freedom in America, from 1933 onward, though he also records Einstein's disappointment in the lack of intellectual life and camaraderie in the U.S., compared with the life that he had in Europe.

Frank makes clear Einstein's excitement and anticipation for future progress with his theory of relativity, in both the special and general forms, and his disappointment with the way in which the quantum theory was evolving. He rightly emphasizes Einstein's later rejection of the ontological view of atomism, replacing it with an ontology based on the continuous field concept, and his hope that eventually quantum mechanics would emerge from a deterministic field theory based on the view of the theory of general relativity. However, Frank seems to maintain the idea that Einstein retained the epistemological stand of logical positivism (as Niels Bohr and Werner Heisenberg interpreted the quantum theory), rather than the actual stand of realism that he took—the idea that there is a real world, independent of the existence of human observers, or what they may say about it from their observations and measurements.

HOFFMANN makes more clear than the other biographers why Einstein rejected the Bohr view of quantum mechanics as well as his rejection of Bohr's reply to the "thought-experiment" conducted by Einstein, Podolsky, and Rosen. Hoffmann also includes more detail on Einstein's discussions with fellow students during his college years and during his time at the Swiss Patent Office, indicating how discussions in his college years with Konrad Halbicht and Maurice Solovine seemed to have had a great deal of influence on his later thinking in physics, and the extreme value to his physics development that Michelangelo Besso had during Einstein's time at the Swiss Patent Office, and many more years of correspondence with him.

CLARK, who is not a professional physicist, provides a very complete chronological document, certainly well-researched, focusing in great detail on Einstein's life and rich in anecdotes.

PAIS is quite detailed regarding the developments of Einstein's physics, from the early considerations of spontaneous and induced emission of radiation from excited atomic systems, the photoelectric effect (leading Einstein to the concept of wave-particle dualism for radiation), ideas of statistical mechanics and quantum statistics (today referred to as "Bose-Einstein statistics"), thence to his development of the theory of special and general relativity, including some mathematical exposition of Einstein's attempts to construct a unified field theory.

Unfortunately, Pais' discussions of Einstein's views of the Copenhagen approach are patronizing, not revealing the real conflicts Einstein had with the conventionally accepted views. Einstein's thoughts on this subject are clearly revealed in many of his publications, including his "Autobiographical Notes" (see below). Pais gives the false impression that Einstein's opposition to the Copenhagen view was not objective at all, but rather based on his own conservatism. Further, Pais does not seem to see the difference between Einstein's concept of a unified field theory (which he pursued during the greater part of his career as a theoretical physicist) and the contemporary "unified theories" of elementary particle physics, such as the recently discovered "electroweak" theory in quantum field theory. The latter view of a unified theory is indeed quite contrary to Einstein's conception.

The biographies by Infeld and Lanczos, each a former collaborator of Einstein, focus primarily on the theory of relativity. INFELD gives more discussion to explaining ideas of special relativity theory to non-specialists, and somewhat less discussion of general relativity, which he interprets as a theory of gravitation. (In contrast, Einstein saw the theory of general relativity as a general theory of matter, with its successful results in gravitation only as a first stage of the theory.) Some of Infeld's explanation of special relativity formulas, for example the Lorentz transformations that led Einstein to the prediction of the twin paradox, reveal Einstein's belief in the effect of relative motion on the aging of a physical body, a view that is still controversial. Einstein himself seems to have changed his mind about such a physical effect later on in his career. For example, in his "Autobiographical Notes," Einstein says, " . . . Strictly speaking, measuring rods and clocks would have to be represented as solutions of the basic equations (objects consisting of moving atomic configurations), not as it were, as theoretically self-sufficient entities."

LANCZOS focuses more on the aspects of the theory of general relativity, providing very clear explanations for the relations between curved space-time geometry and the dynamical properties of matter. He also brings out many of the aspects of Einstein's personality that motivated his attitudes in his research.

The biography by WHITROW is a transcription of 25 short BBC interviews with scholars who were intimately acquainted with Einstein's lifework in theoretical physics, as well as his philosophical and ethical attitudes, and who had personal interviews with him. These scholars include the philosophers Bertrand Russell and Karl Popper, the physicists/mathematicians P. Bergmann, W. B. Bonner, C. Lanczos, E. Straus and J. A. Wheeler, the historian of science I. B. Cohen, and Einstein's son, a hydraulic engineer, H. A. Einstein. Whitrow's book brings out much of Einstein's anticipations for a unified field theory in the final analysis, as well as the continuous field concept to replace the atomistic ontology. There is also discussion of Einstein's dissenting opinion about the Copenhagen interpretation of quantum mechanics. These interviews are brief and primarily anecdotal, but they do provide an enlightening glimpse of Einstein the man, the physicist, and the philosopher.

Finally, to learn about Einstein's own views of his lifework (though not about his personal life) his "Autobiographical Notes" are strongly recommended, as well as his "Reply to Criticism," both published in SCHILPP's 1949 work. This gives the most accurate accounting of Einstein's own views in physics as they developed from the earlier to the more mature stages, encompassing the two major revolutions of modern physics, the quantum and relativity theories. Though he was very instrumental in the formulations of both of these developments in science, Einstein indicates here why he spent a great deal of his career in pursuing further the relativity revolution, toward the discovery of a unified field theory, and why he rejected the path followed by the quantum theorists in accordance with the Copenhagen school.

—Mendel Sachs

EISENHOWER, Dwight D., 1890–1969; American military and political leader, 34th president of the United States.

Adams, Sherman, *Firsthand Report: The Story of the Eisenhower Administration.* New York, Harper, 1961.

Ambrose, Stephen E., *The Supreme Commander: The War Years of General Dwight D. Eisenhower.* New York, Doubleday, 1970; London, Cassell, 1971.

Ambrose, Stephen E., *Eisenhower* (2 vols.). New York, Simon and Schuster, 1983–84; London, Allen and Unwin, 1984.

Brendon, Piers, *Ike: His Life and Times.* New York, Harper, 1986.

Burk, Robert F., *Dwight D. Eisenhower, Hero and Politician.* Boston, Twayne, 1986.

Davis, Kenneth S., *Soldier of Democracy: A Biography of Dwight Eisenhower.* New York, Doubleday, 1945.

Donovan, Robert J., *Eisenhower: The Inside Story.* New York, Harper, 1956.

Eisenhower, David, *Eisenhower: At War, 1943–45.* New York, Random House, and London, Collins, 1986.

Gunther, John, *Eisenhower, the Man and the Symbol.* New York, Harper, and London, Hamilton, 1952.

Hatch, Alden, *General Ike: A Biography of Dwight David Eisenhower.* New York, Holt, 1944; as *General Eisenhower: A Biography of Dwight David Eisenhower,* London, Skeffington, 1946.

Kornitzer, Bela, *The Great American Heritage: The Story of the Five Eisenhower Brothers.* New York, Farrar Straus, 1955.

Larson, Arthur, *Eisenhower: The President Nobody Knew.* New York, Scribner, 1968; London, Frewin, 1969.

Lee, R. Alton, *Dwight D. Eisenhower, Soldier and Statesman.* Chicago, Nelson-Hall, 1981.

Lyon, Peter, *Eisenhower: Portrait of a Hero.* Boston, Little Brown, 1974.

McCann, Kevin, *Man from Abilene.* New York, Doubleday, 1952.

Miller, Francis T., *Eisenhower: Man and Soldier.* Philadelphia, J. C. Winston, 1944.

Moran, Relman, *Dwight D. Eisenhower: A Gauge of Greatness.* New York, 1969.

Neal, Steve, *The Eisenhowers: Reluctant Dynasty.* New York, Doubleday, 1978.

Parmet, Herbert S., *Eisenhower and the American Crusades.* New York and London, Macmillan, 1972.

Pusey, Merlo J., *Eisenhower, the President.* New York, Macmillan, 1956.

Sixsmith, E. K. G., *Eisenhower as Military Commander.* New York, Stein and Day, and London, B. T. Batsford, 1973.

*

Though recognition came late to Dwight David Eisenhower—he remained obscure beyond his 50th birthday—successive roles as commander of American forces in Britain, Supreme Commander of Allied forces, Army chief of staff, president of Columbia University, head of NATO, two-term president of the United States, and best-selling author insured a plethora of biographical attention. The earliest books written about him, such as those by MILLER and HATCH, are useful only in documenting his rise to public notice, but DAVIS' volume remains valuable for its insights regarding Eisenhower's boyhood, a formative period also emphasized by many later biographers. Davis should be supplemented with KORNITZER's study, which includes verbatim interviews with each of the five Eisenhower brothers, and NEAL's more sophisticated work, which is enhanced by contributions from Milton Eisenhower. Despite their meager beginnings, all six of the Eisenhower boys (one of whom died early) had, in their various ways, extraordinarily successful careers.

Once Eisenhower had become the Republican presidential nominee (and almost certain winner) in 1952, campaign biographies inevitably appeared. GUNTHER is only a collection of magazine pieces, whereas McCANN approaches hagiolatry. Both are primarily of interest now for what they tell us about the image-making of that year. Both PUSEY and DONOVAN review the first presidential term sympathetically. The unfairly maligned Eisenhower presidency as a whole was then absolved by ADAMS (Ike's former chief of staff) in his *Firsthand Report*. Another Republican defense, LARSON's is not a standard biography but a topically arranged apologetic. Objectivity cannot be taken for granted in any of these works. Preferable instead, for most purposes, is PARMET's nearly 700-page chronicle of both Eisenhower terms.

Generally speaking, one should view with distrust almost all the books published about Eisenhower during his lifetime. A major reason is that few of them attempted to be objective. The earliest sought to eulogize a military hero; later ones, to sell or smear a party. There are also partial memoirs of Ike written by staff members and other close associates during both his military and his presidential years (like the Sherman Adams book cited). Whether by associates, journalists, party hacks, or bureaucrats, few of these works approach the standards of professional history. A second major reason why most of these books are obsolete is that their source materials were inadequate. All reputable investigators now make extensive use of such resources as those housed in the Dwight David Eisenhower Presidential Library in Abilene, Kansas, for example, but these collections—or most of them—were unavailable to researchers during Eisenhower's lifetime. Later workers also have Eisenhower's own memoirs, *Crusade in Europe* (1948), *The White House Years* (1963), *At Ease* (1967), plus diaries and letters, in addition to corroborating memoirs from Eisenhower associates, a substantial body of

Eisenhower scholarship on specific topics, diminished partisanship, and the enhanced perspective. While Eisenhower's stature as a military leader has always been extremely high, his presidency (despite its eight years of peace and prosperity) remains more controversial. Increasingly, however, informed historians see the Eisenhower of the White House years as the same low-key, shrewd tactician as the Eisenhower of the war years.

Because of the voluminous source material now available, recent biographical studies of Eisenhower have often limited themselves to specific topics or phases of his career. Of these less than comprehensive works, an outstanding example is AMBROSE's 1970 volume, which devotes more than 700 pages to a detailed examination of Ike's activities and military opinions from December 1941 to May 1945. A great strength of this study is that much of its substance derives from Eisenhower's own papers, a published selection of which was co-edited by Ambrose. It is, however, indicative that this finely researched volume contains maps but (except for a frontispiece) no pictures; there is very little in it about Eisenhower's personal life or any nonmilitary aspect of his existence. The result, therefore, is military history rather than biography.

A second treatment of the war years, by SIXSMITH, is more interesting for its perspective than for its facts. A British author with childhood memories of the necessary but sometimes resented American "occupation" of southern England during the planning of the D-Day invasion of 6 June 1944, Sixsmith covers Eisenhower's early years briefly, dealing primarily with World War II and ending with the German surrender. Sixsmith utilized the then recently published Eisenhower *Papers* and interviewed some important participants (including General Omar Bradley), but did not go to America to consult the Eisenhower Library. Though professedly impartial, Sixsmith clearly admires the bald, grinning, look-you-in-the-eye American general who made some military mistakes, to be sure, but whose absolute integrity, humanity, impartiality, selfless devotion, and masterly handling of difficult people (e.g., General Patton) saved the free world.

David EISENHOWER (Ike's grandson) offers an even more elaborate treatment of the campaign, with nearly 1000 pages devoted to a period of less than three years (1943–45). This is the first volume of an intended three, the other two to concentrate on Eisenhower's presidential years. Having intended originally to deal *only* with the presidential years, David Eisenhower soon realized that much of his grandfather's thinking with regard to global politics and national roles and strategies derived significantly from his wartime experiences. This volume, drafted originally as a massive chronology, is therefore a prolegomenon to those which will deal with Ike's political career. Surprisingly, David learned little about the war from childhood talks with his grandfather, who rarely discussed it. In any event, he describes the conflict as Ike understood and experienced it from day to day, emphasizing the military and political challenges and with what fine leadership he met them. (Criticism is reported but not endorsed.) Chapters 1–5 begin with the preparations of 1943 and culminate with the D-Day invasion; 6–8 focus on the subsequent campaign in France; 9–10 then conclude the resistance. Wartime experiences, David argues, led his grandfather to seek the presidency.

Admirable as these dutifully researched studies are, most nonspecialist readers will prefer a comprehensive, one-volume life. The easiest introduction to Eisenhower—concisely written, strikingly illustrated, and properly uplifting—is MORAN's, written quickly but competently by an Associated Press reporter upon news of Eisenhower's death. This relatively short book—in large format with brief, factual chapters, and a fine collection of photographs, including some in color—was of course intended as a tribute, for Ike's millions of admirers to cherish. Though responsibly informative, it is uncritical and rather protective. Ike, we learn, was a selfless American who always served when asked.

The next major comprehensive biography after Moran's was LYON's, which devotes more than 900 pages to Ike's wartime and presidential years, with only a brief, unoriginal glance at earlier periods in his life. Despite its subtitle, this is not a hero-worshiping book. In well written, balanced accounts, Lyon accepts the hero and his critics as equals; he does not, therefore, hesitate to fault Eisenhower (for political indecisiveness, especially), whose handling of the Cold War as President—in contrast to his wartime victories—seemed to Lyon a great failure.

Another, even more critical biography, by British author BRENDON, concentrates on the presidential years and their most significant problems, including Senator McCarthy, John Foster Dulles and his foreign-policy influence, Richard Nixon, the incessant presidential golfing, the Suez crisis of 1956, civil rights agitation (in Little Rock and elsewhere), Cold War paranoia, and the U-2 incident involving pilot Gary Powers. Though Eisenhower was the first of our television presidents, Brendon complains, he was made to seem an ailing, incoherent senior citizen, vacillating, inept, and unsophisticated. The Eisenhower years, it is alleged, were characterized by materialism, conformity, and urban decay. As revisionist history, however, Brendon's is less than successful. For a more balanced account, and one of the briefest, see BURK, who offers easy access to basic information and a useful bibliographical essay. For longer but still basic treatment, prefer LEE's well-written if somewhat juvenile comprehensive biography in almost 400 pages. Its final chapter, "Verdict of History," usefully surveys Eisenhower historiography.

AMBROSE has written the most satisfactory comprehensive biography of Eisenhower to date (though perhaps too flattering), comprising two large volumes. Volume one, covering Eisenhower's life from his birth in 1890 (with family history before that) to his election victory in 1952, necessarily reviews wartime episodes treated at greater length by Ambrose in 1970, but the perspective here is entirely different. We now see Eisenhower as a *personality* shaped by his upbringing and later significant experiences. Given at times to rages that he gradually learned to control, Ike was ambitious, thin-skinned, stubborn, culturally unsophisticated, naive—and immensely likable. Thus, war becomes in part a study of relationships. Volume two deals with the presidential and retirement years. Ambrose attempts throughout to present events and persons as Ike saw them, thereby to describe and explain the man rather than to judge him. Yet Ambrose clearly shows his admiration for his subject. Let all who today live in freedom, Ambrose admonishes, not forget how much we owe to Dwight David Eisenhower.

—Dennis R. Dean

EISENSTEIN, Sergei, 1898–1948; Russian film director and theorist.

Barna, Yon, *Eisenstein*, translated by Lise Hunter. Bloomington, Indiana University Press, and London, Secker and Warburg, 1973 (originally published, Bucharest, 1966).

Moussinac, Leon, *Sergei Eisenstein*, translated by D. Sandy Petrey. New York, Crown, 1970 (originally published by Éditions Seghers, Paris, 1964).

Seton, Marie, *Sergei M. Eisenstein: A Biography*. London, Bodley Head, and New York, A. A. Wyn, 1952.

Swallow, Norman, *Eisenstein: A Documentary Portrait*. London, Allen and Unwin, 1976; New York, Dutton, 1977.

*

The authors of all four biographical works on Eisenstein shamelessly bow before his brilliance, while the pictures they render of the man and artist seem to imply that obeisance is the very least he deserves. Yet each volume has its own value.

French film writer MOUSSINAC befriended Eisenstein in the late 1920s and corresponded with him until his death in 1948. "To be in the presence of Eisenstein was to be in the presence of genius," he avows. His book is therefore a paean to the director, which he attempts to sing mostly by presenting portions of their extensive, theory-laden correspondence. Unfortunately, the translation is not the best, and as a biography the book is very sketchy. While Moussinac is willing to detail Eisenstein's creative disappointments in Hollywood and Mexico, he says little about his intellectual formation during childhood, or about the complexity of his adult personal life. The book is helpful, however, for its "Texts and Documents" section, which includes Eisenstein's own views on montage, sound, music, and color, selected assessments of his work and influence, and a helpful "bio-filmography."

Perhaps the most readable of all these biographies, by SWALLOW, was adapted from a 1970 BBC television film on Eisenstein. Swallow collaborated with G. V. Alexandrov, who served as Eisenstein's assistant on several films, including *Battleship Potemkin* and *Que Viva Mexico*. Together the authors construct a brisk narrative of Eisenstein as he reads and thinks and plays, and subsequently bursts upon the theatrical and cinematic scenes with unrivaled creativity and innovation, to the astonishment of those around him. The book relies heavily on extensive interviews Swallow conducted with a score of Eisenstein's associates, making this book a kind of oral biography. Although Swallow rarely intrudes, his occasional analyses of individual films are insightful. Throughout, he focuses on the artist above all, and gives little information regarding the contexts in which he worked.

The serious scholar, therefore, will have to look elsewhere. A much fuller treatment of Eisenstein's work can be found in BARNA's biography. Barna's concern is the artistic process; he wishes "to trace less the events or the facts than that exciting 'inner adventure,' the biography of Eisenstein's creation." One might complain, once again, that this approach leaves so much unsaid about Eisenstein's life. But here was a man consumed by his work, such that it might safely be said that the man *was* his work. In this light, Barna does a magnificent job of charting Eisenstein's artistic development, his successes and failures, and his legacy.

Eisenstein's childhood, in Barna's eyes, was his "training period," the experiences of which "shed a revealing light on Eisenstein's mature years as an artist." That childhood was characterized by the voracious reading that gave him nearly encyclopedic knowledge of many subjects, the constant clowning that would inform his stagecraft, and the painful experiences with his parents that would impress him so deeply that they "found an echo in all his films." Barna then insightfully discusses Eisenstein's official entry into the emerging Soviet cinema, via the Proletkult Theatre under the tutelage of Valeri Pletnyov and Vsevolod Meyerhold. His work with the stage, Barna convincingly argues, prefigured his move to the medium of film.

Barna's biography is probably the best documented and most thorough of the four. Barna bases his study on a vast store of material that Eisenstein's earlier biographers did not have at their disposal, including variant scripts, stenographic records of his lectures, Eisenstein's own analyses of his work, and notes written at the time of filming. Barna boldly takes exception with Marie Seton's biography (see below) for being "obsolete and in many ways contradicted by the immense amount of biographical material made available in recent years, or still unpublished."

He is probably right, but SETON's work has a few merits of its own. She became a close friend of Eisenstein in the 1930s, and much of her biography comes from the material he dictated to her. It is an attempt to portray the man, not just the director and theorist; for, as Seton remarks, "the understanding of a great artist as a human being is more important than the creation of a formal record of his achievement." This may be true, and Seton does render Eisenstein a fuller human being than does Barna. However, she transcribes his version of his life with little probing, and her entire account seems somewhat under the spell of her admiration for him. Seton's work, therefore, can be read as a subjective and adoring glimpse at the man, while Barna's is the more useful as a rigorous treatment of his development as an artist and theorist. For those who do not wish to delve so deeply, Swallow provides a good, informative read.

—Martin Thies

ELEANOR OF AQUITAINE, 1122?–1204; queen consort of Louis VII of France and of Henry II of England; mother of kings Richard I and John of England.

Kelly, Amy R., *Eleanor of Aquitaine and the Four Kings.* Cambridge, Massachusetts, Harvard University Press, 1950; London, Cassell, 1952.

Kibler, William W., editor, *Eleanor of Aquitaine: Patron and Politician.* Austin, University of Texas Press, 1976.

Pernoud, Régine, *Eleanor of Aquitaine,* translated by Peter Wiles. London, Collins, 1967; New York, Coward-McCann, 1968 (originally published as *Aliénore d'Aquitaine,* Paris, A. Michel, 1965).

Walker, Curtis Howe, *Eleanor of Aquitaine.* Chapel Hill, University of North Carolina Press, 1950.

*

Few biographies of Eleanor of Aquitaine have been written in English. Some of these, such as Rosenburg's 1937 account, are incredibly misleading, giving the same weight to the myths that surround Eleanor as they do to historical facts. Biographers have, for the most part, relied on background sources such as the *Rolls Series,* J. P. Migne's *Patrologia latina,* and a number of French chroniclers for clues to Eleanor's time and her associates as indicators of her personality. During the 19th century, the best short account of her life was written by T. A. Archer and can be found in the *Dictionary of National Biography,* (vol. XVII, 1889). The section on Eleanor in Agnes Strickland's, *Lives of the Queens of England, from the Norman Conquest,* (6 vols., London, 1864–65) is a romanticized version of her life but useful for dates.

The difficulty with the lack of reliable firsthand sources causes the personality of Eleanor to elude 20th-century biographers. KELLY's work will likely remain as the seminal study of the life of Eleanor. She offers her account of Eleanor as "a study of individuals who set their stamp upon the events of their time, rather than as a study of developing systems of politics, economics, or jurisprudence." She also incorporates the broader source material to provide a detailed assessment of the 12th century. Sometimes, however, Eleanor gets lost in the detailed accounting of her background and entourage. The work would have been made stronger by devoting more space to the canonical issues involved in the queen's divorce from Louis and her later marriage to Henry. That criticism aside, Kelly's work remains one of the few that does not mythologize Eleanor at the expense of historical accuracy. Kelly combines the Gothic overtones of the life of Eleanor with careful attention to the sources, providing a scholarly yet readable account.

WALKER's biography, published the same year as Kelly's, is another attempt to grapple with the question, Who was Eleanor of Aquitaine? Walker tells a straightforward story and deliberately avoids the complications of 12th-century court life that makes Kelly's work the more comprehensive of the two. Though it serves as a fairly informative treatment of Eleanor's life, Walker's biography is not as compelling as Kelly's; and perhaps because he wished to make his work more readable to the laymen, Walker is vague in some of the important historical details. Additionally, what he cannot determine from the sources about Eleanor, he simply guesses—a practice in which Kelly also engages, though her guesses are based on the most careful reading of the sources. With Walker, one is not so sure.

PERNOUD's excellent biography succeeds in portraying Eleanor's personality more clearly, perhaps due to the appearance of source material unavailable to earlier biographers. Pernoud's Eleanor is vivacious, intelligent, persuasive, argumentative, and articulate. Pernoud's historical account, in common with those by Kelly and Walker, reads a little like a romance novel. An antidote to this kind of heroic treatment, so common in the lives of Eleanor, may be found in KIBLER's edition of articles covering Eleanor and her era. This collection embodies some of the seminal research done on the twelfth century, and many of the articles elucidate the life of Eleanor. Most particularly, Elizabeth A. R. Brown's "Eleanor of Aquitaine: Parent, Queen and Duchess," chapter one of Kibler's work, is an excellent source for the life of Eleanor. Her provocative thesis that Eleanor's motivations and activities can be explained through the use of psychoanalytical theory is certainly a product of the 1970s. She is, however, one of the few recent scholars to contribute to a better understanding of Eleanor that does not portray her as a romanticized character in a work of historical fiction.

Other articles important in sketching out the details of Eleanor's life are Amy Kelly's "Eleanor of Aquitaine and her Courts of Love" (*Speculum*, vol. XII, 1937), F. M. Chambers' "Some Legends Concerning Eleanor of Aquitaine" (*Speculum*, vol. XVI, 1941), and H. G. Richardson's "The Letters and Charters of Eleanor of Aquitaine" (*English Historical Review*, vol. 74, 1959).

—Kay Rogers

ELGAR, Sir Edward, 1857–1934; English composer.

De-La-Noy, Michael, *Elgar, the Man*. London, A. Lane, 1983.

Kennedy, Michael, *Portrait of Elgar*. London and New York, Oxford University Press, 1968; 3rd edition, 1987.

Maine, Basil, *Elgar: His Life and Works* (2 vols.). London, G. Bell, 1933; one–volume edition, Bath, Chivers, 1973.

McVeagh, Diana M., *Edward Elgar: His Life and Music*. London, Dent, 1955.

Moore, Jerrold N., *Edward Elgar: A Creative Life*. Oxford and New York, Oxford University Press, 1984.

Moore, Jerrold N., *Spirit of England: Edward Elgar in His World*. London, Heinemann, 1984.

Young, Percy M., *Elgar, O.M: A Study of a Musician*. London, Collins, 1955.

*

The enigma that was Edward Elgar—the music and the man—has aroused much curiosity; the major biographies accordingly reveal a common theme. Ranging from the earliest studies that deal almost exclusively with Elgar's musical development to those portrayals in which the "primary aim" of the author is "to understand the personality of the artist" (De-La-Noy), *all*, nevertheless, attempt to trace the processes of this self-taught composer's musical imagination.

MOORE's *Spirit of England* is the only biography in which Elgar's life is not approached chronologically. Instead, chapter by chapter, Moore studies the circumstances that nurtured the composer's creativity: family, friendships, homes, towns, and landscapes. Although this is not a conventional "life and times" (Elgar remains throughout the focus of attention), Moore effectively evokes something of the social and spiritual values prevalent in England at the turn of the century. The text is comparatively short, yet the content is by no means superficial. On the contrary, Moore's ideas are thoroughly researched and his approach is convincing, well-written, and attractively packaged.

For those who require a more detailed account, MOORE has obliged with *A Creative Life*, which shares a similar orientation.

Extending to more than 800 pages, it is by far the most comprehensive account available of Elgar's life. This biography contains an impressive quantity of previously unpublished material drawn from a variety of sources, notably correspondence, diaries, and sketches.

Moore's belief that "a creative life can have no general significance apart from its works, and works have no cumulative significance outside a worker's life," in his appropriately named biography, prompted him to maintain a strict chronological progression, despite the detail with which he treats both life and music (500 musical examples are interspersed throughout the text). Although some of the musical relationships that the author frequently highlights as he traces a lifelong development may seem a little tenuous, his method of organization provides a unique insight into Elgar's creative processes. Moore's biography is superlative in this respect.

Both De-La-Noy and Kennedy (in the third edition of the latter's biography) acknowledge Moore's scholarship and, taking advantage of material that has only recently come to light, produce accurate though considerably more compact accounts. KENNEDY was the first author to inquire beyond Elgar's public image, revealing in his subject a complex and not entirely endearing personality. This study, based on the accounts (some published) of those who knew the composer, includes a fairly detailed assessment of the ways in which Elgar expressed himself both in words and in music. Kennedy's tone is tinged with realism, yet remains unbiased. Discussion of the music is mostly descriptive and includes only a handful of musical examples (a particularly attractive feature to those who are not familiar with musical terminology); nevertheless, it is clear that Kennedy considers the nature of the composer's creativity to be an essential part of his appraisal. This particular dimension is notably absent from the study by DE-LA-NOY, who professes to being no musician. His attempt to understand the artist without taking due consideration of Elgar's creative expression somehow misses the point, and, coupled with the fact that De-La-Noy does not reserve value judgement, Elgar (and certain others of his circle, for that matter) is presented in rather a poor light.

With regard to the earlier biographies, the work of YOUNG, the first Elgar scholar to work extensively with source material, should not be overlooked. Young's study contains a significant amount of correspondence that is not published elsewhere. McVEAGH's account of Elgar's life, although less stylish than those so far considered, is nevertheless concise and accurate and will be useful to those requiring an introductory text. McVeagh's approach is notable for the insight that it yields into Elgar's conception of his music. Although her commentary is rather technical, she retains throughout the second section of her book a sensitivity to the experiences, enthusiasms, and attitudes of the composer. Particular attention is drawn to her discussion of Elgar's approach to orchestration in Chapter XIV (Moore also writes an excellent chapter on this aspect of the composer's work in *Spirit of England*), as well as her comments on his compositional techniques.

MAINE is the only author to have worked extensively with Elgar himself; consequently his study relies to a lesser degree on documentary evidence. It is worth noting, however, that much of the first-hand information about Elgar's life contained in this work has been incorporated, with acknowledgment, in the more recent biographies.

Considering Maine's position, the insight that he provides into Elgar's personality is disappointing. He himself acknowledges the difficulties (his own words are "imposed conditions") of writing a biography of a living subject; this problem would perhaps explain why he confines his discussion to Elgar's public image, a treatment of the composer also characteristic of the two other early biographies.

The division of the earlier biographies—by Maine, Young, and McVeagh—into life and works (all of which further categorize the works by genre) has certain advantages in terms of reference and cross-reference. It is as a reference volume that Moore's *A Creative Life* falls short of expectations; the index is not as detailed as would have been anticipated in a work of this magnitude. The methods employed by Kennedy are much more effective. Neither does *A Creative Life* contain a bibliography (although references are recorded accurately in footnotes). Attention is once again drawn to Kennedy's book in this respect, which is further distinguished by the fact that it contains several useful appendices, including a chronological list of works (published and unpublished) and a list of recordings that Elgar himself conducted. Several of the other biographies contain similar information, but that which Kennedy provides is by far the most comprehensive and accurate.

—Sally MacGregor

EL GRECO. See **GRECO, El.**

ELIOT, George [*born* Marian Evans], 1819–1880; English writer.

Blind, Mathilde, *George Eliot*. London, W. H. Allen, and Boston, Roberts, 1883.

Browning, Oscar, *Life of George Eliot*. London, W. Scott, 1890.

Bullett, Gerald, *George Eliot: Her Life and Her Books*. London, Collins, 1947; New Haven, Connecticut, Yale University Press, 1948.

Crompton, Margaret, *George Eliot, the Woman*. London, Cassell, and New York, T. Yoseloff, 1960.

Cross, J. W., *George Eliot's Life as Related in Her Letters and Journals, Arranged and Edited by Her Husband* (3 vols.). Edinburgh and London, Blackwood, and New York, Harper, 1885.

Dewes, Simon, *Marian: The Life of George Eliot*. [n.p.], Rich and Cowan, 1939.

Dodd, Valerie A., *George Eliot: An Intellectual Life*. New York, St. Martin's, and London, Macmillan, 1990.

Gardner, Charles, *The Inner Life of George Eliot*. London, I. Pitman, 1912.

Haight, Gordon S., *George Eliot and John Chapman, with Chapman's Diaries*. New Haven, Connecticut, Yale University Press, and Oxford, Oxford University Press, 1940.

Haight, Gordon S., *George Eliot: A Biography*. Oxford, Clarendon Press, and New York, Oxford University Press, 1968.

Hanson, Lawrence and Elizabeth Hanson, *Marian Evans and George Eliot: A Biography*. London and New York, Oxford University Press, 1952.

Laski, Marghanita, *George Eliot and Her World*. London, Thames and Hudson, 1973; New York, Scribner, 1978.

McKenzie, K. A., *Edith Simcox and George Eliot*. London, Oxford University Press, 1961.

Redinger, Ruby V., *George Eliot: The Emergent Self*. New York, Knopf, 1975; London, Bodley Head, 1976.

Sprague, Rosemary, *George Eliot: A Biography*. New York, Chilton, 1968.

*

After a brief sketch of George Eliot by BLIND, which lacked notes or index, came the three volumes by Eliot's husband, CROSS, of which Gladstone is supposed to have said: "It is not a life—it is a reticence." One can sympathize with Cross' predicament. There had been a strong tendency among the mid-Victorian elite to idolize George Eliot, as woman and as writer. Her irregular association with Lewes had been elevated in the minds of some to an unapproachable spiritual glory, which led naturally to disillusionment when she chose to please herself in the last year of her life by marrying a man young enough to be her son. Cross' reticence is extreme and leads at times to well-meant dishonesty in suppressing facts and altering the text of letters. Behind the reticence is intense personal feeling, unstated but unhidden. Cross' book is less a monument to a very impulsive and inconsistent woman than to a phase of secularist culture and its rather unconvincing hagiographies.

BROWNING, a worshipper of more temperate and detached feelings, acknowledges the value of Cross' work, but introduces some new material in the form of unpublished letters. He hails Eliot's association with Lewes as a "true marriage," quoting, as many later writers were to do, Feuerbach's lofty remarks on the superiority of a union that ignores social and legal considerations. Browning is the first to analyze the paradox of Eliot's conscious rejection of Christian doctrine and the reverent and sympathetic tone of her treatment of religion in her books. He is the first, too, to see in her a "strong, passionate nature," and so unobtrusively plays his part in demythologizing Cross' holy portrait. In a striking passage, Browning describes Eliot's funeral, which he attended, and recalls the presence at it of her brother Isaac, from whom she had been estranged for so long.

GARDNER sees Eliot as "in advance of her time" (we may find a certain irony in the unthinking progressive assumptions). She was a teacher and moralist for transitional times. The transition Gardner means seems to be something like that between Arnold's "two worlds," between an old and new religious consensus. He sets Eliot especially in the context of Victorian religious controversy, suggesting that it may have been unfortunate that a narrow Evangelical piety, rather than the broader influence of the Oxford Movement, gripped her impressionable adolescence. He sees her as a prophet of some shadowy future religious synthesis, and he finds a special significance in *Romola* as the place where she gave utterance to "her inmost thought of her own act of rebellion."

DEWES' book is written in racy style with short stacatto sentences. He much exaggerates "persecution, slander and misunderstanding," apparently because phrases like this were thought conventionally appropriate at the end of the perversely anti-Victorian phase of English culture. Eliot's late marriage to Cross is seen as a search for reputation, while her love for Lewes is described in purple prose reminiscent of the Hollywood scriptwriters of the period.

All this time some aspects of Eliot's life had remained hidden from view. In 1940, the publication by HAIGHT of Chapman's diaries, and the inevitable reassessment of Eliot's relations with him, and thus of parts of her character, inaugurated a new phase. Many years later, after editing the letters, Haight returned with a full-scale biography. It is painstaking and scholarly, and extremely accurate about facts. Plausibly (and in this he is followed by most subsequent writers), Haight finds a pattern repeated in each of Eliot's associations with male friends. He describes it as "intellectual friendship drawn by over-ready expansiveness into feelings misunderstood." The unsatisfactory feature of what remains the most generally useful book on George Eliot is its sketchy knowledge of the intellectual background. Haight overrates the influence of Comte and is inclined to be taken in by the pretensions to intellectual preeminence of the third-rate figure, Herbert Spencer. His partial failure is testimony, no doubt, to the wide range of expert knowledge the ideal biographer in this case would require.

BULLETT sees Eliot as a woman who always needed to be needed and characterizes her youthful rectitude as "solemn if reluctant." Unlike several later writers, though having the evidence of Chapman's diary before him, Bullett interprets her relation to Chapman as technically innocent, and the jealousy excited in his other women as the effect only of her naivety. He tellingly adds his own italics to Eliot's words in a letter about her engagement to Cross: "He . . . sees his happiness in the dedication of his life to me," commenting acidly that she would perhaps not have seen the point of the addition.

The HANSONs follow Haight in his critique of Cross and are eager to "demythologize," presenting Eliot as a passionate child and a priggish young woman. They stress her loneliness and the strength of influence of friends upon her. They see Eliot as possessed of "the mind of a man—an exceptional man" and "the heart of a woman, with none of the physical advantages that would have promised a woman's reward." The authors are terse about Eliot's position in the 1870s as a "goddess on a pedestal," and point out the irony of the "second marriage" to Cross, which so much scandalized her positivist admirers. CROMPTON, on the whole, adds little to this.

McKENZIE's book is a valuable monograph on a minor but very interesting aspect, the extraordinarily strong appeal which, entirely against her own wishes and sentiments, Eliot made to women of Lesbian tendencies. Edith Simcox was the most extreme case, writing of loving her in three ways, "idolatrously . . . in romance wise, . . . with a child's fondness for a mother." The impression left is that George Eliot found devotion of this kind at once tiresome and reassuring. The book has an introduction by Haight.

SPRAGUE stresses Eliot's uncompromising tactlessness in dealing with her father at the time of her loss of faith, and partly redresses the balance of previous biographers' treatment of the family. But Sprague's book is apt to miss or confuse finer points,

as in its odd defence of the marriage to Cross: "In 1880, a man nearing 40 was considered a full-grown man, old enough to cope in the world." Sprague thus ignores the point noted by contemporaries, the advanced age of the bride. LASKI's work is mainly a study of background, houses, family settings, and genealogy.

REDINGER's volume is full and elaborate, but the author does not altogether make clear in what way she intends to supersede or elaborate the work of Haight. Like other biographers, Redinger sees as the key to the emotional side of George Eliot's character her urgent need to be all things to someone. She sees the painful experience with Chapman as having initiated a personality change. "He was punishing her . . . and this treatment evoked a positive response from the masochistic streak in her." She questions the assumption of Haight and other biographers that an ardent George Eliot was rebuffed by Herbert Spencer, considering it at least possible that she rejected him. Redinger considers that Eliot's evasion of the over-importunate attentions of Edith Simcox may have been one of the motives for her surprising decision to marry Cross. Also, perhaps, she was tired of being on a pedestal. Redinger is not free from the fault into which several other biographers occasionally fall, that of inferring biographical facts from events in the novels.

DODD's book is a careful and well-documented study of George Eliot's intellectual formation up to the time when she began writing fiction. It stresses Carlyle and various continental influences, including Comte and German philosophy.

—A. O. J. Cockshut

ELIOT, T(homas) S(ternes), 1888–1965; American-born English poet and critic.

Ackroyd, Peter, *T. S. Eliot: A Life.* New York, Simon and Schuster, and London, Hamilton, 1984.

Bush, Ronald, *T. S. Eliot: A Study in Character and Style.* New York and Oxford, Oxford University Press, 1983.

Gordon, Lyndall, *Eliot's Early Years.* New York and Oxford, Oxford University Press, 1977.

Matthews, Thomas S., *Great Tom: Notes Toward the Definition of T. S. Eliot.* London, Weidenfeld and Nicolson, and New York, Harper, 1974.

Sencourt, Robert, *T. S. Eliot: A Memoir.* New York, Dodd Mead, and London, Garnstone Press, 1971.

*

The first two biographies of Eliot considered here come from men who knew the poet personally. One, Robert Sencourt, had a past similar to Eliot's. Eliot had put St. Louis and Boston behind him in order to live and write in England; Sencourt had left New Zealand with a similar purpose in mind. T. S. Matthews, too, had both a personal and a literary association with Eliot—an advantage to a biographer of Eliot, whose presence was, as these and other writers show, a mixture of gaiety and enigma.

SENCOURT's volume of recollections is supplemented by much careful conversation with those who could provide background on Eliot's St. Louis and Harvard days, as well as his early English years. Sencourt also gives us a clear and sufficiently tasteful account of Eliot's first marriage and a sympathetic summary of his entrance into the Church of England. Sencourt provides essays on the intellectual climate of Eliot's Unitarian background, on the philosophical attitudes that were important for Eliot in his prolonged student days, and of course on the Anglo-Catholicism that Sencourt shared fully with his friend.

MATTHEWS' *Great Tom* is another early effort to estimate Eliot's achievement and character. Matthews operates under the same difficulties Sencourt faced: many documents relating to Eliot's life were not yet available to him. Matthews' book, however, is factually more rich than Sencourt's, with a fuller presentation of Eliot's early days in Missouri and his years at Harvard. The difficulties of Eliot's marriage receive more precise chronicling, and the relative peace of his later, Anglo-Catholic years is depicted, if not fully approved of.

Matthews' account is not, as was Sencourt's, chiefly reverent in tone. He is, by turns, deeply admiring of Eliot's achievement in poetry and at best indulgent toward his dramatic work. As for Eliot's uneasy approach to religion, Matthews asks, "What is it about churches like St. Stephen's [Eliot's London church] that is attractive to some, repellant to others? What is there, of the same sort of alternating current, that turns people on and off about the Church of England, or any other Christian sect? Why do Christians hate each other so? Is there such a thing as religion?" Occasional outbursts of this sort disturb the cheerful surface of Matthews' narrative. Such protests are indeed common in a half-century of comment on Eliot's intellectual and religious attitudes.

Of particular interest is Matthews' concluding essay on Eliot's makeup. Here we see the biographer moving from fact to fairly complex psychological interpretation. Matthews starts with one more comment on Christianity: "For most of us—except, of course, the saints—Christianity is a threadbare covering, the dogged repetition of a threadbare creed." After this introduction Matthews moves on to portray Eliot as a man of taste and talent.

GORDON's work, part biography, part literary analysis, is an account of Eliot's mental growth. In Gordon's confident narrative, Eliot's youth is not marked simply by his fretful adoption and abandonment of freshly-encountered intellectual attitudes met in the work of such men as Bertrand Russell and F. H. Bradley. There is in Eliot, Gordon suggests, a yearning that finds its final satisfaction in Christian writers, from Augustine to Lancelot Andrews and beyond. Through these writers Eliot was able to detach himself from the company headed by Russell, his one-time master and friend.

Thanks to this insight of Gordon's, Eliot's early years take on a coherence that other biographers do not always see. If Eliot is an enigma (and Gordon does not pretend to full comprehension), he is, in Gordon's highly unified book, an enigma that is in a constant process of resolving itself. While Sencourt was respectful of Eliot's final pose, he did not (as Gordon does) try to see the pose as a gesture that is a summary of previous gestures rather than a careless cancellation of them.

BUSH's work effects, for attentive readers, an impressive immersion in all the intellectual currents through which Eliot moved. Bush has access to materials that earlier writers could not draw on, and he uses these materials with firmness. Bush's

judgment is both instructed and detached, and he never indulges, as did Matthews, in self-righteousness at Eliot's expense. Bush studies the poems both in themselves and in relation to what can be known of Eliot's mental states at the time of their composition.

Bush, like Matthews and others, often detects a basic discontinuity in Eliot, an abundance of fresh starts. He does not follow Eliot into his dramatic works; the variation in Eliot's poetic path is a sufficient challenge, and Bush takes up this challenge so well that the reader of his study will return to the poetry with fresh illumination.

ACKROYD sets forth all the events in Eliot's life that force him, and the reader, to face the hard questions about Eliot. He not only addresses the intellectual problems that vexed Eliot, from questions of perception and moral values to theological mazes, but gives careful treatment to Eliot's personal life. He studies, for example, Eliot's earlier responses to sex, as well as his attitude on this subject into marriage. Ackroyd also considers and rejects Eliot's supposed homosexuality. He provides a vivid picture of the London literary scene and its relation to other such scenes on the European continent and, to an extent, in the United States.

Ackroyd's narrative never disintegrates into mere recording of the facts, however. He takes up subjects with which readers of Eliot and Eliot criticism are familiar: the state of modern poetry and the fragmentary condition of modern culture. Here Ackroyd often moves from the overt subject—Eliot's mind—to a covert one: the mind of the biographer. But such commentary never transforms the biography into propaganda for a private point of view. And through all this background material and theoretical discussion, the physical presence of Eliot is always felt—the manner in which he visited with his friends or stood on a lecture platform.

Ackroyd's perception of Eliot as a man of great personal as well as artistic complexity might find its best expression in the following statement: "Throughout his life Eliot brought the anguish of his difficult and divided nature to the surface of his poetry, just as in oblique form he analyzed it in his prose. His predilection for order, as well as his susceptibility to disorder, were immense, and in the jarring, crushing equilibrium, his life and work were formed." Much of this judgment would be acceptable to the writers of the other studies discussed here. Though they respond variously to the challenge of Eliot, the challenge obscurely persists and provokes new studies of the man who, in a sense, haunts the present century.

—Harold H. Watts

ELIZABETH I, 1533–1603; English monarch.

Bassnett, Susan, *Elizabeth I: A Feminist Perspective*. Oxford and New York, Berg, 1988.
Erickson, Carolly, *The First Elizabeth*. London, Macmillan, and New York, Summit Books, 1983.
Haigh, Christopher, *Elizabeth I*. London and New York, Longman, 1988.

Hurstfield, Joel, *Elizabeth I and the Unity of England*. London, English Universities Press, and New York, Macmillan, 1960.
Neale, Sir John, *Queen Elizabeth I*. London, Cape, and New York, Harcourt, 1934.
Ridley, Jasper, *Elizabeth I*. London, Constable, 1987; New York, Viking, 1988.
Smith, Lacey Baldwin, *Elizabeth Tudor: Portrait of a Queen*. Boston, Little Brown, 1975; London, Hutchinson/Cape, 1976.

*

Lacey Baldwin Smith found more than 60 biographies of Elizabeth in the British Library Catalogue when he came to write his study of her in the mid 1970s. Since then at least another 14 have appeared. Yet a strictly finite amount is known about Elizabeth herself. Few of her private letters survive, and new ones have only very rarely surfaced this century. She is captured for us in the memoirs of many contemporaries; but their purpose is frequently hagiographical and again, new materials are scarce. It is now known that many of the portraits of her were painted—literally—from a mask; Elizabeth was a mistress of disguise. Her public speeches were as contrived and calculatedly unrevealing as those portraits, although the obsession with disguise is itself very revealing of a certain personality type. Anyone who, at the age of three, sees her mother beheaded for adultery, and who then spends her adolescence trying to adapt to the whims of a moody father, her early adulthood trying not to inflame a hostile half-sister and queen has reason enough to entomb herself in dissimulation. In these circumstances, anyone who sets out to read the piles of biographies of the Virgin Queen is going to find a great deal of repetition of theme, anecdote, judgment.

For most of this century one biography has dominated the field. NEALE wrote his biography in the early 1930s, and its shape, structure, and argument inform many that have followed. Neale was Astor Professor of British History in London and the most distinguished Elizabethan historian of his generation. Already in 1934 he had a formidable knowledge of the main archival records of government; his biography is notably secure in rooting the Queen's actions and reactions into the context of events throughout her realm and abroad. It is a book of very obvious biases: a bias toward the rationality of Protestantism and against the obscurantism of Catholicism; a bias toward the genius of the English for toleration, decency, and fair play; and a sexism that would have passed unnoticed 50 years ago but not today. Neale shows affection for the mask that is Elizabeth, and indulgence toward the panic and indecision that can often be heard (muffled) behind the mask. To put it bluntly, Elizabeth can do no wrong. Sometimes Neale's writing exhibits a vacuousness that nowadays carries little conviction.

Neale's biography sticks close to the Queen and to her problems as monarch. It is the most authoritative defence of her. Rarely has anyone been granted so much credit for presiding over the law of unforeseen consequences. Beguiled by her Golden Speeches, and trapped by the afterglow of British imperial Greatness and the myth of the White Man's Burden, Neale sees Elizabeth taming the tiger of Reformation fanaticism and siding with Progress. It is stirring stuff, and still makes a good read except when its unfashionable prejudices peep through.

Of Neale's many imitators, HURSTFIELD is probably the best. Hurstfield was for decades a colleague of Neale, and was his successor in the Astor Chair. At times, this closeness shows. Yet while Hurstfield's biography is equally uncritical, it does attempt more of an overarching interpretation of her achievement. Neale's relentless chronology tells us of one shrewd decision after another, and it tells the story down to the day of her death and then stops. Hurstfield attempts more of a balance-sheet, and finds a key in the following: "there was a theme in Elizabeth's life and reign, and that was the unremitting search to bind the nation in unity after two decades of discord in the time of her father, brother and sister. These views she held with passion, . . . " Paradoxes abound; Elizabeth's arguments with Parliament apparently both represent consensus and show her to be more representative of her people than were the representatives of the people gathered at Westminster. But then everyone accepts that Elizabeth believed in paradox.

Elizabeth's mastery of intrigue, her skilful prevarication, and her restless inactivity as a way of seeing difficulties resolve themselves are all preserved in the recent biography by ERICKSON. Hers is very much a life of the queen, with relatively little coverage of the reign. We only reach her accession on page 167 of a 407-page text; the more personal aspects of her life remain dominant. For example, only two pages are devoted to the religious settlement of 1559 and ten to the suitors for her hand in those early months; and more to the dalliance with the earl of Leicester. The book is thinly researched except on the queen herself, but it reads better than Erickson's previous lives of Elizabeth's father and sister.

A more successful recent life is that by RIDLEY. It is a fatter book, a meatier read, and it is handsomely illustrated. It is also more balanced. Elizabeth is given credit for lacking dogmatism, for "bringing Scotland permanently into the English orbit of influence," and for ending the reign of terror. Ultimately, Ridley accepts that Elizabeth identified with the forces of Progress, though he is also prepared to confront head on her paralysis in the face of difficult decisions, her petulance, her emotionalism, and her petty-mindedness. Yet he invites us to see these for the most part as venial failures. Elizabeth charmed her age and transformed national morale. If she was lucky, it was in large part because she had made her own luck.

There is another view of Elizabeth, a subversive tradition, that sees her as a shrill and hysterical woman, out of her depth, deeply damaged by the traumas of her early life, unable ever to make a binding commitment to anything. This view sees the reign in terms of a limited achievement by capable but harassed ministers frequently having to go behind the queen's back and just as frequently stymied by her refusal to act even when her entire council pleaded with her or brought the full weight of parliamentary pressure to bear. The liveliest and most learned such approach is by HAIGH. He has written his biography thematically, offering chapters on the queen and her throne, the queen and her Church, the queen and her nobility, her council, her court, her Parliament, her military, and her people. Haigh writes with great verve and wit: "Elizabeth I was a bully, and like most bullies, she harassed the weak while deferring to the strong"; "on her throne, Elizabeth was the Virgin Queen; towards the Church she was a mother, with her nobles she was an aunt, to her councillors a nagging wife, and to her courtiers a seductress"; "For Elizabeth Parliamentarians *were* little boys—sometimes unruly, usually a nuisance, and always a waste of an intelligent woman's time." Though Haigh's is an iconoclastic performance, the icon had taken a very powerful hold. Those who want to recognize just how much unproven value-judgment was contained in the traditional view need to read Haigh. It will shock; but it is full of trenchant good sense as well as what many will find rather crass oversimplifications of complex problems.

SMITH wrote his life of Elizabeth shortly after a big, bold psychobiography of Henry VIII. This effort is slighter—in research, in length, and in depth. But it too aims to explode the Gloriana myth. Whereas Haigh wields the fairground mallet, however, Smith sets to work with the chisel. For example, his cool evaluation of Elizabeth's hypnotic words on public stages is far removed from Neale's superlatives. Yet Smith retains an amazed admiration for her and gives a harrowing account of her in old age, lonely, frightened, and weary as "the price of showmanship grew greater." Despite herself, she presided over a triumphant reign.

Finally there is the short, refreshingly straightforward "feminist" study by BASSNETT. In fact, apart from an assertive final sentence proclaiming Elizabeth as "a woman who struggled against anti-feminist prejudice and who has remained a symbol of active female assertiveness for future generations," this book need not deter unliberated readers. It is firmly rooted in a careful sifting of Elizabeth's own words and (more enterprisingly) in her own poems. It is shrewd in its assessments, and for the general reader it is an admirable starting point for the most enigmatic and infuriatingly successful of monarchs.

—John Morrill

ELIZABETH II, 1926–   ; English monarch.

Bocca, Geoffrey, *Elizabeth and Philip*. New York, Holt, 1953.
Brendon, Piers, *Our Own Dear Queen*. London, Secker and Warburg, 1986.
Campbell, Judith, *Queen Elizabeth II: A Biography*. New York, Crown, 1979.
Cathcart, Helen, *Her Majesty the Queen*. New York, Dodd Mead, and London, W. H. Allen, 1962.
Crawford, Marion, *Queen Elizabeth II*. London, Newnes, 1952; as *Elizabeth the Queen*, Englewood Cliffs, New Jersey, Prentice-Hall, 1952.
Dimbleby, Richard, *Elizabeth, Our Queen*. London, Hodder and Stoughton, 1953.
Fisher, Graham and Heather Fisher, *Elizabeth, Queen and Mother: The Story of Queen Elizabeth II and the British Royal Family*. London, W. H. Allen, and New York, Hawthorne, 1964; revised as *Monarch: The Life and Times of Elizabeth II*, London, Hale, 1985; as *Monarch: A Biography of Elizabeth II*, Topsfield, Massachusetts, Salem House, 1985.
Johnston, Laurie, *Elizabeth Enters: The Story of a Queen*. New York, Scribner, 1953.
Lacey, Robert, *Majesty: Elizabeth II and the House of Windsor*. New York, Harcourt, and London, Hutchinson, 1977.
Liversidge, Douglas, *Queen Elizabeth II: The British Monarchy Today*. London, A. Barker, 1974.
Longford, Elizabeth, *Elizabeth R.: A Biography*. London, Weidenfeld and Nicolson, 1982; as *The Queen: The Life of Elizabeth II*, New York, Knopf, 1983.
Michie, Allan Andrew, *The Crown and the People*. London, Secker and Warburg, 1952; as *God Save the Queen: A Modern Monarchy*, New York, Sloane, 1953.
Montgomery-Massingberd, Hugh, *Her Majesty, the Queen*. London, Collins, 1985.
Morrow, Ann, *The Queen*. London, Granada, and New York, Morrow, 1983.
Parker, Elinor Milnor, *Most Gracious Majesty: The Story of Queen Elizabeth II*. New York, Crowell, 1953; revised edition, 1962.

*

There have been over a score of biographies of Elizabeth II since she succeeded her father, King George VI, in 1952. Many of them have been shallow, anecdotal, and aimed at readers interested in royal gossip. One of the first is by JOHNSTON, a readable outline of the young queen's life accompanied by humanizing stories and many photographs. Chattier, breezier, and possibly more authoritative is BOCCA, who focuses on Elizabeth's marriage. The *New Yorker*'s reviewer described Bocca's book as "a mixture of fact and fatuousness," but the author—a veteran British newspaperman—evidently had access to reliable background sources. MICHIE provides another early biography, praised by no less a critic than V. S. Pritchett as being tasteful and well-informed, but panned by the *Times Literary Supplement* for circulating tittle-tattle. DIMBLEBY and CRAWFORD are two more early lives, the latter of special interest because the author was a former governess to Elizabeth and her sister Margaret. Crawford's account of the future queen's girlhood is a primary source (however much the author's role in it is exaggerated), but much of her book is a composite of newspaper reports.

The 10th and 20th anniversaries of Elizabeth's accession to the throne were occasions for further biographies. CAMPBELL, CATHCART, FISHER, LIVERSIDGE, and PARKER are on the whole pedestrian works, best described as factually accurate, pleasantly written, and undemanding of the reader. One of Parker's reviewers hoped that her introduction to the queen's life "[might] lead to the reading of better biographies," but there was none until Elizabeth had reigned for a quarter century.

Queen Elizabeth's silver jubilee finally produced a genuinely interpretive and critical life. LACEY sought but did not receive the crown's imprimatur for his study. Nevertheless, the author—a trained historian as well as a writer for the London *Sunday Times*—conducted an impressive amount of research among those royal relatives, friends, and palace officials willing to talk. The result is a portrait in depth that, while sympathetic on the whole, is far from obsequious. For example, Lacey reproaches Elizabeth for her apparent partisanship during the selection of a new prime minister after the 1956 Suez Crisis, notes her preference for (pre-Margaret Thatcher) Conservative over Labour governments, and implies that British taxpayers may not be getting their money's worth from the increasingly expensive royal family.

Lacey's biography represents the apex of Elizabeth II historiography to the present, but other works have been written more recently from various standpoints. LONGFORD's is the work of a prolific writer of high-quality popularized history and biography, including a good life of Queen Victoria. With her aristocratic and political connections, Lady Longford was better qualified than Lacey to compile and analyze "elitelore" from courtiers and officeholders, but the result is disappointing. Possibly because most of her interviews—including several with Princess Margaret—were off the record, Longford's portrait is one-dimensional. Her book is nevertheless well organized, highly readable, and informative about the queen's public functions and political role. The accompanying photographs are the best to be found in any of the biographies.

MORROW, former court correspondent for the London *Daily Telegraph*, has a whimsical style that is better suited to short newspaper commentaries than to a 250-page book. We are back to anecdotal ephemera, heavy on descriptions of royal tours, ribbon-cutting ceremonies, and female fashions. MONTGOMERY-MASSINGBERD, an authority on the history of British royalty, is a more learned and sophisticated writer than Morrow. Here the acecdotes are polished, rather wicked, and suggestive. If Montgomery-Massingberd can be read on more than one level, BRENDON leaves no doubt about his inclinations. An anti-monarchist and republican, Brendon rates Elizabeth II higher as a horse-lover than as a head of state. In this acerbic, indifferently-researched, and undocumented book, the author takes pot-shots less at the present sovereign than at the whole panoply of royal institutions.

—Don M. Cregier

ELLINGTON, Duke [*born* Edward Kennedy Ellington], 1899–1974; American jazz pianist, composer, and bandleader.

Barclay, Pamela, *Duke Ellington: Ambassador of Music*. Mankato, Minnesota, Creative Education, 1974.

Brown, Gene, *Duke Ellington*. Englewood Cliffs, New Jersey, Silver Burdett Press, 1990.

Collier, James L., *Duke Ellington*. New York, Oxford University Press, and London, M. Joseph, 1987.

Dance, Stanley, *The World of Duke Ellington*. New York, Scribner, 1970; London, Macmillan, 1971.

De Trazegnis, Jean, *Duke Ellington: Harlem Aristocrat of Jazz*. Brussels, Hot Club de Belgique, 1946.

Ellington, Mercer, with Stanley Dance, *Duke Ellington in Person: An Intimate Memoir*. Boston, Houghton Mifflin, and London, Hutchinson, 1978.

Frankl, Ron, *Duke Ellington*. New York, Chelsea House, 1988.

Gammond, Peter, editor, *Duke Ellington: His Life and Music*. New York, Roy Publishers, and London, Phoenix House, 1958.

Gammond, Peter, *Duke Ellington*. Tunbridge Wells, Spellmount, 1985.

George, Don, *Sweet Man: The Real Duke Ellington*. New York, Putnam, 1981; London, Robson, 1983.

Jewell, Derek, *Duke: A Portrait of Duke Ellington*. London, Elm Tree Books, and New York, Norton, 1977.

Lambert, George E., *Duke Ellington*. London, Cassell, 1959; New York, Barnes, 1961.

Montgomery, Elizabeth R., *Duke Ellington: King of Jazz*. Champaign, Illinois, Garrard Publishing, 1972.

Preston, Denis, *Mood Indigo*. Egham, England, Citizens Press, 1946.

Schaaf, Martha, *Duke Ellington: Young Music Master*. Indianapolis, Bobbs-Merrill, 1975.

Tucker, Mark T., *The Early Years of Edward Kennedy "Duke" Ellington, 1899–1927* (2 vols.). Ann Arbor, Michigan, UMI Research Press, 1986.

Ulanov, Barry, *Duke Ellington*. New York, Creative Age Press, 1946; London, Musicians Press, 1947.

*

The definitive biography of Duke Ellington has not yet been written. The existing literature reflects the gradual movement within the study of jazz history—a relatively new discipline—from anecdotal surveys written for the jazz fan to the advent of scholarly inquiry.

ULANOV wrote the earliest significant biography of Ellington. His research included extensive interviews with Ellington's family and bandmembers. Although the book contributes a wealth of information about Ellington's career and personality, its presentation is heavily romanticized; the intended audience is the Ellington fan. The biographies by DE TRAZEGNIS and PRESTON are additional early attempts to chronicle Ellington's blossoming career. They received limited distribution and have been long out of print.

GAMMOND's early work (1958) is a compilation of essays by Stanley Dance, Charles Fox, Peter Gammond, Alun Morgan, and other British jazz journalists. Each writer contributes an essay on a specific period of Ellington's career or a particular facet of his music. These essays are arranged to provide a primarily chronological survey of Ellington's career. The presentations vary from the purely anecdotal to the keenly insightful. LAMBERT recycles material from Ulanov and Gammond into a succint, 88-page survey of Ellington's career, but presents little new information.

DANCE, a celebrated journalist and record producer who enjoyed an extended friendship with Ellington, offers an entertaining and informative collection of "personality portraits" of Ellington and his sidemen. Much of the text is oral history interview that has been sensibly edited. The wealth of firsthand information makes this book an indispensable contribution.

The publication of Duke Ellington's *Music is My Mistress* (1973) was a heralded event in the world of jazz scholarship. Ellington refrained from producing a strictly narrative autobiography and, instead, fashioned an enchanting compilation of observations, reminiscences, song texts, and photographs. In keeping with his famous trait of gracious diplomacy, Duke sugarcoats the events of his life and career—not a single unkind word is mentioned about any person or place. Especially valuable to the researcher are the appendices containing comprehensive lists of honors and awards, compositions, singers, arrangers, and lyricists. Perhaps the book's only flaw is its lack of an index. It is still essential reading for anyone interested in Ellington.

After Ellington's death, three books, by Mercer Ellington, George, and Collier, appeared that exposed hidden facets of Ellington's private life. Of the three, only Mercer Ellington's book withstands the tests of diligent verification and critical rereadings.

MERCER ELLINGTON (with editorial assistance from Stanley Dance) intended that his book complement his father's memoirs and Dance's *The World of Duke Ellington*. He examines Ellington's amorous entanglements, professional shrewdness, self-destructive tendencies, superstitions, and mental toughness. The book is as much a purgative agent for Mercer, who for many years was engaged in a love-hate relationship with his internationally-famous father, as it is a compelling penetration into the inner life of a man who was both a creative genius and a consummate professional. The book won the 1979 ASCAP-Deems Taylor award.

GEORGE is a lyricist who collaborated with Ellington on 11 songs, of which the only hit was "I'm Beginning to See the Light." The unsuspecting reader is led to believe, by George's sycophantic anecdotes, that Ellington and George were the closest of confidants and that throughout the years they spent countless hours together. Conspicuous errors and hearsay disguised as first-person narrative make much of the book suspect, and the "kiss and tell" reports of Ellington's sexual encounters serve no honorable purpose.

COLLIER portrays Ellington as an indolent egocentric who built his career by exploiting others. Prominent scholars and critics denounced the book as "ill conceived" and "mean spirited." Stanley Dance shared his research materials and memories with Collier, but later wrote that Collier's book was a "disaster" and that he could "only regret having been associated with the book in any way." Although the book displays skillful writing and an abundance of research, it is handicapped by its almost exclusive reliance upon secondary sources—Collier never met Ellington in person, nor did he ever hear the Ellington Orchestra. Because Collier believes that Ellington reached his creative peak in the 1930s, Ellington's career receives lopsided coverage. The final three decades of his life are covered in fewer than 50 pages. Perhaps the only service of Collier's book is its attempt to dispel many of the myths and band lore that contribute to the Ellington legend.

Because it was the first strictly narrative biography to be published after Ellington's death, JEWELL's *Duke* is the earliest examination of Ellington's entire career. The book presents little new information, but the accessible writing style and the comprehensive scope make it perhaps the most practical one-volume survey of Ellington's life.

GAMMOND's second contribution (1985) is a handy, pocket-sized study. Gammond, like Collier, believes that Ellington reached his creative peak in the 1930s and 40s and therefore devotes little coverage to the band's later years. Far too many pages of this brief work (76 pages of text) are filled with Gammond's own opinions and conjectures for the book to succeed as an objective examination of Ellington's career.

TUCKER holds the distinction of producing the first scholarly investigation of Ellington. Nearly 500 pages are devoted to scrutinizing the first 28 years of Ellington's life. The results of his exhaustive research are presented in a straightforward literary style that avoids the ostentation so common to academic tomes.

All of his information is impeccably documented. Tucker's monograph is a model study that belongs in every university music library.

Ellington has been a favorite subject for children's books (see those by BARCLAY, BROWN, FRANKL, MONTGOMERY, and SCHAAF), in part because he overcame racial barriers to become the recipient of dozens of awards and honorary degrees, and to have been the esteemed guest of presidents and kings.

In 1988 the Smithsonian Institution acquired Ellington's own archives of music manuscripts, personal papers, photographs, scrapbooks, and memorabilia. After these materials are organized, cataloged, and made available to researchers, the stage will be set for a diligent historian to produce a definitive biography of Duke Ellington.

—Michael Cogswell

EMERSON, Ralph Waldo, 1803–1882; American essayist and poet.

Alcott, Amos B., *Ralph Waldo Emerson: An Estimate of His Character and Genius in Prose and Verse*. Boston, A. Williams, 1882; London, E. Stock, 1889.

Allen, Gay Wilson, *Waldo Emerson*. New York, Viking, 1981; London, Penguin, 1982.

Brooks, Van Wyck, *The Life of Emerson*. New York, Dutton, 1932; London, Dent, 1934.

Cabot, James E., *A Memoir of Ralph Waldo Emerson* (2 vols.). Boston, Houghton Mifflin, and London, Macmillan, 1887.

Conway, Moncure Daniel, *Emerson at Home and Abroad*. Boston, J. R. Osgood, 1882; London, Trübner, 1883.

Cooke, George W., *Ralph Waldo Emerson: His Life, Writings, and Philosophy*. Boston, J. R. Osgood, 1881.

Derleth, August, *Emerson, Our Contemporary*. New York, Crowell-Collier, 1970.

Holmes, Oliver Wendall, *Ralph Waldo Emerson*. Boston, Houghton Mifflin, 1884; London, Kegan Paul, 1885.

Ireland, Alexander, *Ralph Waldo Emerson: His Life, Genius, and Writings*. London, Simpkin and Marshall, 1882.

McAleer, John, *Ralph Waldo Emerson: Days of Encounter*. Boston, Little Brown, 1984.

Rusk, Ralph L., *The Life of Ralph Waldo Emerson*. New York, Scribner, 1949.

Thayer, James B., *A Western Journey with Mr. Emerson*. Boston, Little Brown, 1884.

Woodberry, George, *Ralph Waldo Emerson*. New York, Macmillan, 1907.

Yannella, Donald, *Ralph Waldo Emerson*. Boston, Twayne, 1982.

*

By the time of his death in 1882, Ralph Waldo Emerson had achieved pre-eminent standing among the American writers of his generation. Because of that eminence, he then became the subject of unprecedented literary adulation. No earlier American author (and perhaps none since) had ever inspired such a deluge of published remembrances: COOKE, ALCOTT, and IRELAND were all published in 1882, and CONWAY's volume appeared the following year. Each of these sources (often unavailable in libraries) includes firsthand reminiscences of Emerson by literary persons who knew him. Valuable as their anecdotes often are, however, everything of importance that these books contain has been synthesized into later and better biographies. The chief reason one would have for seeking out and consulting any of them today would be to obtain insights regarding the relationship of the author or editor with Emerson.

Yet five 19th-century books remain useful. The first of these, published while Emerson was still alive, is Frothingham's *Transcendentalism in New England* (New York, Putnam, 1876); together with the same author's *Boston Unitarianism 1820–50* (New York and London, Putnam, 1890), it is a necessary adjunct to any consideration of Emerson's religious and philosophical beliefs. THAYER's *Western Journey* is the only systematic record we have of Emerson's trip to California. HOLMES' *Ralph Waldo Emerson* was among the last of those attempted literary portraits by acquaintances. It differs from the others in that Holmes was himself a highly distinguished American author, whose insights regarding Emerson and his times have proven to be of permanent value and appear frequently in subsequent biographies. Holmes was a good deal less idealistic than Emerson and much more receptive to a purely scientific view of the world (including Darwinian evolution). But he is superior to most of the other early commentators in his attention to Emerson's ideas. It was Holmes who first characterized Emerson's "American Scholar" address as "our intellectual Declaration of Independence." Finally, CABOT's *Memoir*, which was the "official" life (i.e., had the sanction of his survivors), remained a primary source for 60 years. Cabot is notable for the number of Emerson's letters he published, as well as for the synthesis he created, but his work is only of historical importance today.

In 1903, 100 years after Emerson was born, the Centenary Edition of *The Complete Works of Ralph Waldo Emerson*, edited by his grandson Edward Waldo Emerson, began to appear (12 vols., 1903–1904), followed by an edition of his journals. Once they were out, all of the biographies previously mentioned became obsolete. A number of further treatments then appeared. There also appeared editions of Emerson's selected essays and poems with up-to-date biographical introductions—by Brooks Atkinson (1940) and Mark Van Doren (1946), for example. Among the biographical works, WOODBERRY's is often considered the most incisive. BROOKS' biography should be read in conjunction with his two fine original studies, *The Flowering of New England* (1936) and *New England: Indian Summer* (1940). The cultural centrality accorded Emerson by Brooks was then confirmed in Robert E. Spiller, et al, Literary History of the United States (1948). DERLETH's *Emerson* is yet another gracious appreciation by a later writer. Elegant as these works can be, however, they failed to add significant new facts and were not crafted by Emerson specialists. The most recent example of a short introduction to Emerson (intended primarily for students) is YANNELLA's *Ralph Waldo Emerson*.

Another major watershed in the history of Emerson biography was the publication in six volumes of *The Letters of Ralph Waldo Emerson*, edited by Ralph L. Rusk (New York, Columbia University Press, 1939). These letters, together with Emerson's extensive journals (1820 ff., published in two multi-volume edi-

tions) and occasional autobiographical asides (as in *English Traits*), are the most valuable and most comprehensive record of his public and private activities we have. No other major American author, including Thoreau, has left us so full a record of his doings—or, more importantly, his *thoughts*. Limited collections of Emerson's letters had appeared earlier. But the most important of these (Charles Eliot Norton, editor, *Correspondence of Carlyle and Emerson*, 2 vols., 1883) has now been superseded by Joseph Slater's one-volume edition (1964). Letters published by Norton were not republished by Rusk. Though less accomplished than those of some contemporaries, Emerson's letters are fundamental to any understanding of his life.

With the publication of Rusk's edition of Emerson's letters, so much new information became available that all previous biographies again became obsolete. To put the matter plainly, anyone writing on Emerson today should base his discussion, including all matters of fact, on the primary sources (including letters and journal entries) now available or on biographies published since 1939 that have made use of the resources of the Ralph Waldo Emerson Memorial Association's archives, where the original letters and much else are preserved. Though some of the best insights regarding Emerson are also some of the earliest, one should be wary of critical opinions based on inadequate evidence. Broadly speaking, biographies of Emerson published before 1939 were written by amateurs; those published after, by scholars. In any case, the reader should look to see what sources the biographer himself acknowledges and how adequate his documentation (footnotes and bibliography) is.

RUSK, the editor of Emerson's letters, wrote the first really scholarly biography of Emerson. Though more than 40 years old now, Rusk's work has been supplemented but not superseded. Between 1950 and 1980, roughly, Rusk's was unquestionably the finest biography of Emerson ever published—and may still be. Certainly, his trenchwork in finding and editing Emerson's letters gave Rusk an unequalled factual command of Emerson's life. He then presented that life in a responsibly written narrative of just over 500 pages. There are, unfortunately, no photographs (beyond the frontispiece) or maps, and the documentation, while thorough, is hard to follow. His book does not include a conventional bibliography. Beyond these shortcomings, moreover, it is now possible to recognize others. The first is that Rusk, like Cabot and others earlier, stands too much in awe of his subject to see flaws and tensions within Emerson. Biased by the materials available to him, and perhaps somewhat timid as well, Rusk understates Emerson's emotional conflicts, too often dignifying them into unrealistic saintliness. Second, Rusk also understates Emerson's intellectual conflicts, preferring external activity to internal. Yet it is only in retrospect that these flaws become apparent; when first published, Rusk's biography was better on both topics than any previous treatment.

The next major biography of Emerson, with almost 700 pages of text, was written by ALLEN. Like Rusk's, it is conscientiously documented, but, unlike his, includes a few illustrations also. Hoping to find both a popular and scholarly audience, Allen reviews essentially the same life that Rusk had established for Emerson, but with more attention to its intimacies. Allen, moreover, who had previously written biographies of Walt Whitman and William James, is more willing than Rusk to include literary criticism of Emerson's works as well as conventional background information concerning them. Taking advantage of a

30-year difference in perspective, Allen stresses the social and intellectual milieu of which Emerson had been a part. It should be noted that he often reads Emerson in Jamesian terms. Thus, Emerson's essay "The Over-Soul" records what James would later designate "the mystical experience"; similarly, according to Allen, Emerson's "Experience" includes "a clear anticipation of William James' 'Will to Believe.'" It would therefore be a good idea to read Allen's book on James before his biography of Emerson, particularly because his Jamesian reading of Emerson has been widely accepted.

A leading biography now, and in many respects the most satisfactory of all, is McALEER's, which includes almost 700 pages of text, some fine illustrations, adequate source notes, an above-average bibliography, and a good index. Very much aware of Allen's book, McAleer occasionally "corrects" it with a silence audible only to scholars. Though Allen is often the better writer, McAleer goes beyond Allen in both the range and depth of his materials. Less rhetorical and more concrete, McAleer exceeds Allen (and every other biographer except Rusk) in the integrity of his facts. For reliable information regarding Emerson, this is therefore the source of choice. McAleer is also very good on Emerson's ideas, clearly superior to Rusk in this respect and often preferable to Allen. Finally, McAleer is almost certainly unequalled in the depth and shrewdness of his characterizations, as if the first of all biographers to understand Emerson and his circle as personalities.

Unlike earlier biographers of Emerson, McAleer also includes within his primary narrative a series of topical chapters, in which he considers Emerson's relationships with others. The chapters on Emerson's two wives, Ellen and Lidian, seem particularly striking. Many of the others deal with literary relationships, whether contemporary influences like Coleridge, Carlyle, and Wordsworth, or associates and disciples like Very, Alcott, Margaret Fuller, Thoreau, Hawthorne, Dickens, Clough, Howells, and Muir, or early biographers like Conway and Norton. No other biography of Emerson offers similar coverage, making this one something of an Emerson encyclopedia, to be consulted as well as read. For most purposes, it is the first book on Emerson to which one should turn.

—Dennis R. Dean

ERASMUS, Desiderius, 1466?–1536; Dutch scholar and humanist.

Bainton, Roland H., *Erasmus of Christendom.* New York, Scribner, 1969; London, Collins, 1970.
Hyma, Albert, *The Life of Desiderius Erasmus.* Assen, The Netherlands, Van Gorcum, 1972.
Smith, Preserved, *Erasmus: A Study of His Life, Ideals, and Place in History.* New York, Harper, 1923.
Sowards, J. Kelley, *Desiderius Erasmus.* Boston, Twayne, 1975.

*

Still a highly regarded biography of Erasmus, SMITH's 1923 volume sets out to sum up existing and newly discovered information about his subject's life, explore the texture of his "rational piety," and explain the connection between the Renaissance and Reformation by the example of Erasmus' career. Smith amply demonstrates how Erasmus' "undogmatic Christianity" placed greater emphasis on ethical and reasonable as opposed to dogmatic and ritualistic religion. Yet his examination of particular events, especially Erasmus' neutrality in response to issues raised at the Diet of Worms and his break with Luther, illustrates how the thinker's ideas prepared the way for the Reformation, encouraged the movement, and finally repudiated it. Smith writes clearly and persuasively; his chapters on the apprentice years and Erasmus' role in reviving antiquity are especially illuminating. His summarizing chapter, "The Genius of Erasmus and His Place in History," is perhaps the best single account of his subject's impact on followers, "the seekers for reason in religion and for a culture emancipated from the bondage of the past but not ungrateful to the precious heritage of the ages." Smith's three appendices contain useful data about the year of Erasmus' birth, unpublished correspondence with Jean De Pins, and unpublished poems by Erasmus and Gaguin. The book has an excellent selected bibliography and a useful index.

BAINTON's biography is more of a popularized life than Smith's, making heavy use of illustrations and portraits. The text consists of expanded lectures first delivered at the Princeton Theological Seminary during February 1967. Bainton tends to dramatize events, making for readable and stimulating accounts of Erasmus' quarrel with Luther and of his denials of authorship of satires against Pope Julius. Bainton quotes lengthy swatches from the correspondence and diaries of contemporaries, from which one gains a strong impression of the humanist movement. Bainton also provides perceptive analyses of the *Enchiridion* (pointing out how the word admits the meanings "handbook" and "dagger") and *The Praise of Folly.* Bainton's chapters on Erasmus' later career—"No abiding Place" and "The Cultivated Man"—are narrated with a remarkable degree of poignancy and empathy. But Bainton's central motive for writing the biography—to underscore Erasmus' fateful role as mediator between increasingly intolerant Catholics and Protestants—colors his final chapter, "A Voice Crying in the Wilderness." In this chapter we encounter the pleas of the apologist, not the assessment of a detached scholar. The book's extensive bibliography is especially helpful to students, however.

HYMA admits a debt to Preserved Smith in the preface to his slim biography. Hyma's analyses of the works and major events in his subject's life are slight; he also spends an inordinate amount of space criticizing the opinions of other scholars—about Erasmus and his own scholarship. The volume contains neither a bibliography nor an index, thus reducing its usefulness to students and professors alike. Hyma's chapter on the colloquies provides little commentary on them, and it concludes with reproductions of two colloquies translated by Hyma in 1930. The better chapters in this generally disappointing biography discuss the relationship between Erasmus and Sir Thomas More and Erasmus' appointment as a professor at Cambridge. For the latter chapter, however, Hyma relies heavily on D. F. S. Thompson and H. C. Porter, *Erasmus and Cambridge: The Cambridge Letters of Erasmus* (Toronto, University of Toronto Press, 1963).

The Twayne biography by SOWARDS conforms to the format and style prescribed by the series editor and is aimed at college undergraduates. Sowards admits in his forward that he has set out to write, not a comprehensive biography, but rather a literary study. Events in Erasmus' life and in Renaissance society are considered only insofar as they influence Erasmus' writing. Sowards pays close attention to Erasmus' satirical, devotional, scholarly, controversial, and anti-war works. The major advantage of this study is that Sowards paints faithful portraits of the several Erasmuses—the liberal, the conservative, the "moral coward," the heretic—without designating any one identity as canonical: "The reader may draw his own conclusions and interpret him as he likes." The author devises a useful chronology, makes effective use of primary sources, and includes a reliable selected bibliography. The chapters on Erasmus' satirical writings and on his anti-war commentaries are strong. Given Twayne's aim of reaching mainly an undergraduate audience and its limited objectives, Soward's volume performs the required tasks admirably.

—Robert F. Willson, Jr.

ERIKSON, Erik H., 1902–   ; Danish-born American psychologist.

Coles, Robert, *Erik H. Erikson: The Growth of His Work.* Boston, Little Brown, 1970; London, Souvenir Press, 1973.

Roazen, Paul, *Erik H. Erikson: The Power and Limits of a Vision.* New York, Free Press, 1976; London, Collier Macmillan, 1986.

Stevens, Richard, *Erik Erikson: An Introduction.* New York, St. Martin's, and Milton Keynes, England, Open University Press, 1983.

Wright, J. Eugene, *Erikson: Identity and Religion.* New York, Seabury Press, 1982.

*

Erikson's life illustrates many of the life-cycle concepts that fill his books: adolescent "identity crisis," adulthood "psychosocial generativity," and "integrity" during old age. His psychological biographies, particularly of Martin Luther and Mahatma Gandhi, beg for a similar analysis of Erikson's own life. Psychiatrist Robert Coles and political scientist Paul Roazen have written the two major biographical studies. While neither approaches the quality of Erikson's own biographies, both have significant strengths.

COLES wrote the first full-length biography of Erikson. His portrait is meticulous and rich in personal details. Coles devotes separate chapters to Erikson's roots in Europe, emigration to the United States, subsequent move to California, and move back East again; in each chapter he successfully avoids a psychoanalytically reductionistic sketch of Erikson's "personality." Coles also traces Erikson's scholarly development through an engaging chronological review of his publications. Here, however, Coles may have been too thorough: the amount of attention given to Erikson's biographies of Luther and Gandhi seems to be out of proportion (36% of the text). While Coles' treatment of his subject is largely uncritical, Erikson emerges as the author we have come to know through his own books: warm, caring, and wise.

ROAZEN's biography is a well-organized and well-written appraisal of the potency and the limitations of Erikson's theory and, to a lesser degree, of the theorist himself. Roazen's basic approach is to devote a separate chapter to a series of ten topics (e.g., the ego, society, morals and ethics). Roazen reviews an element of Erikson's "vision," and then presents his own critique. Erikson's personal history emerges through the inclusion of biographical material relevant to a particular topic; in the chapter on "youth and identity," for instance, Roazen discusses the relation between Erikson's identity conflict and his Danish-Protestant birth father, Danish-Jewish birth mother, and German-Jewish adoptive father. In contrast with Coles, however, Roazen is more concerned with writing an intellectual biography of a vision than a psychohistorical biography of a life. Roazen is also more critical, less respectful, of Erikson, who comes across here as temperamental, self-deceptive, and preachy. By the end of some 200 pages of text, however, Roazen's negative characterizations have begun to sound like pure projection.

While both Coles and Roazen make, at times, perceptive and poignant biographical contributions, both fundamentally prepare the way for a more thorough and balanced biography of Erikson. Guidance for executing such a future biography is found in Donald Capps' 1987 biographical sketch published in *Thinkers of the 20th Century* (Chicago and London, St. James Press, 1987), which he organizes around critical events in Erikson's life, similar in style to the manner in which Erikson organized his biographies of Luther and Gandhi.

A few of the many other shorter works, and a collection of Erikson's writings, also contribute significant biographical material. Henry W. Maier (*Three Theories of Child Development*, New York, 1965) offers his readers an informative "Thumbnail Sketch of Erikson's Life." This early work has been surpassed by later biographical sketches, but it is still a valuable illustration of how Erikson's life has contributed to the study of human development. STEVENS' introductory exposition of Eriksonian theory is, along with the works of Coles and Roazen, one of the most cited publications on Erikson. Stevens' introductory and concluding chapters, "A Brief Biography" and "The Nature of Erikson's Contribution," together provide an unusually sensitive and rich portrait of the relation between Erikson's life and work. WRIGHT's book on identity and religion begins with a general biographical chapter on Erikson, "An American Stepchild," and concludes with a focused biographical chapter, "Erik H. Erikson: Homo Religious?" Wright's book primarily documents Erikson's impact on the psychological study of religion, but it also makes a significant contribution to understanding the role of religion in Erikson's own life and thought. Finally, Stephen Schlein's edition of Erikson's writings (*A Way of Looking at Things: Selected Papers 1930–80*, New York, 1987) is worthy of note. The articles collected in this volume provide a 50-year bibliographical sweep of Erikson's scholarship, while Schlein's preface and thematic organization provide a similar perspective on Erikson's life.

—John Snarey

FAULKNER, William, 1897–1962; American writer.

Blotner, Joseph, *Faulkner, a Biography* (2 vols.). New York, Random House, and London, Chatto and Windus, 1974; condensed and revised one-volume edition, Random House, 1984.

Faulkner, John, *My Brother Bill: An Affectionate Reminiscence.* New York, Trident Press, 1963; London, Gollancz, 1964.

Minter, David, *William Faulkner: His Life and Work.* Baltimore, Maryland, and London, Johns Hopkins University Press, 1980.

Oates, Stephen B., *William Faulkner: The Man and the Artist.* New York and London, Harper, 1987.

Wasson, Ben, *Count No 'Count: Flashbacks to Faulkner.* Jackson, University Press of Mississippi, 1983.

*

William Faulkner stated in his Nobel Prize acceptance speech that a writer must leave no room in his workshop "for anything but the old verities and truths of the heart, the old universal truths lacking which any story is ephemeral and doomed—love and honor and pity and pride and compassion and sacrifice." Admirable sentiments, suggesting that the speaker is both a good and a quite conventional man. This is however an impression somewhat at odds with the one that comes to readers of Faulkner's fiction and the accounts of his life discussed here. Indeed, the relation between the man and his work has been a continuing challenge to students and biographers of Faulkner. Of the works selected for notice here, three are formal and exhaustive biographies, and two—*My Brother Bill* and *Count No 'Count*—are recollections by persons who knew Faulkner intimately. The two groups of books supplement each other and offer pictures of a man whose writing and whose social behavior remain a partial mystery.

The novels themselves slowly won a wide audience in the United States and other countries. Faulkner's records of the South caught the minds of many readers. In due time, the novelist himself became a figure for reporters to cover. His travels, his years in Hollywood as a screenwriter, his opinions in his later years on the race question—all became matters for public discussion. Readers increasingly began to ask who indeed William Faulkner was and were deeply and often impatiently curious about the relation between the man and his work.

This is the question that is insistent in the books listed here. It meets us at every turn of the formal biographies, and it even crops up occasionally in the two volumes of personal recollections. But in the three full biographies the reader is led, step by step, through the events of Faulkner's literary career and of his personal life. All three writers move back and forth between two mysteries: is there a basic continuity that links together all his fiction? and is Faulkner himself a single, unified man and not several, variously manifesting himself to family and friends? And there is a related perplexity that all three highly competent biographers take up: the relation between Faulkner's invented tales of the South and the tale of the South that was William Faulkner himself. All this constitutes a task that sets biographers to work again and again. No earlier performance is completely acceptable to later reshapers of the various Faulkner problems.

The earliest of the three formal biographies is BLOTNER's impressive two-volume work, which runs to about 1900 pages.

Blotner conducted numerous interviews and examined carefully all the letters available to him. (Later biographers have been able to draw on some files that remained closed to Blotner.) While Blotner reveals much about turn-of-the-century Mississippi, he reveals much more about Faulkner's process of maturing and of his adult life. His schooling was boring to him and fragmentary; his reading in the family libraries open to him was omnivorous and attentive. A few friends were nearby to suggest and encourage, and as he moved away from Oxford (and he always moved away only to return) he met persons who respected his work: writers like Sherwood Anderson and New York agents and publishers and, later, celebrated figures in Hollywood and elsewhere.

Blotner adds to these facts of an external sort more personal matters, chiefly the thread of Faulkner's unsatisfactory marriage with a childhood sweetheart. But Blotner properly regards as most important the years in which Faulkner composed his tales and novels. Each important work receives what could be called *its* biography. For example, Faulkner's Christological novel, *A Fable*, rises up again and again in all its several forms, until it is published and reviewed.

Blotner's account leaves in the reader's mind a unified impression of Faulkner and his work. Nearly all that later students of Faulkner will have to reckon with is on Blotner's page, and there are interesting efforts to explain the incoherences in both Faulkner's life and his work. Thanks to Blotner, Faulkner has been fully described if not entirely understood.

Full understanding is the aim of the most recent biographies. Both MINTER and OATES (discussed below by turns) repeat—and more briefly—the materials Blotner includes in his account. Research has indeed enabled the later writers to enter into their records matters that were either unavailable to Blotner or were avoided by him. Chief among these matters are narratives that tell of the most painful sections of Faulkner's marriage and precise accounts of Faulkner's discovery, in Hollywood, in Sweden, and in Rome, of women whose company gave him both sentimental and sensual pleasure. All this Minter and Oates understand as well as may be. Both Minter and Oates delineate a man who expected a full acceptance of his incoherences.

Both biographers, however, speculate on the meaning of Faulkner's discontinuous romances in the light of particular works of fiction. Usually these discussions center on a completed work of fiction; for the processes of false starts and revisions Blotner is the important source of information. Oates' estimates are extremely precise and firm. And Minter certainly gives us pleasure as he lives up to the promise he offers in his introduction: that he will deal fully with the contrasts and incoherences of Faulkner's life against the triumphant and unifying focus of novel after novel. Minter defines his stance in his introduction. "Throughout I try to subordinate critical discussion of Faulkner's writings to the task of sketching the 'mysterious armature' (to borrow Mallarmé's phrase) that binds Faulkner's life and art together. My claim to the reader's attention is specific, then, and it stems from the story I have to tell—of deep reciprocities, of relations and revisions between Faulkner's flawed life and his great art."

Minter's reading of the facts lives up to his stated aim. This is not to say that other students of a psychological bent will repeat the path that Minter traces from man to artist and back again. Oates' deft reading of the same mystery—the man in confrontation with the artist—is just as deft and compelling, and one is reminded of two mental therapists parting company even though they share the same evidence.

It should be added that all three biographers display in differing degrees a narrative skill. This is so even in Blotner's exhaustive book. As for the other two writers, they impose on the differing textures of their sources—letters, gossip, newspaper reports—an easy and effective unity. Each of the biographies is, in its own way, a work of art and no mere compilation.

If one wishes for simpler approaches to Faulkner's presence, two memoirs will serve admirably. Both books are simple and offer stories that do not call for comment and analysis. JOHN FAULKNER—a novelist in his own right—is as much interested in the entire Faulkner household as he is in the youth and maturity of his famous brother. The result is a pleasant contrast to the sometimes relentless pursuit of William Faulkner in the biographies; an easy and open town called Oxford emerges along with an easier and more open William Faulkner. WASSON's volume is like a long chat over glasses of bourbon, truthful in intent and casual in approach. These two modest books are agreeable versions of the milieu that in large part surrounded and supported the great novelist as he worked.

—Harold H. Watts

FELLINI, Federico, 1920–   ; Italian film director.

Alpert, Hollis, *Fellini, a Life*. New York, Atheneum, 1986; London, W. H. Allen, 1987.
Murry, Edward, *Fellini the Artist*. New York, Ungar, and Bembridge, Isle of Wight, BCW Publishing, 1975; revised edition, New York, Ungar, 1985.
Solmi, Angelo, *Fellini*, translated by Elizabeth Greenwood. London, Merlin Press, and New York, Humanities Press, 1967.

*

SOLMI was an early admirer of Fellini, and this two-part introduction to his early career (through *8 1/2*, 1963) reads, at times, like a rhapsody for the genius who "carried the name of Italy into every corner of the world." The book is still one of the best introductions available, however.

Solmi contends that Fellini is neither socialist, Marxist nor neo-realist, as early criticism concluded, but a humanist whose self-reflective films illuminate the human condition. Discovering in Fellini's art evidence of his middle-class background and lack of schooling, Solmi notes that many of the director's film characters are reflections of Fellini, who often identified himself with such characters as Zampano in *La Strada*. With this thesis foremost, Part I begins with Fellini's biography, much of it corroborated by conversations with Fellini, and concludes by delineating the recurring themes in his films. Part II provides the background of the films and emphasizes the biographical connections between them and Fellini's childhood, youth, and adult life. Because of his personal relationship with Fellini, Solmi can

provide many illuminating anecdotes not found elsewhere. Though lacking footnotes, the book includes 28 clear photos, several of Fellini as a child and a young man.

Whether to support or modify events, subsequent biographies rely to some extent on Solmi, whose insistence on the synergetic relationship between Fellini's life and his art is, in retrospect, the position most frequently developed in later Fellini studies. MURRY's book, meant to appeal to the film student, approaches Fellini's life and personality as keys to understanding his art. Recently revised, the three-part work examines *The White Sheik* (1952) through *Fred and Ginger* (1985). Part I, though not a formal biography, gives a brief chronicle of Fellini's life, emphasizing his early years. Part II focuses on Fellini's unusual methods for constructing a film, and in Part III Murry sensitively and systematically explicates 12 of Fellini's films. Fellini's own comments and analysis, here collected and organized, are used to interpret the language and symbols in each film. Taken together, the three parts give a comprehensive picture of Fellini's artistic temperament and personal vision.

Of the three works considered here, Murry's contains the most incisive criticism of Fellini's art. The author explains, for example, that Fellini's "growing egoism" is reflected in the deteriorated quality of his later films. While his primary concern is with the formal characteristics of the "Felliniesque," the importance Murry attaches to autobiography and biography makes his book a useful adjunct to understanding Fellini. Though sparsely documented, the book contains a bibliography, numerous literary allusions, and 18 stills from the films.

ALPERT has written the traditional biography, a straightforward, relatively full account of Fellini's character and of his experiences and activities. Although Fellini did not actively cooperate with Alpert, he did, according to the author, answer queries, correcting some of the supposed facts about his life. Alpert is the only biographer here to acknowledge that Fellini's recollections change over time, making the events of his life difficult to substantiate. Still, Alpert is able to clarify some of the vagueness surrounding Fellini's early life. Through his research, for example, he convincingly demonstrates that Fellini could not have journeyed with Aldo Fabrizi's traveling variety show when he said he did.

Alpert includes biographic sketches of the influential people who affected Fellini. His exploration of Fellini's professional and personal relationship with wife Giulietta Masina is particularly revealing. Alpert gives a number of behind-the-scenes glimpses of the "Maestro" at work, revealing Fellini's need for autocratic control as well as providing insights into his improvisational techniques and his curious methods for selecting actors.

Alpert briefly examines the more important films, using quotations from the most frequently referenced reviews. Like Solmi and Murry, Alpert attempts to establish factual connections between Fellini's life and his art. And like Murry, Alpert identifies two distinct stages in Fellini's development, noting a falling off after *La Dolce Vita* (1960). By the time he made *Satyricon* (1969), he notes, Fellini "kept around him a loyal and devoted corps" of followers and seemed to have forgotten the importance of box office receipts. Alpert is particularly adept at chronicling the ups and downs of Fellini's career and the frustrations he experienced as an artist. Though it will probably not prove to be the definitive Fellini biography, this work is readable and informative. It contains a complete, detailed filmography (with lists of casts) and 26 photographs.

—Alan Pratt

_____

FIELDING, Henry, 1707–1754; English writer.

Battestin, Martin C. and Ruthe Battestin, *Henry Fielding: A Life.* London and New York, Routledge, 1989.

Cross, Wilbur L., *The History of Henry Fielding.* Hew Haven, Connecticut, Yale University Press, 1918.

Dobson, Austin, *Fielding.* London, Macmillan, and New York, Harper, 1883.

Dudden, F. Homes, *Henry Fielding: His Life, Works, and Times.* Oxford, Clarendon Press, 1952.

Godden, G. M., *Henry Fielding: A Memoir.* London, 1910.

Hume, Robert D., *Henry Fielding and the London Theatre 1728–37.* Oxford, Clarendon Press, and New York, Oxford University Press, 1988.

Jenkins, Elizabeth, *Henry Fielding.* London, A. Barker, 1947; Denver, Colorado, A. Swallow, 1948.

Jones, Benjamin M., *Henry Fielding, Novelist and Magistrate.* London, Allen and Unwin, 1933.

Rogers, Pat, *Henry Fielding: A Biography.* New York, Scribner, and London, Elek, 1979.

*

The earliest substantial biography of Fielding has proved something of an obstacle and an irritant to later students. This was the essay on Fielding's "Life and Genius" that Arthur Murphy prefaced to the first collected edition of the novelist's works (8 vols., London, 1762). Issued by Fielding's own publisher, Andrew Millar, only eight years after Fielding's death, this ought to have been definitive. Murphy was a competent man of letters who was to produce acceptable surveys of Johnson and Garrick; though he knew Fielding less intimately, he had some firsthand acquaintance with his subject and was able to consult family and friends. His account is almost bereft of precise dates and falls down in just those areas where subsequent biographers would have liked information. It is a rather flashy performance that had the incidental demerit of spiking what could have been a better work, by a much closer friend of Fielding, James Harris of Salisbury, the author of *Hermes* (1751). Fielding's biography was doubly vexed in that few of his letters survived: indeed, only some 20 items had been published as late as the 1980s, and no truly personal letter emerged until 1989.

19th-century views of Fielding, as with other writers, were influenced chiefly by critics, journalists, and the generalist men of letters who dominated the scene. In this case it was the essays of men like Scott, Hazlitt, and Thackeray that set the tone, and none of them took much interest in advancing the core of biographical knowledge. A few new facts appeared in dispersed notes and queries, but little merged for generations to supply a more adequate picture of Fielding's life than that provided by Murphy. Again, Fielding is not unique in the fact that the best biography of the period was contained in a volume of the En-

glish Men of Letters series, namely that contributed by DOBSON in 1883 (with later revisions). Dobson, necessarily in his time, reacts to Thackeray, and echoes his master's voice in regretting the fate of Fielding's "candour" in *Tom Jones*, which precluded the book's perusal by women or young people. But at least Dobson was able to supply the first effective full-length survey: it is as well to remind ourselves that when Dickens named his son "Henry Fielding" in love and admiration, there was no ordinary half-way decent life available.

Progress in the 20th century has been by fits and starts. After GODDEN's small "memoir" of 1910 (printing hitherto unknown material, some of it now lost), CROSS transformed the scene with his three-volume *History of Henry Fielding* (1918). This was much the fullest and most searching review of the evidence to date, and indeed it remained so until very recently. Much in Cross' treatment is open to debate, especially on questions of intellectual background. His belief in Fielding's debt to the liberal freethinking of Shaftesbury has been open to criticism, and generally Cross makes Fielding more cheerful, untroubled and irreproachably virtuous than today seems plausible. Nonetheless, his work deservedly stood as the standard biography during a long period in which Fielding studies became more sophisticated in critical perspective and more soundly rooted in intellectual history.

The best work to emerge in the interwar years was JONES' survey of Fielding as magistrate, an area where Cross was in need of supplement. Otherwise the field was left to popular biographers such as JENKINS, who did a competent job without expanding the underlying base of biographical knowledge. The same, astoundingly, applies in large part to the lengthy two-volume study by DUDDEN in 1952. This has all the appearance of a major "Oxford" life, but it is too easily distracted into background and padding; the subtitle, *Life, Works and Times*, points to the weakness. On the central issues of Fielding's own life, Dudden had little new to offer, and he did not incorporate all the findings of scholars such as de Castro and Woods. This was an opportunity missed, and left matters much where they had stood in 1918.

Nonetheless, intense scholarly inquiry was proceeding by this time, and its fruits began to appear in learned journals in the 1950s. A new generation of scholars investigated all aspects of Fielding's career; specialists in theatre history revolutionized our sense of his dramatic years. Here the major outcome is represented by HUME's book, a searching and detailed treatment of Fielding's involvement with the London stage. Some of the new findings were used by ROGERS in a short general life (1979), which does not rest on first-order research but seeks to tell the story of Fielding's life in broad outline in the light of the growing body of facts.

All this work, with the exception of Hume's specialist study, has been effectively supplanted by BATTESTIN's monumental new biography. This was in fact written by Martin C. Battestin with Ruthe Battestin, and the archival skills of Ruthe Battestin afford one of the main strengths of the book. Countless new details have been ferreted out from record offices, which provide a far more complete account of Fielding's day-to-day existence than we have ever had before. Much light has been thrown on his years on the judicial bench, and indeed on Fielding's own troubles with the law as plaintiff or (more often) defendant in actions for the recovery of debts. In terms of the public career, the most important materials concern Fielding's relations with his patron, the Duke of Bedford. Different interpretations are possible with regard to this evidence, which was first announced by the Battestins in 1977 and briefly summarized by Rogers, but on most readings it would suggest a less idealized picture of Fielding's conduct as a magistrate, particularly in the events surrounding the Westminster election of 1749. This is not to suggest that Fielding emerges as seriously corrupt or shamefully partisan, simply that he behaved according to the standards of his time and was less of a perfect Edwardian gentleman (in the tough and seamy environment he inhabited) than Cross had implied.

The Battestins' work also includes 26 new letters from James Harris (with a couple in return), which give us our first contact with Fielding in the sphere of personal correspondence. The letters have not been published in full, but it is clear from the extracts now before us that a new dimension has been given to the life of Fielding. Other innovations will be regarded with varying degrees of favor: the suggestion that Henry and his sister Sarah had entered into an incestuous relationship (not very fully documented, from life or literature), and the attribution of numerous *Craftsman* papers in the late 1730s to Fielding. But whatever reservations in detail may be expressed, the new work—whether it becomes known as "Battistin" or "Battestins"—will hold its place as the major life of Fielding for as far ahead as one can see.

—Pat Rogers

FIELDS, W. C. [*born* **William Claude Dukenfield**], 1880–1946; American vaudevillian comedian and film actor.

Taylor, Robert L., *W. C. Fields: His Follies and Fortunes.* New York, Doubleday, 1949; London, Cassell, 1950.

*

TAYLOR's biography of Fields had appeared in a condensed version (as "W. C. Fields: Rowdy King of Comedy") commissioned by and published in the *Saturday Evening Post*, running for eight issues beginning with that of 21 May 1949. The full book was dedicated to Gene Fowler, journalist, memoirist, and biographer, who had given Taylor his notes on Fields. Taylor's style owed something to that of Fowler, the texture of whose mock-heroic and gentlemanly burlesque was particularly evident in his best-selling chronicle of John Barrymore, *Good Night, Sweet Prince* (1944).

W. C. Fields: His Follies and Fortunes has no index, notes, bibliography, or acknowledgements. Few exact sources of written or anecdotal material are given, and only the dates of several letters are recorded. However, the very tone and texture of the work peculiarly complements its subject. Taylor's attitude to Fields is indulgent, his tone familiar. In an urbane, mischievous, affected, and raffishly good-natured style, Taylor provides a consistently amusing account. Taylor's approach is largely uncritical and permissive, with little real variation in tone or

mood. Serious elements receive almost uniformly short shrift, even a jesting dismissal, and Fields' peccadillos are bemusedly forgiven. Taylor pays little attention to the comedian's private life.

Taylor's work features many self-contained scenes, comic turns, and anecdotes. Some passages are pure "business," often an undocumented borrowing from Fields' own fantastic elaboration of incidents. Unceasingly witty, filled with comic asides that may aim to emulate Fields' famous and exaggerated patterns of speech, Taylor's book is pervaded by the kind of mock-heroic and elevated language we associate with W. C. Fields.

Subsequent biographical treatments of Fields have merely abbreviated and selected Taylor's work, which remains the only relatively thorough treatment of the comedian's life. Paul Denscher's "Biography" in *The Films of W. C. Fields* (1966) is, like most of its successors, functional. Carlotta Monti's *W. C. Fields and Me* (1971) is an anecdotal account of the comedian's last 14 years; Blythe Foote Finke's poorly-edited *W. C. Fields, Renowned Comedian of the Early Motion Picture Industry* (1974) selects information from Taylor for young people. Nicholas Yanni's *W. C. Fields* (1974) uses familiar material up to the beginning of Fields' film performances. Fields' grandson, Ronald C. Fields, adds new but only occasional information between documents by Fields in *W. C. Fields by Himself: His Intended Autobiography* (1974). Wes Gehring's scholarly and careful *W. C. Fields: A Bio-Bibliography* (1984) uses Taylor, Monti, and Fowler (a latter-day reminiscence in *Minutes of the Last Meeting*, 1954) in a biographical chapter, and includes a "Chronological Biography"; like Yanni, this record strongly focuses on "Fields' career and his growth as a performer."

An early review of Taylor, in the *San Francisco Chronicle*, observed that the biography lacked accuracy but not entertainment. However, corrections to Taylor's work, except for several small film facts, have not been forthcoming. An inconsequential number of more precise details and dates about Fields' professional careers, in particular, have appeared in such works as histories of vaudeville, of film genres and corporations, and in biographies and autobiographies of a very few of Fields' contemporaries and associates.

—Louis K. MacKendrick

FITZGERALD, Edward, 1809–1883; English poet and translator.

Adams, Morley, *Omar's Interpreter: A New Life of Edward FitzGerald.* London, Priory Press, 1909.

Benson, Arthur C., *Edward FitzGerald.* New York and London, Macmillan, 1905.

Glyde, John, *The Life of Edward FitzGerald.* Chicago, H. S. Stone, and London, C. A. Pearson, 1900.

Jewett, Iran B. Hassani, *Edward FitzGerald.* Boston, Twayne, and London, G. Prior, 1977.

Martin, Robert B., *With Friends Possessed: A Life of Edward FitzGerald.* New York, Atheneum, and London, Faber, 1985.

Terhune, Alfred M., *The Life of Edward FitzGerald*. New Haven, Connecticut, Yale University Press, and London, Oxford University Press, 1947.

Wright, Thomas, *The Life of Edward FitzGerald* (2 vols.). London, G. Richards, and New York, Scribner, 1904.

*

Written only 17 years after the death of FitzGerald, GLYDE's study was the first book-length biography to be published. The principal sources of information for Glyde are his interviews with men and women "who knew [FitzGerald] well, who could describe his habits, who were as familiar with his generosity as with his eccentricity." Limited use is also made of letters written by and to the famous translator; where used, these are noted in the text. This is not a scholarly study, but rather an anecdotal portrait that carefully preserves a positive image of the man. Glyde's style can be characterized as intrusive, with his frequent use of personal pronouns, urging the reader to accept his analysis and conclusions. Although the study does not conform to the highest standards of modern biography, factually it is accurate in its content. Glyde's description and evaluation of FitzGerald's personal library and his inclusion of FitzGerald's will, items that do not appear in any other biographies, add to the interest of this work.

Intending his study to be both critical and comprehensive, WRIGHT declares in the lengthy Preface, "I have been successful beyond my utmost expectations, and for the simple reason that nobody before had taken the trouble to make exhaustive investigations." Despite this assurance, contemporary critics and later biographers of FitzGerald have agreed that this work contains numerous inaccuracies. In addition, Wright's two volumes are padded throughout with many illustrations that are neither essential nor helpful, rambling digressions on Persian, Spanish, and Greek literature, and 16 appendices of various types. In spite of a writing style that arouses little interest or curiosity in the reader, Wright's biography was accepted as the standard against which all others were measured until the publication of Terhune's study in 1947 (see below).

BENSON's study seeks to provide a critical study of the man whose life's work amounted to "a single volume of imperishable quality, . . . a little piece of delicate prose-writing, and many beautiful letters." Benson is simple, direct, and succinct in his writing. He allows FitzGerald to speak for himself through his letters, such as were available for study at that time, and provides interpretation in his discussions of FitzGerald's friendships with prominent contemporaries such as Tennyson, Carlyle, and Thackeray. The tone here is not sentimental but objective. Samples of FitzGerald's poetry, prose, translations, and letters are woven into the narrative and put into context skillfully and without affectation. Benson acknowledges the researches of previous biographers and succeeds in incorporating what is best in each. The result is an honest and respectful assessment of the man and his work.

ADAMs offers "no apology for this short life" of FitzGerald, gathered, like others, from "persons intimately associated with him"; unfortunately, these sources are not always identified. In a striking feature of the book, Adams gives detailed physical descriptions often accompanied by photographs, of the locations FitzGerald visited and places where he resided. Often these col-

lections of images and descriptions resemble nothing so much as the personal travelogue of a FitzGerald devotee. FitzGerald's relationship with his brother, John, is explained through anecdotes, but since the particulars are not documented readers must be cautioned about accepting such speculations. Adams includes in his text long segments of FitzGerald's verse. Seventy-five quatrains from the "Rubaiyat" are used to direct attention to an account of Omar Khayyám himself, this in an unsuccessful attempt to show a special affinity between the two men. Although flawed in a number of respects, this book does furnish useful physical descriptions of places associated with FitzGerald.

The first critical biography to appear was that of TERHUNE. It should be noted that this was also the first to be written with the approval and support of the FitzGerald family. Consequently, manuscript materials, chiefly thousands of letters not used in previous biographical studies, were made available to Terhune. These were later systematically edited and published in four volumes by Terhune himself and a collaborator. The author faces his challenge with the knowledge that "ferreting out the story of a man's life from his correspondence is like reading a closely written manuscript by the light of a flickering candle." Nevertheless, he succeeds in handling the available evidence judiciously and in presenting an objective and authoritative picture of FitzGerald. His careful scholarship, supported by detailed notes, establishes the book as the standard biography of this Victorian man of letters. Though perhaps appreciated most by scholars for its disciplined approach and clarity of expression, this work is appropriate for the widest of audiences. Terhune depicts the events of FitzGerald's life and aspects of his poetry and translations with discrimination. Rightfully, he leaves for future scholars the comprehensive, critical assessment of his subject's writings. Terhune enhances his volume with a bibliography, a map of FitzGerald's native Suffolk, and an explanation of works wrongly attributed to FitzGerald. FitzGerald emerges as an individual well established and secure in his society and circle of friends and at his legitimate rank in Victorian literary history.

If Terhune's impressive study may at first seem intimidating to a popular audience of readers, JEWETT's study is certainly not. Condensed into less than 200 pages is a sketch of FitzGerald's life and a critical introduction to his works. Part of the Twayne "English Author Series," the book succeeds in making the subject's life uncomplicated and accessible, particularly to the non-specialist. In addition to the biographical survey furnished, descriptions of selected writings by FitzGerald, a chronological table, a short annotated bibliography, and a thorough index serve to assist the beginner. Although helpful as an introduction to the man and his work, this slim volume cannot hope to describe fully the character of FitzGerald "as he travels through the centuries."

In an effort to recognize and demonstrate the complexity of FitzGerald's nature, MARTIN draws on the recently-published Terhune edition of the letters. With the firm conviction that FitzGerald did not deliberately deceive others in his correspondence, Martin attempts to prove that his subject is more fully revealed in the deliberate choice of language, and it is "in the relative enthusiasm with which he approaches different subjects, most of all in what he leaves out, that tell us a great deal more than he intended." The most startling example here comes in Martin's revelation that one aspect of FitzGerald's undisclosed life was "the nature of his responses to several of the men who were so important in his life." At the same time, the author argues that FitzGerald was utterly unaware of this side of his nature and concludes that he was not so innocent as naive in his sexuality. While the historical outline provided is accurate, not differing from the standard set by Terhune, Martin's suggestion of FitzGerald's hidden nature, based solely on a forced reading of the correspondence, is the chief shortcoming of his book.

—Robin Grollmus Hanson

FITZGERALD, F. Scott, 1896–1940; American writer.

Bruccoli, Matthew J., *Some Sort of Epic Grandeur*. New York, Harcourt, and London, Hodder and Stoughton, 1981.

Donaldson, Scott, *Fool for Love*. New York, Congdon and Weed, 1983.

Graham, Sheilah, *The Real F. Scott Fitzgerald 35 Years Later*. New York, Grosset and Dunlap, and London, W. H. Allen, 1976.

Koblas, John J., *F. Scott Fitzgerald in Minnesota: His Homes and Haunts*. St. Paul, Minnesota Historical Society, 1978.

Le Vot, André, *F. Scott Fitzgerald: A Biography*, translated by William Byron. New York, Doubleday, 1983; London, A. Lane, 1984 (originally published as *Scott Fitzgerald*, Paris, Julliard, 1979).

Mayfield, Sara, *Exiles from Paradise: Zelda and Scott Fitzgerald*. New York, Delacorte, 1971.

Mellow, James R., *Invented Lives: F. Scott and Zelda Fitzgerald*. Boston, Houghton Mifflin, 1984; London, Souvenir Press, 1985.

Mizener, Arthur, *The Far Side of Paradise: A Biography of F. Scott Fitzgerald*. Boston, Houghton Mifflin, and London, Eyre and Spottiswoode, 1951.

Piper, Henry D., *F. Scott Fitzgerald: A Critical Portrait*. New York, Holt, and London, Bodley Head, 1965.

Sklar, Robert, *F. Scott Fitzgerald: The Last Laocoön*. New York, Oxford University Press, 1967.

Turnbull, Andrew, *Scott Fitzgerald*. New York, Scribner, and London, Bodley Head, 1962.

*

Biographies of F. Scott Fitzgerald often begin by bemoaning the overlapping of his life and his writing. "He used himself so mercilessly in his fiction," Charles E. Shain typically notes, "there is often a complete fusion between his life and his stories" (*F. Scott Fitzgerald*, Minneapolis, University of Minnesota Press, 1961). Personal memoirs of Fitzgerald usually offer some criticism of his work, and critical biographies must at least acknowledge the gossip Fitzgerald's celebrity stirred.

The best of the memoir-cum-biography genre is TURNBULL's *Scott Fitzgerald*. Turnbull, who was 11 when Fitzgerald first rented a house on the Turnbull family property, remembers him fondly—the funny notes Fitzgerald jotted to the boy show off his wit and charm. But other incidents are too plainly seen through a boy's eyes. When T. S. Eliot joined Fitzgerald for dinner at the

Turnbulls' one night, Fitzgerald read some of Eliot's poetry aloud "without hesitation in that moving voice of his that could bring out all the beauty and hint at all the mystery of words"— the praise of an uncritical adolescent. But *which* poems did Fitzgerald read, what phrases did he emphasize, how did he use accents, tone, pace?—all is lost in Turnbull's adoration. Coyly, Turnbull omits many fascinating details, masking several figures in anonymity. Relying too heavily on Fitzgerald's own inaccurate Ledgers (autobiographical notes Fitzgerald wrote years after the events described), Turnbull meticulously records Fitzgerald's peripatetic family's moves, but he characterizes the streets, buildings, and landlords only by mentioning them. In repeating Fitzgerald's lists of homes and neighborhoods, Turnbull delivers mere raw data.

KOBLAS cooks some similar data about Fitzgerald's residences in Minnesota, settling for a load of details about his many boyhood and family dwellings in St. Paul while leaving unexplained the Fitzgeralds' choice to live out of packing crates for half a century. MAYFIELD tries to defend her girlhood friend, Zelda Sayre Fitzgerald, against charges of hindering her husband Scott's career, a task done more dispassionately in Nancy Milford's biography *Zelda* (1970). *Exiles from Paradise* displays Mayfield's too-great acquaintance with foreign languages, throwing up a smokescreen of French, Italian, Latin, and Yiddish snippets for no meaningful purpose. Her title, taken from Voltaire, over-romanticizes their wandering: if indeed the Fitzgeralds were "Exiles from Paradise," where was that paradise? St. Paul? Long Island? The clearest indication that the title refers to any place at all is Mayfield's consistent idealization of Montgomery, Alabama, her hometown and Zelda's, which she describes throughout in terms that would shame the Montgomery Chamber of Commerce: "Montgomery was an international city, coequal with London, Rome or Athens—and in the eyes of its proud citizens, *primus inter pares*." Thus squandering her authority (unless she was referring to London, Ontario; Rome, New York; and Athens, Georgia), Mayfield defends Zelda by telling anecdotes that show her faults instead of the virtues Mayfield intends. Aside from mentioning the name of one of Zelda's girlhood beaux, "Dan Cody" (which Fitzgerald later gave to Gatsby's benefactor), Mayfield's only original contribution is her interview with Edouard Jozan, Zelda's purported French lover.

The entire question of whether Jozan was actually Zelda Fitzgerald's lover or simply a summer acquaintance is a vital one for most of Fitzgerald's biographers. Even literary biographies must speculate on this intimate question because of the central role marital infidelity plays in Fitzgerald's best work. Fitzgerald's lovelife, in fact, is the theme of DONALDSON's fine biography. (Donaldson also sensitively examines other important issues, distinguishing himself as a superb interpreter of letters, texts, and other documents.) Donaldson implies that the affair between Zelda and Jozan probably did take place, while André Le Vot (see below) takes Jozan at his word that the "affair" was merely a brief flirtation. In fact, Le Vot is willing to presume Fitzgerald "had slept with no one else [but Zelda] in the . . . [first] ten years" of their marriage. Donaldson cites Fitzgerald's ambiguous Ledger notations of "significant encounters" with women, conceding that just "how significant these encounters were is difficult to determine."

Graham (see below) believes "Zelda had had a notable affair with a French aviator, and Scott had been unfaithful to her only after 1930," but her reasoning is shaky: Lois Moran, a young actress Fitzgerald certainly pursued in 1927, "afterwards visited him—and Zelda" at their home. MIZENER's reasoning is more philosophical: he "had never acquired the twenties' habit of tolerating casual affairs. . . . His attitude was the attitude of Gatsby towards Daisy." In this assertion, Mizener reveals his biography's essential flaw, by confusing the legends Fitzgerald invented with his own values. As MELLOW demonstrates relentlessly, Fitzgerald's idealization of his characters' lofty values contrasted sharply with his own practices. Read together, Mizener and Mellow provide a balanced view of Fitzgerald's personal life. Oddly, although Mizener's was the first biography, it contains incidents (and some photos) later biographers rarely use: scenes such as the teenaged Fitzgerald drunkenly serenading Montana cowboys may have been excluded from later books because of space considerations or because Mizener's documentation is suspect. (This anecdote, for example, is unsourced. Mellow, Donaldson, Piper, and Bruccoli have particularly thorough source notes.)

As Mizener and Mellow balance each other out, so do the memoirs and the critical accounts. Sara Mayfield's or Aaron Latham's books on Fitzgerald as the drinking man's writer simply cannot be reconciled with scholarly portraits of Fitzgerald as the thinking man's writer. The gossipy biographies play variations on Edna St. Vincent Millay's remark comparing Fitzgerald's talent to a diamond whose owner is ignorant of its true beauty. But both SKLAR and PIPER show how Fitzgerald drew broadly and intelligently from his reading. For them, Fitzgerald's most important relationshps were not with women or with liquor but with editors and other writers, and they treat Fitzgerald's riotous personal life as an impediment to his real, inner life. Through letters and textual evidence, they each show Fitzgerald's mind at work. (Piper's detailed analyses of Fitzgerald's self-editing processes are particularly revealing.) Piper also thoroughly explains the historic sources of Jay Gatsby's underworld career, in sharp contrast with André Le Vot's pompous generalities about American culture of the 1920s.

LE VOT's quirky biography is marred by small and large errors. The small ones include arguing that "Jozan" rhymes with "Buchanan" (in French, they do), stating that Fitzgerald was buried by the William Wordsworth Funeral Parlor (he wasn't, nor did such an absurd establishment exist), and misquoting Edith Wharton's diary notation after tea with Fitzgerald (this error is probably the fault of Le Vot's translator). Larger errors result from the length Le Vot devotes to his hazier ideas, such as the chapter analyzing *The Great Gatsby*'s color scheme. (He claims *Gatsby*—and American literature in general—is dominated by blue and yellow. A better case could be made for white and green, but the best case argues that this is stuff for critical articles, not biography). Essentially, Le Vot oversimplifies American values: stressing the mercantile nature of American literature forces him into making claims such as the "only real tragedy written by an American playwright is *Death of a Salesman*," which even Arthur Miller would dispute.

James E. Miller, in his critical study *F. Scott Fitzgerald: His Art and His Technique* (1964), classifies Sheilah Graham's memoir *Beloved Infidel* (1958) under "Fictional Accounts of F. Scott Fitzgerald." This may be more by way of an acerbic editorial comment than an error: a few years after Miller's book came out, GRAHAM virtually admitted almost as much in *The Real Scott Fitzgerald*, dismissing her earlier memoir as a "romanti-

cized version" formed by "the discreet haze of the times and the gloss of my experienced collaborator, Gerold Frank." Works that rely on *Beloved Infidel*, such as Latham's *Crazy Sundays* (1971), may fairly be considered badly compromised; in Latham's case, his purely fictional account of the impoverished Fitzgerald supporting the successful and wealthy Ernest Hemingway in 1937 damages his credibility in itself.

The subject of so many books, Fitzgerald surprisingly has only one fully satisfying full-length biography, by BRUCCOLI. Judiciously sifting through Fitzgerald's work and that of his contemporaries and influences, Bruccoli presents an overview clearly and impartially. The editor of the *Hemingway-Fitzgerald Newsletter*, Bruccoli has written or edited well over a dozen different Fitzgerald texts, giving him plenty of channels for floating obscure or arguable ideas. The soundest, most seaworthy ideas float through *Some Sort Of Epic Grandeur*. Although discriminating in his use of all the data at his fingertips, Bruccoli does err occasionally on the side of excess: the nine epigraphs on the subject of writers' lives; or the ludicrous (if serious—and I'm afraid it is) afterword by Fitzgerald's impossibly pompous daughter on "The Colonial Ancestors of F. Scott Fitzgerald." (Perhaps the essay's inclusion was Fitzgerald's daughter's price for cooperating with Bruccoli—if so, that price was high, but perhaps worth it.) Bruccoli's biography is the one freest from bias or tendentiousness.

While general readers may value an accessible biography like Turnbull's, readers interested in recent reliable scholarship focussing on Fitzgerald's personal life will want to read Donaldson or Mellow; those primarily interested in analysis of his work will look to Piper or Sklar. (The best corrective to the mostly skewed accounts of Fitzgerald in Hollywood is Gore Vidal's essay, "Scott Fitzgerald's Case," reprinted in his *Second American Revolution* (1982). Budd Schulberg's *roman à clef*, *The Disenchanted* (1936), is also well written, if overly dramatic.) But those interested in both Fitzgerald's life and work have only Bruccoli's *Some Sort of Epic Grandeur*, the one truly comprehensive biography available.

—Steven Goldleaf

FLAUBERT, Gustave, 1821–1880; French writer.

Bart, Benjamin F., *Flaubert*. Syracuse, New York, Syracuse University Press, 1967.
Lottman, Herbert, *Flaubert: A Biography*. Boston, Little Brown, and London, Methuen, 1989.
Sartre, Jean-Paul, *The Family Idiot: Gustave Flaubert 1821–57* (3 vols.). Chicago, University of Chicago Press, 1981–89 (originally published by Gallimard, Paris, 1971–88).
Spencer, Philip, *Flaubert, a Biography*. London, Faber, and New York, Grove, 1952.
Starkie, Enid, *Flaubert: The Making of the Master*. London, Weidenfeld and Nicolson, and New York, Atheneum, 1967.
Starkie, Enid, *Flaubert the Master: A Critical and Biographical Study*. London, Weidenfeld and Nicolson, and New York, Atheneum, 1971.

*

BART has produced a monumental, and nearly definitive, one-volume biography that is the obvious first place to look for authoritative information on the facts of Flaubert's life. Bart has made the most exhaustive use of the new documentary sources that have become available after World War II: original manuscript versions of Flaubert's works, as well as early drafts, notes, and working papers in his own handwriting; and original manuscript versions of his correspondence, from which often expurgated versions had previously been printed. Indeed, the documentation available to Bart's predecessors in the field of Flaubert biography was so limited, and flawed by censorship, that Bart could rightly declare, in his Preface, that "the tens of thousands of sheets of manuscript materials" newly available to scholars have rendered all earlier biographies seriously inadequate, and made the work he had undertaken necessary and overdue. Merely to correct past misrepresentations and misunderstandings, and to record hitherto unknown details of Flaubert's life, Bart was forced to write many more pages, and supply many more footnotes, than a normal biography should require. The result is a volume of some 800 pages that is rather cumbersome to handle and cannot be recommended for casual reading by the general public, even though it is written in a clear, sprightly style that engages and holds one's interest. Major segments of Bart's biography are necessarily addressed to matters of concern primarily to scholarly specialists. It is a critical biography, in the fullest sense, examining Flaubert's life, work, and character as an integrated whole, based on the most complete, reliable evidence available. As such, Bart's biographical study stands alone as the most authoritative work in the field, indispensable for the serious scholar.

SPENCER's was the best Flaubert biography of the immediate post-World War II period, meticulously researched and beautifully written. Today, however, it stands as the perfect illustration of Bart's contention that the huge volume of new documentation emerging in the 1960s has rendered previous biographies no longer adequate. The needs of serious scholars can certainly not be satisfied by Spencer, but his biography is nevertheless by no means obsolete. It still contains much that is both valid and valuable, and is perhaps the most intelligent brief introduction to Flaubert extant. Spencer's biography is an example of scholarly excellence undermined by the chance emergence of evidence not previously known to exist. As a scholarly reference, it has been superseded by Bart, but as a concise literary biography it can still be read with pleasure and profit.

STARKIE's biography, so eagerly awaited because of the high quality of her earlier biographies of French writers, proved a sad disappointment, both for the author and her audience. A few years into the work, the biography was wrenched out of its intended shape by the misfortune of the author's illness, which appeared to be so threatening that she hastily changed course, and recast it as an account limited to Flaubert's early development, up to the completion of his first novel, *Madame Bovary*, in 1857. She published that material under the improvised title, *Flaubert: The Making of the Master*. When the threat of failing health unexpectedly eased, Starkie courageously resumed work on the biography and, with the help of associates, was able to complete a second volume, which recounted the rest of Flaubert's life from the publication of *Madame Bovary* to his death in 1880. The unhappy circumstances of its interrupted composition made of Starkie's biography a study in two parts that did not fit together very well and that showed all too clearly the strain of working against time and physical suffering. Starkie had been unable to travel to France for the necessary archival research during the preparation of the second volume, and, though she had highly competent assistants doing those tasks for her, it proved impossible for her to give this biography the distinctive authority and insight she had shown herself capable of commanding in earlier biographical studies of Baudelaire, Rimbaud, and Gide. Flawed though this two-volume biography of Flaubert is, it remains a vivid and sympathetic account of his life and work, well worth reading for its intelligent and sensitive understanding of Flaubert's qualities both as a writer and a personality. While it falls somewhat short of being either masterful or wholly reliable, it is a richly textured and always engaging narrative that makes a significant contribution to Flaubert studies.

LOTTMAN offers the newest biography of Flaubert in English, and in some respects fills the need for a reliable and readable work of modest proportions intended for the general public. Lottman justifies his undertaking with the prefatory remark: "Perhaps each generation needs a new version of the past," and, like the good journalist-historian that he is, asserts his firm belief that "biography is nothing if it is not history." This operative principle clearly distinguishes Lottman's biography from all others, since it concentrates on giving the verifiable facts of Flaubert's life, resisting any attempt at psychological analysis or critical evaluation, either of Flaubert's conduct or of his creations. The account he gives is chronologically correct, precise, and clear; the research is thorough and carefully documented; the style is fluid and lively, marked by short sentences, short paragraphs, and even short chapters: its approximately 350 pages are divided into ten Parts and 51 Chapters. Since the publication of Flaubert's books are the most dramatic "events" of his relatively uneventful life, Lottman's strictly historical approach to the publications permits him to give a clear and concise account of the origin, contents, and reception of each publication, but forbids him to venture comments that could be construed as interpretation, analysis, or aesthetic appreciation. Lottman shows a sound grasp of current scholarship on Flaubert, and an awareness of the new source materials and manuscripts that have come to light in the last generation, but he makes no claim to being exhaustively informed about *all* of this mass of data. His main concern is to get his facts right, in accordance with the latest findings of scholars. It is a responsible and serviceable biography, enjoyable to read for those who are fascinated by the lives of great men, but of little interest to specialists since it contains no new discoveries.

The most massive and finely-detailed study of Flaubert's life ever published, though not, strictly speaking, a biography, deserves mention as an important source of biographical information. That is the monumental and unique three-volume opus of SARTRE, left unfinished at his death. Sartre devoted more than 20 years to this major study, considering it a methodological experiment to try to find out, on the basis of one specific case, "what we can know about a man," with the tools presently available to us. Given this purpose, Sartre does not hesitate to use the methods of the philosopher, the historian, the literary critic, and the psychoanalyst, bringing their different insights to bear on every scrap of documentary evidence about Flaubert he could find, in order to interpret the way he developed under the influence of his family and his environment, and how he became the kind of writer he was. Sartre makes free use of his own analytical and speculative imagination. If a youthful tale of Flaubert's depicted rivalry between two brothers, or hostility between father and son, the work argues that such themes reflected, and afforded proof of, Flaubert's personal relationship with his own brother or father. By such procedures, Sartre often falls into the trap of subjectivity, arguing from his own prejudices more than from verifiable facts. Indeed, one learns more about Sartre than one does about Flaubert from reading *The Family Idiot*. Nevertheless, Sartre's research is impressively thorough and detailed, and his analytical arguments are often brilliant. In spite of its sometimes fatiguing verbosity—it runs to more than 3000 pages in the original, covers only half of Flaubert's life, and was never completed—the work is fascinating and challenging to read. It makes no claim to being a systematic biography, but it simply cannot be ignored by anyone interested in Flaubert's life.

—Murray Sachs

FLETCHER, John. See BEAUMONT, Francis.

FORD, Ford Madox, 1873–1939; English writer.

Goldring, Douglas, *The Last Pre-Raphaelite: A Record of the Life and Writings of Ford Madox Ford*. London, Macdonald, 1948; as *Trained for Genius: The Life and Writings of Ford Madox Ford*, New York, Dutton, 1949.

Judd, Alan, *Ford Madox Ford*. London, Collins, 1990; Cambridge, Massachusetts, Harvard University Press, 1991.

MacShane, Frank, *The Life and Work of Ford Madox Ford*. London, Routledge, and New York, Horizon Press, 1965.

Mizener, Arthur, *The Saddest Story: A Biography of Ford Madox Ford*. London, Bodley Head, and New York, World Publishing, 1971.

*

Ford Madox Ford left instructions in his will that he should not be the subject of any biography. Such an instruction was unlikely to be followed. During a literary career spanning four decades, he had been the victim of misunderstanding, especially in England, and it was inevitable that biographers would seek to unravel the intricacies of the life and establish his contribution to the literature of the early 20th century.

The first biography, by GOLDRING, followed that writer's *South Lodge* (1943), a memoir reviewing his association with Ford over many years. Indeed Goldring acknowledged that his biography was the fourth book on Ford. In addition to *South Lodge*, two of the women in Ford's life, Violet Hunt and Stella Bowen, had published memoirs. Goldring's biography condenses episodes discussed in these earlier books; the complications arising out of Ford's "marriage" to Violet Hunt, for example, are treated fully elsewhere. While Goldring did not aim for completeness, he does provide a readable account of Ford's life, es-

pecially up to the 1920s. In particular, the pre-Raphaelite ambiance around Ford's childhood, his school years, marriage to Elsie Martindale, editorship of *The English Review* (on which Goldring was assistant editor), and the war years are presented with assurance. Where there are fewer sources, for example for the hectic years in Paris and New York in the 1920s, the narrative seems deficient; and the 1930s, especially the relationship with Janice Biala, are dealt with in a superficial manner. Goldring was unable or unwilling to gain access to American sources that could have enriched the final chapters.

Goldring's purpose, however, was to defend Ford before an English audience. He wrote largely from a sense of loyalty, what he calls "pietas," for his subject and argued that Ford's literary reputation in England had to be restored. The pietas is evident in his defence of Ford's grandiose tendencies, such as claiming to have gone to Eton, and in Goldring's sympathetic treatment of such matters as Ford's financial mismanagement. Naturally, he praises the literature, although little attention is given to anything other than *The Good Soldier* and the Tietjens novels. His focus moreover is on their reception rather than on their literary qualities.

For a discussion of Ford's work within a biographical context one had to wait until MacSHANE's biography. In his preface, MacShane asserts that his emphasis will be on the literary career. Nevertheless, the major episodes in the life are included, in summary fashion usually, but the treatment is generous and lacking the defensiveness found in the Goldring account. MacShane conceded that he was using sources readily available, so he adds little that is new. The reader will again note that the coverage of the personal life in the 1930s is shallow due to the lack of information about the Biala relationship.

The merit of this book lies in its tracing of Ford's development as a writer. MacShane succinctly fills in the backgrounds—the pre-Raphaelite environment, literary London in the early 1900s, the cosmopolitan hubbub of 1920s Paris—and Ford's place in each. The multi-faceted aspects of Ford's career over 40 years are given proper recognition: his editorship of *The English Review* and *Transatlantic Review*, his critical and nonfiction books, such as *The March of Literature*, and his contribution to English poetry in the early years of the century. MacShane devotes primary attention to the novels, especially *The Good Soldier* and *Parade's End*, and he duly provides information on their composition. However, the discussion centres on their themes and techniques (especially the Ford theory of Impressionism) and their place in modern fiction.

MacShane set out with the limited intention of "exploring the extent and scope of [Ford's] literary career," and it was left to the definitive biography, written by MIZENER, to present the complete picture of this complicated life. Unlike his predecessors, Mizener had access to substantial collections of unpublished documents, including Janice Biala's and Violet Hunt's papers. The resulting book is long, 300,000 words plus 80 pages of notes, and the narrative is closely written. Mizener was determined to get the picture right so he concentrates inevitably on detail: on the intricacies of the collaboration with Conrad, for example; on the relationships with women; and on the complicated financial dealings with a host of publishers in London and New York. The weight of detail threatens to overwhelm, especially the minutiae of the continuous haggling over advances, royalties, and loans from publishers, agents and acquaintances.

The facts might finally be laid before the public, but at a price of making Ford an unsympathetic figure and perhaps diminishing his literary achievements.

Such of course was not the biographer's intention. Over 30 novels, nonfiction works, poetry, and Ford's editorships are reviewed. Because of their intrusive impact on the narrative, discussions on novels are mostly contained in an appendix, but separate chapters are devoted to *The Good Soldier* and *Parade's End*. Much of the appendix is taken up with synopses (useful since most novels are out of print) but Mizener's analyses of the major novels have been rightly praised for their critical insights.

Interest in Ford's work and life has not declined in recent years. Several books have been published, including a "psychobiography" (*The Life in the Fiction of Ford Madox Ford*, 1981), by Thomas Moser, who attempts to unravel Ford's psychology and relate it to his novels. The most recent biography is by JUDD, a novelist rather than a biographer, who believes that "biographers are like blind men with sticks." At best they can get a feeling for their subject, but never convey the total picture. His aim is to capture Ford's spirit, and, like Goldring, to correct misunderstandings about his subject and refute the unfavourable portrait in Mizener's book.

Judd describes his method as "a ramble, haphazard, discursive." While generally following the Mizener chronology, he does interrupt the narrative to reflect on the man in general or to speculate on why he acted as he did. Unlike Mizener, however, he avoids unnecessary detail, except during his account of Ford's war service. Like his subject, Judd served in the British army, and these years were clearly of special interest. He quotes lengthy poems in full, but eschews critical analysis of the major novels. Throughout, the tone is relaxed and conversational, and that unfailing admiration of one writer for a greater one makes this a most readable book. Whether this biography or Mizener's becomes the standard biography remains to be seen. One suspects that the life of this multi-faceted man, so often misunderstood, will continue to attract interpreters.

—F. C. Molloy

FORD, Henry, 1863–1947; American inventor and industrialist.

Burlingame, Roger, *Henry Ford: A Great Life in Brief*. New York, Knopf, 1955.

Garrett, Garet, *The Wild Wheel: The World of Henry Ford*. New York, Pantheon Books, and London, Cresset Press, 1952.

Gelderman, Carol, *Henry Ford: The Wayward Capitalist*. New York, Dial Press, 1981.

Greenleaf, William, *From These Beginnings: The Early Philanthropies of Henry and Edsel Ford 1911–36*. Detroit, Wayne State University Press, 1964.

Jardim, Anne, *The First Henry Ford: A Study in Personality and Business Leadership*. Cambridge, Massachusetts, MIT Press, 1970.

Marquis, Samuel S., *Henry Ford: An Interpretation*. Boston, Little Brown, 1923.

Nevins, Allan, with the collaboration of Frank E. Hill, *Ford: The Times, the Man, the Company*. New York, Scribner, 1954.

Nevins, Allan, and Frank E. Hill, *Ford: Expansion and Challenge 1915–33*. New York, Scribner, 1957.

Nevins, Allan, and Frank E. Hill, *Ford: Decline and Rebirth 1933–62*. New York, Scribner, 1963.

Nye, David E., *Henry Ford: "Ignorant Idealist."* Port Washington, New York, Kennikat Press, 1979.

Rae, John B., editor, *Henry Ford*. Englewood Cliffs, New Jersey, Prentice-Hall, 1969.

Richards, William C., *The Last Billionaire*. New York, Scribner, 1948.

Simonds, William A., *Henry Ford: His Life, His Work, His Genius*. Indianapolis, Bobbs-Merrill, 1943.

Sward, Keith, *The Legend of Henry Ford*. New York, Rinehart, 1948.

*

Henry Ford was a nearly universally acclaimed American hero from the time his Model T automobile came out in 1908 at least until the early 1930s. His behavior during his later years—such as his anti-Semitism and his violent opposition to unionization—transformed him into a center of controversy. Not surprisingly, therefore, Ford has been the subject of a formidable body of writing, including personal reminiscences, popular biographies, and scholarly treatments ranging in approach from adulatory to damning.

Ford's own autobiography (*My Life and Work*, 1922), apparently dictated in haphazard fashion to his favorite ghostwriter without any attempt at checking, is unreliable on even the basic facts of his life.

There are any number of eulogies published during his lifetime, including Rose Wilder Lane, *Henry Ford's Own Story* (1917); Sarah T. Bushnell, *The Truth about Henry Ford* (1922); James M. Miller, *The Amazing Story of Henry Ford: The Ideal American and the World's Most Famous Private Citizen* (1922); and William Stidger, *Henry Ford: The Man and His Motives* (1923). The only book falling in this category that retains value is by SIMONDS. Although the work is undocumented, Simonds, who was a longtime associate of Henry Ford, had access to information, especially details about Ford's early life, not available to previous writers.

In contrast with the one-dimensional portrait found in such eulogistic accounts, a number of writers took advantage of their firsthand experience with Ford to attempt more or less balanced appraisals that make significant contributions to illuminating his complex, even contradictory, personality. The most insightful is the account by MARQUIS, an Episcopalian minister who served as head of the company's "Sociological Department" (Ford's experiment in welfare capitalism around the time of World War I) and who was for a time one of Ford's closest intimates. RICHARDS, a Detroit newspaperman who covered Ford for over 30 years, presents a treasure trove of anecdotes about the man. GARRETT, another journalist who was long associated with Ford, praises Ford's resistance to governmental interference with business while simultaneously making perceptive observations about his personality and character.

Most of the anti-Ford accounts are as extreme in their hostility as the eulogies are in their praise—and as thinly based. Examples include E. G. Pipp, *The Real Henry Ford* (1922); Jonathan Leonard, *The Tragedy of Henry Ford* (1932); and Upton Sinclair, *The Flivver King: A Story of Ford-America* (1937). The most substantial of the hostile accounts is by SWARD, a former public relations man for Ford's bitter enemy, the Congress of Industrial Organizations. Sward lacked access to Ford's papers and company records, but he did an impressive amount of research in such public records as newspapers, periodicals and trade journals, and government investigations and reports. His major goal is to debunk Ford's reputation for beneficence and public spiritedness, with his major target for attack Ford's supposed paternalism toward his workers.

BURLINGAME's slender volume apparently is based on the published materials available at the time he was writing, supplemented by personal interviews along with oral history reminiscences collected by the Ford Archives, Dearborn, Michigan. Burlingame makes no pretense to having written the definitive biography, and he is stronger in depicting Ford the man than in explaining Ford's achievements as industrial innovator and business leader. But he was largely successful in offering a balanced portrait that remains the most satisfactory introduction to Ford for the beginning student and general reader. A useful companion piece is RAE's volume. Rae combines excerpts from primary sources, observations by contemporaries, and historians' appraisals to provide a handy overview of the man and his works.

The three volumes by NEVINS AND HILL will remain for the foreseeable future the standard history of the Ford Motor Company. The first volume, covering to 1915, offers a thoroughly researched, detailed, and richly documented account of Ford and his company during their crucial formative years set within the larger context not simply of the automobile industry but of American society of the time. Volume two traces the company's history up through 1933, years in which it continued to grow but lost its primacy within the industry to General Motors. The final volume relates the company's continued decline as Henry Ford became ever more erratic and out-of-touch, and charts its resurgence under his grandson, Henry Ford II.

Partly because of the authors' skill as writers, partly because of the extent to which the Ford Motor Company was an extension of Henry Ford's personality, the volumes avoid the dullness typical of company histories. The authors were given free access to the voluminous records (correspondence, memoranda, and statistics) in the Ford Archives and had the full cooperation of the family. In this sense, the work is an authorized history. But Nevins and Hill received near unanimous plaudits for their balance and fairness. As one reviewer summed up the consensus: "Authoritative, outspoken, utterly absorbing, it is a work that should stand as a model of its genre for years to come" (John Brooks, *New York Herald-Tribune Books*, 4 August 1963). The years since the publication of this landmark work have witnessed a continuing flow of popularized, even sensationalized, accounts of the Ford dynasty. Typically the information about Henry I was drawn largely from the Nevins and Hill volumes, while the treatment of Henry II emphasizes intrigue inside the corporate boardroom and sex outside. Examples include Booton Herndon, *Ford: An Unconventional Biography of the Men and Their Times* (1969); Robert Lacey, *Ford: The Men and the Machine* (1986); and Peter Collier and David Horowitz, *The Fords: An American Epic* (1987).

There are, however, a number of recent studies that do warrant closer attention. GELDERMAN did extensive research in the primary sources to turn up new information supplementing Nevins and Hill. JARDIM has written a heavily Freudian-influenced psychobiography that attempts "to give consistency and meaning to Ford's actions and interests by examining the constant play of unconscious motivation beneath and through the rational, conscious decisions he reached." GREENLEAF's account of Ford's philanthropic involvements shows him as unpredictable and even contradictory in this area as in other spheres. NYE combines an analysis of "Ford's View of the World" with a survey of his changing reputation.

Specialized works shedding light on different aspects of Ford's life are William Greenleaf, *Monopoly on Wheels: Henry Ford and the Selden Automobile Patent* (1961), concerning Ford's successful breaking of the attempted patent monopoly by the "automobile trust"; Barbara S. Kraft, *The Peace Ship: Henry Ford's Pacifist Adventure in the First World War* (1978); and Albert Lee, *Henry Ford and the Jews* (1980), treating Ford's anti-Semitism. Harry Bennett (as told to Paul Marcus) *We Never Called Him Henry* (1951) and Charles E. Sorenson, with Samuel T. Williamson, *My Forty Years with Ford* (1956), are informative memoirs by two of Ford's most important lieutenants.

Two indispensable books for understanding the place Ford held in the American imagination are Ronald M. Wik, *Henry Ford and Grass-roots America* (1972), and David L. Lewis, *The Public Image of Henry Ford: An American Folk Hero and His Company* (1976). Wik describes how Ford was the hero of rural America during the 1920s. Broader in its scope, the Lewis volume is an exhaustively researched account that traces how Americans viewed Ford over his lifetime.

—John Braeman

FORD, John, 1895–1973; American film director.

Anderson, Lindsey, *About John Ford.* London, Plexus, 1981; New York, McGraw-Hill, 1983.

Baxter, John, *The Cinema of John Ford.* London, A. Zwemmer, and New York, A. S. Barnes, 1971.

Bogdanovich, Peter, *John Ford.* London, Studio Vista, 1967; Berkeley, University of California Press, 1968; revised and enlarged edition, Berkeley, University of California Press, 1978.

Ford, Dan, *Pappy: The Life of John Ford.* Englewood Cliffs, New Jersey, Prentice-Hall, 1979.

Gallagher, Tag, *John Ford: The Man and His Films.* Berkeley and London, University of California Press, 1986.

McBride, Joseph and Michael Wilmington, *John Ford.* London, Secker and Warburg, 1974; New York, Da Capo Press, 1975.

Sarris, Andrew, *The John Ford Murder Mystery.* Bloomington, Indiana University Press, and London, Secker and Warburg, 1976.

Sinclair, Andrew, *John Ford*. London, Allen and Unwin, and New York, Dial Press, 1979.

*

BOGDANOVICH provided the pioneering biography in English, arguing that John Ford was one of the greatest, if not *the* greatest, American moviemaker. To praise Ford during the late 1960s was indeed a controversial act. For one thing, Ford was an unabashed patriot, proud of his nation during the controversial days of the Vietnam war. Thus, though one might agree with Bogdanovich that the director's films were complex visual artworks, Ford's politics—far right, in avowed praise of Richard Nixon—could not be confined to simple academic bickering. Thus Bogdanovich's stance must be considered important even though his book really only consists of a sequence of magazine sketches strung together. But its filmography remains a cornerstone for all others. The book was republished in 1978, with some additional material.

ANDERSON's work is similar to Bogdanovich's; both began as magazine articles, and both authors became famous directors in their own right. Indeed in the late 1940s, while in university in England, Lindsey Anderson almost alone outside Hollywood championed Ford's work. His book's strength is its series of interviews with Ford and with many of the actors and writers who collaborated on Ford's best films.

McBRIDE AND WILMINGTON provide another early work, by two veteran journalists. While this work contains invaluable biographical details, it is primarily a critical study of 14 films from Ford's massive body of work. BAXTER is also not so much a biography as an analysis of the great director's major films, a group different from those selected by McBride and Wilmington. This is an entry in the International Film Guide Series. SARRIS offers more sophisticated readings of Ford's greatest films than do McBride and Wilmington or Baxter. This is an art historical reading of the entire opus of John Ford, noting the greatest films, the periods of peak productivity, and the influences of family and national history. Sarris, the longtime critic for the *Village Voice*, does not however succeed in making sense of a 50-year career in the 200 pages he has allotted.

SINCLAIR's book is a more conventional biography. In his relatively short text (short considering that Ford made films from around 1915 well into the late 1960s), Sinclair hits all the high spots. Curiously, however, we find little about Ford's family life (a recurrent theme in his films). But the book has a detailed filmography (built on Bogdanovich), extensive notes, and an index. Sinclair's strength lies in the details he provides about Ford's years in the United States Navy during World War II and how that period influenced his filmmaking after the war, in particular *They Were Expendable* (1945).

DAN FORD's book, another mainstream biography, was written by the grandson of the great director and contains information, including the files and memories of the author's grandmother, unavailable to any other biographer. As a tale told from the point of view of a family member, this book could have been fawning, emphasizing only the image of the rugged, man's man of a filmmaker. Luckily for us Dan Ford did not take such a course. His book offers unique photographs from the family files.

GALLAGHER's bio-critical work seeks to examine Ford's films in terms of the events of his life. Unlike Sinclair or Ford, Gallagher does not simply tell the story of a man's life but attempts an analysis of the man and his work. Still Gallagher goes far beyond Sinclair or Ford in detailing the filmmaker's life. Gallagher includes an appendix listing grosses and earnings from the films, a detailed filmography including unrealized projects and films about Ford, and a select bibliography.

—Douglas Gomery

FORSTER, E(dward) M(organ), 1879–1970; English writer.

Furbank, P. N., *E. M. Forster: A Life* (2 vols.). London, Secker and Warburg, and New York, Harcourt, 1977–78.
McDowell, Frederick P. W., *E. M. Forster*. Revised edition, Boston, Twayne, 1982.
Stone, Wilfred, *The Cave and the Mountain: A Study of E. M. Forster*. Stanford, California, Stanford University Press, and London, Oxford University Press, 1966.
Trilling, Lionel, *E. M. Forster: A Study*. Norfolk, Connecticut, New Directions, 1943, London, Hogarth Press, 1944.

*

No Forster biography appeared until after the end of his long life. FURBANK's authorized biography will remain a basic work, for it benefits from three decades of friendship with its subject and exclusive access to many personal sources. The understated style and sense of humor are very like Forster's own. The structure parallels the life, but the narrative ends at 1953, when Forster had completed work with Eric Crozier on the opera libretto for Benjamin Britten's *Billy Budd* (1951); had published *The Hill of Devi* (1953); had begun his last major book, *Marianne Thornton* (1956); and was approaching the end of a 30-year career as BBC broadcaster on literary subjects. Furbank emphasizes the three most influential friendships, which represent also Forster's loyalties at home and abroad: Syed Ross Masood, who inspired his visits to India; Mohammed el Adl, who represented for Forster the human side of the classical Egyptian tradition; and Robert Buckingham, the London police constable who embodied the solid British virtues of hard work, thrift, and civic responsibility.

Furbank traces the alternating pattern of Forster's sojourns in England and abroad, tracing them as both materials for the works and as bases for lifelong convictions about cultural values and personal relations: *The Longest Journey* (1907) deals with public school, University, and British family conventions; England and Italy inspired *Where Angels Fear to Tread* (1905) and *A Room with a View* (1905); *Howards End* (1910) is both criticism of and tribute to middle-class Edwardian England; *A Passage to India* (1924) is unique in the literature of the British in India. Furbank seeks to counteract the impression that Forster's major canon consists principally of fiction, and, of that, none after 1924, unless one includes the posthumously-published *Maurice* (1971), begun in 1913.

Forster's autobiographical writings are essential complements to any biography of him. His *Commonplace Book*, edited by Philip Gardner (London, Scolar Press, 1985) contains, besides dated commentaries, passages from letters and published works that he found particularly interesting. The *Selected Letters*, edited by Mary Lago and P. N. Furbank (2 vols., London, Collins, and Cambridge, Massachusetts, Harvard University Press, 1983–1985) include 446 of more than 12,000 extant letters, with passages from other Forster correspondence incorporated in annotations. This selection highlights friendships, travels abroad, genesis of the novels, and activities on behalf of artists and writers. *The Hill of Devi* includes India letters from Forster's term as Private Secretary to the Maharaja of Dewas. *Marianne Thornton*, although a "Domestic Biography," of the great-aunt whose bequest enabled him to be an independent writer, is also Forster's indirect account of his background and heritage from the Clapham Group. Of special value are the editorial Introductions to the Abinger Editions of Forster's works published by Edward Arnold (London), which include letters and biographical material unavailable elsewhere.

Because so much of Forster's writing is closely linked to his background, friendships, and experiences, the many critical studies complement biographical and autobiographical sources. For those entering on this subject, McDOWELL provides basic introductory material, including a chapter of biography and an essential bibliography. TRILLING is of particular importance: the liberal imagination has been a continuing theme, and he studies Forster as representative of that outlook. Forster's American readers at that time were "a quiet band," Trilling notes, and his novels, except for *Passage*, "esoteric with us." Trilling wished to stir American readers to further interest in Forster's beliefs in the saving virtues of culture as defined by the arts and by human rights. In fact, Trilling inaugurated the continuing worldwide critical interest in Forster and his work. Forster disagreed with some of Trilling's judgments but found most of them valid and helpful. STONE examines the works with detailed care that illuminates the biography and emphasizes Forster's primary concerns: the nature and fragility of civilization, England's class divisions, and the role of the arts in an urbanized society. He analyzes Forster's misgivings about civilization's future as being less a disillusionment than an "anxiety" that "undergoes many changes in pitch and intensity."

Two books on Forster in India are valuable supplements to both his experience and his Indian novel. G. K. Das, in *E. M. Forster's India* (London, Macmillan, 1977) describes the range of his reactions to Indian culture and politics. Robin Jared Lewis, in *E. M. Forster's Passage to India* (New York, Columbia University Press, 1979) traces his personal involvement with India.

An essential supplement to Forster's works, the autobiographical writings, and the critical studies is *A Bibliography of E. M. Forster*, compiled by B. J. Kirkpatrick: a second, enlarged edition (Oxford, Clarendon Press, 1985) includes, among other additions, a complete listing of his BBC radio broadcasts, many of which include autobiographical material, from scripts in the BBC Written Archives. The *Calendar of Letters of E. M. Forster*, compiled by Mary Lago (London, Mansell, 1985), lists the more than 12,000 letters traced up to 1985, with date and place of writing, number of folios, incipit, and owner as of 1985. Fi-

nally, mention should be made of Forster's "Locked Diary," owned by King's College, Cambridge. Entries up to 1945 are available to accredited scholars.

—Mary Lago

FRANCE, Anatole [*born* Jacques-Anatole-François Thibault], 1844–1924; French writer.

Axelrod, Jacob, *Anatole France: A Life Without Illusions*. New York and London, Harper, 1944.

Dargan, Edwin P., *Anatole France 1844–96*. New York, Oxford University Press, 1937.

Jefferson, Alfred C., *Anatole France: The Politics of Skepticism*. New Brunswick, New Jersey, Rutgers University Press, 1965.

Tylden-Wright, David, *Anatole France*. New York, Walker, and London, Collins, 1967.

Virtanen, Reino, *Anatole France*. New York, Twayne, 1968.

*

AXELROD wrote the first complete biography of Anatole France in English, and was bold enough to express the hope, in his Foreword, that his book "might be accepted as a definitive biography of the French master." His research was certainly extensive and thorough, and his work was probably as "definitive" as a biography could have been at that time. He confidently asserts, in that same Foreword, "I have had access to material known to no other writer before me," by which he clearly meant material supplied by the granddaughter of Anatole France's mistress, Madame de Caillavet—material not in print but part of a private family archive. One result is that Axelrod was able to produce the most accurate and detailed account we have yet had of the intimate association between Anatole France and Madame de Caillavet, which lasted for more than 25 years, and which had so profound an influence on his literary career. Another distinction of Axelrod's biography is its sympathetic and understanding tone, born of Axelrod's personal sense of ideological communion with his subject. As a longtime socialist, Axelrod felt especially drawn to Anatole France's characteristic compassion for the poor and defenseless, and to his espousal of socialist and pacifist ideals during the final decades of his life. While Axelrod strove mightily for a fair and objective portrayal of Anatole France throughout his biography, there is no doubt that his admiration for his subject's political and social views gives an almost hagiographical cast to some of its pages, particularly the account of Anatole France's involvement in the Dreyfus Affair. Axelrod provides neither the definitive biography nor the scrupulously objective analysis he aimed to achieve. His book is nevertheless the biography of choice for the reader who wants the single most reliable and most readable account of Anatole France's life.

Though his account stops at the year 1896, DARGAN has written the most copiously detailed and the most exhaustively researched biography we have. Scrupulously following the most stringent scholarly principles, Dargan made use of all documents and personal sources of information available to him to assure the reliability of his work. When he found such indispensable documentation closed to him, for the last decades of Anatole France's life, he regretfully decided to publish the material he had thus far assembled, taking his story to the year 1896, and postponed his account of the rest until reliable documentation might become available. He did not live to see that happen.

Dargan is a mine of information, the most complete and the most accurate for the period covered. His purpose, in so meticulously collecting every scrap of information he could find, was to write a "psychological biography," the better to understand the man and his work. A volume of more than 700 pages, it is the most substantial biography of Anatole France in print, and had he been able to complete the projected second volume, to cover the period 1896–1924, it would surely have been the definitive biography for which we are still waiting.

TYLDEN-WRIGHT produced his biography a generation after those of Dargan and Axelrod, and benefited by the availability of some new sources of information, mainly letters and personal reminiscences. Tylden-Wright's effort was also directed toward the deciphering of Anatole France's elusive and enigmatic character, and toward the understanding of his often contradictory and unpredictable behavior and the obscure motives behind those actions. That eminently justifiable focus nevertheless produced a biography that, while engagingly written and constantly absorbing, is too frequently marred by bold but unsubstantiated speculation as to the reasons for, or significance of, his utterances or his conduct. There is some evidence, too, that Tylden-Wright's research is less than thorough, for there are factual errors and misspelled names scattered through the volume, which make the work somewhat less reliable. The overall portrayal of Anatole France, however, both as a personality and as a writer, is generally persuasive and marked by a sensitive and sympathetic outlook even when it is most speculative. Approached with a modicum of cautious skepticism, Tylden-Wright's biography will be found both informative and pleasantly readable by all but the most exacting and scholarly students of Anatole France.

Two volumes, not strictly biographies, are worthy of mention for the reliable, though narrowly circumscribed, biographical information they contain. JEFFERSON's study of Anatole France's political ideas gives the fullest and most reliable account of the writer's socialist period, which comprised nearly half of his active career. VIRTANEN makes effective use of the standard "life and works" format in his study of Anatole France's literary career to provide, with meticulous scholarship, the fundamental biographical information needed to understand his achievements as a creative writer. Until a truly definitive biography appears, these two volumes afford a useful supplement, in specified areas, to the existing biographies.

—Murray Sachs

———————

FRANCIS OF ASSISI, Saint, *ca.* 1181–1226; Italian friar, founder of the Franciscan Order.

Boase, T. S. R., *St. Francis of Assisi.* London, Duckworth, 1936; revised edition, Bloomington, Indiana University Press, and London, Thames and Hudson, 1968.

Chesterton, G. K., *St. Francis of Assisi.* London, Hodder and Stoughton, 1923; New York, Doubleday, 1924.

Cuthbert, Father, *Life of St. Francis of Assisi.* London and New York, Longman, 1912.

De La Bedoyère, Michael, *Francis: A Biography of the Saint of Assisi.* New York, Harper, and London, Collins, 1962.

Englebert, Omer, *Saint Francis of Assisi: A Biography*, translated and edited by Edward Hutton. London, Burns and Oates, and New York, Longman, 1950 (originally published as *Vie de Saint François d'Assise*, Paris, A. Michel, 1947).

Fortini, Arnaldo, *Francis of Assisi*, translated by Helen Moak. New York, Crossroad, 1981 (originally published as *Nova Vita di San Francesco d'Assisi*, Milan, 1926).

Goudge, Elizabeth, *Saint Francis of Assisi.* London, Duckworth, 1959.

Green, Julien, *God's Fool: The Life and Times of Francis of Assisi*, translated by Peter Heinegg. New York, Harper, 1985; London, Hodder and Stoughton, 1986 (originally published as *Frère François*, Paris, Éditions du Seuil, 1983).

Jorgensen, Johannes, *Life of Saint Francis.* London, 1907 (originally published as *Den hellige Frans af Assisi*, Copenhagen, Gylendal, 1907).

Longford, Frank Pakenham, Earl of, *Francis of Assisi: A Life for All Seasons.* London, Weidenfeld and Nicolson, 1978.

Mockler, Anthony, *Francis of Assisi: The Wandering Years.* Oxford, Phaidon, 1976.

Sabatier, Paul, *Life of Saint Francis of Assisi.* London, Hodder and Stoughton, and New York, Scribner, 1894.

Smith, John Holland, *Francis of Assisi.* London, Sidgwick and Jackson, and New York, Scribner, 1972.

*

The first biography of St. Francis was written by Thomas of Celano within a few years of Francis' death. Later, Thomas was commissioned to write a second biography, incorporating new material contributed by Franciscan brothers who had been close to Francis. In 1263 St. Bonaventure, then Minister-General of the Order, wrote his *Legenda Major* and subsequently attempted to suppress the earlier works. It is generally agreed that St. Bonaventure's *Life* is a sanitised version of Thomas of Celano's, designed to make Francis fit better into the traditional mould of saintliness and to smooth over the controversies that split the Order after his death. Translations of these early biographies, together with all the other sources for Francis' life, have been published in a single volume entitled *St. Francis of Assisi: Writings and Early Biographies: English Omnibus of the Sources for the Life of St. Francis*, edited by Marion Alphonse Habig (3rd revised edition, Chicago, Franciscan Herald Press, 1977). Each source printed in this collection is accompanied by a critical introduction.

The seminal work for the modern study of St. Francis' life is SABATIER's 1894 biography, a work of brilliant scholarship that draws particularly on sources predating Bonaventure. A

French protestant curé, Sabatier writes as a Christian believer but an outsider to the Roman Catholic faith. His fierce condemnation of the Catholic Church for perverting the purity of the Franciscan ideal caused his book to be placed on the Index. The great debate that ensued turned on the markers Sabatier had laid down: the Rule in its original and subsequent forms, particularly with reference to property and learning, Francis' "Testimony," and the role and motivations of Cardinal Ugolino, later Pope Gregory IX. As well as the ecclesiastical background, Sabatier vividly presents the secular history of the age, emphasising how, through the mercantile activities of his father, Francis would have been aware of the major political events, cultural influences, and religious ideas of his day.

The first part of the 20th century saw the publication of four other scholarly works which, together with Sabatier's, established the historical foundation for the numerous undocumented lives that followed. The style of JORGENSEN's book today seems rather high-flown. The work of a scholar who was also a poet, it is concerned above all with Francis' spiritual quest. Father CUTHBERT, a Capuchin friar, is rather more down to earth. In his mild, orthodox Catholic reply to Sabatier's accusations, he defends Ugolino's worldly wisdom in transforming the Order into a body that could survive in the real world, where Francis' idealism would surely have perished. At the same time Cuthbert's narrative retains a sense of the sweetness and romance of the Franciscan legends and is imbued with a feeling for the Italian landscape in which they grew up. There is considerable discussion of the first Rule, of which Cuthbert attempts a reconstruction. On the whole, however, historical debate is confined to the footnotes, allowing the narrative to flow on without interruption. The language is occasionally quaintly archaic.

Writing as Roman Catholic scholars, neither Abbé Omer ENGLEBERT nor Father Cuthbert find any difficulty with including the miracles of St. Francis in their narratives, since they are a matter of faith rather than of historical enquiry. Englebert prefaces his book with a good review of the sources and their relative merits and then allows his narrative, fully footnoted, to proceed with only occasional pauses for discussion. Like Cuthbert, he defends Ugolino and the official church and devotes more attention to the ecclesiastical than the secular background. He provides a very comprehensive bibliography.

FORTINI's enormous work is the fruit of years of exploration of the archives of Assisi and has provided a mine of information for subsequent biographers to draw on. Of the four volumes, the first is a chronological account of Francis' life, while the remaining three are vast compilations of additional information about the town of Assisi, the life of St. Clare, the primary sources, etc. Helen Moak has translated the first volume and incorporated valuable information from the other three in the form of footnotes. Fortini has the close focus of the enthusiastic local antiquarian. The detailed picture he uncovers of the social mores of 12th-century Assisi does much to explain Thomas of Celano's allusions to the dissoluteness of Francis' youthful environment, which Bonaventure was at pains to suppress.

Of the very many undocumented biographies of St. Francis, only a few can be mentioned here. The most famous is CHESTERTON's. It has more the character of a book-length essay than of a traditional biography, conveying in its colourful prose as much about the author and his personal response to his subject as about Francis himself. A Catholic convert, Chesterton

addresses himself directly to the intelligent outsider to the faith and goes straight to the heart of the biographer's problem as he sees it: the mysterious nature of religious experience. The occasional historical inaccuracy along the way perhaps does not greatly matter.

GOUDGE is another popular writer who has tackled St. Francis. Like Father Cuthbert, she provides descriptive scene-setting for her narrative from personal familiarity with the Italian landscape. Again this is the work of a Christian writer and, as with Chesterton, the main thread of the story is Francis' spiritual journey, culminating on Mount Alverna with the imprinting of the Stigmata. The author's sympathies are firmly with Francis on the question of "betrayal" of the Franciscan ideal. Despite her generally devotional tone, Goudge is not afraid to find evidence, in certain episodes, for a certain harsh streak in Francis' character.

BOASE's biography, originally published in 1936, was revised in 1968 to form an accompanying text for a series of lithographs by Arthur Boyd. The artistic licence of the 1960s illustrations bears no relation to the elegant clarity of the rather brief but straightforward, balanced, and attractively readable text. The sources are carefully discussed, the historical background concisely drawn, and the historian's debt to Sabatier fully acknowledged. Michael DE LA BEOYÈRE's 1962 account is rather more loquacious and "popular" in tone but is also well balanced, sympathetic, and attractive.

With the 1970s come new departures. MOCKLER, perhaps because he is primarily a military historian, sees the climax of Francis' life not on Mount Alverna but in the adventure of the crusade. Francis' last years are summarised in a few brief paragraphs; Mockler does not, he says, feel qualified to discuss the mystery of sanctity. Another novelty is the theory that Francis' father was actually a Cathar heretic and that Francis, while rejecting their doctrines, modelled the Rule of his Order on the way of life of the Cathar Perfects. Mockler speculates in Freudian terms on the relationship between Francis and his father and portrays Francis as a highly immature and psychologically unbalanced young man at the time of his conversion. His lively text is supported by copious historical references in the notes following each chapter, and in these he freely admits that some of his theories are no more than speculation.

SMITH delves even more deeply into psychological analysis, this time Jungian rather than Freudian. Francis' conversion is seen as the process by which his "ego-consciousness" is "invaded by the unconscious mind." The experience on Mount Alverna is the culmination of this "take-over bid" by the "anthropos image." Various dreams and illnesses along the way receive psychosomatic interpretations. The portrait of Francis that emerges is by no means always sympathetic; Francis' humility, it is suggested, may have been an excuse for failure to take responsibility, and his solitary quest for personal holiness a betrayal of the trust of the early brothers. As for Ugolino's controversial reforms, Smith sees them as a pragmatic adaptation, "overcoming consumer resistance by changing the product."

With Lord LONGFORD's 1978 study we have a return to a Christian, Catholic perspective and to an emphasis on Francis' spiritual development. The sources are compared and previous biographies neatly reviewed. Throughout the text the views of other writers are referred to and the book seems almost intended as a guide to the contemporary orthodox Catholic view of St. Francis. This impression is strengthened by the fact that the second half of the book is devoted to a discussion of how Franciscan ideals can be applied to contemporary social problems.

GREEN's biography clearly reflects his own love of St. Francis. Written in a rather colloquial style, with a great deal of personal interpretation, it incorporates all the known facts and the historical background, along with a good admixture of legend where this makes for a good tale. As Sabatier wrote, they may not be true in fact but the old stories are certainly true to the Franciscan spirit, and this is justification enough for their inclusion here.

—Isabel Aitken

FRANCIS I. See FRANÇOIS I.

FRANCIS JOSEPH I. See FRANZ JOSEPH I.

FRANCO, Francisco, 1892–1975; Spanish general and dictator.

Coles, Sydney F. A., *Franco of Spain: A Full-Length Biography.* London, N. Spearman, 1955; Westminster, Maryland, Newman Press, 1956.

Crozier, Brian, *Franco.* Boston, Little Brown, 1967; with subtitle *A Biographical History,* London, Eyre and Spottiswoode, 1967.

Fusi, Juan Pablo, *Franco: A Biography,* translated by Felipe Fernandez-Armesto. New York, Harper, and London, Unwin Hyman, 1987.

Garza, Hedda, *Francisco Franco.* New York, Chelsea House, 1987.

Hills, George, *Franco: The Man and His Nation.* New York, Macmillan, and London, Hale, 1967.

Lloyd, Alan, *Franco.* New York, Doubleday, 1969; London, Longman, 1970.

Trythall, J. W. D., *El Caudillo: A Political Biography of Franco.* New York, McGraw-Hill, 1970.

*

A short biography by Joaquin Arrarás, *Franco* (1937), was the first of many eulogistic books published in Spain during Franco's lifetime. COLES' book, the first attempt at a serious biography in English, is badly dated and has nothing of fact or interpretation to make it worth reading today. Like its Spanish predecessors, it casts a kindly light on Franco's life and achievements. Unlike the majority of them, it is carefully researched and well written.

As Franco's life drew to a close, a number of readable and adequate biographies appeared for the general reader. CRO-ZIER, a journalist of anti-communist sentiments, weighed in with a generally balanced and clear portrait that attempted to weigh the pros and cons of Franco's policies. The difficulty of the task is evident from the result. For all the author's care, his political leanings show continually in his favorable assessments, and his lack of any informed understanding of the nature and dynamics of Falangism as well as his uncertain grasp of facts undermine the value of his effort. He also exhibits a tendency to credit his subject with responsibility for social and economic trends that far exceed the power of any individual to create.

HILLS, perhaps because he interviewed Franco and had access to his family papers and Army archives, could not distance himself at all from his subject and prepared a thoroughly polemical and apologetic portrait. Despite the availability of source material, his book makes numerous errors and lacks detail, color, and clarity. Historically at sea and unable to comprehend Falangism, Hills made a hash of his task. More worthwhile than either Crozier or Hills is LLOYD, a minor effort by an author whose broad knowledge of Spain and its historical background is illuminating for the general reader. GARZA is a good short treatment in a series of biographies for young adults.

TRYTHALL was for long the most penetrating and dispassionate study of its subject available in English. Undertaken as a graduate student project in the Iberian Centre of St. Antony's College, Oxford, this book is somewhat less rich in detail than the more journalistic portraits and more often interested in the Franco government and its policies than in the man himself. The author's insight into Spanish history, Falangism, and the workings of the Spanish government, as well as his balanced and scholarly assessments, make this book valuable reading even though the greater availability of source material since Franco's death now makes sounder judgments possible.

FUSI is now the indispensable starting point for any serious consideration of Franco's life. The work of an historian who is director of the Spanish National Library, it is almost telegraphically brief. Nevertheless, it manages to be thorough, clear, and judicious in portraying Franco the man and exceptionally intelligent in summarizing and commenting upon modern Spanish political history.

—Joseph M. McCarthy

FRANÇOIS I [François d'Angoulême], 1494–1547; French monarch.

Knecht, R. J., *Francis I.* Cambridge and New York, Cambridge University Press, 1982.

Seward, Desmond, *Prince of the Renaissance: The Life of François I.* London, Constable, 1973; with subtitle *The Golden Life of François I,* New York, Macmillan, 1973.

*

There is no full account in English specifically devoted to François I before Seward (see below). There are state papers in France, Italy, England, and Belgium; there are various memoirs, as well as the relevant volumes of by now usually obsolete general histories, such as that of Lavisse, and there are some often unreliable biographies in French, but that is all. Michelet's famous *Histoire de France* mythologized the whole subject of the French Renaissance in 1885, and attention is still drawn to L. Madelin's *François Ier, le souverain politique* (1937), which does not attempt biography, and to C. Terrasse, *François Ier, le roi et le règne* (2 vols., 1943–48), which is also chiefly political. Most histories of the reign depend on A. Varillas, *Histoire de François Ier* (2 vols., 1685–86), but certain aspects of it, notably artistic patronage and court life, have been treated piecemeal in both French and English, and all students of history will need to have recourse to J. H. Shennan, *The Parlement of Paris* (1968).

SEWARD's book is much more serious than its appearance would suggest. It is a quarto with a large number of illustrations and almost 40 colour plates. The chapter headings, like the book's title, suggest a work for light browsing. In fact this is a popular, readable, unpretentious, but very knowledgeable and professionally written biography with a helpful bibliography, a genealogy, and a properly compiled index, although the journalistic colourfulness of the writing has to be paid for by imprecision. It leaves no room for the judicious balancing of evidence, although it would be difficult to quarrel with the serried judgments. Moreover, there is a sweetening of anecdotes, which in a biography pitched at this level is not at all out of place. The authorities for the anecdotes exist, even if they are not given here.

Seward pays particular attention to the king's patronage of letters and the arts, a subject to which the illustrations pander. The weaknesses come in assessing the position of the Church, the tensions building up inside it, and its relationship to the universities and the *parlements*. Lyons, for instance, which had neither university nor *parlement*, was a notable refuge for liberals and dissenters. Much instead is made of the king's physical strength and prowess, as of his undoubted personal courage. Seward gives a good account of the battle of Pavia, but he is better on the physical aspects of the military engagement than on the ultimate political implications, so that the attempt to remain as strictly biographical as possible underplays François' political role. This is not the sort of biography to be read for its intellectual historical content, so that it remains weak on the forces leading to Calvin's religious revolution, as it does on the ultimate aims of the foreign policy of a king not quite so uniquely devoted to hunting and womanizing as is suggested.

KNECHT, who has made himself an outstanding authority on the political life and strifes of 16th-century France, is the author of the only serious modern biography of François I available in English, disclaims the role of biographer, preferring that of historian, and laments the absence of any proper history in any language of the unquestionably important reign that saw the peak of the French Renaissance and the accomplishment of the Reformation in France. The distinction he makes between biography, which demands a completeness of documentary evidence that for remote periods seldom exists, and history, which can focus on an absolute monarch and his reign, generally with some documentary sources in state papers, is of course valid. Knecht is in this technical sense an historian rather than a biographer, but what he has written is in fact also a superb biography. His labours coincided with those on the same subject of Jean Jacquart, with whose *François Ier* (1981) Kencht invariably agrees, conceding strength on the economic and social background but

claiming it for certain biographical and other aspects of the subject. It is unusual for two such scholars not to know that they were working on the same subject.

Knecht is severely scholarly where Seward, who does not figure in the former's bibliography, is merely anecdotal. Knecht's bibliography is in fact too vast, including a number of items of only very slight relevance to the history of the reign. This is primarily a political biography, with detailed attention paid to the finances of the kingdom as well as precise information about the king's consultations with his medical advisers. Most modern historians would have preferred heavier reliance on the approach pioneered by such French scholars as Braudel and Mousnier dealing with the general economics of agriculture, transport, and political institutions. We need to know more about good and bad harvests, the years and regions hit by the plague, the causes and extent of inflation, and the constraints on the unification of the kingdom caused by its physical geography.

On the religious question not enough attention is paid to the reasons for the scholastic positions and for the difference between theological debate and popular religion. "Humanism and Heresy" must be the weakest chapter in the book, and Seward is more informative than Knecht on artistic patronage. On heterodox tendencies and the way heresy was dealt with, Knecht does not always rely on the best sources available, even when they are given in the bibliography. The few lines given to the execution of Dolet seem inadequate, and there is no reference at all to the reign's greatest writer, Rabelais.

Perhaps in the end such weakness as there is in Knecht's excellent book is the result of falling between the two stools of biographer and historian. He has written a serious book for scholars and students, yet one that is not quite wide enough in scope to cover the history of the reign. On the other hand it goes well beyond the requirements of a strict biography.

—A. H. T. Levi

FRANKLIN, Benjamin, 1706–1790; American statesman and philosopher.

Aldridge, Alfred Owen, *Franklin and His French Contemporaries.* New York, New York University Press, 1957.

Aldridge, Alfred Owen, *Benjamin Franklin, Philosopher and Man.* Philadelphia, Lippincott, 1965.

Clark, Ronald W., *Benjamin Franklin: A Biography.* New York, Random House, and London, Weidenfeld and Nicolson, 1983.

Cohen, I. Bernard, *Franklin and Newton.* Philadelphia, American Philosophical Society, 1956.

Currey, Cecil B., *Road to Revolution: Benjamin Franklin in England 1765–75.* New York, Anchor Books, 1968.

Faÿ, Bernard, *Bernard Faÿ's Franklin, the Apostle of Modern Times.* London, Sampson Low, and Boston, Little Brown, 1929.

Fleming, Thomas, *The Man Who Dared the Lightning: A New Look at Benjamin Franklin.* New York, Morrow, 1971.

Nolan, J. Bennett, *Benjamin Franklin in Scotland and Ireland, 1759 and 1771.* Philadelphia, University of Pennsylvania Press, and London, H. Milford/Oxford University Press, 1956.

Seavey, Ormond, *Becoming Benjamin Franklin: The Autobiography and the Life.* University Park, Pennsylvania State University Press, 1988.

Van Doran, Carl, *Benjamin Franklin.* New York, Viking, 1938; London, Putnam, 1939.

*

Any examination of Franklin's life necessarily begins with a careful reading of his *Autobiography,* one of the best-known classics of earlier American literature. It was begun at Twyford, England, in 1771, ostensibly as a letter to his son, and continued in segments but was never completed. The Twyford segment extended only to 1730, with Franklin's founding of the Philadelphia Library. He did not resume his narration for 13 years; the third segment was written four years after that, and the fourth was finished only in 1789, a few months before his death. The *Autobiography* as we have it ends with Franklin's 1757 arrival in London, before most of his greatest accomplishments.

Throughout the 19th century, Franklin's autobiography tended to be read literally, as if it were the legend of a national saint. Responses today are more sophisticated, with some critics emphasizing the practical nature of the book—a treatise on how to succeed—and others seeing Franklin as a clever self-promoter who deliberately reinforced his own fame while professing modesty. Still others are attracted to an almost Calvinistic reading, in which Franklin's confessed "errors" appear as momentary deviations from a confidently assumed journey toward secular achievement. Most comprehensive biographies of Franklin comment on his *Autobiography* and generally endorse its accuracy (he wrote almost entirely from memory, and as an old man). Serious study of the book should include a look at SEAVEY's treatment of Franklin's *Autobiography* and his life.

Early biographies of Franklin were largely dependent on the *Autobiography* and such other materials as eventually came into print. The first authorized collection of his works was *Memoirs of the Life and Writings of Benjamin Franklin* (edited by his grandson William Temple Franklin, 3 vols., London, 1818), which contributed new biographical information and some bad texts. This was superseded in turn by *The Works of Benjamin Franklin* (edited by Jared Sparks, 10 vols., Boston, 1840), *The Complete Works of Benjamin Franklin* (edited by John Bigelow, 10 vols., New York, 1887–89), and *The Writings of Benjamin Franklin* (edited by Albert Henry Smythe, 10 vols., New York, 1905–07, with a life of Franklin in Volume X). An as yet incomplete edition of *The Papers of Benjamin Franklin,* by Yale University Press, has reached more than 30 volumes and the period of the American Revolution. All of the major biographies depend heavily on texts and scholarship available in these editions. Their editors, moreover, have often contributed separately to our knowledge of Franklin's life.

Aside from Smythe's, which is responsible but no longer outstanding, FAŸ's is the earliest biography still of value to general readers, based in large part on unpublished manuscript material. Unfortunately, Faÿ is more interesting for his distortions than for his facts. According to him, Franklin (a Mason) was in religion a follower of the 17th-century English Pythagoreans and therefore believed in metempsychosis. He acknowledged, claims Faÿ, a supreme deity who was surrounded with innumerable inferior deities and regarded Christ as nothing more than a major

prophet. In another context, Faÿ emphasizes Franklin's treacherous situation in France, surrounded by spies; his diplomatic success was therefore all the more remarkable. Unpublished letters also revealed hitherto unknown relationships with women—a likely topic, as Franklin had long been known to have had an illegitimate son. For Faÿ more generally, Franklin was the great exemplar of the bourgeois, whose *Autobiography* made his life a pattern for others to follow.

Though it was completed before the Yale edition of Franklin's papers began to appear, VAN DORAN's *Benjamin Franklin* is often considered the definitive life. Its contributions include some new writings, enhanced attention to Franklin as author-printer, an accounting of his finances, analysis of his surreptitious publications, a critical examination of the kite-flying episode, treatment of previously unknown diplomatic, military, and personal episodes, and corrected versions of some that were known. This new information came not only from the major repositories of Franklin manuscripts at the American Philosophical Society, the Historical Society of Pennsylvania, and the library of the University of Pennsylvania, but from commerical records, bank ledgers, and other not formerly consulted materials. In consequence, Van Doran's narrative is noticeably specific.

It is eminently readable as well, having been written by a distinguished literary historian who was also a fine stylist. If we regard Van Doran's conception of Franklin as a bit limited today, it is not because he was content to depict "a great and wise man moving though great and troubling events." Van Doran's Franklin is unquestionably more complex than this, but his book seems more a factual biography than a psychohistorical analysis. Whatever Franklin may have been in private, his public image is convincingly presented. Whether for reading or reference, therefore, Van Doran can still be recommended highly. The same author subsequently edited *Benjamin Franklin's Autobiographical Writings* (New York, 1945) and two volumes of Franklin's correspondence.

FLEMING's "new look" at Franklin is less scholarly in terms of original research but is nonetheless carefully footnoted, employs a reasonable bibliography, and was the first major biography to make use of the Yale edition of Franklin's works (the first 14 volumes only). By this time it was also possible to cite the collected papers of other, related American figures (Adams, Jefferson, Madison, and Washington) and to incorporate a number of specialized studies concerning Franklin. Fleming assumes that his readers know only the Franklin of the *Autobiography,* a self-made man who had just become world-famous, who scarcely mentions the scientific work that made him so, and who of course said nothing about the American Revolution and the Constitutional Convention still to come. "Beyond the *Autobiography,*" Fleming declares, "there is another Franklin—the mature man who, more than any other single person, presided over the birth of the American republic." His account therefore begins in 1752, only five years before the *Autobiography* ends.

By now, certain problematic aspects of Franklin's life had become well known and were variously interpreted by his biographers. During the 20 years Franklin lived in London, for example, he was virtually a husband to his landlady, Margaret Stevenson; her pretty daughter Mary ("Polly") later became a favorite correspondent. Since Franklin at the time had a wife in Philadelphia patiently awaiting his return, there has been a good deal of speculation regarding his private relationships. Though Franklin readily acknowledged his illegitimate son William, the mother's name has never been established. Franklin's uneven relationship with William (to whom the *Autobiography* is addressed) led ultimately to a breach between them; explanations of it differ. There has been less contention regarding his scientific accomplishments, in part because so few biographers are qualified to discuss them. His religious opinions, a good deal less spectacular than Faÿ supposed, have not been emphasized in recent work. But it *has* been popular to stress how much Franklin accomplished in his old age, the post-*Autobiography* portion of his life. In whatever biography you choose, notice the number of pages still left to read after arriving at 1776, the year in which Franklin turned 70.

Most of the papers relevant to Franklin's Revolutionary War activities (activities that all regard as being of extreme importance) have not yet been published. When they are, further interpretations will appear regarding a number of important issues and relationships. A standard center of controversy, differently interpreted by almost every biographer, has been Franklin's relationship with Silas Deane (sometimes called "America's first diplomat") who came to France in hopes of gaining eventually forthcoming support for the Revolution. Besides Franklin, the other involved person was Arthur Lee, who vilified both Franklin and Deane in letters of dubious reliability. It is certain that Edward Bancroft, a man whom both befriended, was in fact a British spy. (An interesting attempt to penetrate the complicated intrigues of those years is Cecil B. Currey, *Code Number 72: Ben Franklin, Patriot or Spy?*, 1972.) As Currey points out, such eminent Revolutionary American leaders as John Adams and John Jay distrusted Franklin's diplomatic endeavors in France. Finally, there are still inadequately understood episodes at the very end of Franklin's life, including his specific contributions to the Constitutional Convention (and the Constitution itself).

The most significant comprehensive biography of Franklin since Van Doran's is that of CLARK, which includes more than 400 pages of text, 70 pages more of documentation, and the most detailed index of any. Its British author, an experienced biographer of several famous names, found some new information in British archives but relied otherwise on the Yale Edition, previous biographies of Franklin, and other already published sources. What one looks for in Clark, therefore, is the presumably disinterested perspective of one for whom Franklin was unquestionably a great man but not a national hero. Actually, his perspective is still nationalistic, but British rather than American. Like other recent biographers, he claims to have created a more complex, more life-like Franklin who was subject to both shortcomings and contradictions. It is not the Franklin to which most readers of the *Autobiography* are accustomed.

Finally, one should note that the impressive range of Franklin's accomplishments, together with changing fortunes of the three nations (America, England, and France) with which he was associated, has encouraged a large number of less than comprehensive biographies. Among these more limited works, the most rewarding are ALDRIDGE (1957), ALDRIDGE (1965), COHEN, CURREY, and NOLAN.

—Dennis R. Dean

FRANZ JOSEPH I, 1830–1916; Emperor of Austria.

Harding, Bertita, *Golden Fleece: The Story of Franz Joseph and Elizabeth of Austria.* Indianapolis, Bobbs-Merrill, and London, Harrap, 1937.

Marek, George R., *The Eagles Die: Franz Joseph, Elizabeth, and Their Austria.* New York, Harper, 1974; London, Hart-Davis MacGibbon, 1975.

Murad, Anatol, *Franz Joseph I of Austria and His Empire.* Boston, Twayne, 1968.

Redlich, Joseph, *Emperor Francis Joseph of Austria: A Biography.* New York and London, Macmillan, 1929.

*

Though much has been written about the life of Emperor Franz Joseph I, only a very few sources are available to English-language readers. Of those works in German, E. C. Corti and Hans Sokol, *Der Alte Kaiser Franz Joseph I* (1955), remains the most detailed study of the emperor's life. Heinrich Ritter von Srbik's essay entitled "Franz Joseph I: Charakter und Regierungsgrundsätze" (in *Aus Österreich's Vergangenheit: Von Prinz Eugen zu Franz Joseph,* 1949) is a valuable treatment of the character and principles of government of the monarch who ruled for more than two-thirds of a century. Oswald Redlich's article, "Franz Joseph" (in *Neue Österreichische Biographie 1815–1918,* 1928), paints the emperor as having limited initiative in public affairs, remaining for the most part absorbed in daily routines.

According to REDLICH, Franz Joseph was a foe of nationalism and liberalism and opposed the transformation of Europe into a series of closed national states. Redlich claims that the emperor, an autocrat, retained to the end his "primitive conception" of the ruler whose will is always the strongest political force in his realm. Redlich's book asks whether the destruction of the Austro-Hungarian realm was really an act of creative policy for the liberated peoples and for Europe as a whole, though Redlich refrains from giving an answer. With an index but no bibliographical notes, this work remains one of the better researched biographies of Franz Joseph.

MURAD focuses more on the biography and personality of Franz Joseph, on his relations with Empress Elizabeth and other relatives, than on domestic and international problems. Useful as an introduction, Murad's work contains some notes and an index, though it makes little recourse to primary sources. MAREK, too, focuses on the lives of his subjects rather than on the complex historical events surrounding them. However, the historical background—wholly inadequate in Marek's treatment—is important for understanding the course Franz Joseph's life took. Marek does provide a usable bibliography. HARDING's earlier work is a readable account for a popular audience, though it has little if any scholarly value. Harding has also written on Maximilian, younger brother of Franz Joseph, the pretender to the throne of Mexico who was defeated and executed.

Several other sources, not specifically biography, contain material that sheds light on the life of Emperor Franz Joseph. These include Otto Ernst, editor, *Franz Joseph as Revealed by His Letters* (translated by Agnes Blake, 1927); Edward Crankshaw, *The Fall of the House of Habsburg* (1963); Gordon Brook-Shepherd, *The Austrian Odyssey* (1957), emphasizing the civilizing mission of the Habsburg Empire; Robert Kann, *A History of the Habsburg Empire 1526–1918* (1974), and *The Multinational Empire* (2 vols., 1964).

—Alfred D. Low

———————

FREDERICK II [the Great], 1712–1786; king of Prussia.

Asprey, Robert B., *Frederick the Great, Magnificent Enigma.* New York, Ticknor and Fields, 1986; Tunbridge Wells, Kent, Costello, 1988.

Barker, Thomas M., *Frederick the Great and the Making of Prussia.* New York, Holt, 1971; London, 1972.

Carlyle, Thomas, *The History of Friedrich II of Prussia* (10 vols.). London, Chapman and Hall, and New York, Scribner, 1858–65.

Duffy, Christopher, *The Army of Frederick the Great.* New York, Hippocrene Books, and Newton Abbey, David and Charles, 1974.

Dupuy, Trevor N., *The Military Life of Frederick the Great of Prussia.* New York, F. Watts, 1969.

Gaxotte, Pierre, *Frederick the Great,* translated by R. A. Bell. London, G. Bell, 1941; New Haven, Connecticut, Yale University Press, 1942 (originally published as *Frédéric II,* Paris, Fayard, 1938).

Gooch, G. P., *Frederick the Great: The Ruler, the Writer, the Man.* New York, Knopf, and London, Longman, 1947.

Hegemann, Werner, *Frederick the Great,* translated by Winifred Ray. London, Constable, and New York, Knopf, 1929 (originally published as *Fridericus; oder, Das Konigsopfer,* Hellerau, J. Hegner, 1924).

Hubatsch, Walther, *Frederick the Great of Prussia, Absolutism and Administration.* London, Thames and Hudson, 1975 (originally published by Grote, Cologne, 1973).

Johnson, Hubert C., *Frederick the Great and His Officials.* New Haven, Connecticut, Yale University Press, 1975.

Kittredge, Mary, *Frederick the Great.* New York, Chelsea House, 1987.

Macaulay, Thomas Babington, *The Life of Frederick the Great.* New York, Delisser and Procter, 1859.

Reddaway, William F., *Frederick the Great and the Rise of Prussia.* London and New York, Putnam, 1904.

Wright, Constance, *A Royal Affinity: The Story of Frederick the Great and His Sister Wilhelmina von Bayreuth.* New York, Scribner, 1965; London, Muller, 1967.

*

Of the numerous German historians who have dealt with the life and deeds of Frederick the Great, Leopold von Ranke was the first competent scholar. His *Neun Bücher Preussischer Geschichte* was published in 1847–49, bringing the account down to 1756. He not only gave his due to Frederick William I, Frederick's father, assigning him a place of honor, but also expressed his admiration for the son. A leading representative of the Prussian School was Heinrich von Treitschke (*Deutsche Geschichte im Neunzehnten Jahrhundert,* 1879–94). To him Frederick was the greatest figure in Germany since Gustavus Adolphus. The prosperity of Silesia under Frederick's rule showed that the province had found "its natural master."

In the 19th century Frederick II was glorified by German national-minded, *kleindeutsch*-oriented historians, though he was not a precursor of German nationalism and did not even fully appreciate the developing late 18th-century German literature. He was sharply criticized by the *grossdeutsch*-oriented Austrian or pro-Austrian historians. Among the latter sharply critical of Frederick II was Onno Klopp (*König Friedrich II,* 1867). Not as critical of the Prussian king as Klopp was Max Lehmann (*Friedrich der Grosse und der Ursprung des Siebenjärigen Krieges,* 1894). Lehmann pointed to Frederick's recorded ambitions in 1752, his first Political Testament passages which Bismarck had wanted suppressed. The most authoritative German account of Frederick came from the pen of Reinhold Koser (*Geschichte Friedrichs des Grossen,* 4 vols., Stuttgart, 1912–14). Though an admirer of Frederick, he was not uncritical of him. In Koser's view, the young king "warmed" his ambition to seize Silesia "at the holy fire of patriotism." Koser also acquitted Frederick from taking the offensive in 1756. The author admitted failures in Frederick's economic policy and in the political field by trying to do everything himself. Prussia's gain turned out ultimately to be a German gain, claims Koser, from the perspective of the newly unified German state.

The ex-Kaiser William II, while in his *Memoirs* praising Frederick as a German hero, criticized him for the "French spirit" at Sans-Souci—as about a century earlier the nationalist Ernst Moritz Arndt had done. HEGEMANN considered it as a "world tragedy" that Frederick was held up as a model for kings everywhere. The traditional view of the Prussian king was restated in 1936—the era of the Third Reich—"unblushingly," as the historian G. P. Gooch remarked, by Gerhard Ritter (see below), who conceded that with Frederick the Great "hard raison d'-état" took form "among us Germans."

One of the first English authors on Frederick II was his admirer Thomas CARLYLE. The noted essayist and historian expounded his philosophy of history also in the ten-volume work on Frederick the Great, the last volume ending with the battle of Rossbach. Though according to Carlyle Frederick was no hero of the faith, he displayed many positive qualities. Following Ranke, Carlyle saw in the father Frederick William I not a crude and irascible tyrant but a hero. Carlyle began his work on Frederick rather late, at the age of 56, and preoccupied himself with it for the next 14 years, relying on printed sources rather than on German archives. Bismarck wrote Carlyle on the occasion of his 80th birthday that he had presented to Germans the great king of the Prussians in his complete form, "like a living monument." The work was widely acclaimed in Germany; Prussians and Germans in general greatly appreciated the unexpected moral support in their struggle for hegemony in Germany. In 1874 Carlyle became the recipient of the German order *Pour le Mérite.*

Measured by modern critical standards, Carlyle's work on Frederick the Great is the high point of apologetic writing. The highly exaggerated praise of the king, the often bombastic language, the direct appeal to the reader to take the side of Frederick, and the relentless criticism of his opponents leave no doubt that the king was the author's hero whose virtues must be extolled and whose faults, if any, suppressed or minimized. Carlyle advised his readers to relinquish the view that Frederick was "ambiguous" and inclined to "lying and artfulness." Yet he was not uncritical toward the French colony of jokers the king had gathered around his table, noting that Frederick's love of wisdom was not deep enough, while he appreciated wit too highly. Turning in conclusion to the reader, Carlyle thus summed up: "In all yearbooks of every faith you will find only with difficulty a king of human beings who has fulfilled his duty more loyally."

There is hardly a greater contrast in the assessment of the Prussian monarch than that between Carlyle and MACAULAY. Macaulay's small book on Frederick II is a brilliant work focussing on the king's character and policies, but picturing him with both his foibles and talents. Considering Germany's only incipient literary development, Macaulay found the crown prince's and later king's admiration for French writers not surprising. He nevertheless held that Frederick as a result of his neglect of the German language had no full command of any language. The author found in Frederick's voluminous *Memoirs* neither deep reflection nor vivid writing. The crown prince's refutation of the *Principe* of Macchiavelli, his *Anti-Macchiavel*, was, according to Macaulay, an edifying "homily against rapacity, perfidy, arbitrary government, unjust war, in short, against almost everything for which its author is now remembered among men." But when Frederick ascended the throne nobody had the least suspicion that a "tyrant of extraordinary military and political talents, of industry more extraordinary still, without fear, without faith and without mercy" was to begin his rule.

The Hohenzollerns, and Frederick chief among them, have been extolled by hundreds of German historians as the pioneers of a solid and triumphant Germany. According to REDDAWAY, the reviewing of the life-work of Frederick without either sympathy or the bias of German patriotism raised the question whether Frederick deserved to be placed among the great. In his view, Frederick as a thinker fell "very far short of greatness." Yet though he witnessed the American Revolution and died within three years of the great Revolution in France, he had no suspicion that the framework of the world might change. His judgment of Voltaire and of the young Goethe showed that he regarded literature and learning not with an open mind. In foreign policy he was successful and in economic practice his failure was qualified. Far from training the Prussian bureaucrats, he continued to treat them like schoolboys who deserved to be flogged.

Reddaway considered it part of the Hohenzollern legend that Frederick was the conscious or semi-conscious architect of the modern German Empire. In reality, he thought and acted on behalf of the aggrandizement only of Prussia. By his single will he shaped the course of history and completed the fusion of provinces into the Prussian state. His victories gave the state prestige, and the growth of Prussia consecrated the very acts by which it was accomplished. Reddaway's book contains an index, but no footnotes.

RITTER's biography originated in a series of lectures he delivered at the University of Freiburg in 1933–34 and which he first published with hardly any revisions in 1936. Though they lack footnotes, the lectures were undoubtedly based on thorough research. An admirer of Frederick, the noted conservative historian was by no means uncritical toward the king. Frederick's reign, he claimed, gained "worldwide significance." The monarch "triumphed" because he "combined in his person all the courage, daring, and military expertise that could be found in

Prussia." Clearly a man of action rather than an administrator, his domestic policies "conspicuously lacked in innovation." They were even more conservative than those pursued by his father and great-grandfather or those of his younger contemporary Joseph II of Austria. The historical judgment on his administration policies must remain in doubt.

Ritter did not consider Frederick II a true precursor of German nationalism of the 19th or 20th centuries. Frederick also played no part in the great intellectual awakening beginning in the middle of the 18th century. He turned the Academy at Berlin into a society of French wits and writers. He repeatedly asserted that race and religion of the newcomers to Prussia were of no concern to him. About Frederican warfare, Ritter, a specialist in German military history, observed that "his practical genius matched the clarity and depth of his theoretical understanding."

Only after World War II did Ritter admit that he had often uncritically accepted "the necessity of states giving full reign to their drive for power." For too long, Ritter then conceded, have German historians praised violence if it proved successful. The Frenchman Pierre GAXOTTE's study was less encumbered by the patriotic approach to Frederick than were those by most German historians. Gaxotte notes that the Prussian army, composed of natives and foreigners, drawn in by the certainty of high pay and good food, were kept by implacable discipline and the fear of terrible punishments. He further notes that during the Seven Years War, "Frederick and Prussia endured seven terrible years of agony, suffering, and danger." It was because he surmounted all this that Frederick seemed so great to the men of his time. Gaxotte describes in lively prose Federick's relations with Voltaire, Maupertuis, and other Frenchmen and Germans at Sans-Souci. This work, a useful introduction to Frederick's life and reign, is provided with an index; it has no footnotes, though includes some bibliographical notes.

One of the best, most balanced books on Frederick the Great is by the noted English historian, GOOCH. According to Gooch, none of the makers of history has been the object of more conflicting evaluations than Frederick II, who hoisted Prussia into the rank of great powers and unwittingly paved the way for a united Germany under Prussian leadership. The part played by Germany in staging and waging two World Wars has sharpened Gooch's distaste for the "father of Prussian militarism." The author admits that Frederick dedicated his life to the service of Prussia. Trained in a hard and rigorous school, his gentler instincts were frozen during the impressionable years of adolescence. He struck his contemporaries as a "superman, ruthless and sarcastic," difficult to love and impossible to trust.

Gooch saw in Frederick a unique and many-sided personality, "at once fascinating and repulsive." What Germans, especially German historians, have thought of Frederick II is of peculiar significance, wrote Gooch in the wake of World War II, "in view of their craving for leadership, their political romanticism, their worship of efficiency and their intellectual glorification of war." Frederick's immense prestige, as seen from the standpoint of European history, is not the least important aspect of his life's work.

In the view of JOHNSON, Frederick's leadership of a minor state in war and peace was "remarkable." While dazzling Europe by his military and literary exploits, his role in the administration of the state had allegedly remained obscure. An absolutist, though an enlightened one, he is supposed to have made all important decisions. The book is provided with a bibliography and an index.

According to HUBATSCH, only few among Frederick's contemporaries and even admirers really understood him. Hubatsch, trying to defend the monarch, points to the growth of the Prussian population, "in spite of heavy losses in the wars," and praises Frederick's administrative activities, about which allegedly "little" has been written. The king's conception of the state was also "little understood" by many contemporaries. The work is based on the printed series of archival materials, the *Act Borussica,* complemented by other unprinted materials. It is provided with tables, detailed biographical notes, and an index.

The work by ASPREY is a well-written study designed for the general reader, relying on many secondary German and non-German sources as well as primary sources, including Frederick's 46-volume collection of his political correspondence, military writings, and other materials. Illustrations and maps add to the work. While focussing on his wars, Asprey does not neglect Frederick's peace-time policies and activities. The complex character of Frederick, his intellect, wit, as well as his self-seeking desire for glory, emerge clearly in this work. Frederick is pictured with all his contradictions. What is missing is a concluding overall assessment of Frederick the Great and of his lasting accomplishments.

KITTRIDGE's work on Frederick the Great is introductory. The preface, "On Leadership," by Arthur M. Schlesinger, has no connection with Frederick. DUFFY claims that though Frederick did not foresee the ultimate result, he set Prussia on the path of aggression that led first to the temporary unification of a prussianized Germany and ultimately to ruin, the partition of 1945. BARKER's selection of readings from other well-known works is useful, as is in a rather different way WRIGHT's study, which makes lavish use of Frederick's confidences with his sister Wilhelmina. Many historians read Wilhelmina out of court as an authority, since she said many unkind things about her brother, thereby irritating many of his biographers. DUPUY, a retired colonel in the U.S. Army, author of numerous short treatises on military heroes throughout history, offers a useful introduction to military aspects of Frederick's reign.

The noted journalist Rudolph Augstein (*Preussens Friedrich und die Deutschen,* 1986) considers himself only a "private historian," who has in mind "not so much a 'debunking' of this most fascinating human being of his century," but rather a "demasking, a demythologizing" of German historians seeking for meaning in history. According to Wilhelm Treue (*Preussens Grosser König: Leben und Wirken Friedrichs des Grossen,* Freiburg, 1986), Frederick has also from today's perspective great importance for the history of his country, of Austria, Germany, and Central Europe, indeed as an ally of England even for world history.

—Alfred D. Low

FREUD, Sigmund, 1856–1939; Austrian psychiatrist, founder of psychoanalysis.

Brome, Vincent, *Freud and His Early Circle.* London, Heinemann, 1967; New York, Morrow, 1968.

Clark, Ronald, *Freud: The Man and the Cause.* New York, Random House, and London, Cape/Weidenfeld and Nicolson, 1980.

Freud, Ernst, Lucie Freud, and Ilse Gribrich-Simitis, editors, *Sigmund Freud: His Life in Pictures and Words,* translated by Christine Trollope. New York and London, Harcourt, 1978 (originally published by Suhrkamp, Frankfurt am Main, 1976).

Gay, Peter, *Freud: A Life for Our Time.* New York, Norton, and London, Dent, 1988.

Homans, Peter, *The Ability to Mourn: Disillusionment and the Social Origins of Psychoanalysis.* Chicago and London, University of Chicago Press, 1989.

Isbister, J. N., *Freud: An Introduction to his Life and Work.* Cambridge, Polity Press; New York and Oxford, Blackwell, 1985.

Jones, Ernest, *The Life and Work of Sigmund Freud* (3 vols.). New York, Basic Books, 1953–57; London, Hogarth Press, 1956. One-volume abridgement, Lionel Trilling and Steven Marcus, editors, New York, Basic Books, 1961.

Klein, Dennis B., *Jewish Origins of the Psychoanalytic Movement.* New York, Praeger, 1981; Chicago and London, University of Chicago Press, 1985.

McGrath, William J., *Freud's Discovery of Psychoanalysis: The Politics of Hysteria.* Ithaca, New York, Cornell University Press, 1986.

Roazen, Paul, *Freud and His Followers.* New York, Knopf, 1974; London, A. Lane, 1976.

Robert, Marthe, *From Oedipus to Moses: Freud's Jewish Identity,* translated by Ralph Manheim. New York, Anchor Books, 1976; London, Routledge, 1977 (originally published by Calmann-Lévy, Paris, 1974).

Sachs, Hanns, *Freud: Master and Friend.* Cambridge, Massachusetts, Harvard University Press, 1944; London, Imago, 1945.

Schur, Max, *Freud: Living and Dying.* New York, International Universities Press, and London, Hogarth Press, 1972.

Wittels, Fritz, *Sigmund Freud: His Personality, His Teaching, and His School,* translated by Eden and Cedar Paul. New York, Dodd Mead, and London, Allen and Unwin, 1924 (originally published by E. P. Tol, Leipzig, 1924).

*

Freud himself was sometimes suspicious of biography, telling the writer Arnold Zweig, who was contemplating a biography of the pioneer psychoanalyst, "Anyone turning biographer commits himself to lies, to concealment, to hypocrisy, to flattery, and even to hiding his own lack of understanding, for biographical truth is not to be had, and even if it were it couldn't be used." Even so, Freud's first colleagues were not deterred from biographical studies. Short and interesting books by WITTELS and SACHS, though now seen to have errors of fact, were based on personal knowledge of their subject (as was Jones' landmark contribution, see below).

The study of Freud's life has been shaped by access to his voluminous private papers. Jones' biography is based on his unique relations with the original Freudian circle and the critical primary materials he assembled. Even today, though many more letters and other materials are public or are available to scholars, limits on the accessibility of important documents means that even the most complete biographies, as Gay himself notes, have significant gaps.

With the publication of JONES' authoritative biography in the years surrounding the celebration of the centennial of Freud's birth, also a time of public acclaim for psychoanalysis, the basic structure of Freud's life was set out for the psychoanalytic and other scholarly communities and for the public as well (the Lionel Trilling and Steven Marcus abridgement of Jones' work helping with the last group especially). Yet Jones' desire to protect Freud's reputation—he had the approval of Freud's daughter Anna, who was even more cautious than Zweig about biography—meant that important subjects would not get the treatment they deserved despite the space available in the traditional (or Victorian) three-volume format. Jones' *Freud* is more than ample in its documentary aspect but less so in others. As the psychoanalyst and art historian Ernst Kris said of it: "Everything human and personal is treated wisely and almost with tenderness. Only the thinker Freud, the man in battle with his task, was not sufficiently done." Kris himself made an important contribution to the biographical study of Freud with his extensive introduction to *The Origins of Psychoanalysis: Letter to Wilhelm Fliess by Sigmund Freud* (New York, Basic Books, 1954).

The first of Jones' volumes ends with the publication in 1899 of Freud's *The Interpretation of Dreams*. It appropriately stresses Freud's relations with Josef Breuer and Wilhelm Fliess, as well as Freud's unique "self-analysis." In Volume Two Freud is presented as an isolated hero of clinical innovation and as an organizer of the budding international psychoanalytic movement. From the point of view of the loyalist Jones, Freud's opponents like Jung and Adler appear as misguided antagonists of scientific progress in psychology. Jones' firsthand account of Freud's work habits and family life is invaluable. One chapter in the last volume is titled "Fame and Suffering," an apt summary of Freud's old age when he triumphed over his long struggle with cancer to produce major studies, especially of relations between psychoanalysis, social and historical themes, and practices in anthropology, literature, and other fields. About half of this last volume is dedicated to textual commentaries, though several are now dated in light of recent research.

Since Jones' work an enormous literature on Freud's life and work has appeared. Gay (see below) asserts that it is nearly "out of control." Some of it is subversive in intention, at least in the sense that it tries to free Freud biography of Jones' hagiographic motive and to recover the contributions of other psychoanalysts. ROAZEN offers a broad survey based on interviews with many important participants in the psychoanalytic movement. ISBISTER's book depends on recent (and controversial) research on Freud's life suggesting less than heroic qualities. Still, most writers are loyal to the "authorized" Freud. CLARK's balanced and thorough biography offers ample evidence of Freud's debt to biology and of his fierce independence as well. He follows Freud closely through his early medical career and the series of collaborations in which his theory developed. Like Gay later, Clark documents the domestic, social, and medical environments in which Freud and psychoanalysis developed. He is detailed and reliable on the years of discovery and then the expansion of the international psychoanalytic community.

Freud was often contemptuous of his critics inside and outside the psychoanalytic movement, and Clark retells the stories of his breaks with Adler, Jung, and Rank with justice to all sides. A few figures, like the idiosyncratic German analyst and novelist Georg Groddeck and the American psychologist James Putnam, get from Clark the attention they deserve and have been denied by other biographers. On the other hand, despite considerable emphasis on Freud's devotion to his family, Clark never gets beyond Anna Freud's role as a chaperon for her father in his old age and their flight from the Nazis to London. He acknowledges the range of influence of psychoanalysis on intellectual life, but his comments on "The Freudian Age" include only the most rudimentary points.

The spirit of GAY's authoritative biography is conveyed by the headnote he chose from Freud's brief biographical study of Leonardo: "There is no one so great that it would be a disgrace for him to be subject to the laws that govern normal and pathological activity with equal severity." Accordingly, Gay, who in addition to being one of the most distinguished and prolific historians of his generation has also been trained as a psychoanalyst, offers an account of Freud's life that matches its subject's psychological complexity and narrative gift. He admits to trying for accuracy rather than for startling effects, a frequent temptation for psychoanalytic biographers.

Gay seamlessly weaves together an account of Freud's life and the social and political environment of his time with astute critical readings (rarely mere summaries) of his work. He provides detailed and interpretively rich accounts of every state in Freud's life. The biography's organization and its extensive bibliographic essay constitute in themselves a short course in how to think about both the life of Freud and his impact on 20th-century life. For example, Gay displays the extraordinary counterpoint of the hardships of Freud's life and his family's during World War I in Vienna against the composition of some of his most important essays on psychoanalytic technique. And Freud's work during the immediate postwar years reflects in Gay's treatment the developmental logic of his science: the aggression that Freud had observed in European society, and the personal grief over the death of one of his daughters. Gay does not pretend, finally, to be able to penetrate the essence of Freud's achievement, nor should he have to: "In the end, unsatisfactory as it sounds, one comes back to Freud's own disclaimer that before creativity the psychoanalyst must put down his arms. Freud was Freud."

Gay's biography includes many photographs, but inquirers into Freud's life will also want to consult an impressive collection of photographs of Freud, his family, colleagues, and others bearing on the history of the psychoanalytic movement, and of places, artworks, and documents related to psychoanalysis, compiled and edited by FREUD, FREUD, AND GRIBRICH-SIMITIS. This volume also includes a useful biographical introduction by Kurt Eissler. Other biographers focus on periods in Freud's life or significant themes to explore in them: the early years and the Viennese political environment in both BROME and McGRATH (following on the influential biographical essays in Carl Schorske's *Fin de Siècle Vienna: Politics and Culture* [New York, Vintage Books, 1981]); religion and ethnic identity in the works by ROBERT and KLEIN; Freud's middle years and the origins of his "social texts" in the volume by HOMANS.

The biography by SCHUR is certainly of enduring interest, written as it was by Freud's personal physician (he was also a psychoanalyst) in his last decade. The work derives from Schur's dissatisfaction with Jones' presentation of Freud's medical history and his attitudes toward death and dying. It is a complete biography in that it reviews the essentials of Freud's background, early years, professional ascendance, and analytic discoveries and colleagueship. In its second half, however, special attention goes to Freud's illness and the place of death as a psychological problem. Other biographers (following Jones again) demonstrate Freud's scientific courage in his early and middle years. Schur's unique relationship with Freud makes his careful judgments of his character in late life indispensable.

Three influential works of interpretation with biographical overtones deserve mention: Philip Rieff, *The Mind of the Moralist* (New York, Viking, 1959); John Murray Cuddihy, *The Ordeal of Civility* (New York, Basic Books, 1974); and Frank Sulloway, *Freud, Biologist of the Mind* (New York, Basic Books, 1979).

—Steven Weiland

_____

FROST, Robert, 1874–1963; American poet.

Burnshaw, Stanley, *Robert Frost Himself.* New York, G. Braziller, 1986.

Mertins, Louis, *Robert Frost: Life and Talks-Walking.* Norman, University of Oklahoma Press, 1965.

Morrison, Kathleen, *Robert Frost: A Pictorial Chronicle.* New York, Holt Rinehart, 1974.

Pritchard, William, *Frost: A Literary Life Reconsidered.* New York, Oxford University Press, 1984.

Sergeant, Elizabeth Shepley, *Robert Frost: The Trial by Existence.* New York, Holt Rinehart, 1960.

Sutton, William A., editor, *Newdick's Season of Frost: An Interrupted Biography of Robert Frost.* Albany, State University of New York Press, 1976.

Thompson, Lawrence, *Robert Frost* (3 vols.; vol. III with R. H. Winnick). New York, Holt Rinehart, 1966–76.

Thompson, Lawrence and R. H. Winnick, *Robert Frost: A Biography* (condensed into one volume by E. C. Lathem). New York, Holt Rinehart, 1982.

Van Dore, Wade, *The Life of the Hired Man.* Dayton, Ohio, Wright State University Press, 1986.

Walsh, John E., *Into My Own: The English Years of Robert Frost.* New York, Grove, 1988.

*

Accounts of Robert Frost's long life divide into those published before and after his death; they also divide into memoirs by acquaintances and friends (Burnshaw, Mertins, Morrison, Sergeant), and formal biographies taking a scholarly approach (Newdick, Thompson, Pritchard, Walsh).

Frost's first authorized biographer, Robert Newdick, died in 1939; his work was completed by SUTTON. Newdick had gathered enough material to draft 13 short chapters on Frost's early

life that are accurate and respectful without being adulatory; these were not published until 1976, along with 150 pages of Newdick's research findings, confusingly arranged, not always reliably transcribed, but often remarkably interesting. For example, Newdick obtained a good many very personal recollections from Frost's high school classmates and from his students in New Hampshire. This book leaves one regretting Newdick's untimely death, especially in light of the work produced by his successor.

THOMPSON became the authorized biographer in 1939, under the condition that nothing be published before Frost's death. The huge three-volume biography, the third volume finished by Winnick after Thompson died, was adumbrated in the *Selected Letters of Robert Frost* (edited by Lawrence Thompson, 1964) and abbreviated and diluted in E. C. Lathem's one-volume edition of 1982. The full work remains an essential tool for Frost scholars although it must be used with the utmost caution. Over his many years of close association with Frost, Thompson appears to have conceived an animus against his subject so strong as to have disqualified him from writing the biography he felt committed to complete. Peter Ackroyd has called the result "an elephantine work of scholarship which by dint of repetition suggests that Frost was a self-obsessed, paranoid, manipulative and positively sinister human being." Despite his bias, Thompson collected enormous amounts of significant as well as trivial primary materials, and his three cumbersome and graceless books are stuffed with them, both in the text and the several hundred pages of footnotes (omitted from Lathem's condensation). The caution one exercises in reading Thompson is in distinguishing fact and information from interpretation. Thompson applied to Frost a reductive psychoanalytic method derived from Karen Horney (cf. Burnshaw, p. 229), and virtually every page is murky with speculations and suppositions about Frost's unconscious motives and the hidden meanings of his words and actions. Thompson writes with a leaden ear, having missed Frost's essential messages about the "sound of sense" in prose and verse.

A valuable though limited corrective to Thompson is MORRISON's *Pictorial Chronicle.* When Elinor Frost died in 1938, Mrs. Morrison replaced her as Frost's housekeeper and business manager—in fact, as his Muse. Her account of his later years is, therefore, the closest extended firsthand view we have, and her picture is far more charitable than Thompson's, though by no means idolizing. The numerous pictures (Frost was a photographer's dream), with informative captions, tell much of the story, but Morrison's first-hand reports of major events in Frost's last 25 years are invaluable, especially his relations with President John F. Kennedy. His trip to the Soviet Union is more fully described in solid short books by F. D. Reeve, *Robert Frost in Russia* (1963), and Frederick B. Adams, *To Russia with Frost* (1963). Morrison writes clearly and matter-of-factly; her account of Frost's life and career emphasizes that "the chief characteristic that underlay . . . all his achievements was his native intellectual power."

Two recent scholars, Pritchard and Walsh, have begun more substantially to alter the assessment of Frost left by Thompson. PRITCHARD, an experienced critic of modern literature, bases his "reconsideration" of Frost's life on Thompson's information but gives Frost more benefit of the doubt. He also provides some new materials, including selections from the Frost notebooks.

His avowed purpose is to release Frost from Thompson's rigid explantory categories, and in this he succeeds. Pritchard alternates sections of biography with literary criticism in chapters sketching each phase of Frost's life. Like most critics, he devotes more attention and sympathy to the early poetry than to the later, but his biographical account covers the whole span.

WALSH's is a breakthrough biography. Dissatisfied with Thompson, for reasons he forcefully explains, Walsh from the start worked directly and ingeniously from many primary sources that the supposedly indefatigable Thompson had failed to discover or that were not available before his death. Walsh brings us closer than any other biographer has done to imagining and understanding what sort of man Frost was when he went to England, how he approached his stay there, what he did and thought and wrote, and how important the English years were to his later career and reputation. This is the best book-length biography of Frost yet published.

Still useful among the memoirs by friends and acquaintances are those by Burnshaw, Mertins, and Sergeant, though all have severe limitations. MERTINS was a California book collector who met Frost in 1932 and pursued his acquaintance over the next three decades. In the course of recording, in superfluous detail, every meeting and exchange between them, Mertins includes over 20 letters and many allegedly verbatim transcripts of conversations, which contain numerous comments on individual poems as well as much biographical information to check against other sources. Frost's words are always set off from Mertins' extensive and frequently banal comments, and while Mertins' reliability as a transcriber has been questioned by scholars, the passages he attributes to Frost at least sound true to Frost's style of speaking as recorded elsewhere. He is Frost's most dogged Boswell.

SERGEANT was another admiring friend who had Frost's complicity in compiling her biography, which he allowed her to publish before his death, to the annoyance of his official biographer, Thompson. Although it is a less professional scholarly effort—the extensive quotations are not footnoted—and continually adopts its subject's views of the events of his life, Sergeant's biography is considered by some who knew Frost to present a truer image of his mind and personality than Thompson's version.

BURNSHAW took on Thompson head to head, having been the editor who handled Frost's last book of verse and Thompson's first volume of biography. According to Burnshaw, Frost explicitly begged him to "save me" from Thompson, but *Robert Frost Himself* is almost as much about Stanley Burnshaw himself, although it makes some valid if spotty corrections of Thompson and directs the reader to Thompson's papers in the Frost Collection of the University of Virginia Library. Though Burnshaw provides some authentic glimpses of Frost at work, he writes in a spiteful style at times, with many unconvincingly-worded direct quotations surprisingly devoid of interest. Similar values and limitations mark VAN DORE's volume, a memoir with many comments and letters by Frost.

Three books essential to an understanding of Frost are Margaret Bartlett Anderson, *Robert Frost and John Bartlett: The Record of a Friendship* (1963); William R. Evans, editor, *Robert Frost and Sidney Cox: Forty Years of Friendship* (1981); and *The Letters of Robert Frost to Louis Untermeyer* (1963). Each provides fairly loose and selective biographical accounts. However, the primary value of each is in its large collection of Frost's letters, supplementing Thompson's *Selected Letters*, in which a good many of these are included. Frost's prose is at least as great as his verse, as all his letters show; much of the time he's as funny as good Mark Twain. The published letters have provided many readers with their first glimpses of Frost outside his poems; the view is often startlingly at odds with the popular misconceptions of Frost as a kindly old New England farmer-poet—a misconception that Frost's own self-publicity helped to create. In all three volumes his wit and erudition are evident, as well as his mischief and sting, and a complex, vivid personality emerges that Thompson had failed to pin down with his dogmatic analysis. The Untermeyer collection does the most to alert the reader to Frost's intellectual sophistication and power, and it occasionally lets us see into the well-shielded depths of his private sorrows.

Among the numerous biographical and critical essays and articles on Frost, a few with new materials and well-informed interpretations are notable, particularly those by his granddaughter, Lesley Lee Francis (articles in *Massachusetts Review*, *South Carolina Review*, and elsewhere), who has had access to private family papers. There are also some short yet extremely revealing pieces by fellow poets and writers. Of particular note are chapters by C. P. Snow in *Varieties of Men* (1968) and Donald Hall in *Remembering Poets* (1977). Frost's shrewdest Boswell, the New England poet Robert Francis, provides crisply written insights and authentic sounding conversations from two periods of Frost's life (1933–35 and 1950–59), in *Frost: A Time to Talk: Conversations and Indiscretions Recorded by Robert Francis* (1972).

Two film biographies deserve mention. *A Lover's Quarrel with the World* (Holt, 1967) shows Frost at home and in public in his last years, with most of the soundtrack in his own voice, reading or reciting his poems, lecturing, and talking. *Voices and Visions* (The New York Center for Visual History, 1988) attempts a full-length interpretive biography, with a script by Margot Feldman, editor of a comprehensive collection of Frost's notebooks not yet in print. The latter film is heavy on interpretations of the life and the poems by several modern poets and critics who tend to get in Frost's way. The earlier, black and white documentary provides a more moving, thoughtful, and less academic view.

Robert Frost appears well on his way to becoming America's national Bard, and like Shakespeare's his reputation will inevitably fluctuate while views of his life and works proliferate. (The canon of Frost's writings is far from being fixed; his prose is scattered, and the textual integrity of the intended standard edition of his poetry by E. C. Lathem [1969] has been called into doubt.) In time, biographies of Frost's whole life will meet the scholarly standards expected for major authors, but until everyone who knew him has died, there will continue to be excitement and uncertainty—a mixture of dread and anticipation—whenever a new biography of Frost is announced.

—John Ridland

FULLER, (Sarah) Margaret [Marchioness Ossoli], 1810–1850; American writer and lecturer.

Allen, Margaret, *The Achievement of Margaret Fuller*. University Park, Pennsylvania State University Press, 1979.

Anthony, Katherine, *Margaret Fuller: A Psychological Biography*. New York, Harcourt, 1920.

Bell, Margaret, *Margaret Fuller, a Biography*. New York, Boni, 1930.

Blanchard, Paula, *Margaret Fuller: From Transcendentalism to Revolution*. New York, Delacorte Press/S. Lawrence, 1978.

Chevigny, Bell Gale, *The Woman and the Myth: Margaret Fuller's Life and Writings*. Old Westbury, New York, The Feminist Press, 1976.

Chipperfield, Faith, *In Quest of Love*. New York, Coward-McCann, 1957.

Higginson, Thomas Wentworth, *Margaret Fuller Ossoli*. Boston, Houghton Mifflin, 1884.

Howe, Julia Ward, *Margaret Fuller*. Boston, Roberts, and London, Allen, 1883.

Stern, Madeline B., *The Life of Margaret Fuller*. New York, Dutton, 1942.

Wade, Mason, *Margaret Fuller: Whetstone of Genius*. New York, Viking, 1940.

Watson, David, *Margaret Fuller: An American Romantic*. Oxford, Berg, and New York, St. Martin's, 1988.

*

Several early biographies are going to have limited use for the serious researcher. HOWE's served as a sympathetic portrait written by a close friend, which sought interestingly enough to recreate Fuller's personality with very little critical commentary on her works. Like the Anthony and Bell biographies, Howe provides a quasi-fictionalized, sentimental account of Fuller as a failed romantic—talented, idiosyncratic—who finds passion, revolution, and redemption as an expatriate in Italy. Little else is offered pertaining to the wider context of social, cultural, or feminist history.

According to ANTHONY, her book attempts to cut through the "mood of evasion" conveyed by earlier biographers by applying "modern psychological analysis." Her overtly Freudian interpretation of Fuller's life is often too narrow and speculative. Fuller's "inner life" is the focus of this study, not the surrounding social and historical events that would give the reader some cultural context. BELL's biography also has limited usefulness. Although the work is adequately researched, Bell's tendency is to semi-fictionalize events, dialogue, and Fuller's thoughts has led reviewers to label this biography overly "romanticized and eulogistic" and "not sufficiently mature to be a critical document."

Of the early biographies the general consensus is that HIGGINSON's is the best source for what we know of the details of Fuller's life and times. Even though Higginson was a childhood friend, he places less emphasis on romanticizing Fuller's personality and more on the specific details of the American phase of her life.

Although STERN's work falls into the same category of semi-fictional biography as several of those previously mentioned, this book, according to bibliographer Joel Myerson in his *Mar-*

garet Fuller: A Secondary Bibliography (New York, B. Franklin, 1977), has "the most detailed and best researched life of Fuller" and it is particularly "strong in describing Fuller's environment." He further writes, "[Stern's] biography is best for published material on people and events surrounding Fuller (through 1942) but occasionally specific items in the text are nearly impossible to trace in the general bibliographical notations." A later work by CHIPPERFIELD falls into the sentimental category; it idealizes Fuller's personality as a romantic heroine while often ignoring the wider critical, social, historical, and political contexts. Although the book has been described by some reviewers as "an excellent character study," others have complained of its "gushing sentimentality."

WADE's biography has been criticized for its pseudo-Freudian analyses of Fuller's sexual and political enlightenment in Italy, or what Wade terms her "feminization," and his neglect of some of the difficulties in her life that feminists would label essential to any biography. Bibliographer Myerson described it as a "good introductory biography" but reviewers called it "uneven," particularly in Wade's rendering of the Italian years.

Fuller's feminism holds analytical potential and becomes critically important to later feminist biographers. By far one of the most useful such studies is CHEVIGNY's, which includes not only a biography but a selection of writings by Fuller, commentaries by contemporaries on Fuller, and excellent bibliographical references. This collection is designed to "trace the struggle to conceive and act out of free womanhood." Chevigny examines carefully the many identities Fuller assumed in an effort to self-actualize. Her roles as friend, transcendentalist, teacher, editor, literary critic, feminist, social critic, journalist, and radical are discussed in individual chapters. Each chapter includes a wide variety of materials—reminiscences, journal entries, letters, fragments of fiction, essays, and reportage.

BLANCHARD seeks to examine "the life of a woman who in the past fought on a heroic scale against the open and hidden forces that worked against her in society . . ." Those patriarchal forces, which Blanchard contends still work against women today, become the focus in her analysis of Fuller's education, isolation, political and social activism and, most important, her distorted reputation. Blanchard argues that Fuller became a "legendary bogeywoman symbolizing a threat not only to the male ego, but to the family and thus to the social order." This biography seeks a deeper understanding of the differences between "the real and the phantom Margaret," and provides an extensive discussion of Fuller's transcendentalism, social activism, and her Italian years.

ALLEN's biography is mainly concerned with Fuller's ideas and her achievements. Through her research, Allen discovered the "sometimes deliberate obfuscation" of Fuller's reputation, and she devotes an entire chapter to exploring the creation of the "Myth of Margaret Fuller." Allen correctly argues that Fuller has been relatively unnoticed as a woman of ideas since her death. Other biographies, she contends, romanticized her life and the tragedy of her death. Chapter II explores the reasons for this disproportionate neglect. Allen states that Fuller's papers had been mishandled from the start, some destroyed by Carlyle at Emerson's request, others "ruthlessly bluepenciled, chopped and altered by Emerson, Channing and Clarke."

WATSON structured his study in an attempt to clarify "critical and historiographical problems" that have made Fuller "a victim of successive and contradictory acts of appropriation and partial reinterpretation.'' He believes her aims and her achievement have been distorted by certain groups of scholars—by the editors of the memoirs, by contemporary critics and artists like Hawthorne and James, by her biographers in the more sympathetic tradition of Higginson through Chippenfield, and by the feminist scholars of the last decade. With this in mind, he has framed his study by separating analyses of Fuller's life, work, and reputation to allow her to "speak for herself." He examines her roles as romanticist, feminist, journalist, and socialist. Although he often criticizes the feminist scholarship, he borrows freely from their works to create this mostly derivative work.

—Maria F. Bruno

GAINSBOROUGH, Thomas, 1727–1788; English painter.

Hayes, John, *Gainsborough: Paintings and Drawings*. London, Phaidon Press, 1975.
Lindsay, Jack, *Thomas Gainsborough, His Life and Art*. New York, Granada, 1982.
Waterhouse, Ellis, *Gainsborough*. London, Spring Books, 1958; revised 1966.
Whitley, William T., *Thomas Gainsborough*. London, J. Murray, and New York, Scribner, 1915.
Woodall, Mary, *Thomas Gainsborough, His Life and Work*. London, Pheonix House, and New York, Chanticleer Press, 1949.

*

Still considered to be a prime source is WHITLEY's 1915 life of Gainsborough, which, as John Hayes wrote, was "based on years of patient and immensely fruitful documentary research which . . . radically transformed Gainsborough studies" (*Apollo*, June 1982). Strictly biographical, by a writer who was essentially a chronicler, Whitley's volume made no claim to assess Gainsborough as an artist. It seems that in the interest of somehow protecting Gainsborough's reputation, Whitley left out or glossed over a considerable amount of evidence that the artist was, according to Ellis Waterhouse, "in spite of an endearing and recklessly kind-hearted nature, . . . basically a raffish and rather irresponsible person. An honest study of his letters make this clear enough'' (*Burlington Magazine*, March 1982).

Indispensable for a proper study and appreciation of Gainsborough and his art is WATERHOUSE's book which, in the words of one critic, is "so authoritative and lavishly illustrated as to seem calculated to discourage any undertaking on comparable lines" (*Apollo*, March 1986). It contains the most complete survey of his paintings and drawings in a single volume, almost all uniformly fine reproductions.

Both WOODALL and HAYES have written general art-and-life works in addition to their many individual specialized studies of Gainsborough's oeuvre. Both have also edited volumes of his letters (Hayes' is still to appear), a *corpus* of which has been

compared to that of Gainsborough's brilliant contemporary, Laurence Sterne. An intimate familiarity with his writings greatly affects each of these biographies, lending an immediacy to the texts. Hayes, in particular, has "let [Gainsborough] speak in his own words, often idiosyncratic but wholly to the point.''

Hayes' survey is the more up-to-date, encompassing the results of his research for individual *catalogue raisonées* of Gainsborough's drawings, prints, and landscapes. As Hayes states in the introduction, he "sought to bring into focus, from the various detailed studies of aspects of his work I have made over the last twenty years, my feelings about Gainsborough, both as man and artist." He has succeeded. The chapter on Gainsborough's personality is unparalleled in the literature. If there be any criticism, it would be for the almost unceasing lavish praise heaped upon the artist.

Critics, including Waterhouse and Hayes, have been uniform in their praise of LINDSAY's book, which is both a biography and an art historical assessment. Though he does not reveal any new material, Lindsay takes into account all previous literature and writes in a lively style. The most difficult of Lindsay's hypotheses concerns the most personal of Gainsborough's art, his landscapes. In his review, Hayes cautions the reader that what Lindsay has to say about the landscapes, much of it derived from the highly controversial ideas of Ronald Paulson, needs further study. For those who want to see the paintings and drawings referred to so eloquently in Lindsay's text, a copy of Waterhouse and the catalogues of Hayes are necessary accompaniments.

—Faya Causey

GALILEO [Galileo Galilei], 1564–1642; Italian astronomer and physicist.

Allan-Olney, Mary, *The Private Life of Galileo*. Philadelphia, Keystone, 1869; London, Macmillan, 1870.
Brodrick, James, S. J., *Galileo: The Man, His Work, His Misfortunes*. New York, Harper, 1964.
De Santillana, Giorgio, *The Crime of Galileo*. Chicago, University of Chicago Press, 1955.
Drake, Stillman, *Galileo at Work: His Scientific Biography*. Chicago, University of Chicago Press, 1978.
Drake, Stillman, *Galileo*. Oxford, Oxford University Press, and New York, Hill and Wang, 1980.
Fahie, John J., *Galileo, His Life and Work*. New York, J. Pott, and London, J. Murray, 1903.
Gebler, Karl von, *Galileo Galilei and the Roman Curia*, translated by Mrs. George Sturge. London, C. K. Paul, 1879 (originally published in 2 vols. by J. G. Cotta, Stuttgart, 1877).
Geymonat, Ludovico, *Galileo Galilei: A Biography and Inquiry into His Philosophy of Science*, translated by Stillman Drake. New York, McGraw-Hill, 1965 (originally published by G. Einaudi, Turin, 1957).
Redondi, Pietro, *Galileo: Heretic*, translated by Raymond Rosenthal. Princeton, New Jersey, Princeton University Press, 1987; London, A. Lane, 1988 (originally published by G. Einaudi, Turin, 1983).

Ronan, Colin A., *Galileo*. London, Weidenfeld and Nicolson, and New York, Putnam, 1974.

Taylor, F. S., *Galileo and the Freedom of Thought*. London, Watts, 1938.

*

Galileo was controversial during his lifetime, and the debate around him has continued unabated in the three-and-a-half centuries since his death. At issue are three central questions: to what extent did Galileo *prove* the superiority of the Copernican system to that of Ptolemy? did he actually perform most of the physical experiments he describes in his writings? how and why did his condemnation by the Roman Inquisition come about? His biographers all have their opinions about these issues, and this lends a polemical air to many biographies. Protestant historians, for example, have often used Galileo as a stick with which to flog Papists and Inquisitors in the name of Reason; some Catholic apologists have portrayed Galileo as a strong-headed fanatic whose hubris eventually attracts the reluctant participation of a harried Roman curia.

Many of the earlier biographies are little short of hagiographic. All of the pre-20th-century biographies are dated; the only one of them that still has any real interest is that of ALLAN-OLNEY, which (as its title specifies) is based primarily on the letters between Galileo and his daughter. Allan-Olney quotes these letters at great length, infusing character and color into a man who is so often portrayed as aloof and impersonal. The other early biographies, even GEBLER's careful analysis of Galileo's trial, have been superseded, particularly in light of the wealth of new Galileo research available to the 20th-century scholar.

FAHIE is the first biographer to have access to the complete edition of Galileo's works, edited by Antonio Favaro (*Opere*, 20 vols., Florence, 1890–1909). His biography is marred by a number of rather minor factual errors, and perhaps even more so by his portrayal of Galileo's clash with the Church, which he focuses on to the detriment of Galileo's earlier life. In Fahie's view the Church silenced Galileo on account of a stubborn refusal to recognize the obvious truth of the Copernican system; it was his punishment for showing the Church its own ridiculousness. His Galileo is aloof and haughty, contemptuous of the Pope and his men.

TAYLOR's work serves as something of a corrective to this view. For Taylor, it is Galileo's method, not the substance of his teachings, that gets him into trouble. Galileo is the "apostle of the scientific method," who was fighting "the battle for the freedom of thought." Taylor's biography is less focused on Galileo's trial and its aftermath, more on the development of his thought. He portrays Galileo as an "exact and scrupulous experimentalist." While acknowledging that some scientists (e.g., Tycho Brahe) opposed Copernicus on sound scientific grounds, Taylor blames Galileo's persecution on Dominican and Jesuit intellectuals who saw in his *Dialogues concerning the Two Principal Systems of the World* "a challenge which could not be answered by argument and must be smothered by force, if their system was to survive."

DE SANTILLANA's account focuses on the trial and on what led up to it. For him, it is not the Church per se that persecuted Galileo, but jealous enemies in the intellectual establishment—in particular, rival university professors. Galileo was resented not only because his ideas in physics and astronomy threatened the very foundation of the Aristotelian system, but also (perhaps even more so) because he circumvented the academic bureaucracies by writing, in simple Italian, treatises that were seen to lampoon the theories of leading intellectuals. Jesuit academics are here the main culprits; they make the inquisitorial censors drag their feet in granting Galileo permission to publish the *Dialogues*. They compel Pope Urban VIII into taking action against Galileo, while the pope himself is naively duped. The Church becomes the unwitting pawn of academic in-fighting.

The Jesuit BRODRICK seems to have written, to an extent, as a reply to De Santillana's charges against his order. He focuses on Galileo's astronomy (to the detriment of his physics) and portrays him as a "crusader for Copernicanism" who came to Rome naively expecting to convert the Church. Galileo used "underhanded maneuvers" to obtain the censor's permission to publish the *Dialogues*, and thus "hoodwinked" Urban, who, being "a very proud prelate," brought his large store of personal wrath down on Galileo's head. Urban, "of whom so little good can be said," is the culprit here; the Jesuits are innocent bystanders.

GEYMONAT's position is perhaps more balanced than that of any of his predecessors. His study is part biography, part inquiry into Galileo's role in the history of philosophy. He makes no attempt to excuse the Church's intransigence, but he puts it into the context of the religious and political concerns of Urban VIII's papacy. Geymonat also takes pains to point out that those who supported the Ptolemaic system over the Copernican had reason not to be convinced by Galileo's arguments; in the context of 16th-century astronomy, Copernicus' system created as many problems as it solved. The phenomenon Galileo considered as the most convincing proof of the earth's rotation—the tides—are in fact caused not by the earth's movement but by the gravitational attraction of the moon and sun; here the pre-Galileo theory was much closer to the truth.

DRAKE is one of the foremost names in modern Galileo scholarship; most of his numerous articles and books deal with Galileo, and his numerous translations include many of Galileo's works as well as Geymonat's biography. In addition, he has produced two of the best and most readable biographies available. *Galileo at Work* (1978) is a 400-page study of the man and the development of his scientific ideas. *Galileo* (1980) is a brief (100-page) overview of his life; it contains a good bibliography of available books in English. Both of these books are well written, and Drake is very much on top of the scholarship. He does an excellent job of throwing cold water on the excesses of both the traditional hagiographers and some of the revisionists. Galileo, he makes clear, was not a "Copernican zealot": his earliest works, in fact, attempted to *refute* Copernicus, and he showed no signs of belief in the sun-centered system before the age of 30. Galileo was not a modern empiricist in an Aristotelian wilderness; important advances in scientific theory had been made throughout the Middle Ages, and Galileo's contemporaries were not all idiots and Aristotle-worshippers. Nevertheless, as Drake points out, his differences with the intellectual establishment of the time were broad and fundamental; his physical experiments and his astronomical observations undermined Aristotelian orthodoxy in both method and substance. However, he was neither irreligious nor anti-clerical; he long enjoyed the friendship and protection of important members of the Jesuits and the Papal curia. He certainly did not pick a fight with the Church. Some of Drake's defenses of Galileo against revisionists seem, however, to go too far; there certainly were problems with some of his theories (e.g., that of the tides); some of the experiments he describes do not, in fact, work the way he describes them. Drake seems at times to take umbrage at the sullying of Galileo's name; at points the reader is left wishing for an objective weighing of the facts instead of an impassioned defense of the great man. As to Galileo's condemnation by the Inquisition, Drake takes a slightly modified tack on De Santillana's thesis. Galileo's real enemies were the Aristotelian professors of philosophy, who saw him trying to destroy their whole intellectual structure. Since the only way to silence Galileo was through the Church, it was these philosophers who first attacked Copernicanism and who persuaded Rome to take action against Galileo.

RONAN has produced a lavishly illustrated, informative, and well-written account for the general reader. He avoids trying to apportion blame for Galileo's tribulations, instead presenting them in terms of his age and his personality. Ronan succeeds in making the story compelling, though readers who really wish to understand Galileo's scientific ideas will be left unsatisfied. "Not only does he omit technical aspects of Galileo's work in astronomy," writes I. B. Cohen (*Times Literary Supplement*, 2 May 1975), "but he glosses over Galileo's most fundamental contributions to science, his conceptual reformation of the principles of motion. The presentation of Galileo's immediate predecessors and teachers as slavish followers of Aristotle is not only out of date by many decades; it so belittles his opponents as to give a false picture of his real intellectual achievement."

One recent book, though not strictly a biography, is worth citing for its novel approach to the issue of Galileo's trial and condemnation. REDONDI claims it was not Galileo's Copernicanism at all that got him in trouble with the Inquisition; it was rather his atomistic physics, which indirectly undermined the principles of the Transubstantiation (i.e., the conversion of the bread and wine of the Eucharist into the body and blood of Christ). This, Redondi points out, seems a minor issue to us today; it is, however, one of the central doctrines of the Catholic church and was far more important to Rome than was all of Aristotle's cosmology. While many Galileo scholars remain unconvinced by Redondi's thesis, it has sparked another round of fascinating (and often heated) debate around the ever-controversial Galileo.

—John Tolan

GALSWORTHY, John, 1867–1933; English writer.

Barker, Dudley, *The Man of Principle: A View of John Galsworthy.* London, Heinemann, and New York, London House and Maxwell, 1963.

Dupré, Catherine, *John Galsworthy: A Biography.* London, Collins, and New York, Coward McCann, 1976.

Fréchet, Alec, *John Galsworthy: A Reassessment,* translated by Denis Mahaffey. London, Macmillan, and New York, Barnes and Noble, 1982.

Gindin, James, *John Galsworthy's Life and Art: An Alien's Fortress.* London, Macmillan, and Ann Arbor, University of Michigan Press, 1987.

Marrot, Harold V., *Life and Letters of John Galsworthy.* London, Heinemann, 1935; New York, Scribner, 1936.

Sauter, Rudolf, *Galsworthy the Man: An Intimate Portrait.* London, P. Owen, 1967.

*

BARKER, like most of Galsworthy's biographers, uses the earlier authorised biographies by MARROT (the "official biography" published in 1935, a eulogistic work written with the assistance of Galsworthy's wife), and of R. H. Mottram, a long-standing friend (*For Some We Have Loved,* London, 1936), neither now readily available. Barker's printed sources also include M. E. Reynolds' *Memories of John Galsworthy* (1936) and the memoirs of Galsworthy's wife Ada. He is informative on Galsworthy's marriage to Ada but does not comment on Galsworthy's relationship with Margaret Morris, the actress and dancer who acted in and directed some of Galsworthy's plays. Their correspondence and her book about it (*My Galsworthy Story,* 1967), are revealing sources which are used by Dupré (see below), who traces the complexities of Galsworthy's apparently straight-forward life.

SAUTER, Galsworthy's nephew, offers a more personal tribute, promoting the image of Galsworthy as the blameless and upright man. Sauter was very close to Galsworthy, traveled with him, and was almost a surrogate son. His sources are the many letters Galsworthy wrote to him in his boyhood and youth, and also those Galsworthy wrote to his niece Vi. Sauter's views on those of Galsworthy's works that were considered to be based on his own family and his wife Ida's first marriage are of interest; the family did not wish Galsworthy to publish them lest they be considered *romans à clef.* Despite Sauter's claim that he wishes to show Galsworthy's "inner self," his biography deals not with the inner but with the outer man.

DUPRÉ reconsiders Sauter's information and also uses the unpublished memoirs and letters of Mrs. Dorothy Ivens. Dupré stresses the significance of Galsworthy's early years, using the biographies of Marrot and Mottram for the schooldays of this serious youth, but she corrects details concerning Ada Galsworthy's birth and background. She devotes considerable attention to the diary of Galsworthy's sister Lilian, remarking that "No other document gives so complete a picture of the family from which Galsworthy came." From the memoirs of his sister Agnes Ridgeway (*Elstree Memories*), Dupré discerns "almost alarming perfection of both character and appearance"; Dupré also incorporates the memoirs of Galsworthy's sister Mabel Reynolds. In addition to acknowledging the friendship and influence of such writers as Joseph Conrad, Edward Garnett, and Ford Madox Ford, Dupré cites as the dominant influence of Galsworthy's life his wife Ida, quoting letters, unpublished love poems, and Galsworthy's first novel, *Jocelyn* (1898), to good effect. Ada's notebook provides a picture of the marriage and of the society they moved in.

The "Reassessment" offered by FRÉCHET is mainly of Galsworthy's work, but he also reconsiders aspects of Galsworthy's life, such as "Galsworthy the Sportsman" (Chapter 3). GINDIN, like Dupré, is interested in the "complexity and uneasiness behind Galsworthy's public stance.'' He sees him as an ''outsider,'' and illustrates widely from the Galsworthy Memorial Collection and from Rudolf Sauter's material in the University of Birmingham (from which permission to quote was only given in 1975). Gindin sees Galsworthy's career as neither a triumph (as did Marrot) nor a tragic decline after initial success (as did Dupré). Gindin does not oversimplify complexities, and he usefully reassesses Galsworthy's career, political opinions, critical reception, finances, and reading at each stage of his life. He sees the Margaret Morris episode as evidence of Galsworthy's ''constantly subdued kind of sexuality,'' and considers Galsworthy to be ''separable into three different identities'': the public, hardworking philanthropist, the sceptical, bitter man, and the private persona lived only within his fiction.

—Barbara Hayley

———————

GALT, John, 1779–1839; Scottish writer and Canadian coloniser.

Aberdein, Jennie W., *John Galt*. London, Oxford University Press, 1936.
Aldrich, Ruth I., *John Galt*. Boston, Twayne, 1978.
Gordon, Robert K., *John Galt*. Toronto, University of Toronto Library, 1920.
Gordon, Ian A., *John Galt: The Life of a Writer*. Edinburgh, Oliver & Boyd, and Toronto, University of Toronto Press, 1972.
Moir, David Macbeth (''Delta''), *Biographical Memoir of John Galt*. Edinburgh, Ballantyne and Hughes, 1841.
Scott, Paul Henderson, *John Galt*. Edinburgh, Scottish Academic Press, 1985.
Timothy, Hamilton Baird, *The Galts: A Canadian Odyssey: John Galt, 1779–1839*. Toronto, McClelland and Stewart, 1977.

*

Galt published his *Autobiography of John Galt* in 1833, and his *Literary Life* in 1834. The first concentrates on his career as a colonist, the second on his literary works; both are sometimes inaccurate, but the autobiographies will remain the main source on which any biographies are based. For almost 80 years MOIR's was the only biography of Galt of any standing; Moir knew Galt well, and finished one of his novels for him when Galt was called to Canada. Moir's memoir, often prefixed to Blackwood's editions of Galt's novels, is full of long extracts from Galt's letters to Moir, including letters from Canada. It is well written and balanced, and remains the best short appreciation of Galt's life.

The first serious biography this century, by R. K. GORDON, concentrates on Galt's career with the Canada Company, and much of his work was done from the primary sources available in Toronto; the Canada Company only ceased trading in 1956 when it sold its last acre of land. This book is really a work of historical research, and has few comments evaluating Galt's literary productions; R. K. Gordon was not familiar with many of

Galt's stories and articles in periodicals, yet his book contains information unavailable elsewhere and is admirably concise.

ABERDEIN's remains the best and fullest biography of Galt, and has not been superseded by Ian A. Gordon's book as P. H. Scott suggests. Aberdein captures her subject and provides one of the very few books on Galt that is a pleasure to read, as well as being scholarly and accurate. She used many primary sources, some of which are no longer available, and she is the only writer who has added much to our knowledge of Galt's early life. She also comments on almost every aspect of Galt's career, and her literary judgments are usually sound. She is perhaps slightly too close to her subject and is insufficiently critical of Galt's failings. A genealogy, chronology, and appendices are included, and all are useful; in all, she talks sense, and writes well.

IAN A. GORDON's biography is now the standard reference work. It is admirably economical and accurate and contains much bibliographical information. Ian Gordon has a prodigious talent for organising and communicating facts, and he draws on a great deal of unpublished correspondence. He admits that Galt's extra-literary activities are outside his scope and concentrates on Galt's relationship with his publishers. Gordon does not provide as distinct a psychological portrait of Galt as does Aberdein, and Galt's observation ''I shall not be justly dealt with if I am considered merely as a literary man'' needs to be kept in mind. Gordon also tends, like many Scottish critics, to think Galt is only at his best when dealing with Scottish subjects and settings. Nonetheless, Gordon has done more for Galt studies than anyone else in the last 50 years; fresh biographical information is contained in several of his editions of Galt's novels.

TIMOTHY is a classicist, and the structure of his books and articles on Galt is unusual. However, his odd methods have their benefits, as his biography contains information that other scholars have overlooked (e.g., about Galt's first love, Miss Hamilton). The book is a psychobiography of Galt as an heroic Canadian, and Timothy is not always objective, perhaps because he himself is distinctly related to Galt and hails from Galt's birthplace, Irvine. He undoubtedly knows more about living members of the Galt family and their collections than anyone else; but his insights are often insufficiently documented, although his book was not aimed at a specialist audience. His biography was followed by a second volume on two of Galt's descendants.

ALDRICH's book has the look of a commissioned work, but what it lacks in enthusiasm it makes up for by its workmanlike approach. Aldrich gives summaries of most of Galt's works and of the critical response to them, making her book the best means of getting an overview of what Galt wrote, much of which is hard to find. Aldrich does not appear to have used primary sources to any great extent, but her summaries prove that she has read most of Galt's myriad works—something few writers have done. Her work's main limitation, apart from its lack of original material, is that Galt's numerous periodical contributions are hardly mentioned.

SCOTT's sketch is short but sound and has a useful chapter on Galt's North American and political novels. Aldrich's book gives more detail, but Scott is more engaged, handles his material with greater verve, and places Galt in context more effectively. This is a good book for students of Scottish literature, though it adds little new information.

—Nick Whistler

GAMA, Vasco da, *ca*. 1460–1524; Portuguese navigator.

Hart, Henry H., *Sea Road to the Indies: An Account of the Voyages and Exploits of the Portuguese Navigators, together with the Life and Times of Dom Vasco Da Gama.* New York, Macmillan, 1950; London, W. Hodge, 1952.

Ravenstein, E. G., editor and translator, *A Journal of the First Voyage of Vasco da Gama 1497–99.* London, Hakluyt Society, 1898.

Sanceau, Elaine, *Good Hope: The Voyage of Vasco da Gama.* Lisbon, Academia Internacional da Cultura Portuguesa, 1967.

Stanley, Henry E. J., editor and translator, *The Three Voyages of Vasco da Gama and His Viceroyalty.* London, Hakluyt Society, 1869.

*

The accounts of Vasco da Gama by SANCEAU and HART are limited in scope and in scholarly appeal, and the level of interpretation is unsophisticated. Sanceau has retold the story of the 1497–99 voyage contained in the *Journal* in a readable but popular form. Hart has included da Gama in a survey of Portuguese explorers of the 15th and 16th centuries. Hart tells a story of high adventure, replete with colorful imagery and dramatic writing style. Particularly effective are his descriptions of the wharves of Lisbon and ports of call on the road to the Indies and the exotica of the Orient. Little attempt is made to assess the legacy of this voyage on East-West relations, its impact on the exchange of commodities between Asia and Europe, or an evaluation of his viceroyalty. Nor does Hart dwell on the intrusive role of the Portuguese, let alone the inauguration of what the Indian historian K. M. Panikkar referred to as the "da Gama epoch" of Asian history from 1498 until 1949 characterized by a strong European presence.

The reader is strongly recommended to turn to the original accounts of da Gama's voyages, translated from the Portuguese and available in Hakluyt Society editions that are annotated and include explanatory maps. STANLEY and RAVENSTEIN have produced readable, scholarly editions. The former's is a translation from the *Lendas da India* of the Portuguese historian Gaspar Corrêa, who had firsthand knowledge of India but whose accuracy on the first two voyages may be questioned. Ravenstein completed the first translation into English of the *Roteiro da Viagem* and the appendices, maps, and footnotes are excellent. Clearly there is a need for a well-researched biography, unavailable even in Portuguese, of this remarkable man.

—A.J. R. Russell-Wood

GANDHI, Indira, 1917–1984; prime minister of India, daughter of Jawaharlal Nehru.

Agrawal, C.P., *Indira Gandhi (Then and Now) and Janata.* Chandausi, Hindustan Exporters/Vivek Prakashan, 1978.

Alexander, Mithrapuram K., *Indira Gandhi: An Illustrated Biography.* New Delhi, New Light Publishers, 1968.

Basu, Nirmal Kumar, *Indira of India, Glimpses of Life and Work.* Calcutta, Sanskrit Pustak Bhandar, 1972; as *Indira Invincible,* 1981.

Bhatia, Krishan, *Indira, a Biography of Prime Minister Gandhi.* New York, Praeger, and London, Angus and Robertson, 1974.

Birla, K.K., *Indira Gandhi, Reminiscences.* New Delhi, Vikas, and London, Sangam, 1987.

Carras, Mary C., *Indira Gandhi in the Crucible of Leadership: A Political Biography.* Boston, Beacon Press, 1979.

Drieberg, Trevor, *Indira Gandhi, a Profile in Courage.* New Delhi, Vikas, 1972; New York, Drake, 1973.

Hutheesing, Krishna (Nehru), *Dear To Behold: An Intimate Portrait of Indira Gandhi.* New York, Macmillan, 1969.

Malhotra, Inder, *Indira Gandhi, a Personal and Political Biography.* London, Hodder and Stoughton, 1989.

Masani, Zareer, *Indira Gandhi, a Biography.* London, Hamilton, 1975; New York, T.Y. Crowell, 1976.

Mohan, Anand, *Indira Gandhi, a Personal and Political Biography.* New York, Hawthorne, 1967.

Moraes, Dom F., *Indira Gandhi.* Boston, Little Brown, 1980.

Pande, B.N., *Indira Gandhi.* New Delhi, Publications Division, Government of India, 1989.

Sahgal, Nayantara, *Indira Gandhi: Her Road To Power.* New York, Ungar, 1982; London, Macdonald, 1983.

Sahota, Sohan Singh, *Indira Gandhi, a Political Biography.* Jullundur, New Academic Publishing, 1972.

Sarin, L.N., *Indira Gandhi, a Political Biography.* New Delhi, S. Chand, 1974.

*

A year before her assassination, Indira Gandhi grumbled that "she was unable to recommend" a single biography of herself to any of her friends or relatives, dismissing, in short, the hundreds of books written about her, many by staunch admirers. Since the vast majority of her biographies are hagiography at best, propaganda at worst, she obviously had discriminating taste.

Few political leaders have been as written about in their own lifetime as Indira Gandhi. Of course the fact that she attained the highest office in a land where women are at best second-class citizens excited universal interest and admiration. She also governed a teeming subcontinent, one of broiling passions and insoluble problems. Throughout her long prime ministership (1966 to 1984, re-elected three times and out of office for over a year), she cut a striking figure in her brilliantly colored saris, perpetually the center of controversy, through her own fault or that of others.

Upon Indira Gandhi's election in 1966 to the same office as her father had held, a stream of books about the relatively unknown daughter came out in India and abroad to satisfy curiosity about her. Among them, Indian political journalist MOHAN alone did her justice. Admitting that "very little documentation" existed on her life, he nevertheless managed in three months to interview numerous individuals who knew her, including Indira Gandhi herself. The result is a carefully written, authoritative history of her life, which coincides in so many ways with the history of modern India. Her father, Jawaharlal Nehru, her grandfather, Motilal, and Mahatma Gandhi (no relation of hers) were the founders of modern India. As the daughter, granddaughter, and friend of such illustrious men, Indira Gandhi was drawn into the Indian independence movement from the age of four. Mohan skillfully draws a picture of the rich but lonely girl, who was expected to throw her Western dolls and clothing into a bonfire because they were foreign made; who witnessed the arrests of her parents and grandfather, and whose childhood and youth were abnormal and chaotic. It is a sympathetic portrait of a woman newly elected to office, without exaggeration; but it is lacking in balance, and fails to prepare one to understand her later mistakes as prime minister and her obvious weaknesses.

This imbalance runs like a thread throughout most of her biographies. Indira Gandhi's aunt, Krishna Nehru HUTHEESING (Nehru's sister), published her *Dear to Behold, an Intimate Portrait* ("Dear To Behold," in Hindi, was in fact Indira Gandhi's second or middle name). This work is engagingly written—Hutheesing is a well-established author in her own right—and, like Mohan's secondhand account, is sympathetic without being sentimental. Hutheesing's memoirs are valuable as one of the few primary source accounts of Indira Gandhi's life.

Absorbing as her aunt's reminiscences may be, Hutheesing is too over-protective to be fully objective. A similar drawback can be found in the work of ALEXANDER. Although an educator and Indian political activist, Alexander has done little more than write a simple narrative of Indira's complex life, endowing her with heroic dimensions. Surprisingly, English author and journalist DRIEBERG's volume published several years later, scarcely improves upon Alexander's treatment of his subject. Although an expert on Indian politics and a journalist in India, Drieberg's account is superficial, not based on interviews with those who knew her or with the prime minister herself, and written in an unusually (for a journalist) plodding style. He does not impugn the stereotype that Nehru deliberately groomed his daughter to be his successor, or the (by then) ample criticism of her policies. The sole merit of this book lies in its close, first-hand analysis of the 1966 election that brought Indira Gandhi to power.

Neither SAHOTA nor BASU rises above the level of blatant propaganda in their respective volumes, published in the same year. Some idea of the nature of Sahota's biography can be gleaned from the preface: "I shall not be exaggerating if I say that she is the greatest woman that the world has produced so far." But this comment is outdone by Basu's inarticulately composed remark, "Every Indian and every student of world politics are interested to know her life, which has always been very charming but potent in ingoings right from the beginning" (from a man who claimed to know Indira Gandhi for 33 years). These propagandistic writings nevertheless are indicative of the mood or mindset of many of the educated Indians in that time, and should not be dismissed out of hand; neither should the equally inflated biography by SARIN, well-known political writer in India. Like so many others, this biography begins promisingly, persuading the reader to think that what follows is a balanced, critical study of the famed Prime Minister Gandhi, only to realize that it is no different than the usual one-dimensional flattery.

Unlike the preceding three biographers, however, Sarin has considerable expertise in the highly complicated subject of Indian politics, although his book is still far from being a scholarly work. BHATIA's work is far better in terms of syntax and research, but still mainly a re-hash of well-known facts about Indira Gandhi.

Nearly ten years after Anand Mohan's biography appeared, MASANI published a probing account of Indira Gandhi's life. This unassuming title belies a work that is surprisingly (considering the author's youthfulness) understanding, proving that, as in Mohan's case, a good biography of a woman is not necessarily written by a woman. While the quality of this young Oxford graduate student's writing is below the par of Mohan's, this is made up for in the balanced perspective it offers of its subject, a perspective regrettably absent in previous biographies. Masani considers (unlike some other biographers, who have cited several examples of strong women rulers in ancient and medieval Indian history), that the lot of Indian women has been one of "total subjugation," and he depicts Indira Gandhi as an exception to the rule, although even her own youth and happiness were sacrificed on the altar of the Indian independence struggle. It is interesting to learn that Indira Gandhi was no intellectual, as her father had been; that Oxford had been "irrelevant" to her as a student, and that her marriage to Feroze Gandhi (no relation to the Mahatma) had been a failure possibly as much through her own fault as his. Masani's book would be a well-balanced, solid work were it not for the unevenness of its writing, its indulgence in trivial details, and its self-evident statements. While not biography at its best, it is one of the best of Indira Gandhi.

In June 1975, Indira Gandhi declared an internal state of emergency that lasted 19 months, a move that even her admirers deplored. Her assumption in that time of dictatorial power, the arrest of opposition leaders, and her son Sanjay's emergence as the unpopular Heir Apparent, unleashed a flood of books about her, many of which were highly critical despite official censorship. No more captious a "biography" can be found than that by the law professor, AGRAWAL, ("Janata" in his title referring to the opposition party gathering momentum to unseat Indira Gandhi). Though the author insists that his book is not solely about the state of emergency but also "a reading into Mrs. Gandhi's character since her early childhood till uptodate" (sic), it fails as both biography and political analysis. His reason for writing his book alone leaves one wondering: the author's mother had appeared to him in a dream and directed him to write it. This biased, rambling, and disjointed work is more an illustration of the times and the feelings of educated Indians than a credible account of Indira Gandhi's life and politics. Far more astute and probing is the work by American political scientist CARRAS, also written during the period of emergency rule. Of the plethora of books on Indira Gandhi, only Carras attempts to write a political psychobiography, the book's chief weakness. Not a trained psychologist, Carras makes statements and draws conclusions that are highly speculative. Nevertheless, her vignettes of Indira Gandhi are intriguing, having spent two years in India researching her book, where she also befriended her subject. On the whole, while not for the general reader, Carras' account can be an indispensable source to the serious biographer, though once again it is written by a decided admirer of Indira Gandhi.

Just as indispensable a biography is the work by Indira Gandhi's cousin, SAHGAL, an Indian intellectual and writer whose book emerged out of a paper she delivered at the University of London. Though well-written, it is a tendentious work, doubtless stemming from the fact that Sahgal's mother, Madam Pandit, had been ill-disposed to Indira Gandhi from the moment of her birth by virtue of her intense dislike of Indira Gandhi's mother. Madam Pandit felt slighted and ignored by her famous niece when she assumed the Prime Ministership (an office that this sister of Nehru felt rightfully should belong to her). Yet if some of the facts in this partisan book are true, future biographers definitely will glimpse another side of Indira Gandhi that no other biography (not the most blatantly hostile, which are too emotional to take seriously) reveals.

By far the most beautifully written, intensely vivid, and highly readable biography of Indira Gandhi written in her lifetime is by MORAES. Yet if Gandhi as late as 1983 was dissatisfied with all of her biographies, it is not too difficult to discern why even Moraes is lacking. While he knew his subject and interviewed her on numerous occasions (he found her far more interesting out of office, after her defeat in the elections, than in), he reveals nothing new, except perhaps a despondent Indira Gandhi out of office determined to make a comeback, which she did in 1980. She would most likely have objected to Moraes' depiction of her marriage as her own fault since she had had too little time for her husband Feroze. The author also maintains the usual stereotype of "powerful" Indian women rulers in the past and, once again, upholds the popular view that Nehru had consciously groomed Indira as his successor, with her unquestioning support.

Moraes' work would be surpassed after her assassination in 1984, when a whole new series of works about her was unleashed. Once again they are panegyrics, predictably depicting Indira Gandhi as a martyr and heroine. PANDE's cut-and-dried official biography is no exception. More useful is the volume by BIRLA (son of the industrialist at whose mansion Mahatma Gandhi was assassinated in 1974), which is by no means probing and analytical, but important because of the paucity of authoritative memoirs of the late prime minister. Hardly any biography discusses the highly negative role of her younger son Sanjay in her administration, and Birla, a personal friend of Sanjay's before the latter's death in a stunt flying accident in 1980, is revealing of the personality and character of the "Crown Prince."

Outshining all biographies, however, is the definitive work, appearing five years after Indira Gandhi's assassination, by Indian political journalist, pundit, and critic, MALHOTRA.

Malhotra's purpose, " . . . to break the cycle of hagiography and demonology and present her life story in its entirety," is fulfilled brilliantly. A witness to most of the events he describes and a personal friend of Indira Gandhi's estranged husband Feroze, Malhotra bases his book on at least 30 "off the record" conversations with his subject in her lifetime, and includes the newly published, highly revealing correspondence between Indira Gandhi and a close personal American friend, Dorothy Norman. Hence there is much that is new and original in this work. For instance, we learn that Indira Gandhi went to live with her father not because she wanted to be near the seat of power or because of his desire to groom her for his office, but to escape a miserable marriage to a very likeable but crude man, a skirt chaser who was insanely jealous of his wife's connections and growing success in political life. Malhotra also reveals that the long widowed Nehru had carried on a lengthy liaison with the

wife of the last Viceroy of India, Lord Mountbatten. He also uses Indira Gandhi's letters to Dorothy Norman to prove that the furthest thing from her mind and desires was to become prime minister after her father's death. Unlike other biographers, Malhotra analyzes in depth the deleterious effect of her son Sanjay's influence on Indian politics, a son whom she loved blindly and to whom she could deny nothing. Malhotra criticizes not only Sanjay but the "shenanigans of the goons who became his devotees," as well as his wife, Maneka, who detested her mother-in-law. There is much revealing and original material in this deftly written, scintillating work, whose perspective of the colorful, complex Indira Gandhi is a balanced as it is free from judgment. This is a must for the general reader and the serious biographer as a book that finally does Indira Gandhi justice.

—Sina Dubovoj

GANDHI, Mohandas Karamchand ["Mahatma"], 1869–1948; Indian political and spiritual leader.

Ashe, Geoffrey, *Gandhi*. New York, Stein and Day, and London, Heinemann, 1968.

Brown, Judith M., *Gandhi, Prisoner of Hope*. New Haven, Connecticut, and London, Yale University Press, 1989.

Doke, Joseph, J., *M. K. Gandhi, An Indian Patriot in South Africa*. London, London Indian Chronicle, 1909.

Fischer, Louis, *The Life of Mahatma Gandhi*. New York, Harper, 1950; London, Cape, 1951.

Mehta, Ved, *Mahatma Gandhi and His Apostles*. New York, Viking, 1976; London, Penguin, 1977.

Nehru, Jawaharlal, *Mahatma Gandhi*. Calcutta, Signet, 1949; London, Asia Publishing House, 1965.

Payne, Robert, *The Life and Death of Mahatma Gandhi*. New York, Dutton, and London, Bodley Head, 1969.

Pyarelal (Pyarelal Nair), *Mahatma Gandhi* (5 vols.). Ahmedabad, Navajivan Publishing, 1956–86 (vol. 4, subtitled *The Discovery of Satyagraha*, published by Sevak Prakashan, Bombay, 1980).

Rolland, Romain, *Mahatma Gandhi, the Man Who Became One with the Universal Being*, translated by C. D. Groth. New York and London, Century, 1924 (originally published, Paris, 1923).

Shukla, Chandrashankar, editor, *Reminiscences of Gandhiji*. Bombay, Vora, 1951.

Tendulkar, D. G., *Mahatma, Life of Mohandas Karamchand Gandhi* (8 vols.). Bombay, 1951–54.

*

Indo-American author Ved Mehta (see below), writing about Gandhi in the mid-1970s, noted the existence of at least 400 biographies of the celebrated Mahatma (an honorific title that Gandhi disliked). Since then the number has risen despite the fact that, according to Gandhi's protégé Jawaharlal Nehru, "No one can write a biography of Gandhi, unless he is as big as Gandhi." This insurmountable obstacle did not prevent Nehru (see below) from authoring a biography of Gandhi, adding to the heap. While most biographers of eminent persons humbly state as their objective to demythologize their "larger than life" subjects, in the case of Gandhi, it is well nigh impossible to do so. Indeed biographers' attempts to portray and analyze his greatness invariably fall short and fail to do him justice, perhaps bearing out Nehru's caveat.

While still a young man in South Africa, where Gandhi single-handedly created the basis of his non-violent resistance movement, an obscure Baptist minister in Johannesburg, DOKE, wrote the first biography of Gandhi. A supporter of Gandhi's struggle to end South African oppression of Indians, Doke's 100-page biography (details of Gandhi's childhood and youth he obtained from interviewing him) is a heartfelt and loving tribute to an Indian and a non-Christian who Doke believed was following the will of God. Published in 1909, this intense, eloquent biography, written by an eyewitness of Gandhi's struggles in South Africa, had virtually no resonance abroad.

Awareness of Gandhi's remarkable achievements in South Africa still were confined to India, where Gandhi returned in 1914. In an age without television or satellite broadcasting, his worldwide renown was largely the result of the biography written by the famous man of letters, humanist, and left-wing French intellectual, Romain ROLLAND. Rolland admitted that he had never heard of Gandhi until 1920, when Indian friends informed him of the remarkable Gandhi whose non-violent resistance was rocking the foundations of British colonialism in India. Rolland began writing a series of biographical essays on Gandhi in the early 1920s, chiefly, he confessed, to generate interest in his new journal, *Europe*, where the articles first appeared (and which came out in book form in 1924). Interestingly, the book's eulogistic title belied the critical nature of its contents. Rolland turned out to be no blind admirer of Gandhi, and his book proved, as so many Gandhi biographies, that it was impossible to understand Gandhi. Partly because Gandhi's own account of his life had not yet appeared and Rolland's knowledge of Gandhi's early life and career were sketchy, the book is less a biography than a "critical appraisal" of Gandhism. Rolland's admiration for the Bolshevik Revolution of 1917 prevented him from embracing Gandhi's *ahimsa*, or non-violence. Similarly Rolland's uncritical approval of Western science and technology led him to portray Gandhi as a reactionary more suitable to the Middle Ages than to the progressive 20th century. Since Gandhi's views on virtually every subject were controversial, in India as well as in the West, a Rolland as well as a Nehru would have been shocked to realize that in the late 20th century, Gandhi's championing of village enterprise as opposed to large-scale industrialization, his "return to nature" philosophy and idiosyncratic insistence on recycling raw and household material would be widely acclaimed and accepted. Despite Rolland's typically Western criticism of Gandhi, he presented him in terms that Europeans could understand and admire: a champion of the oppressed (the Untouchables in India, the indentured Indians of South Africa) and a David triumphing over the Goliath of British imperialism. Within weeks of the appearance of Rolland's work, it became a best seller. To present day readers, it is hardly readable, with its rambling, sentimental style and impassioned defense of outdated ideas.

By the time Gandhi's own autobiography came out in serialized form in the late 1920s, his name had become a household word. Of the hundreds of biographies of Gandhi, his own account of his life stands out as perhaps the clearest and truest. *An Autobiography; or, The Story of My Experiments With Truth* (1927) is written in a distinctive spirit of sincere truthfulness and love that makes this book inspirational reading. Gandhi's gift for clarity and concision, for identifying with the evil as well as the good in others, enables the reader to feel the shame he felt when he left his dying father's side to quench his sexual appetite with his young wife; to relive the horror of his brutal physical assault by an angry white in South Africa for daring to ride in a horse-drawn carriage with other whites. Harsh at times though he may be on himself, Gandhi shows no misunderstanding of others, insensitivity, or self-vindication. His autobiography's engaging, humorous writing will enthrall the present day reader as much as it did those of a half century ago.

An avalanche of biographies and memoirs about Gandhi was unleashed after his assassination in 1948. Possibly Nehru was right in claiming that the utmost a writer could achieve in a biography of Gandhi was to conjure up pictures or vignettes of the great apostle of non-violence. Hence there exist no "definitive" biographies of Gandhi, although the best reveal truthful aspects of him and his life that augment our knowledge and help us understand his influence, even if we cannot understand Gandhi the person. Among those who attempted to convey his own vision of Gandhi was NEHRU. As the first prime minister of India after the country achieved independence in 1947, and the father of controversial Indira Gandhi, Nehru was at most a protégé of Gandhi rather than a true disciple. Nehru could not shed, as some of Gandhi's real disciples did, his cosmopolitanism, his Western education, his admiration for socialism and even Russian communism. It is a testimony to Gandhi's "larger than life" qualities that despite these major differences, even the proud, diffident Nehru was not immune to the love that flowed from Gandhi to him and to all who came in contact with him. Nehru's brief biography of Gandhi, written in a spirit of grief and bereavement shortly after Gandhi's death, is remarkable for the depth of love for Gandhi coming from the pen of a man who simply could not accept Gandhi's deep religiosity or, for that matter, his upholding of love and non-violence as the means to all ends. The fact that Nehru could not accept as universal the most fundamental principle of Gandhi's—non-violence—makes Gandhi, rather than Nehru, appear superhumanly tolerant and forgiving. While short on biographical details, Nehru's biography of Gandhi is must reading for the serious biographer, since Nehru was a dedicated follower of Gandhi in his struggle for Indian independence and possessed a personal knowledge of Gandhi's actions from 1916 (the year he first met Gandhi) onwards that few could match. While Nehru portrays Gandhi's greatness as lying mainly in his contribution to India's independence, he is objective enough to admit that Gandhi was impossible to understand—a "colossus."

Gandhi's death not only generated a stream of memoirs by his disciples and countless friends but gave rise to the two most comprehensive, detailed biographies of him, D. G. Tendulkar's weighty eight-volume work, followed by Pyarelal's five-volume account. It is difficult for Western readers to grasp or appreciate the enormous difficulties these Indian biographers faced doing research in a land where major research libraries did not even possess copies of leading Indian newspapers, where communication can be slow or non-existent, and where collecting research materials required a herculean effort. Yet both biographers not only surmounted these and many other difficulties but turned out very authoritative, and in the case of Pyarelal's five-volume study, readable biographies. Both biographers had been Gandhi's longtime disciples and dedicated their lives after his assassination to preserving his memory.

Of all Gandhi biographies perhaps none is more authoritative than TENDULKAR'S eight large tomes. No biographer of Gandhi could claim, as could Tendulkar, that Gandhi had had a hand in his work and "in doubtful cases," was frequently consulted. According to Tendulkar, most of his research and much of his writing were completed at the time of Gandhi's death. Himself an Indian freedom fighter and Gandhian disciple, one would assume that his lengthy biography would be unrivaled, and indeed one finds here a treasure trove of information and primary source material. The many photographs alone, many of them very rare, would make the book worthwhile. An unusual photo of Gandhi depicts him greeting an American black woman officer of the YWCA, and another shows him meeting with Herbert Hoover. Yet in eight lengthy volumes, one would have expected the author to have devoted more than a couple of hundred pages to Gandhi's 21 years in South Africa, more than 50 pages to his childhood and youth, and to have explained how an Afro-American woman came to be greeting Gandhi and why Herbert Hoover had met him. What were Gandhi's views of Stalin, of communism, of Hitler? One must look elsewhere for answers. Hence, in spite of the many page-length (often longer) quotations of Gandhi, Tendulkar's biography can hardly be called readable. It concentrates on the period during which the author was most closely associated with him, while the first half of Gandhi's long life fills out less than a volume.

Presumably PYARELAL (who gave up his surname) felt that Tendulkar had by no means exhausted all that could be said about Gandhi. As his former chief secretary, Pyarelal was approached after Gandhi's death and asked to write an official biography of him, to which, like Tendulkar, he devoted the remainder of his life. Five volumes, the last appearing posthumously in 1986, were the result, and unlike Tendulkar's they are well written and readable. Pyarelal, however, like Tendulkar, offers a long narrative of mainly political events, with little or no analysis, and Gandhi throughout appears one-dimensional. One would assume that the author's unique relationship with Gandhi would have given him special insights, but they fail to surface in this blow by blow account of Gandhi's life that leaves the reader feeling he understands him in the end no better than when he began.

While author Ved Mehta criticized Pyarelal for glorifying Gandhi (the same could be said of Tendulkar), an overview of Gandhi's major biographies and eyewitness accounts shows that even "critical" accounts were not necessarily more objective than those "glorifying" him. This is borne out, for example, by a slender volume containing 48 eyewitness accounts collected by SHUKLA, *Reminiscences of Gandhiji*, published after his assassination and regrettably never re-printed. Despite the editor's goal to avoid "appreciation and eulogy," these fascinating memoirs of Gandhi, from the time of his student days in London until his death, fail notably in this regard. Nevertheless, the images or vignettes of Gandhi all bear the imprint of sincerity and truthfulness, and are a very moving tribute to him. The majority of these memoirs, ranging from the humble to the exalted, attest to

Gandhi's overwhelming personality, to his sense of humor, and to the aura of gaiety surrounding him that children especially seemed to delight in. Despite the hundreds of biographies of Gandhi, few possess the power of *Reminiscences of Gandhiji* to evoke a sense of Gandhi's personality and influence.

Decades after the appearance of *Reminiscences,* the renowned Indo-American writer MEHTA returned to India in search of Gandhi's apostles who might help him find and understand the real Gandhi. The result of his visit was a highly original book, part memoir, part biography. Beautifully written, his quasi-biography conveys more than any other biography in English a real sense of the living Gandhi. With no personal memories of Gandhi, as Nehru and other biographers had possessed, Mehta nonetheless was endowed with an extraordinary sixth sense, highly developed in him possibly as a result of his blindness (a fact he never reveals in any of his numerous writings, including *Mahatma Gandhi and His Disciples*). Mehta seems to see and bring out of his eyewitnesses—former disciples, relatives-,biographers—aspects of their own personalities and revelations that might have been hidden from a more ordinary interviewer, especially a Westerner. In the end, Mehta himself, who begins his search quite open-mindedly and even critical of Gandhi, seems to have fallen under his spell. Far from demythologizing him as he had started out to do, Mehta reveals a man whose tolerance was genuine and whose love for all was never forgotten.

FISCHER, a prolific American journalist, conveys Gandhi's greatness to a Western readership. Appearing in the early 1950s, his book was also the most complete and best documented biography of Gandhi in any language to appear since Gandhi's death. A seasoned journalist who had spent years in Europe, the Middle East, and India, Fischer too fell under Gandhi's spell. Critics faulted the author for his tendency throughout the narrative of "reading motives and thoughts into Gandhi's mind." To other readers, this might well be the biography's strength, especially when contrasted to the essentially arid and lifeless accounts of Gandhi by his eminent Indian biographers. Fisher's carefully documented work is still absorbing to read decades after it first appeared.

A welter of biographies and memoirs of Gandhi appeared in the late 1960s to mark the centenary of Gandhi's birth in 1969. The best among them were written by British authors Geoffrey Ashe and Robert Payne. Distinguished professional writers, their works are gracefully, engagingly written. Neither, however, demonstrates any real understanding or feeling for Gandhi. In the case of ASHE, a serious Catholic writer and journalist, a sympathetic account and compelling atmosphere are all one can hope for in his lengthy, undocumented narrative. PAYNE's work by contrast is carefully researched, the result of having visited India, but it presents the most negative interpretation of Gandhi of any major biography. Gandhi clearly was too controversial and eccentric for Payne to stomach. Payne dwells on Gandhi's authoritarianism, his failure, in Payne's view, as a husband and a father. As Payne presents them, Gandhi's controversial ideas regarding sex and marriage were patently difficult to swallow, the result less of soul searching on Gandhi's part than of the influence of Indian cultural tradition, which for thousands of years had placed the highest value on chastity. Payne's biography, interesting because it is a rare example of a negative assessment of Gandhi, nonetheless fails as a thought-provoking, penetrating analysis.

Far more thoroughly researched, because it was preceded by nearly a lifetime of study and research on Gandhi's life, is the most recent biography of Gandhi by a British scholar and history professor, BROWN. Her work demonstrates that decades after Gandhi's death, when even his disciples have gone and there are few eyewitnesses left to interview, Gandhi's life can still be meaningfully retold, even by a biographer who is non-Indian with no ready command of an Indian language. Brown lacks the literary flair of an Ashe or a Payne, but that is more than compensated by a biography representing scholarship at its most dynamic, written in a clear, concise prose that makes the book fascinating reading for the serious scholar or biographer, though perhaps a bit labored for the casual reader. Still a relatively young writer, Brown brings to her work two decades of scholarship and absorption in the life of Gandhi and Gandhism, with the result that not since Ved Mehta has there been a biography of Gandhi that is as profound and original as this. Quite unlike the one-dimensional accounts given by other major biographers, Brown presents a multi-dimensional Gandhi who was not only a political leader (sparing the reader a blow-by-blow, lifeless account of a Tendulkar and Pyarelal), but a health-conscious practitioner of holistic medicine, an environmentalist, a religious thinker, a husband and father. Brown also examines Gandhi's views toward women in considerable detail. While the historian's analytical eye is evident throughout her study of Gandhi, Brown's biography proves once again that even an historian's well-tested objectivity suffers in the face of Gandhi's extraordinary life and personality.

—Sina Dubovoj

GARCÍA LORCA, Federico, 1898–1936; Spanish poet and playwright.

Adams, Mildred, *García Lorca: Playwright and Poet*. New York, G. Braziller, 1977.
Barea, Arturo, *Lorca: The Poet and His People*. London, Faber, 1944; New York, Harcourt, 1949 (originally published by Losada, Buenos Aires, 1957).
Cano, J. L., *García Lorca: Biografía Ilustrada*. Barcelona, Destino, 1962.
Cobb, Carl W., *Federico García Lorca*. New York, Twayne, 1967.
García Lorca, Francisco, *In the Green Morning: Memories of Federico*, translated by Christopher Maurer. New York, New Directions, 1986; London, Owen, 1989 (originally published as *Federico y su mundo*, edited by Mario Hernandez, Madrid, Alianza Editorial, 1980).
Gibson, Ian, *The Death of Lorca*. London, W. H. Allen, and Chicago, J. P. O'Hara, 1973 (originally published as *La represión nacionalista de Granada en 1936 y la muerte de Federico García Lorca*, Paris, Ruedo Iberico, 1971).

Gibson, Ian, *Federico García Lorca: A Life*. London, Faber, and New York, Pantheon, 1989 (originally published by Ediciones Grijalbo, Madrid, 2 vols., 1985–87).
Honig, Edwin, *Federico García Lorca*. Norfolk, Connecticut, New Directions, 1944; London, Cape, 1968.

*

HONIG observes in the preface to his work, "Few Lorca critics have shown the skill to pass effectively across the dim border between biographical and contextual criticism." The reader may wonder if Honig himself has not fallen foul of this trap; in a chapter entitled "The Juggler" he races through Lorca's life only, it seems, in order to provide a chronology against which to set the bio-critical study that follows. Without providing sources, Honig makes would-be authoritative statements about Lorca's early life. Paradoxically, while assuring us that Lorca sang at the age of two, Honig states that Lorca did not speak until age three, a statement that has since been refuted by Lorca's brother, Francisco. For a summary account of the poet's life the reader would do better to consult COBB. Though elementary, Cobb presents a reliable account of the essential facts in Lorca's life; in common with all the texts in the Twayne series, however, Cobb is apt to oversimplify, and the advanced student may find the assumption of an ab initio approach irritating.

BAREA prides himself on never having known Lorca personally. Correspondingly, his stated aim is to show the significance Lorca's work and persona held for the often forgotten larger contemporary audience. Barea serves as a contrast to accounts that overshadow Lorca's wider appeal with ceaseless lists of famous friends and artistic coteries. His work is not without mistakes (the translator in the introduction is in error over Lorca's first play), and it is biographical more in structure than in detail. Barea's principal interest is in the exposition he provides of Lorca's politicisation to which subsequent critics refer.

Initially, GIBSON's 1973 work, which first appeared in Spanish in Paris due to the strictures of the still prevailing regime, may seem to be Barea's complete antithesis; Gibson writes, "Lorca never joined a political party or identified himself with any particular left-wing group—he was not so politically committed as some left-wing propagandists would have us believe." The work's original title, "Nationalist repression in Granada in 1936 and the death of Federico García Lorca," illustrates another motif that becomes fully apparent in the last chapter, "Propaganda," when we see the conflation of investigation into Lorca's death and an indictment of the Nationalists. Of Neville Edgar's comment on the cowardly reluctance of those involved to assume responsibility for Lorca's death, Gibson writes that it is "of course an apt description of what the regime itself has been doing for the last 30 years." José Luis Vila-San-Juan (*García Lorca, Asesinado: toda la verdad*, Barcelona, Planeta, 1975) has commented of *The Death of Lorca*, "Gibson's ferocious anti-francoism leads him to make certain errors which are exaggerated by his being a foreigner." In Spain, however, where the word "assassinated" was not used to refer to Lorca until 1969 (Manuel Vincent, *García Lorca*, Madrid, 1969), one suspects that it was Gibson's capacity as foreigner that allowed him to interview surviving Granadians who knew Lorca. This aspect of Gibson's work complements Auclair's *Enfances et mort de*

García Lorca (Paris, Seuil, 1968). The first properly investigative study into Lorca's death, Gibson's book (which includes the transcription of an interview with Ruiz Alonso, the man who arrested Lorca) prompted similar studies in Spanish (e.g., José Luis Vila-San-Juan and Eduardo Molina Fajardo, *Los Ultimos días de García Lorca*, Barcelona, 1983) which did not appear, however, until the tail end of, or long after, the regime.

ADAMS gives one the impression that little progress has been made since 1961, when Honig complained in his revised preface that biographers were too keen to play up the legendary magnetic charm, magnanimity and showmanship of the mask rather than "the complex nature of Lorca as a human being." Adams' aim as stated is to correct a deficiency in the attention paid by Lorca's Spanish critics to his North American period. This aim is frustrated by her over-reliance on hearsay and unspecified sources or "unknown spirits with extra-sensory perception of the past." Though able to detail the colour of the sky on any particular day, in the case of more serious matters she uses the dodge of "reasons that must be surmised rather than made clear." Like all Lorca's biographers (Gibson not excluded) Adams is prone, when sources are scarce, to make generalisations about "the Spaniards." Her account is uneven, with undue space dedicated to her own brief meeting with Lorca and Lorca's ten days in Vermont, which are stretched out with descriptions, hard to verify, of Alice Cummings' doughnut-making. Flawed by repetition, often clumsy writing, and the failure to give references for quotes from Lorca's work, Adams is nevertheless readable, if unprecise.

Written between 1959 and 1965, FRANCISCO GARCÍA LORCA's memories of his elder brother did not appear in Spain until 1980. *In The Green Morning* is an abridged version of the original, the translator having deleted those parts he assumes would be of no interest to the English-speaking reader; photographs and an index lacking in the original are, however, added to the English edition. The style, which is humourless in the original, loses little in translation. Presumably the person best able to do so, Francisco provides an eye-witness account of Lorca's childhood and adolescence. Following a genealogy of the Lorca family are anecdotal reports of shared experiences at school and at home. Francisco aims to illustrate the formative influence of Lorca's early life, but one feels that the approach he takes is too guarded for this to be a success. Francisco describes himself as "a man with a poor memory," and his recollections are at times more impressionistic than detailed. Not awed by his subject, he sometimes comments in a straightforward way that challenges the mythical Lorca personality, as when he says that Federico was never one to laugh at himself. The book is divided into biographical and interpretive sections, and the detached style of the biographical half of the book is apt to lead one to forget that it is by Lorca's brother. Though admirable, this objectivity may have been gained at the expense of a deeper inquiry into the still elusive "nature of the man." The question of Lorca's sexuality is completely passed over in his brother's account.

Having dealt with Lorca's death, after a 13 year interval GIBSON returned to Spain and to Lorca's life. Painstaking research, access to correspondence and documents as well as interviews with Lorca's sister, helped to produce a biography that supersedes all previous efforts. The same investigative approach as in *The Death* is employed in *The Life*; in this case the enigma is

Lorca's homosexuality. The passing of the regime has not made *this* an easier subject to research; Gibson writes, "[my] desire to explore the hidden and often tormented side to Lorca's character met with considerable difficulties." The consequent focus on events rather than attitudes may move the reader, as it did George Steiner, to feel that "an otherwise sensitive study ponders on whether or not intercourse did take place with this or that object of Lorca's 'Dionysian Libido.'" Sections from *The Death*, the evocation of Granada, for example, are reworked, though only occasionally does one feel that Gibson is padding. He can be tiresome, however, when critical; he describes Buñuel's grasp of poetry, for example, as rudimentary. But these are minor complaints of a biography one critic labelled as the best written of a Spanish writer.

CANO makes an excellent visual accompaniment to all of the above, none of which is well endowed with photographs. Cano portrays each stage of Lorca's life with abundant photographic materials, and ignorance of Spanish would be no handicap to the enjoyment of this book.

—Ryan Prout

GARIBALDI, Giuseppe, 1807–1882; Italian nationalist leader and soldier.

Davenport, Marcia, *Garibaldi: Father of Modern Italy*. New York, Random House, 1957.
De Polnay, Peter, *Garbaldi: The Legend and the Man*. London, Hollis and Carter, 1960.
Hibbert, Christopher, *Garibaldi and His Enemies: The Clash of Arms and Personalities in the Making of Italy*. London, Longman, 1965; Boston, Little Brown, 1966.
Larg, David, *Giuseppe Garibaldi: A Biography*. London, P. Davies 1934; Port Washington, New York, Kennikat Press, 1970.
Mack Smith, Denis, *Garibaldi: A Great Life in Brief*. New York, Knopf, 1956; London, Hutchinson, 1957 (without subtitle).
Parris, John, *The Lion of Caprera: A Biography of Giuseppe Garibaldi*. New York, D. McKay, and London, A. Barker, 1962.
Ridley, Jasper, *Garibaldi*. London, Constable, 1974; New York, Viking, 1976.
Trevelyan, George M., *Garibaldi* (3 vols.). London and New York, Longman, 1907–11.
Viola, Herman J., *Giuseppe Garibaldi*. New York, Chelsea House, 1988.

*

One could not ask for a much better introduction to Garibaldi's life than that by MACK SMITH. This work combines a very readable style with a gripping narration to produce a work of the first rank. Mack Smith is not only balanced and fair but has a sympathetic understanding of Garibaldi, whom he views as the "very embodiment of the common man." This insight into the secret of Garibaldi's appeal is vital to understanding a man who combined so many seemingly conflicting traits and attitudes. Further, Mack Smith places Garibaldi in a larger context than that merely of Italian nationalist hero. While Garibaldi's role in the creation of the Italian nation is kept primary, the author reveals Garibaldi as "a professional liberator, a man who fought for oppressed people wherever he found them." While such a view is by no means unique, it is important to stress as the temptation to reduce Garibaldi into a less complex and intricate figure is always present. To make him only a "colorful" character involved in Italian politics is to do Garibaldi a disservice.

Still, Mack Smith fails to fully complete this promise, perhaps due to his desire to keep the work brief. Thus, the last two decades of Garibaldi's life are treated in very cursory fashion, as if they were largely anticlimactic to his struggles in the cause of Italian unification. This failing is shared by many other biographers of Garibaldi.

For sheer wealth of detail and brilliance of style, TREVELYAN's trilogy on Garibaldi's role in the Risorgimento is unmatched. The author provides an exciting, vivid, and insightful account of the events from 1848–60, the period dominating most accounts of Garibaldi's life. However, Trevelyan tends toward a type of enthusiasm for his subject that at times gets in the way of his objectivity. While this very fault is one of the reasons this triology is so interesting, it is a defect the reader must bear in mind. Further, historians over the seven decades since these volumes appeared have proven Trevelyan wrong on a number of facts. All this said, the fact remains that one could hardly do better than consult these volumes for understanding the period they cover.

All autobiographies must be treated with great care. So it is with Garibaldi's *Memoirs* (New York, 1931), an interesting and even exciting but seriously flawed work. While Garibaldi seems to have tried to be honest and fair in recounting his life, much of this work was done from memory and often, it appears, "enhanced" by those who collaborated on it. To make matters worse, this autobiography has gone through a number of editions, with facts often changed from version to version. Despite these problems, this work does allow the reader to have some firsthand insight into Garibaldi that might not otherwise be possible. If used carefully in coordination with other more reliable works, this title may be of value to the serious reader. This is particularly true for those who wish to understand the man behind the historical events.

An important corrective to the habit of treating Garibaldi's life as insignificant after 1860 is furnished by RIDLEY, who devotes a great deal of space to the last 20 years of the revolutionary's life. By so doing, his work provides a better-rounded portrait of Garibaldi and does not reduce him to a piece in the puzzle of the Risorgimento. To accomplish this, Ridley was forced to produce a book of a length that may deter the more casual reader. It would, however, be a mistake to let the wealth of detail and information contained in this book to blind one to Ridley's excellent presentation of Garibaldi's life as a complete whole. This work, while lacking Mack Smith's brevity and Trevelyan's passion, has much to recommend it.

A useful title stressing Garibaldi's early life, PARRIS serves as a good source for those who wish to understand the early events and influences that created the "lion of Caprera." Al-

though most of the volume adds little new on the main events of Garibaldi's political career, its emphasis on his formative years make it worthwhile.

Another extremely readable contribution to the study of Garibaldi is provided by HIBBERT. It might be argued that this title is not as serious as Mack Smith's but all the same it paints the main events of Garibaldi's life in detail, producing an interesting picture of this important individual. This is certainly a title that deserves to be consulted by those desiring a more complete understanding of Garibaldi.

VIOLA offers an extremely brief introduction that has little to add to Mack Smith. Still, it is an acceptable first book for the reader new to Garibaldi. LARG, DAVENPORT, and DE POLNAY contribute nothing new to the study of Garibaldi although all three are relatively accurate and might be of use to some readers.

—William A. Pelz

GARLAND, Judy, 1922–1969; American singer and film actress.

Dahl, David and Barry Kehoe, *Young Judy*. New York, Masson/Charter, 1975; London, Hart-Davis MacGibbon, 1976.

Deans, Mickey and Ann Pinchot, *Weep No More, My Lady*. New York, Hawthorn Books, 1972; with subtitle *An Intimate Biography of Judy Garland*, London, W. H. Allen, 1972.

DiOrio, Al, Jr., *Little Girl Lost*. New Rochelle, New York, Arlington House, 1973; London, Robson Books, 1975.

Edwards, Anne, *Judy Garland: A Biography*. New York, Simon and Schuster, and London, Constable, 1975.

Frank, Gerold, *Judy*. New York, Harper, and London, W. H. Allen, 1975.

Meyer, John, *Heartbreaker*. New York, Doubleday, and London, W. H. Allen, 1983.

Morella, Joe and Edward Z. Epstein, *The Films and Career of Judy Garland*. New York, Cadillac Publishing, 1969.

Spada, James, *Judy and Liza*. New York, Doubleday, and London, Hodder and Stoughton, 1983.

Steiger, Brad, *Judy Garland*. New York, Ace, 1969.

Torme, Mel, *The Other Side of the Rainbow with Judy Garland on the Dawn Patrol*. New York, Morrow, 1970; London, W. H. Allen, 1971.

*

Most of the biographies of Judy Garland are works of tear-duct exploitation, many without benefit of research. Such titles as *Weep No More, My Lady; Little Girl Lost*; and *Heartbreaker* are characteristic of books about the performer as pathetic waif. These lachrymose treatments frequently deal only with short periods of the subject's life. DEANS, Garland's last husband, covers only the last two years of Garland's life. However, the author knows his subject well and provides many quite intimate episodes. MEYER describes a two-month love affair the author enjoyed with Garland in her last year. This book is even more "up close and personal" than Deans, with details of sexual encounters, verbatim reports of long conversations and other minutiae of invented or betrayed intimacy. Deans and Meyer partake of tabloid exploitation, since both are revealing, explicit memoirs by young men who were the middle-aged Garland's lovers during her decline.

DAHL and KEHOE focus on Garland's childhood and her parents, with painstaking and essentially trivial research into her local vaudeville performances and her father's childhood and adolescence. This book dwells too long on Garland's youth, but contains some facts otherwise unnoted. The authors offer the alleged homosexuality of Garland's father as the key to her whole life, even though evidence for his predilections are only hearsay, and the authors report that Garland herself never knew about her father's problem. The work is lopsided, wrongheaded, even occasionally ridiculous; still it contains unique material.

TORME details Garland's television work from the point of view of her musical director, who is as interested in discussing his own divorce as in scrutinizing Garland's media achievements and breakdowns. Nevertheless, this insider's look at Judy Garland the entertainer gives real insight into her working habits and her problems. Torme, himself a performer, assesses Garland by standards that are not merely emotional.

DIORIO also takes a career-oriented approach, while presenting the whole course of the subject's life. Written by an acknowledged fan, DiOrio's volume contains an incredible amount of "gush" but also more coverage of newspaper and magazine sources than any other Garland biography. The author emphasizes the usual triumvirate of "innocence, talent and heartbreak," but many facts emerge clearly here, including details about Garland's recording work. The book contains an excellent discography, filmography, and a detailed listing of Garland's television appearances. This book is essentially a lengthy movie magazine article, but rather classy in its dedication to any and all hard facts about the idolized subject.

MORELLA gives an adequate brief account of Garland's life, copiously and beautifully illustrated, with commentary by Arthur Freed, Gene Kelly, and others. The emphasis is upon individual treatments of Garland's films. Since this book is essentially a glorified filmography, every Garland movie appears, including many that receive little mention elsewhere. This biography should be the choice of readers primarily interested in Judy Garland the movie star; her concert career gets short shrift here.

Those who wish to read an account of Garland's whole life, dealing with her personal experiences and her career, have two good choices: Edwards or Frank. EDWARDS' book, a rather novelistic but conscientiously researched biography of the sort always stocked by public libraries, is not as long or detailed as Frank's. A professional biographer, Edwards is slick, swift, and romantic. Interpretations of Garland's life fall easily into the author's simple schema: Judy's "childhood was a nightmare from which she never recovered" and "no woman in theatrical history has been as exploited"; nevertheless her whole life was a search for love. Edwards includes more wide-ranging speculations about Garland's love life and sexual experiences than the other biographers. This penchant, for example, leads the author to consider the possibility that Louis B. Mayer's exploitation of the young Garland at MGM included sexual relations, and motivates Edwards' stress—possibly overstress—on Garland's first romantic involvement (with Tyrone Power). Many details differ from those in other biographies. Edwards claims Garland sus-

pected her father's homosexuality, whereas other sources explicitly deny this. She asserts Garland had an abortion during her first marriage, although Frank says the evidence does not support such a claim. Edwards always discusses the more sensational of two alternatives, even when she brings it up only to dismiss it. Yet her books is not simply sensationalistic. It is a tribute to the author's skills that this book is not simply another little Judy weeper, but provides a reasonably convincing overview of the subject. The book includes a short selection of Garland's youthful poetry—romantic, derivative, and blatant—in an appendix.

For a reader who wants to read only one of the many Judy Garland books available, FRANK's is the best choice. It is the only biography written with the full cooperation of Garland's immediate family—her sister, her children, and four of her five husbands. The writer had complete access to family data, letters, and private papers; yet he produced his book with no editorial supervision from the family. In addition, he interviewed nearly 200 people who played some part in Garland's life, and he had met the subject herself. Frank, writing in a rather punchy journalistic style, avoids the awe-stricken tone of many other Garland biographers, evenhandedly assessing legends and—it must be said—the subject's own lies about herself. Then he insistently demolishes the mythologies that have built up around this cult figure, sparing no one's fantasies, least of all Judy Garland's own. The result is a readable, apparently reliable, view of a great entertainer, with no special attempt to make readers weep over her.

SPADA does an excellent job of combining and summarizing the findings of earlier biographers, but, since this work is a joint biography of Judy Garland and her famous daughter, Liza Minnelli, it is naturally slanted toward Garland as a mother; a large portion of the book is devoted to Minnelli. Of the Garland biographies, this "coffee table" edition is the most attractive book, and it contains by far the best photographs, many of which are not the standard shots.

Readers with an interest in the formulation and preservation of cult figures should take a look at STEIGER, a dreadful little volume, which offers astrology, numerology, handwriting and biorhythm analysis, besides the usual allotment of gushing prose. The author seems to be an astrologist himself, but his book offers no insight into Judy Garland or any other subject; nevertheless Steiger's book is itself an example of the development of the celebrity cult figure (almost always dead) as part of a whole network of superstition and pseudo-religious hype.

—Richard Sears

GARRICK, David, 1717–1779; English actor, theatre manager, and dramatist.

Barton, Margaret, *Garrick*. London, Faber, and New York, Macmillan, 1948.

Davies, Thomas, *Memoirs of the Life of David Garrick*. Dublin, J. Williams, 1780; Boston, Wells and Lilly, 1818.

Fitzgerald, Percy, *The Life of David Garrick*. London, Tinsley Brothers, 1868; revised and updated edition, London, Simpkin and Marshall, 1899.

Kendall, Alan, *David Garrick: A Biography*. London, Harrap, and New York, St. Martin's, 1985.

Knight, Joseph, *David Garrick*. London, Kegan Paul, 1894.

Murphy, Arthur, *The Life of David Garrick*. London, J. Wright, 1801.

Oman, Carola, *David Garrick*. London, Hodder and Stoughton, 1958.

Smith, Helen, R., *David Garrick 1717–79: A Brief Account*. London, British Library, 1979.

Stone, George Winchester, Jr. and George M. Karhl, *David Garrick: A Critical Biography*. Carbondale, Southern Illinois University Press, 1979.

*

The biographies of David Garrick that have appeared over the last 200 years offer considerable variety in method and means. General readers may prefer to sample the more recent treatments by Oman or Kendall, while scholars will typically resort to the longer, more detailed accounts offered by Fitzgerald and jointly by Stone and Kahrl. Readers interested in encountering Garrick firsthand also have his collected *Letters*, (edited by Little and Kahrl, 1963), and the much earlier *Private Correspondence*, (edited by James Boaden, 1831), which consists mostly of letters addressed to the actor. The mass of materials surrounding Garrick's life and his work on the stage has been usefully set out by Gerald M. Berkowitz in *David Garrick: A Reference Guide* (1980).

The first biographers of Garrick were men who knew and worked with him in the theatre. DAVIES, for a time an actor in Garrick's company at Drury Lane, brought out his memoirs of Garrick the year following the great actor's death. Davies' position gives great authority to his testimony in matters of the stage. However, Davies subordinates Garrick's acting—the most striking and original area of Garrick's talent, and that which laid the foundation for his extremely broad engagement in the social and cultural life of 18th-century England—to his managerial and social activities. Davies, who was in a better position than almost any of his contemporaries to document and memorialize Garrick's acting skills, seems to have taken that area of Garrick's talent largely for granted, apparently blind to its novelty. While Davies' disagreements with Garrick over company discipline may have jaundiced certain parts of the book, the appendix in which he lists Garrick's roles is a useful adjunct to the chatty and digressive style that typifies this work.

MURPHY, who wrote plays that Garrick both acted in and staged, was another close associate of Garrick's. Like Davies, Murphy had artistic and personal disagreements with Garrick, which may have left him not always charitable in his assessments of Garrick's character. On the other hand, Murphy is very thorough in unfolding Garrick's dealings with playwrights as a professional group; and he is acute, too, in his critical pronouncements on the new plays Garrick mounted, whereas Davies is at his best in considering Shakespearean and other standard works of the repertory.

The first edition of FITZGERALD's life of Garrick appeared in 1868, followed 31 years later by an expanded version which drew on a number of sources that had come to light during the intervening years. Fitzgerald had been given a veritable archive of materials surrounding Garrick's life by John Foster, who had intended writing his own biography of Garrick to go with his

others on Goldsmith and, later, Dickens. Fitzgerald thus possessed the material for a broader exploration of Garrick's life than had previously been attempted. The documentary mass in Fitzgerald's account effectively replaces the weight of personal familiarity with the actor that animates the accounts by Davies and Murphy.

Although it runs to nearly 500 pages of rather small print, Fitzgerald's book continually unfolds its voluminous materials in striking ways. Even with the advent of more recent scholarship, Fitzgerald remains an authority on such matters as the roles Garrick took at Ipswich during the Summer of 1741, which would serve as trial runs for the actor's epochal debut as Richard III the following October. However, Fitzgerald justifies his own book partly by dismissing the previous biographies as sinks of bitterness, and his assessments of the motives of Davies and Murphy seem overstated and petty.

KNIGHT credits Fitzgerald as the basis for his own book, which lacks, nevertheless, the freshness and vitality of all the previous works. Knight quotes at length from the eyewitness accounts of Garrick served up with great penetration by the German tourist, Georg Lichtenberg; but otherwise, his chronicle of Garrick's career turns too often into mere listing of names, dates, and productions. Nor are his evocations of the actor as clear-cut as Fitzgerald's, an indeterminacy that takes its toll through the course of a book in which chapters are numbered rather than titled, and in which the reader yearns for some more compelling organization. Aiming for Fitzgerald's comprehensiveness, Knight achieves a result more superficial, less integrated, and less satisfying.

BARTON, much more selective than the 19th-century biographers, at the same time provides many more illustrations (capitalizing on the wealth of iconography surrounding the actor's life) than had previously been seen. Barton excels in capturing the personalities of people associated with Garrick, particularly those of women: the dancer Eva-Marie Violette, who became Garrick's wife, and Peg Woffington, the actress Garrick loved at the time of his earliest fame. Barton is weakest in re-creating Garrick's acting, perhaps in her assumption that this had already been done by previous biographers, or simply owing to her primary interest: Garrick's activities as a man about town.

OMAN combines fine writing with an acute sense of English social history as it found resonance in Garrick's life. In just under 400 pages, she offers a view of the actor that brings together many areas of his extremely busy life, in a narrative clearly demarcated in terms of time and of topic. Oman suggests a more complex image of the actor than does Barton. She, too, does not attempt any full-scale re-creations of Garrick's acting, implying that Garrick's interest in society transcended his interest in acting as his life wore on. Whether or not this is true, it represents a novel view, and one which serves Garrick's far-reaching enterprise.

Writing in the bicentennial year of Garrick's death, SMITH offers a brief version of the actor's life, organized both chronologically and thematically. Rich in illustrations, her book clearly reveals its intention to coincide with the British Library's exhibition of Garrickiana in 1979.

STONE AND KAHRL's book, appearing the same year as Smith's, is also lavishly illustrated and represents the most scholarly account to date of Garrick's life. With the most footnotes of any biography, together with the most extensive bibliography, general index, and index to titles of plays and secondary sources, Stone and Kahrl provide much heretofore unpublished material. These include useful appendices documenting Garrick's performances by season (amending Fitzgerald's records, on the basis of more recent scholarly work out of *The London Stage,* 1961 and 1962); listing the numbers of performers in Garrick's company by season; listing the new plays performed under Garrick's management at Drury Lane and under the rival management of Covent Garden theatre; and even an appendix recording Garrick's illnesses. The whole book runs to more than 770 pages, and includes so much material that even an expert reader may find difficulty in sorting through facts. Lacking much narrative definition, Stone and Kahrl's book suffers from its dual authorship; one feels at times the two biographers vying with each other to advance the facts each deems most important.

KENDALL's is the most copiously illustrated of any of the biographies. His text, organized around topics, succeeds in weaving the strands of 18th-century English life into a sense of Garrick's own mission on the stage. Like all other 20th-century biographers, however (except Stone and Kahrl, who include chapters on Garrick's comic and tragic roles), Kendall subordinates Garrick's acting to his other endeavors. Perhaps in order to stake a claim to originality, Kendall asserts that Garrick's was "an unhistrionic personality," and so finds justification for de-emphasizing his acting. In his steady reliance on Garrick's correspondence, though, Kendall finds solid ground for offering interpretations of events commensurate with those advanced or implied by Garrick himself.

—Leigh Woods

GARVEY, Marcus, 1887–1940; Jamaican-born American political activist, proponent of black nationalism.

Cronon, Edward D., *Black Moses: The Story of Marcus Garvey and the Universal Negro Improvement Association.* Madison, University of Wisconsin Press, 1955.

Davis, Daniel S., *Marcus Garvey.* New York, F. Watts, 1972.

Fax, Elton C., *Garvey: The Story of a Pioneer Black Nationalist.* New York, Dodd Mead, 1972.

Lawler, Mary, *Marcus Garvey.* New York, Chelsea House, 1988.

Lewis, Rupert, *Marcus Garvey: Anti-Colonial Champion.* London, Karia Press, 1987; Trenton, New Jersey, Africa World Press, 1988.

Martin, Tony, *Race First: The Ideological and Organizational Struggle of Marcus Garvey and the Universal Negro Improvement Association.* Westpoint, Connecticut, Greenwood Press, 1976.

Nembhard, Lenford, *Trials and Triumphs of Marcus Garvey.* Kingston, Jamaica, Gleaner, 1940.

*

CRONON's *Black Moses* has become the standard biography of Garvey. Vivid and detailed, it concentrates most attention on the short period of make-or-break work during which Garvey sought to consolidate the United Negro Improvement Association's phenomenal success in 1920. Perhaps in this respect the work is centred too much (though not exclusively) on the UNIA in the United States, neglecting somewhat Garvey's massive international following and influence. As some other biographies point out, the anti-colonial struggles in Africa owed much to Garvey's slogan "Africa for the Black man." However, it cannot be denied that it was in America, where the black population had, if not a political voice, at least a measure of disposable income, that Garvey hoped to underpin his grand design. There, he could find the black worker not merely dissatisfied and angry (as blacks were the world over) but with the political will and financial means to demand change. Cronon's explanation of Garvey's astronomical success is exemplary: he reveals how dismally the emergent labour unions failed to include the black worker in their struggle for equality, and how Garvey brilliantly exploited this failure. His UNIA filled the vacuum of black politics, argues Cronon, using the same self-help, grassroots structure as the unions, but adding his own egocentric touches (such as naming himself Grand Potentate and President-in-waiting of the African Republic). Cronon also maintains that Garvey's political programme—apart from the radical demand that blacks be equal to whites in all countries—was politically moderate, and offers in support of this the example of the Black Star Line. The litany of incompetence, official hostility, and corruption that constitutes the steamship company's history is revealing in what it suggests about the overall failure of the UNIA. Cronon's version of events is based closely on the evidence given in Garvey's trial for fraud that followed the line's collapse. It is clear from both this account and many others that Garvey was innocent of the crime for which he was arraigned, but was guilty of gross mismanagement and naivete in running the Black Star Line. In presenting a portrait of the man that embraces both the personal and political aspects of his character, the book benefits immensely from the willing cooperation of Amy Jacques Garvey, who as Marcus' secretary and wife knew a great deal about both aspects. Excerpts from speeches and articles are well chosen to convey the power of Garvey's oratory. Cronon's remains the best and most accessible of Garvey's biographies.

The first biography of Garvey was published in the year of his death by a fellow-Jamaican, NEMBHARD. It lacks the detail of *Black Moses*, and by contrast focuses on Garvey's activities after his release from jail and deportation from the United States. So, with its emphasis on Garvey's wilderness years and its close proximity to his death, it is an elegiac book. It is extremely moving in places, as it surely could not fail to be given the tragic subject matter; and its Caribbean background makes it an invaluable (though by now sadly obscure) text on the life and work of Garvey.

DAVIS looks at Garvey from the vantage of the Black Power movement of the 1960s and 70s, in which much of the rhetoric and symbolism harked back to the Garveyite movement in the 20s. Taking his cue from Amy Jacques Garvey's suggestion that Marcus Garvey inspired both the African liberationists and the "Black is Beautiful" philosophy that came out of the USA, Davis charts the progress of Garveyism as a body of ideas-in-exile. He argues that though Garvey's programme failed, his ideas continued, and that much of contemporary black politics was influenced by him. As a means of assessing Garvey's relevance today, the book works admirably; as a biography, however, it suffers somewhat from an excess of hindsight.

MARTIN describes Garvey's enterprise by means of a broad and detailed account of his political environment. Martin confronts the reader with a staggering mass of information about the structure of the UNIA and that of its opponents; and it is the diversity of the latter that is most staggering of all. Garvey faced opposition from the Communist Party, Labor Unions, black conservatives; from left, right, and centre, black and white. Reading this biography goes a long way toward correcting any impression of Garvey as an unworldy visionary, as might be the conclusion from some other studies. Instead, Martin suggests, Garvey was a consummate politician and popular orator; that he had millions of black working-class supporters in the USA alone demonstrates his skill and energy. Where Cronon cites Garvey's foolhardiness in representing himself in the Black Star Line case as the main cause of his downfall, Martin goes further by claiming that the outcome was a foregone conclusion; his opponents had too great a vested interest in it to allow a fair trial. While this book is light on Garvey's personality, it represents a fine exploration of Garvey as a political being, operating in a fierce and complex political arena.

Of other biographies, the most interesting and useful is by FAX. Published the same year as Davis' biography, it has many of the same concerns, not least of which is to prove Garvey's contemporary importance. It is an impassioned work, ringing with extravagant phrases and almost painfully sincere. Yet it conveys more about the hopes and fears of Garvey's people, the hordes who placed their money and faith in the "Black Messiah" and who lost both in his collapse, than do the more academic books of Cronon and Martin. Compared with those works, Fax's is a lightweight study; but the author no doubt hoped to complete the historical picture with a more personal and committed account of Garvey's life. As such it is memorable and, like Nembhard's *Trials and Triumphs*, extremely moving.

The most recent biography, by LAWLER, is a timely restatement of available work on Garvey. Eminently readable, it covers most of the material available in other works, though it adds little to our understanding of Garvey as a private figure. That said, it has much to recommend itself over another readily-available text, that by LEWIS. Leaden and dogmatic, this offers the reader little by way of objective consideration of the subject, and almost nothing in terms of insight.

—Alan Murphy

GASKELL, Elizabeth, 1810–1865; English writer.

Chadwick, Esther (Mrs. Ellis Chadwick), *Mrs. Gaskell: Haunts, Homes, Stories.* New York, F. Stokes, and London, I. Pitman, 1910.

Chapple, J. A. V., *Elizabeth Gaskell: A Portrait in Letters.* Manchester, Manchester University Press, 1980.

French, Yvonne, *Elizabeth Gaskell.* London, Home and Van Thal, and Denver, Colorado, A. Swallow, 1949.

Gérin, Winifred, *Elizabeth Gaskell: A Biography.* Oxford, Clarendon Press, 1976; New York, Oxford University Press, 1980.

Haldane, Elizabeth, *Mrs. Gaskell and Her Friends.* London, Hodder and Stoughton, 1930; New York, Appleton, 1931.

Hopkins, Annette B., *Elizabeth Gaskell: Her Life and Work.* London, J. Lehmann, 1952.

Payne, George, *Mrs. Gaskell: A Brief Biography.* Manchester, Sterratt, 1929.

Whitfield, A. Stanton, *Mrs. Gaskell: Her Life and Work.* London, Routledge, 1929.

*

All early biographers of Gaskell faced the same problem; a lack of the writer's correspondence. CHADWICK made the first attempt at biography, relying on scanty diary entries and letters. Legal restrictions limited her access to material, however, and as a consequence she structured the work around places of importance to Gaskell. The result is an anti-chronological biography that traces any connection between Gaskell's physical world and her fictional worlds. In 1913, Gaskell's last surviving daughter, Meta, died, leaving instructions for her mother's literary executors to destroy documents in their possession. As a result, letters to her husband and two of her daughters are lost to us. In 1929 WHITFIELD published a "life and work" volume that necessarily focused on the work. Whitfield wrote in the tradition of the cosy amateur biographer: "Let us draw aside the curtain of years and sink our point of view to the moment of our heroine's birth. It is as though the Fates have already mapped out the thread of her life."

HALDANE's 1931 biography follows the Whitfield approach, though Haldane had access to some letters. It is her narrow vision of women rather than problems with sources that limits Haldane's view of Gaskell. We learn, for instance, that "letter writing is one of the arts—possibly not very numerous—in which women may claim to excel." Her title, with its emphasis on friendship, reflects that limited vision: "Men and women are judged largely by the friendships that are made by them." Gaskell, so active in the world of Manchester slums, so provocative a writer, deserves a different basis for judgment.

PAYNE's own experience as Unitarian minister at Knutsford, a place so important to Gaskell, enriches an otherwise brief account of her life. FRENCH's slim, derivative work is based on Chadwick and Haldane. Devoting six pages to the period from Gaskell's birth to her honeymoon, French sketches only an outline of the life lived. By 1952 the availability of correspondence to friends enabled HOPKINS to make the first serious attempt at biography. Better than any earlier work, it too necessarily emphasized Gaskell's work at the expense of her life. In all these biographies people remain flat, and readers gain no sense of Gaskell's world or her remarkable position in it. Early biographers did Gaskell a disservice: they marginalized her.

Some 600 new letters were brought to light by Gaskell's great-granddaughter. Their existence made compelling biography possible for the first time. Readers interested in Gaskell firsthand should read either CHAPPLE's *A Portrait in Letters* or the complete correspondence, edited by Chapple and Pollard, rather than any earlier work.

But for insightful biography, turn to GÉRIN. Family letters to all but one daughter do seem to have been destroyed, but the extant letters allow Gérin to do what no earlier biographer had done: convey a sense of the life lived. Gaskell's correspondence reveals "her high spirits, the sparkle of her style, the zig-zig course of her reasoning, her honesty and want of all affectation, her fun and freedom of thought and expression.''

Gérin came logically to the subject, having written biographies of all four Brontë siblings. Her biography of Gaskell is closer in scope to those of Branwell and Emily Brontë. Readers of her award-winning biography of Charlotte may well be disappointed, since her biography of Gaskell does not reveal the same depth of analysis. This difference simply reflects her subject: Gaskell's life of writing, of competent domesticity, and of urban reform, makes for a direct contrast to Brontë's. Wit and charm characterize Gaskell's life, not passion and suffering.

Gaskell was not, however, the ever ebullient woman earlier biographers had described. Gérin identifies two warring sides to Gaskell's nature: a cheerful temperament and a nervous morbidity. Gérin documents a series of emotional breakdowns, the first coming in response to the death of her nine-month-old son Willie. Other biographers have all noted that this sorrow prompted her to write fiction and that it accounts, in part, for the moribidity of *Mary Barton*. Yet in every biographer's hands before Gérin, Gaskell emerges as the patently good and uninteresting heroine of Victorian fiction—the sort of portrait that Gaskell never drew. Gérin brings the darker, painful side of Gaskell's nature to the surface. In so doing, she explains the emotional makeup of a Victorian woman committed to telling the truth, willing to shock her readers. In important ways Gaskell was at odds with her culture; as Gérin observes, ''In a censorious age she was singularly uncensorious.'' Consequently, she sided with the workers in *Mary Barton* and *North and South,* wrote of seduction, betrayal, and illegitimacy in *Ruth,* and was willing to court libel in telling the truth of the traumas of Charlotte Brontë's life in *The Life of Charlotte Brontë.*

Gérin's portrait of Elizabeth Gaskell makes sense of the artist for the first time. Earlier biographers focused on the ''Cranford'' side of Gaskell's personality and thus could not account for the dark vision in such novels as *Mary Barton* and *Ruth.* Gérin ably demonstrates that Gaskell's art and her life were ''completely integrated.'' As Gaskell was a great biographer herself, a remarkable biographer in that censorious age, it is fitting that her life should be told by such an accomplished biographer.

—Marnie Jones

GAUGUIN, Paul, 1848–1903; French painter.

Becker, Beril, *Paul Gauguin: The Calm Madman.* New York, A. and C. Boni, and London, Cassell, 1931.

Burnett, Robert, *The Life of Paul Gauguin.* London, Cobden-Sanderson, 1936; New York, Oxford University Press, 1937.

Danielsson, Bengt, *Gauguin in the South Seas*, translated by Reginald Spink. London, Allen and Unwin, and New York, Doubleday, 1965.

Gauguin, Pola, *My Father, Paul Gauguin*, translated by Arthur G. Chater. New York, Knopf, and London, Cassell, 1937.

Hanson, Lawrence and Elizabeth Hanson, *Noble Savage: The Life of Paul Gauguin.* London, Chatto and Windus, 1954; New York, Random House, 1955.

Hoog, Michel, *Paul Gauguin, Life and Work.* New York, Rizzoli, and London, Thames and Hudson, 1987 (originally published by Office du Livre, Fribourg, Switzerland, 1987).

Le Pinchon, Yann, *Gauguin, Life, Art, and Inspiration.* New York, Abrams, 1987 (originally published as *Sur les traces de Gauguin*, Paris, Éditions Robert Laffont, 1986).

Perruchot, Henri, *Gauguin*, translated by Humphrey Hare, edited by Jean Ellsmoor. London, Perpetua, 1963; Cleveland and New York, World Publishing, 1964 (originally published as *Gauguin, sa vie ardente et misérable*, Paris, Le Sillage, 1948).

Thomson, Belinda, *Gauguin.* London and New York, Thames and Hudson, 1987.

*

From the first eyewitness account by Charles Morice published in *Les Hommes d'Aujourd'hui* in 1891, both popular and scholarly biographies of Paul Gauguin have appeared through each subsequent generation. Jean de Rotonchamp, *Gauguin* (Weimar, 1906; Paris, 1925) and Charles Morice, *Gauguin* (Paris, 1920) remain the standard lives of Paul Gauguin and form the foundation of many of the studies that followed. In addition, Gauguin's own extensive writings, including his journals *Noa Noa* (Paris, 1901) and *Avant et Après* (Leipzig, 1918; Paris, 1923), his annotated sketchbooks, numerous letters exchanged with his wife, colleagues and long time friend Daniel de Monfried support the more reliable lives.

BECKER's biography, one of the first available to the English reader, casts Gauguin as the archetypal Romantic genius. Marred by its fictionalized style—''Gauguin enters his office, throws his portfolio on the table, and hat on the rack, and slumps down in his chair deeply exhausted''—Becker's life opens in 1883 with a dramatic scene of Gauguin's unhappy routine as a stockbroker, a career that, in Becker's view, prompted him to choose instead the life of an unrestrained avant-garde artist. The treatment of Gauguin's years in Paris, the south of France, and the south Seas fares little better. While supported by extensive passages from the artist's writings, Becker's text dramatizes these difficult years, coloring the artist's struggles through a paradisiac filter and his perception of Gauguin as a ''calm madman.'' Overall, this work is more fiction than biography.

BURNETT supplanted Becker with the most objective and conscientious biography available in English. Until the appearance of Perruchot's text (see below), this was the standard life. Drawing heavily on the French sources of Rotonchamp and Morice, as well as Gauguin's writings and the correspondence then available, Burnett situates his work against the backdrop of social transformations occurring in France during the late 19th century. Here one finds important details of Gauguin's youth, including his family's four-year stay in Peru (1851–56), his career in the merchant marine and navy, and a richly detailed account of life in Tahiti. Burnett objectively records the less positive aspects of the artist's character in a well-organized, somewhat prosaic biography. Quoting liberally from Gauguin's writings (in reliable translations), Burnett does not identify his sources, somewhat limiting this book's value to the scholar.

POLA GAUGUIN's fluid portrait of his father covers much the same material as Burnett, with letters and passages from the journals peppered freely throughout his text. Here, one finds new insights into Gauguin's youth and family history and life in the Gad/Gauguin household during the years of Paul's absence. Palo is surprisingly objective in addressing the less positive aspects of his father's character—including his marital infidelities—and like Burnett, he corrects the idealized image of the Tahitian period with material from Frederick O'Brien's *White Shadows in the South Seas* (1919) and conversations with the French sculptor Paco Durio.

Since Palo barely knew his father, his perceptions derive from his mother's reminiscences and those of family friends, amplified by published studies. The portrait of Paul Gauguin that emerges here differs only slightly from that found in previous works: a man of tremendous independence but "without fanaticism." Gauguin sought that independence in all dimensions of his life, from his religious beliefs to his artistic aims and his views on traditional bourgeois life and culture. For its insights into Gauguin from family and close friends, this work is worth reading.

The HANSON biography, although based on extensive research including newly discovered letters, was written for a popular audience, "for those who, like ourselves, get pleasure and inspiration from a work of art and are eager to know more about the artist." They further the Romantic image of Gauguin as a "noble savage," and like Becker's *Calm Madman*, they indulge a regrettable tendency toward sensationalism. Novelistic in tone, this work explodes factually accurate events into larger-than-life vignettes, woven together by invented dialogue and free translations of Gauguin's writings. the Hansons amplify the character of Mette Gad—the text opens with Gauguin's courtship of the young Danish governess—yet her personality is projected through such a prejudicial view of Gauguin's character that the reader will find their assessment suspect, despite new factual material. Since the authors are not art critics, their portrait deemphasises Gauguin's role as a painter in favor of a personality whose interest rests on its dramatic deviance.

PERRUCHOT's life is a revised and expanded version of his biography of 1948. Offering the most extensive research yet available in English, Perruchot incorporates new information from manuscript material, published secondary sources, and both published and unpublished letters and recollections of family, friends, and colleagues. From this evidence, Perruchot fleshes out Gauguin's artistic evolution; his youth and life in Denmark and France prior to the first Martinique voyage; his connections with contemporary artists; and the social and artistic climate of Arles, Le Pouldu, Paris, and the South Seas. The personality of Mette Gad is given fuller dimension (and she is generally more objectively treated) than in any other source, but certain difficulties—over money matters and the sale of pictures—are at times glossed over in Perruchot's account.

Perruchot's liberal quotations from Gauguin's writings and from the memoirs of friends and associates capture Gauguin's moods, his responses and feelings to new situations and surroundings, yielding a biography with the richest and most textured view of Gauguin's character. This elaborately detailed biography is marred only by the absence of citations for these texts and a slight tendency toward fictionalizing less well-documented events. Perruchot contributes to our understanding of Gauguin's independence as he sensitively sketches a figure who was an enigma even to himself. An extensive bibliography

and chronology as well as contemporaneous photographs further enhance the value of this study. Both the scholar and general reader will find this the single most valuable biography.

DANIELSSON's more narrowly focused and very detailed study of the South Seas' period is invaluable for its frank, unidealized portrait of Gauguin, its insights into the social life and history of the islands during the late 19th century, and for its correction of chronological errors in previous lives and in the Gauguin correspondence edited by Maurice Malinque (*Lettres de Gauguin à sa femme et à ses amis*, Paris, 1946). An anthropologist by training, Danielsson deemphasises artistic analysis in favor of the routine, the friendships, and the petty quarrels that made up Gauguin's day-to-day life in the islands. After interviewing more than 200 officials and residents, Danielsson chose only a tenth of these as reliable witnesses. A cache of yet unpublished letters, newspaper accounts, and official documents (now in the Danielsson Archives, Papeete) also support his reassessment of Gauguin's years in the South Seas. Danielsson is able to claim that Gauguin did not visit Tahiti in 1867 as Perruchot wrote and that the child conceived (and thought to have been born) to his Tahitian wife Teha'amana (Tehura) was aborted. He provides information on and photographs of Gauguin's surviving Tahitian children, along with more specific details on Gauguin's illness (syphilis) and his difficulties with Mette over finances and the sale of paintings. The Gauguin who emerges here, as Danielsson writes in his introduction, is indeed without his false halo. Also valuable in this study are Gauguin's photographs of Tahitian models that may have been used as sources for finished paintings.

Three recent studies written for the non-specialist draw upon material from previous lives; each interweaves biography with artistic analysis. LE PINCHON's lavishly illustrated work retains a somewhat romanticized tone, but of the three it offers the most detailed account of Gauguin's life. Comparable in format, HOOG's fluidly written text assumes a more objective historical stance and includes a useful chronological summary. Of the three this is the most valuable overall study of Gauguin. THOMSON, like Hoog, adds a third ingredient to the mix, the larger artistic context, but this work is marred by a few factual errors (e.g., concerning Gauguin's burial).

—Phylis Floyd

GAULLE, Charles de. See **DE GAULLE, Charles.**

GENGHIS KHAN, *ca.* 1167–1227; Mongol conqueror.

Fox, Ralph, *Genghis Khan*. London, J. Lane, and New York, Harcourt, 1936.
Grousset, René, *Conqueror of the World*, translated by Denis Sinor and Marian Mackellar. Edinburgh and London, Oliver and Boyd, and New York, Orion, 1967 (originally published by A. Michel, Paris, 1944).

Hartog, Leo de, *Genghis Khan: Conqueror of the World*. London, I. B. Tauris, and New York, St. Martin's, 1989 (originally published by Elsevier, Amsterdam, 1979).

Lamb, Harold, *Genghis Khan, Emperor of All Men*. New York, Doubleday, 1927; London, T. Butterworth, 1928.

Martin, Henry Desmond, *The Rise of Chingis Khan and his Conquest of North China*. Baltimore, Maryland, Johns Hopkins University Press, 1950.

Petis de la Croix, F., *The History of Genghizcan the Great*, translated by P. Aubin. London, J. Darby, 1722 (originally published Chez la Veuve Jombert, Paris, 1710).

Vladimirtsov, B. Y., *The Life of Chingis Khan*, translated by D. S. Mirksy. London, Routledge, and Boston, Houghton Mifflin, 1930 (originally published in 1922).

Walker, C. C., *Jenghiz Khan*. London, Luzac, 1939.

*

Genghis Khan, one of the most remarkable figures in world history, has attracted a great many biographers, good, bad, and indifferent. Most of them, unfortunately, fall into the two latter categories. The writing of Genghis' biography makes serious demands on the author, especially of a linguistic nature. The sources are in a large number of languages, of which the most important are Mongolian, Persian, and Chinese. Very few scholars have an adequate reading knowledge of all three languages, and most of the biographers have known none of them, being entirely dependent on translations. There are translations into various languages of the major Mongolian source, the *Secret History of the Mongols*, English versions of two of the Persian sources, Juwayni and Juzjani, and a Russian version of the most important Persian source, Rashid al-Din (whose account of Genghis Khan's life was based on a now lost Mongolian chronicle); but for much of the Chinese material, such as the official history of the Mongol dynasty in China, the *Yüan-shih*, a knowledge of the language is essential. The result of this difficulty is that almost none of the biographies, whatever their virtues in terms of readability or insight, really meet the demands of modern scholarship in terms of a firsthand and critical use of original sources.

PETIS DE LA CROIX was Oriental interpreter at the court of Louis XIV of France. His biography of Genghis Khan, first published in French in 1710, was the first modern European life. It was based, unavoidably, on the limited range of sources that happened to be available to the author—mainly the Persian sources accessible in Louis XIV's library. Considering its pioneering character, it is an impressive piece of work; much of its material and even many of its conclusions remain valid. It exercised a wide influence on the study of the subject, an influence that is perhaps not yet wholly spent. The English translator dedicated his version to the Prince of Wales, the future King George II, and in an unintentionally very funny preface compared George (to his advantage, but only just) with Genghis Khan.

Not all subsequent biographies were as impressive as the first. LAMB was an inveterate biographer whose subjects included, among others, Cyrus the Great, Charlemagne, Omar Khayyam, Tamerlane, and Babur. His books hover on the indistinct borderland between history and fiction, and are characterised by such features as conversations in direct speech. As J. J. Saunders

justly remarked, "his racy, journalistic style is not to everyone's taste" (*The History of the Mongol Conquests*, London, Routledge, 1971), and his information is very far from reliable. Lamb's life has probably been the most widely read of all. The best that can be said for it is that, in common with his other books, it aroused the interest of many readers in a subject that was rather off the beaten track—possibly not an entirely negligible achievement.

VLADIMIRTSOV was a distinguished Russian Mongolist, whose book first appeared in Russian in 1922. It has the virtue of attempting to dig below the surface of events and to examine the social and economic background to the rise of Genghis Khan; and it is based on the fundamental Mongolian source, the *Secret History of the Mongols*. It is still of some value, though it is neither a full nor an especially profound study; nor is it more than very lightly annotated.

FOX was a colourful Marxist whose book, while not an original scholarly contribution, makes extensive use of what was at the time rather inaccessible Russian scholarship, much of it of importance. His book is lively and for the most part accurate.

WALKER added little of substance to what could be learned from the biographies that already existed. But he was a Squadron Leader in the Royal Canadian Air Force, and no doubt because of this he had more understanding than most authors of the purely military aspects of Genghis Khan's career. His book is interesting on matters of tactics and strategy and also includes a number of excellent maps.

GROUSSET wrote what has long been seen, until recently, as the standard biography. The editorial work of the translators, and especially the very helpful and up-to-date bibliography by Denis Sinor, greatly enhances the book's usefulness, though the annotation is still far from adequate. Grousset was an exceptionally fine historian in the French *haute vulgarisation* tradition. His book, a little rhapsodic in approach, is readable and based on very extensive knowledge.

The first modern biography that broke new ground was MARTIN's book. It is based on a very thorough and comprehensive knowledge of the Chinese sources, and provides, in particular, an immensely detailed account of Genghis Khan's campaigns in China—an account that may indeed become a little wearisome, in its unrelenting detail, to readers who are not devotees of military history. Still, this is a study of major scholarly value. It cannot, however, be regarded as a fully rounded biography. Its scope is indicated by its title: it deals with Genghis Khan's early career and his conquest of north China, and touches only briefly—though interestingly—on his campaigns in Central Asia, Afghanistan, and Persia.

So far as Genghis Khan's life as a whole is concerned, the most recent biography, DE HARTOG's, is the best in English. Like so many of his predecessors, de Hartog had no knowledge of the sources in their original languages. An enthusiastic "amateur" student of the subject, he produced what is an example of good amateur history, both readable and well-informed, though stronger as a narrative of events than in terms of analysis. First published in Dutch in 1979, the book was to some extent revised for its English edition. It is based on a careful and extensive study of both translated original sources and a wide range of secondary literature. Hence it provides a helpful conspectus of the state of the field at the time of writing. It has the additional advantage of providing, in its last three chapters, a discussion of the reigns of Genghis Khan's two successors, his son Ögedei and grandson Güyük (1229–1248).

De Hartog therefore provides the best current biography, though scholars will continue to refer to Martin for his detailed Chinese material. But this situation will soon change. In 1983 there appeared Paul Ratchnevsky's *Činggis-Khan sein Leben und Wirken*, a biography that is in a class of its own. Ratchnevsky is a notable Mongolist who is at home in both Mongolian and Chinese (he used the Russian translations for the Persian material provided by Rashid al-Din). His book is firmly based on the full range of original souces, takes account of the important scholarly work of the last 30 years, is well annotated and referenced, and is indeed the only full biography of Genghis Khan to conform entirely satisfactorily to modern scholarly standards. An English translation by Thomas Haining, a former British ambassador to Mongolia, has been completed and is in the press (Oxford, Blackwell). When it appears it will supersede all other biographies in English.

—David Morgan

GEORGE III, 1738–1820; English monarch.

Ayling, Stanley, *George the Third*. London, Collins, and New York, Knopf, 1972.

Brooke, John, *King George III*. London, Constable, and New York, McGraw-Hill, 1972.

Clarke, John, *The Life and Times of George III*. London, Weidenfeld and Nicolson, 1972.

MacAlpine, Ida and Richard Hunter, *George III and the Mad-Business*. London, A. Lane, 1969; New York, Pantheon, 1970.

Pares, Richard, *King George III and the Politicians*. Oxford, Clarendon Press, 1953; with subtitle, *The Ford Lectures Delivered at the University of Oxford*, London and New York, Oxford University Press, 1967.

*

These books are agreed on many points: they destroy the myths of "the old, mad, bad, blind and despised" king; they destroy also the largely American view of him as a reactionary tyrant, conspiring against the liberties of his subjects, British as well as American, the view born of the vulgar polemics of John Wilkes and of the eloquent tirades of Edmund Burke, and used by Bancroft in the 19th century to explain American national origins.

From 1809 onwards George III was, of course, mentally unbalanced and all but blind. Most historians, including Brooke and Ayling, accept the medical findings of MacALPINE AND HUNTER, both psychiatrists, who claimed that the king became a sufferer from a form of madness now know as porphyria: an inherited metabolic disorder endemic in the Stuarts and transmitted to the Hanoverians by the Electress Sophia, granddaughter of James I and mother of George I. It was a physical rather than mental condition, which caused abdominal pain, weakness of the limbs and mental unbalance, marked by rambling speech and hallucinations; for shorter or longer periods after his 50th year, and only from that point, it was to afflict George III with what medical experts could then only describe as madness. MacAlpine and Hunter's diagnosis has been confirmed only in our own time by experts at the British Medical Association. Most historians now accept the diagnosis, but there have been a few dissenters (see correspondence in *Times Literary Supplement* 8, 15, 22, 29 January 1970).

PARES, in a study designed to assess the king's role as manipulator of the House of Commons, draws attention to the remarkable transformation of the lazy and "almost hysterically diffident" youth of the Bute letters, into the energetic, self-confident, and astute figure of the later years. This, in major part, explains how the feeble and short-lived administrations of the 1760s were succeeded by strong and stable administrations. CLARKE's volume purveys the old (now discounted) rumours of the alleged infatuation of the king's mother with Lord Bute, and of George III's supposed involvement with Hannah Lightfoot, the beautiful Quaker.

BROOKE is at his best on the parliamentary scene, even if he allows himself to be swamped by partisan and involved *minutiae*. He furnishes some remarkable pages on Whiggism, one of the best summaries of that little-valued creed. He has, however, a somewhat irritating habit of hunting for contemporary parallels—Lord North "was the Stanley Baldwin or Clement Attlee of his age"—and to this reviewer he too readily assumes the inevitability of American separation. He can be too argumentative at times. As an expert on the House of Commons, he is much too cursory in his treatment of the years between the Stamp Act, the Townshend duties, and the Boston Tea Party: he tells us little on the shaping of the king's views in this decade. His portrait, too, is royal—and aristocratic—centred. Both Ayling (see below) and Brooke fail to portray the complexity and the fascination of the American question; and Brooke in particular seeks a too-popular line. In places, indeed, he is jejune: "Perhaps the fundamental reason why Great Britain lost the American colonies was that King George and Queen Charlotte never visited America." But in its accuracy, sharpness of judgment, and command of British political detail, Brooke's is a masterly and authoritative study of a too much abused king.

AYLING's biography is equally accurate and more readable. His treatment, however, is conventional, and again especially sketchy on the American revolt; he sees "obsolete paternalism at the heart of British errors of policy."

In the biographies of Brooke and Ayling, we have two highly competent and sympathetic studies; and Brooke, the more revisionist, is the more stimulating. From each of them emerges a consensus that, on America, the king had the overwhelming support not only of the House of Commons, but of the lords and of most of the country. From each comes a portrait of an industrious, art-loving and art-collecting, generous, and well-meaning ruler.

—Esmond Wright

GEORGE V, 1865–1936; English monarch.

Gore, John, *King George V: A Personal Memoir.* London, J. Murray, and New York, Scribner, 1941; abridged edition, J. Murray, 1949.

Nicolson, Harold, *King George the Fifth: His Life and Reign.* London, Constable, 1952; New York, Doubleday, 1953.

Rose, Kenneth, *King George V.* London, Weidenfeld and Nicolson, 1983; New York, Knopf, 1984.

*

Among the many books about members of the British royal family, relatively few have appeared on George V. This would not have distressed him. The written word did not much interest him. He read little, and wrote less, perhaps because he wrote painfully slowly. His advisers wrote not only his speeches but his letters. Even the memoir of three teenage years in a Royal Navy ship, ostensibly co-authored by Prince George and his elder brother, was written by John Dalton, an Anglican clergyman chosen by Queen Victoria as tutor to her grandsons. *H.M.S. Bacchante* (2 vols., London, 1886) was misnamed, at least while Dalton was aboard, and the endless pendantry of the tutor's writing suggests why his youthful charges learned so little from him (George V loved but could not spell royal prerogative). A later naval cruise, in which Prince George was accompanied by his wife (the future Queen Mary), is wonderfully described and illustrated in the diary of Petty Officer Harry Price, published in fascimile as *The Royal Tour, 1901* (New York, 1980).

While on the *Bacchante*, Price George did begin a diary, into which he wrote daily until a few days before his death. This diary, which has never been published in its entirety, and access to which has been restricted by his heirs, is the basis for the three most important biographies of George V that have been published.

The first, by GORE, bears the legend "Published by authority of His Majesty the King." George VI, according to Nicolson (see below), charged Gore with writing about only the private life of the king's father, avoiding political matters. This charge, accompanied by the eventual royal imprimatur, suggests that Gore's book contains nothing that offended the royal family. Since Gore follows not only the chronological form of the diary of George V, with occasional extracts from it, but the diary's perspective, his book could fairly be termed entirely sympathetic. His most reliable accounts are of the king's hobbies. George V had two minor enthusiasms, for horse racing and yachting. The former flowed from filial piety, and the latter from his happy early experiences in the Royal Navy (which he left only after his older brother died, leaving Prince George unexpectedly in the direct line of succession). The real passions of George V were his two major hobbies, the unusual combination of philately and hunting birds. As prince and king, George amassed an astonishing number of valuable stamps, and killed an equally astonishing number of birds. The latter achievement is related with special pride by Gore, as well as by James Wentworth Day (*King George V as a Sportsman*, London, 1935). When Gore goes, occasionally, beyond the king's private life, his accounts of political matters are often misleading as well as mistaken. It is regrettable that the popular abridged edition of Gore's book omits his account of George's youth, the most interesting part of his original edition.

In 1948 George VI decided another official biography of his father was needed. This book would, unlike Gore's, focus on the public life of George V. It would not mention anything discreditable, but in exchange for royal censorship its author would gain access to royal archives, including the diary of George V. NICOLSON agreed to write this book, although to him George V was dull and lacking in charm, fatal flaws to Nicolson, who had no mystic feeling about the monarchy. Large sales, public acclaim, and a knighthood for its author followed publication of *King George the Fifth.* Privately, however, its author confided in his own diary his indifference to publication of the book. Nicolson's failure to feel satisfied with his book is understandable. Sometimes the insincerity of his praise for George V shows. The book, whose chapters were written in largely random order, is disjointed. Nicolson's feline grace as a writer appears only occasionally in this mostly narrative book. Most seriously, belatedly realizing that George V had not mattered much politically, Nicolson was left without a distinctive focus. Abandoning a strictly political biography, he adds to George's private life a few confused analytical musings on the power of monarchy in a modern state. Gore (whose book Nicolson read only after he had agreed to write its successor) had already treated George's private life, and at least Gore's praise of his subject was sincere.

While using the royal archives Nicolson took many notes on the diary of George V that he did not use in his book. These notes were later used by ROSE, who also draws on a substantial number of other archival and published sources, including the early biography by Sir George Arthur (*George V*, New York, 1930), although, surprisingly, not the other early books, by Buchan (1935), Dent (1930), and Legge (1918). Dealing with both personal and public matters, as well as their intersection, Rose's book is the best biography of George V. Rose asks more, and more penetrating, questions about George V than do Gore or Nicolson. Sometimes Rose slips, as when he repeatedly acknowledges, but does not try to explain, increasing republicanism in Britain during and shortly after World War I. Rose quotes, slightly imprecisely and in another context, David Lloyd George's later claim that George V "owes his throne to me." This curious remark goes unexamined by Rose.

—Marvin Rintala

GEORGE VI, 1895–1952; English monarch.

Bradford, Sarah, *King George VI.* London, Weidenfeld and Nicolson, 1989; as *The Reluctant King: The Life and Reign of George VI*, New York, St. Martin's, 1990.

Howarth, Patrick, *George VI: A New Biography.* London, Hutchinson, 1987.

Judd, Denis, *King George VI 1895–1952.* London, M. Joseph, 1982; New York, F. Watts, 1983.

Middlemas, Keith, *King George VI.* London, Weidenfeld and Nicolson, 1969.

Thomson, Malcolm, et al, *The Life and Times of King George VI.* London, Odhams Press, 1952.

Townsend, Peter, *The Last Emperor: Decline and Fall of the British Empire.* London, Weidenfeld and Nicolson, 1975; as

Last Emperor: An Intimate Account of George VI and the Fall of His Empire, New York, Simon and Schuster, 1976.

Warwick, Christopher, *King George VI and Queen Elizabeth*. New York, Beaufort, and London, Sidgwick and Jackson, 1985.

Wheeler-Bennett, John W., *King George VI: His Life and Reign*. London, Macmillan, and New York, St. Martin's, 1958.

*

The biographies of King George VI at this time seem to have fallen into a familiar pattern. First, there comes the outright hagiographical material appearing shortly after his death, which should come as no surprise since George VI was genuinely liked by the British people with many of them perceiving his passing as the ending of an historical era. Next comes the inevitable official biography, long, detailed, well researched, and thorough, although too courtly in tone, showing too much awe of the royal subject. Then in the intervening years a number of biographies of George VI have appeared, promising revisionism, shocking personal or family details, psychological insights, or new information about politics and diplomacy. And finally there are the popular books that center on the relationship between father and daughter, George VI and Queen Elizabeth, that appeal to a public hungry for news about the royal family.

Belonging to the first category of hagiography is the pictorial, souvenir remembrance put together by THOMSON, containing Prime Minister Winston Churchill's tribute to the fallen king, the last emperor. An historical curiosity today, it still possesses some value because of the insights and images provided by the photographs of the period and the king. TOWNSEND's study may not be hagiography, but it verges on it. The author served in the royal household for eight years as an equerry (an officer who attends the king), so he can provide a close personal view of the palace and its doings. So close in fact that he had at one time a much publicized relationship with Princess Margaret. Townsend's study is a sympathetic portrait of George VI—appropriately closed with the moving and dramatic phrase, "The King is dead"—as well as an account of the events and personalities in a rapidly changing British Empire.

The official biography of King George V represented a division of labor with the private life entrusted to one author, and the public life going to another. WHEELER-BENNETT in his official biography of George VI will have none of that nonsense, so he deals with both sovereign and man, the public and the private George VI. The author had full access to the Royal Archives. Wheeler-Bennett deals tenderly with this shy, withdrawn man who had a severe speech impediment as a child. But he offers no real psychological insight that would explain his character. The royal role in historical affairs tends to be overplayed, but Wheeler-Bennett nonetheless avoids merely repeating the court calendar. Throughout the narrative there always seems to be a halo floating above the crown. George VI always seemed to be suffering, was always wise, religious, courageous, dutiful, devoted to his country and his family, all the while acting as the "People's King." Such excessive adulation perhaps stems from the circumstances in which George VI ascended to the throne (the unseemly affair of Edward VIII and Mrs. Wallis Simpson still rankled the British, or at least Wheeler-Bennett). Monarchs,

even British monarchs, can be petty and temperamental, though Wheeler-Bennett shows us no such side of George VI.

A number of biographies have appeared since the definitive study by Wheeler-Bennett. The works by MIDDLEMAS and JUDD are not well known in the United States and neither offers much beyond Wheeler-Bennett. Judd records some remarkable anecdotes about the tongue-twisters that the young Duke's speech therapist had him practice to relieve his stammering (a memorable one being, "Let's go gathering healthy heather with the gay brigade of grand dragoons").

HOWARTH in his 1988 study sees a much more earthy and human king than did Wheeler-Bennett. Howarth's biography is methodical and deeply researched, drawing on some neglected Foreign Office papers in the Public Records Office. His major disclosure is the revelation that the Duke of Windsor offered to accept the presidency of a British Socialist republic. He makes other disclosures as well involving Anglo-American relations during World War II, some merely anecdotal, others more substantive.

The most recent biography of George VI is by the biographer of Disraeli, BRADFORD. The author spent four years researching the book and supposedly had access to some previously unpublished letters and documents. She offers a much more complex psychological portrait of George VI than had previously been presented. Bradford reveals that he had a mania for punctuality, an obsession with correct dress, and a propensity for "gnashes," wild, emotional rages. But Bradford is at her best when she shows the deep alienation, and indeed fear, that separated both sons from their father, George V, a petty, mean, denigrating man, and from their aloof mother, Queen Mary. The future Edward VIII and George VI suffered grievous psychological damage from which they never really recovered. Bradford also dwells on the stormy relationship between the two brothers, generated in large measure by their opposite personalities. Here we have a George VI whose character was warped, who was not very intellectual (although he possessed a photographic memory), yet stodgy enough, in an elegant and charming way, to appeal to the British masses. Bradford has produced a modern, readable, well-researched, and well-illustrated biography that has popular appeal without trivializing its subject.

There are several unnoteworthy books dealing with the relationship between George VI and Queen Elizabeth. The best of this lot may be by WARWICK, who also serves as an authorized biographer for members of the royal family. The study listed here consists merely of a series of sketches of the Queen Mother, Queen Elizabeth, and George VI, based almost entirely on secondary sources. Most of this genre of popular royal biography is intended for the coffee table.

—Richard A. Voeltz

GERSHWIN, George, 1898–1937; American composer and pianist.

Armitage, Merle, editor, *George Gershwin*. New York and London, Longman, 1938.

Armitage, Merle, *George Gershwin: Man and Legend*. New York, Duell Sloane, 1958.

De Santis, Florence, *Gershwin*. New York, Treves, 1987.

Ewen, David, *The Story of George Gershwin*. New York, Holt, 1943.

Ewen, David, *A Journey to Greatness: The Life and Music of George Gershwin*. New York, Holt, and London, W. H. Allen, 1956; revised as *George Gershwin: His Journey to Greatness*, Englewood Cliffs, New Jersey, Prentice-Hall, 1970.

Goldberg, Isaac, *George Gershwin: A Study in American Music*. New York, Simon and Schuster, 1931; revised edition, New York, F. Ungar, 1958.

Jablonski, Edward and Lawrence D. Stewart, *The Gershwin Years*. New York, Doubleday, 1958; revised edition, Doubleday, 1973; London, Robson Books, 1974.

Jablonski, Edward, *George Gershwin*. New York, Putnam, 1962.

Jablonski, Edward, *Gershwin*. New York, Doubleday, 1987; London, Simon and Schuster, 1988.

Kendall, Alan, *George Gershwin: A Biography*. New York, Universe Books, and London, Harrap, 1987.

Kimball, Robert and Alfred Simon, *The Gershwins*. New York, Atheneum, 1973; London, Cape, 1974.

Kresh, Paul, *American Rhapsody: The Story of George Gershwin*. New York, Lodestar, 1988.

Mitchell, Barbara, *America, I Hear You: A Story about George Gershwin*. Minneapolis, Carolrhoda Books, 1987.

Payne, Robert, *Gershwin*. New York, Pyramid Books, and London, R. Hale, 1960.

Rushmore, Robert, *The Life of George Gershwin*. New York, Crowell Collier, and London, Collier Macmillan, 1966.

Schwartz, Charles M., *Gershwin: His Life and Music*. Indianapolis, Bobbs-Merrill, and London, Abelard-Schuman, 1973.

*

George Gershwin is considered by journalists and authors to be "good copy" because of his meteoric rise to celebrity, colorful career, and sudden death at the height of his powers. The early biographies, several of which are heavily romanticized, were intended to satisfy the public's appetite for accounts of Gershwin's life. Only in recent years have more objective treatments appeared.

GOLDBERG published his study six years before Gershwin's death. Because the author enjoyed Gershwin's full cooperation in the project, the book includes an abundance of information about Gershwin's childhood and early career. Goldberg (philologist, editor, and author of a respected history of Tin Pan Alley) champions Gershwin as the first composer to produce a uniquely American musical idiom. In spite of its heavy-handed idolatry, Goldberg remains indispensable reading for Gershwin researchers. The revised edition (1958) includes an extensive supplement that examines the final years of Gershwin's life.

ARMITAGE is an impresario, author, editor, and book designer who managed Gershwin's final concerts and produced acclaimed stagings of *Porgy and Bess* after Gershwin's death. His *George Gershwin* (1938) is a reverent collection of essays written by 38 of Gershwin's contemporaries. Although not a narra-

tive biography, this compilation of tributes and reminiscences by other famous musicians (including Irving Berlin, Jerome Kern, Harold Arlen, Paul Whiteman, Walter Damrosch, Arnold Schoenberg, and Serge Koussevitzky) is a unique source of biographical information. Armitage's eye for design is evidenced by the inclusion of 16 elegant photographs of Gershwin and reproductions of 16 of Gershwin's paintings and drawings. Armitage's *George Gershwin: Man and Legend* (1958) presents a fascinating behind-the-scenes look into the years of friendship between Armitage and Gershwin, and charmingly describes the tribulations of a successful impresario. The final chapter is an especially thorough account of the history of *Porgy and Bess*.

EWEN, a prolific writer on popular music and on 20th-century composers, has written biographical dictionaries, general histories, and numerous journal articles. His *Journey to Greatness* (1956) is an accessible and entertaining survey, but a number of scholars, including Jablonski, have criticized Ewen for fabrication and misrepresentation.

PAYNE's popularly oriented biography, written for the paperback trade, contemplates the engaging but unprovable premise that the source of Gershwin's inspiration was his Jewish heritage. (The topic is not without merit—others, including Kresh, also consider this subject.) Unfortunately, Payne's book is flawed by an almost total dependence upon secondary sources (especially upon Jablonski and Stewart's *Gershwin Years*, see below) and by the careless recycling of misinformation.

SCHWARTZ has written four monographs on Gershwin: a Ph.D. dissertation entitled *The Life and Orchestral Works of George Gershwin* (1969), which examines Jewish elements in Gershwin's music; a bibliography; and two biographies. His dissertation presents an abundance of information but lacks focus and style. The study does provide some service by detailing discrepancies between Goldberg, Armitage, Ewen, and Jablonski/Stewart. Schwartz's *Gershwin* (1973), written after he had completed his university studies, is valuable for its wealth of well-researched information and its clarity of composition. Although this work recycles many passages from the 1969 dissertation, Schwartz presents so much new information here that *Gershwin* cannot be considered a mere revision of the earlier work. In addition to rendering biographical particulars, Schwartz speculates on hidden aspects of Gershwin's personality: sexual promiscuity, failure to form a lasting relationship with a woman, self-adulation, and the need to associate with classical masters. The abundance of documented material, presented in a straightforward—although somewhat plodding—literary style, makes this work a useful acquisition for university libraries.

KIMBALL AND SIMON offer a handsome coffee-table book that presents, in chronological order, a fascinating compilation of photographs, diary excerpts, song texts, interviews, excerpts from letters, and insightful commentary by the editors. Like Armitage's 1938 collection of articles, this book is not a narrative biography, but its wealth of material makes it an invaluable source of information on both George and Ira Gershwin. DE SANTIS' brief survey (106 pages, with over 200 illustrations), intended for the general reader, offers no new information.

KENDALL provides a well-intentioned but somewhat amateurish attempt to reassess Gershwin's career. In its effort to be "not just another Gershwin biography," it frequently omits basic information that belongs in every Gershwin biography. For example, the chapter on "Rhapsody in Blue" neglects to mention the famous "Experiment in Modern Music" concert that served as the composition's premiere.

Edward Jablonski (a noted music critic whose output includes an encyclopedia on American music, a biography of Harold Arlen, and dozens of journal articles) has produced the finest investigations of Gershwin. JABLONSKI AND STEWART's *The Gershwin Years* (1958) was produced with the full cooperation of Ira Gershwin, who freely shared his extensive archives with the authors. The result is an engrossing work that can entertain the Gershwin fan as well as satisfy the discerning academic. The revised edition (1973) includes in its appendices an especially cogent evaluation of Gershwin bibliography, discography, and public and private archives.

JABLONSKI has also produced an excellent introductory treatment of Gershwin's life for adolescent readers. Of the biographies in this category, his *George Gershwin* (1962) offers the most in substance and style. Other works for younger readers include EWEN's *The Story of George Gershwin* (1943), RUSHMORE's *Life* (1966), and KRESH's *American Rhapsody* (1988). MITCHELL's 1987 publication would be suitable for elementary school readers.

JABLONSKI's *Gershwin* (1987) is the definitive Gershwin biography. Authoritative and accessible, it presents the fruits of decades of research in a captivating fashion. Thoroughly researched data, a polished prose style, educated speculation, a judicious selection of insightful photography, and a meticulous index are the principle ingredients that make this work a model biography.

—Michael Cogswell

GIBBON, Edward, 1737–1794; English historian.

Carnochan, W. B., *Gibbon's Solitude*. Stanford, California, Stanford University Press, 1987.

Craddock, Patricia B., *Young Edward Gibbon: Gentleman of Letters*. Baltimore, Maryland, Johns Hopkins University Press, 1982.

Craddock, Patricia B., *Edward Gibbon, Luminous Historian, 1772–94*. Baltimore, Maryland, Johns Hopkins University Press, 1989.

De Beer, Gavin, *Gibbon and his World*. London, Thames and Hudson, and New York, Viking, 1968.

Joyce, Michael, *Edward Gibbon*. London and New York, Longman, 1953.

Low, D. M., *Edward Gibbon*. London, Chatto and Windus, and New York, Random House, 1937.

Morison, James Augustus Cotter, *Gibbon*. London, Macmillan, and New York, Harper, 1878.

Mowat, Robert M., *Gibbon*. London, A. Barker, 1936.

Oliver, E. J., *Gibbon and Rome*. London and New York, Sheed and Ward, 1958.

Parkinson, Richard N., *Edward Gibbon*. Boston, Twayne, 1973.

Quennell, Peter, *Four Portraits: Studies of the 18th Century*. London, Collins, 1945; as *The Profane Virtues: Four Studies of the 18th Century*, New York, Viking, 1945.

Read, J. Meredith, *Historic Studies in Vaud, Berne, and Savoy* (2 vols.). London, Chatto and Windus, 1897.

Robertson, J. M., *Gibbon*. London, Watts, 1925.

Swain, Joseph W., *Edward Gibbon the Historian*. London, Macmillan, and New York, St. Martin's, 1966.

Young, G. M., *Gibbon*. London, P. Davies, 1932; New York, Appleton, 1933.

*

Gibbon made half a dozen attempts to write his autobiography, but achieved no version with which he himself was satisfied. The original drafts were first published by John Murray in 1896 (as *The Autobiographies of Edward Gibbon*), but 100 years earlier Gibbon's friend Lord Sheffield had constructed a continuous narrative out of the fragments, and in so doing provided the basis for all subsequent lives of the historian. The task of reconstruction was attempted anew by G. A. Bonnard, and his elaborate editorial work makes his version (*Memoirs of My Life*, London, Nelson, 1966) an indispensable contribution to Gibbon studies.

The earliest standard biography, by MORISON, adheres closely to the narrative established by Sheffield, but amplifies it with materials serving to illustrate the state of the universities and the temper of politics in 18th-century England, along with a certain amount of gossip on the famous love-affair with Suzanne Curchod. Although Gibbon studies have moved on immeasurably since 1878, Morison's book remains an attractive short narrative, interesting in its own right as a Comtist evaluation of the theme of *The History of the Decline and Fall of the Roman Empire*. Morison's emphasis on Gibbon's cool detachment may seem uncontentious enough until one reads the detailed polemic against Morison's book launched by ROBERTSON in his eloquent rationalist vindication of Gibbon as man and historian. Robertson is particularly concerned to question some of the anecdotes that have been told to Gibbon's disadvantage, and which still colour impressions of his character. Some adverse judgment is unavoidable: Robertson, who was a member of Parliament himself, concedes that Gibbon's political career did him no great credit.

Gibbon's long periods of residence in Lausanne make the Swiss context of major importance to biographers, and the pioneer work in this field was undertaken by READ. Most of the material he collects has been incorporated in later studies, and his anecdotes have been subjected to much-needed critical examination, but his book (see vol. 2) continues to be of interest in viewing Gibbon in his Lausanne setting. The same might be said of DE BEER, whose book is particularly well supplied with Swiss material. His scientific interests also help him to evaluate evidence on Gibbon's ill health.

YOUNG's short study is probably still the best of its kind. Concise almost to abruptness, Young outlines the main events of Gibbon's life vividly, and provides an admirable account of the various intellectual influences that affected him. His quotations are peculiarly felicitous: he savours them, and communicates his enjoyment to the reader. Young gives a pungent account of Gibbon's political career, emphasizing that his natural affinities were with the Whig opposition. He makes the most of Charles James Fox's visit to Gibbon in Lausanne, suggesting dryly that the great Whig found himself "cast for the role of Caesar dining with Cicero." Fox, says Young, "played up royally." The book is helpful also in suggesting why Gibbon's account of the early Church aroused such hostility. Young is keenly aware of the emerging public opinion which was to find satisfaction in Scott and Chateaubriand, an environment in which Gibbon could not fail to strike a jarring note.

MOWAT's biography is a competent retelling of the familiar story, but makes no special contribution to Gibbon studies. Its publication was soon followed by LOW's, a major landmark. Low's book is thoroughly researched, following through the work begun in his fine edition of the journal that Gibbon kept in the early 1760s. He dwells with a novelist's appreciation on every phase of the historian's development. He conjures up a picture of a 13-year-old boy, his head full of the *Arabian Nights* and Pope's version of Homer, writing with enthusiam about a visit he had paid to "the Remains of an Ancient Camp." His account of the Suzanne Curchod affair is sympathetic, full, and probably definitive, as is the brief assessment of the ambiguous connection with Mme. Bontemps in Paris. Low enters into Gibbon's conscientious participation in militia service, organizing recruitment and enforcing discipline. Gibbon's political career is seen mainly in terms of his relations with his cousin and patron, Edward Eliot, a relationship conducted with diplomatic skill and a certain barbed courtesy. Low gives a particularly graphic picture of the last period of residence in Lausanne, imaginatively enlarging on informants like Sophie Laroche, and entering into his alarms about the revolution in France. Gibbon's great work, *The Decline and Fall*, is less prominently featured than in most biographies, but Low's brief discussion is perceptive. He argues that, for Gibbon, history was "essentially personal and dramatic": *The Decline and Fall* reminds him of "old engravings of dramatic scenes," the actors expressing their passions with "upturned eyes and streaming hair." He gives a very adequate account of the political and moral preoccupations of the historian, and claims for him an anticipation of "the most progressive thought of our own day."

QUENNELL's short sketch is deftly executed, but retails anecdotes in a dismayingly uncritical way. It may be recommended as an eminently readable version of the Gibbon legend. More serious, but without any particular claim to originality, are the studies by JOYCE and PARKINSON. Both have their centre of interest in admirable reassessments of *The Decline and Fall*; the biographical sections cover familiar ground. SWAIN's study is similar in scope, but makes a more striking contribution to our understanding of Gibbon's life. The chapters on the development of his religious skepticism and on his political career are lucid and full, and are probably the best starting-point for the general reader interested in these issues.

The studies by Oliver and Carnochan are only marginally biographies, but have considerable biographical interest. OLIVER reassesses the life in terms of Gibbon's fascination with his conception of Rome, developing a hint thrown out by Christopher Dawson that he felt, thought, and wrote as a latter-day Roman. He connects the emotional pain that Gibbon must have suffered in the course of his withdrawal from the Catholic Church with the pain of relinquishing Suzanne Curchod: Gibbon avoided such discomfort by taking refuge in the serene detachment that he

identified with the Roman ethos. His devotion to this Rome naturally led him into opposition to the Rome of the Church. CARNOCHAN sees "Gibbon's solitude" as the condition of his creativity and attempts to describe "the dialectic of Gibbon's inner life." Carnochan has a good chapter on the "defensive maneuvers and delaying actions" with which Gibbon encountered the prospect of death.

CRADDOCK's two volumes are the fullest biography to date and unlikely to be superseded in the foreseeable future. She has examined every phase of Gibbon's life with scrupulous thoroughness, and offers a systematic guide to the wealth of biographical material that has become available over the years. She emphasizes the negative associations that family ties had for Gibbon in the earlier part of his life. His traumatically insecure childhood made history—by which the past might seem to be controllable—peculiarly attractive. The actual development of his thinking about history is explained in great detail, with an authoritative analysis of his "apprentice works." She shows, too, how for a long time Gibbon was torn between two possible ways of life, that of the leisured country gentleman, and that of the scholar and historian. Once he had made his choice, Craddock demonstrates (in her second volume), Gibbon was still open to distraction and discouragement, as well as experiencing reinforcement and inspiration in his role. Although the "luminous historian" was not altogether an attractive character, Craddock produces ample evidence to show that he was quite able "to bestow and accept love and kindness when he knew they would not be rejected." The great achievement of this part of Craddock's study is in showing how the development of the historian's outlook reflects changes in his life, in particular his readiness to see merits in historical characters against whom he might well have been prejudiced, such as bishops. She notes the appearance of romantic heroes in the final installment of the history (Saladin, Richard Coeur de Lion, etc.), and suggests a pleasing connection with Gibbon's youthful conversations with his aunt, Catherine Porten.

Craddock's treatments of the major problems of Gibbon's biography—his conversions, his relations with Suzanne Curchod, his political life—are exemplary in their balance and sensitivity. Her account of his various physical infirmities provides vivid evidence of the torture he went through by way of medical treatment in his childhood. One wonders how he ever survived.

—Geoffrey Carnall

GIDE, André, 1869–1951; French writer.

Delay, Jean, *The Youth of André Gide*, translated by J. Guicharnaud. Chicago, University of Chicago Press, 1963 (originally published as *La Jeunesse d'André Gide*, Paris, Gallimard, 1956–57).

Fowlie, Wallace, *André Gide: His Life and Art*. New York, Macmillan, 1965; London, Collier-Macmillan, 1966.

Guérard, Albert, *André Gide*. Cambridge, Massachusetts, Harvard University Press, 1951; 2nd edition, 1969.

Hytier, Jean, *André Gide,* translated by Richard Howard. New York, Doubleday, and London, Constable, 1962 (originally published by E. Charlot, Alger, 1938).

Martin du Gard, Roger, *Recollections of André Gide,* translated by John Russell. New York, Viking, 1953; as *Notes on André Gide,* London, A. Deutsch, 1953 (originally published as *Notes sur André Gide,* Paris, Gallimard, 1951).

O'Brien, Justin, *Portrait of André Gide: A Critical Biography.* New York, Knopf, and London, Secker and Warburg, 1953.

*

André Gide was deeply affected by the regional, cultural, and religious differences of his heritage. Paul Gide, his father, a native of Uzès in Southern France, was a well-known scholar of law. His mother, Juliette Rondeaux, came from Normandy and was strongly influenced by Calvinist and Jansenist doctrines. Gide portrayed himself as "sitting at the crossroads of religions," that is to say, between Rondeaux's Catholicism and Gide's own Protestantism. In 1920 he wrote an article entitled "Heredity" in which he discusses the contradictions he was brought up with that became the source of his need to write: "Nothing could be more different than these two families, nothing more different than these two provinces of France, whose contradictory influences are combined in me. I have often convinced myself that I was forced to create because only through art could I reconcile those discordant elements. . . . "

These contradictory influences in his childhood may explain why Gide remained rather unsettled and why he traveled extensively throughout the world during his life. For a man well known for writing "families I hate you" and "I am not like the others," it is then of the utmost importance to give full consideration to his biography. DELAY's study constitutes the most valuable biographical source on Gide to date due to its extensive and thorough research. This study is based on unpublished documents previously in the possession of Gide's family and friends, on his *Cahier de lecture* and on the notes and corrections for *Si le grain ne meurt* (1926) which include many chronological references not mentioned in Gide's works or *Journal* (1889–1939 and 1939–49). Delay's work also presents a close reading of Gide's correspondence with his mother as well as his literary correspondence with Pierre Louis, Paul Valéry, and Marcel Drouin. Finally, Delay gives an account of his personal conversations with André Gide, to whom he became a close friend in the last years of Gide's life. This biographical material not only presents Gide's life but also illustrates the evolution of his literary production. Delay's biographical work is divided in two major sections, "André Gide before André Walter" (1869–90) and "From André Walter to André Gide" (1890–95). Each section is then divided into two parts and then into subchapters, which are extremely concise and informative for readers who are interested in examining a specific period of Gide's adolescence, as for example "The nervous attacks," "At School with Pierre Louis," or the "Letters from Munich." At times, part of the information or analysis becomes anecdotal or does not seem quite relevant, as in the case of Gide's sexual fantasies and masturbation habits. At least Delay does not attempt to explain away Gide's homosexuality when referring to the latter's precocious sexual games with members of the same sex. For Delay, the drama of Gide's life arose from his spiritual and mystic conflicts rather than from psychological traumas rooted in childhood.

The reader will have to decide whether it is appropriate to read Gide's works from a biographical perspective as Jean Delay proposes when he examines sexual imagery in *Le voyage d'Urien* (1893) or when he discusses the character of Boris (*Les Faux-Monnayeurs,* 1926) who, he claims, embodies Gide's own early sexual conflicts. One should remember, however, that Delay's study was published in 1963 and since then contemporary criticism has moved away from considering biographical information as a reflection of the literary imagination. Literary critics like Serge Doubrovski and Philippe Lejeune in particular have introduced new critical perspectives on the notions of "autobiography" and "autofiction." It is, therefore, debatable whether Delay's approach to *Si le grain ne meurt* as a valid source of biography is truly accurate.

The discussion on the transition that Gide made from life with his family to life in the literary milieux in 1891 is much more interesting when it focuses on Gide's interaction with Valéry, Mallarmé, Claudel, and the symbolist circles. The subchapter "The young symbolist and his friends" successfully depicts the manner in which Gide developed friendships with a wide variety of littérateurs: Oscar Wilde, Marcel Schwob, Bernard Lazare, and Paul Adam to name only a few. Delay notes that "beyond their mutual interest in aesthetics, several were, socially and politically, violent nonconformists," and he emphasizes what an important role Wilde played in Gide's "de-Christianisation and demoralization." Gide is also described from the point of view of other artists, such as Jacques-Émile Blanche, for whom Gide had been a model.

Gide's activities while traveling in Munich, Tunisia, and Italy comprise the most interesting aspects of Delay's biography. The letters Gide wrote reveal that he began reading Goethe in Munich and that he emancipated himself from his mother. Delay argues that his discovery of Goethe began the "great and perhaps most important battle in Gide's life." He also claims that Gide's "inward revolution" had started before embarking upon his trip to North Africa in 1893. The sexual conflict that emerged during his marriage to his cousin Madeleine Rondeaux is presented as an important chapter in his life. Delay remarks that the role of Gide's mother during his education and into his adult life was the main cause for the failure of the marriage. This Delay documents with notes from Gide's journal, in which he wrote: "How often, with Madeleine in the next room, have I mistaken her for my mother."

FOWLIE's study of Gide, although less well documented than Delay's, is generally more synthetic and analytical and serves as a good introduction to Gide's literary life and works. It contains valuable information concerning the reaction of Gide's readers and records step by step his literary production. Fowlie demonstrates how the autobiographical elements in Gide's novels, while only a pretext, yet serve as background to the text. This is confirmed by Gide's initial comments on *La porte étroite* (1909): "Gide expressed the hope that his books would be judged solely from an aesthetic point of view. The only possible solution to moral contradictions is in the aesthetic triumph of the book." Fowlie reads in Gide's continual need to subvert religion and morality nothing less than a profound desire to live according to one's own moral code, that is to say, to be free from the repression of desire. In other words, Fowlie does not consider sexual repression or homosexuality to have played a dominant role in Gide's life. The main focus of his study is then to recognize the autobiographical elements rooted in Gide's novels all the while emphasizing Gide's literary imagination. Again, in regard to *Les Faux-Monnayeurs*, Wallace Fowlie writes: "Everything in the book: characters, situations, themes, is transposed from Gide's life. But the transposition is re-creation and therefore a novel. Gide as novelist feels no need to describe in detail and to explain motivations and events. This is what he means by a 'pure' novel, by a non-Balzacian novel."

Fowlie's 12th chapter, entitled "At Gide's Death," focuses on how Gide achieved his ultimate recognition upon winning the Nobel Prize in 1948. Fowlie examines criticism on Gide's work and life, such as Pierre Herbart's scandalous portrait of Gide in *À la recherche d'André Gide*. He also reviews the development of the publications of Gide's works, particularly the Pléiade Edition of Gide's *Journal* in 1939. Once again Fowlie differs from Delay when he argues that Gide's *Journal*, even though it is accurate, does not give the reader any information relating to the most important problems in Gide's life: "More than in the autobiography, *Si le grain ne meurt*, which in parts seems almost embarrassingly indiscreet, the *Journal* narrates a combat, a spiritual struggle to exorcise a combat."

GUÉRARD presents the question of Gide biography in a more theoretical and analytical manner than Fowlie, with what he calls the "conflict between real experience and its idealization in fiction." Indeed, it would be tempting to read *Le voyage d'Urien* from a psychological and personal perspective since it is the last book Gide wrote before "discovering" his homosexuality. One should note, Guérard writes, that other biographers like Stephen Ullmann (*The Image in the Modern World*, 1960) analyze *Le voyage d'Urien* and *L'immoraliste* without referring to Gide's homosexuality.

Guérard is opposed to the division of Gide's life and works into "periods." Rather, he is concerned with political, religious, and social issues as they relate to Gide's intellectual development, giving special attention to the changing demands of readers. The question of Gide's influence in literature leads Guérard to focus on the cultural differences between the cultural life of France and that of the United States: "The most obvious aspect of Gide's classical influence, though the least apparent to many readers, has been the influence on style. Even *Le voyage d'Urien* shows that subtle interplay of inner mobility and unusual syntax which no translation can reflect." He situates Gide's conflicts in the same sphere as those in which Freud was interested at the same time. *L'immoraliste*, for Guérard, stands out as one of Gide's best novels for the way in which it evolves from being a representation of the self and of neurosis to the staging of a universal conflict. For Guérard, it is essential to take into consideration Michel's sexual conflicts in *L'immoraliste*. In his conclusion, Guérard raises the issue of academic criticism, which has almost completely ignored sexual imagery and gender issues in Gide's novels.

MARTIN DU GARD's *Recollections* takes the form of a diary of his numerous meetings with Gide. Martin du Gard transcribes and analyzes meticulously his conversations with Gide: "Gide seems to be continually playing hide-and-seek with himself, and with his interlocutors. His conversations—broken into parentheses, remininscences, anecdotes and bursts of religious fooling— has the gratuitousness, the unconcern of a game." This work

offers valuable insights into Gide's conception of his works as well as his political convictions. Martin du Gard presents Gide first and foremost as a man of letters and emphasizes Gide's unusual emotional sensitivity and unrest.

HYTIER's biography is a transcription of a conference on Gide's writings, presented in 1938 at the University of Algier. Its first objective is to demonstrate how Gide's poetic works revolve around the questions of desire and spirituality. Hytier presents Gide as a multi-faceted literary figure and examines his contributions as a novelist and a playwright.

O'BRIEN's study successfully juxtaposes Gide's life and works. Throughout his extremely well-annotated study, O'Brien demonstrates how Gide "had categorically placed the ethical question before the social question." The constant use of classical mythology in Gide's works and Gide's fascination for Greek and Latin bucolic poetry constitute the main leitmotiv of O'Brien's study, whose chapters are divided according to the different myths present in Gide's works: "As might be expected, André Gide's interpretation of the myth is a personal one, for he claimed to 'interrogate the Greek fable in a new way,' bringing out its psychological significance. . . . One must not be surprised, then, to see Narcissus contemplating Adam in Paradise, to find Prometheus lecturing to men on the necessity of an eagle, to see an obese and rich Zeus strolling on the Paris boulevards. . . . " O'Brien's study of Gide's two speakers named Corydon, like the shepherds figuring in Theocritus and Virgil, adds to our understanding of Gide's homosexuality: "A cognate reason for writing *Corydon*, he once confessed, was to disavow the false holiness with which his 'disdain for ordinary temptations' clothed him in the eyes of relatives and friends."

—Martine Natat Antle

GINSBERG, Allen, 1926–   ; American poet.

Kramer, Jane, *Allen Ginsberg in America*. New York, Random House, 1968; London, Gollancz, 1970.
Miles, Barry, *Ginsberg: A Biography*. New York, Simon and Schuster, 1989.
Mottram, Eric, *Ginsberg in the Sixties*. Brighton and Seattle, Washington, Unicorn Bookshop, 1972.

*

"*Collected Poems* may be read as a lifelong poem including history, wherein things are symbols of themselves," wrote Allen Ginsberg in the "Author's Preface" to the 1984 compilation of his work. As with perhaps no other writer, Ginsberg's poems themselves provide his most comprehensive and intimate biography. Little is left out. Nevertheless, because he drew so much extra-literary media attention, the line between Ginsberg's personal biography and cultural history has been inevitably blurred, providing fascinating terrain for the biographer.

The earliest biographical portraits were done in the 1960s when, as the author of the then notorious *Howl* (1955) and the alleged guru of a mystifying and often threatening counterculture, Ginsberg was regarded as much as a social phenomenon—a magnet for sensation-hungry journalists—as he was a serious poet. Not surprisingly, then, the first serious biographical treatment of Ginsberg, Jane KRAMER's *Allen Ginsberg in America* (Random House, 1968), catches Ginsberg *in media res* and is necessarily limited to a brief though powerfully significant period of his life. Kramer's study originally appeared as a three-part *New Yorker* portrait, and taking into consideration that its focus is limited to the sixties without benefit of historical perspective, it is a well-informed, highly readable introduction to the man at one exciting phase of his life. The strengths of this acclaimed biography are also its weaknesses. It has the narrative freshness and naivete of an in-process report, contriving anecdote and fact to achieve what its book jacket accurately claims as the "fascinating and varied tapestry of Ginsberg's life, his companions, and the kaleidoscopic, shifting American scene." We see, however, only one side of the tapestry and, of course, only the eye-catching pattern of its center. The fringes and the backing must wait for a treatment less constrained by the dictates of popular interest. After all, Kramer's immensely interesting narrative (it reads like a novel) is aimed at a popular audience who is primarily interested in Ginsberg as a fleeting, albeit intriguing, figure on the sixties' landscape. Well-informed and sympathetic as it is, Kramer's portrait is nevertheless one by an outsider. It is responsible journalism at its best, but it is captive to its time and lacks the scope and perception that only a more retrospective and comprehensive biography can provide.

As its title suggests, Eric MOTTRAM's brief *Ginsberg in the Sixties* suffers from the same limitations as Kramer's, although here, the British scholar manages better to convince us that he gives more of an insider's (and of course non-American) focus on Ginsberg's literary importance. Both books are excellent in their way, but they are clearly superseded by the most recent biography by Barry Miles.

MILES has been a friend of Ginsberg since 1965 and is quite pleased with the sobriquet conferred on him by the press as "Ginsberg's advocate in Britain." Given complete access to Ginsberg's private papers (60,000 plus letters, manuscripts, journals, notebooks, and doodles), along with personal interviews with the poet, his friends, and others who knew him, Miles accurately describes his undertaking as "a rare situation between biographer and subject." Despite his obvious sympathy and admiration for Ginsberg, Miles succeeds in maintaining a reassuring objectivity. In authorizing the biography Ginsberg granted Miles full license and forfeited any veto power even when the two did "not always see eye to eye on what happened." The only condition Ginsberg insisted on was that he review Miles' remarks about Ginsberg's friends for accuracy and for any inappropriate invasions of their privacy. The thoroughness of Miles' investigations can be judged by Ginsberg's response to the five-year process: "I feel like I'm a robot being deprogrammed!"

The result is an unusually frank, detailed chronicle that does not shy away from explicit accounts of Ginsberg's homosexuality, drug use, and personal insecurities. It is a non-judgmental account that seems driven not by a discernible point of view but by facts—voluminous facts, not only of Ginsberg's personal life but of an entire half-century of cultural turbulence viewed from what many might regard as the eye of the hurricane. Like Ginsberg himself this authorized biography is not reticent, apologetic, or always pretty. Much better, it is real, a fascinating

narrative of a rare life woven from a seemingly inexhaustible fund of detailed information. It comes, incidentally, with a 24-page collection of fascinating informal photographs of Ginsberg, his family, and his friends.

—Thomas F. Merrill

GISSING, George, 1857–1903; English writer.

Collie, Michael, *George Gissing: A Biography*. Hamden, Connecticut, Archon Books, and Folkstone, England, Dawson, 1977.

Donnelly, Mabel Collins, *George Gissing: Grave Comedian*. Cambridge, Massachusetts, Harvard University Press, 1954.

Halperin, John, *Gissing: A Life in Books*. Oxford and New York, Oxford University Press, 1982.

Korg, Jacob, *George Gissing: A Critical Biography*. Seattle, University of Washington Press, 1963; London, Methuen, 1965.

Tindall, Gillian, *The Born Exiles: George Gissing*. New York, Harcourt, and London, Temple Smith, 1974.

*

The standard for biographies of George Gissing was set in 1963 with the publication of Korg's critical study (see below). For, from Gissing's death in 1903 to Morley Robert's thinly disguised fictional account of his friend's life in *The Private Life of Henry Maitland* (1912), to the first scholarly monograph by Donnelly in 1954, no extensive use was made of manuscript sources held privately. It was Korg who first made careful and intelligent use of these in his thorough, objective study. The biographical works that followed, authored by Tindall, Collie, and Halperin, take on the more personal tone and convictions of their authors.

The first book-length treatment of George Gissing's life and times appeared 50 years after his death. DONNELLY bases her investigation on the notion that Gissing deserves to be studied "not only as a skilled surgeon at work on Victorian orthodoxy, but also as a novelist of skill." Her intention is to show the gradual maturation of Gissing as man and writer, emphasizing early influences in his life, notably the relationship with his father. Poverty and disgrace, life between the worlds of the wealthy and the poor, marriage and misanthropy, and love and exile are topics Donnelly traces in Gissing's life. She makes little use, however, of important unpublished materials but relies heavily on published editions of Gissing's essays, diaries, and letters. If this book today appears rather naive in its interpretations and use of sources, it nevertheless represents a pioneering effort in the understanding of a complex author.

Using manuscripts held by Yale University, the Berg Collection of the New York Public Library, and the Carl H. Pforzheimer Library, KORG furnishes a clear and well-documented survey of Gissing's life suitable for specialists and general readers alike. He traces Gissing from boyhood to the abrupt end of his formal education at Owens College, through his subsequent travels in America, London, and on the continent, to his death in St. Jean Pied de Port near Biarritz in southwestern France. The study is distinguished by Korg's incisive discussions of Gissing's development as a novelist, his motivation for writing, his professional failures and successes, his relationships with publishers, wives, and a small circle of friends, and his reaction to criticism. Readers of this book will come to an understanding of the autobiographical elements in Gissing's works, but also to the realization that here art does not always equal life. Korg effectively uses biographical material to illuminate changes in Gissing's intellect, tracing his movement from the ideas expressed in "The Hope of Pessimism," to Positivism, through socialism to his philosophical base of agnosticism. Gissing emerges as a complex individual who led his paradoxical life as a man driven to write for money but failing to publish all he writes—or even pursue revisions to make his work publishable; a writer who takes no pleasure from what he writes, yet is driven to the vocation.

TINDALL's book on Gissing is not intended to stand as biography alone. While the first ten pages do present the basic facts and chronology of his life in summary form, Tindall's major task, as stated in her introduction, is to assess Gissing's impact on literature in the second 50 years after his death, and to distinguish "real writing from book-making" through an examination of his life and times. She hopes to dispel various myths surrounding Gissing's life, revaluating them by means of his letters (many of which were unpublished in 1974), his diary, and his novels. In each segment of the book, Tindall poses questions about the circumstances and personal relationships in Gissing's life, analyzes the available evidence, and offers well-argued conclusions. Her analysis is thoughtful and distinctive. She maintains the delicate balance necessary for a detailed examination of fiction vis-à-vis biographical truth, without placing undue emphasis on any one novel or episode within a novel. In trying to create a comprehensive image of Gissing, she offers careful speculation when the details are uncertain and does not impose a contemporary social consciousness on this late Victorian figure. Tindall's work is as much literary criticism as it is traditional biography, and represents a landmark study of this type.

Was Gissing a late 19th-century writer who, though determined, lacked the basic skills to succeed? Or was he a masterly novelist and experimenter, as well as an insightful social critic? COLLIE's biography is an attempt to place Gissing in the second category. He asserts that until 1975 Gissing had been misunderstood and wrongly labeled by scholars and the public as an autobiographical writer who lived in penury instead of as a naturalist; as an author who always wrote the same dull book rather than a composer of varied, experimental pieces; and as a man whose work was conditioned by his experiences, unable to maintain a clinical detachment from his own fiction. This slim volume emphatically describes the adult Gissing as a repressed bohemian who possessed a cynical, sensual, passionate, irrational nature. For evidence, Collie draws on autobiographical elements in Gissing's fiction as well as his letters, while at the same time dismissing as unreliable other evidence from the same sources, especially letters to his family. He strenuously argues that the work of other biographers, naming Korg most often, does not represent the real truth about the man. Collie's book, though one-sided, is a challenging interpretation of a fascinating life.

In HALPERIN's survey the life and times of Gissing are presented in abundant detail. Halperin skillfully puts together the pieces of Gissing's biographical puzzle, focusing on the events of his adulthood and drawing comparisons and contrasts with his contemporaries, particularly Meredith and Hardy. Halperin's treatment is mostly chronological, with discussions and critiques of Gissing's novels interspersed throughout. His criticism, while sound, presumes the reader's familiarity with all of Gissing's works and, unfortunately, detracts from the book's effectiveness. To the author Gissing represents an "observer and recorder of his own time, a novelist of manner, a frustrated teacher, a realist, a classicist, a conservative." Halperin's enthusiasm for his subject leads him to assert that fully a dozen of Gissing's novels are first-rate. He endorses much of Korg's earlier scholarly work and provides some interesting notes on other Gissing biographers. In the preface Halperin gratefully acknowledges the cooperation and assistance of Pierre Coustillas, who allowed him to read in manuscript form his unpublished biography of Gissing (which still has not appeared in print). The new information on Gissing's life provided by Halperin is not substantial enough to place this work ahead of Korg's authoritative study. Rather, this is a book for Gissing enthusiasts; others may find it to be an inflated assessment of the man and his work.

—Robin Grollmus Hanson

GLADSTONE, William, 1809–1898; English statesman and writer.

Bryce, James, *William Ewart Gladstone, His Characteristics as Man and Statesman.* New York, Century, 1898.

Feuchtwanger, E. J., *Gladstone.* London, A. Lane, and New York, St. Martin's, 1975.

Hamilton, Sir Edward Walter, *Mr. Gladstone, a Monograph.* London, J. Murray, and New York, Scribner, 1898.

Magnus, Philip, *Gladstone, a Biography.* London, J. Murray, and New York, Dutton, 1954.

Matthew, H. C. G., *Gladstone, 1809–74.* Oxford, Clarendon Press, and New York, Oxford University Press, 1986.

Morley, John, *The Life of William Ewart Gladstone* (3 vols.). New York and London, Macmillan, 1903.

Ramm, Agatha, *William Ewart Gladstone.* Cardiff, Wales, GPC Books, 1989.

Reid, T. Wemyss, editor, *The Life of William Ewart Gladstone* (2 vols.). London and New York, Putnam, 1899.

Robbins, A. F., *The Early Public Life of W. E. Gladstone.* London, Methuen, and New York, Dodd Mead, 1894.

Shannon, Richard, *Gladstone.* London, Hamilton, 1982; Chapel Hill, University of North Carolina Press, 1984.

*

Gladstone's biography was written dozens of times during his lifetime, becoming a regular part of publishers' lists from the late 1870s. Early biographical accounts tended to be hagiographic and moralistic, producing by the 1890s a mythical image of an "almost superhuman" politician able "to bend circumstances to his will'' (D. A. Hamer, ''Gladstone, The Making of A Political Myth,'' *Victorian Studies*, 1978–79). ROBBINS is representative of biographies with greater balance, based on better research that began to appear during the 1890s. Upon Gladstone's death in 1898, a flood of eulogistic reflections appeared, Bryce, Reid, and Hamilton perhaps being most notable. BRYCE's brief sketch, published first in America, contains the keen observations of an accomplished author and cabinet colleague and is still a useful introduction to Gladstone's character. REID's is a laudatory but informed collection in 12 parts containing contributions from Robbins, Reid, G. W. E. Russell, and F. W. Hirst, and is of considerable interest for the more than 200 illustrations of Gladstone and his milieu that adorn its pages. HAMILTON offers an important memoir by a former private secretary.

Despite the value of previous works, the starting point for all Gladstone scholarship is MORLEY, chosen official biographer in September 1898. Morley was eminent both as man of letters and as politician, serving in Gladstone's final two cabinets (1886, 1892–94) and strongly supporting his Irish home rule and anti-expansionist policies. The first biographer granted access to the massive Gladstone archive, Morley largely retired from political life and devoted five years to his task, publishing the 700,000-word, three-volume biography ''punctually as if by Act of Parliament'' in October 1903. Herbert Gladstone's complaint that it did not present ''for those who did not know Mr. Gladstone a true and complete view of his personality,'' is accurate in the sense that inner struggles clearly represented in the *Diaries* are largely excluded. Nevertheless, Morley's remains the standard biography that must be consulted for detail, and marks the culmination of Liberal tributes to a purposeful and unified career in the development of liberty, both at home and abroad.

The sheer weight of authority and scholarship in Morley inhibited serious attempts to displace him, particularly in light of restrictions on use of Gladstone's diaries. Fifty years later, however, MAGNUS gained limited access and became the first to deal substantively with Gladstone's private life. His account, though restrained and genteel, remains the best single-volume treatment: it is detailed, well illustrated, and gives due attention to what Mrs. Gladstone termed the two sides of the prime minister's nature. FEUCHTWANGER provides an admirable introduction to Gladstone's political career, incorporating 20 years of Victorian scholarship since Magnus, but suffers from an avowed neglect of Gladstone's private, religious, and scholarly life.

The watershed in biographical writing on Gladstone began in 1968 with publication of the first two volumes of Gladstone's *Diaries* (edited by M. R. D. Foot), now brought through 1886 with volumes X and XI (edited by H. C. G. Matthew, 1990). This selection of correspondence and extraordinary daily chronicle (1825–96) has become the touchstone for all Gladstone studies, providing laconic but detailed accounts of books read, people visited, daily habits, and personal ''introspections,'' ''misgivings,'' and ''self-accusations,'' the latter once thought by Gladstone's family to be too sensitive for public consumption. MATTHEW also offers a collection of introductions to the *Diaries*, with two additional chapters and ''an extended biographical essay'' that never pretends to be definitive. It is, nevertheless, the fullest account of Gladstone's fundamental attitudes toward God, politics, family, and self, and necessary reading for an understanding of the inner man. More detailed

and outwardly driven is SHANNON's revisionist account through 1865, an exhaustively researched tale of an ambitious conservative, with scarcely a hint of the aura pervading virtually all Gladstone biographies since his successes of the 1870s. An anticipated second volume (1866–98) is dependent on further publication of the *Diaries*, scheduled for completion in the mid-1990s. Morley, Matthew, and Shannon are necessary to the scholar and, taken together, provide an erudite composite of a complex statesman. RAMM's interpretive essay, too brief to do justice to a long career, is nevertheless notable for its treatment of Gladstone as a man of letters.

—John Powell

GODWIN, William, 1756–1836; English writer and political philosopher.

Brailsford, H. N., *Shelley, Godwin, and Their Circle*. London, Williams and Norgate, and New York, Holt, 1913.
Brown, Ford K., *The Life of William Godwin*. London, Dent, and New York, Dutton, 1926.
Grylls, Roselie G., *William Godwin and His World*. London, Odham's Press, 1953.
Locke, Don, *A Fantasy of Reason: Life and Thought of William Godwin*. London and Boston, Routledge, 1980.
Marshall, Peter H., *William Godwin*. New Haven, Connecticut, and London, Yale University Press, 1984.
Paul, Charles K., *William Godwin: His Friends and Contemporaries* (2 vols.). London, H. S. King, and Boston, Roberts, 1876.
Woodcock, George, *William Godwin: A Biographical Study*. London, Porcupine Press, 1946.

*

No biography of William Godwin was written or published during his long life, nor did any appear until 40 years after his death. This was largely because of the peculiar circumstances of his career, which led to a relatively early fame when he published *An Enquiry Concerning Political Justice* in 1793, followed by notoriety and something approaching ostracism at the height of the anti-Jacobin reaction of the late 1790s. Godwin never again became the centre of attention, and lived the remainder of his life in relative obscurity, from which he emerged during the 19th century less on his own merits than because of his association with the poet Percy Bysshe Shelley.

If no contemporary—not even William Hazlitt, who had written a Life of their common friend Thomas Holocroft—chose to write Godwin's biography, he himself was autobiographically reticent and published nothing approaching a complete memoir of his life. The nearest he came was his *Memoirs of the Author of A Vindication of the Rights of Women* (1798), in which he inevitably appeared as a figure during the period of his companionship with and marriage to Mary Wollstonecraft. It was a moving recollection that offended his conservative contemporaries, but at this time any stick was good enough to beat Godwin with. Coincidentally, the only collection of Godwin's letters published up to now is to be found in *Godwin and Mary* (1966), his correspondence with Wollstonecraft, edited by Richard M. Wardle.

The first biography of Godwin was PAUL's two-volume work that appeared in 1876. Paul had access to Godwin's papers, which had passed after his death into the hands of Mary Wollstonecraft Shelley, and thence into the possession of the Abinger family. What he really produced was a typical 19th-century Life and Letters, with copious extracts from Godwin's correspondence, from his journals, and from his published writings, somewhat shakily united by narrative and commentary rather than by criticism. The very title of the book indicates Paul's view that Godwin might not be interesting enough to stand on his own feet as a subject of biography, but that he might well gather meaning as the focus of a circle including such more celebrated men as Coleridge and Lamb, Hazlitt and Shelley, Bulwer Lytton and Charles Manning, the Tibetan traveler.

A similar approach would govern another, briefer work, BRAILSFORD's volume, which is partly biographical in its treatment of Godwin and is really the first book to attempt a fair treatment of Godwin's behaviour in his relationship with Shelley. In 1926 another biography appeared, by the American scholar BROWN. Since the Abinger archive was now closed to scholars, Brown relied largely on the material already published by Kegan Paul, and tended to make up for lack of new facts about Godwin himself by sketching out the literary background to his life and works; the latter he does not discuss in any depth. Brown's book sets Godwin rather well in his world, but it does not offer a penetrating portrait.

The next biography, by WOODCOCK, was a frankly rehabilitative work, attempting to see Godwin stripped of a century-and-a-half's accretion of prejudice and rumour. Since the Abinger archive remained closed, Woodcock worked largely with familiar material, but he interpreted it in a way that did more justice to Godwin. As well as providing a balanced survey of Godwin's life, Woodcock entered into a close exposition of his political philosophy.

Coming at a time when libertarian theories and sentiments were returning to favour at the end of World War II, Woodcock's book aroused a great deal of attention when it appeared, being widely and favourably reviewed in England and was the first of a spate of books that have accompanied the welcoming of Godwin like a returning exile to his proper place in the history of literature and political thought. Most of these books, appearing from the 1950s onward, were scholarly criticism of ideas and writings, but three can be regarded as biographical. They were written with access to the Abinger archive, which again became available to scholars in the 1950s.

GRYLLS' is a patchy, superficial work that fails to take full advantage of the material now available. LOCKE's study is partly biography and partly critique; flatly written, it is mainly useful for its analysis of the reasons for Godwin's retreat into obscurity after both his fame and his notoriety ended.

In 1984 appeared the largest, the most scholarly, and one of the best-written biographies of Godwin, MARSHALL's *William Godwin*. This is a biography with a thesis: that Godwin for a period was a true revolutionary, an actual anarchist, both in his thought and in his expression of it in writing, and that he never fully abandoned the ideals of his youth to join the reactionary

throng. The thesis, already foreshadowed in Woodcock, is well argued; Godwin's life is warmly and brightly represented even in its hours of apparent defeat. The writings are given fair consideration, and the breadth and complexity of Godwin's ideas are fairly revealed. Godwin is shaken free of the misfortunes and calumnies that have so long concealed his personality and his achievement, and he takes his place as one of the seminal minds of our age. For all its passion of argument, Marshall's *William Godwin* is a reliable and exact biography.

—George Woodcock

GOETHE, Johann Wolfgang von, 1749–1832; German poet.

Bielschowsky, Albert, *Life of Goethe* (2 vols.), translated by William A. Cooper. New York and London, Putnam, 1905–08 (originally published as *Goethe: Sein Leben und seine Werke*, Munich, 1896–1904).

Brown, Peter H., *Life of Goethe* (2 vols.). London, J. Murray, and New York, Holt, 1920.

Browning, Henry C. (A. C. Ritchie), *Life of Goethe: From His Autobiographical Papers and the Contributions of His Contemporaries* (2 vols.). New York, J. Mowatt, 1844.

Calvert, George Henry, *Goethe: His Life and Work*. Boston, Lee and Shepard, 1872.

Dieckmann, Liselotte, *Johann Wolfgang Goethe*. New York, Twayne, 1974.

Düntzer, Heinrich, *Life of Goethe*, translated by T. W. Lyster. London, Macmillan, 1883 (originally published as *Goethes Leben*, Leipzig, 1880).

Eissler, Kurt Robert, *Goethe: A Psychoanalytical Study 1775–86* (2 vols.). Detroit, Wayne State University Press, 1963.

Fairley, Barker, *A Study of Goethe*. Oxford, Clarendon Press, 1947.

Friedenthal, Richard, *Goethe: His Life and Times*. London, Weidenfeld and Nicolson, and Cleveland, World Publishing, 1965 (originally published, Munich, 1963).

Grimm, Karl, *Life and Times of Goethe* (2 vols.), translated by S. H. Adams. Boston, Little Brown, 1880 (originally published as *Goethe*, Berlin, 1877).

Hatfield, Henry C., *Goethe: A Critical Introduction*. Norfolk, Connecticut, J. Laughlin, 1963.

Hayward, Abraham, *Goethe*. Edinburgh and London, Blackwood, 1878.

Lamport, F. J., *A Student's Guide to Goethe*. London, Heinemann, 1971.

Lewes, George Henry, *The Life and Works of Goethe* (2 vols.). London, D. Nutt, 1855; Boston, Ticknor and Fields, 1856.

Lewisohn, Ludwig, *Goethe: The Story of a Man*. New York, Farrar Straus, 1949.

McCabe, Joseph, *Goethe: The Man and His Character*. London, Nash, and Philadelphia, Lippincott, 1912.

Nevinson, Henry W., *Goethe: Man and Poet*. London, Nisbet, 1931; New York, Harcourt, 1932.

Reed, T. J., *Goethe*. Oxford and New York, Oxford University Press, 1984.

Robertson, John George, *Goethe*. London, Routledge, and New York, Dutton, 1927; revised as *The Life and Work of Goethe 1749–1832*, London, Routledge, and New York, Dutton, 1932.

Sime, James, *Life of Johann Wolfgang Goethe*. London, W. Scott, 1888.

Thomas, Calvin, *Goethe*. New York, Holt, 1917.

*

Biography of Goethe has both benefited and suffered from the prodigious mass of biographical information and documentation available from the poet himself and from his contemporaries in the form of correspondence, diaries, conversations, reminiscences, and official documents (only recently has full documentation of Goethe's activities in the Weimar Privy Council become publicly available). Problems have also been created by the unreliability, as objective evidence, of Goethe's own autobiography, a retrospective account appropriately entitled *Dichtung und Wahrheit* (Poetry—or Fiction—and Truth), which in any case covers only the first 26 years of his life; and by the less than total accuracy of J. P. Eckermann's exhaustive accounts of conversations with Goethe in the last decade of his life. The vast amount of material available to biographers and critics has also meant that, more so than with most writers, Goethe's works have traditionally been understood and interpreted in close, even literal, conjunction with his biography—in particular with his various relationships with a long line of women. The image of Goethe has also been modified or distorted, on the one hand by biographers who have presented him uncritically as the Olympian Sage of Weimar, as a German cultural exemplar, and on the other hand by those who, in reaction against hagiographical perceptions, have sought to reveal human, all too human characteristics, even feet of clay, in this intimidating literary figure.

The first English-language biographical account of Goethe, by BROWNING, was a quaint and not entirely accurate compilation from his own autobiography and the contributions of his contemporaries. But the first full account in English, acknowledged even today by biographers and critics as authoritative, was written by LEWES. To be sure, many details of Lewes' work relating to biography, and especially to critical interpretation, have been revised in the light of research and discovery (for example, Lewes was writing well before the discovery of the *Urfaust* manuscript in 1889); but his is still recognised as one of the finest introductions to Goethe. Lewes followed Carlyle in presenting Goethe as sage and moralist, but went very much further than his mentor in his assessment of Goethe's literary and scientific works. Indeed, it was the news that an Englishman was engaged on a study of Goethe that stimulated Heinrich Viehoff, one of the earliest German biographers, to complete his monumental four-volume life (*Goethes Leben*, Stuttgart, 1847–54), the final volume of which appeared the year before Lewes. However, Viehoff did not have access, or did not trouble to gain access, to the private unpublished documentation that Lewes found in Germany; indeed, as Lewes himself points out, Viehoff did not even see fit to visit Weimar, where Lewes had gathered much valuable information from those who had known Goethe. Other accounts in English from the 19th century draw on Lewes and are essayistic studies of Goethe's life and works: they in-

clude the volumes by CALVERT, HAYWARD, and the exiguous *Life of Goethe* by SIME.

In 1912 McCABE published a rather verbose and sentimental study of "the Man and his Character" which draws mainly on the German accounts of Albert Bielschowsky (see below) and Karl Heinemann (*Goethe*, 2 vols., 1895). THOMAS' work of 1917 remains the most substantial, if now rather dated, American introduction to Goethe. BROWN wrote a conventional and unoriginal account of the life, with the works summarised descriptively rather than critically (the study of *Faust*, Part Two, was contributed by Viscount Haldane after the death of the author). ROBERTSON's 1927 study was revised and extended into *The Life and Work of Goethe* (1932)—a still useful reference work that acknowledges Goethe's supremacy as a lyric poet while questioning his achievement in narrative fiction and the validity of his "fatalistic optimism" for 20th-century readers. NEVINSON contributed a popular life of Goethe in 1931 that celebrates—and trivialises—Goethe as "the great liver."

Altogether more stimulating and authoritative is FAIRLEY's subtle and imaginative reading of the man and his thinking which, while it might over-centralise the significance of Charlotte von Stein in Goethe's life and works, does place Goethe firmly in the context of his time. Fairley recognises in Goethe the "malady of introspection" that characterised Goethe's own age and so many later ages; but he charts and defines Goethe's struggle for wholeness and objectivity, for the integration of his poetry and his philosophy with "the problem of living."

LEWISOHN furnishes a "life of Goethe as told in his own words and the words of his contemporaries." HATFIELD's critical introduction and DIECKMANN's Twayne volume are concise and lucid, primarily critical studies of the works rather than biographical. Both REED and LAMPORT offer brief and concise paperback introductions to Goethe's life and works.

FRIEDENTHAL's best-selling historical account of Goethe's life and times appeared in an English version in 1965 and has found a wide readership outside Germany. Written in a deliberately non-scholarly, at times jaunty narrative style, with much use of the historic present, Friedenthal presents a human, fallible Goethe (with whom the reader is encouraged to relax and become familiar) as an antidote to the all too reverential approach of much traditional Goethe biography—particularly in Germany. To be sure, Friedenthal was already pushing at an open door; though negative judgements were not unknown in the previous century, many recent approaches to Goethe have represented a tendentiously hostile reaction to a cultural icon, and in doing so have distorted the image of Goethe at least as much as earlier hagiographical studies did in the opposite direction.

Other German biographies of Goethe, most of which remain untranslated, cannot be dealt with exhaustively in the space available. The first full account during Goethe's lifetime, by Heinrich Döring, appeared as a supplement to Goethe's works in 1828. Early independent biographies by Rosenkranz, Viehoff, and J. W. Schaefer (2 vols., 1851) appeared within two decades of his death; the last two were acknowledged as sources by Lewes. Three major positivist biographies appeared in the years following the foundation of the Second *Reich*, establishing Goethe as the "Olympian," the German cultural exemplar: Karl Goedeke (*Goethes Leben und Schriften*, 1874), GRIMM, and DÜNTZER. A still widely respected and much reprinted comprehensive study of the life and works by BIELSCHOWSKY appeared between 1896 and 1904. Georg Witkowski's more compact illustrated *Goethe* dates from 1899—both these continue in modified form the positivist tradition of the previous three. Friedrich Gundolf's magisterial celebration of Goethe as the German Shakespeare (*Goethe*, 1916) has a whiff of incense about it and bears traces of the biographer's reverent perception of his own master, the vatic magus figure of the poet Stefan George; but for all its high-mindedness, Gundolf's book was profoundly influential in moulding the German image of Goethe. Less hagiographical are the studies of Wilhelm Bode (*Goethes Leben*, 9 vols., Berlin, 1820–27) and Phillip Witkop (*Goethe: Leben und Werk*, Stuttgart, 1931) and, in post-war years, of Richard Benz (*Goethes Leben*, 1949) and Heinrich Meyer (*Goethe: Das Leben im Werk*, Hamburg, 1951). Emil Staiger's three-volume critical study (1952–59), while not primarily biographical, deserves mention as the most comprehensive post-war German chronological survey of the life and works. Richard Friedenthal's version (German edition, 1963) has been mentioned above. Peter Boerner's record of Goethe in pictures and personal documents (1964) is brief but illuminating. The most recent life and works is that of Karl Otto Conrady (1982–85), which aims not at the specialist but at the general reader; it is a readable narrative that seeks to present the light and dark aspects of Goethe's experience and personality, the inner crises, even insecurities, of an outwardly serene and successful writer.

Finally, if only as a curiosity, EISSLER's psychoanalytical profile of Goethe, which suggests provocatively that Goethe's famously passionate love poetry was not matched by corresponding achievement in terms of physical sexuality, has achieved some notoriety; it was not published in German until 1983, 20 years after its appearance in America.

—John R. Williams

GOGOL, Nikolai, 1809–1852; Russian writer.

Magarshack, David, *Gogol: A Life*. London, Faber, 1956; New York, Grove, 1957.

Setchkarev, Vsevolod, *Gogol: His Life and Works*, translated by Robert Kramer. New York, New York University Press, and London, P. Owen, 1965.

Troyat, Henri, *Divided Soul: The Life of Gogol*, translated by Nancy Amphoux. New York, Doubleday, and London, Allen and Unwin, 1973 (originally published as *Gogol*, Paris, Flammarion, 1971).

*

After viewing his remains, Gogol's long-time confidant Sergei Aksakov, himself a writer, commented that on this occasion he had not felt his usual unease at bidding farewell to deceased friends because for him "Gogol was not a person." The remark was a strange one, but somehow it fits a man whose personality and writing are among the most enigmatic in Russian literary history. Even today scholars quarrel heatedly over the interpretation of his works, and none of his biographers has yet plumbed the depths of his character. A thorough analysis of his personal-

ity and his ideas would require more effort than any of his English biographers has yet invested in him, and until now ideological considerations have prevented his Soviet biographers from analyzing him on his own terms.

There is no shortage of material to work with. Gogol was a prolific letter-writer, one who often spoke of his own viewpoints. But, as Troyat puts it justly, he "had never been able to tell the truth about his intentions and actions." When a letter-writer composes eloquent falsehoods about his personal motivations, he places his future biographers at a great (though not insuperable) disadvantage. It is one which his biographers have thus far been unable to overcome.

In short, none of the existing biographies of Gogol in English is entirely satisfactory. The best is probably SETCHKAREV's, but it is the lesser half of a two-part study of Gogol's life and works that runs to fewer than 100 pages, a compass within which it is simply impossible to illuminate fully a personality as complex as Gogol's. Setchkarev ordinarily resists the impulse to allow Gogol to speak for himself, and brings in enough outside material to enable us to grasp the externals of Gogol's life. Being quite aware of his subject's tendency to embroider or even to pervert the truth, Setchkarev takes a deservedly skeptical approach to Gogol's writings, but then extends it to some, like Turgenev, who do not deserve such treatment. In his final decade Gogol became an intensely religious Christian, but in a very peculiar and partly heretical way that repelled many of his friends. Setchkarev is quite interested in the religious element in Gogol's life, but does not allow himself space to evaluate it, and also projects Gogol's later religious notions back onto his earlier career in ways that are not always appropriate. Still, this biography remains the work of a trained specialist and sober scholar.

In his study of Gogol, MAGARSHACK, a well-known British biographer of Russian literary figures, succumbs to the autobiographical temptation with a vengeance. Sympathetic to Gogol, he dedicates considerable space to the religious quest that obsessed him in his final decade. But he constructs his book primarily by stitching together lengthy passages from Gogol's letters—or from his writings, when they have clear biographical implications—while offering only a minimal analysis of his ideas or the views of the other people who impinged on Gogol's life. Thus, when Magarshack discusses Gogol's last book, *Selected Passages from Correspondence with Friends*—a controversial work with a strongly religious orientation—he offers chiefly extensive quotations from it followed by lengthy segments from the critic Vissarion Belinsky's furious rebuttal of Gogol's ideas. Magarshack does emphasize the underlying ideological unity of Gogol's life (like Tolstoy after him, toward the end Gogol condemned his own earlier writings in many respects), but he fails to penetrate below the philosophical surface.

TROYAT's is a more popular work than either Setchkarev's or Magarshack's. It is written chronologically and divided at literary high points: the first section ends with the staging of Gogol's classic comedy *The Inspector General*, the second with the publication of his novel *Dead Souls*, and the last with his death. Generous in his use of exclamations and rhetorical questions, Troyat produces a colorful narrative containing many details for which he lacks direct documentary justification or which contribute little of substance to the biography. For instance, in describing his subject's departure for Western Europe in 1836, Troyat writes: "Deck hands in blue blouses and round straw hats

with ribbons trotted along the deck. Gogol started up the ramp.''
In addition, Troyat's translator has little or no acquaintance with
things Russian, so that the text contains some rather obvious errors, and the portraits of two men who played important roles in
Gogol's life are transposed.

Gogol still awaits his English biographer. The rich materials
he left in his letters and fiction require a subtle interpretation
that no one has yet given them.

—Charles A. Moser

GOLDMAN, Emma, 1869–1940; American anarchist writer
and activist.

Drinnon, Richard, *Rebel in Paradise: A Biography of Emma
    Goldman.* Chicago, University of Chicago Press, 1961.
Falk, Candace, *Love, Anarchy, and Emma Goldman.* New
    York, Holt Rinehart, 1984.
Ganguli, B. N., *Emma Goldman: A Portrait of a Rebel Woman.*
    New Delhi, Allied Publishers, 1979.
Shulman, Alix, *To the Barricades: The Anarchist Life of Emma
    Goldman.* New York, T. Y. Crowell, 1971.
Wexler, Alice, *Emma Goldman: An Intimate Life.* New York,
    Pantheon, and London, Virago, 1984.
Wexler, Alice, *Emma Goldman in Exile: From the Russian Rev-
    olution to the Spanish Civil War.* Boston, Beacon Press,
    1989.

*

Both the public career and private life of Emma Goldman
were remarkably turbulent and complex. The former is characterized by radical activism, which resulted in constant harrass-
ment, countless arrests, and, eventually, deportation from the
United States; the latter, by the many lovers with whom she
lived and worked. This wealth of interesting biographical material has been adequately mined and molded into a half dozen
biographies of varying scope and focus.

GANGULI and SHULMAN have given us the two biographies of least depth and scholarly appeal, though they do nevertheless present sensitive introductory accounts of Goldman's life.
Ganguli's is a slim volume that focuses most on the development
and meaning of Goldman's anarchist political views. His treatments of her early struggles in Lithuania, her coming to anarchism during the labor unrest in the United States, and her
disappointments in Russia and Spain are indeed cursory, but
Ganguli succeeds in unifying these phases of her life in an intellectually stimulating portrait. A third of the book is given to
extended ruminations on women's liberation, anarchism, and the
question of violence and social revolution. Shulman's biography
is good for adolescent readers. It is immensely readable, adequately inclusive, but of little intellectual appeal for the serious
scholar. Shulman simply retells the "story" of this exceptional
woman's life.

In the first full biography of Goldman, DRINNON announces
about his subject at the outset, "I like her and trust her." His is
indeed a sympathetic portrait, but his sympathy does not keep

him from acknowledging Goldman's blind spots. Drinnon's biography is very well researched, a revision of his doctoral dissertation for which he combed all relevant material then
available: published anarchist works, largely unpublished correspondence and other writings held in various library collections,
and the records of the U.S. Departments of State and Justice.
Throughout, Drinnon gives both details and critical perspective
when rendering the key moments of Goldman's public life, such
as the McKinley assassination, the Kersner case, and her deportation trial. He also insightfully charts Goldman's contributions
to the early feminist movement and her relationship to other political radicals and their ideas. Especially helpful is his ability to
set these events of her life in the historical context of the first,
repressive decades of the new century. Though some may consider his frequent editorializing tiresome and intrusive, Drinnon's insights are sound and they help to make this an exciting
and comprehensive biography of a woman and her times.

Drinnon does not entirely neglect the private life of Emma
Goldman, but he only occasionally analyzes the richness and
pain of her many affairs. The best treatment of her private world
is contained in FALK's biography. In 1975, Falk discovered hundreds of Goldman's letters in a dusty Chicago guitar shop. All
were written to Ben Reitman, her lover and manager from 1908
to 1917, who had probably loaned them to her to help her write
Living My Life (1931), her autobiography. Falk uses these letters
as the basis of her biography in an attempt to document the tension Goldman felt between her work and her personal life, and
the struggle to make them consistent with each another. With
regard to Reitman, Falk observes, "Emma cast herself in the
role of the abused but forgiving mother, and Ben as the wayward son. This revealing metaphor became a leitmotif of their
relationship."

Falk's intimate account of their time together is fascinating
and revealing. She records their sexual yearning and their attempts to dismiss civilization's inhibitive "conscience"; she
tells of their mutual tortures when apart and of their gradual
break-up. After Reitman leaves the scene, Falk focuses on some
of Emma Goldman's other lovers, though in less detail. We see
in her narrative the craving and devotion in Goldman's intimate
relationships, and the uncomfortable strain it brought to her public work. During the period of her greatest notoriety in the
United States, Goldman wrote, "If I had to give up everything
and everybody in order to go with Ben I would go, he is the
most compelling element in my life, even if it means living
in Hell."

Though Falk does not entirely neglect the public woman, she
certainly gives her short shrift. A more balanced study of her
life—one that also takes advantage of newly discovered material—can be found in WEXLER's two biographies. These must
be read together because the first documents Goldman's life only
up to her deportation in 1919, which is where the second begins.
Like Falk, Wexler is concerned with the tensions between Goldman's public and private worlds, but Wexler has more success in
keeping the whole woman in view. An historian, Wexler writes
with great authority about the contexts in which Goldman lived
and worked. We learn, for instance, about American industrial
development and immigration, the history of European and
American anarchism, and the blow inflicted upon the latter by
the McKinley assassination. This material helps to clarify and

delineate the world against which Emma Goldman protested and which she attempted to change.

Wexler's second volume focuses on the three most important events of Goldman's last 20 years; her profound personal disappointment with the progress of the Russian revolution, the death of Alexander Berkman, and the time she spent with the Spanish anarchists in the late 1930s. Again, the historical contexts are very helpful, rendering this version of Goldman's later life the best one available. In her treatment of the Russian sojourn, however, Wexler steps out of a purely documentary role to contend that Goldman's critiques (especially in her 1925 volume *My Disillusionment in Russia*) helped to form "an anti-Communist consensus" in the West. One can take or leave this hypothesis, which is incidental to the quality and thoroughness of her narrative.

Wexler's biographies are perhaps richer in detail than Drinnon's but, taken together, they are also much longer and less handy. Both are well researched and well documented, and both render a faithful and complete account of a remarkable life.

—Martin Thies

GOLDSMITH, Oliver, 1730–1774; English writer.

Black, William, *Goldsmith*. London, Macmillan, 1878.

Dobson, Austin, *Life of Oliver Goldsmith*. London, W. H. Scott, 1888.

Forster, John, *The Life and Adventures of Oliver Goldsmith*. London, Bradbury and Evans, 1848; as *The Life and Times of Oliver Goldsmith*, 2 vols., 1854.

Freeman, William, *Oliver Goldsmith*. London, H. Jenkins, 1951; New York, Philosophical Society, 1952.

Ginger, John, *The Notable Man: The Life and Times of Oliver Goldsmith*. London, Hamilton, 1977.

Gwynn, Stephen, *Oliver Goldsmith*. London, T. Butterworth, and New York, Holt, 1935.

Irving, Washington, *Oliver Goldsmith: A Biography*. New York, Putnam, 1849 (revised edition).

Kent, Elizabeth E., *Goldsmith and His Booksellers*. Ithaca, New York, Cornell University Press, and London, Oxford University Press, 1933.

Percy, Thomas, "Memoir of Goldsmith," in *The Miscellaneous Works of Oliver Goldsmith*, vol. I. London, Baldwin, 1801.

Prior, James, *The Life of Oliver Goldsmith* (2 vols.). London, J. Murray, 1837.

Sells, A. Lytton, *Oliver Goldsmith, His Life and Works*. London, Allen and Unwin, and New York, Barnes and Noble, 1974.

Sherwin, Oscar, *Goldy: The Life and Times of Oliver Goldsmith*. New York, Twayne, 1961.

Wardle, Ralph M., *Oliver Goldsmith*. Lawrence, University of Kansas Press, 1957.

*

Of the early biographies PERCY's has particular interest because Bishop Percy, a close friend, was designated by Goldsmith as his biographer. The first full life of Goldsmith was by PRIOR: it was drawn from a variety of original sources and benefitted from Prior's firsthand knowledge of things and people connected with Goldsmith. Though Prior has been corrected by 20th-century scholarship on many details, his beautifully written biography is still valuable for its fullness, balance, fine judgment, and liberal spirit.

FORSTER's full-length biography in one volume (1848), expanded into two volumes with additional information on Goldsmith's contemporaries in 1854, includes new material on its subject's life in London. Forster is mainly responsible for the more graphic details in the familiar, legendary picture of Goldsmith as the man of genius in distress. IRVING's biography is lively but hurried; it does not add to the facts in Prior and Forster, but is an affecting tribute of personal gratitude arising from Irving's childhood delight in Goldsmith. Both Forster and Irving depend heavily on Prior, to the extent that Prior accused both men of plagiarism. BLACK offers a highly coloured and sentimental account of "gentle Goldsmith" that adds nothing factual to Prior.

DOBSON's is probably still the best of the crop of short, impressionistic, popular biographies of Goldsmith down to 1952, of which only GWYNN's deserves any notice. Gwynn stresses Goldsmith's Irishness in a sympathetic character study that displays its subject as the "ugly duckling" of English literature. The narrowly specialized study by KENT reviews what is known of Goldsmith's relations with the more important of his publishers, serving to correct some statements in Forster and the tribe of later biographers who nearly all followed Forster. No less usefully, Katherine Balderston has gathered in the very thin harvest of Goldsmith's letters (*The Collected Letters of Oliver Goldsmith*, Cambridge, 1928). FREEMAN compiled a brief, journalistic, factual account of Goldsmith's life, full of illuminating quotations, but still heavily indebted to Forster (and therefore to Prior) and oddly unsympathetic to Goldsmith's literary achievement.

WARDLE's work amply justifies its claim to be "the first attempt at a scholarly biography of Oliver Goldsmith published in the 20th century." This highly sympathetic, thoroughly researched, and fully documented study does not offer any significant new material, but it provides a clear and copious synthesis of up-to-date scholarship on Goldsmith and his associates, introducing many important details overlooked by Wardle's 20th-century predecessors. Wardle's plain style and clear arrangement make for easy reading; his command of detail is impressive, especially when discussing the hack work and (drawing on Kent) the entanglements with booksellers; Wardle gives here a vivid and intimate sense of the profession of letters as pursued by Goldsmith. He rates Goldsmith very highly for sharp intelligence, breadth of mind, and independence of spirit, as well as for the clarity and ease of style and geniality of temperament that most readers have found. He endorses Johnson's judgment that Goldsmith was "a very great man," and concludes that he is "the most versatile genius of all English literature." The only notable weakness of Wardle's biography for modern readers is in its adherence to an outdated, simplistic dualism between so-called "Classical" and "Romantic" in the literature of Goldsmith's period.

There is no real advance on Wardle in SHERWIN's popularized *Goldy*, but GINGER's useful biography, written out of a full knowledge of the literary, theatrical, and journalistic worlds of the mid-18th century, interestingly presents the argument that the clue to Goldsmith's personality is his "congenital and unnatural inability to feel." Ginger treats Goldsmith's writings perhaps too consistently as covert and unconscious autobiography, but his book is an absorbing and vivid recreation of an unhappier, more tormented Goldsmith than the one to whom we are more accustomed.

SELLS offers the most voluminous study since Wardle but seems to have benefitted very little from Wardle's sound biographical findings. Sells castigates previous biographers of Goldsmith for their inability to distinguish between fact and legend, but his own work slides easily along the scale of conjecture from "it is tempting to suppose" to "one can believe that." Much of the background detail (for instance about ignorant, time-serving clergymen, about Johnson as a character invented by Boswell, or about "pre-Romantic poetry") was outdated even when this book was written.

—James Sambrook

GOLDWYN, Samuel, 1879?–1974; Jewish-American film producer.

Berg, A. Scott, *Goldwyn: A Biography.* New York, Knopf, 1989; London, Sphere, 1990.
Easton, Carol, *The Search for Sam Goldwyn: A Biography.* New York, Morrow, 1976.
Epstein, Lawrence J., *Samuel Goldwyn.* Boston, Twayne, 1981.
Griffith, Richard, *Samuel Goldwyn: The Producer and His Films.* New York, The Museum of Modern Art Film Library/Simon and Schuster, 1956.
Johnston, Alva, *The Great Goldwyn.* New York, Random House, 1937.
Marx, Arthur, *Goldwyn: A Biography Of The Man Behind The Myth.* New York, Norton, and London, Bodley Head, 1976.

*

A barely literate, impoverished teenage runaway from the squalor of Warsaw's late 19th-century ghetto, Schmuel Gelbfisz arrived on the North American shores an illegal alien. At his death, almost 80 years later, he was mourned as the most famous independent producer of classy, literate movies created during Hollywood's richest period.

Throughout his long life, Goldwyn strove mightily to re-invent himself. It is not surprising, then, that most of what has been written about "the Great Goldwyn" is evasive and often fictitious. An early exception is a two-page *New Yorker* profile (25 April 1925) anonymously written by Goldwyn's own press agent, Carl Brandt, which shrewdly assesses its subject as "the celluloid prince." Not until the publication in 1989 of Berg's massive and fanatically researched work (see below) was there a definitive biography.

Goldwyn's autobiography, *Behind the Screen* (1923), was ghostwritten by journalist Corinne Lowe (in affected, old-fashioned prose), originally serialized in *Pictorial Review* and then published as a book that became an immediate bestseller. Of negligible value as a chronicle of his personal life (the first 14 years of his life are dismissed in one sentence, and his parents, first wife, and daughter are never mentioned), it is an interesting source of anecdotes about Goldwyn's early Hollywood working days.

JOHNSTON's work was originally a four-part *Saturday Evening Post* profile (Spring 1937) later published as a 99-page book. Goldwyn loved it. It is pithy and quotable, for example in describing Goldwyn as a "surrealist word painter." Although it concentrates on Goldwyn's personality rather than on his movie-making prowess—hardly a film is named—it does make the point that the essence of his work was "that the intelligence of the audience is never insulted." This sentiment echoes through every Goldwyn study (save Easton, see below).

GRIFFITH's work is "a 48-page panegyric" (to quote arch-enemy Carol Easton) by the curator of the Museum of Modern Art's film library, published in conjunction with the Museum's film cycle honoring Goldwyn. Concise yet pedantic, the pamphlet's pretentious and almost humorless style would kill it but for the brilliant insights and deadpan humor that lurk in the verbiage. Describing the setting of 1939 masterpiece *Wuthering Heights* as "not the moors of Yorkshire, but a wilderness of the imagination" is perfect, and, observing that after Goldwyn protégée Anna Sten "left the Goldwyn studio Miss Sten appeared in six films for other producers to profound public indifference" is delicious. It is worth considering Easton's claim that the honorable scholar Griffith might have been seduced by Goldwyn publicists' ballyhoo into believing every film a gem. But there is no question that Griffith was the first to articulate the notion that Goldwyn was an aesthetic and creative force behind every film he bankrolled. EPSTEIN is the poor man's Griffith, poorly proofread, offering strange hypotheses about the supposed relationship between the producer's personal life and the films he made. It does have a fine annotated bibliography.

1976 saw the publication of two well-written biographies. Their authors' points of view, however, could not have been more divergent. EASTON, bitter and nasty, is a put-down of Goldwyn, his family, his films, and even the folks whose reminiscences are drawn upon. Easton's contempt for those who consented to be interviewed is appalling. (Bruce Humberstone and Sylvia Fine Kaye get quite a drubbing.) But one must admit that the book is hilarious. Goldwyn is left without a shred of dignity. Only Walter Brennan, who steadfastly maintains his loyalty to and affection for his former boss throughout his interview, is spared Easton's savagery. MARX, on the other hand, likes his subject. Breezy and sometimes raunchy—very much the product of a facile gagwriter—his work views Goldwyn as a lovable curmudgeon and a comic legend spouting Goldwynisms, and a man whose contributions to film art are not to be denied. Goldwyn's leap from buffoon to arbiter of impeccable taste is not satisfactorily explained. Howard Dietz (who worked for and was a personal friend of Goldwyn)—interviewed at length—remarks that, "I don't think he knew anything about making movies . . . how he could arrive at the pinnacle of success with so little is beyond me." This paradox nags every Goldwyn biographer. How a man of such obvious limitations could be perceived as a cultural icon remains *the* question.

BERG comes closest to answering it. A remarkable achievement, overwhelming in its scholarship and felicitously presented,

Berg's work was written at the behest of the Goldwyn family. Samuel Goldwyn, Jr., allowed Scott Berg access to a wealth of personal, business, and legal documents hitherto unavailable. At last, Samuel Goldwyn's parents, even his grandparents, his childhood, his siblings, his marriages, relationships with his two children—all spring to life. Virtually no aspect of Goldwyn's 94 years is left unexplored. Even peripheral characters are treated with meticulous attention. Obviously indebted to the cooperation of the Goldwyn family, Berg is nevertheless objective, revealing much that is unflattering (for instance, Goldwyn's refusal in the 1920s to finance his sister Manya's emigration from Poland to Palestine; she and her husband were subsequently murdered in Auschwitz). Yet the overall sense is one of understanding, if not compassion, for Sam Goldwyn, who devoted every waking moment to forging his own destiny while making everyone else's life hell. Although Mordecai Richler found the book "largely nonjudgmental" (*New York Times Book Review*, 28 March 1989), it is replete with shock value. The shocks range from gossipy tidbits about Merle Oberon's $100-a night career, and Billy Wilder's "part-time gigolo" status in 1920s Berlin, to what amounts to a biography-within-the-biography of Sam's second wife, Frances, her loony Jew-hating mother, and the "true love" of Frances' life: the homosexual, and Jewish, director George Cukor. All of them, including Sam, played out their lives in a manner worthy of a blockbuster gothic romance.

The only quibble with a work that appears to leave no stone unturned is its omission of any reference to Goldwyn's attempt, in 1921, to lure Yiddish-American writer Anzia Yezierska (1880?–1970) into his stable of screenwriters. (See Louise Levitas Henriksen, *Anzia Yezierska: A Writer's Life,* New Brunswick and London, Rutgers University Press, 1988.) Berg has missed a grand opportunity to explore the interaction—for they did meet, disastrously—of two Eastern European Jewish immigrants, almost exact contemporaries, whose boundless energy to succeed in the golden land fueled their monomaniacal pursuit of life careers. They were both stymied by but ultimately immortalized for their determination not to compromise their standards. The difference, though, is that Ms. Yezierska died impoverished, Goldwyn a multimillionaire. The parable, yet unwritten, is fascinating.

—Honora Raphael Weinstein

GOODMAN, Benny [Benjamin David Goodman], 1909–1986; American clarinetist and bandleader.

Collier, James L., *Benny Goodman and the Swing Era.* New York, Oxford University Press, 1989.
Connor, D. Russell and Warren W. Hicks, *BG On the Record: A Bio-Discography of Benny Goodman.* New Rochelle, New York, Arlington House, 1969.
Crowther, Bruce, *Benny Goodman.* London, Apollo Press, 1988.
Hammond, John, with Irving Townsend, *John Hammond on Record.* New York, Ridge Press, 1977.

Schuller, Gunther, *The Swing Era: The Development of Jazz 1930–1945.* New York and Oxford, Oxford University Press, 1989.

*

Aside from the mildly interesting paradox that a dour soul like Benny Goodman was responsible for what was, and still is, America's most joyous popular music, there is not much in Goodman's personal and emotional life to intrigue a biographer. What matters, instead, is his prodigious public life as a performer from the age of 13 until the day he died. The best books about him are about his music.

Goodman's autobiography, *The Kingdom of Swing*, with Irving Kolodin (1939), written when he was 30 and at the peak of his popularity, is charming, irreverent, unpretentious, and the source of most of the personal anecdotes repeated in subsequent Goodman biographies. Interspersed among the reminiscences about Goodman's desperately poor Jewish immigrant family, Al Capone's Chicago, and practical hints for those who want to start their own bands, are stodgy essays by Irving Kolodin, who self-consciously purports to illuminate the "vast and ill-studied history" of jazz. *Benny, King of Swing: A Pictorial Biography Based on Benny Goodman's Personal Archives* (1979) is a lovely collection of photos accompanied by a fairly short introductory essay by Stanley Baron.

Kolodin, it turns out, is absolutely right about the fact that our jazz heritage has been (until recently) poorly documented, except on sound recordings. The next book-length study of one of the world's most important jazzmen was not published until 1969 (although it was privately circulated in 1958), 30 years after the autobiography. CONNOR AND HICKS is a pioneer work—the first of the "bio-discography" genre—vast, minutely detailed, and smoothly written. "No attempt has been made to measure Goodman's personal relationships with his associates. The authors leave this to behavioral psychologists . . . or gossips." A monumental chronicle, enriched with rare photographs, it was updated after Goodman's death by Connor alone. The poignant re-telling of Goodman's last year, an improbably busy one after two years of illness and inactivity, concludes thus: "The Kind is Dead. But there is no line of succession, there is no one to replace him. Long Live His Music." The two Connor discographies (here and in *Benny Goodman: Listen to His Legacy,* 1988), compiled with Goodman's assistance, are treasure troves of information found nowhere else, information about, for instance, show-biz gigs (movies and television appearances), material that is ignored by most jazz writers.

HAMMOND—described by Schuller as "indefatigable jazz fan, impresario, recording executive, critic, discoverer and furtherer of most of the major talents of the Swing Era . . . [and] . . . unquestionably the most influential (non-performing) individual in the field" is also less charitably characterized by Collier as "meddlesome, tactless, arrogant and, when his self-righteousness was ablaze, insensitive to anything but the imperious demands of his own crusades"—wrote his own story in 1977 with verve and style. He has much to say in his memoirs about his brother-in-law Benny Goodman, with whose career he was inextricably involved. Hammond was a courageous man of fierce opinions, a great-grandson of Commodore Vanderbilt who championed black causes at a time when lynching was sometimes the price paid for such courage. His musical likes and dislikes were expressed passionately also. Although he was, from the start, a tremendous admirer of Goodman's abilities as a jazzman, and it was he who prodded Goodman into forming the first interracial jazz combo to perform widely in public, he claims that his idea to expand Goodman's career to include classical music performances was "one of the worst ideas I ever had." Hammond is required reading for anyone interested in (as Schuller says) "that remarkable period in American musical history when jazz was synonymous with America's popular music, its social dances and its musical entertainment."

In fewer than 100 pages, CROWTHER gives as good an analysis of Benny Goodman's career and personal "eccentricities" as any, and without resorting to references to unpleasant personal habits, as Collier (see below) does.

It is a relief to read the kind words for Benny Goodman in recent autobiographies by Lionel Hampton (*Hamp: An Autobiography*, 1989) and Peggy Lee (*Miss Peggy Lee: An Autobiography*, 1989), two performers who were closely associated with Goodman. The gratitude both Lionel Hampton and Peggy Lee feel for Goodman is amply expressed. The first two words of Lee's book are, in fact, "Benny Goodman." Hampton plainly expresses his appreciation of the risks Goodman took in hiring black musicians and playing publicly with them in the South: "Goodman once bopped a guy in the head with his clarinet when the guy told him he should 'get those niggers off his show.' Meanwhile, he was getting flack from some critics in the black community who accused him of using blacks. That was nonsense."

SCHULLER and COLLIER (discussed below by turns) are both important scholarly studies of the swing era, and both were reviewed ecstatically. The former was lauded as "a basic text for anyone seriously interested in American music" (by Martin Williams in *American Music*, Spring 1990) and the latter as "as complete a bio of Goodman as we are likely to see." Collier writes in a pleasant, direct style, although with a few grammatical lapses and a strange fondness for the "perfervid." It is a revisionist view of the American Jazz scene, attempting to revive critical interest in dozens of white jazz musicians (Goodman included), many of whom, the author is correct in saying, have been given "short shrift—of no shrift at all—by many jazz writers." Harry James (who, incidentally, is treated reverentially by Schuller), Ben Pollack (who hung himself in 1971), Leon Roppolo (incarcerated in a mental institution from 1925 until his death in 1943), Art Rollini ("who ended his working life as a concrete inspector"), and the critic Otis Ferguson (an early World War II casualty) are a few of those whose neglected reputations Collier tries to rectify.

Schuller, somewhat along the same lines, begins his 42-page chapter, "The King of Swing—Benny Goodman," which opens the second volume of his massive "History of Jazz," with an unabashed appreciation of Goodman's unique talents. He also condemns the critics of the past who took extreme positions regarding Goodman's importance in jazz, who saw things "only in terms of black and white pigmentation—arguments which evade the real complexities of arriving at a fair and true *musical* appraisal." But Schuller then proceeds to imply strongly that

Goodman appropriated, even "exploited," Fletcher Henderson's arrangements, making a great success of them where Henderson had failed. Having his cake and eating it, too, is Mr. Schuller.

The two authors differ, too, in their assessment of Goodman's improvisational talents. Collier frequently cites Goodman's supposed "incoherence" while Schuller marvels at his "fluency of musical ideas." The two writers disagree about Goodman's place in the classical firmament. Collier repeats the tired notion that Goodman's classical performances were competent at best, technically flawless but unexciting. Schuller, who ought to know, praises Benny Goodman's excursions into the classical world, saying "Benny was the first Third Stream musician, moving easily in and out of jazz and classical music, from the Palomar Ballroom to Carnegie Hall. . . . "

All of Benny Goodman's biographers agree that he was a performer of awesome abilities; there is no question of his immortality.

—Honora Raphael Weinstein

———————

GORBACHEV, Mikhail, 1931–   ; Soviet political leader.

Butson, Thos B., *Gorbachev: A Biography*. New York, Stein and Day, 1985.
Medvedev, Zhores, *Gorbachev*. Oxford, Blackwell, and New York, Norton, 1986.
Muraka, Dev, *Gorbachev: The Limits of Power*. London, Hutchinson, 1988.
Schmidt-Hauer, Christian, *Gorbachev: The Path to Power*. Topsfield, Massachusetts, Salem House, and London, I.B. Tauris, 1986.

*

BUTSON, writing the first biography of Gorbachev in 1985, was not only limited by the scant information made available through official Soviet sources, but had little basis on which to interpret Gorbachev's role as the new General Secretary. An assistant news editor for *The New York Times*, Butson journalistically recounts Gorbachev's childhood, schooling, and rise to his position as the head of state. In comparing his subject to past Soviet leaders, Butson assumes that Gorbachev's policies will be predetermined by prior Russian and Soviet ideology, claiming that "the Soviet Union is not likely to forsake the politically expansionist policies it has pursued for more than six decades." This book, while lacking inquisitive investigation into a larger and more diversified field of Soviet sources, is an adequate source for popular audiences curious about this charismatic leader.

SCHMIDT-HAUER, the Moscow correspondent for the West German weekly, *Die Ziet*, is astounded by the difference between Gorbachev and his predecessors. Gorbachev's intelligence, adaptability, frankness, charm, and humor (as well as his spouse) were a welcome change for most in the Western media. Schmidt-Hauer's book does not always remain neutral, however, and the author fails to list any of his sources. Even so, the boo does provide a better understanding of two influential people who affected Gorbachev's development as a young man: Zdenek Mlynar and Gorbachev's wife, Raisa. Schmidt-Hauer and Medvedev were the first biographers to describe the importance of Gorbachev's relationship with these two individuals. The testimony of Mlynar, Gorbachev's Moscow University roommate, who was a former Czech official and leader in the Prague Spring, provides insight into the development of Gorbachev's personality. Schmidt-Hauer also focuses on the intellectual relationship between Gorbachev and his wife and discusses Raisa's doctoral thesis on agriculture and the collective farm. He believes Raisa's sociological work influenced her husband's outlook because "her findings were not always in agreement with the Party's socio-political objectives." Therefore, according to Schmidt-Hauer, "her practical research complemented his own view of the Party." An appendix on economic reform provided by Maria Huber compares the 1965 reform policy to the situation Gorbachev has faced in his attempt to restructure the economy. This book, while an improvement over Butson's, is written not so much for specialists as it is for a larger, educated audience.

The combination of Zhores MEDVEDEV's insight as a former Soviet citizen, and the assistance of his dissident brother Roy (who provides Zhores with both official and unofficial Soviet material), makes this biography a richly detailed one. The scope of the book covers Gorbachev's early life in Stavropol, his education in law and agriculture, through his political career as advanced by Suslov and Andropov. Because of Medvedev's background in agronomy, his book focuses primarily on the significance of agriculture in both Gorbachev's career and the Soviet economy. The specialist of Soviet agriculture will be greatly assisted by Medvedev's numerical detailing of agricultural output during the late 1970s and early 1980s. However, Medvedev's work does have a few minor flaws. For instance, though he states that Gorbachev "is neither a liberal nor a bold reformer," Medvedev does not fully commit himself to this view. He notes that since Gorbachev is only now able to put forth his own programs, it is possible he may "not have yet made his final choice." Because this book was published the same year as Schmidt-Hauer's, the information it provides concerning Gorbachev is similar. While it will be of value to scholars, its glossary will assist the general reader as well. If only one biography of Gorbachev is to be read, this should be it. Medvedev deftly covers the personal and political sides of Gorbachev through a unique understanding of the Soviet system.

MURAKA's book differs from the other biographies most notably in scope and in the types of sources it uses. Concerning the latter, Muraka takes advantage of the new openness developed through *glasnost*. His use of Soviet television and radio broadcasts is significant, as is his ability to cite exhortations now published in official Soviet journals and periodicals. Muraka also makes full use of Medvedev's and Schmidt-Hauer's biographies to substantiate his own views, which he believes will "shake up our received notions." Points of disagreement arise among the other authors concerning the Korean Airline incident, Gorbachev's possible involvement in Khrushchev's removal, Kulakov's death, and reasons why Gorbachev joined the Party. Muraka's noting these differing interpretations in his text and notes makes for interesting reading. Muraka claims his book is not a biography since "there is little information about the early

and personal life of Gorbachev, his intimate friends, views or habits which make a personal biography possible." Nevertheless, Muraka does develop a biographical background for Gorbachev and covers in greater detail the period since Gorbachev's election to General Secretary in March 1985. In this respect, as one reviewer notes, the book is " . . . essentially a political and cultural history of the Soviet Union in the 1980s . . . " (A. Brown, *Times Educational Supplement*, 2 September 1988). This 400-page work is the most pedagogic of the four books reviewed, and will offer the specialist of contemporary Soviet politics insights into Gorbachev's political role throughout the last decade.

Mikhail Gorbachev will continue to interest readers and biographers as the fast pace of events in the Soviet Union, and the changing image of Gorbachev himself, cause people the world over to ask about his actions and his character. Final judgment will, of course, have to be deferred for many years. Among the many biographies coming out in recent months are Strobe Talbott's *Mikhail S. Gorbachev: An Intimate Biography* (1988), and Gail Sheehy's *The Man Who Changed the World: The Lives of Mikhail S. Gorbachev* (1991).

—John J. Dwyer

GORKY, Maxim [*born* Alexey Maximovich Peshkov], 1868–1936; Russian writer.

Dillon, E. J., *Maxim Gorky: His Life and Writings.* London, Isbister, 1902.

Gourfinkel, Nina, *Gorky,* translated by Ann Feshbach, New York, Grove Press, 1960 (originally published as *Gorki par lui-même,* Paris, Éditions du Seuil, 1954).

Habermann, Gerhard, *Maksim Gorki,* translated by Ernestine Schlant. New York, Ungar, 1971.

Hare, Richard, *Maxim Gorky—Romantic Realist and Conservative Revolutionary.* London and New York, Oxford University Press, 1962.

Holtzman, Filia, *The Young Maxim Gorky 1868–1902.* New York, Columbia University Press, 1948.

Kaun, Alexander, *Maxim Gorky and His Russia.* London, Cape, 1931.

Levin, Dan, *Stormy Petrel: The Life and Work of Maxim Gorky.* New York, Appleton-Century, and London, F. Muller, 1965; revised edition, New York, Schocken Books, 1986.

Olgin, Moissaye J., *Maxim Gorky: Writer and Revolutionist.* New York, International Publishers, and London, Lawrence, 1933.

Roskin, Alexander, *Life of Maxim Gorky,* translated by F. M. Fromberg. Moscow, Foreign Languages Publishing, 1944; as *From the Banks of the Volga: The Life of Maxim Gorky,* New York, Philosophical Library, 1946.

Scherr, Barry P., *Maxim Gorky.* Boston, Twayne, 1988.

Troyat, Henri, *Gorky.* New York, Crown, 1989 (originally published by Flammarion, Paris, 1986).

Weil, Irwin, *Gorky: His Literary Development and Influence on Soviet Intellectual Life.* New York, Random House, 1966.

Wolfe, Bertram D., *The Bridge and the Abyss: The Troubled Friendship of Maxim Gorky and V. I. Lenin.* New York, Praeger, and London, Pall Mall, 1967.

*

Because DILLON's obviously incomplete study appeared when Gorky was only 34, it reveals little about its subject. Factual errors and inconsistencies, together with peculiar generalizations about Russia and the Russians, make this an unreliable book. Nevertheless, Dillon provided a useful service at the time by including translations of several Gorky stories within his text to demonstrate his points. A literary curiosity rather than a real biography, this dated book discloses more about the author's thoughts and opinions than it does about Gorky.

Although it too was written during the subject's lifetime, KAUN's pioneering work differs from its predecessor by furnishing an accurate historical background, especially in its detailed descriptions of the various literary, political, and revolutionary movements that influenced Gorky. This long comprehensive biography includes a chronology of life and works and lists sources in the acknowledgements. This remains the best and most complete account of Gorky's life until 1931—in spite of a prediction about his final days that proved to be wrong. All subsequent biographers borrow heavily from Kaun, usually citing him as their primary source after Gorky's own autobiographical trilogy (1915–23, published together as *Autobiography*, 1949).

Kaun corresponded with many people who were involved in episodes of Gorky's life and even includes a letter from Trotsky in one appendix. The other appendix represents the best published account of Gorky's troubled stay in the United States. Kaun also had the advantage of knowing his subject personally, having spent a summer in Italy engaging in daily conversations with Gorky. During that time Kaun clearly became enchanted with Gorky, accepting almost everything the writer said at face value. Consequently, he vigorously defends Gorky against his *émigré* critics and almost becomes his apologist. Kaun seems to sympathize with the revolutionary movement, another factor that predisposes him both to accept and present Gorky mainly in a positive light.

OLGIN's endorsement of revolutionary goals is more overt. Under the basic assumption that Gorky's guiding principle defines literature as a weapon in class warfare, Olgin investigates three creative periods in the writer's career. He pits Gorky against the morbid, backward intelligentsia of the 1880s and discusses him "first and foremost" as a revolutionist proletarian writer. He does admit that Gorky disagreed somewhat with Soviet policy, but dismisses this as irrelevant. Clearly prorevolutionary, Olgin sees only darkness in the Russia of Gorky's autobiography. His somewhat simplistic approach to Gorky is full of unreliable statements and value judgments with no valid bases. However, a summary, with quotations, of the 1932 celebration of Gorky's 40th anniversary as a writer comprises the most useful element of the book.

ROSKIN's blatantly hagiographical essay presents a pastiche of Gorky's life. Told in straight chronological order, this sketchy and highly selective work predictably stresses Gorky's revolutionary attitudes and explores his life made wretched at the hands of the bourgeoisie. While condemning Imperial Russia for its cruelty and widespread poverty, Roskin echoes Gorky by emphasizing his faith in man. Understandably absent from this book are any references to Gorky's doubts about the Bolsheviks or to his estrangement from Lenin. Approximately 90 per cent of the text concentrates on Gorky's life in 1905 but glosses over the sensitive years in a mere 15 pages. Given that Roskin wrote during Stalin's heyday, the omissions and emphases do not surprise.

HOLTZMAN's well-written and lucid overview of Gorky's early life is the first really scholarly study of Gorky in English. As a result, Holtzman finds errors in Kaun and Dillon. With its copious footnotes, helpful index, and excellent bibliography, this book quotes extensively and intelligently from Gorky's works to provide a good analysis of his journalism, reviews, fiction, and the roots of his folklore. Holtzman also discusses works others ignore. She investigates at length Gorky's first love affair with Olga Kaminskaya and explores some of his literary relationships with contemporaries. She seeks in his early life the roots of various aspects of this complex man: journalist, critic, socialist, humanist, Revolutionary romantic, and Socialist realist.

GOURFINKEL also wrote a thematic rather than a chronological biography, approximately a quarter of which consists of pictures. She quotes heavily from Gorky to illustrate significant events in his life. While it is a charming endeavor, it adds no new insights to any scholarship that preceded it. HARE investigates some of the same themes as Holtzman and Gourfinkel in his solid, objective study. Although he provides minimal documentation, Hare's perceptive analyses trace the development of motifs in Gorky's social, political, and literary thought. He sets out to disprove the myths surrounding Gorky and succeeds. Hare's explications of a number of articles from Gorky's later life explain rather than justify some actions for which his harshest critics condemn him.

For LEVIN, on the other hand, Gorky can do no wrong—except for minor lapses. Levin's cloyingly sentimental, convoluted style mars this biography, which occasionally borders on the realm of fiction; he makes Gorky the hero of a melodramatic tale. To this he adds emotional analyses of Gorky's work. Even though mistakes appear in the text, the book is not without merit: it completes Kaun's work. The first edition lacked documentation of sources, a situation remedied in the 1986 edition, which adds ten pages of "updated" footnotes.

WEIL's literary analysis contributes a great deal to understanding Gorky the man as well as the writer. The first biographical chapter places him in his milieu. Analysis of the literature underlines its tendentiousness, while examination of the autobiography probes the author's psychology and demonstrates how Gorky created an artistic work biographical in nature but not totally reliable as a source. Unfortunately earlier biographers, as well as some who follow Weil, use the autobiography as an authoritative source. Weil provides a wealth of informative notes, a chronology, and a good annotated selective bibliography.

WOLFE relies on close reading of the Lenin-Gorky correspondence in his scholarly investigation of the relationship between the two. He succeeds in his goal "to appraise [Gorky's] stature as a writer . . . [and] to throw some light on his character in the years of his freedom by examining the peculiar ambivalence of his troubled and frequently stormy friendship with Lenin." Wolfe objectively discusses conflicts within Gorky and judiciously uses Gorky's life and works to lead up to the special period under scrutiny. The epilogue of Gorky's three portraits of Lenin aptly concludes an excellent book full of fascinatingdetails.

HABERMANN's superficial, cursory monograph, consisting of snippets from earlier biographies, offers nothing new. Its idiosyncratic spellings of proper names probably results from English translations of German renderings of Russian. Devoid of any analysis, it is not even useful as a general introduction to Gorky. Conversely SCHERR does provide an excellent summary of the life and works of Maxim Gorky. Approximately one-fifth of the text concentrates on biography while the rest tries to acquaint the non-specialist with some of Gorky's work. Scherr devotes separate chapters to the stories, pre-revolutionary novels, plays, autobiography, and memoirs; however, he treats all post-revolutionary work in only one chapter. The book is generally well written, on a higher analytical level than is usual in the Twayne series. In addition to an index and chronology, Scherr supplies informative footnotes and a very good selected annotated bibliography.

TROYAT's nicely written, pleasant biography for the general reader relies for the most part on Gorky's autobiography and repeats much found in earlier studies. Not heavy on details, it skims the surface of Gorky's life in straight narrative form, unencumbered by scholarly notes.

On the whole the biographies of Gorky tend to repeat each other and rarely offer new facts—only new configurations. Probably because of the sensitive nature of Gorky's final years, the controversy surrounding his death, and the questions concerning destruction of his personal papers during the Stalin years, his archives have normally been closed to scholars. At present no precise, definitive biography of Maxim Gorky exist.

—Christine A. Rydel

GOULD, Glenn, 1932–1982; Canadian pianist.

Cott, Jonathan, *Conversations with Glenn Gould.* Boston, Little Brown, 1984.
Friederich, Otto, *Glenn Gould: A Life and Variations.* Toronto, L. and O. Dennys, and New York, Random House, 1989.
Kazdin, Andrew, *Glenn Gould at Work: Creative Lying.* New York, Dutton, 1989.
Payzant, Geoffrey, *Glenn Gould: Music and Mind.* New York and London, Van Nostrand Reinhold, 1978.

*

FRIEDERICH was engaged by the Glenn Gould estate, and its executor, J. Stephen Posen, to write, he relates, "what might be described as the 'official' or 'authorized' biography." With some ground rules, which are not named, agreed upon by Friederich and Posen, Friederich received access to Gould's papers housed at the National Library in Ottawa, covering the life and activities, the letters that contain "nothing either confessional or revelatory," and fragments of miscellaneous notes. He also interviewed many of Gould's colleagues and professional associates and studied Gould's published writings and interviews. He amalgamates copious data and has written 334 pages of text besides a Preface. His results are based exclusively on the papers and interviews (since he did not have any personal contact with Gould), and all his sources are carefully documented.

Friederich, self-admittedly, is not a professionally trained musician or scholar. He does not attempt to function with the perceptions of an experienced performer or an active professional member of the music world. He approaches his task, as he says, as a journalist. Friedrich uses his material to report the events of Gould's life and the varied responses of those interviewed. At the same time, he does not hesitate to intersperse his own thoughts and responses throughout, as well as his unbounded admiration for Gould.

The Appendix listing Gould's concerts includes dates, places, and "main works performed." Also provided are a discography by Nancy Canning, a list of C.B.C. radio and television shows, and Gould's published writings, a great part of which are his liner and program notes.

COTT's *Conversations* does not provide dates for individual interviews. As these conversations stand, they convey an unconvincing absolutism on the part of both Gould and Cott. A text of 136 pages, including the author's Introduction, is followed by a discography, a listing of the "C.B.C. private Glenn Gould Tape Collection," radio programs, television programs, and filmography.

PAYZANT's book is constructed chiefly from Gould's printed interviews and published writing. As Andrew Kazdin remarked, "Payzant wrote the book without extensive interviews with Gould (or any of his intimates, such as they were) and based his point of view solely on Gould's writings, recordings and other personal creations, . . . outpourings that Gould had meticulously controlled in the first place."

KAZDIN's volume, while not a biography per se, offers an intimate portrait of Gould unachievable except by close and extended association. Kazdin was Gould's record producer for 15 consecutive years. His data emerges from the unavoidably revealing conditions of a sustained working relationship between performer and producer—a relationship which of its very nature provides revelatory material pertinent to virtually all aspects of Gould's work and personality. Kazdin's reportage and conclusions are supported by extensive documentation. He also includes valuable elucidations of many of the technical processes of recording and record production. Besides an Epilogue and an Appendix entitled "Slaughterhouse Five" having to do with commercial interests in recording, Appendix Two lists the discography.

—Rosalyn Tureck

GOYA Y LUCIENTES, Francisco José de, 1746–1828; Spanish painter.

Chabrun, Jean-François, *Goya,* translated by Maxwell Brown-John. London, Thames and Hudson, and New York, Tudor, 1965 (originally published by Somogy, Paris, 1965).
Gassier, Pierre and Juliet Wilson, *Life and Complete Works of Francisco Goya.* New York, Reynal, 1971; as *Goya: His Life*

and Work, London, Thames and Hudson, 1971 (originally published as *Vie et Oeuvre de Francisco Goya*, Paris, Office du Livre, 1970).

Gassier, Pierre, *Goya, a Witness of His Times*, translated by Helga Harrison. Secaucus, New Jersey, Chartwell Books, 1983.

Glendinning, Nigel, *Goya and His Critics*. New Haven, Connecticut, Yale University Press, 1977.

Gudiol José, *Goya 1746–1828: Biography, Analytical Study, and Catalog of His Paintings* (4 vols.). New York, Tudor, 1971 (originally published by Ediciones Polígrafa, 1969–70).

Hull, Anthony, *Goya: Man Among Kings*. New York, Hamilton Press, 1987.

Klingender, Francis D., *Goya in the Democratic Tradition*. London, Sidgwick and Jackson, 1948.

Licht, Fred, *Goya: The Origins of the Modern Temper in Art*. New York, Universe Books, 1979; London, J. Murray, 1980.

Nordström, Folke, *Goya, Saturn, and Melancholy*. Stockholm, Almqvist and Wiksell, 1962.

Pérez Sanchez, Alfonso E. and Eleanor A. Sayre, *Goya and the Spirit of the Enlightenment*. Boston, Museum of Fine Arts, 1989.

Salas, Xavier de, *Goya*, translated by G. T. Culverwell. New York, Mayflower, and London, Studio Vista, 1979.

Williams, Gwyn A., *Goya and the Impossible Revolution*. London, A. Lane, and New York, Pantheon, 1976.

*

GASSIER's 1983 work is not at all short at 300 pages, and yet it is but a reflection of his masterpiece, the standard reference work at this moment, the 1971 *Life and Complete Works*, by GASSIER AND WILSON. This great and impeccably detailed work also offers a catalog raisonné with 1870 works, compiled by François Lacheval. In the 1983 version, the illustrations are all well printed and carefully chosen, and each of the seven chapters begins its title with the same phrase, "The Time of . . . ", thus subtly underscoring the majestic and chronological march through the major episodes of Goya's life. There is a relatively brief bibliography but no footnotes, although the illustrations are captioned with biographical and critical detail. GUDIOL's major work, also extremely well researched, appeared in an English translation in 1971.

PÉREZ SANCHEZ's beautifully printed catalog of a major exhibition that appeared in Boston, New York, and Spain, presents Goya's life and work as part of the Spanish Enlightenment. Five lengthy introductory essays probe the idea of freedom and the relation of Goya and his circle to Enlightenment attitudes, especially those coming from France. Each catalog entry comprises a detailed discussion with bibliography and illustrations for the person, event, tradition, or social meaning conveyed by the entry. Thus either directly or by inference, Goya's personality is reflected in his choice and construction of each image. A detailed chronology closes the text. Years before, KLINGENDER, in a highly influential work, had explored such an approach in his effort to relate Goya's change of style—both subject and technique—to the socio-political activities of his time.

WILLIAMS interprets Goya's career in terms of the crisis of his deafness (with sexual undertones), representing a turning away from idealism to realism, and sees Goya as strongly influenced by his circle of intellectual and enlightened friends. But Williams over-emphasizes the darkness and pessimism within Goya's new grasp of reality.

Both Licht and Nordström focus on Goya's bleak view of humanity. NORDSTRÖM's unique work concentrates on just this one facet of Goya's life and work—melancholy—and shows parallels in his art to the force of this temperament. This iconographical study underscores the importance of Jovellanos, a leading Romantic author who is considered a vital key to Goya's bleakness. LICHT is broader in his interpretation of the man and the work. He offers Goya as the first painter to present an existential world where a sense of human inadequacy, despair, and nihilism reign. Each chapter treats a major category, such as the portraits or *The Caprichos*, and attempts to trace the evolution of Goya's acknowledgement of the violence, both literal and psychological, that ravaged his world.

HULL intends a more formal biography, with few illustrations and little elaboration on art work. The complex political world surrounding Goya is offered with confidence and conjecture based on Hull's detailed and factual treatment, including portraits of complex historical personalities.

SALAS, a leading Goya authority, presents a relatively brief, biographical-critical survey that is well illustrated. Of high interest is the extensive catalog at the close of the text made up of small monochromatic images. CHABRUN's work is also typical of many pleasant, short but detailed and serious biographies—composed of course because of Goya's continuing fascination. GLENDINNING perceived this vast interest in Goya, which accelerated through the course of the 19th century, and cataloged it. After a brief sketch of the artist's life, his text presents a summary of opinion organized by theoretical category (which invariably becomes chronological): Romantic and Realist attitudes, Racial and Political Approaches, etc. While not an easy course to Goya biography, the sequence of quotes from various works, along with Glendinning's narrative, produces a complex if shifting picture of the artist.

—Joshua Kind

GRANT, Cary [*born* Archibald Alec Leach], 1904–1986; English-born American film actor.

Deschner, Donald, *The Films of Cary Grant*. Secaucus, New Jersey, Citadel Press, 1973.

Donaldson, Maureen and William Royce, *An Affair to Remember: My Life with Cary Grant*. New York, Putnam, and London, Macdonald, 1989.

Godfrey, Lionel, *Cary Grant: The Light Touch*. New York, St. Martin's, and London, R. Hale, 1981.

Govoni, Albert, *Cary Grant: An Unauthorized Biography*. Chicago, H. H. Regnery Company, 1971; London, R. Hale, 1973.

Guthrie, Lee, *The Life and Loves of Cary Grant*. New York, Drake Publishers, 1977.

Harris, Warren G., *Cary Grant: A Touch of Elegance*. New York, Doubleday, 1987; London, Sphere, 1988.

Higham, Charles and Roy Moseley, *Cary Grant: The Lonely Heart*. San Diego, Harcourt and Sevenoaks, New English Library, 1989.

McIntosh, William Currie and William Weaver, *The Private Cary Grant*. London, Sidgwick and Jackson, 1983.

Schickel, Richard, *Cary Grant: A Celebration*. Boston, Little Brown, and London, Pavilion, 1983.

Trescott, Pamela, *Cary Grant: His Movies and His Life*. Washington, D.C., Acropolis Books, 1987.

Wansell, Geoffrey, *Haunted Idol: The Story of the Real Cary Grant*. New York, Morrow, 1984.

*

A great deal has been published about Cary Grant over the past 15 years. Most of the book-length biographies have the same weaknesses and strengths. With one or two exceptions, they tend to be less scholarly and more gossipy. Several read like movie magazine confessions. Nearly all of the biographies are well equipped with photographs, and nearly all feature a filmography of Cary Grant's movies, though only one or two have a bibliography or note section. This lack of bibliographic information on Grant will no doubt be alleviated by Beverley Bare Beuhrer's *Cary Grant: A Bio-Bibliography* (Greenwood Press, 1990) which was unable for review at this writing.

GOVONI takes a non-academic look at Cary Grant's life. He has chapters on Grant's early life, his theatrical career, his film work, and his tempestuous relationships with women. The subject here lends itself to a Populist biography, but Govoni squanders his opportunity with his pointless generalizations—he attempts, and fails, to answer the question, "Who is Cary Grant"—and more importantly with his rather poor writing style. In addition, Govoni appears dated when viewed in the light of more recent (and more competent) biographies. Though among the first to chronicle Cary Grant's life, Govoni is not among the best.

DESCHNER is little better than Govoni. His study is primarily designed for the coffee table, full of pretty pictures and little else of interest. His scrapbook approach chronologically lists Cary Grant's films, presenting cast and credit lists as well as a brief analysis of each film entry. Deschner does have a chapter devoted to Grant's life, and he includes a chapter entitled "Myth and Reality" that attempts in a heavy-handed and vague manner to place Cary Grant in a cultural context.

GUTHRIE emphasizes Grant's film career and his controversial associations with women. He devotes entire chapters of his book to Grant's wives, including Barbara Hutton, Betsy Drake, and Dyan Cannon. His prose is lightweight, and he unfortunately relies more on the "kiss and tell" school of writing than on academic scholarship.

GODFREY is more scholarly in tone. His style is at times dense, yet his points are sound and well researched. Godfrey deals more with the personal history of Cary Grant, especially his early life. This work, one of the finer studies done on Grant, includes a filmography, a bibliography, and detailed notes.

McINTOSH AND WEAVER's thin, conversational narrative makes for easy, if somewhat unscholarly, reading. The authors spend little time with Cary Grant's childhood, choosing instead to focus on the mature actor's life behind his public career.

Though this is not a major study, it is nonetheless entertaining and one of the better popular efforts.

SCHICKEL furnishes another coffee-table scrapbook review of Cary Grant's film career that is profusely illustrated with publicity photos and behind-the-scene shots of Grant at work. Schickel's attitude is perhaps too laudatory (as the title of his book might indicate); his biography is however very well written and quite useful as an in-depth review of Grant's films. Schickel gives the reader useful and perceptive insights into the actor's psychological motivations.

What the other "kiss and tell" biographies of Cary Grant promise and generally fail to deliver, WANSELL more than makes up for. His is the first of the truly contemporary spare-nothing-for-the-imagination studies. Wansell dredges it all up: Grant's four ugly divorces, his obsession with money, his drug use, and his relationships with Randolph Scott and Howard Hughes. Wansell's background is in journalism, and his methodology resembles investigative reporting, centering as it does on an oral history of Grant. Wansell conducted numerous interviews with people who knew (or claimed to know) the actor. His work is very reliable, an essential source for those who wish to get at the man behind Grant's studio image.

HARRIS is among the first biographers to publish after Cary Grant's death, and as such he was among the first to realize the possibility of a truly objective, retrospective view of Grant's life in show business and contributions to the motion picture arts. Such potential, unfortunately, was not realized. Harris is little more than an extension of Wansell, and his work, written on a fourth-grade reading level, seems to underestimate the intelligence of its readers.

TRESCOTT, too, misses an opportunity for ground-breaking scholarship; her books falls squarely in the domain of hero-worship. Trescott deals both with Grant's life and with his work, and she generally relies too much on undocumented information (though in all fairness to Trescott, so do a number of the other Grant biographies). Trescott also provides some cultural perspectives on Cary Grant's cinematic contributions, but not as much as one would desire. Finally, her study contains a detailed filmography, but no bibliography.

DONALDSON's biography of Cary Grant is as much the author's story as it is Grant's. Donaldson was involved in a relationship with the actor from the mid to late 1970s, and her account purports to be an inside view of the man. While Donaldson does comment some on Grant's youth, she, along with Wansell and Harris, again focuses on Grant's love life, his involvement with drugs, and his rocky dealings with women and past wives. Donaldson's version is supported—if the reader is to believe her—by her personal experiences with Grant. Despite a total lack of scholarship, which indeed is not the book's intention, Donaldson provides an intriguing look at Grant's later years.

HIGHAM AND MOSELEY provide the depth of research and analysis lacking in the other Grant biographies. Their investigations, moreover, produce the most explicit descriptions of the actor's life. They are able, for example, to relate in detail Grant's long-standing affair with the actor Randolph Scott. The detailed notes at the end of the book are very useful, describing as they do the methodology employed to substantiate the authors' analysis of Cary Grant (something that many of the other Grant biographers fail to accomplish). Objective, exhaustive, and truly sympathetic to its subject, Higham and Moseley's work is the single best book about Cary Grant.

—Gary Hoppenstand

GRANT, Ulysses S., 1822–1885; American general and political leader, 18th president of the United States.

Badeau, Adam, *Military History of Ulysses S. Grant* (3 vols.). New York, Appleton, 1868–81.

Badeau, Adam, *Grant in Peace: From Appomattox to Mount Mc-Gregor; A Personal Record.* Hartford, Conneticut, S.S. Scranton, 1887.

Cadwallader, Syvanus, *Three Years with Grant,* edited by Benjamin P. Thomas. New York, Knopf, 1955.

Carpenter, John A., *Ulysses S. Grant.* New York, Twayne, 1970.

Catton, Bruce, *U.S. Grant and the American Military Tradition.* Boston, Little Brown, 1954.

Catton, Bruce, *Grant Moves South.* Boston, Little Brown, 1960.

Catton, Bruce, *Grant Takes Command.* Boston, Little Brown, and London, Dent, 1969.

Fuller, J.F.C., *The Generalship of Ulysses S. Grant.* New York, Dodd Mead, and London, J. Murray, 1929.

Fuller, J.F.C., *Grant and Lee: A Study in Personality and Generalship.* New York, Scribner, and London, Eyre and Spottiswoode, 1933.

Gillette, William, *Retreat from Reconstruction, 1869–79.* Baton Rouge, Louisiana State University Press, 1979.

Hesseltine, William B., *Ulysses S. Grant: Politician.* New York, Dodd Mead, 1935.

Lewis, Lloyd, *Captain Sam Grant.* Boston, Little Brown, 1950.

MacArtney, Clarence Edward, *Grant and His Generals.* New York, McBride, 1953.

Marshall-Cornwall, Sir James, *Grant as Military Commander.* New York, Van Nostrand-Reinhold, 1970.

McFeely, William S., *Grant: A Biography.* New York, Norton, 1981.

Pitkin, Thomas M., *The Captain Departs: Ulysses S. Grant's Last Campaign.* Carbondale, Southern Illinois University Press, 1973.

Porter, Horace, *Campaigning with Grant.* New York, Century, 1897.

Smith, Gene, *Lee and Grant: a Dual Biography.* New York, McGraw-Hill, 1984.

Williams, Kenneth P., *Lincoln Finds a General: A Military Study of the Civil War* (5 vols.). New York, Macmillan, 1949–59.

Woodward, W.E., *Meet General Grant.* New York, Horace Liveright, 1928.

Young, John Russell, *Around the World with General Grant.* New York, American News Company, 1879.

*

Any study of Grant's life should begin with his own *Personal Memoirs* (1885–86), a superb work whose literary merit has been praised by such figures as Matthew Arnold, Henry James, and Gertrude Stein. Edmund Wilson claimed that the *Memoirs* were "nothing less than one of the great American books," "perfect in conciseness and clearness, in propriety and purity of language." Written when Grant was dying of throat cancer, the work was intended to repay heavy debts. Written without rancor or apparent bias, it possesses a clear and forceful style. The *Memoirs* begin with a tantalizing if brief account of his ancestry, then moves to his boyhood in Ohio, education at West Point, and courtship of Julia Dent. Though Grant saw combat in the Mexican War, he found the annexation of Texas rooted in a slave-holding conspiracy and the conflict with Mexico unjustified. After a brief summary of his bleak life in the 1850s, Grant gives nearly two-thirds of his narrative over to the Civil War. Here the narrative points to two climaxes: Vicksburg and Lee's surrender at Appomattox.

The *Memoirs* are far from complete. Over 36 years of marriage are neglected, as are the entire post-Civil War years, which include the presidency. In his military narrative, Grant was prone to exaggerate the strength of the enemy while belittling his own. His account of the battle of Chattanooga is inaccurate, and he minimizes his mistakes at Shiloh and Cold Harbor. Fortunately, the edition edited by E.B. Long (1952) covers errors in figures, dates, and names.

Julia Grant's own *Personal Memoirs*, not published until 1975, reveal a more human Grant, a devoted father very much in love with his wife. Much of the account is superficial: Mrs. Grant devotes 30 pages to her husband as president as compared to over 100 on their round-the-world trip. Yet she shows a sharp eye for detail. If at times her behind-the-scenes observations on the Civil War are not accurate, at her best she is most perceptive.

BADEAU's three-volume *Military History* (1868–81) long stood as the official biography, its impenetrable prose appearing to confirm its authority. Early campaigns are slighted; volumes two and three cover only the last year of the Civil War. Badeau had joined Grant's staff in 1864, serving as aide-de-camp and secretary before his appointment as consul to London in 1869. Only Badeau had access to Grant's personal collection of military records. Moreover, Grant offered a critique of each chapter draft. *Grant in Peace* (1887) is far more gossipy, and offers neither political history nor firm narrative.

Superior memoirs include those by CADWALLADER and PORTER. In 1945, Grant biographer Lloyd Lewis discovered a manuscript written by Sylvanus Cadwallader, correspondent for the *Chicago Times* and *New York Herald* who spent four years with Grant in the field. The original manuscript was a rambling, discursive account. Under Benjamin Thomas' expert editing, however, it has become one of the best memoirs to emerge from the Civil War. Though finding Grant far too heavy a drinker, Cadwallader usually presents an admiring portrait, abounding in human detail, sharp insight, and absorbing incident. Porter, a staff officer who drew upon a now vanished diary, also offers an excellent picture of Grant in the last year of the war.

By far, McFEELY's Pulitzer prize-winning biography is the best general study of Grant in close to 50 years. Then a historian at Mount Holyoke College, McFeely finds Grant's story "the quest of an ordinary American man in the mid-19th century to make his mark." Though a failure as peacetime military officer, farmer, minor businessman, and clerk, Grant still wanted to be "taken into account." His chance came during the Civil War, where a combination of luck (West Pointers were suddenly in demand), a ruthless pragmatism, and "an uneven but remarkable degree of self-confidence" permitted him to "make a great mark." Indeed, in a sense, "he became a general and a president because he had nothing better to do." No admirer of his subject, McFeely denies that Grant possessed any "organic, artistic, or intellectual specialness." As president, he could never face the limits of his talents; neither could the confused society that propelled him to the pinnacle of power, and it is this, McFeely suggests, that is the real tragedy.

Yet McFeely has some drawbacks. His anti-war sentiments are too overt and heavy-handed, obviously betraying the impact of the Vietnam War. Porter's account had shown that Grant was not insensitive to the dead or wounded but felt deeply about the casualties. Furthermore, Grant was far more sympathetic to the predicament of American blacks than McFeely would have one believe. At times McFeely is inappropriately flippant, as when he writes that "one of the reasons for war is to have an excuse to do some drinking." McFeely's claims notwithstanding, both Fuller and Catton (see below) show that the ratio of casualties in Grant's armies was considerably lower than that of Lee, or of most generals on either side. WILLIAMS is far superior on Grant's generalship, GILLETTE on Grant's Reconstruction policies (for both, see below). McFeely leaves an inordinate number of factual errors, particularly concerning military matters.

CATTON's *Ulysses S. Grant* (1954) remains the best brief biography, making the man more understandable, admirable, and yet more pathetic than had any previous account. Catton finds in Grant a complex mixture: singularly happy boyhood, hatred of West Point, dislike of abolitionists, military tactics of speed and deception, and disappointing record as president. Space limitations lead Catton to oversimplify such matters as Reconstruction, and he is more at home in discussing Grant the politician than Grant the president. Yet the book remains an eloquent tribute.

LEWIS' account is not only definitive on Grant's early life but offers superb descriptions of the Mexican War campaigns of Zachary Taylor and Winfield Scott. Scott in particular influenced Grant, showing him how to break loose from a supply base and how to turn motly volunteers into excellent soldiers. Scott intensified young lieutenant Grant's taciturn personality and distaste for uniforms. In Lewis' biography, Grant emerges as quiet, unassuming, kindly, courageous, solid, foreshadowing the general to be. Lewis, however, died before his multi-volume project was well underway, and he only was able to take Grant's story down to 15 June 1861, when he was appointed colonel of a volunteer Illinois regiment called "Governor Yates's Hellions." At the request of Lewis' widow and the publisher, Catton completed the project.

In scholarship, psychological understanding, narrative power, and stylistic skill, CATTON matches his predecessor. His *Grant Moves South* (1960) takes the story down to Vicksburg. Given the choice, so Catton notes, Grant strongly preferred destroying enemy armies to capturing enemy terrain. In the process, Catton blasts the widely accepted picture of Grant as butcher and drunk. *Grant Takes Command* (1969) begins with Grant's victory at Chattanooga and ends with Appomattox. Here Catton keeps his articulate and analytical approach, always emphasizing Grant's unshakable self-confidence.

Catton's positive interpretation was not in vogue at the beginning of the 20th century. WOODWARD's volume, a pro-Confederate account both undocumented and unreliable, set the tone. In 1929 the British military historian FULLER was definitely an iconoclast, writing in *The Generalship* (1929) that Grant was "the greatest strategist of his age, of the war, and, consequently, its greatest general." Fuller continues that Vicksburg, not Gettysburg, was the crisis of the war, for it was there that the Confederacy was cut in two. In *Grant and Lee* (1933), Fuller finds that Grant saw the war as a whole far more than Lee ever did. Grant was perenially the grand strategist, Lee the field tactician.

In one of the most authoritative military accounts of the Civil War yet written, WILLIAMS offers five volumes on Lincoln's search for a winning general. Professor of mathematics at Indiana University, Williams had been a field artillery colonel and quartermaster general. His study of Grant was written in the grand style on a grand scale. Williams had only reached March 1864, when Grant was commissioned as lieutenant general, before he died. Williams' Grant is a figure of singular courage, imagination, and judgment. Not the drunk of legend, he was modest, unselfish, decisive, and cared greatly for the men entrusted to him.

MacARTNEY finds Grant wise in his choice of generals, particularly James B. McPherson, Philip T. Sheridan, and William T. Sherman. Both MARSHALL-CORNWALL, a British general, and SMITH, a free-lance writer of popular history, show sympathy to Grant, but offer little not presented far more ably elsewhere. Marshall-Cornwall overlooks recent scholarship and neglects manuscripts; Smith omits such works as Williams and the Grant papers from the bibliography.

Revisionism of Grant's career does not usually extend to the presidency, though CARPENTER's brief account is superior. HESSELTINE's study, written with verve and contempt, condemns nearly every aspect of Grant's character and conduct. An historian at the University of Wisconsin, he writes of Grant, "As he acquired the ideology of a politican, he lost the vision of a statesman." Hesseltine's opening chapter, "Forty Years of Failure," portrays "a plastic person" incapable of creating his own success, but rather destined to be shaped by the events of the day. Grant was "peculiarly ignorant of the Constitution and inept in handling men," and moreover "dogs did not like him." He mistakenly finds Grantism rooted in "industrial magnates" and "masters of capital" and thereby neglects the racial dynamics of Reconstruction.

Race is very much at the center of GILLETTE, a historian at Rutgers University, who is more friendly to Radical Reconstruction than Hesseltine is. Yet Gillette finds Grant's southern policy "a study in incongruity: a curious, confusing, changable mix of boldheadedness and timidity, decision and indecision, activity and passivity, as he shifted between reinforcement and retrenchment, coercion and conciliation." Grant was unable to provide effective policy, clear direction, and strong leadership.

John Y. Simon is in the process of editing *The Papers of Ulysses S. Grant* (Carbondale, Southern Illinois University Press, 1967- ; 14 vols. published as of 1987), which reveal a general who knows his own strengths and those of his subordinates. YOUNG's account offers a massive travelogue of Grant's world tour and includes some Grant reminiscences. PITKIN presents an excellent picture of Grant's "last campaign," his effort to complete his memoirs before his death.

—Justus D. Doenecke

GRAVES, Robert, 1895–1985; English writer.

Graves, Richard Perceval, *Robert Graves: The Assault Heroic 1895–1926*. London, Weidenfeld and Nicolson, 1986; New York, Viking, 1987.
Seymour-Smith, Martin, *Robert Graves: His Life and Works*. London, Hutchinson, and New York, Holt, 1983.

*

Robert Graves' autobiography, *Goodbye to All That*, (London, 1929) is a primary source for the two biographies of Graves. Written in a mood of angry disenchantment with post-war Britain, the autobiography moves from Graves' unhappy formative years at Charterhouse to his stint as an officer in the Royal Welch Fusiliers, fighting in the battle of Loos and the Somme in World War I. As a description of an officer's life in and out of the trenches, and of the muddled mixture of patriotism, bravery, and anti-militarism that motivated so many who fought in the war, it is crammed with relevant incident, detail and opinion. Its style tends toward the documentary, with parts of letters, songs, postcards, newspaper cuttings, diaries, and even a Battalion Order, giving a lively sense of authenticity to the anecdotal narrative of Graves' military exploits, his marriage and domestic circumstances, and his literary acquaintances (with accounts of T. E. Lawrence and Siegfried Sassoon, and passing mention of, among others, Edmund Blunden, John Masefield, and Thomas Hardy). His career up to his departure for Mallorca is dealt with, including his boisterously inefficacious year as a professor at the University of Cairo. Overall the mood of the book is valedictory and tending to repudiate the society that Graves is leaving, as in the revelation of homosexual behaviour at English private schools (with a frank account of his own sentimental attachment to a school colleague), or in the appallingly straightforward depiction of the incompetence of those in charge of running the war, or the gulf between civilian and soldiers' attitudes concerning what was happening at the front.

SEYMOUR-SMITH writes as a long-standing friend and admirer of Graves as man and poet ("I have known Graves—and his wife Beryl—very well since March 1943," he writes in his Introduction). His account of Graves' early life, while reliant on *Goodbye to All That*, is fleshed out with what are obviously latter day reflections and memories culled from conversations with the poet and others. There follows a detailed account of the relationships between Graves, his first wife Nancy, the American poet Laura Riding, and an Irish writer, Geoffrey Phibbs, which resulted in the notorious episode in which Riding jumped from a fourth-floor window in St. Peter's Square, London, followed by Graves jumping from the third floor. Seymour-Smith attempts to explain this farcical and tragic episode through a careful chronological examination of the events surrounding it, along with notes and letters exchanged between the participants. An analysis of the Riding-Graves relationship and their way of life in Deyá, Mallorca, continues through to their final breaking apart in Pennsylvania in 1939. In general Seymour-Smith is less than sympathetic to Laura Riding during this scrutiny, and Riding wrote bitterly to the *Times Literary Supplement* (16 July 1982) complaining of "this literarily and humanly shameful book." The rest of Graves' life, the war years in Britain, and his life on Mallorca up to the poet's 80th birthday, takes up the remaining half of the book, with the poet depicted as ruled by three concerns: the need to make money (resulting in the writing of a large number of prose works of various kinds), his imperative poetic urge, and, connected with this, his yearning for "Muses" in the form of various young women whom he meets in later life, while enjoying the stability of marriage to his second wife, Beryl. Some of Graves' behaviour, attitudes, and opinions, as described by Seymour-Smith, are individual to the point of requiring specially sympathetic explanation, psychological and biographical, from the narrator, and these explanations are not always convincing. Quotations from Graves' poetry are constantly used as points of reference in the developing story.

RICHARD PERCEVAL GRAVES is the poet's nephew, the son of Robert's younger brother John. *The Assault Heroic 1895–1926* is the first of two or three projected volumes, finishing just at the point when Laura Riding enters the life of the Graves family, just before the year in Cairo. The writer had access to family papers in the form of diaries and letters, and Graves' own depiction of his youth is considerably filled out by family memories and descriptions of him. Sometimes the book almost takes the family's side against Graves, for example in detailing his parents' anxious disapproval of his tendency to drift financially during his first marriage. Certainly we are given a new view of Graves as a son and brother. As in Seymour-Smith the development of Graves' dedication to poetry is a focus for the narrative, in this case from earliest times. The writing is more balanced and reticent than Seymour-Smith's account, which is at times partisan in its sympathies.

—Martin Gray

GRECO, El [born Domenikos Theotokopoulos], 1541–1614; Cretan-born Spanish painter.

Brown, Jonathan, *El Greco of Toledo*. Boston, Little Brown, 1982.
Calvert, F. and C. Gascoine Hartley, *El Greco: An Account of His Life and Works*. London and New York, J. Lane, 1909.
Guinard, Paul, *El Greco: A Biographical and Critical Study*, translated by James Emmons. Barcelona and New York, Skira, 1956.
Kelemen, Pál, *El Greco Revisited, Candia, Venice, Toledo*. New York, Macmillan, 1961.
Palomino, Antonio, *Lives of the Eminent Spanish Painters and Sculptors*, translated and edited by Nina Ayala Mallory. Cambridge and New York, Cambridge University Press, 1987.
Stirling-Maxwell, William, *Annals of the Artists of Spain*. London, J. Ollivier, 1848.

Wethey, Harold E., *El Greco and His School*. Princeton, New Jersey, Princeton University Press, 1962.

*

El Greco's biography, like that of all artists, has been shaped and re-shaped by changing tastes in art. El Greco's painting was admired and respected in his lifetime, but it was not well understood by the more conventionally minded contemporaries who wrote about him. Early Spanish critics and theorists were not very interested in facts about El Greco's life, instead giving him relatively short shrift by simply commenting that he "did excellent things" and that he "earned many ducats." The first real biography of El Greco was included by PALOMINO in his early 18th-century history of Spanish art. Palomino included all of the biographical details then known about El Greco, which were few, and he did not really look for more, apparently stymied by a painter whose work was sometimes excellent, but sometimes "ludicrous and contemptible."

The taste for academic classicism during the 18th century further relegated El Greco to obscurity, but the following century discovered in him a highly individual temperament suited to the Romantic sensibility. STIRLING-MAXWELL, like other writers of the time, created a somewhat mad El Greco, "an artist who alternated between reason and delirium, and displayed his great genius only at lucid intervals." Stirling-Maxwell and other 19th-century biographers of El Greco base their work on the meager information provided earlier by Palomino.

The first modern, scholarly biography of the artist, though unavailable in English, was written by Manuel B. Cossio (*Dominico Theotocopuli El Greco*, Madrid, 1908), who added enormously to our knowledge about El Greco through patient archival research. Cossio's book remains a fundamental source for El Greco scholars, but it is not without its own bias. Cossio wrote at a time when Spanish intellectuals found themselves grappling with a Spain so diminished as a world power that even Spanish national identity came into question. The result of this circumstance was Cossio's creation of an El Greco who "achieved greatness through his Spanishness." The English-speaking reader can get a sense of this new version of El Greco in CALVERT AND HARTLEY, whose 1909 biography of the artist was based on Cossio: "El Greco's extreme individuality, and the sincerity with which he imposed his own mannerism on the norms of art, are Spanish traits." A number of writers about Spanish art have been convinced by Cossio's argument and thus treated El Greco as an artist who, although born in Crete and trained as a painter in Italy, did not truly attain greatness until the self-discovery that awaited him in Spain.

Some, however, particularly Greek scholars, have explained El Greco's style as resulting rather from his native heritage and have connected the dynamic impact of his art directly to his Byzantine heritage, thus emphasizing the importance of El Greco's early years. The main thesis of KELEMEN is that "El Greco, both intellectually and artistically, was thoroughly educated in the Byzantine tradition," and that the artist's style was based on Byzantine compositional methods "modulated to conform to Western taste."

WETHEY wrote about El Greco's life and work in a far less biased fashion; his monograph and catalogue raisonné remain the standard reference for all El Greco studies. Wethey was the first modern scholar to recognize in the artist the attributes of a Renaissance humanist. Key to his reassessment of El Greco's intellect was an analysis of El Greco's library, an inventory of which is one of the many documents that now shed light on the painter's life. El Greco's books suggested to Wethey "an essentially scholarly mind with a strong inclination to history, past and present. He enjoyed both religious and profane writings. The only indication of any enthusiasm for the occult is slight and no greater than any intellectual of the day might have displayed."

The most recent, and perhaps final, debunking of the myths of El Greco as madman, Orthodox imagist, or Roman Catholic mystic is in the carefully reasoned essay by BROWN in the catalogue of an important El Greco exhibition. Brown cogently and eloquently uses all of the biographical information that has thus far come to light to place El Greco's artistic accomplishments within the context of Counter-Reformation Italy and Spain. Brown's study, as well as the other essays in this catalogue, reflects the central role of patrons and shows how much the imprimatur of important patrons can reveal about the way the artist—as talent and as intellect—was viewed in his own time.

Another biography of El Greco in English deserves mention: GUINARD is excellent though now somewhat outdated.

—Suzanne Stratton

GREENE, Graham, 1904–   ; English writer

Allain, Marie-Françoise, *The Other Man: Conversations with Graham Green*, translated by Guido Waldman. New York, Simon and Schuster, and London, Bodley Head, 1983 (originally published as *Autre et son Double*, Paris, Belford, 1981).

Atkins, John, *Graham Greene*. London, J. Calder, and New York, Roy Publishers, 1957.

De Vitis, A. A., *Graham Greene*. New York, Twayne, 1964.

Pryce-Jones, David, *Graham Greene*. Edinburgh, Oliver and Boyd, 1963.

Sherry, Norman, *The Life of Graham Greene*. London, Cape, and New York, Viking, 1989.

*

It was only recently, at age 85, that Graham Greene, for half a century one of the world's most celebrated authors, became the subject of a full-scale biography, when the first volume of Norman Sherry's *The Life of Graham Greene* (see below), covering the writer's life from 1904 to 1939, appeared in 1989. The reason for the delay has been Greene's unwillingness to name a writer whom he would be willing to offer the necessary permission to use his writings, published and unpublished, as the basis for a life. The result of this hesitation has been, over recent decades, a good deal of critical writing about Greene, and a modest amount of biographical writing, and that almost entirely by the subject himself.

The relationship between Greene's novels and his life has usually been that of experiencing first and then turning experience into fiction, so that usually we find that Greene has been there already in the terrain of the novel, as a traveler, a journalist, even a member of the highly amateur British intelligence service. He went all the way through the Mexican territory in which he placed *The Power and the Glory* (1940); he was a secret agent in the West African colony where he set *The Heart of the Matter* (1948). Similar situations can be found in Greene's more recent novels; he traveled to experience and he experienced to write.

And very often there was experience left over that he did not transmute into fiction, so that, until the day in 1977 when Greene finally decided to allow Norman Sherry to become his biographer, it was on the novelist himself that we relied for our knowledge of Graham Greene the man. He wrote two notable travel narratives, which are doubly valuable because they contain so many flashback recollections of his life before the journeys began; *Journey without Maps* (1936), describing a quixotic and apparently motiveless journey into the heart of Liberia, and *The Lawless Roads* (1939), narrating a journey into southern Mexico to investigate the persecution of Catholics by anti-Clericals in power. And many years later Greene wrote two brief memoirs: *A Sort of Life* (1971), dealing with his early days, and *Ways of Escape* (1980), in which he talked of the sources in real life many of his novels.

What strikes one, as in so many autobiographies, is that these books by Greene have in fact been containing exercises, means by which he could in some way delay the reckoning with himself and with truth that either confessional autobiography or a full biography by another person might involve. They are curiously detached accounts, stylized in much the same way as his fiction, and one feels that their purpose is concealment as much as revelation; the offering to an inevitably curious public of sufficient information without a full commitment of feeling.

Greene's incommunicability is doubtless the main reason why the numerous books on him appearing between 1950 and 1980—some of them critically excellent—present no more than a sketchy account of his life, or in some cases a psychological study of the writer based on the evidence of his writings. ATKINS published the first study of any biographical interest, providing a sketch of the life and a commentary on Greene's early novels. Other works in this category include the brief study by PRYCE-JONES and the 1964 Twayne volume by De VITIS. This latter treatment offers the combination of simplified biography and appreciative discussion of the works to which one has become accustomed in the Twayne series of introductions to writers: useful for its basic information, but hardly profound or penetrating. More recently, at least a corner of the veil was lifted when ALLAIN published her collection of conversations with Greene, giving us a glimpse of the man we had not before seen.

Having at least partially revealed himself through his autobiographical works and his conversations with Allain, Greene finally found in 1977 the biographer he wanted. SHERRY, whom one could perhaps describe as a liberated academic, had written on the Brontës and Jane Austen, but has made his name with a series of critical and biographical works on Joseph Conrad. For two of these, *Conrad's Eastern World* and *Conrad's Western World*, he had made extraordinary journeys to the actual sites envisaged in the novelist's work, and this, reminding him of his own journey to Mexico in search of the material for *The Power and the Glory*, appealed to Graham Greene, who finally allowed Sherry access to his unpublished correspondence and agreed to answer most of his questions.

Sherry became a biographer of epic dedication. He traveled the hard way in Haiti and Argentina, in Mexico and Paraguay, in West Africa and Japan, in Malaya and Indochina, following in Greene's wandering tracks. He went down with fever in Africa, suffered from gangrene in Panama, and for six months was blind as a result of a tropical infection. At the same time he spent many months working through the accumulations of letters and other papers hoarded, in the manner of the Edwardians and Georgians, by Greene, his friends, and his relatives.

The result is a massive work. The first volume, covering only the first 35 years of Greene's life (approximately two-fifths of it to date) already includes more than 700 pages. Sherry's travels and researches have enabled him to fulfill admirably what should be the main task of a writer's biographer, to relate his books to experience, to place and time, and to suggest how he has transformed the material in pursuing his art, which in Greene's case is mainly fiction. But at the same time he does not neglect the man who became the creator, and delves, clearly with Greene's benign if uneasy approval, into the intimate corners of his subject's life insofar as the documents and what Greene will tell him have allowed. Some of Greene's unease is shared by the reader as he follows—from behind the closet door as it were—the well-documented course of Greene's extraordinary romantic passion for his wife Vivian, which will offer most readers a quite unexpected aspect of the world-wise-and-weary author of the later novels. Volume I of *The Life of Graham Greene* is in fact a model of literary biography, particularly since Sherry, while commenting on the works, does not allow the critical to take over from the biographical side of his task; he balances the two sides admirably.

—George Woodcock

———

GREGORY I [the Great], *ca.* 540–604; Roman saint, pope, and father of the church.

Clark, Francis, *The Pseudo-Gregorian Dialogues* (2 vols.). Leiden, Netherlands, E. J. Brill, 1987.

Dudden, F. Homes, *Gregory the Great, His Place in History and in Thought* (2 vols.). London and New York, Longman, 1905.

Gasquet, F. A., editor, *A Life of Pope Saint Gregory the Great, Written by a Monk of the Monastery of Whitby.* Westminster, Art and Book Company, 1904.

Howorth, Sir Henry H., *Saint Gregory the Great.* London, J. Murray, and New York, Dutton, 1912.

Petersen, Joan M., *The "Dialogues" of Gregory the Great in Their Late Antique Cultural Background.* Toronto, Pontifical Institute of Medieval Studies, 1984.

Richards, Jeffrey, *Consul of God: The Life and Times of Gregory the Great.* London and Boston, Routledge, 1980.

*

The biographies of Gregory the Great lay much emphasis on a phrase from a letter to Bishop Maximian of Syracuse, stating that the *Dialogues* were written at the request of "fratres mei qui mecum familiariter vivunt" (the brethren who live as a "familia"/household with me). Gregory, it is argued by Richards (see below) "lived in common with some of his monks." From here Gregory is seen "to have carried his monastic preferences into the field of personnel policy" and, as a result, "a rival ecclesiastical power base was created in the Roman church." Gregory's personal style, in other words, "marks a decisive bid to reshape the papal power structure along monarchic lines and to use the familial papal household rather than the bourgeoning clerical administration as its centre." The *Dialogues* explain a shift of emphasis in the church toward a power structure with the pope and his curia, later to consist of, or at any rate be headed by, the cardinals, orginally the parish priests of the Roman diocese, at its summit, rather than a college of bishops aided by lay administrators.

From the same phrase quoted at the outset, PETERSEN argues that "the *Dialogues* do not represent a lower level of culture than the other writings of Gregory. The idea that they are simple tales composed for the benefit of a popular audience, as opposed to an audience of learned monks and clergy, is unacceptable." They were written for the "familia." So the *Dialogues*, and Gregory's reasons for writing them, lend papal and saintly authority not only to the way the papal curia developed its hegemony of ecclesiastical power, but also to the doctrine of purgation by fire, the utility of a numerical series of Masses celebrated for the souls of the living and the dead, a quasi-superstitious demonology behind the vicissitudes of daily life, and a spirituality based on the miraculous as commonplace—everything, that is, that coarsened late medieval piety.

In 1987 CLARK exploded a theological and historical bomb when he proved beyond reasonable doubt that the *Dialogues* are spurious, so removing papal authority from a considerable amount of what Catholic theologians have found it most difficult to defend, and from an administrative practice that relied on that authority, and in particular on Gregory's *Dialogues* and the assumed circumstances of their composition, for its validation. Of greater concern here, the destruction of the authority of the *Dialogues* also calls for a completely new assessment of the significance of Gregory's life, attitudes, and activities. While the non-authenticity of the *Dialogues* does not change the events and circumstances of Gregory's day-to-day life, it does change their importance, and perhaps their nature. A new evaluation must now also be made of Gregory's own contribution to monastic life in comparison with that of Benedict, to whose miracles the *Dialogues* devotes one of its four books.

When we consider that Gregory's legend of the good sinner was in 1977 published in eight separate French medieval versions alone, we can begin to realise the immense impact the authority of the *Dialogues* had for medieval piety, and the consequences of its elimination. We now need a new biography of Gregory the Great taking into account the fact that the *Dialogues* are pseudepigrapha, which is the theologically polite term for forgeries. Francis Clark gave notice of his conclusions at the Chantilly colloquy whose acts are published in *Grégoire le Grand* (Paris, 1986), although the editor of the *Dialogues* for the series "Sources chrètiennes," Adalbert de Vogüé, a monk of La-Pierre-qui-Vire, is reported by Clark, who fulsomely acknowledges his help in *The Pseudo-Gregorian Dialogues*, to have remained unconvinced by his arguments, which seem nonetheless irrefutable.

The earliest biography of Gregory the Great available in English, unlikely to be of much interest except to medieval scholars, is that of the monk of Whitby, available in the modern edition of GASQUET. This was written in Yorkshire from information probably supplied by Bede (who himself modeled his direct and simple style on the *Dialogues*) between about 704 and 714, most probably in 713, not long after the first mention of the *Dialogues* at the end of the seventh century. (For the dating of the biography, see B. Colgrave, "The Earliest Life of Gregory the Great," in *Celt and Saxon*, edited by N. K. Chadwick, Cambridge, 1964.) Gregory was the first monk to become pope, which largely explains Bede's strong interest in him a century after his death (discussed in some detail by Paul Meyvaert in *Bede and Gregory the Great*, (1964), and *Gregory, Benedict, Bede and Others* (London, 1977). Few, however, of the medieval biographers have any real idea of the achievement of a pope who largely removed monks from the jurisdiction of local bishops, founded the temporal power of the papacy by using, with whatever personal integrity, the powers of a secular prince, firmly established in practice the primacy of the Roman see, enforced clerical discipline, and enormously boosted the missionary efforts of Christianity.

Dudden (see below) sums up Gregory's achievement as giving energetic practical expression to ideas already existing, consolidating power, and boosting a rapidly developing system, just as his theology coordinated the teaching of Augustine and his predecessors with popular religion, so creating the amalgam the scholastics began four centuries later to fashion dialectically. Richards (see below) adds to the list of Gregory's achievements the unremitting war on heresy and the establishment of a new pastoral tradition to replace the complex theological and spiritual teaching of the east. The early sources for the biography, critically surveyed by Dudden, include Gregory's own writings, the life by Gregory of Tours (538–594), and the scanty treatments by Isidore of Seville (*ca*. 560–636) and Ildefonsus of Toledo (607–667). There are four early medieval lives as well, including that of the monk of Whitby.

There are however only two modern lives of importance to consider, those by F. Homes Dudden (1905) and Jeffrey Richards (1980). The only English biography in between these two is virtually a popularization derived from and dedicated to Homes Dudden by H. H. Howorth in 1912, although Pierre Batiffol's French life of 1928 was published in English translation a year later (*St. Gregory the Great*, translated by J. L. Stoddard, London and New York, 1929).

DUDDEN's biography in two stout volumes, not much short of 1000 pages in all, is a magisterial product of the confident 19th-century Life-and-Times tradition of encyclopedic compilations, undertaken before the 20th century was daunted by scientific advance and forced to retreat into doctoral theses or careful monographs researching minute corners of history and generally published in obscure reviews. Dudden, a fellow of Lincoln College, Oxford, was clearly not a Catholic, but he writes with great sympathy for modern and, remarkably, for medieval Catholicism. He has undertaken to write as complete a picture as he could of the century in which he quotes Gregorovius' *Rome in the Middle Ages* (1894) as saying the Catholic Church "everywhere constituted itself the vital principle" from which first medieval Christendom and then the modern west emerged from the capitulation of antique civilization to the barbarians. The critical bibliography incorporated into the preface missed nothing of importance before 1905, and Dudden is able to draw heavily on one of the early marvels of modern historical scholarship, the

Monument Germaniae Historica, while still naturally having to rely for most texts on Migne's scrambled Patrology, since critical editions scarcely existed of anything but classical texts. Of Dudden's method one could do worse than quote Howorth's accurate dedication, saying that Dudden "has combined . . . the thoroughness and research of Germany with the picturesque and lucid diction of an accomplished scholar."

One of the advantages of the Life-and-Times format, especially for historically remote figures, is that the broad cultural sweep can be deployed wherever there is inadequate evidence for an accurate biographical focus, as is the case with Gregory's childhood. A long chapter surveying "The World of Gregory's Childhood" (53 pages) nutritiously fills the sandwich between the thin slices on "Gregory's Family and Home" (13 pages) and "Gregory's Education" (10 pages). Even in the short chapters the biographical information is necessarily conjectural, drawing on what is known of Roman topography at that date and on the patrician conservative educational struggle to survive a disappearing culture. Dudden is both sensitive to and knowledgeable about the social and economic circumstances of the great mass of the Roman populace in the 540s, during the siege by Totila, but, Gregory's education summarily despatched ("when we meet him next he will be a boy no longer"), a chapter on the Lombard invasion nicely fills in the 15-year gap. The style lurches from time to time, sometimes skirting the fairy story ("The new chieftain . . . had a beautiful daughter, Rosamund, whom Alboin loved, but wooed without success"), and sometimes touching rhetorical pomposity ("Hence about the year 600 the domains of the Fisherman had swelled to great dimensions"), but the information is comprehensive and exact, with best estimates given for quantities and clear expositions of doctrinal and administrative arrangements and innovations.

Dudden openly discusses the historical problems, weighing the evidence almost ponderously, although in the light of Clark's work we can see the historical imagination being forced. In the 35 pages devoted to them, the anecdotes in the *Dialogues* are classified and straight-facedly discussed. Gregory's credulity is criticized, the stories dismissed as historically interesting legends, but the conclusion is drawn: "It is certainly astonishing that the clear-headed man who managed the Papal estates and governed the Church with such admirable skill, should have contributed to the propaganda of these wild tales of demons and wizards and haunted houses, of souls made visible, of rivers obedient to written orders, of corpses that scream and walk. And yet such was the fact. The landlord of the Papal Patrimonies and the author of the *Dialogues* are one and the same person."

We may find it strange that the author of such a fine historical biography should come to such a false conclusion, when the evidence for the authenticity of the *Dialogues* had already been questioned since the Renaissance. Dudden refers to the phrase from the Latin letter quoted above, but he glosses over a discrepancy of dating between 593 and 594, and he fails to examine the reasons adduced in earlier centuries for doubting the *Dialogues'* authenticity, even while admitting that such reasons existed. In the end, however, this monumental biography is still an excellent guide to its subject, to the sixth century, and to the dawn of the Christian Middle Ages, at its best on matters of administrative arrangement, at its weakest when matters of dogma or spirituality have to be discussed in detail.

Of HOWORTH's excellent vulgarization one need only add that it provides unusually clear explanations of technical terms like "Chrismal Mass" and "Indictions," and of such awkward subjects as what "scholasticism" was. Howorth kept back information about the missionary activities of Gregory for a subsequent volume that never appeared.

RICHARDS pays a massive compliment to the breadth of Dudden's scholarship and clarity of vision, saying that "there are substantial parts of his work which it is still impossible to improve on." His book builds on the research activities of the three quarters of a century since the earlier work. The style is of course crisper and more factual, with more information compacted into less space. The author's previous work, *The Popes and the Papacy in the Early Middle Ages 476–752* (1979) puts him in an excellent position to provide the necessary background information. Richards does not, however, realize that Gregory's ignorance of the Greek language did not preclude his expertise in Greek theology, as Petersen has shown to have been the case, and he glosses over the difficulty in dating the *Dialogues*, saying "593–94" in one place, and "593" in two others. He rightly ascribes the widespread acceptance of Benedict's rule to its enthusiastic endorsement in Gregory's *Dialogues*, but the earlier doubts about the authenticity of that work are not even mentioned.

Richards had naturally updated Dudden's work, drawing on secondary sources, particularly Italian sources, published in the interval. Unhappily, he has once again concentrated on the datable and the quantifiable, the administrative arrangements for the consolidation of power and the missionary activities. It is the only recent biography available in English, and it is in many ways excellent. But it is written from inside a peculiarly English tradition that does not seem, even among its monks, to have given rise to serious historians of theology and spirituality on whom biographers need to be able to draw for rounded portraits of religious figures. Sadly it must be said that even if his work is generally good, readable, accurate, and clear, Richards *ought* to have acquired greater expertise in the history of spirituality. If he had, he would have suspected the authenticity of the *Dialogues* before Clark, whose great advantage was to understand late medieval spirituality, and to have studied the theology that supported it.

—A.H.T. Levi

GUTENBERG, Johannes, *ca.* 1390–1468; German inventor of printing from movable type.

Ing, Janet, *Johann Gutenberg and His Bible: A Historical Study.* New York, Typophiles, 1988.
Scholderer, Victor, *Johann Gutenberg: The Inventor of Printing.* London, Trustees of the British Museum, 1963.

*

There is no good full-length biography of Gutenberg in English. The standard biography, Aloys Ruppel's *Johannes Gutenberg: sein Leben und sein Werk* (2nd edition, 1947), has never been superseded nor translated into English. Material for biography is thin, consisting mainly of documentary evidence from lawsuits, and is still very much under debate. The documents have been translated in full by Douglas C. McMurtrie (1941) and summarised in English (Margaret B. Stillwell, *The Beginning of the World of Books, with a synopsis of the Gutenberg Documents*, 1972), but the accompanying interpretations of the evidence have been outdated by more recent research.

The best recent account of what may be deduced about Gutenberg's life is contained in ING's *Johann Gutenberg and his Bible*, which is, however, only available in limited edition and largely devoted to discussion of the Gutenberg Bible. The best approach to a biographical portrait of Gutenberg in English, although no longer fully up to date with the latest research, is SCHOLDERER's *Johann Gutenberg, the Inventor of Printing*, a short booklet published by the British Museum. It is an attractive, chronological narrative, into which the rather complicated legal evidence is incorporated with admirable clarity. The very few hints that the documents afford about Gutenberg's personality are noted, without too much being built upon them. Where the evidence has given rise to controversy, alternative interpretations are discussed. The operation of Gutenberg's press is explained briefly and clearly and the work it produced is illustrated by facsimile reproductions. There are also photographs of a hypothetical reconstruction of the press. Finally, the book contains a good bibliography.

—Isabel Aitken

H. D. See **DOOLITTLE, Hilda.**

HADRIAN, A. D. 76–138; Roman emperor.

Boatwright, Mary T., *Hadrian and the City of Rome.* Princeton, New Jersey, Princeton University Press, 1989.
Coolidge, Olivia E., *Lives of Famous Romans.* New York, Houghton Mifflin, 1965.
Ish-Kishor, Sulamith, *Magnificent Hadrian; a Biography of Hadrian, Emperor of Rome.* New York, Minton Balch, and London, Gallancz, 1935.
Lambert, Royston, *Beloved and God: the Story of Hadrian and Antinous.* New York, Viking, and London, Weidenfeld and Nicolson, 1984.
Perowne, Stewart, *Hadrian.* London, Hodder and Stoughton, 1960; New York, Norton, 1961.
Spartianus, Aelius, *Life of Emperor Hadrian,* translated by William Maude. New York, Cambridge Encyclopedia Co., 1900.
Yourcenar, Marguerite, *Memoirs of Hadrian,* translated by Grace Frick. New York, Farrar Straus, 1954; London, Secker and Warburg, 1955 (originally published by Plon, Paris, 1951).

*

There is a serious lack of materials, both popular and scholarly, regarding Hadrian. Part of the problem lies in the great lack of primary sources. Also, there tends to be much more interest in the existing physical manifestations of Hadrian's reign than in Hadrian himself. Yet, considering the accomplishments of this Emperor, the amount of useful biographical material, most of which dates from the brief period 1955–70, is rather sparse.

Probably the oldest attempt is SPARTIANUS' work from 1900, which is rare and difficult to obtain. ISH-KISHOR somewhat later produced a work that was praised by some historians and deplored by others. To the credit of the author, the work survives on minimal primary material and, in the process, serves well to give one a realistic impression of the emperor and his age. There are some inconsistencies in her history, but otherwise the effort is readable.

YOURCENAR's work, masterfully translated by Grace Frick, is historical fiction, but deserves mention for its overwhelmingly accurate and favorable portrayal of a second-century Roman life as well as its very respectable psychological assessment of Hadrian himself. The work is written like a documentary and requires a minimal amount of background knowledge, but it is otherwise fascinating, easy reading, and does not suffer in the least from being a fictitious story.

As with most other works of this type, that by PEROWNE does little to separate the biography of the man from the history of the age. However, its first few chapters, which chronicle Hadrian's early life and career, are the best, and the least ambiguous. Like Yourcenar, Perowne succeeds at giving the reader a vivid feel for the era, and his work is also interesting, easy reading. However, Perowne's claim that Hadrian was an unorthodox, but effective, statesman and philosopher is largely unsupported. In the later part of the book Perowne becomes somewhat more ambiguous as he attempts to analyze Judaism and Judaic patriotism. *Hadrian* was intended to be read as the third part of a trilogy based on Perowne's arguments on the religious tension of the era; and taken together, the works are a landmark in the study of Judaism and early Christianity.

COOLIDGE's work is actually a collection of biographies, and the effort on Hadrian (and all others, for that matter) is concise, authoritative, and readable. By the nature of the work, the piece is brief and suffers from a lack of illustration, but it will serve well as supplementary reading.

BOATWRIGHT's effort is oriented primarily toward the architecture of the period, and in that aspect it is a landmark work. However, biographical material is scarce and deals solely with Hadrian's interests in the city and its building (in addition to a brief foray into his Greek interests). The work is lavishly illustrated. LAMBERT's recent work is another that succeeds in vividly portraying the era but offers no new insight into Hadrian himself. Indeed, the story is more concerned with Antinous than the emperor himself.

The material dealing with Hadrian is inadequate to derive more than a superficial assessment of the emperor. Unlike efforts aimed at Nero or other infamous Romans, there has been no serious effort to delve into Hadrian's character or to scrutinize his psyche.

—Lawrence M. Enoch

HAMILTON, Alexander, 1755–1804; American statesman.

Cooke, Jacob E., *Alexander Hamilton*. New York, Scribner, 1982.

Emery, Noemie, *Alexander Hamilton: An Intimate Portrait*. New York, Putnam, 1982.

Flexner, James T., *The Young Hamilton: A Biography*. Boston, Little Brown, and Condor, Collins, 1978.

Hacker, Louis M., *Alexander Hamilton in the American Tradition*. New York, McGraw-Hill, 1957.

Hecht, Marie B., *Odd Destiny: The Life of Alexander Hamilton*. New York, Macmillan, 1982.

Hendrickson, Robert A., *Hamilton* (2 vols.). New York, Mason Charter, 1976.

Lodge, Henry Cabot, *Alexander Hamilton*. Boston, Houghton Mifflin, 1882.

McDonald, Forrest, *Alexander Hamilton: A Biography*. New York, Norton, 1979.

Miller, John C., *Alexander Hamilton: Portrait in Paradox*. New York, Harper, 1959.

Mitchell, Broadus, *Alexander Hamilton* (2 vols.). New York, Macmillan, 1957.

Schachner, Nathan, *Alexander Hamilton*. New York, Appleton, 1946.

Stourzh, Gerald, *Alexander Hamilton and the Idea of Republican Government*. Ithaca, New York, Cornell University Press, 1970.

*

In death as in life, Alexander Hamilton has inspired passionate controversy between his defenders and detractors. LODGE's 1882 biography, part of the American Statesman Series, exemplified the worship of Hamilton in vogue at the end of the 19th century, reflecting series editor John T. Morse's claim that Hamilton "was the real maker of the government of the United States." Other early biographical studies include those by Frederick S. Oliver (1906) and Hamilton's grandson, Allan McLane Hamilton (1911), the latter particularly valuable on Hamilton's personal life. These studies were not strong enough to withstand the wave of anti-Hamilton animus during the 1920s and 1930s, when the upward ascendance of Thomas Jefferson's reputation seemed almost to demand a corresponding collapse in Hamilton's standing.

After World War II Hamilton enjoyed a revival of popularity in an era where national strength and prosperity were especially revered. Several biographies published between 1946 and 1962 present Hamilton in a rather favorable light, endorsing his advocacy of national power and economic might as an example of his foresight. SCHACHNER presents a sympathetic yet balanced view of Hamilton in a well-written account that has nevertheless been seriously dated by subsequent scholarship. MITCHELL's richly-researched study suffers from an anti-Jefferson bias, provoked in part, one suspects, by Claude Bowers' journalistic and erratic *Jefferson and Hamilton* (1925), a scathing attack on Hamilton, and by Joseph Charles' assertion that Hamilton was the advocate of the privileged, moneyed aristocracy. Establishing a simplistic dualism between Hamilton and Jefferson—the former an advocate of central control while the latter defended

laissez-faire and decentralization—Mitchell presents Hamilton as the creator of national order and stability.

MILLER presents an account notable for its ability to view Hamilton against the backdrop of events and its awareness of Hamilton's ambiguous legacy, exemplified in his nationalist programs which, far from fostering union, exacerbated sectional conflict. Striving for America as a nation, Hamilton often could not understand Americans as a people, believing that short-sightedness and selfishness could derail his dream of future greatness. Miller's biography ranks in the top echelon of Hamilton scholarship.

HACKER's volume is an exercise in unabashed nationalism, arguing that Hamilton was the father of American industrial power. In contrast to those historians who present Hamilton as the agent of avarice and aristocracy, Hacker argues that Hamilton grasped the fact that only through establishing an environment favorable to capitalism could opportunity and upward mobility be guaranteed. In short, far from protecting privilege, Hamilton attacked it. National wealth led to national welfare, individually and collectively. A vigorous dissent to these positive portrayals was entered by Adrienne Koch. In "Hamilton and the Pursuit of Power" (*Power, Morals, and the Founding Fathers* [1961]), Koch stresses Hamilton's unchecked ambition, hinting that it could lead to an endorsement of totalitarianism in the name of efficiency.

The foregoing biographies marked the maturing of scholarly thought about Hamilton within the framework of historical interpretations about the early national period at mid-century. But new perspectives, emphasizing ideology and political economy, reshaped historians' understanding about the founding period. Among the works most responsible for this redirection of inquiry was STOURZH's examination of Hamilton's understanding of republicanism, derived from Hume and Blackstone. Drawing on Douglass Adair's 1967 essay on "Fame and the Founding Fathers," which in turn borrowed from Stourzh's previous work, Stourzh presents the clearest case yet for Hamilton's ability to link personal fame with national greatness.

McDONALD, drawing on recent scholarship about republicanism and political economy, makes a passionate case for Hamilton. His explication of Hamilton's understanding of political economy makes for informative reading; his emphasis on Hamilton's desire for fame echoes the interpretations of Stourzh and Adair; his assertion that the goals of Hamilton's economic policy was to open up opportunities for capitalism to flourish by destroying barriers to development bears some resemblance to Hacker's argument. But these merits are offset by McDonald's obvious partisanship in favor of Hamilton over Jefferson and John Adams, who seem sinister when they are not dismissed as inept and naive. Exalting Hamilton above his peers, in the spirit of Lodge's century-old celebration, serves only to make McDonald's biases painfully apparent. The result is controversial and stimulating, as McDonald's scholarship tends to be.

A more balanced perspective is offered by COOKE, one of the editors of Hamilton's papers. Drawing connections between private life and public career, Cooke provides an insightful narrative, although critics have protested his forgiving treatment of Hamilton's activities during the administration of John Adams. This is the best brief biography of Hamilton available. Cooke's Hamilton possesses both human strengths and weaknesses; perhaps most notable is his argument that the differences between

Hamilton and Jefferson were far more a product of combative and mutually distrustful personalities engaged in a rivalry for power than a battle over principles and philosophy.

While Cooke makes clear his familiarity with personal psychology, he rarely leans on it too heavily in tracing the development of his subject's personality. The same cannot be said for FLEXNER, who, in a study devoted to Hamilton's career prior to 1790, portrays Hamilton as immature, even childish, especially in his dealings with George Washington. It seems all too clear that this volume represents a somewhat perverse effort to defend Washington from the charge that he was overly influenced if not manipulated by Hamilton by denigrating the general's young aide. This is too bad, for the relationship between Hamilton and Washington is a subject ripe for study.

The accounts by EMERY and HECHT also emphasize issues of personality. The former is a romanticized if readable narrative, in which the image of Hamilton as the tragically flawed hero is taken to extremes, leaving the reader to wonder whether Emery's attraction to her subject blossomed into infatuation. The latter represents a compromise between popular and scholarly biography, spiced with provocative speculations and a willingness to forgive Hamilton's weaknesses in light of his accomplishments. A few random thoughts, throw-away lines that are a bit too clever, and interpretations that stretch evidence, reduce this volume's usefulness. Although HENDRICKSON's narrative, which effusively praises its subject, is marred by several stunning misstatements of fact, it presents some suggestive interpretations about Hamilton's motives. It too is flawed by an overly-romantic view of its subject, tending toward the salacious in discussing Hamilton's relations with women. None of these studies has left more than a small dent in the body of Hamilton scholarship, although their vibrant prose and vigorous argument will prove attractive to readers. One senses that a discerning scholar could mine them selectively for some telling insights into Hamilton's character and behavior.

Hamilton's recent biographers have been well served by the virtually complete edition of *The Papers of Alexander Hamilton* (1961–87), edited by Harold C. Syrett and Jacob E. Cooke. This edition replaces previous multivolume efforts edited by Henry Cabot Lodge and John C. Hamilton. To accompany them Julius Goebel and others have edited Hamilton's legal papers. These massive efforts will assist future biographers who will be drawn to this compelling and challenging personality, for Hamilton remains an absorbing combination of strengths and shortcomings that await fuller treatment.

—Brooks D. Simpson

HAMMETT, Dashiell, 1894–1961; American writer.

Johnson, Diane, *Dashiell Hammett: A Life*. New York, Random House, 1983.
Layman, Richard, *Shadow Man: The Life of Dashiell Hammett*. New York, Harcourt, 1981.
Nolan, William F., *Hammett: A Life at the Edge*. New York, Congdon and Weed, and London, A. Barker, 1983.

Symons, Julian, *Dashiell Hammett*. San Diego, Harcourt, 1985.

*

Although four substantial biographies, several critical studies, and numerous short reminiscences chronicling the life and literary career of Dashiell Hammett have appeared in the last decade and a half, the inner life and driving motivations of the man remain essentially unrevealed. Biographers, grappling with the perplexing contradictions of Hammett's personal history, have been constrained by the censorial presence of his longtime lover and confidante, author Lillian Hellman, who owned the rights to his literary estate and claimed authority over all biographical treatments of his life until her death in 1984. Her own remembrances of Hammett, published primarily in an autobiographical trilogy (*An Unfinished Woman*, 1969; *Pentimento*, 1973; and *Scoundrel Time*, 1976), provide at best an oblique portrait, filtered through the distorting lenses of romantic idealization and literary politics.

LAYMAN's strategy is to present the facts of Hammett's life in a straightforward manner, relying on extensive research from FBI files, army records, court proceedings, correspondence, newspaper inventories, and scores of interviews with Hammett's friends, family, and associates. Despite the voluminous documentation, however, Hammett's essential character remains unilluminated, since Layman expressly refused to draw inferences or speculate about his subject's motivations. While Layman provides a useful history of Hammett's development as a writer of the hard-boiled school, his discussion of the fiction is critically unsophisticated, too often reduced to plot summary and providing little insight into the artist's darkly violent milieu. In spite of its shortcomings, Layman's treatment remains the most thorough of the biographies; working "without . . . assistance and without hindrance" from Hellman, he manages to counterbalance her somewhat self-justifying portrait of Hammett, offering a more full-ranging and equitable account.

NOLAN, in part responding to the enigmas of character left unexplained in Layman, attempts "to bring the man out of the shadows." He examines in particular Hammett's profligate behavior and premature authorial silence, attributing the latter to Hammett's disaffection with his own amoral characters. But the book lacks a cohesive argument: its loosely episodic structure treats significant and trivial events with equal attention, stringing events together with no shaping vision. The biography is compromised as well by its adoring tone. Nolan tends to write unreflectively about his subject, effectively glamorizing Hammett's excesses and leaving the reader with the wish for a more discerning commentator.

SYMONS comes closer to filling that role. His deftly written, unruffled narrative provides a solid overview of Hammett's life, diagnosing the writer's career breakdown and intemperance as "a failure of will," scrutinizing his alliance to the Communist Party in more clear-eyed fashion than previous biographers, and interpreting Hammett's satisfaction with army and prison life as forms of escape from the burden of authorship. Stronger on analysis than evidence, and more interested in the high points of his life than the formative or concluding stages, Symons skirts aspects of Hammett's personal history, leaving too many informational gaps.

JOHNSON's conception of "the biographer as artist" accounts for both the strengths and weaknesses of her ambitious work. Utilizing a rich store of letters, documents, and memorabilia made available to her by Hellman, Johnson strives to portray Hammett's interior life, hypothesizing his thoughts and feelings, and penetrating through his verbal reticence. She offers intimate information, previously undisclosed, about his family life, his relationship with Hellman, his sexuality and premature impotence, his illnesses and addictions, and his political affiliations. Johnson ponders the cycle of defeat and creative failure that plagued Hammett, and she brings something of a feminist consciousness, lacking in the other biographers, to Hammett's masculine ethos, arguing that the prevasive theme of his life and writings was an antipathy to paternal authority.

In spite of its grander objectives, however, Johnson's biography is impaired by its novelistic format and its uncritical point of view. The effort to enter the minds of Hammett and other principals in his life becomes gimmicky rather than revelatory, and the random shifts in tense and point of view become disconcerting. The narrative is alternately flippant and studious, its momentum too frequently interrupted by the inclusion of lengthy, undigested segments from the manuscript material. Faced with the bewildering contradictions of Hammett's personality, Johnson often resorts to cliches and platitudes rather than penetrating explanation, and the portrait of Hammett that emerges is further marred by a naive romanticization of his politics.

Taken together, the four provide considerable information and irregular insights into Hammett's character, but none is a wholly adequate treatment of his life, in part since each leaves the big questions fundamentally unanswered: why the lifelong skepticism and bitterness; the ruinous bouts of drinking, improvidence, and public dissipation; the alienation from family and friends; the contradictions of personal affluence and left-wing politics; the hankering for male institutions like the army, the veteran's hospital, and the penitentiary? And most important, why the agonizing 30-year writer's block? The novice is best served by beginning with Symons, whose solid overview identifies the paramount personal and literary questions to be pursued, with mixed results, in the other three books.

—Liahna Babener

HANDEL, George Frideric, 1685–1759; German-born English composer.

Dean, Winton, *Handel*. London, Macmillan, 1982.
Dent, Edward J., *Handel*. London, Duckworth, 1934.
Deutsch, Otto E., *Handel, a Documentary Biography*. New York, Norton, 1954; London, Black, 1955.
Flower, Newman, *George Frideric Handel: His Personality and His Times*. London and New York, Cassell, 1923.
Hogwood, Christopher, *Handel*. London, Thames and Hudson, 1984.
Keates, Jonathan, *Handel: The Man and His Music*. London, Gollancz, and New York, St. Martin's, 1985.
Lang, Paul Henry, *George Frideric Handel*. New York, Norton, 1966; London, Faber, 1967.
Mainwaring, John, *Memoirs of the Life of George Frederic Handel*. London, Dodsley, 1760.
Rockstro, William S., *The Life of George Frederick Handel*. London, Macmillan, 1883.
Schoelcher, V., *The Life of Handel*. London, Trubner, and Boston, O. Ditson, 1857.
Streatfeild, Richard A., *Handel*. London, Methuen, 1909.
Weinstock, Herbert, *Handel*. New York, Knopf, 1946; revised edition, 1959.

*

With Handel, the music is the biography; the man himself remains elusive. Dent emphasises the scarcity of facts and of personal material: "It is almost impossible to form any idea of his private character and his inward personality." A scatter of letters survives, offering little illumination. Handel's biographers concern themselves with his public career, where there is a wealth of direct and contextual evidence, at the same time drawing, to a greater or lesser extent, on an anecdotal tradition that Mainwaring intitiated immediately after the composer's death.

Handel, both man and music, has caused posterity problems of interpretation. No other serious composer has gained such popular fame and admiration on the strength of one, arguably untypical, work, as Handel has with *Messiah*.

His biographers differ in their concern for his music, in their styles of interpreting the life contextually, and in the place they allow the "worldly" Handel of the operas as against the sacerdotal Handel of the oratorios and church music. MAINWARING's *Memoirs*, published the year after the composer's death, give unusual attention to Handel's childhood and his Italian years, probably because this material was less accessible, and therefore of more interest, to readers familiar with the circumstances of Handel's later life. Mainwaring stands at the head of a tradition that shapes the narrative of Handel's biography through a host of romance motifs: the hostility of the unmusical father (the boy overcame this by smuggling a clavicord into the attic to practise on when the household was asleep); the child's independent character, which led him at the age of seven to pursue and overtake on foot his father's chaise, and demand to accompany him on a crucial visit to the ducal court; the duke's recognition of the precocious talent on chancing to hear Handel play; the apprenticeship to Zachow, with the pupil quickly surpassing his master; travelling to seek his fortune; encounters with rivals and jealous elders; the duel with his friend Mattheson, following a quarrel over who should be playing the harpsichord at an opera performance, when Handel's life is saved only by "the friendly *Score*, which he accidentally carried in his bosom"; the meetings and the competitions in performance skill with the leading composers and virtuosi in Italy; the estrangement from George I, repaired through the device of performing the *Water Music* on the Thames; the risk attached to operatic productions that succeeded or failed, making and losing fortunes; treacherous business partners and tempermental singers; illness and miraculous recovery; final blindness. The list suggests both the delights and the temptations for the biographical enterprise. Subsequent biography has broken free from Mainwaring's agenda with some difficulty, possibly because much in Handel's life does have the extraordinary quality of romance; a composer who can recover a lost fortune with a burst of creative energy, and draw the fashionable public to his next commercial venture, is indeed a romantic figure.

DEUTSCH offers the best corrective for the tradition of tendentious narrative biography. The method of his documentary biography is to present in sequence all available documents, as far as possible letting them speak for themselves. Commentary and narrative linking are kept to a minimum, and where possible draw on 18th-century sources. Although a narrative emerges, it is never the leading concern. Deutsch's strength is that he puts the reader in touch with the rough texture of Handel's life: the projects, the performances, the quarrels, the opinions of the fashionable world, the satirical squibs, opera politics, and public events. Much of this material is lively and highly individual: Hervey's satirical account of a rival's opera in performance, with Handel glowering in the stalls, has the immediacy of something written yesterday. Deutsch's approach sometimes gives unexpected emphasis to episodes: Handel's Oxford visit is entertainingly documented, and the ten-month stay in Dublin turns out to involve much more than the first performance of *Messiah*, which the hindsight of narrative tends to make the focus in other biographies. Deutsch's re-emphases are of course arbitrary, and depend on the availability of documentary material to represent the different episodes of the life. Because few documents exist for Handel's childhood and his German and Italian periods, Deutsch can give little sense of the experiences that formed Handel into the fully accomplished composer and practitioner who arrived in England at the age of 25. Deutsch's is therefore a rich volume of supplementary evidence, to be read gratefully in conjunction with a conventional narrative biography. Since its business is not with the interpretation of the compositions, the volume could claim to be the most purely biographical.

SCHOELCHER's is the first substantial biography in English. It is a thorough and original gathering of scattered evidence, sceptical of the romance-anecdotal tradition. The focus is on Handel's career in England; Schoelcher gives a lively account of the world of opera production, although he writes little about the operas themselves. His enthusiasm for his subject may make him immoderate over Handel himself: his Handel is "a first rank composer and a great and noble man," and he tends to draw on 18th-century anecdote to illustrate the character. He sees in Handel's church music "fire and an active exaltation . . . wholly distinct from the compositions of his predecessors," acknowledging its essentially dramatic impulse.

In his preface to ROCKSTRO, George Grove dismisses Schoelcher as deformed by rampant partiality, by a want of method and technical knowledge, and by an unfortunate style. Rockstro's own text tends to restore the romance elements and to emphasise the Handel of the ceremonial church music and the oratorios at the expense of the opera composer, both matters where Schoelcher had shown a more disciplined judgement. For Handel the man, Rockstro goes to 18th-century memoir sources to stress his benevolence, intelligence, and dignity ("he had been accustomed to associate with Princes, from his childhood"); his scholarship and wit; his deep sense of religion and charity; his choleric and unmalicious demeanour.

The reverential view of Handel as sacred rather than secular did not go unchallenged in the 19th century. Edward Fitzgerald characterised him "a good old Pagan at heart," and Wagner reportedly commented "the fellow was a scoundrel, but a genius

as well." STREATFEILD explicitly detached himself from the Christianising tradition of the Victorians, presenting Handel not as a preacher but as an "artist, with all his embracing sympathy for human beings and his delight in the world around him." In his thorough, literate, and humane biography, Streatfeild is sensitive to the processes and meanings of history, makes convincing assessments of the issues in Handel's career, and is lively on opera and its negotiation with the world of fashion. Streatfeild exhibits an independent turn of phrase and quotation, unobtrusive irony and humour, and a happily unsentimental taste for anecdote. Although scholarship has inevitably overtaken this biography, it was outstanding in its day, and well deserves its modern reprint (London, Greenfield, 1978).

FLOWER's book has become a standard biography. Although fully researched—Flower was a scholar with a remarkable collection of Handeliana—the narrative is constructed essentially around Mainwaring's stereotypes and later legend; scholarship yields to romance and antiquarianism. His prose is too often sentimental and cloying, and events seem sometimes to be presented imaginatively for the sake of the story, as in Flower's account of Handel's death.

DENT, by contrast, is economical and clear, including good reassessments of musical influences on the young Handel, particularly the Italian. He is conscious of the inaccessibility of Handel's operas, and treats them rather distantly himself. WEINSTOCK sets Handel in an historical context, raises pertinent questions, and continues to reassess in a clear-sighted and intelligent way. He provides a full account of the history, and the performing conditions of the operas, and concludes that Handel needs to be rediscovered.

LANG's is the most exhaustive and historically aware modern biography; he deals with facts and issues comprehensively, and is at all points critically intelligent, illuminating, and scholarly. His discussions of such matters as influences, musical styles, and contemporary composers and events is full and sophisticated; indeed, in his anxiety to cover all aspects definitively Lang runs beyond 700 pages. DEAN's monograph is based on his excellent article in *Grove*: it is entirely lucid, accessible, and secure in its judgements. Although it remains a convenient and up-to-date reference summary rather than a full-blown biography, it is in no way flavourless: witness how deftly Dean picks up the old debate of whether Handel continued or stifled the "English" tradition by quoting an anecdote of R. J. S. Stevens from 1775: "When Handel was blind, and attending a performance of the Oratorio *Jephtha*, Mr. (William) Savage, my master, who sat next him, said, 'This movement, sir, reminds me of some of old Purcell's music.' 'O got te teffel,' said Handel, 'if Purcell had lived, he would have composed better music than this.' "

KEATES writes a stylish narrative, and is prepared to come at episodes and issues freshly. He gives attractive accounts of the operas, bringing them to life with glimpses of scenes, and suggesting their dramatic validity: here is a biographer writing in the context of the early music revival, Keates writes with commitment and judgement, and avoids melodrama when discussing such things as Handel's bankruptcy, paralysis, blindness, and death. He concludes with a shrewd summary of Handel's influence and of the history of his reputation.

Finally HOGWOOD, a musicologist and working musician specialising in the music of the period, writes with an ideal balance of scholarship and interpretive vigour. He is up-to-date, draws with discrimination on the researches of the post-war years, and has done his own work independently. Hogwood provides an excellent section on Handel's posthumous reputation and on performance tradition. By displaying anecdotes and observations separately from the main flow of the text, he allows the reader the pleasure of sharing the material without having it intrude on the serious narrative of the biography. This well-illustrated volume sets the standard for the decade.

—Roger Lowman

———

HANNIBAL, 247 B.C.– *ca.* 183 B.C.; Carthaginian general.

Bradford, Ernle, *Hannibal.* London, Macmillan, and New York, McGraw-Hill, 1981.

Cottrell, L., *Enemy of Rome.* London, Evans, 1960.

De Beer, Sir Gavin, *Hannibal: The Struggle for Power in the Mediterranean.* London, Thames and Hudson, 1969; as *Hannibal: Challenging Rome's Supremacy,* New York, Viking, 1969.

Livy, *The War with Hannibal: Books XXI-XXX of The History of Rome from Its Foundation,* translated by A. de Selincourt. London and Baltimore, Penguin, 1965.

Polybius, *The Histories,* translated by W. R. Paton. Cambridge, Massachusetts, Harvard University Press/Loeb Classics, and London, Heinemann, 1922–27.

*

As nothing that might be termed a proper biography of Hannibal has descended to modern times, modern scholars are of necessity forced to search for the man and his character in the two principal surviving accounts of the Second Punic War written in ancient times, namely those contained in Polybius' History and Livy's History of Rome.

POLYBIUS, an Arcadian Greek, was born in 202 B.C., the year of the battle of Zama and Hannibal's final defeat by the Romans. Polybius therefore lived within Hannibal's own lifetime and his account of the Hannibalic War is considered the more reliable not only because of his lengthy sojourn in the Aemilian household (members of this Patrician family played important roles in the Second and Third Punic Wars) but also by virtue of his familiarity with the geography of Hannibal's campaigns. As Polybius himself notes: "On these points I can speak with some confidence as I have enquired about the circumstances from men present on the occasion and have personally inspected the country. . . ."

In addition to this considerable body of firsthand knowledge Polybius has earned a deservedly high reputation as an historian both for his generally scrupulous distinction between the legendary and the factual and for his disciplined enquiry into cause and effect. While he is authoritative in his account of Hannibal's actions and movements, he is much more hesitant when it comes to dealing with the character of his protagonist. He admits that as Hannibal "had to deal with circumstances of such an exceptional and complex nature it is difficult to discuss the man's

character from his actions when in Italy." Although he mentions Hannibal's reputation among the Romans for cruelty, and among his own people for greed, Polybius himself seems little convinced of the validity of these charges, implying that even if Hannibal were guilty of such vices then the blame would lie not in the man himself but in the peculiarly harsh conditions under which Hannibal was forced to live during his lengthy Italian campaign.

Against Roman steadfastness and bravery Polybius tends to emphasise Hannibalic guile, consonant with his belief in the inexorable progress of his adopted nation to world empire, but at numerous points he expresses his open admiration for Hannibal's qualities of leadership and tenacity, evidenced in the latter's ability to stay active and dangerous despite dwindling armies, supplies, and hopes. LIVY, born almost a century and half after Polybius, is a good deal less scrupulous as an historian, so as far as our knowledge of the progress of the Hannibalic War is concerned it is fortunate that he followed Polybius and not vice versa. The emotional patriotism that colours Livy's historical analysis and his sometimes critical failure to separate fact from fiction renders his portrait of Hannibal suspect.

Livy's famous assessment of Hannibal's personality near the beginning of Book 21 displays none of the careful hesitancy shown by Polybius. While more definite in tone, it is also seriously contradictory. One senses that the "inhuman cruelty and more than Punic perfidy" of which Livy accuses Hannibal is more probably the product of Roman propaganda and misunderstanding of Punic customs than a realistic description of the man's character. It is not easy to reconcile such alleged baseness and depravity with the fact, which Livy later freely admits, that Hannibal suffered neither mutiny nor attempted assassination nor even significant desertions from his hard-pressed army. To most subsequent commentators Livy's condemnation appears rather as an index of Rome's fear of a skillful and implacable enemy than as a true portrait of its subject. Indeed Livy seems often to be caught uncomfortably between admiration for Hannibal's prowess and his self-imposed duty of refusing to honour Rome's most dangerous opponent, an impasse from which Livy never satisfactorily extricates himself.

Of the modern biographers here reviewed, COTTRELL resembles Livy in that he chooses to dramatise events and episodes and Polybius in that Cottrell too followed Hannibal's route over the Alps, albeit on wheels rather than on foot. For Cottrell human emotions are the motivating factor in human history, and he therefore dismisses as irrelevant to Hannibal's achievement the vast impersonal forces of history.

This is a very personal journey; the reader is invited *en famille* to share with the writer not only his metaphorical view of events long past but also his literal views from Alpine summit and Tuscan hill. Cottrell is fond of relating the events of the Hannibalic War to more modern European history in order to assist the reader in understanding these events. Cottrell writes movingly of the carnage of Cannae, providing some idea of the scale of this disaster to Roman arms by citing more recent bloodbaths such as Passchendaele (1917).

Cottrell's account is unusual in that he seems to have changed his view of Hannibal during the course of writing, a surprisingly humble admission rarely found in scholarly writings. Initially Hannibal's genius, "like Hitler's, may have been an evil one," but by the end of his book close acquaintance with his subject has led to a much more favourable impression. However, I do not think it fanciful to suggest that the subtext of this account still implies a parallel between Hannibal's attempt to destroy Rome and Hitler's recent attempt to destroy democracy in modern Europe. It is not mere coincidence that the writer mentions his service with the Allied armies in the Italian campaign of 1943–44, reading Arnold's *The Second Punic War* in a hospital bed to the accompaniment of the sounds of modern battle.

This is a charming book, vivid and extremely easy to read, though one might question how far ancient campaigns and politics can be said to resemble those of more recent ages. The subtitle of DE BEER's book indicates both the depth and especially breadth of his assessment of the significance of the Hannibalic War. The writer applies his obviously very considerable and wide-ranging knowledge of the social, linguistic, military, and political history (and pre-history) of the ancient Mediterranean world to provide a most authoritative context for his account. An added strength is the large number of maps, illustrations, and photographs that accompany the text.

De Beer generally follows Polybius but occasionally inserts details from other authorities, sometimes his own, when he deems it necessary. An example of the latter is his lengthy discussion of the precise route taken by Hannibal across the Rhône valley and then over the Alps in which De Beer seeks to resolve once and for all this vexed issue. It is perhaps unsurprising that the author of *Alps and Elephants* (1957) should display such interest in this aspect of Hannibal's campaign, but the length and detail of his argument in favour of a particular route may prove as overwhelming to the casual reader as Alpine avalanches no doubt were to the troops of Hannibal's army, wherever they happened. This criticism excepted, De Beer successfully achieves his stated aim of providing a text that is both accurate and readable.

BRADFORD begins his account with a useful synopsis of the origins and customs of the Carthaginian people. This acts as a preface to Bradford's chief premise, that Carthage was "largely innocent as to the cause of the Punic Wars." According to Bradford, Roman expansionism inevitably provoked Hannibal into his attack on Saguntum (the casus belli) and what amounted to a massive raid in retaliation for Roman interference in Spain and her previous absorption of the Carthaginian colonies in Sicily and Sardinia.

It is not inaccurate to describe Bradford as a partisan for the Punic cause, and thus it is not surprising to find this writer arguing for Hannibal's humaneness (relative to the age in which he lived) in comparison with the brutality of his Roman opponents; it is they rather than Hannibal who display "iron ruthlessness." Bradford dismisses Livy's assertion of Hannibalic perfidy and cruelty: "As will become clear these charges cannot be substantiated and there is no evidence—even in Livy's account—of any of them."

According to Bradford, the true character of Hannibal will always remain obscure, excepting of course those qualities of intelligence, determination, and courage manifested in his actions, because "a man who exercises absolute authority is constrained to assume a pose of invariable reserve." As such Hannibal is "the sphinx whose riddle still eludes us." Bradford's is a thought-provoking book, not least in its somewhat unusual partisanship for the Carthaginian cause. For that very reason however it lacks that objectivity of approach which may be more suited to the general reader.

—D. H. O'Leary

HARDY, Thomas, 1840–1928; English writer.

Blunden, Edmund, *Thomas Hardy*. London, Macmillan, and New York, St. Martin's, 1942.

Brennecke, Ernst, *The Life of Thomas Hardy*. New York, Greenberg, 1925.

Chew, Samuel, *Thomas Hardy, Poet and Novelist*. Bryn Mawr, Pennsylvania, Bryn Mawr College, 1921.

Deacon, Lois, and Terry Coleman, *Providence and Mr. Hardy*. London, Hutchinson, 1966.

Gittings, Robert, *Young Thomas Hardy*. London, Heinemann, and Boston, Little Brown, 1975.

Gittings, Robert, *The Older Hardy*. London, Heinemann, 1978.

Hardy, Evelyn, *Thomas Hardy: A Critical Biography*. London, Hogarth Press, 1953; New York, St. Martin's, 1954.

Hardy, Florence, *The Early Life of Thomas Hardy 1840–91*. London, Macmillan, 1928.

Hardy, Florence, *The Later Years of Thomas Hardy 1892–1928*. London, Macmillan, 1930.

Hedgcock, Frank A., *Thomas Hardy: Penseur et Artiste*. Paris, Librairie Hachette, 1911.

Millgate, Michael, *Thomas Hardy: A Biography*. Oxford and New York, Oxford University Press, 1982.

Weber, Carl, *Hardy of Wessex*. London, Routledge, and New York, Columbia University Press, 1940; revised edition, 1965.

*

From about 1910 until his death in 1928, Hardy was commonly regarded as the most eminent English man of letters of his time. The three studies published during this period, by HEDGCOCK, CHEW, and BRENNECKE—this last the first booklength life—all acknowledge this position, but characteristically Hardy did his best to obstruct their writing, and they are interesting now mainly for his numerous marginal annotations to the copies subsequently lodged in the Dorchester County Museum. The insistent burden of these comments is that no connections can be made between Hardy's own life and the events and characters of his novels; such speculation is dismissed as "unmannerly" and "impertinent," or simply "inaccurate." Later biographers have predictably been unimpressed by these disclaimers.

In 1915 or 1916, in an attempt to forestall other biographers, Hardy began with his second wife Florence the two volumes published under her name in 1928 and 1930, and still ascribed to FLORENCE HARDY when published in one volume as *The Life of Thomas Hardy* (1962). However, the deception was successful only until 1940, when the bibliographer Richard Purdy explained how Hardy had carefully crafted a manuscript version of the text, which was typed by Florence and then destroyed, any corrections either added to the ribbon copy by Florence, or entered by Hardy in a disguised calligraphic hand. Since Hardy was the author of the first 34 chapters, and had a hand in two of the remaining four, it has become customary to refer to the *Life* as an autobiography, but in fact the situation is more complicated. Florence abbreviated the lists of famous people Hardy had met at various dinners and soirées, trimmed his attacks on critics he believed had misrepresented him, and to some extent reduced Emma's presence in the work; she also added a number of anecdotes, supplied mainly by Sir James Barrie, and some letters, including four to Mary Hardy. The typescript passages omitted from the published version of the *Life* are included in Richard H. Taylor, editor, *The Personal Notebooks of Thomas Hardy* (London, Macmillan, 1978); Michael Millgate's *The Life and Work of Thomas Hardy* (London, Macmillan, 1984) tries to present the text as Hardy himself produced it.

The lives that appeared over the next 40 years tend toward celebration, if not outright hagiography. BLUNDEN's work is interesting in revealing the respect in which the younger poet held the elder, and unusual in commenting on Hardy's "innocent cheerfulness." It has the virtues, inconvenient in a biographer, of loyalty and discretion: the *Life* is accepted as the work of Florence Hardy, the suicide of Hardy's closest friend Horace Moule appears merely as a "tragic death," and the unhappiness of Hardy's marriage to Emma Gifford receives only a passing reference to the "curious solitariness" of their later years. EVELYN HARDY is more informative, but unduly partisan. She remarks on "the stressful days" of the childhood of Hardy's mother, but does not uncover the reality of her life as one of seven pauper children. She lauds the lack of ambition of Hardy's father, and credits Hardy with a similar indifference to worldly possessions—a view at odds with various of the *Materials* collected by Cox, and with the conclusions of Gittings in particular. She is generally incautious in trusting the *Life*, accepting, for example, Hardy's spiteful claim that Henry James was rejected by the Rabelais Club as lacking "virility." Caution is further abandoned in order to disparage Emma and justify Hardy. Emma is accused of "belittling" Hardy "in some horrible animal way," and of suffering from "religious mania," while he is seen as responding with unfailing courtesy. The view that Hardy and Florence came to share, that Emma suffered from "delusions," and that there was some hereditary instability in her family, is accepted here. The role of Florence is correspondingly exalted; her own difficult nature is ignored, and she appears as the loyal and self-effacing wife Emma had failed to be. WEBER, even in the revised edition, shares many of these failings, although he makes greater effort at balance. He notes for example that Hardy's susceptibility to a succession of literary ladies must have wounded Emma, just as his infatuation for Gertrude Bugler distressed Florence. But the bias is in Hardy's favour; thus he repeats the canard that Emma asked Richard Garnett to suppress *Jude the Obscure*, with the suggestion that she understood neither her husband nor his work, and complements his account of the Bugler episode by citing Sassoon's reference to Florence's habitual gloominess. While both Weber and Evelyn Hardy make welcome if limited attempts to explore the intellectual context of Hardy's work, both are sketchy and inadequate when dealing with Hardy's sense of his class and social position. It perhaps indicates the character of these works that the figure who seems to Weber nearest to Hardy is not a contemporary, but William Shakespeare.

In the revised edition Weber tries, albeit equivocally, to dis-

miss speculation about Hardy's liaison with his cousin Tryphena Sparks, a story later expanded by DEACON AND COLEMAN into the claim that Tryphena was in fact Hardy's niece, that she became the mother of his child, and that guilt about the relationship dogged the rest of his life. Evidence for these theories range from the negligible to the derisory, as Gittings in particular has shown. They have been an irritant rather than a contribution to Hardy scholarship.

Hardy biography came of age with GITTINGS, the first life based on genuine research. Gittings adds greatly to our knowledge of Hardy's family background, and of the labourers, cobblers, and servants who were his relatives in Puddletown. A main theme of his study is Hardy's loyalty to, or as Gittings often represents it, his inability to escape from these family ties. Gittings is more conscious than earlier biographers of the damage done to Hardy's personality by this conflict, and, indeed, presents a more damaged Hardy than had been seen before. The unflattering image that emerges from the recollections of local people gathered together in the monographs edited by Cox (*Thomas Hardy: Materials for a Study of His Life, Times, and Works*, 1968–71) could be set aside with the reflection that no man is a hero to his valet, but Gittings' study reads at times like a sustained assault on Hardy's character. He writes of Hardy's "ugly fascination" with brutality, his "perverse morbidity" about the hanging of Martha Brown, his "pathological habit of falling in love," his "intractable temperament," and the "tortuous deception" of his outward life. He suggests that Emma's inherited mental imbalance was largely the invention of Florence, whom he sees as another of Hardy's victims (he also describes her as suffering from paranoia). His most serious charge, and the one that most distressed the loyal and faithful among Hardy's readers, is that Hardy tried to "shut his eyes" to the evidence of Emma's last illness, and then "tried to shut the eyes of others" after her death. Gittings' increasingly evident dislike for his subject—Edward Clodd's remark that Hardy had "no largeness of soul" becomes his *leitmotif*—is the main weakness in what is in most other respects a well-informed and intelligent study.

Hardy's admirers have found MILLGATE more sympathetic. As the editor, with Richard Purdy, of the *Collected Letters*, and with access to papers in Purdy's own collection, Millgate was ideally placed to produce his full and thoughtful study. He gives due weight to Hardy's family background, ascribing Hardy's touchiness on the subject to a desire for accuracy rather than to snobbishness. He provides a valuable account of Hardy's relationship with Eliza Nichols, is informative about Hardy's dealings with his editors and publishers, and is more balanced than his predecessors when describing Hardy's relationship with Emma, noting, for example, the mutually accommodating self-sufficiency of their lives in the later years. Even so, he is too tolerant of what he calls "the necessary ruthlessness of an artist," and the suggestion that Emma may have deceived Hardy into marriage by pretending to be pregnant seems as unfounded as it is ungenerous. (This idea, like Gittings' account of the circumstances leading to Moule's suicide, is teased out of *Jude the Obscure*; neither writer is able to resist such inferences, though both are generally scrupulous in admitting them.) Millgate, more sympathetic to Florence than is Gittings, notes that Florence's behaviour was often erratic as well as unhappy. This will certainly, and deservedly, remain the standard life for some time to come, but Gittings' work will also continue to command attention; that being so, it is a matter for regret that Gittings' various claims and suggestions are not discussed directly by Millgate, making cross-reference between the two unnecessarily difficult, and that Millgate provides no bibliography. In other respects, both books are well produced, well illustrated, and lucidly written, accessible to the general reader and the scholar alike.

—Phillip Mallett

HAWTHORNE, Nathaniel, 1804–1864; American writer.

Arvin, Newton, *Hawthorne*. Boston, Little Brown, 1929; London, N. Douglas, 1930.

Baym, Nina, *The Shape of Hawthorne's Career*. Ithaca, New York, Cornell University Press, 1976.

Cantwell, Robert, *Nathaniel Hawthorne: The American Years*. New York, Rinehart, 1948.

Conway, Moncure D., *The Life of Nathaniel Hawthorne*. New York and London, W. Scott, 1890.

Golin, Rita, *Portraits of Hawthorne: An Iconography*. Dekalb, Northern Illinois University Press, 1983.

Gorman, Herbert, *Hawthorne: A Study in Solitude*. New York, G. Doran, 1927.

Hoeltje, Hubert, *Inward Sky: The Mind and Heart of Nathaniel Hawthorne*. Durham, North Carolina, Duke University Press, 1962.

Hull, Raymona, *Nathaniel Hawthorne: The English Experience 1853–64*. Pittsburg, Pennsylvania, University of Pittsburg Press, and London, Feffer and Simons, 1980.

James, Henry, *Hawthorne*. New York, Harper, and London, Macmillan, 1879.

Lathrop, George P., *A Study of Hawthorne*. Boston, J. R. Osgood, 1876.

Martin, Terrence, *Hawthorne*. Boston, Twayne, 1975; revised edition, 1983.

Mather, Edward, *Nathaniel Hawthorne: A Modest Man*. New York, T. Crowell, 1940.

Mellow, James R., *Nathaniel Hawthorne in His Times*. New York, Houghton Mifflin, 1980.

Morris, Lloyd, *The Rebellious Puritan: Portrait of Mr. Hawthorne*. New York, Harcourt, 1927; London, Constable, 1928.

Normand, Jean, *Nathaniel Hawthorne: An Approach to an Analysis of Artistic Creation*, translated by Derek Coltman. Cleveland, Ohio, Case Western Reserve University Press, 1970 (originally published by Presses Universitaires de France, Paris, 1964).

Stewart, Randall, *Nathaniel Hawthorne, a Biography*. New Haven, Connecticut, Yale University Press, 1948.

Turner, Arlin, *Nathaniel Hawthorne: A Biography*. New York and London, Oxford University Press, 1980.

Van Doren, Mark, *Nathaniel Hawthorne*. New York, Viking, and London, Methuen, 1949.

Wagenknecht, Edward, *Nathaniel Hawthorne: Man and Writer*. New York, Oxford University Press, 1961.

Waggoner, Hyatt, *Hawthorne: A Critical Study*. Cambridge, Massachusetts, Belknap Press, 1955; revised edition, 1963.

Woodberry, George, *Nathaniel Hawthorne*. Boston, Houghton Mifflin, 1902.

Young, Philip, *Hawthorne's Secret: An Untold Tale*. Boston, Godine, 1984.

*

Modern biographies of Hawthorne draw upon a rich store of primary materials beginning with Hawthorne's own journals and letters—of intrinsic literary value in their own right, although it has been necessary to return them as nearly as possible to their original state by restoring elisions made by Mrs. Hawthorne. The work of his son Julian and his daughter Rose, as well as reminiscences of friends and acquaintants like James and Annie Fields and Horatio Bridge provide valuable information, necessarily colored by filial affection and friendship. The difficulty presented to Hawthorne scholars therefore is not any lack of primary materials, but the wide variety of reliabilty and interpretive stance.

A case in point is one of the earliest works by Hawthorne's then son-in-law George LATHROP, which helped to fix the early portraits of the writer as existing in a lonely, brooding solitude, acting out "the tragedy of isolation that is the lot of every artist in America." Denying any intention to write a biography, Lathrop presents "my conception of what a portrait of Hawthorne *should be* (emphasis added)"—fair warning that biographical objectivity is not to be expected. CONWAY's *Life* has a good deal more to recommend it, including elegant writing. Though the author is still personally connected to many of the figures in Hawthorne's life, his work is more dispassionate, except when it comes to Hawthorne's politics, since the biographer was active in the movement for emancipation and a staunch supporter of the northern causes in the Civil War.

Two other studies date from the same general period, one a small masterpiece and as revealing about the writer as about his subject. JAMES' *Hawthorne* is a significant document in American literature despite its limitations as biography. Based mainly on Lathrop, and the available edited notebooks, it reveals the realist's prejudice that was to mark the evaluation of Hawthorne for a generation, a prejudice which noted in James' terms Hawthorne's "tendency to weigh moonbeams." This prejudice appears as well in WOODBERRY's book, which appeared about the same time and reinforced early portraits of the writer as lonely, brooding, and haunted by the sense of evil at the heart of life.

Three more biographies appeared in the 1920s, the most significant being ARVIN's well-written psychological study, which again, by applying realistic criteria, finds Hawthorne's accomplishment wanting and reinforces the picture of a writer alienated and essentially estranged from his society. Of the other two, GORMAN's is brief, readable and provides a somewhat romanticized portrait of Hawthorne, but one markedly less idiosyncratic than that by MORRIS, who adopts the peculiar imaginative stance of writing as if he were Emerson.

The 1940s saw a marked shift away from the romanticized portrait of Hawthorne as a brooding genius. As always, Hawthorne's psychology fascinates biographers, but MATHER's approach to "a man with a peculiar personal history" is anecdotal, witty, and ironic, especially valuable in providing a sense of persons and place in Hawthorne's English and European experiences. (The latter are later carefully documented by HULL, just as CANTWELL focused in 1948 on the American years.)

VAN DOREN's major work provides a deeply sympathetic account of Hawthorne's life, though in his extended discussion of Hawthorne's work the author exhibits the realist's discomfort with Hawthorne's allegorical and symbolic tendencies. Van Doren portrays a more normal childhood and a more available mother than the earlier studies had, admiring in the process Hawthorne's personal qualities of reticence, insight, skepticism, and emotional control. STEWART's brief, elegant biography (which Van Doren had read in manuscript) became in 1948 and continued for 30 years to be the bench-mark study of Hawthorne. It has been chiefly responsible for the prevailing sense of Hawthorne as a skeptical neo-orthodox Christian writer, a profound conservative. It remains an important landmark in Hawthorne studies.

The 1960s saw an explosion in Hawthorne biography, beginning with reprints of Lathrop, Conway, Gorman, Morris, and Arvin. This practice suggests among other possibilities, including that of the intrinsic value of these studies, a sense that the definitive "Hawthorne" had yet to appear. Also reprinted in 1963 was WAGGONER's earlier study, which used the biographical materials to read the fiction as written by an idiosyncratic Christian idealist. New studies published at this time included three very different books. The first of WAGENKNECHT's "psychographs" purported to be "a study of Hawthorne's character and personality based on his writings and his letters and journals and on all that has been written about him." Readable and informative, organized under generic headings such as "Family," "Friends," "Reading," etc., this study emphasizes Hawthorne's 18th-century side, the elements of normality and no-nonsenseness, that appear to be equally a part of Hawthorne's complex character. HOELTJE's massive study is quite different, setting out to parallel Hawthorne's inner and outer lives. Almost novelistic in effect, it is a book that uses a great deal of unacknowledged paraphrasing of primary materials, making it difficult to determine where the primary materials leave off and the author's own speculations about Hawthorne's inner life begin.

NORMAND's extremely interesting aesthetic study of "the mental history of Hawthorne" rejects both the earlier portrait of the tormented romantic and realist revisions of it. Normand attempts, with no small success, "to reach beyond and behind the literature to the psychology and aesthetics of artistic creation." Judging his subject "a great intermittent creator and poetic fabulist," Normand places Hawthorne in the larger context of American literary thematic concerns, with the incisive insight that European critics have brought to bear on classic American literature. Normand's book is hardly the place to start to learn about Hawthorne, but for one interested in the aesthetics of literary creation as demonstrated in 19th-century American literature it is an extremely provocative book. A thoroughly American investigation of Hawthorne's development as an artist and of his creative philosophy is BAYM's study, one of her several valuable contributions to our understanding of Hawthorne and of 19th-century American romantics.

MARTIN's brief, incisive, up-to-date volume in the Twayne series (a revision of his 1975 study) attempts a "responsible understanding of Hawthorne's achievement in fiction." His approach emphasizes the dichotomies in Hawthorne's life and themes; the man of affairs—bookkeeper/poet; the actual/the imaginary; damnation/redemption. It includes an excellent chapter on Hawthorne's creative process, and is the place to start for a quick introductory overview of Hawthorne, although the specifically biographical materials are brief.

Briefer still, and probably the last place to start, is YOUNG's book. Really only a biographical sketch, it focuses on materials largely ignored by major biographers: public documents, readily available to Hawthorne and to modern researchers, which record the brother/sister incest in the Manning (maternal) branch of the family in the 17th century. Young's efforts to tie this family scandal to speculation about the writer's relationship with his sister Elizabeth, and his subsequent reading of *The Scarlet Letter* in the light of such suppositions, are ingenious, but remain hypothetical and highly speculative.

Two remaining studies are fulldress biographies with different emphases. MELLOW's book is very long and full of detail about Hawthorne and "the times," with vivid portraits of other people, both intimately involved in and peripheral to his life. Hawthorne appears in the foreground of a very large canvas indeed, which serves to reinforce the tendency of modern biographical approaches to see him as a much less alienated figure than earlier portaits had suggested. While Mellow's study is the first of his proposed four-volume series of biographies of major 19th-century American literary figures (other projected subjects include Margaret Fuller, Thoreau, and Emerson) its focus is historical rather than critical.

The other major modern biography, as definitive as such things are likely to get, is TURNER's *Hawthorne*. Turner sets a threefold task for himself and accomplishes it admirably: "to present the rich variety of Hawthorne's personality and the individuality and complexity of his thought . . . ; to record Hawthorne's lifelong efforts to know the land and the people of his region, to understand the nature and the meaning of the American experience . . . ; [and] to introduce Hawthorne's works into the biographical narrative with the prominence they had in his life." Turner's work is a model of literary critical biography, fixing for the contemporary reader what is the definitive portrait to date of a highly complex and gifted American writer, a human being of enormous integrity and charm.

Finally, as a bonus to modern understanding and appreciation of Hawthorne, GOLIN's study of Hawthorne's portraits reveals the writer as the uncommonly handsome in addition to the uncommonly gifted man who emerges from the pages of his own work as well as from the studies of those who would seek to know him better.

—Susette Ryan Graham

HAYDN, Franz Joseph, 1732–1809; Austrian composer.

Barbaud, Pierre, *Haydn*, translated by Katharine Sorley Walker. New York, Grove, 1959 (originally published by Édition du Seuil, 1957).

Brenet, Michel (Marie Bobillier), *Haydn*, translated by C. Leonard Leese. London, Oxford University Press, 1926 (originally published by F. Alcan, Paris, 1909).

Geiringer, Karl, in collaboration with Irene Geiringer, *Haydn: A Creative Life in Music*. New York, Norton, 1946; 3rd edition, revised and enlarged, Berkeley, University of California Press, 1982.

Gotwals, Vernon, editor and translator, *Joseph Haydn: 18th-Century Gentleman and Genius*. Madison, University of Wisconsin Press, 1963; as *Joseph Haydn: Two Contemporary Portraits*, 2nd edition, 1968 (contains translations of Albert Cristoph Dies, *Biographische Nachrichten von Joseph Haydn*, Vienna, Camesinaische Buchhandlung, 1810; and Georg August Briesinger, *Biographische Notizen über Joseph Haydn*, Leipzig, Breitkopf and Härtel, 1810).

Hadden, J. Cuthbert, *Haydn*. London, Dent, and New York, Dutton, 1902.

Hadow, William H., *A Croatian Composer: Notes Toward the Study of Joseph Haydn*. London, Seeley, 1897.

Hughes, Rosemary, *Haydn*. London, Dent, and New York, Pellegrini and Cudahay, 1950; 5th edition, Dent, 1974.

Jacob, Heinrich Eduard, *Joseph Haydn: His Art, Times, and Glory*, translated by Richard and Clara Winston. New York, Rinehart, and London, Gollancz, 1950.

Landon, H. C. Robbins and Henry Raynor, *Haydn*. New York, Praeger, and London, Faber, 1972.

Landon, H. C. Robbins, *Haydn: Chronicle and Works* (5 vols.). Bloomington, Indiana University Press, and London, Thames and Hudson, 1976–80.

Landon, H. C. Robbins, *Haydn: A Documentary Study*. New York, Rizzoli, and London, Thames and Hudson, 1981.

Landon, H. C. Robbins and David Wyn Jones, *Haydn: His Life and Music*. Bloomington, Indiana University Press, and London, Thames and Hudson, 1988.

Larsen, Jens Peter, with Georg Feder, *The New Grove Haydn*. London, Macmillan, and New York, Norton, 1982.

Nohl, Ludwig, *Life of Haydn*, translated by George P. Upton. Chicago, Jansen McClurg, 1880 (originally published as *Joseph Haydn*, Leipzig, Reclam, 1880).

Redfern, Brian, *Haydn: A Biography, with a Survey of Books, Editions, and Recordings*. London, C. Bingley, 1970.

Somfai, László, *Joseph Haydn: His Life in Contemporary Pictures*, translated by Mari Kuttna and Károly Ravasz. New York, Taplinger, and London, Faber, 1969 (originally published by Bärenreiter, Kassel, 1966).

Stendhal ("as Louis-César-Alexandre Bombet"), *Lives of Haydn, Mozart and Metastasio*, translated and edited by Richard N. Coe. London, J. Murray, 1818 (originally published as *Lettres écrites de Vienne en Autriche, sur le célèbre compositeur Joseph Haydn*, Paris, Didot, 1814).

*

In the early years of the 19th century, the great esteem in which Haydn was held inspired several biographies that conveyed the image of a benign, paternal figure whose personal integrity, humility, and homespun wisdom found reflection in the optimism, innocence, and folk-inspired humor with which his music was felt to be identified. Albert Cristoph Dies' *Biographische Nachrichten von Joseph Haydn*—translated by GOTWALS—describes 30 visits by the author to the aging composer between April 1805 and August 1808. Featuring recollections of memorable incidents from Haydn's life and travels, this account devotes little attention to his music. In portraying Haydn's artistic personality, it underscores Dies' identification with the humanistic, middle-class values of his age. Gotwals' edition pairs Dies with Georg August Griesinger's *Biographische Notizen über Joseph Haydn*, which had appeared serially in the *Allgemeine musikalische Zeitung* 11 (1808–09) before being expanded and published separately in 1810. Like that of Dies, Griesinger's biography rests on the authority of personal acquaintance with the composer. It furnishes a succinct account of his career, including early adventures, Esterházy employment, and London sojourns. Major emphasis falls on the London period and later years in Vienna. Describing him as the founder of an epoch in music, Griesinger comments on Haydn's work habits, his aesthetic outlook, and his assessments of other composers.

Appearing at about the same time as the Viennese authors' work, though not based on personal encounters, Giuseppe Carpani's *"Le Haydine," ovvero Lettere sulla vita e le opere del celebre maestro Giuseppe Haydn* (Milan, C. Buccinelli, 1812) takes the form of 17 letters penned in the years 1808–11. Eschewing chronological narrative, Carpani offers reflections on the composer's life and the nature of his creative achievement, and provides comparisons with predecessors and contemporaries, including artists, poets, and philosophers as well as musicians. For the portion of his volume devoted to Haydn, STENDHAL (under the pseudonym Louis-César-Alexandre Bombet) plagiarized Carpani's biography, translating from the Italian into French with changes and additions. The original publication was revised and published in 1818 under the new title *Vies de Haydn, de Mozart et de Métastase* and translated into English in the same year.

In evident rebellion against popular adoration of Haydn and the stifling, old-fashioned aesthetic that his music seemed to represent, a younger, romantically inclined generation turned its back on the composer and his musical legacy. A telling reflection of this attitude, which helped postpone serious Haydn scholarship until well into the 20th century, was the fact that the age produced no Haydn study comparable to the magisterial 19th-century biographies of Beethoven (Alexander Wheelock Thayer), Bach (Philipp Spitta), or Mozart (Otto Jahn). Confronting the task of writing a major book on Haydn, the archivist Carl Ferdinand Pohl (1819–1887) confessed that he would have preferred to see the job done by his friend Jahn. Pohl's subsequent labors yielded two volumes (1875, 1882) that traced the composer's life and offered an account of his music up to the time of his departure for London in late 1790. (A third volume was eventually supplied by Hugo Botstiber in 1927.) Basing his work on the examination of earlier studies as well as documentary material in Eisenstadt, Vienna, and elsewhere, Pohl followed what Spitta described as an "antiquarian" approach that chronicled Haydn's life and times without furnishing a fresh critical interpretation. He nevertheless succeeded in compiling a wealth of information of value to 20th-century biographers. Despite the book's importance in the history of Haydn scholarship, it has remained untranslated.

Reflecting early signs of a Haydn revival in the waning years of the 19th century, NOHL's *Haydn* was destined to become an especially well-loved and frequently reissued popular biography. Drawing largely on Dies for anecdotal material, Nohl celebrates Haydn as a predecessor of Beethoven, assigns him leadership in the development of symphonic and quartet style, underscores his distinct German character, and attempts to draw connections between the man and his music.

HADOW, derived from two studies by František S. Kuhač (a collection of South Slavonic folksongs and a pamphlet of Haydn), speculates on the composer's ethnic background and cites various melodic correspondences to bolster his thesis about Haydn's alleged Croatian origins. Hadow's argument, which stirred controversy in the decades following its appearance in 1897, was successfully refuted by the German scholar Ernst Fritz Schmid, whose *Joseph Haydn: Ein Buch von Vorfahren und Heimat des Meisters* (Kassel, Bärenreiter, 1934) demonstrated the composer's German origins with the help of elaborate genealogical tables.

HADDEN concentrates on Haydn's life, with special emphasis on the London visits, rather than on description of the music. He transmits the traditional depiction of a modest, pious, industrious artist, unspoiled by success. BRENET's work divides into separate sections on the composer's life and works. It follows the customary interpretation by which the moral content of Haydn's music is understood in terms of the "simplicity, kindness, and tranquil endurance" that formed the basis of his character. Brenet characterizes Haydn as a writer of musical "prose" rather than "poetry," views his operatic and sacred works with condescension, and identifies him as one of the greatest masters of pure music and instrumental scene-painting.

GEIRINGER's first study of Haydn, a monograph prepared in connection with the 1932 bicentennial celebration of his birth, provided the basis for a more substantial biography, first published in 1946 and revised several times in response to advances in Haydn scholarship. A well-balanced, eminently readable account of the composer's life and works, the book offers descriptions of his milieu and portrayals of contemporaries with whom he came in contact. Tracing the stations of Haydn's career and his development as an artist, it quotes extensively but judiciously from his correspondence and other pertinent documents. Discussion of the music distinguishes five style periods: youth (1750–60), a phase of transition (1761–70), a Romantic crisis (1771–80), maturity (1781–90), and consummate mastery (1791–1803). For each period, Geiringer divides Haydn's works by category and gives concise descriptions of stylistic features for each.

Sharply contrasted to Geiringer's scientific approach, JACOB's volume, originally written in German though first published in English, reads more like a novel. In a loose-jointed, leisurely narrative, this book offers vivid portrayals of contemporary figures and locales, biographical anecdotes, and background discussion of 18th-century musical customs. The author attempts to show how Haydn preserved his inner freedom while submitting to outward servitude.

By far the largest, most ambitious study of the composer's life and works, LANDON's *Haydn: Chronicle and Works* follows in Pohl's footsteps by pursuing an antiquarian approach. Each volume distinguishes "Chronicle" chapters, which quote letters and other contemporary documents, from chapters on musical works written during the period in question. Texts of documents are often given both in the original language and in English. While taking pains to place Haydn's music in the context of achievements by predecessors and contemporaries (with particular emphasis on various groups of Haydn imitators), Landon tends to avoid detailed critical or stylistic analysis. The volumes feature many illustrations and a substantial number of music examples. Each has an extensive bibliography, detailed general index, and index of works cited. The first volume, *Haydn: The Early Years, 1732–65*, offers extensive historical and biographical background, while volume two, *Haydn at Eszterháza, 1766–90*, encompasses discussion of the administrative organization of Eszterháza, Haydn's role as composer of vocal music (sacred and operatic), the *Sturm und Drang* movement, Haydn and Viennese society, and the dissemination of Haydn's music abroad. Volume three, *Haydn in England, 1791–95*, draws on the London notebooks in addition to many newspaper announcements, contemporary critiques, and concert programs. Volume four, *The Years of "The Creation," 1796–1800*, encompasses discussion of that work's libretto, sketches (reproduced in transcription), sources, and musical design (including aspects of key structure, symbolism, orchestration, and commentary on individual numbers). The final volume, *The Late Years, 1801–09*, features documents pertaining to early performances of *The Creation* and an extended discussion of *The Seasons*. It reproduces the contents of Haydn's first will and final will, the Elssler catalogue of Haydn's music library, the catalogue of his libretto collection, and the auction catalogue of his artistic effects. An appendix, "Haydn and Posterity: A Study in Changing Values," traces the eclipse of Haydn's reputation through documents from the years following his death. It includes writings by Mendelssohn, Schumann, and Hanslick.

LARSEN constitutes a modified, corrected version of the *Grove* encyclopedia article (1980), complete with Georg Feder's catalogue of Haydn's works and an updated bibliography. In this concise, authoritative study, emphasis is biographical rather than critical. There are chapters on the composer's early life, his activities as Esterházy kapellmeister, the London sojourns, and his later years. Larsen discusses the recently revised views of Haydn's personality and examines his artistic development by summarizing his principal contributions in the major genres: symphony, quartet, opera, mass, and oratorio.

LANDON AND JONES (1988) incorporates material from Landon's *Haydn: Chronicle and Works* and *Haydn: A Documentary Study* (discussed below). Alternating biographical chapters with description of the music in different periods, the book strives for a balanced overview of Haydn's output. Designed specially for the musical amateur, LANDON AND RAYNOR (1972) features the quotation of several short works (keyboard pieces, song, vocal canon) in their entirety.

Doubtless the best of the modern popular biographies, HUGHES furnishes a concise treatment of Haydn's life and works. This oft-revised book (latest edition, London, Dent, 1989) gives a summary of the composer's output, with chapters on non-operatic vocal works, keyboard music, chamber music for strings, orchestral music, and opera. Other studies in this popular vein include REDFERN, which offers a clearly written but superficial discussion of Haydn's life and works. It includes a survey of predominantly non-specialist literature on Haydn available in English or English translation, a survey of editions, and a brief discography. BARBAUD presents a not very coherently organized collection of information and discussion of Haydn's life and his music, with numerous illustrations pertinent to Haydn and his milieu, including contemporary engravings, portraits, and photographs of landmarks.

The two most ambitious iconographical studies to date are LANDON's *Haydn: A Documentary Study* (1981), which encompasses a biographical narrative, 220 illustrations (44 in color), a chronology, and genealogical tables; and SOMFAI, which contains 394 illustrations (black and white) of Haydn, his surroundings, patrons, friends, associates, musical sources, and documents. Many illustrations are supplied with substantial commentary and relevant quotations from contemporary sources such as the Dies and Griesinger biographies, Haydn's correspondence, and newspapers. The book includes an essay on the composer and furnishes a list of authentic Haydn representations as well as an inventory of sources for the illustrations.

—Floyd K. Grave

HAZLITT, William, 1778–1830; English essayist and critic.

Baker, Herschel, *William Hazlitt*. Cambridge, Massachusetts, Harvard University Press, 1962.

Birrell, Augustine, *William Hazlitt*. London, Macmillan, 1902.

Hazlitt, W. Carew, *Memoirs of William Hazlitt* (2 vols.). London, R. Bentley, 1867.

Hazlitt, W. Carew, *Four Generations of a Literary Family* (2 vols.). London and New York, Redway, 1897.

Howe, Percival P., *The Life of William Hazlitt*. London, M. Secker, and New York, G.H. Doran, 1922.

Jones, Stanley, *Hazlitt, a Life*. Oxford, Clarendon Press, and New York, Oxford University Press, 1989.

Maclean, Catherine M., *Born Under Saturn: A Biography of William Hazlitt*. London, Collins, 1943; New York, Macmillan, 1944.

Pearson, Hesketh, *The Fool of Love (a Life of William Hazlitt)*. London, Hamilton, and New York, Harper, 1934.

Uphaus, Robert W., *William Hazlitt*. Boston, Twayne, 1985.

Wardle, Ralph M., *Hazlitt*. Lincoln, University of Nebraska Press, 1971.

*

Apart from the rather scanty "sketch" of Hazlitt's life by his son prefixed to the *Literary Remains* (1836), the first extended biography is by the grandson. In his *Memoirs* (1867), W.C. HAZLITT amplifies an outline of events with letters, anecdotes, and autobiographical passages from Hazlitt's own writings. Although it has been superseded by subsequent biographies, it is still worth consulting for the vivid chapter on "personal characteristics," and not all the anecdotes have found their way into later publications. A similar judgment can be made of W.C. Hazlitt's other compilations, *Four Generations* (1897), *Lamb and Hazlitt* (1899), and *The Hazlitts (1911)*: the first of these remains the best source of information about the essayist's father.

BIRRELL's volume is chatty and amusing, but the author seems to have no great interest in his subject. HOWE, on the other hand, was deeply committed to Hazlitt, knew his writings intimately, and was tireless in clarifying problems and misconceptions. His biography has a permanent value as a lucid narrative of events, providing a convincing picture of an industrious

and sensible man, whose misanthropy and disagreeble habits had been grossly exaggerated. Howe, in his concern to show the Hazlitt whom Lamb described as "one of the finest and wisest spirits breathing," may overlook some of the passion that is a crucial part of Hazlitt's importance as a writer. Even so, Howe provides a useful corrective to the highly-coloured picture drawn by some of Hazlitt's political enemies, including his former friends Wordsworth and Coleridge.

Passion certainly dominates PEARSON's portrait. Where Birrell had seen *Liber Amoris* as "vile kitchen stuff," and Howe is at pains to remind us of Hazlitt's rational "outward demeanour" even at the worst of times, Pearson sees the sadly one-sided love affair with Sarah Walker as central to our understanding of Hazlitt. Although such an approach was worth attempting, Pearson writes popular biography rather than scholarly analysis, and the effect, though lively and acute, tends to be slapdash. His reconstruction of the circumstances, allegedly scandalous, in which Hazlitt was forced to leave the Lake District in 1803 is ingenious, and he convincingly presents the young writer as a victim rather than an aggressor.

MACLEAN examines the same obscure incident in even greater detail, and adds a political dimension that makes excellent sense: an outspoken radical might well offend the sensibilities of country boors, regardless of any amorous exploits. Her whole biography is informed by this kind of sympathetic identification with Hazlitt's principles and convictions. It may be found rather too long, but Maclean needs space to explore the successive phases of her subject's development, meditating on the qualities apparent in the portraits, applying the many confessional passages in his essays to the interpretation of particular episodes, and setting incidents in a context—often political— that amply explains their apparent excess. Some readers have been alienated by what might seem her overprotectiveness, and she is not always successful in her imitations of Hazlitt's more florid utterances. Still, the book is moving in its alertness to his inner life, and particularly in its evocation of his sense of rejection. A by-product of her biography was the construction of an autobiography out of widely scattered passages from his writings: the exercise is deftly performed, and almost succeeds.

BAKER's work is an ambitious attempt to relate the events of Hazlitt's life to his achievement as a writer. The historical milieu is fully presented, with particular attention given to contemporary unitarianism and political radicalism. Baker gives fair exposition of Hazlitt's ideas on politics, metaphysics, literature, and the arts, including lively narratives of the controversies involving Godwin, Mackintosh, Parr, and Malthus. Baker is offended by the attacks on the "apostate poets" Wordsworth, Coleridge, and Southey, with whom Hazlitt had once been intimate. He describes these outbursts as "appalling bad behaviour" inspired by "motiveless malignity." That "motiveless" indicates a certain lack of rapport between Baker and his subject, which sometimes makes the book seem unduly aloof from the strains and stresses of Hazlitt's life. Formidably well informed though Baker is, he does less than might be expected to show the workings of Hazlitt's thought and feeling. The biography remains, however, the best for those who are primarily concerned with Hazlitt's place in the history of ideas.

WARDLE's book, more limited in scope, focuses on the man himself and his successive publications. It is a fairminded reassessment, a little too long, perhaps rather overloaded with quotations. UPHAUS, on the other hand, while mainly concerned with the writings, provides an excellent short account of how Hazlitt developed from his dissenting background.

JONES concentrates on Hazlitt's mature years, beginning his narrative with the marriage to Sarah Stoddart in 1808. Like Howe, Jones scrupulously investigates every scrap of evidence he can find to establish the facts about his subject's contentious existence, and he makes full use of the material that has accumulated since 1922, some of which he publishes for the first time. He has besides a keen eye for material that has long been available but disregarded, like Mary Russell Mitford's splendid account of how Hazlitt delivered his lectures. The great merit of the book is the deep but not uncritical sympathy Jones evidently feels for Hazlitt, combined with a rendering of the political and intellectual milieu that is perhaps as fine as Baker's, though less elaborately deployed. He carefully identifies the distinctive qualities of Hazlitt's character—his love of independence and horror of self-interest, his quest for affection among social inferiors— that made him so vulnerable to scandal-mongers. On the outrageous attacks on the "apostate poets," Jones brings out the real danger in which a subversive journalist like Hazlitt stood in the immediate aftermath of the Napoleonic War, and reminds us that what now seems bad manners was actually a manifestation of political courage. He shows conclusively that much of the image of the irate, misanthropic, unpredictable Hazlitt was the creation of hostile propagandists. But he also shows, as Howe perhaps does not, why the propagandists found Hazlitt such an easy target.

—Geoffrey Carnall

HEARST, William Randolph, 1863–1951; American newspaper publisher.

Carlisle, Rodney P., *Hearst and the New Deal: The Progressive as Reactionary.* New York, Garland, 1979.

Carlson, Oliver, and Ernest Sutherland Bates, *Hearst, Lord of San Simeon.* New York, Viking, 1936.

Chaney, Lindsay, and Michael Cieply, *The Hearsts, Family and Empire: The Later Years.* New York, Simon and Schuster, 1981.

Davies, Marion, *The Times We Had: Life with William Randolph Hearst,* edited by Pamela Pfau and Kenneth S. Marx. Indianapolis, Bobbs-Merrill, 1975; London, Angus and Robertson, 1976.

Littlefield, Roy Everett III, *William Randolph Hearst: His Role in American Progressivism.* Lanham, Maryland, University Press of America, 1980.

Lundberg, Ferdinand, *Imperial Hearst: A Social Biography.* New York, Equinox, 1936.

Older, Mrs. Fremont, *William Randolph Hearst, American.* New York, Appleton-Century, 1936.

Swanberg, W.A., *Citizen Hearst: A Biography of William Randolph Hearst.* New York, Scribner, 1961; London, Longman, 1962.

Tebbel, John, *The Life and Good Times of William Randolph Hearst.* New York, Dutton, 1952; London, Gollancz, 1953.

Winkler, John, *W.R. Hearst: An American Phenomenon.* London, J. Cape, and New York, Simon and Schuster, 1928.

Winkler, John, *William Randolph Hearst: A New Appraisal.* New York, Hastings House, 1955.

*

In one sense, the best place to begin a study of Hearst is with the publisher's own writings, *Selections from the Writings and Speeches* (1948), and *William Randolph Hearst: a Portrait in His Own Words* (1952). *Selections*, edited by E.F. Tompkins, a Hearst editorial writer, includes signed editorials, personal correspondence, broadcasts, and messages. While offering many tips on effective journalism, it gives full vent to his political views. Hence it contains his attacks on the Ku Klux Klan, anti-Semitism, Communism, the World Court, the New Deal, Japanese expansion, the Washington Disarmament conference of 1921–22, sitdown strikes, prohibition, and capital punishment. In this volume Hearst advocates issues ranging from economic protectionism, an informal alliance of English-speaking peoples, and a two-term limit on the presidency, to Japanese exclusion, Irish home rule, independence for India, and a canal through Nicaragua. Hearst's *Portrait in His Own Words,* edited by Edmond Coblentz, longtime supervising editor of the Hearst newspapers, similarly includes Hearst correspondence and excerpts from his editorials. It also contains Hearst's own on-the spot accounts as well as recollections of his upbringing in San Francisco, his time at St. Paul's School in Concord, New Hampshire, and his tenure at the *San Francisco Examiner.* Included also are his accounts of the Spanish-American War, World War I, his expulsion from France in 1930, the 1932 Democratic convention, and his relations with Franklin D. Roosevelt.

The first major biography was an authorized account, for Mrs. OLDER was a close friend of Hearst's. Her husband, who had been editor of Hearst's *San Francisco Call,* wrote the forward in which he finds Hearst's activities constituting "a history of the reform movement in America." Hearst had requested Older himself to write the biography but Older, who felt too old, simply aided in the research. Hearst himself launched the project by sending the couple four trunkloads of letters dating back to his youth.

Hence it is hardly suprising that Mrs. Older presents Hearst through his own eyes, a man who spent his entire life on behalf of "the inarticulate millions" against "privilege and corruption in high places." She exaggerates Hearst's impact on American progressivism, omits certain aspects of his life (e.g., expulsion from Harvard, relationship to Marion Davies, faking Mexican documents), and offers a one-sided account of his rivalry with New York publisher Joseph Pulitzer. Yet she is helpful on family detail and on his role in the Spanish-American War, World War I, and his opposition to the League of Nations.

Also friendly is WINKLER's 1955 work, which—despite its claim to be a "new appraisal"—is but an elaboration of his biography published in 1928. A former staff writer for the *New York Journal,* a Hearst paper, Winkler had access to the files of the Hearst corporation. He finds Hearst the "world genius of journalism," the "king of public opinion," and spokesman for "the toilers and the workers, the plain people of America." Winkler does concede that Hearst's yellow journalism was often "demagogic, disgusting, degrading," and he acknowledges Hearst's role in a German plot to involve the United States and Japan in a dispute over Mexico.

TEBBLE draws liberally on already published material to write a biography both witty and charitable, one that captures the ambiance of the man and his environment. Particular attention is given to the human Hearst: the Lord of San Simeon, lover of Marion Davies, and "the world's greatest collector."

Beginning in 1936, the same year that Mrs. Older published her eulogy, two critical works emerged. LUNDBERG, a Socialist journalist, is the mirror image of Mrs. Older as he seeks to present Hearst in the most unfavorable light possible. In the forward, historian Charles A. Beard said of Hearst, "He will depart loved by few and respected by none whose respect is worthy of respect." The book focuses on Hearst's extensive financial holdings. From the beginning of his career, writes Lundberg, Hearst "wanted to make other people dance as he cracked the whip." Lundberg cites lurid personal ads appearing in *Examiner* columns, the advertisement of quack cures, exploiting his laborer's mines owned at home and abroad, taunting of Japan, and alliance with populist demagogue Charles E. Coughlin.

Much of the volume is reckless. Lundberg claims that Hearst's call to annex Hawaii and retain the Philippines was rooted in his desire to embrace Hearst's personal holdings in the port of San Francisco. According to Lundberg, Hearst's presidential endorsement of William Jennings Bryan in 1896 and 1904 was strictly for circulation purposes. He claims that in 1898 Hearst was bribed by the Southern Pacific Railroad, and that his participation in circulation wars in Chicago during the 1920s initiated the Windy City's system of gang warfare and racketeering. Even his marriage to Millicent Wilson is seen as an effort to gain respectability in his quest for the presidency.

Though CARLSON AND BATES' volume, also published in 1936, is more reliable than Lundberg's, it is critical nonetheless. The authors concede that Hearst originally had been a reformer, and their portrayal of Hearst from 1903 to 1909 as "the millionaire radical" is particularly engrossing. They find the key to his personality lying in an inferiority complex.

For the best biography of Hearst, see SWANBERG's Pulitzer-prize winning account. Rich in detail, and enhanced by interviews, the book is strongest in describing the creation and operation of Hearst's publishing empire, which at its peak in 1923 boasted 22 daily papers, 15 Sunday papers, and nine magazines. Swanberg has little respect for Hearst the politican, who strove for the presidency in 1904, mayor of New York in 1905 and 1909, and governor of New York in 1906. "He could," writes Swanburg, "have been dangerous in high office."

Much of the book's strength lies in its perceptive character study. Given Hearst's "awesome vigor, industry, capability and intellect," Swanberg claims, he might have been the greatest man of his era. Hearst, however, lacked "unshakable integrity," "unswerving principles," and "steadfast beliefs." To Swanburg, his crippling weakness was "instability, vaccilation, his ability to anchor his thinking to a few basic, rocklike truths that were immovable in his heart." Swanberg, however, fails to account for Hearst's shift from reformer to red-baiter, and he stretches matters by claiming that Hearst was the first influential American to recognize the danger of Communism.

One of the most celebrated mistresses of the first half of the 20th century, Marion DAVIES presents some memoirs taped just before Hearst's death. In *The Times We Had*, Davies describes her first meeting with Hearst, the construction of San Simeon, Hearst's supposed affection for the Roosevelts, and his financial problems. But, as CHANEY AND CIEPLY note, nowhere does she touch on her own influence on business organization, the underlying tension between her and members of the Hearst family, her heavy drinking, and "small affairs" with Charlie Chaplin and Dick Powell. Somewhat similar in genre is Fred L. Guiles' *Marion Davies* (1972). Written in gossipy fashion, it engages in amateur psychology (e.g., Hearst as father-figure) and finds the reputation of both Hearst and Davies lastingly and unfairly marred by Orson Welles' film "Citizen Kane" (1941). In this regard, Pauline Kael's *The Citizen Kane Book* (1971) is extremely important, for it notes the strong differences between Welles' Charles Foster Kane and the real Hearst.

In some ways, certain scholarly books are superior to any popular account. LITTLEFIELD analyzes Hearst's progressive policies advocated from 1895 to 1920 as editor, publisher, political candidate and activist. Based on a carefully researched dissertation completed at Catholic University, the book draws on the morgue of Hearst's *New York Journal-American* and on interviews with William Randolph Hearst, Jr. In a generally positive account, Littlefield writes that Hearst was "entitled to more credit than historians were willing to give him." Littlefield places Hearst in the context of the wider progressive movement, stressing his attacks on the trusts and his adoption of such cases as the eight-hour day, the direct election of senators, child and female labor laws, and factory inspection. Even the much maligned Spanish-American War, writes Littlefield, was a "progressive cause," aimed at the liberation of Cuba. Despite the book's revisionism, it has some problems. Hearst's most extravagant statements are permitted to stand without comment. Littlefield skirts Hearst's opportunistic handling of the Archbold letters, a scandal involving the Standard Oil Company. He exaggerates Hearst's importance in the Spanish-American War and in Woodrow Wilson's legislative program, and he ignores major interpretations of progressivism.

CARLISLE's book is also based on a doctoral dissertation, this one submitted to the University of California at Berkeley. It draws on many manuscripts, including that of E.D. Coblentz. Carlisle shows that at the beginning of the New Deal, Hearst was enthusiastic about such measures as public works. When in 1935 Roosevelt sharply increased taxes, created a federal bureaucracy, and sought American membership in the World Court, Hearst's enthusiasm cooled, and by the presidential campaign of 1936 he was attacking Roosevelt's following as a "conglomerate party of Socialists, Communists, and renegade Democrats." Carlisle denies, however, that Hearst was a fascist, pointing out that he opposed racist groups, was never anti-Semitic, and distrusted government by an elite. He sought a deterrent armed force, one that would neither threaten Germany nor help enforce the Versailles settlement, but would keep a wary eye on Japan and the Soviet Union.

—Justus D. Doenecke

HEGEL, Georg Wilhelm Friedrich, 1770–1831; German philosopher.

Kaufmann, Walter, *Hegel: Reinterpretation, Texts, and Commentary.* London, Weidenfeld and Nicolson, and New York, Doubleday, 1966.

Mackintosh, R., *Hegel and Hegelianism.* Edinburgh, T. Clark, and New York, Scribner, 1903.

Singer, Peter, *Hegel.* Oxford and New York, Oxford University Press, 1983.

*

Biographers of Hegel have all had to face the constricting fact that philosophers in the modern, post-Renaissance era, including Hegel, often led relatively uneventful lives and left few private documents other than their mostly professional correspondence. And yet, as Kaufmann (see below) correctly points out, "One cannot understand Hegel's philosophy at all adequately if one ignores his life and times." As Hegel himself said, "Philosophy is its age comprehended in thought." Hegel's career differs outwardly from that of Kant only in that he spent as headmaster of a school in Nuremberg some of the time necessarily passed between eking out an existence as a licensed university teacher or *Privatdozent* and being appointed to a series of increasingly lucrative and important professorial posts. Hegel spent only a relatively brief time as a private tutor in the service of wealthy families.

Yet Hegel married and Kant did not, and not even so massively dedicated a thinker as Hegel can have been other than traumatised by the series of events which occurred in his life between his marriage in 1811 and his sister's final breakdown in 1814, leading to her eventual suicide. Hegel had already had an illegitimate son in 1807 by his landlady at Jena. The first daughter of his marriage to the daughter of an old Nuremberg family, born in 1791 and scarcely half his age, died almost immediately, his brother was killed in Napoleon's 1812 campaign, and his wife bore him two sons in 1813 and 1816. Few surviving documents allow us any insight into his feelings.

The most personal legacies he left for any biographer to work on consist of the minute diary of a hiking trip in the Berner Oberland in 1796, a list of books he bought in 1785 at the age of fourteen, and a careful record of his income and expenditure during the early years of marriage. Less personal, but revealing, are the end-of-year speech-day commencement addresses to the boys of the Nuremberg Gymnasium, justifying for instance the compulsory military training that would naturally have been taken for granted in Kant's Prussia. The real story of Hegel's life can be said to focus on his intellectual development away first from theology and then away from, and his final break with, his colleague Friedrich Wilhelm Joseph von Schelling (1775–1854), who also taught at Jena, with whom Hegel co-edited a philosophical review, and whose publishing activity reached a peak of intensity 20 years earlier than that of Hegel, his elder colleague.

The early biographies of Hegel by K. Rosenkranz (*Das Leben Hegels*, Berlin, 1857), R. R. Haym, (*Hegel und seine Zeit*, Berlin, 1857), K. Köstlin (*Hegel in philosophischer, politischer und nationaler Beziehung*, Tübingen, 1870), available only in German, were all surpassed by Kuno Fischer's two-volume work,

Hegels Leben und Werke (Heidelberg, 1901). Much new material, mostly about Hegel's professional activities, was, however, discovered in the early years of the century, and is incorporated in J. H. Muirhead's perceptive and informative article about Hegel's life and works in the famous 1911 edition of the *Encyclopaedia Britannica* (1910).

The MACKINTOSH biography of 1903, like most successful accounts of the great philosophers, interweaves accounts of life and thought. Enough is said about Hegel's student diversions, snuff, cards, and drinking, to show how the intense schoolboy, earnestly pursuing excellence in classical scholarship and translating Longinus from Greek at the age of 16, relaxed when he was a young man. Mackintosh remains discreet, however, about almost everything else except the stridency of Hegel's denunciations of Catholicism or, some would feel, Christianity. Hegel had earned a scholarship to a Protestant seminary, although he was soon to abandon theology for philosophy. In 1913, of course, European cultural interest focused much more on Hegel as a possible non-believer than on his views as a philosopher of history or of law or economics than it does today, and the interest of the modern reader in pursuit of the precursor of Marx or Sartre, Dilthey or even certain Catholic theological thinkers after World War II will remain unsatisfied by this biography. Mackintosh provides translated selections of letters and reports and of the preface to Hegel's most important work, *The Phenomenology of Mind*. There is an index and a bibliography.

KAUFMANN, too, interweaves an interpretation of the thought with an account of the life, also providing texts with commentaries. There is a brief but useful chronology. Kaufman's strength is in his account of the life, emphasising for instance the importance for Hegel of the death of his mother in 1783, of his relationship with Hölderlin, and of his relative unpopularity as a lecturer. From 11 fee-paying students in 1801, his audience climbed to only 30 in 1804. The move away from Kant's "critical" philosophy is also well analysed. Kaufmann re-translates the preface to the *Phenomenology* and presents it with an excellent commentary. He also gives a documented account of the gestation of the major works and a well-chosen selection of his own translations from the correspondence. He is totally familiar with the thought of his subject and conversant with the secondary material. In addition he makes so careful an attempt to present Hegel's life and the principal lines of his thought to the neophyte that there can be little doubt that Kaufmann offers the best introduction to Hegel available in any language. It is a supremely readable book, with important biographical information scattered throughout, and it is intended to be read and not merely consulted.

SINGER's introductory biographical material is more than usually well presented and depends quite heavily on Kaufmann as well as on two works, each excellent in its way, not considered here because they are only partial biographies, *The Young Hegel*, by Georg Lukács, translated by R. Livingstone (1975), which has an ideological slant to it, and *Hegel's Development*, by H. S. Harris (1972), concentrating on the intellectual development during the early years.

The bibliography of works on Hegel is immense, but there is still room for a straightforward account of the development of his life and thought in the light of the philosophical movements—the philosophy of history for instance—that have subsequently been developed from his still often misunderstood intellectual development.

—A. H. T. Levi

_____

HEIDEGGER, Martin, 1889–1976; German philosopher.

Biemel, Walter, *Martin Heidegger: An Illustrated Study*, translated by J. L. Menta. New York, Harcourt, 1976; London, Routledge, 1977.
Farías, Victor, *Heidegger and Nazism*, translated by Paul Burrell. Philadelphia, Temple University Press, 1989.

*

BIEMEL, a professor of philosophy in Aachen, West Germany, was a student of Martin Heidegger. He has written a well-illustrated book that presents the life of the philosopher in the context of his thought about two central elements: Being and Truth. In this sense the inner and outer life of this thinker are set forth by an examination of seven of Heidegger's works that appeared during the course of his life: *Being and Time*, "On the Essence of Truth," "Letter on Humanism," "The Question Concerning Technology," "The Nature of Language," "The End of Philosophy and the Task of Thinking." This biographical-intellectual exposition is preceded by an excerpt from an essay by Hannah Arendt, who remembers Heidegger's qualities as a teacher and scholar.

Biemel notes that while it is normal in a biography to recite the unusual and dramatic events in the life of the person concerned, with Heidegger "it is not from his life from which we can learn something about his work; his work is his life." The proper understanding of Heidegger requires that we join his life to the thought and sensibility that inform it. By so doing we begin to grasp the forms in which his life is grounded. Biemel's work does however illuminate Heidegger's political error, when for one year he was associated with the Nazi party. In sum, Biemel shows that, like Kant, Heidegger's life is not outwardly exciting. It is its intellectual and spiritual content that lend it significance. In this sense, Heidegger's is one of the most exciting lives of the century.

FARÍAS' biography, originally published in France in 1987, has proven to be a controversial work. In his lopsided, ax-grinding account, Farías seeks any impression, story, or analogy that could implicate Heidegger as a full-blown Nazi and anti-Semite. Farías attempts to convince the world that Heidegger's brief and mistaken involvement with the Nazi party (1933) was a prolonged and deep devotion to Hitler and genocide. He virtually ignores any authors or evidence that suggest a side of the question more fair to Heidegger. He constantly implies that the mind and work of Heidegger were somehow a moving force that sent millions of Jews to their deaths. The tone is one of insinuation and guilt by association. For example, he cites Heidegger's admiration for a 17th-century local priest, Abraham a Sancta Clara, who lived in Heidegger's area of Germany, as evidence that Heidegger was a life-long anti-Semite. This priest was sometimes critical of Jews in his sermons, so Farías draws the conclusion that Heidegger must be an anti-Semite. From the beginning of his one-year involvement with the party as rector of the University of Freiburg, Heidegger attempted to moderate the extreme and racist elements of Nazism. By the end of World War II he had long since terminated his associations with the party, and was a *persona non grata* within the Nazi organization. He was conscripted by Nazi authorities to do forced labor at the end of the war. We would get no impression of these things in Farías' work. Moreover, Farías' claim that the content of *Being and Time* is fascist or a proof of Heidegger's fascism would be both hysterical and absurd to a competent scholar or anyone who had read the book. The "tumultuous reception" of Farías' book (of which the dust jacket speaks) is, I fear, advertisement for a $30.00 volume.

A definitive biography of Heidegger has not been written in either German, English, or French. Farías' work does not even approach this standard, and Biemel's work needs to be amplified and updated by more political and biographical research. But Biemel's work is honorable scholarship, and it will have to suffice until something definitive is written.

—Howard N. Tuttle

_____

HEINE, Heinrich, 1797–1856; German poet.

Prawer, S. S., *Heine's Jewish Comedy*. Oxford, Clarendon Press, 1983.
Robertson, Ritchie, *Heine*. New York, Grove, and London, Halban, 1988.
Sammons, Jeffrey L., *Heinrich Heine: A Modern Biography*. Princeton, New Jersey, Princeton University Press, 1979.
Spencer, Hanna, *Heinrich Heine*. Boston, Twayne, 1982.
Untermeyer, Louis, *Heinrich Heine: Paradox and Poet, the Life*. New York, Harcourt, 1937; London, J. Cape, 1938 (without subtitle).

*

The very titles (or subtitles) of some of the numerous books on Heine that have appeared in English are indicative of the biographers' great fascination with their complex and mercurial subject: *A Life Between Love and Hate* (Ludwig Marcuse), *The Artist in Revolt* (Max Brod), *The Tragic Satirist* (Siegbert S. Prawer), *Poet in Exile* (Antonina Vallentin), *The Strange Guest* (Henry Bernard), *That Man Heine* (Lewis Browne). An important point of contact (or identification) arises from the fact that several of the above mentioned authors were, like Heine, forced to spend a major part of their lives in exile from their native countries.

UNTERMEYER's vividly written, evocative, and well-illustrated biography is still worthy of note because the American poet and anthologist was one of Heine's foremost translators into English. The author sets out to answer these questions: "As a person was Heine a scheming blackguard, a self-deluded scapegrace, a confused liberal, a deliberate evader, or a broken creative spirit triumphing over humiliations and a progressively racking disease? As an author was he a cosmopolitan soul, a

German revolutionary, a French agent, or a specifically Jewish satirist? Was he primarily a wit, a politician, a philosopher-journalist, a complex skeptic, or a simple lyric poet?'' Having overcome his uncritical identification with Heine and recognized the many contradictions in the man and the poet, Untermeyer successfully attempts to elucidate Heine's paradoxes by continually comparing reality with poetic vision, the poet's circumstances and actions, desires and illusions, with his literary rationalizations and transmutations. Some of his chapter titles indicate his awareness of his subject's complexity and his approach as a biographer: "The Restless Spirit," "The Unconverted Convert," "The Harried Lover," "The Willing Exile," "The Unwilling Expatriate," "The Tortured Wit," "The 'Poor, Sick Jew,' " and "The Phoenix." Writing during the Nazi period, Untermeyer aptly concludes that "Heine has continued to be the scholar's puzzle and the politician's nightmare." In an Apppendix he reprints Matthew Arnold's poem "Heine's Grave" and his own empathic "Monolog from a Mattress."

The scholar's puzzle is outlined and largely solved in SAMMONS' book, a work of mature scholarship that is written with admirable authority and in a lively style. By virtue of its authentic and balanced portrait of Heine, it deserves to supersede many of the older biographies listed above. As pure biography this book is unsurpassed, and it also supplies valuable information about the background, the substance, and the special quality of Heine's entire literary output. In cogent fashion and satisfying detail, Sammons presents all the major stages and aspects of Heine's life and creativity: his controversial birthdate, his family background, his boyhood and youth, his schooling and his early loves, his brief and ill-starred business career, his years as a fledgling poet, essayist, and dramatist, his search for a Jewish identity, and the transformation of Harry Heine into Dr. Heinrich Heine; the years of drift and his breakthrough to fame, his departure from Germany after the 1830 revolution, his activities and associations during his early years in Paris, the women in his life, his radical phase in the 1840s, his relationships with Ludwig Börne and Karl Marx, his later poetry, the feud over his inheritance, and his physical collapse and final years in his "mattress grave." In a rather personal final chapter, "Aftermath," the author treats Heine's posthumous reputation and the state of Heine studies in various countries. Displaying an impressive command of both primary and secondary sources, Sammons is an authoritative guide on a number of convoluted paths.

Like most of the titles in Twayne's World Authors Series, SPENCER's book is intended as a readable introduction for the general reader, and in this her balanced and reasonably comprehensive presentation fully succeeds. Spencer clearly describes Heine in his many aspects: "the romantic poet of bittersweet love songs, . . . the irreverent satirist, provocative social commentator, and brilliant and penetrating essayist. Aptly remarking that "in Heine's case, a consistent separation of biographical and literary matters is not only difficult to achieve but is not advisable," she begins with a chronological table as well as a ten-page biographical essay covering Heine's German period and then allows his Paris period (a quarter-century!) to emerge from a discussion of his writings. In general, Spencer's approach is to group Heine's works according to genres, and her quotations from the original German are followed by her own serviceable though unpoetic English renditions. Spencer duly notes the "ver-

itable Heine renaissance" that began with the 100th anniversary of the poet's death and takes cognizance of the latest scholarship by providing, as part of her bibliography, brief comments on the major critical works that have appeared during the past three or four decades.

PRAWER's book is not, strictly speaking, a biography, but it presents such wide-ranging evidence that Heine's life, work, and thought are inextricably intertwined that it belongs in this context. Prawer's title is intended to ring up associations with both *The Divine Comedy* by Dante and *The Human Comedy* by Balzac, authors whom Heine admired, and the author points to the "Balzacian sweep of [Heine's] social overview and the Dantesque vigor of his condemnations." Nor does the author let us lose sight of the fact that "the Jewish comedy in which Heine brought his humor, his wit, his anger, and his compassion to bear was above all the tragicomedy of emancipation, assimilation, and acculturation," and that it therefore encompasses Jewish self-hatred. With a fine eye for the intermingling of the comic and the tragic elements in the poet's life and work, the author invites us to take a holistic approach to Heine by letting an extensive typology of Jewish figures, ideas, and situations—both real and fictitious, historical and contemporary—pass in review before us. Even Prawer's arrangement is Heinesque: Each of his four major sections ("German-Jewish Dilemmas," "Parisian Perspectives," "Roads from Damascus," "Views from a Mattress Crypt") is followed by an Intermezzo. The colorful parade includes both actual figures (the Rothschilds, the Meyerbeers, the Mendelssohns, Börne, Platen, Marcus, Gans, Zunz, Wihl, Weill, Werth) and fictional or semi-fictional characters (Moses Lump, Hirsch-Hyazinth, Gumpelino, Little Samson, Rabbi Abraham). Such facts and fictions are viewed against the background of contemporary Gentile society and also against that of great Jewish figures of the past—from the Biblical patriarchs to Yehuda Halevy, Spinoza, and Moses Mendelssohn. Heine emerges as a brilliant portraitist and cartoonist with a marked satiric sense, and Prawer concludes that even as Heine identified himself as a German and a European, he remained "a Jew by memory and feeling, . . . by decree of history, . . . by community of fate," which subjected him to multifarious tensions and conflicts.

ROBERTSON's little book is an intellectual biography appearing in the series "Jewish Thinkers," but since Heine was not an abstract thinker or a pragmatic philosopher, the empathic non-Jewish author properly presents him less as a Jewish thinker than as a thinker who was Jewish. As he discusses the historical, social, and ideological background of Heine's life and creativity, Robertson lucidly sets forth the poet's attitudes toward Goethe, Romanticism, Young Germany, Saint-Simon, Napoleon, and Marx. Under the rubric "Between Revolutions," the author discusses the activities of the political poet and thinker between the Congress of Vienna and the revolutions of 1848, as well as the attitude of Heine the traveler toward France, England, and America. Robertson suggests that Heine's celebration of the senses increasingly acted as compensation for his constitutional ill health and his self-pitying, self-deprecatory, self-styled "dark west-eastern spleen." The author does not pretend to settle the question of Heine's new-found piety in his "mattress grave," and he closes on a suitably inconclusive note by evoking Heine's poignant image of the poet as *schlemiel*, for Heine really has "no final message transcending the antinomies around which we have seen his thought restlessly circling."

—Harry Zohn

HELLMAN, Lillian, 1905–1984; American playwright.

Feibleman, Peter, *Lilly: Reminiscences of Lillian Hellman.* New York, Morrow, 1988; London, Chatto and Windus, 1989.

Moody, Richard, *Lillian Hellman: Playwright.* New York, Pegasus, 1972.

Rollyson, Carl, *Lillian Hellman: Her Legend and Her Legacy.* New York, St. Martin's, 1988.

Wright, William, *Lillian Hellman: The Image, The Woman.* New York, Simon and Schuster, 1986; London, Sidgwick and Jackson, 1987.

*

MOODY's work, spanning the years in Lillian Hellman's life from 1905 to 1969, is the first biography to be written on the playwright whose career has measured favorably against those of her contemporaries Arthur Miller and Tennessee Williams. Writing shortly after the publication of Hellman's first memoir, *Unfinished Woman* (1969), Moody presents Hellman as "a moral writer" who had no talent for collaboration and maintained an uneasy truce with the theatre for 27 years.

Moody's critical biography sustains a consistent format: each chapter begins with biographical detail and ends with a critical analysis of a play written during that period of Hellman's life. The format explores Hellman's biography and her characteristic dramaturgy influenced by Henrik Ibsen and later by Anton Chekhov. For Moody, Hellman's adaptation of Emmanuel Roblès' novel *Montserrat* in 1949 "signaled a change" in her career. A series of stage adaptations—*Montserrat* (1949), *Candide* (1956), *The Lark* (1956), *My Mother, My Father and Me* (1963)—eventually led Hellman away from the public arena of the theatre and into the private explorations of autobiography where she regarded her life as "an extended chronicle play."

Moody's persistent view of Hellman as a "rare, lean and upright person"—a moralist—has been dispelled by recent biographers. WRIGHT replaces the saintly, often fictive Lillian Hellman portrayed in her three memoirs with a flawed individual who was manipulative, cantankerous, strong-principled, angry, dishonest, lascivious, paranoid, and mercurial. Still regarded as America's greatest "woman" playwright, Hellman is, in Wright's view, a good writer and passionate speaker who wrote one of the American theatre's great plays (*The Little Foxes*, 1939) and set a new standard for autobiography (*Unfinished Woman*, 1969, and *Pentimento*, 1973).

Wright traces the facts and fictions of Hellman's long and complicated life through an historical period when political forces were shaping modern history, especially the American intellectual left in the 1930s. Hellman's life touches on cultural and political issues: Broadway, Hollywood, a world war, McCarthyism, personal fame, success, and failure. She outlived her success as a screenwriter and playwright but reestablished her writer's credentials in the memoirs that were often fictive but never dull or clumsy.

During the two years following Hellman's death, Wright interviewed over 150 people and wrote his "complex and contradictory" biography that melds truth with the fiction of legend. To her admirers, Hellman was a paragon of integrity during her appearance before the Subcommittee of the House UnAmerican Activities Committee, what she later called her "scoundrel time." To her detractors, she was a fabricator and a liar. Wright separates most of the lies, great and small, from the truth in a biography unlike any other book written about Hellman. While Moody had "Miss Hellman" looking over his shoulder (even approving his manuscript), Wright escapes the "official version" of the Hellman story and separates the "woman" from the "image."

In an effort to set the record straight, Wright frequently records two versions of life-shaping events. For example, Hellman's version of her first ("love at first sight") encounter with Dashiell Hammett, in which they left a restaurant and talked all night in a parked car, differs from an eyewitness' version of their meeting. It was not in a restaurant and they did not leave together. Wright conjectures that both versions are essentially true; however, the second meeting where the attraction of the two people was unleashed stuck in Hellman's memory to be described 40 years later.

Wright makes a case for the meeting between Hammett and Hellman as being the most important event of *her* life. Under his influence, Wright argues, Hellman realized herself as a creative artist and a political force. "He was a collaborator," Wright concludes, "in the creation not so much of the plays as of Lillian Hellman herself."

Of the many unverifiable stories that Hellman relates in her memoirs, Wright attributes to Hellman's ability "to distill a diffuse and unsatisfactory reality into a deft literary concentrate." He skillfully separates the woman from the image in a superlatively written biography on a literary figure whose life impinged upon American political and artistic arenas for over fifty years.

In his "reminiscences" FEIBLEMAN regrets that Hellman's friends (at her insistence) refused to talk with Wright; consequently, only her "enemies" were accessible to the unauthorized biographer, resulting in "inaccuracies" which Feibleman fails to identify. *Lilly*, nevertheless, explodes Wright's assumption that Hellman's friendships with young men were "uncomplicated" by eroticism. Feibleman's biographical memoir on Hellman's years between 1963 and her death in 1984 is often lurid in its details of her fierce sexuality and uncontrollable rage. Feibleman, 25 years younger than Hellman, became her close companion in the difficult period of her failing health. Composed from letters, taped conversations, and memories, his portrait of the aging, irascible Hellman prone to uncontrollable temper tantrums exposes an aged woman "raging against the dying of the light."

ROLLYSON's biography purports to be a major work on Hellman. However, in its 613 pages, it offers little new information not already examined by Wright. Furthermore, Rollyson pursues a peculiarly eccentric viewpoint: that Hellman led an incomplete life because she failed to savor her sexuality and her career. "This biography," he asserts, "shows what got in her way." Rather than showing, Rollyson succeeds in obscuring.

Unlike Wright and Feibleman, Rollyson frequently takes his mercurial subject at face value, which the Hellman biographer does at his peril. From her hospital bed she jokingly explained her deficiencies to Feibleman as "the worst writer's block I've ever had." Rollyson reports this incident as, "near death," Hellman "spoke of being blocked." At best in his analysis of Hellman's work, Rollyson flounders when confronted with the many personal fictions that comprise the Hellman legend.

—Milly S. Barranger

HEMINGWAY, Ernest, 1899–1961; American writer.

Baker, Carlos, *Ernest Hemingway: A Life Story*. New York, Scribner, and London, Collins, 1969.

Brian, Denis, editor, *The True Gen: An Intimate Portrait of Ernest Hemingway by Those Who Knew Him*. New York, Grove, 1988.

Fenton, Charles A., *The Apprenticeship of Ernest Hemingway: The Early Years*. New York, Farrar Straus, 1954.

Fuentes, Norberto, *Hemingway in Cuba*, translated by Consuelo E. Corwin. Secaucus, New Jersey, Lyle Stuart, 1984.

Griffin, Peter, *Along With Youth: Hemingway, The Early Years*. New York and Oxford, Oxford University Press, 1985.

Hotchner, A.E., *Papa Hemingway: A Personal Memoir*. New York, Random House, and London, Weidenfeld and Nicolson, 1966.

Kert, Bernice, *The Hemingway Women*. New York, Norton, 1983.

Lynn, Kenneth S., *Hemingway*. New York and London, Simon and Schuster, 1987.

Meyers, Jeffrey, *Hemingway: A Biography*. New York, Harper, 1985; London, Macmillan, 1986.

Reynolds, Michael, *The Young Hemingway*. Oxford, Blackwell, 1986; New York, Blackwell, 1987.

Reynolds, Michael, *Hemingway: The Paris Years*. Oxford and New York, Blackwell, 1989.

*

With the possible exception of Mark Twain, no American writer has lived and died more in the public eye than Ernest Hemingway. But for all the glare of publicity, self-promoted and otherwise, many shadowy areas have required biographical illumination. So complex and often contradictory was his character, so dramatically engaged was his life with major historical currents of the first half of the 20th century, and so important and enduring is his literary art that one can safely predict scores of books on Hemingway to follow the many scores already written.

At present, four biographies deserve to be called major: those by Baker, Meyers, Lynn, and Reynolds. The earliest of these is BAKER's, based on thorough scholarly research and still indispensable. All subsequent biographers are in his debt, not only for *Ernest Hemingway: A Life Story* itself but for the massive file of interviews, correspondence, and other material he compiled during its preparation. Because he wrote an important earlier critical study of Hemingway, Baker eschews criticism in the biography. He likewise deliberately avoids a thesis, for no single key, he believes, will unlock the door to a full understanding of his subject's personality. Instead, Baker provides a straightforward, fact-filled, chronological account of Hemingway's crowded life based on manuscript sources, "including many pages of his unpublished work, approximately 2,500 of his letters, and at least an equal number of letters to him from friends, members of his family, and chance associates." To supplement this documentation, Baker interviewed 162 and corresponded with 240 individuals about Hemingway, and he traveled to many of the places significant in Hemingway's peripatetic career. Baker remains the best source for a full, accurate, and objective account of Hemingway's "life story."

Unlike Baker, MEYERS integrates literary analysis with biographical narrative. Fresh readings based on careful research often result, as in his demonstration that the protagonist of *Across the River and Into the Trees* derives more from Hemingway's World War I friend Chink Dorman-Smith than from his World War II friend Buck Lanham. The strictly biographical material makes extensive use of information coming to light after Baker's book, especially the memoirs of Hemingway's last two loves, Mary Welsh and Adriana Ivancich. Meyers' own new findings include a full account of Hemingway's lover Jane Mason and her psychiatrist Lawrence Kubie, who wrote a suppressed psychoanalytic study of Hemingway, thereby provoking the subject's wrath. Another previously unavailable source is the extensive F.B.I. file on Hemingway, maintained over a period of two decades. As Meyers points out, this shameful record of government surveillance shows that "even paranoids have real enemies." The Meyers book is not without its weaknesses—some inaccuracies, frequently dogmatic psychologizing, facile generalizations, and perhaps excessive emphasis on its subject's negative personal traits—but it does succeed in placing Hemingway firmly in the context of Anglo-American literary history while relating the biographical details. The two concluding paragraphs are genuinely moving.

While neither Baker nor Meyers develops a coherent theory to "explain" Hemingway's life, LYNN's *Hemingway* is a book with a thesis. Stated baldly, this thesis is that Hemingway's character was shaped by the psychological problems, revolving around sexual identity, imposed on him by his mother, Grace Hall Hemingway, who dressed him as a girl during early childhood and treated him and his sister Marcelline, eighteen months older, as twins. Hemingway's writing, Lynn maintains, is a painful effort to purge his psyche of these problems by expressing them, covertly and laconically, in artistic form. As a writer he strove "to cope with the disorder of his inner world by creating fictional equivalents for it." Lynn analyzes almost all of Hemingway's works in reference both to early childhood experience and to his adult career. The result is a unified literary biography, well written and challenging, emphasizing Hemingway's relations to women and his fascination with androgyny. Many readers, however, may suspect that Lynn's reading of both life and work overemphasizes what other biographers have underemphasized and imposes a single thesis too relentlessly to avoid oversimplification.

REYNOLDS' ongoing biography seems destined to become definitive in our time. Assimilating and richly augmenting Baker's pioneering scholarship, more subtle and sympathetic than Meyers and less narrow than Lynn, Reynolds' two biographical volumes to date, in addition to his three other books on Hemingway, make him the preëminent scholar in the field. His emphasis in *The Young Hemingway* and *Hemingway: The Paris Years* lies squarely on the background, formation, and growth of the artist. No one has recreated so successfully the milieu of Oak Park or Paris, and the fully rendered external settings are examined alongside the inward terrain of Hemingway as a child, youth, young man, and journalist-fiction writer, fiercely competitive but in Paris already beginning his long struggle with the genetic family curse of depression. Without losing scholarly objectivity, Reynolds sympathetically identifies with his subject and often brings his reader into Hemingway's very thought processes. If Reynolds completes his biography on the same scale as the first two volumes, as one hopes he will, the whole will be massive, dwarfing other biographies of Hemingway and perhaps approaching the size of Leon Edel's great *Henry James*. And if subsequent volumes resemble the first two, they will be exhaustively researched, meticulously accurate, widely and deeply informative, and beautifully written.

One can only hope that the success of Reynolds' first two volumes will deter GRIFFIN from continuing his projected three-volume life, for *Along with Youth* is a failure. It treats fiction as if it were reliable autobiographical evidence instead of using the biography to elucidate the fiction. It is long on documentation, short on analysis, coherence, and organization. In contrast, KERT's well-organized biographical study of the women in Hemingway's life is a good idea successfully realized. Two works focus on Hemingway early and late. FENTON's treatment of Hemingway's journalistic apprenticeship (1916-23) is still reliable after 36 years. For the Cuban period FUENTES draws on sources generally unavailable to American scholars, including extensive interviews with Hemingway's employees at the Finca Vigía; his mate on the *Pilar*, Gregorio Fuentes; and his physician and close friend, José Luis Herrera Sotolongo. More anecdotal than analytical, the somewhat casual organization of *Hemingway in Cuba* mixes topical and chronological approaches, and the prose is journalistic. Fuentes succeeds in evoking the atmosphere of Hemingway's Cuba and the style of his life there for some twenty years. More controversial is his effort to present Hemingway as a dedicated leftist in complete solidarity with the Castro revolution, but here too Fuentes presents new evidence that must be considered. Valuable appendices print for the first time documents from the Finca Vigía, including numerous letters to and from Hemingway such as a wonderful series of love letters to Mary in late 1944, various bibliographical items from the Cuban press, and a complete inventory of the Finca Vigía in its present state as a Hemingway museum.

Only a few of the many memoirs of Hemingway can be mentioned. BRIAN's skillful compilation is a treasure trove of gossip and commentary by family members, friends, critics, and scholars. For the really true gen (i.e., valid information) one will go to Reynolds or Baker, but Brian's work is fascinating in its refraction of Hemingway's personality through the prisms of many sensibilities. Equally interesting is the readable, if not always reliable, *Papa Hemingway*. A.E. HOTCHNER is Hemingway's Boswell. Like Boswell, Hotchner was a lawyer by training and a writer by inclination who in his 20s met a literary idol old enough to be his father. Like Boswell, Hotchner's almost filial affection for the older man was met with an indulgent paternal fondness. Like Boswell, Hotchner kept journals that recorded in detail his friend's conversations over a period of years. The resulting memoir provides a close, favorable, almost sycophantic perspective on Hemingway's character from 1948 until his death. Hotchner not only visited Hemingway in Cuba, Idaho, and the Mayo Clinic, but saw him in New York and traveled with him in France, Italy, and Spain, often for protracted periods. Not usually inclined to literary talk in his later years, Hemingway spoke freely to Hotchner about his own work and commented on other writers as well. The festive side of Hemingway emerges engagingly in *Papa Hemingway*, but Hotchner also records with considerable pathos the mental and physical deterioration of the final years.

Members of Hemingway's family have not been reticent in recording their memories. In addition to the indispensable but highly subjective books by brother Leicester (*My Brother, Ernest Hemingway*, Cleveland, World Publishing, 1962) and last wife Mary (*How It Was*, New York, Knopf, 1976), two sisters and two sons have published books, and third wife Martha Gellhorn has recalled her unhappy marriage to Hemingway in both nonfiction and fiction. Various friends and sporting companions have likewise swelled the tide of memoirs. Of the making of books about one of this century's most fascinating figures, there would seem to be no end.

—Keneth Kinnamon

HENRI IV [Henry III of Navarre], 1553–1610; French monarch.

Baird, Henry M., *The Huguenots and Henry of Navarre* (2 vols.). London, Kegan Paul, and New York, Scribner, 1896.

Buisseret, David, *Henry IV*. London and Boston, Allen and Unwin, 1984.

l'Estoile, Pierre de, *The Paris of Henry of Navarre, as Seen by Pierre de l'Estoile: Selections from His "Mémoires—Journaux,,"* translated and edited by Nancy Lyman Roelker. Cambridge, Massachusetts, Harvard University Press, 1958 (published as *Mémoires Journaux*, 12 vols., Paris, Librairie des Bibliophiles, 1875–96).

Freer, Martha Walker, *The History of the Reign of Henry IV: King of France and Navarre* (6 vols.). London, Hurst and Blackett, 1861.

Hurst, Quentin, *Henry of Navarre*. London, Hodder and Stoughton, 1937; New York, Appleton-Century, 1938.

Jackson, Lady Catherine H. C. Elliot, *The First of the Bourbons* (2 vols.). London, R. Bentley, and New York, Scribner, 1890.

Mahoney, Irene, *Royal Cousin: The Life of Henri IV of France*. New York, Doubleday, 1970.

Mann, Heinrich, *Young Henry of Navarre*, translated by Eric Sutton. New York, Knopf, 1937; as *King Wren: The Youth of Henri IV*, London, Secker and Warburg, 1937 (originally published as *Die Jugend des Königs Henri Quatre*, Amsterdam, Querido, 1935).

Mann, Heinrich, *Henry, King of France*, translated by Eric Sutton. New York, Knopf, 1939; as *Henri Quatre, King of France*, 2 vols., London, Secker and Warburg, 1938–39 (originally published as *Die Vollendung des Königs Henri Quatre*, Amsterdam, Querido, 1936).

Mousnier, Roland, *The Assassination of Henry IV: The Tyrannicide Problem and the Consolidation of the French Absolute Monarchy in the Early 17th Century*, translated by John Spenser. New York, Scribner, and London, Faber, 1973 (originally published by Gallimard, Paris, 1964).

Pearson, Hesketh, *Henry of Navarre: His Life*. London, Heinemann, 1963; as *Henry of Navarre, The King who Dared*, New York, Harper and Row, 1963.

Péréfixe, Hardouin de Beaumont de, *The History of Henry IV*, translated by J. Dauncey. London, J. Cottrel, 1663; revised as *Memoirs of Henri IV, King of France and Navarre, by the Court Historian of Louis XIV*, Paris and Boston, Grollier Society, [n.d.]; London, Grollier Society, 1904 (originally published, Amsterdam, 1661).

Russell of Liverpool (Edward F. L.), *Henry of Navarre: Henry IV of France*. London, R. Hale, 1969; New York, Praeger, 1970.

Sedgwick, Henry Dwight, *Henry of Navarre*. Indianapolis, Bobbs-Merrill, 1930.

Seward, Desmond, *The First Bourbon: Henri IV, King of France and Navarre*. London, Constable, and Boston, Gambit, 1971.

Slocombe, George Edward, *Henry of Navarre: A Passionate History*. London, Cayme Press, 1931; as *The White Plumed Henry: King of France*, New York, Cosmopolitan, 1931.

Sully, Maximilien de Béthune, *Memoirs of Maximilien de Béthune, Duc of Sully*, translated by Charlotte Lennox (5 vols.). London, A. Millar, 1757 (based on *Mémoires, ou Oeconomies Royales d'estat, domestiques, politiques, et militaires de Henry le Grand*, 4 vols., Rouen, L. Billaire, 1663).

Vioux, Marcelle, *Henry of Navarre: Le Vert-Galant*, translated by J. Lewis May. London, G. Bles, 1936; New York, Dutton, 1937.

Willert, P. F., *Henry of Navarre and the Huguenots in France*. New York and London, Putnam, 1893.

*

Biographers of national heroes are sometimes tempted to embellish their life stories with colorful details rather than straight historical facts. When the hero in question has a multiple reputation, the possibility of turning out one-sided hagiography or proscription, myth or polemic increases geometrically. Henry of Navarre, who became Henri IV of France, was seen variously in his own time as Catholic apostate, Protestant heretic, defender of tolerance, Protector of the Churches, gallant knight, dastardly womanizer, the savior of France, usurper of the throne, creator of French absolutism, and villainous tyrant. His biographers have struggled ever since to sort out the man from his legend, but in varying degrees each writer has been influenced by personal or national ideologies. Modern readers will do well to remain alert to possible distortions.

Even the source material on which biographers of Henri IV are based has the potential to mislead. On the one hand, Henri is the first French king for whom almost complete records are extant; we have access to his personal letters and diplomatic correspondence, the memoirs of his court, his accounts, and his official edicts and decrees. On the other, English-speaking researchers have been handicapped by a lack of reliable transla-

tions of these documents. The most accurate and complete memoir, SULLY's *Oeconomies royales*, have been well-edited in France, but English readers will find only Charlotte Lennox's translation of a paraphrased and rearranged 18th-century edition. The near-contemporary biography by PÉRÉFIXE, bishop and sycophantic court historian to Louis XIV, was translated for the edification of Charles II, Henri's English grandson, and bears the obvious marks of its mirror-of-princes genre. L'ESTOILE, a Catholic parliamentary bourgeoisie, was a French Pepys. He knew Henri's Paris well, kept voluminous memoirs, but displayed little taste for historical accuracy or reasoned judgment. The reader will find in the modern translation by Roelker a pleasantly readable, if somewhat sketchy and linguistically anachronistic condensation of L'Estoile's 12 volumes.

Similarly, a search for English biographies turns up only a handful of reliable works, although untranslated French biographies abound. In the 19th century, multi-volume "histories" of the reign of Henri IV were popular. FREER's work was based on extensive research in the French archives and provided a strictly chronological account. Modern readers may find her Victorian value judgments and heavy-handed use of purple prose somewhat distasteful. Her extensive footnotes are less than useful, both because they are usually in French and because their references no longer correspond to modern archival designations. JACKSON produced a more readable account of Henri's life, with historical facts often relegated to footnotes so as not to interfere with the more colorful narrative. BAIRD, whose work was long considered the "standard" biography, documented his research well, consulting, as he took pains to point out, "every available source of accurate knowledge, whether Protestant or Roman Catholic." The reader must not overlook the fact, however, that Baird's long-term goal was to write the definitive history of the Huguenots—that "valiant people." (Baird also published *History of the Rise of the Huguenots* [2 vols., 1865] and *The Huguenots and the Revocation of the Edict of Nantes* [2 vols., 1895].) As might be expected, he viewed Henri's abjuration of the Protestant faith as "an act as disastrous to public morality as disgraceful to the king himself," and the Edict of Nantes as one of the "grandest monuments of European civilization." For WILLERT, on the other hand, the Huguenots were often motivated "not so much from spiritual conviction as from discontent," both political and social. In Willert's more balanced interpretation, Henri's abjuration was politically expedient and the Edict a limited, but fair and equitable solution to religious persecution.

In the 1930s, English writers saw Henri IV as the ideal French gallant, and their biographies reflected the romantic legends that surrounded his reign. VIOUX concentrated on the lurid and the sensational aspects of the royal court. He emphasized the intrigues, the sexual peccadillos, the scandals; he omitted almost every important historical detail. The *New York Times* (16 May 1937) justifiably labeled the book "historical gossip." In contrast, HURST maintained a certain emotional detachment from a figure with whom he sympathized and conscientiously attempted to separate the legends from biographical fact. As a result, he produced a book that readers of his day found dull. SLOCOMBE's bias is obvious from his titles. His biography was a romantic treatment of a king the author obviously admired. Despite a complete lack of documentation, Slocombe did not produce inaccurate history; his work makes for good reading for those who are curious about the king rather than his reign. Perhaps the best of this group is SEDGEWICK's biography. Although he strove for a popular approach, his story is impartial and accurate, due at least in part to extensive quotes from Henri's letters, a practice that lets the king speak for himself. A brief bibliography testifies to Sedgewick's familiarity with French sources, and despite his claim to have omitted most historical matters in deference to his "romantical, Protestantish or sexually minded" readers, Sedgewick produced a fair and balanced account.

During World War II, interest in Henri IV focused more on his political actions than on his romantic and gallant image. MANN's two-volume fictional account of Henri's life would not normally be included here, except for the fact that literary critics such as Lucáks accused it of being too biographical to be considered fiction. Mann, a German émigré in the 1930s, saw distinct parallels between Henri's France and Nazi Germany. Thus he portrayed Henri as a human and humane king, a force for progress, reason, and tolerance in an age torn by factionalism, bigotry, and inhumanity. There is no historical apparatus in this work and much that is historically inaccurate, such as Henri's frequent meetings with Montaigne. Still, for the reader who wishes to discover what Henri meant to his own people, and why he remains, for many Frenchmen, their favorite king, Mann's two books offer fresh insights.

Among the more recent studies is the readable, if strongly anti-Catholic, study done by PEARSON. This tireless biographer cites few references, although, like Sedgewick, he uses quotes from Henri's personal correspondence to illuminate the character of the king. For the reactions of members of the court to the king's acts, he seems to have relied heavily on the memoir collections of Sully. The problem with doing so is that such memoirs are not necessarily factual, and there is no evidence that Pearson has attempted to verify their judgments. A similarly flawed work is that of RUSSELL, who gives high praise for the man but nothing of substance to back up his judgment. Russell's primary interest is the clash between Protestant and Catholic forces; he has little to say about political administration or international affairs. Because the author has relied on nothing but secondary sources, the book is not likely to be of use to anyone but those who are totally unfamiliar with Henri or his age.

A much better effort comes from MAHONEY, who deliberately disguises her extensive and careful research so as not to put off the general reader for whom she is writing. The endnotes will not satisfy the scholar, nor will her somewhat sketchy coverage of the reign itself. Nevertheless, Mahoney has complete command of her subject. She has consulted not only the usual memoirs and letter collections, but also diplomatic and archival materials from England, Italy, Spain, and the Netherlands. The book reads like a novel, but one with a firm historical substructure. SEWARD's work is better documented, although some readers may well object to its admitted English bias. Because of his insistence on using English translations of sources, albeit after checking them against the French originals, Seward tells us much about Henri the man as seen through English eyes, less about the French king and his country.

The serious scholar will find the most satisfactory coverage in BUISSERET's well-researched biography. Frequent maps point the way through a sometimes unfamiliar landscape, and a glossary provides the same service for an extensively French vocabulary. Character identifications are clearly given throughout, so that the reader remains unconfused by rapidly changing titles of nobility. Extensive appendices, illustrations, and chronological tables supplement the work. Although Buisseret adds little new material to the corpus of biographical data on Henri, he succeeds in giving a clear and balanced interpretation of the reign of this paradoxical king.

For a more analytical account, the specialist reader would do well to move on from general biography to MOUSNIER, who approached the story of Henri's life backward from the moment of his death. Beginning with the assumption that Henri's assassination occurred because he was perceived as a tyrant, Mousnier examines the meaning of tyranny, the political actions that might have qualified Henri as a tyrant, and the effect of his reign on the future of France. While this is not a work to be approached without prior knowledge of the reign, Mousnier's biographical study will reveal the depth of French scholarship in this field and the corresponding dearth of scholarly coverage to date among English writers.

—Carolyn P. Schriber

HENRY IV, 1366–1413; English monarch.

Bruce, Marie Louise, *The Usurper King: Henry of Bolingbroke 1366–99*. London, Rubicon Press, 1986.
Goodman, Anthony, *The Loyal Conspiracy: The Lords Appellant under Richard II*. London, Routledge, and Coral Gables, Florida, University of Miami Press, 1971.
Kirby, John L., *Henry IV of England*. London, Constable, 1970.
McFarlane, Kenneth B., *Lancastrian Kings and Lollard Knights*. Oxford, Clarendon Press, 1972.
Wylie, James H., *History of England under Henry the Fourth* (4 vols.). London, Longman, 1884–98.

*

WYLIE's book was the first scholarly account of Henry IV and his reign. It is by far the fullest and seems certain to remain so. At over 2000 pages, it is truly monumental. Wylie's prime concern was to collect and establish the facts. Rather than harnessing his material to his interpretation, he allowed it to determine what he wrote, scarcely discriminated between what mattered and what did not, and gave a low priority to the explanation of events. The resultant text is so detailed and so lacking in argument that the reader is confused and overwhelmed. Yet it cannot be disregarded. "Not that it is not immensely valuable," wrote McFarlane; "none can deny that it remains a great work of scholarship," wrote Kirby. It contains much on the life of Henry IV, but it does not present such information in a coherent or readily digested form. It is an indispensable work of reference, but it must be approached as such, via the chapter headings and index. It is not a book to be read.

McFARLANE was the most influential English late-medievalist of the 20th century. His biography is clear and concise: one-twentieth the length of Wylie's, infinitely more vivid and readable, and still the best introduction to the king. Published posthumously from a celebrated series of lectures of 1936–53, it sought to make sense of the reign and to correct the constitutional idealism wrongly attributed to Henry IV by Stubbs (*Constitutional History of England in the Middle Ages*, London 1874–78). McFarlane focuses on Henry himself and shows a proper concern for his personal development. Already 33 at his accession, Henry IV lived to be only 47 and was ill for the last five years. "It is dangerous to concentrate on the last 14 years, important though they were. It is more important to remember that he was not brought up as a future king." McFarlane establishes Henry as a great nobleman, "an unrivalled jouster," a "man of action who was also an intellectual," and a "European celebrity" with immense promise as a king. But he was also an unscrupulous opportunist who perjured himself to secure the crown. Thereafter he was always on the defensive against rebels and in parliament, and he was tortured by pangs of guilt. The reign itself is treated sparingly with chapters only on government and parliament and Henry's relations with the nobility and his heir.

Two lives confine themselves to Henry's career before his accession. For GOODMAN he is one of the five Lords Appellant who destroyed Richard II's favourites in 1388. Scholarly and accurate, Goodman draws together disparate material and focuses it on this formative episode in Henry's life. The portrait suffers because Henry's role in it is relatively minor and because it uses only secondary sources. BRUCE, in contrast, offers a popular illustrated account of Henry's early life by a professional biographer. Well-researched and presented in a lively style, it entwines the careers of Henry and his cousin Richard II and presents the revolution of 1399 as an accident that nobody wanted. Sometimes suspect in interpretation, Bruce certainly succeeds in his objective: "to remember Henry of Bolingbroke as he was," as the carefree idol of the people before he became the careworn and defeated king.

The standard biography is by KIRBY, a pupil of McFarlane. Although again beginning in 1366, this work devotes much less space to Henry's early life and motivation—probably too little—and much more to the reign. Here the treatment is chronological, mainstream politics being discussed at length and other themes incorporated as they occur. Accurate and detailed, the product of much research, it is much clearer and more accessible than Wylie's volume and more comprehensive than McFarlane's.

—Michael Hicks

HENRY V, 1387–1422; English monarch.

Allmand, Christopher T., *Henry V*. London, Historical Association, 1968.

Harriss, Gerald L., editor, *Henry V: The Practice of Kingship*. Oxford and New York, Oxford University Press, 1985.

Hutchison, Harold, *Henry V: A Biography*. London, Eyre and Spottiswoode, 1967.

Jacob, Ernest F., *Henry V and the Invasion of France*. London, Hodder and Stoughton/English Universities Press, 1947.

McFarlane, Kenneth B., *Lancastrian Kings and Lollard Knights*. Oxford, Clarendon Press, 1972.

Pugh, Thomas B., *Henry V and the Southampton Plot of 1415*. Gloucester, Gloucestershire, A. Sutton, 1988.

Wylie, James H. and William T. Waugh, *The Reign of Henry the Fifth* (3 vols.). Cambridge, Cambridge University Press, 1914–29.

*

The patriotic image of Henry V propagated by Shakespeare in his *History of King Henry V* originated in the king's lifetime and still strongly influences most modern biographers, who accept or, more rarely, react against it. WYLIE is one of Henry V's rare critics. He judges him anachronistically, by 20th-century standards, and sees him as driven by ambition into deceit. But Wylie's view is buried in a vast assembly of facts: rather "a collection of material for a history than a history in any true sense of the word," as Kingsford said. Following Wylie's death, his third volume was completed by WAUGH on more selective lines and incorporating a more favourable assessment of the king. Wylie is to be sampled rather than read; Waugh is still worth reading.

JACOB and HUTCHISON aim at the general reading public. Jacob is more scholarly, Hutchison more readable. Both accept Shakespeare's patriotic interpretation of Henry V's reign and concentrate on the war to the exclusion of domestic events. Both reject the legend of his disreputable pre-accession career as Prince Hal: "Henry of Monmouth was very far from being the prince of the Boar's Head Tavern," wrote Jacob. Jacob tries to explain what happened and to judge Henry's actions and motives by the standards of his day. However unrealistic, Henry considered himself to be recovering his rightful inheritance lost by John Lackland: "The historical fact of the expansion of the Capetian monarchy meant nothing to him compared with the justice of his own claim." Both admire their subject—an "organizing genius" whose justice had "an Old Testament quality"—and his "formidable achievement," but both question whether his conquest of France was feasible.

ALLMAND reviews earlier work and provides a rounded picture in an extremely brief compass. He emphasises Henry's dynamism, his relentless determination, and his sincere and genuine piety to explain a claim to France that was perfectly genuine and comprehensible at the time. Henry was a remarkable man of impressive achievements, but his mission was an unattainable for himself, had he lived, as it proved for his successor.

If unduly favourable, McFARLANE's short study presents the most vivid insight into Henry's mind. He concentrates on Henry's formative career as Prince of Wales, which lasted longer than his reign, and on his working methods in government. McFarlane relies heavily on Henry's letters, claiming that "to read a man's own words is to know his mind more intimately than at second-hand." He stresses Henry's personal magnetism, vitality, determination, and control over affairs. Like contemporaries, McFarlane thought Henry's potential limitless and refused to write off his chances of ultimate victory. "Take him all round and he was, I think, the greatest man that ever ruled England."

McFarlane influenced HARRISS, whose work comes closest to a modern biography. The volume comprises ten lectures by five authors. Focusing on his reign rather than his life, thematic rather than chronological, he concentrates consistently on the king himself, who is assessed not just as a soldier but as a ruler. Henry is measured against contemporary expectations, which he is shown to have fulfilled. Each thematic chapter is by an expert and the whole is scholarly, up-to-date, and the best portrait we have of the king. But such an approach poses problems. There is no uniform interpretation, some authors being more critical than others, and not all bear out Harriss' summary that the "simple record of Henry V's achievement is sufficient to establish him as a great king."

"Henry V is the only 15th-century English king whose reputation has been enhanced by recent historians," writes PUGH, whose short book is replete with scholarly apparatus and trenchant judgements. Even as prince, Henry has been over-rated; only death saved him from inevitable defeat, and his justice was marred by wilful oppression. His aims were attainable without war, which was against English interests, and his greatest triumph, the Treaty of Troyes, failed even before his own death. Of "limited vision and outlook," he was "an adventurer, not a statesman." Moreover—and this is the heart of Pugh's book—the so-called Southampton Plot (which never actually happened) resulted from Henry's mismanagement of the conspirators. Idiosyncratic in structure and eccentric in focus, Pugh's work is not complete biography, and treats only facets of Henry's career. On the plot itself he is misconceived, and other judgements need careful weighing. Yet he is a useful corrective to Harriss and needs to be read with him.

—Michael Hicks

HENRY VIII, 1491–1547; English monarch.

Erickson, Carolly, *Great Harry*. New York, Summitt Books, and London, Dent, 1980.
Pollard, A. F., *Henry VIII*. London and New York, Goupil, 1902; revised edition, London and New York, Longman, 1905.
Ridley, Jasper, *Henry VIII*. London, Constable, 1984; New York, Viking, 1985.
Scarisbrick, Jack J., *Henry VIII*. London, Eyre and Spottiswoode, and Berkeley, University of California Press, 1968.
Smith, Lacey Baldwin, *Henry VIII: The Mask of Royalty*. London, Cape, and Boston, Houghton Mifflin, 1971.
Starkey, David, *The Reign of Henry VIII: Personalities and Politics*. London, G. Philip, 1985; New York, F. Watts, 1986.

*

Has ever a king or any other statesman been so completely fixed in the scholarly and popular mind by an artist as Henry VIII by Holbein? The bulk, the presence, the mean eyes, and the Renaissance swagger. Biographers have differed about the significance of Henry within his reign; and the significance of the reign within the Tudor century. But Henry's wilful dominance of his age is accepted by all. His personality is something all biographers have agreed on. And Holbein conveys the essence in a few canvasses.

POLLARD produced a biography that dominated the field for more than half a century. Pollard was one of the most influential historians in England, for 30 years Professor of British History at the University of London. He wrote about high politics with a strong biographical bent (he was the author of the leading biography of Cranmer and of a study of the reign of Edward VI even before he turned to Henry VIII). For someone who dominated the field so completely, his work is actually quite sloppy. He seems never to have gone behind the Calendar of State Letters and Papers (which often gives wholly inadequate summaries of the content and even more often a poor sense of the *tone* of the documents) to the originals. Otherwise his reading of sources was broad and his grasp of the national and international context was excellent. Writing in Edwardian Britain, Pollard made Henry sound very un-English. "Surrounded by faint hearts and fearful minds, Henry VIII neither faltered nor failed. He ruled in a ruthless age with a ruthless hand, he dealt with a violent crisis by methods of blood and iron, and his measures were crowned with whatever sanction worldly success can give. He was Machiavelli's *Prince* in action." This deeply anti-clerical king, whose assertion of national sovereignty stemmed from self-interest and not piety, is made to seem uncomfortably as a type for Bismarck—"blood and iron" indeed. All the actors in the dramas of the reign (Wolsey, Cranmer, Cromwell, etc.) are strongly and coherently delineated. The book is marred by a residual anti-catholicism, and Pollard shows no interest in the intellectual currents that influenced the king's actions (or that informed his self-deceptions). Henry's actions are resolutely explained in worldly terms: "the dissolution of the monasteries was in effect, and probably in intention, a gigantic bribe to the laity to induce them to acquiesce in the revolution effected by Henry VIII." Many writers since 1905 have concluded as much, but few have put it so bluntly. The book essentially narrates the reign chronologically and at a leisurely pace. The reign is treated fairly evenly: 228 pages on the first 20 years (1509–29), 210 on the remaining 18 years. Later biographies tend to give about two-thirds of their space to the second half of the reign (the Reformation, the accompanying "Revolution in Government" as it has been called, and five of the six wives were all crammed into the last 15 years).

The modern biography that comes closest to Pollard's in approach and valuation is that of RIDLEY. Ridley is a professional writer and biographer who came to Henry VIII afer writing acclaimed lives not only of great 19th-century statesmen like Palmerston, Garibaldi, and Napoleon III, but of several of the dominant figures of the English and Scottish Reformations: Cranmer, Nicholas Ridley (his own ancestor), and John Knox. This is a well-researched life that recaptures the life of the Court with great vividness and wit. Ridley lacks the depth of knowledge and the immersion in archives to produce a telling or fresh background. Though his is a very conventional account of the *times*, Henry VIII himself comes up bright and clear. Like Pollard's King Henry, he dazzles and repels: "during his 38-year reign, he used the services of others and listened to their advice, but took all the decisions, whether in the hunting field, at the butts in the park of Hampton Court, in the camp at Boulogne, or on his sickbed at Whitehall. He was always the tall, jovial *bon vivant*, with his zest for life, his love of music and the company of ladies, and his cruel piggy eyes."

ERICKSON's biography is longer than Pollard's and Ridley's, but it is also far more historically insouciant. It is based on a thorough reading of the main printed sources (though less widely than are the other lives), but it shows little real understanding of the operations of the Tudor state, the nature of legal process, or of the intellectual traditions of Renaissance Europe. Erickson's is a human interest story; and for those who want a good read about the flesh-and-blood characters who made up a real 16th-century soap opera, this is very well done. Erickson tries, wherever possible, to give period flavour by extensive quotation from the sources (suitably modernized in spelling and punctuation). Nonetheless, her Henry does not dominate the book in the way he does all the others under review here. One never quite feels that Erickson has got inside his skin. He remains a colossus unpredictable even in his unpredictability.

Three other biographies offer the opposite virtue. They are much less thickly textured; they make no attempt to narrate the epic story of Henry's public and private lives. But they are rooted in, and grow out of, an understanding of what made the Tudor state tick. STARKEY offers a short, pithy, and bleak account (167 pages) of a nightmare world of intrigue and double-dealing. Starkey re-creates the mental world of the Court based on his intensive study of the king's Privy Chamber. It is an exercise in Kremlinology, with the imaginative insight of a John le Carré. The final page, cataloguing those unjustly bundled away in show trials to their ugly executions, sums it up: "it is true, of course, that it was the peculiarities of the King's character that made both the rewards and the penalties of the politics so great. But only a few isolated figures like More or Wyatt quarrelled, and then only on paper, with the resulting rules of the game, and even they, when they had the opportunity, played as dirtily as the rest."

SMITH offers a very different approach. In place of the rather glib narrative that moves steadily from year to year, Smith attempts a psychological portrait that begins with Henry's deathbed. His premise is that according to geriatric theory "it is during the final stages of life that a man casts off a portion of the protective shield hammered out during childhood and adolescence and reveals the raw personality beneath." The book takes aspects of that raw personality as revealed in his declining years and uses them to project backwards. Smith's Henry is indeed powerful, assertive, sadistic even; but the assertiveness stemmed from a basically weak personality, one morbidly suspicious, havering on the brink of paranoia, rooted in a deep sexual inadequacy. Henry constantly had to prove to *himself* that he was in charge. This study has divided the scholarly community. Some reviewers picked up too many factual slips for comfort, but others saw it as a triumph of historical imagination. Thus John Kenyon wrote that "as thread after thread is woven into the fabric, the emergent effect is the most complete character study we have of any ruler." It is certainly not a book for those whose sense of the events of the period is hazy. But for those who have a clear grasp of events, it is both challenging and startling.

SCARISBRICK has written the most learned and historically rewarding study of Henry. Again it is not a straightforward biography, but rather a series of brilliant essays on particular events or aspects of the reign. If Smith offers the greatest psychological portrait, Scarisbrick is unrivalled on Henry's intellectual make-up and development. This is a brilliant study of the interplay of Catholic piety, Erasmian humanism and (a poor third) Protestant theology in the mind and conscience of Henry and of those around him. Scarisbrick offers a convincing reinterpretation of the king's relationship with his even larger-than-life Cardinal Thomas Wolsey (radical chic *avant la lettre*), a telling judgment on the taut relationship of the king and Cranmer, and the most convincing account yet (though it hasn't convinced everyone) of Henry's personal responsibility for the nature and timing of the schism from the Roman Catholic Church. Chapters with unpromising titles like "The Canon Law of the Divorce" and "The Royal Supremacy and Theology" turn out to be amongst the most riveting and open up the mental world of the Tudors better than anything else written this century. Scarisbrick writes as a devout Catholic about the king who took the Church in England from its allegiance to the See of Rome. His judgment, just as ambiguous as that of other biographers, is yet less grudging. He sees Henry as a man of boldness, of energy, of vision, a worthy companion to the other colossi of Renaissance Monarchy, the Emperor Charles V and François I of France. He created an unprecedented political integration of his realms, but he divided his people into patterns of religious discord that would endure for centuries. He was a great king whose reign—more obviously than almost any other—marked a watershed in British history.

—John Morrill

HENRY, O. [*born* William Sydney Porter], 1862–1910; American writer.

Arnett, Ethel Stephens, *O. Henry from Polecat Creek.* Greensboro, North Carolina, Piedmont Press, 1962.

Current-Garcia, Eugene, *O. Henry.* New York, Twayne, 1965.

Davis, Robert H. and Arthur B. Maurice, *The Caliph of Bagdad.* New York, Appleton, 1931.

Jennings, Alphonso J., *Through the Shadows With O. Henry.* New York, A. L. Burt, 1921; London, Duckworth, 1922.

Langford, Gerald, *Alias O. Henry: A Biography of William Sidney Porter.* New York, Macmillan, 1957.

Long, E. Hudson, *O. Henry, The Man And His Work.* Philadelphia, University of Pennsylvania Press, 1949.

Maltby, Frances G., *The Dimity Sweetheart.* Richmond, Virginia, Dietz Printing Company, 1930.

O'Connor, Richard, *O. Henry: The Legendary Life of William S. Porter.* New York, Doubleday, 1970.

Smith, C. Alphonso, *O. Henry Biography.* New York, Doubleday, and London, Hodder and Stoughton, 1916.

Williams, William Wash, *The Quiet Lodger of Irving Place.* New York, Dutton, 1936.

*

SMITH's was the first authorized full-length treatment of Porter's legendary career as America's most popular writer of short fiction. Published within six years after his death, it offers a straightforward, sympathetic appraisal of Porter's life and literary achievement, an appraisal firmly based on both a lifelong personal friendship with his subject, dating from their shared boyhood in Greensboro, North Carolina, and on his own scholarly capabilities as Poe Professor of English at the University of Virginia. In his effort to reconcile the man and the artist, however, Smith's exploration of "the O. Henry myth" necessarily remains incomplete and limited by contemporaneity; it was written during a period when O. Henry's literary reputation had achieved its zenith, even among learned critics such as William James and William Lyon Phelps, and thus could hardly have failed to attribute less merit than they to the work of a fellow native son and friend. Although Smith had carefully examined all the essential data made available to him through the scattered commentaries of Porter's publishers, family members, and personal acquaintances, the record he compiled was but a memorable beginning. Having first exposed the zealously guarded secret of Porter's "shadowed years" of imprisonment as a convicted embezzler of bank funds in Texas, Smith's book opened a whole new area for biographical investigation and critical analysis.

JENNINGS, the notorious train robber, added an abundance of specific anecdotal detail to the legend, but despite its flamboyant style and colorful imagery this is a flawed portrayal of both Porter and his alter ego. Yet, like Smith's book, Jennings' is also based on a close personal relationship and a mutual respect of the two men for each other. Jennings first met Porter in Honduras in 1896, when both were "on the lam" from Federal indictment. They spent several months there engaging in madcap activities, later highly fictionalized in some of the stories published in O. Henry's first book, *Cabbages and Kings* (1904); they also shared most of the period of Porter's incarceration in the Ohio Penitentiary encouraging and assisting each other's literary aspirations; and later still they enjoyed brief periods together in New York during the climactic years of Porter's meteoric success. Although Jennings' largely undocumented narrative of Porter's life and works has been justifiably criticised as "fictional to the point of being wholly undependable," there is some value in his many samples of and reverential attitude toward Porter's correspondence and other writings.

Another much briefer but more trustworthy account based on close personal ties is by MALTBY. Privately printed in a small limited edition, this charming reminiscence is focused chiefly on the courtship, marriage, and family life of Porter and his first wife, Athol Estes Roach, from the mid 1880s until her death in Austin, Texas, 27 July 1897. Written many years after those events, the book freshly evokes a classmate's vivid recollections of their youthful escapades, parties, dances, and songfests, as well as of the more somber concerns of family responsibilities, parentage, illness, and despair over threatening death and imprisonment. It also corrects some mistaken assumptions aired about Porter by other commentators and raises several possibilities that others were not aware of: among them, for instance, the fact that Porter's early career in New York might have been vastly enhanced, his life even changed, by a proffered but neglected assignment to edit a book written by Colonel Edward M. House—"who afterward became the Warwick of the Wilson administration." Despite its brevity, *The Dimity Sweetheart* is a significant contribution to biographical O. Henryana.

Along with other sources, Maltby's little book was gratefully acknowledged a year after it appeared by DAVIS AND MAURICE, joint authors of *The Caliph of Bagdad*. This was the most elaborate account yet written of Porter's impact on American literature; a serious attempt to aggrandize their theme within an idealized framework as the progress of a modern Haroun al Rashcid through "Arabian Nights, Flashes of the Life, Letters, and Work of O. Henry." To flesh out their portrait, the authors erected its structure under four headings entitled Aladdin, Sinbad, Haroun, and Scheherezade: ten chapters arranged under the first two headings deal with the known facts of Porter's youth, marriage, and imprisonment; the remaining 14 chapters under the latter two, primarily with the climactic seven years of his life (1903–10), when they knew him personally as the self-anointed "Caliph of Bagdad on the Hudson." Their book thus teems with intimate glimpses of O. Henry at work and at leisure, enjoying his mounting fame and marketability, driving magazine editors wild with his promises, delays, and evasions, yet also producing saleable short fiction at a fantastic pace and spending his money even faster than he earned it. Magazinists themselves, Davis and Maurice knew Porter better than most of his non-journalist friends, and their respect for both his literary genius and his affable personality is evident in their lavish display of his letters and other illustrative material. These alone add a rich flavor to their carefully written if somewhat casual record of "Haroun in his golden prime."

Shortly after *The Caliph* appeared, another journalist, WILLIAMS, published his equally adulatory work, dedicated "to O. Henry enthusiasts everywhere, in the hope that it will bring the personality of William Sydney Porter closer to them." Its contents, organization, and style amply requite the desire; for within its nine chapters Williams succinctly displays the growth of his admiration from the moment when, as a young cub reporter on the New York *Sunday World*, he first met the affably courteous Mr. Porter at a cheap hostelry in 1903, until their last chance encounter seven years later "in front of Trinity Chapel," just a few weeks before Porter's sad funeral service there on 7 June 1910. With less fanfare than Davis and Maurice, Williams covers in 250 pages much the same ground as they, describing carefully Porter's working habits and living arrangements in Irving Place, as well as their many visits together to neighboring saloons and restaurants, and vividly recalling Porter's endless quest for short story material in their conversations and joint social encounters among other associates and strangers alike. How these ordinary places and people became magically transformed yet recognizably real in his fiction is repeatedly documented, as are Porter's monetary gains and losses, his attitude toward himself and the world, his strangely guarded reticence, and his unfailingly opulent generosity. Williams' closing tribute to his departed friend is prophetic: though he knew not the precise haven of O. Henry's spirit, he wrote, "this I know clean of any doubt: the home folks, where he went, love him."

Williams' panegyric brought to an end the biographical eulogies of O. Henry written by individuals who had known him personally; but as new factual data about him came to light, the task his later biographers faced became more challenging, their approach to it more scholarly. LONG's book, for instance, was the first fully impartial study that attempted to draw palpable relationships between the activities and events in Porter's life and the process whereby these experiences became transmogrified within the pages of O. Henry's extraordinarily popular fiction. Long's study, prepared originally as a doctoral dissertation at the University of Pennsylvania, is well documented and firmly based, not only on a thoughtful consideration of all the works noted above (especially Smith's biography); but also on an array of other supplementary sources published in magazines and journals dating from the early 1900s. Written in a plain, straightforward style, Long's book brought up to date the pertinent facts that were known to have marked the progress of O. Henry's expanding international popularity: its only noticeable deficiency is the author's apparent reluctance to undertake a serious qualitative appraisal of even O. Henry's allegedly "best" short stories.

This weakness, however, was adroitly disposed of a few years later with the publication of LANGFORD's biography. Contending that earlier biographers had failed to probe deeply enough into both the ambiance of Porter's two marriages and the evidence of his embezzlement trial, Langford clearly strove to address these problems by combing through every available source of information. His extensive notes and references indicate that he had made a thorough search of all the pertinent unpublished materials housed in library collections at Greensboro, Austin, The University of Virginia, and Harvard University; they also show that he must have read and pondered every scrap of Porter's writing to be found in print. *Alias O. Henry* thus became the most carefully documented and, on controversial matters, apparently still is the most evenly balanced treatment of Porter's life as a whole. Moreover, although Langford's judgment of Porter's character may be questioned at times, there is no doubt of his respect for Porter's artistry: his analysis of the subtle ways in which Porter's character and personality are often reflected in O. Henry's stories can only be admired.

As part of a memorial celebration on the occasion of Porter's 100th birthday, ARNETT's study appeared in Greensboro, North Carolina on 11 September 1962. Her purpose in writing the book, Arnett announced, had been specifically to depict Porter's youthful surroundings and experiences because they "not only shaped his own character, but also provided him with characters that were to come alive again through the medium of his genius, his short stories." As a prominent, longtime resident of the community, Arnett was well acquainted with a host of surviving relatives and friends of the Porter family, and their letters and reminiscences in personal interviews added substantially to the rich store of O. Henry memorabilia available for her use in the Greensboro Public Library and Historical Museum collections. As a result, her book is liberally supplied with important genealogical data and other illustrative features, although analogies drawn between some of them and the characters and events in O. Henry's individual short stories sometimes appear to be rather tenuous. As a tribute to O. Henry, however, the make-up of this displays a unique charm.

Another work that gives added emphasis to Porter's southern heritage as a predominant influence on both content and style in his fiction is CURRENT-GARCIA's *O. Henry*. The aim here, however, is not merely to identify recognizable southern types and their mannerisms, speech patterns, or other peculiarities in many of O. Henry's stories, though these are abundantly present. Rather, this author is primarily concerned with the technical similarities and relationships between a great many of O. Henry's stories and the popular writings of older southern groups, such as the frontier humorists and local color regionalists. O. Henry's stories, he argues, show that both the ideas in them and the methods of presenting those ideas were largely drawn from the rowdy frontier tales and the more sophisticated local color stories, a subtle process of amalgamating techniques from which an original O. Henry style emerged.

Last among the full-length treatments of Porter's life and works—so far—is O'CONNOR's biography. It is a gracefully written tribute to both the man and the artist, the main focus of which, explains the author, "is on those amazing last eight years, the years of O. Henry." But to show how the artist was formed during so brief a period, he adds, it was "necessary to deal as cogently as possible" with the life of Porter, the man. Acknowledging aid received from the works of each of the earlier biographies listed above, O'Connor fulfills his dual purpose by organizing his material under two headings: "The Will Porter Years," a swift summary covering in three chapters of 86 pages the bulk of Porter's experience to 1901; and "The O. Henry Years," in which the remaining nine chapters of the book leisurely recall the wondrous steps along the road of destiny that transformed Federal Prisoner No. 30664 into the fabulous "biographer of New York." Carefully documented and adorned with many artfully arranged references and illustrations, O'Connor's book is a brilliant biographical tour de force.

—Eugene Current-Garcia

HENRY, Patrick, 1736–1799; American statesman and orator.

Axelrad, Jacob, *Patrick Henry: The Voice of Freedom.* New York, Random House, 1947.

Beeman, Richard R., *Patrick Henry: A Biography.* New York, McGraw-Hill, 1974.

Henry, William Wirt, *Character and Public Career of Patrick Henry.* [n.p.], 1867.

Henry, William Wirt, *Patrick Henry: Life Correspondence, and Speeches* (3 vols.). New York, Scribner, 1891.

Mayer, Henry, *A Son of Thunder: Patrick Henry and the American Republic.* New York, F. Watts, 1986.

Meade, Robert D., *Patrick Henry* (2 vols.). Philadelphia, Lippincott, 1957–69.

Morgan, George, *The True Patrick Henry.* Philadelphia, Lippincott, 1907.

Tyler, Moses C., *Patrick Henry.* Boston, Houghton Mifflin, 1887.

Wirt, William, *Sketches of the Life and Character of Patrick Henry.* Philadelphia, J. Webster, 1817.

*

Within two decades of his death Henry was indelibly memorialized by his first biographer, WIRT, a writer of the Parson Weems school. Wirt's life of Henry went through 25 editions to become one of the most popular 19th-century biographies. Dedicated to "The Young Men Of Virginia" as a textbook on "rhetoric, patriotism, and morals," Wirt's exaggerated romanticism created a "giant genius," larger than life and more noble. As the personification of freedom and frontier democracy, Wirt's Henry is a backwoods "plebian" who humbled the haughty Tidewater aristocrats. "In a voice of thunder and with the look of a god," Henry defied King George and sparked rebellion in Virginia.

Based on memory, tradition, and fond anecdotes, Wirt's biography created the image of Patrick Henry all subsequent biographers have had to reckon with. Because none of Henry's speeches had been preserved, Wirt reconstructed them from hearsay, tradition, and conversations with old men who dimly recalled his words. Subsequent scholars have been challenged to distinguish Wirt's flights of fancy from Henry's stunning oratory.

Another challenge for biographers has been the negative or dark image of Henry that emerged simultaneously with the bright hero. Because of the political and personal animosity that festered between Thomas Jefferson and Patrick Henry, many of Jefferson's 19th-century apostles darkened Henry's image as a demagogue committed to fame and wealth, unworthy to be hailed as a glorious patriot.

TYLER, attempting to correct both the bright and dark images of Henry, produced a very fine narrative account, much more restrained than Wirt's. He also defended Henry against his 19th-century critics who demeaned his oratory, patriotism, and character.

One of the most valuable early biographies was written by Henry's grandson, William Wirt HENRY, in 1867. Later, in three commemorative volumes, containing extensive documentary materials, a few letters, and fragments of speeches, Henry presented a richly detailed version in defence of his grandfather (1891).

MORGAN wrote a solid, well-researched biography, quite readable and comfortably balanced. It remained the most popular biography of Henry, even after the publication of AXELRAD's biography in 1947, though it has since been superseded. Axelrad's volume is a well-written "popular" portrait of Henry as a solitary hero of the Revolution. Unfortunately, it lacks sufficient background information to place Henry in a creditable context of time and place. While the colorful narrative may have held the attention of the general reader, it did not address the need for a judiciously balanced biography based on informed use of manuscripts and published materials that had become available in the half century since the works of Morgan and Tyler.

MEADE's work remains the most detailed 20th-century biography of Patrick Henry. The first of his two-volume study is heavily focused on Henry's early years. Dismissing the myth of the "untaught backwoods genius," Meade details Henry's classical education by his father, a product of Aberdeen University. He also depicts Henry's family as well respected, bound by ties of marriage to the established gentry. Henry's later success as a trial lawyer is attributed to his quick mind, uncanny perception of human nature, and remarkable courtroom eloquence.

Mead's second volume covers the years following Henry's return from the First Continental Congress in 1774 until his death in 1799. Focusing on Henry the Virginia politician and American statesman, Meade produced the definitive biography of the practical patriot, insofar as exhaustive research permits. It remained for others to explain the enigmatic and capture the elusive historical Patrick Henry.

BEEMAN focuses on the local and provincial context of Henry's politics, claiming that "interests, not ideology, and instincts, not reason, tended to be the forces that guided his conduct." Beeman presents a less contradictory figure than others have perceived, less transcendent and more ambitious, politically and socially.

MAYER's volume is the most recent and probably the best biography yet. Reflecting recent historiographical trends, Mayer is concerned to understand Henry's particular ability to articulate the fears and aspirations of his fellow Virginians. Focusing on the impact of evangelism in the colony, Mayers develops a convincing portrait of the gentleman revivalist as political orator. He insists this unique merger of religion and politics accounts for Henry's power as a Revolutionary leader and wartime governor.

Henry's post-war career appears less vivid as the man was forced to address the myth he had become, all the while striving to secure status and fortune for his family. Mayer's treatment of Henry's last great campaign for civil liberties at the Virginia Convention conveys the enduring power of the aging Son of Thunder.

—Mary Jo Bratton

HEPBURN, Katharine, 1909–   ; American actress.

Anderson, Christopher, *Young Kate*. New York, Holt, and London, Macmillan, 1988.

Britton, Andrew, *Katharine Hepburn: The Thirties and After*. Newcastle upon Tyne, Tyneside Cinema, 1984.

Carey, Gary, *Katharine Hepburn: A Biography*. New York, Pocket Books, 1975; updated edition, London, Robson Books, 1983; with subtitle *A Hollywood Yankee*, New York, St. Martin's, 1983.

Edwards, Anne, *A Remarkable Woman: A Biography of Katharine Hepburn*. New York, Morrow, 1985; as *Katherine Hepburn: A Biography*, London, Hodder and Stoughton, 1986.

Higham, Charles, *Kate: The Life of Katharine Hepburn*. New York, Norton, and London, W. H. Allen, 1975.

Kanin, Garson, *Tracy and Hepburn: An Intimate Portrait*. New York, Viking, 1971; London, Angus and Robertson, 1972.

Latham, Caroline, *Katharine Hepburn: Her Film and Stage Career*. London and New York, Proteus Books, 1982.

Latham, Caroline, *Katharine Hepburn*. New York, Chelsea House, 1988.

Morley, Sheridan, *Katharine Hepburn*. Boston, Little Brown, and London, Pavilion, 1984.

*

Much to Hepburn's disapproval, several reasonably good biographies have been written of her. She has always rejected the idea of her personal life being presented in print for all to see. The enthusiast of Katharine Hepburn is best advised to begin with ANDERSON for a thorough picture of her early childhood and young adulthood. Hepburn came from a well-to-do family who were known as a bit radical for their time. This influence is important in understanding Hepburn's later life and career choices. Anderson presents a very in-depth look at her beginnings up to her graduation from Bryn Mawr in June of 1928, and he includes a short "Hepburn Family Chronology" which mentions major family events from 1852 to 1988. The "acknowledgements and sources" section contains a list of many good books and archival sources Anderson researched for this study.

LATHAM's two books can provide essential highlights for the reader seeking quick information. Her 1982 book is about as condensed as a story should ever be allowed for such a complicated subject as Katharine Hepburn. The 1988 book is written more for a young adult audience and is useful in that context. HIGHAM must be read with caution. His 232-page biography lends itself too much to a Hollywood gossip approach in its coverage. It gets downright vulgar at times and should not be considered a scholarly work.

BRITTON's work is a textbook-style companion to film studies that presents a feminist viewpoint of Katharine Hepburn's image and choice of characters on the screen. It can generate some worthwhile questions for the serious student.

Another slant on Hepburn's career is offered by MORLEY, the son of actor Robert Morley ("Brother" in *The African Queen*). He gives a British point of view on Hepburn, and he seems to have done his homework on the subject. Morley quotes from some interesting sources who knew Hepburn intimately. The book is well illustrated with photographs accompanied by quotes from journal and newspaper reviews. It is not a very slick format, but it is an effective publication. The illustrated filmography is a nice touch.

CAREY's final updated biography is a very approachable, though unexceptional, work, presented in a clear and readable style. The book has been well researched and may be read with profit.

The best biography currently available of Katharine Hepburn is without a doubt that by EDWARDS. The information is well documented and believable, and the book contains the best film, theatre, television, and radio chronologies available on Katharine Hepburn. Also included is a list of Hepburn's 12 Academy Award nominations and the competition she faced each time. The list of "Main Repositories for Hepburn Material" is essential for any serious researcher. The notes and bibliography sections verify the academic status of this work.

KANIN, a long-time friend of both Katharine Hepburn and Spencer Tracy, provides insights into both individuals that cannot be found anywhere else. Kanin sacrificed his good standing with Hepburn by telling the truth as he saw it at a time when she was unwilling to accept its publication. The result is an honest approach to the Tracy-Hepburn relationship on and off screen. This book, less scholarly than Edwards', proceeds in no particular chronological order, as though Kanin wrote just as the memories occurred to him. Though it contains no index or bibliography, Kanin's memoir remains a good source, well worth the reading.

—Richard C. Dickey

HERBERT, George, 1593 1633; English poet and clergyman.

Bottrall, Margaret, *George Herbert*. London, J. Murray, 1954.

Charles, Amy M., *A Life of George Herbert*. Ithaca, New York, Cornell University Press, 1977.

Chute, Marchette, *Two Gentle Men: The Lives of George Herbert and Robert Herrick*. New York, Dutton, and London, Secker and Warburg, 1960.

Daniell, John J., *The Life of George Herbert of Bemerton*. London, Society for the Promotion of Christian Knowledge, and New York, E. and J. B. Young, 1893.

Eliot, T. S., *George Herbert*. London, Longman/British Council, 1962.

Hyde, A. G., *George Herbert and His Times*. London, Methuen, and New York, Putnam, 1906.

Stewart, Stanley, *George Herbert*. Boston, Twayne, 1986.

Summers, Joseph H., *George Herbert: His Religion and Art*. London, Chatto and Windus, 1953; Cambridge, Massachusetts, Harvard University Press, 1954.

*

Every modern biographer of Herbert uses Izaak Walton's beautifully written *Life of Mr. George Herbert* (1670; reprinted in *Lives*, London and New York, Oxford University Press, 1927). Yet most caution readers about its inaccuracies and fabrications, its royalist and High Church biases, and its portrait of Herbert as not only saintly but almost naively innocent.

Apart from Walton, several 17th- and 19th-century writers wrote brief sketches of Herbert's life. But except for a small book that does little more than repeat Walton—George L. Duyckinck's *The Life of George Herbert* (1858)—the first full-length biography was that by DANIELL. Though now outdated, Daniell's biography was the first based on extensive research into primary sources. In interpreting his materials, however, Daniell generally follows Walton.

About a decade later, HYDE's readable, plentifully illustrated biography appeared. Besides recounting Herbert's life and discussing his views and character, Hyde describes the period's political and religious controversies and several of Herbert's contemporaries. Hyde follows and is sometimes misled by Walton, quoting him at length and accepting his view that Herbert became a priest after the sudden shattering of his hopes for secular employment. Yet convinced of Herbert's early spirituality, Hyde expresses doubts about the traditional picture of Herbert as an ambitious courtier turned churchman. Often factually unreliable, the book nevertheless offers the beginning student helpful background. Hyde's assessment of Herbert's religious position is judicious and balanced.

Writing half a century later when much new information was available, BOTTRALL still relies on Walton. She uses other sources, too, and acknowledges Walton's imperfections, yet he leads her into some errors and omissions. For instance, she is unaware of Herbert's parliamentary service, and she accepts too easily Walton's story of Herbert's shattered hopes. Parts of the book are marred by Bottrall's strong High Church bias. Only a third of it is strictly biographical; the rest deals with Herbert's writing. Bottrall's greatest strength lies in her penetrating remarks on Herbert's character and attitudes, drawn mostly from his writings.

CHUTE's popularized version of Herbert's life provides a colorful sense of literary and historical context as well as an impression of Herbert's attitudes and personality. Though Chute uses Walton, she is aware of his flaws and rejects his notion that Herbert was held back by ambition from service to God. Yet she makes questionable assertions of her own about Herbert's inner life, exaggerating the "rootlessness" and "anguish" he supposedly suffered. Chute's book is unsuitable for scholarly use because, among other shortcomings, it gives no sources for most quotations. But for the general reader, this is a good short biography.

ELIOT's pamphlet mainly discusses Herbert's poetry and his relation to other "metaphysical poets." But Eliot starts with a ten-page account of Herbert's life, presenting with clarity and grace the facts as they were known when Eliot wrote. Perhaps he follows too closely the traditional view of Herbert's "court hopes," but significantly he argues that Herbert's struggle with spiritual desolation was more important than his struggle with ambition. Eliot's account is especially useful for its discussion of Herbert's poetry and its perceptive comments on Herbert as poet and human being.

Now acknowledged as the definitive life of Herbert, CHARLES' volume is cautious, precise, detailed, and carefully documented, providing closely reasoned arguments for revising the dating of some letters, Herbert's writing of his poems, and other events. Charles uses Walton sparingly and skeptically, omitting most of his anecdotes and correcting many of his errors. She makes a special point of overturning his myth of the dashing of Herbert's court hopes by showing that Herbert had applied for ordination as a deacon (and probably been ordained) well before these hopes were supposedly dashed. This biography presents plain factual information, firmly grounded in documents, and makes little attempt to depict Herbert's personality or historical context. For this reason, and because it is addressed to scholars familiar with Herbert, the general reader may find it tedious or confusing. But anyone wanting an accurate account of Herbert's life will find the book indispensable.

In addition to the full-length biographies, three accounts forming part of longer studies are worth looking at. F. E. Hutchinson's introduction to *The Works of George Herbert* (Oxford, Clarendon Press, 1941) includes discussions of Herbert's life, influence, and reputation. Though Charles has since refined our knowledge of details, Hutchinson's account presents the basic facts clearly, succinctly, and (almost always) reliably, including—beginning with the 1945 reprint—information on Herbert's parliamentary service. Hutchinson is sensible and discerning in assessing Herbert's character, and though he sees Herbert as having been temporarily distracted by ambition, he does not overemphasize this view.

Perhaps still the best introduction to Herbert's poetry is SUMMERS' influential book, which includes chapters on Herbert's life, reputation, and religious attitudes. The book, devoted largely to discussing Herbert's poetic theory and practice, argues that Herbert's artistic achievement is closely related to his religious thought and experience. Summers was one of the first to depart markedly from Walton, especially on Herbert's involvement in public affairs and entry into the ministry. Though now superseded in matters of detail, Summers' account of Herbert's life and thought is still required reading for Herbert scholars.

A more recent study, by STEWART, benefits from newly available biographical information and from the rethinking of Herbert's literary and religious affinities. Stewart's very brief (four-page), lucid account of Herbert's life is followed by a longer discussion of changing images of Herbert. Other chapters discuss Herbert's religious attitudes, poetry, and relation to the Little Gidding community and to other poets. Disagreeing with recent studies, Stewart presses—sometimes too hard—his view that Herbert was neither Puritan (or even particularly Protestant) nor Roman Catholic in his sympathies, but a faithful follower of the Church of England with High Church tendencies. Stewart's book, though an important contribution, should be supplemented by other studies.

—Bruce W. Young

HERZL, Theodor, 1860–1904; Austrian writer and Zionist leader.

Bein, Alex, *Theodor Herzl: A Biography*, translated by Maurice Samuel. Philadelphia, Jewish Publication Society, 1940 (originally published by Fiba, Vienna, 1934).

De Haas, Jacob, *Theodor Herzl: A Biographical Study* (2 vols.). Chicago and New York, Leonard, 1927.

Elon, Amos, *Herzl*. New York, Holt Rinehart, 1975; London, Weidenfeld and Nicolson, 1976.

Pawel, Ernst, *The Labyrinth of Exile: A Life of Theodor Herzl*. New York, Farrar Straus, 1989; London, Collins-Harvill, 1990.

*

To Jacob DE HAAS belongs the distinction of being the author of the first major biography of Herzl, certainly the first in English, several shorter studies in German, Hebrew, Yiddish, and French having preceded his work. He was the only biographer who had close personal contact with Herzl throughout his Zionist period. (In fact, when Herzl met the young British journalist and activist in London in 1896, he appointed him as his "honorary secretary.") The relatively uncritical de Haas, who later moved to New York and Boston, credits his subject with "the stature of Kossuth and Garibaldi . . . the moral suasion of Lincoln, the political imagination of Mazzini, and the glamour of Disraeli." In his leisurely exploitation of Herzl's quest for a Jewish homeland, de Haas quotes copiously from Herzl's *Diaries* (then newly published), letters, and other documents as well as presenting his own notes, rare photos, facsimiles, and maps. He has little to say about Herzl's pre-Zionist period and seems uninterested in Herzl's private life and, with the possible exception of the play *The New Ghetto* (1955) and the utopian novel *Oldnewland* (1941), his literary production. With its old-fashioned style, misspellings, and other slips, de Haas' exceptionally handsome volumes contain a somewhat unkempt text, but his moving eyewitness account of Herzl's last days as well as his sensitive final chapter, "The Man and His Fame," together with valuable appendices, have made his work an important reference to this day.

Since its first publication in German (Vienna, 1934) BEIN's magisterial study has been the standard biography of the father of political Zionism. It is a remarkable achievement for a 30-year-old author preparing his own emigration to Palestine, and its appearance in the early Nazi period undoubtedly made a substantial contribution to the self-awareness and courage of German Jews facing a grave identity crisis. This reverent but not hagiographic, balanced, and accurate biography is copiously illustrated with photos and facsimiles. In his prefatory note to the 1962 paperback edition, Bein says that it was his intention to "create [a] clear and objective picture . . . of Theodor Herzl the man, the writer, and the creator of the modern Zionist movement, covering his development, his ideas, and his effective influence." In all this the author has brilliantly succeeded, and his book has never been superseded.

Writing from the perspective of a quarter-century of Israeli statehood, ELON, a Viennese-born journalist living in Tel Aviv, surveys the triumphs and tragedies of Herzl's career from the vantage point of Mount Herzl in Jerusalem, where the leader has lain buried since 1949. Elon gives a lucid exposition of Herzl's childhood and youth (a more detailed and more satisfying treatment of which may be found in Andrew Handler's *Dori: The Life and Times of Theodor Herzl in Budapest, 1860–1878*, University of Alabama Press, 1983), his studies in Vienna, his legal apprenticeship there and in Salzburg, his years as a budding playwright, essayist, and storyteller, his work for the *Neue Freie Presse*, and his gradual evolution of political Zionism from the trauma of the Dreyfus affair and other, more personal experiences that transformed the assimilated Jew and effete litterateur into a wide-ranging *Realpolitiker* and a charismatic if autocratic leader. Displaying a becoming sense of the political, cultural, and social milieu in which Herzl was raised, Elon describes *fin de siècle* Vienna as a place where "many cultural currents of great vigor and originality were fused into a baroque synthesis. . . . The same city, the same decaying crucible of passion and hope, love and hatred . . . produced a Herzl as well as a Hitler—the antidote before the poison." Elon's atmospheric, vividly written book is marred somewhat by a number of stylistic infelicities and factual errors.

The German-born critic and novelist Ernst PAWEL has successfully attempted to present Herzl in his full complexity. His unsparing, sometimes overly speculative exploration of Herzl's psyche and his occasional touches of condescension make his work come closer to a demythologization and debunking than to a hagiographic portrayal. Yet even stripped of heroics and sentimentality, Herzl emerges as "the first Jewish leader in modern times" and "thus far the only one," for his successors have been only politicians. The dedication of Pawel's book, "To the Spiritual Heirs of Ahad Ha-Am," indicates that his sympathies lie with the likes of the Eastern European Jewish thinker who called for a Hebrew-based cultural and spiritual Zionism in principled opposition to Herzl's eminently political, Germanic orientation. Pawel devotes almost a third of his richly detailed, well-illustrated book to Herzl's pre-Zionist period and gives a sensitive, evocative picture of the society and culture of his time and place. Highlighting the self-destructive impulses that often underlie heroic endeavors, he concentrates on Herzl's naive egocentricity, his excessive attachment to his parents, and his singularly unhappy marriage, which adversely affected his wife and his children even after his death. Pawel quotes copiously from

Herzl's writings, principally the *Diaries*, but he rejects Herzl as a playwright and novelist, praising only the feuilletonist. Some egregious statements and carelessness about facts do not seriously affect the value of this exhaustively researched and absorbingly written biography.

—Harry Zohn

HESSE, Hermann, 1877–1962; German writer.

Boulby, Mark, *Hermann Hesse: His Mind and Art.* Ithaca, New York, Cornell University Press, 1967.

Field, G. W., *Hermann Hesse.* New York, Twayne, 1970.

Freedman, Ralph, *Hermann Hesse: Pilgrim of Crisis: A Biography.* New York, Pantheon, 1978; London, Cape, 1979.

Mileck, Joseph, *Hermann Hesse and His Critics.* Chapel Hill, University of North Carolina Press, 1958.

Mileck, Joseph, *Hermann Hesse, Life and Art.* Berkeley, University of California Press, 1978.

Rose, Ernst, *Faith from the Abyss: Hermann Hesse's Way from Romanticism to Modernity.* New York, New York University Press, 1965; London, P. Owen, 1966.

Sorell, Walter, *Hermann Hesse: The Man Who Sought and Found Himself.* London, Wolff, 1974.

Stelzig, Eugene L., *Hermann Hesse's Fictions of the Self: Autobiography and the Confessional Imagination.* Princeton, New Jersey, Princeton University Press, 1978.

Zeller, Bernhard, *Hermann Hesse: An Illustrated Biography,* translated by Mark Hollebone. London, P. Owen, 1972 (originally published by Suhrkamp, Frankfurt am Main, 1960).

Ziolkowski, Theodore, *The Novels of Hermann Hesse.* Princeton, New Jersey, Princeton University Press, 1965.

*

Although MILECK's first book (1958), issued on the occasion of Hesse's 80th birthday, is not strictly a biography and shows signs of dating, it is still a useful publication for students of Hesse. The first section is biographical, particularly important because of Hesse's unpopularity during both world wars, but it perhaps exaggerates the diminution of public interest in his deeply pessimistic outlook on western culture, to be emphasized again in Mileck's later biography. The second section of *Hesse and His Critics* contains critical reactions in articles, pamphlets, and books to Hesse's work, and the third is a classified bibliography of work by and about Hesse. Quotations are not translated, but for the specialist the book is still indispensable.

In his biography proper (1978), Mileck stresses the universality of Hesse's view of life, "transfigured, fantasized, poeticized, dramatized, and symbolized," and Hesse's hurt and fury at his mother's disapproval of the three volumes published before her death. Mileck emphasises the influence, not of Jung, with whom Hesse was on friendly terms, but of Freud, which is important because the works yield "substantially different interpretations" (Stelzig) according to the psychological school by reference to which they are to be considered, and because Jung claimed Hesse, perhaps exaggeratedly, as a disciple. Mileck's probably accurate contention that the conception of *Glasperlenspiel* (*Magister Ludi*) dates from 1927 is valuable because, if that were so, the novel would have to be interpreted more clearly in the light of Hesse's renewed interest in Goethe than has been generally supposed.

FREEDMAN's biography of the same year was not helped by its wholesale dismissal in a review by Peter Gay (*New York Times Book Review*, 21 January 1979), which regarded Hesse as "a fanatical scribbler" who wrote "autobiography practically undisguised," contrasting Hesse unfavourably, but on the whole reasonably, with Proust. Freedman points to the importance for Hesse of his mother's repressed personality in the wake of her father's cruelly wilful destruction of her youthful love for John Barns and to Hesse's excessive dependence on his most recent reading and personal experience for his early fiction. Hesse's ambivalent attitude to World War I is explained as both pacifist and patriotic at the same time, and Freedman brings out well Hesse's post-war relationship to expressionism.

Freedman also emphasizes more than Mileck the importance for Hesse of Jung, and regards *Kurgast* (*A Guest at the Spa*) as the funniest and most penetrating of the fictional and semi-fictional autobiographies. According to Freedman *Steppenwolf*, "the symbolic city," was written a year earlier than normally assumed, in February 1926, while the events recounted in the plot were actually occurring. On *Glasperlenspiel* Freedman is among the harshest of Hesse's critics of the "arid, intellectual style." He regards the characters of what most biographers and critics regard as Hesse's greatest achievement simply as "puppets." The interpretation of the personal history of Hesse and of the books differs therefore considerably, notably between Mileck and Freedman.

The dustcover of ZELLER's pictorial biography is strictly correct in referring to "the first biography" only if it is referred to the original German. As an "illustrated biography" it does not rate very highly, as the pictures are few and poor. This is for the non-specialist, with the poems translated, and there is the occasional grammatical error in a German title. It is a good, short, introductory biography, with a chronology, subsequently surpassed, but which served its purpose reasonably well.

Three books that are not strictly biographies should be mentioned. ZIOLKOWSKI's book on the novels is rich in biographical material, the first full-length study in English. All quotations are in English, and this is probably still the best book on the novels available in English. ROSE's book again devotes most of its space to a critical account of the novels, but is again sufficiently rich in biographical introductory and background material, informatively and concisely presented, to warrant attention in the present context. It is still probably the best brief all-around introduction to Hesse the novelist. BOULBY's excellent monograph on the novels, on which all subsequent biographers will be obliged to draw, is itself however concerned exclusively with critical analysis.

The quickest access to biographical material is provided by FIELD. The first three chapters are almost totally biographical, and there is the usual (for volumes in the Twayne series) chronology, together with notes, bibliography, and index. The work of Mileck, Ziolkowski, and Boulby is explicitly acknowledged, and no acquaintanceship with German is presupposed. The standard German biography, by Hugo Ball, is on the other hand rightly criticized. Hesse himself emerges with his strong links to

the 18th century emphasized, and as the romantic whose rebellion mellowed. The spiritual relationship with Thomas Mann, who put *Steppenwolf* on a par with the best of Gide and Joyce, is well brought out, as is the pessimism about Western democracy and the continued acceptance of the liberal value system on which it is founded.

SORELL's short introductory book is really a plea for a particular interpretation of the fictional works as they appealed to the youth of the 1960s on account of their detached, meditative characteristics. This is an introductory book for students, but very one-sided in its interpretations of the life and works, and with significant errors, as in the date of Hesse's Nobel Prize.

STELZIG's book is precisely about the relationship of autobiography and fiction. It therefore contains a great deal of biographical material, notably pointing to the simultaneous condemnations of Hesse during World War II for opposite and incompatible reasons by sympathizers with and opponents of Nazi Germany. Stelzig offers particularly perceptive insights into Hesse's mind as he analyses the degree, nature, and direction of the fictionalizing process that was operated by Hesse's imagination on his own personal history. The biographical background is in a sense a bonus in a study of literary creation, but it is accurate, perceptive, and fascinating, and for readers seriously interested in Hesse, his life, and the interpretation of his texts, Stelzig offers more than do the best surveys available. He also goes some way to resolving the conflicting accounts in 1978 by Mileck and Freedman.

—A. H. T. Levi

HITCHCOCK, (Sir) Alfred, 1899–1980; English film director; became United States citizen, 1955.

Deutelbaum, Marshall and Leland Poague, editors, *A Hitchcock Reader*. Ames, Iowa State University Press, 1986.

Durgnat, Raymond, *The Strange Case of Alfred Hitchcock; or, The Plain Man's Hitchcock*. Cambridge, Massachusetts, MIT Press, and London, Faber, 1974.

LaValley, Albert J., editor, *Focus on Hitchcock*. Englewood Cliffs, New Jersey, Prentice-Hall, 1972.

Leff, Leonard J., *Hitchcock and Selznick: The Rich and Strange Collaboration of Alfred Hitchcock and David O. Selznick in Hollywood*. New York, Weidenfeld and Nicolson, 1987; London, Weidenfeld and Nicolson, 1988.

Modleski, Tania, *The Women Who Knew Too Much: Hitchcock and His Feminist Theory*. New York and London, Methuen, 1988.

Phillips, Gene D., *Alfred Hitchcock*. Boston, Twayne, 1984.

Rohmer, Eric and Claude Chabrol, *Hitchcock: The First Forty-Four Films*, translated by Stanley Hochman. New York, Ungar, 1979.

Rothman, William, *Hitchcock: The Murderous Gaze*. Cambridge, Massachusetts, Harvard University Press, 1982.

Ryall, Tom, *Alfred Hitchcock and the British Cinema*. Urbana, University of Illinois Press, and London, Croom Helm, 1986.

Simone, Sam P., *Hitchcock as Activist: Politics and the War Films*. Ann Arbor, Michigan, UMI Research Press, 1985.

Spoto, Donald, *The Art of Alfred Hitchcock: Fifty Years of His Motion Pictures*. New York, Hopkinson and Blake, 1976; London, W.H. Allen, 1977.

Spoto, Donald, *The Dark Side of Genius: The Life of Alfred Hitchcock*. Boston, Little Brown, and London, Collins, 1983.

Taylor, John Russell, *Hitch: The Life and Times of Alfred Hitchcock*. New York, Pantheon, and London, Faber, 1978.

Truffaut, François and Helen G. Scott, *Hitchcock*. New York, Simon and Schuster, 1967; London, Secker and Warburg, 1968.

Weis, Elisabeth, *The Silent Scream: Alfred Hitchcock's Sound Track*. East Brunswick, New Jersey, Farleigh Dickinson University Press, 1982.

Yacowar, Maurice, *Hitchcock's British Films*. Hamden, Connecticut, Archon Books, 1977.

*

Most of the studies published about Alfred Hitchcock contain some combination of biographic material and film criticism. Of the few "pure" biographies, the two best are by Spoto and Taylor. SPOTO's 1983 volume is the more controversial of the two. In 1976, Spoto had written what many critics feel is the best critical study of Hitchcock's films: *The Art of Alfred Hitchcock*. This study is a type of tribute to Hitchcock, and Spoto thinly veils his admiration for the famous director. Though it provides some information about Hitchcock's life, it concentrates on analyzing in depth the films from *The 39 Steps* (1935) to *Family Plot* (1976). What makes Spoto's subsequent biography unusual is that, instead of paying tribute as in his earlier effort, Spoto viciously attacks his subject, allowing gossip and innuendo to enter into his writing. Spoto revels in telling anecdotes that illustrate Hitchcock's meanness. He tells how Hitchcock smashed bulbs on his film set to startle people, how he would humiliate actors and actresses (including one incident when Hitchcock slipped a prop man a powerful laxative and then chained him overnight to a camera housed in a deserted studio), how Hitchcock abused his wife and daughter and flirted with his various actresses. Spoto's work descends to the level of tabloid magazines and would perhaps appeal most to cinematic gossipmongers.

However, Spoto is not without value, especially his analysis of the cultural, cinematic, and literary influences on Hitchcock. His discussion of the effect German cinema had on Hitchcock is thoughtful. Spoto's detailing of Hitchcock's early life and first endeavors into the British film industry, and his perceptive analysis of that industry, are sound and revealing. The petty rivalries between Hitchcock and senior British directors, the backwardness of British moviemaking when compared to the American scene, the steady rise in prestige and influence as the public recognized in Hitchcock great talent, the politics of producing movies: all these Spoto examines with skill.

Despite the valuable reviewing of Hitchcock's early efforts at filmmaking, the balance of Spoto's book seems hurried, less thoughtful, more biased, and crudely opinionated. The result is a Dr. Jekyll and Mr. Hyde effort, where one must take the bad with the good.

TAYLOR is the standard review of Hitchcock's life. Less partial than Spoto in his treatment of Hitchcock, Taylor provides a wealth of detailed information about the director without being gossipy. He treats his subject more fairly than does Spoto without sacrificing a complex analysis of Hitchcock's personal character and the relationship of that character to the director's cinematic worldview.

Taylor divides his study into two sections, the first dealing with Hitchcock's film career in Great Britain, the second with his work in America. Taylor also provides an informative, analytical introduction and epilogue, the latter stating in five pages what it takes Spoto to say in 500. The serious student of Hitchcock's life should begin with Taylor.

Several books about Hitchcock deal with specific periods of his life. For example, RYALL examines Hitchcock's years with the British cinema, providing chapters on British film culture, British movies during the 1930s, Hitchcock's role as a thriller genre director, and his broader relationship with the British film industry. Ryall's approach is from the top down, and he provides a superior cultural context in which to review Hitchcock's early films. YACOWAR, also focusing on Hitchcock's British film period, is less concerned with cultural context and attends more to a critical discussion of the director's work.

Another exploration of a specific period of Hitchcock's life in the cinema is the volume by ROHMER AND CHABROL, which concentrates on the British and American studios and producers responsible for the Hitchcock films from 1923 through 1957. Their work, while informative, is somewhat difficult to read at times, though perhaps the stylistic lapses are the fault of the translation.

LEFF looks at the relationship between Hitchcock and the famous independent American producer, David O. Selznick, who was responsible for bringing Hitchcock to Hollywood. Leff meticulously recounts the business and social relationships between these two cinematic giants. Of particular interest are Leff's superior chapter-length discussions of the making of the films *Spellbound* (1945), *Notorious* (1946), and *The Paradine Case* (1947).

SIMONE emphasizes Hitchcock's movies produced during the director's World War II period. Though he offers some background information about Hitchcock's life and work from 1899-1939, Simone focuses mainly on four films, *Foreign Correspondent* (1940), *Saboteur* (1942), *Lifeboat* (1943), and *Notorious* (1946), each title supplying a chapter heading. Simone seeks to analyze the relationship between the war years and Hitchcock's political ideology, and he contends that these four selected films are propaganda that attack fascism and promote democracy. Though Simone's is an academic study, his style is unobtrusive, and his findings are soundly researched and provoking.

The balance of the works about Hitchcock tends to be a hodgepodge blend of biography and critical analysis. The best of these are Truffaut and Scott, Durgnat, and Rothman. TRUFFAUT's AND SCOTT's work is a book-length interview with Hitchcock. Its value is that Hitchcock provides his *own* views about the background of his career in movies, and the director is guided with his extensive discussion by another great director, Truffaut, who is sympathetic to film being perceived as a personal, artistic statement. DURGNAT has a biographical introduction, but the author spends most of his time in a critical review of Hitchcock's films. ROTHMAN takes an important theme in Hitchcock's work, the use and function of vision, and develops an extensive analysis. The problem with Rothman is his lack of biographical support for his thesis and his overt selectivity of Hitchcock films to prove his point.

The weakest of the Hitchcock studies are by WEIS and Modleski. Weis discusses the relationship between Hitchcock's movies and their use of music. Her views lean toward the obvious, though she does give the reader a good deal of background information about Hitchcock's movies. MODLESKI, an example of how *not* to bias one's subject by pounding it into an artifical mold, establishes a feminist approach to Hitchcock and his films that flourishes in conceit and fallacy.

Both LaVALLEY and PHILLIPS offer typical "study guide" fare, balancing their books between the director's life and his work. DEUTELBAUM AND POAGUE provide a collection of essays by various film critics. A number of these essays touch on Hitchcock's life, each with varying degrees of effectiveness.

—Gary Hoppenstand

HITLER, Adolf, 1889–1945; German dictator, founder and leader of National Socialism.

Bullock, Alan, *Hitler, a Study in Tyranny.* New York, Harper, and London, Odhams, 1952; revised edition, 1964.

Fest, Joachim, *Hitler.* New York, Harcourt, and London, Weidenfeld and Nicolson, 1974.

Flood, Charles B., *Hitler: The Path to Power.* Boston, Houghton Mifflin, 1989.

Heiden, Konrad, *Hitler: A Biography,* translated by W. Ray. London, Constable, and New York, Knopf, 1936; as *Der Fuehrer: Hitler's Rise to Power,* translated by Ralph Manheim, Boston, Houghton Mifflin, and London, Gollancz, 1944.

Maser, Werner, *Hitler: Legend, Myth, and Reality,* translated by P. and B. Ross. New York, Harper, and London, A. Lane, 1973 (originally published as *Adolf Hitler: Legende, Mythos, Wirklichkeit,* Munich, Bechthe, 1971).

Payne, Robert, *The Life and Death of Adolf Hitler.* New York, Praeger, and London Cape, 1973.

Stone, Norman, *Hitler.* Boston, Little Brown, and London, Hodder and Stoughton, 1980.

Toland, John, *Adolf Hitler.* New York, Doubleday, 1976.

Trevor-Roper, Hugh, *The Last Days of Hitler.* New York and London, Macmillan, 1947.

Waite, Robert L., *The Psychopathic God, Adolf Hitler.* New York, Basic Books, 1971

*

The first important biography of Hitler, published originally in 1936 and now often available in reprint, was that of HEIDEN, a democratic socialist and bitter political opponent of the Nazi leader. Heiden fled Germany for America, later claiming to have been "the oldest, or one of the oldest, anti-Nazis in the United States." His work, part biography and to some extent history of National Socialism, takes Hitler's story from his youth through the vicissitudes of the 1920s and the "Seizure of Power" in 1933 down through the Blood Purge of 1934. His narrative draws heavily on his own personal recollections and those of his friends. Despite his bitter tone and at times scathing indictments, Heiden's work is still much respected for insights into Hitler's early life and in fact, as eminent an historian as Fest (see below) has occasion to quote him a number of times. Heiden's digressions, such as that on the *Protocols of Zion*, are worth the reader's patience. One only wishes that Heiden could have completed his work.

BULLOCK's biography, appearing first in 1952 and subsequently updated and available in abridged form, remained unchallenged for two decades as the definitive work and still ranks as one of the two best. Though Bullock denies having any particular axe to grind in interpretation, his subtitle, *A Study in Tyranny*, represents his theme and outlook. Those who are interested in Hitler's early life in more than a cursory manner had better look elsewhere, for Bullock, not believing that such an inquiry has much to contribute to our understanding, focuses on Hitler the dictator. In fact, his treatment of the period beginning 1934 emphasizes foreign policy moves and the war itself. Actually, since his work was revised to include documents made available after the first edition, Bullock's work can be read as an excellent account of the road to war and of World War II in Europe.

FEST's work is just as highly esteemed among professional historians. Equally comprehensive, equally monumental, Fest's book differs from Bullock's in that about half of it focuses on the period before Hitler came to power. It thus is able to tell us much about the mood of pre-World War I Vienna, where Hitler spent several years. In fact, what one discovers as particularly noteworthy in Fest's work is his combining of biography with analysis of *Zeitgeist* in several short interpretive essays or "interpolations," which are strategically placed throughout the book. In one of these, perhaps better than a non-German might be able to do, Fest sees a flight from reality in the post-war malaise that nourished the Hitler movement; in another he looks at Hitler's place in history as 1933 began; in another he reflects on his fateful decision for war in 1939; and in a final section he presents a retrospective look at all that Hitlerism meant. Thus, Fest's is not a book for one who wishes really to delve into diplomatic or military history. Rather, it is for the serious reader who wants more to think about than is afforded by say, William L. Shirer's immensely popular history of the Third Reich, *The Rise and Fall of The Third Reich* (1960).

The best popular biography remains the long and vivid narrative by TOLAND who, though not a professional historian, brings the discerning eye of the journalist to his subject. Particularly noteworthy is that his story is enriched by over 200 personal interviews with adjutants and associates of Hitler as well as by the use of some unpublished material. Lacking the biting acerbity of a Bullock or Trevor-Roper, Toland is a more dispassionate, if indeed a neutral observer of phenomena. His portrayal of the vagaries and complexities of Hitler's personality begins with the young Hitler in Vienna as seen through the eyes of his friend Kubizek and ends with the bunker days with the awful and dreadfully mediocre entourage who were present at his *Götterdämmerung*.

Another popular biography is that of PAYNE, who curiously enough also wrote lives of Gandhi and Lenin. His is an engaging and vigorous narrative, and with the war years the view is strictly from Hitler's command post, with the most exciting episode being the Generals' Assassination Plot of 1944. Because it is less carefully researched than the Toland work—there is no documentation, no citation of sources—the reader has cause to beware. A case in point is the repetition of the absurd story, gathered from a spurious source (according to Waite), of a supposed visit by Hitler to Liverpool in 1912. Though Toland makes a fleeting reference to this in his book, Payne devotes an entire short chapter to it.

Another book for the general reader, but with a definite revisionist slant, is STONE's short and quite readable biography. Stone explores such questions as how little Hitler spent on an arms buildup, and of how he had not planned on war with the West—matters either of degree or of half-truth. Earlier on, when he maintains the Reichstag Fire (1933) was very likely accidental and offers little or no proof, the revisionism seems quite out of control. Overall, Stone's book does not add to our knowledge of Hitler in any significant way.

Two books, one by Maser and the other by Waite, while not biographies in the ordinary sense, do provide valuable insights into aspects of Hitler the man. MASER, the distinguished German historian, presents a thematic approach as he examines topics such as Hitler as artist and architect, as soldier for the Reich, etc. Particularly striking is the chapter on family antecedents. Maser suggests that this genealogical problem, which intensely bothered Hitler lest a non-Aryan ancestor be turned up, is not one that exhaustive research has been able to resolve conclusively once and for all. A major theme of the book is that the deterioration in Hitler's physical and mental health from about 1941 seriously affected the conduct of the war. Another section analyzes Hitler as strategist and warlord and shows the Nazi leader's inadequacies as supreme commander and the dilemmas of a General Staff who were not trusted by him. Two unusual appendices are of general interest: one showing the sketchy notes for one of his speeches revealing among other things his hysterical anti-Semitic fulminations; the other being a schedule of daily events and appointments presumably during war time.

The other work, by WAITE, is a study of Hitler's psychopathology. Events and behavioral patterns in Hitler's life are subsumed into long chapters such as "Images and the Man" and "Intellectual World." Where historical evidence is lacking, Waite feels, we can possibly gain a clue as to Hitler's actions through psychology and psychiatry, that is, psychohistory. The result is as fascinating as it is repellent. Topics such as the possibilities of sexual perversion and primal scene trauma are discussed along with broader manifestations such as the urge to destroy and the playing out of private fantasies into becoming public policy. Waite's thesis is that Hitler was a borderline personality between neurotic and psychotic, with serious mental problems but with the ability to function, often brilliantly, in day-to-day situations. Many historians are highly critical of such a psychohistorical approach and question the evidence for this extrapolation of private neurosis into public policy.

By way of contrast TREVOR-ROPER's study narrowly focuses on the last months of Hitler's life in the fantasy world of his bunker. Trevor-Roper was originally assigned by British Intelligence to investigate the circumstances of Hitler's death. Though his findings have been updated in a newer edition, the author sees no reason to change his original conclusion in what started out as a detective story investigation. His style is acerbic yet his peppery judgments in the main have not been challenged. Trevor-Roper's subject emerges as the prime illustration of Lord Action's aphorism that absolute power corrupts absolutely.

FLOOD's recently published work does not attempt to break new ground historically. Rather it is a deft and skillful re-working and re-telling of four years of Hitler's life and work, from the agony and trauma of defeat in 1919 through to the debacle of the Beer Hall Putsch in 1923 and Hitler's imprisonment at the Landsberg fortress. It is a long and detailed book but one that the general reader will find fascinating and compelling. The character portraits of Hitler's associates are particularly vivid and informative. Hitler's organizational abilities and his demogogic skills come through again and again. If there is any particular theme to the book, it is that for many Germans, Hitler represented a spirit of the times, a bundle of frustrations and resentments against the Treaty of Versailles, the allied occupation, and the democratic Weimar system—frustrations for which Hitler found a scapegoat in the Jews. Flood alludes to a conversation in which Hitler, with utmost cynicism, announced that "a battle against the Jews would be as popular as it would be successful." Here a note of balance and caution is needed. Because Flood obviously focuses on Hitler and his circle, one would assume from his book that all of Germany in the 1920s was awash with a virulent and obsessive anti-Semitism, when in fact recent research has shown that anti-Semitism was not a significant factor in Nazi electoral successes. The culmination of Flood's work is a gripping account of the Beer Hall Putsch, often hour by hour, a story of interplay of personalities, of happenstance and might have been. It is the best re-telling of this crucial episode since the appearance of Gordon's monograph on the subject a number of years ago. The book ends with Hitler paroled from prison acknowledging the putsch to have been a grave mistake.

—Robert A. Ryan

HOBBES, Thomas, 1588–1679; English philosopher.

Hinnant, Charles H., *Thomas Hobbes*. Boston, Twayne, 1977.

Mintz, Samuel I., *The Hunting of Leviathan: 17th-Century Reactions to the Materialism and Moral Philosophy of Thomas Hobbes*. Cambridge, Cambridge University Press, 1962.

Reik, Miriam M., *The Golden Lands of Thomas Hobbes*. Detroit, Michigan, Wayne State University Press, 1977.

Robertson, George Croom, *Hobbes*. Edinburgh and London, Blackwood, and Philadelphia, Lippincott, 1886.

Rogow, Arnold A., *Thomas Hobbes: Radical in the Service of Reaction*. New York, Norton, 1986.

*

In his recent biography, Rogow (see below) exaggerates only slightly when he complains that students of Hobbes have done without a full-length biography for the four centuries since the philosopher's birth. Certainly Robertson's 1886 study qualifies as full-length biography, old-fashioned and excessively appreciative though it may be. But Rogow's observation is, nonetheless, at least partly valid: scholars such as Robertson and Leo Strauss (*The Political Philosophy of Hobbes, Its Basis and Genesis*, 1937) have preferred to grapple with Hobbes' philosophical systems than to sort through the meager details of his life. Miriam Reik (see below) emphasizes the difficulty facing someone attempting to exclude treatment of Hobbes' philosophy from a biographical account: "he never *did* much in the active sense: he never went to war, sent ships to the New World, or became Lord Chancellor. He mainly seemed to write and think, read and talk, play tennis and music." Further, we know very little about the first 40 years of his life—the "dark years" before he became a public figure. Naturally, then, his biographers have conceived of Hobbes' life primarily in terms of his intellectual development—the origins of his "mechanical philosophy," his drive toward systematizing his philosophical, scientific, and political analyses.

ROBERTSON certainly deserves credit for shaping the jumble of biographical data transmitted by John Aubrey in his sketchy *Brief Lives* (1813), and for making extensive use of the Hobbes manuscripts at Hardwick. Expanding on his appreciative survey in the *Encyclopedia Britannica* (9th edition, 1881), Robertson argues that the origins of Hobbes' thought can be traced, not from his "mechanical philosophy," but from his early observations of "men and manners." Because of the coincidence of Hobbes' birth with the defeat of the Spanish Armada, Robertson's book set the pattern for virtually every subsequent biography by beginning with an elaborate discussion of the emergence of late 16th-century politics and the Elizabethan roots of Hobbesian thought. For Robertson, the philosopher becomes a sort of heroic force, providing a unifying vision at a time of ecclesiastical conflict, the decline of philosophy, and the decay of discipline at Oxford.

The question that unifies REIK's approach to Hobbes is, "How did the early humanist scholar become, in a seemingly abrupt manner, the author of *Leviathan* and the philosopher whose method is modelled on rigorous scientific thinking?" Reik provides fascinating contextual material on Elizabethan humanist education and conceives of the Hobbes emerging from this background as intellectually driven toward the development of systematic political, scientific, and moral analysis. She imagines his personality to be a mixture of crude dogmatism and amiable companionship. Her "intellectual biography" resists strict chronology and, instead, concentrates for the most part on Hobbes' career—his approaches to humanism, science, moral philosophy, politics, and poetics.

The Twayne *Hobbes* is one of the better representatives of a series that has often produced work that is formulaic and lacking in detail and originality. HINNANT, who has also compiled the useful *Thomas Hobbes: A Reference Guide* (Boston, G. K. Hall, 1980), evaluates the relationship among Hobbes' treatises, their audiences, and their author's career. Like most others who have attempted such a study, Hinnant quickly departs from the business of biographical narrative: only his first chapter is devoted strictly to the facts of Hobbes' life. The subsequent chapters concern themselves more centrally with the philosopher's political theories, his ethics, and his scientific views.

ROGOW's study is a reasonably successful attempt to fuse Hobbesian thought and its historical and biographical contexts. Like Robertson, Rogow makes productive use of Aubrey's sketch and also of Hobbes' own autobiographical account written

in Latin verse. Rogow's detailed and highly readable account suggests a Hobbes who was "timid, fearful, competitive, and inordinately ambitious" and who projected those attributes onto the human condition generally. In addition to providing a valuable discussion of the history of Hobbes' reputation, Rogow puts forth an imaginative and convincing argument for the importance of Hobbes' reading of Euclid in the development of his science of politics.

At a crucial point, however, Rogow's work disappoints: an all-too-brief treatment of the reception of *Leviathan* is interrupted by long bibliographic descriptions of the early editions of the book—material perhaps better suited for an appendix. For an excellent treatment of reactions to *Leviathan*, especially of the critiques of the Cambridge Platonists, students would do well to turn to MINTZ, whose primary focus is not biographical, but who nonetheless provides insight into the relationship between Hobbes and his peers.

In the absence of an accepted standard biography, Rogow's study, supplemented by Reik's and Robertson's, must serve. But the ideal life of Hobbes, conforming to current standards of documentation and specificity and synthesizing more than three centuries of critical reaction, remains an obvious desideratum.

—Richard C. Taylor

HOGARTH, William, 1697–1764; English painter and engraver.

Dobson, Austin, *Hogarth*. New York, Scribner, 1879; revised and enlarged edition, as *William Hogarth,* London, Heinemann, 1907.

Jarrett, Derek, *The Ingenious Mr. Hogarth*. London, M. Joseph, 1976.

Lindsay, Jack, *Hogarth: His Art and His World*. London, Hart-Davis MacGibbon, 1977; New York, Taplinger, 1979.

Nichols, John, *Biographical Anecdotes of William Hogarth*. London, J. Nichols, 1781; 3rd edition, enlarged and corrected, London, J. Nichols, 1785.

Paulson, Ronald, *Hogarth: His Life, Art, and Times* (2 vols.). New Haven, Connecticut, and London, Yale University Press, 1971.

Quennell, Peter, *Hogarth's Progress*. London, Collins, and New York, Viking, 1955.

*

Biographies of Hogart begin with the *Biographical Anecdotes* compiled by NICHOLS (with help from George Steevens and Isaac Reed) from the recollections and information supplied by many different friends and acquaintances of the artist. This book, first published in 1781, was greatly expanded through three editions and is the source of many of the most famous stories about Hogarth. Though this personal information is often fascinating and even indispensable, much of it is also unverifiable. Moreover, as a collection of anecdotes, the book lacks coherence and contains only modest insight into Hogarth the man. It tends to highlight the combative, cantankerous side of

Hogarth's personality, which upset Mrs. Hogarth who was still alive when it was first published. Nevertheless, it contains some essential primary information about the artist, along with the first catalogue of Hogarth's prints and paintings. Despite its general unreliability, therefore, it remains an important point of departure. Nichols' later brief biogaphical essay for the *Genuine Works* (vol. 1, 1808) is based on this material as well as on Hogarth's own autobiographical notes that appeared for the first time in John Ireland's *Hogarth Illustrated* (vol. 3, 1798). Since Ireland rewrote Hogarth's rough notes, the reader interested in the artist's own words can consult them in Joseph Burke's edition of *The Analysis of Beauty* (Oxford, 1955), where they appear unrevised.

The best 19th-century biography is by DOBSON. His book, first appearing in 1879, grew through several editions with the final, and most complete one, coming in 1907. Dobson wove together the known facts of the artist's life into a cogent, dependable account that generally excludes the gossip and questionable assertions of the earlier books. He is sympathetic toward Hogarth as an artist and a man, treating him as a "moralist" who is "unrelenting, uncompromising, [and] uncompassionate," but not savage or self-righteous. Dobson, nonetheless, does not idealize Hogarth, but constructs a balanced portrait, recognizing the artist's weaknesses as well as his strengths. Hogarth was, according to Dobson, "a sturdy, outspoken, honest, obstinate, pugnacious little man who—one is glad to believe—once pummelled a fellow soundly for maltreating the beautiful Drummeress who figures in *Southwark Fair*." As a good Victorian, Dobson slides over some of the more scabrous details in Hogarth's prints as he describes them. The illustrations themselves are limited in number and of rather poor quality, but the book contains an extensive bibliography and a revised and updated catalogue of the works, which has of course since been superseded.

QUENNELL's lively biography recreates much of Hogarth's milieu, especially the London of his time, and describes some of the historical and literary figures of the age. Hogarth is still the center of attention, but Quennell spends a good deal of time detailing the artist's environment, showing how he responded to its poverty, violence, filth, bustling activity, and occasional joys and beauty. His vignettes of various personalities of the time, such as Sir Christopher Wren, John Gay, and David Garrick, supplement and enrich the account of Hogarth's life and give a fuller sense of the artist's world. Quennell's book is rather short on illustrations (only 25 in all, including the endpapers), but they are much improved qualitatively over previous studies. In sum, Quennell paints a vivid picture of Hogarth in this time. This popular biography is still an excellent one for someone who knows little about the period and wants a sound introduction to the life of an artist in 18th-century London.

For a scholarly and detailed account of Hogarth, PAULSON's two-volume set is a magisterial work, the standard life for our time. Paulson has returned to the archives to augment the existing knowledge about the artist from contemporary sources, such as newspapers, letters, and manuscripts, and although he has not radically revised our view of the man, he has fleshed out the portrait in many small but not insignificant ways. Furthermore, Paulson's extensive knowledge of the literature of the time enables him to interpret Hogarth's work with greater literary sophistication than previous biographers.

Paulson takes a leisurely pace as he details Hogarth's struggle from humble origins in London to his eventual position as one of the most respected and admired artists in England. He describes how the artist's character traits that were often considered unattractive, such as his combativeness, were in fact essential to his success. He shows Hogarth variously responding to contemporaries and events, and sometimes translating these reactions into art. For the most part, Paulson shies away from using Freudian or other modern psychological approaches to the artist, remaining sympathetic throughout without losing objectivity or engaging in undue speculation. The many illustrations are a pleasure to examine and come in the text at the appropriate moment when they are under discussion. Though long, Paulson's work is highly readable and successfully integrates Hogarth's life, artistic development, and times into a superb critical biography.

For less detailed biographies that take advantage of Paulson's learning, one can turn to either the JARRETT or LINDSAY books. Both provide solid, informative studies of Hogarth and his career, though neither is as spirited as Quennell. Jarrett stresses Hogarth's use of traditional images, symbols, and emblems in contrast to the usual emphasis on his realism. Lindsay focuses on Hogarth's theory of art as expounded in his *Analysis of Beauty* and applies it to his artistic development. Lindsay also believes that Hogarth helped bring about a new, more critical role for art in English society, without eliminating the celebratory function it had traditionally served. Both Jarrett and Lindsay cover the main events in Hogarth's life, though they are somewhat more abstract and less colorful than Quennell.

—Nicolas H. Nelson

HÖLDERLIN, Friedrich, 1770–1843; German poet.

Constantine, David, *Hölderlin*. Oxford, Clarendon Press, and New York, Oxford University Press, 1988.
Shelton, Roy C., *The Young Hölderlin*. Bern and Frankfurt am Main, H. Lang, 1973.
Stansfield, Agnes, *Hölderlin*. Manchester, Manchester University Press, 1944.
Unger, Richard, *Friedrich Hölderlin*. Boston, Twayne, 1984.

*

The paucity of English-language biographies of Hölderlin is striking, especially in comparison with the number of German-language biographies published in recent years. Donna Hoffmeister reflects this situation by covering only German-language biographies in her otherwise excellent essay: "Hölderlin-Biography, 1924–1982: Transformations of a Literary Life." Hoffmeister neatly sums up the common view in the breadth of studies to be found in the genre: "The compelling consensus in all Hölderlin biographies is that he was simply incomparable."

CONSTANTINE's work has the advantage of being the most up-to-date and comprehensive of all the biographies available in English. A reviewer (*Choice*, February 1989) puts it succinctly: "Although Constantine does not bring to light any significant new data on Hölderlin's life, he has mastered the enormous previous scholarship on the famed and unfortunate writer.'' Constantine not only provides us with detailed biographical information, he also interprets Hölderlin's poems against the background of the poet's life and the prevailing social, cultural, and philosophical climate of his time. Although Constantine makes extensive use of German quotes in his text, there is a translation provided at the back of the book. If the scholar or student were to consult only one biography of Hölderlin, this should be it.

SHELTON's attempt to provide an antidote to the prevalent hagiographic tendency amongst Germans concerning Hölderlin soon degenerates into a highly subjective over-emphasis of his subject's feet of clay. The text is replete with statements such as: ''Already he seems to have been developing an exaggerated respect for learned men''; ''Even now we can see that important elements needed for normal development were missing''; and ''A normal boy would not have reviewed the tragedy of his life merely because his tooth hurt.'' In spite of Shelton's apparent inability to grasp the fact that an artist, and more importantly a great poet, can be both highly creative *and* ''normal'' (Shelton never defines what he considers to be ''normal''), his biography contains useful facts about Hölderlin's life through 1795, that is before the poet met and loved Susette Gontard, whose later death many biographers believe to be the most important event in Hölderlin's life. For readers willing to pick their way through a veritable minefield of speculation and subjective commentary, Shelton's facts are nonetheless accurate.

UNGER refers to Shelton's ''stimulating, if unsympathetic, psychological study of the poet's youth'' in his own useful study of Hölderlin. Although Unger's work is not exclusively biographical, his introductory chapter on Hölderlin's life is factually accurate, based as it is on an eclectic summary of available German-language biographies. Unger avoids Shelton's tendentiousness by accepting the *opinio communis* on Hölderlin's genius and madness.

STANSFIELD's study from 1944 is, like Unger's, not exclusively biographical, although she does follow Hölderlin's life chronologically, with excursions into critical interpretations of the poet's works. Stansfield occasionally lapses into personal comment (such as her reference to Hölderlin's love for his mother as being ''abnormal''), and her book contains inaccuracies and several typographical errors; but this book can be consulted if an overview of Hölderlin's life and major works is all that is required. Considering when Stansfield's work was published and that many Nazis had attempted to co-opt Hölderlin as the quintessential Germanic poet, the study is admirably free of polemic.

—Colin R. Hall

HOLIDAY, Billie [*born* Eleanora Fagan], 1915–1959; American jazz singer.

Chilton, John, *Billie's Blues*. London, Quartet Books, and New York, Stein and Day, 1975.

James, Burnett, *Billie Holiday*. New York, Hippocrene Books, and Tunbridge Wells, Spellmount, 1984.
White, John, *Billie Holiday: Her Life and Times*. Tunbridge Wells, Spellmount, and New York, Universal Books, 1987.

*

Billie Holiday's admirers can count themselves fortunate indeed that her unique voice survives not only in recordings but in the exhilarating and unreliable memoir *Lady Sings the Blues* (1956), prepared with the help of *New York Times* journalist William Dufty during a brief positive phase of Holiday's last few years. As Burnett James says in his otherwise unremarkable study of Holiday's life (see below), ''It tells us, beyond all the critical commentaries and appreciations, . . . beyond the nuance of biography, what Billie Holiday felt and thought about Billie Holiday. That is its real value—and as such it is both absorbing and irreplaceable.'' The book remains the starting point to any appreciation of Billie Holiday's life, a mythical basis on which to hang the raw data of biographical research.

CHILTON's volume rarely deviates from the version of events given by the subject in her own book, except where he can definitely prove that Holiday's memory was at fault. That this should be the case is something of a tribute to her honesty, because *Billie's Blues* is exhaustively researched and in no way seeks to be an apology for Holiday's life. A musician himself, with an encyclopedic knowledge of jazz and a critical respect for Holiday's musical work, Chilton succeeds in making his biography definitive. The professional side of the singer's life is stressed, the personal aspects taking their colour from interviews with other musicians and musical associates. A second section explores more fully her work on record, with detailed and fascinating accounts of how the Billie Holiday we hear today came to be preserved, an often haphazard procedure. That Chilton wants to concentrate on the professional Lady Day is his greatest asset; the autobiography conveys more about her personal self than any amount of acquaintances' recollections. But his approach leads to some odd omissions, not least of which is his virtual silence on the subject of her early life in Baltimore and her relations there. This is the most sensationally described part of the autobiography, and Chilton may have felt that, given the difficulty of researching this part of her life, the story in *Lady Sings the Blues* should be allowed to stand. At one point he practically confesses the enormous difficulties of verifying facts when the only sources would be long-buried.

Of the later biographies, little is added to the picture conveyed in the books already discussed, though WHITE's *Billie Holiday* makes valuable use of a BBC TV documentary *The Long Night of Lady Day* (1972). This programme explored the declining years of her life and included interviews with many of her friends and acquaintances. White, though, chooses to take a larger, more sociological perspective on this individual life. This approach leads him to preface each chapter—dealing at length with her childhood in Baltimore and her early career in Harlem—with a broad survey of American life and politics. He is surely right in pursuing this approach to emphasize the importance of racial discrimination: Holiday was always alert to instances of racism and repeatedly refers to them in her memoir. Some readers may well feel that White is short-changing his subject as a unique personality and performing artist, or that he is using her as a pretext in order to explore issues with which he is better qualified.

JAMES falls between the stools of personal appreciation and biographical sketch, achieving neither. Self-regarding, derivative, and incoherent, his book offers little in either new information or new insight. Non sequiturs abound, such as the detailed account of the life of the musician Chuck Webb, which ends with the revelation that "the careers of Billie Holiday and Chuck Webb did not cross at any significant point." His discussion of Holiday's tragic drug addiction degenerates to simple bathos, and the incoherent structure of the biography makes it difficult to follow.

—Alan Murphy

———————

HOLMES, Oliver Wendell, Jr., 1841–1935; American legal scholar, jurist, United States Supreme Court justice.

Aichele, Gary J., *Oliver Wendell Holmes, Jr.: Soldier, Scholar, Judge.* Boston, Twayne, 1989.
Bent, Silas, *Justice Oliver Wendell Holmes: A Biography.* New York, Garden City Publishing, 1932.
Bowen, Catherine Drinker, *Yankee From Olympus: Justice Holmes and His Family.* Boston, Little Brown, 1944; London, Benn, 1949.
Frankfurter, Felix, *Mr. Justice Holmes and the Supreme Court.* Cambridge, Massachusetts, Belknap Press, 1961.
Howe, Mark D., *Justice Oliver Wendell Holmes* (2 vols.). Cambridge, Massachusetts, Belknap Press, 1957–63.
Meyer, Edith Patterson, *That Remarkable Man: Justice Oliver Wendell Holmes.* Boston, Little Brown, 1967.
Novick, Sheldon M., *Honorable Justice: The Life of Oliver Wendell Holmes.* Boston, Little Brown, 1989.

*

The first biography of Holmes, written by BENT, a journalist, appeared in 1932, the year the justice resigned from the court and three years before his death. Holmes refused to cooperate with the author, forcing Bent to draw his material from published materials. Now dated but very readable, Elizabeth Shepley Sergeant's 1927 sketch of a "Yankee, Strayed from Olympus," published in *Fire Under the Andes* probably influenced Bent, as it did later writers. In that article Sergeant created a view of Holmes that has long endured, that of the independent minded Yankee. Not uncritical of the justice, Bent nevertheless romanticized his portrait, creating a "genteel" New Englander who "freed himself from the group loyalties and prejudices and passions which are a heritage" of that class and, marked by the Civil War, created a faith in duty, the "faith of a soldier." On Bent's canvas Holmes the aristocrat became the democrat; "Never was an aristocrat less class-conscious." That theme proved to be a well turned one for the 1930s, for a few months after Bent's biography appeared, Franklin Roosevelt won the presidential election and launched what many saw as an economic battle of another aristocrat against his own class.

Capturing another theme of the 1930s, Bent painted Holmes as a liberal, citing Holmes' tolerance and open-mindedness, his wisdom (which Bent estimated to be "wider than the market place, deeper than any oil well"), and his determination to be "fair-minded" and keep "aggressively abreast" of his times. But Bent warned that his subject was no "professional liberal" or reformer. These individuals always seem to become "notoriously illiberal at certain points of the compass. . . . " Bent, of course, did not discern such traits in Holmes. The value of Bent's study today is in helping us understand the evolution of opinions about Holmes.

FRANKFURTER in 1938 published his Harvard lectures on Holmes, adding later a sketch written for the *Dictionary of American Biographies*. Drawing from unpublished materials, his personal relationship with Holmes, as well as his position as professor of law at Harvard, Frankfurter is able to give his volume a particular authenticity. Contributing significantly to the efforts by members of the Harvard Law School faculty (for example, Zechariah Chafee, Jr. and his writings on free speech) to build the Holmes myth, Frankfurter reenforced the theme of Holmes as liberal. Later, after his own appointment to the Supreme Court, Frankfurter described Holmes as "the most liberty-alert" justice of all times. Prepared for the layman as well as the legal scholar, Frankfurter's small volume gives an assessment of Holmes widely accepted in the late 1930s.

BOWEN's readable and fast-moving volume came in the midst of an intense struggle among scholars about the meaning of Holmes and his ideas. If the 1930s witnessed his deification, the early 1940s observed a period of Holmes-bashing. Engaged with England and the Allied Powers in a struggle to defend the ideals of Western civilization against Nazism, some scholars in the United States became uncomfortable with the Holmes legacy. In particular, scholars of the natural law attacked Holmes for his relativism, his willingness to accept the will of the majority, and his reliance on force as the ultimate arbiter of disputes. During the world war struggle and the Cold War that replaced it, many believed that justice and law must be joined and that law must be based on a sense of morality. If not, "Hobbes, Holmes, and Hitler," as one writer phrased it, the totalitarian doctrine that might makes right, would erode the very foundation of law in the West.

Insisting that her work was a "narrative, not a discussion," Bowen elevated herself above the heated controversy about the meaning and significance of Holmes and his ideas. She announced that his greatness lay in "his manner of meeting life" and his "genius for living," for "using himself wholly." Her goal was to create a "picture and a translation," to bring the justice "out of legal terms into human terms." To accomplish that end, she concedes that she "often embellished" quotes "deliberately and with purpose." Authenticity was not achieved, she argued, by simply relying on "names and dates"; and when it seemed "necessary to engage the reader's attention," Bowen "invented" the settings for conversations, although she insisted her inventions were a part of the reality. Bowen also warned readers about her sources. Though she consulted the available published materials, she relied on material that "came from people, not books." The currently acceptable descriptions for her sources would be "oral history." Such sources have proven to be invaluable for historians and biographers, but they must be used prudently and always with great caution. A reviewer in the

1940s characterized her volume as an "intimate, loving portrait" of Holmes. More recently it was dismissed as a "fictionalized" account of Holmes and his family.

Bowen kept alive the myth of Holmes the aristocrat as democrat. Her efforts materialized in a Hollywood film, *The Magnificent Yankee*, a 1950 Metro-Goldwyn-Mayer production. During that decade the movement, as one writer phrased it, to "elevate Mr. Justice Holmes from deity to mortality" developed significant momentum.

If Bent, Frankfurter, and Bowen had tried to make Holmes an example, an authority, a guide for the present, HOWE, a professor at the Harvard Law School, sought to establish the justice as an historical figure. Selected as the authorized biographer, Howe wrote an "essay in intellectual history." Probably reacting to much of the literature published about Holmes, Howe felt a greater "responsibility to truth . . . than to romance. . . . " He also viewed preparation of three collections of Holmes' correspondence as "partial fulfillment of my responsibility as biographer": *The Holmes-Pollock Letters* (1941), the Civil War diary and letters, *Touched with Fire* (1947), and the *Holmes-Laski Letters* (1953). Howe's volumes go a long way toward replacing the mythological with the historical Holmes. The man that emerges from these pages is less the liberal of the New Deal era and more the philosophical positivist who had a naive faith that science could ultimately resolve all problems. The Holmes of Howe's creation is a man who could rather easily fall prey to the trap presented by *Buck v. Bell* (1927), when Holmes upheld a Virginia eugenics law providing for the sterilization of persons determined feeble minded.

Limiting her research to secondary works and published correspondence and addresses, MEYER produced a rapidly moving study aimed at the juvenile audience. Besides incorporating unverified stories, although they lend color to her work, Meyer writes from what might be described as the Parson Mason L. Weems' school of history. Holmes always expressed "classic examples of noble thinking, nobly expressed in beautiful, flowing prose," and as a judge he exhibited "detached, impartial, tolerant" characteristics. The virtues of Holmes are magnified, the limitations swept aside, even though his critics do receive some space.

AICHELE's brief biography, 166 pages of text, is the first serious study giving full sweep to the Justice's life to appear in almost 50 years. Aichele's book is highly readable and fast paced, and his scholarship gives the study a tone and feel of reality. The reader gains not only a feel for the man but an estimate of his significance for America and the evolution of law as we move to the end of the century. Aichele achieves that result by consulting unpublished sources and drawing upon the wealth of research conducted by others, not unverified oral histories. Although he includes an excellent essay on sources, his citations, possibly limited by the overall dictates of brevity, are so restricted that the work can be completed without full exposure to the vigorous debate that has swirled about Holmes in legal journals and historical reviews. Even though the study is flawed by inadequate proofing, it is, nonetheless, a good second choice for readers.

NOVICK's study also appeared in 1989 and will likely become the standard biography for lay readers and scholars. The text is more than double that of Aichele's and the notes and bibliography add another 100 pages of valuable material. Drawing from published and unpublished materials, Novick's biography is rich in detail. Novick even attempts to address Holmes' ambitions and motivations, often ignored by others. The result is a readable and illuminating account of both the public and private Holmes, and the biography makes Novick the logical heir to Howe as the leading Holmes scholar.

—Fred D. Ragan

HOOVER, Herbert, 1874–1964; American political leader, 31st president of the United States.

Burner, David, *Herbert Hoover: A Public Life*. New York, Knopf, 1979.

Fausold, Martin L., *The Presidency of Herbert C. Hoover*. Lawrence, University of Kansas Press, 1985.

Hoff-Wilson, Joan, *Herbert Hoover: Forgotten Progressive*. Boston, Little Brown, 1975.

Lyons, Eugene, *Our Unknown Ex-President: A Portrait of Herbert Hoover*. New York, Doubleday, 1948; as *Herbert Hoover: A Biography*, Doubleday, 1964.

Nash, George N., *The Life of Herbert Hoover* (2 vols.; 3 vols. projected). New York, Norton, 1983, 1988.

Smith, Gene, *The Shattered Dream: Herbert Hoover and the Great Depression*. New York, Morrow, 1970.

Warren, Harris G., *Herbert Hoover and the Great Depression*. New York, Oxford University Press, 1959.

Wilson, Carol G., *Herbert Hoover: A Challenge for Today*. New York, Evans Publishing, 1968.

*

LYONS offers an account of Hoover's entire career and depicts Hoover as principled, kindly, and loyal, betrayed by a fickle public. Lyons' book is unfootnoted but extensively researched. He claims Hoover had a happy childhood, became the most prominent student in the inaugural class at Stanford, and married happily. He attributes Hoover's rise as a mining engineer to astuteness, hard work, meticulous attention to detail, and an ability to inspire confidence.

Lyons details Hoover's humanitarian undertakings, and he calls Secretary of Commerce Hoover the most effective at that position in history. He also asserts that Hoover was an effective leader and that his policies were partly successful, attributing the myth of Hoover's failure to poor public relations. Lyons' Hoover is shy, prefers work to publicity, and seldom takes credit for his own accomplishments. He rejects stereotypes that Hoover was callous, cold, and humorless.

Lyons devotes the final third of the book to Hoover's post-presidential career, describing Hoover's work for Truman and Eisenhower. This is one of the best-written books on Hoover, and its chapters on his childhood and his final years are particularly strong. An unabashed defense of Hoover, it eloquently describes his virtues.

FAUSOLD provides the most detailed account of Hoover's presidential policies. Hoover's childhood and personality are discussed briefly, with emphasis on the Quaker religion as a shaper of his views. He characterizes Hoover as an aggressive entrepreneur in business, though ineffective with the press and the public, inflexible, pessimistic, and insufficiently pragmatic. Nonetheless, Fausold's systematic account of Hoover's policies indicates activism.

Fausold views Hoover as a corporatist who balanced government, capital, and labor and firmly believed in states' rights. The chapter on foreign policy credits Hoover with instigating the Good Neighbor Policy and praises the Stimson Doctrine. Fausold feels that Hoover's approach to the Depression was plausible, and concludes that Hoover failed as a president because he was unwilling to experiment. Fausold does not include an account of Hoover's career after 1933 but ends by examining evaluations of Hoover by his contemporaries. Heavily footnoted, the book contains an extensive annotated bibliography.

BURNER considers Hoover's personality flawed, his policies constructive. Summarizing Hoover's childhood and education briefly and emphasizing his Quakerism, he implies that Hoover's early life was less happy than Hoover claimed. A substantial section of the book covers Hoover's career as a mining engineer and humanitarian. Burner devotes chapters to Belgian relief, the Food Administration, the feeding of Europe after World War I, the presidential campaign of 1920, Hoover's tenure as secretary of commerce, and the 1928 campaign. About one-third of the book is devoted to Hoover's presidency and one chapter to his post-presidential career.

Burner views Hoover as an efficiency expert who applied engineering techniques to politics and believed that "the world is resoluable into harmonies," seeking to reconcile labor, capital, and government. No Darwinian individualist, he was a rationalizer of individual initiatives for the common good but had an unrealistic faith in the ability of technology to solve human problems.

Burner provides new information about Hoover as secretary of commerce. He sees Hoover as a benevolent expert, paternalistic despite his faith in individuality. He dispels the myth that President Hoover was incompetent, arguing that Hoover's accomplishments prior to the stock market crash were substantial and that in ordinary times he would have been a reform president.

The study is based on exhaustive research in primary sources. It includes a bibliography of manuscripts (but not of secondary sources) along with extensive footnotes. General readers will find the style dry; scholars will appreciate the emphasis on facts. Hoover is difficult to enliven, and while Burner does not succeed in this, he effectively places him in a historical context.

HOFF-WILSON views Hoover as a progressive out of his element as president. Her thesis is that progressive values shaped Hoover's public service, but that progressivism was conservative in many respects. She traces Hoover's upbringing, the influence on him of Quakerism, the frontier, and the values of rural America. From Quakerism Hoover took a "sense of the harmony and unity of voluntary community cooperation" that he never shed. He expected too much of voluntarism in the crisis of the Great Depression. Hoff-Wilson devotes chapters to Hoover's engineering career, his humanitarianism, his tenure as secretary of commerce, presidential domestic policies, and foreign policy. She

characterizes President Hoover as a "desperate ideologue," compassionate but inflexible. She devotes three chapters to Hoover's life after the presidency, though she includes little about Hoover's private life or personality unless it illuminates his policies. A cross between a popular and scholarly biography, this study will be most useful to college students.

SMITH is entertaining and succinct. One-third of his book is devoted to the campaign of 1932, the march of the Bonus Army, the contrast between Franklin Roosevelt and Hoover, and their conflict during the interregnum. Smith has an eye for picturesque detail and a talent for description, but he attempts no in-depth analysis of Hoover's Depression policies and provides nothing on foreign affairs. Hoover's pre-presidential and post-presidential career are described cursorily, and his upbringing and education are summarized in a few pages. Smith empathizes with Hoover and probes his personality. He concludes that Hoover's failures are attributable to poor oratory, shyness, and an inability to dramatize his actions. This is popular biography, based on secondary and a few primary sources, of most interest to a general audience.

NASH's multi-volume biography of Hoover (two volumes of a projected three have been published) promises to be definitive, based on massive primary research. Nash covers Hoover's childhood, education, mining career, and humanitarian undertakings in greater detail than any other study. Principally narrative, it presents an authoritative analysis of Hoover before his political career. Nash relates details and accounts not widely known. Volume one describes Hoover's orphan upbringing, education at Stanford, and mining career. Nash praises his subject's engineering ability.

Volume two describes Hoover's incredible labors to feed Belgium during World War I. Nash demonstrates that Hoover overcame formidable obstacles in the world's greatest relief effort up until that time. This is a comprehensive study, impeccably documented, but the massive detail and scholarly prose will diminish its appeal among general readers.

WARREN provides a detailed analysis of Hoover's Depression policies. He feels that Hoover has been unfairly maligned for the Depression, but he does not deny Hoover's flaws. Warren depicts Hoover as conscientious and dedicated, claiming that his policies were rational under the circumstances. He rejects the notion that Hoover was cold, reclusive, or cynical, and he finds the ideas for many New Deal programs in Hoover's administration, concluding that Hoover was "the greatest Republican of his generation."

WILSON's biography is highly favorable, based largely on extensive interviews with Hoover's friends. A popular work, it emphasizes Hoover's private life and humanitarian career more than his presidency. The book includes entertaining anecdotes and personal details unavailable elsewhere. Wilson views Hoover as a man "who dedicated all that he was and possessed to his fellowmen and to his ideals for America." Admirers of Hoover will enjoy Wilson, but scholars and students will prefer a more analytical approach.

—Glen Jeansonne

HOPKINS, Gerard Manley, 1844–1889; English poet.

Kitchen, Paddy, *Gerard Manley Hopkins*. London, Hamilton, 1978; New York, Atheneum, 1979.

Lahey, G.F., *Gerard Manley Hopkins*. London, Oxford University Press, 1930.

Mackenzie, Norman H., *Hopkins*. Edinburgh and London, Oliver and Boyd, 1942.

Pick, John, *Gerard Manley Hopkins, Priest and Poet*. London and New York, Oxford University Press, 1942.

Ruggles, Eleanor, *Gerard Manley Hopkins: A Life*. New York, Norton, 1944; London, Bodley Head, 1947.

Thomas, Alfred, *Hopkins the Jesuit: The Years of Training*. London and New York, Oxford University Press, 1969.

*

Since Hopkins was unusually articulate in self-expression and self-description, and since he lived almost the whole of his life in well-defined communities with little privacy, controversy among his biographers has generally turned on certain well-defined cruces of interpretation. These have been the influence of family and early friendships, his conversion to Catholicism, and the relation between his two vocations as priest and poet.

LAHEY stressed especially Hopkins' cultivated family background and the multiplicity of his talents. He might, for instance, have become a distinguished painter. He shows his development at Balliol from the early, theologically minimizing influence of Jowett to Tractarianism and then to Catholicism. He enters a strong plea for Bridges, who seems to Lahey to have been unfairly criticized both as friend and editor. Lahey sees the crucial year 1866 as a contest for allegiance between the High Church Liddon and the Catholic Newman, concluding in the inevitable victory of the latter. An interesting point in his account of Hopkins' life as a Jesuit is the power of his influence, unsuspected by himself, on older friends, particularly Patmore. Two or three words impelled Patmore to burn a poem, a consequence of his criticism Hopkins had not dreamed of and would have regretted. In his account of the late Dublin period Lahey stresses some of the fortuitous causes of depression, his English nationalism, which made him hostile to Irish nationalism, and his unnecessarily severe distress about marking examinations.

PICK's book, stressing the harmonious mingling of the two vocations as priest and poet, is conceived in part as an answer to the suggestions of Protestant and agnostic critics that Hopkins' Jesuit vocation rendered the productions of his literary genius incomplete. In his account of the early Oxford period, Pick stresses the influence on Hopkins of Addis and Pater. He sees the Ignatian exercises as formative not only of spiritual but also of poetic life. Scotus, on the other hand, he sees rather as a writer who confirmed what was already present, at least potentially, in Hopkins' youthful mind. Pick takes issue with Bridges' phrase "the naked encounter between sensuality and asceticism," and, quoting the example of St. Francis of Assisi, rather sees asceticism as a necessary preparation for an intense perception of beauty. He stresses the influence of place and the stark contrast between the beauty of Wales and the dreariness of Liverpool. With the support in a brief preface of the eminent Jesuit Fr. D'Arcy, Pick rejects the interpretation of the miseries from which the "terrible sonnets" emerged as a classic instance of

the Dark Night of the Soul as described by St John of the Cross. He endorses D'Arcy's friendly criticism that Hopkins was scrupulous, overstrained, and too unwilling to accept innocent enjoyments.

RUGGLES' relatively slight work, with few scholarly pretensions, stresses the later influence of Hopkins' school life and his rebellious attitude toward his headmaster. Ruggles' book contains too much vaguely articulated background material, probably drawn from secondary sources.

For MACKENZIE, Hopkins was more thoroughly a priest than a poet. He thinks that Hopkins' asceticism might have become dangerously extreme if not restrained by Jesuit obedience and the good sense of the community. He thinks intimate inner reasons for not writing poetry during the unproductive years were more important than any external discipline or vocational scruples. Mackenzie's judgments are psychologically shrewd; and where they are speculative, they are always worth serious consideration. More than other writers Mackenzie attempts to penetrate beyond Hopkins' own writings and the reminiscences of others to a deeper interpretation.

THOMAS offers a more specialized study of the pattern of Hopkins' life as a Jesuit, with extensive details of the routine he followed and valuable accounts of the lives and personalities of colleagues and superiors. He makes good use of new material in the form of a newly-discovered journal written by Hopkins between 1868 and 1875. In an interesting appendix, Thomas is able to quote from an account written by Hopkins' father of missionary effort in Hawaii, which presents the Catholic missionaries in a much more favourable light than the Protestant. The nature of Hopkins' relation to the order and its discipline has been a point of controversy among Jesuits themselves, as well as elsewhere. Thomas takes a favourable view, dissenting from Fr. Devlin's summary: "He was wounded three times, firstly as a scholar, secondly as a preacher, and thirdly as a writer." This is a useful book, though with a narrower field and less ambitious aim than other lives.

KITCHEN seems to have violated a promise, or at least an understanding, in printing material he was shown in confidence. He is acute in his analysis of Hopkins' devotional life and of the central place within it of the Eucharist. In other matters Kitchen has a tendency to over-interpret comparatively trivial data, especially in relation to Hopkins' supposed "sexual ambivalence." He places great stress on Hopkins' early friendship with Bridges and sees his conversion as a kind of inevitable "divine elopement," thus underrating the strongly logical quality of Hopkins' trained intellect.

—A.O.J. Cockshut

HORACE [Quintus Horatius Flaccus], 65 B.C.–8 B.C.; Roman poet and satirist.

D'Alton, John F., *Horace and His Age*. London and New York, Longman, 1917.

Frank, Tenny, *Catullus and Horace: Two Poets in Their Environment*. Oxford, Blackwell, and New York, Holt, 1928.

Noyes, Alfred, *Portrait of Horace*. London, Sheed and Ward, 1947.

Sedgwick, H.D., *Horace: A Biography*. Cambridge, Massachusetts, Harvard University Press, 1947.
Wilkinson, L.P., *Horace and His Lyric Poetry*. Cambridge, Cambridge University Press, 1945.

*

The main problem facing the biographer of Horace is the lack of reliable sources about him. For an accurate picture of the world in which he lived we can turn to contemporary historical documents. But for an account of the life and personality of Horace himself, we have only Horace's own poetry, which includes much self-reference, and the first-century *Life of Horace* by Suetonius, not an author reputed for his reliability. Therefore, in order to assess the sources well, the biographer of Horace must also be to some degree a literary critic.

A major weakness in the biographies by D'Alton and Sedgwick lies in their failure to appreciate this point. Of the two, D'ALTON's is the less successful as a biography. It claims to study Horace in the light of the influences of his own day, but instead it is more a study of the Augustan age with reference to Horace. D'Alton offers no criticism or even quotation of Horace's poetry. He rashly supposes Horace to be a typical product of his age and dangerously uses Horace's poetry as a sincere testimony to the poet's beliefs and attitudes and consequently to those of the Augustan era. Even as a study of Horace in his world, D'Alton's work is disappointing, because he fails to draw any conclusions about Horace's relationship to the world around him.

SEDGWICK makes little use of modern scholarship and draws chiefly on 19th- and early 20th-century sources, including D'Alton. It is, by his own admission, not a book for scholars. But it is enthusiastic, lucid, and very readable. Quotations are usually (but not always) given in Latin, but where this is the case they are always translated into English as well. Perhaps one of the most attractive features of the biography is that it is inspired by a genuine love of Horace, which while making the book often too uncritical, at least makes it attractive to read. Sedgwick draws on Horace's poetry with naive credulity, giving descriptions that are both vivid and audacious, such as his recurrent picture of Horace reclining under the palm tree sacred to Diana on his Sabine farm. (The question, however, of whether Horace actually owned the farm has long ceased to interest scholars.) Sedgwick's attention to detail is assiduous and often amusing. The list of wines that appear in the works of Horace, complete with notes on their cultivation and taste, is a generous inclusion, but one that has little relevance in a study of Horace. Although Sedgwick gives vivid accounts of contemporary historical events, he, like D'Alton, does not attempt to discuss Horace's relationship to the world around him.

NOYES' work was published in the same year as Sedgwick's, and suffers largely from the same failings. Like Sedgwick, Noyes indulges in imaginative reconstructions of possible scenes in Horace's life, which, though delightful, make no pretence to historical accuracy. Most of this kind of writing, however, is confined to the first chapter. Noyes makes bold and frequent use of comparisons between Horace's poetry and parallel passages in later English poets, and between the events in Horace's life and events in more recent history. His only source appears to be the poetry of Horace, from which he freely draws inferences,

thereby falling into the biographer's trap of trying to reconstruct a poet's life from self-reference in the poet's works. Noyes serves better as an introduction to and commentary on the poems than as a true biography.

FRANK's work, treating both Catullus and Horace, is intelligently written and more scholarly than the three works cited so far. Frank acknowledges the problem of using poetry as his source and frequently hesitates to assume that Horace actually held the opinions he claims to have held. Frank's attitude toward Horace is less emotional than Sedgwick's, and he is not afraid to criticise. Perhaps his most important contribution is to assess Horace within the context of his historical background in a way that both D'Alton and Sedgwick fail to do, often showing Horace's independence from his contemporaries. But Frank's book is not an easy read. His style is too florid for present-day taste and his sentences too long. His arguments lack pointers and summaries so that it is not always easy to see where they lead. Perhaps because of this imprecision Frank does not seem to construct any consistent picture of Horace.

WILKINSON has two aims: to investigate Horace the man and to assess the value and character of his poetry. Wilkinson follows both aims concurrently throughout the book. This is an excellent approach in a biography of Horace, since it allows Wilkinson to explore Horace's life and character through his poetry. And because Wilkinson recognises the limitations of this approach, namely that poetic output cannot always be a reliable indication of the character of the writer, he has wisely directed the final aim of the book toward a greater understanding of Horace's poetry rather than a study of his personality. But the book is nonetheless a biography, and of all the biographies discussed here Wilkinson's offers the most thorough and honest assessment of Horace's character and attitudes. It is free of the romanticism of Sedgwick and the overgeneralisations of D'Alton. The book is intended for the Classical student and includes two excellent indexes and the longest chapter on Horace's character and views, divided thematically into palatable sections. But its appeal is not limited to the scholar, and translations of the frequent Latin quotations are found in footnotes.

—Charlotte Goddard

HOUSMAN, A(lfred) E(dward), 1859–1936; English classical scholar and poet.

Chambers, R. W., "A. E. Housman" in *Man's Unconquerable Mind*. London, Cape, 1939.
Gow, A. S. F., *A. E. Housman: A Sketch*. New York, Macmillan, and Cambridge, Cambridge University Press, 1936.
Graves, Richard P., *A. E. Housman: The Scholar-Poet*. London, Routledge, 1979; New York, Scribner, 1980.
Hawkins, Maude, *A. E. Housman: Man Behind a Mask*. Chicago, H. Regnery, 1958.
Housman, Laurence, *A. E. H.: Some Poems, Some Letters, and a Personal Memoir*. London, Cape, 1937.
Page, Norman, *A. E. Housman: A Critical Biography*. London, Macmillan, and New York, Schocken, 1983.

Richards, Grant, *Housman 1897–1936*. London and New York, Oxford University Press, 1941.

Scott-Kilvert, Ian, *A. E. Housman: A Divided Life*. London, Hart-Davis, 1957; Boston, Beacon, 1958.

Withers, Percy, *A Buried Life: Personal Recollections of A. E. Housman*. London, Cape, 1940.

*

Had Housman been only a classical scholar it is likely that his sole biography would have been a short laudatory memoir by one of his academic colleagues. But he was also a poet of rare quality, whose volume *A Shropshire Lad*, first published in a small edition in 1896, attained great popularity in the early years of the 20th century. This double life, and Housman's own habitual reticence, have posed problems for his biographers.

Perhaps the reader's best starting-point is SCOTT-KILVERT's work. This short biographical essay draws on memoirs published shortly after Housman's death and offers a well-written assessment of Housman as man and poet.

In the years following Housman's death several memoirs appeared, written by men who had known at least some aspect of him. The earliest was by GOW, a colleague who saw much of Housman during his years of intense scholarship (from 1911) at Trinity College, Cambridge. Gow's volume contains the fullest information on Housman's scholarly publications. This "sketch" was followed by the work of LAURENCE HOUSMAN, Housman's brother. His memoir makes good use of selected letters and remains a major source for Housman's early life.

CHAMBERS' work is of particular importance as it was written by a man who, having been Housman's pupil in University College, London, later became Professor of English at the college and so a colleague who knew him well and admired both his classical scholarship and his poetry (and also respected his administrative ability). Chambers covers the years from 1892 to 1911.

Differing in style and approach are Withers and Richards. WITHERS, a friend of the Cambridge years, found Housman an enigma, and his book attempts to understand the combination of the austere professor and the poet of concealed passions. RICHARDS took over the publication of *A Shropshire Lad* in 1898, and his account of business relations with Housman is detailed and full. The two men saw much of each other in the London years, wining and dining, and on several occasions traveled together on the Continent. Richards confesses that his memory for detail may on occasion be faulty, but his 400 pages contain much information on Housman (and aspects of Housman's personality) that no other study can touch. For all its journalistic swagger and anecdotal garrulity, it is an invaluable source, on which later, more formal biographers have drawn heavily.

The 1950s saw two biographies, by WATSON and HAWKINS. Both are "interpretive" and neither very satisfactory. Watson paints a portrait of a man he dislikes, a fussy pedant. Hawkins is something of an idolator but has no firsthand knowledge of the milieu in which Housman operated.

Housman had said, "all that need be known of my life and books is contained in about a dozen lines of the publication *Who's Who*." By the 1970s these dozen lines had expanded to thousands: his notebooks, his manuscripts, his diary were all on deposit in libraries; many old acquaintances had put their memories into print; a full edition of his letters appeared in 1971 (Henry Maas, editor, *The Letters of A. E. Housman*, 1971). It was now possible to contemplate a full biography.

The result was not one work but two, by GRAVES and PAGE. Each has its merits and both must be consulted. Both make full use of the now extensive documentary evidence. Where they differ (when they differ) is in the interpretation of the material. Graves, an Oxford graduate from St. John's College (which had sent young Housman down without a degree, a shock from which he never recovered in spite of his later academic distinction), is particularly good on the early formative family years, his schooling, and on the Oxford scene. On the London years at University College Graves does not improve on Chambers' firsthand account. Graves devotes a whole chapter to Housman's annual trips to the Continent, claiming that one of the main attractions was the ease of homosexual encounters. Page on the other hand finds the "evidence" for these casual affairs totally unconvincing and certainly Graves sets out his narrative on occasion as if it were a romantic novel rather than a strict biography. The austere professor at loose in Paris makes sensational reading. Readers must read both biographies and judge for themselves.

Page's work, subtitled "A Critical Biography," is critical (in the best sense) both of its subject and of previous biographers. The introduction is an admirable essay on the art of biography that comes down heavily against those biographers who feel that all their research notes, important or trivial, must find a place in the final text. He is particularly good on the criteria required for the assessment of evidence both oral and written. As a graduate of Cambridge, Page knows and devotes two full chapters to the Cambridge scene, in which Housman spent the major portion of his life and in which he flowered. The book is rounded off with separate assessments of Housman's contributions to classical studies and to poetry, the latter skillfully avoiding the "elementary but pervasive error" of using the poems as biographical "evidence." While Page's book is the best available on the subject, the serious reader should make use of both Graves and Page.

—Ian A. Gordon

HOWELLS, William Dean, 1837–1920; American writer.

Brooks, Van Wyck, *Howells: His Life and World*. New York, Dutton, and London, Dent, 1959.

Cady, Edwin H., *The Road to Realism: The Early Years 1837–85 of William Dean Howells*. Syracuse, New York, Syracuse University Press, 1956.

Cady, Edwin H., *The Realist at War: The Mature Years 1885–1920 of William Dean Howells*. Syracuse, New York, Syracuse University Press, 1958.

Carter, Everett, *Howells and the Age of Realism*. Philadelphia, Lippincott, 1954.

Eble, Kenneth E., *William Dean Howells*. Boston, Twayne, 1982 (2nd edition).

Firkins, Oscar W., *William Dean Howells: A Study*. Cambridge, Massachusetts, Harvard University Press, 1924.

Gibson, William M., *William Dean Howells*. Minneapolis, University of Minnesota Press, 1967.

Kirk, Clara M. and Rudolph Kirk, *William Dean Howells*. New York, Twayne, 1962.

Lynn, Kenneth S., *William Dean Howells: An American Life*. New York, Harcourt, 1971.

Wagenknecht, Edward, *William Dean Howells: The Friendly Eye*. New York, Oxford University Press, 1969.

*

Howells scholars are blessed with a rich store of primary materials: six volumes of reminiscences, six more of selected letters, in addition to other volumes of correspondence exchanged specifically with Mark Twain and John Hay. While generically different and serving a different function altogether from formal biography, Howells' autobiographic writings and letters are not only a pleasure to read, but prove highly useful in revealing both the man and his times. The earlier books vividly recreate with a rare honesty and objectivity not simply personal experience, but the world of the antebellum Ohio Valley, while the later ones are an invaluable source of information about American literary life in post-Civil War America, a life whose center of gravity was Howells himself. (For Howells' autobiographical writings, see the *Selected Edition*, edited by Ronald Gottesman and others, 1968–   .)

The reprinting of his account of his relationship with Mark Twain (1967) provides one indication of just how valuable these materials have proven to be for the contemporary scholar. In addition, ten volumes of travel books reveal simultaneously carefully wrought accounts of their subjects and the sensibilities of both author and his era. In fact, the virtues of the realist's approach to experience is perhaps nowhere more evident than in Howells' use of the materials of his own life.

It was a life long and full, centrally located in the mainstream of American literature. In the vast Howells bibliography of novels, plays, criticism, travel books, magazine articles, etc., a biographer's work is indeed cut out for him. Consequently, much of the biographical writing about Howells focuses in rather specialized ways on his writing, most specifically close critical readings of novels. Among critical studies useful for their biographical content are George N. Bennett, *William Dean Howells: The Development of a Novelist* (1959), and *The Realism of William Dean Howells 1889–1920* (1973); Olav W. Fryckstedt, *In Quest of America: A Study of Howells' Early Development as a Novelist* (1958); Kermit Vanderbilt, *The Achievement of William Dean Howells: A Reinterpretation* (1968); Clara M. and Rudolph Kirk, *Howells, Traveler from Altruria 1889–94* (1962); George C. Carrington, Jr., *The Immense Complex Drama: The World and Art of the Howells Novel* (1966); William McMurray, *The Literary Realism of William Dean Howells* (1967); and John W. Crowley, *The Black Heart's Truth* (1985). Moving away from the study of specific novels as the primary focus, the most readable, thorough, and eminently useful study of Howells in the larger context of American realism is CARTER's, valuable equally for its understanding of Howells and the literary movement to which he is so central.

Even those studies that take the traditional biographer's stance do so by focusing on that aspect of Howells which makes his life of primary interest to us: his writing, and most specifically, his novels. The approach is set in FIRKINS' early study, deemed useful enough to be reissued in 1963. Subtitled "A Study," it is a somewhat personal tour of Howells' life and works depending on copious quotation from the subject, but providing positive, if rather bland, insight into the state of Howells' literary standing in the decade following his death, a time when reaction to his dominance of the American literary scene was already well underway. BROOKS' volume, published some 35 years later, is well written, easy to read, and anecdotal, but not "definitive" by the author's own admission.

A serious attempt at a definitive biography had already appeared in CADY's two volumes. These provide the structure on which the increasing output of Howells studies, particularly rich in the 1960s, rests, and which any further study of Howells will need to take into account. Cady's scholarship is painstaking and thorough, his understanding of his subject objective yet sympathetic, a model of the biographer's art. Readable and workmanlike, Cady depends primarily, and to good effect, on the careful massing of detail, rather than brilliant insight, to bring his subject to life; but, while careful to document the underlying episodes of nervous prostration that periodically afflicted Howells, he leaves undeveloped the sense that his subject was a much more complex figure than emerges from this estimable study.

Three other books published in the 1960s warrant mention here. Like many in the series, the KIRK volume published by Twayne is a solid, reliable, introductory study, while GIBSON's brilliant monograph in the Minnesota series is a superb example of the kind of precision and succinctness of expression that only vast knowledge of a subject permits. 39 brief pages provide a stunning introduction to Howells, performing masterfully the task of any good introduction by whetting our desire to know more. WAGENKNECHT's study, on the other hand, one of a long series of studies of American writers by this author, is almost too easy to read, facile, and organized in an idiosyncratic manner. While it adds little to our understanding of Howells, it does provide easy access to his life and his work in a sympathetic manner.

Finally, two later studies address two very different but perhaps the most telling questions that remain for the modern reader of Howells. One question is eminently biographical, the other bio-critical. The first is addressed by LYNN in his elegantly written and profoundly sympathetic biography. If it is the role of the successful biographer to provide as thorough and as relevant as possible an account of the circumstances of his subject's life, an insightful evaluation of what that life might have meant to his own time and ours, and an understanding of the multidimensional complexity and ambiguity that underlies his subject's existence, Lynn's study is a major achievement. Howells' life was an unusual combination of the highly public and social and the deeply reticent, and in Lynn's pages we get some idea of what the projection of that urbane, hard-working, courteous, soft-spoken, and large-hearted persona cost, and of the pain out of which the essentially comic vision of Howells was born.

The second late study, by EBLE, is very different, its motive clearly stated: "to furnish an acquaintance with Howells which may lead readers to read his works." Able to take advantage of materials restricted until 1972 and drawing on the scholarship of those involved in preparation of the CEAA edition of Howells' works, Eble's volume is the second in the Twayne series on Howells, and probably the place to begin for the kind of overview that is possible in the brief compass of the Twayne format. Eble makes the most of it, masterfully touching on the significant elements in Howells' life and in his more important work as novelist and critic, concluding with a useful commentary on the status of Howells in our time. For one who has read a novel or two by Howells and is curious to learn more, this could be the place to start, for while brief, its scholarship is impeccable and its insight into Howells both appreciative and judicious. For a more thorough study, Cady and Lynn are indispensible.

—Susette Ryan Graham

HUGHES, (James) Langston, 1902–1967; American writer.

Berry, Faith, *Langston Hughes: Before and Beyond Harlem.* Westport, Connecticut, L. Hill, 1983.

Dickinson, Donald C., *A Bio-bibliography of Langston Hughes, 1920–67.* New York, Archon, 1967; revised edition, 1972.

Emanuel, James A., *Langston Hughes.* New York, Twayne, 1967.

Larson, Norita D., *Langston Hughes: Poet of Harlem.* Mankato, Minnesota, Creative Education, 1981.

Meltzer, Milton, *Langston Hughes: A Biography.* New York, Crowell, 1968.

Rampersad, Arnold, *The Life of Langston Hughes* (2 vols.). Volume one, *I, Too, Hear America Singing* (1902–41), New York, Oxford University Press, 1986; volume two, *I Dream a World* (1941–67), New York and Oxford, Oxford University Press, 1988.

Rollins, Charlemae H., *Black Troubadour: Langston Hughes.* Chicago, Rand McNally, 1970.

Rummel, Jack, *Langston Hughes.* New York, Chelsea House, 1988.

Walker, Alice, *Langston Hughes, American Poet.* New York, Crowell, 1974.

*

Arnold Rampersad's superb life of Langston Hughes (see below), one of the great literary biographies of our time, so far surpasses other biographical treatments of this important and versatile man of letters that it is tempting to dismiss everything else. To do so would be a mistake, however, for the other biographies of Hughes have their uses and audiences. Nor can one overlook Hughes' artfully engaging autobiographies, *The Big Sea* (1940) and *I Wonder as I Wander* (1956). These works must be used with caution, however, for the research of Rampersad and Faith Berry has shown that Hughes, simultaneously private and gregarious as both writer and person, conceals as well as reveals much.

Since some of Hughes' poetry is accessible to very young readers, they are fortunate to be able to make the acquaintance of the poet himself as a child and young man in WALKER's brief volume in the Crowell Biographies series. Only 3280 words in length with large type and ample illustrations, it should readily engage a child's interest. It seems appropriate that a distinguished contemporary writer, who herself benefited from Hughes' help and encouragement as well as from his example, should have written this children's life of a distinguished predecessor, who also wrote delightful children's books. Another book for the very young is LARSON's *Langston Hughes: Poet of Harlem*, but the Walker book is preferable.

Juvenile readers are likewise well served. The first extended life of Hughes was by his friend and collaborator, MELTZER. Readily conceding that his work "is in no sense an official biography," Meltzer uses *The Big Sea* and *I Wonder as I Wander* as his primary sources, supplementing them with conversations with Hughes during the last few months of his life, interviews with some 60 friends and acquaintances, and limited archival research. Lacking access to the vast collection of Hughes papers at Yale, Meltzer focuses on the public side of Hughes' career in this brief life (c. 32,000 words). A longtime student of black history and culture, he writes knowledgeably about racial conflicts in his subject's experience, but is reticent on more private matters and very sketchy on the 1950s and 60s. But Meltzer writes vivid, lively, simple prose, and his is a good book to place in the hands of a teenager.

An older friend of Hughes, the Chicago librarian and children's biographer ROLLINS, wrote the next life of Hughes. Shorter and less well-written than Meltzer's biography, it relies largely on Hughes' autobiographies. Unlike Meltzer, though, the Rollins book is illustrated with reproductions of letters and playbills as well as photographs. The bibliography contains interesting annotations of Hughes' dramatic works, including comments on their suitability for production. The value of *Black Troubadour* is enhanced by a foreword by Gwendolyn Brooks.

RUMMEL's book on Hughes, a volume in the Black Americans of Achievement series, is slickly produced, well informed, and profusely illustrated. Rummel's prose style is not as fluent as Meltzer's, but he has the immense advantage of writing after Faith Berry and the first volume of Rampersad. Like Walker, Meltzer, and Rollins, Rummel understandably highlights the adventurous elements of his subject's peripatetic life. Even if he pays scant attention to the final two sedentary decades in Harlem, Rummel does treat Hughes' adult life with appropriate attention to its political dimensions and its international connections. And readers of all ages will enjoy browsing through the book for its 90 photographs and drawings carefully selected to illustrate Hughes' life and its context.

Turning to works useful to advanced students and scholars, one should note in passing two early books (both published in 1967) that are not biographies but have considerable biographical relevance. EMANUEL's *Langston Hughes* in Twayne's United States Authors series and DICKINSON's *Bio-bibliography* both start with biographical accounts before turning to criticism and bibliography respectively. Both focus more on the literary career than the personal life. Emanuel's is the shorter and better.

The two substantial biographies of Langston Hughes are Berry's and Rampersad's. BERRY's work appeared in 1983 after seven years of intensive research and five years of prior work on Hughes. Like Meltzer and others, though, Berry was not granted permission by the Langston Hughes Estate to use the great repository at Yale. Despite this serious limitation, her book is a creditable performance, drawing as it does on other archives and the help of many friends and scholars of her subject. As the title indicates, *Langston Hughes: Before and Beyond Harlem* de-emphasizes "the limited stereotype of him as the 'bard of Harlem'" and places him in a larger context. Berry is less reliant than prior biographers on Hughes' autobiographical writings; indeed, she takes pains to correct or supplement them where she can. She is especially sympathetic to Hughes the political militant, having earlier collected some of his radical writings in *Good Morning, Revolution*. Conscientiously disclaiming an attempt to write a definitive life, Berry provided a book that advanced Hughes studies in the mid-1980s and is still worth reading.

In his will Hughes designated his old friend Arna Bontemps as his biographer, and Bontemps in his last years was organizing the material at Yale indispensable to the task. The death of Bontemps in 1973 halted this project, and George Bass became executor of the Hughes Estate. Bass was slow in selecting a scholar to receive what Faith Berry has called "the keys to the kingdom," but when he finally made his choice it was an inspired one—Arnold Rampersad. Beginning work on Hughes in 1979, RAMPERSAD published less than a decade later the second and final volume of *The Life of Langston Hughes*, one of the few literary biographies that truly deserves to be called definitive. Among its many merits, the most immediately obvious is its scope and detail. Its two volumes run close to 1000 pages and more than 500,000 words. Rampersad utilizes fully the collection of Hughes Papers at Yale, a gargantuan accumulation, as well as information from more than three dozen other archives in this country and Europe. Interviews were held with some 125 friends and acquaintances of Hughes, and scores of other people provided assistance of various kinds. The task of organizing such a mass of detail from so many sources was formidable indeed, but Rampersad succeeds brilliantly. The resulting narrative is full and rich without seeming cluttered, moving along easily and vividly in supple prose. Many hiterto unknown, concealed, or misinterpreted aspects of Hughes' personality and literary career are set straight in lucid and persuasive fashion. Rampersad is respectful to his subject but not awed by him. He shows us a Hughes troubled under his cheerful exterior by an unhappy childhood, emotional detachment, uncertain sexual orientation, and political compromise. In treating these difficult issues Rampersad is balanced and careful, but not timid, in marshalling evidence and showing where it leads. Laughing to keep from crying and always strapped for money, Hughes doggedly kept faith with the great goal of his tireless literary activity over five decades: "My seeking has been to explain and illuminate the Negro condition in America and obliquely that of all human kind." In his brilliant explanation and illumination of the life and work of Langston Hughes, Arnold Rampersad has written an exemplary biography.

—Keneth Kinnamon

HUGO, Victor, 1802–1885; French writer.

Edwards, Samuel, *Victor Hugo: A Tumultuous Life*. New York, D. McKay, 1971; with subtitle *A Biography*, London, New English Library, 1975.

Grant, Elliott M., *The Career of Victor Hugo*. Cambridge, Massachusetts, Harvard University Press, 1945.

Josephson, Matthew, *Victor Hugo: A Realistic Biography of the Great Romantic*. New York, Doubleday, 1942.

Maurois, André, *Olympio: The Life of Victor Hugo*, translated by Gerard Hopkins. New York, Harper, 1956; as *Victor Hugo*, London, Cape, 1956 (originally published by Hachette, Paris, 1954).

Richardson, Joanna, *Victor Hugo*. New York, St. Martin's, and London, Weidenfeld and Nicolson, 1976.

*

EDWARDS gives an intense and somewhat hyperbolic account of Victor Hugo's life, including the main events in his literary and his political careers. The fact that he quotes from Hugo's political speeches more than from his poetry or other imaginative writings indicates the emphasis he has given to his fast-moving narrative: it is a celebration of the patriot and the political liberal more than of the great writer. No serious scholarly research underlies this biography, and the author's ideas about literature are relatively simplistic, as may be seen by his description of Hugo's celebrated humanitarian fantasy, *Les Misérables* (1862), as "an extreme form of realism." Often exaggerated and misleading so far as historical fact is concerned, the Edwards biography is not a volume to be consulted by students, but it affords a most exciting, even entrancing, view of its subject. The author's evident admiration for Hugo as an inspirational public figure, and his rapid-paced journalistic style, turn this biography into what one reviewer called "excellent high-class soap opera," a joyous entertainment for the general reader, but only distantly related to the truth.

By contrast, GRANT gives a sober and very responsible account of Hugo's career, emphasizing his work as a writer, but also giving the most accurate and the most objective analysis of his role and attitudes in the political arena—a topic on which Grant did pioneering scholarly investigation. In his Preface, Grant notes that the appearance of Josephson's biography of Hugo, while he was working on his own book, deterred him from writing a complete biography himself, which would have been redundant, and led him instead to concentrate on the course of Hugo's public career, explaining his political evolution from monarchist to republican, and analyzing the thematic and aesthetic features of his creative writing, based on Grant's own close reading of all the texts, supplemented by the best available scholarship of his predecessors in the field. Grant's volume, as much critical study as biography, continues to be worth consulting on many points because of the thoroughness of his research in the primary sources then available. On the other hand, so much new material (letters, notebooks, memoirs, unpublished manuscripts, etc.) has come to light since the publication of Grant that, on many other points, Grant has been superseded.

JOSEPHSON brought highly-developed skills as a popular biographer and social historian to bear on his life of Victor Hugo. He saw in Hugo an exemplary case of the very private literary artist who, finding his work hampered by an external threat—

revolution, war, or a despotic ruler—enters the public arena to regain artistic freedom, and it is that theme Josephson emphasizes in his biography. Though not a trained scholar, Josephson had the wisdom to enlist the help of scholars to assure a responsible presentation of the verifiable facts of Hugo's life. Because he was writing during the period of World War II, Josephson could not resist giving his narrative a kind of emblematic slant, making of Hugo's life a symbol of the struggle for democracy in France in the 19th century, while pointedly noting that Hugo's life could be a source of inspiration for those who despaired of the fate of France in the dark days of the German occupation after 1940, when he did the bulk of his writing on Hugo. Circumstances thus gave Josephson's biography an unexpected patriotic cast that may sound a bit forced today. Still, Josephson's writing is lively, and his warm admiration both for Hugo and for French culture is genuinely engaging. It is popular biography at its best, detailed, reasonably accurate though mildly tendentious, constantly absorbing and eminently readable. For the general reader, unconcerned with scholarly precision or completeness, and satisfied to gain a vivid impression of the whole man, Josephson's *Victor Hugo* is certainly the biography of choice.

MAUROIS, on the other hand, provides the most densely detailed and closely studied account of Victor Hugo's life presently available in one volume, in any language. A justly celebrated biographer, Maurois' trademark is the exhaustive and meticulous attention to accuracy of detail, combined with an intelligent and sensitive effort to know and understand his subject as completely as possible, as though from within. Like his landmark biographies of Shelley, Byron, and George Sand, Maurois' account of the life of Hugo strives to give the reader, as nearly as may be, the sense of what it must have been like to *be* Victor Hugo. Psychological penetration is the principal thrust of his biographical method. In his Foreword, Maurois lists the many overt contradictions in Hugo's ideas and in his behavior to explain why "we need to know the story of his life if we are to understand his tormented genius to the full." Maurois expressly disclaims any intention of discussing Hugo's ideas on poetry, on politics, or on religion, nor does he plan to explore the origin of those ideas, since such work has already been thoroughly done by his scholarly predecessors. Instead, he says, "what I have done here is to write a life, nothing more and nothing less," by which he clearly means that his book is a "pure" biography, focused on factual truth and free of the critical analyses and disputes that occupy scholars in their investigations. Nevertheless, he acknowledges his heavy debt to scholars who, by their methods, have established what is verifiable about Hugo's life, and modestly describes his own task as biographer to be "to reduce to order, with a lively sense of my duty to the cause of truth, all that is now known about the life of this great man."

Implied in Maurois' view of the biographer's role is a dual effort: the painstaking accumulation of every truth about the subject's life established by the work of scholars or recorded in authenticated documents, followed by the orderly presentation of those truths in such a manner as to allow the reality of a highly complex personality to emerge for the reader. That is indeed what Maurois' biography of Hugo accomplishes. The truly massive compilation of small, even trivial, details of his life are all carefully documented; and it is evident that Maurois has not personally done the research but has coordinated and collected the work of others to form the bedrock of his biography, and to make it the most complete and most reliable account of Hugo's life in print. At the same time, the narrative is given unity and coherence by the controlling wisdom and sensibility of the biographer, who understands the creative imagination, and who has discerned, by dint of close study of the facts, a meaningful pattern in the flow of events in Hugo's long life. Not everyone will agree with Maurois' heroic view of Hugo as "the greatest of all French poets," but all must agree that Maurois' biography is, to date, the most thorough, and therefore the most indispensable account of Hugo's life for the serious student. Since Maurois writes with clarity, grace, and enthusiastic verve that sustains the reader's interest, consulting this monumental biography, always rewardingly informative, is also an aesthetic pleasure.

Writing 20 years after Maurois, RICHARDSON has wisely made her Hugo biography not a rival but a complement to Maurois' imposing volume. She has made use of new information and new material available since 1956, and has undertaken the kinds of analytical evaluations that Maurois declined to address. Quite correctly, she calls her work "the first critical biography of Hugo in English," and points out in her introduction the many reasons for saying that it is impossible to admire Hugo "without reservations, or without regrets." Richardson has given us a full, and quite objective, portrait of a great literary and political figure, whose influence dominated 19th-century France and has continued to be a vital factor throughout the 20th century as well. Richardson combines the best elements of the scholarly biography and the popular biography: using the very best sources, but without getting bogged down in scholarly minutiae or jargon, telling her story directly and forcefully, but without exaggeration or rhetorical flourishes, remaining true to the facts without fearing to express moral or aesthetic judgments when called for, and supplying meticulous documentation in the notes and bibliography without inflating her narrative with insignificant details. Richardson's biography is compact—300 pages—compared to Maurois', which is nearly twice as long. Maurois' is *the* indispensable reference volume, but if one can only read a single biography of Hugo, the wisest choice would be Richardson's, because it is the most succinct and the most up-to-date, while preserving a fundamental integrity.

—Murray Sachs

HUME, David, 1711–1776; Scottish philosopher and historian.

Burton, John H., *Life and Correspondence of David Hume.* Edinburgh, W. Tait, 1846.
Flew, Anthony, *David Hume: Philosopher of Moral Science.* Oxford and New York, Blackwell, 1986.
Greig, J.Y.T., *David Hume.* London, Cape, and New York, Oxford University Press, 1931.
Mossner, Ernest Campbell, *The Forgotten Hume: Le Bon David.* New York, Columbia University Press, 1943.
Mossner, Ernest Campbell, *The Life of David Hume.* Edinburgh, Nelson, and Austin, University of Texas Press, 1954.
Price, John V., *David Hume.* New York, Twayne, 1968.

*

In at least two important respects, students of David Hume fare better than those of most other 18th-century philosophers: they have at their disposal a biography that is indisputably the standard and an accompanying collection of letters that are varied and richly suggestive of the time and of the controversies in which Hume engaged—a collection that is itself biography, a detailed and vital self-portrait. Two 20th-century Hume scholars, Mossner and Greig, assume a foremost position.

GREIG was a well-regarded novelist when he wrote his colorful biography, which he published one year before the appearance of the two-volume *Letters* (Oxford, Clarendon Press, 1932). In both his biography and in the collection of letters, Greig modernizes, enlivens, and improves the accuracy of Burton's stuffy but fact-filled tomes. With a surprisingly off-hand and engaging style, Greig attempts in his biography to define more precisely the nature of Hume's skepticism. The book provides valuable background on the Scottish religious atmosphere from which Hume emerged; for the most part, though, it concerns itself more with the details of Hume's life than with an analysis of his philosophy—a departure from the usual treatment of 18th-century philosophers. In fact, with subtle humor Greig recognizes the typical gap between treatment of life and discussion of philosophy when he invites his readers to ignore his first chapter, which concerns itself exclusively with Hume's philosophy. Like most biographies of the time, however, it is under-footnoted (by current standards) and has been clearly surpassed by Mossner's *Life*.

MOSSNER's *The Forgotten Hume* represents the critic's early exploration of the philosopher's personality. It is a carefully researched examination of Hume's humanity, the Hume revealed in his literary friendships. The philosopher's controversial support of the playwright John Home, best known for his tragedy *Douglas* (1757), forms an admirable chapter in Hume's life, and Mossner describes this friendship purposefully. His description of Hume's relationships with Boswell and Johnson is equally rich with detail. An "intimate biography," the book is especially enlightening in its discussion of "Hume's Hume"—the philosopher's self-perception as revealed in *My Own Life* (1927) and in his letters. The lively prose and careful research represented here clearly anticipates the standard biography Mossner produced a decade later.

In *The Life*, MOSSNER comes more directly to the crux to which Greig humorously alludes: "A critical problem faces the biographer who has chosen to treat of a man of letters remembered chiefly as a thinker: shall he treat of his subject's thought as well as of the external facts of his life?" In describing his own handling of that problem, Mossner observes that "the man predominates, but the ideas provide the rationale of his actions." Mossner's Hume is a man motivated by his desire for a life of letters, for literary expression. At the same time, Hume is depicted as an intellectual revolutionary fighting a ceaseless battle against the rationalistic traditions of his forebears. The tremendous specificity of the biography occasions tedium, for example, in the minute account of Hume's education; but the work more frequently delights, as it does in Mossner's account of the philosopher's response to the Jacobite Rebellion of 1745. Notably, Mossner contributed to the editing of *New Letters of David Hume* (Oxford, Clarendon Press, 1954); he recognized, as did Greig, the remarkable extent to which the man is revealed in his letters.

The most important predecessor of Greig and Mossner is BURTON, whose extensive use of Hume's papers set the pattern for Mossner. Burton's Hume is a persevering writer, stymied by the cold reception of his peers—a man whose "stoic severity of thought" is inflamed by the "fire of literary ardour." Burton finds Hume "disrespectful" and "insincere" on the subject of religion. In his preface, Burton seeks to reassure those who had heard rumors that the publication of the Hume papers would create personal scandal for the family members of prominent Scottish clergymen.

It is unlikely that Mossner's study will soon be surpassed, and PRICE admits as much in his mostly superfluous Twayne volume. Price concentrates on Hume's public controversies and depicts him as an enigma, an "original" who defies analysis and who, in spite of his links with the London literary establishment, must be seen as removed from that society.

FLEW, another important Hume scholar, includes some biographical analysis in his impressive new study. He stands in awe of the incredible robustness of Hume studies, yet wonders why more attention has not been paid to the philosopher's life. One obvious answer is the success of Mossner's study, which remains a barrier to another full-length treatment. However, the letters are so remarkably complex and diverse that biographical analyses of their content, style, and contexts would surely be welcome additions.

—Richard C. Taylor

HUXLEY, Aldous (Leonard), 1894–1963; English writer.

Bedford, Sybille, *Aldous Huxley: A Biography* (2 vols.). New York, Knopf, and London, Chatto and Windus, 1973.
Huxley, Laura Archera, *This Timeless Moment: A Personal View of Aldous Huxley*. New York, Farrar Strauss, 1968; London, Chatto and Windus, 1969.
Thody, Philip, *Huxley, a Biographical Introduction*. New York, Scribner, and London, Studio Vista, 1973.

*

There is much in the extensive work of Aldous Huxley to stimulate curiosity as to what manner of man he was. Researchers and biographers have been greatly assisted by the collection of Huxley letters assembled by Grover Smith (New York, 1969). But guidance through such a collection is needed, and this comes from the works discussed below.

All biographical works on Huxley are overshadowed by BEDFORD's large book. Bedford combines a wealth of material with some fine critical assessments of Huxley's works that will challenge the reader to reexamine them. Throughout her work, Bedford is in pursuit of the "real" Aldous Huxley: a man who took up and put down a wide range of topics. He was a man, Bedford argues, who remained himself, whatever direction he followed.

One is naturally curious to know how Bedford, a considerable novelist in her own right, was in a position to write so full a report. In the first place, she enjoyed a lifelong friendship with the Huxleys. Moreover, Bedford was obviously in contact with many of Huxley's old friends, for the book is full of letters between Huxley and his many correspondents. Sometimes Bedford quotes too generously from these letters, but there is in fact seldom an entry of this sort that does not give one a chance view of Huxley at work or in vivid contact with contemporaries like D. H. Lawrence or Gerald Heard. In all this Bedford never indulges in pointless gossip. Whatever she includes appears because it is a line or stroke in the portrait being drawn of the chief figure. If her treatment is minute and precise, that is because Huxley is a figure who demands careful consideration.

From this aim Bedford seldom wavers, even when she occasionally exercises a novelist's privilege and fills out a scene that is but scantily recorded, or remarks on the unfolding of Huxley's uncertain movements; on one hand, his agnosticism and cynical estimates (both lifelong tendencies) and, on the other hand, the beliefs that Huxley came to feel were necessary for him.

LAURA ARCHERA HUXLEY's book is rightfully personal and intimate throughout. As Huxley's second wife, Laura Huxley reconstructs conversations that she had with Huxley on psychological and psychic matters, often verging on the religious. Mrs. Huxley moves through the shared years without great attention to chronology, and the result is a touching and controlled portrait of a man at once kind and intellectually voracious.

THODY's work is no brief replay of Bedford's large study. Instead, it centers on matters that Bedford touches only in passing, concerned as she is with the events (social contacts, publishing, and film activity) that absorbed much of Huxley's energy. Thody offers a continuous and illuminating account of the various stages through which Huxley passed during his career. This journey, as Thody represents it, was never completed but was made up of constant re-workings of earlier attitudes that had been, at some point, expressed with an air of finality. Thody's account is highly successful; all of Huxley's intellectual gestures are made elements in a career that expresses the variety and the ambiguity of 20th-century life.

The three works treated here are not flat repetitions of each other. Bedford's careful presentation of fact and of all that gathers itself around the facts is suitably filled out by the warmth and intelligent affection of Mrs. Huxley's *This Timeless Moment* and by Thody's densely compacted study of the Huxley mind at its unremitting work. All this, along with Grover Smith's edition of Huxley's correspondence, puts the reader in clear contact with the man he has met glancingly in Huxley's many and widely varied works.

—Harold H. Watts

HUXLEY, Thomas Henry, 1825–1895; English biologist.

Ainsworth-Davis, James R., *Thomas H. Huxley*. London, Dent, and New York, Dutton, 1907.

Ashforth, Albert, *Thomas Henry Huxley*. New York, Twayne, 1969.

Ayres, Clarence, *Huxley*. New York, Norton, 1932.

Bibby, (Harold) Cyril, *T. H. Huxley, Scientist, Humanist, and Educator*. London, Watts, 1959; New York, Horizon Press, 1960.

Clark, Ronald W., *The Huxleys*. New York, McGraw-Hill, and London, Heinemann, 1968.

Di Gregorio, Mario A., *T. H. Huxley's Place in Natural Science*. New Haven, Connecticut, and London, Yale University Press, 1984.

Huxley, Aldous, "T. H. Huxley as a Man of Letters," in *Huxley Memorial Lectures 1925–32*. London, Macmillan, 1932.

Huxley, Leonard, *The Life and Letters of Thomas Henry Huxley* (2 vols.). London, Macmillan, and New York, Appleton, 1900.

Huxley, Leonard, *Thomas Henry Huxley: A Character Sketch*. London, Watts, 1920.

Irvine, William, *Apes, Angels, and Victorians: The Story of Darwin, Huxley, and Evolution*. New York, McGraw-Hill, 1955; with subtitle, *A Joint Biography of Darwin and Huxley*, London, Weidenfeld and Nicolson, 1955.

Irvine, William, *Thomas Henry Huxley*. London, Longman, 1960.

Leighton, Gerald, *Huxley: His Life and Work*. London, Jack, and New York, Dodge, 1912.

Mitchell, P. Chalmers, *Thomas Henry Huxley: A Sketch of His Life and Work*. New York, Putnam, 1900; 2nd edition, London, Methuen, 1913.

Paradis, J. G., *T. H. Huxley: Man's Place in Nature*. Lincoln, University of Nebraska Press, 1978.

Peterson, Houston, *Huxley, Prophet of Science*. London and New York, Longman, 1932.

*

The work of Thomas Henry Huxley, a brilliant scientist and writer in his own right, has been largely overshadowed by that of Charles Darwin. Indeed, Huxley is often referred to as "Darwin's bulldog." Fortunately, there are several good biographies that examine the life, work, writings, and thoughts of this exemplary scientist. The scholarly treatments are generally based on Huxley's published writings, his son Leonard Huxley's classic work, *The Life and Letters of Thomas Henry Huxley* (see below), and the Huxley Papers preserved at the Imperial College of Science and Technology. Many interesting biographical sketches were written by colleagues, friends, and family members; these include the early works by AINSWORTH-DAVIS and LEIGHTON.

ASHFORTH provides a concise, scholarly biography that follows its subject from "Young Scientist" to "Last Years" and includes a chronology, footnotes, bibliography, and index. The emphasis is on Huxley's ideas about evolution, education, metaphysics, politics, and theology rather than on his personal life. Although Huxley is best remembered as Darwin's most zealous advocate, after 1870 Huxley produced a prodigious body of writings dealing with every aspect of English civilization and culture. Ashforth demonstrates that this great body of work made Huxley one of the most influential men of his generation. AYRES sees Huxley as one of the most remarkable figures of the 19th century. With chapter headings such as "Saint Darwin and Pope Huxley" and reminiscences from his father, the Reverend W. S. Ayres, Ayres tries to restore the dramatic aspects of

Huxley's life. Ayres demonstrates how successful Huxley was when he sharpened his "claws and beak" to do battle for science and vanquish all humbugs. The book contains a bibliography of principal sources, biographies, and related texts.

As noted in the foreword by Sir Julian Huxley, BIBBY's work appeared in the centenary year of the birth of the modern theory of evolution. Bibby makes it clear that Huxley was much more than the greatest protagonist of Darwin's theory, and he provides insights into Huxley's character, the great range of his interests and achievements, and places him directly in the context of Victorian culture, society, educational policy, and science. Bibby also provides a selected list of Huxley's publications, portraits of Huxley at many stages of his life, a detailed Conspectus of Huxley's Life and Times, and references. Bibby has also published *Scientist Extraordinary: The Life and Scientific Work of Thomas Henry Huxley, 1825–95* (1972), *The Essence of T. H. Huxley* (1967), and *T. H. Huxley on Education: A Selection from His Writings* (1971).

CLARK's entertaining and readable book examines the transmission of genius through three generations of Huxleys. The popular biographer presents a fully detailed account of "the world's reigning dynasty of the mind." The story begins with an examination of T. H. Huxley as biologist, educational administrator, humanist, and popularizer of the theory of evolution. In addition to Aldous and Sir Julian Huxley, Clark brings to life less well-known but gifted descendants. The book is divided into three major parts: 1) The Founding of a Family; 2) Development of a Dynasty; 3) The Huxleys' Place in Nature. It also includes a bibliography, family tree, 16 pages of photographs, and an index.

DI GREGORIO's book is well researched and rich in the expected scholarly apparatus, including an extensive bibliography of published and unpublished materials and a list of Huxley's writings. Fortunately, it is quite well written and worthy of its colorful protagonist. Di Gregorio examines the remarkable way in which a self-taught man of the lower middle class became one of the most powerful scientists in class-conscious Britain, president of the Royal Society, and founder of a dynasty of scientists and writers. The book deals primarily with Huxley as a scientist and is not a comprehensive analysis of all his views. Although addressed primarily to historians of science, the book should also be of interest to scientists and general readers with some prior knowledge of evolutionary theories.

Huxley's descendants have provided many fine studies of the life and work of the founder of this illustrious clan. The standard biography is *The Life and Letters of Thomas Henry Huxley*, composed by his son LEONARD HUXLEY. Although this might have been the obligatory two-volume biography, the Huxley gift for literary exposition and the subject's colorful life and character make this a readable and rewarding biography for those with the stamina to make their way through more than 1000 pages. For a more concise account, the reader should turn to Leonard Huxley's *Thomas Henry Huxley: A Character Sketch*. "T. H. Huxley as a Man of Letters," by his grandson ALDOUS HUXLEY, is one of seven tributes to Huxley collectively published as the *Huxley Memorial Lectures* in 1932.

One of the best studies of Huxley's place in history is IRVINE's sympathetic, scholarly, well-written, and witty biography of Darwin and Huxley. Irvine explores Huxley's gifts as orator and writer and his passion for science, as well as the re-

markable contrast between Huxley's love of controversy and Darwin's retreat to the privacy of his country home and loving family. Good use is made of excerpts from letters, scientific correspondence, and diaries. Irvine is also the author of a biographical essay, *Thomas Henry Huxley*, which captures the essence of the life, work, and character of his subject in only 37 pages. This essay should inspire the reader to seek out Huxley's own works in order to experience what Irvine calls "one of the most satisfactory combinations of 18th-century clarity with 19th-century elevation and vividness."

In contrast to Irvine's brevity, MITCHELL's work is almost 300 pages long. It is based on published sources, which in Huxley's case are extensive and colorful, but it tends to be a rather laudatory biographical exercise. The text marches predictably from "Birth" or "Death," though with thoroughness and attention to detail. An outstanding account of Huxley's social and philosophical views can be found in PARADIS. This scholarly book, with its notes and selected bibliography, is not the story of Huxley the man but rather an exploration of Huxley the scientist in the context of the "New Victorian Idea of the Scientist." PETERSON's work is a portrait of the "Gladiator-general and maid-of-all work" who "stalked through his age with fire in his eye . . . ready to do battle with anyone who would . . . interfere with the sacred cause of science." Peterson's biography is largely based on the work of Leonard Huxley.

Many other books about Huxley explore rather specialized aspects of his work and influence, including E. Clodd, *Thomas Henry Huxley* (1902) and *Pioneers of Evolution From Thales to Huxley* (1897); Janel Elizabeth (Hogarth) Courtney, *Freethinkers of the 19th Century* (1920); A. J. Marshall, *Darwin and Huxley in Australia* (1970); A. Smith Woodward, *The Place of T. H. Huxley in Anthropology* (1935); and W. H. Thompson, *Professor Huxley and Religion*, (1905).

Readers who want to learn more about Huxley should turn to his published journals and autobiographies. The autobiographies of Charles Darwin and Thomas Henry Huxley were published in one volume (*Autobiographies*, Oxford and New York, 1974), edited by Gavin De Beer, who also provides a valuable critical introduction, explanatory notes, bibliography, and chronologies for the lives of Darwin and Huxley. Although Huxley himself described autobiographies as "essentially works of fiction," his autobiography is well worth reading for the insights it gives us into the workings of his mind.

—Lois N. Magner

IBSEN, Henrik, 1828–1906; Norwegian playwright and poet.

Bradbrook, M. C., *Ibsen, The Norwegian: A Revaluation.* London, Chatto and Windus, 1946.

Downs, Brian W., *Ibsen: The Intellectual Background.* Cambridge, England, The University Press, 1946.

Gosse, Edmund, *Henrik Ibsen.* New York, Scribner, 1907.

Heiberg, Hans, *Ibsen: A Portrait of the Artist,* translated by Joan Tate. Coral Gables, Florida, University of Miami Press, and London, Allen and Unwin, 1969.

Jaeger, Henrik B., *Henrik Ibsen, 1828–88: A Critical Biography*, translated by W. M. Payne. Chicago, A. C. McClurg, 1890.

Jorgenson, Theodore, *Henrik Ibsen: Life and Drama*. Northfield, Minnesota, St. Olaf College Press, 1945.

Knight, George Wilson, *Henrik Ibsen*. New York, Grove, and Edinburgh, Oliver and Boyd, 1962.

Koht, Halvden, *Life of Ibsen*, translated by R. C. McMahon and H. A. Larsen. New York, American-Scandinavian Foundation, and London, Allen and Unwin, 1931; revised edition, translated and edited by Einar Hangen and A. E. Santaniello, New York, B. Blom, 1971 (originally published by Aschehoug, Oslo, 1928).

Meyer, Hans Georg, *Henrik Ibsen*, translated by Helen Sebba. New York, Ungar, 1972 (originally published by Friedrich, Velber, 1967).

Meyer, Michael, *Ibsen: A Biography*, New York, Doubleday, 1971; London, Penguin, 1974.

Zucker, A. E., *Ibsen, the Master Builder*. New York, Holt, 1929; London, Butterworth, 1930.

*

KOHT has an interesting history of editions. As originally written in 1928–29 (English translation 1931), Koht stressed Ibsen's contribution to the struggle for intellectual freedom throughout the arts, exemplified in the Free Theatre Movement. A second edition (1954, never translated) changed the focus to Ibsen's dramaturgy and sensitivity to dramatic characterization. "Ibsen the poet, rather than Ibsen the thinker, became the center of attention," according to the translators' note to the 1971 version. This edition is not purely Koht's work, but includes the translators' comments and inferences. Its working copy was read by Koht before his death in 1965 and approved by Sigmund Skard, Koht's son-in-law and literary executor; while it features parallel original and translated passages from Ibsen's plays, the translations are in prose, with no attempt at a poetic rendition of the original. In the earlier version, Koht defines the battleground for all subsequent dialectics: intellectualism vs. feeling, psychological portraiture vs. aesthetic invention, Norwegian in exile vs. pan-European citizen. It is difficult to separate Koht's opinions from those of the translators, who are unfair to George Bernard Shaw's championing of Ibsen in England, renaming his study "The Quintessence of Shavianism." Strong in paralleling fictive characters with persons from Ibsen's life, but making many assumptions that often disregard the creative mind's ability to synthesize and transform, the biography is too strong-minded and self-conscious to be the final word on Ibsen.

MICHAEL MEYER, who wrote the first completely researched biography since Koht's, combines excellent scholarship with style; even his chapter titles are provocative. He emphasizes another dialectic: was Ibsen writing for a theatre of imagination or for the real world of commercial and artistic theatre? Meyer comes down on the side of practicality, seeing Ibsen as "a man writing for the theatre rather than for the printed page." He regards Koht's work as "narrowly nationalistic" and points out that Koht was not a man of the theatre. Particularly valuable here are Meyer's discussions of Ibsen's directing, the Dresden years, and his reaction to Tolstoy, Strindberg, and other contemporaries. Enumerating three great contributions (the breakdown of social barriers, Ibsen's rejection of the Scribean artificialities

of plot, and his understanding of human character, especially feminine), Meyer argues well that "the drama owes more to him than to any other dramatist since Shakespeare." With 60 fascinating illustrations, caricatures, portraits, and manuscript facsimiles, Meyer's remains the best biography for the general reader and the theatre scholar.

The first significant study of Ibsen, JAEGER's work is valuable because the author knew Ibsen and interviewed him regarding his Bergen years. However, Jaeger could not take advantage of the published letters of 1904 or of facts revealed only after Ibsen's death. He felt Ibsen had to return to Norway to write his best modern dramas and sees Ibsen's life as a gradual progression of a man who had "never taken a leap [but] progressed from point to point logically."

GOSSE, writing just after Ibsen's death, concentrates on "that movement of intellectual life in Norway which has surrounded him and which he has stimulated," and consequently returns again and again to his nationalism as it fluctuates from exile to reunion, ending in a public funeral attended by the King of Norway, "to the sound of a people's lamentation." Typical of biographies of this period, it evaluates its subject's characteristics, chronicling changes in "character" as he moved through his life and career. A final chapter discusses his "intellectual characteristics," concluding that no great writer of his century was "so bitter in dealing with human frailty." This work lacks index, footnotes, bibliography or other aids to further study; it is sparsely illustrated.

HEIBERG begins with the idea that the Norwegian character was formed in large part by Ibsen's having given his art, at exactly the time he did, to Europe. His plays, often inspired by political and social events around him, reflect Norway's struggle for self-identity through moral construction; they are "Christian propaganda," a response to the Danish critics who smothered Norwegian nationalism, and as such his plays are constant statements of principle. Heiberg uses the notion of Ibsen's intense national spirit in his early work as a touchstone to the entire canon, and to his travels; in Rome, for example, he "was very hospitable, particularly to Norwegians." From his self-imposed exile to his politically significant return, Ibsen's life and work, in Heiberg's interpretation, were strongly tied to his Norwegian origins.

BRADBROOK, too, even in her subtitle, stresses Ibsen the Norwegian, stating her purpose "to restore Ibsen to his background, and thereby to reveal his true proportions." She quotes Ibsen's response to a German who did not understand *Rosmersholm*: "He who would know me fully must know Norway." Dividing her study into aspects of the writer's impulses—the poet, the humanist, the moralist, etc.—Bradbrook treats the literature as a life-long biography of his thinking; her work is more a literary excursion into the biographical clues in the canon than a biographer's exercise in primary research.

JORGENSON begins with a chapter entitled "The Personal Self," expounding on the ego, Christianity, the supernatural, Plato, the ancient law of the Hebrews, and modern scientific naturalism, to get at his insightful premise: "The entire inner structure of [Ibsen's] works is that of a master builder, a little god who makes order out of chaos." Ibsen's childhood sets the "basic pattern of his own personality" from which spring his characters. What Jorgenson calls "the driving power" of Ibsen's early life in Norway, together with the intellectual climate where his youthful experiences combined with his creativity, explains the prolific nationalist output of Ibsen's first writing. Each of his creative periods has at its base the equivalent passage in his own life; from the prodigal Peer Gynt through the pillars of truth and freedom, to the sublimation of human passions, Ibsen's life and art described each other. A final chapter, "An Epitome," recapitulates the parallels period by period. Altogether Jorgenson offers a thoroughly convincing argument that the man's life and art were one.

ZUCKER relies heavily on the memoirs and recollections of people who knew Ibsen—relatives, acquaintances, even his first biographer Koht, believing the 20-year remove may have freed his friends from restraint. Ibsen trained his willpower early, never wrote to his parents from Grimstad while serving his apprenticeship as apothecary, age 15–21, indulged in clever pranks, and drew caricatures of his classmates. Keeping literary analysis to an absolute minimum, Zucker dwells on childhood anecdote as though every remembered incident presages the man's greatness. He describes Ibsen's life as a dedication to "the cult of the solace of memory," and sees the transition from poetry to drama as a "great leap." Master builder Solness is a self-portrait, since Ibsen viewed playwriting as architecture. Zucker's bibliography credits Gosse, Jaeger, Koht, and the essays of Georg Brandes.

Approaching Ibsen's life as "dissolved in his work," KNIGHT writes from early lecture notes at Leeds, taking on the scholar-teacher tone of the New Critic. Fairly short biographical place-marks introduce longer "elucidations" of the major plays by period, concluding with a brief essay on death, morality, Christianity, suicide, and Nietzsche. HANS GEORG MEYER, whose work is part of a series on World Dramatists, offers critical analysis rather than biography, but he supplies several insights into Ibsen's dramatic themes and techniques as he moves through the canon. DOWNS puts Ibsen in a broader European perspective, helpful in differentiating Ibsen's innovations from his traditional borrowings.

—Thomas J. Taylor

IGNATIUS OF LOYOLA, Saint, 1491–1556; Spanish mystic, founder of the Society of Jesus (Jesuits).

Brodrick, James, *Saint Ignatius Loyola, the Pilgrim Years.* London, Burns and Oates, and New York, Farrar Straus, 1956.

Dalmases, Cándido de, *Ignatius of Loyola, Founder of the Jesuits: His Life and Work,* translated by J. Aixalá. St. Louis, Institute of Jesuit Sources, 1985 (originally published as *El Padre Maestro Ignacio,* Madrid, Editorial Católica, 1979).

Dudon, Paul, *St. Ignatius of Loyola,* translated by William Young. Milwaukee, Bruce Publishing, 1949 (originally published by Beauchesne, Paris, 1934).

Harvey, Robert, *Ignatius Loyola: A General in the Church Militant.* Milwaukee, Bruce Publishing, 1936.

Hollis, Christopher, *Saint Ignatius.* London, Sheed and Ward, and New York, Harper, 1931.

Liversidge, Douglas, *Ignatius of Loyola, the Soldier-Saint.* New York and London, F. Watts, 1970.

Marcuse, Ludwig, *Soldier of the Church: A Life of Ignatius of Loyola,* translated and edited by Christopher Lazare. London, Methuen, and New York, Simon and Schuster, 1939.

Maynard, Theodore, *Saint Ignatius and the Jesuits.* New York, P. J. Kennedy, 1956.

Papasogli, Giorgio, *Saint Ignatius of Loyola,* translated by Paul Garvin. New York, Society of St. Paul, 1959.

Purcell, Mary, *The First Jesuit, Saint Ignatius of Loyola.* Dublin, Gill, 1956; Westminster, Maryland, Newman Press, 1957; revised edition, Chicago, Loyola University Press, 1981.

Rahner, Hugo, *The Spirituality of Saint Ignatius of Loyola: An Account of its Historical Development,* translated by F. J. Smith. Chicago, Loyola University Press, 1953 (originally published as *Ignatius von Loyola und das geschichtliche Werden seiner Frömmigkeit,* Graz and Vienna, A. Pustet, 1947).

Rose, Stewart, *St. Ignatius Loyola and the Early Jesuits.* London, Burns and Oates, and New York, Catholic Publications Society, 1891.

Sedgwick, Henry Dwight, *Ignatius Loyola: An Attempt at an Impartial Biography.* London, Macmillan, 1924.

Thomson, Francis, *Saint Ignatius Loyola.* London, Burns and Oates, 1909; New York, Benzinger, 1910; revised edition, edited by J. H. Pollen, Burns and Oates, 1962.

*

Iñigo López or, as he came to call himself, Ignatius, himself dictated to one of his early disciples, González da Cámara, what has unfortunately come to be known as his "autobiography." This account is limited to spiritual events in Ignatius' life and to the nature of his mystical vision, later elaborated in various works by his most trusted lieutenant, Jéronimo Nadal, whose emphasis differs from that of four other important contemporary biographical sources, all members of the Order, Polanco, Lainez, Maffei, and Ribadeneira. The *Autobiography,* described recently as the account "of a master of discernment . . . sifting, interpreting, controlling the events, the thoughts, the motions in his soul," is available in English translation with Nadal's prologue and an introduction and commentary by J. N. Tylenda (1985), and there are also English editions by William J. Young (1956), John C. Olin, editor, translated by J. F. O'Callaghan (1974), and Pramanando Divarkar (1983). Like all the other writings of and about Ignatius, including his very bulky business correspondence, the dictated *Acta,* to give them their proper title, have been scrupulously edited by the Jesuits in their massive series of historical documents in many languages, the *Monumenta historica Societatis Jesu* (Madrid and Rome, 1894–   ), put out by the Institutum historicum Societatis Jesu and associated with its review, the *Archivum historicum.*

The available biographies reflect the controversial reputation acquired from its earliest years by the Society of Jesus and are frequently either brief and not very penetrating hagiographies or veiled attacks anchored in historical myths. Research into the nature and originality of Ignatius' spirituality dating from the early 1960s has resulted in a radically transformed understanding of its relationship to other Renaissance spiritualities like illuminism, the evangelical humanism of Erasmus, the spiritualities of

Luther, Calvin, and Zwingli, and classical humanism. Scholars have also noted the flexibility of Ignatius' spirituality and the overriding importance of the direct religious experience, "the discernment of spirits," which is at its core. The results of this research have not yet worked their way through to any full-scale biography. Of those available in English, only Brodrick and Dalmases (see below), both Jesuits, are at all reliable. A further English-language biography with new archival material is expected from Philip Caraman, also a Jesuit.

A rather perfunctory but admiring *Life of Saint Ignatius* appeared in English in 1889, having been translated from a French translation of the German original. The earlier native English biographies resound with ideological warfare and are written in a counter-reformatory perspective. The work of ROSE is a product of the Victorian "life-and-times" tradition that wrongly gives the impression that the inspiration Ignatius left his Order, which was always in fact to appear on the Church's advanced liberal pastoral wing, was combatively anti-Protestant, a still common view that does violence to all the evidence of religious and intellectual history.

Rose was followed by THOMSON whose *Saint Ignatius Loyola* was a work of obvious piety. There followed in 1924 what was advertised by its author, SEDGWICK, as "an attempt at an impartial biography." The desperate efforts to be fair make the biography now faintly comic as well as hopelessly out of date. In 1927 there was a short and hagiographic English adaptation of the classic biography by Astráin from within the Order and then, in 1931, HOLLIS, a Catholic layman, published his more general but lightweight biography, anecdotally attempting to sketch his subject against a superficially conceived Renaissance setting. An unsure guide to both Ignatius and his period, this biography is still readable, and a more polished and urbane product than its immediate successors: the English biography by HARVEY and the French attempt at making a "new start" on Ignatius' life by DUDON, whose patronisingly concessive attitude is summed up in his remark, "Detestable as was the remedy proposed by Luther. . . . " The last pre-war biography was MARCUSE's short and popular *Soldier of the Church*.

PURCELL's *The First Jesuit* is a popular book that respects the sources but romanticises them; it is hagiographical in its point of view. More serious is MAYNARD's work, also of 1956. In spite of its learning and breadth of sympathy, however, it is now clearly also dated. The short biography by PAPASOGLI appears overtly proselytising, while that by LIVERSIDGE, is really too short to be useful. Liversidge, who has also written biographies of Lenin, Stalin, and Peter the Great, offers no particular insights into the character or historical role of Ignatius. What is of great expertise is the 1953 account of the development of Ignatius' spirituality by RAHNER, which narrates how experience forged from the initial committed enthusiasms of Ignatius the flexible and responsive instrument that his spirituality became. Unhappily, it could not take account of the subsequent research that revealed the importance of Ignatius' experience beside the Cardoner river in the autumn of 1522.

Unhappily, too, it is not possible to write unequivocally in praise of the two remaining biographies that do have claims to serious attention. The earlier, by BRODRICK, was followed in a second volume by an account of the young Society of Jesus. Both were expected to be definitive English-language works, on the model of the author's early biography of St. Peter Canisius,

an early German Jesuit known above all for his educational activity. It is a known fact, which also emerges from the pages of his biography, that Brodrick, who always writes well, with a twinkle in his eye, and is a serious historian, did not feel real sympathy with what he took to be the intense Spanish mystic who founded his Order. The result is therefore disappointing; a job well done, a duty engagingly accomplished, readable certainly, clearly intelligent, but neither riveting nor penetrating.

Brodrick's historical touch is also unsure, as in his uncritical acceptance that the celebrated preacher Gérard Roussel was a Lutheran (which in 1533 he certainly was not), and in his account of Cop's famous sermon on the beatitudes on 1 November 1533. Brodrick side-steps the once disputed but long ago resolved question about who wrote the sermon, reaction to which caused the outbreak of the French Reformation. He must have known that the choice of text was provocative *only* because it announced a homily on the gospel of the day and not on account of its moral message. At this crucial point, when Ignatius was at Cop's college, Brodrick lets his historical curiosity flag and misses a series of important points about what took place. Though popular and readable, Brodrick blurs detail, giving only a rather wearied and sometimes erroneous account of events.

DALMASES' work, similarly, but with less excuse, fails to appreciate the significance of some of the events he narrates, such as the substitution of his thoroughly Erasmian nephew for the reactionary head of Ignatius' college during the critical years. Surprisingly Dalmases also misses the crucial importance of the Cardoner experience for Ignatius' later life, although it was elaborated in a number of the *Archivum historicum* to which Dalmases himself contributed. His biography scores neither on the interpretation of historical events nor on spiritual or psychological penetration, but on account of its helpful index, notes, bibliography, and survey of the state of the young Society in the year of its founder's death. This is good institutional biography, the sources used with scholarship but not at the expense of readability. Dalmases is particularly strong on statistics of votes, on dates, people, places, decisions, and foundations. His is a less engaging but factually more informative book than Brodrick's.

—A. H. T. Levi

IRVING, Washington, 1783–1859; American writer.

Bowden, Mary Wetherspoon, *Washington Irving*. New York, Twayne, 1981.

Bowers, Claude G., *The Spanish Adventures of Washington Irving*. Boston, Houghton Mifflin, 1940.

Boynton, Henry W., *Washington Irving*. New York, Houghton Mifflin, 1901.

Cater, Harold Dean, *Washington Irving at Sunnyside*. Tarrytown, New York, Sleepy Hollow Restorations, 1957.

Hellman, George, *Washington Irving, Esquire, Ambassador at Large From the New World to the Old*. New York, Knopf, 1925; London, Cape, (192?).

Hill, David J., *Washington Irving*. New York, Sheldon, 1879.

Irving, Pierre Monroe, *The Life and Letters of Washington Irving* (4 vols.). New York, Putnam, and London, Reeve, 1862–64.

Johnston, Johanna, *The Heart That Would Not Hold: A Biography of Washington Irving*. New York, M. Evans, 1971.

McClary, Ben H., editor, *Washington Irving and the House of Murray: Geoffrey Crayon Charms the British 1817–56*. Knoxville, University of Tennessee Press, 1969.

Reichart, Walter A., *Washington Irving and Germany*. Ann Arbor, University of Michigan Press, 1957.

Wagenknecht, Edward, *Washington Irving: Moderation Displayed*. New York, Oxford University Press, 1962.

Warner, Charles D., *Washington Irving*. Boston, Houghton Mifflin, 1881.

Williams, Stanley T., *The Life of Washington Irving* (2 vols.). New York, Oxford University Press, and London, H. Milford, 1935.

*

To date, the biography of Washington Irving against which all others must be measured is the definitive two-volume critical-historical work by WILLIAMS. The book is based on Irving's manuscripts, journals, notebooks, commonplace books, travel notes, memoranda, and letters. It contains extensive appendices, notes, supplemental studies, and an excellent index. Original and revised manuscripts of Irving's published texts were gleaned from public and private sources in Europe and the United States, and Volume II is followed by extensive notes. The biography also includes the then newly discovered Journal of Emily Foster (1820–23). Williams places Irving in the context of the literary criteria of his own time, managing what could be dusty scholarship in a most readable way: "Irving's career, in contrast to his writing, had that volume and variety which entitle him to be remembered, through a full biography, as a famous American; this, despite his modesty, his caution, and the slenderness of his talents, he was. Lacking force and concentration, his life experience, nevertheless, ranged freely over that past to which we now look back with mingled feelings of superiority and longing. Irving, as Poe said, pioneered in the democracy—in literature, history, travel, politics, and diplomacy."

The Williams biography corrects information and misinformation from the authorized first biography of Irving by his nephew, PIERRE IRVING, who had a family interest in preserving the popularity and love Washington Irving inspired in the general public as "Geoffrey Crayon," as acquaintance of such British writers as Sir Walter Scott and Charles Dickens, and as an elder statesman, Ambassador to Spain under President Van Buren. With a Victorian sensibility, Pierre Irving romanticized his uncle's engagement to Matilda Hoffman, who died of tuberculosis at age 18, insisting that Washington Irving's undying love for Matilda was the reason he never married. Even though flawed, Pierre's biography is important enough that every responsible biographer has been forced to react to it.

Elisions and distortions in Pierre Irving's quotations (especially concerning Irving's mature relationship with Emily Foster) were discovered by HELLMAN, who attempted to create a fuller understanding of Irving's character and art. Hellman acknowledges a debt to the nephew, but adds original journals and notebooks from 1804 to 1842, unpublished letters by Irving in the Library of Congress and State Department files, correspondence between Irving and his best friend, Henry Brevoort, books and private papers held at Sunnyside, Irving's home, and unpublished journals by Irving's contemporaries. In addition, Hellman edited two volumes, *Letters of Washington Irving to Henry Brevoort* (1915) and the *Letters of Henry Brevoort to Washington Irving* (1916) and, with W. T. Trent, the *Journals of Washington Irving* (1919).

Hellman's work is additionally superior to BOYNTON's sentimental book-length sketch (similar to his article, "Irving" in John Macy, editor, *American Writers on American Literature*, New York, Tudor, 1934). Nevertheless, Hellman falls considerably short of Williams, attempting as he does to portray a rounder human being without stress on anything detrimental: "Irving . . . believed in enjoying life and in making life as pleasant as possible for others. He was not the exponent of morality but the proponent of good will. He was an observer, not a teacher; and he cared much more to observe and to enjoy than to be taught. . . . He was fond of dancing and of masquerades; passionately fond of the theatre, and pleasantly fond of flirtation. He was much more interested in people than in institutions. . . . "

HILL's early biography is similar in scope to Boynton's, though longer, the chief source of information being extracts from the "charming" *Life and Letters* by Pierre M. Irving, which Hill describes as "less popular than it deserves to be." The book is comprised primarily of entertaining and laudatory anecdotes; Hill makes no attempt at interpretation. Similarly, WARNER's book, which was written to commemorate the centenary of Irving's birth, attempts to place Irving in the context of a canon of newly developing American literature. More objective in tone than Hill or Boynton, Warner nevertheless also depends largely on the Pierre Irving biography. He does not claim additional scholarly sources in this work, which was probably intended for a general audience.

Several biographies limit their explorations of Irving's life to geographically defined phases. BOWERS claims some original discoveries of memorabilia relating to friends Irving met in Spain. Bowers' interpretation of these discoveries seems suspect, for the resulting book is an entertaining series of fictionalized romantic accounts of Irving's sojourn in Spain. As Executive Director of Sleepy Hollow Restorations, CATER was in a unique position to write of Washington Irving's New York home at Sunnyside and the years Irving spent there. The slim volume, possibly prepared as a souvenir, is entertainingly written, well illustrated, and based on reliable scholarly sources. REICHART focuses entirely on Irving's tour of Germany and Austria in 1822–23 to gather material for a "German Sketch Book," as well as the six months Irving spent in Dresden after having met the Fosters. Guided by Williams and his own extensive research in Germany, he balances perspectives on the Emily Foster matter. Reichart also made use of the Irving-Livius adaptation of Weber's comic opera *Abu Hassan*, and the collection of German books Irving brought to America. Also of special interest is McCLARY's study of Irving's relationship with his British publisher, John Murray II, with additional background on both figures. The study focuses on the correspondence between the two men in the context of a running commentary, with seven vignettes as introductions to each chapter.

WAGENKNECHT's book, published in 1962, the same year as Reichart's, attempts to create a "moderate" portrait of Washington Irving, a man too highly lauded by Pierre Irving and, he feels, too highly criticized by S. T. Williams. Wagenknecht makes use of all previous scholarship with the addition of several unpublished dissertations listed in the Preface. His intention is not to supplant Williams' definitive biography, but to focus attention on Irving's personality.

The most recent works on Irving's life are JOHNSTON's biographical novel aimed at a popular audience, and BOWDEN's study for Twayne. BOWDEN's effort is principally literary criticism, but each chapter is prefaced by a biographical sketch of Irving's life as it was when he wrote the works discussed. The study attempts to show Irving as a staunch Jeffersonian—disgusted by monarchies, fond of behind-the-scenes political maneuvering.

—Helen Killoran

ISHERWOOD, Christopher (William Bradshaw), 1904–1986; English-born American writer.

Finney, Brian, *Christopher Isherwood: A Critical Biography.* London, Faber, and New York, Oxford University Press, 1979.

Fryer, Jonathan, *Isherwood: A Biography.* London, New English Library, 1977; New York, Doubleday, 1978.

Lehmann, John, *Christopher Isherwood: A Personal Memoir.* London, Weidenfeld and Nicolson, and New York, Holt, 1987.

Piazza, Paul, *Christopher Isherwood: Myth and Anti-Myth.* New York, Columbia University Press, 1978.

Schwerdt, Lisa M., *Isherwood's Fiction: The Self and Technique.* London, Macmillan, and New York, St. Martin's, 1989.

Summers, Claude J., *Christopher Isherwood.* New York, Ungar, 1980.

*

A definitive biography of Christopher Isherwood? Not yet—and maybe not ever. Isherwood, who died in 1983 (after the available biographies were published), defies most attempts at categorization, just as his works blur the traditional distinctions between genres. To psychoanalytic theorists of the multiple self, Isherwood's personality would make an intriguing case study, for in his novels, essays, biographies, memoirs, travelogues, and diaries, Isherwood reveals himself to be a man intent on scrutinizing, evaluating, describing, and reshaping his own psyche.

The only truly satisfactory starting place is Isherwood's own work, which, in addition to such semi-autobiographical works of fiction as those collected in *The Berlin Stories* (1946), include at least half a dozen autobiographical volumes. For a roughly chronological perspective, readers might wish to adopt the following agenda: *Kathleen and Frank: The Autobiography of a Family* (1971), *Lions and Shadows: An Education in the Twenties* (1938), *Christopher and His Kind 1929–39* (1976), *Journey to a*

War (with W. H. Auden, 1939), *The Condor and the Cows: A South American Travel Diary* (1949), *My Guru and His Disciple* (1980), and *October* (1980). The late journals are being edited by Don Bachardy, who is also the editor of the recent collection entitled *Where Joy Resides: A Christopher Isherwood Reader* (1989).

Two full-length biographies of Isherwood have been written, by FINNEY and FRYER. Finney's book seems more scrupulous in its detail, dates, exact quotations, and the like; he is quite meticulous in citing unpublished correspondence, for example. However, the interview section of Finney's bibliography is dotted with errors in pagination, issue numbers, dates and article titles. Both books succeed in summarizing the twists and turns of Isherwood's career and relationships, although perhaps too much attention is paid to strict chronology, at the expense of the narrative voice. Finney and Fryer were each encouraged by Isherwood, who granted the authors a number of interviews during their work. Fryer provides few footnotes, but his appendices identify the pseudonyms in *Lions and Shadows* and the scene-by-scene authorship of Isherwood's dramatic collaborations with Auden.

The impatient reader, wishing quickly to ascertain the rough outlines of Isherwood's life, should consult the chronology and short biographical first chapter in SUMMERS' work. Summers offers a straightforward analysis of Isherwood's major concerns, and his final chapter provides an excellent introduction to the autobiographical elements of Isherwood's work. Similarly, PIAZZA's and SCHWERDT's analyses, interweaving biography and biographical (or archetypal) criticism, are both provocative and instructive. Piazza focuses on the rebellious, self-ironic streak in Isherwood's life and work, whereas Schwerdt, using an Eriksonian model, explores both the nature of the self and the metaphor of the self in Isherwood's fiction. For an intimate portrait of Isherwood, readers may consult the memoir by publisher John LEHMANN.

—Mark T. Bassett

IVAN IV [the Terrible], 1533–1584; ruler of Russia.

Bobrick, Benson, *Fearful Majesty: The Life and Times of Ivan the Terrible.* New York, Putnam, 1987; Edinburgh, Canongate, 1990.

Graham, Stephen, *Ivan the Terrible: The Life of Ivan IV of Russia.* New Haven, Connecticut, Yale University Press, 1933.

Grey, Ian, *Ivan the Terrible.* Philadelphia, Lippincott, and London, Hodder and Stoughton, 1964.

Payne, Robert and Nikita Romanoff, *Ivan the Terrible.* New York, Crowell, 1975.

Platonov, Sergei, *Ivan the Terrible*, edited and translated by Joseph L. Wieczynski. Gulf Breeze, Florida, Academic International Press, 1974 (originally published as *Ivan Groznyi*, Leningrad, 1923).

Skrynnikov, Ruslan G., *Ivan the Terrible*, edited and translated by Hugh F. Graham. Gulf Breeze, Florida, Academic International Press, 1981 (originally published as *Ivan Grozny*, Moscow, Nauka, 1975).

Troyat, Henri, *Ivan the Terrible*, translated by Joan Pinkham. New York, Dutton, 1984; London, New English Library, 1985 (originally published by Flammarion, Paris, 1981).

Von Eckhardt, Hans, *Ivan the Terrible*, translated by Catherine Alison Phillips. New York, Knopf, 1949 (originally published as *Ivan Schreckliche*, Vittorio Klostermann, Frankfurt am Main, 1941).

Waliszewski, K., *Ivan the Terrible*, translated by Lady Mary Loyd. London, Heinemann, 1904 (originally published as *Les Origines de la Russie Moderne, Ivan le Terrible*, Paris, Plon-Nourrit et Cie., 1904).

*

The biographies of Ivan IV can be divided into two major groups: those that dwell on the psychological explanations of Ivan's character and relate his rule to his mental and emotional make-up, and those that tend to focus more intensely on the events of Ivan's reign set against the historical background of both Russia and Europe. The first set of books reads almost like historical novels, and though they grip the reader with enthralling and horrifying tales of Ivan's excesses, they do not provide sufficient historical analysis of his rule, relying instead on a sensational and anecdotal presentation of Ivan and his reign. The authors of the second group of biographies are more reluctant to use psychology to explain, illuminate, or simplify Ivan's reign. As Bobrick states, "I cannot claim to have resolved the fundamental contradictions that must baffle any biographer of Ivan IV. On the contrary, I learned to live with them—even as his contemporaries did."

GRAHAM wrote the earliest detailed biography of Ivan in English that applies psychological insights to the character of the Tzar. It is a straightforward account of his life and times that portrays Ivan as cruel, not mad. "He seldom lost his head, but remained coolly rational, and sometimes witty in the midst of his barbarities." Ivan's age was a violent one and his atrocities are compared to those of Catherine de' Medici and the Duke of Alva. Graham draws on the accounts of English travelers and the Russian historians Karamzin, Soloviev, and Klyuchevsky for his readable, if unexciting, account.

GREY provides vibrant descriptions of medieval Moscow and a solid summary of earlier Russian history in short, clearly written chapters with footnotes at the bottom of the pages. The Tzar is portrayed as tragic; his egoism denied him the humility required of a successful ruler. An adequate bibliography is included.

PAYNE AND ROMANOFF's book is a "good read" for the less scholarly, although it offers an excellent geneology, chronology, glossary, and bibliography. Maps are sprinkled throughout the work, and Ivan's character is analyzed through a series of portraits. The Tzar is portrayed as a madman who used the *oprichnina* and other means to destroy his country and was unequalled in cruelty until the 20th century.

TROYAT offers a colorful and dramatic portrait of Ivan and his exploits, reminiscent of the Tzar in Eisenstein's film, as well as good descriptions of Moscow, its markets, the terem, and the wretched situation of women. The most psychological of all the works, Troyat ascribes Ivan's excessive cruelty to his passion for sexual excitement and fulfillment as well as his identification with an omnipotent God whose omniscience rationalized the Tzar's own license.

Although VON EKHARDT is a little too romantic in attributing much of Ivan's cruelty and strange behavior to the loss of his first wife, Anastasia, he also justifies the Tzar's terroristic tactics as necessary in building a powerful centralized state, free from attacks by Russia's neighbors and responsive to the mass of Russian people, not just the boyars. In this way von Ekhardt's work, though rather turgid in translation, bridges the gap between the more romantic or psychological biographies and the more analytical ones.

PLATONOV's study offers a rationalist account of Ivan's reign, though he infers that psychology and even pathology may provide some insight into the Tzar's deeds. Unlike many of his Soviet contemporaries, Platonov was not interested in the philosophy of history, relying instead upon the facts and events of Ivan's reign to explain the Tzar's rule. His work includes an invaluable essay by Richard Hellie summarizing the Russian and Soviet historiography of Ivan IV.

SKRYNNIKOV, like Platonov, is skeptical of the psychological interpretation that attributes Ivan's later actions to his childhood traumas. Rather, he states that "a turbulent time placed its distinctive stamp upon the character and fate of those who were part of it. Ivan the Terrible was very much a man of this time." Skrynnikov regards Ivan as a strong ruler who strengthened the centralized autocracy, attempted to equalize the privileges of the gentry and the boyars, and created the *oprichnina* to subdue those nobles who resisted moving to Kazan. In evaluating the effects of the *oprichnina*, Skrynnikov points out that though it impeded Russia's development in the second half of the 16th century, it did not ultimately alter the structure of Russian government. With its excellent historiographical and bibliographical notes and its short but clearly written chapters, Skrynnikov's work is an indispensable—if dispassionate—study.

WALISZEWSKI's heavy style, with its long sentences and often archaic expression of ideas, should not discourage the reader from exploring this excellent source on Ivan and his times. The author provides rich details about life in 16th-century Russia. Descriptions of the Tzar's profligate banquets, his gargantuan capacities, his mockery of foreign dignitaries, and his life at Alexandrov Sloboda, a mixture of "Sodom and Cythera," enliven this long, dense, but fascinating biography. Waliszewski emphasizes that Ivan was a man of action, stronger in practice than in theory. He reflected the "material greatness and brute force" of his epoch as did Peter the Great, Russia's other great reformer. An extensive bibliography enriches this fine source.

BOBRICK's study continues where Waliszewski left off and stands as the most up-to-date, clearly written biography of Ivan IV. Geneologies, a list of Russian rulers and metropolitans, illustrations, maps, and an extensive bibliography make this source valuable to both the casual and serious scholar. Rich anecdotes, vignettes, and short character studies enliven this account, which is based on the latest research. Bobrick stresses that Ivan consolidated the power of the monarch, extended Russia's territory, and reached out to the West. In sum, he presents a picture of Ivan as "cruel—and 'terrible'—and great."

—Mary Rossabi

IVES, Charles, 1874–1954; American composer.

Burkholder, J. Peter, *Charles Ives: The Ideas Behind the Music.* New Haven, Connecticut, and London, Yale University Press, 1985.

Cowell, Henry and Sidney Cowell, *Charles Ives and His Music.* New York, Oxford University Press, 1955.

Perlis, Vivian, *Charles Ives Remembered: An Oral History.* New Haven, Connecticut, Yale University Press, 1974.

Perry, Rosalie S., *Charles Ives and the American Mind.* Kent, Ohio, Kent State University Press, 1974.

Rossiter, Frank R., *Charles Ives and His America.* New York, Liveright, 1975; London, Gollancz, 1976.

Woolridge, David, *From the Steeples and Mountains: A Study of Charles Ives.* New York, Knopf, 1974; as *Charles Ives: A Portrait*, London, Faber, 1974.

*

COWELL wrote the first book-length biography of Ives, published one year after the composer's death. Of all Ives' biographers, Henry Cowell (himself a composer) was closest to him professionally and personally, and his book, co-authored with his wife, Sidney Cowell, can be considered an "official" biography. Though it includes some discussion of Ives' music, Cowell's book remains an inestimably valuable biographical document, drawing on conversations with Ives, Ives' wife, and on Cowell's own personal acquaintance with the composer. Cowell is, of course, far from objective, since he presents Ives as Ives himself wished to be seen: as a lonely rebel working apart from the professional European musical establishment, rooted in the New England intellectual and cultural tradition, anticipating the major innovations of the 20th century. Cowell is thus the foundation for the still-prevalent Ives "myth" and a standard against which subsequent views must be measured.

The Ives centenary year, 1974, brought forth three significant biographical works by Perlis, Perry, and Woolridge. These were followed in 1975 by ROSSITER, the first truly revisionist study and important for seeing Ives in a new light. Rossiter, a social rather than musical historian, views Ives as a social conformist who fell increasingly out of touch with the modern industrial world. Ives, in Rossiter's view, retreated into an idealistic fantasy of heroic, "masculine" music to challenge the commercialism and aesthetic weakness he saw around him, unconsciously asserting his own masculinity. Rossiter's study verges on psycho-biography and his analysis may be overdrawn; but despite the unreconciled dichotomy he sees between Ives' advanced music and his reactionary world-view, Rossiter holds Ives' musical achievements in great esteem.

PERRY comes closer to the conventional view, emphasizing Ives' indebtedness to Emersonian Transcendentalism and citing examples from his musical works to illustrate his philosophical sources. She places Ives squarely in the American intellectual tradition characterized by optimism and democratic idealism, not sensing the uneasy psyche that Rossiter perceives. Her view is a well-stated, intelligent reassertion of the Ives "myth."

WOOLRIDGE presents a wild and idiosyncratic embroidery bristling with value judgments, personal impressions, hearsay, and assertions of fact unsupported by evidence. Though at times brilliant and entertaining, Woolridge must nevertheless be taken with more than a grain of salt.

PERLIS gives us, not a biography in the strict sense, but an "oral history"—raw biographical material consisting of interviews with Ives' family, friends, and associates. Informal and anecdotal, it portrays Ives' personality more vividly than any formal biography, and for that it is surpassed only by Ives' own *Essays before a Sonata* (1920) and *Memos* (1972). Perlis is more objective than Cowell had been, and her book serves, in passing, to correct some aspects of the Ives "myth" (note particularly the interview with Elliott Carter, an early Ives protege who became an outstanding composer in his own right). It is also copiously and well illustrated.

The most recent biography is BURKHOLDER's, in many ways the most penetrating study so far. Burkholder takes particular issue with Perry, showing that Ives achieved maturity before turning to Transcendentalism, and emphasizing the influence of Ives' family and especially his teachers in shaping his artistic development. Burkholder deepens our insight into Ives' music and personality and places our understanding of Ives' career on a more solid foundation.

Many fundamental aspects of the Ives "myth" are now being questioned, especially his own testimony concerning the influence of his Yale education, the dates of composition and revision of his works, his familiarity with contemporary European music, and his public relations strategies. The next biography can be expected to confront a new, more complex image of this quintessentially American composer.

—Martin Picker

JACKSON, Andrew, 1767–1845; American general and political leader, 7th president of the United States.

Bassett, John S., *The Life of Andrew Jackson* (2 vols.). New York, Macmillan, 1911; revised edition, 1916.

Curtis, James C., *Andrew Jackson and the Search for Vindication.* Boston, Little Brown, 1966.

Davis, Burke, *Old Hickory: A Life of Andrew Jackson.* New York, Dial Press, 1977.

James, Marquis, *Andrew Jackson* (2 Vols.). New York, Bobbs-Merrill, 1933–37.

Latner, Richard B., *The Presidency of Andrew Jackson: White House Politics 1829–37.* Athens, Georgia, The University of Georgia Press, 1979.

Parton, James, *Life of Andrew Jackson* (3 vols.). New York, Mason Brothers, 1860.

Remini, Robert V., *Andrew Jackson.* New York, Twayne, 1966.

Remini, Robert V., *Andrew Jackson and the Course of American Empire, 1767–1821.* New York, Harper and Row, 1977.

Remini, Robert V., *Andrew Jackson and the Course of American Freedom, 1822–1832.* New York, Harper and Row, 1981.

Remini, Robert V., *Andrew Jackson and the Course of American Democracy, 1833–45.* New York, Harper and Row, 1984.

Remini, Robert V., *The Life of Andrew Jackson.* New York, Harper, 1988 (one-volume edition of the above three-volume work).

Remini, Robert V., *The Legacy of Andrew Jackson: Essays on Democracy, Indian Removal, and Slavery.* Baton Rouge, Louisiana State University Press, 1988.

Rogin, Michael Paul, *Fathers and Children: Andrew Jackson and the Subjugation of the American Indian.* New York, Knopf, 1975.

Sumner, William Graham, *Andrew Jackson.* Boston, Houghton Mifflin, 1882.

Ward, John W., *Andrew Jackson: Symbol for an Age.* New York, Oxford University Press, 1955.

*

As one of the central figures in American history during the first half of the 19th century, Andrew Jackson has not lacked for attention. To satisfy public interest in his life, as well as to advance his political fortunes, Jackson's close associates John H. Eaton and John Reed issued a biography in 1817. Another biography completed during Jackson's lifetime by Amos Kendall in 1844 reflects Kendall's Democratic roots. But it was left to PARTON, one of America's most prominent biographers in the mid-19th century, to produce the first noteworthy study of Jackson's life. His three volumes are valuable today primarily as source material, for Parton had access to many of Jackson's contemporaries and uncovered much about Jackson's early life. They also remain quite readable and absorbing for the modern reader. SUMNER'S brief volume in the American Statesmen Series is highly critical of the Hero of New Orleans as a person and for his policies, evidence of Sumner's advocacy of Social Darwinism and laissez-faire.

The first study reflecting the impact of professional scholarship is BASSETT'S sound and sober biography, sympathetic to Jackson as a representative of "the common man" and the democratic westerner. JAMES celebrated Jackson's life in a lively two-volume biography that was as passionate and fiery as its subject; it won a Pulitzer Prize in 1938. While it still makes for enjoyable reading, it should not be mistaken for an accurate or balanced account. Both biographies contributed to maintaining Jackson's status as a popular hero and an advocate of democracy.

Although the nature of "Jacksonian Democracy" and the issues that dominated Jackson's presidency were major topics of debate among scholars from the 1940s to the early 1960s, no biography reflecting these concerns appeared. Arthur M. Schlesinger, Jr., argued for Jackson's centrality in his time in *The Age of Jackson* (1946), a wonderfully written book that errs in mistaking Jackson for Franklin Delano Roosevelt. Schlesinger's Jackson resembles the Jackson portrayed by Bassett and James, although he is shorn of much of his western characteristics, for Schlesinger wished to emphasize class over section as the primary cleavage in American politics. Before long scholarly debate over the meaning of Jacksonian Democracy became almost detached from study of Jackson himself. One volume that did address Jackson's meaning to his age is WARD's fine study of how Jackson's image was shaped to conform to American values about nature, providence, and will, serving as a vehicle of definition. However, it was linked only tangentially to the main debates over Jacksonian Democracy.

Jackson's reputation came under fire in the 1970s as historians attacked his association with slavery and his advocacy of Indian removal. Representative of this new hostility are two studies that make use of psychological notions about behavior to understand Jackson. ROGIN's examination of Jackson and the Indians is long on passionate anger and short on sympathy for the Hero of New Orleans, but its efforts to link Jackson's personality and private life with his politics and policies are absorbing if sometimes strained. In a well-written, compact study, CURTIS portrays Jackson as a man sensitive to slights, afraid of death, and driven by a desire for revenge, with a tendency to view political differences as personal challenges. In so doing he minimizes the extent to which Jackson actually believed in the positions he advocated, and comes close to reducing politics to a matter of personality and psychology. Of these two studies, Curtis' is the more persuasive, for it is somewhat more limited, while Rogin's agenda-ridden assault obscures some acute insights.

While personality and psychology are essential components of a good biography, they must be set in context. LATNER emphasizes ideology and issues as far more important motivations, presenting a rather detailed and enlightening exploration of Jackson's relationship to his advisors, and emphasizing the influence of Western interests in administration policy. Jackson emerges as an able politician, in control of events, using his powers as president to further his image of the good society. In contrast, DAVIS' 1977 biography, while written with accustomed verve, made little impact on historians' understanding of him; in some ways it is reminiscent of James' effort.

REMINI is Jackson's most prolific and preeminent biographer. His brief 1966 study of Jackson defended Old Hickory's image as a hero of democracy. A three-volume effort followed, which expanded on this theme at great length, although Remini did pause to note Jackson's role in Indian removal. In many ways the second volume is the most remarkable, for in it Remini insists that Jackson's decision to remain in public life after his defeat in the 1824 presidential contest was motivated by his belief that corruption had corroded the ideological foundations of American republicanism. Jackson was determined to restore the new nation to the pure state envisioned by the Farmers; he was "a man of republican principle and purpose who devised a program of reform by which he believed he could best protect and perpetuate the liberty of the American people." Throughout the trilogy, based upon extensive archival research and written with verve and conviction, Remini asserts Jackson's central role in the evolution of American politics during the first half of the 19th century. A one-volume condensation, *The Life of Andrew Jackson*, appeared in 1988; Remini's thoughts on several pivotal issues in Old Hickory's career are best summarized in *The Legacy of Andrew Jackson*, originally given as the Walter Lynwood Fleming Lectures at Louisiana State University in 1984.

Jackson's correspondence and papers are currently being edited by a team of scholars under the direction of Harold Moser at the University of Tennessee. A microfilm collection that supplements the Library of Congress' collection of Jackson papers is currently available. Moser's predecessors, John S. Bassett and J. Franklin Jameson's multivolume *The Correspondence of Andrew Jackson* (1926–35) will remain valuable until the modern edition is complete.

—Brooks D. Simpson

JACKSON, Stonewall [Thomas Jonathan Jackson], 1824–1863; American Confederate general.

Bowers, John, *Stonewall Jackson: Portrait of a Soldier*. New York, Morrow, 1989.

Chambers, Lenoir, *Stonewall Jackson* (2 vols.). New York, Morrow, 1959.

Cooke, John E., *Stonewall Jackson: A Military Biography*. New York, Appleton, 1866.

Dabney, Robert L., *Life and Campaigns of Lieut.-Gen. Thomas J. Jackson*. New York, Blelock, 1866.

Davis, Burke, *They Called Him Stonewall: A Life of Lt. General T. J. Jackson, C.S.A.* New York, Holt Rinehart, 1954.

Henderson, G. F. R., *Stonewall Jackson and the American Civil War* (2 vols.). London, Longman, 1898; one-volume edition, New York, Grosset and Dunlap, 1943.

Jackson, Anna Mary, *Life and Letters of General Thomas J. Jackson*. New York, Harper, 1892.

Tate, Allen, *Stonewall Jackson: The Good Soldier*. New York, Minton Balch, 1928.

Vandiver, Frank E., *Mighty Stonewall*. New York, McGraw-Hill, 1957.

*

The two best early biographers of Jackson, Cooke and Dabney, began writing before the war was over. Both men worshiped Jackson and, consequently, both found it difficult to separate man from myth. Yet they produced quite different books. COOKE, a Virginia novelist and Confederate staff officer who had known Jackson, was carried by his emotions to begin writing within days of Jackson's death. He finished his task in less than three months, but, recognizing the thinness of his effort, almost immediately began work on an expanded volume. Cooke's account of military affairs is gripping, and he provides an insider's view of Confederate military operations that is strengthened by personal observations by Jackson's contemporaries. Yet even the revised edition, with its meager coverage of Jackson's pre-war life, remains a biography only in the narrowest sense.

DABNEY, a Presbyterian minister and Confederate officer, had served briefly on Jackson's staff. He fashioned his biography over a three-year period, during which Anna Jackson, who had asked Dabney to undertake the labor, granted him several interviews and access to much of the general's correspondence. Still, the book is imperfect. Dabney spends too much time justifying the Lost Cause, and he makes numerous errors of fact. He ignores Jackson's military failures and depreciates "those *bizarre* traits" that popular fancy had attributed to Stonewall. Indeed, Dabney states unequivocally that his "prime object" is to "portray and vindicate [Jackson's] Christian character." His narration of military affairs lacks the charm and power of Cooke's.

Still, Dabney remained preeminent for over 30 years. During that time, Mrs. JACKSON gave the world her unique view of Stonewall's life, but the principal value of her work is the long excerpts she provides from private letters. HENDERSON, a British soldier and military historian, was the next serious biographer. He relied heavily on Dabney for information about Jackson's antebellum life, but his knowledge of military affairs and access to a wealth of war records and reminiscences published

after Dabney's book allowed Henderson to place Jackson's life in firmer perspective. His analysis of Jackson's military career, while containing some errors, is still the best one available. Henderson, like Dabney, sees Jackson as "a Christian hero," and he refuses to admit that Jackson ever made a tactical error; but unlike either Dabney or Cooke, he understands the complexities of war and, while writing from a southern perspective, avoids the sin of sectional partisanship. Finally, Henderson's colorful and exciting prose nearly matches Cooke.

It was another 30 years before TATE, the southern poet and essayist, tried his hand. His "narrative" of Jackson's life is lively and entertaining, but it lacks serious analysis. Tate is a little more critical than earlier writers of Jackson's military errors, such as the Seven Days; but he, too, portrays Jackson primarily as a southern Cromwell, motivated largely by a relentless religious faith and pursuit of earthly perfection. More disturbing from a scholarly perspective, Tate tends to paraphrase quotations (without even identifying his sources) and to insert imagined conversations.

Not until the 1950s did Jackson again undergo biographical scrutiny. Then, as the centennial of the Civil War grew near, three biographies appeared. First and least is the offering by DAVIS, a North Carolina journalist and novelist. While admiring Jackson, Davis seeks to extract him from legend. He succeeds on one level by devoting nearly a third of the book—more than any other writer—to Jackson's antebellum life. Davis writes with verve, and he does not hesitate to criticize Jackson, particularly for the damaging military effects of his secretive nature. Yet, except for this fine-tuning, Davis does not contribute much to our understanding of Jackson.

Three years later, VANDIVER, the only trained historian to attempt a full-scale biography, completed the most satisfying single volume on Jackson. Vandiver is also the only biographer fully to document his interpretation. His style can be plodding, however, and his research, while impressive, is not exhaustive. He cannot match Henderson's tactical analysis of battles or his evaluation of strategic situations. Yet Vandiver does provide new information about the antebellum years, particularly Jackson's time at VMI. He is more critical of Jackson's military performance than any previous writer, and he shows Jackson to have been a poor administrator and a frequently tyrannical commander. In the end, Vandiver probably satisfies because he provides the best available delineation of Jackson's personality. In Vandiver's pages we probably find Jackson as his contemporaries knew him.

At the end of the 1950s, CHAMBERS, a North Carolina journalist whose great-grandfather presided over Jackson's second marriage, produced the longest (over 1000 pages in two volumes) and most complete biography. Chambers' announced intention is to account for the whole man, and particularly to show how the first 37 years of Jackson's life account for the climactic final two. He devotes slightly less space than does Davis to those first years, but he is more perceptive. He writes vividly, and his evaluation of individuals is balanced. His conclusions are firmly rooted in scholarship, he corrects some longstanding errors of fact, and he fills in many gaps in Jackson's early life, particularly the Mexican War years. Rather than excuse Jackson's military and personal failings, he explains them. One even senses that he improves on some aspects of Vandiver's evocation of Jackson's elusive character.

Most recently, novelist and free-lance writer BOWERS, a Tennessean, has contributed a highly readable but intellectually deficient look at Jackson. His book is a biography insofar as it re-creates the life of a real person, but Bowers admits that many conversations in his narrative are fictitious. Without notes or a bibliography, the book does not clearly distinguish fact from fiction.

—Daniel E. Sutherland

JAMES I, 1566–1625; English monarch.

Lee, Maurice, *Government by Pen*. Urbana, University of Illinois Press, 1980.

Mathew, David, *James I*. London, Eyre and Spottiswoode, 1967.

McElwee, William, *The Wisest Fool in Christendom: The Reign of King James I and VI*. London, Faber, and New York, Harcourt, 1958.

Willson, David H., *King James VI and I*. London, Cape, and New York, Holt, 1956.

*

James VI and I is an easy man to understand, but a difficult man to judge. He was one of the most open of kings. He was the first intellectual to sit on the throne since Alfred the Great in the ninth century. He wrote extensively—about politics, religion, and about many contemporary issues such as demonology and what he saw as the filthy new habit of tobacco-smoking—and many of his speeches (spoken from the heart) and even more of his letters (especially his private letters to close friends) have survived. He is thus an easy king to write about. But his achievement remains deeply controversial. Historians of his reign have tended to be far more charitable to him than have his biographers.

WILLSON's is a full scholarly biography, and a consistently hostile one that remorselessly contrasts the high ideals that James proclaimed in his writings and the shabby reality of his lazy and lackadaisical performance. Like many other biographers, Willson discusses the shocking circumstances of James' early life: his mother's connivance in his father's murder and subsequent abdication and flight, James' strict education and reaction against many aspects of the political theories of his mentors, and his dangerous years as king of an unruly Scotland before his inheritance of the English throne. Thereafter, Willson offers a fundamentally unsympathetic account of a king who failed to grasp his opportunities, gave himself up to a life of rather squalid leisure and who weakened respect for the monarchy. He was "a baffling combination of learning and pedantry, shrewdness and folly, lofty aspirations and contemptible practice." Willson allowed himself to be overinfluenced by the bilious but vivid character assassination penned in the 1620s by Anthony Weldon, a courtier disappointed of advancement, but this very fully researched biography, offering authoritative judgments on the age as well as the man, has proved highly influential.

McELWEE's biography is less scholarly, less well researched, and less authoritative about the background. But it offers a more balanced portrait and in some ways one easier to read and follow. Its title is very apt. It was Henri IV of France, James' contemporary (assassinated in 1610), who first called James "the wisest fool in Christendom." This drew attention to James' learning and to his lack of judgment, to his sophisticated diagnoses of political problems and to his lack of tact and diplomacy in solving them. McElwee sees him as a king who inherited a creaking state apparatus and who failed to find remedies to those deep-seated problems, but also as a canny king who was a sound Protestant and who spared England the costs of vainglorious foreign adventures. He was a king who inspired affection; as McElwee remarks "a curious note of sincerity pervades many of the conventional panegyrics which marked his death." Despite having previously written a study of the Essex Divorce scandal and the murder of Sir Thomas Overbury (the greatest and seediest scandal to rock James' court), McElwee's biography serves as a healthy corrective to the stern judgments of the more scholarly Willson.

MATHEW's biography is eccentric but at times brilliantly illuminating. Mathew was himself a larger-than-life character, an Oxford based Catholic priest (eventually an archbishop *in partibus infidelium*) of vast girth and grubby clothes who wrote extensively on early modern history. He was by nature an essayist, one for whom writing constituted a stream-of-learned-consciousness. There was nothing orderly about his books. He simply wrote about what he knew and what interested him, leaving yawning gaps in his narrative. In this book the chapter headings reveal his interests. There are 39 chapters making up the 330 pages of text. For the early years of James' reign in England the chapter titles are "Church and State," "The House of Commons," "Sir Walter Raleigh," "the Gunpowder Plot," "Father Garnet's Trial." Mathew was far more interested in James' attitude to the Catholics than to the Puritans; to Spain than to Parliament; to Renaissance civilization than to the Exchequer. A chapter called "Ecclesiastics" begins with an almost wholly irrelevant vignette about the fate that befell Marc Antonio de Dominis when he defected back to Rome after a sojourn in England under James' patronage; continues with the ecclesiastical problems created when the archbishop of Canterbury accidentally killed a gamekeeper while out hunting; discussed the rise of bishop John Williams; and ends with the religious pilgrimage of James' queen. In the midst of this odd mixture is much learning and some beautiful writing. Mathew is a delight to read and the final impression is rich and satisfying. But one has to abandon the search for completeness and coherence. It is a book to dip into rather than to read from cover to cover. It is a book that proves that idiosyncrasy can be highly effective.

Although all these biographies offer accounts of James' early life in Scotland and of his government of his native land up to his inheritance of the English throne in 1603, they all largely ignore the continuing story of his rule of Scotland in the last 25 years of his life. This major lacuna is filled by LEE's study. "Here I sit and govern Scotland by pen," James declared in a speech to his English Parliament; and Lee sees how, and how effectively he managed it. It is a study that reinforces an uneasy feeling raised by the other biographies: how can so skillful a ruler of Scotland have been so inadequate a ruler of England. Lee came to this study having written two major studies of

Scottish politics and administration during the later 16th century, and *Government by Pen* is a shrewd and very thoroughly researched study of effective absentee kingship. It is an essential supplement for anyone who wants to get a full sense of James' aspirations and achievements.

—John Morrill

———————

JAMES II, 1633–1701; English monarch.

Ashley, Maurice, *James II*. London, Dent, and Minneapolis, University of Minnesota Press, 1977.
Clarke, J. S., *Life of James II, King of England* (2 vols.). London, Longman, 1816.
Miller, John, *James II: A Study in Kingship*. Hove, East Sussex, Wayland, 1977.
Turner, Francis C., *James II*. London, Eyre and Spottiswoode, and New York, Macmillan, 1948.

*

Studies of James II are complicated by the events of two Revolutions, those of 1689 and 1789. The Revolution of 1689 in England generated powerful myths about the procurement of civil and religious liberty, which in turn generated some of the most effective historical polemics produced by the 19th century, above all Thomas Babington Macaulay's *History of England* with its invective against James' Catholic tyranny overthrown at the Glorious Revolution. The violence of the French Revolution of 1789 caused the destruction of many archives, not the least of which was the private archive of James II, containing many hundreds of his letters and the personal journals he kept from the age of 16 (viz from the date of his father's execution) to his death. This has created handicaps from which all subsequent biographers have suffered.

CLARKE was the librarian to the Prince Regent, i.e., to the Royal House that displaced the Stuarts. In 1816, with the assistance of the Romantic novelist Sir Walter Scott, he published a version of James II's Memoirs based on some genuine and some corrupt transcripts of documents from the destroyed Jacobite archive. This cobbled together semi-autobiography is fundamental to any new life of James but is fraught with difficulties. The best advice that modern authors have offered is that it is most reliable for the years before 1660 (when James was a commander in the armies of France and Spain) and for the years 1678–85 (during the period of the Exclusion Crisis, the parliamentary attempt to prevent James II from succeeding his brother as king because of James' Roman Catholicism). It is strongest on James' military interests and concerns, but it has to be the starting point for a discussion of his beliefs.

TURNER's is the longest and fullest of the modern biographies. It was the first 20th-century biography to shake itself free from the intellectual pall that Macaulay had thrown over the later 17th century. It benefitted from the rethinking of the period as a whole that had taken place in the 1930s and 1940s by historians like Sir George Clark and David Ogg; and it benefitted even more from a thorough reading and rethinking of the printed sources, and a careful study of selected manuscript collections.

Turner did not use the formal governmental papers in the Public Record Office, and therefore his study remains essentially a study of James as a politician and as a Catholic bigot. 60 pages are devoted to his childhood and exile (1633–60); 170 pages to his career during the reign of his brother (1660–85); 220 to his three and a half year reign (1685–88); and 50 pages to his attempts to regain his throne and to his decline into religious melancholia.

ASHLEY is a veteran writer on the 17th century and has published more than 20 books on the subject. His biography of James followed hard on the heels of a life of Charles II and a study of the Glorious Revolution. There is, in truth, a great deal of overlap between this biography and those two previous books. Ashley had also written two biographies of Oliver Cromwell and he was, at the time he wrote this study, President of the Cromwell Association. His sympathies were far more with the Lord Protector's strenuous puritanism and libertarianism than with later Stuart divine right monarchy. His study has all the hallmarks of experience. It is nicely arranged, elegantly written, and has a good eye for the apt quotation. It is Whiggish in its preconceptions (James was doomed from the outset of the reign because he espoused illiberal and un-British causes, especialy Roman Catholicism). The book paints him in dark if not pitch-black colours. It is an easier read than the study by Miller, which appeared the following year, and it is a strongly delineated portrait of a man bent on self-destruction; but it lacks subtlty.

MILLER's is by far the best-researched biography. Miller came to write his biography after completing a doctorate (published as *Popery and Politics 1660–1688*) on the force of anti-catholicism in later Stuart England. He had been deeper into the archives, specifically those of local and central government relating to the implication of policy, than anyone else. His study is much more effective than others in discussing the effects of James' policies and the extent to which it was not the policies themselves so much as widespread misunderstanding of them that caused him to fall. James is portrayed as a king who stretched his prerogative to the limit, but who was not an advocate of a continental-style absolutism. Furthermore, James did not intend or seek the forced conversion of his peoples to catholicism. He intended to create conditions of civil and religious equality for Catholics and Protestants such that conversions to Rome took place naturally and in vast numbers. He was ruthless as to the means he adopted to make this possible; but there was no intention to create a Catholic tyranny. Miller's book, like Turner's, adopts a narrative frame and a chronological order, with the same proportions being alloted to the various stages of James' life. The study of the period before James' accession is also notable for its very harsh judgments on Charles II's political skills.

—John Morrill

———————

JAMES, Henry, 1843–1916; American writer; became British subject, 1915.

Bosanquet, Theodora, *Henry James at Work*. London, Hogarth Press, 1924.

Edel, Leon, *Henry James: The Untried Years, 1843–70.* Philadelphia, Lippincott, and London, Hart-Davis, 1953.

Edel, Leon, *Henry James: the Conquest of London, 1870–81.* Philadelphia, Lippincott, and London, Hart-Davis, 1962.

Edel, Leon, *Henry James: The Middle Years, 1882–95.* Philadelphia, Lippincott, 1962; London, Hart-Davis, 1963.

Edel, Leon, *Henry James: The Treacherous Years, 1895–1901.* Philadelphia, Lippincott, and London, Hart-Davis, 1969.

Edel, Leon, *Henry James: The Master, 1901–16.* Philadelphia, Lippincott, and London, Hart-Davis, 1972.

Edel, Leon, *Henry James: A Life.* New York, Harper, 1985.

Edgar, Pelham, *Henry James: Man and Author.* London, G. Richards, 1925; Boston, Houghton Mifflin, 1927.

Hyde, H. Montgomery, *Henry James at Home.* London, Methuen, and New York, Farrar Straus, 1969.

Le Clair, Robert Charles, *The Young Henry James, 1843–70.* New York, Bookman, 1955.

Nowell-Smith, Simon, editor, *The Legend of the Master: Henry James.* London, Constable, 1947; New York, Scribner, 1948.

Page, Norman, editor, *Henry James: Interviews and Recollections.* New York, St. Martin's, and London, Macmillan, 1984.

*

While the five-volume Edel biography is the definitive life of James, many less ambitious though quite valuable works preceded and often contributed to its making. Notable among these is BOSANQUET, an intimate portrait by the woman who was employed by James as his secretary on 10 October 1907 and worked with him intermittently for the rest of his life. Her memoir benefits both from her extraordinary access to the minutiae of James' working life as well as from the fact that she was no career secretary but a writer herself: before she went to work for James, Theodora Bosanquet (even her name is like that of a Jamesian heroine) had tried her hand at both poetry and fiction and had published essays in periodicals. Her prose tends to be florid yet quite insightful; small wonder, then, that Edel quotes Bosanquet frequently and to good effect.

EDGAR wrote at a time when bookish lives such as James' were often thought to lack content. Therefore, while some reviewers of this bio-critical study praise its author for giving more attention to the works than to the man, others complain that James' personality is inadequately portrayed. Both types of reviewers are correct, of course, in identifying Edgar as a biographical critic who found little of compelling interest in his subject's life. LE CLAIR covers James' first three decades, with special emphasis on family relations, particularly the influence of Henry James Sr. and the "devotion, the lifelong friendship" between Henry and his brother William. Aware of Edel's psychological interest in James (the first of Edel's five-volume biography had appeared two years earlier), Le Clair notes in his preface his attempt to write "as objectively as possible" and insists on his "constant effort . . . to avoid psychoanalysis." HYDE, too, in his account of the 40 years James spent in England, avoids psychologizing and concentrates on the externals of his life, his relations with Edmund Gosse, Edith Wharton, Ford Madox Ford, and a host of lesser-knowns, and the importance to James of his various residences, especially Lamb House in Rye, Sussex, where he spent his final years.

Two invaluable collections of anecdotes and vignettes flesh out the portrait of James found in the other book-length studies. The epigraph to NOWELL-SMITH's introduction is from Hugh Walpole and describes James as he is often viewed by his acolytes: "A quite legendary figure, a sort of stuffed waxwork from whose mouth a stream of coloured sentences, like winding rolls of green and pink paper, are for ever issuing." Nowell-Smith quotes more than 150 of James' contemporaries in a way that emphasizes the social creature and conversationalist. Inevitably, of course, many of these tales show a private James not all that different from the magisterial author, as in Edith Wharton's account of a lost James spinning sentence after endless sentence around a befuddled old man from whom he is trying to get directions to the King's Road in the town of Windsor, only to be told, after a seemingly interminable amount of confusion, that " 'Ye're in it.' " PAGE, too, emphasizes James' style of conversation, telling how one acquaintance recorded that James always spoke as though he were reading proof, and how another observed that he said everything three times: first he felt for the right word, then tried it out, then accepted it (though "it was always exactly the right word in the beginning"). Since James' personal and professional selves come closer to being identical than those of almost any other author, the Nowell-Smith and Page collections, though intimate, brim with metaphors useful to James' critics.

EDEL's five-volume biography is not only exhaustive within the field of James studies but is considered one of the classics of biographical writing, often spoken of in the same breath as Boswell's life of Johnson. As the foremost authority of James, Edel has attracted the kind of admiration and scorn accorded celebrities in every field. The reasons for the admiration are clear, since he has written extensively on every aspect of James' life and work in a clean yet masterful style that discriminates closely while avoiding jargon. Edel has also made available for the first time a great number of unpublished documents. The reasons for the scorn are less evident, although a certain amount of it has been attributed by disinterested scholars to professional jealousy over Edel's control of these manuscript materials, notably the thousands of letters that would comprise a 50-volume edition were they to be published. Edel has released approximately 1000 of these letters in an edition of four volumes; his detractors accuse him of selectively publishing letters that support only his own view of the relation between Henry and William James as described in the five-volume biography, a view decidedly less sanguine than that of Le Clair.

Volume I covers James' childhood and youth, the heady nature of life within a family dominated by the eccentric Henry James Sr., the patchwork education of the five James siblings, the author's early writings and first experiences of Europe. Because Edel is a psychological critic, human relations are underscored, as, for example, James' innocent worship of his cousin Minny Temple, who died young and served as model for such Jamesian heroines as Isabel Archer in *The Portrait of a Lady* and Milly Theale in *The Wings of the Dove*. But the greatest emphasis is given to the friendly yet competitive relationship between Henry and his slightly older brother William, the future philosopher-psychologist who always seemed to his younger brother to be a little more accomplished, and, because he was a husband and a father in addition to being a scientist, perhaps even a little more "manly." According to Edel, Henry and William were like Jacob and Esau in the Old Testament story of fraternal struggle over birthright and a father's blessing, with Henry/Jacob as the younger "dweller in tents" and William/Esau as the active one, the cunning hunter. This paradigm is used by Edel throughout all five volumes of biography, both to explain the relationship between the two brothers and to elaborate on the heroic second-born characters in James' fiction whose elder siblings have either died or revealed themselves as scoundrels.

The second volume takes James' life up through the appearance of *The Portrait of a Lady*. The years covered by Volume III are those in which James grappled with overtly political topics, as evidenced by *The Bostonians*, *The Princess Casamassima*, and *The Tragic Muse*; this is also the period in which James undertook his misguided effort to write plays. "The treacherous years" are dealt with in Volume IV, which begins with the catastrophic failure on 5 January 1895 of his play *Guy Domville* and details James' professional and personal problems in the months that followed.

The final and most lengthy volume of this biography examines James' emergence into what Louis Auchincloss (*The Nation*, 23 April 1960) refers to as his period of "high, golden light." With insight and painstaking attention to detail, Edel shows how James reaped the harvest of his theatre years, putting aside the awful memories and incorporating the lessons of the theatre in what were to be his finest novels. In this ultimate volume Edel also sketches a full portrait of James as the apotheosis of his own social ambitions, the magisterial wit and critic who was friend to such established personages as Mark Twain and Joseph Conrad as well as an avuncular presence to a girlish Virginia Woolf and her circle.

Over the years, Edel's work has been rewarded by a number of prizes and honors, including the National Book Award and the Pulitzer prize, both in 1963, for Volumes II and III of the biography. But Edel has also drawn a certain amount of criticism from readers put off by his insistence on a psychological motivation for each of James' acts—that his writing for the theatre was an unconscious "masculine" attempt to compete with William James, for example, which is why the *Guy Domville* disaster was so devastating to him. It seems improbable that, as Robert Garis believes (*Hudson Review*, Spring 1970), Edel's "strange prestige . . . may discourage better minds from trying"; no multi-volume biography is likely to appear in the next few decades, but certainly future ages will interpret James according to the fashion of their day. The most obvious objection to Edel's life of James, its sheer length, has been countered by Edel himself: in 1985 he produced a one-volume condensation of the longer work.

—David Kirby

JAMES, William, 1842–1910; American psychologist and philosopher.

Allen, Gay Wilson, *William James: A Biography*. New York, Viking, and London, Hart-Davis, 1967.

Bjork, Daniel W., *William James: The Center of His Vision*. New York, Columbia University Press, 1988.

Feinstein, Howard, *Becoming William James*. Ithaca, New York, Cornell University Press, 1984.

Myers, Gerald E., *William James: His Life and Thought*. New Haven, Connecticut, Yale University Press, 1986.

Perry, Ralph Barton, *The Thought and Character of William James* (2 vols.). Boston, Little Brown, and London, Humphrey Milford/Oxford University Press, 1935.

Taylor, Eugene, *William James on Exceptional Mental States: The 1896 Lowell Lectures*. New York, Scribner, 1983.

*

Interpretation of William James began as early as 1907, gathering momentum after his death in 1910. Early sketches praised James' contributions as an American philosopher or eulogized his many personal and intellectual qualities. One exception to this mainstream treatment was Santayana's objection to James as philosopher (in *Character and Opinion in the United States*, New York, 1920). Critical of James' "raids" into metaphysics and his failure to build a traditional philosophical structure, Santayana portrayed James as too solidly a product of Guilded Age American culture to make a truly substantial philosophical contribution. Notwithstanding Santayana's objections, commentators throughout the 1920s and 1930s continued to view James as the philosophical father of a broad pragmatic movement advocating progressive change in American institutions.

PERRY's two-volume biography remained, until recently, the most comprehensive account of James' personal and intellectual development, despite its lack of any substantial criticism of either James' life or mind. Perry argues that James was first and foremost a philosopher who offered a pragmatic alternative to the prevailing British empiricism and German idealism. His portrait of James as a sensitive, troubled young man who moved from art, to natural science, to psychology, and finally to his true calling, philosophy, is still widely accepted.

The centenary of James' birth in 1942 brought a harvest of adoring scholarship, maintaining that James' fundamental contribution still lay in the philosophical field of morally responsible pragmatism. A few dissenting voices, however, began to express different emphases that were still decades away from full expression. These interpreters, such as Jacques Barzun ("William James as Artist," *The New Republic*, 15 February 1943) and Aron Gurwitsch ("William James' Theory of the 'Transitive Parts' of the Stream of Consciousness," *Philosophy and Phenomenological Research*, June 1943), explored James' interest in art, his discovery of pure experience, his radical empiricism and his contributions to phenomenology. Throughout the 1950s and 1960s Jamesian scholarship investigated his familial connections and influence on other prominent Americans, such as Oliver Wendell Holmes, Jr. and Franklin D. Roosevelt, as well as continued enhancement of his reputation as a pragmatic philosopher.

The first full-scale biographical alternative to Perry appeared in 1967. ALLEN makes significant use of family correspondence to give a detailed account of James' extensive European travels. His book does not, however, develop intellectual matters and Perry remains far superior in that regard. Treatment of James advanced markedly in 1968 with the appearance of Cushing Strout's psychoanalytic approach, which presented James for the first time in the context of an oedipal conflict ("William James and the Twice-Born Sick Soul," *Daedalus*, vol. 97, pp. 1062–82). Drawing from Erik Erikson's concept of identity crisis, Strout maintained that young William was troubled by vocational indecision stemming from his father's role as an "inner court of tribunal." Not until after Henry Sr.'s death was William free to develop his own original philosophy, pragmatism. Since Strout's article, much biographical interest in James has centered on his oedipal-vocational difficulties.

FEINSTEIN, building on Strout's theme, argued that an intergenerational father-son conflict had not originated with Henry Sr. and William, but rather with Henry Sr. and his own father, William James of Albany. Henry Sr.'s father never accepted his son's liberal Protestantism and Henry Sr. himself never resolved a satisfactory career choice. Thus, any vocation William might embark upon (painter, natural scientist, psychologist, or philosopher) was disapproved of by Henry Sr. Feinstein offers the first book-length interpretation of William James as thwarted from his true calling as an artist, and hence became a major alternative to Perry.

Discounting oedipal conflict theory, S.P. Fullinwider ("William James' Spiritual Crisis," *The Historian*, 1975, vol. 13, pp. 39–57) interprets James' melancholia and neurasthenia as symptomatic of an existential struggle. James regained mental health not so much by resolving father-son conflicts as by working out a creative psychology in *The Principles of Psychology*. Fullinwider notes that James' scientific psychology was not just a developmental stage to his pragmatic and pluralistic metaphysics but the major key to the resolution of understanding the connection between his emotional and intellectual life.

Recent interpretation has been aided by TAYLOR, who reconstructed James' personal library. Taylor tracked down hundreds of books that contain James' own marginalia, and in so doing has provided a missing link between the publication of *The Principles of Psychology* in 1890 and *The Varieties of Religious Experience* in 1902. Taylor shows that James did not abandon science to move toward "mysticism" after 1890 as Perry and others had assumed.

MYERS' volume is the most comprehensive analysis of James' intellectual contribution since Perry. Myers explicates both the historical and intellectual context of James' major ideas and also offers critical commentary. His work does not, however, balance James' life and thought in chronological progression, as would a conventional biography. The work makes it impossible to view James as merely a pragmatist, demonstrating that both his science and his philosophy were too deeply interwoven in the intellectual development of the modern western world.

BJORK presents a more traditional full-scale biography, the first to make full use of the extensive correspondence between James and his wife, Alice Howe Gibbens James. Bjork also characterizes James as fundamentally an interdisciplinary thinker, thus breaking with those studies that depict James as primarily a philosopher, psychologist, or artist.

Anyone interested in William James should be aware of the introductory essays and annotated versions of his publications in *The Works of William James*, edited by Frederick Burkhardt (Cambridge, Massachusetts, Harvard University Press, 1975–   ). Up to 1989, 15 volumes had appeared. For the most complete annotated bibliography of works about James, see Ignas K. Skrupskelis', *William James: A Reference Guide* (Boston, G.K. Hall, 1977).

—Daniel W. Bjork

JEANNE D'ARC. See **JOAN OF ARC.**

JEFFERS, Robinson, 1887–1962; American poet.

Adamic, Louis, *Robinson Jeffers: A Portrait.* Seattle, University of Washington Bookstore, 1929; new edition, with foreword by Garth Sherwood Jeffers, C. and J. Robertson, Covelo, California, 1983.

Bennett, Melba Berry, *The Stone Mason of Tor House: The Life and Work of Robinson Jeffers.* Los Angeles, Ward Ritchie Press, 1966.

Carpenter, Frederic I., *Robinson Jeffers.* New York, Twayne, 1962.

Karman, James, *Robinson Jeffers: Poet of California.* San Francisco, Chronicle Books, 1987.

Powell, Lawrence C., *Robinson Jeffers: The Man and His Work.* Los Angeles, Primavera Press, 1934.

Sterling, George, *Robinson Jeffers: The Man and the Artist.* New York, Boni and Liveright, 1926.

*

Although Robinson Jeffers is a major voice among 20th-century American poets, he never achieved the preeminence of his contemporaries T. S. Eliot, Ezra Pound, Wallace Stevens, or William Carlos Williams. He is rather more of a cult figure attracting a coterie of intensely loyal followers who have secured for his home at Carmel, California, a place on the National Register of Historic Places and made it a shrine. Every fall a Jeffers festival is held there with poetry readings, lectures, and discussions, while a few yards away the Pacific Ocean breaks against the rocky coast of the Monterey Peninsula. This is Jeffers country, the setting of his short lyrics as well as his long narrative poems.

The definitive biography of Jeffers has yet to be written, and until this lacuna is filled one must make do with two incomplete biographies, letters, reminiscences, diaries, a newsletter by and for his *aficionados*, and other odds and ends. Perhaps the place to begin the study of Jeffers' life is with KARMAN's *Robinson Jeffers*, the most recent of the biographical works. Karman is a competent writer who spent two years as resident scholar for the Tor House Foundation, the trust that administers the Jeffers estate. While Karman is a great admirer of Jeffers and somewhat beholden to the Jeffers family and the directors of the Foundation, his book is reasonably objective. Its strengths lie in the excellent integration of Jeffers' poetry into the story of his life and its attention to the friends who were important to Jeffers and his development as a poet. These aspects, however, take up a good deal of space, and the entire book contains only 143 pages of text. It is impossible to do justice in such short space to a life that extended from 1887 to 1962 and produced a body of poetry that in the definitive edition, which happily has been ably edited by Tim Hunt, runs to two thick volumes. Karman deals more candidly than previous writers with Jeffers' marital infidelities and Una Jeffers' attempt to commit suicide in Taos in 1938, but he glosses over and barely mentions the great hue and cry that greeted Jeffers' anti-war poetry in *Be Angry at the Sun* (1941) and *The Double Axe and Other Poems* (1948). When Jeffers linked Franklin D. Roosevelt and Hitler in the same poem, his work seemed treasonous to many readers, and when he refused to describe Hitler as absolute evil, people concluded he was a fascist and simply stopped reading him. His books went out of print and his reputation withered. Now that we have passed through the Korean War and the trauma of Vietnam, Jeffers' fierce anti-war stance seems far less radical and his reputation has made a comeback. These are matters that some future biographer will have to deal with fully. For the time being this subject may be pursued in Alex A. Vardamis' *The Critical Reputation of Robinson Jeffers: A Bibliographical Study* (1972).

The only other full-scale biography of Jeffers is BENNETT's *Stone Mason of Tor House*. This book, which appeared four years after Jeffers died, is the authorized biography written by a longtime family friend. It is much more complete than Karman's work (and about two-thirds longer), but Bennett worked with the handicap of being too close to her subject. Whoever writes the definitive biography will be greatly indebted to Bennett for gathering materials that might otherwise have been lost. But Bennett is captivated by the personality of Una Jeffers and treats the 37-year marriage between Robinson and Una as an idyllic relationship. That Una was vastly important to Jeffers, and that without her he might never have become a major poet, is incontestable, but it was a stormy relationship at times, and the definitive biographer will need more objectivity in handling the marriage. Although Bennett's biography had the approval and help of Jeffers' sons, the manuscript was never submitted to them to read. For a two-page list of Bennett's errors, see *Robinson Jeffers Newsletter*, no. 35 (May 1973), pp. 4–5.

The life of Jeffers cannot be assessed adequately without dealing fully with Una Jeffers. The impact she had on everyone she came in contact with was remarkable, as Edith Greenan's *Of Una Jeffers* (1939) makes clear. This memoir of Jeffers' wife (and, of course, of Jeffers too) is by the woman who became the second wife of Una's first husband. That Greenan was devoted to Una is in itself a rather astonishing fact. Another memoir that one should not miss is that of Mabel Dodge Luhan, the lion-hunter of Taos, who collected Jeffers among the notables she lured to New Mexico. Her little book, *Una and Robin*, was written in 1933, but Una would never let her publish it, and the 36-page pamphlet remained in manuscript until 1976. It is an intimate picture of the domestic life of the Jeffers. Mabel managed to get the Jeffers to Taos for some weeks seven times in the 1930s, a surprising feat considering Jeffers' fierce attachment to Carmel and an utter disinclination to travel anywhere.

Although most of Jeffers' friends would have said that Una did most of the letter-writing for the family, there are a good many Jeffers letters extant, and Ann N. Ridgeway's *The Selected Letters of Robinson Jeffers, 1897–1962* (1968) contains much

biographical information. Also available, though in a rare limited edition, is Charles Kafka's collection of the love letters entitled *Where Shall I Take You: The Love Letters of Una and Robinson Jeffers* (Covelo, California, Yolla Bolly Press, 1987). Una's diaries, mostly unpublished, provide more biographical data, but a portion, edited by Jeffers after Una's death, came out in 1924 as *Visits to Ireland*. Jeffers supplied biographical data in his introduction to *Jeffers Country* (1971), the picture collection that Jeffers and Horace Lyon put together in the 1930s but never published. These are photos of the Carmel/Big Sur area that Jeffers wrote about. There also is biographical material in the preface Jeffers wrote for Sidney S. Alberts' *Bibliography of the Works of Robinson Jeffers* (1933). Anyone searching for biographical information should not overlook the *Robinson Jeffers Newsletter*, which began publishing in 1962.

Two books by scholars and two by writers complete this summary of materials for Jeffers' biography. POWELL, an early admirer and personal friend, wrote a dissertation on Jeffers at the University of Dijon in 1932 and later published *Robinson Jeffers: The Man and His Work*. This is mostly a critical study, but it also contains biographical information. CARPENTER's first chapter in the familiar Twayne series is a very good 34-page account of Jeffers' life and times. STERLING, the San Francisco poet who was a good friend of Jeffers, wrote the first book on him in 1926. It is a generous and sympathetic portrait that Lawrence Powell compares to William D. O'Connor's passionate defense of Whitman in *The Good Gray Poet*. Finally, there is an engaging essay on Jeffers by ADAMIC. Originally published in 1929, it has been reprinted as a pamphlet with an introduction of reminiscences by Garth Jeffers.

—James Woodress

JEFFERSON, Thomas, 1743–1826; American political leader, third president of the United States.

Adams, Henry, *History of the United States during the Presidencies of Thomas Jefferson and James Madison* (9 vols.). New York, Scribner, 1889–91.

Bedini, Silvio A., *Thomas Jefferson: Statesman of Science*. New York, Macmillan, 1990.

Bowers, Claude G., *Jefferson and Hamilton: The Struggle for Democracy in America* (3 vols.). Boston, Houghton Mifflin, 1925–45.

Brodie, Fawn N., *Thomas Jefferson: An Intimate History*. New York, Norton, and London, Eyre Methuen, 1974.

Cunningham, Noble, *In Pursuit of Reason: The Life of Thomas Jefferson*. Baton Rouge, Louisiana State University Press, 1987.

Dabney, Virginius, *The Jefferson Scandals: A Rebuttal*. New York, Dodd Mead, 1981.

Kimball, Marie, *Jefferson* (3 vols.). New York, Coward-McCann, 1943–50.

Koch, Adrienne, *The Philosophy of Thomas Jefferson*. New York, Columbia University Press, 1943.

Levy, Leonard W., *Jefferson and Civil Liberties: The Darker Side*. Cambridge, Massachusetts, Belknap Press, 1963.

Malone, Dumas, *Jefferson and His Time* (6 vols.). Boston, Little Brown, 1948–81.

Matthews, Richard K., *The Radical Politics of Thomas Jefferson: A Revisionist View*. Lawrence, University Press of Kansas, 1984.

McDonald, Forrest, *The Presidency of Thomas Jefferson*. Lawrence, University Press of Kansas, 1976.

McLaughlin, Jack, *Jefferson and Monticello: The Biography of a Builder*. New York, Holt, 1988.

Miller, John C., *The Wolf By the Ears: Thomas Jefferson and Slavery*. New York, Free Press, 1977.

Peterson, Merrill D., *Thomas Jefferson and the New Nation: A Biography*. New York and London, Oxford University Press, 1970.

Peterson, Merrill D., *Thomas Jefferson: A Reference Biography*. New York, Scribner, 1986.

Tucker, Robert W. and David C. Hendrickson, *Empire of Liberty: The Statecraft of Thomas Jefferson*. New York, Oxford University Press, 1990.

Wills, Garry, *Inventing America: Jefferson's Declaration of Independence*. New York, Doubleday, 1978; London, Athlone, 1980.

*

Jefferson's early biographers, George Tucker (1837) and Henry S. Randall (1858), provided laudatory life-and-times accounts of their subject. Of these, Randall's study remains the most valuable to the scholar, because it is based in part upon now-lost Jefferson manuscripts and interviews with Jefferson's descendants and personal acquaintances. John T. Morse issued a severely critical study in 1883 as part of the American Statesman Series; in light of Morse's declared preference for Hamilton, the tone of this small volume should not have been a surprise.

By far the most important work on Jefferson during the 19th century was the portrait of him offered in ADAMS' multivolume history. Adams' work featured Jefferson as a central character, and his emphasis on the contradictions and tensions between philosophy, principles, and practice in politics shaped much of the agenda for many subsequent biographers. Most useful in tracing the evolution of Jefferson's reputation during these years (and later) is Merrill Peterson's *The Jeffersonian Image in the American Mind* (1960), which presents a wealth of fascinating information on the Virginian's standing in the American consciousness.

Through the early 20th century, as Americans celebrated Jefferson's archrival, Alexander Hamilton, Jefferson received mostly negative treatment at the hands of historians. But the revival of the Democratic party and changes in historical interpretation of the politics of the early republic brought renewed interest, as biographers viewed their subject in a more positive light. Perhaps the pivotal work was that of BOWERS, a writer who leaned heavily in the direction of the Democratic party and used his popular historical studies to endorse his political preferences. Between 1925 and 1945 he produced a three-volume hagiography that masqueraded as biography, presenting Jefferson as the apostle of democracy and liberalism. Deficient as scholarship, the series succeeded as propaganda, rehabilitating Jeffer-

son's reputation while refurbishing his status as a symbol of the Democratic party, despite James Truslow Adams' effort to demonstrate Jefferson's conservatism *(The Living Jefferson, 1936)*.

Subsequent biographies reflected more scholarship and less partisanship. Although they only address Jefferson's life prior to 1790, KIMBALL's three volumes, although often overlooked, are still informative and carefully researched, if sometimes excessively detailed. Most impressive has been the six-volume biography of MALONE. Often praised as the definitive biographical treatment of Jefferson, this monumental effort is absorbing for those who take the time to peruse its 3000 pages. Yet its very length and detail make it difficult to extract underlying themes or to form a coherent picture, and critics have noted that Malone's affection for his subject, which grows with each volume, sometimes spills over into a determined defense.

PETERSON (1970) and CUNNINGHAM have written single-volume interpretations of Jefferson. The former, while sometimes dry, is an impressive effort to treat Jefferson's varied interests while offering a balanced commentary on his accomplishments and shortcomings in politics, while the latter is a valiant effort to explore all the facets of Jefferson's life in a concise format. Both present an overwhelmingly favorable view of their subject, despite attempts to maintain detachment and balance. By far the most controversial biography is that by BRODIE, who employed psychological concepts in an effort to gain insight into connections between Jefferson's public and private selves. Her revival of the story that Jefferson carried on a romantic liaison with his slave Sally Hemings excited much debate, as other Jefferson scholars rushed to defend the Sage of Monticello; DABNEY offers the best summary of the case for the defense, although Miller's comments (see below) are helpful.

In recent years some scholars have explored Jefferson's political philosophy in an effort to explicate its main tenets and assumptions. Carl Becker's explication of the Declaration of Independence as derived from the philosophy of John Locke *(Declaration of Independence*, 1922) gained such widespread acceptance as to become commonplace. KOCH's study took a broader look at Jefferson the political philosopher, drawing together much information and integrating it in an analysis that is still useful. It stresses the degree to which Jefferson sought to realize his ideas in practice, while making clear that Jefferson was not limited to Locke, but borrowed freely from many sources, including the Bible and the Enlightenment, in devising his own perspective grounded in natural rights and natural law. WILLS broke with both of these views in arguing for the primacy of the Scottish Enlightenment thinkers in Jefferson's philosophy, dissenting from the view of Jefferson as liberal individualist in favor of Jefferson as communitarian who viewed society as an organic whole. Less publicized was Morton White's similar conclusion in *The Philosophy of the American Revolution* (1978), although he identified different strands of Scottish thought as exercising influence upon Jefferson's thought. In contrast, MATTHEWS emphasizes Jefferson's radical democratic notions of social change and community in a slender volume that provoked much controversy and debate when it appeared. Other scholars, including Lance Banning, Drew McCoy, and Joyce Appleby, have contributed to this debate in their own examination of the notion of political economy in the early national period. One interesting question raised by this recent debate is whether Thomas Jefferson is properly labeled a "Jeffersonian"; another remains whether Jefferson sought to realize his ideas in formulating policy.

Indeed, the tension between principles and political practice has been a main theme of Jefferson biography, especially during the Virginian's presidency. Adams' study set the tone. In a powerful work LEVY questions Jefferson's commitment to civil liberties, pointing out that Jefferson, despite his fierce opposition to the Alien and Sedition Acts, had no qualms about instigating seditious libel suits to silence his opponents. As Levy frankly admits, his study offers but one side of the case, and thus does not come to grips with all of Jefferson's ambiguous legacy. Even more unrelenting in its attack on Jefferson is McDONALD's study of his presidency. Resembling a legal brief drawn up by a Federalist lawyer coached by Alexander Hamilton, this indictment is more provocative than persuasive, although McDonald's explication of the contradictions in Jefferson's thought and practice deserve consideration.

Adams' influence continues to be evident in recent studies, especially the explication of Jefferson's political economy offered by Drew McCoy in *The Elusive Republic* (1980) and in the interpretation of Jefferson's diplomacy offered by TUCKER AND HENDRICKSON. The latter is a provocative if not entirely new exploration of the contradictions within Jefferson's thought and between his principles and practice, highlighting the use of Hamiltonian means to pursue Jeffersonian ends in acquiring Louisiana and implementing his embargo policy. While many of the arguments advanced by Tucker and Hendrickson will be familiar to most scholars, their volume serves as an admirable interpretive synthesis of scholarship on Jefferson's foreign policy.

Jefferson's prominence in political events during the American republic's first 50 years sometimes obscures his many other interests. Indeed, the diversity of his mind has proven difficult to capture in a single unified study. MILLER's examination of Jefferson's relationship to slavery is a dispassionate and reasonable discussion of Jefferson's efforts to reconcile his belief in human equality with his belief in racial inequality; most important is his assertion that in later life Jefferson overlooked his earlier qualms about slavery as he became a staunch supporter of southern interests. Two rewarding studies that explore other major facets of Jefferson's life are McLAUGHLIN's suggestive if sometimes questionable analysis of Jefferson's personality as reflected in his work as the architect of his home, Monticello, and BEDINI's recent look at Jefferson's scientific interests.

Through the first half of the 20th century, biographers relied on Paul Leicester Ford's edition of Jefferson's writings, which appeared between 1892 and 1899. Since 1950 many scholars have turned to *The Papers of Thomas Jefferson*, initiated by Julian Boyd, and in recent years edited by Charles Cullen and John Cantazariti. As of 1990 this mammoth undertaking had reached 24 volumes, extending to the end of 1792; it had taken 40 years of publication to cover 49 years of Jefferson's life. Much of the annotation that accompanies each document, some of it voluminous in itself, contains essential biographical information. Also not falling strictly within the confines of narrative biography is PETERSON's "reference biography" (1986), a collection of comprehensive and insightful essays on many facets of Jefferson's life, which in its diversity of subject headings suggests the difficulty inherent in composing a complete yet manageable biography.

—Brooks D. Simpson

JEROME, Saint, *ca.* 347–*ca.* 420; Christian scholar and father of the church.

Kelly, John N., *Jerome: His Life, Writings, and Controversies.* New York, Harper, and London, Duckworth, 1975.

Martin, Mrs. Charles, *Life of St. Jerome.* London, Kegan Paul, 1888.

Mierow, Charles C., *Saint Jerome: The Sage of Bethlehem.* Milwaukee, Bruce Publishing, 1959.

Monceaux, Paul, *St. Jerome: The Early Years*, translated by F. Sheed. London, Sheed and Ward, 1933 (originally published by B. Grasset, Paris, 1932).

Steinmann, Jean, *Saint Jerome and His Times*, translated by Ronald Matthews. Notre Dame, Indiana, Fides Publishers, 1959 (originally published by Éditions du Cerf, Paris, 1958).

*

Until the publication of Kelly's monograph on St. Jerome, no comprehensive, scholarly biography of this Doctor of the Church was available to English-speaking readers. Fundamental works of earlier, continental scholarship, such as those by Grützmacher (1901-08), Cavallera (1922), Penna (1949), Antin (1951), Favez (1959), Chaffin (1961), and Testard (1969), remain untranslated. This state of affairs is especially surprising given Jerome's prominence in the history of early Christianity. To be sure, a number of full-length biographies in English were available before 1975, but these are popular in nature.

MARTIN's work is representative of such studies of the late 19th century. While the author does provide an adequate overview of events in Jerome's life, the book's obvious hagiographical tone, as well as its lack of critical apparatus, detracts from its usefulness. One theme, however, marks this book out from similar works. As Martin states in her preface, "Upon one phase of this influence—that which [Jerome] possessed with the noble and distinguished women whom he spiritually directed—I have dwelt more particularly, hoping that in so doing I may add my mite of encouragement to the great movement for the mental emancipation and intellectual progress of the weaker sex which this century has inaugurated."

Another popular study intended for a general readership is that by MONCEAUX. As its title indicates, the book treats only the early years of the saint's life and career, to about the year A.D. 378. It is especially this period which, in Monceaux's opinion, requires historical reassessment. Basing his work on the detailed and authoritative researches of Grützmacher and Cavallera, he reconstructs the turbulent life of the young Jerome in lively fashion. The short chapters are well organized and concisely written. Textual references are usually provided only for translations of primary source material. An especially appealing characteristic of the book is the inclusion of medieval and Renaissance artistic representations of Jerome with accompanying descriptions.

In MIEROW's biography, intended for the educated, reading public, Jerome the scholar, correspondent, controversialist, and ascetic seems to come alive. The author skillfully interweaves chronological narrative and description with relevant passages from the saint's own writings, allowing Jerome to speak for himself. Mierow views his subject as an individual marked by paradox. Indeed, Jerome was a master of the literary traditions of pagan Rome though always uncomfortable with their implications; a man of the senses who chose the life of asceticism, a cosmopolitan who lived much of his life in the world of desert and monastery, and a man of profound charity who could hate with unmatched fervor. Mierow's biography is a balanced assessment of this difficult and controversial historical figure.

STEINMANN's study, more comprehensive and scholarly than Mierow's work, encompasses much of the previous academic research on the life and times of Jerome. Unfortunately, the lack of a bibliography leaves the more curious reader with few avenues for further exploration. The author, in his conclusion, acknowledges an affection for the figure of Jerome: "His epic tempers, his tendernesses, and above all his masterly offensiveness enchanted me." Despite this attitude, the tone of the work is not hagiographical. Steinmann is clearly at home in the world of late antiquity and does an admirable job of portraying both saint and society. At times the English translation is awkward (as shown in the quotation above) but does not seriously disrupt reading. A noteworthy aspect of the book is Steinmann's evaluation of Jerome as biblical translator and exegete.

A new level of excellence in Jerome scholarship was reached with the publication of KELLY's authoritative biography in 1975. English readers in particular have benefited. Kelly's careful research, masterful interpretations, and readable style all contribute to the ultimate success of the work. Its title, *Jerome: His Life, Writings, and Controversies*, is truly descriptive, since this book is much more than a conventional biography. Kelly emphasizes not only Jerome's character and the events of his life, but also the saint's intellectual and religious development as the "Christian Cicero" and his lasting contributions to Christianity. Especially enlightening are Kelly's discussions of Jerome's impact on such Christian traditions and issues as asceticism, biblical translation and exegesis, women, heresy and orthodoxy, Mariology, and pilgrimage. The author consistently furnishes primary source documentation for his conclusions and references to the secondary literature within the text; a separate bibliography is not included in the book. Kelly's presentation is chronologically based, with helpful topical digressions interspersed within the chapters. Jerome emerges here as a passionate, complex figure, both hero and anti-hero, a man superhuman in his labors and all too human in his faults. Kelly is sympathetic without being reverential, critical without being patronizing. This is a fine piece of scholarship that should remain the standard account for years to come.

—Craig L. Hanson

JESUS CHRIST, *ca.* 6 B.C.–*ca.* 30 A.D.; Jewish religious reformer.

Anderson, Charles C., *Critical Quests of Jesus*. Grand Rapids, Michigan, Eerdmans, 1969.

Barton, Bruce, *The Man Nobody Knows*. Indianapolis, Bobbs-Merrill, and London, Constable, 1925.

Bishop, Jim, *The Day Christ Died*. New York, Harper, and London, Weidenfeld and Nicolson, 1957.

Bornkamm, Günther, *Jesus of Nazareth*, translated by Irene and Fraser McClusky with James M. Robinson. New York, Harper, and London, Hodder and Stoughton, 1960 (originally published by Kohlhammer, Stuttgart, 1956).

Bosworth, Edward Increase, *The Life and Teaching of Jesus According to the First Three Gospels*. New York, Macmillan, 1924.

Bultmann, Rudolf Karl, *Jesus and the Word*, translated by L. P. Smith. New York, Scribner, and London, Collins, 1958.

Bultmann, Rudolf Karl, *Jesus Christ and Mythology*. New York, Scribner, 1958; London, SCM Press, 1960.

Bultmann, Rudolf Karl and Karl Kundsin, *Form Criticism: Two Essays on New Testament Research*, translated by F. C. Grant. New York, Harper, 1962.

Carpenter, Humphrey, *Jesus*. New York, Hill and Wang, 1980; Oxford and New York, Oxford University Press, 1980.

Denny, Walter Bell, *The Career and Significance of Jesus*. New York, T. Nelson, 1934.

Dibelius, Martin, *Jesus*, translated by Charles B. Hedrick and Frederick C. Grant. Philadelphia, Westminster Press, 1949 (originally published by W. de Gruyter, Berlin, 1939).

Dickens, Charles, *The Life of Our Lord*. New York, Simon and Schuster, and London, A. Barker, 1934 (first publication; written 1846–49).

Dodd, Charles Harold, *The Founder of Christianity*. New York, Macmillan, 1970; London, Collins, 1971.

Edersheim, Alfred, *The Life and Times of Jesus the Messiah* (2 vols.). London, Longman, and New York, A.D.F. Randolph, 1883.

Enslin, Morton Scott, *The Prophet from Nazareth*. New York, McGraw-Hill, 1961.

Fiske, Charles and Burton Scott Easton, *The Real Jesus*. New York, Harper, 1929.

Glover, T. R., *The Jesus of History*. New York, Harper, 1916; London, S.C.M. Press, 1917.

Grant, Michael, *Jesus: An Historian's Review of the Gospels*. New York, Scribner, and London, Weidenfeld and Nicolson, 1977.

Harrison, Everett Falconer, *A Short Life of Christ*. Grand Rapids, Michigan, Eerdmans, 1968.

Kissinger, Warren S., *The Lives of Jesus: A History and Bibliography*. New York and London, Garland, 1985.

Klausner, Joseph, *Jesus of Nazareth: His Life, Times, and Teaching*, translated by Herbert Danby. New York, Macmillan, and London, Allen and Unwin, 1925 (originally published as *Yeshu ha-Nostri*, Jerusalem, 1921).

Laymon, Charles M., *The Life and Teachings of Jesus*. New York, Abingdon Press, 1955.

Maus, Cynthia Pearl, *Christ and the Fine Arts*. New York, Harper, 1938.

Neander, August, *The Life of Jesus Christ in its Historical Connexion and Historical Development*, translated by J. M'Clintock and C. E. Blumenthal. New York, Harper, 1848; London, H. G. Bohn, 1851 (originally published, Hamburg, 1837).

Oursler, Fulton, *The Greatest Story Ever Told*. New York, Doubleday, 1949.

Papini, Giovanni, *Life of Christ*, translated by Dorothy Canfield Fisher. New York, Harcourt, 1923; as *Story of Christ*, London, Hodder and Stoughton, 1923 (originally published as *Storia di Cristo*, Florence, Vallecchi, 1921).

Paterson-Smyth, John, *A People's Life of Christ*. New York, F. H. Revell, 1920.

Pearson, Charles Wilson, *The Carpenter Prophet*. Chicago and New York, H. S. Stone, 1902.

Putney, Max C., *The Man of Galilee*. New York, Exposition Press, 1955.

Renan, Ernest, *The Life of Jesus*. London, Mathieson, 1863; revised edition, translated by J. H. Allen, Boston, Roberts, 1896; translated by William G. Hutchinson, London, W. Scott, 1897 (originally published as *Vie de Jésus*, Paris, M. Lévy, 1863).

Schweitzer, Albert, *The Quest of the Historical Jesus: A Critical Study of Its Progress from Reimarus to Wrede*, translated by W. Montgomery. London, A. and C. Black, 1910; New York, Macmillan, 1922 (originally published as *Von Reimarus zu Wrede*, Tübingen, J. C. B. Mohr, 1906).

Sinclair, Upton, *A Personal Jesus: Portrait and Interpretation*. New York and Philadelphia, Evans, 1952; London, Allen and Unwin, 1954.

Stauffer, Ethelbert, *Jesus and His Story*, translated by Richard and Clara Winston. New York, Knopf, 1960; translated by D. M. Barton, London, SCM Press, 1960.

Strauss, David F., *Life of Christ*. New York, Vale, 1843; as *The Life of Jesus Critically Examined*, translated by George Eliot, London, Chapman, 1846; New York, C. Blanchard, 1855 (originally published as *Das Leben Jesu, kritisch bearbeitet*, 2 vols., Tübingen, C. F. Osiander, 1835–36).

Warschauer, Joseph, *The Historical Life of Christ*. New York, Macmillan, 1927.

*

It is reported that 60,000 lives of Jesus were written in the 19th century alone. This flood, the result of widespread interest and deep methodological difficulty, has since then only slightly abated.

Before proper biographies of Jesus could even be attempted, it was necessary to establish the need for a uniquely rigorous evaluation of the materials, especially the canonical Gospels. Enlightenment groundwork rationalized the miracles and provided piecemeal critiques of the religious ethos and the historical reliability of the Scriptures. It was STRAUSS' detailed but taut argument of 1835 that exposed beyond doubt the strongly mythic character of the Gospels and launched the search—still underway—for an historically reliable account of Jesus. Strauss was the first to publish an examination of the entire traditional range of the life of Jesus. He attempted systematically to separate the historical elements from the unhistorical by segregating all that was contrary to the "known and universal laws which govern the course of events," all that was self-contradictory or contra-

dicted by another account, all that was unrealistically poetical, all that was tendentious. This is not a biography so much as an attempt to determine the scientific possibility for an historical life of Jesus. Strauss did not by any means conclude, as some have thought him to have done, that Jesus was a complete fiction, but he found that the Gospels were so heavily mythopoeic that very little in them could pass as reliable evidence: the general outlines of a preacher's life; of events, the Crucifixion; Jesus' special Messianic-eschatological consciousness (see below). Strauss' work, it should be noted, proved offensive to the establishment, and he lost all hope of a career in theology. His influence, however, has been lasting, and all subsequent work lies in his shadow.

In 1906 SCHWEITZER surveyed the entire problem, beginning with Strauss' predecessors and discussing over 300 books. No ordinary bibliographic survey, Schweitzer's book is truly critical, dedicatedly judging the validity or fallaciousness of the works chosen for comment. One must admire, for example, the sequence devoted to the 19th century "liberal lives," as Schweitzer accumulates evidence for his overall finding that each one in its own way gratuitously projected its own social and religious hopes backwards onto Jesus. Schweitzer's discussions, furthermore, are alive with incisive wit, as, for example, on the clerical opposition to Renan's life of Jesus: "Whatever wore a soutane and could yield a pen charged against Renan, the bishops leading the van." One is reminded here of the critical prose of A. E. Housman. In clarity and strength of argument, Schweitzer's book is a work of genius, a masterpiece of intellectual history.

Acquaintance with both Strauss and Schweitzer is urged for the reader who wishes to appreciate the controversies and achievements that underlie the other works surveyed here. To bring the matter up to more recent date, one may use the outline-surveys in ANDERSON and KISSINGER. Neither one is judgmental. Anderson's discussions are far better, his bibliography more discriminating.

Narrative is conceivable, if at all, only for the last part of Jesus' life, and his ministry presents severe chronological uncertainties. How many years did it cover? Which episodes, if any, are true, and in what order did they occur? The Passion provides the best field for tight narrative. Hence arises the focus of BISHOP, who, as in his other "Day Somebody Famous Died" books of creative quasi-journalism, novelizes often. We are given a day-by-day, hour-by-hour countdown, with many imaginary conversations among characters both historical and imaginary. The effect is not unlike that of a Passion play. In all ways, with or without fantasy, hopeful biographers have been forced to make a more or less—often less—judicious choice among the Gospels for selection and ordering of events.

Critical work on the origins and nature of the Gospels has proved anything but comforting for biographers. The "old quest" that began with Strauss bequeathed the generally accepted hypothesis that Matthew and Luke each separately used *Mark* as a source. Where they agree, therefore, there are not three witnesses but only one, and its two copies. To *Mark*, Matthew and Luke made additions from a non-narrative source. Nor, it appears, is even *Mark* a witness, since the "form-criticism" dating from *ca.* 1919 shows that Mark wove traditional unconnected episodes and sayings into a quasi-narrative. The synoptic Gospels, therefore, only *seem* to reflect a biographical tradition, and the narrative format is only a late stage of the lore concerning Jesus. Where *John* comes from is an even shadier matter. Scholarship must declare that when we look for evidence of Jesus we find only evidence of the early Christian community and that a biography is "not possible." The Gospels were, like Paul of Tarsus, concerned only with the crucified Christ, not with the living Jesus. It is perfectly possible to hold that the Crucifixion is the sole undoubtable event. Nor have extrabiblical materials (New Testament apocrypha and pseuepigrapha, pagan authors, Josephus, the Dead Sea Scrolls, the Coptic papyri) added anything to our historical knowledge of Jesus.

The "new quest" arising in the 1950s has sought to undo this heavily negative legacy by reminding us of persistent agreement on the general outline of Jesus' life and by identifying features in the portraits of Jesus that are idiosyncratic (such as calling God "Abba" and using parables), hence unlikely to arise from evangelical mythification. They are, be it noted, still emulating the caution of Strauss.

Even if we cannot have an historically sound narrative of Jesus' life, perhaps it is still possible to gain some authentic insight into his parlance and thought. Books treating the life of Jesus may be grouped according to how they answer the question, What goals did Jesus have for his ministry? What, in other words, did he mean by the "Kingdom of God"? Amid the numerous issues, this question speaks most to the recoverable history of Jesus' interest in his own life and is therefore the most interesting single test for *biography*. The books, regardless of era, present two radically disparate answers:

A. Jesus intended to usher in God's complete and final changing of the world. To follow Jesus was not to strive to make this world better, but to prepare for a new world coming soon. This "apocalyptic" or "eschatological" Jesus was the kernel that remained for Strauss after his severe winnowing of the sources. It has been a difficult view to propagate, partly because it implies that Jesus failed, partly because it emerges from a strange and distant world-view.

SCHWEITZER reaffirmed it as the only viable historical viewpoint, the only one that withstands a subtractive scientific approach to the sources and also, because of its very alienness, satisfies hermeneutic requirements. Schweitzer's last chapter is eloquent in stressing how perplexing to our age must be the authentic account of Jesus: "He will not be a Jesus Christ to whom the religion of the present can ascribe . . . its own thoughts and ideas. Nor will He be a figure which can be made by a popular historical treatment so sympathetic and universally intelligible to the multitude. The historical Jesus will be to our time a stranger and an enigma."

The life of Jesus is a problem in ancient history, and one might think that historians of antiquity today would tackle it. Not so, however; they have indeed duly devoted their energies to Christianity, its growth and transformation of the Roman Empire, but the source-criticism and the rest of the problematic about Jesus himself has been carried out by the theologians. GRANT, one of the few to espouse an apocalyptic Jesus, is also one of the few ancient historians to focus on Jesus. He has appropriate accessories—maps, notes, glossary—and he conveys a sound and clear sense of the milieu: within a great empire, a small province with a history of internal tensions. Grant is well regarded for his other popular books on the ancient world (e.g., *The World of Rome*) and *Jesus* is comparable to them. It appears, however, to confirm Schweitzer's warning, because Grant's attempts (especially in chapters 5 and 6) to explain this

Jesus merely issue in variously phrased iterations of the question, "Who did he think he was?" Grant is, however, quite in order in his feeling that Jesus himself found this a difficult question to answer in words. Elucidating the semiotics of Jesus' actions is a task that still needs doing.

WARSCHAUER claimed to be elaborating Schweitzer's suggestions, to be explicating the enigma, but he actually ended up with a Jesus of the type described in the next section. ENSLIN and CARPENTER are commendable specimens of the few who have genuinely followed up on Schweitzer. Carpenter, lucid, terse, and accessible, is especially to be recommended to the reader who would read along this line, hoping to meet a Jesus whose demands on us will escape our understanding at the first meeting, and the second, and perhaps even the last.

B. Jesus intended to initiate an ongoing spiritual regeneration, offering himself as a perpetual example and guide. This view leads more straightforwardly to the establishment of a familiar church, and is therefore orthodox, majority interpretation, often adopted from habit.

Innocent of controversies, DICKENS rewrote Luke for his children with the utmost simplicity and brevity. The pathos, however, is Dickens' own touch, and Jesus is presented as a child misunderstood by a hardhearted adult world.

To Strauss NEANDER furnished early opposition, invoking parapsychology to explain the miracles as authentic if not supernatural events. He mistook the strength of Strauss' case and never managed adequate rebuttal. He must, however, be praised for his magnanimity. The Prussian government saw a threat in Strauss' book and asked Neander to recommend whether it should be banned; Neander insisted that it should not be banned and that it must be opposed only through open debate.

RENAN produced a noteworthy response to Strauss, one which can fairly be called the first biography of Jesus. Renan caused a furor by declining to confirm the miracles, and no other book on Jesus has been so often reprinted, reissued, and translated. A praiseworthy introduction on sources and critical method is followed by a connected story marred by arbitrariness, fancifulness, and sentimentality (Schweitzer called it "Christian art in the worst sense"). On the other hand, Renan deserves credit for including the topography of Palestine and its historical framework; thus he decisively placed a human Jesus in a real place at a real time. Renan is responsible for introducing many such features that became standard in all such *exempli gratia* attempts to construct a narrative. Renan's Jesus begins as a simple and placid soul, presiding over a gentle group in Galilee, devoted to pastoral admiration of the beauties of creation. This idyll is shattered by intolerant harassment from the priestly establishment. Jesus, embittered, resorts to ever more demonstrative acts, culminating in the *démarche* on Jerusalem and tragic debacle. Criticisms aside, Renan's account remains unsurpassed in its strength of style and its ability to open up a distant and entrancing world. It is still the one to be recommended to the reader who must have a narrative and is willing to suspend historiographical strictness.

Enlightenment rationalism is strong in PEARSON. GLOVER is more dogmatic than one expects from an ancient historian and slips into sermonizing. PATERSON-SMYTH's account is tender like Renan's, but it reads like a collection of sermons, a genre to beware of. PAPINI, earnest but reasonable, wears his erudition lightly. BOSWORTH's Jesus begins as a type A but develops into a B. For FISKE AND EASTON, too, gradualism wins out over urgency in Jesus' program. Advertising executive BARTON, reacting against the "meek little Jesus" image, replaced it with a sturdy but subtle leader—the ideal personnel manager or CEO. DENNY is designed for Bible study, with recurrent denials of the dreaded apocalyptic view. Also aimed at youth, MAUS illustrates a Lucan narrative with an abundance of the most saccharine mediocrities in devotional visual art and verse. EDERSHEIM's two heavy volumes are basically a Gospel commentary made remarkable and still useful by copious inclusion of Rabbinic and Talmudic documents. Both KLAUSNER and STAUFFER, worthy but briefer successors, have a very deft way with Judaic materials. Like PUTNEY, OURSLER is heavily novelistic (but no improvement on Renan); his title is symptomatic of the hyperbole that so often arises in the more popular books.

The social reformer SINCLAIR saw in Jesus a kindred spirit, often frustrated by the world's slowness to repent; he too novelizes somewhat, though his account consists chiefly of long quotations from the Gospels, interrupted by personal anecdotes. One may regard this as another "liberal life" of the kind criticized by Schweitzer.

DODD argues that Jesus saw *himself* as the Kingdom Come. The changing of the world was indeed on time, complete, and fulfilled in one man. Let all others take example, with less hope of success. This sleight-of-hand in describing Jesus' position, called "realized eschatology," has been applauded by many as the ultimate solution in squaring the circle, and is glibly adopted by LAYMON and HARRISON.

In DIBELIUS one meets the first systematic application of form-criticism, which in BULTMANN's analysis causes biographical facts about Jesus to dwindle almost to a vanishing point. What remains as historical is purely the message of Jesus' preaching (the "kerygma"): a call to liberating commitment. BORNKAMM, moving amid the "new quest," salvages more facts, while also taking an existentialist position: Jesus in life displayed engagement of unparalleled intensity. In this group of presentations a reader can have a minimalist biography while still being gripped and stirred by the small but potent authentic historical kernel.

—John Wickersham

JOAN OF ARC [Jeanne d'Arc], *ca.* 1412–1431; French national heroine and saint.

France, Anatole, *Life of Joan of Arc*, translated by Winifred Stephens. London, J. Lane, and New York, Dodd Mead, 1923 (originally published as *Vie de Jeanne d'Arc*, Paris, Calmann-Lévy, 1908).

Gies, Frances, *Joan of Arc: The Legend and the Reality*. New York, Harper, 1981.

Guérin, André and Jack Palmer White, *Operation Shepherdess: The Mystery of Joan of Arc*. London, Heinemann, 1961.

Guillemin, Henri, *The True History of Jeanne d'Arc*, translated by H. J. Salemson. London, Allen and Unwin, 1972; as *Joan, Maid of Orleans*, New York, Saturday Review Press, 1973 (originally published as *Jeanne dite Jeanne d'Arc*, Paris, Gallimard, 1970).

Lang, Andrew, *Maid of France*. London and New York, Longman, 1908.

Lucie-Smith, Edward, *Joan of Arc*. London, A. Lane, 1976; New York, Norton, 1977.

Michelet, Jules, *Joan of Arc; or, the Maid of Orleans*. New York, Stanford and Delisser, 1858 (originally published as *Jeanne d'Arc*, Paris, Hachette, 1853).

Pernoud, Régine, *Joan of Arc, by Herself and Her Witnesses*, translated by Edward Hyams. London, Macdonald, 1964; New York, Stein and Day, 1966 (originally published by Edito-Service, Geneva, 1962).

Sackville-West, Vita, *Saint Joan of Arc*. New York, Doubleday, and London, Cobden-Sanderson, 1936.

Scott, W. S., *Jeanne d'Arc*. London, Harrap, and New York, Barnes and Noble, 1974.

Sermoise, Pierre de, *Joan of Arc and Her Secret Missions*, translated by Jennifer Taylor. London, R. Hale, 1973 (originally published as *Missions Secrètes de Jehanne la Pucelle*, Paris, R. Laffont, 1970).

Smith, John Holland, *Joan of Arc*. London, Sidgwick and Jackson, and New York, Scribner, 1973.

Warner, Marina, *Joan of Arc: Image of Female Heroism*. New York, Knopf, and London, Weidenfeld and Nicolson, 1981.

*

Patriotic legend gave way to historical study of Joan of Arc after the publication in 1841–49 by Jules Quicherat of almost all the documentary evidence pertaining to her, chiefly the records of her trial in 1431 and the rehabilitation hearings in 1450. The trial records have been translated into English by W. P. Barrett in *The Trial of Joan of Arc* (1931). MICHELET's biography was the first to be based on this evidence. Written at a time of deep political division in France, its tone reflects the fervent republican patriotism of its author and retains the aura of the legend.

A long tradition of sceptical reaction to the legend, chiefly exemplified by Voltaire, was renewed in 1908 by Anatole FRANCE, who used the new evidence to argue that Joan was merely a deluded peasant girl, whose hallucinations were manipulated for their own ends by cynical ecclesiastical politicians. With LANG's somewhat emotional defence of Joan, also drawing on Quicherat's work, the main lines of 20th-century historical debate were drawn, closely following those of traditional controversy.

SACKVILLE-WEST's 1936 biography is the best of many traditional sympathetic biographies from the earlier part of the century and is still worth reading. The style is somewhat old-fashioned and discursive, and the author is not afraid to enter imaginatively into the mind of her heroine, but she bases her arguments on the documentary evidence to produce a memorable and psychologically convincing portrait. The difficult problem for the biographer of Joan's "voices" is fully discussed but ultimately allowed to remain mysterious.

The sceptical approach re-emerged in a new form in the 1960s and 70s. Revitalising an old tradition, some writers now asserted that Joan was not really a peasant girl but the bastard daughter of Queen Isabelle and Louis of Orleans, secretly brought up in the country and summoned in 1429 to the aid of the political party loyal to the Dauphin. This theory was used to explain how Joan gained influence with the Dauphin and was able to master the alien world of royal court, politics, and war. In one version of the story, instead of being sacrificed to the English, she survived to marry and bear children in Spain, her place at the stake having been taken by a substitute. Here Joan is again portrayed as the instrument of others, and her "voices" are explained away. Variations of this theory are to be found in the biographies by SERMOISE and GUÉRIN AND WHITE.

A new element entered 20th-century debate with the application of psychoanalytic theory to Joan's "case." LUCIE-SMITH offers a Freudian interpretation of her "voices," according to which they were the result of repressed incestuous relationships within her family. Initial incestous attraction to her father was transferred to fuel her "obsession" with the Dauphin. Possible lesbian tendencies are also hinted at, of which Joan's adoption of male clothing is seen as one manifestation. These suggestions are made within the context of a full chronological biography and an extensive historical background, but the documentary evidence is overlaid with much speculation. In general questions of personality, Joan is not given the benefit of any doubt.

Other biographies of the 70s are those by Guilleman, Smith, and Scott. SMITH rather begs the question of the "voices," while giving the general impression that they must have been psychologically generated. Joan does not emerge as a real military leader and her actual historical role is depicted as relatively minor in comparison with the symbolic importance with which she was later endowed. SCOTT accepts the "voices" unquestioningly and is surprisingly sentimental and old-fashioned in tone. Pleasing traditions are reported alongside historical facts and particular interest is taken in tracing Joan's steps on her various journeys through France. Appendices include discussions of Joan's personality and the English view of her, and an extensive bibliography. GUILLEMIN adopts a friendly and patronising tone toward a poor simple country girl, exploited by political schemers and kept in the dark by the real military leaders, but he defends her "voices" as true revelations to which Joan responded with joyful and obedient love.

With PERNOUD, a professional archivist, we have a rigorous return to the sources. Insisting on history as an exact science, she adopts a new approach to building up a biography. Each chapter of her book consists of questions and answers reproduced from the records of Joan's trial and the rehabilitationprocess, relating to successive stages in her life. The testimony of Joan herself and other witnesses is interspersed with comments by the author, and each chapter ends with a "Commentary" summing up the evidence and drawing conclusions. In the course of these commentaries, the various "conspiracy" and "bastard" theories are firmly refuted. The argument is lively and there is no lack of psychological insight to illuminate the sense, irony, candour, insolence, etc., of the bare recorded words of Joan and the other witnesses. The excitement of actual contact with original documents is well conveyed.

Another new element in more recent biographical treatments of Joan is the feminist viewpoint. WARNER's study is not a conventional chronological biography. Divided into two sections, the book's first part is devoted to the historical Joan while the second deals with the way in which her legend developed after her death. In part one, the author's aim is to portray Joan in terms of the culture of her time and to explain what it meant to

her, her supporters, and her enemies that she adopted—and succeeded in—a man's role. With considerable erudition, Warner discusses the significance of such aspects of Joan as her virginity, her adoption of male dress, and the conventions of chivalry. Parallels are drawn in depth with other female saints and mystics. The mediaeval fear of the diabolically supernatural is also discussed to show how her enemies arrived at their interpretation of her actions.

GIES' 1981 portrait is a straightforward, scholarly, and sympathetic biography, prefaced by a good discussion of the sources and concluding with a review of earlier treatments of her life. Gies is also concerned with Joan's adoption of a traditional male role and defends her against what she sees as the predominantly male viewpoint, which has tended to detract from her real military achievements and their importance to subsequent French history. Here Joan certainly does not appear as anyone's pawn. On the crucial question of the "voices," the author does not consider psychological explanations offered by other biographers to be adequate. She believes that they were real for Joan and, for herself, acknowledges their essential mystery.

—Isabel Aitken

JOHN OF THE CROSS, Saint [San Juan de la Cruz; *born* Juan de Yepes y Álvarez], 1542–1591; Spanish mystic and poet.

Brenan, Gerald, *St. John of the Cross: His Life and Poetry* (poetry translated by Lynda Nicholson). London, Cambridge University Press, 1973.

Bruno de Jesus-Marie, Father, *St. John of the Cross*, edited by Father Benedict Zimmerman, London, Sheed and Ward, and New York, Benziger, 1932 (originally published by Les Petits-fils de Plon et Nourrit, Paris, 1932).

Crisógono de Jesús Sacramentado, Father, *The Life of St. John of the Cross*, translated by Kathleen Pond. London, Longman, and New York, Harper, 1958.

Cristiani, Léon, *St. John of the Cross: Prince of Mystical Theology*. New York, Doubleday, 1962.

Heriz, Paschasius (Paschasius of Our Lady of Mount Carmel), *Saint John of the Cross*. Washington, D.C. 1919.

Lewis, David, editor, *Life of Saint John of the Cross of the Order of Our Lady of Mount Carmel*. London, T. Baker, 1897.

Peers, E. Allison, *Spirit of Flame: A Study of St. John of the Cross*. London, SCM Press, 1943; New York, Morehouse-Gorham, 1944.

Peers, E. Allison, *Handbook to the Life and Times of St. Teresa and St. John of the Cross*. London, Burns and Oates, and Westminster, Maryland, Newman Press, 1954.

Sencourt, Robert, *Carmelite and Poet: A Framed Portrait of St. John of the Cross, with His Poems in Spanish*. London, Hollis and Carter, 1943; New York, Macmillan, 1944.

Sisters of Notre Dame, Mount Pleasant, Liverpool, *Life of St. John of the Cross, Mystical Doctor*. London, Baker, and New York, Benziger, 1927.

*

The earliest lives of St. John of the Cross are the 17th-century works of Fathers José de Jesús María (1628), Jerónimo de San José (1641), and Francisco de Santa María (1655). Late 19th- and early 20th-century biographers continue to rely exclusively on these sources. LEWIS, for example, assumes that José de Jesús María, as appointed annalist of the Carmelite Order, had access to all of the documentation necessary for his work. His study, as well as those of HERIZ and the SISTERS OF NOTRE DAME, is largely hagiographical. The latter two are in fact intended to assist in the spiritual edification of their readers.

BRUNO DE JESUS MARIE is the first modern biographer to shed new light on the life of St. John of the Cross. Unlike his immediate predecessors, he takes as his primary source the processes of beatification located in Rome. Moreover, he breaks with the hagiographical tradition and attempts a more objective analysis. In particular, he highlights the crucial role that St. John of the Cross played in the Carmelite Reform Movement. Nevertheless, he often admits to reconstructing details of place and circumstance not contained in his original sources. This lends to his work a certain novelistic quality that ultimately detracts from the rigor of his analysis.

The goal of SENCOURT is to "frame" St. John of the Cross in the context of his time and culture. In so doing he refers not only to the biographies of Bruno and his predecessors but to more recent studies of the nature and origin of Spanish mystical literature and thought. Despite the historical and critical sources cited, this work is directed not so much to an audience of scholars as to what are described in the preface as "spiritually minded persons."

The work of PEERS, like that of Sencourt, is only partially biographical. While the first half of *Spirit of Flame* (1943) deals with the life of St. John of the Cross, the second half analyzes his poetry and mystical doctrine. In the first section of his *Handbook* (1954), Peers places the biographies of St. Teresa and St. John of the Cross within the context of the Carmelite Reform Movement. In the second section, which many scholars will find useful, Peers gives a brief biographical sketch of the principal persons mentioned in the writings of the two saints or those closely connected with them personally.

Notwithstanding the merits of the aforementioned works, the most significant and most exhaustive biography of St. John of the Cross to date is that of CRISÓGONO DE JESÚS SACRA-MENTADO. Not only has he undertaken a scrupulous analysis of all of the existing documentation, some of which came to light after the publication of Bruno's work, but he brings to his subject a wealth of theological and historical knowledge. Crisógono is particularly successful in integrating the life of St. John of the Cross into the cultural history of 16th-century Spain as well as the Carmelite Reform Movement. Sections such as the one dealing with the religious formation and novitiate of St. John of the Cross remain unsurpassed in Sanjuanist biographies. Readers of the English translation, however, will be disappointed to learn that translator Kathleen Pond has chosen not to reproduce all of the footnotes contained in the original Spanish version. She has also omitted the author's comments on the manuscripts and other works listed in the references.

Most of the significant historical research since that of Crisógono has focused on the manuscripts of St. John of the Cross and not on his life. The work of CRISTIANI, for example, adds little to the existing biographical corpus. The study by

BRENAN, on the other hand, is of interest for several reasons. Rather than reject the miraculous occurrences that fill the pages of traditional hagiographies, Brenan often attempts to place them in a psychological context. Thus, during the celebrated escape from prison, it is not the Virgin Mary but "a voice in his head" that said to St. John of the Cross, "Be quick, be quick." Brenan, moveover, speculates on the possible Semitic origins of St. John of the Cross. He finds intriguing that many of his paternal ancestors were either silk merchants or canons of Toledo Cathedral, occupations usually held by "New Christians." Though Gómez-Menor raised the question of St. John's background several years earlier in *El linaje familiar de Santa Teresa y San Juan de la Cruz* (Toledo, Gráficas Cervantes, 1970), Brenan is the first to indicate to English-speaking readers what will clearly be one of the directions of future research into the life of St. John of the Cross.

—Robert Richmond Ellis

JOHN PAUL II [*born* Karol Wojtyla], 1920–   ; Polish pope.

Blazynski, George, *John Paul II: A Man from Krakow*. London, Weidenfeld and Nicolson, 1979; as *Pope John Paul II*, New York, Dell, 1979.

Craig, Mary, *Man from a Far Country: An Informal Portrait of Pope John Paul II*. London, Hodder and Stoughton, and New York, Morrow, 1979.

Longford, Frank Pakenham, Earl of, *Pope John Paul II: An Authorised Biography*. New York, Morrow, and London, M. Joseph, 1982.

Malinsky, Mieczyslaw, *A Life of My Friend John Paul II*. London, Burns and Oates, and New York, Seabury Press, 1979.

*

The two fullest biographies of John Paul II available are those by Mary Craig and George Blazynski, both written immediately after the pope's election. The two books take different approaches. BLAZYNSKI begins with a long perspective of Poland's history and the Church's historic role as custodian of Polish nationhood. He then moves on to a detailed discussion of Church-State relations during the post-war years, brought right up to date by the author's own talks with the Polish Episcopate. In this account Karol Wojtyla does not figure; as Polish Primate, Cardinal Wyszynski is the key protagonist on the side of the Church. Blazynski goes on to sketch a portrait of Polish national psychology, moulded, as he sees it, by the twin influences of oppression and religious faith. Only after these preliminaries does he embark on an account of Wojtyla's life. This he does by amassing information from people who knew Wojtyla at different stages of his career. The result is a portrait built up from anecdote and reminiscence. While this affords much detail, glimpses of personal relationships, and memorable insights into personality, it does not provide a coherent picture of a man developing in his historic context. To some extent this is remedied in the closing chapters. One of these, entitled "Wojtyla the Man," draws the anecdotal threads together to produce a rounded picture of Wojtyla's personality. Another, "Cardinal Wojtyla Speaks," uses extensive quotations from Wojtyla's own writings and pronouncements to explain his views and stances on various issues of importance. Here the emphasis is more on Polish than worldwide problems, but such controversial topics as contraception and divorce are also considered.

CRAIG adopts a broader and more integrated approach. After a couple of chapters devoted in journalistic style to the excitement of the election, she turns to an account of Wojtyla's life seen against the perspective of contemporary history. She emphasises the influence of Wojtyla's experiences, particularly during the years of the Nazi occupation, on the development of his thought, quoting from his poetry and other writings. She also discusses the influence of his theological and philosophical studies, particularly his interest in St. John of the Cross and St. Thomas Aquinas and in reconciling these with modern thinkers such as Martin Buber, Gabriel Marcel, and Max Scheler. The impact of the Second Vatican Council on Wojtyla's thinking is particularly stressed and his own contribution to the debate discussed. As Wojtyla advances to ever higher office in the Polish Church, his attempts to put the precepts of the Council into practice are followed. The Church's continuing struggle with the Communist government is seen from Wojtyla's perspective. Meanwhile his growing knowledge of and contribution to international church affairs is described, showing how he came to be seen as a suitable candidate for the highest office. A concluding chapter poses some of the questions raised by the appointment of a Polish pope and assesses John Paul II's likely response to important issues in the light of his past career.

A third book published in immediate response to the papal election is MALINSKY's. This is chiefly a book of personal reminiscence, written by a contemporary who knew Wojtyla well, particularly during their late adolescence and young manhood. Malinsky met Wojtyla at a religious discussion group and later followed him into the priesthood. Malinsky's own memories are supplemented by those of other acquaintances whom he has interviewed. Alternating with chapters of reminiscence are chapters describing the author's own rise to public importance in 1978, as one of the few people able to provide the media with interviews about the unknown Polish pope.

Lord LONGFORD's book, subtitled "An Authorised Biography," was written in connection with the pope's visit to Britain in 1982. It is a glossy production, full of photographs, among the most interesting of which are old sepia portraits from the pope's childhood. After an opening discussion of the papacy from the time of John XXII and the Second Vatican Council, Longford gives a brief and concise résumé of Wojtyla's life up to the time of his election to the papacy, drawing on both Mary Craig and Blazynski and emphasising Wojtyla's stand on issues of particular concern to the contemporary Catholic. The three years between the election and the papal visit to Britain are covered in detail. In this blow-by-blow account of the pope's various journeys, Longford pauses to comment on the more controversial papal pronouncements, but he does not offer any overall assessment of the papacy to date. After his own audience with the pope in 1981, Longford is able to give a personal im-

pression of the man, but does so only briefly. A chapter entitled "The Man and the Message" sums up the pope's chief concerns and a final epilogue traces the history of Catholicism in Britain and sets the papal visit in this context.

—Isabel Aitken

JOHNSON, Lyndon Baines, 1908-1973; American political leader, 36th president of the United States.

Bornet, Vaughn D., *The Presidency of Lyndon B. Johnson.* Lawrence, University of Kansas Press, 1983.
Caro, Robert A., *The Years of Lyndon Johnson.* Vol. 1: *The Path to Power,* New York, Knopf, 1982; London, Collins, 1983. Vol 2: *Means of Ascent,* New York, Knopf, 1990.
Conkin, Paul, *Big Daddy from the Pedernales: Lyndon Baines Johnson.* Boston, Twayne, 1986.
Dugger, Ronnie, *The Politician, the Life and Times of Lyndon Johnson: The Drive for Power, from the Frontier to Master of the Senate.* New York, Norton, 1982.
Kearns, Doris, *Lyndon Johnson and the American Dream.* New York, Harper, and London, Deutsch, 1976.

*

Lyndon B. Johnson was probably the most controversial American president, perhaps the most controversial politician, of the 20th century. Accurately described by biographer Paul Conkin as "larger than life," Johnson found his presidency enmeshed in rapid domestic social change as well as America's longest and, to many, most unpopular war. Moreover, his pre-presidential career was often mired in controversy, usually involving allegations that Johnson was an unprincipled wheeler-dealer who too often operated on the ethical dark side.

Unlike John F. Kennedy, who inspired, at least in the period immediately after his death, a series of immensely positive biographical studies bordering on hagiography, most accounts of Johnson's life and presidency are either largely negative, balanced, or fraught with ambiguity. One major exception, understandably, is Johnson's own memoir, *The Vantage Point* (1971). This "court reminiscence" barely touches on Johnson's pre-presidential life and career. Rather, the central focus is on the presidency, more specifically on the connection between Johnson's policies and those of his predecessor. The dominant theme of *Vantage Point* is continuity. Johnson saw himself, both in domestic and foreign policy, carrying out Kennedy's grand design. In addition, Johnson sought to prove that a Southerner not only could govern a divided nation but could implement a liberal reform program. Ultimately *Vantage Point* will stand as a useful source for future biographers.

By far the most comprehensive and balanced academic account of the Johnson presidency is provided by BORNET. Bornet's straightfoward study focuses on the official actions of the administration in domestic and foreign affairs. He argues that many of Johnson's goals were noble and that his performance, especially in the area of civil rights, was nothing short of spectacular. Nonetheless, Johnson's domestic agenda, particularly the War on Poverty, promised more than it delivered. And he failed in Vietnam by not initiating a fundamental reassessment of Kennedy's policy and by deceiving the public. Bornet's summing up is a model of balance and thoughtfulness: "The presidency of Lyndon B. Johnson will inevitably be remembered— and ought to be—for the characteristics of its central figure; for the unintentional but substantial damage that it did with some catastrophic policies abroad and erroneous policies at home; and especially for the many worthwhile changes it embedded deeply in legislation, in the lives of millions, and in American society."

Bornet's dispassionate account of the Johnson presidency stands in stark contrast to DUGGER's passionate assault on Johnson's rise to political power. Although *The Politician* covers the period up to the 1950s, as Johnson expanded his mastery of the senate, Dugger makes disparaging allusions to Johnson as president. This biography is clearly characterized by an emphasis on the negative. Although Dugger pays lip service to Johnson's virtues—especially his compassion—he focuses on his ruthlessness, crudeness, and vindictiveness. In sum, according to Dugger, Johnson was single-mindedly devoted to a relentless search for political power—a drive that included inumerable lies and clear vote manipulation, particularly in the Texas senatorial election of 1948. Finally, Dugger sees in Johnson's early career the seeds of a fundamental hawkishness in foreign affairs. He concludes his work ominously: "If the holocaust comes and if there is still a human history, the global American hawkery of the Johnson Period will be understood as a principal cause of World War IV."

If Dugger is negative, occassionally vicious in his account of Johnson's early life, KEARNS, a political scientist, highlights the ambiguities, one might say the personal devils that hounded Johnson for much of his life. Kearns had unusual special access to Johnson, especially as a presidential assistant and, from 1969–73, as a part-time live-in visitor and confidante at the Johnson ranch. Relying largely on her numerous frank and personal conversations with her subject, Kearns paints Johnson as a tragic hero. She argues that the "very patterns of behavior and belief responsible for his greatest successes contained within them the seeds of his ultimate failure." The great value of Kearns' account is its wealth of intimate details that Johnson poured out to her. While some might disagree with her penchant for psychobiography, one finds personal insights here available in no other work.

Kearns obviously knew Johnson intimately and wrote her biography from both a personal and disciplinary perspective. CONKIN, a professional historian, offers by far the best biography of Johnson from a purely academic perspective. Although Conkin is no "psycho-historian," he does suggest that Johnson's childhood and early career helped form certain key personality traits: impulsiveness, insecurity, determination, emphasis on personal loyalty, and the seemingly contradictory desire both to conciliate and dominate.

Conkin quite self-consciously wants more to describe than to explain or judge. He admits that it is impossible for him either to hate or love Johnson, whom he sees as an enormously complex man, profoundly influenced by his youth in the Texas hill country and by his deep need for "the emotional support and intimacy of an extended family." In his assessments of the major issues arising during Johnson's presidential administration, Conkin is fair, balanced, and largely positive. In his civil rights

and Great Society initiatives, Johnson showed immense compassion. To Conkin, " . . . at least briefly, in the mid-60s, the federal government did try to be generous. Big Daddy saw to that." The Vietnam tangle revealed Johnson not as a war criminal but as a tragic figure. Conkin emphasizes Johnson's agony as he made decisions that drew America further into the war. Johnson "deeply felt" both the necessity to stay the course in Vietnam and the pain and suffering that such a decision entailed.

If Conkin's is the best brief biography of Johnson, CARO's massive study will be the most complete. Two volumes of a projected multi-volume series have appeared, taking Johnson's story only up through the 1948 Texas senatorial election. The sheer mass and sweep of Caro's account is remarkable. This is life-and-times biography at its best, as Johnson himself often disappears amidst descriptions of friends, enemies, even the hill country of Texas.

Caro clearly does not like Lyndon Johnson. Reviewer James Patterson rightly says that Caro paints Johnson as "manipulative, domineering, sycophantic, aggressive, . . . desperately competitive, . . . secretive, hypocritical, self-serving, superambitious, and opportunistic" (*Journal of American History*, September 1983). It would seem from this list that Johnson had few if any positive qualities. Yet for all his negative portraiture, Caro does recognize Johnson's strengths. He begins his second volume with twin images—one of Johnson's famous Voting Rights speech before Congress in 1965, another of Johnson's attitudes toward anti-Vietnam War protestors. While Johnson's role in the war represented the "darker" threads of his life and career, his commitment to civil rights was one of the "bright threads." In other words, although Caro certainly spends considerable space following the dark side of Johnson, the light surely shows through as well. When Caro's mammoth project is completed, we will have not only the most complete biography of Lyndon Johnson, but a monument to the biographer's art.

—Anthony O. Edmonds

JOHNSON, Samuel, 1709–1784; English writer and lexicographer.

Bate, Walter Jackson, *Samuel Johnson*. New York, Harcourt, 1977; London, Chatto and Windus, 1978.

Boswell, James, *Life of Samuel Johnson* (2 vols.). London, H. Baldwin, 1791; revised edition, 1793, 1799; edited by R. W. Chapman, London and New York, Oxford University Press, 1953.

Clifford, James L., *Young Samuel Johnson*. London, Heinemann, 1955; as *Young Sam Johnson*, New York, McGraw-Hill, 1955.

Clifford, James L., *Dictionary Johnson: Samuel Johnson's Middle Years*. New York, McGraw-Hill, 1979; London, Heinemann, 1980.

Hibbert, Christopher, *The Personal History of Samuel Johnson*. London, Longman, and New York, Harper and Row, 1971.

Hill, G. B., *Johnsonian Miscellanies*. Oxford, Clarendon Press, and New York, Harper, 1897.

Hodgart, Matthew J. C., *Samuel Johnson and His Times*. London, Batsford, 1962.

Kaminski, Thomas, *The Early Career of Samuel Johnson*. New York, Oxford University Press, 1987.

Kingsmill, Hugh, *Johnson without Boswell: A Contemporary Portrait of Samuel Johnson*. London, Methuen, and New York, Knopf, 1940.

Krutch, Joseph W., *Samuel Johnson*. New York, Holt, 1944; London, Cassell, 1948.

Stephen, Leslie, *Samuel Johnson*. London, Macmillan, and New York, Harper, 1878.

Wain, John, *Samuel Johnson: A Biography*. London, Macmillan, 1974; New York, Viking, 1975.

*

Johnsonian biography neither starts nor ends with Boswell, but he is unquestionably its center. Modern scholars debate with Boswell, correct and adjust, often supplement his findings; but no one can doubt that this is a major classic in literary biography, a book that will survive whatever new material should come to light.

Even in Johnson's lifetime there were sketches, anecdotes, collections of Johnsoniana (chiefly bons mots by the great man), and satirical surveys of his career. After his death in 1784 a number of magazines brought out short lives, of which the most interesting is perhaps that by Thomas Tyers. In 1785 Boswell produced his *Journal* of the Hebridean trip he had made with his friend 12 years earlier. It was in many ways a trial shot for the great biography he planned, and it remains one of the most absorbing accounts of Johnson in full flight we possess. Quicker off the mark in producing their full-dress accounts were Hester (Thrale) Piozzi, with her *Anedoctes* (1786), and Sir John Hawkins with his *Life* (1787)—the latter has appeared in a deft modern abridgment by B. H. Davis (1961). Both are illuminating and stronger than Boswell in certain specialized areas—Piozzi, in particular, knew certain intimate sides of Johnson better than her rival biographer. The other significant item from this early period is Arthur Murphy's *Essay* on the "life and genius" of Johnson—again, this benefits from a close firsthand acquaintance with its subject.

What sets BOSWELL's *Life* apart is a combination of qualities, literary and human. It is incomparably the fullest of the early biographies, replete with personal detail, especially for Johnson's last years. It embodies a full scan of his writings, cites a generous selection of his letters, and reports his conversations with extraordinary vividness and directness. Its simple chronological structure is organized more cunningly than is sometimes supposed, while its management of authorial viewpoint set standards that modern biographers must even today struggle to emulate. It combines a superb narrative with sharp character sketches, and it illuminates a whole age as well as an individual at the center of 18th-century culture. No biography succeeds better in presenting a rounded, convincing, and lovable personality: while we may quarrel with details, and suspect that Boswell's own prejudices creep in at times, we can only marvel at the warmth and richness of coloring that suffuse the entire book.

Inevitably Boswell dominated the landscape for a century or more. The most influential 19th-century accounts of Johnson tend- ed to appear as reviews of new editions of Boswell; above all in the essays of Macaulay (1831) and Carlyle (1832). Macaulay's is generally regarded today as a caricature, though its sharply etched lines do allow some essential truths to be stated shortly. A more temperate account of Johnson's life was written by Macaulay for the *Encyclopaedia Britannica* (1859), though this had less impact on prevailing views. A number of memoirs and journals appeared in the 19th century that provided new data, including Letitia Hawkins' *Anecdotes* (1832) and Fanny Burney's *Diary* (1842–46), but no substantial new life appeared for many decades. Perhaps the most respected book from the period remains STEPHEN's short study for the English Men of Letters series. This is usually seen as a Victorian re-reading of Boswell, but it has its own sanity and a largely sympathetic cast of mind.

The shadow of Boswell continued to hang over Johnsonian studies as the Victorian era gave way to the concern of the new century. The scholar G. B. HILL, mainly known as editor of Boswell, produced important work of his own, including a collection of *Johnsonian Miscellanies* (1897), which consists of extracts from contemporary sources, excluding only Boswell. Specialized inquiries illuminated Johnson's relations with figures such as Hester Thrale and Fanny Burney, and there were several popular guides to his life, but as late as the 1930s there was little by way of fundamental reassessment of Johnson's personal and literary identity. For this it was necessary to wait until the appearance of KRUTCH's fine work in 1944, which could be termed the first recognizably modern biography. This was partly a matter of loosening the grip of Boswell, partly a matter of looking harder at Johnson's earlier career (Boswell himself only enters in the eighth of 17 chapters, a more fitting proportion than had usually been achieved), and partly a matter of intense scrutiny of the relevant material, including Johnson's own writings. Krutch is the first item among those so far mentioned that can be studied today not just for historical interest (again, with the inevitable exclusion of Boswell), and it supplies a judicious overview of most aspects of the man and the work.

In the past 40 years, the pace has quickened. There has been considerable industry both in scholarly production and in popular, or semi-popular, treatment of Johnson. In the latter category the most interesting items start as far back as KINGSMILL, who provides another sample of contemporary sources; then comes a good brief survey by HODGART, covering the various stages of Johnson's writing career with neat economy; and an effective study of Johnson's "personal history" by HIBBERT. There are several other brief lives aimed at a broad reading public, which embody original research and do not warrant detailed listing here, though they mostly supply a reasonably accurate picture of their subject.

In the scholarly area, three enterprises stand out. CLIFFORD produced two installments of a planned longer work that together constitute the fullest and most reliable account of Johnson's life, year by year, that we have. *Young Samuel Johnson* covers the first 40 years of the life and is by far the best general treatment of this phase, a section where Boswell was at his least impressive. *Dictionary Johnson* was a much needed rehearsal of the middle years from 1749 to 1763: a good deal remains obscure, but Clifford has filled out our knowledge to great effect. His is a sober, factual, but never boring narrative that constitutes the "standard" account for Johnson in these decades preceding his first acquaintance with Boswell.

Two very different works appeared in the 1970s to supply a new depth and engagement in Johnsonian biography. WAIN's study is a splendid example of its kind: a sympathetic, detailed, and sensitive approach, uncluttered by academic baggage, acutely alert to the tone and message of Johnson's utterances. Wain begins with sections on the Midlands background and the Grub Street experiences, areas which (as a professional man of letters born and raised close to Johnson's childhood home, and as a bright Oxford student quitting the cloister when young) Wain is well placed to understand and evaluate. While Wain does not claim to work from original sources, he has kept up with the march of scholarship and is able to provide skillful translations of Johnson's Latin verse, which calls for the hand of a poet rather than a scholar. There are few books on Johnson that give a better all-round sense of the man and his milieu.

A more radical, challenging, and contentious reading is offered by BATE in his monumental biography. Bate had earlier written of Johnson's as a "life of allegory," and this approach is here extended into a full-length psychological study. Bate, more finely attuned to the inner springs of Johnson's melancholy than Wain, emphasizes rather the miseries and grandeurs of a literary life. Bate is strongest on such matters as Johnson's painful upbringing, his lost years of obscurity, the trials of his marriage (underplayed, it is now felt, by Boswell), and the irresolute "straggling" that marked much of Johnson's career before he found his true subjects, in the *Dictionary* and beyond. This is certainly the key biography for an assessment of the darker side of Johnson, and it incorporates some profound engagements with Johnson's personal writing—diaries, sermons, and letters in particular. Some might feel that it deals less successfully with the convivial, sportive and exuberant aspects of Johnson's personality, but overall it stands as a major landmark in the field.

Among many recent specialized works, the most significant increment to Johnsonian biography is perhaps a study of the early career by KAMINSKI. This fills out the work of previous scholars on Johnson's years in and around Grub Street, when he worked on the *Gentleman's Magazine*, and it suggests that he was not as indigent as has generally been supposed. The tradition is thus worthily maintained as we reach the bicentenary of the greatest of English literary biographies.

—Pat Rogers

JOLSON, Al, 1886?–1950; Jewish-American entertainer.

Freedland, Michael, *Jolson*. New York, Stein and Day, 1972.
Goldman, Herbert G., *Jolson: The Legend Comes to Life*. New York and Oxford, Oxford University Press, 1988.
Jolson, Harry, *Mistah Jolson: As Told to Alban Emley*. Hollywood, House-Warven, 1951.
McClelland, Doug, *Blackface to Blacklist: Al Jolson, Larry Parks, and "The Jolson Story"*. Metuchen, New Jersey, Scarecrow, 1987.
Oberfirst, Robert, *Al Jolson: You Ain't Heart Nothin' Yet*. San Diego, A. S. Barnes, and London, Tantivy Press, 1980.
Sieben, Pearl, *The Immortal Jolson: His Life and Times*. New York, F. Fell, 1962.

*

The most charismatic stage performer of the 20th century has inspired a largely disappointing assortment of biographies which are, nevertheless, more reliable than the illusory tales that appeared during the subject's lifetime. (See, for example, "Jolson: alchemist of the emotions," *American Hebrew*, September 1929, and "Al Jolson" in Harry T. Brundidge, *Twinkle, Twinkle, Movie Star!* New York, Dutton, 1930.)

Older brother Harry's autobiography, JOLSON, published a year after Al's death, is also a vital source of information about Al's personal and early professional life. The mixture of love and resentment that characterized Harry Jolson's relationship with his brother make this a fascinating, sometimes pathetic, and perhaps not wholly objective, document. But it is movingly written, especially in its descriptions of the Yoelson family's life in the now-vanished world of Eastern European Jewry, and, in marked contrast to other titles herein cited, it is very funny and a pleasure to read. Its depiction of vaudeville life, a forgotten chunk of theatrical history, is marvelous.

Another chatty account by one who knew Al Jolson personally, SIEBEN is (according to Herbert Goldman, who interviewed Pearl Sieben for his book, see below) the work of a stagestruck "groupie" who in the early 1940s talked her way into her idol's confidence and apparently based her biography (written 20 years later) on the memory of what Jolson told her. Sieben lacks the charm of Harry Jolson—and needs a good proofreader as well—but hers is the first of the biographies to deal, although clumsily, with Jolson's formidable neuroses.

An index, finally, graces the next biography to appear, FREEDLAND's "richly detailed, enthusiastic, even adulatory" account (*Best Sellers*, December 1972), which is "drawn mostly from the recollections of Jolson's peers and contemporaries" (*Library Journal*, November 1972). Freedland writes smooth, confident prose that nevertheless resorts to the deplorable use of "dialogue"—usually of the semi-grammatical, "dese-dem-dose" variety. Sieben, Oberfirst, and Goldman rely on profane (and inane) dialogue also, substituting for style and vivid writing. Freedland maintains an ironic distance, unique among Jolson biographers, from his subject. He is strongest in his coverage of Jolson's career, offering brief, intelligent comments about the stage productions and films, and he is mercifully succinct on the subject of Jolson's marital history. Freedland quips, "when the 'other woman' in the man's life turns out to be an audience, an incomparable love story emerges."

In describing the 1946 film biography, "The Jolson Story," OBERFIRST is also aptly describing his own work: "the thin line of Al's real life was embellished with fancy incidents that were more or less fictionalized." Oberfirst's book contains a hodgepodge of irrelevancies and lies, vaguely pornographic descriptions, spurious Yoelson family vignettes, extensive bedtime "conversations" between Al and his various wives (Goldman is partial to these dialogues also), and an inordinate number of references to meals ingested. There is a ludicrous depiction of 19-year-old Ruby Keeler, whose purported innocence captivated middle-aged Jolson. It is well known that she was actually the adolescent mistress of one of the Prohibition era's most powerful gangsters. To Oberfirst's credit, there is a fine segment (information not revealed elsewhere) about Jolson's relationship with the fledgling William Morris Theatrical Agency; an excellent discography (although the film- and stageographies are poor); an attempt to analyze Jolson's unique musical style; and rare photographs (no captions, alas) that say more about the man's enormous gusto and impishness than the purple prose does.

Jolson buffs will be pleased with McCLELLAND's *Blackface to Blacklist*, which examines the period 1945–50, when the two film biographies were made and Jolson experienced a brief but spectacular comeback. Amusing, bitchy, overly fond of the word "ironic," the author presents a balanced view and rights some old wrongs such as "Jolson-bashing"—which has always been fashionable according to interviewee Phil Silvers. McClelland also does a good job of explaining the "almost orgasmic euphoria" that characterized Jolson's performances before live audiences. Readers familiar with the journal "Films in Review" will recognize the mix of solid research, trivia, affection, and gossip.

The most ambitious and best researched study, by GOLDMAN, is fascinating in its accumulation of unsavory details about Jolson's private life and habits. The author contends that Jolson was an Oedipal wreck, forever moored in his childhood because of his mother's early death. His subsequent relationships with women were fraught with problems, among them wife-beating and bisexuality. Despite these revelations, one must agree with the reviewer in the *Village Voice* of December 1988: "There's just enough tantalizing material to keep us curious . . . but in spite of [the work's] subtitle, the legend remains as lively as a wet sock." Not the fault of Al Jolson, let it be said, for he remains the icon of American popular music during its golden age. A man of fierce energies and brash confidence, emblematic of early 20th-century America, his definitive biography has yet to be written.

—Honora Raphael Weinstein

JONES, John Paul, 1747–1792; Scottish-born American naval officer.

Abbott, John S., *The Life and Adventures of Rear-Admiral John Paul Jones, Commonly Called Paul Jones*. New York, Dodd Mead, 1874.

Buell, Augustus C., *Paul Jones: Founder of the American Navy* (2 vols.). New York, Scribner, and London, K. Paul, 1900.

Crawford, Mary (MacDermot), *The Sailor Whom England Feared: Being the Story of Paul Jones, Scotch Naval Adventurer and Admiral in the American and Russian Fleets*. London, Eveleigh Nash, and New York, Duffield, 1913.

DeKoven, Mrs. Reginald [Anna], *The Life and Letters of John Paul Jones*. New York, Scribner, and London, T. W. Laurie, 1913.

Golder, F. A., *John Paul Jones in Russia*, New York, Doubleday, 1927.

Johnson, Gerald W., *The First Captain: The Story of John Paul Jones*. New York, Coward-McCann, 1947.

Lorenz, Lincoln, *John Paul Jones: Fighter for Freedom and Glory*. Annapolis, Maryland, United States Naval Institute, 1943.

Mackenzie, Alexander Slidell, *The Life of Paul Jones* (2 vols.). Boston, Hilliard Gray, 1841; condensed version, under the pseudonym "Edward Hamilton," Aberdeem, G. Clark, and London, W. Brittain, 1848.

Malcolm, Sir John (?), *Memoirs of Rear Admiral Paul Jones . . . Compiled from his Original Journals and Correspondence* (2 vols.). New York, Oliver and Boyd, and London, Simpkin and Marshall, 1830.

McCulloch, John Herries, *The Splendid Renegade*. New York, Grosset and Dunlap, 1928.

Morison, Samuel Eliot, *John Paul Jones: A Sailor's Biography*. Boston, Little Brown, and London, Faber, 1959.

Sands, Robert, editor, *Life and Correspondence of John Paul Jones, Including His Narrative of the Campaign of the Liman*. New York, A. Chandler, 1830.

Sherburne, John Henry, *The Life and Character of the Chevalier John Paul Jones, A Captain in the Navy of the United States, during their Revolutionary War*. New York, Wilder and Campbell, 1825.

Thomson, Valentine, *Knight of the Seas: The Adventurous Life of John Paul Jones*, New York, Liveright, 1939.

*

Though the subject of numerous chapbook writers, especially in England, Jones was not the subject of a full-length biography until SHERBURNE's book appeared in 1825. Sherburne served as Register of the U.S. Navy, had access to many government documents, and borrowed letters from men like Thomas Jefferson who had corresponded with Jones. The result was a fuller, more accurate portrait of Jones than had previously appeared. Sherburne set the tone for American writers for the next three-quarters of a century when he called Jones "an example worthy of imitation" and praised his "chivalric spirit and undaunted valor, . . . active disposition and nautical skill." Jones was venerated as one whose "labors . . . for the furtherance of the American cause [were] incessant, . . . " a view shared by ABBOTT in his volume in the American Pioneers and Patriots series. This view of Jones as a hero of the War for Independence, a man of bravery, honor, and patriotism, contrasted sharply with his image among British authors, where he remained a corsair at best. The heading in Rudyard Kipling's poem "The Rhyme of the Three Captains" (1890) referring to "the exploits of the notorious Paul Jones, an American Pirate"; naval historian J. K. Laughton's article entitled "Paul Jones, the Pirate," (*Fraser's Magazine*, January 1878); and Sir Winston Churchill's calling Jones a "privateer" in *The Age of Revolution* (1957), all reflect the persistence of this view in Britain.

Janette Taylor, Jones' niece and heir to a large collection of his papers, arranged biographies by MALCOLM and SANDS that, while not changing the prevailing view of Jones, did publish a large number of his papers, particularly the journal he wrote concerning his service in the Russian navy. MACKENZIE, an American naval officer, wrote travel literature and a biography of Oliver Hazard Perry before writing his study of Jones. Its strength is its descriptive narrative, and, though weak on analysis, it does avoid the stringing together of document transcriptions that makes the works by Malcolm and Sands choppy.

At the turn of the century BUELL published his highly unreliable biography of Jones. Like earlier writers he devoted the majority of his work to descriptions of naval operations and battles, but in keeping with the Progressivism of the era he was interested in the development of institutions and managerial skills. Thus Buell spoke of Jones' "undiminished earnestness for professional improvement" and quoted his ideas on officer education and proposals for naval administration. When Buell lacked documentation for the events and ideas he wished to describe he simply fabricated, and the result is a mixture of fact and fiction that continues to mislead readers to this day. Buell's work spawned, and served as the basis for, other equally unreliable biographies, such as CRAWFORD's.

The discovery of Jones' body in Paris, its return to America by U.S. warships and entombment beneath the chapel at the U.S. Naval Academy in Annapolis, heightened interest in his life and inspired a number of works about him, most important of which is DeKOVEN's. In her preface DeKoven notes that "The fame of Paul Jones has been the sport of romance and the plaything of tradition" and promised that she would "present a final and truthful estimate of his life and character." The result is the most accurate and most complete biography of Jones to that time. It is of the life and letters genre and repeats a number of anecdotes about Jones for which there is no documentary evidence, but it omits the clearly apocryphal stories recounted by virtually every previous biographer except Malcolm, Sands, Mackenzie, and Sherburne. Gracefully written, it stood for 30 years as the standard biography of Jones.

Several rather romantic biographies appeared, such as those by McCULLOCH and THOMSON, whose titles are indicative of their content. Thomson has the distinction of adding several inventions of her own to the myths surrounding Jones. When GOLDER located a series of documents in Russian archives, he used them for his study of Jones' service in the Black Sea.

LORENZ's biography supplemented but did not completely replace DeKoven's. Drawing on sources not available to DeKoven, Lorenz substituted narration for the long quotations favored by DeKoven and produced a more readable, if still very long, 846-page biography. Writing during World War II, Lorenz heralded Jones' "passion for freedom and action" and found few faults with him.

The dustjacket of JOHNSON's biography sums up his view: Jones "was the first true professional among our naval officers, and as such, the first to understand that the navy as an implement of peace may be no less valuable than it is as a weapon of war. . . . Paul Jones won his fights against the British and the Turks, but the fight of the man of genius to get his ideas accepted goes on forever. His ideal of the naval officer not merely as a combatant but as an instrument to serve the nation's purpose is perhaps more valuable today than it was in his time."

Admiral MORISON's biography best combines accuracy, readability, and brevity. Keenly aware of the problem of separating "the real Jones" from the mythical, he wrote in the preface to his 1959 Pulitzer Prize-winning work: "If a story conflicts with known facts about Jones, I reject it; if it fits in with or supplements ascertained facts, and is intrinsically probable, I tell it." He says that he has "not taken up space and the reader's

time to refute all the nonsense that has been written about Paul Jones," but he does devote six appendices to refuting some of the more enduring Jones legends. The result is a lively biography based as much on the author's assessment of Jones as on the documentary record. Morison's Jones is a skilled seaman, an intrepid warrior, a master tactician, and an inspiring leader, who "accomplished what he did through sheer merit, persistence, and force of character." Jones was also egotistical, quarrelsome, short of temper, and "a hard person to get along with." Morison is particularly adept at evoking a mood, and his clear depictions of life at sea, combined with the intrinsic interest in Jones, made his book a best seller. Almost constantly in print for over three decades, it remains the standard by which any further biography of Jones will be measured.

—James C. Bradford

———————

JONSON, Ben, 1572–1637; English playwright and poet.

Chute, Marchette, *Ben Jonson of Westminster*. New York, Dutton, 1953; London, R. Hale, 1954.

Herford, C. H., "Life of Ben Jonson," in vol I of *Ben Jonson* (11 vols.), edited by C. H. Herford and Percy Simpson. Oxford, Clarendon Press, 1925–63.

Linklater, Eric, *Ben Jonson and King James*. London, Cape, and New York, H. Smith, 1931.

Miles, Rosalind, *Ben Jonson: His Life and Work*. London and New York, Routledge, 1986.

Palmer, John, *Ben Jonson*. London, Routledge, and New York, Viking, 1934.

Riggs, David, *Ben Jonson: A Life*. Cambridge, Massachusetts, and London, Harvard University Press, 1989.

Smith, Gregory, *Ben Jonson*. London, Macmillan, 1919.

Steegmuller, Francis (Byron Steel), *O Rare Ben Jonson*. New York, Knopf, 1927.

Swinburne, Algernon C., *A Study of Ben Jonson*. London, Chatto and Windus, and New York, Worthington, 1889.

Symonds, John A., *Ben Jonson*. London, Longman, and New York, Appleton, 1886.

*

Our extensive knowledge of the facts of Ben Jonson's life, at least by contrast with the elusiveness of Shakespeare's, has served to discourage modern biographers from the wilder realms of apocryphal anecdotage. However, the existence of the nearest we shall ever get to an "interview" with a Jacobean dramatist, in the form of the *Conversations* disjointedly recorded by Drummond of Hawthornden, has posed almost as many problems as it has resolved—not least with regard to Jonson's views on Shakespeare, so elided in some editions of the *Conversations* as to provide ammunition in that unhelpful league-tabling of reputations which, for too many years, displaced serious consideration of Jonson, whether as man or as artist. Anyone wishing to assess for themselves the contemporary view of the dramatists will find the material assembled in the two volumes of Gerald Eades Bentley's *Shakespeare and Jonson: Their Reputations in the Seventeenth Century Compared* (1945). Unfortunately, as Bentley concludes, the fact that on the evidence "Jonson was evidently more popular than Shakespeare" precipitated several centuries of demolition work on Jonson by those concerned to reverse the verdict. Thus, by contrast with the subtle distortions and unsubtle vilifications of Rufus Chetwood's *Memoirs of the Life and Writings of Ben Jonson* (1756), the earlier thumbnail sketches to be found in such old faithfuls as Fuller's *Worthies* (1662), Winstanley's *Lives* (1687), and Aubrey's *Brief Lives* (1690), seem almost amiable in their inaccuracies.

Despite Coleridge's interest in the dramatist, as revealed in the first volume of his *Literary Remains* (1836), and a pioneering but pedestrian full-length study by SYMONDS in 1886, it was SWINBURNE's *Study of Ben Jonson* in 1889 that proved the most influential of these, the earliest modern approaches. Swinburne is refreshing in his idiosyncratic preference for some of the lesser-known plays, but essentially he perpetuated a reach-me-down romantic portrait of a man regretfully lacking in "natural taste" and incapable of infusing his plays with "light." Though Jonson was among "the giants of energy and invention," it was, of course, Shakespeare—up there among "the gods of harmony and creation"—who reigned supreme. Coleridge's comparable view of a "surly" if "robust" figure was no less capable of expansion by unsympathetic critics into the "brutish pedant" perceived by Bernard Shaw. STEEL's heavily fictionalized account follows, rather ploddingly, in such well-worn tracks.

That monument of the Samuel Smiles school of literary history, the "English Men of Letters" series, founded by Henry Morley in 1877, finally admitted Jonson to its ranks in 1919—a belated but not ungracious acknowledgement of his status, in the respectful but somewhat muted tones of SMITH. Ironically, the same year saw the publication of the essay on Jonson by T. S. Eliot in *The Sacred Wood*, which was seminally responsible for his revaluation as a writer, and for the biographical rethinking this entailed. Then, in 1925, came the first of the 11 volumes of Herford and Simpson's massive edition of the collected works: this included a good reprint of the *Conversations*, together with other original documentation essential to any consideration of Jonson's life, and also a substantial biographical essay by C. H. HERFORD himself—a scrupulously objective and, for its time, authoritative account with regard to the facts, though in its value judgments it still seems heavily influenced by 19th-century preconceptions, sustaining the Swinburnian version of the writer as variously "hearty," "gregarious," and a "rugged individualist."

Thus, while critics largely followed Eliot's lead in trying to find new ways into Jonson's plays, biographers at first lagged behind, and even Herford continued to look in vain (or improbably) for a "sympathetic" Jonson, as the critics had once sought, no less vainly, for "sympathetic" characters in his plays. Typically, PALMER's study of 1934 bemoaned the lack of any "deep sense of spiritual values" alike in the person and the plays. Critically, the corollary could only be such a notorious put-down as Edmund Wilson's "Morose Ben Jonson," included in his *The Triple Thinkers* (1938), which remains heavily dependent on Victorian values, for all its casual veneer of Freudian sophistication. Thankfully, however, this proved a dead end rather than a new beginning, and now biographers, too, began to

look for a new, perhaps no less cussed, but more complex yet more comprehensible version of their man.

As early as 1931 had come a little-remembered biography by LINKLATER, which has the simple virtue of being prepared to like its subject, warts and all. Unfortunately, it also displays the predictable defects of being written by a novelist. Thus, all too imaginatively visualizing Jonson's declining years, Linklater rather typically sums up: "Day after day Ben studied his own writings, and peopled them with memories. Night came heavily to shut them out, and sometimes he was loth to wake. Time on its heavy feet went curiously fast." This book, on its own quite sprightly feet, remains eminently readable, if such flights of fancy be forgiven, and its cavalier regard for factual niceties borne steadily in mind. Like Marchette Chute's better-known and widely available study, it continued the necessary process of humanizing a figure that had for so long been presented as at best improbably Falstaffian, at worst grotesque and forbidding.

CHUTE's book is entitled *Ben Jonson of Westminster* by way of complement to her earlier *Shakespeare of London*, and it sustains the relish for local colour that the careful boundary-marking suggests. For a popularization, it is a chunky volume, and well balanced in its then-unfashionable attention to Jonson's activities as a masque writer as much as to his work as a dramatist. But unhistorical comparisons still creep in. "Unlike Shakespeare," she writes, "Jonson could not accept things as they were and settle down to write for ordinary people." Almost every phrase begs a question, and invites qualification if not repudiation. Chute is at her weakest in presenting judgments in the guise of facts, but fairly reliable when it comes to the facts themselves. She largely avoids psychological conjecture, and prefers to take Jonson at his own estimation: the result is a straightforward narrative, which seems almost to affirm the earlier confidence of Gregory Smith that "there are no mysteries, or at least great mysteries, in his literary career," and "even his personality stands forth fresh and convincing." Chute seems to agree: Jonson only got angry, she claims, "when his fellow playwrights jeered at him." After Edmund Wilson's anal erotic, the view is both attractive and corrective: but, or so later biographers have felt, it is also insufficiently complex to represent the "real" Ben Jonson.

In a primarily literary-critical work, *Ben Jonson: His Vision and His Art* (1981), Alexander Leggatt includes a chapter on "The Poet as Character," which examines Jonson's assumption of a *persona*, halfway between the deliberate jester's mask of a Shaw and the casual trademark of a Hitchcockian personal appearance. Is there a self-portrait to be discerned beneath—and if so, is it of an "essential" person, or an existential self-creation? The two most recent biographies come up with contrasting answers, though the earlier, by MILES, addresses the question only indirectly. As she says, she has "tried to let Jonson speak for himself": while recognizing that he is a considerably more complicated character than he would have had us believe, she presents the dissembling as largely a conscious process—"half-hopeful, half-rueful," as she puts it. Jonson's main preoccupations are presented first as earning his ever-precarious living, and next with preserving his reputation for posterity. Though she discerns "more than a touch of paranoia" in the conversations recorded by Drummond, Jonson had, she concludes, "tried to be an amiable guest."

RIGGS takes this "amiable guest" as but one half of the "potential" Jonson, who could no less readily be presented as a "notorious reprobate and public nuisance," and he sets out to "study the interplay of reckless self-assertion and rationalistic self-limitation in a single life." The result is a book well-grounded in historicist analysis when that seems appropriate, but not less open to psychological speculation as to the roots of Jonson's behaviour in childhood experience—dangerous ground, since this is the area of his life of which we know least (through deliberate concealment, as Riggs would argue). Ironically, the dual approach converges best as a way into the plays rather than the person—perhaps appropriately, since this biography both aims for and achieves a definition of Jonson as an *author* after the modern manner. Riggs' biography is thus the first to be discernably touched by recent developments in literary theory, to the extent that Jonson is invested with occupying what Foucault called the "privileged moment of individualization" in the history of English literature. Establishing a "proprietary claim to his own writings" is thus perceived as no less crucial to Jonson's life than it was to his *Works*—and that description of his collected writings, so pretentious to the contemporaries of a "mere" playwright, is here presented as the first creation of an "authorized" text in a very specific and appropriative sense.

—Simon Trussler

JOSEPH II, 1741–1790; Holy Roman emperor, co-regent and emperor of the Habsburg Empire.

Beales, Derek, *Joseph II* (2 vols. projected). Cambridge and New York, Cambridge University Press, 1987– (first volume subtitled *In the Shadow of Maria Theresa 1741–80*).

Blanning, T. C. W., *Joseph II and Enlightened Despotism*. London, Longman, and New York, Harper, 1970.

Padover, Saul K., *The Revolutionary Emperor: Joseph II of Austria*. New York, R. O. Ballou, and London, Cape, 1934; revised edition, London, Eyre and Spottiswoode, 1967.

*

PADOVER, after more than half a century since its publication, remains the only full-length life of Joseph II in English. It is divided into three unequal sections: "The Crown Prince" (two chapters), "The Co-Regent" (four chapters), and "The Autocrat" (11 chapters). There are eight portraits, two maps, two appendices illustrating the governmental structure of the Empire, and a detailed bibliography.

The enduring popularity of this biography is doubtless due to its easy style and the frequent quotations from documentary sources. Unfortunately, the origin of the documentary extracts is hardly ever given. There are only three footnotes in the entire text of 290 pages: one refers to the Paris 1882 edition of Voltaire's works, and the only other two relate to letters of Lafayette in an American collection. This absence of attribution is the more serious as approximately a quarter of Padover's extracts come from a collection of letters—known as the Constantinople collection—that is almost certainly spurious; since 1868, German historians have treated them as suspect. Padover's lack of footnotes prevents the reader from distinguishing the false from the authentic. The effect is to give too much credit to the French Enlightenment in the formulation of Joseph's ideas, and to exaggerate the extent to which he differed from his mother.

BEALES provides a corrective to both these misconceptions. As the first historian to acquaint English readers with the spuriousness of the Constantinople letters, Beales understands the importance of scholarly detective work. There is no lack of footnotes here! But readers should not be put off by the apparatus of scholarship: though this is a weighty volume in every sense of the term, Beales wears his learning lightly, with more than a touch of humour.

The first volume of a projected two, the work covers the first 39 years of Joseph's life, up to his mother's death in 1780 and his assumption of sole power. Beales stresses how little Joseph's education was influenced by the ideas of the French *philosophes*, how much his interest in expanding the army was implanted in the days when Maria Theresa was planning a war of revenge against Prussia, and how much of the reforming impulse of the co-regency came from Kaunitz and his circle. Beales concedes the revolutionary import of Joseph's *Reveries* (1763). The emperor later claimed to have jettisoned these proposals, and, although Beales thinks Joseph never lost sight of the basic aims there expressed, he points to the absurdity of regarding Joseph as "the Enlightenment enthroned."

In examining Joseph II's political subservience to his mother, Beales reminds us that "he was the co-regent; she was the ruler." Joseph even had to secure his mother's agreement to the arrangements for his daughter's education. Yet his achievements during the co-regency were not confined to reducing the number of horses in the imperial stables. He achieved a substantial reduction in the national debt through a scheme to reduce the rate of interest paid on government bonds, he achieved changes in the membership and structure of the *Staatsraat*, he threw his weight behind the abolition of torture, and he helped to secure the partial abolition of internal customs duties.

In what is probably his most important chapter, Beales shows that the policy of making the church serve the interests of the state—known to historians as "Josephism"—does indeed reveal the emperor's decisive influence long before he became sole ruler. Volume 2, dealing with Joseph's last ten years of frenetic activity, is still to come. Meanwhile Beales argues that Joseph did not possess "the over-weening self-confidence with which he is often credited," and that he declined Maria Theresa's offer to abdicate in his favour because "he genuinely felt unsure of himself." Yet he was totally committed to serving his people without pompous display, and wished to be "a soldier sovereign, a bureaucrat monarch, a citizen king."

BLANNING, a Fellow of the same Cambridge college as Beales, provides a brief study of Joseph within the context of Enlightened Despotism. It is in a series designed for senior high-school pupils and university students, and is not a true biography. In keeping with the scheme of the series, the text contains frequent references to a detailed bibliography and to an appendix of documentary extracts. There is at least one quotation from a bogus letter: it appears on page 64 and derives from Padover. Blanning differs marginally from Beales in giving Joseph less credit for "Josephism," and perhaps puts more emphasis on the humanitarian motives of Joseph's reforms. Blanning does not like Joseph, but he accords him grudging admiration: "The relentless emphasis on duty opened up a prospect as grim as Joseph's personality, but it was service for a quite specific cause—for the material welfare of the community, not for some metaphysical concept such as God, *Volk,* or Classless Society."

—Stuart Andrews

———

JOYCE, James, 1882–1941; Irish writer.

Bradley, Bruce, *James Joyce's Schooldays.* Dublin, Gill and Macmillan, and New York, St. Martin's, 1982.

Costello, Peter, *James Joyce.* Dublin, Gill and Macmillan, 1980.

Ellmann, Richard, *James Joyce.* New York, Oxford University Press, 1959; revised edition, New York and London, Oxford University Press, 1982.

Sullivan, Kevin, *Joyce Among the Jesuits.* New York, Columbia University Press, 1958.

*

The standard set by ELLMANN in his massive and detailed work has not been surpassed, nor has it been possible for later biographers of Joyce to add significantly to his chronological account or to deepen his characterisation. The book is also written in an attractively engaging style. While Ellmann respects Joyce as a writer and admires his persistent struggle to overcome the difficulties of his life, he is able to view him critically both as a man and as a writer. Some doubts have been cast on Ellmann's gullibility, that is, his apparent readiness to believe what Irish informants tell him, but on balance it is clear that Ellmann weighs such information when he can against verifiable sources. Given Joyce's obsessive need to feed off his own experience and to make use of relatives, neighbours, and friends throughout his work, Ellman had no choice but to pursue biographical information from the same and similar sources. The encyclopedic detail that results and that he shaped into an absorbing portrait are a tribute to Ellmann's powers of organisation and his ability to use such material effectively. Added to his mastery of organisation is his sophisticated critical handling of all of Joyce's work. He is about to relate Joyce to sources and analogues, understanding the associative nature of Joyce's mind, which drew upon everyday events, however incidental, and upon more general cultural experience, such as his readings and his musical taste. The result is a constantly engaging and engaged biography.

Based on the idea that Joyce's Catholicism is fundamental to his growth as a man and a writer, SULLIVAN's book is a valuable account of the subject's educational years that holds its place in Joyce scholarship despite Ellmann's monumental work. It is not a study of influence, nor an assessment of Joyce's Catholicism, but a definition of Joyce's relationship with the Jesuits, including his years at university. It shows what Joyce's education consisted of and relates it to his work, particularly *Portrait of the Artist as a Young Man.* It is reliably and helpfully factual and written with detachment and style.

BRADLEY's is an even more painstaking and accurate account. It fills in the record of Joyce's time at Clongowes Wood College and at Belvedere College in greater detail on the basis of documents already known but now more fully exploited and on the basis of newly discovered material. Modestly, but fairly, Bradley claims that his book merely complements both Sullivan and Ellmann and that it is essentially a series of historical footnotes to *Portrait of the Artist.* Nevertheless it is scrupulously reliable and helpful.

COSTELLO inevitably draws upon Ellmann but provides some additional information and some corrections. His work also provides useful critical evaluations of the various works. It is objective but finds no fault with the master and is written for popular consumption. Brenda Maddox, for her biography of Nora Joyce (*Nora: A Biography of Nora Joyce,* London, 1988; as *Nora: The Real Life of Molly Bloom,* Boston, 1988), draws heavily on Ellmann, but her detailed account of Joyce family life as experienced by Nora provides different perspectives on James Joyce as well, in addition to some fresh information. Maddox relates her portrait of Nora to her husband's work.

—Maurice Harmon

———

JULIUS CAESAR, 100 B.C.–44 B.C.; Roman statesman, general, and writer.

Balsdon, J. P. V. D., *Julius Caesar: A Political Biography.* New York, Atheneum, 1967; as *Julius Caesar and Rome,* London, English University Presses, 1967.

Bradford, Ernle, *Julius Caesar: The Pursuit for Power.* New York, Morrow, and London, Hamilton, 1984.

Bruns, Roger, *Julius Caesar.* New York, Chelsea House, 1987.

Buchan, John, *Julius Caesar.* New York, D. Appleton, and Edinburgh, P. Davies, 1932.

Duggan, Alfred L., *Julius Caesar.* New York, Knopf, and London, Hutchinson, 1955.

Ferrero, Guglielmo, *Life of Caesar,* translated by A. E. Zimmern. London, Allen and Unwin, and New York, Putnam, 1933 (originally published as vols. I and II of *Grandezzsa e decadenza di Roma,* 5 vols., Milan, Treves, 1902–07).

Fuller, J. F. C., *Julius Caesar: Man, Soldier, and Tyrant.* New Brunswick, New Jersey, Rutgers University Press, and London, Eyre and Spottiswoode, 1965.

Gelzer, Matthias, *Caesar: Politician and Statesman,* translated by Peter Needham. Cambridge, Massachusetts, Harvard University Press, and Oxford, Blackwell, 1968.

Grant, Michael, *Julius Caesar.* New York, McGraw-Hill, and London, Weidenfeld and Nicolson, 1969.

Gunther, John, *Julius Caesar.* New York, Random House, 1959.

Kahn, Arthur D., *The Education of Caesar: A Biography, a Reconstruction.* New York, Schocken, 1988.

Komroff, Manuel, *Julius Caesar.* New York, J. Messner, 1955.

Massie, Allan, *The Caesars.* London, Secker and Warburg, 1983; New York, F. Watts, 1984.

Matthews, Rupert O., *Julius Caesar.* Hove, UK, Wayland, 1988; New York, Bookwright Press, 1989.

May, Robin, *Julius Caesar and the Romans.* Hove, UK, Wayland, 1984; New York, Bookwright Press, 1985.

Meier, Christian, *Caesar.* Berlin, Severin and Siedler, 1982.

Walter, Gérard, *Caesar: A Biography,* translated by E. Craufurd. New York, Scribner, 1952; London, Cassell, 1953.

*

BUCHAN's 1932 work is well written and concise, and it succeeds in portraying Julius Caesar within his milieu. However, it is not intended for the casual reader as it presumes some detailed prior knowledge of Roman society and history. FERRERO, writing at the same time, presents a more readable, gripping story intended for a less scholarly audience. However, the book is somewhat less complete in its portrayal of Julius Caesar's personality, and certain aspects of Roman history are not well presented. DUGGAN's work succeeds where Ferrero's fails. Duggan gives the reader a concise, readable biography with objective criticism and excellent treatment of controversial issues. GUNTHER's 1959 book is similar, but written for a much younger audience (grades 5–9).

WALTER's work was the most comprehensive biography of Caesar to appear up to the time of its publication. The book is long and tedious in places but generally readable, and is aimed at general readership. It is well documented and accurate, but in places the author's apparent dislike for his subject is manifest.

KOMROFF's effort, also from the mid 1950s, deals with certain aspects of Caesar's career, particularly his western campaigns. In this it is incomplete as a biography but would serve well as a supplementary tool for further reading.

The decade of the 1960s was a sort of revisionist era for studies on Julius Caesar. A number of authors have stepped back to take a fresh view of the available literature. BALSDON does a good job of weighing and evaluating most of the ancient criticism regarding Caesar. In this he is rather successful in refuting the traditional Plutarchian viewpoints in a readable, brief manner. FULLER wrote of Caesar in a similar manner but took his thesis farther in showing the emperor as somewhat less competent than has commonly been believed. Also from this period, GELZER provides the best effort so far at chronicling the upheavals and intricacies of Roman politics in Caesar's time. This work serves well to set the background for any study of Caesar. GRANT, at the end of the decade, produced another good, solid account of Caesar aimed at general readership. This work, like most from the period, is to be commended for its objectivity.

MASSIE's book is intended to serve as an introduction to and popular history of the first of the Roman emperors, including Julius Caesar. Its best features are its brevity and its treatment of some of the more popular misconceptions regarding Rome's first emperors. BRADFORD's work is a more detailed account that concentrates on the more ruthless and nefarious aspects of Caesar's personality.

Several more recent works have appeared that add little to the already existing research. MATTHEWS' work is graphic in its depiction of the violence of the era, but it offers little else. The book fails to get at the substance of its subject and in no way presents a complete picture of Caesar. BRUNS' account is more sedate in nature and intended for a younger, general audience. While readable, it does not say anything that is not stated in other sources. Similarly intended for a young audience is MAY's

work, which is far too brief to be effective. Poor quality of illustrations and periphery treatment of major themes make this work of little use.

Somewhat better are the works by MEIER and KAHN, which present opposing viewpoints as to the driving forces behind Caesar's personality and character. Kahn is an ardent admirer of Caesar, while Meier is more subdued. Both, however, present convincing arguments.

Duggan remains a good starting place for a quick account, while Walter serves well for more detailed reading. Any of the works produced in the 1960s will provide an interesting counterpoint.

—Lawrence M. Enoch

———

JUNG, Carl Gustav, 1875–1961; Swiss psychiatrist; founder of analytical psychology.

Bennet, E. A., *C. G. Jung.* London, Barrie and Rockliff, 1961; New York, Dutton, 1962.

Brome, Vincent, *Jung: Man and Myth.* New York, Atheneum, and London, Macmillan, 1978.

Donn, Linda, *Freud and Jung: Years of Friendship, Years of Loss.* New York, Scribner, 1988.

Hannah, Barbara, *Jung: His Life and Work: A Biographical Memoir.* New York, Putnam, 1976; London, M. Joseph, 1977.

Homans, Peter, *Jung in Context: Modernity and the Making of a Psychology.* Chicago, University of Chicago Press, 1979.

Jaffé, Aniela, *From the Life and Work of C. G. Jung,* translated by R. F. C. Hull. New York, Harper, and London, Hodder and Stoughton, 1971 (originally published by Rascher, Zürich, 1968).

McGuire, William and R. F. C. Hull, *C. G. Jung Speaking: Interviews and Encounters.* Princeton, New Jersey, Princeton University Press, 1977; London, Thames and Hudson, 1978.

Stern, Paul J., *C. G. Jung: The Haunted Prophet.* New York, Braziller, 1976.

Van der Post, Laurens, *Jung and the Story of Our Time.* New York, Pantheon, 1975; London, Hogarth Press, 1976.

Wehr, Gerhard, *Portrait of Jung: An Illustrated Biography,* translated by W. A. Hargreaves. New York, Herder, 1971 (originally published as *C. G. Jung in Selbstzeugnissen und Bilddockumenten,* Reinbek bei Hamburg, Rowohlt, 1969).

Wehr, Gerhard, *Jung: A Biography,* translated by David M. Weeks. Boston, Shambhala, and New York, Random House, 1987 (originally published as *Carl Gustav Jung: Leben, Werk, Wirkung,* Munich, Kösel-Verlag, 1985).

*

Recorded and edited by Aniela Jaffé and translated from the German by Richard and Clara Winston in 1963, Jung's autobiography, *Memories, Dreams, Reflections* is considered by all of Jung's biographers to be the *sine qua non* of writing his life. Most writers acknowledge that it underwrites the subsequent biographical enterprise about Jung. Typical is Barbara Hannah's comment that Jung's autobiography "will always remain the deepest and most authentic source concerning Jung." However, British child psychiatrist Donald Winnicott acknowledges Jung's "exceptional attainment," but concludes with many psychoanalysts that although Jung "reached the centre of his self" (represented symbolically by his preoccupation with mandalas), his accomplishment was a "blind alley if looked at as an achievement for a remarkable and truly big personality," since it was an "obsessional flight from disintegration" (review in *International Journal of Psychoanalysis*, vol. 45, 1964).

Three biographies remain paramount as scholarly chronicles of Jung's life and work, aspects that all biographers find difficult to separate. Also useful as grist for sustaining the chronicle of Jung's life is one important biographical source book.

BENNET presents "key aspects" of Jung's work to assist "in the setting of his personality." Bennet's biography is as close as we get to an official, authorized life of Jung, who read the manuscript and "made some suggestions and corrections in his own handwriting." Thus, we are told to assume that Bennet's statements are "in accordance" with Jung's views. Portions of correspondence between Bennet and Jung are included in the text. Bennet is the first to try to set straight the public record regarding Jung's 1912–13 break with Freud and to defend Jung against charges that he was a Nazi sympathizer. Bennet also rebuts the critical view of Ernest Jones, biographer of Freud, that Jung's interest in paranormal phenomena was unscientific.

HANNAH's "biographical memoir" is not slanted like Bennet's account toward Jung's work, focusing rather on Jung himself. Hannah shows how Jung "first lived his psychology and only much later formulated in words what he had lived." Fresh information about Jung's grandparents from Aniela Jaffé's appendix (exclusive to the German edition) to *Memories, Dreams, Reflections* is supplied in English for the first time. Hannah also shows a unique appreciation of the influence of Swiss geography on Jung. She includes her unusual 1934 pencil sketch of Jung in a withdrawn mood which he himself requested and helped her to sketch. Jung indicated that the portrayal of his withdrawn, introverted mood was something important "that none of the other portraits have." By contrast, a photograph of a robust, outgoing Jung smoking his pipe and leaning against the stone door jamb at Bollingen in January 1961 is the frontispiece in Bennet's work. Thus, archetypal differences between men and women, which Jung's life and work first identified, subtly make their way into biographies about him written by his pupils. This is a book of internal appreciation of Jung.

BROME is 20 years removed from the living Jung but, like Bennet, he invokes personal contact with Jung, beginning in 1938, as the basis for his biographical endeavor. Depicting key aspects of Jung's work is less pressing to Brome than underscoring the creative achievement of an outstanding man. Conversation with Jung continually "came back," one is told, to the author's "immature ideas and ambitions"; the interchange was "laced with quips and jokes." Brome, steering a careful course between hero-worship and character assassination, uses Jung's thought to enhance his humanity. Jung "materialized in the flesh" the "timeless figure of his own creation—the Old Wise Man." Brome's tendency to romanticize Jung as the soul's oracle, or "holy man," is skillfully tempered by references to Jung the "scientist" and, more significantly, to Jung's humanizing displays of "vanity" and to his delight in assuming the bubble-

popping role of the "*gamin.*" Brome presents a careful review of the controversial affair between Jung and Antonia Wolff, first described by Barbara Hannah and Paul Stern, considering it in terms of Jung's psychology and the role played by Jung's wife, Emma. This fills the void left by Bennet's notable failure even to mention the now legendary liaison in which the feminine (*anima*) was successfully activated in Jung's consciousness. Brome's Appendix II on Jung's bibliographical sources both psychological and mythological is helpful. No visual material is included in the book.

McGUIRE AND HULL compile 55 "interviews and encounters" presenting different kinds of testimony "from and about Jung." These range from the youthful memories of Albert Oeri, Jung's boyhood friend, to Charles Lindbergh's report of a visit with Jung, to more theoretical talks by Jung himself about such topics as "The 2,000,000-Year-Old Man" and reports about Jung by the likes of Esther Harding and Mircea Eliade. This collection is rich in biographical bits provided by those who were affected by Jung and by their own high hopes for how his work would affect the post-nuclear age. The diversity of people attracted and devoted to Jung is amply demonstrated in this valuable biographical source book, itself testimony to the attraction of Jung's great personal and spiritual vitality.

JAFFÉ clarifies themes of Jung's thought and describes his style of working. The "peculiarity" of his method, Jaffé asserts, was in his returning to basic problems and rethinking old questions and then giving "new and differentiated answers" to them. One wonders whether this was indeed so peculiar. Nevertheless, as Jung's secretary and pupil, Jaffé could clarify what Jung said on such topics as parapsychology, alchemy, and his relationship to National Socialism. Interesting details of Jung's everyday life appear in the section, "From Jung's Last Years." Jaffé furnishes a unique insider's view of Jung's personal style.

WEHR's *Portrait of Jung* (1971) is a popular, scholarly, and easily accessible treatment of Jung as a researcher of the unconscious. Unlike his more recent and much longer work (see below), this biography is relatively short (173 pages). Jung is copiously quoted (with references) on both his life and work, including his dreams and visions, which, Jung said, were "the *prima materia*" of his scientific work. Fifty-five photographs and plates are included throughout the text, almost as if to punctuate the imagistic medium in which Jung worked in order to understand dreams and visions. Useful attention is given to Jung's understanding (or mistaken understanding) of Eastern religions, which Wehr correctly suggests was the basis for the psycho-cultural principle of "synchronicity." Unlike most other biographers, Wehr notes the intellectual and cultural influence of Jung's life and the power of his ideas. This fine but little known biography has not received the attention it rightly deserves.

VAN DER POST has high hopes that Jung's influence will rekindle in humankind an appreciation of its primal past. Jung becomes a man for all people, whose lives are exemplified and culminated in Jung's creative achievement. Van der Post, South African author, statesman, and godfather of Charles, Prince of Wales, goes further than any biographer to humanize Jung, this based on a "non-psychological relationship" or "friendship" with Jung. Instead of launching directly into Jung's life, van der Post begins with his own childhood in the South African bush. Van der Post's novels about growing up in South Africa are virtual case studies of Jung's psychological worldview. The bush and its native inhabitants represent the collective unconscious, while the author himself stands for a conscious assimilation of the personal, spiritual impact he understands Africa to represent. Such individuation is offered by van der Post, through the medium of Jung's impact on him, to the rest of us. The biography served as the basis of a BBC production narrated by van der Post, entitled "The Story of Carl Gustav Jung." A most sensitive, imaginative biography, it also brinks on devotion. It is the most recent, most accessible, and most rewarding biography of Jung for the intelligent, non-specialist reader.

HOMANS, emphasizing Jung's work, like van der Post collapses Jung into contemporary times, albeit for the additional purpose of using psychoanalytic theory to discuss narcissism (viz. Ellenberger, Erikson, Kohut) and psychohistorical themes. Jung is a paradigmatic case study of recovery amidst the loss of religious transcendence and the vital Protestant culture that supported it in the modern West. Jung undergoes a "creative illness" and forms an "identity" in terms of his "psychological discovery" of archetypes. The decline in power of traditional Christianity gives rise to "psychological man," which Homans argues Jung epitomizes. This is due to Jung's creative psychological resolution of two unconscious narcissistic processes, namely, the infantile belief in the omnipotence of the "self" and the tendency to idealize the "Other" (in the first instance, one's mother). Jung's ideas are outcroppings of "the Protestant psychologic," or the socio-cultural ethos in which Jung was reared and spent his life. If he could not warm to identifying with the Christ of Christianity and to express his narcissistic processes there, then his creative effort was to locate all that Christ represented in the past dynamically within himself in the present. This he did by articulating the process of individuation and the *telos* of the archetype of the self. Jung created "a unique and highly effective solution to the universal psychological needs for idealization and merger," which went unmet in the cultural vacuum left by an attenuated Protestantism.

Homans' psychological analysis of Jung's life far and away surpasses attempts by other biographers. Jung remains a man for our times: "By creating his unique system of ideas Jung has given many people a means of conceptualizing, ordering, and reflecting meaningfully on their own inner struggles." This biography is for scholars with technical knowledge of the history of dynamic or "depth" psychology and hermeneutics.

STERN casts Jung as a prophet whose "revelation" of the "Reality of the Soul" came at a period that was not yet ready for his "gospel of inwardness." Stern believes that Jung saw himself as "herald of the dawning Age of Aquarius—an age of mutants bound to usher in radical changes in modes of human feeling and thought." If the reader remains unconvinced of Jung's status as a prophet, then one must agree that his "compelling" case illustrates the "creative uses of incipient madness." Stern uses Erik Erikson's work on the characteristics of the "great man" to underscore the positive, even laudatory, clinical protocol of the prophet. This point of view is the flipside of Winnicott's diagnosis and represents the most daring (some might say strained) interpretation of all the biographies. Jung's life is portrayed as a battle against his "unruly demons," which culminates in the creation of the C. G. Jung Institute in 1948, described by Stern as "Carl Jung's Mystical Body." The religious feeling like that generated by van der Post's biography

is, perhaps, rendered wooden by Stern's thematic, religious (Christian) reductions. Nevertheless, this book makes for a lively read and has inspired Christian theologians to open their hearts and minds to Jungian thought.

WEHR (1987) updates his earlier work along a similar thematic line, this time in 550 pages. Wehr identifies Jung as the man who asked "Again and Again, the Religious Question" (Chapter 18). Wehr, who has published on depth psychology, anthroposophy, and Christian spirituality, and has edited the works of Jakob Böhme, links Jung with this mystic and with Rudolf Steiner, founder of anthroposophy, by means of opening epigraphs. Jung the introvert, Wehr claims, resisted autobiographical and biographical presentations during his life. He preferred to dwell on the "superindividual," or the "transpersonal." Jung's intuition of the "unboundedness of the soul" (Heraclitus) must be taken seriously by the biographer, the outer facts of Jung's life notwithstanding. Wehr is the only biographer to discuss the Germanic psychological research context of Jung's work. This is done, however, by including in the list of psychologists such figures as Count Hermann Keyserling, founder of the Darmstadt "School of Wisdom," and Berlin neurologist and psychiatrist, J. H. Schultz, originator of "Autogenic Training." Also unique is the inclusion of criticism of Jung, including that of Eugen Bleuler, Karl Jaspers, Ernst Bloch, and others.

Wehr dispels the hagiographical legend that Jung's mysticism radiated from his teutonic blue eyes by pointing out that Jung's eyes were, in fact, brown. Seen in no other biography (Donn's omission of it is surprising) is a photoplate of Jung's letter of 6 January 1913 to Freud, marking the end of their collaboration and friendship. At the end of the biography are three essays by Wehr, unusual for their presence but helpful for locating Jung in current discussion about modern spirituality and East/West psychology. First, "Western Consciousness and Eastern Spirituality" asks whether Jung's interpretations of Eastern religious texts were results of accurate scholarship or simply unwitting reductions of oriental worldviews to Jung's Western preoccupations and "search for the Holy Grail." Wehr suggests that Jung's life and work will benefit "contemporary religious and spiritual seekers," but mostly because of Jung's connections between Eastern thought and Rosicrucianism, Gnosticism, and the mystical path of the West. The second essay, "C. G. Jung in Dialogue and Dispute," opens the controversial interchange initiated by the charge of Jewish theologian, Martin Buber, that Jung's gnosticism pointed to an "eclipse of God in our time." Other contentious engagements also are described, making Jung appear less the universal reconciler of all things psychological and more as the focus of intellectual heat and debate. Finally, "Prolegomenon to a History of Jung's Influence" is unusual in that Jung is turned into an advocate for Christianity. Popular opinion is that Jung eschewed the antiquated religion of his clergyman father. However, Wehr suggests that what was (in Jung's words) "antiquated" was Christianity's "conception and interpretation." Jung, argues Wehr, affirmed his faith in Christianity by saying that modern people would be wise to meditate on "Christian premises." This biography sets the stage for reading Jung as a quiet saint in a modern pluralistic religious context, in which "New Age" thought is predominant and religious seekership rife.

DONN writes a circumscribed thematic biography about the Freud-Jung relationship. It is the best biography to date about that relationship, itself the *sine qua non* of Jung's creativity. Donn relies on interviews with other Jung biographers (and people associated with them), including E. A. Bennet's wife, Sir Laurens van der Post and his wife, Franz Jung (Jung's son), Aniela Jaffé, and William McGuire. She also availed herself of the little known Jung Biographical Archive in the Francis A. Countway Library of Medicine in Boston, where she was aided by Richard Wolfe. The theme of the "lost comrade" offers a splendid glimpse into Jung not only as the man of warmth and personality, but also as the co-producer of dynamic psychology, itself a major force in the 20th century. Jung (and Freud) bore witness to the "mystery of the human spirit." This was the "terrible beauty" of the psyche, and Freud and Jung, "lived it . . . alone." Photographs of Jung and the female colleagues in his life, not usually seen in other biographies, are included.

For scholarly introductions to Jung, the biographies by Bennet, Hannah, and Brome, along with the biographical source book by McGuire and Hull, are best in that they sustain better than other biographies the objective chronicle of Jung's life. The personal, interpretive biographies by Jaffé, Wehr, van der Post, Homans, Stern, and Donn present Jung's life according to specific overall themes. All the biographies waver to some degree between Jung's life and his thought. Of all the works, the most gracious and commodius invitation into Jung's life and thought for the intelligent reader is van der Post's. To date, a truly critical biography of Jung has yet to be written.

—Richard A. Hutch

JUSTINIAN I, 483–565; Byzantine emperor.

Baker, George P., *Justinian*. New York, Dodd Mead, 1931; London, Nash and Grayson, 1932.

Barker, John W., *Justinian and the Later Roman Empire*. Madison, University of Wisconsin Press, 1966.

Browning, Robert, *Justinian and Theodora*. London, Weidenfeld and Nicolson, and New York, Praeger, 1971.

Bury, John B., *A History of the Later Roman Empire from the Death of Theodosius to the Death of Justinian* (2 vols.). London, Macmillan, 1923.

Gibbon, Edward, *The History of the Decline and Fall of the Roman Empire* (6 vols.). London, W. Strahan and T. Cadell, 1776–88; edited by John B. Bury, 7 vols., London, Methuen, and New York, Macmillan, 1909–14.

Holmes, William G., *The Age of Justinian and Theodora* (2 vols.). London, G. Bell, 1905–07.

Ure, Percy N., *Justinian and His Age*. London, Penguin, 1951.

*

The outstanding historical figure of the Roman emperor, general, theologian, lawgiver, and builder Justinian I has long attracted the attention of historians and their readers. Among the earliest modern accounts written in English is GIBBON's classic 18th-century treatment of the reign of Justinian and his consort, Theodora, in chapters 40–44 of his *magnum opus*. Gibbon here clearly exhibits the rationalist skepticism concerning Christianity that characterizes and ultimately weakens his work throughout. Despite this criticism, however, the author provides a picture of the sixth century that is in most respects accurate and certainly compelling. His characterizations of the emperor, drawn from the historian Procopius, are mostly negative but tinged with a grudging respect. Gibbon first treats Justinian's origins, early years, elevation to the throne, and imperial administration, and then in later chapters describes his role in foreign affairs and his lasting contributions to Western jurisprudence. As a stylist Gibbon has few equals, and his work is both great literature and great history. *The History of the Decline and Fall of the Roman Empire*, originally published in 1776–88, is best consulted in the edition by Bury.

The first monographic treatment of Justinian to appear in English was that of HOLMES. Although the two volumes comprise over 750 pages, most of Volume I covers the pre-Justinianic empire of the sixth century. Like Gibbon, Holmes views this century as a period of stagnation during which "civilization was on the decline, and progress imperceptible, but the germs of a riper growth were still existent, concealed within the spreading darkness of mediaevalism." While Holmes' familiarity with the primary sources enables him to improve on Gibbon's earlier account, as a narrator he does little to compel the reader's interest.

Much more satisfying is BURY's study, the culmination of years of painstaking original research. Volume II is devoted to the reign of Justinian. Bury emphasizes primarily political and military history; economic, social, and cultural issues receive less coverage. Still, his is a balanced survey, comprehensive in scope and rich in detail. The author's portrayals of the leading figures of the age are especially memorable. It is a tribute to Bury's intimate knowledge of the inner workings of the later Roman Empire and his powers of historical interpretation that most of his judgments are still accepted by scholars today. The book is well organized and written in clear, readable prose.

BAKER, who had previously written successful biographies of Constantine, Hannibal, Tiberius, and Sulla, sets out in his popular biography to trace the career of Justinian, the great man, "whose story may enlarge our conceptions of the ideals which men may entertain, and the programmes to which they may elect to work." Baker stresses above all the emperor's unique ability to serve as a catalyst for the other strong personalities of his age: Justin I, Belisarius, Narses, Anthemius, Tribonian, John of Cappadocia, Procopius, and, most notably, Theodora. For most historical detail and interpretation, Baker, to his credit, closely follows Bury. But the reader must still beware the occasional non-historical embellishment. The tone is decidedly popular, the narrative fast-moving. The language seems almost too colloquial, as when Theodora, during the emergency of the Nika rebellion, is made to say, "We have got to get a move on quick."

A more scholarly study by the English classicist URE was published posthumously in 1951. Organized in a topical manner, this volume treats in succession the wars, bureaucracy, church, secular society, laws, literature, leading individuals, and art and architecture of Justinian's reign in a lucid, concise fashion. A series of illustrations accompany and enhance the text. The author makes effective use of quotations from primary sources and is clearly successful in placing before his readers "a portrait of a great emperor and an account of his age as we have it recorded by contemporary writers."

BARKER's book marks a rather different approach to the figure of Justinian. Intended for general readers and students, it serves admirably as a reliable introduction to both Justinian's life and the entire period of the late Roman/early Byzantine Empire. The author devotes substantial sections of his work to setting the historical stage for Justinian's reign, as well as presenting the aftermath and consequences of his policies and actions. The organizational format is mostly chronological. Barker's use of the categories "old problems" and "new projects" for describing and analyzing imperial priorities and responsibilities of the emperor (chapters III–IV) is particularly helpful. The text is supplemented by a chronological summary of Justinian's reign, historical lists of emperors, patriarchs, popes, foreign monarchs and imperial exarchs, illustrations (with extensive notes), an annotated bibliography of primary and secondary sources, and a full index. This volume offers the interested layperson a perfect entry to the Justinianic epoch.

BROWNING's monograph represents the latest and most authoritative biographical treatment of Justinian to date. Drawing on previous scholarship, including the work of the continental scholars Diehl (1901), Stein (1949), Vasiliev (1950), and Rubin (1960), the author draws a convincing portrait of both ruler and society. This study is more detailed and better balanced than those by Ure and Barker. Browning here shows himself to be a master of historical interpretation and lively narrative. The Mediterranean world of the sixth century emerges in all its excitement and color, and the decisive role of religion in the life of Justinian and his subjects is rightly emphasized. The book is beautifully illustrated, with over 150 plates, many in color, allowing the reader to glimpse something of the majesty of the art and architecture commissioned by this ruler. The revised edition of 1987 unfortunately lacks most of the original's illustrations.

—Craig L. Hanson

KAFKA, Franz, 1883–1924; Austrian writer.

Bauer, Johann, *Kafka and Prague*, translated by P. S. Falla. New York, Praeger, and London, Pall Mall, 1971.

Brod, Max, *Franz Kafka: A Biography*, translated by G. Humphreys-Roberts. New York, Schocken Books, 1947 (originally published by Heinr. Mercy Sohn, Prague, 1937).

Citati, Pietro, *Kafka*. New York, Knopf, and London, Secker and Warburg, 1990.

Hayman, Ronald, *Kafka: A Biography*. New York, Oxford University Press, 1982.

Heller, Erich, *Franz Kafka*. New York, Viking, 1974.

Mailloux, Peter, *A Hesitation Before Birth: The Life of Franz Kafka*. Newark, University of Delaware Press, 1989.

Pawel, Ernest, *The Nightmare of Reason, A Life of Franz Kafka*. New York, Farrar Straus, and London, Harvill, 1984.

Spann, Meno, *Franz Kafka*. Boston, Twayne, 1976.

Stern, J. P., editor, *The World of Franz Kafka*. New York, Holt, and London, Weidenfeld and Nicolson, 1980.

*

BAUER's volume, with many wonderfully mood-creating photographs by Isidor Pollak, and framed by quotes from Kafka's work, provides a good introduction to Kafka's life and work and is in a sense most Kafka-like of the available studies: it is atmospheric; one can see Kafka's Prague. For example, the pictures of the Workers' Accident Insurance Office for the Kingdom of Bohemia indicate an interesting blending of modern bureaucracy, the Monarchy, and urban indifference. Little wonder, then, that Bauer draws a direct link between Kafka's life and art. The book provides a brief chronology and a bibliography.

STERN's collection of essays has greater coverage of Kafka, his work, and his world. All of the essays are helpful, but especially meritorious is Allan Blunden's "A Chronology of Kafka's Life," which is quite detailed. (It should be noted that all the biographies discussed in this essay except Citati's have a good chronology, an essential item in reading and understanding Kafka.) As with all artists, scholars and intellectuals differ over the significance and meaning of Kafka's art; therefore the commentaries by such writers as J. P. Stern, Walter Benjamin, Bertolt Brecht, and Georg Lukács are particularly informative in this volume.

While Kafka's literary persona is dark and aloof, reflecting certain aspects of his biography and character, he was after all only human. BROD's work reveals a nervous, super-sensitive individual who until his tragic death had the capacity to laugh at himself. Kafka asked Max Brod, his literary executor, to destroy all of his unpublished writings after he died. Of course Brod did not do it. If he had, Kafka would not "exist" today as an icon of 20th-century modernism, with his artistic attack as an iconoclast against the assumed notions of automatic progress and rationality. Brod argues quite correctly that in not following Kafka's instructions he realized Kafka's ultimate desire to be read and appreciated. His biography and other literary efforts saved Kafka's writings and thereby created Kafka's reputation. Meanwhile, during his life Kafka's "energy was directed inwards only and . . . manifested itself as stubbornness, a passive tenacity. Herein perhaps lay the fatal weakness of his life. He suffered and kept silent." Brod's judgment remains valid. With appendices of brief writings and two reminiscences, this biography is important as a pioneer document in the works on Kafka. It helped create his reputation.

HAYMAN's book is a workman-like biography, as solid and straightforward as a biography of Kafka can be. The strong chronological table in this book allows the reader to reach a clear understanding of the self-absorbed Kafka. Hayman's main strength is his emphasis on Kafka's day-to-day life. However, he does not discuss Kafka's writing in sufficient detail.

HELLER's work provides a different emphasis. Heller states in his Preface, "Kafka's works, not the incidents of his life, are the focus of this study: or rather Kafka's life only insofar as it *is* his writing." Heller's Kafka is one whose art (and maybe ultimately his life) turned on the trinity of suffering, guilt, and fear. Heller's book, part of the Modern Masters Series edited by Frank Kermode, contains a short bibliography that provides several key items for understanding Kafka's life and work.

The most recent biography that stresses Kafka's art is CITATI's. Disdaining chronology, this book assumes the reader is a close student of Kafka's life and has read his writings: it is a good book for the specialist. The author makes some interesting semi-cryptic statements, such as, "In Kafka Plato's cave has become a modern railroad tunnel" and "He is the combination of Faust and Ulysses in the heart of our century." At the same time Citati uses such standard incidents from Kafka's life as his "ironic dream" of opening a restaurant in Palestine. And he relates the chilling moment when Kafka, as he lay dying, said: " 'Don't go away.' 'No I'm not going away,' his friend Klopstock replied. With a deep voice, Kafka answered back: 'But I'm going away.' " Kafka was an artist to the end. Though an interesting treatment, Citati's book is not the place to begin understanding Kafka.

On the other hand, SPANN is an excellent introduction to Kafka's life and work. The book's thesis is simple: the reasons for Kafka's unhappiness are external. Spann's is possibly the best of the brief biographies. PAWEL develops the same thesis in greater detail. He discusses how Kafka's life and more particularly his art anticipated the moral horrors (totalitarianism, the death camps) that became a reality after Kafka's death in 1924. Understandably, Pawel notes, Kafka's literary reputation overshadows his human life. In a semi-demonic manner, Kafka's personality challenges his biographers to find the "real" Kafka independent of his art.

Finally, MAILLOUX's biography is a good balance of this problem of art and life. In a book of nearly 600 pages, the solution is still problematic. "No writer is more contained in his writing than Franz Kafka." Kafka had a massive need for self-revelation, which is expressed in his writings by an "almost complete identification of salvation with confession." Mailloux's strength lies in his intelligent separation of Kafka's fictional from his autobiographical writing for biographical understanding but allowing the two to melt together in appreciating Kafka's art. Finally, Mailloux's volume has an excellent last chapter—"Epilogue: Life after Death"—that deals with the creation of Kafka's literary reputation and what happens to Kafka's friends (Max Brod died in Israel in 1968) and family (Kafka's three sisters died in Nazi death camps). Little wonder that in reading Kafka's biographies and writings a sense of depression hangs over the entire enterprise.

—Donald K. Pickens

KANDINSKY, Wassily, 1866–1944; Russian painter.

Derouet, Christian and Vivian Endicott Barnett, *Kandinsky in Paris 1934–44*. New York, Solomon R. Guggenheim Museum, 1985.

Grohmann, Will, *Wassily Kandinsky: Life and Work*, translated by Norbert Guterman. New York, Abrams, 1958; London, Thames and Hudson, 1959 (originally published by Du Mont-Schauberg, Cologne, 1958).

Le Targat, François, *Kandinsky*. New York, Rizzoli, 1987 (originally published by A. Michel, Paris, 1986).

Poling, Clark V., *Kandinsky: Russian and Bauhaus Years*. New York, Solomon R. Guggenheim Museum, 1983.

Röthel, Hans Konrad and Jean K. Benjamin, *Kandinsky*. Oxford, Phaidon, and New York, Hudson Hills Press, 1979.

Weiss, Peg, *Kandinsky in Munich: The Formative Jugenstil Years*. Princeton, New Jersey, Princeton University Press, 1979.

*

GROHMANN, author of the standard monograph on Kandinsky, maintained a friendship with the painter from 1923 until his death in 1944. This association, together with material from the Gabriele Münter Archives in Munich, and generous quotations from the artist's letters and writings, inform this major, lavishly illustrated work. Building on his earlier *Wassily Kandinsky* (Paris, 1930), this volume is richer in biographical detail and includes supplemental material of art historical significance: for example, Kandinsky's House Catalogue of paintings. But, as Kenneth Lindsay discovered (*Art Bulletin*, December 1959), Grohmann's friendship often obscures a deeper, scholarly assessment of the artist. While sensitive to subtleties of character, Grohmann "fails to relate the main periods [of Kandinsky's career] to their background and surroundings." Kandinsky appears an isolated genius, "who did not reflect what was going on outside the studio." Grohmann's treatment of Kandinsky's life is weighted more heavily on the years of his development toward abstraction, the later Munich period (1908–14, 108 pages), and is weakest on the Paris years (1934–44, 27 pages). Rich in primary documentation, and with the fullest discussion of Kandinsky's personal life, this remains the standard biography.

WEISS focuses on Kandinsky's years in Munich (1896–1914) for her scholarly, illustrated study of the artist's developing career. In preparing her research, Weiss consulted the artist's wife, Nina, who made available letters, documents, and other material. Weiss also explored the archives of the Städtische Galerie in Lenbachhaus, Munich, which houses the Gabriele Münter Archives, the most comprehensive collection of Kandinsky's sketchbooks, notebooks, and works of art from the Munich period. Translating numerous letters (from both German publications and unpublished sources), Weiss offers the English reader a wealth of documentation on this critical period of Kandinsky's life.

From this study emerges new information on Kandinsky's early training with the Yugoslav artist, Anton Azbe (1897–99), who ran a private atelier in Schwabing, the Bohemian quarter of Munich; Kandinsky's friendships with the Jugenstil artist Hermann Obrist; and the influence of August Endell and Adolf Holzel on his developing theories of abstraction. Kandinsky's crucial relationship with the poet Stefan George (perhaps as early as 1907), his training with the Munich Secessionist Franz Stuck (1899-1900), and his activities within the Phalanx Society and the Munich Artist's Theater are all elaborately detailed and clarified for the first time. As Reinhold Heller notes in his review (*Art Journal*, Summer 1980), Weiss' success is in breaking down the portrait of an isolated artist-hero first presented by Grohmann, but "she largely ignores questions of personality and psyche." Focusing on Kandinsky's associations within the artistic circles of Munich, Weiss offers few insights on his private life. Kandinsky's relationship with Gabriele Münter (beginning in 1902) is mentioned in cursory fashion, while his marriage to his cousin Ania Chimiakin (1892) and his divorce from her (in 1911) are merely cited in the chronology.

RÖTHEL offers the non-professional a satisfying look at the highlights of Kandinsky's life and career. With an introductory essay and 48 plates, each accompanied by a short prose entry, this lavish publication also makes available to the scholar new material from Gabriele Münter's diaries and entries from the artist's notebooks, in a reliable, although less detailed, study of Kandinsky's life.

POLING focuses on the period after Kandinsky's return to Russia in 1915 and his years teaching at the Bauhaus, in the second of three publications accompanying exhibitions at the Guggenheim Museum, which highlighted chapters in Kandinsky's life and career. While stressing the painter's aesthetic evolution, Poling offers important biographical material on the years 1915–33. Kandinsky's role in the Russian avant-garde, the development of his writings on art, his teaching methods at the Bauhaus (derived from published interviews), new information from Nina Kandinsky's memoirs (Munich, 1977), Kandinsky's correspondence with Katherine Dreier, Will Grohmann (from the Grohmann Archive in Stuttgart), and with artists and associates at the Bauhaus, are woven into this scholarly, well-documented and well-illustrated text. This publication is also valuable in making available to the English reader important material from German publications. An in-depth chronology summarizes key events in Kandinsky's life during these years.

DEROUET, in the third Guggenheim exhibition catalogue, focuses on Kandinsky's last years in Paris. This largely biographical essay incorporates analysis of his artistic development within the cultural and historical context of Paris in the 1930s and 1940s. Building on Grohmann, Derouet fleshes out this neglected chapter in Kandinsky's biography with substantial new information from Nina Kandinsky's memoirs, the Kandinsky Archives at the Centre Pompidou in Paris, correspondence in the New York Historical Society and in private collections (such as letters Kandinsky exchanged with Christian Zervos). These are translated into English and offered intact in the text. A detailed chronology summarizing the significant events of Kandinsky's last decade appears at the end of the catalogue.

Derouet offers new information on Kandinsky's politics, his prolonged hope of returning to Germany, and his relationships with critics and dealers, such as Christian Zervos and Jeanne Bucher. Kandinsky's ties to Arp, Miró, and the Surrealists are amplified as Derouet makes available to the English reader letters and other material culled from numerous French and German publications. The Kandinsky who emerges here is a skeptical, somewhat reclusive artist who "wished to keep aloof from the atmosphere of intrigue that flourished in the Paris art world." However, he is also seen as the artist who fought hard to establish and maintain his place in the history of abstract art.

LE TARGAT offers the English reader a summary account of the highlights of Kandinsky's life in a more popular, illustrated book. A mere 20 pages in length and without footnotes, Le Targat's essay nonetheless captures essential details from the major studies of Kandinsky's life and is supplemented by a lengthy chronology. The final pages include revealing information on Nina Kandinsky and her relations with Parisian dealers after her husband's death.

—Phylis Floyd

KANT, Immanuel, 1724–1804; German philosopher.

Cassirer, Ernst, *Kant's Life and Thought*, translated by James Haden. New Haven, Connecticut, and London, Yale University Press, 1981 (originally published by B. Cassirer, Berlin, 1918).

Jaspers, Karl, *Kant*, translated by Ralph Manheim (part of the author's *The Great Philosophers*, edited by Hannah Arendt). London, Hart-Davis, and New York, Harcourt, 1962.

Paulsen, S., *Immanuel Kant: His Life and Doctrine*. London, J. C. Nimmo, and New York, Scribner, 1902 (originally published by Frommanns, Stuttgart, 1898).

Scruton, Roger, *Kant*. Oxford and New York, Oxford University Press, 1982.

Wenley, R. M., *Kant and His Philosophical Revolution*. Edinburgh, T. and T. Clark, and New York, Scribner, 1910.

*

One of the chief difficulties facing the biographer of Kant is the multitude of anecdotes, for some of which Kant is himself responsible, that caricature him and camouflage the utterly dedicated thinker. Few of his biographers have appreciated the intensity of Kant's dedication to what he felt until nearly the end of his life to be his unfulfilled mission. The three *Kritiken* were not published until 1781, 1788, and 1790.

Naturally enough the early biographers could not fully have realised the strength or object of their subject's motivation. Kant had a satirical bent to his mind that was not going to reveal it, and his first biographer, Ludwig Ernst Borowski (*Darstellung des Lebens und Charakters Immanuel Kants*, Königsberg, 1804), had his sketch of Kant's life and character read and emended by Kant himself. Borowski was a disciple who had attended Kant's first lecture in 1755 in Professor Kypke's house. In 1804, too, the year of Kant's death, appeared a sketch compiled from his letters to a friend, Reinhold Bernhard Jachmann (*Immanuel Kant geschildert in Briefen an einen Freund*, Königsberg, 1804). In both sources he concealed his most intimate concern. The following year saw the publication of F. T. Rink's sketchy "Aspects" (*Ansichten aus Immanuel Kants Leben*, Königsberg, 1805).

In 1860 came the regrettably hagiographic and unreliable *Kantiana* by Reicke (Königsberg, 1860), and much the same may be said of Emil Arnoldt's account of Kant's youth and the first five years of his teaching (in *Gesammelte Schriften* edited by Otto Schöndörffer). There is a further German biography by F. W. Schubert in Kant's Complete Works (*Sämmtliche Werke*, edited by K. Rosenkranz and F. W. Schubert, Leipzig, 1842), and there is also a composite account of the life, drawn largely from Borowski and Jachmann, by Kant's faithful friend and nurse-companion, E. A. C. Wasianski (Halle, 1902), noting Kant's week-by-week decline during his final years.

Apart from the innumerable philosophical analyses of Kant's texts, sometimes so complex that a sentence with a singular subject ends up a page later with a plural verb, there are two English-language publications of 1882, J. H. W. Stickenberg's *The Life of Immanuel Kant*, dependent on the German sources already mentioned, and W. Wallace's volume, *Kant*, in the "Blackwood's World Classics" series. Both books are weak and now out of date.

WENLEY's 1910 volume is strongly marked by its date, but has a an old-fashioned thoroughness and non-technical readability that still commend it. As an attempt to set Kant and his thought in their period, domestic, academic, and social, with a clear exposition of what Kant was trying to do, in however obsolete an idiom, this book is still well worth recommending, although its judgements on intellectual history are naturally no longer reliable.

There are also relatively modern popular treatments of Kant with biographical introductions: Scruton's *Kant* in the often excellent Oxford "Past Masters" series, and the much more commendable volume by Karl Jaspers. SCRUTON is not an historian, but a teacher of philosophy, so that it scarcely surprises if his biographical introduction is poor. Unfortunately he also has to simplify the philosophy almost to annihilation in order to present it acceptably. Even a thinker as accomplished as JASPERS, a well-known philosopher himself, is satisfactory only for those who want the briefest of introductions. Obviously neither Scruton nor Jaspers adds anything to the career details or the biographical anecdotage.

The two serious biographical essays, those by Paulsen and Cassirer, an important neo-Kantian philosopher in his own right, both interweave accounts of the life with analyses of the doctrine. Given the relative uneventfulness of Kant's career, these works' date does not much affect their value.

PAULSEN is particularly good on the background circumstances, with exact details of Kant's university career, his lecture time-table, and his financial circumstances, including poverty. He points convincingly to Kant's fear of responsibility as the root cause of his failure twice to propose marriage when the indications are that he wanted to and would have been accepted. In the end he never married. Paulsen also brings out Kant's financial caution. Having once had to sell his books to safeguard his small savings against sickness or old age, Kant did not set up house with a man-servant and a cook until the 1780s, when the first *Kritik* had finally appeared.

The outstanding biography remains CASSIRER's. The 1981 edition has an authoritative introduction by the Kantian scholar Stephan Körner. Cassirer himself developed his own attitude to what we now call the history of ideas from Kant through Dilthey, and sees Kant's philosophical development in a controversial way, as a progress from ontology to epistemology toward a philosophy of symbolic forms rather than as the slow development of a properly critical method applied to different parts of the subject, principally epistemology, ethics, and aesthetics. Cassirer also holds, as Hegel did, that the philosopher cannot be separated from his works, which is why his biography is interleaved with the interpretation of Kant's philosophy. The interpretation itself is stimulating and personal, though it probably goes

too far in linking moderation in life-style to moderation in solutions to philosophical problems.

On the biographical side, Cassirer emphasizes the frivolity of the young Kant while expunging many of the mere anecdotes. Hamann thought Kant so caught up in social "diversions" that he would never produce the great works he was undoubtedly nurturing. Cassirer brings out well the fundamental harmony between Kant, with his meticulously timed activities, and Rousseau, who threw away his watch. He is also good on Kant's domestic circumstances when young, the satirical mind he exhibited in the 1766 *Träume eines Geistersehers* ("Dreams of a Seer"), and the background of 18th-century Prussia, built on "iron discipline, self-restraint, and renunciation."

Undoubtedly the most fascinating aspect of Cassirer's biography is devoted to Kant's intellectual development, necessarily difficult reading for those not versed in the reaction of Hume and Locke against Descartes and the need for a new philosophical method to replace the ultimately non-"critical" analyses of Descartes, whose proof of the objectivity of phenomena had come to be seen as inadequately based. We still require however a good biography of Kant that recounts his life, pierces his ambition, traces the development of his personality and his thought, and competently assesses his philosophical achievement.

—A. H. T. Levi

KEAN, Edmund, 1789–1833; English actor.

FitzSimons, Raymund, *Edmund Kean: Fire from Heaven.* London, Hamilton, and New York, Dial, 1976.

Hawkins, Frederick W., *The Life of Edmund Kean* (2 vols.). London, Tinsley Brothers, 1869; New York, B. Blom, 1969.

Hillebrand, Harold Newcomb, *Edmund Kean.* New York, Columbia University Press, 1933.

Molloy, J. Fitzgerald, *The Life and Adventures of Edmund Kean, Tragedian* (2 vols.). London, Ward and Downey, 1888.

Playfair, Giles, *Kean.* New York, Dutton, and London, G. Bless, 1939.

Playfair, Giles, *The Flash of Lightning: A Portrait of Edmund Kean.* London, W. Kimber, 1983.

Procter, Bryan Waller, *The Life of Edmund Kean.* London, E. Moxon, 1835.

*

Kean's biographers have often focused on the actor's personal life in preference to, and at times to the near exclusion of, his acting. This is not surprising, given Kean's frequently scandalous adventures and his penchant for exploiting early modern journalism in ways that maintained him in the public eye well after he had passed his prime on the stage. A large quantity of gossip, therefore, surround Kean, and part of any biographer's challenge lies in testing his gossip against a Kean driven to embroider or invent the facts of his life and against the veracity of the literary men who could make money by invoking his name and his inveterate unreliability.

HILLEBRAND's biography, published on the centennial of Kean's death, remains the most objective and carefully researched account of the notorious actor's life and career. Though lacking in flair, Hillebrand's writing is largely devoid of the moral posturing that figures so prominently in all the other lives of Kean, and his concluding chapter offers the clearest overall assessment of Kean's acting. Hillebrand is not, however, immune from the tendency inherited from Romanticism to conceive of the actor as the direct function of his own personality, and to assume that great art is impossible without great suffering. The stories of Kean's suffering, whether or not they are based in fact, make very compelling reading.

PROCTER, Kean's first biographer, was a playwright who knew Kean from the stage and from London society. Published only two years after Kean's death, Procter's chatty book sets out to entertain a readership hungry for more of the scandals reported daily while the actor was still alive. Though he warns readers of Kean's unreliability as a source for facts, Procter goes on to repeat some of Dean's more dubious stories, in addition to those told by several others that strain credibility. Procter is especially lively and reliable in exploring the theatrical tradition Kean challenged at the time of his debut, and he has a sharp eye for the social firmament in which Kean moved.

HAWKINS, while crediting the authority of Procter and other English theatre historians, uses sources that were unavailable to Procter. He also makes liberal use of theatrical reviews printed in the London newspapers during Kean's prime. While on the one hand Hawkins merely had more time than Procter to collect random memoirs and other printed notices of Kean (which grew less reliable the longer after his death they appeared), Hawkins is nonetheless deft at assembling scattered information to evoke the salient features of many of Kean's characterizations. Sometimes, in his skill at re-creating, Hawkins misleads by suggesting that he was himself present at performances given before he was born.

MOLLOY's two-volume life exhibits the author's affinity for the sensational elements in actors' lives. Relying more on hearsay even than Procter or Hawkins, Molloy tries to reenact climactic events in Kean's life through a point of view he imagines for his subject, ascribing lines of dialogue to the actor and his fellows many years after the incidents in question transpired.

PLAYFAIR's first life of Kean (1939) is not so steeped in a Victorian lexicon as are the 19th-century biographies. However, in his desire both to champion and defend the actor, Playfair launches into several fantastic treatments of the psychologies of Kean, of his wife Mary Chambers Kean, and of several of Kean's cronies and sexual companions. Playfair's brand of psychology is often biased and simplistic in its need to exculpate Kean, and his endowment of historically remote personages with very specific motives savors of the apparently irresistable tendency to render Kean's life a play, and to treat him and others as dramatic characters.

PLAYFAIR's 1983 book, which claims studious resort to the Winston diaries (compiled during Kean's career by a minor functionary at Drury Lane theatre), reasserts its author's earlier endorsement of Kean as perhaps the greatest actor who ever lived. A good deal shorter than Playfair's earlier book, this second biography shows greater narrative focus. But such brevity comes partly as the function of even more narrow and idiosyn-

cratic readings of Kean than Playfair advanced earlier; his assessment of Kean seems to grow more sympathetic as his estimation of Mary Kean, for example, grows harsher.

As a playwright who has dramatized Kean's life, FITZSIMONS as a biographer is often guilty of schematizing the actor's life to conform to his own sense of narrative and dramatic expediency. (Kean is the subject of at least two other plays, the most famous by Jean-Paul Sartre.) However, FitzSimons is very good at exploring manifestations of Kean's craving for attention and his later obsession with maintaining his popularity. The only biography to include a bibliography, FitzSimons' treatment also introduces modern medical testimony into his discussions of Kean's long physical decline and the emotional symptoms that attended it.

—Leigh Woods

KEATS, John, 1795–1821; English poet.

Bate, Walter Jackson, *John Keats*. Cambridge, Massachusetts, Harvard University Press, and London, Oxford University Press, 1963.

Bush, Douglas, *John Keats: His Life and Writings*. New York, Macmillan, and London, Collier-Macmillan, 1966.

Colvin, Sidney, *Keats*. London, Macmillan, and New York, Harper, 1887.

Colvin, Sidney, *John Keats: His Life and Poetry, His Friends, Critics, and After-Fame*. New York, Scribner, and London, Macmillan, 1917.

Gittings, Robert, *John Keats*. Boston, Little Brown, and London, Heinemann, 1968.

Hewlett, Dorothy, *Adonais: A Life of John Keats*. London, Hurst and Blackwell, 1937; 3rd edition, New York, Barnes, and London, Hutchinson, 1970.

Houghton, Richard Monckton Milnes, *Life, Letters, and Literary Remains of John Keats* (2 vols.). London, Moxon, and New York, Putnam, 1848; revised edition, 1867.

Lowell, Amy, *John Keats* (2 vols.). London, Cape, 1924; Boston, Houghton Mifflin, 1925.

Rossetti, William Michael, *Life of John Keats*. London, W. Scott, 1887.

Ward, Aileen, *John Keats: The Making of a Poet*. New York, Viking, and London, Secker and Warburg, 1963.

*

Though several of Keats' associates projected biographies immediately upon his death, squabbles between them prevented a major biography until MILNES took up the task, which largely consisted in winning over those associates and procuring their materials, something he was apparently quite good at, though other projects delayed his biography until 1848. Previous to this, Leigh Hunt had portrayed Keats in a section of *Lord Byron and Some of His Contemporaries* (1828) and in John Gorton's *General Biographical Dictionary*, also published in 1828. However, in Charles Brockder Brown's view, Hunt's accounts unfairly pictured Keats as a ''whining, puling boy.''

Brown finally wrote his own "Life of John Keats" for a lecture at the Plymouth Institution in 1836, and he eventually contributed it, along with many other important materials, to MILNES. In addition to these documents, Milnes was able to obtain important matter from John Hamilton Reynolds, Edward Holmes, Cowden Clarke, John Jeffrey (Georgiana Keats' second husband), John Taylor, Joseph Severn, Richard Woodhouse, and others who knew Keats well.

Milnes' biography expressly rejected the image of Keats' personality as that of a sensual weakling and did much to establish Keats' future literary reputation. There were, however, some flaws. In the first publication of the book, Milnes stated that Benjamin Bailey, one of Keats' closest friends, was dead, which he was not. Bailey subsequently forwarded to Milnes additional information for a revision of the biography, minus the literary remains, in 1867. Milnes also omitted mention of Fanny Brawne, and mistakenly (or on purpose) assumed that Keats' fiancee was, instead, a woman named Charmian. In spite of these flaws, the biography helped spur the renewed interest in Keats coming from the pre-Raphaelite brotherhood, especially that of Dante Gabriel Rossetti, and such poets as William Morris and Elizabeth Barrett Browning. Two shorter biographies of Keats appeared in 1887, COLVIN's volume for the English Men of Letters Series, and ROSSETTI's for the Great Writers series. They are important today mainly as indicaters of how high Keats' reputation had become.

COLVIN would subsequently write his major work on Keats (1917), perhaps the most factually correct biography prior to those by Bate and Ward in 1963, and containing some materials no longer available (e.g., a Woodhouse notebook destroyed in a fire in 1882). Colvin connected Keats' poetry to its Elizabethan sources, indicated his influence on subsequent Victorian poets, and attempted to reveal Keats' inspiration, interpret his symbolism, and place him within the critical and poetical context of the times.

Two other biographies from the first half of the 20th century also stand out above the rest. LOWELL's, though valuable in shedding new light on such concerns as Keats' relationship with Fanny Brawne, is simply too long. Her chapter on "Endymion" alone is 144 pages. Enthusiasm is fine, but in this case, it has resulted in a labyrinth of psychology, literary criticism, and questionable new materials (e.g., two poems, "The Poet" and "Gripus") that is hard to disentangle. Nevertheless, for the serious scholar with some spare time, the book offers an almost daily account of Keats' adult life, observing his friendships, outlining important influences on his development, and drawing some convincing conclusions about the birth of his poems and philosophy. It was a major biography at the time, and would be of greater value today if better biographies had not superseded it.

HEWLETT's biography, shorter and more readable than those by Lowell and Colvin, places Keats in his time and details contemporary reactions to his three volumes of poetry. Though it is, perhaps, overfilled with excerpts from letters and Keats' poems, it still manages to preserve Keats' life as a unity, and it has an excellent index. Fourteen brief appendices in the 1970 edition correct and enlarge on some aspects in light of more recent scholarship.

WARD's biography, winner of the 1964 National Book Award for arts and letters, deals mainly with the development of Keats as a person and how that influenced and was integrated with the emergence of Keats the poet. In addition, there is some excellent discussion of political and public events of Keats' time (e.g., England's concern over a French invasion), some interesting interpretations of the poems (e.g., seeing "Endymion" as an allegory about sex) and some incisive observations on his imagery (e.g., the images of medicine and disease in "Isabella"). For all this, the book remains essentially a biography focusing on the life rather than the poetry.

BATE's biography, winner of the Pulitzer Prize for biography, is not only the best critical biography of Keats, but is one of the best ever written on any poet. Whereas Ward is concise and speculative, Bate is exhaustive. At times his promises of what is to come in Keats' development, and, thus, in the biography, cause the reader to wish he would move along more quickly to the brilliant final year, which, since it has been built up so much throughout the book and since most readers already know it is the center of any consideration of Keats, is not dealt with in as much detail as it deserves (partially because there is not as much correspondence from Keats during that time for Bate to draw on). There is also a tendency to romanticize (e.g., Keats' rise from poverty is seen in terms of the standard Dickens characters). The close relationship of the three brothers is also a bit overdone, especially when the facts show that John Keats was constantly placing his pursuit of poetry before concern for his sickly brother Tom, and George left for America as soon as he was old enough, and when he returned briefly to England, he barely bothered to visit with John, and, in fact, without telling John, took what was, for them, a great deal of money he had gotten from Abbey back to America.

However, whatever minor flaws there may be, the biography easily overcomes them. Bate offers excellent insight into Keats' developing philosophy of poetry (involving Keats' theories of Negative Capability, the equation of Truth and Beauty, and the embracement of the imagination and its relation to empathy), gives a precise analysis of the techniques Keats employed, both his development and subsequent use of them (e.g., Keats' complex interplay of long and short vowels in "Eve of St. Agnes" and "Hyperion"), and demonstrates the strong influences of Spenser, Shakespeare, and Milton, as well as the not always positive influences of Keats' contemporaries. The book contains appendices on "Family Origins," "The Length of Keats' Apprenticeship," and "The Keats Children's Inheritance." There are also some black-and-white photographs and drawings.

BUSH's biography is not of the scope or insight of either Ward or Bate and suffers in its dealings with Keats' poetry. Nevertheless, it is a clearly presented and easily read book that offers insights and scholarship—a good introduction for the beginning scholar or general reader. A brief list of suggestions for further reading is included.

GITTING's biography, much more scholarly than Bush's, offers more careful research into the facts of the non-literary influences on Keats (e.g., family background, apprenticeship in medicine, possible experiences with venereal disease, and the ever debatable relationship with Fanny Brawne).

There are several partial biographies. Morris Marples, *Romantics at School* (1967), is a highly readable study of Wordsworth, Coleridge, Southey, Byron, Shelley, and Keats during their days at a boys' school. Nelson S. Busnell, *A Walk After John Keats* (1936), offers a daily account of Keats' Scottish tour in 1818 and includes some illustrations and excerpts from Keats' works. Timothy Hilton, *Keats and His World* (1971), is notable mainly for its collection of portraits, maps, engravings, photographs, and reproductions of manuscripts. Somewhat tangential but also useful are three books by Joanna Richardson, *Fanny Brawne: A Biography* (1952), *The Everlasting Spell: A Study of Keats and His Friends* (1963), mainly dealing with Dilke and Charles Brockder Brown, and *Keats and His Circle: An Album of Portraits* (1980), 163 portraits of Keats, his family and friends. Three books dealing with Keats' medical training, his disease, and his use of scientific terminology, are Sir William Hale-White, *Keats as Doctor and Patient* (1938), Walter A. Wells, *A Doctor's Life of John Keats* (1959), and Donald C. Goellnicht, *The Poet-Physician: Keats and Medical Science* (1984), the first two referred to in Bate's discussion of Keats' sickness.

One other extremely important source of biographical material deserves mention: H. E. Rollins, *The Keats Circle: Letters and Papers, 1816–1878* (Cambridge, Massachusetts, Harvard University Press, 1948; supplemented by *More Letters and Poems of the Keats Circle*, 1955; published together under the title *Keats Circle*, 1965). These volumes include the texts of some 400 letters and other documents, including Brown's "Life," letters from Woodhouse, and other materials Lowell had collected for her biography.

—Harry Edwin Eiss

KENNEDY, John Fitzgerald, 1917–1963; American political leader, 35th president of the United States.

Davis, John H., *The Kennedys: Dynasty and Disaster*. New York, McGraw-Hill, 1984; London, Sidgwick and Jackson, 1985.

Manchester, William, *One Brief Shining Moment: Remembering Kennedy*. Boston, Little Brown, and London, Joseph, 1983.

Parmet, Herbert S., *Jack: The Struggles of John F. Kennedy*. New York, Dial, 1980.

Parmet, Herbert S., *JFK: The Presidency of John F. Kennedy*. New York, Dial, 1983.

Schlesinger, Arthur M., Jr., *A Thousand Days: John F. Kennedy in the White House*. Boston, Houghton Mifflin, and London, Deutsch, 1965.

Sorenson, Theodore C., *Kennedy*. New York, Harper, and London, Hodder and Stoughton, 1965.

Wills, Gary, *The Kennedy Imprisonment: A Meditation on Power*. Boston, Little Brown, 1982.

*

With the exception, perhaps, of Franklin Roosevelt, John F. Kennedy is the most studied, analyzed, and dissected American public figure of the 20th century. This remarkable level of attention derives in part from Kennedy's youth and the image of youthful energy that surrounded his presidency, in part from the chaotic events of the 1960s. However, it was, probably, his tragic assassination and the surrounding events, all reported by tele-

vision, that did the most to create both public and scholarly fascination.

The Kennedy literature is certainly large; in a recent study of Kennedy's image, Thomas Brown (*JFK: History of an Image*, Bloomington, Indiana University Press, 1988) cites over 200 books that deal partially or wholly with Kennedy's life, especially his presidential administration. Some, like Maude Shaw's *White House Nannie* (1966), are largely gossipy fluff. Others, like Victor S. Navasky's *Kennedy Justice* (1971), focus narrowly on one aspect of his administration. A few, including Victor Lasky's *It Didn't Start with Watergate* (1977), are little more than vicious polemics.

A few biographical studies clearly stand out, however, because they are comprehensive, or because they have helped establish "The Kennedy Myth," or because they are representative of their type. These biographical accounts fit roughly into three basic categories: those serving the enshrinement of Kennedy; those attempting a revision of the Kennedy myth; and those offering more objective, balanced accounts.

Not surprisingly, most of the initial post-assassination studies were memoiristic panegyrics, usually written by friends who played official roles in the Administration. The most famous and influential of these is SCHLESINGER's *1000 Days*. Schlesinger, who served as an advisor to Kennedy, especially on Latin American affairs, writes beautifully, if incompletely, about Kennedy the President, especially the foreign policy of his administration. For Schlesinger, Kennedy's most admirable quality was his ability to grow. Learning from the mistakes of the Bay of Pigs Invasion, for example, he became an intelligent leader during the Cuban Missile Crisis and a wise one with his American University Address in which he sought "a world safe for diversity." Words like "pragmatic" and "tough-minded" dot Schlesinger's text. Moreover, Schlesinger highlights what he sees as Kennedy's flair—his sense of style, grace, youth—which helped energize a generation. Filled with intimate detail (*not* including information about Kennedy's private sexual encounters, however), *1000 Days* stands as a crucial source for future biographers.

SORENSEN's *Kennedy,* much like Schlesinger's work, serves as both a fascinating first-hand account and a hymn of praise. Although not a full-scale biography (Sorensen begins his study in 1946), *Kennedy* does look at both the public and private JFK. Sorensen was closer to Kennedy than was Schlesinger, and he knew him longer, first joining his Senate staff in 1953. As Special Counsel to the president and chief speech-writer, he shared some of Kennedy's most intimate moments. Indeed, along with Robert Kennedy, Sorensen became the President's alter ego.

Because of this closeness, according to historian Frank Freidel, "Sorensen writes from firsthand knowledge about most of the major concerns of the Kennedy administration" (*American Historical Review*, January 1967). While Schlesinger could write at length about his role in Kennedy's relatively tangential Latin American policy, Sorensen was "there" for the major events—the Bay of Pigs, the Cuban Missile Crisis, the Nuclear Test Ban Treaty, the American University Speech. His memoir is filled with revealing incidents—Kennedy's off-hand remark about Jupiter missiles during the Cuban Crisis; Kennedy's private judgment that the Berlin question was far more vital than problems with Castro; an account of a private luncheon with the Soviet ambassador prior to the discovery of Soviet missiles in Cuba—all of which makes for interesting reading and provides primary source material for the biographer.

Despite differences in personal perspectives, Schlesinger and Sorensen come to much the same conclusion: John F. Kennedy was a great man and great president. Sorensen concludes his memoir with a revealing anecdote. One of the doctors who tried futilely to save Kennedy's life that day in Dallas was heard to remark: " 'He was a big man, bigger than I thought.' " Sorensen concurs: "He was a big man—much bigger than anyone thought—and all of us are better for having lived in the days of Kennedy."

If the 1960s witnessed the creation of the Kennedy legend, in the 1970s and early 80s a number of revisionist studies appeared that began to demolish the positive myth. Although not essentially biographical in nature, studies like Richard Walton, *Cold War and Counterrevolution* (1972); Bruce Mirhoff, *Pragmatic Illusions* (1976); and Henry Fairlie, *The Kennedy Promise* (1973), examined critically Kennedy's alleged accomplishments. Walton argues that JFK was a macho cold warrior who needlessly brought the world to the brink of destruction, while Mirhoff sees his domestic initiatives as the failure of a very conventional politician. Fairlie contends that in both foreign and domestic policy the reality did not live up to the promise.

The most notable attempt to deflate the myth is by WILLS. Wills, a journalist and political thinker, "meditates" on Kennedy's life, his family, his foibles. The central message of this complex and often speculative work is clear: Kennedy males achieved power by breaking rules, and power became an end in itself, not a structure through which public good might be accomplished. For Wills, the central symbol of the Kennedy failure was Joseph's and John's private relations with women. From Kennedy Senior's constant womanizing to John's (by the mid-1970s) well-publicized liaison with a Nazi-connected European beauty queen and later a Mafia-connected woman, Wills suggests that private behavior in essence crippled Kennedy as a public leader. He concludes his study by comparing Kennedy to another assassinated leader, Martin Luther King, Jr., much to Kennedy's disadvantage.

In the 1980s both panegyrics and critiques continued to appear. MANCHESTER wrote the ultimate commendatory work—a lavish coffee-table book, beautifully illustrated. Manchester makes Schlesinger and Sorensen seem almost critical. His dedication is "To David Powers Who Fought with him Upon St. Crispin's Day," while his opening epithet quotes Sir Thomas Malory on Sir Launcelot. If Wills meditates on power, Manchester gushes over perfection. He concludes by comparing Kennedy to the star Capella: "It is brilliant, it is swift, it soars. Of course, to see it you must lift your eyes. But he showed us how to do that."

At the other end of the spectrum is DAVIS' gossipy book. Davis, a reporter and cousin of Jackie Kennedy, looks at the whole family, although he focuses on John. Much like Wills, he concludes that hubris was the trait that ultimately destroyed the Kennedys. Even more than Wills he deals with sleaze and slime—sexual encounters, wiretapping, plots and counterplots. Although Davis grants that the Kennedys "have borne their misfortunes with dignity and grace," one can't help but conclude from his account that they brought much of this suffering on themselves—and on their nation.

Fortunately, the 1980s also witnessed the publication of one balanced major academic biography of John Kennedy—by far the most complete, well-researched, and fair biographical study. PARMET's two-volume account balances material on Kennedy's private life and public career. He has done an especially fine job of documenting his medical problems, creating a sympathetic understanding for a man who experienced almost constant pain. While Parmet recounts Kennedy's sexual encounters, he does not sensationalize them as do many of JFK's more virulent critics.

Like many revisionists, Parmet is critical of the Kennedy Presidency, especially of his domestic record, citing his failure to move a Democratic congress to enact the Party's social reform agenda. While he admits that JFK was a cold warrior, however, he asks us to look beyond this simplistic concept. It would have taken a remarkable and prescient leader indeed to transcend the clear cold war consensus of the early 1960s. Moreover, Kennedy's powerful rhetoric of idealistic service did energize many young people in the 1960s. Historian Alan Winkler is on target when he says, "Parmet's two-volume account of Kennedy is the most even-handed treatment to date" (*Reviews in American History*, March 1984). Indeed, a reader forced to choose among the multitude of studies of John Kennedy could do no better.

—Anthony O. Edmonds

———————

KEPLER, Johannes, 1571–1630; German astronomer.

Caspar, Max, *Kepler*, translated by C. Doris Hellman. London and New York, Abelard-Schuman, 1959 (originally published as *Johannes Kepler*, Stuttgart, W. Kohlhammer, 1948).
Koestler, Arthur, *The Sleepwalkers: A History of Man's Changing Vision of the Universe*. New York, Macmillan, and London, Hutchinson, 1959.

*

In the age of space exploration, Johannes Kepler, the discoverer of the three laws of the planetary motions, is known to students everywhere. In fact, his name may be found in virtually every high school earth science text book, while his use of data in calculating positions for the planet Mars is still under investigation and discussion not only in the professional publications, but also in the daily newspapers (see for example *The New York Times* [23 January 1990], pp. C1, C6). Yet, although we have thousands of publications dealing with every aspect of Kepler's life and work (*cf.*, for example, one of the latest additions to Kepler's bibliographies, namely Martha List's "Bibliografia Kepleriana, 1967–1975" in *Vistas in Astronomy*, Vol. 18 [Oxford and New York, Pergamon Press, 1975], pp. 957–1010), there is only one scholarly and reliable full-length biography of him in English, by CASPAR, ably translated from the German by C. Doris Hellman. Max Caspar is to this day recognized as the greatest Kepler scholar of all time, and his work is superior to all the earlier attempts at writing Kepler's *vita*. As Caspar states in his Preface, in order "to portray and evaluate not only Kepler's life but also his intellectual contribution, it is necessary to have studied at least his principal works, difficult as they are.'' That condition has been met by Caspar, who, in addition, studied newly discovered material that brought to light additional knowledge dealing with Kepler's life and works. Thus he was able to correct, as he calls them, ''false or at least slanted statements, which one author took from another, because he neglected to go back to the sources.''

The English translation is vastly superior to its German original, in that the translator omitted, or corrected in the footnotes, nearly all of Caspar's misstatements. Moreover, by the addition of citations and explanatory footnotes, she changed a book, aimed by its author primarily at the general public, into a superb scholarly work. Although Hellman's English rendering of the German original is uniformly good, still there are a few places where the exact English equivalent of certain German expressions has escaped her. For example, Kepler's son Ludwig became Königsberg city physician (''Stadtphysikus,'' in Caspar's original), and not ''city physicist,'' as Hellman has it.

A part of KOESTLER's *Sleepwalkers*, containing a biography of Kepler, is entitled ''The Watershed.'' That part has also been published separately in an expurgated version (*The Watershed*, New York, 1960; London, 1961). Koestler, a best-selling novelist, writes ''with such verve, brilliance and display of scholarship'' (as one reviewer noted in *Isis*, Vol. 50 [1959]), that it is small wonder his work has become ''a standard book for the lay public, including many philosophers and historians of ideas.'' Yet while Koestler's *Sleepwalkers* is undeniably appealing to the general readership, it is marred by a variety of misstatements as well as by frequent twisting or even suppression of facts in order to prove his theses. Thus, for example, in order to support his contention that Galileo's behavior toward Kepler was unfriendly, Koestler omits the fact that in 1611, when Kepler was looking for a new employment, it was Galileo who, as Casper pointed out, ''had publicly recommended him to the council of Venice to whose sovereign rule Padua belonged'' for the professorship at the University of Padua.

At the time that Koestler wrote and published *The Sleepwalkers* and *The Watershed*, it was generally believed, as Koestler observes, that ''the Lutherans, not the Catholics, had been the first to attack the Copernican system. . . . The Catholics, on the other hand, were uncommitted.'' It was only in 1973 that the eminent Italian scholar Eugenio Garin, in his article ''Alle Origini della Polemica Anti-copernicana'' (*Studia Copernicana VI*, Wroclaw, 1973), disclosed that the closest theological adviser of Pope Paul III, Bartolomeo Spina, Master of the Sacred and Apostolic Palace, intended to condemn Copernicus' *De revolutionibus orbium coelestium*, but he could not accomplish that on account of his illness and subsequent death. Spina's friend, Giovanni Maria Tolosani, in an appendix to his treatise ''On the Truth of the Holy Scripture,'' completed the task undertaken by Spina. That tract was later utilized by the Dominican preacher who initiated the attack on Galileo (*Studia Copernicana VI*, p. 31).

Several of Koestler's erroneous statements are corrected in Edward Rosen's notes to *Kepler's Conversation with Galileo's Sidereal Messenger* (New York and London, 1965).

—Erna Hilfstein

KERN, Jerome, 1885–1945; American musical and film composer.

Bordman, Gerald M., *Jerome Kern: His Life and Music*. New York and Oxford, Oxford University Press, 1980.

Ewen, David, *The World of Jerome Kern, a Biography*. New York, Holt, 1960.

Freedland, Michael, *Jerome Kern*. London, Robson Books, 1978; New York, Stein and Day, 1981.

Green, Stanley, *The World of Musical Comedy*. 4th edition, San Diego, A. S. Barnes, and London, Tantivy Press, 1980.

Kreuger, Miles, *Showboat: The Story of a Classic American Musical*. New York, Oxford University Press, 1977.

Lamb, Andrew, *Jerome Kern in Edwardian England*. East Preston, West Sussex, A. Lamb, 1981; revised and enlarged edition, Brooklyn, Institute for Studies in American Music, 1985.

Wilder, Alec, *American Popular Song: The Great Innovators 1900–50*. London and New York, Oxford University Press, 1972.

Wodehouse, P. G. and Guy Bolton. *Bring on the Girls: The Improbable Story of Our Life in Musical Comedy*. New York, Simon and Schuster, 1953; London, H. Jenkins, 1954.

*

Until recently, EWEN has been the standard biography on Jerome Kern. This prolific writer on music has an engaging writing style and organizational ability that make this book no less appealing to the general public than are his numerous other works; however, its brevity (146 pages), lack of extensive research, and honorific stance hardly make it satisfactory for the reader who wants information in some depth about the important issues of Kern's life: his sophistication as a popular song composer and the various phases of his role in the development of the American musical theater. Before launching into Kern's biography, Ewen has two introductory chapters that attempt to address these issues in a very superficial way. Several useful indexes provide handy information about the location of Kern's songs in musicals, movies, and on recordings.

FREEDLAND's biography comes nearly two decades after that of Ewen. It is about the same size, is even more lightweight, and offers very little new information or evaluation. Written in the intimate manner of a story, Freedland uses numerous anecdotes and direct quotations. The reader is subjected repeatedly to Freedland's emphasis on the awesomeness of Kern's talent, the enormity of his ego, and the boundlessness of his energy and sociability.

BORDMAN is thus the lone substantial Kern biography, is three times the size of Ewen or Freedland, and is based on substantial independent research. The book's organization is relentlessly chronological, and the author's often excellent evaluative insights are difficult to discover among the many details of Kern's life. A distinguished historian of the American musical, Bordman assesses Kern's role in this regard very adequately. The book also has some worthy discussion of the music itself, drawn largely from Wilder (see below). As a result, Bordman offers a relatively balanced view of Kern as a man of the theater and as a composer.

All three biographies lack documentation and bibliography. One is not surprised in the cases of Ewen and Freedland, which are meant for the nonspecialist. The depth and scholarly quality of Bordman, however, make these omissions noticeable. The reader wants to know *where* the author got this or that information and *how* he arrived at some of his conclusions. Regrettably, none of the three biographies deals with Kern sufficiently in the context of other leading popular composers of the time: Gershwin, Berlin, Porter, and Rodgers, to name a few.

A few books, not primarily biographies, are of high quality in their discussion of aspects of Kern's career. Foremost is WILDER, whose chapter on Kern in his remarkable study of American popular song clearly shows Kern's role as the first and perhaps the foremost of America's great 20th-century popular songwriters. Wilder both develops Kern's role in relation to other composers of his day and analyzes many Kern songs in some detail. The four style periods for the songs—the interpolations of pieces into other writers' shows, principally English (1902–15); the Princess Theatre shows, which some consider the beginning of a distinctive American music theater genre (1915–27); the great classic, *Showboat*, and the following musicals (1927–35); and the movie years (1935–45)—correspond to the basic divisions of Kern's career.

WODEHOUSE AND BOLTON have many anecdotes about their association with Kern in such Princess Theatre shows as *Very Good, Eddie* (1915), *Oh, Boy!*, *Oh, Lady, Lady!* and others. Much of this material has found its way into the biographies mentioned above. LAMB discusses in great detail the numerous visits Kern made to London during the years 1905–15 as a representative of the Harms publishing firm and his association with the British theater. One wishes that Kern's entire career would be studied with this rigor in some future full-length biography. KREUGER's study of *Showboat* treats Kern's crucial role in the evolution of Ferber's novel into perhaps our most important musical and is filled with pictures from all of the important versions. Each of the works discussed in this essay, excepting Wilder, includes pictures of Kern at various times in his life, as well as pictures of his family, his associates, and his musicals.

—William K. Kearns

KEROUAC, Jack, 1922–1969; American writer.

Charters, Ann, *Kerouac: A Biography*. San Francisco, Straight Arrow Books, 1973; London, Deutsch, 1974.

Clark, Tom, *Jack Kerouac*. New York, Harcourt, 1984.

Gifford, Barry and Lawrence Lee, *Jack's Book: An Oral Biography of Jack Kerouac*. New York, St. Martin's, 1978; as *Jack's Book: Jack Kerouac in the Lives and Words of His Friends*, London, Hamilton, 1979.

Jarvis, Charles E., *Visions of Kerouac*. Lowell, Massachusetts, Ithaca Press, 1973.

McNally, Dennis, *Desolate Angel: Jack Kerouac, the Beat Generation, and America*. New York, Random House, 1979.

Nicosia, Gerald, *Memory Babe: A Critical Biography of Jack Kerouac*. New York, Grove Press, 1983; London, Viking, 1985.

*

A life that has been transformed into legend is perhaps the hardest to get at, but it also attracts a host of voices eager to tell the story. Since Kerouac's untimely death in 1969, the tale of his life has inspired at least a half dozen biographical accounts, from the conventional and scholarly to the idiosyncratic and impressionistic.

Of these, three are what most would call standard biographies, and each in its own way contends for the title "definitive." CHARTERS wrote the first, which was published just four years after Kerouac's death. Her work is particularly valuable because her primary source was Kerouac himself. During the last three years of his life, he corresponded with Charters and provided her with journals, letters, manuscripts, and notes. Her other resources included Kerouac's mother and a relatively close affiliation with some of the other members of the Beat gang: William Burroughs, Gary Snyder, Robert Creeley, Charles Olson, and Allen Ginsberg, to whom the book is dedicated. Charters was enjoying their work and antics as early as 1956, when she first met Kerouac, so her biography is extremely informed, and nothing since has yielded a radically different vision of Kerouac's life.

Relying so heavily on the assistance and testimonies of Kerouac's friends, Charter's biography is inevitably a chronicle of the Beats and not just Kerouac alone. Charters barely touches the writer's childhood, and devotes little space to his alcoholic dissolution in the 1950s and '60s. The work essentially begins with Kerouac meeting Burroughs and Ginsberg in New York, and ends with the publication and media aftermath of *On the Road* (1957). But these choices of focus are sound: Kerouac lived in terms of his friends and lived to write about their lives and their spirit. Although Charters does not delve deeply into the cultural context in which the Beats howled, she does faithfully render their travels and relationships.

McNALLY attempts to cover some of the ground that Charters misses. He tells a much fuller story of Kerouac's childhood: the neighborhood pranks with boyhood friends, early romances, his relationship with his family, all of which can help a reader to understand the man and the writer. Similarly, McNally's narrative renders Kerouac a more rounded character as he struggles through his later years. Most important of McNally's contributions are his attempts to provide historical perspective. Unlike Charters, McNally worshipfully approaches Kerouac as one of the saviors of a world doomed to ecological and spiritual apocalypse. "I regard these alienated American prophets as my spiritual and intellectual ancestors," he declares in the Preface. Thus, he does not hesitate to editorialize upon presidential administrations, the advertising media, or nuclear testing if he thinks such cultural critique will help to portray Kerouac as he perceives him. At times his insights seem flip, but they may be appreciated nevertheless.

Though Charters and McNally dredge Kerouac's largely autobiographical fiction to render the story of his life, neither delves into much critical analysis of the works themselves. NICOSIA's biography is the only one that does this. For all Kerouac's major publications, Nicosia provides a mini-essay that explicates the text. Some of his analyses are sound and conservative autobiographical notations, and others verge on the obfuscatory. For instance, he belabors the ancestry of *On the Road*, tracing it through Melville, Twain, Whitman, London, and Dos Passos, and goes on to discuss the repetitions of "cosmic moments" and the networks of "overlapping motifs" he sees in the novel. Such insights may or may not be helpful, depending upon the critical affinities of the reader. Nevertheless, Nicosia's biography is the storehouse of detailed information on Kerouac. Two times the length of either of the previously discussed works, it might be less easily read and enjoyed, but it will certainly serve as a primary resource for any serious Kerouac scholar.

Of the remaining biographies, CLARK's is the most thorough and readable. This work, clearly not meant as a tool for exhaustive, academic research, is "intended primarily for readers who may not be familiar with the fuller biographies," as its dust jacket announces. Even so, Clark has done *his* research and presents a fair, if cursory, portrayal of the writer. Not a critical biography, it sticks to Kerouac's life as it is found in his journals, letters, fiction, and in the comments and literary work of his fellow writers. And though Clark does not delve deeply into broader historical matters, he does quote from articles of the time that criticized, praised, or otherwise commented on practices or members of the Beat movement, and thereby gives the reader some cultural perspective on Kerouac and his work. Clark's bibliography and notes are quite thorough.

GIFFORD AND LEE set out to breathe some rambling, Kerouac immediacy into their oral biography, hoping to provide "a reading of the man himself through the people he chose to populate his fiction." They succeed in rendering a host of fresh, firsthand perspectives of the writer; specifically, those of Carolyn Cassady, Gregory Corso, Lucien Carr, Ginsberg, Peter Orlovsky, and Burroughs, to name a few. These are the people who knew Kerouac best, and their impressions and anecdotes are illuminating. The authors perform their task well, but the pitfalls of writing an "oral biography" are hard to avoid: individual remembrances are not probed or contested; sometimes they are repetitive, digressive, and verbose; and most of the time, they appear only loosely stitched together with traditional biographical narrative. These shortcomings aside, Gifford and Lee's work is enjoyable in its very informality. At the very least, they have published a set of individual memoirs that are rich resources in themselves, as is the "Character Key" they include at the book's conclusion.

JARVIS' work is probably the least consequential of the Kerouac biographies because it treats his life in an impressionistic manner. Jarvis offers few notes, and he speaks in the first person throughout; at times he seems too interested in telling stories of his own repartee with Kerouac, in which he condescendingly poses as a teasing father. All this aside, there is some valuable information in this personal account, if the reader can get past a wholly intrusive author.

—Martin Thies

KEYNES, John Maynard, 1883–1946; English economist.

Harrod, Roy F., *The Life of John Maynard Keynes.* New York, St. Martin's, and London, Macmillan, 1951.

Hession, Charles H., *John Maynard Keynes: A Personal Biography of the Man Who Revolutionized Capitalism and the Way We Live.* New York, Macmillan, and London, Collier Macmillan, 1984.

Moggridge, Donald E., *Keynes.* London, Macmillan, 1976; revised edition, 1980.

Moggridge, Donald E., *Maynard Keynes: An Economist's Biography.* London, Routledge, 1991.

Skidelsky, Robert, *John Maynard Keynes: A Biography.* London, Macmillan, 1983– ; New York, Viking, 1986– (volume I, *Hopes Betrayed, 1883–1920*; other volumes projected).

*

Although biography is never an easy task, writing the biography of John Maynard Keynes seems a particularly difficult one. What does one do with a person who was trained as a mathematician (at Cambridge), wrote an international best-seller on contemporary politics (*The Economic Consequences of the Pence*), and is widely acknowledged as the pre-eminent economic theorist of the 20th century? And what if he was also a bisexual, intimate of the Bloomsburies, husband of a great ballerina, driving force behind the creation of Britain's Art Council, and the architect of the international monetary system that lasted from the end of World War II to 1972? It won't help either that he had a long and important career as an economic adviser to the Treasury after starting a Civil Service career in the India Office. One could clearly do quite a bit with this person, but one could also just as clearly do it badly (even with the best of efforts).

Fortunately, Keynes' first biographer was a person of interests not unlike Keynes' own. Raised in a family with connections to the theatre, HARROD was an eminent Oxford economist who had studied under Keynes as a young man and corresponded with him extensively during the composition of Keynes' great work, *The General Theory*. But if Harrod's skills as England's greatest reciter of Shakespearean verse helped to put him in good stead as the biographer of "Keynes the arts patron," his interest and experience in policy-making were not so useful. Harrod's book is an excellent guide to the chronology of Keynes' life and is impressive in its breadth, but it also distorts significant parts of his life in order to make him more acceptable as an authority on policy; Keynes' interests in philosophy, for instance, are downplayed because of their possible link to his early homosexuality. Many of his later positions on economic policy are likewise altered or sanitized to make them more consistent with Harrod's own.

Harrod's book was rushed into print in 1951, and in retrospect it is amazing that it could cover so much only 5 years after Keynes' death. After all, the important omissions and glosses all seem to be intentional rather than from ignorance or misunderstanding. Just how well Harrod did is made clear when one considers the speculative and unsatisfactory biography by HESSION. The major novelty in Hession's work is his consideration of Keynes' sexuality, so the work might seem a fair corrective to Harrod's omission on this count. Hession focuses on what he calls Keynes' androgyny and attempts to link this to his creativity. His attempt has not met with critical success and is not particularly compelling.

A much more successful attempt at incorporating Keynes' sexuality into a broader understanding of his life is the first volume of SKIDELSKY's biography. Although this first installment covers only the period 1883–1920, it paints a much fuller picture of Keynes' early life; it allows not only his homosexuality during this period but includes the first substantial consideration of Keynes' early philosophical work. Skidelsky's style is rich and intimate and, in fact, he often sounds like Keynes' onetime paramour Lytton Strachey in his *Eminent Victorians*. The reward for this stylistic flair has been rave critical reviews, but there would appear to be problems under the surface. It could easily be alleged that in his drive to uncover Keynes' personal life, Skidelsky has missed much of Keynes' attachment to his parents and their presuppositions about the world. His treatment of Keynes' early philosophical work is similarly confused when he tries to link the influence of G. E. Moore and Edmund Burke in Keynes' early essays. The most troublesome aspect of the work, however, may be its attempt to associate Keynes' early work in the philosophy of probability with his concern over uncertainty in his later work in economic theory. Such a link certainly exists, but Skidelsky has hung his star on an interpretation of Keynes made by the economist G. L. S. Shackle; as this interpretation has many exegetical problems and little currency among economists, Skidelsky has set himself a difficult task in his subsequent volumes. His task will not be made any easier by his apparent difficulty with economic theory; in the one treatment important to this early period of Keynes' life, the quantity theory of money is handled very awkwardly and in an appendix. Keynes was many things besides an economist, but putting his economics aside in an appendix leaves the uncomfortable sense that the focus is not at the center of the picture.

The reader looking for a balanced picture is not without recourse, however. Two books by MOGGRIDGE, the editor of Keynes' 30-volume *Collected Writings*, provide outstanding treatments of Keynes' life. The second edition of his short biography (1980) in an excellent introduction to a complex life. The first edition of the book (1976) did not have the benefit of many documents still covered by the 30-year rule of Britain's Public Record Office, or the explosion of Bloomsbury scholarship, but the second edition brings the reader substantially up to date. The limits imposed by this book's brevity are all removed in Moggridge's new long biography (1991). Here we have *all* the aspects of Keynes' full life without a loss of focus or proportion. No one knows Keynes' own writings more intimately than his editor, and no one has made better use of the extensive secondary literature dealing with each of the aspects of Keynes' life. Here we have a full consideration of everything from Keynes' undergraduate essays and his little black book recording sexual encounters to recently released public documents and the extensive literature on early 20th-century history. Moggridge is an economic historian by profession, and this adds to his appreciation of detail and background events. As a result of his extensive background and long work on the project, Moggridge has produced the best work yet on Keynes' life.

—B. W. Bateman

KHRUSHCHEV, Nikita, 1894–1971; Soviet statesman and premier.

Breslauer, George W., *Khrushchev and Brezhnev as Leaders*. London and Boston, Allen and Unwin, 1982.

Crankshaw, Edward, *Khrushchev: A Career*. New York, Viking, 1966; as *Krushchev: A Biography*, London, Collins, 1966.

Khrushchev, Sergei, *Khrushchev on Khrushchev: An Inside Account of the Man and His Era*, edited and translated by William Taubman. Boston, Little Brown, 1990.

McCauley, Martin, editor, *Khrushchev and Khrushchevism*. Bloomington, Indiana University Press, and London, Macmillan/University of London, 1987.

McNeal, Robert H., *Lenin, Stalin, Khrushchev: Voices of Bolshevism*. Englewood Cliffs, New Jersey, Prentice-Hall, 1963 (also published as *The Bolshevik Tradition*).

Medvedev, Roy A., *Khrushchev*, translated by Brian Pearce. Oxford, Blackwell, 1982; New York, Anchor/Doubleday, 1983.

Werth, Alexander, *Russia under Khrushchev*. New York, Hill and Wang, 1962.

Wolfe, Bertram, *Khrushchev and Stalin's Ghost*. New York, Praeger, and London, Atlantic Press, 1957.

*

In the current days of *perestroika* and *glasnost*, there has been a resurgence of interest in the figure of Nikita S. Khrushchev, eventual successor of Josef Stalin, and the man whose infamous "Secret Speech" to the Soviet Twentieth Party Congress in 1956 set off a wave of reform now likened to the policies of Mikhail Gorbachev. Khrushchev—politician, farmer, and diplomat—is an intriguing man, and one of the first Soviet officials to visit the United States.

WOLFE focuses on the "text, background, and meaning of Khrushchev's secret report to the Twentieth Congress on the night of February 24–25, 1956." As biography, the material is naturally limited. However, since most would agree that it was this speech that catapulted Khrushchev into international fame, with ramifications that are still being discussed, Wolfe's book is important. Wolfe expertly organizes his material, and the picture that emerges is a Khrushchev with a need to distance himself from the excesses of the past, coupled with a determined pragmatism to propel the Soviet Union into the future.

WERTH attempts to place Khrushchev in the broader tradition of the Bolshevik Party and tries to find a substantive linkage between the policies of V. I. Lenin and those articulated by Khrushchev. He distorts the social conditions in the Soviet Union that allowed Khrushchev to rise to prominence, even speaking of the "benevolence" of both Stalin and Khrushchev. All in all, Werth's book emerges as a confusing pattern of semi-apology about the Soviet Union, a bit like many books published by sympathizers in the 1930s. As biography, the material is weak and lacks coherence. Most of the sources are questionable, and the book reads more like an exercise in tolerance than a factual biography.

Thankfully, this is not so with McNEAL. Although his study is not purely a biography, it is nevertheless a valuable resource for material on Khrushchev and Communist Party history during his tenure. Indeed, Khrushchev often appears almost as a "boy-scout" party member, loyal to the extreme, and with a deterministic vision for the future of Soviet society. McNeal's style is extremely readable, and he documents each interpretation with appropriate examples. One might quibble with his interpretation of the "logic" of the Purges, but other scholarly works have addressed that question to a greater degree. The book is most valuable for non-specialists and undergraduates, although it should not be neglected in upper division courses.

CRANKSHAW, a knowledgeable and interesting interpreter of the Soviet period, offers a biography of the bureaucratic career of Nikita Khrushchev. The book deals primarily with the years prior to 1957, and it traces Khrushchev's life from youth to political maturity. In the scholarly vein, Crankshaw's treatment of Khrushchev's early years remains one of the most accurate accounts available. The final portion of the book, dealing with Khrushchev's career after Stalin's death in 1953, is less thorough, but nonetheless interesting. Some reviewers have mentioned that Crankshaw is not always historically accurate; readers would benefit from gaining a general background in Soviet history prior to reading this book.

The basis for Khrushchev's own *Khrushchev Remembers* (translated and edited by Strobe Talbot, 1970) remains rather murky. These reminiscences, taped and transcribed over several years while he was in exile, are of limited scholarly use, but they do provide interesting and enjoyable reading. It is a testament to Khrushchev's character that he seems to have been involved in a little bit of everything, and the book itself often reads like a hodgepodge of random conversations carefully reconstructed to paint a positive picture of its author. In addition, Khrushchev seems to be acting out something of a literary vendetta against those who removed him from power, concentrating on the years 1953–64. As a biographical reference tool, the book is useful in its psychological assessment of Khrushchev's state of mind and thoughts on the past. As historical biography, however, it should be carefully scrutinized for omissions and inaccuracies.

A provocative response to Khrushchev's own memoirs is the book by MEDVEDEV, a writer known primarily to the west for his scholarly work on the Stalinist era from a Soviet point of view. His book on Khrushchev contains little that is new, and, as might be expected, is rather one-sided. Medvedev deals briefly with the years from 1894 to 1953, devoting most of the book to the tumultuous period 1953–64. Medvedev believes that the 1956 speech was Khrushchev's "finest hour," and Khrushchev emerges as a frank but fair leader with certain character flaws (e.g. egotism) that would eventually lead to his downfall.

In a sophisticated analysis of the leadership qualities of Soviet leaders in the post-Stalin era, BRESLAUER is much like Wolfe in his bureaucratic biography. While it is difficult to separate the material on Khrushchev from the material on Brezhnev in this volume, and though it contains a great deal of political analysis of actions and attitudes that has little to do with standard biography, Breslauer does fill a needed segment of material on the political aspects of Khrushchev's leadership style. He successfully challenges many of the remaining suppositions about Khrushchev's lack of political acumen, showing that Khrushchev was a shrewd, but not erudite, politician.

Interest in Khrushchev renewed in the 1980s: McCAULEY's collection is a product of a March 1985 conference at the University of London. The conference was held to assess Khrush-

chev's contributions to Soviet history and to analyze and determine the effects of the policies known as "Khrushchev-ism," considering contemporary developments within the Soviet Union. The material is scholarly, designed for the graduate student or specialist with more than a basic knowledge of Soviet history. It also focuses on the role Khrushchev played in Soviet political development. The work is not biography in the strictest sense, yet each contribution deals with certain aspects of Khrushchev's character and attitudes toward a variety of subjects. The volume could have benefited by providing more historiographical data within the individual articles themselves, in order to help the reader place the submissions into a larger historical picture. However, McCauley includes some much needed reinterpretations of Khrushchev the man and leader, with particular emphasis on new material not available to earlier biographers.

The newest biography of Khrushchev is by his favorite son, SERGEI KHRUSHCHEV. The book deals primarily with the final seven years in Nikita Khrushchev's life, and it is biography and recollection with a purpose. Father and son were obviously close, and it is likely that Sergei wishes to paint a flattering picture of his father. Sergei mentions that his primary purpose is to remove the "myths and fables" from previous works. However, he seems to replace them with more of his own, further obfuscating the facts. What emerges is a saintly Khrushchev, the family man, the considerate peasant philosopher, and the man who was surreptitiously removed from power just as he was about to change the face of the Soviet Union. As with Nikita's own work, *Khrushchev on Khrushchev* will likely appeal primarily to the non-specialist, for while it is an interesting account, it is more entertaining than credible. With the drastic changes that are occurring within the Soviet system, there has never been a better time to wish for a new, freshly documented, and scholarly biography of the precursor to the Gorbachev phenomenon, Nikita Khrushchev.

—Kelvin Richardson

KIERKEGAARD, Søren, 1813–1855; Danish philosopher and religious writer.

Lowrie, Walter, *Kierkegaard* (2 vols.). New York and London, Oxford University Press, 1938.

Lowrie, Walter, *A Short Life of Kierkegaard.* Princeton, New Jersey, Princeton University Press, 1942; London, Oxford University Press, 1970.

Thompson, Josiah, *Kierkegaard.* New York, Knopf, 1973; London, Gollancz, 1974.

*

LOWRIE's two-volume study (1938), amply documented by long excerpts from Søren Kierkegaard's journals and unabashedly apologetic, remains the standard biography in English. Lowrie's mastery of Danish, his recourse to the 18 notebooks of Kierkegaard's private journals ("the most voluminous that ever were written"), and his unremitting faithfulness to his subject's perspective on his life—evidenced by his insistence on adopting Kierkegaard's division of his life found on loose, nearly discarded pieces of paper—make this an unusually sensitive and sympathetic biography. Despite apologies for being, if not one of the "Professors" into whose hands Kierkegaard has fallen "as a topic of objective interest," a parson representing that very Christendom Kierkegaard so vehemently criticized, Lowrie sees himself as the "lover" whom Kierkegaard said would come in time. This intense love affair with the subject of the biography constitutes both its strength and its weakness, as Lowrie himself recognizes. Noting the necessity of making a "clear sweep" of the book's pedantry, Lowrie attests the advantage of this truncation in that "no one will suspect it of presuming to be a complete exposition of Kierkegaard's thought or an adequate explanation of his life." Lowrie had so completely identified with the poet-philosopher-religious author that he wished originally to organize the biography as a series of unresolved pseudonymous opinions, leaving the reader free to choose among them.

But Lowrie had to abandon this original plan and opted instead for what some would see as an inordinate use of lengthy quotations from Kierkegaard's own writings. So abundantly does Lowrie quote from his subject's voluminous work that he concedes and perhaps boasts that his biography has turned into autobiography. In his own defense, Lowrie states that if he had foreseen the translation of these works in the near future, he would not have allowed the quotations to comprise two-fifths of the book.

Lowrie, however, was the first to accord Kierkegaard the acquaintance and acclaim he deserves in the English-speaking world, and non-speakers of Danish continue to owe him a great debt. For those readers seeking to become acquainted with the philosopher's thought as well as his life, this is still the best biography with which to begin.

Although to some extent he is dependent on Danish and German biographies to date, Lowrie is to be credited for the ingeniousness with which he has ferreted out of Kierkegaard's method of "indirect communication" in the pseudonymous works and in his journals the details of his deeply disturbed existence. For example, he divined the meaning of "The Great Earthquake" as his father's revelation to him of his sinful relations with the servant-maid who became his father's wife shortly after his first wife died. Such penetrating conclusions as this, which Kierkegaard sought to mask, make Lowrie's study especially perspicacious. On the other hand, Lowrie's treatment of Kierkegaard's engagement to Regina, while not constituting a complete defense of the philosopher's shameful conduct, still seeks to produce pity and conciliation rather than condemnation of Kierkegaard and falls far short of the balanced, critical approach demanded by the topic. Lowrie limply adds at the end of the Regina chapter, "This is what is described to-day as the Sublimation of Eros," a Freudian judgment unwarranted by his own approach and clearly out of keeping with his subject's own views of the aesthetic stage of life and the conscious *choice* of the ethical.

LOWRIE's second study (1942), completed only four years after the first, sees him applying the necessary discipline to prune some of the too lengthy excerpts from Kierkegaard's writings. He is still, however, in large part allowing his subject to speak for himself, and the division according to Kierkegaard's own periodization of his life largely remains, though headings such as "The Great Earthquake," "The Path of Perdition," and "The Great Parenthesis," have been supplemented by a fuller treatment of the setting of Kierkegaard's entire life, 19th-century Copenhagen. Lowrie's basic interpretations of aspects of Kierkegaard's life have not changed.

THOMPSON's 1973 biography has benefited from his year's stay in Copenhagen and use of the Kierkegaard Archives in the Royal Library there. From the Archives he has drawn on letters of Kierkegaard's classmates, his father's papers, his brother's *Journal*, and even marginalia found in books from Kierkegaard's library. What distinguishes this biography from Lowrie's, however, is not so much this somewhat broader base of research but the absence of the reverent, almost hagiographical tone that nearly cloyed in Lowrie's study. Thompson's only reference to Lowrie avers that he made Kierkegaard into "a kind of modern religious hero." In contrast, Thompson chastens Lowrie's romantic excesses and is far more unsparing in his treatment. He sees Kierkegaard as "wrapped in a veil of self-consciousness," with a "masochist's love for his own suffering," and capable of outright deception of Regina. To overcome his "fundamental estrangement" from himself, his body, and the world, Kierkegaard, according to Thompson, attempted to encounter himself by re-creating himself in his characters and pseudonyms. In acknowledging the importance of the "earthquake entry" in Kierkegaard's *Journal*, Thompson does not dwell on its possible meaning with reference to the sin of Kierkegaard's father, but sees it as the philosopher's "attempt at creating a personal myth." Thompson's psychologically penetrating, less sympathetic, even at times unsympathetic portrait of Kierkegaard does much to correct and balance Lowrie's too apologetic study. Yet perhaps when Thompson identifies Kierkegaard with Johannes the Seducer of *Either/Or*, Volume I, he may have gone too far. Unlike Lowrie here, Thompson fails to see that Kierkegaard's ability to draw the character of such a cold, dispassionate seducer puts him beyond its hold on him. Thompson's faster-paced biography offers the much needed note of critical judgment while sharing in many of the overall conclusions also reached by Lowrie. At the same time, however, it lacks the theological depth of insight arrived at through Lowrie's much fuller use of Kierkegaard's own thoughts. In this respect, at least, Kierkegaard is his own best interpreter.

—Maria R. Lichtmann

KING, Martin Luther, Jr., 1929–1968; American clergyman and civil rights leader.

Bennett, Lerone, *What Manner of Man: A Biography of Martin Luther King, Jr.* Chicago, Johnson, 1964; revised edition, New York, Johnson, 1976.

Branch, Taylor, *Parting the Waters: America In the King Years, 1954–63.* New York, Simon and Schuster, 1988; with subtitle *Martin Luther King and the Civil Rights Movement*, London, Macmillan, 1988.

Clayton, Edward J., *Martin Luther King: The Peaceful Warrior.* Englewood Cliffs, New Jersey, Prentice-Hall, 1964.

Colaiaco, James A., *Martin Luther King, Jr.: Apostle of Militant Non-violence*. New York, St. Martin's, and London, Macmillan, 1988.

Davis, Lenwood G., *I Have a Dream: The Life and Times of Martin Luther King, Jr.* Chicago, Adams Press, 1969.

Downing, Frederick J., *To See the Promised Land: The Faith Pilgrimage of Martin Luther King, Jr.* Macon, Georgia, Mercer University Press, 1986.

Fairclough, Adam, *To Redeem the Soul of America: The Southern Christian Leadership Conference and Martin Luther King, Jr.* Athens, Georgia, The University of Georgia Press, 1987.

Garrow, David J., *Bearing the Cross: Martin Luther King, Jr., and the Southern Christian Leadership Conference.* New York, Morrow, and London, Cape, 1988.

King, Coretta Scott, *My Life with Martin Luther King, Jr.* New York, Holt Rinehart, 1969; London, Hodder and Stoughton, 1970.

King, Martin Luther, Sr., *Daddy King: An Autobiography.* New York, Morrow, 1980.

Lewis, David L., *King: A Critical Biography.* New York, Praeger, and London, A. Lane, 1970; revised as *King: A Biography*, Urbana, University of Illinois Press, 1978.

Lincoln, C. Eric, editor, *Martin Luther King, Jr.: A Profile.* New York, Hill and Wang, 1970.

Miller, William R., *Martin Luther King, Jr.: His Life, Martyrdom, and Meaning for the World.* New York, Weybright and Talley, 1968.

Oates, Stephen B., *Let the Trumpet Sound: The Life of Martin Luther King, Jr.* New York, Harper, 1982.

Peake, Thomas R., *Keeping the Dream Alive: A History of the Southern Christian Leadership Conference from King to the 1980s.* New York, P. Lang, 1987.

*

The first generation of biographies of Martin Luther King, Jr., were hagiographies written by close personal friends or for young children. BENNETT is the earliest account of King's life and is still of some value. An historian who was a schoolmate of King's at Morehouse College, Bennett wrote admiringly, and though he provided useful details about King's early life as well as about his dress and demeanor, he was able to furnish neither a critical evaluation nor complete documentation. Another warm portrait by a friend, MILLER, similarly avoided examining King's ideas or scrutinizing his actions closely. CLAYTON, the Public Relations Director of the Southern Christian Leadership Conference, painted a reverential picture of King for young people, while LINCOLN collected an uneven but interesting set of essays by people who knew King or were well versed in the civil rights movement (none of them, however, from the more militant wing). Unquestionably the best personal memoir is by CORETTA SCOTT KING, a widow's recollections that, however unscholarly and loyal, are enormously valuable for the detail they provide on King's family life and for the personal viewpoint they afford on events such as the Birmingham bus boycott and the freedom concerts in which she took an important role. The next best is by MARTIN LUTHER KING, SR., in which Martin Jr. appears in the role of successful son in a family committed to nonviolent struggle for civil rights.

The first biographer to provide at least a tentatively critical analysis of King, DAVIS raised some questions on the nature and adequacy of King's leadership but did not push them very far. LEWIS is well worth reading because of his careful depiction of the southern matrix in which King's personality and ideas matured. Lewis' attempt at a critique is marred by continuous straining to demonstrate that King was forced slowly and reluctantly into his leadership positions by the pressure of events and by those around him.

The first truly thorough and scholarly biography of King was OATES' amply-detailed, well-researched, and well-written work by an academic biographer and historian. Although its lack of a full bibliography and its use of notes only for quotations is annoying to researchers, it is and will remain for some time the most complete, balanced, and readable life of King. DOWNING offers a psychohistory based on the six-stage personality of James Fowler's faith development theory and on Erik Erikson's homo religiosus. As is the case with many psychohistorians, Downing pays especially close attention to the use of primary sources associated with early childhood and family experiences and is less concerned with adult development and intellectual influences. His work is also marred by digressing at times into a study of Fowler's theory rather than of King's personality. Most recently, COLAIACO has presented an interesting work of synthesis, less a biography than a study of King's nonviolent protest campaigns prepared from published sources by an intellectual historian.

The most significant books to appear on King study him in the context of his work with the Southern Christian Leadership Conference. GARROW's *Bearing the Cross*, based on over 700 interviews and on FBI and CIA files, is the most complete study of King's leadership. Scholarly and balanced, it is the most informative portrait of the relationship of the man to the movement he headed. While its focus is primarily on King's political life and activity, it deals fully with his personality and interior struggles. PEAKE's book, less successful as a biography and more competent as organizational history, concentrates on King's ideas and influence rather than on his personality. FAIRCLOUGH, a British academic, carefully distinguishes King from the organization and concentrates on delineating the nature of King's radicalization in the late 1960s as he moved toward black power and a trenchant critique of American society as a whole. BRANCH is unsurpassed in portraying the role of the black church in the development of King and his movement. Concerned to portray as accurately as possible the differing personalities of the secondary actors as well as the main ones in the Southern Christian Leadership Conference, Branch sees King primarily as a moral and religious leader rather than as a political figure. Taken together, these last four books constitute as full a picture of King's civil rights crusade as we are likely to have.

—Joseph M. McCarthy

***

KIPLING, Rudyard, 1865–1936; English writer.

Amis, Kingsley, *Rudyard Kipling and His World*. London, Thames and Hudson, and New York, Scribner, 1975.

Birkenhead, Frederick Winston Furneaux Smith, 2nd Earl of, *Rudyard Kipling*. London, Weidenfeld and Nicolson, and New York, Random House, 1978.

Carrington, Charles, *Rudyard Kipling: His Life and Work*. London, Macmillan, 1955.

Fido, Martin, *Rudyard Kipling: An Illustrated Biography*. New York and London, Hamlyn, 1974.

Mason, Philip, *Kipling: The Glass, the Shadow, and the Fire*. London, Cape, and New York, Harper, 1975.

Wilson, Angus, *The Strange Ride of Rudyard Kipling: His Life and Work*. London, Secker and Warburg, 1977; New York, Viking, 1978.

*

Only one of Rudyard Kipling's three children survived him. (The deaths of the other son and daughter were the major events of his adult life.) Elsie Kipling, later Mrs. George Bambridge, became the custodian of Kipling's memory, and, more importantly, of the Kipling papers. After the death of Kipling's widow, Elsie became responsible for commissioning an official biography. Two writers had attempted the project while Mrs. Kipling was still alive, but abandoned the work, at least in part because Mrs. Kipling's supervision proved too exacting. A third considered the project after Mrs. Kipling's death, but could not come to terms with Mrs. Bambridge. Lord Birkenhead (see below), who met Kipling's daughter through her husband, accepted the commission soon after the end of World War II. (Captain Bambridge died before the manuscript was complete.) Birkenhead signed a contract that gave complete control to Mrs. Bambridge, giving her the right to delete any passage or document from the final work, as well as the ownership of the copyright. The work seemed to progress well, and Birkenhead completed a draft in 1948. On reading the manuscript, Mrs. Bambridge judged it "so bad a book that any attempt at palliative measures . . . is not feasible" and forbade its publication entirely. (She was supported in this decision by T. S. Eliot, who may not have realized that he was shown only a rough draft.) Birkenhead accepted a financial settlement but continued to work on his biography. It was not published until after both he and Mrs. Bambridge had died, and it is impossible to tell how close the published version, which Birkenhead revised in the 1960s, is to the rejected original.

Birkenhead was succeeded as official biographer by CARRINGTON, whose work appeared in 1955. Carrington evidently got on well with Kipling's daughter. His book ends with a memoir by Mrs. Bambridge, and he graciously suggests that she deserves credit as part author. The biography was generally well received, and Carrington's is in every way the most important of Kipling's biographies. All others rely on it: even Birkenhead quotes Carrington on several occasions. Carrington covers every period of Kipling's life, especially those painful periods that are not touched on in Kipling's fascinating but reticent autobiography, *Something of Myself* (1937). He carefully describes the various worlds in which Kipling moved: the artistic circle of the MacDonald sisters (two of Kipling's aunts were married to the painters Edward Burne-Jones and Edward Poynter), the Anglo-Indian society of Lahore and Simla where Kipling spent his formative years as a young writer, the rural Vermont town where Kipling made his home for a few years after his marriage, Af-

rica during the Boer War, Sussex where he finally settled. Carrington offers more a chronicle of the many activities of Kipling's life than a portrait of his character, but a clear picture of an intensely sensitive man who feels himself an outsider in whatever society he enters nevertheless emerges from the book. Carrington does not press psychological interpretations, but he quotes the very passages that a more psychoanalytical critic might make much of, leaving the reader to evaluate them. Carrington's comments on Kipling's works, while sensible, do not probe very deeply.

When BIRKENHEAD's biography appeared in 1978, it proved to be an interesting work, and it is of especial value because Birkenhead was able to interview friends of Kipling's who died before Carrington began his research. Kipling's sister, most notably, gave Birkenhead a good deal of assistance. Birkenhead does not reveal any great, dark secret about Kipling that might account for the book's suppression. It is not hard to see, however, why Mrs. Bambridge might have thought it a very bad book. Birkenhead is full of small touches that seem to put Kipling in a disreputable light. He stresses what a loud obnoxious child his relatives found the three-year-old Kipling, he speculates on whether the schoolboy Kipling had sexual relations with village girls, he retells stories in which the young journalist Kipling seems cocky and rude, and recounts several incidents that make Kipling seem timid. (He mentions a physical fear of horses several times.) What was perhaps more troubling for Mrs. Bambridge, Birkenhead suggests that Kipling's life was darkened in his later years by strains in his marriage and by his wife's periods of "neurotic depression." Birkenhead also tends use extreme formulations for his descriptions. For example, he describes Kipling's attitude to his cousin Stanley Baldwin, the Prime Minister, as "contempt," while other accounts do not suggest that their undoubted political disagreements soured the personal relationship between the two to any great extent. If Carrington sometimes seems muted, Birkenhead always uses the highest tones. Birkenhead often gives a better picture of some part of Kipling's life—his first visit to England, for example—but Carrington does more justice to the range of Kipling's varied activities throughout a long life.

WILSON takes most of his facts from Carrington, but he corrects some misperceptions from earlier works on Kipling. He shows, for example, that the position Kipling's father held as art instructor in Bombay was a humbler one than has been recognized. Wilson's real purpose, though, is to show the interrelation of the real world Kipling knew and the fictive worlds created in his work. Some of the most stimulating sections of the book are Wilson's impressionistic accounts of the worlds evoked in Kipling's fiction: the India of *Kim* and the early stories, the enduring England presented in *Rewards and Fairies*. The emphasis on the relationship between the places Kipling experienced and worlds he creates in his fiction leads to some departures from chronology: all the Indian material is treated together, though Kipling continued to write of India long after he left. Wilson's critical judgments are always insightful, and he makes more useful connections between Kipling's life and work than other biographers. Kipling's readers often argue about whether his great achievements were the early, Indian stories or the later, more experimental works. Wilson intends in part to return the emphasis to the early works.

MASON also takes all his biographical facts from Carrington. Like Wilson, his book's main interest is in the interaction of life and work. Mason is not so skillful a writer as Wilson, but his comments are often illuminating. (His Indian background, like Wilson's colonial childhood, seems to have sharpened his understanding of Kipling.) Unlike Wilson, he takes the later stories as the crown of Kipling's work.

AMIS' book on Kipling is a disappointment. As Wilson shows, one novelist considering the life of another can be fascinating, but Amis includes only a few passages that are more than a repetition of biographical information from Carrington. Amis does include a number of interesting photographs.

FIDO's work is also extensively illustrated, and also takes most of its information from Carrington. It is, however, quite a readable account of Kipling's life. Fido does contain some speculation that seems unsupported. For example, Fido suggests that Kipling gave *The Light that Failed* its final, unhappy ending because his first love, Flo Garrand, was unimpressed by the happy ending that united figures based on Kipling and herself. Other writers accept that the unhappy ending was, as Kipling said, his original intention. But as a sketch of Kipling's life, Fido is quite enjoyable.

—Brian Abel Ragen

KLEE, Paul, 1879–1940; Swiss painter.

Giedion-Welcker, Carola, *Paul Klee*, translated by Alexander Gode. New York, Viking, and London, Faber, 1952.

Grohmann, Will, *Paul Klee*. New York, Abrams, and London, L. Humphries, 1954 (originally published by Kohlhammer, Stuttgart, 1954).

Ponente, Nello, *Klee: Biographical and Critical Study*, translated by James Emmons. Cleveland, Ohio, World Publishing, 1960.

San Lazzaro, Gualtieri di, *Klee: A Study of His Life and Work*, translated by Stuart Hood. New York, Praeger, and London, Thames and Hudson, 1957.

*

GROHMANN's *Paul Klee* serves as the foundation, the touchstone work, from which other biographies and partial biographies on Klee are judged. An acquaintance and obvious admirer of Klee, Grohmann presents a man who devoted his life to his aesthetics, so much so that the aesthetics and the life became indistinguishable. Here is a Klee who made a conscious decision at a young age to pursue a career as an artist, debating only between art and music as his medium, and in many ways combining the two.

The book is divided into three main sections: Klee's life, his work, and his teaching. Grohmann draws not only on his own acquaintance with Klee for the biography; Klee's own diaries, which, as Grohmann points out, deal more with aesthetics than social matters, are quoted from to reveal Klee's thoughts at various stages of his life. In addition, Felix Klee, Paul Klee's son, serves as a source, as well as several records of Klee's personal

correspondence, records of private conversations, and his essays, lectures, and notes on art (including his lecture notes from the Bauhaus). Klee's early drawings, some supplied by Klee himself, are also included, as well as many reproductions of sketches and several of the more important works, some in color. Clear black-and-white photographs of Klee, his family, his studio, and members of the Bauhaus, a brief biographical data page, Klee's own brief autobiography, and several indexes are included as well. It is a highly complimentary monograph, which, interestingly, does not manage, or really even attempt, to reveal the enigmatic mind of Klee. Grohmann continued to issue new books on Klee, but they are little more than rewrites of this central study.

GIEDION-WELCKER's book on Klee, by an expert in Modern Art who also knew Klee personally, is, once again, divided into three parts, in this case, Klee's early years, his later years as a theorist and teacher, and his contributions to artistic expression. It is a less hero-worshipping view than Grohmann's, but not much less, and, once again, does not really get into the human side of Klee. The translation by Gode flows well, and the indexed bibliography is excellent. There are also many black-and-white and a few color reproductions.

SAN LAZZARO's study, translated in an uneven style by Stuart Hood, one where casual language is interspersed with needlessly esoteric language, and where serious insights are interspersed with unsubstantiated comments about Klee's influences and views. San Lazzaro is obviously familiar with Giedion-Welcker's study and fortunately is not afraid to question some of her views. Though uneven, this biography gives a more human view of Klee, discussing such aspects as his sexual indiscretions and struggles as an adolescent and the truth that he did not know from the beginning where he and his art were going. San Lazzaro also makes claims for Klee's position as one of the major figures of modern art. Several reproductions, both in black-and-white and color, are included and indexed by year. PONENTE, also well aware of Giedion-Welcker's study, offers a decent introduction to Klee that is filled with small color reproductions of Klee's works.

Several other studies of Klee, more concerned with his art and theories of aesthetics than with his life, include brief biographies or biographical references. One such is Norbert Lynton, *Klee* (1964), which draws, as do all the studies, on Klee's own writings and on his early life to explain his development as a painter. It includes 50 excellent color reproductions. Werner Schmalenback, *Paul Klee* (1969), translated by Susan Bellamy, includes a brief biography interspersed with art criticism. Hans L. Jaffe, *Klee* (1971), offers a good brief biography. Douglas Hall, *Klee* (1977), is a decent brief biography, along with some reproductions. Denys Chevalier, *Klee* (1971), translated by Eileen B. Hennessey, is a fair brief biography, also including some reproductions. Marcel Marnat, *Klee* (1974), translated by Wade Stevenson, includes a brief biography and an analysis of Klee's works, along with many reproductions. A recent book by O. K. Werckmeister, *The making of Paul Klee's career, 1914–20* (1989), is a highly scholarly study of six years of Klee's life within the context of the socio-political environment of the time.

Since Klee kept a meticulous record of his views on art and his progress, his own writing has served as the major source for biographies about him. *The Diaries of Paul Klee: 1898–1918*, edited by Felix Klee and translated into English in 1964, record his development and his theories from the age of 19 until he was 40, and offer the serious reader endless ideas on art and life, and, though they are not as personal as most diaries, an insight into Klee himself. *Paul Klee: The Thinking Eye; the notebooks of Paul Klee*, edited by Jurg Spiller (1961), serves as an excellent companion to the diaries. It is a detailed record, with diagrams and illustrations, of Klee's theories as he developed and presented them during his years of teaching at the Bauhaus, taken from his own "Pedagogical Sketchbook" and the notes of Petra Petitpierre, one of his students. It is difficult reading, meant only for the serious student.

As with many modern European artists, much of the writing about Klee is not yet available in English. Some acclaimed works include Leopold Zahn, *Paul Klee: Leben, Werk, Geist* (1920), Wilhelm Hausenstein, *Kairuan, oder eine Geschichte vom Maler Klee* (1921), and Rene Cervel, *Paul Klee* (1930).

—Harry Edwin Eiss

LAFAYETTE, Marie–Joseph–Paul–Yves–Roch–Gilbert du Motier, Marquis de, 1757–1834; French general and statesman.

Bernier, Olivier, *Lafayette, Hero of Two Worlds*. New York, Dutton, 1983.

Gerson, Noel B., *Statue in Search of a Pedestal: A Biography of the Marquis de Lafayette*. New York, Dodd Mead, 1976.

Gottschalk, Louis, *Lafayette* (6 vols.). Chicago, University of Chicago Press, 1935–73.

La Fuye, Maurice de and Emile Albert Babeau, *Apostle of Liberty: A Life of La Fayette*, translated by Edward Hyams. New York, T. Yoseloff, and London, Thames and Hudson, 1956 (originally published as *La Fayette: soldat de deux parties*, Paris, Amiot-Dumont, 1953).

Latzko, Andreas, *Lafayette: A Life*, translated by E. W. Dickes. New York, Doubleday, and London, Methuen, 1936 (originally published by Rascher, Zürich, 1935).

Loth, David G., *The People's General: The Personal Story of Lafayette*. New York, Scribner, 1951.

Sedgwick, Henry Dwight, *La Fayette*. Indianapolis, Bobbs-Merrill, 1928.

Tower, Charlemagne, Jr., *The Marquis de La Fayette in the American Revolution* (2 vols.). Philadelphia, Lippincott, 1894.

Woodward, William E., *Lafayette*. New York, Farrar and Rinehart, 1938; London, Cresset Press, 1939.

*

TOWER was the first biographer to attempt a study of Lafayette based on manuscript sources. Though not a professional historian, the retired businessman provided a solid, well-documented two-volume study of Lafayette's activities during the American Revolution that has led to the book's being reprinted several times. While the more recent study by Gottschalk has identified selected errors of factual detail in Tower, motives and character during the most popular and famous period of Lafayette's life appear to be more accurately assessed in Tower than in Gottschalk.

In a series of six volumes, GOTTSCHALK chronicled Lafayette's life until the summer of 1790. The first modern scholar to concentrate on Lafayette, Gottschalk brought a method and approach to the study of the Frenchman that was greatly affected by the perspective of the academic generation that dominated the post-World War I world of scholarship. These men questioned human motivation in light of their own loss of idealism and sought to use the tools of the infant study of psychology to analyze and interpret human action. They carried into their studies a prejudice against monarchy, military figures, and the pre-Revolutionary nobility, depicting them as effete and useless social parasites.

Gottschalk's first volume is an extended essay analyzing Lafayette's motives for involvement in the American Revolution. In it he raises the lack of a strong father figure as an explanation for Lafayette's rebellious nature and his inability to deal with authority. He concludes that Lafayette came to America not due to his belief in the cause but rather because of "a growing dissatisfaction with his lot at home, an increasing desire to achieve glory, and a traditional hatred of the English." Amassing a huge collection of primary research on Lafayette's life both on his own and with the assistance of graduate students, Gottschalk soon found himself riding a scholarly tiger. The slim first volume was followed by a series of volumes increasingly packed with details on shorter periods of Lafayette's life. R. R. Palmer characterized the sixth and final volume as "strictly narrative and chronological," describing the life day by day (*American Historical Review*, December 1974). Despite the outdated Lasswellian psychology on which the original volume was formulated, Gottschalk's series has remained a masterly compendium of detail on Lafayette's first 33 years unlikely to be supplanted for its depth.

Efforts to summarize Lafayette's life in one volume have been much less successful because Lafayette continued to be politically active for over 50 years until his death in 1834, a period of intense and significant change throughout Europe and the Americas, the "two worlds" of which he was a hero. As a result of this complex and extended lifetime, biographers have found it difficult to reflect that story in a single volume. SEDGWICK in 1928 concentrated his energies on three episodes in Lafayette's long life: the American Revolution, the French Revolution of 1789, and the French Revolution of 1830. Gottschalk in a review suggested that "with more critical discrimination he might have written a splendid biography" (*The Nation*, 4 July 1928). Sedgwick's dependence on three periods misleads the reader from viewing the entirety of Lafayette's life as a consistent, solid commitment to a lifelong agenda. In reaction to this approach, LATZKO concentrates on this lifelong commitment by stressing sweeping themes rather than details in his biography, which led Albert Guerard to conclude, "It is not great history; it is not great literature" (*Books*, 2 February 1936). A reviewer for the *Boston Transcript* (1 February 1936) took a different view, terming it "one of the few biographies of Lafayette which had enduring value." The work clearly reflects the world of 1930s Europe in which the principles of Western-style democracy were themselves subject to an uncertain future.

WOODWARD was the first popular biographer affected by Gottschalk. He depicts Lafayette as doing his best with limited success to rise above "the prejudices of his class." He sees the Frenchman as "avid of fame and glory" in the negative sense those two words acquired in the 20th century in contrast to the way Lafayette's world would have understood them. Gottschalk's colleague Geoffrey Bruun complimented the work as "often surprisingly authentic" (*Books*, 20 November 1938). Historian Crane Brinton agreed, suggesting that it would give Americans "a more realistic view" of Lafayette "than is now readily available" (*Saturday Review of Literature*, 3 December 1938).

The post-World War II era brought with it an increased interest in the "star," the personality, and in this setting LOTH proposed to offer a biography presented as a "personal story" of Lafayette. The details of Lafayette's life with his wife, several possible mistresses, and a cast of famous personages from Washington to Bonaparte make that life a ready subject for a movie-style, fact-to-face study. Reviewers disagreed on Loth's success at the task, from historian Richard Brace who styled the work "a sensitive account" (*Chicago Sunday Tribune*, 25 May 1951) to Frances Winwar who saw the attempt as "weak" (*New York Times*, 10 June 1951).

The typical 20th-century French perspective on Lafayette's life is made available to English readers through a translation of LA FUYE AND BABEAU. Because of Lafayette's flight from France in 1792 to escape execution at the hands of the Jacobins and his associations with Louis-Philippe in 1830, Lafayette's role in French politics has always been a subject of controversy. Castigated by the French left and right, his life has generally appeared in such biographies as a pathetic comedy. La Fuye and Babeau's effort caused reviewer Brian Chapman to ask why they "would choose to write a biography about a man who clearly makes them want to snigger" (*Manchester Guardian*, 17 February 1956). Marcus Cunliffe expressed it more forcefully. The book's "wit and vitality are admirable: its irresponsibility is deplorable" (*The New Statesman and Nation*, 17 March 1956). Again the prevailing scholarly disdain for Lafayette appeared in Geoffrey Bruun's defense of the book: "Their aim, in which they have succeeded, is to offer a candid estimate of La Fayette's virtues and defects and by doing so to make clear how inexorably his character influenced his destiny" (*New York Times*, 30 September 1956).

As part of the bicentennial of the American Revolution, GERSON published his popular biography of Lafayette with a curious mixture of the important and trivial. Gerson reflects the quandary the modern biographer faces in reconciling the two major views of Lafayette, the traditional image of him as a hero and the more recent one seeing him as the idealistic but bumbling simpleton. F. J. Gallagher in his review of Gerson put it this way: "[He] constantly emphasizes his hero's great popularity and influence among the people of France. Why then did he accomplish so little and . . . prove such a naive and incompetent politician?" (*Best Sellers*, December 1976). In similar fashion, the biography by BERNIER reflects the same quandary. An anonymous reviewer noted, "As a French historian, this reviewer has tended to view Lafayette as mostly froth and little substance. Bernier does little to change that terse evaluation despite his affection for his subject" (*Choice*, March 1984). Though Bernier cites French archival sources in his bibliography, he does not indicate their specific impact on his interpretation, which appears similar to those by Gerson and other recent biographers. The most reviewer Thomas Schaeper could say was

that "the book fills a need for a new one-volume account of Lafayette's life in English" (*Library Journal*, 1 November 1984).

The sad truth is that none of these recent attempts in English has come anywhere near the mark of Etienne Charavay's 1898 study, *Le Général La Fayette*, which continues to be the best biography, though available only in French.

—Robert Rhodes Crout

LAMB, Charles, 1775–1834; English essayist and critic.

Ainger, Alfred, *Charles Lamb*. London and New York, Macmillan, 1882.

Anthony, Katharine, *The Lambs*. New York, Knopf, 1945; London, Hammond, 1948.

Barnett, George L., *Charles Lamb*. Boston, Twayne, 1976.

Blunden, Edmund, *Charles Lamb: His Life Recorded by His Contemporaries*. London, Leonard and Virginia Woolf, 1934.

Cecil, Lord David, *A Portrait of Charles Lamb*. London, Constable, 1983; New York, Scribner, 1984.

Courtney, Winifred F., *Young Charles Lamb 1775–1802*. New York, New York University Press, and London, Macmillan, 1982.

Craddock, Thomas, *Charles Lamb*. London, Simpkin and Marshall, 1867.

Gilchrist, Anne, *Mary Lamb*. London, W.H. Allen, and Boston, Roberts, 1883.

Johnson, Edith C., *Lamb Always Elia*. London, Methuen, 1935; Boston, M. Jones, 1936.

Lucas, E.V., *The Life of Charles Lamb* (2 vols.). London, Methuen, and New York, Putnam, 1905; revised edition, London, Methuen, 1921.

Marrs, Edwin W., Jr., *Letters of Charles and Mary Lamb*, vol. 1. Ithaca, New York, Cornell University Press, 1975.

Masson, Flora, *Charles Lamb*. London, T.C. Jack, and New York, Dodge, 1913.

May, James Lewis, *Charles Lamb: A Study*. London, G. Bless, 1934.

Morley, F.V., *Lamb Before Elia*. London, Cape, 1932.

Procter, Bryan Waller (pseudonym of Barry Cornwall), *Charles Lamb: A Memoir*. London, E. Moxon, and Boston, Roberts, 1866.

Ross, Ernest C., *The Ordeal of Bridget Elia: A Chronicle of the Lambs*. Norman, University of Oklahoma Press, 1940.

Talfourd, Sir Thomas N., *Letters of Charles Lamb, with a Sketch of His Life*. London, E. Moxon, 1837.

Talfourd, Sir Thomas N., *Final Memorials of Charles Lamb*. London, E. Moxon, 1848.

Ward, A.C., *The Frolic and the Gentle: A Centenary Study of Charles Lamb*. London, Methuen, 1934.

Williams, Orlo, *Charles Lamb*. London, Duckworth, 1934.

*

As "Elia" in the *London Magazine* in the early 1820s, Lamb became widely known as an engaging and idiosyncratic character, whose writings contained much disguised autobiography. Anecdotes about him proliferated, and were recorded in texts such as P.G. Patmore's *My Friends and Acquaintance*, Crabb Robinson's diary, and B.R. Haydon's autobiography. BLUNDEN's collection sets many of these anecdotes in a chronological series, creating a vivid picture of the shy, perverse, stammering humorist, whose originality and warmth have exerted an enduring appeal.

The first systematic biography was by TALFOURD. The *Sketch* the accompanied his 1837 edition of the letters was very slight, constrained as it was by the fact that Lamb's sister Mary was still alive. Not until after her death in 1847 did Talfourd write the *Final Memorials*, which gives a more complete account, including the traumatic experience of Mary killing her mother, and of the periods of insanity that punctuated her life after that. Talfourd emphasises the devotion with which Charles cared for his sister, and presents the "eccentric wildness" of his humour, and his "violent changes from the serious to the farcical" as a reaction against the sombre tenor of his life. A feature that still makes this biography worth consulting is the chapter describing the various members of the Lamb circle, including some less familiar figures such as Dyer, Thelwall, and Barnes.

PROCTER organises his memoir along similar lines, although he plays down the bizarre element in Lamb's conversation and makes him appear something of a Victorian sage. He does this so successfully, in fact, that he seems to have dissuaded Thomas Carlyle from his notoriously adverse assessment of Lamb as a repulsive alcoholic, with a "ghastly make-believe of wit." CRADDOCK's life is equally sober, emphasising Lamb's role in the sharply divided politics of pre-Victorian England. Craddock presents Lamb as a remarkable reconciler, maintaining friendly contact with radicals and conservatives. Even more tending toward the hagiographical is GILCHRIST's life of Mary, where again the emphasis is on the Lambs' friendships, and the pathos of the mutual devotion of the afflicted brother and sister.

AINGER provides a crisp narrative of Lamb's life, introducing an account of his writings that underlines the essayist's "acute and almost painful sympathy." He appreciates the special flavour of Lamb's retorts and puns, where the enjoyment of the wit can be "overpowered by our admiration of its beauty." In chapter five Ainger discusses the effect Lamb had on different observers. In spite of his strong championship, however, Ainger helps one to feel just what it was that so disgusted Carlyle in Lamb's "diluted insanity."

LUCAS' definitive life necessarily overshadows the work of earlier biographers. His acquaintance with Lamb's own writings, and with writings about him, has never been equalled. Like all his predecessors and successors, Lucas feels impelled to quote extensively from the letters and anecdotes, but the tact he shows in organising this material into a compelling narrative is remarkable, and leaves the reader with an impression as coherent as that of Talfourd or Procter, but with a wealth of minute particulars that Lucas' predecessors do not begin to match. The appendices (omitted from the revised edition) include an annotated list of books known or conjectured to have been possessed by Lamb: the annotations incorporated some of his marginalia. The elaborate index makes Lucas still an indispensable work of reference on Lamb and his circle.

MASSON's short book (appearing eight years after Lucas') and the centenary offerings by WARD and WILLIAMS, retell the familiar story competently, but make no claim to special attention. Another centenary study, by MAY, is confessedly subjective in its approach, and is more concerned with the writings than the life. Two other books appearing at about this time, though, develop an assessment of the writer's persona that is more sophisticated than Lamb's contemporaries, and indeed Lucas himself, had supposed. MORLEY underlines the contrast between the liveliness of the young Charles and the complex man who had to cope with the effects of his sister's insanity. He contends that the characteristic humour of "Elia" is a way of coming to terms with a reality he despaired of altering, relating this to such episodes as the failure of *John Woodvil* and the rejection of his proposal of marriage to Fanny Kelly. Lamb, Morley suggests, is one of "the most artful dodgers in literature." JOHNSON, by contrast, sees the Elian essays as the consummation of Lamb's full, rich life, the product of a mind that was "keen, subtle, and discriminating," fostered by a tradition of literary achievement in the East India Company's headquarters where Lamb was a clerk. Johnson's book, incidentally, contains one of the best accounts of Lamb's relationship with the orientalist Thomas Manning.

Charles' life is so closely bound up with Mary's that she necessarily figures largely in all the biographies. ROSS, however, was the first biographer since Gilchrist to retell the whole story from Mary's point of view. His narrative is deliberately restrained and factual. One of his main contributions is to show the precise extent of Mary's periods of illness, and he emphasises how much of her life was normal and productive.

The emphasis on Mary is followed up in ANTHONY's study, but where Ross is sober and cautious, Anthony is almost flamboyantly willing to engage in dramatic reconstruction. Her empathy with Mary sometimes produces excellent results: the retelling of the story of her mother's murder is both vivid and convincing, and where Lucas simply records the fact that David Pitcairn was the Lambs' doctor at the time of the killing, Anthony notes Pitcairn's association with Alexander Crichton, and cites this doctor's work on mental derangement to illustrate the enlightened medical practice that probably governed Mary's treatment in the asylum. Anthony points to Mary's essay on needlework as a pioneering feminist document, and makes a lively defence of her robustly independent friend Sarah Stoddart, who married the not altogether appreciative Hazlitt. Her portrayal of the relationship of brother and sister touches on the possibility of unmanageable unconscious feelings that may have contributed to Mary's continuing periods of illness. Anthony makes the further claim that Charles was in love with his young protégé Emma Isola, but as Ross showed in a brief monograph (Charles Lamb Society, 1950), this claim is difficult to substantiate.

BARNETT's study is primarily an introduction to Lamb's writings, but his many years' work in the field helps to make the short biographical section a model of its kind. He includes some new material, for example on Lamb's frustrated love for Ann Simmons.

COURTNEY's biography, covering the years up to 1802, is more ambitious than any since Lucas'. Although she makes no claim to supersede Lucas, she looks at several areas of Lamb's life that had not previously attracted much attention. She is particularly helpful in examining the political dimensions of Lamb's earlier years, when he was branded as an associate of the Jacobins, earning for himself a place in Gillray's *Anti-Jacobin* cartoon mocking the Theophilanthropist cult in revolutionary France. Courtney looks at Lamb's connection with the *Albion* newspaper, and in an appendix reprints the text of one of his contributions, an essay entitled "What is Jacobinism?" Other matters on which Courtney offers fresh insight include the significance of Lamb's stammer, the office routine of the East India House, and the characteristics of Quakerism as Lamb would have seen it in his association with Charles Lloyd. The book also retells some of the more piquant episodes of Lamb's life with great zest, for example the performance and damnation of Godwin's tragedy *Antonio*. Courtney is presently at work on a second volume.

CECIL writes a full and sensitive assessment of Lamb's personality, providing an acute analysis of how he responded to the burden of Mary's recurrent illness, conveying something of "the shimmering, shot-silk texture of Lamb's conversation," or "the strange blend of the homely and the eerie which composed the atmosphere pervading the Lambs' household." The illustrations in Cecil are particularly valuable, including a fine set on Christ's Hospital in Lamb's time. For the general reader who wants to understand the enduring appeal of Lamb's character, this is the best study.

A final word should be reserved for the edition of the letters of the Lambs undertaken by MARRS. It merits inclusion here because of the excellent biographical introduction, prepared to provide a framework for the letters themselves. Any reader who wants a plain outline of events and a factual account of the Lambs' friends and correspondents will find it most readily here. The scrupulous editing and ample annotation are themselves a major contribution to the biography of the Lambs.

—Geoffrey Carnall

LANE, (Sir) Allen, 1902–1970; English publisher.

Morpurgo, Jack E., *Allen Lane, King Penguin: A Biography.* London, Hutchinson, 1979.
Williams, W. E., *Allen Lane: A Personal Portrait.* London, Bodley Head, 1973.

*

Both biographies of Sir Allen Lane, by MORPURGO and WILLIAMS, were written in the decade after his death (and in his widow's lifetime) by former Penguin colleagues. Williams was for many years a close adviser, then Chief Editor. To underpin his independent stance, he stresses his modest Penguin pay and his own senior positions in cultural politics (he became Secretary-General of the Arts council). His 1956 account, *The Penguin Story*, gives a slanted view of the American operation and is dismissed by Morpurgo as "complacent." Williams' later book is not a full biography, but focuses on its author's experience of Penguin's early years. Ironically, it is published by the firm founded by John Lane and managed by his cousin Allen until shortly before its liquidation in 1937. It is dedicated "to my god-daughter, . . . eldest daughter of Allen Lane," who had married Morpurgo's son.

The two accounts of Lane himself are not essentially different: he emerges as energetic, opportunistic, unreliable to the point of cowardice or unfairness in his human relationships, yet spontaneously generous; his inability to develop a long-term strategy through delegation and collaboration is seen as one reason for the final rapid loss of Penguin's independence. Both authors portray him as more at home on his farm than with literature or ideas; his interest in the physical qualities of Penguins, the design and typography that became distinctive features, is traced to his inheritance from his Uncle John and the 90s tradition of the Bodley Head. (Morpurgo's opening chapter is in effect a useful brief history of that firm, to help "place" Allen Lane's rise and achievement.) Williams gives a surprisingly unclear account of the setting-up of Penguin, while the merger with Longman is not germane to his more personal memoir. Morpurgo, writing later and more fully, amplifies or corrects some well-known stories, such as the early support given to Penguin by Woolworths. (Williams' firsthand authority, however, would seem to support his account of early editorial meetings taking place in various offices and followed by general policy discussion at a Spanish restaurant, whereas Morpurgo has the manuscripts appear at table.) Morpurgo gives, properly, more generous recognition to the early editorial direction of the Pelicans by Krishna Menon, and to the later brilliance of Pevsner. Of Williams himself, he gives an elaborate and decidedly ambivalent account, recognising his industry, practical usefulness to Penguin (sometimes serving it as well as his official master), his careerism, and his failure ultimately to square up to Lane's most arbitrary actions.

Williams' account of his friend is more intimate and less frank: his discreet hints are entertainingly supplemented by Morpurgo's anecdotes of Lane's "enthralling pastime" of womanising, of his interest in astrology and reliance on graphology, and of the Lane brothers' hearty bachelor life with its devotion to the ceremonious conference centre of the communal bathroom. Morpurgo discusses the King Penguin series, Penguin in America (with details of fallings-out), the *Lady Chatterley* trial, and the internal company contests of Lane's last years. (Although not a business historian, he has useful accounts of the firm's operations and personnel.) Finally, he has a detailed though inevitably partial report of the struggle after Lane's death to determine control of the company, in which his daughter-in-law played a prominent and ultimately unsuccessful role. Lane emerges from both books as interesting for his achievements rather than his personality; the more detached and detailed account by Morpurgo will therefore be for almost all purposes the one to consult.

—Ian McGowan

LAWRENCE, D(avid) H(erbert), 1885–1930; English writer.

Aldington, Richard, *D. H. Lawrence: Portrait of a Genius, But . . . .* London, Heinemann, and New York, Duell Sloane, 1950.
Brett, Dorothy, *Lawrence and Brett: A Friendship.* Philadelphia, Lippincott, and London, M. Secker, 1933.

Burgess, Anthony, *Flame into Being: The Life and Work of D. H. Lawrence*. London, Heinemann, and New York, Arbor House, 1985.

Bynner, Witter, *Journey with Genius: Recollections and Reflections Concerning the D. H. Lawrences*. New York, Day, and London, P. Nevill, 1953.

Callow, Philip, *Son and Lover: The Young Lawrence*. London, Bodley Head, and New York, Stein and Day, 1975.

Carswell, Catherine, *The Savage Pilgrimage: A Narrative of D. H. Lawrence*. London, Chatto and Windus, and New York, Harcourt, 1932.

Chambers, Jessie, *D. H. Lawrence: A Personal Record*. London, Cape, 1935; New York, Knight, 1936; edited by J. D. Chambers, New York, Barnes and Noble, 1965.

Corke, Helen, *D. H. Lawrence: The Croydon Years*. Austin, University of Texas Press, 1965.

Delany, Paul, *D. H. Lawrence's Nightmare: The Writer and His Circle in the Years of the Great War*. New York, Basic Books, 1978; Brighton, Sussex, Harvester, 1979.

Delavenay, Emile, *D. H. Lawrence: The Man and His Work. The Formative Years 1885–1919*, translated by K. M. Delavenay. London, Heinemann, and Carbondale, Southern Illinois University Press, 1972.

Kingsmill, Hugh, *D. H. Lawrence*. London, Methuen, 1938; as *The Life of D. H. Lawrence*, New York, Dodge, 1938.

Lawrence, Ada and G. Stuart Gelder, *Young Lorenzo: Early Life of D. H. Lawrence*. Florence, Orioli, 1931; revised edition, as *Early Life of D. H. Lawrence*, London, M. Secker, 1932.

Lawrence, Frieda, *Not I, But the Wind . . . .* New York, Viking, 1934; London, Heinemann, 1935.

Luhan, Mabel Dodge, *Lorenzo in Taos*. New York, Knopf, 1932; London, Secker and Warburg, 1933.

Merrild, Knud, *A Poet and Two Painters: A Memoir of D. H. Lawrence*. London, Routledge, 1938; New York, Viking, 1939.

Meyers, Jeffrey, *D. H. Lawrence: A Biography*. New York, Knopf, and London, Macmillan, 1990.

Moore, Harry T., *The Priest of Love: A Life of D. H. Lawrence*. New York, Farrar Straus, and London, Heinemann, 1974.

Murry, John Middleton, *Son of Woman: The Story of D. H. Lawrence*. London, Cape, and New York, Cape and Smith, 1931.

Murry, John Middleton, *Reminiscences of D. H. Lawrence*. London, Cape, and New York, Holt, 1933.

Nehls, Edward, editor, *D. H. Lawrence: A Composite Biography* (3 vols.). Madison, University of Wisconsin Press, 1957–59.

Neville, George Henry, *A Memoir of D. H. Lawrence*. Cambridge and New York, Cambridge University Press, 1981.

Philippron, Guy, *D. H. Lawrence: The Man Struggling for Love 1885–1912*. Brussels, CPD and Formation Loveral, 1985.

Sagar, Keith, *The Life of D. H. Lawrence: An Illustrated Biography*. London, Methuen, and New York, Pantheon, 1980.

Sagar, Keith, *D. H. Lawrence: Life into Art*. New York, Viking, and London, Penguin, 1985.

Schneider, Daniel J., *The Consciousness of D. H. Lawrence: An Intellectual Biography*. Lawrence, University of Kansas Press, 1986.

Trease, Geoffrey, *The Phoenix and the Flame: D. H. Lawrence: A Biography*. New York, Viking, 1973; as *D. H. Lawrence: The Phoenix and the Flame*, London, Macmillan, 1973.

*

Not since the death of Byron had an English writer inspired such a flood of reminiscences as poured out shortly after D. H. Lawrence died. NEHLS' brilliantly conceived and executed *Composite Biography*, which draws on several such memoirs, remains the most balanced and helpful work on Lawrence's life to date. Nehls assembled his massive three volumes of published and unpublished accounts with great skill and scholarship, providing a battery of ancillary material in his scrupulously researched biographical and bibliographical notes and lists. The contents are artfully arranged, both chronologically and thematically, and with such unobtrusive tact that no running commentary is required. The multiple perspectives gathered in these volumes offer a broad look at Lawrence's life and speak directly to readers, without any overt editorial intrusion to manipulate their responses. A wide-ranging reference work as well as a delightful companion for browsing, this multifaceted "composite" portrait is the one biography of Lawrence that deserves to be called indispensable.

Among the many personal narratives collected in Nehls, a few deserve special notice of their own, since they often reveal more about Lawrence than do the formal biographies. Readers may wish to pursue at greater length some of the following.

The writer's sister, ADA LAWRENCE, was early in the field with her brother's early years lovingly recreated (with help from a journalist) in a pleasant, homespun patchwork made up of many authentic pieces, such as local names of places and people that were adopted or adapted in the fiction. CHAMBERS, Lawrence's childhood sweetheart, provides a more literary and even more fascinating account of the background to *Sons and Lovers*. Though her attempt to "correct" the fiction with fact is misguided, if understandable (as the model for Miriam she felt she had been unfairly represented in the novel), she supplies a wealth of factual detail as well as a beautifully presented emotional history. Her record of their shared reading has proved both a scholarly help and a salutary corrective to the idea of the uneducated miner's son. CORKE extends the story to Lawrence as a young fellow teacher, recreating, with something of a novelist's freedom, Lawrence's speech and thought.

MURRY's psychologically unbalanced polemics, with their narrowly Freudian and transparently self-exculpatory views of Lawrence as misogynist and misanthrope (bewilderingly juxtaposed with a groveling worship of Lawrence as "a hero of love"), did considerable damage to Lawrence's reputation. Murry's is the typical case of the biographer who reveals more about himself and his own neuroses and limitations than about his subject. Although Murry was an acute literary critic, even his critical estimations of Lawrence's writings are too often skewed by his personal attacks.

Murry provoked passionate retaliation from disciples and champions of Lawrence, especially CARSWELL, whose direct personal response, while unsystematic, is more balanced and attractive than Murry's. BRETT, Lawrence's most loyal disciple (she followed him to America), touchingly addresses Lawrence as "you" throughout her sometimes unreliable but always vivid and affectionate reconstruction of their friendship. The most eccentric account (apart from some of Murry's morbid ravings) comes from LUHAN, the admirer who invited Lawrence to America. Though her book about Lawrence in New Mexico misrepresents and maligns everyone, including herself, Luhan's vivacity and descriptive energy give her writing something of Lawrence's own liveliness and trenchant vigour.

Nowhere is Lawrence's writing style more evident than in the most widely appealing of these early personal responses, the splendid book by Lawrence's wife (herself portrayed unsympathetically by Brett and Luhan). FRIEDA LAWRENCE writes with powerful immediacy of their stormy but rewarding life together, from their dramatic elopement to a moving description of Lawrence's death. She persuasively rebuts what she sees as uninformed distortions of Lawrence and herself, triumphantly vindicating their marriage.

Frieda emerges well from both MERRILD's evenhanded and BYNNER's anti-genius portrayals of the Lawrences in America in the 1920s. Neither of these unsycophantic memoirists was as extensively acquainted with Lawrence or his work as their testimonies imply: Merrild was driven to the expedient of adapting passages from Lawrence's books (read after the event) as an imaginative way of representing Lawrence's "conversation," while Bynner's for the most part spiteful and envious hatchet-job appeared so long after his brief "journey" that many of his feats of memory are equally suspect. NEVILLE's 1930s memoir of pre-1912 Lawrence, well represented in Nehls, appeared in an expanded version in 1981. Neville makes an interesting late addition to the early accounts, especially in this close friend's analysis of Lawrence's sexual development, where Neville explicitly takes issue with Murry.

Of the significant biographers treating Lawrence's development up through World War I, DELAVENAY, though sadly outdated and at times mechanical, is still useful in his tracing of influences on Lawrence. Delavenay's speculations, often revealing his own ideological hobby-horses, nevertheless prompt some stimulating suggestions. CALLOW's mature, objective account is written in a novelistic style that, while pleasant to read, unfortunately belies the author's thorough research. DELANY, too, is notable for his thoroughness; his specialized study offers a detailed treatment of Lawrence during the crucial War years. PHILIPPRON's basic study to 1912 is too modest to offer much challenge, while SCHNEIDER's fancifully internalized approach results more in an introduction to Lawrence's reading and thought than in biography.

Fuller treatments of Lawrence's life come from novelists Richard ALDINGTON and Anthony BURGESS. While neither of these authors reveals anything substantially new, their novelistic approaches, along with their genuine sympathies for their subject, make for lively, interesting reading. TREASE, on the other hand, whose novelistic inventiveness makes him unreadable as well as unreliable, cannot be recommended. Nor can KINGSMILL, who is entirely derivative, despite his reputation as an iconoclast. Kingsmill does make some attempt to link the life with the works, however.

MOORE has been rightly praised for eschewing any special bias and attempting to cover all aspects of Lawrence's life in a calmly objective way. His treatment is straightforward and lucid, both structurally and stylistically. For many years Moore's has been regarded, not undeservedly, as the "standard" life. However, his work seems likely to diminish in value owing to limitations both in scholarship and insight. Moore makes no effort to link life with works, and his patient assembling of the material has a certain air of the dutiful cataloguer who is not always sure how best to select and display, analyze and interpret the multitudinous facts he has accumulated. Even so, when biographers of Lawrence (as of many another) are so often eager to demonstrate their own talents, it is refreshing to find a modest servant of his subject offering, despite some inaccuracy and misunderstanding, decently solid if sometimes stolid fare rather than flashy but insubstantial fireworks.

SAGAR's documentary Life (1980) is a thoroughly reliable guided tour, as sensible—and at times as pedestrian—as Moore's, but more sound. Sagar makes extensive use of unpublished or scattered documents, including many of Lawrence's letters. The wealth of attractive illustrations outweighs the text, however, so some may prefer Sagar's Life into Art (1985), with its judicious and critically sensitive handling of the works and the life in fruitful interaction with each other. MEYERS' recent work, on the other hand, is lurid, crass in its handling of issues like homosexuality, and tries to force interpretations that the evidence does not support.

With the exception of the Composite Biography, which is of permanent value, all these biographies, good, bad, and indifferent, will be superseded in the 1990s with the publication of the exhaustive three-volume Cambridge Biography: D. H. Lawrence 1885–1930, by David Ellis, Mark Kinkead-Weekes, and John Worthen. This will embody the latest research, with both reinterpretations and new discoveries, and will lay claim to being not only the standard but the definitive biography for many years to come. The first volume, D. H. Lawrence: The Early Years 1885–1912, will be published by Cambridge University Press in 1991.

—Michael Herbert

LEE, Robert E., 1807–1870; American Confederate general.

Anderson, Nancy S. and Dwight Anderson, *The Generals: Ulysses S. Grant and Robert E. Lee*. New York, Knopf, 1988.

Bradford, Gamaliel, *Lee the American*. Boston, Houghton Mifflin, 1912.

Cooke, John Esten, *A Life of Gen. Robert E. Lee*. New York, Appleton, 1871.

Davis, Burke, *Gray Fox: Robert E. Lee and the Civil War*. New York, Rinehart, 1956.

Dowdey, Clifford, *Lee*. Boston, Little Brown, 1965.

Freeman, Douglas Southall, *R. E. Lee: A Biography* (4 vols.). New York, Scribner, 1934–35.

Jones, John W., *Personal Reminiscences, Anecdotes and Letters of General Robert E. Lee*. New York, Appleton, 1874.

Lee, Robert E., Jr., *Recollections and Letters of General Robert E. Lee*. New York, Doubleday, 1904.

Long, Armistead L., *Memoirs of Robert E. Lee*. New York, Stoddart, 1886.

Mason, Emily V., *Popular Life of General Robert E. Lee*. Baltimore, J. Murphy, 1872.

McCabe, James D., *Life and Campaigns of General Robert E. Lee*. Atlanta, Georgia, National, 1866.

Page, Thomas N., *Robert E. Lee: Man and Soldier*. New York, Scribner, 1911.

Sanborn, Margaret, *Robert E. Lee* (2 vols.). Philadelphia, Lippincott, 1966–67.

White, Henry A., *Robert E. Lee and the Southern Confederacy*. New York, Putnam, 1897.

Winston, Robert W., *Robert E. Lee: A Biography*. New York, Morrow, 1934.

Young, James C., *Marse Robert: Knight of the Confederacy*. New York, Henkle, 1929.

*

Among the earliest biographers of Lee, McCabe, Cooke, and Mason are the least distinguished. McCABE, a Virginia writer, provides excellent newspaper commentary on Lee and useful estimates of Lee by his contemporaries, but he devotes a total of only 40 pages to the years before and after the Civil War, and even the war years constitute little more than a chronicle of the Army of Northern Virginia. Within this chronicle, Lee is clearly the hero of the Confederacy. COOKE, a Virginia novelist and Confederate staff officer, follows a similar formula. The result is an engaging book, made still useful by Cooke's personal observations of Lee during the war. Cooke also lends a critical dimension absent from McCabe by questioning some of Lee's military decisions, especially at Gettysburg. Still, Cooke's Great-Man-on-Horseback approach provides only glimpses of the real Lee. MASON, a friend of the Lee family, profited from Mrs. Lee's willingness to provide details about the general's domestic life and access to his private papers. Mason tells us far more about the antebellum and postbellum years than either McCabe or Cooke, and she is the first biographer to include excerpts from Lee's correspondence. She writes gracefully, but her grasp of military affairs is superficial.

The best early work is an unorthodox one by JONES, a Virginia theologian and Confederate chaplain who became intimate with Lee after the war. His topically organized book, with its mixture of anecdote, personal observation, tributes by contemporaries, and extended quotations from Lee's personal correspondence (made available by Mrs. Lee, to whom the book is dedicated), is less biography than source book. It includes errors of fact, and the writing is stilted, but Jones reveals many hitherto unknown aspects of Lee's life and character. With chapters entitled "His Social Character," "His Christian Character," and "His Love for Children," Jones seeks to reveal the inner man. In 1906, he assembled a second volume, *Life and Letters of R. E. Lee*, which includes some unpublished antebellum letters. The entire volume is suspect, however, because Jones altered passages in the letters—concerning such topics as slavery and Mormonism—that lessened Lee's Olympian stature.

LONG's work is not entirely his own. His publishers thought Long, a Confederate general and wartime intimate of Lee, had slighted Lee's private life for military affairs. Seeking balance, they supplemented his manuscript with portions of McCabe's biography. Long's style is lackluster, but he corrects errors and clarifies misconceptions that had found their way into earlier books. Long's achievement is all the more remarkable in that he wrote this "Memoir" over a period of 15 years after he had gone completely blind. It is far superior to the efforts of WHITE, whose book is fairly accurate but pedestrian in both style and content.

The effort of Lee's son, Robert E. LEE, Jr., is a landmark. The work has weaknesses, however. For instance, Lee begins his narrative in 1846, when his father was nearly 40 years old, and nearly two-thirds of his book focuses on the postwar years. He includes excerpts from unpublished letters, but he has edited them, like Jones, to remove any hint of prejudice or human frailty. Still, the whole is revealing. Lee's unpretentious style shows his father to be a plain, unassuming man who had greatness thrust upon him. Lee stresses his father's character, but he also portrays him as an unselfish patriot whose love of country led him to accept the South's defeat and to promote rapid restoration of the Union. Previous biographers had used Lee to embody the finest qualities of the Old South and, in essence, to justify the Lost Cause. After 1904, Lee the American, the hater of slavery and secession, is emphasized.

The next two Lee biographers, PAGE and BRADFORD, employed the new image, although Page almost miscalculated. The Virginia novelist first published his biography in 1909 under the title *Robert E. Lee: Southerner*. Two years later, he issued a much revised edition that emphasized Lee's character, the postwar years, and the nationalist theme. It is a sprightly volume, and while offering little new information about Lee, it is the first work to explore Lee's relations with the Confederate government. Bradford, a New Englander and the first non-Virginian to attempt a life of Lee, made a cottage industry out of writing biographies. He was particularly well known for his psychological approach to his subjects. Yet Bradford, whose brief, slipshod volume on Lee is filled with errors of fact and quotation, acknowledged privately that Lee remained an enigma to him. Identifying an obstacle that bedevils all Lee biographers, Bradford complained, "He secreted himself and his soul instinctively to such an extent that he left nothing that was really self-revealing."

Nothing worthy of note appeared on Lee for nearly two more decades. YOUNG's hero-worshiping biography seemed unoriginal even when published in 1929. It may be judged by Young's conclusion that Lee's "purity of thought and deed amounted to the virginal." WINSTON, a North Carolina lawyer with previous biographies of Jefferson Davis and Andrew Johnson to his credit, wrote a concise if uninspiring volume five years later. He, too, offers a romanticized interpretation of Lee "the man," and is none too careful with the accuracy of his quotations.

Yet 1934 proved a signal year for Lee biographies, for it witnessed publication of the first of FREEMAN's four volumes. From that day to this, all Lee biographers must begin with Freeman. His magisterial style sweeps the reader along on an epic journey in the life of a man, a section, and a nation. That is not to say it is a flawless journey. Freeman, a Virginia newspaper editor, offers few new insights into Lee, merely an immaculately embroidered account of what was already known. He argues that Lee's life may be summed up in three words: "Character is invincible." Yet he avoids meticulous analysis of either Lee's character or personality. Lee was "a simple soul," contends Freeman, "humble, transparent, and believing." Freeman acknowledges Lee's stature as an American hero, but he is not squeamish about resurrecting the Virginian's reputation as the noblest Confederate. Freeman admits that Lee made mistakes as a general, but he also insists that many of his mistakes resulted from admirable traits, like amiability, loyalty, and tenderness of heart. Ultimately, any evaluation of Freeman rests on his closeness—both in sympathy and birth—to his subject. As historian T. Harry Williams writes, Freeman is "a Virginia gentleman writing about a Virginia gentleman."

Only four works written since Freeman merit attention. DAVIS, a North Carolina journalist and novelist, portrays Lee as a "crafty and wily commander." To his credit, he acknowledges Lee's occasional petulance, peevishness, and temper. Yet Davis is clearly in awe of Lee, and he goes out of his way—by giving selective quotations—to protect Lee's reputation. His treatment of Lee during the Civil War years tends to degenerate into a general history of the Eastern campaigns.

DOWDEY, a Virginia journalist and novelist, provides the best single-volume biography. His style is lucid and sprightly, his scope adequately balanced between the Civil War and the rest of Lee's life. Dowdey even uses some new sources—especially a cache of antebellum letters—that add to our understanding of Lee's early years. Unfortunately, he carries the nationalist theme too far. Dowdey wants to dramatize Lee's life in the context of the "total history of the Republic," but he is not sufficiently familiar with that history to pull it off, a fact demonstrated by numerous factual errors. He also gets into trouble by presenting Lee not just as a man of moderation after the war, but as an active foe of the Radical Republicans.

Despite its length, SANBORN's work is superficial. A movie critic and translator, Sanborn, like so many others, sets out to explore Lee "the man." She claims to have based her research on unexplored manuscript collections, yet most of her references are to published sources, and many interpretations are outdated. She openly confronts the Lee family scandals, Lee's motives in marrying Mary Custis and his fondness for young women. Yet she fails to explain the forces and events that shaped Lee. She offers the best chronological balance of any writer (only a third on the Civil War), but in doing so she fails to develop adequately the eventful war years. Sanborn's prose is vivid but sometimes cumbersome. Her tone is sympathetic but too often romantic.

The most recent biography, by Nancy S. and Dwight ANDERSON (a journalist and political scientist), is actually a dual biography of Lee and Ulysses S. Grant. The chapters on Lee are littered with factual errors, and the authors tend to use their imaginations rather than historical records to dramatize events. The postwar lives of both men are dispensed with in eight pages.

Generally, the best biographies of Lee have been written by Virginians, although that, as suggested by Professor Williams, may explain their limitations, too. Curiously, those historians who have been most critical of Lee have never attempted formal biographies. Perhaps as a consequence, someone has yet to capture the essence both of Lee the legend and Lee the man.

—Daniel E. Sutherland

LEIGH, Vivien, 1913–1967; English stage and film actress.

Dent, Alan, *Vivien Leigh: A Bouquet.* London, Hamilton, 1969.

Edwards, Anne, *Vivien Leigh: A Biography.* New York, Simon and Schuster, and London, W. H. Allen, 1977.

Robyns, Gwen, *Light of a Star.* London, L. Frewin, 1968; South Brunswick, New Jersey, A. S. Barnes, 1970.

Vickers, Hugo, *Vivien Leigh.* London, Hamilton, 1988; Boston, Little Brown, 1989.

Walker, Alexander, *Vivien: The Life of Vivien Leigh.* London and New York, Weidenfeld and Nicolson, 1987.

*

ROBYNS' biography, published the year after Vivien Leigh's death, romanticizes Leigh's life by misrepresenting and oversimplifying the history of a complex and deeply troubled individual. Likewise, DENT, a British drama critic and Leigh's friend for 25 years, celebrates the actress' beauty, fame, shrewdness, ambition, and accomplishments as stage *and* film actress in a biography limited by an unwillingness to explore her private life. ("In the Spring of 1953 Vivien had a bad breakdown," he writes.) Dent's source materials are largely his observations, along with testimonials from colleagues and friends.

Written ten years following the actress' death, EDWARDS' biography, the first of note, concentrates largely on Vivien Leigh's film career. The biography begins in 1938 with the filming of the "burning of Atlanta" for *Gone With the Wind,* even before the role of Scarlett O'Hara was cast. Edwards focuses on Leigh's dual personality that made her an "extraordinary and powerful personality and a desperate unconquerable survivor," while also making her the ideal choice for Margaret Mitchell's heroine, Scarlett O'Hara, and in later years for Tennessee Williams' Blanche DuBois in *A Streetcar Named Desire.* Edwards traces Leigh's emotional battle with depression from the six-year-old convent girl left by her parents in England while they returned to India to the adult woman who leaves husband and child for career and stage idol, Laurence Olivier. Edwards pursues a correlation between the major screen roles (Scarlett O'Hara, Anna Karenina, Blanche DuBois, Cleopatra) and the emotional turmoil in Leigh's personal life. While this is not a psycho-biography, the thread of Edwards' narrative is the duality of personality noted by friends and acquaintances in a woman reputed to be the "most beautiful in the world."

Following the re-release of *Gone With the Wind* in 1968, the films' video-release in 1978, and Laurence Olivier's memoir (*Confession of an Actor,* 1982), two biographies appeared—by Walker and Vickers. These are reappraisals of Vivien Leigh's personal life and public career based on information long withheld by friends and colleagues.

Olivier's publication of his autobiography, which was often shocking in its portrayal of Leigh, proved advantageous to film-critic Alexander WALKER. Once Olivier broke the silence, so to speak, intimate friends testified "to the Vivien whom *they* had known." Walker gained access to information previously withheld by John Gliddon (Leigh's first agent), Jack Merivale (companion of her last seven years), Suzanne Farrington (her daughter), Rosemary Geddes (her secretary), friends, and colleagues. Thus, Walker was enabled to expand on Leigh's relationships with Alexander Korda, Robert Helpmann, Noel Coward, Katharine Hepburn, Peter Finch, Jack Merivale, and

Olivier himself. For the first time, Walker documents the erosion of the Oliviers' marriage as Laurence Olivier's creative (and sexual) energies soared into his becoming the "king of actors" while Vivian Leigh's career diminished into delirium and despair and an untimely death from tuberculosis at age 53. Walker makes a case for the stage (and later, screen) role of Blanche DuBois in *A Streetcar Named Desire* as being the fatal role that tipped Vivien Leigh into "madness." Nor does he ignore pressures of career, aging, manic-depression, alcohol, tuberculosis, and Olivier's success. While the public celebrated her screen performance as Blanche DuBois (for which she won an "Oscar" Award for best actress), Walker perceives in that performance the delirium and despair that echoed throughout the last seven years of her life. He makes a convincing case for Leigh's choice of screen roles in her later years (Blanche DuBois, Karen Stone, Mary Treadwell) and their relationship to her own clinical manic-depression.

VICKERS, designer Cecil Beaton's literary executor, set about a mere two years later to unravel the considerable mythology surrounding Vivien Leigh as romantic star on the one hand and manic-depressive case study on the other. Like Walker, Vickers had access to letters and diaries of relatives and friends (chiefly those of her mother Gertrude Hartley and her life-long friend, barrister Oswald Frewen). Only Laurence Olivier and his correspondence remained inaccessible.

Vickers' biography covers the same territory as Walker's, with few exceptions. All biographers agree that Leigh's abandonment at age six in a convent school in a country separated from her parents by two continents was the childhood trauma that shadowed her life. Biographical debate centers on the dramatic role(s) first revealing the manic-depressive syndrome that hindered her stage and film career and finally drove Olivier from her life. Vickers traces the manic-depressive behavior from episodes as early as the filming of *Gone With the Wind*; Walker, like the majority of biographers, cites as pivotal the stage role of Blanche DuBois, in which the character's "delirium and despair" echoed in the actress' private life. Leigh's major biographers also agree that Olivier abandoned the marriage when her instability affected his career. Both Walker and Vickers are definitive in their search for the truth about Leigh's significant stage and film career, the progressive overshadowing of her stage career by Olivier's, and the twin illnesses which impacted upon her second marriage, her career, and finally her life.

—Milly S. Barranger

LENIN, Vladimir Ilyich, 1870–1924; Russian revolutionary, founder of the Bolshevik Party.

Balabanoff, Angelica, *Impressions of Lenin*, translated by Isotta Cesari. Ann Arbor, University of Michigan Press, 1964.

Carrère D'Encausse, Hélène, *Lenin: Revolution and Power*, translated by Valence Ionescu. London and New York, Longman, 1982 (originally published by Flammarion, Paris, 1979).

Cliff, Tony, *Lenin* (4 vols.). London, Pluto Press, 1975–79.

Conquest, Robert, *V. I. Lenin*, edited by Frank Kermode. New York, Viking, 1972.

Deutscher, Isaac, *Lenin's Childhood*. London and New York, Oxford University Press, 1970.

Dutt, R. Palme, *Life and Teachings of V. I. Lenin*. New York, International Publishers, 1934.

Fischer, Louis, *The Life of Lenin*. New York, Harper, and London, Weidenfeld and Nicolson, 1964.

Gourfinkel, Nina, *Lenin*, translated by M. Thornton. New York, Grove, 1961; as *Portrait of Lenin, an Illustrated Biography*. New York, Herder, 1972 (originally published by Éditions du Seuil, Paris, 1959).

Hill, Christopher, *Lenin and the Russian Revolution*. London, Hodder and Stoughton/English University Presses, 1947; New York, Macmillan, 1950.

Hollis, Christopher, *Lenin*. Milwaukee, Bruce Publishing, 1938; with subtitle, *Portrait of a Professional Revolutionary*, London and New York, Longman, 1938.

Krupskaya, Nadezhda, *Reminiscences of Lenin*, translated by B. Isaacs. Moscow, Foreign Language Publishing, 1959.

Lewin, Moshe, *Lenin's Last Struggle*. New York, Pantheon, 1968; London, Faber, 1969.

Lukacs, Georg, *Lenin: A Study on the Unity of His Thought*, translated by N. Jacobs. London, NLB, 1950; Cambridge, Massachusetts, MIT Press, 1971 (originally published by Malik, Vienna, 1924).

Page, Stanley W., *Lenin and World Revolution*. New York, New York University Press, 1959.

Payne, Robert, *The Life and Death of Lenin*. New York, Simon and Schuster, and London, W. H. Allen, 1964.

Shub, David, *Lenin, a Biography*. New York, Doubleday, 1948; revised edition, London and Baltimore, Maryland, Penguin, 1966.

Shukman, Harold, *Lenin and the Russian Revolution*. New York, Putnam, and London, Batsford, 1967.

Theen, Rolf H. W., *Lenin: Genesis and Development of a Revolutionary*. Philadelphia, Lippincott, 1973; London, Quartet, 1974.

Treadgold, Donald W., *Lenin and His Rivals: The Struggle for Russia's Future 1898–1906*. New York, Praeger, and London, Methuen, 1955.

Trotsky, Leon, *The Young Lenin*, translated by Max Eastman. New York, Doubleday, 1972; London, Penguin, 1974.

Valentinov, Nikolay, *Encounters with Lenin*. New York, Rausen, 1953; London and New York, Oxford University Press, 1968.

Volskii, N. V., *The Early Years of Lenin*, translated and edited by Rolf H. W. Theen. Ann Arbor, University of Michigan Press, 1969.

Williams, Albert Rhys, *Lenin: The Man and His Work*. New York, Scott and Seltzer, 1919.

Zetkin, Klara, *Reminiscences of Lenin*. New York, International Publishers, 1934.

*

Often portrayed as either a power-hungry tyrant or an almost perfect saint, Lenin has been the subject of biographies that are almost always extremely partisan. In spite of this difficulty, there exists a wealth of material that allows the careful reader to come to an independent evaluation. Relatively balanced is FISCHER, who emphasizes the period of the 1917 Revolution and after. He notes that Lenin did what he had to do in order to achieve socialism. This meant Lenin abandoned ideas presented in his *State and Revolution* in order to maintain power, "but in power he was not guided by books."

Written by a Russian Social-Democrat, SHUB's work is well researched, very readable, and mainly balanced. This title contains much firsthand information that gives it a flavor missing from many other works. It comes as no surprise, of course, that the author concludes that the bulk of the Russian people were for moderate socialism and "against Lenin and against the Bourgeoisie."

In contrast, CLIFF is openly a supporter of Lenin, although not an uncritical one. This four-volume work makes no claim to "objectivity," but rather is a wealth of information and analysis written from a radical standpoint. What makes this work so interesting is that it is not an exercise in hero worship like that of DUTT, but rather a frank account of Lenin's life, including what Cliff finds to be his mistakes. Thus Lenin becomes human— neither monster nor saint. Cliff's Marxist analysis sees the degeneration of the Russian Revolution as primarily a result of its isolation, which "led to the consolidation in the power of the bureaucracy in Russia and . . . completely obliterated the communist parties as tools of revolution." As objective conditions changed, so did the consequences of Lenin's errors. The author argues that "Lenin's mistakes in 1917 were overcome by the sweep of the revolution. Now, in 1921–23, . . . each 'mistake' by the leadership was not made good by events, but accentuated by them."

LEWIN focuses only on the end of Lenin's life but takes much the same tack as Cliff. He cites Lenin's opposition to Stalin and his fight against the growing Party bureaucracy as evidence that to the end Lenin remained true to his revolutionary socialist beliefs. Further, the reader sees the human tragedy of a dying Lenin unable to stop developments that will pervert his life's work. HILL provides another friendly and well-done study that focuses on the events of 1917 and after.

Far less sympathetic treatments can be found in PAGE and SHUKMAN. For the former, Lenin was constantly "reshaping Marxism to fit his emotional structure," while the latter sees the Bolshevik leader as incapable of "settling political conflict by any other means than physical violence." Meanwhile, CONQUEST provides a brief, readable and critical introduction, as does PAYNE. A more recent scholarly study of note is to be found in THEEN.

More thoughtful than many, CARRÈRE D'ENCAUSSE offers a sophisticated interpretation of Lenin as a man who saw the "Revolution as synonymous with *Westernisation*." Clearly linking Lenin to his Russian roots, this work maintains that both the man and the movement he led can only be understood within its specific historical context.

From a Roman Catholic viewpoint, HOLLIS argues that Lenin could have been a saint if only he had believed in God. Sadly, he notes, Lenin "had none of the Christian mysticism which sees all souls as of equal value in the sight of God." Less kind is TREADGOLD, who portrays Lenin as a man who manipulated his gullible allies to serve his own evil ends. This was done by telling people "the message they wish to hear, although their own real message they reserve until their power is solid enough. This message is destruction of national independence and agricultural smallholding."

An American eyewitness to the Russian Revolution who saw Lenin as almost flawless, WILLIAMS is useful mainly as an illustration of the enthusiasm the Bolsheviks inspired in some sections of the American left. Still, Williams' volume contains many colorful stories and some interesting—if uncritical— insights into Lenin's role in the Revolution.

Equally uncritical but far more disappointing is ZETKIN, a founding member of the German Communist Party, whose work could have been a valuable source of information on Lenin. Unfortunately, it is marred by a lack of analysis and a clear tendency toward hero worship. Since this book was produced when Stalin was in control in Moscow, Zetkin may well have felt unable to be frank in her judgments.

It is no surprise that the memoirs of Lenin's wife KRUPSKAYA is completely laudatory. All the same, this volume is a basic source of information about the personal side of the Bolshevik leader. The reader learns, for example, of the shock Lenin felt when one of Marx's daughters committed suicide. The picture of a Lenin with normal feelings and doubts is a valuable correction to the view that he was an unfeeling political machine.

Another personal reminiscence of use, authored by a former associate who broke with Lenin in the 1920s, is furnished by BALABANOFF. Written decades after Lenin's death, this work finally concludes that he was a brutally ruthless man. All the same, Balabanoff pays homage to Lenin's moral courage and admits that causing suffering "ran counter to his nature."

A biased view of Lenin is contained in VALENTINOV, who nonetheless provides some worthwhile information about the emotions of Lenin as a young man. VOLSKII's work on the early Lenin has merit, although neither of these can compare with the more thoughtful treatment offered by DEUTSCHER. The latter is both highly readable and offers a number of interesting comments on the pre-revolutionary Lenin. In addition, TROTSKY's *Young Lenin* provides information by one who worked with Lenin and is marred by neither excessive zeal nor undue hostility.

A classic Communist interpretation of Lenin's thought is given in LUKACS. This slim volume maintains that "Lenin not only re-established the purity of Marxist doctrine after decades of decline and distortion by vulgar Marxism, but he developed, concretized, and matured the method itself."

By way of contrast, the more casual reader may be well served by GOURFINKEL. This title contains numerous pictures and a very brief and readable text for those who wish to acquaint themselves with only the basics of Lenin's life.

—William A. Pelz

LENNON, John, 1940–1980; English singer, songwriter, and musician.

Baird, Julia, *John Lennon, My Brother*. New York, Holt, and London, Grafton, 1988.
Blake, John, *All You Needed Was Love: The Beatles After the Beatles*. New York, Perigee Books, and Feltham, Hamlyn, 1981.

Castleman, Harry and Walter J. Podrazik, *All Together Now*. Ann Arbor, Michigan, Pierian Press, 1975.

Castleman, Harry and Walter J. Podrazik, *The Beatles Again?* Ann Arbor, Michigan, Pierian Press, 1977.

Castleman, Harry and Walter J. Podrazik, *The End of the Beatles?* Ann Arbor, Michigan, Pierian Press, 1985.

Coleman, Ray, *John Winston Lennon*. London, Sidgwick and Jackson, 1984; New York, McGraw-Hill, 1985.

Cott, Jonathan and Christine Doudna, editors, *The Ballad of John and Yoko*. New York, Doubleday, and London, M. Joseph, 1982.

Davies, Hunter, *The Beatles: The Authorized Biography*. New York, Dell, and London, Heinemann, 1968.

Fawcett, Anthony, *John Lennon: One Day at a Time*. New York, Grove, 1981.

Goldman, Albert, *The Lives of John Lennon*. New York, Morrow, and London, Bantam, 1988.

Green, John, *Dakota Days*. New York, St. Martin's, 1983.

Hampton, Wayne, *Guerrilla Minstrels: John Lennon, Joe Hill, Woody Guthrie, Bob Dylan*. Knoxville, University of Tennessee Press, 1986.

Lennon, Cynthia, *A Twist of Lennon*. London, Star Books, 1978; New York, Avon, 1980.

McCabe, Peter, *John Lennon: For the Record*. London and New York, Bantam, 1984.

Mellers, Wilfred H., *The Music of the Beatles*. New York, Schirmer, 1973.

Noebel, David A., *The Legacy of John Lennon: Charming or Harming a Generation*. Nashville, Tennessee, T. Nelson, 1982.

Norman, Philip, *Shout! The Beatles in Their Generation*. New York, Simon and Schuster, 1981; as *Shout! The True Story of the Beatles*, London, Corgi, 1982.

Ono, Yoko, *John Lennon: The Summer of 1980*. New York, Putnam, 1983; London, Chatto and Windus, 1984.

Pang, May, *Loving John*. New York, Warner, and London, Corgi, 1983.

Peebles, Andy, *The Last Lennon Tapes*. New York, Dell, 1983.

Sauceda, James, *The Literary Lennon: A Comedy of Letters*. Ann Arbor, Michigan, Pierian Press, 1983.

Schaffner, Nicholas, *Beatles Forever*. New York, McGraw-Hill, 1978.

Shotton, Pete, *John Lennon in My Life*. New York, Stein and Day, 1983; London, Hodder and Stoughton, 1984.

Solt, Andrew and Sam Egan, *Imagine: John Lennon*. New York, Macmillan, and London, Bloomsbury, 1988.

Thomson, Elizabeth and David Gutman, editors, *The Lennon Companion: 25 Years of Comment*. London, Macmillan, 1987; New York, Schirmer, 1988.

Wiener, Jon, *Come Together*. New York, Random House, 1984; London, Faber, 1985.

*

Through the completely mythic fame he achieved with the Beatles, his avant-garde (some would say eccentric) personal lifestyle, and through his art—poems, drawings, musical performances and compositions (he probably would have included his personal lifestyle in this category)—John Lennon continues to fascinate. Yet these three aspects of Lennon have yet to be worked into a complete biography. Many of the books mentioned here are not biographies but contain important biographical information for anyone who might be willing to take up the task of writing a truly scholarly biography of Lennon. Those who want to read one comprehensive biography of Lennon should choose either Goldman or Coleman, as even the other important biographies cover only periods of Lennon's life and work.

Both the Goldman and the Coleman books contain information covering Lennon's entire lifetime, both books are well researched, and both books try to discuss the three themes—fame, lifestyle, and art—I have mentioned above. GOLDMAN's book has come under heavy attack from many people who look at Lennon's murder as a martyrdom and hope to raise his life to the status of saint. Goldman has also been attacked on a more scholarly basis. His biographical style is often judgmental, and he is prone to give his own commentary when reporting biographical information. He also at times clearly states his revulsion of Lennon's lifestyle, and this has led him to negative speculation concerning Lennon's activities. For instance, if Lennon is unaccounted for for a few days in Hong Kong, Goldman fills in that he was possibly spending his time with male prostitutes. While many have tried to discredit Goldman's entire work, 95% of his research seems to be easily corroborated by existing information and sources, with some of the controversial personal information corroborated by Lennon himself on tape, on film, and in print.

COLEMAN's book is an important piece of the Lennon puzzle, especially as it provides new information on the years 1970–80. It also attempts to discuss Lennon's fame, lifestyle, and art. Though it completely avoids dealing with controversial parts of Lennon's life, it does try to give perspective to some of the outrageous and undocumented claims made by other Lennon biographers.

SHOTTON was a friend of Lennon's from boyhood through 1971, and his book gives important firsthand information about these times in Lennon's life. PANG's book gives a personal account centering on the "lost weekend" Lennon experienced for 12–18 months in Los Angeles in the mid 1970s. GREEN's volume also fills in facts from Lennon's somewhat reclusive 1975–80 period. And WIENER's well-researched biography includes important details about Lennon's political involvement from 1972–80, with special notice given to the FBI and INS files on Lennon (26 pounds of files, much still classified).

The following eight biographies, while more limited in scope, do add important details and can be used for reference and further study and to gain varying perspectives on the events of Lennon's life.

Lennon's half sister, Julia BAIRD, states that her motivation for writing *John Lennon, My Brother*, was to correct negative statements made about her family in the spate of biographies published after his murder. Though she seems to have little firsthand knowledge of her brother, she does provide some useful material. FAWCETT's book seems to hold out a promise for another book while failing to achieve its own aim. Fawcett, one of Lennon's personal assistants, instead of focusing on the time he actually spent with Lennon, unsuccessfully tries to get at the "big picture" of Lennon's career. NORMAN's *Shout*, a clear biography of the Beatles, presents coherent and researched information. THOMSON AND GUTMAN's collection of articles about Lennon and the Beatles contains important biographical sources for those interested in further research. CYNTHIA LENNON (Lennon's first wife) is fairly tough going stylistically but gives important information about the period of the late 1950s through 1967. BLAKE's work gives useful information concerning especially the years 1970–80. SCHAFFNER's *Beatles Forever* is one of the best biographies on the Beatles and contains well-documented biographical material on Lennon. It is a highly readable best-seller. Finally, DAVIES' authorized biography of the Beatles covers Lennon's life through 1967, though it contains plenty of omissions from those periods due primarily to the volume's authorizers.

A final category of material with biographical significance includes a variety of sources, from photographic essays to chronological discographies to music criticism to interviews. These books represent the grey area of biography, but they are important sources for further research and are particularly important for a figure who was a master at using the media. This category contains 12 books.

CASTLEMAN AND PODRAZIK's continuing series of Beatles discographies contains chapter by chapter biographical highlights along with dates, and could provide a useful outline for research. Their actual discographies are themselves exhaustive and potentially excellent tools. ONO's mostly photographic work does contain brief biographical comments by each of the photographers involved who worked with Lennon. SAUCEDA's critical discussion of Lennon's work, accompanied as it is with biographical facts, is also useful. SOLT AND EGAN's book of photos that coincided with the release of the film *Imagine* is also interesting in the vein of Ono's book. McCABE's book, based on *Penthouse* interviews conducted in 1971, contains an interesting biographical foreword, and the interview itself is significant. MELLER's work of Beatle criticism is one of the few serious books devoted to such. COTT AND DOUDNA's work contains interviews and biographical sketches and is a good potential research source for future explorations. PEEBLES' book documenting what appears to be Lennon's last interview for radio conducted two days before his murder is a fine book (Lennon closing the interview with a "pip, pip, toot, toot"). Including NOEBEL's work in this selection certainly places it firmly in a biographical grey area, but his point of view in discussing Lennon is different from that of most other writers. Noebel believes that what he describes as Lennon's hedonistic lifestyle and art have been terribly destructive forces in contemporary society. Though this book is stylistically almost unreadable due to logical inconsistencies and repeated unresolved digressions, there is probably work to be done in this area, since different points of view are what make biographical studies complete. And, finally, HAMPTON's analysis of Lennon from the point of view of a political scientist deals in a thoughtful way with all of the major themes of Lennon's life.

The current (1990) body of biographical material on John Lennon, though considerable, might lead some to infer, due to its incomplete state, that the subject is not material for scholarly investigation. Is Lennon's art worthy of such analysis and study? It was a question often posed to Lennon, directly and indirectly, often by the press. Carol Lynn Corbin, in *John Lennon* (1982), singles out the following bit of dialogue:

> Reporter: How do you rate your music?
> Lennon: We're not good musicians, just adequate.

> Reporter: Then why are you so popular?
> Lennon: Maybe people like adequate music.

—Craig Cotter

LEONARDO DA VINCI, 1452–1519; Italian painter, sculptor, architect, and engineer.

Brown, John W., *Life of Leonardo da Vinci.* London, W. Pickering, 1828; published with Leonardo's *Treatise on Painting,* translated by J. F. Rigaud, London, Bell, 1877.

Clark, Kenneth, *Leonardo da Vinci.* Cambridge, Cambridge University Press, and New York, Macmillan, 1939; revised edition, London and New York, Viking, 1988.

Cottler, Joseph, *Man with Wings: The Story of Leonardo da Vinci.* Boston, Little Brown, 1942; London, Harrap, 1945.

Douglas, R. Langton, *Leonardo da Vinci: His Life and His Pictures.* Chicago, University of Chicago Press, 1944.

Eissler, K. R., *Leonardo da Vinci: Psychoanalytic Notes on the Enigma.* New York, International Universities Press, 1961; London, Hogarth Press, 1962.

Franzero, Carlo Maria, *Leonardo.* London, W. H. Allen, 1969 (originally published by Rizzoli, Milan, 1968).

Freud, Sigmund, *Leonardo da Vinci: A Psychosexual Study of an Infantile Reminiscence,* translated by A. A. Brill. New York, Moffat Yard, 1916; London, K. Paul, 1922; as *Leonardo da Vinci and a Memory of His Childhood,* translated by Alan Tyson, London, Penguin, 1963; New York, Norton, 1964 (originally published as *Eine Kindheitserinnerung des Leonardo da Vinci,* Leipzig, Deutike, 1910).

Gould, Cecil, *Leonardo: The Artist and the Non-Artist.* London, Weidenfeld and Nicolson, and New York, New York Graphic Society, 1975.

Gronau, Georg, *Leonardo da Vinci,* translated by Frederic Pledge. London, Duckworth, and New York, Dutton, 1903.

Hahn, Emily, *Leonardo da Vinci.* London, E. M. Hale, and New York, Random House, 1956.

Henrie, Jacqueline, *Leonardo da Vinci: Italian Artist, Inventor, and Engineer.* Edinburgh, W. and R. Chambers, 1977.

Heydenreich, Ludwig H., *Leonardo da Vinci.* New York, Macmillan, and London, Allen and Unwin, 1954 (originally published, Berlin, 1943).

Hollyer, Belinda, *Leonardo da Vinci.* London, Macdonald, 1975.

Keele, Kenneth D., *Leonardo da Vinci and the Art of Science.* London, Priory Press, 1977.

McCurdy, Edward, *The Mind of Leonardo da Vinci.* London, Cape, and New York, Dodd Mead, 1928.

McCurdy, Edward, *Leonardo da Vinci the Artist.* London, Cape, 1933.

Monk, C. H., *Leonardo da Vinci.* London and New York, Hamlyn, 1975.

Ripley, Elizabeth, *Leonardo da Vinci, a Biography.* New York, Oxford University Press, 1952.

Rosenberg, Adolf, *Leonardo da Vinci,* translated by J. Lohse. London, Grevel, 1903 (originally published by Velhagen and Klasing, Bielefeld and Leipzig, 1898).

Rowden, Maurice, *Leonardo da Vinci.* London, Weidenfeld and Nicolson, and Chicago, Follett, 1975.

Santi, Bruno, *Leonardo da Vinci.* London, Constable, 1978 (originally published by Scala, Florence, 1975).

Taylor, Rachel Annand, *Leonardo the Florentine: A Study in Personality.* London, Richards Press, and New York, Harper, 1928.

Vallentin, Antonina, *Leonardo da Vinci: The Tragic Pursuit of Perfection,* translated by E. W. Dickes. New York, Viking, 1938; London, Gollancz, 1939.

Vasari, Giorgio, *Lives of the Artists* (2 vols.), translated by George Bull. London and New York, Penguin, 1965 (originally published as *Le Vite de piu eccellenti architetti, pittori et scultori italiani,* Florence, 1550, 1568).

Wasserman, Jack, *Leonardo.* New York, Abrams, 1975.

Zubov, V. P., *Leonardo da Vinci,* translated by David Kraus. Cambridge, Massachusetts, Harvard University Press, 1968 (originally published, Moscow, 1962).

*

The legacy of Leonardo's notebooks, in their distinctive mirror-writing, and of his extant *Treatise on Painting,* provide scholars with a wealth of material from which to glean information despite the lack of any contemporary biography of the artist. The nearest we come to this is VASARI's *"Life"* of Leonardo, which is anecdotal in the extreme, perhaps due to the lack of finished works by him available for discussion. The resulting picture of Leonardo is colorful and attractive, although its reliability as fact must remain doubtful. It is more valuable as a statement of how Vasari and his generation reacted to the diverse talents of Leonardo then as an accurate portrayal of the artist's life and works.

Leonardo's notebooks were first published in Italian (and then in translation) in 1883. Before that date relatively little was known about the artist except what was written by him in his treatise on painting, and virtually nothing was known about his discoveries in the scientific field. It seems incredible that BROWN could claim in 1828, when writing a biography that was to accompany Rigaud's translation of Leonardo's *Treatise,* that no biography of Leonardo existed. His attempt to rectify this state of affairs in fact relies heavily on the one exception to this statement, Vasari, whose anecdotes he repeats almost verbatim with little recourse to original observation.

By the beginning of the 20th century, Leonardo the artist was better understood, although he was still neglected as a scientist. The works by ROSENBERG and GRONAU, both published in English in 1903, refer to Leonardo almost exclusively in artistic terms. Both writers find it difficult to reconcile themselves to the prickly issue of his illegitimacy, but here the similarity ends. Rosenberg's biography is excessively eulogistic where Gronau's, divided according to Leonardo's principal artistic works, avoids Vasari and is dry and factual. Gronau's interpretation of Leonardo's infant vision of a kite descending upon him as a messenger sent from above to awaken his artistic genius, contrasts sharply with Sigmund Freud's analysis.

FREUD, in 1910, wrote a psychoanalytical study of Leonardo using what was to become a new method of approach to biographics of creative artists. He sees Leonardo as a victim of sexual repression, an "obsessional neurotic," whose sexual inhibitions are manifest in his art. For Freud, the kite vision refers to Leonardo's homosexuality. The novelty of Freud's approach remains thought-provoking despite subsequently proven inaccuracies. EISSLER wrote a criticism of Freud, adding to it his own conclusions that in turn take their place among the biographical material on Leonardo. Eissler's "presentation of disconnected suggestions" will not perhaps be of much interest to the general reader since they do not form the chronological sequence expected of biographies. The author's observations are, however, stimulating in their polemic stance and notable for their reliance on minute attention to the details of the facts available.

Between the wars, writers appear anxious to view Leonardo in the context of his time and surroundings instead of as an isolated figure. This approach is common to the writings of both Taylor and McCurdy, although their treatments of Leonardo prove thereafter to be divergent. TAYLOR's lyricism becomes pedantic as we are asked to imagine a field where "the blood red poppies are lavishly split everywhere . . . here a young man caught and held a girl among the vines, wild satyr and Maenad in the triumphal Renaissance day—and the love child of their fortunate moment was Leonardo da Vinci." Imaginative reconstruction of events is taken to its most fanciful limits, and Freudian issues, though touched on, are inadequately discussed. McCURDY's approach (1928), in comparison, is firmly based on Leonardo's own writings (which McCurdy studied at considerable length) and provides a wider, more thorough view of the artist. The historical background is also prominent here. A further book by McCurdy (1933) includes a useful survey of the Italian biographical material of Leonardo.

DOUGLAS' book is less comprehensive than McCurdy's. Although Douglas is swift to point out differences between our own and Renaissance attitudes in order to help the reader guard against prejudice, he can also make misleading statements that are often delivered with such assurance that they become too easy to read as fact. Much more reliable is the short biographical section in HEYDENREICH's work, which offers a balanced view of Leonardo in all his roles before providing a survey of his artistic and scientific work and a Catalogue Raisonné.

Vallentin, Cottler, and Franzero all employ a less formal method of approach, furnishing the reader with more imaginative and lively accounts of Leonardo's life. VALLENTIN grounds her work firmly in the documentary evidence available, while at the same time making an attempt to imagine specific situations in Renaissance life. The pessimistic image of Leonardo as the solitary, misunderstood genius is mercifully not overexposed and is balanced by Vallentin's probes into Leonardo's spirit of inquiry. COTTLER attempts to reconstruct not only events, but also dialogue in what becomes, to some extent, a biographical novel. Cottler's factual inaccuracy and misplaced modern dialogue are grating, while Leonardo emerges in melodramatic mystery as a "man obsessed with the mad belief that he could fly." This pitch of narrative was evidently impossible to maintain after the completion of the *Mona Lisa,* where the book ends somewhat abruptly with only slight references to Leonardo's final years in France. FRANZERO's descriptive narrative again almost creates the atmosphere of a novel. Curious use of quotations from Leonardo's notebook, and a tendency to treat Vasarian anecdote as fact, have a somewhat confusing effect.

The books by SANTI, MONK, and WASSERMAN make extensive use of colour illustrations, with short biographical sections preceding the plates. While Monk's text can be irritating, that of Santi is more factual. Wasserman's is the most satisfactory of the three, providing a wide, balanced view of Leonardo's personality and interests without overemphasising the mysterious faustian qualities made much of by other biographers.

Most biographers of Leonardo tend to discuss him too much in terms of art alone, neglecting his contribution to the field of science. The Russian V. P. ZUBOV is a refreshing exception to this rule. His 1968 publication looks at Leonardo the experimental scientist, examining the workings of his mind, his thought processes, his views on nature and mathematics, and the relationship between his scientific and creative leanings. Zubov is anxious to put Leonardo in context among the scientific thinkers of his day; for him it is wrong to "archaize or modernize" Leonardo by associating him too much with the past or with our own time, although comparisons with both are welcome and necessary. He concludes that Leonardo's individuality lay in his distance from the 16th-century norm of book learning and in his adoption of what we would term a more modern empirical approach: knowledge through experience and experiment.

Rowden and Gould, both writing in 1975, identify a need to reassess Leonardo in the light of their own generation. ROWDEN sees Leonardo as a "stranger to the Renaissance feeling" whose drive came from his curiosity and thirst for knowledge instead of the material thirst for riches, status, and security fostered by the majority of Renaissance courtiers. Contradictions in the text make this work somewhat unsatisfactory. GOULD's work is more successful, placing Leonardo's painting firmly in its artistic and historical context as a background against which the artist's life can be viewed. Gould realises his overemphasis of the artistic at the expense of the scientific elements of Leonardo's output, going some way to redress the balance in his concluding chapter, which relates one sphere of activity to the other.

For a useful and reliable approach to Leonardo's many-faceted creativity, CLARK's recently republished book is invaluable, since it encompasses most approaches to Leonardo excepting that of pure formal analysis of his paintings, which is, in any case, of little relevance to biography. "The conflict between his aesthetic and his scientific approach to painting" is highlighted here, and while the book does not offer much in the realm of historical depth, Clark's chronological presentation of Leonardo's artistic development creates an informative guide to Leonardo's preoccupations, discoveries, and inventions.

A number of biographies for the younger reader have also been published, starting with that of RIPLEY in 1952. The language of this biography is now too dated to be of interest to children today, although the book is well illustrated. HAHN's volume is unattractive in this respect and presents a confusing lack of reliable information among a welter of anecdote. A better balance is achieved in the more scientifically oriented book by KEELE, which is both informative and well illustrated. HENRIE and HOLLYER write for the younger and much younger child respectively in books designed to be read by the children themselves.

—Alison Leslie

LESSING, Doris, 1919–   ; Iranian-born English writer.

Brewster, Dorothy, *Doris Lessing*. Boston, Twayne, 1965.
Fishburn, Katherine, *Doris Lessing: Life, Work, and Criticism.* Fredericton, New Brunswick, York Press, 1987.
Knapp, Mona, *Doris Lessing*. New York, Ungar, 1984.
Sage, Lorna, *Doris Lessing*. London and New York, Methuen, 1983.

*

FISHBURN's concise, detailed, well-written biographical chapter places Lessing's works in the context of her life. Lessing herself described her early experiences as formative in her profession as writer. Her role as an outsider all her life, enabling her to become a social critic, was insured by the alienation brought on by parental influence. Fishburn describes Lessing's childhood spent with a mother who suffered in her marriage to an unrealistic husband who became a victim of his own unrealized dreams. Fishburn then examines the consequent appearance in Lessing's work of the effects of her life on the Southern Rhodesian farm. She characterizes Lessing as having learned much about racism from the apartheid society in which she was reared.

Fishburn describes later influences in Lessing's life, such as two failed marriages, Communist party membership and subsequent disenchantment with it, and Sufism, which contributes to Lessing's sense of herself as an outsider, one "in the world, not of it." Fishburn's biological chapter is a useful source for the reader who desires a brief, timely, and concisely detailed account of Lessing's life.

KNAPP gives further evidence of the interrelationship between Lessing's life and work. Her chapter entitled, "The Business of Being an Exile: Doris Lessing's Life and Works," attests to the sense of alienation Lessing herself describes as originating in her childhood. The reader may consult this chapter for a slightly fuller account of the details of Lessing's life. Knapp describes Lessing's distaste for conventional femininity, as well as her absorption of her father's idealism and sense of fantasy and justice, as originating in her childhood and lasting throughout her life. Knapp traces Lessing's early hatred of the pitiable conditions of black Rhodesians and the white colonialist mentality to her years in the veld, and shows how her hatred of formal schooling is reflected in her contempt for social conformity. Knapp intimates that the influences of Lessing's involvement in and breaking away from Marxism can be seen in the themes of her later works, when she changes from writing about the individual measured against the collective to the individual's sense of his own inner reality. Lessing's interest in Sufism in the 1960s is shown to be merely an outcome of a life-long mystical tendency, and *The Golden Notebook* is mentioned as her most "Sufi" book, as described by Lessing herself. Knapp points out that Lessing repudiated feminism as a cause in itself, however greatly she was revered by feminists for *The Golden Notebook*— a book that insists there can be no feminist cause independent of social and political ones.

Chapter One, "Africa," of SAGE's critical biography gives a detailed exposition of Lessing's early life in Africa until her departure for England. Sage skillfully weaves the biography with the writing, showing the influences on her writing of Lessing's stay in Africa. Most importantly, the five-novel sequence *Children of Violence* is described as the project by means of which Lessing planned to come to terms with her African past; it was, in Sage's words, "a study in social, sexual, and cultural vagrancy forged out of her own life-history." Displacement and change as recurrent motifs in Lessing's life and writing, as well as her concern with white domination of blacks and social processes, are shown to have their origin in her African past.

In Chapter Two, "England," Lessing's years and work in England after 1949 are described as she confronts, in Sage's words, a "dismayingly blocked, passive British post-war culture." Like her character Martha Quest in *Children of Violence*, Lessing became involved with communism. Like Raymond Williams, she tried to construct a connection between realism and revolutionary history. Eventually she left the Communist party and parted with Williams and embarked on a period in which for her, in Sage's words, "history was suddenly structureless." Sage writes that Lessing felt at home in England during the 60s because of the fragmentation and apocalyptic tone appearing in the culture. *Briefing for a Descent into Hell* (1971) and *The Summer before the Dark* (1973) were early exercises in speculative fiction, a form new to her and which she developed more fully later. Sage explains how in the 60s and early 70s, Lessing moved from realism and communism toward fantasy and science fiction.

BREWSTER offers the reader yet another view of how Lessing's life informs her fiction and other writings. For example, Martha Quest, a character in the *Children of Violence* series, is described as Lessing herself. Brewster gives particulars of Lessing's early life and her parents' endeavors in Southern Rhodesia, found in Lessing's first novel, *The Grass is Singing*, and she shows how her short novel *Eldorado* is based on her father's unrealistic dreams of wealth. Her mother, Maude Tayler, and her garden in the South African home are recalled in Lessing's story "Flavors of Exile," and Brewster relates how Lessing's recollections of the family house appear in *Going Home*, an account of Lessing's return visit to Rhodesia in 1956. To further illustrate the relation between the life and the fiction, Brewster points out that many characters from the high veld appear in Lessing's short novels and stories. *Going Home* is characterized as a personal narrative noting political and social changes occurring in Salisbury. Lessing's concern with apartheid during her 1956 visit to Rhodesia led to further writing; explicit details occurring during the visit are given and Lessing's status during the visit as a "prohibited immigrant" is described.

In light of Lessing's rich life, it is surprising that no book-length biography of her has yet been written. That is partly the result of her own wishes, according to Knapp. Knapp cites as the major autobiographical sources *Going Home* (1957) and the essays and interviews collected in *A Small Personal Voice* (1974). For the moment, the best and most reliable biographical accounts are those by Fishburn and Sage.

—Rosemarie A. Battaglia

LESSING, Gotthold Ephraim, 1729–1781; German critic and dramatist.

Brown, F. Andrew, *Gotthold Ephraim Lessing*. New York, Twayne, 1971.
Garland, Henry B., *Lessing: The Founder of Modern German Literature*. Cambridge, England, Bowes, 1937.
Rolleston, Thomas William, *The Life of Gotthold Ephraim Lessing*. London, W. Scott, 1889.
Sime, James, *Lessing: In Two Volumes with Portraits*. Boston, J. R. Osgood, and London, Trübner, 1877.
Stahr, Adolf, *The Life and Works of Gotthold Ephraim Lessing* (2 vols.), translated by E. P. Evans. Boston, W. V. Spenser, 1866.
Zimmern, Helen, *Gotthold Ephraim Lessing: His Life and Works*. London, Longman, 1878.

*

The earliest Lessing biography is by STAHR. This work is difficult to obtain and largely uncritical, replete with anecdotes of unknown origin, and lacking a critical apparatus or bibliography. Stahr summarily treats Lessing's major publications in chronological order. Books 11 and 12, "Lessing as Philosopher" and "Lessing as a Theologian," give special emphasis to viewing Lessing's work in these areas as an integrated whole, but Stahr's long and wearying text is not notably useful.

James Russell Lowell, in his chapter on Lessing from *Among my Books* (1878), writes a devastating criticism of Stahr, faulting his lack of critical judgment, his "haystacks of praise and quotation," all presented without dates, and his lack of reference to Lessing's milieu or historical traditions. Lowell himself offends in his use of the term "manly" to describe Lessing, a puzzlingly vague, unhelpful term, which may have been used first by John Stuart Blackie (*The Foreign Quarterly Review*, July 1840), when he called Lessing "the very beau-ideal of manliness."

Around the time of the centenary of Lessing's death, three further biographies appeared, the two-volume treatment of his life and works by Sime; then a largely derivative, nicely written, but undistinguished echo of Sime by Zimmern; and Rolleston's shorter volume, appearing about 12 years later. Of these books, SIME's is certainly the most commendable. It is written in a felicitous, if courtly, style, selects very good quotations from Lessing's letters to his family, exhibits careful scholarship, full treatment of necessary detail, plot summaries, and evaluations of Lessing's polemical writing. Very significant in Sime's book are *Laocoon* and *Nathan the Wise* along with the *Hamburg Dramaturgy*, reflecting the tastes of the day. Sime treats the controversies of Lessing's life as part of Lessing's abstract zeal for truth, as does Zimmern, except at the end of his life, where both agree that he was perhaps too touchy. Sime's book is full of admiration and sympathy for Lessing and ends with some very nice anecdotes. The only small advantage of ZIMMERN's text is that her chapter headings include the dates of events treated and give Lessing's age at those times. Sime analyses Lessing's major writings at much greater length.

ROLLESTON begins his text, as do the previously mentioned biographers except Stahr, with a chapter on the temper of the times. He gives some detail of Lessing's early life not present in

Sime or Zimmern, and also provides a nice summary of events in Western Europe when Lessing published his *Writings* in 1753: "that great awakening and expansion of the human spirit which manifested itself in England and Germany in the form of a literary renascence, and in France as a tremendous political convulsion." Generally, however, Rolleston's text contains no particular element to recommend it more highly than Sime's.

Aside from several shorter studies treating aspects of Lessing's writings, the next biographical text to appear was the comparatively brief book by the English critic GARLAND. Still a reliable text, which uses a four-part organization ("Lessing's Life," "Lessing as Critic," " . . . as Dramatist," and, finally, "Lessing and Religion"), it treats only major works, without bibliography or notes. Garland provides a readable narrative, which evaluates and orders the works, i.e. "dramatic apprenticeship" versus "the masterpieces," and praises the man, perhaps too highly: "Lessing's interests and activities were of the most diverse character. He remains unsurpassed in his versatility. He is that rare literary figure, the jack-of-all-trades and master of all."

The most recent, and most useful, Lessing biography, by BROWN, contains a helpful chronological table to give a quick overview of life and publications, an annotated, selected bibliography (in which Stahr, Sime, Zimmern, and Rolleston do not appear), and careful summaries of most of Lessing's writings. The style is modern and fluid, and the references are of additional assistance. The disadvantage of a text in a series such as Twayne is that biography is cursory as well as prefatory, while the necessity for summaries that inform a novice reader simply does not allow for the kind of critical study of one or several texts that might challenge an informed reader. The almost too even-handed setting forth of statements about one work after another gives little indication as to which part of Lessing's oeuvre speaks most eloquently to a contemporary audience. Although Brown's text is a useful tool, it is (intentionally) less biography than it is simply a handbook to introduce Lessing to a general readership of literate users.

Not one of the six texts currently available in English provides an authoritative, modern, and accessible biography. In no text does any difference of opinion arise concerning the major outlines of Lessing's life or his literary accomplishments. All are uniformly positive and all rather dated. Even the so-called "standard Lessing biography," by Erich Schmidt, published in German between 1884 and 1892, is soon to celebrate its own centenary. For a thorough, if quaintly phrased, biography, there is Sime; for more useful texts, Garland, and, most suitably, because also annotated, Brown.

—Erlis Glass

LEWIS, C(live) S(taples), 1898–1963; English writer.

Carpenter, Humphrey, *The Inklings: C. S. Lewis, J. R. R. Tolkien, Charles Williams, and Their Friends.* London, Allen and Unwin, and Boston, Houghton Mifflin, 1978.

Green, Roger L. and Walter Hooper, *C. S. Lewis: A Biography.* London, Collins, and New York, Harcourt, 1974.

Gresham, Douglas, *Lenten Lands: My Childhood with Joy Davidman and C. S. Lewis.* New York, Macmillan, 1988; London, Collins, 1989.

Griffin, Henry W., *Clive Staples Lewis: A Dramatic Life.* San Francisco, Harper, 1986; as *C. S. Lewis: The Authentic Voice,* Tring, Lion, 1988.

Hooper, Walter, *Through Joy and Beyond: A Pictoral Biography of C. S. Lewis.* New York, Macmillan, and London, Collier Macmillan, 1982.

Sayer, George, *Jack: C. S. Lewis and His Times.* San Francisco, Harper, and London, Macmillan, 1988.

Wilson, A. N., *C. S. Lewis: A Biography.* New York, Norton, and London, Collins, 1990.

*

It is now nearly 30 years since C. S. Lewis died, and during this time his critics have managed to be as prolific as he himself was. But a distinguishing characteristic of nearly all work on Lewis is that it tends to center as much on the man as it does on his writings. What was true while Lewis was alive is true even now—the figure behind such creations as Uncle Screwtape and Aslan is as absorbing as *Screwtape* and the *Chronicles* themselves are. As A. N. Wilson (see below) notes, "a taste for Lewis is, in large part, a taste for reading about him." The result is that biographical sketches abound, and so before turning to the main-line biographies it is worthwhile acknowledging the important material on the fringes.

Three collections of reminiscences are worth looking at: Jocelyn Gibb's *Light on Lewis* (London, 1965) includes essays by Owen Barfield and Neville Coghill, while James T. Como's *C. S. Lewis at the Breakfast Table* (New York, 1979), a much larger collection, features sketches by two biographers (Hooper and Sayer, see below), as well as Hooper's important bibliography of Lewis' work. *In Search of C. S. Lewis*, edited by Stephen Schofield (South Plainfield, New Jersey, 1983), again featuring Sayer as well as Malcolm Muggeridge, consists of shorter entries, some of which are interviews and letters. None of these collections should be ignored.

Short biographical sketches such as those in Chad Walsh's *Apostle to the Skeptics* (New York, 1949) and Richard B. Cunningham's *C. S. Lewis: Defender of the Faith* (Philadelphia, 1967) have been superseded in later critical works, among them Margaret Patterson Hannay's *C. S. Lewis* (New York, 1981), which includes a decent though broadly construed chronology, and Jon Peters' *C.S. Lewis: The Man and his Achievement* (Exeter, 1985). The thoroughgoing Lewis reader will look to Hooper's *They Stand Together* (London, 1979), an incomplete collection of Lewis' correspondence with Arthur Greeves, or to Clyde S. Kilby's and Marjory Lamp Mead's *Brothers and Friends* (San Francisco, 1982)—the diaries of Lewis' brother, Major Warren Hamilton Lewis. Kilby and Mead include a scrupulous chronology of Warren's life, which was inextricably linked, as Lewis readers know, to Lewis' own. Before Hooper's collection appeared, Warren published selected letters along with his own memoir in *Letters of C. S. Lewis* (New York, 1966). The biographical sketch, greatly reduced by Christopher Derrick from a manuscript entitled "C. S. Lewis: A Biography," has proven to be an important source for later biographers.

Roger L. Green was a reader of the Narnia books during their composition and was appointed by Lewis to be his biographer.

Walter Hooper, who served as Lewis' personal secretary in the months before his death, had designs on writing a biography of his own. GREEN AND HOOPER collaborated to produce the first biography, and a good one at that, which draws extensively from Lewis' autobiographical *Surprised by Joy* (London, 1956), from his letters, and from what is known as *The Lewis Papers* (a family archives of sorts prepared by Warren). Green and Hooper are careful to acknowledge what sources they have to work with and insist that theirs is *a* biography, not a conclusive one; and they are right about this. As insiders, they give close attention to Lewis' personality but never rid themselves of that *insider-ness* that tends to leave a reader suspicious. Such suspicions are not unfounded, and readers do well to consult Sayer or Wilson along with Green and Hooper's volume. Carefully attuned, though, to such things as the topical nature of Lewis' fiction as well as to the development of his intellectual career, Green and Hooper have a good biography to their credit—one written with an eye and ear for literary sensitivity.

HOOPER's 1982 biography, pictorial and anecdotal, is a quickly-moving account, one central strength of which is its ability to show Lewis' wit and sense of humor. Hooper provides here a shorter and less involved version of his and Green's earlier work, and those who have read Green and Hooper will hear echoes and see almost duplicate passages in this later book. But here is a quicker, easier, more impressionistic entry into Lewis' life.

Among the most enjoyable studies on Lewis is one by an established biographer, CARPENTER, whose book, while not concerned exclusively with Lewis, recognizes him as the hub of that intriguing circle of friends to which Owen Barfield, J. R. R. Tolkien, and Charles Williams belonged. Carpenter's sensible book admittedly strays from pure biography insofar as it attempts to write a collective one, but seeing Lewis from the perspective of a biographical approach into the lives of his friends is an illuminating vantage point indeed. The Lewis that Carpenter constructs in *The Inklings* is not at all inaccurate, at least according to Owen Barfield's testimony in his recent *Owen Barfield on C. S. Lewis* (Middletown, 1989)—another book on the fringe of biography worth the time it takes to read.

In one chapter Carpenter tries to imagine and reconstruct a meeting of the Inklings. Such is the dramatic nature of GRIFFIN's endeavor—a long para-biography that is altogether worth reading, though not the first, second, or even third place the reader interested in biography proper should turn. Wilson finds several inaccuracies in Griffin, but says nothing about what a more imaginative approach is capable of apprehending. Griffin's work is not ungrounded, and the mimetic (or, one might say, episodic and cinematic) quality of the "dramatic life" has the effect of making Lewis' own concerns very present—of letting Lewis speak, as it were, for himself. Griffin, more than any other biographer, brings to the fore Lewis' social awareness and generosity as well as his popularity in the United States. This is, in many ways, a distinctly American biography, the emphases of which are social, religious, and intellectual.

GRESHAM, the younger of Lewis' stepsons, prides himself on having waited for the distance of time to lend his book the prudence that those published immediately after Lewis' death presumably lack. But the truth is that apart from Lewis' name on the cover, Gresham's book wants appeal. It is, strictly speaking about Gresham himself, whose life is far less interesting than Lewis' and certainly not worth writing about except for the fact that Lewis had a part in it. The Lewis scholar should pay his homage, but the general reader may pass this book by.

SAYER seriously begins the task of Lewis demystification. Sayer's telling transcriptions of interviews with Warren, as well as his use of Warren's million-word diary (which Green and Hooper did not have at their disposal), mark his work as an important sequel to previous biographies. A former student of Lewis', Sayer also heeds Warren's criticism of *Surprised by Joy*, implicitly recognizing that the only genre more tenuous than biography is autobiography. We find in Sayer the prudence of a dispassioned approach to the odd and inexplicable relationship Lewis had with his father as well as to the "mystery," as Muggeridge calls it, of Lewis' sexuality—a topic Green and Hooper have been criticized for treating too delicately. Although there is new biographical material available that Sayer did not have access to, and that Wilson could have but did not use, still Sayer's is arguably the most balanced, most reliable biography written.

WILSON takes the task of demystification even further, and his biography, though not without its share of errors, is, on top of being an important account, a good read plain and simple. Clearly, his emphasis on the humanity rather than the divinity of Lewis is a reaction to earlier efforts at mythologizing. Wilson objects to Hooper's insistence on the perpetual virginity of Lewis, claiming that we do Lewis a disservice if we make him into a "plaster saint." Consequently, Wilson has no trouble maintaining that Lewis and Mrs. Moore were lovers and that Lewis and Joy Davidman were, shall we say, more than good friends before they were married (though this latter is based on a dubious oral account). He also gives a sensible account of the famous Anscomb encounter, finding himself under no compulsion to believe that Lewis actually won this debate. And with Sayer, Wilson distrusts Lewis' interpretation of his own early life in *Surprised by Joy*.

But Wilson considers it part of his task to pass literary judgment and to analyze Lewis' life. He offers some rather confident but shaky evaluations of Lewis' fiction and makes little effort to extricate himself from a tendency to psychoanalyze (often almost laughably) Lewis' family life—specifically, the death early in Lewis' life of his mother, and its effect on his subsequent relations with other women, as well as the friction between Lewis and his father. This is territory across which Sayer treads more cautiously, and a number of readers will no doubt think that Wilson has done irreparable damage to Lewis' reputation. Still, the book is a welcome addition to the corpus. Wilson's greatest strength is not as a biographer, critic, or psychoanalyst, but as a writer—as a spinner of a very good, if occasionally erroneous, tale.

The authoritative biography that Green and Hooper claimed not to have written remains unwritten, because in truth no such thing exists. Since the work of Sayer and Wilson we may hope that something approaching an authoritative collective body of biographies exists; we are fast approaching the time when "the later the better" will not in any sense be true, since the living memory of Lewis will soon lie buried with him.

—Jason R. Peters

LEWIS, Sinclair, 1885–1951; American writer.

Lewis, Grace Hegger, *With Love From Gracie: Sinclair Lewis 1912–25.* New York, Harcourt, 1955.

Schorer, Mark, *Sinclair Lewis: An American Life.* New York, McGraw-Hill, and London, Heinemann, 1961.

Sheean, Vincent, *Dorothy and Red.* Boston, Houghton Mifflin, 1963; London, Heinemann, 1964.

Van Doren, Carl, *Sinclair Lewis: A Biographical Sketch.* New York, Doubleday, 1933.

*

During his lifetime Sinclair Lewis attracted much notoriety, but no full-scale biography appeared until Schorer's monumental volume. Early delineations (really promotional booklets) include *The Significance of Sinclair Lewis* (1922) by Stuart Pratt Sherman and *Sinclair Lewis* (1925) by Oliver Harrison (actually Lewis' Harcourt editor and bosom friend, Harrison Smith, who in 1952 edited *From Main Street to Stockholm: Letters of Sinclair Lewis 1919–30*). VAN DOREN, another valued Lewis ally, exalts the novelist as part of recent history; the second half of the book, descriptive bibliography by Harvey Taylor, is neither complete nor always accurate. Only about a third of Van Doren's section (20 pages) is biographical, profiling in dulcet prose "Red" Lewis' appetite for life, Sauk Centre background, career at Yale, and early free-lancing adventures.

Pestered by reporters and scholars after her first husband's death, Grace LEWIS decided to write (rather rewrite) in the form of a factual domestic memoir her earlier novel of their union, *Half a Loaf* (1931). Besides recalling once more scenes of her marriage; perusing her photographs, letters, and manuscripts (now at the University of Texas); and talking to family, friends, and acquaintances, the memoirist also mailed out questionnaires to persons who remembered the Lewises as a couple. In spritely first-person she retells of the first meeting in a New York freight elevator (she working for *Vogue*, he for Doran Company), their marriage on the strength of his first novel, *Our Mr. Wrenn* (1914), the beginning of his fabulous success with *Main Street* (1920), and their later separation and divorce. Particularly fascinating is her depiction of Lewis' overbearing father, herself as model for the heroine of *Main Street*, the excitement over *Babbitt*, the Lewis-de Kruif estrangement, Lewis' failure to write his contemplated labor novel, and the foreshadowing of his serious drinking problem. Forced by their roving life to throw away many of her husband's letters to her about his writing, she nevertheless gives memorable glimpses of Lewis at work (obsessive) and at play (Fool to Her Majesty). But as the volatile novelist became increasingly self-centered, demanding, and cold, he was unable to give his fashion-conscious and continental-minded spouse the candlelight gentility and stability she craved. Mingled with her chic little poses and decorative name-dropping are touches of bitterness, even spite. If the biographer's book memorializes Sinclair Lewis, it also pays tribute to their son, Wells (killed in World War II), and to Gracie herself (wounded on the marital battlefield by a writer to whose development she vitally contributed).

SCHORER's 687-page "official" biography, prodigiously researched and artfully written, is indispensable, required reading for Lewis scholars and the general reader interested in Lewis'

life. Given first and exclusive access to all the Sinclair Lewis papers (now at Yale University), the noted University of California professor-novelist-critic (himself from a small midwestern town) spent more than nine years writing his massive biography, "often a dogged process, full of ennui and pain. . . ." Schorer scrutinized Lewis' books, stories, articles, manuscripts, letters, diaries, and other personal papers. Besides conferring with Grace Hegger Lewis, Dorothy Thompson (Lewis' second wife), and Marcella Powers (the young companion of Lewis' later years), Schorer read everything available on Lewis as writer, worker, student, walker, traveler, lover, husband, father, mimic, lecturer, teacher, actor, drinker, friend, foe, and much more. In converting thousands of particulars into illuminating and moving narrative, Schorer re-creates not only the tragic curve of Lewis' life—small town, college, climb, success, decline, fall—but also the portrait of an era. Though Lewis often insisted that his village boyhood had been had been more or less typical, Schorer brilliantly maintains otherwise. The conflict of values in Lewis' life and art, Schorer argues, stems from his always having felt himself an outsider, gawky, lonely, ugly, the butt of jokes. His early exhibitionism—buffoonery, reading, writing—began as a defense against rejection, especially by his father, brother Claude, and peers. Because Lewis wrote little serious subjective autobiography, Schorer fails to render his inner world adequately. In the end, the biographer ties his view of the writer's appallingly bleak and barren interior to the words the doctor in Italy wrote on Sinclair Lewis' death certificate: "paralysis of the heart." Despite Schorer's compensatory underestimation of a perhaps once overvalued Lewis; despite his New Critical patronizing of Lewis the writer and his urbane caricaturing of Lewis the man; despite his possibly fixing on Lewis' ugliness and oddities in order to exorcise his own demons; and despite his book's inevitable errors of recollection and transmission, Schorer's big study has not only stimulated new interest in Sinclair Lewis but has become itself an impressive contribution to American literary biography.

In the late 1950s the celebrated political journalist Dorothy Thompson, reviewing her papers, anticipated writing her autobiography, with adequate coverage, of course, of her disastrous marriage to Sinclair Lewis from 1928 to 1942. After her death in 1961, SHEEAN, old hand at popular biography and longtime friend of both parties, read Dorothy's papers and her penciled emendations (now at Syracuse University). Limiting himself (with effort) to Dorothy and Red's romantic courtship and bathetic union, Sheean quotes without much question or comment lengthy extracts from Dorothy's private diaries and from her letters sent and unsent. Thus Sheean reveals more details about this marriage made in hell than does Schorer, to whom Sheean refers often and with respect. Where Schorer quotes judiciously from Red Lewis' Caravan-in-England articles in the *New York Herald Tribune*, Sheean transcribes whole sections of Dorothy's honeymoon diary. Because she is represented by many entries from her intermittant diaries and emotional letters (and Lewis only by a few scrappy letters to Dorothy) Sheean's double portrait is conspicuously imbalanced and partisan. The more Dorothy (as junketing prima donna) fulfills her "historic mission," the more Red (as writer in decline) takes to drink and vile behavior. Of particular interest is Sheean's notion that America's "greatest" novelist and America's "greatest" journalist worshipped the images of love, making avowals in absentia, and finding ways to stay apart. Apparently no two witnesses agree about the ten-day party Dorothy threw in Semmering, Austria: Schorer says that a disgusted Red left alone; he also says that the party wound up in Hungary. Sheean says that Lewis went off to Italy with Dorothy's sister; and Dorothy's diary reveals that she, in one of her Sapphic moods, wound up with the *mondaine* Baroness Hatvany. Most disconcerting, however, is Sheean's lax research. He dates one undated letter, for example, as written either a month earlier or a year later, "depending on when Wells passed his entrance examination at Harvard." Impenetrable mystery! Elsewhere he writes that Harry Maule left Doubleday for Random House "in (about) 1940." As Sheean popped in and out of the lives of Dorothy and Red, so he pops in and out of this biography, casually matching his recollections against Dorothy's utterances.

—Martin Bucco

LINCOLN, Abraham, 1809–1865; American political leader, 16th president of the United States.

Barton, William E., *The Life of Abraham Lincoln* (2 vols.). Indianapolis, Bobbs-Merrill, and London, Arrowsmith, 1925.

Beveridge, Albert J., *Abraham Lincoln 1809–58* (2 vols.). Boston, Houghton Mifflin, and London, Gollancz, 1928.

Charnwood, 1st Baron (Godfrey Rathbone Benson), *Abraham Lincoln*. London, Constable, and New York, Holt, 1916.

Herndon, William H. and Jesse W. Weik, *Herndon's Lincoln: The True Story of a Great Life* (3 vols.). Chicago, Belford Clarke, 1889.

Holland, Josiah G., *Life of Abraham Lincoln*. Springfield, Massachusetts, G. Bill, 1866.

Lamon, Ward H., *The Life of Abraham Lincoln: From His Birth to His Inaugeration as President*. Boston, J. R. Osgood, 1872.

Luthin, Reinhard H., *The Real Abraham Lincoln, a Complete One-Volume History of His Life and Times*. Englewood Cliffs, New Jersey, Prentice-Hall, 1960.

Masters, Edgar Lee, *Lincoln the Man*. New York, Dodd Mead, and London, Cassell, 1931.

Nicolay, John G. and John Hay, *Abraham Lincoln: A History* (10 vols.). New York, Century, 1890.

Oates, Stephen B., *With Malice Toward None: The Life of Lincoln*. New York, Harper, 1977; London, Allen and Unwin, 1978.

Randall, James G., *Lincoln, the President* (4 vols.). New York, Dodd Mead, and London, Eyre and Spottiswoode, 1945–55.

Sandburg, Carl, *Abraham Lincoln: The Prairie Years* (2 vols.). New York, Harcourt, and London, Cape, 1926.

Sandburg, Carl, *Abraham Lincoln: The War Years* (4 vols.). New York, Harcourt, 1939.

Stephenson, Nathaniel W., *Lincoln: An Account of His Personal Life*. Indianapolis, Bobbs-Merrill, 1922.

Tarbell, Ida M., *The Early Life of Abraham Lincoln*. New York, McClure, 1896.

Tarbell, Ida M., *The Life of Abraham Lincoln*. New York, Doubleday, 1900.

Thomas, Benjamin P., *Portrait for Posterity: Lincoln and His Biographers*. New Brunswick, New Jersey, Rutgers University Press, 1947.

Thomas, Benjamin P., *Abraham Lincoln: A Biography*. New York, Knopf, 1952; London, Eyre and Spottiswoode, 1953.

*

Because of the impact Abraham Lincoln had on the United States as president during the Civil War, the impact he had on the world as the emancipator of the slaves, and the final shock of his assassination, more words have been written about him than about any individual other than Jesus or possibly Napoleon. Despite this mass of literature, much of the information about him is shrouded in myth and folklore. Over the past 125 years, the social issues of the times have influenced the viewpoints of many of his biographers, as have the accessibility to people who were intimately acquainted with him and the availability of Lincoln document collections.

Before Lincoln's assassination, campaign biographies predominated. The little that was known about his background and early life was supplied by Lincoln himself in three short autobiographical statements. It was not until after his death that HOLLAND, a New England editor and publisher, issued the first serious biography. It was a widely read, laudatory work, and set the pattern for many future biographies.

Herndon, who had been Lincoln's law partner, objected to Holland's depiction of Lincoln as a "religious man," and he soon began to gather data on Lincoln from various sources, many of them unreliable, for his own biography. In 1869, LAMON, an Illinois lawyer and friend of Lincoln, was able to aquire transcripts and notes from Herndon for a biography of his own. Lamon's *Life*, ghost-written by Chauncy Black, Lamon's law partner's son, not only reflects some of Herndon's personal bias from the notes, but betrays Black's own antagonism toward the Republicans and Lincoln.

In 1889, HERNDON pulled his notes and lectures together, and, with Jesse W. Weik, was able to publish his biography. Herndon's work unfortunately did nothing to improve the image of Lincoln's early life as it had been misrepresented and, in fact, created more misconceptions by overemphasizing the Ann Rutledge story and by denigrating Lincoln's wife and marriage. Herndon's redeeming value, however, is his insight into Lincoln's personal tastes and habits and the development of Lincoln's political life during the period before his election to the presidency.

Within the year NICOLAY AND HAY brought out their 10-volume biography. This massive work was the high point of Lincoln scholarship before the turn of the century. Since Nicolay and Hay were secretaries to Lincoln during the Civil War, their work is openly partisan and emphasizes Lincoln's role in the political and administrative history of the time. It is still a basic source for Lincoln scholars.

During the next few years TARBELL wrote two successful Lincoln biographies. Tarbell was a journalist whose work stemmed from articles she wrote for *McClure's Magazine*. She had to do some of her own research since she was one of the first biographers who had not known Lincoln personally.

Lord CHARNWOOD's one-volume work has been noted for its readability, analysis, and fairness, and was declared by many to have been the best one-volume biography of its time. Its drawback, however, is its inclusion of many spurious quotations and anecdotes derived from earlier works such as Herndon's.

The 1920s and 30s brought forth several new biographies of note, by Baron, Beveridge, Stephenson, and Masters. A leading trend in biography at that time was "debunking," and each one contributed to this theme in some way. BARTON was a Lincoln collector and authority on Lincoln's paternity, lineage, and religion, but he is out of his depth when discussing matters after 1860. STEPHENSON was a scholar and professional historian, and in many ways the first modern psycho-historian. While his book was popular at the time of its publication, it is little read today. BEVERAGE was a U.S. Senator from Indiana who held strong imperialist and reformist views. He had access to the Herndon papers, and while he tended to accept some of Herndon's erroneous judgments, his biography is still one of the better for Lincoln's early political life. The most "debunking" book of the period, however, was by MASTERS. Masters was a lawyer, poet, and Democrat with strong political prejudices. He was outright hostile to Lincoln and rude in his description of the man. Although the book received much criticism from Lincoln admirers and scholars, it still rates recognition if one is looking for a less laudatory view of Lincoln.

When the topic of Lincoln biographies is brought up, most people think of the sizable six-volume work by SANDBURG. The biography, in reality, consists of two works, each somewhat different in approach. *The Prairie Years* expounds a lyric and somewhat impressionistic approach to the man. The second group, *The War Years*, is more documentary in its approach and reflects the more pragmatic aspects of Lincoln's life. Sandburg later published a one-volume condensation of this work.

THOMAS' excellent analytic work (1947) reviews the various biographers of Lincoln and examines how their approaches reflected the needs of the time and how they utilized Lincoln as a symbol. In 1952, with this background, he published his own one-volume biography, which has lasted through the years as an excellent, readable, and balanced account of Lincoln's life. Thomas was a Lincoln scholar and a trained historian who lived in Lincoln's home town. He had access to modern research resources and was able to translate the flavor of the land and community from whence Lincoln came. The book was immensely popular, and it supplanted the lyrical one-volume biography by Lord Charnwood.

Lincoln scholarship received its biggest conducement with the publication of the *Collected Works* (edited by R. P. Basler, 9 vols., 1953–55). This monumental and scholarly collection, and its supplement, is the definitive edition of Lincoln's letters, state papers, and miscellaneous writings. It contains materials hitherto unavailable to early scholars and started off a new period of scholarly research and analysis on Lincoln. The accurate texts and meticulous annotations not only provide many new insights into his life and activities but also set a standard for historical research that has influenced other works of this kind.

One of the more distinguished and well-researched works to result from the new data is the four-volume study by RANDALL. Randall is probably the most distinguished of all Lincoln scholars to write a biography, and historians rate his as the best on the years of Lincoln's Presidency.

LUTHIN's one-volume, comprehensive biography, despite its lack of access to the late spate of Civil War research, is still worth reading. The biography was painstakingly researched and contains one of the most extensive bibliographies of pre-1960 literature on Lincoln. It is a collector's and scholar's delight. The narrative is straightforward and factual but is in no way as eloquent as the Thomas or Sandburg volumes. In Luthin's conservative eyes, Lincoln leaned toward conservatism.

OATES' new, definitive, one-volume biography has caught the attention of the public and scholars alike. Writing from a modern historian's point of view, Oates benefits from having access to modern documentation and the recent analysis and revaluation of Lincoln and his role brought on by the Civil War Centennial and the Civil Rights Movement. Oates was not a Lincoln admirer to begin with, so he did not bring with him the baggage of previous biographers. An experienced biographer, he is able to produce a very readable one-volume biography that is well balanced and interpretive in all aspects of Lincoln's life. His work is written in a style that appeals to scholar, Lincoln buff, and layman alike.

Lincoln is an exceptional person in American history and deserves a fair and serious reading. The general reader will prefer the readability of Thomas; more adventurous readers will gain much from Oates. Lincoln buffs will like the bibliography in Luthin. Scholars will prefer the Randall volumes. With these beginnings, most readers will be led back to some of the earlier and historical biographies as well as the vast amount of other literature dealing with Lincoln and the Civil War.

—Robert James Havlik

LINCOLN, Mary Todd, 1818–1882; wife of Abraham Lincoln.

Baker, Jean H., *Mary Todd Lincoln: A Biography*. New York and London, Norton, 1987.

Evans, William A., *Mrs. Abraham Lincoln: A Study of Her Personality and Her Influence on Lincoln*. New York, Knopf, 1932.

Helm, Katherine, *The True Story of Mary, Wife of Lincoln*. New York and London, Harper, 1928.

Keckley, Elizabeth, *Behind the Scenes; or, Thirty Years a Slave and Four Years in the White House*. New York, G. W. Carleton, 1868.

Neely, Mark E., Jr. and R. Gerald McMurtry, *The Insanity File: The Case of Mary Todd Lincoln*. Carbondale, Southern Illinois University Press, 1986.

Randall, Ruth P., *Mary Lincoln: Biography of a Marriage*. Boston, Little Brown, 1953.

Sandburg, Carl and Paul M. Angle, *Mary Lincoln: Wife and Widow*. New York, Harcourt, 1932.

Turner, Justin G. and Linda Levitt Turner, *Mary Todd Lincoln: Her Life and Letters*. New York, Knopf, 1972.

*

Mary Todd Lincoln was one of the most tragic and misunderstood wives of a United States president. Her background and personality created much controversy during her lifetime, and controversy continued even after her death. With the resurgence of interest in her life, stimulated by the publication of her letters in 1972, a clearer, more rational view of this complex and fascinating woman is now coming forward.

During Lincoln's presidency, criticism of Mary's way of dress and her need for attention and approval, compounded by the tragic death of a son and the later assassination of her husband, all added grist to the rumor mills and created poor publicity. In 1868, after Lincoln's death, KECKLEY published a ghost-written memoir that revealed letters and confidences from Mary Lincoln, all of which contributed to her poor image. Mary's subsequent commitment to a private sanitarium by her son, in 1875, only added to her misery. Even more disastrous to her reputation was the publication, seven years after her death, of *Herndon's Lincoln*, by William H. Herndon and Jesse W. Weik (Chicago, 1889). Herndon, who was Lincoln's law partner, and Mary had a mutual dislike for each other, and his book did much to deprecate her and her marriage to the president.

It was not until 1928 that a defense of Mary Lincoln was written, by HELM. Helm was the daughter of Mary Lincoln's half sister, Emily Helm, on whose diary much of the work is based. Her book, while revealing some important insights into Mary Lincoln's family life, is not altogether reliable, however, because of Emily's Southern sympathies and her feelings against the president during the Civil War. Her daughter's book, however, tries to emphasize the genteelness of Mary Lincoln's Kentucky background.

EVANS, a medical doctor, attempted a clinical study of Mary's personality and an etiology of her illnesses. SANDBURG AND ANGLE's brief book contains some of Mary Lincoln's letters that were new to historians at that time. The first scholarly volume on Mary Lincoln was by RANDALL, the wife of the eminent Lincoln scholar, Dr. James G. Randall. Her long book, though well documented, is overly protective and determined to prove that Abraham and Mary were a devoted married couple.

The greatest contribution to research on Mary Lincoln was the publication of her letters in 1972 by TURNER. The book contains over 600 letters, with numerous footnotes interspersed between thoughtful and readable comments. The thoroughness of the collection is indicated by the fact that few new letters have appeared since its publication. Turner's volume stimulated numerous new works and interests in Mary Lincoln. Notable are several plays treating incidents in her life, as well as studies of her insanity trial, the best of which is by NEELY AND Mc-MURTRY.

The best new biography to make use of the material Turner published is by BAKER. Baker brings many talents to her work. Her interests are both in the history of women and local history, and she is thus able to interpret Mary Lincoln as a unique woman in her time and place, as she was. In light of this new, readable book, scholars will need to reassess the real effect Mary had on her husband. For the non-scholar or Lincoln buff, the book will provide a fresh modern approach to a much maligned woman.

—Robert James Havlik

LINDBERGH, Charles Augustus, 1902–1974; American aviator.

Davis, Kenneth S., *The Hero: Charles A. Lindbergh and the American Dream*. New York, Doubleday, 1959; London, Longman, 1960.

Luckett, Perry D., *Charles A. Lindbergh: A Bio-Bibliography*. New York and London, Greenwood, 1986.

Mosley, Leonard, *Lindbergh: A Biography*. New York, Doubleday, and London, Hodder and Stoughton, 1976.

Ross, Walter S., *The Last Hero: Charles A. Lindbergh*. New York, Harper, 1968; revised edition, 1976.

*

Anyone interested in learning about the life of Charles Lindbergh would be well advised to begin with LUCKETT's book. It contains both a detailed chronology and a concise biography. In addition Luckett provides an extensive bibliography that lists Lindbergh's own autobiographical writings (and those of his wife) along with a great many works about him by others. In the latter category the reader will find books that deal with restricted aspects of the man's life, such as the Paris flight and the kidnapping of his son, but in this essay I consider only the three comprehensive biographies that have appeared thus far. For the time being they contain the most complete accounts we have. Readers should bear in mind, however, that none of their authors were permitted access to Lindbergh's personal papers, the most extensive collection of which is housed in the Sterling Library at Yale University.

DAVIS, the first writer to take a long view of Lindbergh's life, sees his task as "that of assembling in one place heretofore scattered materials, testing them for authenticity, and then weaving them together in a continuous narrative." He succeeds admirably in doing this, providing an 80-page bibliographic essay that reveals the extent of his sources, and establishing a dominant point of view to which he adheres consistently throughout. Davis' starting point is the acknowledgment that Lindbergh was unquestionably a great hero. What led to his attainment of that stature, and what brought about his fall from eminence? These are the implicit questions for which his biography provides answers.

Through his account of Lindbergh's lonely childhood we learn that the boy's estranged mother and father each encouraged the development in him of "bravery, fortitude, self-reliance, all the strengths required for independence and self-sufficiency." These, of course, are the very qualities, combined with his technical skill, that enabled Lindbergh to make his solo flight to Paris in 1927. Yet while the deed itself was solitary, the recognition of it was public, and the latter was necessary for the development of the "hero" phenomenon. Likewise, the subsequent withdrawal of mass attention led to the collapse of the hero *qua* hero. Intending to "show how he [Lindbergh-as-hero] was created and how undone in 20th-century America," Davis sets the story he has to tell about the man's individual life within a detailed context of the social and political life of America during the 1920s and 1930s.

The very strength of Davis' book, however, imposes a limitation upon it. Having understood Lindbergh as an historical exemplar of the pattern of experience described by Joseph

Campbell in *The Hero with a Thousand Faces*, Davis is able to provide an extremely satisfying account of Lindbergh's rise and fall. Yet this story comes to an end with American's entry into World War II, when Lindbergh's reputation was eclipsed because of the strong isolationist stand he had previously taken. For the remaining years of his subject's life, up to the time of the book's publication, all Davis can do is append an "Envoi." In this final chapter he acknowledges that "the man who survived his heroism continued intensely alive, intensely active," and that he even "became more interesting than ever to those who would view his life as a process of education." But Davis himself pursues this process no further.

Despite his knowledge that Lindbergh preferred not to have a biography written, ROSS undertook the task because of his conviction that the man was owed another look, that he had "the right to be judged by today's truths, his whole life, and not just by what happened 30 or 40 years ago, and what people thought then." His purpose is to clarify the record by writing a dispassionate account of Lindbergh's life. Davis had largely accomplished this before, but his book, published 15 years before Lindbergh's death, looks at the subject through a particular lens. Making use of no such theoretical framework, Ross instead works simply from the accumulation of "known data and verifiable fact" and is not much given to speculation about Lindbergh's character. He is a conscientious biographer, and the reader can rely on him to be both accurate and fair. At the same time one finds in his work a dutiful quality that is embodied in a rather wooden and sometimes awkward writing style. In one place, for instance, he mentions that Lindbergh's reported paranoia concerning the public was "based on a number of persistent reality factors."

Ross begins his biography with a composite portrait of Lindbergh called "Snapshots," follows this with a chapter devoted to Lindbergh's paternal and maternal forebears, and then turns to a chronological treatment of his life. His unwillingness to elaborate on matters of record is exemplified by his treatment of Lindbergh's wedding, which is presented in two brief paragraphs. Characteristically, Ross makes no attempt to put the reader *there;* what he provides instead is a detached, factual report of the event.

The most significant of Ross' interpretive comments appears at the very end. Moving toward a conclusion, he considers changes in Lindbergh's outlook that took place after he moved into relative obscurity, changes that enlarge upon the process of self-education mentioned by Davis. Then, in the chapter entitled "A Free Man," Ross offers the following summary judgment: "An inner-directed man in an increasingly other-directed world, Lindbergh may be more heroic for us today in his anti-heroism, doing exactly what he decided was his duty, than as the doer of glamorous deeds. We can find in his untrammeled way of life at least a vicarious counterpoise to our own. More than ever, these days, it is heroic to be oneself." In this passage Ross extends the notion of the hero as defined and developed in Davis' work. Yet surely there are many unheralded Americans who, despite the pressures of mass society, persist in following their own paths in their individual lives. It cannot be in this private sense that Lindbergh is to be considered "the last hero."

In the same year that a revised edition of Ross' book was published, MOSLEY's biography appeared. One might therefore fear much duplication, but fortunately this turns out not to be

the case. For one thing, although Ross made factual corrections and other changes in his work, he did not—except for the addition of a two-page Afterword—enlarge it. The body of the book contains exactly the same number of pages as the original edition of 1968. Mosley, on the other hand, has a good deal more to say about Lindbergh's life after World War II than does either Ross or Davis, and this difference significantly alters our sense of the trajectory of that life.

It is Mosley's angle of vision, however, that chiefly accounts for the different impression made by his biography. Davis and Ross, despite the ways in which their books differ, both tend to view Lindbergh from afar. (This remains true of Ross even though he includes a separate chapter near the end called "Family Life.") Mosley, on the contrary, makes every effort to see him up close. He was helped in this regard by drawing upon Lindbergh's *Wartime Journals* (1970), and the diaries and letters of Harold Nicolson, a close friend of the Morrow family, which permitted him to say more than earlier biographers had about the private lives and opinions of Charles and Anne. Moreover, Mosley made greater use of Anne's published writings and apparently also of interviews with friends of the family, both of which enabled him to weave still more of their domestic lives into his treatment of Charles' public career. The result is a more integrated, well-rounded portrait of the man than is provided by either Ross or Davis.

Mosley's different approach is reflected in his style, which is generally more informal than that in either of the other two books. This can occasionally be irritating, such as when he says that Lindbergh was "bugged" by his lack of facility with languages, or when he anachronistically uses the word "peacenik" to identify Lindbergh's isolationist position prior to the entry of the United States into World War II. On the whole, though, the style is appropriate to the author's treatment of his subject. Contrary to Luckett, who criticizes Mosley for "laboring a bit too hard to reinterpret Lindbergh's life, to fight against seeing him as an American hero," I find Mosley's book refreshing. He does not hesitate to admire Lindbergh's genuine accomplishments, but neither is he reluctant to confront his failings and mistakes. The latter are particularly evident in Mosley's handling of Lindbergh's activities prior to 7 December 1941, in which we are presented with the well-documented portrait of an individual who was at best politically naive. Mosley's chief concern, in other words, is to depict a man rather than an American icon. For a more detailed portrayal of that man we must await the publication of two biographies currently in progress. One, by Raymond Fredette, was authorized by Lindbergh himself before his death; the other, by A. Scott Berg, was sanctioned much more recently by Anne Morrow Lindbergh.

—Peter Heidtmann

LISZT, Franz, 1811–1886; Hungarian composer and pianist.

Beckett, Walter, *Liszt*. London, Dent, and New York, Farrar Straus, 1956; revised edition, Dent, 1963.
Burger, Ernst, *Franz Liszt: A Chronicle of His Life in Pictures and Documents*, translated by Stewart Spencer. Princeton,

New Jersey, Princeton University Press, 1989 (originally published by List, Munich, 1986).

Corder, Frederick, *Ferenz Liszt*. London, Kegan Paul, and New York, Harper, 1925.

Hamburger, Klára, *Liszt*, translated by Gyula Gulyás, translation revised by Paul Merrick. Budapest, Corvina, 1980.

Huneker, James, *Franz Liszt*. New York, Scribner, and London, Chapman and Hall, 1911.

László, Zsigmond and Béla Mátéka, *Franz Liszt: A Biography in Pictures*, translated by Barna Balough, translation revised by Cynthia Jolly. Budapest, Corvina, and London, Barrie and Rockliff, 1968.

Legány, Deszö, *Franz Liszt and His Country 1869–73*, translated by Gyula Gulyás, translation revised by Bertha Gaster. Budapest, Corvina, 1983.

Newman, Ernest, *The Man Liszt*. London, Cassell, and New York, Scribner, 1935.

Perényi, Eleanor, *Liszt: The Artist as Romantic Hero*. Boston, Little Brown, and New York, Weidenfeld and Nicolson, 1974.

Pourtalés, Guy de, *Franz Liszt: L'Homme d'Amour*, translated by Eleanor Stimson Brooks. New York, Holt, 1926; as *Franz Liszt: Man of Love*, London, T. Butterworth, 1927 (originally published as *La Vie de Franz Liszt*, Paris, Gallimard, 1925).

Ramann, Lina, *Franz Liszt: Artist and Man*, translated by E. Cowdery. London, W. H. Allen, 1882 (originally published as volume one of *Franz Liszt als Künstler und Mensch*, Leipzig, Breitkopf and Härtel, 1880).

Sitwell, Sacheverell, *Liszt*. London, Faber, and Boston, Houghton Mifflin, 1934; revised edition, London, Cassell, and New York, Philosophical Library, 1967.

Taylor, Ronald, *Franz Liszt: The Man and the Musician*. London, Grafton, and New York, Universe Books, 1986.

Walker, Alan, *Franz Liszt: The Virtuoso Years 1811–47*. London, Faber, and New York, Knopf, 1983; revised edition, Ithaca, New York, Cornell University Press, 1987; London, Faber, 1989.

Walker, Alan, *Franz Liszt: The Weimar Years 1848–61*. London, Faber, and New York, Knopf, 1989.

Walker, Alan, *Franz Liszt: The Final Years: "Une Vie Trifurquée" 1861–86* (to be published).

Watson, Derek, *Liszt*. London, Dent, and New York, Macmillan/Schirmer, 1989.

*

Heinrich Heine called it "Lisztomania." The phenomenon that was Liszt has generated a vast inventory of comment, argument, and fabrication, yet there are lacunae that leave much behavior unexplained. Liszt scholarship has been late to mature; among the biographical works, generally speaking, newer is better.

RAMANN was authorized by Liszt but directed by his second mistress, the Princess Carolyne von Sayn-Wittgenstein. The work is partitioned chronologically into three volumes; only the first, covering to 1840, has received English translation. The hand of the Princess is too apparent: Liszt is depicted as hero-saint, and the Comtesse Marie d'Agoult, his first mistress, is castigated. Though Liszt provided Ramann with extensive data, the composer can scarcely be blamed for the flattering tone of

the book or, indeed, its blatant falsehoods. Later writers, notably Alan Walker, have made far better use of Ramann's source material.

Three other early works are hopelessly inaccurate. HUNEKER's is a hodgepodge of biography, reminiscence, and musical criticism, all outdated. POURTALÉS, at least, discovers some principal themes of the Liszt story, but his style is so rhapsodical as to be almost unreadable. CORDER dwells on Liszt's activities as professional musician, giving little attention to his personal life; Marie and Carolyne are barely mentioned, for instance. When Corder was a student in Germany he met Liszt, and some of the firsthand musical observations are engaging. Little else in the book can be recommended. Peter Raabe's *Franz Liszt: Leben und Schaffen* (1931), still untranslated, was the first major scholarly work on Liszt. Although hardly definitive, its appearance indicated that Liszt had become deserving of serious inquiry; no longer could legend and anecdote pass for biography.

Two books from 1934, still widely read, are more ambitious than all the pre-Raabe works except Ramann. SITWELL is beautifully written, in a vaguely Victorian style, and grants fair coverage to the major points of Liszt's life. Sitwell is persuasive about Liszt the man and evinces a remarkable, prescient sympathy for the music. However, factual errors abound, even in the revision of 1955. Nothing is documented in the modern manner. Readers requiring truth must look to a more recent source, though Sitwell remains thoughtful and evocative. NEWMAN should be avoided. The work purports to be a psychological examination of Liszt's affairs with Marie and Carolyne. Newman submits that Liszt was interested only in women and in social-climbing; the events of Liszt's life, no matter how inimical to this idea, are interpreted accordingly. Much of the "factual" matter does not survive casual scrutiny (a whole chapter on Liszt's student Olga Janina is wrong). Instead of merely debunking Ramann's "St. Francis" myth, Newman contrived a cruel polemic. It would be difficult to imagine another biography, of anyone, so thoroughly negative.

The first half of BECKETT's volume is biography; the second comprises discussions of the music, essays on Liszt as pianist and author, a catalogue of works, etc. Like most of the earlier writers, Beckett relies chiefly on secondary sources. Unfortunately, he seems to rely most heavily on Newman. Though he concedes Newman to be "rather ruthless," Beckett has confiscated a good deal of Newman's psychological method. He perpetuates the simplistic view of Liszt as "half demon, half angel" and reproduces many of Newman's mistakes. Beckett is not gratuitously malicious, but neither does he present a temperate picture. The musical discussions are too superficial to be useful.

PERÉNYI attempts to trace the Romantic threads of Liszt's life to their origins in 1830s France. In the first third of the book Perényi considers the political, literary, and artistic currents that may have influenced Liszt's development. The author's scope is broad, and some intriguing (though speculative) notions emerge. The rest of the book, devoted to Liszt's personal alliances, is unsuccessful. Applying a sort of deconstructive technique to the correspondence, Perényi may render a precise judgment from a line or two in a letter. Since neither she nor anyone else has read all the letters, the procedure seems miscalculated. Moreover, Perényi exhibits no particular understanding of Liszt's music; her argument, thus, is skewed from the outset. Perényi's thesis is inventive, but she makes a poor case for it in this scattered, extravagant book.

The most impressive biographical works have appeared since 1980. WALKER's huge but lucid *Franz Liszt*, when complete, will eclipse Raabe as the major scholarly study. Following the Ramann model, Walker has spread his work among three volumes. Final assessment must await Volume III (which may appear by 1993), but clearly Walker has examined more source material than anyone else. Virtually everything is documented; revelations abound. Volume I opens with a superb overview of the Liszt literature, then considers Liszt's youth and his "Glanz" period as traveling virtuoso. Walker offers the fullest account of Liszt's childhood and is the first to explore, in requisite detail, Liszt's relationship with his father. Liszt's concert itinerary is given in its most exhaustive form to date. Volume II, more complex and discursive than the first, presents Liszt as Weimar Kappellmeister, tireless champion of the avant-garde. Here are Liszt's relationships with Carolyne and his children, his chimerical association with Wagner, and the hostilities between the "New German School" and the Brahms-Schumann circle. Walker surveys Liszt's conducting activities, an area that has been neglected until now. Astute inspection of the music is dispersed throughout both volumes; effects of the life on the art (and vice versa) are thereby exposed. Walker is patently pro-Liszt, and perhaps a few of his conclusions about Liszt's conduct fail to convince. His book, however, is the capstone of contemporary Liszt scholarship and doubtless will serve as the standard biography for many years.

Two other recent works benefit from modern scholarship. WATSON is the declared successor to Beckett but marks a conspicuous advance over his forebear. His prose is clear, his research is careful, and he seems to have no particular psycho-historical ax to grind. Like Beckett, only the first half of Watson is biography; the other half contains separate discussions of many of Liszt's important works. Liszt emerges as a consistent, accessible character, and the myriad aspects of his life receive balanced treatment. Watson's handling of the music, more description than analysis, will be especially useful to the non-specialist. At present this may be the most dependable single-volume introduction to Liszt and his music. TAYLOR's biography is slightly more elaborate than Watson's, and his too-brief musical discussions are embedded in the narrative. Taylor, more equivocal about Liszt than Watson, displays some troubling aesthetic premises. For example, Liszt's frequent revision of his own works is said to demonstrate a lack of "creative stamina." The works of his last years are "barren" and "led nowhere." Perhaps such notions have not been completely discredited, but they are outmoded. Taylor seems uncomfortable with the "incomplete" nature of Liszt's life and art. Readers with a similar outlook (i.e., Brahmsians) will find the book serviceable, despite the few errors of fact that have crept into the account.

Lately Hungary has furnished an abundance of Liszt material, and at least two books have been translated into English. HAMBURGER is more journalistic than most of the other biographers and indulges little in psychological conjecture. However, the emphasis is always on Liszt as Hungarian, so familiar events emerge in fresh colors. Hamburger's national perspective extends to her intricate musical discussions, which, unfortunately,

often are presented in text-only format. LEGÁNY expends an entire book on five years of Liszt's life, the period of Liszt's Hungarian "repatriation." Part of every year of Liszt's *vie trifurquée* was spent in Pest; what did he do there? Legány answers the question in exceptional detail, though this is no mere diary. Liszt's seeming transformation from prodigal to nationalist is presented as a cultural phenomenon. Neither Legány nor Hamburger has been perfectly translated, but both are worthy correctives to the accepted cosmopolitan perspective.

BURGER's pictorial volume contains 650 illustrations (portraits, photographs, scores, letters), many rare or obscure, all generously documented. For each year of Liszt's life there is a calendar of his activities, a list of compositions, and a biographical essay. The text is sound, despite a modest error or two. Stewart Spencer's translation is superb, and Alfred Brendel has contributed an imaginative forward. For its breadth as well as its exquisite quality of manufacture, Burger's work is a significant addition to the Liszt corpus. It supersedes a similar volume by LASZLO AND MÁTÉKA which, though creditable for its time, is neither as extensive nor as well documented.

—Bruce Murray

LIVINGSTONE, David, 1813–1873; Scottish missionary and explorer in Africa.

Adams, H. G., *The Weaver Boy Who Became a Missionary*. New York, R. Carter, 1868.

Blaikie, William Garden, *The Personal Life of David Livingstone*. London, J. Murray, and New York, F. H. Revell, 1880.

Campbell, Reginald John, *Livingstone*. London, E. Benn, 1929; New York, Dodd Mead, 1930.

Chambliss, J. E., *The Life and Labors of David Livingstone*. Philadelphia, Hubbard Brothers, 1875.

Coupland, Sir Reginald, *Livingstone's Last Journey*. London, Collins, 1945; New York, Macmillan, 1946.

Debenham, Frank, *Way to Ilala: David Livingstone's Pilgrimage*. London and New York, Longman, 1955.

Finger, Charles Joseph, *David Livingstone: Explorer and Prophet*. New York, Doubleday, 1927.

Gelfand, Michael, *Livingstone the Doctor: His Life and Travels: A Study in Medical History*. Oxford, Blackwell, 1957.

Helly, Dorothy O., *Livingstone's Legacy: Horace Waller and Victorian Mythmaking*. Athens, Ohio, and London, Ohio University Press, 1987.

Horne, Charles Silvester, *David Livingstone*. London and New York, Macmillan, 1913.

Hughes, Thomas, *David Livingstone*. London and New York, Macmillan, 1889.

Hume, Edward, *David Livingstone: The Man, the Missionary and the Explorer*. London, A. Melrose, 1904.

Huxley, Elspeth, *Livingstone and His African Journey*. London, Weidenfeld and Nicolson, and New York, Saturday Review Press, 1974.

Jeal, Tim, *Livingstone*. New York, Putnam, and London, Heinemann, 1973.

Johnson, Harry Hamilton, *Livingstone and the Exploration of Central Africa*. London, G. Philip, 1891.

Listowel, Judith, *The Other Livingstone*. Lewes, Sussex, J. Friedmann, and New York, Scribner, 1974.

Livingstone, William Pringle, *The Story of David Livingstone*. New York and London, Harper, 1930.

Lloyd, B. W., editor, *Livingstone 1873–1973*. Cape Town, C. Struik, 1973.

Maclachlan, T. Banks, *David Livingstone*. Edinburgh and London, Oliphant Anderson, and New York, Scribner, 1901.

Martelli, George, *Livingstone's River; a History of the Zambezi Expedition 1858–64*. New York, Simon and Schuster, 1969; London, Chatto and Windus, 1970.

Northcott, Cecil, *David Livingstone: His Triumph, Decline and Fall*. London, Lutterworth Press, and Philadelphia, Westminster Press, 1973.

Pachai, Bridglal, editor, *Livingstone: Man of Africa: Memorial Essays 1873–1973*. London, Longman, 1973.

Ransford, Oliver, *David Livingstone: The Dark Interior*. New York, St. Martin's, and London, J. Murray, 1978.

Roberts, John S., *The Life and Explorations of David Livingstone, LL.D.* London, Adam, 1874.

Seaver, George, *David Livingstone: His Life and Letters*. London, Lutterworth Press, and New York, Harper, 1957.

Shepperson, George, editor, *David Livingstone and Africa*. Centre of African Studies, University of Edinburgh, 1973.

Simmons, Jack, *Livingstone and Africa*. New York, Macmillan, 1954.

*

As was the custom in his day, Livingstone was a prolific correspondent, journalist, and diarist. David Chamberlin (1940) quotes Livingstone's youngest daughter as remarking "I can only remember him as always writing letters." These papers, deposited in archival collections in the British Isles and various locations in Africa, afford Livingstone's biographers a wealth of primary source material with which to begin their work.

A Livingstone biographer must begin with the accounts published by Livingstone of his expeditions, such as *Notes on a Tour to the River Sesheke* (Cape Town, 1852), *Missionary Travels and Researches in South Africa* (London, 1857), and *Narrative of an Expedition to the Zambesi and its Tributaries* (London, 1865). These have been supplemented by several collections of Livingstone's letters and journals. Horace Waller, *The Last Journals of David Livingstone* (London, 1874) is itself the subject of a recent book by HELLY because of the manner in which Waller promotes the Livingstone legend through his judicious use of excisions and emendations. Livingstone's Zambesi journals are professionally and accurately presented in J. P. R. Wallis' two-volume edition, *The Zambesi Expedition of David Livingstone, 1858–1863* (London, 1956). Other edited collections of Livingstone's correspondence include Maurice Boucher, *Livingstone Letters 1843–72* (Johannesburg, 1985), David Chamberlin, *Some Letters from Livingstone 1840–72* (London, 1940), R. Foskett, *The Zambesi Doctors: David Livingstone's Letters to John Kirk* (Edinburgh, 1964), and Isaac Schapera, *David Livingstone: Family Letters 1841–56* (London, 1959) and *Livingstone's Missionary Correspondence 1841–56* (London, 1961). Schapera has also edited *Livingstone's African Journal 1853–56* (London, 1963).

George Shepperson, *David Livingstone and the Rovuma* (Edinburgh, 1965) is an edited version of Livingstone's notebook of his attempt to navigate the Rovuma River in 1862. William Monk, *Dr. Livingstone's Cambridge Lectures* (Cambridge, 1858) collected Livingstone's famous Cambridge lectures into a single volume shortly after they were delivered. The most recent collection of Livingstone papers is by Timothy Holmes, *David Livingstone: Letters and Documents 1841–72* (Bloomington, Indiana, 1990). The majority of documents in this collection are being published for the first time.

Although the publications of these documents has now made them widely available to scholars, the man who probably had the most unlimited and extensive access to all of the Livingstone papers was his first official biographer, BLAIKIE. Commissioned by the Livingstone family shortly after the missionary's death, Blaikie received the full cooperation of Livingstone's wife, children, sisters, and a large number of his friends and associates in the preparation of this biography. Glowing in his portrayal of his subject, Blaikie, like many of Livingstone's biographers who followed, concentrates predominantly on the missionary activity. Nevertheless, the work is a solid piece of scholarship and remained the standard biography until well into the 20th century.

ROBERTS' work, which appeared in more than 20 editions between 1874 and 1913, is unexceptional in its content and scholarship, although it is well illustrated. Most Livingstone biographies written in the late 19th and early 20th centuries are hagiographic in their approach to the subject, rarely cite their sources, and are rather pedestrian in style. The anonymous *Livingstone's Africa* (Philadelphia, 1872), based primarily on Livingstone's published accounts and Stanley's dispatches, is typical of this genre, as are JOHNSON, MACLACHLAN, and HUME. ADAMS' heroic portrayal of Livingstone went through several editions with continuous updates after the first edition appeared in 1868. HORNE provides a straightforward "narrative of the facts" and is quite readable for that reason.

HUGHES' biography was second only to Blaikie's in popularity in its day and is probably the best account for the general reader from this period, though it contains little new information that the scholar would find of interest. The same is true for the study by CHAMBLISS, who intended it for "popular patronage" and therefore found little need to make "frequent mention of authorities." An explorer himself, FINGER writes sympathetically of Livingstone's adventures although, as he himself admits, his book adds "nothing to the information about Livingstone." WILLIAM LIVINGSTONE focuses primarily on Livingstone's religious activities.

CAMPBELL was the first biographer since Blaikie to render a scholarly, full-scale treatment of Livingstone. He sought to correct Blaikie's omission of the "faults and weaknesses" of the great man and thus offers a somewhat more critical account than the earlier work. Campbell delimits his study by focusing on Livingstone's personal life and his Christian philanthropy and gives little attention to the scientific, political, commercial, or imperial aspects of Livingstone's career. This work complements but does not replace Blaikie.

Between 1930, the year Campbell's book was published, and 1973, the centenary of Livingstone's death, a few studies appeared that highlighted different facets of Livingstone's life. DEBENHAM, emeritus professor of Geography at Cambridge, describes Livingstone's importance as a geographer in a well-written study that is profusely illustrated with drawings, maps, diagrams, charts, and samples of Livingstone's handwriting. GELFAND, a medical doctor himself, is concerned with Livingstone the healer of bodies as well as the saver of souls. The author of a number of publications about disease in Africa, Gelfand looks at this generally neglected aspect of Livingstone's life both in terms of its importance to the Christian missionary endeavor and of its significance for medicine and disease eradication in Africa. Like Debenham's study of Livingstone the geographer, Gelfand's portrayal of Livingstone the doctor is a major contribution to our knowledge about the multi-faceted man. COUPLAND's scholarly account, based on the last journals and the private papers of the missionaries Waller and Kirk, is an objective study of Livingstone's last years and his final journey in search of the sources of the Nile.

SIMMONS offers a brief but solid biography, perhaps the best short introduction to Livingstone's life. SEAVER's biography uses Livingstone's own words so often that the work is nearly a Livingstone autobiography. Still, this is the most comprehensive and scholarly biography to appear after Blaikie and Campbell. It surpasses these two authors in detail and draws on previously unavailable source material and newly discovered documents. The work suffers, however, from the lack of critical analysis and assessment of Livingstone's life and work and is frustratingly error ridden. MARTELLI seeks to correct what he perceives as the "excessive adulation" that characterizes previous biographies. His study concentrates on the Zambezi Expedition of 1858–64, which by all accounts was a disaster, and portrays Livingstone in a highly unflattering light. Unlike previous journeys where Livingstone was alone except for his African porters, here Livingstone is the leader of a large expedition and must interact with his fellow travelers and take their opinions under consideration. Because of the number of European participants on this journey, Martelli was able to draw on a dozen eyewitness accounts, some of which had never before been available. The result is a highly readable, intelligently researched and written depiction of a great man with his share of human faults and weaknesses. In the end, Livingstone emerges as perhaps an even more heroic figure than in other accounts.

The 1973 centenary witnessed the publication of a number of Livingstone biographies. Three important essay collections that appeared at this time, SHEPPERSON, LLOYD, and PACHAI, are also well worth the reader's attention. The most lavishly illustrated of all Livingstone biographies is HUXLEY. Although there is no new factual information in this volume, it is the best source for illustrations and photographs of Livingstone and the people and places in his life. NORTHCOTT's relatively short biography makes use of Livingstone's correspondence with his father-in-law and fellow missionary, Robert Moffat. LISTOWEL has written a skillfully documented and highly original study of major significance that demonstrates how Livingstone failed to acknowledge the efforts and discoveries of four Europeans who accompanied him on his journeys. While acknowledging Livingstone's greatness, Listowel shows how his jealousy of other Europeans and his desire for glory caused him to take the credit for discoveries and exploits that rightfully belonged to others. This work covers new ground that is not discussed anywhere else.

JEAL's study replaced all previous works to become the standard biography of Livingstone. Jeal makes use of the new material that appeared in the decade prior to 1973, such as the editions of letters and journals by Schapera and Wallis. He is also writing a decade after the independence movement had swept through Africa and thus is able to look back more objectively on the colonial era than had the previous biographers who were part of that era. Jeal portrays Livingstone as a man of contradictions, admired and praised in spite of his failures, whose most important contribution may have been the moral basis for imperial expansion that he instilled in his successors. RANSFORD, an anesthetist and amateur African historian, promotes the thesis that Livingstone suffered from a manic-depressive disorder known as cyclothymia. Although Ransford's biography is well written, well researched, and well illustrated, it is not totally convincing in its psychobiographical thesis and therefore leaves the reader somewhat frustrated. While not equal to Jeal, Ransford's work must be read by anyone seeking more than a superficial understanding of Livingstone.

—Roger B. Beck

LLOYD GEORGE, David, 1863–1945; Welsh politician, prime minister of Great Britain.

Beaverbrook, Max Aitken, Baron, *The Decline and Fall of Lloyd George: And Great Was the Fall Thereof.* London, Collins, and New York, Duell Sloane, 1963.

Campbell, John, *Lloyd George: The Goat in the Wilderness 1922–31.* London, Cape, 1977.

Carey Evans, Lady Olwen, *Lloyd George Was My Father.* Llandysul, Wales, Gomer Press, 1985.

Cregier, Don M., *Bounder from Wales: Lloyd George's Career before the First World War.* Columbia, University of Missouri Press, 1976.

Davies, Alfred T., *The Lloyd George I Knew: Some Side-Lights on a Great Career.* London, H. E. Walter, 1948.

Davies, William Watkin, *Lloyd George 1863–1914.* London, Constable, 1939.

Dilnot, Frank, *Lloyd George: The Man and His Story.* London, T. F. Unwin, and New York, Harper, 1917.

Du Parcq, Herbert, *Life of David Lloyd George* (4 vols.). London, Caxton, 1912–13.

Edwards, John Hugh, *David Lloyd George: The Man and the Statesman* (2 vols.). New York, J. H. Sears, and London, Waverly, 1929.

George, W. R. P., *The Making of Lloyd George.* London, Faber, and Hamden, Connecticut, Archon Books, 1976.

George, William, *My Brother and I.* London, Eyre and Spottiswoode, 1958.

Grigg, John, *The Young Lloyd George.* London, Eyre Methuen, 1973; Berkeley, University of California Press, 1974.

Grigg, John, *Lloyd George: The People's Champion 1902–11.* London, Eyre Methuen, and Berkeley, University of California Press, 1978.

Grigg, John, *Lloyd George: From Peace to War 1912–16.* London, Methuen, and Berkeley, University of California Press, 1985.

Jones, Jack, *The Man David: An Imaginative Presentation, Based on Fact, of the Life of David Lloyd George from 1880–1914*. London, Hamilton, 1944.

Jones, Thomas, *Lloyd George*. London, Oxford University Press, and Cambridge, Massachusetts, Harvard University Press, 1951.

Kinnear, Michael, *The Fall of Lloyd George: The Political Crisis of 1922*. London, Macmillan, and Toronto and Buffalo, New York, Toronto University Press, 1973.

Lloyd George, Frances, *The Years that are Past*. London, Hutchinson, 1967.

Lloyd George, Richard, 2nd Earl, *Lloyd George*. London, F. Muller, 1960; as *My Father, Lloyd George*, New York, Crown, 1961.

Mallet, Charles, *Mr. Lloyd George: A Study*. London, E. Benn, and New York, Dutton, 1930.

McCormick, Donald, *The Mask of Merlin: A Critical Story of David Lloyd George*. London, Macdonald, 1963.

Morgan, Kenneth O., *David Lloyd George: Welsh Radical as World Statesman*. Cardiff, University of Wales Press, 1963.

Murray, Basil, *L. G.* London, Low Marston, 1932.

Owen, Frank, *Tempestuous Journey: Lloyd George, His Life and Times*. London, Hutchinson, 1954; New York, McGraw-Hill, 1955.

Raymond, E. T., *Mr. Lloyd George*. London, Collins, and New York, G. H. Doran, 1922.

Rowland, Peter, *Lloyd George*. London, Barrie and Jenkins, 1975; as *David Lloyd George: A Biography*, New York, Macmillan, 1976.

Sylvester, A. J., *The Real Lloyd George*. London, Cassell, 1947.

Sylvester, A. J., *Life with Lloyd George: The Diary of A.J. Sylvester 1931–45*, edited by Colin Cross. London, Macmillan, and New York, Barnes and Noble, 1975.

Taylor, A. J. P., editor, *Lloyd George: Twelve Essays*. London, Hamilton, and New York, Atheneum, 1971.

Thomson, Malcolm, *David Lloyd George: The Official Biography*. London and New York, Hutchinson, 1948.

Wrigley, Chris, *David Lloyd George and the British Labour Movement: Peace and War*. Hassocks, Harvester Press, and New York, Barnes and Noble, 1976.

*

Few politicians, in Britain or elsewhere, have had such political longevity as David Lloyd George. Much valuable biographical data about Lloyd George therefore appears in biographies of other senior British politicians, especially Winston Churchill (his closest friend), Stanley Baldwin (his worst enemy), and H. H. Asquith (first his colleague and then his enemy). Since Lloyd George was in high office throughout World War I and the ensuing Paris Peace Conference, books about non-British politicians, especially Woodrow Wilson and Georges Clemenceau, are also often helpful sources.

The literature explicitly on Lloyd George is itself dauntingly large. Part of that was written by Lloyd George himself. Especially when out of Cabinet office he liked to write policy-oriented books that included relevant autobiographical nuggets. Among the most interesting of these are his book on post-1918 German reparations (*The Truth about Reparations and War Debts*, 1932), and, on broader diplomatic matters, *Where are We Going?* (1923). His most important autobiographical book is his six-volume *War Memoirs* (1933–36) defending his actions during World War I. This defense is a skilled solicitor's brief, carefully reasoned and worded, drawing appropriately if selectively on contemporary documents as well as personal recollections. Lloyd George's accounts of his performance as Chancellor of the Exchequer (until May 1915), as the first Minister of Munitions (until mid-1916), and as Prime Minister (from December 1916) persuasively demonstrate that the enormous popular and scholarly respect for his performance as a wartime Minister was and is justified. He is much less persuasive, however, in defending his failure as, briefly in 1916, War Minister to stop the slaughter of the British Army on the Western Front. He is least persuasive in arguing that it was German violation of Belgian neutrality that led him in August 1914 to shift (decisively, within and for the British Cabinet) away from British neutrality, causing the emerging European war to become World War I.

Largely missing from the *War Memoirs* are emotions. Since Lloyd George was a man of many passions, as a politician and as a human being, this lack is a serious deficiency. Compensating for the icy rationalist tone of his autobiographical books are the various passions candidly revealed in his personal letters, published in two well-edited, if brief, volumes. Kenneth O. Morgan's edition (*Lloyd George: Family Letters 1885–1936*, 1973) includes, besides a few entries from a diary Lloyd George kept in his youth, mostly letters written from 1890 to 1902 by Lloyd George to Margaret Lloyd George, his first wife. A. J. P. Taylor's edition (*My Darling Pussy: The Letters of Lloyd George and Frances Stevenson 1931–41*, 1975) includes letters written to Frances Stevenson, his secretary and, for three decades until she became his second wife, his mistress.

This bifurcation of personal correspondence suggests Lloyd George's private life was complicated. It was. Even the substantial literature by and about his family members is initially confusing. Lloyd George and his only, younger, brother, WILLIAM GEORGE, could not agree on a common surname, or much else. In his 90s William George published his bitter masterpiece of sibling rivalry. Its author resented, especially, that in the brothers' law firm William George had been expected to do all the work that David Lloyd George had attracted to the firm. Still resentful, but much more reliable on the young Lloyd George, is the later book by William George's son, W. R. P. GEORGE, who draws heavily on family papers denied to many other authors. Lloyd George's legitimate children, all with his first wife, resented, in varying degrees, his infidelity to their mother. By the time her recollections were published, his nonagenarian daughter, Olwen CAREY EVANS, had somewhat mellowed toward her wayward father. Emyr Price's book on Lloyd George's most gifted child (*Megan Lloyd George*, 1983), who had a distinguished parliamentary career, reveals Lloyd George as a loving father as well as an unfaithful husband. The most unforgiving family accounts are by Lloyd George's oldest son, Richard Lloyd George. Writing as Viscount Gwynedd, his biography of his mother (*Dame Margaret*, 1947) aims primarily at tearing down his father, without revealing the reason for that aim. Writing later as RICHARD LLOYD GEORGE (2nd Earl), the son reveals, in his biography of his father, the reason for his hatred of his father. Richard was the first author to describe (luridly, at that) Lloyd George's sex life. Thus challenged,

FRANCES LLOYD GEORGE, by now a dowager Countess, responded with publication of her demure but valuable memoirs and later of her less demure and even more valuable diary (expertly edited by Taylor). The Stevenson material is generally more reliable on the latter half, and that by other members of his family on the first half, of Lloyd George's career and life.

Lloyd George arouses almost as strong feelings among biographers who were not members of his family. Among his enthusiasts is DU PARCQ, author of the first substantial biography, who had access to many but not all family papers dealing with his subject's youth. Always precise (he was a barrister) and generally well organized, du Parcq's first three volumes (the fourth is an excellent selection of Lloyd George's speeches) remain the most important single published source for the first 50 years of Lloyd George's life. The sharpness of Lloyd George's mind and the complexity of his personality need a biographer capable of both intellectual sophistication and human understanding. Du Parcq had both, in high degree (he later became a distinguished judge), and most of du Parcq's successors have failed to possess one, or both, of these capabilities to the degree du Parcq did.

Of the remaining admiring biographies, the most valuable, despite its inelegant style and excessive length, is EDWARDS' two volumes. Edwards, a journalist and minor politician who saw Lloyd George in heroic terms, lacked du Parcq's intellectual sophistication, but as a faithful disciple of his subject collected, and uncritically included, much information that can be interpreted in more than one way. The human side of Lloyd George is illuminated much more effectively than is the political career, although Edwards exaggerates greatly the poverty of the young Lloyd George. Almost as verbose are Thomson and Owen. THOMSON, a former member of Lloyd George's staff, was asked by Lloyd George's widow to write an official biography. The uninspiring as well as unrevealing result suggests that the Countess Lloyd-George of Dwyfor chose poorly. By far the most interesting part of Thomson's book is its extensive introduction by the Countess. OWEN's book is much more impressive intellectually than is Thomson's. Owen displays a real understanding of his subject, especially of Lloyd George's youth. Many readers, unfortunately, may lack the patience to wade through Owen's almost endless purple prose. Much shorter and less theatrical are the equally generous accounts by DILNOT and MURRAY. Neither author presents any intellectual challenges, but both provide some nice human touches. Dilnot also provides some unintended humor by glowingly describing the happiness of Lloyd George's first marriage. Murray uses some unconventional photographs and includes a distinctive preface by his subject, who claims not to have read Murray's book or, indeed, any biography of himself. Whatever the truth of the unusual claim, Lloyd George probably accurately stated his own view when he added that all biographies (not only those about him) should have a slight bias in favor of the subject.

This appeal has been met with deaf ears from many of Lloyd George's biographers. Some are openly hostile. Typical of such books published during his lifetime is that by MALLET, an Asquithian Liberal who vigorously attacks Lloyd George as insincere and disloyal and therefore unworthy of continued membership in (let alone leadership of) the Liberal Party. Worthy or not, Lloyd George continued as Leader of the Liberal Party even after Mallet's attack, which was intellectually sharp but unsupported by sufficient biographical data to be effective. After Lloyd George's death, the openly hostile biographies became even more open. The most extreme example is doubtless the book by McCORMICK, which, in entirely direct language, accuses Lloyd George of violating virtually every Biblical commandment and therefore having undermined the moral structure of British politics. McCormick's sweeping indictment is much weakened by his own numerous factual imprecisions and lack of intellectual judgment.

Much more dangerous to Lloyd George's reputation are those biographies that are not so open in their hostility. SYLVESTER, who served on the staff of an aging Lloyd George, is ostensibly admiring in his biography, but he persistently digs in his knife with many conversational quotations of dubious reliability. Sylvester's diary, helpfully edited by Cross, is more reliable, suggesting that Sylvester deeply resented Frances Stevenson's greater influence with their common master, who thereby incurred Sylvester's wrath. The books by ALFRED DAVIES and WILLIAM DAVIES are typical expressions of another kind of anger with Lloyd George: the assumption that the young Lloyd George, who appeared to be a spokesman primarily for Welsh interests in British politics, was replaced by an older Lloyd George who in some way betrayed Wales by expanding his political horizons. Alfred Davies writes in old age, almost entirely from memory, and is largely unpersuasive in his attack. Watkin Davies, much sharper intellectually, is more persuasive in arguing that Lloyd George's initial idealism was undermined by arrival on a larger stage. This attack exaggerates the primacy of Wales for even the youthful Lloyd George. An important scholarly variation on this theme is the brief elegant biography by MORGAN.

Among the biographies that strive, relatively successfully, for objectivity, three, those by Raymond, Thomas Jones, and Rowland, are useful and interesting. RAYMOND's book, written while Lloyd George was still prime minister, is intelligent and incisive and can still be read with much profit. Raymond's Lloyd George is, however, entirely motivated by emotion rather than thought. THOMAS JONES, who as a senior civil servant had extensive official dealings with Lloyd George, uses, surprisingly, only published sources. Jones is so judicious and impartial that blandness is never far, although there are occasional human touches. ROWLAND uses substantial archival materials in an attempt to let the story tell itself, with the result that his Lloyd George is virtually without context.

The most effective placing of Lloyd George into his various contexts is achieved by GRIGG in his three volumes, which are also models of biographical fairness. Objectivity does not lead Grigg into bland detachment, however. Throughout he is visibly and passionately engaged in determining the truth about Lloyd George. His three volumes therefore raise the study of Lloyd George to new levels of intellectual and human understanding of their subject. By far the best books ever published about Lloyd George, their only real deficiency flows from the denial of access for their author to the William George collection of family papers, and this deficiency is serious only in Grigg's treatment of Lloyd George's youth.

Helpful addenda to Griggs' incomplete masterpiece are several more specialized books. CREGIER gives a careful summary of several major policy themes of Lloyd George's early political career. BEAVERBROOK describes, dramatically but relatively reliably, the high-politics events leading to Lloyd George's resignation from the prime minstership in 1922. Beaverbrook has valuable documentation, made easier by his purchase from the Lloyd George estate of many of Lloyd George's papers. More prosaic, but perhaps more balanced, than Beaverbrook's book is KINNEAR's scholarly book on the same events. CAMPBELL is well documented and sensible on Lloyd George after 1922. The volume of essays edited by TAYLOR includes a sampling of much of the better historical scholarship on Lloyd George. Another serious specialized scholarly work is that by WRIGLEY, who nevertheless exaggerates Lloyd George's distance from the British labor movement.

Lloyd George appears frequently in fictional works. The unusual book, fact pretending to be fiction, by JACK JONES is far more illuminating psychologically than are many of the more conventional biographies. Much more negative is the portrait of an omnipotent prime minister drawn in Arnold Bennett's novel, *Lord Raingo* (1926). For this venomous attack Lloyd George, characteristically, forgave Bennett. What Lloyd George would have made of Chester Nimmo, the central character in Joyce Cary's novel, *Prisoner of Grace* (1952; published after Lloyd George's death) is more problematical. Cary apparently intended to criticize Lloyd George but instead created a dynamic, passionate, and fascinating character, very much like his intended victim.

—Marvin Rintala

LOCKE, John, 1632–1704; English philosopher.

Aaron, Richard I., *John Locke*. London and New York, Oxford University Press, 1937.

Bourne, Henry R. F., *The Life of John Locke* (2 vols.). London, King, and New York, Harper, 1876.

Cranston, Maurice, *John Locke: A Biography*. New York, Macmillan, and London, Longman, 1957.

Grant, Ruth W., *John Locke's Liberalism*. Chicago and London, University of Chicago Press, 1987.

King, Lord Peter, *The Life of John Locke, with Extracts from His Correspondence, Journals, and Common-Place Books*. London, H. Colburn, 1829.

Wood, Neal, *The Politics of Locke's Philosophy: A Social Study of "An Essay Concerning Human Understanding."* Berkeley and London, University of California Press, 1983.

*

Given the central importance of Locke to 18th-century studies, critical interest in his life has been disappointingly slight, although the completion of the eight-volume *Correspondence* (edited by E. S. de Beer, Oxford, Clarendon Press, 1976–) will surely stimulate production of at least one more full-length biography. The Lovelace Collection of Locke manuscripts, including correspondence, journals, notebooks, and drafts, was first made publicly available at the Bodleian in 1948. Before that time, Locke scholars were forced to rely on two severely limited works. KING, descendant of Locke's cousin Sir Peter King, produced a wholly unacceptable jumble of inaccurately transcribed letters and poorly written, judgmental prose. His critics accused King of displaying his "crude politics" and of using the Locke papers to reveal his own political leanings. As Bourne, Locke's first serious biographer, noted: "Lord King, notwithstanding the title of his work, seems to have made no effort at all to string [the documents] together in any order, or to combine them with such information as he could procure from other sources."

BOURNE's two-volume *Life*, which suffered from the anti-Catholic bias of its author, nevertheless represented a significant improvement over King. It revealed a great deal of new information, in spite of the inaccessibility of parts of the Lovelace collection. Bourne's account is chatty and affable, and it is oddly defensive on the subject of Locke's religious convictions: "There can be no doubt that Locke, being in the best sense of the term a very religious man, had during these years [1672–75] much intercourse with many of the foremost and worthiest religious thinkers, writers, and workers of his time." On the *Essay Concerning Human Understanding*, Bourne is careful and convincing in his description of the composition, the ordering of arguments, and the reception of the work. He is also fascinating in his accounts of Locke's relationships with Newton and Boyle. At the center of the biography, though, is Bourne's defense of Locke's "reasonable" Christianity.

With the complete Lovelace Collection available to him, but without the benefit of the edited letters, CRANSTON wrote the commonly accepted standard biography. His prose is inelegant—choppy and verbally elementary, though one critic more charitably labeled it "plain dealing." But it is mostly accurate and replete with valuable contextual material: Cranston makes productive use of contemporary pamphlets and other ephemeral material. His Locke is patient, affectionate, and loyal, though also secretive. The biographer admits that his subject's personality remains elusive; in fact, the book never fully offers much original insight into Locke's character, beyond the argument that Locke was not, as some have claimed, "a man unaffected by the more tender emotions," but was capable of deep "sentimental" attachments. Nor does Cranston spend much time on Lockean philosophy. In fact, he provides very little discussion of Locke's writings. Even the *Essay Concerning Human Understanding* is passed over cursorily. The strength of the book is its background detail: a portrait of the Puritan trading class, from which Locke emerged, is rendered convincingly, as is a description of Oxford in the 1650s. However, the biography that satisfactorily blends the man and his ideas—one that adequately sorts through the complexities of the religious history of the period—remains to be written.

Because of the dearth of purely biographical materials on Locke, readers might turn to three other works that reflect the interconnectedness of Locke's life and works. AARON studies the development of Locke's religious views. Although only one of his three parts is devoted to biography, his explications of Locke's prose are engaging. He suggests a Locke whose writings reflect a "cool, disciplined" exterior at a time in England of "bitter conflict and narrow zeal." Aaron admires Locke's "balanced" and "tolerant" attitudes and writes that the philosopher navigated successfully the passage from an Age of Enthusiasm to an Age of Reason. WOOD's study makes extensive use of the Locke correspondence edited by de Beer. Sophisticated in his use of modern literary theory, Wood employs, in part, Marxist theory in his approach to Locke's outlook, his intentions, and his audiences. He summarizes his position: "Philosophers . . . are far from being neutral spectators of the 'game' of human life. As participants in that life, the meaning of their philosophy and its implications for action can only be fully grasped by establishing its links with the social context." In the absence of any single biographical study that fully grapples with Lockean politics, GRANT's recent book helps fill a void. Her study places Lockean philosophy in the context of the history of liberal political theory and discourses on the nature of legitimate and illegitimate power.

—Richard C. Taylor

LONDON, Jack [John Griffith London], 1876–1916; American writer.

Barltrop, Robert, *Jack London: The Man, the Writer, the Rebel*. London, Pluto Press, 1976.

Hedrick, Joan, *Solitary Comrade: Jack London and His Work*. Chapel Hill, University of North Carolina Press, 1982.

Labour, Earle, *Jack London*. New York, Twayne, 1974.

London, Joan D., *Jack London and His Times: An Unconventional Biography*. New York, Doubleday, 1939; revised edition, Seattle, University of Washington Press, 1968.

O'Connor, Richard, *Jack London: A Biography*. Boston, Little Brown, 1964; London, Gollancz, 1965.

Sinclair, Andrew, *Jack: A Biography of Jack London*. New York, Harper, 1977; London, Weidenfeld and Nicolson, 1978.

Walker, Franklin, *Jack London and the Klondike: The Genesis of an American Writer*. San Marino, California, Huntington Library, 1966.

*

In between the restricted release of Jack London's letters in 1965 (*Letters from Jack London*, edited by King Hendricks and Irving Shepard) and the massive three-volume edition published in 1988 (*Letters of Jack London*, edited by Earle Labour, Robert C. Leitz, III, and I. Milo Shepard), the effort to reconstruct the life of Jack London has increased in breadth and depth. Eschewing the popularizing and fictional tendencies of the Irving Stone biography (*Sailor on Horseback*, 1938), London's recent biographers have tried to take the measure of the man against the cultural and psychological conditions that marked his life. If biography is the "prism of history," as biographer and historian Barbara Tuchman has written, then we are beginning to understand the full spectrum of both Jack London and his times. On the other hand, those biographers who have attempted to throw light on Jack London still puzzle over how to explain the contradictions of a man who combined socialism and racialism, rough realism with sentimental romanticism, and working-class crudeness with bourgeois refinement. Thus, in trying to explain the range of hues that color the character of their subject, the biographers under consideration cast their own particular stylistic and interpretive shadows over the figure of Jack London.

While all the biographers are quick to admit that Jack London was a man of his time, the sources and methods they use to reconstitute his life reveal as much about themselves as they do about London. BARLTROP's own background as a boxer, roustabout, working-class autodidact, and socialist provides a parallel life from which the examination of London assumes, at times, a quest for self-examination of class attitudes and political values. Thus, Jack London is ultimately determined to have failed as an interpreter and representative of the class struggle. However, Barltrop's biography is not a mere marxist polemic but an effort to sort out the myth that London constructed and the way that myth was reinforced in the writings of Jack's second wife, Charmian Kittredge, and in Stone's biography. For example, Barltrop disputes the mythopoetic accounts of London's early departure from the University of California that are perpetuated by both. Incorporating London's letters and contemporary accounts of London's writings, Barltrop's biography does develop a sense of how the contrasts in London's life are more than a blight on the socialism that London espoused.

While Barltrop does try to connect London's politics and writings to the intellectual climate of the times, his work is thin by the standards of JOAN LONDON's excellent biography. First published in 1939 and reissued in 1968 with a new introduction by the author, this biography renders a sensitive and perceptive study of a father whose personal life kept his daughter at a certain distance. Overcoming that distance with sympathy and insight, Joan London helps to reveal the way in which Jack's friends and family influenced both his thinking and his writing. Her portraits of some of Jack's earliest political mentors, such as George Speed and Austin Lewis, plus her analysis of the role of Benjamin Kidd's *Social Evolution* (1894) on her father's ideology of racialist socialism and determinism, not only get beyond the platitudinous and pedestrian generalizations that mark some of the other biographies, but also greatly expand our knowledge of those factors that aid our understanding of the personal and political life of Jack London.

While O'CONNOR's study shares Joan London's emphasis on environmental factors in explaining Jack's contradictions, his biography is curiously lacking in the kind of primary source material and interpretive sweep found in Joan London. Perhaps because O'Connor did not have access to London's letters and library, he tries to compensate by trying to separate out the mythic and fictional components of the Stone biography. Nonetheless, a rather protective tone about the myth and legend of Jack London remains.

In noting O'Connor's restricted biography, SINCLAIR goes to great lengths to sort out the man and the myth. In particular, he dwells on the various theories of London's death, weighing the contentions of suicidal versus accidental death. There is a rather morbid and obsessive quality to this exploration of the end of London's life that suggests both the desire for narrative closure and the search for the kind of symmetry that Tolstoy saw in the life and death of his characters in *War and Peace*. While Sinclair does an excellent job in situating London in the cultural milieu of the California frontier, thus creating a means to locate London's boasting and drive for eternal youth and upward mobility in a cultural context, his psychological speculations leave much to be desired. From his attribution of mother fixation to his obfuscation of London's misogynistic tendencies, Sinclair too often seeks a too neat psychological packaging.

As a direct contrast to Sinclair, especially on the interpretation of London's sexual politics, HEDRICK's feminist and critical study of London's "divided consciousness" seeks to account for the public and private split. Viewing London's life and writings through the lens of gender and class, Hedrick contends that the conflation and confusion of gender and class in London's fiction mirrors his own fear and loathing of women and the lower class. While Hedrick's insights into London's sexual politics, especially as seen in *The Iron Heel* (1908), add immeasurably to our understanding of the story and the biographical context out of which it emerged, the drive to explain all the contradictions of London through class and gender threatens to treat his life as a series of social problems.

Much of those mini-biographies found in longer works that deal with the myth of success, such as Kenneth Lynn's *The Dream of Success* (1955), and California dreaming, such as Kevin Starr's *Americans and the California Dream* (1973), adduce London's life as grist for their interpretive mill. While there is much in that life that calls for a cultural hermeneutic, there is also much that requires just a simple sorting out of fact from fiction. While WALKER's biography is limited to time that London spent in the Klondike, it is a welcome yeoman effort to separate the myths London constructed around his Klondike experience from the actual events. LABOUR's brief and critical literary study also helps in spots to separate the myth from the man even while propagating London the writer as a Jungian myth-maker. While Labour's attempt to elevate London's writings to the ranks of first-class American fiction does not always succeed, he does present a thoughtful categorization of London's life and literature, including a selected and annotated bibliography.

Other snapshots of Jack London's life, whether in the breezy South Seas travelogue of Martin Johnson (*Through the South Seas with Jack London*, 1913) or Russ Kingman's *Pictorial Life* (1979), help to capture the quixotic adventure that London lived. More recent studies, including John Perry's *Jack London, an American Myth* (1981) and Carolyn Johnston's *Jack London, an American Radical?* (1984), may begin to sort through both the fleeting moments and the life-long travails of Jack London to produce a more inclusive portrait. It would, however, be folly to suggest that any biography of London could be definitive. It is a measure of the man and his prolific work, as well as the problematic of the biography as prism, that there will always be the open question of how one reconstructs his life and times.

—Francis Shor

LONGFELLOW, Henry Wadsworth, 1807–1882; American poet.

Arvin, Newton, *Longfellow: His Life and Work*. Boston, Little Brown, 1963.

Austin, George L., *Henry Wadsworth Longfellow, His Life, His Works, His Friendships*. Boston, Lee and Shepard, 1883.

Carpenter, George R., *Henry Wadsworth Longfellow*. Boston, Small Maynard, 1901.

Fields, Annie, *Authors and Friends*. Boston, Houghton Mifflin, 1896.

Gorman, Herbert S., *Victorian American: Henry Wadsworth Longfellow*. New York, G. H. Doran, and London, Cassell, 1926.

Hatfield, James T., *New Light on Longfellow, with Special Reference to His Relations with Germany*. Boston, Houghton Mifflin, 1933.

Hawthorne, Hildegarde, *The Poet of Craigie House: The Story of Henry Wadsworth Longfellow*. New York and London, D. Appleton, 1936.

Higginson, Thomas W., *Henry Wadsworth Longfellow*. Boston, Houghton Mifflin, 1902.

Hilen, Andrew, *Longfellow and Scandinavia*. New Haven, Connecticut, Yale University Press, 1947.

Johnson, Carl L., *Professor Longfellow of Harvard*. Eugene, University of Oregon Press, 1944.

Kennedy, W. Sloane, *Henry W. Longfellow: Biography, Anecdote, Letters, Criticism*. Boston, D. Lothrop, 1882.

Longfellow, Samuel, *The Life of Henry Wadsworth Longfellow, with Extracts from His Journals and Correspondence* (3 vols.). New York, Houghton Mifflin, 1886–87.

Macchetta, Blanche Roosevelt Tucker, *The Home Life of Henry W. Longfellow*. New York, R. W. Carleton, 1882.

Norton, Charles Eliot, *Henry Wadsworth Longfellow: A Sketch of his Life together with Longfellow's Chief Autobiographical Poems*. Boston, Houghton Mifflin, 1907.

Peare, Catherine Owens, *Henry Wadsworth Longfellow: His Life*. New York, Holt, 1953.

Robertson, Eric S., *Life of Henry Wadsworth Longfellow*. London, W. Scott, 1887.

Thompson, Lawrance, *Young Longfellow 1807–43*. New York, Macmillan, 1938.

Underwood, Francis H., *Henry Wadsworth Longfellow: A Biographical Sketch*. Boston, J. R. Osgood, 1882.

Wagenknecht, Edward, *Longfellow: A Full-Length Portrait*. New York, Longman, 1955.

Wagenknecht, Edward, *Henry Wadsworth Longfellow: Portrait of an American Humanist*. New York, Oxford University Press, 1966.

Whitman, Iris L., *Longfellow and Spain*. New York, Instituto de las Españos en los Estados Unidos, 1927.

Williams, Cecil B., *Henry Wadsworth Longfellow*. New York, Twayne, 1964.

Williams, Stanley T., "Longfellow," in Vol. II of *The Spanish Background of American Literature* (2 vols.). New Haven, Connecticut, Yale University Press, 1955.

*

UNDERWOOD, the first biographer of Longfellow, was encouraged by Longfellow himself. The laudatory sketch is intended for a general readership, relying as it does on recollections by Longfellow's acquaintances and containing a good many qualifying adverbs and adjectives. KENNEDY's volume claims to be a pie baked with many anecdotal huckleberries, some but not all previously published, and demonstrating "the luster and perfume" of a "pure life." Included is previously unpublished juvenilia of "quiet beauty and tender purity of sentiment," newspaper reviews, and lots of tributary verses.

Three other reminiscences rely on anecdotal charm: NORTON's biography, a 40-page sketch with autobiographical poems, depends on Samuel Longfellow's biography throughout. FIELDS, the wife of Longfellow's publisher, characterizes Longfellow as "a seer of beauty in common things and a singer to the universal heart." MACCHETTA writes a "humble and affectionate tribute," which scholars must suspect on two counts: sentimentality and the author's claim that Longfellow himself "corrected" much of what she wrote.

Longfellow was also involved in AUSTIN's biography: "I very carefully gathered from his lips my memoranda." Longfellow died before the work was finished, so Austin enlisted the help of a friend, John Owen, who, somewhat romantically, became ill the day the book was completed and died shortly thereafter. Austin's work is "a clear but popular picture of the poet's life," which nevertheless avoids Longfellow's entire private life and all his correspondence, substituting instead anecdotes of unnamed mutual friends. The book does include illustrations and manuscript facsimiles.

CARPENTER's biography employs anonymous anecdotes focused on the poet's 50th and 60th years. HAWTHORNE's book is a popularized life in novel form complete with dialogue in quotation marks. PEARE's effort is also a fictionalized life but directed at children. Any of these biographies would entertain a general reader unconcerned about scholarly accuracy.

Oddly, there is no truly definitive biography of Longfellow. The authorized biography, written by Henry's brother Rev. SAMUEL LONGFELLOW, was published in two volumes that contained an extensive treatment of journals and correspondence (except for the final 15 years). A subsequent three-volume edition added material including reminiscences of friends, "table talk," and an index. The letters and journals are provided with the briefest introductory of transitional commentary by the author. This biography constituted the undisputed authority for 50 years until Thompson (see below) exposed some unfortunate editing. However, it remains an important consideration for academic work.

Of additional use to scholars is HIGGINSON. Starting with Samuel Longfellow's volumes, Higginson adds letters from Longfellow's first wife, material from the "Harvard College Papers" relating to Longfellow's academic career, as well as extracts from the earlier writings intended to show the poet's "lifelong desire to employ American material and help the creation of a native literature. . . . " A genealogical appendix and index complete the text.

GORMAN's biography—with its interesting feature of having been written in the present tense—is admittedly selective. His thesis is that the greater part of Longfellow's intellectual sustenance was drawn from the Old World. Comparing him to Henry James, Gorman contradicts Higginson, saying that the "real Longfellow" was as much Victorian English as American. Gorman acknowledges debts to Austin, Underwood, Higginson, and to *Random Memories* (1922) by Ernest Wadsworth Longfellow.

THOMPSON was the first to challenge Samuel Longfellow, whose omissions and modifications were apparently intended to conceal details of conflict, certain romances, prejudices, influences, trials, and disappointments. Thompson's work is based on unpublished material from Longfellow's Craigie house and other papers that cover the first 30 years. Thompson deliberately avoids literary criticism, instead following the text with scholarly notes and an extensive index.

Likewise, WAGENKNECHT's *Full-Length Portrait* (1955) challenges Samuel Longfellow and modern critics, too, especially Gorman, whose biography he calls "a very bad book" that uses "the poet as a stick with which he might beat the Victorians," and claiming that Gorman "added nothing of his own except cheapness." Further, Wagenknecht accuses Thompson of research "with a jaundiced eye." To help make his case he, too, adds previously unpublished manuscripts. After this biography went out of print, Wagenknecht wrote a new one, *Portrait of an American Humanist* (1966), the original substantially rewritten, subtracting many quotations but adding new material. He refers scholars to the then forthcoming edition of Longfellow's letters by HILEN and an edition of the journals by Robert Stafford Ward.

Meanwhile, S. T. WILLIAMS, author of the definitive biography of Washington Irving, had written of Longfellow as Spanish translator and leader of the New England Hispanophiles. He focused on Spanish influences including Cervantes, the poet's Spanish travels, and his Spanish writings including the semiautobiographical "Castle in Spain," *Evangeline*, and others. Williams' book depends in part on WHITMAN's study, which in turn makes use of Samuel Longfellow and Gorman. Though Whitman lists studies of the influence on Longfellow of France, Germany, and Italy, she confines her chronicle to the role played by Spain in Longfellow's development as a poet, drawing from unpublished marginalia, journals, diaries, letters, and allusions to Spanish literature. Whitman concludes that Spain had the largest share in teaching the poet his art. Similarly, HATFIELD depends on the Rev. Samuel's "excellent work" and studies a vast enough collection of documents at Craigie House to freely claim that previous works on the German influence on Longfellow were "immature utterances," and that Germany had the largest share in teaching the poet his art.

HILEN's book is an account of Longfellow's travels in Sweden and Denmark and of his study of Icelandic literature. Hilen adds new information, including Longfellow's Scandinavian journal and a number of letters. For Longfellow's academic career consult JOHNSON, who treats the poet's years as Smith Professor at Harvard from 1834–54. Longfellow's tenure corresponded with Harvard's years of change from a conservative provincial college to a national university. Johnson's documentation is based on a thorough, accurate treatment of college records on which Johnson used modern scholarly editorial techniques.

ARVIN's combination of biography and criticism competently redigests most of the works mentioned above as well as *Final Memorials of Henry Wadsworth Longfellow* (1887) by Samuel Longfellow, *Literary Friends and Acquaintances* (1900) by William Dean Howells, and *Mrs. Longfellow: Selected Letters and Journals of Fanny Appleton Longfellow* (1956), edited by Edward Wagenknecht. CECIL B. WILLIAMS also divides his effort for Twayne into biographical and critical parts. In addition to the usual sources, he mentions as helpful Hilen's edition of the *Diary of Clara Crowninshield* (1955), her personal journal of a trip to Europe chaperoned by Mr. and Mrs. Longfellow in 1835–36. Either Arvin's or Cecil Williams' book should serve the student well as an overview of Longfellow's life and works.

—Helen Killoran

LOPE Félix de Vega Carpio. See **VEGA CARPIO, Lope Félix de.**

LORCA, Federico García. See **GARCÍA LORCA, Federico.**

LOUIS IX, 1214–1270; French monarch and saint.

Joinville, Jean, Sire de, *Life of St. Louis,* translated by R. Hague. New York and London, Sheed and Ward, 1955; in *Chronicles of the Crusades,* translated by M. Shaw, London and Baltimore, Maryland, Penguin, 1963 (originally *Histoire de Saint Louis,* 1309; edited by Natalis de Wailly, Paris, 1868).

Jordan, William C., *Louis IX and the Challenge of the Crusade: A Study in Rulership.* Princeton, New Jersey, Princeton University Press, 1979.

Knox, Winifred, *The Court of a Saint.* London, Methuen, 1909.

Labarge, Margaret Wade, *Saint Louis: The Life of Louis IX of France.* London, Eyre and Spottiswoode, 1968; as *Saint Louis: Louis IX, Most Christian King of France,* Boston, Little Brown, 1968.

Perry, Frederick, *St. Louis (Louis IX of France): The Most Christian King.* New York and London, Putnam, 1900.

*

When Louis IX died in 1270, he was universally known and regarded as "Saint" Louis, although his official canonization did not take place until 1297. The son of the redoubtable Blanche of Castile, Louis was organiser of two crusades, builder of the Sainte-Chapelle in Paris, and on the whole, but not unreservedly, politically successful. As king and saint he offers an important subject for the often opposed traditions of secular and ecclesiastical history, and since he was also a colourful figure in his own right, he has not lacked for biographers, and they have not lacked for sources.

His biographers, however, have been overwhelmingly interested in either the king or the saint, in spite of what Voltaire wrote about Louis IX in his *Essai sur les moeurs*: "His piety, which was that of an anchorite, did not deprive him of any of the virtues of a king. . . . he knew how to reconcile the profoundest politics with the strictest justice, and perhaps was the only sovereign who deserved this praise. . . . it is not in the power of man to carry virtue to a greater height." Biographers of Louis IX have also tended to write either for a popular readership, like Labarge, or for a more academic one, like Jordan (for both see below). In spite therefore of all the interest generated by Louis IX, or perhaps because of the confusions generated by hagiography on the one side and chauvinism on the other, there exist few authoritative attempts by historians to write a comprehensive life. As a result the standard work is still the 17th-century, six-volume life by Le Nain de Tillemont (edited by J. de Gaulle, 6 vols., Paris, 1849), which had the advantage of drawing on a number of important sources since lost. There have naturally been other studies treating incidentally of

important aspects of Louis' life, such as histories of the crusades, of the Cathars, and of the Inquisition. These include Steven Runciman's *The Medieval Manichee* (Cambridge, 1947), J. Strayer's *Medieval Statecraft and the Perspectives of History* (edited by J. Benton and T. Bisson, Princeton, 1971), Robert Fawtier's *The Capetian Kings of France* (translated by L. Butler and R. J. Adam, London, 1960), and a multitude of works by French historians, hagiographers, and journalists that have never been translated or thought to deserve translation. There are also several standard treatments, such as that to be found in the *Cambridge Medieval History* (vol. 6).

Until recently the biography accepted as most authoritative was Henri Wallon's *Saint Louis et son temps* (2 vols., Paris, 1876), a work whose translation would have been welcome. The difficulty with Le Nain de Tillemont's treatment, in spite of its impressive accumulation of apparently accurate biographical detail, is that it pre-dates the scientific study of history as the 19th century knew it and preserves a fundamentally clerical point of view. Henri Wallon's biography, which had several 19th-century editions, also pre-dates much of the work on medieval sources. Wallon did not for instance know Deslisle's survey of Louis' provincial administration in the 24th volume of the *Recueil des Historiens des Gaules et de la France* (Paris, 1904).

The first authoritative biography of Louis IX was written by his contemporary and intimate friend, Jean de JOINVILLE (1224–1317). Joinville, the hereditary Seneschal of Champagne and the king's close confidant, was asked to write his life by Jeanne, Queen of Navarre, wife of Louis' grandson Philip IV ("le Bel," 1268–1314). Joinville had taken part in the king's first crusade (the seventh, 1248–54), but refused to accompany him in 1270 on the eighth crusade, on which the king died from the plague. Joinville later gave evidence to the inquiry in 1282 that led to the formal canonization. He wrote in old age, no doubt adding a gloss to his recollections, but his work contains vivid anecdotes, brutal descriptions, and skillful portraits. Like most medieval chroniclers, he is better at detail than at overall vision and judgement, but no one seriously interested in Louis IX should avoid reading him. The narrative is swift, and there is a dry humour that makes reading this work agreeable. The *Histoire* is of course indispensable reading for serious historians of medieval France. There are other contemporary or near-contemporary sources for biographical detail, notably the *Grandes Chroniques de France* (edited by J. Viard, 10 vols., Paris, 1920–53). Translated from Latin, this was the first important historical work in French, and the first French book printed in France (January 1476, in the "old style" of dating). The chronicle of Louis IX's reign is by Guillaume de Nangis, a monk of St-Denis.

PERRY's book of some 80,000 words, the only biography of Louis IX written in English prior to World War II, deals with the disputes over authority between Louis and Blanche of Castile, with the war with England, and with the seventh crusade, devoting only its final quarter to foreign policy, internal affairs, Louis' personal life, and the final crusade. It is therefore a straightforward account of the reign, its politics, and the first of its two crusades. Perry offers some imaginative reconstruction of events and reactions, but the interpretive element does not go beyond what is reasonable. One hopes that today's university students do not need to be talked down to quite as obviously as when Perry remarks, "The piety of the time was manifested in the building and endowing of abbeys and churches. . . . " The book is clear, easy to read, contains few notes and no bibliography, but it is still more than an introductory guide to medieval French history.

For that we must turn to the work by KNOX, a delightfully romanticized book which, for all its bibliography, its real awareness of historical and geographical problems, and its proper index, still contains engagingly reported conversations. But behind the less than wholly successful attempts to write as if the subject were Robin Hood, and the Holy Land Sherwood Forest, lurks a genuinely well-informed historian. No one else gives quite such explicit instructions on where to find printed editions of relevant primary sources. It is a pity that the over-writing sometimes spoils the well-informed, if over-confident, judgements of an historian well endowed with what we have come to call empathy. The fold-in map is better than Perry's, and the information is remarkably accurate, but the book unfailingly reads like an effort to turn medieval sources into the script of a period film.

For serious historians and other readers who want the results of the most sophisticated research, two French volumes must at least be mentioned, both compiled for the seventh centenary in 1970 of Louis IX's death. A still up-to-date account of the results and trends of contemporary research is to be found in the *Siècle de Louis IX* (edited by P. Labal, Paris, 1970: the title alludes to Voltaire's celebrated *Siècle de Louis XIV* in praise of the Sun-King), and the *Septième centenaire de la mort de Saint Louis* (Paris, 1976). These volumes contain contributions about the monarch or the reign that vary in quality and intention. Some throw new light on economic or social affairs, while others address questions that have now long been debated, like Louis' attitude to the Jews. Le Nain's *Vie* is defended, and the origins of the relationship between the university and the king, so important for the hegemony of doctrinal rectitude later imposed by Paris, but never by Oxford, are newly investigated. What we are told suggests that there is not a lot of recoverable information still to be discovered about the ruler.

Of the two remaining biographies, that by LABARGE is popular in style although still soundly based on historical research. It contains an index and a bibliography, a helpful table of dates, reasonably apt illustrations, and some plans, as of the routes taken by the crusader's fleets in 1248 and 1270. Inevitably the hastily sketched background has imperfections, and Labarge is guilty of some irritating naiveties, as when she remarks, "the Christian ideal of sanctity was generally admired and respected in the 13th century, even though most medieval men did not attempt to approach holiness." However, the book is well informed, well written, accurate, and readable, with a critical appendix on the medieval sources.

While Labarge does not neglect the crusade, she diminishes its importance in the total context of Louis' reign. Her account of the regency of Blanche of Castile, of the king's youth, of his subjugation of the rebellious feudal lords, his relations with the Pope, the English, and the Germans, the preparations for the crusade and the events that comprised it scarcely take us beyond the halfway point. Labarge claims that from his return in 1254, Louis' "emphasis on peace and justice within his realm would make him the most sought after arbitrator in Europe." His weakness was the spiritual conviction that he should undertake the crusade of 1270, from which he either could not or would not see that there was no political advantage to be gained. What im-

presses about Labarge is her grasp of the realities of the European power struggle and the complexities of the administrative arrangements for governing France rather than her mastery of the social, economic, or ecological realities. Not much is made of the king's simplification of his own household arrangements or his ascetic cut-backs on domestic expenditure. Indeed, there is little real attempt to explain the popular dislike of the 1270 crusade. The biography remains however an excellent introduction to the history of at least the reign, especially in its explanation of the administrative arrangements for the government of France. The account of Louis' settlement with the English, which, although cautiously welcomed at the time, led in the end to the hundred years' war, is a judicious and balanced as the scope of a popular biography admits.

JORDAN has written an outstanding account of Louis' reign, the first and so far the only attempt at a synthesis of recent historical research using the best of modern scientific historical method, with its emphasis on whatever hard economic or social facts are available. What is modestly presented as an "interim portrait" of the king, in spite of its suffering from the limitations acknowledged by the author, is likely to remain the definitive synthetic account of the reign for some time to come, certainly as far as pure biography goes. Jordan's weakness is his deliberate decision to focus the book on the crusade of 1248–54, and the controversial view that it was this crusade's failure that produced "a profound crisis" in the king, of which the outcome was "the creation of the 'ideal' medieval monarchy." It will not really be clear until a convincing "psycho-biography" is written whether the king seriously acknowledged the political failure of the seventh crusade. If he did, why did he persist so obdurately in mounting a further one? If he did not, could there not have been other factors contributing to the style of his internal reforms?

Such questions inevitably raise the further matter of the king's sanctity, with which Jordan is not primarily concerned. How far was the motivation for political acts finally spiritual? How far did social concern activate administrative reformatory endeavour? Was Voltaire right or merely generous when he saw in Louis IX the reconciliation of the strictest justice with the profoundest politics? Like all really good biographies, this one penetrates into the mind of its subject sufficiently far to leave the reader uncertain about the ultimate motivating springs of behaviour. Even if it were true that the saint took over from the ruler, except insofar as the achievement of justice required the imposition of government (as remains at least a serious possibility), the sheer weight of facts adduced and the application of a proper historical method make this a very distinguished, if unremittingly academic biography.

—A. H. T. Levi

LOUIS XI, 1423–1483; French monarch.

Champion, Pierre, *Louis XI* (2 vols.). New York, Dodd Mead, and London, Cassell, 1929 (originally published by H. Champion, Paris, 1927).

Hare. Christopher, *Life of Louis XI* [n.p.], 1907.
Kendall, Paul Murray, *Louis XI, the Universal Spider*. New York, Norton, 1970; London, Allen and Unwin, 1971 (without subtitle).
Tyrell, Joseph M., *Louis XI*. Boston, Twayne, 1980.

*

The bad character attributed to Louis XI for centuries after his death was firmly imprinted on the imagination of the English-speaking world by Sir Walter Scott's *Quentin Durward* (1823). Christopher Hare, in his 1907 biography (see below), devotes an interesting chapter to tracing the political and personal motives of writers who defamed Louis XI, in his own day and subsequently. The one contemporary writer who acclaimed Louis' greatness was Philippe de Commines, a man who had been a trusted courtier and beneficiary of the king. Writing after the king's death, Philippe claimed to be motivated only by a desire to record the truth. His *Memoirs*, written between 1489 and 1498, have been a major source for historians ever since. Recently, however, doubt has been cast on Commines' good faith by the German historian Karl Bittman.

With the publication between 1885 and 1905 of Louis XI's vast surviving correspondence, a second major source became available to historians. The insight this afforded into Louis' personality and motives told in his favour. HARE, the first English historian to draw on the new evidence, presented a king who could be harsh and devious but only in the interests of his people, who owed their survival as a nation to his care and wisdom. Many French historians also came to Louis' defence. CHAMPION's major two-volume biography of 1927 has been translated into English.

The best biography of Louis XI available in English is KENDALL's. To the sources previously explored, he adds extensive contemporary Italian diplomatic correspondence, describing the shrewd Italians, well-versed in Renaissance statecraft, as the "journalists" of Louis' court. Kendall is obviously fascinated by the mind of his subject and the complexity of his subject's personality, trying to put aside the perspective of hindsight long enough to observe how Louis grappled on the spot with each successive problem of his reign. Kendall's book is a large scholarly volume but written with an energy and vivacity that give the narrative great momentum, while the copious notes to each chapter are almost equally inviting. There are several interesting appendices, including one in which Philippe de Commines is defended against Bittman and other critics. There is also an extensive bibliography.

TYRRELL's account is much briefer and less scholarly in tone. Tyrell allies himself with the anti-Commines camp, placing great importance on Bittman's findings. His comments about the earlier works on Louis, which he lists in his fairly extensive bibliography, reflect this judgement.

—Isabel Aitken

LOUIS XIV, 1638–1715; French monarch.

Cronin, Vincent, *Louis XIV*. London, Collins, 1964; Boston, Houghton Mifflin, 1965.
Erlanger, Philippe, *Louis XIV*, translated by Stephen Cox. London, Weidenfeld and Nicolson, and New York, Praeger, 1970 (originally published by La Table Ronde, Paris, 1960).
Michel, Prince of Greece, *Louis XIV: The Other Side of the Sun*, translated by Alan Sheridan. London, Orbis, and New York, Harper, 1983 (originally published by O. Orban, Paris, 1979).
Mitford, Nancy, *The Sun King*. London, Hamilton, and New York, Harper, 1966.
Norton, Lucy, *The Sun King and His Loves*. London, Folio Society, 1982.
Ogg, David, *Louis XIV*. London, Oxford University Press, 1933; New York, 1959.

*

All biographies of Louis XIV have been influenced by two classic works: Voltaire's *The Century of Louis XIV*, which was first published in 1751, and the *Memoirs* of Saint-Simon, which first began to appear in 1788 although they were written much earlier, some 20 or 30 years after the king's death in 1715. Voltaire regarded Louis XIV as a great man, one who helped to modernize France, who possessed both judgment and taste. Saint-Simon saw him rather as a monster of egoism, immoral and deceitful, surrounding himself with mediocre advisers who were usually taken from the middle class.

Doubtless because of the literary qualities of Saint-Simon, and because Louis was remembered as an enemy of England and as the representative of an unacceptable despotism, most English biographers were hostile to Louis. This was the case of what was for many years the standard biography in English, that by Arthur Hassall (*Louis XIV*, New York, 1895).

OGG, a distinguished Oxford historian whose biography was very widely read, still reflects some of these views. As Ogg narrates the main events of the reign and sets them in the background of European history as a whole, he gives an unflattering picture of the king. He describes him as acting capriciously at times when other men would have behaved more scrupulously. Thus Louis' persecution of the Huguenots and of the Jansenists is explained by the influence of the Jesuits and of Madame de Maintenon (whom he married secretly, probably in 1684), as well as by a superstitious sentiment that God was no longer favouring him and that he should do something to placate the Deity. Just as the attack on the Huguenots by the revocation of the Edict of Nantes was a violation of a most solemn commitment, so the king showed little regard for fundamental laws. He threatened security of property by an edict declaring his superior lordship over all territory in the kingdom (1692), and he threatened the principle of monarchy itself by ruling that his illegitimate children could succeed to the throne. Louis could have done much, given his power and his strong personality, but he neither re-invigorated nor remoulded the institutions of his country. Ogg accepts that he was probably popular, although he argues that it is difficult to be sure about this, since Louis neither suffered a serious illness nor was the target of assassination attempts, which would have provided the occasion for popular sentiments to be expressed.

CRONIN concentrates more than does Ogg on the details of Louis' life, from the circumstances of his birth to parents who had been childless for 22 years of marriage, to the circumstances of his death four days short of the age of 77. But he presents the king in a favourable light. While it is true that he was surrounded by many loyal and hardworking men who concerned themselves with the details of government, Cronin believes that the many beneficial changes that took place in France would never have occurred without a ruler who could conceive great schemes and who had the will to carry them out. He approves the title that was bestowed upon Louis by the municipality of Paris in 1678, that of Louis the Great.

Cronin suggests a number of explanations for Louis' persecution of the Huguenots. There was the desire for unity, since unity got rid of disorder (in religion as in gardens), the conviction that unity was more efficient than diversity (so that the Comédie Française was in 1680 given exclusive acting rights in Paris), and the belief in the old coronation oath whereby the monarch swore that he would extirpate all heretics. But Louis, like Madame de Maintenon, wanted to convert rather than to persecute, and the revocation of the Edict of Nantes appears rather as a reluctant acceptance of the fact that there were Protestants who refused to be converted. Cronin says that Louis took an interest in theology and in spiritual affairs and that these tempered his extravagance and his love of luxury. We are presented with a man who was painfully conscious of a conflict of loyalties: between his private and his public life, between his own fulfillment and the welfare of France, between a passion for glory and a sense of humility before God's will.

MITFORD concentrates on the character of the king without suggesting that he was subjected to personal dilemmas. She sees him as secretive, cruel, one who often inspired terror, who was always attracted to clever and amusing people, found it easy to forgive women, and was only once in his life moved by the death of a relative or friend. We are presented with a mass of detailed, personal characteristics: the consuming of vast quantities of food, his persistent sexual appetite, a dislike of scent, a vaguely Jewish appearance (he probably had Jewish and Moorish blood through his Aragon ascendants). Louis' daily routine, we learn, left only a short time for work with ministers, and he never wished to confide in too many. On foreign policy he concentrated on the details of frontiers; on the persecution of the Huguenots he did not know what was really happening; he was surrounded by schemers and plotters; at the end of his life he was bored and sad. When Mitford recalls Lord Macaulay saying that France had over surrounding countries at once the ascendancy Rome had over Greece and the ascendancy Greece had over Rome, she does not explain this in terms of Louis XIV's biography, but leaves the matter in abeyance.

ERLANGER leads one into a different form of speculation, since central to his biography is his belief that Louis enjoyed being disconcerting. Thus he inflicted affronts on the pope, encouraged Molière to write mockingly about ecclesiastics, and frequently brought the Catholic zealots to heal. Yet he persecuted both the Protestants and the Jansenists. His foreign policy was also rich in contrasts, since he did not wish to adhere to any fixed system of alliances but simply wanted France's presence to be felt everywhere. All this was in line with the suggestion that Louis was essentially preoccupied with his greatness and was determined to outshine any example or rival. Therefore a shifting quality emerges in all his actions. While condemning

the revocation of the Edict of Nantes as a disaster, Erlanger hints that amongst the several reasons that explain this action, including the need to seize Protestant wealth, was the desire for popularity, the misguided idea of following the prejudices of the masses so as to receive their acclamation.

Erlanger gives considerable importance to Louis' health (more than other biographers do). He suggests that he worked too hard and suffered from headaches. Consequently he was subjected to painful treatments of laxatives, bloodletting and, for other ailments, surgery. It was when he was undergoing the most considerable discomfort and anxiety that his regime was at its most brutal. Yet Erlanger maintains that behind the illnesses, the secret ambitions, the lack of scruples, and the inexhaustible desire for flattery, Louis always remained a careful calculator, protecting his realm as a good landowner seeks to protect his property by wise extensions.

Very different is the picture given by PRINCE MICHEL of Greece. Just as for him the court is nothing but a brothel, frequented by those who are immoral, thieving, childish and, invariably, filthy, so Louis is an untalented man who has succeeded in imposing himself on his country where more intelligent predecessors have failed. He has done this, not only by ruining all those who surrounded him by appealing to their vanity and cupidity and by causing them to neglect their estates, but also by establishing in his court an inhuman and obsessive ballet that gave an image to posterity and made a mark on his century. He was fearful of truth, hypocritical, and secretive. His mind was narrow and superficial. When Louis died it was as if the cage in which the old potentate had for so long imprisoned France had suddenly been opened and there was general rejoicing.

With NORTON we are back with the king and his five loves: four women and a house with a garden. It was the last that was the greatest. He had, we are told, a cold and selfish heart. But we are also told that he was a very great king. All biographers have to choose between the individual who is covered by the ornate trappings of a unique court and the individual who has to contemplate the realities of his existence and those of the French people. None has altogether succeeded.

—Douglas Johnson

LOWELL, Amy, 1874–1925; American poet.

Benvenuto, Richard, *Amy Lowell*. Boston, Twayne, 1985.

Damon, S. Foster, *Amy Lowell: A Chronicle*. Boston, Houghton Mifflin, 1935.

Flint, F. Cudworth, *Amy Lowell*. Minneapolis, University of Minnesota Press, 1969.

Gould, Jean, *Amy: The World of Amy Lowell and the Imagist Movement*. New York, Dodd Mead, 1975.

Gregory, Horace, *Amy Lowell: A Portrait of the Poet in Her Time*. Edinburgh and New York, T. Nelson, 1958.

Ruihley, Glenn Richard, *The Thorn of a Rose: Amy Lowell Reconsidered*. Hamden, Connecticut, Archon Books, 1975.

Wood, Clement, *Amy Lowell*. New York, H. Vinal, 1926.

*

Except for the little Twayne volume, no biography of Amy Lowell has appeared since 1975. Amy's place in the annual bibliographies now has been taken by her more famous relative, Robert Lowell. This development makes clear that Amy Lowell's reputation has faded badly, and few followers of contemporary American poetry expect a revival of interest in her poetry. BENVENUTO's slim study contains a good 30-page biographical chapter, mostly drawn from previous biographies, but he makes little effort to resuscitate Lowell's fame and is chiefly interested in giving her a fair and detailed reading, ''to suggest the scope and limitations of her art, and to acquaint the reader with poems that ought not to be neglected any longer.''

RUIHLEY's book did make an effort to put Lowell back into the forefront of 20th-century poetry. His work is sympathetic and written with a vigorous sense that Lowell has been unjustly neglected in the last generation. Chapters one, two, four, and five contain mostly biography, but the book is a blend of biography and criticism. One comes away feeling, however, that Lowell never was as good as Ruihley thinks she was.

GOULD's biography of Lowell will have the most appeal for readers in the 1990s. Although one is apt to bridle at biographies of women writers that use the author's first name as the title, Gould's book is well researched and reasonably objective. Gould tends to run to clichés and often invents conversation, but she is able to bring in the pathos of Lowell's life without getting mawkish. This is, of course, a very sympathetic biography, but it has the merit of dealing rather straightforwardly with Lowell's relationship with her long-time friend and companion, Ada Dwyer Russell, making clear that it was a lesbian relationship, though she never uses the term.

Gould is probably the last biographer of Amy Lowell able to draw on both written and oral sources. She interviewed a number of people who knew Lowell, notably Mrs. August Belmont, who was close to Lowell, and Ada Russell. Gould also was aided by Robert Frost's daughter, Leslie Frost Ballantine, John Farrar, and others. Thus this biography contains some additional material not in Damon's earlier and bulkier life (see below), but unfortunately there are no notes to aid readers who want to know where specific pieces of information came from.

For the fullest account of Amy Lowell's life one must go to DAMON, the first real biographer and the most comprehensive one: his book runs to 773 pages. Damon was a close friend of Lowell's, having met her about ten years before her death, and was often a guest at her Brookline, Massachusetts, estate. He had access to her papers, and the help of Ada Russell, who survived Lowell. The available documentation was extensive: eight full cabinet drawers of letters sent and received, scrapbooks of newspaper clippings (Lowell subscribed to clipping services), diaries, journals, and school notebooks. Damon also had the advantage of working with Lowell's circle of friends.

Damon's book is the work of a scholar (he was a professor at Brown), carefully done and cogently written. It often quotes extensively from letters, both to and from Lowell, but the book is old-fashioned biography which makes no effort to probe beneath the surface of Lowell's life. It is not very lively reading, but it's a vast storehouse of information. It is somewhat better documented than Gould's book, as Damon has supplied footnotes for some of his sources, but in reality the supply of sources is meager.

Although Amy Lowell's poetic reputation has faded greatly, she was an indefatigable entrepreneur of modern poetry, and in this regard she retains a significant place in the history of 20th-

century American verse. She corresponded with and associated with all the important people. Gould's book does an adequate job of dealing with Lowell's relationships with Ezra Pound, D. H. Lawrence, Harriet Monroe, Robert Frost, Louis Untermeyer, and many others, but Damon's accounts are much fuller. His treatment of Lowell's battles for Imagism are important source material for this period. His view of Lowell herself, however, suffers from lack of perspective and too close a friendship, which made him overrate his subject.

GREGORY's work is about one-third the length of Damon's, but it covers the essential material and offers a rather cool assessment of Lowell's achievement. FLINT's contribution to Lowell biography is one of the pamphlets in that excellent series on American writers published by the University of Minnesota Press. Though it is only 45 pages in length, it contains a good, objective summation of Lowell's life and work and is an appropriate place to begin a study of Amy Lowell. WOOD's volume, published the year after Lowell died, is a hostile, disparaging book that can well be ignored.

—James Woodress

LOWELL, James Russell, 1819–1891; American writer and editor.

Beatty, Richmond C., *James Russell Lowell*. Nashville, Tennessee, Vanderbilt University Press, 1942.

Duberman, Martin B., *James Russell Lowell*. Boston, Houghton Mifflin, 1966.

Greenslet, Ferris, *James Russell Lowell: His Life and Work*. Boston, Houghton Mifflin, 1905.

Greenslet, Ferris, *The Lowells and Their Seven Worlds*. Boston, Houghton Mifflin, 1946.

Hale, Edward Everett (1822–1909), *James Russell Lowell and His Friends*. Boston, Houghton Mifflin, 1899.

Howard, Leon, *Victorian Knight-Errant: A Study of the Early Literary Career of James Russell Lowell*. Berkeley, University of California Press, 1952.

McGlinchee, Claire, *James Russell Lowell*. New York, Twayne, 1967.

Scudder, Horace, *James Russell Lowell: A Biography*. Boston, Houghton Mifflin, and London, Gay and Bird, 1901.

Wagenknecht, Edward, *James Russell Lowell: Portrait of a Many-Sided Man*. New York, Oxford University Press, 1971.

*

James Russell Lowell was at the peak of his fame when he died a century ago, but steadily during the advancing decades of the 20th century his reputation has diminished. Early biographers accepted as a given that Lowell was one of the great men of his age. He had been a major poet, an essayist of charm and wit, a humorist, a distinguished professor at Harvard, an able editor of the *Atlantic* and the *North American Review*, and he had capped his career with a diplomatic post as minister to both Spain and England.

The three biographies that appeared in the years immediately following Lowell's death all have been superseded, but they have historic interest as pioneering efforts. HALE's book came out before the turn of the century and should have been better than it is. Hale was a student at Harvard behind Lowell and had a long personal relationship with him. He apparently had no zest for the hard work involved in writing a real biography and contented himself with a chatty memoir. His book is entertaining and anecdotal, but it is of little value today.

SCUDDER, who was one of the later editors of the *Atlantic* that Lowell first headed when it began publication in 1857, wrote what might be called the official biography. He compiled two volumes of material put together in the leisurely Victorian fashion with many long quotations from letters. As Lowell was a prolific letter writer and thousands of his letters have survived, the documentation was extensive. But Scudder conceived of his biography as a tribute to Lowell, and it is not in the least an objective treatment of the man. While Scudder concentrates on heaping up the details of Lowell's life rather than analyzing them, he was still the first to research Lowell's life in detail, and subsequent biographers all owe him a considerable debt.

GREENSLET's 1905 biography is fashioned out of the materials gathered by Scudder and is about one-third as long. Coming 14 years after Lowell's death, it puts its subject into better perspective and is in general a better-written book. The great slabs of raw material loaded into Scudder's biography have been processed and offered in a more savory concoction. But Greenslet also avoids analysis and writes in his preface: "I have, indeed, endeavored to make Lowell, so far as possible, tell his own story, and be his own interpreter." After 40 years as a distinguished editor at Houghton Mifflin, GREENSLET returned to Lowell in his *The Lowells and Their Seven Worlds* and devoted a couple of chapters to James Russell along with other members of that illustrous clan.

It was not until 1966 that we had a full, objective, well-written biography of Lowell. DUBERMAN's book will no doubt stand as the definitive biography for a long time to come, and there would seem to be no need for anyone else to attempt the project. Duberman has gone to manuscript sources and put a vast amount of time and effort into uncovering much more primary material than any other biographer of Lowell has managed to find. The bibliography of manuscript and printed sources is extensive, and the notes run to over 100 pages. This is a scholarly, readable biography.

Duberman did not begin his work on Lowell with any illusion that Lowell was a great poet or that his accomplishments as critic, antislavery leader, professor, or diplomat seemed very important in the second half of the 20th century. Duberman writes, "What I have wished to do is to restore him as a man. It is Lowell's qualities as a human being which have most attracted me, and which most warrant rehabilitation. . . . the assumption underlying this book is that there is more to Lowell (and to many men) than their 'accomplishments'—and more that is of lasting importance."

Appearing about the same time as Duberman's impressive biography was McGLINCHEE's little volume, which is one of the poorest that the uneven Twayne Series has brought out. It is bland and superficial and of little use to anyone. Another unsatisfactory though not superficial book is BEATTY's contribution to Lowell studies. This book was written by a Southerner who didn't know the Civil War was over. Its anti-Northern bias is pervasive, and Beatty can't seem to forgive Lowell for being a Yankee and an abolitionist. Throughout the book there is a running commentary of snide remarks.

The final two books left for discussion are much more important. HOWARD's work, as the subtitle indicates, is a limited study of Lowell's early career. It is, however, a first-rate study by a distinguished scholar. Howard writes in his forward: "My purpose . . . was to discover the extent to which a meticulous examination of an individual's entire literary output, within the human context of its origin, could improve one's understanding of the individual himself and of the age in which he lived." WAGENKNECHT's book, the only work on Lowell in the last two decades, is what the author calls a "psychograph," or character portrait. The portrait that emerges from this well-written study is that of a man who had too many talents and never focused on one thing to do superbly well in it. Nothing about Lowell is simple, however, says Wagenknecht, who believes some of Lowell's contemporaries overestimated him because of his charm. Lowell was a human who seems more important than the sum of what he did. In this Wagenknecht and Duberman are in agreement.

—James Woodress

LOWELL, Robert, 1917–1977; American poet.

Axelrod, Stephen Gould, *Robert Lowell: Life and Art.* Princeton, New Jersey, Princeton University Press, 1978.

Hamilton, Ian, *Robert Lowell: A Biography.* New York, Random House, 1982; London, Faber, 1983.

Heymann, C. David, *American Aristocracy: The Lives and Times of James Russell, Amy, and Robert Lowell.* New York, Dodd Mead, 1980.

Meyers, Jeffrey, *Manic Power: Robert Lowell and His Circle.* New York, Arbor House, and London, Macmillan, 1987.

Meyers, Jeffrey, *Robert Lowell: Interviews and Memoirs.* Ann Arbor, University of Michigan Press, 1988.

*

When Hamilton (see below) published the first full-length biography five years after Lowell's death, the outlines of his subject's life were well known from his poetry, interviews, and critical studies of his art; these are still good introductions to Lowell biography. His fourth collection, *Life Studies* (1959), in which he abandoned poetic formalism for a more colloquial free verse, marks the shift to a directly personal, even documentary poetic. In that volume Lowell provided biographers with a model for the inseparability of his life and work by including a fragment of his autobiography as a bridge between poems in the older style and the newer "confessional" ones. Although Lowell never completed his autobiography (another section was published in *Collected Prose*, 1987), he viewed his 40 years' output as a "journey of the soul."

It is not surprising, then, that criticism of Lowell's poetry incorporates information about his life. AXELROD's study, the first book on Lowell to appear after his death, is explicitly biographical in being based on the premise that Lowell's poetry is dedicated to "the mind's experience of itself and its world." Although his subtitle suggests a balance between life and art and his avowed purpose is to tell us "how it was" for Lowell, Axelrod's emphasis is finally critical and interpretive; he uses biographical details, including unpublished manuscripts and letters, primarily to illuminate Lowell's poetry. In the belief that "the artist's existence becomes his art," he pays particular attention to Lowell's politics, his relation to American literary tradition, and the overall shape of his career.

HEYMANN's strategy of viewing Lowell in relation to his Boston Brahmin clan is effective because the innovations of Robert Lowell's work, which changed the direction of American poetry toward the informal and personal, seem all the more remarkable in the context of that conservative family. Although he emphasizes Lowell's turbulent life, Heymann attempts a valuation of his poetry, concluding that Robert's worthiness to be considered alongside his illustrious relatives derives from his early volumes (through *Life Studies*). These represent his "aristocracy of achievement." Contrasting this valuable work with Lowell's troubled personal history resulted in the title for this section, "Noble Savage," which takes up over one-third of his group biography. William Pritchard turned the implied criticism of Lowell's messy personal life back on Heymann, finding the "gossipy character" of his approach offputting, and concluding that the biographer's "style seems not quite aristocratic enough for its subjects" (*New York Times Book Review*, 3 August 1980).

Although Lowell's life was spent in public view as the leading poet of his generation, HAMILTON's comprehensive biography provided readers with much new material, some of it sensational or painful, depending on one's attitude toward "confessional" biography. One revelation was that Lowell fought manic-depressive illness most of his life, with one sign of the onset of a manic episode being sudden sexual infatuation. Doubtless it is such details that made the book popular even with those uninterested in poetry. Those who were interested praised Hamilton's comprehensive research and the care he took to show the selfless loyalty of Lowell's intimates (especially second wife Elizabeth Hardwick) to a troubled and difficult man. Hamilton seems to have interviewed everyone who knew the poet well and to have read all the Lowell manuscripts as well as much of the correspondence of this decidedly literary circle.

Hamilton spends only two chapters on Lowell's childhood and adolescence while devoting more than half the book to his last two decades. He neither assesses the value of Lowell's work nor determines his place in modern poetry. In Richard Ellmann's words, Hamilton's method is "close inspection rather than large perspectives" (*New York Times Book Review*, 28 November 1982). He lets his sources speak for themselves and presents conflicting reviews of controversial volumes of poems without siding with either view. In some sections, Hamilton seems to be narrating only to link the many extracts from interviews, correspondence, and Lowell's own manuscripts and conversation. Occasionally he steps in to look at transformations and revisions of particular poems, printing early drafts in order to study his subject's working methods. A poet himself and former editor of two journals, Hamilton received high marks for these analyses; to John Simon the best parts of his book "read like the beginnings of a variorum edition of Lowell's poetry (*New Republic*, 27 December 1982).

In all Hamilton's is a curiously detached biography that takes its shape from the external events of Lowell's life—his troubled family relations, religious crises, erratic politics, bouts of mental

illness and alcoholism, and turbulent marriages—rather than from following the course of his intellectual and poetic development (an approach that would be of interest primarily to scholars). As Helen Vendler pointed out in her favorable review, Hamilton has not written the intellectual biography of Lowell that scholars need (*New York Review of Books*, 2 December 1982). Other critics noted the absence of a sense of Lowell's inner life, and Bernard McCabe lamented the lack of serious discussion of the philosophical underpinnings of such matters as Lowell's conversion to Roman Catholicism (*The Nation*, 26 February 1983). He also complained about Hamilton's neglect of "the rich cultural ambiance" in which Lowell moved. Calling it a "dangerously unserious" work, he faulted especially Hamilton's "basic failure to relate the life to the work in useful ways." But Jean Strouse admired Hamilton's "seamless weave of life story and literary criticism, his calm, sharp assessments, and his refusal to idealize or 'explain' Lowell's genius or his pain" (*Newsweek*, 15 November 1982).

MEYERS' group biography of Lowell and his contemporaries (1987) complements Hamilton's looser depiction of a group of intelligent, competitive writers by focusing on Lowell's relations with poets Randall Jarrell, John Berryman, Theodore Roethke, and (in an epilogue) Sylvia Plath. Meyers relies on published biographies and memoirs—including Eileen Simpson's *Poets in Their Youth* (1982), a group memoir featuring many of the same figures. Robert Von Hallberg said that despite Meyers' lack of originality his "subject is a great one: how a group of talented American poets cultivated neurosis and brought their lives to disaster, somehow in the name of what was taken in the years following World War II as the demands of poetry itself" (*New England Quarterly*, December 1988).

Published interviews are another source of the connections between Lowell's personal and public lives; 20 are reprinted in MEYERS' edited collection (1988), including Norman Mailer's portrait of Lowell as political poet and activist (originally published in *Armies of the Night*, 1968) and 16 tributes and essays (one an essay-review of Hamilton). This compilation of memoirs by some of our century's best writers and extensive transcriptions of the conversation of one of its most articulate poets is valuable in its own right, and it supplements each of the other biographical studies, including Hamilton's definitive biography.

—Phyllis Frus

LOYOLA, Saint Ignatius. See IGNATIUS OF LOYOLA.

LUCE, Clare Boothe, 1903–1987; American playwright, politician, and diplomat.

Hatch, Alden, *Ambassador Extraordinary: Clare Boothe Luce.* New York, Holt, 1956.
Henle, Faye, *Au Clare de Luce: Portrait of a Luminous Lady.* New York, Daye, 1943.

Lawrenson, Helen, *Stranger at the Party*. New York, Random House, 1975.

Shadegg, Stephen, *Clare Boothe Luce: A Biography*. New York, Simon and Schuster, 1970; London, Frewin, 1973.

Sheed, Wilfrid, *Clare Boothe Luce*. New York, Dutton, and London, Weidenfeld and Nicolson, 1982.

*

The first comprehensive biography, that by HENLE, was written while Mrs. Luce was only 40. It has valuable information on her ambitious mother, a former chorus girl, and her profligate father, a professional violinist; her education at St. Mary's School in Garden City, Long Island, and Castle School in Tarrytown; unfortunate marriage to millionaire George Browkaw; her stint as an editor of *Vanity Fair*; second marriage to publisher Henry R. Luce; her most successful play, *The Women* (1937); and role as roving correspondent in World War II. Henle's is often fawning and she does find "plenty of evidence" for Clare's "charity and thoughtfulness." She does, however, find Mrs. Luce "shrewd, cynical, hard and calculating, an opportunist, a careful engineer of her own destiny who puts self-advancement above all else."

HATCH's life, which includes material on Luce's ambassadorship, is even more friendly than Henle's, though it is also more superficial. Using prose that gets increasingly heady, Hatch combines an adoring tone with a grating style. He refers to Clare as "brilliant, yet often foolish, . . . tough as a marine sargeant, but almost quixotically kind to unfortunates, . . . with the mind and courage of a man and exceedingly feminine instincts." Hatch can only conclude that "Probably the reason no one understands her is because she does not understand herself."

The next full biography, that by SHADDEG, retraces familiar ground while adding material on Luce's role as congresswoman from 1943 to 1947, her conversion to Roman Catholicism, and the death of her husband. It is a friendly account, written by a conservative advertising executive, free-lance writer, and erstwhile braintruster for Senator Barry Goldwater. Considering Clare "one of the giants of our time," Shaddeg had free access to her unpublished papers and benefitted from her personal reminiscences. Although often a competent work, the book (as Lawrenson points out) garbles the chronology of her early life, greatly exaggerates her role in the passage of the National Industrial Recovery Act, and claims that she "transformed her resentment" over the death of her daughter on to her husband, who had "never suffered a defeat." Moreover, it leaves major topics unanswered, such as her mercurial marriage to Henry and the rationale for her political shift from Willkie Republicanism to the Goldwater brand.

In many ways, SHEED's account is the best. A family friend from his boyhood, novelist Sheed offers more a memoir than a biography. The novice reader might feel like a playgoer who missed the first act, something not helped by the fact that Sheed is candid in admitting that he has pulled his punches: "Does one blow the secret, or leave a gaping hole in her character? I do a bit of both." Yet at its best, this rambling, impressionistic account is the most perceptive we have, for it is the only one that explores Clare's marriage to Henry, the Roman Catholic milieu of the 1950s, and her political conservatism. He attempts to refute the acid description of Clare's career given by *Vanity Fair* editor LAWRENSON in a chapter entitled "The Delicate Monster."

E. H. Swanberg, in his life of Henry Luce (*Luce and His Empire*, 1972), notes how Clare's husband puffed her plays and managed her congressional campaign. He is critical of Clare's role of ambassador and of her outright enthusiasm for the Diem family and the American effort in Vietnam. John Kobler (*Luce: His Time, Life, and Fortune*, 1968) sees Clare as the true initiator of *Life* magazine, which was supposedly patterned on a memo she had written for Conde Nast three years earlier. He also notes that Henry pushed his wife on President Eisenhower for the Italian post.

—Justus D. Doenecke

LUTHER, Martin, 1483–1546; German theologian and church reformer.

Bainton, Roland, *Here I Stand: A Life of Martin Luther*. Nashville, Tennessee, Abingdon Press, 1950; London, Hodder and Stoughton, 1951.

Boehmer, Heinrich, *Martin Luther: Road to Reformation*, translated by John W. Doberstein and Theodore G. Tappert. Philadelphia, Muhlenberg Press; London, Thames and Hudson, and New York, Meridian, 1957 (originally published as *Der Junge Luther*, 2 vols., Flamberg, Gotha, 1925).

Bornkamm, Heinrich, *Luther in Mid-Career 1521–30*, edited by Karin Bornkamm, translated by Theodore Bachmann. Philadelphia, Fortress Press, and London, Darton Longman, 1983 (originally published by Vandenhoeck and Ruprecht, Göttingen, 1979).

Brecht, Martin, *Martin Luther: His Road to Reformation 1483–1521*, translated by James L. Schaaf. Philadelphia, Fortress Press, 1985 (originally published by Calwer, Stuttgart, 3 vols., 1981–87).

Dickens, A. G., *Martin Luther and the Reformation*. Mystic, Connecticut, L. Verry, and London, English Universities Press/Hodder and Stoughton, 1967.

Edwards, Mark U., Jr., *Luther's Last Battles: Politics and Polemics 1531–46*. Leiden, Netherlands, and Ithaca, New York, Cornell University Press, 1983.

Erikson, Erik H., *Young Man Luther: A Study in Psychoanalysis and History*. New York, Norton, and London, Faber, 1958.

Fife, Robert, *The Revolt of Martin Luther*. New York, Columbia University Press, 1957.

Haile, H. G., *Luther: An Experiment in Biography*. New York, Doubleday, 1980; as *Luther: A Biography*, London, Sheldon, 1981.

Mackinnon, James, *Martin Luther and the Reformation* (4 vols.). London and New York, Longman, 1925–30.

Oberman, Heiko A., *Luther: Man Between God and the Devil*, translated by Eileen Walliser-Schwarzbart. New Haven, Connecticut, Yale University Press, 1989 (originally published by Severin and Siedler, Berlin, 1981).

Rupp, Gordon, *Luther's Progress to the Diet of Worms*. London, SCM Press, and Chicago, Wilcox and Follett, 1951.

Schwiebert, E. C., *Luther and His Times*. St. Louis, Concordia
    Publishing House, 1950.
Smith, Preserved, *The Life and Letters of Martin Luther*.
    Boston and New York, Houghton Mifflin, and London, J.
    Murray, 1911.
Thiel, Rudolf, *Luther*, translated by Gustav K. Wiencke.
    Philadelphia, Muhlenberg Press, 1955.
Todd, John M., *Martin Luther: A Biographical Study*. New
    York, Paulist Press, and London, Burns and Oates, 1964.

*

Authenticated information about the personal life of Martin
Luther is limited, but that has not inhibited biographies, based
as they are on his place in theological inquiry and religious reform, and on his abundant writings on these matters. The psychoanalyst Erikson in his controversial study (see below) asserts
that Luther's "role in history, and above all his personality, remain ambiguous on a grandiose scale." The ambiguity derives
not only from the paradox of scarcity and abundance in the primary sources but from the varied purposes and points of view
that have been brought to the subject over more than four centuries. Biographies published by religious presses, essentially for
the faithful, co-exist with academic studies aimed at scholars,
though some of the most useful and influential biographies actually represent both aims.

The many biographies—most are in German and the Scandinavian languages—vary in their theological orientations, the
older and polemical Catholic studies of Luther facing obvious
difficulties in point of view, with even such recent works as
TODD's showing ambivalence about him. There is disagreement too about the relative emphasis to be given to Luther's
background in the late Medieval period in relation to his role
in the early Renaissance, to the social and political nature of
the Lutheran movement, and to the nature of his legacy across
the many nationalities that came to have large Protestant
populations.

Rupp (for whose full-length study see below) has provided a
good survey of early Luther biography in "The Luther of Myth
and the Luther of History" (*The Righteousness of God: Luther
Studies* [London, 1953]). And he says elsewhere of MACKIN-
NON's massive effort that "He commits the one unforgivable
sin in Luther study, which is to make Luther dull." Conversely,
THIEL offers, in his words, a Luther "continually visited by
earthquakes of the soul." His biography is organized around
Luther's roles as "Heretic," "Warrior," etc. FIFE's lengthy and
scholarly study, in contrast again, is deliberate and thorough,
leaving more room for the reader's judgments of Luther's character and work. SCHWIEBERT's is another ambitious volume
having the virtue of comprehensiveness (it offers a good map of
the biographical and historical terrain, and it includes a useful
section on the university environment) even if it is lacking in the
interpretive subtleties of more recent studies.

BAINTON's biography, certainly the one most widely read
and cited in English, is an example of the mingling of sophisticated scholarship and adept popularization. The reputation of
this study derives in part from Bainton's authority as a leading
church historian and partly from his talent for conveying the
meaning of Luther's convictions for readers with non-sectarian

interests. His book is artfully constructed and well illustrated
with woodcuts and engravings representing Luther's milieu. It is
organized into many short vivid sections.

Here I Stand makes little of Luther's childhood, adolescence,
and university education in philosophy and theology. Instead,
Bainton begins with Luther's sudden entry into the monastery at
the age of 20 and then addresses his choice of a complementary
vocation as a professor of the Bible in Wittenberg. Even though
Luther's marriage and other personal matters are well treated in
the text, Bainton reminds us that "the great outward crises of
his life which bedazzle the eyes of dramatic biographers were to
Luther himself trivial in comparison with the inner upheavals of
his questing after God." Still, as his book's title suggests, Bainton makes the drama of Luther's heresy the centerpiece of his
biography.

As with all other biographers, Bainton stresses Luther's great
capacity for work and the innovations he offered not only in
theology but in the personal example of modern religiosity. In
this biography the chief subject is the unity of Luther's work and
life in his mature years; though Luther's last 16 years get merely
ten pages. Bainton's great virtue is that despite biographical neglect of nearly a third of Luther's life (the early and late years),
he presents a convincing portrait of his dominating religious motivations and his *Anfechtung*, a German term roughly translat-
able in Luther's case as inner turmoil, panic, and desolation at
the idea of personally facing God. This notion is the source of
continuity in his account of Luther's life.

BOEHMER presents a different view, that the early Luther
suffered from problems of faith while the mature churchman agonized over problems associated with the theological professions. BORNKAMM and HAILE are among the few biographers
focussing on Luther's middle years, where the narrative drama
must depend less on well-known personal turning points and
more on the consolidation of theological ideas and institutional
structures. Bornkamm writes with unusual self-consciousness
about the need to balance personal and theological materials. He
regards his book as a continuation of Boehmer's, and he offers a
compelling portrait of the solitary Luther fashioning a spiritual
legacy. Bornkamm is not reluctant to speculate about Luther's
feelings and reactions to people and events. Haile concentrates
on Luther in his 50s, when his "ever shifting irony" and "raucous humor" came to reflect an influential thinker also "pun-
gently alive" to his followers. This unusual biography seeks to
speak from within Luther's mid-life contemplation on his experience. Haile writes with considerable urgency, believing as he
does that Luther is more than a mere religious figure: he is a
"classical" one in the challenges his life and thought present to
ordinary human thinking and behavior. As its title makes plain,
EDWARD's study fills out the story of Luther's life, concentrating on his bitter controversies beyond Wittenberg.

ERIKSON's controversial book is perhaps the only one that
rivals Bainton's in its broad appeal, though many readers come
to it out of historical and psychological rather than theological
interest. It represents the preoccupation of scholars with Luther's
youth, or at least the period that ends with the Diet of Worms.
Erikson's is an exemplary text in what is sometimes called
"psychohistory," a putative synonym for psychological biography. Indeed, in an introductory chapter Erikson makes the
question of biographies of Luther a central part of his subject.

He is critical of several from the 20th century: one in English, a primitive psychological study by SMITH, the others still untranslated.

Though it contains accounts of Luther's study of Occamism and other philosophical trends, the bulk of Erikson's treatment reflects his belief in the general neglect in all biographies of the psychology of work. Hence he organizes his account of Luther's early years (especially the seemingly difficult relation with his father Hans) and choice of a career around the psychoanalytic theory of developmental stages and the making of ego-identity in late adolescence. Erikson also stresses Luther's erudition, his talents as a lecturer and writer, part of his devotion to words and the Word. And the great theological reformer is ultimately aligned with the secular hero Freud as a figure in Western intellectual history who radically confronted conventional ideas.

Erikson's biography prompted a debate that continues to the present. Bainton has been one of his chief antagonists, asserting the problems entailed in the paucity of clinical data (something Erikson himself had acknowledged), disputing translations and interpretations of key statements and events, questioning the stage-specific distinctions made about Luther's mental state (Bainton finds *Anfechtung* throughout), and altogether casting doubt on the role of psychology in religious and historical biography. Erikson's book is in a sense specialized, but by virtue of its author's stature and the affiliation of its argument to significant trends in 20th-century thought and life, *Young Man Luther* demands attention from anyone interested in the life of Luther.

The brief but influential study of RUPP stands to the side of this dispute. It preceded Erikson's volume, but even in a 1964 preface to a new edition Rupp ignores recent biographical controversies and instead addresses scholarly differences on theological points. His book is an admiring and scholarly account of the development of Luther's theology prior to the posting (in 1517) of his Ninety-Five Theses at the Castle Church in Wittenberg. It reflects the need to supplant the view that Luther's earliest theological stirrings, and hence the Protestant Reformation too, were merely negative and destructive. By calling for the reorientation of Luther biography, Rupp shows how the theological and institutional reformers in Luther emerged together in the role of the professor, that being essential, in Rupp's view, to any understanding of his subject. Still, even in his brief study Rupp (like Bainton) seeks to convey his belief in Luther's accessibility, both in his time and ours.

DICKENS, like Rupp a succinct and artful prose stylist, accepts the need to think psychologically about Luther even while elucidating his ideas. He has a useful chapter on Luther's last years, and he also situates Luther's achievement in the European setting and in the centuries that followed. BRECHT's biography takes Boehmer's as its model. It is painstaking in its efforts to combine up-to-date scholarship on theological issues, readability, and a certain partisanship. It was written, Brecht says in stressing his reliance on new international, multidisciplinary, and ecumenical research, by a Protestant church historian, "who owes much to his confrontation with the reformer."

OBERMAN's biography reflects the virtues of many of its predecessors: it is another essential book that anyone interested in Luther will want to consult, not least for its unusual opening section in which the complex political environment of early 16th-century German and Roman Catholicism is vividly portrayed. It is dedicated to Bainton and in some ways resembles his in design (including many illustrations) as well as in its strong authorial voice. Oberman is more sympathetic to psychological interpretations of Luther, but he refreshingly stresses the role of Luther's mother Margarethe and her family in the making of her son's identity. Oberman presents Luther's earliest schooling with great skill and attention to the philosophic and theological disputes—as part of the general monastic climate—that preceded and then were submerged in the Reformation itself. But as his subtitle suggests, Oberman is especially interested in Luther's lifelong struggle with the devil. By rejecting the mythologizing of a path from medieval superstition to enlightened evangelical faith, this biography restores an important element of Luther's life and thought.

Luther's place in history means that the story of his life and work appears in many books on religious, historical, social, and even economic themes. Typical is Steven Ozment's *The Age of Reform, 1250-1550: An Intellectual and Religious History of Late Medieval and Reformation Europe* (1980), in which Luther's "mental world" is also elucidated as a complex combination of personal motives and trends in the history of religion and ideas generally.

—Steven Weiland

LUXEMBURG, Rosa, 1871–1919; German revolutionary and Socialist leader.

Abraham, Richard, *Rosa Luxemburg: A Life for the International.* Oxford and New York, Berg, 1989.
Basso, Lelio, *Rosa Luxemburg: A Reappraisal*, translated by D. Parmée. London, Deutsch, and New York, Praeger, 1975 (originally published by Feltrinelli, Milan, 1973).
Cliff, Tony, *Rosa Luxemburg.* London, Bookmarks, 1959; revised as *Rosa Luxemburg: A Study*, London, Socialist Review, 1968.
Ettinger, Elzbieta, *Rosa Luxemburg: A Life.* Boston, Beacon Press, 1986; London, Harrap, 1987.
Frölich, Paul, *Rosa Luxemburg: Ideas in Action*, translated by J. Hoornweg. London, Pluto Press, 1972 (originally published, Paris, 1939).
Geras, Norman, *The Legacy of Rosa Luxemburg.* London, NLB, 1976.
Nettl, J. P., *Rosa Luxemburg* (2 vols.). London, Oxford University Press, 1966; abridged edition, London and New York, Oxford University Press, 1969.

*

Although one of the earliest studies, NETTL remains the definitive work. This work covers not only Luxemburg's political history but also her personal history. Based on exhaustive research of both German and Polish sources, Nettl clearly restores Luxemburg to her place in the history of socialism as developing "an alternative revolutionary Marxist tradition against other claimants." At the same time, Nettl provides a clear vision of the person behind the politics.

A close collaborator of Luxemburg, FRÖLICH's work is inspired and exciting but suffers from its obvious bias in favor of its subject. Still, there is a great value in the insights given about Luxemburg and in revealing the emotions of her co-thinkers: "it was rumoured in the proletarian districts of Germany that the news of her murder was not true, that she was alive, that she had managed to escape. . . . People did not want to believe that so much will-power, enthusiasm, and intellectual strength could have been wiped out by a rifle-butt."

A more detailed focus on Luxemburg's personal life is to be found in ETTINGER. Drawing on Luxemburg's personal letters, this volume delves into the person more than the thinker. Ettinger makes no attempt "to give a comprehensive analysis of her writings." Rather, Luxemburg is treated as "a person of flesh and blood, with strengths and weaknesses, triumphs and nightmares. Brilliant and courageous, she was still racked by doubts, insecurity, and disappointments inevitable in the life of a woman who transcended her time." This approach makes Ettinger useful for those who are more interested in Luxemburg as a woman in a man's world than as a socialist in a capitalist world.

Brief and centered on Luxemburg's political teachings, CLIFF is notable for his attempt to explain complex theories in simple language. Although not based on firsthand research, Cliff serves as a notable introduction to Luxemburg's "main permanent contribution to the international socialist movement."

A more developed study of her thought, particularly her internationalist beliefs, is contained in ABRAHAM. While it adds little that isn't in Nettl it is very readable and does a great service in stressing Luxemburg's importance in fighting against war and nationalism. Further, Abraham manages to be understanding to his subject yet retain his critical judgement.

BASSO devotes his work to the study of Luxemburg's philosophical contribution to Marxist theory. While not a biography in the sense of Nettl, this work may be seen as an intellectual biography of Luxemburg. Basso certainly sees her importance in that "Luxemburg's thought and method can and must become an intellectual guide for the labour movement."

Much like Basso, GERAS wants to explore Luxemburg's importance as a theorist and focuses on four topics: capitalist breakdown, Russian Revolution, mass strikes, and socialist democracy. After raising as many questions as he tries to answer, Geras concludes that those who wish to understand revolutionary politics "could begin by reading Rosa Luxemburg."

—William A. Pelz

LYELL, (Sir) Charles, 1797–1875; English geologist.

Bailey, Edward, *Charles Lyell*. London and New York, T. Nelson, 1962.

Bonney, Thomas G., *Charles Lyell and Modern Geology*. London, Cassell, and New York, Macmillan, 1895.

Lyell, Katharine M., editor, *Life, Letters, and Journals of Sir Charles Lyell, Bart.* (2 vols.). London, J. Murray, 1881.

Wilson, Leonard G., *Charles Lyell, the Years to 1841: A Revolution in Geology*. New Haven, Connecticut, Yale University Press, 1972.

*

Lyell's first biographer was his sister-in-law, KATHERINE M. LYELL, the younger daughter of Leonard Horner; she married Charles Lyell's military brother, Henry. Her *Memoir of Leonard Horner* (2 vols., London, 1890) and *Life of Sir Charles Bunbury* (2 vols., London, 1906) both supplement the more important *Life, Letters, and Journals of Sir Charles Lyell*. The latter includes an autobiographical account of Lyell's boyhood, large extracts from his private journals, and selected letters (from among the large number still extant) to his wife, family, and friends. The quality and utility of the collection are considerably enhanced by Lyell's skill as a writer. Unfortunately, even two volumes are insufficient to encompass large portions of Lyell's life, including his frequent travels. A scientifically important trip to Madeira in 1853, for example, would be lost to us had not Charles Bunbury, who accompanied Lyell, described it in letters of his own. Some of the letters that Katharine did publish, moreover, were silently edited by her, with unannounced deletions and some mistakes. As was usual in the life and letters genre, editorial intrusion is otherwise minimal. There is therefore no attempt at objective analysis or psychological insight.

BONNEY's short biography of Lyell is based primarily on the *Life, Letters, and Journals*, together with additional information from Lyell's numerous books and scientific papers. As its title indicates, the book has two purposes: first, to present a concise account of Lyell's life; and, second, to detail the rise of "modern geology," which he equated with the uniformitarianism of Lyell's *Principles of Geology* (1830–33) and related publications. (Uniformitarianism holds that the geological causes active in the past are, in kind and degree, precisely those which we see around us today. Other theorists had assumed a geological past totally unlike the present.)

Chapters one through four in Bonney cover Lyell's life from birth to the publication of the third volume of the *Principles* in 1833. A conscientious historian, Bonney includes what facts he had. But, not having access to Lyell family papers, he has necessarily to guess at the significance of numerous details. A good deal of pleasant (but not necessarily accurate) commentary results with improvisation generally identified as such. In other respects, Bonney is often reduced to paraphrasing Lyell. He is concise and occasionally insightful, but the limitations of his scanty sources naturally become his own.

Chapter five is a lengthy examination and evaluation of Lyell's *Principles* (the first volume of which appeared in June 1830, not January as both Bonney and Lyell himself attest). There were more textual changes of significance in the early editions of the *Principles* (which had 12 editions in all) than Bonney indicates. In other respects, too, the entire discussion is now unhelpful and obsolete, not even a reliable guide to Lyell's reputation as it existed at the time. By 1895, in particular, two of Lyell's most central beliefs—the immense age of the earth, and the uniformity of geological causes—were seriously in question. Bonney thus overlooked a good deal in regarding Lyell as the first modern geologist.

The remainder of the book contains good accounts of Lyell's two major visits (of four) to North America—episodes scarcely noticed in the *Life, Letters, and Journals.* As in that earlier account, however, the last decades of Lyell's life are poorly represented, and his important relationship with Charles Darwin (whose theories were also in trouble by 1895) is little more than alluded to. Bonney's "Summary" generalizes eloquently about Lyell and is now the most valuable portion of this largely superseded book.

As yet, BAILEY's is the only other completed biography of Lyell. Like Bonney's, it is a short, rather basic life written by an admiring geological successor from fairly obvious source materials. Unfortunately, one has to guess at the materials he used because he provides neither footnotes nor a bibliography. Only published sources were consulted. By way of recompence, photographs, maps, and drawings abound. Though superficial, uncritical, and badly written, Bailey's is a responsible, if dated, introduction. One finds here better treatments than Bonney's concerning geological background (emphasizing Lyell's indebtedness to his Scottish predecessor, James Hutton) and the Lyell-Darwin relationship, among others. Important friends and influences like Gideon Mantell and Roderick Murchison are characterized briefly, but the Madeira trip, like some other episodes, is sketchier. Lyell's final decade is dismissed in about two pages. By way of conclusion, an oversimplified "Epilogue" uncritically lists Lyellian positions now considered modern. Continuing the established tradition of unabashed admiration, this biography too should be treated with caution.

WILSON's far more massive life of Lyell, the first to be attempted by a properly trained historian, was not, unfortunately, continued beyond its initial volume. Having appeared in 1972, it stands on the threshold of significant changes in perspective as to the development of modern geology as a whole. As a result, some of its judgments now seem overstated while its inclusion or omission of topics appears to be inexact. The book is also uneven in literary quality; eloquent and moving in some places, turgid and unfinished in others. The editing is noticeably uneven. A further commonly expressed criticism is that Lyell himself appears throughout as little more than a geological calculating machine, without the normal passions and frailties of flesh and blood. Extensive portions of this lengthy work, moreover, are devoted to geological background, in which Lyell and his life tend to get lost amid sweeping reviews of the science of geology.

Despite these flaws—all of them real—Wilson's is still the most valuable biography of Lyell that we have, for two reasons. First, Wilson was an extremely diligent, impressively intelligent researcher who thought through historical problems in an original manner and followed them to the end. His book, therefore, contributes greatly to our understanding of geology in Lyell's time and necessarily clarifies many aspects of his own accomplishments. Later scholarship has been significantly influenced by Wilson's discoveries. Second, Wilson alone was granted access to the hitherto unused and unavailable Lyell family papers, a resource so fundamental as to plunge all previous biographies into obsolescence. His book, therefore, abounds in new, significant material. Equally original photographs, drawings, and maps enhance the text, together with an outstanding bibliography. The index, unfortunately, is occasionally inadequate.

—Dennis R. Dean

MacARTHUR, Douglas, 1880–1964; American military leader.

Blair, Clay, Jr., *MacArthur.* New York, Doubleday, and London, Futura, 1977.

Fredericks, Edgar J., *MacArthur: His Mission and Meaning.* Philadelphia, Whitmore, 1968.

Gunther, John, *The Riddle of MacArthur: Japan, Korea, and the Far East.* New York, Harper, 1951.

Higgins, Trumbell, *Korea and the Fall of MacArthur.* New York, Oxford Universtiy Press, 1960.

James, D. Clayton, *The Years of MacArthur* (3 vols.). Boston, Houghton Mifflin, 1970–85.

Kelley, Frank R. and Cornelius Ryan, *Star-Spangled Mikado.* New York, R. M. McBride, 1947.

Kelley, Frank R. and Cornelius Ryan, *MacArthur, a Man of Action.* New York, Doubleday, 1950; as *MacArthur: A Biography,* London, W. H. Allen, 1951.

Kenney, George C., *The MacArthur I Know.* New York, Duell Sloane, 1951.

Lee, Clark and Richard Henschel, *Douglas MacArthur.* New York, Holt, 1952.

Manchester, William, *American Caesar: Douglas MacArthur 1880–1964.* Boston, Little Brown, 1978; London, Hutchinson, 1979.

Mayer, Sydney L., *MacArthur in Japan.* New York, Ballantine, 1973.

Miller, Francis T., *General Douglas MacArthur: Fighter for Freedom.* Philadelphia, J. C. Miller, and London, Angus and Robertson, 1942; as *General Douglas MacArthur: Soldier Statesman,* Philadelphia, J. C. Winston, 1951.

Petillo, Carol M., *Douglas MacArthur: The Philippine Years.* Bloomington, Indiana University Press, 1981.

Rovere, Richard H. and Arthur M. Schlesinger, *The General and The President.* New York, Farrar Straus, 1951; as *The MacArthur Controversy and American Foreign Policy,* New York, Farrar Straus, 1965.

Smith, Robert, *MacArthur in Korea: The Naked Emperor.* New York, Simon and Schuster, 1982.

Spanier, John W., *The Truman-MacArthur Controversy and the Korean War.* Cambridge, Massachusetts, Belknap Press, 1959.

Whan, Vorin E., editor, *A Soldier Speaks: Public Papers and Speeches of General of the Army Douglas MacArthur.* New York, Praeger, 1965.

Whitney, Courtney, *MacArthur: His Rendezvous with Destiny.* New York, Knopf, 1955.

Willoughby, Charles A. and John Chamberlain, *MacArthur, 1941–51.* New York, McGraw-Hill, 1954; with subtitle *Victory in the Pacific,* London, Heinemann, 1956.

Wittner, Lawrence S., editor, *MacArthur.* Englewood Cliffs, New Jersey, Prentice-Hall, 1971.

*

Despite an already extraordinary military career (including first in his class at West Point), MacArthur did not become a prominent public figure until World War II. The earliest book about him still of any importance is MILLER's, which in its 1944 version includes an introduction by Lowell Thomas. MacArthur's stature was then enhanced by the occupation of Japan and by the Korean War, as the titles of KELLEY AND RYAN's two books make clear. A more complex portrait emerges from GUNTHER, whose work, based on previously published magazine sketches, became a best-seller. It is valuable today primarily for its first four chapters.

In 1951 President Truman (who had once served in the Army under MacArthur, without having ever met him) abruptly relieved the by now five-star general of his Korean command, not for incompetence but for insubordination. This controversial action culminated in a triumphant return to the United States for MacArthur and a burst of unpopularity for Truman. Many articles and books about the MacArthur-Truman debacle appeared, together with biographical defenses of MacArthur. Among the latter were books by MILLER (1951, revision of his 1942 work; see bibliography); KENNEY; LEE AND HENSCHEL; WILLOUGHBY AND CHAMBERLAIN; and WHITNEY. All of these books were written (or reissued) in response to the Truman action, and almost all of them were highly sympathetic to MacArthur. This is particularly true of the Willoughby and Chamberlain volume, as MacArthur himself reviewed and to some extent guided its "semi-official" text. Lee and Henschel provide a picture book with some new information on MacArthur's early life, a period that most of the others neglect. Kenney and Whitney were both close associates of MacArthur's, with Whitney being the closest of all. While one-sided in his admiration, Whitney knew MacArthur as few others did. MacArthur almost certainly had a direct hand in this book also.

The one work among these that chose not to adulate was ROVERE AND SCHLESINGER, a critique rather than a biography, written by two prophetic liberal historians. It has had an important influence on subsequent biographies. Throughout MacArthur's long and very distinguished career (he was the most decorated soldier in American history), mental brilliance, prodigious memory, physical courage, and devotion to duty were inarguably evident, and are conceded by virtually all who have written about him. But, as Rovere and Schlesinger point out, MacArthur was also (for many) remote, austere, imperial, and even arrogant. Lacing the common toughness and charisma that did so much to elevate Dwight D. Eisenhower (once his subordinate) to military and political heights, MacArthur made other people feel little—and they despised him for it.

The damage done to MacArthur's public image (of which he was extremely sensitive) by his dismissal from command in Korea was compounded by the publication of former president Truman's memoirs in 1955 and 1956. A much-noticed publication, it tended to overshadow those by Willoughby/Chamberlain and Whitney, in which MacArthur and his loyalists had roundly condemned the man from Missouri. Truman was capable of extremely blunt invective, some of it unprintable, and in this case defended his dismissal of MacArthur with ringing vigor. Two responsible but less noticed books, by SPANIER and HIGGINS, attempted more scholarly analysis, but the eventual by-product was SMITH's vitriolic defense of the dismissal that MacArthur "so richly deserved."

In 1964, the year of his death, MacArthur's autobiographical *Reminiscences* (New York, McGraw Hill, 1964) became a best-seller among the public but was less well received by critics and professional historians. Many of the latter suspect that Cornelius Whitney contributed significantly to the book; perhaps MacArthur dictated it to him. In any case, this version of events must be read. What emerges from it, besides a number of new

and occasionally charming anecdotes, is the self-portrait of an extremely able man who never doubted his own motives and who never admitted to a mistake.

His 1951 dismissal, MacArthur said, had taken place just when victory was within his grasp; he also pointed out that in testimony before Congress, every member of the Joint Chiefs of Staff had repudiated Truman's charge of insubordination. Truman himself, a man of violent temper and paroxysmal rages, had been confused, bewildered, and stupid. WHAN's collection represents a more dignified farewell. Excerpts from several of the speeches, and from books about MacArthur, are usefully collected by WITTNER, whose volume is essentially a casebook.

Among recent biographies, not all of them comprehensive, one may note FREDERICKS, MAYER, BLAIR, and PETILLO. The most popular book on MacArthur in recent years has been MANCHESTER's *American Caesar*. Interesting as it can be, however, anyone seriously interested in the facts should prefer the definitive, three-volume biography by James, which is the one work on MacArthur (together with his *Reminiscences*, perhaps) that is now indispensable.

No other biographer of MacArthur (most of whom were either associates or journalists) can compare with JAMES in the quality of his research. The center for all such endeavors is the MacArthur Memorial archives in Norfolk, Virginia (where he is also buried); much of the remaining documentation is to be found in War Department collections in Washington, D.C. But pertinent materials illuminating such a varied career as MacArthur's remain extremely widespread; in 20 years of research, James managed to find most of them, not to mention dozens of still-living persons who had known MacArthur personally. He has also fully mastered the secondary literature. The result is a somewhat militaristic but otherwise impeccably factual account of MacArthur that, if anything, concedes too much to his critics. Volume I (1970) covers the years 1880–1941, by which time MacArthur—at 60, remarkably fit both physically and mentally—had entered upon his period of greatness. Volume II (1975) is devoted entirely to 1941–45, the Pacific campaign of World War II. Finally, Volume III, subtitled "Triumph and Disaster" (the other two volumes do not have such titles), considers his years as Supreme Commander in Japan, his generalship in Korea, and the post-dismissal years of frustrations and decline. All in all, James' is one of the finest biographies of any 20th-century American that we have.

—Dennis R. Dean

MacDIARMID, Hugh [*born* Christopher Murray Grieve], 1892–1978; Scottish poet.

Bold, Alan, *MacDiarmid: Christopher Murray Grieve, a Critical Biography*. London, J. Murray, 1988; Amherst, University of Massachusetts Press, 1990; revised and enlarged edition, London, Paladin Paperbacks, 1990.

Boutelle, Ann E., *Thistle and Rose: A Study of MacDiarmid's*

Poetry. Edinburgh, Macdonald, 1980; Lewisburg, Pennsylvania, Bucknell University Press, 1981.

Buthlay, Kenneth, *Hugh MacDiarmid (Christopher Murray Grieve)*. Edinburgh, Oliver and Boyd, 1964; revised and enlarged edition, Edinburgh, Scottish Academic Press, 1982.

Duval, K. D. and S. G. Smith, editors, *MacDiarmid: A Festschrift*. Edinburgh, Duval, 1962.

Gish, N., *Hugh MacDiarmid: The Man and His Work*. London, Macmillan, 1984.

Glen, Duncan, *Hugh MacDiarmid and the Scottish Renaissance*. Edinburgh, W. and R. Chambers, 1964.

Kerrigan, Catherine, *Whaur Extremes Meet: The Poetry of Hugh MacDiarmid*. Edinburgh, Thin, 1983.

Morgan, Edwin, *Hugh MacDiarmid*. London, Longman/British Council, 1976.

Scott, P. H. and A. C. Davis, editors, *The Age of MacDiarmid: Essays on Hugh MacDiarmid and His Influence on Contemporary Scotland*. Edinburgh, Mainstream Publishing, 1980.

Watson, Roderick, *Hugh MacDiarmid*. Milton Keynes, Open University Press, 1976.

*

Because of his uncompromising support for both Scottish Nationalism and Communism, and the fact that the poet's first "period"—1922–32—consisted mainly of poetry in Scots, MacDiarmid's first biographer, GLEN, necessarily devotes much attention to setting him into the context of the 20th-century Scottish Renaissance literary revival movement, which MacDiarmid founded with the support of his former English teacher, the composer Francis George Scott (see the present writer's *Francis George Scott and the Scottish Renaissance*, Edinburgh, 1980). As MacDiarmid was still alive when Glen's book was published, Glen's approach is that of persuasive advocate, and unsavoury facts are glossed over or omitted. Nevertheless, Glen remains a valuable contemporary sourcebook for MacDiarmid students.

MacDiarmid's omission from the British Council's series of studies of great *Writers and Their Work* was corrected by MORGAN's monograph, a lively brief account both of the man and his work, including the prose books. A similar but more extensive introductory volume was provided by WATSON in the same year for the students of the Open University. The first serious critical account is BUTHLAY's, though its biographical aspect is of secondary importance. Buthlay is, however, the most knowledgeable and balanced critic of MacDiarmid's work.

By far the fullest biographical material on MacDiarmid is contained in *The Letters of Hugh MacDiarmid*, edited by Alan Bold (London, 1984), and in Bold's subsequent biography. *The Letters* are more truly self-revealing than the poet's own prolix and posturing autobiography, *Lucky Poet: A Self-Study in Literature and Political Ideas* (London, 1943). *The Letters* contain editorial introductions to those who feature in the correspondence, thus revealing MacDiarmid's variable relations with some of his contemporaries.

Given that BOLD became a friend of the then elderly poet in 1962, his biography is remarkably detached. He reveals for the first time many of the facts of MacDiarmid's tempestuous career that could not be mentioned while he was still alive. He does not gloss over the less unpleasant aspects of his behaviour or character, but simply records what happened. Bold does not go soft on MacDiarmid's extensive unacknowledged borrowings, in prose and verse (though it would take a dubious lifetime's research to uncover them all); nor on the poet's habit of pretending extensive knowledge in subjects of which he knew very little. The book, which is well illustrated, deals factually with the many literary and political controversies in which MacDiarmid engaged and which he sometimes provoked. The most celebrated of these was the dispute with Muir over the latter's claim that since the Reformation, Scotsmen have felt in one language, Scots, and thought in another, English. Bold states the facts of the ensuing dispute (Muir's theory seeming to strike at the very heart of MacDiarmid's lyrical and satircal achievement in Scots) without judgmental comment.

Two collections of essays, each by several hands, throw light on particular aspects of MacDiarmid's life. In the DUVAL AND SMITH *Festschrift*, a gift to the poet on his 70th birthday, Douglas Young provides interesting commentary on the evolution of MacDiarmid's nationalism, while David Craig examines the flawed dichotomy at the roots of the poet's Communism. In the SCOTT AND DAVIS collection, brought together after the poet's death, Stephen Maxwell takes a broader look at the poet's nationalism and George Bruce provides a balanced verdict on the MacDiarmid-versus-Muir *fracas*.

Of the rapidly growing number of MacDiarmid studies, three have biographical significance. GISH offers no theories but relates the man and the work in a straightforward manner. KERRIGAN sets out to place MacDiarmid as "a great poet in the Romantic tradition," and consequently concludes that his political activities, "radical as they were, rested on the ideals of the great Victorian reformers, . . . always related to securing an improved quality of life for all."

BOUTELLE, while providing much lively and by no means uncritical comment, advances two unsubstantiated theories. She suggests that the abrasive and arrogant public MacDiarmid (as opposed to Grieve, the courteous private person) developed his belligerency in childhood because he was jealous of Andrew, his younger brother. Reviewing Boutelle's book in *The Scotsman*, Bold observes that "there is no real evidence in the supposition that the pseudonym Hugh MacDiarmid was invented to protect Grieve from personality defects." Boutelle is even wider off the mark in referring to "the Garden of Eden that was Langholm" (the small Border town where MacDiarmid was born). As Bold puts it, MacDiarmid was simply not "an Eden-questing poet like Edwin Muir."

In due course a biographer will emerge who did not experience the remarkable force of the poet's personality and who will therefore be able to interpret fact more freely. For obvious reasons, this is unlikely to be the long-promised official biography by Duncan Macmillan and the poet's son, Michael Grieve, if it ever appears. It is back to Bold, both as editor and as biographer, for the fullest and frankest account of one of Scotland's three greatest poets—the others being William Dunbar and Robert Burns.

—Maurice Lindsay.

MACHIAVELLI, Niccolò, 1469–1527; Italian political philosopher and statesman.

De Grazia, Sebastian, *Machiavelli in Hell*. Princeton, New Jersey, Princeton University Press, and London, Harvester Wheatsheaf, 1989.

Ridolfi, Roberto, *The Life of Niccolò Machiavelli*, translated by Cecil Grayson. Chicago, University of Chicago Press, and London, Routledge, 1963.

Ruffo-Fiore, *Niccolò Machiavelli*. Boston, Twayne, 1982.

Skinner, Quentin, *Machiavelli*. Oxford, Oxford University Press, and New York, Hill and Wang, 1981.

Strauss, Leo, *Thoughts on Machiavelli*. Seattle, University of Washington Press, 1958.

Villari, Pascuale, *The Life and Times of Niccolò Machiavelli*, translated by Linda Villari. London, T. F. Unwin, and New York, Scribner, 1898.

*

One of the main reasons why "the problem of Machiavelli . . . will never be closed" (as Benedetto Croce remarked in "Una questione che forse non si chiuderia mai: la questione del Machiavelli," *Quaderni di critica*, 1949) is that scholars disagree on the importance of Machiavelli's biography. One school of opinion, influential since Machiavelli's days, maintains that Machiavelli the man is much less important than Machiavelli the author. The other school strongly believes that Machiavelli's "ideas cannot be properly understood in isolation: we must know the story of his life" (J. H. Hale, *Machiavelli and Renaissance Italy*, 1960). In fact, Giuseppe Prezzolini (*Machiavelli*, translated by Gioconda Savine, 1967) has even claimed that "Machiavelli's life is itself one of his masterpieces."

Throughout his life—divided into 28 years of near total obscurity, 14 years of intense political and diplomatic activity, another 14 years of productive retirement, and the last two years back into professional life and disappointment—Machiavelli's fate was bound inextricably with the history of Florence. Hence Machiavellism, though transcending Machiavelli himself, must be studied through the experiences that shaped his ideas and provided him with the raw materials for his work.

Of the modern biographies of Machiavelli, those by Oreste Tommasini (*La vita e gli scritti di Niccolò Machiavelli*, 2 vols., Rome, 1883–1911) and VILLARI have not been satisfactory. The former lacks substance and scholarship, while the latter, though informative, is tendentious. Written within a few years of the unification, Villari's Machiavelli emerges as the forerunner of the Italian *Risorgimento* and the symbol of a new Italy. Of the numerous biographical studies since the 1950s, several stand out. Nicolai Rubinstein's seminal paper of 1956 provides definitive information on Machiavelli's entry into the service in the Florentine chancery. His dispatches from the court of Emperor Maximilian I in 1508 have been examined by R. Jones, who demonstrated that Francesco Vettori coauthored many of the reports hitherto supposed to have been the products of Machiavelli's pen only. Several specialist articles provide new information on Machiavelli's relations with the Orti Oricellari circle (Felix Gilbert), with Girolamo Savonarola, who actually inspired Machiavelli's millennial world-view (Donald Weinstein), Cesare Borgia (F. Biondolillo) and Piero Soderini (Guido Hurlimann and Sergio Bertelli), with whom the secretary was always

friendly and yet of whom occasionally critical, and on Machiavelli's religiosity (Ridolfi and E. Levi). Finally, new findings are made in Machiavelli's correspondence—"secret" as well as "undated" and "unaddressed"—which provides, in an autobiographical manner, as it were, fresh insights into his thoughts and moods. These studies are variously discussed by Skinner (see below), Eric W. Cochran ("Machiavelli: 1940–1960," *Journal of Modern History*, XXXIII, 2, 1961), Cecil H. Clough (*Machiavelli Researches*, Napoli, Instituto orientale, 1967), Vincenzo Romano ("Profilo biografico del Machiavelli," *Cultura e scuola*, IX, 1970, especially the bibliographical note), Gilbert ("Machiavelli in Modern Historical Scholarship," *Machiavelli nel V° centenario della nascita*, Bologna, Biblioteca di cultura, 1973), and John H. Geerken ("Machiavelli Studies since 1969," *Journal of the History of Ideas*, XXXVII, 2, 1976).

Machiavelli's first straightforward biography comes from RIDOLFI. It has, as the author claims, brought to light "certain important facts . . . and corrected errors solemnly repeated by scholars for years." However, his excessive concentration on Machiavelli the "quintessential Florentine" has perpetuated the enigma of Machiavelli by conjuring up his image as a poet in whose *Il principe* "new political theories rewoven on the fabric of a dream, rise . . . to the realm of poetry." This minor caveat notwithstanding, Ridolfi's *Life* remains the standard authority. SKINNER's *Machiavelli* provides the best short biography that incorporates the fruits of new research. RUFFO-FIORE's volume, less comprehensive, provides another brief introduction to Machiavelli's life and contains a useful bibliography.

Machiavelli's notoriety, the product of centuries of prejudice and misunderstanding, was rekindled by the late Leo STRAUSS. His Machiavelli, the doctor of the damned, was subjected to an acrimonious debate (see the Communication section of *Political Theory*, III, 4, 1975). The latest salvo in this academic war has been delivered by the Rutgers political scientist Sebastian DE GRAZIA, whose Machiavelli is at once complex and colorful. The new Machiavelli is a trenchant critic of classical humanism (cf. Q. Skinner and Russell Price, editors, *Machiavelli: The Prince*, 1988), even an anti-humanist, and yet a humanist *par excellence* in his attitude to writing, which he considered to be the spur of action. Above all, de Grazia's Niccolò, like the Machiavelli of the *Risorgimento*, appears as a supreme patriot who wrote that "the greatest good that one can do, and the most gratifying to God, is that which one does for one's country."

—Narasingha P. Sil

MADISON, James, 1751–1836; American political leader, 4th president of the United States.

Brant, Irving, *James Madison* (6 vols.). Indianapolis, Bobbs-Merrill, 1941–61.

Brant, Irving, *The Fourth President: A Life of James Madison*. Indianapolis, Bobbs-Merrill, and London, Eyre and Spottiswoode, 1970.

Gay, Sydney H., *James Madison*. New York, Houghton Mifflin, 1884.

Hunt, Gaillard, *The Life of James Madison*. New York, Doubleday, 1902.

Ketcham, Ralph, *James Madison: A Biography*. New York, Macmillan, 1971.

McCoy, Drew R., *The Last of the Fathers: James Madison and the Republican Legacy*. Cambridge and New York, Cambridge University Press, 1989.

Rakove, Jack N., *James Madison and the Creation of the American Republic*. Glenview, Illinois, Scott Foresman, 1990.

Rives, William C., *History of the Life and Times of James Madison* (3 vols.). Boston, Little Brown, 1859–68.

Rutland, Robert A., *James Madison: The Founding Father*. New York, Macmillan, and London, Collier Macmillan, 1987.

Schultz, Harold S., *James Madison*. New York, Twayne, 1970.

Smith, Abbott E., *James Madison, Builder: A New Estimate of a Memorable Career*. New York, Wilson-Erickson, 1937.

*

The first scholarly biography of James Madison was written by RIVES, an acquaintance and fellow Virginia politician. While writing his history Rives had access to original letters and documents, from which he quoted copiously. (Many years later missing Madison letters were found mixed in with Rives' papers.) Along with Philip R. Fendall, Rives also edited the first collection of Madison's papers, *Letters and Other Writings of James Madison* (4 vols., 1865).

Although Rives' biography remains impressive in terms of scholarship and detail, unfortunately it was never completed. The last of the three volumes stops in 1797 at the end of George Washington's term in office. In his preface to the first volume Rives observed that his work "belongs more, perhaps, to the department of History than of Biography." This is an accurate assessment. Throughout Rives concentrates on politics; at times Madison is not even directly present, and there is very little personal material. Rives' affection for his subject is obvious; he refers to him as "one of the purest and most elevated characters that ever adorned humanity." He is aided in this analysis by the fact that he never wrote a planned fourth volume and therefore did not deal with Madison's later and more controversial career.

Very different is the biography written by GAY. Though much of his work is based on that of Rives, Gay is clearly hostile to his subject. His Madison is a somber, timid person, lacking imagination, wit, or humor. The Virginian's movement in the 1790s into the "opposition" was "unfortunate." Madison's political thought was inconsistent, he was a "party politician and not a statesman," a poor president, and an incompetent wartime leader. His status would have been higher if he had never been president. Gay, along with other 19th-century historians, clearly sympathized with the Federalists and reflected their portraits of the opposition Jeffersonian-Republicans.

While more even-handed in his discussion of Madison, HUNT also reflected the influence of the Federalists. Biographers, he implies, should be charitable and forgive Madison for his opposition to Hamilton! His biography is both longer and more scholarly than Gay's. This is not surprising since Hunt also edited a nine-volume set of *The Writings of James Madison* (1900–10), in which he expunged comments too racy or thought to reflect poorly on Madison. Hunt includes aspects of Madison's private as well as public life, and pictures him as an even-tempered individual with a warm sense of humor. Throughout the book he de-emphasizes Madison's nationalism, arguing that he always

saw the union as a compact of states, but never approved of nullification. Like Gay however, Hunt sees Madison as subservient to "Jefferson's stronger personality," primarily a scholar, and an uninspiring war-time leader who did a poor job of "selecting and commanding men."

SMITH pictures Madison as a conservative southern aristocrat, an unpopular, colorless individual who had a "great reputation for cogency and logic, but little or none for human feeling." Madison was neither a consistent nationalist nor constant in his interpretation of the Constitution. Throughout his career, Smith argues, Madison's "scholarly and bookish nature unfitted" him for a true understanding of foreign affairs. He wrongly insisted on principles of neutral rights, opposed impressment, and did not comprehend the lack of support among his own people. Smith clearly concurs with Federalist views of Republican policies, and sympathizes with England. His Madison is a weak president who during wartime "failed to exert a powerful moral and political leadership."

BRANT set out to rescue Madison from his detractors. What started as a brief biography became a 23-year project that expanded to a massive, detailed, and scholarly six-volume work. Brant examines every aspect of Madison's life, public as well as private, and sets it within the history of his times. He also takes to task previous historians for their various errors (whether in the form of statements or omissions). Brant's research is prodigious, and writers on Madison since his volumes appeared have acknowledged their debt to him. At times, though, his work is overwhelming: he includes, for example, extended discussions of the true origins of Madison's mother's and wife's names, as well as of political ideas and policy decisions. Brant himself was aware of this problem and in 1970 prepared a one-volume rendition of the larger work that leaves out all the scholarly disputations and condenses extended discussions of background information. While briefer and more readable, *The Fourth President* only cites chapters in the larger work, so that a scholar wanting to go back to the sources must consult the multi-volume biography.

While Brant's full biography is still the most detailed and best scholarly interpretation of Madison, it is not without problems. Brant is too fond of his subject and defends him at every turn. While he acknowledges highs and lows from the 1780s to the end of Madison's life, Brant portrays Madison as a consistent nationalist. He even sees the Virginia Resolution of 1798 as a political "weapon" behind which "Madison's nationalism, though buried, was as much alive as it ever was." He admires Madison as secretary of state, defends his policies as president, and blames others for his wartime travails. Madison was his own man—Jefferson's partner, not his "office boy"—and has been greatly "underrated" by historians. Madison's enemies (Patrick Henry, Charles Pinckney, etc.) become Brant's. The Madison that emerges from this work, when not obscured by the extensive narrative, is far from the "dry and serious" figure sketched by Henry Cabot Lodge and previous biographers. Brant's Madison is scholarly and shy, but also warm, humorous, and appealing.

Two other one-volume studies of Madison appeared about the same time as Brant's. SCHULTZ's brief work, part of the Twayne series on American figures, is a political biography that does not deal with social history or Madison's personal life. While recognizing Brant's efforts, Schultz's interpretation often goes back to previous authors. For Schultz, Madison was primarily a practical politician whose "views on specific policies came first"—constitutional arguments were "derivative and secondary." By the time he became secretary of state, Madison was past his "prime," and as president he was constricted by his previous experiences as a Congressman—he deferred to Congress and consequently appeared indecisive. During the War of 1812 his strategy was wrong, he failed to direct activities clearly, and he was unable to arouse the nation. While observing that some of the criticism of Madison as a wartime president has been too strong, Schultz for the most part agrees with it.

KETCHAM's book is much longer and more balanced. It contains a great deal of social history, as well as descriptions of Madison's personal life. Grounded in Brant, the ongoing modern edition of the *Papers of James Madison* (William T. Hutchinson, et. al., editors, 15 volumes to date), and extensive use of manuscript materials, Ketcham reaches his own conclusions about Madison while he paints a wonderful three-dimensional picture of the Virginian. He discusses the political philosophy behind Madison's ideas and emphasizes that Madison was consistently a republican while not always a nationalist. Here he and Jefferson were "coarchitects and coexecutors of a Republican policy." He is not as quick as Brant to defend Madison as president, though he does see him as thoughtful and effective, taking a principled but "subtle" stand, while being hampered by his own republican values. Ketcham's work is the most balanced and judicious one-volume biography of Madison.

Three recent biographies of Madison reflect historians' current interest in the ideology of republicanism; all deal primarily with politics. RUTLAND's book is written for a popular audience in a sprightly style that makes extensive use of colorful metaphors. His Madison emerges as a "man of character," a patriot, and a dedicated republican. Although a shy scholar, Madison was neither Jefferson's subordinate (an idea put forth by Hamilton and later "followed by gullible historians") nor a weak president [though he is also described as "not forceful" in that office). Rutland follows Ketcham's picture of Madison as primarily a republican, seeing this as his source both of strength and of weakness while president. During the War of 1812 "Madison was a spectator rather than an active participant," and his concept of war was out of date. Although early writers such as Henry Adams were too critical of Madison, Rutland agrees he reached his peak in 1791, and was inconsistent as both a nationalist and a supporter of states sovereignty at different times in his career. Though written in an appealing style, this is an uneven book in quality and in its handling of Madison.

McCOY concentrates on Madison from his retirement in 1817 to his death in 1836. But McCoy, whose book is organized topically rather than chronologically, also flashes back to Madison's earlier experiences, as well as ahead to those of some of his "disciples" (Edward Coles, Nicholas P. Trist, and William C. Rives). McCoy concentrates on Madison's "emotional" commitment "to a republican dream." He offers well-developed discussions of Madison's conservatism, his views on economic development, and especially his opinions on slavery. McCoy agrees that Madison's career peaked in the early 1790s, but he sees him as consistently committed to "fundamental values and purposes" while "some of his specific views" changed.

The most recent biography of Madison, by RAKOVE, is part of the Library of American Biography series containing brief summaries of the lives of significant figures. Rakove's work is the most up-to-date and readable brief biography available. The emphasis here is on Madison as a practical politician whose very sense of purpose and being stemmed from his public life. Madison's "talent" was "a rigorous political intelligence" and an ability to let logic yield to reality when necessary without losing his "integrity." Madison was a republican who could "apply bookish learning to real problems" whether in the Constitutional Convention or later. Rakove criticizes Madison the president for his weak policies and poor administration but praises him for preserving republican principles at a difficult time. Here his assessment is less harsh than Ketcham's, while he shares, with Brant, Ketcham, and McCoy, the notion that Madison was in some way consistent in his beliefs.

—Maxine N. Lurie

MAGELLAN, Ferdinand, *ca.* 1480–1521; Portuguese navigator.

Guillemard, Francis H. H., *The Life of Ferdinand Magellan and the First Circumnavigation of the Globe 1480–1521.* New York, Dodd Mead, and London, G. Philip, 1890.

Nowell, Charles E., editor, *Magellan's Voyage Around the World: Three Contemporary Accounts.* Evanston, Illinois, Northwestern University Press, 1962.

Parr, Charles McKew, *So Noble a Captain: The Life and Times of Ferdinand Magellan.* New York, T. Y. Crowell, 1953; with subtitle *Life and Voyages of Ferdinand Magellan*, London, R. Hale, 1955.

Roditi, Edouard, *Magellan of the Pacific.* London, Faber, 1972; New York, McGraw-Hill, 1973.

Zweig, Stefan, *Conqueror of the Seas*, translated by Eden and Cedar Paul. New York, Viking, 1938; as *Magellan, Pioneer of the Pacific*, London, Cassell, 1938 (originally published as *Magellan: Der Mann und Seiner Tat*, Vienna, H. Reichner, 1938).

*

Literature on Magellan falls into two categories: studies that unabashedly limit themselves to the circumnavigation voyage of 1519–21, and biographies that, while purporting to tell the Magellan story in a "life and times" format, focus disproportionately on the voyage, struggle valiantly to flesh out meagre authenticated biographical details by references to contemporary events, or dwell at length on navigational techniques, geographical theories, or international rivalries for domination of the spice trade.

Three contemporary accounts of Magellan's voyage, already available in English translations (as *The First Voyage Round the World by Magellan*, translated from the accounts of Pigafetta and other contemporary writers by Henry Stanley, London, 1874), but here republished in a highly readable and well-annotated account, comprise NOWELL's elegant volume. These are the fundamental eyewitness account by the Venetian Antonio Pigafetta, Maximilian of Transylvania's report on his interviews conducted with survivors on their return to Spain, and the account by the Portuguese historian Gaspar Corrêa, who had firsthand knowledge of oriental trade. Nowell makes no claims of completeness for the narratives, but his scholarly introduction and conclusion, together with notes and bibliography, make this a superb introduction to Magellan and his age. That the text should be complemented with charts and maps enhances its value.

Biographers of Magellan face the problem that little is known of his years prior to his service in Portuguese India. Even Pigafetta's indispensable account of the circumnavigation reveals little of the character, personality, or values of this complex person. A great favorite of children's literature of the "great discoverers" and "men of adventure" ilk, Magellan has received little attention from serious biographers. GUILLEMARD's life of Magellan and account of the circumnavigation has stood the test of time. Whereas the bulk of the book is a retelling of the voyage, this is done uncommonly well and Guillemard's observations are illuminating and revealing. He has assembled the available data on Magellan's early life and service in India and North Africa. Appendices contain valuable information on genealogy, Magellan's wills, and the provisioning and personnel of his fleet. Maps, index, and notes are of high quality and helpful to the reader. This is a gem of a book, unfortunately long since out of print.

ZWEIG's account was motivated by his curiosity, while bound for South America, for those in whose wakes he was sailing and their life on board. The result is heavily dependent on Pigafetta and well larded with adulation for Magellan and the author's personal views. This is a readable and popular account, but it cannot withstand critical or scholarly scrutiny.

PARR's view of the voyage as a commercial venture to break the Portuguese hold on the spice trade, and his exhaustive analysis of political machinations and maneuverings by venture capitalists with Venetian interests in mind preceding the voyage, make demands on readers whose interests lie exclusively with Magellan, who only appears center stage in the second quarter of this 423-page book. The retelling of the voyage relies heavily on Pigafetta. The author's views on Sebastian del Cano and his assertion that Magellan visited the Philippines on a prior occasion are debatable. Although the author has based his account on archival and printed primary and secondary sources, the inexplicable absence of footnotes undermines the credibility of some assertions.

RODITI adds little to our previous knowledge of Magellan and has steered clear of controversy in this very readable biography. He acknowledges his debt to the Visconde de Lagôa's two-volume biography of Magellan (Lisbon, 1938) as well as to Pigafetta. Roditi has reached a balance between the "life" and the "times"—with more on navigation and geography than is necessary—and inevitably the retelling of the voyage occupies the lion's share of this 271-page book. Roditi sets Magellan in historical context of Luso-Spanish rivalries, without overwhelming the reader with details. He has strived to tell the story of Magellan prior to 1519 as page in the queen's household, clerk, and royal service in India and Malacca. Roditi himself admits the shortcomings of the evidence and of a methodology that depends on highlighting the major events in the early history of Portuguese India in which Magellan may or may not have par-

ticipated. Roditi's description and interpretation of Magellan's fatal decision to meddle in local politics in the Philippines emphasizes a less publicized episode of the voyage, but his attribution to Magellan of a sudden burst of missionary zeal is unconvincing. There are errors of fact and the reader should accept more critically than does the author certain Portuguese sources. Roditi's biography, together with the firsthand accounts in Nowell, will familiarize the reader with the "state of the art" of Magellania and provide an insight into this major figure in terms of the significance of his achievement but with full realization that a satisfactory and full biography of Magellan still remains to be written.

—A. J. R. Russell-Wood

MAHLER, Gustav, 1860–1911; Austrian composer.

Bauer-Lechner, Natalie, *Recollections of Gustav Mahler*, translated by Dika Newlin, edited and annotated by Peter Franklin. Cambridge and New York, Cambridge University Press, 1980 (originally published by E. P. Tal, Leipzig, 1923).

Blaukopf, Kurt, *Mahler*, translated by Inge Goodwin. London, A. Lane, and New York, Praeger, 1973 (originally published as *Gustav Mahler*, Vienna, Molden, 1969).

Blaukopf, Kurt, editor, *Mahler: A Documentary Study*, translated by Paul Baker. New York, Oxford University Press, 1976 (originally published as *Mahler: Sein Leben, sein Werk und seine Welt*, Vienna, Universal Edition, 1976).

Cardus, Neville, *Gustav Mahler: His Mind and His Music*. London, Gollancz, and New York, St. Martin's, 1965.

De la Grange, Henry-Louis, *Mahler*. New York, Doubleday, 1973 (the first volume of *Gustav Mahler, Chronique d'une Vie*, 3 vols., Paris, Fayard, 1973–84).

Engel, Gabriel, *Gustav Mahler: Song-Symphonist*. New York, Bruckner Society of America, 1932.

Gartenberg, Egon, *Mahler: The Man and His Music*. London, Cassell, and New York, Schirmer, 1978.

Holbrook, David, *Gustav Mahler and the Courage To Be*. London, Vision Press, 1975.

Kennedy, Michael, *Mahler*. London, Dent, 1974.

Lea, Henry A., *Gustav Mahler: Man on the Margin*. Bonn, Bouvier, 1985.

Lebrecht, Norman, *Mahler Remembered*. London, Faber, 1987; New York, Norton, 1988.

Loschnigg, Franz, *The Cultural Education of Gustav Mahler*. Madison, University of Wisconsin Press, 1976.

Mahler, Alma (Alma [Schindler] Mahler Werfel), *Gustav Mahler: Memories and Letters*, translated by Basil Creighton. London, J. Murray, and New York, Viking, 1946; revised edition, edited by Donald Mitchell, London, J. Murray, and Seattle, University of Washington Press, 1968 (originally published by Allert de Lange, Amsterdam, 1940).

Mitchell, Donald, *Gustav Mahler: The Early Years*. London, Rockliff, 1958; revised edition, London, Faber, and New York, University of California Press, 1980.

Mitchell, Donald, *Gustav Mahler: The Wunderhorn Years*. London, Faber, 1975; Boulder, Colorado, Westview Press, 1976.

Mitchell, Donald, *Gustav Mahler: Songs and Symphonies of Life and Death*. London, Faber, and Berkeley, University of California Press, 1985.

Reik, Theodor, *The Haunting Melody: Psychoanalytic Experiences in Life and Music*. New York, Farrar Straus, 1953.

Reilly, Edward R., *Gustav Mahler and Guido Adler: Records of a Friendship*. Cambridge and New York, Cambridge University Press, 1982.

Walter, Bruno, *Gustav Mahler*, translated by James Galston. London, K. Paul, 1937; revised edition, with biographical essay by Ernst Krenek, New York, Greystone Press, 1941 (originally published by H. Reichner, Vienna, 1936).

*

A fundamental consideration in planning any artist's biography is the relative emphasis to be placed on two elements: works of the artist and more traditional biographical aspects. In the case of Gustav Mahler, this consideration seems especially significant; two enormous biographies, both of them lifelong labors of love, illustrate the principle. MITCHELL demonstrates an intimate and comprehensive knowledge of Mahler's music and life in his three-volume set. Written over a 30-year span, Mitchell's perspective evolves from predominately biographical to almost exclusively analytical. The first volume divides into a discussion of Mahler's early years and his early compositions. The first section covers Mahler's childhood years and corrects errors found in many earlier biographies. The second section is quite balanced in regard to source materials and analysis; it contains many helpful cross-references to the first section. By the time Mitchell's second volume appeared, the domination of the music over biographical considerations was firmly established; the middle period of the composer's life is covered chronologically, but primarily as a consequence of Mitchell's interest in specific works. With the increase in the relative importance of the music, the level of the reader's technical skills in music must also increase. Volume three contains analyses of some of Mahler's late works, literally abandoning any pretense of biography, but therein is found some of the best reading available on Mahler's music. A fourth volume is planned.

Between Mitchell's first and second volumes, DE LA GRANGE published the first volume of his three; this was partly responsible for the former's change of emphasis. No other biography relates details of Mahler's life as comprehensively as Mitchell covers the early years (1860–81) or as thoroughly as De la Grange covers the composer's entire life. De la Grange has made available the largest body of information on Mahler, including exclusive anecdotes and source material. His narrative is fluent and perceptive and does not veer off into analytical discourse; it is the standard by which the accuracy of all earlier writings on Mahler may be judged. Unfortunately, only the first of three volumes is readily available in English.

Several personal reminiscences are available in translation, but all of them are limited by their authors having known Mahler for only a portion of his life. One of the most fascinating is by BAUER-LECHNER, who had no pretenses about worshiping Mahler. She knew Mahler from his years as a conservatory student until he met Alma Schindler and claimed to be his near-constant companion between 1893 and 1901. Her recollections contain extended quotations from conversations, and her experiences are related vividly and in great detail. Indeed, the amount of detail has at times raised questions about the accuracy of some of her citations. The recollections were first released following the author's death (they were not intended for publication), and the diary-like style freely reveals the author's idiosyncracies and prejudices. Because Bauer-Lechner was a musician, her book is unique in the quality of musical insights relating to this part of Mahler's life.

As Bauer-Lechner left Mahler's life, Alma Schindler entered it, and not long afterward, she married him. Although written by someone who was a fairly accomplished composer, Alma MAHLER's book exhibits a devoted wife's perspective, so that in the selection and presentation of details it is accordingly protective and guarded. The somewhat maternal tone that results is carried to the extreme whenever another composer, particularly Richard Strauss, intersects Mahler's life. It is the letters in Mahler's volume that reveal the most about the composer, but they have been carefully screened to present the best possible picture of both the composer and his wife.

The relationships that both Mahler and Bauer-Lechner maintained to the composer were personal, but the perspectives of both Reilly and Walter are based upon professional relationships. WALTER's book, published on the 30th anniversary of Mahler's death, attempts to reproduce an assistant's memory of Mahler as he followed the composer-conductor from city to city. Not only had Walter's memory faded by the time of writing, but his work omits painful aspects of the author's strained relationship with Mahler's wife and sister. Walter attempts to establish that his relationship with Mahler was an intimate one, and his eagerness to verify it more than once casts doubt upon his veracity. REILLY's work contains two principal sections: a translation of a short Mahler biography originally published in 1914 by Guido Adler, and an essay by Reilly on the relationship of Adler and Mahler. While Adler knew Mahler longer than anyone except his sister Justine, he saw him infrequently, and very few letters exist that would confirm a close relationship. While claiming intimacy, Adler's essay invariably resorts to musical analysis to fill most of its pages. Reilly's essay is much more informative and well written, but it is a biography of Adler rather than of Mahler.

Mahler's meeting with Sigmund Freud (August 1910), coupled with his well-known interest in philosophy, has inspired an entire genre of psychobiographical studies that includes Blaukopf (1969), Holbrook, Loschnigg, Reik, and Lea. The most idiosyncratic of these is by REIK, who takes Mahler's meeting with Freud as a starting point for relating musical experiences to psychological experiences. Those who read this work expecting to learn a great deal about Mahler will be disappointed. A handful of Mahler's works are discussed as they relate to various aspects of his personality, but the main thrust of the book is the exercise of an analytical technique on Mahler and a few other composers. BLAUKOPF's *Gustav Mahler* (1969) is a fairly conventional biography that is peppered with psychological insights. The primary focus is on Mahler's music and its subsequent reception by the public, with Blaukopf relating his evaluation of how the music and its reception affected Mahler. Even though significant details of Mahler's life are slighted, this work is effectively organized and is perhaps the most interesting and revealing of all the single-volume studies.

The musical focal point for HOLBROOK is Mahler's Ninth Symphony, but the study is concerned primarily with Mahler's passions and motivations. Every available resource was consulted in an effort to bring to the reader a picture of what motivated the composer; both the method and the result are impressive. Holbrook does not constitute a suitable introduction to Mahler, but for those with some knowledge of Mahler's life and musical style, it will add considerable insight into the final years of the composer's life.

LOSCHNIGG's book is mentioned here because it is the only work in English that underscores the social, creative, and cultural environment of Mahler's youth. The author brings to his work an eastern-European perspective that on occasion almost turns into arrogance. Loschnigg's work is successful in providing a thorough overview of Mahler's environment; it discusses most of the significant writings that were in circulation prior to the turn of the century and provides insights into Mahler's Jewish heritage that are not available elsewhere. Loschnigg's work, however, is tainted by a manifest desire to discredit de la Grange.

LEA, another of the psychobiographical studies, treats Mahler as a man without a country, who is unable to affirm the world as it is. The biography traces Mahler's spiritual torment directly to his social environment. We are convincingly shown how this torment is expressed through Mahler's music.

The most common biography of Mahler is of the "man-and-his-music" variety. All of these fall between Mitchell and de la Grange in terms of whether they emphasize more the man or the music, and all of them fall short of Mitchell and de la Grange in terms of scholarship and thoroughness. GARTENBERG's book is the most conventional, and it is also the most complete. In spite of its division into two equal sections entitled "The Man," and "The Creator," a minimal amount of theoretical expertise is required to grasp this work; thus it makes a suitable general introduction to Mahler. CARDUS offers a work-by-work overview of Mahler's music with a brief biographical statement before each section. Taken as a whole, the biographical narrative is not distinctive. Cardus' outlook is that of one who first discounted Mahler, then came to see the light. ENGEL, like Loschnigg, writes from a European perspective. This work draws almost exclusively on Mahler's letters and claims to be the first biography by a person who did not know the composer. Because Engel's sources are limited, his perspective is also limited. In fact, when he wrote his biography, at least half of Mahler's currently known letters were not available. KENNEDY is more useful as a guide to Mahler's music than to his life, but his is one of the most easily read volumes on the composer and does manage to preserve a slender thread of biographical material from beginning to end.

Lebrecht and Blaukopf (1976) both paint enchanting portraits of Mahler through the presentation of source materials. LEBRECHT provides a relatively brief collection of writings by Mahler's contemporaries. The excerpts are lengthy enough to be individually helpful, but the greatest value of this work is in making available between two covers a wide range of perspectives.

While most of the biographies discussed above contain several plates of photographs, programs of music performances, and other documents, BLAUKOPF's 1976 volume is almost exclusively devoted to plates. The notes that accompany the photographs, etc., are well researched and contain much information not found elsewhere.

—Jeffrey Hopper

MAILER, Norman, 1923–   ; American writer.

Mills, Hilary, *Mailer: A Biography*. New York, Empire Books, 1982; London, New English Library, 1983.
Manso, Peter, *Mailer: His Life and Times*. New York, Simon and Schuster, and London, Viking, 1985.

*

Norman Mailer has been well served by these biographies written during his lifetime. Strictly speaking, Manso's book is oral history, while Mills follows the standard narrative approach, offering some original and perceptive observations on the relationship between Mailer's personal life and his work.

Rather than presenting his view of events, MANSO, who worked on Mailer's 1969 New York City mayoralty campaign, skillfully allows the book's 150 contributors to speak instead. He has done a superb job of editing and arranging these selections from conversations and interviews with a comprehensive range of family, friends, and professional acquaintances. Thanks to Manso's skill, all who converse in this book—starting with Mailer's formidable mother, to his Harvard roommates, *Village Voice* partners, fellow writers, members of his entourage and fashionable society, literary critics, editors, three of his six wives, and even Mailer himself—speak in their own distinctive voices.

Because Manso does not distill this information (except insofar as he stage-manages it), offering no interpretations, to some extent his method makes biographers of all his readers. Caught in the conversational crossfire, the reader feels as if she is actually listening to the book's contributors talk, giving their often contradictory opinions and versions of events. Hearing these differing perspectives, the reader forms her own conclusions about Mailer's turbulent life.

But since Manso's method depends extensively on the juxtaposition of individual points of view, the reader misses hearing Mailer's first, third, fourth, and fifth wives' side of the story, especially since his second wife's contributions are so eloquent. Neither Manso nor Mills explains the reasons for not interviewing Mailer's children, nor do they confront the issue of the possible compromise to their research this omission engenders.

An even more serious lapse is the omission of substantial information on Mailer's relationship with his father, a figure virtually absent from both books. There are hints (no more) that the subject may be painful for Mailer and his family—all the more reason for the biographer to confront the problem.

Manso quotes sparingly but always illuminatingly from Mailer's published work and unpublished letters, and the familiar portraits as well as a multitude of well-chosen, rarely-seen photographs accompany the text. Manso's method works particularly well in the sections on Mailer's 1960 stabbing of his second wife during a possible psychotic breakdown, and on Mailer's meetings with the Kennedys, leading to his ground-breaking essay "Superman Comes to the Supermarket." Rare and revealing tidbits include a McCarthy-era affadavit Mailer wrote to the Civil Service Commission defending his father, an account of his construction of a "Lego City" made out of thousands of interlocking plastic children's blocks, and recollections contributed by Diana Trilling, Shelley Winters, and Lillian Hellman.

Both books cover the difficulties and censorship battles preceding publication of the *Naked and the Dead* (1948) and the revisions and negotiations involved in the publication of *The Deer Park* (1955), though Mailer's own account of the latter in *Advertisements for Myself* (1959), with its comparison of successive drafts of the manuscript, is essential.

MILLS' detailed account of Mailer's Harvard years and the burgeoning there of his literary persona is insightful, as is her brief analysis of *The Naked and the Dead*. She also adds valuable details to the story of the editorial problems involved in *Esquire*'s publication of "Superman Comes to the Supermarket." Although Mills begins her book with bravura, opening with the contentious 1982 press conference following Mailer's testimony at Jake Henry Abbot's murder trial, by the second half of the book, however, Mills follows the fluctuations of Mailer's stock with the "literary establishment" as if his celebrity and financial success were more important than his artistic achievements. Finally, Mills' biography is respectable, informative, reliable, and readable, but Manso's is alive. Manso makes the reader feel as if he knows Mailer firsthand.

—Carolyn Yalkut

MAIMONIDES, Moses [Moses ben Maimon], 1135–1204; Jewish philosopher and physician.

Heschel, Abraham Joshua, *Maimonides: A Biography,* translated by Joachim Neugroschel. New York, Farrar Straus, 1982 (originally published by E. Reiss, Berlin, 1935).
Zeitlin, Solomon, *Maimonides: A Biography.* New York, Bloch, 1935; revised edition, 1955.

*

There was no full biography of Maimonides available in English between that by Israel Abrahams and David Yellin (Jewish Publication Society, 1903) and those of HESCHEL and ZEITLIN (discussed below by turns), both first published to commemorate in 1935 the eighth centenary of Maimonides' birth. Unhappily the Abrahams/Yellin volume, like the German *Moses ben Maimon* by Münz (1912), was rendered obsolete by the discovery of much new primary material, particularly that published by Asaff and Mann, which has thrown altogether new light on Maimonides' career. Both the biographies noted here have been updated since their original publication, Heschel's by bringing the translated material into conformity with modern scholarly norms, identifying references and illusions, and Zeitlin's by its author's 1955 preface to the second edition, in which he reiterates his conviction, which has been disputed, that the *Mishne Torah* was intended to provide Jewry with a constitution for its future state.

Heschel's biography is both popular and romantic. Heschel had called on the publisher Erich Reiss in East Berlin in March 1935 with a friend's manuscript and found himself immediately commissioned by the publisher to write a book himself. We may assume that on account of the date the subject matter was immediately agreed upon, and the *Maimonides,* stylistically rich but short on research, was out before the end of the centenary year. Heschel was 28 when he wrote it. He wanted himself to translate it into English, but never had time. He did in fact see drafts of the first and last chapters of an English translation earlier than that by Neugroschel. Germaine Bernard published a French translation in 1966, and Heschel's widow has contributed a foreward to the 1982 English translation referring to the difficulties in translating the work's "poetic prose." Heschel's book is not so much a straight biography as an almost poetic meditation on Maimonides' life and thought, concentrating on the strong sense of race necessary for Jewish survival almost anywhere in Europe, north Africa, or the middle east in the 12th century.

Zeitlin on the other hand does attempt formal biography, although the verifiable historical facts remain few and the legends are often nebulously transmitted. Zeitlin accepts that Maimonides' family stayed in and around Cordoba disguised as Arabs after 1148 when the puritanical sect of Islamic fundamentalists, the Almohedes, forced Jews and Christians alike to choose between Islam and exile. Maimonides, his father, his young brother David, and his sister did not leave Spain for Fez until 1159. Zeitlin's account is uncritical and often too defensive, perhaps on account of the potential unpopularity of his central contention about the fundamental nationalism of his subject, but he does sketch the circumstances and events of the life, drawing where possible on Maimonides' own account as reported in the *Sefer Haredim,* whose authenticity Zeitlin convincingly defends. By 1165 or 1166, shortly after his father's death, Maimonides was in Egypt where he was acknowledged to be leader and the chief scholarly authority of their community by the Jews of Cairo.

No mention is made in the records of Maimonides' father after the departure from Morocco, when Moses himself briefly and surreptitiously visited the Holy Land. We know only of Maimonides' financial dependence on his brother, David, who traded in gems and was drowned at sea with his precious cargo in 1174, after which Moses had to keep his family by practising as a doctor. He became personal physician to Saladin and married the sister of Ibn al Māli, one of the royal secretaries. His son Abraham was born in 1186. It was, according to Zeitlin, soon after his brother's death that opposition broke out between the faction led by Samuel ben Ali, which believed in a purely spiritual Jewish leadership, and that led by Maimonides, which wished to appoint a new political Exilarch in succession to Daniel, who had just died.

Although Zeitlin seldom gets beyond well-informed hagiography and writes in a popular style, without bibliography, he does gather together what is known and what may reasonably be conjectured about his subject's life. Unfortunately the book, primarily written for Jews, assumes too great a familiarity with Jewish medieval history and its sources. A good bibliography with places and dates of publication, and above all the full names of books and authors, would have made his work much more useful. It is regrettable, too, that so little is made of Maimonides' awareness of the problems bequeathed to the medieval theologians of Islam, Judaism, and Christianity alike by Aristotle. Maimonides' solution to the problems, apparently concerning with the eternity of the world but actually chiefly concerned with personal immortality after death, over which Averroes, Avicenna, Aquinas, and Scotus agonized, was in fact radical. Either scripture and philosophy could be harmonized or, if they could not, then either the scriptural statement was allegorical or Aristotle was wrong.

Maimonides was one of the very great 12th-century thinkers. He may have been profoundly Jewish, but his metaphysical problems were part of the West's common heritage from antiquity through Islam. Unhappily the development of Christianity in western Europe has ensured that far more research has been poured into the work of the Christian scholastics than into that of non-Christian philosophers and theologians. We need more scholarly exegesis than we have of Judaism's greatest medieval philosopher, and his colourful life and high profile warrant a fuller biography than those currently available.

—A. H. T. Levi

MALCOLM X [*born* Malcolm Little], 1925–1965; American civil rights leader.

Breitman, George, *The Last Year of Malcolm X: The Evolution of a Revolutionary*. New York, Merit Publishers, 1967.
Clarke, John Henrik, editor, *Malcolm X: The Man and His Times*. New York, Macmillan, 1969.
Goldman, Peter, *The Death and Life of Malcolm X*. New York, Harper, 1973; London, Gollancz, 1974.
Lomax, Louis E., *To Kill a Black Man*. Los Angeles, Holloway House, 1968.

*

While Malcolm X's *Autobiography* (1965) remains unsurpassed in broad historical import, it can now be profitably supplemented by nearly half a dozen general and specialized biographical studies. Such works vary considerably in scholarly merit, style, and composition; a few are intended exclusively for juvenile readers. Others, however, are rich in rare insight, information, and interpretation. The best and most useful of these are the handful prepared by scholar-journalists and contemporaries of Malcolm X.

BREITMAN, probably best known for his earlier excellent collection of speeches, *Malcolm X Speaks* (1965), prepared the present concise and probing little book as an addendum to *The Autobiography of Malcolm X*, a work Malcolm himself considered revising during the last stages of preparation. Splendidly written, though not scrupulously balanced, it examines Malcolm's changing ideas and philosophy between 1964 and 1965, the period when he left the Nation of Islam and began to chart his own course as an independent, free-thinking black leader. The book is carefully researched, as reviewers have noted, but

rests largely on an analysis of speeches contained in *Malcolm X Speaks*. An appendix, comprising about one-fourth of its content, is particularly important; also useful is the extensive list of related sources (printed and audio). These features, coupled with Breitman's conspicuous, though skilfully drawn, Marxist profile of Malcolm—a black nationalist on the way to becoming a socialist revolutionary just prior to his death—make the book both valuable and informative. The book offers readers a particularly relevant and intellectually based discussion of black nationalist thought.

LOMAX's undocumented, fast-moving, impressionistic book is both a sympathetic tribute to Malcolm (Lomax's friend of many years) and the retrospective, personal musing of yet another black social critic of American racism. The main value of this work, however, is its full sketch of both Malcolm X and Martin Luther King, Jr., and the comparative perspective Lomax offers on their lives and martyrdom. Lomax makes the controversial claim that ''had both men lived longer they probably would have traversed 180 degrees to become as one.'' *To Kill a Black Man* also includes five speeches and an interview with Malcolm from *When the Word is Given* (1963), Lomax's earlier publication on the Nation of Islam and Elijah Muhammad.

CLARKE's six-part edited collection of articles and documents is—and will likely remain—one of the more valuable and illuminating of all printed sources on Malcolm X. In large part, it examines the underpinnings of the modern day Malcolm legend. Among the 21 contributors are university professors, activists, reporters, writers, and the widow of Malcolm, Mrs. Betty Shabazz. Though the volume lacks any notes, it offers a rich and varied assortment of perspectives which, taken together, combine the intimacy of personal observations and reflections with objective data to give readers a fascinating and remarkably warm portrait. The content of the book, in fact, will allow readers to ponder much of Malcolm's life story through ''personal views,'' the words of Malcolm X himself, and the diverse assessments of people who knew him or were influenced by his ideas and leadership during the 1960s.

Readers will discern some common threads in the works of Clarke and Breitman regarding Malcolm's shifting ideology after his trips to Africa and the Middle East, his tenacious commitment to ''black unity and self-defense,'' and his hazy, though determined, quest to internationalize the black struggle. However, the two books differ considerably in perspective and interpretation. Beginning with its introduction, which rejects Breitman's narrow focus, Clarke's edited work offers a broad chronological view—an odyssey from Malcolm Little, to Malcolm X, and, finally, to El-Hajj Malik El-Shabazz. Additionally, Clarke emphasizes the spirit of the times as a major determinant in the development of Malcolm's overall leadership growth and maturity. As a whole, the publication is richer in research possibilities than in elaborate details. Yet revealed throughout the wide mixture of African-American and African voices is a magnificent glimpse of Malcolm X—his stature, appeal, and meaning—both at home and abroad.

GOLDMAN's illustrated, documented, and clearly written biographical study is a provocative counterpoint to previous works on Malcolm X. Broadly, it characterizes Malcolm X as little more than a confused, bitter, and prophetic man who in death assumed an unfortunate but exalted leadership status, born largely of distortion, exaggeration, and misunderstanding. Goldman's book, however, is problematic. Though premised on an impressive number of primary and secondary sources, it lacks balance, is thin on the chronological narrative of Malcolm's life while excessively overburdened in other areas. In large part, moreover, the entire study tends to center more on discrediting Malcolm's radical or revolutionary image than with understanding the man and his times. Readers, consequently, may well learn more from this book about what Malcolm X was not than about what he actually was. A cogent and more recent account of Goldman's views, adapted largely from *The Death and Life of Malcolm X*, is his "Malcolm X: Witness for the Prosecution," included in John Hope Franklin and August Meier, editors, *Black Leaders of the 20th Century* (1982).

—David C. Dennard

MALLARMÉ, Stéphane, 1842–1898; French poet.

Fowlie, Wallace, *Mallarmé*. London, D. Dobson, and Chicago, University of Chicago Press, 1953.

Gill, Austin, *The Early Mallarmé* (2 vols.). Oxford, Clarendon Press, 1979–86.

Mauron, Charles, *Introduction to the Psychoanalysis of Mallarmé*, translated by Archibald Henderson, Jr. and Will L. McClendon. Berkeley, University of California Press, 1963 (originally published by La Baconnière, Neuchâtel, 1950).

Michaud, Guy, *Mallarmé*, translated by M. Collins and B. Hunez. New York, New York University Press, 1965; London, P. Owen, 1966 (originally published by Hatier-Boivin, Paris, 1953).

St. Aubyn, Frederic C., *Stéphane Mallarmé*. New York, Twayne, 1969; revised edition, 1989.

*

It is a curious fact that, although Stéphane Mallarmé is now recognized throughout the world as one of the most original and influential poets of the 19th century, there should still be no proper biography of him in English. He himself once wrote that it is the work which "better than anything else reveals the man," and it is as if authors in English had taken this dictum all too much to heart. The gap is all the more noticeable as English-language studies of his writings are relatively numerous and as there have been detailed and remarkable biographies in other languages. The standard work is the massive *Vie de Mallarmé* (Paris, Gallimard, 1941) by Henri Mondor, the distinguished French surgeon who was also the founding father of Mallarmé studies. Magnificently written (it was largely responsible for Mondor's election as a member of the French Academy) and based on an unrivaled knowledge of Mallarmé and all he wrote, it is so thorough that no one has yet attempted to produce anything to supersede it. First published in 1941 and several times reprinted, it has unfortunately never been translated into English. Almost as weighty is the long essay on the man and his work in German by Kurt Wais, *Mallarmé*, first published in 1938 but extensively revised and greatly enlarged in 1952. But this too remains untranslated.

Even in critical books in English summing up the man and his works, the place accorded to biography is very small. This is the case with FOWLIE, who devotes fewer than 20 pages to "The Man" before going on to characterize Mallarmé's work. The biographical section of ST. AUBYN's volume in the Twayne's World Authors Series is equally summary, this as a matter of policy on the grounds that there is no need to know anything of the poet's life in order to appreciate his poetry. Only in MICHAUD's work is the balance more even, partly because that was the principle of the Connaissance des Lettres series in which the book originally appeared, but also because Michaud, one of the leading authorities on French Symbolism, believed that, in Mallarmé's case at least, it was impossible to dissociate the study of the words from the study of the man. The result is a lucid and informative account of both.

On the other hand, Michaud's work is made almost entirely dependent on the life in the psychoanalytical study by MAURON, the founder of the French school of "psychocriticism." This is not of course a complete biography; Mauron's thesis is that Mallarmé's life and writings were conditioned by the traumas of losing first his mother and then his young sister when he was still a boy. The examination of these bereavements thus leads Mauron into an analysis of the poetry. The book originally appeared in French in 1950, but for the English version, Mauron added a new introduction maintaining that his method had retained all its scientific validity, and an extra chapter integrating into his argument material newly discovered since the original publication.

A vastly different approach is exemplified in what is by far the most substantial contribution in English to the study of Mallarmé's life, the two volumes of GILL's meticulous investigation of the early Mallarmé. Part of Gill's case, supported by scrupulous sifting of a mass of evidence, is that much of what Mallarmé wrote, or indeed felt, is the direct result of his assimilation and imitation of literary models, notably Victor Hugo, to such an extent that many of his love-letters to his German fiancée Marie Gerhard are lifted from a section of *Les Misérables*. For Gill, however much Mallarmé may have grieved for his sister, he also saw her death as an ideal occasion for the composition of elegiac poetry. But it would be unjust to regard these two rich and penetrating books, the product of a lifetime of devotion to Mallarmé, as concerned with propounding a single view of him. They are an exploration, as rigorous and fair-minded as it is humane, of everything to do with the young Mallarmé's life, attitudes, and writings, and there is nothing remotely comparable to them in any other language. Unfortunately, they only take us up to 1864, when Mallarmé was no more than 22 years old and his greatest poetry was still to come.

Maybe it is because Mallarmé's life was outwardly uneventful, split between an unexciting career as a schoolmaster teaching English and a vertiginous inquiry into the limits of art, that he has not yet had in English the biography he deserves. But Mondor has demonstrated that a life of Mallarmé can be a work of art in its own right, so perhaps we can hope, especially now that Professor Lloyd Austin has completed the mammoth task, begun by Mondor, of publishing all Mallarmé's correspondence.

—A. W. Raitt

MALTHUS, Thomas (Robert), 1766–1834; English economist and sociologist.

Bonar, James, *Malthus and His Work*. London, Macmillan, and New York, Harper, 1885.

James, Patricia, *Population Malthus: His Life and Times*. London and Boston, Routledge, 1979.

Levin, Samuel M., *Malthus and the Conduct of Life*. New York, Astra Books, 1967.

Nickerson, Jane Soames, *Homage to Malthus*. Port Washington, New York, Kennikat Press, 1975.

Petersen, William, *Malthus*. Cambridge, Massachusetts, Harvard University Press, and London, Heinemann, 1979.

Winch, Donald, *Malthus*. Oxford, Oxford University Press, 1987.

*

Ever since the publication of his "Essay on Population" in 1798, Malthus has been a controversial figure. As Winch (see below) observes, "Malthus' position has probably generated more vituperation . . . and misunderstanding than that of any comparable figure in the history of social and political thought." In outlining his concerns that unchecked population growth could outstrip food supplies, and thus give rise to widespread starvation and death from malnutrition on an epidemic scale, Malthus gave offense to almost all of his contemporaries. On the one hand, he challenged Adam Smith's optimistic view of economic growth and, as Robert Heibroner puts it, "In one staggering intellectual blow Malthus undid all the hopes of an age oriented toward self-satisfaction and a comfortable vista of progress" (*The Worldly Philosophers*, 1953). Then, in addition, he challenged the generosity and concern of liberal thinkers by declaring that the provisions of the Poor Law would only prolong the suffering of the starving members of the labouring class. And finally he rejected the utopian proposals of left-wing authors who offered the prospect of an ideal society if only the menace of capitalism could be overcome. No wonder that Carlyle described him as a spokesman of the dismal science of illth, while at a later date, as Ronald L. Meek reports, Marx attached him as a shameless sycophant of the ruling classes, for whom the hatred of the English working class was entirely justified (*Marx and Engels on the Population Bomb*, 1971).

Despite these adverse reactions, Malthus has attracted many followers over the past 200 years both in the field of population studies (demography) and economics. Currently available works that focus primarily on his contributions to demography include those by LEVIN, NICKERSON, and the opening chapter of WINCH. All explore the neo-Malthusian concerns over the rapid growth of world population, which stood at 3.3 billion when Levin's work was published and is now approaching the 6 billion mark. They speculate as to ways in which population growth might be reduced, and explore the consequences of unchecked expansion that could lead to a depletion of global supplies of the food and raw materials essential to life. Economic commentaries on Malthus' work extend across the spectrum from Marx to John Maynard Keynes. Marx, who rejected Malthus' notions of natural checks on population growth, attributed the misery of the working class to the accumulation of private capital in the hands of the ruling class, and dismissed his

economic theories as an empty apologia for capitalism. On the other hand, Keynes praised the "Essay on Population" as a work of youthful genius and observed that the world would be a much wiser and richer place if only the 19th-century economists had pursued Malthus' demand-side approach rather than the more speculative approach taken by Ricardo (*The Collected Writings of John Maynard Keynes*, Vol. 8, "Essays in Biography," 1972). As the bicentennial of the publication of the Essay approaches, it will be interesting to note whether Cambridge will follow Keyne's expectation that Malthus will be remembered at his Alma Mater with undiminished regard. In the meantime, all readers are urged to read the Essay, if only to refute D. V. Glass' assertion that no work has been so much discussed by persons who do not seem to have read it (J. A. Banks and D. V. Glass, *Introduction to Malthus*, 1953).

Detailed critiques and assessments of Malthus' work by various authors over the years are assembled in readily available form in the four-volume *Thomas Robert Malthus: Critical Assessments*, edited by John Cunningham Wood (London, Croom Helm, 1986). Serious scholars will welcome this publication, which includes detailed notes and a section, in volume one, entitled "The Life of Thomas Robert Malthus and Perspectives on His Thought," as well as a series of articles on Specialized Topics featured in Volume four.

BONAR's classic study includes separate sections on the Essay, Economics, Moral and Political Philosophy, along with a brief Biography and a review of critical responses to Malthus' views on population. Bonar summarizes these critical viewpoints and claims that Malthus was offering a strong appeal to personal responsibility, and that he had faith in our power to conquer nature by obeying her.

PETERSEN notes that his work is complementary to the full biographical study that JAMES was due to publish at or about the time that his book was ready for publication. Thus it is no surprise to note that his study offers a scholarly review of Malthus' publications, including 16 pages of notes and 30 pages of works cited, while James features a detailed account of his life and times. Both works offer a serious introduction to an understanding of malthus, and serve to correct some inaccuracies in earlier publications. James in particular goes into great detail in her coverage of Malthus' background and career, including his years of service at the East India College at Haileybury, right up to reviews of his obituaries in the London press following his death on 29 December 1834. James comes down heavily in favor of her subject, commenting that she found him to be as interesting and lovable as his friends described him.

—George Thomas Potter

———

MANET, Édouard, 1832–1883; French painter.

Cachin, François and Charles S. Moffett, *Manet 1832–83*. New York, Metropolitan Museum of Art/Abrams, 1983.

Courthion, Pierre and Pierre Cailler, editors, *Manet by Himself and His Contemporaries*, translated by Michael Ross. London, Cassell, and New York, Roy, 1960 (originally published by Pierre Cailler, Geneva, 1953).

Duret, Théodore, *Manet and the French Impressionists*. Philadelphia, Lippincott, and London, G. Richards, 1910 (originally published by H. Floury, Paris, 1902).

Perruchot, Henri, *Manet*, translated by Humphrey Hare. London, Perpetua, and Cleveland, World Publishing, 1962 (originally published as *La Vie de Manet*, Paris, Hachette, 1959).

*

DURET's study was the first authoritative biography of Manet to appear in English. In a chronological overview of Manet's career framed by the historical context within which his aesthetic evolved, Duret interweaves reminiscences from Antonin Proust (*Édouard Manet, Souvenirs*, Paris, 1913) with his own memories of a long-time friendship. The reader will find letters exchanged between Manet and the author, details of the public and critical reception of his art, the names of models and sitters (not completely accurate), and firsthand accounts of the artist's working methods. Although little documentation is given (the text is not footnoted), Duret's skillfully written portrait reveals Manet as an instinctive artist and a Parisian gentleman: "Manet was a Parisian of the Parisians, both in his habits and his attitude towards life." A tendency to perceive Manet's early career and youth through the lens of his maturity—as when Duret writes of the years spent in Thomas Couture's studio, "Manet was possessed of a strong sense of individuality, and was dominated by the impulse which urges all men of original character to follow an independent course"—results in a mere six pages covering the six years Manet passed under Couture's tutelage. Duret emphasizes the period of Manet's radical output (1863–74), which he finds marked by continual struggle for acceptance within official circles: "Honours, official positions, academic distinctions . . . seemed to be due to him also. To see others wearing the laurels which he was unable to obtain, filled him with bitterness." Overall, Duret offers a revealing firsthand account of Manet's personality.

COURTHION allows Manet himself, and his contemporaries, to articulate the key passages of his life. This lengthy study includes, in part one, annotated letters from Manet and published and unpublished correspondence and reminiscences from his contemporaries: Antonin Proust, Charles Baudelaire, Albert Wolff, Emile Zola, Théodore Duret, Berthe Morisot, and Stéphane Mallarmé, among others. Completing the chronological documentation are extracts from the biographies of Duret, Jacques de Biezt (Paris, 1884), Edmond Bazire (Paris, 1884), Antonin Proust (Paris, 1913), and Adolphe Tabarant (*Manet: Histoire Catalographique*, Paris, 1931), with additional material extracted from memoirs published in French periodicals. In part two Courthion collects critical essays and key passages from contemporary critics on Manet's aesthetic, as well as later historians on Manet's influence. Also included in this volume are primary documents, such as Manet's birth certificate and last will and testament. While Courthion's text parallels that of Émile Moreau-Nélaton (*Manet raconté par lui-même*, Paris, 1926), the latter, unavailable in English, remains the definitive biographical reference on Manet. For the English reader, however, Courthion stands as the most scholarly and comprehensive resource.

In a competent biography, PERRUCHOT offers the English reader new information from Adolphe Tabarant's *Manet et ses oeuvres* (Paris, 1947), adding material from unpublished correspondence between Berthe Morisot and Stéphane Mallarmé, Eva Gonzales (Manet's pupil), and letters in the Bibliothèque Nationale. Perruchot expands on Duret with a fuller discussion of Manet's youth and early career, corrects and clarifies (from Tabarant's research) the identity of Manet's subjects, and amplifies the personalities in Manet's circle. Perruchot was first to make available to the English reader details of Manet's youthful liaison with his future wife Suzanne Leenhoff, intimating that her son, Léon-Édouard Köella Leenhoff, was Manet's own child. (Tabarant, who interviewed Léon extensively in preparing his manuscript, was first to propose Manet's paternity.) Recent publications, however, suggest that Léon may have been the offspring of Suzanne by Manet's father (Kathleen Adler, *Manet*, London, 1986). If there is a flaw in Perruchot, it is, as John Rewald discovered (*History of Impressionism*, New York, 1961), a tendency to "infuse the artist's life with adventures of a sentimental character . . . ," as, for example, the implication of a romance between Manet and painter Berthe Morisot: "Manet's art, and Berthe's, too, were nourished by their unavowed love, their communion of thought." But in Perruchot's readable and generally reliable biography, Manet appears "a bourgeois, a wit, a dandy, and a man about town, an *habitué* of Tortoni's and the friend of beautiful *demi-mondaines*, such was the man who revolutionized the painting of his time.

CACHIN's recent exhibition catalogue, while primarily a critical study of the artist's oeuvre, is also a valuable resource for the study of Manet's life. The analysis of individual paintings, rich in biographical detail, correlates both old and new material (published articles and books as well as documents from the primary archives in Paris and the Tabarant archives in the Pierpont Morgan Library). Cachin's comprehensive, annotated chronology summarizes (and clarifies conflicting facts) from both published and newly discovered material. The entries incorporate several important letters from Manet, with fifty letters to Zola from 1866–82 published here for the first time. These are offered in the original French, along with an English translation and annotations in Appendix I. A second appendix includes all the primary materials (including unpublished letters and other documents) relating to the "Maximilian Affair" (1867–69), and the bibliography here is comprehensive. Cachin's introduction sketches a revealing portrait of Manet, who "remains one of the most enigmatic, least classifiable artists in the history of painting."

John Rewald's detailed *History of Impressionism* (4th edition, New York, 1973) remains a valuable, scholarly reference on the events of Manet's life and his history within the Impressionist circle.

—Phylis Floyd

MANN, (Paul) Thomas, 1875–1955; German writer.

Bürgin, Hans and Hans-Otto Mayer, *Thomas Mann: A Chronicle of His Life*, translated by Eugene Dobson. University, University of Alabama Press, 1969 (originally published by Fischer, Frankfurt am Main, 1965).

Hamilton, Nigel, *The Brothers Mann: The Lives of Heinrich and Thomas Mann, 1871–1950 and 1875–1955*. London, Secker and Warburg, 1978; New Haven, Connecticut, Yale University Press, 1979.

Léser, Esther H., *Thomas Mann's Short Fiction: An Intellectual Biography*, edited by Mitzi Brunsdale. Cranbury, New Jersey, and London, Associated University Presses, 1989.

Mann, Erika, *The Last Year of Thomas Mann*, translated by Richard Graves. New York, Farrar Straus, 1958; as *The Last Year: A Memoir of My Father*, London, Secker and Warburg, 1958 (originally published as *Das letzter Jahr: Bericht über meinen Vater*, Frankfurt am Main, Fischer, 1956).

Mann, Katia, *Unwritten Memories*, edited by Elisabeth Plessen and Michael Mann, translated by Hunter and Hildegarde Hannum. New York, Knopf, and London, Deutsch, 1975 (originally published as *Katia Mann: Meine ungeschreibenen Memorien*, Frankfurt am Main, Fischer, 1974).

Reich-Ranicki, Marcel, *Thomas Mann and His Family*, translated by Ralph Mannheim. London, Collins, 1989 (originally published by Deutsche Verlags-Anhalt, 1987).

Winston, Richard, *Thomas Mann: The Making of an Artist 1875–1911*. New York, Knopf, 1981; London, Constable, 1982.

*

WINSTON, who with his wife translated Mann's *Letters*, *Diaries*, and other works, produced an admirable biography. He was the first English biographer with access to Mann's diaries, which were sealed until 1975. Unfortunately, only the diaries from 1918–21 and 1933–55 survive, and Winston did not live to reach the period they covered.

The work Winston completed is engaging and thorough, conceived and written with knowledge of Mann's entire life. The narrative draws on all sources to describe Mann's artistic development. Those works that mark a significant development in Mann's art, or that can be seen in a biographical light, are more thoroughly investigated—but never at the expense of narrative momentum. Winston's only flaw is a tendency to blur the dates in Mann's life when he is on the trail of a significant biographical theme. Three are foremost: Mann's fictional sources, his sexuality, and his relationship with his brother Heinrich.

Mann depended largely on autobiographical material for his fiction, at a time when this was still rare. When *Buddenbrooks* (1900; English translation, 1924) was attacked as a *roman à clef*, Mann defended his position: "I don't say: The novelist has the right to do portraits of people. Such a right cannot be proved. I do say: Important writers through the ages have assumed that right." Such comments only intensified scrutiny of Mann's work—which strengthened his obsession with defending it. While the issue may seem obscure, it was important to Mann and deserves the full treatment Winston gives it.

Winston died before he could treat Mann's sexuality. Mann's life and art both show he often felt strong homosexual attraction. He explained in his diary: "Although erotic, [the attraction] requires no fulfillment at all, neither intellectually nor physically."

As Winston tells it, much of the early tension between Thomas and Heinrich Mann was in Thomas' head. From an early age Thomas saw Heinrich, his elder by four years, as both

teacher and competitor. Thomas, a slow and cautious writer, envied Heinrich his prolific output. Heinrich's easy skill and Thomas' high standards fed a political debate that broke open the brothers' friendship at the start of World War I—also beyond the period Winston lived to cover.

Fortunately, it is at that point that HAMILTON's dual biography of Heinrich and Thomas hits its stride. Although the brothers were not all that mattered in each other's lives (as Hamilton sometimes seems to believe), they were undoubtedly central. Hamilton's book is often summary, as might be expected of an attempt to cover two long and significant lives—of prolific writers, at that—in a single medium-length volume; but Thomas, whose life is better documented, generally commands the structure of the narrative. Hamilton relies heavily on the letters of both Heinrich and Thomas; Thomas' diaries were not available when he wrote.

The book concentrates on politics, nearly to the exclusion of Thomas' and Heinrich's other writings from 1930 on. The brothers were reconciled in 1922, and together they led the German émigré community during the Nazi era. To Hamilton, Heinrich is an original and inventive writer, never at rest, with an uncompromising respect for democratic principles. Thomas, too, lived more and more motivated by political decisions—such as his return to Europe in 1952 in face of the all-too-familiar witch-hunts of American anti-communism.

The details of Thomas Mann's political and other activities are provided by BÜRGIN AND MAYER, whose book is simply a chronological listing of the events of Mann's life, day-by-day or month-by-month. Mann's words are used whenever possible. Missing are Mann's intellectual development (since ideas cannot be dated) and the great biographical "issues." The result is dry as dust, but complements the later, more polemical chapters of Hamilton's biography. The text, however, is plagued by small errors and inconsistencies.

In addition to the revealing *Letters* (1975) and *Diaries* (1983) Thomas Mann completed two autobiographical works, both limited in very different ways. His *Sketch of My Life* (1930), written after he received the Nobel Prize in 1929, is a brief and incomplete essay. It is significant for its discussion of Mann's early attraction to the work of Nietzsche and Schopenhauer—intellectual in the first case, aesthetic and spiritual in the second. Mann's *Story of a Novel* (1961) retells the author's activity during the period 1943–47, the years in which he wrote *Doctor Faustus*. The book lists dates and concerns of work on particular chapters, but omits any sense of the broad thematic construction of the novel. It does, however, provide a clear picture of Mann's position within the German émigré community and of his political views during four critical years.

The Manns were a family of writers. Son Klaus was an important and original novelist and playwright, son Golo a great historian, and daughter ERIKA MANN a journalist. She wrote a loving but oddly lifeless memoir of her father; some of the details she provides of Mann's activities during the last year of his life are available nowhere else. KATIA MANN, Thomas' wife, contributed her reminiscences at the age of 90. Her book (transcribed from television interviews: "there must be one person in this family who doesn't write") is very readable, but hardly a store of new information. Much is given over to setting straight old misunderstandings and unsubstantiated rumors.

These works and others relating to Thomas Mann and his family are reviewed in essays collected in REICH-RANICKI's book. Since the works are all diaries, letters, and memoirs, the criticism makes important contributions to biography. Foremost, however, is Reich-Ranicki's stated project of "demonumentalization." This becomes clear in his treatment of the quarrel between Heinrich and Thomas. "It should not be forgotten that both brothers were not only excitable but exceedingly neurotic." Heinrich, in Reich-Ranicki's portrait, is almost entirely lacking in talent; Thomas' insecurities about his own work fed on his distaste for Heinrich's. Thomas brought himself under control, and by World War II had taken over the role of German political conscience Heinrich had played after World War I. "Heinrich's political writings bear witness to a total, occasionally touching dilettantism and missionary zeal; those of Thomas remained to the end of his life the reflections of a non-political man."

Many works of Mann criticism contain biographical elements, but few contribute anything not found in the volumes already discussed. However, LÉSER's volume—though occasionally awkward in style and poorly proofread—is valuable for its tracing of Mann's intellectual development. His short fiction (although he wrote little after "Death in Venice" in 1912) is thoroughly analyzed in light of his developing worldview and the influences of Nietzsche, Wagner, and especially Schopenhauer. Winston recognized this as a worthwhile aspect of biography, and Léser's book complements his limited work.

—Matt Rowe

MANSFIELD, Katherine [born Kathleen Mansfield Beauchamp], 1888–1923; New Zealand-born English writer.

Alpers, Antony, *Katherine Mansfield: A Biography*. New York, Knopf, 1953; London, Cape, 1954.

Alpers, Antony, *The Life of Katherine Mansfield*. London, Cape, and New York, Viking, 1980.

Baker, Ida, with Georgina Joysmith, *Katherine Mansfield: The Memories of L. M. Taplinger*. London, 1971.

Berkman, Sylvia, *Katherine Mansfield*. New Haven, Connecticut, Yale University Press, 1951; London, G. Cumberlege/Oxford University Press, 1952.

Boddy, Gillian, *Katherine Mansfield, the Woman and the Writer*. Victoria, Australia, and New York, Penguin, 1988.

Fullbrook, Kate, *Katherine Mansfield*. Brighton, Harvester, and Bloomington, Indiana University Press, 1986.

Hanson, Claire and Andrew Gurr, *Katherine Mansfield*. London, Macmillan, and New York, St. Martin's, 1981.

Mantz, R. E., with John Middleton Murry, *The Life of Katherine Mansfield*. London, Constable, 1933.

Meyers, Jeffrey, *Katherine Mansfield: A Biography*. London, Hamilton, and New York, Braziller, 1978.

Tomalin, Claire, *Katherine Mansfield: A Secret Life*. London, Viking, 1987; New York, Knopf, 1988.

*

In spite of Mansfield's high profile as an innovative 20th-century short-story writer (her impact on the short story was as significant as Joyce's impact on the 20th-century novel) and despite the posthumous publication of her personal *Journal* and many of her letters, she has proved to be an elusive subject for biographers, who have tended to produce a succession of legends rather than an accurate and documented life story. There are several reasons for this. Her 35 years of life fall into two separate parts, divided almost equally between New Zealand, whence came the source material for her best stories, and Europe, where she wrote her best work. A biographer to do her justice must know both her backgrounds at first hand, but even those few biographers who have done the necessary travel have not always managed to avoid the trap of adducing her vivid New Zealand stories as primary biographical evidence. They are fiction, based on memories certainly, but created artefacts.

Mansfield died young, with only two volumes of her mature stories printed. Four more volumes of her prose and two volumes of her letters were published after her death, the material in them edited, selected, and (as it was later to be discovered) manipulated by her husband, John Middleton Murry, to create the rarified spirit who became the first Mansfield legend.

The earliest biography was by MANTZ, who visited New Zealand and was able to collect anecdotal material from some of Mansfield's contemporaries, though not from any of the Beauchamp family. The remainder of Mantz's book was derived from Murry's 1927 edition of the *Journal* and his 1928 edition of the Letters, Murry giving her no direct access to the Mansfield papers on which these were based. Mantz created the second Mansfield legend, the rebellious adolescent who abandoned family and birthplace for the literary life overseas.

BERKMAN had no access to Mansfield papers, but her scholarly appraisal of all available printed sources and access to one of Mansfield's sisters produced a more sober account. Her book remains the best biography of Mansfield as a working writer. It is still a standard work for the record of Mansfield's numerous appearances in the periodicals of her day.

ALPERS was a New Zealand journalist who spent some years in England working on his 1954 publication, the first biography based on a knowledge of Mansfield's two countries. A good investigative journalist, Alpers succeeded in gaining much new material from many in the UK who had known Mansfield (notably Ida Baker and George Bowden, Mansfield's first husband). Alpers met Murry, who revealed nothing of the documents he held.

Alpers was on occasion led astray by his informants, notably concerning Mansfield's relations with her New Zealand family, and he accepted without question the Mantz "rebellious adolescent-legend. His appendix (entitled "Money Matters") on Mansfield's finances led to a third Mansfield legend, the penurious artist unsupported by a wealthy banker father, a legend which is the reverse of the truth but which still persists in many later biographical essays and books.

The death of John Middleton Murry in 1957 opened up a new landscape in Mansfield studies. Her letters to him (and later his letters to her) were acquired by the Turnbull Library (now the research library of the National Library of New Zealand in Wellington). An even more important acquisition was the considerable collection of Mansfield manuscripts and notebooks (some of them going back to her early teens), which Murry had inherited and which he had jealously guarded. With these documents in the public domain, it was at last possible to get behind the accumulated legends. The task is still in process.

One of the first discoveries was that Murry was not only an interfering editor, but on occasion a fabricator. There never had been a Mansfield *Journal* nor a Mansfield *Scrapbook*. Both volumes were skilful manipulations of Mansfield documents. It is fair to say that not one page of the 1927 *Journal* nor of the so-called "definitive" edition of 1954 can be trusted. Texts are altered; pieces of short stories are printed as if they were genuine personal "diary" entries; undated sheets are given specific dates and inserted to conform with the idealised portrait that Murry was intent on depicting. The published Journal, on which every Mansfield biography had hitherto been based, was no base.

In the past 20 years or so further biographical material has appeared. Ida BAKER, Mansfield's close companion (and frequently bugbear) published her account of her friend in 1971. Baker was by then an old woman, and she had had contact only with isolated segments of Mansfield's life. The book is ghosted by a younger writer. As the testimony of a contemporary, however, it cannot be ignored, though it must be read with caution.

During the same period there has been a spate of publications, letters, diaries, and memoirs of the literary figures with whom Mansfield had associations in England, notably D. H. Lawrence and Virginia Woolf. These have often added sidelights to the Mansfield portrait.

There is by now almost a Mansfield industry. Her letters are appearing in an excellent scholarly edition edited by O'Sullivan and Margaret Scott, who is also engaged on the mammoth task of editing the mass of papers in the Turnbull Library. It is doubtful if a really authoritative biography can be done until all this accurate documentation has been completed.

This has not deterred the biographers. MEYERS produced an academic biography in 1978, dutifully covering well-known ground. The 1988 centenary of Mansfield's birth sparked off a whole group of short biographies, including two feminist biographies, by HANSON AND GURR and FULLBROOK. The best of these shorter biographical studies is probably the unassuming but accurate work by BODDY. The most sensational book is by TOMALIN. Though highly praised in the press, it is full of errors of fact and some unsubstantiated guesswork.

A quarter century after his 1954 biography (which he now insisted on dismissing as a young man's book done for the money), ALPERS returned to Mansfield. Now a professor in Canada, his talent for investigative journalism did not desert him. He made full use of the Bloomsbury archives and other English literary memoirs that are now available. He pursued Mansfield's medical history and traveled to her old haunts in England and Europe. The result is the fullest and most detailed biography of Mansfield yet written. It will more than satisfy the general reader and can be recommended as the fullest available biography.

The serious Mansfield scholar must still approach it with some caution. Curiously enough, Alpers is strong on the English and European material but inadequate on Mansfield's early New Zealand years, on which a great deal of useful new information had been published in the 60s and 70s in shorter studies published in research journals and elsewhere. There is also valuable Beauchamp family documentation now for the first time available. A really authoritative biography of Katherine Mansfield has yet to be written.

—Ian A. Gordon

MAO TSE-TUNG, 1893–1976; Chinese ruler, founder of the People's Republic of China.

Baum, Richard, *Prelude to Revolution: Mao, the Party, and the Peasant Question 1962–66*. New York, Columbia University Press, 1975.

Carter, Peter, *Mao*. London, Oxford University Press, 1976; New York, Viking, 1979.

Ch'en, Jerome, *Mao and the Chinese Revolution*. London and New York, Oxford University Press, 1965.

Ch'en, Jerome, editor, *Mao Papers: Anthology and Bibliography*. London and New York, Oxford University Press, 1970.

Chou, Eric, *Mao Tse-Tung: The Man and the Myth*. London, Cassell, and New York, Stein and Day, 1982.

Cohen, Arthur A., *The Communism of Mao Tse-Tung*. Chicago, University of Chicago Press, 1964.

Devillers, Philippe, *Mao*, translated by Tony White. New York, Schocken Books, and London, Macdonald, 1969.

Fitzgerald, C. P., *Mao Tsetung and China*. New York, Holmes and Meier, and London, Hodder and Stoughton, 1976.

Goodstadt, Leo, *Mao Tse-tung: The Search for Plenty*. London, Longman, 1972; as *China's Search for Plenty: The Economics of Mao Tse-tung*, New York, Weatherhill, 1973.

Han, Suyin, *The Morning Deluge: Mao Tsetung and the Chinese Revolution 1893–1954*. Boston, Little Brown, and London, J. Cape, 1972.

Han, Suyin, *Wind in the Tower: Mao Tsetung and the Chinese Revolution 1949–75*. Boston, Little Brown, and London, J. Cape, 1976.

Hawkins, John N., *Mao Tse-tung and Education: His Thoughts and Teachings*. Hamden, Connecticut, Linnet Books, 1974.

Hsiao, Yü, *Mao Tse-tung and I Were Beggars*. Syracuse, New York, Syracuse University Press, 1959; London, Hutchinson, 1960.

Karnow, Stanley, *Mao and China: From Revolution to Revolution*. New York, Viking, 1972; London, Macmillan, 1973; with subtitle *Inside China's Cultural Revolution*, London and New York, Penguin, 1984.

Leys, Simon, *The Chairman's New Clothes: Mao and the Cultural Revolution*, translated by Carol Appleyard and Patrick Goode. London, Allison and Busby, and New York, St. Martin's, 1977.

Lifton, Robert Jay, *Revolutionary Immortality: Mao Tse-tung and the Chinese Cultural Revolution*. New York, Random House, and London, Weidenfeld and Nicolson, 1968.

MacFarquhar, Roderick, et al, editors, *The Secret Speeches of Chairman Mao: From the Hundred Flowers to the Great Leap Forward*. Cambridge, Massachusetts, Council on East Asian Studies/Harvard University Press, 1989.

MacGregor-Hastie, Roy, *The Red Barbarians: The Life and Times of Mao Tse-tung*. London and New York, T. V. Boardman, 1961.

Meisner, Maurice, *Mao's China*. New York, Free Press, 1977; revised as *Mao's China and After: A History of the People*, New York, Free Press, and London, Collier/Macmillan, 1986.

Pálóczi-Horváth, Gyorgy, *Mao Tse-tung: Emperor of the Blue Ants*. London, Secker and Warburg, 1962; New York, Doubleday, 1963.

Payne, Robert, *Mao Tse-tung, Ruler of Red China*. New York, Schuman, 1950; London, Secker and Warburg, 1951; revised as *Portrait of a Revolutionary: Mao Tse-tung*, London and New York, Abelard-Schuman, 1961.

Pye, Lucian W., *Mao Tse-Tung: The Man in the Leader*. New York, Basic Books, 1976.

Rice, Edward E., *Mao's Way*. Berkeley, University of California Press, 1972.

Rue, John E., *Mao Tse-tung in Opposition 1927–35*. Stanford, California, Stanford University Press, 1966.

Schram, Stuart, *The Political Thought of Mao Tse-tung*. New York, Praeger, and London, Pall Mall Press, 1963.

Schram, Stuart, *Mao Tse-tung*. New York, Simon and Schuster, and London, Penguin, 1966.

Schram, Stuart, editor, *Mao Tse-tung Unrehearsed: Talks and Letters 1956–71*. London, Penguin, 1974; as *Chairman Mao Talks to the People*, New York, Pantheon, 1975.

Schwartz, Benjamin, *Chinese Communism and the Rise of Mao*. Cambridge, Massachusetts, Harvard University Press, 1951; revised 1958.

Shih, Bernadette P. N., *Mao: A Young Man from the Yangtze Valley*. Port Washington, New York, Ashley Books, 1974.

Snow, Edgar, *Red Star Over China*. New York, Random House, 1938; revised and enlarged, New York, Grove, and London, Gollancz, 1968.

Snow, Edgar, *The Other Side of the River: Red China Today*. New York, Random House, 1962; London, Gollancz, 1963; revised as *Red China Today*, New York, Random House, and London, Penguin, 1970.

Snow, Edgar, *The Long Revolution*. New York, Random House, 1972; London, Hutchinson, 1973.

Solomon, Richard H., *Mao's Revolution and Chinese Political Culture*. Berkeley, University of California Press, 1971.

Terrill, Ross, *Mao: A Biography*. New York, Harper, 1980.

Uhalley, Stephen, Jr., *Mao Tse-tung, a Critical Biography*. New York, F. Watts, 1975.

Wilson, Dick, editor, *Mao Tse-tung in the Scales of History: A Preliminary Assessment*. Cambridge and New York, Cambridge University Press, 1977.

Wilson, Dick, *Mao, the People's Emperor*. London, Hutchinson, 1979; as *The People's Emperor, Mao: A Biography of Mao Tse-Tung*, New York, Doubleday, 1980.

*

Every biographer of Mao begins with the account offered in SNOW's *Red Star Over China* (1938), and with good reason. It contains the only autobiographical account of Mao's early years on record and hence is by far the single most important source covering his life. Snow, an American journalist, interviewed Mao in 1936 at Mao's Yenan headquarters. Here Mao describes in somewhat wry humorous fashion the first 43 years of his life—his antipathy toward his father, a prosperous peasant; love of his mother, who protected him from his father; his rebellion against farm life; love of romantic novels; early education; discovery of Marxism; break with the Koumintang; and the Long March. Snow's later volume, *The Other Side of the River* (1961), offers more autobiographical data, though it is by no means as thorough and contains many errors of detail and omission.

HSIAO, Mao's schoolmate and friend at Tungshan Higher Primary School, offers an account of Mao's life from the time he began his schooling until the Chinese Party was founded in 1931. Writing some 40 years after the event, and at the time a bitter opponent of Mao's regime, Hsiao-Yü presents Mao's character as a mixture of arrogance, cruelty, and stubbornness, a picture that no doubt has elements of truth. If the book has some tedious spots, it is particularly interesting in describing a trip Hsiao-Yü made with Mao in the summer of 1917, when as mock mendicants they walked through several districts around Tungting Lake.

Of the many general biographies of Mao, SCHRAM's *Mao Tse-Tung* (1966) is still the best. An American who was director of the Soviet and Chinese section of the Fondation Nationale des Sciences Politiques in Paris, Schram offers a detailed account, with much attention to ideology. He stresses Mao's anti-Western nationalism as well as his faith that the human will could transform both external and human nature. Carrying his story to 1966, Schram sees the budging Cultural Revolution as Mao's deliberate and nostalgic attempt to relive the May Fourth period, recapture his own youth, and create in his lifetime something more lasting than the pyramids, even at the expense of his own efforts to modernize China.

Also excellent is British historian CH'EN's *Mao and the Chinese Revolution* (1965), which integrates theory with Ch'en's personal experiences, the nature of Chinese society in the 1920s and 30s, and China's revolutionary wars. Ch'en finds Mao's greatest contribution to Marxist thinking in his adoption of the Chinese tradition of peasant culture to Marxist-Leninist aims. Writing in 1965, when Mao's career was far from over, Ch'en claims that "it seems premature to judge him, his contribution, or his place in history." Ch'en denies that the Long March of 1934–36 was pre-planned; rather, at each stage, it had a different destination in view. The best-documented of all the books on Mao, Ch'en's book includes 37 of Mao's poems.

One of the more stimulating studies comes from PYE, who uses psychological techniques to understand Mao's personality. Pye sees Mao given to extolling contradictions and prone to high-risk decision-making. He notes that Mao's closeness to his mother gave him strong feelings of narcissism. The young Mao resented the domination of his father, Mao Shun-sheng, but he felt superior to Shun-sheng and was aware of his ability to outwit him. In a sense, the book is both stimulating and misleading, for Pye concentrates so much on Mao's early childhood that the rest of his quite eventful life does not appear to affect his personality and thought.

Several general biographies have updated such accounts. In a highly respected volume written after Mao's death, foreign correspondent TERRILL sees much of Mao's life in positive terms. Mao unified China and restored its pride. Taking large steps toward social modernization, Mao left his China sufficiently independent to possess the sixth largest economy in the world. Yet Mao was far less gifted as manager than as iconoclast, teacher, and warrior. Seeing Mao the ruler as distinct from Mao the guerrilla leader, Terrill writes, "China might have been better off had he died 20 years earlier than he did." At best a "semi-intellectual," Mao outlived his usefulness to his nation.

In an account more superficial than Terrill's, WILSON (1979), editor of the *China Quarterly*, portrays Mao as a "barrack-room philosopher," who failed because he set his sights too high. By discussing his prolific sexual activities in Yenan and the four-letter earthiness of his language, Wilson humanizes Mao. Drawbacks include paraphrased conversations as direct quotation, thinness on Mao's political and military thought, and a failure to integrate Mao's psychology, education, and adherence to communism.

Other general biographies vary in scope and competence. PÁLÓCZI-HORVÁTH offers a general life that, like Terrill's, divides Mao's life into two distinct stages. Before he assumed power, says Pálóczi-Horváth, Mao was a supreme realist, but once he assumed control, he became a rigid Marxist-Leninist ideologue impressed by his own dogma. The book is particularly strong in its use of documents captured from the Russian embassy in Peking in 1927. Journalist PAYNE's biography contains many errors but includes a personal interview with Mao held in 1946. RICE offers a hostile account of Mao's career, extensively documented and revealing an extraordinary number of primary and secondary sources. FITZGERALD, an Australian historian, offers a lucid biography aimed at the general reader, but the book is marred by a pro-Mao bias. More respected for its balance is the elementary account by CARTER.

CHOU, a Chinese journalist who knew many communist leaders before he broke with Mao's regime in 1961, also contains weaknesses. Chou presents Mao as an organizational genius, but also a man who continually showed his contempt for human life. Chou assails Mao for failing to show filial piety, for his contentious personality and marital infidelity, the massive purges in the Kiangsi area in 1930, the desertion of army units during the Long March, and the cost of several thousand lives during the rectification campaign of 1942.

British journalist MacGREGOR-HASTIE offers a hero-worshipping volume that betrays little knowledge of China and less of Mao. Despite the title "critical biography," UHALLEY, an historian at the University of Hawaii, claims that Mao's authoritarian regime was necessary to promote the welfare of the peasants, but fears that "the system possesses the potential for much tyranny if a less nobly motivated and humane leader succeeds Mao." HAN's two-volume biography so internalizes Mao's perceptions that it is totally uncritical. She writes, for example, that Mao gave the Chinese people "that liberation of mind which is true liberty." Although Han writes with the skill of a novelist, she ignores major works of scholarship, particularly if they do not reinforce her preconceived notions. SHIH has written a fictionalized narrative from the perspective of Mao's supposed "fifth daughter," born to Mao and Ho Tze-chen in 1935 at Pao-an after the Long March. The mythical conversations and stilted narration are almost disastrous enough to convey a certain charm.

Any examination of Mao's ideology should begin with Mao's own *Selected Works* (5 vols.), frequently printed by China's Foreign Language Press. MacFARQUHAR's collection of speeches shows Mao thinking out loud and unrehearsed. SCHRAM's *Political Thought* (1963) offers excerpts of Mao's political philosophy in fluent English. Schram notes Mao's political debt to Lenin and Stalin but stresses the populist strain in his thought, the immense role of the peasantry, and "voluntarism." Schram has also edited Mao's speeches of 1956 to 1971. CH'EN's *Mao Papers* (1970) has collected Mao's statements on the cultural Revolution and lists his total corpus as well. DEVILLERS has selected the most significant of Mao's works along with a useful sketch of his life. Director of Southeast Asia Studies at the Centre d'Études des Relations Internationales, Paris, Devillers em-

phasizes that Mao saw lengthy armed struggle essential to creating a new China.

SCHWARTZ, a Harvard scholar, relied on Chinese, Japanese, and Russian sources to analyse with brilliance the indigenous roots of Mao's political strategy, doing so at a time when Stalinist historiography was giving the Russian dictator all the credit. In his preface to the second printing, Schwartz finds Mao exercising complete leadership of the Chinese Communist movement in 1935, not in 1933, as he originally stated. RUE supplies new data for the late 1920s and early 1930s, but only challenges Schwartz on minor matters. He shows how bitterly Mao had to fight for survival within his own party. SOLOMON presents Mao as an innovator who attempted to institutionalize the revolutionary conflict by mass participation and criticism. He notes how Mao cleverly used several strands of Chinese culture, especially attitudes toward leaders, to overcome the deep-seated aversion to conflict.

Several books deal with specialized aspects of Mao's thought. GOODSTADT unsuccessfully attempts to show that Mao's works provide a distinctive and coherent framework of economic analysis. HAWKINS organizes Mao's fragmentary remarks on education. COHEN surveys Mao's doctrines on such topics as revolution, transition to communism, dictatorship of the proletariat, and contradictions within socialist society. He finds Mao a derivative thinker, not an original one. WILSON's anthology (1977) is superior, with chapters by such leading scholars as Schram and Schwartz on Mao in a variety of roles: philosopher, Marxist, political leader, soldier, teacher, economist, patriot, statesman, Chinese, and innovator.

Much work has concentrated on Mao's rule. That by MEISNER, an historian at the University of Wisconsin, is the most scholarly, giving an almost encyclopedic treatment of Mao's activities. Meisner sees Mao as creating a modern nation-state, a modern educational system, and at least the beginnings of industrialization. He finds, however, that Mao's political methods and ideology became anachronistic in the very modernization process he fostered, for his doctrines were unsuited to modern Chinese conditions.

BAUM traces the struggle, both political and ideological, between Mao and Liu Shao-ch'i over the Socialist Education Movement that immediately preceded the Cultural Revolution. LEYS, a Belgian specialist in Chinese art, presents a simplistic indictment of Mao, but does include the text of a Mao speech "explaining" the Cultural Revolution to foreign visitors. The American journalist KARNOW finds Mao, the "poet" of revolution, unable to adjust to the "prose" of stable administration. "Consumed by an obsessive urge," the anachronistic old man was making his last leap toward utopia. LIFTON, a Yale psycho-historian, explains the Cultural Revolution in terms of Mao's obsession to have his works outlive him, or what Lifton calls "symbolic immortality." All of SNOW's books are rich in Mao interviews. Snow's *Long Revolution* (1971) contains the celebrated interview of January 1965 declaring that Chinese troops would not intervene in the Vietnam War.

—Justus D. Doenecke

MARCUS AURELIUS. See **AURELIUS, Marcus.**

MARIE ANTOINETTE, 1755–1793; French monarch.

Asquith, Annunziata, *Marie Antoinette*. London, Weidenfeld and Nicolson, 1974; New York, Taplinger, 1976.

Castelot, André, *Marie Antoinette*, translated by Denise Folliet. London, Vallentine Mitchell, 1957.

Cronin, Vincent, *Louis and Antoinette*. London, Collins, and New York, Morrow, 1974.

Haslip, Joan, *Marie Antoinette*. London, Weidenfeld and Nicolson, 1987; New York, 1988.

Hearsey, John, *Marie Antoinette*. London, Constable, and New York, Dutton, 1972.

Huisman, Philippe and Marguerite Jallut, *Marie Antoinette*. New York, Viking, and London, Stephens, 1971.

Loomis, Stanley, *The Fatal Friendship: Marie Antoinette, Count Fersen and the Flight to Varennes*. London, Davis-Poynter, and New York, Doubleday, 1972.

Seward, Desmond, *Marie Antoinette*. New York, St. Martin's, and London, Constable, 1981.

Zweig, Stefan, *Marie Antoinette: The Portrait of an Average Woman*, translated by Eden and Cedar Paul. New York, Viking, and London, Cassell, 1933 (originally published by Insel, Leipzig, 1932).

*

Early accounts of Marie Antoinette's life were divided, as one historian puts it, between "hagiography and demonology." ZWEIG's 1933 biography, still influential despite its age, aims at redressing this, as its subtitle suggests. The approach is both somewhat romantic and somewhat Freudian, focusing on the Queen's unsatisfactory marriage with Louis XVI, her love affair with the romantic Fersen and her sublimation from ordinary woman to tragic heroine through the circumstances of her last months. The sympathetic and compelling portrait Zweig created has been a challenge to later biographers.

CASTELOT's biography displays no such obvious angle or sympathy but is a chronological account with a fairly close focus and a wealth of detail. Anecdotes and even conversations are frequently reproduced from the sources, chiefly from Mme. de Campan's detailed *Mémoires de la vie privée de Marie Antoinette*, and there are lavishly descriptive set pieces, such as the wedding of Marie Antoinette and the Dauphin and the coronation of Louis XVI. HEARSEY's biography uses much the same material and approach, but his less generous inclusion of detail allows the story-line to emerge more clearly. He furnishes his book with an historical appendix, in which events in Marie Antoinette's life are listed chronologically against political events and landmarks in art and thought.

Other biographers, whose focus is less close, manage successfully to integrate this background material into the main fabric of their work. CRONIN in particular, devotes two separate chapters to "The Tenor of the Age," dealing with science and the arts, and religion and philosophy respectively. Because his book is a double biography of both the king and queen, affairs

of state are naturally given prominence. Cronin champions both Louis and Antoinette, making a critical reappraisal of traditional evidence to show that previous biographers have not made allowance for the negative bias of contemporary sources, including the much-used letters of Mercy, Maria Theresa's ambassador to the French court. Cronin even suggests that Zweig may have suppressed evidence that would have contradicted his theory of an extremely late consummation of the marriage. In attempting to rescue Louis' reputation as a politician, he diminishes Antoinette's as a meddler. Cronin portrays Louis as protective toward Antoinette, wisely realising that as an Austrian she was bound to be unpopular, and therefore deliberately keeping her out of politics. In almost every political crisis—the dismissal of Turgot, the affair of Cardinal Rohan and the necklace, etc.—Cronin puts the king's behaviour in the most favourable light and plays down the influence of the queen. The relationship between the two emerges as closer and more rewarding than Zweig and others allow. The Fersen affair is touched on lightly and delicately. On the whole, Cronin's account is humane and sensible, although some of the queen's more extravagant behaviour and its consequences are passed over rather fleetingly.

With SEWARD we have a return to Louis as an "amiable freak" and as a concomitant, Antoinette appears once more as influential politically, but Seward makes a positive case for the queen as a genuine, albeit unsuccessful, politician. While dismissive of the king, Seward is sympathetic to the queen, drawing attention to the serious side of her character, her personal religion, and portraying her as a fundamentally healthy German woman, unhappily caught in a diseased and corrupt French court—the source of the pornographic scandal that finally brought about her downfall. He deals at more length than Cronin with her faults and follies, but shows her gradually maturing. The Zweig view of Fersen as a romantic hero is not shared by Seward, who sees him as "complicated and neurotic." There is less discussion of the sources than Cronin provides and less historical background, but a sound and independent view emerges through an attractively written narrative.

HASLIP is not unsympathetic to her subject but more detached and more traditional in her criticisms than Cronin and Seward. She portrays a frivolous and foolish woman and tries to explain her failings through an understanding of her early life. While Seward's heroine is robust, strongminded and capable of an intelligent appraisal of politics, Haslip's, like Zweig's, is a very ordinary woman, wholly unable to grasp her real situation and matured only by the terrible circumstances of her life's end. Haslip makes the opposite judgement of Seward about her capacity for forming successful personal relations, for example with her daughter and the king's sister, Madame Elizabeth.

LOOMIS' book is focused, as its subtitle suggests, on one particular episode in the queen's life, but this is placed in the context of her life as a whole and used as the basis for a study of her personality. Again, it is a double portrait, but in telling Fersen's side of the story, his hopes and plans for saving the queen and her family, Loomis illuminates the politics and diplomacy of Europe at the time. He adopts the same critical attitude to the sources and to Zweig's interpretation of them as Cronin, maintaining, for example, that no one can prove that Fersen was ever the queen's lover. As with Cronin and Seward, the author's engagement with and sympathy for his characters comes across well and makes for entertaining reading.

HUISMAN AND JALLUT's approach is completely original. Their aim, essentially, is to illuminate Marie Antoinette's personality through an exploration of her taste, "her own concept of happiness." A full account of her life is given, with numerous quotations from the sources, but the emphasis is on the culture that the queen enjoyed or inspired, and the book is richly and beautifully illustrated with reproductions and photographs.

ASQUITH's biography is one of Weidenfeld's Great Lives series. It reworks the traditional material in a very readable form with the emphasis on swift-moving narrative, and is well illustrated throughout.

—Isabel Aitken

MARLOWE, Christopher, 1564–1593; English playwright and poet.

Bakeless, John, *Christopher Marlowe: The Man in His Time.* New York, Morrow, 1937.

Bakeless, John, *The Tragicall History of Christopher Marlowe* (2 vols.). Cambridge, Massachusetts, Harvard University Press, and London, Oxford University Press, 1942.

Boas, F. S., *Marlowe and His Circle: A Biographical Survey.* Oxford, Clarendon Press, 1929.

Boas, F. S., *Christopher Marlowe: A Biographical and Critical Study.* Oxford, Clarendon Press, 1940.

Eccles, Mark, *Christopher Marlowe in London.* Cambridge, Massachusetts, Harvard University Press, 1934.

Ellis-Fermor, Una M., *Christopher Marlowe.* London, Methuen, 1927.

Henderson, Philip, *And Morning in His Eyes.* London, Boriswood, 1937.

Henderson, Philip, *Christopher Marlowe.* London and New York, Longman, 1952.

Hilton, Della, *Who Was Kit Marlowe?* London, Weidenfeld and Nicolson, and New York, Taplinger, 1977.

Hoffman, Calvin, *The Murder of the Man Who Was "Shakespeare".* New York, J. Messner, 1955.

Hotson, Leslie, *The Death of Christopher Marlowe.* London, Nonesuch Press, and Cambridge, Massachusetts, Harvard University Press, 1925.

Ingram, John H., *Christopher Marlowe and His Associates.* London, G. Richards, 1904.

Kocher, Paul H., *Christopher Marlowe: A Study of His Thought, Learning, and Character.* Chapel Hill, University of North Carolina Press, 1946.

Levin, Harry, *The Overreacher: A Study of Christopher Marlowe.* Cambridge, Massachusetts, Harvard University Press, 1952; London, Faber, 1954.

Lewis, J. G., *Christopher Marlowe: Outlines of His Life and Work.* London, W. W. Gibbings, 1891.

Norman, Charles, *The Muses' Darling: The Life of Christopher Marlowe.* New York, Rinehart, 1946; London, Falcon Press, 1947.

Poirier, Michel, *Christopher Marlowe.* London, Chatto and Windus, 1951.

Ross Williamson, Hugh, *Kind Kit: An Informal Biography of Christopher Marlowe.* London, M. Joseph, 1972; New York, St. Martin's, 1973.

Rowse, A. L., *Christopher Marlowe: A Biography.* London, Macmillan, 1964; with subtitle, *His Life and Works*, New York, Harper, 1964.

Tannenbaum, Samuel A., *The Assassination of Christopher Marlowe: A New View.* New York, Tenny Press, 1928.

Williams, David Rhys, *Shakespeare: Thy Name is Marlowe.* New York, Philosophical Library, and London, Vision Press, 1966.

Wraight, A. D., *In Search of Christopher Marlowe: A Pictorial Biography.* London, Macdonald, and New York, Vanguard Press, 1965.

Zeigler, Wilbur G., *It Was Marlowe: A Story of the Secret of Three Centuries.* Chicago, Donohue, 1895.

*

The image of Christopher Marlowe has been remoulded by each new generation of his critics, with his biographers usually in rather belated pursuit. Yet his life and work have until relatively recent years been regarded as inseparable, the one infallibly illuminating the other. The brevity of the life and the multiplicity of "meanings" potential in the works have added to the innocent reader's impression of an elusive author, of whom one keeps catching a glimpse down some new alley in a maze of distorting mirrors.

Here, we can do no more than mention the existence of such source materials as the 'Baines libel' (pervasively influential, whether or not it be believed) and other contemporary hearsay concerning Marlowe's alleged atheism. Together with extracts from other early considerations of the dramatist down to 1896, these are conveniently assembled in *Marlowe: the Critical Heritage*, edited by Millar Maclure (1976), which, despite its title, deals as much with the man as his writings—the two generally being haplessly conflated. The 19th century saw its Marlowe, even in his premature death, as a precursor of their own romantic poets—a free-thinking and free-spirited individualist, at one with such of his heroes (so perceived) as Tamburlaine and Faustus. Alexander Dyce's biographical preface to his pioneering edition of the collected works (1850) and Sidney Lee's article on Marlowe for the *Dictionary of National Biography* stand as safe cornerstones to the Victorian conception of their man.

Swinburne wrote on Marlowe with more communicated enthusiasm, in sources as varied as an essay for the *Encyclopedia Britannica* and four verse quatrains in *Astrophel and Other Poems*. However, his fullest consideration came in 1908, in a volume significantly entitled *The Age of Shakespeare*—for Swinburne was representative in his belief that Marlowe's ultimate distinction was his occupation of a lower rung on some Darwinian ladder of dramatic evolution, his destiny duly fulfilled by guiding Shakespeare "into the right way of work." It is ironic, but not perhaps surprising, therefore, that the first full-length biography, by ZEIGLER, should have been largely devoted to demonstrating to its own satisfaction that Marlowe did not die in that notorious "tavern brawl," but lived on to write those very plays that are attributed to Shakespeare. Such a view now seems so quaint that the later contentions to the same effect of HOFFMAN and WILLIAMS, which continued the controversy into the 1960s, may best be disposed of here—the very air they breathe redolent of the 1890s, when, if other writers were not trying to prove that Marlowe (among others) was Shakespeare, they were, like LEWIS, trying to build him a memorial of his own. Let us leave such irrelevancies along with the raked-over bones of Marlowe and Shakespeare, to rest in peace.

Despite the well-intentioned but now redundant endeavours of INGRAM in 1904 to rescue "the brightness of Marlowe's name," which for three centuries had been "damned by libel and slander," the appearance in the late 1920s of major studies by ELLIS-FERMOR and BOAS—the former more concerned with the works, the latter with the background to the life—were probably most influenced by T. S. Eliot's essay in *The Sacred Wood* (1920), and by the renewal of interest occasioned by HOTSON's brief but revelatory account, published in 1925, of his researches into the long-undiscovered proceedings of the inquest into the dramatist's death. TANNENBAUM in 1928, while readily acknowledging his debt to Hotson, was only the first, however, to question the credibility of the verdict in this politically murky business, suggesting the complicity of Raleigh in a deliberate plot to murder Marlowe as he slept. He concluded that "the coroner was influenced by certain powers not to inquire too curiously into the affair." Subsequent biographers have, one suspects, been persuaded less by the ample but one-sided evidence than by their own prejudices about the trustworthiness of "official enquiries." In 1934, ECCLES added new evidence, notably concerning Marlowe's friendship and misadventures with the poet and Walsingham camp-follower, Thomas Watson.

In 1940, BOAS produced a further volume, now more closely directed to the poet and his works rather than their background: it remains an excellent summation of a state of knowledge that has not in substance (as distinct from emphasis and interpretation) been much supplemented since. Boas' is a reliable, slightly cautious account—but eminently more readable than the two studies by BAKELESS between which its first appearance was sandwiched. Of these, the first and shorter at least gives some impression of enjoying its subject. Such works of solid, sometimes stolid scholarship had the cumulative effect (though it generally formed no part of their stated intention) of underpinning the emerging critical view of Marlowe not as the aspiring individualist of old, but as a half-way respectable representative of the spirit of Christian humanism, the plays now being understood as condemning worldly ambitions and portraying their invariable disappointment.

KOCHER's study of 1946 brings yet another version of the dramatist into focus: while clarifying, in particular, what "atheism" actually implied for the Elizabethans, it also draws the clearest picture yet of the sheer range of Marlowe's interests and associations. A refurbishing of the view of Marlowe as iconoclast follows—the extremes of rebellion now, however, to be commended where they were once condemned. And so, as Alfred Harbage put it, the posthumous charges against Marlowe of everything from "smoking to sodomy" and "from coining to catholicism" were "no longer kept under wraps or cautiously discounted," but "produced with a flourish, like a recommendation." The Marlowe who thus appealed to the radical spirit of the immediate post-war world is vividly redrawn in relation to his plays in LEVIN's study in 1952: more a work of criticism than a strict biography, it nonetheless still sees the poet's personality as the key to understanding his dramaturgy. Although Levin's Marlowe is a complex, darkly introspective figure, the original title of his book, *The Overreacher*, provided an instant image that clung irresistibly to the man until generations of students had reduced it to a cliché.

The more familiar, romantic Marlowe lives on and dies young again in NORMAN's revealingly titled *The Muses' Darling*, a fictionalized account leaning coyly on the present tense in its desperate striving for verisimilitude, while POIRIER keeps alive the vision of the representative Renaissance man, full of youthful confidence in humankind and doubt in God. ROWSE proceeds to squeeze his subject into his own inimitable if not altogether accurate Elizabethan world picture, filled with explorers of the high seas and adventurers of the human spirit. Rowse essentially uses the works as evidence for the life—somewhat suspect sources for an historian, one would have supposed. HENDERSON's two books on Marlowe are the best of this subsequently worked-out vein, and far more critically perceptive about the plays, though they still lay undue stress on the sensational elements in Marlowe's life, and sometimes confuse conjecture with actuality. Henderson sees Marlowe as essentially a lyric poet, exploring his own ideas and ambitions in what are made to appear, in view of their intensely subjective focus, essentially undramatic plays.

The romantic-rebellious and the orthodox Christian images of Marlowe thus rubbed shoulders on the shelves for a good many years, their implicit contradictions unresolved. The continuing inseparability of criticism from biography is perhaps best illustrated by the debate over the comic scenes in *Doctor Faustus*: for long regarded as later interpolations or, if Marlowe's, as unfortunate concessions to the groundlings, they now began to be understood as integral to the play. Their ironic commentary on the main plot thus reflected not only a more complex dramaturgy, but a more detached and reflective writer, a cynical outsider rather than an involved, aspiring Renaissance man—and a less evidently attractive subject for popular biography. WRAIGHT's account of 1964 is in fact more substantial than its own subtitle, "a pictorial biography," might suggest: aimed at the general reader, it nonetheless achieves an exemplary integration between text and iconography, and displays an "historicist" awareness ahead of its academic time. More recently, ROSS WILLIAMSON took delight in the doubts over Marlowe's death, working backwards through a multiplicity of identities (Shakespeare's, thankfully, not among them). The imaginary conversations Ross Williamson invents for his subject are more credible than most of their kind, though this may appear less of a virtue to the scholar than to the general reader. HILTON's study raised hopes in its title that she too had recognized the problem of her subject's multiplying identities: but such hopes were quickly dashed by answers that rely on guesswork, and by so self-conscious a sympathy with Marlowe that he is addressed as Kit throughout.

If serious biography seems of late to have lost interest in Marlowe, this is perhaps in part because recent critical writings have tended—some might say, at last—to detach the dramatist not so much from his background as from the possession of his plays. One of the latest full-length studies, by Simon Shepherd (1986), even abandons as irrelevant the old search for "authoritative" texts of the plays, and virtually throws out the author along with his "authority." Critically, the intention is to prioritize the collective, theatrical decisions that the surviving texts are seen as representing, over the "elitist" assertion of an individual artist's integrity: but biographically the consequence is that "Christopher Marlowe" becomes simply a form of shorthand for an almost arbitrary *persona* who might as well have been called "the *Faustus* author." Always an elusive figure, Marlowe is now threatening to disappear altogether within infinite folds of text and context.

—Simon Trussler

* * *

MARVELL, Andrew, 1621–1678; English poet.

Birrell, Augustine, *Andrew Marvell.* London and New York, Macmillan, 1905.

Bradbrook, M. C. and M. G. Lloyd Thomas, *Andrew Marvell.* Cambridge, Cambridge University Press, 1940.

Craze, Michael, *The Life and Lyrics of Andrew Marvell.* New York, Barnes and Noble, and London, Macmillan, 1979.

Hunt, John Dixon, *Andrew Marvell: His Life and Writings.* Ithaca, New York, Cornell University Press, and London, P. Elek, 1978.

Legouis, Pierre, *Andrew Marvell: Poet, Puritan, Patriot.* Oxford, Clarendon Press, 1965; 2nd edition, 1968.

*

BIRRELL first identifies a real problem in writing about Marvell: not much is known about Marvell's private life. To deal with this problem, Birrell evolved various strategies: he mines Marvell's poetry for its biographical significance; he adduces more fully documented lives contemporary with and parallel to Marvell's; he provides a great deal of historical background; and, above all, he relies on Marvell's letters, especially the lengthy series Marvell wrote to his constituents when he was MP for Hull, from 1659 to his death.

Birrell so roots Marvell's life in the history of his times that the book sometimes reads more like a history than a biography. But the times were interesting, after all, and Birrell's use of well-selected primary material—about 40% of the book is direct quotations—does bring the times to life. Furthermore, Birrell was a lawyer, and his balanced appraisal of Marvell's character and achievement makes sense. Seeing Marvell as neither fanatic nor doctrinaire, Birrell accedes to the then-new revaluation of Marvell as an important poet, confesses that he takes "great pleasure in Marvell's [verse] satires," and praises Marvell's prose style. Though to some extent superseded by the later works, this is still a solid short biography, well worth reading.

BRADBROOK AND THOMAS offer a critical biography, with heavy emphasis on "critical." Unlike Birrell, who used Marvell's poetry to illumine his life, Bradbrook and Thomas use Marvell's life to illumine his poetry. The intent throughout is to interpret Marvell's writings in terms of the literary, social, intellectual, and cultural habits of his era. The book opens with a brief sketch of Marvell's career, then devotes chapters to his early poetry (up to and including the Nunappleton period), to his later religious and political poetry, to his most famous prose

work (*The Rehearsal Transpros'd*, 1672), and to his minor prose works and his letters. Three appendices treat the question of his alleged marriage, give details about his journey to Russia, and suggest a possible intellectual debt to Spinoza.

Bradbrook and Thomas' study is both comprehensive and pithy. While the authors touch on everything Marvell wrote, their comments are unusually compact (this book is shorter even than Birrell's). Marvell's greatest strength as a writer, they claim, is his deceptive straightforwardness ("it is more usual to read him incompletely than to misread him") owing to subtle workmanship. His greatest weakness is that his work too often depends on circumstances. Deft, dense, demanding, this is not a book for beginners but for readers familiar with the period and with Marvell's life. It is also important because its judgments still carry weight, a half century later, with students of Marvell's poetry.

LEGOUIS' work is the closest thing we have to a standard biography of Marvell. Unfortunately, there are major differences between the French version (*André Marvell*, Paris, 1928) and the 1968 English version (done by Legouis himself). The French version, which was his dissertation, is twice as long as the English version (500 as opposed to 250 pages). What's missing from the English version is a lot of theory, a fair amount of evidential quotation, many details about Marvell's life, some 1,500 footnotes (the more important ones were incorporated into the English version), and an impressive bibliography. As partial compensation, the English version fixes errors, includes a few new facts about Marvell's life and has an appendix discussing books and articles published between the first (1965) and second (1968) editions. The remarks below refer to the English version, more readily available than the French.

The book proceeds chronologically. After a brief chapter on Marvell's early life and an even briefer chapter on his poetical masters, there are richly detailed chapters on his lyrical poetry, his political poetry, his sojourn in Parliament, his verse satires, his controversial prose, and his reputation. Legouis conflates the strengths of Birrell and Bradbrook/Thomas: even more historically informed than the former, he is also at least as critically perspicacious as the latter. Further, his style, though academic, is as clear as Birrell's and much more discursive than that of Bradbrook and Thomas. If this book has a flaw, it might be that the three parts of the subtitle do not receive equal weight—the Poet receives somewhat more attention than the Patriot; the Puritan much less attention than the Patriot.

HUNT's biography was published on the tercentenary of Marvell's death. Although clearly derivative—most of the quotations in Hunt's book also appear in one of the earlier biographies—Hunt still manages to innovate. First, Hunt divides Marvell's life into smaller pieces, i.e., ten chapters. Second, he manages to add further details to our understanding of ground already covered by his predecessors, most strikingly in the chapter on Marvell's first trip abroad. Third, from hints in the previous biographies about oppositions in Marvell's personality and poetry, Hunt develops a full-blown portrait of Marvell as "multiplicitous": he finds in Marvell's poetry a double vision that parallels various antimonies in Marvell's character, for instance, "a recognition both of essential principles and of expediency" when Marvell had to make political decisions.

Hunt's most obvious innovation is his inspired use of over 60 black-and-white illustrations, "to image," as he puts it in his preface, "the people and places in Marvell's life; and to provide a visual anthology of the cultural artifacts of the 17th century." So we see not just the obligatory portrait of Marvell, but also, for instance, a portrait of Milton (Marvell's best-known friend) and a picture of a cabinet of curiosities (to illustrate a point about Marvell's poetry). Lively, accessible, and profusely illustrated, this book seems designed for the general reader, though even specialists will no doubt find interesting angles and unusual connections.

CRAZE's volume is misleadingly titled. This book is actually an edition of 40 of Marvell's lyric poems, preceded by a 25-page biography. Nonetheless, the brief biography is an accurate and well-written compendium of the little we know for certain about Marvell's life, with special attention, naturally, paid to dating Marvell's poetry.

—Todd H. Sammons

MARX, Karl, 1818–1883; German political philosopher and socialist.

Berlin, Isaiah, *Karl Marx: His Life and Environment.* London, T. Butterworth, 1939.

Callinicos, Alex, *The Revolutionary Ideas of Karl Marx.* London, Bookmarks, 1983.

Foner, Philip S., *When Karl Marx Died: Comments in 1883.* New York, International Publishers, 1973.

Gemkow, Heinrich, *Karl Marx: A Biography.* Dresden, Verlag Zeit im Bild, 1968 (originally published by Dietz, Berlin, 1967).

Kettle, Arnold, *Karl Marx: Founder of Modern Communism.* London, Weidenfeld and Nicolson, 1963.

Liebknecht, Wilhelm, *Karl Marx: Biographical Memoirs,* translated by E. Untermann. Chicago, C. H. Kerr, 1901 (originally published as *Karl Marx, zum Gedächtniss,* Nürnberg, Wörlein, 1896).

McLellan, David, *Karl Marx: His Life and Thought.* New York, Harper, and London, Macmillan, 1973.

McLellan, David, *Karl Marx.* New York, Viking, and London, Fontana, 1975.

Mehring, Franz, *Karl Marx: The Story of His Life,* translated by Edward Fitzgerald. New York, Covici Friede, 1935; London, J. Lane, 1936 (originally published by Soziologische Verlagsanstalt, Leipzig, 1933).

Nicolaevsky, Boris and Otto Maenchen-Helfen, *Karl Marx: Man and Fighter,* translated by Gwenda D. and Eric Mosbacher. Philadelphia and London, Lippincott, 1936.

Padover, Saul K., *Karl Marx: An Intimate Biography.* New York, McGraw-Hill, 1978.

Rühle, Otto, *Karl Marx: His Life and Work.* translated by Eden and Cedar Paul. New York, Viking, and London, Allen and Unwin, 1929 (originally published by Avalun-verlag, Hellerau-bei-Dresden, 1928).

Schwarzschild, Leopold, *The Red Prussian: The Life and Legend of Karl Marx,* translated by M. Wing. New York, Scribner, 1947; London, Hamilton, 1948.

*

McLELLAN's brief *Karl Marx* (1975) serves as a useful introduction, while his *Karl Marx: His Life and Thought* (1973) is clearly one of the better complete biographies available. The latter gives a lively and surprisingly balanced account, avoiding the political prejudice that mars so many works on Marx. In addition, McLellan makes able use of previously unpublished works by Marx and the unedited Marx-Engels correspondence. Lack of access to such material is clearly a weakness in many of the earlier biographies.

McLellan deals with three aspects of Marx: personal, political, and intellectual. This is a great undertaking as so many works have been content merely to focus on a single side of the multifaceted Marx. Thus, the reader is given clear insights into Marx's beliefs, yet the personal side behind the thinker is never far away. The passion Marx felt while writing *Capital* is revealed, as is the love he felt for his wife and children. While his work is extensively documented and footnoted, McLellan does not allow details to impede his story. Equipped with a chronological table, genealogical chart, an excellent critical bibliography, and useful index, this title would serve well both the general reader and the serious scholar.

Although now dated and written without full access to the evidence available to the modern researcher, MEHRING's was for decades the classic biography of Marx. Notwithstanding these limitations and Mehring's obvious loyalty to the cause of socialism, this remains a wonderful work, rich in insights and detail. Mehring personally knew Marx's daughter, Laura Lafarague, and was her editorial representative when a collection of the Marx-Engels correspondence was first proposed.

Mehring's work reveals the attitude and logic of left-wing German Social Democracy, of which Mehring was a leader. In fact, he often fought fellow party members over questions concerning what Marx had said or meant. This results in a clear, one might say crisp, understanding of Marx, both as abstract thinker and human being.

LIEBKNECHT not only knew Marx but considered him a close friend, despite the fact that the Marx-Engels correspondence has revealed that Marx was not always his greatest admirer. More a series of sketches than a full-blown biography, Liebknecht's work remains useful mainly for the colorful stories it relates about Marx. While such incidents as late-night drinking and tossing stones at gas lights in a London street tell us little if anything about Marx the thinker, they do allow us to glimpse the man behind the theories. Further, to read the reflections of one of the founders of German Social Democracy, and to realize the distance between that party and Marx, is still of value.

NICOLAEVSKY AND MAENCHEN-HELFEN suffer from many of the same faults as Mehring but still manage to give an excellent account of Marx's life. They focus most attention and detail on Marx's involvement in the 1848–49 revolutions and his struggles in the International Workingmen's Association. Less attention is paid to the economic theories since the purpose of the work is to show Marx as "the strategist of the class struggle." This work has benefited from a number of documents and letters that appeared after World War I. Still, any number of points that remain vague in this work have been clarified in McLellan. Extremely readable and utilizing a great deal of quotation, this volume is worth consulting.

FONER's book collects various responses, newspaper articles, and tributes that appeared when Marx died in 1883. This expertly edited volume gives the reader a feel for the reactions to Marx by various people and institutions, particularly those within the labor movement. The book is best read after one is already somewhat familiar with Marx's life.

KETTLE is lucid, fair, and brief, an excellent introduction to Marx for the reader who wishes to grasp the essentials, though unsuitable for the more advanced student of Marx. Likewise, BERLIN provides a valuable introduction, though it lacks the depth of other biographies. Still, as an absorbing and well-written work, it cannot be discounted. A more in-depth treatment is given by PADOVER, whose work is certainly worth consulting even if it has little new to say.

Unlike other biographers cited, CALLINICOS attempts to focus on Marx's ideas more than his life. The author does so "to rescue Marx from the distortions he has suffered; to present, in as clear and simple a manner as possible, his basic ideas." In this attempt the author is very successful, although the result is a work that appears more one-dimensional when contrasted with more complete treatments.

The works by Rühle, Gemkow, and Schwarzschild are all seriously flawed in one manner or another. RÜHLE's biography reveals the danger of practicing psychology without a license. While much of his information is sound, his attempts to psychoanalyze Marx are unsuccessful. His conclusion is filled with statements such as, "Unquestionably Marx was a neurotic," and he stresses Marx's "inferiority complex." The author was once a Social Democratic deputy in the Imperial German Reichstag who ended his life as an artist in Mexico. GEMKOW's work was written under the authority of the Institute for Marxism-Leninism in East Berlin and sadly is marred by the political trends then current in the German Democratic Republic. Here Marx is too much an idol and too little a man, and he is given credit (some would say blame) for events that took place years after his death. On the other hand, SCHWARZSCHILD clearly sets himself the task of turning Marx into a monster. Drawing heavily—and selectively—on the Marx-Engels correspondence, the author attempts to "correct" the positive image set out by previous biographers.

—William A. Pelz

MARY I [Mary Tudor], 1516–1558; English monarch.

Erickson, Carolly, *Bloody Mary*. New York, Doubleday, and London, Dent, 1978.

Loach, Jennifer, *Parliament and the Crown in the Reign of Mary Tudor*. Oxford, Clarendon Press, and New York, Oxford University Press, 1986.

Loades, David M., *The Reign of Mary Tudor*. London, Benn, and New York, St. Martin's, 1979.

Loades, David M., *Mary Tudor: A Life*. Oxford and New York, Blackwell, 1989.

Prescott, Hilda F. M., *Spanish Tudor, Life of Bloody Mary*. London, Constable, and New York, Columbia University Press, 1940; as *Mary Tudor*, London, Eyre and Spottiswoode, 1952; New York, Macmillan, 1953.

Ridley, Jasper, *The Life and Times of Mary Tudor*. London, Weidenfeld and Nicolson, 1973.

Tittler, Robert, *The Reign of Mary Tudor*. London and New York, Longman, 1983.

Waldman, Milton, *The Lady Mary: A Biography of Mary Tudor*. London, Collins, and New York, Scribner, 1972.

*

For nearly two generations, PRESCOTT's portrait of Mary I has been the standard life, dispelling earlier harsh judgments of the queen by James Froude in *The Reign of Mary Tudor* (1910) and A. F. Pollard in *Political History of England, 1547–1603* (1913). Using mostly printed sources and few manuscripts, Prescott, in beautiful narrative fashion with footnotes, analyzes Mary's harassed and embittered childhood, her betrayal, forced on her by her father in 1536, of her mother's and her own principles, the persecution of heretics during her own reign, and her rather pathetic marriage and early death. The focus is rightfully on Mary, though occasionally Prescott awkwardly tosses in a bit of "new" social history. She argues that if Mary became more Spanish than English, it was "her fathers doing." Prescott depicts Anne Boleyn as vicious and dangerous, Thomas Cromwell as a "deep, conscienceless schemer," and Catherine of Aragon as a loving and pious mother. Prescott exculpates Mary for the Protestant burnings at Smithfield, blaming Papal Legate Reginald Pole and Lord Chancellor Stephen Gardiner. They persuaded her that, especially after Thomas Wyatt's rebellion, "Spanish style" orthodoxy was needed to return England to the Roman Catholic way, but Prescott asserts that the real trouble was the queen's marriage to Philip II of Spain. Philip used Mary's affection to declare war on France, where the English lost Calais and Mary lost her subjects' respect.

Three popular biographies of Mary appeared in the 1970s: Waldman, Ridley, and Erickson. WALDMAN focuses on Mary's life before her accession to the throne, and although his style is readable, his work provides no footnotes or bibliography for the serious student. Personalities emerge as either good or evil, except Henry VIII who is both. Waldman argues that Henry restored Mary after 1537 only because of public opinion, and that Cromwell was frightened by Mary's obduracy. RIDLEY's undocumented, illustrated work draws largely on Prescott. Too many events are handled simplistically (e.g., Cromwell's fall), but there are some tidbits for Tudor fanciers. While Ridley lauds the wisdom of Mary's decisions to expel Protestant refugees and to lower taxes, he is critical of Mary's treatment of heretics, pointing out that she burned 283 Protestants in only five years, compared to five executed in 44 Elizabethan years. He notes the irony of her punishments: a recanting Cranmer, never her enemy, was burnt; the menacing Norfolk and Richard Rich were appointed to Queen Mary's Privy Council. Ridley exonerates Philip II from a charge of callousness, suggesting that the Spanish monarch had pressing business outside England. ERICKSON, a writer of Tudor biographies for book club audiences, relies heavily on Prescott and a few manuscripts, producing a lively narrative unblemished by many footnotes. Despite an unfortunate title, the book casts Mary as a woman warped by life, not as one inherently murderous. More skillfully than Prescott, Erickson colors her story with meaningful social and cultural observations.

Revisionists have examined Mary's life and reign and have found it not nearly as "sterile" as Pollard suggested. TITTLER blames Mary's mistrust of Englishmen on her "peculiar apprenticeship," and touts her bravery and decisiveness at the death of Edward VI. He attributes her lack of popularity to her disdain for public relations and accuses the Spanish Dominicans and an out-of-touch Pole of railroading the queen into the burnings. Downplaying the martyrs, Tittler insists that had her reign been longer, Mary's policies might have worked. Neither was the campaign in France the disaster bemoaned by critics; the loss of Calais had little economic or military significance. Tittler disagrees with Pollard's estimation that a mid-Tudor crisis occurred. He characterizes Mary's relations with Parliament as full of compromise and cooperation. LOACH also emphasizes the smoothness of Marian Parliamentary relations and the legislative productivity achieved. Mary was a courageous and sincere leader, as her claiming the throne in 1553 shows. Her supporters weren't just outsiders, but included Catholics and conservatives. Mary did not make a fatal error when she assumed that Catholicism was still a political force. Loach disagrees with Loades about Mary's marriage and its effect on the war with France. She argues that Parliament was keen on the war and seethed with residual enmity from the Hundred Years War. The crown's business continued to get done and there was little political fallout. Armed with an extensive bibliography and helpful appendices, Loach favorably compares Mary's Parliaments with those of her father.

Beginning in 1979, LOADES has crafted the definitive, scholarly work on Mary's life and reign, debunking the Spanish Tudor image by noting that the queen never learned to speak the language of her mother. Mary's submission in 1536 bothered her conscience, but she blamed Anne Boleyn and Cranmer for her troubles, not Cromwell. Though no revisionist, Loades asserts that Mary's policy was coherent from the start, showing good sense and discrimination, though she was easily influenced. Loades characterizes Mary's mind as "limited, conventional and obstinate," but she was generous in rewarding service. Loades discusses the other players involved as well as her religious and financial policies in detail drawn from an extensive bibliography. His book contains illustrations, maps, and a listing of Mary's Privy Council. He concludes that Mary unwittingly divided her conservative support and paralyzed it as a political force.

Drawing on many manuscript sources at the Public Record Office and the British Library, Loades has recently published the definitive, scholarly biography of Mary, which includes a glossary, appendices dealing with Mary's household and will, and the most complete bibliography available. His content footnotes make fascinating suggestions for future research. The mid-16th century was not a time for strong women, and Mary's life must be considered against that background. Women were to be either married or in a religious community; for most of her life, Mary Tudor was neither. Once queen, "Mary's limitations as a ruler were imposed by her gender." Loades appreciates, like Waldman, the influence of Juan Luis Vives on Mary's education, but concludes that her curriculum didn't "take." The book is particularly strong on the *annus mirabilis*, 1553, when Mary received a papal absolution for her earlier submission, started Catholic restoration, negotiated the marriage treaty with Philip, and quashed Wyatt's rebellion. Like Ridley, Loades is effective when dealing with Mary's phantom pregnancies and the impact of Philip's departures. When casting about for comparisons in this balanced account, Loades finds the closest parallels to Mary in the rule of Charles I. He concludes that Mary's life was shaped by the "dictates of her conscience," creating a sort of martyrdom for the Tudor queen.

—Elizabeth Lane Furdell

MARY QUEEN OF SCOTS [Mary Stuart], 1542–1587; Scottish monarch.

Cowan, Ian B., *The Enigma of Mary Stuart*. London, Gollancz, and New York, St. Martin's, 1971.

Donaldson, Gordon, *Mary Queen of Scots*. London, English Universities Press, 1974.

Fraser, Antonia, *Mary Queen of Scots*. London, Weidenfeld and Nicolson, and New York, Delacorte, 1969.

Henderson, T. F., *Mary Queen of Scots, Her Environment and Tragedy* (2 vols.). London, Hutchinson, and New York, Scribner, 1905.

Strickland, Agnes, *Lives of the Queens of Scotland* (8 vols.). London and Edinburgh, Blackwood, 1850–59; New York, Harper, 1851–59 (Mary occupies vols. III to VII).

Wormald, Jenny, *Mary Queen of Scots: A Study in Failure*. London, G. Philip, 1988.

Zweig, Stefan, *The Queen of Scots*, translated by Eden and Cedar Paul. London, Cassell, 1935; as *Mary, Queen of Scotland and the Isles*, New York, Viking, 1935 (originally published as *Maria Stuart*, Vienna, H. Reichner, 1935).

*

Queen Elizabeth I, in a verse on the defeat of the Northern Rebellion, referred to Mary Queen of Scots as "the Daughter of Debate"; the description was apt, and has remained so. Historians of Scotland and historical biographers are as far as ever from agreement on the subject of Mary Queen of Scots, but now that the heat has gone out of religious debate, discussion concerning the queen's life and reign turns on the interpretation of the evidence. The debate began immediately after Mary's fall from power, with *A Defence of the honour of the right highe, mightye and noble Princesse Marie Quene of Scotland,* by John Leslie, Bishop of Ross (1569), which was followed by a fierce attack on her in *Ane detectioun of the doinges of Marie Quene of Scottes,* by George Buchanan, published in both Scots and Latin (1571). The manner of Mary's death gave her defenders an enormous advantage, since it enabled them to present her to posterity as a martyr. *Martyre de la Royne d'Escosse,* by Adam Blackwood (Paris, 1587) was the first of many hagiographical writings.

COWAN's work is not a biography but a study of biographical, historical, and literary attitudes to Mary Queen of Scots. His book is a good starting point for biographical study, for the introduction details all the major works on Mary and traces the course of Marian writings from the virulent polemics of the 16th century to the scholarly though still heated debates of the 19th century. He goes on to trace the development of genuine biographical writing, up to 1971. Cowan's ensuing chapters, chronologically and thematically arranged, contain selected quotations from the books discussed (including the plays of Schiller and Swinburne), which illustrate the diversity in the interpretations of Mary's character.

An early and honourable attempt at straightforward biography was given in STRICKLAND's *Lives of the Queens of Scotland* (1850–59). Strickland was a Victorian lady who presented Mary as an exemplar of the Victorian ideal of virtuous womanhood. Though this interpretation now appears quaintly anachronistic, the author's scholarly use of the collections of documents and letters then newly available remains impressive, and her work is still a pleasure to read for its minute detail and for its insights.

HENDERSON's two-volume biography is a solid but readable work, detailed, conscientious, and remarkably free from bias. It remained the definitive biography of Mary Queen of Scots for more than half a century and is still very well worth reading.

ZWEIG's work is addressed to the general reader and, though well researched, lacks the reference notes and bibliography required of the modern biographer. It is a good example of the "psychological interpretation" school of biography that flourished in the 1930s. The author's Austrian Jewish background freed him from the Anglo-Scottish tendency to partisanship in writing of Mary Queen of Scots, and from the Catholic or Protestant tendency to religious bias. Zweig's Mary is a femme fatale who was led to crime and to her downfall by impulsive passion. His interpretation may be out of fashion, but his narrative is compelling.

FRASER's book is outstanding as a personal biography of Mary, though the political background is by no means neglected. Fraser stated her aims as "First, being possessed since childhood by a passion for the subject of Mary Queen of Scots, I wished to test for myself the truth or falsehood of the many legends which surround her name. . . . Secondly, for the sake of the general reader, I hoped to set Mary anew in the context of the age in which she lived. . . . In the end my two aims converged, and I found myself with the single object of showing with as much accuracy as is possible in the light of modern research, what Mary Queen of Scots must have been like as a person."

Fraser is triumphantly successful in presenting a sympathetic portrait of her subject; less successful, perhaps, in persuading the reader that Mary was innocent of any involvement in the murder of Darnley, of an adulterous liaison with Bothwell, and of authorship of the controversial "Casket Letters." However, most readers may follow Zweig in finding Mary worthy of sympathetic interest without requiring her to be morally blameless.

Fraser presents Mary as an attractive character, unusually tolerant and merciful for her period, affectionate and tenderhearted, devoted to children and animals, loyal to her friends, and capable of inspiring devotion in her servants. However, she shows that Mary was also capable of demanding the death penalty for those who offended her—for example, the impassioned

Chastelard, who hid in her bedchamber, and was pardoned for his first offence, but paid for the second with his life. Fraser, however, demonstrates Mary's general distaste for executions by describing her collapsing when forced to witness that of Sir John Gordon. Fraser cites many examples of Mary's physical and emotional collapse at moments of stress. This lifelong weakness makes the courage with which she faced her own execution all the more remarkable, and Fraser's description evokes the horror—and the political outrageousness—of this event. Fraser demonstrates the sincerity of Mary's conviction that she died as a Roman Catholic martyr.

The familiar image of Mary Queen of Scots is of the captive queen dressed with austere elegance in black and white. Fraser's attention to the details of Mary's wardrobe shows that in her earlier life in France and Scotland Mary had a predilection for dresses of white or gold; she also wore scarlet, orange, and yellow. Fraser also describes Mary's wearing for her execution a petticoat of crimson or dark red, the liturgical colour for the commemoration of martyrs.

DONALDSON portrays Mary sympathetically and considers that "her residence in France was no bad apprenticeship" (though Fraser has shown that her education there was intended to prepare her to be Queen Consort of France and not ruler of Scotland, to which she would not have returned if her French husband, King Francis II, had lived). Donaldson believes that Mary showed acumen in accepting the Scottish Reformation as a *fait accompli* while reserving for herself the right to practice the Catholic faith. According to Donaldson, during the early years of her personal rule, while she accepted the guidance of her halfbrother Lord James Stewart (Donaldson prefers this spelling; other biographers prefer "Stuart") and of Maitland of Lethington, "Mary's policy in all her doings was such as to win support from fairminded men and from all whose minds were not closed to the consideration of her merits." Donaldson claims that Mary's good record as a "politic ruler" was not forgotten despite the disastrous marriage to Darnley, the scandals of the murders of Rizzio and of Darnley, and the ultimate scandal of her marriage to Bothwell by Protestant rites. To the good record of Mary's earlier years Donaldson imputes the strength of the support that rallied to her after her escape from Lochleven. Donaldson compares the Eleven Days of Mary Stewart to the Hundred Days of Napoleon: "in her marvellous Eleven Days, Mary seems to have mustered between 5000 and 6000 men." Nonetheless, Langside was Mary's Waterloo. Donaldson produces another Napoleonic parallel when he compares Mary's relations with her last gaoler Sir Amias Paulet to Napoleon's relations with his unsympathetic custodian Sir Hudson Lowe: "a policy of irritating pinpricks on one side, a succession of grievances and complaints on the other." However, Paulet's honourable ("scrupulous" is Donaldson's word) refusal to assassinate his prisoner secretly gave her the opportunity to demonstrate "calm, courage and dignity" at her death. Donaldson concludes that "a review of Mary's career, with its record of political acumen, tolerance, expediency and opportunism, makes it impossible to regard her as a martyr for a cause which in fact she adopted wholeheartedly only when all else had failed."

WORMALD's book states its conclusion in its subtitle. Wormald explains her line of enquiry as follows: "The business of the historian is not to love or hate Mary Stuart, to judge her as a saint or a criminal, but to ask about the success or failure of her rule.'' Where Donaldson sees Mary as prudently accepting guidance from her half-brother and her secretary of state (''The Politic Ruler''), Wormald sees her as almost abandoning her responsibilities to them (''The Reluctant Ruler''). Wormald produces some damning evidence of Mary's negligence; for example, the sederunts (attendance lists) of her privy council demonstrate the rarity of her attendance (17 times out of 54 in 1561–62; 5 out of 50 in 1564; 12 out of 62 in 1566). Wormald considers the religious situation to have been very much more fluid than does Donaldson; in her view, since the success of the Scottish Reformation was far from assured, Mary abrogated her responsibility in failing to attempt the restoration of Catholicism: ''Even at the level of preserving social order, no monarch could afford to allow religious division to run riot.'' Wormald does not agree with Fraser and Donaldson in seeing Mary's tolerance as admirable. She remarks, ''the suggestion that Mary Queen of Scots showed the attractive virtue of tolerance in an intolerant age emerges as wholly anachronistic. Her indifference not only to her kingdom but to the religion of her kingdom was not attractive; it was extraordinary, and it was profoundly irresponsible.'' In Wormald's view, after demonstrable incompetence and irresponsibility had been followed by scandal and debacle, the formation of a Queen's Party after Mary's escape from Lochleven illustrated ''ideological commitment'' to the monarchy, and not personal support.

By the time the narrative reaches Mary's execution, Wormald is sufficiently out of sympathy with her subject to write that the executioner ''botched his job; it took him two blows of the axe to kill her, and three to get her head off, and he then suffered the shattering experience of picking up the head to display it according to accepted ritual, only to find that what he was holding was a wig, while the head itself dropped from his hands.'' Wormald recovers from her sympathy for the executioner to conclude that Mary was a tragic figure ''because she was one of the rare—strangely rare—cases of someone born to supreme power who was wholly unable to cope with its responsibilities.'' Wormald has made a strong case that the failure of Mary Queen of Scots resulted from her own incompetence, and a future biographer will be hard pressed to answer it.

For the serious student of the reign of Mary Queen of Scots, the earlier writings discussed in Cowan's *Enigma of Mary Stuart* are required reading. For the general reader, Fraser's biography remains the most enjoyable. Almost certainly, the interest aroused by it will compel the reader to go on to read Donaldson and Wormald, and to look forward to the next biography.

—Caroline Bingham

MATISSE, Henri, 1869–1954; French painter.

Barr, Alfred H., Jr., *Matisse, His Art and His Public.* New York, Museum of Modern Art, 1951; London, Secker and Warburg, 1975.

Flam, Jack D., *Matisse: The Man and His Art 1869–1918* (2 vols. projected). Ithaca, New York, Cornell University Press, and London, Thames and Hudson, 1986.

Schneider, Pierre, *Matisse*, translated by N. Taylor and B. S. Romer. New York, Rizzoli, and London, Thames and Hudson, 1984 (originally published by Flammarion, Paris, 1984).

*

There is no authorized biography, properly speaking, of Matisse. The first full-scale scholarly monograph on the artist, by BARR, was published when Matisse was 81 years old. This text alternates biographical material—much of it new in 1951 and based on questionnaires to the artist and to those close to him—with a stylistic history of Matisse's work in all media: painting, drawing, printmaking, sculpture, and decorative projects. As the title indicates, Barr's pioneering study is also a record of the artist's patronage throughout his lifetime and includes a list of works by Matisse in public museums in English-speaking countries. Barr's book is also notable for the, to that date, most complete bibliography of books and articles by and about Henri Matisse, compiled by Bernard Karpel, Librarian of the Museum of Modern Art. This comprehensive text has other superb collateral material, notably translations of several of Matisse's important statements on art, including ''Notes of a Painter'' (1908), and his hitherto unpublished studio instruction (1908), gathered by his patron and pupil, Sarah Stein. In short, Barr's work remains the indispensable study of the artist's career.

Before Barr's book, several monographs by friends or colleagues of Matisse included important biographical material. Notable among these are: Marcel Sembat, *Henri Matisse et son oeuvre* (Paris, 1920; the first real monograph on the artist), Florent Fels, *Henri-Matisse* (Paris, 1929), and Raymond Escholier, *Henri Matisse* (Paris, 1937). Immediate post-Barr publications include: Gaston Diehl, *Henri Matisse* (Paris, 1954; abridged version in English, New York, 1958) and Raymond Escholier, *Matisse, ce vivant* (Paris, 1956, followed by a free English translation, *Matisse, from the Life*, London, 1960). Mention must also be made of an important biographical note by the artist himself, published in *Formes*, no. 1, January 1930, which appeared just before the series of international retrospective exhibitions of 1930–31. These exhibitions acknowledged a career that no one could then predict would continue, with unabated innovation, for another 23 years.

After the artist's death in 1954, Barr's study was completed or—on specific points—corrected, as new date and documentation became available. It was not until 1970, however, during the centenary year of Matisse's birth (he was born on 31 December 1869), that a new biographical portrait of the artist appeared, in Pierre Schneider's *Henri Matisse, exposition du centenaire* (Paris, 1970), a catalogue accompanying the large retrospective exhibition at the Grand Palais, and published by the Réunion des Musées Nationaux. Schneider, a friend of the artist's son-in-law, Georges Duthuit, and daughter, Marguerite Duthuit-Matisse, provided an updated chronology of Matisse's life and a new interpretation of his oeuvre.

SCHNEIDER's work was expanded in his definitive monograph on the artist, *Matisse*, a luxurious and leisurely exposition of the author's lifetime meditation on Matisse as a man and artist. Although the 752-page text provides new biographical material, hitherto unpublished letters and journals entries, the work is thematically rather than chronologically ordered, so that biographical information must be excavated from the text, except for the short section at the end (pages 715–740), which is specifically biographical.

Concurrent with Schneider's 1970 centenary catalogue is Louis Aragon's *Henri Matisse: Roman* (2 vols., Paris, 1971), an anthology of previously published essays on Matisse. The texts are enriched by the annotations and comments originally made by the painter and are enlarged by personal anecdotes about him. Immediately after the centenary exhibit, two collections of Matisse's writings appeared: Dominique Fourcade, editor, *Henri Matisse: Écrits et propos sur l'art* (Paris, 1972) and Jack D. Flam, editor, *Matisse on Art* (London and New York, 1973). The French anthology is indexed by topic or theme as well as proper names and contains valuable additional material in the extended footnotes. Flam's collection is in a flexible English translation and contains a fine introductory overview of the artist's aesthetic and intellectual development, as well as informative notes for each text. Neither anthology is exhaustive and each contains material that the other omits.

In 1986, the first book of FLAM's two-volume artistic biography was published. As the parallelism of the text suggests, Flam's book is the first serious successor, 35 years later, to Barr's complete treatment of Matisse's life and oeuvre. Whereas Barr was more concerned with the reception of the artist's work, its patrons and current locations, Flam integrates biographical and psychological insights with interpretations of Matisse's works, both individually and in their historical development. His text incorporates all the post-Barr scholarship on the artist, is meticulously documented, and contains a fine bibliography of the most essential Matisse literature; Flam corrects data on the artist's life and on specific works. After Barr, this is perhaps the most essential biographical work on Matisse; the second volume is eagerly awaited.

New biographical material on Matisse has been engendered by major exhibitions on specific periods of his life. The most important of these catalogues are: Jack Cowart, Jack D. Flam, Dominique Fourcade, and John Hallmark Neff, *Henri Matisse: Paper Cut-outs* (St. Louis and Detroit, 1977); Jack Cowart and Dominique Fourcade, *Henri Matisse: The Early Years in Nice, 1916–30* (Washington and New York, 1986); and Jack Cowart, Pierre Schneider, John Elderfield, et al, *Matisse in Morocco: The Paintings and Drawings, 1912–13* (Washington and New York, 1990). In addition, Matisse's secretary-model during his late years, Lydia Delectorskaya, has published an eye-witness record of the years 1935–39 in *L'apparante facilité: Peintures de 1935–1939* (Paris, 1986).

A complete biography is sorely needed of this important 20th-century artist. There are many unpublished letters,uncollected and untranslated writings and interviews, and family records that are as yet untapped sources for such a biography. The artist's grandson, Claude Duthuit, assisted by Wanda de Guébriant, is the director of the Archives Henri Matisse, which is producing a catalogue raisonné of the artist's work. To date, the following volumes have appeared: Marguerite Duthuit-Matisse and Claude Duthuit, *Henri Matisse: Catalogue raisonné de l'oeuvre gravé établi avec la collaboration de Françoise Garnaud* (2 vols.,

Paris, 1983) and Claude Duthuit, *Henri Matisse: Catalogue raisonné de l'oeuvre illustrée établi avec la collaboration de Françoise Garnaud* (Paris, 1989).

—Catherine C. Bock

MAUGHAM, (William) Somerset, 1874–1965; English writer.

Calder, Robert L., *Willie: The Life of W. Somerset Maugham.* New York, St. Martin's, and London, Heinemann, 1989.

Cordell, Richard A., *Somerset Maugham: A Biographical and Critical Study.* Bloomington, Indiana University Press, and London, Heinemann, 1961.

Curtis, Anthony, *The Pattern of Maugham: A Critical Portrait.* London, Hamilton, and New York, Taplinger, 1974.

Kanin, Garson, *Remembering Mr. Maugham.* London, Hamilton, and New York, Atheneum, 1966.

Maugham, Robin, *Somerset and All the Maughams.* London, Longman/Heinemann, and New York, New American Library, 1966.

Maugham, Robin, *Escape From the Shadows.* London, Hodder and Stoughton, 1972.

Maugham, Robin, *Conversations with Willie.* London, W. H. Allen, and New York, Simon and Schuster, 1978.

Morgan, Ted, *Somerset Maugham.* London, Cape, 1980; as *Maugham: A Biography*, New York, Simon and Schuster, 1980.

Nichols, Beverly, *A Case of Human Bondage.* London, Secker and Warburg, 1966.

Pfeiffer, K. G., *W. Somerset Maugham: A Candid Portrait.* London, Gollancz, and New York, Norton, 1959.

Raphael, Frederic, *Somerset Maugham and His World.* London, Thames and Hudson, 1976.

*

Maugham always tried to discourage would-be biographers. He detested the idea of his life being written, put a clause in his will refusing permission for any biography or publication of his correspondence, and asked his friends to destroy letters he sent them. In his last years he made regular bonfires of personal documents and letters in the attempt to safeguard his privacy. He feared that, after his death, the image of himself he had sedulously cultivated over a lifetime would be shattered. Inevitably, the studies and biographies that appeared while he was still alive told only a small part of the story. CORDELL's book, an expansion of an earlier critical study (1937), is unreliable because Maugham, who read the proofs, supplied deliberately misleading information. PFEIFFER, who published his book despite Maugham's vigorous objections, was, according to the latter, "full of absurd inaccuracies," although equally annoying to him were the sometimes unflattering critical judgments.

Maugham's death in 1965 was the signal for a series of unauthorised biographies. First in the field was ROBIN MAUGHAM, the writer's nephew and the son of his brother Viscount Maugham, distinguished lawyer and Lord Chancellor whom Maugham described as "a perfectly odious man." He had much greater affection for Robin, whom he advised about his literary career and upon whom he settled a handsome trust fund. Robin's first volume, *Somerset and All The Maughams*, traces the family history of the Maughams back to the 17th century, throws up some interesting genetic discoveries, and includes reminiscences of people still alive at the time who could remember Maugham as a boy in Whitstable. The book offers understanding analyses of Maugham's devotion to his mother, who died when he was a child, of his long-time relationship with his lover Gerald Haxton, of his ambivalent feelings about the school where he spent an unhappy boyhood, and of his resentment toward the "intellectuals" who never accepted him as a serious writer. The book's second section is a personal memoir in which Robin introduces what has now become the well-known image of his uncle as a bitter misanthrope and heartless monster declining into a graceless senility. Much of the narrative consists of dialogue which, one suspects, has been skillfully re-created with a number of fictional touches, for Robin was also a professional novelist. This trait is even more apparent in his later volumes, *Escape From The Shadows* and *Conversations With Willie*, especially in the latter. It has since been revealed that many of the reported conversations with Maugham were fabricated with the aid of a researcher. All of Robin's personal writing about his uncle must, therefore, be treated with reserve.

KANIN, a playwright and screen writer, and his wife, the actress Ruth Gordon, knew Maugham personally during the war years he spent in the United States. The volume is affectionate, often amusing in a Boswellian fashion, and concentrates on anecdotes and Maugham's table talk without venturing into deeper subjects. If the evidence is to be believed, the book gives a fair picture of the novelist at one stage in his life. The same cannot be said of NICHOLS' book. Nichols was a frequent guest in Maugham's home and knew him well. He also was fond of Syrie, Maugham's wife, and became outraged by what he regarded as Maugham's harsh treatment of her. This led him to give a shrill portrayal of Maugham as a wholly wicked and malicious old man. Nichols was a professional journalist and could write vividly, but his exaggeration often makes one suspect the truth of his statements.

CURTISS is more scholarly, although his book is more a critical appraisal than a biography. RAPHAEL offers a readable and shrewd life of the subject, very well illustrated and contained within handy limits. While he bases himself on printed sources alone, he succeeds in presenting a convincing portrait. He only met Maugham once, but his account of the meeting is so arresting that he immediately conjures up the man himself. His book, with its illuminating glances at the novels and plays, is especially interesting because Raphael is himself a creative writer and is able to approach Maugham as a fellow-practitioner. He is also perceptive on Maugham's homosexuality and on the ambiguous nature of the worldly success that left him oddly unsatisfied. Maugham's marriage, a key event in his life, is treated sympathetically, and Raphael does well to remind us that Maugham was capable of subtle and friendly relations with women.

The first full-length scholarly biography was written by MORGAN. Despite the embargo on publication of letters and documents, Morgan was given permission by Maugham's literary executor to use material hitherto suppressed. He also had access to Maugham's daughter, who, up to then, had refused to meet prospective biographers. The result is the fullest, most authoritative, and most amply documented biography to date. Morgan

tends, however, to look on Maugham's black side. In his interpretation of the facts he seems to prefer whichever reading puts Maugham in an unfavourable light. In this way the picture of Maugham as a thoroughly unpleasant character, first popularised by his nephew Robin, is perpetuated.

While CALDER was not allowed access to the embargoed unpublished material, he did have the advantage of cooperation from Alan Searle, Maugham's companion for many years, who had held aloof from Morgan. Calder's *W. Somerset Maugham and the Quest For Freedom* (1972) had earlier thrown light on the author's career by revealing the true identity of the heroine in *Cakes and Ale* and by recounting Maugham's espionage activities during World War I. In *Willie*, the name by which Maugham was known to intimates and with which he signed letters to friends, Calder's aim was clear: to give a picture of the man behind the mask and to show that Maugham, depicted elsewhere with the emphasis on his more disagreeable qualities, could also be a warm, affectionate and courteous human being. To a great extent he does redress the balance. One feels that here is a more credible and better-rounded picture. Calder uses his raw material with judiciousness. The homosexuality is seen as a major element in Maugham's character and is explored with informed sympathy, both in its influence on his personality and on his work. The deep psychological reasons behind the urbane facade Maugham erected to protect himself against the cruel outside world are delicately and surely probed. In addition, the plays and novels are fully analysed and neatly dovetailed into the narrative of the life. This is an integrated portrait based on an immaculate network of references. If you want a reliable bird's-eye view of Maugham, then Raphael is recommended. For the most complete and balanced account, Calder is well worth attention.

—James Harding

MAUPASSANT, (Henri-René-Albert-) Guy de, 1850–1893; French writer.

Boyd, Ernest, *Guy de Maupassant: A Biographical Study*. New York and London, Knopf, 1926.

Ignotus, Paul, *The Paradox of Maupassant*. London, University of London Press, and New York, Funk and Wagnalls, 1966.

Jackson, Stanley, *Guy de Maupassant*. London, Duckworth, 1938.

Lerner, Michael G., *Maupassant*. London, Allen and Unwin, and New York, G. Braziller, 1975.

Sherard, Robert H., *The Life, Work and Evil Fate of Guy de Maupassant (Gentilhomme de Lettres)*. London, T. Werner Laurie, and New York, Brentano's, 1926.

Steegmuller, Francis, *Maupassant: A Lion in the Path*. New York, Grosset and Dunlap, 1949; as *Maupassant*, London, Collins, 1950.

Wallace, A. H., *Guy de Maupassant*. Boston, Twayne, 1973.

*

The most important biographies of Maupassant, by Maynial (1906) and Morand (1942), have never been translated. The earliest life in English is by SHERARD which, in spite of its eulogistic reception in France, is something of a curiosity. Sherard knew Maupassant, defends him against the accusation of womanizing on the grounds that he was always the pursued and only ever once the pursuer, and excuses "his lies, his boasting, his fondness for salacious conversation, his cruelty to animals . . ." on the grounds of his syphilis. He puts the commencement of insanity at 1890 and points out that Maupassant's mother first suspected the symptoms from the autobiographical sketches and self-criticism in *Sur l'Eau* (1885).

Since Maupassant's mother found it too painful to reveal all she knew about her son, and since he was too tempting a target for caricaturists and those who bore him ill will, no properly documented biography can now ever be written. In the circumstances, Sherard's hand-wringing, moralizing, extended sermon by someone close enough to Maupassant to have played football with a cushion embroidered for him by a lady is of greater interest than it would otherwise deserve to be. Of Adrienne Legay, the original of Boule de Suif in Maupassant's short story, Sherard writes "The dying 'dressmaker' *was* the Legay woman. Adrienne, like that other Adrienne, the Lecouvreur one, gay, gay. Gay by name, once gay by nature and gay by trade!" The reader has to wade through a lot of that to find out that she died of poverty owing her lodging-house keeper seven francs. Adrienne Lecouvreur was the famous 18th-century actress.

BOYD's biography of the same date is better informed and better written, although the element of fictionalization is still strong. Boyd is perceptive in tracing the parallel between the literary evolution and the personal development and leaves the reader with a clear idea of why Maupassant has achieved his standing among 19th-century French writers. It is a careful biography, but not intended to be a scholarly one.

JACKSON got the idea for his biography, he tells us, by failing to find a book by Maugham in a London public library and then discovering no Maupassant further along the Mau. . . shelf. " 'No call for his work,' announced the librarian, 'with a hint of disapproval.' " Jackson, surprised at the erroneous assumption of pornography, has written a fictionalized re-creation of the life rather than a strict biography, but he draws on letters from Maupassant to his mother hitherto untranslated. Jackson says he admires Sherard, but he writes a great deal better, although his text still suffers from a surfeit of exclamation marks, bursting like pimples from the page. His book is less distinguished than Boyd's, erring on the side of discretion and more defensive in tone than would today be considered necessary.

STEEGMULLER's work has serious scholarly pretensions, although the scholarship does not impede readability. Such conjecture as the book contains is plausible and properly sign-posted. The awkward issues, like the date of the onset of insanity and its cause, and the nature and pace of the final disintegration, are firmly confronted, although there is more than a hint of cosmeticizing the sexual side of the life, if not of the gossip. The most notable contribution of this biography is its treatment of Maupassant's relationship with his master, Flaubert. Its weakest point, in spite of an outstanding treatment of the short story *La Parure* ("The Necklace"), is the lack of even enough critical comment to give a neophyte reader any real idea of why Maupassant's literary talent is so highly esteemed, and where its limits lay.

IGNOTUS has written the most scholarly of the available biographies, although the treatment is not strictly chronological, the notes are spasmodic, and there is no bibliography. There is however an extended and useful chronology of Maupassant's life, which suggests 1874 as the most likely year for the contraction of syphilis. Given the madness of his brother Hervé, who died from the same disease, the unlikely possibility is also considered that the disease could have been congenital, passed from the mother in the womb. Given the paucity of archival material here, too, we have a re-creation of the life, but one that commands belief and is particularly good on the literary historical background, the dinners at Trapp's and the relationships with Flaubert, Zola, and Edmond de Goncourt. Ignotus has written a sound, reliable, readable account of his subject's life, with enough detail to give solidity to the necessarily speculative judgements.

WALLACE's volume for Twayne has the virtues associated with that series, a chronology, index, bibliography, and notes, although the notes are indecently sparse and the constraints imposed by the series weigh here more heavily than usual. The biographical portion is so brief and schematic that such major formative or disruptive influences on Maupassant's life as the Franco-Prussian war and the Paris literary salons are mentioned only casually, and the volume reads like the product of a duty perfunctorily discharged. Headings like " 'Making It' as a Writer" set the rather shallow tone. Like Ignotus, Wallace thinks, surely with reason, that Maupassant's syphilis in its early hallucinatory stages actually enhanced his perceptions and literary skills.

LERNER writes in 1975 that "it is some years since a study of Maupassant in English has appeared," although Jackson, Steegmuller, Ignotus, and Wallace are all in his own bibliography. "All the fresh evidence available," which, he claims, justifies his book, amounts to the 1973 edition of the correspondence of which Lerner does not anyway make extensive use, and to which he does not refer when quoting from letters. The biography concludes with the unexciting statement that "Guy de Maupassant's life was thus highly representative of the changes in France in the latter half of the last century and of the greatness and weakness of the society he lived in." Of course, and it is true of any of his contemporaries, too, even those who did not produce six novels and 200 short stories in eleven years.

—A. H. T. Levi

MAZZINI, Giuseppe, 1805–1872; Italian patriot and revolutionist.

Barr, Stringfellow, *Mazzini: Portrait of an Exile*. New York, Holt, 1935.

Griffith, Gwilym O., *Mazzini: Prophet of Modern Europe*. New York, Harcourt, and London, Hodder and Stoughton, 1932.

Hales, E. E. Y., *Mazzini and the Secret Societies: The Making of a Myth*. New York, P. J. Kenedy, and London, Eyre and Spottiswoode, 1956.

Hinkley, Edyth, *Mazzini: The Story of a Great Italian*. New York, Putnam, and London, Allen and Unwin, 1924.

King, Bolton, *Mazzini*. London, Dent, and New York, Dutton, 1902.

Salvemini, Gaetano, *Mazzini*, translated by I. M. Rawson. London, Cape, 1956; Stanford, California, Stanford University Press, 1957.

*

Mazzini's intense political activity produced an inordinately large correspondence which, along with some autobiographical works prepared in the early 1860s, provide the biographer with what is very nearly an embarrassment of riches. Much of the material first became available in English toward the end of the 19th century in *Life and Writings of Joseph Mazzini* (6 vols., 1890–91). The first serious biography in English, by KING, came a generation after Mazzini's death. A student of the history of Italian unity, King wrote his book to estimate the significance of Mazzini's life and work for the crystallization of Italian national sentiment. However, his work has not withstood the test of time. HINKLEY drew heavily on King in a style at once awkward and colorful, approached her subject with an awe verging on adoration, and marred her presentation by excessive emotionalism and too frequent quotation. Despite this, and despite the fact that her book neither broke new ground nor provided much insight into the intricacies of Italian politics, it still merits reading because of the thoroughness with which it explores the years Mazzini spent in England.

GRIFFITH's work is in many ways the best biography of Mazzini available in English. Written by an experienced biographer in an uneven and excessively mannered style, uncritically approving of Mazzini, it has never been bested in its portrayal of his personality. Though the book is organized around the evolution of Mazzini's thought and the nature of his influence, Griffith's emphasis is always on the personal characteristics of an individual he obviously found admirable in every respect. BARR's book also repays reading, as a biography that is historically sound, careful about the complexities of the age, and brilliantly narrated. It is especially effective in conveying what Mazzini was like as a person, even though the presentation suffers somewhat because Barr was so consciously setting up Mazzini's life and thought as a contrast to the career and politics of Benito Mussolini.

HALES remains the most scholarly evaluation of Mazzini's role in the achievement of Italian unity. Written by an English academic who had previously published a biography of Pius IX and was especially well informed on the role of the Roman Catholic Church in Italian politics and diplomacy, it includes a particularly insightful chapter on Mazzini's theology. In fact, the book is very politically and ideologically sophisticated while never losing sight of Mazzini's daily life. Its chief value is that, of all the books on the subject, Hales' most nearly balances the man and his ideas and approaches an ideal of dispassionate scholarship in evaluating both. For those primarily interested in Mazzini's ideas, SALVEMINI furnishes a critique that is sometimes excessively pointed, side by side with a short biography that is most useful when discussing Mazzini's student days.

—Joseph M. McCarthy

McCARTHY, Joseph R., 1908–1957; American politician.

Anderson, Jack and Ronald May, *McCarthy: The Man, the Senator, the "Ism"*. Boston, Beacon Press, 1952; London, Gollancz, 1953.

Buckley, William F., Jr. and L. Brent Bozell, *McCarthy and his Enemies: The Record and its Meaning*. Chicago, H. Regnery, 1954.

Cook, Fred J., *The Nightmare Decade: The Life and Times of Senator Joseph McCarthy*. New York, Random House, 1971.

Feuerlicht, Roberta Strauss, *Joe McCarthy and McCarthyism: The Hate that Haunts America*. New York, McGraw-Hill, 1972.

Griffith, Robert, *The Politics of Fear: Joseph R. McCarthy and the Senate*. Lexington, University of Kentucky Press, 1970.

Landis, Mark, *Joseph McCarthy: The Politics of Chaos*. Selingsgrove, Pennsylvania, Susquehanna University Press, 1987.

O'Brien, Michael, *McCarthy and McCarthyism in Wisconsin*. Columbia, University of Missouri Press, 1980.

Oshinsky, David M., *A Conspiracy so Immense: The World of Joe McCarthy*. New York, Free Press, and London, Collier Macmillan, 1983.

Reeves, Thomas C., *The Life and Times of Joe McCarthy: A Biography*. New York, Stein and Day, and London, Blond and Briggs, 1982.

Rovere, Richard H., *Senator Joe McCarthy*. New York, Harcourt, 1959; London, Methuen, 1960.

Thomas, Lately (Robert V. P. Steele), *When Even Angels Wept: The Senator Joseph McCarthy Affair—A Story Without a Hero*. New York, Morrow, 1973.

*

The first biographies of Senator Joseph McCarthy were published during the height of "McCarthyism," the early 1950s, when McCarthy was accusing large numbers of government officials, even including President Dwight Eisenhower, of disloyalty, subversion, or insufficient zeal in prosecuting subversives. Not surprisingly, these early works seem quickly written and polemical. The ANDERSON AND MAY book provides basic information about the early years of McCarthy's life, but the authors' real purpose is to expose his methods and to warn of his threat to individual liberties. The polar opposite is the BUCKLEY AND BOZELL defense of McCarthy as a patriot concerned with serious internal threats to national security. Both of these books seem quaint, if not a bit silly, today, but for different reasons. The Anderson and May book warns us to examine the evidence before quickly accepting charges that a political leader is subversive or a government department infiltrated with treasonous personnel. The Buckley and Bozell work suggests that internal subversion is such a threat that extreme efforts are warranted. Neither book shows a great concern for understanding the life of Joe McCarthy.

ROVERE's 1959 biography is the first real effort to understand McCarthy rather than use the events of his life to make an argument about McCarthyism. Rovere's effort to describe McCarthy's life is a warmly personal effort that uses Rovere's perceptions and experiences in Washington as a reporter during the McCarthy era to provide a context for the basic facts. Although

Rovere clearly has little use for McCarthy's shenanigans, the author avoids adopting a self-righteous attitude. Rovere knows that politicians are rarely saints, but that McCarthy went beyond a plausible description of both reality and common decency. Despite the enormity of McCarthy's sins, Rovere writes gracefully and without a shrill tone. He seems to sense that the facts are both fascinating and sufficiently shocking so that there is no need to tell readers that they should be shocked.

A limitation of Rovere's biography is that the description of McCarthy's childhood is sketchy, as is his life outside of politics. The biography focuses almost entirely on the last 8 years of his life: from his 1950 discovery of internal Communism as an issue to his death in 1957. Also, Rovere is a journalist, not a scholar, so readers who expect voluminous citations will be disappointed. Nevertheless, scholarship since publication of the Rovere biography has done little damage to the accuracy of his assertions. The book reads as freshly as it did in 1959 and remains the outstanding journalistic biography of Senator McCarthy.

GRIFFITH's volume is the first scholarly account of Senator McCarthy's life. Using the methods of an historian, Griffith argues that the key to understanding McCarthy's position in American politics is the failure of the Senate to condemn him before 1955 despite the Senator's egregious behavior. Griffith attributes this delay in the Senate's controlling McCarthy to the latter's role in the Republican Party's drive for power. In making a good case for this position, the book focuses more on the Senate than on McCarthy. Winner of the Turner Award as that year's outstanding book in American history, the book nevertheless fails to provide much information on the man. For readers who want to read about the Senate in the 1950s, this is an outstanding book; for those who want a good biography of McCarthy, look elsewhere.

The three biographies published in the early 1970s, by Cook, Feuerlicht, and Thomas, respectively, add little to earlier works. The COOK and FEUERLICHT volumes are similar in style: litanies of McCarthy abuses and expressions of disgust that other politicians, who presumably knew better, let McCarthy persist in calumny for so long. Although Cook, unlike Feuerlicht, generally documents his assertions, they share the same righteous hatred of McCarthy. One difference is that Cook at least perceives that the original McCarthy has made us aware of the evils of McCarthyism; Feuerlicht disagrees. She subtitles her book *The Hate that Haunts America* and includes an epilogue entitled "He Lives" that details civil liberties abuses of the first Nixon administration. Even with the knowledge we now have of the Watergate abuses, an equating of the Nixon era with the horrors of the McCarthy-era accusations seems difficult to defend. McCarthy cost people their careers and ruined lives. In any event, both these biographies are much more concerned with McCarthyism than with McCarthy.

THOMAS' biography is less shrill, yet more melodramatic, than those by Cook and Feuerlicht. As with most other McCarthy biographies, Thomas focuses more on the Senate proceedings than on other elements of McCarthy's life and, again typically, his early years are particularly neglected. Although generally accurate, the book lacks documentation.

Thomas writes in the "you-are-there" style of the breathless replay of the news. The conceit used throughout the narrative is that McCarthy can best be understood as a modern pirate: dangerous, fascinating, living for the moment, and amoral. The problem is that the metaphor does not work because, despite the pirate chapter headings, McCarthy still appears as a weak blusterer and pathological liar rather than a brave if misguided outlaw. Despite the melodramatic style, the book fails to provide a sense of the drama of the witch-hunts. The author proclaims that there is great adventure here rather than allowing the reader to reach this conclusion through the excitement of the tale. Unlike Cook and Feuerlicht, Thomas does not moralize about the situation, but, perhaps as a consequence, the significance of McCarthy and his actions are left vague. We know that Thomas regards his topic as quite important, but we are not provided with good reasons to share his enthusiasm. Read Rovere instead.

The biographies of the 1980s are much more scholarly and dispassionate than are the earlier works. The first to appear, by O'BRIEN, is a useful addition because it focuses on the senator's life outside of Washington. O'Brien argues that a key to understanding McCarthy's rise to power was his ability to manipulate newspaper coverage in Wisconsin and the media's naiveté and irresponsibility in dealing with him. O'Brien also looks at McCarthy's impact in Wisconsin, arguing that Wisconsin may have escaped "red scare" waves of hysteria precisely because McCarthy could not afford to attack his constituents. Also, McCarthy may have inadvertently aided the Democratic Party in his home state by providing a target that helped party organizers to attract new members. This is McCarthy material absent from the other biographies.

O'Brien was the first biographer since Anderson and May to go to Wisconsin to interview McCarthy's classmates, friends, and colleagues. O'Brien's work also is the first since Anderson and May's to attempt to describe McCarthy's childhood and adolescence. Though a well documented and original contribution, it is not a definitive biography. O'Brien perceives no central theme that links the young McCarthy, the older McCarthy in Wisconsin, and Senator McCarthy in Washington. The book is typical of many biographies written by academic historians in that no clear rationale appears for the inclusion of some facts and the exclusion of others. The book, however, is well written and, with its attention to McCarthy in Wisconsin, an important contribution.

Thomas Reeves and David Oshinsky also travelled to Wisconsin to interview friends and associates of the late senator. With over 800 pages, REEVES' book is McCarthy's first full-length scholarly biography. Concentrating on McCarthy as a politician, Reeves provides a detailed accounting of the senator's pronouncements and behavior. The style, however, is tedious, with little attention to providing a perspective on the facts.

OSHINSKY's book has the documentation and completeness of Reeves', but does a better job of placing McCarthy in the context of the times. Oshinsky is able to describe the drama of the events of the era without falling into a righteous moralizing. This book also succeeds in giving the reader a sense of Joe McCarthy as a real person with both strengths and weaknesses. Oshinsky is able to maintain a balanced perspective while accurately describing despicable behavior. Perhaps such a book could not have been written until a quarter-century had passed since McCarthy's death. For a short, graceful account of McCarthy and his era, read Rovere. For a longer, well-written, well-documented, and complete account, read Oshinsky.

Finally, LANDIS provides a brief application of political psychology concepts (derived from Maslow, Piaget, Merelman, and Barber) to the life and times of Joseph McCarthy. Landis uses secondary materials for his information on McCarthy, then applies psychological theories of needs and motivations to attempt to understand both McCarthy and the roots of demagoguery in American politics. Landis successfully avoids psychobabble to provide plausible explanations for both McCarthy's behavior and the reactions of political elites. Not a full biography by any means, Landis' book is nevertheless a well-written and original contribution.

—Robert E. O'Connor

McCULLERS, Carson, 1917–1967; American writer.

Carr, Virginia Spencer, *The Lonely Hunter: A Biography of Carson McCullers.* New York, Doubleday, 1975.

Evans, Oliver, *Carson McCullers: Her Life and Work.* London, P. Owen, 1965; as *The Ballad of Carson McCullers: A Biography*, New York, Coward McCann, 1966.

*

The life of Carson McCullers would seem to be the ideal vehicle for the writer of biography. It is the story of a girl from a small town in Georgia who grew up to be a phenomenally successful and even controversial novelist and dramatist; who counted among her close friends some of the most famous writers and other celebrities of her times; and whose personal life, including the suicide of her husband and a series of debilitating strokes and other ailments, could be called tragic. Thus it might be surprising that only two studies of her life have appeared to date—surprising, until one considers the fact that one of the works is so excellent and so thorough that revisionists will probably continue to be discouraged from launching a new study of Carson McCullers for some time.

EVANS, the first writer to undertake a biography of McCullers, was a friend of his subject, and therein lies the key to both the strengths and the weaknesses of his work. Clearly he had access to important information provided by McCullers, her family members, and her friends, and his portrait of her is enriched by personal details to which he was privy. There is an immediacy about his accounts of her mature life, and she comes alive in many anecdotes because of Evans' direct knowledge of the writer and other people involved in her story.

In a sense this position makes Evans' book what might be termed an "official biography." The author of such a biography is almost always in an awkward position, for blessed as he may be with inner-circle knowledge, he is usually heir to a considerable amount of obligation such access entails, especially if he is close to his subject. The result in Evans' case is an almost schizophrenic approach to his topic. Often he refers to the novelist by her first name, calling her Carson naturally and unaffectedly in some of the best and most touching parts of the work. Within the next paragraph, however, he will sometimes switch to the much more formal "Mrs. McCullers," and the result of such juxtaposition is troublesome for the reader.

Since McCullers was still living at the time of the publication of this biography, even though her writing career was for all practical purposes finished, her last novel already in print, Evans was probably considerably impeded in what he could write about the personal details of her unorthodox life. Understandably, he writes best about the early years, giving a convincing picture of her growing up in small-town Georgia and pointing out the parallels between her own life and the lives of protagonists Mick and Frankie in *Member of the Wedding* (1946) and *The Heart Is a Lonely Hunter* (1940), respectively. The troubled later years of McCullers' marriage, her husband's suicide, her love life, and her complex medical problems are recorded, but without the candor a great biography requires.

Evans is a sound critic whose evaluations of the works and critical analyses of motifs and themes in the novels and short stories are valid and reliable, and this is the greatest strength of his book. He reads McCullers as author well, and his study is significant if for no other reason than that it contains the first serious sustained critique of the body of her fiction. Evans was himself a poet, and his prose style is elegant and readable, with an almost casual flow to the narrative. The reader comes away from Evans' book with a credible portrait of McCullers as artist, even though much is left unsaid.

CARR never knew Carson McCullers, and when she began her biography, the novelist had been dead for a year. Carr thus had the decided advantage of objectivity that Evans had lacked. She also had access to Evans' work, of course, and was able to interview him. As a consequence, her portrayal of the novelist is more accurate and candid. This is not to say by any means that Carr conveys a negative impression; indeed, her book brings to life a more positive, because more believable, character than Evans was able to do. Freed from the "official" biographer's built-in restraints, she could recreate the novelist in all her complexity.

The result of Carr's efforts is truly a model of the biographer's art, a study of Carson McCullers that is not likely to be superseded in quality and detail. Carr spent seven years in research, writing, and rewriting, first on a dissertation devoted to the novelist, then on *The Lonely Hunter.* The finished work is a long, closely detailed, exhaustive look at McCullers' life and works. Clearly no significant site associated with McCullers was left unvisited, no available family member, friend, or associate of the subject left uninterviewed in the production of this layered, complex, and intriguing recreation of a very remarkable and even paradoxical life. Tennessee Williams, who provided the introduction to this biography, once referred to McCullers as an "iron butterfly," and Carr examines both these contradictory elements of the novelist's character with close attention. She does not avoid the controversial personality traits that sometimes made McCullers a difficult friend or associate, but the final image that emerges is of a woman and artist who was appealing and lovable despite her faults. Carr obviously feels an affinity for her subject, whom she seems to have come to know personally in the course of her research. Ironically, Evans, who did know McCullers in the flesh, seems to be separated from her by a distance that results, presumably, from his reluctance to reveal those unpleasant aspects of her life he must have known. On the other hand, McCullers comes alive in the pages of Carr's book as if being remembered by a friend.

Readers who might approach such a lengthy work with some misgivings are soon won over by the author's narrative style. Carr writes a flowing, comfortable prose even in the more complicated sections of the book in which she analyzes individual novels and stories or traces motifs from work to work. Her particular gift as a biographer is her ability to bring to bear on the writing some of the techniques of a fiction writer. She dramatizes various scenes from McCullers' life, drawing from the memory of those who knew the author, and although it must be granted that such a method relies to some extent on the imagination, the overall impression, once again, is of intense credibility.

If such an ideal as the definitive biography existed, one would be tempted to bestow that accolade upon Virginia Spencer Carr's *The Lonely Hunter*. In all probability, there is more to be said about Carson McCullers's life; only the future can reveal that. Oliver Evans' study certainly has its virtues, not the least being its contribution to Carr's work, but it is finally to *The Lonely Hunter* that the scholar of McCullers must turn for enlightenment and understanding of a complex writer.

—W. Kenneth Holditch

MEAD, Margaret, 1901–1978; American anthropologist.

Bateson, Mary C., *With a Daughter's Eye: A Memoir of Margaret Mead and Gregory Bateson*. New York, Morrow, 1984.
Cassidy, Robert, *Margaret Mead: A Voice for the Century*. New York, Universe Books, 1982.
Freeman, Derek, *Margaret Mead and Samoa: The Making and Unmaking of an Anthropological Myth*. Cambridge, Massachusetts, Harvard University Press, 1983; London, Penguin, 1984.
Howard, Jane, *Margaret Mead: A Life*. New York, Simon and Schuster, and London, Harvill, 1984.

*

Margaret Mead was the only anthropologist so well known to the general public that she could be referred to as an American institution. Unlike many scientists, Mead was passionate about making scientific knowledge serve useful purposes. It is not surprising that such a colorful figure should be the subject of numerous articles and biographies, including some rather controversial assessments of the "Mead mythology."

CASSIDY emphasizes the public aspects of Mead's life and work rather than the personal. According to Cassidy, this book can be read as a continuation and completion of Mead's autobiography, *Blackberry Winter* (1972). Cassidy deals with Mead as scientist and humanist, and his well-written biography provides valuable information for those interested in Mead's career, the evolution of American anthropology, and the way Mead related her anthropological field work among primitive cultures to problems of contemporary America. Another emphasis is Mead's concern with—and eagerness to prescribe for—the

American family. Cassidy provides notes to his chapters and a chronologically arranged bibliography of Mead's major works. However, for a complete guide to Mead's writings the reader should consult Joan Gordan's definitive bibliography, *Margaret Mead: The Complete Bibliography 1925–75* (The Hague, Mouton, 1976).

FREEMAN's *Margaret Mead and Samoa* received extraordinary media coverage prior to publication, with its broad claims to represent a turning point in anthropology and a refutation of "a towering scientific error." However, many scientists and reviewers considered the hoopla about the book to be quite disproportionate to its actual content and quality. Freeman's rhetoric seems calculated to create its own myths about Mead, Franz Boas, Samoa, anthropology, and the old nature-nurture debate. Freeman, Professor of Anthropology at Australian National University, contends that Mead's classic description of Samoan adolescence was based on false evidence and deliberate distortion.

Freeman's book has a vindictive tone and reiterates the same examples again and again to beat Mead's errors into the ground. It is interesting to note that Freeman knew Reo Fortune, Mead's second husband, during the miserable period of his life after Mead left him. Fortune was said to have been deeply hurt and wanted to prove that everything Mead said was wrong. Supporters of Mead called Freeman's book "badly written and deeply destructive" to anthropology as a whole. The attack on Mead has generated many rebuttals. For example, see Lowell D. Holmes, *Quest for the Real Samoa: The Mead-Freeman Controversy and Beyond* (1986). Holmes, who did a study of American Samoa in the 1950s at least in part to evaluate Mead's work, reported differences but agreed with her basic idea that adolescence in Samoa was less stressful and traumatic than in America. Holmes also said that Freeman's claim that he could not get access to important court records until 1981 was nonsense.

It is interesting to see how different authors treat the same incident in Mead's career. Both Cassidy and Freeman note that Franz Boas did not offer any substantive criticism of Mead's *Coming of Age in Samoa* (1928). To Cassidy this shows Boas' wisdom, to Freeman it is the mark of a tired 70-year old man who was happy to find confirmation of his own ideas in a rather weak piece of research.

In contrast to Cassidy and Freeman, HOWARD, a reporter, writer, and lecturer, is primarily interested in Mead's personal life and her complex relationships with family, peers, friends, and disciples. According to Howard, this carefully nurtured network of relationships was the core of Mead's personal life. Howard spent five years collecting materials and interviewing some 300 persons in order to create this rich but nuanced portrait. Her book is overwhelmingly detailed in its discussion of Mead's complex relationships, gossipy in a well-documented way, lively and well paced, but written with a sense of balance and humor that make Freeman's book appear excessively tedious, spiteful, and dogmatic.

BATESON eschewed interviews with other anthropologists and ignored documents housed in archives at the Library of Congress and the University of California at Santa Cruz, deciding instead to write a memoir based on her own perceptions and experience. Even an index was deliberately omitted to avoid giving the memoir "a spurious air of systematicity." Bateson chose to honor her parents by speaking honestly in her own voice, out of her own feelings. Her book depicts the relationship between the daughter and her parents, as Bateson recalls it, rather than Margaret Mead's entire life.

Ironically, while Freeman believed that his revelations would cause Mead's work to be banished into oblivion, the controversy has instead created a resurgence of attention. The details of Mead's work might be in dispute, but there is no doubt, as all her biographers show, that Mead herself remains a fascinating subject.

There are also several brief accounts of the life and work of Margaret Mead written specifically for young readers: Julie Castiglia, *Margaret Mead* (1989; grades 5–12); Susan Saunders, *Margaret Mead: The World Was Her Family* (1987; grades 2–6). For young adults the following biographies are recommended: Jacqueline Ludel, *Margaret Mead* (1983; grades 7 and up); Edward Rice, *Margaret Mead: A Portrait* (1979; grades 7 and up); Edra Ziesk, *Margaret Mead* (1990; grades 7–12).

—Lois N. Magner

MEDICI, Catherine de'. See **CATHERINE DE' MEDICI.**

MEDICI, Lorenzo de', 1449–1492; Florentine statesman and cultural patron.

Armstrong, E., *Lorenzo de' Medici and Florence in the 15th Century.* New York and London, Putnam, 1896.

Brinton, Selwyn, *The Golden Age of the Medici: Cosimo, Piero, Lorenzo de' Medici 1434–94.* London, Methuen, 1925; New York, Small Maynard, 1926.

Hook, Judith, *Lorenzo de' Medici: An Historical Biography.* London, Hamilton, 1984.

Roscoe, William, *Life of Lorenzo de' Medici.* Liverpool, J. M'Creery, 1795; edited by William Hazlitt, London, D. Bogue, 1846.

Ross Williamson, Hugh, *Lorenzo the Magnificent.* London, M. Joseph, and New York, Putnam, 1974.

Rubinstein, Nicolai, *Lorenzo de' Medici: The Formation of His Statecraft.* Oxford, Oxford University Press, 1977.

Sturm, Sarah, *Lorenzo de' Medici.* New York, Twayne, 1974.

*

ROSCOE's *Life* was originally published in 1795 and met with immediate critical acclaim, in contrast with Roscoe's later attempt (1805) at a biography of Lorenzo de' Medici's son, Leo X. The *Life* became a lucrative best-seller and was speedily translated into Italian, then German and French. Some of the critical reaction to this work now seems a little over-enthusiastic. One reviewer put Roscoe in "the very first rank of English classical [sic] historians"; Hazlitt, who wrote the preface to the popular 1846 edition, was even more rapturous, placing the book "among the standard works of English literature."

A pronounced Italophile, Roscoe was clearly attracted to Lorenzo as a fellow poet and patron of the arts and of civic culture. But in addition to his own activities as a cultural patron, the engaging and all too versatile William Roscoe had other interests and ideals. He was a pioneer campaigner against the slave trade and held decidedly liberal (and unitarian) views. Why was this liberal drawn to de' Medici, widely seen as the prime foe of Florentine liberty and described by the Italian republican historian Villari as determined "to crush any lingering remains of liberty. . . . "? Perhaps the answer lies in a new biography of Hazlitt (Stanley Jones, *Hazlitt: A Life From Winterslow to Frith Street,* Oxford, Clarendon Press, 1989), which reveals that Roscoe was a "Bonapartist," a not uncommon combination with the kind of Whiggery that Roscoe espoused. Was Roscoe captivated by Lorenzo de' Medici as a proto-Bonaparte? That is indeed possible, but in fact Roscoe fell under the spell not of Lorenzo the authoritarian politician but of *il magnifico,* the poet and patron. Consequently, Roscoe devised his own liberal reconstruction of de' Medici: "The approximate suppression of the liberties of Florence, under the influence of [Lorenzo de' Medici's] descendants, may induce suspicions unfavourable to his patriotism, but it will be difficult, not to say impossible, to discover . . . anything that ought to stigmatize him as an enemy of the freedom of his country." Perhaps Villari had Roscoe in mind when he decried those who "condoned" Lorenzo's political sins "in virtue of his patronage of letters and art."

ARMSTRONG's work was one in the 17 volumes of Putnam's Heroes of the Nations series—a collection with a strong predilection for military figures and wielders of power. Armstrong made "little claim to original research" and included Roscoe in his sources. His work is lavishly illustrated with black-and-white Medici portraits, assorted examples of Renaissance art, and reproductions of medals and coats of arms. Armstrong had straightforward and downright views, but also important insights into such themes as the key importance of family in Renaissance Italian social and political life and Lorenzo's manipulation of popular culture for political ends. With his sharp sense of contrast between Italian and "English and American" cultures and his dismissive attitude to "the masses" and "the inherent vices of Italian democracy," Armstrong shed few tears about the alleged eclipse of Florentine liberty under de' Medici, seeing this unsentimentally as part of a widespread process in late medieval Italy in which urban republics one after another "accepted despotism as preferable to chronic strife." And Lorenzo was for Armstrong what he had been for Guicciardini, "the agreeable tyrant."

Armstrong's calm acceptance of the historical necessity for the Medicean system stands in vivid contrast with Villari's republican fulminations against Lorenzo that appeared in English in the year Armstrong's book was published. But Armstrong is obviously fascinated by Lorenzo as a man of destiny, with a magnetic "stamp of personality," and astonishing *virtù* and versatility. Indeed, Armstrong speculates that, had he lived, Lorenzo might have been able to save Italy from the catastrophe of invasion in 1494—from "Plundering Frenchmen," "drunken clownish Swiss and Germans," and "bloodthirsty Spanish savages." These phrases are typical of Armstrong's powerful, rather choleric, style and indicate how far English historical prose had travelled from Roscoe's measured cadences.

Over half of BRINTON's *Golden Age of the Medici* is devoted to Lorenzo, and the chapter that opens the main section on him has the revealing title, "The Springtime Returns." What was for Brinton "this happy period in the story of Florence"—the 1470s and 80s—is characterised by the flowering of the Renaissance under the influence of Hellenism and under the patronage of the Medici. Typical results were Botticelli's masterpieces, *The Birth of Venus* and *Primavera*. Even so, there was a stark contrast—and Brinton captures it brilliantly—between the gaiety of the courtly culture sponsored by *il magnifico* and the grim and ruthless supression of a liberation movement (1472) in subject Volterra (where Lorenzo had financial interests as a capitalist proprietor). Brinton, indeed, has a certain gift for the evocation of horror, as in his account of the Pazzi Conspiracy (1478) against the Medici, though in truth the coming together in this incident of sacrilege, vendetta, gangsterism, and bloodshed provide the narrative historian with unrivaled opportunities for scenic description.

Brinton is essentially a narrator when it comes to events and an analyst when it comes to the study of the extraordinary effusion of great works of art that appeared in his *Golden Age of the Medici*; he is totally aware of the intimate relationship, in works such as Benozzo's *Journey of the Magi*, between Mediceanism and great art. He is also able (partly using Fritz Schultze) to reconstruct the Platonic thought of the likes of Plethon and Ficino and, with his gift for scenic reconstruction and vivid writing, manages to capture brilliantly the atmosphere of those rather precious philosophic seminars typical of the intellectual life of Lorenzan Florence. Because of his fascination with artistic and cultural achievements in the Florentine Renaissance under the Medici, Brinton, like Armstrong, is inclined to take a tolerant, or what he would have seen as a realistic, line over the erosion of constitutional government at a time when "Republican institutions were becoming practically impossible in Italy." Brinton believed, or professed to believe, that government by the people was the "highest form of political expression," but, possibly influenced by the corporate hostility to party politics fashionable in some quarters in the 1920s, he suggests that the "stable citizen" would often opt for something less risky than free institutions. In this Brinton would seem to cast Lorenzo de' Medici as a civilised *duce*.

Brinton's "golden age" approach to Lorenzo was extended to a high degree by ROSS WILLIAMSON. Published in 1974, this study, with its surprising suggestion of a homosexual relationship between Lorenzo and both Poliziano and Michelangelo, reflects the greater openness towards such matters in England following the legalisation of adult homosexuality. On the political front, Williamson tries to cut through the web of traditional, and to his way of thinking irrelevant, ideological argument about Lorenzo in relation to forms of government, though is claim that Lorenzo was "devoid of any ambition for himself" seems to come close to political hagiography. Williamson writes colourfully and unrestrainedly: for example, his Savonarola is a "sex-obsessed egomaniac." This handsomely produced volume contains an illustration on or facing nearly every page.

STURM sets out on what she admits is the difficult task of dealing with Lorenzo the "man of letters" apart from the "man of action." In examining de' Medici the writer, she fully captures the paradoxical and even contradictory nature of the man who could convey both the sensuality of the Carnival Songs and the piety (admittedly stilted and unoriginal) of the religious verse. Although Sturm is not primarily concerned with Lorenzo

the politician, she has at least to make some reference to this aspect of an individual who in himself brought together the two Renaissance archetypes of action and intellect. To imply, she suggests, that artistic patronage was consciously used to subserve entirely distinct political ends points to a conceptual divorce between activities that was not there in Lorenzo. Poet and politician, philosopher and man of action, Platonist and Christian, sensualist and *dévot*, Sturm's Lorenzo in the end represents not contradiction but fusion.

A leading expert on Florentine politics in the Renaissance, RUBINSTEIN, in a brief but highly detailed essay, eschews earlier value-laden debate about whether or not Lorenzo was a "tyrant" and concentrated on the way in which his authority in Florence was consolidated. This took place, Rubinstein shows, largely as a result of the pressure to consolidate direction of Italian inter-state relations in the hands of single individuals. The conduct of foreign policy in the tense 1470s and 80s required decision-making to be both flexible and instantaneous, while authoritarian states such as Milan expected to do business with identifiable individuals. Thus inter-state relations, Rubinstein argues, created Lorenzo's strong executive power.

HOOK writes clearly, elegantly, and learnedly for a student and lay readership. Influenced by the 20th-century retreat from "great man" history, she is keen to show Lorenzo as being shaped by, rather than shaping, his times. Hook covers Lorenzo's background, deals with five phases of his political career, and examines his roles as patron and writer. She has no illusions about her subject—his cruelty, vindictiveness, arrogance, moodiness, and rashness—but she offers analysis in 15th-century terms, rather than ideological judgement by 20th-century standards, of his exercise of power. Her Lorenzo, weak, frail, and all too human, is also undeniably great, and her account of him is probably the finest and certainly the most readable of those reviewed here.

—Michael A. Mullett

MEIR, Golda, 1898–1978; Israeli prime minister.

Martin, Ralph G., *Golda: The Romantic Years*. New York, Scribner, 1988; London, Piatkus, 1989.
Meir, Menahem, *My Mother, Golda Meir: A Son's Evocation of Life with Golda Meir*. New York, Arbor House, 1983.
Syrkin, Marie, *Golda Meir Speaks Out*. London, Weidenfeld and Nicolson, 1973.

*

Golda Meir, one of the founders of Israel who broke through sexual barriers and established a precedent for women leaders everywhere to follow, may have also set a precedent in 1975 with the publication of her autobiography *My Life*, which recalls in disarming and candid prose her difficult adolescence, education as a Zionist, and long career as Israel's labor minister, foreign minister, and prime minister, particularly during the precarious days of the Yom Kippur War of 1973. Unlike many political autobiographies, *My Life* is not an "as-told-to" puff piece, nor a ghostwritten best-seller, but rather an honest summation—well illustrated—of Meir's Zionist convictions, the significance of Israel as the land of the Jews, and an oftentimes painful account of the private price exacted by a very demanding public life. Meir admirably widens the scope of this book to include the inner political struggles within Israel, her forthright appraisal of the various leaders she worked with on the world stage, and the frequently uncomfortable relationship between Israel and the United States.

Similarly, SYRKIN's volume, while somewhat proselytizing, also contains valuable biographical material conveyed through a series of interviews, press conferences, and speeches given by Meir from the late 1950s to the early 1970s. On matters of Nazi persecution and Hitler's proposed "final solution"—the execution of all Jews in Europe—Meir writes with a haunting and somber prose that is perhaps surpassed only by Elie Wiesel and Primo Levi.

Of important anecdotal value is MENAHEM MEIR's account, written by Golda Meir's son. Meir proposes to reveal the woman behind the legend, and he largely succeeds. However, this book is less effective as political history and is obviously suspect in its objectivity.

MARTIN's *Golda* is by far the most thoroughly researched and documented biography of Meir to date. Martin, who has written biographies of Winston Churchill and John F. Kennedy, takes Meir from her childhood in Russia and the U.S. to the years in which she lived in a kibbutz in Tel Aviv. He also covers Meir's work trying to establish Israel as a nation of Jews, and the first days of Israel's existence as a nation in 1948. Martin skillfully blends oral interviews with archival material to present an authoritative biography that is, to date, the only such biography of Meir available.

It is also a strength of *Golda* that Martin evokes, in language both literary and historical, important events in Meir's life and in the struggle for Israel's independence. He convincingly illustrates her horror over the mistreatment of exiled Jews and her rigid militance in making Israel as mighty as possible in the months leading up to its formal declaration of independence and recognition by the United States. Martin, through well-placed dialogue, shows how Meir worked with, and sometimes outmaneuvered, such forceful leaders as David Ben-Gurion and Winston Churchill, sometimes in such a macho Machiavellian fashion that Ben-Gurion later remarked that Meir was "the only man in my cabinet."

Yet Martin also reveals for the first time the tender and sensitive letters Meir wrote to her husband and, later, to her lover, giving readers a glimpse of Meir never before seen by her public. With its rich supply of anecdotal and original source material, as well as an abundance of oral interviews, *Golda* is a first rate political biography of a woman frequently shrouded in myth.

—Garry Boulard

MELVILLE, Herman, 1819–1891; American writer.

Allen, Gay Wilson, *Melville and His World*. New York, Viking, 1971.

Anderson, Charles Roberts, *Melville in the South Seas*. New York, Columbia University Press, 1939.

Arvin, Newton, *Herman Melville*. New York, W. Sloane, and London, Methuen, 1950.

Bixby, William, *Rebel Genius: The Life of Herman Melville*. New York, D. McKay, 1970.

Davis, Merrell R., *Melville's Mardi—A Chartless Voyage*. New Haven, Connecticut, Yale University Press, 1952.

Freeman, John, *Herman Melville*. New York and London, Macmillan, 1926.

Gilman, William H., *Melville's Early Life and Redburn*. New York, New York University Press, 1951.

Howard, Leon, *Herman Melville: A Biography*. Berkeley, University of California Press, 1951.

Leyda, Jay, *The Melville Log: A Documentary Life of Herman Melville, 1819–1891* (2 vols.). New York, Harcourt, 1951; revised edition, with supplement, 1969.

Metcalf, Eleanor Melville, *Herman Melville: Cycle and Epicycle*. Cambridge, Massachusetts, Harvard University Press, 1953.

Miller, Edwin Haviland, *Melville*. New York, G. Braziller, 1975.

Mumford, Lewis, *Herman Melville*. New York, Harcourt, and London, Cape, 1929; revised edition, with subtitle *A Study of His Life and Vision*, New York, Harcourt, and London, Secker and Warburg, 1962.

Sealts, Merton M., Jr., *Melville as Lecturer*. Cambridge, Massachusetts, Harvard University Press, 1957.

Sealts, Merton M., Jr., *The Early Lives of Melville: 19th-Century Biographical Sketches and Their Authors*. Madison, University of Wisconsin Press, 1974.

Weaver, Raymond, *Herman Melville, Mariner and Mystic*. New York, G. H. Doran, 1921.

*

Herman Melville's career as an author began auspiciously: his first two works (*Typee*, 1846; *Omoo*, 1847) were popular successes; he published ten books in roughly his first ten years of writing. But then he announced his withdrawal in the portrait of a deaf-mute in *The Confidence-Man* (1857), "stealing into retirement, and there going asleep and continuing so, . . . courted oblivion." For the last 34 years of his life, Melville published virtually no fiction. He so successfully "courted oblivion" that the brief entry on him in *The Condensed American Cyclopaedia* (1877) makes no mention of *Moby-Dick* among the list of his publications. By 1900, he received a one-sentence treatment in the 600-page *Literary History of America* by Barrett Wendell.

It is not surprising, therefore, that no book-length biography of Melville appeared until 30 years after his death and that the few 19th-century biographical sketches of Melville were easy to collect in a slim volume published in 1974 by SEALTS. The book contains a sampling of entries from the biographical dictionaries, sketches written shortly after Melville's death by three of his acquaintances, and brief reminiscences by his wife and two of his grandchildren.

The centennial of Melville's birth in 1919 stimulated renewed interest in his works and led to publication of the first full-fledged biography in 1921. WEAVER claims authenticity for his study through access to previously unpublished family records.

But the biography is essentially a transmutation of the fictions of Melville's early works into the "facts" of Melville's life. The first chapter establishes the standard profile of Melville for the next two decades: he experienced a "discreditable" neglect by his contemporaries; his "most complex" fictional character was "Herman Melville"; "blighted by disillusionment," he eventually came to see the writing of books as "an irrelevancy." Roughly half the rest of the book describes Melville's experiences as a seaman, drawn largely from the fictionalized accounts of his sea-going experiences (*Typee, Omoo, Redburn, White-Jacket*), which Weaver reads as factual travel narrative. One brief chapter is devoted to the last 35 years of Melville's life. FREEMAN appears to be equally indebted to Weaver and to Melville's early fiction for the information in the four chapters of his book that he devotes to Melville's life.

MUMFORD's book, the first critical biography of Melville, is often discredited for reinforcing the myth of Melville as a defeated "titan," deemphasizing the known facts of Melville's life, and accepting Melville's fiction as an accurate account of his experience. Despite those drawbacks, it is a highly suggestive account of Melville's life and works. The reader already acquainted with the essential facts of Melville's life will delight in the brilliant commentary throughout the book—certainly a reflection of Mumford's life-long ability to do what Melville did so well, look beyond the facts.

The "facts," however, were eventually bound to come out, and with them, the de-mythicizing of the persona created by the "Melville revival" of the 1920s. Most of those facts appeared between 1939 and 1960, a large number in four books that studied particular periods of Melville's life. Focusing on Melville's sea-going adventures from 1841 through 1844, ANDERSON shed light on his South Sea experiences, his tour of duty on a U.S. frigate, and his extensive borrowings from travel books. Anderson's painstaking research cast doubt for the first time on the autobiographical nature of Melville's books that deal with the experiences of that period. GILMAN concentrates on the period 1819–41, providing much information on family history, genealogy, and influences. His close examination of the circumstances surrounding Melville's voyage to Liverpool as an ordinary seaman in 1839 leads Gilman to conclude that Melville "romanticized freely" in his account of the trip in *Redburn*. DAVIS highlights the beginning of Melville's career as an author (1844–48) with particular attention to influences on *Mardi*. The three-year period (1857–60) when Melville (having abandoned his career as an author) attempted to make a living as a lecturer is clarified by SEALTS (1957) in a study of reviews and excerpts from the lectures in the newspapers.

All four of these books, in addition to establishing more precisely the facts of Melville's life, make public previously unpublished documents. METCALF (Melville's granddaughter) provides additional documentary information in her collection of passages from family letters and diaries and her account of her own recollections and of family anecdotes. A complete edition of the 271 known letters by Melville was published by Merrell R. Davis and William H. Gilman, *The Letters of Herman Melville* (1960). About 40 additional letters have since been found. The most comprehensive collection of documents on Melville's life appeared in the centennial year of the publication of *Moby-Dick*, 1951. While not, strictly speaking, a biography, LEYDA's massive chronological compilation of facts has been

mined by every major Melville scholar since its publication. Leyda states in the introduction to this "documentary life" that his purpose is to "give each reader the opportunity to be his own biographer of Herman Melville." The thousands of excerpts from diaries, letters, reviews, etc., are of principal interest to the serious student of Melville but make good reading for the Melville enthusiast engaged in the kind of speculative biography Leyda encourages in his introduction. A new and expanded edition of *The Melville Log* is being prepared by Hershel Parker.

Collaborating with Leyda and often sharing sources, HOWARD published the most comprehensive and authoritative narrative biography of Melville in the same year. Like Mumford's book, it is a critical biography but, unlike Mumford's, attentive to the details of Melville's life and informed by the wealth of information accumulated in the intervening 20 years. It quickly established itself as the definitive biography of Melville in its time. Its strength is as a narrative of facts; its weakness, in its limited critical range. Both of these factors might be explained by Howard's assertion that he "made no statements of fact or probability which are not reasoned conclusions based upon the best available evidence." When he does indulge in critical commentary, Howard often leaves the reader disappointed. He seems almost as unappreciative of the subtleties of *Pierre* and *The Confidence-Man* as Melville's contemporaries were. The bulk of his treatment of *Moby-Dick* focuses on literary influences and compositional technique. His resolve to stick to the facts—while it is admirable and results in the most accurate account of the circumstances of Melville's life published to date—restricts his judgments and conclusions and results in an often plodding recitation of mundane activities and minor events. Nevertheless, narration of facts is what Howard did best, and it is the reason his book is still the most reliable biography for the general reader.

It is certainly more reliable than the "popular" biography by BIXBY, which reverts to reading Melville's fiction as autobiography and tries to capitalize on the social unrest of its time (it was published in 1970) in its emphasis on Melville as a "rebel." ALLEN's "studio book," published the following year, is a slim but adequate sketch intended as text for a pictorial biography.

Two additional studies fall in the category of psychobiography. ARVIN's interpretation of Melville's life emphasizes the influence of the "tormented psychology" of Melville's patrician family, "the frightening sense of abandonment" Melville experienced when his father died, and the "inward stresses" from his "intense and contrarious relationship" with his mother. Although Arvin's interpretations are often conventionally Freudian, he is at his best when he enlarges his critical perspective, as he does in his brilliant analysis of *Moby-Dick*, which examines the organizational principles of the novel and its movements, language, and symbolism in the light of tragic and epic tradition, taking into account the literal, psychological, moral, and mythic dimensions of meaning. Like Mumford, Arvin is less interested in the external facts than in Melville's states of mind, so he often condenses periods and events in Melville's life that don't suit his purpose. Despite these limitations, the reader with a taste for biography that probes its subject's psyche will find this an engaging and thoughtful account of the conflicts in Melville's life and the "infirm well-being" he eventually attained.

Taking his cue from the prominent role of Ishmael in *Moby-Dick*, MILLER returns to the notion advanced by Weaver that

Melville's major fictional character was "Herman Melville," but not in the role of a picaresque mariner, as Weaver portrayed him. Rather, Melville's "self-dramatization" is as "the rejected Ishmael" in a family whose life history seemed to Melville to parallel the biblical story of Abraham. Miller speculates on the roots of Melville's association of his father, Allan, with the banishing Abraham; his brother, Gansevoort, with the usurping Isaac; and his mother, Maria, with both the emasculating Sarah and the loving Hagar. He contends that Melville projects his desire for fatherly acceptance in portraits of classically muscular but delicate male figures whose "Apollonian aura" of attractiveness draws attention to them. He argues that Melville's self-dramatizations vacillate between the Apollonian hope for restoration and an Ishmaelian acceptance of the harsh reality of rejection. In this scheme, Melville's relationship with Nathaniel Hawthorne becomes the crucial event of his life, in which the pattern of rejection by the father is repeated. Miller's thesis received a large amount of negative commentary at the time his book was published. It remains, however, a provocative and fascinating account of the inner workings of Melville's mind and, ultimately, of the motives for his art. It is not likely to be the last attempt to plumb the depths of Melville's psyche for, despite Metcalf's judgment that "the core of the man remains incommunicable," the ambiguities of Melville's life and works continue to fix and fascinate his readers.

—Joseph Flibbert

* * *

MENCKEN, H(enry) L(ouis), 1880–1956; American journalist and editor.

Bode, Carl, *Mencken.* Carbondale, Southern Illinois University Press, 1969.

Goldberg, Isaac, *The Man Mencken: A Biographical and Critical Survey.* New York, Simon and Schuster, 1925.

Kemler, Edgar, *The Irreverent Mr. Mencken.* Boston, Little Brown, 1950.

Manchester, William, *Disturber of the Peace: The Life of H. L. Mencken.* New York, Harper, 1951.

*

Most of these books reverently chronicle the Mencken myth. Goldberg and Kemler were Mencken's friends; Manchester became one. Although Manchester's book is the best-written—as he has demonstrated in his subsequent starry-eyed popular histories, Manchester knows how to tell a good story—only Bode's biography is penetrating and wise. Bode is balanced, dependable, and fair, painstakingly thorough and meticulously documented.

Mencken essentially ghosted the books by GOLDBERG and KEMLER. A model of cooperation and accessibility, Mencken typed two hundred pages of biographical information for Goldberg. Inundated, Goldberg never realized how much, in all those thousands of words, Mencken had managed to leave out. Thus, while seeming to give his biographer free rein, Mencken actually tied blinders to Goldberg's eyes, and led him by the nose.

Later Mencken made his side of the story equally available to Kemler. As a result, virtually interchangeable passages on the learned Menckenii (as Mencken preferred calling his German ancestors), his happy childhood, and his early years as a reporter and editor appear in Goldberg's and Kemler's books. Mencken alone succeeds in turning this material to good use: he recycled the hyperbolic and ironic notes he'd written 15 years earlier for his richly comic but not entirely factual memoirs (3 vols., 1940; *Happy Days, Newspaper Days,* and *Heathen Days*). Though neither Goldberg nor Kemler ever recovered from the influence of the material Mencken supplied, Goldberg's prose especially suffers. His style, a failed homage to Mencken's, succeeds only in being overworked and difficult to read.

Goldberg's book, written years before some of Mencken's most noteworthy achievements, includes such curiosities as an X-ray of Mencken's skull and hard-to-find selections of his early work—poetry, short stories, and the Baltimore *Herald* columns, *Untold Tales.* (Yet even these finds have been superseded by Bode's excellent 1973 collection of Mencken's early work, *Young Mencken.*)

Kemler is more readable than Goldberg. But the thesis he announces boldly—that Mencken is a failed skeptic—is never developed. What remains is a biography of Mencken as a man of action rather than a man of ideas. Since Kemler's concept of action is chiefly social engagements, practical jokes, and the pronouncing of *bon mots*, his biography degenerates into mere chronology, leaping from highpoint to highpoint in Mencken's varied career. Kemler's book lacks a necessary intellectual dimension.

MANCHESTER is lively and colorful. He begins promisingly. He has a gift for depicting scenes dramatically and for capturing atmosphere, particularly that of Baltimore and early 20th-century America. His pace is brisk, and at least some of his vivid adjectives are his own, even though he, too, falls under the spell of Mencken's distinctive phrasing. Manchester's account of the intricate legal maneuvering in the Hatrack case—the censorship battle Mencken fought after his triumphant coverage of the Scopes trial—is the clearest available.

Manchester, however, is prone to sentimentality. In writing about Mencken's marriage, he seems to feel obliged, out of respect for Mencken, to be dazzled by Sara Haardt. The epithet Manchester used so effectively years later to describe Jacqueline Kennedy—"camellia beauty"—appears first here to characterize Haardt, whom Manchester never saw. But Manchester's ability to write sympathetically succeeds in the book's conclusion. His account of Mencken after the 1948 stroke that left him aphasic is evocative and moving.

Alone among these biographies, BODE's book has depth and breadth. He provides a considered assessment of Mencken because he discusses Mencken as a writer. Bode's discussions of Mencken's books, particularly those on Nietzsche and on religion, are the most satisfying, and he has the surest grasp of the philosophical foundations as well as the flaws of Mencken's criticism.

Kemler and Goldberg gasp in wonder at Mencken's meteoric rise from cub reporter to editor, and merely list Mencken's successively impressive job titles, as if *biography* were synonymous with *résumé*. Only Bode tells us what Mencken did as an editor, and places Mencken's accomplishments in American journalism history. Bode's tempered and just estimation of Mencken's early journalism, the Free Lance columns, and so-called Monday Articles, makes Goldberg's, Manchester's, and even Kemler's work (for all its professed reservations) seem like book-length blurbs.

As insightful as Bode is, in a sense there has not yet been a definitive biography of Mencken. Ernest Boyd's *H. L. Mencken* (1925), often erroneously cited as a biography, is in fact an early critical essay. In her memoir *The Constant Circle: H. L. Mencken and His Friends* (1968), Haardt's friend Sara Mayfield capitalizes on the coincidence that they (along with Zelda Fitzgerald and Tallulah Bankhead) happened to come from the same hometown and social milieu. Mayfield's sentimental, derivative, defensive, gossipy, and unreliable book is useful only for its account of the terms of Mencken's will and the disposition of his papers after his death. For a glimpse into Mencken's personal life, Mencken's letters and diary are far more dependable and revealing than Mayfield's cliche-ridden panegyric.

The 1989 publication of Mencken's diary (*The Diary of H. L. Mencken*), sealed for 25 years after his death, reveals a deficiency in all Mencken biography. In particular, the diary rekindles debate on his supposed racism (the subject of Charles Scruggs' engrossing study, *The Sage in Harlem*, 1984) and his anti-Semitism. Charles Fecher, the redoubtable critic who vigorously defended Mencken against charges of anti-Semitism, now says editing the diary has changed his mind.

Though it relies extensively and often brilliantly on biographical detail, Guy Forgue's *H. L. Mencken: L'homme, l'oeuvre, l'influence* (1967) is ultimately a comprehensive critical work. Forgue's is a splendid book, probably the best on Mencken to date, so much so that its psychological insights surpass even those of Mencken's best biographer, Carl Bode. It is lamentable that Forgue's monumental accomplishment remains untranslated.

—Carolyn Yalkut

MENDEL, Gregor (Johann), 1822–1884; Austrian botanist and monk; founder of genetic science.

George, Wilma, *Gregor Mendel and Heredity*. London, Priory Press, 1975.

Iltis, Hugo, *Life of Mendel*, translated by Eden and Cedar Paul. New York, Norton, and London, Allen and Unwin, 1932.

Orel, Vitezslav, *Mendel*, translated by Stephen Finn. Oxford and New York, Oxford University Press, 1984.

Sootin, H., *Gregor Mendel, Father of the Science of Genetics*. New York, Vanguard, 1959; London, Blackie, 1961.

*

ILTIS wrote the first and most comprehensive biography of the Augustinian monk whose concept of heredity has become the central theme of biological research. Despite the appearance of many recent studies of the history of genetics, this book remains the definitive biography of Gregor Mendel. Iltis provides detailed information about Mendel's ancestry, birthplace, and education. In addition to discussing at length Mendel's discovery of the laws of inheritance, Iltis describes Mendel's studies of plant hybridization, horticulture, apiculture, and meteorology, as well

as Mendel's activities as abbot of the Augustinian monastery, which took up so much of his time and energy.

Iltis, a teacher of natural history and proud native of Brno, Czechoslovakia, recalls reading Mendel's classic monograph in the museum library at a time when its significance was still unknown. He later embarked on the collection of "Mendelia" as a means of honoring the memory of this once obscure investigator. After publishing a number of short articles and popular essays on Mendel's life and work, Iltis was finally able to complete the first full biography of Mendel, based on materials at the Brno Mendel Museum (including some Iltis had collected and donated himself).

The difficulties in preparing a biography of this remarkable scientist were considerable. Unfortunately for biographers, Mendel never kept a diary, and his surviving letters reveal little of a personal nature. Because he was a priest, Mendel had to be extremely cautious in expressing his philosophical views. He seems to have been very reserved in his relationships with his clerical and monastic colleagues. During the closing years of his life, although surrounded by his monastic brothers, he led a solitary and rather gloomy existence. Failing to appreciate his scientific work, his successors at the monastery destroyed the few documents he left behind. Within 20 years of his death, he had been virtually forgotten and almost all reliable biographical material lost.

Fortunately, Iltis was able to secure some letters and photographs from Mendel's nephews. Other biographical information was provided by members of the monastery community, university professors, colleagues, acquaintances, and pupils. The book contains a portrait of Mendel and ten other illustrations including diagrams illustrating the principles of Mendelian inheritance.

The *Life of Mendel* begins with the usual account of "Home and Ancestry." Since so little is known of Mendel himself, much is made of the history and geography of the area surrounding Mendel's birthplace, the village of Kuhländchen in Moravia, an area that was then Austrian Silesia, now Czechoslovakia. Some surprisingly personal early documents did survive, such as two poems composed by Mendel as a schoolboy and lovingly preserved by his sister. Iltis provides insight into Mendel's studies and failure to pass his examinations, his love of teaching, gardening, and beekeeping, his studies of meteorology, and his correspondence with Carl von Nägeli.

One of the most difficult facts for a biographer of Mendel to account for is the way in which his remarkable discovery remained in obscurity from 1865 until 1900. Iltis struggled with this puzzle just as every historian of science has in the years since this charming and sensitive biography was published. Many accounts of "Mendel and his era" or the "origins of genetics" exist, but the inner life of Gregor Mendel and the source of his genius remain a mystery.

Although SOOTIN includes no preface or introduction in his work to identify its intended audience, his simple prose and "you-are-there" conversational style suggest that it is suitable for junior high or high school students. In simple terms, Sootin presents the inspirational story of the boy from a poor family who through hard work and sacrifice becomes a scientist. The book is based on the comprehensive biography by Iltis.

GEORGE's book, in fewer than 100 profusely illustrated pages, traces the basic facts of Mendel's life and places his work within the history of biology. George, a lecturer in Zoology, Genetics, and history of Science at the University of Oxford, emphasizes how Mendel's ideas remained outside the mainstream of science for some 40 years. Written clearly and precisely, the short text provides a glossary, chronological chart, suggested readings, index, and over 50 well-chosen illustrations. The book is suitable for young adults and general readers unfamiliar with the science of genetics. Explanations of Mendel's experiments, and those of his precursors, are presented clearly and simply, without insulting the reader's intelligence.

 OREL, the most recent biographer of Mendel, is eminently qualified to reflect on Mendel's life and work. Orel is the editor of the *Folia Mendeliana*, published annually by the Moravian Museum, and Chairman of the Gregor Mendel Department of Genetics in the Moravian Museum, Brno. Both Orel and Iltis are especially interested in explicating the factors, both personal and cultural, that motivated Mendel's scientific interest in plant breeding, hybridization, and the mechanism of heredity.

Orel's biography draws on new studies of Mendel published in German and other languages, as well as on original articles published in the *Folia Mendeliana*. Although brief, the book is lucid, informative, and accurate. It covers the intellectual background in Mendel's native country, his education at the University of Vienna, his experiments on peas and other plant species, the innovative nature of his experimental methods, and the implications of his research for Darwin's theory of evolution. Orel sensitively describes the conflicts that claimed so much of the Abbot's energy, as well as Mendel's continued interest in horticulture, apiculture, and meteorology.

Reading the biographies by Iltis or Orel should dispel this myth of Mendel's complete isolation from the scientific community and provide more insight into Mendel within the intellectual climate that initially nourished, but eventually ignored, his work.

Readers interested in studies of Mendel's experiments and the evolution of genetics should find the following books of interest: William Bateson, *Mendel's Principles of Heredity* (1913); J. H. Bennet, editor, *Experiments in Plant Hybridisation. Mendel's Original Paper in English Translation with Commentary and Assessment by the Late Sir Ronald A. Fisher Together with a Reprint of W. Bateson's Biographical Notice of Mendel* (1965); R. Alexander Brink and E. Derek Styles, editors, *Heritage from Mendel* (1967); Roland M. Nardone, editor, *Mendel Centenary: Genetics, Development, and Evolution* (1968; the paper by Conway Zirkel, "Mendel and His Era," provides biographical data and an analysis of the neglect of Mendel's work); R. C. Olby, *Origins of Mendelism* (1967; chapter 5, "Gregor Mendel," is an excellent biographical essay that reflects on Mendel's life from his student days in Vienna to his work as Abbot of his monastery).

—Lois N. Magner

MENDELSSOHN-BARTHOLDY, Felix, 1809–1847; German composer and pianist.

Benedict, Julius, *A Sketch of the Life and Works of the Late Felix Mendelssohn-Bartholdy*. London, J. Murray, 1850.

Devrient, Eduard, *My Recollections of Felix Mendelssohn-Bartholdy and His Letters to Me*, translated by N. Macfarren. London, R. Bentley, 1869 (originally published by J. J. Weber, Leipzig, 1869).

Elvers, Rudolf, editor, *Felix Mendelssohn: A Life in Letters*, translated by Craig Tomlison. New York, Fromm International, 1986 (originally published by Fischer, Frankfurt am Main, 1984).

Grove, George, "Mendelssohn," in *A Dictionary of Music and Musicians* (4 vols.). London and New York, Macmillan, 1890.

Hensel, Sebastian, *The Mendelssohn Family (1729–1847) from Letters and Journals* (2 vols.), translated by C. Klingemann. London, Low Marston, and New York, Harper, 1881 (originally published by B. Behr, Berlin, 1879).

Hiller, Ferdinand, *Mendelssohn: Letters and Recollections*, translated by M. E. von Glehn. London, Macmillan, and Cincinnati, Ohio, J. Church, 1874; revised edition, New York, Vienna House, 1972 (originally published as *Felix Mendelssohn-Bartholdy Briefe und Erinnerungen*, Cologne, Du Mont-Schauberg, 1874).

Jacob, Heinrich Edvard, *Felix Mendelssohn and His Times*, translated by Richard and Clara Winston. London, Barrie and Rockliff, and Englewood Cliffs, New Jersey, Prentice-Hall, 1963 (originally published by Fischer, Frankfurt am Main, 1959).

Jenkins, David and Mark Visocchi, *Mendelssohn in Scotland*. London and New York, Chappell, 1978.

Köhler, Karl-Heinz, "Mendelssohn," in *The New Grove Dictionary of Music and Musicians* (20 vols.), edited by Stanley Sadie. Sixth edition, London, Macmillan, and New York, Norton, 1980; in *The New Grove Early Romantic Masters 2*, 1985.

Kupferberg, Herbert, *Felix Mendelssohn: His Life, His Family, His Music*. New York, Scribner, 1972.

Lampadius, W. A., *The Life of Felix Mendelssohn-Bartholdy*, translated, with supplementary material, by W. L. Gage. New York, F. Leypoldt, and Boston, D. Ditson, 1865; London, Reeves, 1876; revised and expanded edition, Boston, D. Ditson, 1887.

Marek, George R., *Gentle Genius: The Story of Felix Mendelssohn*. New York, Funk and Wagnalls/T. Y. Crowell, 1972; London, R. Hale, 1973.

Petitpierre, Jacques, *The Romance of the Mendelssohns*, translated by G. Micholet-Coté. London, Dobson, 1947 (originally published as *Le Marriage de Mendelssohn*, Lausanne, Payot, 1937).

Polko, Elise, *Reminiscences of Felix Mendelssohn-Bartholdy: A Social and Artistic Biography*, translated by Lady Wallace. London, Longman, and New York, Leypoldt, 1869.

Radcliffe, Philip, *Mendelssohn*. London and New York, Dent, 1954.

Rockstro, William S., *Mendelssohn*. London, Low Marston, and New York, Scribner, 1884.

Schumann, Robert, *Memoirs of Felix Mendelssohn-Bartholdy*, edited by G. Eismann, translated by James A. Galston. Rochester, New York, 1951.

Stratton, Stephen S., *Mendelssohn*. London, Dent, and New York, Dutton, 1901; revised edition, 1934.

Werner, Eric, *Mendelssohn: A New Image of the Composer and His Age*, translated by Dika Newlin. New York, Free Press, 1963; as *Felix Mendelssohn*, London, Collier-Macmillan, 1963.

Young, Percy M., "Mendelssohn," in *The Grove Dictionary of Music and Musicians*, edited by Eric Blom. Fifth edition, London, Macmillan, and New York, St. Martin's, 1954.

*

Biographical notices about Felix Mendelssohn-Bartholdy began to appear early in his career; in 1825, when he was 16, the *Quarterly Musical Magazine and Review* published this report from Paris: "artists and connoisseurs . . . are of unanimous opinion that he is deeply founded in his art, and holds forth the finest promise of future excellence." Mendelssohn's leading position in German music during the 1830s and 1840s ensured his place in 19th-century musical biographies; his celebration as an extraordinary musical prodigy and his death at the age of 38 encouraged comparisons with Mozart, a process that hastened the production of biographies. Mendelssohn's death in 1847 was viewed as a calamity of the first order not only in Germany but in England, a country the composer often visited between 1829 and 1847. Following his death, Mendelssohn was lionized, and his life and career subjected to a type of hero-worship. The most remarkable result of this development was Elizabeth Sheppard's popular historical romance *Charles Auchester* (1853), in which Mendelssohn was idealized as Seraphael. As late as 1869 Polko (see below) could still write as a closing eulogy, "Never did a more ideal man, or more ideal artist tread this earth than our beloved and never-to-be-forgotten Felix Mendelssohn!"

Inevitably, a reaction occurred, and its effects were felt in the Mendelssohn literature. At least three factors seem to have influenced the ensuing negative reassessments of the composer. First, as the grandson of Moses Mendelssohn, the distinguished 18th-century Jewish philosopher, Mendelssohn was a victim of anti-semitism (though he converted to the Lutheran faith in 1816, and his family adopted Bartholdy as a second surname). Wagner penned a scurrilous attack on Mendelssohn, and in the 20th century, the Nazis banned his music and destroyed his statue in Leipzig. Second, by the middle of the 19th century Mendelssohn's refined style—in many ways derivative of such earlier masters as J. S. Bach, Mozart, and Beethoven, and therefore labelled by some critics as "neo-classical"—was judged to be incongruent with the "progressive" direction of Wagner's and Liszt's *Zukunftsmusik* ("Music of the Future"). And third, the reaction toward the end of the century against the Victorian age found a ready target of criticism in Mendelssohn, whose music was now perceived as cloyingly sentimental.

A starting point for Mendelssohn biography was provided by BENEDICT's brief sketch; in 1865 an English translation of LAMPADIUS, a more substantial German biography originally published in 1848, appeared. Prepared by W. L. Gage, the English version included as supplementary sketches several accounts by contemporaries of the composer. An expanded German edition of Lampadius followed in 1886, and this, too, was translated; Gage described the revision as "large enough to hold all that one *need* to know regarding this gifted man, and yet

piquant enough to stimulate the reader to go on into yet larger reaches of knowledge."

Many of the 19th-century studies of Mendelssohn took the form of collections of the composer's letters to and memoirs by his closest friends. The so-called *Reisebriefe*, with letters from Mendelssohn's grand tour of Germany, Austria, Italy, Switzerland, and France (1830–32), were released in 1861 by his brother, Paul Mendelssohn-Bartholdy (English translation, 1862). A supplementary volume, with letters from 1833 to 1847 and an incomplete catalogue of the composer's works by Julius Rietz, appeared in 1863 (translation, 1868). In the preface to the latter, Mendelssohn's brother revealed a primary criterion for the selection of letters: "no letter addressed to any living person has been published without express permission readily accorded." Unfortunately, those letters that were published typically appeared in heavily edited or incomplete versions.

Similarly, the several volumes of memoirs published by Mendelssohn's contemporaries suffered considerably from editorial inaccuracies and are not always reliable. POLKO is undoubtedly the worst offender in this regard (the English translation, however, does include in an appendix several letters unavailable elsewhere). DEVRIENT contains what is probably a highly embellished account of Mendelssohn's revival of Bach's *St. Matthew Passion*. HILLER offers stimulating accounts of Mendelssohn's relationships with Chopin and Liszt. His work, the 1972 edition of which includes an excellent introduction by Joel Sachs and also identifies several of the figures whose names were suppressed in the first edition, was published primarily to counter attacks on the composer; as Hiller explained, "Gold cannot be tarnished." *Goethe and Mendelssohn* (London, 1872), by Carl Mendelssohn-Bartholdy, recounts the composer's friendship with the German poet laureate and includes several of Mendelssohn's letters in an appendix. A somewhat more accurate transmission of Mendelssohn's correspondence obtains in *Letters of Felix Mendelssohn to Ignaz and Charlotte Moscheles* (New York, 1888). In the preface the editor and translator, Felix Moscheles (son of the composer Ignaz Moscheles) informs us that "many passages occur in which prominent musicians of those days are unreservedly criticised, . . . I trust they will be none the less interesting now that time has judged between the critics and those criticised." ROCKSTRO's biography, colored by personal reminiscences, includes several anecdotes about Mendelssohn's extraordinary musical abilities.

HENSEL's work has enjoyed an illustrious publication history. Hensel, the son of Mendelssohn's sister Fanny Hensel, broadens the scope of this "family biography" to include the composer's grandfather, parents, siblings, and other relatives. Based largely on the family correspondence and diaries, Hensel's work is marred by uncritical readings of the letters; many letters appear in a heavily edited form, and some are conflated, so that scholars are still compelled to consult the original autographs (a sizeable collection of which is preserved in the New York Public Library). Still, Hensel remained an influential biographical account of the composer; by 1924 it reached its 18th edition.

The foundation for modern Mendelssohn research was set by GROVE, whose lengthy study of the composer appeared in the first *Dictionary of Music and Musicians* in 1890, and then reappeared in subsequent editions of 1900, 1920 (with revisions by F. G. Edwards), and 1940; for the 1954 edition of the *Dictionary* a new Mendelssohn article by YOUNG was prepared, to "bring the Dictionary into line with modern requirements and modern research," though Grove's original article had been reissued as recently as 1951. Grove subjected his work to an unprecedented critical standard. In 1879 he visited Berlin and Leipzig to examine firsthand the composer's substantial *Nachlass* and to interview members of his family and friends. The resulting monograph offered a careful, remarkably accurate account of Mendelssohn's life but also a meticulous consideration of his portraits and drawings, letters (Grove declared Mendelssohn's calligraphy a "work of art"), method of composition, piano and organ playing and skill at extemporization, and many other aspects of his life—all carefully examined from the basis of documented sources. Grove also produced a detailed catalogue of Mendelssohn's works with specific dates of composition, a considerable improvement over earlier catalogues.

Surprisingly few English biographies of Mendelssohn were produced during the early decades of the 20th century. When STRATTON's book, first published in 1901, was reissued in 1934, the following note was appended in the preface: "Mendelssohn, in his time the most successful of the 'master musicians,' is now the most neglected, a fact which we will tactfully account for by a mysterious law of compensation." Reliable biographies from later in the century include works by RADCLIFFE, who attempts to present Mendelssohn's life and works "coloured neither by the exaggerated hero-worship by which they were first surrounded nor by the equally exaggerated denigration that followed," and JACOB, who, viewing Mendelssohn as a "child of Early Victorianism," adopts a non-chronological approach. Less exacting biographies accessible to a broad audience include those by MAREK, which examines the view of Mendelssohn as a "polite man writing polite music," and KUPFERBERG, which lacks a bibliography and list of sources consulted.

The major full-length Mendelssohn biography in English remains that by WERNER. Founded largely on a multitude of primary documents previously unavailable to biographers, Werner's work drew attention to a number of unpublished compositions, many of them from Mendelssohn's early career. A central concern of the biography is to trace the ongoing conflict in Mendelssohn's life between German culture and his Jewish ancestry. The concluding chapter reexamines the shifting tides of Mendelssohn's posthumous reputation. More recently, KÖHLER offers a convenient short biography: its reissue in 1985 incorporated a number of corrections, a substantial bibliography, and an itemized list of works. ELVERS' work is primarily organized as a selection of letters from 1820 to 1847. Many of the letters are published for the first time, and all are accurately transcribed. The volume includes biographical notes and a year-by-year chronology of Mendelssohn's life.

A final group deserving mention comprises specialized biographical studies. PETITPIERRE treats Mendelssohn's marriage to Cécile Jeanrenaud and includes illustrations from the couple's wedding diary. The 1951 edition of SCHUMANN presents a facsimile and translation of Robert Schumann's memoirs of Mendelssohn. The well-illustrated volume by JENKINS AND VISOCCHI treats Mendelssohn's 1829 sojourn in Scotland. Still unfulfilled, however, are several basic *desiderata* in Mendelssohn scholarship: complete critical editions of his letters and music, and a scholarly thematic catalogue, for example. Until these gaps are filled, our view of Mendelssohn will continue to remain incomplete and imperfect.

—R. Larry Todd

————————

MERTON, Thomas, 1915–1968; American religious writer, poet, and Trappist monk.

Furlong, Monica, *Merton: A Biography*. New York, Harper, and London, Collins, 1980.
Mott, Michael, *The Seven Mountains of Thomas Merton*. Boston, Houghton Mifflin, 1984; London, Sheldon, 1986.
Rice, Edward, *The Man in the Sycamore Tree: The Good Times and Hard Life of Thomas Merton: An Entertainment with Photos*. New York, Doubleday, 1970.

*

With its beautiful photographs taken by the author, RICE's biography is, as its sub-sub-title calls it, more "An Entertainment" than a biography. But this friend of Merton's from Columbia University, who had worked with him on the student magazine there, does provide a personal angle missing in the other biographies.

FURLONG assembled materials for her biography through personal interviews, review of Merton's voluminous correspondence, and study of many of his works on the monastic and contemplative life. The starting point for any biographer, she tells us, is Merton's own 1948 autobiography, *The Seven Storey Mountain*, written several years after his entrance into the Cistercian Abbey of Our Lady of Gethsemane in Bardstown, Kentucky. Furlong counts herself "among those who regard Thomas Merton's life as a victorious one," and that tone pervades her biography. She disagrees with the only previous biographer, Ed Rice, who saw Merton's final trip to Asia as a "desperate dash for freedom" from an order that had continually thwarted and persecuted him. She avoids the temptation of idealizing Merton into a kind of saint, seeing him instead as "the normal man he was with his fair share, perhaps more than his fair share, of human frailties." For example, she does not whitewash Merton's getting a girl pregnant while at Cambridge, but sees his "excruciating sense of guilt" as a key to his decision to enter the monastery.

She raises a crucial question to guide her biography: What did it mean to be a monk in the 20th century? Furlong's spiritual sensitivity and innate common sense combine to produce special insights in answering this question. Like Merton himself, she recognizes the falsity of the world-condemning postures in his autobiography. She sees him becoming a true monk by moving toward the simplicity of being human and toward the discipline of self-acceptance and self-forgiveness. Furlong's biography amply documents Merton's many struggles with his superior, Dom James Fox, providing a balanced view of their painful relationship. She is to be credited for emphasizing the importance of the feminine to Merton in his realization of the Hagia Sophia aspect of God not only in his understanding and his dreams but in his life. However, because she did not have access to the restricted journals, she passes over 1966, the year of his love affair with a nurse, as a "rather quiet time in Merton's life." In Furlong's fully documented account of the sometimes sharp, confrontational series of letters between Merton and theologian Rosemary Ruether, there is a strong sense of Merton's renewed loyalty to his monastic vocation. With her touching final comment that at Polonnaruwa, where he experienced his own "inner clarity" exploding from the statues of the Buddhas, his life had become a "perfect circle," we get a final demonstration of Furlong's conviction that his life had indeed been victorious.

MOTT, an Anglican poet and novelist, became Merton's official biographer in 1978 when John Howard Griffin, who had been appointed to the position upon Merton's untimely death in 1968, became too ill to continue. Mott never met Thomas Merton; thus his biography attains a degree of distance from its subject. Neither does it appear that Mott traveled within the extremely wide literary and religious circles established around the contemplative monk. Yet Mott's nearly 700-page study compensates for this lack of personal acquaintance with the subject by access to Merton's many volumes of journals, including those restricted for a 25-year period after his death. Mott has also made use of Merton's letters—to roughly 1800 correspondents—held at the Thomas Merton Studies Center at Bellarmine College, Louisville, Kentucky. In addition, he has conducted interviews with monks who studied under Merton as Novice Master and with publishers of Merton's more than 50 books, including James Laughlin and Robert Giroux. Mott's thoroughness in tracking down the innumerable sources necessary in compiling the research for this biography is commendable.

The result is a study replete with journalistic detail of such a sensory nature that one can come away from it able to reconstruct whole scenes of Merton's life. The book is written in what the *New York Times Book Review* calls "clear, unpretentious and vigorous prose" (23 December 1984). Its seven chapters are ambitiously, if sometimes contrivedly, structured to represent seven mountains in Merton's geographical and spiritual journey, three from his childhood, three from his American and monastic experience, and the last from his Asian journey. Thus, he continues to employ the metaphor Merton himself used in the autobiography of the seven mountains of purgatory. Mott sees Merton as writing not only a continuous autobiography throughout his works but also as being an anti-autobiographer, and thus his study of the life especially captures the sense of irony and humor so present in Merton's character. He admits to the difficulty of writing about such an exceedingly complex man, often letting Merton interpret himself. He moves gently but thoroughly over the details of Merton's love affair, the most shocking episode to emerge from this biography and from his exclusive reading of the restricted journals. He concludes generously that by it Merton was changed forever, never again talking "of his inability to love and be loved."

From Mott's biography, we get the impression of a spirituality fully integrated into the events and relationships of Merton's life. This impression may, however, be the result of Mott's literary orientation, which gives this biography a tendency to emphasize the poetry and literary relationships at the expense of Merton's enormous corpus of works on spirituality. This tendency may have given rise to Donald Grayston's judgment that

"the biography which takes with full seriousness Merton's achievement as a spiritual theologian remains to be written" (*Christian Century*, 10 April 1985). Still, with its profusion of detail and judicious use of sources, Mott's biography fleshes in an important side of Merton the man and will probably remain the definitive biography for a long time to come.

—Maria R. Lichtmann

METTERNICH, Klemens Wenzel Nepomuk Lothar, 1773–1859; Austrian statesman.

Auernheimer, Raoul, *Prince Metternich, Stateman and Lover.* New York, Alliance Book Corporation, 1940.

Bertier de Sauvigny, Guillaume de, *Metternich and His Times*, translated by Peter Ryde. London, Darton Longman, 1962 (originally published by Hachette, Paris, 1959).

Cartland, Barbara, *Metternich, the Passionate Diplomat.* London, Hutchinson, 1964.

Cecil, Algernon, *Metternich 1773–1859: A Study of His Period and His Personality.* London, Eyre and Spottiswoode, and New York, Macmillan, 1933.

De Reichenberg, Frederick, *Prince Metternich in Love and War.* London, M. Secker, 1938.

Du Coudray, Helene, *Metternich.* London, Cape, 1935; New Haven, Connecticut, Yale University Press, 1936.

Grunwald, Constantin de, *Metternich*, translated by Dorothy Todd. London, Falcon Press, 1953 (originally published as *La Vie de Metternich*, Paris, Calmann-Lévy, 1938).

Herman, Arthur, *Metternich.* London, Allen and Unwin, and New York, Century, 1932.

Malleson, George Bruce, *The Life of Prince Metternich.* London, W. H. Allen, and Philadelphia, Lippincott, 1888.

Milne, Andrew, *Metternich.* London, University of London Press, and Totowa, New Jersey, Rowman and Littlefield, 1975.

Palmer, Alan Warwick, *Metternich.* London, Weidenfeld and Nicolson, and New York, Harper, 1972.

Sandemann, George Amelius Crawshay, *Metternich.* London, Methuen, and New York, Brentano, 1911.

Von der Heide, John T., *Klemens von Metternich.* New York, Chelsea House, 1988.

*

The publication of Metternich's memoirs in the early 1880s (*Memoirs of Prince Metternich*, 5 vols., 1880–82) began the detailed investigation of his life. This collection of autobiographical notes, documents, and letters was released under the supervision of Metternich's son Richard and the archivist and historian Alfons von Klinkowström. All subsequent biographies are to some extent based on this collection. Not long after its appearance in Austria, parts of these memoirs dealing with the period up to 1835 were translated into English by Mrs. Alexander Napier. This edition is unfortunately incomplete and marred by poor translation.

MALLESON, a British military historian specializing in the history of India who also wrote on central European topics, published his work a few years after the appearance of the memoirs. This work followed closely the interpretation of Metternich as a reactionary suppressor of nationalistic aspirations. The outline of this interpretation had been laid down in the work of the influential German historian Treitschke. In 1911 SANDEMANN, another English historian, produced a more balanced treatment that is however based on relatively little archival material.

Interest in Metternich and his thought after the dissolution of the old European diplomatic system and the Austro-Hungarian Empire after World War I resulted in a spate of biographies. Metternich was seen as the leading force in a stable international system based on universal values, something for which many at that time were searching.

Heinrich Srbik's three-volume study, *Metternich, der Staatsmann und der Mensch* (Munich, 1925–54), remains the standard biography. Srbik placed Metternich in his intellectual and political context. He created the picture of a conservative statesman trying to sustain Austria's position in Europe and following a coherent theoretical program while doing so. Based primarily on published sources, Srbik's work offered a fundamentally new picture of Metternich that contrasted sharply with earlier views of the man. This new picture produced a number of responses from biographers writing in English.

Cecil, Herman, and Du Coudray all reflected and popularized Srbik's theses. CECIL, an English nobleman, concentrated on the European nature of Metternich's thought, neglecting to a large degree the Austrian domestic situation. Cecil wrote in the preface that the work is "a study by an Englishman of this old friend of England." His work is a compact study of Metternich as an internationalist.

Srbik lambasted HERMAN on a number of occasions for writing an abridged, popularized version of his work without properly acknowledging it. This judgement has been sustained by others. Herman's work is a popularization of Srbik's views written in an awkward style and providing next to no academic apparatus.

DU COUDRAY's work is in many ways also simply an English popularization of Srbik's ideas, but it is better written. The author, like Cecil and Herman, tended to heroize Metternich. She sees the crucial point of his career not in his fight against Napoleon, but in his later attempts to erect a new European system.

The Baltic emigré GRUNWALD wrote perhaps the best work of the inter-war period that has appeared in English. It is based to a large extent on original archival research, especially in the Metternich family archives (now in Prague), contains a useful bibliography, and offers a view of Metternich as seigneur.

After the war, BERTIER DE SAVIGNY, a French international relations specialist, produced a compilation of Metternich's thoughts that provides many previously unpublished documents and a very favorable view of Metternich's intentions. The English edition adds material not available in the original French version. The brief study by MILNE can be seen as a partial antidote to the tendency to discuss Metternich in a positive light. Only covering part of Metternich's life, this short essay (189 pages) echoes on many points the traditional Liberal or nationalistic criticisms of Metternich as out of touch with his time.

Instead of stressing the period after the Congress of Vienna like many of the authors of the 1930s who were interested in the cosmopolitan nature of Metternich's "system" and thought, PALMER emphasizes the importance of the French Revolution and the early period of Metternich's career. Palmer's work is a complete, studied survey of the literature on Metternich. Research for the book included some archival work with the immense amount of primary sources left to us by Prince Metternich. This book is probably the definitive one-volume English biography of the Austrian statesman.

Many books have been written that concentrate on Metternich's relations with women. Those by AUERNHEIMER, CARTLAND, and DE REICHENBERG sensationalize the subject and make few pretensions that they wish to handle the topic objectively or for the purpose of understanding Metternich's actions and mentality. Auernheimer's book is interesting more for the fact that the author was imprisoned in a concentration camp and could only publish his work in exile after his release. It first appeared in Austria after the war.

Metternich's relations with women and his use of them in diplomacy (one need only think of Marie Louise, the Habsburg princess who became Napoleon's Empress of the French, and Leopoldine, her sister, who Metternich sent to become Empress of Brazil) are indeed important subjects for serious historical research. Egon Caesar Corti in his *Metternich und die Frauen* (2 vols., 1948–49), has sketched out some of the ways this could be done.

VON DER HEIDE's brief, well-illustrated book is well suited to the task of introducing young adults to many of the important themes touched on in the literature on Metternich. Emphasizing the years of the French Revolutionary and Napoleonic wars, this work deals in a clear manner with the foreign policy issues facing the Austrian statesman.

—Joseph F. Patrouch

MICHELANGELO [Michelangelo Buonarroti], 1475–1564; Italian sculptor, painter, architect, and poet.

Allen, Agnes, *The Story of Michelangelo*. London, Faber, 1953.

Brandes, Georg, *Michelangelo: His Life, His Times, His Era*, translated by Heinz Norden. London, Constable, and New York, Ungar, 1963.

Condivi, Ascanio, "Life of Michelangelo," in *Michelangelo: Life, Letters, and Poetry*, translated by George Bull. Oxford and New York, Oxford University Press, 1987 (originally published as *Vita di Michelangiolo Buonarroti*, Rome, 1553).

De Tolnay, Charles, *Michelangelo* (5 vols.). Princeton, New Jersey, Princeton University Press, 1943–60.

Duppa, R., *Life of Michel Angelo Buonarroti*. London, J. Murray, 1806.

Einem, Herbert von, *Michelangelo*, translated by Ronald Taylor. London, Methuen, 1973 (originally published by Kohlhammer, Stuttgart, 1959).

Finlayson, Donald Lord, *Michelangelo the Man*. New York, T. Y. Crowell, 1935.

Gower, Lord Ronald Sutherland, *Michael Angelo Buonarroti*. London, G. Bell, 1903.

Grimm, Herman, *Life of Michelangelo*, translated by F. E. Bunnett (2 vols.), Boston, Little Brown, 1865; 5th edition, Boston, Little Brown, and London, Dent, 1896 (originally published as *Leben Michelangelos*, 2 vols., Hanover, 1860–63).

Harford, John, *The Life of Michael Angelo Buonarroti*. London, Longman, 1857; revised edition, 1858.

Hibbard, Howard, *Michelangelo*. New York, Harper, 1974; London, A. Lane, 1975.

Holroyd, Charles, *Michael Angelo Buonarroti*. London, Duckworth, 1903.

Leites, Nathan, *Art and Life: Aspects of Michelangelo*. New York and London, New York University Press, 1986.

Liebert, Robert, *Michelangelo: A Psychoanalytic Study of His Life and Images*. New Haven, Connecticut, and London, Yale University Press, 1983.

Morgan, Charles H., *The Life of Michelangelo*. London, Weidenfeld and Nicolson, and New York, Reynal, 1960.

Murray, Linda, *Michelangelo, His Life, Work, and Times*. London, Thames and Hudson, 1984.

Nardini, Bruno, *Michelangelo: His Life and Works*, translated by Isabel Quigly. London, Collins, 1977 (originally published as *Incontro con Michelangelo*, Florence, Giunti, 1972).

Ripley, Elizabeth, *Michelangelo*. New York, Oxford University Press, 1953.

Rizzatti, Maria Luisa, *The Life and Times of Michelangelo*, translated by C. J. Richards. Philadelphia, Curtis, 1967; London, Hamlyn, 1968 (originally published as *Michelangelo*, Milan, Mondadori, 1965).

Rolland, Romain, *The Life of Michel Angelo*, translated by Fredric Lees. London, Heinemann, and New York, Dutton, 1912 (originally published as *Vie de Michel-Ange*, Paris, Hachette, 1907).

Salvini, Roberto, *The Hidden Michelangelo*, translated by Catherine Atthill. Chicago, Rand McNally, 1976; Oxford, Phaidon Press, 1978 (originally published as *Michelangelo*, Milan, Mondadori, 1976).

Saponaro, Michele, *Michelangelo*, translated by C. S. Richards. New York, Pellegrini and Cudahy, 1950; London, P. Owen, 1951 (originally published by Garzanti, Milan, 1947).

Schott, Rudolf, *Michelangelo*, translated by Constance McNab. London, Thames and Hudson, and New York, Tudor, 1963.

Stone, Irving, *The Agony and the Ecstasy*. New York, Doubleday, and London, Collins, 1961.

Strutt, Edward C., *Michelangelo*. London, G. Bell, 1904.

Symonds, John Addington, *The Life of Michelangelo Buonarroti* (2 vols.). London, J. Nimmo, and New York, Scribner, 1893.

Vasari, Giorgio, *Lives of the Artists*, translated by George Bull (2 vols.). London and New York, Penguin, 1965 (originally published as *Le Vite de piu eccellenti architetti, pittori, et scultori italiani*, Florence, 1550, 1568).

Wilson, Charles, *Life and Works of Michelangelo Buonarroti*. London, J. Murray, 1876; 2nd edition, 1881.

*

More has been written about Michelangelo than about any other artist, perhaps due to the exceptional volume of surviving documentation for an artist of this period. Biographical study is aided by a considerable number of letters in the artist's hand, his poetry, and other letters written to him. There are also three contemporary biographies of Michelangelo, two of which are by VASARI. Michelangelo is the only living artist to have been included in the first (1550) edition of Vasari's "Lives," where he is seen as the peak of artistic achievement. In the second edition (1568), which includes the lives of many more contemporary artists, this position remains undisputed. Although he is invaluable as a chronicler of Michelangelo, Vasari must be read with caution and the propogandist element of his writings must be taken into account. The commemoration of the role in artistic patronage played by Vasari's Medici employers is very much part of the author's intention, and this can lead to some distortion of the truth. The reasons given by Vasari for Michelangelo's departure from Rome in 1506 are quite different from those to be found in Michelangelo's letters and in the writings of his second biographer, Condivi: the correspondence shows the Medici Pope in a considerably less complimentary light.

CONDIVI, a pupil of Michelangelo, was urged to write a biography of his master in answer to Vasari's 1550 publication. Says Condivi, "some . . . on the one hand have said things about him that never happened, and on the other have left out many of those most worthy of being recorded." Condivi's work is no literary masterpiece and is both subjective and biased in Michelangelo's favour. Since it in fact amounts to autobiography, the artist being alive and well into his seventies, this is hardly surprising. In this respect, it is most valuable as an insight into what Michelangelo himself viewed as the high points and low points in his artistic career. Vasari's second edition takes this "Life" by Condivi (1553) as its starting point, including details of the artist's interests, appearance, and health as well as those of his creative production. Condivi's work first appeared in its entirety in an English translation in HOLROYD's 1903 volume.

Biographers before the 1870s, when the Buonarroti archives were finally made available for study in their entirety, faced the vexing problem of attempting to reconstruct Michelangelo's life from Vasari and Condivi and a much smaller selection of letters and poems. DUPPA attempts such a synthesis of the information available to him, including his own opinions of Michelangelo's works. Doubtful attributions and the as yet unobtained archival material make this book very out of date. Also unknown until 1863 was the fact that many of Michelangelo's sonnets were written to young men as opposed to women. In 1623, when the poetry was first published by Michelangelo's great-nephew, certain amendments to the texts were made in order that misunderstandings of Michelangelo's neo-platonic concepts of love should not be made. Consequently, HARFORD's *Life*, which discusses the poetry at some length, has also been rendered invalid. GRIMM, writing in 1865, benefits from the first of these discoveries yet seems unwilling to take issue with the findings. While he is right to question Vasari's accuracy, his distaste for this early biographer often leads him to digress, indeed digression in a historical vein often obscures Grimm's narrative.

WILSON was the first English writer to examine the newly available documents from the Buonarroti archives. Basing his account of Michelangelo's life on the Italian Aurelio Gotti's findings, as well as on his own observations of the archival material, Wilson provides a full account. The detail does, however, become laborious, and Victorian prejudices are allowed to colour the narrative without adequate consideration of Renaissance values. Of Pope Julius II's tomb, Wilson says, "Monuments of this class now remaining are regarded rather with pity and distaste than with any other feeling, hiding, as they often do, real merit or commemorating incapacity under forms of foolish allegory." In this book homosexual implications are not discussed, while Vittoria Colonna is viewed almost as a Pre-Raphaelite muse ("on her death he lost all control of himself"). Michelangelo is very much made to conform to the "great and good" Victorian ideal.

The authoritative work by SYMONDS was long held to be the standard biography of Michelangelo. Symonds' aim was to give an account of Michelangelo's life and works, concentrating on his personality without digression into history and comparative artistic theory. This object is achieved in a thorough and businesslike fashion, with few of Wilson's Victorian intrusions, in an attempt to come as close to the truth as possible through examination of the documentary evidence. Aside from painting, sculpture, architecture, and poetry, Symonds addresses the question of Michelangelo's sexuality with no qualms, although he is careful in introducing the subject to his readers. While this work remains important, it is now largely outdated by advances in the study of Michelangelo.

No author really challenged Symonds for half a century. In the intervening period a somewhat unreliable succession of biographies appeared, starting with GOWER's contribution to the "Great Masters in Painting and Sculpture" series. Gower's judgements are traditional and his tendency to generalise is irksome even in the context of a book intended for general readership. Gower forgets the Pope Julius II tomb (which as we see in Condivi was so important to Michelangelo), after only a few pages, without proper consideration: "Gladly does one dismiss this sepulchre of Pope Julius and all the trouble it caused its great creator." STRUTT, in a small book on Michelangelo, has no space for historical depth, and background tends to confuse fact and anecdote. ROLLAND provides his readers with a melodramatic account, peppered with exclamation marks, of Michelangelo's life. For him Michelangelo represented a "poignant contradiction between an heroic genius and a will which was not heroic, between imperious passions and a will which willed not." The modern reader, accustomed to less flamboyant modes of expression, may find it difficult to take this biography seriously. However, Rolland's use of source material is more intelligent than might appear at first glance, and his book certainly makes entertaining reading. This is more than can be said for FINLAYSON's book, which fails to realise its aim to uncover the fundamental *man* in Michelangelo. "The subjective approach is helpful, but dangerous," he proclaims. His alternative approach is to quote extensively from the documents. However, he uses these indiscriminately and makes no observation on their context. The result is not satisfactory.

BRANDES provides a biography whose "critical judgements and insights remain valid," according to the note written by his translator 42 years after the book originally appeared. Sweeping statements and a tendency toward the pedantic hamper what is otherwise the only really informative biography from the years before the publication of DE TOLNAY's extensive five-volume work. This covers considerably more ground than the strict biography as it investigates documents (which are here published) and includes a critical catalogue of works as well as a list of lost

works and false attributions. Tolnay's biographical input is based first in Michelangelo's letters and poems and second on the work of contemporary biographers (Vasari and Condivi). Tolnay's book, direct and not at all anecdotal, is very much intended for the scholar as opposed to the general reader. However, while it is an important academic achievement and provides a most comprehensive survey of Michelangelo, it tackles certain areas without inspiration and fails to question such important issues as the enigmatic Medici sculpture garden: who really taught Michelangelo the mechanics of sculpture?

Several biographies of considerably less depth follow in the 1950s and 60s. SAPONARO seems to want to equate Michelangelo with Christ. He is "a man who has seen God" among other things, and it is difficult to evaluate Saponaro's intentions here. Both ALLEN and RIPLEY write for the younger reader. MORGAN makes some exaggerated claims for Michelangelo—"he was perhaps the best educated man of his times"—in his appraisal of the artist as the ideal Renaissance "uomo universal." However, Morgan's historical background and grasp of contemporary events and personalities are masterful. SCHOTT on the other hand prefers to ignore circumstance: "It is probably correct to assume that external happenings meant little to [Michelangelo]; feeling, thought, achievement and meditation were more real to him than most of the actual events of his life." Contradictions confuse this attempt at "detailed analysis of Michelangelo's inner vision." RIZZATTI provides a brief biographical sketch in what is predominantly a life of Michelangelo in pictures. The result is a good visual biography.

One of the more scholarly biographies of Michelangelo in recent years is by von EINEM. This work assumes considerable knowledge in an attempt to "absorb the modern view of the role of criticism into a biographical work in the old sense." The book (written in 1959 and revised and updated in 1973) looks at the point of origin of each commission in order to try to understand it fully while at the same time examining the true relationship between the execution of the commission and the manifestation of Michelangelo's creativity. The details in this biography are carefully researched and included in footnotes where they would otherwise spoil the flow of what is a stimulating and absorbing work that is not afraid to ask questions.

HIBBARD provides a basic, accessible overview of the artist and his achievement for the general reader who requires a balanced and reliable account. NARDINI is anecdotal and lacking in depth, using sources indiscriminately without reference. SALVINI's biography centres on conflict and morality in Michelangelo. Unfortunately, his approach is subjective and his answers do not seem to be based on logical assimilation of the documentary evidence.

Both LIEBERT and LEITES adopt a psychoanalytical approach to Michelangelo and his work. Leites is not strictly biographical, his work forming part of the Psychoanalytic Crosscurrents series. Liebert's aims are to reveal Michelangelo's inner life and to evaluate the contribution of psychoanalytic study to the understanding of artistic images as a complement to the research of the art historian. The result is an interesting exploration of the choices Michelangelo makes in his work based on the realisation that a valid study of Michelangelo in these terms must be founded on the direct evidence of his writings and his drawings.

MURRAY's book is the most recent attempt at a documentary biography, taking into account contemporary politics and society. Her book is well balanced and sensible and makes extensive use of quotations. This book is also most stimulating visually, with full page illustrations augmented by margin sketches. Finally, no survey of biographies of Michelangelo would be complete without mentioning STONE's biographical novel, *The Agony and the Ecstasy*. Although his imaginative reconstruction of events and dialogue does rely heavily on artistic license, the book is based on fact and makes very entertaining reading.

—Alison Leslie

———————

MIES VAN DER ROHE, Ludwig, 1886–1969; German-born American architect.

Blake, Peter, *The Master Builders: le Corbusier, Mies van der Rohe, Frank Lloyd Wright*. New York, Norton, 1976.

Carter, Peter, *Mies van der Rohe at Work*. New York, Praeger, and London, Pall Mall, 1974.

Drexler, Arthur, *Ludwig Mies van der Rohe*. New York, Braziller, and London, Mayflower, 1960.

Hilberseimer, Ludwig, *Mies van der Rohe*. Chicago, P. Theobald, 1956.

Hochman, Elaine S., *Architects of Fortune: Mies van der Rohe and the Third Reich*. New York, Weidenfeld and Nicolson, and London, Fourth Estate, 1989.

Johnson, Philip C., *Mies van der Rohe*. New York, Museum of Modern Art, 1947.

Schulze, Franz, *Mies van der Rohe: A Critical Biography*. Chicago and London, University of Chicago Press, 1985.

Spaeth, David, *Mies van der Rohe*. New York, Rizzoli, and London, Architectural Press, 1985.

Tegethoff, Wolf, *Mies van der Rohe: The Villas and Country Houses*, translated by Russell M. Stockman, edited by William Dyckes. New York, Museum of Modern Art, 1985.

Zukowsky, John, editor, *Mies Reconsidered: His Career, Legacy, and Disciplines*. Chicago, Art Institute, and New York, Rizzoli, 1986.

*

DREXLER's relatively early work on Ludwig Mies van der Rohe is one of the weaker volumes in the "Masters" series. Its illustrations are lackluster, but its true failing is that the author utterly underestimates Mies van der Rohe's significance, both in terms of his work and of his influence on architecture as a whole. Part of a wave of anti-Mies van der Rohe sentiment prevalent at the time, Drexler's book fails to place the architect in the realm that the series title promises and is of dubious value as a biography.

JOHNSON's work is very heavily oriented toward Mies van der Rohe's work. The smattering of biographical material is incomplete and only echoes that which is found in similar works. The HILBERSEIMER book is not biographical in nature, either, but is worthwhile for its illustrations and for its critical interpretations of Mies van der Rohe's work. BLAKE's volume gives a

good, brief history of Mies van der Rohe's career. The work succeeds in its limited space in giving a readable account of the social forces behind, and those resulting from, the architect's work.

Mies van der Rohe's centennial year (1986) sparked renewed interest in the architect. During this period, the three most successful and useful biographical works appeared. Taken together, they serve as useful reassessments of the architect's career and contributions to modern architecture.

SCHULZE published the first complete, full-length biography on Mies van de Rohe. In most aspects, the work is conservative and does not seek to create or change any particular image of the architect. Schulze chronicles Mies van der Rohe in terms of the four commonly recognized, distinct phases of his career. Schulze also relies heavily on the efforts of previous authors for an interpretation of Mies van der Rohe's various buildings, to the degree that the quality of his effort is a reflection of the varying quality of the resources used. The major contribution of Schulze's book is its investigation of events and desires in the architect's life that were manifested in his work. For this and other reasons, it is not only the first but the most complete biography yet of Mies van der Rohe. While Schulze gives peripheral treatment to a few projects that demand more attention and in other places simply fails to make an important connection, overall his effort must be commended. Schulze's tone and style are neutral and objective, which sets this book apart from most previous efforts.

TEGETHOFF's work, often reviewed with or compared to the Schulze book since they were published in the same year, is really a different sort of effort. Tegethoff is rather blatant in his adoration of the architect. His book, not a complete chronicle of Mies van der Rohe's life, addresses particular aspects of the architect's career and attempts to define the nature of the work rather than the nature of the man. In this, it is not wholly convincing, nor is the book light reading. There are many illustrations, but for the most part they are poorly placed at the end of the book. CARTER's book is a somewhat older effort that is similar in nature, though less hagiographical and easier to read.

SPAETH's interest in Mies van der Rohe predates the centennial period. His bibliography, *Ludwig Mies van der Rohe: An Annotated Bibliography* (1979), contains more than 700 entries citing monographs, periodical articles, and other items. While not in itself a biography, the work is indispensable as a research tool. Spaeth's 1985 book is outstanding in its portrayal of Mies van der Rohe's career. Because Spaeth studied under Mies van der Rohe, the book might seem to be something of a reaction to the movement against Mies van der Rohe after his death, though this is not the case. As with his earlier biography, Spaeth manages to give an objective account of the architect's life and career. Profusely illustrated, Spaeth's book is well balanced and recommended for introductory or advanced reading.

ZUKOWSKY's volume of essays, dating from the same period, is of value since it contains some important biographical materials presented by competent and authoritative writers, the most notable contribution coming from Spaeth. The work contains information regarding Mies van der Rohe's youth. Perhaps most attractive to educators and architects, this book will be worthwhile for the lay reader as well.

HOCHMAN's recent book is a very interesting, well-documented history of Mies van der Rohe's struggle with Hitler and the Third Reich. Essentially a period piece, it contains enough biographical material to warrant attention.

For the average reader, Schulze is the starting place for readings on Mies van der Rohe's life. For a more balanced treatment of the man and his architecture, Spaeth is recommended, with Tegethoff as a supplement.

—Lawrence M. Enoch

MILL, John Stuart, 1806–1873; English philosopher and economist.

Bain, Alexander, *John Stuart Mill: A Criticism with Personal Recollections.* London, Longman, and New York, Holt, 1882.

Borchard, Ruth, *John Stuart Mill, the Man.* London, Watts, 1957.

Courtney, W. L., *Life of John Stuart Mill.* London, W. Scott, and New York, F. Whittaker, 1889.

Ellery, John B., *John Stuart Mill.* New York, Twayne, 1964.

Glassman, Peter, *J. S. Mill: The Evolution of a Genius.* Gainesville, University of Florida Press, 1985.

Hayek, F. A., *John Stuart Mill and Harriet Taylor.* Chicago, University of Chicago Press, and London, Routledge, 1951.

Kamm, Josephine, *John Stuart Mill in Love.* London, Gordon and Cremonesi, 1977.

Mazlish, Bruce, *James and John Stuart Mill: Father and Son in the 19th Century.* New York, Basic Books, and London, Hutchinson, 1975.

Packe, Michael St. John, *The Life of John Stuart Mill.* New York, Macmillan, and London, Secker and Warburg, 1954.

Pappe, H. O., *John Stuart Mill and the Harriet Taylor Myth.* London, Cambridge University Press, and Parkville, Melbourne University Press, 1960.

Spencer, Herbert, et al, *John Stuart Mill: His Life and Works.* New York, Holt, 1873.

Stillinger, Jack, editor, *The Early Draft of John Stuart Mill's Autobiography.* Urbana, University of Illinois Press, 1961.

*

In 1873, a year after Mill's death, his *Autobiography* was published. Though he was a prolific writer, most of Mill's other works do not currently command a wide readership. Mill's *Autobiography*, however, has retained its popularity through several editions to the present day. The original 1873 edition was taken from a transcript copied by Mill's stepdaughter Helen Taylor and others. With the subsequent discovery of a final draft of the *Autobiography* in Mill's own hand, some later editions (such as that edited by Jack Stillinger, Boston, Houghton Mifflin, 1969) have drawn upon that manuscript in reissuing the work. The differences between these two versions are minor. More substantive differences exist between these versions and an earlier draft rediscovered in 1959. The early draft, written nearly 20 years before Mill's death, includes the editorial suggestions of Mill's wife Harriet. Thus one can compare not only this early draft with the final version, but different versions of the early draft, allowing for Harriet's influence.

The *Autobiography* focuses mainly on Mill's early life, with less than a third of the text devoted to the last half of his life. Mill's purpose in writing this work, argues Alan Ryan, was to make a public document of his views on the upbringing to which he was subjected. It was not his intention to provide a detailed factual account of his private life. Mill, referred to as "the manufactured man" by his contemporaries for the intensive educational regime with which his father, Benthamite James Mill, molded him intellectually, wrote what Thomas Carlyle called the "autobiography of a steam engine": without self-revelation and without passion. Indeed, a comparison of the early and final drafts shows that Mill deleted or softened some of the more revealing, harsher comments, particularly concerning his family.

Within weeks of Mill's death, Herbert SPENCER, Henry Fawcett and others published a memorial volume of 12 brief sketches depicting various aspects of Mill's personal and professional life. This was followed in 1882 with a biographical work by Alexander BAIN. Bain, a longtime friend of Mill's, also published a biography of James Mill in the same year. However, Bain's work on John Stuart Mill was not intended as a complete biography. It is instead an examination of Mill's "character and writings" based upon Bain's personal recollections. Bain reinforces the image of Mill as the saint of rationalism, open-minded but austere. Bain's account of Mill's platonic relationship with Harriet Taylor from their first meeting until their marriage two decades later is accompanied by the comment that Mill was "below average" in the "so-called sensual feelings" with "no difficulty controlling the sexual appetite." Mill's work was certainly influenced by Harriet, but her influence was not the result of sexual captivation. While Bain dismisses the description of Harriet's intellectual contributions given in the *Autobiography* as hyperbole, he admits that Harriet often played the role of catalyst in stimulating Mill's writing.

The *Autobiography*, Bain's works, and the recently published reminiscences of Mill's contemporaries (particularly those of Caroline Fox) served as the basis of COURTNEY's 1888 biography. Bain's interpretation of Harriet's impact on Mill is reiterated, though Mill's relationship is seen essentially as an "infatuation" with a "clever woman." On the whole, Courtney's work does little to improve on the earlier biographical images of Mill.

In the 1890s, Mill's correspondence with d'Eichtal and Comte appeared, followed in 1910 by Hugh Elliot's two-volume edition of other correspondence. Additional information on Mill's private life became available in the 1920s when, with the death of Mill's niece, a collection of his papers and letters were put up for auction. Little use was made of these new sources until HAYEK's study appeared in 1951. In Hayek's view, the new material contradicted the prevailing opinion of Bain and others that Harriet's contributions to Mill's writings were relatively minor. On the contrary, Mill's description in the *Autobiography* of Harriet's influence was accurate. The Hayek work is more an annotated collection of letters than a biography, intended by Hayek to "fill a gap" until the definitive biography was written.

PACKE's definitive biography appeared in 1954, with an introduction by Hayek. Packe's comprehensive command of the biographical raw materials provides the first multi-dimensional view of Mill the scholar and the man. As Robbins has noted, the book's readability is artificially enhanced to some degree by the artistic license Packe invoked to give color to otherwise colorless facts. Moreover, given the documentation, it is difficult at times to discern where fact stops and speculation begins. Despite this and other minor difficulties, the Packe biography remains the standard work on Mill.

BORCHARD's brief biography continues in the tradition established by Hayek and Packe, emphasizing Harriet's role in Mill's work. Borchard, who assisted Hayek in his research on Mill, provides an accessible if somewhat romantic introduction to Mill's life. An equally brief introductory account is also provided by ELLERY, who does not subscribe to the Hayek view on Harriet's influence.

The controversy surrounding Harriet's influence is continued in PAPPE's short essay characterizing the Hayek interpretation as a myth. Using the same sources as Hayek, Pappe makes the case that "Mill without Harriet would still have been Mill." Using the early draft of the *Autobiography*, STILLINGER bolsters Pappe's position, noting that while Harriet displayed style and a sense of propriety in altering Mill's work, there is nothing in those alterations to justify Mill's description of her intellectual powers.

The issue is examined once again in KAMM's work. Kamm argues that Mill's attitude toward Harriet and other women was rooted in his family life. Feeling his mother to be intellectually inferior, Mill searched for female alternatives to provide the intellectual atmosphere which his mother was unable to create either for Mill or his father. Kamm identifies a series of dominant women in Mill's life, the two foremost, of course, being Harriet and her daughter Helen. Those women, in turn, shaped Mill's basic opinions on women's rights and other related issues. While the focus of Kamm's study is innovative, most of the evidence marshalled in support of the central thesis is familiar from earlier biographies.

The Mazlish and Glassman works are psychoanalytic efforts. MAZLISH argues that generational conflict in the 19th century was at least equal in importance to class conflict in effecting social change. His psycho-history takes the father-son relationship of James and John Stuart Mill as a case study in 19th-century generational conflict. Thus the Mills become the prototypic protagonists in the Victorian Oedipal conflict. GLASSMAN analyzes Mill's writings to show how they were used therapeutically to repair the psychological damage wrought by his father during childhood. Rather than remaining crippled from his grotesque childhood, Mill succeeded in rebuilding his sensibilities over the course of his life.

—Roger S. Hewett

MILLER, Arthur, 1915–   ; American playwright and essayist.

Carson, Neil, *Arthur Miller.* New York, Grove, and London, Macmillan, 1982.

Hayman, Ronald, *Arthur Miller.* New York, Ungar, 1972; 2nd edition, London, Heinemann, 1973.

Huftel, Sheila, *Arthur Miller: The Burning Glass.* New York, Citadel, and London, W. H. Allen, 1965.

Moss, Leonard, *Arthur Miller.* New York, Twayne, 1967.

Nelson, Benjamin, *Arthur Miller: Portrait of a Playwright.* New York, D. McKay, and London, P. Owen, 1970.

*

In the absence of a full biography, Arthur Miller's own *Timebends: A Life* (1987) serves to introduce the writer's personal background to readers of his work. It is, however, a fairly intellectual recapitulation of the facts, stylistically creative, very much a continuation of the writer's expression as well as a reliable sourcebook for future biographers. Miller's mother gave him the desire "to move on, to metamorphose," and his life is told here as a series of sea-changes, turnings both unpredictable and total. Miller avoids self-examination, preferring instead, like his photographer wife Inge Morath (to whom the autobiography is dedicated), to observe. He is gentle of Marilyn Monroe's memory, stern with the Commie-hunters, and justly proud of what the theatre world has done for his dramatic canon, modest in size by contrast with his contemporaries, but large in human sensibility. His acquaintance and more intimate familiarity with such persons as Elia Kazan, Orson Welles, Lee J. Cobb, and John Huston serve better to illuminate his associates than himself. Particularly valuable in filling in the chaotic years between *View from the Bridge* (1955) and *After the Fall* (1964), this autobiography is, as all good ones are, a full-length portrait of modern history.

Some other works touch on Miller's life, but no protracted biography presents itself. Despite NELSON's stated purpose to place the works in a biographical context, more that half of his book is play analysis. He sees Miller's work as influencing all American drama, and he examines the plays in the context of Miller's intellectual experiences. Some interesting and insightful anecdotes help delineate Miller's personality as it emerges from the Jewish community into the theatre world at large; particularly useful are details of Miller's early education, job experiences (leading to *Memory of Two Mondays*, for example), and prize-winning but unproduced early works. The production history of *All My Sons*, which won the New York Drama Critics' Circle Award over Eugene O'Neill's *The Iceman Cometh* in 1947, includes details of Miller's move to Connecticut in the wake of his new success; subsequent public biographical information, such as his marriage to Marilyn Monroe in 1956, only serves to fill out what is essential literary criticism.

CARSON follows Miller's dramaturgy through the canon as a continuing inquiry into "the problems raised by the coexistence of kindness and cruelty." Carson is better at providing early biographical information than at examining Miller's career after *Death of a Salesman*, at which point the book becomes theatrical overview. The opening chapter of HUFTEL is biographical, but the rest is criticism with a good portion of biographical material interspersed. Particularly valuable is the cast list of openings and important productions of every Miller play to date (*Incident at Vichy* is last). HAYMAN begins with an interview with Miller, but focuses on the relationship between productions and ideal realizations of Miller's canon. Hayman provides some information on writing habits, playwriting courses at Michigan, approaches to characterization, and even Miller's response to the "hippie" movement active at the time of the interview, but his work is not biographical in the private sense. The work includes a chronology, lists of stage productions, cast lists, bibliography, and index. The first chapter of MOSS ("The Man") and another on early works constitute all the biographical information here; the body of the study is protracted literary analysis, with alarmingly little attention to production.

—Thomas J. Taylor

MILLER, Henry, 1891–1980; American writer.

Brown, J. D., *Henry Miller*. New York, Unger, 1986.
Martin, Jay, *Always Merry and Bright: The Life of Henry Miller*. Santa Barbara, California, Capra Press, 1978; London, Sheldon Press, 1979.
Perlès, Alfred, *My Friend Henry Miller: An Intimate Biography*. London, Spearman, 1955; New York, J. Day, 1956.
Winslow, Kathryn, *Henry Miller: Full of Life*. Los Angeles, J. P. Tarcher, 1986.

*

PERLÈS' memoir was the first full-length biographical work to appear on Miller. Perlès (Carl in *Tropic of Cancer*) first met Miller in 1928. As Miller's boon companion in Paris throughout the 1930's, he was in a good position to report on Miller's activities at the time Miller was writing his most important works. The biography is particularly strong on providing intimate details and analyses of the relationships that existed between the people whom Miller was to transform into thinly veiled fictional characters. Perlès' style is anecdotal, full of overblown metaphors; his tone is nostalgic. While he can, at times, be critical of Miller—especially concerning his love life—he generally prostrates himself before the master's genius. The book, written many years after some of the incidents occurred, may miss a fact here or there, but it is highly successful in capturing the heady atmosphere of Miller's Paris years. Even though Perlès visited Miller in California while he was writing the biography, Miller's life there receives only passing attention. On the whole, Perlès' portrait is warm and affectionate and tends toward hero worship. It includes a bibliography of Miller's works.

MARTIN's book, published 24 years later, is the standard biography of Miller to date and probably will remain so for some time. Martin spoke with Miller himself but failed to convince him that such a biography was needed or desirable. Nevertheless, Miller did not stand in the way, and Martin had access to and interviewed many of Miller's friends and acquaintances. Distrusting the autobiographical details in Miller's work, Martin relies heavily on Miller's letters, diaries, early drafts, and unpublished works. His research sources include over 100,000 pages of manuscript material in over 23 libraries and private collections, including those at UCLA, the Huntington Library, the San Francisco Public Library, Brooklyn Public Library, New York Public Library, and many other university libraries. Martin is a meticulous scholar, and his biography is thoroughly documented. Yet Martin does more than just uncover facts and dates. He tries as much as possible to view the world through Miller's consciousness. His book, he says, "is parallel to Miller's life; it

exhibits the process of Miller's life." Instead of extracting Miller's life from his work, Martin clings "to the moment, the mundane trifle, rooms, streets, houses, and especially to all those instances of the tentative grasping toward self-understanding which would eventually lead to the creative work." He seeks to remain "as close as possible to the life as it was lived, and to catch Miller at the point just before his imagination buries his origins." In writing Miller's life, Martin recreates and celebrates it so that his account reads as smoothly as a novel. Martin's book is certainly the most balanced of all the Miller biographies, though, as one reviewer pointed out (*Choice*, April 1979), it is strongest in evoking the joys and nostalgia of Miller's Brooklyn boyhood. Like Perlès, Martin tries his hand at psychoanalysis. Whereas Perlès sees Miller as a masochist, however, Martin views him as the victim of a cold, dominating mother who rejected his need for love. Although this Freudian analysis underlies Martin's view of Miller's sexuality, it is not dwelt upon excessively. Martin's biography is reliable, well written, and richly detailed. Martin is certainly sympathetic to Miller as a man and an artist, but he is not blind to Miller's faults, both personal and literary. His work succeeds, to the extent that any biography can, in separating the life from the legend, in revealing the author behind his fictional persona. The work includes extensive notes and identifies valuable collections of primary source material.

WINSLOW first met Miller in 1944 when he came to live in Big Sur. She quickly became one of his disciples and, after moving to Chicago in 1948, she opened "M, The Studio for Henry Miller," where she sold Miller's books and watercolors for the next ten years. The biography is especially worthwhile in detailing Miller's California years, his growth as a water-colorist, and his involvement in various limited edition and small press publications. It is also strong on the censorship battles fought over Miller's work in the 1950s and 60s. Winslow depends on her diaries, notebooks, correspondence, and published interviews with Miller, and on mutual friends like Emil White and Bern Porter for much of her information. Many conversations are reported verbatim. While no doubt the sentiments they express are accurate, one questions the biographer's ability to recall such conversations word for word. Winslow also relies heavily on Miller's own work. As a result, especially in terms of Miller's earlier life, her biography reads like capsule summaries of *Black Spring*, *Tropic of Capricorn*, and *Tropic of Cancer*. Winslow provides a selected bibliography of primary and secondary sources.

BROWN's book is a good general introduction to Miller and his work and is especially suited to students seeking a brief overview. Brown's sources include earlier biographies, especially Perlès and Martin, and literary criticism. Almost half of the book concentrates on the Paris years, perhaps because Brown published an earlier essay on Miller in *American Writers in Paris 1920–1939* (*Dictionary of Literary Biography*, vol. 4, 1980). Brown places Miller in the tradition of American autobiography set by Benjamin Franklin, Henry Adams, and Walt Whitman. He skillfully weaves the facts of Miller's life with an exploration of the major literary themes of his work: life, love, death, freedom, and the puritan conscience. For Brown, Miller's "greatest achievements were as a surrealist, as a vernacular humorist, as a transcendentalist, and as an autobiographer. In these four respects,'' Brown concludes, ''Miller ranks with the best writers of this century.'' His volume includes a chronology and primary as well as secondary bibliography.

—William M. Gargan

MILTON, John, 1608–1674; English poet.

Hill, Christopher, *Milton and the English Revolution.* London, Faber, 1977; New York, Viking, 1978.

Masson, David, *The Life of John Milton* (7 vols.). London, Macmillan, 1859–94; revised edition, 1881–1896.

Parker, William Riley, *Milton: A Biography* (2 vols.). Oxford, Clarendon Press, 1968.

Pattison, Mark, *Milton.* London, Macmillan, and New York, Harper, 1879.

Saurat, Denis, *Milton, Man and Thinker.* London, Cape, 1924; New York, L. Macveagh/Dial Press, 1925.

Tillyard, E. M. W., *Milton.* London, Chatto and Windus, and New York, Barnes and Noble, 1930.

Wilson, A. N., *The Life of John Milton.* Oxford and New York, Oxford University Press, 1983.

*

Milton gave several accounts of himself, notably in *An Apology against a Pamphlet* and the *Defensio Secunda* in reply to detraction. These are admirably free from sneaking modesty and convey a lofty idea of his character. Drier and more anecdotal accounts were written after his death: a life by Edward Phillips, Milton's nephew, as well as an anonymous life and Aubrey's vivid, unreliable notes. As ''Miltonolatry'' grew in the 18th century, further information was gleaned from those who had known him, and the accumulated lore was worked into short lives and notices prefatory to editions of the works. The tendency was to idealize the harsh outlines of Milton's character, a tendency particularly marked in Richardson's life (1734). Against this hallowing of Milton's memory Johnson set his face. His *Life of Milton* (1799) interprets the evidence unfavourably to deliver a morose but wonderfully trenchant portrait, whose main feature is pride. Not all of Johnson's views can be discounted as bias. Later attempts, for example, to explain Milton's pamphleteering rarely see so clearly how self-disfiguring his insolence is.

When he wrote his biography, MASSON had the 19th-century discovery of many official records of Milton's stint as Latin Secretary to work into the accumulated materials. He did not, however, limit himself to a narrative of Milton's life, but aimed also at ''a continuous Political, Ecclesiastical and Literary history through Milton's whole time.'' His six large volumes contain some lumber. The literary history lacks critical edge. Masson's taste in poetry is secondhand Palgrave and his commentary on the poems is at best summaries of their contents. Some of the historical detail might have been spared. Nothing is gained from an account of the battle of Luncarty, included only because Thomas Young, Milton's tutor, hailed from those parts. But the

reader who has leisure to take in imaginatively Masson's magnificent compilation of facts will come away with a lively impression of the scene of Milton's life, from the enumeration of the furniture of a scrivener's office, from the list of the men at Cambridge in Milton's time, or from the vigorous narration of historical events, even remote ones such as Montrose's campaign. As for Milton's character, Masson's portrait has a Victorian appreciation of its idealism, a Victorian tact too that can imply the defects of such a character. And he has the imagination and fairness to be appalled when he discovers, as he thinks, that Milton must have conceived *The Doctrine and Discipline of Divorce* on his honeymoon. He has a breadth of outlook that gives him assurance in treating the world of men among other men and a vein of fancy that at least does not detract from his subject.

The length of Masson's biography is the excuse PATTISON claimed for his short one. He has no new facts, but he has new interpretations, among them that Mary Powell refused to consummate the marriage. His bracing observations include a list of Milton's botanical errors and the firm assurance that the *De Doctrina* is written without the ''average aquaintance of Christian antiquity which formed at that day the professional outfit of the episcopal divine.''

In the century before Parker's biography (see below) many interpretive lives appeared. Two stand out. SAURAT tries to replace the image of Milton the sour puritan with Milton the revolutionary, stresses the gaudy days that he used to enjoy as a bachelor and puts him in the company of pantheists, Cabbalists, and hermetics. His interpretation, like Johnson's, is that Milton's ruling passion was pride, only for Saurat pride is the source of Milton's moral beauty. He still has the power to make one think more seriously about Milton's creativity than most of those whose scholarship is less wild.

TILLYARD's *Milton* became a standby of those Milton studies that lived to resist the 20th century. He avoids anything so assertive as a general thesis, of course, but holds that *Paradise Lost* is the work of a revolutionary deeply disillusioned with human possibility. He asks some sensible questions but generally gives shallow answers. His critical commentary is most alive with Latin or minor poems rarely discussed.

Meanwhile academic research, especially in America, was sifting the evidence, correcting and even adding to the details from which a biography might be written. J. Milton French brought together the old material and the new in *The Life Records of John Milton* (1949–58), and Parker undertook the writing of the definitive academic biography.

PARKER's first volume tells the story of Milton's life, as Parker conceives it. His second, even longer, volumes consists of short essays for each chapter of volume I, discussing the case for the story he tells, these followed by notes that summarize and weigh the scholarship on points of detail. It includes a princely index. Appendix I lists Milton's publications, 1628–1700; Appendix II lists 17th-century editions of his works. Anyone wishing to study the facts of Milton's life and what scholars have made of them will find this volume indispensable. By relegating discussion of the evidence to this second volume, Parker can tell a much brisker tale than he could otherwise, as readers of Masson's leisurely unravellings of doubtful matters will appreciate.

Parker makes some bold departures from his predecessors. For instance, he has Milton write Sonnet XXIII, ("Methought I saw . . . ") for Mary Powell in 1653, not for Katherine Woodcock in 1658, and *Samson Agonistes* in 1647/48, not in the late 1660s. His reason for changing these and other traditional datings is "to challenge the spurious authority of mere repetition and to inspire the reconsideration of pertinent data." It is one thing, however, to challenge received opinion in scholarly journals, quite another to incorporate one's opinion, knowing it is no more than an opinion, in a biography. Parker, of course, admits that his conjectures are conjectures and sets out the uncertainties fairly in his separate volume of notes. But the impression in the narrative volume is too positive. The unwary reader might take Parker's "challenges" as facts; the scholar will think he is having his way without having won the argument. Parker's unorthodox dating of Sonnet XXIII, for example, is too easily assimilated to his view that Milton's reconciliation with Mary grew into a happy marriage. A more serious flaw is Parker's attitude to Milton. "Let me say at once that I like Milton as a person" sounds a sensible line to take. But Parker's liking makes his subject small. He fondles the young Milton, and one cannot feel that his bright, callow young man will become anything more than a learned, tolerably genial and opinionated professor of literature at a great Midwestern university. He deprecates Milton's brutality in controversy but does not allow us to see how astonishing his violence is. Though Parker's style is spry and direct, its vigour goes to defending rather than searching out the man. It palliates, softens, and diminishes. Nor does Parker's *Life* shed much light on the poetry, either indirectly by showing us the growth of a mind or directly in his sections of critical commentary. As a reliable source of information about Milton's life Parker's biography has triumphantly supplanted Masson's, but it has not been thought the last word where understanding of the man is concerned.

HILL also likes Milton. But his book, not so much a biography as, like Saurat's, an essay on the life and work of a revolutionary, argues for Milton's connection with the radical "third culture," whose part in the English Revolution Hill has made it his business to rescue from the disregard of historians and of Miltonists like Parker. His way is not to analyse closely, but rather to associate Milton with a cloud of libertarian witnesses. And still his extraordinarily sharp eye for radical traces in Milton's writing together with his command of the historical background make this openly political reshaping of the image of the man intellectually the most stimulating reading of the life at present.

WILSON's biography is a gentlemanly affair, with its interest in Jacobean church furnishings, aristocratic sodomy and the sheer beauty of Milton's early poems ("To have written such things must have been akin to receiving a divine visitation"). It rides on the back of others' scholarship, elegant, desultory, yet not negligible. Wilson has a novelist's knack of making human situations clear to himself, and so his scouting of the stories of Milton's rustication from Cambridge and of his daughters' having to read to him in languages they didn't understand carries weight. Perhaps too it is a novelist's gift to feel keenly with what is ridiculous or unlikeable about a character: speaking of Milton's vindication of his looks in the *Defensio Secunda*, he writes, "This sounds more like Sir Walter Eliot than some 'great

deliverer' from the Book of Judges. There is something, precisely because of that fact, poignant and moving about those public displays of private vanity." At any rate Wilson often writes with more insight, more genuine sympathy, than Milton's more solid biographers.

—David Reid

MIRABEAU, Honoré-Gabriel Riqueti, comte de, 1749–1791; French orator and revolutionary.

Barthou, Louis, *Mirabeau*. New York, Dodd Mead, and London, Heinemann, 1913.
Dumont, Étienne, *The Great Frenchman and the Little Genevese*, translated by Elizabeth Seymour. London, Duckworth, 1904 (originally published as *Souvenirs sur Mirabeau*, Paris, 1832).
Vallentin, Antonina, *Mirabeau*, translated by F. W. Dickes. New York, Viking, and London, Hamilton, 1948.
Warwick, Charles, *Mirabeau and the French Revolution*. Philadelphia, Lippincott, 1905; London, T. F. Unwin, 1909.
Welch, Oliver J., *Mirabeau: A Study of a Democratic Monarchist*. London, Cape, 1951; Port Washington, New York, Kennikat Press, 1968.

*

DUMONT's book is mainly a collection of notes on events and persons of the period, which Dumont intended to develop into a comprehensive historical work. Unfortunately this was a goal he never realized. As it stands, this "biography" is neither definitive nor complete. It does provide portraits of many revolutionaries including Sieyès and Talleyrand, as well as information concerning factions such as the Feuillants and Girondins. The book is concerned only with the years immediately preceding the French Revolution and the early years of the Revolution. Although a friend of Mirabeau, Dumont was more critical of the statesman than sympathetic. This criticism prompted Lucas de Montigny, son of Mirabeau, to produce his *Mémoires* (8 vols., 1834–35) to serve as a corrective to the image of Mirabeau presented by Dumont. The latter is a work of filial piety. Dumont's work received much attention when it was published. The eminent 19th-century British historian Macaulay described it in the following terms: "This is a very amusing and very instructive book; but even if it were less amusing and less instructive it would still be interesting as a relic of a wise and virtuous man. . . . Till now Mirabeau was to us . . . not a man, but a string of antitheses. Henceforth he will be a real human being" *Edinburgh Review* (July 1832).

WARWICK's book, intended as a series of lectures, is neither a sound biography nor a clear summary of the events of the French Revolution. It lacks a bibliography and footnotes, though here and there such sources as Mirabeau's newspapers and Dumont's work are quoted secondhand. There is too much polemic and personal impression and too little analysis. The Duc d'Orléans, for example, is described as "the wretched liar," while the Marquis de Mirabeau is called "the old ruffian" and "the conceited old pedant" without justification. Clearly, Warwick has not come to grips with his subject. As Fred Morrow Fling wrote in his review for the *American Historical Review* (October 1905), the book "has all the failings and qualities of the writings of the enthusiastic amateur. [Warwick] offers nothing that is new; the book is repetitive and the writing style is popular rather than scholarly."

BARTHOU, as a politician himself—he was prime minister of France—scrutinizes Mirabeau's political career. This is chiefly a biography of political principles. Half the book is devoted to the years before Mirabeau's election to the Estates-General. It cannot be regarded as a work of profound research, although Barthou does use primary material such as Mirabeau's personal letters and speeches. The original French does contain a complete bibliography, but regrettably the English translator has not bothered to reproduce it. Once again, footnotes are lacking. Barthou is best at describing Mirabeau as a statesman. This is a complete survey that is both candid and critical.

A journalist by training, VALLENTIN has written a popular biography that lacks continuity and balance. Over half the book deals with Mirabeau's pre-revolutionary career. The author fails to provide a clear account of Mirabeau's role in the French Revolution, the most significant aspect of his life. She goes into tremendous detail on family, love affairs, marriages, lawsuits, which could easily have been dealt with in half the space. The sensational rather than the serious aspects of Mirabeau's life are emphasized. A bibliography consisting of the standard sources of Mirabeau, including some primary material, is provided.

WELCH's biography is a clearly written life, times, and thought of Mirabeau. It is the most scholarly book to appear in the English language to date. In his Preface, Welch states that his is not intended to be a "full biography of Mirabeau." He justifies his work on the grounds that Mirabeau "is one of history's great failures, but his failure is more interesting than most men's successes." This is a well-reasoned account of Mirabeau's life that indicates a sound knowledge of the period and takes an analytical rather than narrative approach.

The primary sources for this biography consist of Mirabeau's printed correspondence, including the "Notes to the Court," which contain important information on the last two years of Mirabeau's life. Also consulted are Mirabeau's speeches, memoirs of a number of revolutionaries as well as the standard French work of the period, Louis de Loménie's *Les Mirabeau* (1889–91).

Welch writes from the standpoint of an Actonian liberal. He is in agreement with Acton's interpretation that France possessed a weak king. Welch concludes that Mirabeau failed because Louis XVI was unable to make a policy decision on his own. Mirabeau, he claims, "was a monarchist without a monarch." There is much emphasis on the idea that Mirabeau, who "could have been a supreme demagogue," opted for "liberty." Had Mirabeau succeeded, the monarchy would have been preserved as an integral part of the French state. Welch's explanation for Mirabeau's failure to create a viable constitutional monarchy for France because he lacked a party is pure Actonian liberalism. He argues that the Constituent Assembly suspected Mirabeau of playing a double game and that the Court neither trusted nor understood him.

Despite the central role that Mirabeau played in the early years of the French Revolution, the only scholarly modern study of his life and thought in English remains that of Welch. The most recent study of this interesting revolutionary figure, entitled *Mirabeau* by Guy Chaussinard-Nogaret, published in French in 1986, has yet to be translated.

—Leigh Ann Whaley

MOHAMMED, *ca.* 570–632; Arab prophet and founder of Islam.

Andrae, Tor, *Mohammed: The Man and His Faith*, translated by Theophil Menzel. New York, Barnes and Noble, 1935; London, Allen and Unwin, 1936 (originally published by Vandenhoeck and Ruprecht, Göttingen, 1932).

Bodley, Ronald V., *The Messenger: The Life of Mohammed*. New York, Doubleday, and London, R. Hale, 1946.

Cook, Michael, *Muhammad*. Oxford and New York, Oxford University Press, 1983.

Dermenghem, Émile, *The Life of Mahomet*, translated by Arabella Yorke. London, Routledge, and New York, Dial, 1930 (originally published by Plon, Paris, 1929).

Glubb, John B., *The Life and Times of Muhammad*. New York, Stein and Day, and London, Hodder and Stoughton, 1970.

Goldziher, Ignác, *Mohammed and Islam*, translated by Kate Seelye. New Haven, Connecticut, Yale University Press, 1917.

Hamidullah, Muhammad, *Muhammad Rasulullah: A Concise Survey of the Life and Work of the Founder of Islam*. Paris, Centre Culturel Islamique, 1974.

Haykal, Muhammad, *The Life of Muhammad*, translated by Ismail al Faruqi. Philadelphia, North American Trust Publications, 1976 (originally published in Cairo, 1935).

Ibn Ishaq, Muhammad, *The Life of Muhammad*, edited by Abd al-Malik Ibn Hisham; translated by Alfred Guillaume. London and New York, Oxford University Press, 1955.

Lings, Martin, *Muhammad: His Life Based on the Earliest Sources*. New York, Inner Traditions International, and London, Allen and Unwin/Islamic Texts Society, 1983.

Margoliouth, David S., *Mohammed and the Rise of Islam*. London and New York, Putnam, 1905.

Muir, William, *The Life of Mohammed from Original Sources* (4 vols.). London, Smith Elder, 1861; revised edition by T. H. Weir, Edinburgh, J. Grant, 1923.

Newby, Gordon D., *The Making of the Last Prophet: A Reconstruction of the Earliest Biography of Muhammad*. Columbia, University of South Carolina Press, 1989.

Rodinson, Maxime, *Mohammed*, translated by Anne Carter. New York, Pantheon, and London, Lane, 1971.

Watt, William M., *Muhammad at Mecca*. Oxford, Clarendon Press, 1953.

Watt, William M., *Muhammad at Medina*. Oxford, Clarendon Press, 1956.

Watt, William M., *Muhammad: Prophet and Statesman*. London, Oxford University Press, 1961.

Watt, William M., *Muhammad's Mecca: History in the Quran*. Edinburgh, Edinburgh University Press, 1988.

Widengren, Geo, *Muhammad, the Apostle of God, and His Ascension*. Uppsala, Sweden, Lundeguistska Bokhandeln, 1955.

*

As might be expected, the figure of Mohammed has attracted a vast literature in the modern period. Indeed, a bibliography compiled in 1965 includes 1548 different titles dealing with the founder of Islam, and much research has been published since then. Both Muslim and non-Muslim scholars and popularizers have been active, often differing widely in their aims, assumptions, selection of data, modes of presentation, and conclusions. In the following sections, a descriptive sampling of the most influential and significant works available in English has been provided. The focus is on the historico-critical scholarship of Western specialists, though representative works of traditional Muslim biography have received attention as well.

One of the earliest modern treatments to appear in English was MUIR's massive biography. Although a work of considerable technical erudition, it is weakened by the author's unsympathetic attitude toward his subject and by his use of what is today termed "psychological reductionism," or the explanation of religious phenomena in terms of psychic categories. This account is best consulted in the edition by Weir.

A more popular biography by the Oxford orientalist MARGOLIOUTH, though intended for the educated reading public, lacks the scholarly reference material and copious notes of Muir's work. Nevertheless, it furnishes, according to the standards of the day, an accessible overview of Mohammed's life and times. Margoliouth emphasizes military and political events and, like Muir, is somewhat at odds with his subject, which makes for difficulties of interpretation.

A central theme in GOLDZIHER's monograph is the distinction between the Mohammed of history and the Mohammed of pious Muslim fiction, as embodied in much of the *hadith* (traditions). Unfortunately for the modern historian, he says, "the pious legends about the ideal Mohammed early take the place of the historical man." Goldziher is more critical of the *hadith* as a source for Mohammed's biography than are many Western researchers today. His work has been rejected in Muslim circles as a transparent attempt to undermine the entire edifice of Islam.

DERMENGHEM's finely-crafted popular biography has been warmly received by Muslims and non-Muslims alike. Here it is the author's intention "to draw as accurate a portrait of Mahomet as possible, as he appears to me after watching him live again in the hearts of his adherents and in the tales from the books." This is a well-informed, balanced, and sympathetic work, whose lack of scholarly apparatus does not detract from its impressionistic but authentic re-creation of life in Mohammed's time.

Another classic study, by the Swedish scholar ANDRAE, deftly explores the psychological and religious aspects of Mohammed's persona. Andrae accepts the authenticity of the prophet's mystical experiences as recorded in the Quran. His historical reconstruction of the setting for Mohammed's life and career and his discussions of the contemporary religio-cultural milieu of the Christian Near East are especially valuable.

In 1935 one of the most influential of the modern Muslim biographies of Mohammed appeared in Arabic. HAYKAL's treatment represents traditional Islamic scholarship updated for a new, literate audience of believers. Although it purports to be a "scientific study [written] according to the modern western method," in fact it is an effective apologetic for the centuries-old image of the prophet. The scholarship of earlier Western specialists, the so-called "Orientalists," is vigorously attacked and rejected.

BODLEY's account, on the other hand, is intended for a Western audience, and "more for people who want to know something about Mohammed and Islam than for oriental scholars or students of theology." The author, a British military officer, brings to his task a personal familiarity with the nomadic lifestyle of the Middle East and a genuine sympathy for the people and their religion. Although he admits to consulting works of earlier scholars, he envisions his own contribution in very different terms: "But, while these [books] confirmed and coordinated what I had picked up among my nomad Arabs, the basic thoughts of my story of Mohammed's life originated among the snowy peaks of Kashmir and on the golden wastes of the Sahara." This attempt to depict Mohammed as he was understood by Muslims of Bodley's day is clearly successful.

In 1953 the first of WATT's authoritative studies of the prophet was published. *Muhammad at Mecca* sets forth the historical background of Mohammed's life and explores his early career. A later volume, *Muhammad at Medina* (1956), carries the story forward to his death. In the words of the author, "the two together are intended to constitute a history of the life of Muhammad and of the origins of the Islamic community." Watt brings to his work not only an intimate acquaintance with the sources, both primary and secondary, but also a willingness to approach the material from different perspectives. Sociological and economic factors are given new prominence in his systematic reconstruction of the prophet's times, and the traditional Muslim sources for Mohammed's life are revaluated in the light of contemporary scholarship. In 1961 an abridged and refined version of these volumes was issued as *Muhammad: Prophet and Statesman*. For most readers, this is still the best introduction to the prophet's life. Watt has continued to work in this field, his latest contribution being *Muhammad's Mecca: History in the Quran* (1988). Its purpose is "to obtain from the Qur'an as much historical material as possible for the Meccan period of Muhammad's career."

In the view of WIDENGREN, a specialist in comparative religions, the figure of Mohammed can best be explored and understood within the context of "celestial messenger" typologies characteristic of ancient Near Eastern religions. Widengren's provocative thesis has met with considerable criticism but is acknowledged as having opened new avenues of thought and research.

The appearance of HAMIDULLAH's biography in 1959 (originally published in French) marked an important step in the development of modern Muslim scholarship in this field. The work has as its focus the emergence of Mohammed as head of the early Islamic state. As a devout Muslim educated in the European university system, Hamidullah is perhaps uniquely qualified to bridge the gap between the dominant scientific historicism of Western specialists and the traditionalism of Muslim researchers. But while the author demonstrates an extensive knowledge of both the original Arabic sources and the secondary literature of the West, he unfortunately accepts the former with absolute, uncritical confidence while discarding the latter as biased or irrelevant. Consequently, Mohammed himself emerges as a mere hagiographical figure. Despite these criticisms, Hamidullah's work does have value for the Western reader: first, as a guide to important but little-known primary source material; second, as a convenient compilation of previous traditionalist scholarship on the prophet; and third, as a personal and highly-articulate expression of Muslim piety.

The French Islamicist RODINSON broke new ground with his penetrating study of Mohammed. Incorporating modes of inquiry from both earlier and contemporary Western scholars, especially Watt, Rodinson focuses on the psychological evolution of the prophet in the context of the tensions and changing needs of his own society. Indeed, the author argues that it was this inner evolution that "shaped Muhammad into an instrument capable of formulating and communicating an ideology that corresponded to the needs of the time and the milieu." Rodinson has been criticised for his underplaying of the prophet's religious inspiration and originality, but his overall thesis is well argued and persuasive, and the picture he furnishes of early Meccan and Arabian society is valuable.

A different perspective is offered in GLUBB's more popular biography. The author, a British army officer who served extensively in the Middle East, emphasizes the military aspects of the prophet's career. His reconstructions of early Muslim campaigns and battles are perceptive, if occasionally overdrawn. Numerous chronological tables, genealogical charts, identification lists of people discussed in the text, and maps enhance this book.

COOK's *Muhammad* is a recent, accessible study of the prophet. In this slim volume the author provides a concise examination of the life and thought of the founder of Islam. Cook is especially concerned with assessing the nature and reliability of the traditional biographical sources, and cautions that in the past some of these have been accepted too readily. His style is simple and straightforward, and readers interested in discovering Mohammed for the first time will find this book helpful.

Finally, for those who wish to approach the study of the prophet through the reading of early Arab biographies, there exist several good possibilities. The best choice, perhaps, is the *sira* (biography) composed by the eighth-century author IBN ISHAQ, which survives in epitomized form in the edition of Ibn Hisham (*ca.* 830). This lengthy account (almost 800 pages in Guillaume's translation) contains much material of earlier date, such as the recorded sayings of Mohammed, recollections of his activities, descriptions of his military campaigns, compilations of early poetry, and the like. To be sure, the "historical" Mohammed is here already partially obscured by the Mohammed of legend and hagiography. But perhaps, as the contemporary Islamicist Annemarie Schimmel has stated, "the charisma of a true religious leader can be better recognized from such legends than from the dry facts of his life, facts that are always likely to be interpreted by the biographer according to his peculiar viewpoint." The *sira* of Ibn Ishaq became acknowledged as authoritative by the Islamic community, and consequently most modern biographical efforts by Muslim scholars have this material as their centerpiece. Guillaume's translation is easy to follow, and his introduction and accompanying notes provide the reader with

a firm basis for understanding the text. Recently, NEWBY has offered a reconstruction of the missing portions of Ibn Ishaq's account, based on quotations from Quranic commentators.

LINGS' work on the prophet, as the book's subtitle indicates, is not a modern, critical biography, but rather a compilation and translation of early source materials (including Ibn Ishaq) dealing with the life and times of Mohammed. Lings arranges his sources in a chronological manner, with some topical digressions; his translation is rendered in a clear prose style. Unfortunately, the author does not supply the sort of reference material that would enable a general reader fully to understand or appreciate these sources.

—Craig L. Hanson

MOLIÈRE, Jean-Baptiste Poquelin, 1622–1673; French playwright and actor.

Fernandez, Ramon, *Molière: The Man Seen Through the Plays*, translated by W. Follett. New York, Hill and Wang, 1958 (originally published as *La Vie de Molière*, Paris, Gallimard, 1929).

Howarth, W. D., *Molière: A Playwright and His Audience*. Cambridge and New York, Cambridge University Press, 1982.

Lewis, D. B. Wyndham, *Molière: The Comic Mask*. London, Eyre and Spottiswoode, and New York, Coward-McCann, 1959.

Palmer, John, *Molière: His Life and Works*. London, G. Bell, and New York, Brewer and Warren, 1930.

Tilley, Arthur A., *Molière*. Cambridge, England, The University Press, 1921.

*

TILLEY's carefully written study in conventional biographical manner takes over and dilutes some of the then current notions about Molière the man and his view of life. Thus Molière gravitates toward the circle of young sceptics surrounding Gassendi, becomes a freethinker though advocating a modest, unambitious and wholesome philosophy in his plays. Disliking any assumption of superiority in things intellectual, moral, or spiritual, Molière impatiently lumps together religious hypocrites and religious busybodies. His values are articulated by his commonsensical female servants. A warm-hearted and jealous man, he puts his misanthropic humour into Alceste. His serious side is increasingly evident in the plays after *Le Misanthrope* (predominating over source material in *George Dandin*), *Amphitryon*, *L'Avare*. Molière the man however is not in complete harmony with Molière the dramatist, since his jealous heroes invariably suffer comic deflation. Tilley offers a good introduction to the man and his work from the standpoint of a conservative critic using the material of the time.

PALMER's descriptive biography devotes much space to Molière's origins and childhood at Rue St. Honoré, and evinces salutary scepticism about the mass of legends and half-truths with which the early years are entwined. Thus the story of Molière's introduction to the theatre by his maternal grandfather is treated as apocryphal, as is Grimarest's account of his education at the Collège de Clermont. Following in the footsteps of G. Michaut, Palmer refuses to embellish Molière's provincial peregrinations or to speculate about amative relationships with actresses in his troupes. The circle of his male friends is more fully described. The vexed issue of Molière's marriage is treated judiciously, with Molière presented as a generous and faithful husband and Armande as an actress of real but superficial charm, by no means the coquette of defamatory contemporary satires. No attempt is made to read Molière's life into the plays, which are seen as creative reactions to life's misadventures rather than as direct revelations of a frustrated husband. As a man, Molière is seen as jealous, melancholy, and not especially sympathetic to religion. Yet his opinions in the plays are moderate. Even in the most personal of his plays, he displays a capacity to laugh at what he himself might have become in Alceste were he deprived of the sense of humour incarnated in Philinte. In the reasoners he creates a reaction to his own impulsive nature.

A resolutely rational comic genius emerges, never allowing his private woes to cloud a comic vision mocking the excessive application of logic to life. His gift for self-detachment allows him to apply common sense to society: thus excessive credulity as well as excessive scepticism toward religion is satirized, as is any inflamed sense of self-righteousness. While Molière refused to surrender his judgement in temporal things to spiritual experts, Palmer views nothing in his life or work as being inconsistent with the profession of a Catholic Christian. With its conventional chronological approach to the subject, this biography remains one of the fullest and most readable available in English.

LEWIS offers a comprehensive and highly subjective account of Molière's life and plays in which it is not always easy to distinguish fact from fiction. Sources such as Grimarest, Le Boulanger de Chalussay and the satire against Molière's widow in *La fameuse comédienne* are widely used, on which critics in the tradition of G. Michaut would not place excessive reliance. The result is a vibrant, readable, and romanticized book written in a racy manner. There are colourful evocations of Molière's youth and the dramatic ending to his life, lurid accounts of his friendships with the actresses in his troupes, and fictional conversations between the playwright and the king about forthcoming comedies such as *Le Tartuffe*. The bittersweet relationship between Molière and his wife looms large, with ample space devoted to her affairs. Her attempts to keep the troupe afloat in the face of competition after his death rehabilitate her in the author's eyes, and she is viewed as the necessary grain of sand in Molière's life producing the pearl of comedy. Molière is seen as the generous but suffering creator, plagued by the incessant pressures of work and unfavourable circumstances. His sufferings spill over into the plays to lend them an increasingly sombre hue. The book conveys romantic colour and the spirit of the stage, often at the expense of accuracy.

Reacting against contemporary orthodoxy to the effect that little was known about Molière the man, and influenced by Freudian psychology, FERNANDEZ's double premise is that a connection must exist between the artist and his work and that it is the legitimate task of criticism to find the creator's personality through his art form. Molière's plays therefore trace the stages of his experiences: his marriage to a woman two decades his junior is foreshadowed in *L'École des Maris*, reflected in *L'École des Femmes*, and dramatized in *Le Misanthrope*. To identify

Molière however with a particular character is simplistic, as Fernandez discerns in Molière a sharp conflict between temperament and reason, portrayed in opposing characters whose clash originates comedy. Much of the dramatist is revealed through irascible comic heroes, and wisdom remains for Molière an ideal fruit of reflection. Art allows him to give unrestricted rein to his temperament, which he is able to indulge with impunity in the guise of comic caricature.

On stage his warring tendencies fuse into poetic harmony of opposites as comedy becomes for him the complete vehicle for self-expression. Fernandez's attitude to the often controversial sources of Molière's life is eclectic and latitudinarian. He deems it just as wrong to dismiss the stories surrounding Molière's life as it is to believe them literally. Myth surrounds great men because it alone symbolizes aspects of truth. A complex, solitary figure emerges with no firm friendships with members of his own sex, drawn by his sensuous nature and by circumstances into a preponderantly feminine entourage. Insecure and needing the friendship of younger people in the latter part of his life he transfers his affections from his wife to his young acting protégé Baron.

Jealous, anxious, taciturn, an ambitious go-getter like Racine, unlike him however Molière allows his energy to overflow into generosity toward others. Fernandez's analysis of Molière's comic vision is one of the most influential parts of the study. A new comedy founded on an invariable comic potential in humanity is located in the divorce between aspiration and reality, instinct and theory. It was Molière's genius to perceive that individual but unvarying constant in his fellows and to engineer situations pointing up the clash of individually expressed lucidity and blindness. The moral teaching resides in the judgement producing such situations rather than in the conventional expression of wisdom. As his comic vision broadens to include apparently uncomic elements, the corrective power of comedy is nullified by the pressure of cynical worldly values. This is by far the most suggestive and penetrating biography of Molière available.

HOWARTH's study is thematic and mainly historical in nature, although the aesthetic dimension to the plays is taken into account. It is situated in the line of R. Bray, with emphasis on Molière's theatrical virtuosity, his debt to Italian popular comedy, the necessity of viewing Molière as the director of a troupe involved with everyday problems of the theatre and divided between his work for the town and that for the court. These twin loci are reflected in comic drama with plot and characters on the one hand, and an art form based on fantasy for the court on the other. Social considerations such as the status of the actor, the strata of the audiences attending the plays, the function of the *honnête homme* in shaping values within his theatre are important features. The evolution of comedy is traced by means of key characters who originate in farce and develop into paradoxical fusions of the ridiculous and the serious.

Howarth does not regard Molière's use of satire as particularly incisive, though he does find depth in his social comments in *George Dandin* and *Amphitryon*, which Howarth sees as uncomfortable plays on uncomfortable topics. He claims that Molière put forward a valid, consistent view of human nature, and that his purpose was not to scourge particular vices but rather to regenerate audiences as social beings through the restorative process of laughter. It is Molière the humanist rather than the moralist or philosopher who emerges in this well-rounded and cautious study.

—Robert McBride

MONET, Claude, 1840–1926; French painter.

Gwynn, Stephen, *Claude Monet and his Garden: The Story of An Artist's Paradise.* New York, Macmillan, and London, Country Life, 1934.

Joyes, Claire, *Monet at Giverny.* London, Matthews Miller Dunbar, and New York, Mayflower, 1975.

Mauclair, Camille, *Claude Monet,* translated by J. Lewis May. New York, Dodd Mead, 1924; London, Bodley Head, 1925 (originally published by F. Reider, Paris, 1924).

Mount, Charles Merrill, *Monet: A Biography.* New York, Simon and Schuster, 1966.

Weeks, C. P., *Camille: A Study of Claude Monet.* London, Sidgwick and Jackson, 1962.

*

MAUCLAIR's 64-page book, the first biographical sketch of Monet available to the English reader, appeared prior to the artist's death and was followed shortly thereafter by Lila Cabot Perry's more narrowly focused "Reminiscences of Claude Monet from 1889 to 1909," (*The American Magazine of Art,* March 1927). In his popular, illustrated text, which contains little first-hand information and no documentation, Mauclair lyrically sketches the highlights of Monet's life and career, with an emphasis on his developing style and aesthetic outlook.

GWYNN's highly romanticized study offers the English reader material culled from the standard French biographies of Gustave Geffroy, *Claude Monet, Sa vie, son temps, son oeuvre* (Paris, 1924) and Marthe de Fels, *La Vie de Claude Monet* (Paris, 1929), but it draws most heavily on George Clemenceau's reminiscences of Monet's last 30 years (*Claude Monet, le nymphéas,* Paris, 1928). True to his introductory statement, Gwynn prefers the flavor to the specifics of the painter's life: "My concern, writing for an English-speaking public, is rather with the scene and the setting . . . " Despite new photographs of Monet's gardens at Giverny and discussions with his step-daughter, Blanche Hoschedé Monet, this biography, like Clemenceau's, suffers from a panegyric on the artist's late works and from the absence of scholarly detail or documentation.

WEEKS' popular, very readable portrait, first published in 1960 as *The Invincible Monet,* but revised and corrected in this later edition, relies heavily on material from Geffroy's standard French life. Focusing on Monet's place within the Impressionist group, Weeks balances his portrait with sketches of the Parisian painters, critics, and collectors whom Monet counted among his associates, and published criticism of the artist's work. Some new letters support this biography but they are often quoted from or summarized in the text, which is not footnoted. Although more detailed than any previous study of Monet's life in English, this text attributes feelings and attitudes to the artist (and to other members of his circle) without documentation. The Monet portrayed here is a romantic figure continually struggling for

funds to support his beleaguered family, whose success finally was the result of "great courage and determination." The Giverny years (1883–1926) are "deliberately compressed" in this account.

MOUNT's *Monet: A Biography,* the only substantial, scholarly study in English, is flawed, as John Rewald states in his review (*Artnews,* January 1968) by the author's biased assessment of Monet's character, by several inaccurate translations of French texts, and a few historical errors (such as naming Gambetta "President of France"). Despite these faults, Mount uncovered new material on Monet's mistress and first wife, Camille Doncieux (first published in his "New Materials on Claude Monet—The Discovery of a Heroine," *Art Quarterly,* Winter 1962). The discovery of her marriage contract and documents on the Doncieux family reveal Camille to have been a well-bred woman of the bourgeoisie. Mount also documents more extensively than any previous author the personality and genealogy of the painter's father, Claude Auguste Monet, including his irregular birth, his adoption by Claude Eulalie Perroty, and his marriage. In these circumstances Mount finds the source of "the artist's neurotic youth." Here, Monet's troubled relationship with his father is brought to light and amplified.

Mount's well-documented 400-page text makes available to the English reader substantial detail from the standard French biographies of Gustave Geffroy and Marthe de Fels, along with published interviews between Monet and his contemporaries. Both published and newly discovered letters are offered complete in the text, and chronological errors in the correspondence recorded in Gaston Poulain's *Bazille et ses Amis* (Paris, 1932) are corrected. One finds, however, Mount's opinionated tone overshadowing his valuable research. He describes Monet's arrival in Paris with " . . . his entire baggage the slapdash arrogance of a fledgling who refused to learn the basic disciplines of his craft." Statements such as " . . . the dowry of another woman Monet seduced [Alice], the wife of his patron Ernest Hoschedé, permitted him to achieve his final enormous position in French art," caution the reader to evaluate his assessments with care. Nevertheless, Mount's documentation suggests an opportunism in Monet's character that is not always flattering to the image of this important artist.

JOYES' well-documented essay on Monet's years at Giverny draws on both published and unpublished material of the period, including journals, letters, and other archival records from Jean-Pierre Hoschedé, Alice Hoschedé Monet, Blanche Hoschedé Monet, and Jim Butler (the grandson of Mme. Alice Monet), with contributions from Jean-Marie Toulgouat, all residents of the Monet household during his lifetime. Period photographs of the gardens, the house, and of the Monet family further enhance the value of this publication. Correcting Clemenceau's highly personal and romantic reminiscences of Monet's late career, this short, scholarly essay offers a more balanced view and new insights into the artist's family life at Giverny.

John Rewald's detailed *History of Impressionism* (4th edition, New York, 1973) remains a valuable, scholarly reference on the events of Monet's life and his history within the Impressionist circle.

—Phylis Floyd

MONROE, James, 1758–1831; American political leader, fifth president of the United States.

Adams, John Quincy, *The Lives of James Madison and James Monroe, Fourth and Fifth Presidents of the United States.* Boston, Phillips Sampson, 1850.

Ammon, Harry, *James Monroe, The Quest for National Identity.* New York, McGraw-Hill, 1971.

Cresson, W. P., *James Monroe.* Chapel Hill, University of North Carolina Press, 1946.

Gilman, Daniel C., *James Monroe.* Boston, Houghton Mifflin, 1883.

Morgan, George, *The Life of James Monroe.* Boston, Small Maynard, 1921.

Styron, Arthur, *The Last of the Cocked Hats: James Monroe and the Virginia Dynasty.* Norman, University of Oklahoma Press, 1912.

*

ADAMS' dual biography of Monroe and James Madison treats each man separately, and the portion devoted to Monroe is divided into two parts. The first is the eulogy Adams delivered in Boston on 25 August 1831, an elegantly written tribute to Monroe that nicely surveys the main events of his career. The second is an administrative history and unfortunately rather dry. It makes much use of Monroe's speeches and messages to Congress. For example, the text of Monroe's message on internal improvements is given in its entirety. Missing is a discussion of the Monroe Doctrine, which Adams himself did much to create; it is given only parenthetical mention. Nonetheless, this is a fascinating work by a man who knew personally and worked with his subject.

GILMAN, writing for the original American Statesmen Series, was the first historian to write a biography of Monroe. He also incorporates many of Monroe's letters into the text and suffers the same wearisome results as Adams. For example, an entire chapter summarizes Monroe's presidential addresses. Many of the letters included are not even Monroe's but were considered by Gilman to be relevant to the times. Gilman's main concern throughout the text is to stress Jefferson's influence on Monroe. As the work was published before an edition of Monroe's papers was available, most of the information was obtained from the Gouveneur manuscripts. Though the book offers an excellent chronology at the beginning, considering the paucity of sources it is no wonder there is little of Monroe the man in this biography.

The first well-written, detailed life is that of MORGAN, who made excellent use of the Monroe papers edited by Stanislaus Murray Hamilton and published from 1898 to 1903. Though it offers too much detail and too little analysis, this uncritical work served its purpose for both general reader and scholar of commemorating the centennial of the Monroe Doctrine. Morgan offers little on the events of Monroe's presidency; especially notable by their absence are the acquisition of Florida and the Missouri controversy. He prefers instead to concentrate on Monroe's diplomatic career, where any excuse is offered for Monroe's errors. Morgan's is a simplistic work and, though engagingly written, out of date for modern scholars. Nevertheless it offers a starting point for a study of Monroe as diplomat.

Published within a year of each other were two very different works, those of Styron and Cresson. STYRON's book, though nicely written, is simply a life-and-times work in which Monroe gets lost amidst discussions of the Constitutional Convention (at which Monroe was not a member) and military strategy. The reader can go pages in the text without coming across anything about Monroe. Opinionated and overgeneralized, its 450-plus pages are divided into only four chapters, making it unnecessarily difficult reading. CRESSON, on the other hand, provides a useful book for both general reader and historian. Borrowing much from Morgan, this book is better as it offers a separate and detailed study of each of the main issues that confronted Monroe while he was president. Cresson portrays Monroe as a man of the West, and is critical of his subject where he needs to be. He notes the influence of Jefferson and the negative effects of Monroe's desire to pursue a military career. Overall, Cresson, who did not live to see his book completed (though it was substantially finished when he died), provided the most worthwhile study of Monroe until the 1970s.

AMMON has definitely written the best biography for the scholar. Recently re-issued in paperback, this book will remain the standard life of Monroe for many years. Ammon makes use of all relevant manuscript material and does an excellent job of giving the reader an objective look at his subject. He is admirable on Monroe's period in the Confederation Congress, as governor of Virginia, and on the social life of the times. The Jefferson-Madison-Monroe triumvirate is very well analyzed, and Monroe accurately emerges the least abstract and most pragmatic of the three. The Monroe-Armstrong rivalry in Madison's cabinet, the Richmond Junto, and the relationship between Monroe and Congress while he was president receive talented appraisal. Ammon recognizes that Monroe was among the first to understand that the Republican Party could no longer remain agrarian, and that to become president of all the people meant to sacrifice party loyalty as a means of accomplishing presidential objectives. Such concepts are either ignored or given only cursory notice in other biographies. Ammon's book is charmingly written, well organized, and definitive, and as there has not emerged any new manuscript material on Monroe in some time (and none is likely to), this will be the best biography of Monroe for some time.

—Daniel Dean Roland

MONROE, Marilyn [*born* Norma Jean Baker], 1926–1962; American film actress.

Guiles, Fred L., *Legend: The Life and Death of Marilyn Monroe.* New York, Stein and Day, 1984; as *Norma Jeane*, London, Grafton, 1985.

Mailer, Norman, *Marilyn: A Biography.* New York, Grossett and Dunlap, and London, Hodder and Stoughton, 1973.

McCann, Graham, *Marilyn Monroe.* New Brunswick, New Jersey, Rutgers University Press, and Cambridge, England, Polity Press, 1988.

Riese, Randall and Neal Hitchens, *The Unabridged Marilyn: Her Life from A to Z.* New York, Congden and Weed, 1987.

Rollyson, Carl E., Jr., *Marilyn Monroe: A Life of the Actress.*
    Ann Arbor, Michigan, UMI Research Press, 1986; London,
    Souvenir Press, 1987.
Slatzer, Robert F., *The Life and Curious Death of Marilyn Mon-
    roe.* New York, Pinnacle House, 1974; London, W. H.
    Allen, 1975.
Steinem, Gloria, *Marilyn.* New York, Holt, 1986; London, Gol-
    lancz, 1987.
Summers, Anthony, *Goddess: The Secret Lives of Marilyn Mon-
    roe.* London, Gollancz, and New York, Macmillan, 1985.
Zolotow, Maurice, *Marilyn Monroe.* New York, Harcourt,
    1960; London, W. H. Allen, 1961.

*

As photographer Eve Arnold notes in her memoir (*Marilyn Monroe: An Appreciation*, 1987), one collector claims to own 600 different Monroe books. Theoretician Graham McCann (see below) estimates that there are some 50 biographies, photo books, and documentaries of Monroe's life. So much has been published that a researcher may feel overwhelmed by the abundance of material. Yet only a few volumes are needed to gain an introduction to the woman who was christened "Norma Jeane."

Most writers concur that the definitive biography is by GUILES. In his preface, Guiles reminds readers that *Legend* is more than a mere revision of Guiles' 1969 biography, *Norma Jean*, since the later book reveals a clearer understanding of both Monroe and the forces that transformed her into myth. (The UK edition of the new book still carries the title *Norma Jeane*.) In addition, the second book draws on newly conducted interviews and on recent research into the events surrounding Monroe's death.

Guiles' biography is comfortable to read; it is composed of six sections that are further divided into many short chapters. The narrative voice is credible and fluid, in the tradition of Victorian biography. Guiles' book is arranged chronologically, and despite the lack of notes has proven to be accurate in most details. The filmography provides a wealth of information on Monroe's 29 completed films, including studio, director, producer, release date, screenwriter and source, cast (with character names), musical score composer, photographer, short plot summaries, and excerpts from contemporary reviews.

ZOLOTOW was able to interview Monroe herself several times during his work. His 1960 account was the first serious biography to be published, but because of its early date it is necessarily incomplete, and it contains no notes or bibliography. Zolotow is often vivid and dramatic, frequently quoting entire conversations, though his style is plagued with occasionally wooden language and a self-conscious tone. Nevertheless, his biography is to be recommended for casting a bright and lively spotlight on Monroe's personality.

For a complete discussion of Monroe's decline and death, readers must turn to the work of British investigative reporter Anthony SUMMERS. Inspired by a 1982 criminal inquiry into the circumstances of Monroe's death, Summers interviewed approximately 600 persons. His findings are carefully scrutinized throughout the text, particularly in his lengthy final section on the Kennedys. Summers theorizes that the FBI participated in a cover-up after Monroe's death in order to shield Robert Kennedy, who was present when she died, in an ambulance en route to a Santa Monica hospital. The widely publicized enigma of her suicide (or homicide), Summers admits, has not been fully solved. He reprints several documents and meticulously cites the sources of his information—a boon to researchers—but his prose is largely uninspired. (Summers' preface neglects Guiles, citing Zolotow's book as definitive.)

Every biographer is bound to consider Monroe's version of her life, *My Story* (1974). First serialized in one of London's "yellow" newspapers in 1954 and ghost-written by screenwriter Ben Hecht, the narrative ends with Monroe's concert appearance, earlier that year, for a group of G.I.s stationed in Korea. Guiles and Zolotow generally accept the book as factual, whereas others question Monroe's discussion of her childhood (notably Mailer, who coined the term "factoid" to describe the inaccurate results of a faulty memory or a redefined self).

The most detailed analysis of Monroe's acting career is ROLLYSON's *Life of the Actress*. Although Rollyson relies on Guiles for the chronology of events, his narrative concentrates on Monroe's professional growth as an actress, her acting teachers Natasha Lytess, Michael Chekhov, and Lee Strasberg, and the "creative dynamic . . . of her urge to become the artist of her own self-transformation." Beginning with *Clash by Night* (1952), each film role is analyzed in depth. Rollyson also provides a succinct history of *My Story* and reprints Monroe's last interview, published in *Life* Magazine, on 3 August 1962.

A gold mine for trivia buffs is found in RIESE AND HITCHENS' *Unabridged Marilyn*, a "personality encyclopedia" collecting "every known fact about Marilyn Monroe." The book's filmography is supplemented by anecdotal entries under each film title. Riese and Hitchens offer the most detailed discography available. And readers will be fascinated by their eccentric lists: books about Marilyn Monroe, quotations from various persons, Monroe's restaurants, doctors, illnesses, homes, fashions, schools, songs, (nick-) names. For the 22 films released beginning in 1948, Riese and Hitchens provide excerpts from contemporary reviews. Three short studio biographies are reprinted in their entirety (from 20th-Century Fox 1946 and 1951, and RKO 1951).

SLATZER's memoir, the first detailed account of the contradictions surrounding Monroe's "suicide," reprints various pertinent documents (birth and death certificates, marriage certificates, Monroe's autopsy report, her will, claims against her estate, etc.). Slatzer's work, despite his folk style, awkward repetitions, and "pop" chapter titles, is a useful compendium of private conversations; however, the book is also controversial, partly because Slatzer claims to have been briefly married to Monroe.

Other memoirs by Monroe's associates range from the warm nostalgia of photographer Sam Shaw and poet Norman Rosten (*Marilyn Among Friends*, 1987) to the near-pornography of Ted Jordan (*Norma Jean: My Secret Life with Marilyn Monroe*, 1989). Most researchers will find these specialized biographies of little immediate usefulness. An occasional exception might be made for a work like playwright Arthur Miller's autobiography (*Timebends*, 1987), which describes his relationship with Monroe in detail, or for journalist James Goode's account of the filming of Monroe's last complete film (*The Story of "The Misfits,"* 1963). Also of limited use are the numerous photograph anthologies, many of which are complemented by a biographical narrative. (Interested readers should consult one of the available bibliographies for more information.)

MAILER's *Marilyn*, despite its notorious self-indulgence, is a *tour de force* of style and design. His is a metaphorical and melodramatic voice, both aphoristic and graphically frank, shameless and romantic, territorial and wistful. Mailer combines the biographer's imperative for factual accuracy with the novelist's latitude for imagining "the interior of . . . a closed and silent life." As a result, his "novel biography" offers "a literary hypothesis of a *possible* Marilyn Monroe who might have lived and fit most of the facts available." As Mailer explains in an "afterword," his text was originally contracted as a preface to Larry Schiller's book edition of Monroe images by 24 renowned photographers. But the narrative seized Mailer's imagination. Like his novels, *Marilyn* employs a sophisticated narrative structure. In contrast to most biographers, Mailer considers *Some Like It Hot* Monroe's finest film (not *Bus Stop*).

STEINEM's biography, intended to accompany George Barris' photographs, is composed of six related essays, each written to stand independently of the rest. Steinem's biography gives Monroe's life universal significance, approaching the subjects of posterity and reputation, the "inner child," the economic and sexual politics of Monroe's profession, Monroe's relations with women and with men, the female body, and the transformations of Monroe's image in recent decades. Because Steinem relies heavily on Guiles and Summers, supplemented by few interviews and little biographical theory, some writers wish to discredit the book. However, Steinem's personal vision exemplifies the mixed reactions of feminists toward Monroe, who constructed a public identity appearing to endorse the male definition of the archetypical Female.

McCANN's "anti-biography" is provocative reading, but his specialized vocabulary and antagonistic assumptions restrict the book's usefulness. In eight chapters he focuses on myth-making, biographers' shortcomings, images, film, public opinion, Miller and Mailer, mourning, and posterity. McCann's Monroe—like Steinem's—becomes an occasion to enunciate private theories about the nature of interpretation. According to McCann, the men [*sic*] who write about Monroe face "two fundamental problems of distance: the distance between men and women, and the distance between the researcher and the deceased subject." In the most intriguing chapter, "Marilyn in Focus," McCann explores the notion that "the photographic image of Marilyn Monroe inhabits various contexts: cultural contexts of spectatorship; institutional, social, and historical contexts of production and consumption." Oddly, McCann claims to be feminist—even though his denunciation of Steinem's work is strongly paternal. McCann's self-righteous indignation in Chapter 2 ("On Writers and Their Inelegance") will dismay many readers.

—Mark T. Bassett

MONTAIGNE, Michel (Eyquem) de, 1533–1592; French writer.

Dowden, Edward, *Michel de Montaigne*. Philadelphia and London, Lippincott, 1905.

Frame, Donald M., *Montaigne: A Biography*. New York, Harcourt, and London, Hamilton, 1965.

Lowndes, M. E., *Michel de Montaigne: A Biographical Study*. Cambridge, Cambridge University Press, 1898.

Sichel, Edith, *Michel de Montaigne*. London, Constable, and New York, Dutton, 1911.

Tetel, Marcel, *Montaigne*. New York, Twayne, 1974.

Willis, Irene Cooper, *Montaigne*. New York, Knopf, 1927.

*

The best biography of Montaigne in any language, and one of the classics of modern biographical writing, is Frame's *Montaigne: A Biography* (see below). However, in addition to the biographies to be discussed, readers of French and intellectual historians should be made aware at least of four other works: Maturin Dréano, *La Pensée religieuse de Montaigne* (1937), which establishes the seriousness of Montaigne's Catholicism after the more rationalist readings current in French academic circles during the first quarter of the century; H. Friedrich, *Montaigne* (1949), originally published in German and subsequently translated into French, particularly good on Montaigne's attitude to death; Craig Brush, *Montaigne and Bayle* (1966), not a biography, but the only major study to understand the theology of the longest chapter of Montaigne's *Les Essais*; and A. Trinquet, *La Jeunesse de Montaigne* (1972), a very thorough biography indeed of the formative first 25 years of Montaigne's life. There is of course a vast list of titles concerned with the composition, moral content, historical interest, evaluation, and analysis of *Les Essais* and the *Journal de voyage*. In addition to Frame's other two books on Montaigne (*Montaigne's Discovery of Man*, 1955, and *Montaigne's "Essais": a Study*, 1969), there is a good analysis of *Les Essais* by Richard Sayce, *The Essays of Montaigne: A Critical Explanation* (1973).

All the biographies of Montaigne stem from Grün's *La Vie publique de Montaigne* (1855), Bonnefon's *Montaigne, l'Homme et l'oeuvre* (1893), and Malvezin's *Michel de Montaigne, son origine, sa famille* (1875). The English biography by LOWNDES draws on these sources and is of interest only as an early, carefully written summary of knowledge about Montaigne's life available at the turn of the century. Of the other biographies available in English, DOWDEN's is also inevitably out of date, in spite of being the product of serious reading intelligently digested, and although its judgements on Montaigne's experiences and attitudes are sensitive and reflective. SICHEL, depending in 1911 on Strowski, one of the earliest historians to point to the development of Montaigne's thought, is again now out of date. She portrays only the good-natured, unsystematic, studious semi-recluse, but she rightly puts more emphasis on Montaigne's Christianity than was usual at this period in France, even if she also over-emphasizes the satirical content of his work and puts Montaigne at the head of a tradition that includes La Rochefoucauld, Voltaire, and Anatole France.

WILLIS wrote simply as a non-scholarly enthusiast to advertise the merits of Montaigne, prompted by an essay of Virginia Woolf's originally printed in *The Times Literary Supplement*. She is well informed, especially about the political roles Montaigne played, but her book has now outlived its usefulness. No further attempt was made to make a biography of Montaigne available in English for nearly 40 years.

FRAME's exemplary biography rightly emphasizes the importance to Montaigne of his domestic life and of his marriage in 1565 to a wife of Jewish descent, Françoise de la Chassaigne, who bore him six daughters of whom only one, Léonor, survived. Frame holds that Montaigne amply fulfilled the roles expected of him inside and outside marriage and brings out his consciousness of rank. He was the first member of his family to drop the bourgeois name "Eyquem" from his full title, and his attitude to his estates, which he neither augmented nor diminished, was partly determined by his lack of a male heir. Frame goes into the social standing and financial position of the rural landowners struggling against the policies of Catherine de' Medici, striving to maintain both their social standing and the purchasing power of their assets when the value of the currency dropped by two thirds during the course of the century.

Frame has traced the fortunes of Montaigne's mother's and his father's families, and we have the notaried deeds to give us dates of births, deaths, and marriages. There are some references to Montaigne in the works of his contemporaries. But overwhelmingly the biographical evidence has to be extracted from *Les Essais* and the *Journal de voyage* themselves, which means decoding the often self-deprecatory and deliberately falsified expressions of attitude he left us. This is what Frame, with the aid of a detailed analysis of the changes Montaigne made or contemplated in the text of *Les Essais*, has done superbly well. Others who have attempted parts of the same task include Frieda S. Brown, *Religious and Political Conservatism in the "Essais" of Montaigne* (1963).

The best scholarship never impedes readability, and Frame himself hoped that the nonspecialist may read his biography "with interest, the scholar, with confidence." He has succeeded with the help of a clearly presented series of chronologically based chapters. Endpapers indicate the route of Montaigne's principal journey to Italy, and Frame's examination of the "Bordeaux manuscript" yields important conclusions for Montaigne's relationship with his *fille d'alliance* (adoptive daughter), Marie le Jars de Gournay, who made significant changes in Montaigne's references to her when she edited *Les Essais* after his death.

Finally, TETEL's volume of 1974 contains a smaller proportion of biographical to analytic material than is usual for the Twayne series, although there is the always useful chronology of Montaigne's life. The English-speaking reader in search of a biography of Montaigne has really no choice but Frame who, happily, has written a classic.

—A. H. T. Levi

MONTESQUIEU, Charles-Louis de Secondat, Baron de, 1689–1755; French political philosopher and lawyer.

Loy, J. Robert, *Montesquieu*. New York, Twayne, 1968.
Shackleton, Robert, *Montesquieu: A Critical Biography*. London, Oxford University Press, 1961.

Shklar, Judith N., *Montesquieu*. Oxford and New York, Oxford University Press, 1987.

*

While a vast bibliography exists on Montesquieu's political thought, deceptively presented in *The Spirit of the Laws* (1748; translated and edited, with biographical and bibliographical introductions by Anne M. Cohler, Basia Carolyn Miller, and Harold Samuel Stone, 1989), and while much has been written on Montesquieu's social satire, his life was sufficiently uneventful to have attracted few biographers. There is however one outstanding biography, "the standard reference for Montesquieu's biography," as the editors of *The Spirit of the Laws* say, SHACKLETON's *Montesquieu* of 1961. It has components of social and intellectual history, is clear and well written if formally academic in presentation, draws copiously on original sources, and necessarily illustrates the political, social, and personal constraints endured by its subject on account of the potentially subversive nature of his thought.

Shackleton's work is in its way the model for an academic biography; well written, researched in great depth, immensely knowledgeable about its subject's personal and social circumstances and the intellectual traditions on which he drew. Shackleton is as interested in Montesquieu's everyday life, his house, his travels, his contacts, his income, his friends, and his position in society as in his political theory, his reading, his social and political vision, and his place in the history of letters. Shackleton does not emphasize the often-repeated claim that Montesquieu was the "founder of sociology," which he would have regarded as bombastically imprecise. He has however produced a fascinating portrait of a serious political visionary with time and means to read and think. He publishes photographs of the places with which Montesquieu was connected, writes with sardonic humour and assured mastery of the intellectual history of his period, and gives clear and accurate accounts of such subjects as Spinozism, natural law, 18th-century freemasonry, Montesquieu's friends, and the thought of important earlier legal theorists. Shackleton's exposition of Montesquieu's thought is masterly. His weakness is the common failure to notice Montesquieu's constant mental references to the scholastics.

LOY, who also wrote a book on Diderot, published his *Montesquieu* in Twayne's World Authors series, and he necessarily derives much from Shackleton's "essential study . . . [the] most complete and careful treatment in English by an eminent scholar," to which Loy notes 15 references in his index. Loy includes notes and a bibliography, but he is much less formally academic in his approach. He seeks to inform those who want to know about Montesquieu and his work, but "does not claim to add significantly to Montesquieu scholarship." He does not expect his readers to love, or even to like, Montesquieu, and he draws too on non-biographical critical treatments of aspects of his subject's thought and influence, notably on F. T. H. Fletcher, *Montesquieu and English Politics 1750–1800* (1939). The book intelligently adapts the available material to fit with workmanlike precision into the series of biographies in which it is published.

Also available in English is SHKLAR's study, which presents Montesquieu's personality and work in a different and less reliable light. This work's importance is not primarily biographical, and it does not intend to present new information.

—A. H. T. Levi

MONTGOMERY, Bernard Law [1st Viscount Montgomery of Alamein], 1887–1976; English general and field marshal.

Barnett, Correlli, *The Desert Generals.* London, W. Kimber, 1960.

Brett-James, Antony, *Conversations with Montgomery.* London, W. Kimber, 1984.

Chalfont, Alun, *Montgomery of Alamein.* London, Weidenfeld and Nicolson, and New York, Atheneum, 1976.

Hamilton, Nigel, *Monty* (3 vols.). London, Hamilton, and New York, McGraw-Hill, 1981–86.

Howarth, T. E. B., editor, *Monty at Close Quarters, Recollections of the Man.* New York, Hippocrene Books, and London, Secker and Warburg, 1985.

Lamb, Richard, *Montgomery in Europe, 1943–45, Success or Failure?* London, Buchan and Enright, 1983.

Lewin, Ronald, *Montgomery as Military Commander.* New York, Stein and Day, 1971.

Montgomery, Brian, *A Field Marshal in the Family.* London, Constable, 1973; New York, Taplinger, 1974.

Moorehead, Alan, *Montgomery, a Biography.* London, Hamilton, and New York, Coward McCann, 1946.

Thompson, R. W., *The Montgomery Legend.* London, Allen and Unwin, 1966.

Thompson, R. W., *Montgomery.* New York, Random House, 1974.

*

Since the publication of Moorehead's book in 1946 there has been a steady stream of memoirs, military histories, and biographies attempting to evaluate Montgomery both as man and military leader, culminating in the definitive, massive three-volume study by Hamilton. The earlier work by the popular, prolific author MOOREHEAD is not based primarily on printed documents (although Montgomery did authorize him to examine some of his files), but rather on the author's own observations of Montgomery and conversations with associates. Moorehead provides a readable, journalistic, but not overly critical, account of the life of Montgomery down to 1946.

Montgomery's own *Memoirs* (1958), serialized in advance by *Life* magazine, reveal better than any other source his own personality. Anyone who reads them will discover a difficult, cantankerous, opinionated, conceited, and arrogant person. Not heavy on operational facts, these memoirs reveal the character flaws of Montgomery that will so fascinate his biographers. Colonel Brian MONTGOMERY, the field marshal's brother, wrote a very revealing anecdotal biography of "Monty" with the full use of family papers. Writing with restraint and sensitivity, Colonel Montgomery believes that the death of Monty's wife affected him profoundly for the worse for the rest of his career,

and in part explains his irascible character and inability to get close to anyone, even members of his family. The book contains many revealing personal details about the field marshal that will be mined by biographers.

Montgomery's reputation as a military commander has also produced some controversy. BARNETT's account of the desert campaign of 1940–43 is a forthright polemical work in favor of Wavell and Auchinleck, against Churchill and especially Montgomery, whose generalship he views as being very overrated. LEWIN, in a volume on Montgomery for a series on military commanders, presents a much more balanced view of his generalship. Although aware of his shortcomings, Lewin acknowledges Montgomery as "a great commander" and a "modern general." Based completely on secondary sources, Lewin emphasizes the lively accounts of Montgomery's military action. The well-documented study by LAMB centers on Montgomery's stormy relationship with Eisenhower. Lamb, while censuring Montgomery for behind-the-scenes conniving to get his way, does present a strong case that his superiors, Lt. General Brooke and Sir James Grigg, encouraged him to seek sole command when that was impossible politically.

THOMPSON's *Montgomery* (1974) is intended for the popular reader or World War II "buff." The book is lavishly illustrated with photographs and lucidly written, though it lacks an index. Thompson is totally uncompromising toward his subject's temperamental weaknesses and character defects. For instance, he refers in his description of Montgomery's arrival in north Africa to "an act of boarish vulgarity and rudeness unworthy of the worst type of Warrant Officer." Yet anyone familiar with Thompson's earlier work, *The Montgomery Legend* (1967), will not be surprised at his unflattering opinion of Montgomery.

CHALFONT finds at least some redeeming qualities in Montgomery, who in fact encouraged Chalfont to write the book. Although based on secondary sources, especially drawing heavily on Moorehead's earlier biography, Chalfont's book can still be recommended to readers who wish an introduction to Montgomery without having to wade through the close to 3,000 pages presented by Hamilton.

HAMILTON had full access to all Montgomery's papers, letters, diaries, documents, and the uninhibited help of all the members of his family, colleagues, and friends. While undoubtedly the "official" biographer, Hamilton is unflinching in his search for the truth behind Montgomery. His three-volume biography is dense with detail. The first volume covers Montgomery's life down to 1942. In the second installment, covering the war years 1942–44, Hamilton presents a revisionist view of Montgomery as one who was capable of bold and adventurous planning but who was often let down by cautious subordinates. Hamilton, however, does not ignore the personal characteristics of his subject, detailing his uncaring attitude toward his family. The third and final volume comes in at over 1,000 pages. Again, Montgomery as a military commander is frequently portrayed in a new and favorable light; Hamilton appears to take shots at some of the "American" anti-Montgomery literature, such as the work by Thompson, though Hamilton shows how in his waning years Montgomery's personality flaws became even more pronounced. Hamilton's books are written for a wide audience, and scholars may find some of the footnotes and references inadequate. Even so, this triple set should remain the standard biography of Montgomery for a very long time.

Two other recent works should be mentioned. That by BRETT-JAMES consists of a set of conversations the author had with Montgomery. Of much more interest and worth in understanding Montgomery is the set of recollections edited by HOWARTH, especially the contributions by Dr. R. Luckett (unfortunately expurgated) and L. F. Trueb concerning Montgomery's sexuality, or lack of interest in it, and how that influenced his career and character.

—Richard A. Voeltz

———————

MOORE, George, 1852–1933; Irish writer.

Brown, Malcolm, *George Moore: A Reconsideration.* Seattle, University of Washington Press, 1955.
Cunard, Nancy, *G. M.: Memories of George Moore.* London, Hart-Davis, 1956.
Goodwin, Geraint, *Conversations with George Moore.* London, E. Benn, 1929; New York, Knopf, 1930.
Hone, Joseph, *The Life of George Moore.* London, Gollancz, and New York, Macmillan, 1936.
Hone, Joseph, *The Moores of Moore Hall.* London, Cape, 1938.
Mitchell, Susan, *George Moore.* Dublin and London, Maunsel, and New York, Dodd Mead, 1916.

*

George Moore was lucky in his first and only major biographer. HONE was a man of taste, with a good general knowledge of literature, art, and music, who was also well known in Irish literary circles. He writes an objective and faithful account of Moore's life, being careful not to repeat events already familiar from Moore's own autobiographical writings, of which there are several. At the same time he calls attention to Moore's inventions and omissions in such matters. While he does not devote much space to literary criticism, he directs our attention to literary influences, both particular and general. Hone's literary judgments are well founded and while the approach is not psychological, his interpretations of Moore's complex personality are carefully weighed.

Hone moves steadily through the major phases of Moore's life—the Parisian years in which he knew the French impressionist painters, the salons and the naturalistic novelists, the London years in which he pioneered the naturalist movement in London, the Dublin years in which he participated in the Irish Literary Revival, the return to London and his achievements as a stylist in his later years.

Hone is at times drily ironic at Moore's expense but avoids the temptation, to which many succumb, to see Moore as an object of ridicule. He provides sympathetic treatment for a complex, chameleon-like character. The difficulty in seeing Moore clearly arises in large part from the autobiographical writings, the existing self-portraits, the delightfully puzzling enigmas that Moore created. Not only did he puzzle over the problematical

nature of self-knowledge, but he created so many versions of himself, so many protective masks, that it is virtually impossible to write a convincing, objective biography. So far Hone is the only one to make the attempt. But it is time for another, more modern one.

Some supplementary and more general information about Moore's background may be found in HONE's 1938 volume on the Moore family. MITCHELL's book, while witty and caustic, is somewhat too negative. It needs to be balanced with other views, such as those found in GOODWIN's imitative *Conversations.* Though most of the pre-Hone material, found in various memoirs of Moore, is trivial and anecdotal, the volume by Lady CUNARD, to whom Moore felt able to speak frankly about himself and his writings, is an exception.

Moore's years in France are well described by Georges-Paul Collet (*George Moore et la France*, Paris, 1957). Another French writer, Jean Noel (*George Moore: l'Homme et l'Oeuvre*, Paris, 1966), relies on Hone for biographical material but offers his own psychological explanations for the man and the work. BROWN wrote the first modern scholarly work on Moore and makes good use of biography in his critical revaluation.

Future biographers of Moore will need to get behind the writer's public image, since the enigma of Moore's personality is too challenging to be ignored. The reasons for his creation of a multiple self need to be addressed. His relationships with women cry out for investigation. Moore's letters to his mother offer scope for discussion. A modern biographer will also be faced with the daunting knowledge that Moore cannot be relied upon, though that in itself should not be the deterrent it apparently has been since the publication of Hone's book.

—Maurice Harmon

———————

MOORE, Henry, 1898–1986; English sculptor.

Berthoud, Roger, *The Life of Henry Moore.* London, Faber, and New York, Dutton, 1987.
Compton, Susan, *Henry Moore.* London, Royal Academy of Arts/Weidenfeld and Nicolson, and New York, Scribner, 1988.
Grohmann, Will, *The Art of Henry Moore.* New York, Abrams, and London, Thames and Hudson, 1960.
Hall, Donald, *Henry Moore: The Life and Work of a Great Sculptor.* New York, Harper, 1965; London, Gollancz, 1966.
Hedgecoe, John, editor and photographer, *Henry Moore* (text by Henry Moore). London, T. Nelson, 1968; as *Henry Spencer Moore*, New York, Simon and Schuster, 1968.
Jianou, Ionel, *Henry Moore*, translated by J. Skelding. New York, Tudor, 1968 (originally published by Arted, Paris, 1968).
Packer, William, *Henry Moore: An Illustrated Biography.* London, Weidenfeld and Nicolson, and New York, Grove, 1985.
Read, Sir Herbert, *Henry Moore: A Study of His Life and Work.* London, Thames and Hudson, 1965; New York, Praeger, 1966.

Russell, John, *Henry Moore*. London, A. Lane, and New York, Putnam, 1968; revised edition, London, Penguin, 1973.

＊

The Henry Moore industry has been in full swing now for several decades. Since Herbert Read wrote the first book on Moore in 1933 (a critical study of his works), literally hundreds of studies of him have appeared, a surprisingly large number of them claiming to have some relevance to his biography—surprisingly large, considering that Moore, a sculptor (a profession that has not traditionally attracted great numbers of biographers), led what many would consider a studiously uninteresting life. His artistic output was by any standards enormous; he lived much of his life in the quiet surroundings of rural England; he did not belong to or ever attempt to found any "school"; his travels and his associations with other artists, writers, and intellectuals were minimal when compared to those recorded in the lives of so many artists. None of these factors suggests a particularly colorful life to write about.

The biographies of Moore reflect, and often duplicate, this blandness. Most of them are appreciations of the man and his art, charting the external circumstances of his life in an almost obligatory fashion. Most biographers have acknowledged the lack of substance upon which to base a truly compelling narrative of Moore's life. His inner life, according to many who knew him, was apparently as uncomplicated and placid as his outer life, and so we have a series of books portraying a warm, generous man quietly practicing his craft, patiently moving from work to family in untroubled regularity.

Yet reasons exist for suspecting that all was not as it appeared in Moore's life. Passages in Moore's *Henry Moore on Sculpture: A Collection of the Sculptor's Writings and Spoken Words* (edited by Philip James, London, 1966) and in the more autobiographically revealing *Henry Moore: My Ideas, Inspiration, and Life as an Artist* (with John Hedgecoe, 1986) suggest relevant biographical details that all his biographers have strangely ignored, or at most glanced at superficially, failing in either case to treat Moore's life in light of the often rich psychological implications found in these works. His remarks, recorded in the 1986 book, about the death of his athlete sister ("I blame myself. . . . I encouraged her to go farther and farther and train harder and harder and then she died of heart failure. It upset me for years"), or of his aged grandmother ("I had a grandmother whom I used to have to go and see every Saturday or Sunday. . . . I hated it . . . to me she was terribly revolting. But there we were, it was part of the pattern of life"), have received no rigorous commentary, though they contain suggestions that ought to inform any effort to understand Moore's life as well as some of the manifestations of his art. Even the most complete biographical treatment of Moore's life, by Berthoud (see below), avoids penetrating Moore's mind in any revealing fashion, maintaining the by now familiar pattern of "Great Man" narratives.

GROHMANN's book is essentially a descriptive/critical guide through Moore's work, with many fine reproductions and some photographs of Moore not found elsewhere. Grohmann frequently, however, offers incisive comments about Moore's life while analyzing his artistic practice, illuminating corners of Moore's character almost one feels by accident. Still, Grohmann's writing more often strains for profound statement than it

eases naturally into genuine and intelligent insight. He examines such central elements as the Reclining Figure, claiming "that there must be reasons why the theme of the 'Reclining Figure' has preoccupied Moore throughout his life" at the beginning of a chapter one hopes will throw some light on these reasons. Unfortunately, what follows are lengthy descriptions of the sculptures, with little effort to follow the potentially rich biographical path implied in Grohmann's opening remark. Erich Neumann's book, *The Archetypal World of Henry Moore* (translated by R. F. C. Hull, New York, Pantheon, 1959), though not a biography, provides a valuable framework for understanding such "preoccupations." Neumann, drawing on Jungian psychoanalytic theory, examines important recurring images—which Jung had called archetypes—in Moore's work. Future biographers would do well to consider Neumann's work on Moore's sculptures as they try to account for Moore's character and the outward motions of his life.

Readers should avoid JIANOU's volume, largely a catalog of sculptures with black-and-white photographs and a brief chronology. It contains an introductory chapter entitled "Henry Moore, His Life and Wok" (sic), which lays out, with no regard to Moore's culinary tastes, a few of the basic features of his life as these are revealed in *Henry Moore on Sculpture*, from which Jianou quotes to an absurd degree.

HALL's admiring portrait opens with an in-depth look at a particular day—23 December 1963, during the period of Moore's work on the major sculpture entitled *The Locking Pieces*—before giving way to a more conventional chronological approach to Moore's life. In this first section, which itself makes Hall's book still valuable, Hall brings us into the studio to watch the sculptor at work. While Hall recreates what he witnesses to what some will call dramatic effect, he is extremely good at noticing and describing in precise language the details of Moore's work. From this, and from Hall's equally fine recreation of life at the Moore residence, a portrait of the sculptor emerges that reveals much about his character and temperament.

Hall is skilled at capturing the many elements of Moore's life—his working habits, his relations with his family, his intellectual milieu—that make that life interesting to us. The rest of Hall's narrative is serviceable, though clearly his gift as a biographer is in bringing to life what he sees and hears. In broad strokes, he outlines Moore's early days in Castleford, identifies early influences, and follows the progression of events in a conventional manner, staying mostly on the surface without relating Moore's outer life to his inner. This book is valuable as an example of one craftsman (Hall is a well-known American poet) observing and learning from another working in a different medium.

READ's book, appearing in the same year as Hall's, rehearses the bald details of Moore's life in a reliable manner and in a relatively short space. Read was Moore's friend and associate over a long period, and he had Moore's cooperation and approval in the preparation of his book. His treatment is almost wholly uncritical; while he does add some remarks suggesting that he has taken Neumann's insights to heart, he makes none that suggest he is willing to examine Henry Moore's life in light of those insights. Read's volume contains some fine illustrations, most of them from the sculptor's own photographs.

RUSSELL, another close friend of Moore, offers, like Read, a book primarily useful as a guide to Moore's work for a general audience. His remarks on Moore's life are unsurprising, often evasive, as though Russell regretted having to combine biographical treatment with his often very illuminating critical commentary. He skirts, for example, the personal guilt Moore expressed over the death of his sister, pointing only to the advantages the young Henry gained upon becoming the youngest family member. On Moore's childhood generally, Russell is dismissive: "If there were traumatic incidents, no one knows of them." Russell's comments on influences, and on Moore's work generally, carry authority. His is the only book on Henry Moore to reproduce works by other sculptors—Rodin, Gaudier-Brzeska—to demonstrate possible influences on Moore.

One cannot say of Henry Moore that he was an uncooperative subject for biographers. He was unusually receptive to visitors—photographers, writers, admirers who simply wanted to meet him—and allowed an even more unusual degree of access to his private papers. HEDGECOE was among the many who enjoyed Moore's hospitality, and he returned the favor by producing one of the finest early photographic collections of Moore's work. Hedgecoe, who took over 12,000 photographs of Moore, his family, and his work (about 800 of them included here), combines illustration and commentary (the latter supplied by Moore himself) in a delightful, lighthearted, and suggestive manner. While this work serves primarily to extend our understanding of Moore's art (explaining for instance why he began to incorporate strings into his sculptures in the 1930s), it provides incidentally valuable insights into Moore's mind and character.

PACKER's "illustrated biography," appearing 17 years after Hedgecoe's collection, is less successful. Less generous in the number of photographs (100, taken by Gemma Levine), the work suffers as well from a bland and unrevealing text. We learn very little about Moore's childhood or adult relationships, and next to nothing about the personality and intellect behind some of the most striking visual images of the 20th century. One has to wonder why this book was produced: it does not approach the scope of Hedgecoe's work or of the fine volume by David Finn, *Henry Moore: Sculpture and Environment* (New York, Abrams, 1977). Finn's book, which contains a foreword by Kenneth Clark and some commentary by Henry Moore, will be of interest to readers capable of following some rather technical discussions concerning the relationship between Moore's works and the locations where they may be seen. Stephen Spender's *In Irina's Garden, with Henry Moore's Sculpture* (London, Thames and Hudson, 1986) is a wonderfully atmospheric volume, with photographs by David Finn, that will be of interest to all who want visual insight into the sculptor's environment. Two essays, "Henry and Irina," by Spender, and "Reminiscences," by Irina Moore, the sculptor's wife, add to the book's quiet congeniality. Gemma Levine's *With Henry Moore: The Artist at Work* (New York, Times Books, 1978) again emphasizes the importance of environment to Moore's work. Levine's book includes photographs of Moore *ca.* 1977, in his studio and on his grounds, walking among his sheep and his sculptures.

All previous collections of Moore's work take a back seat to the highly impressive catalog by COMPTON. This work is a boon to Moore scholars, lay readers, and future biographers. The biographical material to be found here is not of an immediately revealing nature; the work is not organized or intended as a biography but as a comprehensive catalog of Moore's works. In this capacity it succeeds almost without reservation: the repro-

ductions, which encompass drawings, carvings, paintings, lithographies, in addition to the sculptures, are exquisite. The range of interest and obvious mastery exhibited in these smaller works will surprise the viewer who thinks of Moore only as the creator of gigantic forms dominating an entire English landscape. Even so, Compton's achievement represents one of the richest sources yet published for information relating to the life of Henry Moore. The texts accompanying the individual entries, though necessarily brief, are precisely written and replete with relevant data about Moore's life, background, and psychological makeup. The catalog contains three introductory essays on Moore's art, including one by Peter Fuller entitled "Henry Moore: An English Romantic," which traces the rough edges of Moore's life through the stages of his career, citing influences ("in Moore's work there is always at the back of his mind the memory of Michelangelo and the Greeks"), noting shifts in perspective, and arguing the thesis implied in the essay's title that Moore was not a pioneer of modern sculpture. Compton's book, a model of its kind, also supplies a chronology and list of major exhibitions.

Of BERTHOUD, author of the one truly full-scale biography of Henry Moore and the most recent work to appear on him, it is not possible to write with much satisfaction. Those who have waited for a full biography of Moore, one that would examine and make sense of the known facts and tendencies of his life—his passions and preoccupations—in such a way as to throw light on his artistic achievement, must continue to wait. If earlier biographers were reticent about describing Moore's private life—other than what could be observed in the sitting room or the studio—Berthoud has done nothing to expand our sense of Moore as a man of strong and apparently conflicting emotions. Berthoud too was a friend of the Moore family for over 30 years, and this perhaps explains why he avoids any consideration of Moore's sexual life in light of the pervasive, and often rather strange, sexual imagery found in his work. Berthoud instead moves from commission to unveiling to state honor, for the most part denying the reader any insight into the inner life and vision of the artist with which Berthoud's almost unlimited access to archives and extensive interviews with Moore's friends and associates would have supplied him. Berthoud's book will be an important source for the biographer willing to approach Moore as a man whose personal insecurities (here hinted at, though they are consistently denied) have implications for his artistic achievement, and whose greatness as an artist deserves a more probing, less admiring and obligatory, biographical treatment than any he has yet received.

—Gerhard Glière

MORE, Sir Thomas, 1478–1535; English statesman, writer, and saint.

Bridgett, T. E., *Life and Writings of Sir Thomas More*. London, Burns and Oates, 1891.
Chambers, R. W., *Thomas More*. London, Cape, and New York, Harcourt, 1935.

Fox, Alistair, *Thomas More: History and Providence*. Oxford, Blackwell, and New Haven, Connecticut, Yale University Press, 1982.

Guy, John, *The Public Career of Sir Thomas More*. New Haven, Connecticut, Yale University Press, and Brighton, Sussex, Harvester Press, 1980.

Kenny, Anthony, *Thomas More*. Oxford and New York, Oxford University Press, 1983.

Marius, Richard, *Thomas More: A Biography*. New York, Knopf, 1984; London, Dent, 1985.

Martz, Louis M., *Thomas More: The Search for the Inner Man*. New Haven, Connecticut, and London, Yale University Press, 1990.

McConica, James, *Thomas More: A Short Biography*. London, H. M. Stationery's Office, 1977.

*

Many facts about More's life have only recently been ascertained, partly on account of the projected publication of *The Yale Edition of the Complete Works of St. Thomas More* (New Haven, Connecticut, and London, 1963–) following on the publication of the *Correspondence* (edited by Elizabeth F. Rogers, Princeton, 1947). More's attitudes certainly changed when, after his political defeat with the faction of Catherine of Aragon and his loss of the chancellorship in 1532, he no longer had a public tightrope to walk and could withdraw from balancing his private convictions against his public duties. Even now, though, the sources do not permit an exact assessment of whether the fourth indictment of treason, on account of which More was condemned, was in fact technically proven, even as that crime was defined in the 1534 Act of Treasons.

The question of More's guilt matters to two groups of his biographers: those mostly early apologists who present More's writings and personal positions as an important obstacle to what was to become the English Reformation, and those who present him chiefly as a lay martyr to the Catholic faith and to papal supremacy. The best analysis of the trial currently available is given by Marius (see below), who builds on J.D.M. Derrett in "The Trial of Sir Thomas More," printed in *Essential Articles for the Study of Thomas More*, edited by R. S. Sylvester and G. P. Marc'hadour (1977).

Since More's public position was so prominent, his activities have also been extensively treated by historians of politics, diplomacy, statecraft, and the administration of justice in Tudor England. His social satire, *Utopia* (1516), to which the best guide is by J. H. Hexter (*More's "Utopia": The Biography of an Idea*, Princeton, 1952) has caused many different forms of social and political theory to be attributed to him, as for instance by the pioneer socialist Karl Kautsky (*Thomas More and his "Utopia": With an Historical Introduction*, 1927). As the co-translator of Lucian with Erasmus, the author of the Platonizing social criticism to be found in his *Utopia* and his strong defences of Erasmus, with whom he is often said to have enjoyed a virtual identity of views and attitudes during at least the first two decades of the 16th century, More has also attracted the attention of historians of English Renaissance humanism. In addition he has frequently been portrayed, as in the famous Holbein portrait later destroyed by fire but for which the 1527 sketch still

exists in the Basle Kunstmuseum, as the model father and family man, "A Man for All Seasons" in the phrase coined of him by Erasmus and borrowed by Robert Bolt for the dramatisation of his life.

There is an early pen portrait of More by Erasmus in a 1519 letter replying to the humanist and future reformer Ulrich von Hutten, who had asked for one. A sketch of his life was written by his son-in-law, William Roper, in about 1557 (published 1626 and re-edited by E. V. Hitchcock in 1935) as a tribute, to be worked into a fuller biography by a family friend, Nicholas Harpsfield (edited by E. V. Hitchcock, 1932), who corrects some of Roper's errors. There is a third hagiographical biography of 1588, in Latin, by Thomas Stapleton (translated by Philip E. Hallett, 1928).

Interest in More was never extinguished, but the embers were rekindled by the Oxford Movement and Frederick Seebohm's *The Oxford Reformers* of 1867 associating More with Erasmus and Colet, who had been spiritual director to them both. More had been declared a martyr in 1579 and was beatified in 1886. In 1891 BRIDGETT's biography, while still hagiographic, delved into the primary sources and uncovered hitherto neglected facets of More's personality. In 1935, the year of the canonisation (after which biographers and others have to choose between "Sir" and "Saint," according to their point of view, or incur the possible embarrassment of avoiding any title at all), appeared *Thomas More* by R. W. CHAMBERS, for long the standard biography and a strong and religiously impartial defence of More's refusal to submit to tyranny. Chambers ignores the religious and theological passion underlying the polemic and perhaps some of the legal decisions. In the previous year Enid M. G. Routh had published *Sir Thomas More and his Friends 1477–1535* (London, 1934). Slighter accounts have subsequently appeared, like William Edward Campbell's *Erasmus, Tyndale, and More* (1949), Russell Ames' *Citizen Thomas More and his "Utopia"* (1949), and E. E. Reynolds' *The Field is Won* (1968), which gives a clear but not very profound account of its subject's life. It appeared under the title *The Life and Death of St. Thomas More* in 1978.

The Yale project to publish *The Complete Works* under the executive editorship of the late R. S. Sylvester and subsequently of Clarence Miller was conceived in 1958 and has so far been executed with rigorous scholarship. Its launching roughly coincided with a recrudescence of interest in Tudor parliamentary history and produced much fundamental research on More. Important material has appeared in the review *Moreana*, in *Essential Articles for the Study of Thomas More* (notably by M. Hastings, J. McConica, R. O'Sullivan, G. R. Elton, and J. D. M. Derrett), in *St. Thomas More: Action and Contemplation*, edited by R. S. Sylvester (1972), and in the volumes of *The Complete Works*.

Apart from Marius, there is a full-length study by John Guy (see below), an important account of More's intellectual career and controversial writings by FOX, and two short but excellent works by McCONICA and KENNY. A hostile account is to be found in Jasper Ridley's *The Statesman and the Fanatic* (1982), and there is an English chronology of the life in *L'Univers de Thomas More* (1963) by Germain Marc'hadour. Several other studies are important for More's biography but tangential to it, such as J. J. Scarisbrick, *Henry VIII* (1968), where the detailed and original account of the canon law of the royal divorce is flawed by an unfamiliarity with the practice which always transcended the written texts; J. McConica, *English Humanists and Reformation Politics* (1965); Margaret Mann Phillips, *Erasmus and His Times* (1967); R. Pineas, *Thomas More and Tudor Polemics* (1968); S. J. Greenblatt, *Renaissance and Self-Fashioning: From More to Shakespeare* (1980); and Robert P. Adams on English humanists under Henry VIII, *The Better Part of Valor* (1962). In 1961 R. W. Gibson and J. Max Patrick edited *Saint Thomas More: A Preliminary Bibliography*.

More's official papers never entered the government's archives and have not survived, so that GUY's researches among the Chancery Proceedings and other state papers at the Public Records Office have resulted in a much fuller picture than was hitherto available of More's role in the royal service, as councillor under Wolsey, and as diplomat and royal secretary as well as judge and lawyer. Guy incidentally also illuminates More's attitude to his family and his fairness, even generosity, of spirit, although he is harsh in his presentation of More's attitude to the six heretics executed during his chancellorship.

Owing much to G. R. Elton, Guy treats More's career from its beginnings to 1532 but concentrates chiefly on the period of the chancellorship, which lasted only from 1529–32. He succeeds not only in illuminating the relationship between Wolsey and the lay compromise candidate for the chancellorship who succeeded him, but also and more generally the way in which the administration of justice was changing in England and the role played by More in its socio-legal adaptation from the canon law and equity tradition of the clerical chancellors to that of the lay chancellors drawn from a Common Law background. More added "practical realism to Wolsey's idealism" in the administration of justice. His 31 months in office, writes Guy, "was a magisterial performance." The biography is outstanding, too, in its appreciation of the political difficulties faced, in the end unsuccessfully, by More.

MARIUS, also clearly influenced by Elton among others, writes for the non-professional and pays little attention to the theological minutiae, thinking no doubt rightly that the issues involved were more broadly important than do the majority of historians, who regard the theological disputes as mostly technical. Marius has produced an admirably readable as well as a scholarly if popular biography that emphasises the possible influence on More's activity of a sexuality he found it hard to suppress. His biography presents a personal interpretation that does not belong to the history of ideas or value systems and plays down the community of feeling even between the More of *Utopia* and the Erasmus of the series of long essays on social topics inserted into the 1515 Froben edition of the *Adagia*.

More is emphasised more as "a master of evasion" as illustrated by his defence of the satirical *Julius exclusus*, which Marius attributes to Erasmus without discussion, although the attribution was still contested at the date at which he was writing. The interest of Marius' work lies in his reading of More's personality, and the conflicts it undoubtedly contained, rather than on his uncovering any new historical evidence. The scholarship is up-to-date, but the intention is clearly as much to interpret More's character as to narrate his activities.

MARTZ's recent work is a disappointingly slight volume of only 112 pages, much heralded before its appearance as "an antidote to revisionist charges" and "a sound rebuttal of negative criticism." Dedicated to Richard Sylvester, the book makes clear its intention to repudiate the picture of More presented by Elton and developed by Marius. In fact it confines itself to showing that More's harshness on heresy and heretics was just a feature of the age he lived in. The explicit attempt to reinstate the image of the gentle, humanist, "man for all seasons" is too insubstantial to dent the Elton-Marius packaging. Martz achieves little more than an announcement that the debate is still going on.

The centenary of More's birth was celebrated in 1977–78 by an exhibition at the National Portrait Gallery in London, whose highly scholarly catalogue, by J. B. Trapp and Hubertus Schulte Herbrüggen, German editor of recently discovered letters of More, contains much detailed and important biographical information. In 1978 a symposium at Georgetown University occasioned further important reassessments of More's personality and achievements, without excluding from consideration the "hidden violence," particularly in the anti-Lutheran polemic, which, taken in conjunction with the much-emphasised serenity, affection, and evenness of temper, leaves an enigma in More's character unresolved by any biographer.

—A. H. T. Levi

MORGAN, John Pierpont, 1837–1913; American banker and art collector.

Allen, Frederick Lewis, *The Great Pierpont Morgan.* New York, Harper, and London, Gollancz, 1949.

Canfield, Cass, *The Incredible Pierpont Morgan: Financier and Art Collector.* New York, Harper, and London, Hamilton, 1974.

Hovey, Carl, *The Life Story of J. Pierpont Morgan.* New York, Sturgis and Walton, 1911; London, Heinemann, 1912.

Jackson, Stanley, *J. P. Morgan: A Biography.* New York, Stein and Day, 1983; as *J. P. Morgan: The Rise and Fall of a Banker*, London, Heinemann, 1984.

Satterlee, Herbert L., *J. Pierpont Morgan: An Intimate Portrait.* New York, Macmillan, 1939.

Sinclair, Andrew, *Corsair: The Life of J. Pierpont Morgan.* Boston, Little Brown, and London, Weidenfeld and Nicolson, 1981.

Taylor, Francis Henry, *Pierpont Morgan As Collector And Patron 1837–1913.* New York, Pierpont Morgan Library, 1957; revised edition, 1970.

Wheeler, George, *Pierpont Morgan and Friends: The Anatomy of a Myth.* Englewood Cliffs, New Jersey, Prentice-Hall, 1973.

Winkler, John K., *Morgan The Magnificent: The Life of J. Pierpont Morgan 1837–1913.* New York, Vanguard Press, 1932.

*

HOVEY's rather pallidly written volume, the only biography written while Morgan was alive, presents a basically favorable sketch of Morgan's business career. Hovey finds that "the moral axis upon which [Morgan's] career turns as a whole, is a natural passion for sound, well-founded business, without logical flaws or sapping weakness." Hovey also points out that to Morgan a sound business was one with a minimum of competition, as the banker "discovered long ago that competition is waste, is war in its worst effect. Hovey includes brief accounts of the patrician banker's art collection and charities, and has occasional comments on his personality (remarking, for example, on his "taciturnity" and "love of mental privacy"). But the author all but ignores Morgan's private life. Hovey had the advantage of being able to interview eyewitnesses who have long since departed. Because of this, and because of painstaking research, his work continues to be useful to serious students of Morgan's career.

In certain respects WINKLER's biography is an advance on Hovey's. Written in a lively style, Winkler's book offers a fuller and more stimulating account of Morgan's family background. He suggests, for example, that Morgan's maternal grandfather exhibited traits like "imagination, dash," "initiative akin to recklessness," and above all an "insatiable love of the beautiful" that appeared later in the grandson. Again, Winkler remarks on some of Morgan's beliefs, prejudices, and dislikes (E. H. Harriman, for one); comments shrewdly on his personality; and devotes space to the banker's private life. Indeed, Winkler has several paragraphs concerned with Morgan's "adventures in romance," which, he claims, "were many and varied."

If Winkler's discussion of Morgan's private life and personality is fuller and more spirited than Hovey's, his account of Morgan's business career is more familiar. Like Hovey, Winkler covers such topics as Morgan's role in the reorganization of the nation's railroads, the 1895 gold bond sale, and the formation of United States Steel in 1901. Both authors, deeply impressed by Morgan's achievements, declare him a financial "genius." Neither writer, it should be said, employs footnotes, or has seen fit to attach a bibliography to his study.

SATTERLEE's volume is the amplest biography of the Wall Street magnate. Since he was Morgan's son-in-law, and since the banker "sanctioned" his study, Satterlee had access to Morgan's diaries, notes, and correspondence, as well as to relatives and friends. The result is a lengthy—roughly a quarter of a million words—detailed chronicle of Morgan's privileged youth, schooling, business career, family life, travels, charities, public service, art collections, and even medical problems. The book is arranged in a tight, chronological framework, rolling along from month-to-month, and year-to-year. In a typical six- or seven-page segment, Satterlee might discuss—and without any changes in emphasis—a business problem, one of Morgan's charities, additions to his art collection, and preparations for an ocean voyage. The biography has no organizing theme and contains little interpretation of Morgan's character.

Here and there, it is true, Satterlee does offer some suggestive comments. Perhaps the single most insightful such comment occurs when the author relates Morgan's "passion for order" to his love of the game of solitaire. "When he played cards with others it was whist," writes Satterlee, "that was his favorite game." But when alone "it was natural that he should try to create order among the cards," insists the author, "by shuffling and to build them up in the orderly sequence of suits." Morgan "always wanted to substitute a pattern for disorder," concludes Satterlee, and that "was undoubtedly why he loved all games of solitaire."

Unfortunately, such observations are infrequent. Satterlee, a devoted admirer of his father-in-law, rarely probes or questions. He is at times inaccurate, or at any rate incomplete, in his dis-

cussion of business matters (as, for instance, in his truncated account of the International Mercantile Marine). And some subjects, including Morgan's financial worth, are left untouched. Still, his biography is, and will remain, a prime source for Morgan scholars.

ALLEN has produced a graphic, tight-knit, objective portrait of J. P. Morgan. Allen steers a middle course between the "Morgan-praisers" (like Satterlee), and the "Morgan-depraisers," as he labels Morgan's detractors. The author appreciates Morgan's accomplishments, and acknowledges that "he was a man great in character and force, whose influence was in many respects salutary." Allen, for instance, demonstrates how Morgan's courage and imperious will were instrumental in carrying out the 1895 gold bond sale. Yet Allen also argues that Morgan "represented a trend in the direction of economic affairs which had to be altered for the good of the country." Quite simply, Morgan had become too powerful. As the Pujo Committee report revealed in 1913, Morgan and his circle held 341 directorships in 112 corporations with a total capitalization of $22 billion.

Allen has some astute observations concerning Morgan's style of life and character. "Morgan was by nature a duke of industry, pursuing the life of an unostentatious gentleman on a majestic scale," writes Allen. Morgan "didn't care for balls, cotillions" or "social emulation." Rather, observes Allen, this "proper" New Yorker "preferred solid comfort, solid dinners, [and] solid people." Of course, the "solid comfort" included a country estate on the Hudson, a thousand acre "place" in the Adirondacks, a small "fishing box" at Newport, a "country seat" outside of London, and a 302-foot ocean-going yacht. Allen points out, too, that Morgan could be brusque, but also "truly courteous"; and that though the banker lived royally, he was also given to "sudden acts of good will."

In his research, Allen—the first biographer to list his sources—reviewed diaries, account books and certain company records, and interviewed Thomas W. Lamont, a surviving Morgan associate. But since many company records and family documents were unavailable to him, Allen is able to shed little new light on Morgan's financial career. Nonetheless, he has written a readable and satisfying biography.

TAYLOR provides a competent review of Morgan's career as a collector. Taylor sees Morgan as "the greatest figure in the art world that America has yet produced." Between 1890 and 1913, Morgan collected manuscripts, books and various objects of art—paintings, frescoes, jewelry, sculpture, porcelains, furniture, altar pieces, and tapestries—valued by the London *Times* in 1913 at $60 million. This collection, much of which was divided between the Metropolitan Museum and the Morgan Library (itself a work of art), was, according to Taylor, of very high quality. Apparently Morgan and the experts he consulted were rarely fooled. Taylor suggests that of the 4000 objects from Morgan's collection given to the Metropolitan, "something well over ninety per cent" are on permanent exhibition. And he adds that an "even higher percentage of excellence is true of the collection of the library."

After quickly rehashing Morgan's business career, CANFIELD focuses on Morgan as a collector of art. He hardly exhausts the subject, and in fact adds little to Taylor's pioneering effort. Canfield (who attended Groton with Morgan's grandson) believes that "Morgan had an extraordinary eye for art." He further suggests that Morgan "was so formidable that few dealers dared to cheat him." Canfield also observes that Morgan's collection was "diverse." The book's many photographs and colored plates offer convincing testimony to this observation.

WHEELER, writing in the Matthew Josephson "Robber Baron" tradition, concentrates on Morgan's business career. From the Hall carbine affair, through the 1895 gold bond sale, on to the Pujo Committee hearings, Wheeler has little but criticism for Morgan's motives and actions. Morgan was no angel, and made his share of business mistakes, but he was not the arrogant, hypocritical, greedy, lawless, second-rate banker depicted in this book.

SINCLAIR pleasingly presents familiar material for a popular audience. Here and there he spices his narrative with details of Morgan's life and career neglected by previous biographers. Sinclair also adds a Freudian touch when discussing such subjects as Morgan's extraordinary first marriage to a woman dying of tuberculosis, and his relationship to his father, Junius (whose death "liberated his son," according to the author). Still, Sinclair's biography, which is based largely on secondary sources, breaks no new ground.

JACKSON, a London barrister, relies even more heavily on secondary sources. Jackson contributes nothing to our knowledge of Morgan's character and career, but he does put forth some racy and at times tasteless speculation about Morgan's sex life. "His mistresses, so often seasoned theatrical veterans," writes Jackson, "must have needed dramatic talent in order to swoon convincingly in the arms of an elderly and obese lover with a monstrous nose and smoke-laden lungs that wheezed under pressure like a bagpipe." Such earthiness entertains, but fails to enlighten.

—Richard Harmond

MORISOT, Berthe, 1841–1895; French painter.

Adler, Kathleen and Tamar Garb, *Berthe Morisot*. Ithaca, New York, Cornell University Press, and Oxford, Phaidon, 1987.

Higonnet, Anne, *Berthe Morisot: A Biography*. New York, Harper and Row, and London, Collins, 1990.

Rey, Jean Dominique, *Berthe Morisot*, translated by Shirley Jennings. Naefels, Switzerland, Bonfifi Press, 1982.

Rouart, Dennis, *The Correspondence of Berthe Morisot*. New York, Wittenborn, 1957 (originally published by Quatre-Chemins Editart, Paris, 1950); as *Berthe Morisot: The Correspondence with Her Family and Her Friends*, edited, with introduction and notes, by Kathleen Adler and Tamar Garb, London, Camden Press, 1986.

Stuckey, Charles F. and William P. Scott, with Suzanne G. Lindsay, *Berthe Morisot, Impressionist*. New York, Hudson Hills, and London, Sotheby's, 1987.

*

A key reference for the study of Morisot's life and times remains the compilation of her correspondence by her grandson, Denis ROUART. Rouart draws on a wealth of letters exchanged within the Morisot family and letters Berthe shared with her friends (Puvis de Chavannes, Edgar Degas, Édouard Manet, Auguste Renoir, and Stéphane Mallarmé). As Adler and Garb point out in their new edition, however, the material is neither unbiased nor complete, and "it is certain that letters, unpublished here, exist."

Rouart weaves passages from Morisot's correspondence into a biographical narrative that connects and elaborates on events referenced in the letters. The new edition includes extensive notes, clarifies ambiguities in Rouart's chronology, and corrects some errors of date. Letters cited in the text are now dated, and a chronology of significant events in Morisot's life has been added to Rouart's original text.

Rouart's collection offers firsthand accounts of Mme. Morisot's encouragement and concern over her daughter's independence and burgeoning career, the early training of Berthe and her sisters in the studios of Guichard and Corot, the informal apprenticeship with and modeling sessions for Édouard Manet, events in Paris during the War of 1870 and the Commune, Berthe's conflicting feelings about marriage, her late espousal to Eugène Manet, and the birth and youth of her daughter Julie. From Berthe's intimate viewpoint, the social circles in which she moved come to life: the Thursday evening salons of Madame Morisot and Madame Manet, the preparations and machinations surrounding the Impressionist exhibitions, and, throughout, her steadfast commitment to painting. Anecdotes colorfully illuminate the personalities of her circle (Manet, Degas, Puvis de Chavannes, Mallarmé), the critical reception of her work (and the work of her colleagues) at the Paris Salons and the Impressionist exhibitions, but as Rouart notes in the preface, "Her letters almost never touch on fundamental questions." And, as Adler and Garb stress in the introduction, it is the personality of "Rouart's Morisot" who appears in this collection. Nancy Mathews reiterates this conclusion in her review (*Women's Art Journal*, Spring/Summer 1989): "Morisot . . . has remained undocumented because her heirs have guarded her reputation. The Rouart family has closely controlled access to her, allowing only excerpted letters . . . to be published . . . [which] has contributed to her being neglected and misunderstood for most of the century since her death."

REY, in a popular, illustrated study of Morisot's art, draws heavily on Rouart and two French texts by Monique Angoulvent (*Berthe Morisot*, Paris, 1933) and Armand Fourreau (*Berthe Morisot*, Paris, 1925), as well as on Julie Manet's diary (*Journal 1893–99*, Paris, 1979), which contains new information about Morisot's last years. Although this is not a scholarly book, it offers a reliable, readable assessment of key events in Morisot's life, the development of her artistic career, and her role within the Impressionist circle.

STUCKEY's lengthy essay for the catalogue of a major retrospective exhibition is the most comprehensive and thoroughly documented biography of this artist yet available. While drawing on previous studies by Angoulvent, Fourreau, and others, as well as letters in Rouart, Stuckey discovered new material, including correspondence from Degas, Mme. Morisot, Mallarmé, and Puvis de Chavannes (now in a private collection). These indicate that Morisot joined the first Impressionist exhibition a few months later than once believed, and newly discovered letters exchanged between Berthe and Puvis de Chavannes in the early 1870s intimate a romantic liaison, which her parents opposed.

These sources, in addition to Morisot's notebooks from 1885–95, Julie Manet's diary, the Durand-Rueil archives, and research from the substantial exhibition catalogue entitled *The New Painting: Impressionism* (Geneva, 1986), support Stuckey's correction and clarification of works Morisot sent to the Salon and the Impressionist exhibitions, the identity of her sitters, as well as his elaboration of her aesthetic development. Here, Eugène Manet, Morisot's husband, emerges slightly from the shadows of his famous brother and wife. We learn that Eugène identified himself in his marriage license as a "landowner," and that in the mid-1870s his financial difficulties may have contributed to Morisot's concern with selling her work (letters from the Morisot family around 1875 express concern over his employment). Stuckey also clarifies Morisot's friendship with Stéphane Mallarmé beginning in 1874 and with Claude Monet after Édouard Manet's death, and the origins of a myth that the 18th-century painter Fragonard was a distant relative of Morisot on her father's side. (Mallarmé's preface to an exhibition catalogue of 1896 first cited this relationship, but the publication of Mary Cassatt's correspondence in 1984 clarified the origins of the story.) If one were to read only one biography of the artist, this is certainly the most scholarly, comprehensive, but also readable source.

ADLER AND GARB balance their thematic study of Morisot's art with rich biographical detail based on Rouart, Julie Manet's diary, and published reminiscences and correspondence from Morisot's associates. Friendships with Mary Cassatt (based on recently published correspondence), Renoir, and Mallarmé; the social context in which Morisot's work evolved; and published criticism of her art, are fleshed out in this text. Drawing on the memoirs of Mallarmé, de Renier, and Paul Valéry, Morisot appears "a muse, a sphinx-like figure, an intent and reserved personality whose grace and remoteness combined to produce extraordinary charm." Although such authorities are quoted throughout, the text provides no footnotes, and one wishes for more scholarly documentation. Moreover, as Barbara Scott notes in her review (*Apollo*, October 1987), the authors' feminist slant sometimes results in irritating and subjective comments, such as: "Mallarmé's letter to Morisot reveals that her physical appearance was rarely forgotten, and that the obligation to compliment and flatter her as a woman was almost always present." Nancy Mathews (*Women's Art Journal*, Spring/Summer 1989) also finds here "rather heavy-handed reminders of conventional thinking about [a woman's] sphere in the 19th century (which does not seem quite relevant to Morisot)." Nevertheless, Adler and Garb's decision to position their study of the artist's life and career within the social context of 19th-century France results in new insights into Morisot's life and artistic development.

HIGONNET's life of Morisot will likely become the standard. Access to the Morisot family letters, still owned by the artist's descendants, coupled with new material from Impressionist scholarship, enables Higonnet to clarify Morisot's personality and history more fully than any other writer had done. This engaging, fluid text explores the struggles and accomplishments of an artist who was also a woman in a society structured to curb her freedom. A feminist historian, Higonnet yet avoids the judgmental tone assumed by Adler and Garb. Instead, she sensitively probes the issues with an eye always on Morisot's own perceptions of her situation. Generous citations from letters and journals

support this biography's in-depth treatment of Morisot's friendships within the Impressionist circle, with the sculptress Marcello, and with her mentor, Éduard Manet. Here we learn more about Morisot's difficulties with her family in the early 1870s, her political views during the Commune, her bouts of depression and melancholy, and her struggle during the 1890s to preserve and promote the Impressionists' achievements. Eugène Manet here emerges fully as a personality, as do Morisot's sisters, Yves and Edma. Written for the specialist and non-specialist alike, this illustrated study is marred only by the absence of notes for all the texts cited.

—Phylis Floyd

MORRIS, William, 1834–1896; English poet, designer, and socialist.

Arnot, R. Page, *William Morris: A Vindication*. London, M. Lawrence, 1934.

Bloomfield, Paul, *The Life and Work of William Morris*. London, A. Barker/Royal Society of Arts, 1934.

Boos, Florence, editor, *William Morris' Socialist Diary*. London and New York, Journeyman Press, 1985.

Burne-Jones, Georgiana, *Memorials of Burne-Jones*. London, Macmillan, 1904.

Cary, Elisabeth, *William Morris: Poet, Craftsman, Socialist*. New York and London, Putnam, 1902.

Clark, Fiona, *William Morris: Wallpapers and Chintzes*. London, Academy Editions, and New York, St. Martin's, 1973.

Clutton-Brock, A., *William Morris: His Work and Influence*. London, Butterworth, and New York, Holt, 1914.

Compton-Rickett, Arthur, *William Morris: A Study in Personality*. London, H. Jenkins, and New York, Dutton, 1913.

Crow, Gerald, *William Morris: Designer*. London and New York, Studio Publications, 1934.

Drinkwater, John, *William Morris: A Critical Study*. London, M. Secker, and New York, M. Kennerly, 1912.

Dunlap, Joseph R., *The Book That Never Was*. New York, Oriole Editions, 1971.

Dunlap, Joseph R., *The Introductions to the Collected Works of William Morris*. New York, Oriole Editions, 1973.

Faulkner, Peter, *Against the Age: An Introduction to William Morris*. London, Allen and Unwin, 1980.

Glasier, J. Bruce, *William Morris and the Early Days of the Socialist Movement*. London and New York, Longman, 1921.

Grennan, Margaret R., *William Morris: Medievalist and Revolutionary*. New York, King's Crown Press, 1945.

Henderson, Philip, *William Morris: His Life, Work and Friends*. London, Thames and Hudson, and New York, McGraw-Hill, 1967.

Jackson, Holbrook, *William Morris: Craftsman, Socialist*. London, A. C. Fifield, 1908.

Kelvin, Norman, *The Collected Letters of William Morris, 1848–88* (2 vols.). Princeton, New Jersey, Princeton University Press, 1984–87.

Kirchhoff, Frederick, *William Morris*. Boston, Twayne, 1979.

Lindsay, Jack, *William Morris: His Life and Work*. London, Constable, 1975; New York, Taplinger, 1979.

Mackail, J. W., *The Life of William Morris* (2 vols.). London and New York, Longman, 1899.

Meier, Paul, *William Morris: The Marxist Dreamer*, translated by F. Grubb. Hassocks, Sussex, Harvester Press, 1978 (originally published as *La pensée utopique de William Morris*, 2 vols., Paris, Éditions sociales, 1972).

Morris, May, editor, *The Collected Works of William Morris* (24 vols.). London, Longman, 1910–15.

Morris, May, editor, *William Morris: Artist, Writer, Socialist* (2 vols.). Oxford, Blackwell, 1936.

Noyes, Alfred, *William Morris*. London, Macmillan, 1908.

Parry, Linda, *William Morris Textiles*. New York, Viking, and London, Weidenfeld and Nicolson, 1983.

Peterson, William S., *A Bibliography of the Kelmscott Press*. Oxford, Clarendon Press, 1984.

Sewter, A. C., *The Stained Glass of William Morris and His Circle* (2 vols.). New Haven, Connecticut, Yale University Press, 1974–75.

Shaw, George Bernard, *William Morris As I Knew Him*. New York, Dodd Mead, 1936 (originally published in vol. 2 of *William Morris: Artist, Writer, Socialist*, edited by Mary Morris, Oxford, Blackwell, 1936).

Silver, Carol, *The Romance of William Morris*. Athens, Ohio University Press, 1982.

Sparling, H. Halliday, *The Kelmscott Press and William Morris, Master Craftsman*. London, Macmillan, 1924.

Stansky, Peter, *William Morris*. Oxford and New York, Oxford University Press, 1983.

Thompson, E. P., *William Morris: Romantic to Revolutionary*. London, Lawrence and Wishart, 1955; revised edition, New York, Pantheon, 1976; London, Merlin Press, 1977.

Thompson, Paul, *The Work of William Morris*. London, Heinemann, and New York, Viking, 1967; revised edition, London, Quartet Books, 1977.

Thompson, Susan Otis, *American Book Design and William Morris*. New York, R. R. Bowker, 1977.

Watkinson, Ray, *William Morris as Designer*. London, Studio Vista, and New York, Reinhold, 1967.

Weekly, Montague, *William Morris*. London, Duckworth, 1934.

*

BOOS, one of the most active and astute scholars now working on William Morris, has remarked that Morris' "achievements routinely exhaust the energies of his biographers." She's absolutely right. To cover only his literary achievements, the editors of *The Dictionary of Literary Biography* called upon three different guest experts: Joseph Dunlap, K. L. Goodwin, and Frederick Kirchhoff, to write major essays on Morris in, respectively, *Victorian Novelists After 1885* (*DLB*, vol. 18, 1983); *Victorian Poets After 1850* (*DLB*, vol. 35, 1985); and *Victorian Prose Writers After 1857* (*DLB*, vol. 57, 1987). Dunlap's essay opens with the following point: Morris' "life was one of constant creativity as designer, craftsman, writer, translator, lecturer, calligrapher, merchant, medievalist, socialist, typographer, printer, environmentalist, and pioneer in architectural preservation." In each of these 13 fields, Morris' contributions were im-

portant, often very influential; and it follows that anyone desiring precise or technical information about Morris' achievements in one or more of these fields must perforce consult works other than traditional biographies. One would, for instance, have to read WATKINSON on Morris and design, and—to break that field into narrower categories—SEWTER on Morris and stained glass, PARRY on Morris and textiles, CLARK on Morris and wallpaper, DUNLAP (1971) and SUSAN THOMPSON on Morris and the book arts, and so forth. SPARLING and PETERSON must be consulted on the Kelmscott Press, Meier and E. P. Thompson (see below) on Morris' radical politics, Silver and Faulkner (see below) on his romances, and so on. And there are also many exhibition catalogues, monographs, collections of letters (see KELVIN), editions (see Boos, and May Morris, below), and memoirs (see Burne-Jones and Shaw, below) that contain significant biographical data.

The most important of the traditional biographies was written by MACKAIL, a poet and classical scholar who was also the son-in-law of Morris' closest friend. This is the official biography, and all subsequent biographers (nearly 30) are indebted to it—and most of them have mined it freely. Because he had "unreserved access" to unpublished materials, to personal letters—most no longer extant—to journals and diaries; and becuase of his many conversations with relatives and intimate friends, including of course Georgie and Edward Burne-Jones, whose daughter he had married in 1884, Mackail's lengthy and judicious narrative is of prime importance. It moves with steady eloquence from descriptions of Morris' parents and boyhood to somber evocations of the atmosphere at Morris' simple funeral, which Mackail had attended. Here occur for the first time the now hackneyed anecdotes about Morris' precosity—reading all of the Waverly novels by the age of seven, for example—restless energy, and bad temper; and here are the stories about the "brotherhood" at Oxford, who exulted over Chaucer and Malory, who started a literary magazine, who journeyed to France to visit medieval cathedrals and painted Arthurian murals under Rossetti's easy eye. Here also are the stories about their marriages and the decorations at Red House that inspired the formation of Morris and Company. Other stories, notably about Morris' marital problems, are left untold, or only hinted at: "In the verses that frame the stories of *The Earthly Paradise*, there is an autobiography so delicate and so outspoken that it must needs be allowed to speak for itself." (Modern biographers have not been so discreet: HENDERSON and LINDSAY write openly of Janey's affair with Rossetti and of Morris seeking consolation with Georgie Burne-Jones and Aglaia Coronio.) Mackail remains indispensable for the year-to-year record and for his balanced and full discussions of Morris' poetry, translations, and retellings of classical stories. Although he was not as opposed to Morris' politics as some recent critics have suggested, Mackail does imply that it was more normal for Morris to translate Homer than to speak out against capitalism.

To get the full account of the significance of Morris' political activities and writings, one must turn to E. P. THOMPSON, who used sources either not available to Mackail (archives in Holland) or ignored by him (all of the journalism in *Commonweal* and *Justice*) to trace the "transformation" of Morris from an "eccentric artist and literary man into a Socialist agitator." The Morris who emerges from these pages is a true revolutionary thinker, one who tempered Marxist ideas about historical necessity with his own ideas about the importance of human desire finding outlets in joyful work (hence art) and in fellowship, of prime importance in Morris' thought. He was not, as many biographers have suggested (see Glasier, below), a "mere muddle-headed convert to Marxism." In a revised second edition, E. P. Thompson omits sections with "pat political sentiments," but he adds a 65-page postscript in which he reviews the intervening 20 years of Morris criticism. He praises MEIER's exhaustive survey of the development of Morris' socialist thought, but he argues that Morris' ideas about alienation and the like grew out of his own experiences, without benefit of Marx or Engels.

Between Mackail and E. P. Thompson, the most significant additions to the biographical record occur in BURNE-JONES' *Memorials* (as much about Morris as it is about her husband, since the two were the closest of friends for 45 years and collaborators on important projects from stained glass for Morris and Co. to the Kelmscott Chaucer), and in MAY MORRIS's introductions to each of the 24 volumes of *The Collected Works*. (These introductions have been re-issued in a two-volume set; see DUNLAP, 1973.) Since she had worked closely with her father on designs and patterns, and had shared his sympathies and friends, May Morris speaks with unique authority about the people and events that inspired and shaped particular works. And she quotes extensively from previously unpublished letters and manuscripts. A two-volume supplement (1936), again important for its long introductions, appeared 25 years later; the second volume opens with SHAW's memoir (also published separately), famous for its insider's view of Morris' political activities, especially during the 1880s, and for its discussion of Morris' socialist writings, the "best books in the Bible of socialism."

After Mackail the first full biography is CARY's. She promises "to reveal the man and his work as they appeared to the outer public." Her discussions of the poetry, of Morris' pioneering work with the Society to Protect Ancient Buildings and at the Kelmscott Press, are adequate, but she laments his political work and writings, asserting that "he had not a reasoning mind" and that socialism raised havoc with his "aesthetic life." Such themes were picked up by a majority of subsequent biographers, creators of the "Morris myth" attacked by Arnot (see below) and finally laid to rest by E. P. Thompson. A strong bias against Morris' politics is apparent in NOYES' biography, written for a general audience. Noyes claims that "socialism means the substitution of death for life," and so ignores or misreads the socialist romances, insisting that the "essential factor in Morris' career is the poetic spirit in him." His commentary on the poetry is often helpful, if over-blown (he says that *Sigurd* is a greater epic than *Paradise Lost*). Slightly less dyspeptic about Morris' politics, COMPTON-RICKETT promises to "deal particularly with the personal equation," and so he sought interviews with many of Morris' colleagues. There are fresh anecdotes here, and sane discussions of the poetry and design work, but Morris is labeled an "aesthetic reformer" and again the socialist writings are presented with a conservative bias. Perhaps the most damaging estimation of Morris' socialism came from a fellow-socialist, GLASIER, who insisted that Morris did not understand Marx, nor did he want to. This book is valuable for its eyewitness accounts of factional disputes and of lecture tours to Scotland and elsewhere, but it did more to undermine Morris' modern reputation as a socialist thinker than any other

book; that is why E. P. Thompson devoted so many pages to debunking Glasier.

There are early biographies that provide good general introductions to Morris and that are neutral about his politics. One such is DRINKWATER, who pays close attention to Morris' literary output and concludes that for Morris "art was gospel, and all his social teaching and activity were but an effort to bring his gospel to pass upon earth." Another is by CLUTTON-BROCK, who sees Morris as "the chief representative of that aesthetic discontent which is peculiar to our time." This study is generally reliable and fulfills its aim of introducing new readers to the "greatness" of Morris. Not all of the early biographers were biased against Morris' socialism. JACKSON's short study, a volume in the Social Reformer's Series, stresses the connections between Morris' craftsmanship and his politics, between his idealization of the middle ages and his hatred of modern civilization. Jackson's discussion of Morris' antipathy to both anarchists and Fabians is acute, as is his analysis of *A Dream of John Ball*.

The centenary year, 1934, saw the publication of two general and faintly hagiographic introductions, by BLOOMFIELD and WEEKLY; both provide adequate surveys of the life and works. This was also the year that ARNOT, in response to "an orgy of canonization" and outrageous claims by diverse politicians, made his strong and convincing claims that Morris was not a dreamy reformer but a scientific, revolutionary socialist. CROW, in a volume sponsored by *Studio* magazine, replete with fine illustrations and full-page color plates, celebrated Morris' centenary with a solid discussion of his achievements as a designer; the book also has a concise and reliable biographical sketch.

Since 1934, several biographies have appeared. The most important, by E. P. Thompson, focuses on Morris' political development. That focus caused him to skirt the early and late prose romances, as well as the translations and design work. Readers interested in such matters should consult books by Grennan, Silver, Henderson, Lindsay, Paul Thompson, and Faulkner.

In the first of these, GRENNAN examines the "interrelations of Morris' medievalism and his socialism," offering specific discussions of major events and people in his life and astute analyses of most of his writings, including the socialist lectures. But she also says, following Glasier, "of the Marxian theory of value he understood little and cared less."

SILVER provides thorough and reliable discussions of all of Morris' literary works, pointing out how each of them uses romantic conventions and motifs. Since she employs Freudian and Jungian terms, her discussions, particularly of the late prose romances, often break new ground and offer fresh insights.

HENDERSON's book, because he worked with newly released correspondence (e.g., the Jane Morris-Rossetti letters), contains a wealth of new material and is a necessary supplement to Mackail. Henderson stresses the centrality of Morris to his time. His many associations with important artists, poets, and politicians, and his work with many organizations and causes, are here displayed so fully that it becomes apparent that Morris is also a central figure for our time.

LINDSAY follows both Mackail and Henderson in his discussions of the major writings and achievements, but he reiterates throughout the importance of Morris' childhood and "how much his whole hope for the future, for a happy and brotherly world, is linked to his childhood memories." Moreover, bonds that he formed then with his sister Emma affected his marriage and his attitudes toward Rossetti. Lindsay is also provocative in his claims for the signal importance of Morris' socialist writings and his significance as a Marxist thinker, ''indeed apart from Lenin, the only one who never lost or diluted his sense of the vital unity of political, economic, aesthetic, and moral factors.''

PAUL THOMPSON's biography is significant for its summaries and evaluations of recent research on Morris' achievements and reputation as a designer, pointing out that ''Morris is less important in the evolution of the modern movement than had previously been thought.'' His discussions of the literary works are enhanced by references to the decorative arts. The book includes a useful gazeteer that lists the museums, churches, and private homes where many of the works discussed in the text can still be seen.

FAULKNER offers a trenchant introduction to Morris, his times, his work, and his continuing relevance, demonstrating the ways that Morris in his poetry and prose, in his design work, and of course in his lectures, was continually ''against the age.'' Faulkner uses contemporary responses and reviews to good effect and provides stimulating and sensible evaluations of the early poetry and of the classical translations.

KIRCHHOFF's book is limited to Morris' literary development; it opens with a biographical sketch that highlights Morris' rebellion against the values of his middle-class family. To them his marriage to the ''uneducated daughter of an Oxford stableman must have seemed the final humiliation,'' and they did not attend the wedding—a fact not noted by previous biographers. It becomes here part of a psychological backdrop against which Kirchhoff offers new readings of the literary works. Another short introduction, one that uses a political rather than a psychological approach, is STANSKY's volume in Oxford's ''Past Masters Series.'' Cogent and clear, this survey of Morris' life and the diversity and significance of his work is wholly reliable and recommended for readers just embarking on a study of William Morris, the versatile Victorian.

—Gary L. Aho

MORSE, Samuel Finley Breese, 1791–1872; American inventor and painter.

Cikovsky, Nicolai, Jr., editor, *Lectures on the Affinity of Painting with the Other Fine Arts.* Columbia, University of Missouri Press, 1983.

Larkin, Oliver W., *Samuel F. B. Morse and American Democratic Art.* Boston, Little Brown, 1954.

Mabee, Carleton, *The American Leonardo: A Life of Samuel F. B. Morse.* New York, Knopf, 1943.

Prime, Samuel Irenaeus, *The Life of Samuel F. B. Morse, L. L. D.* New York, D. Appleton, 1875.

*

Morse's biographers have followed two different paths in describing his life. Most of the early commentators stressed his role as an amateur scientist who invented and developed the

telegraph. Now in the 20th century, Morse's biographers have focused primarily on his role as an artist.

The first type of approach was taken by James D. Reid in *Telegraph in America: Its Founders, Promoters, and Noted Men* (1879). Reid reserved his greatest accolades for Morse, though he did recognize the importance of Joseph Henry, Alfred Vail, and Leonard D. Gale. Van Buren Denslow and J. M. Parker in *Thomas A. Edison and Samuel F. B. Morse* (1877) equate the importance of both men in the development of American science.

Roger Burlingame, the frustrated novelist, took a different tack. In his *March of the Iron Men: A Social History of Union through Prevention* (1938), Burlingame minimized the importance of Morse and his inventive skills. He noted that many other inventors had played a greater role in providing the ingredients for a successful telegraph. In particular he emphasized the activities of Joseph Henry. Correctly, Burlingame recognized that Morse's contributions had been eliminated at the very moment the telegraph became commercially successful.

But while some contemporaries like Horace Greeley, the editor of the *New York Tribune*, insisted that Morse was nothing more than a greedy monopolist, such was not the commonly held view. Generally, he was accepted as an unusually gifted man. That viewpoint was presented in W. J. Youmans' assessment in ''Samuel Finley Breese Morse,'' in *Pioneers of Science in America* (1896). At least one 19th-century contemporary of Morse, however, did center his attention on the importance of Morse to American art. Henry T. Tuckerman provided this view in his *Artistic-Life: or Sketches of American Painters* (1847). This conception of Morse reappeared in Tuckerman's *Book of Artists* (1867). But in general, it was Morse the inventor who was portrayed during the 19th century, and usually these assessments were positive.

The Morse progeny wanted a positive view of their father. The family commissioned an authorized biography to be written by a member of the prominent New England family, Samuel Irenaeus PRIME, who gave the family what it wanted. Unfortunately, Prime's book was replete with factual errors. In this first biography of Morse, the telegraph dominated and Morse's role as an artist and politician were given little attention. Morse's youngest son, Edward Lind Morse, tried to balance this discrepancy in his edition of his father's letters (*Samuel F. B. Morse: Letters and Journals*, 1914).

By far the most comprehensive of Morse's biographies is that by MABEE. Mabee does not ignore Morse the inventor, but he demonstrates that Morse was much more than an inventor. This scholarly and fully researched work proved to be the necessary corrective to the earlier published version of Morse's life. While the view of Morse as an American Leonardo may be overdrawn, Mabee nonetheless provides a comprehensive assessment of Morse the man, the artist, the inventor, and the politician. Mabee's biography is the definitive study at the present time.

If the 19th century saw Morse the inventor, the 20th century has come to stress the importance of Morse the artist and his impact on American art. William Francklyn Paris in his *The Hall of American Artists* (1952) elaborated the importance of Morse in his role as founder and President of the National Academy of Design. LARKIN, Professor of Art at Smith College, demonstrated that Morse played a critical part in providing a more democratic tradition for the arts. This work benefited from access to Carleton Mabee's notes on Morse's artistic works and for the most part relied on secondary sources.

The role of Morse as an artist interested in taking art to the public is stressed in CIKOVSKY's edition of Morse's lectures delivered at New York University in the 1820s and 1830s. Cikovsky includes a biographical sketch that again underlines Morse's role as an artist. This publication is useful in fully understanding Morse the artist. William Dunlap covered some of this ground in his earlier work, *History of the Rise and Progress of the Arts of Design in the United States* (1954).

Paul J. Staiti in his doctoral dissertation, "Samuel F. B. Morse and the Search for the Grand Style" (Unpublished Ph.D. dissertation, University of Pennsylvania, 1979), also sees Morse as a bridge between the elitist European tradition and the post-1812 war American nationalist viewpoint. The dissertation's major arguments have been published in two articles: "Samuel F. B. Morse in Charleston, 1818–1821" (*South Carolina Historical Magazine* 79 [1978]), and more cogently in "Samuel F. B. Morse's Search for a Personal Style: The Anxiety of Influence" (*Winterthur* 16 [1981]). In much the same vein as Staiti, David Tatham evaluates Morse's 1832 painting, *Gallery of the Louvre* (see his "Samuel F. B. Morse's *Gallery of the Louvre*," *American Art Journal*, 13 [1981].

While most of his biographers have emphasized Morse the inventor, or Morse the artist, Morse the politician and anti-immigrant publicist has been neglected by all his biographers except Mabee. A fuller explanation of Morse's hostility to the foreign-born, especially the Catholics among them, can be followed in Francis J. Connors, "Samuel Finley Breese Morse and the Anti-Catholic Political Movements in the United States" (*Illinois Catholic Historical Review*, 1927).

But of all the facets of Morse's career, his role as an artist diminished as he wandered off into politics and invention; he reflected the changes that occurred in his lifetime, a lifetime that saw the basic transformation of a rural agrarian lifestyle to an urban industrial framework that relied on his communication network. The best overall study of Morse that demonstrates these alterations remains that of Carleton Mabee.

—Thomas J. Curran

MOSES BEN MAIMON. See MAIMONIDES.

MOTHER TERESA, 1910–   ; Albanian-born Roman Catholic missionary in India.

Clucas, Joan, *Mother Teresa*. New York, Chelsea House, 1989.
Doig, Desmond, *Mother Teresa: Her People and Her Work*. New York, Harper, and London, Collins, 1976.
Egan, Eileen, *Such a Vision of the Street: Mother Teresa—The Spirit and The Work*. New York, Doubleday, and London, Sidgwick and Jackson, 1985.
Le Joly, Edward, S.J., *Mother Teresa of Calcutta: A Biography*. San Francisco, Harper, 1985.
Muggeridge, Malcolm, *Something Beautiful for God: Mother Teresa of Calcutta*. New York, Harper, and London, Collins, 1971.
Porter, David, *Mother Teresa: The Early Years*. Grand Rapids, Michigan, W. B. Eerdmans, and London, SPCK, 1986.
Serrou, Robert, *Teresa of Calcutta: A Pictorial Biography*. New York, McGraw-Hill, 1980.
Spink, Kathryn, *The Miracle of Love: Mother Teresa of Calcutta*. San Francisco, Harper, 1981; as *For The Brotherhood of Man under the Fatherhood of God: Mother Teresa of Calcutta*. New Molden, Surrey, Colour Library International, 1981.

*

DOIG, a journalist for the *Statesman*, a Calcutta newspaper, was the first writer to draw attention to Mother Teresa by describing her charitable work to the city's poor. His poignant and sensitive writing reveals a deeply religious woman as she first touches him and ultimately the world. Written in the first person, Doig's book presents an honest account of his own impressions and, through numerous quotations, those of the people closely associated with Mother Teresa. As an Indian, Doig can provide unique observations on the city's inability to cope with its starving masses, and his background material on the historical and sociological aspects of poverty in Calcutta is valuable. Doig interviewed many people, but where two people give conflicting accounts of the same incident, the author makes no attempt to clarify the matter. The usual anecdotes are related, sometimes differently than in other biographies, and minimum attention is given to Mother Teresa's life before she came to India. Doig adequately explains matters of religion, though he often lacks the depth of other biographers in this regard. Although he is a crusader and longtime friend of Mother Teresa, Doig includes noticeably little material coming directly from her. Along with the outstanding photographs by Raghu Rai, the book includes a table of chronology.

EGAN's biography is most thorough. As an official of Catholic Relief Services, Egan is close to her subject in her work of providing food to thousands of starving Indians. The information is copious due to the extensive notes Egan took since she first met Mother Teresa in 1955. Egan relates many more conversations with and remarks by Mother Teresa than do other works. She has had the advantage of traveling at various times with her subject as she established her sisters in countries throughout the world. She offers a comprehensive description of Mother Teresa as a sister of Loreto, drawing on interviews with people of early associations (most of whom are only mentioned by other biographers). The impact of Fr. Van Exam, the Archbishop of Calcutta, and the Medical Missionary Sisters in Patna on Mother Teresa's preparation for going out alone to minister to the poor is extremely enlightening. Egan sets forth her disagreements with some of Mother Teresa's policies, along with the latter's replies. Egan's writing is clear and direct, and the many black-and-white photographs are helpful, particularly those showing Mother Teresa as a young girl. Appendices include a letter to Desai, Prime Minister of India, an excerpt from a talk by Mother Teresa, the Rule of the Missionaries of Charity, a list of the foundations established outside India, and the addresses of various Co-Workers associated with Mother Teresa. There is also an index. If only one book on Mother Teresa were to be read, this should be it.

LE JOLY offers an accurate and well-defined picture of Mother Teresa from his own perspective. As a longtime spiritual director to the Missionaries of Charity, Le Joly has an insider's view, and as a priest he has a deeper understanding of the spirituality that motivates his subject to accomplish her goal of helping the poorest of the poor. The writing is clear and straightforward. Interviews with people closest to Mother Teresa provide some information not contained in other biographies. Le Joly gives several accounts of hostile reactions by the poor toward Mother Teresa's sisters, information which is also missing from other books. Background material on Mother Teresa before she came to India as a nun is minimal; Le Joly is primarily interested in offering a spiritual perspective, which he does better than anyone else. Because the book comprises two previously published works (*Servant of Love*, 1977; *Messenger of God's Love*, 1983), there is considerable repetition. To be fair, the reiterated events are presented each time from a different slant; however, the recurrence of familiar material is irksome. The black-and-white photographs, some taken by Le Joly himself, are selective. The meditative aspect of this book may not be of interest to all scholars, but for those who desire a well-rounded portrait of a woman consecrated to God, it should not be overlooked.

SPINK writes mainly about Mother Teresa's Co-Workers, an international organization comprised of lay people from all religious denominations as well as unbelievers. Only one quarter of the book recounts Mother Teresa's early years as a sister of Loreto, when she heard a "call" to go out to the poor. The chapters on the growth of the two religious orders founded by Mother Teresa, one for men and another for women, are presented through the letters of the sisters and brothers who were sent out from India to work among the poor in other countries. Also, the inclusion of letters written by Mother Teresa to her Co-Workers is a unique contribution to this book. The world map showing the locations of the hundreds of established missions is a helpful aid. Likewise, the many photographs, mostly in color and depicting the work of Mother Teresa and her helpers, offer a clear elucidation of the subject matter. The author's sensitive portrayal of the group within the Co-Workers called the Sick and Suffering, who contribute to Mother Teresa's efforts with their prayers, makes reading this book worthwhile. Spink is a nondenominational Christian, and she brings to the subject a refreshing viewpoint. This book is valuable for its in-depth explanation of auxiliary groups devoted to assisting Mother Teresa in her missionary endeavors. Included are addresses of worldwide establishments for those wishing to inquire about the work of Mother Teresa or that of her Co-Workers.

PORTER's description of the early life of Mother Teresa as an Albanian in Yugoslavia is of inestimable value to the serious scholar. The author's information is based heavily on his translation of an Albanian's biography of Mother Teresa, which offers a unique presentation of her homeland, family, and local church. Through his focus on the subject's formative years, Porter defines how her deep religious convictions and love for the poor were inculcated in her from an early age. Included are several accounts, written by the subject herself, of Mother Teresa's encounters with the poor of Calcutta. Also, the extensive material contributed by Mother Teresa's brother adds to a fuller understanding of the subject. Some rare black-and-white photographs of the Bojaxhiu family are shown.

CLUCAS' biography, while based on other writings about Mother Teresa and written for young adults, must be considered. The material is clearly written, especially the historical background explaining the partitioning of India and its contribution to the poverty of Calcutta. It is mainly a factual account of Mother Teresa's life, starting with a fitting description of her parents and the impact they had on the formation of her character, and ending with a description of her opening a hospice for AIDS-stricken patients. Concise and informative, this well-researched account is told without the usual variations on overused anecdotes. Many excellent black-and-white photographs are incorporated throughout the text. Included are a table of chronology, a list of books for further reference, and an index.

SERROU, a journalist for *Paris Match*, offers a pictorial biography with a text that is informative, astute, and broad in scope. Because the author's sources are mostly secondary, and because Serrou occasionally speculates on how his subject might have thought or felt, this book cannot be given the highest of recommendations. However, the account of Mother Teresa's impact on children and the descriptions of the top awards she has received are more extensive than those found in other biographies. The historical account of Yugoslavia during Mother Teresa's lifetime is well done. Serrou's account of the formation of the Loreto Congregation gives some insight into how Mother Teresa's early awareness of the poor was nurtured. He includes direct quotations from Mother Teresa's brother, Lazar Bojaxhiu, who, at the age of 72, not only reflects on his childhood with his sister, but also gives his impressions of her present-day accomplishments. Of interest is Lazar's refutation of the popular description of his sister as being of peasant stock. The many photographs, some in color, document well the work of Mother Teresa. The Constitution of the International Association of the Co-Workers of Mother Teresa comprises the appendix.

MUGGERIDGE's short but highly dramatic account emphasizes the impact Mother Teresa has had on other people, including himself. Written in a first-person narrative voice, the book relates Muggeridge's observations on Mother Teresa, mostly while he is making a film on her and her work. Included is a rare interview in question-and-answer form that is not found in other biographies. The writing is both informative and brilliant, and the black-and-white photographs, although unusually dark, are uncommon.

—Patricia Grassi

MOUNTBATTEN, Louis [1st Earl Mountbatten of Burma], 1900–1979; English admiral.

Hough, Richard A., *Mountbatten: Hero of Our Time*. London, Weidenfeld and Nicolson, 1980; New York, Random House, 1981.

Smith, Charles, *Fifty Years with Mountbatten*. London, Sidgwick and Jackson, 1980; as *Lord Mountbatten: His Butler's Story*, New York, Stein and Day, 1980.

Terraine, John, *The Life and Times of Mountbatten*. London, Hutchinson, 1968.

Ziegler, Philip, *Mountbatten: The Official Biography*. London, Collins, and New York, Knopf, 1985.

*

HOUGH's biography of Mountbatten was the best among the several books published shortly after the British admiral was killed by an I.R.A. bomb in 1979; it remained the finest treatment until Ziegler's book (see below) appeared five years later. Hough had been at work on this biography when Mountbatten was killed, and his careful research (he had been given access to the Royal Family and its archives) and smooth narrative are in evidence throughout. An "authorized," though not a definitive, biography, it provides an informal, largely appreciative view of Mountbatten that does not, however, neglect his faults. It can still be of use to those seeking a relatively brief, mostly reliable glance at the admiral's private life, and would make a nice accompaniment to Lord Mountbatten's own *Mountbatten: 80 Years in Pictures* (1979); the latter book contains a simple, anonymously written text that could well be disregarded, though the photographs, most of them from Mountbatten's own archives, make the book useful.

ZIEGLER's massive "official" biography stands as the definitive life, and it is unlikely to be superseded for a long time to come. Beautifully written, fair, sound in its judgments, Ziegler's work will serve both specialists in modern British history and general readers who enjoy reading about the lives of colorful figures. Ziegler examines in much greater detail than any previous biographer both the public and the private Mountbatten, showing us a man of scrupulous manners, dazzling good looks, and considerable personal and national achievements, though at the same time revealing his arrogance, vanity, and obsession with his royal lineage. He leaves us finally with the impression of one who fell far short of greatness, even though his life was full of adventure and he was adored by many in his own country as a hero. Ziegler's book provides a useful, extensive bibliography.

The earlier biographies of Mountbatten are almost all adulatory, though some of them provide useful pictorial memoirs or private glimpses of the man. TERRAINE's book, another illustrated biography prepared with its subject's cooperation, was written, as Mountbatten notes in the preface, to give his grandchildren "some idea of what their grandfather had done." SMITH, Mountbatten's personal butler and valet for almost 50 years, provides a light, domestic view of his hero. His book is useful for its many anecdotes spanning most of Mountbatten's career. Those seeking any discussion of politics or life outside the Mountbatten household will need to look elsewhere, however.

—Noelle A. Watson

MOZART, Wolfgang Amadeus, 1756–1791; Austrian composer.

Blom, Eric, *Mozart*. London, Dent, 1935.

Bory, Robert, *The Life and Works of Wolfgang Amadeus Mozart in Pictures*. Geneva, Éditions Contemporaines, 1948.

Burk, John N., *Mozart and His Music*. New York, Random House, 1959.

Davenport, Marcia, *Mozart*. New York, Scribner, 1932; London, Heinemann, 1933.

Davies, Peter J., *Mozart in Person: His Character and Health*. New York and London, Greenwood Press, 1989.

Deutsch, Otto Erich, *Mozart: A Documentary Biography, 1765–1891*, translated by Eric Blom, Peter Branscombe, and Jeremy Noble. Stanford, California, Stanford University Press, and London, Black, 1965 (originally published as *Mozart: die Dokumente seines Lebens, gesammelt und erläutert*, Kassel, Bärenreiter, 1961).

Einstein, Alfred, *Mozart: His Character, His Work*, translated by Arthur Mendel and Nathan Broder. London and New York, Oxford University Press, 1945.

Fischer, Hans Conrad and Lutz Besch, *The Life of Mozart: An Account in Text and Pictures*. London, Macmillan, and New York, St. Martin's, 1969.

Ghéon, Henri, *In Search of Mozart*, translated by Alexander Dru. New York, Sheed & Ward, 1934 (originally published as *Promenades avec Mozart*, Paris, Desclée de Brouwer, 1932).

Hildesheimer, Wolfgang, *Mozart*, translated by Marian Faber. New York, Farrar Straus, 1982 (originally published by Suhrkump, Frankfurt am Main, 1977).

Holmes, Edward, *The Life of Mozart*. London, Chapman and Hall, and New York, Harper, 1845; revised edition, London, Dent, 1921.

Hussey, Dyneley, *Wolfgang Amade Mozart*. London, K. Paul, and New York, Harper, 1928.

Hutchings, Arthur, *Mozart: The Man, the Musician*. New York, Schirmer Books, and London, Thames and Hudson, 1976.

Jahn, Otto, *Life of Mozart* (3 vols.), translated by Pauline D. Townsend. London, Novello, 1882 (originally published as *W. A. Mozart*, Leipzig, Breitkopf and Härtel, 1856–59).

Keys, Ivor, *Mozart: His Music and His Life*. New York, Holmes and Meier, and London, Elek, 1980.

King, Alec H., *Mozart: A Biography, with a Survey of Books, Editions, and Recordings*. London, C. Bingley, 1970.

Landon, H. C. Robbins, *1791: Mozart's Last Year*. London, Thames and Hudson, and New York, Schirmer Books, 1988.

Landon, H. C. Robbins, *Mozart: The Golden Years, 1789–91*. London, Thames and Hudson, and New York, Schirmer Books, 1989.

Levey, Michael, *The Life and Death of Mozart*. London, Weidenfeld and Nicolson, and New York, Stein and Day, 1971.

Niemetschek, Franz, *Life of Mozart*, translated by Helen Mautner. London, L. Hyman, 1956 (originally published as *Leben des K. K. Kapellmeisters Wolfgang Gottlieb Mozart*, Prague, Herrlische Buchhandlung, 1798).

Ottaway, Hugh, *Mozart*. London, Orbis, 1979; Detroit, Wayne State University Press, 1980.

Sadie, Stanley, *Mozart*. London, Calder and Boyars, and New York, Vienna House, 1965.

Sadie, Stanley, *The New Grove Mozart*. London, Macmillan, 1982; New York, Norton, 1983.

Schenk, Erich, *Mozart and His times*, translated by Richard and Clara Winston. New York, Knopf, and London, Secker and Warburg, 1959 (originally published as *Wolfgang Amadeus Mozart: eine Biographie*, Vienna, 1955).

Turner, W. J., *Mozart: The Man and His Works*. London, Gollancz, and New York, Knopf, 1938.

*

Mozart poses great challenges for the biographer, who must not only confront the child-composer's incomprehensible growth from prodigy to consummate genius, but who must also account for his phenomenally large and diverse musical output, an oeuvre whose qualities of transcendent perfection defy rational criticism and analysis. Most difficult of all is the task of finding an integral link between the superhuman artistic personality embodied in the music and the flawed human being represented in the surviving correspondence. (This invaluable source of biographical information, comprising more than 600 letters, is available in an excellent translation by Emily Anderson, *The Letters of Mozart and His Family* [3 vols., London, Macmillan, 1938; 2nd edition, 2 vols., New York, St. Martin's, 1966].) It is fair to say that a coherent synthesis has remained beyond reach to this day, and it is hoped that a major biography by Maynard Solomon, currently in progress, will succeed at least partially in furnishing a unified picture of the man and his accomplishment.

Among the early accounts of Mozart's life, NIEMETSCHEK bears scrutiny in light of the closeness of the writer to his subject. Drawing on letters, recollections of acquaintances and other eyewitnesses, and information obtained from Mozart's widow, Niemetschek offers a colorful picture of the composer's astonishing accomplishments and a rather idealized portrayal of his character. Especially enlightening are the references to the reception of Mozart's music in the last decade of the 18th century. Though not readily accessible to modern readers, HOLMES possesses enduring value as an early, authentic account of the composer's life. Its authority rests in part on the author's access to Mozart letters that had been used by Georg Nikolaus von Nissen (the husband of Mozart's widow), whose sprawling Mozart biography, still untranslated, was first published in 1828.

The work of a philologist and archaeologist, JAHN's monumental, mid-19th-century contribution represents an unprecedentedly high standard of accuracy in biographical detail. Maintaining an objective distance from his subject, Jahn gathers information from a vast array of primary sources. Works in various genres are discussed in strategically placed digressions from the chronological narrative, but the treatment of the music is nevertheless the least satisfying aspect of the book, and no attempt is made to connect Mozart's life with the substance of his musical output.

Constituting a response to the inadequacy of Jahn and other 19th-century biographers in addressing Mozart's music, the immense, still untranslated *Mozart, sa vie musicale et son oeuvre* by Théodore de Wyzewa and Georges de St. Foix (1912–46) has cast a long shadow on 20th-century Mozart biography and criticism. This five-volume work focuses on Mozart's practice, especially evident in the earlier years of his creative development, of imitating and then assimilating the music of contemporaries with which he came into contact. The authors succeeded in identifying hitherto unperceived patterns of continuity, evolution, and change in Mozart's style, and their work prompted considerable revision in the accepted chronology of his compositions.

EINSTEIN, evidently sensing the near impossibility of encompassing an authoritative critique of Mozart's career, personality, and artistic accomplishment within standard biographical format, chose to organize his book as a series of essays, some primarily biographical, some critical, some bent on drawing connections between the composer and his oeuvre. Written by one of the most knowledgeable of Mozart experts, the book retains its indispensability for the scholar as well as the general reader. There are gaps, and the writer's aphoristic style often leaves the reader wishing for elaboration, but the scope is nearly comprehensive. A chapter is devoted to each of the major genres, and the biographical essays, including those on Freemasonry and Catholicism, relationships with women, and relationships with contemporary musicians, are filled with insights that aid comprehension both of the composer's life and the sources of his artistic inspiration.

Several 20th-century handbooks have met the challenge of presenting a biographical synopsis and a summary overview of works. BLOM's book, having gone through numerous editions, has retained its value as an authoritative resource and has furnished a model for subsequent life-and-works treatments. Using his own translations of excerpts from the Mozart correspondence, and drawing on the German scholar Hermann Abert's expanded revision of the Jahn biography, Blom places more emphasis on the unfolding of events in Mozart's life than on the interaction of personalities. In treating the music, he offers descriptive summaries of major accomplishments within each genre, as well as numerous music examples. Though resembling Blom in both scope and format, BURK lacks the earlier book's insights into either the music or the composer's personality. A clearly written though bland narrative features extensive quotations from the letters. The second half of the book lists works chronologically by genre and offers thumbnail descriptions in the manner of program notes. SADIE (1965) updates Blom's book and compresses more information into a smaller space than most other biographies. His treatment of the music is indebted to Wyzewa and St. Foix. There are many illustrations (all in black and white), and several handy appendices, including a "dating table" that links Köchel numbers with dates of composition. While drawing heavily on his earlier book, Sadie's 1983 volume encompasses a good deal of revision in response to recent research. Betraying its origins as an encyclopedia article (for the New Grove Dictionary), it furnishes quick access to essential information on life and works. Despite additional features (e.g., information on Mozart's ancestry, an expanded bibliography, and a more elaborate work-list), the book lacks the earlier handbook's coherence, and its format affords Sadie less opportunity for critical discussion of the music.

Among 20th-century biographies whose vantage point is more literary than musical, HUSSEY stands as an early representative. Engagingly written and reasonably strong on factual detail, the book offers limited insight into Mozart's personality and has little to say about his music. DAVENPORT offers an idealized portrait that brings the man into line with lofty ideals manifested in the music. Written with conviction in a polished literary style, the book features the novel device of imaginary conversations (set off in single quotes) among Mozart and his contemporaries. TURNER, placing special emphasis on a careful reading of the Mozart correspondence, seeks to correct the misguided, idealized portrayals of earlier biographers. His work's greatest strength is its account of Mozart's early travels, with extended quotes from the correspondence in Turner's own translation. LEVEY's curiously melodramatic account of Mozart's life concentrates on the operatic works. Exploring the circumstances of their creation, their plots, and the interaction of their characters, the author finds telling reflections of the composer's own personality and inner life. Sensitively written and well informed, KEYS' book offers occasionally perceptive commentary on individual works in the course of a well-conceived biographical narrative. LANDON (1988), inspired by the success of the Peter Shaffer play *Amadeus* and the subsequent film, cites letters, other contemporary documents, and references to recent scholarly literature in assembling a singularly detailed account of events in the last year of Mozart's life.

Rising above the limited aspirations of the popular biographies cited above are three books that merit special notice. GHÉON, reflective, poetic, and emotionally intense, strives to communicate something of the author's insight into Mozart's musical genius. Distinguishing between the bourgeois ambitions of his outer life and the transcendent spirit represented by his music, Ghéon offers at least a partially convincing portrayal of the artist's musical personality. SCHENK, by contrast, avoids aesthetic evaluation in favor of a rigorous, factual exploration of Mozart's life that attempts to combat the perpetuation of unsubstantiated anecdotes from earlier biographies. Schenk's work contains numerous illustrations and many quotations from the correspondence. Doubtless the most unconventional of Mozart biographies, HILDESHEIMER's is also the one most indebted to the principles of Freudian psychology. Consisting of a single, extended chapter—in effect a kind of stream of consciousness—the book divides into topical discussions that generally range from one to five pages. Avoiding both factual narrative and criticism of individual compositions, the author attempts to reach a level of understanding on which Mozart's behavior and the artistic outpouring of his compositions are seen to stem from the same source.

DEUTSCH, though not strictly speaking a biography, furnishes an indispensable biographical resource. Consisting of pertinent documents from 1712 (an official record of the wedding of Mozart's maternal grandparents) to 1891 (an excerpt from Johanna von Bischoff's memoir), it complements the collected letters as a compendium of source material. KING offers a handy guide for the Mozart enthusiast that surveys English-language books on the composer, editions, and recordings, and includes 50 pages of excellent biographical narrative.

Chief among English-language iconographical volumes is HUTCHINGS' elegant, large-format pictorial biography with 320 illustrations, 170 in color. Interspersed with the biographical narrative and accompanying illustrations are pictorial essays (in color) on such topics as Mozart's portraits, his family, his tours, rulers and residences, and Freemasonry. This book complements the earlier, more comprehensive treatment by BORY, which has 500 black-and-white illustrations, chronologically ordered according to their relevance to the events of Mozart's life. The more compact volume by FISCHER AND BESCH adorns a biographical account with a selection of well-chosen depictions of landscapes, architectural landmarks, portraits, and facsimiles of manuscripts. Related in scope is OTTAWAY, which occupies a position halfway between a popular biography and a picture-book. LANDON's 1989 effort is in some respects a sequel to the author's earlier book, but the balance weighs more heavily in favor of pictures. Though cluttered by digressions into such subjects as the late 18th-century Viennese piano, the text is informative, up-to-date, and attractively written.

Final mention may be made of a recent and significant contribution by DAVIES, a specialist in internal medicine. Examining the vicissitudes of Mozart's life in a harsh, clinical light, this painstakingly researched, highly original book proceeds from an arrestingly vivid account of the Mozart family's illnesses to an inquiry into the composer's financial affairs, his proclivity for gambling, and his sexual exploits. Psychological exploration reveals signs of emotional disorders in the child and manic-depressive behavior in the adult. The ghastly manifestations of Schönlein-Henoch Syndrome are implicated in the composer's tragically premature death.

—Floyd K. Grave

———

MUHAMMAD. See MOHAMMED.

———

MUIR, John, 1838–1914; Scottish-born American naturalist.

Bade, William F., *The Life and Letters of John Muir*. Boston, Houghton Mifflin, 1924.
Clarke, James M., *The Life and Adventures of John Muir*. San Diego, Word Shop Publications, 1979.
Cohen, Michael, *The Pathless Way: John Muir and American Wilderness*. Madison, University of Wisconsin Press, 1984.
Fox, Stephen, *John Muir and His Legacy*. Boston, Little Brown, 1981.
Turner, Frederick, *Rediscovering America: John Muir in His Time and Ours*. New York, Viking, 1985.
Wolfe, Linnie, *Son of the Wilderness: The Life of John Muir*. New York, Knopf, 1945.

*

W. Somerset Maugham once remarked that a novelist is under enormous pressure to make characters unitary when, in reality, people are inconsistent and contradictory. For the sake of making a character understandable, the author must hide the contradictions and inconsistencies. There is a similar pressure evident in biographies of Muir: a pull to make him a unitary identity, a representative of one way of thinking. But Muir came of age at a time when certain distinctions were not made—between scientist and Romantic, biologist and geologist, professionally trained naturalist and educated layman, farmer and environmentalist, preservationist and conservationist—so that he pursued goals which, by modern standards, seem inconsistent. His story is difficult to tell in such a way as to make clear the conflicting interests and approaches he had toward nature. It is easier to characterize him as a mountain hermit, or wood sylph, or martyr for the environmental cause.

Somewhat ironically, the biography least given to smoothing over Muir's contradictions is the first book-length biography. BADE, perhaps because he tries much less than other biographers to make an argument, gives some consideration to those parts of Muir's life that are often ignored: his early childhood in Scotland, for example, or his success as a farmer. Bade's approach is extremely conventional; he narrates Muir's life, relying almost exclusively on Muir's letters and autobiographies, with little if any insightful analysis. Bade's work is primarily of interest for the letters published in it that are otherwise unavailable; as more of Muir's unpublished writings become available, its interest will diminish.

Like Bade, WOLFE uses thoroughly conventional biographical methods, relying uncritically on Muir's own version of events. Although occasionally inaccurate on minor points (such as the correct names of Acts of Congress), she goes into somewhat more detail about some of Muir's political activities, thereby giving the reader a better understanding of the difficulties Muir faced in his political causes. Her analysis of those events is not very deep, and it is certainly true that Muir's opponents tend to come off as slightly villainous, but the book is highly readable.

CLARKE himself gives the best description of his book. It is "a narrative made up, except for a few interpretive passages, almost entirely of actions and circumstances recounted by Muir himself." Clarke defends this decision by saying that Muir was "a modest and irreproachable witness." The story is told in chronological order, broken into seven sections entitled: Boy, Wanderer, Geologist, Ecologist, Explorer, Husbandman, Activist. As Clarke sees Muir's entire life leading up to his "Activist" years, the book tends to discount Muir's other aspects. One might mistakenly infer, for example, that not only was Muir's being a geologist merely a stage toward greater things, but that he stopped being a geologist when he became an explorer. In short, Clarke emphasizes Muir the visionary, at the expense of Muir's very practical side.

FOX uses Muir as the beginning of his history of the 20th-century conservation movement. It is interesting for the reader to see the similarities between Muir and those people whom Fox suggests followed him. Beginning with Muir, however, means that Fox is necessarily very weak on the historical, intellectual, or political movements that led up to Muir. He is especially weak on Emerson, Humboldt, and the influence of Romanticism and pantheism in general.

COHEN's elegant and eloquent work is significantly different from the others. Cohen emphasizes Muir's philosophical development, especially his wilderness ethic, with empathy and insight; he is less interested in Muir's political activities or personal relations. The structure is not strictly chronological; it is like a mountain hike with occasional pauses and digressions into, for example, the process of writing the book, Cohen's own experiences climbing, and comments on other biographies. Cohen is impressive and persuasive on the connections (especially stylistic) to Thoreau, although less strong on the influence of pantheism. His attempt to place Muir in the American tradition is slightly flawed by his uncritical use of the questionable theses of Roderick Nash and Lynn White, Jr.

TURNER's book is an excellent complement to Cohen's. Turner, an accomplished biographer, effectively balances attempts to discern Muir's motives and psychology with well-told narrations of Muir's adventures. The book is thorough, backed by well-reasoned interpretations and impressive use of original sources. Due to his use of Muir's unpublished papers, Turner narrates events unfamiliar to Muir's readers (such as his trip to Manchuria or Young's version of events in Alaska). Although he does not accept Muir's version of events uncritically, he is still highly sympathetic to Muir and, hence, partisans of Muir's opponents (such as Gifford Pinchot) may feel they get short shrift.

Most of Muir's writings were essentially autobiographical. He was an accurate observer and a dramatic and compelling storyteller, although tending to view disputes as stark oppositions between right and wrong and generally ascribing the worst possible motives to his opponents. By relying uncritically on Muir's version of events, Bade, Wolfe, Clarke, and Fox each share certain weaknesses. In the first place, Muir's writings generally inspire admiration of him, and such admiration, although well-deserved, can turn biographies into hagiographies. Second, although Muir was honest, any one version of political or scientific disputes is necessarily limited. Thus, a biography that relies uncritically on Muir's version is necessarily as limited as Muir's own writings, while not necessarily as exciting. A biography that does little more than place his writings in a historical context does not give a reader much more that he would get simply reading Muir. Cohen and Turner, however, by describing events left out of Muir's published writings, looking critically at influences on Muir, and placing Muir in a tradition, provide a context for understanding Muir, his writings, and his significance.

—Patricia Roberts

MUNCH, Edvard, 1863–1944; Norwegian painter.

Benesch, Otto, *Edvard Munch*, translated by Joan Spencer. London, Phaidon, 1960.

Deknatel, Frederick B., *Edward Munch*. New York, Museum of Modern Art/Chanticleer, 1950.

Eggum, Arne, *Edvard Munch; Paintings, Sketches and Studies*, translated by Ragnar Christophersen. New York, Potter, 1984 (originally published in Norway by J. M. Stenersens, 1983).

Heller, Reinhold, *Munch, His Life and Work*. London, Murray, and Chicago, University of Chicago Press, 1984.

Hodin, J. P., *Edvard Munch*. London, Thames and Hudson, and New York, Praeger, 1972.

Langaard, Johan H. and R. A. Revold, *Edvard Munch, Masterpieces from the Artist's Collection in the Munch Museum in Oslo*, translated by Michael Bullock. New York, McGraw-Hill, 1964 (originally published by C. Belser, Stuttgart, 1963).

Selz, Jean, *E. Munch*, translated by Eileen B. Hennessy. New York, Crown, 1974.

Stang, Ragna T., *Edvard Munch: The Man and His Art*, translated by Geoffrey Culverwell. New York, Abbeville Press, and London, Fraser, 1979 (originally published by H. Aschehoug, Oslo, 1978).

Stenerson, Rolf, *Edvard Munch, Close-up of a Genius*, translated and edited by Rolf Stenerson. Oslo, Gyldendal, 1969 (originally published by Wahlstrom and Widstrand, Stockholm, 1944).

Timm, Werner, *The Graphic Art of Edward Munch*. Greenwich, Connecticut, New York Graphic Society, and London, Studio Vista, 1969.

*

STENERSON's small book first appeared in Stockholm in 1944, the year of Munch's death. In an informal account, Stenerson, a personal friend and a collector of Munch's work, gives us reports of actual conversations and anecdotal material that point up Munch's loneliness and fears. He describes Munch's strange personal habits and his relationships with his friends, though, as Langaard (see below) cautions, there is some embellishment.

DEKNATEL published the first major work on Munch written in English. The author, who visited Norway and consulted with Norwegian scholars, had access to an impressive number of publications in English and Norwegian, and the work is thoroughly documented. Well-written and informative, with good illustrations, it was planned to accompany a Munch exhibition in the United States.

BENESCH, in an excellent translation from the German, is more analytical, and he theorizes about the events that affected Munch. His work is accurate and detailed and provides notes referring to the illustrations. Approximately half of the book consists of color plates.

LANGAARD AND REVOLD, respectively director and keeper of the Munch Museum in Oslo, between them know more about Munch than anyone. Before the Munch archives were transferred to the museum, the authors had access to the artistic remains at Ekely, where the painter died. This publication benefits from access to primary sources and its authors' impressive scholarship. It is well documented and contains extracts from Munch's diary and more important writings. In the preface, Langaard and Revold state that their purpose, besides giving a comprehensive survey of Munch's work, is to convey an idea of his rich artistic personality. They feel that the most important source of information remains his art. They present a balanced, accessible view of Munch. The work includes colored plates, a list of exhibitions, and a bibliography, but it lacks an index.

TIMM explores the symbolism and psychological overtones revealed in Munch's graphic work. He also gives an account of Munch's life and thought and describes the events in his life that most influenced him. A running commentary adjacent to the numbers of the reproductions expands these events to discover the background.

HODIN, an art historian who was decorated by the Norwegian government for his work on Munch, offers us a detailed, comprehensive and conscientious study of the painter. Hodin had access to primary sources and visited Munch in 1938. Yet his work does not come to grips with its subject. In a review, critic Peter Gay (*American Scholar*, Autumn 1972) claims that Hodin is too timid in the private dimension, and is more concerned with Munch's paintings and prints than his life and career.

SELZ, in an inexpensive monograph, gives us the essential biographical information, noting the important influences in Munch's life and remarking on his neurotic preoccupations. The text is scholarly, reflecting recent research, and is illustrated by well-chosen reproductions. Yet his emphasis is primarily on Munch's relationship to German Expressionism, and he is not much interested in events after Munch's breakdown and treatment by Dr. Jacobson.

STANG's book, in an excellent translation from the Norwegian, is one of the three best on Munch. Stang, former director of the Oslo Municipal Collections, which include the Munch Museum and Archives, had access to almost everything available on Munch, much of it previously unpublished. She calls Munch "the most revealing of artists" and claims that his paintings illustrate his life. For this reason, she begins the book with a series of self portraits, with quotations from Munch's own writings attached. The readable text gives the story of his life and background, using extracts from his diaries, letters, and recorded conversations. The book is meticulous and scholarly, with 20 pages of detailed notes and a comprehensive bibliography. The later part of Munch's life is left undeveloped, but Stang was organizing the documentation at the time of her death.

Ten years after Stang's death, when more documentation was available, two books were published, by Eggum and Heller. EGGUM, the chief curator of the Munch Museum, had intimate access to the personal documents, paintings, and drawings, many of them previously unpublished, that illustrate his work. Eggum's approach is wide-ranging. Building on Stang's scholarship, he relates Munch's despair and anxiety and chronicles his development through various stages. He has some new material on the later period, although more needs to be made available.

HELLER, the leading American Munch specialist, had access to the Munch Museum and Archives, and consulted with Stang and Eggum, to whom he acknowledges his debt. Heller moves through the episodes of Munch's life providing insight into his major relationships and documenting his erotic life. He digs more deeply into his subject in the 1890s, a period where he has done the most research. His knowledge of the Norwegian background is most useful, as the Norwegian writers tend to take this for granted. Again, more work needs to be done on the later documentation.

The Eggum and Heller volumes are scholarly and well researched, with visual and textual documentation. Both make liberal use of quotations from the artist's writings. Both have bibliographies and excellent notes, although Heller's are more explanatory. Eggum includes twice the number of pictures and puts equal weight on the sketches. Reviewer John Boulton Smith (*Apollo*, May 1985) calls both books good, reliable, sensible works that tend to complement each other.

—Patricia Brauch

MURROW, Edward R(oscoe), 1908–1965; American broadcast journalist.

Kendrick, Alexander, *Prime Time: The Life of Edward R. Murrow*. Boston, Little Brown, 1969.

Persico, Joseph E., *Edward R. Murrow: An American Original*. New York, McGraw-Hill, 1988.

Smith, R. Franklin, *Edward R. Murrow: The War Years*. Kalamazoo, Michigan, New Issues Press, 1978.
Sperber, A. M., *Murrow: His Life and Times*. New York, Freundlich Books, 1986; London, M. Joseph, 1987.

*

In light of the reverence with which Edward R. Murrow is regarded, it is not surprising that he should have been the subject of four biographies in the first 15 years after his death. Three of these biographies are comprehensive, attempting to record Murrow's life from birth to death. One other, by Smith, concentrates on the war years from 1937 through 1946, when Murrow was stationed in London for CBS. All four are extensively researched and well written.

SPERBER's biography, however, stands above the rest. It collected many honors after it was published in 1986: it was a finalist for the Pulitzer Prize; became a Book-of-the-Month Club selection; was named a Notable Book of the Year by the New York Times; and received the prestigious Kappa Tau Alpha-Frank Luther Mott Research Award as the best journalism-related book of 1986.

Sperber's interest in Murrow was stimulated by the broadcaster's famous exposé of Senator Joe McCarthy in 1954. Her nearly 13 years of research tapped previously unavailable sources. She used the Federal Freedom of Information Act to obtain files from the Department of State, the United States Information Agency, and the Federal Bureau of Investigation—files that had previously been closed. She also had access to archives of the BBC, CBS, the Emergency Committee in Aid of Displaced German Scholars, and the private papers of Mrs. Edward R. Murrow, among other sources. Sperber's use of these primary sources was extensive—too extensive, in fact, to be published in their entirety. For example, her chapter on the Emergency Committee ran to 400 typescript pages and had to be cut to 60 pages for the book. Her research is blended nicely into a well-written narrative, and the result is readable, cohesive, and credible. Sperber's is the definitive work on the life of Edward R. Murrow.

PERSICO seems to be more concerned with drawing a picture of Murrow than describing the broadcaster's world. For example, in a bit of fanciful hyperbole, Persico focuses on Murrow's relationship with Pamela Churchill: "His personal life was a confusion of forbidden happiness, guilt, self-reproach, and indecision. He was torn between a wife he loved and a woman with whom he was wildly in love." Sperber, on the other hand, refers rather casually to the relationship: "It was a relationship entirely in the open and a radical departure for a man who formerly wouldn't so much as be photographed without his wedding ring." Persico's book, one feels, could be adapted for the screen more easily than Sperber's. But his scholarship is thorough, including interviews with 109 of Murrow's colleagues and citations from Murrow's FBI files, which had been opened through Sperber's FOI inquiries.

KENDRICK's might be regarded as the most authoritative of the three comprehensive works because Kendrick was one of Murrow's "boys" who had worked for Murrow during the war years. But Kendrick did not use many of the sources cited by Sperber and Persico, and his scholarship simply is not as thorough. Readers will notice certain omissions in Kendrick's biog-

raphy. For example, there is no mention of Pamela Churchill, the woman with whom Murrow was "wildly in love." In fact, Kendrick does not even mention himself, an omission so self-effacing as to be a distortion. His work also lacks any citation of his sources. Still, Kendrick's personal relationship with Murrow gives *Prime Time* a special significance.

SMITH's short biography (150 pages) concerns only Murrow's experience during the war years. (The books by Kendrick and Persico are about 550 pages each, and Sperber's book is more than 800 pages long.) Smith's book, published posthumously in 1978, is based mainly on interviews conducted in 1971 with Murrow's London colleagues. Inexpensively produced in a paperback edition by the university where Smith taught, the book incorporates original research that contributes to one's understanding of Murrow's values and the development of his reputation.

Despite the availability of a definitive biography like Sperber's, and a narrative biography like Persico's, one cannot appreciate Edward R. Murrow fully unless one listens to records of those wartime broadcasts from London and views the kinescopes of his television programs. And even then, one wishes to know more.

—Whitney R. Mundt

MUSSOLINI, Benito, 1883–1945; Italian Fascist leader and dictator.

Bordeux, V. J. (Mrs. Sofia De Bonis), *Benito Mussolini, the Man*. London, Hutchinson, and New York, G. H. Doran, 1927.
Borghi, Armando, *Mussolini: Red and Black*. London, Wishart, 1935.
Collier, Richard, *Duce! A Biography of Benito Mussolini*. New York, Viking, 1971; as *Duce! The Rise and Fall of Mussolini*, London, Collins, 1971.
Fermi, Laura, *Mussolini*. Chicago, University of Chicago Press, 1961.
Gallo, Max, *Mussolini's Italy*, translated by Charles L. Markmann. New York, Macmillan, 1973; London, Abelard-Schuman, 1974 (originally published by Perrin, Paris, 1964).
Gregor, A. James, *Young Mussolini and the Intellectual Origins of Fascism*. Berkeley, University of California Press, 1979.
Halperin, Samuel William, *Mussolini and Italian Fascism*. Princeton, New Jersey, Van Nostrand, 1964.
Hibbert, Christopher, *Mussolini*. New York, Ballantine, 1972; London, Pan Books, 1973.
Joes, Anthony J., *Mussolini*. New York, F. Watts, 1982.
Kirkpatrick, Ivone, *Mussolini: A Study in Power*. New York, Hawthorn, 1964; as *Mussolini, Study of a Demagogue*, London, Odhams, 1964.
MacGregor-Hastie, Roy, *The Day of the Lion: The Life and Death of Fascist Italy*. London, Macdonald, 1963; New York, Coward-McCann, 1964.
Mack Smith, Denis, *Mussolini*. London, Weidenfeld and Nicolson, 1981; New York, Knopf, 1982.

Megaro, Gaudens, *Mussolini in the Making*. Boston, Houghton Mifflin, and London, Allen and Unwin, 1938.

Monelli, Paolo, *Mussolini: An Intimate Life*, translated by Brigid Maxwell. London, Thames and Hudson, 1953; as *Mussolini: The Intimate Life of a Demagogue*, New York, Vanguard, 1954.

Mussolini, Rachele Guidi, *Mussolini: an Intimate Biography*. New York, Morrow, 1974; as *The Real Mussolini*, translated by C. Huach, Farnborough, U.K., Saxon House, 1974 (originally published as *Mussolini sans masque*, Paris, Fayard, 1973).

Pini, Giorgio, *The Official Life of Benito Mussolini*, translated by Luigi Villari. London, Hutchinson, 1939 (originally published as *Benito Mussolini, la sua vita*, Bologna, L. Cappelli, 1926).

Sarfatti, Margherita, *The Life of Benito Mussolini*, translated by Frederic Whyte. London, T. Butterworth, and New York, F. A. Stokes, 1925.

Seldes, George, *Sawdust Caesar*. New York, Harper, 1935; London, A. Barker, 1936.

*

Biographies of Mussolini generally fall into four categories: hagiographies; workmanlike narratives; portrayals of Mussolini as an opportunist with no consistent principles; and accounts that regard Mussolini as a genuine revolutionary.

Representative of the first group, which should be read with caution, is SARFATTI's biography. It is a romantic and not always accurate account by an adoring associate. Sarfatti seeks to portray Mussolini not only as the archetypal Italian and Roman, but (along with Lenin) as one of the two dominant figures of the post-war period. Sarfatti paints a picture of an idealist sensitive to injustice, an avid reader influenced by ideas, a nationalist searching for an original Italian conception of life, and an ethical revolutionary working to transform the Italian state. She also attempts to refurbish Mussolini's lineage, dismisses his anticlericalism, and covers up his early socialism.

If Sarfatti plays fast and loose with the facts, her book is still more useful than the other hagiographic accounts. BORDEUX, although borrowing much from Sarfatti, manages to create an even more adulatory account of a man tirelessly working to save Italy from Bolshevist disaster. PINI's biography is an official account by a Fascist sympathizer and the editor of Mussolini's own newspaper. As such, it is an unabashed glorification, which results in the virtual apotheosis of Mussolini. Finally, the account by RACHELE MUSSOLINI, the Duce's widow, casts him as a popular, romantic hero opposed to Fascist violence, forced into an alliance with Hitler by the British and French, and determined to avoid war. Perhaps the only factual accuracy in the entire book is her reluctant admission that her beloved husband had affairs with several women.

Typical of the narrative accounts, COLLIER focuses on Mussolini's personality in a well-written, fast-paced account rich in anecdotes. This Mussolini emerges as a near-anarchist who is impulsive, vindictive, and cruel, a man who sees revolution and social change only in terms of violence, yet who also has an enormous capacity for work and a passion for efficiency. Collier sketches a solid portrait of Mussolini the man, but says little of interest about Mussolini the ideologist or national leader.

In an episodic biography designed to illustrate the linkage between contemporary Italian society and Mussolini's career, FERMI, the widow of the famous exile physicist, also spotlights Mussolini's personality. Not quite a full-blown psychological portrait, Fermi nonetheless looks for the "true" Mussolini. Admitting that she was at the time a member of the politically apathetic Italian middle class, Fermi discovers in Mussolini a complex personality, full of contradictions and of unanswered questions. Unfortunately, Fermi's account is ultimately unsatisfactory, never proving the promised insights into Mussolini's character. Hers is a standard portrait of the Duce, with little to distinguish it from other narrative biographies.

Slightly different is GALLO, who attempts to portray Mussolini as a product of Italian culture and tradition, a man who embodied the defects and qualities of a complex and contradictory people. Although regarding Mussolini as the creator of Fascism, Gallo ultimately sees it as representative of a deep vein within the Italian character. Gallo's account, however, is rather disjointed, highly descriptive of the problems of a developing nation and the chaos produced by World War I, but unhelpful for understanding Mussolini or Fascism. Nor is HIBBERT particularly useful for arriving at a fuller comprehension of Mussolini. The largest portion of his book is devoted not to a study of Mussolini or Fascism, but to his foreign policy and World War II. Finally, truer to its title, MONELLI relates many details of the Duce's private life, including his various affairs, in a gossipy exposé.

One of the first accounts to appear in English depicting Mussolini as a power-hungry opportunist was that of BORGHI, a former anarchist associate of Mussolini forced into exile by the Fascist government. This is a scathing attack that portrays Mussolini as nothing more than a cowardly gangster, a hypocrite selling out to the highest bidder. In his rage, however, Borghi falsifies the historical record at least as much as the hagiographers. Much the same could be said about SELDES, the leftist American journalist whose polemical assault on Mussolini owes much to Borghi (although not credited). While bandying about a number of then-fashionable psychological concepts, Seldes in essence sees Mussolini as nothing more than a weak and fearful man trying to be strong, his revolutionary ideas based only on personal resentment. Far the most useful of these contemporary works is by MEGARO, a Harvard historian who makes a serious attempt to cut through the veil of myth to understand the "true" Mussolini. Basing his account on primary and "untapped" sources, Megaro sees Mussolini's early life as the key to understanding him. Megaro's exploration of the sources of Mussolini's thought, the manner in which his ideas were shaped by Marx, Pareto, Nietzsche, and Sorel, is the strong point of the book, even if it fails to note the consistency in the Duce's core ideas. Still, Megaro's work caused a sensation at the time by revealing the leftist past that Mussolini was trying to cover up.

Of the post-war accounts, that by MacGREGOR-HASTIE is curiously flat and uninteresting, especially so since the author was an active Laborite, married the daughter of a formerly prominent Fascist, and interviewed a cross-section of Mussolini's friends and enemies. It is hard to discern the point of this book, since it clearly fails as both serious analysis and as popular biography. HALPERIN's short survey, on the other hand, is decidedly serious, aimed at an undergraduate audience and composed about equally of analysis and documents. Halperin equates

Fascism with Mussolinism, seeing in it nothing but Mussolini's drive for power, opportunism, and cynicism. An essentially uncommitted man ideologically, the movement he created thus lacked the potency of Socialism or Nazism. While charging Mussolini with inconsistency, Halperin is guilty of the same crime. He admits that Mussolini began with some convictions, did not completely forsake them all, was especially influenced by Syndicalist ideas, and that his basic strategy aimed at wooing the workers to Fascism. Halperin's account is tinged by excessive class analysis, seeing Mussolini not only as a class traitor, but also as a virtual stooge of big industrialists.

More useful is KIRKPATRICK's extensive biography, which aims, if not at the scholar, then at the serious reader. The author, a British diplomat stationed in Rome from 1930 to 1933, had the opportunity to meet and observe Mussolini. Based on records of his conversations with the Duce, memoirs, diaries, and diplomatic documents, Kirkpatrick searches for an explanation of Mussolini's character, motivation, and conduct. The picture Kirkpatrick gives is of a restless, ambitious, resentful, and aggressive man, one whose radicalism sprang not from intellectual sources but from a private sense of indignity and frustration. A dabbler in ideas, Mussolini saw the Italian Socialist Party only as a convenient organization through which to realize his individual goals. Nor was he ever guided by well-defined principles or convictions, remaining a restless man who charted no course but drifted uncertainly on the current of events. Kirkpatrick paints a portrait of a classic opportunist, a man willing and able to move in any direction in order to realize his ambitions, one who relied on willpower and intuition, who was adventurous without knowing precisely what to do, and whose system consisted of action. Not surprisingly, Kirkpatrick's account is knowledgeable on foreign policy, while less satisfactory on domestic affairs.

MACK SMITH's biography is generally recognized as the finest one-volume account available. Based on a thorough study of the sources, with an exhaustive bibliography, it is both a narrative history and an informed psychological portrait and assessment of Mussolini. Thus, it is suitable for the general reader but detailed enough for the specialist. Although admitting that Mussolini was a man of great talents, a complex individual greatly admired in his time by Italians and foreigners alike, Mack Smith nonetheless depicts the Duce as a mean-spirited schemer with no principles or coherent policy, skilled only in deception. To Mack Smith, Mussolini saw ideas only as a means by which to further his career, his radicalism reflecting his own personal bitterness and resentment. Driven by ambition, Mussolini exhibited skill as a journalist and as a politician. As a leader, however, Mussolini was an actor, an improvisor, instinctive and impulsive, turning to action when he did not know what else to do, fostering the cult of the Duce to enhance his own personal power. In the end, Fascism was not a doctrine but only a technique for winning power. All in all, Mack Smith paints a devastating portrait of Mussolini, but not always a consistent one. Indeed, Mack Smith grudgingly acknowledges that Mussolini was influenced by the ideas of Marx, Sorel, Nietzsche, and Darwin, while conceding that he maintained fixed ideas about struggle, revolution, and the notion of creating a new Italian character. In the end, Mack Smith's explanation for Mussolini's success rests excessively on the Duce's "instincts," while his assessment of Fascist doctrine fails to show that it was any more inconsistent than that of other rev-

olutionary movements. Mack Smith's is thus an exhaustive portrait, but one that understates the value of ideas to Mussolini, as well as the consistency of core concepts in Fascism.

Lurking behind those authors who see in Mussolini a consistent revolutionary thinker is the figure of Renzo De Felice, whose multi-volume biography of Mussolini not only accepts him as an authentic revolutionary, but asserts as well that the Fascist regime had genuine consensual support up until the late 1930s. Unfortunately, De Felice's work has not yet been translated into English. Suffice it to say that no serious student of Mussolini or Fascism can afford to ignore De Felice.

Two biographies do, however, provide the flavor of De Felice's arguments. The first, by GREGOR, argues that Fascism possessed a theoretical and ideological substance that was both interesting and sophisticated. Gregor disagrees with the conventional wisdom that Mussolini had few, or any, ideological convictions—or that Fascist ideology was totally contradictory. Gregor seeks to trace the intellectual development of Mussolini's political convictions, discovering an evolving system of thought rather than a synthesis of contradictions. To Gregor, Fascism developed out of the crisis of classical Marxism, which was vague and porous enough as an ideology to accommodate all the theoretical elements put together by Mussolini to fashion his revolutionary ideology. In essence, then, Gregor posits a Mussolini moving from revolutionary socialism to Fascism by way of a "national syndicalism." Gregor's synoptic account of the thought of various syndicalist theorists and how their ideas affected the young Mussolini provides a welcome corrective to those who see Mussolini as merely an opportunist indifferent to ideology. In addition, Gregor points to some of the modernizing aspects of Fascism that appealed to vital segments of the Italian population. Ultimately, however, Gregor strains credulity by seeing too much systemization, and too direct a line from Marxism to Syndicalism to Fascism, in Mussolini's thought.

JOES parallels the arguments of Gregor, trying to synthesize for the non-specialist reader the newer scholarship on Mussolini's life and the Fascist movement. Joes argues that Mussolini's was another revolution, not a counter-revolution, and that the Fascist regime pointed the way to the modernization of Italy. This is, however, a curiously uneven biography. Most of his insights Joes owes to Gregor or De Felice, while seeming to accept at face value some of the dubious assertions of Sarfatti. Moreover, he makes lame assertions for the extent of Mussolini's influence on "developmental dictatorships" in the present-day Third World.

—Stephen G. Fritz

NABOKOV, Vladimir, 1899–1977; Russian-born American writer.

Boyd, Brian, *Vladimir Nabokov: The Russian Years*. Princeton, New Jersey, Princeton University Press, and London, Chatto and Windus, 1990.
Field, Andrew, *Nabokov: His Life in Part*. New York, Viking, and London, Hamilton, 1977.

Field, Andrew, *VN: The Life and Art of Vladimir Nabokov*. New York, Crown, 1986; London, Macdonald, 1987.

Hyde, George M., *Vladimir Nabokov: America's Russian Novelist*. Atlantic Highlands, New Jersey, Humanities Press, and London, M. Boyars, 1977.

Lee, Lawrence, *Vladimir Nabokov*. Boston, Twayne, and London, G. Prior, 1976.

Quennell, Peter, editor, *Vladimir Nabokov, His Life, His Work, His World: A Tribute*. London, Wiedenfeld and Nicolson, 1979; New York, Morrow, 1980.

Ross, Charles S., *Vladimir Nabokov: Life, Work, and Criticism*. Fredericton, New Brunswick, York Press, 1985.

*

Sure to become the standard in Nabokov biography is BOYD, the first of whose projected two volumes appeared in the Fall of 1990. Initial reaction to this study has been positive, an encouraging sign in an area of scholarship that has been the scene of considerable controversy. Previous studies have been criticized for being entirely too superficial, speculative in their conclusions, or harsh in tone. With its reliance on evidence gleaned from an examination of Nabokov's private papers as well as an astonishing array of archival material from around the world, Boyd's promises to be the first truly critical biography of this important literary figure.

Although a literary critic by training, Boyd has been particularly praised for his expanding the discussion of Nabokov's life and work into the broader context of the highly politicized Russian émigré community massed in the cultural centers throughout Europe. According to Robert Alter, writing in *The New Republic* (15 October 1990), with the publication of this first volume dealing with Nabokov's life to 1940, "it is now possible to get a clear picture of Nabokov's relation to Russian political and cultural history, and the various currents of European emigration." Perhaps Boyd's major contribution is his reconsideration of Nabokov as very much connected to the culture that produced him, and not the aloof, sometimes hostile figure he has frequently been portrayed to be.

In addition to Boyd there are two major biographies of Nabokov, both written by the same person. FIELD's 1977 work grew naturally out of his much admired and praised critical study, *Nabokov: His Life in Art* (1967). The positive reception this book enjoyed established Field as a leading Nabokovian and helped secure him access to the subject, who then generously cooperated in the preparation of the first biography. Although Nabokov and his biographer had a serious falling out as the book was being readied for press, with threats of legal action forcing its author to rewrite significant portions, Field provided the first important biographical treatment, other than the subject's own autobiography *Speak, Memory* (1951; revised edition, 1966). Field's full-scale study (1986, see below) attempts to complete the record.

Limited as it is by its rambling, conversational manner, Field's 1977 work yet creates an impression of the living presence of Nabokov within its very pages. Compiled from a substantial archive of tape recorded interviews, and supported by an examination of private correspondence, together with a mass of information gathered from friends and associates, the book is a kind of running narrative with Nabokov's own words (presented in bold type) woven into Field's commentary. Despite its unconventional structure, as well as what seems at points to be very speculative observations, Field offers a wealth of detail about Nabokov's life—much of which had not been previously revealed in print. In addition to the glimpses of the subject as a struggling writer in exile in Berlin and Paris between the wars, of particular interest is the information Field presents about the Nabokov family's genealogy and its complex connections to the Russian aristocracy in the days before the Bolshevik Revolution. Field considers the degree to which the loss of this world finds its way into Nabokov's fiction. However, readers wishing to learn something about the origin and genesis of his novel *Lolita* (1955), the masterpiece of his years in America, will be somewhat disappointed. Although there is some discussion of the American period, the study focuses primarily on Nabokov's early life and career as an émigré writer in Europe prior to his immigration to the United States in 1940.

While many reviewers praised Field for bringing forward so much new information, they frequently complained about an awkwardness in his style. According to J. D. O'Hara reviewing for the *Nation*, "Andrew Field writes like someone gossiping over a back fence in backwoods New Jersey, backwardly" (9 July 1977). To this objection must also be added the book's limited utility. It is not indexed, and none of its information is documented except in the most general sense within the text itself.

FIELD's subsequent study (1986) completes the record of Nabokov's life and is much more conventional in its format. It does provide an index, though information is in places hard to cross reference, and the notes are sparse considering the book's length. Much of the documentation that is provided relies on Field's private archive, which he reports will one day find a home in an unspecified university manuscript collection. Of course, this work is based in large part on the earlier book, and it incorporates long passages verbatim. There is, however, a significant difference in tone between the two portraits. Whereas the earlier study presents the subject as a master illusionist blurring the lines between art and reality, the latter portrait is a more deflated view of a man who becomes the victim of his own self-creation. Indeed, there is a much more strident thesis to this book—that of Nabokov as Narcissus, driven by very deep-seated personality difficulties, who ultimately abandons the great compulsions of his genius, and compromises his art. The portrait that emerges of the subject's final years is that of a man isolated and aloof, who wore his fame badly. According to Field, this Nabokov/Narcissus retreating to Switzerland following his success in America, "wandered from the perfect pool and turned into a garden-variety egotist, one with the powers of a giant, true, but still entirely different from what he had been before."

Reviewers of *VN: The Life and Art of Vladimir Nabokov* were quick to point out the hostility so evident throughout its pages. There were also, again, complaints about the author's eccentric prose style, a style that does at times create some confusion. Another complaint, one raised by Joel Conarroe, is that in this more scholarly study Field fails to penetrate below his own narrow and jaundiced perspective of Nabokov's public person. Conarroe remarks that, "for the conjuror who gave us *The Gift, Pnin, Pale Fire* and other works of genius, this, surely, is prose too feeble, praise too faint" (*New York Times Book*

Reviews, 2 November 1986). Nonetheless, the portraits presented by Andrew Field when judiciously used will remain important resources.

Among less extensive, though some would argue more balanced, treatments of Nabokov's life, two basic sources are ROSS and LEE. Although Ross' critical judgments are quite idiosyncratic, particularly for so brief a study, his general overview of Nabokov's life and work provides quick orientation for the beginning student. Also directed toward the student is Lee's 1976 study, which like all the biographies in the Twayne series offers a short overview of the subject's life, together with critical analysis of his major work, supported by selected primary and secondary bibliographies.

Although intended as a work of literary analysis, HYDE presents general biographical information interspersed through this important contribution to Nabokov criticism. Because it was published the year of Nabokov's death, Hyde was the first scholar to consider the totality of his life and work. Furthermore, because Hyde's fundamental thesis is the way in which memory (or the life remembered) is central to the novelist's work, this book seems an almost necessary complement to any discussion of Nabokov's life.

Those interested in a more personal perspective would do well to consult QUENNELL's collection of reminiscences and critical essays by friends, associates, and scholars. Included are memoirs of Nabokov as teacher and mentor by Alfred Appel, Jr. and Hannah Green, his last interview, and a moving tribute by Nabokov's son Dimitri. The portrait that emerges here is much more human than that often associated with the subject in the final years of his life.

The biographical record is further supported by two editions of letters. *The Nabokov-Wilson Letters* (1979), edited by Simon Karlinsky, a leading scholar of Russian literature, presents selected correspondence between Nabokov and Edmund Wilson, who together represent two of the most powerful voices in modern literature. *Vladimir Nabokov: Selected Letters 1940–77* (1989), selected and edited by Dimitri Nabokov and Matthew J. Bruccoli, provides a more comprehensive collection of letters from throughout most of the novelist's adult life. Both collections are annotated and indexed and will be useful for both the scholar and the interested general reader, offering important adjuncts to existing biographies and undoubtedly those of the future.

—Paul H. Carlton

NAPOLEON I [*or* Napoleon Bonaparte], 1769–1821; Corsican-born French general and emperor.

Aubrey, Octave, *Napoleon: Soldier and Emperor*, translated by Arthur Livingstone. Philadelphia, Lippincott, 1938.

Barnett, Corelli, *Bonaparte*. London, Allen and Unwin, and New York, Hill and Wang, 1978.

Bergeron, Louis, *France under Napoleon*, translated by R. R. Palmer. Princeton, New Jersey, Princeton University Press, 1981 (originally published as *Episode Napoléonien*, Paris, Éditions du Seuil, 1972).

Bruun, Geoffrey, *Europe and the French Imperium 1799–1814*. New York, Harper, 1938.

Castlelot, André, *Napoleon*, translated by Guy Daniels. New York, Harper, 1971 (originally published by Perrin, Paris, 1968).

Chandler, David G., *The Campaigns of Napoleon*. London, Weidenfeld and Nicolson, and New York, Macmillan, 1966.

Chandler, David G., *Napoleon*. London, Weidenfeld and Nicolson, and New York, Saturday Review Press, 1973.

Cronin, Vincent, *Napoleon*. London, Collins, 1971; as *Napoleon Bonaparte: An Intimate Biography* New York, Morrow, 1972.

Fisher, H. A. L., *Napoleon*. London, Oxford University Press, 1912; New York, Holt, 1913.

Fournier, August, *Napoleon I: A Biography*, translated by A. E. Adams. New York, Holt, and London, Longman, 1911.

Glover, Michael, *The Napoleonic Wars: An Illustrated History 1799–1815*. London, Batsford, and New York, Hippocrene Books, 1979.

Holtman, Robert B., *The Napoleonic Revolution*. Philadelphia, Lippincott, 1967.

Hutt, Maurice, editor, *Napoleon*. Englewood Cliffs, New Jersey, Prentice-Hall, 1972.

Jones, R. Ben, *Napoleon: Man and Myth*. London, Hodder and Stoughton, 1977; New York, Holmes and Meier, 1978.

Kircheisen, Friedrich Max, *Napoleon*. London, G. Howe, 1931; New York, Harcourt, 1932 (originally published as *Napoleon I: Sein Leben und seine Zeit*, 9 vols., Munich, G. Muller, 1911–31).

Lachouque, Henry, *The Anatomy of Glory: Napoleon and His Guard, a Study in Leadership*, translated by Anne S. K. Brown. Providence, Rhode Island, Brown University Press, 1961; London, Arms and Armour Press, 1978 (originally published as *Napoleon et la Garde Impériale*, Paris, Bloud and Gay, 1957).

Laing, Margaret Irene, *Josephine and Napoleon*. London, Sidgwick and Jackson, 1973; New York, Mason Charter, 1974.

Lefebvre, Georges, *Napoleon*: vol. 1, *From 18 Brumaire to Tilsit 1799–1807*, translated by Henry F. Stockhold; vol 2., *From Tilsit to Waterloo 1807–15*, translated by J. E. Anderson. London, Routledge, and New York, Columbia University Press, 1969 (originally published as *Napoleon*, Paris, Presses Universitaires de France, 1936).

Markham, Felix M., *Napoleon and the Awakening of Europe*. London, English Universities Press, and New York, Macmillan, 1954.

Markham, Felix M., *Napoleon*. London, Weidenfeld and Nicolson, and New York, New American Library, 1963.

Maurois, André, *Napoleon, a Pictoral Biography*. London, Thames and Hudson, 1963; New York, Viking, 1964.

Rose, J. Holland, *The Life of Napoleon I*. London and New York, Macmillan, 1902.

Tarle, Evgenii V., *Bonaparte*, translated by John Cournos. New York, Knight, and London, Hodder and Stoughton, 1937.

Thompson, J. M., *Napoleon Bonaparte: His Rise and Fall*. Oxford and New York, Oxford University Press, 1951.

Tulard, Jean, *Napoleon, the Myth of a Saviour*, translated by Teresa Waugh. London, Weidenfeld and Nicolson, 1984 (originally published by Fayard, Paris, 1977).

*

In the nearly 200 years since Napoleon's seizure of power, over 2000 monographs have been published investigating every aspect of his life and influence. Added to this are the several hundred thousand scholarly articles and many fictional accounts that further augment the vast amount of material available to the reader. The works discussed below have been selected from this wide range of sources. They consist of the most valuable popular and scholarly biographies as well as the best of the military chronicles.

Beginning with the early biographies of Napoleon, FOURNIER's study is one of the best and most highly regarded of the early works. It is bright and readable and contains a mass of material, including printed contemporary sources. The only defect is that the author, as an Austrian, attempted to defend the policy of Austria, and in so doing tended to distort the events.

ROSE's is a classic work. When published it was regarded as the best biography of Napoleon by an English scholar. It is well-organized, well-written, and well-documented—a good example of historical literature. Based on new materials from official British records, the papers of the London Record Office, it offers a balanced view of the Emperor. The first ten chapters cover the years before 1800.

KIRCHEISEN's *Napoleon* is an abridgement of a monumental nine-volume work first published in German. It is a less thorough study than that of Rose, but more entertaining to read. While Fournier and Rose based their biographies on documents, Kircheisen worked from printed sources, notably German and Austrian. His work is especially good for covering the campaigns in which these two nations were engaged against the French. Napoleon is not idolized as he had been in many early French accounts; Kircheisen presents a balanced view. Intended for the general reader, the work includes no notes or appendices. The author concludes: "Napoleon came and vanished like a meteor. He had destroyed more than he had created, but at least he had roused the old Europe from its lethargy and pointed the way to a future union of nations." The translation is excellent and reads as though the work had been written in English.

Among the more accurate and interesting popular biographies are those of Aubrey, Fisher, and Cronin. AUBREY, who is a French authority on the subject, surveys the life of Napoleon from his early days in military college to his death. FISHER concentrates on the man himself and his character. This book, not meant for readers interested mainly in Napoleon's military campaigns, is an excellent introductory biography—simple, brief, and direct.

In his preface, CRONIN defends his biography of Napoleon on the grounds that he discovered new material: the Notebooks of Alexander de Mazis, Napoleon's best childhood friend; the letters of Desiree Carey, an early lover; the memoirs of Louis Marchand, Napoleon's valet; and General Bertrand's St. Helena diary. Based upon these and other primary sources, Cronin has written an intimate portrayal of Napoleon's personal life. As J. H. Plumb remarks, "The portrait of Napoleon is profound in its understanding and moving in it presentation" (*New York Times Book Review*, 12 March 1972). Topics covered include Napoleon's love affairs, his diet, and his innermost thoughts. The book is written in a very chatty and informal style that is easy to read.

MAUROIS provides a study of Napoleon's career that is illustrated with pictures and caricatures from the work of David, Goya, Phillippoteaux, and others. It is a fine edition of a pictorial biography, with 168 illustrations. The text, consisting of a short account of Napoleon's career and character, is sketchy and incomplete. CASTLELOT's popular biography is a somewhat rambling and erratic "rise and fall" of Napoleon. Beginning with his boyhood in Corsica to his death in exile, the book focuses on romances and military exploits.

HUTT has compiled a useful and interesting anthology for those previously unacquainted with Napoleon. Geared to the student and general reader, this slim volume consists of a selection of Napoleon's own statements reflecting his image of himself, insightful comments made by contemporaries, and finally interpretations by 19th- and early 20th-century French historians.

LAING's book is primarily a study of Josephine, but it is useful for Napoleon himself in that it demonstrates the extraordinary influence she exercised over him. The book is based mostly on their letters, which are quoted extensively throughout the text. Their marriage and divorce is considered in terms of personal emotions. This is a lavishly illustrated book that provides the reader with a visual panorama of the period and therefore is recommended for popular collectors.

One of the more recent short biographies is that by JONES. In 221 pages, the author has attempted to demonstrate the peculiar conditions that allowed Napoleon's career to take place. This is a well-reasoned assessment of Napoleon's career as general, administrator, and diplomat. It is well written and includes a bibliography of recent works and a chronology at the end of each chapter.

TARLE, a Russian soldier, is a specialist in the Continental System. In his very clear biography of Napoleon, he makes use of sources unavailable to the Western historian. This enables him to expound Russian policy effectively and to treat the Russian side of the 1812 campaign in a manner superior to that of most French and British writers. It is a complete and scholarly biography.

BRUUN's work is an attempt to get beyond the traditional confines of political and military history without entirely neglecting them. These are discussed alongside developments in the economic, financial, social, religious, cultural, and artistic spheres. A book designed for students and general readers, it is clearly written and relatively unbiased. As George Dutcher remarks, "Bruun neither worships nor detests Napoleon: he distributes credit and blame with an equal hand" (*Journal of Modern History*, April 1939). Bruun also discusses the personality of Napoleon and the national history of France in this compact volume.

THOMPSON, a leading authority on the French Revolution, interprets Napoleon's career in the light of the Revolution. As Thompson states, "His greatest triumph was not Europe but the French Revolution." He is interested in the Napoleon who codified the laws and institutions created during the Revolution. Beautifully written in a classical style, his work is a brilliant piece of scholarship, not intended for the beginner. Thompson relies for the most part on the famous *Correspondance* published by order of Napoleon III between 1858–70.

MARKHAM has produced two worthwhile studies, both of which are based on primary sources, including Napoleon's *Mémoires* and *Correspondance*. His short *Napoleon and the Awakening of Europe* (1954) is more a biography than its title suggests. It is the story of an adventurer, "a great man of history." The Emperor is portrayed as the last of the Enlightened despots and a typical child of the Romantic movement. Interesting details concerning Napoleon's life in exile on St. Helena shed light on his character. As Alfred Cobban claims, it is an "excellent book . . . and notably well-written" (*English Historical Review*, 1954).

MARKHAM's *Napoleon* (1963) is a longer (292 pages) and more scholarly study of his subject's political and military career. Markham provides the reader with a balanced and comprehensive examination of Napoleon's achievements both domestic and foreign, and he is especially good on Napoleon's later years. Interesting details on the state of Napoleon's health and personality add a personal touch. Markham tends not to regard Napoleon as a military dictator, but as an "enlightened despot." Interesting and carefully chosen illustrations enhance the attraction of this very readable biography.

HOLTMAN begins by telling the reader what his book is not about: "The present volume is not concerned with passing judgement, with showing whether Napoleon was good or evil." Rather his aim is to "examine the elements of the Napoleonic revolution and see how they came about." In ten brief chapters, Holtman surveys the institutional changes and domestic innovations that characterized Napoleon's rule. Geared to the educated layman and university student, Holtman convincingly demonstrates how Napoleon's ideas and politics had their origins in the Enlightenment and in the French Revolution. This book is particularly useful for anyone interested in Napoleon's reforms in education, law, and religion. Holtman concludes that as a founder of modern Western civilization, Napoleon permanently changed Europe.

The biography by LEFEBVRE, the French Marxist historian, has accurately been described by most reviewers as a "classic" and a "masterpiece." This work is not geared to the general public, but to the student and scholar, and it is not intended as a biography per se, but as a general survey of the Napoleonic period. Lefebvre is at his best when discussing the material aspects of French life, such as the economy and the Continental system.

BARNETT, a distinguished military historian, focuses on Napoleon's military career and interprets his victories in a very critical light. Although he recognizes Napoleon's military genius, he argues that Napoleon made many tactical errors that ultimately led to his defeat. Napoleon's victories are explained in terms of luck. Barnett also argues that the Napoleonic legend is little more than skillful propaganda on the Emperor's part. This is a biography strongly recommended for students of history.

In the tradition of the Annales school, BERGERON has written an excellent social history of France under Napoleon. Neatly divided into two parts, the work's first section examines the social structure, economic activity, and demographic trends of the period. Part II is concerned with the opposition Napoleon faced, which Bergeron tends to exaggerate. This is a superb study of French attitudes or *mentalités*. The distinguished historian of the French Revolution, R. R. Palmer, has done a fine job of translating the text. He has, however, shortened the footnotes and omitted items from the original bibliography, which may frustrate those in search of original sources.

From the large selection of books concerned with the exclusively military side of Napoleon, there are a number of exceptional examples. In his popular history, GLOVER outlines the wars of the French Revolution, Consulate, and Empire. In an attractively produced volume of 232 pages, the author has included 97 black-and-white and 12 full-paged colour illustrations.

There are also seven maps, a chart on the different types of warships, and sketches of various weapons. Glover succeeds in interweaving the diplomatic, economic, and naval with the simple military aspects of warfare. His work is a joy to read for those interested in Napoleon's battles.

LACHOUQUE's book is an outstanding contribution to the history of the Napoleonic wars that will be of interest to collectors and students. In a lively narrative, Lachouque describes the birth, life, and death of the Imperial Guard. His account is constructed around quotations from the letters and reports of the participants. The 173 illustrations, 90 of them in colour, are of excellent quality. Many had never been published before. The book also contains 14 maps and plates of the general's great battles. Lachouque does not, however, contribute anything new to our knowledge of Napoleonic warfare. His is an examination of the past through the eyes of a soldier rather than those of an historian.

Both of CHANDLER's books deal with Napoleon's military exploits. His *Campaigns* (1966), a colossal study of 1172 pages, analyses and critiques the "art of war" as developed by Napoleon. Every campaign led by Napoleon is examined in detail. Included is a helpful glossary of military terms in an appendix. It is a useful book for professional historians, students, and general readers. Chandler's second and much shorter book (1973), in the Great Commanders series, emphasizes Napoleon's military record. While Napoleon's role in French politics is played down and his domestic reforms as First Consul and later as Emperor are dealt with in a cursory fashion, the book's last chapter provides a good summary of his character.

The most recent biography to appear in English is TULARD's *Napoleon*. Tulard, a well-known scholar of the period, sees Napoleon as a talented outsider. His thesis is that the real beneficiaries of Napoleon's 16-year rule were the notables: the bourgeoisie who had purchased church lands. They created the "saviour" on 18 Brumaire and they withdrew their support in 1814 when Napoleon exceeded their plans for France. Tulard is a master of his subject. His book includes an impressive annotated bibliography of 97 pages. Unfortunately, Teresa Waugh's translation of Tulard is full of factual errors. In the words of Norman Hampson, "This is emphatically not a book that may be safely used by anyone without access to the original text" (*Times Literary Supplement*, 5 October 1984).

1989, the year of the bicentenary of the French Revolution, was not a popular year for Napoleon if one judges by the number of publications. The only one to appear was that by the French revolutionary historian, Jean-Paul Bertaud, *Bonaparte prend le pouvoir, la République, meurt-elle assassinée?* This book has yet to be translated into English.

—Leigh Ann Whaley

NAPOLEON III [Charles Louis Napoleon Bonaparte], 1808–1873; French emperor.

Arnaud, René, *Second Republic and Napoleon III*, translated by E. F. Buckley. New York, Putnam, and London, Heinemann,

1930 (originally published as *La Deuxième République et le Second Empire*, Paris, Hachette, 1929).

Aronson, Theo, *The Fall of the Third Napoleon*. London, Cassell, and Indianapolis, Bobbs-Merrill, 1970.

Bierman, John, *Napoleon III and His Carnival Empire*. New York, St. Martin's, 1988; London, J. Murray, 1989.

Cheetham, F. H., *Louis Napoleon and the Genesis of the Second Empire*. London and New York, J. Lane, 1909.

D'Auvergne, Edmund Basil Francis, *Napoleon the Third: A Biography*. London, Nash and Grayson, and New York, Dodd Mead, 1929.

Guedalla, Philip, *Second Empire*. New York, Putnam, and London, Constable/Hodder and Stoughton, 1922.

Guerard, Albert Léon, *Napoleon III, a Great Life in Brief*. New York, Knopf, 1955.

Jerrold, Blanchard, *Life of Napoleon III* (4 vols.). London, Longman, 1874–82.

Ridley, Jasper, *Napoleon III and Eugenie*. London, Constable, 1979; New York, Viking, 1980.

Sencourt, Robert, *Napoleon III: The Modern Emperor*. New York, Appleton-Century, and London, E. Benn, 1934.

Simpson, Frederick A., *The Rise of Louis Napoleon*. New York, Putnam, and London, J. Murray, 1909; revised edition, London and New York, Longman, 1925.

Simpson, Frederick A., *Louis Napoleon and the Recovery of France*. London and New York, Longman, 1923.

Smith, W. H. C., *Napoleon III*. London, Wayland, 1972; New York, St. Martin's, 1973.

Thompson, James Matthew, *Louis Napoleon and the Second Empire*. Oxford, Blackwell, 1954; New York, Noonday, 1955.

*

While Louis Napoleon's place in world history falls far beneath that of Napoleon Bonaparte, leaving him the subject of considerably less commentary, the biographical material on him is still enormous. Much about his life is contained in the numerous books treating the Second republic and the Second empire (books that have been largely excluded from consideration here), and accounts continue to be given of particular aspects or phases of Napoleon III's life and career.

A fairly early work written in English, now superseded, may still deserve some mention out of historical interest. JERROLD was too favorably inclined toward Louis Napoleon to provide anything like a balanced assessment. However, he was able to benefit from the many private papers given to him by the royal family; all subsequent biographers remain in his debt.

At the time of their publication, each of SIMPSON's two books (1909, 1923) represented the finest biographical narrative and soundest historical research on Louis Napoleon and his age to have appeared in English. They remain valuable today as the first real scholarly work done in English on Napoleon III and for their accurate and balanced assessments of the Second empire. Simpson in each case conducted wide-ranging research into unpublished source materials, including some of Louis Napoleon's letters written in exile. *The Rise of Louis Napoleon* (1909) covers the first 40 years of his subject's life, from the fall of the First empire to the beginning of the Second. It succeeds in portraying Louis Napoleon's positive qualities without falling into

adulation, and it avoids the tone of ridicule some historians adopted after Victo Hugo (*Napoléon le Petit*, 1852). It contained the most complete bibliography then available (updated in 1925 after Simpson's second book came out), and an impressive array of notes and appendices. CHEETHAM's book, published in the same year and claiming to cover exactly the same time period, pales miserably by comparison, failing like Jerrold to convey any sense of a rounded human being, and adopting a generally laudatory tone.

SIMPSON's second book, *Louis Napoleon and the Recovery of France* (1923), picks up where the earlier work left off. Here, however, Simpson looks more generally at events during the Second republic; his focus on the life of Louis Napoleon, while still sharp, is not as consistent as it is in the first book. Yet this is hardly a criticism, since the events of the age demand close scrutiny in any consideration of the emperor's life. Nor is it a very great criticism to admit that Simpson's writing sometimes fails to bring to life the fast-paced events he describes; he opts always for sound historical writing over flashy effect. Both of Simpson's books, while they exhibit the highest standards of academic scholarship, should still be useful for general readers wanting to know both the man and his period.

Whatever his faults, GUEDALLA cannot be criticized for serving up stodgy academic prose. His *Second Empire*, the one book claiming to cover such wide ground that must be considered in a survey of Louis Napoleon biographies, bristles with wit and irony, brilliance of detail and elegance of style. Its title notwithstanding, Guedalla's work actually begins during the First empire, with a lengthy section entitled "Bonapartism" (which Guedalla includes both to set up the events of the Second empire and to trace the growth of the Napoleonic legends), before following the career of Napoleon III in sections entitled "The Prince," "The President," and "The Emperor." His book has been widely regarded as a masterpiece of literary historical writing, after the fashion of Lytton Strachey and Hillaire Belloc. Guedalla's command of his subject is also extraordinary. Events come alive on his page—not just through colorful imaginings but in a very high degree of depth and accuracy—as they have in no other treatment before or since. One might complain only that Guedella's abiding wit sometimes blinds the reader to the extreme seriousness of events during this period. Readers who prefer a more conventional, generally solid and reliable account of Napoleon within the republic and the empire should read ARNAUD.

D'AUVERGNE in 1929 provided a brief, reliable introduction to Napoleon III, shying away from political events in favor of a more personal view of the man. Five years later SENCOURT's volume appeared. Sencourt had been appointed the "official" biographer of the wife of Louis Napoleon (*The Life of the Empress Eugénie*, 1931), and was thereby given access to family documents unavailable to previous biographers. His *Napoleon III* exhibits wide learning, gained not just from the private documents but from a careful reading of all previously published accounts. Sencourt's writing, less accomplished than Guedalla's, is nonetheless both lively and accessible; it does not belie the historian's exhaustive research.

GUERARD's "Great Life in Brief" replaced D'Auvergne's earlier work as the finest short introduction to the emperor. Factual to the core, generally unbiased, and vividly written, Guerard's volume relates authoritatively the main outline of events in

Louis Napoleon's life during the central decades of the 19th century in France. While the book will still serve some readers as an adequate "last stop" biography of Napoleon III, perhaps its greatest use is in preparing the reader for more comprehensive, or more specialized, studies.

THOMPSON's amiable life and times is one of the more notable such efforts since Guedalla. Its warm, unpretentious prose and obvious affinity for its subject will recommend it to readers seeking a solid, accessible, yet broadly based overview of Louis Napoleon and his era. While Thompson is generous in his treatment of Louis Napoleon, he manages to elicit an aspect of the emperor that many other English biographers since the 19th century have missed, or else deemphasized: that of a man who fell somewhat short of greatness, whose ambitions for himself and his nation were compromised by vanity (Thompson points out how Louis sought glory through the name "Napoleon"), mediocrity, and bad luck.

SMITH, drawing on much recent literature on the Second empire, focuses on Louis Napoleon's career after 1830; he dispenses with the first 22 years of his life in just six pages. The work will be of value primarily to those interested in the political dimensions of Louis Napoleon's reign, especially with regard to foreign policy. ARONSON provides a popular account of the final days of the Second empire. In so doing, he paints a sympathetic portrait of the Bonapartes against the "brutal" Prussians. No new information is offered here. Neither does the most recent broad view of Napoleon III within his empire break any new ground: BIERMAN tells his story in an admirably straightforward, journalistic manner, although he fails to make much sense of the events he retells and is given to some flamboyant, often baseless, descriptions of mood and character.

Several biographies attempt to cover the lives of both Louis Napoleon and the Empress Eugénie; several others devoted just to the latter necessarily throw light on the former. In addition to Sencourt's biography of the empress, noted above, an outstanding biography of her comes from Harold Kurtz (*The Empress Eugénie*, 1965). Of the joint biographies, most, such as those by David Duff (*Eugénie and Napoleon III*, 1978) and Alyn Brodsky (*Imperial Charade: A Biography of Emperor Napoleon III and Empress Eugénie*, 1978), are not worth investigating. RIDLEY, an experienced biographer of English monarchs, has proven most successful in this category. His extremely readable book covers the period from Napoleon III's birth in 1808 to Eugénie's death in 1920 (in England, where she had resided in exile since 1870). This work, far and away the most scholarly study of the emperor and empress together, is still written with a popular audience in view.

Finally, mention should be made of a few of the recent specialized studies that shed further light on Louis Napoleon's character. All such books assume on the part of the reader basic knowledge of both the emperor and the age. David I. Kulstein (*Napoleon III and the Working Class: A Study of Government Propaganda under the Second Empire*, 1971) demonstrates the wide-ranging and "modern" techniques Napoleon III and his officials used to control public opinion. S. C. Burchell (*Imperial Masquerade: The Paris of Napoleon III*, New York, 1971; in the UK as *Upstart Empire*, London, 1971) looks very broadly at the mood and the major figures in Paris during the Second empire. Burchell's scope includes politics, art, architecture, music, and

morals. While he attempts no major arguments, he provides for the general reader a sense of the disparity between the richness of cultural life and the poverty within the regime during this period.

David Henry Pinkney (*Napoleon III and the Rebuilding of Paris*, 1958) has written the best account of this major phase in Napoleon III's reign. It is a fascinating story, and the picture we get of Napoleon III and Haussmann working together to make over the city is illuminating. Roger L. Williams (*The Mortal Napoleon*, 1972) examines the various illnesses Napoleon III suffered and speculates on how they affected his rule. One final book should be mentioned here, by George Peabody Gooch (*The Second Empire*, 1961). Its valuable biographical essays on numerous figures of the period (including, of course, Napoleon III), blended with an impeccable historical approach, make this still a useful reference work for scholars and students.

—Noelle A. Watson

NATION, Carry (Amelia), 1846–1911; American temperance advocate.

Asbury, Herbert, *Carry Nation: The Woman with the Hatchet.* New York, Knopf, 1929.

Beals, Carlton, *Cyclone Carry: The Story of Carry Nation.* Philadelphia, Chilton, 1962.

Madison, Arnold, *Carry Nation.* Nashville, Tennessee, T. Nelson, 1977.

Taylor, Robert Lewis, *Vessel of Wrath; The Life and Times of Carry Nation.* New York, New American Library, 1966.

*

The full biographies of Carry Nation are all meant to be popular and lack the paraphernalia of scholarship. For basic factual data they all depend to varying degrees on Nation's curious autobiography, *The Use and Need of the Life of Carry A. Nation* (Topeka, Kansas, F. M. Steves, 1904). The first part recounts her birth, marriage, travels, etc., and the latter part is devoted to reprints of articles, reports, poetry, and opinions concerning alcohol and various opinions others had of her.

ASBURY, who wrote the first and best biography, although some of the other biographies evidence greater research in newspapers, is the only source of any real substance available to authors. The scion of a devoutly religious American family that dates back to colonial times, Asbury attributes Nation's reform zeal to the dissipation of Charles Gloyd, her first husband. He was what she came to despise—a drunkard, cigarette smoker, and member of the Masonic Lodge. All of the biographies repeat Gloyd's habits as influencing Nation but assign varying degrees of importance to them. Asbury, however, writes: "She loved Gloyd to distraction, but he made her desperately unhappy." He believes that this unhappiness and a life of difficulty with her second husband, David A. Nation, produced a brooding, morose, fanatical woman, who became obsessed with the notion that God called her to oppose demon rum and a host of its associates.

In Asbury's opinion, Carry Nation transformed temperance from a reasonable course into a prohibitionist movement. She, of course, had the energy and political *savoir faire* to help prohibition be established. Writing in the 1920s, he concludes that without prohibition there would have been no speakeasies, bootleggers, crime, or corruption, and that temperance or some other rational solution to the over-consumption of alcohol might have been achieved.

TAYLOR neither approves nor condemns Carry Nation's prohibitionist stand. He does, however, trivialize her effort. In the last paragraph of his study he notes that the recognition she sought eluded her until long after her death. Then at mid-century in Wichita, Kansas, where she suffered her first arrest for bar smashing, "a handsome inscribed fountain was erected, a testimonial not long afterward knocked down and smashed by an errant, oversized beer truck." Taylor also provides a list of people and things that she considered as her enemies. They are, in the following "approximate order," alcohol, tobacco, sex, politics, government, the Masonic Lodge, William McKinley, Teddy Roosevelt ("a blood-thirsty, reckless, cigarette-smoking rummy"), and William Jennings Bryan.

Like other biographers, Taylor notes that insanity ran in Nation's family and that she had visions as a child, but he says that her "mental weakness" was hardly the cause for her reforming zeal. She was, he avers, "a complex, memorable person touched by genius." Environment had more to do with what she became than did her mental instability. She lived in odd times in the backwater areas of extremism—Kentucky, Missouri, Texas, and Kansas.

In Kansas Carry Nation encountered the cruelty of drunken frontiersmen. Moreover, David Nation remained a ne'er-do-well loafer, a lawyer without clients, and a preacher without a flock. She was not insane but was approaching menopause when she began her hatchet-wielding crusade against booze. Taylor, who despite what is at times a tongue-in-cheek presentation, shows great empathy for Carry, concluding that the above circumstances gave her great energy and that, once accustomed to fame, she was sustained by her belief that she was creating a better community.

BEALS, who was raised in Medicine Lodge, Kansas, the town with which Nation is most associated, claims that Carry Nation "baby-sat" with his mother, and that his father, who edited the local newspaper, *The Index*, was often the object of Carry's scorn because of his evenhandedness, which Nation viewed as cowardice. Beals explains her zealotry as resulting from childhood religious experiences in Kentucky among blacks, from her reaction to the failed marriage to Gloyd, from her requited love and desire for attention, from a hard life in frontier Texas and Kansas that caused insomnia and hallucinations, and from a character that reveled in responsibility. Beals invents quotations in his informal, breezy presentation and claims that he relied in part on stories common within his family. He does provide a two-page bibliography.

All of the authors agree with those contemporary assessments of Nation that she was the leading force behind prohibition early in this century and that the 18th amendment to the United States Constitution was something of a monument to her violent reformism. But Beals, who notes that she was deeply spiritual, honest, and believed in people, is nevertheless her harshest critic. "She was," he writes, "the Hitler of morals, the Joe McCarthy of personal conduct."

The most recent biography, that of MADISON, is the least satisfying. Madison could have drawn upon a wealth of scholarship about Nation that appeared in the 1960s and 70s in academic journals or a number of excellent monographs on the temperance and prohibition movements, but he apparently did not. Consequently, he has added nothing to the three earlier studies. He points out that the tragic flaw of Nation's life as a self-righteous crusader was that she never understood the biological or psychological aspects of alcoholism. However, he believes that, to her credit, she had the answer to alcoholism, i.e., the only way to stop being an alcoholic is to stop drinking.

—Robert S. La Forte

NEHRU, Jawaharlal, 1889–1964; Indian nationalist and prime minister.

Crocker, W. R., *Nehru: A Contemporary's Estimate*. London, Allen and Unwin, and New York, Oxford University Press, 1986.
Gopal, Sarvepalli, *Jawaharlal Nehru: A Biography* (3 vols.). London, Cape, 1975–84; Cambridge, Massachusetts, Harvard University Press, 1976–84.
Mukerjee, H., *The Gentle Colossus: A Study of Jawaharlal Nehru*. Calcutta, Manisha Granthalaya, 1964; Oxford and New York, Oxford University Press, 1986.

*

GOPAL's trilogy outweighs, literally and metaphorically, all other studies of Nehru. His insight as a senior Foreign Affairs official coupled with his academic rigour and status result in an informed "insider's" view. He is neither detached nor dispassionate—probably an impossibility for any Indian of the Independence generation—but neither is he a hagiographer. His interpretations are often sharp and contentious but he provides a minutely detailed factual record.

Volume 1 (1889–1946) covers Nehru's life to the brink of Indian Independence; it could well be subtitled "the making of Nehru." Gopal illuminates his subject's character, attitudes (secularist, atheist, and Anglicised), and obsessions with a knowledge that only a fellow Indian of Oxbridge background could convey. He traces Nehru's conversion from an apolitical dilettante (who had once criticised Fenner Brockway's "extremism") to a passionate nationalist leader from Amritsar (1919) onwards. Hindu religiosity repelled Nehru, and Gopal faithfully traces his contretemps with Ghandi: Nehru said in 1934, "our objectives are different, our ideas are different, our spiritual outlook is different and our methods are likely to be different."

Gopal details Nehru's fascination with the Soviet Union and admiration for Stalinist industrialisation, later adapted as a role model for India. He also reflects Nehru's obsessive mistrust in being summarily dismissive of the persistent and genuine British attempts to reach a constitutional formula for Independence. Cripps, Wavell, and the British military effort against the Japanese in Assam and Burma are all given short shrift. The least satisfactory feature of this volume, however, is its failure to assess fairly those Muslim leaders who opted for partition in 1947. Gopal's sympathy with Nehru diminishes his objectivity in portraying the mutual incomprehension and mistrust which ten years earlier foreshadowed the inevitability—and bitterness—of partition.

Volume 2 (1947–56) covers the agonised birth of independent India and Nehru's growth into a major global figure. Gopal's account of the bloodshed of 1947 is doubtless accurate as to fact but it reads as a partisan account. Neither on Partition nor on Kashmir is Pakistan's case fairly stated. The account of Nehru's role as an Asian leader and international arbiter is written with relish. Canada's St. Laurent is quoted as describing the 1957 meeting of Nehru and Eisenhower as between "probably the two most important statesmen in the World." Gopal suggests that Nehru drew sustenance from popular idolatry and he assuredly played up to the international gallery as an arbiter between nations. The contrast between his attitudes over Suez and Hungary in 1956 demands but gets no adequate explanation, though it is evident that Nehru was himself uneasy over his position. The whole flavour of Nehru's "moral ascendancy" in the 1950s is perfectly illustrated by Gopal's quotation of Nehru's comment on a request for Indian fighting troops for Korea: "our moral help is a big enough thing which outbalances the petty military help of some other countries."

After lauding the "zenith" of Nehru's role in world affairs, Volume 3 (1957–1964) turns to a catalogue of failures, bitterness, and finally humiliation at the hands of the Chinese whom Nehru had wooed so assiduously. Confronted with communalism, casteism, and corruption Nehru became, asserts Gopal, "very sensitive to India being the country most sunk, most undeveloped, most backward . . . because of caste chiefly, plus poverty." The final years must be recorded as a tragedy. Nehru's moralising did not conceal his deceit and brute force over the occupation of Goa, although Gopal endeavours to exculpate him. His domestic prestige was shattered in 1962 on the Himalayan borders and after that his "purpose and authority shrivelled."

CROCKER spent two tours as Australia's High Commissioner (i.e, ambassador) to Delhi during Nehru's premiership and had also served in India during the War. He is thus no political neophyte. Whilst clearly finding much to admire in Nehru, Crocker leaves the lasting impression of a reasoned and effective exercise in demythologising, a necessity because the legend propogated by Nehru's devotees had become absurdly inflated. Crocker's main concern is with the period of Nehru's political supremacy. He makes the point that as a Brahmin Nehru was an hereditary expositor of dogma. As a secularist he ardently propounded political and social dogma from 1920 until his death. For 25 of these years "to destroy the British Raj was the beacon light of his existence," and in Crocker's view the violence incited by the Independence movement inculcated the deadly tradition of Indian political violence for which Nehru bore much of the responsibility. Finally, suggests Crocker, by the time of his death Nehru could view India as "a prospect littered with ruins," with Kashmir, Goa, the Chinese humiliation, Hindu revivalism, communal violence, and corruption as massive mementos of failure. Although the British Raj had underrated Nehru before Independence, in Crocker's view the world subsequently overrated him. Crocker's biography is prefaced by a noteworthy foreword by Ar-

nold Toynbee, which encapsulates the contradictory yet reconcilable aspects of Nehru's personality.

As the title of his book implies, MUKERJEE was devoted to Nehru. This work is basically a Hindu Nationalist's partisan eulogy and lacks both the scholarly definitiveness of Gopal and the sharp judgement and perception of Crocker. Mukerjee suggests that the decade from 1932 "was the most radiant phase of Nehru's life"—the period of closest collaboration with Ghandi and Rajagopalachari, Nehru's only compeers. This biography scarcely has any validity as a commentary on Nehru's leadership as prime minister, either domestically or in world affairs. It also has a perniciously anti-Western bias: "the Western World looked askance at every step of India's struggle for completion and consolidation of her Independence." And there is an extraordinary gullibility, so that Mukerjee, rejoicing in Nehru's persistence in five-year plans in emulation of the Soviet Stalinist example, asserts that by 1964 the Soviets had created an affluent society! The chief recommendation of this book is that it is the sort of account many Indians believe, but it should only be considered as a supplementary work with the authentic feel of popular mythology.

—D. H. O'Leary

NELSON, Horatio [Viscount Nelson], 1758–1805; English admiral.

Bryant, Sir Arthur, *Nelson*. London, Collins, 1970.

Clarke, J. S. and J. MacArthur, *The Life of Admiral Lord Nelson*. London, T. Bensley, 1809.

Mahan, Alfred Thayer, *The Life of Nelson* (2 vols.). Boston, Little Brown, and London, Low Marston, 1897; abridged one-volume edition, London and New York, Penguin, 1942.

Oman, Carola, *Nelson*. New York, Doubleday, 1946; London, Hodder and Stoughton, 1947.

Southey, Robert, *The Life of Nelson*. London, J. Murray, 1813; New York, Eastburn Kirk, 1814.

Warner, Oliver, *A Portrait of Lord Nelson*. London, Chatto and Windus, 1958.

*

CLARKE AND MacARTHUR's massive opus was intended as an instant official biography. It provides the most compendious collection of facts and anecdotes culled from contemporary sources, including a memoir of Nelson's life up to 1799 provided by the subject himself. Both authors knew or served Nelson personally and their tenor verges on hagiography, deliberately concentrating almost wholly on his unique achievements as a naval commander at the cost of suppressing the reality of the Admiral's human frailty and complex personality. The liaison with Emma Hamilton is given only the most cursory attention, and the work is recognisably written to a specification intended to satisfy the national and social prejudices of the day. Since it fully reflects the Francophobia and wartime zeal that characterised Britain during the Napoleonic era, its judgements and assertions need to be viewed with caution. Nonetheless it is an invaluable contemporary source robustly reflecting the ethos of Nelson's own day.

SOUTHEY was commissioned to write a popular biography and freely pillaged Clarke and MacArthur for material on the naval aspects, where he is also too uncritical (he was writing before the end of the Napoleonic Wars whilst Trafalgar was still viewed as the national salvation—Waterloo had not yet happened). However, Southey made the first attempt to convey Nelson's "abnormally sensitive and emotional nature" and his yearning for praise and affection. Though more reticent about the Hamilton affair than the then known facts required, Southey is frank about the "shameful consequences" of Nelson's besotted involvement in Neapolitan affairs as a result of the Hamilton connexion, and he condemns Nelson's role in the judicial execution of the Republican Caracciolo.

Echoing the sentiments of his day, Southey is sometimes absurdly abusive of the French (as was Nelson); when he was writing Imperial France still posed a threat to the existence of every other European power and every other system of government. Inevitably the fear of this threat produced a national phobia that Southey faithfully echoes. So great was the impact of this portrayal of the great seaman that it earned the unique compliment of distribution by the American authorities throughout the United States' infant navy—an endorsement it never achieved in the Royal Navy, which remained sceptical about a layman's account of professional matters.

MAHAN, writing at the end of the 19th century, benefitted both from his professional discernment and from the industry of the numerous scholars who had examined the archives in the intervening decades. Moreover, as an American Mahan does not betray the Francophobia that had distorted the earlier British biographies. Mahan is particularly strong in his lucid accounts of Nelson's major battles, illustrating his intuitive strategic grasp and fearless recognition of the fine line dividing danger from opportunity. (Nelson rarely if ever fought a major action with numerical advantage on his side; he sought tactical advantage at the point of impact.)

In contrast to Southey, Mahan delves deeply into the component parts of Nelson's personality and their influence on his unequalled leadership as a fleet commander. His analysis is sufficiently complete to note Nelson's own confession that many of his officers far exceeded him in pure seamanship (a view confirmed by Codrington), and he makes clear how difficult a subordinate Nelson could be even to a distinguished and successful commander like Keith, whom he "disobeyed, defied and thwarted." Mahan condemns the Hamilton affair as a "flagrant moral aberration" but does not allow this moral censure to affect his estimate of Nelson's genius as commander and strategist.

The 1942 English abridged edition of Mahan (one volume) retains intact the material relating to Nelson's naval years but omits much detail of his early life and domestic matters relating to his family. As an abridgement it is a faithful reflection of the key material in the original work.

OMAN's biography of 1947 ranks high for scholarship and comprehensiveness among the modern works. It is thoroughly researched, factually almost faultless, and written from the perspective of a century and a half of digested research and documentation. (Ms. Oman's prefatory note provides in itself a valuable survey of Nelsoniana.) The result is an impressively complete character study. Nelson's sensitive temperament and emotional involvements are skilfully dissected with a rare degree of detachment from moral judgement. Nevertheless, the final impression of this authoritative biography is that it is stronger on the analysis of character than on the strategic insight and foresight that made Nelson a uniquely successful fighting leader.

In contrast, WARNER, a distinguished naval specialist, provides a deeper insight into Nelson's supreme professional gifts and utilises a wider range of sources than had other biographers (for example the betting book at Brooks' Club and the archives of the Society for the Promotion of Christian Knowledge) to deepen the reader's understanding of the climate within which the Admiral operated. The characteristics that made Nelson a difficult subordinate (to Keith and Parker in the Mediterranean and Baltic) and troubled his relationships with his near-contemporaries Troubridge, Saumarez, and Sidney Smith are fully brought out. This is probably the most authoritative and comprehensive of the modern biographies, stemming from the author's deep understanding of the essentials of sea-power and Nelson's key contribution to naval supremacy.

BRYANT's very readable 1970 biography is lightweight by comparison with Oman and Warner. It is largely derived from the naval contents of Bryant's earlier works on the Napoleonic Wars, and though admirably accurate in describing the victories of the Nile, Copenhagen, and Trafalgar, it adds nothing and omits much that is essential to an understanding of Nelson elsewhere than on the quarterdeck. It is an almost unashamed return to the hagiography that typifies the earliest British biographies portraying Nelson virtually as a demi-god. Though a stirring and heroic tale, it lacks the depth necessary to rank it among the acknowledged leaders.

—D. H. O'Leary

NERO [Nero Claudius Caesar Drusus Germanicus], A.D. 37–68; Roman emperor.

Abbott, Jacob, Nero. New York, Harper, 1881.

Bishop, John, Nero, the Man and the Legend. London, R. Hale, 1964; San Diego, A. S. Barnes, 1965.

Grant, Michael, Nero: Emperor in Revolt. New York, American Heritage, and London, Weidenfeld and Nicolson, 1970.

Griffin, Miriam, Nero: The End of a Dynasty. London, Batsford, 1984; New Haven, Connecticut, Yale University Press, 1985.

Henderson, Bernard W., The Life and Principate of the Emperor Nero. London, Methuen, and Philadelphia, Lippincott, 1903.

Ronalds, Mary Teresa, Nero. New York, Doubleday, 1969.

Warmington, B. H., Nero: Reality and Legend. London, Chatto and Windus, 1969; New York, Norton, 1970.

Weigall, Arther. Nero, the Singing Emperor of Rome. New York, Putnam, 1930; as Nero, Emperor of Rome, London, T. Butterworth, 1930.

*

Any attempt to arrive at an accurate assessment of the life history of a figure as ancient as Claudius Nero Caesar is handicapped by the vast chronological remoteness of the character and the need to treat increasingly older source material with skepticism. In the case of Roman figures, primary sources tend to be heavily biased toward either favor or disfavor of the figure, or else they are completely absent. In the case of Nero, nearly all primary source material stems from the works of Seneca or, more commonly, Tacitus and Suetonius, which are universally recognized as biased and negative. The earlier attempts at characterizing Nero do not escape this negative portrayal. However, beginning with Henderson's attempt and culminating in Griffin's work in 1985, there was an increasing attempt among biographers to de-emphasize or disprove the villainous or insane aspects of the emperor's personality.

Three older works served as the basis for readers until the Nero revival in the late 1960s. ABBOTT's work is interesting and readable, but it must be treated with some reserve as there is a complete lack of notes and bibliography. Furthermore, this work reads almost as if it were a firsthand account of Nero's life with much of the dramatic embellishment of a grocery store romance novel.

HENDERSON's account is somewhat less emotional than Abbott's and is much more particular in its attention to sources. Like the much later work by Griffin, Henderson relies heavily on the ancients, but he supplements his work with much English and foreign-language material from contemporary sources. Henderson's is a typical historical work of the turn of the century, complete with maps and sparse illustration.

WEIGALL's well-documented volume is the first significant work to attempt to separate Nero from lies and misconceptions regarding his personality and reign. The work offered, at the time of its appearance, a fresh and enjoyable new perspective on Nero. However, despite Weigall's credentials as a noted scholar with a significant record, his effort fails to convince the reader fully of the author's thesis. Like those by Abbott and Henderson, this account is very readable but suffers from an almost total lack of illustration.

WARMINGTON's book is not strictly a biography but contains enough material on Nero's life to be of value. The first few chapters chronicle Nero's rise to power, and others elucidate the history of his reign. The overall intent of the work is to evaluate Nero in the context of his reign and in the context of the events of the second century as a whole. Warmington's intention is to differentiate between facts and legend and invalidate the idea that Nero himself is solely responsible for the political chaos of his time. In this, Nero suffers somewhat in diminished aura; but Warmington's approach is excellent in that it manages to get at the true nature of his subject's complex political and personal relationships. The author makes judicial use of his carefully chosen sources and in sum achieves his aim. The work is aimed at the student and non-specialist and thoughtfully contains translations and explanations of all Latin verse, though it is of value to all levels of study. It contains a few errors, especially in the chronological tables, but these do not significantly detract from the overall value of the work.

GRIFFIN also pays heavy tribute to ancient sources, especially Tacitus, to the almost total exclusion of more modern interpretations of Nero. Her effort is more biographical in nature, giving a complex psychological analysis of Nero combined with an essay into the man's nature in the context of a Julio-Claudian nobleman. The work does an excellent job of relating personality considerations to Nero's actions and the history of his reign. The overall effect is to present the reader with a great deal of understanding rather than a complete revaluation of Nero. Unfortunately, Griffin does not achieve full objectivity, though her attempt to do so is apparent. The book is rather heavy reading and presupposes some knowledge of Roman society and social structure, yet it is recommended for its successful, clear approach to a very complex problem and its in-depth attention to ancient sources. The earlier BISHOP work is similar in approach and could be used as an alternative if Griffin's book is unavailable.

GRANT's work is interesting, if not for the writing itself then for its lavish illustrations. The text is biographical and intended for an astute audience. Grant attempts to portray Nero as a brutal hero who was only a reflection of his era, no more nefarious or unusual than others of his time. There is an obvious positive bias toward Nero in the work, but there is enough objectivity and documentary support to make the effort plausible and worthwhile. To the detriment of the work, the large number of illustrations include several that have little if anything to do with the text. This is not enough to warrant disregard of this title, however, for Grant's work is a must.

RONALDS' book is an attempt at historical fiction, centering on court intrigue in the reign of Nero. Rather than attempt judiciously to prove a point about Nero's troublesome character, Ronalds instead slaughters fact and fiction alike in a manner that will not contribute anything but discomfort to the serious student.

—Lawrence M. Enoch

NERUDA, Pablo, [*born* **Nefatlí Ricardo Reyes Basoalto**], 1904–1973; Chilean poet and diplomat.

Agosín, Marjorie, *Pablo Neruda*, translated by Lorraine Roses. New York, Twayne, 1986.

Bizzaro, Salvatore, *Pablo Neruda: All Poets the Poet.* Metuchen, New Jersey, Scarecrow Press, 1979.

Duran, Manuel and Margery Safir, *Earth Tones: The Poetry of Pablo Neruda.* Bloomington, Indiana University Press, 1981.

Pring-Mill, Robert, *Pablo Neruda: A Basic Anthology.* Oxford, Dolphin Book Company, 1975.

*

Despite international acclaim, to date Neruda has had no English-language biographer; nor even have translations of the book-length biographies in Spanish appeared (Aguirre, *Las Vidas de Pablo Neruda*, Santiago, 1967; Szmulewicz, *Pablo Neruda*, Santiago, 1975; Teitelboim, *Neruda*, Madrid, 1984). Neruda, whose poetry has been dubbed autobiographical (a label pertinent to *Memorial de Isla Negra*, 1964, translated by Alastair Reid as *Isla Negra: A Notebook*, 1982), once said "If you ask what my poetry is, I must say, I don't know; but if you ask my poetry it will tell you who I am!'' However, this remark does not account for the scarcity of non-subjective accounts of Neruda's life available to the reader of English.

In the absence of anything even approaching a comprehensive biography of Neruda in English, his own version of his life as found in the *Memoirs* and *Passions and Impressions* has a monopoly over material available to the reader. The *Memoirs* (translated by Hardie St. Martin, 1977) are essentially a reworking of ten essays Neruda prepared in the early 1960s for publication in the Brazilian journal, *O Cruzeiro Internacional*; the additional material, which Neruda dictated in the last months of his life, includes a commentary on the 1973 coup with which the book closes. Structured chronologically with chapters broken into short segments by sub-headings, the book is entertaining and easy to read; Neruda's direct prose style appears to survive translation. His use of his works as landmarks suggests his tendency to address himself to the poet-persona rather than to the private self. The majority of critics has found the *Memoirs* to be guarded and unrevealing; Selden Rodman's response is typical: "No-one could read the *Memoirs* and find out anything about Neruda's private life or what really motivated his poetry and his politics" (*National Review*, 18 March 1977). Since Neruda confesses nothing, the original title (literally "I confess having lived") must be taken ironically. The reader is likely to be particularly disappointed if hoping for information concerning Neruda's personal relationships or his attitude to women. No more than names are furnished for the women who inspired his most popular works. Referring to one of his later wives Neruda comments, "Delia del Carril, sweetest of consorts . . . my perfect mate for 18 years." With the sparing references to them Neruda merely enumerates his wives as if they were secretaries. As if by way of disclaimer Neruda begins by saying "there are gaps here and there and sometimes [these memoirs] are forgetful, because life is like that." The curious reader should bear this in mind.

Pablo Neruda 1904–73: Passions and Impressions (edited by Matilde Neruda, translated by Margaret S. Peden, 1983) is a somewhat arbitrary compilation of essays and speeches of the 1960s; it could be regarded as a supplement to the *Memoirs* and as a comprehensive account of the poet's activities. The translation maintains the straightforward and sincere tone of the original, and Binding seems unduly harsh in describing *Passions* as "self-congratulatory rhetoric . . . too often the effusions of a self-important windbag" (*New Statesman*, 25 November 1983). Neruda illustrates the development of his own aesthetics and politics when he claims, "I have assumed the poet's time-honoured obligation to defend the people, the poor and the exploited."

Part two of BIZZARRO's work is biographical and begins to compensate for the lacunae of the *Memoirs*. One chapter each is dedicated to interviews the author held with Delia Del Carril and Matilde Urrutia; the conversations are reconstructed rather than transcribed since both women were reluctant for the interviews to be taped. Carril presents her perspective on Neruda's time in Spain, their return together to Chile, and their underground phase after Videla's betrayal and outlawing of the communist party. Little can be gleaned from this chapter, however, on the non-factual circumstances of their relationship, particularly those pertaining to Neruda's separation from Carril. Mat-

ilde Urrutia's paraphrased conversation details Neruda's last days and the circumstances of his death. Urrutia refutes the rumours put to her questioning the authenticity of the *Memoirs'* last pages and the Nixonicide tract. Bizzarro concludes that writer and subject are inseparable; one suspects an apology for the scant biographical material when he writes, " . . . the poems have only one subject: Pablo Neruda.''

The first chapters of both Agosín and Duran provide rapid-fire accounts of Neruda's life. AGOSÍN provides a self-avowed summary of the above cited full-length biography by Neruda's niece, Margarita Aguirre; its brevity leads inevitably to oversimplification, though the repetition is unexpected.

Agosín's commonplaces regarding Neruda's early response to nature are repeated by DURAN, whose work is otherwise superior in the realm of brief biography. Using Neruda's often hectic itinerary as a base, Duran nevertheless presents a clear chronology. Despite its brevity, this account manages to emphasize Neruda's involvement in politics and diplomacy as well as literature. Obvious admiration for his subject does not prevent Duran from conveying the inconsistency of "a communist who filled his houses with material objects purchased with royalties from capitalist countries."

Although intended primarily as a chronology of Neruda's works, PRING-MILL's introduction succeeds in presenting what is more than a biographical sketch. Next to Duran it is the most satisfactory brief account; readers uninterested in literary interpretation, however, would do better to consult Duran as a biographical introduction. Readers desiring biographical information on specific stages of Neruda's life are referred to Woodbridge and Zubatsky's *Pablo Neruda: An Annotated Bibliography of Biographical and Critical Studies* (New York, Garland, 1988), the index of which is itself arranged as a chronology. Biographical material in English-language journals, although not nonexistent as is the case for full-length studies, is still scarce.

—Ryan Prout

NEWMAN, John Henry, 1801–1890; English theologian, cardinal, and writer.

Atkins, Gaius Glenn, *Life of Cardinal Newman*. New York, Harper, 1931.

Dessain, Charles S., *John Henry Newman*. London, Nelson, 1966; 3rd edition, New York and Oxford, Oxford University Press, 1980.

Hollis, Christopher, *Newman and the Modern World*. London, Hollis and Carter, 1967; New York, Doubleday, 1968.

Ker, Ian, *John Henry Newman: A Biography*. Oxford, Clarendon Press, and New York, Oxford University Press, 1988.

Lapati, Americo D., *John Henry Newman*. New York, Twayne, 1972.

Martin, Brian, *John Henry Newman: His Life and Work*. London, Chatto and Windus, and New York, Oxford University Press, 1982.

May, J. Lewis, *Cardinal Newman: A Study*. London, G. Bles, 1929; New York, Longman, 1937.

O'Faolin, Sean, *Newman's Way: The Odyssey of John Henry Newman*. New York, Devin-Adair, and London, Longman, 1952.

Sencourt, Robert, *The Life of Newman*. London, Dacre Press, 1948.

Trevor, Meriol, *Newman* (2 vols.). London, Macmillan, 1962; New York, Doubleday, 1962–63.

Trevor, Meriol, *Newman's Journey*. Huntington, Indiana, Our Sunday Visitor Press, 1985.

Ward, Masie, *Young Mr. Newman*. New York, Sheed and Ward, 1948.

Ward, Wilfrid, *The Life of John Henry Cardinal Newman* (2 vols.). London, Longman, 1921.

*

Guy Bedouelle has observed that two complications can ruin the biography of a great historical figure: too much information or too little information. Biographers of John Henry Cardinal Newman find their works complicated by tens of thousands of pages of Newman's writings in the form of autobiography (see the *Apologia Pro Vita Sua*, 1864), theology, homilies, controversial tracts, novels, poetry, and correspondence. The result is that Newman biography often takes extreme forms. Either writers attempt to include every detail recoverable—and the biographies become voluminous—or writers willfully ignore significant facts—and the biographies become short caricatures. Paradoxically, those biographers who aspire to comprehensiveness rarely produce works that adequately deal with Newman's intellectual development, but those who are content with a narrow field of sources often claim to provide *the* definitive explanations of this development in its entirety. Overall, a lack of balance seems to afflict most Newman biography.

Three works justly stake claim to being the most extensive treatments of Newman's personal life, those by Wilfrid Ward, Trevor, and Ker. The oldest of these—WILFRID WARD—is the main influence on most subsequent biographies and, though it depends on a smaller field of sources than its heirs, still retains its usefulness (after nearly a century) because of the way it paints the multidimensionality of Newman's character. The portrait that emerges is one of a man who challenged the *Zeitgeist* of 19th-century England, a man engaged in a "relentless war against . . . 'Liberalism.'" Newman wore his contradictions clearly marked. So devoutly religious as to border on superstition, he was a man with a keen belief in a providential mission, sensitive to the coldness of ecclesiastical authority, dutiful, somewhat effeminate, friendly, honest, disaffected with authority, Socratic in argument, a hater of wooden scholasticism, and a keen observer of human nature. But, despite the length at which it treats Newman's Catholic career, Ward's work is flawed on a number of counts. Though over 1200 pages long, it treats the first 45 years of Newman's life in a single chapter (a defect that Ward's daughter, MASIE WARD, attempted to remedy in her own work, which is a personal and intellectual biography of Newman before his conversion to Roman Catholicism). Wilfrid Ward's reliance on only those letters and journals that were available in the first two decades of the 20th century hopelessly dates his work, and the personality it conveys is as often the personification of Ward's own causes as it is representative

of Newman's concerns. Finally, Ward provides no deep interpretation of Newman's intellectual development.

TREVOR (1962–63) has attempted to update Ward's study of Newman by using the available sources in the Birmingham and London Oratories. The result is the most complete biography of Newman the man. Written in an entertaining style, this two-volume work covers the Anglican career of Newman as well as his life after his conversion to Roman Catholicism. Particularly valuable are the corrections she makes to the legends surrounding Newman, the descriptions of Newman's Oxford years in the company of Whately, Keble, Froude, and Pusey, and the light she sheds on his most controversial years as a Catholic. Evident on every page is her appreciation of Newman, an appreciation helped in its romanticism by the fact that her work written in one of the cottages at Littlemore (Newman's original retreat just prior to his break with the Church of England). Like Ward, Trevor has no pretense of writing an intellectual biography, though Newman's ideas do seem to hover in the background. Trevor's remains the best available personal biography, incomplete as it is without an intellectual biography to augment its narrative.

More accessible to the reader who does not feel up to the challenge of its 1,200 pages is the condensed version of Trevor's two-volume work. *Newman's Journey* (1985) is an attempt to keep what was essential in the larger work without sacrificing the humanity of Newman's day-to-day existence. As in the earlier set, Newman comes off as a highly complex figure, a positive zeal hidden beneath his gentle demeanor. Particularly good are the descriptions of Newman as a naive administrator (a characteristic that lost him the Catholic University in Ireland and eventually resulted in the division of the Oratory) and of his career before the age of 45. Equivalent in quality to its parent work, *Newman's Journey* is the best short personal life of Newman.

KER's shorter work was written to correct the defects of Ward and Trevor. The result is a 762-page life that weaves together personal, intellectual, and literary biography. Helped by the Birmingham archivist Dessain, Ker accomplishes a description of Newman that in large measure dispels the myth of Newman's hypersensitivity, humorlessness, and sadness. Emphasis here is not on Newman's clerical femininity but on the sinewy masculinity of Newman's temperament, his intellectual toughness and pragmatism. Frequent, too, is the use of long quotations that might have been excerpted. Ker's observation that Newman's psychology included oppositions in complementary balance is not original, having been anticipated both by Ward and Trevor. What is original, however, is Ker's characterization of these opposites. Newman emerges as a figure who, like Thomas Aquinas, was a synthetic thinker: "conservative and liberal, progressive and traditional, cautious and radical, dogmatic yet pragmatic [and] idealistic but realistic." Ker also sheds new light on the rhetoric and imagery in the writings of Newman; Newman emerges as a satiric writer of the first order, a man of letters in the ranks of Arnold, Carlyle, and Ruskin. Newman's prophetic anticipation of Vatican II also receives treatment not possible in the earlier lives.

In addition to the three great, magisterial biographies of Newman, three much shorter works were written to capture the process of Newman's personal development. All fail in varying degrees. The best of these is a recent treatment by MARTIN, which focuses chiefly on the personal life of Newman but includes a final chapter containing a rapid-fire rehearsal of Newman's important works and their purposes. Newman is sketched, tritely, as a brilliant, saintly, and gentle 19th-century controversialist.

Much older, and perhaps more focused, is ATKINS' biography, which attempts to gauge the influence of Newman on Roman Catholicism, Anglicanism, and Protestantism, achieving its aim only in the most general terms. There is little originality here. Newman is portrayed as a powerful personality wrestling with the impossibility of faith in a culture gripped by modernity. Newman's great discovery, according to Atkins, is that modern faith implies both an appreciation of development and an approach to religion that is neither excessively rationalistic or fideistic. This biography also suffers because it is dated and not based on the complete field of sources.

Deserving mention because of its eccentricity is O'FAOLIN's characterization of Newman's personal development as a "lone, stark intellectual and spiritual struggle" driven in part by his "perverse" relations to his family. O'Faolin's intent is, as he puts it, "to humanize" (read debunk) the Newman legend. The impious and ironic result is not psychohistory, but a gossipy life of Newman critical of Newman's own perceptions but credulous of the claims of his family. It interprets Newman as egotistical, impersonal, and something of a "genius/blessed nuisance." Although a bit refreshing both for his originality and crank quality, O'Faolin represents no discernible strain of scholarly consensus.

The final group of Newman biographies is defined by their intent to describe Newman's intellectual pilgrimage and explain its enduring significance. Sharing this common intent, they are usually heavily reliant upon Newman's theological work and the autobiographical narrative of that intellectual odyssey presented in the *Apologia Pro Vita Sua*. This work, however, is problematic because, as Henry Tristram has observed, it read alone is "an obscure work without a considerable apparatus of explanatory matter." The better intellectual biographies rely upon the complete field of available sources, instead of taking the narrative in *Apologia* at face value.

A very tightly organized and succinct work in this vein is offered by LAPATI. Written as a "compact résumé" of Newman's career and thought, it has no pretense of being a "definitive and complete study," but stands as an invitation to Newman's original writings. In this it succeeds very well. Lapati confirms Newman's universal talents as well as the complexity and contradictory personality frequently mentioned by other biographers. But Lapait's work is most useful for the compact way it relates the significance of Newman's ideas to the history of Western civilization. Particularly enlightening are his discussions of Newman and interdisciplinary studies, Newman's anticipation of the role of the laity in the Roman Catholic Church, and Newman's theology in the context of church history and the history of philosophy.

Similar in purpose, except that it is almost solely concerned with the contemporary relevance of Newman, is HOLLIS. Though he employs the peculiar biographical method of highlighting the content and contemporary significance of Newman's thought against biographical episodes—the latter often getting minimal treatment—Hollis insightfully portrays Newman as a visionary who, well ahead of his time, anticipated the challenges posed by secularization, ecumenicity, evolutionary epistemol-

ogy, and increasing freedom of conscience and inquiry. According to Hollis, Newman answered by forging a middle way between rationalism and Ultramontane authoritarianism and by warning that any *aggiornamento*—such as that later advocated by John XXIII—must be approached judiciously.

The most doctrinaire approach to Newman's intellectual biography is provided by DESSAIN. Written by the well-known archivist of Newman's Birmingham Oratory, this is a life with a thesis—namely, that Newman's own intellectual odyssey from Protestantism to Roman Catholicism is a movement from error to truth, a movement from an imperfect understanding of revealed religion to its perfection. At Dessain's hands Newman's intellectual development becomes a biographical demonstration of the superiority of Roman Catholicism to other Christian churches. Though perhaps offensive in its apologetic intent, Dessain's work is grounded in the primary sources and has interesting chapters that set Newman's major works in historical context. It is, however, flawed by the imposition of a thesis that cannot be proven on the basis of the historical documents alone.

SENCOURT also deserves mention as a solid intellectual biography that traces some of the intellectual influences on Newman's thought. The rhetoric of Cicero, the language of the Book of Common Prayer and the King James Bible, the philosophy of Aristotle, the theology of the Patristics and of Thomas Aquinas all contributed their share, making Newman a sort of recapitulation of Western culture, a man in whom style and substance fused to form a peculiar blend of ancient and modern wisdom.

Finally, the work by MAY is best described not as biography but as a Platonic meditation on Newman's writings. Taking these writings and their circumstances as his meditative themes, May reflects upon what relevance Newman's thought holds for him. The result is a highly personal interpretation of Newman's significance that is speculative, lyrically written, and reminiscent of some of the poems of Wordsworth. Although not informative in the sense of typical biography, May is worth reading as a speculative and aesthetic appreciation of the mind of Newman.

—Thomas Ryba

NEWTON, Sir Isaac, 1642–1727; English physicist, mathematician, theologian, and alchemist.

Andrade, Edward Neville da Costa, *Sir Isaac Newton*. London, M. Parrish, 1950; New York, Doubleday, 1958.

Brewster, Sir David, *Life of Sir Isaac Newton*. London, J. Murray, and New York, Harper, 1831.

Brewster, Sir David, *Memoirs of the Life, Writings, and Discoveries of Sir Isaac Newton* (2 vols.). Edinburgh, Constable, 1855.

Christianson, Gale E., *In the Presence of the Creator: Isaac Newton and His Times*. New York, Free Press and London, Collier Macmillan, 1984.

De Morgan, Augustus, *Newton: His Friend, and His Niece*. London, E. Stock, 1855.

De Morgan, Augustus, *Essays on the Life and Work of Newton*. Chicago and London, Open Court, 1914.

Manuel, Frank E., *A Portrait of Isaac Newton*. Cambridge, Massachusetts, Belknap Press, 1968; London, F. Muller, 1980.

More, Louis Trenchard, *Isaac Newton: A Biography*. New York and London, Scribner, 1934.

Stukeley, William, *Memoirs of Sir Isaac Newton's Life, Being Some Account of His Family and Chiefly of the Junior Part of His Life*, edited by A. Hastings White. London, Taylor and Francis, 1936.

Westfall, Richard S., *Never at Rest: A Biography of Isaac Newton*. Cambridge and New York, Cambridge University Press, 1980.

*

When Newton died in 1727, he was the most famous philosopher of nature in the world and generally recognized as the most intelligent human being of modern times. Yet he had throughout life remained so aloof, so remote from ordinary social contact that no one rushed forward to preserve memories of him—except the French, for Bernard de Fontenelle and Voltaire published biographies. Quite properly, Newton's work received more attention than he did. Thus, Henry Pemberton and Colin Maclaurin, former associates of Newton, published important explications of the *Principia*, and Newton's collected works appeared in both Latin and English editions.

The most interesting and least known part of Newton's extremely uneventful life (from which romance, friendship, and travel were all conspicuously excluded) in his childhood. What scraps of information we have regarding it were collected from still-living witnesses in their old age by William STUKELEY, the antiquary, who around 1752 compiled his gleanings into a narrative that was known and utilized in manuscript by later biographers but published in its own right only in 1936. Virtually everything of importance that we know about Newton's life prior to his university years comes from Stukeley, including the famous story of how the fall of an apple led Newton to speculate on gravitation. Stukeley also recorded, as an eyewitness, Queen Anne's knighting of Newton at Cambridge on 16 April 1705 and a series of anecdotes relevant to the last decade of Newton's existence.

BREWSTER's *Life* (1831), published a century after Newton's death, was the first biography of him intended for popular consumption. One of the earlier books to apotheosize a scientific hero, it appeared just when science was coming to be recognized as an independent intellectual activity, and immediately created a sensation. Upon reading Brewster, for example, Wordsworth feelingly revised a passage in his autobiographical poem *The Prelude* (not published till 1850) to celebrate Newton's commemorative statue at Cambridge, calling it "The marble index of a mind for ever/Voyaging through strange seas of thought, alone." Brewster's book also stimulated the publication of others, including a new explication of the *Principia* by Wright (1833); a biography of Flamsteed by Baily (1835), in which Newton's conduct was severely criticized; and an edition of the Newton-Cotes correspondence by Edleston (1850), which not only allowed Newton to speak for himself through rarely preserved personal letters but also included a wonderfully detailed chronology of Newton's life by Edleston that greatly aided the much more sophisticated biographies to follow.

The success of his 1831 *Life* notwithstanding, Brewster began work on an expanded version six years later. He was the first of Newton's major biographers to be allowed access to a large body of Newton manuscripts known as the Portsmouth Papers, held in private hands. He also knew of Stukeley's manuscript and of other important materials collected but never published by Newton's nephew, John Conduitt. These valuable new resources, together with Brewster's specialized knowledge of optics, then became part of the massive, two-volume *Memoirs* (1855), still the standard work for many. The first three chapters deal with Newton's childhood and his university years as student, fellow, and professor; chapters IV through X concern his optics; XI–XIII deal with astronomy (including gravitation), the modern history of which is also reviewed. Brewster's summary of *Principia* appears in Chapter XII. Volume II continues with Newton and calculus (XIV–XV) but soon becomes increasingly miscellaneous, partly because Brewster tried to incorporate newly discovered information that more properly belonged in volume I. Chapters XVIII and XX are devoted to quarrels with Flamsteed; XXII, to that with Leibniz. Newton's friendship with Charles Montague, his appointments as Warden and later Master of the Mint, and his relationship with Catherine Barton (his niece) are rather hurriedly discussed in chapters XIX and XXI. The Royal Society, of which Newton became president for life, appears in several chapters, as do Newton's interests in alchemy, chronology, and theology. The concluding chapters narrate his infirmity and death, assert the permanence of Newton's scientific reputation, and extol Newton's character and modesty. It was Brewster who first published (from a scrap in the Portsmouth Papers) Newton's memorable self-assessment: "I do not know what I may appear to the world, but to myself I seem to have been only like a boy playing on the seashore, and diverting myself in now and then finding a smoother pebble or a prettier shell than ordinary, whilst the great ocean of truth lay all undiscovered before me."

In his monumental work, Brewster acknowledged the considerable assistance he had received from other scholars, notably Joseph Edleston and Augustus De Morgan. It is probably not too much to say that all subsequent biographies of Newton combine Brewster's with various responses to the eye-opening charges of deficiency made against it by DE MORGAN. In opposition to Brewster's twin idealizations of Newton (in 1831 and 1855), De Morgan emphasized the less flattering realities of Newton's temperament and character, particularly with regard to Flamsteed and Leibniz. Though he did not originate the charge, De Morgan also tellingly questioned Newton's conduct with regard to his niece and Charles Montague (Earl of Halifax), the implication being that Newton had in effect sold Catherine to Montague in order to obtain preferment at the Mint. Finally (and less controversially), De Morgan established that Brewster had been somewhat disingenuous in discussing Newton's religious opinions.

Despite these and other objections to his work, Brewster's success as a biographer of Newton was so entirely convincing that no effort of consequence was made to supersede him for more than 70 years. And even then, MORE's *Isaac Newton* of 1934 remains essentially a 20th-century version of Brewster, with up-dated techniques, additional facts, a more documentary approach, and a properly critical (but occasionally pompous) spirit. Several brief sources utilized by Brewster are given fully here, particularly letters. Overall organization is also superior, making information easier to find and to account for. In addition, More's interpretive passages are usually cogent and lucid, providing useful background information where relevant. An academic physicist by profession, More was the first of Newton's biographers to write under the influence of a developed field called the history of science.

Excepting a few letters, however, and some additional facts in already known sources, More found little that was new. Since Newton's scientific accomplishments were now well understood, it seemed that any further insights regarding their enigmatic creator would have to involve new perspectives. A pioneer in this regard was MANUEL, who approached Newton somewhat gingerly in *The Eighteenth Century Confronts the Gods* (1959), discussed nonscientific aspects of his work in *Isaac Newton, Historian* (1963) and *The Religion of Isaac Newton* (1974), and attempted a composite view (though largely ignoring science) in *A Portrait of Isaac Newton* (1968). The recent publication of Stukeley's 1752 notes on Newton had once again called attention to the latter's childhood. Adopting a psychoanalytical approach, Manuel found the key to Newton's entire life in his having been deprived of a living father before birth and in the remarriage of his mother when he was only three. It cannot be said that this new insight has found universal acceptance, but Manuel provocatively raised an issue too plausible to be ignored. The three parts of his well-written book deal respectively with Newton's life in Lincolnshire, Cambridge, and London.

Between the appearance of Manuel's book and Westfall's, several important new sources of information became more easily available, including multi-volume editions of Newton's correspondence (1959–1977) and mathematical papers (1967–1980), together with a study of his library by John Harrison (1978). Moreover, a large amount of nonbiographical scholarship on Newton had also appeared, much of it exhibiting the kind of expertise of which only specialist historians are capable. Unlike his predecessors, WESTFALL was specifically a historian of *science*, and as a long-productive Newton scholar he had not only his own expertise to rely on but that of a whole group of similarly equipped colleagues, in what had become something of a Newton industry. The result of this in-part collective endeavor was a 900–page volume of meticulous scholarship requiring 20 years to produce.

For most professional historians of science, Westfall's is now the standard biography of Newton. Though many of its source materials were available to earlier biographers, these materials have since been edited and explicated by superbly qualified scholars. Thanks to the excellence of preceding major biographies, Newton's life was now in extremely good order (though still lacking details we would like to have) and contained few surprises. Being American (like More), Westfall was perhaps less likely to insist on Newton's Britannic virtues. The study of him had, in any case, become a relatively dispassionate international—and, to some extent, interdisciplinary—endeavor. Westfall therefore began his book with Copernicus and other such intellectual predecessors before turning to Newton himself, scientific ancestors being of more importance than familial ones. Unlike his predecessors, moreover, Westfall freely invoked mathematics and mathematical diagrams in this section and throughout his book, though one can get along without them.

There are 15 chapters in all, one of them devoted exclusively to the *Principia*.

The most recent major biography of Newton is CHRISTIANSON's, which Westfall generously helped to foster. Like his, it is comprehensive, but shorter by almost 300 pages and wholly devoid of mathematics; the approach, therefore, is somewhat more popular, though Westfall actually has more illustrations. Not surprisingly, Christianson is less demanding to read than Westfall, but also less authoritative. As throughout the biographical tradition, Christianson evaluates Newton's childhood, unexpected rise to genius, reticence, quarrels, oddity, and emotional sterility. Like Westfall, he endorses Manuel's contention that the remarriage of Newton's mother was traumatic for him. Catherine Barton, he affirms, was in fact Halifax's mistress, though more important to Newton's life than has previously been supposed. The charge that Newton in any way sold his niece to Halifax is not supportable, we are assured. In religion, as others had previously established, Newton was not a Trinitarian, though British law required him to be.

Admirable as they are, the major biographies of Newton are all exceptionally long. A well regarded short treatment, by a physicist and Newton scholar, is ANDRADE's, which reviews science before Newton in a chapter and then devotes seven more to his life, one of which is entirely about the *Principia*. There are diagrams but no other illustrations. Also worthwhile, and perhaps to be preferred, is I. Bernard Cohen's authoritative discussion of Newton in the *Dictionary of Scientific Biography* (1990). The *Newton Handbook*, edited by Derek Gjertson (1987), is often convenient for preliminary research.

—Dennis R. Dean

NICHOLAS II, 1868–1918; Russian czar.

Aleksandr Mikhailovich, Grand Duke of Russia, *Once a Grand Duke*. New York, Farrar and Rinehart, and London, Cassell, 1932.

Botkin, Gleb, *The Real Romanovs*. New York, F. H. Revell, 1931.

Krug Von Nidda, H. R. L., editor, *I Am Anastasia*, translated by Oliver Coburn. New York, Harcourt, 1958.

Massie, Robert K., *Nicholas and Alexandra: An Intimate Account of the Last of the Romanovs and the Fall of Imperial Russia*. New York, Atheneum, 1967; London, Gollancz, 1968.

Richards, Guy, *The Hunt for the Czar*. New York, Doubleday, 1970; London, P. Davies, 1971.

Trufanoff, Sergei, *The Mad Monk of Russia, Iliodor*. New York, Century, 1918.

Vyrubova, Anna, *Memories of the Russian Court*. New York, Macmillan, 1923.

Yusupov, Prince Felix, *Rasputin*. New York, Dial Press, 1927.

*

General studies of the entire Romanov dynasty point out the inherent weakness in Nicholas II, a "reluctance to rule," that eventually caused the Romanovs' downfall. The intimacy of MASSIE's treatment of the Romanovs both obstructs and informs his portrait of the tragic family. Massie is so sympathetic is his view of their personalities that the reader takes sides without realizing the bias with which the facts are arranged. The gentle, charismatic Nicholas II, beside his reclusive, misunderstood wife, seems innocent of all charges, a victim whose accident of inheritance placed him in the center of ruthless forces entirely outside his control. By far the most complete study of the last of the Romanovs, Massie's work places the "love story" inside a full-length examination of the forces—from the primitive peasantry's love of the idea of a fatherly protector to the churning factions of violent dissatisfaction with the idea of monarchy, demonstrated in the unrest in the cities—that moved Russia away from an imperialist past toward a modern socialist state. The work is best for details of the circle of events and associates on both sides of the monarch/socialist split.

Even members of his own family, such as ALEKSANDR, admit Nicholas' weakness as a decision-maker, understanding but not entirely excusing his part in the downfall of imperial Russia. Aleksandr points out again and again that neither he nor any other sane member of the court could change Nicholas' mind on any matter of importance. Because of his military responsibilities, Aleksandr is strongest in discussing political strategy, the causes and effects of the establishment of the first Duma after the 1905 riots, and the details of the Russian army's involvement and tactics in the Balkan theatre of World War I. A maturity of style and clarity of thought lend a calm truthfulness to his version of international events.

All the memoirs and autobiographies of Nicholas' courtiers seem to revolve around him the same way the life at court did during his lifetime. VYRUBOVA is predictably an insider's condemnation of all her detractors and a justification of her own power within the imperial family; in many respects she fails to explain her interference in affairs and never takes blame for the results of her meddling. Her account adds little that is not questionable regarding the Empress, Rasputin, or the family. Many studies on Rasputin, such as YUSUPOV's (1927), are in essence examinations of the Rasputin/Empress Alexandra relationship, exploring also to what degree Nicholas II ruled or did not rule during the last days of the empire. TRUFANOFF's book is wonderfully written, by a rival to Rasputin, giving the best picture of the religious background of Nicholas' and Alexandra's obsession with the other, more famous, mad monk. BOTKIN, the son of the Romanov's house doctor who died with the Romanovs at Ekaterinburg, is particularly valuable for his candor and essentially unpolitical viewpoint. Near Anastasia's age, Gleb Botkin grew up in close proximity with the daughters, which, especially coupled with his father's anecdotes, provides an intimate look at daily life at court, without the self-serving reconstruction of the facts found in Vyrubova. Botkin survived the Revolution and wrote his book, actually a series of books, in America. He believes that the claimant Anna Anderson is indeed the youngest daughter of the Czar, and much of his account verifies her claim. The Czar is painted as a gentle, feeling man, but unsuited to the rigors of leading a great nation through crisis.

RICHARDS, in the process of examining evidence for a scenario in which the Romanovs survived the massacre at Ekaterin-burg, offers a readable synopsis of the major influences in the Romanov court, on the way to his close analysis of the details of the last year, 1918. Other "Anastasia" books, gnawing at the remote possibility of a survivor, also give basic biographical background for the family. Anastasia's autobiography, edited by KRUG, an autobiography in name only, has been rejected as pure fiction by Anna Anderson herself.

—Thomas J. Taylor

NIETZSCHE, Friedrich (Wilhelm), 1844–1900; German philosopher.

Andreas-Salomé, Lou, *Nietzsche*, translated by Siegfried Mandel. Redding Ridge, Connecticut, Black Swan Books, 1988 (originally published as *Friedrich Nietzsche in seinen Werken*, Vienna, Konegan, 1894).

Brinton, Crane, *Nietzsche*. Cambridge, Massachusetts, Harvard University Press, 1941.

Copleston, Frederick, *Friedrich Nietzsche: Philosopher of Culture*. London, Burns and Oates, 1942; New York, Barnes and Noble, 1975.

Danto, Arthur C., *Nietzsche as Philosopher*. New York, Macmillan, 1965.

Del Caro, Adrian, *Nietzsche Contra Nietzsche: Creativity and the Anti-Romantic*. Baton Rouge, Louisiana State University Press, 1989.

Heidegger, Martin, *Nietzsche* (4 vols.), edited by David Farrell Krell. New York, Harper, and London, Routledge, 1979–87.

Hollingdale, R. J., *Nietzsche: The Man and His Philosophy*. Baton Rouge, Louisiana State University Press, and London, Routledge, 1965.

Kaufmann, Walter, *Nietzsche: Philosopher, Psychologist, Antichrist*. Princeton, New Jersey, Princeton University Press, 1950.

Kennedy, John M., *The Quintessence of Nietzsche*. London, T. W. Laurie, 1909; New York, Duffield, 1910; as *Nietzsche*, T. W. Laurie, 1914.

Knight, A. H. J., *Some Aspects of the Life and Work of Nietzsche, and Particularly of His Connection with Greek Literature and Thought*. London, Cambridge University Press, 1933.

Mügge, Maximilian A., *Friedrich Nietzsche: His Life and Work*. London, T. F. Unwin, 1909; 3rd edition, New York, Brentano's, 1915.

Nehamas, Alexander, *Nietzsche: Life As Literature*. Cambridge, Massachusetts, and London, Harvard University Press, 1985.

Reyburn, H. A., *Nietzsche: The Story of a Human Philosopher*. London, Macmillan, 1948.

*

Although several outstanding critical works have been produced on Nietzsche—most notably Kaufmann's, Hollingdale's, and Danto's—and continue to be produced—recent studies by Nehamas and Del Caro, for example—the state of scholarly biography is lamentable. Like the political movements that have misappropriated his philosophy, many of those who have written about Nietzsche's life and works have had an ideological axe to grind, or they have been more concerned with retrieving the philosopher's reputation from the brutal misuse of the Nazi propagandists than they have been with recounting factually the details of his life. Critics and biographers have typically taken one of the following positions: 1) Nietzschean philosophy ought to be seen as a part of one of a number of intellectual movements (romanticism, anti-romanticism, existentialism, classicism, psychoanalysis, analytical philosophy—to name a few); 2) the philosopher's attack on Christianity is or is not as monstrous as it might seem; 3) Nietzsche is or is not to blame for World War II. Someone looking for a reliable and straightforward biographical narrative must cull through a maddening variety of approaches, none of them—in the strictest sense—"straight" biography.

ANDREAS-SALOMÉ's book is an unreliable, self-serving account written by a close companion of Nietzsche. She draws heavily on their encounters in 1882 and describes his radical isolation from the world. Her central thesis is that Nietzsche wrote only for himself, with no pretensions of public influence: "He describes only himself and transposes his own self into thoughts." As Kaufmann and others have proven, her work, though a lively firsthand account, is replete with errors and reveals ultimately more about herself than about the philosopher.

Three early 20th-century studies are especially noteworthy: MÜGGE's book corrects a number of biographical inaccuracies introduced by Andreas-Salomé and by Nietzsche's sister, who produced a biased, almost unusable account. Mügge also sets the pattern for speculation on the degree to which Nietzsche's illness influenced his writings, and his book provides an early and remarkably thorough bibliography. KENNEDY's book is an early sympathetic treatment, perhaps excessively appreciative. Like most of his contemporaries, Kennedy felt compelled to address centrally Nietzsche's challenge to Christianity, an impulse the critic/biographer applauds as "a healthy sign of the times of the de-Christianising, if one may use the word, of the Church of England." While his book makes the crucial point that Nietzsche attacked the very sort of German culture he has been blamed for fostering, Kennedy unfortunately rehearses many of the cultural and religious stereotypes of his day while singing praises to the philosopher and testing out his own modernist leanings. KNIGHT's focus is on Nietzsche's career as a classical scholar. While admittedly "not the most important side of his life," Knight finds Nietzsche's philological studies bearing significantly on the development of his *Weltanschauung*. The discussion of the scholars of Greek who influenced him and the course of his classical scholarship further enables Knight to place Nietzsche in the Hellenistic tradition.

The HEIDEGGER study, a compilation of lecture notes, is seldom primarily biographical, yet it offers frequent insight into the development of a Nietzschean "habit of mind." The climax of the study seems to be Heidegger's discussion of the "overturning of Platonism" and the "raging discordance between art and truth" that he finds in Nietzschean philosophy. He traces the genesis of the "doctrine of return" and the origins of Nietzschean metaphysics.

The zenith of interest in Nietzsche's life and works occurred, of course, before, during, and immediately after World War II. Much of this torrent of biographical and critical analysis was a product of anti-German rage, with Nietzsche a convenient focal point and scapegoat. BRINTON, for example, in his laudable attempt to place the philosopher "in the more general currents of 'opinion'" of his time, promises not to engage in what he calls "Hun-baiting." Part of the Makers of Modern Europe biographical series, this work is error-filled and unreliable—in fact, it is one of the most pretentious examples of the species of "Hun-baiting" Brinton promises to avoid. For instance, he writes, "Nietzsche, like the Nazi leaders, was never really housebroken." Brinton's Nietzsche is a man "charged with the full energy of hatred"—a madman in the making throughout his life.

A fairer and more accurate book produced during this period is COPLESTON's study. Only in part biographical, this work is a remarkably sympathetic treatment of a philosopher who had been vilified in the popular imagination as the inspiration for Naziism. An overriding concern in the work's biographical sections is the philosopher's departure from Christianity—an obvious impediment to his popular acceptance and a virtual obsession with early critics. Copleston also provides a sympathetic and well-written description of the anguish and illness of Nietzsche's later years.

Psychologists have taken a great deal of interest in the philosopher and his personal torments. A professor of psychology at the University of Capetown, REYBURN makes the bold claim that more than any other modern philosopher, Nietzsche's doctrines were a product of "his own personal needs, likes, dislikes, powers and insufficiencies." In developing this thesis, however, the author resorts more often to fictionalized speculation than to original biographical psychoanalysis. One particularly entertaining example occurs when Reyburn recounts Nietzsche's adolescent participation in "Germania," a sort of "Dead Poets Society," as if the psychologist were a participating member of the club. Like many studies of the period, it is stimulating but distorted by the particular political and intellectual agendas of its author.

The best and most current work on Nietzsche has been written by philosophers more interested, naturally, in placing him in the context of philosophical movements and in understanding his contradictions and paradoxes than in the details of his life. HOLLINGDALE seems to set out to produce biography, and his work is accurate and—as Kaufmann rightly notes—"sympathetic, informed, and well written." Its focus, however, is on Nietzschean philosophy, discussed in the context of his life. Kaufmann calls Hollingdale the first decent biographer of Nietzsche in English, but his work falls short of the demands of modern critical biography.

KAUFMANN is still probably the most respected and often cited authority on Nietzsche. *Nietzsche: Philosopher, Psychologist, Antichrist* is a seminal work; it is a reliable, factual, and entertainingly quarrelsome account of Nietzsche's life, written by the principal modern translator of his works into English. It also successfully incorporates (and in many instances disposes of) previous scholarship. Such a task is daunting, as Kaufmann notes: writers as diverse and profound as Thomas Mann, Freud, Camus, and Heidegger have written on Nietzsche, and students of literary theory might well add Derrida to this list. In the text of his work, in long critical footnotes, and in a highly useful annotated bibliography, Kaufmann is delightfully ruthless in his dismissal of shoddy scholarship and competing points of view. For Kaufmann, the life serves as a backdrop for a discussion of Nietzschean thought, which he sees as close to the "temper of existentialism.'' Kaufmann's disciples remember fondly his course on Nietzsche and existentialism at Princeton, and his work remains a pivotal part of the scholarship.

DANTO, a respected philosopher, was criticized by Kaufmann for taking biographical and philosophical snippets out of context and basing his analysis on these rather than on the whole body of work. Danto's book is an attempt to link Nietzsche with analytical philosophy. In so doing, he attempts to separate philosophy and biography by making an argument analogous to that made by formalist literary critics: Nietzsche is a philosopher ''whose thought merits examination on its own, independent of the strange personality and the special cultural circumstances of its author.'' Despite Kaufmann's attack, Danto's book has been too influential to ignore.

Two recent works have reasserted and explored the interconnectedness of Nietzsche's life and philosophy. NEHAMAS examines the apparent contradictoriness of Nietzschean philosophy and the man's life, and he structures his study around a number of partially fathomable paradoxes. He also makes the still-necessary observation that ''being interested in Nietzsche [is] not being interested simply in a raving, ranting anti-Semitic, pro-Aryan irrationalist.'' DEL CARO returns to an idea first taken up at the turn of the century and distorted by mid-century critics: Nietzsche's place in our understanding of a German character and Germanic tradition. The author deconstructs Nietzsche's ''campaign to disassociate himself from romanticism'' and shows how well the various phases of his life can be measured against romantic traditions. Del Caro also provides a valuable discussion of Nietzsche's reading, focused especially on his reading of the romantic philosophers. The argument is compelling, if somewhat skewed by the demands of its thesis. The book continues a tradition of study on the intellectual origins of Nietzschean thought to which Knight, Heidegger, Kaufmann, and others have made significant contributions.

In spite of the critical attention Nietzsche has garnered—even by those whose fame rivals the philosopher's—a reliable modern biography remains a desideratum. In most of the best studies that have appeared so far, the life has played a secondary role in attempts to systematize Nietzschean thought. Scholars have attempted with mixed results to integrate life and works. Perhaps the corpus is so vast and the philosophy so complex and controversial that a would-be biographer would do well to avoid attempts to synthesize fully the author's biography and his philosophy and to concentrate on an accurate presentation of the verifiable details of his life.

—Richard C. Taylor

NIGHTINGALE, Florence, 1823–1910; English pioneer in nursing.

Andrews, Mary R. S., *A Lost Commander: Florence Nightingale.* New York, Doubleday, 1929.
Boyd, Nancy, *Josephine Butler, Octavia Hill, Florence Nightingale: Three Victorian Women Who Changed Their World.*

London, Macmillan, 1982; as *Three Victorian Women Who Changed Their World*, New York, Oxford University Press, 1982.
Cook, Sir Edward, *The Life of Florence Nightingale* (2 vols.). London, Macmillan, 1913.
Cooper, Lettice, *The Young Florence Nightingale.* New York, Roy, 1960.
Goldsmith, Margaret L., *Florence Nightingale: The Woman and the Legend.* London, Hodder and Stoughton, 1937.
Hume, Ruth F., *Florence Nightingale.* New York, Random House, 1960.
Smith, F. B., *Florence Nightingale: Reputation and Power.* New York, St. Martin's, and London, Croom Helm, 1982.
Strachey, Lytton, *Florence Nightingale.* London, Chatto and Windus, 1938.
Willis, Irene Cooper, *Florence Nightingale.* New York, A. L. Burt, 1931; with subtitle, *A Biography for Older Girls*, New York, Coward-McCann, and London, Allen and Unwin, 1931.
Woodham-Smith, Cecil, *Florence Nightingale 1820–1910.* London, Constable, 1950; New York, McGraw-Hill, 1951.
Woodham-Smith, Cecil, *Lonely Crusader: The Life of Florence Nightingale.* New York, McGraw-Hill, 1951.

*

The life and work of Florence Nightingale have been examined in dozens of biographies and hagiographies and hundreds of essays and articles. Few biographers have had the endurance to fully explore the embarrassment of riches available for the study of this remarkable woman. Unfortunately, many biographies of Nightingale fit Strachey's description of the traditional ''British Standard Biography'' full of disorganized, undigested masses of material, with a tone of ''tedious panegyric'' betraying a lack of insight and detachment.

Throughout her long life, Nightingale habitually recorded almost every idea, opinion, emotion, and vagrant thought. More important for posterity, she seems to have kept every scrap of paper adorned with these ''private notes.'' COOK, author of her official two-volume biography, had to wade through a mountain of unsorted materials: diaries, notebooks, scraps of private notes, official documents, letters she received, and copies of letters she wrote to others. Other members of her family shared this obsession, but Cook did not have access to all of these materials. Cook's *Life of Florence Nightingale* remains a monument of industry and insight worthy of its subject.

A man of remarkable patience and industry, Cook produced a biography that is accurate, well balanced, and sensitive to historical context. He also provides an unrivaled guide to Nightingale's social, religious, political, and medical context. Although Nightingale was involved in numerous conflicts that aroused strong emotions, Cook tactfully conveys a sense of all the personalities involved. Nightingale emerges as a strong figure, of great intelligence, tough and tenacious. Her ability to map out strategy and mobilize support are major themes of this sensitive but unsentimental biography.

As Cook discovered while preparing his biography, after Nightingale retreated from public life, a legendary figure was created. Most books written about her were about the legend rather than the reality. Cook discusses this problem in some detail in his introductory chapter; his biography presents the real as opposed to the legendary figure. Cook's conclusions are complex, subtle, but unflinching as to Nightingale's faults and virtues. Nightingale emerges as a logician rather than a sentimentalist, a complex woman of strong passions rather than a ministering angel of compassion.

Since until the recent wave of new scholarship on the history of nursing almost all subsequent works on Nightingale and nursing were based largely on Cook's biography, readers with the stamina to work their way through both volumes should go straight to the source. Of course, many changes in nursing, medicine, and the concept of "woman's work" have occurred since Cook's biography was published. Nevertheless, his work remains the standard to which all others must be compared.

GOLDSMITH's biography is based on Cook's, but it is quite lively and has the virtue of being much more manageable in size. Goldsmith provides a bibliography, but no notes or index. The book is a well-paced, unsentimental assessment of Nightingale's life and work by the author of biographies of Christina of Sweden, Mesmer, Madame de Staël, Sappho of Lesbos, etc.

SMITH's study of "reputation and power" is not a complete biography, but it is a serious and scholarly analysis of Nightingale's "thoughts in action." Instead of writing a conventional biography, Smith attempts to discover why and how Nightingale assumed the career of reformer, and he analyzes how she selected her strategies and fought her battles. In addition to bringing his new perspective to bear on the Nightingale Papers, he has examined collections that were unavailable to Cook and unused by Woodham-Smith (see below). The book examines Nightingale's character and public life, her work at Scutari, and the battle for the reform of army medical and sanitary services. Smith focuses an unmercifully bright light as well on the less noble aspects of Nightingale's battle to gain her own way and assert her opinions, in spite of contrary evidence or the equally valid beliefs of others.

WOODHAM-SMITH's *Florence Nightingale* (1950) has been denounced by scholars as the most pretentious of the various recensions of Cook's standard biography. Written in a popular style, the work is sometimes misleading and rather superficial. Although the text is heavily based on Cook's work, Woodham-Smith asserts that her access to sources unavailable to Cook for his "admirable official life" allowed her to be the first to present a complete picture of Nightingale. The story begins with a very detailed account of the family, focusing especially on matters of wealth and position, and relies heavily on Nightingale's "private notes" to explore her "inner life and feelings."

BOYD brings the perspective of historian as well as biographer to bear on the lives of three remarkable social reformers. Boyd argues that religion provided Nightingale with her goals: vision, courage, and single-minded determination. Boyd's essay makes an interesting contrast to that of Strachey.

In his well-known collection of biographical essays, *Eminent Victorians* (1918), STRACHEY selected Nightingale as a "woman of action" whose life was illustrative of the richness of the Victorian Age. The study of Nightingale was later published separately. Strachey's goals were brevity, accuracy, and impartiality. Primarily, he wanted to demonstrate that the real Miss Nightingale was more interesting than the legendary one, but far less attractive. In this cogent essay, Strachey argues that if Nightingale had died on the way back from Scutari, the legend would remain unchanged, but her great work would scarcely have begun.

Many apparently full-length adult biographies of Nightingale would be better suited to young readers. HUME's illustrated biography is, however, clearly intended for young girls. The writing is lively and humorous and Hume takes pains to do away with sentimental myths when possible; this is not the insipid, cloying, inspirational story usually aimed at young girls.

WOODHAM-SMITH's *Lonely Crusader* (1951) is an abridged edition of her full-length biography. In writing for young girls, the author deleted some of the more upsetting, graphic details of Scutari and political matters. But the usual biographical details, from ancestry to death, are provided.

The biography by WILLIS is obviously based on the work of Cook, but it is simple enough for young girls and falls into the category of books that provide motivational role-models for young women. Willis emphasizes a view of Nightingale as politician and social revolutionary, and she explores the economic and social problems facing Victorian women, who had to fight for the right to perform meaningful work. Today's young women will probably find the biography sentimental and old-fashioned, with its exhortations about work, public spirit, charity, and self-sacrifice.

ANDREWS' *Lost Commander* is an old-fashioned story of Nightingale from youth to death, written in the conversational "you-are-there" mode thought appropriate for young readers. The emphasis is on the heroic elements of the Nightingale legend, especially the dreadful conditions she faced and conquered in Scutari.

COOPER's account is another "you-are-there" story of the young Florence, following her up to the moment in 1837 when she first heard the voice of God calling her to special service. Written expressly for young readers, it is based on Nightingale's diaries, notes, letters, and an autobiographical essay Nightingale wrote as a French exercise. It puts the emphasis on the legendary Florence who nursed pets, relatives, babies, and the poor with precocious skill. An epilogue deals briefly with Nightingale's struggle to become a nurse and with the Crimean years.

Many brief accounts of the life of Nightingale have been written for use in elementary school. These include: Angela Bull, *Florence Nightingale* (1985); Charlotte Gray, *Florence Nightingale: The Determined English Woman Who Founded Modern Nursing and Reformed Military Medicine* (1989); Ann D. Johnson, *The Value of Compassion: The Story of Florence Nightingale* (1986); Donnali Shor, *Florence Nightingale* (1987); Dorothy Turner, *Florence Nightingale* (1986); Lee Lyndham, *The Lady with the Lamp: The Story of Florence Nightingale* (1970).

Those interested in Nightingale might also wish to consult Brian Abel-Smith, *A History of the Nursing Profession* (1960). This book is of great importance in stimulating recent critical reinterpretation of nursing history. *Rewriting Nursing History* (1980), edited by Celia Davies, intends primarily to make nurses more critical of what has passed for the history of nursing. Much nursing history has been written in a vague, congratulatory mode, showing exceptional individuals engaged in the great battle to lead nursing from the dark ages into modern times. In her prime, Nightingale was probably too tough and skeptical to accept the histories in which the legend figured more prominently than reality.

Zachary Cope's *Florence Nightingale and The Doctors* (1958) was written to illuminate the relationship between Nightingale and the medical profession. It shows the magnitude of her influence and the assistance she received from doctors with whom she collaborated. Most of the book consists of letters and excerpts of letters. The chapter "Miss Nightingale's general attitude towards doctors" provides especially valuable insights into Nightingale's complex character and network of associations. Although obviously not a complete biography, this work makes a fine addition to the literature on Nightingale.

Many of Nightingale's letters and essays have been published, and her classic *Notes on Nursing: What It Is and What It Is Not* (1859) remains in print. Nightingale's essay *Cassandra*, first published in 1979 with an introduction by Myra Stark and an epilogue by Cynthia Macdonald, is of special interest.

—Lois N. Magner

NIJINSKY, Vaslav, 1890–1950; Russian ballet dancer.

Beaumont, Cyril, *Vaslav Nijinsky*. London, C. W. Beaumont, 1932.

Bourman, Anatole, *The Tragedy of Nijinsky*. New York and London, Whittlesey House/McGraw-Hill, 1936.

Buckle, Richard, *Nijinsky*. New York, Simon and Schuster, and London, Weidenfeld and Nicolson, 1971.

Nijinsky, Romola, *Nijinsky*. London, Gollancz, 1933; New York, Grossett and Dunlap, 1934.

Nijinsky, Romola, editor, *The Diary of Vaslav Nijinsky*. London, Gollancz, 1937.

Nijinsky, Romola, *The Last Years of Nijinsky*. London, Gollancz, and New York, Simon and Schuster, 1952.

Parker, Derek, *Nijinsky, God of the Dance*. Wellingborough, Northamptonshire, Equation, 1988.

Reiss, Françoise, *Nijinsky: A Biography*, translated by Helen and Stephen Haskell. New York, Putnam, and London, A. and G. Black, 1960 (originally published as *Nijinsky; ou, La Grâce*, Paris, Plon, 1957).

*

As Richard Buckle points out, Nijinsky's life can be summarised as "ten years growing; ten years learning; ten years dancing; thirty years in eclipse." The handsome young Nijinsky, probably the greatest dancer the world has ever known, dazzled Europe with his genius for a brief decade and then spent the rest of his life in a deepening twilight of mental illness and schizophrenia. The earliest important publication about him is by BEAUMONT, the English balletomane, though this is really no more than an expert monograph.

A key biography is, of course, that by ROMOLA NIJINSKY, the Hungarian dancer who became Vaslav's wife after a courtship conducted by her with skill and diplomacy under the very nose of his powerful protector Diaghilev. *Nijinsky* was among the tasks she undertook to earn money for herself and her husband during the long years of his decline. Obviously it was in her interest to make the book as colourful as possible so as to attract a wide readership, and naturally she champions her husband

against those whom she considers to be his enemies, the prime villain in her eyes being Diaghilev. On the other hand, the book gives authoritative details about Nijinsky's youth and early upbringing that are not available elsewhere. In 1937 she translated and published her husband's diary, which he had kept while they were living in Switzerland during the winter of 1918–19. It is a very moving document that charts the razor's edge between normality and madness. Finally, in 1952, she published after his death *The Last Years of Nijinsky*. This briefly recaps the events of his career and then takes up the story where she left it at the end of her earlier biography to complete the account of their wanderings through war-torn Europe before coming to rest in England, where Nijinsky eventually died. *The Last Years* is a sad, though somehow uplifting, tale of their restless travels, of Nijinsky's steady decline, and of the many desperate attempts made, all in vain, to cure him. Romola Nijinsky includes no bibliographies in her books since she was writing from personal knowledge and family documents. Allowance must also be made for the intensity of her personal feelings, which a more objective view of other characters in the story might have softened. Her account of the courtship of Nijinsky is perhaps a little romanticised since in later years she claimed that at the time she did not think of marrying him. Subsequent research also shows inaccuracies in her account of the South American tour in 1917. Other discrepancies in small matters of fact are not difficult to find, and her inborn enmity for Diaghilev tends to colour the narrative on occasion. However, her two biographies comprise an intimate picture that no one else could have drawn. They recreate the magic of the Russian Imperial Ballet and the hothouse atmosphere of the Diaghilev troupe. Among the unique episodes she describes is the heart-breaking scene where the dying Nijinsky attempts a final *port-de-bras* from the *Spectre de la Rose*, one of his most famous ballets.

BOURMAN, a fellow student of Nijinsky at ballet school and a member of the Ballets Russes, sought to capitalise on his acquaintance, which he made out to be closer than it really was. Many of his anecdotes are unreliable, and some of them were accepted by REISS, whose book must therefore be treated with reserve. PARKER's book is short but pithy and concentrates on Nijinsky as a dancer.

The classic biography is BUCKLE's. While writing it he was able to consult both Romola and Nijinsky's sister Bronislava, both of whom approved of his interpretation. "I know Vaslav would have loved it," Romola told him, and Bronislava described his book as "wonderful." Many other eyewitnesses were alive at the time of Buckle's writing who helped to give him information about crucial events. He was even able to go one better than Romola by utilising the reminiscences of her daughter Kyra, who, as a child of three, saw her father dancing. The book has a substantial bibliography and a close-knit system of references at the back that gives sources for all major quotations and statements. A particularly valuable feature is the detailed descriptions of individual ballets in which Nijinsky appeared, all of which help to fill out the picture. Buckle also goes deeply into the enigma of Nijinsky, who, offstage, was an unimpressive and inarticulate figure, yet who, the moment he started dancing, became metamorphosed into a being of wonder. An appendix includes a psychoanalytical appraisal of Nijinsky's mental illness that goes a long way to explain the mystery of his character by throwing light on his creative instinct, his persecution complex, and his relationship with Diaghilev. The essential reading about

Nijinsky is, therefore, to be found in Romola's two books, for the sake of their firsthand account, and in Buckle for his enthusiastic, heavily documented and all-embracing approach.

—James Harding

NIXON, Richard (Milhous), 1913–   ; American political leader, 37th president of the United States.

Abrahamsen, David, *Nixon vs. Nixon: An Emotional Tragedy.* New York, Farrar Straus, 1977.

Ambrose, Stephen E., *Nixon: The Education of a Politician 1913–62.* New York and London, Simon and Schuster, 1987.

Ambrose, Stephen E., *Nixon: The Triumph of a Politician 1962–72.* New York and London, Simon and Schuster, 1989.

Brodie, Fawn M., *Richard Nixon: The Shaping of His Character.* New York, Norton, 1981; Cambridge, Massachusetts, and London, Harvard University Press, 1983.

Cavan, Sherri, *20th Century Gothic: America's Nixon.* San Francisco, Wigan Pier Press, 1979.

Costello, William, *The Facts about Nixon: An Unauthorized Biography.* New York, Viking, 1960; with subtitle *A Candid Biography,* London, Hutchinson, 1960.

De Toledano, Ralph, *Nixon.* New York, Holt, 1956; London, Sidgwick and Jackson, 1957.

De Toledano, Ralph, *One Man Alone: Richard Nixon.* New York, Funk and Wagnalls, 1969.

Henderson, Charles P., Jr., *The Nixon Theology.* New York, Harper, 1972.

Hoyt, Edwin P., *The Nixons: An American Family.* New York, Random House, 1972.

Keogh, James, *This Is Nixon.* New York, Putnam, 1956.

Kornitzer, Bela, *The Real Nixon: An Intimate Biography.* Chicago, Rand McNally, 1960.

Lurie, Leonard, *The Running of Richard Nixon.* New York, Coward McCann, 1972.

Mazlish, Bruce, *In Search of Nixon: A Psychohistorical Inquiry.* New York, Basic Books, 1972.

Mazo, Earl, *Richard Nixon: A Political and Personal Portrait.* New York, Harper, 1959.

Mazo, Earl and Stephen Hess, *Nixon: A Political Portrait.* New York, Harper, 1967.

Morris, Roger, *Richard Milhous Nixon: The Rise of an American Politician.* New York, Holt, 1990.

Parmet, Herbert S., *Richard Nixon and His America.* Boston, Little Brown, 1990.

Spalding, Henry D., *The Nixon Nobody Knows.* Middle Village, New York, J. David, 1972.

Voorhis, Horace J., *The Strange Case of Richard Nixon.* New York, P. S. Eriksson, 1972.

Wills, Garry, *Nixon Agonistes: The Crisis of the Self-Made Man.* Boston, Houghton Mifflin, 1970.

Woodstone, Arthur, *Nixon's Head.* New York, St. Martin's, and London, Olympia Press, 1972.

*

After almost a decade without a fresh Nixon biography, at the end of the 1980s Stephen Ambrose, Herbert Parmet, and Roger Morris wrote well-researched, thoroughly documented books. The 18 previously published biographies are less carefully documented, but often entertaining. Each falls into a particular biographic type: admiring portrait, exposé, phychobiography, and mirror-of-the-times.

Perhaps surprisingly in light of their subject's questionable ethics well before the Watergate revelations, eight of the 18 early biographies tell an admiring story of the life of Richard Nixon. All appeared before the Watergate scandal brought President Nixon to resign from office in 1974. The KEOGH and SPALDING biographies, although 15 years apart, are joyful campaign biographies that tell an admiring story of the rise of their hero. Topics that might prove embarrassing are avoided. DE TOLEDANO, author of 1957 and 1969 biographies, is more aggressive in his support of his hero. De Toledano does not ignore embarrassments, such as Nixon's unethical campaign tactics in 1950 against Helen Gahagan Douglas, but turns them on their head. For example, he reaches the strange conclusion that the Douglas campaign calumniated Richard Nixon.

The four other favorable biographies are more temperate in their treatment. Both KORNITZER and HOYT emphasize genealogical research and Nixon's youth. They pay little attention to his years as a Washington politician. The two MAZO biographies are broader, attempting to explain both the private Nixon and the political leader. Though Mazo's books are the most balanced of the admiring early biographies, the author's glowing conclusions regarding the character and wisdom of Nixon do not seem warranted by the facts. Mazo's Nixon seems lacking in authentic feelings and beliefs. This portrayal of Nixon's beliefs as difficult to ascertain or plastic runs through most of the biographies.

WILLS, author of one of the two mirror-of-the-times biographies, argues that Nixon's alleged lack of strongly held views is exactly the key. Wills makes an intriguing argument that Nixon is the last classical liberal, a self-made man willing to mold himself into whatever the marketplace decrees. For Wills, Nixon represents both what is best and worst in America; to understand him is to understand America in the post-war era. Rambling and poorly organized, the book still presents a brilliant and stimulating argument even though it is less about Nixon *per se* than the Nixon era.

The other mirror-of-the-times work is CAVAN's sociobiography, an effort to understand Nixon as a product of American culture interacting with personal life-cycle forces. She describes his worldview as gothic: life as mortal combat between good and evil. The book covers the origins of this view, its impact on both Nixon's public and private lives, and its consequences for American politics. All this sounds a bit extreme, but Cavan carefully and effectively argues the utility of the gothic notion for understanding America and Nixon. The book is well written and well documented, although it offers nothing new except the gothic interpretation. Readers who admire Richard Nixon will not enjoy this book, but even those readers will be unable to dismiss her arguments out of hand.

Of the five psychobiographies, three appeared in 1972, before the Watergate revelations. All conclude that Nixon is a dangerous neurotic. HENDERSON sees Nixon's life as an effort to reconcile his moral convictions and pious views with his actual behavior, an effort which resulted in a psuedo-patriotism that became Nixon's religion. WOODSTONE, a British journalist, is less careful with evidence than is Henderson and less theoretical in his conclusions. Woodstone simply warns us that Nixon is an unstable anal-compulsive. With much more careful language and seemingly without malice, MAZLISH reaches the same conclusion. In 1978 AMBRAHAMSEN wrote even more strongly in Freudian terms that Nixon is a psychopathic personality.

The last of the psychobiographies, BRODIE's 1981 book, is the most thorough and the least constrained by Freudian assumptions and language. Based on primary and secondary written sources as well as interviews, her work shows extraordinary care for factual accuracy. Brodie does not simply present Nixon's character, but traces the evolution of its elements. This is the book for readers who want a scholarly, interesting psychobiography that avoids Freudian clichés.

The three exposé biographies are critical narratives that focus on Nixon's campaigns for office. COSTELLO uses the public record to chart Nixon's rise. Although occasionally Costello weakens his case by attributing motives to his subject, the book mostly is a deadly critique because of its direct presentation of Nixon's ruthless, dishonest, and cruel behavior. The books by Voorhis and Lurie chronicle Nixon's willingness to appeal to the dark side of public opinion. VOORHIS, the congressman whom Nixon defeated in 1946, tries to avoid charges of bias by a hyper-factual presentation. The result is a boring account that emphasizes deceitful campaign charges and policy failures during Nixon's first administration. LURIE portrays Nixon as unprincipled, dishonest, and motivated almost entirely by a drive for power. The author's disgusted and nasty tone, and his unwillingness to credit the Nixon administration with any accomplishments, weaken the force of his often valid criticisms.

The three recent biographers have benefited from the passage of time. Passions have cooled since the Vietnam war ended. Nixon seems to us more moderate in his politics since a stridently conservative president has held the office. Still, to the biographer's advantage, many key figures from Nixon's life are yet available for interviews. Although all three men have produced good, well-documented books, none succeeds in explaining how Nixon changed from a well-behaved, pious Quaker youth into a mature world leader who seemed to understand nothing of the difference between right and wrong. Each author focuses his attention on other issues.

AMBROSE has written the first two volumes of a projected three-volume study. Concluding the second volume with Nixon's landslide re-election victory of 1972, Ambrose portrays Nixon as intelligent and tenacious, though at the same time self-doubting, dishonest, and unable to trust others. Ambrose lets the reader reach these conclusions by providing facts rather than interpretations. Despite the vile Nixon that emerges, Ambrose is fair to his subject: Nixon and his supporters are allowed to present their understanding of events. Although Ambrose does not ignore troublesome events in Nixon's life, neither does he dwell on them, and he gives much attention to Nixon's accomplishments. Readers who want a thorough narrative with a Nixon that is neither the devil nor an angel should read this book. Because the facts of Nixon's life are so interesting, this pithy narrative is engrossing.

PARMET is more favorable to his subject. The problem with this biography is that the author fails to give adequate attention to the dark side of the record. For example, Parmet devotes only four pages to the Watergate scandal. What Parmet does report is done well, but by selective inclusion Nixon appears better than he deserves. Parmet is right that future historians will credit the Nixon presidency with major accomplishments. What Parmet forgets is that future historians will also remember Nixon's appeals to fear and prejudice, and the horrors of Watergate.

MORRIS' biography is the first of a projected three volumes. Over 1000 pages, the book concludes with the 1952 Checkers speech that enabled Senator Nixon to remain on the ticket with presidential candidate Eisenhower. In its scope, detail, and drama, Morris' work is most similar to the biographies of Robert Caro.

Morris focuses on Nixon's personal traits as demonstrated in his early campaigns and in the Hiss case. These adventures are understood in the context of California politics and culture. The author makes an intriguing case that Nixon has the same roots that manifested themselves in Ronald Reagan and the sagebrush rebellion in the 1980s. Without malice, Morris describes the development of Nixon's character and captures the flavor of his early years.

The Morris book is the definitive biography of the early stages of Richard Nixon's life. Ambrose provides a fine narrative through 1972, and Brodie furnishes the outstanding psychobiography.

—Robert E. O'Connor

O'CASEY, Sean, 1880–1964; Irish playwright.

Cowasjee, Saros, *Sean O'Casey: The Man Behind the Plays.* London, Oliver and Boyd, and New York, St. Martin's, 1963.
Fallon, Gabriel, *Sean O'Casey, the Man I Knew.* London, Routledge, and Boston, Little Brown, 1965.
Hunt, Hugh, *Sean O'Casey.* Dublin, Gill and Macmillan, 1980.
Krause, David, *Sean O'Casey: The Man and His Work.* London, MacGibbon and Kee, and New York, Collier Macmillan, 1960; revised edition, Macmillan, 1975.
Krause, David, *Sean O'Casey and His World.* London, Thames and Hudson, and New York, Scribner, 1976.
Margulies, Martin B., *The Early Life of Sean O'Casey.* Dublin, Dolman, 1970.
O'Casey, Eileen, *Sean,* edited by J. C. Trewin. London, Macmillan, 1971; New York, Coward McCann, 1972.
O'Connor, Garry, *Sean O'Casey: A Life.* London, Hodder and Stoughton, and New York, Atheneum, 1988.
O'Riordain, John and E. H. Mikhail, editors, *The Sting and the Twinkle: Conversations with Sean O'Casey.* London, Macmillan, and New York, Barnes and Noble, 1974.

*

Anyone who tries to write the life of Sean O'Casey is faced with his voluminous and unreliable autobiography in which he sometimes altered the course of events, ignored dates, exaggerated or diminished the importance of people or events in accordance with his own creative urge. O'CONNOR faces up to this fact manfully, going to alternative sources of information whenever he could, in records, in the recollections of others, in contemporary material. He writes a quickly moving, lively biography that succeeds in not being overawed or cajoled by its subject.

While O'Connor provides much useful factual information, he is less successful in assessing O'Casey's character or intellectual life. The area between the autobiographies, the plays, and the verifiable biographical facts remains to be explored for its psychological potential.

Understandably, EILEEN O'CASEY's biography of her husband is more personal than O'Connor's and has much information about their everyday lives, domestic matters, and relationship. Unfortunately, although she had the advantage of living with her subject for many years, her book is unreflective and shallow.

MARGULIES bases his work in large part on interviews and conversations with those who knew O'Casey and had significant contacts with him or his family. He also makes good use of contemporary records for information on education and on births and marriages. Wisely, he does not rely on the autobiographies. Margulies, a lawyer, shows an ability to handle material in an objective, detailed, and reliable manner. He gives a particularly useful account of O'Casey's extended family and of O'Casey's various political allegiances up to 1920.

KRAUSE (1960; 1975) begins with biography, focusing on the Dublin years in an attempt to get at the origins of O'Casey's discontent. The enlarged later edition has an additional chapter that reassesses the life and work. Krause has also compiled a pictorial biography of O'Casey (1976). COWASJEE's volume has numerous factual errors, most of which have been corrected or omitted in later editions, although the author's critical method has not improved. FALLON had the advantage of knowing O'Casey well in the 1920s and 30s, and while he is informative for this period, he is less reliable on O'Casey's later life. The volume collected by O'RIORDAIN AND MIKHAIL, consisting of interviews and personal memories, is a useful but not always reliable work. Contributors include Lillian Gish, Brooks Atkinson, Gerard Fay, Lady Gregory, and Paul Shyre.

HUNT's book is a useful summarizing and compressed account that draws from the previous biographies. Written by a man who was associated with the Abbey Theatre for many years and was at one time a play-director, its judgments on the plays are reliable, but necessarily brief. It combines a rehearsal of the facts of O'Casey's life with attention to the books that O'Casey found important. While the treatment is objective and workmanlike the book on the whole is deficient in its appraisal of the man and the work.

—Maurice Harmon

O'CONNOR, (Mary) Flannery, 1925-1964; American writer.

Coles, Robert, *Flannery O'Connor's South*. Baton Rouge, Louisiana State University Press, 1980.
Fickett, Harold and Douglas R. Gilbert, *Flannery O'Connor: Images of Grace*. Grand Rapids, Michigan, Eerdmans, 1986.
Getz, Lorine M., *Flannery O'Connor: Her Life, Library, and Book Reviews*. New York, E. Mellen, 1981.
Magee, Rosemary M., editor, *Conversations with Flannery O'Connor*. Jackson, University Press of Mississippi, 1987.
McKenzie, Barbara, *Flannery O'Connor's Georgia*. Athens, University of Georgia Press, 1980.

*

Of the available biographies, FICKETT AND GILBERT's is most comprehensive in presenting O'Connor's life and works. The work includes a detailed life history, a broad discussion of O'Connor's writing and an appended pictorial section. Fickett surveys O'Connor's Southern and family background, her early training in writing at Iowa and Yaddo, and her correspondence, all from the standpoint that "a correlation must exist between the fascination of the work and the life out of which that work was created." Fickett goes on to examine O'Connor's two novels, popular short stories, and major non-fiction writing to explain to the general reader how O'Connor's faith and understanding of grace ceaselesssly inspired and directed her vision. Gilbert's brief "Images" at the end of the book provides a chronological panorama of pictures depicting O'Connor at home and at school, with colleagues and acquaintances. While the photographs gathered here are interesting, those in McKENZIE's book provide a more thorough photographic presentation of Milledgeville and surrounding countryside.

Compared to Fickett and Gilbert's pictorial biography, COLES' work reads as sound scholarship, almost to a fault. A professor of psychiatry and medical humanities at the time he published his work, Coles' research of O'Connor's life betrays a strong psychological bias. He describes in detail the region and people of rural Georgia in the late 1950s and early 1960s, adding to his observations an account of his brief acquaintance with Flannery and Regina Cline O'Connor, as well as interviews Coles conducted with many citizens of Milledgeville. Making connections between O'Connor's work and the demographics of her region, Coles attemts to explain how regional factors influenced themes in her fiction. While he provides some acute and original insights into the Southern culture, including comments on certain regional issues—Southern and Catholic—that O'Connor struggled with, such observations are infrequent, and at times Coles semeems more concerned about demography than about O'Connor. This source provides more of a social-psychological perspective of Southern identity than an examination of O'Connor's life, and therefore its usefulness as biography is remote and limited.

GETZ examines primary material catalogued until 1980 from the Flannery O'Connor Memorial Room at Georgia College. Concerned mostly with O'Connor's intellectual interests, Getz opens her book with "Flannery O'Connor's Literary Biography," then goes on to list the holdings of her subject's personal library (usefully preserving O'Connor's annotations and inscriptions). The list of book reviews with Getz's introduction in Part III is also valuable. (For a more detailed critical bibliography of O'Connor's library, see Arthur F. Kinney, *Flannery O'Connor's Library: Resources of Being*, 1985.)

Although Sally Fitzgerald's collection of O'Connor's vast correspondence (*The Habit of Being*, 1978) cannot be considered a self-contained biography, scholars typically consult it to augment readings of O'Connor's fiction. The letters relay O'Connor's thoughts on work-in-progress, characters and characterizations, art and Catholicism, travels and colloquiums, and her own declining health. After a largely anecdotal introduction, Fitzgerald classifies the correspondence into four Parts, each part opening with editorial comments on pertinent events in O'Connor's personal and professional life.

O'Connor's life-long friend and primary curator of her letters, Fitzgerald is however sometimes unreliable as a scholar. This shortcoming hinders her selection (she does not include, for example, any of the letters O'Connor wrote to her mother), as well as her editorial annotations of the correspondence. Thus, although Fitzgerald offers explanations of O'Connor's views on art and religion, the most reliable biographical information is best gleaned from the letters themselves. The investigative reader will also wish to consult *Mystery and Manners* (1969), edited by Sally and Robert Fitzgerald. This volume examines O'Connor's perspective on the art of fiction and reprints lectures and essays by O'Connor encompassing the relationship between reader-critic-writer, the role of religion in fiction, the value of the grotesque, and the unique truths of Southern history and culture.

MAGEE's volume challenges the position that interviews are of little help toward understanding O'Connor or her fiction. These 22 interviews, originally appearing in magazines, journals, and newspapers, exhibit (according to Magee) "remarkable consistency and coherency with O'Connor's other published works," and uniquely capture her grace, idiom, and vitality. The biographical content in Magee is, however, general and repetitive as interviewers ask similar questions about O'Connor's writing methods, characters, religion, and home life, to all of which O'Connor provides carefully constructed and terse responses.

—Jacqueline Lauby

O'CONNOR, Frank [*born* Michael John O'Donovan], 1903–1966; Irish writer.

Matthews, James, *Voices: A Life of Frank O'Connor.* New York, Atheneum, and Dublin, Gill and Macmillan, 1983.
Sheehy, Maurice, editor, *Michael/Frank: Studies on Frank O'Connor.* New York, Knopf; London, Macmillan; and Dublin, Gill and Macmillan, 1969.
Wohlgelernter, Maurice, *Frank O'Connor: An Introduction.* New York, Columbia University Press, 1977.

*

MATTHEWS has written the only biography of Frank O'Connor yet available. It is exceedingly long—450 pages—and excessively detailed. The account covers the whole of O'Connor's life from his birth in Cork in 1903 to his death in Dublin in 1966 and makes use of all available sources, the published work, journals, letters in public and private places, and information from those who knew him. Nevertheless, Matthews' work is seriously flawed.

The information contained in *Voices* is not always accurate or reliable. The subject is swamped in detail, with the result that the broad outline of O'Connor's career is not firmly drawn, nor are the significant moments of his life sufficiently identified and

discussed. The influential figures in his life, such as AE, W. B. Yeats, Daniel Corkery, Sean O'Faolain, are not examined to determine the nature of their influence, both literary and personal.

Furthermore Matthews is unable to see his subject with critical detachment. O'Connor's merits as a writer, which were considerable, are over-praised, his flaws, which were also considerable, are virtually ignored. The critical evaluations are often inadequate, sometimes wrong. Similarly, O'Connor's character, which was complex, with many valuable but also many unattractive qualities, does not receive a measured and balanced assessment. The treatment both of the writer and of the man is superficial. In treating personal relationships the book too often descends into gossip.

Finally, Matthews' research is not thorough. Documentary evidence is not provided for some of the essential facts. No attempt seems to have been made to get in touch with contemporary witnesses to the earlier years. The autobiographical writings and the fiction are used with insufficient caution as evidence for the biography. One of the primary faults with Matthews' book is that it does not provide an historical, social, cultural, or intellectual context for the life. The impoverished childhood, the Cork ambience, the Gaelic Revival, the emergence of nationalism, the nature of post-revolutionary society, what was going on in Irish literature before and during O'Connor's time are not considered. Such background would provide an essential element in any attempt to understand and evaluate Frank O'Connor and his writing.

WOHLGELERNTER points out that his introduction is neither a "life and works" nor a "reader," but a biography of the mind in that it tries to outline O'Connor's work against the confusion of modern Irish life. The book's first chapter provides a biographical summary. SHEEHY's volume, primarily a critical study, contains some biographical material.

Any biographer draws gratefully from the two lively autobiographies, *An Only Child* (1961) and *My Father's Son* (1968). The first deals with the period up to 1923, and the second continues on from there. The volumes relate O'Connor's deep affection for his mother, his troubled relationship with his father, and his experiences with significant people and events in Ireland.

—Maurice Harmon

O'HARA, John, 1905–1970; American writer.

Bruccoli, Matthew J., *The O'Hara Concern.* New York, Random House, 1975.
Farr, Finis, *O'Hara.* Boston, Little Brown, and London, W. H. Allen, 1973.
MacShane, Frank, *The Life of John O'Hara.* New York, Dutton, and London, Cape, 1980.

*

Of his three full-scale biographies, John O'Hara would have preferred Finis Farr's attempt, the most uncritically admiring. Frank MacShane's lively biography and Matthew J. Bruccoli's authoritative version bow less frequently and less deeply in O'Hara's direction than Farr's does.

Literary biographers are often mesmerized by their subjects' writing styles. Aping their subjects' prose makes biographers often seem more foolish than clever. O'Hara's stylistic traits, such as the waves of detail he washed over his readers, have earned him praise for sharp observation and censure for caring too much about trivia. (Attacked for his promiscuous embracing of details, O'Hara at the same time—often in the same stories—offended some readers with his brevity, particularly in ending his stories before reaching an explicit conclusion.) Farr and, to a much lesser degree, MacShane fill their prose with O'Haran detail in an attempt to describe O'Hara's style by re-creating it.

FARR encourages his reader to skim, for example, by listing ten full pages of items, relevant and otherwise, in O'Hara's cluttered study. (Like some panorama of Neanderthal man's native habitat, O'Hara's study has been preserved and is on exhibit in the Penn State library.) After informing us that O'Hara (like several million other Americans) enjoyed ordering from mail-catalogues, Farr supplies the items he liked to order, the mail-order companies he favored, and their mailing addresses as well.

Farr's overfondness for detail betrays his book, finally, as lapses in the telling of one anecdote show: in 1903, O'Hara's father got into a street fight. Farr—not quoting anyone—concludes: "Dr. O'Hara hit that Dutch son of a bitch so hard that he fell unconscious in the gutter." That sort of enthusiasm might be more appropriate coming from Dr. O'Hara's son and, indeed, John O'Hara is probably Farr's source for this story. (Farr's sources are undocumented.) But O'Hara wouldn't be born until two years after this fight. And even if Farr's source *had* witnessed the fight, he or she certainly couldn't have provided him reliably with the verbatim dialogue Farr directly quotes here. Novelist O'Hara's gift for colorful fictionalizing is admirable, but biographer Farr's is not.

O'Hara also exalted his own considerable importance in the literary hierarchy of his day. (He insisted that there *was* such a hierarchy and that he stood atop it.) Farr benignly observes this point of view, and indeed preserves and embellishes it: Farr's first chapter attributes O'Hara's literary quality to nothing less than "the mystery of genius"; his last chapter asserts "O'Hara *did* tell the truth about his time, as he saw it, better than anyone else." In treating O'Hara with such unfailing generosity, Farr does manage to capture his more amiable personal qualities, like his devotion to his family. Farr quotes moving and perceptive messages on familial loyalty from *A Rage to Live* (1949) and *Ourselves To Know* (1960), the last of which concludes with uncharacteristic O'Haran modesty: "There were a lot of things I didn't know."

MACSHANE's versions of O'Hara's professional and personal eccentricities are highly entertaining; apparently O'Hara spoke to his cleaning lady and his publisher with equally unprovoked irascibility. MacShane dots his text with his own literary judgments: inexplicably dubbing *The Lockwood Concern* (1965) "successful" but *The Instrument* (1967) "hasty and superficial," and decreeing *Ten North Frederick* (1955) to be "generally a better novel than *A Rage to Live*" because its "central character survives until the end." (MacShane's critical criterion here is questionable, only partly because many readers consider Sidney Tate's death to be, in fact, the death of a supporting character.) Elsewhere, MacShane expresses pointed judgments, telling of the comical (but to O'Hara deadly serious) grudges O'Hara freely bore. (No fewer than three of O'Hara's contemporaries, according to MacShane, claimed to have originated the epithet

that best captures O'Hara's touchiness: "master of the imagined slight.") He also makes many intelligent judgments on more literary matters, like O'Hara's reasons for rejecting the closed-ended story, and the quintessential O'Hara problem, that of writing interesting fiction about dull people.

BRUCCOLI mildly consigns his differences with O'Hara to footnotes. Without editorial comment, one such note simply cites in full the ludicrous inscription O'Hara, a "staunch Yankee fan," wrote in *A Family Party* and sent to the Yankees' catcher: "To Lawrence 'Yogi' Berra—On all occasions, but especially on the occasion of his 300th home run—in admiration." Literary discrepancies are also handled decorously: although O'Hara claimed the proofs of Fitzgerald's *Tender is the Night* as a "treasured possession," Bruccoli records they "were not found among his books after his death." (Having read Fitzgerald's proofs, he probably had sent them back for Fitzgerald's use, and embellished the memory into physical possession.)

There is not a great difference between Bruccoli's book and MacShane's but every small advantage is Bruccoli's. All three books have many photographs—Bruccoli distributes his throughout his text—and Bruccoli's is the handsomest and the best organized: printed on thick high-quality paper, it includes maps of O'Hara country on the back and front inside covers, a listing of O'Hara's complete published work (essentially a shorter version of his book-length bibliographic study, *John O'Hara: A Checklist*, 1972), and critical reaction to O'Hara's work. Bruccoli's apparatus (with an index of over twice the number of entries that MacShane includes) is impeccably complete. Bruccoli also published *John O'Hara: A Descriptive Bibliography* (1978).

A final clue to the thoroughness of these three books may be seen in O'Hara's use of Alexander Pope's work, which he alludes to in three novel titles, a fact MacShane notes accurately. Farr catches only one allusion, while Bruccoli not only points out all three but also finds a fourth that O'Hara considered using (for *Ten North Frederick*). O'Hara's friends may enjoy Farr's book, and his fans will like MacShane's, but his serious readers will find Bruccoli's indispensable.

—Steven Goldleaf

O'KEEFFE, Georgia, 1887–1986; American painter.

Castro, Jan Garden, *The Art and Life of Georgia O'Keeffe*. New York, Crown, 1985; London, Virago, 1986.

Hoffman, Katherine, *An Enduring Spirit: The Art of Georgia O'Keeffe*. Metuchen, New Jersey, Scarecrow Press, 1984.

Lisle, Laurie, *Portrait of an Artist: A Biography of Georgia O'Keeffe*. New York, Seaview, 1980; revised edition, Albuquerque, University of New Mexico Press, 1986; London, Heinemann, 1987.

Pollitzer, Anita, *A Woman on Paper: Georgia O'Keeffe*. New York, Simon and Schuster, 1988.

Robinson, Roxana, *Georgia O'Keeffe: A Life*. New York, Harper and Row, 1989.

*

The life of Georgia O'Keeffe presents an absorbing subject for a biographer. Her first solo exhibition held in New York at the gallery "291" in 1917 signaled the public debut of a long and productive career, and until her death at 98, her art and life remained inextricably intertwined. A leading member of the first generation of American moderns, her work comprises abstract, floral, architectural, and landscape themes, and through her lengthy residence in New Mexico, she became particularly identified with the Southwest. She had many connections to a wide range of important American intellectuals, and her sustained relationship with Alfred Stieglitz was one of the most significant artistic alliances of the 20th century.

Few American artists have been the object of such considerable popular and scholarly interest, and O'Keeffe's bibliography is extensive. But this fiercely independent and intensely private artist resisted written examination of her life. She said in 1976, "Where I was born and where and how I have lived is unimportant. It is what I have done with where I have been that should be of interest." It was not until 1980 that LISLE published the first biography of the artist. Typically, O'Keeffe refused to provide any assistance to the author, informing her: "You are welcome to what you find." Although Lisle used few archival sources, her book, revised and reissued following the artist's death, is solid, factual, and readable, and its straightforward approach corrected much previously published misinformation concerning the artist.

Lisle's volume has been largely supplanted by ROBINSON's compellingly written and thoroughly researched biography of 639 pages (as compared to Lisle's 408 pages). Conducting many interviews, the author also made effective use of extensive primary sources, and the result is a richly textured chronicle of this fascinating woman's life. Grounding her topic in contemporary feminist criticism, Robinson includes many quotations from letters and period sources that give authority and depth to her narrative. The personal and professional complexities of her 50-year association with Alfred Stieglitz are convincingly discussed. While Robinson's volume is clearly the more substantive, both authors make many perceptive if differing observations, and those eager for the fullest information might well wish to read both. Until such time as scholars have full access to all research materials, Robinson's volume will likely remain the definitive biography. One major archival cache of some 1800 letters and telegrams O'Keeffe and Stieglitz exchanged, now in the Collection of American Literature at Yale University's Beinecke Rare Book and Manuscript Library, have been restricted until 2011, 25 years after the artist's death.

Other studies of O'Keeffe's life are less satisfactory. One of the most interesting is by POLLITZER, who met the artist in 1914 and began her biographical memoir in the early 1950s. But in 1968 publication was indefinitely delayed when the artist, who had initially cooperated with the project, refused permission to publish the letters she and Pollitzer had written. The book provides a vivid record of their long friendship, which began while they were still students, and is particularly good for an understanding of the critical years 1914–17, the period to which is devoted more than half of the book. The 40 black-and-white photographs are especially valuable in conveying a sense of O'Keeffe's early visual milieu.

Excellent color reproductions are the main strength of CASTRO's volume, but, frustratingly, they are poorly integrated with her all too general and conventional text. Also unsatisfactory is HOFFMAN's book, based on her 1976 Ph.D. disserta-

tion. The author aimed to emphasize O'Keeffe's art rather than her life, but, nevertheless, her format remains largely biographical and chronological. It is further marred by careless editing and misleading generalities. The reproductions are poor in quality and the work makes little contribution to our understanding of O'Keeffe. An annotated bibliography occupies 50 of the book's 185 pages, but it is deceptive, for it consists largely of short articles and reviews published in periodicals and newspapers; Hoffman disappointingly consulted little archival material.

Except for the pictures published in Castro's book, none of the biographies, illustrated as they are solely with black-and-white photographs, can do justice to the actual works of art. Interested readers may wish to supplement their study by consulting several other sources for visual material. A good place to start is O'Keeffe's own *Georgia O'Keeffe* (New York, Viking, 1976), which reproduces 108 works in excellent color. While it is by no means an autobiography, the work includes many of the artist's own memories and observations concerning her work. Even better is *Georgia O'Keeffe: Art and Letters* (Washington, D.C., National Gallery of Art, 1987) by Jack Cowart, Juan Hamilton, and Sarah Greenough, the catalogue accompanying the first major exhibition to be mounted after her death, and which marked the centennial of her birth. Reproducing 120 works in superior color, it also includes a thorough chronology and bibliography. The most significant part of the book comprises a selection of 125 letters spanning the years between 1915–81 edited by Greenough, who wrote the excellent accompanying notes. O'Keeffe was a lively correspondent, and her letters give an animated and direct sense of the artist, unobscured by scholarly analysis and historical fact.

Real-life stories have always fascinated children, and two juvenile biographies of O'Keeffe have been published. Lisle notes the worth of such exemplars in the foreword to her own volume: "My interest in biography began in childhood, when I voraciously read the pumpkin-colored 'famous people' books for beginning readers." Best is Michael Berry's *Georgia O'Keeffe, Painter* (New York, Chelsea House, 1988). Published as part of a 50-volume series on American Women of Achievement, it is accompanied by an introduction by Matina S. Horner, President of Radcliffe College. Factual yet lively in approach, Berry addresses honestly issues relating to the fact that Stieglitz was married and had a daughter when he and O'Keeffe began living together, and also discusses his involvement with other women. A well-chosen selection of photographs reproduces works of art by O'Keeffe and her contemporaries, images of the artist, and telling period photographs. Less satisfactory is Beverly Gherman's admiring *Georgia O'Keeffe: The "Wideness and Wonder" of her World* (New York, Athenaeum, 1986), whose more predictable text fails to convey much of what constitutes the fundamental interest of the life of one of America's most distinctive artists.

—Betsy Fahlman

OLIVIER, Laurence, 1907–1990; English actor.

Barker, Felix, *The Oliviers: A Biography*. London, Hamilton, and Philadelphia, Lippincott, 1953.

Bragg, Melvyn, *Laurence Olivier*. London, Hutchinson, 1984; New York, St. Martin's, 1985.

Cottrell, John, *Laurence Olivier*. Englewood Cliffs, New Jersey, Prentice-Hall, and London, Weidenfeld and Nicolson, 1975.

Darlington, William A., *Laurence Olivier*. London, Morgan-Grampian, 1968.

Fairweather, Virginia, *Olivier: An Informal Portrait*. New York, Coward-McCann, 1969.

Holden, Anthony, *Laurence Olivier*. New York, Atheneum, 1988; London, Collier, 1990.

Kiernan, Thomas, *Sir Larry: The Life of Laurence Olivier*. New York, Times Books, 1981.

*

Each of the biographies of Sir Laurence Olivier published so far was written during his life, so each reaps a harvest of anecdote and recent recollection, liberally sprinkled with gossip, and each inevitably stands a bit in awe of a personage who was both an imposing celebrity and one of the great thespians of all time. All the books are based on newspaper reports, television talk, other actors' books, and interviews with those who can enliven particular episodes with selectively remembered facts. (There is no comprehensive interview with Olivier himself.) From such a foundation the reader will not expect balanced appraisals of the man, judicious assessments of his impact on the theatre, or even historically conscious reviews of the many parts he played. An approach to these larger issues must wait until the stardust has settled, by which time, hopefully, the complete personal and professional papers of Olivier will be available for scrutiny. For now we must be content with summaries of his life and career, and attempts to capture his fascinating but beguiling personality.

Much was written about Olivier long before the end of his career, but four of those preliminary sketches have something to recommend them to the introductory reader. BARKER ably reviews the professional careers of both Olivier and his second wife, Vivien Leigh, though he ignored their dramatic personal lives. DARLINGTON, like Barker an English drama critic, focuses on the great Shakespearean roles of the late 1930s and 40s that established Olivier's reputation. FAIRWEATHER was press agent for the National Theatre during Olivier's tenure there as its first artistic director. Her anecdotal book is chiefly useful for the warm appreciation of Joan Plowright, Olivier's third wife, whom other biographers have contrived to treat in only the most superficial fashion. BRAGG's volume describes the interviews that led to a BBC television profile of Lord Olivier. It boasts the best collection of photographs.

COTTRELL, a British journalist, wrote the first extensive biography, which attempts to mention all his many plays and films, as well as the directing, producing, and managerial efforts of Olivier. It is briskly written in a pleasing style that moves along with such grace that it is not until the end one realizes a rich smorgasbord has been reduced to a mere beef stew. The emphasis is on the deeds and progress of a great actor, rather than an analysis of the complex man behind the mask, though Cottrell points out how deliberately Olivier combined just the right amount of publicity with mystery to cultivate a legend during his own lifetime. The book summarizes much press coverage of Olivier's acting.

Taking a more analytical approach enables KIERNAN to rechart the geography of Olivier's life into a series of peaks and valleys, some with far greater significance than others. An American freelance writer of admirable breadth, Kiernan uses extensive interviews to piece together an explanation of career cogently related to character and circumstance. From this perceptive author we learn where Olivier picked up some of his best ideas and techniques, and we get by far the best picture of Olivier's first wife, Jill Esmond, who taught him much about the craft of an actor. Vivien Leigh stalks through this life as an adventurous predator, though insufficient allowance is made for her mental illness.

Unquestionably the most absorbing life of Olivier is his own autobiography, *Confessions of an Actor* (New York, Simon and Schuster, 1982). On the one hand it is amazingly candid (embarrassingly so, many friends felt) about numerous topics: his awkward wedding night with Jill Esmond, whom he married mostly to pacify his libido; his difficult relationship with their son, Tarquin; his delight in showing off, which matured into a hugely competitive ego; his early effeminacy, and his later marital infidelities; his many unsuccessful ventures in the theatre; and, most surprising of all, his horrific experience of stage fright for five and a half years, at a time when he was widely hailed as the greatest actor of his time.

For all its candor Olivier's confession disguises as much as it reveals, and is obsessed with depicting Mr. Nice Guy, who has a good word for everyone, even the likes of Peter Finch, the first to cuckold him. His frankness in relating Vivien's manic depression seems admirable at first, yet when contrasted to the self-deprecating humor and stylish evasiveness with which he handles his own shortcomings the morbid details of her illness seem unnecessarily grim. Perhaps he was being petty, perhaps vengeful, but in either case the image of the much abused husband does nothing to deter his adoring public. Similarly, his complaints about the Board of the National Theatre sound like special pleading. An objective assessment of Olivier's work there is lacking.

Though his wording is sometimes too florid, his narrative is constructed with imagination and force, like so many of Olivier's memorable stage creations. His perspective on the theatre in England is irreplaceable and invaluable, and his comments on people (I found those on Marilyn Monroe and Winston Churchill especially delicious), at least when he chooses to give them, more than meet the demands of curiosity.

Coming last, HOLDEN can fill in many of the gaps left by previous writers, including several important omissions by Olivier himself. He does this job well, though in fleshing out various incidents and aspects Holden must traverse much of the same ground already covered by others, often using the same examples and quotations. The banquet of narrative detail expands, but too much of it must be swallowed undigested, without the elixir of fresh insight. Holden's is the most sympathetic treatment of Vivien Leigh, perhaps too sympathetic. There is an undercurrent of antagonism toward Olivier regarding Vivien, a chivalrous but overbold defense of a fallen lady, which, in defiance of Holden's own evidence, blames Olivier for much of her hardship.

—Mike F. Foster

O'NEILL, Eugene, 1888–1953; American playwright.

Alexander, Doris, *The Tempering of Eugene O'Neill.* New York, Harcourt, 1962.

Boulton, Agnes, *Part of a Long Story.* New York, Doubleday, and London, P. Davies, 1958.

Bowen, Croswell, *The Curse of the Misbegotten.* New York, McGraw-Hill, 1959; London, Hart-Davis, 1960.

Carpenter, Frederic I., *Eugene O'Neill.* New York, Twayne, 1964.

Clark, Barrett H., *Eugene O'Neill.* New York, McBride, 1926.

Clark, Barrett H., *Eugene O'Neill: The Man and His Plays.* New York, Dover, 1947.

Coolidge, Olivia E., *Eugene O'Neill.* New York, Scribner, 1966.

Frenz, Horst, *Eugene O'Neill,* translated by Helen Sebba. New York, Ungar, 1971 (originally published by Colloquium-Verlag, Berlin, 1965).

Gassner, John, *Eugene O'Neill.* Minneapolis, University of Minnesota Press, 1965.

Gelb, Arthur and Barbara Gelb, *O'Neill.* New York, Harper, and London, Cape, 1962; revised edition, 1974.

Leech, Clifford, *Eugene O'Neill.* New York, Grove, 1963.

Sheaffer, Louis, *O'Neill: Son and Playwright.* New York, Little Brown, 1968; London, Dent, 1969.

Sheaffer, Louis, *O'Neill: Son and Artist.* New York, Little Brown, 1973; London, Elek, 1974.

Skinner, Richard Dana, *Eugene O'Neill: A Poet's Quest.* New York, Longman, 1935.

*

In an interesting but slightly embarrassing example of "dueling biographies," Gelb and Sheaffer, writing and revising at essentially the same time (Sheaffer cites Gelb in his bibliography, however), try to outdo each other in exhaustive attention to detail and their ability to interpret and discover the true O'Neill underneath the debris of his huge canon and the witness of vast troops of hangers-on, acquaintances, wives, and sons. Taking a good, even an important, figure and raising him to the status of sainthood, Sheaffer and the Gelbs spend too much of their own lives gathering into thick volumes everything that had ever been said about O'Neill, an essentially reclusive and private man. The two biographies taken together are longer than O'Neill's entire canon.

SHEAFFER's first volume (1968) takes O'Neill's life to 1920 and his first play produced on Broadway, *Beyond the Horizon.* Sheaffer allows no detail to be missed, having interviewed everyone who ever remotely came into contact with O'Neill. The problem lies in his interpretation of the facts, which are wedged into Sheaffer's own axiom that "O'Neill is the most autobiographical of playwrights"; in this view, virtually every character in O'Neill's plays is, according to Sheaffer, drawn from life almost without change, a supposition that requires a tautological explanation for both fictive and real characterization. Understandably, Sheaffer gets bogged down in details, taking too much time describing secondary characters and thereby losing the train of narrative.

Sheaffer's second volume (1973) covers the rest of O'Neill's life, and is even more detailed, since more of his associates were still alive and labored to remember even their most occasional brushes with the great man (the desk clerk on duty when O'Neill's body is carried out is even quoted). Sheaffer's problem, then—to sort out, organize, and interpret the information—is even more difficult. His treatment of O'Neill's final hospital stay, with the parade of visitors screened by Carlotta, is a model of exhaustive and essentially pointless biographical craft. Comparing Gelb with Sheaffer on several points reveals a stubbornness on both their parts to interpret the facts to their liking.

GELB, in one volume, takes a chattier, more "in-crowd" tone, moving in and out of O'Neill's career and life with more style and less distance; the work is readable in a way that Sheaffer's is not, and more a portrait of the theatrical times than purely a biography. However, by interspersing factual observations with supporting material from another time and place, the Gelbs have muddied the biographical waters. Such phrases as "on another occasion," and "later," which refer to untraceable sources, give a softness to the whole study, so that one feels the information is unreliable, slanted by the Gelbs toward their own inclinations. It would not, for example, hold up in court. Continuing the biography well past O'Neill's death with an epilogue on Carlotta, who lived another 17 years as O'Neill's self-appointed hagiographer, Gelb explains her death at 81: "Her heart had worn out." Discrepancies of facts between Sheaffer and Gelb (who really painted or carved or etched exactly what inscription in the beam of O'Neill's apartment in Provincetown? what exactly was written on the sign outside his door? etc.) can be resolved by flipping a coin, but Sheaffer's portraits of O'Neill's friends and acquaintances are stiff and unrewarding compared to Gelb's. The epilogue mentions the production of *More Stately Mansions,* but not of *Hughie,* performed in 1964 and included in the Gelb chronological table of O'Neill's published plays. Other than an index, no critical apparatus is offered.

CLARK, the official biographer, gives his first book (1926) an immediacy and calmness that affords a clearer image of O'Neill than any of his subsequent biographers could hope for. Clark tells the anecdote of the simple-minded boy in Provincetown who asked O'Neill what was "beyond the horizon," and remarks, "It exemplifies O'Neill's utter simplicity of character, a thing most of his friends apparently cannot understand." Clark's 1947 work is in one sense a new edition of the earlier study, but it benefits from 21 more years of insight into the man's maturer work. Clark incorporates into the text a critical survey of the canon to date. Referring to the "temporary retirement" of 1934–46, Clark rightly avoids making too much of the details, and relies mostly on personal letters to him from O'Neill during this time; not dwelling on the numerous illnesses and changes of address, Clark concentrates on those mentions of literary progress that best inform the reader about O'Neill's period of "almost incredible activity."

COOLIDGE's "swift pace" too often becomes merely a hasty assembly of sparse facts glued together with a romantic writing style that O'Neill would have abhorred: "That old shed had seen many a cargo hauled in through the great door at its seaward end." The transitions from marriage to marriage, especially from Agnes to Carlotta, read like a soap opera. Coolidge parallels O'Neill's career with the progress of the Provincetown Players; while all other biographers see this period as a beginning but not the fount of all his work (that was reserved for his family), Coolidge shares even her last paragraphs with Jig Cook and Susan Glaspell.

ALEXANDER concentrates on "the unresolved family drama" that shaped O'Neill by devoting a chapter each to his mother, father, brother Jamie, Jimmie "Tomorrow" Byth, and "the old foolosopher," Terry Carlin. A psychological study more than a literary analysis, Alexander tries to penetrate O'Neill's superficial coldness by positioning an emotionally draining insecurity underneath. Like Sheaffer's first volume, this work ends with O'Neill, "a beginner with prospects," on the threshold of Broadway success. BOWEN, working from the premise that a curse was laid on the O'Neill family, draws a portrait of the entire family, with assistance by Shane O'Neill, and concludes that at the base of the family's problems lay a hereditary inability to communicate love to one another. SKINNER's volume is not strictly biography but is interesting because it makes something of the order in which O'Neill's plays were written (to 1933), and sees a "moral" order and struggle between good and evil in the canon. An analysis from a Catholic viewpoint, it attempts, not always successfully, to find in the plays the author's working out of large moral problems. In response to Skinner's request, O'Neill wrote down an exhaustive chronology of his writing from draft to draft, a document that, allowing for some inaccuracy of memory, serves well to outline O'Neill's work habits and aesthetic progress through the canon. BOULTON, O'Neill's second wife, records in touching detail the exciting years, especially 1917–19, just before his Broadway success and the entrance of Carlotta into their lives; her "frankly personal" remembrances are cited in subsequent studies, without giving her sufficient credit for having lived through them.

CARPENTER follows the Twayne Series format, introducing the brief facts of O'Neill's life, and then moving on to an overview of his accomplishments. The chronology is disappointingly sparse; the work includes notes, bibliography, and index. FRENZ offers a concise introduction, part of the Modern Literature Monograph series from Ungar; personal and literary information is smoothly blended, with chronology, list of works, bibliographical notes, and index added. LEECH provides a brief introduction, moving quickly from personal history to literary interpretation; he cites important previous scholarship, including Gelb, and adds a valuable bibliography. GASSNER offers a 48-page pamphlet in the American Writers series for high schools.

—Thomas J. Taylor

OPPENHEIMER, J(ulius) Robert, 1904–1967; American physicist.

Chevalier, Hakron, *Oppenheimer: The Story of a Friendship*. New York, G. Braziller, 1965; London, A. Deutsch, 1966.
Goodchild, Peter, *J. Robert Oppenheimer: Shatterer of Worlds*. London, BBC Books, and Boston, Houghton Mifflin, 1980.
Kunetka, James W., *Oppenheimer: The Years of Risk*. Englewood Cliffs, New Jersey, Prentice-Hall, 1982.
Michelmore, Peter, *The Swift Years: The Robert Oppenheimer Story*. New York, Dodd Mead, 1969.

*

It is perhaps a sign of the uncomfortable feelings aroused by the paradoxical figure of Oppenheimer that MICHELMORE's biography was published in 1969, 25 years after the fruition of the Manhattan project, and more than 10 years after the security hearings. Even so, this book is hampered by the still-restricted files that prove in later works Michelmore's contention that Oppenheimer was not a security risk but an avidly loyal U.S. citizen. Michelmore, though, never doubts this fact. The Oppenheimer of this biography is "Oppie": all-round Emersonian fixit, who negotiated the narrow straits between conflicting interests and personalities to produce in the nuclear weapon a synthesis of terrible theoretical power and mundane *realpolitik*. Michelmore investigates the early life of his subject, providing for the first time a glance at the deep insecurities that underlay the apparent arrogance; though whether for reasons of delicacy or ignorance, he skirts the problems the younger Oppenheimer had with profound and sometimes suicidal depression, as well as in his relations with women. He presents us with not so much the man behind the name as the guy in the hat, a romantic cowboy with a PhD.

For many years, despite his celebrity, there was relatively little biographical material on Oppenheimer. The memoirs by his friends make fascinating reading, especially that of CHEVALIER, whose attempt to get Oppenheimer to pass secrets through him to Communist agents was the centrepiece of Oppenheimer's security hearing.

GOODCHILD's biography is a companion to the excellent BBC drama-documentary film on the life of Oppenheimer, and is both thoroughly researched and well narrated. Unlike Michelmore, Goodchild is expansive on the technical details of Oppenheimer's work, and succeeds (with the aid of diagrams and photographs) in conveying to the lay reader some idea of the physical complexity of his wartime task. Goodchild reminds us that the Bomb was referred to in the development stages as "the gadget," and that the two used against Japan were the only two in existence: such was the atmosphere of make-do that prevailed in Los Alamos. Building on Michelmore's research into Oppie's private life, Goodchild also provides an outline of his subject's personality. It is characteristic of Oppenheimer, however, that this remains just an outline, as crude in its way as the blow-up diagrams showing what made the bomb. With the security documents available to Goodchild, the amount of information on Oppenheimer reaches a critical mass; it is to his credit that this biography is both concise and comprehensive.

KUNETKA's study is more restricted, choosing to cover only "The Years of Risk" during Oppenheimer's work on the Manhattan Project. Perhaps acknowledging the enigmatic quality of his subject, Kunetka further limits himself to collating known facts in the case, stating that his book "is neither a study of his psyche nor a definitive statement about his life: no work so close to the events and the individuals could be." Unfortunately, Kunetka's dogged refusal to stray from the historical documents leads him to excruciating dullness. Although he amasses and presents coherently a great deal of material, he takes no risks. For example, of Oppenheimer's crippling rivalry with Edward

Teller (father of the H-Bomb or Super), which contributed to his downfall, Kunetka states that it was "the result of differing philosophies and perhaps because of secret competition." This could scarcely be less informative.

Oppenheimer stands at the dark centre of the cloud of fear that his creation spread across the world: a paradox, an ascetic and unworldy innocent who created the greatest terror ever experienced by humanity, a decent and honest man accused of treachery, a genius made to look a fool. The definitive biography of this great scientist remains to be written.

—Alan Murphy

ORWELL, George [born Eric Arthur Blair], 1903–1950; English writer.

Atkins, John A., *George Orwell, a Literary Study.* London, J. Calder, 1954; as *George Orwell: A Literary and Biographical Study*, New York, Ungar, 1954.

Crick, Bernard, *George Orwell, a Life.* London, Secker and Warburg, and Boston, Little Brown, 1980.

Gross, Miriam, editor, *The World of George Orwell.* New York, Simon and Schuster, and London, Weidenfeld and Nicolson, 1971.

Stansky, Peter and William Abraham, *The Unknown Orwell.* London, Constable, and New York, Knopf, 1972.

Stansky, Peter and William Abraham, *Orwell: The Transformation.* London, Constable, 1979; New York, Knopf, 1980.

Woodcock, George, *Crystal Spirit: A Study of George Orwell.* Boston, Little Brown, 1966; London, Cape, 1967.

*

The biographical case of George Orwell is an unusual one, since Orwell himself gave instructions in his will that no biography of him should be written. For 30 years, from his death in 1950 until the appearance of Bernard Crick's *George Orwell, a Life* (see below) in 1980, the ban was sustained by Sonia Brownell Orwell, his widow and literary executor, through the simple device of refusing—to those she suspected of biographical intent—permission to quote from Orwell's works and letters. However, Orwell's will was not a legally valid prohibition against discussing the facts of his life, and the result of the situation during the three decades after his death was a spate of shadow lives and quasi-biographies.

Perhaps the most important and the most ambiguous of these interim productions was the great four-volume *Collected Essays, Journalism and Letters of George Orwell* (1968), edited by Sonia Orwell herself with the aid of Ian Angus, keeper of the Orwell Archive at University College, London. With its quite elaborate notes, this in fact amounted to a kind of skeleton biography in which the events of Orwell's life were being described mostly in his own words, with his characteristic concealments and evasions, so that those who read it began to look with a more critical eye on his "autobiographical" writings, *Down and Out in Paris and London* (1933), *The Road to Wigan Pier*

(1937), and *Homage to Catalonia* (1938), which critical examination have shown to be partly fiction and at best manipulated fact.

The result of the ban on actual biographies was a series of hybrid books on Orwell, whom his friend Julian Symons once declared to be even more interesting as a man than as a writer. Orwell in fact made so deep a personal impression on those who knew him that there seemed an irresistible urge to call up his ghost in writing. ATKINS, who had worked with Orwell on the editorial staff of *Tribune*, managed to get away in 1954 with a sketchy and superficial biography that made no use of the extensive correspondence then being accumulated in the Orwell Archive. Indeed, it was more a memoir celebrating a friendship than a real biography, and later on books that were more frankly memoirs were published by Laurence Bradner, who had worked with Orwell at the BBC (*George Orwell*, 1954); by Christopher Hollis, who had been at Eton with him (*A Study of George Orwell*, 1956); and by Richard Rees, who had edited the *Adelphi* in the 1930s when it published Orwell's early work (*George Orwell: Fugitive from the Camp of Victory*, 1961). None of these books is either a real biography or truly criticism, though they have contributed material a biographer might use.

Sonia Orwell tended to be gentle with Orwell's old friends, provided they did not set about writing full biographies. WOODCOCK was fortunate in the same way in his *Crystal Spirit*, a key work that begins with a long chapter of recollections of Orwell and uses biographical material extensively in the remaining "critical" chapters, for which Sonia Orwell approved ample quotations. The prohibitions she might have raised have been evaded by other writers through such means as producing collections of reminiscent essays that together amount to a shadow biography, such as the volume edited by GROSS and described as "a composite picture of the man, his society, and his career from his schooldays to *Nineteen Eighty-Four*." The work includes recollections from 18 people who had known Orwell in childhood, in his Burmese days, and in a variety of later situations.

Scholars who did not belong to Orwell's world of acquaintance tended to be seen as outsiders and to receive more rigorous treatment in the interpretation of the Orwell will, and the result was the publication of two very curious but also very valuable semi-biographical volumes. Two Americans, STANSKY AND ABRAHAMS, a history professor and a publisher's reader, combined in an extraordinary work of enquiry into Orwell's past from his childhood to the end of the Spanish Civil War. They sought out people still alive who had known Orwell in a great variety of circumstances. They delved deeply into the Orwell Archive and into literary sources outside Orwell's writing. But they never received permission to quote to any extent from Orwell's books and letters, and the result was two somewhat crippled volumes; *The Unknown Orwell* (1972) deals with Eric Blair's youth until, on the publication of *Down and Out in Paris and London* in 1933, he publicly assumed the name of "George Orwell," while *Orwell: The Transformation* (1979) covers the period when the persons of George Orwell became consolidated between 1933 and 1938, and was baptized, as it were, in the blood and fire of Spain.

They are strange books, for the relative absence of Orwell's voice lends a ghostly sense of indirection to a story told mostly in voices other than the hero's. But they give an order to Orwell's earlier years, offer much essential and new material, and, with the exception of the *Collected Essays, Journalism and Letters of George Orwell*, they are certainly the most important of the pre-biographical works on Orwell. But their very appearance showed the absurdity of trying to maintain the ban on a biography. In fact, even during the 1960s Sonia Orwell had begun to realize how untenable the will had become. She tried to stave off a final decision by announcing that Malcolm Muggeridge would be the official biographer, with a shrewd feeling—which was justified—that Muggeridge would never stay the course of completing so ambitious a work. Later, Orwell's English publishers suggested Julian Symons as a possible biographer. For obscure reasons of her own, Sonia rejected him, and picked instead a political scientist, Bernard Crick.

CRICK's qualifications for the task were not evident at the time, for he did not move in literary circles and he had never written a biography before. But he turned out a fortunate choice for a first biographer. He was a conscientious researcher, not afraid to listen to the views of others, and he had no difficulty untangling the obscurities of Orwell's political thinking and the way it affected his life. He had enough literary acumen to make his statements on Orwell's writing acceptable, yet he did not burden his narrative with critical theorizing, which fitted in with Orwell's own "plain man" approach to literature. He was too young to have known the London literary world of the 1930s and 1940s in which Orwell had operated, and perhaps he did not listen enough to the surviving denizens of that world. But he benefitted greatly from the sweeping permission he had been given to quote freely from Orwell's letters and other writings, and he avoided the pressures to become an "official" rather than an "authorized" biographer, so that there were a number of points at which he seemed in disagreement with Sonia Orwell and the interpretations she might have wished to see presented.

Crick's *George Orwell* is a substantial, clearly (if flatly) written work, well argued and well narrated, even if occasionally it fails to catch the spirit of the man or his times. It amply fills the existing gaps in the reading public's knowledge of Orwell, and even Orwell's contemporaries, though they might be critical about details, thought that it provided a valid assessment of Orwell as man, writer, and political thinker, seen a generation after his death. It was said by more than one critic that no further Life of Orwell would be needed for a long time, and in fact nothing rivaling Crick's book has appeared during the past decade, though as we enter the 1990s reports are circulating that the Orwell Estate has approved an even larger "official" biography.

—George Woodcock

OWEN, Wilfred, 1893-1918; English poet.

Hibberd, Dominic, *Owen the Poet*. Athens, University of Georgia Press, and London, Macmillan, 1986.
Owen, William Harold, *Journey from Obscurity: Wilfred Owen 1893–1918* (3 vols.). London and New York, Oxford University Press, 1963-65.
Stallworthy, Jon, *Wilfred Owen*. London, Oxford University Press/Chatto and Windus, 1974; New York, Oxford University Press, 1975.
Welland, Dennis, *Wilfred Owen: A Critical Study*. London, Chatto and Windus, 1960; revised edition, 1978.
White, Gertrude, *Wilfred Owen*. New York, Twayne, 1969.

*

HAROLD OWEN's work is a unique, three-volume memoir of his older brother Wilfred; although essentially an autobiography, it is the most thorough account available of Wilfred Owen's early life. The story of both brothers' lives is traced candidly from their early history. Harold Owen excels in conveying the poet's personality and in suggesting something about his inner life before World War I. There are many rich and illuminating details here about Wilfred Owen that can help us to understand the peculiar qualities of his poetry written during the war. Harold treats his brother's two years at Dunsden vicarage, during which time the poet was considering taking Holy Orders, and we are left with a clearer sense of the person behind some of the very lofty verses written in the trenches. The first two volumes contain more detail on Wilfred, while the third, which ends with a gesture toward Harold's own setting off to be an artist in London, is necessarily more limited owing to the brothers' different courses during the war.

STALLWORTHY's biography, the standard work on Owen, draws on Harold Owen's memoir as a chief source, as well as original research into unpublished materials and interviews with Owen's family and friends. The book is also important for its analysis of Owen's "transformation" by the war (he offers many detailed observations of the war itself) and its sound critical study of his poetry. Stallworthy offers the finest account of Owen's life for both the general reader and the scholar. His book contains a bibliography and an index.

HIBBERD deals with Owen's development as a poet; his biography focuses on literary influences and sources of themes and imagery. It includes details not found in Stallworthy's book, especially analyses of Owen's earlier work. It includes notes, a general index as well as an index of poems, and other appendices, making it especially useful to Owen scholars. Two other monographs on Owen, by WELLAND and WHITE, contain criticism of his poetry and brief biographical information.

—Noelle A. Watson

PAINE, Thomas, 1737–1809; English-born American political philosopher and writer.

Aldridge, Alfred Owen, *Man of Reason: The Life of Thomas Paine*. Philadelphia, Lippincott, 1959; London, Cresset, 1960.
Conway, Moncure, *The Life of Thomas Paine* (2 vols.). New York and London, Putnam, 1892.
Edwards, Samuel, *Rebel! A Biography of Thomas Paine*. London, New English Library, and New York, Praeger, 1974.
Hawke, David F., *Paine*. New York, Harper, 1974.

Philip, Mark, *Paine*. Oxford and New York, Oxford University Press, 1989.

Powell, David *Tom Paine: The Greatest Exile*. London, Croom Helm, and New York, St. Martin's, 1985.

*

Aldridge (see below) wrote the first life of Paine to display impartial scholarship. Earlier biographers were either too hostile or too adulatory. The first two, George Chalmers (*Life of Thomas Paine*, London, 1791) and James Cheetham (*Life of Thomas Paine*, New York, 1809), were contemporaries of Paine and were maliciously critical. Aldridge describes Cheetham's book as "the first muck-raking biography in American literature." The years 1819–20 saw three favourable biographies published in London (by Richard Carlile, Thomas Rickman, and William Sherwin), and in 1892 came CONWAY's two-volume life, which for the first time investigated the original documentary sources of Paine's years in Paris. But Conway also was too prejudiced in Paine's favour, depicting Gouverneur Morris as deliberately plotting to prolong Paine's stay in the Luxembourg prison.

By contrast ALDRIDGE, besides citing much material that was unknown to Conway, seeks to present a balanced portrait. His intention is, he explains, "not to please either Paine's idolators or his enemies, but to gather and present documentary evidence." Aldridge is indeed judicious in his weighing of evidence. He will not allow frequently repeated stories if he cannot find corroborative evidence, and he even questions Paine's claim that he escaped the guillotine only because the executioner's mark was scrawled by mistake on the *inside* of his cell door. Here is an author who evidently *can* resist a good story.

For the same reason Aldridge devotes little space to Paine's life before he arrived in America in November 1774, since almost all the details stand on the solitary testimony of George Chalmers—though Paine admittedly had ample opportunity to refute them and apparently did not do so. From Paine's arrival in America, however, Aldridge skilfully blends documentary evidence into his narrative and frankly indicates where the documents appear contradictory. Thanks to his own research in the French archives, Aldridge is well placed to emphasize Paine's trans-Atlantic links, arising out of France's interest in the War of Independence. He deals adroitly with the Dean affair, which led to Paine's resigning his post as secretary of the Foreign Affairs Committee of Congress. The middle 200 pages of the book focus directly or indirectly on the French connection with a postscript of some 40 pages devoted to Paine's largely unhappy years after his final return from France in November 1802.

In 1974, the bicentennial of Paine's first arrival in America, two biographies were published of similar scope to Aldridge but with somewhat different flavours. HAWKE puts slightly more emphasis on the American years and less on Paine's time in France. He differs from Aldridge by regarding Paine as a prophet who reflected the opinion of the age rather than leading and shaping it. He sees Paine as "one of those men who achieve distinction by embodying the spirit of the society in which they live, rather than deviating from it or going beyond it." Aldridge, while emphasizing Paine's originality, is content to quote Paine's own judgment that "he was at a loss to know whether he was made for the times or the times made for him."

EDWARDS, the other bicentennial biographer, sees Paine as a child of the Enlightenment, while listing the liberal causes that he was the first to espouse: the emancipation of women (a generation before Mary Wollstonecraft Godwin), the emancipation of slaves, the need for the new United States to develop a national identity, the abolition of dueling, the prevention of cruelty to animals, the establishment of national and international copyright laws, and the introduction of equitable divorce laws. Edwards seems to be more concerned with the man than with the revolutionary, and perhaps the "rebel" of his title highlights this. He certainly has a keener eye for human detail, and he allows himself a glance at Paine's love-life—particularly the four years he spent with the widow Martha Daley in Philadelphia.

Edwards, a novelist as well as an historian and a biographer, writes with rather more spirit than Hawke and Aldridge. But he also differs from them in giving much longer extracts from his documentary sources, as in the case of the first *Crisis*, which he describes as Paine's "most celebrated work." Apart from the extended quotations in the text itself (including some of Paine's verse compositions!), Edwards adds a 16-page appendix of longer excerpts, mainly from the *Rights of Man*.

POWELL's book, with only 13 chapters, is also generous with extended quotations from Paine's writings, but as a biography it is flawed by having a substantial admixture of fiction. One's confidence in the work is jolted on the very first page of the preface when "deist" appears as "diest." Powell then goes on to explain that his method is to "recreate something of the background in which Paine grew up and attempt to interpret his imagined response to all that he saw and heard." Powell recognises that his approach "will offend the historical purists," but he impatiently disparages "that handful of academics who, inheriting the leisured practices of the 18th century, have the time to indulge in their specialisation, careless of wider audiences."

Powell's earliest chapters are, in his own engaging phrase, "weighted towards the speculative," but even when there is no shortage of documentary evidence, the narrative is still peppered with such unhelpful and unhistorical phrases as: "Recalling Voltaire, Paine laughed wryly . . . "; " . . . shrugging off the thought, he turned into the State House"; " . . . remembering Rhode Island, Paine poured himself another rum and wrote. . . ." Powell would have done better to let Paine's own words speak for him. As Joel Barlow, a contemporary, observed on the occasion of Paine's death: "His own writings are his best life."

PHILIP's slim volume of 125 pages could not be expected to quote extensively, but most of the references to the phrases he does quote frustratingly refer to the volume and page of the *Life and Major Writings of Thomas Paine*, edited by Philip S. Foner (1948). No clue is given to the actual pamphlet from which the quotation comes. This is all the more irritating as the book is concerned less with Paine's life and personality (which are summarily treated in the first chapter) than with his ideas, and we need to see how his ideas evolve chronologically. The three main chapters are chronological, dealing successively with his American pamphlets, the *Rights of Man* and the *Age of Reason*; but few readers are likely to have Foner's two volumes at their elbow. Philip's distinctive contribution is his detailed analysis of the *Age of Reason*—a work normally given perfunctory treatment by biographers. His conclusion is that Paine's case against

Christian orthodoxy is a telling one, but that the existence of a God is no guarantee that God is a moral being: religious revelation is needed to tell us that!

Philip is not interested in Paine's personal habits: "The question of whether there is anything of value in his political theory or theology cannot be determined by the level of alcohol in his bloodstream or by how frequently he washed his clothes." He is interested in the interrelation between Paine's political ideas and the rhetorical skills he deploys to publicize them. Philip thinks we should see Paine as a revolutionary democrat rather than as a liberal—though he embodied much of modern liberalism. His talent was to teach the ordinary reader and citizen to question all received wisdom and to demand a full share in government. Philip's concluding judgment on Paine is that "as a political philosopher his status may not be as great as that of other writers, but as a committed and practising democrat, it is difficult to believe that it has been equalled."

—Stuart Andrews

* * *

PARKER, Charles, Jr. [Charlie; "Bird"], 1920–1955; American jazz musician and composer.

Giddins, Gary, *Celebrating Bird: The Triumph of Charlie Parker*. New York, Beech Tree Books, and London, Hodder and Stoughton, 1987.

Harrison, Max, *Charlie Parker*. London, Cassell, 1960; New York, A. S. Barnes, 1961.

Koch, Lawrence O., *Yardbird Suite: A Compendium of the Music and Life of Charlie Parker*. Bowling Green, Ohio, Bowling Green State University Press, 1988.

Priestley, Brian, *Charlie Parker*. Tunbridge Wells, Kent, Spellmount, and New York, Hippocrene Books, 1984.

Reisner, Robert, *Bird: The Legend of Charlie Parker*. New York, Citadel Press, and London, Quartet, 1962.

Russell, Ross, *Bird Lives! The High Life and Hard Times of Charlie Parker*. New York, Charterhouse, and London, Quartet, 1973.

*

In a brief synthesis, HARRISON submits that the "bebop" style that Parker heralded sprang from both favorable conditions and the developments among certain young big band musicians. He credits that style with having the complexity and depth of classical music, hence placing Parker among the leading figures in American culture. He is careful not to glorify the all-too-often seedy club forum, indicating that this setting had its origins in general exclusion of Black artists from the concert hall. Lack of appreciation as a serious musician fed Parker's alienation and drug use; ignored and unduly criticized, the artist "found it necessary to seek oblivion from time to time." Though weak on social context, particularly on the changes in the nation and among Blacks, Harrison does suggest that Parker reflected "the insecurity and anxiety of the post-war world." While containing certain minor errors and limited by the paucity of then-available sources, the treatment is sensitive and poignant.

Harrison would have benefited if REISNER's oral history had appeared earlier; it is a treasury for all later biographers. Among the 80 interviews collected here can be found moving and revealing assessments. The artist's mother, second wife (Doris), fellow musicians, and others provide insights into his youth, music ("Bird contributed more and received less than anybody"), personality, addictions ("He had the oldest face I ever saw"), influence and intelligence, his sensitivity to discrimination and his appreciation of European classical music. Occasional inconsistencies and irregularities in these accounts reflect both Parker's many-sided character as well as differences among those he impressed. Regrettably, the contributions are organized alphabetically, making biographical navigation difficult. Though the work cannot be used by itself, it contains an enormous amount of relevant material.

RUSSELL's book on Parker is the masterwork, though it is flawed in a number of areas. It is the best conceived and the only truly full-length life story. Russell draws upon both Reisner's and his own interviews, substantial research, and his relationship with the subject: he had been Parker's producer for a period. Parker had been the apex of Russell's previous work on the significance and growth of jazz in the Southwest; quite deservedly here, he becomes the focus. Flowing from Russell's view of the close relationship between artist and society and from his grasp of the burdens of Black artists, the book is accessible and comprehensible. The author portrays the young Parker as a product of Kansas City's African-American "musical culture," drawing a parallel with Mozart's emergence in Salzburg. Depicting the atmosphere in Kansas City, Russell gives a good picture of Parker's informal studies in the hum and drive of the Reno club and its featured Basie orchestra. Russell lucidly explains the revolution embodied in bebop. He supports the generally accepted view that Parker's innovations peaked in the mid-to-late 1940s, then ebbed as Parker's health deteriorated. Parker's environment throughout is shown to have been racist and discriminatory: Russell had been among a growing number of whites in the 1930s and 1940s opposed to segregation, and thus his treatment here is emphatic and revealing. Russell notes the irony of creating art in a drinking establishment as symptomatic of the pressures, frustrations, and exploitation brought upon so thoughtful a musician as Parker. Under such conditions, "the appetite for toxicants becomes understandable." Moreover, Parker developed under inhospitable social and political circumstances, in which conformity and commercialism were officially exalted; Russell contends that a man of Parker's originality and "real talent" stood little chance of acceptance or survival. At points, the author's view of the Black condition is skewed. For example, Parker's tendency to have many unstable sexual affairs is ascribed first of all to "his class and ethnic background," a debatable assumption. The book has several minor factual errors, and the author's over-identification with the sentiments of Parker's fourth and last wife (Chan) tend to undermine his objectivity in assessing the furor and tussle over the artist's demise and estate. Nevertheless, no work makes clearer Parker's centrality to American music.

PRIESTLEY's work, like Harrison's, is a contribution to a series of small handbooks. Short on detail, the work seems intended for those already familiar with the subject. Employing Reisner, Russell, and his own interviews and research, Priestley supplies the basic facts of Parker's life. Several passages tend to confuse the narrative, including references to Parker's "Oedipus complex" and astrological sign. Though there is little new here—other than the important disclosure of Parker's sympathy with African independence groups in the 1940s—the book successfully evokes Parker's "disorganization" and "rootless confusion," while documenting the triumph of his "musical legacy."

GIDDINS' narrative is more broadly accessible. The well-known critic effects a coup in Parker biography in his discovery of and conversations with Parker's first wife (Rebecca), whose reminiscences of the Kansas City period break new ground. Further, Giddins consults others not contacted by previous biographers: Roland Hanna, Al Cohn, John Lewis. Giddins criticizes Russell as overdramatic, warning against both "fast-Freud analyses" and sole attribution of Parker's problems to the racist milieu. He recognizes Parker's substantial "self-destructive impulses" and "gluttonies." His evocation of the social context is at times more helpful than Russell's, outlining the post-war scene for Blacks (who demanded democracy at home), for whose "discontent" Parker's music "set the most comprehensive tone. . . ." Nor does Giddins neglect to mention that those who then came of musical age were "of the first generation born during the Harlem Renaissance." He is the only biographer to discuss Parker's appearance at a benefit for Smith Act victim Benjamin Davis, a leading Black Communist, though he fails to indicate Parker's evident principle in so appearing or in being seen there with the maligned and blacklisted Paul Robeson or Parker's other support for civil liberties. Though short on musical analysis, the book's new information and reinterpretation are valuable.

With KOCH, Parker's work finds the studious and serious attention it has long awaited. Though the book is inappropriate for the newly interested, it is valuable as a detailed discussion by a scholar of innovations who provides an exhaustive examination of every recording. The attempt to put all this in the context of Parker's life is superficial and suffers from abrupt transition to the main task. Koch is at his best in showing the state of Parker's mind and health as evidenced in performances at every stage of his career. He criticizes Russell's errors, but notes that Russell and other "middle-class" whites rallied to Parker's side at critical moments, signifying that "the man and his music were not at all racial but rather universal." For Parker's addictions Koch blames objective factors, which he does not fully explore, as well as Parker's character defects. In the latter instance, Koch puts forward controversial arguments regarding Parker's "doting mother," his lack of a "stronger father figure," his "childish openness," and his low self-esteem, generally devoid of all but superficial contextual contributing factors. Since the author could not have injected too much hard biography without diluting his musical focus, those who might hope for a clear treatment of Parker's life may be disappointed. The fact remains, however, that Koch's work is essential to understanding what Parker really accomplished.

—Daniel Rosenberg

PARKER, Dorothy, 1893–1967; American writer.

Keats, John, *You Might As Well Live: The Life and Times of Dorothy Parker.* New York, Simon and Schuster 1970; London, Secker and Warburg, 1971.

Meade, Marion, *Dorothy Parker: What Fresh Hell Is This?* New York, Villard, 1987; London, Heinemann, 1988.

*

Parker has been the subject of only two biographies and very little serious critical study at all, except for Arthur F. Kinney's *Dorothy Parker* (New York, Twayne, 1978). This critical and biographical neglect mirrors the self-deprecation of Parker and many of her characters, the frivolous contexts of many of her tart short stories, and the flippant cynicism of her verse (she never called it "poetry") and bon mots ("You can lead a horticulture but you can't make her think."). If she doesn't proclaim herself a serious writer, why should anybody take her seriously?

Parker is also a secretive biographical subject. She obscured significant relationships, ceasing to acknowledge her first husband, Edwin Pond Parker, long before they were divorced, and concealed her origins so thoroughly that, as Meade says, she "gave the impression that she had no family ties whatsoever, even though her close relationship with her sister, Helen, lasted a lifetime." Moreover, Meade notes, "Parker herself left no correspondence, manuscripts, memorabilia, or private papers of any kind." She allegedly told her friend Lillian Hellman that she wished "never to be the subject of a biography." The biographer's problems are further complicated by Parker's alcoholism, which kept her from sustaining the literary distinction she attained early in her career and indeed from writing much at all during her last 25 years. She was an unreliable recorder and interpreter of the events of her life, "drunk half the time" in her 60s and full of excuses for why she wasn't writing, or meeting deadlines, or showing up for the class she taught at Cal State, or paying bills—a classic example of the celebrity destroyed by her own success.

So any Parker biographer would have to depend on the kindness of others—Parker's friends, publishers, denizens of the Algonquin Round Table, descendants of her second husband, bisexual actor Alan Campbell—for interviews, photographs, reviews, surviving correspondence, publishers' records. The biographer must also look to Parker's works, which speak for themselves now, in the 1990s; in a sotto feminist voice missed by the male reviewers of the 20s and 30s when most of her poetry and short stories were published.

KEATS embarked on Parker's biography shortly after his subject's death, interviewing some 50 people in order to "present the facts as well as the legend while they are still fresh in living memories." Although Keats, a journalist despite his poetic namesake, makes no claim to have written "an authorized or definitive biography," he has focused on explaining "a time and a woman in terms of each other." Keats has succeeded admirably in demonstrating that Parker was "a quite serious and creative artist . . . at the very center of New York's intellectual life in the twenties and early thirties"—"America's intellectual adolescence." Her stories, poems, and reviews, says Keats, helped to create both a national taste and a national style that "called for one to go through life armed with a wry, hard suspicion," ready to acknowledge excellence but equally ready "to express an informed contempt" for the bogus—"meanwhile being just as ready to have a damned good time at every opportunity." Her own life, like her vision of existence, was "an inextricable tangle of disaster and joy."

Keats untangles the snarls of Parker's complex persona and makes sense of the myriad of complicated relationships in Parker's social and professional life. He appropriately focuses on her *New Yorker* literary milieu and on her writing, offering brief, sympathetic explanations of her choice of subjects, style, and point of view. Thus his five-page discussion of "Big Blonde," winner of the O. Henry award for 1929, anticipates contemporary revisionist feminist criticism in interpreting the central character, Hazel Morse, as a symbol of exploited womanhood, lured to self-destruction by a series of men who find their solace in her escalating drinking and easy sexuality: "It was the great fiction of the twenties that women could and should be the great pals of men. . . . Dorothy Parker had plainly said how little fun there was for a woman . . . [particularly] when the fun chiefly amounted to drinking too much in speakeasies."

The sparkle, wit, and fast pace of Keats' somewhat superficial biography is a fitting reflection of its subject. On the contrary, MEADE's work, in endeavoring to be the biography of record by including every scrap of available information, moves with deliberation and seriousness, its proportioning apparently determined as much by the amount of material Meade unearthed in consulting some 200 people and 70 libraries as by its importance. In general, the narrative of the events of Parker's vivid, vigorous life is enhanced rather than encumbered by the myriad of specific details from a variety of sources. Typically, Meade's account of Parker's possible Communist Party affiliation is derived from FBI records (Parker knew the agents "meant trouble—because they were wearing hats"), newspaper accounts, *The Congressional Record*, an oral history interview with Dorothy Parker, and interviews and letters from Dalton Trumbo, S. J. Perelman and others. Parker's political activism rates some 30 closely-printed pages, quadruple Keats' emphasis.

As a literary biographer, however, Meade gives Parker's works disproportionately short shrift. Although she acknowledged that "Big Blonde" is "possibly the finest story [Parker] ever wrote" (why hedge?), Meade simply identifies the central character in this, "the most intensely autobiographical" of all Parker's fiction, by her many roles: "wholesale dress model, good sport, wife, ex-wife, swell drinker, animal lover, unsuccessful suicide, and big blonde." She devotes the rest of her half-page discussion to the story's enhancement of Parker's literary reputation. Because Meade's treatment of Parker's writing is so subdued, it is hard to determine why she was attracted to her subject. The biography's odd subtitle, *What Fresh Hell Is This?*, indicates Meade's dour disposition toward Parker—a disconcerting stance toward a comic writer. "Even ordinary occurrences," says Meade, "the doorbell, a ringing telephone—made her wonder 'What fresh hell is this?' " Meade certainly underplays some of Parker's best lines in her thoroughgoing treatment of the Rise (rapid) and Fall (prolonged) of Dorothy Parker—a cautionary tale.

Thus although both biographies are of value, we await the

work that combines Keats' sympathetic verve with Meade's factual infrastructure.

—Lynn Z. Bloom

PARKMAN, Francis, 1823–1893; American historian.

Doughty, Howard, *Francis Parkman*. New York, Macmillan, 1962.
Farnham, Charles H., *A Life of Francis Parkman*. Boston, Little Brown, and London, Macmillan, 1900.
Gale, Robert, *Francis Parkman*. New York, Twayne, 1973.
Wade, Mason, *Francis Parkman: Heroic Historian*. New York, Viking, 1942.

*

The history of North America, and particularly Canada and the northeastern part of the United States, was the driving concern of Francis Parkman. This Harvard educated historian and novelist is known and respected for the accuracy and detail of his work. Several biographies have been written over the years from a variety of perspectives based on his memoirs, letters, and journals. While these sources are voluminous, certain aspects of Parkman's life remain obscure. His journal entries reveal little about the private inner life of the man.

The earliest biography of Francis Parkman, by FARNHAM, contains all the naivete of a turn of the century biography written as an attempt at apotheosis. Part of its charm consists in its insights about the 19th century world in which Parkman lived. Farnham relies heavily on direct quotations from Parkman's letters, diaries, and other writings. While this practice lends a degree of authenticity to the biography, the large number of quotations becomes burdensome. Farnham devotes little space to critical observations about Parkman as an historian or novelist, but instead renders a highly romanticized account of Parkman as an heroic figure who rises out of his Puritan background to become an adventurous bearer of cool logic and rationalism to the chaos of the wilderness. At the same time, Farnham emphasizes the psychological problems facing Parkman, and depicts the pathos of his later years burdened by recurring illness that crippled his work. Also stressed here is Parkman's significant role in recording the French and Indian wars with simplicity, accuracy, and vividness. Farnham defends his subject's stoic, judgmental, patristic, and anti-democratic traits. Despite his apologetic romanticism, however, Farnham remains the classic early source on Parkman's life.

WADE, who has written perhaps the most balanced biography of Parkman, adds fresh materials from Parkman's journals. Wade argues that Parkman, one of America's greatest historians, has received too little attention, largely because he is associated with an older, more romantic concept of history and has written novels. Wade sketches the early formation of Parkman's interest in history, his aristocratic background as a Boston Brahmin, and his strong sense of "manhood" manifested in numerous adventures to Oregon and throughout the northeast. He portrays Parkman as a man of his time and gains strong support from

Parkman's diaries to trace his ambivalent encounters with nature and Native American populations. Wade also argues that Parkman became actively anti-Catholic in his later years, and notes how Parkman was a victim of doctors who suggested that any kind of hard work, including writing, would lead to madness. A section entitled the "dungeon of the spirit" illustrates the extensive physical suffering endured by Parkman, particularly in his later years. Wade argues that Parkman was the last of the Brahmins, that he conducted meticulous research, distrusted secondary sources (which was rare in his day), and was an outstanding writer. Wade considers Parkman, moreover, to be the greatest historian of Canada's early days. At the end of Wade's biography is a good list of Parkman's writings.

DOUGHTY's biography of Parkman is less romantic than the two earlier ones. This extensive work, though adding little new information to the previous biographies, contains several valuable appendices, including those on Parkman's religious beliefs and his views on slavery and abolition. Some well-written chapters review Parkman's extensive writings on the French and Indian wars. Doughty is neither an historian nor a professional scholar, however, and his biography fails to evaluate successfully Parkman's contributions to the field of history.

A more recent and concise biography of Francis Parkman is that of GALE. This volume is unique because one half is devoted to Parkman's life while the other is a thorough, systematic, biographically-oriented review of the man through his many writings. Less overwritten than the other biographies, Gales's volume is particularly valuable as an evaluation of Parkman's contributions to history. Gale is critical of the earlier biographies for their unbridled romanticism. He labels Parkman a "literary historian" whose extensive writings, comprising about 7000 pages, represent an important contribution to the field of literature. According to Gale, Parkman " . . . writes so much better than the average professional, academic historian that critics from the ranks of history teachers tend to dismiss him as outmoded." An excellent critical and annotated bibliography at the end of this volume is useful for students.

Overall the biographies of Francis Parkman are somewhat disappointing since they do not probe very deeply. None manages to grapple effectively with Parkman's implicit racism, his strong, almost neurotic compulsion for "masculinity," and his explicit anti-clericalism. Parkman's example challenges historians to continue to debate the problem of objectivity in historical studies. While Parkman was clearly a pioneer whose research was painstaking, he leaves a rather distorted view of European and Native American history in North America. None of the biographies addresses this issue successfully. A more current biography needs to be written.

—James J. Preston

PARKMAN, Charles Stewart, 1846–1891; Irish nationalist leader.

Foster, R. F., *Charles Stewart Parnell: The Man and His Family*. Atlantic Highlands, New Jersey, Humanities Press, and Hassocks, England, Harvester Press, 1976.

Haslip, Joan, *Parnell: A Biography*. London, Cobden-Sanderson, 1936; New York, F. A. Stokes, 1937.

Lyons, F. S. L., *Charles Stewart Parnell*. New York, Oxford University Press, and London, Collins, 1977.

Parnell, John H., *Charles Stewart Parnell: A Memoir*. New York, Holt, 1914; London, Constable, 1916.

*

The account written in 1914 by J. H. PARNELL, Parnell's brother, gives a friendly and heroic portrait of the subject. Its greatest strength comes from the inside knowledge of the Parnell family, which had a long and distinguished history in Irish politics even before the union with Britain. The work also provides an insider's view and knowledge of how Parnell thought during the critical periods in the development and implementation of the Irish Nationalist strategy. The appendices give a great deal of interesting information about the industries of the Parnells' home town, personal superstitions, family in America, and financial problems. The closeness of the author and the subject has made this an important source for later biographers when discussing Parnell's early life and travels and how they influenced his thoughts and actions. Parnell writes in a familiar tone, giving his work the feel of an intimate monologue, but often sacrificing objectivity.

The Parnell family has been as much a subject of interest with historians as has Charles Stewart Parnell's political career. FOSTER focuses almost exclusively on the Parnell family and the private life of Charles Stewart. On the occasions that it ventures into politics it deals primarily with local affairs, seldom venturing beyond the communities in which the Parnells lived. While it provides an excellent picture of the Parnell family, its usefulness to those studying Charles Stewart's political career is limited. This is a very well-documented work that offers good background data on the Parnell family, but readers are assumed to have prior knowledge of the events in Britain and Ireland during the 18th and 19th centuries.

HASLIP's work reads like a well-researched novel. While Halslip presents Parnell in a positive light, she does look seriously at his flaws (pointing out, for example, that Charles was the most "spoilt" of the Parnell children, a situation to which even his nurse contributed). The work deals well with Parnell's early life, especially when discussing his relationship within his family. The majority of the work covers his political career, but it is in dealing with the personal Parnell that Haslip, attempting to correct previous works, gives a feel for what kind of man he was. Haslip states that Parnell was "pure in his relationships with women," not a "sensuous libertine," as other writers had held. Haslip's work sets a good basis from which to begin serious research into Parnell's life and politics.

LYONS provides the best work that combines both the life and career of Parnell. It uses primary sources and earlier biographies well to develop Parnell's early life, but focuses on his political career and his efforts to gain Home Rule, even when discussing the family. This is shown by the discussion of the Parnell family's participation in the Grattan Parliament, and the fight to prevent its surrender to England. The strongest, and largest, part of the work covers the period from 1875 to Parnell's death. Lyons develops well the events that led to the Pigott Affair, describing how it made Parnell a folk hero in England and almost assured passage of Home Rule by the next Liberal government. In his handling of the O'Shea Affair, Lyons examines how these events led to the collapse of the efforts to pass the Home Rule bill and brought about Parnell's fall from Irish leadership.

Overall this is a very well-written and extremely well-documented work. Lyons' use of Parnell's letters, of private papers of those with whom Parnell had dealings, of the memoirs of political contemporaries, and of earlier biographies of Parnell makes this one of the foremost biographies of Parnell. The work's weakness is that it treats Parnell as a hero. While Lyons points out his subjects flaws, he dismisses them as making Parnell more human and memorable. Lyons underestimates the effect Parnell's personal and political errors had on Anglo-Irish relations both then and now.

—Donald E. Heidenreich, Jr.

PASCAL, Blaise, 1623–1662; French mathemetician, scientist, and religious philosopher.

Bishop, Morris, *Pascal, the Life of Genius.* New York, Reynal and Hitchcock, 1936; London, G. Bell, 1937.

Cailliet, Émile, *Pascal: The Emergence of Genius.* New York, Harper, 1961.

Mesnard, Jean, *Pascal, His Life and Works,* translated by G. S. Fraser. London, Harvill Press, and New York, Philosophical Library, 1952 (originally published by Boivin, Paris, 1951).

Mortimer, Ernest, *Blaise Pascal: The Life and Work of a Realist.* London, Methuen, and New York, Harper, 1959.

Steinmann, Jean, *Pascal,* translated by Martin Turnell. New York, Harcourt, and London, Burns and Oates, 1965 (based on revised and augmented French edition, Bruges, Desclée de Brouwer, 1962).

*

All biographers of Pascal are indebted to Gilberte Périer, who published a life of her brother in 1684. Manuscript copies of this work are said to have circulated in France some years earlier. The text, which is usefully included in Martin Turnell's translation of the *Pensées* (1962), is well worth reading despite some ambiguities and Mme Périer's general tendency to see her brother in the most favourable light possible.

Despite its age and a certain incompatibility between author and subject, BISHOP's remains one of the most detailed biographies of Pascal in English. While acknowledging the value of Mme Périer's testimony, Bishop properly warns against "the exaggerations that family pride intrudes unwittingly into an oft-told tale." Bishop is particularly informative on Pascal's achievements as a physicist and mathematician, discussing the work on scientific methodology, the vacuum, atmospheric pressure, the calculus of probabilities, the cycloid, etc., with a particularly clear account of Pascal's theories concerning the construction and operation of the calculating machine. On the other hand, Bishop is very critical of Pascal's religious development, describing him as being, at the age of 25, "a spiritual prig, con-

vinced of his own grace, but doubtful of the grace of all others." This judgment, a question of opinion rather than of fact, was no doubt encouraged by Bishop's determination to see Pascal as a thorough Jansenist, combined with Bishop's strong dislike of Jansenism with its "icy theology," "crabbed dourness," and "fundamentalism." In the end, this attitude leads Bishop to pass an unenthusiastic verdict on Pascal's intended *apologia,* though he admires the *Pensées* to the extent that they reveal "the emotional faith of a great Christian." Though this is not the only point at which Bishop comes close to self-contradiction, he nevertheless shows a fine detachment and penetration in his account of Pascal's so-called "worldly period," his mystical experience of 23 November 1654, his campaign against Jesuit laxism, etc.

Some of CAILLIET's rather old-fashioned and patronizing phrasing suggests an unreliable and romanticized biography. He uses such phrases as: "Let us now wend our way to the Pascal home" or "What a reverent spirit it was that molded the mind of this gifted child." However, despite such excruciating prose, Cailliet knows his subject well and was familiar with the latest research at the time he published his biography. He provides a reasonably detailed account of Pascal's life up to 1656 and the publication of the *Provincial Letters,* but after that date biography gives way increasingly to Cailliet's enthusiastic advocacy of Pascal's religious ideas. Cailliet appears to interpret Pascal's thought from a Protestant point of view, though he is concerned to emphasize that Pascal died asserting his loyalty to the Church of Rome and expressing a horror of heresy. Though he is weak on the subject of Pascal's achievements as a scientist and mathematician and does not adequately explain such events as the Saint-Ange affair, Cailliet is worth reading for his repeated description of Pascal as a "man of the Bible." He contrasts Pascal's Bible-based theology with the theology of scholasticism and provides details of Pascal's use of various biblical translations, including the Polyglot Bible of Vatable. Cailliet's repeated assertion that the key to understanding the Bible is to be found within it, and not elsewhere, points to the fundamentalist position which colours various aspects of his biography.

Unlike Bishop, MORTIMER is firmly of the view that Pascal was not a Jansenist. Like Cailliet, he is filled with enthusiasm for his subject, though without falling into hagiography. Mortimer's is an eminently readable biography, though readers should be on their guard against various inaccuracies of names, dates, etc. Also, Mortimer is inconsistent in his use of quotations from Pascal: some are translated, but many are left in the original French. Nevertheless, the treatment of Pascal's life and intellectual background is lively and fresh, with very precise summaries of the competing doctrines of grace current at the time. Mortimer provides thoughtful and detailed accounts of Pascal's intellectual relationships with Montaigne and Descartes. The strictly biographical material in this study occupies approximately the first three quarters of the book and is followed by useful accounts of Pascal's theory of knowledge and conception of man.

STEINMANN conveys, in lively prose, much information concerning the intellectual and social context of Pascal's life, covering such matters as the scientific controversy with the Jesuit Père Noël. Steinmann is keen to correct the picture of a gloomy, Jansenist Pascal, dismisses the idea—accepted by many biographers—of a romantic attachment between Pascal and Mlle de Roannez, and claims that studying Pascal taught him "to love the Bible and to love and respect Port Royal.'' On the *Provincial Letters* and *Pensées* Steinmann provides more lengthy and sophisticated analyses than the other biographers mentioned above.

MESNARD, too, offers much acute analysis of Pascal's writings. The greatest living authority on Pascal, Mesnard has written the most reliable biography of his subject, based as it is on particularly extensive documentation. As a result, his biography includes details that are largely ignored by other scholars, such as the early hostility of the Pascal family to the monastic life, Pascal's horror from a relatively early age of popular uprisings, and the influence in Rouen of Jean Guillebert. In addition, we have a very rational view of the Saint-Ange incident, a clearer picture than usual of Pascal's ''worldly period,'' and a most useful discussion of the date, nature, and consequences of his differences with Arnauld and Nicole toward the end of his life. Not least, Mesnard rejects the view of a largely neurotic Pascal and argues strongly for the integrated nature of his personality. He concludes: ''All critical efforts to divide Pascal from himself have ended in failure. We cannot radically oppose the scientist to the man of the world, or the scientist or the man of the world to the Christian; Pascal was always, in various fashions, a scientist, a man of the world, *and* a Christian.''

—John Cruickshank

PASTERNAK, Boris (Leonidovich), 1890–1960; Russian writer and translator.

Barnes, Christopher, *Boris Pasternak: A Literary Biography* (Volume I, 1890–1928). Cambridge, Cambridge University Press, 1989.

Fleishman, Lazar, *Boris Pasternak: The Poet and His Politics.* Cambridge, Massachusetts, Harvard University Press, 1990.

Hingley, Ronald, *Pasternak: A Biography.* London, Weidenfeld and Nicolson, and New York, Knopf, 1983.

Levi, Peter, *Boris Pasternak.* London, Hutchinson, 1990.

Mallac, Guy de, *Boris Pasternak: His Life and Art.* Norman, University of Oklahoma Press, 1981; London, Souvenir Press, 1983.

Pasternak, Evgenii, *Boris Pasternak: The Tragic Years 1930–60,* translated by Michael Duncan. London, Collins Harvill, 1990.

Payne, Robert, *The Three Worlds of Boris Pasternak.* London, R. Hale, and New York, Coward-McCann, 1961.

Ruge, Gerd, *Pasternak: A Pictorial Biography.* London, Thames and Hudson, and New York, McGraw-Hill, 1959.

*

Early biographies of Pasternak, those by Ruge and Payne, were produced in the immediate aftermath of the *Doctor Zhivago* and Nobel Prize affairs. They drew their information largely from Pasternak's two hypnotic but wayward and lacuna-ridden autobiographies, *Safe Conduct* (1931), and *Essay In Autobiography* (1957; also known as *I Remember*). They also used material from standard literary histories and the recent Western and Soviet press. (An interesting detailed study of the Zhivago-

Nobel episode is Robert Conquest's *Courage of Genius,* 1961.)

RUGE's study is a short, profusely illustrated, and popular account by a professional journalist who had met Pasternak in the 1950s. PAYNE's book is a full-length, belletristic and somewhat romanticised narrative of Pasternak's life. It contains some perceptive observations on his writings and devotes two whole chapters to discussion of a selection of poems and short stories, as well as several other translated quotations; as much as any subsequent commentator, Payne successfully conveys the ''feel'' of Pasternak's Russian to an English reader. However, owing to the shortage of secondary source material, lack of access to archives, and the impossibility of researching a disgraced writer in the USSR, Payne's account—especially of the 1930s and 40s—is somewhat threadbare. And his view of the ''late'' Pasternak of the 1950s is based mainly on what was ''visible''—press reportage, eyewitness accounts, etc.

MALLAC's later study is altogether more ambitious and thoroughly researched. Amply illustrated, partly with family photographs of various periods, and with an extensive bibliography, Mallac's book also contains an extended discussion of Pasternak's philosophical and aesthetic theory. Solemnly workmanlike as a biographical account, it is nevertheless seriously faulted in some respects and quickly became obsolete. Mallac had made little effort to consult the by then available Soviet archival and eyewitness sources, and he went into print too early to use the highly revealing correspondence with Olga Freidenberg, published in 1981, the memoirs of Aleksandr Pasternak (Boris' brother), and the researches of Lazar Fleishman. His account also contains some poorly assimilated background material and draws on a ''continental'' frame of scholarly reference that sometimes confuses rather than clarifies. Drawing heavily still on Pasternak's eccentric autobiographies and accepting too readily his own self-assessments. Mallac is short on information concerning many features of Pasternak's personal and literary life, especially in his ''middle period,'' and his acceptance of Pasternak's inflated estimation of *Doctor Zhivago*'s significance led to an unbalanced appointment and ''end-loading'' of page space.

HINGLEY's life of Pasternak followed on an earlier quadripartite biographic and literary study of Pasternak, Mandelstam, Tsvetaeva and Akhmatova (*Nightingale Fever*, 1981). It is vigorously written, with humour and with a refreshing lack of Mallacian hagiographic reverence: ''[Pasternak] was, let the fact be faced, a man who liked to muddle things—a process to which he brought the creative flair of genius.'' And à propos of Tsvetaeva's enthusiasm at Pasternak's apparent ''inarticulacy of the truly great'': ''It is tempting to argue that there were occasions on which he projected the inarticulacy of the truly inarticulate''! Although, like Mallac, Hingley's book appeared too early to make use of several valuable source materials published in the USSR and the West in the 1980s, it has none of the other work's faults; it offers a coherent portrait of Pasternak and still remains the best shorter introduction to his life and work.

Writing for the Pasternak centenary in 1990, LEVI offers the interesting personal view of an Oxford University professor of poetry. Though presented as a biography, however, his book is more of an inspired, and often brashly subjective, extended essay on Pasternak's life and work. Levi communicates the infectious enthusiasm of a true *amateur*, and he has some interesting and original views about Pasternak's masterpieces as well as some of his lesser-known works. As a source of factual information on Pasternak, though, the book is unreliable. It reveals the author's patchy knowledge of Russian language and literary history; it contains several internal inconsistencies, garbles names, and contributes new myths and errors where it should have clarified.

FLEISHMAN is the most erudite of modern Pasternak scholars. His biography follows three earlier books written in Russian (*Stat'i o Pasternake*, 1977; *Boris Pasternak v dvadtsatye gody*, 1981; *Boris Pasternak v tridtsatye gody*, 1984). It deals with the writer, concentrating on his ties with his epoch, literary, social, and political milieu, rather than on his works. (For anyone interested specifically in the works and the artistic evolution of Pasternak, the best monograph remains Henry Gifford, *Pasternak: A Critical Study*, 1977.) Fleishman's emphasis on Pasternak as a writer deeply implicated with the issues of his times contrasts with earlier "ivory tower" views of him prevalent in the USSR and the West, which coloured the accounts by Mallac, Hingley, and others, and which were partly encouraged by Pasternak's lifelong air of distraction, by the selectivity and reticence of his autobiographies, and by his artistic silences during the worst years of Stalinism. Fleishman gives a scrupulously documented, fresh account, concentrating, however, on Pasternak's specifically artistic activities, allegiances, tastes, and opinions. His private and family life tend to be aired cursorily and insofar as they impinge on his literary existence.

Fleishman's book and the two works by Barnes and Evgenii Pasternak are the most authoritative and detailed studies of Pasternak's life to date, and they presuppose a more than casual interest and curiosity on the part of the reader. The latter two books are, respectively, parts one and two of quite separate works, although in view of the periods they embrace they can be read in sequence. BARNES distributes attention between Pasternak in private, the public author, and cultural and historical background. There is descriptive treatment of Pasternak's works as well as of their critical reception, with complete translated poems used as chapter-heads. The author had access to family and other archive materials both in Moscow and abroad, and new details are added, in particular to our picture of Pasternak's early unpublished writings, his doings during the revolution, his amorous involvements, and family life during the 1920s. The book breaks off with deliberate inconclusiveness in 1928; volume two has yet to appear.

EVGENII PASTERNAK's book is in fact only the second, translated, part of a full-length biographical study published in Russian: *Boris Pasternak. Materialy dlya biografii* (Moscow, 1990). As the elder son of his subject, the author has the unique knowledge and insight of an eyewitness, and also possesses a fine understanding of even the most recondite literary texts plus a fingertip knowledge of family archive materials. His narrative makes ample use of quotation, and the verse extracts have been well rendered into English by the poet Craig Raine and the author's cousin, Ann Pasternak Slater. After the surmise and conjecture that supported earlier accounts of these darker years of Pasternak's life, this inside view is of special value. As the translator Michael Duncan comments, the author "has let his father be his own witness and has kept his own authorial presence in the background." Indeed, the sobriety of this account and its avoidance of partisanship, special pleading, or over-dramatisation are extraordinary and make even the title of this

volume seem sensational: with characteristic modesty Evgenii Pasternak subheads his own Russian text only as "Materials for—or towards—a Biography."

—Christopher J. Barnes

PASTEUR, Louis, 1882–1895; French chemist and microbiologist.

Compton, Piers, *The Genius of Louis Pasteur*. New York, Macmillan, 1932; London, A. Ouseley, [n.d.].

Cuny, Hilaire, *Louis Pasteur: The Man and His Theories*, translated by Patrick Evans. New York, P. S. Eriksson, 1963; London, Souvenir Press, 1965.

Dolan, Edward F., *Pasteur and the Invisible Giants*. New York, Dodd Mead, 1958.

Dubos, René, *Louis Pasteur: Freelance of Science*. Boston, Little Brown, 1950; London, Gollancz, 1951.

Dubos, René, *Pasteur and Modern Science*. New York, Anchor Books, 1960; London, Heinemann, 1961.

Duclaux, Émile, *Pasteur: The History of a Mind*, translated by Erwin F. Smith and Florence Hedges. Philadelphia, W.B. Saunders, 1920 (originally published by Charaire, Sceaux, 1896).

Holmes, S. J., *Louis Pasteur*. New York, Harcourt, and London, Chapman and Hall, 1924.

Nicolle, Jacques, *Louis Pasteur: The Story of His Major Discoveries*. New York, Basic Books, 1961; as *Louis Pasteur: A Master of Scientific Enquiry*, London, Hutchinson, 1961 (originally published by La Colombe, Paris, 1953).

Paget, Stephen, *Pasteur and After Pasteur*. London, A. and C. Black, 1914.

Vallery-Radot, René, *The Life of Pasteur*, translated by Mrs. R. L. Devonshire. New York, Doubleday, and London, Constable, 1919.

*

The life of Louis Pasteur has been examined in minute detail by several biographers. Pasteur's family and disciples preserved a wealth of material, some of which has only recently become available to historians. Only a few biographers have been adequate to the task of understanding Pasteur's work and putting his life into its proper context. Many biographies are essentially reworkings of a few standard works simplified for a general audience or are reflections of partisan viewpoints. The biographies by Dubos, Duclaux, and Vallery-Radot are the most valuable.

DUBOS (1950), the eminent microbiologist and experimental pathologist, offers a lucid and gracefully written assessment of Pasteur's life and work. Dubos is uniquely qualified to assess the work of Pasteur; in addition to his scientific work he is the author of many thoughtful books on science and the human condition. This is an excellent biography for those who want to gain an appreciation of scientific method and theory from a master of science. Moreover, Dubos' biography dispels many of the myths that have grown up around Pasteur's legacy and presents a well-reasoned view of Pasteur as an ecologist struggling to formulate a scientific theory of global eco-systems, in contrast to the simplistic version of "man versus microbe" found in popular accounts of the germ theory of disease. Dubos is one of the only biographers to help us understand not only what Pasteur did, but what he dreamed of doing and could not.

The introductory chapter, "The Complexities of Genius," is an especially insightful examination of the general question of scientific genius and the specifics of Pasteur's ideas and methodology. While Dubos often seems to defer to Duclaux's analysis of Pasteur's thoughts and methods (see below), he is more objective in his presentation of the larger context of late 19th-century science.

Dubos' second biography of Pasteur, *Pasteur and Modern Science* (1960), is a masterpiece of condensation. This book is brief, informative, and understandable without being condescending as it surveys Pasteur's family background, education, professional advancement, and major concepts and discoveries.

Although even the translators of DUCLAUX's biography admit that Duclaux's style loses much in English, the obvious admiration and devotion lavished on this translation render it still graceful, lucid, and fascinating. This brilliant intellectual biography was written by one of Pasteur's closest associates. After Pasteur died, Duclaux succeeded his mentor as director of the Pasteur Institute. His remarkable book provides insights into Pasteur's ideas and methods unavailable in any other source. Despite the sympathy and intellectual affinities shared by Duclaux and Pasteur, the disciple was independent enough to assess his mentor's strengths and weaknesses with a fair degree of objectivity.

Duclaux was not concerned with the chronology of external events in Pasteur's life, details of which could be assembled by any biographer, but with the origin and development of Pasteur's scientific discoveries. The book includes an annotated list of persons mentioned in the text. Despite the fact that Duclaux was also uniquely qualified to discuss Pasteur's personality traits, he deliberately limited the scope of his analysis to Pasteur's scientific ideas and their significance. Scholars who have studied Pasteur's life very closely think that Duclaux probably made the right decision. Pasteur's scientific ideas were exciting for their originality and boldness, but his beliefs and behavior in social, religious, familial, and political matters were generally conservative and conformist.

As Sir William Osler notes in the introduction, VALLERY-RADOT's *Life of Pasteur* is indeed a "well-told story" of both the life and the work of Louis Pasteur. This extraordinarily detailed text has been the major source for a long line of derivative biographies which, in turn, accept Pasteur as "the most perfect man who has ever entered the Kingdom of Science."

Pasteur's devoted son-in-law, Vallery-Radot presents a remarkably complete record of the life and work of the man to whom he devoted much of his own life. In creating this portrait of Pasteur, Vallery-Radot quotes extensively from Pasteur's notebooks, lectures, and correspondence, including many unpublished documents. Some modern critics charge that Vallery-Radot's work borders on hagiography and that it created the myth of Pasteur as isolated genius and embattled hero. Indeed, out of devotion and love, Vallery-Radot abandoned objectivity and created a romantic hero surrounded by hostile, ignorant, even vicious opponents.

Nevertheless, this indispensable biography remains the fullest account of the life and work of Pasteur. Vallery-Radot provides a wealth of detail concerning Pasteur's personal and professional life, the evolution of his ideas, and his research and its reception by admirers and critics. By devoting much of the book to quotations from Pasteur's letters and other documents, Vallery-Radot provides a sense of intimacy between subject and reader. On the other hand, the book lacks scholarly apparatus, is sometimes obscure concerning dates, and is weak on historical background.

Among the second tier of Pasteur biographies, CUNY's work is particularly valuable. While the first section contains conventional biographical data, Part Two provides a chonrological outline of Pasteur's life, a glossary, a short bibliography, and selected examples of Pasteur's writings, including informal notes and reflections, correspondence, and formal scientific papers.

COMPTON's biography lacks all forms of scholarly apparatus, from footnotes to index. When Compton dubs one of the keenest minds of the 19th century "the scientist of the heart," the reader can expect an excess of sentimentality embedded in a predictably plodding journey through ancestors, early years, education, fermentation, spontaneous generation, hydrophobia, and death.

Several biographies appear to be written for young adults, although the authors fail to specify the intended audience. For example, DOLAN's book is written in the simplified, conversational "you-are-there" style that is generally adopted in biographies for young readers. Dolan is the author of similar biographies of Edward Jenner and Alexander von Humboldt. However, young adults interested in biographies of scientists are probably sophisticated enough to appreciate Dubos' brief *Pasteur and Modern Science*.

HOLMES, a professor of zoology at the University of California, does say that his brief biography of Pasteur is written for students and general readers who are not equipped to study more comprehensive biographies. The text is heavily based on the works of Vallery-Radot and Duclaux. Written with obvious admiration, and no claims for originality, it provides a simple, straightforward, old-fashioned survey of Pasteur's work and a similar view of his personality.

PAGET's book was written during World War I and the author makes much of the fact that the United States and France were fighting against common enemies. Thus, the book was conceived as an appropriate tribute to Pasteur and the principles of international scientific cooperation. Although Paget's book provides only a brief outline of the life of Pasteur, it is a valuable guide to the rapid diffusion of his ideas and the progress made in medical microbiology between the death of Pasteur and World War I.

NICOLLE's book is part of the "Science and Discovery Series" written by scientists and expert interpreters of science to allow students and general readers access to the world of scientific research. Nicolle's very readable account focuses on ten of Pasteur's major studies: rabies, anthrax, chicken cholera, silkworm diseases, diseases of wine, fermentation, the brewing of beer, the formation of vinegar, the spontaneous generation debate, and stereochemistry. Nicolle's father and uncle were Pasteur's associates at the Pasteur Institute, where the author lived for some time. While Nicolle deals only briefly with Pasteur's life, he provides an informative discussion of Pasteur's methods of investigation and patterns of thought.

Readers interested in the results of more recent scholarship on Pasteur and in a preview of critical biographies yet to be written should consult Gerald L. Geison's entry on Louis Pasteur in the *Dictionary of Scientific Biography* (New York, Scribner, vol. X [1974] pages 350–416). *World's Debt to Pasteur: Proceedings of a Centennial Symposium Commemorating the First Rabies Vaccination*, edited by Hilary Kaprowski and Stanley Plotkin (New York, A. R. Liss, 1985), includes several informative biographical essays: Gerald Geison, "Pasteur: A Sketch in Bold Strokes"; Maya Starr, "Pasteur as a Painter"; and Cyril Ponnamperuma, "Louis Pasteur and the Origin of Life." Starr also provides a list of museums where Pasteur's paintings can still be seen. Bruno Latour's intriguing book, *The Pasteurization of France* (translated by Alan Sheridan and John Law, 1988) shows how the complex interactions between Pasteur's work and other forces led to action against disease. A comparative appreciation of Pasteur by the great zoologist I. I. Mechnikov (*The Founders of Modern Medicine: Pasteur, Koch, Lister*, 1939) is also well worth reading. *The Pasteur Fermentation Centennial 1857–1957* (New York, 1958) includes valuable biographical essays by Pasteur's grandson, L. Pasteur Vallery-Radot ("Pasteur as I Remember Him") and René Dubos ("Pasteur in His Time").

There are also many brief accounts of the life and work of Louis Pasteur written specifically for use in elementary school, including: Rae Bains, *Louis Pasteur* (1985); Spencer Johnson, *The Value of Believing in Yourself: The Story of Louis Pasteur* (1976); and Francene Sabin, *Louis Pasteur: Young Scientist* (1983).

—Lois N. Magner

PATRICK, Saint, *ca.* 389–461; apostle of Ireland.

Bieler, Ludwig, *The Life and Legend of St. Patrick: Problems of Modern Scholarship*. Dublin, Clonmore and Reynolds, and London, Burns Oates, 1949.

Bury, John B., *The Life of St. Patrick and His Place in History*. London and New York, Macmillan, 1905.

Hanson, Richard P. C., *Saint Patrick: His Origins and Career*. Oxford, Clarendon Press, and New York, Oxford University Press, 1968.

Hanson, Richard P. C., *Life and Writings of the Historical St. Patrick*. New York, Seabury Press, 1983.

MacNeill, Eoin, *St. Patrick, Apostle of Ireland*. London and New York, Sheed and Ward, 1934; revisied edition, edited by John Ryan, Dublin, Clonmore and Reynolds, 1964.

O'Rahilly, Thomas Francis, *The Two Patricks: A Lecture on the History of Christianity in Fifth-Century Ireland*. Dublin, Dublin Institute for Advanced Studies, 1942.

Ryan, John, editor, *Saint Patrick*. Dublin, Radio Eireann/Stationary Office, 1958.

Stokes, Whitley, editor and translator, *The Tripartite Life of Patrick with Other Documents Relative to That Saint* (2 vols.). London, HMSO/Eyre and Spottiswoode, 1887.

Thompson, E. A., *Who Was St. Patrick?* Woodbridge, Boydell Press, 1985; New York, St. Martin's, 1986.

Todd, James H., *St Patrick, Apostle of Ireland: A Memoir of His Life and Mission*. Dublin, Hodges Smith, 1864.

*

The Venerable Bede, writing in 731 the earliest "History of the English Church and People," gives no hint of the life or the mission of Patrick. Rather he makes specific that of Palladius, purportedly sent by Pope Celestine I to serve as first bishop of the Scotti (by which the Irish were then known), and dated by the eighth year of the Roman emperor, Theodosius II (431).

The issue of "the two Patricks," or the uncertainty relative to Patrick's chronology, arose already, according to Todd (see below), with annotations upon the "Memoir of Patrick" by Tirechan, equally preserved in the *Book of Armagh* (whose copy was made by Ferdomnach the scribe in 807; see *The Patrician Texts in the Book of Armagh*, edited, with introduction, translation, and commentary, by Ludwig Bieler, Dublin, 1979). Bury (see below) understood the "Memoir" to constitute "the earliest extant document" for the "Life of Patrick" and dated it after 657, the year of the death of bishop Ultan of Ardbraccan in Meath, of whom Tirechan was a "disciple."

In the later seventh century another "Life of Patrick" had been written by Muirchu Maccu Machteni, also partially preserved in the *Book of Armagh*, which began that process of conflation, confusion, and conviction by which hagiography both reveals and blocks what ever little can be known of an essential personality who becomes the center of meaning for a people's subsequent history. Muirchu had himself complained of finding difficult his way among "the conflict of opinion and the very many conjectures of very many persons" (see *St. Patrick: His Writings and Muirchu's Life*, edited and translated by Allan B. E. Hood, with an introductory note by John Morris, 1978).

The so-called "Tripartite Life" of the later ninth century, a lengthy Irish-language source consisting of three homilies on Patrick, first printed by STOKES (1887), in which, as Hanson (see below) has commented, "folklore and pious imagination have run riot," compounds the unknown by having Patrick visit Rome when Celestine was bishop (422-432), study with Germanus (*ca.* 375–437/446) first at Rome and then at Auxerre (bishop from 418), and live as a monk at Tours under Martin (*ca.* 316–397). Its multiplicity of Patricks remains "a source of much embarassment," as Todd noted.

Autobiographically, there survive two short works: the *epistola*, a "letter to the soldiers of Coroticus" which demands from a petty Christian British chieftain the return of kidnapped converts; and the *confessio*, the defence of Patrick's mission against critics within the same "British" church. John Morris (*St. Patrick: His Writings and Muirchu's Life*) noted these to be "the only documents that have survived from the *dicta*, three brief "utterances" ascribed to Patrick.

All these have long been known, and editions with commentary, or discussions constituting "biographies" with varying quantities of edited materials included, came from the hands of TODD, Stokes, and Bury. While critically reviewing the evidences with massive works of erudition, each tried to salvage from post-Patrick "lives" enough to identify "his place in history." The recent editions have settled for the "genuine" Patrick of *epitola* and *confessio* (see R. P. C. Hanson and Cécile Blanc, *Saint Patrick: Confession et Lettre à Coroticus*, Paris, 1978); or with *dicta* and the *vita* by Muirchu (see Hood and Morris, 1978); or separately with the Patrician texts in the *Book of Armagh* (see Bieler, 1979).

BURY's stature as an historian of the later Roman empires, both east and west, meant that his "epoch-making work," with which Thompson (see below), to the neglect of Todd, thought "modern study of Patrick began," was assumed to have solved the basic issues relating to Patrick's life and mission. As O'Rahilly (see below) was to note, the volume "set the fashion for a whole generation." Its appendices exceed its narrative, providing bibliographic notes on sources, annotated notes on chapters, and 21 excursuses. The larger setting of any discussion of "Patrick" becomes the problematic of Britain and the British Church in the fifth century.

By contrast, a simple kind of "Life of St. Patrick" without any academic paraphernalia, written for the faithful, and devoted to *Patricius peccator* ("Patrick the sinner"—the opening words of both *epitola* and *confessio*), comes from MACNEILL, writing within "the traditional view" as defined by RYAN. Another Irishman, O Croinin, in praising Thompson, subjects this kind of effort to severe criticism by noting that the "effusions on the subject of St. Patrick (By John Ryan and his school of Irish Catholic apologists) represent a dark chapter in modern Irish historiography." Yet Ryan had intended to bring MacNeill up-to-date in 1964, and, equally sympathetic, BIELER tried to survey "Patrician scholarship past and present," whose origins he knew to lie "in the tense atmosphere of Reformation and Counter-Reformation" over which Patrick-study, like Ireland itself, also divides. D. A. Binchy, in "Patrick and His Biographers: Ancient and Modern" (*Studia Hibernica*, edited by G. MacNiocaill, 1962), sought to narrate all the chapters in Irish historiography, with a critique of all Patrick's biographers.

O'RAHILLY's slim volume attempted to cut through to the basics, beginning from the names as they would have existed in the fifth century, and to show in development of Todd that, as written in the annotations to Tirechan, *Patricius Palladius* must be distinguished from *Patricius secundus*. The former, commonly Palladius, had served out his mission from the year 431 to his death in either 457 or 461; while the latter, by whom one commonly means St. Patrick, arriving not earlier than the death of the former, served in an alternate fashion until his death in 491/2. The former's mission was recalled later in the memory of the Irish people, but not his name, so that the two were conflated in spite of the chronological difficulties of so long an interim and a "Moses-like" imitated age of 120 years.

Careful attention to precise linguistic detail, to the exact wording of text, and to the annals of the Irish kings, makes the set of notes as extensive as O'Rahilly's original lecture so that he forms a watershed in Patrick studies. Yet the works coming after, like those written before, continue to divide over, while attempting to refine further, the interpretation of the slim body of data. Binchy also preferred the later years.

HANSON (1968), have reassessed the sources, makes Patrick's date the climaxing chapter before his summary conclusion. He settles for the earlier years, *ca.* 390–460. For Hanson, "the only valid source of information about Patrick is the works of Patrick himself." The volume's appendices, which place in parallel columns the Irish annals and discuss the "high king,"

add valuable supplements. In his English translation with running explanatory commentary, and brief statements about historical background, Patrick's career, and "character and mind," Hanson's 1983 *Life and Writings* reiterated his conclusion and preference for the earier dates.

Conclusions, however, oscillate with cycles of text republication. The volumes by Hanson and Blanc or Morris and Hood take their place beside the earlier achievements. Yet THOMPSON, working from Hanson's edition, refused to arrive at any absolute dates. Like his title, Thompson's book more frequently asks questions than provides answers. The "problem of Patrick" is not concluded.

—Clyde Curry Smith

PATTON, George (Smith, Jr.), 1885–1945; American general.

Anders, Curt, *Warrior: The Story of General George S. Patton.* New York, Putnam, 1967.

Ayer, Fred, *Before the Colors Fade: Portrait of a Soldier.* Boston, Houghton Mifflin, 1964; London, Cassell, 1965.

Blumenson, Martin, *Patton, The Man Behind The Legend.* New York, Morrow, 1985.

Essame, H., *Patton: A Study in Command.* New York, Scribner, 1974; as *Patton, The Commander*, London, Batsford, 1974.

Farago, Ladislos, *Patton: Ordeal and Triumph.* New York, I. Obolensky, 1963.

*

Farago's massive biography of 885 pages replaced a number of earlier and superficial biographies written by friends and military subordinates of Patton. For those students interested, they were: William Bancroft Mellor, *Patton: Fighting Man*, 1946; Colonel Brenton Greene Wallace, *Patton and His Third Army*, 1946; James Wellord, *General George S. Patton, Jr.*, 1946; Alden Hatch, *George Patton: General in Spurs*, 1950; Harry H. Semmes, *Portrait of Patton*, 1955; Milton F. Perry and Barbara W. Parker, *Patton and His Pistols*, 1957; and Jack Pearl, *Blood and Guts Patton*, 1961. Well intentioned as these early works were, they lacked objectivity and classified sources, and they tend to create a legendary image of Patton as a flamboyant leader of superhuman proportions.

FARAGO, a professional historian, provides a needed corrective to their deficiencies. He spent 12 years of research to write a comprehensive, factual, and objective biography, which overall presents a favorable picture of Patton but does not gloss over his flaws. The strength of Farago's biography lies in its use of basic source material rather than personal recollection. He corrected many of the myths surrounding Patton by the expert use of heretofore unavailable sources as the *Wehrmacht Kriegelagebuch* (German High Command War Diary), memoirs of both German and American generals, Patton's papers, declassified documents from the War Department, and Pentagon and National Archives. His coverage of Patton's childhood, education, military career, and tactical concepts are related in a smooth-flowing prose accompanied by careful analysis and expert insights. Students wishing to know about any phase of Patton's life and career will find it covered in detail. His character, military prowess, controversial opinions, and relationship with other Allied generals are all discussed. Ample quotes from Patton's writings, speeches, orders, and informal statements reveal Patton's personality as both audacious and humble, a theme that Farago stresses. Having stood the test of time, Farago's biography is the magnum opus of Patton's biographers and remains the definitive work. Students will find it both interesting and challenging. It is the biography that the movie *Patton* is based on; George C. Scott's Oscar-winning performance is consequently a very accurate portrayal.

AYER's biography has considerable merit, but in a limited way. As a nephew of Patton, Ayer was in a unique position to write a knowledgeable firsthand account of the personal side of Patton's life. Obviously, as a relative, he saw his uncle as a heroic figure. This very subjectivity, however, allows him to reveal many intimate facts relating to Patton's boyhood, education, family life, and pre-World War II military career. Many family stories, anecdotes, and private incidents are revealed that were not available to other biographers. Particularly note-worthy is the supportive and protective role played by Patton's wife, Beatrice (Ayer) Patton, in nurturing the general's career. This highly personalized portrait of Patton is further enhanced by many photographs from Ayer's private collection. Ayer does correct some myths about Patton, noting, for instance, that he carried ivory-handled pistols, not pearl-handled as other biographers state (even Farago makes this mistake). Ayer provides a good description of Patton's frustrations in the last days of his life, since he served as an aide to Patton during this period. He also gives an account of the fatal injury Patton received in the collision of his jeep with a truck. Patton's World War II exploits, however, are treated in a rather cursory manner, and the conflicts with Eisenhower are presented solely from Patton's point of view. Moreover, the book lacks any footnotes, sources, or bibliography, and is written in an amateurish style that is over-laudatory of Patton. But it has an "inside story" quality that is authentic. The Foreword by General Bradley presents an interesting capsule characterization of Patton that merits attention.

ESSAME, a professional historian specializing in military affairs and author of five books on World War II and one on World War I, focuses primarily on the leadership qualities of Patton. In Essame's judgment, based on his intense interpretive analysis, Patton ranks with the great military chieftans of the world, such as Napoleon, Stonewall Jackson, Hannibal, and Frederick the Great. The maverick quality of Patton's character makes for an interesting discussion within the context of his audacious attack philosophy of military command. A particularly notable portion of Essame's biography contains very favorable appraisals of Patton's skill as an army commander by such German generals as Guderian, Manstein, and Rommel, who all fought against him. By contrast, mixed appraisals are presented by generals Bradley, Eisenhower, and Montgomery, who fought with him. A detailed analysis of this whole matter of inter-Allied stress is presented at length. Despite Patton's reputation as a disciplinarian and the "Blood and Guts" accolade, Essame presents new evidence that Patton was also very considerate of his troops' health and well-being. The major value of Essame's biography remains the excellent explanation and analysis of Pat-

ton's military techniques. Students will find it very absorbing reading.

ANDERS, one of the editors of the *Army Times*, bases his biography on the thesis that Patton was a "complex man," who was daring in combat but a careful student of military history. Though it presents a factually correct overview of Patton's life and career, the work lacks any real scholarly analysis. It is a superficially written, popularized version suitable for the beginning student.

BLUMENSON, a professional historian with great expertise on World War II (having written 11 books about it) and editor of *The Patton Papers* (2 vols.), offers a concise but comprehensive biography of Patton. Blumenson uses data from the Patton papers to "revise and clarify" previous biographies without attempting to supplant them. He attempts to achieve this goal by generous quotes from the Patton papers, but he is not entirely successful. His greatest weakness is lack of footnotes; hence the reader does not know from what documents he is making the citation. This tends to weaken his methodological goals by only amplifying Patton's views without further clarification or revision. The real value of Blumenson is that he can place Patton's role in World War II in proper perspective because of his general knowledge of the big picture. Blumenson, like Ayer, served on Patton's staff during the last months of his life, and he too includes some personal recollections. He is particularly edifying concerning Patton's relations with the Russians. Though written 21 years later, Blumenson's book does not displace Farago's as the standard biography, but remains the second best life of Patton.

—Frederick H. Schapsmeier

PAUL, Saint [*born* Saul of Tarsus], d. *ca.* 65 A.D.; apostle of the Gentiles.

Bornkamm, Günther, *Paul,* translated by D. M. G. Stalker. New York, Harper, and London, Hodder and Stoughton, 1971 (originally published as *Paulus,* Stuttgart, W. Kohlhammer, 1969).

Conybeare, William John and John Saul Howson, *The Life and Epistles of St. Paul* (2 vols.). London, Longman, and New York, Scribner, 1854.

Deissmann, (Gustav) Adolf, *Paul: A Study in Social and Religious History,* translated by William E. Wilson. London, Hodder and Stoughton, 1912; revised and enlarged edition, London, Hodder and Stoughton, 1926; New York, Harper, 1927 (originally published as *Paulus, eine kultur und religiongeschichtliche Skizze,* Tübingen, Mohr, 1911).

Glover, Terrot R., *Paul of Tarsus.* London, SCM Press, and New York, G. H. Doran, 1925.

Goodspeed, Edgar Johnson, *The Meaning of Ephesians.* Chicago, University of Chicago Press, 1933.

Goodspeed, Edgar Johnson, *Paul: A Biography Drawn from Evidence in the Apostle's Writing.* Nashville, Tennessee, Abingdon Press, 1947.

Hock, Ronald F., *The Social Context of Paul's Ministry: Tent-Making and Apostleship*. Philadelphia, Fortress Press, 1980.

Jewett, Robert, *A Chronology of Paul's Life*. Philadelphia, Fortress Press, and London, SCM Press, 1979.

Johnson, Sherman, *Paul the Apostle and His Cities*. Wilmington, Delaware, M. Clazier, 1987.

Knox, Wilfred L., *St. Paul*. London, P. Davies, and New York, T. Nelson, 1932.

Lüdemann, Gerd, *Paul, Apostle to the Gentiles: Studies in Chronology*, translated by Stanley Jones. Philadelphia, Fortress Press, and London, SCM Press, 1984 (originally published as *Paulus der Heidenapostel I: Studien zur Chronologie*, Göttingen, Habilitationsschrift, 1977).

MacDonald, Dennis R., *The Legend and the Apostle: The Battle for Paul in Story and Canon*. Philadelphia, Westminster Press, 1983.

Morton, Henry C. V., *In the Steps of St. Paul*. New York, Dodd Mead, and London, Rich and Cowan, 1936.

Nock, Arthur Darby, *St. Paul*. New York, Harper, 1937; London, T. Butterworth, 1938.

Ogg, George, *The Chronology of the Life of Paul*. London, Epworth, 1968.

Pagels, Elaine Hiesey, *The Gnostic Paul: Gnostic Exegesis of the Pauline Letters*. Philadelphia, Fortress Press, 1975.

Pollock, J. C., *The Apostle: A Life of Paul*. New York, Doubleday, and London, Hodder and Stoughton, 1969.

Ramsay, Sir William M., *St. Paul the Traveller and the Roman Citizen*. New York, Putnam, 1879; London, Hodder and Stoughton, 1895.

Ramsay, Sir William M., *The Cities of St. Paul: Their Influence on His Life and Thought*. London, Hodder and Stoughton, 1907; New York, A. C. Armstrong, 1908.

Schweitzer, Albert, *Paul and His Interpreters: a Critical History*, translated by William Montgomery. London, A. and C. Black, and New York, Macmillan, 1912 (originally published as *Geschichte der Paulinischen Forschung*, Tübingen, Mohr, 1911).

Schweitzer, Albert, *The Mysticism of Paul the Apostle*, translated by William Montgomery. London, A. and C. Black, and New York, Holt, 1931 (originally published as *Die Mystik des apostels Paulus*, Tübingen, Mohr, 1930).

Stendhal, Krister, *Paul among Jews and Gentiles*. Philadelphia, Fortress Press, 1976; London, SCM Press, 1977.

Tabor, James D., *Things Unutterable: Paul's Ascent to Paradise in Its Greco-Roman, Judaic, and Early Christian Contexts*. Lanham, Maryland, University Press of America, 1986.

*

Most figures of the New Testament remain ambiguously enigmatic. While this is not less so for "the Apostle" Paul, he is the one personality of whom a competent Hellenistic historian set out a significant degree of biographical information. Luke, in the second volume of his accounts of earliest Christianity, which came to be called "The Acts of the Apostles," provides the initial biographical information, derived from a source close to Paul as illustrated by its "we" passages (16: 10–17; 20: 5– 21: 26; 27: 1– 28).

Biographically the collection of epistles written by Paul are basic; from within also come scattered autobiographical hints—

often, to be sure, in the form of defensive responses to his critics. For Paul a very early word description of his physiognomy survives, in *The Acts of Paul and Thecla* (1: 7).

Much of the discussion of Paul falls into a commentary format upon the various epistles included within the New Testament. From the ancient church these include works by Origen, Theodore of Mopsuestia, John Chrysostom, Jerome, and Ambrosiaster. Such literature has assumed prodigious proportions since the application of the critical method to the New Testament by the French Oratorian priest Richard Simon (1638–1712).

Much less attention has been paid to corresponding materials of the Apocrypha to the New Testament—the variety of "Acts" (including those of Peter), other "Epistles" (including another correspondence with the Corinthian church, and the ones between "Paul and Seneca"), and, as MacDonald (see below) calls it, an "Apocalypse of Paul." Ancient commentators on the Pauline epistles from outside the developing Tradition have received attention from Pagels (see below).

Considering the apparent significance of Pauline epistles for what later became the canon of the New Testament, and of his major role in the establishment of Hellenistic churches, remarkably little is actually known of Paul's early life. A similar statement, though based on a smaller literary corpus, has to be said about Peter. The two must be considered together, for what is known begins to tie them to each other and to Rome, so that the Tradition speaks of "Paul and Peter" or "Peter and Paul." The "Second Epistle of Peter" first records the Pauline epistolary collection (3: 15–16).

A basic collection of information is included in Eusebius of Caesarea (*ca.* 260–340). The translator G. A. Williamson made the observation: "Believing that Paul died before Peter, Eusebius puts Paul first whenever he has their deaths in mind. But we find Peter put first in quotations from Dionysius (of Corinth) and Irenaeus (of Lyons), who are referring to his arrival in Rome, which they believed to be prior to Paul's, as did Eusebius" (*Eusebius: The History of the Church from Christ to Constantine*, translated with an introduction by G. A. Williamson, 1965; revised edition, 1989).

If Paul's death was undocumented, his thought, however, was crucial. It had been said by Adolf Harnack that "no one understood Paul but Marcion—and Marcion misunderstood him." Marcion brought together an abridged Gospel of Luke and what he called an "Apostolicon" (ten expurgated Pauline epistles, excluding Timothy and Titus, whose origin remained for later solution, and Hebrews, which was often identified with Paul for lack of any other author). Brief "Marcionite Prologues" to the letters of Paul appear in most manuscripts of the Latin Vulgate, translated from Greek originals.

While Paul, or at least the interpretation of Paul, became central to the Reformation, the separation of Paul as a person worthy of biographical attention is a post-Enlightenment occurrence. Jaroslav Pelikan opens the introduction to his 18 verbal illustrations of ways to describe *Jesus Through the Centuries* (1985) with a quotation from the beginning of Albert Schweitzer's *The Quest of the Historical Jesus* (1910): "But it was not only each epoch that found its reflection in Jesus; each individual created Him in accordance with his own character. There is no historical task which so reveals a man's true self as the writing of the Life of Jesus."

The same affirmation applies to Paul, as SCHWEITZER himself says in the preface to *Paul and his Interpreters:* "The present work forms the continuation of my History of the Critical Study of the Life of Jesus." The study of written "lives" of Jesus or of Paul convinced Schweitzer that a biography could not be accomplished. Jesus and Paul lived in an era, under the mode of a "thorough-going" Jewish eschatology, alien to the Hellenizing which emerging Christianity underwent, and of continuing value only with respect to "a deeply ethical and perfected version of the contemporary Apocalyptic." Schweitzer's own version of the resulting description of Paul, his thought, its meaning, and the contemporary significance, appeared under the title *The Mysticism of Paul the Apostle.* By contrast TABOR returned Paul to a first-century context with its common ideological irrelevancies of ascents into "heavenly" realms.

Within the English-speaking world, the most widely studied work on Paul published in the 19th century, which marked the beginning of "modern" understanding, was that of CONYBEARE AND HOWSON. At the end of the century RAMSAY's own itineraries of inscriptional gathering and archaeological site inspection, especially in Asia Minor, led to two important surveys (1879, 1907) which added new dimensions to Pauline evaluation.

The image of Paul in the biographical studies of the 20th century hinges on another factor: what is the amount of evidence accepted as genuinely from Paul? (This issue is raised in Raymond Collins, *Letters That Paul Did Not Write: The Epistle to the Hebrews and the Pauline Pseudepigrapha,* 1988). GLOVER still accepted the fragments of apparent Pauline biography in the so-called "Pastoral Epistles" (those addressed to Timothy or Titus rather than some urban "church"; so named by Paul Anton of Halle in 1726) as credible.

DEISSMANN had treated the epistle labeled "to the Ephesians" as though it were the missing letter "to the Laodiceans" (Colossians 4: 16). He had difficulty with the "conventionalized, stiff and unletter-like" Pastorals, though he had not yet cut them out of biographical construction, and he speculated on what a relation of Paul to Seneca could have been, even if it were not. KNOX was uncertain of Ephesians.

GOODSPEED (1933), following the German scholar Adolf Jülicher's suggestion of 1904, saw the possibility that "Ephesians" was created anonymously but imitatively of Paul, as an "introduction" when the Pauline corpus was gathered in response to the appearance of Luke's "Acts of the Apostles." The Pastorals belonged to another generation responding to Marcion's use of Paul. NOCK tended to agree, and there is little to distinguish his impression of Paul from that of GOODSPEED (1947).

BORNKAMM rejects not only the Pastoral Epistles and Ephesians, but also Colossians and Second Thessalonians; STENDAHL agrees and finds Bornkamm's position "the best available general introduction to Paul." MacDONALD, by close reference to the apocryphal "Acts of Paul and Thecla," shows how the Pastoral Epistles, which distorted Paul's thought, were successful in attaining canonical status; the issue joined was the shaping of Paul's perspective on women in the church.

PAGELS identifies the image of Paul within the exegesis of Pauline epistles by the second-century Naassenes, Valentinians, and other "gnostic" writers, now also known from Nag Hammadi texts. She demonstrates how Paul, "the opponent of gnostic heresy," could have his letters, including Ephesians, Colossians, and Hebrews, as well as Romans, Corinthians, Galatians, and Philippians, claimed as "a primary source of gnostic theology." Such understanding helps her explain how the image of Paul took the turn found in the Pastoral Epistles.

The decision on authenticity of the "Pastorals" also affects the question of the end of Paul's life. JEWETT belongs with those who reject them. His treatise, a methodological inquiry into chronology rather than straight biography, demonstrates how thoroughly the biographer must look at the complex evidence of the apparent chronological data in the sources as well as subjecting all previous studies, including OGG (1968) and LÜDEMANN (1977) to a retesting.

HOCK maintains the maximum distinction of Pauline and "deutero-Pauline" epistles; the latter, when associated with Luke's "Acts," provide an "unqualified positive view of work" not only as a feature of Paul's emphasis upon self-support, but also in contrast to Graeco-Roman intellectual tendencies to stigmatize artisans. This treatise emphasizes the artisan side of Paul's occupation, to which only Deissmann previously attended. Hock sees Paul here in the context of other itinerant philosophers and their means of support, but tends to neglect the named fellow-laborers and fails to note the ease of movement of the citizen Paul throughout the Roman Empire, engaging in that trade.

JOHNSON tries to gain new perspective on Paul by reexamining in detail the cities from within the Pauline itineraries as revealed by contemporary archaeology; while Johnson updates Ramsay, and is more thorough on Paul as thinker and preacher in those cities, his work is no less popular than MORTON's of a half-century earlier. POLLOCK likewise drove the route and thought of Morton's "travelogue," but also of Sholem Asch. For those who remain unimpressible by scholarship, Saul the persecutor become Paul the protagonist is the basis for Asch's biographical fiction (*The Apostle,* 1943).

—Clyde Curry Smith

PAVLOVA, Anna, 1881–1931; Russian ballerina.

Algeranoff, Harcourt, *My Years with Pavlova.* London, Heinemann, 1957.

Dandré, Victor E., *Anna Pavlova.* London, Cassell, 1932.

Franks, Arthur H., editor, *Pavlova, a Biography.* London, Burke, and New York, Macmillan, 1956; as *Pavlova in Art and Life,* New York, Blum, 1972.

Hyden, Walford, *Pavlova: The Genius of the Dance.* London, Constable, 1931.

Kerensky, Oleg, *Anna Pavlova.* London, Hamilton, and New York, Dutton, 1973.

Lieven, Prince Peter, *The Birth of Ballets-Russes,* translated by L. Zarine. London, Allen and Unwin, 1936.

Money, Keith, *Anna Pavlova: Her Art and Life.* London, Collins, and New York, Knopf, 1982.

*

The cryptic, popular DANDRÉ was Pavlova's manager (though she was the disciplinarian) and ostensibly her husband too, though their marriage is not proven. His biography is close-range, giving evidence that he was avaricious and should have restrained his wife from working so hard.

By contrast, LIEVEN's attitude is balanced, and his description of Pavlova, encapsulated in a mere four 1/2 pages in a book about Diaghilev's company, is valuable for his knowledge and perception of her work. "She was a born genius. . . . Such rare phenomena as she and Nijinsky appear only once in a century."

KERENSKY's all-round and "modern" account breaks silence over many previously unspoken aspects of Pavlova: her illegitimacy and probably Jewish father; her religious outlook; her promiscuity and sexuality; her unfulfilled desire for motherhood; her physical defect in that direction and unwillingness to accept normal sexual practices; her preference to be seen in public with "gay" young men; her extravagant adoration of children. Kerensky emphasizes her simple, childlike nature and includes good pictures.

ALGERANOFF (an Englishman) was Pavlova's principal character-dancer and often her partner. He was one of many young people from audiences so won over by her art that they became dancers themselves. (Frederick Ashton in South America and Robert Helpmann in Australia were others). Algeranoff's lively and informative biography, important because it is by a dancer, gives the best indication of life in her company with its constantly hectic tours. Algeranoff describes how Pavlova's personality held him in thrall from 1921 and consistently until her death: "Such beauty of line, poise and balance, such nobility—I realised the meaning of the term 'Imperial Artist.' " There are piquant examples of her humour and generosity to senior members of her company.

HYDEN became Pavlova's musical director after Theodore Stier and is the preferred author of two books written from the rostrum. Hyden's criticisms are sometimes severe: "She was an erratic performer. She would become entranced with her own bodily rhythm." She was musically ignorant and "instead of dancing to the music, she wanted the music to be played in time to her." She was "ruthless, selfish, mean" towards her *corps de ballet*. But Hyden insists: "She was a mystic of the dance. . . . Only the dance mattered." Hyden offers the best account of Pavlova's amazing *Giselle:* She acted "with such realism that not only did she hold the audience spell-bound, . . . but she affected the girls in the *corps de ballet* to such an extent that some of them, with tears running down their cheeks . . . completely broke down."

MONEY, a photographer as well as a writer, charts Pavlova's life in hundreds of evocative photographs and an exhaustive text. The useful list of her tours is not found elsewhere. The book is very well produced and adds considerably to our understanding of Anna Pavlova.

FRANKS has gathered a symposium of different views from experts: Sol Hurok, the impresario; Michel Fokine, the choreographer of *The Swan*; Laurent Novikov, one of Pavlova's classical partners; Ram Gopal, who taught her Indian dancing; and Philip Richardson, grand old man of dancing organisations in Britain.

Franks contributes his own penetrating biographical study and has also included, in translation, Pavlova's *Pages of my Life*. This is all too short and simple, though her wistful ending may mean more than just the words: "When, a small child, I was rambling over there by the fir trees, I thought that success meant happiness. I was wrong. Happiness is like a butterfly which appears and delights us for one brief moment, but soon flits away."

—Alan Jefferson

PENN, William, 1644–1718; English Quaker, founder of Pennsylvania.

Brailsford, Mabel R., *The Making of William Penn*. London and New York, Longman, 1930.

Buell, Augustus C., *William Penn as the Founder of Two Commonwealths*. New York, Appleton, 1904.

Dunn, Mary M., *William Penn, Politics and Conscience*. Princeton, New Jersey, Princeton University Press, 1967.

Endy, Melvin B., *William Penn and Early Quakerism*. Princeton, New Jersey, Princeton University Press, 1973.

Fantel, Hans, *William Penn: Apostle of Dissent*. New York, Morrow, 1974.

Graham, John W., *William Penn, Founder of Pennsylvania*. New York, Stokes, 1916.

Hull, William I., *Eight First Biographies of William Penn in Seven Languages and Seven Lands*. Swarthmore, Pennsylvania, Swarthmore College, 1936.

Hull, William I., *William Penn: A Topical Biography*. London and New York, Oxford University Press, 1937.

Illick, Joseph E., *William Penn, the Politician: His Relations with the English Government*. Ithaca, New York, Cornell University Press, 1965.

Janney, Samuel M., *The Life of William Penn: With Selections from His Correspondence and Autobiography*. Philadelphia, Friends Book Association, 1851.

Peare, Catherine O., *William Penn: A Biography*. London, D. Dobson, 1956; Philadelphia, Lippincott, 1957.

Wildes, Harry E., *William Penn*. New York, Macmillan, 1974.

*

A complex man who lived a long and active life, William Penn's many-faceted character eluded many of his biographers. Some historians were able to chronicle one or another aspect of his life, but few could capture the fullness of Penn's humanity. He was at once a man of action and a seeker of contemplation. He fused the sacred and the profane, the religious and the political in his "Holy Experiment." Though he is the subject of many biographies, few authors have inscribed him as the man of multifarious actions and thoughts.

HULL's scholarly collection of the first eight biographies (1936) summarizes early Penn writers. Perhaps the earliest, and in some ways the most influential, work in English is Joseph Besse's two-volume collection of Penn's writings, *A Collection of the Works of William Penn* (London, 1726), which contains a full compilation of the works and a useful life. Other items in Professor Hull's assemblage include Penn biographies by Mason L. Weems, William Sewel, and Gerard Croese. The volume includes works written in English, Dutch, Latin, German, French, Spanish, and Italian; it contains useful illustrations and an epitome of Penn's life.

JANNEY produced a clearly written, well-documented, and generally reliable work in the mid-19th century. He pays particular attention to Penn's religious and political tracts and reproduces many of his letters. This biography follows the "life and letters" fashion of the times by containing liberal excerpts from contemporary documents. For many years, this was considered the standard biography of Penn.

Several biographies appeared at the turn of the century, all essentially in the mold of Joseph Besse and all particularly focused on the apparent double-sided split in Penn's life: Quaker and cavalier or statesman and courtier. BUELL's work is a laudatory—and unreliable—account of Penn's colonial activities. GRAHAM's biography features a clear chronology, a study of Penn portraiture, and a summary of the various refutations of T. B. Macaulay's aspersions upon Penn.

In the 1930s several other biographies were published, and two of these deserve special mention because they broke with the prevailing pattern. BRAILSFORD deals mainly with Penn's formative influences (until 1681), especially his childhood and Quakerism. She notes the importance of Moise Amyrant (Penn's teacher in France), whose calls for religious liberty had a profound effect on young Penn. But the central figure in his life is Admiral Penn, to whom Brailsford gives a sympathetic and favorable portrayal. She traces the influences that formed the younger Penn's character and finds a singular parallel in the lives of father and son.

HULL's *Topical Biography* (1937) is original in approach and painstaking in research. Hull deals with 30 topics in Penn's life and character, each topic treated consecutively from start to finish. His novel treatment attempts to give weight to little-known or previously ignored aspects of Penn's life. Hull paints a balanced picture, acknowledging Penn's failures and defects while giving due praise for his genuine greatness. Hull writes: "As a founder of the Society of Friends, and of a great American commonwealth; as an eloquent and convincing preacher, and a successful champion of religious toleration; as a learned scholar and author of classic literature, and a law-giver and international statesman of the highest mark: no other personality in American colonial history looms so large or shines so brightly. . . ."

PEARE presents an excellent synthesis in an engaging style. She describes Penn as martyr, spokesman, and administrator. Her work is a balanced presentation of the personal, the political, and the religious. Based on thorough research and a wealth of documentation, Peare's scholarship is of the highest order. She writes with feeling and sympathy and without mushiness or blind idolatry. She presents the complexities and paradoxes of Penn's character in a manner to elicit the total person in a balanced portrait. Her dramatic handling of history and her clarity of focus are worthy of her subject. Also containing a nearly complete bibliography of Penn's writings, this scholarly biography is the definitive work.

ILLICK criticizes all biographies of Penn for their almost exclusive attention to his connection to the Society of Friends and his role in the cause of religious toleration, to the general neglect of his political career. Illick treats Penn's provincial failure and his imperial success. He writes of Penn's political life as both a creative and defensive statesman, an aggressive and be-

leaguered proprietor, an indiscreet and perplexed courtier, and a frustrated fugitive. Illick asserts that, except for the first years of William III's reign, Penn's success in retaining his colony against various governmental attacks was largely the result of his influence with prominent statesmen. Illick's scholarship encompasses a broad range of sources.

DUNN's biography brings out the relationship between Penn's ideas and his actions as mirrored in his voluminous writings. According to some historians, Dunn's eloquent work is the best available guide to the political thought of Penn. Clearly and perceptively, she analyzes Penn's ideas on toleration, government, and social organization. Her work is a biography of Penn's mind, keenly penetrated. Penn emerges as a man possessed of one dream—establishing the principle of religious toleration. If Penn appears to be waffling—he first supported Parliament and then the king—it is because his actions are taken out of context. He favored the center of power he thought most apt to grant toleration. (Vincent Buranelli, *The King and The Quaker*, Philadelphia, University of Pennsylvania Press, 1962, arrives at the same conclusion.) Dunn's work is a splendid performance in all regards, and deals skillfully with the dual forces that made Penn an aggressive, eloquent, and determined exponent of reform.

ENDY's work joins together the man and the movement. His account of Penn's religious thought, its influence on his political thought and actions, and the significance of his life and thought to the Quaker movement is a thorough analysis of primary sources and contemporary scholarship. Endy convincingly shows that Penn was a gifted, innovative spokesman for the Quaker vision. In the process of providing context, he tends to accentuate continuities between Penn and early Quakerism. This solid interpretation is not only a definitive study of Penn's religious thought, but also a major contribution to the understanding of early Quakerism.

FANTEL's work, intended for general readers, describes Penn's conversion from cavalier to Quaker, his codifying of Quaker theology, and their influence on political, social, and religious institutions in England and America. Fantel, a refugee from Nazi Germany, idealizes Penn as the apostle of freedom. He relies on secondary sources, and many of his assertions are ahistorical leaps of faith rather than sound hypotheses based on documentary evidence. Yet Fantel does achieve his goal to provide a popular biography on a theme of current concern.

WILDES' more comprehensive work offers a portrayal of both the public and the private man, touching on Penn's childhood and education, his two marriages, and his relationship with his children. In 50 chapters and nine appendices, (including material on portraits, ancestry, family, publicity, Mather hoax, grave commemorations, writings and biographies) Wildes probes into Penn's life and interests. He makes extensive use of primary sources, and his book shows the results of his painstaking research. He has made logical deductions (so labeled) as to what Penn did based on actions Penn had taken in similar circumstances. The author eschews the stereotype of the flawless proprietor and presents Penn realistically. Yet the work is a regression in some respects because it ignores the fruits of recent scholarship. There are, unfortunately, careless errors in documentation, quotation, and factual detail, which render the volume less than reliable. Still, this work will probably give many readers a novel appreciation for Penn. This may be one of the most detailed biographies, though hardly one that renders all others obsolete. The search for the well-rounded biography of the human William Penn goes on.

—Jacob L. Susskind

PEPYS, Samuel, 1633–1703; English diarist and public official.

Barber, Richard, *Samuel Pepys, Esquire*. London, G. Bell, and Berkeley, University of California Press, 1970.

Bradford, Gamaliel, *The Soul of Samuel Pepys*. Boston, Houghton Mifflin, and London, Cape, 1924.

Bridge, Sir Frederick, *Samuel Pepys: Lover of Musique*. London, Smith Elder, 1903.

Bryant, Sir Arthur, *Samuel Pepys* (3 vols.). Cambridge, University Press, and New York, Macmillan, 1933–39.

Bryant, Sir Arthur, *Pepys and the Revolution*. London, Collins, 1979.

Cleugh, James, *The Amorous Master Pepys*. London, Frederick Muller, 1958.

Drinkwater, John, *Pepys: His Life and Character*. London, Heinemann, and New York, Doubleday, 1930.

Emden, Cecil Stuart, *Pepys Himself*. London and New York, Oxford University Press, 1963.

Hearsey, John E. N., *Young Mr. Pepys*. New York, Scribner, and London, Constable, 1973.

Hunt, Percival, *Samuel Pepys in the Diary*. Pittsburgh, Pennsylvania, University of Pittsburgh Press, 1958.

Kirk, Rudolf, *Mr. Pepys Upon the State of Christ-Hospital*. London, Oxford University Press, and Philadelphia, University of Pennsylvania Press, 1935.

Lubbock, Percy, *Samuel Pepys*. London, Hodder and Stoughton, and New York, Scribner, 1909.

Lucas-Dubreton, Jean *Samuel Pepys: A Portrait in Miniature*, translated by H. J. Stenning. London, A. M. Philpot, 1924; New York, Putnam, 1925 (originally published as *Petite Vie de Samuel Pepys, Londonien*, Paris, Payot, 1923).

Marburg, Clara (Clara Marburg Kirk), *Mr. Pepys and Mr. Evelyn*. London, Oxford University Press, and Philadelphia, University of Pennsylvania Press, 1935.

Moorhouse, Esther Hallam (Meynell), *Samuel Pepys, Administrator, Observer, Gossip*. London, Chapman and Hall, and New York, Dutton, 1909.

Nicolson, Marjorie Hope, *Pepys' Diary and the New Science*. Charlottesville, University Press of Virginia, 1965.

Ollard, Richard, *Pepys: A Biography*. New York, Holt, and London, Hodder and Stoughton, 1974.

Ponsonby, Arthur, *Samuel Pepys*. London and New York, Macmillan, 1928.

Smith, John, *Life, Journals, and Correspondence of Samuel Pepys, Esq., F.R.S.* (2 vols.). London, R. Bentley, 1841.

Tanner, J. R., *Mr. Pepys. An Introduction to the Diary, Together with a Sketch of his Later Life*. London, G. Bell, and New York, Harcourt, 1924.

Taylor, Ivan, *Samuel Pepys*. New York, Twayne, 1967.

Trease, Geoffrey, *Samuel Pepys and his World*. New York, Scribner, and London, Thames and Hudson, 1972.

Wheatley, Henry B., *Samuel Pepys and the World He Lived In*. London, Bickers, and New York, Scribner, 1880.

Wilson, John Harold, *The Private Life of Mr. Pepys*. New York, Farrar Straus, 1959; London, R. Hale, 1960.

*

On 26 May 1703, John Evelyn noted, "This day died Mr. Samuel Pepys, a very worthy industrious and curious person, none in England exceeding him in knowledge of the Navy. . . . He was . . . learned in many things, skilled in music, a very great cherisher of learned men" (quoted in Tanner). This summation, the earliest biographical sketch, was the general estimate of Pepys until the early 19th century. From 1819, however, a different Pepys emerged, when SMITH began deciphering Pepys's shorthand *Diary*. Richard Lord Braybrooke published editions of Smith's deciphering efforts between 1825 and 1848–49. The *Diary* remained abridged and expurgated until editors Mynors Bright (1875–79) and Henry B. Wheatley (1893–99) published successively more of Pepys' frank entries. By 1900, as Ollard notes, one could "know more about Pepys than about any other individual Englishman of his time." He has become the most well-known 17th-century diarist, and the number of biographies attests to his popularity.

Before 1900, only WHEATLEY had provided a book-length life. While Smith merely prefaces his edition of Pepys' correspondence with an introductory sketch (as does Lord Braybrooke in his editions of the *Diary*), Wheatley studies the wider world in which Pepys moved, including chapters on the Court, the Navy, contemporary manners, and on Pepys' life before, during, and after the *Diary*. Wheatley's work was the standard for many years, and it went through at least five editions by the early 1900s.

After publication of the relatively unexpurgated *Diary*, several analyses of the "private" Pepys were published between 1900 and 1925. Most are based almost entirely on the *Diary*. MOORHOUSE's relatively full and clear life owes much to Wheatley and to published collections of "Pepysiana." It is useful as a balanced introduction to many aspects of Pepys' professional life. LUBBOCK's book is part of a standard biography series (as are Ponsonby and Taylor, described below). In addition to the usual chronicle of the *Diary* years, Lubbock discusses his later life, with the Popish Plot and Pepys' library receiving attention at the expense of his official career. BRIDGE uses the *Diary* to portray Pepys as a musician (vocalist, composer, and listener), while he discusses mainly other Restoration composers and players. BRADFORD relies on Moorhouse and on the *Diary*. This self-styled "psychographic," topical study includes an important examination of Pepys' enigmatic religious beliefs but is otherwise unmemorable. LUCAS-DUBRETON, a biographer of Napoleon, offers an overwritten novelistic foray into Pepys' moods and actions during the *Diary* years. Though the volume asks insightful questions, its readiness to resort to guesswork makes it useful only as a guide to further research.

Between the First and Second World Wars Pepys was revived as "Savior of the Navy," or, rather, the witty and open Pepys of the *Diary* was reunited with his later, more prosaic incarnation as Secretary of the Admiralty. TANNER paved the way, first with an important series of lectures (*Samuel Pepys and the Royal*

Navy, 1920) and catalogs of Pepysian manuscripts, which highlight his important role in the Naval Office. Tanner inherited Wheatley's notes and "engaged upon a larger life," but the brief introduction cited here is the only book-length biography he produced. Tanner mainly considers the *Diary* years topically, including: Pepys' position, wife, friends, food, books. Several chapters, that on Pepys' sermon-going and that comparing his official and private styles for example, remain the most thorough discussions of particular aspects of the diarists' life. The last chapter, "Later Life of Pepys," is more than a "sketch." It quotes extensively from important sources, and it notes mistakes in earlier editions of correspondence. Tanner is a delight to read and proves the author to be, as Ollard says, "the doyen of Pepysian scholars." What is lacking is extended discussion of Pepys' beliefs and motivations.

A much fuller narrative is found in the three volumes (1933–39) of BRYANT, the other major work of the Augustan Age of Pepys studies. Bryant's well-documented narrative remains the standard work of reference. Bryant employs the vast array of personal manuscripts and admiralty documents that reveals Pepys' day-to-day actions (uncovering, for example, the extent of his near-blindness *circa* 1670). Because he also provides a clear narrative of high politics, his lengthy study is accessible to students minimally familiar with the period. But it is not a complete biography; it ends with Pepys' dismissal in 1689 and includes nothing on the last decade of his life. Bryant's *Pepys and the Revolution* (1979) is simply half of the third volume of the trilogy followed by a few pages of uninformative epilogue. Unlike the original volumes, it is not self-contained (including, for example, unexplained references to his Tangier voyage). The failure to incorporate recent revaluations of the Glorious Revolution by J. R. Jones and others date this repackaged work.

Compared with Tanner and Bryant, other interwar biographies are less substantial. PONSONBY and DRINKWATER rely heavily on Tanner. Ponsonby, a scholar of 17th-century diaries, sticks closely to the *Diary*. His discussion of the contemporary assessment of Pepys both before and after publication of the *Diary* is useful. Drinkwater is a good, readable, and popular-style biography of the "public" Pepys, buttressed by some research in manuscripts that were more fully mined by Bryant. Finally, KIRK and MARBURG are companion monographs (the authors are husband and wife) that are limited in scope but rewarding. Kirk briefly and clearly covers Pepys' governorship of a mathematical school for poor boys. Pepys' stormy relationship with the schoolmasters adds insight into the mind and morality of the first modern bureaucrat. Marburg examines the friendship and correspondence of Evelyn and Pepys more exhaustively than Ponsonby had done. The diarists' intertwined "publick" roles and private lives are discussed in two lengthy chapters.

By the 1950s, many aspects of Pepys had been recovered: the *Diary* published more or less intact, his reputation as founder of the modern navy established, much of his correspondence published, and the extent of his famous library documented if not fully cataloged. With this scholarly appratus, and with Bryant as a guide to his life, a flurry of monographs on Pepys from particular points of view have appeared. Least satisfactory of these studies are Cleugh, Taylor, and Wilson. All are based on the *Diary*. CLEUGH offers a popular, if unexciting, study of the earthy side of the *Diary*. TAYLOR, a topical study looking at Pepys on the Court, music, theatre, and other subjects, is marred by extremely poor editing. WILSON's narrative is notable only for a final chapter on the life of Mary Skinner, Pepys' companion during his final years.

EMDEN and HUNT both look chiefly at the *Diary* years. Emdem's is a brief study of Pepys' character that neglects to use Bryant's more thorough exploration of this period. Hunt also provides some insight into his character in a collection of "Pepysiana." NICOLSON's volume, composed of three distinct lectures, is a profound investigation of Pepys' interest in science during the early years of the Royal Society. The narrative of Pepys' connection with the Royal Society, however, remains unwritten.

Recently, a Renaissance of Pepys studies has begun, led by Robert Latham, the Pepys Librarian. A new, definitive *Diary*, edited by Latham and William Matthews (1970–83), has a *Companion* (vol. X, 1983) of some 1700 entries, including many substantial essays. The essay on "religion" adds to Bradford, that on "music" supplements Bridge, and "Royal Society" expands on Nicolson. Latham has also begun editing a new multi-volume *Catalogue of the Pepys Library at Magdalene College* (1978–   ). Yet the last 20 years, with one important exception, has not been a boon period for biographers. The life prefacing the new edition of the *Diary* is wan and uninformative. HEARSEY appears unaware of the new edition of the *Diary* in progress. Despite the title, it studies mainly the young man of the *Diary* years. Barber and Trease are notable more for their illustrations than for their texts. BARBER, an exhibition catalog, links portraits with the narrative of the life of Pepys. The student will value this brief visual "making of the man." TREASE is a brief and clear updating of Wheatley and is an undemanding pictorial introduction to Pepys.

The most recent biography and the first to make use of the new edition of the *Diary* (then in progress) is by OLLARD. The author, an expert on the Restoration navy, is well qualified to provide a fresh Pepys. Ollard builds on the work of Wheatley, Tanner, and Bryant and presents a full-length biography of Pepys' complete life. It often defers to Bryant's fuller descriptions, while correcting minor points within the notes. To Ollard, Pepys was a great man whose "deepest springs of action were artistic" and whose greatest work of art was "the professionalising of the naval officer." But this is no idealized portrait. It shows the young man of the 1660s swaying to the winds of "faction" and "crude personal gain"; and Ollard is at odds with Bryant in stressing the hard edge of Pepys—his "mercilessness" could at times be "repellent." The work includes a splendid recreation of naval affairs, but its greatest feat is to illuminate Pepys' thought. Unlike Bryant, Ollard assumes some knowledge of the period and remains focused on Pepys. The constant use of anachronistic, metaphorical illustration and namedropping—"rush-hour traffic of middle age," Le Corbusier, *A Doll's House*—is perhaps less than scholarly; but it makes for "a very worthy, industrious and curious" biography.

—Newton E. Key

PERÓN, Juan Domingo, 1895-1974; Argentine political leader.
PERÓN, (Maria) Eva Duarte, 1919-1952; Argentine actress and political leader.

Alexander, Robert J., *Juan Domingo Péron: A History*. Boulder, Colorado, Westview Press, 1979.

Barnes, John, *Evita: First Lady, A Biography of Eva Péron*. New York, Grove, and London, W.H. Allen, 1978.

Crassweller, Robert D., *Péron and the Enigmas of Argentina*. New York and London, Norton, 1987.

Fraser, Nicholas and Marysa Navarro, *Eva Perón*. New York, Norton, and London, Deutsch, 1980.

Main, Mary Foster (Maria Flores), *The Woman with the Whip: Eva Perón*. New York, Doubleday, 1952; revised as *Evita*, New York, Dodd Mead, and London, Severn House, 1980.

Page, Joseph A., *Perón: A Biography*. New York, Random House, 1983.

Taylor, Julie M., *Eva Perón: The Myths of a Woman*. Chicago, University of Chicago Press, 1979; as *Evita Perón*, Oxford, Blackwell, 1979.

*

Juan Domingo Perón ruled Argentina during one of the most frenetic periods in that troubled country's history. His second wife, Eva Duarte Perón, captured the imaginations of her countrymen and women with her charismatic personality and obvious flair for popular leadership, virtually running the ministries of health and labor after her husband became president. Each has received considerable treatment at the hands of biographers in English, though curiously no single biography exists that adequately covers both lives. Readers seeking comprehensive accounts of the two will have to turn to more than one of the works discussed below.

ALEXANDER attempted the first complete life of Juan Perón in English. Though now superseded, it satisfied the popular need for information about the founder of *peronismo* at the time of its publication. Alexander tried unsuccessfully to assess the president's policy failures and dictatorial approach to government, though his overview of the social and economic conditions in Argentina throughout the 20th century may still be useful to some readers.

PAGE has written what many still regard as the definitive biography of Juan Perón, although serious students wanting a full picture of the man should read both Page and the more recent work by Crassweller (see below). Page covers in greater depth and detail than Alexander every stage of Perón's life and career. He also provides a more extensive and sympathetic treatment of Eva Perón than any other biographer of the president. Page reminds us of the obstacles Eva Perón faced as a woman in her husband's political movement, and points out that after her death Juan Perón took measures never to allow another figure to become so visible in his party. With a straightforward prose style, serviceable bibliography and index, and thoroughly researched and documented sources (Page worked on this book in Argentina at a time when journalists and writers there were routinely "disappeared"), Page's work should satisfy most readers looking for a comprehensive biography of the former Argentine president.

CRASSWELLER provides a nice complement to Page's book. Attempting to place Juan Perón within the context of Argentine history and politics—something that Page does not stress—Crassweller demonstrates how the president was a product of Hispanic traditions as well as a representative of the pampa. This shifting back and forth between the man and his environment helps to illuminate aspects of his personality and style of leadership that a straight chronological account of his life cannot capture. Crassweller's book is equipped with the most complete and up-to-date bibliography available of literature on Perón.

Eva Perón provided her own version of her life in *Evita by Evita* (1978); this somewhat self-aggrandizing account can still be read profitably in conjunction with the biographies of her. A notable contrast to the view put forth in the autobiography (and later by Barnes, see below) is found in MAIN's study, originally published in 1952 and updated, with a new foreword and epilogue, in 1980. These additions touch more favorably on some of Eva Perón's accomplishments, though the central text, which remains virtually unchanged from the original edition, takes a mostly negative stance.

BARNES has provided a generally balanced portrait of "Evita," and it is as readable as any produced thus far. Barnes maintains his objectivity throughout most of the study, treating Eva Perón sympathetically but not failing to note her faults. His book, as well as that by FRASER AND NAVARRO, will serve adequately the needs of general readers. The latter work is better researched and contains a more complete bibliography. It is also a more accurate and penetrating historical examination of Eva Perón within her milieu. Barnes gives us more of the private Evita (the one who loved soap operas), Fraser and Navarro more of the populist leader who, despite the grievous consequences of some of her actions, made significant contributions to her people.

Less a biography than an anthropological study in mythmaking, TAYLOR examines the differing views of Eva Perón held by those in her own culture and, incidentally, in ours—an approach that anyone who has seen the Broadway musical *Evita* would benefit from, if only to gain insight into the ways popular culture can distort reality. Taylor provides a few pages of straight biography and some by way of furnishing necessary historical background, in neither case saying much of note. The book is valuable for its treatment of what Eva Perón represented to different people and, by extension, for the light it throws on her personality. Eva Perón was never indifferent to the ways in which she was viewed.

—Noelle A. Watson

PETER, Saint, d. *ca.* 65 A.D.; first bishop of Rome.

Barnes, Arthur S., *St. Peter in Rome and His Tomb on the Vatican Hill*. London, S. Sonnenschein, 1900.

Barnes, Arthur S., *The Martyrdom of St. Peter and St. Paul*. London, Oxford University Press, 1933.

Brown, Raymond E., K. Donfried, and J. Reumann, *Peter in the New Testament: A Collaborative Assessment by Protestant and Roman Catholic Scholars*. Minneapolis, Augsburg Press, 1973; London, G. Chapman, 1974.

Cullmann, Oscar, *Peter: Disciple, Apostle, Martyr: A Historical and Theological Study*, translated by Floyd V. Filson. London, SCM Press, and Philadelphia, Westminster Press, 1953; revised and expanded edition, 1962.

Elton, Godfrey, *Simon Peter*. London, P. Davies, 1965; New York, Doubleday, 1966.

Findlay, James A., *A Portrait of Peter*. New York, Abingdon Press, and London, Hodder and Stoughton, 1935.

Foakes-Jackson, Frederick John, *Peter, Prince of Apostles: A Study in the History and Tradition of Christianity*. New York, G. H. Doran, and London, Hodder and Stoughton, 1927.

Karrer, Otto, *Peter and the Church: An Examination of Cullmann's Thesis*, translated by Ronald Walls. Edinburgh and London, Nelson, 1963 (originally published by Herder, Freiburg, 1963).

O'Connor, Daniel W., *Peter in Rome: The Literary, Liturgical, and Archaeological Evidence*. New York, Columbia University Press, 1969.

Robertson, Archibald T., *Epochs in the Life of Simon Peter*. New York, Scribner, 1933.

Smith, Terence V., *Petrine Controversies in Early Christianity: Attitudes Toward Peter in Christian Writings of the First Two Centuries*. Tübingen, Mohr-Siebeck, 1985.

Toynbee, Jocelyn and John Ward-Perkins, *The Shrine of St. Peter and the Vatican Excavations*. London and New York, Longman, 1956.

Walsh, John Evangelist, *The Bones of St. Peter: The First Full Account of the Search for the Apostle's Body*. New York, Doubleday, 1982; London, Gollancz, 1983.

*

All of the figures of the New Testament remain ambiguously enigmatic, but none more elusive than "the Disciple" Peter, called "one of the strangest facts of history," upon whom came to rest the Western Tradition of "Apostolic Succession." R. M. Grant noted the divergence developed already in each "Gospel" and the role portrayed by or assigned to Peter relative to "the Gospels in the first two centuries" and to "Origen and the Life of Jesus" (*The Earliest Lives of Jesus*, 1961).

Simon, whom Jesus surnamed Peter, appears in all four canonical gospels, and heads the lists of "The Twelve" when these are given (Mark 3: 16–19; Matthew 10: 2–4; Luke 6: 14–16 and Acts 1: 13). He is known to have been married. His calling as "disciple" is associated with the prior action of his brother Andrew. The one biographical study of the latter (P. M. Peterson, *Andrew, Brother of Simon Peter*, 1958) documents further how both brothers began, in contexts of Galilean opposition to Rome, as disciples of John the Baptist. This relationship was first clarified, not only concerning them but also concerning Jesus, from a careful reading of John 3: 22–4: 3, by M. Goguel (*Vie de Jésus*, 1932; English translation, 1933), whose work was an important base for Cullmann (see below). The study of Andrew also shows how little was ever known of any except Paul and Peter, James and John, and James brother of Jesus. The early church resumed interest in "the Twelve" too late to recover the originals, even the most important, or their individual fate. Instead there was spawned the legendizing accounts in the "Apocryphal New Testament" (see *The New Testament Apocrypha*,

edited by E. Hennecke and W. Schneemelcher, translated by R. Wilson, 2 vols., 1963–66).

Luke, in the second volume of his accounts of earliest Christianity, which came to be called "The Acts of the Apostles," provides some additional biographical information. However, aside from the epistles themselves, written in the name of Peter, much of the discussion of Peter falls into a commentary format upon the "Acts" or the several epistles, including Paul's to the Galatians and Corinthians. Attention has been paid to the variety of "Acts," other "Gospels," the "Preaching," and an "Apocalypse"—all identified by the name of Peter, by SMITH (see also below) in an academic work of first magnitude following the precedent set by Foakes-Jackson (see below).

In the early period, considering the apparent significance of Petrine epistles for what later became the canon of the New Testament, and in spite of extensive debate concerning their authenticity, remarkably little is known of Peter or his relation to them. A similar statement, though based on a larger literary corpus, has been said about Paul. The two must be considered together, for what is known ties them to each other and to Rome, so that the Tradition speaks of "Paul and Peter" or "Peter and Paul." The so-called "Second Epistle of Peter" first identified the Pauline epistolary collection (3: 15–16).

Basic information comes from Eusebius of Caesarea (*ca.* 260–340). The translator G. A. Williamson made the observation: "Believing that Paul died before Peter, Eusebius puts Paul first whenever he has their deaths in mind. But we find Peter put first in quotations from Dionysius (of Corinth) and Irenaeus (of Lyons), who are referring to his arrival in Rome, which they believed to be prior to Paul's, as did Eusebius" (*Eusebius: The History of the Church from Christ to Constantine*, translated with an introduction by G. A. Williamson, 1965; revised edition, 1989).

Neither Peter nor Paul appears in the first-century Jewish historian, Josephus, even though the latter writes from Rome and knows of John the Baptist, Jesus, and James the brother of Jesus (*Josephus: Complete Works*, translated by William Whiston, 1960); nor in the second-century Greek critic of Christianity, Celsus, who knows of John the Baptist, Jesus, and some New Testament-like material (*Celsus on the True Doctrine: A Discourse Against the Christians*, translated by R. Joseph Hoffman, 1987); nor in the Roman historians of the period, Tacitus (*Complete Works*, edited by Moses Hadas, 1942) and Suetonius (*Twelve Caesars*, translated by Robert Graves, 1957), who know of Christians and the Christian movement. Celsus does know that Jesus "collected around him ten or eleven unsavory characters—tax collectors, sailors, and the like."

Christian authors demonstrate how quickly real biographical information on Peter and Paul disappeared before the end of the first Christian century even within the developing Tradition, the result of "attitudes" related to "Petrine controversies," as Smith has noted. Clement of Rome (traditionally bishop, 88–97), in a letter to the church at Corinth, speaks vaguely of the opposition to, yet ultimate reward of, both. Ignatius of Antioch (martyred *ca.* 112) knows the combination as having apostolic authority that he lacked. Hippolytus of Rome (*ca.* 170–*ca.* 235), in a list of the "twelve" apostles, gives supposed itinerary of preaching, plus a developing traditional statement on the mode, place, and relative time of death—first for Peter, and last (13th!) for Paul. Jerome (*ca.* 347–419/20), in his "Lives of Illustrious

Men," develops minibiographies for Peter (first) and Paul (fifth) that are dependent as much on sources outside as those inside the New Testament.

In contrast, by the later second century the primacy of the bishop of Rome, as "successor to the Apostles" with special reference to Peter, was developing, and it was strengthened in the fifth century with the acquisition by "the See of Peter" of the defunct ancient Roman title of *pontifex maximus* (by Leo the Great, bishop 440–461). Throughout the medieval period the power of the Petrine office was formidable, the reality of Peter inconsequential.

A separation of Peter as a person worthy of biographical attention is a post-Enlightenment occurrence. On the other hand, liturgically speaking, the cemeteries called by the names of Peter and Paul, as known to Eusebius, were known already at least from the time of the writer Gaius, "who was living while Zephyrinus was Bishop of Rome" (199–217). It is the rediscovery of the tomb, if not the bones, of "Saint Peter" that has sparked renewed attention to him biographically. Pre-excavation perspectives are illustrated: by BARNES (1900, 1933), official Roman Catholic from the era before dialogue; by FOAKES-JACKSON, academically critical but thorough; and by ROBERTSON or FINDLAY, both popular, though Robertson includes an extensive list of earlier "lives."

All the recent authors belong to a cluster arising from one study. CULLMAN, aware that in comparison to "monographs on Paul" there were "but few scholarly works on Peter," began the new discussion as "*a contribution to the science of history*" (his italics), in particular that dealing "with the beginnings of the Christian faith and the Christian Church," especially where such might be informed by "a historical study concerning the Apostle Peter." That he knew of the Vatican excavations by their preliminary reports gave his work additional freshness. Yet he also meant, in an era of increasing Protestant-Roman Catholic dialogue, to come in his final chapter to the whole doctrinal question.

A stringent Roman Catholic response was made by KARRER, who emphasized the "primacy of Peter" over any concern for historical biography. The stimulus provided required extensive revision by Cullmann in 1962, "which shows the course of the debate, deals with the criticisms, and clarifies the presentation." The volume edited by BROWN, DONFRIED, AND REUMANN engaged 11 participants in theological conversation focussed upon Peter as found in each divergent portion or book of the New Testament. Any "biography of Peter" is an essay in the history of Christian doctrine, but for a survey of all the Petrine literary connections, with the advantage of past bibliographic mastery, SMITH remains historically superior.

Based on a thorough survey of the excavations conducted from 1939, TOYNBEE AND WARD-PERKINS intended to satisfy both "the classical and archaeological specialist and the general reader," while providing technical documentation, couched in language intelligible especially to the English-only reader. They arrived at no conclusions relative to Peter, though the question of his presence in Rome, especially relative to what exists beneath St. Peter's Church, was not avoided.

O'CONNOR brought the fully evaluated evidence from literature, liturgy, and archaeology to bear on the issue of Peter in Rome, in three areas: his residence, his martyrdom, and his burial. Bibliography alone comprehends "over 525" titles in-

volving all pertinent citations from whatever date in whatever language. O'Connor arrives at four summary statements "more plausible than not" relative to Peter's biography. This might remain the one best book on the archaeology.

WALSH, while knowing the preceding volumes and related scholarship, plus some newer results from the excavations, combined in a very popularly written style a devotional concern, identifiable in the heavily laden modifiers, with a tale told in suspenseful detective fashion. He arrives, as does Appendix A, at "the surviving skeleton of St. Peter."

There is a special sense in which none of these studies can provide a biography of "Saint Peter." The imaginative mind of the late 19th and mid 20th centuries has therefore taken recourse to the same imaginative base that fired the 2nd century, so that even the Apocryphal Acts of Peter lived again in some very popular fiction: "*Quo Vadis?*" *A Narrative of the Time of Nero*, written by Henryk Sienkiewicz and translated from the Polish by Jeremiah Curtin, has been available in English since 1896; and *The Big Fisherman*, by Lloyd Cassel Douglas, appeared in 1948, with movie script in 1959. ELTON devotionally fictionalized how Peter "might have told" about his life with Jesus.

—Clyde Curry Smith

PETER I [the Great], 1672–1725; Russian czar.

Grey, Ian, *Peter the Great, Emperor of All Russia*. Philadelphia Lippincott, 1960; London, Hodder and Stoughton, 1962.

Klyuchevsky, Vasili, *Peter the Great*, translated by Lilian Archibald. London, Macmillan, 1958.

Massie, Robert, *Peter the Great, His Life and World*. New York, Knopf, 1980; London, Gollancz, 1981.

Sumner, Benedict H., *Peter the Great and the Emergence of Russia*. London, English Universities Press, 1950; New York, Macmillan, 1951.

*

KLYUCHEVSKY's work was first published in 1910 as volume 4 of the author's five-volume *History of Russia*, which was a reworked version of lectures delivered at the University of Moscow over the preceding 20 years. After almost a century, this remains the best biography of Peter. Its origin as a series of lectures is reflected in its crisp style, with few long sentences and a wealth of colourful detail likely to appeal to undergraduate audiences.

In spite of being part of a history, Klyuchevsky's book reads very much as a biography. It begins with Peter at the age of two, playing with toy drummers, and describes how his education started at the age of five, when Zotov became his tutor. The two opening chapters are based on the court records of Peter's pastimes in those early years and cover such details as the kindling of his interest in the navy and his passion for fireworks, drunken orgies, blasphemous ceremonies, and dangerously realistic mock battles. Peter's physical characteristics, reinforced by reference to two portraits (including the famous Kneller portrait, which appears as a frontispiece), and his restless temperament, which made it "impossible to remain a mere spectator," are graphically depicted.

In examining the impetus of Peter's reforms, Klyuchevsky emphasizes both their origin in earlier reigns and the contemporary imperatives that shaped the form they now took. The outbreak of the Great Northern War in 1700 is seen as "unexpected"—an unwelcome diversion that interrupted consolidation against the Turks in the south—and Peter's desertion of his army at Narva is explained as the result of a wish to avoid embarrassing the commander of the doomed Russian army. Klyuchevsky shows little concern for wars or diplomacy, however: there are no narratives of battles, and the whole saga of events between Narva and Poltava is condensed into five pages. What does interest him is the impact of the Swedish wars on the social, economic, and administrative development of Russia, and three-quarters of the book is devoted to this theme.

The tenth and final chapter attempts an assessment. An historiographical survey of the shifts in Peter's reputation concludes with the view that, whether or not Peter's reorganization of Russian society amounted to a revolution, it was largely opportunist: "He regarded everything he did as an immediate necessity rather than a reform, and did not notice how his actions changed both people and established systems." Peter is thus seen as a reformer by accident, and his attempt to conduct war and reform simultaneously is viewed as self-defeating: war slowed up reform, and reform prolonged the war by provoking protest and disunity at home. This last chapter partially compensates for the lack of a bibliography. A map, a family tree and a glossary usefully supplement the text.

GREY is twice as long as Klyuchevsky and sets a far more leisurely pace. The dust jacket carries a quotation from an American reviewer, claiming that this biography "combines some of the best elements of the diary, the novel and the formal history." The novelistic flavour is detectable in the prominence given to such incidents as Peter's confrontation with Sofia after the second *streltsi* revolt, the emotional scene at the death of the Scotsman General Patrick Gordon, Charles XII's grotesque behaviour in cutting off animals' heads and throwing them out of the palace windows, Peter's love-match with Catherine (his second wife), his bizarre relations with his son Alexei, Menshikov's posing as a pie-vendor to appease the czar's anger, and Peter as unsolicited pilot of the first merchant ship to enter St. Petersburg.

But Grey's book is not just bedside reading. He devotes 50 pages to Peter's interest in the navy and to the importance of his European tour. The creation of St. Petersburg—"transplanting Novgorod to the Gulf of Finland"—is well described, while there is a compelling account of how the catastrophic loss of artillery at Narva was made good. The largest section of the book (some 75 pages) is devoted to war, rebellion, and diplomacy, culminating in a detailed account of the battle of Poltava. In contrast to Klyuchevsky, Grey sees the attack on Sweden in 1700 as carefully prepared for—diplomatically, if not militarily. And Grey devotes only three chapters (out of 41) to Peter's programme of reform after Poltava—Klyuchevsky's principal focus. Grey does not attempt a final verdict on Peter, perhaps because his biography is itself an apologia. True to the chronological scheme of the book as a whole, the concluding chapter merely records the last months of the czar's life.

Grey does provide chapter notes and a bibliography of more than 70 titles, of which about 30 are available only in Russian. These include Bogolovsky's five-volume life published in the 1940s, Luppov's history of the building of St. Petersburg (1957), Tarle's work on the Russian navy (1949) and Voskresenky's edition of the legislative acts of Peter the Great (1945). But of the total of 75 titles, only 25 have been published since 1910—the year Klyuchevsky's life appeared. Grey has not superseded Klyuchevsky: the two biographies are complementary.

Readers who are deterred by Grey's 490 pages may prefer the much briefer SUMNER. Published in 1951 as one of the titles in the popular EUP series edited by A. L. Rowse, it reached its eighth impression in 1972 and has stood the test of nearly 40 years. Its theme is simply stated at the outset: "Peter the Great was decisive in the long process of transforming medieval Muscovy into modern Russia." He is portrayed as one of the four great rulers of the period, the other three being Louis XIV, Frederick the Great, and Catherine the Great.

Of the book's 10 chapters, only the first is concerned with the sort of personal details that proliferate in the other biographies. This is much more a story of Russian regeneration and expansion, and Sumner quotes Peter's own words after Poltava: "Now the final stone has been laid of the foundation of St. Petersburg." Equal weight is given to foreign policy and internal reform, and the last ten pages give a verdict that coincides broadly with Klyuchevsky.

The latest life of Peter is by far the longest. MASSIE's book has more than 900 pages, including index, maps, and many illustrations. Yet it adds little to our picture of Peter. Admittedly this is a portrait of Peter and his world, but that world is described with some self-indulgence. The opening chapter, a description of Old Muscovy, ends emotively: "Russia is a stern land with a harsh climate, but few travellers can forget its deep appeal, and no Russian ever finds peace in his soul anywhere else on earth." Of the 62 chapters that follow, among the best are those on Sophia and the *streltsi*. There are 120 pages on the period before Peter is czar, 130 on the Grand Embassy, and 226 on the Great Northern War. Chapter 40, "The Sultan's World," is a description of the Ottoman Empire from the inside, reconstructed from the Russian Ambassador's despatches, that includes a digression on the Sultan's harem.

Massie provides a graphic account of the building of St. Petersburg and a portrayal of court life derived from the pen of Friederich Christian Weber, the Hanoverian ambassador. But Massie, a master of narrative with little interest in analysis, is not ready, even after 850 pages, to attempt an assessment of Peter. Instead, he resorts to Pushkin's phrase, "eternal toiler on the throne of Russia," and applauds Peter's energy in a poetically rhetorical question: "How does one judge the endless roll of the ocean or the mighty power of the whirlwind?"

—Stuart Andrews

PETRARCH [Francesco Petrarca], 1304–1374; Italian poet.

Bergin, Thomas G., *Petrarch*. New York, Twayne, 1970.

Bishop, Morris, *Petrarch and His World*. Bloomington, Indiana University Press, 1963; London, Chatto and Windus, 1964.

Foster, Kenelm, *Petrarch, Poet and Humanist*. Edinburgh, Edinburgh University Press, 1984.

Mann, Nicholas, *Petrarch*. Oxford and New York, Oxford University Press, 1984.

Tatham, Edward H. R., *Francesco Petrarca, the First Modern Man of Letters: His Life and Correspondence* (2 vols.). London, Sheldon Press, and New York, Macmillan, 1925–26.

Trinkaus, Charles, *The Poet as Philosopher: Petrarch and the Formation of Renaissance Consciousness*. New Haven, Connecticut, and London, Yale University Press, 1979.

Whitfield, John H., *Petrarch and the Renascence*. Oxford, Blackwell, 1943.

Wilkins, Ernest Hatch, *Life of Petrarch*. Chicago, University of Chicago Press, 1961.

*

Petrarch is so massively important a figure in the history of European culture, and his life, works, and travels so various, that it is a pity there is really only one biography available in English worthy of serious consideration, the 1961 *Life of Petrarch* by Ernest Hatch Wilkins (see below), drawing on that author's earlier three-volume academic study of the poet's life and works. Unfortunately Wilkins does not concern himself with those facets of Petrarch's life most likely to be of interest to the modern reader: Petrarch the inaugurator of the Renaissance whose Roman and Florentine loyalties, grafted on to his experience at the Avignon papal court, created in him a new sensibility and led him toward a life-time's cultural effort obviously obsessed by the figure of Augustine a millenium before.

Earlier English-language biographies are still to be found, like the 1775 *Life of Petrarch* in two volumes by Susanna Dobson that is adapted from a French model by Jacques de Sade. Other notable early treatments include T. Campbell's two-volume *Life and Times of Petrarch* (1843), or H. C. Hollway-Cathrop's *Petrarch, His Life and Times* (1907). All of these works are marked by the ways in which their period sought to produce encyclopedic volumes in which the individual achievements of the subjects of biographies were seen against very broad cultural backdrops.

The first recognisably modern biography in English, unhappily incomplete, is TATHAM's two-volume *Life and Letters*. This work is slow, meandering, and lacking in concision. The lack of incisiveness and penetration goes with a tendency to moralise, notably about Petrarch's "pessimism." The book is more readable than reliably informative, and the judgements now need modifying and sharpening.

The elegant volume by WHITFIELD contains more on Petrarch's historical background than on his life. Its main thrust is in its presentation of the way in which the classical past was reborn through the leadership of Petrarch after what we call the "middle ages," summed up in the chapter heading "Ancient and Modern against Medieval." There is an excellent introduction along with notes, an index, and a bibliography, with some quotations left in Italian.

WILKINS concentrates on Petrarch's personality and draws very heavily on his letters. Wilkins is not really a cultural historian. The Petrarch he offers us in the academic works (*Petrarch*

in Provence, 1351–53; Petrarch's Eight Years in Milan, 1353–61; Petrarch's Later Years, 1361–74), as in the *Life*, is as much the gardener, fisherman, and botanist as the renewer of antique culture, the poet, and the moralist. Above all, however, Petrarch emerges as a loyal personal friend and a passionate devotee of letters. The difficulty with Wilkins' *Life* is that it is based on too great a knowledge of the letters and day-to-day concerns and does not stand back enough to make a serious estimate of what each detail contributes to Petrarch's total achievement. Wilkins almost admits to being overwhelmed by the literary problem, writing of Petrarch, "We know more about his experiences in life than of any human being who had lived before his time." There is some speculative reconstruction, some evocation of scenes, but Wilkins' study is mostly a sketch of activities, travel, and daily life, season by season. It is a fairly short book, intended to be popular, with an index, a list of Petrarch's works, and all quotations now translated.

Of BISHOP's *Petrarch and His World* a later Petrarch biographer has written that it adds to the "almost impeccable bones" of Wilkins "a great deal of elegant and entertaining (but not always reliable) flesh," a judgement with which one has to agree. Bishop's book, which originated as a series of lectures in Indiana, recreates Petrarch's life and emphasises the role Florence played in Petrarch's imagination. A bibliography, notes, and an index denote the trappings of academic presentation, but some fairly banal quotations from other modern historians belie it. Bishop's readability beckons as fatally as the sirens' song because his grasp of intellectual history is horrifyingly superficial, as on the Averroism, which "accepted astrology, which being deterministic, rules out free will," or on the pope's fear of the "dangers of the high style in business." Nothing is quite so simple as that. On the other hand Bishop is good on Petrarch's hesitancy on whether art exists for beauty and delight or for its civilizing function, and on his views about poetic inspiration. He recognises the affectations of inconsequence and triviality in the Laura poems and rightly quotes at length from the *Secretum*, Petrarch's "spiritual purge," although he elsewhere underplays the importance for Petrarch of Augustine.

BERGIN's volume in Twayne's World Author series has an index and an annotated bibliography and is in its way excellent, setting Petrarch's life more easily now against the unusually complicated cultural background of his period. Only the poems, when quoted, are left in Italian, but the analysis and criticism, although they do crowd out the narration of the life itself, are of high quality. As a book for the general reader, this one scores highly in its presentation of the chronology and in its informed account of the historical background. It is a concise and recommendable account of Petrarch, the man and the artist.

The five essays by TRINKAUS are short and not really biographical. They attempt to reinforce their author's well-known interpretation of the intellectual history of the Renaissance, which he sees in terms of the transformation of thought patterns leading to a new sort of self-conception, with poetry and rhetoric creating "an intimate bond between reason and emotion." The importance of Petrarch's intellectual and spiritual activity in the context of the formation of a specifically Renaissance sensibility may well interest those curious about Petrarch's life.

Two works remain for consideration. FOSTER's book in the Writers of Italy series is workmanlike, short, and learned, with the quotations from the poetry left in Italian, but more devoted to criticism than to biography. MANN's *Petrarch* in the Oxford Past Masters series is a short, elegant, accurate, and totally up-to-date account of Petrarch although it, too, is not strictly a biography. It is a beautifully written little book, containing an excellent guide to modern scholarship, and is always precise and clear about its subject, on whom Mann, Director of the Warburg Institute, is himself one of the major world authorities.

—A.H.T. Levi

PHILIP II, 382 B.C.–336 B.C.; king of Macedon.

Andronikos, Manolês and Harry Deng, *Philip of Macedonia.* New York, Jupiter Books, 1984.

Cawkwell, George, *Philip of Macedon.* London and Boston, Faber, 1978.

Ellis, J. R., *Philip II and Macedonian Imperialism.* London, Thames and Hudson, 1976.

Hatzopoulos, Miltiades B. and Louisa D. Loukopoulos, editors, *Philip of Macedon.* London, Heinemann, 1981.

Hogarth, David G., *Philip and Alexander of Macedon: Two Essays in Biography.* London, J. Murray, 1897.

∗

Philip appears to have received no direct biography in antiquity, though he obviously comes in for considerable attention within the sources pertinent to his most famous son, Alexander the Great, so much so that the classic reference is to the *Two Essays in Biography* by HOGARTH. This was a first attempt to correct the biographical gap and to balance the relative estimate of the father and son.

The biographical source for Alexander accorded greatest reliability is that of Arrian (*The Life of Alexander the Great by Arrian*, translated by Aubrey de Selincourt, 1958), since it was based upon the contemporary accounts of two of Alexander's generals: Ptolemy and Aristobulus. But it has little to say about Philip, since, beginning from the latter's death, it becomes the "Anabasis" or itinerary of Alexander's Persian conquest.

On the other hand Plutarch covers a number of those contemporary with Philip, within which his life requires reference, even if as a foil: Agesilaus, Timoleon, Pelopidas, Phocion, Demosthenes, and especially Alexander. In addition, Plutarch wrote, without a parallel, a life of the Persian king, Artaxerxes II. With the exception of the latter, translations of those "lives" are easiest obtained in *The Age of Alexander* (with historical introduction by G. T. Griffith, 1973).

Contemporary with Philip were historians, as well as orators or rhetoricians—we might even say "politicians"—some of whose speeches directly assailed or praised Philip. N.G.L. Hammond, writing in the *Oxford Classical Dictionary* (1949), noted "the nationalist Demosthenes saw in Philip a perfidious despot, the Panhellenist Isocrates and Ephorus a leader of Greece, and the individualist Theopompus the greatest man Europe had ever known." Specific examples of Isocrates (436 B.C–338 B.C.) and Demosthenes (384 B.C–322 B.C.) are best found in *Greek Orations*, edited by W. Robert Connor (1966), which also includes

"the letter of Philip" noted for its sarcastic and scornful response to Demosthenes, thereby providing one autobiographical hint of Philip himself.

The works of the historians Ephorus of Kyme (*ca.* 405 B.C–330 B.C.) and Theopompus of Khios (born *ca.* 378 B.C.), both pupils of Isocrates, survive only in fragments. These are derived from later summarizers who are not always in sympathy with their perspectives on Philip, or are unduly impressed by Alexander, or are simply of so much later date.

For original inscriptions found at classical Greek sites, which include the alliance of Philip with the Chalcidians of 356 B.C., and the king's peace made with representatives of all the Greek city-states after their defeat at the battle of Chaironeia in 338 B.C., translations are available in John Wickersham and Gerald Verbrugghe, *Greek Historical Documents: The Fourth Century B.C.* (1973). While neither the orations nor the inscriptions can be considered biography in some restricted sense, they do provide perspective on Philip and on the opinions about him by his contemporaries. They have come to be used as the bases for any modern "historical biography."

The most noteworthy development since 1977 was the discovery of the royal Macedonian tombs near Vergina, wherein, among the actual remains from Tomb II, was a preserved skull, recognizable by 1983 as Philip's, from the loss of the right eye which the king had suffered, according to Theopompus, "when he was struck by an arrow while inspecting the siege-engines and the protective sheds at the siege of Methone." Biographical concern has been renewed out of these archaeological considerations.

Just before the excavations began, ELLIS had closed a gap relative to the lack of full-scale studies of Philip's reign, especially of the political expansion of Macedonia. Ellis considers that Philip's military skill is matched by his diplomatic adroitness, of which Alexander inherited the former, but had no opportunity to demonstrate the latter. CAWKWELL's work had nearly been completed when the excavation news arrived. It represents a good summary of all that had previously been said about Philip. Slimmer than Ellis' volume, this study focuses more on the career—again to Philip's advantage over Alexander.

Both Ellis and Cawkwell had been revised by G. T. Griffith, who, during the same period, was working with N.G.L. Hammond through the second volume of a *History of Macedonia* (1979). All three works shun the more anachronistic views that Macedonian expansion could be accounted for simply in terms of either the king's ambitions or his ideals. Their divergence concerning Philip hinges on their several interpretations of how he overcame the inherent weakness of, and gained external stability for, Macedon.

Others have reemphasized from a close study of a fragment by the Peripatetic biographer Satyrus (3rd century B.C.) Philip's seven political marriages. These marriages return consideration to the excavations; for within the tombs was evidence of more than one female presence. All of the major recent biographers, including Andronikos, Cawkwell, Ellis, Griffith, Hammond, among others, were assembled in the volume edited by HATZOPOLOUS AND LOUKOPOULOS, each contributing an essay on some aspect of Philip's life. This volume contains some spectacular color plates and would make a splendid sampler for the general reader. ANDRONIKOS AND DENG continued the updating of the revised biography within this larger pictorial format.

—Clyde Curry Smith

PHILIP II, 1527–1598; Spanish monarch.

Cadoux, C. J., *Philip of Spain and the Netherlands: An Essay on Moral Judgments in History*. London, Lutterworth Press, 1947.

Gayarré, Charles, *Philip II*. New York, W. J. Middleton, 1866.

Grierson, Edward, *The Fatal Inheritance: Philip II and the Spanish Netherlands*. London, Gollancz, and New York, Doubleday, 1969.

Lynch, John, *Spain under the Habsburgs* (2 vols.). Oxford, Clarendon Press, and New York, Oxford University Press, 1963–69.

Mattingly, Garrett, *The Armada*. Boston, Houghton Mifflin, 1959; as *The Defeat of the Spanish Armada*, London, Cape, 1959.

Merriman, R. B., *The Rise of the Spanish Empire in the Old World and the New* (see volume IV, "Philip the Prudent"). New York, Macmillan 1918–34.

Parker, Geoffrey, *Philip II*. London, Hutchinson, and Boston, Little Brown, 1978.

Petrie, Sir Charles, *Philip II of Spain*. London, Eyre and Spottiswoode, and New York, Norton, 1963.

Pierson, Peter, *Philip II of Spain*. London, Thames and Hudson, 1975.

Rule, J. C. and J. TePaske, editors, *The Character of Philip II: The Problem of Moral Judgments in History*. Boston, Heath, 1963.

Walsh, William T., *Philip II*. London and New York, Sheed and Ward, 1937.

*

The intention of GAYARRÉ's work is to provide an insight to the persona of Philip II. The intellect and cultural preferences of the man are examined in the light of historical events rather than as arising out of them. It is this emphasis that makes Gayarré's work of interest. Often verbose, opinionated, and subjective (though perhaps this is its appeal), the book reflects the era in which it was written more accurately than the mood of the era about which it was written.

Many works written before this century betray an anti-Catholic bias in their evaluation of Philip II. This problem has been examined by RULE AND TEPASKE, whose book contains a useful and substantial bibliography and is interesting for the angle it adopts in assessing the various characters that have been assigned to Philip II by his biographers. CADOUX's work can be seen to have inherited this traditional prejudice as Cadoux seeks to portray Philip as a monstrous tyrant with no inclination to serve his subjects. It is a typically subjective account and

counteracts WALSH's earlier work, which comes from the opposite camp and yet equally lacks historical objectivity and discernment.

MERRIMAN, in the fourth volume of his larger work on the Spanish empire, has long held a primary place among the studies of Philip II. His evaluation of Philip has only been built on by subsequent historians. The style of the book is not flamboyant nor is it even compelling, yet Merriman establishes Philip's character accurately: an unimaginative, constant, prosaic figure who rarely departed from the norm of his behaviour. Merriman does, however, fall into the trap of attributing to Philip many policy initiatives that should rightly be assigned by the historian to his ministers and advisers. Overall this is a wide-ranging and thorough study, tracing Philip's achievements in the context of Spain, its empire abroad, and the realms governed outside the Spanish context. Merriman goes further to examine Philip in the light of the role he played on the broader European stage, as a statesman operating in an unstable and war-torn Europe.

MATTINGLY, a student of Merriman, demonstrates a similar understanding of Philip in his work. However, Mattingly's analysis is perhaps more searching, his attempt to establish Philip more carefully made. Mattingly makes a deeper psychological analysis to uncover an inherent hesitancy that was to give rise to the bland prudence of Philip established by Merriman. Mattingly uses this by way of an explanation for Philip's diligence in attending to his state papers.

PETRIE gives a sympathetic view of Philip in a popular, highly regarded biography. PIERSON in his more recent work gives a conservative Philip, determined and successful in maintaining the status quo with no grand scheme realised because, except perhaps in his later years, he had conceived none. In this work Pierson brings the human Philip to the fore, emphasising his family role and evaluating his development from childhood to old age as few other biographers have attempted. He explains Philip's conservatism and intransience in terms of his religious ideology.

While not strictly a biography, the work by LYNCH is again well thought of by other biographers and is repeatedly referred to. This is a sophisticated if not lengthy study of the reign that essentially adopts Merriman's view of Philip. It is perhaps a good place to start a study of the man.

Another place to start might be with GRIERSON's book. A novelist as well as an historian, Grierson has written an account that is readable and even compelling. Grierson is anxious to sustain the interest of his reader, of whom he does not presume a vast degree of knowledge of 16th- and 17th-century Europe. His emphasis is therefore on arguably the most romantic aspect of Philip's reign—the revolt of the Netherlands—aptly named "the fatal inheritance." This Grierson views in the traditional way, as a rebellion against the tyranny of Spain. Although he does not concern himself with the evolution of Philip's character from childhood, he is sympathetic while remaining objective in his appraisal, and he often adopts a psychological mode of analysis.

More recently still, PARKER, a recognised and respected authority on the history of European Habsburg lands of and around Philip's reign, has written a challenging work on Philip. His sources include letters and contemporary accounts of his subject, and he presents an objective, yet again sympathetic, portrait. Parker forwards the view that Philip's attitude to his affairs arose not merely from a religious, ideological standpoint, but also from a constitutional one. Parker maintains that for Philip, Protestantism was synonymous with rebellion and disunity; thus his devotion to Catholicism in all spheres of life was reinforced by his political perceptions of the evils of Protestantism. In his epilogue, Parker also gives an interesting summary of "Philip II, in Myth and Legend."

—Rebecca C. Pilcher

PIAF, Edith, 1915–1963; French cabaret singer.

Berteaut, Simone, *Piaf: A Biography*, translated by June Guicharnaud. New York, Harper, 1972 (originally published by Opera Mundi, Paris, 1969).

Bret, David, *The Piaf Legend*. London, Robson Books, 1988.

Crosland, Margaret, *Piaf*. New York, Putnam, and London, Hodder and Stoughton, 1985.

Lange, Monique, *Piaf*, translated by Richard S. Woodward. New York, Seaver Books, and London, W. H. Allen, 1981 (originally published as *Histoire de Piaf*, Paris, Éditions Ramsay, 1979).

*

Much of the biographical material on Edith Piaf, of course, has appeared only in French. In fact, two of the works currently to be found in English are translations, and one of those (Berteaut) is out of print. Only within the past five years have biographies written in English been published. Still, the range of the books available in English offers something for anyone's needs.

The first is BERTEAUT's *Piaf*, a personal "how tough it was for us kids" approach by Edith's supposed half-sister. Crosland (see below) dismisses that claim but grants that Simone and Edith were close as teenagers. She also notes omissions and falsification of incidents by Berteaut. At times, moreover, a reader must be careful to determine whether the "I" is Edith or Simone. Although Berteaut makes for an emotional, sometimes soapy read, the tone of the book still gives what is perhaps the most authentic feeling for Piaf's life, especially the early years. Details such as their wearing new clothes until they were dirty and then replacing them because of a lack of laundry facilities somehow ring true.

LANGE's *Piaf*, larger in format than the others, also contains many more photographs to document the various stages of Piaf's life. It is correspondingly short on text, but the photos, many of which appear here only, are themselves adequate compensation. Sometimes Piaf's expressive face tells its own story. Some of the photos are of other celebrities or of events that capture the spirit of the times, but they are not mere fillers. If one is looking for a pictorial biography in English, Lange is it.

The best-researched and documented biography, however, is CROSLAND's, the first to be originally written in English. As mentioned above, it points out some of the problems with Berteaut, and the whole tone of the book shows a dual concern—for the subject and for the facts. It is, for example, the only book discussed here to contain a bibliography. Also included are a discography, a checklist of songs (titles, composers, lyric-writers,

recording companies, and dates), and a filmography. One is not surprised to learn that Crosland has written biographies of Colette and Cocteau as well. A reader seeking a single, reliable treatment of Piaf's life should choose Crosland.

The recent entry in the field is BRET, whose work is the shortest (161 pages for the biography as such), but it is concise rather than superficial. The author, described as an authority on the *chanson*, has a particular interest in Piaf as singer and in her songs. Included are a discography by year from 1935–63, a filmography, and theatre productions in which Piaf appeared. Also listed are film and theatre tributes to Piaf, revues honoring her music, and British radio and television biographies. Bret deals with Piaf from the perspective of a sincere, knowledgeable, and genuine longtime fan.

Except for the reservations about Berteaut as expressed by Crosland, most of these books will supply the essential facts about Piaf, as best they can be determined. But each also offers something of its own special flavor to suit the reader's taste. The scholar or serious reader will chose Crosland, whose bibliography shows a familiarity with a range of materials in both French and English. The general reader has the choice of Berteaut's street-wise emotion, Lange's photos, or Bret's tribute.

—Robert E. Burkhart

PICASSO, Pablo, 1881–1973; Spanish painter and sculptor in France.

Barr, Alfred M., *Picasso: 50 Years of His Art*. New York, Museum of Modern Art, 1946.

Boeck, Wilhelm, *Picasso*. New York, Abrams, and London, Thames and Hudson, 1955.

Brassaï, *Picasso and Company*. New York, Doubleday, 1966; London, Thames and Hudson, 1967.

Chipp, Herschel, *Picasso's "Guernica": History, Transformations, Meanings*. Berkeley, University of California Press, 1988; London, Thames and Hudson, 1989.

Cirlot, Juan-Eduardo, *Picasso, Birth of a Genius*. New York, Praeger, and London, Elek, 1972.

Crespelle, Jean-Paul, *Picasso and His Women*, translated by Robert Baldick. New York, Coward McCann, and London, Hodder and Stoughton, 1969 (originally published as *Picasso, les femmes, les amies, l'oeuvre*, Paris, Presses de la Cité, 1967).

Duncan, David Douglas, *The Private World of Pablo Picasso*. New York, Harper, 1958.

Elgar, Frank and Robert Maillard, *Picasso*, translated by Francis Scarfe. New York, Praeger, and London, Thames and Hudson, 1956; revised and enlarged edition, New York, Tudor, and London, Thames and Hudson, 1972.

Gedo, Mary, *Picasso: Art as Autobiography*. Chicago and London, University of Chicago Press, 1980.

Gilot, Françoise and Carlton Lake, *Life with Picasso*. New York, McGraw-Hill, 1964; London, Penguin, 1966.

Glimcher, Arnold and Marc Glimcher, *Je Suis le Cahier: The Sketchbooks of Picasso*. New York, Atlantic Monthly Press, and London, Thames and Hudson, 1986.

Huffington, Arianna Stassinopoulos, *Picasso, Creator and Destroyer*. New York, Simon and Schuster, and London, Weidenfeld and Nicolson, 1988.

Laporte, Geneviève, *Sunshine at Midnight: Memories of Picasso*, translated by Douglas Cooper. London, Weidenfeld and Nicolson, 1975 (originally published as *Si tard le soir, le soleil brille*, Paris, Plon, 1973).

Leighton, Patricia, *Reordering the Universe: Picasso and Anarchism, 1897–1914*. Princeton, New Jersey, and London, Princeton University Press, 1989.

McCully, Marilyn, *A Picasso Anthology: Documents, Criticism, Reminiscences*. London, British Arts Council/Thames and Hudson, 1981; Princeton, New Jersey, Princeton University Press, 1982.

McKnight, Gerald, *Bitter Legacy: Picasso's Disputed Millions*. New York and London, Bantam, 1987.

O'Brian, Patrick, *Picasso, a Biography*. New York, Putnam, and London, Collins, 1976.

Olivier, Fernande, *Picasso and His Friends*, translated by Jane Miller. New York, Appleton-Century, and London, Heinemann, 1964 (originally published by Stock, Paris, 1933).

Penrose, Roland, *Picasso: His Life and Work*. London, Gollancz, 1958; New York, Harper, 1959; 3rd edition, Berkeley, University of California Press, 1981.

Penrose, Roland and John Golding, editors, *Picasso in Retrospect*. New York, Praeger, and London, Elek, 1973.

Sabartès, Jaime, *Picasso: An Intimate Portrait*. New York, Prentice-Hall, 1948; London, W. H. Allen, 1949.

Schiff, Gert, *Picasso: The Last Years, 1963–73*. New York, G. Braziller, 1983.

*

Among the important comprehensive works on Picasso, that of PENROSE (1958) is considered a triumph for a large biography, produced both by a longtime friend and within the subject's lifetime. Penrose attempts an objective view (with few photographs and little critical analysis) of the flow of events in the artist's life. Yet some have complained that Penrose was overly discreet, thereby distorting his discussion.

BOECK focuses on Picasso's art, though the extensive notes to his text supply anecdotal details, many of which have since become legend. Jaime Sabartès, Picasso's secretary and life-long friend, supplied a 60-page introductory essay entitled "Thoughts about Picasso." The work also contains a classified catalog with over 500 illustrations. Boeck, like many other later writers, acknowledges his debt to BARR, who had provided a critical- biographical text and 500-item catalog. Earlier, SABARTÈS had himself published his charming recollections, covering the early years of the century in the first half of the book, with the latter half telling of the years 1935–41, when Sabartès came to live in Picasso's house and became his secretary, which he remained until his death.

ELGAR AND MAILLARD present a critical survey of Picasso's works (written by Elgar) and a biographical survey in the form of short paragraphs, often a year-by-year listing of important events and illustrated only by artwork pertaining to that time (written by Maillard). There are no illustrations at all in O'BRIAN's 500-page book intended for the intelligent non-

specialist. It contains neither bibliography nor footnotes and offers few critical or interpretive comments. O'Brian feels the importance of Picasso's early life and presents it in great detail: the first half of the text brings his life only up to World War I.

BRASSAI was a well-known Hungarian photographer who began a close acquaintance with Picasso in 1943, when the text begins. His focus is the period 1943–47, and his method, relayed in the introduction by Penrose, was to make notes after a visit to Picasso and then place them in a box that came to be labeled "Conversations with Picasso." Each entry, with a specific date, narrates Brassai's and Picasso's conversation, as well as those with other notable personalities who visited Picasso.

DUNCAN, the best-known American photographer to work with Picasso, began his friendship with him in 1956 and has produced several notable books in the category of visual biography. In *The Private World of Pablo Picasso*, which contains a brief text, Picasso is portrayed as the charming genius at play with friends and family and at work: many of Duncan's photographs have become standard Picasso iconography.

Several of the many women in the artist's life have composed memoirs of their time with him. CRESPELLE's text is a light-hearted survey of Picasso's two wives and many companions. OLIVIER, the fabled first important woman, evokes an innocent world of the pre-World War I loves of the still little-known artist. She excludes her own relationship with Picasso. LAPORTE, through her quiet charm, seemed to attract the devotion and protection of Picasso's circle. Her work is little known.

The work of GILOT, Picasso's companion from 1943 to 1953 and mother of two of his four children, has been hailed as "one of the most agonizingly honest . . . and most haunting accounts of the life of a painter in the history of art." With apparently inexhaustible memory, Gilot re-creates the artist's attitude and tone and offers detailed interpretations. Some among Picasso's inner circle tried to stop publication of Gilot's biography; her revelations of negative character qualities of an international figure were taken as indiscretions.

While Gilot's text is generally considered to be fair-minded, the comprehensive biography by HUFFINGTON, who held long consultations with Gilot, provides a dark picture of the older Picasso, whom Huffington had never met. Her minutely-researched book evoked massive publicity at its appearance, partially because of its alleged distorted image of Picasso, but also through more calculated actions of the publishing industry to enhance the celebrity status of the already well-known author. The book contains elaborate footnotes and a detailed bibliography. (A lengthy and very useful condensation of the text appeared in *The Atlantic*, June 1988.)

In the current critical climate, with its turn away from form invention as the foremost determinant of value, LEIGHTON is among those who emphasize Picasso's intellectual and emotional commitments—in her case, to the radical political thought at the century's turn. She shows, through a reading of early figurative works, and even the heretofore-held purely decorative collages of 1913–14, that these paintings reveal a revulsion toward the bourgeois industrial world in decay, together with a utopian hope of renewal. The approach of GEDO is psychoanalytical; she speculates on the life-long influences of the artist's youth and family relationships. She proposes that Picasso's art always depended on partnerships and that he was always able—as reflected in his more vital stylistic periods—to maintain connections to an important individual and group. Gedo also emphasizes the destructive aspect of Picasso's relationships with women.

A documentation of this early life is found in CIRLOT's catalog of Picasso's donation, to the city of Barcelona, of a collection of almost 1000 of his drawings and paintings produced from 1894 to 1904. Under the care of family members since at least 1917, they form one of the most complete records in history of the early development of an artist. Cirlot's text details five critical areas of development, with larger illustrations in color and smaller black-and-white images included to present the totality of the collection. Similarly, GLIMCHER looks at the often lost world of creative process. While the text is comprised of six essays that trace the meanings of the six complete sketchbooks (offered in the original exhibition), selected pages from other sketchbooks are also shown, along with a catalogue raisonné, with one illustration each, accounting for the surviving 175 Picasso sketchbooks, ranging in time from 1905 to 1962. The title of the exhibition came from the phrase Picasso himself wrote onto sketchbook number 40.

A multifaceted view of the artist is found in McCULLY; in eight sections that span Picasso's entire career, McCully has collected all manner of documents—periodical articles, letters, catalog entries, etc.—to present a Cubist-like picture. She supplies introductions to each larger chronological section and to the individual entries.

Exemplary of several books now available that treat one of Picasso's best-known works and no doubt the 20th century's single most discussed work, CHIPP presents a detailed documentary view of the Spanish Republic and the Destruction of Guernica on 26 April 1937. Picasso's politics are discussed, and the many contemporary photographs include the famous set by Picasso's mistress of that time, Dora Maar, which show ten states of the mural-sized canvas on its way to completion. Another fine blend of critical and biographical treatment is found in the volume by PENROSE AND GOLDING (1973), where seven illustrated essays present Picasso's work from early to late.

In SCHIFF, the catalog of an exhibition, and many others within the past two decades, there is found a careful revision of the previous feeling of decline in Picasso's final three decades of work. Putting aside the expected unevenness in an enormous output, Schiff's essay examines the themes and creative problems of old age, and argues the qualities of greatness beyond mere poignance.

The destructive aspect of Picasso, asserted by Huffington and others, is largely responsible for the world-famous drama that ensued after Picasso died intestate. McKNIGHT wrote his short book after conversations with several members of the family; in it, their personalities, both the damaged and the healthy ones, are shown in complex legal workings to establish heirs. The book includes a family tree.

The 1535-item listing in Ray Anne Kibbey, *Picasso: A Comprehensive Bibliography* (1977), divides works on Picasso by type of publication—monograph, catalog, essay, etc. Further material is covered in a detailed index. The long-awaited four-volume biography by John Richardson, *The Life of Picasso* (New York, Random House) is to begin publication in 1990.

—Joshua Kind

PIERO DELLA FRANCESCA, *ca.* 1420–1492; Italian painter.

Clark, Kenneth, *Piero della Francesca*. London and New York, Phaidon Press, 1951; 2nd revised edition, 1969.

Ginzberg, Carlo, *The Enigma of Piero*, translated by Martin Ryle and Kate Soper. London, Verso, 1985 (originally published as *Indagini Su Piero*, Turin, Guilio Einaudi, 1981).

Hendy, Philip, *Piero della Francesca and the Early Renaissance*. New York, Macmillan, and London, Weidenfeld and Nicolson, 1968.

Longhi, Roberto, *Piero Della Francesca*, translated by Leonard Penlock. London and New York, F. Warne, 1931 (originally published, Florence, 1927).

Vasari, Giorgio, *Lives of the Artists* (2 vols.), translated by George Bull. London and New York, Penguin, 1965 (originally published as *Le Vite de piu eccelenti architetti, pittori, et scultori italiani*, Florence, 1550, 1568).

Venturi, Lionell, *Piero Della Francesca*, translated by James Emmons. Geneva, Skira, 1954.

*

The earliest account of Piero's life can be found in VASARI, and in this instance subsequent scholars agree that the assertion of the facts of place and patrons can be relied on as a starting point for investigation. No single work on Piero is devoted strictly to the details of his life, for there are not enough recorded references to produce a standard biography.

By far the most scholarly investigation of Piero is LONGHI's classic. It covers all the known facts of Piero's life and his association with the councilors in his home of Borgo San Sepolcro, as well as documenting his works in Arezzo, Ferrara, and for the Duke of Urbino. This work proposed the illuminating premise that Piero was one of the founding artists of the whole European tradition of painting because his artistic vision merged the painting styles of Florence, Bruges, and Venice. Since its translation into English in 1931, it has proven to be the basis for most subsequent analytical research. Written in a polished academic style, it offers not only biographical information, but theories on the artistic interpretation of the underlying themes of the works. All illustrations are in black and white.

CLARK's volume offers the general reader a clear look at the biography as well as the circumstances of the works without losing the audience in a maze of academic footnotes. Clark incorporates some of the research compiled by Oreste del Buono and Pier Luigi de' Vechhi in *L'Opera completa di Piero della Francesca* (1967), and he strongly suggests that Piero's artistic reputation in Florence was more important than previously thought due to his early works. Clark links the arrival of a diplomatic mission from Constantinople with Piero's virtuosity at depicting exotic Eastern costumes in his fresco cycles.

Because of Clark's flowing literary style, the reader can more completely understand the relationship between the subjects of Piero's works and the known biographical notations. There are both black-and-white illustrations and clear color plates that are conveniently arranged for the reader's information.

HENDY offers the first scholarly edition originally done for an English-speaking audience. However, he focuses primarily on the works themselves and weaves the biographical thread through minute descriptions of religious and historical themes. The literary style of Clark's volume is much to be preferred to

Hendy's for its clarity as well as for the more logical arrangement of fact and theory. Hendy's work would serve for those readers interested in direct comparison of a biographical entry to a given work, such as a specific journey to Urbino and the details found in the ''Flagellation of Christ.'' In addition, the many color plates included in this volume aid the reader's understanding of the arguments made in the body of the text.

VENTURI's account briefly summarizes Piero's life while adding psychological interpretations of the artist's intent as found in the compositional elements of the artworks themselves. Venturi based his observations on the Humanistic principle of the Cult of Man espoused by Coluccio Salutati and Leonardo Bruni, which, in Venturi's judgment, Piero embraced in his life as evidenced by the subjects of his art. The artist's depiction of the fortunes of the wealthy and powerful can be directly correlated to Piero's growing artistic reputation and the esteem in which he was held in Borgo San Sepolcro and the rest of Italy. Venturi's work can be viewed as a scholarly speculation concerning the theoretical, artistic, and biographical connections in Piero's life. The small number of color plates in the work contributes to its overall academic theme.

By far the most interesting work on Piero della Francesca published to date, which includes both biography and investigative artistic theory, is by GINZBERG. Although it is written for scholars and contains long explanatory footnotes for guidance through the arguments, the work is fascinating because Ginzberg is neither a professional biographer nor an art historian. Rather, he is a general historian who here writes from the stated purpose of demonstrating how to use works of art as larger historical resources rather than as narrow interpretations of the contents as evidence of the painter's state of mind. For Ginzberg the question is one of proper focus, and in this larger framework, the small body of facts that are known about Piero's life form a core that can be used to frame a more substantial view of the society in which he lived.

Ginzberg's book includes black-and-white photographs of specific architectural elements, sculptures, prints, and artifacts to bolster theories concerning artistic references to specific historical elements found in the paintings. The contents are organized around historical topics following the chronology of Piero's life; this combined with a lucid writing style make this the most pleasurable work yet produced on Piero della Francesca.

—Linda K. Varkonda

—————

PINTER, Harold, 1930–   ; English playwright.

Hayman, Ronald, *Harold Pinter*. London, Heinemann, 1968; New York, Ungar, 1973.

Hinchliffe, Arnold P., *Harold Pinter*. New York, Twayne, 1967; reissued, New York, St. Martin's, 1975; London, Macmillan, 1976.

Thompson, David T., *Pinter, the Player's Playwright*. New York, Schocken, and London, Macmillan, 1985.

*

The best source of biographical information on Harold Pinter, in the absence of a full biography, can be found in several interviews and reviews, especially around the time of his successes with *The Birthday Party* (1958) and *The Caretaker* (1960). Notable for biographical material are Mel Gussow's article in the *New York Times Magazine* (5 December 1971), L. M Bensky's interview in *Paris Review* (1966), and Joan Bakewell's interview in *Listener* (November 1969). THOMPSON, hardly a full-fledged biography, nevertheless offers some connection between the playwright's life and work, and gives three opening chapters to Pinter's early repertory experience, his development as an actor (under the stage name David Baron), his Irish apprenticeship, and his first attempts at ''play-writing.'' The rest of the text, essentially an analysis of Pinter's dramaturgy, sprinkles anecdotes from previous interviews among the criticism. An appendix lists his roles from 1949–59. HAYMAN offers a study of the plays, the only biographical information being a list of stage and broadcast productions with dates. HINCHLIFFE, despite its protracted notes, bibliography, and index, is not a biography but a critical overview.

—Thomas J. Taylor

—————

PITT, William [the younger], 1759–1806; English statesman.

Ehrman, John, *The Younger Pitt: The Years of Acclaim*. London, Constable, and New York, Dutton, 1969.

Ehrman, John, *The Younger Pitt: The Reluctant Transition*. London, Constable, and Stanford, California, Stanford University Press, 1983.

Jarrett, Derek, *Pitt the Younger*. New York, Scribner, and London, Weidenfeld and Nicolson, 1974.

Mackesy, Piers, *War Without Victory: The Downfall of Pitt 1799–1802*. Oxford, Clarendon Press, and New York, Oxford University Press, 1984.

Reilly, Robin, *Pitt the Younger*. London, Cassell, 1978.

Rose, John Holland, *Life of William Pitt*. London, Bell, 1923; New York, Harcourt, 1924.

Rosebery, Archibald, *Pitt*. London and New York, Macmillan, 1891.

Stanhope, Philip Henry, 5th Earl, *Life of the Right Honourable William Pitt* (4 vols.). London, J. Murray, 1861–62.

Tomline, George, *Memoirs of the Life of the Right Honorable William Pitt* (3 vols.). London, J. Murray, 1821.

Wilson, Philip W., *William Pitt, the Younger*. London, Stanley Paul, 1928; New York, Doubleday, 1930.

*

The central problem facing biographers of Pitt the Younger is an embarrassment of biographical and historical riches, the product of a life fully and publicly chronicled, and a historical context of international scope. Evidence of this phenomenon can be seen in the labors of Ehrman, who toiled in the complexities and vagaries of late 18th-century parliamentary documents for

14 years between publishing the first and second volumes of his planned three-part biography. However, Ehrman was not alone in confronting—not always successfully—the problem of writing a biography of a man constantly at the center of the world stage without writing simultaneously the history of world affairs during the same period. Virtually every biographer of Pitt has found himself concerned more fully with the details of revolution and war, radical social change, economic upheavals, and parliamentary intrigue than—specifically—with the daily life of the man who so profoundly influenced these events. As Reilly (see below) observes, for all his public stature, Pitt was in many ways a private man: a poor correspondent, his letters provide little insight into his character. While the biographies of Ehrman and others have produced remarkably sophisticated analyses of the politics of late 18th-century England, they have found the task of capturing Pitt's essential personality an elusive one.

Although Ehrman is recognized as the unquestioned authority on Pitt's life, several others have contributed significantly to the field. Although consistently inaccurate, TOMLINE's three-volume *Memoirs* gives a lively account beginning with the military triumphs of the elder Pitt in the Seven Years' War. As almost all subsequent biographers point out, Pitt was born at the peak of the elder Pitt's popularity, on the heels of a series of military successes in what Donald Greene calls the "Great War for Empire." The first important 20th-century account is Lord ROSEBERY's, which relies in part on STANHOPE's four-volume *Life*, the standard for 19th-century readers. Rosebery sees Pitt as a victim of circumstances, a man propelled prematurely into world prominence who exhausted himself fatally in ultimately futile attempts to maintain personal glory. His Pitt is passionately anti-war, yet unable to prevent its onslaught: "To no human being, then, did war come with such a curse as to Pitt, by none was it more hated or shunned."

Perhaps the most prominent scholar of Pitt in the early part of the 20th century was ROSE, whose two-part *Life* (William Pitt and National Revival, William Pitt and the Great War) was the standard for decades. In his own popular biography, which adds very little to Rose, Wilson finds a fault in Rose's book that continues to plague biographers: "The massive tomes of Dr. J. Holland Rose contain an elaborate analysis of Pitt's period, but are only incidentally biographical of Pitt himself." Indeed, Rose's book might more accurately have been titled "The Politics of Empire in the Late Eighteenth Century." Still, Pitt is certainly its central, unifying figure, and Rose provides a still useful account of ministerial crises and reform efforts. One of the central dramatic motifs in the book is the ever-present fear of national bankruptcy, with Pitt's attempts to endure from crisis to crisis. For WILSON, too, the most "astonishing fact about William Pitt is that without success he was able to survive." Wilson's book, stylish yet unscholarly, expresses amazement at Pitt's enduring reputation in the face of "supreme vicissitudes."

Two other popular biographies deserve mention: JARRETT's work is facile and unoriginal, but its fascinating illustrations justify its place on the coffee table. REILLY's is probably the best of this breed—lively though excessively appreciative and unscholarly. He begins with an odd and self-damning admission: "This is not a work of deep original research. It is an attempt to assemble and interpret material, much of it already published . . . . " One wonders about the need for such a study, especially in light of the work of Ehrman, but Reilly's book is better researched and more stylishly written than his overly humble preface would suggest. He does, however, concentrate too heavily on the career of Pitt the Elder and insufficiently on the prime ministry of Pitt the Younger.

EHRMAN was the first biographer of Pitt to recognize and assimilate the Namierite contribution to our understanding of the political complexities and factionalism of late 18-century parliamentary politics. As Ehrman comments, "no one can now assume that Pitt began his career within the structure of a definite two-party system" (although he fails to point out that the anti-Namierites have established a cottage industry of their own). This first volume takes the reader through the events of the year 1785. Making use of important primary sources, such as the Chatham Papers at the Public Record Office in London, Ehrman traces Pitt's career from his appointment as Chancellor of the Exchequer at the age of 23 and his assumption of the position of Prime Minister the following year to the apex of his success in the late 1780s. The author provides the "flavor" of the times with minute, perhaps even obsessive, particularity; the reader is treated, for example, to "the course and temper of a parliamentary session," a session to which, for unnervingly long spells, Pitt is uninvited.

Ehrman's second volume was received with conspicuously less rapturous applause than the first. His reviewers emphasized not only the length of time it took Ehrman to produce this volume, which took readers to the end of 1796, but also the tedium of much of its detail and the all-too-obvious fact that Ehrman "loses" Pitt for long sections of his biography. Carl B. Cone provides a fair-minded assessment: "Disappointing as biography, this is nevertheless a magisterial book, a superb presentation of the foreign and domestic problems that Pitt, his government, and Britain faced in this period." Ehrman regards Pitt, during this period, as optimistic and self-confident, in spite of his having been unprepared to go to war with revolutionary France. The biographer faults Pitt for his love of power, which led in part to an overly ambitious military strategy. The book gives scrupulously detailed accounts of the management of the war and lively analyses of Pitt's relationship with the press. It also details many of the reform movements of the early 1790s. In these sections, the biography of Pitt becomes a narrowly focused political history of England: the story of England's struggle to manage the dangerous influx of "French ideas." In spite of all the detail Ehrman provides, "Pitt the man" never fully emerges. The book's critics have rightly challenged the assumption that Pitt's public life revealed his private character. And they were understandably disappointed by the thinly depicted relationship between Pitt and King George III.

In lieu of the final book in the Ehrman series, MACKESY's study is useful. Light on detail, it is an account, designed for the non-specialist, of Pitt's "downfall" in the years 1799–1802.

If the Ehrman series is completed, it will stand in the way of further full-length biographies of Pitt. Still, a book that somehow manages to focus on Pitt's life and personality, isolated from the global conflicts in which he played a vital role, would be a valuable addition.

—Richard C. Taylor

PLATH, Sylvia, 1932–1963; American poet.

Butscher, Edward, *Sylvia Plath: Method and Madness.* New
York, Seabury Press, 1976.

Stevenson, Anne, *Bitter Fame: A Life of Sylvia Plath.* Boston,
Houghton Mifflin, 1989.

Wagner-Martin, Linda W., *Sylvia Plath: A Biography.* New
York, Simon and Schuster, 1987; London, Chatto and Windus,
1988.

*

When Sylvia Plath died, her husband, the poet Ted Hughes,
from whom she was separated but not divorced, became the executor of her literary estate and appointed his sister, Olwyn, literary agent. He also destroyed one of Plath's journal notebooks
and reported a second such manuscript missing. Several collections of Plath's manuscripts are housed in the Lily Library at
Indiana University and in the Smith Library Plath Collection,
where one group of papers is sealed until the year 2013 and another until after the deaths of Plath's mother and brother.

For literary biographers, this situation presents serious, often
insurmountable, problems. Denied access to the sealed manuscripts at Smith College, researchers are obliged to rely on the
memories of Plath's friends and relatives and on her published
letters and creative work, without knowing just what fraction of
her total output that represents. Further, to obtain permission to
quote from various manuscripts or to express personal interpretations of events in Plath's life, biographers must negotiate with
her literary estate, controlled by people from whom Plath was
estranged at the time of her death.

The first biographer willing to work under these conditions
was BUTSCHER. By the time he published his book, Plath had
been dead for 13 years, but Ted Hughes had not yet published
her *Collected Poems*. To complicate matters further, the Plath
estate proved uncooperative, forcing Butscher to piece together a
version of Plath's life largely from interviews with her friends,
many of whom knew Plath only slightly and for a very short
time. The result is a preponderance of detailed descriptions of
trivia: 1950s-style dating, minor physical ailments, and men-
strual cramps, for example.

Butscher becomes something of an amateur psychologist in his
approach to Plath, which is often critical and judgmental. He
frequently refers to her as a "bitch goddess," a term he admits
will distress some readers. In his preface he justifies his choice
of this term: "No doubt the appellation 'bitch goddess' as occasionally applied to Sylvia Plath . . . will disconcert some readers, but it struck me as a fitting description of the persona who
rages through the poetry of *Ariel* and *Winter Trees*. . . . " Ironically, in his analysis of Plath's verse, Butscher devotes less time
to the later work, *Ariel* and *Winter Trees*, where this raging persona is almost tangibly present, than he does to her much less
ferocious early work, which he finds largely disappointing.

Method and Madness received mixed reviews, but most of
Plath's readers were grateful for any information that could help
dispel the mystery that had surrounded both her life and her
death. Olwyn Hughes, on the other hand, was not grateful; nor
was she pleased with the book. When the *New York Review
of Books* published a favorable review, Ms. Hughes promptly
responded in a letter to the editor, printed in the 30 September
1976 issue. Butscher's biography of Plath, she insists, is "not
worthy of critical attention." It is merely a "rubbishy hotch-
potch."

WAGNER-MARTIN's biography was the second to appear.
Drawing on previously unavailable journals and letters, Wagner-
Martin explores the roots of the emotional instability and severe
bouts of depression Plath endured all her life. Her father's death
when she was eight, her complicated relationship with her
mother, and her relentless struggle to be both perfect scholar/
poet and perfect wife/mother are presented as the major sources
of trauma. Because the extremes of rage, anguish, and joy Plath
experienced in her personal life are consistently expressed in her
poetry and fiction, such an investigation into Plath's complex
emotional life is necessary to a thorough understanding of her
work.

Wagner-Martin includes detailed accounts of the sources of
many poems, especially the later ones, generally considered to
be Plath's best work. Olwyn Hughes, who was initially cooperative, took exception to the biographer's analyses of these
sources. In her preface, Wagner-Martin reports that when she
insisted on presenting a point of view other than that of Ted and
Olwyn Hughes, they refused to grant her permission to quote
from Plath's unpublished writing. Instead of quoting, then,
Wagner-Martin paraphrases several passages, many of which
cast suspicion on Hughes. The reader cannot avoid speculating
on the reasons behind his secretiveness, his destruction of
Plath's last journal, and his explanation of what happened to the
draft of her last novel, which he says "disappeared somewhere
around 1970."

The latest biography of Plath, written by the poet Anne
STEVENSON, was the first to be fully authorized by the
Hughes family. Stevenson herself acknowledges Olwyn Hughes'
"unstinting help" in producing "almost a work of dual authorship." Indeed, this biography reads like a treatise on Plath's
malice and vindictiveness as seen through the eyes of Olwyn and
Ted Hughes. Stevenson proceeds from the premise that even as a
child Plath was ungrateful, possessive, and unjustifiably critical
of everyone in her life. The tone is relentlessly condemnatory
toward Plath. Even Ted Hughes' adultery with Assia Wevill is
blamed on Plath's irrational jealousy, Stevenson seeming to
agree with Assia's opinion that "the attraction between Ted and
herself would [not] have developed into an affair . . . had Sylvia
behaved differently." Ted Hughes, on the other hand, is presented as a long-suffering and supportive saint of a husband,
who simply could no longer cope with his wife's twisted behavior. The possibility that mental and emotional illness caused
much of Plath's angry, spiteful outbursts is given short shrift.
Instead, the biographer—and presumably the Hugheses—likens
Plath to a spoiled, rude child, who was "fiercely antagonistic,"
"unforgiving," "brutal," filled with "uncontrollable rage."

Stevenson discusses the source material for nearly all of
Plath's poems in some detail, but her critical analysis of the poems themselves is often cursory and even dismissive. A characteristic example is Stevenson's handling of the poem "Ariel,"
which, she rightly asserts, "in the canon of Sylvia's work . . .
is supreme." The explication she offers, however, is merely that
Plath "rehearses the whole spectrum of her color imagery" in
the poem.

The book ends with three appendices, reminiscences of Plath by three former acquaintances, none of whom is more sympathetic toward Plath than the biographer is. Moreover, their inclusion at the end of the book is redundant, since the contents of each is paraphrased within the biography itself.

—Sheryl L. Meyering

POE, Edgar Allan, 1809–1848; American writer.

Allen, Hervey, *Israfel: The Life and Times of Edgar Allan Poe.* New York, G. H. Doran, 1926; London, Gollancz, 1935.

Asselineau, Roger, *Edgar Allan Poe.* Minneapolis, University of Minnesota Press, 1970.

Bittner, William R., *Poe: A Biography.* Boston, Little Brown, 1962; London, Elek, 1963.

Bonaparte, Marie, *The Life and Works of Edgar Allan Poe: A Psychoanalytical Interpretation*, translated by John Rodker, with a foreword by Sigmund Freud. London, Imago, and New York, Humanities Press, 1949.

Buranelli, Vincent, *Edgar Allan Poe.* Boston, Twayne, 1961.

Fagin, N. Bryllion, *The Histrionic Mr. Poe.* Baltimore, Maryland, Johns Hopkins University Press, 1949.

Gill, William F., *The Life of Edgar Allan Poe.* New York, C. T. Dillingham, 1876; fourth revised edition, London, Chatto and Windus, and New York, W. J. Widdleton, 1878.

Harrison, James A., *Life and Letters of Edgar Allan Poe* (2 vols.). New York, T. Y. Crowell, 1902.

Ingram, J. H., *Edgar Allan Poe: His Life, Letters, and Opinions* (2 vols.). London, J. Hogg, 1880.

Knapp, Bettina L., *Edgar Allan Poe.* New York, Ungar, 1984.

Krutch, Joseph W., *Edgar Allan Poe: A Study in Genius.* New York, Knopf, 1926.

Lindsay, Philip, *The Haunted Man: A Portrait of Edgar Allan Poe.* London, Hutchinson, 1953; New York, Philosophical Society, 1954.

Phillips, Mary E., *Edgar Allan Poe, the Man* (2 vols.). Philadelphia, J. C. Wilson, 1926.

Pope-Hennessy, Una, *Edgar Allan Poe 1809–49: A Critical Biography.* London, Macmillan, 1934.

Quinn, Arthur H., *Edgar Allan Poe: A Critical Biography.* New York, Appleton-Century, 1941.

Rans, Geoffrey, *Edgar Allan Poe.* Edinburgh, Oliver and Boyd, 1965.

Robertson, John W., *Edgar A. Poe: A Study.* San Francisco, Brough, 1921.

Shanks, Edward B., *Edgar Allan Poe.* New York and London, Macmillan, 1937.

Sinclair, David, *Edgar Allan Poe.* Totowa, New Jersey, Rowman and Littlefield, and London, Dent, 1977.

Smith, C. Alphonso, *Edgar Allan Poe: How to Know Him.* Indianapolis, Bobbs-Merrill, 1921.

Standard, Mary N., *The Dreamer: A Romantic Rendering of the Life-Story of Edgar Allan Poe.* Philadelphia, Lippincott, 1925.

Thomas, Dwight and David K. Jackson, *The Poe Log: A Documentary Life of Edgar Allan Poe.* New York, G. K. Hall, 1987.

Wagenknecht, Edward, *Edgar Allan Poe: The Man Behind the Legend.* New York, Oxford University Press, 1963.

Weiss, Susan A. T., *Home Life of Poe.* New York, Broadway, 1907.

Winwar, Frances, *The Haunted Palace: A Life of Edgar Allan Poe.* New York, Harper, 1959.

Woodberry, George E., *Edgar Allan Poe.* Boston, Houghton Mifflin, 1885.

Woodberry, George E., *The Life of Edgar Allan Poe: Personal and Literary, with His Chief Correspondence with Men of Letters.* Boston, Houghton Mifflin, 1909.

*

Drawing much of his information from the correspondence entrusted to Rufus W. Griswold, a man inclined to falsify materials, WOODBERRY nevertheless wrote the first important biography of Poe (1885), purposely leaving out incidents he thought best forgotten. He later revised and expanded this biograpy into a large two-volume work (1909) that included Poe's major correspondence with important men of letters, added many of the incidents originally left out, and presented the views of others, even though he disagreed with them. The biography, still worth reading, is generally scholarly and accurate, though many details have since been revised due to the availability of new materials.

Another early biography now interesting mainly from an historical perspective, is by INGRAM. Ingram consulted many who had known Poe, gained access to some materials unavailable to Woodberry, and generally tried to produce a scholarly work. However, since many of the people who had supplied him with information were still alive when the book was published, certain facts had to be suppressed. Woodberry claimed the work was filled with lies.

GILL, the first American biographer, was able to gain some firsthand accounts, but he was not very discriminating between fact and fiction. WEISS wrote a sympathetic biography that offered some interesting insights, including admissions of some of Poe's failings, but she too failed to distinguish fact from fancy when using the accounts of others.

In addition to compiling a 17-volume canon of Poe's works that remains important, HARRISON wrote the best of the biographies to come out in the early 1900s, a two-volume work, the second volume consisting of Poe's correspondence. Also included is Poe's own brief autobiography, which is completely inaccurate. (Poe's own distortions of his life have continually blunted attempts to sort out the truth about him.) Harrison had access to a few materials not available to Woodberry, and his biography is generally good and enthusiastic.

Many biographies appeared in the 1920s, most of them more concerned with romanticizing Poe than presenting the facts. The best of these is by ALLEN, whose work remains an important view of the human side of Poe. It is a heavily documented, detailed account drawn from original sources, which allows Allen to point out flaws in previous biographies (e.g., footnote 210, "Poe did *not* give the place of his birth as Woodberry states vol. I, 1909, page 32"). Several photographs of Poe, places he lived and studied, manuscripts in his handwriting, and the like, complement Allen's writing, which carefully recreates the world in which Poe lived.

With all of its detailed documentation drawn from original and painstaking research, Allen's biography, nevertheless, romanticizes Poe and gains much of both its value and its weakness from its psychological theorizing. Basing his views on the supposition that Poe's weak heart and nervous exhaustion caused him to take opiates, Allen suggests that Poe's loss of sexual energy and the "sadistic trend" in much of his work are the result of drugs. Allen's well-considered analysis, though conjecture, is regarded as the best of this type of approach to an understanding of Poe. However, it must be remembered that Allen, in pursuing his psychological portrait, was willing to accept unsupported rumors.

Other, lesser biographies from this time include works by STANDARD, an example of pure romance that has little to do with true biography; KRUTCH, an interesting psychological study based on theories that Poe's genius was the result of an abnormal condition of nerves; PHILLIPS, a large collection of materials, including many photographs, but poorly written; SMITH, a decent introduction to Poe that deals with his humor and social interests; and ROBERTSON, a psychological study.

Biographies from the 1930s continued the psychological interpretations of Poe and are notable today mainly as historical documents. POPE-HENNESSY used the Valentine Museum Letters released in 1925 in addition to the previous biographies of Woodberry, Harrison, Allen, and Krutch to write a highly sympathetic biography that, among other things, compares and contrasts Poe with Coleridge. SHANKS, includes a short, critical biography and discusses Poe's influence on the French writers, but offers nothing new on Poe's life.

The most important scholarly biography on Poe comes from QUINN. His determined efforts to separate fact from fiction provide the first real insights into the extent of Griswald's indulgence in forgery, thus offering a new perspective from which to understand the real Poe. In Quinn, Poe the drug addict becomes Poe the man with a weakness for alcohol, but innocent when it comes to drugs: "Poe was not a drug addict. On this point we have direct testimony. . . . Indeed, the best negative argument lies in the fact that Poe was so little acquainted with the effect of laudanum that he either took or said he took at least an ounce of the drug in Boston in 1848, which his stomach immediately rejected. 'I had not calculated on the strength of the laudanum,' are not the words of a drug addict."

Conscientious as Quinn was and highly respected as his biography is, other critics have pointed out a lack of objectivity. Philip Lindsay, for example, while praising Quinn's biography in the introduction to his own book on Poe, states: "While disproving many of the slanders against Poe, in his donnish enthusiasm [Quinn] attempts to belittle his subject into a plaster saint and therefore his study, invaluable though it is, turns out to be a failure when we seek to find the essential Poe. The scholarship remains to be admired and respected; only Poe himself has disappeared under its weight." Quinn's extreme concern for substantiating the facts also forced him to leave out statements and reminiscences from Poe's contemporaries, perhaps a necessary omission in a strictly factual biography, but a loss when trying to understand the subject of that biography. With this in mind, the biographies of Quinn and Allen complement each other well.

Though little new data has been uncovered since Quinn, new interpretations of that data have resulted in a continuous stream of new biographies. BONAPARTE, including an introduction written by Sigmund Freud, offers a strongly Freudian perspective. FAGIN presents Poe as an actor, unable to act on stage because of his separation from his parents and upbringing as a Southern gentleman, thus acting in his writing, very much aware of its theatrical effects. LINDSAY gives a psychological study, claiming that Poe was tormented by his Anima. WINWAR, writing a biography aimed at the general public, suggests, once again, that Poe was an opium addict. BURANELLI attempts to show how Poe's life directly influenced his work, and concludes that Poe's objectivity is remarkable considering his personal/psychological problems.

BITTNER offers a highly readable summary of Poe's life. In the Preface, he states "My foremost intention has been to interpret the facts of Poe's life and show how and why he wrote what he did." Bittner reduces Poe to a normal man who led a sensible and unpretentious life. The work has a journalistic rather than a scholarly trust. WAGENKNECHT adopts a more scholarly approach to present an informal biography appealing to the non-specialist. It deals with Poe the man while avoiding psychological theorizing; its most interesting portion addresses Poe's theories on art. RANS and ASSELINEAU both offer brief introductory biographies.

SINCLAIR's work, aimed at the non-scholar, attempts to capture the essence of the man. Sinclair claims not to know if Poe should be considered a genius, but praises Poe's ability to "chart the disintegration of the soul." KNAPP attempts to unravel Poe from a Jungian perspective and interprets his tales in relation to the archetypes of the anima, the shadow, and the mythical quest, claiming that Poe was able to penetrate the secrets of the individual and collective unconscious. It is more a critical study of Poe's work than a biography.

THOMAS AND JACKSON supply a massive, detailed documentation of the facts of Poe's life as they were recorded in contemporary documents, including Poe's letters, reviews of his publications and lectures, photographs, newspaper accounts, and even business directories. In addition, there are biographical notes on many of Poe's acquaintances, relatives, and colleagues, but no real narrative, theorizing, or evaluating.

—Harry Edwin Eiss

POLO, Marco, 1254?–1324?; Venetian merchant and traveler.

Balazs, Étienne, et al, *Oriente Poliano*. Rome, Instituto Italiano per il Medio ed Estremo Oriente, 1957.

Blunck, Hildegard, *Marco Polo: The Great Adventurer,* translated by Isabel and Florence McHugh. London, Blackie, 1966.

Collis, Maurice, *Marco Polo*. London, Faber, 1950; New York, New Directions, 1960.

Cordier, Henri, *Ser Marco Polo: Notes and Addenda to Sir Henry Yule's Edition*. London, J. Murray, and New York, Scribner, 1920.

Hart, Henry, *Marco Polo: Venetian Adventurer.* Norman, University of Oklahoma Press, 1967.

Humble, Richard, *Marco Polo.* New York, Putnam, and London, Weidenfeld and Nicolson, 1975.

Komroff, Manuel, *Marco Polo.* New York, J. Messner, 1952.

Moule, Arthur and Paul Pelliot, translators and annotators, *Marco Polo: The Description of the World* (2 vols.). London, Routledge, 1938.

Moule, Arthur, *Quinsai, with Other Notes on Marco Polo.* Cambridge, Cambridge University Press, 1957.

Olschki, Leonardo, *Marco Polo's Asia.* Berkeley, University of California Press, 1960.

Pelliot, Paul, *Notes on Marco Polo* (2 vols.). Paris, Adrien-Maisonneuve, 1959–63.

Rugoff, Milton, editor, *The Travels of Marco Polo.* New York, Modern Library, 1953.

Yule, Henry, *The Book of Ser Marco Polo, the Venetian, Concerning the Kingdoms and Marvels of the East* (2 vols.). Third edition, revised by Henri Cordier, London, J. Murray, and New York, Scribner, 1903.

*

The monumental two-volume work by MOULE AND PELLIOT supersedes all previous English-language translations of Marco Polo's account of his travels, which is also the most comprehensive source on his life and career. Based on a meticulous study and evaluation of the various editions of Polo's book, the translation offers the first complete version of the superior Franco-Italian manuscript and a transcription of the Latin Codex found in the Cathedral Library at Toledo and deals as well with 15 other manuscripts and printed texts. Moule, the principal translator, also provides a geneology of the Polo family, notes on the Polos' mansion in Venice, and a chronology of Marco's travels. PELLIOT, who is on occasion criticized for his overly detailed and pedantic articles, nonetheless yields a treasure trove of information on Polo and the places he visited. Pelliot identifies unusual transcriptions, personal names, and locations mentioned in the Polo text and places historical and contemporary events and customs in proper context. Though much of the philological data in the book is highly specialized and will appeal principally to scholars, the general reader will find it a useful reference work, particularly on historical figures and on the rare and precious products of 13th-century Asia. The entries on Genghis Khan, on cotton, and on the Central Asian towns of Khotan and Kashgar are lengthy and could be considered monographs in their own right.

YULE's was for more than 60 years the authoritative translation of Polo's book. The work begins with an introductory notice on Polo himself, and the translation is interspersed with valuable illustrations of the sites that the Venetian traveler saw on his way to Khubilai Khan's court in "Cambaluc" (near modern Peking). Contemporary maps, representations of Chinese and Persian coins, and reproductions of paintings enliven the book and supplement the notes to the translation, which provide colorful information (on yaks, Nestorians and Jacobites, fish in the Caspian Sea, "naked barley," and wild sheep) not covered in Pelliot. The antiquarian interest of the notes matches the somewhat archaic language of the translation. CORDIER corrects and adds to Yule's notes, incorporating the research findings of the late 19th century. Most of the entries are specialized, and some are included in Pelliot. RUGOFF's edited work is representative of popular translations of Polo. Translated into modern colloquial English and thus accessible to the general reader, it nonetheless scarcely provides background for Marco's travels or biographical sketches of Marco or consideration of textual problems.

OLSCHKI is a classic study, based on a lifetime of research and exhaustive sifting of sources—of the social, religious, and political conditions encountered and described by Marco on his travels in Asia. An exceptionally readable and lively book, it reveals remarkable erudition. Yet Olschki is blessed with a graceful and lively style that appeals to a wide audience. A notable feature is the chapter on "Aspects of Nature—Animal, Vegetable, Mineral . . . ," which offers botanical, geological, and zoological identifications from Marco's book. The collection by BALAZS, et al, which consists of papers read at a conference commemorating the seventh centenary of Marco's birth, complements Olschki, emphasizing Marco's reports of the Asian lands he either traveled through or heard about. The essays on Japan, India, Central Asia, and Iran compare Marco's observations with actual conditions as documented in indigenous sources. Similarly, MOULE's 1957 book is composed of brief sketches seeking to ascertain the veracity of Marco's accounts and comparing them with the descriptions found in the Chinese histories. It demonstrates that Marco's report on Quinsai (or, in Chinese, Lin an or Hang-chou, the capital of the Southern Sung dynasty, 1127–1279), and his anecdotes about the assassination of Khubilai Khan's finance minister Ahmad, dovetail with the written records in the Chinese gazetteers and dynastic histories.

HART offers a straightforward and reliable account of Marco's life and travels that is particularly valuable for its sections on the European background. Relying upon an extensive examination of the major secondary sources, Hart provides a credible and well-organized narrative of Marco's early life as well as his career after his return from China. His relatively skimpy accounts of the Mongol conquest and of China are simplistic and, on occasion, inaccurate. HUMBLE's sumptuously illustrated book accords more attention to China than does Hart and is also more riveting and dramatic; but it too is prone to error and misinterpretation in its treatment of China and derives most of its information from Moule/Pelliot and Yule.

The other biographies are also dependent on the researches and translations of Moule, Pelliot, and Yule, but in addition they inject highly questionable information and incidents into their narratives. Both BLUNCK and KOMROFF offer breathless prose and often invent dialogues between Marco and the rulers and clerics he encountered on his journeys. Komroff's book is simply written and would appeal to children. COLLIS is more circumspect in his narrative and does not fictionalize his biography. Yet he too lacks expertise on Asia, and mistakes and misinterpretations creep into his book.

The dramatic potential of Marco's adventures has attracted writers of fiction and playwrights. The Italian novelist Italo Calvino is the latest to receive inspiration for a novel from Marco's travels and in particular the Venetian merchant's conversations with Khubilai Khan (*Invisible Cities*, 1974). Eugene O'Neill in his play *Marco's Millions* (1927) also shows the remarkable influence Marco has had on imaginative literature. The French Sinologist Jacques Gernet has used Marco's book, together with Chinese works, to write a fascinating social history of the city of Hang-chou, entitled *Daily Life in China on the Eve of the Mongol Invasion, 1250–1276* (1970). Though it reads like a novel, it is meticulously researched and scrupulously accurate.

—Morris Rossabi

POMPEY [Gnaeus Pompeius Magnus], 106 B.C.–48 B.C.; Roman general and statesman.

Anderson, William S., *Pompey, His Friends, and the Literature of the First Century B.C.* Berkeley, University of California Press, 1963.

Greenhalgh, Peter A. L., *Pompey, the Roman Alexander.* London, Weidenfeld and Nicolson, 1980; Columbia, University of Missouri Press, 1981.

Greenhalgh, Peter A. L., *Pompey, the Republican Prince.* London, Weidenfeld and Nicolson, 1981; Columbia, University of Missouri Press, 1982.

Holliday, Vivian L., *Pompey in Cicero's Correspondence and Lucan's Civil War.* The Hague, Mouton, 1969.

Leach, John, *Pompey the Great.* London, Croom Helm, and Totowa, New Jersey, Rowman and Littlefield, 1978.

Seager, Robin, *Pompey: A Political Biography.* Oxford, Blackwell, and Berkeley, University of California Press, 1979.

*

The earliest surviving source for Pompey is Cicero. A kind of biographical portrait can be culled from Cicero's *Orations*, but HOLLIDAY has shown that Cicero's *Correspondence* provides "a quasi-diary" from the year 68 B.C. to his own death, wherein Pompey is first mentioned in 65 B.C., and then undergoes variable evaluation as appropriate to ever-changing situations.

After the revenge for Julius Caesar's assassination, it was more advantageous to give a "Pompeian, not Caesarian" tone to the falsely perpetuated, but dead, Republic. Marcus Annaeus Lucan (39–65 A.D.), writing a poetic history *de bello civili* ("on the civil war"), with access to Cicero's letters, continued in his seventh book the reshaping of Pompey into a tragic hero who died "in defense of Rome, the Senate, the Republic, and *Libertas*"—each of which also have been regarded as "the hero" of Lucan's work. Holliday's evaluation concluded, along with Matthias Gelzer (*Pompeius*, 1949) and Jules Van Ooteghem (*Pompée le Grand*, 1954), that Pompey deserved the epithet *Magnus* as "builder of the Empire," even if he were unequal to Caesar in politics or war. Final sections summarize the views of both ancient and modern biographical statements; the book itself requires familiarity with Latin.

The Jewish historian Josephus (*ca.* 37–100 A.D.) in his *Antiquities of the Jews* (book XIV), provided a non-Roman perspective on Pompey as "conqueror of the East." *The Lives of the Twelve Caesars* by Suetonius incorporated in the first section on Julius Caesar information on Pompey, from a "republican" perspective.

But the primary biographer of Pompey was Plutarch in his series of parallel "lives" of notable Greeks and Romans (see

Fall of the Roman Republic: Six Lives by Plutarch, translated by Rex Warner, 1958). Pompey was paired with Agesilaus (444 B.C.–360 B.C.), a king of Sparta, though more for contrast than for similarity. Plutarch also covered ten other contemporaries of Pompey, each of whose "lives" must be read to complete the biography of the other: Caius Marius (157–86), Sulla (138–78), Sertorius (*ca.* 125–72), Crassus (*ca.* 112–53), Lucullus (110–56), Cicero (106–43), Julius Caesar (102/101–44), Cato "Minor" (95–46), Brutus (85–42), and Antony (83–30). The English translator Rex Warner considers Plutarch "the last of the Greek classical historians" and "the first of modern biographers." He also notes "Plutarch's narrative skill in repeating himself so seldom even when he is dealing in two or more Lives with precisely the same events." The account of Pompey illustrates, according to Plutarch, "his modest way of life, his record as a soldier, his eloquence, his trustworthy character, and the easy way he had of dealing with people." Pompey's life is not quite the stuff of tragedy. Yet Shakespeare began his *Julius Caesar* with reference to Pompey's murder in Egypt after his army's defeat at Caesar's hands in the battle near Pharsalus in Thessaly.

German scholarship took over in the 19th century, and the plethora of personalities considered "prosopographically" form the bases for modern academic biographies: in German that of Matthias Gelzer (*Pompeius*, 1949), and in French the full account of Pompey and his age by Jules Van Ooteghem (*Pompée le Grand*, 1954), to both of whom all others refer. No translations of these biographies exist.

ANDERSON's slim volume is an illustration of the academic at work, propounding three theses, each supported by reference to predecessors and sources, and by pursuasively argued hypotheses to fill the gaps. Each is based on common prosopographical assumptions. The first thesis, in relation to Pompey's life, considers his five marriage alliances, the offspring and their alliances, those whom Pompey appointed as his military officers, and those who held magistracies during the two decades of his greatest influence. The second deals with the "confidential friends," those sharing the secrets of the general. In the third Anderson turns to a less obvious set and speculates on the thin but visible threads of evidence originating with Pompey's youthful education and intellectual connections, to find those poets and writers of whom Pompey became a patron in the decade when he was least in power. Thereby Anderson lays the foundation for a Hellenistic-style court in Republican Rome, with Pompey as the legitimate Roman Alexander. Plutarch had matched Caesar with Alexander; contemporary thought might find Pompey a more suitable example justifying their common epithet: "the Great."

LEACH opens, "To Romans of later generations the three decades between the dictatorships of Sulla and Caesar were the age of Pompey the Great." Since there existed no full study comparable to those for Cicero and Julius Caesar, in spite of the prominence of both Pompey and the period as standard for English public school boys, Leach set out to "re-examine the life and career of Pompey" chiefly through the words of the sources, with his own translations. He makes minimal but trenchant references to the proliferation of academic literature, though his bibliography identifies most modern material. He adds in translation the lesser known or less commonly available classical texts that refer to Pompey (Appendix B), after a carefully worded but compact identification of "the documentary sources" and the location of their most accessible texts with translations (Appendix A). For those beginning a look at Pompey, Leach provides the more helpful guide.

A common need sets in motion multiple responses. SEAGER, belaboring the absence of a proper biography of Pompey in English, though depreciating Leach in passing, writes a tightly knit, well-documented account of those facets of and events in Pompey's "political" life, omitting his earlier "military" roles. Seager's work is of value to scholars, though it is unclear how much he really gets beyond Anderson and the "politics of friendship" in whose mode he stands. The story of Pompey is measured against the more extensively covered and better-known lives of Caesar and Cicero. A political emphasis could not be otherwise.

GREENHALGH's two-volume study can be read and appreciated by scholars and general readers alike. Generous quotation of sources, in an English translation of quality to match his biographical prose, gives one the flavor of the materials from Pompey's own lifetime. The two volumes divide in such a way that "the Roman Alexander" who conquered without subverting Rome is succeeded by "the Republican Prince" who failed without ceasing to be princely. The convenient division of the Triumvirate of 59 B.C. with Marcus Crassus and Julius Caesar, which Greenhalgh described using the ancient name given by Marcus Terentius Varro (116 B.C–27 B.C.), "Three-headed Monster," forebodes the change in fortune that is the definition of Pompey's life and the death-knell of the Republic as well. For specialists, Greenhalgh has packed somewhat inconveniently at the rear of each volume, with no connecting linkage more than an emboldened phrase or name, extensive annotated notes to each chapter.

—Clyde Curry Smith

POPE, Alexander, 1688–1744; English poet.

Ault, N., *New Light on Pope.* London, Methuen, 1949.

Clifford, James L. and Louis Landa, editors, *Pope and His Contemporaries: Essays Presented to George Sherburn.* Oxford, Clarendon Press, and New York, Oxford University Press, 1949.

Gurr, Elizabeth, *Pope.* Edinburgh, Oliver and Boyd, 1971.

Johnson, Samuel, "Pope," in *The Lives of the English Poets.* London, 1781.

Mack, Maynard, *Alexander Pope: A Life.* New Haven, Connecticut, and London, Yale University Press, 1985.

Sitwell, Edith, *Alexander Pope.* London, Faber, and New York, Cosmopolitan, 1930.

Spence, J., *Anecdotes, Observations, and Characters of Books and Men.* London, W. H. Carpenter, 1820; edited by J. M. Osborn, 2 vols., Oxford, Clarendon Press, 1966.

Stephen, Leslie, *Alexander Pope.* London, Macmillan, and New York, Harper, 1880.

Wimsatt, W. K., *The Portraits of Alexander Pope.* New Haven, Connecticut, Yale University Press, 1965.

*

Compared with many other English poets, Pope has been the subject of remarkably few biographies. Only one major life of him appeared in his own century, and the next century found the lives of poets like Keats and Shelley and Byron more exciting. It is only in the last hundred years that Pope as a subject for biography has come into his own.

Pope's considerable output, originally published as a series of separate items in book and in pamphlet form, was gathered together into a collected edition seven years after his death, and this edition, edited by Warburton (1751), offers some biographical information. Further biographical material on Pope was collected in manuscript notes by SPENCE (d.1768), the manuscript remaining unpublished till 1820.

JOHNSON, the first Pope biographer, had access to some of Pope's contemporaries and to both the Warburton edition and the Spence manuscript. Johnson used all these sources as the basis for his biography of Pope, which appeared in his *Lives of the Poets*, 1783. Johnson was not attempting to produce the modern kind of fully documented biography. His life of Pope was designed (as were all his lives of the poets) as a short introduction to an edition of the poetry; but his blend of biographical information and critical assessment of Pope's personality and work—a great writer judging another great writer—meant that Johnson's remained for long the standard life of Pope. It is still a significant piece of work.

Interest in Pope, which had waned in the latter part of the 18th century and reached a low point in the Romantic period, was revived in the mid-19th century, leading to the production of a great ten-volume edition of his works, edited by W. Elwin and W. J. Courthope (1871–89). This edition is of particular importance since it printed not only Pope's poetry but many of his letters, which had not been available to Johnson. Courthope's life of Pope is in volume five and makes full use of this new material.

The best 19th-century life of Pope (and the most accessible) is by STEPHEN, who had a special affinity with the 18th century, on which he wrote extensively. His life of Pope appeared in two variant forms, as a separate book in 1880, and as a long detailed biographical article in the *Dictionary of National Biography*, the volumes of which appeared at intervals from 1885 to 1900. The Life is readily available in later reprints of the *DNB*, of which Leslie Stephen was the editor. His long biographical article is a model of its kind and is still one of the best lives of Pope, comprehensive and full.

The first part of the 20th century witnessed another slump in Pope's reputation, but by the 1930s he had been rediscovered by SITWELL. Her biography, while it adds no new information and is based on limited reading of her predecessors, is a striking tribute to a poet from a poet of a very different nature.

New information was to come from a team of scholars on both sides of the Atlantic who among them elevated Pope studies to a new plane. The great 11-volume *Twickenham Edition of the Poems of Alexander Pope* (1938–68) established the text of his poetry and cleared up many hitherto unilluminated passages in Pope's life and times. SHERBURN's 1934 work became the classic new biography. It was confined to Pope's early career, bringing the life story up to 1727, when much of Pope's best work had still to be written. A second volume was planned but Sherburn turned to edit in five volumes *The Complete Correspondence of Alexander Pope* (1956), and a full modern biography of Pope had to wait for some years and another author. Meantime various aspects of Pope's life were being dealt with in books and periodical articles. Notable studies include those by AULT, CLIFFORD AND LANDA, WIMSATT, and GURR. This last work provides an excellent short introduction to Pope's life.

The definitive life of Pope was to come from MACK, who had 20 years earlier contributed an important essay on Pope, entitled "A Poet in His Landscape: Pope at Twickenham," to the volume edited by F. W. Hilles and Harold Bloom, *From Sensibility to Romanticism* (1965). Mack, like Ault, had been one of the Twickenham editorial team of Pope's works. His massive and masterly *Alexander Pope: A Life* is unlikely to be surpassed for a long time to come. It is the work of a fine biographical writer and represents the culmination of half a century of exacting research work by Pope scholars in England and America.

—Ian A. Gordon

PORTER, Cole (Albert), 1892?–1964; American composer and lyricist.

Eells, George, *The Life That Late He Led: A Biography of Cole Porter.* New York, Putnam, and London, W. H. Allen, 1967.
Ewen, Daniel, *The Cole Porter Story.* New York, Holt, 1965.
Hubler, Richard G., *The Cole Porter Story.* Cleveland, World Publishing, 1965.
Kimball, Robert, *Cole,* with biographical essay by Brendan Gill. New York, Holt, 1971; London, M. Joseph, 1972.
Schwartz, Charles, *Cole Porter: A Biography.* New York, Dial Press, 1977; London, W. H. Allen, 1978.

*

SCHWARTZ has written the definitive book on Cole Porter's life and works. Schwartz, who also wrote *Gershwin: His Life and Music* (1973), knew intimately the world and lifestyles of American popular composers. His biography of Porter is comprehensive, based on solid and wide-ranging research, and sympathetic without the uncritical adulation typical of so many other works. It contains 33 excellent photographs, an alphabetical listing of Cole Porter songs and other musical compositions, selected bibliography and discography, and an index, all of them first-rate.

Schwartz examines Porter in much more detail than previous biographers had, pointing out several inconsistencies in his character that the biographical film *Night and Day* (in which Cary Grant played the role of Porter) failed to note. Porter, according to Schwartz, was on the one hand the personification of "worldliness, savoir faire, [with] even a touch of cynicism," and at the same time "mawkish," perhaps owing to his intense fondness for listening to the radio soap operas, often interrupting his busy schedule to do so. Schwartz also portrays a "tough-as-nails Cole," pointing for example to his aggressive relationship with Jack Warner during the filming of *Night and Day.* Another indication of the "high degree of inconsistency in Cole Porter's

makeup," Schwartz notes, is seen in his frequenting of shabby, greasy waterfront bars inhabited by sailors and burly labor types, an image that stands in sharp contrast to the beautiful houses and estates with which he is often associated. But the figure who emerges from Schwartz's biography is sensitive, compassionate, devoted to his mother, given to showering his friends—or sometimes young men who simply "struck his fancy"—with expensive gifts. To read Schwartz is to get to know all sides of Cole Porter.

Before Schwartz, some of the best insights into Cole Porter's background came from the autobiographical writings of his contemporaries, and these remain of value. Particularly, Richard Rogers (*Musical Stages: An Autobiography*, 1975) praised Porter's ability to write both music and lyrics and concluded that this was most unusual for "an Episcopalian millionaire who was born on a farm in Peru, Indiana." EWEN's biography, difficult to find, contains some worthwhile insights into Porter's character, but it tries to cover too much ground in too little space and is generally adulatory and superficial.

HUBLER's *Cole Porter Story* ("as told to Richard G. Hubler") contains a warm, reflective introduction by Arthur Schwartz, the producer of the movie *Night and Day.* The introduction itself makes the volume worthwhile, highlighting Porter's generous efforts to help other songwriters whose work he admired. Arthur Schwartz also points out that with the exception of *Anything Goes* and *Kiss Me Kate,* "Porter's scores received luke-warm reviews," and that the press was chilly toward such classic songs as "Just One of Those Things." Hubler's text is only 140 pages long, with a list at the end of the 470 songs Porter wrote. The few photographs are excellent and not reproduced elsewhere. Porter's story as told to Hubler is filled with romance, money, fame, and adventure. It is lively reading with an authentic touch not found in other works.

EELLS in 1967 called his book a "definitive biography," and while it is a valuable contribution to Cole Porter literature, his claim is exaggerated. Writing just after the composer's death, Eells makes some interesting, detailed observations gleaned from extensive interviews with Cole Porter's family and associates. Eells sees Porter as an "outsider"—witty, full of bon mots, yet an aloof figure in society. Unlike Charles Schwartz, he considers that Porter was "aristocratic in appearance," that he was never one of the crowd and indeed "didn't seem to want to be." Eells concludes, however, that Cole Porter was "the greatest composer of light music that America has produced."

KIMBALL's picture biography is a must for Porter fans, for several reasons. The photographs are excellent and include some not found in other books. The volume contains interesting newspaper excerpts describing Porter's accomplishments as well as several letters Porter wrote to other celebrities. Kimball also reproduces the lyrics to some of the best Porter songs, but the real value of his book lies in its rich portrayal of the famous social life enjoyed by Cole and his wife Linda. Kimball also makes some shrewd observations on Porter's background. The biographical essay by Brendan Gill includes an analysis of Porter's philosophy of life.

—Nicholas Christopher Polos

PORTER, Katherine Anne, 1890–1980; American writer.

Givner, Joan, *Katherine Anne Porter: A Life.* New York, Simon and Schuster, 1982; London, Cape, 1983.
Hendrick, George, *Katherine Anne Porter.* New York, Twayne, 1965; revised edition, 1988.
Lopez, Enrique H., *Conversations with Katherine Anne Porter: Refugee From Indian Creek.* Boston, Little Brown, 1981.

*

GIVNER has written the authoritative biography of Katherine Anne Porter. She has drawn extensively on Porter's correspondence, in addition to her own interview with Porter and her acquaintances, to portray a complex, charismatic, and difficult figure. Beginning with the knowledge that Porter invented many of the stories about her life, Givner's approach throughout is to present Porter's version of an event and supplement it with other evidence. Although as a result the presentation of facts may at times be overwhelming, the reader gains not only a comprehensive view of the significant moments in Porter's life but also some insight into her own method and motive for exaggeration and self-invention. Givner starts with a description of Porter's own attempts to create her family tree and immediately proceeds with her own corrective, a description of Porter's paternal grandfather, giving considerable attention to Porter's family, Givner develops the thesis that it was these troubled relationships that resulted in Porter having a weak sense of identity, which motivated her to create fantasies about herself and to be deeply insecure regarding both her work and her friendships. From the Prologue and Epilogue that frame the actual biography and emphasize the critical importance of Porter's fiction, we learn that Porter asked Givner to write her biography because she liked Givner's critical interpretations of her fiction.

LOPEZ offers the only other comprehensive account of Porter's life, beginning with her birth and ending shortly before her death, but he himself does not claim to offer an objective view, nor does he pretend that all the details of his story are accurate. The book grew out of interviews that Lopez conducted with Porter beginning in 1965; he compiled Porter's own reminiscences in a chronological narrative, which he then read to her so that she could correct or amplify. The few additional interviews with her former acquaintances serve to amplify rather than to verify the narrative. As a result, the book is highly anecdotal, and it consistently and uncritically presents Porter's own point of view; because it includes only those events and experiences that Porter herself had time and inclination to recall for the purposes of their conversations, Lopez's work implicitly reveals what was most significant to Porter. Its single theme, introduced in the book's subtitle, is Porter's restlessness and sense of homelessness. Lopez includes some discussion of her essays and fiction, but does not offer a full interpretation of all her fiction; like Givner he reads her stories as direct transcriptions of Porter's experiences. Because its methodology and perspective complement Givner's, this biography provides a useful complementary perspective on Porter's experience of her own life.

HENDRICK's biography of Porter was the first full-length biography, but because it was based largely on Porter's own misinformation it contains many errors (although Porter herself was angered by the biographical basis for Hendrick's interpretations

of her fiction). A revised edition, written with his wife Willene Hendrick and published in 1988, has acknowledged and corrected these errors, and offers a condensed, readable overview of Porter's life and fiction.

—Judith Lee

PORTER, William Sydney. See **Henry, O.**

POUND, Ezra (Loomis), 1885–1972; American poet and critic.

Carpenter, Humphrey, *A Serious Character: The Life of Ezra Pound.* London, Faber, and Boston, Houghton Mifflin, 1988.
Flory, Wendy S., *The American Ezra Pound.* New Haven, Connecticut, Yale University Press, 1989.
Norman, Charles, *Ezra Pound.* New York, Macmillan, 1960.
Stock, Noel, *The Life of Ezra Pound.* London, Routlege, and New York, Pantheon, 1970.

*

Although there is a superabundance of published material on Pound, there is no satisfactory biography of him. His own voluminous output includes two unsatisfactory autobiographical essays, *Indiscretions* (1923) and *Patria Mia* (1950), together with many interviews and impressions from 1946 onwards, the fullest of which is by Donald M. Hall. There are early testimonies by Ford Madox Ford and Richard Aldington, the *EP/DS Letters* between Pound and his wife-to-be, Dorothy Shakespeare (edited by Omar Pound and A. Walton Litz, 1985), and portraits by Wyndham Lewis and Gaudier-Brzeska. There are lapidary paragraphs by Yeats in *The Oxford Book of Modern English Verse* and *A Packet for Ezra Pound*; the moving memoir, *Discretions* (1971), by Pound's daughter Mary de Rachewiltz; and some fine pages in Kenner's grand work, *The Pound Era* (1971). *Pound as Wuz* (1987), by James Laughlin, is friendly and full of good anecdotes. Peter Ackroyd's brief photographic biography, *Ezra Pound and His World* (1980), is a success. There are more ambitiously hostile or partisan biographical/political studies by C. David Heymann (1976) and E. Fuller Torrey (1984). There are the correspondences *Pound/Ford* (edited by Brita Lindberg-Seyersted, 1982) and *Pound/Joyce* (edited by Forrest Read, 1967). Julien Cornell, Pound's lawyer in Washington, has given his account in *The Trial of Ezra Pound* (1966). L. Doob has edited Pound's Rome Radio broadcasts. The journal *Paideuma* is a mine of information. But Pound has so far best been seen from limited angles. There is nothing to compare with Peter Ackroyd's *T. S. Eliot: A Life.*

There are only three biographies that attempt to cover the whole life to the date of their writing, those by Charles Norman, Noel Stock, and Humphrey Carpenter. NORMAN wrote a light journalistic account, readable and adequate so far as it goes, but external and with no special access to unpublished sources.

STOCK is an Australian journalist, a former disciple of Pound, who put the poet's papers in order at Brunnenburg in the early 1960s and compiled a well-documented and dutiful biography, from which Stock's gradual failure of sympathy with Pound's ideas and poetics becomes evident. Based on genuine knowledge of family papers, it is honest, modest, and reliable as to dates and Pound's reading, but deliberately limited and incomplete, and rather flat and factual to read.

CARPENTER's 1988 biography must for the present supersede all previous efforts because of the amount of new information it contains. A large and comprehensive volume, it is able to take advantage of many sources unavailable to Stock, and to deal with Pound's private life in a way that was not possible in the poet's lifetime or immediately after his death. Carpenter is a literary journalist who had previously written satisfactory biographies of J. R. R. Tolkien, C. S. Lewis, and W. H. Auden, as well as handbooks to children's literature. His experience as a biographer has helped him. It must have been thought that the difficult job of writing the life of so controversial a poet had to be left to someone outside the poet's circle of admirers. However, Carpenter does not understand Pound's poetry at all well, and he stated on BBC radio that he had begun from the premise that Pound was mad. This is a depressingly common English prejudice to which Carpenter returns at the end of the volume, and which is visible in his choice of illustrations. Pound seems to have been an unsympathetic and almost unintelligible personality to Carpenter, who approaches him primarily as a curious human and cultural phenomenon rather than as a poet, whereas it is difficult to see why anyone might want to read about Pound if they had not been drawn to him through his poetry and especially *The Cantos*. Biographers ought to resist commissions to write lives of authors whom they neither understand nor admire. One wonders why Carpenter was offered the commission. The result is another contribution to the cause of Anglo-American misunderstanding (see Hugh Kenner's *A Sinking Island*, 1988), the effect of which will be to perpetuate the disappearance of Pound from (English) men's memory, which was noted by the poet himself in *Hugh Selwyn Mauberley* (1920). Humphrey Carpenter is as uncomprehendingly English a biographer of Pound as could be imagined, the real counterpart of Philip Larkin's fantasy American academic, "Jake Balokowsky, my biographer" (in his poem "Posterity").

Like Stock, Carpenter uses as his backbone Pound's not very revealing letters to his family. He has not sat down and read all the material at Yale and elsewhere. He has not even read all of Pound's literary output. Charity might say that, in view of these handicaps, Carpenter has done surprisingly well; but the book resembles a long and ultimately unsuccessful game of Pin the Tail on the Donkey. The biography improves in the period 1920–58: Carpenter has written on the Americans in Paris in the 1920s, and his command of the cultural field is much stronger in this period. He is the best source on Pound's correspondence with Eliot and Yeats, having had access to both sides of their letters, and he writes well on Pound and music and Pound and radio. His quotations seem reliable, though his system of reference is not very helpful.

Of the earlier part of Pound's life Carpenter writes with less comprehension and sympathy, and less neutrality: the opening chapters contain intrusive judgements indicating a failure of understanding and even of interest, especially in regard to Pound's

literary aspirations. His account of the Kensington milieu in which Pound worked is strangely thin, and his literary assessments here are (as throughout the biography) of little value where they are not simply mistaken. He makes no attempt to understand Pound's life's work, the *Cantos*, and has read very little of the literary criticism on Pound. The progress and production of *The Cantos* could have been much illuminated by a biographer, but Carpenter does not attempt this. *The Cantos* appear here as an intrusion into the life of a loafer, crank, and publicist. Carpenter is unable to make any sense of Pound's last years in Italy and abandons connected narrative and final assessment in fragmentary despair. Superficially readable, Carpenter's becomes an unwieldy and finally an incoherent book.

Pound's extraordinary private life, especially his inability to commit himself completely to a single woman, intrigues Carpenter greatly, though he is not without tact. Carpenter presents Pound's whole career, literary as well as otherwise, in terms of this inability to make the total commitment often demanded in his work. But Carpenter does not look at the poetry, where Pound's attempt upon the absolute is made. The psychological side to Pound's exceedingly difficult "case" is examined at length but without success. FLORY's *The American Ezra Pound* addresses at a more profound level Pound's frustrated longing for absolute commitment. In the words of a *TLS* reviewer, "it offers us an intelligibly complex human being, one who might plausibly have written the *Cantos*, whereas the somewhat loathsome buffoon of Carpenter's biography is inconceivable as a poet of lyrical tenderness. Flory's achievement is to portray a deeply flawed man who needed, wanted and failed to find psychiatric treatment but who may, in the spare luminosity of the *Drafts and Fragments*, in the aphasia he had threatened so long before, have somehow puzzled out his own salvation. She leads us to hope so."

—M. J. Alexander

PRESLEY, Elvis (Aaron), 1935–1977; American singer.

Cotton, Lee, *All Shook Up: Elvis Day-by-Day*. Ann Arbor, Michigan, Pierian Press, 1985.

Crumbaker, Marge, with Gabe Tucker, *Up and Down with Elvis Presley*. New York, Putnam, 1981; London, New English Library, 1982.

Dundy, Elaine, *Elvis and Gladys*. New York, Macmillan, and London, Weidenfeld and Nicolson, 1985.

Geller, Larry, *If I Can Dream: Elvis' Own Story*. New York, Simon and Schuster, and London, Century, 1989.

Goldman, Albert, *Elvis*. New York, McGraw-Hill, 1981; London, Penguin, 1982.

Gregory, Janice and Neal Gregory, *When Elvis Died*. Washington, D.C., Communications Press, 1980.

Hammontree, Patsy Guy, *Elvis Presley: A Bio-Bibliography*. Westport, Connecticut, Greenwood Press, and London, Aldwych, 1985.

Hopkins, Jerry, *Elvis: A Biography*. New York, Simon and Schuster, 1971; London, Open Gate Books, 1972.

Hopkins, Jerry, *Elvis, the Final Years*. New York, St. Martin's, and London, W. H. Allen, 1980.

Marsh, Dave, *Elvis*. New York, Times Books, and London, Elm Tree, 1982.

Presley, Priscilla Beaulieu (as told to Sandra Harmon), *Elvis and Me*. New York, Putnam, and London, Century, 1985.

Tharpe, Jac L., editor, *Elvis: Images and Fancies*. Jackson, University Press of Mississippi, 1979; London, Star, 1983.

West, Red, Sonny West, and Dave Hebler (as told to Steve Dunleavy), *Elvis, What Happened?* New York, Ballantine, 1977.

*

It is hard to imagine that there remains anything, whether true or false, to be said about Elvis Presley that has not already been said. Since his death in 1977 literally hundreds of books have been printed under the guise of "the real truth about Elvis." Many of these publications so stretch journalistic decorum that Presley biography should probably have its own entry in Webster's dictionary, under which there would have to be the subheadings, according to degree of accuracy, of "tabloid truths," "my-life-with-Elvis" or "as told to" truths, and "good research"—factual truths.

GOLDMAN's is perhaps the most well-known of the biographies published before Priscilla Presley's 1985 work (see below). Labeled the "graverobber" of Lenny Bruce and John Lennon, Goldman transcends the above categories because, as it has come to be known, his is both a "told to" as well as self-researched book. Presley bodyguard Lamar Fike was Goldman's chief insider to this overwritten, pompous biography which, while often compelling and entertaining, is worthless as research material because the author chooses never to cite his sources or provide documentation. Also, because Goldman psychoanalyzes nearly every Presley tale without any secondary back-up or clinical reference, his prose becomes the same egoistic self-aggrandizing that he criticizes his subject for.

Like Goldman's, the many other "as told to" books are long on entertainment and spectacle and lacking in journalistic correctness. The WEST book is significant because of its eerie timeliness, published just days before Presley's death, and because of its trend-setting love/hate mudslinging. The first of its kind, West's book would set the standard for scandal to which all other insiders would respond. Of course, all these books claim to tell the truth (although it seems odd that most need a "ghostwriter" to make the truth sound worth telling), and all retell the same stories from different perspectives and with conflicting details. Red West perhaps knew Presley longer than any of the other biographers and for that reason his story seems more poignant. But, like most others, West and his cohorts had a "score to settle" and for that reason truth can become indiscernible.

For an opposing, but no less entertaining, version see the GELLER biography. A sequel to his 1980 "truth" book, to which Dave Marsh referred as the "funniest" of Presley biographies, this is Elvis' hairdresser and "spiritual advisor" claiming to tell the story that Elvis himself would have written. Concentrating mostly on Elvis' (and Geller's) metaphysical obsessions, Geller, though he may have tried to make Presley a more likeable man by showing his preoccupation with new-age hocus pocus, succeeds only in portraying him as all the more weird.

Of the remaining more well-known "told to" books, the more neutral are those by Priscilla Presley (as told to Sandra Harmon) and CRUMBAKER AND TUCKER. Tucker was a Colonel Parker crony and this book, although the title implies Elvis, is mostly about the Colonel. Parker was Presley's longtime manager and the person, many believe, who made Elvis and, in the end, wrecked him. Although Parker was a very secretive man and much of his personal life still remains a mystery, Tucker may well be as close to him as we'll ever get (although he too had a score to settle).

PRISCILLA PRESLEY'S book is perhaps the best-known of all the Presley biographies. Elvis is made to be a Svengali here, which should come as no surprise since the two first got together when Elvis was in the army and Priscilla was only 14. One would think that when the bride of Elvis comes clean there would be some startling revelations. Possibly because the book seems to be mostly a reaction to stories told in previous books, the revelations are few. Mostly useful for its insight into the first few years of their relationship—from Germany to just before marriage—this quick read is entertaining for its schoolgirl tone but redundant as research material.

Among other, related sources, many "history of rock and roll" type books contain relatively detailed accounts of Presley and his music. The two most usually cited are *The Rolling Stone Illustrated History of Rock and Roll*, edited by Jim Miller (1976; revised edition, 1980), and Greil Marcus' *Mystery Train: Images of American Rock and Roll* (1975). Along with MARSH, Marcus and Miller stick mostly to the music because that is what they know best. Read Marcus for a good, short analysis of Elvis as myth, how that myth was transformed in the last years before his death, and how it originated. Like Marsh, Marcus writes from the "purist" perspective, meaning that he is one who believes Elvis was at his artistic peak before he went to RCA Records in 1956. While Marcus and Marsh devote about the same amount of text to Presley, Marsh's book is in the "oversized picturebook" category. The best of its kind for its combination of visual illustration and insightful, if limited, text, the Marsh book is artfully crafted with rare, enlarged black-and-white and color photographs of Elvis and those closest to him.

Probably the best and most factual under the "good research" category are the two HOPKINS books, although DUNDY has done a beautiful job, too. Because of Goldman's downfalls, Hopkins remains "the source" for the most basic and complete Presley information. But while Hopkins remains the standard for information, Dundy will be the standard for analysis. Where Goldman seems like armchair psychology, Dundy gives the impression of truly knowing the psyche of Presley through vast historical research and accurate demythologizing. She is conscientious enough to point out all possibilities and then to direct the reader to those that seem most probable. The only problem here is that the book only reaches to the time of Gladys' death.

Another "good research" book comes from Neal and Janice GREGORY, who put together a chronicle of how the media saw Presley's death. Objective in their outlook, and without purveying the Elvis myth, the Gregorys subvert the ordinary run of Elvis reportage to give something different and valuable.

Also important is THARPE's collection of mostly non-academic essays written by academics. Culled from *Southern Quarterly*, although many essays are heavily regional, all are worthwhile and very well-written insights into the Presley myth as an every day cultural reality. And while there are many sources for discographies, filmographies, bibliographies, etc., COTTON and HAMMONTREE take the research and data one step further. Cotton's book contains a detailed day-by-day account of the public life of Presley to coincide with the most comprehensive discographies and filmographies to date. Hammontree is most useful for her encapsulated and succinct biographical notes and her bibliographical essay, which discusses much of the literature on Presley.

It should be noted that the books listed here represent a small sampling of all that has come to be Presley biography. In most cases, they are the sources most usually cited in scholarly research on the topic. They are not to be misunderstood as all sources, or even as the only types of sources. The category of "hero-worship" biography, headed up by May Mann's *Elvis and the Colonel* (1975; as *The Private Elvis*, 1977), has not been included in this survey. All sources on Presley, however ridiculous they are, yet hold some interest because of the nature of the Presley myth. Every week a glossy tabloid runs an outrageously bogus account of Elvis spotted at the Burger King or coming out of a spaceship. While such accounts are easily dismissable as yellow journalism or sensationalism, sensationalism remains the hallmark of the Presley myth. Sensationalism is synonymous with the name Elvis Presley.

—Michael Rodriguez

* * *

PROKOFIEV, Sergey, 1891–1953; Russian composer and pianist.

Gutman, David, *Prokofiev.* London, Alderman, 1988.
Hanson, Lawrence and Elizabeth Hanson, *Prokofiev, a Biography in Three Movements.* New York, Random House, and London, Cassell, 1964; also published as *Prokofiev, the Prodigal Son: An Introduction to His Life and Work in Three Movements,* London, Cassell, 1964.
Kaufman, Helen, *The Story of Sergei Prokofiev.* Philadelphia, Lippincott, 1971.
Nestyev, Israel V., *Sergei Prokofiev, His Musical Life,* translated by Florence Jonas. New York, Knopf, and London, Faber, 1946; revised as *Prokofiev,* Stanford, California, Stanford University Press, 1960.
Robinson, Harlow L., *Sergei Prokofiev: A Biography.* New York, Viking, and London, R. Hale, 1987.
Samuel, Claude, *Prokofiev,* translated by Miriam John. London, Calder and Boyers, and New York, Grossman, 1971 (originally published by Éditions du Seuil, Paris, 1960).
Savkina, Natalia, *Prokofiev: His Life and Times,* translated by Catherine Young. Neptune City, New Jersey, Paganiniana Publications, 1984.
Seroff, Victor, *Sergei Prokofiev: A Soviet Tragedy.* New York, Funk and Wagnalls, 1968; London, Frewin, 1969.

*

Some aspects of Prokofiev's life have been slow to come to light due to Soviet censorship of materials and the understandable reluctance of family and friends still living in Russia to speak frankly. Thus, readers about Prokofiev's life will find themselves unusually dependent on the interpretations of individual authors. Unfortunately, these often come with political overtones, so the reader must be cautious.

The account by ROBINSON stands above all others for its comprehensiveness, currency of information, and relative lack of bias. In scrupulous but engrossing detail, the author ferrets out personal information that appears nowhere else. (Most books minimize details of Prokofiev's two marriages because of shortage of data and the awkward lack of any divorce record.) Robinson takes an evenhanded view of the man, acknowledging both good and bad—Prokofiev's unbounded optimism as well as his rudeness. What makes Robinson's account so compelling is the judicious incorporation of just enough of the political and historical setting to enlighten the reader without interrupting the story. The author also offers some provocative insights, noting, for example, Prokofiev's greater success in portraying pictorial concepts in music (the ballet and film scores) than in conveying literary ideas (opera). Musical discussions are usually general and kept subordinate to the narrative. In addition to material culled from Prokofiev's own autobiography and memoirs by the immediate family (read in the original Russian), the author also includes fine musical commentaries by well-known performers (Sviatoslav Richter and David Oistrakh) and recent statements by Prokofiev's two sons. The book contains complete documentation, a list of works, bibliography, and chronology.

Several of the other narratives are seriously distorted by political bias. NESTYEV, a Soviet musicologist, was the government's choice as Prokofiev's first and "official" biographer. Both the biographical and musical sections of the narrative are badly marred by Nestyev's adherence to the Communist party position. He views any years Prokofiev spent outside the Soviet Union as detrimental to his creative activity and determines the success of each work based on how well it reflects Soviet realism (or avoids "modernism") rather than on its intrinsic merit. Unfortunately, prejudice also damages the final chapter in the book, which summarizes Prokofiev's musical style, and the detailed descriptions of several musical works unknown in the West.

SEROFF's account, intended as a corrective to that of Nestyev, is equally biased, but in the opposite direction. He sees the government as persecuting Prokofiev in his personal and public life and even suggests that Prokofiev's last eight years of poor health may have come from the repeated disappointments after his return to Russia. Seroff's account has an immediacy that stems from the use of numerous well-chosen anecdotes, told in breezy fashion. Documentation is at a minimum, as is discussion of the music (the index omits compositions). Some of Seroff's speculations toward the end of the book seem unlikely in light of Robinson's new information, but they are thought-provoking to say the least. Read the book, but cautiously.

The HANSONS' generalized account also attempts to set Nestyev's record straight, but in the process it introduces other shortcomings. The authors, believing oral responses to be less honest than written ones, avoided consulting living acquaintances of Prokofiev. Thus, their information comes solely from written sources, none of which is documented. Accuracy also may be an issue here, for Robinson specifically refutes one of their most colorful anecdotes that claims Prokofiev sat with his back turned to the speaker Zhdanov at an infamous condemnatory conference of 1948. The prose is flowery, and the authors are sometimes naive. For example, they describe the personalities of Prokofiev and his parents by turning to a photo of the family taken when Prokofiev was only one year old, and claim to recognize particular qualities in the faces. The American edition is preferable to the British one (which accidentally omits the seven ballets in the catalogue of works), for the editor at least makes an effort to control wordiness. The musical description is on an elementary level, and little appears in this account that does not show up more effectively in Seroff's narrative.

Among the shorter chronicles, GUTMAN's is preferable for its currency and lack of political bias. Gutman uses numerous passages of direct quotations, but they are often new and always illuminating. His discussions regarding ''socialist realism'' and Prokofiev's rivalry with Stravinsky are particularly noteworthy. He did considerable research for his brief but good musical descriptions (partially documented), and he has no hesitation in correcting evaluations when necessary. Readers using any account other than Gutman's should consult *The New Grove Russian Masters 2* (New York and London, Norton, 1986) for a concise updating of biographical information that corrects even the New Grove dictionary article of 1980.

SAMUEL, as the only French author, had access to materials Prokofiev left in France when he returned to Russia, and this source gives a particularly good picture of the Parisian years. A fine chapter on Prokofiev's personality, ''PRKF'' (his secret code for his diaries omitted all vowels), appears part way through the narrative, and the musical descriptions are excellent, sometimes extending to interesting details of the ballet and opera plots. Drawbacks of the book include lack of updated information and personal details, plus some typographical errors in dates.

The short KAUFMAN narrative is geared to young readers of secondary school level and omits discussion of the music. Elaborations border on the fanciful, and some of the details do not jibe exactly with accounts in the recently published English edition of Prokofiev's autobiography. Readers, in fact, who want to draw their own conclusions about Prokofiev's personality would do well to consult this lively autobiography that covers the years 1891–1909 (*Prokofiev by Prokofiev: A Composer's Memoir*, translated by Guy Daniels, New York, Doubleday, 1979).

The recent SAVKINA account should be avoided. It has a strong pro-Soviet bias and omits any reference to the 1948 Soviet condemnation of Prokofiev's music. In addition, the translation is inept, musical references are imprecise, and no personal details are provided.

—Courtney Adams

PROUDHON, Pierre-Joseph, 1809–1865; French journalist and social theorist.

Brogan, D. W., *Proudhon*. London, Hamilton, 1934.

Lubac, Henri de, *The Unmarxian Socialist: A Study of Proudhon*, translated by R. E. Scantlebury. London, Sheed and Ward, 1948 (originally published as *Proudhon et le Christianisme*, Paris, Éditions du Seuil, 1945).

Woodcock, George, *Pierre-Joseph Proudhon: A Biography*. New York, Macmillan, and London, Routledge, 1956; with subtitle *His Life and Work*, New York, Schocken Books, 1972.

*

Unlike his rival and sometime friend Karl Marx, Pierre-Joseph Proudhon, the pioneer of anarchism, did not make a great impression in the English-reading countries. From the publication in 1872 of Saint-Beuve's *P.-J. Proudhon, Sa Vie at Sa Correspondance*, there has been in France a fairly constant stream of new works on Proudhon, but books in English have been few in number and tardy in coming.

The first was BROGAN's *Proudhon*, published in London in 1934 when events in Spain were creating a revived interest in anarchism. A brief introductory work, it presented to a readership unfamiliar with the French writer the main facts of his life and the main aspects of his teaching. In accordance with the biographical fashions of the time, it stresses Proudhon's inconsistencies and the more comic aspects of his life.

Not until after World War II did another book on Proudhon appear in English. This was de LUBAC's *The Unmarxian Socialist*, in Scantlebury's somewhat misleading translation of *Proudhon et le Christianisme*, which had appeared in Paris in 1945. De Lubac was a Jesuit priest, one of the liberally inclined Catholic intellectuals of post-Resistance France who found Proudhon's thinking attractive as an alternative to Marxism. His book is a biography, but a biography with a purpose, seeking to counter the crudely reactionary attacks by past Catholic writers on Proudhon. De Lubac suggested that there was much in common between Proudhon's struggle with God and that of the Christian existentialists like Kierkegaard who, as de Lubac remarked, called God ''the mortal enemy'' and declared ''Christianity exists because there is a hatred between God and man.'' *The Unmarxian Socialist* certainly saw Proudhon from a new point of view, but it was inevitably informed by de Lubac's search for the common ground between Proudhonism and Christianity, and for this reason cannot be seen as a comprehensive biography.

The first such biography in English, and the only one to date, is by WOODCOCK. Woodcock had traveled extensively on research in France, where Proudhon lived most of his life, and in Belgium, where he spent a brief exile during the Second Empire, and had read Proudhon's books and papers with the sympathetic but not entirely uncritical eye of a student of anarchism. His book sets Proudhon clearly in his many worlds—as a peasant child in the Jura, as a journeyman printer, as a journalistic voice during the revolution of 1848, as a political and socialist theoretician, and as a kind of partyless prophet who never cut his links with the working class and who was one of the notable precursors of the International Workingmen's Association (the First International), which began to emerge in 1864, the year of Proudhon's death.

At the same time as he narrates Proudhon's life, Woodcock reconstructs the political and literary world of France during the revolutionary 1840s and the Second Empire, with its native political agitators and its groups of exiles, notably Bakunin and Kropotkin, with whom Proudhon was in touch. Because so little of Proudhon's writing had by the 1950s been translated into English, Woodcock describes and comments extensively on his books, so that his book is as much an intellectual biography as a life in the ordinary sense.

In addition to these books there are mainly biographical chapters on Proudhon in recent histories of anarchism, such as George Woodcock's *Anarchism* (1962) and James Joyce's *The Anarchists* (1964), and also in Daniel Guérin's *Anarchisme*, whose English version (*Anarchism*, translated by Mary Klopper), appeared in 1970.

—George Woodcock

PROUST, Marcel, 1871–1922; French writer.

Albaret, Céleste, *Monsieur Proust*, translated by Barbara Bray. London, Collins and Harvill, and New York, McGraw-Hill, 1976 (originally published by Laffont, Paris, 1973).

Appignanesi, Lisa, *Femininity and the Creative Imagination: A Study of Henry James, Robert Musil and Marcel Proust*. New York, Barnes and Noble, and London, Vision Press, 1973.

Barker, Richard H., *Marcel Proust: A Biography*. London, Faber, and New York, Criterion, 1958.

Bersani, Leo, *Marcel Proust: The Fictions of Life and Art*. New York, Oxford University Press, 1965.

Brée, Germaine, *The World of Marcel Proust*. London, Chatto and Windus, and Boston, Houghton Mifflin, 1967.

May, Derwent, *Proust*. New York, Oxford University Press. 1983.

Miller, Milton L., *Nostalgia: A Psychoanalytic Study of Marcel Proust*. Boston, Houghton Mifflin, 1956; London, Gollancz, 1957.

Painter, George, *Proust* (2 vols.). London, Chatto and Windus, and Boston, Little Brown, 1959–65; revised and enlarged as *Marcel Proust: A Biography*, Chatto and Windus, 1989.

Quennell, Peter, *Marcel Proust 1871–1922: A Centennial Volume*. London, Weidenfeld and Nicolson, and New York, Simon and Schuster, 1971.

Rivers, J. E., *Proust and the Art of Love*. New York, Columbia University Press, 1980.

Shattuck, Roger, *Proust*. London, Fontana, 1974.

Thody, Philip, *Marcel Proust*. London, Macmillan, 1987; New York, St. Martin's, 1988.

*

The best and most complete work on Proust's life in either English or French remains the two-volume study by PAINTER. Painter sets out from the presupposition that almost all the incidents in Proust's 1,240,000-word novel *A la recherche du temps perdu* (1913–27) have their origin in Proust's own life. The biography is based on a detailed study of an enormous amount of printed material and is unlikely to be superseded. It has had the unusual honour for a book by an English critic about a French writer of being translated into French. Admirers of Proust as a literary creator nevertheless find Painter's insistence on treating the novel as a kind of autobiography rather tiresome at times. Painter was the first to query the view that Proust was exclusively homosexual, to look at his heterosexual affairs and his claims that he enjoyed consummated heterosexual affairs. This leads him to argue that Proust's equation of love and jealousy is not therefore as pathological as most critics have argued but represents a reliable account of human sexual experience in general. Painter nevertheless gives considerable detail about Proust's homosexual and sado-masochistic practices, a view sharply contradicted by the hagiographic account by Proust's housekeeper, ALBARET.

RIVERS gives a more balanced account of Proust, both as a man and a writer. MAY's shorter book in the *Past Masters series* also provides a valuable corrective to both approaches by pointing out how much of Proust's apparent account of himself in *A la recherche du temps perdu* is part of the creation of a personal myth. Readers interested in seeing the world Proust took as his model should read QUENNELL's collection of articles; Anthony Powell's on Proust as a soldier is especially interesting. (Powell's own ten-volume series *A Dance to the Music of Time* [1951–72] is an ironically presented English equivalent of Proust). A valuable, detailed, and more straightforward critique to compare with Painter is BARKER's biography.

Proust has proved an irresistibly attractive target for Freudian analysis, and MILLER's is the most useful volume in this context. An equally interesting approach is that of APPIGNANESI, who compares Proust with other writers. The most recent study of Proust for the general reader, THODY emphasizes Proust's inability to form satisfactory human relationships with other people and presents his great novel as being at one and the same time a dream world and a consolation for personal failure.

All books on Proust discuss his obsessive relationship with his mother and the element of self-satire in his creation of the character of Le Baron de Charlus. The collection of essays edited by Larkin B. Price, *Marcel Proust: A Critical Panorama* (1973) is a valuable introduction to the literary theories connected with Proust, as is Jean Cocking's *Proust: Collected Essays on the Writer and his Art* (1982), and a very interesting early work by Samuel Beckett, *Proust*, first published in Paris in 1931, is most useful for its unconscious account of Beckett's own development. It contains the judgement "Proust's style was generally resented in French literary circles. But now that he is no longer read, it is conceded that he might have written even worse than he did." Beckett's prediction has not turned out to be true.

BERSANI's is the best study of the relationship between the individual Proust and the fictional Marcel. SHATTUCK's volume is a shorter but equally intriguing introduction, dwelling on Proust's remodelling of experience into a satisfactory whole. BRÉE's work is a sound, scholarly account that prefers the more accurate but less poetic English title of *A la recherche du temps perdu* as *In Search of Time Lost*.

Proust was an indefatigable correspondent who wrote an average of three letters a day. Philip Kolb has been editing his letters since 1960 and has now reached the year 1917, five years before Proust's death. Readers wishing for a shorter account of Proust's fictional world and its relationships to the society of its time should read Terence Kilmartin's *A Guide to Proust* (London,

1983). This provides reference to Scott-Moncrieff's revised translation of *Remembrance of Things Past*, which Kilmartin published in three volumes in the same year and which also contains a valuable index of places and people.

—Philip Thody

PUCCINI, Giacomo, 1858–1924; Italian composer.

Carner, Mosco, *Puccini: A Critical Biography*. London, Duckworth, 1958; New York, Knopf, 1959; revised edition, London, Duckworth, and New York, Holmes and Meier, 1974.

Dry, Wakeling, *Giacomo Puccini*. London and New York, J. Lane, 1906.

Fiorentino, Dante del, *Immortal Bohemian: An Intimate Memoir of Giacomo Puccini*. London, Gollancz, and New York, Prentice-Hall, 1952.

Greenfeld, Howard, *Puccini: A Biography*. New York, Putnam, 1980; London, Hale, 1981.

Greenfield, Edward, *Puccini: Keeper of the Seal*. London, Arrow Books, 1958.

Jackson, Stanley, *Monsieur Butterfly: The Story of Giacomo Puccini*. New York, Stein and Day, 1974; with subtitle, *The Story of Puccini*, London, W. H. Allen, 1974.

Marek, George Richard, *Puccini: A Biography*. New York, Simon and Schuster, 1951; London, Cassell, 1952.

Seligman, Vincent, *Puccini Among Friends*. London and New York, Macmillan, 1938.

Specht, Richard, *Giacomo Puccini, The Man, His Life, His Work*, translated by Catherine Alison Phillips. London, Dent, and New York, Knopf, 1933 (originally published by M. Hesse, Berlin-Schoneberg, 1931).

Weaver, William, *Puccini: The Man and His Music*. New York, Dutton, and London, Hutchinson, 1977.

*

The first biography of Puccini in English was DRY's hastily written book published just one year after Puccini's visit to London. Mainly notable for quotes from conversations the author had with the composer and for reproducing some snapshots Puccini gave the author, it is otherwise of little value. Dry is totally sympathetic to his subject, and the bulk of the book contains uncritical essays on Puccini's operas through *Madama Butterfly*.

Shortly after Puccini's death in 1924, several Italian biographies appeared, written by his friends: the journalist Fraccaroli (Milan, 1925), Marotti (Florence, 1926), and his librettist Adami, who edited the first volume of Puccini's letters (the *Epistolario*) in 1928. These works were sentimental, affectionate reminiscences that had a total disregard for accuracy, especially in the dating of letters and spelling of names.

Viennese journalist SPECHT based his work almost entirely on these hero worshippers, having himself met the composer only once during a party in Vienna. Specht relates the standard tales, embellishing them along the way in a romantic and florid style. Specht also attempts a Freudian analysis of Puccini's character, yet he is the only biographer who suppresses any mention of the suicide of Doria, one of Puccini's maids, and the resulting scandal that so shocked the composer. The English translation is idiomatic. More importantly, the translator has provided footnotes that explain people and events known when the book was written but later forgotten, and refer to the original Italian texts by Fraccaroli and Marotti, from which Specht often paraphrases freely.

MAREK's work is a serious and complete biography written in English. Eminently readable, this fluent account of Puccini's life was based on solid research. Marek traveled to Italy where he interviewed surviving friends and relatives of the composer, including Puccini's chauffeur. Marek weaves the musical triumphs and failures into the narrative, but provides no analyses of the operas, offering instead a chatty discussion of the plots. He did bring forward for the first time unpublished letters from Puccini to the Englishwoman Sybil Seligman as well as those to and from Puccini's publisher, Ricordi. Marek's straightforward writing effectively incorporates many direct quotations from letters that are properly documented. The portrait of the composer's wife, Elvira, is one of the most revealing available.

The standard scholarly work on Puccini's life and operas was written, in English, by the Viennese-born musicologist CARNER. Using many and varied quotations from Puccini's letters, Carner draws a complete portrait of Puccini's professional life, yet he offers only fleeting glimpses of his private life and few personal revelations. Carner, like his countryman Specht, also indulged in Freudian psychoanalysis, for which he received much criticism. Carner theorized that Puccini had a "mother-fixation" that caused him to compose the kind of operas he did. Carner used original sources to research the composer's life and ancestry. A detailed technical analysis of each opera takes up approximately one third of the book and sheds new light on points of characterization. The second edition, which incorporates letters discovered after the original publication date, is not otherwise substantially revised, although it should supersede the first edition.

Unlike Marek and Carner, Dante del FIORENTINO knew Puccini personally. Father Dante, an Italian-born priest assigned to a Brooklyn, New York, parish, met Puccini for the first time when the latter was about 50 years old. Because of this, the chapters on Puccini's early years suffer from hearsay since most of the information came from Fiorentino's uncle, Don Antonio, a musician and poet. Other personal episodes are related through stories of friends and neighbors. Few dates are mentioned and fewer quotations from letters are included. An unpretentious book that neither adds to the factual knowledge on Puccini's life nor provides any analyses of the music, its colorful, vivid writing nonetheless offers a tolerant, amused look at the composer from a front row seat, without the hero worship. To find hard facts look to other biographers; to know the flavor of the times and the man, read Father Dante.

SELIGMAN offers a selection of letters written by Puccini to the author's mother, Sybil. Their correspondence extends only over the latter part of Puccini's life, from 1905 on. The letters had never been published in the original Italian—only in these translations by Seligman. None of Mrs. Seligman's letters to the composer are included to provide a more well-rounded view, although Seligman does include informative annotations throughout.

JACKSON had unrestricted access to the correspondence between Puccini and Sybil, yet he fails either to capture or enlighten their relationship. Instead of quotations from letters or contemporary sources, the author presents the composer's life in his own words, and consequently his work reads like an historical novel. Source materials are frequently distorted to portray Puccini as Jackson sees him, and he presents anecdotes and newspaper clippings as fact without documenting most of them. Although much emphasis is placed on Puccini's supposed and real amorous adventures, no new documents and very few old ones are cited as a basis for fact. Jackson avoids any analysis of the music, thereby missing an important part of his subject's character.

GREENFELD includes the first detailed account of Puccini's serious love affair with a law student, known only as Corinna or "the Piemontese." Greenfeld incorporates for the first time many newly discovered letters and successfully establishes the social world in which the composer lived and worked. The writing style, however, is uneven, at times embarrassingly sentimental.

Both Greenfield and Weaver offer concise accounts of Puccini's life. GREENFIELD presents a clearly ordered progression of facts on Puccini's life, condensed effectively into 95 pages. The rest of the work is a perceptive analysis of the music. WEAVER offers a picture book with well-reproduced photographs; the many opera pictures reflect Metropolitan Opera (New York City) productions. A few minor inaccuracies slip through, but the basic facts are sound without offering much historical detail or musical description.

—Sharon G. Almquist

PURCELL, Henry, *ca.* 1659–1695; English composer.

Arundell, Dennis, *Henry Purcell*. London, Oxford University Press, 1927.

Cummings, William H., *Henry Purcell*. London, Sampson Low, 1881; revised edition, New York, Haskell House, 1969, with a foreword by Francesco Berger.

Dupré, Henri, *Purcell*, translated by C. A. Phillips and A. Bedford. New York, Knopf, 1928 (originally published by F. Alcan, Paris, 1927).

Holland, Arthur Keith, *Henry Purcell: The English Musical Tradition*. London, G. Bell, 1932.

Holst, Imogen, *Henry Purcell: The Story of his Life and Work*. London, Boosey and Hawkes, 1961.

Westrup, Jack A., *Purcell*. London, Dent, and New York, Dutton, 1937; edited by N. Fortune, Dent, 1980.

Zimmerman, Franklin B., *Henry Purcell 1659–95: His Life and Times*. London, Macmillan, and New York, St. Martin's, 1967; revised edition, Philadelphia, University of Pennsylvania Press, 1983.

*

"A life of Henry Purcell is of necessity a slender record," wrote Westrup in 1937. His judgment is confirmed by this short

series of slim volumes, most of which rely on extensive reproduction of documentary sources and critical analysis of the music to achieve book length. Elementary facts about Purcell's life are still not established: we do not even know the exact date or place of his birth. Some facts have been so recently discovered—Purcell's parentage, for example—that they are given accurately only in the most recent study. Little is known, moreover, about the personality behind the diverse musical output. Only the public figure, the series of official positions held and commissions fulfilled are recorded in these biographies, and all the authors cited have spent considerable time and space explaining the social, religious, and political institutions within which Purcell worked. The Chapel Royal, London theatres, and the momentous changes at court provide the framework for the life of a busy practical musician.

CUMMINGS is the grandfather of Purcell biography. That his book should have been reissued so recently is remarkable in view of the many inaccuracies it contains. Much of his book is plain wrong: he erroneously identifies the year of Purcell's birth and unwisely compounds his mistaken identification of Purcell's birthplace by adding a drawing of the house, sending at least one scholar (Dupré) on a wild goose chase round Chelsea (in Purcell's day, a small village outside London). Nevertheless, Cummings' scholarship is still highly regarded and his strength lies in his ability to invoke a wide range of sources—for whatever purpose. For instance, he does not disguise his aim to paint an agreeable portrait of the composer, and in order to discredit anecdotes of Purcell's "low associations" as frequenter of taverns and composer of bawdy songs, he sifts the more disreputable stories (originating in Hawkins' *General History*, London, 1776) and ingeniously assembles contrary evidence. The most enjoyable aspect of the book for today's reader is its wealth of quotations from the 17th and 18th centuries, presenting a lively impression of the period, but all dates must be cross-checked in Zimmerman.

ARUNDELL shows clearly the problems of working with such thin biographical material. Only 27 pages are devoted to "Purcell and his family," though a biographical thread runs strongly through the musical commentary. (Music figures largely in this account and there are many music examples.) Arundell is most illuminating when he relates the music to political events of the day. He is best on the dramatic music, communicating the hectic pace and innate superficiality of Restoration theatre. Arundell requires a more musically literate readership than Cummings, and his judgments are sharper in dealing with the fragmentary evidence.

Significantly WESTRUP judges Arundell's study "excellent." (Westrup is Arundell's heir, just as Zimmerman is Cummings.) His focus is on the music, and there is no better writer on the elusive confluence of French, Italian, and native English traditions. In a lucid and at times racy account, Westrup is generally reliable on Purcell's life, though he defends a now discredited theory of Purcell's parentage. His strongly-expressed opinions required a triumph of tact on the part of Fortune's editing, which refers the reader to the latest evidence in Zimmerman rather than tampering with Westrup's forcefully-argued theories.

If Westrup is always an exhilarating read, ZIMMERMAN can be plodding; but Zimmerman attempts much more, both in coverage and objectivity. His masterly study ranges widely over life in 17th-century England, and includes a fascinating chapter on political subtexts in Restoration anthems. The latest facts of Purcell's life are carefully set out, supported by a substantial selection of documents. He includes a valuable critical iconography and reproduces many of the portraits. Zimmerman is clearheaded in his distinction between qualities perceptible in the music—energy, humour, tenderness, melancholy—and the unknown personality of the composer. Without attempting to draw groundless conclusions about Purcell's character, Zimmerman offers a generous collection of contemporary eulogies for the reader's own interpretation. A disappointing aspect is that there is no systematic review of earlier studies, pointing up their errors. This serious-minded study updates but does not altogether replace Cummings, Arundell, and Westrup, and a guide through the discrepant accounts is badly needed.

By no stretch of the imagination can DUPRÉ be called essential reading. Yet it would be a pity to miss it. The French viewpoint, though appearing to English readers as a distortion, has its own value in setting Purcell within the European tradition, and this book offers a perceptive comparison between Purcell and Lully. Dupré takes Cummings as his main source but sifts conflicting accounts (of, for example, Purcell's birthplace) with an engaging enthusiasm. His manner is deceptively relaxed: some hard historical thinking lies behind this investigation. The student of reciprocal influences between London and Paris should read this book, though as pure biography it remains a charming oddity.

HOLLAND writes from an exclusively English perspective and aims to set Purcell in his national tradition. His sources are Cummings and Arundell but his approach is interdisciplinary, incorporating both an excellent overview of the literary materials Purcell worked with, and offering a useful account of the interworking of music with spectacle. Holland's breadth of coverage is available in no other study; he addresses the well-read amateur, and his re-creation of the late 17th-century scene affords a thoroughly enjoyable read.

Purcell, as one of the few great English composers, has attracted a small group of biographies addressed to children. He is, however, an inappropriate candidate for simplification, since sophisticated historical judgement is called for in assessing the slender facts. Most of these simple narratives can be ignored, but HOLST tackles the job honestly and without condescension. She provides a clear digest of the known facts (Westrup seems to be her principal source) but makes disappointingly little use of documents. Without quotations from the period, hers is a dry account, lacking the gusto, the extravagance, and the intensity that characterise both the century and Purcell's music.

—Patricia Howard

RABELAIS, François, *ca.* 1483–1553; French writer.

Febvre, Lucien, *The Problem of Unbelief in the 16th Century: The Religion of Rabelais*, translated by Beatrice Gottlieb. Cambridge, Massachusetts, and London, Harvard University Press, 1982 (originally published by A. Michel, Paris, 1942).
Frame, Donald M., *François Rabelais: A Study*. New York, Harcourt, 1977.

Krailsheimer, A.J., *Rabelais and the Franciscans*. Oxford, Clarendon Press, 1963.
Lewis, D. B. Wyndham, *Doctor Rabelais*. London and New York, Sheed and Ward, 1957.
Plattard, Jean, *Life of François Rabelais*, translated by C. P. Roche. London, Routledge, 1930; New York, Knopf, 1931 (originally published as *Vie de François Rabelais,* G. van Oest, Paris and Brussels, 1928).
Powys, John Cowper, *Rabelais, his Life*. London, Bodley Head, and New York, Philosophical Library, 1948.
Putnam, Samuel, *François Rabelais, Man of the Renaissance: A Spiritual Biography*. New York, H. Smith, and London, Cape, 1929.
Smith, W. F., *Rabelais in His Writings*. Cambridge, Cambridge University Press, 1918.
Tilley, Arthur, *François Rabelais*. Philadelphia and London, Lippincott, 1907.

*

Strictly speaking, there are no biographies of Rabelais. Not enough of the facts about his life are known. There is an enormous bibliography on the popular but exceedingly complex works, whose interpretation has been strongly disputed and is not yet agreed. However, some sort of spiritual and intellectual itinerary can be reconstituted from allusions in the works, of whose dates of publication only that of *Gargantua* is still disputed. Much even of the biography still depends on decoding the humour and the allusions to datable events. In common with many Renaissance humanists, Rabelais has been made into a rebellious priest, a virtual atheist, and a strong ally of the reformers, reflecting the prejudices or the dated circumstances and fragmented learning of the commentators. The interpretation of the biographical data was radically changed with the publication of Lucien Febvre's 1942 study (see below); since then we have had strongly religious interpretations (Krailsheimer), even quasi-Anglican readings (Screech), and a famous book by Mikhail Bakhtin emphasising the non-serious, carnivalesque side of Rabelais (*Rabelais and His World*, 1968). We shall be concerned not with the unending flow of volumes devoted to the interpretation or the techniques, genres, allusions, and structures of Rabelaisian fiction, but with those parts of those books that lay reasonable emphasis on the physical, intellectual, and spiritual aspects of Rabelais' life—chiefly Tilley, Powys, Plattard, Febvre, Krailsheimer, and Frame.

The early lives of Rabelais are founded on the biography by Rathery prefacing the edition of the works issued by himself and Burgaud des Marets in 1857 and 1858. This is the biography drawn on by TILLEY in 1907, whose book devotes some hundred pages to the life. Since Tilley wrote with grace and informed scholarship and, unlike so many modern scholars, was neither patronising nor pedantic, it is regrettable that he is now hopelessly out of date. His erudition remains impressive, but he is no longer a sure guide to the interpretation of either the life or the works, about both of which there was still a good deal to discover. SMITH's volume still shows how biographical material can be extracted from the works, with their private jokes and allusions, and especially from the lists of plants, almost all from Pliny, and the other physiological and medical references that demonstrate the humanist direction in which Rabelais wished medical science to advance. There is much here for various historical specialists (on "blasons" for instance) as well as for historians of science.

PUTNAM's volume is padded with important background material, particularly concerning the position of women in society. His crypto-Protestant Rabelais has now given way to the anti-Lutheran humourist, and no one today could accept Putnam's view of humanism, so that his book has become merely a historical landmark in Renaissance historiography. Neither of his immediate successors, John Cowper Powys and D. B. Wyndham Lewis, is a professional scholar, although Wyndham Lewis has written a number of other biographies, among them four concerned with the Renaissance. POWYS devotes much of his book to selections and interpretation, and his style is too arch to invite the page-flicking reader to do more than browse. His facetious tone is a discouraging way of concealing sneers and inaccuracies: "The Grey Friars had got into the habit of condensing into the most tasteless and ridiculous text-books the daring speculations of their great metaphysicians, Duns Scotus and Bonaventura." Doubtful facts are produced like rabbits from hats, with exclamation marks appended, yet the book is pleasant enough to read, providing the impressionist historical sketches are not found too irritating. Much derives from Plattard (see below).

LEWIS has written one of the fictionalized re-creations in which he specialises, generally confusing the reader with his own brand mixture of serious erudition and speculative fireworks. His book is dangerously entertaining, and sometimes simply wrong, as in making 1534 the date at which François I withdrew his favour "for the growing Calvinist groups at home." There was no such thing as "Calvinism" in 1534. Most scholars will regret the seductive flippancy of style that seasons the brew of important insights and occasional disinformation.

PLATTARD's biography undoubtedly still gives the best account of the historical facts, although its date explains a residual anti-clericalism that has now to be discounted, even if it already departs from the frankly rationalist Rabelais of the French academic tradition represented by scholars like Lefranc and Busson, writing shortly before or after World War I. Plattard gives us a clear account of the events and achievements of the life, but he was unhappily not aware of the dependence of Rabelais on Erasmus, brought out, for instance, by Walter Kaiser in his *Praisers of Folly* (1963). Plattard is still indispensable, but KRAILSHEIMER's study, showing Rabelais' continuing dependence on his religious and specifically Franciscan training (or, for those who have French even better, his *Religion de Rabelais* of 1967) should be read for its quite different interpretations of Rabelais' mind.

FEBVRE's book, a thoroughgoing attack on Plattard's 1922 view that Rabelais' book is anti-Christian, is taken gently to task in a famous review by Marcel Bataillon for holding that atheism in the modern sense simply could not and did not exist in the 16th century. But Febvre demonstrates the fundamental Christianity of Rabelais in a book at once comprehensive and penetrating, one of the great works of intellectual history to have been written in the 20th century. The biography, even spiritual, of Rabelais is however tangential to his purposes.

FRAME's book is mostly interpretive, although it does succinctly present the biographical facts. The weakness of the extremely competent treatment of Rabelais is the all-too-usual

ignorance among intellectual historians of what was ultimately at stake in the late medieval theological disputes among the scholastics. Professor Frame's is the best currently available general introduction to the understanding of Rabelais in English.

—A. H. T. Levi

RACHMANINOV, Sergei Vasilyevich, 1873–1943; Russian composer, pianist, and conductor.

Bazhenov, Nikolai, *Rachmaninov*, translated by Andrew Bromfield. Moscow, Raduga, 1983.

Bertensson, Sergei and Jay Leyda, *Sergei Rachmaninoff: A Lifetime in Music.* New York, New York University Press, 1956; London, Allen and Unwin, 1965.

Culshaw, John, *Sergei Rachmaninov.* London, D. Dobson, 1949.

Lyle, Watson, *Rachmaninoff: A Biography.* London, W. Reeves, 1938.

Norris, Geoffrey, *Rakhmaninov.* London, Dent, 1976.

Piggott, Patrick, *Rachmaninov.* London, Faber, 1978.

Riesemann, Oskar von. *Rachmaninoff's Recollections Told to Oskar von Riesemann.* New York, Macmillan, and London, Allen and Unwin, 1934.

Seroff, Victor I., *Rachmaninoff.* New York, Simon and Schuster, 1950; London, Cassell, 1951.

Threlfall, R., *Sergei Rachmaninoff: His Life and Music.* London, Boosey and Hawkes, 1973.

Walker, Robert, *Rachmaninoff: His Life and Times.* Tunbridge Wells, Kent, Midas Books, 1980; Neptune City, New Jersey, Paganiniana Publications, 1981.

*

The first substantial biography of Rachmaninov, by RIESEMANN, was completed during the composer's lifetime and therefore took no account of his final years; in fact it offers only scant and schematic coverage of the period after Rachmaninov left Russia in 1918. The book is based on extensive quoted passages of reminiscence, as told to the author by Rachmaninov, and contains much authentic detail. But there are a number of careless factual errors and misrepresentations by Riesemann. On seeing proofs of the book, Rachmaninov objected to the title and to several passages in the text, and he himself paid the publisher's charges for alteration and removal of some episodes (e.g., self-congratulatory statements attributed to him). A somewhat uncritical, admiring tone in fact pervades much of von Riesemann's own otherwise very readable account.

According to Leff Pouishnoff's foreword, LYLE died before completion of his somewhat uncritical biography, though this is not immediately obvious. He evidently used von Riesemann extensively as a source, but without acknowledgement, and the narrative becomes very sketchy after an indignantly anti-Soviet account of Rachmaninov's emigration. The book concludes with a record of some platitudinous conversations between Lyle and the composer, and a rapture-ridden survey of Rachmaninov's gramophone recordings.

CULSHAW has only 18 pages of biographical outline in a nine-chapter study of Rachmaninov's works. But both biographically and musicologically, the book is important in providing the first balanced critical evaluation of Rachmaninov in English. Culshaw stresses mainly the period before Rachmaninov's emigration, however. Indeed, on the whole, "Rachmaninov's life is not in itself one of the most interesting in music; highlights there are, but he was far too preoccupied with his music, his family and himself to take a vital interest in the changing world around him. . . . after his arrival in America in 1920 his life became little more interesting than that of any touring virtuoso."

SEROFF is the first biographer combining musical expertise with a close knowledge of Russian-language sources; and alongside the usual list of Rachmaninov's works, he offers a detailed bibliography. Like Culshaw, Seroff gives a more cursory survey of the 1920s and 30s. And within this period he seems to allot undue prominence to Rachmaninov's letters to Vladimir Vilshau (Wilshaw) in Moscow, his few late compositions, and his anathematisation and subsequent rehabilitation in the USSR. Otherwise, however, this is recommendable as the first objective, full-length critical biography.

A good shorter biographical study that avoids the inconsistencies of Seroff's later chapters is NORRIS' book in the Master Musicians series. Norris makes discriminating use of much recent Russian and English memoir and critical material, dividing his 211 pages almost equally between biography and a survey of Rachmaninov's works. As with Seroff, the émigré chapters are slimmer than the Russian ones. This proportionment is followed, too, in BAZHENOV's full-length biography of over 300 pages, the only Soviet study available in English. The story is sympathetically told, but Bazhenov's passages of social and historical background are predictably shrill: Rachmaninov's decision to emigrate is presented as a tragic mistake, and Bazhenov avoids the full truth and invents Rachmaninov's private thoughts à propos of the Soviet boycott in teaching and performing his works after 1931.

BERTENSSON AND LEYDA's monumental biography is the first to carry a proper apparatus of endnotes and references, a full *catalogue raisonné* of works, discography, and a very adequate index. This is by far the most complete and balanced biography, and all subsequent chroniclers have been, and will remain, in the two authors' debt. However, unlike some shorter studies (e.g. Walker), there is little attempt to incorporate any descriptive or evaluative comment on Rachmaninov's compositions; the book's forte lies in its excellently focussed montage of quoted sources.

Of the shorter, more recent studies, the least interesting (though nevertheless quite sound) is THRELFALL's 75-page booklet. It relies heavily on Bertensson and Leyda and divides Rachmaninov's career into an introduction and successive chapters on "The Student," "The Composer," "The Pianist," followed by a conclusion and list of compositions. PIGGOTT provides a 110-page survey specifically of Rachmaninov as a composer. There is thus little discussion of his émigré period. There seem to be too many pages of musical example in relation to text, and the latter, in any case, tends to be descriptive rather than critical. For instance, Piggott records the "flop" of the Piano Concerto No. 4 without any attempt to explain or analyse the reasons. WALKER's work is in the genre of illustrated life and times, and some of the photographic material relates only

tangentially to Rachmaninov himself. however, this 133-page account succeeds splendidly in combining biography with a descriptive and critical discussion of Rachmaninov's compositions and his recorded legacy as a performer. Within its scope Walker's book is highly recommendable, and an excellent short introduction to its subject.

—Christopher J. Barnes

RACINE, Jean, 1639–1699; French playwright.

Brereton, Geoffrey, *Jean Racine: A Critical Biography.* London, Cassell, 1951.
Clark, A. F. B., *Jean Racine.* Cambridge, Massachusetts, Harvard University Press, 1939.

*

There are only two biographies of Racine available in English that continue to merit attention, and both of them antedate the still definitive and radically new French biography by Raymond Picard, *La carrière de Jean Racine* (Paris, 1956). However, the career of France's greatest dramatist is controversial enough to make it worth the effort of the anglophone world to come to terms with the still unsolved biographical problems behind a cultural achievement perhaps rightly regarded by the French as without parallel.

CLARK's biography is well organised, intelligent, and sometimes perceptive, but now badly out of date. Clark is also at times badly out of his depth. The opening chapter, "The Age of Racine," does not highlight as it might have done the tidal wave of reactionary cultural pessimism about man and society of the period from about 1655 to about 1685, but takes one or two of its elements of apparently direct later relevance to the biography, Jansenism and the much talked of outbreak of poisoning associated with the name of La Voisin. In spite of what Clark aptly notes as "the tough carapace of erroneous emphasis" and "barnacles of pedantry" in earlier critical work, his own account of Jansenism sins equally by simply eluding the issues at stake with an avalanche of adverbs (mainly depends, practically all) and misapprehensions. Since Clark thinks that Racine's "Jansenism" caused him to stop writing for the secular stage after *Phèdre,* the theological errors are serious, particularly since putting them right would have shown the general thesis to have been quite unsustainable.

On matters of literary criticism and biographical detail, Clark's book contains too many facile or simply erroneous judgements, as on the rupture with Molière, where Racine has subsequently been shown to have behaved unforgiveably. No serious literary historian could even in 1939 regard Corneille as "pathetically" unable "to grow old gracefully," and no serious critic could at any time have written "The motto of Racine's time is supposed to have been 'Le *moi* est haïssable.'" Unhappily, too, Clark does not understand the bitter struggles between the two leading cultural, and not merely dramatic, factions of Racine's time, the groups we know as the partisans of the *modernes* and those of the *anciens*. Racine's dramatic career is in consequence seen in a series of false perspectives, which in turn lead to a misunderstanding of what the plays are fundamentally about.

Elements of Racine's biography have been treated in A. A. Tilley, *Three French Dramatists* (Cambridge, 1933), Martin Turnell, *The Classical Moment* (London, 1947), and V. Orgel, *A New View of the Plays of Racine* (London, 1948), but since the appearance of the Picard biography it can be seen that none of these works gets near the centre of the subject. Their interest has become merely historical. The heady traditional mixture of fantasy, myth, and literary historical convention proved too strong for all three writers.

Not enough had changed by the time BRERETON's critical biography appeared in 1951. Although the facts as known have been well researched, the conclusions are wrong, as again on the behaviour that occasioned the break with Molière, played down by Brereton, the exculpation of Racine from complicity in the death of Du Parc, in which Brereton ignores important evidence of protection in high places, the importance of the importation of the newly invented character of Aricie into the Phaedra legend, and the connection between the opposition to *Iphigénie* and that to *Phèdre et Hippolyte*, the original title of Racine's play, a fact of which Brereton seems unaware but which is important in view of Pradon's play of the same name put on two days later. There is no reference to what was so urgently at stake between the partisans of the *modernes*, including the still "pathetic" Corneille, and those of the *anciens*. The dispute was much more savage than Brereton suggests, and although part of it was fought out between the two major theatrical companies, what was ultimately at issue had to do not with pleasing an audience but with the nature of human perfectibility and human society, a hugely important battle in which Racine's side was in the end resoundingly defeated.

Brereton writes well, but his biography must have been weak even in 1951, although that is difficult to judge since it was not widely reviewed in France. Today it must be regarded as simply misleading. There is no even nearly adequate biography available in English. Were one to be written, it would still have to decide whether Racine's depictions of female passion depended on his intimate personal relationships with his actresses, or were their cause. It could also contribute much to our understanding of the intellectual, social, religious, and literary history of the period from which modern western democracy emerged. It was after all the party that defeated Racine's that elaborated the view of man and society to be enshrined 100 years later in the Declaration of Independence and the Declaration of the Rights of Man.

—A. H. T. Levi

RALEIGH (*or* Ralegh), Sir Walter, 1554–1618; English soldier, navigator, and courtier.

Adamson, J. H. and H. F. Folland, *The Shepherd of the Ocean: An Account of Sir Walter Raleigh and His Times*. London, Bodley Head, and Boston, Gambit, 1969.

Anthony, Irwin, *Raleigh and His World*. New York and London, Scribner, 1934.

Birch, Thomas, *The Life of Walter Raleigh*. London, 1739; reprinted in Raleigh's Works, Oxford, Oxford University Press, 1829.

Bradbrook, Muriel C., *The School of the Night: A Study in the Literary Relationships of Sir Walter Raleigh*. Cambridge, Cambridge University Press, 1936.

Buchan, John, *Sir Walter Raleigh*. Oxford, Blackwell, 1897.

Cayley, Arthur, *The Life of Sir Walter Raleigh*. London, Cadell and Davies, 1805.

Edwards, Edward, *The Life of Sir Walter Raleigh* (2 vols.). London, Macmillan, 1868.

Edwards, Philip, *Sir Walter Raleigh*. London, Longman, 1953.

Greenblatt, Stephen Jay, *Sir Walter Raleigh: The Renaissance Man and His Role*. New Haven, Connecticut, Yale University Press, 1973.

Harlow, V. T., *Raleigh's Last Voyage*. London, Argonaut, 1932.

Hume, Martin A. S., *Sir Walter Raleigh: The British Dominion of the West*. London, T. F. Unwin, and New York, Longman, 1897.

Irwin, Margaret, *That Great Lucifer: A Portrait of Sir Walter Raleigh*. New York, Harcourt, and London, Chatto and Windus, 1960.

Magnus, Sir Philip, *Walter Raleigh*. London, Collins, 1952.

Oakeshott, Walter F., *The Queen and the Poet*. London, Faber, 1960; New York, Barnes and Noble, 1962.

Oldys, William, *The Life of Sir Walter Raleigh*. London, 1736; reprinted in Raleigh's *Works*, Oxford, Oxford University Press, 1829.

Pope-Hennessy, Sir John, *Sir Walter Raleigh in Ireland*. London, K. Paul, 1883.

Quinn, David B., *Raleigh and the British Empire*. London, Hodder and Stoughton, 1947; New York, Macmillan, 1949.

Ross Williamson, Hugh, *Sir Walter Raleigh*. London, Faber, 1951.

Rowse, A. L., *Raleigh and the Throckmortons*. London, Macmillan, 1962; as *Sir Walter Raleigh: His Family and Private Life*, New York, Harper, 1962.

Sélincourt, Hugh de, *Great Raleigh*. London, Methuen, and New York, Putnam, 1908.

Stebbing, William, *Sir Walter Raleigh: A Biography*. Oxford, Clarendon Press, 1899.

Strathman, Ernest A., *Sir Walter Raleigh: A Study in Elizabethan Skepticism*. New York, Columbia University Press, 1951.

Thompson, Edward John, *Sir Walter Raleigh: The Last of the Elizabethans*. London, Macmillan, 1935; New Haven, Connecticut, Yale University Press, 1936.

Wallace, Willard M., *Sir Walter Raleigh*. Princeton, New Jersey, Princeton University Press, 1959.

Williams, Norman Lloyd, *Sir Walter Raleigh*. London, Eyre and Spottiswoode, 1962.

*

Raleigh's career has been the subject of a good deal of controversy during his lifetime and since. Those who have taken the trouble to write his biography, however (and there have been many), are, by and large, his stout defenders. His principal detractors tend to be students of the general history of Elizabethan and Jacobean England whose work reflects the deep ambiguity with which Raleigh's contemporaries regarded him. This striking difference in the perception of Raleigh has persisted for a long time.

The first genuine biography worthy of the name, and done on a generous scale, was by OLDYS (1736), who presented the courtier and the Renaissance man in a clearly favourable light. Oldys carefully collected the published literature and pamphlets of Raleigh's day, went through Raleigh's own writing, told all the best stories, retailed Raleigh's wit, of which there was much, and provided a convenient quarry for the legion of amateur biographers who were to follow. In brief, he provided a basic model of the favourable view of Raleigh. Almost a century later the Oxford edition of Raleigh's works reprinted Oldys' life by way of preface, and threw in BIRCH's briefer sketch for good measure. Thus, well down to the mid-19th century, Oldys' account was the authoritative life. The Napoleonic Wars stimulated a taste for lives of British naval heroes, and CAYLEY's work filled that niche.

In the mid-19th century, EDWARD EDWARDS' two-volume work broke new ground as the rise of history as a profession demanded more systematic documentation. While his biography is now largely superseded by modern scholarship, the second volume, containing virtually all of Raleigh's extant correspondence, has retained its value ever since. Subsequent biographers have pillaged these conveniently collected sources. Edwards' work, the dominant biography for the later Victorians, was challenged however in its favourable view of Raleigh by S. R. Gardiner, then leading historian of early Stuart England. Gardiner's *History of England . . . 1603–1642* (revised edition, 10 vols., 1883–84) took some time to establish itself as the authoritative history of the reign of James I. It began appearing piecemeal in the 1860s. By the 1880s when it was completed it provided the definitive narrative of its period for scholars, down to the 1960s. Though no admirer of King James, Gardiner reflected the judgement of his sources and found Raleigh rash, dangerous, and foolhardy, his difficulties with the king and his predecessor, the great Elizabeth, clearly much his own fault. Gardiner's influence within the historical profession was formidable, and no serious student of Raleigh's public career can afford to ignore his critical account, which provides necessary balance to a score of adulatory biographies.

There are only four significant late-Victorian works on Raleigh's career of any value after Edwards and Gardiner. POPE-HENNESSY's study of the Irish phase was the first work to address one particular aspect of Raleigh's career. Though Raleigh's time in Ireland was far less glamorous than his adventures at sea or in the Americas, it was a significant and relatively neglected part of his story. At the time Pope-Hennessy was writing, Britain was struggling to repress Irish nationalism; thus there was perhaps less embarrassment about Raleigh's harsher methods subduing the Irish than a later age would feel. In the last decade of the century STEBBING produced a fine scholarly assessment in one volume surveying the whole career. His work is still widely referred to. HUME emphasises the colonial projector and the doughty warrior combating the Spanish Empire. Hume's background in Spanish history, and his pioneering work with Spanish documents, serves him well. He explores stories, which turned out to be exaggerated, that the Spanish

ambassador at the court of King James had a personal grudge as well as a political objection to Raleigh's fatal behaviour in Guiana. Hume's emphasis on Raleigh as empire builder struck a resonant chord with British readers at the height of the empire's power. Perhaps the most enduring piece of late 19th-century scholarship on Raleigh, of great use to 20th-century readers, is Thomas N. Brushfield's *Bibliography of Sir Walter Raleigh* (1886), the product of a lifetime of study. This remains enormously helpful for everything published up to the time of its second edition (1908).

The 20th century has produced a great mass of writing about Raleigh. One persistent stream of this has been popular biography, books written essentially because the authors have taken a fancy to Raleigh as a fascinating and complicated subject, not because they present much new material. While most of these books are usually respectful of the body of facts they have to deal with, most lack much sense of the context in which Raleigh lived and worked. BUCHAN wrote good adventure yarns for children. Raleigh, the man of action, was a natural subject for him. SÉLINCOURT provided a fuller, pleasing, popular account for those who had no time for Stebbing. In the 1930s ANTHONY wrote an interesting, readable account of Raleigh as exponent of Machiavelli, and THOMPSON produced the best one-volume scholarly account since Stebbing, strongly defending Raleigh. After World War II, WILLIAMSON, MAGNUS, and the skillful novelist IRWIN, whose costume novels of the period had a devoted following, also produced brisk popular surveys. Williamson had done some similar history in the period that gives his brief account some plausibility, and Irwin makes the most of her shrewd psychological insights—James' resentment of Raleigh for his influence over Prince Henry, for example. Magnus' brief volume is slight, not as good as his lives of Kitchener and Burke. All of the popular accounts exist essentially to tell a very well-known tale for the amusement of readers who might as easily be seeing the MGM version. While there is no harm to reading them, these works add little or nothing to the sum of knowledge about Raleigh.

The best scholarly biography in one volume written in the 1950s was by WALLACE, whose work remains the most convenient, well-documented account of its length.

Some serious professional research has been done on Raleigh in this century mostly since 1945, along two general lines: on his role in the building of the first British empire, and on his place in literary history. On the first, the basic works are by HARLOW and QUINN as part of their distinguished careers in the general field of early British exploration and colonization. A good deal of work was done on Raleigh's writing as exemplary material for studies of the English Renaissance. Ignoring a great flood of narrow literary study, there are a number of works focusing on Raleigh as a literary figure that are of general biographical interest. BRADBROOK offers an influential yet esoteric interpretation (which mirrored the suspicions of the Elizabethans, that Raleigh was an atheist), and set off a modern scholarly debate. STRATHMAN took issue, arguing that Raleigh was not an atheist but a skeptic, and placed him nicely in the intellectual milieu of his day. OAKESHOTT uses the poems to explore Raleigh's strained and complicated relationship with the queen, a strategy that was soon taken up by some of the popular biographers. GREENBLATT considers Raleigh as a figure inventing and presenting himself to the world through his writing—a self-construction through rhetoric. The most widely used one-volume scholarly biography devoted to Raleigh as a literary figure is by PHILIP EDWARDS (1953), whose book is the standard life for that purpose.

In a different vein, while nothing new has turned up about Raleigh's public career, ROWSE's study of the local and private background is based on new material on Raleigh's in-laws, the Throckmortons. Working from his own deep knowledge of Raleigh's native west country, Rowse has added something fresh to a familiar story. Although there has not been a concise scholarly work since Wallace, the current contenders for short, reliable accounts directed at the general reader would seem to be ADAMSON AND FOLLAND, who have shrewd things to say about Raleigh's military career and write with some imagination, and WILLIAMS, who quotes very liberally from the documents. Christopher Armitage (*Sir Walter Raleigh: An Annotated Bibliography*, 1987) and Jerry Leith Mills (*Sir Walter Raleigh: A Reference Guide*, 1986) each provide some bibliographical guidance on the work done since Brushfield. The emphasis in these works is literary rather than historical.

—S. J. Stearns

RAPHAEL [*born* **Raffaello Sanzio**], 1483–1520; Italian painter.

Bortolon, Liana, *The Life and Times of Raphael*, translated by Barbera Paterson. London, Hamlyn, 1968 (originally published as *Raffaello*, Verona, Mondadori, 1965).

Cartwright, Julia, *Raphael*. London, Seeley, and New York, Macmillan, 1895.

Crawford, Virginia M., *Raphael*. London, Catholic Truth Society, 1902.

Crowe, J. A. and G. B. Cavalcaselle, *Raphael: His Life and Works* (2 vols.). London, J. Murray, 1882–85.

Dryhurst, A. R., *Raphael*. London, Methuen, 1905; New York, Dodge, 1906.

Duppa, Richard, *Life of Raffaello Sanzio*. London, J. Murray, 1816.

Fischel, Oskar, *Raphael*, translated by Bernard Rackham. London, Spring Books, 1948.

Grimm, Herman, *The Life of Raphael*, translated by Sarah Holland Adams. Boston, Cupples and Hurd, 1888; London, Gardner, 1889 (originally published as *Das Leben Raphaels*, Berlin, W. Hertz, 1886).

Jones, Roger and Nicholas Penny, *Raphael*. New Haven, Connecticut, and London, Yale University Press, 1983.

Knackfuss, H., *Raphael*, translated by Campbell Dodgson. London, Grevel, and New York, Lemcke, 1899 (originally published as *Raffael*, Leipzig, Velhagen and Klasing, 1898).

Lavery, Felix, *Raphael*. London, Sands, 1920; New York, F. A. Stokes, [n.d.].

McCurdy, Edward, *Raphael Santi*. London and New York, Hodder and Stoughton, 1918.

Müntz, Eugène, *Raphael, His Life, Works, and Times*, translated by Walter Armstrong. London, Chapman, 1882; revised edition, 1896 (originally published by Hachette, Paris, 1881).

Oppe, Adolf Paul, *Raphael*. London, Methuen, 1909; revised edition, edited by Charles Mitchell, London, Elek, and New York, Praeger, 1970.

Passavant, J. D., *Raphael of Urbino and His Father Giovanni Santi*, translated by Harwood. London and New York, Macmillan, 1872 (originally published in 3 vols. by F. A. Brockhaus, Leipzig, 1839–58).

Pope-Hennessy, John, *Raphael*. New York, Harper, 1970.

Quatremère de Quincy, *History of the Life and Works of Raffaello*, translated by William Hazlitt from the 3rd French edition. London, H. G. Bohn, 1856 (originally published, Paris, 1824).

Ripley, Elizabeth, *Raphael*. London, Oxford University Press, and Philadelphia, Lippincott, 1961.

Santi, Bruno, *Raphael*, translated by Paul Blanchard. London, Constable, 1977 (originally published as *Raffaello*, Florence, Scala, 1977).

Scott, McDougall, *Raphael*. London, G. Bell, 1909.

Staley, (John) Edgcumbe, *Raphael*. London, G. Newnes, and New York, F. Warne, 1904.

Strachey, Henry, *Raphael*. London, G. Bell, 1900.

Thompson, David, *Raphael, the Life and the Legacy*. London, BBC, 1983.

Vasari, Giorgio, *Lives of the Artists* (2 vols.), translated by George Bull. London and New York, Penguin, 1965 (originally published as *Le Vite de piu eccellenti architetti, pittori, et scultori Italiani*, Florence, 1550, 1568).

Wolzogen, Alfred Baron von, *Raphael Santi, His Life and His Works*, translated by F. E. Bunnett. London, Smith Elder, 1886 (originally published by F. A. Brockhaus, Leipzig, 1865).

*

Biographical studies of Raphael are hampered by the fact that the artist was not recorded in any documents until he was 17 years old. Consequently our only guide to his childhood is VASARI, who was not personally acquainted with Raphael, since he was only eight when the artist died. This makes even Vasari's version of events secondhand. Surprisingly, there are no other contemporary biographies of Raphael, which seems strange given his evident popularity during his short lifetime and the high regard in which he was held by men in the most influential circles. Although we have no evidence with which to refute Vasari's account, his known predilection for anecdotal detail leads us to doubt his accuracy. He views Raphael as the pinnacle of artistic achievement whose skill is equalled only by Michelangelo. Vasari goes so far as to say that "Artists as outstandingly gifted as Raphael are not simply men, but, if it be allowed to say so, mortal gods."

Since documentation of Raphael continues to be scarce well into the 19th century, biographies before that date must rely heavily on the information provided by Vasari. This is clearly evident in DUPPA's 1816 publication intended as an introduction to Raphael for the traveller in Europe, particularly the visitor to Rome. This book also contains character sketches of "The most Celebrated Painters of Italy" by none other than Sir Joshua Reynolds. Vasari is also prominent in QUATREMÈRE DE QUINCY's *Raffaello* (1824 original). This undivided chronological narrative does consider Raphael in terms of his social position and character as well as his role as artist and architect. However, the style of language is old-fashioned by modern standards and a bogus document is quoted on the circumstances of Raphael's death.

PASSAVANT, to whom the Roman and Medici archives remained closed, laments the lack of a "complete and truthful biography" of Raphael. Passavant is willing to probe the more problematic areas of Raphael's life, and he provides detailed notes to aid the scholar in reference and cross-reference. Adolf Oppe (see below) referred to Passavant's book as the "Foundation for all modern study on Raphael," and one of its strongest points is its insight into the other figures who were in contact with Perugino's studio at the time when Raphael was also involved in its activities. Like Passavant, WOLZOGEN provides careful notes and always acknowledges his sources, although his aim is to provide a concise biography for the general reader. Where Wolzogen is brief and avoids unnecessary detail, CROWE AND CAVALCASELLE stretch their biography to two volumes and 15 chapters. The value of their work lies in its use of every scrap of available information. "No one as yet," they say, "has convincingly traced the progress of the artist." Their account includes considerable reference to other artists and to time past and contemporary. Yet despite the undoubted importance of the work, its length is excessive and its language can be pedantic and unnecessarily effusive: "Raphael! At the mere whisper of this magic name, our whole being seems spellbound." The account of Raphael's life published by MÜNTZ in the same year is, like Crowe and Cavalcaselle's, notable for its historical depth. It is less exhaustive and more imaginative in approach, usefully evaluating the artistic currents that could have affected Raphael on his arrival in Rome.

Neither Grimm nor Knackfuss approaches the scope of Crowe and Cavalcaselle. Both authors are willing to question traditional viewpoints. GRIMM attacks Passavant for inventing much of Raphael's youth. Some factual inaccuracies damage Grimm's own credibility, as does his frequent use of quotations without any form of reference. Despite its sometimes clumsy translation, KNACKFUSS' work belies a more intelligent and practical approach to the lack of facts concerning Raphael's youth, relying for the most part on simple logic: Raphael could only have learned a limited amount from his father, who died when the boy was only 11 years old.

At the turn of the century, several smaller biographies of Raphael were published. STRACHEY's contribution to the "Great Masters in Painting and Sculpture" series does not go beyond the essential basics of biography, including only what is necessary to make a study of Raphael's art coherent, and with no intention of making original judgements. CRAWFORD's tiny, unillustrated biography is intended for a religious-minded readership. This is evident in her portrayal of Pope Julius II as a great patron of the arts—a far cry from Machiavellian perceptions of this prince of temporal as well as spiritual power. SCOTT's evaluation of this position is altogether more realistic, as is his acknowledgement of the basic lack of biographical material on Raphael. CARTWRIGHT does not conceive of Raphael as an original genius in the same mold as Michelangelo and Leonardo, although she concedes that "for the vast majority of the human race, Raphael will always remain the greatest and most popular of painters." Cartwright's account is remarkably full for a book of its size, including as it does translated letters and de-

tails of Raphael's will. It can, however, tend toward the apocryphal without questioning the sources. DRYHURST covers much the same ground as Cartwright, although his approach deals more in terms of paintings than of personality. Dryhurst also comments on the state of restoration of the works and includes a bibliography that is more comprehensive than one would expect from a book of this size.

Two more ambitious biographies appeared before World War I. STALEY's volume includes the first comprehensive set of illustrations. However, the text is undisciplined and written in a somewhat romanticised style that would be of limited appeal to the serious scholar. By comparison, OPPE's book is straightforward and without pretension. His candid analysis is based on the facts available to him, and he resolutely refuses to idealise Raphael's childhood. "Raphael was not born in the atmosphere of the noble court," he states, where many other authors have been keen to see Raphael enjoying the refined surroundings associated with Castiglione's *Courtier* from the earliest age, despite the fact that he was born into the family of a second-rate painter who did not have many associations with the court at Urbino. Oppe's refreshing account of Raphael appeared in a new edition, edited by Charles Mitchell, in 1970.

Between the wars, only three biographies appeared in English (in fact the third was not released in translation until 1948), and after that interest in Raphael fell into a decline until the late 1960s. McCURDY assembles a clear account of Raphael and his times that is useful for general reading, although there is nothing new here. He makes the by now obvious observation that "Such personalia as have survived the intervening centuries seem curiously few, when we consider the immediate greatness of his fame." The lack of primary documentation to shed light on Raphael's personality cannot be escaped, although it seems that LAVERY would like to deny it when he claims that his will be the "first chronologically coherent record of Raphael's life since the days of Vasari, . . . " In fact Lavery does not realise his objective satisfactorily. His schematic approach fails when it is confronted with the lack of factual material, and his discussion of modern purchases and sale prices seems out of place here.

The third of these biographies, FISCHEL, is the most comprehensive of this group and includes a Catalogue Raisonné of Raphael's works. Fischel traces Raphael's life through his painting, hoping to show what influences he was prey to at different times in his life. Religious, academic, and artistic currents contemporary with Raphael are all investigated, and Raphael is considered in all his roles: as artist, architect, and papally appointed archaeologist. For the first time a proper enquiry is made into who, among Raphael's circle, Vasari could have known and talked to in order to write his "Life" of Raphael, in what amounts to a full account of the artist's life.

RIPLEY's biography for children, and BORTOLON's pictorial record of Raphael's life, which in fact has illustrations of a rather mediocre quality, are both minor works. Of a more substantial nature is POPE-HENNESSY's *Raphael*, which attempts to do some justice to Raphael after this period of neglect. While it is useful to students of Raphael, it is not strictly biography, based as it is on a series of lectures given by the author at New York University. While the illustrations in SANTI are of good quality, the text is somewhat confusing since it assumes knowledge of other writings on Raphael without providing notes or a bibliography from which these references could be followed up.

From the present decade, we have an important book by JONES AND PENNY that aims to present "an account of Raphael's achievements and ambitions as painter, architect, archaeologist and entrepreneur." While this book centres really on the purposes for which Raphael's art was designed, and would not therefore normally come under the heading of biography, it represents a well-illustrated and coherent presentation of Raphael and his art in context. Finally, THOMPSON has published a book based on a series of programmes produced by the BBC to celebrate the 500th anniversary of Raphael's birth. Although it is designed very much with the general readership in mind, as an introduction to Raphael, it presents a reliable picture of Raphael's world and makes good use of contemporary documentation.

—Alison Leslie

RAVEL, Maurice, 1875–1937; French composer.

Myers, Rollo, *Ravel: Life and Works.* New York, T. Yoseloff, and London, G. Duckworth, 1960.
Nichols, Roger, *Ravel.* London, Dent, 1977.
Nichols, Roger, editor, *Ravel Remembered.* London, Faber, 1987; New York, Norton, 1988.
Orenstein, Arbie, *Ravel: Man and Musician.* New York, Columbia University Press, 1975.
Stuckenschmidt, Hans H., *Maurice Ravel: Variations on His Life and Work,* translated by Samuel R. Rosenbaum. Philadelphia, Chilton, 1968; London, Calder and Boyers, 1969 (originally published by Suhrkamp, Frankfurt am Main, 1966).

*

MYERS' book, subtitled "Life and Works," was the first substantial biography of Ravel to appear in English. There had, of course, been a number of good French biographies prior to this, but Myers, a distinguished writer on French music and, indeed, something of a pioneer (his was the earliest English biography of the avant-garde composer Erik Satie at a time when the latter was by no means the celebrated figure he is now), was the first to give a full and authoritative account aimed at an Anglo-Saxon readership. As a lifelong Francophile who spent much of his time in France, Myers is very much at home with the social, artistic, and literary background to Ravel's life. He is also a man of the world who can sympathize with Ravel's complex personality. Myers makes no claim to present Ravel in a new light, relying only on printed sources. His aim was to establish the connection between the uneventul life of the introverted Ravel, whose everyday existence was ordinary in the extreme when compared with that of the tumultuous Liszt or Wagner, and the intense inner life of the composer, made up of secret tensions, desires, ambitions, and disappointments. Although at the time Myers wrote not a great deal was known about Ravel's private life, Myers succeeded to a great extent in finding the link he sought and in showing how Ravel's music did in fact project the inner man, despite the composer's ostensibly cold and objective attitude toward the music he composed. A useful bibliography completes Myers' agreeable book, although the discography is now out of date and in need of revision. Both STUCKENSCHMIDT and ORENSTEIN are apt to be ponderous compared with the light but firm touch of Myers.

An examination of Myers' bibliography and that of NICHOLS 17 years later shows how little new material had emerged during the intervening period. Nichols follows the hallowed life/works arrangement used by Myers and includes the usual "Master Musicians" calendar tabulating important events in the life, an analytical work list, and a handy "Personalia" identifying the major names mentioned. He makes good use of conversations with people acquainted with Ravel during his lifetime, and, something of a "scoop," prints a hitherto unpublished extract from the Prix de Rome entry Ravel composed as a student. His account of the life includes more detail than Myers', especially on the sexual and psychological aspects. He also breaks new ground in showing that Ravel did not die of syphilis or a brain tumour, as has been suggested elsewhere, and offers a plausible medical explanation of the ailment that clouded his last years with aphasia and the tragic inability to communicate.

NICHOLS is also the editor of a book that, while not a conventional biography, gives the best available portrait of Ravel to be enjoyed by readers who do not necessarily have much technical knowledge of music. *Ravel Remembered* is made up of judiciously chosen passages from the recollections of friends and colleagues who knew him well. These reminiscences begin with memories of him as a 14-year-old student and end with his entry into the hospital for the operation that failed to save him. Among those quoted are the pianists Alfred Cortot, Ricardo Viñes, and Marguerite Long; the composers Honegger, Poulenc, Falla, Milhaud, Stravinsky, and Vaughan Williams; and the writers Farque, Colette, Cocteau, and Jules Renard. In this way we are given unique firsthand accounts of the man at successive stages of his life as seen by those who were close to him. Much of this material has never before appeared in English and helps to correct the popular image of Ravel as a cold and distant dandy. A very full chronology binds the narrative together by listing the important incidents throughout his life and placing them in the context of other developments in the arts and contemporary political and social affairs. With the aid of Myers and Nichols, the reader will get a very good idea of the man Ravel and his fascinating personality.

—James Harding

REAGAN, Ronald W., 1911–   ; American actor and political leader, 40th president of the United States.

Boyarsky, Bill, *The Rise of Ronald Reagan.* New York, Random House, 1968; as *Ronald Reagan: His Life and Rise to the Presidency,* New York, Random House, 1981.
Brown, Edmund G. (Pat), *Reagan and Reality: The Two Californias.* New York, Praeger, 1970.
Brown, Edmund G. (Pat) and Bill Brown, *Reagan: The Political Chameleon.* New York, Praeger, 1976.

Cannon, Lou, *Ronnie and Jesse: A Political Odyssey*. New York, Doubleday, 1969.

Cannon, Lou, *Reagan*. New York, Putnam, 1982.

Dallek, Robert, *Ronald Reagan: The Politics of Symbolism*. Cambridge, Massachusetts, and London, Harvard University Press, 1984.

Dugger, Ronnie, *On Reagan: The Man and His Presidency*. New York, McGraw-Hill, 1983.

Edwards, Anne, *Early Reagan*. New York, Morrow, 1987; with subtitle, *The Rise of an American Hero*, London, Hodder and Stoughton, 1987.

Van der Linden, Frank, *The Real Reagan: What He Believes, What He Has Accomplished, What We Can Expect from Him*. New York, Morrow, 1981.

Wills, Garry, *Reagan's America: Innocents at Home*. New York, Doubleday, 1987; London, Heinemann, 1988.

*

Ronald Reagan had not even left the presidency before former members of his administration had published their own accounts of the Reagan years. In many of these books Reagan himself has a minor role as the authors portray a detached president manipulated by advisers. There are, however, a number of Reagan biographies that suggest that the president's style, including passivity and avoiding blame, has long accompanied a particular vision both for himself and the nation.

The three earliest biographies appeared during Reagan's first term as governor of California. Each of these biographers wrote a second book years later as Reagan gained in national prominence. What emerges from these books, and from more recent biographies, is strong evidence of the stability of Reagan's views since he began touring for General Electric in the 1950s. All share a similar portrayal of Reagan as offering simple solutions that appealed to whites fearful of the cultural and social changes of the 1960s.

Reagan biographies, beginning with those of BOYARSKY, a reporter for the *Los Angeles Times*, are unusually strong reminders that one reader's exposé is another's positive portrayal. Boyarsky's 1968 book shows us a Ronald Reagan stridently critical of student demonstrators, insensitive to minorities and to the poor, but remarkably attuned to the concerns of suburban homeowners. Reagan appears to have little patience for the details of public policy, makes frequent misstatements of fact, and wants to reschedule his inauguration on the advice of an astrologer. Whereas liberals may view the book as a devastating critique that exposes Reagan's conservative anti-intellectualism, conservatives may view Boyarsky's Reagan as just what the country needed. Stanton Evans, in an essay for the conservative *National Review*, wrote that there is "little unflattering" to Reagan in the book, unless the reader is a liberal.

The Boyarsky biographies are superficial but readable histories of Reagan's ascent into politics. The 1968 book stops with his election to the governorship of California; the 1981 book continues through his governorship, with brief material on what he would probably do as president. Both books share the theme that Ronald Reagan is essentially a product of reaction to the social problems of the 1960s. The first half of each book is so similar that many passages have the same wording. The second book shows no evidence of additional research into Reagan's life

prior to his becoming a candidate for governor in 1966. What the second book does add is a thorough description of Reagan's governing style in California. Despite his rhetoric, he was willing to compromise with adversaries. Also similar to his Washington years, he gave his subordinates in office great latitude with little supervision. The material about Reagan's approach to executive management would fit as easily into a description of his presidency as of his governorship.

CANNON's 1969 book is an intriguing idea: a dual biography of Ronald Reagan and the late Jesse Unruh, then the Democratic leader of the California State Assembly. When the book was written, expectations were that the stridently conservative Reagan would face the traditional progressive liberal Unruh in the 1970 gubernatorial election in California. This contest did take place, with Reagan, who had compromised on many matters, defeating Unruh, who had campaigned as a pragmatic liberal. Nevertheless, the book still seems like a good idea. Both candidates emigrated to California, rose from humble backgrounds, and developed strong commitments to a political ideology.

A reporter, Lou Cannon covered Reagan for two decades both in California and Washington. His 1982 biography is readable, well written, and thoroughly documented. The problem is that the almost 500 pages of information, interesting as they are, still do not add up to a definitive portrait. The book answers the *what* about Reagan, but not the *why*. Cannon shows Reagan to be intuitively perceptive in understanding popular fears and aspirations, yet intellectually lazy. What is missing from Cannon's biography is a focus on the role of Reagan's strong conservative ideology, which serves to insulate him from questioning his own thinking and policies. The problem may be in Cannon's profound ambivalence toward his subject. The reporter considers Reagan a friend and reports that Reagan somehow just belonged in the White House (p. 411). Yet, Cannon reports so much about Reagan that suggests that the latter was unfit for the presidency. Cannon has not reconciled, neither personally nor as a biographer, the two Reagans: the warm and charming Irishman and the misinformed, insensitive ideologue.

Former California Governor Pat BROWN has no ambivalence in his two Reagan biographies. The first, published in 1970, exposes Reagan as an anti-intellectual prejudiced against higher education, blind to the problems of the poor and minorities, and given to simplistic answers to complex problems. Written four years after Reagan defeated him to become governor, Brown documents his charges. The second book, published in 1976, provides further evidence from Reagan's years as governor. The "chameleon" in the title refers to Reagan's practice of presenting his views to the public only when they are popular. Brown catalogues numerous astounding comments Reagan made in semi-public settings while he was governor.

Both books barely qualify as biographies as they are quite weak in describing Reagan's life before he became involved in California politics. Essentially, both books are warnings that Reagan is, well, Reagan. Although Brown's charges are accurate, he weakens the force of both books by an outraged tone and by gratuitously comparing Reagan's record with his own as governor. Again, as with other Reagan books, one writer's warning of danger to the nation may be read as praise of the politician by readers who do not share the writer's goals and values.

The biographies of the 1980s have an enormous range. VAN DER LINDEN's book is a worshipful account of the 1980 campaign interspersed with Reagan trivia. Van der Linden presents numerous tidbits of information without analysis or explanation of their significance. Readers who want to know Reagan's eating habits and his memories of his first trip to the dentist should read this book.

In contrast, DUGGER's book is "not a personal biography, but a policy biography." It has a chapter on Reagan's life, a chapter on his style of government, and the remaining 600 pages cite his positions on issues, one chapter to each issue. Dugger was able to procure transcripts of 500 five-minute radio commentaries Reagan made from 1975–79. The resulting presentation shows a glib conservative with many extreme views. Although this book might have been interesting reading in 1983, by now its utility is limited to researchers who want to know Reagan's policy stands in the 1970s.

The Leamer and Edwards biographies are gossipy accounts with weak documentation. LEAMER's book, based on hundreds of interviews, presents a great deal of trivia about the Reagans' Hollywood years as well as their prior backgrounds. The relevance of this material for understanding Reagan's presidency and other significant aspects of his life, such as his shift to conservatism, is unclear.

EDWARDS' book stops at 1966, the year of Reagan's first gubernatorial campaign. She argues in a documentary style, mostly with anecdotal evidence, that Reagan's shift to conservatism came from his clashes with Communism during his union days. She ignores the abundant evidence that Reagan emerged primarily as a reaction to the frustrations and the cultural challenges of the 1960s.

The two most recent biographies attempt to explain Reagan and his politics by focusing on his childhood and by placing his life in a framework of the American social tradition. DALLEK's book is a well-written, well-documented exploration that tries to fit Reagan's childhood into an account of his political success. Dallek depends on secondary sources to build an argument from psychoanalytic theory that Reagan's attitudes stem from his efforts to cope with his alcoholic father. Dallek views Reagan's politics as intended to accomplish symbolic victories: to restore traditional values and enhance the self-esteem of his followers. Dallek is distressed that Reagan is unwilling to assess the actual impact of his policies on the country.

Dallek's book has the problem of most psychoanalytic biographies: the author's interpretations exceed the information at hand. Readers who accept psychoanalytic theory will find the book valuable; others will simply dismiss it.

WILLS' biography focuses on Reagan's self-image and the role of his conception of America's past in developing that self-image. Wills argues convincingly that to understand Reagan with all his contradictions is to go far toward understanding America. Wills says that Reagan does not just present a set of values, but embodies American values. Reagan is always acting, but he is playing himself—so it is authentic.

Wills has written a brilliant biography. His research into Reagan's life is exhaustive, but he does not supply facts without signaling their significance. His purpose is not to tell us that Reagan is often misinformed (we know this already), but to explain why to so many Americans, and to Reagan himself, it does not matter that he is misinformed. Wills' explanations are not always simple, but they are consistently logical, interesting, and provocative. Regardless of one's opinion of Reagan and the Reagan years, *Reagan's America* is the choice for readers who want to know Reagan and, through understanding him, know themselves a bit better.

—Robert E. O'Connor

REICH, Wilhelm, 1897–1957; Austrian psychologist.

Cattier, Michel, *The Life and Work of Wilhelm Reich*, translated by Ghislaine Boulanger. New York, Horizon, 1971 (originally published by La Cité, Lausanne, 1969).

Mann, W. Edward and Edward Hoffman, *The Man Who Dreamed of Tomorrow: A Conceptual Biography of Wilhelm Reich*. Los Angeles, Tarcher Press, 1980.

Reich, Ilse Ollendorff, *Wilhelm Reich: A Personal Biography*. London, Elek, and New York, St. Martin's, 1969.

Sharaf, Myron, *Fury on Earth: A Biography of Wilhelm Reich*. New York, St. Martin's/Marek, and London, Deutsch, 1983.

Wilson, Colin, *The Quest for Wilhelm Reich*. New York, Doubleday, and London, Granada, 1981.

Wyckoff, James, *Wilhelm Reich: Life Force Explorer*. Greenwich, Connecticut, Fawcett, 1973.

*

Biographies of Reich tend to reflect something of the fanaticism with which he was associated, especially toward the end of his furious life. James WYCOFF's *Life Force Explorer*, and MANN AND HOFFMAN's *The Man Who Dreamed of Tomorrow* are typical in this respect. The latter contains a foreword from Reich's daughter and successor, Eva, which outdoes the main text in its hagiographical excess. Despite their subtitle, Mann and Hoffman include only one chapter of straight biography, devoting the rest of the book to a survey of Reich's ideas. A bonus for the reader is an appendix that gives full instructions and a plan to build an orgone accumulator of you own.

A notable exception to this tendency toward uncritical adulation, and an excellent introduction to the life of this undeniably great (and possibly mad) man, is WILSON's work. It begins with a warning. Frustrated at the unavailability of original documents, the author adds a caveat to his introduction, claiming that it is "not intended as a biography of Reich, . . . [who] had no intention of allowing anyone to write a frank and fully documented biography." This refers to the infamous clause in Reich's will, sealing the archives for 50 years after his death. (Wilson is not alone in his resentment: Myron Sharaf [see below] relates bitterly that his own notes, appropriated by Reich for his archives, will not be available to him until 2007!) However, despite the disclaimer, Wilson's book serves both as an introduction to the work and as a concise biography. The author maintains a sceptical, though open-minded, attitude to his subject that is rare among such studies. Wilson is careful not to fall into the trap of identifying valid work in the first part of Reich's life and simply rubbishing his later experiments; though he does suggest that in his final few years, obsessed by his struggle with the Food and Drug Administration, Reich verged on paranoia.

Another exception is ILSE OLLENDORFF-REICH's "Personal Biography," which is less personal than the reader might expect from Reich's wife, colleague, and confidante of several years. Very little is given to convey a sense of their life together. The impression is that the couple were united by their mutual interest in his work, and indeed the marriage broke down under the strain of the FDA campaign against Reich and his explosive reaction to it. The experience understandably cooled her passion for orgone research, allowing her to examine it in a detached manner; similarly, Reich is presented coolly and referred to by surname only. She remained loyal to him, however, and this book is a touching and penetrating study of Reich from one who knew him intimately, but who perhaps preferred not to tell all.

There are two main biographical works devoted to Reich that explore both his work and personality in detail. CATTIER's is an adequately researched and competent biography that gives the known facts plainly and with some measure of objectivity. But SHARAF's *Fury On Earth* looks set to become the definitive text. Sharaf opens his book with a comprehensive account of his own involvement with Reich, a tumultuous relationship that lasted ten years and stemmed from a family crisis scarcely less bizarre than Reich's own. Having declared his position in fulsome and sometimes painful detail, Sharaf then sets out to cover the life of his subject. The author's own relationship with Reich is intrinsic to the text, which acts for Sharaf as a cathartic mechanism, reliving in his subject's life (with which he identified completely in his formative years) something of his own. While retaining belief in Reich's genius, Sharaf is not afraid to criticise his one-time mentor, defining him as an "extraordinary mixture of greatness, pettiness and vindictiveness." True to his Freudian origins, Sharaf analyses Reich's work as a manifestation of latent psychological content. Often this approach offers astonishing insight into the hidden background, as, for example, when he identifies a 1920 paper as a secret autobiographical fragment, in which Reich is disguised as "the patient." As that paper deals with Reich's mother's suicide and Reich's own part in that tragic affair, it is no wonder that Reich never referred to it in his other work. Reich's relationship with Freud, which mirrored Sharaf's own with Reich nearly 30 years later, is explained in similar terms. Such a synthesis of passion and analytical detachment is rare in any book, and in a study of Reich it is unprecedented. Until 2007, when the Reich archives are finally opened, there is unlikely to be another biography as exhaustive and satisfying.

—Alan Murphy

REMBRANDT (Harmenszoon van Rijn), 1606–1669; Dutch painter.

Alpers, Svetlana, *Rembrandt's Enterprise: The Studio and the Market*. London, Thames and Hudson, and Chicago, University of Chicago Press, 1988.

Benesch, Otto, *Rembrandt: A Biographical and Critical Study*. Geneva and New York, Skira, 1957.

Haak, Bob, *Rembrandt: His Life, His Work, His Time*. New York, Abrams, and London, Thames and Hudson, 1969.

Rosenberg, Jacob, *Rembrandt: Life and Work*. Cambridge, Massachusetts, Harvard University Press, 1948; revised edition, London, Phaidon, and Greenwich, Connecticut, New York Graphic Society, 1964.

Schwartz, Gary, *Rembrandt: His Life, His Paintings*. London and New York, Viking, 1985.

Strauss, Walter L. and Marjon van der Meulen, *The Rembrandt Documents*. New York, Abaris Books, 1969.

White, Christopher, *Rembrandt and His World*. London, Thames and Hudson, and New York, Viking, 1964.

*

Nearly everything we know about Rembrandt's early youth is derived from one source, a 350-word biography written in 1641 by Jan Orlers, the first biographer of Rembrandt. A few passages from the biography of Constantijn Huyghens, secretary to the Stadtholder, written between 1629 and 1631, give us some additional information concerning Rembrandt's early Leiden period (between 1625 and 1631) and his collaboration with Jan Lievens. Most early biographers comment on his Amsterdam period, his success, his extravagance, his falling out of grace, and his bankruptcy. Joachim von Sandrart (1675), for instance, stressed that Rembrandt's house was filled with highborn children for instruction and training, but criticized Rembrandt for not knowing how to keep his station and for always associating with the lower orders. Arnold Houbraken (3 vols., 1718–21) amplified Sandrart's biography in many aspects by also emphasizing that when Rembrandt was in Amsterdam pupils literally flowed to him from all sides. The master leased a warehouse on the Bloemgracht, where each of his pupils had his own space. Here too we find the value-laden comment that Rembrandt, in the autumn of his life, kept company mostly with common people. Flippo Baldinucci (1686), who received his information on good authority, called Rembrandt a most temperamental man who was inclined to disparage everyone. He also described Rembrandt's extravagance and his activity as a collector. Some of this material is available in English in *The Rembrandt Documents* (see below).

Little consideration has been given to the negative criticisms voiced by Rembrandt's contemporaries. From the 19th century onward, the perception of Rembrandt's sacred genius has been so great that negative evidence either does not penetrate or is minimized.

As early as the 1880s, continuous archival research of Abraham Bredius together with De Vries and the Amsterdam archivist De Roever laid the foundation for our present knowledge of Rembrandt's biography. The first issues of the Dutch art historical journal *Oud Holland*, established in 1883, published a number of new documents with comments in Dutch relating to Rembrandt's life and the lives of his contemporaries. By the beginning of the 20th century so much had been published on Rembrandt by Bredius, De Roever, and De Vries that Cornelis Hofstede de Groot felt ready to publish his compilation on the third centenary of Rembrandt's birth (*Die Urkunden über Rembrandt*, 1906). However, despite the rich biographical documentation available to him, Hofstede de Groot's book lacked the necessary archival annotation, leaving these texts isolated and devoid of contextual reference points. The first biography of Rembrandt based on solid archival evidence would not come until the 1930s, from the deputy librarian at the Amsterdam University, Hendrik F. Wijnman.

The biographies by BENESCH and ROSENBERG take the traditional view of Rembrandt, emphasizing the power of his senses and the violence of his temperament, which gave way to the humility and spirituality of Rembrandt's late period. Tragic events influenced the inner change of Rembrandt's human and artistic outlook, but the revelatory episode with Geertge Dircx, whom Benesch earlier described laconically as "an hysteric," is described by Rosenberg as an "unfortunate relationship." Here, too, we find the older notion that Rembrandt's increasing use of chiaroscuro with less regard for naturalistic effects caused dissatisfaction and contributed to the decline of his reputation, resulting in his disillusionment and, finally, financial and psychological collapse.

Wijnman was the first to uncover the unsavory story of Rembrandt and Geertje Dircx, which was mentioned in detail in the Dutch translation of WHITE's monograph on Rembrandt. This is an exceptional case, as van Eeghen rightly remarked in her 1965 review of White's book, where the Dutch translation is preferable to the original English edition. In general, however, White's biography, as well as that of HAAK, leaves Rembrandt exclusively in the world of art and art theory, a creature of the studio and the bookshelf. Van Eeghen made many new additions and significant corrections to Rembrandt's biography in many articles published in *Amstelodamum*. Her article of 1956 is revelatory in providing something Hofstede de Groot's edition lacked: archival annotation and context, thus making the Rembrandt documents truly comprehensive.

In 1979, STRAUSS AND VAN DER MEULEN, with the assistance of Dudok van Heel and P. J. M. de Baar, published an updated version of Hofstede de Groot's 1906 edition of the Rembrandt documents. It contains all published and several unpublished documents with both the original Dutch transcription and complete English translations. Many of the documents published by Hofstede de Groot and Strauss were first discovered by Bredius, whose massive work (*Künstler-Inventare*, 7 vols., The Hague, 1915–22) also provided information for the period after Rembrandt's death.

SCHWARTZ's recent biography of Rembrandt presents a chronological, integrated, and complete account of his life and work. Prior to Schwartz, almost none of Rembrandt's biographers had succeeded in breaking with the powerful tradition that sees him as a sensitive human being with great spiritual depths. That Rembrandt, the protégé of Remonstrant patrons, lacked support in Leiden can be attributed entirely to politics, but in Amsterdam entirely to personal causes. The Geertge Dircx tragedy shows him as a bitter, vindictive person. His dealings with patrons, including Lodewijk van Ludick and Jan Six for instance, show him to be underhanded and untrustworthy even to his friends, and arrogant to those who admired him. In short, Schwartz concludes, Rembrandt was not only overly attached to his money, but he had a nasty disposition and an untrustworthy character.

ALPERS aims to locate Rembrandt's idiosyncrasies in his artistic production, by which she means the studio practice and his relationship to the market. As far as Rembrandt's biography is concerned, Alpers argues that the studio was for Rembrandt a world in which life had to be reenacted. She interprets Rembrandt's biography in relation to patrons, to tradition, and to the marketplace. In other words, Alpers proposes to account for three problematic features of Rembrandt's pictures—their idiosyncratic paint structure, obscure subject matter, and uncertain authenticity—by peculiarities of his biography, especially the conditions of production and the character of their marketing. To be sure, Rembrandt got on badly with his potential patrons, failed to complete his works on time, and ran into debt. Alpers sees something Protestant about his rejection of authority, as well as his discovery of artistic freedom. Her argument revolves around Rembrandt's turning art into a commodity to be exchanged in the marketplace.

—Hans J. Van Miegroet

RENOIR, Pierre-Auguste, 1841–1919; French painter.

Renoir, Jean, *Renoir, My Father*, translated by Randolph and Dorothy Weaver. Boston, Little Brown, and London, Collins, 1962 (originally published as *Renoir: Souvenirs de mon père*, Paris, 1948).

Vollard, Ambroise, *Renoir, an Intimate Record*, translated by Harold L. Van Doren and Randolph Weaver. New York, Knopf, 1925 (originally published as *La Vie et l'oeuvre de Renoir*, Paris, 1919).

White, Barbara E., *Renoir, His Life, Art, and Letters*. New York, Abrams, 1984.

*

The biographies of Pierre-Auguste Renoir by Vollard and Jean Renoir (see below), long understood as the old and new testaments of Renoir studies in English, are supplanted by White's document. Vollard and Jean Renoir's priviledged communications with the artist accorded their biographies primary source status; Vollard was one of Renoir's dealers and Jean Renoir was the second of the artist's three sons. Additionally, Vollard and Jean Renoir achieved recognition beyond their associations with Renoir, Vollard as author of other artists' biographies and as a well-known member of Parisian art circles, and Jean Renoir as an internationally successful film maker.

WHITE, a professor at Tufts University, approaches the biography as an historian trained in documentary research. Her meticulous use of letters, diaries (especially Julie Manet's), manuscript fragments, published reviews, and public records establishes a precise chronological outline of Renoir's life not found in the impressionistic portrayals of the artist by Vollard and Jean Renoir. White's use of written and painted documents and the arrangement of her text create a portrait of Renoir also not seen before in the many art historical studies based almost entirely on his paintings. Dividing the life into clusters of years associated with significant events in Renoir's life, White gives her chapter-headings appropriate chronological and topical titles such as "1890–99, Marriage, Acclaim, and Illness." A useful year-by-year outline of Renoir's life follows the endnotes and precedes the extensive bibliography. The numerous color illustrations are superb. In addition, many previously unpublished letters are cited in the endnotes. Among the most significant new letters are those from the Parisian Bibliothèque Centrale du Louvre, Bibliothèque d'Art et d'Archéologie, collections of Durand-Ruel, Maurice Bérard, and Denis Rouart, as well as some from the Pierpont Morgan Library in New York.

Major themes discussed by White, about which she has new information, are Renoir's personal relationships, his interactions with aristocratic and middle-class private patrons, and the government arts establishment. White's tracking of Renoir's ideas about his theory of art during the 1880s, which took naturalistic asymmetry as its organizing principle, comes as a surprise to readers accustomed to Vollard's and Jean Renoir's representations of Renoir's opposition to theoretical systems of art. Renoir was a friend of contemporary authors including Stephane Mallarmé and Octave Mirabeau, as well as painters Claude Monet and Berthe Morisot. White characterizes the Renoir of these friendships as a man of warmth and humor who is sometimes insecure and provincial in manner, yet on the other hand able to maintain close ties to aristocratic patrons including the Bérards of Paris and Wargemont.

Occasionally White's formal analysis of paintings gets in the way of the flow of the text, but for the most part her discussion of artworks aids readers in understanding the impact of Renoir's goals and experiences on the development of his art and life. The unwieldly size and reflective surface of the pages of White's volume make this otherwise useful and informative work difficult to read. Nonetheless, readers who persevere find, for instance, that it is only here and in French municipal records that one can locate precise references to birth certificates of Renoir's children and his own marriage certificate.

The compelling biographies of VOLLARD and JEAN RENOIR are important sources of the mythology of impressionism; both present versions of Renoir tempered by what each author saw in him. Vollard's Renoir is an aristocratic though earthy artisan, with a vast knowledge of the history of art and royalist-catholic-traditionalist political inclinations. Jean Renoir describes his father as a liberal artisan who had aristocratic forebears but did not accord honor to claims of merit through birth. Both authors concur on the importance of sensation and instinct in Renoir's worldview, and as a corollary they have him describe his pathway through life as that of a "cork floating in a stream." Neither seems to be aware of the way Renoir plotted his entry into the Salon of 1879 or of his complex understanding of the working of the government patronage system as revealed in White's biography. All three authors agree in their heroic portraits of Renoir in the 1890s, when he achieved fame and financial stability but was crippled with rheumatoid arthritis. The wit, kindness, and courage of the man and his devotion to his art provide inspiring conclusions for each biography.

—Alice H. R. H. Beckwith

RHODES, Cecil John, 1853–1902; British industrialist, politician, and philanthropist in South Africa.

Baker, Sir Herbert, *Cecil Rhodes: By His Architect.* London, Oxford University Press, 1934.

Flint, John E., *Cecil Rhodes.* Boston, Little Brown, 1974; London, Hutchinson, 1976.

Fuller, Thomas Elkins, *The Right Honourable Cecil John Rhodes, a Monograph and Reminiscence.* London and New York, Longman, 1910.

Gross, Felix, *Rhodes of Africa.* London, Cassell, 1956; New York, Praeger, 1957.

Jourdan, Philip, *Cecil Rhodes: His Private Life by His Private Secretary.* London and New York, J. Lane, 1911.

Le Sueur, Gordon, *Cecil Rhodes, the Man and His Work.* London, J. Murray, 1913; New York, McBride Nast, 1914.

Lockhart, J. G. and C. M. Woodhouse, *Cecil Rhodes: The Colossus of Southern Africa.* London, Hodder and Stoughton, and New York, Macmillan, 1963.

McDonald, James Gordon, *Rhodes: A Life.* London, P. Allen, 1927; New York, McBride, 1928.

McDonald, James Gordon, *Rhodes: A Heritage.* London, Chatto and Windus, 1943.

Michell, Sir Lewis, *Life and Times of the Right Honourable Cecil John Rhodes 1853–1902* (2 vols.). New York and London, M. Kennerley, 1910.

Millin, Sarah Gertrude, *Cecil Rhodes.* New York and London, Harper, 1933; revised as *Rhodes*, London, Chatto and Windus, 1953.

Plomer, William, *Cecil Rhodes.* New York, D. Appleton, and London, P. Davies, 1933.

Roberts, Brian, *Cecil Rhodes: Flawed Colossus.* London, Hamilton, 1987; New York, Norton, 1988.

Rotberg, Robert I., with Miles F. Shore, *The Founder: Cecil Rhodes and the Pursuit of Power.* New York and Oxford, Oxford University Press, 1988.

Stead, W. T., editor, *The Last Will and Testament of Cecil John Rhodes.* London, "Review of Reviews" Office, 1902.

Stent, Vere, *A Personal Record of Some Incidents in the Life of Cecil Rhodes.* Cape Town, M. Miller, 1925.

Williams, Basil, *Cecil Rhodes.* London, Constable, and New York, Holt, 1921.

*

After Rhodes' death, his friends and associates offered their own accounts of his life and their particular role in it. Most, but not all, are simply the recorded memories of men who idolized Rhodes and shared his dreams. STEAD was a close friend who published Rhodes' last will and testament more as an act of homage than scholarship. Nevertheless, by tracing the changes in Rhodes' successive wills and adding his own personal reminiscences, Stead illuminates Rhodes' thoughts on God, the British Empire, the nature and future of mankind and the establishment of the scholarships that bear his name. This is not a comprehensive biography, but it can be read with pleasure and unexpected reward. FULLER's personal account of his association with Rhodes is written mainly from memory, is generally anecdotal, and is prone to inaccuracies and errors. JOURDAN and LE SUEUR, personal secretaries to Rhodes, record bits of conversation and everyday events, based on their notes and memory, about life around "the Old Man." STENT's biography is valuable for its being the most reliable account of the Great Indaba in the Matopo Hills in 1896 that ended the rebellion in Matabeleland.

McDONALD (1927) describes Rhodes' life as he witnessed it for 12 years, relying mainly on Michell and Williams (see below) to fill in the biographical details. His second volume (1943) studies the effect of Rhodes' work for "humanity and especially for the British race," during his lifetime and for 40 years following his death. BAKER was responsible for putting Rhodes' dreams into material reality. This short account offers a unique insight into the empire builder's thinking and, most interestingly, his love of nature.

MICHELL wrote the first full-scale biography of Rhodes. A close friend, the executor and trustee of Rhodes' will, Michell had access to all of Rhodes' papers. He views Rhodes as a great man and is sympathetic toward his ideas and actions. His only criticism is that the famous philanthropist was too indiscriminate with his almsgiving. Michell relates a number of personal anecdotes about Rhodes but also quotes extensively from the documents made available to him. The text is intelligently written and relatively free of errors.

WILLIAMS is more critical and occasionally finds fault with Rhodes' actions, but concludes that "with all his grievous faults" Rhodes was a great man. Like Michell, Williams was acquainted with Rhodes and thus writes from firsthand knowledge about many of the events in Rhodes' life. He also makes use of as many published and unpublished sources as were available at the time. He lists these in an extensive "Note on Sources" at the end, but regretfully includes no footnotes. The work, though shorter than Michell's, places Rhodes' life in the much broader context of British imperial and Cape colonial politics than does the earlier volume.

PLOMER did not know Rhodes and it does not appear that he would have liked him if he had. This biography characterizes Rhodes as "a major prophet of capitalist imperialism," and is an indictment of both the man and the British imperial spirit of the times. It is not a tirade, however, and Plomer methodically and carefully supports his arguments and also gives credit where it is due for the shrewdness, personal charisma, drive and courage that were also part of Rhodes' character. A controversial study for its time, the work is still well worth reading.

MILLEN, best known for her fiction writing, offers nothing extraordinary or new in her Rhodes biography, but she tells the story effectively and efficiently. Like a true novelist, Millen gets inside her main character's mind and sees and describes the world from his vantage point. GROSS' book is neither as well written nor as sympathetic to Rhodes' perspective as Millen's. A journalist, Gross had access to more documentary material than any previous biographer, spent 12 years preparing the work, and presents some important new material. The result is a solid work of biography that yet suffers from its lack of footnotes or bibliography.

The volume written by LOCKHART AND WOODHOUSE, while long considered the standard biography of Rhodes, is restrained and humdrum. This is a full-length, fully documented, detailed biography that regrettably was written with a much smaller vision than their subject, the "Colossus of Southern Africa," possessed. While FLINT's biography is not as detailed, it does seek to ask more challenging questions and arrives at a

number of controversial conclusions. Flint's support for his arguments is not always convincing, but this shortcoming does not detract from the overall importance of his book. The first major Rhodes biographer of post-independence Africa and post-unilaterally independent Rhodesia, Flint writes in a style and manner that recognizes the African side of the African history equation.

ROBERTS offers "a biography of Cecil Rhodes, not a history of his times." He is concerned with Rhodes' personality, his personal development, and his motivation. This is a masterful biography that will remain required reading for many years.

ROTBERG, an historian and vice president of Tufts University, in collaboration with SHORE, who teaches psychiatry at the Harvard Medical School, has produced a monumental study that took him longer to research and write (24 years) than the time that Rhodes spent in South Africa (22 years). The book touches on every aspect of Rhodes' life and tackles most of the major questions, although the conclusions are not always satisfactory. The contribution by Shore, an investigation of Rhodes' psyche, will no doubt alienate some readers and confuse others, but the investigation is interesting if somewhat uneven. This will probably remain the definitive Rhodes biography, for it is hard to imagine that enough new information will come to light to substantially alter the facts presented here.

—Roger B. Beck

RICHARD I [Richard Coeur de Lion], 1157–1199; English monarch.

Bridge, Anthony, *Richard the Lionheart*. London, Grafton, 1989; New York, M. Evans, 1990.

Gillingham, John, *The Life and Times of Richard I*. London, Weidenfeld and Nicolson, 1973.

Henderson, Philip, *Richard, Coeur de Lion: A Biography*. London, R. Hale, 1958; New York, Norton, 1959.

Howser, Harry Steven, *Richard I in England*. Tangelwuld, Garland, 1986.

Norgate, Kate, *Richard the Lion Heart*. London, Macmillan, 1924.

*

Over the years, public opinion of Richard and his life has generally been favorable. He was a flamboyant, romantic leader who led armies into the Crusades and who rivals King Arthur and Robin Hood as an object of public admiration. The most recent biographical study, by BRIDGE, presents this positive view of Richard's life and personality. In this work, written for the general reader, Bridge concludes that "Far from being little more than a bone-headed soldier—a brutal oaf good at nothing but killing his fellow man—he was a subtle, complex and many sided man." This point of view is also echoed in GILLINGHAM's study, which records the various opinions of many authors, from Bishop Stubbs to Winston Churchill, in an effort to present a picture of the "real Richard."

The position taken by both Bridge and Gillingham is at variance with William Stubbs' view that Richard was a bad king who had no ambition but to fight and kill the infidels (*Chroni-*

cles and Memorials of the Reign of Richard I, London, 1864). Since Stubbs' comments, published over 100 years ago, are not readily available to the general reader, Bridge provides a useful reference to his position in the final chapter of his work.

HOWSER echoes the more critical views about Richard in his study, which focusses primarily on the very short period of time—just six months in 1194—in which he was resident as king in England. After reciting the variety of offenses that Richard perpetrated against the people, the Church, and the State, Howser states that the "reign was a disaster for the country and for the English people," which was only redeemed by the fact that his contemptuous actions gave impetus to the barons' revolt that led to the confrontation with King John at Runnymede in 1215.

Perhaps the closest approach to a standard biography of Richard is NORGATE's work, published in 1924. Although this book is out of print, it is still obtainable in some collections, and provides a very full, somewhat old-fashioned account of Richard I's life and times. In references to Richard's personal lifestyle, Norgate notes that he had homosexual inclinations, and notes also Stubbs' criticism that he was a bad husband to his queen, Berengaria of Navarre, whom he married in Cyprus in 1191. Similar emphasis on his sexual interests is of course featured in Chapter 2 of James Graham's study, *The Homosexual Kings of England* (1968), in which all sides of Richard's character are briefly reviewed.

Many other more general works include interesting brief accounts of Richard's life and times. In particular, Poole's comments in volume III of *The Oxford History of England* (*From Doomesday Book to Magna Carta, 1087–1216*, 1951, pp. 347–384), which should be readily available in most academic libraries, offers a good introduction to the topic.

Last, but by no means least, there is HENDERSON's scholarly study, originally published in 1958. Like the other works reviewed above, Henderson quotes the comments of earlier authorities and debates the pros and cons of Richard's life in an effort to assess his stature. This leads him to claim that "when all is said . . . one feels instinctively in the presence of greatness, . . . " and that Richard "possessed in a unique degree the qualities of warrior and poet."

—George Thomas Potter

RICHARD II, 1367–1400; English monarch.

Du Boulay, F. R. H., and Caroline M. Barron, editors, *The Reign of Richard II*. London, Athlone Press, 1971.

Hutchison, Harold F., *The Hollow Crown: A Life of Richard II*. London, Eyre and Spottiswoode, and New York, Day, 1961.

Palmer, John J. N., *England, France, and Christendom, 1377–99*. Chapel Hill, University of North Carolina Press, and London, Routledge, 1972.

Senior, Michael, *The Life and Times of Richard II*. London, Weidenfeld and Nicolson, 1981.

Steel, Anthony, *Richard II*. Cambridge, Cambridge University Press, 1941.

Tuck, Anthony, *Richard II and the English Nobility*. London, E. Arnold, 1973; New York, St. Martin's, 1974.

*

During his reign, Richard II engaged in a bitter struggle with the opposition group known as the Lords Appellant, and after he was deposed by the last surviving Appellant (Henry IV) the conflict continued among chroniclers and historians. Most opinions from the time of his deposition to this century were hostile to him; then certain discoveries and reinterpretations led to a more favorable estimate, which some recent scholars are now modifying.

The Life and Reign of King Richard the Second (1681), by someone known simply as "A Person of Quality," is unlikely to be available to many readers, but it conveniently symbolizes the traditional view of the king. Quite literally "Whig history," it condemns the king as a precursor of the Stuart royalism its anonymous author evidently opposed. As stated in its introduction, this work is chiefly based on the chronicles of Henry Knighton and Thomas Walsingham, together with the articles justifying Richard's deposition. As Walsingham is among the most hostile of the contemporary chroniclers, and the charges against Richard at his deposition are of course partisan, it is not surprising that these sources produced a picture of Richard as an unsuccessful tyrant.

This view gathered increasing weight from the later work of Stubbs in the 19th century and Tout in the early 20th, both of whom regarded Richard as a threat to the development of free parliamentary institutions, a position that remained essentially intact in May McKisack's standard survey *The Fourteenth Century* as late as 1959.

Meanwhile a more sympathetic view of the king was gradually emerging, beginning with the (still untranslated) French life, *Richard II* (Paris, 1864), by Henri Wallon, who favored Richard as the proponent of peace with France. Wallon's 19th-century work had no new documentation to support its interpretation, and it was largely ignored until Clarke and Galbraith brought new sources to light in the 1920s and 30s (in articles largely collected in Maud V. Clarke's *Fourteenth Century Studies*, Oxford, 1937). This research and other new work on the reign was embodied in the volume by STEEL, which for the moment remains the standard biography. Steel followed Clarke and Galbraith in using the Dieulacres Chronicle to support previously neglected French sources in rejecting the official account of Richard's deposition, and used his own work on the exchequer and on parliament to present a more favorable understanding of the king's financial and political position. His best-known and most controversial contribution, however, is his attempt at psychobiography, which presents the king as increasingly divorced from reality and ultimately a "mumbling neurotic." This view, not generally accepted, is largely secondary to Steel's real value as a synthesis of the scholarship of his day, and for providing a more impartial, to some degree sympathetic, view of the king.

Much more sympathetic is HUTCHISON, who writes as a fierce partisan of the king, finding grounds to defend, or at least mitigate, even Richard's most notorious actions. This attitude carries with it a hostile review of the "Merciless Parliament," which undoubtedly strained the law to destroy the young king's friends; Hutchison, unlike most of the king's present-day admirers, believes Richard plotted revenge on his enemies for the next ten years, a revenge Hutchison regards as justified. This view of Richard's plans has not won wide acceptance, but Hutchison's evidence deserves consideration, whatever one's opinion of Richard's justification. Hutchison's sources are essentially Steel's, and he adopts much of Steel's material while firmly rejecting Steel's psychological interpretation (a point on which most scholars would agree with Hutchison).

Hutchison is the high tide of Ricardian sympathy, and thereafter an ebb set in, signaled by some of the articles collected in DU BOULAY AND BARRON (a festschrift for May McKisack). Opinions among the authors vary: Barron herself sees Richard's handling of his quarrel with London as more successful than most scholars had supposed, while Palmer argues that Richard was not the gentle aesthete some of his admirers imagined, but a tough-minded politician who forced French concessions by serious threats of war. On the other hand, Tuck uses a study of royal patronage in the early part of the reign to show that some of Richard's advisers (such as Simon Burley), whom Hutchison and Steel had defended as veteran administrators unjustly accused, were in fact profiting inordinately from their positions, as the Appellants charged.

TUCK expanded this point in his monograph, which is more an analysis of Richard's political relations with his baronial opposition than a biography. Tuck's thesis is that Richard's defeat resulted from his failure to handle the nobility, and specifically his excessive generosity to a dangerously narrow circle of friends and supporters. This view serves as an important corrective to the enthusiasm of Hutchison, and at the moment Tuck's work is probably the best comparatively recent treatment of the reign.

PALMER, like Tuck, is not strictly a biography, being rather a study of Richard's diplomacy. But many of Palmer's points have important implications for the general history of the reign. That the first attempt at a peace policy with France, before the Appellant episode, was a failure, and that the Appellants' war policy came closer to success than has previously been realized, are facts as significant for the early part of the reign as Palmer's better-known thesis that a full-fledged peace with France (based on the transfer of Aquitaine to the duke of Lancaster) was barely aborted in 1393 is for the latter part of the period. Although Palmer's interpretation (and often re-dating) of scattered foreign correspondence does not provide as firm support for his theories as some would require, his book provides a whole series of important new perspectives on Richard's situation and intentions.

In contrast to these specialized works, SENIOR aims to provide a broad picture of the reign. One of a series of royal biographies for a popular audience, it has handsome illustrations, but the accompanying text is not trustworthy even for the general reader for whom it is intended. To say the earl of Northumberland died fighting the Scots, when he in fact died fighting against the English king as a rebel with Scottish support, is not the sort of statement that inspires confidence in a work of any level, however popular.

The absence of a satisfactory full-scale biography of Richard in the years since Steel has attracted the interest of several scholars, and a new life by Nigel Saul (anticipated from Methuen) may supersede much of the work cited here, while the king's intellectual and cultural interests are also the subject of an ongoing study by George Stow.

—John L. Leland

RICHARD III, 1452–1485; English monarch.

Gairdner, James, *History of the Life and Reign of Richard the Third*. London, Longman, 1878; revised edition, Cambridge, Cambridge University Press, 1898.

Griffiths, Ralph and James Sherborne, editors, *Kings and Nobles in Later Medieval England: A Tribute to Charles Ross*. Gloucester, Gloucestershire, A. Sutton, and New York, St. Martin's, 1986.

Hammond, Peter, editor, *Richard III: Loyalty, Lordship, and Law*. London, Richard III and Yorkist History Trust, 1986.

Hicks, Michael, *Richard III as Duke of Gloucester: A Study in Character*. Peasholme Green, York, St. Anthony's Press, 1986.

Horrox, Rosemary, *Richard III and the North*. Hull, Hull University Press, 1985.

Horrox, Rosemary, *Richard III: A Study in Service*. Cambridge and New York, Cambridge University Press, 1989.

Kendall, Paul Murray, *Richard III*. London, Allen and Unwin, 1955; New York, Norton, 1956.

Myers, Alec, "The Character of Richard III," in *English Society and Government in the 15th Century*, edited by C. M. D. Crowder. Edinburgh and London, Oliver and Boyd, 1967.

Petre, James, *Richard III: Crown and People*. London, Richard III Society, 1985.

Potter, Jeremy, *Good King Richard? An Account of Richard III and His Reputation 1483–1983*. London, Constable, 1983.

Ross, Charles, *Richard III*. London, Eyre Methuen, and Berkeley, University of California Press, 1981.

Rowse, A. L., *Bosworth Field and the Wars of the Roses*. London, Macmillan, and New York, Doubleday, 1966.

Seward, Desmond, *Richard III: England's Black Legend*. London, Country Life, 1983; New York, Watts, 1984.

*

GAIRDNER's was the standard critical life of Richard III until Ross. Long unrivalled for his mastery of documents and the period, but rather dull in his presentation, Gairdner cautiously confirmed the worst interpretations of Richard's career and character devised by Sir Thomas More in about 1516 and promulgated by Shakespeare. Of those later lives that take a similar line, probably those most worthy of attention are ROWSE, "who confirmed Shakespeare's view using only Shakespeare's sources," and SEWARD, who made Richard's quincentenary the occasion for a deliberately controversial denunciation. Only Gairdner has any lasting value.

More favourable interpretations of Richard III date back only to the early 17th century and carried little weight until after World War II. Brilliant though the works of Buck (1619), Walpole (1768), and Markham (1906) were, they relied overwhelmingly on the ingenious reassessment of old sources rather than the discovery of new ones and thus scarcely dented the Shakespearian orthodoxy. The 20th century has witnessed a remarkable upsurge in the popularity of Richard III through the combined efforts of academic historians, enthusiastic amateurs, and romantic novelists. The Richard III Society was founded in 1924 to rehabilitate Richard and now encourages much new research and publication, notably through its quarterly journal *The Ricardian*.

MYERS critically examines the traditional interpretation. In particular he shows that Richard's supposed responsibility for killing Henry VI and his son Prince Edward was not a contemporary charge, but a later accretion. It is now a commonplace that such Tudor historians as More, Vergil, and Shakespeare blackened Richard III and thus justified the accession of Henry VII. Historians contemporary with Richard were more favourable, and Richard should be seen through their eyes. Myers praises Richard for the quality of his government.

KENDALL has been labelled by Ross as the "high water mark of Ricardian apologia," but his is nevertheless the most influential of 20th-century lives. In many ways Kendall was a pioneer. He was the first historian to give weight to Richard's career before his accession, stressing his consistent loyalty to Edward IV and his beneficial rule as Lord of the North. To Kendall it was obvious that Richard could not have changed his whole character when he succeeded as king. He also minimises the battle of Bosworth in 1485, indicating in particular the similar fate that nearly befell Henry VII in 1487. KENDALL uses an unprecedentedly wide range of sources, notably the York civic records and Richard's signet letter book (MS Harley 433), and argues ingeniously and at length both in his text and in his luxuriant footnotes. Fluent and lively, as befitted a Professor of English Literature, Kendall is imaginative, romantic, and fanciful, particularly about Richard's infancy. He always takes the most favourable line, and his exhilarating style can sometimes lead the unwary into mistaking speculation for fact.

ROSS superseded both Kendall and Gairdner. A professional historian in the McFarlane tradition and author of the standard life of Edward IV (1974), Ross uses few new sources—perhaps only the *Ballad of Bosworthfield*—and does not work extensively on what was unexplored in manuscript, though he does re-examine thoroughly all that was known, whether in print or not. He draws on the Ricardian tradition wherever appropriate. Like Myers before and Horrox after, Ross dwells less on the old murder charges than on Richard's performance as king. He does treat Richard's early career but comes to less flattering conclusions. To avoid charges of Tudor propaganda, he relies principally on contemporaries less hostile but nevertheless critical of Richard. While playing down the murder of the princes, he still holds Richard responsible, and overall his verdict on Richard is unfavourable. Sober, elegant, lucid and balanced, Ross is now the standard critical life.

The pace of publication quickened markedly with the quincentenary celebrations orchestrated by the Richard III Society and has continued thereafter. The resultant publications are both supportive and critical of Richard III. In addition to Seward's popular life (mentioned above), one other, by Potter, and four collections of essays, edited by Griffiths and Sherborne, Hammond, Horrox (1985), and Petre, were all published between 1983 and 1986. POTTER offers not so much a straight life as a review of Richard III's life and reputation through the Great De-

bate that has gone on since his death. Written in a terse, abrupt, and forceful style, Potter critically examines Richardian historiography and rejects many past contributions, often justifiably but sometimes over-summarily. As befits the chairman of the Richard III Society, Potter is unashamedly Ricardian and revisionist and opposed to traditionalists and anti-Richards. Hence his emphasis on Richard's loyalty, the quality of his rule, which "was motivated by concern for the poor and helpless," the favourable comments gleaned from fundamentally hostile sources, and the frequent arguments from the silence of the sources. Yet he also strives for balance. After showing that Richard's reasons for bastardising the princes could have been true, Potter admits that the variety of alternate claims casts doubt on the validity of any one. While accepting Ross's argument from the Croyland chronicle that Richard was hated in his own lifetime, he makes much of the chronicler's failure to accuse Richard of any of the major crimes usually alleged against him. If Potter deploys little new evidence, he reviews the old in a stimulating and novel way, and his book makes an original contribution that deserves to be read.

PETRE republishes many short articles from *The Ricardian*. Generally factual, never hostile, and variable in quality, these present the king from many different angles: through his appearance, relations with his nobility, his times, etc. Also a Richard III Society publication, HAMMOND contains more substantial pieces by professional historians on such topics as the precontract and Richard's self-image as king. More critical and coherent are the volume edited jointly by GRIFFITHS AND SHERBORNE and HORROX's 1985 edition of papers. The former, a posthumous festschrift to Charles Ross, contains excellent scholarly assessments of Richard's relations with the Hungerfords, with the Church of York, and County Durham. Shorter, coherent and critical, Horrox (1985) comprises five interim statements by professional academics on Richard's career in the north. These cover his claim to be a northern king and his relations with the city of York. All four volumes need to be taken with HICKS, who views Richard's early life as a whole through his surviving cartulary, identifies him as duke as a ruthless egotist, and argues that his ducal career was about to collapse in 1483. All five add to or refine the conclusions of Ross, whose work is rapidly becoming out of date.

HORROX (1989) concentrates on Richard's relations with his retainers. She had already published the most important records of the reign and is the acknowledged expert on both rule and retinue. The book is not an easy read, but at many points it supersedes previous works. If not primarily a biography, it inevitably reveals much about Richard in its detailed examination of the basis of his power and rule. If not unsympathetic, it considers that his usurpation miscalculated the reactions of the Yorkist political establishment and largely explains his fall. Horrox writes, "In dynastic terms his usurpation was a disaster: Richard destroyed the House of York. He also destroyed himself; and Halle, the most perceptive of the later Tudor writers, is surely right to see his reign as a tragedy."

—Michael Hicks

RICHARDSON, Samuel, 1689–1761; English writer.

Dobson, Austin, *Samuel Richardson*. London and New York, Macmillan, 1902.

Downs, Brian W., *Richardson*. London, Routledge, and New York, Dutton, 1928.

Eaves, T. C. Duncan and Ben D. Kimpel, *Samuel Richardson: A Biography*. Oxford, Clarendon Press, 1971.

McKillop, Alan D., *Samuel Richardson, Printer and Novelist*. Chapel Hill, University of North Carolina Press, 1936.

Thomson, Clare, *Samuel Richardson: A Biographical and Critical Study*. London, H. Marshall, 1900.

*

In 1804 Anna Laetitia Barbauld published an edition of Richardson's letters in six volumes. As a preface she included over 200 pages of biography incorporating all that was known about the writer then and for a hundred years thereafter. During the latter part of the 19th century a number of prominent literary figures wrote intelligently about Richardson: Leslie Stephen in *Hours in a Library* and in the introduction to a deluxe edition of the novels; Augustine Birrell in *Res Judicatae*; Andrew Lang in *Letters on Literature*; Henry Duff Traill in a dialogue between Richardson and Fielding as part of *The New Lucian*. THOMSON was the first, though, to produce a book-length study. While she relied heavily on Barbauld's account, she also combed six folio volumes, with their more than 800 letters to and from the novelist, housed in the Victoria and Albert Museum. From Charterhouse Chapel archives she demonstrated that Richardson had married the daughter of John Wilde, his master, rather than the child of Allington Wilde, as some biographers had claimed. Since Richardson's novels were more often talked about than read, Thomson included critical discussions aimed at those unfamiliar with the texts, and she concluded with a chapter on Richardson's influence.

Writing for the "English Men of Letters" series, DOBSON turned to the same materials as Thomson, yet his book differs from hers in a number of ways. His familiarity with the 18th century allowed him to place Richardson and various of his correspondents firmly in their age, so that Richardson's daily life becomes vivid. Criticism of the fiction is sparse, and Dobson devotes only four pages to considering Richardson's influence on foreign writers. Unlike Thomson, Dobson includes no bibliography, but both works are well indexed and very readable. Despite their age, they remain good general introductions to the author.

DOWNS, in his volume for the "Republic of Letters" series, offers a concise overview of Richardson's life, which he presents in the opening 58 pages, then turns to criticism of the novels, from which he quotes frequently. Like Dobson, Downs sets Richardson in his time, and this book adds new material on the life as well as new insights into the fiction. The section on Richardson's influence remains useful. Like the earlier works, it aims at the general reader and provides a good introduction to the man and his works, even though Downs shows little sympathy for Richardson's Puritan, bourgeois values.

Despite McKILLOP's title, his book was not designed primarily as a biography. As he wrote, "The present work . . . centers on the origins, publication, and reception of Richardson's three

great novels, though of course his personality and associations must figure largely in the account." Nonetheless, it became the standard life for several decades and remains another fine introduction. For in a lengthy appendix McKillop included "The Records of Richardson's Life and Business," offering much biographical information. In addition to reviewing the manuscript letters at the Victoria and Albert Museum and Richardson's publications, he examined the Stationers' Register, Guild Hall records, Parliamentary journals, and contemporary accounts in magazines, books, and pamphlets. Richardson appears as a shrewd businessman as well as an important and influential writer; McKillop traces this influence across Europe into the early 19th century.

Some reviewers found McKillop's account too detailed for the general reader. This reservation certainly applies to EAVES AND KIMPEL's definitive biography. The scholarship is exhaustive; for example, in the course of 15 years' research the authors examined 147 parish records to determine where and when Richardson was born. As John Carroll wrote in *Review of English Studies* (New Series), "The authors prefer hard fact to conjecture, common sense observations to ingenious theorizing" (vol. 23 [1973], 505). The account relies heavily on and quotes extensively from Richardson's letters, many of which Eaves and Kimpel discovered. Richardson thus is allowed to speak for himself. This Richardson is conservative, orthodox, unspeculative, and generous. Eaves and Kimpel concede, though, that all their details cannot explain how a dull, puritanical printer could create the English novel, plumb the psyche of a teen-aged servant girl, or portray so vividly the psychological depths of Clarissa.

Most of the book deals with the last 20 years of Richardson's life, after he turned author. The first 50 years are covered in 86 pages, while over 500 treat the remainder. The work concludes with four excellent chapters that summarize Richardson's personality, thoughts, reading, and achievement. Those seeking an overview of the man would do well to read this section and then turn to some less detailed account. An 80-page appendix gives the date, correspondent, and source of all of Richardson's known letters. In sum, the work is a biography for scholars, a reference work for anyone seeking information on the father of the English novel.

—Joseph Rosenblum

RICHELIEU, Armand-Jean du Plessis, Duc de, 1585–1642; French cardinal and statesman.

Auchinloss, Louis, *Richelieu*. London, M. Joseph, and New York, Viking, 1973.

Bergin, Joseph, *Cardinal Richelieu: Power and the Pursuit of Wealth*. New Haven, Connecticut, and London, Yale University Press, 1985.

Burckhardt, Carl, *Richelieu and His Age* (3 vols.), translated by Bernard Hoy. London, Allen and Unwin, and New York, Harcourt, 1970 (originally published as *Richelieu*, 4 vols., Munich, 1933–67).

Church, William, *Richelieu and Reason of State*. Princeton, New Jersey, Princeton University Press, 1972.

Elliott, John H., *Richelieu and Olivares.* Cambridge and New York, Cambridge University Press, 1984.

Erlanger, Philippe, *Richelieu and the Affair of Cinq-Mars*, translated by G. and H. Cremonesi. London, Elek, 1971; as *The King's Minion*, Englewood Cliffs, New Jersey, Prentice-Hall, 1972 (originally published as *Cinq-Mars*, Paris, Librairie Académique Perrin, 1962).

Lodge, Richard, *Richelieu.* London and New York, Macmillan, 1896.

Marvick, Elizabeth Wirth, *The Young Richelieu: A Psychoanalytic Approach to Leadership.* Chicago and London, University of Chicago Press, 1983.

O'Connell, D. P., *Richelieu.* London, Weidenfeld and Nicolson, and Cleveland, World Publishing, 1968.

Ranum, Orest, *Richelieu and the Councillors of Louis XIII.* Oxford, Clarendon Press, 1963.

Tapié, Victor-Lucien, *France in the Age of Louis XIII and Richelieu*, translated and edited by D. Lockie. London and New York, Macmillan, 1974 (originally published as *La France de Louis XIII et de Richelieu*, Paris, Flammarion, 1952).

Treasure, G. R. R., *Cardinal Richelieu and the Development of Absolutism.* London, A. and C. Black, and New York, St. Martin's, 1972.

Wedgewood, C. V., *Richelieu and the French Monarchy.* London, Hodder and Stoughton/English Universities Press, 1949; revised edition, New York, Collier, 1962.

*

Biographers of Richelieu have diverged in their approach, some continuing to follow the cardinal's own line that his personal biography should fuse with the historical destiny of France, others concentrating on individual incidents in his political career, or on specialised aspects of his life or character. Inevitably the early biographers were French. Of the English historians, LODGE in the 19th century produced a faithful, although now somewhat dated account in the tradition of the purely political and personal biography. There are unfortunate lapses of style, and in his conclusion Lodge uncritically accepts what would have been Richelieu's own assessment of his historical position: "The statesman who has been hailed by the almost unanimous opinion of later generations as the grandest figure among those who have contributed most to the greatness of France." In an appendix Lodge also comes firmly but wrongly out against the authenticity of Richelieu's *Testament politique*, adding however, that, if it were ever proved to be authentic, "many results of his rule, which are now attributed to intelligent purpose, would have to be regarded as the product of change."

The monumental six-volume study of Richelieu by Hanotaux and La Force (1893–1947) has remained untranslated, so that BURCKHARDT's German *Richelieu*, reduced from four to three volumes in translation, is, despite its faults, the fundamental study in English. There are factual inaccuracies: Richelieu was not, for instance, born at the Château de Richelieu. Champagne's triple portrait was intended for a sculptor to work from and did not just "dispense entirely with the décor normally demanded by contemporary taste in representative art." The information on which Burckhardt relied for such chapters as those on Richelieu's personal life has now been very largely superseded, particularly since the publication of the inventories taken after

the cardinal's death of the contents of the Palais Cardinal and his favourite Château de Rueil and of his personal papers. The biography is uneven in quality, with a narrative pace that broods too ponderously, for instance, over the Montmorencys and the subject of duelling. The second and third volumes appeared in translation only after a gap of 30 years, since Burckhardt's history had been interrupted by World War II. The complete notes and references are to be found only in the German original.

WEDGEWOOD's is a less serious although attractively written work, and it provides a perceptive introduction to the whole period. It may well be the best biography for readers who are not professional students of history, and it is both carefully researched and reliable. RANUM's volume on the other hand represents a different type of study, concentrating not on the general sweep of historical narrative but on the day-to-day government of France through the secretaries of state and "Surintendants" of finance who worked for Richelieu's ministry in the last seven years of his life. Ranum concentrates on the flexibility between the duties of what today would be regarded as the separate state departments of finance, justice, and foreign affairs, and analyses the functions of the major officers involved.

O'CONNELL's *Richelieu* is again different. It is fictionalized to read like an historical novel, as its style makes clear. O'Connell describes how Richelieu obtained from Rome the necessary dispensation to be ordained priest and consecrated bishop before the canonical age: "The pudding-faced Borghese Pope, Paul V, was at first cold towards the young man who claimed his attention, but wily and experienced though he was, fell victim—the first victim—to Richelieu's skill as a professional charmer." Another similarly lightweight treatment is that of ERLANGER, which deals with the four-year period culminating in the execution of the king's former favourite, only months before the deaths of the king and Richelieu themselves. It is a readable but fanciful account and depends on a few old and not always reliable sources, such as contemporary memoirs notorious for political or personal bias.

With TREASURE, we have a more seriously intended and better written study in spite of some factual and printing errors. But this book alone still does not offer the reader a complete picture. Treasure presupposes too much general knowledge of the period and of European geography, referring at least twice to "the passes of the Val Telline" before giving their position and explaining their significance.

CHURCH does not retell Richelieu's political career but analyses the power, politics, and morality of the 17th-century French state, copiously using and examining in detail contemporary pamphlets, judicial writings, tracts and treatises, memoirs, and Richelieu's own correspondence. In particular he analyses Richelieu's own *Mémoires* and his *Testament politique*. These documents were written by a series of secretaries and pamphleteers under Richelieu's supervision, and were an apologia for his position. the *Mémoires* remained incomplete on his death, unlike the *Testament*, which was more a record of his achievements. An English translation of the *Testament* has been available in English since 1695. Church provides a very full and useful bibliography. AUCHINLOSS intended his *Richelieu* for a very different audience. He gives a novelist's lively and fairly brief romp through the cardinal's career. This book is chiefly to be recommended for its extraordinarily wide and vivid illustrations, many of which are rarely found elsewhere.

TAPIÉ has written an enormously useful book for any student of 17th-century France, concentrating not so much on Richelieu's career itself as on its historical perspective. The very able translator and editor has added extra notes and considerable bibliographical material, so that the initially rather daunting size of the book can be cut down by nearly a third to produce an accurate and lively account of the reign. The work contains a chronological table and seven maps of contemporary Europe.

The three most recent studies address quite different areas of Richelieu's life and career. The title of MARVICK's book gives an adequate indication of its contents. The author delves into family background, relationships, and empathies in order to explain the cardinal's eventual career. Although it is a serious account, the application of psychoanalytical theories, however interesting they may be, is not totally convincing. Much of the chapter entitled "Gaining Self-Mastery" seems to be based on supposition, and, in particular, Marvick's descriptions of the "imaginary links" with members of Richelieu's family, from childish fantasising to sub-conscious transference in adulthood, seem forced.

ELLIOTT's book is never less than firmly centred on fact. It brilliantly encapsulates the shared characteristics and fortunes of the two statesmen whose lives and careers were interwoven in the political history of Europe. The Cardinal-Duke of Richelieu and the Count-Duke of Olivares, principal minister of the King of Spain, were born within a couple of years of each other, died at almost the same age, were both third sons of noble fathers employed in royal service, and worked non-stop for nearly 20 years in the service of their respective monarchs. Elliott notes that "they shared many of the same problems; they came up with many of the same answers; and in the end they reached the conclusion that the world was too small to contain them both." As a psychological study of how each reacted to his upbringing, his royal master, and his fellow politicians, the analysis is succinct and well written.

Finally, BERGIN's study of Richelieu's fortune is a meticulously detailed and researched piece of work. Richelieu's income rose from 55,000 livres in 1621 to over 1,000,000 livres 20 years later. Bergin points out that not enough is known about Richelieu's expenditure on patronage of the arts to allow this study to be fully comprehensive, but he rightly stresses Richelieu's personal frugality as opposed to the spectacular public display, and Bergin's analysis rises well beyond an arid display of figures, sums, and totals. From a complex first chapter detailing the history, income, and landed wealth of the Richelieu family, Bergin moves on to a discussion of the ways in which the cardinal was to manage his own fortune, which he built up relying not solely on land, but drawing on his various offices as minister, governor, and "surintendant" of the admiralty and maritime commerce.

—Honor Levi

RILKE, Rainer Maria, 1875–1926; Austro-German poet.

Batterby, K. A. J., *Rilke and France: A Study in Poetic Development*. London, Oxford University Press, 1966.

Butler, E. M., *Rainer Maria Rilke*. Cambridge, Cambridge University Press, and New York, Macmillan, 1941.

Fuerst, Norbert, *Phases of Rilke*. Bloomington, Indiana University Press, 1958.

Heerikhuizen, F. W. van, *Rainer Maria Rilke: His Life and Work*, translated by Fernand G. Renier and Anne Cliff. London, Routledge, 1951; New York, Philosophical Library, 1952 (originally published by F. G. Kroonder, Bussum, 1946).

Hendry, J. F., *The Sacred Threshold: A Life of Rainer Maria Rilke*. Manchester, Carcanet New Press, 1983.

Holthusen, Hans Egon, *Portrait of Rilke: An Illustrated Biography*, translated by W. H. Hargreaves. New York, Herder, 1971 (originally published as *Rainer Maria Rilke in Selbstzeugnissen und Bilddokumenten*, Hamburg, Rowohlt, 1958).

Leppmann, Wolfgang, *Rilke: A Life*, translated by Russell M. Stockman, in collaboration with the author. New York, Fromm International, and Cambridge, Lutterworth, 1984 (originally published by Scherz, Bern, 1981).

Mason, Eudo C., *Rilke*. Edinburgh and London, Oliver and Boyd, 1963.

Prater, Donald, *A Ringing Glass: The Life of Rainer Maria Rilke*. Oxford, Clarendon Press, and New York, Oxford University Press, 1986.

Salis, Jean Randolphe de, *Rainer Maria Rilke: The Years in Switzerland; A Contribution to the Biography of Rilke's Later Life*, translated by N. K. Cruikshank. London, Hogarth Press, and Berkeley, University of California Press, 1964 (originally published by von Huber, Frauenfeld, 1936).

Schoolfield, George C., *Rilke's Last Year*. Lawrence, University of Kansas Libraries, 1969.

Wydenbruck, Nora, *Rilke, Man and Poet: A Biographical Study*. London, J. Lehmann, 1949; New York, Appleton-Century, 1950.

*

LEPPMANN has written the most detailed and well-documented biography of Rilke available in English. Although not intended for the general reader—"Leppmann's obsession with incorporating every known fact and facet of Rilke's life in his text renders his work cumbersome to the casual reader"—this may well "remain the standard reference on Rilke's background, career, and legacy for a great many years to come" (*Choice*, November 1984). Leppmann's lightness of style (at least in the English version) does not always meet with reviewers' approval, and he occasionally lacks taste, as for example when he makes the unnecessary (and wholly undeserved) comparison between Rilke and Hitler as being two representatives of *homo austriacus*.

HENDRY makes an attempt at a fusion of Rilke's life and work, but then loses the biographer's detachment to such an extent that he can no longer distinguish between fact and creative output. Hendry's biography is mostly valuable as a surface introduction to Rilke and would probably not benefit anyone other than the general reader or, at most, the undergraduate who needs background information. The quotes are in German and English. The "select" bibliography has too many gaps and is not completely reliable.

For the reader looking for information on Rilke's life who does not want or need constant reference to his work, PRATER has provided the facts in a book that is "conservative, self-effacing, neutral, without brilliance" (*New York Times Book Review*, 21 September 1986). Prater takes an objective look at Rilke's life and is a useful antidote to the many mythologizers. BUTLER, on the other hand, is an unreliable demythologizer who seems intent on destroying not only the myth surrounding Rilke, but also any respect for him as a man or a poet. Butler's problematic relationship with her subject can be seen already in the introductory chapter: "Since the whole of his work is one long unremitting effort to represent life and the universe in the terms of his own strange philosophy, . . . in reality he recognized only the god of art and Rainer Maria Rilke his prophet."

HEERIKHUIZEN's dated contribution might be accurately described as an interpretation and criticism of Rilke's life and work from the standpoint of a disciple. Many would take issue with such claims as "[Rilke] explores the latent possibilities of the German tongue more fully than any poet before or after him." This work is not easily accessible to the reader who is looking only for facts, and it is heavily philosophical in nature. The translation is at times quaint and at times unintelligible. HOLTHUSEN suffers too in a translation that is often wooden. Quotations from Rilke's works are unfortunately given only in English. With no index and only a scant bibliography, this biography could not be used for scholarly research or even serious study. On the other hand, interesting photographs and sympathetic treatment of Rilke and his milieu make it a good read for the Rilke *aficionado*.

MASON provides a "sensible, informative and unawed introduction to the poet" (*Critical Quarterly*, 1966), but the work is lacking in detail and is too short to be anything other than a brief overview.

WYDENBRUCK, who knew the poet and his friends personally, is still useful as a source of "inside" information, although her work is now dated. Most German quotes are immediately translated, and biographical information is made relevant to Rilke's *oeuvre*. Her debunking of some of the myths concerning Rilke's snobbishness (he was apparently delighted to find out that one branch of the family was descended from miners in Corinthia—no aristocracy there) is refreshing.

FUERST, whose work offers no bibliography, footnotes, or index, is mostly concerned to uphold the thesis implied in his title. As one reviewer noted, "Since in this book Rilke is taken fervidly and naively at his face value and no overall interpretation is attempted, the author naturally finds it a simple matter to divide the poet's work neatly into eight separate 'phases' and to deal with his life equally tidily in eight brief sentimentalizing vignettes" (*German Life and Letters*, vol. 13, 1960). Fuerst's book is of little value to either the scholar or the general reader.

Batterby, Salis, and Schoolfield all look at specific aspects of Rilke's life with varying degrees of detail and success, but should not be overlooked by the serious student or scholar who wishes more information on the individual areas covered. BATTERBY's thesis is based on the effect of the French language, its structure and sound, on Rilke's creative use of his own language, and also gives useful, chronologically ordered background information on the importance of many French figures to the poet. SCHOOLFIELD covers more than Rilke's last year in spite of the title of this short work (73 pages). Although Schoolfield's intention appears to be to bring Rilke's eulogizers back down to earth, it is often difficult to know when objectivity

has become sarcasm. Schoolfield drily repeats reports of those who claim to have felt by extrasensory means that Rilke had died (probably aware that such tales had also circulated after the death of Christian Morgenstern) and seems to have fun with the different versions given of Rilke's last words on his deathbed. The *Modern Language Journal* (1972) review concludes: "*Rilke's Last Year* sums up the findings of previous research in an unprecedented fashion, and offers, moreover, noteworthy hypotheses and insights, which all future biographers will have to contend with." SALIS' work was probably important in 1936, its original year of publication in German, largely because it directed attention to Rilke's later period and paved the way for a full appreciation of the poet's mature work. Although occasionally bordering on the bathetic, Salis' personal comments are still important, coming from someone who knew Rilke personally.

—Colin R. Hall

RIMBAUD, (Jean-Nicolas-) Arthur, 1854–1891; French poet.

Bonnefoy, Yves, *Rimbaud*, translated by Paul Schmidt. New York, Harper, 1973 (originally published as *Rimbaud par lui-même*, Paris, Éditions du Seuil, 1961).

Carré, Jean-Marie, *A Season in Hell: The Life of Rimbaud*, translated by Hannah and Matthew Josephson. New York, Macaulay, 1931 (originally published as *La Vie aventureuse de Jean-Arthur Rimbaud*, Paris, Plon, 1926).

Chadwick, C., *Rimbaud*. London, Athlone Press, and Atlantic Heights, New Jersey, Humanities Press, 1979.

Fowlie, Wallace, *Rimbaud, the Myth of Childhood*. London, D. Dobson, 1946; as *Rimbaud*, Chicago, University of Chicago Press, 1965.

Hackett, C. A., *Rimbaud*. London, Bowes, and New York, Hillary House, 1957.

Hackett, C. A., *Rimbaud: A Critical Introduction*. Cambridge and New York, Cambridge University Press, 1981.

Hanson, Elisabeth, *My Poor Arthur: An Illumination of Arthur Rimbaud*. London, Secker and Warburg, 1959; New York, Holt, 1960.

Petitfils, Pierre, *Rimbaud*, translated by Alan Sheridan. Charlottesville, University Press of Virginia, 1987 (originally published by Juliard, Paris, 1982).

Rickword, Edgell, *Rimbaud, the Boy and the Poet*. London, Heinemann, and New York, Knopf, 1924.

St. Aubyn, Frederic Chase, *Arthur Rimbaud*. New York, Twayne, 1975; revised edition, 1988.

Starkie, Enid, *Arthur Rimbaud in Abyssinia*. Oxford, Clarendon Press, 1937.

Starkie, Enid, *Arthur Rimbaud*. London, Faber, and New York, Norton, 1938; revised edition, London, Faber, and New York, New Directions, 1961.

*

Writing the life of any lyric poet almost inevitably raises the problem of the imbrication of his creative activities in the verifiable events of his life. With Rimbaud the problem is especially acute, not only because of the highly personal obscurity of much of his poetry, but also because of the uncertainty that continues to surround the chronology of composition of his major works. The result is that no book on Rimbaud, even those that purport to be purely critical studies, can avoid tackling certain biographical issues. Did *Les Illuminations* precede *Une Saison en enfer*, as was traditionally thought? Or was the order reversed, according to the theories propounded by Henri Bouillane de Lacoste in the 1940s? Or were some of the *Illuminations* written before *Une Saison en enfer*, some at the same time, and some afterwards? Up to the present, no one has been able to give definitive answers to these questions, so that it remains unsure whether *Une Saison en enfer* is a farewell to poetry generally or just to a certain type of poetry. In addition to difficulties of this sort, Rimbaud's extraordinary life—recognized as a genius while still in his teens, shot and wounded by an equally celebrated poet, becoming a complete apostate from literature, and finally spending the last 15 or so years of his short existence as a wandering adventurer in Europe, the Far East, and eventually the Middle East—poses unique psychological enigmas as well as constituting a fascinating and exciting story.

It is thus even harder in Rimbaud's case than in others to separate biographies in the normal sense of the word from essays intending to concentrate on the works. The first full-length attempts to recount the whole of his life, apart from partial and unreliable memoirs from those who had known him personally, came in the 1920s. Oddly, the first of these, by RICKWORD, was written in English rather than in French. This is a straightforward account of the facts as they were known at the time, but it contains neither bibliography nor critical apparatus, and there is a liberal sprinkling of mistakes in the transcription of French. CARRÉ, a respected French academic, published his biography in the same year. Though both these works were valuable in their time, so much has been discovered since then that they can hardly be recommended as trustworthy guides nowadays.

The other pre-war biography marks a date in Rimbaud studies. This is the life of Rimbaud by STARKIE, first published in 1938 and preceded by her book on Rimbaud in Abyssinia (1937), which is dissociated from the more general enterprise because the amount of new material she had unearthed would have overweighted it. There have been several editions of the biography, the most recent of them in 1961, which is substantially different from the original version. Starkie's work on Rimbaud is based on extensive and original research, and it remains such an authoritative statement that it was translated into French as recently as 1982. Not everyone would agree with the emphasis she puts on Rimbaud's readings in alchemy and occultism, and she attaches crucial importance to the sexual trauma supposedly suffered by Rimbaud with soldiers while on an escapade to Paris in 1871 which, though eminently plausible, remains no more than a hypothesis. On his activities in the Middle East, more is known now than at the time of the revisions of her biography, notably after the publication in 1965 of Rimbaud's correspondence with the Swiss engineer Ilg: to that extent one may prefer the *Rimbaud in Ethiopia* (1979) of Duncan Forbes, who lived and worked in the area for years and who by consulting documents not available to Dr. Starkie has been able to add to and occasionally correct her information—in particular casting serious doubt on her contention that Rimbaud may have been involved in the slave-trade as well as in gun-running.

The only other full-length biography in English is that by HANSON, published in 1959 after the first two versions of the life by Starkie, which, incredibly, is ignored in Hanson's remarkably selective bibliography. *My Poor Arthur* (so called because that is how Mme Rimbaud latterly referred to her son) is on the whole a brisk and reasonably well informed narrative of external facts with (as in the Hanson biography of Verlaine) speculation about a character's thoughts or feelings sometimes presented as fact. It has other, more damaging weaknesses too: it says nothing of interest about the poetry, it is superficial about Rimbaud's psychology, largely ignores his sexuality, fails to supply references for its quotations, and never attempts any scholarly discussion of the many mysteries and obscurities of Rimbaud's life. Moreover, rendering "Avis aux amateurs" as "Note to lovers," when it means little more than "Take note," hardly inspires confidence in its translations. So, though it is very readable, it is much inferior to Dr. Starkie's work in terms of thoroughness and reliability.

So far as the other books are concerned, BONNEFOY's study is not in any sense an orthodox biography: it is essentially a personal meditation by one poet on the life and writings of another. It is consequently not something one would consult to verify factual information, the more so as it sums up in no more than a dozen pages Rimbaud's life after he renounced poetry. But up to that point it operates on a broadly chronological basis, considering life and poetry together in a sequence of chapters from birth to about 1874. Its attraction and value reside in the sensitively intuitive understanding of the wellsprings of both Rimbaud's poetic creativity and his restlessly tormented existence.

There is even less straight biography in the other works in English concerning Rimbaud. Most of them include a biographical summary but spend most of their time examining the poetry (though, for the reasons given above, this necessarily entails some treatment of biographical questions). The two books by HACKETT, an outstanding international authority on Rimbaud, are particularly good, despite their relative brevity, and CHADWICK and ST. AUBYN can also be recommended. FOWLIE too is interesting, despite some dubious generalisations and the absence of any sort of critical apparatus.

The most recent addition to the canon of lives of Rimbaud in English is happily also one of the most thorough and judicious. This is PETITFILS' straightforward account based on extensive knowledge of the research available at the time of its original publication in French in 1982. Petitfils tends to play down Rimbaud's homosexuality, and he is not always well served by his translator. Even so, this remains a useful work of reference that tells its story clearly and at times movingly.

—A. W. Raitt

RIVERA, Diego, 1886–1957; Mexican painter.

March, Gladys, *Diego Rivera: My Art and My Life*. New York, Citadel Press, 1960.
Wolfe, Bertram D., *Diego Rivera: His Life and Times*. New York, Knopf, and London, R. Hale, 1939.

Wolfe, Bertram D., *The Fabulous Life of Diego Rivera*. New York, Stein and Day, 1963.

*

WOLFE's 1963 work is the accepted standard biography of Rivera. Unlike Wolfe's 1939 portrayal of his friend and art mentor, the later biography presents Rivera's entire life; it is more accurate and more celebratory. The collection of Wolfe's papers (Woodrow Wilson Archives, Stanford University) documents his close friendship with Rivera and his extensive biographical research.

The Fabulous Life of Diego Rivera presents Rivera's politics and art as inseparable, and Wolfe gives apologia for the work that is devoid of political content. Wolfe was a newspaper writer with leftist views when he met the artist in 1922. He wrote extensively on various aspects of Russian communism and was appointed an advisor to the U.S. State Department. He influenced Rivera's political activities in the 1920s and 30s, and consequently his work emphasizes this aspect of the artist's life.

Wolfe's political acuity is not always matched by an aesthetic sensibility. He was not knowledgeable in art and, in fact, learned all that he knew from Rivera. His presentation of Rivera's art relies primarily on descriptions of subjects rather than on critical analysis or treatment of them as aesthetic objects. He does, however, verbally present beautiful images of the pre- and post-revolutionary Mexico as if seen through the artist's eyes, and he conveys a deep enjoyment and understanding of Rivera's work. Wolfe (1963) remains a rich source of information, insights, and analyses of Rivera's life.

The biographers of Rivera—Wolfe and March in the United States, Antonio Rodriguez and Loló de la Torriente in Mexico—were his friends, and they all relied heavily on conversations with the artist to gather information about his life. Wolfe's introduction (1963) describes the problem of this method: " . . . he was always bent on telling his tale with such skill, with such show of frankness and taken-for-granted assent with a knowing wraith of a smile and snorts of certitude, with such elaborate underpinning of supporting detail, that one found it hard not to become an accomplice, hard not to act as though both speaker and listener believed." In the same introduction, Wolfe asks himself if there are errors, and he replies, "Surely there must be."

Rivera excelled at weaving tall tales about his life, which even he probably believed, and Wolfe is the most willing of the artist's biographers to point out Rivera's exaggerations. In addition to Wolfe, three writers have attempted to correct previous exaggerations. Jean Charlot, a French artist and writer ten years younger than Rivera, participated in the *Mexican Mural Renaissance* (1963). He wrote in a forceful and eloquent voice of the early development of the Union of Technical Workers, Painters, and Sculptors and their mural projects of the 1920s. Charlot gives greater detail to Wolfe's 1963 description of the formation of the Union and of Rivera's leadership, which was not easily won. He also corrects the myth, prevalent in Mexican biographies, of Rivera's successful use of ancient Mayan fresco recipes in the Secretariat of Education Murals. Ramón Favela's text for the Phoenix Art Museum's 1984 exhibition catalogue *Diego Rivera: The Cubist Years* thoroughly documents the artist's prominence in the Cubist circle. He carefully constructs Rivera's contribution to Cubist painting and thoroughly analyses his work. Lawrence Hurlbert's publication *The Mexican Muralists in the United States* (1989) sheds more light on Wolfe's already very detailed account of the controversy surrounding the Rockefeller Center Mural. He points to Nelson Rockefeller's encouragement of Rivera's leftist concerns, and to his belief that Communism was a future reality for the United States.

MARCH's volume is cataloged by the Library of Congress as a Rivera autobiography. It is, however, written in the first person by March, who developed the essay from interviews with the artist during March's frequent trips to Mexico. The work was not read or reviewed by Rivera and was published three years after the artist's death. Still, this "autobiography" is written in an engaging, conversational, narrative style. The vignette-like chapters are organized chronologically, and Rivera's life is presented without critical or "introspective" analysis, a technique that perpetuates the legends in an easily readable fashion. (The Mexican equivalent to March is by Luis Suarez, *Confesiones de Diego Rivera*, Mexico City, 1962.)

—Linda Downs

ROBESON, Paul, 1898–1976; American actor, singer, and civil rights activist.

Duberman, Martin B., *Paul Robeson*. New York, Knopf, 1988; London, Bodley Head, 1989.

Gilliam, Dorothy B., *Paul Robeson: All American*. Washington, D.C., New Republic, 1976.

Graham, Shirley, *Paul Robeson: Citizen of the World*. New York, J. Messner, 1946.

Robeson, Eslanda Goode, *Paul Robeson, Negro*. New York, Harper, and London, Gollancz, 1930.

Robeson, Susan, *The Whole World in His Hands: A Pictorial Biography of Paul Robeson*. Seacaucus, New Jersey, Citadel Press, 1981.

*

Duberman's 1989 biography of Robeson (see below) is clearly the definitive work on this figure, but it is also a work that has generated a significant amount of political controversy. The earlier works—one half of which are written by members of the Robeson family—all suffer from a lack of rigorous analysis and a paucity of research. Nevertheless, most of these works have their value, if for no other reason than their summary judgments.

ESLANDE GOODE ROBESON's work appeared in 1930, just as Robeson was achieving international prominence as a performer. The author, the subject's wife, offers a remarkably disingenuous portrait to the reader. Mrs. Robeson's work illustrates aspects of Robeson's married life that no other biographer can reproduce. It varies from outright worship to shockingly matter-of-fact criticism—including mention of his sexual infidelities. It also provides a contemporary perspective on American race relations in the first decades of the 20th century, a view that helps one to comprehend the subsequent actions of Robeson.

GRAHAM, the wife of W. E. B. Du Bois, offers a largely anecdotal work, with her anecdotes often being of dubious veracity. One reviewer, George Streator, in *The New York Times* of 18 August 1946, noting the thinness of Graham's biography, remarks, "It takes much more than a procession of famous names greeting Paul in public to complete the picture." Duberman, accurately I think, calls this book "largely imagined."

GILLIAM also treats Robeson in a somewhat perfunctory manner. The author, a reporter and editor for the *Washington Post*, began this project when asked to write an obituary of Robeson. It is an unauthorized biography, written with the facility of a journalist, and relies solely on secondary published materials. This method limits Gilliam's knowledge of the particulars of Robeson's life. Her vision is neither probing nor notably astute. Yet, her use of secondary sources is far ranging for a book of this type: she employs scholarly works on African-American history to inform her discussion of Robeson's constant trials of bigotry; she uses appropriate sources to discuss Robeson's particular plight as a black actor, and her knowledge of American politics in the era immediately after World War II provides a reasonable basis for her discussion of the subject's political difficulties. Thus, although, as Edward Mapp noted in his 15 October 1976 review in *Library Journal*, "Gilliam's biography is an accurate but truncated account of the artists life," this book is an adequate source for a reader interested primarily in Robeson's public life and not desiring the meticulous detail of Duberman.

The written text of SUSAN ROBESON's pictorial biography of her grandfather can be avoided. It expresses primarily a granddaughter's devotion. However, the photographs of this work provide a compelling representation of Robeson's varied and remarkable life. Indeed, when coupled with Duberman's exhaustive writings they seem able to bring Robeson virtually to life. We see Robeson pictured with figures as diverse as Oscar Hammerstein and Jomo Keyatta, with Ethel Waters and Nikita Khrushchev. The book well provides a visual enactment of the ascension and decline of this man.

DUBERMAN has written a lucid and thorough biography that is unlikely to be superseded for some time. It is composed almost entirely from manuscript sources, including the Robeson family archives, that have not been made available to any previous biographer. Duberman also interviewed some 135 friends and associates of Robeson. Indeed, since if Robeson had survived he would be 92 years old, the timing of Duberman's interviews with his contemporaries is fortuitous: likely no subsequent biographer will have this opportunity. Also, the author makes extensive use of files obtained from the F.B.I. under the Freedom of Information Act; though he cautions that these records released were by no means complete and seem destined to remain partial. Duberman explains, "the F.B.I. lawyers told . . . that some 56 volumes out of a probable 103 in the Robeson file of the New York Field Office had 'unaccountably disappeared.'"

With the rigor of a trained historian, Duberman molds these sources into a work that seems to capture Robeson's public and private life. He has uncovered its focal narrative: Robeson's burgeoning leftist political passions, which grew from his persistent confrontation with American racism, both de facto and de jure. These incidents were as personal as being told, in his short career as a lawyer, that he would never be allowed to try a case

before a judge "for fear his race would be a detriment," and as generalized as being denied lodgings at segregated hotels. As Robeson saw the pervasive and insidious effects of discrimination, he idealized a world without such sentiments and actions. This led to his embracing the egalitarian hope of socialism and his idealization of the Soviet Union. With sympathy, but without apology, Duberman explains why Robeson did not publicly denounce Stalin's duplicitousness and barbarism. He also shows his readers in convincing detail the torments of a man denounced during the anti-communist hysteria of the 1950s.

The political passions that Robeson inspired, both love and hate, recur in responses to Duberman's book. Those somewhat sympathetic toward Robeson tend to accept Duberman's treatment. Those who feel that Robeson was the embodiment of anti-Americanism scorn Duberman's work for its absence of explicit outraged judgment. The left of center *Nation* exclaims, "It is the wonderful achievement of Martin Bauml Duberman to have captured the greatness of Paul Robeson" (20 March 1989); while the rightist *New Leader* denounces it as "a tendentious, ultimately dishonest book." The latter view, however, is rarely echoed with the same fervor; for example, even the conservative *Commentary* commends Duberman's "prodigious research" (May 1989). Whether one feels that Robeson was a victim of his own blindness or afflicted by the myopia of others, this book remains the encyclopedic and thoroughly conceived biography of record.

—Stanley Corkin

ROBESPIERRE, Maximilien (-François-Marie-Isadore de), 1758–1794; French lawyer and revolutionary.

Hampson, Norman, *The Life and Opinions of Maximilien Robespierre.* London, Duckworth, 1974.
Jordan, David P., *The Revolutionary Career of Maximilien Robespierre.* New York, Free Press, and London, Collier-Macmillan, 1985.
Lewes, G. H., *The Life of Maximilien Robespierre.* London, Routledge, and Philadelphia, Carey and Hart, 1849.
Mathiez, Albert, *The Fall of Robespierre and Other Essays.* London, Williams and Norgate, and New York, Knopf, 1927 (originally published as *Autour de Robespierre,* Paris, Payot, 1925).
Rudé, George, *Robespierre: Portrait of a Revolutionary Democrat.* London, Collins, and New York, Viking, 1975.
Thompson, J. M., *Robespierre* (2 vols.). Oxford, Blackwell, 1935; New York, D. Appleton, 1936.

*

The earliest biography of Robespierre was written by a Frenchman calling himself Le Blond de Neuvéglise, although that was almost certainly not his name, and was published in Germany in 1795. When G. H. Lewes, the consort of the English novelist George Eliot, came to write his work in 1849, he found that he had only two predecessors in English. The one was an anonymous and violent attack entitled *History of Robespi-*

erre, Personal and Political, which appeared in London in 1794. The other was an incomplete life by the Chartist, James Bronterre O'Brien (*Life and Character of Robespierre*, 1837). O'Brien had known the old conspirator, Buonarotti, and he had seen him shed tears at the mention of the very name of Robespierre. He was therefore a great admirer of the French revolutionary and in a further, though again incomplete, life (*Elegy on The Death of Robespierre*, 1857), he referred to him as god-like and praised not only his virtuous character but also his wisdom.

LEWES' interest in Robespierre had been kindled by the 1848 revolution in France and by the great histories of the Revolution by Lamartine, Michelet, and Louis Blanc, which had just appeared. Lewes was particularly indebted to Lamartine, but Louis Blanc lent him some letters written by Robespierre in his youth that show him in a surprisingly poetic mood. Lewes was the first to publish these letters, which were all the more valuable since most of Robespierre's papers were destroyed at the time when he was guillotined or when the monarchy was restored in 1814 and 1815.

Lewes was a serious and conscientious biographer. He was critical of some of the more imaginative of his sources. He did not, for example, repeat the story of the young Robespierre having a love affair with a seamstress in his native town (which he calls "the dismal town of Arras"), although he does lend some credence to the story that the Robespierre family was of Irish origin (probably named Robert Spiers).

The main problem that confronts any biographer of Robespierre was realised by Lewes. How can one understand someone who is so blatantly self-contradictory, the advocate of freedom who organized a tyrranical witch-hunt? Lewes seeks to be reasonable, and to recognise the many varied characteristics of his subject. He describes him as ambitious and fanatical, honest and self-denying, the Incorruptible as he was always called. Endowed with a powerful intellect, he is shown to be vain and lacking in generosity and greatness. The conclusion is not so much critical as hostile.

Toward the end of the 19th century, the study of the French Revolution became more scientific, with a concentration on archives. A Robespierre Society was founded in 1908 that published his writings and speeches and all documents relating to him. The cult of Robespierre was led by MATHIEZ. Because of his early death, Mathiez never wrote the biography that he had planned, but he produced several collections of biographical essays that sought, in his words, to improve our knowledge of the man who incarnated everything that was best in revolutionary France. Robespierre was not, in the eyes of the polemical Mathiez, the blood-stained puppet of legend, but a just and clear-sighted statesman who lived for the good of his country.

In 1935, the Oxford historian J. M. THOMPSON, believing that it was unlikely that any new documents would emerge, thought that it was time to write the definitive life and to call a truce between those who claimed that Robespierre was a dictator with the guillotine at his disposal and those who saw him as the most virtuous of heroes. For Thompson this was not a man who directed the Revolution but one who followed it and who, doing so, embodied more than any other the revolutionary spirit of the French people. He wrote what was, and remains, the most careful study of Robespierre's life and career, a fully documented analysis that considers all the issues. From time to time he is disappointed, as when he finds mere rhetoric and a certain ordi-

nariness where he hoped to find genuine passion and great talent. But as he merges his biography into the history of the Revolution, he finds that Robespierre always identifies himself with the collective conscience of France.

Thompson rarely puts forward as fact something for which he does not have reliable evidence. However, one such occasion is when the schoolboy Robespierre had to give a Latin speech of welcome to Louis XVI as he visited the college at Arras. Thompson writes that the king looked kindly at the little boy who was one day to demand his death, reflecting a desire to suggest personal drama that is always tempting to the biographer but in this case has no solid evidence to support it.

Thompson points out that most of those who simply gave a physical description of Robespierre were men who, either by conviction or by policy, were his enemies. Yet he thought that one could establish with reasonable certainty what he looked like, and in the same way he claimed that one could both understand and agree about him. Robespierre himself believed that he could reconcile contradictory ideas. He was always rational and cautious and possessed all the virtues of the democrat, the prophet, and the puritan. But an unhappy childhood and a political experience that was dominated by opposition made him cold, suspicious, and ruthless.

HAMPSON does not think that there can be any general agreement about Robespierre. He set out to write a biography but he found that he was unable to put together in one conventional synthesis all the many ambivalences that characterise Robespierre. While accepting the assumption that there is not likely to be any important new discoveries about him (an assumption that has proved to be true so far, with the exception of an early discussion about the legal condition of bastards, which was discovered and published in 1971), Hampson found it impossible to come to conclusions about his subject. He therefore adopted a novel approach to biography, setting his work within the framework of a university class in which there is a constant discussion between the tutor (who acts as the narrator, providing the facts) and three characters who appear as students. They are a Marxist, a civil servant, and a clergyman. Hampson tells us that they all utter opinions he himself shares, however differing they are. At the end they agree that while they might not have learned all they wanted to know about Robespierre, at least they have learned a lot about each other.

RUDÉ does not have many doubts about the Incorruptible. He portrays Robespierre as the champion of popular sovereignty, the upholder of democracy, and the outstanding leader of the Revolution at every stage of its most vigorous and creative years. But Rudé, perhaps surprisingly, introduces personal issues for which the evidence is doubtful—for example, that Robespierre met (or perhaps glimpsed) Rousseau when the philosopher was near the end of his life, and that Robespierre was ill or fatigued during the critical weeks before his overthrow in July 1794 and did not therefore defend himself as he might have done. A Marxist interpretation of the Revolution thus goes alongside a biographer's assessment of chance and accident in an individual's life.

JORDAN avoids some of the problems of the biographer by insisting on Robespierre's role in the Revolution. This can, he suggests, be understood only by examining Robespierre's thought and his words, and their evolution as the years progressed. This is therefore an intellectual biography, showing how

Robespierre came to identify himself with the Revolution and how he became identified with it, to his cost, but also to his fame.

—Douglas Johnson

ROCKEFELLER, John D(avison), 1839–1937; American industrialist and philanthropist.

Hawke, David F., *John D.: The Founding Father of the Rockefellers.* New York, Harper, 1980.

Nevins, Allan, *John D. Rockefeller: The Heroic Age of American Enterprise* (2 vols.). New York, Scribner, 1940.

Nevins, Allan, *Study in Power: John D. Rockefeller, Industrialist and Philanthropist* (2 vols.). New York, Scribner, 1953.

Tarbell, Ida M., *History of the Standard Oil Company.* New York, P. Smith, 1950.

*

The most recent biographer of Rockefeller is HAWKE, who was provided with total access to the Rockefeller family and business papers housed at the Rockefeller Archives in Pocantico Hills, New York. While applauding the careful preservation of massive letter books, ledgers, and personal papers relating to the founding father of this dynasty, Hawke, in "Traps that Await the Biographer of John D. Rockefeller" (*American Industrialization, Economic Expansion and the Law*, edited by Joseph R. Frese and Jacob Judd, 1981), alerts future historians to the need to analyze carefully such available documentation. He points out that John D. quite frequently sought to color the record for posterity. Historians are familiar with the frequent instances of selective memory demonstrated by public figures when they characterize their own activities. Rockefeller was no exception. While very reticent in public, Rockefeller did let the mask slip when he once compared himself to Napoleon. Hawke portrays a man who is far more complex than described either by Ida Tarbell or Allan Nevins (see below). Any biographer of Rockefeller must treat the founding of the petroleum industry in the United States and, in particular, the creation of the Standard Oil Empire. In this context, the difficulty lies in distinguishing the private Rockefeller from the public one.

While Hawke attempts to strike a balance in portraying Rockefeller in his family, philanthropic, and private moments, NEVINS in his multivolume studies concentrates on Rockefeller the industrialist. In creating the Standard Oil complex, Rockefeller brought many innovative ideas to American industrialization. He created a petroleum kingdom that controlled every operation from the drilling of the natural resource to the final stage of product sales throughout the world. Such a creation not only entailed foresight, daring, and business acumen but also, on occasion, ruthlessness. Nevins attempts in both major studies to demonstrate that business ruthlessness did not necessarily equate with personal callousness and perversity.

With the vast wealth accumulated from his enterprises, Rockefeller sought to create channels by which some of his private wealth could contribute to public improvement. Nevins ably depicts Rockefeller as one of the great philanthropists of the late 19th and early 20th centuries. Nevins provides details regarding the creation of the philanthropic machinery that has come down to us in the form of universities, medical centers, missionary activities, nature preserves, medical educational reforms, and myriad programs in the arts and humanities. Using his extensive knowledge of business history and of Rockefeller, Nevins condensed his previously published voluminous writings into nine double-columned pages for a model Rockefeller sketch that appeared in a *Supplement* to the *Dictionary of American Biography.*

The only published work of what may loosely be described as "autobiographical" in nature originally appeared as a series of articles published in 1908–09 in a magazine called the *The World's Work,* then collected and printed in book form in 1909. The published Frank N. Doubleday arranged to meet and converse with Rockefeller in Augusta, Georgia. Doubleday then had his notes transcribed, sent them to Rockefeller for revisions and approval, and afterwards prepared the material for publication. Rockefeller discussed his philanthropies, personal friends, his early business activities, and the concept of "benevolent trust," somewhat similar to Andrew Carnegie's "Gospel of Wealth." Rockefeller's *Random Reminiscences of Men and Events* (1984) may be based somewhat on Rockefeller's recollections, with much assistance from the professional writer, Doubleday.

The doyenne of Rockefeller biographers was TARBELL, who set out to provide a full-scale study of the creation of Standard Oil and, at the same time, to depict Rockefeller in his true colors. Tarbell, in seeking to obtain as much insight as possible into her subject's character, followed him to church one Sunday in Cleveland. She described his face as exhibiting "concentration, cruelty, and craftiness," and she found him "altogether indescribably repulsive." She then wrote the classic account of Standard Oil. Her account of the creation of the oil giant has withstood the test of time, while her characterization of Rockefeller as a money-grabbing, miserly, and vicious businessman has been somewhat softened by Nevins and Hawke in their biographies. Both of these writers concurred in their view that it is extremely difficult to understand the private Rockefeller because of an evasiveness in his correspondence and, certainly, in his public appearances. For a contemporary study of the man and his industrial creation, Tarbell still must be read, while Nevins provides the most thorough study of all phases of Rockefeller's business and charitable activities. Hawke portrays him as a person "who is quite understandable and very human."

—Jacob Judd

RODIN, Auguste, 1840–1917; French sculptor.

Champigneulle, Bernard, *Rodin*, translated by J. Maxwell Brownjohn. New York, Abrams, and London, Thames and Hudson, 1967 (originally published by A. Somogy, Paris, 1967).

Cladel, Judith, *Rodin: The Man and His Art*, translated by S. K. Star. New York, Century, 1917.

Cladel, Judith, *Rodin*, translated by James Whitall. New York, Harcourt, and London, K. Paul, 1937 (originally published as *Rodin, sa vie glorieuse, sa vie inconnue*, Paris, Grasset, 1936).

Descharnes, Robert and Jean-François Chabrun, *Auguste Rodin*. New York, Viking, and London, Macmillan, 1967.

Grunfeld, Frederic, *Rodin: A Biography*. New York, Holt, and London, Hutchinson, 1987.

Rilke, Rainer Maria, *Rodin*, translated by Jessie Lemont and Hans Trausil. London, Grey Walls Press, 1946; New York, Fine Editions Press, 1954 (originally published as *Auguste Rodin*, Berlin, J. Bard, 1902).

*

In the preface to his 1987 biography of Rodin, Grunfeld (see below) correctly observes that "the last real Rodin biography based on original research" was CLADEL's 1936 *Rodin*. As important as Cladel's works are, they suffer from a limited scope and a subjective viewpoint. This is especially obvious in the earlier *Rodin: The Man and His Art* (1917), which provides a modest biography focusing on three major periods in the artist's life. This work is heavy with the presence of Rodin as a ghost writer. More substantive is the 1936 book (English translation, 1937), where the author's long-time association with Rodin and her access to family and friends provides a wellspring of information and observation. Both books are lively and highly readable and communicate a deep, sincere appreciation for Rodin as a man and an artist. A review of the literature on Rodin's life since Cladel's publications confirms that subsequent authors have relied heavily on her and consequently contribute to the myth of the artist as a grand master.

GRUNFELD successfully addresses the task of allowing the "documentary record to speak for itself" and as a result produces a multifaceted and human portrait of Rodin. Impressive in its scope, the book presents a detailed and well-documented study of Rodin's life and art set in the broader context of French society of the late 19th and early 20th centuries. Grunfeld is particularly effective at integrating Rodin's life experiences with his artistic development and draws many pertinent, thought-provoking, and potentially controversial connections between his art and his life. In accomplishing this task, Grunfeld includes many quotes from Rodin's comtemporaries, a technique that creates an authenticity and relevance. The book contains a remarkably thorough bibliography and extensive notes that will serve researchers well despite the fact that Grunfeld uses an unconventional and somewhat awkward system of coding his references. The text is written in a lively, interesting style and is intelligently, but not lavishly illustrated. Grunfeld has clearly produced the definitive biography of Rodin, and it is not likely to be challenged in the near future. The book will serve the scholar and general reader alike, but at 670 pages, it will prove formidable to some.

DESCHARNES AND CHABRUN produced their book as a tribute to Rodin on the 50th anniversary of his death. They acknowledge in the preface that the book is neither a cataloge raisonné nor a complete biography. Nonetheless, the scope of the publication is large and based on significant research and documentation. As is customary, the authors acknowledge the centrality of Judith Cladel's work on Rodin, which they characterize as "the key source for all Rodin biographies." However, they draw on sufficient additional sources, including artists' commentaries, reports from the press of the times, and subsequent Rodin literature to achieve a fairly realistic and balanced view of Rodin as an "artist of enormous strength" but "a man with his share

of weakness." This book is organized around the major works of art that punctuated Rodin's artistic career, i.e., *The Gates of Hell*, *The Burghers of Calais*, *The Monument to Balzac*. As a biography, the book is thorough and well researched. While it lacks the detail of Grunfeld, it is nonetheless accurate and does an excellent job of capturing the flavor of the times. The text is well written and substantially enhanced by over 450 high quality illustrations (more than 60 in color) that are pertinent to the biography. The book is supported by an exceptionally fine bibliography and good notes, and it will continue to be an important source for researchers and general readers alike.

CHAMPIGNEULLE's biography of Rodin is highly readable and accessible to a broad public. The author approaches his subject in an informal and amicable fashion that depends largely on Judith Cladel and Rodin's own commentary as reported by proponents such as Paul Grell and Rainer Maria Rilke. Consequently, the text is occasionally gratuitous and lacks a substantive connection with the broader aspects of Rodin's times. On the other hand, Champigneulle delivers a fine sense of the personality of Rodin largely by organizing his text around themes that illustrate the artist's emotional highs and lows. Chronological in structure, the text makes excellent use of Rodin's major works by providing pace and context for the telling of his life's story. Champigneulle's rendition of the development of *The Burghers of Calais* and *Balzac* are particularly engaging. This biography is flawed by its strong dependence on limited sources, a lack of original research, and minimal scholarly references. It is, however, written in a lively and fluid style, well illustrated, and genuinely sensitive to the significance and contributions of its subject.

RILKE's brief book-length "essay" on Rodin has become a standard reference for research into the character and values of this great artist. While not properly a biography, the book does offer a meaningful view of the legend of the grand master by touching on, as Rilke sees them, the epochs of Rodin's development. Already a world-famous writer, Rilke served as Rodin's secretary for several years, late in the sculptor's life. This employment enabled him to provide sensitive commentary on Rodin which, while admittedly poetic and elegiac, is an excellent psychological portrait of this important artist.

—John A. Day

_____

ROETHKE, Theodore, 1908–1963; American poet.

Seager, Alan, *The Glass House: The Life of Theodore Roethke*. New York, McGraw-Hill, 1968.

Sullivan, Rosemary, *Theodore Roethke: The Garden Master*. Seattle, University of Washington Press, 1975.

Meyers, Jeffrey, *Manic Power: Robert Lowell and his Circle*. New York, Arbor House, and London, Macmillan, 1987.

*

Seager's book provides the primary biographical resource for Roethke scholarship. It is chronologically arranged, descriptive, and complete except for minor omissions. Sullivan augments

Seager by probing the psychological resources of Roethke's creativity, and Meyers adds the times to the life. Together, they present a composite portrait of the man and artist.

Sullivan and Meyers accept Seager's identification of the three significant events in the poet's life: his childhood experience in his father's greenhouse, his father's death, and his manic-depressive illness. Roethke left no autobiography, but he discussed these events in scattered prose fragments that are collected in good editions of his selected letters, notebooks, and essays. (See *On the Poet and His Craft: Selected Prose of Theodore Roethke*, 1966, and *Selected Letters*, 1968, both edited by Ralph J. Mills, Jr.)

SEAGER was Roethke's lifelong friend and sometime colleague. When Roethke died, his widow asked Seager to write this authorized biography. His sympathetic portrayal does not prevent a balanced depiction of the bad with the good, however. He credits Roethke's character with candor and sincerity, but he also corrects several exaggerations that Roethke repeated about his "tough guy" background. Throughout, Seager measures the "ordinariness" of Roethke's upbringing, education, and teaching assignments against his "extraordinariness" as a poet. He describes a normal relationship between father and son, but documents Roethke's fear and guilt following his father's death, which made him "shield the best part of himself from the public" and made him overly ambitious for public recognition and praise.

Seager is convinced that Roethke's first mental breakdown was self-induced to heighten perception and create mystical visions. Seager himself witnessed one of Roethke's breakdowns and in an Appendix provides a description of the shock treatments he endured, but Seager offers little clinical analysis of the illness or its relation to Roethke's art.

Seager applies his novelist's skills to produce a graceful narrative. He quotes extensively from letters and reviews but little from the poetry. Though it includes an index to proper names, the work provides no footnotes or bibliography, and several early quotations lack attribution. However, this reliable biography is indispensable for its personal accounts of Roethke's conduct and for the understanding a fellow-writer brings to his subject.

In her study of Roethke's poetry, SULLIVAN keeps the individual personality of Roethke before us to demonstrate how personal experience is transformed into art. The poetry, she argues, is only partially autobiographical since there is little of the public side of the man in the work, and any personal allusions become archetypal and symbolic. Her caveats against reducing poetry, however personal, to autobiography are worth any biographer's consideration.

Sullivan pays close attention to the death of Roethke's father as central to his creative imagination, the subject of a major poem, and the psychic source of much of the emotion in his poetry. Because the greenhouse poems "were a deliberate cultivation of his past," she probes his childhood for their source. She accepts Roethke's poetry as "spiritual autobiography" and his madness as a source of his mysticism, but she rejects his poetry as a private myth. Her comparison of the life with the poems reveals the difference between the man and his art. She relies on Seager and the published letters and notebooks (apparently there is little new to be learned from the unpublished papers), but she makes more critical use of biography than does Seager.

MEYERS has written a "group biography" of five mid-20th-century poets whose central figure was Robert Lowell and includes Randall Jarrell, John Berryman, and Roethke (Meyers adds Sylvia Plath in an Epilogue). He discovers several parallels: all of them pursued self-destruction through alcohol, suicide or madness, all had fathers who died or abandoned them, all suffered mental breakdowns, all supported themselves by teaching and public readings, all cultivated public reputations and awards, and all were fiercely competitive, even "imitating each other." Meyers argues that they "used their art to justify their mania," that their mania reflected the ugly materialism and tension in post-war and cold-war America, and that their art was an attempt to escape from their culture.

In reviewing Roethke's life, Meyers repeats Seager's account of the father's death. He attaches great importance to Roethke's self-induced neurosis and documents from Roethke's own writings that the poet self-consciously identified with a tradition of the mad artist that begins with Plato's *Ion* and continues through the Romantics, Dostoevsky, Rimbaud, and Nietzsche.

Meyers' parallel lives reveal provocative similarities among these poets without, however, devoting equal attention to their differences. In this short study, the biographical analyses are brief and the explanations of cultural influence are sometimes truncated. However, the focus on the times provides an historical context for Sullivan's criticism and Seager's chronology.

—Donald C. Irving

ROOSEVELT, Eleanor, 1884–1962; American political activist, wife of Franklin D. Roosevelt.

Flemion, Jess and Colleen M. O'Connor, editors, *Eleanor Roosevelt: An American Journey*. San Diego, California, San Diego State University Press, 1987.

Hoff-Wilson, Joan and Marjorie Lightman, editors, *Without Precedent: The Life and Career of Eleanor Roosevelt*. Bloomington, Indiana University Press, 1984.

Lash, Joseph P., *Eleanor and Franklin: The Story of Their Relationship Based on Eleanor Roosevelt's Private Papers*. New York, Norton, 1971; London, Deutsch, 1972.

Lash, Joseph P., *Eleanor: The Years Alone*. New York, Norton, 1972; London, Deutsch, 1973.

Lash, Joseph P., *Life Was Meant To Be Lived: A Centenary Portrait of Eleanor Roosevelt*. New York and London, Norton, 1984.

*

Perhaps no historian on earth knows more about Eleanor Roosevelt than LASH, who has written about the former first lady in at least three well-received books and in numerous popular and scholarly articles. If only two books could be read about Eleanor Roosevelt they would surely be Lash's *Eleanor and Franklin* and the companion volume, *Eleanor: The Years Alone*.

In both works, Lash borrows liberally from the private letters, notes, and diaries kept by Eleanor Roosevelt throughout her adult life to present a convincing, highly readable portrait of a woman often mistreated in her private life but nonetheless considerate and concerned about those less fortunate than herself in her public life.

Both books underline a public perception of Mrs. Roosevelt as an energetic progressive who advanced issues dealing with workers' rights, civil rights, and the brotherhood of man long before it was considered to be the proper thing to do. While Lash's *Eleanor and Franklin* covers the frequently painful years of her marriage to Franklin Roosevelt, and is thus sometimes a rather disquieting reading experience, *Eleanor: The Years Alone* is a book of joy, detailing Mrs. Roosevelt's frenetic global activities in the years after FDR's death in 1945, her growing influence throughout the world in the 1950s, her status as the most popular woman in the United States in the early 1960s, as well as her unusually great influence within the national Democratic Party. As a quick read that in many ways summarizes the work of the above mentioned books, Lash's *Life Was Meant To Be Lived* is a lavishly illustrated coffeetable book, elegantly written, that provides a snapshot overview of Mrs. Roosevelt's life and career.

While all of Lash's works on Roosevelt are revealing and sympathetic, and though together they still represent the definitive source for information on Mrs. Roosevelt, none of them is very well documented, nor do they bring with them a scholar's perspective explaining why certain things Mrs. Roosevelt did were historically important. But this is surely a flaw that any historian would find with any work intended for mass consumption. As a source of information for issues and events covering the range of Mrs. Roosevelt's life, Lash's books are still the most important literary works available.

Of less significance are the many books examining certain aspects of Eleanor Roosevelt's life and career. Two collections of essays written by several hands are nonetheless noteworthy: *Eleanor Roosevelt*, edited by Flemion and O'Connor, and *Without Precedent*, edited by Hoff-Wilson and Lightman. Each book is a series of essays presenting scholarly evidence of Mrs. Roosevelt's early civil rights activism, her support of and involvement with the United Nations, and her role as an unknowing, but nonetheless powerful, feminist figure. Not surprisingly, however, the writing in both books, owing to the large number of contributors, is uneven, and both books rely too heavily on secondary source material.

FLEMION AND O'CONNOR's volume is helpful because it presents evidence of Eleanor Roosevelt as a cultural icon. Of particular interest is the large political cartoon collection from the early 1930s to Mrs. Roosevelt's death in 1962, which both shows her as a figure of inspiration and vilification and gives testimony to how thoroughly Mrs. Roosevelt captured the public's imagination in her lifetime. Of less interest are two facile essays written by Mrs. Roosevelt's sons, James and Elliott Roosevelt, which have the markings of ghostwriters about them, and a separate essay by Senator Edward Kennedy on Mrs. Roosevelt and John F. Kennedy that seems somewhat self-serving.

The work by HOFF-WILSON AND LIGHTMAN is more academic in its subject matter and is largely an interpretive sourcebook for Roosevelt scholars. All of the essays in this book are thoroughly researched and thoughtfully written, and they raise an interesting question: why haven't historians approached the life and career of Mrs. Roosevelt with such scholarly precision?

While Lash obviously comes the closest, he is still far from giving us the sort of thick, compelling biography that C. Vann Woodward wrote on Tom Watson or Arthur Schlesinger on John F. Kennedy. *Without Precedent* opens new avenues of thought on Mrs. Roosevelt's career and leaves the reader feeling that the best book on Eleanor Roosevelt has yet to be written.

This Is My Story (1937), Eleanor Roosevelt's autobiography published at the height of President Roosevelt's popularity, is a curious work, taking us from Eleanor Roosevelt's childhood to the earliest days of the Roosevelt administration. Although pleasant and engaging, the work is also revealing for what it, by obvious necessity, neglects—her troubled private life and emotionally painful marriage to Franklin. In one passage, Mrs. Roosevelt declares a preference for fiction over non-fiction because the "author can really tell the truth without hurting anyone and without humiliating himself too much." Sadly, that thought may say more about Mrs. Roosevelt than she imagined. *This Is My Story* is a book without any scholarly documentation, but it is, nevertheless, of substantial interest because it tells us how Eleanor Roosevelt thought her life should be presented for public viewing.

—Garry Boulard

ROOSEVELT, Franklin Delano, 1882–1945; American political leader, 32nd president of the United States.

Burns, James M., *Roosevelt* (2 vols.). New York, Harcourt, 1956–70.

Davis, Kenneth S., *FDR* (3 vols.). Vol. 1, New York, Putnam, 1972; Vol. 2, New York, Random House, 1985; Vol. 3, New York, Random House, 1986.

Freidel, Frank B., *Franklin D. Roosevelt* (4 vols.). Boston, Little Brown, 1952–73.

Freidel, Frank B., *Franklin D. Roosevelt: Rendezvous with Destiny*. Boston, Little Brown, 1990.

Miller, Nathan, *F.D.R.: An Intimate History*. New York, Doubleday, 1983.

Morgan, Ted, *F.D.R.: A Biography*. New York, Simon and Schuster, 1985; London, Grafton, 1986.

Ward, Geoffrey C., *Before the Trumpet: Young Franklin Roosevelt, 1882–1905*. New York, Harper, 1985.

Ward, Geoffrey C., *A First Class Temperament: The Emergence of Franklin Roosevelt*. New York, Harper, 1989.

*

FREIDEL's monumental four-volume work remains the standard Roosevelt biography. It is based on exhaustive research in manuscript collections and printed sources, and is informed by numerous personal interviews. Although the author points to several flaws in Roosevelt's makeup, such as his readiness to compromise in the name of expendiency, his overall approach is one of admiration. Freidel denies the popular notion that Roosevelt was a lightweight until his struggle with infantile paralysis transformed his character. The man all along combined great inner reserves with a strong sense of destiny, according to Freidel. His character was tested rather than shaped by his illness.

The volumes are particularly valuable for their analyses of the political structures within which Roosevelt operated and the issues he dealt with. Freidel emphasizes how much Roosevelt's governorship of the State of New York foreshadowed his presidency, noting his formation as governor of what later would be called the "Brains Trust" to advise him in his presidency, and how his use of radio broadcasts anticipated his "Fireside Chats." Well written for the most part (though the author has a distressing tendency to employ slang that has not worn well), these books are models of scholarship to which most subsequent biographers acknowledge their indebtedness.

Despite its enduring value, Freidel's multi-volume work has become dated in some respects. It is a traditional political biography with fewer than 100 pages devoted to the period before Roosevelt first ran for public office. Freidel treats Roosevelt's personal life with a delicacy later writers have considered unnecessary. Matters of more recent interest, such as Roosevelt's views about minorities and women and the effects of his policies on these groups, are given relatively little attention.

FREIDEL's latest, single-volume biography (1990) is the capstone of his lifetime interest in FDR. Like his earlier volumes, *Rendezvous* is an admiring though not uncritical analysis based on thorough research in primary sources. Interpretations are conventional, particularly in the realm of foreign policies. Lack of a bibliography makes it impossible to determine whether Freidel has ignored much recent scholarship on FDR, or considered and rejected it. The book is well written, factually reliable, and provides broad coverage.

WARD's brilliantly written volumes complement Freidel's work. Ward emphasizes Roosevelt the person: the milieu in which he was raised, his relationships with family and friends, and his thinking about a range of issues beyond politics. Ward's treatment of Roosevelt's relentless efforts to overcome the effects of polio and of his complicated relationship with Eleanor are unlikely to be surpassed. Eleanor as an individual figures prominently. The books are based on a wide range of souces, some previously untapped, and are remarkable for their even-handedness. They provide as well an elegant contribution to social history. Freidel himself has characterized Ward's contribution as "a truly first class study."

DAVIS intends his work for a general audience. Although he has done some research in primary sources, he has relied greatly on published accounts. The result is good popular history: providing here a sampling of social attitudes, there an extended analysis of larger issues with which the general reader may be unfamiliar. Davis offers vivid portraits of those close to Roosevelt, such as Louis Howe. Davis is excellent on Roosevelt's governorship of New York State and on his intellectual development over the years. He attempts no major reinterpretations of earlier works such as Freidel's. The volumes, moreover, are slightly marred by Davis' tendency to overwrite and to attribute to individuals motives and emotions that can only be guessed.

BURNS' two volumes span Roosevelt's entire life, though the author devotes only a few pages to Roosevelt's early years. Burns, a distinguished student of American political processes, emphasizes Roosevelt's leadership role as president functioning within the American political system. On domestic affairs,

Burns depicts his subject as a master politician who was unable to conquer the Depression because he was intellectually incapable of devising long-range strategies and temperamentally incapable of rising above partisan concerns. Roosevelt's foreign policy is treated extensively in the latter part of the first volume and throughout the second. Burns praises Roosevelt's goal of creating a lasting peace at the end of World War II, but again faults him for being unable to transcend political expediency to attain it. He regards as particularly damaging Roosevelt's failure to push for the creation of an early second front against Nazi Germany, thereby incurring Soviet distrust of Anglo-American motives.

There are two good, single-volume biographies of Roosevelt written for the general reader. As MILLER's subtitle suggests, his is an anecdotal account that strives to convey the flavor of Roosevelt's personality. The author does offer interpretations, however, and explains his reasons for disagreeing with previous writers. Miller is highly laudatory of Roosevelt the person and the president. MORGAN's book, more detailed and more vividly written, reveals the author's admiration for his subject on nearly every page. He subscribes to the idea that Roosevelt's struggle with polio wrought a nearly miraculous transformation in a man who previously was not "big enough." Faulting several of Roosevelt's character traits, Morgan nonetheless credits him with Herculean accomplishments in both the domestic and world arenas.

Franklin Roosevelt was president during two of the most traumatic periods in American history: the Great Depression and World War II. Because of the magnitude of these events, scores of studies have appeared, covering particular aspects of Roosevelt's career, that fall outside the realm of biography. Arthur M. Schlesinger, Jr.'s magisterial work on the depression and the New Deal (*The Coming of The New Deal*, Boston, Houghton Mifflin, 1958) is indispensable reading for those seriously interested in the man and his times. Of the multi-volume biographies, only Burns' deals with the coming of World War II and the course of that conflict. Because a great deal of new material has become available since Burns wrote, Waldo Heinrichs' volume on FDR and Japan (*Threshold of War: Franklin D. Roosevelt and American Entry into World War II*, New York and Oxford, Oxford University Press, 1988), and Robert Dallek's on Rooseveltian foreign policy (*Franklin D. Roosevelt and American Foreign Policy 1932–45*, New York, Oxford University Press, 1979), should be consulted.

—Robert James Maddox

ROOSEVELT, Theodore, 1858–1919; American political leader, 26th president of the United States.

Bishop, Joseph B., *Theodore Roosevelt and His Time* (2 vols.). New York, Scribner, 1920.

Blum, John M., *The Republican Roosevelt*. Cambridge, Massachusetts, Harvard University Press, 1954.

Burton, David H., *Theodore Roosevelt*. New York, Twayne, 1972.

Busch, Noel F., *T. R.: The Story of Theodore Roosevelt and His Influence on Our Times.* New York, Reynal, 1963.

Charnwood, 1st Baron (Godfrey Rathbone Benson), *Theodore Roosevelt.* Boston, Atlantic Monthly Press, and London, Constable, 1923.

Chessman, G. Wallace, *Theodore Roosevelt and the Politics of Power.* Boston, Little Brown, 1969.

Gardner, Joseph L., *Departing Glory: Theodore Roosevelt as Ex-President.* New York, Scribner, 1973.

Grantham, Dewey, *Theodore Roosevelt.* Englewood Cliffs, New Jersey, Prentice-Hall, 1971.

Hagedorn, Hermann, *Roosevelt in the Badlands.* Boston, Houghton Mifflin, 1921; London, A. Melrose, 1924.

Harbaugh, William H., *Power and Responsibility: The Life and Times of Theodore Roosevelt.* New York, Farrar Straus, 1961; Oxford, Oxford University Press, 1975.

Lorant, Stefan, *The Life and Times of Theodore Roosevelt.* New York, Doubleday, 1959.

McCullough, David, *Mornings on Horseback.* New York, Simon and Schuster, 1981.

Morris, Edmund. *The Rise of Theodore Roosevelt.* New York, Coward McCann, and London, Collins, 1979.

Pringle, Henry F., *Theodore Roosevelt, a Biography.* New York, Harcourt, and London, Cape, 1931.

Putnam, Carleton, *Theodore Roosevelt: A Biography* (vol. 1, *The Formative Years*). New York, Scribner, 1958.

Robinson, Corinne Roosevelt, *My Brother Theodore Roosevelt.* New York, Scribner, 1921.

Roosevelt, Nicholas, *Theodore Roosevelt: The Man as I Knew Him.* New York, Dodd Mead, 1967.

Thayer, William R., *Theodore Roosevelt.* New York, Grosset and Dunlap, and London, Constable, 1919.

Wagenknecht, Edward, *The Seven Worlds of Theodore Roosevelt.* New York, Longman, 1958.

*

THAYER leads off Roosevelt biography. His book, subtitled "an intimate biography," contains good coverage of Roosevelt's life and work, mixing heavy doses of admiration with occasional negative comment. Thayer speaks authoritatively, too much so at times, as though he had been at Roosevelt's elbow. He sees his subject as both he and Roosevelt wanted him to be remembered. BISHOP's two-volume study also enjoys the advantages—and many of the disadvantages—of being done by someone close to Roosevelt. It is, however, a more contextualized and scholarly treatment than Thayer's, based on personal and official correspondence and other materials relating to Teddy Roosevelt's public career. The resulting detail is generous and remains useful, though its claims should be weighed against later, better informed accounts. Lord CHARNWOOD added a third entry to early Roosevelt biography. His book, less factual than the foregoing, is an impression of what the man was like, conveying a sense of personality important for understanding Roosevelt and helpful for rounding out the picture of a man admired and written about by his own generation.

PRINGLE's Pulitzer Prize-winning *Roosevelt* marks a distinct change in the way scholars and others came to view Roosevelt. Adulation gives way to ridicule, impressions are replaced by the muckraker's fondness for foibles designed to dull the luster of a reputation, while professed objectivity is as slanted as the formidable bias of Thayer and Bishop. Pringle writes in high style, a feature that no doubt adds to its influence on the popular as well as the scholarly perception of Roosevelt. The *Works of Theodore Roosevelt* had been available to Pringle but not the 5000 pieces of correspondence later published in the *Letters of Theodore Roosevelt,* a careful selection from the 150,000 letters preserved. After these were published, Pringle brought out a revised edition of his biography and announced that having read all the published letters "word for word," his original judgments were confirmed. More importantly, Pringle had persuaded a whole generation that Roosevelt was a mixture of "adult greatness . . . with the quality of being a magnificent child."

Exactly 30 years later, HARBAUGH challenged and in the process largely demolished the image of Roosevelt left by Pringle. Harbaugh the historian rewrote what Pringle the journalist had set down, and Harbaugh's has proved to be the best and the most durable of all Roosevelt biographies. By making use of the *Letters* as well as other archival correspondence, drawing on the *Works,* and consulting the full range of secondary literature in books and articles, Harbaugh developed a believable hero who was still intensely human. The study is balanced, comprehensive, and historically sound, largely because it rests on firm scholarly foundations. Harbaugh's biography proved to be an ice-breaker, as a large number of monographs and special studies dealing with Roosevelt began to flow freely thereafter.

CHESSMAN's biography tends to simplify Roosevelt by using the theme, "the politics of power." His understanding of the early political life of Roosevelt as governor of New York is unmatched, and this insight adds strength to his general proposition about power and politics. Despite the catch phrases used as chapter headings, Chessman provides a straightforward account, informed but stylistically unexciting. At best it is a basic introduction to a great life. BURTON's biography, written up in lively prose, is the first to treat the mind of Theodore Roosevelt, examining his ideas, his public philosophy, and his understanding of history as central premises in his life and work. Unlike WAGENKNECHT's analysis of the "seven worlds" of Roosevelt—a trailblazing account that prefers to keep "the facts" of his life apart from his values, his principles, and his outlook—Burton integrates as consistently as Wagenknecht separates. Wagenknecht's book, biographical without being conventional biography, is an indispensable work.

Roosevelt's life awaits the multi-volume study that it deserves. PUTNAM planned four volumes but completed only volume one. Covering Roosevelt's life to 1886, Putnam offers a thorough treatment of the first 28 years. His is, however, a ponderous book, more to be consulted than read through, though especially worthwhile for learning the particulars of Roosevelt the western rancher and fledgling eastern politician. In Putnam's hands Roosevelt comes across as an earnest young man, his earnestness in fact tending to crowd out other aspects of his personality. In contrast, MORRIS' first volume of a projected three-volume life captures the total Roosevelt, taking the story down to September 1901, when Roosevelt assumed the presidency. Morris' scholarly account—though perhaps less scholarly than Putnam's—is written with verve. His book also has the advantage of taking events 15 years beyond those covered in Putnam, providing a broader scope for looking at the "many selves" that characterize the man who became the first modern president. Morris also won a Pulitzer Prize for volume one.

Other biographers have covered important segments of Roosevelt's life. MCCULLOUGH covers the first three decades, GARDNER the last decade. They contrast the bright promise of the early years with the somber ending of a great career. McCullough's rendering of the father-son relationship is persuasive and important, for Roosevelt never lost love and respect for his father's ideals. No biographer can safely neglect this consideration. As a social biographer, viewing the life as an expression of social manners and morals, of conventions and conflicts, McCullough is a master. Gardner's description of the last ten years of the ex-president's life makes for exciting reading, only to be tinged with sadness at the end, when the Great War had shattered Roosevelt's hope for international peace and order. Gardner appears very definitely on Roosevelt's side as he recounts successes and frustrations, but his views are moderately expressed and his historical grasp is sound.

Biographies written by relatives, though of some value, must be used with caution. Corinne Roosevelt ROBINSON's story provides a charming portrait without pretending to be more than a tribute to a much loved brother. Written in the emotional backwash of Roosevelt's death, it draws on memories and memoirs that insist on recognizing the private side of a public man. Nicholas ROOSEVELT comes at his subject differently: his account turns out to be much less a series of impressions and more a serious effort to supplement the historical record.

BUSCH's popular approach is well written and goes into some detail to explain Roosevelt's position in affairs of state. Busch purports to define the influence of Roosevelt on our times and claims that had Roosevelt been president in 1914, there would have been no general war in Europe. However, this is speculation rather than history, interesting to read as speculation often is, but falling short of persuasion.

BLUM demonstrates that not all valuable investigations require weighty documentation. His brief work, though biographical, is more interpretive than narrative, and his insights are uncanny. Blum was the first to observe that while for some men power corrupts, Roosevelt's lack of power after 1910 distorted his judgments. Blum, who combines history, politics, and biography, assumes that the reader has a working knowledge of Roosevelt in public affairs. A good short book for beginners is GRANTHAM's "Great Lives Observed" approach. Nicely organized around well-chosen selections from Roosevelt's own writings, those of his contemporaries and the opinions of historians, Grantham's book provides many leads for those who want to learn more about the "Republican Roosevelt." HAGEDORN's account of Roosevelt in the Badlands is a convincing story of a significant interlude, while LORANT's pictorial biography, as big and robust as Roosevelt himself, should be consulted by every student and admirer of Teddy Roosevelt.

—David H. Burton

ROSSETTI, Christina Georgina, 1830–1894; English poet.

Battiscombe, Georgina, *Christina Rossetti: A Divided Life.* New York, Holt, and London, Constable, 1981.

Bell, Mackenzie, *Christina Rossetti: A Biographical and Critical Study.* London, Hurst and Blackett, and Boston, Roberts, 1898.

Packer, Lona Mosk, *Christina Rossetti.* Berkeley, University of California Press, 1963.

Sandars, Mary Frances, *Life of Christina Rossetti.* London, Hutchinson, 1930.

Sawtell, Margaret, *Christina Rossetti: Her Life and Religion.* London, Mowbray, 1955.

Stuart, Dorothy Margaret, *Christina Rossetti.* London, Macmillan, 1930.

Thomas, Eleanor Walter, *Christina Georgina Rossetti.* New York, Columbia University Press, 1931.

Zaturenska, Marya, *Christina Rossetti: A Portrait with Background.* New York, Macmillan, 1949.

*

The numerous memorial poems and essays written upon the death of Christina Rossetti testify to the esteem in which she was held by her contemporaries. For someone whose life could be regarded as constrained and reclusive, Rossetti and her poetry influenced and impressed a great many people. William Michael Rossetti, the poet's brother, had originally intended to write a biography of his sister but relinquished the responsibility when Mackenzie Bell, poet and family friend, indicated a desire to write Christina's life. William Michael supported Bell's efforts willingly, giving interviews and suggestions and access to family papers. And, as a separate project, he wrote a family memoir, *Some Reminiscences of William Michael Rossetti* (1906), about his siblings Christina, Dante Gabriel, and Maria Francesca, providing an interesting supplement to the Bell biography.

BELL's biography draws deeply on his friendship with Christina and the Rossetti family. It is a careful and caring work, a devoted and affectionate portrait, much respectful of its subject, who herself had encouraged the young Bell's poetic aspirations. As narrator, Bell is omnipresent, mixing formal and anecdotal writing styles, sometimes to odd effect; one gets as much a sense of his personality as of Rossetti's. To his credit, though, Bell also quotes liberally from Rossetti's letters and poems and thereby allows her to speak for herself. Bell's true value as a biographer is most apparent, however, in his intimate description of the last years of Rossetti's life, when he knew her best. He carefully describes her behavior and idiosyncracies, her acquaintances and activities, and the agonies of her final illness.

Despite Bell's extreme and curious discretion regarding the intimate concerns of his subject, his biography is an invaluable part of the life-studies of Christina Rossetti. His critical evaluation of her poetry is not particularly insightful; his talent, rather, is in his abundant presentation of the seemingly mundane and trivial incidents in the life of a person he knew and cared about and whose talent and beliefs he respected. Readers get from him a perspective no other biographer could give; his wealth of detail is the source all other biographers must go to in order to begin Rossetti's life.

Although Christina Rossetti was the subject of several critical and biographical essays in the years immediately following the publication of Bell's biography, no other full-scale life-studies were produced until the centenary of her birth. With that centennial celebration, starting in 1930, there appeared a plethora of articles and appreciations (notably Virginia Woolf's "I Am Christina Rossetti," reprinted in the *Second Common Reader*, 1932) as well as three full-length biographies.

SANDARS had the inestimable benefit of full access to the Rossetti family. They told her their personal recollections and family anecdotes, and they must have been terribly disappointed with the work that resulted, for Sandars' biography is a mess. Her purpose seems to be to prove that Rossetti is the greatest religious poet of all time, if not the greatest poet; but she does not demonstrate this belief, only states it. She cannot tell a story (scenes are left incomplete), confuses dates and family names, and blurs the chronology of events. She frequently refers to and assumes reader familiarity with persons and events that have not been introduced into the narrative. Sometimes she provides translations of Italian verses, and sometimes not. She strangely concludes that Rossetti's melancholy aspect was the result solely of her family's loving support of her literary talent. Nor can much be said for Sandars' prose style, which is repetitive and redundant and awkwardly constructed. All this is more than sad because Sandars squandered a unique opportunity and did a disservice to her subject.

Such is far from the case with the 1930 biography by STUART. Although it is part of the English Men of Letters series, it wears its scholarship easily. This is a good biography. Stuart's prose is lively and colorful, and she skillfully and succinctly handles many complex bits of information involving history, habits, and personalities. The work is, however, very much a life of the *poet*, and Rossetti's poetry therefore informs its organization: the poems provide the chronology and the chapter headings. The periodic back-and-forth chronology that this necessitates can be confusing and somewhat constrains the life-narrative, but Stuart is such a good writer that Rossetti's personal story seldom gets lost in the critical assessment of the poetry.

Stuart's objective is to interweave the life with the poetry. At the outset she observes that Bell's biography "was written too soon after [Rossetti's] death for her portrait to be set in its right perspective." Accordingly, Stuart maintains a personal distance as narrator: she is observer, not participant; pain, joy, and sorrow are described but not felt. Because of this, Rossetti's personality remains elusive; there are few set-pieces to establish character, perhaps due to Stuart's expressed awareness of the danger of ascribing too much autobiographical import to creative writings. While such distance might seem an impediment to a good biography, Stuart nevertheless gives a vivid sense of the Rossetti family personality and background, provides precise, evocative descriptions of a place and time now gone, and presents a wealth of fascinating sidelights that are worth further investigation in their own right. (She does not, unfortunately, provide translations of the French and Italian texts she quotes.) Rossetti the poet is Stuart's story, and she tells it well.

THOMAS' biography is clearly delineated: the first 120 pages are the life story, and the remaining 90 pages are literary criticism. Within the limited space of those 120 pages, Thomas presents an admirably clear narrative and provides a useful historical and cultural context for her subject. Her perspective, like Stuart's, is slightly removed emotionally but is still sympathetic and good-natured. She is adept at the telling detail, giving, for example, a sense of Rossetti family life by describing the books that the Rossetti children read. Thomas is also careful to point out that the themes of death and sorrowful love are hardly unique to Christina Rossetti but were popular themes of the day and that, because of this, assumptions about Rossetti's state of mind must be carefully made.

As a side note, readers may be interested to know that the poet Sara Teasdale was preparing a biography of Rossetti for publication by the Macmillan Publishing Company in 1932 (and some bibliographies list it as having been published then). But Teasdale decided to do further research and wanted to interview Rossetti's nieces in England. While there she contracted pneumonia and died in 1933, leaving the manuscript incomplete. Margaret Haley Carpenter, in her biography of Teasdale, quotes extensively from the unfinished manuscript, including the provocative statement: "A person who knew Christina, but who insists on remaining nameless, told me that the poet loved deeply a man who was married—a facet of her emotion that has never caught the light—but that she would not have his love at the cost of sorrow to his wife."

ZATURENSKA combines Rossetti's life story with critical evaluations of her writings. It also includes substantial considerations of the personalities surrounding Rossetti and the Pre-Raphaelites. In itself this is not a bad procedure, and Zaturenska, herself a poet, creates vivid scenes, although she does not so much tell Rossetti's story as describe her world. Personalities, rather than the progress of a life, are prominent in this biography. Sometimes Rossetti gets lost in the crowd, but Zaturenska does trust her subject's own words and allows Rossetti to present herself as both personally strict and engagingly vain. Unfortunately, Zaturenska also trusts Violet Hunt's alleged biography of Elizabeth Siddal, the wife of Dante Gabriel Rossetti. (Helen Rossetti Angeli nicknamed her "Violent Hunt.") Hunt's book is a remarkably unreliable source for any sort of factual material, mixing as it does gossip, animosity, inaccuracies, and pure fantasy in the guise of biography. Zaturenska particularly uses Hunt in her depiction of Rossetti's engagement to Collinson and in her interpretation of "Goblin Market." The use of Hunt does, therefore, call into question Zaturenska's research and the reader should be cautious in accepting everything the biographer says. For Zaturenska's is an unabashedly sympathetic portrait of Rossetti; so much so that she succumbs to grandiose claims about Rossetti's literary accomplishments, claiming at one point that Rossetti's later, rather severe Anglican poems set the pattern for T. S. Eliot's poetry. An argument may presumably be made for this opinion, but Zaturenska does not elaborate. Still, this sort of authorial enthusiasm can provide entertaining if somewhat skeptical reading.

SAWTELL put forth the proposition in her biography that Rossetti planned to elope with the married Collinson, who had wed after Rossetti had broken her engagement with him. (Teasdale's statement about Rossetti's love for a married man was not widely known until Carpenter's Teasdale biography came out in 1960.) Sawtell, however, does not try to tell an intimate story, despite her intriguing suggestion; her principal interest is in Rossetti's religious development as it is revealed in her poetry. (Religion was profoundly important to Rossetti and is a legitimate part of a biographical study of her.) But Sawtell uses the poems to jump to conclusions about Rossetti's state of mind, and she does not try to maintain any sort of narrative flow; she jumps back and forth in time and relies excessively on paraphrases of William Michael Rossetti's memoirs. Like Zaturenska, Sawtell uncritically uses Violet Hunt's book on Siddal as a primary source. Her biography also contains errors of fact: for example, she states that Dante Gabriel Rossetti is buried in the family grave at Highgate Cemetery while he is actually buried where he died, at Birchington-on-Sea. Although some of the religious/poetical explication may be useful in approaching Rossetti's poetry, Sawtell's biography is more analysis than engaging narrative and contains little that is original.

With PACKER, life and interest return to Rossetti biography. Packer's book is beautifully written and incorporates extensive new and original research. Rossetti's personality shines through Packer's descriptions of her depth of feeling and fondness for whimsy, her love of family and her religious agony. Packer fully describes and elucidates the illnesses that dogged Rossetti throughout her life. She reasonably implies that Rossetti's reclusiveness was in part due to the change that Graves' disease wrought on her appearance, darkening and toughening her skin and making her eyes protrude. The torment, both mental and physical, of Rossetti's final fight with cancer is painfully and sympathetically conveyed.

But there is a major problem with Packer's biography, and it involves an alleged secret lover. Speculation concerning Rossetti's loves, known or secret, are part of most biographies about her. Packer conjectures that Rossetti was in love not only with Collinson and Cayley but with William Bell Scott, a married man and a life-long friend of the Rossettis. In her introduction Packer makes this rather distressing disclaimer: "In advancing my hypothesis, which I believe approximates the truth, I have supported it by a detailed and carefully constructed edifice of indirect evidence in the hope that when the small pieces of the puzzle are all fitted together, the total design . . . will be revealed. For this and other reasons [which are left unstated], I have not considered it necessary to qualify every statement made in the course of my narrative or to supply documentary 'proof' for every speculation hazarded." For such a proposition, documentation is most necessary. Unfortunately Packer bases her whole narrative, her whole point of view, on her William Bell Scott theory. Rossetti's actions and reactions are presented and evaluated solely in relation to Scott. Packer even goes so far as to suggest that William Michael Rossetti falsified records. Her basis for this hypothesis is that neither Collinson nor Cayley was worthy of Rossetti's true affection and so, since the poems seem to indicate some sort of love agony, there must have been some other, secret, unattainable love. Scott seems the likely candidate; he was a family friend, he was known to Rossetti, he was a poet and painter (of mediocre ability), and he was married. Packer uses Rossetti's poems, along with their dating, as her "proof"; she can offer no other evidence. Packer's need for Rossetti to have a secret lover leads her into conundrums: "It is unlikely that a poet as subjective as Christina would conceive this poetry in an emotional vacuum; consequently, we can only surmise that it was addressed to someone who does not appear on the record." But Rossetti was "ultra" subjective; she visited Italy, her beloved father's home, and wrote *no* poem about it.

Packer's preoccupation with Scott as an inspirational source, her exclusive reliance on a conjecture that she cannot really substantiate, undermines her otherwise careful and forceful scholarship. The Scott hobby-horse leads her into a mire of "must haves" and "would haves" that are exacerbated by misreadings and by taking facts and poetry out of context. Sadly, Packer died shortly after the publication of her biography and before the discovery of the Penkill Papers, which show that the dates ascribed to many of Rossetti's poems were erroneous (Packer's Scott theory used poem dates as its justification). In addition, the Penkill Papers indicate that Rossetti was on friendly terms with both Scott's wife and his mistress, which begs the question of whether Rossetti would be willing to be a "third" woman. Packer's biography is still the most satisfying to read, but it must be read with caution. BATTISCOMBE's narrative suffers as a life-story because so much of it is spent disputing Packer's Scott theory. In providing a counterpoint to Packer's readings of Rossetti's poetry and interpretations of events in Rossetti's life, however, Battiscombe is quite successful. She writes clearly and makes careful, well-considered observations. As she demonstrates, guilt, death, love, and loss were consistent themes of Christina Rossetti's work throughout her life; none was necessarily predominant in any one particular period. Poetry can be very misleading as biographical material, and Battiscombe stresses and makes the case for the importance of documentary evidence in the writing of a life.

—Elizabeth Dominique Lloyd-Kimbrel

ROSSETTI, Dante Gabriel, 1828–1882; English poet and painter.

Angeli, Helen Rossetti, *Dante Gabriel Rossetti: His Friends and Enemies.* London, Hamilton, 1949.

Benson, Arthur C., *Rossetti.* London and New York, Macmillan, 1904.

Caine, Hall, *Recollections of Dante Gabriel Rossetti.* London, E. Stock, 1882; Boston, Roberts, 1883.

Cary, Elisabeth Luther, *The Rossettis: Dante Gabriel and Christina.* London and New York, Putnam, 1900.

Dobbs, Brian and Judy Dobbs, *Dante Gabriel Rossetti: An Alien Victorian.* London, Macdonald and Jane's, 1977.

Doughty, Oswald, *Dante Gabriel Rossetti: A Victorian Romantic.* New Haven, Connecticut, Yale University Press, and London, F. Muller. 1949.

Dunn, Henry T., *Recollections of Dante Gabriel Rossetti and His Circle.* London, E. Mathews, and New York, J. Pott, 1904.

Grylls, Rosalie Glynn, *Portrait of Rossetti.* Carbondale, Southern Illinois University Press, and London, Macdonald, 1964.

Knight, Joseph, *Life of Dante Gabriel Rossetti.* London, W. Scott, 1887.

Sharp, William, *Dante Gabriel Rossetti: A Record and a Study.* London, Macmillan, 1882.

Waugh, Evelyn, *Rossetti: His Life and Works.* London, Duckworth, and New York, Dodd Mead, 1928.

Winwar, Frances, *Poor Splendid Wings: The Rossettis and Their Circle.* Boston, Little Brown, 1933.

*

SHARP's study of D. G. Rossetti was the first to appear. The appendix has an interesting catalogue of Rossetti's pictorial works. Though the book is flawed by a lack of objectivity, Sharp's discussions of Rossetti's work are worthwhile. KNIGHT's life of Rossetti is really more of a long eulogy, not considered by either he or the Rossetti family to be the needed biography. Knight states that "an exhaustive biography of Rossetti is not yet to be expected, since few men are equal to the task of estimating fully his work in two different branches." These early biographies are interesting mainly for their historical perspective or as sources for future biographies.

CARY's biography of Dante and Christina, readable but not thorough, contains several illustrations, a list of Rossetti's important writings, paintings, and drawings (many of the dates are listed with a question mark), and an index. DUNN was a pupil of Rossetti and one of those who lived at the house on Cheyne walk. His *Recollections* present the views of a close associate in a simple, straightforward style. It contains a preface by William Michael Rossetti, a fastidious collection of notes, in contrast to the easy-flowing style of the narrative itself, and a few illustrations. In the same year BENSON published his sympathetic biography and study of Rossetti's works.

CAINE, a close friend of the poet, offers a firsthand account of Rossetti's final years, and his work remains valuable for that reason. However, it exaggerates and sensationalizes, and it cannot be trusted. WAUGH's study is more concerned with an analysis of Rossetti's paintings than necessary, and he refuses to draw the desired inferences about his subject, leaving a mixed impression. Violet Hunt's biography of Elizabeth Siddal (*Wife of Rossetti*, 1932) paints Rossetti in very negative terms as a terrible husband who pushed his wife to suicide. It is filled with gossip, old photographs and documents, and many unsubstantiated claims. It is generally considered suspect today.

Not long after the publication of Hunt's work, ANGELI, the daughter of Dante's brother William, came to a strident defense of Dante Gabriel: "This book is written with the object of contradicting misstatements and correcting misapprehensions regarding Dante Gabriel Rossetti's character and life, more particularly in his relations with his friends and fellow-artists." The appendices contain correspondence supporting Angeli's position and raising questions about Hunt's claims.

WINWAR's biography has the feel of a novel about it and is considered suspect in terms of accuracy. Though it is about the Pre-Raphaelite movement in general, Rossetti is the main character it deals with. Frank Laurence Lucas' *Ten Victorian Poets* (1940) includes an entertaining introduction to Rossetti in a brief biography. Robert Rosenbaum's *Earnest Victorians* (1961) offers a brief view of Rossetti during his Pre-Raphaelite years, drawing on Rossetti's own diaries and letters and some of the early biographies of him.

DOUGHTY's lengthy biography (712 pages) is generally considered the best; it is certainly the most thorough. Doughty attempts to dig through the legends surrounding Rossetti and develop theories based on evidence and facts. This approach leads to a reinterpretation of Rossetti's later sonnets as reflecting his relationship with Mrs. Morris (wife of William Morris) and his "morbid tendency" to "anxiety" and "at least some aspects of paranoia," overturning the traditional view that Rossetti's wife was the inspiration for the sonnets. Of course, the facts can be and have been interpreted differently by other scholars, and Doughty's claim that his major source for his inferences wished not to be revealed obviously hurts his argument.

Doughty's text is arranged chronologically and presents the Victorian background in detail, which, in turn, draws the reader into the life. This detailed background is indicative of the wide-ranging scholarship and thorough study of a massive amount of material that went into Doughty's work. It includes some of Rossetti's portraits among its illustrations, substantial notes and index sections, and a good select bibliography. Though some of the conclusions are controversial and the later years are sketchy, this remains an indispensable biography. However, other, less lengthy biographies by Grylls and Dobbs (see below) are useful for moderating and updating some of Doughty's views.

GRYLLS, using some previously unavailable letters between Rossetti and Mrs. Morris and some previously unpublished materials uncovered by Lady Mander (including some sketches by Rossetti), offers a highly sympathetic biography that pointedly disagrees with some of Doughty's conclusions (such as his negative view of Mrs. Morris). Included are a chronology, a book list, an index, sources and references, and several appendices, mainly detailing Rossetti's various relationships, including that with Jane Morris, and one containing Rossetti's Last Will and Testament.

DOBBS offers an excellent biography that deals well with Rossetti's relationship with his parents and offers some solid discussions of the Pre-Raphaelite Brotherhood. Though attempts are made to place Rossetti in his environment, this is not so well done as in Doughty, nor are the surrounding personalities handled as clearly. At times, theories are put forth without much support. Nevertheless, Dobbs furnishes a good, concise biography, the one to read if a quick, clear picture is desired. There are a few black-and-white illustrations, notes, and an index.

Among the several partial biographies, family biographies, and memoirs, R. L. Mégroz, *Dante Gabriel Rossetti: Painter Poet of Heaven in Earth* (1928), employs Rossetti's biography in a good discussion of his ideas and work. Robert Cooper, *Lost on Both Sides: Dante Gabriel Rossetti, Critic and Poet* (1970), includes biographical material in a generally poorly supported attempt to deal with Rossetti as a critic. R. D. Waller, *The Rossetti Family* (1932), centers on the career, personality, and literary aspirations of Dante's father. Though not a biography of Dante Gabriel, it does present valuable family context. Many black-and-white pictures of the family and its lodgings are included. Horace Gregory's *The World of James McNeill Whistler* (1959), discusses the relationship between Whistler and Rossetti during the years when "Rossetti in his deepest fits of melancholia believed himself persecuted by Lewis Carroll and felt that he was an object of ridicule in *The Hunting of the Snark*." Stanley Weintraub's *Four Rossettis: A Victorian Biography* (1977) includes well-reproduced illustrations, sources, and an index, in his study that dwells on the sexual/religious schism running through the family.

W. Holman Hunt's *Pre-Raphaelitism and the Pre-Raphaelite Brotherhood* (2 vols., 1906) offers an insider's view of the Pre-Raphaelite movement, partially flawed by its author's need to address his own grievances with Rossetti. It is, nevertheless, a lengthy, detailed account by one of the founding members, and is filled with excellent illustrations.

William Michael Rossetti was a prolific writer, art critic, and propagator of his brother's memory, and many of his works are extremely valuable in understanding Dante Gabriel. William's own thick, two-volume autobiography, *Some Reminiscences of William Michael Rossetti* (1906), supplies excellent background and some direct discussion of Dante Gabriel. He also edited and added an important memoir to the two-volume *Letters of Dante Gabriel Rossetti* (London, 1895).

—Harry Edwin Eiss

ROSSINI, Gioacchino (Antonio), 1792–1868; Italian composer.

Derwent, G. H. J., *Rossini and Some Forgotten Nightingales.* London, Duckworth, 1934.

Edwards, H. Sutherland, *The Life of Rossini.* London, Hurst and Blackett, 1860; revised as *Rossini and His School,* New York, Scribner, and London, Low Marston, 1881.

Harding, Robert, *Rossini.* London, Faber, 1971; New York, T. Y. Crowell, 1972.

Osborne, Richard, *Rossini.* London, Dent, 1986; Boston, Northeastern University Press, 1990.

Stendhal (Marie Henri Beyle), *Life of Rossini,* translated by Richard N. Coe. London, Calder and Boyars, and New York, Orion Press, 1970 (originally published as *Vie de Rossini,* Paris, 1824).

Till, Nicholas, *Rossini, His Life and Times.* Tunbridge Wells, Kent, Midas Books, and New York, Hippocrene Books, 1983.

Toye, Frances, *Rossini: A Study in Tragi-Comedy.* London, Heinemann, and New York, Knopf, 1934.

Weinstock, Herbert, *Rossini: A Biography.* New York, Knopf, and London, Oxford University Press, 1968.

*

The earlist biography of Rossini dates from 1824, written by the French novelist STENDHAL. Despite this biography's having been completed when Rossini himself was only 32 years old, the analysis covers the most crucial period of the composer's early years and includes almost everything that is of lasting musical value in Rossini's work with the exception of *Le Comte Ory, Guillaume Tell,* and the collection of miscellaneous musical satires and cameos entitled *Peches de Vieillesse,* which are amongst the few masterpieces of Rossini's later years. Though unreliable as a purely biographical source and heavily coloured by Stendhal's own personal enthusiasm for Rossini's music, Stendhal's biography remains useful for its contemporary standpoint as it traces the paths and circumstances that account for the composer's popularity within his own lifetime. Stendhal lived for eight to ten years in the same towns and cities as Rossini and was, therefore, in a position to judge the success and failure of individual works. Coe's 1970 translation presents the original text in its complete and unabridged form with all its "footnotes, digressions and irrelevancies, . . . for only by such a translation can the true flavour of Stendhal's masterpiece be preserved." Coe briefly covers the remaining period of Rossini's life in his preface to the translation, mentioning the major works and influences on the composer in his later years.

EDWARDS' biography appeared one year after the composer's death and was the first to be written in English. Although this is a more purely biographical account than Stendhal's and covers the entire period of Rossini's life, it is awkwardly written and less charming to read.

Two distinctive biographies were published simultaneously in 1934 by Toye and Derwent. From their constant references to Radiciotti's Italian account (*Gioacchino Rossini: vita documentata, opere ed influenza su l'arte,* Tivoli, 1927–29), one can assume that both writers were given impetus to produce up-to-date English biographies by that continental contemporary. Lord DERWENT, a keen Italophile of the 1930s, dedicated his book to Henri Beyle (Stendhal). In his foreward he acknowledges Stendhal's historical and biographical inaccuracies but states that these are unimportant in light of the author's enthusiasm ("the delight and fury of Stendhal's interest in Rossini were too absolute for him to trouble over details, . . . I would give all his inexactness for one ounce of the vitality exuded by the merest of his footnotes"). Derwent's book aims to rectify and apologise for Stendhal's previous errors and, in addition, to establish a view of Rossini as a composer inspired by Stendhal. Derwent's account makes flamboyant reading; biographical detail is enshrined in a dense padding of narrative description and subjective commentary and the account is further coloured by Derwent's constant praise and admiration of Stendhal.

TOYE takes a more objective standpoint and in fact criticizes Radiciotti for portraying Rossini as a heroic figure. Toye's narrative creates a happy medium between detail and essential fact, relating numerous anecdotes from Rossini's life with a tongue-in-cheek humour. He is primarily concerned with a biographical account; an analytical approach to the music is confined to the last chapters of the book, where Toye does little more than allude to Rossini's influence, innovations, and style.

HARDING's coffee-table book should be avoided. It offers no detailed account beyond a pictorial potpourri of events within the composer's life, which the author tries wittily and chattily to convey, without success.

All early biographies have been superseded by more trustworthy accounts, the most reliable of which are by Weinstock and Osborne. WEINSTOCK incorporates new material that only came to light with recent research and presents an authoritative picture of opera in Rossini's day. This is the most scholarly of modern biographies written in English, and is divided into chapters that assess successive periods of the composer's life rather than individual operas. It is purely biographical and extensive in its detail behind the planning and first performance of each opera. Weinstock refrains from analysis or comment on Rossini's style and maintains the role of historian throughout.

OSBORNE's account is less purely historical. In the first part (up to page 125) he traces Rossini's career and the evolution of his personality, examining the composer's relations with the leading musicians of his time and the changing pattern of influences and successes down to the present day. Osborne devotes the second point to an analytical assessment of Rossini's operas, though this is kept necessarily general in order to conform to the aims of the Master Musicians series. Biography and analysis are, therefore, dealt with separately, and it is possible to absorb one without having to sift through the other. This account is more comprehensive and less detailed than Weinstock's and is specifically aimed at those who require only a general background to the composer and his works.

A preoccupation with sociological detail characterizes TILL's biography. Using illustrations, contemporary accounts, and documents, Till attempts to explain the reasons for Rossini's popularity and fame. He views the composer's life and works within the context of the period and, in so doing, draws a persuasive picture of musical life in Italy and Europe in the years that followed Napoleon's death. Though not specifically biographical, it is an interesting study by an opera producer (as distinct from a scholar) that succeeds in establishing an understanding of Rossini's approach to dramatic writing.

—L. J. Maxwell-Stewart

ROUSSEAU, Henri, 1844–1910; French painter.

Rich, Daniel C., *Henri Rousseau.* New York, Museum of Modern Art, 1942; revised edition, 1946.

Shattuck, Roger, *The Banquet Years: The Arts in France 1885–1913: Alfred Jarry, Henri Rousseau, Erik Satie, Guillaume Apollinaire.* New York, Harcourt, and London, Faber, 1958; revised as *The Banquet Years: Origins of the Avant-Garde in France 1885 to World War II,* New York, Vintage, 1968; London, Cape, 1969.

Vallier, Dora, *Henri Rousseau.* New York, Abrams, and London, Thames and Hudson, 1964 (originally published by Flammarion, Paris, 1961).

Werner, Alfred, *Rousseau/Dufy.* New York, Tudor Publishing, 1970.

*

VALLIER's *Henri Rousseau* remains the most important monograph on Rousseau. Sorting through the often fictionalized accounts of Rousseau and such contemporaries and friends as Apollinaire and Jarry, all of whom purposely distorted the facts of Rousseau's life in pursuit of their art and philosophy, Vallier presents as accurate a biography of Rousseau as is likely to appear.

Vallier points out that, though some documentation can be affirmed, such as Rousseau's birth certificate, court records of his petty thefts as a youth, military records offering a description of his physical appearance (the indication of a scarred left ear has caused much speculation), marriage certificates, programs of performance, photographs, a few of his letters, and records of his exhibitions, many of the more famous incidents revealing what he was like remain a mixture of fact and fantasy. For example, Vallier indicates that Rousseau claimed to have fought in the Mexican War, and that Apollinaire supported the claim, but that it has since been established by Henri Certigny that this could not have been true.

Vallier's study also offers color reproductions and analyses of Rousseau's works, excerpts from the two plays he wrote, lists of the works he exhibited at the Salon des Independants, the Salon d'Automne, and the other exhibitions, a chronology of his life, a bibliography, and an index of names.

While not devoted specifically to Rousseau, SHATTUCK's volume gives an excellent overview of Rousseau's world by concentrating on four representative men of the *avant-garde* in France from 1885–1918. As with Vallier, Shattuck concerns himself with sorting out the legends from the reality. And as with Vallier, he must finally offer probable truths. What exactly was Rousseau's part in the famous fraud perpetrated by Sauvaget, for which Rousseau was put on trial? Shattuck points out that it all comes down to how one judges Rousseau's personality and mind set. Was Rousseau simply naive, innocent, as he portrayed himself throughout his life? Or was he an extremely clever con-artist? Shattuck claims, as does Vallier, that Rousseau's own personality and the personality of the *avant-garde* make it extremely difficult, perhaps impossible, ever to know for sure.

Shattuck further discusses this mixture of legend and reality that surrounds Rousseau as it appears in the infamous banquet for Rousseau at Picasso's studio, a wild party, either a joke on Rousseau or a tribute to him, or quite possibly an example of the Dada activities to come. Once again, Vallier discusses the same incident with similar views.

Shattuck's book has several reproductions of Rousseau's work and some photographs of Rousseau, but they are of poor quality, not nearly as well done as those in Vallier's book. Shattuck's book also has a decent bibliography, but only more valuable than Vallier's in that it includes more materials on the time period, which, in general, is what Shattuck offers to complement Vallier.

WERNER, contributing editor to *Arts Magazine,* has a small book out called *Rousseau/Dufy* that includes a biography of each. Werner portrays Rousseau as a naive man, devoted to his art, who manages to recapture a childhood vision. The book includes several color reproductions of Rousseau's work. Neither the biography nor the reproductions are close to the quality of Vallier's.

RICH's study of Rousseau was prepared to accompany an exhibition of his work arranged in 1942 by the Art Institute of Chicago and the Museum of Modern Art in New York. It pictures Rousseau not as a naive eccentric but as an artist significant in his own right. Some black-and-white and two-color reproductions are included, but they are of poor quality. A brief bibliography and a chronology are also included. The biography is brief but well thought out, and it can serve as a good introduction to Rousseau and some of his work.

Many anthologies and other works on modern art include brief discussions of Rousseau and his work. One of the better treatments is *A History of Modern Art: Painting, Sculpture, Architecture* (1968), by H. H. Arnason. There are also several important works on Rousseau in French that have received wide acclaim: W. Uhde, *Henri Rousseau* (1914), C. Zervos, *Henri Rousseau* (1927), and H. Certigny, *La Vérité sur le Douanier Rousseau* (1961).

—Harry Edwin Eiss

ROUSSEAU, Jean-Jacques, 1712–1778; Swiss-born French writer and philosopher.

Blanchard, William H., *Rousseau and the Spirit of Revolt: A Psychological Study.* Ann Arbor, University of Michigan Press, 1987.

Cranston, Maurice, *Jean-Jacques: The Early Life and Work of Jean-Jacques Rousseau 1712–54.* London, A. Lane, and New York, Norton, 1983.

Crocker, Lester, *Jean-Jacques Rousseau* (2 vols.). New York, Macmillan, 1968–73.

Green, F. C., *Jean-Jacques Rousseau: A Critical Study of His Life and Writings.* Cambridge, Cambridge University Press, 1955.

Grimsley, Ronald, *Jean-Jacques Rousseau: A Study in Self-Awareness.* Cardiff, University of Wales Press, 1961.

Grimsley, Ronald, *Rousseau and the Religious Quest.* Oxford, Clarendon Press, 1968.

Guéhenno, Jean, *Jean-Jacques Rousseau* (2 vols.). London, Routledge, and New York, Columbia University Press, 1966 (originally published as *Jean-Jacques,* Paris, Grasset, 1948–52).

*

Rousseau's enigmatic personality, his uncertain attitude to both nature and social organization, his psychological maladjustment, the apparent contradictions between liberal and totalitarian elements in his political thought, the sheer comprehensiveness of his written output, and his passionately felt need for self-revelation have attracted an unusually large number of biographers, many of whose works are available in English. Rousseau's status among English-language readers is evidenced by the fact that his vast correspondence of some 6000 letters in 35 volumes is being edited in England by R. A. Leigh (1965–).

Little attempt was made in the 19th century to reconcile the "romantic" Rousseau, who seemed to extol the unbridled rights of the individual to act in communion with an inner prompting, and the political theoretician who, however much he intended to follow Locke's liberalism, was thought partly to have laid the foundations for a dictatorial tyranny such as was seen during the French Revolution. Toward the end of the century the liberal and positivist reactions to Romanticism prompted a re-examination of Rousseau's work based on greater knowledge and less hostility (Lord Morley, 1873; Fauguet and Lanson, 1899). From 1905 onward appeared the series of *Annales* of the Société Jean-Jacques Rousseau, although a long series of hostile analyses was still to appear until after World War I (Lemaître, Seillière, Gide, Daudet, Maurras, Ducros) alongside the now sometimes obsolete defences (Frederika Macdonald, Dumur, Mornet, Baldensperger).

The attacks continued to flow from famous pens, especially on the Catholic side, in books that are still read (J. Maritain, 1925; F. Mauriac, 1929). C. A. Fusil thought Rousseau a charlatan in a famous trilogy (1923, 1929, 1932) and P. Carton thought him paranoid as recently as 1937. Meanwhile the biographical facts were being carefully assembled by Courtois (1923), Richebourg (1934) and by several important contributors to the *Annales.* Interest was also intensifying outside France. Much new biographical information as well as new critical assessments came from introductions and notes to editions of the works, notably in England from the authoritative edition by C. E. Vaughan of *The Political Writings of J.-J. Rousseau* (1915). Two other fundamental works, not available in English, should be mentioned, P. M. Masson's *La Religion de Rousseau* (1916) and R. Derathé's *Rousseau et la science politique de son temps*

(1951). An edition of the letters was published in 20 volumes from 1924 to 1934. By 1941 a survey of work on Rousseau by A. Schinz ran to 400 pages.

The first serious modern biographies available in English are the *Rousseau* of C. E. Vulliamy (1931), followed by R. B. Mowat (1938) and, dwarfing its predecessors in scholarship, comprehensiveness, and readability, the two volumes by GUÉHENNO. Guéhenno sets out more faithfully than most from Rousseau's own autobiographical accounts of himself and of the events of his life, adding in evidence of his thought from the two *Discours, La Nouvelle Heloíse,* and *Emile* and of his daily preoccupations from the *Correspondance,* giving a strictly chronological account of his life that does not draw on evidence later in date than that from the period reached in the biography. Guéhenno set out to reconstitute a life in narrative, and he has produced one of the great biographies of the last half-century, combining lightly carried scholarship of a very high order with a human sympathy for its subject, understanding and narrating the humiliations and the triumphs, moving us to admiration and pity for Rousseau and responding sensitively to the vibrating passion of the self-revelatory prose, especially when, as we know from elsewhere, Rousseau has falsified the self-revelation. Guéhenno is also admirably restrained in his exposition of Rousseau's tortured psychology and the roots in his childhood of the attitudes and ineptitudes that Rousseau preserved throughout the vicissitudes of his later life.

What gives this biography its stature is the accumulated scholarship underlying the evocative portrait of Rousseau as he ages from the small boy to the prematurely old man. It is not unusual for biographers to reconstruct places, atmospheres, and events after the manner of historical novelists, hoping that their conjectures about situations and feelings have not led them too far astray. Guéhenno could, on the other hand, have quoted a reference for virtually every sentence he writes. The style is elegant, the touch light, the tone authoritative, and there is nothing of mere conjecture in the reconstitution of Rousseau's dreams and anxieties. All French passages appear in translation.

GREEN's work is also important, more speculative than Guéhenno on the psychology of its subject and its intrusion into the writings, as also on the social constraints Rousseau clearly felt. Green is particularly strong on Rousseau's insights into his own moral state, and on the importance to him of his bladder condition, although neither the psychology nor the physiology is considered to have had more than incidental relevance for Rousseau's thought in either its fictional or its non-fictional expression. Although Green's biography has been criticized for going in places beyond what can be supported by evidence, he is not merely fanciful. The apparent contradictions in the final text of *Du contrat social,* which Rousseau himself thought "une oeuvre à refaire," do however confuse Green, and he shows an inexact grasp of the genesis of that work as well as a lack of awareness of some of the 16th-century intellectual traditions on which Rousseau depended, including those of Montaigne and Althusius.

The two books by GRIMSLEY can be seen as an attempt to right the anti-rationalistic bias of P.-M. Masson's three volumes on Rousseau's religion half a century earlier. Grimsley's earlier work (1961) starts off with two chapters out of eight devoted to the early psychological development and, although the intention is autobiographical—"to trace the development of self-awareness''—Grimsley's method is inadequate. He tends to illustrate his interpretations rather than conclude from his analyses, inevitably ending up by blurring the portrait of his subject. He concentrates naturally on the personal writings, going so far as to skirt the necessarily sterile debate about the ''existentialism'' of Rousseau's philosophy. Grimsley's second biographical essay (1969), primarily devoted to Rousseau's ''religion,'' complements its predecessor and has a more direct relevance to Masson, much as J. H. Broome's semi-biographical *Rousseau: A Study of His Thought* (1963) also complements Grimsley's earlier work in a different direction, concentrating on Rousseau's worldview as expressed piecemeal throughout his major works rather than on his personal experience as such.

Rousseau's psychological make-up is the avowed focus of BLANCHARD's study. Blanchard regards Rousseau's psychology as the key to his ''politics of revolution'' and claims that Rousseau's ''childhood sado-masochism'' evolved into the ''moral foundation for his adult personality.'' The resulting biography, mixing Freudian categories with sociology, interprets Rousseau's character somewhat superficially as centered on a ''peculiar groveling arrogance.'' Perhaps Blanchard's error was the deliberate avoidance of psychoanalytical terminology. The whole tenor of his argument requires expertise in psychoanalytical theory and practice.

CROCKER's two-volume biography of Rousseau forms part of Crocker's depiction of the whole French Enlightenment spread over a number of works. This biography is less well written and less well informed than Guéhenno's, but it refers openly to a wide variety of sources, and its wider perspectives allow Rousseau's life to serve as a link connecting comments on all aspects of the history of ideas in 18th-century France. Crocker makes frequent reference to psychological and sociological concepts. Although a fascinating picture of Rousseau emerges from these volumes, Crocker does not make clear exactly where Rousseau's greatness lay or how fiercely original his theoretical writings sometimes were. The psychological explanations adduced are inferior substitutes for the closer academic or literary analysis called for by so powerful and original a subject.

CRANSTON's book on Rousseau is the work of an accomplished biographer whose work on Locke is a classic of the genre. The few French quotations are not translated, but the book is learned, intelligent, thoroughly readable, and based on a deep understanding of the period. Cranston is understandably dismissive of the ''kind of patronizing psychological explanation'' from earlier biographies too dependent on Rousseau's own *Confessions*, and he successfully provides a more ''systematically reasonable'' biography, as factual as possible, based on the original sources rather than the accumulated folklore. The text is refreshingly factual without being weighted down by detail, but it may be considered somewhat too detached and cool for its colourful and tormented subject. Excellently informed, perfectly balanced, dry almost to a fault, it suffers only from an excessive lack of that passion that on the whole spoiled the attempts of so many previous biographers.

—A. H. T. Levi

RUBENS, Peter Paul, 1577–1640; Flemish painter.

Avermaete, Roger, *Rubens and His Times*, translated by Christine Trollope. New York, A. S. Barnes, and London, Allen and Unwin, 1968 (originally published by Éditions Brepols, Brussels, 1964).

Baudouin, Frans, *Pietro Paulo Rubens*, translated by Elsie Callander. New York, Abrams, 1977.

Burckhardt, Jacob, *Recollections of Rubens*, edited by H. Gerson, translated by Mary Hottinger, R. H. Boothroyd, and I. Grafe. London, Phaidon, 1950.

Cabanne, Pierre, *Rubens*, translated by Oliver Bernard. New York, Tudor, and London, Thames and Hudson, 1967 (originally published by A. Somogy, Paris, 1966).

Cammaerts, Émile, *Rubens, Painter and Diplomat*. London, Faber, 1932.

Edwards, Samuel, *Peter Paul Rubens: A Biography of a Giant*. New York, D. McKay, 1973.

Fletcher, Jennifer, *Peter Paul Rubens*. London, Phaidon, and New York, Praeger, 1968.

Held, Julius S., *The Oil Sketches of Peter Paul Rubens, A Critical Catalog* (2 vols.). Princeton, New Jersey, and London, Princeton University Press, 1980.

Held, Julius S., *Rubens and His Circle*. Princeton, New Jersey, and London, Princeton University Press, 1982.

Michel, Emile, *Rubens, His Life, His Work, and His Time* (2 vols.). London, Heinemann, and New York, Scribner, 1899.

Muller, Jeffrey M., *Rubens: The Artist as Collector*. Princeton, New Jersey, and London, Princeton University Press, 1989.

Ripley, Elizabeth, *Rubens: A Biography*. New York, H. Z. Walck, 1957.

Wedgwood, C. V., *The World of Rubens 1577–1640*. New York, Time-Life Books, 1967.

White, Christopher, *Rubens and His World*. New York, Viking, and London, Thames and Hudson, 1968.

White, Christopher, *Peter Paul Rubens, Man and Artist*. New Haven, Connecticut, and London, Yale University Press, 1987.

*

The enormous number of essays and books covering the life and works of Peter Paul Rubens constitutes a small cottage industry in itself. Of these, the 15 volumes listed above offer the best selection available in English.

A two-volume work of 1899 by MICHEL presents a stately account of Rubens' life interwoven with commentary on the most important works. Michel's principle reference is the 1681 version of *La vie de Rubens* by R. de Piles, which was based on the memoirs of Phillip Rubens, nephew of the artist. This fascinating volume gives a glimpse of the type of opinionated biographical investigations that have been discarded in most modern analyses. A case in point is Michel's speculation that the figures in the small *Visitation* found in the Borghese Palace could be identified as the parents of Rubens' first wife, Isabella Brandt. Although there is no documentation for this supposition, Michel's passionate eloquence convinces the reader of its truth; and sadly, therein lies the main flaw of the work. Sources are rare, and it is difficult to discern facts among the theories. For the scholar, Michel's work is a valuable reference tool for the comparison of styles and methods in historical biography, but one must look to more modern research texts to find complete documentation. For today's reader, the randomly placed sepia reproductions lend little to the text, for they are copies of engravings of the paintings. However, the work serves to provide a starting point for serious Rubens studies by recounting the main elements of his life in a literary style.

AVERMAETE, on the other hand, states that his purpose is to strip away the myths surrounding the life of Rubens in order to reveal the true man. The result is a negative assessment of Rubens' personality and achievements in the artistic and diplomatic world of the 17th century that completely contradicts the documented accounts of the artist's contemporaries. This book stands outside the mainstream of Rubens biography in viewing the artist as a cynical manipulator, when all other accounts of Rubens indicate the opposite. Avermaete's theory is based on his belief that the misadventures of Jan Rubens, the painter's father, with Anna of Saxony, wife of William the Silent, caused the painter to spend his life distancing himself from those sordid adulterous circumstances. As with Michel, there are no footnotes or bibliography included with this book, so documented instances bolstering the author's conjectures are not provided.

Among the best biographies for the general reader is WHITE's *Rubens and His World* (1968), a shorter version of the later, more scholarly *Peter Paul Rubens, Man and Artist* (see below) by the same author. With its lively voice and precise accounts of the many events in Rubens' life, this work offers an excellent choice. White thoughtfully includes in this volume illustrations of influential patrons along with comparative illustrations placed at reasonable intervals in the text. Good color plates with crisp black-and-white reproductions coupled with a chronology of the life help make this one of the best beginning references.

EDWARDS, too, has produced a memorable biography, but his volume concentrates on the ramifications of the events in the artist's early life. It stresses the strength of Rubens' mother, Maria Pypelinckx Rubens, in facing the unrelenting danger that followed the family from the time of Jan Rubens' adultery until the death of this foolish man. Edwards concludes that Rubens' successes in both the artistic and political sphere were based on the lessons of bravery and confidence learned from the example of his mother's actions during this unfortunate period. This thought-provoking work sadly lacks documentation and leaves many questions unanswered about the nature of the evidence for Edwards' premises. CAMMAERTS glosses over these same incidents and chooses to concentrate on the artistic and diplomatic triumphs. The author's glowing references to Rubens' fame helps a general reader to realize the importance of the artist's place in official diplomatic circles as well as his elevated status at many of the European courts. In contrast, RIPLEY's volume reduces Rubens' life to the proportions of a formula film script, with virtue and compassion rewarded with fame, riches, and two beautiful wives.

For detailed, in-depth studies of Rubens' life that include documentation and bibliographic references, two important works can be recommended, those of Baudouin and White (1987).

BAUDOUIN, curator of the Rubens House at the time of publication, provides an exciting look at the biographical facts of Rubens' life combined with a thorough understanding of the modern aesthetic criteria from which his life and works can be examined. His stated aim is to produce a work that will "lead to closer contact with the personality of the man and with his art." Baudouin succeeds eloquently. The text flows smoothly between the tasks of linking Rubens' life with artistic developments of the Baroque era. He carefully points out the importance of the Roman years in shaping not only the Mannerist elements in the paintings but the deliberate Italianate customs adopted for Rubens' own life in Antwerp and Steen. As in all good scholarly volumes, the excellent color plates and the small black-and-white pictures correspond directly to the individual discussions in the text. An extensive documents list, a bibliography, and several indexes are provided for the serious reader.

WHITE (1987) also provides excellent notes in his volume, although the text is not as detailed as that of Baudouin. White focuses here on the interrelationship between Rubens and his patrons, citing evidence of mutual agreement and respect between the artist and the Archduke Albert and the Archduchess Isabella at their court in Brussels and the subsequent benefits of these friendships in Rubens' life. White also clearly explains the artist's commitment to the Jesuits and the tenets of Counter Reformation with its need for dramatic ecclesiastical compositions of the highest degree. Rubens was a devout Catholic, faithful throughout his life to church doctrine. Individual art works supporting this theme are scattered among those represented in the excellent color plates.

The remaining volumes offer biographical information in conjunction with stylistic analysis of Rubens' paintings. BURCKHARDT concentrates on examining the pictures from an historical perspective, commenting on their importance in Rubens' career advancement. Burckhardt's elegant writing style and his inclusion of a selection of letters from the artist's hand make this book a joy to read. However, true to the scholarly customs of the time, scant mention of sources beyond the sampling of letters is available. WEDGWOOD's work is part of the Time-Life series on great artists, with both the writing style and the content aimed at the general reading public. However, one of the virtues of this series is its succinct coupling of biographical information with explanations of the works, resulting in a good basic reference. In addition to Wedgwood, the volume by FLETCHER, with its 50 color plates, edited chronology, and selected catalog, is specifically aimed at the budding reader who is interested in the life of this great painter. A lucid style combined with an orderly arrangement of biographical detail make this a valuable source.

CABANNE stresses the early Manneristic elements in Rubens' art and explains how his true international style evolved from his assimilation of techniques learned from studying the masterpieces in Italy combined with his training in the strong Northern tradition of detailed representation. Cabanne's critical comments are interspersed with specific events from Rubens' life. Some black-and-white illustrations and color plates, a short bibliography, and footnotes are included.

The role of the artist as collector is examined in depth in MULLER's volume. Clearly researched with extensive notes, the book focuses on Rubens' status in Antwerp and the importance to his career of his reputation as an expert on the antique. The examples cited by Muller to bolster his arguments are marred only by the unfortunate placement of the illustrations at the book's conclusion. Otherwise, Muller offers a unique perspective on an important aspect of Rubens' personal and professional life.

HELD's two works center on Rubens' paintings. *Rubens and His Circle* (1982) incorporates 15 articles covering major issues in the works. In it Held examines the sources of Rubens' themes that are repeated time and again in the portraits, the mythological paintings, and the private religious works that were produced without commission restrictions. The two-volume edition of Held's *The Oil Sketches of Peter Paul Rubens* (1980) is also an important source for scholarly interpretation of connections between Rubens' life and his paintings. Meticulously researched and superbly organized, the edition provides extensive notes for the serious scholar as well as carefully chosen examples of the oil sketches for comparison. Held's studies help us to understand the correlation between Rubens' life and times and his works. No investigation of the artist's life could be complete without reading the works of Julius Held.

—Linda K. Varkonda

RUSKIN, John, 1819–1900; English critic, essayist, and social theorist.

Benson, Arthur C., *Ruskin: A Study in Personality.* London, Smith Elder, and New York, Putnam, 1911.

Collingwood, W. G., *The Life and Work of John Ruskin* (2 vols.). London, Methuen, 1893.

Cook, E. T., *The Life of John Ruskin* (2 vols.). London, Allen, and New York, Macmillan, 1911.

Evans, Joan, *John Ruskin.* London, Cape, and New York, Oxford University Press, 1954.

Hilton, Tim, *John Ruskin* (2 vols.). New Haven, Connecticut, and London, Yale University Press, 1985- (volume I subtitled *The Early Years 1819–59*).

Hunt, John Dixon, *The Wider Sea: A Life of John Ruskin.* London, Dent, and New York, Viking, 1982.

Larg, David, *John Ruskin.* London, P. Davies, 1932; New York, Appleton, 1933.

Leon, Derrick, *Ruskin, the Great Victorian.* London, Routledge, 1949.

Lutyens, Mary, *Millais and the Ruskins.* London, J. Murray, and New York, Vanguard, 1967.

Quennell, Peter, *John Ruskin: Portrait of a Prophet.* London, Collins, and New York, Viking, 1949.

Wilenski, Reginald H., *John Ruskin: An Introduction to Further Study of His Life and Work.* London, Faber, and New York, F. A. Stokes, 1933.

Wingate, Ashmore K. P., *Life of John Ruskin.* London, W. Scott, 1910.

*

Few 19th-century lives present as many problems for the biographer as that of Ruskin. *Praeterita* (3 vols., 1886–89) is a great autobiography, but also a misleading one; the subtlety of the man's mind, the powerful ambivalence of his emotions, and the notoriety of his marital affairs combine to make a balanced judgment difficult. COLLINGWOOD, Ruskin's private secretary, published while Ruskin was still in the grip of his final madness. He sees him as a noble victim of his own passionate, prophetic spirit. Images of Jacob wrestling with the angel, and Savonarola denouncing sin are used to proclaim him too great and wonderful for the time; and, like several later writers, Collingwood sees the late essay *The Storm-Cloud of the 19th Century* as at once emblematic of his overburdened descent into madness, and illustrative of his prophetic protest against industrial England. He sees it as paradoxical that Ruskin, while he really followed the traditions of his parents, grieved them by seeming not to. His treatment of Ruskin's marriage to Effie is hasty and unconvincing, presenting it as an arranged match that Ruskin never desired.

WINGATE's comparatively slight work is favourable to Ruskin's father, and distinctly hostile to Effie. It has a rapidly dated Edwardian modernity and superiority to the Victorians. BENSON, a prolific writer, and a clever man, probably did not pursue any deep researches, saw Ruskin as a moralist above all, though at the same time, rather oddly, asserting that in youth he "gave the Philistine public what it wanted." This public, he thought, failed (except for a few more perceptive spirits) to recognize a "passionate emotion and a sincere fidelity to truth, only obscured by natural dogmatism and rigid Calvinistic training." It is a view that fails to take full account of Ruskin's long and complex development.

COOK, the editor of the enormous Library edition of Ruskin's works, produced the standard two-volume life, which appeared, for a time, to be definitive. It coincided also with a period of unfashionableness for Ruskin as for other great Victorians, when his art criticism, especially, was despised or ignored. It was hardly surprising that no very notable work followed for some 20 years. Cook sees Ruskin's father as the source of his artistic interests, and his mother the source of his religion. But he shows his gradual rejection of his mother's extreme Protestantism, and emergence, under the influence of Italian religious art and the spirit of Assisi, into a "religion of humanity," which included a lively appreciation of Catholicism. Cook plays down the story of the marriage and annulment, assessing the emotional residue as small.

In 1929, copious new sources of information began to become available, when Helen Viljeon found at Brantwood unknown diaries and letters. This discovery, and the publication a little later of WILENSKI's psychological analysis of Ruskin's madness, inaugurated a new period in Ruskin studies, and later writers have generally seen him as altogether more enigmatic and mysterious than earlier ones.

The effects of all this were felt only gradually, however. LARG's volume is only a sketch, with facts taken from Cook. But the post-war revival of literary interest was reflected in a renewal of biographical enquiry. QUENNELL saw Ruskin as marred permanently by his childhood need both for love and friendship. Effie is presented as a bemused but patient victim of his emotional incapacity. Quennell is the first writer to stress the guilt of masturbation as a destructive influence. Because, his argument runs, Ruskin could not avoid this deep association between guilt and pleasure, he was unable to link love and pleasure in a normal way; hence both his refusal to consummate the marriage and his immensely powerful but frustrated emotions about young girls. He is sympathetic and eloquent in his account of the concluding madness.

LEON's book was unrevised at his death, but, when allowance is made for this, it is still fair to say that it has an undeserved reputation. The reader is put off by silly chapter headings like "The Sun is God"—an extraordinary soubriquet for Ruskin's devoutly Protestant phase—or "The Fair Maid of Perth." In judgment Leon is curiously timid, giving no coherent view at all of the disputed points, such as the influence of parents, the marriage, and the causes of madness. When Ruskin is obviously being sophistical, as in his paradoxical defence of Governor Eyre, Leon allows his arguments to stand uncriticized.

EVANS, one of the editors of Ruskin's diaries, wrote as an art critic, and thus gives less weight than some would judge right to the social criticism. She is perhaps too inclined at certain points to rely on the evidence of *Praeterita*. But, if these are blemishes at all, they are minor ones. Her book is the best since Cook, and, in some ways, an advance on him. She can be severe, as when she says: "Rome was too great for Ruskin's comprehension. He was remarkably ill-read in its ancient history, and remarkably prejudiced in his attitude to Popery." Ruskin's mother is seen as a constantly lurking and baleful presence; she notes and convincingly interprets the "breathless" character of the letters to Effie during the engagement period, and sees Effie as waiting anxiously, and for a long time patiently, for signs that her husband was becoming less dependent on his parents. She makes a poignant contrast between the power of Ruskin's intellect and the futile bickerings that ensued. Ruskin, she thinks, unconsciously desired a child-wife, when really Effie was more mature than he. Her Ruskin is at all times selfish, and never more so than in his passion for Rose La Touche. She stresses his devotion to the Bible through all his vicissitudes of belief, but sees his reading of it as fostering a lonely and superstitious kind of religion, which proved a powerful check on Catholic impulses.

HUNT takes his title from Tintoretto's painter's view of the sea. His book is, in the main, an intellectual history. It suffers from a self-conscious and now dated modernity, with extensive quotations from 20th-century poets. Hunt sees Ruskin as manipulating his public influence with great deliberation, and seems to underrate the sturdy independence of Ruskin's character, well shown in his contempt for gossip and scandal at the time of the annulment proceedings. LUTYENS provides a useful subsidiary study of the marriage. She writes as the editor of Effie's letters and is more interested in Effie and Millais than in Ruskin himself. She stresses Millais' suspicion of Ruskin's motives, which some, including Gladstone, thought to be unjustified.

HILTON's work cannot be properly judged until his second volume is published, since he says that his main stress will fall on the later years, which he considers less known and less well understood than the early ones. He is clearly aiming at a new synthesis, and believes that the authority of Cook and the great Library Edition of Ruskin's works is still harmful to true understanding.

—A. O. J. Cockshut

RUSSELL, Bertrand (Arthur William), 3rd Earl Russell, 1872–1970; English philosopher, mathematician, and social critic.

Ayer, Alfred Jules, *Bertrand Russell as a Philosopher*. London, Oxford University Press, 1972; as *Bertrand Russell*, New York, Viking, 1972.

Clark, Ronald W., *The Life of Bertrand Russell*. New York, Knopf, and London, Cape/Weidenfeld and Nicolson, 1975.

Crawshay-Williams, Rupert, *Russell Remembered*. Oxford and New York, Oxford University Press, 1970.

Gottshalk, Herbert, *Bertrand Russell: A Life*, translated by Edward Fitzgerald. London, J. Baker, 1964; New York, Roy, 1965 (originally published by Colloquium Verlag, Berlin, 1962).

Hardy, Geoffrey H., *Bertrand Russell and Trinity*. Privately printed, Cambridge, 1942; London, Cambridge University Press, 1970.

Kallen, Horace M. and John Dewey, *The Bertrand Russell Case*. New York, Viking, 1941.

Kuntz, Paul G., *Bertrand Russell*. Boston, Twayne, 1986.

Russell, Dora, *The Tamarisk Tree: My Quest for Liberty and Love*. London, Elek, and New York, Dutton, 1975.

Tait, Katherine, *My Father, Bertrand Russell*. New York, Harcourt, 1975; London, Gollancz, 1976.

Vellacott, Jo, *Bertrand Russell and the Pacifists in the First World War*. London, Harvester Press, 1980; New York, St. Martin's, 1981.

Wood, Alan, *Bertrand Russell, the Passionate Skeptic: A Biography*. London, Allen and Unwin, 1957; New York, Simon and Schuster, 1958.

*

Bertrand Russell's prolific career and intriguing life have presented researchers with an embarrassment of riches. At the same time, however, biographers have had to confront the formidable task of reconciling the public Russell with the private man, while attempting to place their subject within an historical framework seemingly inadequate to contain him. Most biographers, evidently daunted by the challenge, have opted to focus on discrete aspects of either Russell's life or his works, without managing to connect one with the other.

AYER's study, part of the Modern Masters series, provides a concise and simplified interpretation of Russell's writings, yet it is not a simplistic work. Nor should its brevity be construed as a sign of superficiality. As Wykeham Professor of Logic at Oxford, Ayer is well qualified to tackle the job before him. Not surprisingly, he concentrates on Russell's intellectual contributions while devoting only 27 pages to an actual biography. As a result of his efforts, Ayer has succeeded in making Russell's complex philosophy accessible to the general reader. Arguably, however, Russell had already done that himself. Still, Ayer offers a convenient survey that is a good starting point for undergraduates.

GOTTSHALK's work is, on the other hand, a feeble walk through a tangled subject. Though he tries to attain a balanced perspective, the result is tentative and unsatisfying. It is sad and ironic that Gottshalk views Russell with such obvious reverence, when his work fails to persuade the reader of Russell's significance. He provides no clarifying or supportive evidence for many of his statements. For example, Gottshalk writes that Russell "sought to make mathematical logic the basis of philosophy," but instead of expanding on this important point, he undermines it by merely adding that Russell's view has subsequently come into doubt. Apparently, the reader is expected to accept such statements on faith, a notion that would have been anathema to Russell.

Stylistically, Gottshalk's work is cumbersome, but this may be the fault of the translation. There is a disturbing dearth of citations—a problem, curiously enough, that is shared by a number of Russell's biographers. Further, the work provides neither an index nor a bibliography. Because of these shortcomings, Gottshalk is not recommended.

As a self-styled corrective to the problem of viewing Russell and his work as separate entities, KUNTZ offers the most recent intellectual biography of the philosopher. A professor of philosophy at Emory University, Kuntz, like Ayer, capably analyzes Russell's achievements. But he is not an historian and despite his good intentions, he also fails to produce a complete and unified vision. Indeed, Russell's long and extraordinarily productive life has been absurdly encapsulated into a mere six-page chronology. Nevertheless, this is a scholarly monograph, predicated on a wide reading of the source material. It is, perhaps, too advanced for the general reader, for whom Ayer is still the best introduction. For a more specialized readership, though, Kuntz merits attention.

Another group of studies concentrates not on Russell's works but rather on particular events in which he played a significant part. While not biographies per se, they deserve brief mention because they provide researchers with some clues to the puzzle of Russell's life. The best study among this group is VELLACOTT's. While she offers a well-researched history of pacifism in Britain, Vellacott also paints an insightful portrait of Bertrand Russell as he entered a new stage in his life, that of social activist and public man. G. H. HARDY, the eminent Cambridge mathematician, wrote a short account of the breach that occurred between Russell and Trinity College following Russell's pacifist activities during World War I. Though written first as a pamphlet for private circulation, it is useful to scholars as it sheds light on a widely misunderstood episode in Russell's life. In a related vein, KALLEN AND DEWEY focus on the issues of Russell's academic freedom and civil rights, which they argue were violated as a result of the philosopher's controversial opinions.

The next group of works includes personal memoirs. CRAWSHAY-WILLIAMS, a longtime friend of Russell's, penned his remembrance for the purpose of refuting allegations that Russell, for all his benevolent public demeanor, was a cold, unfeeling individual, a brilliant mind bereft of any real understanding of people. Even more than Crawshay-Williams, TAIT provides the reader with direct access to the very private Russell. Though his daughter, Tait reveals an ambivalence in her portrait that is absent in more hagiographic studies, Crawshay-Williams among them. This lends Tait a greater credibility. Her vision is of a complex, enigmatic man who, though intimidating, inspired great loyalty and love. She points out that Russell's friendships with men were often warm, easy, and of long duration, which further helps to explain Crawshay-Williams' perspective. On the other hand, Russell's relationships with women, though numer-

ous, were not as close or as satisfactory, a view supported in the memoirs of Russell's second wife, DORA RUSSELL. Tait shows that a wide and painful gulf also existed between Russell and his children. It is clear that she earnestly strives for a truthful picture of her father, however unflattering it might be. It is therefore disturbing that she relies so heavily on his voluminous *Autobiography* (3 vols., 1967–69) for her own understanding, for despite Russell's lifelong search for objective truth, his autobiography, like all others, reveals a selective memory and, by definition, a strong bias. What is more annoying is that Tait does not cite the passages she has taken from his writings. Though some reviewers have regarded Tait's memoir to be rather frivolous and more revealing of the author than of her father, her book is useful in fleshing out the hitherto sketchy figure that has been drawn of Russell the man.

The final corpus of works comprises standard biographical studies, the most comprehensive and scholarly being CLARK's. In over 700 pages, Clark covers virtually every aspect of Russell's life and career, finally bringing together the man and his work in a useful historical context. This monograph is based on an extensive use of primary and secondary source materials, some of which have been previously unobtainable. It is, and probably shall remain, the definitive biography of Russell. WOOD, a student of philosophy and a protégé of Russell, offers yet another adulatory tribute. It is an engaging work, predicated on a great deal of anecdotal material gleaned from conversations with Russell's contemporaries as well as from Wood's own acquaintance with the philosopher. Despite this wealth of personal material, and perhaps from a sense of loyalty to Lord and Lady Russell, very little insight is gained into Russell's domestic life. Only the public man is discussed. As is true of several of the other books mentioned above, Wood does not encumber his account with documentation—a maddening omission. The great weaknesses of this biography are Wood's poor skills at historical interpretation coupled with his inability to move beyond his personal biases. These flaws undercut the entire book. Though Wood does make a contribution to an understanding of Russell, it is neither the first nor the best choice.

—Donna Price Paul

SADAT, Anwar al-, 1918–1981; Egyptian president.

Fernández-Armesto, Felipe, *Sadat and His Statescraft*. London, Kensal Press, 1982.

Heikal, Muhamad, *Autumn of Fury: The Assassination of Sadat*. New York, Random House, and London, Deutsch, 1983.

Hirst, David and Irene Beeson, *Sadat*. London, Faber, 1981.

Israeli, Raphael, with Carol Bardenstein, *Man of Defiance: A Political Biography of Anwar Sadat*. New York, Barnes and Noble, and London, Weidenfeld and Nicolson, 1985.

Narayan, B.K., *Anwar el Sadat: Man with a Mission*. New Delhi, Vikas Publishing House, 1977.

Shoukra, Ghali, *Egypt, Portrait of a President 1971-81: The Counter-Revolution in Egypt; Sadat's Road to Jerusalem*. London, Zed, 1981.

Sullivan, George, *Sadat: The Man who Changed Middle-Eastern History*. New York, Walker, 1981.

*

The biographies of Anwar al-Sadat are for the most part clustered around the year of his assassination. Written by countrymen, friends, and Middle East experts, they are all by necessity political biographies, dealing more or less effectively with Sadat's impact on world history. FERNÁNDEZ-ARMESTO weighs Sadat's "historical standing" in grand tones; a chapter on the background of Egypt goes back to the pharoahs of the 18th dynasty. Drawing exclusively on published sources, Fernández-Armesto focuses on Sadat's accomplishments after 1973. His book is generally readable and accurate, with an interesting account of the assassination and its causes, but it offers little new insight and is more favorable than it needs to be in order to provide a balanced assessment of the man. This perhaps owes to the author's heavy reliance on Sadat's autobiography, *In Search of Identity* (1977), a book whose historical value cannot be denied, especially for its accounts of Egypt's relations with the U.S. and the Soviet Union. What it says of biographical interest, however, must be taken with caution, as Sadat often seems more concerned with pressing his points than with relaying accurate information.

HEIKAL, a once-close friend of Sadat's and well-known Egyptian journalist, claims in the preface to his book that it is not a biography or a book about Egypt; his apparent motive for writing it is to assure that a misunderstood Sadat will not be forgotten. That claim notwithstanding, Heikal seems more intent on resurrecting Pan-Arabism and nonalignment. His critical evalution of the Sadat era is at times heavy-handed, and he writes more to reveal Sadat's negative impact on Eygpt, and to defend his own position, than to analyze his subject fairly. Heikal does offer a detailed description of events leading to the assassination, underscoring the widespread opposition to Sadat's measures to seek peace with Israel. The book is well written and offers much firsthand information.

British journalists HIRST AND BEESON, like Hcikal, emphasize the harm of Sadat's leadership to Egypt, carrying to an extreme their portrait of a hypocritical, traitorous Sadat. The authors clearly lack Heikal's understanding of the Arab world; their aim is to show that the West chose to believe in a Sadat that did not actually exist, and that Sadat nurtured this misconception to his own ends. SHOUKRI takes a somewhat different route to arrive at similar conclusions. Looking more generally at the "counter revolution" under Sadat, Shoukri sides with the Leftist opposition in Egypt who offered "democratic" solutions to some of the problems Sadat faced. Shoukri provides valuable insight into Sadat's character by showing him vacillating between opposing viewpoints before adopting the one that emerged the strongest.

ISRAELI, a professor at the Hebrew University, presents a more sympathetic portrait of Sadat. As a Jewish writer, Israeli provides interesting evidence of the impact Sadat made on intellectuals in Israel. His biography offers a readable chronological approach to Sadat's life while at the same time relating aspects of his rule to his village upbringing.

Two briefer portraits of Sadat that do not argue any thesis may be useful for students seeking the rough outline of his life.

NARAYAN, desirous of promoting an understanding of Sadat, gives a comparatively simplistic account of his economic and political policies. He does provide some useful historical background. SULLIVAN's book contains some interesting photos, but his text is unremarkable.

The memoirs of Sadat's wife and daughter may be of some interest to students of Sadat. Jehan Sadat, in *A Woman of Egypt* (1987), is an unreliable witness to her husband's presidency. At 478 pages, this work is a curious mix of undigested history, travel guide, and hyperbole. Mrs. Sadat seems most intent, with some reason, on describing her own work on behalf of Egyptian women. Camelia Sadat's *My Father and I* (1985) is better written and relates the shifting relations between the author and her father. This work is more valuable for its insights into a "traditional" Moslem woman trying to find fulfillment than for its treatment of Anwar Sadat.

Finally, some of the more recent economic and political studies of Egypt should be named, since they include treatments of Sadat's policies with implications for his biography. These are: Raymond W. Baker, *Egypt's Uncertain Revolution under Nasser and Sadat* (1978); John Waterbury, *The Egypt of Nasser and Sadat: The Political Economy of Two Regimes* (1983); and Derek Hopwood, *Egypt, Politics and Society 1945-81* (1982). No student of Sadat or the Middle East should fail to read former President Jimmy Carter's sensitive and well-informed book, *The Blood of Abraham: Inside the Middle East* (1985).

—Noelle A. Watson

SALINGER, J(erome) D(avid), 1919–   ; American writer.

French, Warren, *J. D. Salinger*. New York, Twayne, 1963; revised edition, 1976.

French, Warren, *J. D. Salinger, Revisted*. Boston, Twayne, 1988.

Grunwald, Henry A., editor, *Salinger: A Critical and Personal Portrait*. New York, Harper, 1962; London, P. Owen, 1964.

Hamilton, Ian, *In Search of J. D. Salinger*. New York, Random House, and London, Heinemann, 1988.

Lundquist, James, *J. D. Salinger*. New York, Unger, 1979.

*

Despite its many deficiencies, Hamilton is to date the most extensive biographical treatment of this elusive figure, adding to and correcting the record as earlier presented by Grunwald, French and Lundquist. Of course, the problem all of Salinger's biographers have faced has been his outright refusal to provide information, or even verify any details, about his life. Throughout his career, and especially since his virtual retirement from the literary scene in the mid-1960s, Salinger has jealously guarded his privacy, and on occasion actively obstructed those who have attempted to publish even the most seemingly innocuous information about him as it has surfaced.

In light of such reclusive habits, it is little wonder that much about Salinger's life remains a mystery. Nevertheless, the essential outline has been known since GRUNWALD's 1962 book, primarily a collection of previously published essays (mostly reviews) by such noted writers and critics as John Updike, Alfred Kazin, and Leslie Fiedler. In an introductory biographical section, Grunwald provides a concise though incomplete sketch of Salinger's life—the details of which have formed the basis of all subsequent portraits. Published at the height of Salinger's fame when he had achieved an almost cult status among a whole generation of young American readers, Grunwald is nonetheless a well-balanced treatment of both Salinger and his work. Though now considerably dated, it still offers an interesting perspective on Salinger, his unique fiction, and the attention he once commanded.

Despite his considerable following, there was no full-scale scholarly treatment of Salinger until FRENCH (1963), who like Salinger's other biographers was forced to collect most of his information from scattered published sources. The virtue of this volume and its subsequent revision is that it provides the basic facts about Salinger's life in an accessible critical framework designed to illuminate the fiction. Such a structure is particularly appropriate for Salinger, who as most of his critics have noted is among the most autobiographical of writers. French's work conforms to the Twayne series standards, combining general biography with criticism. Like all the volumes in this series, the study is well documented, adequately indexed, and provides both a primary bibliography and an annotated checklist of secondary sources. French's more recent rewrite of his original study (1988) updates the biographical record with what information has become available and adds to the bibliography. French is primarily interested here in reconsidering his earlier critical judgments—attitudes he developed and refined over a period of 25 years of active scholarship.

Similarly, LUNDQUIST presents the basic biographical record as a prelude to a discussion of Salinger's fiction, though Lundquist's book is generally inferior to French's. Useful as basic introductions, both of these studies are limited primarily by their being intended for the general reader or student, rather than in-depth considerations directed toward the serious scholar.

HAMILTON undertakes a much more ambitious enterprise, which regrettably becomes grounded in Hamilton's own frustrations with publishing the book he had originally conceived and written. Based in large part on information he had turned up from unpublished letters obtained through publicly accessible manuscript collections, the original version was successfully challenged in court by Salinger and prevented from publication. In a landmark legal decision that has had far-reaching impact in the publishing industry, the courts affirmed a writer's privilege of copyright for unpublished material, forcing Random House to withdraw the book and Hamilton to rewrite most of it.

Recast as a "search" for the mysterious Salinger, this study projects Hamilton's profound disappointment that his search has failed to uncover Holden Caulfield, the puckish hero of *The Catcher in the Rye* (1951), in the personality of his very stubborn creator, who insists upon his privacy. Hamilton reveals this disappointment in a moment of sober reflection: "I think the sharpest spur was an infatuation, an infatuation that bowled me over at the age of 17 and which it seems I never properly outgrew. Well, I've outgrown it now. The book I fell for has at last broken free of its magician author."

Although many of the reviews complained that Hamilton failed to turn up much that was new, he does add much to the record. In fact, he should be applauded for what he was able to discover and document considering the difficulties he encountered. In addition to the information gleaned from an examination of unpublished (and disputed) letters, Hamilton interviewed many of Salinger's former and present associates—and insofar as they were willing to talk, a number of new things about his early life and career are revealed. Where this information is appropriately documented and objectively presented, it provides a useful context for understanding Salinger's life. However, throughout this entire study too much is qualified by "seems" and "probably," and Hamilton consistently reports information credited to sources who will not allow themselves to be identified.

A more serious objection to Hamilton is his intrusiveness. Indeed, the final chapter of what is a fairly slim volume deals exclusively with Hamilton's legal entanglement with Salinger, and hardly conceals his bitterness. Reviewers were quick to point out this lapse of scholarly distance. As Mordecai Richler notes, this study "is tainted by a nastiness born of frustration perhaps, but hardly excused by it. Mr. Salinger is never given the benefit of a doubt. He is described as a 'callow self-advancer' " (*New York Times Book Review*, 5 June 1988).

Certainly a writer of Salinger's stature and talents is a much more complex individual than the portrait Hamilton presents, and he deserves a more objective treatment. However, given his demonstrated contempt for biography, as well as all forms of scholarship, it is likely that Ian Hamilton's bitter assessment of a man somehow unworthy of his own considerable achievements will have to stand for a long time to come.

—Paul H. Carlton

SAND, George [*born* **Amandine-Aurore-Lucie Dupin;** *later* **Baronne Dudevant],** 1804–1876; French writer.

Atwood, William G., *The Lioness and the Little One: The Liaison of George Sand and Frédéric Chopin*. New York, Columbia University Press, 1980.

Barry, Joseph, *Infamous Woman: The Life of George Sand*. New York, Doubleday, 1976.

Cate, Curtis, *George Sand: A Biography*. Boston, Houghton Mifflin, and London, Hamilton, 1975.

Dickenson, Donna, *George Sand: A Brave Man, The Most Womanly Woman*. Oxford, Berg, and New York, St. Martin's, 1988.

Gribble, Francis, *George Sand and Her Lovers*. London, E. Nash, and New York, Scribner, 1907.

Howe, Marie Jenny, *George Sand: The Search for Love*. New York, J. Day, 1927.

Jordan, Ruth, *George Sand: A Biography*. London, Constable, 1976; as *George Sand, a Biographical Portrait*, New York, Taplinger, 1976.

Maurois, André, *Lélia, The Life of George Sand*, translated by Gerard Hopkins. New York, Harper, and London, Cape, 1953 (originally published by Hachette, Paris, 1952).

Sanders, Mary F., *George Sand*. London, Holden, 1927.

Schermerhorn, Elizabeth W., *The Seven Strings of the Lyre: The Romantic Life of George Sand, 1804–76*. Boston, Houghton Mifflin, and London, Heinemann, 1927.

Seyd, Felizia, *Romantic Rebel: The Life and Times of George Sand*. New York, Viking, 1940.

Winegarten, Renee, *The Double Life of George Sand, Woman and Writer: A Critical Biography*. New York, Basic Books, 1978.

Winwar, Frances, *The Life of the Heart: George Sand and Her Times*. New York and London, Harper, 1945.

*

The titles listed immediately situate the problem with George Sand biography: for almost a century after her death, biographers viewed Sand as a pathological case study. The resulting works, generally unscholarly although several include bibliographies, reveal a curious mix of prurient interest in Sand's psychosexual existence and moralistic distance from the subject. Within this school of biography, two approaches prevail. Whereas GRIBBLE uses superficial assumptions of cultural difference to justify his approach ("French literary lives as a rule are interesting; English literary lives as a rule are not"), SANDERS adopts a universal moral standard to judge—and condemn—her subject ("George Sand is too near our own time to be forgiven"). HOWE is the first to write from a feminist perspective, viewing Sand as controversial because she embodied qualities that were normative for men, not women. Both SCHERMERHORN (1927) and SEYD (1940) acknowledge the help of Sand's only surviving descendant, a granddaughter. WINWAR's work is a popular biography that offers no new perspective.

MAUROIS was both a prolific biographer and a theoretician of biography. The combination of solid scholarship and highly readable style has made his biography of Sand a classic; for many years, it was the standard work. Maurois' approach is unabashedly Freudian. Although he claims to adopt a sympathetic attitude toward his subject (thereby providing a corrective to the previous hostility that characterized most biographies), his view of Sand is predicated on a primal childhood drama: Sand "lost her father, tried to fill his place with a mother whom she adored, and, consequently, developed a masculine attitude . . . " As a result of his uncritical acceptance of masculinity as a normative value rather than as a social construct, Maurois is ultimately dismissive of Sand's genuine contributions. Furthermore, his insistence on Sand's masculinity and her refusal to "submit to a master" lead him to contradictory conclusions: she was at once an emancipated woman who helped shape her times and a woman dominated by the desire to return to the unfettered world of her childhood. Though Maurois' approach is dated, his biography remains a powerful and informative work.

Four full-length English-language biographies of George Sand were published in the 1970s to commemorate the centennial of Sand's death. JORDAN takes an exact counterpoint stance to Maurois' view, seeing Sand as "an elemental woman" who was the product of her times; her unconventional views and behavior were not indicative of feminism or a rejection of male authority but reflected the self-indulgence of an egocentric and somewhat spoiled woman. Unlike Maurois, however, Jordan makes no attempt to assess Sand's literary merit.

CATE's view of Sand derives from his own discomfort with the women's liberation movement of the 1970s. Though its scholarly apparatus is extensive, this work suffers from Cate's inability to detach himself from his own environment. He even goes so far as to align Sand with his own views, claiming that she "would have been . . . critical of those who today have been promoting lust and license as a necessary forward step on the road to the final 'emancipation' of man- and woman-kind. . . ." Charged language such as this detracts from the credibility of his work.

The other two works that appeared during the 1970s can be viewed as binary opposites. BARRY sees Sand as an androgyne who transcended male/female stereotypes and whose life represented the ultimately successful quest for wholeness. WINEGARTEN represents her as a person who was aware of herself in two distinct capacities, as "a woman and a human being," and who did not always succeed in understanding herself. Though Winegarten's title suggests an anti-feminist attitude, her work is in fact the best reflection of biographies written from the perspective of women's studies: she provides important gender context through discussion of such topics as birth control and women's education. Despite a lengthy bibliography, Winegarten's work is the only one from the 1970s that is popular rather than scholarly. ATWOOD's entire focus is on the liaison of Sand and Chopin. Though the detailed and informative account sheds much light on this period of Sand's life, the author's interest is in Chopin rather than in Sand.

DICKENSON's work is not a full-length biography. Her intent is to provide the first English-language introduction to Sand and her works. The merit and originality of this brief study reside in the author's reference to the most recent psychological and feminist theoreticians (such as Michel Foucault or Sandra Gilbert and Susan Gubar). Furthermore, she systematically challenges long-standing myths and theories about Sand, presenting each as a question/chapter title. This is a valuable contribution to Sand studies that assumes prior knowledge of Sand's life.

—Amy B. Millstone

SANDBURG, Carl, 1878–1967; American poet.

Callahan, North, *Carl Sandburg, His Life and Works*. University Park, Pennsylvania State University Press, 1987.

Crowder, Richard, *Carl Sandburg*. New York, Twayne, 1964.

Detzer, Karl, *Carl Sandburg: A Study in Personality and Background*. New York, Harcourt, 1941.

Durnell, Hazel, *The America of Carl Sandburg*. Washington, D.C., University Press of Washington, 1965.

Golden, Harry, *Carl Sandburg*. Cleveland, World Publishing, 1961.

Sandburg, Helga, *A Great and Glorious Romance: The Story of Carl Sandburg and Lilian Steichen*. New York, Harcourt, 1978.

Weirick, Bruce, *From Whitman to Sandburg*. New York, Macmillan, 1924.

*

CALLAHAN updated his first portrait of Sandburg (*Carl Sandburg, Lincoln of Our Literature*, 1970) to produce a full-length biography that is far more comprehensive than any published before or since. Though his work is limited to 236 pages, Callahan manages to encompass a good deal of the striving, the failures, the bull-dog determination, and the strong belief in self of a man who lived to be 89 and was enormously productive for most of his working years.

Callahan's easy narrative is interrupted by direct quotations that, while pertinent in many instances, weaken the continuity. This technique, along with the use of anecdotes, does manage to highlight the individuality of the man at the expense of his serious message. To a large extent, Callahan writes about what Sandburg said rather than why he said what he did.

Despite his own exhaustive research, Callahan would be the first to acknowledge that Sandburg's prodigious output and the diversity of his achievement awaits and deserves considerably more study. Even with the assistance and full cooperation of Carl Sandburg and his family, Callahan had to be aware of how much more there was to the man than he had been able to capture. The praise and criticism directed at whatever Sandburg wrote needs to be sorted and evaluated. The mass of articles, monographs, pamphlets, scholarly papers, and short studies written about him both while he was alive and since his death need to be considered. There is also the matter of Sandburg's yet unpublished letters and possibly some poems and other writings that need review. Until such time as all of this is available, the Callahan work will probably remain the most complete biography of Sandburg available.

A strong running companion to the Callahan biography is CROWDER's overview of the poet, his works, and their critics. All of Sandburg's major works had been written by the time this book was published. Crowder was thus able to evaluate the poet's major output and consider both the harsh critics as well as those who found lasting merit in what Sandburg wrote.

Crowder's estimate of Sandburg's literary work is fair and thorough. While his masterful volume may be too brief to be called a full biography, it still serves as an ideal frame upon which one could be built. What Crowder has been able to cover and say about Sandburg, his poetry, and his critics is impressive in its range. His book, one of the Twayne series on United States authors, is an excellent and useful guidebook for college students and contains a comprehensive bibliography of primary and secondary sources. In a final judgment, Crowder believes "that to have read Sandburg is to have been in the company of a profoundly sincere American and of a craftsman capable of communicating pity, scorn, brawn, beauty, and abiding love."

WEIRICK's early work contains a final chapter devoted to Sandburg that is warm in praise for the poet. The biography by DETZER, even though it is called a "study in personality and background," is more of a friendly and laudatory tribute to Sandburg with no real attempt to get behind the man and his works. Detzer's approach was to quote poems and letters, tell of Sandburg's speaking schedules, and list the honors that came to Sandburg and how he received some of them. This book, which is out of print, does explain something, though not all, of the Carl Sandburg story to the reading public.

DURNELL did not attempt a full biography of the poet so much as to position him in the American literary scene. She considered both the critics who praised the poet and the "New

Critics" who viewed his work as "an assault on the English language." The book by GOLDEN cannot be considered anything more than light reading, full of anecdotes and not a few factual errors. It does not harm the Sandburg image and should be regarded as the work of a friend rather than a serious biography.

The work by HELGA SANDBURG contributes significantly to a greater understanding of the poet through a sensitive and compassionate portrait by his daughter. Growing up and living in the home where she could observe a father who was destined for world-wide recognition offered Helga insights other biographers could never hope to acquire. Intimate and revealing details that she was able to extract in private conversations with her mother, for example, would never have been revealed to anyone else. The gentleness and fairness of Sandburg are never better captured than in his own home.

While not a biography, the 640 letters by Carl Sandburg edited by Herbert Mitgang (1968) certainly deserves consideration for the extensive biographical material they contain. The poet's easy-to-read letters reflect how he thought on a wide range of topics. Mitgang has arranged the letters in chronological order with no more commentary than is needed. Sandburg said that "letter writing is writing," and his style, quick humor, and concerns are reflected in all, no matter who he was writing to. As Mitgang observes, "the letters explain a great deal about his life and work."

—Robert A. Gates

SANGER, Margaret, 1883–1966; American pioneer of the birth-control movement.

Drogin, Elasah, *Margaret Sanger: Father of Modern Society*. Coarsegold, California, CUL Publications, 1979.

Gray, Madeline, *Margaret Sanger: A Biography of the Champion of Birth Control*. New York, R. Marek, 1979.

Kennedy, David M., *Birth Control in America: The Career of Margaret Sanger*. New Haven, Connecticut, Yale University Press, 1970; London, Yale University Press, 1971.

Lader, Lawrence, *The Margaret Sanger Story and the Fight for Birth Control*. New York, Doubleday, 1955.

*

GRAY's long, intimate biography is presented as an attempt to discover exactly what Margaret Sanger felt and believed about her private and public lives. Sources for the biography include 200 boxes of letters, diaries, and campaign records that Sanger donated to Smith College, and almost 200 boxes of materials in the Library of Congress. Gray claims that she began her search knowing almost nothing about Sanger except for her reputation as the founder of the birth control movement. Her enlightenment began through interviews with Sanger's oldest son, Dr. Stuart Sanger, who gave Gray access to formerly restricted letters and diaries. Interviews with Sanger's relatives, former secretaries, neighbors, maids, lovers, and widows of former lovers added intimate details. Further information came from a grandson, Alexander Sanger, who had written an honors thesis in history at Princeton about Sanger's association with the Industrial Workers of the World and had photocopied all the issues of Sanger's magazine *The Woman Rebel* before they mysteriously disappeared from the New York Public Library.

From her interviews and studies of the archives, Gray discovered the private life that Sanger had hidden in order to protect her cause and public image. Gray concludes that Sanger felt compelled to preserve materials that would later allow a biographer to tell the true story.

Gray's chatty biography opens with the usual consideration of ancestors and growing up. Despite her obvious admiration for her subject, Gray also seems to delight in exposing Sanger's self-made myths—especially about the sources of her ideas on birth control. Tedious descriptions abound of Sanger's lovers, their wives, and their wives' lovers, as well as of the houses and apartments Margaret decorated with her wealthy second husband. More about birth control and less trivia about Sanger's lovers, clothing, houses, servants, and dinner menus would have made for a better balanced book.

Sanger pressured one of her lovers to write her biography, but he wisely resisted. Eventually Sanger wrote two autobiographies, *My Fight for Birth Control* (1931) and *Margaret Sanger: An Autobiography* (1938). Both books omit many aspects of her private life and underestimate the contributions others made to the birth control movement. Reading a critical biography is an essential antidote to the heavy dose of self-promotion found in the autobiographies. One of the great virtues of Gray's book is the trouble she takes to point out many of the false statements and claims Sanger made in her autobiographies.

Begun as a doctoral dissertation, KENNEDY's scholarly biography emphasizes Sanger's public life and traces the birth control movement's change from radicalism to conservatism. His chapters "Birth Control and American Medicine" and "Birth Control and the Law" are especially valuable. Although Kennedy never fails to point out Sanger's "foibles and vanities," he demonstrates her remarkable energy and achievements. Kennedy's scholarly criticism and objectivity is tempered with sympathy for the difficulties Sanger faced in her public and private life. This readable book is valuable both as biography and as social history. Ironically, in view of the conflict between Sanger and the Catholic Church, Kennedy's book was awarded the John Gilmary Shea Award of the American Catholic Historical Association as well as the Bancroft Prize in American History.

Kennedy explores the relationship between Sanger's character and the nature of the birth control movement in America between 1912 and World War II. The emphasis is on the context of Sanger's work rather than her personal life. Kennedy's book is limited in scope from the perspective both of geography and time; it essentially leaves the story with World War II and omits consideration of the history of birth control movements in Europe and Sanger's influence on the international birth control movement.

Like Gray, Kennedy exposes some of the myths that Sanger created and the way in which she ignored or suppressed historical facts to justify her actions and make the cause exclusively hers. Nevertheless, Kennedy seems to accept some myths that

Gray rejects, such as Sanger's claim that she boarded a ship bound for England from Canada with a false name and no passport. Gray argues that Sanger made up this story to accent her bravery and protect her radical friends who had provided her with a false passport.

LADER's popularized biography of Margaret Sanger, despite its lack of index and bibliography, is a well-written work that provides appendices with valuable information on the Planned Parenthood Federation of America. While this biography is very readable and well paced, it accepts Sanger's own version of events too uncritically. Unlike Kennedy, Lader describes Sanger's work in Japan and China. In dealing with Sanger's personal life, Lader takes note of some of her lovers, but generally refers to them as "admirers." For those interested in the details of these relationships readers must consult Gray. When his book was reprinted in 1975, Lader added a new preface but kept the biography unedited and unrevised to preserve the mood and excitement of the 1950s, when Sanger was at the height of her career. The book ends with the birth control pill at the experimental level and world population exploding.

In DROGIN's passionate attack on the birth control movement, Sanger is compared to Hitler and Planned Parenthood is equated with the horrors of genocide, racism, immorality, and the general decay of society. Drogin, the founder of Catholics United for Life, argues that the modern decline of morality coincides with and was actually the consequence of the work of Margaret Sanger, the "father of modern society." The last section contrasts the evils of Sanger with the virtues of the Catholic Church in general and Monsignor John A. Ryan in particular. A comparison of Drogin's account of Sanger's life and theories with those found in the more scholarly studies demonstrates her superficiality, selective and misleading use of sources, obvious bias, and the dangers inherent in accepting Sanger's own inflated view of her importance in the birth control movement.

Sanger's autobiographies and her other major books remain important sources. In addition to her *Autobiography* and *My Fight for Birth Control* see also *The Pivot of Civilization* (1922) and *The New Motherhood* (1922). Those who are interested in reading more about Margaret Sanger while obtaining a broader and more objective perspective might choose among the following titles: Linda Gordon, *Woman's Body, Woman's Right: A Social History of Birth Control in America* (1976); Gloria Moore and Ronald Moore, *Margaret Sanger and the Birth Control Movement: A Bibliography 1911–84* (1986); James Reed, *From Private Vice to Public Virtue: The Birth Control Movement and American Society since 1830* (1978); and Emily Taft Douglas, *Margaret Sanger: Pioneer of the Future* (1960).

There are also several brief accounts of the life and work of Margaret Sanger written specifically for young readers. The following titles are recommended for grades seven and up: 1) *Margaret Sanger: Mini-Play* (1978); Moira D. Reynolds, *Margaret Sanger, Women's Leader for Birth Control* (1982); and Elyse Topalian, *Margaret Sanger* (1984).

—Lois N. Magner

SARTRE, Jean-Paul, 1905–1980; French writer and philosopher.

Brée, Germaine, *Camus and Satre: Crisis and Commitment.* New York, Dell, 1972.

Cohen-Solal, Annie, *Sartre: A Life,* translated by Anna Cancogni. London, Heineman, and New York, Pantheon, 1987.

Gerassi, John, *Jean-Paul Sartre: Hated Conscience of His Century;* volume I, *Protestant or Protester?* Chicago, University of Chicago Press, 1989.

Hayman, Ronald, *Writing Against: A Biography of Sartre.* London, Weidenfeld and Nicolson, 1988.

Thody, Philip, *Jean-Paul Sartre: A Literary and Political Study.* London, Hamilton, 1960.

Thody, Philip, *Sartre: A Biographical Introduction.* London, Studio Vista, and New York, Scribner, 1971.

Thompson, Kenneth and Margaret Thompson, *Sartre: Life and Works.* New York and Bicester, England, Facts on File, 1984.

*

Sartre gave a vigorous account of his childhood in *Les Mots* (Paris, 1963; as *Words*, London, 1964), the only one of his books to be praised in the Russian Literary Press. According to a remark by his mistress, Simone de Beauvoir, Sartre's mother, who inherited the longevity of the Schweitzer family, considered her son's account of his childhood as a lonely and unhappy little boy to be quite unfounded. *Words* ends when Sartre is ten years old and his mother remarries. The account that Anne-Marie Sartre said she herself was writing has, nevertheless, not been published. The image of the young Sartre thus stands uncorrected as a child who suffered even more from the early death of his father than did the other French writers, such as Barthes, Camus, Gide, Péguy, Racine, Saint-Exupéry, and Zola, who began life by losing their fathers.

The most complete if somewhat hagiographic account of Sartre's life as a writer and political activist is in the five volumes of Simone de Beauvoir's autobiography: *Les Mémoirs d'une jeune fille rangée* (Paris, 1958; as *Memoirs of a Dutiful Daughter*, New York, 1959); *La Force de L'Age* (Paris, 1960; as *The Prime of Life*, New York, 1962); *La Force des choses* (Paris, 1963; as *The Force of Circumstance*, New York, 1964); *Tout compte fait* (Paris, 1972; as *All Said and Done*, New York and London, 1974); and *La Cérémonie des adieux* (Paris, 1981; as *Adieux: A Farewell to Sartre*, New York, 1984). A lively corrective can be found in the long account by COHEN-SOLAL. This is based on very detailed research into the archives of Sartre's various schools and universities and on interviews with some 500 people who knew Sartre. There are some splendid photographs of the man who qualifies as the ugliest of the great writers of France, but photograph number 13 suggests that his beautiful mother, *née* Anne-Marie Schweitzer, passed on to him the rather full lips of the Schweitzer family. The photographs of Sartre with Simone de Beauvoir, as well as with some of his other numerous mistresses, confirm the view that it must have been his mind that made him so attractive. The photograph of the enormous crowd that followed his funeral cortège in 1980 recalls how high an opinion the French have of their writers, even when they have behaved like Sartre and done their best to destroy almost every aspect of official French society. Unlike Sartre's *Words*, Cohen-Solal's work dwells on his constant ill health, and attributes the loss of his sight in one eye not, as Sartre did, to a leukoma, but to a neglected stye. A more devastating account of Sartre's personality emerges from HAYMAN's biography. This stresses his extensive selfishness, describing how Simone de Beauvoir looked after him when he was old, incontinent, and blind, only to receive a posthumous kick in the teeth on discovering that he had made his mistress and adopted daughter, Arlette El-Kaim, his sole literary heir. Like Cohen-Solal, Hayman writes at considerable length about Sartre's attempt to find a political party that would correspond to his view that France and the world needed a total revolution. Both books are very good on the great success of Sartre's political life, his struggle against French colonialism, though neither author talks very much about the value of Sartre's ideas or the literary merit of his books. These are more thoroughly analysed by BRÉE and by THODY.

The first volume of GERASSI's work on Sartre gives a very full account from the inside of Sartre's life up to 1939. Gerassi, an enthusiastic supporter of the left, is the son of a close friend of Sartre who inspired part of the portrait of Gomez in the four-volume novel *The Paths to Freedom*. His work is most informative on attitudes and personalities of the left in Europe and America but less useful for the student than THOMPSON's *Life and Works*.

A full account of Sartre's books can be found in *The Writings of Jean-Paul Sartre* (edited by M. Contat and M. Rybalka, Evanston, Northwestern University Press, 1974). A list of what other people have said about Sartre is in François H. Lapointe, *Jean-Paul Sartre and His Critics: An International Bibliography, 1938–1975* (Philosophy Documentation Center, Bowling Green State University, Ohio, 1981). Hazel E. Barnes was the best American critic of Sartre's ideas, and her *Sartre and Flaubert* (University of Chicago Press, 1982) is equally interesting on both writers.

—Philip Thody

SATIE, Erik, 1866–1925; French composer.

Gillmor, Alan M., *Erik Satie.* Boston, Twayne, and London, Macmillan, 1988.

Harding, James, *Erik Satie.* London, Secker and Warburg, and New York, Praeger, 1975.

Myers, Rollo H., *Erik Satie.* London, Dobson, 1948; revised edition, New York, Dover, 1968.

Templier, Pierre-Daniel, *Erik Satie,* translated by Elena L. and David French. Cambridge, Massachusetts, MIT Press, 1969 (originally published by Éditions Riéder, Paris, 1932).

*

Once a neglected master, Satie has recently emerged as a cult figure, the subject of numerous publications. Although current authors may be thorough in their documentation and include work catalogues, bibliographies, and discographies, they are not necessarily the best biographers.

For scope and currency the GILLMOR volume leads all others. Working from an impressive number of sources (the bibliography has 25 pages), the author provides a comprehensive treatment that intertwines Satie's life with his works. There is obvious virtue in the wealth of detail that accompanies the introduction of each individual and event in Satie's life, but there is also a loss. The "sense of the man" disappears in this scholarly approach. From the standpoint of the music, however, there is no rival to Gillmor. Perceptive, detailed analyses take account of information from manuscript as well as printed sources, and careful documentation is apparent throughout. Even though the discussion is often technical, the casual reader will still find useful insights here.

TEMPLIER, the first biographer, gives us a vivid and compelling portrait of the man by including numerous well-chosen quotations from the writings of Satie and others and also through the use of ample illustrations (85 photos, sketches, and various facsimiles). More importantly, however, this source brings up a number of significant questions with which later writers must come to terms. For example, was it only after Debussy's death that Satie could become truly free to explore his own potential? Templier divides his highly readable narrative into sections on the life, the man, and his works. Although he is quick to acknowledge that the last section lacks detail, it still offers some original views. Templier also has a special advantage over the other biographers in his direct contact with Conrad Satie, brother of the composer. Readers using only this account, however, should consult either the New Grove article on Satie (1980) or the slightly altered reprint in *The New Grove Twentieth-Century French Masters* (New York and London, 1986) for updated information.

For the general reader who can make a time commitment, the more extensive HARDING account is a good choice. In common with the other current treatment by Gillmor, it has a no-nonsense approach and describes Satie's fondness for alcohol and his subsequent death from cirrhosis of the liver. The narrative is engrossing, and the author permits himself the leisure to explore facets of Satie's life in considerably more detail than did Templier (although without documentation). Musical discussions are brief, non-technical, and subordinated to the events in Satie's life, so that the biographical thread is not lost. The author takes positions, but not extreme ones; and he offers some fine characterizations, such as his reference to Satie as an awkward friend, a deadly enemy.

MYERS' biographical account is disappointing. Although he acknowledges reliance on Templier, the extent of Myers' duplication goes beyond simply organization of the material (the life, the works, and the man) and sometimes includes Templier's phraseology and perceptions as well. Myers is also pushing a position. He sees Satie as unjustifiably neglected and a significant influence on "some of the greatest composers of the century." Myers misses no chance to put in a laudatory word.

The reader treads a bumpy path through Myers' section on Satie's life, for digressions are frequent. They take the form of quotations praising Satie, elaborations on particular artistic movements (such as dada) with which Satie was connected, or simply discussions of the music that creep into the biographical section. Although quotations from Satie's own writings are usu-

ally welcome, in this source they are sometimes in English and sometimes in French without translation. In his zeal to claim fame for Satie, Myers indulges in overstatement; for example, the degree of influence he believes Satie had on Stravinsky is exaggerated in this reader's opinion.

These drawbacks aside, however, Myers provides excellent musical evaluations and some fine perceptions. He has, for example, a good answer for those who question the composer's sincerity: Myers simply points out Satie's three years' study at the Schola Cantorum, undertaken with some difficulty late in life. The appendices give sections from Satie's *Memoirs of an Amnesiac* and the scenario by J. P. Contamine de Latour for their ballet *USPUD* (all in French).

Three additional sources add important information on Satie. *Satie Seen through his Letters* by Ornella Volta (translated by Michael Bullock; London and New York, Marion Boyars, 1989) was not examined in its entirety by any of the biographers discussed here. The volume contains the only mention anywhere of Erik's second sister, Diane, who died young, and gives the most thoroughgoing account of Satie's death and the reactions to it. Although portions of Satie's writings appear in almost all the biographies, the most complete edition in English is that of Nigel Wilkins, editor and translator of *The Writings of Erik Satie* (London, Eulenburg Books, 1980). It conveys in a way no other volume does the variety and character of Satie's interests, and includes numerous sketches and examples of Satie's calligraphy. Finally, Roger Shattuck's *The Banquet Years: The Origins of the Avant-Garde in France, 1885 to World War I* (London, 1955; revised edition, New York, Vintage Books, 1968) has a valuable 73-page discussion of Satie. It gives all the significant biographical facts, but subordinates them to the focus indicated in his subtitle. This well-written treatment calls attention to some important general aspects of the music, such as Satie's reliance on extra-musical ideas in his works and the rather extraordinary blend of boldness and timidity (sometimes referred to as "provocation and boredom") in his music.

—Courtney Adams

SAVONAROLA, Girolamo, 1452–1498; Italian religious reformer.

De la Bedoyère, Michael, *The Meddlesome Friar: The Story of the Conflict between Savonarola and Alexander VI.* London, Collins, and New York, Hanover House, 1957.

Horsburgh, E. L. S., *Girolamo Savonarola.* London, Methuen, and Boston, Knight, 1901.

Lucas, Herbert, *Fra Girolamo Savonarola: A Biographical Study Based on Contemporary Documents.* London, Sands, and St. Louis, Herder, 1899.

Ridolfi, Roberto, *The Life of Girolamo Savonarola*, translated by Cecil Grayson. London, Routledge, and New York, Knopf, 1959 (originally published as *Vita di Girolamo Savonarola*, Rome, Angelo Belardetti Editore, 1952).

Villari, Pasquale, *History of Girolamo Savonarola and of His Times*, translated by L. Horner. London, Longman, 1863; as *Life and Times of Girolamo Savonarola*, translated by Linda

Villari, London, T. F. Unwin, and New York, Scribner, 1889 (originally published as *La storia de Girolamo e de' suoi tempi*, 2 vols., Florence, Le Monnier, 1859–61).

Weinstein, Donald, *Savonarola and Florence: Prophecy and Patriotism in the Renaissance.* Princeton, New Jersey, Princeton University Press, 1970.

*

A product of the strong republican strand in the *Risorgimento*, VILLARI's account of Savonarola is, significantly, dedicated to Gladstone, "Champion of Italian Freedom." Villari's Savonarola emerges as a liberal—indeed, a republican—statesman "to be ranked among the greatest founders of republican states." Savonarola, for Villari, is the restorer of a medieval Italian communal liberty providing much of the historical legitimation of the *Risorgimento* but in "general decay" in the age of the Medici. Villari sees Lorenzo de' Medici as a seductive but malign force whose amoral blandishments led into a political tyranny whose only counterweight was Savonarola's combination of frugal civic virtue and austere republicanism. Himself a political refugee from a decadent monarchy, Villari emphasises—some would say over-emphasises—confrontation between the "republican" Savonarola and the would-be monarch Lorenzo de' Medici.

Essentially, then, Villari's Savonarola is a "statesman" who "during the first year of his political life" relegated his "visionary ideas" to "the background." Villari's relative marginalisation of what was in fact Savonarola's central visionary messianism has been reversed in modern scholarship, by Weinstein (see below). Villari, though, is absolutely clear on Savonarola's Catholic inspiration and orthodoxy: he was "unswervingly faithful to the dogmas of his faith," and he collided with a papacy—that of Alexander VI—whose hunger for power was the real enemy of Catholic faith.

Villari's work brings together his own researches with those of a group of scholars in relatively liberal Florence, the "new *Piagnoni*," who saw Savonarola, patriot, liberal, and reformist Christian, as the spiritual and political prophet of the *Risorgimento*. Villari's great and scholarly biography is ably translated by Linda Villari into a suitably stately, late-Victorian English prose.

LUCAS' study was described by a later biographer, de la Bedoyère (see below), as "one of the most interesting examples of the Jesuit character and of Jesuit scholarship," and a "kindly expressed, but severe, indictment" of its subject. Lucas' fine scholarly work forms part of a debate between Ludwig Pastor and Savonarola's defender, Paolo Luotto. Lucas establishes Savonarola's fundamental theological orthodoxy and denies that he was a doctrinal herald of Protestantism. Lucas faults Savonarola on the issue of "obedience."

Writing in the aftermath of the declaration of papal infallibility, Lucas could not help but be influenced by the intense papalism that saw the Vatican compensating for its loss of territory in Italy by emphasising its power over the Church. In addition, Lucas belonged to a religious order, the Society of Jesus, whose vow of unreserved obedience to the papacy had been part of the Counter-Reformation's authoritarian reaction to the Protestant challenge. Lucas, then, tends to see Savonarola as a defective Catholic because Savonarola did not seem to share that high pa-

palism that a 19th-century Catholic would see as the essential prerequisite of orthodoxy. The crucial case against Savonarola, upheld by Lucas, was that the friar had called for the deposition of the simoniac Pope Alexander. Savonarola had thereby committed the "constructive heresy and schism" of dissent and revolt; Villari's protestations of his innocence were swept aside, and the fact that Savonarola was a "great and good man," even a harbinger of the Catholic renewal of the 16th century, only deepened his tragedy. Lucas writes in a sometimes heavy Gibbonian style, dignified rather than vivid.

These two great 19th-century studies of Savonarola were inspired by what were in effect variant Catholicisms: on the one hand, Villari's anticipation of Christian democracy, on the other Lucas' 19th-century Jesuit equation of orthodoxy with acceptance of papal absolutism (though it was combined with scholarly balance and considerable human sympathy). Both these works incorporate extensive primary textual material.

HORSBURGH's relatively brief volume is part of the Oxford textbook series of biographies, devoted largely to figures perceived as standard-bearers of human progress. The work, popular and frequently re-published, offers a useful, plainly written introduction to the subject. Horsburgh stresses Savonarola's Catholic orthodoxy, including his overall allegiance to the papacy. The friar was not, for Horsburgh, a "herald of the Reformation," though he did anticipate something of which the Reformation was a part: private judgement and individual discrimination.

RIDOLFI's *Life* was a celebration of the quingentenary of the birth of its hero, whom the biographer regards as a martyr. A Florentine civic patriot, Ridolfi refers to some of the others of the friar's biographers as French or German, but to his predecessor Villari as a Neapolitan and to himself as a Florentine. Somewhat dismissive of Villari, Ridolfi depicts him as a brash foreigner who disrupted the quiet sympathy of the 19th-century Tuscan "new *Piagnoni*" and fashioned a Savonarola in his own image—a progressive, a "civil prophet" and "civil innovator," rather than Ridolfi's "great man of God." Ridolfi aims to give Savonarola back to Florence and to Catholic spirituality. These two tasks of restitution are closely linked, with Savonarola as a patron saint of Florentine civic patriotism. Ridolfi's key appendix, "Summary Account of the Cult . . . of Savonarola" includes a narrative of various attempts made, usually with a Florentine initiative, to canonise the friar. Although Ridolfi expressly disowns the intention of promoting Savonarola's "cause" for canonisation—"this aspect of the subject is not my concern"—his disavowal reads rather like a strategy to make his advocacy more effective. Ridolfi's *Life* is translated into clear, colloquial English but is, sadly, free of scholarly apparatus of any kind.

DE LA BEDOYÈRE's account of Savonarola, focusing particularly on his clash with Alexander VI, forms a Catholic tragedy, written in the tradition of Lucas. No longer the moral monster of legend, Alexander is seen as weak and self-indulgent, his flawed character actually upholding the rights of the human sinner in the "fold of Christ," while Savonarola overlooked the need for Christian charity. The pope's remarkably indulgent handling of the friar met with the latter's "fierce refusal to compromise." But underlying these temperamental differences between the zealot and the man of affairs was the moral issue of Savonarola's obedience as a priest, not to the man Rodrigo Borgia, but to the impersonal "proper authority" of the Church. The friar failed that test and, although he was saintly, he could never be a canonised saint.

Three major chapters of WEINSTEIN's study have to do with a feature that Villari found embarrassing—Savonarola as the "visionary" prophet of apocalyptic drama, as distinct from Villari's projection of the liberal herald of ordered progress. Weinstein anchors Savonarola in a set of essentially medieval assumptions, especially about Florence's manifest destiny. Florence's apparently miraculous escape from the potential catastrophe of 1494 set off in Savonarola's mind a chain of expectations about a glorious future for the city. Not only was Savonarola able to tell the Florentines what they wanted to hear about themselves, but he was also able to inform this bourgeois and commercial republic that its pursuit of wealth was by no means inconsistent with a messianic role. Weinstein's work makes an exciting and fast-paced read, and it moves forcefully through the dramatic changes in Savonarola's views. With a superb scholarly range, Weinstein makes the very best of his extraordinary subject.

—Michael A. Mullett

* * *

SAYERS, Dorothy L., 1893–1957; English writer.

Brabazon, James, *Dorothy L. Sayers: A Biography.* London, Gollancz, and New York, Scribner, 1981.

Dale, Alzina Stone, *Maker and Craftsman: The Story of Dorothy L. Sayers.* Grand Rapids, Michigan, Eerdmans, 1978.

Hitchman, Janet, *Such a Strange Lady: An Introduction to Dorothy L. Sayers.* London, New English Library, 1975; with subtitle *A Biography of Dorothy L. Sayers,* New York, Harper, 1975.

Hone, Ralph E., *Dorothy L. Sayers: A Literary Biography.* Kent, Ohio, Kent State University Press, 1979.

Tischler, Nancy M., *Dorothy L. Sayers: A Pilgrim Soul.* Atlanta, Georgia, John Knox Press, 1980.

*

Dorothy L. Sayers disliked reporters and biographers; critics she could cope with, provided they did not descend to "chit chat." A 50-year moratorium before any "life" should be written was her rule, more honoured in the breach than the observance if her own (unfinished) study of Wilkie Collins is taken into account.

There lies one of the problems facing any biographer of Sayers—the built-in contradictions. Add to that a "best seller" reputation based on a fictional world that keeps on (apparently) overlapping with areas of her known life, throw in a son born out of wedlock to someone who had become one of the authentic voices of the church in the darkest days of World War II, and one can see the temptation to get writing long before the half-century is up.

This temptation, coupled with pressure from publishers, was too much for HITCHMAN. Despite not having access to family papers, she was able to build on her researches for a BBC series

about this "strange lady" and produced a journalistic good read, which cannot however be taken alone as an adequate introduction to her subject. It is not just a question of lacking the authority that access to private papers would have given her. Imprecisions abound. Les Roches (the school where Miss Sayers worked with Eric Whelpton) might have been "snobbish" but was certainly not "equivalent to Eton" and is as far removed from Southern France as Normandy can make it! American readers must be particularly cautious in relying on Hitchman for interpreting British custom and practice. Like bagpipe music, it is stirring stuff and grand in its way, but always slightly out of tune.

While Hitchman was preparing her biography, HONE was researching the Sayers archives for a much more authentic and scholarly book, aimed at the serious student rather than the general reader. But he too was denied access to the family papers, and in particular the questions surrounding the years 1920–26 (between her return from Normandy and her marriage) remain matters for conjecture rather than assertion—or should have remained. Hone is apt to be dogmatic: "It is certain," he says, "that Dorothy had an affair with . . . John Cournos." Later we find that "undoubtedly Dorothy believed Cournos was the father of her child." It seems that Hone knew about, but was unable to consult, the Cournos-Sayers papers at Harvard. "Read with care" must be the verdict on this section, but elsewhere Hone's treatment of his subject stands up to comparison with any other study.

He is adept at finding the right quotes from Sayers' extensive correspondence, each one depicting another characteristic and carrying forward the intellectual exposition. The chapter dealing with her work across the years 1936–44 (which encompass the major part of her religious writing and broadcasting) is central to his presentation of his subject. The theme "integrity of work over-riding and redeeming personal weakness" belongs, says Sayers, to both her novel *Gaudy Night* and her play *The Zeal of Thy House*, and Hone relates this theme to Sayers herself. He probably would not have seen the memorial tablet in St. Anne's Soho, with its text "The only Christian work is good work well done," but he arrived at the same conclusion as those who raised this memorial.

DALE's *Maker and Craftsman* does not stand comparison with Hone in terms of scholarship and breadth of reference. Aimed at a younger audience, it deals with the private life sympathetically but in a distinctly unprobing manner. One suspects that Sayers would have approved of that, but her battles with the BBC attract the same reticence, and that would surely not have gone uncensured. Stylistically the book is at odds with its subject. It is gentle and warming: quite unlike C. S. Lewis' verdict that conversation with Sayers had "zest and edge," attractive to those who "like a high wind." But for the Wimsey enthusiast seeking an introduction to the sterner stuff, this is a good starting point.

TISCHLER's portrait of a "pilgrim soul" makes a distinctive approach with which the reader will either be engaged or exasperated. It is certainly ingenious. Bunyan's Pilgrim has numerous distractions and personal adversities on his way to the Celestial City, and Sayers is made to pass the same way. There is an early warning of Tischler's lack of judgment: "By almost any measurement . . . one of the giants of the first half of the 20th century" must rank as enthusiasm in overdrive! Inevitably there are some inaccuracies and anachronisms in interpreting issues such as the women's movement, racism, antisemitism, and Protestant-Catholic differences in the England of 50 years back, but full credit is due to Tischler for bringing these issues to our notice in this stimulating investigation.

The essential version for both the serious scholar and for the well-informed reader is the "authorised life" by BRABAZON. As Anthony Fleming (Sayers' son), points out in his preface, had it not been for the earlier books, written without access to the private papers "this book would not have been written." Now we have no need to speculate or assert, for Brabazon sets the record straight with the full story, complete with supporting documentation; he conceals only the name of Fleming's father. Much is clarified by reference to the unpublished, semi-autobiographical fragment "Cat o' Mary," and in matters relating to church activities in London, Brabazon had special insights, having served with Sayers as churchwarden in Soho. An excellent Foreword by P. D. James reminds us how lucky we are to have this biography 27 years ahead of the schedule Sayers herself decreed.

—David L. Howard

SCHILLER, (Johann Christoph) Friedrich von, 1759–1805; German poet and playwright.

Carlyle, Thomas, *Life of Schiller*. London, 1825.
Düntzer, Heinrich, *Life of Schiller*, translated by Percy E. Pinkerton. Boston, F. A. Niccols, 1902.
Garland, Henry B., *Schiller*. London, Harrap, 1949; New York, McBride, 1950.
Mann, Thomas, "On Schiller," in *Last Essays*. New York, Knopf, and London, Secker and Warburg, 1959.
Nevinson, Henry W., *Life of Friedrich Schiller*. London, W. Scott, 1889.
Passage, Charles E., *Friedrich Schiller*. New York, Ungar, 1975.
Thomas, Calvin, *The Life and Works of Friedrich Schiller*. New York, Holt, 1901.
Willson, A. Leslie, editor, *A Schiller Symposium*. Austin, University of Texas Press, 1960.

*

While literally dozens of German biographers have examined Schiller's life in every detail, English-language translations are few. DÜNTZER is most thorough and authoritative, containing chapters covering the life in short time spans, usually two years per chapter but occasionally concentrating on important six-month periods. Illustrations consist of photoengravings from paintings, sparse but strikingly romantic. The translation by Percy E. Pinkerton retains some of the archaic diction of the original—"forsooth" and "ere," for example—but stays readable and informative.

Best of the English originals is by THOMAS, reprinted by popular demand in 1970, containing a strong appendix outlining the biographical material not available in English, citing Korner

as the first (1812), "a mere sketch." Particularly valuable here, if slightly Edwardian in their reserve, are Calvin's insights into Schiller's limited talents as a poet, and later poets' debt (notably Heinrich Heine) to Schiller's "sensualized" and even "indecent" literary "defiance of conventional morality."

CARLYLE's work, known more as part of his own canon than as a reliable account of Schiller, is based on not always reliable information (Schiller's letters and personal papers not being available to him as they were for later biographers, after F. Jonas published a seven-volume collection in 1892), but maintains its importance because it incorporates the English view of German Romanticism into Carlyle's own remarkable theories of poetry and the essay form. Goethe introduces the German translation of the original edition (1825). MANN contributes a modern essay on Schiller's importance in a continuum of German literature leading to Mann himself.

NEVINSON tells Schiller's story without letting the feverish charm of the subject interfere with a clear-headed, not always flattering, view. Nevinson's style is oddly anecdotal, and his treatment of Schiller's life is sparse in places. The five years after Schiller's move to Weimar, for example, are described: "The time was indeed almost entirely divided between the labour of composition and the relaxation of illness, so that there remains but little biographical incident to record." He does point out, however, that Schiller wrote four great dramas and many adaptations from French works during this period.

GARLAND, like Nevinson, treats Schiller as "a credible person, not the carefully posed, statuesque figure which too often does duty for him." The kind of scholarship prevalent just after World War II (Garland's work was published in 1949) called for a reductive personalization of great figures, revealing the human being under the larger-than-life historical image. Despite such an effort, however, Garland still views Schiller as "liable to [be swept] away from a standpoint of cool detachment," citing the playwright's tendency to misquote or near-quote, "relying on his remarkable memory to give him the spirit of the original." Garland translates letters and conversations in the text, providing the German and French originals in an appendix.

PASSAGE follows a critical rather than biographical outline, concentrating on Schiller's dramatic work. Passage's treatment benefits from modern criticism and scholarship and contains some still photos from fairly modern productions of Schiller's plays. Passage's bibliography and index are also helpful.

WILLSON's edited volume of essays commemorating the bicentenary of Schiller's birth offers noteworthy studies that tie Schiller's work and biography into a larger context. Essentially critical in nature, these essays nevertheless attempt to place Schiller's works in a biographical framework.

—Thomas J. Taylor

SCHOENBERG, Arnold, 1874–1951; Austrian-American composer.

MacDonald, Malcolm, *Schoenberg*. London, Dent, 1976.

Neighbor, Oliver, "Arnold Schoenberg," in *The New Grove Second Viennese School*. New York, Norton, and London, Papermac/Macmillan, 1983.

Newlin, Dika, *Schoenberg Remembered: Diaries and Recollections*. New York, Pendragon Press, 1980.

Reich, Willi, *Schoenberg: A Critical Biography*, translated by Leo Black. London, Longman, and New York, Praeger, 1971 (originally published as *Arnold Schönberg oder der konservative Revolutionär*, Vienna, Frankfurt, and Zürich, F. Molden, 1968).

Smith, Joan Allen, *Schoenberg and His Circle: A Viennese Portrait*. New York, Schirmer, and London, Collier Macmillan, 1986.

Stuckenschmidt, Hans H., *Schoenberg: His Life, World, and Work*, translated by Humphrey Searle. New York, Schirmer, and London, Calder, 1977 (originally published by Atlantis, Zürich, 1974).

Wellesz, Egon, *Arnold Schoenberg: The Formative Years*, translated by H. Kerridge. London, Dent, and New York, Dutton, 1925; reprint, with new preface, London, Galliard, and New York, Galaxy, 1971 (originally published by E. P. Tal, Vienna, 1921).

*

Much has been written on Arnold Schoenberg—in essays, compositional and stylistic analyses, aesthetic and historical studies, and oral history projects—and scattered throughout these writings, as well as in editions of letters and memoirs, a great deal of disparate biographical material on the composer has gradually become available. Yet even today, almost 40 years after his death, very few, and certainly no definitive, book-length biographies exist. It is tempting to attribute this at least in part to the influence of Schoenberg's own opinion as stated in a 1920 letter to Alban Berg, "my biography as such is highly uninteresting and I consider the publication of any details embarrassing. A few place names, dates of composition, there's really nothing more to say. . . . It would be interesting to outline my development through the music."

Certainly the earliest biography of Schoenberg available in English tried to do just that. WELLESZ, whose 1921 German original won Schoenberg's approval, appeared in English translation in 1925. The 1971 revision (which differs merely in the inclusion of a new introductory chapter and slight revision of the concluding pages), discusses Schoenberg's career and works no further than the early 1920's, ending with the Wind Quintet, op. 25. Since Wellesz studied with Schoenberg and was loosely affiliated with the Vienna circle of disciples, the biographical information can be assumed to have come primarily from the composer himself. Schoenberg's direct influence is likewise recognizable in the tone in which Wellesz deals with questions of stylistic development and historical orientation. Clearly partisan, Wellesz's work obviously stems from a time when Schoenberg's ultimate significance within musical evolution was still fiercely debated. The book, which separates the biographical and analytical chapters, is narrowly focused on Schoenberg the man and composer, and makes no attempt to provide a broader social/historical setting. What gives this book its lasting significance (and no doubt led to its re-issue) is the immediacy of the prose, most particularly in the chapter "His Teaching," which is cast throughout in the present tense.

A comparable sense of immediacy, incidentally, is transmitted by the memoirs of NEWLIN, one of Schoenberg's students from the American years. This is a breezy, entertaining account of almost daily contact with the composer between 1939 and 1941. SMITH's volume likewise offers intriguing recollections of musicians who knew and worked with Schoenberg throughout his life; unfortunately the material, drawn principally from personal interviews, is presented without critical editorial correction of factual errors.

Although REICH, too, was associated with Schoenberg's Vienna circle, his book, which covers Schoenberg's entire life and oeuvre, cannot claim the merits of Wellesz's. Based on a German-language original of 1968 (new annotational material is credited to the translator, Leo Black), the book proceeds generally chronologically, but, despite continuous running heads that identify the time periods under discussion, it suffers from haphazard and often confusing organization. Indeed, much of the content seems dictated by the serendipitous availability of sources, which are strung together rather capriciously. Today many of those sources are more coherently accessible in the biographies by Neighbor and Stuckenschmidt (see below), and in collections of letters (*Letters of Arnold Schoenberg*, edited by Erwin Stein, translated by Eithne Wilkins and Ernst Kaiser, London and New York, 1964; *Arnold Schoenberg, Wassily Kandinsky: Letters, Pictures, and Documents*, edited by Jelena Hahl-Koch, translated by John Crawford, London, 1984; and *The Berg-Schoenberg Correspondence*, edited by Juliane Brand, Christopher Hailey, and Donald Harris, New York, 1987).

MacDONALD's work, the first biography to appear originally in English, is part of the Master Musicians Series and makes no claim to being a comprehensive biography; MacDonald himself terms the book a "fairly impressionistic account," but with its two helpful appendices (a two-column timeline and an annotated "Personalia") it can serve as a limited general introduction. Like Wellesz and Neighbor, MacDonald separates biographical from analytical discussion. In the first quarter of the book MacDonald, primarily on the basis of secondary sources, attempts to identify some of the social, intellectual, political, and emotional forces that determined Schoenberg's path. This is not always satisfactory, as when he spends an inordinate amount of time on the difficulties of Schoenberg's first marriage or willfully misinterprets Schoenberg's 1921 statement about having insured the supremacy of German music for the next hundred years.

NEIGHBOR provides the most recent biographical contribution to Schoenberg scholarship. His book incorporates the most significant work up to 1980, when the *New Grove Dictionary of Music and Musicians*, in which this essay first appeared, went to press. The biographical portion of the essay presents in plain prose the basic facts of Schoenberg's life. It is followed by a short section on "Personality and beliefs" and—by far the largest part of the essay—a descriptive discussion of Schoenberg's music. This last section, too, is chronologically organized and brings in much supportive biographical information. Neighbor offers a readable, straightforward, and factually accurate introduction to Schoenberg; the bibliography is still the most current available.

STUCKENSCHMIDT's work, while flawed in a number of ways, remains since its publication the principal source for

Schoenberg in both English and German, and will no doubt remain the standard secondary source for some time to come. Stuckenschmidt, too, was personally associated with the composer and includes information based on personal experiences and knowledge. More important, he was able to draw on a wealth of primary sources from the major repositories of Schoenberg material, including documents then still in the possession of the family. Stuckenschmidt is especially valuable in his discussion of the many significant creative and personal relationships between the composer and his contemporaries in music and the other arts; the appendix includes a number of translated documents. If the mass of sometimes undigested detail occasionally threatens to swamp the reader, this book nonetheless provides the most comprehensive and varied account of Schoenberg's life and activities presently available.

—Juliane Brand

SCHOPENHAUER, Arthur, 1788–1860; German philosopher.

Bridgwater, Patrick, *Arthur Schopenhauer's English Schooling* London and New York, Routledge, 1988.

Copleston, Frederick, *Arthur Schopenhauer: Philosopher of Pessimism,* London, Burns Oates, 1946.

McGill, Vivian J., *Schopenhauer: Pessimist and Pagan.* New York, Brentano's, 1931.

Wallace, William, *Life of Arthur Schopenhauer,* London, W. Scott, and New York, Lovell, 1890.

*

A new scholarly biography of Arthur Schopenhauer is an obvious desideratum; scholars have had little else than reprints of old-fashioned, unsatisfactory, late 19th- and early 20th-century accounts of the philosopher's life. The starting point for studying the biographical details, though unavailable in an English translation, is still William von Gwinner (*Schopenhauers Leben*, 3rd edition, Leipzig, 1910). One of Schopenhauer's disciples, Gwinner gained access to the bulk of the philosopher's personal papers and compiled the first important account. Gwinner takes particular notice of Schopenhauer's writing in French, which he argues is a tribute to Voltaire and the tradition of biting French satire. Gwinner also describes Schopenhauer's belief that people should not suppress their personal idiosyncrasies at the risk of madness—a belief, he argues, that anticipates Freudian psychology. In addition to his intimate knowledge of the philosopher, Gwinner had at his disposal Schopenhauer's library, which had been willed to him.

WALLACE finds Schopenhauer "more akin to the English than to the German philosopher." Schopenhauer writes in the English manner of using "ordinary language" rather than the German fashion of employing a "technical dialect." Wallace makes much of the philosopher's Dutch heritage, as opposed to his upbringing in Danzig. Of particular interest is the discussion of the German academic hierarchy and how it provided a context for the development of Schopenhauer's philosophy. Schopenhauer's attack on the historical method is analyzed, and the author

clearly sides with his subject in the debate with Hegel: "History, in the strict sense, is but a handmaid to science and philosophy: her function is accessary and illustrative."

McGILL added substantially to Gwinner's work. He had additional documentary material with which to work (letters, posthumous papers, and other evidence provided by Schopenhauer's students and acquaintances), and he constructed the first important biography in English. In spite of his working with fresh primary material, however, McGill produced a highly dramatized and unscholarly book, more nearly hagiography than objective biography. His presentation of the conflict between Schopenhauer and the German university professors, analogous to that between Socrates and the Sophists, is highly romanticized and subjectively described. McGill's Schopenhauer is an *enfant terrible*, an "angry young man," an alienated intellectual never able to find peace within himself. An entertaining account, particularly of the debate with Hegel, it yet suffers from the author's overconfidence in his ability to look into the heart of his subject, whom he conceives to be the apotheosis of unsatisfied desire. Of Schopenhauer's "Weimar period," for example, McGill writes: "The owls hoot, the windows rattle, no light can penetrate the ominous blackness. Arthur feels that the day will never come. He is alone and forgotten and the bright flash of a friendly eye seems infinitely distant and precious."

COPLESTON's study excels at placing Schopenhauer in the history of philosophy—a continuum the author constructs that stretches from Hume to Kant to Hegel. Like most other biographers, he tends—at least until his conclusion—to be highly sympathetic to his subject in his revolt against "the exaggerated and doctrinaire optimism of Hegel." The study discusses Napoleon's influence on the European culture that spawned Schopenhauer's thought. It is particularly helpful in its treatment of the publication history of *The World as Will and Idea* (1819). Copleston's Schopenhauer mistrusts democratic revolution and faces constant frustration as he is "opposed to the spirit of the time" in his pessimism. The author observes: "The optimistic and democratic revolution of 1848 awakened no sympathy in Schopenhauer's heart; he disliked and mistrusted it, not least because he feared it might result in the loss of his own property. All that he desired of a government was that it should preserve law and order." The second half of the book moves beyond biography to explicate Schopenhauer's theory of knowledge and his philosophical systems. In a curiously apologetic and dogmatic conclusion, Copleston rejects Schopenhauer's pessimism and urges the reader to find the solution to life's dilemmas "at the feet of the Crucified Redeemer. Who died and rose again, that we might live."

BRIDGWATER's book makes an impressive start toward a modern, detailed biography. It concentrates on Schopenhauer's formative experiences in England. The study attempts to define the philosopher's "image of England and the influences and experiences which formed that image, notably his visit to England in 1803 and that term which he then spent at an English boarding school." He details Schopenhauer's reaction against his English headmaster and against his "anglomaniac" father heavily influenced by a strong British presence in Danzig. Bridgwater rather brazenly attempts to reconstruct the "British character" in 1800. To understand Schopenhauer, Bridgwater argues, one must understand the life and philosophy of Richard Jameson, Schopenhauer's English schoolmaster, and of Thomas Lancaster, for three months in 1803 Schopenhauer's headmaster. The book provides a useful account of education at the turn of the century, but it more accurately concerns the contexts from which Schopenhauer's habits of mind were formed rather than the philosopher's life itself. Bridgwater also includes a transcription of Schopenhauer's English diary, a fascinating account of the young man's London experiences from 23 May 1803 to 8 November 1803. Theatre historians might find the journal of particular interest, as it details his theatre-going: particular accounts of productions of Drury Lane and Covent Garden theatres and of Italian opera make the journal a lively and valuable resource.

Bridgwater's study is a stylish first step toward the sort of modern scholarly study that might help revivify Schopenhauer studies. That no standard biographical study exists bears witness to the neglect from which Schopenhauer has suffered in recent decades.

—Richard C. Taylor

SCHUBERT, Franz (Peter), 1797–1828; Austrian composer.

Brown, Maurice J. E., *Schubert: A Critical Biography.* London, Macmillan, and New York, St. Martin's, 1958.

Brown, Maurice J. E., *The New Grove Schubert.* London and New York, Macmillan, 1980; revised edition, New York, Norton, 1983.

Deutsch, Otto E., *Schubert: A Documentary Biography.* London, Dent, 1946; as *The Schubert Reader: A Life of Franz Schubert in Letters and Documents,* New York, Norton, 1947 (originally published as *Franz Schubert: die Dokumente seines Lebens,* Munich, G. Müller, [n.d.]).

Deutsch, Otto E., *Schubert: Memoirs by His Friends,* translated by R. Ley and J. Nowell. New York, Macmillan, and London, A. and C. Black, 1958 (originally published as *Schubert: die Erinnerungen seiner Freunde,* Leipzig, Breitkopf and Härtel, 1957).

Flower, Newman, *Franz Schubert: The Man and His Circle.* New York, F. A. Stokes, and London, Cassell, 1928.

Frost, H. F., *Schubert.* London, Low Marston, and New York, Scribner, 1881.

Hilmar, Ernst, *Franz Schubert in His Time,* translated by R. G. Pauley. Portland, Oregon, Amadeus Press, 1988 (originally published by Böhlau, Vienna, 1985).

Hutchings, Arthur, *Schubert.* London, Dent, and New York, Dutton, 1945.

Kobald, Karl, *Franz Schubert and His Times,* translated by Beatrice Marshall. New York, Knopf, 1928 (originally published by Amalthea, Zürich, 1928).

Marek, George R., *Schubert.* New York, Viking, 1985; London, R. Hale, 1986.

Osborne, Charles, *Schubert and His Vienna.* New York, Knopf, and London, Weidenfeld and Nicolson, 1985.

Schauffler, Robert H., *Franz Schubert: The Ariel of Music.* New York, Putnam, 1949.

Wechsberg, Joseph, *Schubert: His Life, His Work, His Time.* New York, Rizzoli, and London, Weidenfeld and Nicolson, 1977.

Woodford, Peggy, *Schubert: His Life and Times.* New York, Two Continents Publishing, and Tunbridge Wells, Kent, Midas, 1978.

*

Schubert's life is one of the shortest of all the great composers. The pool of biographical material is as a result quite shallow; the same information has now been rehashed many times over.

Many of the biographies, particularly the ones from the first half of the 20th century, conclude with chronological lists of Schubert's music that often encompass a significant portion of the book. Recent scholarship has shown that many of the lists ascribe incorrect dates to Schubert's works. (The most accurate list available is Brown's *New Grove Schubert* [1983], discussed below.) The updating of the Schubert work-list is representative of a larger process that continues in biographies of the last 40 years as nearly every work written on Schubert since World War II claims to correct misconceptions perpetuated by the earlier biographies. We are still waiting, however, for the first work that will provide an extended and balanced view of the composer.

DEUTSCH's documentary biography (English translation, 1946) upon which all subsequent biographies have depended, is an annotated collection of documents by and about Schubert. Nearly 2000 individual selections are arranged chronologically; many of them bear specific dates. Taken as a whole, this work will help formulate the most complete picture of Schubert's life. Deutsch intersperses his comments throughout the work, but there is much conjecture, especially in regard to Schubert's early years. A wide range of topics is covered by the documents that include Schubert's birth records (as well as those of his grandfather and father), his school records, plates of his letters and music, and even selections from the diaries of his friends. Special treasures include the scripts of satirical plays that were read at the famous Schubertiads. A weakness of Deutsch's compilation is that he failed to weed out some irrelevant documents. The result is a massive collection with many individual entries that bear only a superficial or remote connection to the composer. If the reader is willing to sift through seemingly endless entries such as the numerous quotations from Franz von Hartmann's diary, helpful information can be obtained. Deutsch's later work (1958) is similar in format.

While billed as "Memoirs by his Friends," this work actually serves as an addendum to the 1947 *Reader.* The earlier work is here supplemented with additional records, notices, and plates. The tone of Deutsch's comments is more scholarly in this second volume which, while it could not be used to form a continuous picture of Schubert's life, does provide some of the most arresting information about the composer; in this regard see especially the excerpts from Louis Schlösser and Albert Stadler.

Brown, as the primary author of the articles on Schubert in both the 1954 and 1980 editions of the *Grove Dictionary of Music and Musicians,* has emerged as a second key figure in Schubert biographical studies. BROWN's *Critical Biography* (1958), both dedicated and indebted to Deutsch for much of its background material, forms the leading edge in the renewal of interest in Schubert in the second half of the 20th century. The organization of the book is bound closely to the conception and composition of Schubert's individual works. This means that biographical information is considered significant only as it helps to date or explain Schubert's music. Absent are effusive descriptions of the Schubertiads that characterize many of the other Schubert biographies, and instead we find only brief references to these famous gatherings. Brown's central arguments are grounded in an encyclopedic knowledge of Schubert's oeuvre. Thus, while his purely biographical discourses cannot be relied upon for a complete picture of the composer's life, they are some of the best available writings for learning about the composition of specific works. This aspect of Brown's work is enhanced by timely references to the music of other composers, so that Schubert's music, and to a lesser extent Schubert's life, are placed in an historical context. While this may seem to be a conspicuous goal of the biography of any composer, most biographies of Schubert do not even attempt it.

BROWN's *New Grove Schubert* (1983) is a revision by Eric Sams of the extended article on Schubert in the *New Grove Dictionary of Music and Musicians* (1980). This book provides much information in a very small space, and the bibliography and work-lists are among the best currently available. Because it is based on a dictionary entry, there is very little of a speculative nature about the book. It attempts to dispel myths about Schubert primarily by omitting all reference to them.

FROST's book in the *Great Musicians* series diligently searches for evidence of genius and strength of character in Schubert's letters and in well-known anecdotes about Schubert's life. There is practically no discussion of music, but rather specific works are treated as signposts along the way to the composer's tragic death. There is some evidence that Frost would not have been capable of discussing Schubert's music adequately even if he had wanted to do so. Frost's writing is dated to the point of being quaint, and his viewpoint is more distracting than quaint; it might even be considered disruptive as it contains what can only be classified as racial slurs and imputations. HUTCHINGS' volume in *The Master Musicians* series divides into three parts: biography, music, and appendices. The latter section is the most beneficial portion of the work. It includes a time-line of Schubert's life, a catalogue (incomplete) of his works, a section called "personalia" that provides a brief biographical statement on most of Schubert's friends and noteworthy contemporaries, a bibliography that for its time is quite good, and a list of poets whose work Schubert set to music. The biographical section only touches on highlights of Schubert's life, but does include some anecdotes not found in most studies. While some musical analysis is attempted, it is not performed very rigorously.

SCHAUFFLER's work is organized with the same three sections as HUTCHINGS', but the third adds a discography (now very much outdated). The perspective is that of a professional performer (cellist). Relying a good bit on Deutsch, Schauffler's writing style is clever and quite lively but sometimes goes too far, achieving a cute style that is on occasion overbearing. Schauffler takes a psychobiographical approach, and his work contains a large amount of musical analysis as well.

WOODFORD is fun to read. An entertaining blend of anecdotes, plates, and citations from letters and other documents, this is a work that could incite interest from beginning to end. While Woodford depends almost completely on the work of other scholars (and quotes from them freely), her goal is apparently not to furnish new information about Schubert but rather to present a concise and lively picture of the composer's life. This is one of the most useful all-purpose introductions to Schubert and his music.

KOBALD comprises six independent topical essays, each depicting a different facet of Schubert's milieu: "The Vienna of Biedermeier," "Schubert's Life," "The Artist and his Work," "Feminine Influence in Schubert's Life," "Schubert and Schwind," and "Schubert's Friends." The most distinctive and forward looking is the one on "Feminine Influence." Mysteries concerning the precise nature of Schubert's love life (or lack of it) are here explored in some depth. The essay goes so far as to point out the discrepancies between the ardor and passion of his music and his apparent lack of romantic interest in women. (Maynard Solomon has recently suggested that Schubert's romantic interests were homosexual, but this idea has not yet found its way into any English biographies.) Dominating the essay are brief portraits of the women whose lives intersected Schubert's. Kobald's work is worth considering if only for this one essay.

As much as any biography of a composer could, FLOWER passes over any discussion of Schubert's music. The result is that a somewhat distorted picture is drawn, since Schubert spent perhaps as much time composing as any great composer. Flower provides many quotations from the Luib correspondence. (Until his death, Luib had planned to be the first biographer of Schubert.) This is a work that gives much attention to the sights, sounds, and smells of Schubert's life.

HILMAR offers eight individual essays that portray some aspect of Schubert and his environment. Written from an extremely skeptical point of view, this biography seeks to dispel many of the traditional notions about Schubert that have persisted from the years immediately following his death until the present day. Hilmar attempts to penetrate deeply into Schubert's psyche and often appears to have succeeded. The lack of discussion about Schubert's music is in this case clearly by choice and not due to a lack of musical expertise on the part of the author. For those who already have a picture of Schubert, Hilmar may be the best choice for refining and developing that image.

Seemingly designed to arouse a debate, MAREK surveys most of the currently available biographies of Schubert and presents the most controversial aspects of his life: his sexual activity, his relationship to Beethoven, his criminal record (mentioned only in this source), and his personality as it was manifested in public. Marek's writing style is lively and sharp, and his discussion of why Schubert never composed a successful opera is especially fascinating. The two major problems with Marek are that he does not seem to have consulted primary sources and that his chosen secondary sources are all treated as gospel.

As his title claims, OSBORNE successfully weaves well-known aspects of Schubert's life into the fabric of early 19th-century Viennese culture. A lack of new information about Schubert keeps the reader at some distance from the composer's personality; the book never warms up to the man. Here we are looking down on Vienna from such a distance that we can see almost everything, but can hear nothing.

The strength of WECHSBERG's volume lies in its plates. Herein are the greatest number (and the finest quality) of reproductions of materials that relate to Schubert, including photographs, manuscripts, and art work. Many of the plates are beautiful, and the photographs of Vienna (as well as other relevant cities) are vivid and well chosen. The text is heavily dependent upon the works of Deutsch and does not advance the general body of knowledge about Schubert.

—Jeffrey Hopper

—————

SCHUMANN, Robert, 1810–1856; German composer.

Bedford, Herbert, *Robert Schumann: His Life and Work.* London, K. Paul, and New York, Harper, 1925.

Boucourechliev, André, *Schumann,* translated by Arthur Boyars. New York, Grove, 1959 (originally published by Éditions du Seuil, Paris, 1956).

Brion, Marcel, *Schumann and the Romantic Age,* translated by Geoffrey Sainsbury. New York, Macmillan, and London, Collins, 1956 (originally published by A. Michel, Paris, 1954).

Chissell, Joan, *Schumann.* London, Dent, 1948.

Fuller-Maitland, J. A., *Schumann.* London, Low Marston, and New York, Scribner, 1884.

Litzmann, Berthold, editor, *Clara Schumann: An Artist's Life* (2 vols.), translated and abridged by Grace E. Hadow. London, Macmillan, 1913 (originally published by Breitkopf and Härtel, Leipzig, 3 vols., 1902–08).

Niecks, Frederick, *Robert Schumann,* edited by Christina Niecks. London, Dent, and New York, Dutton, 1925.

Ostwald, Peter, *Schumann: The Inner Voices of a Musical Genius.* Boston, Northeastern University Press, 1985; as *Schumann: Music and Madness,* London, Gollancz, 1985.

Patterson, Annie Wilson, *Schumann.* London, Dent, and New York, Dutton, 1903.

Plantinga, Leon B., *Schumann as Critic.* New Haven, Connecticut, and London, Yale University Press, 1967.

Reich, Nancy B., *Clara Schumann: The Artist and the Woman.* Ithaca, New York, Cornell University Press, and London, Gollancz, 1985.

Schauffler, Robert Haven, *Florestan: The Life and Work of Robert Schumann.* New York, Holt, 1945.

Taylor, Ronald, *Robert Schumann: His Life and Work.* New York, Universe Books, and London, Granada, 1982.

Walker, Alan, *Schumann.* London, Faber, 1976.

Wasielewski, Joseph Wilhelm von, *Life of Robert Schumann,* translated by A. L. Alger. Boston, Ditson, 1871 (originally published as *Robert Schumann: Eine Biographie,* Dresden, R. Kunze, 1858; 4th edition, Leipzig, Breitkopf and Härtel, 1906).

Young, Percy, *Tragic Muse: The Life and Works of Robert Schumann.* London, Hutchinson, 1957; 2nd edition, London, Dobson, 1961.

*

Much remains to be done before a definitive biography of Schumann can be written in any language. However, the large collections of primary material—unpublished letters, diaries, and other documents—pertaining to Schumann are gradually being published in German by the VEB Deutscher Verlag, Leipzig (2 volumes so far). There is also a great deal of research and new material published in German sources that English-speaking biographers have not yet used.

WASIELEWSKI, the first biographer, knew Schumann well as a teacher in Leipzig and as a conductor in Düsseldorf. He interviewed many people to gather great quantities of information, letters and other papers, but the important informant, Clara Schumann, eluded him. Wasielewski was a good observer and a good judge of his material, although he does not always give the information a modern reader would like. He includes many letters and a valuable medical death report that he solicited. Though his was the first biography to be translated into English, his important, enlarged 4th edition (1906) has never appeared in English. Wasielewski's music analysis reflects Schumann's (and the 19th century's) attitude in that it considers his symphonies and chamber works (large-scale works) the most significant. Works generally most admired today, the piano music and songs, he labels as minor and specifically criticizes the piano music for lacking form.

NIECKS also had direct and extensive contact with friends and acquaintances of Schumann and with Clara Schumann herself. Niecks was a careful researcher and his well-balanced, objective account remains the best biography in English, though some information is now dated. He relies partly on Wasielewski's 3rd edition, but his new discoveries supplement that work significantly. He did not finish his intended 2 volume project, a biography and a music analysis; his widow finished just the biography. Therefore, discussions of the music, interwoven into the biographical narrative, describe only its historical context, including quotes that illuminate the process of composition and some reviews.

FULLER-MAITLAND had no direct connection to the original sources. His relatively brief biography relies on Wasielewski, although he admires Shumann's more intimate works. He is the first to divide his biography into separate "life" and "works" sections, and he has strong opinions about the value of each work. Fuller-Maitland reflects the English attitude of his time in resisting Schumann's symphonies, yet he had an historian's eye: "with the broader views of art which are now gaining ground among us, we may be sure that these Symphonies will increase year by year in popularity, until they are accepted at their true value."

LITZMANN's multi-volume biography of Clara Schumann makes extensive use of unpublished diaries and correspondence of the Schumann family, including large portions of letters and other material quoted directly. Since Robert figures very prominently in this account, the book is essential to Schumann biography. The first English edition is an abridged but reasonably accurate translation.

Several biographies are slanted toward portraying Schumann within a 19th-century romantic sweep. BEDFORD, in a short, popular-style story, sets the historical stage well and gives a breezy but not particularly new account. BOUCOURECHLIEV also places Schumann well and points out the contradictions in his character, but provides few facts. Schumann's life becomes a series of romantic adventures doomed by his "romantic" insanity. BRION also sets a stage for the period and gives a good sense of Schumann's literary connections but whitewashes the characters into romantic symbols. PATTERSON, who knew the daughter, Eugenie Schumann, and used Schumann correspondence and Wasielewski as her sources, concentrates heavily on anecdotes from Schumann's life. Her flowery writing style becomes wearisome, and she displays no critical judgement in her discussion of the music.

A more substantial biography that sticks closer to the facts with less of the author's personal slant is CHISSELL's, in which the life and works are treated separately. The life is a solid, straightforward repetition of known facts, and the music analyses are brief descriptions of the works including historical facts about them. This is not an especially reflective or analytical book, but it is a reliable account. There are few footnotes, a fact common to all the Schumann biographies. YOUNG is less useful, providing little new information and organizing his book in a puzzling mixture of historical-sequence chapters and interrupting subject-chapters, such as "Clara" and "Music for Voices." He accepts, rather than examines, the precept that Schumann's piano works are his greatest accomplishment, and his accounts of the music are laced with personal judgment. WALKER, on the other hand, writes a small, simple book, accurate and easy to read, that focuses only on the most important events of Schumann's life. He goes to the heart of the main Schumann controversies: the hand injury, the supposedly faulty metronome, the seeming dual personality, the medical problems, the Clara-Robert-Wieck dispute, and Schumann's decline with its effect (or lack of effect) on his artistic production. Walker has copious musical examples embedded into this entertaining account based on recent research.

Two writers use 20th-century psychological and medical analysis to study Schumann's character. The conclusions in these books are extremely subjective. SCHAUFFLER's very readable account professes to paint an objective picture of Clara and Robert. Schauffler has reread the early source material to do so, but his strong viewpoints cloud the narrative. He is particularly negative toward Clara, but he overinterprets them both and ascribes to them motives and feelings of doubtful validity. One musical description suffices to demonstrate his flamboyant writing style: "the finale works up to the brazen motto, then takes off from Earth into a western blaze of glory." OSTWALD is the most recent biographer with a medical approach, and he is well qualified to focus on these issues in Schumann's life, both mental and physical. While he provdes much good information, Ostwald stretches credibility to the limit as he practices 20th-century psychiatry on the long-dead Schumann. His conclusions seem speculative at best.

Two books approach Schumann's life from original perspectives. PLANTINGA describes Schumann as a critic by tracing his activity and his writings for the *Neue Zeitschrift für Musik*. Although this aspect occupied Schumann's entire adult life, it has barely been touched on in other biographies. Because of Plantinga's clear, perceptive writing and the many quotes from original sources to support his facts, his is one of the most important recent books, which gives fresh insight into Schumann. Another new perspective on Schumann is provided by REICH, who uses primary sources, many of them previously unknown, to present her case. Her book on Clara Schumann shows that the couple's lives were so interwoven that she in effect writes a biography of Robert also. The book casts their marriage and interactions in a new light that provides an unusually sympathetic and well-rounded view of Robert within this relationship.

TAYLOR's recent book, without footnotes (though it gives a generalized source list and extensive bibliography), retells Schumann's story in an integrated way, discussing music and life together. Taylor has studied the letters and original sources, but he uses few quotes in the narrative, choosing rather to distill the information in his own words. He considers musical works as events within the narrative and does not analyze them separately. The postscript has a good summary of the changing fate of Schumann's music. He places the smaller pieces and symphonies in modern perspective, reversing Schumann's and Wasielewski's assessment of them. Taylor's biography has more synthesis and reflection than Chissell's, and while Niecks remains the best biography in English, this up-to-date, readable book is worth studying while we await a truly comprehensive biography.

—Camilla Cai

SCHWEITZER, Albert, 1875–1965; Alsatian theologian, musician, and missionary physician.

Marshall, George and David Poling, *Schweitzer: A Biography*. New York, Doubleday, 1971.
McKnight, Gerald, *Verdict on Schweitzer: The Man Behind the Legend of Lambaréné*. London, F. Muller, and New York, J. Day, 1964.
Seaver, George, *Albert Schweitzer: The Man and His Mind*. New York, Harper, 1947; London, A. and C. Black, 1948.

*

SEAVER's workmanlike intellectual biography is one of three books written by the author on his subject, whom he regards as one of the great Christian leaders of his generation and "probably the most gifted genius of our age as well as its most prophetic thinker." Quoting extensively from Schweitzer's autobiographical writings, Seaver clearly sets forth the various stages in the European career of the philosopher, theologian, musicologist, organist, organ-builder, preacher, and teacher before detailing his medical studies and the four periods of his activity at his hospital in Africa. Characterizing Schweitzer as "a pioneer with a passion for ultimate truth" and identifying his prime motivation as a desire "to give substance to form," Seaver concludes that "his life and thought are all of a piece." The biographer attempts to show that Schweitzer enriched several branches of learning, making an original and even revolutionary contribution to each. The second part of Seaver's book is devoted to an examination of Schweitzer's works and thought, including *The Quest of the Historical Jesus* (1910) and its reception in England, the monumental study of J. S. Bach, and the ethic of Reverence for Life. An Appendix contains several brief essays by Schweitzer, including the address he delivered at Frankfurt when he received the Goethe Prize there in 1928. Seaver's book is thoughtfully documented but dully written, and the 30 illustrations are rather poorly reproduced.

Appearing several years after Schweitzer's death, the copiously illustrated biography of MARSHALL AND POLING, which includes an appreciative Foreword by Schweitzer's daughter Rhena, has the advantage of covering its subject's entire life span. Its 23 vividly written chapters are replete with revealing anecdotes, and the well-documented biography presents an extensive bibliography, a decade-by-decade list of Schweitzer's activities and achievements, and even a graphic record of medical activities at Lambaréné. The reverent but not hagiographic authors present Schweitzer as a man who called his time "a period of spiritual decadence of mankind," who longed for a "depth of human experience that included involvement with others," and in his lifelong clash with orthodoxy "made the ultimate protest with a creative burst of assistance and affection for the sick and forgotten and lost." Schweitzer's decision to work in Africa is seen as a rational rather than a religious or mystical choice. With the exception of brief chapters on "Albert Schweitzer's Ethics" and "The Man Within," which outline some salient features of the doctor's intellectual and spiritual legacy, the authors seem more interested in the tensions and conflicts in Schweitzer's life than in his thought. Presenting Schweitzer not as a reclusive idealist but as a world citizen, they tell the absorbing story of his life against the background of world events. As they delineate Schweitzer's affinity and identification with Goethe, they relate his life and thought to such great contemporaries as Martin Buber and Dietrich Bonhoeffer, "two men who refused to accept the parochial limitation of religion," and the Arizona magnate Larimer Mellon, who emulated *le grand docteur* by becoming a physician and founding a hospital in Haiti.

On the face of it, McKNIGHT's book deserves some attention as a corrective to hagiographic accounts of a living legend, but the British journalist's muckraking book is little more than a pathetic attempt to demythologize and debunk his subject, to provide a counterpoint (or counterpoise) to "hymns of adulation and hyperbole," to break through the curtain of "mystery and suppression" in Lambaréné, and present Schweitzer "in the round" for the first time. His book is a welter of feebly substantiated charges and half-truths made doubly unpalatable by the author's hit-and-run tactics and snide tone. His very chapter headings are revealing: "Saint or Bigot?", "Women and the Lure," "Eccentrics' Goal," "Why Men Don't Stay," "The Tragedy of Mme Schweitzer," "Is Schweitzer a Christian?", and "How Good a Doctor?" Impugning Schweitzer's motives at every turn, McKnight paints him as an egocentric, parsimonious, crabbed old schoolmaster who stubbornly resists change and impedes progress, an autocratic, paternalistic man who patronizes the natives, an uncaring husband and father, and one who surrounds himself with strange animals and even stranger people ("Schweitzerines," McKnight states, are apt to be "jaded socialites with a charitable urge"). Identifying medicine as "the field in which [Schweitzer] has shown the least talent," the author claims that Schweitzer had done only a minimal amount of doctoring. Lambaréné is seen as just "a backdrop with living 'props' against which he could conduct his experiment in ethical living," and Schweitzer's hospital and quarters, whose woeful sanitary conditions are seen as partly due to his undue reverence for the life of the insect population, constitute "a jungle sore suppurating into the fresh body of emergent Africa." The irreverent McKnight even faults Schweitzer, to whom he repeatedly refers as a "negro doctor" (*sic*), for conversing in "guttural" and "throaty" German while pretending not to know English.

The Bibliography in the Marshall-Poling book lists McKnight

as "Victor Knight," a slip that assumes Freudian significance when one considers that in *An Understanding of Albert Schweitzer* (1966) George Marshall devotes a chapter to a rebuttal of McKnight.

—Harry Zohn

SCOTT, Sir Walter, 1771–1832; Scottish writer.

Buchan, John, *Sir Walter Scott*. London, Cassell, and New York, Coward McCann, 1932.

Carswell, Donald, *Sir Walter: A Four-Part Study in Biography*. London, J. Murray, 1930.

Chambers, Robert, *Life of Sir Walter Scott*. New York, W. Stodart, 1832; Edinburgh, W. and R. Chambers, 1871.

Crawford, Thomas, *Scott*. Edinburgh, Oliver and Boyd, 1965.

Johnson, Edgar, *Sir Walter Scott: The Great Unknown* (2 vols.). New York, Macmillan, and London, Hamilton, 1970.

Lockhart, J. G., *Memoirs of the Life of Sir Walter Scott, Bart*. Edinburgh, R. Cadell, and Philadelphia, Carey Lea, 1837.

Pearson, Hesketh, *Walter Scott: His Life and Personality*. London, Methuen, and New York, Harper and Row, 1954.

Pope-Hennessy, Una, *The Laird of Abbotsford*. London and New York, Putnam, 1932.

Wilson, A. N., *The Laird of Abbotsford: A View of Sir Walter Scott*. Oxford and New York, Oxford University Press, 1980.

*

It used to be said that the two greatest biographies in the English language were Boswell's *Life of Johnson* and LOCKHART's *Life of Scott*. While the reputation of the former stands as high as it ever did, Lockhart has been "found out." The best that can be said for Lockhart's book is that it presents biography in what was then a new manner, the combination of the use of Scott's letters and his later *Journal*, displaying considerable narrative artistry. Lockhart knew Scott intimately and loved and admired him, a personal quality that comes across warmly to the reader.

That said, as the author of what must now be regarded as the authoritative life (Edgar Johnson, see below) puts it: "the work is seriously distorted by misunderstanding and bias and riddled by mis-statements extending even beyond ignorance of the facts to deliberate invention and falsifications." A case in point is Scott's deathbed remark, "be a good man," which was almost certainly not said by Scott, but in a letter to Lockhart by a lady who was urging him to show that Scott made a pious end. Lockhart's work is still therefore of value because of the reflected personal relationship, and is a quarry for slants (if sometimes biased) on contemporary characters, but it has little value as reliable biography.

CHAMBERS' book, like all but the most recent studies, does not reflect the modern scholarly editions of the letters or the journals. (For these see H. J. C. Grierson, editor, *The Letters of Sir Walter Scott*, London, 1932–38, along with J. C. Corson, *Notes and Index to Sir Herbert Grierson's Edition of "The Letters of Sir Walter Scott,"* Oxford, 1979; and W. E. K. Anderson, Editor, *The Journal of Sir Walter Scott*, Oxford, 1972.) Chambers writes, moreover, in what must now be considered a fairly old-fashioned style. CARSWELL's study is of some interest in that it relates Scott's life to the lives of his friends James Hogg, the poet and novelist, Joanna Baillie, the author of unactable (and, nowadays, unreadable) plays, and John Gibson Lockhart, Scott's son-in-law.

Dame Una POPE-HENNESSY's study presents the curious theory that some of the later novels, including *The Fair Maid of Perth,* were written early in Scott's career and merely revised when he ran out of fresh ideas toward the end of his life. As Scott was a notoriously reluctant reviser, her theory seems unusual in itself rather than probable in fact.

BUCHAN's biography, though written without benefit of later scholarship on the *Letters* and *Journal,* is a splendidly readable account; a factual novel, so to say, in which the author's empathy with his hero is obvious. Buchan also has the advantage of a good knowledge of Scottish affairs in Scott's time and after. It would be difficult to finish this book without gaining a strong impression of Scott's goodness as a man, as well as of his skill as a storyteller.

PEARSON, an experienced popular biographer, presents his subjects in a characteristic and easily recognisable mould. (His other subjects have included Wilde, Dickens, Disraeli and Whistler.) His method is to portray his characters very much "in the round," using their own words frequently, but usually without reference to where his quotations and opinions are to be found. His *Walter Scott* has the advantage over all its predecessors of his having been the first biographer to have access to the Grierson edition of the *Letters* (though not to Carson's supplemental volumes) and to the 1939–46 three-volume edition of *The Journal* (which replaced the inexact two-volume edition of 1891, itself replaced in 1972 with Anderson's edition).

There is no doubt about the ease with which Pearson's narrative flows, and even less about his powerful evocation of a very great man. Since Scott himself was a natural producer of aphorisms, no one will quarrel with Pearson's exercise of a similar gift. In two respects, however, he is likely to annoy some readers. While his claim for which seven of Scott's 26 novels are his greatest is interesting, not everyone will agree with his dismissal of *Waverley;* or with his view that *The Heart of Midlothian,* generally reckoned by Scottish readers to be Scott's finest achievement, is not of the first order.

Even more curious are some of his snap judgments on Scott's contemporaries. Describing the famous occasion in Edinburgh when the 15-year-old Scott met Burns at the home of Professor Ferguson, father of Scott's school friend Adam Ferguson, Pearson claims that Burns' "revolutionary views and drunken habits and low associates" discouraged Scott from seeking a later meeting. "The man who insisted on taking a bottle of brandy to bed with him when staying in a friend's house was not the ideal companion for one who preferred a book of poetry in that situation," writes Pearson. But there is not the slightest evidence that Burns ever did any such thing, and plenty to suggest that by the standards of the age he was not an outstandingly heavy drinker.

More astonishing still is Pearson's dismissal of James Hogg, the Ettrick Shepherd: "Hogg is chiefly remembered today not as the writer but as the inciter of a great poem: Wordsworth's lines on his death." Such a verdict is absurd when pronounced on one whose poems are currently available in several selections; whose novels and tales are currently reappearing in critical editions;

whose fictional masterpiece *The Private Memoirs and Confessions of a Justified Sinner* has been more or less constantly in print for the past 100 or so years, and for whom a *Collected Edition* is now being actively mooted. Students of English literature may be equally surprised to find that all the blank verse of Congreve and Otway is "uninspired," as is "most of Dryden."

JOHNSON's splendid two-volume biography became at once the standard scholarly life of Scott, and is likely to remain so in the foreseeable future. Johnson occasionally interrupts his well-annotated narrative flow to provide critical accounts of the work accomplished by his author during the period just written up. His critical powers are acute but generous, his understanding of the Scotland of Scott's time, profound. Johnson's work is, without doubt, essential to anyone who wishes seriously to understand Scott and Scotland, and the continuing relevance today of so much of Scott's output. Unfortunately, Johnson's book is out of print at this writing.

WILSON comes nearer than most to meeting the popular need. His book arises quite frankly out of affection for Scott and his work. Wilson's narrative style is every bit as compelling as Buchan's even though he arranges his work thematically, with such headings as "The border Minstrel," "Scott's Religion," and "Scott and the Critic," rather than by means of strictly chronological narrative.

There has been a revival of Scott scholarship since World War II. The views of some of the scholars are examined, and most of the scholars listed, in CRAWFORD's *Walter Scott.* His view of Scott is politically somewhat that of the Left: "Scott's difficulties as an artist were due not so much to any defect of life in the Scottish people—this was an age of industrial expansion and political and social ferment—as to his Toryism, his pathological fear of radical weavers and contemporary mobs, combined with a refusal to put art first, and a disastrous compromise with the market." While there is some truth in such a view, the impression this undoubtedly useful book ultimately leaves is perhaps of the great beast hardly visible beneath the swarm of critical parasites, each blooded with his own pin-prick viewpoint. The fact remains that at the end of the day, Scott was the generous creator of a larger number of unforgettable characters in British literature than any other writer except Shakespeare; a fact which Buchan, Johnson, and Wilson all readily acknowledge.

—Maurice Lindsay

SCRIABIN, Alexander Nikolayevich, 1872–1915; Russian composer and pianist.

Bowers, Faubion, *Scriabin. A Biography of the Russian Composer* (2 vols.). Tokyo, Kodansha International, 1969.

Bowers, Faubion, *The New Scriabin: Enigmas and Answers.* New York, St. Martin's, 1973; Newton Abbot, David and Charles, 1974.

Hull, A. Eaglefield, *A Great Russian Tone-Poet: Scriabin.* London, K. Paul, 1916; New York, Dutton, 1918.

Swan, Alfred J., *Scriabin.* London, J. Lane, 1923.

*

By comparison with some other Russian composers, Scriabin has fared poorly at the hands of English biographers, partly as a result of changing tastes down the decades. Hull and Swan produced their monographs when Scriabin was a recently deceased avantgardist, still in vogue, not yet upstaged by more advanced forms of modernism, and whose aura of *fin-de-siècle* mysticism did not yet work to his discredit.

HULL was an English musicologist and early Scriabin devotee. His monograph begins with an 81-page biographical sketch. Published immediately after Scriabin's death, it lacks perspective but conveys its author's enthusiasm. As Hull admits, there are some gaps and speculation in his account; he was writing before the appearance of any reliable source materials. Nevertheless, he is well informed on the general outlines of Scriabin's life, about his works and the Russian and Western musical and cultural setting. The study is dated by its romantic rhetoric, and there is a certain naïveté in the gush about "Moscow the Golden, the mother of the mighty Russian race." Even at the end Scriabin could not be left to die, but "passed through the veil which hides the greatest of all mysteries."

Writing seven years later, SWAN is better informed than Hull and has used recent Russian sources such as Yulii Engel's useful chronology of Scriabin's life (1916) and the monographs by Evgenii Gunst (1915), V. G. Karatygin (1915), and Leonid Sabaneyev (1922)—all of which remain untranslated. Like Hull, Swan treats the life and works separately, with a mixture of *engagé* enthusiasm and schoolmasterliness in his account of "our author's" advancement as composer. Within limits of space (57 pages) he gives a balanced, accurate account of Scriabin's life. In part two, he treats Scriabin's "mystery" theme as not self-sufficient, though looming paramount as a source of musical inspiration, and he follows the development of Scriabin's ideas in tandem with his musical evolution.

BOWERS' outwardly impressive two-volume work (1969) was produced for the upcoming centenary, registering a general revival of interest in Scriabin. However, the author proves inadequate to his task. To judge by the slipcase, which is wallpapered with manuscript facsimiles of Scriabin's uncompleted *Preliminary Action* that are nowhere properly discussed in the book, Bowers had access to a wealth of valuable materials but has largely squandered the opportunity of producing a truly authoritative work. Footnotes peter out after page 95 in volume I, and there is no bibliography—only a catalogue of works, select discography, and an (incomplete) index.

Bowers is evidently an ardent "Russia-fancier": his second chapter, on "Atmosphere," introduces a series of sensationalised vignettes of Russian composers. The abnormality of Scriabin, particularly in a Freudian sense, obviously intrigues Bowers, who also over-responds to the hothouse sensuality of some of the music, pointing out for instance the "erotic, even erectile meaning" of the *Poème Languide*! It is generally in these "evocative" terms that the music is described, rather than in a manner to satisfy a musically literate reader.

Undoubtedly Bowers has some familiarity with Russian language and culture, but his knowledge is not close or accurate enough to prevent a fair sprinkling of linguistic howlers, garbled names, and other errors. He also seems unable to decide for whom he is writing. He caters simultaneously to a reader who needs translations of even elementary foreign expressions—"mouton" (sheep), "dolce far niente" (the sweetness of doing

nothing)—yet who takes in his stride such arcane terms as: fulgurous, scintillant, titanomachy, languinous, manvantara, hypnoidal, gravid, orchidaceous, and patulous. The better passages of Bowers' work are those where he himself stands back and quotes *in extenso* from other sources: Scriabin's correspondence, concert reviews, reminiscences by other observers, and so forth. Since the two-volume format permits a fairly leisurely narrative pace, the book contains a wealth of raw source material (much of it translated for the first time) that students and possible future biographers could find useful. As a detailed guide to what Scriabin wrote, played, or otherwise did in any particular period, Bowers' book has no rival. But Scriabin still awaits a biographer able to digest, conceptualise, and present the full range of information now available.

Bowers also produced a sequel volume (1973), responding to the encouragement of friends that he write a short critical biography after the earlier rambling assemblage of materials. There is a short introduction by Vladimir Ashkenazy that mentions only the importance of Scriabin and sounds no fanfare for Bowers' offerings. Five chapters rehearse the outline of Scriabin's life and include new information that was "withheld" earlier. But most of it is anecdotal, certainly interesting to read, but not the stuff of serious biography. There is Bowers' familiar display of errors, with even a few more added to what was earlier correct.

Though not biography in any true sense, Boris de Schloezer's *Scriabin: Artist and Mystic* (Berkeley, California, and Oxford, 1987) offers an absorbing glimpse into the composer's artistic personality. In the absence of any truly satisfactory biography in English, however, one can only recommend more competent works in other languages, notably (in Russian) V. Delson, *Skryabin. Ocherki zhizni i tvorchestva* (Moscow, 1971).

—Christopher J. Barnes

SETON, Mother Elizabeth Ann Bayley, 1774–1821; American religious leader and saint.

Celeste, Sister Marie, *Elizabeth Ann Seton: A Self-Portrait; A Study of Her Spirituality in Her Own Words.* Libertyville, Illinois, Franciscan Marytown Press, 1986.

Celeste, Sister Marie, *The Intimate Friendships of Elizabeth Ann Bayley Seton, First Native-Born American Saint.* New York, Alba House, 1989.

Dirvin, Joseph, *Mrs. Seton: Foundress of the American Sisters of Charity.* New York, Farrar Straus, 1962; revised edition, 1975.

Kelly, Ellin M., *Numerous Choirs: A Chronicle of Elizabeth Bayley Seton and Her Spiritual Daughters.* Evansville, Indiana, Mater Dei Provincialate, 1981.

Melville, Annabelle, *Elizabeth Bayley Seton.* New York, Scribner, 1951.

*

Elizabeth Seton was clearly one of the most influential Catholic women in antebellum America. Yet during the 19th century scholars for the most part ignored her. The Rev. Charles I. White knew Elizabeth Seton's sister Catherine, herself a nun, who provided both reminiscences and letters. In 1853 White published his *Life of Elizabeth A. Seton*, a laudatory account that explained little of Mother Seton's motivations.

In much the same vein Seton's grandson Robert, through his connections with his grand-aunt Catherine and his own reputation as an author, was able to obtain a large amount of primary materials from the Sisters of Charity that had been unavailable to White. Robert Seton edited *Memoirs, Letters, and Journal of Elizabeth Seton* (1869).

The same year, Mme. Helene De Barbery published a biography of Seton in Paris. This French work was eventually translated by Joseph B. Code as *Elizabeth Seton* (1927). Code provided a later study of Mother Seton's letters, entitled *Letters of Mother Seton to Mrs. Julianna Scott* (1928), and also edited *Daily Thought of Mother Seton* (1960). None of these works provides much detailed information concerning Elizabeth Seton's life.

The Catholic author Agnes Sadlier provided a readable biography, *Elizabeth Seton, Foundress of the American Sisters of Charity* (1905). Other books came from the Rev. Leonard Feeney, Mary Coyle O'Neil (1940), and Katherine Burton (1946). But all of these works provide no footnotes and contain imaginary conversations for which no historical documentation exists.

The Sisters of Charity themselves created a book on Mother Seton from the notes of her favorite confessor, the Rev. Simon Gabriel Brute. The work, published in 1884, also is without any scholarly apparatus.

The first scholarly biography of Mother Seton, by MELVILLE, remains the definitive work. Melville has utilized all of the primary sources available. Her study presents Seton undergoing a series of crises and examines her response to the will of God, especially her willingness to accept a number of harsh personal losses in family and friends. It is an excellent piece of work, and has yet to be superseded.

A number of efforts have been made to explain the influences that directed Mother Seton. The Rev. William Brennan, in *The Vincentian Heritage of Mother Seton and Her Spiritual Daughters* (1963), stresses the role of St. Vincent De Paul's rule, which Mother Seton utilized for her new community (1812). Mary Kathleen Flanagan, in her doctoral dissertation presented to the Union Theological Seminary in 1978, emphasizes the role of Seton's pastor, the Rev. John Henry Hobart, pastor of Trinity Church, New York. (He later became the Episcopal Bishop of New York.) In the same vein is Rose Marie Laverty's *Loom of Many Threads: The English and French Influences on the Character of Elizabeth Ann Bayley Seton* (1958), published by the Sisters of Charity. While this work is useful in that it alerts the reader to a wide variety of factors that had an impact on Mother Seton's life, it does not add anything substantial to Melville's work. While DIRVIN does provide more detail on Mother Seton and her husband William's trip to Leghorn, Italy, his study, well-written and thoroughly researched, does not replace the work by Dr. Melville.

KELLY has tried a new tack in her approach to Mother Seton. A professor of medieval English literature at De Paul University, Kelly provides a chronicle of yearly events that she judges had an impact upon and may have affected the options available to Mother Seton. The approach, utilizing the traditional medieval chronicles, does indicate factors that could, and perhaps did, influence Mother Seton. Kelly also joined with Melville to edit a volume of the writings of Elizabeth Seton (*Elizabeth Seton: Selected Writings*, 1987), for which Melville wrote a short biographical account of Mother Seton. With annotations of Mother Seton's most significant comments and letters, this is a useful collection of her written work.

Another member of the Sisters of Charity, CELESTE (1986) offers a biography using Mother Seton's own words, where practical. In the same way she uses Mother Seton's letters to structure her *Intimate Friendships* (1989). Celeste's studies introduce us to the vast number of friends that Seton was able to maintain despite her transition from wealthy New York mother to a poor religious founder in Maryland. They are also beneficial since they provide us with the requisite documentation.

—Judith M. Curran

SÉVIGNÉ, Marquise de [born Marie de Rabutin-Chantal], 1626–1696; French writer.

Aldis, Janet, *Queen of Letter Writers: Marquise de Sévigné, Dame de Bourbilly*. London, Methuen, and New York, Putnam, 1907.
Tilley, Arthur A., *Madame de Sévigné: Some Aspects of Her Life and Character*. Cambridge, Cambridge University Press, 1936.
Williams, Charles G. S., *Madame de Sévigné*. Boston, Twayne, 1981.

*

Madame de Sévigné's life would never have been written were it not for the letters, mostly to her daughter, commenting on literary, cultural, religious, social, and political matters at and around the court of Louis XIV and, through the extended self-portrait, affording posterity an unaffected insight into the social history of the period through the life and concerns of an affectionate, active, and amused young widow. Apart from the three rather light and now obsolete biographies discussed below, there are no full-length biographies of Madame de Sévigné in English, only the customary dictionary articles and pages in literary histories devoted more to the literary and historical interest of the letters than to the life. There are also two selections from the letters with substantial biographical material, Arthur Stanley's *Madame de Sévigné, Her Letters and Her World* (1946) and H. R. Allentuch, *Madame de Sévigné: a Portrait in Letters* (1963). However, none of these works really confronts the serious social, historical, literary, or personal issues raised by the letters of this passionately devoted, lively, charming, talkative, socially important, and seriously religious woman.

All the biographical information available even in French, whether in separate book-length studies, in long essays published in connection with editions of the letters, or in articles devoted to individual details or aspects of Madame de Sévigné's life, must now be checked against the monumental 5000-page, three-volume edition of the *Correspondance* by Roger Duchêne (Paris, Bibliothèque de la Pléiade, 1972–78). Its notes overflow with relevant, readable, but scholarly historical detail and as much biographical information as even the most specialist reader can hope to obtain without recourse to any major new 17th-century sources that may remain to be discovered.

Duchêne is also the author of three straight biographical works, *Mme de Sévigné* (1968), *Mme de Sévigné et la lettre d'amour* (1970), and *Madame de Sévigné ou la chance d'être femme* (1982), a full-scale and narrative rather than evocative account of its subject's life, with a bibliography and somewhat scanty notes but without the massive indices of the *Correspondance*. Jacqueline Duchêne, who compiled the indices for the three volumes of letters, has herself written the life of Madame de Sévigné's daughter, to whom most of the letters were addressed (*Françoise de Gringnan ou le mal d'amour*, 1985).

The ALDIS biography is now so out of date as to be of value almost only for its Edwardian values and its quaintness. It is sensible and literate, makes no pretence to be other than an amateur attempt to convey enthusiasm, but is now little more than a time-filler. By 1936 TILLEY could produce the slim but now professional by-product of his literary historical work, quoting in French, with an index and chronology, dealing mostly with what the Marquise had to say about her friends, the news and gossip of the day, her houses, and the books she read. Tilley himself claims that "This is not a life of Madame Sévigné. It is merely an attempt to bring out in fuller detail than hitherto certain aspects of it."

The 1981 volume by WILLIAMS accords with the norms of the Twayne series to which it belongs. Williams holds that his subject's literary fortunes have been "unusually at the mercy of editors, chance and the prejudices or sympathies of class and temperament of later readers," no doubt a distorted and misleading echo of Duchêne, from whom Williams derives much. He provides an index, notes, and a bibliography, and sensibly synopsizes some of the letters by subject matter. He is sensitive to the value system of the Marquise and sketches in, from Duchêne, of whose work he provides a selective popularisation, some of the important social history, as of the postal system that conveyed the letters.

Future biographers need to explore the religion of the Marquise, the nature of her psychological makeup and of her affection for her daughter, and what her intimate letters reveal about the social history of the life of the aristocracy at and around the court of Louis XIV, rather than Madame de Sévigné's tastes or her position in literary history alongside the authors of memoirs and other forms of self-revelation more stylized than her own.

—A. H. T. Levi

SHAKESPEARE, William, 1564–1616; English playwright and poet.

Adams, Joseph Quincy, *A Life of William Shakespeare*. Boston, Houghton Mifflin, and London, Constable, 1923.
Bentley, Gerald E., *Shakespeare: A Biographical Handbook*. New Haven, Connecticut, Yale University Press, 1961.
Chambers, E. K., *William Shakespeare: A Study of Facts and Problems* (2 vols.). Oxford, Clarendon Press, 1930.
Chute, Marchette, *Shakespeare of London*. New York, Dutton, 1949; London, Secker and Warburg, 1951.
Dowden, Edward, *Shakespeare: A Critical Study of His Mind and Art*. London, H. S. King, and New York, Barnes and Noble, 1875.
Eccles, Mark, *Shakespeare in Warwickshire*. Madison, University of Wisconsin Press, 1961.
Lee, Sir Sidney, *Life of William Shakespeare*. London and New York, Macmillan, 1898.
Malone, Edmond, *Shakespeare*. London, 1790.
Rowe, Nicholas, *Some Account of the Life, etc., of Mr. William Shakespear* (in *The Works of Mr. William Shakespear*). London, 1709.
Rowse, A. L., *William Shakespeare: A Biography*. London, Macmillan, and New York, Harper, 1963.
Schoenbaum, S., *William Shakespeare: A Documentary Life*. Oxford, Clarendon Press, and New York, Oxford University Press, 1975.

*

John Aubrey, a traveling antiquarian, was the first to record information about Shakespeare's life. His 1680 "biography," published in *Brief Lives*, is a rambling aggregation of details, based primarily on conversations with William Beeston, the son of an actor who knew the playwright. Aubrey records such misinformation as the story that John Shakespeare was a butcher and the legend that apprenticed Will delivered speeches "in high style" when he killed a calf. From this source comes the legend that Shakespeare "in his younger years" served as a schoolmaster.

It took a fellow playwright inspired by Shakespearean drama to attempt the first biography, however. ROWE's 40-page *Account* appeared as a preface to his 1709 edition of Shakespeare's plays. Rowe depended heavily on the recollections of Thomas Betterton, an aged actor famous for his interpretations of Hamlet and Richard III. Betterton visited Stratford frequently to gather trivia about Shakespeare's life there. Rowe dutifully records the tale of the playwright's alleged poaching of deer from the estate of Sir Thomas Lucy and his subsequent banishment. We also learn about Shakespeare's acting career that "the top of his Performance was the Ghost in his own *Hamlet*." Rowe commented not only on his subject's life but also critically on his work. He praises Shakespeare's natural genius and dismisses as a failing of the age his habit of mixing comedy and tragedy.

Rowe's *Account* influenced many readers and editors—especially Samuel Johnson and Alexander Pope—in the 18th century, when Shakespeare's popularity and literary reputation grew. Not until MALONE, an assiduous scholar, published his *Shakespeare* in 1790 did the world have an ambitious effort at biography based on contemporary records. Malone traces John Shakespeare's career as a bailiff and recites information about Mary Arden and her family. He also proffers his opinion that Shakespeare possessed a rudimentary knowledge of the law and could have served as a clerk for some country attorney. Malone discredits the deer-poaching and schoolmaster legends but faithfully reports hearsay evidence that Shakespeare began his London career as a prompter's assistant. Malone gives readers an accurate estimate of the worth of the Shakespeare estate at his death and relates details about New Place, the Stratford house Shakespeare purchased for his retirement.

While Malone's was the first biography to employ records rather than rumor, it was not a full "life" in the modern sense of the word. The first such treatment was DOWDEN's 1875 study. Dowden, a scholar at Trinity College, Dublin, found in Shakespeare's plays evidence of "the growth of his intellect and character from youth to full maturity." Dowden argues that Shakespeare created characters whose struggles played out his own inner conflict. Hamlet is thus Shakespeare trying to avoid the destructive effect of excessive thought; Romeo, on the other hand, represents the dangers of too much passion. After achieving the status of a middle-class Stratfordian, the playwright emerged as a Prospero—self-assured, somewhat detached, optimistic.

Dowden's subjective reading of the corpus, especially his division of the plays into four distinct "periods," continued to influence readers and critics in the late 19th and early 20th centuries. For him and for others who read the plays and the sonnets, the texts were guideposts to real or imagined events in Shakespeare's life.

LEE, an Oxford graduate appointed to the editorship of the *Dictionary of National Biography* in 1891, attempted to counter subjective approaches like those of Dowden and others by publishing a *DNB* article in 1897, followed by a full biography in 1898. Lee admits to seeing "traces of personal emotion and . . . experience" in the sonnets, but concludes that the poems were "to a large extent undertaken as literary exercises." The reliable biographer, Lee believed, must uncover and compile facts, not invent them; his goal is to rescue the memory of his subject from oblivion. Yet for all the rich documentation of Lee's article and biography, he communicates many of the legends without questioning their authenticity. The poaching incident and expulsion, the claims that Justice Shallow is a caricature of Lucy, that Southampton gave the poet 1000 pounds, that the novice Shakespeare held horses for playhouse patrons—these fables are dutifully recorded. The legend has become inextricably bound up with the man and his work in Lee's biography.

ADAMS' 1923 book, the first biography of note by an American scholar, moves away from the legend/work nexus, placing Shakespeare in the context of Elizabethan London's theatrical scene. Much space is devoted to physical descriptions of the Theatre and Globe, the conventional spaces Shakespeare was required to work in. Adams pays little attention to the works as literature.

The first modern scholar to attempt an exhaustive compilation of biographical evidence was CHAMBERS, whose two-volume work is still highly regarded by scholars. Freed from the curse of Bardolatry, Chambers discusses the state of grammar-school teaching in Shakespeare's day, the makeup of Elizabethan acting companies, and the careers of actors and managers. Chambers' study is significant for its establishment of a reasonable chronology for the plays, and Chambers also argues convincingly that William Herbert, 3rd Earl of Pembroke, was the "W. H." of the sonnets. The second volume collects all the relevant documents about Shakespeare's life. The major drawbacks of Chambers' biography are his uninviting style and the sheer bulk of detail.

The late 1940s saw the publication of readable, popular biographies of Shakespeare. CHUTE's book is the most engaging of these efforts. Chute refrains from seeking biographical truths in the sonnets and legends, weaving her tale instead with primary texts from the period. She concentrates on life and manners in Stratford and London, takes up the subject of Shakespeare's grammar-school training, and depicts the popular theatrical scene on the Bankside. Chute does not attempt a critical analysis of the plays or sonnets; her goal is that of the historical novelist, which she admirably achieves.

Relying as well on "surviving documents," BENTLEY's 1961 account seems aimed more at students than general readers; it has the feel of a reference work rather than a biography. ECCLES likewise uses documents unearthed by Malone, Halliwell-Phillips, and Chambers to write his 1961 assessment of Shakespeare's life in Warwickshire. Eccles pays special attention to Shakespeare's friends and associates, arguing that his Stratford roots are essential to an understanding of his growth as a writer.

No doubt the most controversial of recent popular biographies is ROWSE's 1963 volume. Rowse, who defends his approach as "historical," devotes much space to the sonnets, where he finds compelling "evidence" about Shakespeare's career. Relying on references to contemporary events in the poems, he concludes that the Earl of Southampton was the youthful boy praised for his beauty, that Marlowe was the Rival Poet, and that William Hervey, husband to the Countess of Southampton, was the "W. H." who took the sequence to the printer. These discoveries were not new, but Rowse defiantly declared that they were "proved" by his historical method. In a later volume, Rowse demonstrated "beyond a doubt" that the mysterious Dark Lady was in fact Emilia Lanier, whose vision Shakespeare reportedly called up on his deathbed. Few if any of Rowse's often romantic assertions are documented by reliable records.

By far the most dependable—and readable—Shakespeare biography to date is SCHOENBAUM's 1975 life. The author attempts to sort legend and fact, pointing out here and in *Shakespeare's Lives* (1970) how many biographers tend to create Shakespeare in their own images. Schoenbaum includes over 200 facsimiles of records and manuscripts, some of which bear only tangentially on Shakespeare's life but provide an historical backdrop. His narrative addresses such questions as the Lost Years, the mystery surrounding Shakespeare's birth into the London theatrical world, his association with the Southampton circle, and his return to Stratford and purchase of New Place. About these subjects Schoenbaum offers reasoned comments based on documents whose authenticity is unquestioned. He conjectures only infrequently, as when he suggests that the traveling Queen's Men, their company reduced by one man (William Knell, killed in a duel) in the summer of 1587, may have recruited the 23-year-old Shakespeare for their Stratford performance. The suggestion is intriguing and plausible, based as it is on acting-company records. For this reason and others cited here, Schoenbaum's biography stands out as the most scholarly, definitive treatment of the playwright's life (if not his works) yet produced.

—Robert F. Willson, Jr.

SHAW, George Bernard, 1856–1950; Irish playwright and critic.

Brown, Ivor John Carnegie, *Shaw in His Time*. London, Nelson, 1965.

Chappelow, Allan, *Shaw the Villager and Human Being: A Biographical Symposium*. London, Skilton, and New York, Macmillan, 1962.

Chappelow, Allan, *Shaw "The Chucker-Out": A Biographical Exposition and Critique*. London, Allen and Unwin, and New York, AMS Press, 1969.

Colbourne, Maurice, *The Real Bernard Shaw*. Toronto, Dent, 1930; Boston, B. Humphries, 1931; London, Dent, 1939; New York, Dodd Mead, 1940; London, Dent, and New York, Philosophical Library, 1949.

Dervin, Daniel, *Bernard Shaw: A Psychological Study*. London, Associated University Presses, and Lewisburg, Pennsylvania, Bucknell University Press, 1975.

DuCann, Charles G. L., *The Loves of George Bernard Shaw*. London, A. Baker, and New York, Funk and Wagnalls, 1963.

Ervine, St. John, *Bernard Shaw: His Life, Work, and Friends*. London, Constable, and New York, Morrow, 1956.

Harris, Frank, *Bernard Shaw: An Unauthorized Biography Based on Firsthand Information*. New York, Simon and Schuster, and London, Gollancz, 1931.

Henderson, Archibald, *George Bernard Shaw, His Life and Works: A Critical Biography*. London, Hurst and Blackett, and Cincinnati, Stewart and Kidd, 1911; New York, Boni and Liveright, 1918.

Henderson, Archibald, *Bernard Shaw: Playboy and Prophet*. New York, D. Appleton, 1932.

Henderson, Archibald, *George Bernard Shaw: Man of the Century*. New York, Appleton-Century, 1956.

Holroyd, Michael, *Bernard Shaw: The Search for Love 1856–98*. New York, Random House, and London, Chatto and Windus, 1988.

Holroyd, Michael, *Bernard Shaw: The Pursuit of Power 1898–1918*. New York, Random House, and London, Chatto and Windus, 1989.

Irvine, William, *The Universe of G. B. S.* New York, Whittlesey House, 1949.

Minney, R. J., *Recollections of George Bernard Shaw*. Englewood Cliffs, New Jersey, Prentice-Hall, 1969.

O'Donovan, John, *Shaw and the Charlatan Genius: A Memoir*. London, Oxford University Press, and Dublin, Dolmer Press, 1965; Chester Springs, Pennsylvania, Dufour Editions, 1966.

Patch, Blanche, *Thirty Years with G. B. S.* London, Gollancz, and New York, Dodd Mead, 1951.

Pearson, Hesketh, *Bernard Shaw: His Life and Personality*. London, Collins, 1942; as *George Bernard Shaw: His Life and Personality*, New York, Harper, 1942; revised and enlarged edition, New York, Atheneum, 1963.

Pearson, Hesketh, *G. B. S., a Full-length Portrait*. London and New York, Harper, 1942.

Pearson, Hesketh, *G. B. S., a Postscript*. London, Collins, and New York, Harper, 1950.

Pearson, Hesketh, *G. B. S., a Full-length Portrait, and a Postscript*. New York, Harper, 1952.

Pearson, Hesketh, *Bernard Shaw: A Biography*. London, Macdonald and Jane's, 1975.

Peters, Margot, *Bernard Shaw and the Actresses*. New York, Doubleday, 1980.

Rattray, Robert F., *Bernard Shaw: A Chronicle*. New York, Roy, and London, Dobson, 1951.

Rosset, B. C., *Shaw of Dublin: The Formative Years*. University Park, Pennsylvania State University Press, 1964.

Shaw, Charles Macmahon, *Bernard's Brethren*. New York, Holt, and London, Constable, 1939.

Weintraub, Stanley, *Private Shaw and Public Shaw: A Dual Biography of Lawrence of Arabia and Bernard Shaw*. London, Cape, and New York, Braziller, 1963.

Weintraub, Stanley, *Journey to Heartbreak: The Crucible Years of Bernard Shaw 1914–18*. New York, Weybright and Talley, 1971; as *Bernard Shaw 1914–18: Journey to Heartbreak*. London, Routledge, 1973.

Weintraub, Stanley, *The Unexpected Shaw: Biographical Approaches to George Bernard Shaw and His Work*. New York, Ungar, 1982.

Winsten, Stephen, *Days with Bernard Shaw*. London, Hutchinson, 1948; New York, Vanguard, 1949.

Winsten, Stephen, *Shaw's Corner*. New York, Roy, and London, Hutchinson, 1952.

Winsten, Stephen, *Jesting Apostle: The Private Life of Bernard Shaw*. London, Hutchinson, 1956; and New York, Dutton, 1957.

*

"I have a horror of biographers," said Shaw. Thus in his plays, as in his music and drama criticism, Fabian socialist tracts, diverse essays, innumerable letters to the editor, and particularly in biographies by "disciples" (Shaw's label for Henderson) ranging from Harris to Pearson to Winsten in which he collaborated shamelessly (though sometimes secretly) with the authors, Shaw endeavored to prove that "The best authority on Shaw is Shaw." Indeed, the memoir by Shaw's Australian cousin, CHARLES SHAW, prints Shaw's manuscript commentary in red ink on facing pages, though the putative author's entire style bears the distinct Savian stamp, as does the writing throughout the works by HARRIS and Pearson. Holroyd, Shaw's benchmark biographer, asserts that Shaw did this "not for facile self-aggrandizement, but to provide his ideas with the endorsement of biographical authority." Not only did Shaw, as Holroyd says, "encumber" his biographers with advice, he was also a far better writer than they were, and couldn't resist livening up works that buried revealing nuggets amidst a dross of trivia. Regrettably, Shaw overlooked RATTRAY's unassimilated pastiche of biographical information, history, and criticism, arranged in unyielding chronological order.

In the last quarter-century of his life, venerated as a cross between a "British institution and a national monument," Shaw largely succeeded in sculpting his own image as an insouciant, irreverent genius capable of making sage pronouncements on every conceivable subject, from anarchy to Neitzsche to vegetarianism to women. Such collaboration pervades HENDERSON's bulky, undigested tomes, which Shaw not only "richly aided and carefully scrutinized" but wrote substantial segments of, as Holroyd says, "the left hand turgid, the right hand fantastical." Henderson, a University of North Carolina mathematics professor, explains in *Bernard Shaw: Playboy and Prophet*, an expansion of *George Bernard Shaw, His Life and Works*, that ''I learned the meaning of [Shaw's] plays, the purport of his philosophy, and the objects of his life not from my viewpoint alone, but from his own,'' remaining faithfully wedded to Shaw's ''millions of words, spoken or written,'' and turning out interpretations of Shaw's ''life, character, and significance'' for over 50 years of their acquaintance. Thus Henderson regards Shaw as the embodiment of the Neitzschean superman and the Life Force, ''Playboy of the Western World [and] Prophet of a new and better day.'' Shaw's writings incorporate Carlyle's ''dour ferocity,'' Ruskin's esthetics, Bunyan's valor, Blake's mystic vision, Swift's satire. . . . Shaw is ''the Irish Tolstoy,'' ''The Irish Molière,'' ''Voltaire perfected,'' a contemporary Cervantes, a jolly Santa Claus ''who brings . . . good cheer to this present world of doubt.'' No wonder that in a century with, as Holroyd says, ''forty-four declining years to run,'' Henderson apotheosized Shaw as *Man of the Century*, ''a true genius: inexplicable, untraceable, unmanageable, unpredictable, incalculable''—''close to the Kingdom of God.''

Numerous works by other acquaintances trivialize Shaw in their very attempts to demonstrate his genius; proximity breeds idolatry rather than insight. Thus PEARSON's anecdotal volumes, clones of *Full-Length Portrait* (1942), assert that Shaw's greatness lies ''in his irrepressible gaiety of spirit'' and ''eccentric personality'' rather than in his political and social philosophy. *Postscript* (1950) claims that Shaw's ''only form of self-indulgence was overwork,'' and includes Shaw's own anticipatory obituary. CHAPPELOW's compilations, *Shaw the Villager* (1962) and *Shaw ''The Chucker-Out''* (1969), give the villagers at Ayot St. Lawrence their say, including Shaw's neighbors, household staff, doctors, and pubkeeper, as does Winsten's *Shaw's Corner*. Their predictable consensus, that beneath the public Shaw's arrogance and ''rapier wit'' lurk private Shaw's ''humanity and humility,'' is a view shared by WINSTEN, another neighbor, about whose sentimental, inaccurate *Days* (1948) the dramatist commented: ''In hardly any passage . . . has Mr. Winsten's art not improved on bare fact. . . . '' The thesis of the less admiring *Jesting Apostle* (1956) is that although in another era Shaw might have been more of a saint and less of a jester, the 19th century had ''turned the mystic that he was by nature into a harsh realist'' lacking in sympathy for the human race. MINNEY and PATCH offer additional personal recollections—the latter particularly entertaining and, for once, not superintended by Shaw.

The most notable exception among the works by Shaw's friends and neighbors is ERVINE's swiftly-moving, well-researched interpretation of Shaw's personality, work, and friendships with H. G. Wells, William Morris, Beatrice and Sidney Webb, and others. Ervine, the author of 21 Irish Renaissance plays, six novels, and biographies of three other Edwardians, did not allow his 40-year friendship with Shaw to impinge on his independence of mind, although his personal perorations on topics ranging from the Welfare State to Lamarckianism present distractions in this otherwise engaging work. That Shaw was safely dead when this work was published doubtless enhanced the biography's integrity, for Ervine says, ''in the whole of our friendship, I never quoted his words without his consent.'' Carlos Baker, in the *Saturday Review*, said ''Shaw is lucky to have a biographer as wise and kindly, acidulous and

crotchety, realistic and witty as he was himself''; that judgment still stands.

Colbourne and Irvine offer biographical approaches to Shaw's works. COLBOURNE, a producer and actor, sees Shaw's essentially serious work as flawed by the comedy of a self-created alter ego, and judges his plays on their theatricality and audience reaction. IRVINE interprets Shaw's life and works in their political and historical contexts.

Try as he might to become his own posthumous Pygmalion, even nonagenarian Shaw could not have the last word. Indeed, the biographies by scholars free of Shaw's interference, notably Weintraub, Dervin, Peters, and particularly Holroyd, have served their complex, controversial subject far better than any works written during his lifetime, except for BROWN's derivative work. They have provided many documented corrections of earlier biographers' inventions and embellishments, and have dispelled legends created by Shaw himself. It is a tribute to these authors that, amidst the incessant labors of the Shaw industry (whose products number around 10,000 and are still growing), these writers have many new things to say, and they say them with zest, elegance, and affection but without the hero worship that contributes to their predecessors' turgid unreliability.

WEINTRAUB's first work (1963) is a scholarly but very readable delineation of the casual friendship between two legendary self-promoting figures, G. B. S. (''Public Shaw'') and T. E. Lawrence (''of Arabia''), who enlisted in the Royal Air Force as ''Private Shaw.'' Here Weintraub disproves the rumor that Lawrence was Shaw's son. Although Weintraub's *Journey to Heartbreak* has been superseded by Holroyd's coverage in volume 2 of the impact of World War I on Shaw, in *The Unexpected Shaw* Weintraub illuminates many paradoxes and contradictions of Shaw's life and work. For instance, he analyzes ''the paradox that Shaw's Irish countrymen, disenchanted with his clowning at their expense and his incessant search for compromise solutions which would leave the land of his birth united with the despised other island, should find in his unlikely person the makings of a staunch and outspoken Irish patriot.'' The first half of DERVIN's ''sensible, sensitive,'' non-jargony Freudian analysis of Shaw offers clinical observations of the playwright; the second half applies Freudian theory to his plays.

It is fitting that Shaw's first feminist biographer, PETERS, should write a sympathetic study of the most important women in his life—actresses—and their influence on his work: Janet Achurch, Ellen Terry, Florence Farr, Lillah McCarthy, Mrs. Patrick Campbell, and others—relationships DUCANN treats with speculation and irritating coyness. The ''New Drama,'' claims Peters, ''was very much the drama of the New Woman.'' Shaw as a feminist not only asserted that ''The stage is the only profession in which women are on equal terms with men,'' but proceeded to prove it by writing plays that dared to break the stereotypes and present women as fully-dimensional human beings, even at times ''unamiable.''

The first two volumes of the three that constitute HOLROYD's herculean 15-year effort to interpret Shaw's life and work have been published to deserved critical acclaim. One reviewer, Anthony Burgess, predicts that when completed it will be ''one of the three great literary biographies of the century'' (*Atlantic*, October 1988), the other two being Ellmann's lives of Joyce and Wilde. Volume one embeds Shaw's developmental years as a brilliant critic of music, drama, and art, and as a writer of bad novels in the social matrix of his ambiguous Dublin childhood and in the London political matrix of Fabian socialism in which, as Robertson Davies says, "he learned much about government and even more about governors" (*New York Times Book Review*, 30 October 1988). Was he, for instance, as ROSSETT ponders, the son of the alcoholic George Carr Shaw or the son of his mother's great and good friend, successful musician George Vandeleur Lee, whom O'DONOVAN argues broke up the Shaws' marriage? Volume one ends with Shaw's cautious courtship and marriage, at 41, to heiress Charlotte Payne-Townshend. Volume two alternates chapters dealing with Shaw's unorthodox, asexual marriage and friendships (never liaisons, says Holroyd) with actresses; his political activities to the beginning of World War I; and the writing of his major plays, *Man and Superman*, *Major Barbara*, and *Pygmalion*. In these two volumes Holroyd has unsentimentally re-created the many roles that Shaw himself played, in public and in private. But unlike Shaw's contemporary biographers, who could or did not discriminate between Shaw's essence, his acting, his self-promotion, and his ambiguous self-analyses ("As a matter of fact," said Shaw, "I am overrated as an author. Most great men are."), Holroyd provides the information and the perspective to help us not only understand, but interpret, this complex figure with confidence and pleasure.

—Lynn Z. Bloom

SHELLEY, Mary Wollstonecraft, 1797–1851; English writer.

Dunn, Jane, *Moon in Eclipse: A Life of Mary Shelley*. London, Weidenfeld and Nicolson, and New York, St. Martin's, 1978.

Grylls, R. Glynn, *Mary Shelley: A Biography*. London and New York, Oxford University Press, 1938.

Marshall, Florence A., *The Life and Letters of Mary Wollstonecraft Shelley* (2 vols.). London, R. Bentley, 1889.

Nitchie, Elizabeth, *Mary Shelley, Author of "Frankenstein."* New Brunswick, New Jersey, Rutgers University Press, 1953.

Spark, Muriel, *Child of Light*. Hadleigh, Essex, Tower Bridge Publications, 1951; revised as *Mary Shelley: A Biography*, New York, Dutton, 1987; London, Constable, 1988.

Sunstein, Emily W., *Mary Shelley: Romance and Reality*. Boston, Little Brown, 1989.

*

Nineteenth- and early 20th-century biographies of Mary Shelley were constrained by limited access to the author's manuscripts. Studies of her life have suffered both from this overprotective measure and from the attacks by her detractors, begun by Edward John Trelawney, who misrepresented her as too conventional to have been a proper companion for the idealized poet Percy Shelley, distortions biographers have since worked to correct. In recent years, their revisionary efforts have been aided by the growth of feminist literary criticism and the appearance of excellent editions of Mary Shelley's letters (3 vols., edited by Betty T. Bennett, Johns Hopkins University Press, 1980, 1983,

1988) and journals (2 vols., edited by Paula R. Feldman and Diana Scott-Kilvert, Oxford, Clarendon Press, 1987). As a result, we have begun to see Mary Shelley for what she was: one of the most important women writers and intellectuals of the 19th century.

MARSHALL's was the first official biography, authorized by Lady Jane Shelley in 1882. It still reads clearly, though as a kind of patchwork of narrative and long quotations from the letters (which, due to Lady Shelley's control, are neither complete nor always accurate). Marshall recognizes the central problems: the overshadowing of Mary Shelley's life by Percy's, and the outright falsifications by Trelawney. But she could not avoid an overly defensive posture, feeling compelled to explain "why any separate Life of her should be written at all." Marshall cogently summarizes the ways in which Shelley has been misrepresented, but she still reaches a conventionally sexist conclusion: "it is probably that no woman of like endowments and promise ever abdicated her own individuality in favour of another so transcendently greater." Overall, Mary Shelley is made to seem the handmaiden to genius, her later life treated as relatively unimportant.

The first full-fledged scholarly biography appeared almost 50 years later: GRYLLS had access to a wider range of primary materials and used them well to produce what immediately became the standard work. Though her interpretations of the life are generally perceptive, they are still marred by gender stereotypes. Mary Shelley was "an Individual," Grylls asserts, but this individuality is then used primarily to prove her "worthy" to be the wife of the poet. She was supposedly the victim of a "conflict between the feminine and the artist" within herself, according to Grylls, but it was her husband Shelley who "fanned the small flame of the artist in her. . . ." Indeed, the union with Shelley is romanticized in almost metaphysical terms: "The important thing is that in essentials Mary and Shelley were at one." The effect of all of this is to absorb Mary Shelley's identity into Percy Shelley's, and it is not surprising, therefore, that Grylls offers little reinterpretation of Mary Shelley's later life as a widow.

NITCHIE's slim volume took advantage of the wider accessibility of manuscripts and added some original research: appendices include parts of separately published articles, as well as texts of previously unpublished Mary Shelley poems. But the interpretation is *too* balanced in its assessments, as when Shelley is said to be "neither angel nor devil, full of faults, full of merits: brave in spite of her self-pity, liberal in her views in spite of her compromises with society, endowed with intellectual powers that command respect in spite of their limitations and with imagination capable of creative achievement in spite of her later taming of it to meet the taste of the reading public." Ultimately, such rhetoric is merely noncommittal.

DUNN's is a popular biography aimed at the general reader (though with notes and index). As the image of "Eclipse" in the title might imply, it too is unwittingly bound to the notion that Shelley was a "secondary" figure. Dunn says she wishes to "draw Mary from her obscurity, to rescue her from the brilliance of her husband and the force of Shelley biography, . . . to give her a justly independent and vivid existence." But the language of this wish cannot escape the idea of Mary Shelley as a *dependent* figure in need of "rescuing" (rather than someone simply requiring a fair representation in history). The book over-simplifies and conventionalizes the life, based on the highly reductive premise that, "ultimately, [Mary Shelley's] ambitions were modest and domestic; the committed love of family and friends was all she really desired."

SPARK's is a biography (with an added critical section) by a popular novelist. Short, accessible, and engaging, it will be useful for many general readers. The book is a revised version of an earlier work, *Child of Light* (1951), but it actually retains many of the limitations of the original. For example, Spark cites Betty T. Bennett in her revised discussion of a biographical question that had troubled her in the 1951 version, but the citation is of little use. Bennett's updated, clearer interpretation of the question is simply embedded awkwardly in Spark's text—in one sentence and one qualifying footnote—with the bulk of the discussion left unchanged. Spark's limited revisions are of more serious consequence when it comes to Shelley's later career and the myth of her supposed drive for social respectability. She acknowledges in the preface that her own views have changed on this issue, yet chapter ten still accuses Shelley, just as the 1951 version had, of compromising her principles because of "her desire for status." The point is that Spark's 1987 book—not substantially different enough from the 1951 version—appeared on the scene already out of date, not really having taken advantage of the criticism and scholarship of the intervening years.

SUNSTEIN, on the other hand, an independent scholar who has written on Mary Wollstonecraft, makes full use of recent studies, including important feminist readings. Rather than collapse Mary Shelley's life into her husband's, Sunstein begins by assuming her autonomy and historical significance. Her special contribution, therefore, is her detailed treatment of the "English years"—the last half of Shelley's life, after the death of her husband. But she also offers insight on the earlier years, stressing for example Shelley's early ambition. The young girl was educated in the Godwin home to desire learning *and* fame, was, as she herself said, "nursed and fed with a love of glory." Though she undoubtedly sublimated some of her own ambition to the furthering of her husband's reputation, Shelley never completely lost the sense that she was the exceptional child of a noble intellectual union.

Even late in life, as Sunstein shows, Mary Shelley continued her literary and scholarly pursuits, including her exemplary editing of Percy Shelley's works. She did moderate her political views, and came to desire a place in society for her son. But she was as much interested in suitable intellectual companionship as in simple status. What stands out in Sunstein's illuminating portrait is Shelley's defiance of mere convention where friendship was concerned—especially the friendship and welfare of other women. In fact, she showed great courage in the face of the immense social pressures of Victorian England, not to mention financial pressures from the Shelley family. As Sunstein rightly observes: "Hers was in the stoic tradition."

The style is clear, though Sunstein does at times resort to over-casual narrative devices, such as repeatedly referring to Thomas Jefferson Hogg as "Jeff" (instead of the more likely "Hogg" or "Jefferson"). But these are minor irritations in this historically sound narrative, firmly based on primary materials. The book includes a complete check-list of Mary Shelley's works, including some newly attributed or potentially attributable to the author, and a review of the history of Mary Shelley studies, placing Sunstein's own effort in context. The notes are thorough, the index is useful, and even the illustrations are of more than antiquarian interest, in this generally excellent biography, by far the best now available on Mary Shelley.

—Steven E. Jones

SHELLEY, Percy Bysshe, 1792–1822; English poet.

Blunden, Edmund, *Shelley: A Life Story*. London, Collins, 1946; New York, Viking, 1947.

Dowden, Edward, *The Life of Percy Bysshe Shelley* (2 vols.). London, K. Paul Trench, 1886; revised and abridged one-volume edition, 1896.

Hogg, Thomas Jefferson, *The Life of Percy Bysshe Shelley* (2 vols.). London, E. Moxon, 1858; edited by Edward Dowden, London, Routledge, and New York, Dutton, 1906.

Holmes, Richard, *Shelley: The Pursuit*. London, Weidenfeld and Nicolson, 1974; New York, Dutton, 1975.

Hunt, Leigh, *Lord Byron and Some of His Contemporaries*. London, H. Colburn, and Philadelphia, Carey Lea, 1828.

Maurois, André, *Ariel: The Life of Shelley*, translated by Ella D'Arcy. New York, Appleton, 1924; as *Ariel: A Shelley Romance*, London, J. Lane, 1924 (originally published by Grasset, Paris, 1923).

Medwin, Thomas, *The Life of Percy Bysshe Shelley* (2 vols.). London, T. C. Newby, 1847; revised 2nd edition, edited by H. Buxton Forman, London and New York, Oxford University Press, 1913.

Peacock, Thomas Love, *Peacock's Memoirs of Shelley With Shelley's Letters to Peacock*, edited by H. F. B. Brett-Smith. London, H. Frowde, 1909.

Peck, Walter E., *Shelley, His Life and Work* (2 vols.). Boston, Houghton Mifflin, and London, E. Benn, 1927.

Trelawney, Edward J., *Recollections of the Last Days of Shelley and Byron*. London, E. Moxon, and Boston, Ticknor and Fields, 1858; revised as *Records of Shelley*, Byron, and the Author (2 vols.), London, Routledge, and New York, Dutton, 1878.

White, Newman Ivey, *Shelley* (2 vols.). New York, Knopf, 1940; abridged one-volume edition, as *A Portrait of Shelley*, New York, Knopf, 1945; London, Secker and Warburg, 1947.

*

No literary figure's biographical history is more vexed than Shelley's. Vilification during his lifetime led to defensive hagiography after his death, including restrictions on access to many of his manuscripts until the 20th century. Ridiculed or beatified (sometimes simultaneously) in early accounts, this politically radical and intellectually formidable poet was eventually mythologized by Matthew Arnold as an "ineffectual angel."

After he drowned in 1822, Shelley's widow Mary began the process of editing his works and shoring up his reputation. The editorial work was exemplary, but she was prevented by the poet's father from publishing a biography. The earliest "lives" of Shelley were written by school or college friends (Medwin,

Hogg), later companions for a time (Trelawney), or literary allies (Peacock, Hunt). Most of these had axes to grind and distorted the poet's image one way or another. They are required reading for scholars and entertaining for others, but as biography, they must be read with a healthy skepticism.

MEDWIN, Shelley's cousin and Eton schoolmate, offers valuable accounts of the poet's early reading and interests. His memories of incidents or dates are sometimes confused or simply wrong, but not deliberately distorted. But he is unreliable when it comes to the important years of Shelley's adult life as a poet, after 1816. HOGG, a later companion, was expelled from Oxford along with Shelley over a pamphlet on atheism, was the third party in several of Shelley's romantic *ménages*, but later became a respectable barrister, with a deep ambivalence toward the poet he had known. Hogg's *Life* is a notorious account of himself, mainly, with Shelley made to play an often unattractive supporting role. It was begun with the imprimatur (and manuscripts) of the heirs, Sir Percy and Lady Shelley, but was suppressed due to their disapproval. Shelley's characteristics and actions are exaggerated—either caricatured or romanticized—and the letters are intentionally misquoted. Despite its entertaining accounts (especially of Oxford days), Hogg's story remains unreliable.

TRELAWNEY, a flamboyant raconteur who befriended the Shelleys during their last days in Italy, was not only an adventurer but a fictionalizer of his own life and the lives of others. He rearranged some of the facts of Shelley's last days, including details of the cremation on the beach at Viareggio, and began in earnest the depictions of the poet as effeminate, ethereal, and otherworldly. (His distortions of the role played by Mary Shelley have troubled her biographers ever since.)

PEACOCK, a close literary friend of Shelley's in England, had playfully satirized him in his novels. His *Memoirs*, which first appeared in magazine installments, were not intended as a full biography, but as a timely correction of the errors in previous ones (especially Hogg's), and this purpose overshadows the purely biographical function. He was especially quick to defend Shelley's first wife, Harriet, against the disparagements of Lady Jane Shelley.

HUNT was one of Shelley's staunch literary and political allies, and a close friend. His book was also written partly in reaction to Hogg's distortions. It offered another perspective on Shelley's last days in Italy, but also added to the etherealization of the poet's image.

All of these early works are more or less loosely discursive, personal memoirs. The first serious, full-length biography appeared with the official authorization of Lady Jane Shelley in 1886, written by DOWDEN. Dowden was a prominent university professor and was sympathetic to his subject, but his authorized biography had to deal with Lady Shelley's heavy restrictions of the primary materials, as well as the piety she all but demanded toward the poet. In Dowden's case, the value of being close to the subject's lifetime, of being able to interview those who knew him, is often outweighed by the drawbacks of the same historical situation. Too little distance can be more limiting than too much, especially when the subject is the focus of partisan controversy and his reputation under proprietary control. Dowden's Shelley is rarefied by all these pressures into an Ariel-figure, the inspiration for Arnold's famous "ineffectual angel" characterization.

In the 20th century, this ineffectual Shelley was packaged for popular consumption in MAUROIS' purely fictionalized life. This straw-poet became the target of much literary criticism, which found in Shelley's poetry the weak and insubstantial features of his supposed personality. PECK's work, though solid, scholarly, and informative (it includes 19 textual and biographical appendices), was naturally affected by the then-pervasive underestimate of Shelley's worth. And, though Peck was a skilled editor of Shelley who knew his works well, he did not yet have access to some crucial documents, especially the journals of Mary Shelley and Claire Clairmont.

The standard scholarly biography has deservedly remained WHITE's, which had the twin historical advantages of greater access to important manuscripts and greater distance from Shelley's Victorian and modern defenders and detractors. White's book is a model of responsible and judicious scholarship, its goal a "fidelity to fact"—though in the full realization that absolute recovery of factual truth is impossible. This historian's perspective leads to meticulous, fully documented research, and the work provides a clear chronology that makes it a useful reference tool. A reader can refer to the thorough index, follow dates in running headings, check details in the expository notes, and quickly grasp something of the texture of Shelley's life at a particular moment.

White's narrative is well written, if not always in an exciting style. As he confesses, his historian's caution leads to qualifiers (e.g., "apparently," or "probably") that tend to impede the flow of the story. But this is preferable to the racy but ungrounded fictionalizations of so many other biographers. Only the decades that followed, which witnessed a boom in Shelley scholarship and the further availability of even more important manuscripts (Shelley's rough draft notebooks, for example, in 1948), could have led to the need for a new biography, not to replace White so much as to continue the kind of valuable work he had begun. White provided an abridged, one-volume *Portrait* in 1945. On the whole, this volume would be a better choice than BLUNDEN's book, which is aimed at the general reader but cannot match White's scholarship. Blunden's style is also uncomfortable, often breezily condescending (as when referring to Shelley's friend Catherine Nugent as "one of those women whose reward is in heaven" or to the poet as "Unfortunate Shelley!").

It was over 25 years before a truly substantial biography for a general audience appeared; HOLMES' 1974 work is a lively, award-winning narrative that seeks to depict Shelley as a human being, complete with his darker side. Within some serious limitations, Holmes does this well. For many general readers, he provides a readable and engaging story complete with love-triangles, violent pistol battles, and gothic terrors in the night, all of it generally factual: Holmes never merely novelizes. But as my list implies, he often emphasizes the lurid and exciting over other features in the story, thus subtly distorting the picture. His Shelley is too relentlessly "romantic" to be true, and in at least one case—the mystery of Shelley's "Neapolitan child" (or foster child)—Holmes' speculative conclusion (involving Claire Clairmont and the Shelleys' maid) is simply unconvincing. (He withdrew part of his "solution" to this mystery in *Footsteps*, see below.)

The title's "pursuit" makes a very personal reference to Holmes' own pursuit of the ghost of Shelley across Italy and nearly two centuries. As he makes clear in his later entertaining book, *Footsteps: Adventures of a Romantic Biographer* (New York, Viking, 1985), Holmes is himself a romantic, seeking a transhistorical intimacy with his subject. A telling phrase in *The Pursuit* declares that, often, "Shelley's life seems more a haunting than a history." This rather sentimental notion of the biographer's relationship to his subject is what makes Holmes' enthusiasm about Shelley infectious; it is also ultimately his greatest limitation. Though Holmes claims in *Footsteps* to have moved beyond the desire for a merely "subjective intimacy," his biography is missing a true respect for history's *dis*continuities. The past always recedes beyond our grasp. We can never fully recover it, much less find ourselves intimates of its long-dead actors. This distance cannot be eliminated by even the most intense imaginative sympathy. Holmes reasonably notes, both in the biography and in *Footsteps*, that Shelley's era of revolution and turmoil has obvious parallels with his own—particularly the 1960s. But he too easily assumes that this gives him an insider's view of the Shelley circle, thus collapsing the immense (and potentially instructive) differences between 1798 and 1968.

The reader whose interests are scholarly and historical must supplement Holmes' well-told tale with other specialized work: two books by Kenneth Neill Cameron that combine biography with literary criticism, *The Young Shelley: Genesis of a Radical* (London, 1951), and *Shelley: The Golden Years* (Harvard, 1974); and the excellent bibliographic, historical, and biographical essays collected with primary documents in the multi-volume *Shelley and his Circle: 1773–1822* (edited by K. N. Cameron and Donald H. Reiman, 8 vols., 1961–86). In both we see a Shelley who was politically and socially engaged in his own times, a public as well as private figure. Neither ineffectual nor angelic, this poet remains embedded in the past that we can never fully know, but he appears more practical and worldly than most of his biographers have shown.

—Steven E. Jones

SHERIDAN, Richard Brinsley, 1751–1816; Irish dramatist and politician.

Bingham, Madeleine, *Sheridan: The Track of a Comet*. London, Allen and Unwin, and New York, St. Martin's, 1972.

Butler, E. M., *Sheridan: A Ghost Story*. London, Constable, 1931.

Darlington, W. A., *Sheridan*. London, Duckworth, and New York, Macmillan, 1933.

Earle, William, *Sheridan and His Times by an Octagenarian, who Stood by His Knee in Youth and Sat at His Table in Manhood*. London, J. F. Hope, 1859.

Fitzgerald, Percy, *The Lives of the Sheridans*. London, R. Bentley, 1886.

Foss, Kenelm, *Here Lies Richard Brinsley Sheridan*. London, M. Secker, 1939; New York, Dutton, 1940.

Gibbs, Lewis, *Sheridan: His Life and His Theatre*. London, Dent, 1947; New York, Morrow, 1948.

Glasgow, Alice, *Sheridan of Drury Lane: A Biography*. New York, F. A. Stokes, 1940.

Hunt, Leigh, "Biographical and Critical Sketch," in *The Dramatic Works of Richard Brinsley Sheridan*. London, E. Moxon, 1840.

Moore, Thomas, *Memoirs of the Life of the Right Honourable Richard Brinsley Sheridan*. London, Longman, and Philadelphia, Carey and Lea, 1825.

Oliphant, Margaret, *Sheridan*. London, Macmillan, and New York, Harper, 1883.

Rae, W. Fraser, *Sheridan: A Biography*. London, R. Bentley and New York, Holt, 1896.

Rhodes, R. Crompton, *Harlequin Sheridan: The Man and the Legends*. Oxford, Blackwell, 1933.

Sanders, Lloyd C., *Life of Richard Brinsley Sheridan*. London, W. Scott, and New York, Scribner, 1890.

Sheridaniana; or, Anecdotes of the Life of Richard Brinsley Sheridan, His Table Talk and Bon Mots. London, Henry Colburn, 1826.

Sherwin, Oscar, *Uncorking Old Sherry: The Life and Times of Richard Brinsley Sheridan*. New York, Twayne, and London, Vision, 1960.

Sichel, Walter, *Sheridan, from New and Original Material: Including a Manuscript Diary by Georgiana, Duchess of Devonshire*. London, Constable, and Boston, Houghton Mifflin, 1909.

Smyth, William, *Memoir of Mr. Sheridan*. Leeds, J. Cross, 1840.

Watkins, John, *Memoirs of the Public and Private Life of the Right Honourable Richard Brinsley Sheridan, with a Particular Account of His Family and Connexions*. London, H. Colburn, 1817.

*

It would indeed be hard to recall anyone so unfortunate as Sheridan in his biographers; nor would it be easy to find a more dissatisfied set of critics than those authors on the subject of each other's attempts. The chief difficulty the biographer of Sheridan had to encounter was the task, not so much of discovering the truth about him, as of cutting it free from the monstrous entanglements of misunderstandings, prejudices, and flat falsehoods with which it is overgrown. Sheridan had no Boswell, and not even a Lockhart or a Forster.

WATKINS, who wrote the first life of Sheridan, had little personal knowledge of him, and Watkins' work, though published as early as 1817, has little value. Watkins was a political opponent and detractor and his *Memoirs* has fallen into oblivion. MOORE, at the request of Sheridan's second wife, wrote what may be called the official biography, founded on the fullest information, with the help of all that Sheridan had left behind in the way of papers, and all that the family could furnish—along with Moore's own personal recollections. However, it is not a very characteristic piece of work and greatly dissatisfied the friends and lovers of Sheridan. Moore was never on intimate terms with Sheridan, and did not meet him until after 1800. Besides, he was sometimes misinformed and ungenerous, and was too much in awe of the great personages of whom he had to write to do justice to his friend's political career. With the professed intention of making up for the absence of character in Moore's *Memoirs*, a small volume called *Sheridaniana* was published the year after, which is full of amusing anecdotes, but little, if any, additional information. SMYTH, who was tutor to Sheridan's son Tom between 1792 and 1796, acceded to a request of Miss Cotton when he became Professor at Oxford and wrote his *Memoir* of Sheridan. Smyth's brief sketch concerns only the latter part of Sheridan's life, but it is usually creditable as to fact and is the most lifelike and, in many respects, the most touching contemporary portrait that has been made of Sheridan.

Scarcely an edition of Sheridan's plays has been published (and they are numberless) without a biographical notice. The most noted of these is perhaps the ''Biographical and Critical Sketch'' of HUNT, which does not, however, pretend to cast any new light, and is entirely unsympathetic. Hunt undertakes to explain the waste of Sheridan's gifts, remarking his early habits of delay, his animated spirits, and his love of luxury. EARLE, the ''Octagenarian,'' promised to afford new information and to correct earlier biographies; but his work, except for certain dubious and not very savoury stories of the Prince Regent period, failed to do so. OLIPHANT was approached by the editor of the ''English Men of Letters'' series, and in her biography of Sheridan she rises in all the outraged virtue of a Victorian matron confronted with Sin. Sheridan's next biography, provided by FITZGERALD, is full of inaccuracies. SANDERS, like Mrs. Oliphant, was approached by the editor of a literary series. In his biography he acknowledges that Sheridan the man was certainly a riddle. Sanders' biography was followed by that of RAE, who wrote at the insistance of a great-grandson of Sheridan. Although Rae undertook the task of writing a full and unprejudiced account, he omitted much and is sometimes monotonously laudatory. Thirteen years after Rae came SICHEL, who published important new material which threw a great deal of fresh light on the subject.

Subsequent biographies of Sheridan are usually reliable. BUTLER sought to locate Sheridan's character and sifted the traditions attaching to his life. DARLINGTON deplored the moralistic bias of Oliphant, the carelessness of Fitzgerald, and the panegyric of Rae. He declared an effort to be objective while yet being sympathetic. RHODES attempted to show Sheridan in the round, as he appeared to his own generation. FOSS organized the life of Sheridan around broad categories of experience, achievement, and states of being. GLASGOW rendered Sheridan's life in the form of a play. GIBBS recounted Sheridan's life on the basis of his ''three careers.'' SHERWIN set Sheridan's life against a backdrop of an age of drinking, gambling, debt, money-worship, conversation, scandal, and literature. BINGHAM based an account of Sheridan's life on the theory that he sought recognition as a gentleman.

—E. H. Mikhail

SHOSTAKOVICH, Dmitri, 1906–1975; Russian composer.

Kay, Norman, *Shostakovich*. London and New York, Oxford University Press, 1971.

Martynov, Ivan, *Dmitri Shostakovich: The Man and His Work*, translated by T. Guralsky. New York, Philosophical Library, 1947.

Norris, Christopher, editor, *Shostakovich: The Man and His Music*. London, Lawrence and Wishart, and Boston, M. Boyars, 1982.

Rabinovich, Dmitri, *Dmitry Shostakovich, Composer*, translated by George Hanna. London, Lawrence and Wishart, and Moscow, Foreign Language Publishing House, 1959.

Roseberry, Eric, *Shostakovich: His Life and Times*. New York, Hippocrene Books, and Tunbridge Wells, Midas Books, 1982.

Sollertinsky, Dmitri and Ludmilla Sollertinsky, *Pages from the Life of Dmitri Shostakovich*. New York, Harcourt, and London, R. Hale, 1981.

*

The numerous biographies of Dmitri Shostakovich have all sought to come to terms with the composer's artistic dimensions. One difficulty has been the way they coupled his personality with his adroitness in achieving a blend of political axioms in the compositional techniques of his music. Unfortunately, the corpus of material on the life of Shostakovich is far from complete, forcing the scholar to choose between stilted Soviet accounts and appreciative, but incomplete, Western versions. Progress Publishers' 1981 version of the life of Shostakovich (*Shostakovich: About Himself and His Times*) is little more than a series of the composer's most popular vignettes, but *Testimony: The Memoirs of Dmitri Shostakovich* (1979) serves as the transition work into more balanced historical scholarship.

MARTYNOV's work, written in the winter of 1942, is one of the earliest biographies of the composer. Concerning itself more with the war years and the impact they had on Shostakovich as a composer and State musician, it offers a largely one-sided presentation. Martynov does not deal effectively with Shostakovich's music, viewing the composer more as a citizen of the State than as an artist. Chronologically organized, the book is nevertheless filled with generalizations and rife with commentary about the difficulties Shostakovich overcame in order to fulfill his role within the Soviet Union.

Similarly flawed, the 1959 biography by RABINOVICH, like so many of the mass-produced biographies of famous Soviet citizens, is more propaganda than substance. Although Rabinovich is more thorough in his treatment of Shostakovich's musical nature, he tends to place socio-political events in an overly generalized format, using the language of the musicologist in order to describe the impetus for Shostakovich's political feelings. Indeed, although one might agree that Shostakovich was the master of the musical tragedy, it seems rather simplistic to isolate musical genius from creativity.

Shostakovich's 1981 account of his life, published by the Soviet publisher Progress, is filled with laudatory statements about Soviet musicality and society, and was presumably hurriedly published in response to the Western version of *Testimony* (1979). Progress organized the book as a series of diary entries, but edited it so heavily as to eliminate any mention of derogatory or critical remarks about the Soviet government. In fact, it appears almost sanitized.

Shostakovich's *Testimony* is one of the strongest, most interesting, and complete accounts of the composer's life. During the Stalinist era, the official Soviet press portrayed Shostakovich as the prime example of the true Soviet artist. However, *Testimony* ''lets the official mask slip,'' and Shostakovich makes powerful statements about artistic and cultural life under Stalin, concluding that it was almost impossible for any great artist to remain in the Soviet Union. Musicologist Solomon Volkov edited and smuggled the material for *Testimony* abroad, determined that the world know the truth about both Shostakovich and the degree of state domination of Soviet artistic life. Additionally, one of the great strengths of this book is its complete honesty when dealing with sensitive subjects. Shostakovich notes that, instead of service to the State and his own artistic genius, it was the terror and disillusionment of the Stalinist system that forced him into composition. Through his music, Shostakovich retreated from political squabbles, but he was never above suspicion from the ever-diligent organs of Soviet State Security. *Testimony* is, therefore, a marvelous example of biographical social history. Although Shostakovich was never able to reveal his disillusionment with the state during his lifetime, readers are fortunate that they can delve into his sensitivity and acumen on a broader base of subject matter.

The volume by NORRIS collects nine submissions by musicians, musicologists, and musical writers. Some of the inclusions deal specifically with Shostakovich's musical technique, particularly as a symphonist, but the most valuable and interesting contributions to biography are the articles by Norris himself and Robert Stradling. Both authors deal specifically with the way in which Shostakovich the musician was shaped by, and reacted to, the politics of the Soviet system. Both believe that the strength of Shostakovich's compositions often lay in the very struggle he sought to overcome. As such, much of the material collected by Norris is valuable as a secondary biography, and gives the reader numerous insights into the composer's thoughts and personality.

Dmitri and Ludmilla SOLLERTINSKY have collected letters and reminiscences about Shostakovich from his colleagues, both in the Soviet Union and abroad. Chronologically arranged, beginning in 1906 and ending with the composer's death in 1975, the book spans several generations of commentary about Shostakovich. As biography, the material is valuable for researchers who desire to compare Shostakovich's thoughts about a particular event or person with those of other commentators or biographers. This material is particularly interesting for its range of interpretations about Shostakovich, but it is naturally biased toward the composer.

One of the most balanced biographies of Shostakovich is by ROSEBERRY. Although not extremely detailed, it nevertheless brings together a myriad of source materials and attempts to analyze various interpretations of the composer's life. It is impossible for biographers writing since Shostakovich's *Testimony* to ignore this account, and Roseberry accepts it with one or two exceptions. Roseberry's style is cogent and effective. However, since his book was a submission for a *Life and Times* series, it should be approached as an initial biography and not as a thorough scholarly study.

KAY, while not having access to *Testimony*, nevertheless offers a detailed, though limited, analysis of the composer and his major works. His book contains ample musical illustrations but lacks an index. Its strength lies in Kay's determination to combine social and artistic biography. Of all the works under review, Kay's holds the most promise for future scholarly material. One might hope that with the advent of *perestroika* the scholarly community will see a resurgence in the study of Shostakovich,

and with it a large, comprehensive biography to add to the limited useful literature on the subject. For the time being, however, one should probably begin with Kay and Roseberry, move to Shostakovich's *Testimony*, and supplement the rest with a critical eye.

—Kelvin Richardson

SIBELIUS, Jean, 1865–1957; Finnish composer.

Arnold, Elliott, *Finlandia: The Story of Sibelius*, illustrated by Lolita Granahan. New York, Holt, 1941.

Ekman, Karl, *Jean Sibelius: His Life and Personality*, translated by Edward Birse. London, A. Wilmer, 1936; New York, Knopf, 1938 (originally published by Bokförlaget Natur och Kultur, Stockholm, 1935).

Gray, Cecil, *Sibelius*. London, Oxford University Press, 1931.

Johnson, Harold Edgar, *Jean Sibelius*. New York, Knopf, 1959.

Layton, Robert, *Sibelius*. London, Dent, and New York, Farrar Straus, 1965.

Layton, Robert, *Sibelius and His World*. New York, Viking, and London, Thames and Hudson, 1970.

Levas, Santeri, *Sibelius, A Personal Portrait*, translated by Percy M. Young. London, Dent, 1972; Lewisburg, Pennsylvania, Bucknell University Press, 1973 (originally published by Söderström, Helsinki, 1957–60).

Newmarch, Rosa, *Jean Sibelius*. Boston, Birchard, 1939.

Ringbom, Nils-Eric, *Jean Sibelius: A Master and His Work*, translated by G. I. C. de Courcy. Norman, University of Oklahoma Press, 1954 (originally published as *Sibelius*, Helsingfors, H. Schildt, and Stockholm, A. Bonniers Förlag, 1948).

Tawaststjerna, Erik, (2 vols.), *Sibelius*, translated by Robert Layton. Berkeley, University of California Press, and London, Faber, 1976–86 (originally published as *Jean Sibelius*, Helsinki, Otava, 1965, 1967, 1972).

Törne, Bengt de, *Sibelius: A Close-Up*. London, Faber, 1937; Boston, Houghton Mifflin, 1938.

*

Most of the biographies of Sibelius were written during the composer's long lifetime. The official biography appeared in 1935, written by Sibelius' countryman, EKMAN. Ekman spent several days talking with the composer in preparation for writing. Much of the book is in Sibelius' own words and presents the composer as he would like to be seen. Almost an autobiography, Ekman's work offers no critical judgements, giving instead an outline of Sibelius' life. There are no analyses of the music, and the translation is fluent and readable.

English music critic GRAY offers a basic biography, consisting mainly of facts and dates, that still gives an entertaining account of the man and his background. Gray used Finnish composer and critic Erik Furuhjelm's work (Borgå, 1916, not translated into English) as a basis for the biography. The book contains useful musical analyses spiced with Gray's strong personal opinions.

Another English music critic and champion of Sibelius, NEW-MARCH had known Sibelius since 1905, and her book includes personal reminiscences. Subtitled in some printings "A Short History of a Long Friendship," this simple chronicle is enhanced by letters and anecdotes. About one third of the book is devoted to a musical analysis of Sibelius' 7th symphony.

TÖRNE, a student of Sibelius, filled his book with anecdotes and conversations he had with "the Master." Törne's sincere hero worship gives a fragmentary view of Sibelius' artistic personality and musical abilities, some of which is relevant, but much more of which is important only to the devotee. Still, Törne does supply firsthand information and has been much quoted in later works. Törne dwells at length on discussions he had with the composer on orchestration, which would be of interest to the person with some technical knowledge of music.

RINGBOM, the manager of the Helsinki Orchestra, knew what Sibelius meant to the Finns and had firsthand knowledge of the sources of Finnish influence on Sibelius. Even so, most of the book is devoted to sketchy analyses of themes, romantically interpreted. Ringbom acknowledges his debt for the biographical material to Ekman and Furuhjelm and uses extensive quotations, inadequately referenced, from these other biographers. No new insights are forthcoming, while the music "analyses" resemble programme-like notes and make up the greater part of the work. Repeated references to "The Master" show that this biography was molded in the worshipful, uncritical tradition.

Unlike Ringbom, LEVAS provides no references to the music at all. Levas was Sibelius' secretary for 20 years, not a musician. Loosely constructed, this chatty, discursive, reverential book uncovers no new information on Sibelius and is valuable mainly for Levas' purely personal impressions. The translation does not read smoothly.

JOHNSON, an American who spent two years in Finland on a Fulbright Grant, painstakingly gathered material from archives and libraries as well as the composer's family, colleagues, and friends, yet chose not to interview the 90-year-old composer himself. Johnson felt that Sibelius, who was distrustful of all writers, would not accurately remember specific facts of his own life. Johnson's book is a reaction to hero worship; he attempts to crack open the Finnish national hero shell that surrounded Sibelius for a glimpse beneath. Sibelius is portrayed in an objective, if unsympathetic, manner. The narrative is a well-written account of the facts of Sibelius' life and brings forth some weak or petty traits in Sibelius' character that are contradictions to the official legend as presented in Ekman, and the uncritical adoration of Ringbom, Törne, and Newmarch. Sometimes, however, Johnson goes too far in his seeming attempt to destroy the Sibelius legend and becomes merely negative or arbitrary. Johnson offers a penetrating analysis of the problems of the creative artist coming to grips with his own style.

LAYTON used sources in the Sibelius Museum at Turku to produce his 1965 book. The biographical sketch is brief and takes up only the first four chapters of the book. None of the composer's letters, writings, or any extended contemporary recollection is included. Even the familiar anecdotes are omitted. The end result is an accurate summary missing that all-important third dimension that is the man. The remainder of the book is an attempt at a close analysis of Sibelius' music. Especially useful are the appendices that include a calendar, catalog of works, personalia, and bibliography.

LAYTON's 1970 book is an illustrated biography that gives a well-written, simplified view of the composer's life. The pictures formerly appeared in Ikka Oramo's *Jean Sibelius-Kuvaelämäkerta* (Helsinki, Kustannusosakeythiö Otava, 1965). The reproduction of the pictures is generally good, although some are indistinct. This easy-to-read volume provides an excellent introduction to the composer.

The major critical and scholarly biography of Sibelius is the monumental work by TAWASTSTJERNA. As of 1986, two volumes had been published in English that cover the composer's life through 1914; additional volumes are in preparation. For the first time Sibelius' widow and daughters gave a biographer unlimited access to Sibelius' personal diaries, manuscript sketches, and letters. Tawastjerna also interviewed family members and, for example, was able to use love letters to document Sibelius' engagement. What emerges is an objectively presented, detailed day-to-day chronicle of Sibelius' life and career. Sibelius the man is at last revealed. A discussion of the composer's music is interwoven in the narrative. The book, originally written in Swedish, receives a readable and scholarly translation from Robert Layton, who enhances the text with footnotes to aid the non-Scandinavian reader. There are some minor errors in musical examples and printing that do not otherwise mar the excellent presentation.

ARNOLD's work is an enthusiastic biography for children. Readable and sympathetic, Arnold presents a full-length portrait of the composer. Written during World War II, the book emphasizes the nationalistic aspects of Sibelius' music.

—Sharon G. Almquist

SIDDHARTHA GAUTAMA. See BUDDHA.

SIDNEY, Sir Philip, 1554–1586; English writer, statesman, and soldier.

Addleshaw, Percy, *Sir Philip Sidney*. London, Methuen, and New York, Putnam, 1909.

Bill, Alfred H., *Astrophel; or, the Life and Death of the Renowned Sir Philip Sidney*. New York, Farrar and Rinehart, 1937; London, Cassell, 1938.

Boas, F. S., *Sir Philip Sidney, Representative Elizabethan: His Life and Writings*. London, Staples Press, 1955.

Bourne, Henry R. Fox, *Sir Philip Sidney: Type of English Chivalry in the Elizabethan Age*. New York, Putnam, 1891.

Buxton, John, *Sir Philip Sidney and the English Renaissance*. New York, St. Martin's, and London, Macmillan, 1954.

Connell, Dorothy, *Sir Philip Sidney: The Maker's Mind*. Oxford, Clarendon Press, 1977.

Denkinger, Emma Marshall, *Immortal Sidney*. New York, Brentano's, 1931.

Greville, Fulke Lord Brooke, *Life of the Renowned Sir Philip Sidney.* London, 1652; revised as *Sir Fulke Greville's Life of Sir Philip Sidney*, edited by Nowell Smith, Oxford, Clarendon Press, 1907.

Howell, Roger, *Sir Philip Sidney: The Shepherd Knight.* Boston, Little Brown, and London, Hutchinson, 1968.

Kimbrough, Robert, *Sir Philip Sidney.* New York, Twayne, 1971.

Lloyd, Julius, *The Life of Sir Philip Sidney.* London, Longman, 1862.

Moffet, Thomas, *Nobilis; or, A View of the Life and Death of a Sidney* and *Lessus Lugubris*, translated and edited by V. B. Heltzel and H. H. Hudson. San Marino, California, Huntington Library, 1940.

Myrick, Kenneth, *Sir Philip Sidney as a Literary Craftsman.* Cambridge, Massachusetts, Harvard University Press, 1935; 2nd edition, 1965.

Osborn, James M., *Young Philip Sidney 1572–77.* New Haven, Connecticut, and London, Yale University Press, 1972.

Symonds, John Addington, *Sir Philip Sidney.* London and New York, Macmillan, 1886.

Wallace, Malcolm W., *The Life of Sir Philip Sidney.* Cambridge, Cambridge University Press, 1915.

Warren, C. Henry, *Sir Philip Sidney: A Study in Conflict.* New York, T. Nelson, 1936.

Wilson, Mona, *Sir Philip Sidney.* London, Duckworth, 1931; New York, Oxford University Press, 1932.

Zouch, Thomas, *Memoires of the Life and Writings of Sir Philip Sidney.* York, Wilson, 1808.

*

GREVILLE provides an early and influential life by a close friend and ardent admirer of Sidney. However, this hagiography was composed some three decades after Sidney's death, contains a large proportion of political discussion, and has been questioned especially on the details of Sidney's military activities and death, for which Greville was not present. MOFFET, though not published until 1940, gives another contemporary portrait, focusing on Sidney at university and Sidney's death. LLOYD and ZOUCH are obsolete, rarely encountered, and included here only for the sake of completeness.

BOURNE revised and expanded his *Memoir of Sir Philip Sidney* (1862) for his 1891 volume in the "Heroes of the Nations" series. The best by far of the 19th-century lives, this was the standard biography until superseded by Wallace. It includes much information drawn from examination of archival and manuscript sources. The subtitle, "Type of English Chivalry in the Elizabethan Age," indicates Bourne's approach and attitude. ADDLESHAW avowedly owes much to Bourne, and is of interest today only as an early deflater of the Sidney myth. Addleshaw passionately makes the case that Sidney was not (as his early admirers claimed) "without spot," but was, for all his virtues, "a prig and a bigot," especially in his attitudes toward Catholics. SYMONDS, written in 1884 for the English Men of Letters series, draws from Bourne and other predecessors to produce a "sketch" of Sidney's "brief life," with opinions on Sidney's works. The book adds no new biographical material and indeed now is perceived as too erroneous to be of use. DENK-INGER, also written for the popular market, despite lacking

scholarly originality or apparatus and being in parts outdated, is nevertheless rather successful in its apparent aims; it is very readable and accessible to the curious layman. The narrative of Sidney's life and works (emphasis on the former) is enlivened with many details of his social and historical milieu. WARREN and BILL are both derivative; Bill especially can be misleading and should be avoided.

WALLACE, a substantial work of scholarship that remains the standard biography today, includes much previously unknown detail on Sidney's continental connections. Additionally, new details about the years 1565–66 are derived from the Account Book of Thomas Marshall, discovered by Wallace at Penshurst. A transcript of the Account Book, published as an appendix, lists every expenditure for young Philip during the period in question, including boot-cleaning, pens, cloth and tailoring, "horse-meat," and the like.

WILSON is generally well regarded for thorough scholarly apparatus, though not for any significant original contributions or for what has been called her "romantic" picture of Sidney. OSBORN, making use of 76 previously unknown letters to Sidney, focuses closely and about as completely as possible on the period of Sidney's Grand Tour; such important matters as his presence at the St. Bartholomew's Day massacre and his German diplomacy are newly illuminated. For the period in question this is clearly the standard work, supplanting even Wallace. BOAS, aiming at "giving an all-round presentation of Sir Philip," remains a readable, usably compact survey of Sidney's life and works. The chapter on Sidney's translation of *The Trewnesse of the Christian Religion* illumines a relatively neglected corner of Sidney's work. KIMBROUGH, in the usual Twayne format and modest length, provides another balanced, accurate and very usable survey of Sidney's life and works.

BUXTON offers a literary biography focusing on Sidney's importance as a literary patron, inspiring and influencing work by writers in England and abroad. Though focusing on Sidney's poetry, MYRICK is important biographically for making the case that in his life, as well as his works, Sidney was a conscious exemplum of the *sprezzatura* defined by Castiglione in *The Book of the Courtier* (1528). HOWELL in contrast provides a professional historian's thoroughly documented biography with modest attention to Sidney's writings. Howell focuses on Sidney as a political creature, and is especially important for attention to the nurturing (by Sidney and his contemporaries) of the myth of Sidney as Protestant hero-knight. Seeing 1579–80 as the period crucial to Sidney's literary shaping of himself, CONNELL gives a biographical approach to the literature with close attention to "reconstruction" of Sidney's actions and thoughts during that time.

—C. Herbert Gilliland, Jr.

———————

SINATRA, Frank, 1915–   ; American singer and film actor.

Goldstein, Norm, *Frank Sinatra: Ol' Blue Eyes.* New York, Holt Rinehart, 1982.

Kelley, Kitty, *His Way: The Unauthorized Biography of Frank Sinatra.* New York and London, Bantam Books, 1986.

Lake, Harriet, *On Stage: Frank Sinatra*. Mankato, Minnesota, Creative Education, 1976.

Rockwell, John, *Sinatra: An American Classic*. New York, Random House, and London, Elm Tree, 1984.

Shaw, Arnold, *Sinatra: Twentieth Century Romantic*. New York, Holt Rinehart, 1968.

Shaw, Arnold, *Sinatra: The Entertainer*. New York, Delilah Books, 1982.

Sinatra, Nancy, *Frank Sinatra: My Father*. New York, Doubleday, and London, Hodder and Stoughton, 1985.

Taylor, Paula, *Frank Sinatra*. Mankato, Minnesota, Creative Education, 1976.

Wilson, Earl, *Sinatra: An Unauthorized Biography*. New York, Macmillan, and London, W. H. Allen, 1976.

*

All of Sinatra's biographers give the same basic information; the difference lies in their at times tacit view of Sinatra. The most recent, KELLEY, also provides the most detailed and definitive life; it is the one Sinatra brought a two-million dollar lawsuit to stop the publication of, and no wonder. It reveals many new facts, carefully documented, and sheds unfavorable light on others. Kelley reveals that Dolly Sinatra, Sinatra's mother, was not only tough, profane, funny, and loud, but that she was arrested for performing illegal abortions (the only biography to reveal this). Kelley does mention Sinatra's generosity to friends and his good works, but she is explicit about the careful coaching of his first bobbysoxer fans to squeal and faint, about his friendship with mobsters, his womanizing, and his beating up (or having others beat up) those he felt had insulted him.

Sinatra emerges as one confident to the point of arrogance, with a quick, fierce temper. Kelley also gives details of Sinatra's band singing days and his movies. The account is gossipy, readable, and seemingly reliable, although Kelley seems not to have liked Sinatra. Even his good qualities are presented with a negative tinge: "Frank's spontaneous acts of kindness laid the foundation for his reputation as a generous, giving man and provided his press agents with what they needed at other times to cover his atrocious behavior."

WILSON, also sued by Sinatra over his biography, provides many details of Sinatra's life, with a fair balance of positive and negative incidents. Wilson quotes negative stories mainly from the media, but a few from other sources, again mentioning Sinatra's power, arrogance, brawls, womanizing, and coarse language. Wilson, a Broadway columnist, was barred from a Sinatra show after reporting one of Sinatra's brawls, but he claims that that did not affect this book. He says that Sinatra has a "conflicting dual personality" and is "deliberately masochistic," which seems a fair summing-up. He says, "[Sinatra] has more likability than anybody I ever met. If there's such a word as unlikability, he has that too, but when he turns on his likability, you think you must have been wrong about him ever being unpleasant."

NANCY SINATRA presents a lavishly illustrated coffee-table book which, as might be expected from a loving daughter who says, "My dad is my hero," is a warm, wonderful, perhaps understandably naive love letter with many, many photos. She relates the problems of his children, the horrors of Frank Junior's kidnapping, and the pleasures of his touring band days, always putting the best face on everything. Her mother, Sinatra's first wife, "knew she would always be his wife," even after, presumably, his three other marriages. Sinatra's crude ethnic jokes are presented as amusing, his appearance before the Select Committee on Crime to determine if he was a friend of mobsters as a "travesty," and Ava Gardner, for whom Sinatra left Nancy Sr., as "the most beautiful woman I ever saw in my life." The only break in her adoration came when, at 14, she learned that while on the road he was sleeping with other women, but that too is explained away. The style is at times clichéd but easy reading; she quotes only upbeat stories from her siblings and Sinatra's friends and co-performers.

SHAW (1968) is a positive book that focuses on Sinatra's career. Sinatra's "courage" becomes for Shaw a key word. While Shaw does mention Sinatra's "ambivalence" in discussing his life, he explains away Sinatra's difficulties. The book goes to the end of Sinatra's marriage to Mia Farrow. Shaw's later work (1982) is "not a biography, not a life story, but a retrospective cameo." It offers an adoring consideration of Sinatra's career as a singer and actor. Shaw's attitude is expressed thus: "In his music, he endures. The ineluctable, unconquerable, inescapable romantic endures."

Both ROCKWELL and GOLDSTEIN have comparatively little text and many photos, and both are mostly positive. Rockwell is largely a career study emphasizing Sinatra's singing selections and style. He claims that at first Sinatra's key opponents who linked his career with the mob came from the "near-rabid right." He does admit that the yelling bobbysoxers may at first have been planted, which Goldstein denies, claiming that the buildup was "real." Neither biography is all that worthwhile unless the reader is a rabid Sinatra fan. The TAYLOR and LAKE books both idolize Sinatra, are very thin on text, and are apparently aimed at quite young teenagers, who should not bother with them.

—Janet Overmyer

SINCLAIR, Upton, 1878–1968; American writer.

Bloodworth, William A., Jr., *Upton Sinclair*. Boston, Twayne, 1977.

Dell, Floyd, *Upton Sinclair: A Study in Social Protest*. New York, G. H. Doran, 1927.

Harris, Leon, *Upton Sinclair: American Rebel*. New York, Crowell, 1975.

Sinclair, Mary Craig, *Southern Belle*. New York, Crown, 1957.

Yoder, Jon A., *Upton Sinclair*. New York, Ungar, 1975.

*

Works on Upton Sinclair tend to combine narrative biography and criticism of his works. For Sinclair, however, a close relationship existed between his life and his novels, the bulk of his work after the years of apprenticeship having been conceived of as an instrument designed to bring about social change. Thus, influential novels such as *The Jungle, King Coal,* and *Oil* involved what now would be called investigative reporting cast into fictional form.

During Sinclair's lifetime only DELL, a prominent novelist and sympathetic friend, wrote anything about Sinclair still worth reading. This is not to say that Sinclair was ignored during his lifetime. As an anti-establishment rebel and ardent social activist, he was written about a great deal, pro and con. Dell's book is an adequate account of Sinclair's career to 1927. Dell treats his subject kindly, and he has the merit of having collected his material when fresh—much of it from Sinclair himself. His book is written with style and charm.

Since Sinclair's death in 1968 at the age of 90, three writers have tried to supply the need for an objective biographical study of this controversial character. Two of them are short studies, parts of a series, and while they are competent treatments of Sinclair, they are quite brief. The first to appear was YODER's volume, which tries to sum up Sinclair's life and work in 134 pages—an impossible task, as Sinclair during his nine decades produced over 80 books, and his papers, when given to the Lily Library at Indiana University, came to eight-plus tons of material. Yet Yoder is a reliable place to start a study of Sinclair.

BLOODWORTH's volume is more useful, as it runs to 178 pages and includes, in the standard format of the Twayne Series, a chronology and an annotated secondary bibliography. Bloodworth, like Yoder, tries to steer a mid-course between praise and blame: "I have rather consciously tried to slant my discussion in the direction of understanding and explanation, not attack or defense." Since Sinclair considered his most important role that of novelist, Bloodworth concentrates on the most important novels; but Sinclair's importance as a novelist belongs to history, and there is little likelihood that there ever will be a Sinclair revival.

The nearest thing to a definitive biography of Sinclair is HARRIS' book, and it will serve as the standard work for the foreseeable future. This is a full-length biography that does justice to its subject. It contains full notes and is based on a thorough mining of original sources. Sinclair was an unknown writer until 1905 when he published *The Jungle*, but thereafter, writes Harris, "he was America's most important writer; that is, he was more responsible than any other writer for changing the view Americans had of themselves, their rights, and their reasonable expectations." Although this sounds like hyperbole, it may well be true, but Harris adds that none of the ideas Sinclair propagandized were originated by him, and he is under no illusion that Sinclair's novels were great additions to *belles lettres:* "I chose to write Upton Sinclair's biography first because it was such an extraordinary life. But also it seemed to me to indicate that within the American system, given enough energy, change for the better is possible." However, Harris has not tried to prove anything in his book, and he treats Sinclair with admirable objectivity.

Anyone interested in Sinclair should not overlook his two autobiographies, *American Outpost* (1932) and the updated *Autobiography of Upton Sinclair* (1962). Papers documenting Sinclair's early career were lost in a fire in 1907, and all biographers have had to rely on Sinclair for material antedating the fire. But for the balance of his life, Sinclair on Sinclair is a rich source. In addition, MARY CRAIG SINCLAIR's *Southern Belle* is the memoir of Sinclair's second wife and covers her life with Sinclair from 1913 until its publication date in 1957.

—James Woodress

SITWELL, Dame Edith, 1887–1964; English poet.

Elborn, Geoffrey, *Edith Sitwell: A Biography.* London, Sheldon Press, and New York, Doubleday, 1981.
Glendinning, Victoria, *Edith Sitwell: A Unicorn among Lions.* London, Weidenfeld and Nicolson, and New York, Knopf, 1981.
Pearson, John, *Facades: Edith, Osbert, and Sacheverell Sitwell.* London, Macmillan, 1978; as *The Sitwells: A Family's Biography*, New York, Harcourt, 1979.
Salter, Elizabeth, *Edith Sitwell.* London, Oresko Books, 1979.

*

SALTER, secretary and close friend of Edith Sitwell, provides an excellent account, in a fairly brief text, of her subject throughout her life, of her family and friends, and of her publications. The individual quality of this work, however, lies in its excellent illustrations showing Edith Sitwell from girlhood to old age, in photographs, portraits, sketches, and sculptures, with commentaries relating these to the poet's life. PEARSON, though treating the three Sitwells, gives a good account of Edith as a troubled woman and writer. Pearson uses unpublished source material from the Humanities Research Center at the University of Texas at Austin as well as Sitwell family letters.

ELBORN is concerned to redress the imbalance between the public persona and the writer: "Many fervent admirers who saw her on television recall with affection her clothes, rings, hats, but have never read a line of anything she wrote. The personal trappings loved by the general public did not particularly amuse the academic critics." Elborn sees Sitwell's life as a conflict between vulgar self-advertisement and outstanding poetic ability, between the vitriolic critic and the kind, loyal, supporting friend. He considers that she should be treated with caution; she believed her own legends, and said, "the public will believe anything—so long as it is not true." He elaborates on Sitwell's dictum that "bad publicity is better than no publicity at all." Elborn, like other biographers, is hampered by the fact that the letters between Sitwell and the Russian artist Pavel Tchelitchew are sealed until the year 2000, but he gives a sympathetic account of her love for him. He presents her as shy, ugly, uneasy, and describes the uneasy atmosphere at Renishaw, the Sitwell house; Edith is projected as an "unwanted, unloved child, born into the wrong world," the family as dissatisfied with everything outside its own circle. He treats Sitwell's literary and artistic circle well, using Salter and Pearson judiciously.

GLENDINNING wrote at the same time as Elborn, so the two writers use similar sources but not each other's biographies. Glendinning writes particularly well about Sitwell's childhood and her relationship with her brothers, her mother, and her father. She uses the memoirs of Osbert and Sacheverell Sitwell to advantage and quotes extensively from both Edith Sitwell's unpublished novel and her autobiography, *Taken Care Of* (1965), though she is careful only to suggest the likenesses between the fictional and the factual "heroines." Her ability to summon up atmosphere is demonstrated in descriptions of Sitwell's poetry readings, notably those of "Façade," with William Walton's music, and her readings during World War II. She describes Sitwell's not always happy involvement with the "poetry scene," and the way in which the poets of that scene shifted around her during her long career. Glendinning gives full and sympathetic treatment to Sitwell's encouragement of young poets, some of whom were second rate, though she also encouraged such writers as Dylan Thomas. Sitwell's reception by the critics, often hostile, and the sales of her books, some unsatisfactory, some, such as *English Eccentrics* (1933) and *Aspects of Modern Poetry* (1934), successful, are dealt with in detail, as are her literary and personal feuds, like that provoked by Wyndham Lewis' *The Apes of God* (1930), which makes fun of Edith and her brothers. Glendinning devotes much thought to Sitwell's psychological makeup—the lack of confidence engendered by her parents, her unexplored sexuality. Glendinning claims that "most of the nervous energy that is part of sexuality went into her poetry, her loyalties, and her crusades; the undischarged residue ate into her heart." She points out that Sitwell's own emotions are reflected in her work, as in, for example, her description in *English Eccentrics* of Margaret Fuller, which relates to her own unhappy love for Tchelichew, and its sexual ambiguity. Glendinning quotes Sitwell's description of Fuller as epitomising herself: "She lived, indeed, a life full of noble ideals, backfisch nonsense and moonshine, silly cloying over-emotionalised friendships and repressed loves (friendship being often disguised as love, and love as friendship), extreme mental and moral courage, and magnificent loyalty to her ideals, friends and loves." The biographer comments: "Yet self-knowledge, at one remove, was as far as [Sitwell] could go: she was unable to act on the self-knowledge, and so free herself."

—Barbara Hayley

SMITH, Adam, 1723–1790; Scottish economist and moral philosopher.

Campbell, R. H. and A. S. Skinner, *Adam Smith*. London, Croom Helm, and New York, St. Martin's, 1982.

Fay, Charles R., *Adam Smith and the Scotland of His Day*. Cambridge, Cambridge University Press, 1956.

Haldane, R. B., *Life of Adam Smith*. London, W. Scott, 1887.

Hirst, Francis W., *Adam Smith*. London and New York, Macmillan, 1904.

Rae, John, *Life of Adam Smith*. London and New York, Macmillan, 1895; expanded edition, New York, A. M. Kelley, 1965.

Scott, William R., *Adam Smith as Student and Professor*. Glasgow, Jackson, 1937; New York, A. M. Kelley, 1965.

West, E. G., *Adam Smith: The Man and His Works*. Indianapolis, Liberty Press, 1976.

*

All of Smith's biographers have had to contend with the rather meagre amount of primary material on Smith's personal and, to a lesser extent, professional life. Smith was a poor correspondent, lived a reclusive life, and was largely successful in having his notes and manuscripts destroyed by his literary executors. The brief presentation by Dugald Stewart to the Royal Society of Edinburgh in 1793 offers the most complete contemporary account of Smith's life and works. It is a laudatory and respectful

biographical sketch that only hints at the "tendency to absence" of which Smith was sufficiently notorious that even his obituary in the London *Times* recalled Smith's absent-minded plunge into a tanning pit while in the midst of conversation.

HALDANE takes advantage of Alexander Carlyle's autobiography, Boswell's biography of Johnson, Smith's correspondence with David Hume, and other published accounts of those who knew Smith adding depth and perspective to the Stewart outline. Unfortunately, the description of Smith's life represents less than a third of Haldane's work. The remaining two thirds are given over to a review of Smith's works and an evaluation of their merit by "modern" (1887) standards.

The 1895 work by economist John RAE stands as the first comprehensive biography of Smith. Utilizing the Glasgow College records, the correspondence of Hume and Carlyle, and other unpublished materials, Rae's biography quickly became the definitive work on Smith. The chronicle of Smith's work on *The Theory of Moral Sentiments* and *The Wealth of Nations* is repeated in greater detail without overwhelming the larger story of Smith's life as an academic and bureaucrat successfully securing appointments as college professor and administrator, tutor to the Duke of Buccleugh, and customs commissioner to support his scholarly pursuits. Despite the wealth of material—including most of the famous, if not always accurate, personal anecdotes—Rae's description fails to give the reader a feeling for Smith as a human being. No doubt this is partially due to the enduring shortage of material on Smith's personal life. But it is also due in part to Rae's affected style, which has been referred to as "artistic" or "old fashioned" by its critics. Regrettably, this style may make the work less accessible for the modern reader. Nevertheless, the Rae biography remains the standard work on Smith. The 1965 reprint of Rae's work includes Jacob Viner's informative "Guide to John Rae's Life of Adam Smith," which brings the reader up to date on the biographical material discovered since 1895.

Following directly in the wake of Rae's biography, HIRST refers to Rae's work as "exhaustive," having "cropped the ground so close that little seemed to have been left . . . to glean." The 1895 discovery of a version of Smith's Glasgow lecture notes by Edwin Cannan is offered by Hirst as justification for a new biography. These notes may bolster the argument that the basic elements of *The Wealth of Nations* were present in rough draft form before Smith encountered Turgot and the Physiocrats during his trip to France as tutor to the Duke of Buccleugh. But they do not provide sufficient cause for preferring Hirst's briefer, less well documented account to that of Rae.

SCOTT does not provide a full biography, confining himself to the period before Smith's European excursion in 1764. However, unlike Hirst, Scott provides more than enough additional material to justify the effort. Scott's thorough search of university records from Glasgow and Edinburgh yielded an early draft of *The Wealth of Nations* and other previously unpublished materials. Scott's work is not intended for the general reader. Over two thirds of the book is devoted to documents while the remainder, as Keynes noted in his lengthy 1938 review, seems at times to be more a history of Glasgow University than a biography of Smith.

Much as Scott enhanced our understanding of Smith through a detailed description of the academic environment in which he worked. FAY's approach is to describe the Scotland in which

Smith lived. Fay is a cautious scholar. Where, for example, Rae notes dramatically that Smith's European tour ended when one of his charges, Hew Scott, was "assassinated in the streets of Paris," Fay, while not necessarily disagreeing, comments that the statement "needs better evidence." This cautious approach, the heavy reliance upon quotation, and an idiosyncratic format make Fay's account less a biography than a set of detailed notes on Smith.

WEST's biography, while more accessible to the modern general reader than any of the earlier works, adds nothing fresh to our knowledge of Smith's life. It is a derivative work, repeating, often verbatim and uncritically, the accounts previously provided by Rae and others. Regarding the death of Hew Scott, for example, West reiterates without attribution Rae's assertion that Scott "was assassinated in the streets of Paris," ignoring the more recent doubts raised on that matter. West's occasional attempts to set Smith in a modern ideological context by referring to conservative thinkers such as Hayek, Friedman, Buchanan, and Tullock detract from the central purpose of the book, but to a far lesser degree than in the Haldane biography.

As contributors to the Glasgow edition of Smith's works commemorating the bicentennial of *The Wealth of Nations*, CAMPBELL AND SKINNER provide the best available source of recent research on Smith. Half the length of Rae's account, it is a brief, readable biography based on solid scholarship. Campbell and Skinner have no pretensions of writing the definitive biography of Smith. Theirs is meant as an introduction to Smith's life and works. The complete biography intended to complement the Glasgow edition of Smith's works is being written by Ian Simpson Ross. This biography, whose imminent publication has been heralded for more than a decade, is now reputedly reaching completion.

—Roger S. Hewett

———————

SMITH, John, *ca.* 1580–1631; English colonist in America.

Barbour, Philip L., *The Three Worlds of Captain John Smith*. Boston, Houghton Mifflin, and London, Macmillan, 1964.

Bradley, A. G., *Captain John Smith*. London, Macmillan, 1905.

Chatterton, E. Keble, *Captain John Smith*. New York, Harper, and London, J. Lane, 1927.

Emerson, Everett H., *Captain John Smith*. New York, Twayne, 1971.

Fletcher, John Gould, *John Smith—Also Pocahontas*. New York, Brentano's, 1928.

Gerson, Noel Bertram (writing as Paul Lewis), *The Great Rogue: A Biography of Captain John Smith*. New York, McKay, 1966.

Gerson, Noel Bertram, *The Glorious Scoundrel: A Biography of Captain John Smith*. New York, Dodd Mead, 1978.

Hillard, George Stillman, *Captain John Smith*. New York, Harper, 1902.

Paine, Lauran B., *Captain John Smith and the Jamestown Story*. New York, Hippocrene Books, and London, Hale, 1973.

Simms, William G., *The Life of Captain John Smith, the Founder of Virginia*. New York, A. L. Burt, 1846; 7th edition, Philadelphia, Potter, 1867.

Smith, Bradford, *Captain John Smith: His Life and Legend*. Philadelphia, Lippincott, 1953.

Vaughan, Alden T., *American Genesis: Captain John Smith and the Founding of Virginia*. Boston, Little Brown, 1975.

Wharton, Henry, *Life of John Smith, English Soldier*. 1685; translated by Laura Polanyi Striker, Chapel Hill, University of North Carolina Press, 1957.

Woods, Katharine Pearson, *The True Story of Captain John Smith*. New York, Doubleday, 1901.

*

There have appeared some 30 comprehensive, adult biographies of John Smith over the course of the past 300 years, but only a few have done more than simply relate what Smith himself presented in his *The True Travels, Adventures, and Observations of Captain John Smith in Europe, Asia, Africa, and America* (1630). The essential question with which Smith's biographers have had to deal is the veracity of his accounts of his adventures, from his fighting the Turks in Transylvania to his rescue from execution by the young Indian maiden, Pocahontas. Those who would deny Smith's truthfulness take their lead from Thomas Fuller, who, in 1662, dismissed Smith from his *Worthies of England*, giving little credence to anything Smith had written. Two centuries later, and an ocean away, Albert Bushnell Hart classified John Smith among the ranks of "American historical liars" and was seconded in his assertion by a number of literary worthies, including John Gorham Palfrey, Edward Neill, Charles Deane, and Henry Adams, none of whom attempted to provide any substantive biographical analysis. Those who did take up their pens to explore Smith's life generally defended him, though to varying degrees.

WHARTON provides one of the earliest biographies of John Smith. Written in 1685 in Latin, it has only recently (1957) been made available to us in English translation by Laura Polanyi Striker. Striker adds an essay on the treatment of John Smith in 17th-century literature and an appendix by Richard Beale Davis, who discusses early American interest in Wharton's manuscript. Wharton, the scholar/divine, presents the best of late 17th-/early 18th-century historical scholarship, which was influenced by the rejection of scholasticism and the impact of the development of experimental science.

The most useful of the 19th-century biographies is that by SIMMS. Simms makes it clear from the start that, with the exception of some references to works of the 16th and 17th centuries on exploration and colonization, he is presenting Smith's *True Travels*, employing as much of Smith's own language as possible. His success in using, and at the same time making more readable, Smith's words, as well as his penchant for the dramatic and heroic, can be measured by the book's several editions. As Simms puts it, the details of Smith's adventures are few, but the imagination will depict them in the "most glowing terms," and the poet and painter will make them their own.

The first three decades of the 20th century produced several good biographies. WOODS' account, which includes useful maps and appendices of documents, devotes over half of its pages to Smith's two and one-half years in Virginia. The author intends a dispassionate rendering of the "true story" of this remarkable man with "absolute fairness" to all concerned. She seeks to substantiate Smith's account of himself, as far as possible, by addressing key elements in Smith's autobiography in the context of the manners and customs of the times, thereby demonstrating Smith's "thorough credibility" and stilling "once and for all those disturbing voices that have of late years been busy in aspersing his memory."

HILLARD's biography is substantially similar in content and purpose to that of Woods. He does add a unique chapter on the "state of public feeling" in England with regard to the colonization of America, as well as a comparatively sophisticated assessment of Smith's administration in Virginia.

Though no less substantive than Woods' or Hillard's accounts, and covering essentially the same ground, BRADLEY's biography is better written. Smith's greatest contributions, Bradley argues, were his enthusiastic belief in colonization as a source of future greatness for England and his "passion for the welfare of Virginia," for which he received "neither reward nor recognition."

CHATTERTON's biography, written some two decades after the three previously noted books, is somewhat more scholarly. Chatterton argues that any acceptance of Smith's truthfulness relies on the validity of his account of his experiences in Transylvania. As Chatterton puts it, if he fails in this, Smith stands, as charged, "a liar and a braggart." Chatterton seeks to substantiate Smith's narrative by arguing that in his account Smith wrote of events of which he had no knowledge other than his own experience; contemporary accounts existed but were unavailable to him. Of particular value is Chatterton's brief account of the historiography that had dominated accounts of Smith's life during the previous seven decades.

Appearing in 1928, FLETCHER's book was touted as belonging to the "new biography." In some ways, it does break with those preceding it, but it does not compare in its modernity to those that would follow. The author addresses a readership that is, he suggests, more than ever before "suspicious," and that, not without reason, has come to expect "pap instead of fact, bias instead of history, and eulogy instead of biography." Most strikingly, as one would not expect from the title of the book, Fletcher asserts that he intends to show how "incidental and unimportant," relatively speaking, was that phase of Smith's career connected with Virginia.

BRADFORD SMITH's study is seminal in that it is he who launches the substantive rehabilitation of John Smith's career in modern scholarship. Taking a page from Chatterton, Bradford Smith suggests that if one were able to prove the truth of John Smith's account of what would appear to be the most fanciful of his adventures—his exploits in Hungary and Transylvania—all else would have to be believed. Bradford Smith employs Laura Polanyi Striker in his efforts, from whose research he constructs his chapters on Smith's Eastern European adventures. Striker provides substantial verification of the details of Smith's account—including names, places, and events—from a number of Magyar, Latin, Italian, and German sources on Hungarian history, studied for the first time for that express purpose. The substance of her defense is presented in an appendix, "Captain John Smith's Hungary and Transylvania." An updated and more thorough analysis appears in Striker's and Smith's "The Rehabilitation of Captain John Smith" (*Journal of Southern History*, XXVIII [1962]).

If Bradford Smith's biography is seminal, BARBOUR's *Three Worlds*, a detailed and heavily documented narrative of John Smith's career—as a "soldier, slave, and fugitive over the face of Europe"; "wise, patient, and energetic founder of a New World"; and "adventurer, home in England, to tell the truth about his other worlds"—is definitive, at least thus far. Compared to the work of Smith and Striker, to whom he is deeply indebted, Barbour's only original contribution lies in "the hints and clues" he finds in a few important documents, especially period maps, hitherto ignored. More important is Barbour's unequaled comprehensive analysis and synthesis of manuscript sources and secondary literature. (Barbour has also edited what is now the definitive edition of the writings of Smith, *The Complete Works of Captain John Smith 1580–1631* [3 vols, Chapel Hill, University of North Carolina Press, 1986].)

EMERSON's study does not provide any original biographical information, referring instead to Barbour's work as the definitive source for that information. He nevertheless provides some useful insights, finding in Smith's writing, for example, the portrait of "a complex, striking personality, . . . a tough-minded dreamer, a practical idealist." Smith's vision of America was what might be considered "the characteristic one," Emerson writes: "Excited by the possibilities of life in the New World, where a man's status might depend on his own endeavors," Smith provided an answer to the question St. Jean de Crevecoeur posed some 150 years later: "What then is the American, this new man."

VAUGHAN is also heavily indebted to Bradford Smith, as well as to Barbour and Emerson. Limiting his account to Smith's life in Virginia, Vaughan argues that Smith became a symbol of the English vanguard in the New World, and he "traces the transformation of the errant dream of a soldier of fortune into an early American social order." In a manner similar to Emerson, Vaughan defends Smith's place in the Library of American Biography series not only on the merits of his contributions to the colony's survival, but also because in Smith "perhaps. . . young America found a prototype of itself; bold, energetic, and optimistic; at the same time brash, intolerant, overly proud of its achievements, and overly solicitous of approval."

Among the best of the recent biographies, written unabashedly for an adult popular audience, are the books of GERSON, who also uses the pseudonym Paul Lewis. Gerson, a prolific writer of over 60 works of fiction and nonfiction, is responsible for both *The Great Rogue* and *The Glorious Scoundrel*. Both are heavily indebted to Bradford Smith; neither to Philip Barbour. *The Glorious Scoundrel* is largely a retelling in briefer form of *The Great Rogue*, its references suggesting additional research limited to a handful of sources on Indian culture.

Like Gerson, PAINE is an accomplished popular writer, though most of her work prior to *Captain John Smith* was on witchcraft and the occult. To her credit, she cites among her sources both Bradford Smith and Philip Barbour, as well as the useful but now dated work by W. F. Craven, *The Southern Colonies in the 17th Century* (1944). Otherwise, there is little to recommend her book over Gerson's. More so than Gerson, Paine's is a retelling in modern language of Smith's personal story, with little else to help the reader understand the man or his times.

—Bryan F. Le Beau

SMITH, Joseph, 1805–1844; American religious leader.

Andrus, Hyrum Leslie, *Joseph Smith, the Man and the Seer.* Salt Lake City, Utah, Deseret Book Company, 1960.

Beardsley, Harry M., *Joseph Smith and His Mormon Empire.* Boston, Houghton Mifflin, 1931.

Brodie, Fawn McKay, *No Man Knows My History: The Life of Joseph Smith, the Mormon Prophet.* New York, Knopf, 1945; revised edition, 1971.

Bushman, Richard L., *Joseph Smith and the Beginnings of Mormonism.* Urbana, University of Illinois Press, 1984.

Cannon, George Q., *The Life of Joseph Smith, the Prophet.* Salt Lake City, Utah, Juvenile Instructor Office, 1888.

Conkling, J. Christopher, *A Joseph Smith Chronology.* Salt Lake City, Utah, Deseret Book Company, 1979.

Evans, John Henry, *Joseph Smith: An American Prophet.* New York, Macmillan, 1933.

Gibbons, Francis M., *Joseph Smith: Martyr, Prophet of God.* Salt Lake City, Utah, Deseret Book Company, 1977.

Hill, Donna, *Joseph Smith, the First Mormon.* New York, Doubleday, 1977.

Madsen, Truman G., *Joseph Smith the Prophet.* Salt Lake City, Utah, Bookcraft, 1989.

Nibley, Preston, *Joseph Smith, the Prophet.* Salt Lake City, Utah, Deseret News Press, 1944.

Riley, I. Woodbridge, *The Founder of Mormonism: A Psychological Study of Joseph Smith.* New York, Dodd Mead, 1902; London, Heinemann, 1903.

Smith, Lucy Mack, *Joseph Smith's History, by His Mother.* London, 1853; Salt Lake City, Utah, Modern Microfilm, 1970.

Stewart, John J., *Joseph Smith: The Mormon Prophet.* Salt Lake City, Utah, Mercury Publishing Company, 1966.

Taves, Ernest H., *Trouble Enough: Joseph Smith and the Book of Mormon.* Buffalo, New York, Prometheus Books, 1984.

*

Few lives of only 39 years have been as full as that of Joseph Smith; fewer yet have been as controversial. As Smith himself is quoted as having said to his followers the year he died: "I don't blame anyone for not believing my history. If I had not experienced what I have, I could not have believed it myself." Smith was as capable of arousing the most bitter enmity in others as he was of inspiring the greatest loyalty. His critics, therefore, appeared from the start, portraying him, among other things, as a lecherous rogue or as the victim of paranoid delusions. Nearly all of his biographers, the most of those discussed herein, however, have been Mormons who, to varying degrees, extoll his virtues. Non-Mormon biographers included below are Riley, Beardsley, Brodie, and Taves.

Common to all his biographers is Smith's own account of his life and work, *History of the Church of Jesus Christ of Latter-day Saints.* The second most common source is his mother's, LUCY MACK SMITH's, biography. Published in England by Church Apostle Orson Pratt, it was touted by Pratt as containing information never before published on "the private life and character" of Joseph Smith and recommended by Church newspapers to all Mormons. In 1865 Brigham Young nevertheless suppressed the book as having been published without permission of the Church leadership and as containing several serious errors. The reprint referred to here is a surviving copy of the original. It is preceded by a history of the text as well as a detailed analysis of changes made in the authorized "revised" edition of 1901.

CANNON addresses "Saints" as well as non-church members, in order that the former may find "joy" in their "beloved Prophet" and the latter may gain a better understanding of Smith as their "benefactor." Although often uncritically flattering, it is the first detailed biography of Joseph Smith. It works from a substantial number of firsthand accounts and includes a useful introduction to Mormon belief in the "Apostacy" from the word of Christ and the Restoration under the "Choice Seer," Joseph Smith.

Often cited as the first of the modern non-Mormon accounts, RILEY's biography is marked by a general discounting of religious causation and by a unique, for its time, reliance on physiological psychology. Riley concludes that Smith's visions were the result of epilepsy, and that his sensuality, vanity, and self-conceit suggest an inherited psychic degeneracy. He is the first to demolish the 19th-century theory that the *Book of Mormon* was Sidney Rigdon's plagiarized version of a novel by Solomon Spaulding. He revives Alexander Campbell's belief that contemporary cultural influences accounted for *The Book of Mormon* and is the first to suggest that Ethan Smith's *View of the Hebrews* (1823) and Josiah Priest's *Wonders of Nature and Providence* (1825) were its sources.

Two useful biographies appeared in the 1930s. BEARSDLEY generally follows the psychological approach of Riley, concluding that Smith suffered from dementia praecox and exhibited symptoms of paranoia, schizophrenia, an inferiority complex, delusions of grandeur, delusions of persecution, and an abnormal sexual interest. Beardsley's popular prose and penchant for the dramatic result in a more entertaining text than Riley's. EVANS sets out to provide another "scientific treatment," but, in contrast to Riley and Beardsley, he assumes that Smith was what he and his followers claim he was—a prophet and seer. He seeks to rescue Smith from the unflattering portraits provided by the previous two writers. The book is useful as well for citing the words of Smith's contemporaries, showing the zeal with which they accepted Smith's leadership.

"Joseph Smith is the only person who is competent to relate the singular and marvelous experiences [of] . . . his life." Thus writes NIBLEY in his introduction to *Joseph Smith, the Prophet*, and such is the sum and substance of his book. It is almost exclusively a blend of excerpts, edited and annotated into narrative form, from Smith's *History of the Church* and his mother's *Joseph Smith's History*. It condenses some eight volumes of personal remembrances into one volume intended for a modern and sophisticated but not scholarly audience.

Much like Riley's biography, BRODIE's represents another leap forward in scholarship. Also reminiscent of Riley's approach, Brodie advances a psychoanalytic interpretation of Smith's behavior as well as a portrait of Smith as the product of his cultural environment. Brodie accepts Riley's negation of the Spaulding theory, but she lays aside his physiological psychology for a more straightforward view of Joseph Smith as an ingenious myth-maker who absorbed ideas from his cultural environment. Her major premise is that Smith's "assumption of the role of a religious prophet was an evolutionary process, that he began as a bucolic scryer, using the primitive techniques of the folklore common to his area, most of which he discarded as he evolved into a preacher-prophet.'' The second edition offers no new theories, but Brodie's research into archives not available to her in 1945, as well into the considerably greater body of literature of clinical psychology, provides a more substantive defense of those theories.

ANDRUS' book is useful, if brief (140 pages of text), in that the author tends to let those who knew Joseph Smith, including those who participated in his spiritual manifestations, speak for themselves. Especially effective is Andrus' use of little known incidents, those usually left out of more scholarly studies, which provide a more personal insight into Smith's character. He challenges those who would label Smith a mere dreamer, an epileptic, a spiritualist, a mystic, or a deceiver. Andrus is also the author of an instructive dissertation, *Joseph Smith, Social Philosopher, Theorist, and Prophet* (Ann Arbor, Michigan, University Microfilms, 1955).

STEWART writes that Smith is ''probably the most explained and the least understood person in American history.'' He argues that Smith, ''the Prophet and Seer of the Lord, has done more, save Jesus only, for the salvation of man in this world, than any other man that ever lived in it.'' Why, then, the negative charges? Stewart suggests that they are the creation of ministers who disdained of losing followers to Smith, politicians who feared Smith's political activities, apostates who were either disillusioned by or excommunicated from the Church, and those who simply misunderstood Smith. Generally, such attacks, Stewart writes, tried to show that Smith's teachings and practices were a departure from such cherished American traditions as the separation of church and state, the sanctity of private property, monogamous marriage, freedom of the press, or of organized religions, then extant.

Both GIBBONS and HILL will satisfy the faithful, as both writers accept the role of Joseph Smith as seer and prophet. Yet, neither presents the life of Joseph Smith without critical content. Gibbons emphasizes the necessity of realizing the difference between Joseph Smith the prophet and Joseph Smith the fallible, imperfect man—a distinction of which Smith himself, Gibbons argues, reminded his followers. Hill concludes that Smith was, in the end, ''an inspired spiritual leader who had ordinary human failings.'' Gibbons discusses the controversies surrounding Smith's life and teachings in some detail and concludes that it was the startling impact of Smith's message, more so than his character or personality, that gave rise to hostility. Such hostility, he adds—even Smith's martyrdom—only served to strengthen the Church. Hill, in contrast, does not dwell on controversy—in such matters, ''there can be no answer that will satisfy everyone,'' she writes—but, instead, points to a unity of the various aspects of culture, evident not only in the important social and religious forces to which Joseph was responding and to which he contributed, but also in the expectations of those who followed him. Any dichotomy between the secular and sacred, often assumed by other, especially non-Mormon, biographers, Hill suggests would have been unrecognizable to Joseph Smith.

The importance of TAVES' work lies not in its biographical details but in his discussion of the origins of *The Book of Mormon.* Taves uses a stylometric quantitative analysis of style to determine single or multiple authorship and the likely identity of the author or authors. He considers such evidence as the frequency, preferred position, and pairing of words, as well as the internal consistency of *The Book of Mormon* and its consistency in relation to three other texts known to have come from the pen of Joseph Smith. Taves finds that there is no evidence of multiple authorship of *The Book of Mormon,* and that Smith was likely its author.

Although more narrowly focused than any of the other biographies discussed herein, BUSHMAN's study merits some attention as a scholarly and exacting study of the first 25 years of Joseph Smith's life, especially the critical ten years from 1820 to 1830, from Smith's first vision to his move to Kirtland, Ohio. Bushman argues that Smith is best understood ''as a person who outgrew his culture,'' that he was not just the sum total of the historical forces acting upon him. Bushman's goal is to ''recognize the unusual as well as the common'' in Smith's early work, to tell how Mormonism unloosed itself from its immediate locale in those critical first years, and to portray as accurately as possible what it had become by the time the Prophet, his family, and his followers left New York for Ohio, early in 1831.

MADSEN, an authority on Mormon Doctrine, does not attempt a comprehensive biography, but instead expounds on several aspects of Smith's life and character: Smith's first vision, his personality, his spiritual gifts and attributes, his various earthly trials, his abilities as speaker and teacher, the Kirtland temple experience, doctrinal developments in Nauvoo, and his martyrdom. Each chapter is based on one of a series of lectures Madsen presented at Brigham Young University, which were made available to the general public on audiocassette. To the printed text, Madsen adds over 50 pages of notes and bibliography.

Those seeking a ''ready reference'' guide to the life of Joseph Smith would do well to consult CONKLING's *Chronology.* It includes the basic facts of Smith's life—the who, what, where and when, if not why—with little elaboration or interpretation. For further reading, Conkling adds an extensive bibliography.

—Bryan F. Le Beau

SMOLLETT, Tobias George, 1721–1771; Scottish writer.

Anderson, Robert, ''Life,'' in *Miscellaneous Works of Tobias Smollett, M.D.* Sixth edition, London, 1820.

Basker, James G., *Tobias Smollett: Critic and Journalist.* Newark, University of Delaware Press, and London, Associated University Presses, 1988.

Boucé, P.-G., *The Novels of Tobias Smollett,* translated by A. White and P.-G. Boucé. London and New York, Longman, 1976 (originally published as *Les Romans de Smollett,* Paris, Didier, 1971).

Chambers, Robert, *Smollett: His Life and a Selection from His Writings.* Edinburgh, W. R. Chambers, 1867.

Hannay, David, *Life of Tobias George Smollett.* London, W. Scott, 1887.

Kahrl, G. M., *Tobias Smollett, Traveler-Novelist.* Chicago, University of Chicago Press, 1945.

Knapp, Lewis M., *Tobias Smollett: Doctor of Men and Manners.* Princeton, New Jersey, Princeton University Press, 1949.

Martz, Lewis L., *The Later Career of Tobias Smollett*. New Haven, Connecticut, Yale University Press, and London, Oxford University Press, 1942.

Melville, Lewis (L. Benjamin), *The Life and Letters of Tobias Smollett*. London, Faber, 1926.

Moore, John, editor, *The Works of Tobias Smollett, M.D., with Memoirs of His Life*. London, B. Law, 1797.

Smeaton, Oliphant, *Tobias Smollett*. Edinburgh, Oliphant Anderson, and New York, Scribner, 1897.

*

Of the many early lives of Smollett only ANDERSON's and MOORE's are notable: Anderson's (greatly expanded between 1794 and 1820) is the fuller, but Moore's contains a valuable psychological portrait drawn from firsthand knowledge. Three Victorian Lives still deserve attention. CHAMBERS is the first biographer to make a really scrupulous distinction between the ascertainable facts of Smollett's life and speculation based on the novels. HANNAY uses his knowledge of naval history to give the fullest, most accurate, and most vivid account of Smollett's maritime career. SMEATON's biography is unfortunately undocumented, so we have no means of determining whether its mass of new information (including, uniquely among all the biographies, Smollett's birthdate) is based on guesswork or on documents now unavailable.

The rather pretentious contribution by MELVILLE is for the most part a synthesis of earlier biographies. It does contain some documents not conveniently available in other accounts of Smollett, but transcriptions are too often inaccurate; with virtually no references, the work as a whole is unreliable. The specialized, sound, thorough, scholarly studies by MARTZ, on Smollett's generally forgotten Grub-Street activities, and by KAHRL, on Smollett's travels, have a predominantly literary-critical focus, but reflect some light on their subject's biography.

The fully documented, highly accurate account by KNAPP is indubitably the standard biography. With unparalleled thoroughness it painstakingly corrects the factual and interpretative errors of earlier biographies and provides very full and fair evaluations of a mass of new material: Knapp is prepared to remain in doubt even over such important matters as Smollett's religious views or philosophical outlook where the evidence on final evaluation appears to be inconclusive. His somewhat dry narrative sticks close to documented facts, but a distinctive portrait of Smollett emerges that fully rehabilitates his character from the Victorian stereotype. Though Knapp continues to stress Smollett's pride and independence, he also shows a kindlier, more humanitarian figure than the familiar irascible satirist. In a rare indulgence in psychological analysis, Knapp finds that Smollett's personality was shaped by two powerful forces, "at times mutually antagonistic, but, in the long run, essentially interlocking and complementary"; Smollett was in many respects "a typical rationalist, a typical satirist, and a conventionally aristocratic gentleman of the mid-18th century." A firm believer in decorum, social order, and subordination, he was also in many respects "a man of ebullient and violent feelings which often escaped from the leash of reason; a person repeatedly unconventional for his times in romantic self-confession, and a very generous humanitarian." Though scholars in the 1990s are by no means convinced that rationalism was in any way typical of the mid-18th century, this

character sketch is well judged. Knapp demonstrates that Smollett's standing in the literary and social worlds was from the beginning much higher than was thought by biographers who believed that *Roderick Random* was more autobiographical than now seems to be the case. However, he somewhat overstates his claims on behalf of Smollett's absolute leadership in literary circles during the interregnum between Pope and Johnson. Knapp's definitive biography is rounded off with a chapter of criticism of Smollett's novels that is much inferior to the rest of the volume. Knapp has also edited a collection of Smollett's letters (*The Letters of Tobias Smollett*, Oxford University Press, 1970), which conveniently gathers together from a variety of sources 103 letters by Smollett, only three of them printed for the first time. The volume is excellently annotated.

BOUCÉ leaves no stone unturned in his exploration of Smollett's novels: the first part of his mostly literary-critical study is biographical and psychological, and though he does not add significantly to the facts in Kapp, he offers some insights that are particularly useful in the light of Knapp's great caution over making psychological assessments of Smollett. BASKER is the first critic to offer a really detailed survey of Smollett's long and successful career as a journalist, a career in which, Basker says, "we perceive a more widely knowledgeable and ambitious intellect than we have usually thought of [Smollett] as being." Basker concludes that Smollett is a founding father of the literary-critical establishment: "the first man of letters really to fill the role of review journal editor, inventing and defining it as he went along, and as such he is a forefather of all the review critics and editors since." Upon this narrow definition of a literary-critical establishment, Basker provides an acceptable modification of Knapp's claims concerning Smollett's leadership in literary circles.

—James Sambrook

SOLZHENITSYN, Alexander, 1918–   ; Russian writer.

Burg, David and George Feifer, *Solzhenitsyn*. New York, Stein and Day, and London, Hodder and Stoughton, 1972.

Scammell, Michael, *Solzhenitsyn: A Biography*. New York, Norton, 1984; London, Hutchinson, 1985.

*

Writing a biography of a living figure is not easy. Part of the difficulty is insuperable, for the subject's life is not yet complete, and therefore cannot be viewed as a whole. Moreover, the biographer is part of the subject's own time, and is therefore prey to all its prejudices and blind spots. To be sure, the biographer of a living person also enjoys certain advantages: he may know his subject personally, and sometimes quite well, or at least he may obain direct information through questions which the biographer himself formulates. In sum, he may form an unmediated impression of the subject of his researches.

Solzhenitsyn's biographers labor under most of the disadvantages of writing about a contemporary figure with few of its advantages. This applies particularly to BURG AND FEIFER, who researched and wrote their study at a time when Solzhenitsyn was still locked in fierce struggle against the recalcitrant Soviet authorities and consequently took an exceedingly dim view of biographies of individuals living under Soviet conditions: in a statement of December 1971 Solzhenitsyn stigmatized biographies of living persons as "unceremonious and amoral," and described biographers as in principle little better than KGB agents gathering information for an internal intelligence dossier. Under such circumstances Burg and Feifer could not approach Solzhenitsyn personally, or gather information about him at all easily through official channels; nor could they learn much about him from Solzhenitsyn's friends. However, persuaded that Russian wrtiers are the "voices—often the only ones—of civilized conscience," Burg and Feifer would not be discouraged, and eventually produced an extensive treatment of Solzhenitsyn based primarily on published materials. They treat Solzhenitsyn as a public, cultural, and political phenomenon; of his inner life they necessarily have little to say.

SCAMMELL's book, published 12 years later, builds on the strengths of the earlier biography. At nearly 1,000 pages of text, it has the scope to incorporate major points from Solzhenitsyn's autobiograpical essay *A Calf Was Butting an Oak* (where he expounded his strong views of events in which he had been personally involved) into a biographical framework, and then to expand that, first into literary history, and finally into literary politics. Since Solzhenitsyn is nothing if not a serious writer, most of his works or pronouncements have occasioned extensive, sometimes acrimonious debate on great questions of our day. Scammell is thoroughly familiar with these disputes and supplies the reader with ample information on the controversies in which Solzhenitsyn has been involved. In analyzying the reception of *One Day in the Life of Ivan Denisovich*, for instance, he not only recognizes the book's esthetic and political worth, but also understands that the reaction to it at the time of its publication had to do with "that sphere of human existence where morality and faith converage and whose workings are beyond our conscious understanding." In such areas Scammell takes much the same approach as Burg and Feifer, but goes beyond them both quantitatively and qualitatively.

In addition, Scammell has more material with which to work: he discusses Solzhenitsyn's dramatic expulsion from the Soviet Union in early 1974, his settling in the United States, and his important speeches in the West. He has had the opportunity to hear him speak and also to visit his Vermont home, if not to become personally acquainted with him. Thus Scammell's Solzhenitsyn is not merely an emanation of the printed word, but a living presence. When Solzhenitsyn departs this life, his definitive biographer will have to incorporate and pass beyond Scammell, just as Scammell has done for Burg and Feifer.

—Charles A. Moser

SPINOZA, Benedict de (*born* Baruch Spinoza), 1632–1677; Dutch philosopher.

Martineau, James, *A Study of Spinoza*. London, Macmillan, 1882.

Pollock, Frederick, *Spinoza: His Life and Philosophy*. London, C. K. Paul, 1880; 2nd edition, London, Duckworth, and New York, Macmillan, 1899.

Roth, Leon, *Spinoza*. London, E. Benn, and Boston, Little Brown, 1929.

Scruton, Roger, *Spinoza*. Oxford and New York, Oxford University Press, 1986.

Wolf, A., "Life of Spinoza," printed with *Spinoza's Short Treatise on God, Man, and His Wellbeing*, edited and translated by A. Wolf. London, A. and C. Black, 1910.

*

Ever since Bayle published his highly unreliable and tendentious account of Spinoza as an atheist in the *Dictionnaire historique et critique* (1697, revised 1702), biographers have been wary of writing accounts of the life and thought of so contentious a figure. A Jew born in Amsterdam of a family of *marronos* fleeing persecution in Portugal, Spinoza had, however, been excommunicated from his own synagogue for his opinions. Spinoza's first biographer, like Kant's, knew him well although, unlike Kant's, he was no disciple. He was German minister of the Lutheran congregation at The Hague, Johannes Köhler ("Colerus"), and his little book, the chief authority for Spinoza's life, was published in Dutch with a sermon against Spinozism in Amsterdam in 1705. An inaccurate French translation of 1706 immediately gained currency, and there was an English translation of the same year (*The Life of Benedict de Spinosa, by John Colerus*, London, 1706). A German translation from the French in 1723 bears a portrait whose caption says that Spinoza carried his damnation written on his face. The biography does not disguise Köhler's liking and even admiration for Spinoza the man, and Pollock, in what is certainly still the best biography available in English (see below), prints the English translation of Köhler from the French as an appendix to his second edition in 1899.

Background material has subsequently been brought to light, notably by K. O. Meinsma, and all the early lives and documents have been collected and published in a German edition by J. Freudenthal, *Die Lebensgeschichte Spinozas in Quellenschriften, Urkunden und nichtamtlichen Nachrichten* (1899). Little of biographical note has changed the picture since Pollock's second edition, and his attitude to the very differing degrees of trustworthiness in his sources has on the whole adequately filtered the wide variety of material at his disposal. The additional material in Freudenthal's own biography (*Spinoza: sein Leben und Seine Lehre*, Stuttgart, 1904) has been incorporated into Wolf's *Life* of 1910 (see below). However, the proscriptions to which Spinoza's works were subjected, and the obloquy in which his opinions were held by Hume, held back any proper appreciation of his philosophical stature for a century, until a famous conversation between Lessing and Jacobi in 1780, and the reassessment brought about by Lessing, Goethe, Herder, Novalis, Schleiermacher, Schelling, and Herder.

MARTINEAU's biography unhappily clashed in date with Pollock's, and had to be extended into a fuller work because it had become too long for the series into which it had been intended to fit. The biographical section of some 100 pages gives the background of the Jewish persecution on the Iberian peninsula in picturesque detail, with rhetoric to match. All sorts of conjectural judgements are implied or even explicitly made, but for an informed sketch of the *marranos* communities in the Low Countries, and a probable account of Spinoza's intellectual development, Martineau is still worth reading, partly no doubt on account of his leisurely pace.

Martineau maintains with some plausibility that Spinoza's native language was not Portuguese but Spanish. He recounts the adventurous early years, the lens-grinding, the possible liaison with one of the Van den Ende daughters, the relationship with the liberal Calvinist Arminian wing, the excommunication from the synagogue, and the attempt on Spinoza's life, all with commendable fidelity to the sources. The intemperance of language is less commendable in a formal work of this sort. Even in 1882 it was unnecessary to refer to a letter from a pupil to Spinoza as "a curious specimen of arrogant commonplace and sacerdotal vulgarity," much as one might still like to have such directness of expression in one's quiver. Martineau is especially strong on Spinoza's scientific preoccupations, his differences with Boyle, the frugalities of Spinoza's lifestyle, and the sources of his small income.

POLLOCK's biography makes more systematic use of Spinoza's correspondence. The biographical content of the book is naturally affected by the decision to print Köhler's text as an appendix, so relieving the author of the task of narrating the day-to-day domestic details of Spinoza's existence. The circumstances of his change of name from Baruch to Benedict, and of his renunciation of his father's inheritance, in spite of clear need, because it was disputed by his two sisters, are clearly set out, as is the way in which, having followed Descartes in becoming a practicing optician, his lens-making opened the doors to his acquaintanceship with Leibniz and Huyghens.

WOLF's 100-page life prefaces his edition of the posthumous *Short Treatise*, a preliminary sketch for the *Ethics*. The biography is more detailed than those of Martineau and Pollock on such matters as Spinoza's health and his circle of friends, although much of the information, particularly financial, still necessarily comes from Köhler. Pollock had dismissed the existence of a "J. M. Lucas," supposed to have written a hostile and very early biography that is said to have appeared with the early atheist tract *de tribus impostoribus* ("On the Three Imposters"), although he admitted that Köhler seemed at some points to depend on an even earlier source. Wolf resurrects Lucas but does not deal with the objections raised by Pollock, and he has a different doctor from Köhler attending Spinoza on his sudden death at the age of 44. Wolf's lack of more than a single passing reference to Pollock, who is however listed in his bibliography, is frankly disquieting and makes it difficult to accept his account of Spinoza's death and other matters.

SCRUTON's brisk and over-simplified introductory biographical remarks echo Pollock's phrases but Wolf's conclusions, and are anyway too cavalier about the historical subtleties to carry weight. A sentence beginning "The Spanish monarchy's intolerable combination of spiritual tyranny and secular arrogance . . ." represents too sweeping a judgement to stand unqualified and unexplained. Scruton's presentation of Spinoza's philosophy is equally peremptory, and his assertion that there is a biography by J. M. Lucas makes one wonder if the volume is not somewhat perfunctory. ROTH has a very brief introduction to Spinoza's "Life and Character" and "General Outlook," and

his chapter on the works is informative. Roth's warning against taking as authentic the *Short Treatise* published by Wolf is timely, in spite of its "valuable illustrations for the authoritative doctrine."

We still clearly need a competent biographer but, as so often, there is comparatively little documented evidence to go on, only a great swell of surmise. For non-professional readers looking for some account of the philosophy itself, an introduction such as that to be found in F. C. Copleston's nine-volume *A History of Philosophy* (vol. 4) is preferable to any others available in English. Unhappily the paucity of reliable sources and the abundance of scurrilous anecdote makes it unlikely that we shall see the properly reliable, up-to-date biography we need.

—A. H. T. Levi

———

STAËL, Madame Germaine de, 1766–1817; French writer.

Andrews, Wayne, *Germaine: A Portrait of Madame de Staël*. New York, Atheneum, 1963; London, Gollancz, 1964.

Goldsmith, Margaret, *Madame de Staël: Portrait of a Liberal in the Revolutionary Age*. London and New York, Longman, 1938.

Herold, J. Christopher, *Mistress to an Age: A Life of Madame de Staël*. Indianapolis, Bobbs-Merrill, 1958; London, Hamilton, 1959.

Winegarten, Renee, *Madame de Staël*. Leamington Spa, Warwickshire, and Dover, New Hampshire, Berg, 1985.

*

GOLDSMITH is particularly interested in Madame de Staël as one of the first specimens of a new kind of self-reliant woman created by the French Revolution. She admires especially Madame de Staël's political liberalism, which made her a life-long foe of oppression in any form, and her independent-mindedness, which enabled her to play a political role in her own right, and not as the appendage of any man. Goldsmith presents Madame de Staël as a woman of exceptional intellect, able to see both sides of any question, generous to her opponents, but always drawn to the side of freedom and liberty. Goldsmith is certainly more interested in Madame de Staël's politics than in her literary works, and while she shows herself to be well-informed and generally accurate about the facts of her life, she is at no pains to be scholarly in a detailed way, and does not strive for a complete biography. Her book is an admiring portrait of an exemplary modern woman, aimed at the general reader, preferably of liberal and feminist sympathies. But so much new information has come to light in the half-century since it was published that, for all its attractive qualities of style, tone and point of view, it cannot help but seem outdated.

ANDREWS accurately labels his biography a "Portrait," to indicate the impressionistic technique he adopted for telling Madame de Staël's story in a sequence of scenes rather than as a continuous and detailed chronological narrative. His Foreword warns the reader that he has purposely simplified her life (about which we have too much information, and in which too many minor figures played a role) in order to allow her personality—the true source of her greatness, according to Andrews—to emerge as the central focus of his work. One may speculate that Andrews chose to simplify Madame de Staël's life, in part at least, for the additional reason that he wanted his work to be defined as belonging to a different category than that of the complete biography—a category virtually preempted five years earlier by Christopher Herold's masterful biography, with which Andrews knew his own work could not hope to compete. Whatever the motive, Andrews makes no attempt to be thorough or scholarly, arguing that as a novelist and literary critic, Madame de Staël is no longer read and is of merely historical interest, whereas in her role as an explorer and adventuress in the world of European cultural values she remains a vital influence. His ''portrait'' is therefore pieced together from a series of specific episodes or moments in her life when some aspect of her extraordinary personality could be seen in action. Andrews devotes scant attention to the qualities or character of those who shared her intellectual or emotional life. Rather he treats the various members of her circle as so many catalysts, each of whom chanced to reveal a different side of her nature. The effect of the method is to treat the reader to a kind of selective pageant of Madame de Staël's intellectual adventures, from which a lively sense of her character and manner does indeed emerge. Since the book is engagingly written and briskly paced, it is an attractive way to ''get to know'' its subject, but it will not satisfy those readers who desire a systematic account of her life.

HEROLD has produced the most compendious and the most thorough modern biography of Madame de Staël, and while he carefully and correctly disclaims any pretensions to definitiveness, his work is the nearest thing we have so far to a complete and definitive biography. It is in a class by itself because of its rare combination of meticulous scholarship and graceful writing style, and it is really the only biography to read or to consult for the truly serious student. A volume of some 500 closely-printed pages must necessarily seem daunting to some and will be suspected, by the general reader at least, of telling more about Madame de Staël than anyone might reasonably want to know. Yet Herold manages to give his narrative a light touch, avoiding the ponderous solemnity of some academic scholarship, and giving every paragraph a refreshing sparkle with the leavening of wit and the perspective of irony. Footnotes are rare, and sources are identified in a very sensible (and readable) ''bibliographic essay'' rather than a dry alphabetical list. The enormous erudition that underpins this biography is pleasantly masked by the urbanity of its tone and the nimble grace of its style. Herold is more than just reliably accurate: he weaves the factual details together artfully into a rich evocation of the age that formed the background for Madame de Staël's life, and he offers as well an intelligent and finely perceptive interpretation of what her life meant for her age and for posterity. Herold's is a model among intellectual biographies, and amply fulfills the goal he had set himself, to provide ''a new synthesis'' in a general biography of Madame de Staël, ''a fully rounded one, which would restore her to life in the public mind.''

WINEGARTEN has written a small-scale intellectual biography of Madame de Staël that does not claim completeness as its objective. It is a biographical essay, in effect, giving all the main facts of the life and discussing or analyzing the significance of those facts from the perspective of the modern reader, and in the context of the history of ideas. Winegarten's scholarship is careful and thorough, but remains hidden below the surface of a thoughtful and smooth-flowing narrative. There are no footnotes, and only a very select bibliography. The main emphasis is on Madame de Staël as a literary figure and as an independent-minded feminist, sensitive both to the problems of the social role of women and to the importance of literature in the political struggle for freedom. In just over 100 pages, Winegarten provides a succinct but authoritative account of Madame de Staël's bustlingly active and influential life, and a most intelligent assessment of the present state of her reputation. The book hardly qualifies as a full-dress biography, even for the casual reader, but it does constitute an excellent introduction for those who want to know who Madame de Staël was and what her life signified.

—Murray Sachs

STALIN, Joseph, 1879–1953; Russian revolutionary and Soviet leader.

Carrère d'Encausse, Hélène, *Stalin, Order through Terror*, translated by Valence Ionescu. London and New York, Longman, 1981 (originally published by Flammarion, Paris, 1979).

Deutscher, Isaac, *Stalin: A Political Biography*. London and New York, Oxford University Press, 1949; revised edition, 1967.

Djilas, Milovan, *Conversations with Stalin*, translated by M. B. Petrovich. New York, Harcourt, and London, Hart-Davis, 1962.

Fischer, Louis, *The Life and Death of Stalin*. New York, Harper, 1952; London, Cape, 1953.

Hoxha, Enver, *With Stalin: Memoirs*. Tirana, 8 Nentori Publishing, 1979.

Liversidge, Douglas, *Joseph Stalin*. New York and London, F. Watts, 1969.

McNeal, Robert H., *Stalin: Man and Ruler*. New York, New York University Press, and London, Macmillan/Oxford University Press, 1988.

Medvedev, Roy A., *On Stalin and Stalinism*, translated by Ellen de Kadt. New York and Oxford, Oxford University Press, 1979.

Payne, Robert, *The Rise and Fall of Stalin*. New York, Simon and Schuster, 1965; London, W. H. Allen, 1966.

Slusser, Robert M., *Stalin in October: The Man Who Missed the Revolution*. Baltimore, Maryland, and London, Johns Hopkins University Press, 1987.

Smith, Edward E., *The Young Stalin: The Early Years of an Elusive Revolutionary*. New York, Farrar Strauss, and London, Cassell, 1967.

Souvarine, Boris, *Stalin: A Critical Survey of Bolshevism*. New York, Longman, 1939; London, Secker and Warburg, 1940.

Trotsky, Leon, *Stalin: An Appraisal of the Man and His Influence*, edited and translated by Charles Malamuth. New York and London, Harper, 1941; revised edition, New York, Stein and Day, 1967; London, MacGibbon and Kee, 1968.

Tucker, Robert C., *Stalin as Revolutionary 1878–1929*. New York, Norton, 1973; London, Chatto and Windus, 1974.

Ulam, Adam B., *Stalin: The Man and His Era.* New York, Viking, 1973; London, A. Lane, 1974.

Warth, Robert D., *Joseph Stalin.* New York, Twayne, 1969.

*

Until the archives of the Soviet Union are opened to scholarly investigation, it is unlikely that we will have a complete picture of Stalin. In addition, the nature of his life was such that objectivity is difficult for even the most fair-minded of authors to maintain. Thus, biographies tend to be extremely critical or, in contrast, undisguised hero worship. As the latter appear so completely unreliable, they are not dealt with in this essay.

Among the early attempts at evaluating Stalin is the work by SOUVARINE, which appeared before World War II. Long considered a classic biography, it suffers from its age and lack of access to information disclosed since 1956. Yet when Souvarine finds Stalin to be "cunning, crafty, treacherous, but also brutal, violent, implacable and set always on the exclusive aim of holding the power he has confiscated by an accumulation of petty means," he is expressing a view common to most writers on Stalin.

DEUTSCHER, for instance, holds that Stalin drew upon "that wide assortment of chicanery and trickery by which rulers of all ages and countries had held their people in subjection." Unlike Souvarine, Deutscher sees Stalin not as the logical result of Bolshevism but rather as its opposite. In this view, Stalin is the man who arises when the revolution has stalled and the stalemate between competing classes allows for a strong man to emerge. Therefore, Deutscher sees Stalin's role as similar to that of Cromwell in the English Revolution and Napoleon in the French Revolution.

In much the same vein, Stalin's arch-rival TROTSKY sees him as the creature of the bureaucracy and those who desired "order." Even Stalin's obvious political skill is made to be secondary to his role as representative of a bureaucratic caste. Therefore, Trotsky argues that Stalin "took possession of power, not with the aid of personal qualities, but with the aid of an impersonal machine. And it was not he who created the machine, but the machine that created him."

Although one would not expect balance from an author who was to be murdered by order of the subject of his biography, Trotsky attempts to be fair and objective when placing Stalin in the broader context of Russian history. Further, this work contains insights only available to one who knew Stalin personally.

Two other biographies of interest have been written by people who knew Stalin at a later period. DJILAS' work contains a great deal of worthwhile information written from the vantage point of a Yugoslav Communist turned dissident. Still, Djilas did not have sufficient contact with Stalin to know many facets of his career. In addition, the book suffers from its lack of an overall theoretical framework to allow the reader to make sense of Djilas' observations. Djilas remains most useful to those already familiar with Stalin's life. Those who seek a brief and popular introduction should consult LIVERSIDGE or WARTH.

HOXHA's memoirs are worthwhile mainly in that they reveal the type of admiration Stalin inspired (or demanded) from his supporters. Written by the leader of Albania, this work is an attempt to refute the "slanders" spread by "revisionists" about the noble Stalin. Also, it was doubtless an effort to increase Hoxha's political stature as a revolutionary theorist.

For a critical evaluation by a Soviet historian, one will find MEDVEDEV of much value. Drawing on conversations with many who knew Stalin, as well as archival material unavailable to most non-Soviet scholars, Medvedev confirms the opinions of many early scholars, including Deutscher. Even in this case, however, it is clear that much is still buried about Stalin's past, which forces Medvedev to theorize at a number of critical points.

If it has been difficult to discover the whole truth about Stalin the leader, it has been nearly impossible to recreate his early activities. In this strikingly difficult task, SMITH does a great service by examining Stalin's youth despite the fact that Stalin had most evidence about his early years destroyed. Smith creates a credible picture of Stalin's youth and its formative influences from what the author admits is fragmentary evidence. He concludes that an atmosphere of "chaos and crime" molded Stalin's personality rather than an adherence to political ideals. Another excellent book on this period is furnished by TUCKER, who labors under the same difficulties as Smith.

The role Stalin played during the crucial events of 1917 is detailed by SLUSSER, who finds that, Soviet claims to the contrary, Stalin was a marginal figure in events largely shaped by men like Lenin and Trotsky. While this is neither surprising nor inconsistent with other aspects of Stalin's life, it remains important given that Stalin always claimed the legacy of Lenin to justify his policies.

Although adding nothing new in terms of fact, CARRÈRE D'ENCAUSSE has given the evidence a unique interpretation. She views Stalin as the reflection of two conflicting currents within Russian society. Thus, the Marxist desire for modernization comes head to head with traditionalist suspicion of the West. This conflict, Carrère D'Encausse argues, "appeared in [Stalin's] choices" and explains the seeming contradictory course of action he pursued: "Swinging continually between these two poles, he ended with an incomplete formula which tried to reach modernization without Westernization and which in the last resort was a mixture of industrial progress and barbarism."

Another notable interpretative work comes from McNEAL, who reopens many aspects of the historical discussion concerning Stalin. McNeal challenges dominant scholarship that has long given a low estimate of Stalin's originality and often overlooked his political abilities. Moreover, McNeal places Stalin in a historical context of violent social conflicts and argues that "he flourished in this environment and his success cannot be understood apart from the context of class hatred." While admitting that Stalin's crimes are too extreme to be excused, McNeal makes the case for understanding him as representative of feelings present in a large segment of Russian society.

Among other available treatments, that by FISCHER is of some value and quite readable. Still, it lacks the type of insight present in Deutscher or the provocative thesis of McNeal. Likewise, PAYNE gives great detail in his massive work but fails to reach the level of sensitivity or nuance of other volumes.

ULAM is less useful inasmuch as he attempts to use Stalin as a club with which to beat Marxism. Neither totally fair-minded nor attentive to contrasting interpretations, Ulam assumes a moralistic and often shrill tone in his work. Thus, he finds Stalin taking "the half-truths and half-myths of dogma and [turning] them into palpable reality in the lives of millions."

—William A. Pelz

STANLEY, Sir Henry Morton, 1841–1904; British-American journalist and explorer.

Anstruther, Ian, *I Presume: Stanley's Triumph and Disaster*. London, G. Bles, 1956; as *Dr. Livingstone, I Presume?*, New York, Dutton, 1957.

Busoni, Rafaello, *Stanley's Africa*. New York, Viking, 1944.

Ellis, James J., *Henry Morton Stanley*. London, Nisbet, and New York, T. Whittaker, 1890.

Farwell, Byron, *The Man Who Presumed: A Biography of Henry M. Stanley*. London, Longman, and New York, Holt, 1957.

Hall, Richard Seymour, *Stanley: An Adventurer Explored*. London, Collins, 1974; Boston, Houghton Mifflin, 1975.

Hird, Frank, *H. M. Stanley: The Authorized Life*. London, Stanley Paul, 1935.

Little, Henry W., *Henry M. Stanley: His Life, Travels, and Explorations*. London, Chapman and Hall, and Philadelphia, Lippincott, 1890.

Reddall, Henry F., *Henry M. Stanley: A Record of His Early Life and Struggles*. New York, Bonner, 1890.

Sterling, Thomas, *Stanley's Way: A Sentimental Journey Through Central Africa*. London, Hart-Davis, and New York, Atheneum, 1960.

Symons, A. J. A., *H. M. Stanley*. New York, Macmillan, and London, Duckworth, 1933.

Wassermann, Jacob, *Bula Matari: Stanley, Conqueror of a Continent*, translated by Eden and Cedar Paul. New York, Liveright, 1933; as *H. M. Stanley, Explorer*, London, Cassell, 1933 (originally published by S. Fischer, Berlin, 1932).

*

Sir Henry Morton Stanley was a hypersensitive, secretive man who camouflaged biographical facts that he considered discreditable. These facts included illegitimacy, a humble and humiliating childhood, turncoating in the American Civil War, jilting by two intended brides, dubious motives and methods as an African explorer and imperialist, and a lifelong record of quarrelsome and abusive behavior. After Stanley's death his widow was equally circumspect in the revelation of biographical details. As editor of the posthumous *Autobiography of Henry Morton Stanley* (1909), Lady Stanley took pains to protect the explorer's self-created image. She also searched out and bought up embarrassing documents that might challenge this image. It is hardly surprising that for many decades there was no satisfactory biography.

While Stanley lived, biographical works reflected what the explorer wanted the public to know about him—no more, no less. There were several publications of this sort, of which only ELLIS, LITTLE, and REDDALL are cited as representative examples. These three popular biographies, among others, were

written to capitalize on public interest in Stanley's last great African expedition (1887–89)—to rescue Emin Pasha, governor of the Southern Sudan, from the Mahdists. They were upstaged by Stanley's own account, *In Darkest Africa*, also published in 1890. There is nothing in these lives that is not better said in articles, books, and speeches by Stanley himself. Ellis' book particularly is heavily padded with Stanley's own words, and only Little makes some use of the writings of other African explorers and travelers. These biographers' treatment of Stanley is wholly uncritical.

Public interest in African exploration was already declining when the *Autobiography* was published, and revelations about atrocities in Belgian King Leopold II's Congo Free State—which Stanley had helped to create—cast a shadow over the explorer's memory. Curiosity about Stanley's career did not revive until the 1930s. WASSERMANN, a German novelist, led off with what the author calls a "psychographic" portrait of "Bula Matari" (Rock Smasher), as the explorer's Zanzibari porters nicknamed him. Although no different from previous biographies in its dependence on Stanley's own "facts" (many of them falsified), Wassermann's life is notable for its perceptive psychological insights. Wassermann also had uncanny skill making intuitive guesses—for example, about Stanley's romantic attachments and his relationship with his foster father—later borne out by more diligent research. The Stanley who emerges from Wassermann's pages is a flawed but still heroic figure. The flaws are deftly smoothed away by SYMONS, the English journalist best known for the literary detective work that uncovered the truth about the eccentric author Frederick William Rolfe ("Baron Corvo"). No such detection is evident in Symons' life of Stanley, which reworks the familiar material without distinction, enlivened only by frequent digs at Wassermann's speculations.

Although Lady Stanley destroyed many threatening documents, a substantial cache—including journals of the African expeditions and hundreds of letters—survived at Furze Hill, the explorer's Surrey estate. In the early 1930s some of these personal papers were made available by Stanley's adopted son, Major Denzil Stanley, for an authorized biography intended to humanize the Rock Smasher. HIRD, the writer who delivered the "authoritative life," was evidently not Denzil Stanley's first choice, and his work is not impressive. Unscholarly and sycophantic, Hird's biography nevertheless is the first to use the Furze Hill archive, and Hird quotes extensively from this trove. His was to be the standard life of the explorer for over 20 years and the only adult biography in English published during this period except for that of BUSONI, a heavily fictionalized potboiler.

In the 1950s two significant reappraisals of Stanley appeared, although neither was the long-awaited definitive study. ANSTRUTHER, a former diplomat, used the Stanley family records and other manuscript sources to try to reconstruct the hidden phases of the explorer's early life, but his book is primarily a vividly-written, detailed analysis of the background, incidents, and consequences of Stanley's search for David Livingstone in 1871. Biographical events after Stanley's return to the United States in 1874 are only summarized. FARWELL's contribution is a full-length, well-proportioned life based exclusively on published sources, including the many academic studies of European imperialism in Africa published since the 1930s. Farwell is more successful than other biographers in putting Stanley's achievements in the historical context of late 19th-century international politics, but he rehashes the conventional myths about Stanley's personal life. In addition to these major works, STERLING in the late 1950s personally retraced the routes of Stanley's four African expeditions and uses his travelogue as a skeleton upon which to hang a stereotyped popular biography.

HALL, an English journalist specializing in Africa, in the early 1970s exhaustively researched and perceptively wrote the first, much-needed biography of Henry Morton Stanley based wholly on original sources. He wisely jettisoned as evidence all existing secondary material and worked entirely from manuscript documents at Furze Hill and in British and Belgian archives. Patiently following up cryptic scattered clues in Stanley's unpublished writings, Hall solved most of the mysteries of Stanley's private life, including his parentage and two failed betrothals, and at last demolished the myths fabricated by the explorer and his widow. (In an interesting postscript, Hall explains, step by step, "How I Found Stanley.") But while generally a model biography—painstakingly researched, competently written, well-illustrated, thoroughly indexed—Hall's book is not without major defects. There is little analysis of Stanley's activities as King Leopold's agent in the Congo, of his role in the complicated diplomacy of central African partition (especially the Berlin Conference of 1884–85), or—curiously, in view of Hall's background—of the impact of Stanley's administration of the Congo upon the Congolese people. The author's flashback narrative technique, while generating suspense for the casual reader, is confusing for those seeking information. While there are detailed endnotes for each chapter, there are few specific citations. And the dual indexes of "persons" and "places," although very complete in these respects, entirely leave out "subjects." Although today clearly the biography of first resort, Hall's is not likely to be the final word on Stanley.

—Don M. Cregier

STEELE, Sir Richard, 1672–1729; English writer and theatre manager.

Aitkin, George Atherton, *The Life of Richard Steele.* London, Isbister, and Boston, Houghton Mifflin, 1889.

Connely, Willard, *Sir Richard Steele.* New York, Scribner, 1934.

Dobson, Austin, *Richard Steele.* London, Longman, 1886.

Winton, Calhoun, *Captain Steele: The Early Career of Richard Steele.* Baltimore, Johns Hopkins University Press, 1964.

Winton, Calhoun, *Sir Richard Steele, MP: The Later Career.* Baltimore, Johns Hopkins University Press, 1970.

*

DOBSON served as a corrective to two earlier portraits of Steele, one by Thomas Babington Macaulay, the other by William Makepeace Thackeray. Macaulay, reviewing a biography of Joseph Addison (*Edinburgh Review,* July 1843), and in his own *Life and Writings of Addison* (1852), indulged his love of paradox and antithesis at Steele's expense: "He was one of those people whom it is impossible either to hate or re-

spect. . . . His life was spent in sinning and repenting; in inculcating what was right, and doing what was wrong." Thackeray's essay on Steele, in *Lectures on English Humorists,* while kinder, was no less a distortion, with its often repeated, condescending "poor Dick." A more balanced portrait appeared in the *Quarterly Review* of March 1855, by John Forster, with whose assessment Dobson agrees. Conceding Steele's weaknesses, Dobson observes that "there have been wiser, stronger, greater men, [but] his virtues redeemed his frailties. He was thoroughly amiable, kindly, and generous."

Through his study of manuscripts at Blenheim and elsewhere, Dobson was the first to establish the date of Steele's birth, and to report in book form Aitkin's earlier discovery of Steele's first marriage. Dobson also introduced a number of Steele's letters to the reading public and includes much commentary by Steele's contemporaries. The student seeking details is apt to be disappointed, for Dobson's narrative is fast-paced, better for an overview than for close study of specifics; but his work is highly readable and replete with fascinating anecdotes.

AITKIN's two-volume, illustrated work appeared soon after Dobson's and remains—likely *will* remain—the standard Life. Aitkin was the first to examine the material in the Public Record Office, where he found documents concerning Steele's lawsuits that reveal much about his finances and theatrical affairs. The Probate Registry at Somerset House yielded the name of Steele's first wife (Margaret Ford Stretch), and careful examination of manuscripts in the British Museum and the Bodleian turned up much previously unused material. Aitkin also interviewed people who had connections to Steele's family. The result is a biography rich in detail. Aitkin quotes generously from Steele's own writings, more extensively even than Dobson had. Aitkin also provides five useful appendices, including a list of performances of Steele's plays and a lengthy bibliography of works by and about Steele.

In the 45 years that elapsed between Aitkin's study and CONNELY's, important new information surfaced about Steele. Connely could draw, for example, on a previously unknown report by Daniel Defoe in 1714 that led to Steele's expulsion from Parliament. He also used newly-found letters, such as the Steele-Newcastle correspondence (1714–24), and other material that allowed him to supplement, though not supersede, Aitkin. For example, he includes new information about Steele's natural daughter, Elizabeth, and his relations with the Tonson family.

Though some reviewers complained about its often burdensome wealth of detail, Connely's book is less than half the length of Aitkin's, and his writing is sprightly. Connely, like his subject a journalist, was also an enthusiastic and careful scholar, visiting every place in Great Britain where Steele had been and, as Connely said, seeking for five years "to know Steele as a human being." He incorporates many amusing stories, offers sketches of Addison, Swift, Richard Savage, and George Berkeley, presents a fine portrait of "Prue," Steele's second wife, and vividly recreates the age. Here are Steele's £30 wig and the 370 alehouses of Steele's Oxford. If one were to read only one life of Steele, this should be it, for Connely shows all aspects of a multifaceted man. As the *Nation* (2 January 1985) observed, Steele's "improvidence, his wining and dining, his political enthusiasms, his love, his gossip, his wit, his sentiment, are all carefully presented."

WINTON's two volumes, as their subtitles suggest, focus on Steele's career, particularly his political activities. Intended for a general audience, the study is, in A. R. Humphreys' words, "interesting without eccentricity, scholarly without pedantry, and civilized without ostentation" (*Modern Language Review*, October 1968). Sparser in detail than Aitkin (Winton covers the period to 1714 in about 200 pages to Aitkin's 500), Winton suppresses anecdotes he regards as unreliable, such as the stories Richard Savage related to Samuel Johnson. Yet Winton occasionally indulges in some questionable statements of his own, referring to Steele as an example of the Irish temperament, claiming that he showed an "uncharacteristic" fusion of life and work, that he was "out of harmony with most of the literary canons of his day"; and he raises some questions in the appendices (was Steele a Freemason? a homosexual?) that remain unresolved. Nonetheless, Winton's emphasis on the social and political aspects of Steele's life contributes to our overall picture of him, and the biography remains a good second choice for general reader and scholar alike.

—Joseph Rosenblum

STEIN, Gertrude, 1874–1946; American writer.

Bridgman, Richard, *Gertrude Stein in Pieces*. New York, Oxford University Press, 1970.

Brinnin, John Malcolm, *The Third Rose: Gertrude Stein and Her World*. Boston, Little Brown, 1959; London, Weidenfeld and Nicolson, 1960.

Greenfeld, Howard, *Gertrude Stein: A Biography*. New York, Crown, 1973.

Hobhouse, Janet, *Everybody Who Was Anybody: A Biography of Gertrude Stein*. New York, Putnam, and London, Weidenfeld and Nicolson, 1975.

Mellow, James R., *Charmed Circle: Gertrude Stein and Company*. New York, Praeger, and London, Phaidon, 1974.

Rogers, William G., *When This You See Remember Me: Gertrude Stein in Person*. New York, Rinehart, 1948.

Rogers, William G., *Gertrude Stein Is Gertrude Stein Is Gertrude Stein*. New York, T. Y. Crowell, 1973.

Sprigge, Elizabeth, *Gertrude Stein: Her Life and Work*. New York, Harper, and London, Hamilton, 1957.

Wilson, Ellen, *They Named Me Gertrude Stein*. New York, Farrar Straus, 1973.

*

ROGERS' 1948 biography of Gertrude Stein begins in 1917, when Rogers—then a young United States soldier in southeastern France—met Stein and Alice B. Toklas. The book continues through Stein's death and is marked by a surprising wealth of detail about her life abroad, her 1934–35 United States lecture tour, her relationship with Toklas, and her writing. Based partly on her correspondence with Rogers ("Kiddy") and his wife ("Mrs. Kiddy"), the book has a vividness that other biographies were not to attain. It is a modest but effective recounting of the Stein life both private and public. Rogers also treats Stein's past, but largely through what she herself said about it; and he weaves

throughout his own assessment of her various writings. The book's validity is increased because Toklas helped with the final manuscript.

SPRIGGE, a British biographer, prepared a useful and reasonably accurate first full biography of Stein. By visiting the manuscript and letter collections at the University of California at Berkeley and at Yale University, Sprigge learned much about Stein's life; she also knew her work. She places Stein in the context of her family and her relationship with Toklas, often citing Stein's own recounting of her life in *The Autobiography of Alice B. Toklas* (1933) and *Everybody's Autobiography* (1937). Her frequent reliance on Stein's prose gives her work a mannered, abrupt pace, which tends to make the reader question why descriptions are so cryptic. Her emphases echo those of Stein in her own autobiographical works and omit many areas that could shed light on the development of Stein's personality. Sprigge wrote a biography that Stein herself would have approved, though such an aim might not have given readers the best possible biography of the writer.

BRINNIN's was the second complete biography of Stein, in that it began with her birth and unusual childhood and continued through her death. It quickly overshadowed Sprigge's work and remains in print today. Although Brinnin writes with authority, he has little: he never knew Stein, and he relied for much of his information on gossip and apocrypha. The "legends" he perpetuated have become set in stone, even though Stein's manuscript and letter collections contain quantities of contradictory evidence. In 1959, when Brinnin published his book, the art of biography was less rigorous than it is now; most reviewers seemed unaware that he had used comparatively few of the many sources available to him.

The product in large part of Brinnin's fancy, *The Third Rose* consistently misrepresents Stein and her work, leaving readers with the idiosyncracies rather than the tough core of Stein's ambition. In Brinnin's view, one of the most important writers of the 20th century was a woman who lived by whimsy and—because she was female—could not be trusted to know what she was attempting. Brinnin says in his preface that his aim as biographer was "to strip away the undergrowth of subjectivity that hedged expressions of her true personality" (one wonders why Stein's own accounts, the subjectivity, couldn't be trusted in helping to reveal whatever her "true" personality was: evidently Brinnin knew and Stein didn't). Another of his aims was "to relate her creative life to aesthetic standards and movements which she regarded with indifference or altogether ignored." As her papers show, Stein was indifferent to very little. One reason she did survive artistically was her networking; nowhere does she even pretend disdain for literary connections.

The greatest objection to Brinnin's biography is his undervaluation of Stein's writing. He misreads some of what he comments on, omits much of her work, and claims that her "influence" on the current literary scene is "all but nil." Rather than treat her work seriously, Brinnin gives us clever, simpering phrases: "no one who has browsed for long in the marvelous meadows of her monotone has failed to come back with a daisy." Stein's 40 years of writing is much diminished by Brinnin's cavalier treatment. He also seems to be unaware of what she produced during the last decade of her life, because he presents her career after the successful reception of *The Autobiography of Alice B. Toklas* as pandering to the literary market place.

ROGERS' second book on Stein (1973) was a broader treatment than the first but still far from a definitive biography. The short studies by both GREENFELD and WILSON were so reductionary that they might have been written for adolescent readers. Wilson repeated already well-known anecdotes with a somewhat incongruous emphasis on Stein's fatness and her sexual naivete. Greenfeld did little better. The paucity of new or even valid information in these books is even more puzzling in light of the fact that Richard BRIDGMAN had, in 1970, published his important critical study, *Gertrude Stein in Pieces*. While not a biography, Bridgman's book is a storehouse of information about Stein's childhood, schooling, and young adulthood, making extensive use of materials in the Bancroft Library collection at Berkeley. Not noticeably sympathetic with either Stein or her writing, Bridgman compiled an immense amount of data that should have been useful to all subsequent biographers.

In what stands as the definitive Stein biography, MELLOW's work makes good use of all existing materials and previous treatments. His *Charmed Circle* is a model for conscientious and insightful biography. Its chief advantage is that it gives the by-now familiar anecdotes enough context for Stein's life to appear significant and ebullient rather than merely idiosyncratic. Anchored firmly in modernist and post-modernist times, Stein's aesthetics—and the work that exemplified her concepts of art and writing—are understandable. And Mellow treats Stein as more than a competent entrepreneur of high modernist art, which the designation of her "circle" might have suggested; he showed the way Stein's writing was informed by graphic art movements and the way her life was centered on exploring areas of art that she thought were integral to her own aesthetics. Mellow added a number of important details to the portrait of Stein that had been emerging through the 1970s, including the importance to her of Otto Weininger's *Sex and Character* (1906), and her political views during World War II (her translations of Marshal Pétain's speeches; the warning to Stein and Toklas to move or be put into a concentration camp).

HOBHOUSE let Stein's own writing create a biography for her (though the question of an appropriate role for the biographer remains unasked). The Hobhouse biography includes many more photographs than other Stein biographies: the Stein archives were at least providing some new material for the seemingly endless treatments of Gertrude Stein's life. Hobhouse portrays Stein's generation as influenced a great deal by British Decadence, especially by the ideas of Oscar Wilde. She also draws extensively on the memoirs of people who had known Stein, or had been contemporaries with her, such as Bravig Imbs, and earlier biographers such as Rogers. While her work adds little new information, it is a more accurate composite than some of the biographies published earlier in that decade.

—Linda Wagner-Martin

STEINBECK, John, 1902–1968; American writer.

Benson, Jackson J., *The True Adventures of John Steinbeck, Writer*. New York, Viking, and London, Heinemann, 1984.

Gannett, Lewis, *John Steinbeck: Personal and Bibliographical Notes*. New York, Viking, 1939.

Hedgpeth, Joel, editor, *The Outer Shores, Parts I and II*. Eureka, California, Mad River Press, 1978–79.

Kiernan, Thomas, *The Intricate Music: A Biography of John Steinbeck*. Boston, Little Brown, 1979.

O'Connor, Richard, *John Steinbeck*. New York, McGraw-Hill, 1970.

St. Pierre, Brian, *John Steinbeck: The California Years*. San Francisco, Chronicle Books, 1983.

Valjean, Nelson, *John Steinbeck, the Errant Knight: An Intimate Biography of His California Years*. San Francisco, Chronicle Books, 1975.

*

For a literary celebrity whose career lasted nearly 40 years, John Steinbeck has excited curiously little biographical activity to date. The reasons may not be hard to pin down: after the success of *The Grapes of Wrath* (1939), Steinbeck became simultaneously a household name who consorted with famous politicians and entertainment figures, and an individual increasingly anxious to preserve his private life from unwanted intrusions. Moreover, for many years Steinbeck was something of a pariah among the elitists of the eastern literary establishment and academe, and thus serious attention to the relationship between his life and his considerable output has been delayed until relatively recently. GANNETT's early account of the writer managed to satisfy some curiosity, but his work is brief and incomplete, however fair. O'CONNOR's biography of Steinbeck, written shortly after his death and intended for young readers, has been allowed to stand as the first reliable account of the writer's life, though it is an account understandably lacking in desirable detail.

One thing Steinbeck seems always to have had in abundance is good and intelligent friends, though for the most part these have been also careful to distance themselves from any hint of blind acceptance of anything the writer published, especially after he left California. In fact, one account of the works, by ST. PIERRE, focuses entirely on the California-based works, neatly implying in the process the assumption common in the Golden Bear State that Steinbeck's work suffered when he left there for the East in the 1940s. St. Pierre's volume adds little to what was already known about Steinbeck's life, however. Almost a decade before, VALJEAN had contributed a book animated by a breezily anecdotal, firsthand sketch of the writer that demands the reader's trust. Other friends have written works in which Steinbeck appears as a biographical creation of genuine and reliable interest. HEDGPETH, for instance, a marine biologist, is particularly well equipped to discuss the ideas Steinbeck shared, or at any rate discussed, with his friend Edward F. Ricketts (another marine biologist), and which he consequently paraded in his fiction.

There have been a number of books concentrating on Steinbeck's personal literary turf, as is common enough with American writers. But such accounts of the history of Cannery Row, the topography of the Monterey-Salinas area, and the houses Steinbeck lived in are logically too esoteric for inclusion here. In 1979, KIERNAN published the first full-length biography of Steinbeck meant for adult readers. It has little to say of critical interest, and has often been attacked in print for being insufficiently researched and factually questionable. Perhaps this deficiency springs from the fact that Kiernan was trying (with success) to publish his work before the man who was in fact to write the definitive life of John Steinbeck published his.

BENSON's definitive *True Adventures* represents the labor of over a decade. The pains Benson took in compiling what turned out to be a massive biography of 1100 pages involved more than the usual chores of the biographer, such as conducting interviews with often elusive subjects and trying to sort fact from invention, innuendo, and a comforting nostalgia. As was well publicized when the volume appeared, Benson had secured the cooperation of Elaine Steinbeck, the writer's widow, who gave him access to papers and photographs that helped fill in many a gap in the story of the man's career. However, that cooperation meant that the Estate could, as it eventually did, object strenuously to the inclusion of certain materials that the widow or Steinbeck's sons thought might be damaging to reputations. Viking, the publisher, passed along the pressure from the Estate to Benson, who was forced to make a considerable number of deletions and revisions. (As a result of this extra anxiety, Benson's great work is also a rarity among biographies, for one of the excisions took with it the event of the subject's birth!) The saga of Benson's ordeal is recounted in his later *Looking for Steinbeck's Ghost* (1989), which is that rare commodity, the biography of a biography, in effect; the attentive reader of both books will be able to fill in some of the gaps created by the fear of legal action over the original biography.

In spite of those gaps, however, no significant challenge to Benson's achievement has been made. Should time remove the original obstacles to their inclusion, moreover, the "missing" data will hardly change the impression of the writer Benson has created, nor create any sense of distortion on the biographer's part. The Estate has, after all, forbidden the republication of Steinbeck's Vietnam War reportage for reasons similar to those used to tax Benson's patience, but even this is a subject covered—and rather judiciously—by means of generalized description and letter-quotation in Benson's treatment. Benson is, for that matter, especially good at filling in the missing details of the writer's life both before and after the better-known period of his Californian existence: surviving members of Steinbeck's childhood and university crowd have provided information that fleshes out what little we knew about the era. Benson also amplifies the period of Steinbeck's celebrity, when he went eastward with his third wife and learned to hobnob with figures from the world of entertainment (to the detriment, many think, of his output). Benson, not overpowered by his subject as is so often the case, is hardly Steinbeck's uncritical admirer as he makes his reasonable way through the products of an entire career; and on the other hand, the stylistic influence of Steinbeck on Benson could hardly be said to have hurt Benson himself: 1100 pages go by without lagging.

Most of the truly biographical works on Steinbeck include photographs, and Benson's is no exception. His text is fully indexed, with voluminous annotation kept to the back pages where there is never any obtrusion (unless a requested one) upon the act of reading the text. However, Benson, a scholar who wears his scholarship lightly, does not burden his readers with unneeded references to prior criticism in his text itself; essentially, he is telling the story of the Steinbeck career, including when possible some statement of what was in the writer's mind as he approached each new work. Setting intention against accom-

plishment naturally makes for a certain amount of evaluation, and Benson hardly shirks this task. His assessments are fresh and fair, even when the reader does not agree with them. Indeed, just as Benson's style can be said to resemble Steinbeck's in its deceptive accessibility, so too is his biography like Steinbeck's works in appealing to serious lay readers and specialists alike.

Even granting the thoroughness of Benson's account, there has obviously been a relative paucity of formal Steinbeck biographies. But the happy fact is that for a writer so recently deceased, there has been an unusually plentiful publication of complementary texts in the form of journals and collections of letters, with no doubt more of these to come. With respect to the journals Steinbeck habitually kept as he wrote a particular work (as a means of "warming up" for the day), we have had since 1969 the *East of Eden* volume, called *Journal of a Novel* (1969). These daily entries, addressed to Steinbeck's editor Pascal Covici, have had a great deal to do with the ongoing critical reappraisal of that novel. More recently, Robert DeMott has edited and annotated the journals Steinbeck kept during the writing of his acknowledged masterwork, *The Grapes of Wrath*. With photographs and a detailed introductory section, DeMott's *Working Days* (New York, Viking, 1989) makes for an especially valuable companion volume for the 50th anniversary edition of the novel itself. Not incidentally, DeMott also published the increasingly useful study of the books which Steinbeck owned and/or read or alluded to in his fiction; this volume (*Steinbeck's Reading: A Catalogue of Books Owned and Borrowed*, New York, Garland, 1984) is a most useful tool for research aimed at understanding the progression of Steinbeck's thinking.

Finally, among the collections of letters, one, *Steinbeck and Covici* (1979), is distinguished by its concentration on one of the most significant relationships between writer and editor of all time. Just as Steinbeck wrote his *East of Eden* letters to Pascal Covici, he stayed in fairly constant touch with the man about his projects, his feelings, and his evolving thinking. "Pat" Covici replied in kind, and journalist Thomas Fensch's heavily annotated edition of their correspondence is a valuable biographical tool. A year earlier, a limited-run collector's volume was issued; *Letters to Elizabeth* (1978) documents Steinbeck's side of an equally important relationship, that with his longtime literary agent, Elizabeth Otis. Yet the most all-inclusive selection of letters is *Steinbeck: A Life in Letters* (1975), edited by Steinbeck's widow and by Robert Wallsten. These encompass nearly all of the writer's life, and what with their annotation they do indeed represent what their collective title promises—a provisional sort of biography/autobiography in the absence of Benson's thenforthcoming work, and a complementary text once it had finally appeared. Indexed but not illustrated, this volume, with over 900 pages, is rich in Steinbeckiana, as the writer opens himself up to family, friends, and the celebrities he was to meet in increasing numbers—including American presidents and their wives. Steinbeck was an avid letter-writer, and those chosen for these three collections are only a part of the letters that survive. Doubtless some have been excluded by reason of the repetitions that creep into the correspondence of all such persons; but the reader of *Life in Letters* should be aware that, in addition, silent elisions have been made, presumably for the sorts of considerations that delayed and affected the Benson volume. Steinbeck wrote a fine letter, however, and this book establishes the significance of that

side of his writing career to the degree that the epistolary Steinbeck ranks with Hemingway among Americans.

—John Ditsky

* * *

STENDHAL [*born* **Marie-Henri Beyle**], 1783–1842; French
writer.

Alter, Robert, with Carol Cosman, *Stendhal: A Biography.*
   London, Allen and Unwin, 1980.

Green, F. C., *Stendhal.* Cambridge, Cambridge University
   Press, 1939

Hemmings, F. J. W., *Stendhal, a Study of His Novels.* Oxford,
   Clarendon Press, 1964.

Josephson, Matthew, *Stendhal; or, the Pursuit of Happiness.*
   New York, Doubleday, 1946.

May, Gita, *Stendhal and the Age of Napoleon.* New York, Columbia University Press, 1977.

Richardson, Joanna, *Stendhal: A Biography.* London, Gollancz,
   and New York, Coward McCann, 1974.

Strickland, Geoffrey, *Stendhal: The Education of a Novelist.*
   London and New York, Cambridge University Press, 1974.

Tillett, Margaret G., *Stendhal: The Background to the Novels.*
   London and New York, Oxford University Press, 1971.

Wakefield, D., *Stendhal: The Promise of Happiness.* Bedford,
   Bedfordshire, Newstead Press, 1984.

Wood, Michael, *Stendhal.* Ithaca, New York, Cornell University Press, and London, Elek, 1971.

*

Although inevitably much of the biographical work on Stendhal has been published in French and much of the interest in him
as a major author has naturally been concerned with literary
analysis, Stendhal, an anglophile, has been the subject of much
commentary in English. The standard two-volume biography by
Stendhal's editor, Henri Martineau (*Coeur de Stendhal*, 1952–
53), is available only in French. While good on fact, it is correctly described by the American Robert Alter, author of the best
available full biography (see below), as "debatable or deficient
in its interpretive views." The first biography in any language
was in English, Andrew Paton's *Henri Beyle* of 1874, chiefly
remarkable because Stendhal's novels were not highly esteemed
until after this date, when Taine drew attention to them in the
early 1880s and romantic ideals of heroism had finally given
way to the ironic or naturalistic description of life as the raw
material of literature.

The next English biography was GREEN's 1939 volume,
drawing on the recently completed Martineau edition of the
works (79 vols., 1927–37). Only when he was 34 did Beyle
choose the name Stendhal from among the spectrum of pseudonyms he used, and most of his works are relevant to his efforts
to define a personal philosophy and to understand the cohesive
force binding together the different facets of his personality.
Green therefore has no difficulty in showing that the life is unusually important for an understanding of the work and in tracing the evolution of "his strange and complex mind," unusually

fascinating as well as unusually difficult. In view additionally of
the sheer bulk of Stendhal's output, Green rightly sets the discussion of the literary qualities of the works at the points during
the life at which they were composed, powerfully illuminating
the significance of the novels in the process, and accurately pinpointing the autobiographical inspiration of parts of them.
Green's is not an academic biography, but a right-minded, perceptive, and readable account of Stendhal.

JOSEPHSON, whose "large, well-meaning, lumbering, and
often inaccurate 1946 volume" (Alter) comes with an index, a
bibliography, and some notes, regarded Stendhal as his favourite
author, although he also wrote biographies of Rousseau, Hugo,
and Zola. Alter is harsh; Josephson's readable biography gives
details of the unexciting circumstances of a life that outwardly
looks like having been a decorous failure, and Josephson undertakes a reasonably accurate account of the novels, though his
analysis of them is independent of considerations about their
composition. RICHARDSON's 1974 *Stendhal* is what Green
would have called a *biographie romancée*, entertainingly readable, but of only marginal interest to readers interested in more
than an assiduous and intelligent, but superficial, literary entertainment, executed with an irritating archness of style, as when
she claims, "His most interesting novel remains the story of his
life . . . ."

Ten years earlier had appeared HEMMINGS' study of the
novels, which although it is not biography, must be mentioned
here if only because it is the first source to which every anglophone student of Stendhal is automatically referred. It is reliable, informed, unexcited and unexciting, and it falls at the same
hurdle as most of the biographies, failing to detect the deliberately laid false scents and covered-up tracks and penetrate to the
fascinating interplay of an intellect and a sensibility at cross purposes beneath them.

TILLETT's study contains much biographical material but is
resolutely literary in its allusions and frame of reference. She
has indeed illuminated the background to Stendhal's novels, although some attention is given also to his other works. Her writing is meticulous and her insight shrewd. She warns readers that
Stendhal has left the most important things out of his *Journal*:
what he felt on listening to Mozart, on reading Tasso, on being
awakened by a barel organ, or giving his arm to the mistress of
the moment. Tillett also has the ability to extract what is important from the significant detail, and her book has the serious
student in mind. WOOD's *Stendhal* is both more scholarly and
less literary, although what literary criticism it does contain is
sharper. Stendhal here is never merely literary, but "sends us
back to reality." No doubt also intended for students, Wood's
volume is perhaps accessible to a wider audience than Tillett's. It
contains notes.

STRICKLAND argues that Stendhal in the end achieved what
he set out to acquire: a thorough insight into human behaviour
and motivation and into the "astonishing intelligence of his
art," which Stendhal obtained through the process rather misleadingly referred to as "education" in the title of Strickland's
books. Much is made of the faults of construction in Stendhal's
novels, their imperfect artistry and sense of incompletion, also
emphasized by Richardson. Strickland examines Stendhal's quest
above all for clarity. The view he convincingly argues allows
him to draw copiously on the history of European literary and
even philosophical traditions. The theme of "education" be-

comes a well-chosen thread around which to narrate and analyze the development of Stendhal's central literary ambition.

MAY dutifully makes use of the available scholarship but falls unhappily at the usual hurdle. What is the cohesive force binding together the elusive personality Stendhal himself spent a lifetime exploring and in which he found so many different things? May is defeated by the complexity of his subject and lacks any fresh unifying or critical vision.

ALTER, who, with the help of his wife, has written the best full biography, has written also on Henry Fielding, on modern Hebrew literature, and on literary criticism. His properly critical biography is aware of all the complexities and pitfalls, and the biographical craftsmanship is impeccable. When scenes are set, Alter depends not on fancy but on research. Stendhal's life is re-created but not romanticized, and its account is interspersed with an analysis of the novels. This volume makes at any rate a serious contribution to the as yet unwritten definitive biography.

WAKEFIELD's ambitions are more limited but better fulfilled. He concentrates on Stendhal's reaction to the arts, particularly the visual arts, and gives us over 80 pages of apposite glossy illustrations to just over 100 of text, seeing behind *La Chartreuse de Parme* "Correggio's personality and atmosphere suffused, . . . the charm, grace and undulating movement." Wakefield sees through Stendhal's posture as the "rich epicurean and dilettante" he toyed with wanting to become, notes that he had "too much imagination and too little hard practical sense for a good businessman," and recalls how Proust noticed the symbolic patterns and obsessive repetitions in Stendhal's work.

Wakefield watches Stendhal defining the conditions for the enjoyment of art, follows Victor Brombert (*Stendhal et la voie oblique*, 1954), in examining Stendhal's attempts to put his readers off the track by disguising his deepest emotions, and emphasizes the importance for his subject of music as well as painting. Outwardly, Stendhal was born poor, stayed poor, never married, and realized none of his ambitions. Did he deliberately antagonize those who could have helped him, "preferring solitude and reverie to the ceaseless efforts needed to realize worldly ambitions"? Oddly limited in its subject matter, although still biographical, Wakefield's is the best book on Stendhal in English.

—A. H. T. Levi

STERNE, Laurence, 1713–1768; English writer.

Cash, Arthur H., *Laurence Sterne* (2 vols.). London, Methuen, 1975–86.

Connely, Willard, *Laurence Sterne as Yorick*. London, Bodley Head, 1958.

Cross, Wilbur L., *The Life and Times of Laurence Sterne*. New York, Macmillan, 1909; 3rd edition, New Haven, Connecticut, Yale University Press, and London, Oxford University Press, 1929.

Fitzgerald, Percy H., *The Life of Laurence Sterne* (2 vols.). London, Chapman and Hall, 1864; revised, London, Downey, 1896.

Hartley, Lodwick, *This is Lorence: A Narrative of the Reverend Laurence Sterne*. Chapel Hill, University of North Carolina Press, 1943; as *Laurence Sterne: A Biographical Essay*, 1968.

Melville, Lewis (Lewis S. Benjamin), *The Life and Letters of Laurence Sterne* (2 vols.). London, S. Paul, 1911.

Sichel, Walter S., *Sterne: A Study*. Philadelphia, Lippincott, and London, Williams and Norgate, 1910.

Traill, Henry D., *The Life of Laurence Sterne*. New York, Harper, 1882.

Yoseloff, Thomas, *A Fellow of Infinite Jest*. New York, Prentice-Hall, 1945; as *Laurence Sterne: A Fellow of Infinite Jest*, London, F. Aldor, 1948.

*

William Makepeace Thackeray sharply attacked Sterne in *The English Humourists of the Eighteenth Century* (1853). The first edition of FITZGERALD's book responded to this negative portrait with a kinder interpretation; it also glossed over certain matters, such as the question of Sterne's marital fidelity, that have continued to vex even Sterne's admirers. Fitzgerald retraced Sterne's French travels and so provides useful details on this subject. On other topics Fitzgerald's grasp of fact is sometimes less certain: he missed by nine months the publication date of the first volumes of *Tristram Shandy* and erroneously introduced the king of Denmark into the audience for Sterne's last sermon. In 1896 Fitzgerald, after reading the *Journal to Eliza*, revised his view of Sterne, painting a portrait much like Thackeray's. Useful now primarily as a reflection of the Victorian attitude toward Sterne, in its day Fitzgerald's study introduced new letters as well as extracts from the then unpublished *Journal to Eliza*.

For his volume in the English Men of Letters series, TRAILL drew heavily on the first edition of Fitzgerald. Like so many later biographers, Traill concentrated on the last years of Sterne's life, after the Yorkshire parson turned author and awoke to find himself famous. As a biography Traill's book adds nothing, but many of his comments on the novels retain their validity.

Though still clouded with Victorian sensibility, CROSS' life immediately became the definitive study and remained so until the 1970s. His Sterne is Shandean: in the revised third edition he writes, "[Sterne] feels, he imagines, and he at once perceives the incongruities of things as ordered by man or by nature; but he does not think, nor has he any appreciation of moral values." Cross shows Sterne in his age, discusses his reading, and places him among his contemporaries. The second and third editions incorporated new discoveries; especially significant are those made by Cross' student Lewis Perry Curtis about Sterne's political activities and his relations with his uncle, Jaques Sterne, Dean of York. Still useful are the reprint of Sterne's Letter Book (from the Morgan Library), the bibliography of first (and occasionally later) editions of Sterne's works, and a list of Sterne manuscripts and their locations.

SICHEL's study drew heavily on Fitzgerald and Cross, often without proper acknowledgment. Cross claimed that the new information here would have sufficed to make up "a letter to a weekly periodical, but not quite enough for a magazine article" (*The Dial*, 1 September 1910). Sichel provided two new Sterne letters, incorporated the research of Emily J. Climenson into the relationship between Elizabeth Montagu and Sterne's wife, Elizabeth Lumley, added information on Sterne's relationship with Catherine Fourmantel and Elizabeth Vesey, and, perhaps most important, made Sterne's *Journal to Eliza* available to an audience larger than that which had purchased the 12-volume Cross edition of Sterne's *Works and Life* (1904). Sichel also offered the observation that Sterne is the father of impressionism. Sichel's view of Sterne harkens back to Thackeray, questioning whether, for all his professed sentiment, Sterne felt anything at all.

Like Sichel, MELVILLE reprinted the *Journal to Eliza*; he also included all or part of some 200 letters by Sterne. His aim was to allow his subject to speak for himself, and the result is a readable but incomplete biography whose chief merit now lies in the various portraits it contains. Until L. P. Curtis published Sterne's *Letters* (1935), though, it offered the most extensive selection.

After the spate of Sterne biographies around 1910, no new lives of Sterne appeared until the 1940s, when two popular biographies were published. Neither HARTLEY nor YOSELOFF sought to uncover new material; both are lively, concise, and sympathetic to their subject. Hartley has the added advantage of accuracy and is the ideal choice for the general reader or, indeed, anyone seeking an overview of Sterne's life. Edward Wagenknecht described the work as "a narrative of admirable sprightliness, and a critical study illuminated by most unstodgy wisdom" (*New York Times Book Review*, 20 June 1943). Hartley's exuberant tone is thoroughly 18th century, though some may find the informality—Sterne is called "Laurie"—excessive. CONNELY, too, aims at a general audience; he treats only the last nine years of Sterne's life, the period in which he produced the novels. Connely presents a clear and readable depiction of the social scene of the 1760s in England and on the Continent and gives the reader the public Sterne.

Those wanting more information than the previous three titles contain will turn to CASH's well-written, definitive, two-volume biography. Cash does not add much new information—volume two prints seven previously unpublished letters and locates 11 others—or even new interpretations. But as Jeffrey R. Smitten writes of the first volume, "Virtually every bit of information about Sterne's early and middle years (to early 1760) is brought forth, its truth weighed . . . , and at last placed carefully into the total context of Sterne's life" (*Review of English Studies*, May 1977). Cross' Shandean eccentric is replaced by a more realistic, deeper figure. For example, where Cross saw in Sterne's slovenliness a disregard for convention, Cash detects depression. Cash presents a hard-working cleric and fully explains 18th-century Anglican practices as well as the politics of York Minster. One thus understands Sterne's activities and so better appreciates the life and works. The emphasis falls on the last eight years of Sterne's life (the first volume extends from 1713 to 1760, the second from 1760 to 1768); this imbalance is justified because Sterne remains of interest primarily because of the fiction he produced at the end of his career. The biography is sympathetic without whitewashing Sterne's faults. Cash maintains, for instance, that Sterne's liaisons with various women went beyond the exchange of letters and claims that this philandering caused Mrs. Sterne's madness. Footnotes are where they belong—at the bottom of the page—and the work is well indexed (though the volumes are not cross-indexed). All serious students of Sterne will read Cash with attention to his details and gratitude for his graceful style and thoroughgoing scholarship.

—Joseph Rosenblum

STEVENS, Wallace, 1879–1955; American poet.

Bates, Milton, *Wallace Stevens: A Mythology of Self*. Berkeley and London, University of California Press, 1985.

Brazeau, Peter, *Parts of a World: Wallace Stevens Remembered, an Oral Biography*. New York, Random House, 1983.

Lensing, George A., *Wallace Stevens: A Poet's Growth*. Baton Rouge, Louisiana State University Press, 1986.

Morse, Samuel French, *Wallace Stevens: Poetry as Life*. New York, Pegasus, 1970.

Richardson, Joan, *Wallace Stevens* (2 vols.). New York, Beech Tree Books, 1986–88.

Stevens, Holly, *Souvenirs and Prophecies: The Young Wallace Stevens*. New York, Knopf, 1977.

*

MORSE's short critical biography concentrates on the development of Stevens' poetic career, presented in 15-year periods. This pioneering biographic study focuses on the growth of the poet's mind, intellectual influences, and the development of Stevens' *oeuvre*. In this foreword, Morse writes, "It seemed, then, that a book which tried to bring into focus some of the apparent contradictions and inconsistencies, as well as the steadfast convictions [Stevens] expressed in his life and work, would be of value to the reader attracted to the poetry and interested in knowing something about the poet himself." Combining biography and critical comment, Morse's study presents a life *through* poetry.

HOLLY STEVENS, the poet's daughter, offers a biographical portrait of the young Wallace Stevens from the journals he kept for ten years, beginning with his sophomore year of college. Spanning a time period from Stevens' boyhood to 1915, when he produced his first mature poems, this book is useful as a developmental portrait of the young poet, especially since it quotes extensively from Stevens' letters and journals, allowing the poet to tell his own story. These entries cover Stevens' Harvard years, his bachelor life in New York City, his courtship of Elsie Kachel, and his early attempts at poetry. *Souvenirs and Prophecies* is delightful to read as a portrait of an artist in the making.

Some of the most interesting personal glimpses of Stevens are found in BRAZEAU's work. Subtitled an "oral biography," this book contains reminiscences and anecdotes from more than "150 writers, scholars, business associates, neighbors, friends, and members of Stevens' family" who consented to be interviewed. It is especially useful for its account of the Hartford years: of Stevens' family life and of his work as an insurance executive with the Hartford Accident and Indemnity Company, where he served as vice-president and expert on surety bonds. Stevens comes across as a capable businessman, but cold, reserved, and distant. He apparently kept his creative life, business life, and family life carefully separate.

BATES calls his work, not a biography, but "a study of how one poet transcended biography by transferring it into fables of identity—what he called 'mythology of self.'" Bates focuses on the development of Stevens' voice and persona. His literary biography illustrates how Stevens recreated his sense of himself and mythologized his experience through his poetry. Incorporating what he calls an "historical approach," Bates traces Stevens' development from college student, to journalist, to law yer, to insurance executive. The book offers perceptive insights about how Stevens balanced his business and creative life.

LENSING's is another recent critical biography. Lensing examines Stevens' "exceptionally long gestation as a poet, a period of time, in fact, that absorbs the first half of his life." He shows how "these protracted apprentice years account for the birth of the modern poet in middle age." Lensing's study traces three formative influences in Stevens' adult life: a conventional but intense religious faith, a growing fascination with the pastoral beauty of the Reading, Pennsylvania countryside, and a gift for writing. He examines various literary influences: Spenser, Pater, Keats, the French Symbolists, the Imagists, translations of Japanese and Chinese lyrics, and contemporaries such as William Carlos Williams and Marianne Moore. As a solitary writer, Stevens made extensive use of his notebooks, his reading, his correspondence with friends, and his interest in art.

The definitive biography of Stevens is RICHARDSON's two-volume *Wallace Stevens*. In the first volume, Richardson addresses the central question of why Stevens felt there was a distinction between the self he commanded "on paper" and the self he presented "in reality." She examines the paradoxes in Stevens' personality: his combination of logical and imaginative ability, his skill as a "verbal sleight-of-hand man who could simultaneously conceal and reveal what lay beneath the surface of things as they are—all 'on paper,'" without feeling that he could command himself "in reality." Why did his self-doubts and insecurities remain with him throughout his life—about his poetry, his business acumen? His life seemed a progressive alienation of his intelligence from his native soil. Richardson's biography tries to "honor the choices" Stevens made in his life. She attempts to trace the development of Stevens' consciousness, balancing reason and imagination. She presents Stevens as a major philosophical poet, committed to the use of reason to construct a "supreme fiction," but understanding the limits of reason. For him, "poetry was a cure of the mind."

In her second volume, Richardson notes, "While the first volume of this biography traced the course of the poet's development, this second and final volume follows him through his maturity to the final 'Good night' he spoke softly to his daughter from his deathbed." Richardson deals extensively with the contradictions in Stevens' temperament and the mysteries of his reclusive personal life. Through his poetry, she affirms, Stevens learned to affirm life while facing the void. From his mentors, William James and George Santayana, he discovered the strength of the "will to believe" and the adequacy of poetry as "the supreme fiction." This final volume focuses on Stevens' accomplishments: his poetry, his family life, his equanimity in facing his final illness, and his reconciliation with religion.

—Andrew J. Angyal

STEVENSON, Robert Louis, 1850–1894; Scottish writer.

Balfour, Sir Graham, *Life of Robert Louis Stevenson*. London, Methuen, and New York, Scribner, 1901.

Calder, Jenni, *RLS: A Life Study*. London, Hamilton, 1980; as *Robert Louis Stevenson: A Life Study*, New York, Oxford University Press, 1980.

Calder, Jenni, editor, *Stevenson and Victorian Scotland*. Edinburgh, Edinburgh University Press, 1981.

Furnas, J. C., *Voyage to Windward: The Life of Robert Louis Stevenson*. New York, Simon and Schuster, 1951; London, Faber, 1952.

Guthrie, C. J., *Robert Louis Stevenson: Some Personal Recollections*. Edinburgh, W. Green, 1920.

Hammerton, John A., editor, *Stevensoniana*. New York, Wessels, and London, G. Richards, 1903; revised edition, Edinburgh, J. Grant, 1907.

Low, W. H., *A Chronicle of Friendships*. London, Hodder and Stoughton, and New York, Scribner, 1908.

Masson, Rosaline O., *I Can Remember Robert Louis Stevenson*. Edinburgh, Chambers, and New York, F. A. Stokes, 1922.

Masson, Rosaline O., *Life of Robert Louis Stevenson*. Edinburgh, Chambers, and New York, F. A. Stokes, 1923.

Osbourne, L., *An Intimate Portrait of R. L. S.* New York, Scribner, 1924.

Saposnik, Irving S., *Robert Louis Stevenson*. New York, Twayne, 1974.

Steuart, J. A., *Robert Louis Stevenson: Man and Writer: a Critical Biography*. London, Hodder and Stoughton, 1924.

*

The nature of Stevenson biographies, of which there are too many, has altered over the years as more information has come to light, as his letters (severely pruned in early editions) have become available to scholars, and as the one-time adulation of his personality has given way to a more informed assessment of his life and of his literary achievement. There are numerous popular studies of his life and works. Only the more significant biographies are discussed in this analysis.

It was Stevenson's original intention that his biography should be written by his one-time collaborator and friend of his Edinburgh years, W. E. Henley. But the two men fell out (Stevenson's understandably protective wife Fanny had rejected Henley as a bad influence) and the plan fell through. Instead Stevenson left instructions that the task should fall on Sydney Colvin, who had been instrumental in introducing Stevenson to magazine editors at the outset of his career.

Colvin published a version of Stevenson's letters from Vailima (Samoa) the year after his death (*Vailima Letters*, 1895), and four years later a two-volume, heavily edited selection of letters to family and friends (1899). But Colvin delayed for so long working on the planned biography that Stevenson's wife and son-in-law reassigned the job to BALFOUR, a Stevenson cousin who had spent some years with them in Samoa. The result is a dutiful but bland two-volume biography which, though outdated, is still useful, particularly in its appendix listing Stevenson's appearances in periodicals.

The Balfour biography produced an angry protest from Henley, who had been a companion of Stevenson in his wilder (and then unrecorded) Edinburgh days, but in general it was well received by the many readers for whom Stevenson the romantic vagabond and author of *Treasure Island* had become something of a cult figure. The next 20 years produced a whole crop of biographical memoirs from devotees and associates, including HAMMERTON, LOW, GUTHRIE, and OSBOURNE. This period came to a close with a gathering of a final set of reminiscences by MASSON in 1922, followed by her full-length biography in 1923.

What early biographers did not recognise was the contrived autobiographical nature of most of Stevenson's early writing. Twentieth-century readers meet his works in bound books and in impressive multi-volume library sets. But for a number of years his original readers encountered him not in books but in monthly magazines like the *Cornhill* or *MacMillan*. Before he published his first "real" book he had become quite well known for his highly personal essays, personal travel notes, personal impressions of his reading and his upbringing. The "hero" of all these is a posturing romantic bohemian, a carefree gallant wanderer, wanting to be admired, and writing in a carefully contrived prose style always demanding attention. It was a persona that readers and acquaintances came to accept and, having accepted it, to perpetuate.

Stevenson was made of tougher material. The stresses under which he laboured, his chronic invalidism and taste for low life as an antidote to his Victorian Edinburgh middle-class milieu, his religious doubts (in a Victorian calvinist society), stern parental disapproval, and yet financial dependence on his father even after he became a married man—these do not figure greatly in early biographies. They represent a different side of Stevenson and go some way toward explaining his interest in Long John Silver and Deacon Brodie and Dr. Jekyll and Mr. Hyde and his later realistic involvement with Pacific politics, which his admirers tended to deplore as out of character.

Biographies since the 1920s have been more searching. Much of the basic documentation is now on public deposit and is yielding new material. It has been shown, for example, that Colvin heavily censored the letters from Samoa (pasting pieces of paper over words and phrases that indicate Stevenson's anything but romantic view of his situation).

The first of the new biographies was by STEUART. Its general tenor can be judged from Steuart's downright statement, "Henley was right; their Stevenson is not the Stevenson of reality at all." The book is a deliberate reply to the Stevenson cult and is somewhat over-written; yet later biographical studies owe much to Steuart. He replaced the myth of the romantic gallant adventurer with a balanced portrait of a man with "strength and weakness, gaiety and gloom," but above all (as Steuart's integration of the life and works displays) of a hard-working writer of tenacity and great personal courage, whose writing improved in quality and depth as he threw aside the posturings of his early magazine journalism. It is significant that Stevenson's later work is receiving increasing critical attention.

Of the later biographies the most important is by FURNAS. Steuart, writing in Edinburgh, is more familiar with the Scottish background—an important element in Stevenson's mature work—but Furnas, writing from America (though after considerable travel and time spent in almost every place Stevenson had inhabited) is fuller, particularly on the Stevensons in America and on the final years in the Pacific. Furnas makes judicious use of documents published and unpublished; his book is the first biography to distinguish accurately between what is ascertainable fact and what are mere probabilities or surmises. With its

first-rate bibliography of sources, no other biography of Stevenson can rival it.

There have been numerous books written on Stevenson since, most of them a blend of biography and literary criticism. Noteworthy additions to the biographies have been the short but well-researched volume by SAPOSNIK and that by CALDER (1980). Jenni Calder was able to make full use of all her predecessors, and her elegant "life study," as she calls it, is able to offer the pace and structure of a good novel and yet be a biography, without sacrifice of accuracy or scholarship.

Of particular importance is CALDER's 1981 work, an edited series of papers given at a Stevenson symposium held in Edinburgh in 1980. It contains an essay by Furnas on the effect of "exile" on Stevenson (which can be read as an appendix to his 1952 biography) and an account of the writing of the first Graham Balfour life (in a paper written by Balfour's son, who had full access to all the relevant papers). This little book is a must for all readers of Stevenson biographies.

—Ian A. Gordon

STEWART, James, 1908–   ; American film actor.

Basinger, Jeanine, *The "It's a Wonderful Life" Book.* New York, Knopf, and London, Pavilion, 1986.
Eyles, Allen, *James Stewart.* New York, Stein and Day, 1984.
Robbins, Jhan, *Everybody's Man: A Biography of Jimmy Stewart.* New York, Putnam, and London, Robson Books, 1985.
Thomas, Tony, *A Wonderful Life: The Films and Career of James Stewart.* Secaucus, New Jersey, Citadel Press, 1988.

*

ROBBINS' book is based on interviews with more than 150 people who knew James Stewart; all of them liked him, and many of them tell "cute" and/or endearing anecdotes about him. This hagiography (it is really not an adequate biography) based on their praises of Stewart is very limited in its appeal: only "fans" need consult it. Robbins becomes so wrapped up in extolling Stewart's folksy virtues that he neglects to mention some of the star's most important films (notably *The Man From Laramie*). There are more serious omissions: Anthony Mann, who directed Stewart in eight major films containing some of the actor's most distinguished performances, is cited once, and in that citation he simply says that Stewart is a skilled horseman and then discusses Stewart's relationship with his horse. Since the westerns Stewart made with Mann reflect a darker side of Stewart's character, Robbins studiously avoids discussing them in any depth.

In fact, he avoids any subject that might intrude upon the heroic, wholesome, and virtuous all-American life he wants to present: to Robbins the subject is always "Jimmy," who lived a wonderful, but completely innocuous, life. In this treatment of Stewart's relationships with women, for example, there is no hint of either sex or romance. "Everybody's Man" is also nobody's in Robbins' account. However, many of Stewart's "dates" were themselves famous people whose biographies give a very different picture of the young man about Hollywood. For examples, see biographies of Marlene Dietrich and Olivia De-Havilland. Photographs in this volume are numerous, but many are rather small and ordinary.

EYLES provides a much fuller treatment with ample discussion of Stewart's films and more general awareness of the hero's "dark" side. This work is still primarily honorific, but Eyles seems to underestimate or at least mis-estimate Stewart's achievements as an actor, while admiring him as a human being. Stewart seems stronger and more adult in this account, in which he is called "James" occasionally as well as "Jimmy." The pictures in Eyles' book are an improvement over those in Robbins' volume, but the index in Eyles bears no relationship to page numbering in the text.

Anyone wishing to ascertain the facts of Stewart's life and read a balanced account of all his films should consult THOMAS. The biographical essay is very short, but its terseness is actually an improvement over the other biographies: Thomas' book contains all the facts as they appear in other biographies, but it avoids the accolades. Thomas admires Stewart too, but he does not make his admiration the primary subject of his book. Since this is a "films of" book, it provides discussion and stills for all of Stewart's many films. For Thomas, Stewart's life is primarily a career, and, since it is a very impressive and significant career, this work actually praises Stewart more highly by indirection than those books that set out to do nothing else but sing his praises.

BASINGER provides some interesting biographical details of Stewart in the context of *It's a Wonderful Life*, tracing the entire production history of one of his most famous films, and the one, incidentally, with which biographers most frequently identify him. This "coffee table" book contains conscientious scholarship and beautiful photographs.

Finally, mention should be made of some excellent articles about Stewart that appear in a special issue of *Film Comment* (March/April 1990) devoted primarily to Stewart. Those dealing with his extraordinary acting ability and his relationship to Anthony Mann are especially important.

—Richard Sears

STIEGLITZ, Alfred, 1864–1946; American photographer, publisher, and gallery director.

Lowe, Sue Davidson, *Stieglitz: A Memoir/Biography.* New York, Farrar Straus, and London, Quartet, 1983.
Norman, Dorothy, *Alfred Stieglitz: An American Seer.* New York, Random House, 1973.

*

LOWE's biography is written from the viewpoint of a loving but distant grand-neice possessed of a strong sense of family loyalty. It is predictably full of information about the Stieglitz family, its houses, its ancestry, and anecdotes and descriptions of the personalities of its members. The book proceeds from a description of Alfred Stieglitz's early environment to an account of his early professional work and important colleagues such as Edward Steichen. It contains a surprisingly honest account of his failed first marriage. As a whole, it concentrates on the artist's work and the professional conflicts engendered by insiders and outsiders to Stieglitz's artistic circle, with particular mention made of the collaboration and discord surrounding the relationship of Steichen to Stieglitz. More occasionally, Lowe provides us with her own first-hand descriptions of family interaction at their Lake George retreat as well as her visits to Stieglitz's New York galleries. Within this context, she presents us with intriguing examples of Stieglitz's family favoritism, such as allowing his niece Georgia Engelhardt to exhibit in the 291 Gallery, a sidelight that contrasts with the overall portrait of a man who is rigidly committed to principles, the chief of which is a belief in excellence. She also uses Stieglitz's apparently lifelong precarious health to justify what appears to others as a kind of self-righteous despotism. With the exception of the attention paid to Stieglitz's relationship to Georgia O'Keefe, Lowe dismisses the women in Stieglitz's life and presents an essentially male personal and professional world. The overall style of the book, which appears to be factually accurate, is one of personal dialogue out of which the portrait of the artist as part of a family emerges. An extensive chronology at the end provides the reader with a reference source and indicates the quality of Lowe's research.

NORMAN's book, the only other extant book-length biography of Stieglitz, possesses a similar first-person tone. In this case, however, the text consists primarily of excerpts from conversations Stieglitz had with the author between 1927 and 1946, when they met almost daily. Norman supplies the connective tissue for this discourse, which focuses on the chronological development of Stieglitz's professional life. Stieglitz emerges as a perspicacious artist and impresario for modern art whose world centers on people's commitment to him and his battle to establish photography as a fine art. Norman builds up his character largely through complementary anecdotes as well as many quotes from his letters, both of which are selected to highlight the aphoristic quality of his speech as well as its declarative style. A portrait emerges of an individual who knew his own mind and had a sense of his extraordinary destiny from a very young age. The book emphasizes his later contacts with various artists and contains lavish page-size reproductions of his work. Toward the end of the volume, Norman provides a chapter-length section containing her notes on Stieglitz as well as a chronology of Stieglitz's life and an appendix listing exhibits held at the various galleries he founded and directed. Norman has written two other contributions to Stieglitz biography, *An Introduction to an American Seer* (1960), and *Beyond A Portrait* (1984), but *Alfred Stieglitz: An American Seer* remains her only book-length treatment of the subject.

For additional information on Stieglitz's conversations, one may consult Herman Seligman's *Alfred Stieglitz Talking* (1966), while *America and Alfred Stieglitz* (1934), edited by Waldo Frank, contains a series of essays relating to Stieglitz and his cultural milieu, some of which contain biographical and critical information. William Homer's *Alfred Stieglitz and the American Avantgarde* (1977), has one chapter on Stieglitz's formative years, authored by Nancy Newhall. All in all, however, Lowe's book remains the most complete and evenhanded artistic biography, while, despite its panegyrical tone, Norman's book remains a useful source of anecdotes and quotations.

—Diana Emery Hulick

STOWE, Harriet Beecher, 1811–1896; American writer.

Fields, Annie, editor, *Life and Letters of Harriet Beecher Stowe*. Boston, Houghton Mifflin, and London, Low Marston, 1897.

Gilbertson, Cathrene, *Harriet Beecher Stowe*. New York, Appleton-Century, 1937.

Johnston, Johanna, *Runaway to Heaven*. New York, Doubleday, 1963.

Stowe, Charles Edward, *Life of Harriet Beecher Stowe from Her Letters and Journals*. Boston, Houghton Mifflin, and London, Low Marston, 1889.

Stowe, Charles Edward and Lyman Beecher Stowe, *Harriet Beecher Stowe: The Story of her Life*. Boston, Houghton Mifflin, and London, J. Nisbet, 1911.

Wilson, Forrest, *Crusader in Crinoline: The Life of Harriet Beecher Stowe*. Philadelphia, Lippincott, 1941; London, Hutchinson, 1942.

*

CHARLES STOWE, the youngest child of Harriet Beecher Stowe, compiled the letters under the careful eye of his mother, who directed the portrayal of her life as she wished it preserved. Therefore, this work (1890) makes no claims to objectivity and in fact touches only briefly and delicately on the criticisms and scandals that affected Harriet Beecher Stowe. Even in those letters we see Harriet adamantly defending her brother Henry Ward Beecher in the sensational adultery scandal and also stubbornly defending her own article and book "vindicating" Lady Byron for exposing Byron's incestuous affair. But the most important controversy drawing out her moral indignation was, of course, the slavery issue itself, and then the effect of *Uncle Tom's Cabin* (1852). Charles Stowe's 500-page work is fairly extensive, beginning with the early years of his mother and ending with the aging celebrity's letter of 1887 to her brother, where she said she had come "within sight of the River of Death," nine years before her death. Although the book is strictly a praise of Harriet Beecher Stowe, it is valuable for the spirited letters of the Stowe family, generously quoted, and for the personal association of the author with his subject.

More concise and popularly written is the 1911 memorial biography, prepared jointly by CHARLES AND LYMAN BEECHER STOWE. This is in some respects Charles Stowe's earlier work rewritten. Similarly, it traces Harriet's development as teacher, writer, wife, mother, and celebrity. The authors frankly assert their purpose of portraying how Harriet Beecher Stowe's experiences appeared to her and "how she appeared to herself." This portrait is highly readable, carrying a steady narrative pace, unlike Charles' earlier biography, which consisted mainly of letters. The *New York Times* observed that this work was "a remarkably real and vivid picture of the woman herself,

of [her] environment . . . and of the conditions which compelled her to do nearly all of her literary work at a tremendous disadvantage" (11 June 1911). Other reviewers noted the detailed accuracy of the book.

Building on the work of Charles Stowe is that of FIELDS, a close friend of Harriet Beecher Stowe. Fields adds "many letters and much new material" to produce another valuable contemporaneous biography. The author strikes a balance between narration and quotation from the documents, resulting in a pleasant, smooth style. The reader expecting objectivity from an author outside the Stowe family will be disappointed. Fields remains in total awe of her subject and, like Charles Stowe, overlooks the flaws of Harriet's extremely complex character.

GILBERTSON's biography does not add much new material but attempts to present a more balanced account than the early hagiographical works. Gilbertson succeeds in portraying Stowe sympathetically yet without bias or adulation, placing her subject within the mid 19th-century religious context. *Commonweal* declared that "if the rest of the book were as thorough, as detailed, and as truly illuminating as the analysis of religion, this biography . . . would be a masterpiece" (18 June 1937). Gilbertson also details the sources of many of the characters and settings of Stowe's novels and analyzes *Uncle Tom's Cabin* in terms of its author's personal suffering. With no documentation or complete bibliography, the book is for the general reader who wants a balanced overview of Stowe in relation to her times. The author moves swiftly through her story in a little over 300 pages, without getting caught up in the details of Stowe's various emotional traumas.

By far the outstanding biography of Stowe is WILSON's definitive study. Drawing on previous biographies, unpublished letters, reminiscences of contemporaries, and newspaper files from all over the country, Wilson has written what L. W. Eshleman called the "best biography of an American that [he] ever read" (*Commonweal*, 28 March 1941). Most reviewers praised the book's narrative vigor, its vivid re-creation of 19th-century America, its fairness, and its painstaking research reflected in the long bibliographic summary for each chapter. Wilson's portrayal of members of the Beecher family, especially Lyman and Henry Ward Beecher, are masterful, as is his sympathetic treatment of the lazy, scholarly Calvin Stowe. He shows his deep understanding of Harriet Beecher Stowe as he points out her ambivalent views and contradictory behavior. Though he gives little attention to the actual style and content of her works, he does describe the rich background in which Stowe is "always moving, speaking and gesturing through her own times" (*New York Times Book Review*, 16 March 1941).

A readable popular biography derived mainly from secondary sources, JOHNSTON's work aims "to reassess and reinterpret the facts already known," to portray Stowe as revealed in her own writings (over 30 published books), and to summarize the doctrines of Calvinism that so greatly influenced her subject. Johnston attempts to present Stowe as a woman first and a literary figure second. The book adequately captures the background of Stowe's writings, her family, and her era. Johnston provides some useful insights into Stowe's behavior (for example, her rebellion against Calvinism and her contradictory feelings about the abolitionist movement), but if one expects from this book's perspective some treatment of Stowe's attitudes toward the women's movement, there is little or none. Overall, this fairly lengthy work projects an imaginative view of a famous, historical woman.

—Marlene A. Hess

STRACHEY, Lytton, 1880–1932; English writer and biographer.

Beerbohm, Max, *Lytton Strachey.* Cambridge, Cambridge University Press, and New York, Knopf, 1943.

Boas, Guy, *Lytton Strachey.* London, Oxford University Press, 1935.

Bower-Shore, Clifford, *Lytton Strachey: An Essay.* London, Fenland Press, 1933.

Ferns, John, *Lytton Strachey.* Boston, Twayne, 1988.

Holroyd, Michael, *Lytton Strachey: A Critical Biography* (2 vols.). London, Heinemann, 1967; New York, Holt, 1968; revised one-volume edition, London, Heinemann, 1973.

Johnstone, J. K., *The Bloomsbury Group: A Study of E. M. Forster, Lytton Strachey, Virginia Woolf, and Their Circle.* London, Secker and Warburg, and New York, Noonday Press, 1954.

Kallich, Martin, *The Psychological Milieu of Lytton Strachey.* New Haven, Connecticut, College and University Press, 1961.

Sanders, Charles R., *Lytton Strachey: His Mind and Art.* New Haven, Connecticut, Yale University Press, 1957.

Srinivasa Iyenagar, K. R., *Lytton Strachey: A Critical Study.* London, Chatto and Windus, 1939.

*

Strachey's fame rested on his skill at writing biography, and his success rested on the rather scandalous air created by those biographies. It is curious then that, for a long generation after his death, his own biography remained unwritten and, when it finally appeared, it did so in an air of scandal. Perhaps he would have been even more amused, if he could have read it, to find it done on the same massive scale as the solemn Victorian biographies his own mocking work had done so much to kill off.

During his lifetime little was known and less was said about Strachey's personal history, though a good deal of work was published about his writing, most of it narrowly critical in scope. In the decade after his death this tradition continued. If a good deal of the earlier critical comment had been sharply divided about the merits of his biographical technique, once he was safely dead the critics writing about his work defended him as a brilliant stylist. BOWER-SHORE's brief essay and BOAS' pamphlet are examples of this. SRINIVASA IYENAGAR's book at least covered the whole body of work systematically for the first time, but with no more than a nod in the direction of the author's life. Of all the work done in this period only BEER-BOHM's slender and mildly envious Rede Lecture has retained any slight independent value for biographical purposes as it was, in part, a personal memoir by a contemporary who knew Strachey, though not intimately. Most of what Beerbohm had to say dealt, again, with prose style.

In the years after World War II, perhaps due to the growing interest in the Bloomsbury Circle and, more particularly, in Virginia Woolf, Strachey's work—still distinct from his life—continued to be a subject of study though his reputation was, temporarily, in decline. JOHNSTONE devoted some attention to him in the context of his membership in the Bloomsbury group. SANDERS' study was the culmination of all the preceding work, the longest and by far the fullest study devoted to a careful scrutiny of all Strachey's published writing and to attempting a full accounting of unsigned pieces. This was supported for the first time by some biographical detail, which, rather unhelpfully, focused as much on the ancestry and Strachey family background as on the author himself. Sanders' work was soon followed by KALLICH's attempt to deal with the body of Strachey's writing from a psychoanalytic point of view. Unfortunately for Kallich the standards of reticence still prevailing in the later 1950s meant that a central fact of Strachey's private life, his homosexuality, was unacknowledged in print. Strachey himself, during his lifetime, was candid and unapologetic about his private affairs but none of this was public knowledge. Kallich's study of Strachey's psychological milieu, along with much else that had been written about him by those who did not know him, was soon dramatically superseded.

Strachey's brother, James, the psychoanalyst and translator of Freud's collected works into English, himself a member of the Bloomsbury set in good standing, had inherited and carefully preserved Lytton's manuscripts and a great mass of his personal correspondence. For a good many years he did not make this generally known. By the early 1960s he was prepared to see the material used in the writing of a biography. He was fiercely loyal to his brother's literary reputation, but he was also determined to have a truthful and completely frank version of Lytton's life. A straightforward telling of the life story with an unblushing account of his homosexuality had been unthinkable in the past. However, in the changing climate of the 1960s it seemed possible, and many of the people who might have been embarrassed by the revelations to be found in the Strachey correspondence were, by then, dead. Nevertheless Boas, when offered the opportunity of using the material, declined, thinking the private material far too scandalous to be published. At the time, it must be remembered, homosexual acts were still a criminal offense in Britain. In 1962 James Strachey offered the use of his archive to Michael Holroyd, whose life of Hugh Kingsmill had given him something of a reputation as a literary biographer. Holroyd, casting about for a new subject in his field, eagerly accepted. In 1965, while he was still working on the project, a parliamentary commission proposed the decriminalization of homosexual acts between consenting adults, and this soon became the law of the land.

Though James Strachey died before HOLROYD's biography was completed, his judgment that the climate had changed sufficiently to allow his brother's life story to be told honestly proved correct. Though in its initial reception much attention was paid to the sexual revelations, the work's frankness clearly went far beyond mere scandal, and it has set a tone for biographical candour in literary and artistic biography that has, a generation later, become the rule rather than the exception. Once the initial fuss was over and the novelty of combining great frankness about the private life of a literary figure with a serious study of his work had vanished, Holroyd's biography could be seen simply for what it was: a fine study of a complicated and elusive writer and a rich and carefully detailed examination of the whole literary scene of which he was an important part.

It takes nothing away from Holroyd's gifts as a biographer to acknowledge that he had been singularly fortunate in his subject—as he was the first to say—not only because Strachey was interesting both as a writer and a person, but also because Holroyd had stumbled on one of the great caches of 20th-century literary papers. This existed for two reasons: the Strachey family preserved its manuscripts with extraordinary care (some of Lytton's childhood letters survived) and, because Strachey loathed the telephone, he normally communicated with his friends—in the best Victorian tradition—in writing. Holroyd made splendid use of this vast mass of letters and other material that gave to his account of Edwardian and Georgian literary life an unparalleled richness. His work is unlikely to be replaced for the foreseeable future, and his only rival on the subject of Strachey is Strachey himself in the autobiographical remains edited by Paul Levy (*The Really Interesting Question and Other Papers*, London, 1972), and in another selection edited by Holroyd (*Lytton Strachey by Himself: A Self Portrait*, London and New York, 1971).

FERNS' volume for the Twayne series is the most recent attempt at an overall critical assessment of Strachey; it contains some biographical material and useful bibliographical appendices. For an extensive treatment of works on Strachey published prior to 1981, see Michael Edmonds, *Lytton Strachey: A Bibliography* (New York, Garland, 1981).

—S. J. Stearns

STRAUSS, Richard, 1864–1949; German composer.

Del Mar, Norman, *Richard Strauss: A Critical Commentary on His Life and Works* (3 vols.). London, Barrie and Rockliff, and Philadelphia, Chilton, 1962–72.

Finck, Henry T., *Richard Strauss: The Man and His Works.* Boston, Little Brown, 1917.

Jefferson, Alan, *The Life of Richard Strauss.* Newton Abbot, England, David and Charles, 1973.

Jefferson, Alan, *Richard Strauss.* London, Macmillan, 1975.

Kennedy, Michael, *Richard Strauss.* London, Dent, 1976; revised edition, 1988.

Kennedy, Michael, "Richard Strauss," in *The New Grove Turn of the Century Masters.* London, Macmillan, and New York, Norton, 1985.

Krause, Ernst, *Richard Strauss: The Man and His Work.* London, Collet's, 1964 (originally published by Breitkopf and Härtel, Leipzig, 1955).

Marek, George, *Richard Strauss: The Life of a Non-Hero.* New York, Simon and Schuster, and London, Gollancz, 1967.

Newman, Ernest, *Richard Strauss.* London, J. Lane, 1908.

Schuh, Willi, *Richard Strauss: A Chronicle of the Early Years 1864–98*, translated by Mary Whittall. Cambridge and New York, Cambridge University Press, 1982 (originally published by Atlantis, Freiburg and Zürich, 1976).

*

Richard Strauss was only 44 years old when NEWMAN's work appeared, the first English-language biography of the composer. It remains one of the most fascinating and probing studies of Strauss' musical personality. The book was written as part of the series *Living Masters of Music*, which was intended not only to present a composer's life and works, but aspects of his private, daily life. Newman, who did not know Strauss personally, entrusted the latter aspect of the book to Alfred Kalisch, who was one of Strauss' earliest champions in England. His prefatory essay ("Richard Strauss: The Man") offers a personality sketch of Strauss at the time of *Salome*.

Kalisch was, no doubt, an enthusiastic devotee of Strauss' music, but Newman's opinion of the composer was not nearly so uncritical. On the one hand Newman acknowledges that Strauss was the "greatest composer living today," yet on the other he observes that in Strauss (especially the more recent Strauss) one finds an unsettling combination of genius and charlatan. Strauss the genius composed "high-minded" works such as *Guntram* and *Tod Und Verklärung*; he was a worthy heir to Liszt and Wagner. Strauss the charlatan had created *Symphonia Domestica* and *Salome*, hollow works that represented the victory of calculation over creativity. Newman's biography, which was published just before the premiere of *Elektra* (1909), ends on an inconclusive note: "His next opera [*Elektra*] . . . will probably show whether he is going to realize our best hopes or our worst fears." Newman's review of *Elektra* following its London premiere (1910) left no doubt that Strauss had allegedly continued in the wrong direction.

FINCK's lengthier study continues the genius-or-charlatan tack of Newman, although the preface by Percy Grainger ("Richard Strauss: Seer and Idealist") clearly places Strauss in the category of the former. This first American biography of Strauss, full of witty anecdotes about the composer and his music, is a less serious work than Newman's. The biography covers Strauss' work through *Josephslegende* and even includes a chapter on Strauss in America, which chronicles the composer's 1904 American tour and provides selected stories pertaining to the reaction to Strauss in the United States from the turn of the century through 1916. While hardly a probing study of the composer, the book serves as an interesting example of Strauss' reception in early 20th-century America.

It was not until after World War II that the next Strauss biography in English appeared: the translation of KRAUSE in 1964. Of the biographies in English, Krause's was unprecedented in thoroughness and scope when it appeared. Now in his 80s, Krause, an East Berlin music critic, remains one of the most important writers on Strauss alive today. Although his contribution can be divided roughly into a life and works format, Krause's interpretive biography goes far beyond the norm, for he is above all interested in the relationship between Strauss and the cultural-historical events that informed his creative life. Whether he examines an aspect of Strauss' biography, personality, or one of his works, we are always made aware of this broader context.

Krause does not delve into technical detail when discussing Strauss' music, and only rarely relies on musical examples in his study. However, his observations about Strauss' music and aesthetics are keen; they get to the very core of the composer's creative thought. Krause's political views are clear, and we find traces of east-bloc political jargon from time to time, but—because of his directness and lucidity—these instances in no way interfere with our understanding and appreciation of the composer. Some of the most interesting parts of the book concern Strauss and politics, his working methods, his musical style, and his personality. The original 1955 German edition was corrected and updated in two subsequent editions (1963 and 1980); the English version, including the American reprint (1969), is based on the 1963 edition. This book, along with Del Mar's study of Strauss, represents an important first stop for any novice who desires a thorough knowledge of the composer.

DEL MAR's comprehensive three-volume study, a project completed over a ten-year period, complements Krause in a felicitous way, for Del Mar's approach is purely musical, and his work is liberally filled with musical examples. Del Mar is a successful conductor and critic, and his contribution is, no doubt, the standard reference source in English for just about any work by Strauss. He discusses nearly all of Strauss' works in chronological order, imparting important biographical information along the way. His basic approach is to provide the historical context for the work, followed by an analysis consisting mainly of presenting principal motives, themes, and their derivations. Thereafter, Del Mar often summarizes the work's reception history.

MAREK's controversial treatment of Strauss has not aged well over the past quarter of a century. Unlike Del Mar's study, it constitutes a purely biographical approach, and within that framework Marek offers his opinions of Strauss the man, his works, and his contemporaries. Marek, who had been an executive at RCA Records, believes that Strauss' artistic powers declined significantly after *Der Rosenkavalier*, and he dismisses a number of works that have prospered since his book appeared. The more recent successes of *Die Frau ohne Schatten* and *Arabella*, not to mention the revivals of other later operas, require us to reevaluate Marek's opinion. His polemical chapter on Strauss during Germany's period of national socialism has been criticized for unscholarly techniques in its negative portrayal of the composer. Recent research on German music and musicology in the 1930s and 40s contradicts a number of Marek's negative anecdotes that flourished shortly after World War II.

JEFFERSON follows the same format as Marek, but he presents the composer more sympathetically. He has written a number of specialized books on Strauss, but this biography was written (to quote Jefferson himself) "[to be] easily digested by those who know the subject as well as those who may not yet do so." He admits that his work contains "a great deal of material which has been stated before." And, although his admission is quite true, the volume still makes for pleasant reading ideal for the non-specialist. In 1975, Jefferson published a brief "coffeetable" biography filled with photographs of the composer and his world as well as color reproductions of more recent operatic stagings.

KENNEDY's life-and-works format presents a warm and sympathetic view of Strauss and his music. Kennedy's work is brief and reliable and was written for *The Master Musicians* series, edited by Stanley Sadie. A critic for the London *Daily Telegraph*, Kennedy is an enthusiastic advocate of Strauss' music, including many of his lesser-known later works. Most of the errors and omissions that appeared in the original edition were rectified in the 1988 paperback edition. Kennedy's contribution for *Grove* presents a condensation of his earlier study, and it includes a thorough, up-to-date bibliography by Robert Bailey. For

someone desiring a quick overview of the composer, Kennedy has an advantage over such works as Marek or Jefferson, for Kennedy includes brief musical descriptions and examples.

Most of the biographies mentioned above were written by music critics and journalists; they were intended for amateurs and specialists alike. None of them are source-critical studies. Musicologists, thus, eagerly awaited the work of SCHUH (and its subsequent translation), which represents the first documentary biography of the composer in the English language. Schuh is a meticulous scholar, whose comprehensive knowledge of Strauss sources remains unmatched today. He was a friend of Strauss since the 1930s, and his biography of the composer had been a work in progress for many decades. Indeed, before his death, he was only able to complete the first volume (over 500 pages); it takes Strauss' career up to his move to Berlin in 1898.

Schuh's work—an encyclopedic study based on letters, diaries, essays, contemporary reviews, and personal recollections—perhaps goes too far in the opposite direction from the other studies. He intentionally avoids interpreting the wealth of material that he presents. Indeed, an interpretive word or two might have helped the reader get through much of this abundant material, which is carefully footnoted, unlike most of the other biographies. Schuh once informed the present writer that because of unusual circumstances the German edition went to press "more or less uncorrected;" many of the textual errors were rectified in the English edition.

This formidable study, which proceeds for the most part chronologically, is not easy reading, but it serves as an unsurpassed source for biographical information on Strauss through the age of 34. It is a pity that Schuh was unable to finish what was to be the second and final volume. His surviving draft of volume two apparently covered the remainder of Strauss' career and got as far as the mid 1920s. Thus, it includes some of the composer's most important works, such as *Salome*, *Elektra*, *Der Rosenkavalier*, *Ariadne auf Naxos*, and *Die Frau ohne Schatten*. Schuh left the uncompleted manuscript with longtime friend and Strauss scholar Franz Trenner, but at present it remains unclear how and by whom this final volume will be finished.

—Bryan Gilliam

STRAVINSKY, Igor (Fedorovich), 1882–1971; Russian-American composer.

Asaf'yev, Boris, *A Book about Stravinsky*, translated by Richard French. Ann Arbor, Michigan, UMI Research Press, and Epping, Bowker, 1982 (originally published, 1929).

Boucourechliev, André, *Stravinsky*, translated by Martin Cooper. New York, Holmes and Meier, and London, Gollancz, 1987 (originally published by Fayard, Paris, 1982).

Dobrin, Arnold, *Igor Stravinsky: His Life and Times*. New York, T. Y. Crowell, 1970.

Druskin, Mikhail, *Igor Stravinsky: His Life, Works, and Views*, translated by Martin Cooper. Cambridge and New York, Cambridge University Press, 1983 (originally published, Leningrad, 1979).

Kobler, John, *Firebird: A Biography of Igor Stravinsky*. New York, Macmillan, 1988.

McLeish, Kenneth and Valerie McLeish, *Stravinsky*. London, Heinemann, 1978.

Onnen, Frank, *Stravinsky*, translated by M. M. Kessler-Button. Stockholm, Continental Books, 1948.

Routh, Francis, *Stravinsky*. London, Dent, 1975.

Siohan, Robert, *Stravinsky*. New York, Grossman, 1965; London, Calder and Boyars, 1966 (originally published by Éditions du Seuil, Paris, 1959).

Tansman, Alexandre, *Igor Stravinsky, the Man and His Music*, translated by Therese and Charles Bleefield. New York, Putnam, 1949.

Tierney, Neil, *The Unknown Country: A Life of Igor Stravinsky*. London, R. Hale, 1977.

Vlad, Roman, *Stravinsky*, translated by Frederick Fuller. London and New York, Oxford University Press, 1960; 3rd edition, 1978.

White, Eric W., *Stravinsky: The Composer and His Works*. Berkeley, University of California Press, and London, Faber, 1979.

Young, Percy M., *Stravinsky*. London, E. Benn, and New York, D. White, 1969.

*

Any unrevised biography of Stravinsky written before the composer's death in 1971 is obviously incomplete. But more importantly, writers of studies that predate 1952 were unaware that the composer would turn to serial technique in his third style period. Stravinsky composed major works well into the 1960s, and unrevised studies give an incomplete picture of the composer's life and *ouevre*.

Earlier biographers relied almost exclusively on Stravinsky's autobiography, *Chroniques de ma vie* (2 vols., 1935-36), which has been translated into English and was written with the help of the composer's friend, Walter Nouvel. Although factually accurate, this book paints a primly proper picture of the composer, who at the time of writing had just put his name forward as successor to Paul Dukas for the Académie des Beaux-Arts, and may have wanted to present himself in as doctrinaire a fashion as possible. For this reason, some of the earlier biographers (Tansman and Onnen) present the composer as an austere monument, rather than the witty and urbane young man that emerges in the more recent accounts (Tierney and Boucourechliev). This is partly because the better later biographers were able to draw on a wider variety of materials, including a vast amount of important data from interviews published by Stravinsky and his amanuensis Robert Craft, who began a long series of written collaborations with the composer in 1959 with *Conversations with Igor Stravinsky*. The problem with the Craft "dialogues" as a whole is revealed by a statement Stravinsky made to his agent, Deborah Ishlon, in one of his letters (later published by Vera Stravinsky and Robert Craft in *Stravinsky in Pictures and Documents*, London, 1978): "[Craft] did write the book [*Conversations*], it is his language, his presentation, has imagination, his memory. . . . It's not a question of simple ghost-writing but of somebody who is to a large extent creating me. . . . " In 1972, shortly after his death, Stravinsky's personal manager, press representative, and nurse, Lillian Libman, published *And Music at*

the Close, an account of the years she spent in the Stravinsky household (1959–71), which some of the more recent biographers (notably Boucourechliev) have used to check the veracity of Craft's material. Interestingly enough, certain discrepancies have appeared that may never be resolved.

BOUCOURECHLIEV's work stands out as perhaps the best of the "life and works" approaches to have emerged in recent years, taking advantage of all the clarifying material now available. His chronological approach is clear and his analyses of Stravinsky's works are illuminating. There is an almost ideal balance between biographical account, stylistic criticism, and analytical writing in this approach. One of the fascinating things about Boucourechliev's book is that it is the first biography to reveal information about Stravinsky's secretive love life, which included 3 extramarital affairs. This highly personal information was curiously absent in earlier volumes (both White and Vlad for example). The substantial amount of time Stravinsky spent away from his first wife, in the company of others such as Diaghilev, Cocteau, Njinsky or Picasso, might lead one to speculate about the composer's relationship to his first wife. White and Vlad had insinuated that Stravinsky's absences from the family were due to his first wife's frail health, which may be partly true; there are indications that Stravinsky had a morbid fear of illness in others, but only Boucourechliev and, later, Kobler (see below) reveal the fact that Stravinsky began his relationship with his second wife, Vera, in 1921, and provide the explanation that he then balanced both relationships simultaneously (or at least in alternation) until 1939, when Catherine Stravinsky died, allowing Igor to marry Vera in 1940.

TIERNEY offers the most complete and up-to-date life and times of the composer. Drawing on an impressive amount of secondary material, including recent biographies of Rimsky-Korsakov (Stravinsky's teacher), Diaghilev, Njinsky, Cocteau, Debussy, Satie, and others, Tierney provides a vivid picture of the composer's Paris days, and then, by drawing skillfully on the Craft material, tells us much about the composer's later years. The problem with this book is that when there is little to draw on, Tierney will embellish what is known in highly impressionistic terms. For example, he surmises that since Stravinsky lived in the country as a young boy (even though he was too straight-laced to tell us about it in his own *Chroniques*), he must surely have been a nature lover, spending hours gazing at snow-covered rooftops, or lying above the river, watching tug boats and indulging in the "escapades" that all young boys indulge in. Tierney paints a picture of the composer's youth that is only 50% verifiable—the rest is biographical novel. He also goes off on many tangents, such as detailed accounts of the Russian Ballet, that have little to do with the topic at hand and cause the reader to lose sight of the man himself. It is to Tierney's credit that he doesn't indulge in Diaghilev-bashing, which is something Boucourechliev does in an almost homophobic manner. Tierney's portraits of Stravinsky's friends and the stormy relationships he forged with them are presented in a more three-dimensional, less prejudicial fashion here. He points out that the friendship between Stravinsky and Diaghilev, though it ended tragically, had great depth and influenced the soul as well as the career of the composer. This is in direct contrast to Boucourechliev's refrain about Diaghilev's evil possessiveness or White's dryly factual approach, which leaves no impression of the people involved at all. Particularly interesting are the accounts Tierney includes of Stravinsky's collaborations with Njinsky, Cocteau, and Picasso, a drawback being that these accounts leave little or no room for stylistic or analytical commentary about Stravinsky's compositions.

WHITE's account is divided into "The Man," an analytical survey of his compositions, appendices that include Stravinsky's correspondence and writings, a bibliography, and a list of compositions. The actual biographical material is not very extensive, nor very personalized. White uses Craft and others more to verify dates of compositions and facts about collaborations than to offer any illumination about the personality or psychology of the composer. The section called "The Man" should be called "The Career," because it does not really tackle any of the personal issues that Tierney, Boucourechliev, or Kobler confront. The same information found in part one of this book appears (with slight rewording) as the New Grove biography on Stravinsky in the "Modern Masters" collection (basically a reprint of the New Grove entry on Stravinsky).

VLAD's book is notable because of the amount of attention the author, a serial composer himself, paid to Stravinsky's later works. Vlad draws on most of the earlier biographical sources and includes Craft's contributions. Interestingly, this book has the opposite problem of so many other accounts, in that Vlad's analyses of the serial works are more insightful than those of the neo-classical period. The stance seems to be that Stravinsky finally found himself with serialism after much thrashing about. Although there are quite a few musical examples, there is not much detail (and no photographs) of the composer's personal life.

One of the first monographs about Stravinsky to be translated into English was by TANSMAN. Aside from being woefully incomplete, his book is, as the Polish composer/pianist/conductor admits, "conceived in the form of a eulogy." He consciously avoids "overtechnical terms that might make the reading too arduous." The main body of the work is devoted to criticism (but always in the form of praise) and assessment of the composer's artistic temperament (in which Tansman gullibly parrots Stravinsky's pretentious and often self-contradicted *Poétique Musicale*), followed by a life and works section that only goes up to 1948. The biographical information is mostly all to be found in Stravinsky's *Chroniques*. There are no notes or bibliography, few musical examples, and only one photograph.

ONNEN clearly states that in his book "Stravinsky's life is reduced to a series of compositions with a bare enumeration of the details related to them" because "the events connected with his individual existence have had, at most, a very indirect influence on his musical work." There are some fascinating photos in this book that don't seem to appear elsewhere and were probably obtained from Soulima Stravinsky, who was consulted by Onnen, but the text amounts to nothing more than liner notes to the works up to 1947.

SIOHAN's life-and-times approach includes brief descriptions of the world events and artistic movements that surrounded Stravinsky's life (until 1962) and surmises how these events affected the music, even though Stravinsky denies that external events influenced him. It is highly speculative and sometimes believable, but the Tierney book, more carefully rendered and more complete, makes this earlier study obsolete. Siohan includes an attractive chronological table as an appendix, with

photos of art posters that place Stravinsky's life and works in context with other figures and events.

DRUSKIN, one of today's most prominent Soviet musicologists, has written a book that owes much to his teacher, ASAF'YEV, whose own earlier critical essay has been translated and reprinted after almost 50 years of suppression. Whereas Asaf'yev's volume contains surprising insights for a book of its time, Druskin's work seems to be colored by the author's background and therefore lapses into occasional political bias. Too often, viewpoints are asserted but not clearly demonstrated, as is the case with Druskin's claim that the architecture of St. Petersburg and the poetry of Pushkin had an influence on Stravinsky's music. The central point of the book is that Stravinsky remained essentially Russian in spite of his uprooted personal history. Some critics have found the book to be little more than an elaboration of Asaf'yev's original stance, stated somewhat less convincingly. Biography is not central to Druskin, although like Onnen, he puts the works in the context of Stravinsky's life. Druskin provides no photographs and no musical examples.

Written just before the composer's death, in non-technical language, DOBRIN's biography is oriented toward young audiences and takes a life-and-times approach. ROUTH's contribution to the Master Musicians series is brief but refreshingly detached, managing to avoid the eulogy trap better than any of the short accounts of Stravinsky's career. Two other slim thumbnail sketches are to be found in YOUNG and the more complete and preferable McLEISH. These are both hardly more than pamphlets, taking no more than an hour to digest.

Reviewers have praised KOBLER's work for being the first popular biography of Stravinsky. Using information gleaned from interviews with the composer's family and friends, Kobler provides clarification of and further insight into Stravinsky's love affairs and marriages. Other officially approved versions (notably the Craft materials) have ignored these aspects of Stravinsky's life. Although weak in the area of musical commentary (the author is a non-musician), this is the only work on Stravinsky written by a professional biographer. Kobler reveals little-known details about Stravinsky's flirtation with Fascism, his religious nature, and other previously unknown personality traits.

—John J. Carbon

STRINDBERG, August, 1849–1912; Swedish playwright and novelist.

Brandell, Gunnar, *Strindberg in Inferno*, translated by Barry Jacobs. Cambridge, Massachusetts, Harvard University Press, 1974.

Johnson, Walter Gilbert, *August Strindberg*. Boston, Twayne, 1976.

Lagercrantz, Olof, *August Strindberg*, translated by Anselm Hollo. New York, Farrar Straus, and London, Faber, 1984 (originally published, Stockholm, 1979).

McGill, Vivian Jerauld, *August Strindberg, the Bedeviled Viking*. New York, Brentano's, and London, N. Douglas, 1930.

Meyer, Michael, *Strindberg: A Biography*. New York, Random House, and London, Secker and Warburg, 1985.

Ollen, Gunnar, *August Strindberg*, translated by Peter Tirner. New York, Ungar, and London, Corrimer, 1972 (originally published by Friedrich, Velber, 1968).

Sprigge, Elizabeth, *The Strange Life of August Strindberg*. New York, Macmillan, and London, Hamilton, 1949.

Strindberg, Freda (sic) Uhl, *Marriage with Genius*. London, Cape, 1937.

*

MEYER's biography is authoritative and complete, with the kind of scholarship and readability Meyer brought to his Ibsen study in 1971. Particularly good at sorting out fact from fiction in Strindberg's own "autobiographical" writing, Meyer makes the most of the published letters, whose editing was virtually the life's work of Torsten Eklund, and the many unpublished letters still residing in Swedish archives. Despite or because of the overwhelming details, however, and in the absence of a stated thesis or approach to the life, Meyer offers little real insight into Strindberg's anguished personality; the result is clinical observation without diagnosis. The book contains 54 illustrations, including some of Strindberg's paintings.

LAGERCRANTZ offers, not the exhaustive study of Meyer, but a full biography, with a carefully neutral tone that almost but not quite disguises opinion. Absent are literary analyses, gossip, and the sense of frantic duality in Strindberg's private life; his marriages and divorces appear unfortunate but normal, and his madness is reduced to the suggestion that "it seemed to [Strindberg] that hallucinations, fantasies and dreams possessed a high degree of reality."

Without explanation, McGILL calls Strindberg "John" (his actual first name) for 125 pages, before changing abruptly to "Strindberg" for the remainder of this strong but uneven biography, which concentrates on the necessary presence of conflict in Strindberg's life. Nowhere among the days of this account is there a peaceful interlude when the dualities—devil and saint, doting husband and misogynist, egomaniac and paranoic, great writer and madman—allow a moment's rest. Two telling chapters, "Naturalism" and "Beyond Naturalism," are important interpretations for future theatre scholarship; however, his awkward explication of the work (especially *A Dream Play*, really a plot summary more than an interpretation), demonstrates McGill's limitations in truly understanding how his subject used his own life in his writing. He discusses Siri von Essen's sexual eccentricities with a candor seldom found in this decade.

SPRIGGE divides Strindberg's life into periods of about two–six years each, drawing on letters, works and previous studies, mostly in Swedish; she saves an "interpretation" for a short final chapter. The thrusts of her theses are that Strindberg's work is largely autobiographical, and that attempts to classify him by contemporary psychological terms "would be to make of him one of the 'strong,' 'either-or' characters he refused to create and certainly never became. He must be left as a 'both-and,' . . . " Sprigge's strong point is her ability to see how Strindberg weaves the events of his own life into his art, notably in her discussion of *A Dream Play*. The book contains only eight illustrations, but one can understand Strindberg's intense attraction to Harriet from the stunning portrait of her in *Easter*. Three appendices and an index help the reader through the material.

FREDA STRINDBERG, the writer's second wife, with whom he spent four short but chaotic years (1893–97), was herself "emotional," and, with the help of Ethel Talbot Scheffauer, takes her hyperbolic turn at explaining Strindberg's "personality and his genius, . . . his astounding versatility, his winged intuition, his sensitive, kindly spirit . . . " The biography reads like the fragment of the novel *Sun*, which they tried to write together early in their relationship and which opens this biography as an abbreviated self-portrait of the "spirit" of the pair. Adding lofty prose passages to a series of diary entries, hurried telegrams, loving letters, and passionate remonstrances and forgivenesses, Freda (spelled Frida in most other studies, and the way she signed her name on an 1892 photograph) works her way through the stormy years that include Strindberg's "Inferno." Her description of the birth of her daughter, in which somehow Strindberg emerges the suffering hero, is a great lost piece of feminist accidental parody. More an effusion of her own pounding heart than a reliable look at Strindberg, it serves future biographers better than itself. There is no question, however, that Freda did her share toward driving Strindberg to the madhouse: "Thou and I alone are different," she claims, a conclusion the reader will reach as well.

Also concentrating on a specific period (roughly 1890–1900) is BRANDELL, examining the external influences on Strindberg's life that led to the chaotic "conversion" to "creedless mysticism" that marked his later literary output. Brandell brings to his task a good understanding of the literary climate of Scandinavia, which Strindberg first criticized and rejected, and then led into the 20th century.

Two general studies deserve attention: JOHNSON summarizes the important biographical events against the background of Strindberg's major literary output; by dividing the book's chapters according to genres—Strindberg the autobiographer, the scholar and scientist, the poet, the story teller, the dramatist and historian, etc.—Johnson keeps the literary criticism behind the biographical portrait, admirably illuminating both. After a brief chapter on Strindberg's time and work, OLLEN moves through the canon with short plot descriptions. The best chapter, on the premieres of the stage productions, completes the book, not exactly criticism and not exactly biography, but a valuable fact-finder on Strindberg.

—Thomas J. Taylor

———

STUART, Mary. See **MARY QUEEN OF SCOTS.**

———

SULLIVAN, Louis (Henri), 1856–1924; American architect.

Andrew, David S., *Louis Sullivan and the Polemics of Modern Architecture*. Urbana, University of Illinois Press, 1985.

Bush-Brown, Albert, *Louis Sullivan*. New York, Braziller, and London, Mayflower, 1960.

Connely, Willard, *Louis Sullivan as He Lived: The Shaping of American Architecture, a Biography*. New York, Horizon, 1960.

Morrison, Hugh, *Louis Sullivan: Prophet of Modern Architecture*. New York, Norton, 1935.

Twombly, Robert, *Louis Sullivan: His Life and Work*. New York, Viking, 1986; Chicago and London, University of Chicago Press, 1987.

Wit, Wim de, *Louis Sullivan: The Function of Ornament*. Chicago, Chicago Historical Society, and New York and London, Norton, 1986.

*

Louis Sullivan was the first American architect to gain world renown and to have a major influence on his successors, particularly Frank Lloyd Wright. As such he should stand at the forefront of scholarly biographical effort. Unfortunately, this is not the case. Like other architects, Sullivan has had no dearth of homage paid to his buildings and ideas, but materials regarding his life and career are few. Most of what is available is very dated. MORRISON's book, the first full-length work on Sullivan, is now more than 50 years old. Considerable research has been done since then, invalidating much of Morrison's content.

The BUSH-BROWN work is part of (and not the best of) the Masters of World Architecture series. There is very brief attention to Sullivan's early years before the work turns to a critique of the architect's various phases and periods. The book is far more useful for its more than 100 plates and illustrations.

CONNELY's book, dating from the same year as Bush-Brown's, constituted a more comprehensive biography than any previous work. His effort is well documented and sheds much light on a man who at the time was relatively unknown. It is of interest now for its lively, almost dramatic style. While it is particularly weak regarding the architecture itself, a description of such was not Connely's intent.

Three much more recent works must be considered as recommended reading on Sullivan.

WIT's book is actually a catalog to an exhibit of Sullivan's work. Biographical material is present but sketchy and non-specific, intended only as background. However, the book is the single most outstanding collection of illustrations regarding Sullivan's buildings and other works and deserves mention.

ANDREW attempts to grapple with the popular myths that have built up around Sullivan, particularly those that revolve around his social life and how it affected and interacted with his career. In this effort Sullivan does not fare well. However, much of Andrew's debunking effort is based on the idea that there is only one interpretation of architecture, and this is not the case. Andrew should be read not as fact but only as one opinion.

If TWOMBLY's biography of Frank Lloyd Wright can be considered well done, then his later effort on Sullivan is far better. Twombly reexamines all the research on Sullivan since the publication of Morrison's book, and he reassesses the architect in a critical but objective manner that has not been apparent in any works since. Twombly presents a shrewdly accurate psychological profile of Sullivan, including an interesting but mostly unconvincing argument regarding the sexual undertones of Sullivan's works. In a readable, well-documented account, Twombly has created the best biography yet of this architect. Unfortu-

nately, the caliber of the author's effort is not matched by the efforts of the publisher. The illustrations are poorly presented and in general are too small, which contributes to such a lack of clarity that they rarely do the subject justice. While Twombly is by far the best of the lot, his work should be supplemented by Wit for its lavish and well-presented illustrations.

—Lawrence M. Enoch

SUN YAT-SEN, 1866–1925; Chinese revolutionary leader.

Bruce, Robert, *Sun Yat-Sen*. London, Oxford University Press, 1969.

Buck, Pearl S., *The Man Who Changed China: The Story of Sun Yat-Sen*. New York, Random House, 1953; London, Methuen, 1955.

Linebarger, Paul, *Sun Yat-Sen and the Chinese Republic*. New York and London, Century, 1925.

Martin, Bernard, *Strange Vigor: A Biography of Sun Yat-Sen*. London, Heinemann, 1944.

Restarick, Henry B., *Sun Yat-Sen, Liberator of China*. New Haven, Connecticut, Yale University Press, and London, Oxford University Press, 1931.

Schiffrin, Harold Z., *Sun Yat-Sen and the Origins of the Chinese Revolution*. Berkeley, University of California Press, 1968.

Sharman, Lyon, *Sun Yat-Sen, His Life and Its Meaning: A Critical Biography*. New York, J. Day, 1934.

*

Both Peking and Taipei continue to claim Sun Yat-sen as their own presiding genius. This political ambiguity is unsurprising since Sun himself was a complex and contradictory man who presented many different faces to the world during his eventful life. This is clearly apparent in the dozen or so English biographies available to the contemporary reader. An unusually large proportion of these are actually hagiographies—testimony not only of the very considerable charm Sun exercised on contemporary or near-contemporary observers, but also of the danger that seems particularly to beset biographers of Sun: coming to the subject already armed with a particular interpretation and forcing or ignoring facts that fail to fit neatly into it.

LINEBARGER's work appeared just before Sun's death and is therefore the first work dealing with Sun's whole life. Linebarger, an American who regarded himself as an intimate friend of Sun, was an open partisan of the Nationalist's cause and of Sun in particular. Consequently, his book is hagiography rather than biography, presenting Sun to his Western readers as a Christian leader of almost Biblical probity and rectitude. The style of writing—religiose, sentimental, and highly coloured—may arouse strong distaste in the contemporary reader. As an objective analysis of Sun's political career, or of his significance in Chinese history, this work is virtually worthless. Its value lies primarily in the many reminiscences scattered throughout the narrative, and secondly (unintentionally) as an example of that powerful, attractive force that Sun certainly seems to have possessed and used to advantage in this case.

In a similarly romantic vein, though written a generation later, is the biography by BUCK. As in the work of Linebarger, a strong moralising tone pervades, although Buck's style is not as florid. The Sun she gives to the reader is a Christian gentleman of impeccable pro-Western and anti-Communist credentials. No serious attempt is made to assess the subject's political importance, nor is Sun in any way brought to life as a man. The simplistic and brief sketches of Chinese political history provided are too often distorted by Buck's own dual requirement of compression and political acceptability. The crude and unattractive line drawings with which the book is furnished merely contribute to the juvenile and immature tone of the whole.

Of much more value to the serious student of Sun is RESTARICK's biography. The author produces a careful and meticulous account of Sun's public and private life. The particular value of this work is in the host of personal memories of Sun that Restarick has tracked down, especially those relating to Sun's Hawaiian sojourns. Restarick's style is almost invariably restrained, factual, and precise, complementing his declared aim of correcting popular myths and inaccuracies about Sun. Although his portrayal is sympathetic, Restarick is quite willing to point out Sun's well-developed capacity for fraud and deceit when it proved expedient. As an ex-cleric Restarick is too uncritical of the opportunistic element in Sun's Christianity and consequently overly shocked by his bigamous marriage to Soong Ching-Ling.

SHARMAN's contribution was, until comparatively recently, regarded as the standard biography. Sharman felt a passionate attachment to China and concern for its future. Her declared aim in writing the biography was to counter the demi-god myth growing up around Sun, fostered by a Kuomintang more eager to use Sun to confirm its own disputed legitimacy than to preserve an accurate record of him. As a result, Sharman's account of Sun is often critical of his motives and of the impracticability of many of his grand plans. Clearly, however, Sharman feels a tremendous admiration for Sun as a man. Although she provides much background detail for the Western reader, her overall grasp of Chinese history and of her subject's place in it is poor.

MARTIN's account is very readable, leavened with plenty of contextual and historical detail, although his limitation to English-language sources necessarily obscures his view of Sun. Martin fails in adequately coming to grips with the realities of Sun's political positions and with the various manoeuvreings Sun was forced in consequence to make.

The two biographies which do tackle this thorny issue are those of Bruce and Schiffrin. BRUCE's study, like Pearl Buck's, is short, but any similarity between the two stops there. The aims of Bruce's book are to place Sun in a larger historical and international context and to provide a simple account of the facts of his life. Although Bruce's approach is also influenced by the need for compression, his exposition of the course of China's decline during the 19th century and of the resulting political conditions under which Sun had to work is both wide-ranging and perceptive. The result is a balanced and objective view of Sun responding to the national and international pressures brought inexorably to bear on him by the history of his own country. Inevitably the private life of Sun loses out in such a scheme, but for anyone seeking a brief and concise account of Sun's political passage amid the shoals of contemporary politics, this biography should be especially suitable.

SCHIFFRIN's is the most authoritative of the biographies here reviewed, although its scope is limited to the years up to 1905. Drawing on an extremely wide range of sources, including many works in Japanese and Chinese, Schiffrin gives the reader a very detailed and illuminating exposition of the social and political problems faced by Sun in the first half of his career. Schiffrin's style is somewhat dry, and he does assume in the reader some prior knowledge of the subject, but his account nevertheless makes for an excellent exposé of the realpolitik governing Sun's quite literal movement toward undisputed leadership of the Revolutionary Movement. Not least valuable is Schiffrin's scholarly investigation of the Reform/Revolutionary factions and of Sun's movement from the one to the other; and of the other major personalities who were allied with or in opposition to Sun.

Schiffrin's is an extremely well researched work full of acute observation and intelligent commentary, though the author's very considerable erudition tends to obscure Sun's forceful personality. It is required reading for any student needing a detailed account and analysis of Sun's rise and of the circumstances that influenced Sun in the first half of his career.

—D. H. O'Leary

SWIFT, Jonathan, 1667–1745; Anglo-Irish writer.

Craik, Henry, *The Life of Jonathan Swift*. London, J. Murray, 1882; revised edition in 2 vols., London, Macmillan, 1894.

Delany, Patrick, *Observations upon Lord Orrery's Remarks upon the Life and Writings of Dr. Jonathan Swift*. Dublin, R. Main, and London, W. Reeve, 1754.

Downie, J. A., *Jonathan Swift: Political Writer*. London and Boston, Routledge, 1984.

Ehrenpreis, Irvin, *The Personality of Jonathan Swift*. London, Methuen, and Cambridge, Massachusetts, Harvard University Press, 1958.

Ehrenpreis, Irvin, *Swift: The Man, His Works, and the Age* (3 vols.). London, Methuen, and Cambridge, Massachusetts, Harvard University Press, 1962–83.

Ewald, William B., *The Masks of Jonathan Swift*. Oxford, Blackwell, and Cambridge, Massachusetts, Harvard University Press, 1954.

Ferguson, Oliver W., *Jonathan Swift and Ireland*. Urbana, University of Illinois Press, 1962.

Forster, John, *The Life of Jonathan Swift*. London, J. Murray, 1875; New York, Harper, 1876.

Greenacre, Phyllis, *Swift and Carroll: A Psychoanalytical Study of Two Lives*. New York, International Universities Press, 1955.

Johnson, Samuel, "Swift," in *Lives of the English Poets*. London, 1781.

Johnston, Denis, *In Search of Swift*. Dublin, Hodges Figgis, and New York, Barnes and Noble, 1959.

Landa, Louis A., *Swift and the Church of Ireland*. Oxford, Clarendon Press, 1954.

Le Brocquy, Sybil, *Cadenus: A Reassessment in the Light of New Evidence of the Relationships between Swift, Stella, and Vanessa*. Dublin, Dolmen Press, 1962.

Nokes, David, *Jonathan Swift, a Hypocrite Reversed: A Critical Biography*. Oxford and New York, Oxford University Press, 1985.

Quintana, Ricardo, *The Mind and Art of Jonathan Swift*. London and New York, Oxford University Press, 1936; revised edition, 1953.

Quintana, Ricardo, *Swift: An Introduction*. London and New York, Oxford University Press, 1955.

Swift, Deane, *An Essay upon the Life, Writings, and Character of Dr. Jonathan Swift*. London, C. Bathurst, 1755.

Wilde, William, *The Closing Years of Dean Swift's Life*. Dublin, Hodges and Smith, 1849.

*

Biographers of Swift have always been tempted by the difficulty of his personality, by his often extreme desire for anonymity and disguise, and by the mysteries of his life. Many have tried to analyse his admittedly complex personality. Others have speculated on whether he contracted a secret marriage with Esther Johnson ("Stella") or whether his relationship with Hester Vanhomrigh ("Vanessa") was a physical one.

Swift's first biographer was Lord Orrery in 1752, seven years after Swift's death. This disapproving and sometimes malicious work set the scene for over a century of attacks on Swift's person, his work (especially the fourth book of *Gulliver's Travels*), and his alleged misanthropy and scatology. Swift's friend Patrick DELANY and his nephew DEANE SWIFT defended him in 1754 and 1755. Dr. JOHNSON joined in the attack (Swift was "not a man to be loved or envied"); often hostile to Swift, Johnson revealed more about himself than about Swift. Sir Walter Scott, in his introduction to Swift's *Works* (1814), was characteristically generous, recognising Swift's excellence as a writer.

Francis Jeffrey, reviewing Scott's edition of Swift's works, attacked Swift, regarding him as a political apostate (*Edinburgh Review*, September 1816). Hazlitt, in his *Lectures on the English Poets* (1818), wrote perceptively of Swift's imagination, indignation, and impatience, describing him as a genius in an essay that attempted a balanced view. Then followed two damaging attacks by influential 19th-century writers whose prejudices guided the general view of Swift down to the 20th century. Lord Macaulay in 1833 described Swift as "an apostate politician, a ribald priest, a perjured lover." William Makepeace Thackeray, in *The English Humorists of the 18th Century* (1853), virtually invented the gloomy Dean, stressing Swift's misanthropy. He also drew attention to Book IV of *Gulliver's Travels* as "filthy," expressing horror at Swift's morals, failing also to appreciate Swift's irony.

Later in the 19th century appeared FORSTER's *Life*. Although only the first volume ever appeared, Forster provided a sound view of Swift's life and personality, collecting and reproducing everything he could find about Swift, leaving us with a mine of useful details about the Dean's public life up to 1711. Forster dispelled the theory of Swift's political apostasy, dismissing it because of his understanding of Swift's devotion to the High Church position in religion and politics. CRAIK drew on Forster's unused material to publish his two-volume *Life*, which became the standard work until Ehrenpreis (see below) a century later. Craik attempted to separate Swift from his many personae.

Advances in medical science enabled the publication of work on Swift's supposed madness and deafness; it was seen that even his apparent madness was the result of Ménières Syndrome. Sir William WILDE, father of Oscar Wilde, was the first to treat of Swift's medical history in an article of 1847, followed by a book in 1849.

The view of the misanthrope Swift persisted, however, to the present day, and at the base of this was the problem of Swift's "scatology." Not surprisingly, several Freudian readings of Swift appeared in the middle of the present century. GREENACRE offered a rather extreme view of Swift and Lewis Carroll based on a Freudian reading. Then in 1959 Norman O. Brown wrote his essay "The Excremental Vision," which contested the validity of many psychoanalytical interpretations dismissing suggestions that Swift was insane (*Life Against Death: The Psychoanalytical Meaning of History*, 1959).

The last 50 years have seen an increase in books on Swift. Nearly all biographies of him are also critical works since it is always helpful to place his life and writings side by side. QUINTANA (1936) was revised in 1953, providing a sound critical biography; his smaller *Introduction* of 1955 supplemented this. EHRENPREIS (1958) presents excellent biographical essays, as does EWALD in dealing with the many personae that Swift employed in his writing.

In 1942 Herbert Davies, the doyen of Swift studies, wrote an elegant life of Stella, which also threw light on Swift (*Stella: A Gentlewoman of the 18th Century*). LE BROCQUY, however, presents a number of theories about the relationship of Swift to his women friends that have received no critical support.

Before moving to the definitive biography of Swift it is important to mention the rather eccentric biography by JOHNSTON. This presented Swift's life as a series of detective puzzles to be "solved": Swift's parentage and origins, his "marriage," his relations with women. The result is highly exciting reading, although Johnston's findings have won little support. Nevertheless, he tackled a number of confusing areas of Swift's life that more orthodox biographers have ignored.

Several narrow areas of Swift's life have been thoroughly documented and well presented. LANDA's coverage of Swift's dedicated commitment to the Church of Ireland is unlikely to be bettered; similarly FERGUSON's account of Swift's life and work in Ireland. DOWNIE has produced a sound study of Swift's life in politics.

EHRENPREIS published the first volume of his definitive life in 1962, the third and last volume in 1983. Angus Ross and David Woolley in their Oxford Authors edition of Swift describe it as "a monumental work based on an impressive grasp of the documents and work; the most substantial modern biography of Swift. Unless any further material comes to light this superbly written work will remain the authoritative biography." Ehrenpreis chose to exclude many of the traditional anecdotes about Swift and he avoided speculation on doubtful incidents.

Ehrenpreis includes a certain amount of discussion of Swift's work, but NOKES combines life and work to produce an extremely readable and intensely critical work. He attempts "to walk a middle path by offering some fresh points of interpretation of Swift's life and works without losing the general reader in academic groves that have sprouted into thickets." He also chose, he says, "to reinstate some of these anecdotes [about Swift's life] . . . because they have played such an important part in the transmission of Swift's reputation through the ages that to have omitted them would have been to ignore an important element in the enigmatic record of a man who deliberately cultivated false images of himself." In *The Year's Work in English Studies* Stephen Copley writes: "[Nokes'] account of the events of Swift's life, and of the controversies surrounding various aspects of it, treads a nice line between scholarliness and readability, and carves a distinct place for itself, without being overshadowed by the monumental labours of Irvin Ehrenpreis."

Two comprehensive collections of Swift's voluminous correspondence contain a wealth of useful biographical information and insights into Swift's personality and thinking. These are E. Elrington Ball, editor, *The Correspondence of Jonathan Swift, D. D.* (6 vols., London, 1910–14), and Harold Williams, editor, *The Correspondence of Jonathan Swift* (5 vols., Oxford, 1963–65).

—Bernard Tucker

SWINBURNE, Algernon Charles, 1837–1909; English poet.

Gosse, Edmund, *The Life of Algernon Charles Swinburne.* New York and London, Macmillan, 1917.

Henderson, Philip, *Swinburne: Portrait of a Poet.* New York, Macmillan, and London, Routledge, 1974.

Lafourcade, Georges, *Swineburne: A Literary Biography.* London, G. Bell, and New York, Morrow, 1932.

Watts-Dunton, Clara, *The Home Life of Swinburne.* London, A. M. Philpot, and New York, Stokes, 1922.

*

Although Swinburne, a man of neurotic personality, is often regarded by literary historians as the *enfant terrible* of the Victorian Period, he was widely loved by those who knew him personally. After his death a spate of more or less hagiographic reminiscences of him appeared, the most valuable being that by WATTS-DUNTON because of her long association with Swinburne at The Pines. Instead of a sense of the complex personality and larger development one would expect of a biography, the main value of this work is the intimate and fascinating glimpses it provides of Swinburne's personal habits and routine at The Pines. Of special interest are the chapters "Swinburne as a Bibliophile" (his love of his books was visceral and his treatment of them reverential), "Swinburne the Dickensian" ("He admired Scott. He venerated Hugo. He loved Dickens," the author tell us), and "The Passing of the Poet"; alone in the library Watts-Dunton opened the dead poet's eyelids to view his remarkable eyes for one last time.

Swinburne's impish sense of humor, his capacity for using billingsgate, his warmth toward his friends and his extreme distaste for strangers, his daily walks and afternoon siestas are all conveyed in clearly written anecdotes. Though written *con amore*—the author feels privileged to have known Swinburne—this book is something more than an idealized portrait. Here we see in passing Swinburne's too-high trousers, his peculiar way of walking, his theoretical championing of the working class while in practice "the needs of the people troubled him no more than the claims of the equator." Still, the only shrill note in Watts-

Dunton's book is when she defends "the Bard," as Swinburne was called affectionately at The Pines, against his detractors.

GOSSE's was the first major biography of Swinburne, and after more than 70 years it remains of primary importance. The product of eight years of effort, this is a meticulously researched work of scholarship, enhanced by the author's personal knowledge of Swinburne and virtually unlimited access to the recollections of those who knew him best. Organized into nine chapters chronologically arranged and buttressed by four appendices, this book examines in greater detail than any of the other English biographies the vicissitudes of Swinburne's life and many of his significant relationships, particularly those with James McNeill Whistler and Benjamin Jowett in the 1870s. Gosse's ability to re-create significant moments in Swinburne's life vividly, freezing them in time for posterity, is the hallmark of this biography. Swinburne's childhood meetings with Samuel Rogers and William Wordsworth and his meeting many years later with Walter Savage Landor are unforgettably recalled. A scene that especially stands out is of the young Swinburne on a Sunday evening in the summer of 1862 reciting "Les Noyades" before a distinguished group that included the Archbishop of York and the horrified reaction that ensued.

As one would expect of a co-editor of Swinburne's complete works, a considerable portion of Gosse's work is devoted to Swinburne's writings. Though his criticism of the poetry and plays is undiscriminating in its lavish praise, the chapter on "Poems and Ballads," which in Gosse's words "turned the pudic snows of Mrs. Grundy's countenance to scarlet," is valuable. Gosse traces the publishing history and critical and moral reaction that followed the publication of that revolutionary volume in the contest of the contemporary milieu. Nowhere else is Gosse's erudition put to more constructive use. Unfortunately, Gosse scarcely notices *Lesbia Brandon*, but his evaluation of Swinburne's criticism is of a high order. In writing this life Gosse was under pressure from Swinburne's family to withhold information that would illuminate the darker aspects of the poet's character. Hence, the influence of the Marquis de Sade and Swinburne's alcoholism and sexual degeneracy are not addressed.

As fine a biography as Gosse's is, LAFOURCADE's is in some ways superior. In sharp contrast to Gosse's mannered, ornate style, Lafourcade's writing is always clear and direct. More importantly, Lafourcade, whose study appeared 15 years after Gosse's, was able to make use of previously unpublished materials and redress the omissions of the earlier biographies. (His two-volume *La Jeunesse de Swinburne* was published in 1928 and is widely regarded as the standard life). *Swinburne: A Literary Biography* is the first life in English to come to grips with Swinburne's aberrations, and if it lacks the density of detail of Gosse, it compensates by presenting a more complex and complete portrait of the poet. Lafourcade makes use of the autobiographical novels, *Lesbia Brandon* and *A Year's Letters* to elucidate Swinburne's strained relationship with his father and he takes note of the matters of Sade's influence, flagellation and alcoholism.

This book is arranged chronologically in eight chapters. The first, "Semel Et Semper," touches on Swinburne hardly at all but rather explores the poet's aristocratic background, devoting much space to the fascinating grandfather Sir John Edward Swinburne. In "Childhood" attention is given to Swinburne's cosmopolitan education at the hands of his mother, who ironically shielded her son from too much Byron. All of this prepares for Lafourcade's fresh view of Swinburne not as the last Victorian but as essentially a modern writer, more akin to Proust and Joyce than to Tennyson or Hardy. This is a literary biography with a strong emphasis always on the forces that shaped Swinburne's sensibility as a writer. Lafourcade's ability to recreate the ambiance of Swinburne's milieu is unequalled. This book must rank with Gosse's as indispensable.

Of the more recent biographies of Swinburne HENDERSON's is unquestionably the best. Making judicious use of Cecil Lang's great edition of Swinburne's letters, Henderson is able to shed new light on Swinburne's relationships with Adah Menken, his cousin Mary Gordon, and the Pre-Raphaelites. One of the major strengths of this work is Henderson's firm grasp of Swinburne's relations with the other writers of the period and especially their reactions to him. As the title indicates the main focus is on Swinburne as poet. Henderson's approach to the poems combines textual analysis with a heavily Freudian biographical emphasis. If his readings are not always convincing, they are never boring. His treatment of the novels is sensitive and informative, but he essentially ignores Swinburne's criticism. The book is organized into 12 very readable, chronological chapters, each focusing on a significant phase of the poet's life or writings. There are also 12 period photographs and illustrations, which enliven the volume. This is a fine piece of work, but it does not supplant Gosse and Lafourcade.

—Robert G. Blake

SYNGE, John Millington, 1871–1909; Irish poet and playwright.

Bourgeois, Maurice, *John Millington Synge and the Irish Theatre.* London, Constable, 1913; New York, Blom, 1965.

Carpenter, Andrew, editor *My Uncle John: Edward Stephens' Life of J. M. Synge.* London, Oxford University Press, 1974.

Gerstenberger, Donna L., *John Millington Synge.* New York, Twayne, 1964.

Greene, David H. and Edward M. Stephens, *J. M. Synge 1871–1909.* New York, Macmillan, 1959.

Mikhail, E. H., editor, *J. M. Synge: Interviews and Recollections.* London, Macmillan, 1977.

Skelton, Robin, *J. M. Synge and His World.* London, Thames and Hudson, and New York, Viking, 1971.

Skelton, Robin, *The Writings of J. M. Synge.* London, Thames and Hudson, and Indianapolis, Bobbs-Merrill, 1971.

*

Since J. M. Synge was an intensely private man who died at the age of 38 after only a few productive years as a dramatist, his biography is inevitably limited in scope. Unlike his contemporaries, such as George Moore or W. B. Yeats, he did not engage in a significant manner with the intellectual or literary issues of the day. His journalism is mainly devoted to his travels in various parts of rural Ireland, and these writings are of interest as observations on a way of life and a people that he portrayed in his plays. His biographer has therefore to confine himself to a relatively uncomplicated account of his life—the theatre, the plays, the involvement with the running of the Abbey Theatre, his one significant love affair. Since he was privately educated as a boy and was an indifferent university student and since he traveled to Europe to learn languages and to study at the Sorbonne, staying in boarding houses and small hotels, there is not much evidence, apart from his own notebooks and letters, on which to base a study of his growth and development. Nevertheless, GREENE, using the manuscript by STEPHENS (see below), wrote an objective, informative, and even-tempered account of the life. He makes judicious use of available documents and traces Synge's life with particular effectiveness when dealing with his actual writing and with his involvement with W. B. Yeats, Lady Gregory, and others in running the Abbey Theatre.

The Edward Stephens biography, edited by CARPENTER, was written between 1939 and 1949. This massive manuscript, here reduced to reasonable length, was also available to David Greene, who made liberal and prudent use of it, but essentially wrote independently of it. Stephens believed strongly in the importance of family background in shaping his uncle's work; he never saw the plays in performance. Although the book is of some interest for what it tells about Stephens, it is not of major significance for what it says about Synge. Stephens identifies rather too closely with his subject on the basis of similarity of background, a comparable religious crisis, and a mutual love of landscape. The book provides an intimate account of Synge, his family, and the immediate rural setting, but Stephens' judgments are not always acceptable.

A number of critics, beginning with BOURGEOIS, whose book has been mistakenly called a biography, have discussed Synge's relationship with W. B. Yeats. They focus on the idea that Yeats was influenced by Synge in his theories of personality and that Synge's example caused him to strive for greater realism in his own style. GERSTENBERGER develops this idea, as does SKELTON's *Writings of J. M. Synge*, particularly in relation to the poetry. Skelton's *J. M. Synge and His World* has no new biographical information of significance, but it gives a good summary of the life and has a most interesting collection of photographs.

MIKHAIL provides a useful collection of usually brief memoirs by many who knew Synge, such as W. B. Yeats, Stephen McKenna, Oliver St. John Gogarty, Padraic Colum, Lady Gregory, George Moore, and James Stephens. These contemporary sources of information are useful. W. B. Yeats, in fact, wrote frequently about Synge. His "Preface to the First Edition of The Well of the Saints" and "J. M. Synge and the Ireland of his Time," both in *Essays and Introductions* (1961), are particularly interesting.

—Maurice Harmon

TAGORE, Rabindranath, 1861–1941; Indian writer and philosopher.

Hay, Stephen, *Asian Ideas of East and West: Tagore and His Critics in Japan, China, and India.* Cambridge, Massachusetts, Harvard University Press, 1970.

Kripalani, Krishna, *Rabindranath Tagore: A Life.* New York and London, Oxford University Press, 1962.

Mukherjee, Sujit, *Passage to America: The Reception of Rabindranath Tagore in the United States 1912–41.* Calcutta, Bookland, 1964.

Roy, Basanta Koomar, *Rabindranath Tagore: The Man and His Poetry.* New York, Dodd Mead, 1915.

Thompson, Edward J., *Rabindranath Tagore: His Life and Work.* Calcutta, Association Press (YMCA), and London, Oxford University Press, 1921.

Thompson, Edward J., *Rabindranath Tagore: Poet and Dramatist.* Oxford, Oxford University Press, 1926.

*

Although he had been a major figure on the Bengali literary, educational, and political scene since the 1890s, Tagore was generally unknown even outside of Bengal until he won the Nobel Prize for Literature in 1913. This followed private publication in England in 1912 of *Gitanjali (Song-Offerings)*, his prose-poem versions of selections from several collections of his Bengali lyrics. The award created a sensation because he was the first Asian to win that or any comparable international award. With British-Indian relations becoming increasingly tense, that literary event assumed political importance and affected approaches to both biography and criticism. In order hurriedly to introduce Tagore to the world at large, many contemporary writers incorporated fulsome praise with background and interpretation. Thus, because Tagore had become a symbol of India's ability to compete culturally on the international scene, interpretations as well as biography were often less than objective.

ROY's English-language work, written in New York for a primarily American audience, coincided with the year of Tagore's knighthood, which he later renounced in protest against the Amritsar Massacre of 1919. Roy's biographical material is thin and his interpretations are unoriginal. Many other studies followed. Those by Indians tended toward hagiography; those by Western writers suffered from ignorance of Tagore's courses and contexts. Western eagerness to embrace the stereotype of Wise Man from the East also hampered objectivity.

The important contemporary exception is THOMPSON's two studies based on his experience as teacher of English literature in Bengal from 1910 to 1921, on his study of Bengali language and literature, and on personal friendship with Tagore. They are a significant contribution to an understanding of connections between Tagore's life and work. The 1921 book explains these connections for non-Indian readers. In 1926 Thompson expanded his study of the major poems and plays, their sources and symbolism. Because they had become accustomed to less critical assessments, many Bengalis and Tagore himself thought Thompson disloyal, and those friendships languished for many years. The books are still reliable assessments of a great writer whose work was sometimes uneven because so often experimental.

KRIPALANI's biography coincided with the centenary celebrations in 1961. It benefits from personal knowledge and a more modern approach to biography, although it is still not as complete or as objective as is desirable for a figure of Tagore's status.

Some of the most reliable views of Tagore are in books dealing with his international travels. MUKHERJEE provides a straightforward account of Tagore's American travels. Not a detailed biography, it is a useful source of information about dates and itineraries, as well as contacts abroad. HAY's study is thoroughly scholarly and puts Tagore's complicated relations with Asian admirers, and his effects on attitudes toward both East and West, into the perspective of political tensions: Tagore is a spokesman for India caught among great changes that would eventually affect the world. The correspondence with William Rothenstein (*Imperfect Encounter: Letters of William Rothenstein and Rabindranath Tagore 1911–1941*, edited by Mary Lago, Cambridge, Massachusetts, Harvard University Press, 1972), who was the prime mover of Tagore's literary career in the West after meeting him in India in 1910, traces that career and its complications as seen through their eyes.

Autobiographical works (in often unsatisfactory translations) often lack detail but provide general background to supplement more factual studies. Tagore's *My Boyhood Days* (1940) and *My Reminiscences* (1917) are episodic memoirs rather than systematic autobiography. *Glimpses of Bengal Life* (1921) comprises letters written during his years as overseer of family estates in East Bengal. It is valuable for descriptions of places, people, and country life that inspired many of his best short stories and supplied the atmosphere for many of his poems.

Rabindranath Tagore: A Bibliography, compiled by Katherine Henn (Metuchen, New Jersey, Scarecrow Press, 1985) lists English-language sources, translations, articles, and biographical materials by and about Tagore, up to 1985. An adequate English-language biography, however, is still to be written. Nevertheless, scholarly work since the 1940s, and Satyajit Ray's films based on Tagore's fiction, provide essential departures for such a project. Studies on Tagore and Bengali cultural history in scholarly publications such as the *Journal of Asian Studies* indicate the increase in depth and thoroughness of such work. Careful study of Ray's films using Tagore's fiction reveals the extent of coordination between his life and his writings. The film *Charulata*, for instance, based on the novella *The Broken Nest* (1901), has as background Tagore's own literary encouragement from a sister-in-law whose life ended tragically.

In choosing non-violent rather than violent political action, and literature as his method of commenting on the events of the time, Tagore in many ways set a lonely course for himself. That loneliness drove him abroad in search of likeminded audiences, and it is an underlying theme of the studies by Thompson and Hay, and of the Rothenstein-Tagore correspondence. It is an essential theme of any Tagore biography, for in defining his role in what has been called the Bengal Renaissance, he had to find a new and constructive middle road between exclusive orthodoxy and complete rejection of indigenous values and traditions. Thereby he set a working model for future Indian relations with the West.

Tagore biography in Bengal is now becoming more objective. His influence and example have been so pervasive there that several generations of biographers and critics have had to pass before genuine objectivity could be achieved. Translations of current work in Bengal will make possible the full English-language biography that is needed.

—Mary Lago

TAYLOR, Elizabeth, 1932– ; English-born American film actress.

David, Lester and Jhan Robbins, *Richard and Elizabeth*. New York, Funk and Wagnalls, and London, A. Barker, 1977.

Kelley, Kitty, *Elizabeth Taylor: The Last Star*. New York, Simon and Schuster, and London, M. Joseph, 1981.

Maddox, Brenda, *Who's Afraid of Elizabeth Taylor?* New York, M. Evans, and London, Hart-Davis MacGibbon, 1977.

Robin-Tani, Marianne, *The New Elizabeth*. New York, St. Martin's, 1988.

Sheppard, Dick, *Elizabeth: The Life and Career of Elizabeth Taylor*. New York, Doubleday, 1974; London, W. H. Allen, 1975.

Waterbury, Ruth, *Elizabeth Taylor*. New York, Appleton-Century, and London, Hale, 1964.

*

KELLEY has written the definitive biography thus far in a clear, straightforward narrative style, quoting dialogue often from the more than 400 people she says she has interviewed, which lends the book credibility. She is relatively evenhanded, beginning and ending the biography by saying that "Elizabeth Taylor was indeed the last of her kind"—a movie star of such magnitude and glamor.

Kelley does seem to take care to bring out negative facts; she quotes producer Pandro Berman: "A director has to get [her acting] out of her. She can't give it spontaneously and naturally like a fine actress can." Kelly does not accept the story that Taylor just grew an extra three inches to play the lead in *National Velvet*, although several authors do. She quotes some of Taylor's coarse language, mentions her affairs with several men other biographers do not, and slobbers much less over the Taylor-Burton affair than many others. She reveals that Taylor was pregnant when she married Mike Todd; others go along with the story of premature birth. No detail is too small to be included. When Taylor was a child, Kelley tells us, she sent a Valentine to her father and forgot to sign it, but she did sign one sent to Donald Crisp; the message is included.

SHEPPARD's bias is revealed at the beginning: "This work . . . is a celebration, a personal tribute to a presence that has enriched my life." In this loving biography that bubbles with admiration, Sheppard relates the plots of all of Taylor's films, and in prose that is just slightly above that of fan magazines, he puts the best face on her life. He says, "To this day, Elizabeth is still a voracious reader," contradicting Kelley's comments on her reading. Taylor's bad movies were the result of "bad scripts." Sheppard also presents details that he could not know: "Elizabeth flushed scarlet and silently begged in vain for a magic power that would enable her to vanish instantly."

Though MADDOX conducted no interviews with Taylor, she writes in a chatty, vastly admiring tone, of how Taylor's life influenced her own. Thus, despite certain details of Taylor's life—she is seen as the product of her stage mother, the studios, and the media—her movies are discussed in terms of her sexuality and growth. ROBIN-TANI very briefly discusses Taylor's life up to Richard Burton's death, focusing primarily on her life afterwards: her stay at the Bette Ford clinic, her weight loss, her recovery from grief, her new male friends, and her work for AIDS patients. She, too, is adoring and chatty: "The new Elizabeth Taylor is an amazing, wondrous woman. She is truly back—better and more beautiful than ever before." This is the only biography to discuss what happened to Taylor's grown-up children. WATERBURY too uses gushy fan-magazine prose; she includes much dialogue in a simplistic style aimed perhaps at early teens, and ending with the Taylor-Burton marriage. DAVID AND ROBBINS discuss adoringly the Taylor-Burton affair, again in an easy-reading style, defending the scandal the pair caused by pointing out that today their relationship would not have been shocking.

Taylor, in her autobiography simply entitled *Elizabeth Taylor* (1964), relates in guileless prose the story of outstanding moments in her life, putting the best construction on people and events. Her early romances, she says, were "childish"; her comments on her husbands before Burton are circumlocutious and non-vindictive. She tells the story of her physical growth to play *National Velvet* as fact. She is proud of a few movies—notably *A Place in the Sun*, *Giant*, and *Who's Afraid of Virginia Woolf*—and of her poetry reading with Burton.

She comes across as a somewhat naive, friendly, open, likable woman who can say, "I know it's incongruous for me to say it, but I don't believe in divorce," about which she has an "enormous guilt complex." She is still married to Burton at the book's conclusion and shortsightedly predicts, "Richard and Elizabeth as actors and celebrities are going into semi-retirement in a few years." She is sure that this marriage will endure.

—Janet Overmyer

TCHAIKOVSKY, Peter Ilyich, 1840–1893; Russian composer.

Bower, Catherine Drinker and Barbara von Meck, *Beloved Friend: The Story of Tchaikowsky and Nadejda von Meck*. London, Hutchinson, and New York, Random House, 1937.

Brown, David, *Tchaikovsky: A Biography and Critical Study* (3 vols. published). London, Gollancz, and New York, Norton, 1978, 1982, 1986.

Evans, Edwin, *Tchaikovsky*. London, Dent, and New York, Dutton, 1906.

Garden, Edward, *Tchaikovsky*. London, Dent, and New York, Octagon Books, 1973.

Gee, John and Elliott Selby, *The Triumph of Tchaikovsky: A Biography*. London, R. Hale, 1959; New York, Vanguard, 1960.

Hanson, Lawrence and Elizabeth Hanson, *Tchaikovsky, the Man behind the Music*. New York, Dodd Mead, 1966.

Hoffman, Michel, *Tchaikovsky*, translated by Angus Heriot. London, J. Calder, 1962.

Kendal, Alan, *Tchaikovsky: A Biography*. London, Bodley Head, 1988.

Newmarch, Rosa, *Tchaikovsky: His Life and Works*. London, J. Lane, 1900; revised edition, with Edwin Evans, London, W. Reeves, and New York, Scribner, 1908.

Schallenberg, E. W., *Tchaikovsky*, translated by M. M. Kessler-Button. London, Sidgwick and Jackson, 1940.

Tchaikovsky, Modest, *The Life and Letters of Peter Ilich Tchaikovsky*, edited and introduced by Rosa Newmarch. London, J. Lane, and New York, Dodd Mead, 1905 (originally published 1902).

Warrack, John, *Tchaikovsky Symphonies and Concertos*. London, British Broadcasting Corporation, 1969; Seattle, University of Washington Press, 1971.

Weinstock, Herbert, *Tchaikovsky*. New York, Knopf, 1943; London, Cassell, 1946.

Wheeler, Opal, *The Story of Peter Tchaikovsky*. New York, Dutton, 1953; London, Faber, 1954.

Yoffe, Elkhonon, *Tchaikovsky in America*, translated by Lidya Yoffe. Oxford and New York, Oxford University Press, 1986.

Young, Percy M., *Letters to His Family*. London, D. Dobson, 1981.

*

Tchaikovsky has suffered greatly at the hands of his early biographers. Despite the overwhelming number of surviving letters, diaries, reviews and documents all in Tchaikovsky's hand, biographers have managed to misquote and therefore often grossly misrepresent the composer's character and subsequently misinform the reader. Even relatively recently, further documents and letters have been discovered shedding new light on Tchaikovsky's life and creating a need for new and more true-to-character biographies to be written.

This history of inadequate biographies begins with Tchaikovsky's own brother, MODEST TCHAIKOVSKY, whose book unfortunately set a standard for other biographers to follow. It is, in essence, a biography of Modest Tchaikovsky as he saw himself had he possessed his brother's compositional skills. He does not present an even view of his brother but concentrates on specific incidents and characteristics that obscure the vigorous, plain-spoken side of Tchaikovsky's nature.

Translated by Rosa NEWMARCH, Modest's biography for many years represented the standard account in English of the composer's life. Newmarch, however, does not provide a literal translation of Modest's work but an abbreviated version in which the quotes from Tchaikovsky's letters are bowdlerized. Newmarch consistently emphasises the composer's homosexual tendency to the degree that she portrays him as nervous yet gentle and even feminine by nature. Newmarch's other publications on Tchaikovsky include an earlier biography of 1900, written in a similar vein, and a joint publication, based on a 1900 work, with Edwin Evans in 1908. This is divided so that the first 111 pages are devoted to a biography by Newmarch with the remaining chapters, by Evans, concentrating on an analysis of selected works and a study of Tchaikovsky as a music critic and composer in relation to his contemporaries in music and the other arts.

The definitive biography to date is BROWN's study in four volumes (the last volume not yet published). Brown, who wrote the *New Grove* article on Tchaikovsky, here divides the volumes into narrowly chosen periods: *The Early Years 1840–74*, including his early travels in the West, his friendships and his love affair with the prima donna Desirée Artot; *The Crisis Years 1874–78*, covering his marriage to Antonina Milukova, his attempted suicide, and his long and strange relationship with his benefactress, Nadeshda von Meck (by mutual agreement they did not meet and on the occasion of his convalescence at her country house, she provided him with a timetable of her comings and goings so that they might avoid a chance meeting); and *The Years of Wandering 1878–85*, which concentrates on Tchaikovsky's journeys around Europe and longing for his homeland.

As a biographer Brown presents a sane and balanced portrait concentrating on Tchaikovsky's relationship with his musical contemporaries Balakirev, Cui, the Rubinsteins, Mussorgsky, and Rimsky-Korsakov. The study is integrated with a discussion of the music which, in light of earlier misrepresentative writings, proves of double importance to an understanding of the man behind the music. The book is not restricted to pure biography and is a scholarly account. Its main asset is its concentration on specific periods, offering the serious reader detailed and isolated studies. Although the sheer volume of this study may discourage the general reader seeking a synopsis, Brown's style of writing is compelling and often humorous; consequently the work is enjoyable to read.

Brown's approach differs from that of his predecessors, probably in large part because he had access to an important Russian text on Tchaikovsky printed in 1940 but suppressed before publication and consequently little known. It was only when Alexandra Orlova emigrated from Russia in 1979, bringing with her a copy of *pisma krodnim* (a selection of letters from the composer to his family, collected in the first of a projected two volumes edited by Vladimar Zhadanov, Moscow, 1955), that this information became available to Western biographers. Orlova, who worked at the Tchaikovsky museum at Klin before emigrating, has been working on her own publication due to appear as *Tchaikovsky, Day by Day: A Biography in Documents* (to be published by Ann Arbor as number 18 in the series *UMI Russian Musical Studies*).

Of other recent Western biographers who have benefited from this revelation KENDAL is the most important. His biography, which is also the most recent, concentrates on the mystery surrounding the death of Tchaikovsky and the question of whether it was self-inflicted. He shows a strong concern for Tchaikovsky's chamber music, encouraging the reader to discover it for himself, and he argues for greater standards of editing and publishing so that the music does not suffer from the anachronistic encrustations and impurities of modern additions.

Four introductory works aim to clear Tchaikovsky's name and to present a less biased picture. WEINSTOCK's book, considering its relatively early date, is particularly trustworthy. Weinstock is especially concerned to present an objective account, uncoloured by his personal enthusiasm for the composers' music. The HANSON collaboration of 1966 never lays claim to being a definitive study; its only aim was to act as a stopgap until a more extensive work was published. The authors wished to amend Tchaikovsky's reputation and to persuade the reader that his music deserved a higher appreciation than it was currently earning. The study does not extend to an analysis of the music but aims rather to a general discussion of the background to his works; the intention being to get closer to the music through a study of the man. In an attempt to show the more introspective and gentle side of Tchaikovsky's temperament, however, the authors are sometimes guilty of the type of angled biography that they themselves criticize in earlier writers.

Like the Hanson biography WARRACK's account aims at the general rather than the scholarly reader. Warrack states to this effect in his introduction: "I have not assumed any musical knowledge beyond that which most concert-goers may be expected to possess nor even the ability to read music." The book tends toward the coffee-table category of biographies and the text is liberally interspersed with photographs and reproductions of paintings. The narrative concentrates on conveying Tchaikovsky as "lonely, touchy, emotionally frail and tormented by his homosexuality." Though a melodramatic account that prefers to create a good read rather than plainly deliver the facts, the work is interesting for the slant Warrack gives on the social context of Tchaikovsky as a Russian composer.

GARDEN's book replaces the earlier EVANS account of 1906 for the *Master Musicians* series. Garden has the general reader/ student in mind, and his approach is similar to the other Tchaikovsky biographies of this type. The account has a strong musical bias, so that biography and analysis are combined throughout.

Of the general type of biography with neither a particular slant nor any great virtue of style are those books by GEE AND SELBY, HOFFMAN, and SCHALLENBERG. They do not leave a great mark but are substantial in themselves.

An unexpected and enchanting biography can be found in WHEELER's *Story of Peter Tchaikovsky*. The book is exactly what it claims to be: a fable, intended as a storybook for children, elaborating on details from Tchaikovsky's childhood. It contains small piano pieces in an appendix aimed to encourage the young pianist.

A number of books present biographical details from particular periods in Tchaikovsky's life, quoting letters and documents that could be of interest to the reader who wishes to study the evidence for himself. The most comprehensive of these is YOUNG's collection of 1981. YOFFE collected extracts from contemporary newspaper accounts as well as Tchaikovsky's diaries and letters to illustrate the composer's visit to America in 1891 for the opening of Carnegie Hall. This is an interesting psychological portrait of Tchaikovsky during the last three years of his life. Yoffe reveals a man of great passion who, despite feeling homesick, was flattered by the attention and acclaim of his hosts and intrigued by the American way of life. Yoffe's own text is sparse in this mostly documentary account.

As a documentary account, the collaboration of BOWER AND VON MECK (grand-daughter to Nadeshda von Meck) fails on a number of points. First, it includes only a quarter of Tchaikovsky's letters to his benefactress, in which all revelations of intimacy have been cut out. Second, not one letter from Nadeshda to Tchaikovsky has been included. Third, the volume is coloured by excessive anachronistic narrative and family anecdote. This can only be recommended as a light, historical account.

—L. J. Maxwell-Stewart

TEILHARD DE CHARDIN, Pierre, 1881–1955; French Jesuit philosopher and paleontologist.

Barbour, George B., *In the Field with Teilhard de Chardin.* New York, Herder, 1965.

Cristiani, Léon (Nicolas Corte), *Pierre Teilhard de Chardin: His Life and Spirit*, translated by Martin Jarrett-Kerr. New York, Macmillan, and London, Barrie and Rockliff, 1960.

Cuénot, Claude, *Teilhard de Chardin: A Biographical Study*, translated by Vincent Colimore. Baltimore, Maryland, Helicon, and London, Burns and Oates, 1965 (originally published by Éditions du Seuil, Paris, 1962).

De Terra, Helmut, *Memories of Teilhard de Chardin.* New York, Harper, and London, Collins, 1964.

Grenet, Paul, *Teilhard de Chardin: The Man and His Theories*, translated by R. A. Rudorff. New York, Paul S. Eriksson, 1961; London, Souvenir Press, 1965.

Grim, John and Mary Grim, *Teilhard de Chardin: A Short Biography.* Chambersburg, Pennsylvania, Anima Books, 1984.

Lubac, Henri de, *Teilhard de Chardin: The Man and His Meaning*, translated by René Hague. New York, Hawthorne Books, and London, Burns and Oates, 1965 (originally published as *La Prière de Père Teilhard de Chardin*, Paris, Fayard, 1964).

Lukas, Mary and Ellen Lukas, *Teilhard: A Biography.* London, Collins, and New York, Doubleday, 1977.

Raven, Charles E., *Teilhard de Chardin: Scientist and Seer.* New York, Harper, and London, Collins, 1962.

Speaight, Robert, *The Life of Teilhard de Chardin.* New York, Harper, 1967.

*

By the time of his death, Teilhard's reputation as a scientist was considerable. His Legion of Honor citation claimed that "in the realm of paleontology and geology he may be considered one of the glories of France." Throughout his life he had been developing a theory of cosmic evolution in essays he circulated to friends in mimeographed form because of Vatican disapproval of his ideas. Posthumous publication of his *chef d'oeuvre*, *Le phénomène humain* (1955; as *The Phenomenon of Man*, 1960) revealed his challenging vision of teleological evolution and generated enormous interest in his life history. The appearance over two decades of 13 volumes of theoretical and autobiographical pieces as well as several collections of his letters afforded an impressive resource for biographers. Despite this interest and these resources, a truly critical and scholarly biography has not yet appeared. Even the best of the biographies now available are strongly apologetic.

CRISTIANI's was the first biography of any consequence available in English and is worth mentioning because it established the course followed by a number of subsequent authors of using a thin and episodic narrative of Teilhard's life as a skeleton to be fleshed out by a synthetic account of his thought. Cristiani's use of a pseudonym is one index to the difficulty Teilhard's early defenders had in brooking the Roman Catholic theological establishment, and his method of reviewing what others had said—pro and con—about *The Phenomenon of Man* by way of limiting his need to take a stand is another. RAVEN followed the same procedure of subordinating the life to the thought but wrote with more boldness since he was Anglican rather than Roman Catholic and was more thorough and insightful in regard to English critics of Teilhard. Similar in construction, both GRENET and LUBAC show how quickly it became possible to approve of Teilhard's life work. Lubac is especially useful because he, himself a Jesuit and a brilliant theologian, had long been not only a friend and admirer of Teilhard but had been asked by Teilhard to provide a critique of his ideas and suggestions for textual alterations that would make them more palatable to ecclesiastical authorities.

The most comprehensive and consequential biography of Teilhard yet to appear is by CUÉNOT. A close personal friend and admirer of Teilhard, Cuénot was one of the coterie entrusted with Teilhard's unpublished works and personal papers. Surprisingly, his book conveys little of the day-to-day habits and personal characteristics of its subject and is especially unhelpful about the details of Teilhard's troubled relationship with theological authorities in Rome. Instead, Cuenot assembled an extensive and careful chronology of Teilhard's deeds, works, and travels as well as a strong account of the correlation between his life circumstances and his intellectual work interlarded with revealing quotations from letters and autobiographical statements. Tinged with a sense of awe that forecloses any rigorous critique, it nonetheless remains the indispensable biography. Similarly worshipful in tone, undocumented, and written in journalese, LUKAS complements Cuénot by addressing the things Cuénot most neglected: Teilhard's charm, his friendships, and the politics of his relationships with his Jesuit superiors and other Church authorities.

The best biography for general readers is SPEAIGHT, a singularly well-informed book by an author thoroughly familiar with the intellectual cross-currents of European Catholicism who also wrote biographies of Georges Bernanos, Eric Gill, François Mauriac, and Ronald Knox. Less ambitious than Cuénot, more attuned to biography and less to exposition of Teilhard's ideas, it is ideal for the non-specialist. Those needing only a brief overview of Teilhard's life will find GRIM sufficient.

Some reminiscences by friends are useful in rounding out the portrait of Teilhard the man and scientist. DE TERRA, a German geologist, met Teilhard in 1933, maintained a lifelong friendship with him, and invited Teilhard to visit his research sites in Southeast Asia. His portrait of a sympathetic friend and gifted scientist lacks insight into Teilhard's religious mysticism and worldview. The same is true of the brief memoir by BARBOUR, a Scottish geologist who worked with Teilhard in China.

—Joseph M. McCarthy

TENNYSON, Alfred, Lord, 1809–1892; English poet.

Fausset, Hugh I'Anson, *Tennyson: A Modern Portrait*. New York, Appleton, and London, Selwyn and Blount, 1923.

Martin, Robert B., *Tennyson: The Unquiet Heart*. Oxford, Clarendon Press, and New York, Oxford University Press, 1980.

Nicolson, Harold, *Tennyson: Aspects of His Life, Character, and Poetry*. Boston, Houghton Mifflin, and London, Constable, 1923.

Richardson, Joanna, *The Pre-eminent Victorian: A Study of Tennyson*. London, Cape, 1962.

Ricks, Christopher, *Tennyson: A Biographical and Critical Study*. Berkeley, University of California Press, and London, Macmillan, 1972; revised edition, 1989.

Tennyson, Charles, *Alfred Tennyson*. London and New York, Macmillan, 1949.

Tennyson, Hallam Tennyson, Baron, *Alfred Lord Tennyson: A Memoir by His Son* (2 vols.). London and New York, Macmillan, 1897.

*

It is inevitable that Tennyson, who dominated his age as has no poet before or since, should be the subject of so many biographies; inevitable, too, that these biographies both trace and affect the continuing reassessment of his place in English literature. Long before his death in 1892, he had become a legendary figure for Victorian England, accorded a reverence only slightly less than Victoria's in the public mind. His first biographer, his son, HALLAM TENNYSON, following Tennyson's wishes, constructed a two-volume *Memoir* designed to perpetuate his Laureate image. With the self-effacement that typified his relationship with his father, Hallam organized the *Memoir* around letters to and from Tennyson, as well as reminiscences he solicited from Tennyson's wide circle of friends and acquaintances, keeping his own connecting commentary as brief as possible on the principle that Tennyson and his friends could speak best for themselves. As a result, the *Memoir* remains the single richest published repository of biographical documents on Tennyson.

It must be used with care, however. Tennyson dreaded the thought of his private life brought to public view, and Hallam suppressed important aspects of his father's life before 1850, when he was named Poet Laureate. Hallam and his mother, Emily, Lady Tennyson, examined 40,000 documents, selecting and carefully editing materials, then burning about three-fourths of them, including Tennyson's letters from Arthur Henry Hallam, the great friend of his Cambridge years whose early death haunted Tennyson his entire life. (Hallam's father also burned Tennyson's letters to Hallam.) The *Memoir* is thinly disguised hagiography, stressing aspects of Tennyson dear to his reading public: his wide ranging knowledge, his religious convictions, his technical perfection, his sense of public responsibility, his concern with political and social issues, and the respect and friendship of the great men and women of his time. It minimizes internal conflicts, early family problems, and frustrations about his art before the public success of *In Memoriam* (his elegy for Arthur Henry Hallam) and the Laureateship.

By the 1920s Tennyson, along with Victorian England, was in eclipse. Reasons are not far to seek. The most obvious, world war, along with revolutions in modern art, led to a repudiation of the Empire, and of the poet who had been its primary voice, and whose art virtually defined Victorianism. FAUSSET's and NICOLSON's biographies, both appearing in 1923, are the first to make claims for Tennyson's poetry in light of post-Victorian ideas about the nature and function of art, and both use the same strategy. They attempt to demonstrate that Tennyson's poetry arises directly out of his life, and they contend that what is lasting in Tennyson must be carefully disentangled from those aspects of his poetry that appealed so powerfully to his reliance on Hallam's *Memoir* for their limited information about Tennyson's formative years. The second, with somewhat different emphases in each biography, isolates a lyric, subjective poetry from the poetry of public statement, and asserts that all too frequently Tennyson was misled by the pressures of his time into a betrayal of his lyric gifts. Such a division is of more interest now as a record of shifting aesthetic priorities during the early 20th century than it is as a lasting and reasoned assessment of Tennyson's art.

In terms of influence on Tennyson's reputation, Nicolson's biography is the more important. In fact, none of the major subsequent biographies engages Fausset, while all, explicitly or implicitly, respond to Nicolson's evaluation of Tennyson's poetry. Nicolson is largely responsible for the creation of the "two voices" of Tennyson: the Laureate voice of public responsibility, speaking to religious, political, scientific, socio-economic, and patriotic issues; and the lyric voice of "pure" poetry. Thus, for instance, Marshall McLuhan ends his introduction to *Alfred Lord Tennyson: Selected Poetry* (1961), a collection aimed at the college market, with a reprise of Nicolson: "The Victorians were enthusiastic about a mainly nonexistent Tennyson who had sold his artistic soul for a pot of message. We are free to discover the Tennyson who Hallam was assured had surpassed Shelley and Keats in the sophisticated art of impressionism."

The first biography to make use of important source materials not in the *Memoir* is Sir CHARLES TENNYSON's *Alfred Tennyson*. As the poet's grandson, he is understandably discreet in his treatment of Tennyson, but it is his biography that introduces materials relating to difficulties in Tennyson's early years: psychological, family, and economic problems resulting from Tennyson's father's being disinherited in favor of his younger brother, more detailed information about the "ten year's silence" from 1832 to 1842, years in which Tennyson, stunned by Hallam's death, and stung by harsh reviews of his *Poems* (1833), refused to publish, and material about Tennyson's relations with his various publishers, and his earnings. Sir Charles' aim is to construct a narrative of Tennyson's life that fills in gaps in Hallam's *Memoir*, and while there is some attempt to bring biographical information to his discussion of the poetry, his analysis of Tennyson's art is restrained, as is his treatment of Tennyson in relation to his historical period. As a detailed narrative of Tennyson's life, however, it remains essential.

RICHARDSON's is the first biography that attempts to see Tennyson as representative and symbol of his age. Against recent scholarship that brings more sophisticated historical, cultural, and literary methodology to bear on the period, her treatment both of Tennyson and Victorianism seems dated. She does, however, attempt to lay to rest the ghost of Nicolson's two-voiced poet whose lyric gifts were compromised by his commitment to Victorian ideology, and she insists that Tennyson's Victorianism was not a cultural graft but a characteristic part of his identity. While her aim is laudable, her work suffers from her committed advocacy for an era she feels has been unjustly dismissed.

RICKS' *Tennyson* is the logical offshoot of his edition of Tennyson's complete poems for Longman (1969, revised 1987). It is

the first important critical biography since Nicolson, and is informed both by Ricks' intimate knowledge of Tennyson's poems in their manuscript and printed variants, and by biographical materials unavailable to earlier biographers. Moreover, Ricks' reading of the poems is acute, close, and sensitive, and while it makes no overt use of current critical theory, it is responsive to texts as complex negotiations between self and society, and between the poet and his received tradition. Ricks assumes that the formative years for Tennyson's personality and poetry were the years before the Laureateship, and that his later career is primarily a refinement—sometimes a vulgarization—of his earlier poetic tendencies, and occasionally a coming to terms with traumatic issues from his past. He reads *Maud* (1855), for instance, as Tennyson's effort to exorcise his father, the taint of inherited madness, his frustration in his engagement to Emily Sellwood by her family's rejection of him as unsuitable, and family tensions caused by his grandfather and his parvenu uncle Charles, while he is careful to underline Tennyson's technical skills in constructing a narrative made up of individual lyric poems. For readers primarily interested in the relationship between poetry and biography, Ricks remains the soundest and the most readable.

At present, the standard biography is by MARTIN. Benefitting from materials not included in Sir Charles' biography, and unhampered by his familial reticence, it is the most detailed, as well as the most searching life of the poet. Like Sir Charles, Martin concentrates much of his attention on the pre-Laureate Tennyson, although he gives detailed and full space to the years of fame. His discussion is supported by medical and psychiatric research in an effort to understand in contemporary terms the severe behavioral symptoms of Tennyson's father, and to account for Tennyson's obsessive concern with his own mental and physical health before 1850. Martin also deals directly with Tennyson's sexuality, an important question in recent studies of Tennyson because *In Memoriam*, the longest elegy in English, commemorates an intimate male friend. He concludes that Tennyson was not prompted by strong heterosexual or homosexual urges, not because he was an inhibited Victorian prude (although Tennyson had a prudish streak), but because it was not his nature.

Martin is also much more frank than Sir Charles in his willingness to expose negative aspects of Tennyson's personality: his intense concern with financial matters in regard to publication, his selfishness and egotism, which sometimes caused him to take friends too much for granted, a strain of the parvenu obvious in the Gothic bad taste of his second home, Aldworth, and ironic in light of his scorn for the Victorian Gothic castle of his arriviste uncle, Charles, and his need for adulation. What other biographers have passed over as the acceptable eccentricities of poetic genius, Martin treats as the evidence of a prickly and difficult, if sometimes lovable, man. Until new primary source material is found, Martin's biography will continue to give the fullest portrait of Tennyson.

—James L. Hill

TERESA OF AVILA, Saint, 1515–1582; Spanish Carmelite and mystic.

Clissold, Stephen, *St. Teresa of Avila.* London, Sheldon Press, 1979.

Lincoln, Victoria, *Teresa: A Woman.* Albany, State University of New York Press, 1984.

Papasogli, Giorgio, *St. Teresa of Avila,* translated by G. Anzilotti. New York, Society of Saint Paul, 1959.

Walsh, William Thomas, *St. Teresa of Avila: A Biography.* Milwaukee, Bruce Publishing, 1943.

*

There is no shortage of hagiographies on the life of St. Teresa of Avila. Written in numerous languages as part of the large cult of devotion that has sprung up over the years, these accounts are often scanty, exaggerated, and naive, while others follow a long established and highly sophisticated Catholic hagiographic tradition. Of St. Teresa of Avila, also known as Teresa of Jesus, one of the most important figures of 16th-century Spain, there are surprisingly few true biographies.

One of the most extensive biographies of St. Teresa was written by PAPASOGLI, an Italian Catholic whose treatment of the saint is somewhat romantic. Preferred by the Catholic hierarchy as it carries the imprimatur of Francis Cardinal Spellman, Archibishop of New York, Papasogli's biography contains an excellent section about the stages of spiritual maturation outlined by St. Teresa in *The Mansions of the Interior Castle.* He stresses her extensive work in the founding of new Carmelite convents throughout Spain, her practices of self-moritifcation, her many profound religious ecstasies, and the final crowning experience of a spiritual marriage to Christ. Papasogli notes the extraordinary early canonization of Teresa: a mere ten years after her death the necessary papers were collected for introducing her cause in Rome; in 1614, 32 years following her death, Teresa of Avila was beatified, then canonized eight years later in 1622. The author omits the elaborate and bizarre struggle that ensued among different factions over her relics.

An older, more scholarly, biography was written by WALSH. This best-selling version of St. Teresa's life is the finest treatment available, even today. It is well written, thorough, comprehensive, and critical. Unlike the Papasogli volume that borders on hagiography, Walsh has written a penetrating biography based on St. Teresa's letters, treatises, and the depositions of witnesses for her beatification and canonization. The volume is very long (nearly 600 pages) yet provides an excellent historical context that helps the contemporary reader to comprehend the complex world in which Teresa's mysticism flowered. Walsh stresses the tests of Teresa's visions, her trials under the scrutiny of the Spanish Inquisition, and the important influence of St. Teresa as a reformer of the Carmelite holy order. He insists that the lives of saints must not be concealed or glossed over by biographers, and argues that the weaknesses and faults of the saints improve people's ability to identify with them as models.

CLISSOLD's more recent biography, briefer and less scholarly than Walsh's, treats the life of St. Teresa in a straightforward story fashion, offering little analytical insight. The general tone of Clissold reflects the late 20th-century psychological approach to biography: Teresa is considered in terms of her personal motivations, her family background, and her psychological needs. Unfortunately the author does not probe deeply enough to render a satisfactory study of Teresa. Clissold explores the agony and ecstasy of Teresa's powerful mystical life, with its often burdensome and embarrasing instances of levitation, spiritual ecstasies similar to drunkenness, visions, and locutions. All of these religious expressions reached complete closure with Teresa's famous mystical marriage to Christ. One of the most interesting contributions of this volume is its final chapter, which discusses some of the more curious aspects associated with Teresa's relics. Not only was one of her arms removed, but by the middle of the eighteenth century '' . . . the right foot, the left eye, part of the upper jaw and much of the neck had gone. The head had been severed and several of the ribs and other bones and pieces of flesh had been ripped out, and the heart also.''

The most remarkable biography was written by LINCOLN, a novelist, scholar, and feminist. This volume, unique in that it is neither hagiography nor pure biography, is written like a novel based on the life of Teresa of Avila. Lincoln is critical of earlier, usually antiseptic, lives of the saints, and this revisionist view of St. Teresa portrays her as a semi-liberated woman. Lincoln's life of Teresa is a well-written and moving document. Although it provides a human view of the saint, it is neither vulgar nor deliberately iconoclastic. Indeed, the exploration of Teresa's humanity only serves to deepen an understanding of her extraordinary spirituality.

The recent biographies of St. Teresa of Avila reveal a new way of perceiving the lives of saints. While saints remain models of high spiritual achievement, modern readers require insights into both their weaknesses and strengths. Recent research on the life of St. Teresa reveals several qualities that were either missing from or deliberately left out of previous biographies; that Teresa had a Jewish background in her famly and that she was not a virgin were discovered only recently. Today these points can only enhance rather than prejudice perceptions of her. While the new biographies place the heroic virtues of saints within the larger context of their human failings, a truly penetrating contemporary biography of St. Teresa has yet to be written.

—James J. Preston

TERESA, Mother. See **MOTHER TERESA.**

THACKERAY, William Makepeace, 1811–1863; English writer.

Carey, John, *Thackeray: Prodigal Genius.* London, Faber, 1977.

Monsarrat, Ann, *An Uneasy Victorian: Thackeray the Man 1811–63.* London, Cassell, and New York, Dodd Mead, 1980.

Peters, Catherine, *Thackeray's Universe: Shifting Worlds of Imagination and Reality*. London, Faber, and New York, Oxford University Press, 1987.

Ray, Gordon N., *The Buried Life: A Study of the Relation between Thackeray's Fiction and His Personal History*. London, Oxford University Press, 1952; Cambridge, Massachusetts, Harvard University Press, 1982.

Ray, Gordon N., *Thackeray* (2 vols.). London, Oxford University Press, and New York, McGraw-Hill, 1955–58.

Stevenson, Lionel, *The Showman of Vanity Fair: The Life of William Makepeace Thackeray*. London, Chapman and Hall, and New York, Scribner, 1947; revised edition, New York, Russell, 1968.

*

RAY's authoritative and authorised two-volume biography (1955–58) encompasses much earlier work, including his own *The Buried Life* (1952), which investigates Thackeray's life in relation to his work, with more emphasis on the latter, though providing useful insights into the former. For that earlier book Ray had used his own edition of Thackeray's life and writings, *Letters and Private Papers* (4 vols., 1945–46); in the intervening years he had found 700 letters written by the author, mainly to his publishers, Bradbury and Evans, and George Smith, to Eyre Evans Crowe and Sir Jonathan Frederick Pollock. Ray also uses the Brookfield papers, 250 letters, including exchanges between Thackeray's mother, aunts, and grandmother about life in India, and the reminiscences of his daughter, Lady Ritchie. Henry Silvers' manuscript diary of conversations at the Punch table, 1858–70, provides journalistic information. The first volume of this biography has as its subject the "unfurnished man," the second "the furnished man." Ray quotes Carlyle's aphorism "For one man who can stand prosperity, there are a hundred that will stand adversity," and analyses Thackeray's reaction to that challenge. Volume I contains evidence for attribution of articles to Thackeray and relates Thackeray's ways of regarding fashionable life in fiction, eschewing the "serious" evangelical approach, in which the reprehensible upper classes are "terrible examples," and the approach of extreme radicals, who drew their villains from the peerage and their heroes from the hardworking lower classes, and likewise that of the actual or would-be fashionable themselves, to whom "high life" offered the culminating pleasures of existence. Thackeray avoided these and displayed the glamour of fashionable life within its own frame, suggesting "the doubts which occur to the thoughtful onlooker once fashionable life is viewed in a larger context." Ray shows Thackeray as at once part of the fashionable life and detached from it. *Cornhill Magazine* enabled Thackeray to present his ideal of the "middle class gentleman" to a far wider and more influential audience than had his earlier work, states Ray in Volume II; he dismisses the legend that Thackeray was merely "devoted to society" after *Vanity Fair*, and "indifferent to former familiars." Thackeray however felt himself at home in upper class society and with success was returning to it "after 15 years of exile." Ray assembles a detailed and revealing picture of Thackeray's character and way of life, his formality and high spirits, during this period.

CAREY uses Ray's edition of the *Letters and Private Papers*, and Ray's two volumes, with the life somewhat less predominant than the novels. He gives a good indication of Thackeray's interests—food, drink, "commodities," theatre—along with a vivid account of Thackeray's social surroundings, his background, and the context in which he worked. His principal argument is that the work is not as variable as has been thought, with *Vanity Fair* not very different from the other novels. He considers that "The emphasis should be on Thackeray's personality, for it is enduringly appealing, and permeates all his best work."

MONSARRAT, in racy, conversational, narrative style, uses the Biographical Introductions written by Lady Ritchie (Thackeray's daughter Anne), Mrs. Brookfield's collection of Thackeray's letters, Anthony Trollope's *Thackeray* (1912), and *The Life of William Thackeray*, by Herman Merivale and Frank T. Marzials (1891). She is informative on Thackeray's publishing history, his contracts, articles for Punch and other magazines; she also devotes attention to Thackeray's social class.

The second version of STEVENSON's biography includes alterations made after reading Ray's four-volume edition of the *Letters and Private Papers of William Makepeace Thackeray* (1945–46) and his two-volume biography of Thackeray. Stevenson presents a very human Thackeray, first as "the waif from India," far from his mother, with evidence of his childhood letters, involved in family and literary squabbles. He too asks the question, "can authors be gentleman?" and is excellent on the details of Thackeray's journalism, as well as his publishing and financial affairs.

To PETERS, who also owes much to Ray, there is no schism between the writer and the work: "To Thackeray the modern idea that a text should, or even could, be studied without reference to its author would have been inconceivable." Peters tries to keep a balance, to identify raw materials without suggesting that each novel is a "covert autobiography." She defies the notion of Thackeray as "one of the great unread, unreadable monuments of 19th-century fiction—a view still widely held in spite of the scholarly rescue of Gordon Ray, Robert Colby, . . . [and] John Carey." Colby's work (*Thackeray's Canvass of Humanity: An Author and His Public*, 1979) focuses on the work rather than on the life.

—Barbara Hayley

THATCHER, Margaret (Hilda), 1925–   ; English prime minister.

Abse, Leo, *Margaret, Daughter of Beatrice: A Politician's Psycho-Biography of Margaret Thatcher*. London, Cape, 1989.

Arnold, Bruce, *Margaret Thatcher: A Study in Power*. London, Hamilton, 1984.

Harris, Kenneth, *Thatcher*. London, Weidenfeld and Nicolson, and Boston, Little Brown, 1988.

Lewis, Russell, *Margaret Thatcher: A Personal and Political Biography*. London and Boston, Routledge, 1984.

Young, Hugo, *One of Us: A Biography of Margaret Thatcher.* London, Macmillan, 1989.

*

All extant biographies of Margaret Thatcher are inevitably incomplete, so further "updated" biographies are likely while she remains on the scene. The assessments hereunder relate only to biographies available by early 1990, roughly the midpoint of her third administration.

LEWIS' biography is an exaltation of her political genius. Lewis, a former Director of the Conservative Political Centre, shares similarly modest origins and is of Thatcher's generation. An early convert to her "new Toryism," his work is as damning about her displaced Conservative rivals (the "wets") as it is about her opponents. Chronological and factual, Lewis provides scant critical insight into her personality or philosophy. He tends to be assertive rather than analytical, in the style of Thatcherite "conviction politics." Racily readable though poorly edited, this biography conveys the viewpoint of a true believer.

By contrast ARNOLD eschews chronology. Instead he analyzes his subject's behaviour in specific situations and seeks to discriminate between the reality and appearance of her political achievements. Emphatically not "one of us," Arnold portrays her as consistent chiefly in her rhetoric and relentless pursuit of power. Whilst admiring her political skills and determination ("the raw materials of greatness") he asserts that her "consistent certainty" is seriously flawed, confusing subjective personal judgement with moral righteousness. In a challenging but contentious final chapter he draws an Orwellian picture of authoritarianism in the ascendant. This is a well-researched and provocative analysis, the precise converse of Lewis' hagiography.

HARRIS seeks to put Thatcherism into the perspective of a wider time-span, comparing her with Atlee in making a clear philosophical break with hitherto accepted policies, her aim being to reverse those changes introduced in 1945–51 and subsequently subsumed into consensus "Butskillite" soft politics. He sees her as "aggressive, challenging and radical." She was a "dissident outsider" in the context of traditional Tory paternalism who became leader in succession to Heath more by accident than design. (The late decision of Keith Joseph to stand aside, and of Whitelaw not to contest the first ballot, presented her with an unexpected opportunity she was swift to seize.) Harris sees her 1983 re-election as the key to her subsequent political mastery; she had overcome party disharmony and poor economic performance to become the strongest British party leader of modern times, rewarded by a third victory in 1987. Harris' final chapter somewhat prematurely eulogises what appeared then (1988) to be her triumphant economic success: events since have cast doubt on this judgement. Nonetheless this biography conveys the authority, assertiveness, and vigour of her political reformation.

YOUNG provides the most thorough and detailed coverage of Thatcherite development up to her third election victory (1987). His own left-of-centre bias gives a critical edge to his assessment, though he is even more unsparing than other biographers of her rivals.

Like Harris, Young portrays Thatcher as an outsider or anti-establishment figure, and in her first years as a leader not infre-

quently isolated by conviction and stark radicalism from much of her cabinet. Like Arnold he sees her as developing into an ideologue of dictatorial temperament, gradually displacing those colleagues she inherited from Heath: only three of the major party figures of 1976 survived in her Government by 1988. Young gives a convincing account of her distrust of the Civil Service mandarins—except for an inner circle within her Downing Street domain—and her distaste for the Foreign Office, the Church establishment, and the intellectual "chatterers." All of these she sees as lacking in conviction and determination characteristic of the debilitating effect of consensus politics. Young offers an extremely illuminating account of the Westland affair and her disposal of Heseltine's challenge to her authority. Young uses the Nassau Commonwealth Conference of 1985 to illustrate what he regards as her narrow but fierce nationalism. This is probably the most incisive albeit critical biography to date.

The former Labour M.P. Leo ABSE calls his avowedly antipathetic study "A politician's psychobiography." It thus belongs to a different genre from the "straight" biographies already mentioned. Abse defines Mrs. Thatcher as the unwitting but compulsively hyperactive victim of a sense of maternal alienation, suffering since childhood from unconscious phallic deprivation and still unreconciled to the dictates of her female chromosomes. Although lacking formal qualifications in clinical psychology (Abse is a lawyer), this is not his first essay into the psychology of politicians. Given his political stance, he lacks clinical detachment but provides novel interpretations of Thatcherite attitudes ranging from her allegedly uneasy relationship with the Queen to her patronage of "the Finchley Jews" (Abse is himself Jewish, but coming from a Welsh Labour stronghold dislikes the nouveau-riche metropolitan variety). A fascinating forensic examination that certainly challenges the uncritical adulation of the "true believers," though falling far short of the target proclaimed in the cover blurb: that of destroying the Thatcher myth.

—D. H. O'Leary

THOMAS AQUINAS. See AQUINAS, Saint Thomas.

THOMAS À BECKET, Saint, *ca.* 1118–1170; English martyr, archbishop of Canterbury.

Barlow, Frank, *Thomas Becket.* London, Weidenfeld and Nicolson, and Berkeley, University of California Press, 1986.
Knowles, David, *Thomas Becket.* London, A. and C. Black, 1970; Stanford, California, Stanford University Press, 1971.
Speaight, Robert, *Thomas Becket.* London and New York, Longman, 1938.
Winston, Richard, *Thomas Becket.* New York, Knopf, and London, Constable, 1967.

*

Immediately following Thomas à Becket's death, a spate of hagiographical and often inaccurate and hazy biographies were written about him. These focused almost exclusively on his exciting murder. The contemporary Latin *Lives*, which were written mostly by men who knew the archbishop, can be found in *Materials for the History of Thomas Becket, Archbishop of Canterbury*, edited by J. C. Robertson (1875–85). Among the contemporaries who wrote about Becket were John of Salisbury, Edward Grim, Anonymous II, Benedict of Peterborough, William of Canterbury, William fitzStephen, Anonymous I, Alan of Tewkesbury, Herbert of Bosham, and Quadrilogus II. These biographies are described and translated into English in a selection by D. C. Douglas and G. W. Greenaway in *English Historical Documents II* (1953).

John of Salisbury, noted as a scholar and author, provides an eyewitness account to Becket's murder as does Edward Grim, although Grim's account is poorly organized and contains vague details. Anonymous II's life of Becket covers the period from approximately 1172–73 and contains pro-King overtones. Both Benedict of Peterborough and William of Canterbury published collections of miracles attributed to Becket. These collections were later used as documentation to justify Becket's sainthood. Benedict of Peterborough was an eyewitness to Becket's murder; William of Canterbury was present but only until the violence began, at which time he fled the cathedral. William fitzStephen provided a life which included Becket's time as royal chancellor, indicating that fitzStephen knew him since at least 1162. Additionally, fitzStephen is the first to draw upon the Gilbert Foliot collection of letters rather than the usual Canterbury archives. Anonymous I essentially repeated the information of previous accounts whereas Alan of Tewkesbury published Becket's letters with a *vita* prefaced at the beginning of the edition. Herbert of Bosham, a student of Peter Lombard and a theologian, wrote his history of Becket after most of his contemporaries (1184–86). Lastly, Quadrilogus II (1198–99) is a compilation by Elias of Evesham of the lives written by John of Salisbury, Benedict of Peterborough, William of Canterbury, Alan of Tewkesbury, and Herbert Bosham.

While scholars have examined many aspects both of the Becket controversy and of his times, biographies throughout the centuries have been few, and all of them depict Becket as either a saint or a villain. For a fairly neutral assessment, Kate Norgate's short account of Becket in the *Dictionary of National Biography* (1898) is especially useful for a quick synopsis of his life as is her section on Becket in *England under the Angevin Kings* (2 vols., London, 1887).

SPEAIGHT's work is based primarily on the Latin *Lives* and on several 19th-century biographies, such as J. A. Giles' *The Life and Letters of Thomas à Becket, now first gathered from the contemporary historians* (2 vols., London, 1846), W. H. Hutton's *St. Thomas of Canterbury* (London, 1889), and Father Morris' *The Life and Martyrdom of St. Thomas Becket* (London and New York, 1859). All of these works provided a pro-catholic bias, casting Becket as a saint, and ignore Becket's human characteristics. Speaight's work is also in this biased tradition but is at least generally readable and historically reliable.

WINSTON's work on Becket is among the first and most accurate of the 20th-century biographies. Winston also relied mostly upon 12th-century documents such as those found in the *Materials*, but he does not include the normative judgments made by his predecessors. Winston concludes that "the quality that stands out in Thomas was his devotion to duty, to the 'flock' that had been committed to his charge." Winston further argues that Becket's quick induction into sainthood was a result of the thousands of miracles attributed to him as well as the love people had for him throughout his life. His biography, although reliable as a history and providing some insight into the personality of Becket, lacks the acumen of works by Knowles and, later, Barlow (see below).

Published in the year of the 800th anniversary of the murder of Thomas à Becket, KNOWLES' biography is impressive in its detail, accuracy, and overall excellent scholarship. His life of Becket is set against the backdrop of 12th-century English politics, and he also provides an evaluation of modern research on the controversy between Becket and King Henry II. Most importantly, Knowles presents a balanced account of Becket, although ultimately he is a stalwart supporter of him. As he concludes his discussion on the death of Becket, Knowles writes "Archbishop Thomas, at that particular moment, and in the largely accidental circumstances that brought about his murder, died for the freedom of the spiritual authority of the Church, and he died declaring that he knew this and was willing to meet death in this cause."

BARLOW's is the most recent and scholarly account of the life of Thomas à Becket. He deliberately avoids treating the historical period and works to provide a narrative of Becket's life and personality. Carefully assessing all possible evidence, Barlow leads the reader to a better understanding of who Becket was. Unlike previous biographers, Barlow does not judge Becket as either a saint or a villain. As a result, Becket is seen as human, perhaps misguided, almost certainly self-centered, but also devoted and capable of great sacrifice. Barlow's rendering of Becket does not have the single-minded focus on the murder as did the accounts of Becket's contemporaries, nor does it pretend to understand the man at places where the sources are unclear. To date, the works by Barlow and Knowles remain the most scholarly and judicious accounts of Thomas à Becket's life.

—Kay Rogers

THOMAS, Dylan, 1914–1953; Welsh poet.

Ackerman, John, *Dylan Thomas: His Life and Work*. London and New York, Oxford University Press, 1964.

Ackerman, John, *Welsh Dylan*. Cardiff, J. Jones, 1979.

Brinnin, John Malcolm, *Dylan Thomas in America*. Boston, Little Brown, 1955; London, Dent, 1956.

Davies, James A., *Dylan Thomas's Places: A Biographical and Literary Guide*. Swansea, C. Davies, 1987.

Ferris, Paul, *Dylan Thomas*. London, Hodder and Stoughton, and New York, Dial, 1977.

Fitzgibbon, Constantine, *The Life of Dylan Thomas*. London, Dent, and Boston, Little Brown, 1965.

Gittins, Rob, *The Last Days of Dylan Thomas*. London, Macdonald, 1986.

Jones, Daniel, *My Friend Dylan Thomas*. London, Dent, and New York, Scribner, 1977.

Michaels, Sidney, *Dylan*. New York, Random House, and London, Deutsch, 1964.

Read, Bill, *The Days of Dylan Thomas*. New York, McGraw-Hill, and London, Weidenfeld and Nicolson, 1964.

Sinclair, Andrew, *Dylan Thomas: No Man More Magical*. New York, Holt, 1975; as *Dylan Thomas: Poet of His People*, London, M. Joseph, 1975.

Thomas, Caitlin, *Leftover Life to Kill*. London, Putnam, and Boston, Little Brown, 1957.

Thomas, Caitlin with George Tremlett, *Caitlin: A Warring Absence*. London, Secker and Warburg, 1986; as *Caitlin: Life with Dylan Thomas*, New York, Holt, 1987.

*

In a statement that she insisted be placed in BRINNIN, the first book-length biographical study of Dylan Thomas, Caitlin Thomas pointed to the need for a biography with "a longer and, I hope, deeper understanding of the changing man hidden inside the poet," and pledged herself to writing such a book. Brinnin, as host and organizer of Thomas' reading tours, was in a position to offer an eyewitness narrative of Thomas' time in America, but it was precisely in such circumstances that Thomas most thoroughly hid the man within the public persona of "the poet." Shy, distrustful, and ultimately bored among intellectuals on college campuses, Thomas' behavior in America was outrageous and tragically self-destructive, a complete dramatization of the figure of the Bohemian poet. Despite recognizing a "loneliness" in Thomas that he cannot reach, Brinnin does not offer the insight into the inner Thomas that his own professional skill as a critic of Thomas' poetry should have allowed. Instead he records every detail that he witnessed of Thomas' cross-country drunkenness and sexual posturing, producing in the process an unintentionally sensationalistic book that helped create the powerful Thomas legend that influenced the behavior of the next generation of poets.

In 1957, CAITLIN THOMAS made her first attempt at carrying out her pledge to reveal the man behind the public persona of the poet; but, as her title indicates, the focus is on her attempts to find a new life after her husband's death, and only the early chapters say much about Dylan Thomas. Nevertheless, despite her florid over-writing, she reveals personal traits of Thomas such as his intuitive quickness of mind, his impatience with wordy intellectual speculation, his need for quiet routine and for friends and family, especially when working, and his total dedication to the craft of poetry.

Throughout the 1960s the legend of Thomas grew, and his death in America came to represent the destruction of a poetic sensibility by American celebrity worship and exploitation. The dramatized biography by MICHAELS put this figure on the stage as played by Alec Guinness, in a play drawing on incidents recorded in the volumes by Brinnin and Caitlin Thomas. The play has considerable power, enhanced by frequent use of Thomas' poetry, but the dialogue no longer rings true, except of course when it is taken directly from Brinnin or Caitlin. Michaels would have needed access to more of Thomas' let-

ters than were yet available to get the speech of the private Dylan right.

ACKERMAN's first book (1964) now seems mistitled, because it is in fact a fine critical study but not a true biography. Ackerman wished to place Thomas in a Welsh context that would contribute to an understanding and appreciation of the poetry, and, the facts of the early life in Wales not then being well known, Ackerman had to set forth some version of the "life." One would not now turn to Ackerman's first book for biographical information. In 1979, Ackerman drew on the letters and other materials that had become available since Thomas' death more than 25 years earlier to write *Welsh Dylan*. This book succeeds in creating a useful context for the poetry and presents evidence that Thomas' inspiration by no means flagged toward the end of his short life. As with the first book, it is less important as biography than as criticism, but the photographs in the book are especially well chosen to provide visual images for readers of the poetry.

Based on interviews and correspondence with Thomas' friends, READ's short biography remains valuable. It emphasizes the professional life of Thomas—as poet, journalist, film writer, radio broadcaster—and presents without sensationalism both the Welsh and London aspects of Thomas' life. Read makes use of important and unique accounts of Thomas from such key individuals in Thomas' life as his political mentor, the socialist grocer Bert Trick. Finally, the photographs in the book, by Rollie McKenna and others, offer exceptional insight into the circumstances and flavor of the personal as well as the professional life.

FITZGIBBON's authorized biography was the first based on full access to the surviving materials, particularly the letters. Although Fitzgibbon is better at presenting the London context than the Welsh one—because London is where he was most closely associated with Thomas—this is a full portrait that reproduces many of the important letters at unusual length. Fitzgibbon is perhaps too much at pains to contradict the "roaring boy" legend that the visits to America created. He argues that Thomas was not an alcoholic, describes a relatively stable relationship with Caitlin, and shows a life of ordinary rather than outrageous incident.

With the appearance of Fitzgibbon, the outline of the life of Thomas and most of the details were firmly established, and no new book-length biography appeared for a decade. SINCLAIR's graceful but brief retelling of the life in 1975 uses the published sources and adds nothing new. It is, in fact, a picture book, more handsome than Read's and with arresting photographs that say much about both man and milieu. JONES is right to declare that his book is not a biography at all, lacking as it does any sustained narrative, but Jones' views on a subject like Thomas' drinking must be considered seriously by anyone attempting to decide whether to label him alcoholic. Jones' discussion of Thomas' dislike of writing that is self-consciously "literature" and his recognition that Thomas produced a counterfeit Dylan for the world confirm Caitlin's insights.

Impeccably researched, using every possible manuscript source and interviewing widely, FERRIS produces a sympathetic but not worshipful portrait that depicts the emergence of Thomas from a Welsh adolescence that never ceased to be an element in Thomas' behavior. The misbehaving Thomas is not denied, but

Thomas is less "roaring boy" than awkward youth with a need for admiration. Ferris integrates the autobiographical content of Thomas' short stories into the biography more skillfully than any other biographer. He is painstaking about footnoting and identifying all new material. Ferris is convincing in fixing the cause of Thomas' death on medical error rather than Thomas' own admittedly dangerous excesses. This is the indispensable biography. Ferris also edited Thomas's *Collected Letters* (London, Dent, 1985), which supersedes Fitzgibbon's *Selected Letters* (London, Dent, 1966). The letters can be read as an engrossing autobiography if one remains aware that Thomas creates several counterfeit Dylans here as he did in life.

GITTINS offers a probably unnecessary retelling of the last days of Thomas' life, working from published materials that include Brinnin and Ferris. Thomas the poet does not seem to interest Gittins, so the account is one of the least sympathetic even though there is a useful "Prologue" that establishes that Thomas was in flight from serious financial and personal problems on his last visit to America. Gittins tends to approach Thomas from the point of view of Liz Reitell, with whom Thomas had an affair, but he does not appear to have any new source of information, writing in a journalistic manner without any documentation. More valuable is DAVIES, who provides an account of Thomas' references to the places in his life with photographs of many of them: it offers an unusual geography of a life.

TREMLETT taped and edited 50 hours of interviews with CAITLIN THOMAS, thereby permitting Caitlin to escape the self-consciousness about style that marred her previous book. Ten years a recovering alcoholic in the Alcoholics Anonymous organization, Caitlin says that the role of alcohol in Thomas' life cannot be overemphasized. She tells an at times appalling tale of their life together, marked by physical violence that she most often initiated and in which she did the more severe damage. She does not hide her own infidelities, even when they now present her in an unflattering light. With her knowledge of Dylan's affair with Liz Reitell in New York, there is a note of bitterness throughout. Yet the private Dylan does emerge here, and one sees the pattern of life in Laugharne within which he was most contented and most productive. There was no intellectual relationship between Caitlin and Dylan, for that was not what Dylan sought, but the poetry itself, both in the process of its creation and in the act of reading it aloud, permeates this version of the life. It is not so full an account as Ferris', from which Caitlin herself learned facts new to her, but it is the necessary last word in the biography of Dylan Thomas.

—Victor N. Paananen

THOREAU, Henry David, 1817–1862; American writer.

Bazalgette, Léon, *Henry Thoreau, Bachelor of Nature*, translated by Van Wyck Brooks. New York, Harcourt, 1924; London, Cape, 1925 (originally published as *Henry Thoreau, Sauvage*, Paris, Reider, 1914).

Bridgman, Richard, *Dark Thoreau*. Lincoln, University of Nebraska Press, 1982.
Canby, Henry Seidel, *Thoreau*. Boston, Houghton Mifflin, 1939.
Channing, William Ellery, *Thoreau, the Poet-Naturalist*. Boston, Roberts, 1873; edited and enlarged by F. B. Sanborn, Boston, Goodspeed, 1902.
Derleth, August, *Concord Rebel: A Life of Henry David Thoreau*. Philadelphia, Chilton, 1962.
Harding, Walter R., *The Days of Henry Thoreau*. New York, Knopf, 1965.
Hough, Henry Beetle, *Thoreau of Walden*. New York, Simon and Schuster, 1956.
Lebeaux, Richard, *Young Man Thoreau*. Amherst, University of Massachusetts Press, 1977.
Salt, Henry S., *Life of Henry David Thoreau*. London, R. Bentley, 1890; revised edition, London, W. Scott, 1896.
Sanborn, Franklin B., *The Life of Henry David Thoreau*. Boston, Houghton Mifflin, 1917.
Schneider, Richard J., *Henry David Thoreau*. Boston, Twayne, 1987.

*

Recognition came slowly to Thoreau, in part because only *A Week on the Concord and Merrimack Rivers* and *Walden* were published during his lifetime, together with some miscellaneous (often anonymous) poetry and prose. Most of the latter appeared in *The Dial*, a short-lived publication of very limited circulation. Even so, when Thoreau died, obituaries of him appeared in newspapers and magazines throughout New England and as far south as New York. Seven previously unpublished essays by him were featured in the *Atlantic Monthly* during the next two years. Similarly, no fewer than six posthumously reconstructed books—*Excursions in Field and Forest, The Maine Woods, Cape Cod, Letters to Various Persons, A Yankee in Canada,* and *Anti-Slavery and Reform Papers*—were in print by the end of 1866, having been edited by his sister Sophia, William Ellery Channing, and Ralph Waldo Emerson. Thoreau's immense journal, often considered his greatest achievement, appeared in various excerpted forms but not fully (or nearly so) until 1906, when a 20-volume *Works* appeared. Thoreau's reputation as a major American author was not securely established before then.

Emerson's obituary of Thoreau (1862), published first in the *Atlantic Monthly* and later in the *Excursions* volume, is still necessary reading. In writing it, Emerson used excerpts from Thoreau's as yet unpublished journals copied out by CHANNING. The latter combined intimate personal knowledge of Thoreau with access to his private writings to create his volume of reminiscences, parts of which were published in the newspaper *Boston Commonwealth* in 1864, the complete and revised version not appearing until 1873 (to be supplemented and reissued by F. B. Sanborn in 1902). Channing's book, not a conventional biography, is primarily thematic rather than narrative in organization. Chapters VIII and IX, moreover, are an incongruous later insertion, a fictitious dialogue among Channing, Emerson, and Thoreau supposedly intended to delineate Thoreau but actually meant to pad the book. Despite its shortcomings with regard to both substance and fact (Channing made no use of public records, for example), this first major discussion of Thoreau is invaluable for its insightful recollections, which are often expressed as anecdotes. Chapter II, ''Manners,'' includes an unforgettable characterization of Thoreau as a homely, etherial but alert eccentric. A number of his poems are also reprinted in passing.

The first real biography of Thoreau, by the British writer SALT, is primarily chronological in organization, but includes thematic chapters also. The revised version is notable for its significantly expanded section on Thoreau's parents and the history and geography of Concord. Musketaquid, we learn, means ''grass-ground'' river. Salt was also the first to emphasize a series of topics since accepted as central to Thoreau's development, including his Harvard education, his relationship with Ellen Sewall, the publishing opportunity afforded him by *The Dial*, his association with Emerson and Channing, and the influence of his brother, John. *Walden* and ''Civil Disobedience'' are seen to be at the center of Thoreau's reputation; when Thoreau went to jail for a night, his mother and aunts (not Emerson) paid the tax to get him out. Salt also considers Thoreau's relations with the issues of slavery and the Civil War. (The hut at Walden Pond was probably not a haven for runaway slaves, in part because few of them sought to reach Canada by that indirect way; the main route went through Ohio.) Salt rarely documents his facts, but he includes a valuable bibliography of 19th-century writings by and about Thoreau.

SANBORN, a long-time Thoreau scholar responsible for the 1902 edition of Channing's biography, did not quite live long enough to see his own life of Thoreau into print; the version that we have may not, therefore, represent his final intentions. On the whole, it is a less polished, less evenly balanced biography than Salt's, but does include significant new information—about Thoreau's French Huguenot ancestors and the family's pencil-making activities, for example. More significantly, Sanborn reprints a number of Thoreau's earliest essays (most of them college assignments), which give little hint of the stylistic mastery later to come. A catalog of Thoreau's library is here published for the first time. Though Sanborn had known Thoreau and his family personally, he is indebted to Channing for a number of facts and anecdotes. Attesting to the growth of Thoreau's fame and reputation, Sanborn notes that Thoreau's works were now being taught at schools and colleges throughout the United States and that his haunts in and near Concord were often described, photographed, and visited. Of all the Concord authors, he stated, only Louisa May Alcott was more often read.

BAZALGETTE's biography made some use of Thoreau's newly published journals but lacks proper bibliographic apparatus and is not fundamentally a work of scholarship; it even omits a table of contents. Written in a grandiose, heroic mode then popular among the French, Bazalgette's *Sauvage* is emotional, dramatic, and intended for a naive audience; it is not a reliable source of facts and has little to offer the readers of today.

CANBY's *Thoreau*, on the other hand, is both scholarly and readable, one of the two best biographies of Thoreau ever published. This attractive, well illustrated book is divided into two parts. Book One, ''Adventurer in Life,'' begins with Concord and the Thoreau family, then follows Henry from birth through the publication of *Walden* in 1854. Book Two, ''Naturalist and Nature Writer,'' considers his remaining years in a partly chro-

nological, partly thematic arrangement. A final chapter usefully discusses Thoreau's influence (on such figures as Tolstoy, Gandhi, and Yeats) and the growth of his reputation; originally the possession of a literary cult, he came to be recognized as of world class, perhaps the greatest of all poet-naturalists. Canby's notes are extensive, and he includes a very competent bibliography. As scholarship, the book is masterly throughout.

From his predecessors, Canby took whatever value they had to offer (and these debts are sometimes understated); he combines the vitality and color of Channing's anecdotes (for example) with the orderliness of Salt's less vivid approach. In addition, he was familiar with all of the major editions of Thoreau's works then available. Unlike any of his predecessors, Canby utilized extensive collections of still-unpublished Thoreau manuscripts at half a dozen research libraries and even some remaining in private hands. Unlike some of his predecessors, Canby never saw Thoreau in life. His methodology and his motives were therefore somewhat different.

From Canby we learn how Thoreau pronounced his name (Thorrow or Thorough); Canby then analyzes extensively Thoreau's relationship with Emerson (Thoreau may have been present at the ''American Scholar'' speech), posits an influence on Thoreau of Carlyle and *Sartor Resartus*, and examines what Thoreau gained (or sought) from his extensive reading in Oriental religious works. Canby also has some very interesting speculations about Thoreau (a lifelong bachelor) and his relations with women—not only Ellen Sewall, with whom he was obviously in love, but also and more surprisingly two older women, Lucy Jackson Brown and her sister, Lidian Jackson Emerson! The latter was, of course, Ralph Waldo Emerson's second wife, whom Thoreau served as man of the house on more than one occasion when Emerson himself was away for an extended period.

Perhaps Canby's most distinguished contribution to Thoreau studies is his two-part analysis of *Walden*, first as an episode in Thoreau's life and then as an eventually successful literary project. However strange or cranky Thoreau's withdrawal from human society may have seemed to his contemporaries, it was more in accord with Thoreau's Oriental reading than even Canby appreciates. Yet Thoreau was never so isolated while at his cabin as *Walden* itself would indicate. His mother and sisters came to see him at least once a week, for example, bringing a supply of baked goods with them. Male friends like Emerson and Channing were also frequent guests, the latter staying once for a week. Thoreau himself went regularly into town, often for meals, and even abandoned Walden Pond temporarily to roam as far away as Maine. *Walden* itself, Canby declares, ''was, and is, a book for anyone interested in how to live a good life and open to the appeals of wild nature, good books, good talk, provocative thinking, and the companionship of an interesting mind.'' Stressing self-reliance, the reduction of life to its essentials, the joy of peaceful labor, and a peculiarly idealistic form of traditional Yankee pragmatism, *Walden* is the very essence of Thoreau's benevolent message to humanity.

Since Canby, a number of popular lives of Thoreau have appeared. As introductions, they tend to be adequate but largely interchangeable. Among such books, one might note HOUGH, DERLETH, a popular Wisconsin author, and SCHNEIDER, whose book is intended primarily for students and includes a particularly useful bibliography. LEBEAUX's *Young Man Thoreau* stands somewhat apart from these, however, offering a behavioristic analysis of Thoreau from his birth to the death of his brother John in 1842. Another, earlier "analysis" of Thoreau's personality (seen as cold and pessimistic) was attempted by BRIDGMAN. Interesting as these alternative characterizations are, they have not been widely accepted.

At present, the standard biography of Thoreau is HARDING's. While fortunate to have had so able a predecessor as Canby, Harding collected an even greater store of knowledge; it came from the research libraries, newly discovered private sources, and an amazing deluge of scholarship that had appeared since 1939, made possible by an adequate biography and increasingly sophisticated editions of Thoreau's own works. Much of the new information Harding presents is fairly peripheral to Thoreau himself—often, the family history of his associates. But such depth gives his work considerable stability. Thus, Harding writes with an assurance scarcely available to any earlier Thoreau biographer.

Though occasionally reduced to conjecture himself, Harding is often critical of certain earlier interpretations, usually Canby's. He doubts, for example, that Thoreau stayed around at Harvard to hear Emerson's "American Scholar" address and does not endorse so extreme a version of Thoreau's undoubted attractions to the older Jackson sisters. Harding is also less emphatic (or perhaps less astute) regarding Carlyle and the Orient as influences. All in all, he probably understates Thoreau's oddity, both psychological and intellectual. Canby and Harding, therefore, need to be read together. But to appreciate his mind and personality there is still no alternative to reading Thoreau himself, especially in his journal.

—Dennis R. Dean

TINTORETTO [*born* Jacopo Robusti], 1518–1594; Italian painter.

Bell, Mrs. Arthur, *Tintoretto*. London, G. Newnes, and New York, F. Warne, 1905.

Bensusan, S. L., *Tintoretto*. London, T. C. and E. Jack, and New York, F. A. Stokes, 1908.

Holborn, J. B. Stoughton, *Jacopo Robusti, called Tintoretto*. London, G. Bell, 1903.

Newton, Eric, *Tintoretto*. London and New York, Longman, 1952.

Osler, W. Roscoe, *Tintoretto*. London, Low Marston, and New York, Scribner, 1879.

Osmaston, F. P. B., *The Art and Genius of Tintoret* (2 vols). London, C. Bell, 1915.

Phillipps, Evelyn March, *Tintoretto*. London, Methuen, 1911.

Ridolfi, Carlo, *Life of Tintoretto and of his Children, Domenico and Marietta*, translated by C. and R. Enggass. University Park, Pennsylvania State University Press, 1984 (originally published as *La Vita de G. Robusti detto il Tintoretto*, Venice, 1642).

Stearns, Frank Preston, *Life and Genius of Jacopo Robusti Called Tintoretto*. London and New York, Putnam, 1894.

Tietze, Hans, *Tintoretto*. London, Phaidon, and New York, Oxford University Press, 1948.

Vasari, Giorgio, *Lives of the Artists* (2 vols.), translated by George Bull. London and New York, Penguin, 1965 (originally published as *Le Vite de piu eccellenti architetti, pittori, et scultori Italiani*, Florence, 1550, 1568).

*

VASARI, so important as a biographer of Renaissance artists, virtually ignores Tintoretto, whose life merits only a brief summary contained in the "Life" of a Venetian contemporary Battista Franco (1498–1561). All biographies of Tintoretto thus depend on RIDOLFI's account of the artist's life written in 1642—the nearest we have in a contemporary account. Ridolfi was acquainted with Tintoretto's son Domenichino and would have known other friends of the artist, but his work, written half a century after Tintoretto's death, inevitably contains secondhand accounts of Tintoretto's life that would have acquired a certain gloss by this date. While Ridolfi, whose work has recently been translated, presents a relatively sound factual outline, details can be unreliable, and although his work is as close as we can get to Tintoretto in terms of character, we must be aware that Ridolfi's account is prone to bias, particularly in discussing Tintoretto's motivation and relationships with others. This trait is perhaps most evident in its references to Titian's supposed jealousy of the young artist, which is taken as fact by later biographers.

Tintoretto's first biographer in the English language, OSLER draws our attention to Ridolfi's weakness in this respect, but otherwise refers to him as a "careful and reliable authority." Osler's aim, stated in his preface, is to assist the Englishman in his study by presenting ideas from other European writers rather than making any judgements of his own. He thus relies heavily on Ridolfi and his other European sources, writing in a lyrical style in an attempt to create a Venetian atmosphere. The end result places too much emphasis on anecdote, without serious consideration of the admittedly scant source material available to him. In some instances his comments are extreme: Tintoretto's wife Faustina is described here as a "tyrant in her home." The concluding sentence of Osler's book perhaps best sums up the flavour of his writing: "Now the creative harmonies sound through the inner deep; and if they often recede far, yet the shimmer on the distant sounds is the sea; and the sea-echoes sing *art is wide*."

STEARNS' judgement of "Mr. Osler's little book" as "good so far as it goes" sets the somewhat condescending tone the author adopts with respect to his sources and precedents. While his intention to write a full and original account of Tintoretto is admirable, his work is marred by this superior approach and some factual inaccuracies. It is perhaps revealing that Stearn's book does not appear in the bibliographies of subsequent writers on Tintoretto. More valuable is HOLBORN's abridged version of what was originally to have been a more ambitious work. Bold claims are made here, and the issue of Tintoretto's premature departure from Titian's workshop is inadequately debated. However, Holborn is prepared to accept the essential importance of Ridolfi as our nearest-to-contemporary biographer of Tintoretto despite his inaccuracies and subjective approach in the absence of more conclusive evidence of his character and working methods.

Holborn's book is not improved on by the other two works on Tintoretto of this decade. Mrs. BELL, writing in 1905, is altogether too fulsome in her praise of the artist and fails to refer to the precise sources of her material. BENSUSAN's short text does contain some worthwhile observations but is of little practical use since few attempts are made here to date the artist's works.

Like Holborn, PHILLIPPS maintains that Tintoretto's personality can be traced through his works. Consequently much of her book is taken up by a survey of Tintoretto's paintings with only two strictly biographical chapters at the beginning of the volume. Unlike the Victorian biographers, Phillipps is prepared to consider her subject out of an heroic context. In her view, Tintoretto's was a "remarkably uneventful life, with none of the wanderings and vicissitudes that make such biographies as those of Michelangelo or Leonardo so picturesque." In general terms Phillipps makes a conscientious attempt to imagine Tintoretto's life in terms of its events in the context of their time, and while not all of her conclusions are based on documentary evidence, Tintoretto does, for the first time since Ridolfi, emerge with an identifiable personality.

OSMASTON, writing in 1915, still claims that there is "no authoritative or adequate English biography of Jacopo Robusti," although he does make some concessions to Phillipps. His own contribution consists of two volumes that are in fact predominantly devoted to art criticism with some biographical material. He sees Ridolfi's erroneous dating of Tintoretto's birth as evidence of his complete lack of authority and accuracy and views him merely as an "enthusiast for his subject." His own approach to Tintoretto's life is oddly contradictory. While he treats speculation in the face of insufficient documentary evidence with contempt, he himself continually includes quotations without reference, which damages his own credibility as a reliable authority.

TIETZE is also keen to base his account of Tintoretto on known fact, and he improves markedly on Osmaston by steering clear of anecdote and by acknowledging his sources. His conclusions are based on careful examination of the evidence before him. The result is reliable although short due to the lack of information about the artist. Most of the book is taken up with stylistic analysis and a catalogue of the artist's work.

NEWTON's book, written in 1952, bowing to the lack of documentary evidence on Tintoretto's life, hopes to place Tintoretto in the context of his own generation. His reading of Ridolfi is both careful and imaginative. He points out the dangers of viewing Tintoretto from the 20th century without proper consideration of his circumstances in his own time: Tintoretto's position after his dismissal from Titian's workshop is not equivalent to a modern art student denied a place at college. Newton perhaps oversteps the mark by claiming that Tintoretto was "the first self-made artist, the first of a race of inspired amateurs who are so familiar today." His book centres more on Tintoretto's artistic achievement in the context of the history of art than on Tintoretto the man. The artist remains something of an enigma, and in the face of the continued lack of documentary evidence no biography of Tintoretto has been published since.

—Alison Leslie

TITIAN [born Tiziano Vecellio], ca. 1488–1576; Italian painter.

Cecchi, Dario, Titian, translated by N. Wydenbruck. London, J. Calder, 1957; New York, Farrar Straus, 1958 (originally published as Tiziano, Milan, Longanesi, 1955).

Crowe, Joseph A. and G. B. Cavalcaselle, Titian: His Life and Times (2 vols.). London, J. Murray, 1877.

Gronau, Georg, Titian, translated by Alic M. Dodd. London, Duckworth, and New York, Scribner, 1904.

Hope, Charles, Titian. London, Jupiter Books, and New York, Harper, 1980.

Kennedy, Ruth Wedgewood, Novelty and Tradition in Titian's Art. Northampton, Massachusetts, Smith College, 1963.

Morassi, Antonio, Titian. Greenwich, Connecticut, New York Graphic Society, 1964.

Nash, Jane C., Veiled Images: Titian's Mythological Paintings for Philip II. Philadelphia, Art Alliance, and London, Associated University Presses, 1985.

Panofsky, Erwin, Problems in Titian, Mostly Iconographic. New York, New York University Press, 1969.

Phillips, Claude, The Earlier Work of Titian. London, Seeley, and New York, Macmillan, 1897.

Phillips, Claude, The Later Work of Titian. London, Seeley, and New York, Macmillan, 1898.

Pope, Arthur, Titian's "Rape of Europa." Cambridge, Massachusetts, Harvard University Press, 1960.

Riggs, Arthur Stanley, Titian the Magnificent and the Venice of His Day. Indianapolis, Bobbs-Merrill, 1946.

Rosand, David, Titian. New York, Abrams, 1978.

Rosand, David, Titian: His World and His Legacy. New York, Columbia University Press, 1982.

Skårsgård, Lars, Research and Reasoning: A Case Study on a Historical Inquiry: Titian's "Diana and Actaeon." Goteborg, Akademiforlaget, 1968.

Vasari, Giorgio, Lives of the Artists (2 vols.), translated by George Bull. London and New York, Penguin, 1965 (originally published as Le Vite de piu eccellenti architetti, pittori, et scultori Italiani, Florence, 1550, 1568).

Walker, John, Bellini and Titian at Ferrara. London, Phaidon Press, 1956.

Wethey, Harold, The Paintings of Titian (3 vols.). London, Phaidon Press, 1969–75.

*

Thanks to Titian's unusually long life and prestigious career, as well as his personal flare for self-promotion, we know more about this Venetian artist's life, work, and self-image than we do about most Renaissance masters. Biographical references in works by Dolce, Sansovino, Michiel, Tizianello, and Aretino give us glimpses of the master's life from his admiring contemporaries; unfortunately, however, these passages generally tend to be anecdotal and, one supposes, somewhat biased rather than scholarly or historical in their approaches.

This is also true even of the most important Renaissance biography of Titian, that found in VASARI's monumental Lives of the Artists. Vasari's book is our major source for knowledge of most Renaissance artists. In the case of Titian, Vasari had the advantage of dealing with a living contemporary whom he apparently had met personally, so in some respects the biography of Titian relies less on speculation and hearsay than do many of Vasari's biographies of earlier artists. At the same time, however, his biography of the Venetian master is colored by his own Florentine biases, which favored line over color, anatomical precision over sensuality, and accuracy over fantasy. Consequently, though recognizing Titian's importance as the major Venetian painter of his century, Vasari was also careful to point out what he regarded as the master's failings in relation to his own Florentine contemporaries, especially Michelangelo. This forms the basis for his most famous anecdote about the two masters: according to Vasari, he went once with Michelangelo to visit Titian while the Venetian was working in Rome. Although the two rivals were mutually complimentary in each other's company, Vasari relates that on the way home from the meeting Michelangelo remarked that it was a pity that the Venetians had never learned to draw and therefore could not achieve true artistic greatness.

Titian remained popular throughout the 17th, 18th, and 19th centuries, and therefore appears in the major surveys of those periods, particularly that by Ridolfi. On the whole, however, this writer merely repeats the information from Vasari's text. It was only in the later 19th century that a different approach was taken. In 1877 CROWE AND CAVALCASELLE set out to remedy what they saw as the largely anecdotal and semi-fictitious treatment of Titian's earlier biographers by publishing a massive two-volume scholarly text. These authors attempted for the first time to assemble and organize all the existing documents and correspondence relating to Titian's life and art in a chronological order. On the basis of these resources, they wrote a thoughtful, probing essay on Titian's life and production. Though their work is now, as one might expect, in some ways outdated, and although additional documents have been turned up since they published their text, Crowe and Cavalcaselle's work remains our leading biographical reference for Titian and an essential source for any scholar working on this artist. Their work far excels the other major but rather dry 19th-century biography of the artist by Northcote.

Perhaps in part because Crowe and Cavalcaselle did such a thorough job, the major 20th-century writers have focused more on scholarly analyses of Titian's works rather than biographical reviews. Those who have written biographies have for the most part merely rewritten Crowe and Cavalcaselle's text, abridging it or trying to make its style more readable. Typical of such efforts is RIGGS' volume, whose title alone gives an indication of Riggs' laudatory approach. In his foreword Riggs mourns that "Titian has been thus far neglected as a great human being. . ." —an evaluation of his character that, judging from much existing documentary evidence that Titian was avaricious and opportunistic, even the most fervent admirers of the Venetian's art might question.

If Riggs seems somewhat unscholarly in his enthusiasm to appeal to "non-technical minds of those many who recognize beauty but do not always analyze its expression," CECCHI is far more so. His biography of Titian is really an historical novel, kept lively through fast-moving dialogue, but only loosely based on the artist's actual life.

Indeed, to study Titian seriously, one must turn away from strict biographical texts to scholarly monographs that focus on his works but still give at least some insight into his biography as well. Until recently, most of these were written by German or Italian scholars, and many are still unavailable in English. In the last few decades, however, there have been a number of important contributions by American and English scholars to Titian scholarship. The most ambitious of these is WETHEY's three-volume treatment of Titian's work, with separate essays and catalogs devoted to his portraits, religious paintings, and mythological subjects. Though marred by occasional inaccuracies, Wethey's text is generally informative. The work's greatest value, however, is its catalog entries, which are among the most thorough ever devoted to the work of any artist. Other monographs on Titian available in English include those by GRONAU and MORASSI.

More recently, several important new books on Titian have appeared. HOPE's monograph is marked by the author's usual lively and original approach as well as his interest in demythologizing the artist by insisting upon simple interpretations for his works. His book also provides insight to aspects of Titian's life, especially his relations with his patrons. ROSAND, who is widely recognized today as the leading Titian scholar in the United States, has been responsible for two important works in recent years, a monograph on the artist, and a collection of essays by a group of international scholars who discuss in their work not only Titian himself, but also the world in which he lived and his influence on later artists. All three of these works should prove to be indispensable sources for future scholars.

During the past century a number of works focusing on a single period or even a single work in Titian's long career have also appeared. Included among these are two monographs by PHILLIPS on the earlier and later works of Titian, POPE's study of The Rape of Europa, and WALKER's discussion of the cycle of paintings created by Bellini and Titian in Ferrara for Alfonso d'Este. KENNEDY, in a series of lectures that were later published, traces Titian's use of antique sources in his art. More recently, SKÅRSGÅRD has produced a rather self-conscious look into his own methodology of art historical inquiry, but has offered disappointingly little convincing new material on the subject of his inquiry, Titian's Diana and Actaeon. NASH focuses on the group of mythological paintings Titian produced for Philip II of Spain. In the process she reexamines documents associated with the commission and offers new interpretations for the works. The most important and far-reaching of these concentrated studies, however, is PANOFSKY's Problems in Titian. This book, based on a series of lectures Panofsky delivered at the Metropolitan Museum of Art, includes five essays on Titian's paintings as well as seven shorter discussions of the artist. It serves as a marvelous example of Panofsky's important contributions to iconological studies. Though not strictly speaking biographies, works such as these are indispensable to any serious student of Titian's life and work.

—Jane Nash Maller

TITO, Marshal [born Josip Broz], 1892–1980; president of Yugoslavia.

Auty, Phyllis, *Tito: A Biography*. London, Longman, and New York, McGraw-Hill, 1970.

Bilainkin, George, *Tito*. London, Williams and Norgate, 1949; New York, Philosophical Library, 1950.

Carter, April, *Marshall Tito: A Bibliography*. Westport, Connecticut, and London, Meckler, 1989.

Dedijer, Vladimir, *Tito Speaks: His Self Portrait and Struggle with Stalin*. New York, Simon and Schuster, 1952; London, Weidenfeld and Nicolson, 1953.

Djilas, Milovan, *Tito: The Story from Inside*, translated by Vasilije Kojic and Richard Hayes. New York, Harcourt, 1980; London, Weidenfeld and Nicolson, 1981.

Draskovich, Slobodan M., *Tito, Moscow's Trojan Horse*. Chicago, H. Regnery, 1957.

Maclean, Fitzroy, *Josip Broz Tito: A Pictorial Biography*. New York, McGraw-Hill, and London, Macmillan, 1980.

Zilliancus, Konni, *Tito of Yugoslavia*. London, M. Joseph, 1952.

*

Although dated by the fact that Tito lived the better part of a decade after its appearance, AUTY remains in many ways the best biography available. Her somewhat favorable evaluation of Tito is currently under attack as the darker side of her subject's life begins to be revealed. All the same, Auty is balanced, fair, and shows an appreciation for an extremely complex historical figure. This title is clearly the best introduction to the life and work of Tito, although it is far from definitive.

For an invaluable and surprisingly fair view of Tito by one of his former comrades, DJILAS is unsurpassed. Besides giving an interesting and noteworthy analysis of Tito's political development, Djilas is able to comment on Tito the man. This work reveals, for instance, that Tito had only a superficial knowledge of most things and that even "his knowledge of Marxism was meager." Rather than becoming a revolutionary out of intellectual conviction, Tito, so Djilas argues, "was born a rebel," who found Communism a doctrine that fit his personality.

On the political side, Djilas argues that Tito created a system of "state capitalism" molded in his own image. Although serious political differences forced a split between Djilas and Tito, Djilas comments that he "loved and respected Tito . . . more as the years went by." This intertwining of the political and the personal makes Djilas a remarkable work that provides insights into Tito other biographies don't.

DEDIJER, one-time editor of the Communist Party newspaper *Borba*, was a close associate of Tito who like Djilas broke over ideological differences. Unfortunately, his work was written before the split, for it is clearly unobjective. Still, it is of use inasmuch as it reveals the official view of Tito promoted in the early 1950s. Further, there is much valuable information contained in it, although the reader has to remember the slant of the author. Of little use is DRASKOVICH, who is both outdated and extremely biased. He argues rather unconvincingly that Tito's split from the Soviet bloc is part of a vast conspiracy directed against the free world by Moscow. This book's prime value is that it shows the mentality of the 1950s red scare, but it reveals

little if anything of interest about Tito. Both BILAINKIN and ZILLIANCUS are too dated to be significant as their subject outlived the writing of these volumes by 30 years.

For the serious student of the first president of post-World War II Yugoslavia, CARTER provides an extremely useful and well-organized introduction to the sources available. This work is to be recommended to those who are engaged in more in-depth research projects rather than individuals who seek a more general knowledge of Tito's life and work. On the other hand, MACLEAN gives a visual introduction to Tito that may allow the general reader to gain a basic understanding of Tito Before turning to Auty or Djilas.

—William A. Pelz

TOCQUEVILLE, Alexis (-Charles-Henri-Clérel de), 1805–1859; French statesman and writer.

Boesche, Roger, *The Strange Liberalism of Alexis de Tocqueville*. Ithaca, New York, Cornell University Press, 1987.

Drescher, Seymour, *Dilemmas of Democracy, Tocqueville and Modernization*. Pittsburgh, University of Pittsburgh Press, 1968.

Gargan, Edward T., *Alexis de Tocqueville: The Critical Years 1848–51*. Washington, D.C., The Catholic University of America Press, 1955.

Goldstein, Doris S., *Trial of Faith: Religion and Politics in Tocqueville's Thought*. New York, Elsevier, 1975.

Hereth, Michael, *Alexis de Tocqueville: Threats to Freedom in Democracy*, translated by George Bogardus. Durham, North Carolina, Duke University Press, 1986 (originally published by Kohlhammer, Stuttgart, 1979).

Jardin, André, *Tocqueville: A Biography*, translated by L. Davis and R. Hemenway. New York, Farrar Straus, and London, Halban, 1988 (originally published as *Alexis de Tocqueville 1805–59*, Paris, Hachette, 1984).

Lawlor, Mary, *Alexis de Tocqueville, in the Chamber of Deputies, His Views on Foreign and Colonial Policy*. Washington, D.C., The Catholic University of America Press, 1959.

Mayer, J. P., *Alexis de Tocqueville, A Biographical Essay in Political Science*. New York, Viking, 1940.

Zetterbaum, Marvin, *Tocqueville and the Problem of Democracy*. Stanford, California, Stanford University Press, 1967.

*

JARDIN offers an excellent full-length biography of Alexis de Tocqueville, well researched, definitive, and thorough; the first 50 pages are devoted to family and background. Tocqueville's ideas, such as his use of history to explain the present and his conception of the role of religion and education in republican institutions, receive admirable attention. Jardin treats Tocqueville's political career, especially the matter of Algiers, in detail, and he offers a brief study of other French visitors to the United States, noting particularly the influence of Chauteaubriand. Jardin makes extensive use of Tocqueville's letters both published and unpublished. The book is definitely intended for the scholar as it requires a knowledge of French history and politics.

MAYER, in the only other full-length biography of Tocqueville, has written a book more for the general reader. Mayer emphasizes the religious nature of Tocqueville's political philosophy, providing little detail of his parliamentary work or of his tenure as foreign minister. His discussion of such concepts as "democracy" and "equality" are unfortunately influenced by the times (1939–1940) and thus the work occasionally has a lecturing tone. In general this is a very uncritical biography that ascribes Tocqueville's failures to his virtues.

Other works, not strictly historical biographies, offer excellent discussions of aspects of Tocqueville's life. Of these, GARGAN offers a biographical study of Tocqueville's entry into politics after the revolution of 1848 and the role he played in drafting the constitution for the Second French Republic. Gargan notes the relationship between Marx and Tocqueville in their observations of the times. LAWLOR focuses on Tocqueville's role as an active legislator in the Chamber of Deputies. Through an analysis of his speeches, the four most noteworthy of which she includes in the text (the eastern question, right of search, slavery in French colonies, and policy in Algiers), Lawlor emphasizes Tocqueville's impassioned nationalism and urgent practicality.

Of the many intellectual biographies, HERETH offers the best introduction to Tocqueville's thought. He attempts to situate Tocqueville in the tradition of political rhetoric and to show the limits of this tradition by concentrating on his subject's urgent necessity to create a civic ethos compatible with democratic social norms. The beginning of the book focuses on Tocqueville's search for order and stability as the basis for freedom. Part two looks at Tocqueville as a political citizen. Part three takes an interesting glance at Tocqueville's ideas on the conquest of Algeria by the French—an attitude in stark contrast to his ideals of self-determination, freedom, and republican government. Hereth also studies Tocqueville's choice of a political career instead of a life of contemplation. His critique rests on a distinction between political rhetoric and political philosophy.

BOESCHE seeks to understand "the true spirit of the age" in which Alexis de Tocqueville lived. He believes that Tocqueville was influenced heavily by his own generation and that he must be studied in this context. Unlike Hereth, who believed Tocqueville was able to disconnect himself from his historical moment and therefore look at it objectively, Boesche concentrates on the anxieties of the age and their influence on his subject. He discusses the intellectual currents of Tocqueville's generation, including art, philosophy, and literature. Boesche argues that Tocqueville rejected the romantic solutions to the problems of bourgeois culture. Tocqueville's ambivalence, his pessimistic yet somehow hopeful analysis of humankind's ability to create political freedom, is well presented.

DRESCHER seeks to study Tocqueville's pattern of intellectual development, citing as the main struggle in his subject's mind that between central themes and peripheral concerns. He views Tocqueville as a writer on practical politics and is also concerned to uncover the sources of Tocqueville's thought in the social and intellectual environment of the day. ZETTERBAUM draws on four of Tocqueville's essays to find the theoretical structure of his political philosophy and to show its failure. Tocqueville is observed to be more calculating and less neutral than is usually thought. Tocqueville's creation of the "salutary myth"

of unavoidable democracy is well argued. Zetterbaum insists that Tocqueville knew that human nature must change before democracy can succeed. Both studies are very readable but are intended primarily for the scholar.

GOLDSTEIN emphasizes the role of religion in Tocqueville's writing and politics but not in his personal life. She looks closely at other elements of Tocqueville's era and avoids making religion an all-encompassing aspect of Tocqueville's political thought. Tocqueville combined faith, truth, and utility, and he saw religion and political participation as two elements of good society. The influence of religion is most obvious, Goldstein argues, in Tocqueville's recognition of providence as a guiding force in history and his willingness to judge human action in moral and spiritual, rather than merely economic, terms. Goldstein's writing style is unfortunately prosaic and repetitive.

—Daniel Dean Roland

TOLSTOY, Leo [Count Lev Nikolayevich Tolstoy], 1828–1910; Russian writer.

Asquith, Cynthia, *Married to Tolstoy*. London, Hutchinson, 1960; Boston, Houghton Mifflin, 1961.

Bulgakov, V. F., *The Last Year of Leo Tolstoy*, translated by Ann Dunnigan, New York, Dial Press, and London, Hamilton, 1971.

Courcel, Martina de, *Tolstoy, the Ultimate Reconciliation*, translated by Peter Levi. New York, Scribner, and London, Collier Macmillan, 1988 (originally published by Hermann, Paris, 1980).

Edwards, Ann, *Sonya: The Life of Countess Tolstoy*. New York, Simon and Schuster, and London, Hodder and Stoughton, 1981.

Gustafson, Richard F., *Leo Tolstoy: Resident and Stranger*. Princeton, New Jersey, Princeton University Press, 1986.

Kenworthy, John C., *Tolstoy, His Life and Works*. London, W. Scott, 1902.

Kuzminskaya, Tatyana A., *Tolstoy as I Knew Him*, translated by Nora Sigerist et al. New York, Macmillan, 1948.

Leon, Derrick, *Tolstoy, His Life and Works*. London, Routledge, 1944.

Maude, Aylmer, *The Life of Tolstoy* (2 vols.). New York, Dodd Mead, and London, Constable, 1910.

Nazaroff, Alexander I., *Tolstoy, the Inconstant Genius*. New York, F. A. Stokes, 1929; London, Harrap, 1930.

Noyes, George R., *Tolstoy*. New York, Duffield, 1918; London, J. Murray, 1919.

Perris, G. H., *Leo Tolstoy, the Grand Mujik*. London, T. F. Unwin, 1898.

Rolland, Romain, *Tolstoy*, translated by Bernard Miall. New York, Dutton, and London, T. F. Unwin, 1911 (originally published as *Vie de Tolstoy*, Paris, Hachette, 1911).

Simmons, Ernest, *Leo Tolstoy*. Boston, Little Brown, 1946; London, J. Lehmann, 1949.

Tolstoy, Alexandra, *Tolstoy, a Life of My Father*, translated by Elizabeth R. Hapgood. New York, Harper, and London, Gollancz, 1953.

Tolstoy, Sergei, *Tolstoy Remembered by His Son*, translated by M. Budberg. London, Weidenfeld and Nicolson, 1961; New York, Atheneum, 1962.

Tolstoy, Tatyana (T. L. Sukhotina-Tolstoy), *Tolstoy Remembered*, translated by Derek Coltman. New York, McGraw-Hill, and London, M. Joseph, 1977.

Troyat, Henri, *Tolstoy*, translated by Nancy Amphoux. New York, Doubleday, 1967 (originally published by Fayard/Hachette, Paris, 1965).

Wilson, A. N., *Tolstoy*. New York, Norton, and London, Hamilton, 1988.

*

Biographies written while Tolstoy was still alive have the special advantage of seeing the man and his importance, while still in the making. The emphasis in books by contemporaries tends to be on the later years and on Tolstoy as the moral and religious teacher. We have to remind ourselves that Tolstoy's impact in the last decade of the 19th century and the first of the 20th century was immense.

MAUDE's large work on Tolstoy is one of the best and most complete. Maude knew Tolstoy, followed his teachings, and presented them to the world with intimate knowledge of the man and with a scholar's thoroughness and intelligence. In addition to an historical overview of Tolstoy the man, Maude includes in the second volume chapters on special topics such as "Dukhobors," the religious sect that Tolstoy helped emigrate to Canada and for whom he wrote *Resurrection*, "Patriotism," "Non-Resistance to Evil," and "Sex."

ROLLAND, the distinguished French writer, also wrote his *Tolstoy* from the vantage point of intimate firsthand knowledge of Tolstoy, from the experience of the same historical age, and from enthusiastic sympathy for his teachings. Rolland's book is very different from Maude's in approach and style. Rolland's writing is lyrical, emotional, and very personal. It lacks Maude's objectivity, but gives us some sense of how powerfully Tolstoy affected distinguished contemporaries. Rolland's emphasis is on the later Tolstoy and on his world view, with chapters on "Reality," "Art and Conscience," "Science and Art."

KENWORTHY's work is a primary source of how Tolstoy influenced English opinion. The state of English life, by way of contrast to Tolstoy's views on society, is very much on Kenworthy's mind. Kenworthy's reconstruction of the history of English Tolstoyan communes may be of particular interest to the reader. Such communes were established in many countries, but there is very little firsthand reportage by the participants in such communes. PERRIS' biography, written too while Tolstoy was alive, lacks something of Kenworthy's missionary zeal and his account of the special influence of Tolstoy on English life. It is moral and personal and concerned with the effect of Tolstoy's teaching on different cultures. The book has a dated and archaic quality without the redeeming virtues of firsthand knowledge.

Biographies written by Tolstoy's children and relatives form a special category of works written from firsthand knowledge that function as source material. One would expect special knowledge from those who lived with Tolstoy on a day-to-day basis. But as one goes through the various volumes written by his sons and daughters, one is impressed with how intimacy can blind and how distance can reveal. What is lacking in most of these studies is a sense of perspective: one is lost in details that may have seemed important to the child but are of limited interest to the student of Tolstoy. When the authors attempt some perspective, it is likely to be borrowed from the biographies of others. Some of this is baffling, but the impression is inescapable that the children did not know Tolstoy very well. They knew the father, but not necessarily the genius, and they knew the father and writer from their own special points of view.

Sometimes this perspective, as with ALEXANDRA TOLSTOY's volume, is marred by generations of struggle, quarrels, and competition with others who knew her father. Her volume is large, detailed, and important, and one will certainly want to go to it for certain facts, especially those dealing with Tolstoy's last years, his agonies over his will, his relations with Chertkov, and especially his relations with his wife. But one will also want to be cautious, if not about the facts, then about the way they are presented. Still, by comparison with the biographies by Tolstoy's sons, Alexandra's work comes over as substantial and important.

SERGEI TOLSTOY's biography of his father is slight and impressionistic, adding little to what was already known about Tolstoy. The book was published in Russian a half-century after the facts he observed and noted, and the strain of memory tends to rob the facts of some of the intimacy and freshness that one finds in the volume written by his eldest daughter, TATYANA TOLSTOY. This work, interrupted by Tatyana's death, is based on her childhood diaries, and though undoubtedly supplemented and modified by memory and distance, the work retains much of the freshness of facts and impressions recorded while they were occurring.

Perhaps the best of the "family" biographies is by Tatyana KUZMINSKAYA, Tolstoy's sister-in-law, a lively and attractive person, whom Tolstoy deeply loved and admired. Hers is a biography not only of Tolstoy but of herself also, a fact that seems to add rather than detract from our knowledge of Tolstoy. The facts she gives us of her life and her family broaden the context in which we see and hear Tolstoy.

There are, too, dozens of "reminiscences" of Tolstoy, especially of his last decades, written by friends, visitors, and those in the service of the Tolstoys. BULGAKOV was a young secretary hired by Tolstoy in his last year to help him with his correspondence and other clerical details. He lived with the family, and set down in simple and vivid detail, with no special axe to grind, the events of Tolstoy's last extraordinary year, including the day that Tolstoy fled from the family estate and the reaction of his wife to his leaving. Bulgakov's work is fascinating reading and is excellent primary source material.

Of scholarly biographies published since Tolstoy's death, SIMMONS' work is something of a classic. Simmons approaches his subject in a dry, objective, and detailed fashion, with concern for a full and scrupulous accounting of the facts and with little or no intrusion of his own views. The biography is not lively, but it is reliable and helpful.

TROYAT's work is the very opposite. Troyat is himself a prestigious French writer of fiction and biography, and his work on Tolstoy is very readable. Indeed, it reads somewhat like a novel, incorporating the drama and vividness of Tolstoy's own extraordinary life. Troyat has the principal facts of Tolstoy's life correct, but there is a substantial amount of embellishment of the actual events. Troyat imaginatively reconstructs conversations he could not have known about and feelings he could not possibly know. Simmons gives us only facts; Troyat gives us facts and conjectures. For the average sophisticated reader, Troyat's work is a good introduction to Tolstoy, but it is of uncertain value for the specialist.

NOYES' biography is also useful by way of introduction. It has been around since 1918 (reissued in 1968) and has worn well. It communicates all the basic facts in a responsible way, but it is somewhat outdated in light of the scholarship and criticism that has appeared in the more than half-century since Noyes wrote. The same can be said of NAZAROFF's work, which is outdated and incomplete and has not worn as well as that of Noyes. LEON's work provides less of an overview than do Noyes', Simmons', and Troyat's biographies, but it has some interesting material on Tolstoyan colonies and Chekhov's visits to Tolstoy.

Of recent works on Tolstoy, one must give without any hesitation the laurels to A. N. WILSON's monumental work on Tolstoy. Wilson is a distinguished man of letters who has written an extraordinary work on Tolstoy, not so much because of original and new material, but because of the width of his background and the force of his intelligence. It is a biography that concentrates on the meaning of Tolstoy, that is, on the legacy of his teachings on the moral, social, and philosophical life. Wilson has been powerfully affected by Tolstoy, and his prose resounds with the emotion of this impact. But with three-quarters of a century of distance, he is able to see that impact with considerable objectivity. What we have is a work with the scholarship of Simmons, the imagination and talent of Troyat, and the sense of immediate impact conveyed by Maude. Wilson does not permit his emotions to "imagine" parts of Tolstoy's life as Troyat has done.

One wonders why COURCEL wrote her recent biography, even more why it has been translated. It is a competent work but rehearses all the known material and adds nothing new by way of perspective or approach. GUSTAFSON's work is largely an analysis of Tolstoy's ideas in his post-conversion period, and as such a basic biography only in the sense that we consider the cartography of Tolstoy's ideas as part of his biography.

Finally, mention should be made of two works that deal with Tolstoy's relationship to his wife, Sophia or Sonia. These relations were, at least in the last decade, not only complex but also painful and difficult. Mention of Tolstoy's relationships with his wife are to be found in one way or another in all the biographies, but these two—by ASQUITH and EDWARDS—are detailed examinations of them, and they attempt, moreover, to see the relationships from a point of view more sympathetic to the wife. Both works are less than scholarly. The Asquith volume is well written, and Edwards' work, though it is fairly well researched and bears the fruits of much cooperation from the Tolstoy foundation in upstate New York, still breaks very little new ground. It has something of a journalistic air and suffers from an inadequate knowledge of the rest of Tolstoy, that is, his works and his times.

—Edward Wasiolek

TOSCANINI, Arturo, 1867–1957; Italian conductor.

Chotzinoff, Samuel, *Toscanini: An Intimate Portrait*. New York, Knopf, and London, Hamilton, 1956.
Haggin, B. H., *Arturo Toscanini: Contemporary Recollections of the Maestro*. New York, Da Capo, 1989.
Horowitz, Joseph, *Understanding Toscanini*. New York, Knopf, and London, Faber, 1987.
Marek, George, *Toscanini*. New York, Atheneum, 1975; London, Vision Press, 1976.
Matthews, Denis, *Arturo Toscanini*. Tunbridge Wells, Kent, and New York, Hippocrene Books, 1982.
Nicotra, Tobia, *Arturo Toscanini*, translated by Irma Brandeis and H. D. Kahn. New York, Knopf, 1929.
Sacchi, Filippo, *The Magic Baton*. London, Putnam, 1952; revised and abridged edition, London and New York, Putnam, 1957.
Sachs, Harvey, *Toscanini*. Philadelphia, Lippincott, and London, Weidenfeld and Nicolson, 1978.
Stefan, Paul, *Arturo Toscanini*, translated by Eden and Cedar Paul. New York, Viking, and London, Heinemann, 1936 (originally published by Reichner, Vienna, 1935).
Taubman, Howard, *The Maestro: The Life of Arturo Toscanini*. New York, Simon and Schuster, 1951.

*

Well before the end of Toscanini's unprecedented 68-year career, biographies of him were attempted. Two such books that turn up frequently in second-hand stores are by Nicotra and Stefan. Both have the obvious limitation of incompleteness, Toscanini's last concert occurring a quarter of a century after Nicotra's work and 18 years after Stefan's. Furthermore, both are poorly documented and occasionally inaccurate. Still, each offers something of value, particularly NICOTRA, who includes a number of quotations of Toscanini himself about works in his repertory and provides details of programs led by the conductor during his earliest years in Italy (1886–1908) that cannot be gleaned elsewhere.

STEFAN's work, although published in 1936, virtually ignores Toscanini's years with the New York Philharmonic (1926–36), perhaps because the author, as a European journalist, did not come to the United States until 1941. But even aspects of Toscanini's European career that Stefan observed, such as the conductor's Salzburg years (1934–37), are treated far too sparsely. Although its organization is loosely chronological, Stefan's book is encumbered with much subjective digression. The most valuable aspect of this slim volume (aside from its many photographs of Toscanini conducting at Salzburg and in Vienna) is its occasional quotations of Toscanini himself and its recollections of some of his performances.

Far more detailed is TAUBMAN. Written 15 years after Stefan, his work incorporates discussion of Toscanini's years at NBC (1937–54). Free of Stefan's digressions, it offers straightforward biography from the conductor's childhood onward. But the major problem with Taubman, aside from an incompleteness resulting from Toscanini's still being active at the time the book was published, is that he uses his subject as a primary source for information. Although Toscanini's memory for music was photographic, his recall of dates, places, and other details of his life was fallible. Consequently, for all the useful information Taubman offers, his work is often inaccurate and untrustworthy.

The same is even truer of CHOTZINOFF. Carelessly written and gossipy, it has egregious factual errors and makes the sophisticated Toscanini sometimes look like a puerile fool. Certainly not biography in the strict sense of the term, Chotzinoff purports to be a character sketch, but contrary to its subtitle, it is neither "intimate" nor a "portrait." Rather it comprises a series of loosely strung together incidents, some of which (such as the description of Toscanini's last concert) falsify history.

SACCHI's volume suffers from an unidiomatic English translation. It reads awkwardly and, being a shortened version of the original Italian edition, lacks completeness. But its author has witness to Italian musical life for the first half of this century and knew Toscanini. Thus his recollections of that life and his quotations of the conductor give this flawed translation dimension and value.

When MAREK's book first appeared, it was heralded for correcting a number of inaccurate generalizations often made about Toscanini, prime among them that his interest in the arts was confined primarily to music. But the book suffers from careless scholarship and is blemished with many factual errors. Moreover, Marek's style is pretentious, with quotations from well-known poets, for instance, directing more attention to its author than to his subject. And as biography, the volume is far from complete, narrowing its focus to major portions of Toscanini's career and thus leaving huge gaps in his life. Yet in spite of these shortcomings, Marek's book is useful for providing information not to be found elsewhere. But all of its facts should be treated as suspect and verified wherever possible by referring to Sachs.

Standing alone in terms of accuracy, completeness, clarity of style, and value as a research tool is the work of SACHS. No other biography approaches its thoroughness, its wealth of quotations from primary sources, its storehouse of information, and its cogent objectivity. Unique among all of Toscanini's biographers, Sachs is too young to have heard the conductor in the concert hall or the theater. Perhaps it is this distancing from his subject that enabled him to flesh it out with such impartial dimension. All aspects of the conductor's life and career—from his familial roots to his grave—are traced. What is more, Sachs' occasional critical judgments prove revealing, as in the concluding chapter that epitomizes Toscanini's talent as having produced "communication at a level undreamed of by most performers." Also invaluable are the book's appendices, which include lists of all works currently known to have been in Toscanini's repertory, with dates supplied for many of the conductor's important operatic productions. In short, this biography should remain definitive until the revelation of previously suppressed material enables Sachs to produce a new, expanded edition.

The most recent biography, by MATTHEWS, is far shorter and considerably less comprehensive than Sachs's work, from which it has clearly benefited. Here is a well-written overview centered on Toscanini's professional life, but touching on his early years in Parma and the response of critics to the conductor. Alone among biographies, Matthews' book contains a comprehensive discography of the Toscanini recordings that, save for a few recently issued items, is complete; it includes pointed critical commentary about the recordings by Ray Burford. Unlike other biographers, Matthews had a distinguished career as pia-

nist and pedagogue and thus occasionally brings to his writing a refreshing angle of vision. If not the last word in scholarship, then, Matthews is eminently readable, informative, and often insightful. HAGGIN's 1989 reprint brings together two of the author's justly admired books, *Conversations with Toscanini* (1959) and *The Toscanini Musicians Knew* (1967), both ably edited and revised by Thomas Hathaway. Though not a true biography, this source offers insight into the conductor's art from a critic and from many musicians who knew Toscanini.

Finally, a note about a book that is easy to mistake for biography at a superficial glance. HOROWITZ's *Understanding Toscanini* is a speciously argued, inadequately researched, overwritten book that raises many relevant questions about musical life in the United States, but treats Toscanini with contempt and with a disdain for accuracy and thoroughness that is irresponsible. Although often stimulating, this book must be read with full awareness of its bias.

—Mortimer H. Frank

TOULOUSE-LAUTREC, Henri (-Marie-Raymond de), 1864–1901; French painter.

Adriani, Götz, *Toulouse-Lautrec*. London and New York, Thames and Hudson, 1987.
Castleman, Riva and Wolfgang Wittrock, *Henri de Toulouse-Lautrec, Images of the 1890s*. New York, Museum of Modern Art, 1985.
Desloge, Nora, *Toulouse-Lautrec, the Baldwin Collection*. San Diego, San Diego Museum of Art, 1988; Seattle and London, University of Washington Press, 1989.
Goldschmidt, Lucien and Herbert Schimmel, editors, *Unpublished Correspondence of Henry de Toulouse-Lautrec*, translated by Edward B. Garside, with notes and biographical essays by Jean Adhémar and Theodore Reff. New York, Phaidon Press, 1969.
Huisman, Philippe and M. G. Dortu, *Lautrec by Lautrec*, translated and edited by C. Bellow. New York, Galahad Books, 1964 (originally published by Bibliothèque des Arts, Paris, 1964).
Mack, Gerstle, *Toulouse-Lautrec*. New York, Knopf, and London, Cape, 1938.
Perruchot, Henri, *Toulouse-Lautrec*, translated by Humphrey Hare. New York, Collier, 1962 (originally published as *Vie de Toulouse-Lautrec*, Paris, Hachette, 1958).
Stuckey, Charles F., *Toulouse-Lautrec: Paintings*. Chicago, Art Institute, 1979.

*

The now half-century old work by MACK was the first full-length biography of Toulouse-Lautrec in English. The minute description of art work, not illustrated, invests the book with an almost pre-modern aura; yet Mack's careful research and documentation, of both the surrounding locale and personalities of Lautrec's world, as well as for the artist himself, produce a warm and sympathetic tone and permit the book's current use by authorities as well as the general public.

PERRUCHOT's is a far more recent text that takes a witty, more ironic tone. The extensive bibliography, none of it in translation, reveals the sources that supplied Perruchot's incidental, conversational accents of intimate studio, cabaret, brothel, and family scenes. It would appear that nothing anecdotal in this volume was invented.

The DESLOGE catalog of the Baldwin Collection of the San Diego Museum of Art offers sensitive entries for the 108 works, almost all lithographs. Biographical detail in the catalog is balanced with aesthetic discussion. Of special interest is the concise introductory biographical essay by Julia Frey, from whom a full-length biography of Lautrec is forthcoming. (Her work will apparently draw on unpublished material from the Lake Collection at the Humanities Research Center, University of Texas, Austin.) This essay and that of Phillip Dennis Cate, ''Parades, Paris and Prostitutes: Thematic Concerns of Lautrec and his Contemporaries,'' are illustrated with contemporary photographs of Lautrec and others of his world. Frey has also contributed an introductory essay, ''Henri de Toulouse-Lautrec: A Biography of the Artist,'' to CASTLEMAN AND WITTROCK's catalog for the Museum of Modern Art.

ADRIANI provides a catalog of a West German exhibition in which Lautrec is show as painter and portraitist. (This book is in every respect more extensive than Adriani's previous work, *Toulouse-Lautrec, The Complete Graphic Works*, London, Thames and Hudson, 1986.) Through a careful documentation of the 130 works discussed—Lautrec made about 600 paintings—each with its own bibliography, the artist's attachments and mode of life are portrayed. The inclusion of a narrative chronological biography with previously unpublished photographs completes a satisfying approach.

In another catalog of an exhibition of paintings, STUCKEY in his introductory essay, ''Models and Spectators in the Art of Lautrec,'' sets the tone of the probing analytical comments that accompany the 109 items spanning Lautrec's entire career. The care and time that Lautrec took to produce the most casual effects—the pose of his figures against their settings, the nature of that environment, the use of innuendo in visual punning—present the artist as utterly devoted to his art. As well, biographical detail given for the portrait sitters is presented as relevant for an understanding of Lautrec's character and his interests.

Such sense of intimacy is only intensified in the work by HUISMAN AND DORTU, which reads like a view into a collection of Lautrec's memorabilia. This is so because the co-author, Mme. M. G. Dortu, inherited all the pictures and files of Lautrec's personal friend and dealer, Maurice Joyant. And so the juxtaposition here of the artist's works together with personal photographs of models, friends, and family, beginning with three-year-old Lautrec himself, is vital in setting forth a Lautrec far closer to reality than the depraved artist still generally imaged by the public through hearsay and faction. Appended are a brief chronology, a map of Lautrec's Paris showing the residences of his circle, and an illustrated catalog of his graphic work (since superseded by several more recent works).

Adding to our understanding of Lautrec through his letters (which comprise nearly all of his writing), GOLDSCHMIDT AND SCHIMMEL have translated a group of letters that have about them the feeling of dutiful family talk; some even suggest that his relationship to his father was loving. Nonetheless, Lautrec is seen here as close to his family. Aside from a precise life chronology, essays with further character implications are

provided by Jean Adhémar and Theodore Reff. Another aspect of Lautrec's life of art—his professional and business sense—is given in the collection published by Herbert D. Schimmel and Phillip D. Cate, *The Henri de Toulouse-Lautrec and W. M. B. Sands Correspondence* (New York, 1983). Sands was an English printer and publisher who had dealings with Lautrec.

—Joshua Kind

TROLLOPE, Anthony, 1815–1882; English writer.

Pope-Hennessey, James, *Anthony Trollope*. Boston, Little Brown, and London, Cape, 1971.
Sadleir, Michael, *Anthony Trollope: A Commentary*. New York, Houghton Mifflin, 1927; as *Trollope: A Commentary*, London, Constable, 1945.
Super, Robert Henry, *Trollope in the Post Office*. Ann Arbor, University of Michigan Press, 1981.
Walpole, Horace, *Anthony Trollope*. London and New York, Macmillan, 1928.

*

One of the first signs of a Trollope revival in the 20th century was the appearance of Michael Sadleir's biography in 1927 (see below). There has been a persistent body of readers of the novels ever since. Perhaps this is so, as a recent biographer (Pope-Hennessey) points out, because Trollope's work offers a welcome contrast to the violence and moral ambivalence of the 20th century.

Sadleir's book was the spearhead of a revival; POPE-HENNESSEY represents its persistence. Both writers draw on much the same body of material. First of all, there is Trollope's *Autobiography* written late in the novelist's life. There are also letters from publishers and critical reviews of the novels, and both biographers draw on the surviving family correspondence. Both Pope-Hennessey and Sadleir trace Trollope's difficult progress toward novel-writing. Trollope spent years as an underling at the British Post Office. Finally, while a supervisor in Ireland, Trollope began his writing, first with tales of Irish life and then, with great success, the books that told of contentious life in an English cathedral town, the Barsetshire series.

Pope-Hennessey's biography supplements the flow of fact with two sorts of material. First, he makes a successful attempt to define Trollope's own character—the fits of temper that perhaps expressed youthful frustrations, and the well-curbed attempts to enjoy something more romantic than a quiet Victorian marriage. Pope-Hennessey links Trollope's political conservatism with his taste for fox-hunting, a chief pleasure of the class that finally opened its gates to the novelist. Second, Pope-Hennessey provides a sensitive and cultivated reading of Trollope's works. But his analyses do not go to murky psychological depths in Trollope. Instead, he sees Trollope as a man very much at one with the society that surrounded him and bought his works of fiction.

SADLEIR's inspection of the *Autobiography* and the other materials leads him to a gentler view of Trollope's character. Sadleir is evidently concerned to restore the novelist's general reputation. For in the 1920s, Trollope was thought to represent Victorian prudery and hypocrisy. And Trollope's accounts of his methods of writing—so many words every fifteen minutes—was a far cry from the artistic care of later times. Sadleir argues that the Victorian era was more complex than the early 20th century had judged, and that Trollope scanned his chosen sections of his world with subtlety and precision. This latter point is underlined by the concluding section of Sadleir's book, where an analysis of the great merits and the considerable faults of Trollope is offered.

Three other books supplement the two biographies. The *Autobiography* (2 vols., 1883), as Pope-Hennessey points out frequently, gives us a record of Trollope's lonely childhood (his parents were involved in their own travels and literary efforts), and may be read profitably alongside the interpretations of it made by Pope-Hennessey and Sadleir. But the narrative is an interesting tale in its own right. SUPER focuses on Trollope's many years of public service. WALPOLE's volume in the English Men of Letters series pulls together one man's impression of Trollope's work. Walpole had, in his day, the kind of reputation Trollope had enjoyed. For this reason and others, Walpole is a good companion to the on-going reading of the works of a man who was, in more than one sense of the phrase, a great Victorian.

—Harold H. Watts

TROTSKY, Leon, 1879–1940; Russian revolutionary and Marxist theorist.

Carmichael, Joel, *Trotsky: An Appreciation of His Life*. New York, St. Martin's, and London, Hodder and Stoughton, 1975.

Cliff, Tony, *Trotsky: Towards October 1879–1917*. London, Bookmarks, 1989.

Deutscher, Issac, *The Prophet Armed: Trotsky 1879–1921*. London and New York, Oxford University Press, 1954.

Deutscher, Issac, *The Prophet Unarmed: Trotsky 1921–29*. London and New York, Oxford University Press, 1959.

Deutscher, Issac, *The Prophet Outcast: Trotsky 1919–40*. London and New York, Oxford University Press, 1963.

Eastman, Max, *Leon Trotsky: The Portrait of a Youth*. New York, Greenberg, 1925; London, Faber, 1926.

Hallas, Duncan, *Trotsky's Marxism*. London, Pluto Press, 1979.

Howe, Irving, *Leon Trotsky*. New York, Viking Press, 1978; as *Trotsky*, London, Fontana, 1978.

King, David, *Trotsky: A Photographic Biography*. Oxford and New York, Blackwell, 1986.

Mandel, Ernest, *Trotsky, a Study in the Dynamic of His Thought*. London, NLB, 1979.

Payne, Robert, *The Life and Death of Trotsky*. New York, McGraw-Hill, 1977; London, W. H. Allen, 1978.

Serge, Victor and Natalia Sedova-Trotsky, *The Life and Death of Leon Trotsky*, translated by Arnold Pomerans. New York, Basic Books, and London, Wildwood House, 1975 (originally published by Amiot Dumont, Paris, 1951).

Van Heijenoort, Jan, *With Trotsky in Exile*. Cambridge, Massachusetts, Harvard University Press, 1978.

Warth, Robert D., *Leon Trotsky*. Boston, Twayne, 1977.

Wistrich, Robert S., *Trotsky: Fate of a Revolutionary*. London, Robson Books, 1979; New York, Stein and Day, 1982.

Wyndham, Francis and David King, *Trotsky: A Documentary*. New York, Praeger, and London, A. Lane, 1972.

*

Despite the volume of recent literature written about Trotsky, DEUTSCHER's trilogy remains the most complete and worthwhile work available. Although Deutscher is certainly partial to Trotsky, he remains fair and objective while allowing his reader to note his own prejudices. In addition, he manages to intertwine Trotsky the man with Trotsky the revolutionary in such a manner that a complete picture emerges of his complex subject. The author draws upon, not only Trotsky's papers and published writings, but also Tsarist police records and the seemingly countless memoirs of Trotsky's associates and friends.

Deutscher's first volume, *The Prophet Armed*, benefits greatly from the Tsarist records in particular. Deutscher is able to give the reader a picture of Trotsky first being influenced by and later influencing events in Russia. The context in which Trotsky develops into a revolutionary is drawn with precision. Further, Trotsky the adult revolutionary is shown reacting to the impact of other radicals and world-historic events such as World War I.

When Deutscher details the role of Trotsky in the Russian Revolution of 1917, he manages to do justice to both the complexity of the event and the role played by his subject. Of great interest is how Trotsky is shown after the revolution accepting undemocratic actions in the name of realism while little realizing that he was helping to pave the road for his own defeat and the betrayal of the revolution by Stalin.

In *The Prophet Unarmed*, Deutscher discusses the events that ultimately led to Stalin's dictatorship of the Soviet Union and Trotsky's exile. In so doing, he reveals Trotsky's strengths while showing him "in his many moments of irresolution and indecision." In addition to written records, Deutscher uses numerous interviews with important figures who knew Trotsky in this period, such as Heinrich Brandler, Alfred Romer, Max Eastman, and Natalya Sedova Trotsky.

In his final part of the trilogy, *The Prophet Outcast*, Deutscher "relates the catastrophic *denouement* of his drama." Trotsky's exile and assassination mark a new period where he "appeared to stand quite alone against Stalin's autocracy." Deutscher shows the tremendous strain the man who had once been second only to Lenin felt as he wandered about the world only slightly ahead of Stalin's agents. In telling of this tragedy, Deutscher continues to paint Trotsky as a multifaceted individual with great strengths and fatal weaknesses.

Extremely flattering and obviously biased, SERGE AND SEDOVA-TROTSKY's work is important in that it tells Trotsky's story from the viewpoint of those who supported him. Further, it contains a number of personal insights supplied by Trotsky's widow that have escaped more neutral biographers. This volume's main emphasis is on the Trotsky of 1917–40, particularly the period of exile. Less self-serving than one would normally expect from an autobiography, Trotsky's own *My Life* (1960) tells his own story up till 1929 and reveals what he thought about the key events of the Russian Revolution and the power struggle with Stalin. Inasmuch as it gives the reader a clear vision of the manner in which Trotsky viewed himself and his role in history, this title is of great value.

CLIFF's book is the first of a projected three volumes that will attempt a revision of Trotsky's role in revolutionary history. The author faults Deutscher for being "fatalistic" and for having a concept of "socialism from above." Even Trotsky's autobiography is flawed because it underplays the importance of his "tremendous contributions where he differed from Lenin." Cliff writes from the perspective of "a disciple of Trotsky of over a half a century's duration."

Much like Cliff, HALLAS is a devoted follower of Trotsky's ideas, which he attempts to outline in his work so as to make them easily understood by the general public. As an introduction to Trotsky's political beliefs, this title has much to recommend itself. Another work to focus on Trotsky's ideas is MANDEL's more scholarly and nuanced study, also by a self-proclaimed follower of Trotsky's political beliefs.

In a completely different approach, CARMICHAEL focuses on Trotsky the man rather than Trotsky the revolutionary. The author seeks to correct what he sees as the overemphasis on "Trotskyism" to the exclusion of Trotsky. His work is motivated by the belief that all previous accounts "have been warped by excessive identification with his ideas."

As a general introduction to Trotsky's life and the various controversies surrounding it, HOWE's volume is excellent. Although not comparable to Deutscher, Howe does an excellent job of presenting a balanced portrait that is both readable and scholarly. WARTH is a much shorter introduction that may appeal to the reader who wants brevity. Both KING and WYNDHAW are interesting, although they add little to more in-depth treatments.

For a study of the early Trotsky, EASTMAN, though dated and rather one-sided, is to be recommended. For details of Trotsky's day-to-day life during exile, one would do well to consult VAN HEIJENOORT. WISTRICH is useful for stressing Trotsky's Jewish background. PAYNE is quite readable but has little to say that isn't said in more depth and with more power elsewhere.

—William A. Pelz

TRUMAN, Harry S., 1884–1972; American political leader, 33rd president of the United States.

Clemens, Cyril, *The Man from Missouri: A Biography of Harry S. Truman.* New York, J. P. Didier, 1945.

Daniels, Jonathan, *The Man of Independence.* Philadelphia, Lippincott, 1950.

Dayton, Eldorous L., *Give 'em Hell Harry: An Informal Biography of the Terrible Tempered Mr. T.* New York, Devin-Adair, 1956.

Ferrell, Robert H., *Harry S. Truman and the Modern American Presidency.* Boston, Little Brown, 1983.

Ferrell, Robert H., *Truman: A Centenary Remembrance.* New York, Viking, and London, Thames and Hudson, 1984.

Gies, Joseph, *Harry S. Truman: A Pictorial Biography.* New York, Doubleday, 1968.

Gosnell, Harold F., *Truman's Crises: A Political Biography of Harry S. Truman.* Westport, Connecticut, Greenwood Press, 1980.

Helm, William P., *Harry Truman: A Political Biography.* New York, Duell Sloan, 1947.

Jenkins, Roy, *Truman.* New York, Harper, and London, Collins, 1986.

McNaughton, Frank and Walter Hehmeyer, *This Man Truman.* New York, Putnam, 1945; London, Harrap, 1946.

Miller, Merle, *Plain Speaking: An Oral Biography of Harry S. Truman.* New York, Putnam, and London, Gollancz, 1974.

Miller, Richard L., *Truman: The Rise to Power.* New York, McGraw-Hill, 1986.

Pemberton, William E., *Harry S. Truman: Fair Dealer and Cold Warrior.* Boston, Twayne, 1989.

Powell, Gene, *Tom's Boy Harry.* Jefferson City, Missouri, Hawthorn Publishing, 1948.

Robbins, Charles, *Last of his Kind: An Informal Portrait of Harry S. Truman.* New York, Morrow, 1979.

Steinberg, Alfred, *The Man from Missouri: The Life and Times of Harry S. Truman.* New York, Putnam, 1962.

Truman, Margaret, *Harry S. Truman.* New York, Morrow, 1972; London, Hamilton, 1973.

*

Harry S. Truman was a controversial president and remains a controversial and popular figure for biographers. In addition to the 17 full biographies reviewed here, many other books cover only selected aspects of Truman's life.

The first biographies, both published shortly after Truman became president in 1945, have a "gee whiz" quality about them that seems quaint and almost embarrassingly naive to the readers of the 1990s. Neither the CLEMENS book nor the McNAUGHTON AND HEHMEYER biography shows any skepticism regarding Truman's comportment during his years with the notorious Pendergast machine in Missouri. Both books tell a simple story of an innocent farm boy whose rise to the presidency has an Horatio Alger aura about it. Both books depend on personal interviews, are anecdotal, and do not provide citations.

HELM's biography similarly uses "insider" information without citation. Helm is more willing, however, to delve into potentially embarrassing topics and to portray a more balanced view. Helm's Truman was neither an innocent propelled toward the presidency by natural forces nor a dishonest political hack. Truman worked with the Pendergast machine just as the other Democratic politicians in Missouri worked within the system. Truman also emerges in this biography as a positive actor, not merely a lucky commoner who just happens to advance through the efforts of others.

POWELL's biography has none of the balance of the Helms book. The "Tom" in the title is Thomas Pendergast. Powell's thesis is that Truman functioned as a lackey for the corrupt Pendergast. This Truman shares the passivity of the Truman of the 1945 books, but none of the quality of noble innocence. What all four biographies of the 1940s have in common is an absence of documentation for their characterizations of Truman before his presidency.

Among the early biographies, that by DANIELS holds up the best. Daniels has a theme: Truman's life as an "everyday man" rising to the challenges of leadership. Using both written sources and numerous interviews, the 384 pages are a thorough description of Truman's life prior to his decision to go into politics, his years as a Missouri politician, and his Washington experiences through the 1948 presidential election victory. Truman granted Daniels several interviews himself, encouraged associates to speak with the biographer, and suggested changes in the manuscript that Daniels made. In light of Truman's involvement with the work, it is not surprising that Daniels shows admiration for the president. This admiration, however, does not become adulation as Daniels depicts a man, not a saint. Although Daniels does not use citations, the massive scholarship in the 40 years since this book was published supports the accuracy of his work.

The other Truman biography of the 1950s is DAYTON's collection of undocumented charges and innuendoes. The book is poorly written, angry, and inaccurate. Truman is cartoonishly portrayed as a corrupt buffoon. Even readers who despise Harry Truman will find this book's treatment of him excessive.

The only full Truman biography of the 1960s—and the first to use the resources of the Truman library—is STEINBERG's 1962 *Man from Missouri*. Written in a journalistic style without citations, Steinberg continues in the admiring tradition of Daniels in his ready willingness to accept Truman's version of events. Nevertheless, the book is a warm account of Truman's family experiences and an accurate and detailed accounting of his presidency. Particularly valuable is the description of Truman's years as a farm worker and soldier during World War I.

The other 1960s book is GIES' disappointing "pictorial biography." The prose is a simple summary of information available elsewhere with no original interpretations. In a book called a "pictorial biography" weak prose might be forgiven, but the poor selection of pictures is surprising. Many of the shots are obviously staged public relations photographs. Others are familiar shots (e.g., Pearl Harbor under attack, troops goose-stepping before Hitler) that are tangential to Truman's life. The book is neither informative nor interesting.

Although fewer in number, the photographs in MARGARET TRUMAN's 1973 biography are more revealing of her father than are the pictures in the Gies book. The rest of her biography is similarly revealing of the character and temperament of a father she obviously loved. Readers who want intimate stories of a strong family man will enjoy this book. Although the strength of the book is the author's personal experiences with her father, there is also much material regarding his policy positions and motivations. She angrily attacks unnamed revisionist historians who criticized her father for fomenting the Cold War, supporting J. Edgar Hoover, and other alleged misdeeds. This book is by no means an objective, dispassionate biography, but a warm paean by a loyal and loving daughter.

Besides publication of Margaret Truman's book, 1973 witnessed a second unusual Truman book. Although Merle MILLER called his book "an oral biography," the work can more accurately be described as a creative portrait than a biography. In 1961 and 1962 the author spent hours interviewing Truman for a television series that was never produced. A decade later Miller collected these interviews into a book composed primarily of the edited transcripts. In addition, there are a few pages of interviews with friends from the president's youth and from his Washington years (e.g., Dean Acheson), and Miller's reactions, questions, and feelings interspersed throughout the in-

terviews. What emerges is an unusually entertaining presentation of a refreshingly guileless, straight-talking politician. The book catches the Truman spirit and style well, although it does not serve as good history. Miller avoids hard questions, does not pursue lines of inquiry well, and fails to note inaccuracies. In this book, as in several of the biographies noted above, Truman seems to have played a large role in writing his own biography.

ROBBINS follows the Miller oral model. Robbins interviewed Truman during the summer of 1953 as part of a project to help Truman with an article. The author returned in 1977 to gather additional information, including some of Truman's preliminary autobiographical notes. The resulting brief book is a supplement to Miller's more comprehensive oral history and has the same strengths and weaknesses: warm, friendly, and uncritical.

Beginning in 1975 the private presidential papers of Harry S. Truman became available at the Truman Library. With this information available and Truman generally remembered as an outstanding president, six biographies appeared in the 1980s. The first of these was GOSNELL's 656-page narrative of Truman's political career. This biography is the antithesis of the Merle Miller book; Gosnell carefully describes how Truman made decisions, organized his staff, worked as party leader, and performed the other political tasks of his life. Using primary sources, the work is a thorough, if dry, description of Truman's political life.

In 1983 and 1984 the historian Robert FERRELL published two biographies. The first brief book focuses on Truman's political life from his first elected office through retirement. Despite the title, the book is weakest in describing Truman's presidency. Perhaps too much is attempted for too few pages. The second book focuses instead on Truman's development from a poorly educated farm worker to a world leader. Particularly impressive in the second book is a wonderful collection of candid photographs that are well integrated into the text.

Both books suffer from Ferrell's worshipful attitude toward his subject. Ferrell avoids dealing with the strongest criticisms of the revisionists. Although he claims to have made extensive use of the Truman papers, there is no documentation in the text even for dubious attributions. These books offer little beyond the earlier biographies.

British author and politician Roy JENKINS presents an admiring, yet more balanced view in his cogent 232-page biography. He focuses more on Truman's role in creating the post-World War II world system than do other biographers. Nevertheless, Jenkins accurately and adequately describes both Truman's personal and political lives. Using secondary sources entirely, Jenkins has produced an extremely well-written, entertaining biography.

Another impressive work is Richard MILLER's thoroughly documented history of Truman's rise to national prominence. Miller shows Truman as a professional big-city politician who cooperated with the Pendergast machine. Although not personally corrupt, Truman was not the innocent, small-town politician portrayed in the earlier biographies. Miller's Truman faced the problem of balancing two sets of obligations: to the machine and to the public. The book reads like good investigative reporting, with Miller's thorough documentation not inhibiting the telling of an intriguing tale. The book will not satisfy readers who want a full biography, but it is the definitive explanation of Truman's rise.

The most recent biography should be the choice for readers who want a cogent, well-written synthesis that captures both the essence of the man and the progression of his life. PEMBERTON's book has 178 pages of text, a useful four-page chronology, and over 40 pages of notes and references. Pemberton is an historian who carefully documents his interpretations, yet boils down the mass of documents into its essence. His view shows balance, and when the evidence is inconclusive on a point, he is willing to say so. He addresses revisionist criticisms, at times in agreement, at times in disagreement, and often in between.

Readers who want a warm, anecdotal, supportive biography will be pleased with Margaret Truman's work. Those who want to read Truman's self-image entertainingly presented should read Merle Miller's oral biography. Readers who want to focus on Truman's rise to power will find Richard Miller's book fascinating, and those who want an emphasis on the presidential years should read Jenkins' brief biography. For a cogent, well-documented, and interesting presentation of both the man and his life, readers will find the Pemberton book satisfying.

—Robert E. O'Connor

TURGENEV, Ivan, 1818–1883; Russian writer.

Lloyd, John A. T., *Ivan Turgenev.* London, R. Hale, 1942.
Magarshack, David, *Turgenev: A Life.* London, Faber, and New York, Grove, 1954.
Schapiro, Leonard, *Turgenev: His Life and Times.* Oxford, Oxford University Press, and New York, Random House, 1978.
Troyat, Henri, *Turgenev,* translated by Nancy Amphoux. New York, Dutton, 1988 (originally published as *Tourgeniev,* Paris, Flammarion, 1985).
Yarmolinsky, Avrahm, *Turgenev: The Man, His Art and His Age.* New York and London, Century, 1926; revised edition, New York, Collier, 1961.

*

"You will find my whole biography in my works," Turgenev once wrote. By that he meant, not that his fiction was unusually autobiographical, but rather that his life and his writing were so intimately intertwined that neither could be properly understood without the other. Although nearly any biography—particularly of modern figures—must incorporate autobiographical elements, biographers of talented writers should guard against excessive reliance on their subjects' own words lest they produce something more like autobiography than biography.

On the whole Turgenev has attracted good biographers, although one of them, LLOYD, succumbs to the temptation of drawing too heavily on his fiction. After a general introduction, in his second chapter Lloyd focuses on the personality of Turgenev's mother, who exerted considerable influence on him, in a chattily atmospheric chapter consisting largely of quotations from Turgenev's own writing. The next chapter, based mostly on Turgenev's short story "First Love," sketches Turgenev's youth-

ful emotional involvements, and still another chapter on his earlier years leans heavily upon "Spring Torrents," a work written much later. In short, if Lloyd's biograpy reads well, we should thank Turgenev rather than Lloyd for that circumstance.

For many years YARMOLINSKY's remained the standard biography of Turgenev in English. Published in 1926, after Yarmolinsky had conducted extensive research in Soviet libraries and archives under the difficult conditions prevailing in the early 1920s, it was later revised, and then republished more than once. Yarmolinsky never forgets that Turgenev was a writer as well as a man (though not a "remarkably strange or amazing" one, as he rightly comments), and discusses his literary works and contemporary reactions to them at the appropriate length in the appropriate places. Yarmolinsky pictures Turgenev as a characteristic personality of his time: once we understand him, we will also understand the Russian mind of his day, especially as revealed in its finest literature. Yarmolinsky is surely correct here, for Turgenev created fascinating canvases of the society within which he moved, portrayals which, moreover, his contemporary readers normally recognized as objective.

If Yarmolinsky's book is even now the best single treatment of Turgenev as cultural figure, SCHAPIRO's still has some advantages over it. Principally, Schapiro benefits from the Soviets' efforts during the 1960s to bring out the first serious attempt at a complete scholarly edition of Turgenev's fiction and most especially his correspondence. The gargantuan effort invested in the gathering of his letters from correspondents scattered across Europe and America has greatly eased the work of Turgenev's biographers. As a beneficiary of this labor, Schapiro has made excellent use of the collected edition, as well as numerous scholarly contributions to have appeared since Yarmolinsky wrote.

Schapiro's biography was a bit of a surprise, since he had been known earlier for a book on the Communist Party of the Soviet Union and other works dealing with the history and politics of this century. But he had long been interested in Turgenev, though with a tilt toward Turgenev's view of politics generally, and cultural politics in particular. Turgenev's correspondence contains many remarks on current political events to which his biographers had paid relatively little attention. So in this book—which Sharipo cautiously dubs a "portrait" rather than an interpretation—the author sets out to elucidate what remains of the "enigma" of Turgenev's life, and to discuss his political ideas. Schapiro always remains close to his source materials in formulating judicious evaluations. He displays restraint in introducing evidence from Turgenev's fiction, and even when he cites the much more reliable biographical evidence taken from letters, he evaluates it on the basis of his assessments of Turgenev's relationships with his correspondents. Schapiro also discusses Turgenev's fictional works at the proper points, but of the major biographies Schapiro's is focused most closely upon the man as we know him through non-fictional documentation. In this respect Schapiro and Lloyd stand at opposite poles.

Two works have appeared by scholars who have written biographies of many other Russian writers, and who seem more interested in biography as such than in Turgenev as an individual. MAGARSHACK (also a translator) devoted one of his earlier biographical efforts to Turgenev. Magarshack takes the long view of Turgenev's life, searching for common threads running through it, organizing his study, not along a straight chronology, but in large chunks of time within which he does not strictly observe chronological order (three of his chapter headings are geographical, where geography is closely linked with chronology: Courtavenel, Baden-Baden, and Bougival). Magarshack understands that fictional works can provide keys to biographical truth in the emotional and psychological spheres, though not usually in the arena of historical fact. He has assimilated his material thoroughly, and undergirds some stimulating biographical generalizations with persuasive argumentation. For example, he maintains—and quite reasonably, in my view—that a Turgenev committed for 40 years to another man's wife, the famous singer Pauline Viardot, on occasion had to resent his enslavement. At another point Magarshack writes that "Turgenev always required the passage of time to form a just appreciation of the character of a man," to which the corollary is that Turgenev's first impressions of people were often wrong, or at the least subject to drastic revision. Overall Magarshack offers a very worthwhile treatment of Turgenev's life, and does not yield to the tug of Turgenev's own pen. He sees Turgenev through the eyes of contemporary friends and enemies in addition to Turgenev's own, and as objectively as he can.

The French scholar TROYAT occupies much the same niche in French intellectual life as does Magarshack in the British, but he is less thorough. Troyat's biography is quite short for such a well-documented life, which means that it cannot provide very detailed information. For example, Troyat is understandably interested in Turgenev's links with French culture, but the scope of his book does not permit him to develop the topic properly. He provides brief summaries of Turgenev's fictional works, which he sometimes does not understand thoroughly (cf., his discussion of "Clara Milich"). It is also unfortunate that the book's translator from the French evidently knows nothing of Russia, so that the English version contains errors that could easily have been eliminated by a knowledgeable editor. But in the final accounting Troyat takes a clear view of his subject. He sympathsizes with Turgenev without idealizing him.

A Russian writer who finds three such English biographers as Yarmolinsky, Magarshack, and Schapiro is indeed fortunate. In life, Turgenev always sought to be even-handed, but for some reason he made many personal enemies among his contemporaries. Among his biographers, though, who know him more intimately than most of his contemporaries did, and are not subject to immediate political pressures, he has no enemies.

—Charles A. Moser

TURNER, J(oseph) M(allord) W(illiam), 1775–1851; English painter.

Anderson, John, Jr., *The Unknown Turner: Revelations Concerning the Life and Art of J. M. W. Turner.* New York, privately printed, 1926.

Falk, Bernard, *Turner the Painter: His Hidden Life.* London, Hutchinson, 1938.

Finberg, A. J., *The Life of J. M. W. Turner, R.A.* Oxford, Clarendon Press, 1939; 2nd revised edition, 1961.

Gage, John, editor, *Collected Correspondence of J. M. W. Turner with an Early Diary and a Memoir by George Jones.* Oxford, Clarendon Press, and New York, Oxford University Press, 1980.

Hamerton, Philip Gilbert, *The Life of J. M. W. Turner, R.A.* London, Seeley Jackson, and Boston, Roberts, 1879.

Lindsay, Jack, *J. M. W. Turner. His Life and Work.* London, Cory Adams, and Greenwich, Connecticut, New York Graphic Society, 1966.

Reynolds, Graham, *Turner.* London, Thames and Hudson, and New York, Abrams.

Thornbury, Walter, *The Life of J. M. W. Turner, R.A., Founded on Letters and Papers Furnished by His Friends and Fellow Academicians* (2 vols.). London, Hurst and Blackett, 1862; revised edition in one volume, London, Chatto and Windus, and New York, Holt, 1877.

Wilton, Andrew, *Turner in his Time,* London, Thames and Hudson, and New York, Abrams, 1987.

*

Innumerable books have been written on the subject of Turner's art, each of them containing a certain amount of biographical material in connection with his paintings. However, there are very few biographies of the artist, and none of them is wholly satisfactory. The earliest, that by THORNBURY, has many drawbacks: its arrangement is often thematic rather than strictly chronological; there are occasional long passages with no direct relevance to Turner; and it has no index. The book also contains both repetitions and contradictions, the inevitable result of having been compiled in a hurry by an over-worked professional journalist and writer. Its chief virtue is that it was written only a decade after Turner's death, so that Thornbury was able to obtain firsthand information and quotations from many of Turner's friends and colleagues. Thornbury also quotes extensively from the artist's own letters, some of which are known only from these transcriptions. The book includes a chronologically arranged list of Turner's exhibited works (based on the entries in the catalogues of the Royal Academy), lists of those works in private collections at the time of writing, the text of Turner's will, and an account of the notorious legal proceedings over the will that took place in the 1850s. Furthermore, it is becoming increasingly clear that many of Thornbury's apparent fabrications are based on fact, so that his book is of cardinal importance to Turner scholars. However, neither its style nor its arrangement makes it really suitable for the general reader of today.

In the biography by the Victorian artist and art critic HAMERTON the reader will find dates, quotations, and anecdotes coupled with a real and valuable sensitivity to Turner's art (an attribute missing from Thornbury's book, where this crucial dimension was supplied by extensive quotations from the works of Ruskin). On the other hand, it is hard to see how appreciation of Turner's art has been furthered by FALK's biography, written in a chatty style with much emphasis on the painter's sexual life. LINDSAY's biography is coloured by his own lifelong Marxism, but it is both shorter and simpler than Finberg's book (see below), while at the same time containing a great deal of useful material. Readers should be strongly warned against consulting ANDERSON's book (fortunately this was printed in a limited edition of only 1000 copies). This reproduces innumerable works that have no connection whatsoever with Turner, much of its biographical material is in total conflict with that found in other biographies of Turner and appears to be the product of fantasy, and the lengthy "tour diary" from which it quotes is indubitably spurious.

Thornbury's biography attracted much criticism as soon as it was published, Turner's friends resenting not only its inaccuracies of fact but even more the impression it gave of the artist in his later years as a miserly old eccentric living in dirt and squalor and enjoying both drink and the company of unsuitable women. A very substantial biography that redresses the imbalance and portrays Turner as a serious and hard-working genius is that written by FINBERG, whose approach is sober, meticulous, and scholarly. His book is an essential reference work for anyone interested in Turner, giving, so far as is possible, a day-by-day account of the artist's doings. However, it is rather monotonous in its narrative and some readers may find it too dense and detailed to be read for more than a chapter or two at a time. Finberg was engaged in research on Turner for over 30 years (he died in 1939, just before the first edition of his book was published, so that the second edition was supervised by his widow). His biography of Turner was preceded by a mammoth undertaking, the publication of the two-volume *Inventory* (1909) of the 20,000 or so works on paper belonging to all periods of Turner's career and found in his studio when he died (the "Turner Bequest," now housed in the Clore Gallery for the Turner Collection, at the Tate Gallery in London). In the course of this work Finberg assigned definite or provisional dates to all of Turner's sketchbooks and drawings on loose sheets of paper in the Bequest and allocated these to particular tours known or thought to have been made by the artist in Great Britain and on the Continent. Finberg's biography is, naturally, based on the definitive chronology established through this important work. Occasionally in his biography he corrected errors of dating made in the *Inventory* (e.g., he reassigned one sketchbook from Turner's first tour of Italy in 1819 to his second tour in 1828), and he was sometimes forced to reserve judgement over the dating of particularly difficult material. In recent years many of Turner's tours have been studied in far more detail than was possible for Finberg, but his chronology has received remarkably little modification, the most notable instance relating to Turner's second visit to Venice, which is now generally dated to 1833 rather than 1835. Despite these criticisms of style and the presence of a very few accidental misdatings, Finberg's biography is certainly the one that the serious reader should consult for solid information on Turner himself, together with explanatory historical material and frequent relevant quotations such as contemporary comments on Turner's exhibited paintings.

Readers wanting a briefer account of Turner's career than Finberg's would do well to consult that by REYNOLDS. This has a reliable and easy-to-read text by an expert on British 19th-century painting and also has the advantage of containing a large number of illustrations, many in colour.

In the past 20 years there have been many good books and exhibition catalogues on Turner, but biography has not in general been their prime purpose. GAGE's edition of what little remains of Turner's correspondence is a tool for serious scholars, Turner's difficult prose having minimal appeal for the general reader. The book begins with a transcription of the manuscript "Recol-

lections of Turner" by his friend George Jones, R.A. (a useful source also used by Thornbury); however, the "Diary of a Tour in Wales in 1792," which Gage also reproduces, has subsequently been shown to be definitely not written by Turner.

WILTON's *Turner in his Time* is less historically oriented than its title suggests and comes close to being a straightforward biography of Turner for a general audience, based as far as possible on contemporary accounts. A lively text is accompanied by many illustrations, including attractive colour plates, and there are useful chronologies summarizing Turner's artistic output, activities, and journeys. There is also a list of the books in Turner's own library. However, Wilton's book has no footnotes crediting his modern sources, a fact that will endear it to the general reader but may irritate those who disagree with some of its pronouncements or suspect it of occasional carelessness.

—Cecilia Powell

TWAIN, Mark [*born* Samuel Langhorne Clemens], 1835–1910; American writer.

Benson, Ivan, *Mark Twain's Western Years*. Stanford, California, Stanford University Press, and London, Oxford University Press, 1938.

Brashear, Minnie, *Mark Twain, Son of Missouri*. Chapel Hill, University of North Carolina Press, 1934.

Brooks, Van Wyck, *The Ordeal of Mark Twain*. New York, Dutton, 1920; London, Heinemann, 1922; revised edition, 1933.

Clemens, Clara (Mrs. Ossip Gabrilowitsch), *My Father, Mark Twain*. New York, Harper, 1931.

DeVoto, Bernard, *Mark Twain's America*. Boston, Little Brown, 1932.

Emerson, Everett, *The Authentic Mark Twain: A Literary Biography of Samuel L. Clemens*. Philadelphia, University of Pennsylvania Press, 1984.

Ferguson, DeLancey, *Mark Twain: Man and Legend*. Indianapolis, Bobbs-Merrill, 1943.

Henderson, Archibald, *Mark Twain*. London, Duckworth, 1911; New York, F. A. Stokes, 1912.

Hill, Hamlin, *Mark Twain: God's Fool*. New York, Harper, 1973.

Howells, William Dean, *My Mark Twain: Reminiscences and Criticisms*. New York, Harper, 1910.

Kaplan, Justin, *Mr. Clemens and Mark Twain: A Biography*. New York, Simon and Schuster, and London, Penguin, 1966.

Kaplan, Justin, *Mark Twain and His World*. New York, Simon and Schuster, and London, M. Joseph, 1974.

Lauber, John, *The Making of Mark Twain: A Biography*. New York, American Heritage Press, 1985.

Lauber, John, *The Inventions of Mark Twain*. New York, Hill and Wang, 1990.

Meltzer, Milton, *Mark Twain Himself: A Pictorial Biography*. New York, T. Y. Crowell, 1960.

Paine, Albert Bigelow, *Mark Twain: A Biography: The Personal and Literary Life of Samuel Langhorne Clemens* (3 vols.). New York and London, Harper, 1912.

Sanborn, Margaret, *Mark Twain: The Bachelor Years*. New York, Doubleday, 1990.

Wagenknecht, Edward, *Mark Twain: The Man and His Work*. New Haven Connecticut, Yale University Press, and London, Oxford University Press, 1935; 2nd edition, Norman, University of Oklahoma Press, 1961; 3rd edition, Norman, 1967.

Wecter, Dixon, *Sam Clemens of Hannibal*. Boston, Houghton Mifflin, 1952.

*

The number of biographies of Twain is small considering the fascination his life and works have held for readers worldwide. There is no "definitive" biography. A limitation of many studies of Twain is their partiality, a characteristic found in the first biography of note, by HENDERSON, whose susceptibility to his subject's charm led to somewhat inflated critical judgment and to a denial of the pessimism of Twain's last years.

PAINE's three-volume study is partial in a second sense as well, for besides monumentalizing the man whom he served as secretary, authorized biographer, and literary executor, Paine devoted one-third of his text to Twain's relatively unproductive last decade at the expense of balanced coverage. Paine also neglected Twain's literary career in favor of his other activities, relying for this narrative on the *Autobiography* (2 vols., 1924)—that is to say, on Twain's recollections, which Paine took down from Twain's conversations and later edited. Later biographers have found Paine indispensable, for he gathered and preserved materials and information from the Clemens family and acquaintances that might otherwise have been lost; and because of his intimacy he appears to have represented Twain as he wished to be perceived. Paine's lack of verification of some of Twain's embellishments or inaccurate memory means that there are many errors, but because Paine allowed no one access to the papers during his lifetime, the work of correction had to wait. For good and ill, he established the basis of subsequent Twain biography with his emphasis on his subject's strong personality and elevated character and his reliance on anecdotal reminiscence rather than investigation of primary materials. Paine wrote for the general reader, and the narrative's entertainment value is high.

More limited in focus but valuable additions to the biographical record are reminiscences by Twain's close friend HOWELLS and his daughter Clara CLEMENS. Both provide intimate glimpses of the writer as the center of his close-knit family, and they offer anecdotes that reveal his contradictory personality (gentle and temperamental, bitter and humorous); understandably they show Twain in a rosy light.

The image of Twain as great writer beloved by the common people (Howells called him the "Lincoln of our literature") was bound to be attacked as part of the revolt by artists and critics against the genteel tradition in the arts and the materialism of the Gilded Age in which it flourished, for both aspects of the surrounding culture seemed to have limited Twain's art as well as his spirit. BROOKS launched the attack in a controversial psychoanalytical study in which he tried to account for the "miscarriage in [Twain's] creative life" (Brooks values highly only a few works, including *Huckleberry Finn* and *Tom Sawyer*), and the pessimism and misanthropy of his later years. He singles out as causes of Twain's "wound" a traumatic scene at his father's deathbed and the hostile environment of his child-

hood and the Western frontier; and he lists as symptoms Twain's submission to the refined standards of taste represented by his wife, provincial New England society, and Howells' highmindedness and his capitulation to the degraded values of an increasingly acquisitive culture. Brooks' powerful conception of Twain's dual personality inevitably affected successive Twain biographers, if only in stirring them to argue against it. It has gradually been corrected or refined as psychoanalytical criticism has become more sophisticated, as Twain's historical background has been scrutinized, and as autobiographical materials have become available to scholars.

The strongest rebuttal to Brooks came from historian DeVOTO, who called his book an "essay in the correction of ideas" and in turn was accused of being overly tendentious. His thesis is that, rather than being deformed or thwarted by his background, Twain was a frontier humorist who "worked out in obscure newspapers the first formidable realism . . . in our literature." In offering this introduction to Twain's works and "how they issue from American life," DeVoto evokes the frontier world of Twain's first three decades, with its wealth of folk traditions and its occasions for "anxiety, violence, supernatural horror"—the raw humor that some critics believe needed suppressing.

BRASHEAR argues with Brooks by insisting that the "heroic character of his early environment" in northeast Missouri and the "epic quality of life" there actually fomented Twain's genius. She also wants to counteract the legend (which Twain himself encouraged) that his was a natural, "unliterary" talent that bloomed preternaturally among the "western wilderness." In positing this positive cultural environment capable of nourishing him, Brashear notes the formative influence of Twain's uncle's farm and the steadily advancing frontier. She emphasizes the importance of his printing apprenticeships and newspaper experience, speculates about what books he might have read on the basis of what would have been available in the town library or bookstores, and treats his river pilot days insofar as they provided material for his literary ambitions.

WECTER offers an exhaustive picture of Hannibal and the first 18 years of Twain's life; his researches led him to question the "literary resources" available to the youth, calling the "basic culture" of Hannibal "literate but not literary." Had Wecter lived to finish the projected two-volume biography, it would doubtless have been definitive, as he was literary executor of Clemens' estate and had visited every important Twain setting. He meticulously describes Hannibal, provides detailed ancestry, and covers the writer's education thoroughly.

Twain's years as a silver miner and reporter in Nevada and California are covered in BENSON; here the two counterposed tendencies in Twain's character are his ability to "rough it" and his attraction to the more sophisticated cultural life available in California and on his voyage to the Sandwich Islands. He sees Twain teasing his readers with jokes and hoaxes, while at the same time protesting against "sham, hypocrisy, humbug" and developing a keen sense of loyalty and fair play.

Another important "partial" biography is provided by HILL, who treats Twain's last decade in gruesome, tragic, or sympathetic detail, depending on how convincing one finds his depiction of Twain as a "domestic tyrant, self-centered and vindictive, who makes psychological cripples of his wife and children" (John Tuckey, *American Literature*, March 1974). Hill uses notebooks kept by Twain's secretary to tell of the years of his decline. According to one reviewer, it is "not a pretty story," but it is "splendidly, grippingly written and excellently documented" and supports the " 'DeVoto school,' which seeks to explain much of the pessimism in his later works as a result of Twain's personal misfortune" (*Choice*, December 1973).

WAGENKNECHT takes a middle ground in the controversy, following Brooks in emphasizing Twain's self-dramatization and conceding that his personality, rather than his art, makes him a mythical figure on the American landscape. Like DeVoto he finds the frontier enabling rather than limiting, but he believes that Twain transformed what he found there; to him Twain was a conscious artist influenced by literary sources as well as vernacular ones. Wagenknecht concludes that Olivia Langdon Clemens' influence on her husband was not "determinative," for "there was too much virility in him to permit himself to be pushed very far from his native bent." As revised to account for new scholarship, this "centenary portrait" is a satisfying introduction.

If Wagenknecht produced the first worthwhile study of the whole of Twain's life, in the view of many scholars FERGUSON supplanted it. Focusing on Twain's "career as a writing man," Ferguson interweaves much new material that had come to light (he bases his discussion of the composition of *Huckleberry Finn* on his own collation of the manuscripts), quoting Twain whenever possible, and relating his works to literary tradition. He asserts that Twain's best books are those organized around journeys, which provide structure and continuity. The main drawback of this work for students is its lack of footnotes (and, unfortunately, its unavailability, for it is out of print).

EMERSON offers another literary biography, one that has been criticized for its "strong reluctance to take on non-literary matters" (*TLS*, 1 February 1985). He weaves many unpublished or inaccessible writings into his story of the "disappearance" of the "authentic" Mark Twain; he clearly prefers the comic persona of the earlier work. Critics disagree over the extent to which Emerson shapes his thesis convincingly, with Foster Hirsch complaining that the biography "disappears under a blizzard of dates, facts, plot summaries and nerveless exposition" (*America*, 7–14 July 1984) and T. A. Shippey grateful for Emerson's clearly stated and "plausible" thesis—"that Mark Twain cracked, both as a writer and as a man, somewhere around the year 1885" (*TLS*, 1 February 1985).

One of the most popular biographies of any American literary figure is KAPLAN's *Mr. Clemens and Mark Twain* (1966), which begins when Twain is 31 years old and leaving the West. Kaplan justifies this starting point by saying that Clemens wrote the best accounts of his first three decades; what interests him is the "central drama of his mature literary life," his "discovery of the usable past." This Pulitzer Prize-winning study is so densely packed and so well written that readers may be seduced into thinking they "know" Twain as he really was, but academic reviewers have criticized its preference for psychological over political and social explanation and its disproportionate emphasis on Twain's disappointments, humiliations, rages, and financial difficulties. They concede the provocativeness of Kaplan's interpretations and admire the comprehensiveness of his study and his assimilation of the scholarship, while criticizing his book's inadequate documentation and Kaplan's failure to acknowledge previous work.

Perhaps because Kaplan's widely read life omits discussion of Twain's formative years, two recent books focus on this signifi-

cant period. In *The Making of Mark Twain* (1985) LAUBER drew on then-unpublished letters and their editorial apparatus (two volumes, appearing in 1988 and 1990, take Twain up to 1868) to help him sort out false from valid anecdotes and examine incidents, such as Samuel Clemens' pledge to his mother at his father's deathbed, which Brooks drew on for his theory (Lauber concludes it probably never happened). SANBORN covers the same period, but her study is much more detailed (it is longer by a third) and no less readable. She quotes directly from Twain's letters and 11 notebooks (covering the period 1853–68) to allow him to tell his story in his own words as much as possible, and she examines the autobiographical transformations in his published works. She also counters some by-now hardened pictures such as that of his mother as a stern and unreasonable moral guardian; and she concludes from the evidence in Twain's letters during his intense courtship of Olivia Langdon that "had this near-fanatical desire for reformation and acceptance" by her and her family continued, his genius would have been stifled, but "his wild humor, the very thing they were trying to root out," saved him.

LAUBER's second biography (1990) is not a continuation of the first but an assimilative study of Twain's "entire life and career," with special attention paid to the composition and reception of *Huckleberry Finn*, which he considers Twain's most important "invention." Although Lauber provides a suitable introduction to the life by using Twain's own writings, as in his earlier volume the notes are sparse. (Skimping on citations is evidently a trend in recent commercial biographies, for Sanborn, too, gathers her sources in a narrative summary for each chapter; but she at least provides a bibliography.) As Guy Cardwell said in a review of Lauber's 1985 study, a satisfactory biography of the whole of Clemens' life must be postponed until the new Twain texts are "complete" (*New York Times Book Review*, 24 November 1985). Until then, the reader can enjoy Wagenknecht's or Emerson's account or read Sanborn and Kaplan in succession.

There are also two pictorial biographies. MELTZER includes more than 600 contemporary illustrations, many of them previously unknown, to compile a brilliantly researched picture of Twain's world. KAPLAN's *Mark Twain and His World* (1974) offers both color prints and a readable narrative.

—Phyllis Frus

VALÉRY, (Ambroise-) Paul (-Toussaint-Jules), 1871–1945; French poet.

Grubbs, Henry A., *Paul Valéry*. Boston, Twayne, 1968.
Mackay, Agnes Ethel, *The Universal Self: A Study of Paul Valéry*. Toronto, University of Toronto Press, and London, Routledge, 1961.

*

Throughout his life, Valéry devoted some time every day to the writing of his *Cahiers*, in which he expressed his point of view about his biography: "I do not keep, I have never kept a record of my days. What do I care about my biography?'' This statement alone reveals that Valéry left us little biographical information.

As announced in the preface, GRUBBS' study is meant to give the American reader a complete picture of Valéry's life and works. Its biographical sources come mostly from the *Introduction biographique* written by Agathe Rouart-Valéry, Valéry's daughter. Grubbs' study opens with a detailed chronology of Valéry's life: his birth in Sète, his education at the Lycée in Montpellier, his early collaboration with Pierre Louÿs in 1890, his election to the Académie Française in 1925, and his important speech (''Discours sur Voltaire'') at The Sorbonne in 1944. The first chapter is a thoroughly detailed account of Valéry's upbringing. It puts a special emphasis on his discovery of Mallarmé, whom he met in 1890. Grubbs presents Valéry first and foremost as a writer and thinker and traces his development as the ''official poet of France.'' He thus chooses not to emphasize biographical details, ignoring for example Valéry's marriage to Jeannie Gobbillard in 1900, his journey to the Riviera, and the official ceremonies he attended and numerous lectures he gave.

Grubbs' argument regarding Valéry's choice in 1922 to abandon literature suggests that the young poet was ''faced with the necessity of choosing between literary creation (Orpheus) and the cultivation of his own mind (Narcissus).'' This point of view is supported by Valéry's correspondence with Albert Thibaudet and André Gide. Grubbs portrays Valéry's experiences in Paris through the *Cahiers*, which reveal how Valéry continued to develop his talent while facing the necessity of earning his living (Only a small part of these *Cahiers* were published during Valéry's life; they have since been published in their entirety by the Centre National de la Recherche Scientifique, Paris, 29 vols., 1957–61).

For Grubbs, Valéry's return to poetry in 1923 is marked by the publication of the sonnet ''Orphée.'' Grubbs' study thoroughly examines Valéry's hesitations regarding the writing of poetry, and he presents remarkably well Valéry's opposition to poetic inspiration (in the traditional sense of the term) and his disdain for the ''parasitism of critics'' as well as biographical approaches to poetry. Grubbs' principal contribution is to delineate step by step Valéry's poetic search as shown in the transcripts of the poet's lectures and in various texts published in *Commerce*, the literary review Valéry edited with Léon-Paul Fargue and Valéry Larbaud from 1924 to 1932.

MACKAY's study offers a more detailed account of Valéry's life, in particular his childhood. She takes into consideration the region of Sète where Valéry was born, discussing its history and the crucial role it played in Valéry's life. ''I am happy,'' Valéry wrote, ''to have been born in a place where my first impressions were those that came from facing the sea and from being in the midst of human activities.'' Moreover, Mackay meticulously documents Mallarmé's Tuesday afternoons at the ''Rue de Rome,'' which were attended by Valéry on a regular basis. Mackay reminds us how Valéry was the first one to see Mallarmé's ''Un coup de dés'' and claims that no other poet at the time understood Mallarmé's poetics so well. In particular, she discusses Valéry's scholarly article on ''Un coup de dés'' in a chapter entitled ''Poetry in Paris.'' This chapter recreates the atmosphere of Valéry's entourage, which was composed of poets and painters, and underlines their passion for music: '' 'We were nourished on music,' Valéry confessed, and 'our heads filled with literature; we dreamt only of extracting from language al-

most the same effects which purely sonorous causes produced on our nervous system.' ''

The remaining chapters of Mackay's book are devoted to a textual analysis of the entire body of Valéry's works and in particular to the evolution of Valéry's idea of ''pure poetry.'' Her critical study is supported by extensive quotes from poems in French. Valéry, she writes, ''invites us to consider a science of ideas and an art of treating them.'' Mackay is a good reader of the texts, and she successfully demonstrates the lyrical and musical qualities of Valéry's poetry. However, her thematic approach is antiquated in comparison to more sophisticated models of literary criticism. Therefore, the reader interested in contemporary critical issues might consider examining more recent studies.

Finally, given the limited number of biographies of Valéry in English, the reader will find the most interesting and insightful biographical information on Valéry in the final volume of Jackson Matthews' translation and edition of *The Collected Works of Paul Valéry* (15 vols., Princeton, 1956–75). This final volume includes excerpts from the *Cahiers* selected by Valéry and a record of his lectures as well as the Valéry-Fourment and the Valéry-Gide correspondence. The opening chapters, ''Autobiography'' and ''Moi,'' provide more accurate recollections of Valéry's childhood than do the biographies presented above. The chapter entitled ''My early days in England'' offers interesting and detailed biographical material on Valéry's education, including the memoirs about his philosophy professors and his travels. The chapter entitled ''Memories of Paul Valéry,'' by Pierre Féline, traces the beginning of Féline's friendship with the poet in Montpellier, where Valéry was studying law. Finally, the two-hour interview held in 1921 with Paul Valéry by S. Bach presents Valéry's perspectives on his own literary production as well as on the writers of his generation.

—Martine Natat Antle

VAN DYCK, Sir Anthony, 1599–1641; Flemish painter.

Brown, Christopher, *Van Dyck*. Oxford, Phaidon, 1982; Ithaca, New York, Cornell University Press, 1983.

Cust, Lionel, *Anthony van Dyck: An Historical Study of His Life and Work*. London, G. Bell, 1900.

Martin, J. R., and G. Feigenbaum, *Van Dyck as a Religious Artist*. Princeton, New Jersey, Princeton University Art Museum, 1979.

*

Throughout the centuries, many colorful legends have emerged, or have been created, concerning Van Dyck's life. One of the most persistent was that of his aristocratic descent, an assumption that finally came to rest with the publication of the archival research of F. J. Van de Branden, unequivocally proving that Van Dyck's father was in fact a silk merchant. Another unfounded claim has it that Van Dyck was trained by his mother, which was first mentioned by C. De Bie. Many anecdotes are also known concerning Van Dyck's turbulent, amorous life in England, first written about by Lord Conway in a letter of 22

January 1636 to the Count of Strafford, repeated later by Richard Symonds and varied endlessly in many Van Dyck biographies, including those by G. P. Bellori (1672), J. von Sandrart (1675), R. de Piles (1715), A. Houbraken (3 vols., 1718–21), and, in English, H. Walpole (*Anecdotes of Painting in England*, 4 vols., 1765–71). Even CUST still held that women were the fatal attraction of Van Dyck's life and that he wasted on them his health and money, a view echoed in Glück's German biography (*Van Dyck: Des Meisters Gemälde*, 2nd edition, 1931), which was criticized by Van Puyvelde (*Van Dyck*, 1950). Guiffrey (*Antione van Dyck: sa vie et son oeuvre*, 1882) also expressed another widely held belief that Van Dyck's decadence in his mature years spoiled his talent. Several Dutch and German scholars have argued along similar lines.

Less speculative is the statement made by all the early chroniclers of Van Dyck's life that Van Dyck went directly from Van Balen's studio to that of Rubens. His association with Rubens may not have been an apprenticeship as was often believed, even in 20th-century scholarship, but should probably be regarded as a collaboration between a young, talented master and an older, established artist.

An anonymous 18th-century biography in French was probably written by the Flemish antiquarian J. F. M. Michel and is now in the Bibliothèque du Louvre, Paris. It is by far the most detailed account of Van Dyck's Italian years. The manuscript was commented upon by Michiels (*Van Dyck et Ses Eleves*, 1882), who dated it between 1769 and 1775, and more recently by Brown (see below). Its importance lies in the fact that the author of the account had access to letters, now lost, written by Van Dyck's host in Genoa, Cornelis de Wael, to his fellow-Fleming, Lucas Van Uffelen, who lived in Venice. Additional information on Van Dyck's Italian years after he left Antwerp on 3 October 1621 may be found in the master's Italian sketchbook. This sketchbook, which is now in the British Museum, London, is the most important artistic document of Van Dyck's Italian years. Brown rightly stresses that, as far as can be judged, Van Dyck seems to have used his sketchbook principally between his arrival in Rome in February 1622 and his departure from Sicily in September 1624. One of the most striking aspects of the Italian sketchbook is the virtual absence of drawings after the Antique, which confirms a similar remark made by von Sandrart in his 1675 biography of Van Dyck.

Many comments in this unfinished manuscript were also meant to correct Descamps' biography of Van Dyck (3 vols., 1753–63). Descamps' own claim to be more reliable than Van Dyck's earlier biographers is, however, questionable. For instance, he is blatantly wrong in claiming that a 13-year-old Van Dyck was in Rubens' atelier, where he had made corrections in Rubens' famous *Descent of the Cross* of 1612, an anecdote first mentioned by Weyerman in 1729. In later biographies of Van Dyck the very same anecdote reappears in a different guise. According to Mensaert, Van Dyck corrected not the *Descent* but Rubens' *Virgin and Saints* in the Augustinian Church in Antwerp. Also, Descamps erroneously assumes that Van Dyck's preference for portraits originated in this period when Rubens, who had grown increasingly jealous of his young apprentice, advised him to relinquish history painting and stick to portraits instead. Already in the 19th century these and similar biographical stories were rightly regarded by Michiels as sheer fantasy. Van

Dyck is thought of almost exclusively as a portraitist, a common misunderstanding. His often neglected activities as a religious artist were clarified in the catalog by MARTIN AND FEIGENBAUM.

BROWN's book on Van Dyck's life and art is the first comprehensive account of Van Dyck to appear in English since Cust's monograph of 1900. Brown has incorporated many results of modern scholarship and he deals with the life and work of the artist in a very clear manner. Contrary to what is quite often the case in previous studies about Van Dyck, the English period does not overshadow Van Dyck's Antwerp and Italian years. Also, greater attention has been given to Van Dyck's early success as a painter of sacred and mythological subjects, for which there was little demand at the court of Charles I in England. However, little is known about Van Dyck's pupils and assistants or about the organization of his studio at any point of his career.

—Hans J. Van Miegroet

VAN GOGH, Vincent, 1853–1890; Dutch painter.

Barrielle, Jean-François, *The Life and Work of Vincent van Gogh*, translated by Virginia Golen. Seacaucus, New Jersey, Chartwell Books, 1984.

Bernard, Bruce, editor, *Vincent by Himself: A Selection of Van Gogh's Paintings and Drawings Together with Extracts from His Letters*. Boston, Little Brown, and London, Orbis, 1985.

Burra, Peter J. S., *Van Gogh*. London, Duckworth, and New York, Macmillan, 1934.

Cabanne, Pierre, *Van Gogh*, translated by Daphne Wordward. London, Thames and Hudson, 1963; 1st American edition translated by Mary I. Martin, Englewood Cliffs, New Jersey, Prentice-Hall, 1963 (originally published by A. Somogny, Paris, 1961).

Du Quesne-Van Gogh, Elisabeth Huberta, *Personal Recollections of Vincent Van Gogh*, translated by Katherine S. Dreier. Boston, Houghton Mifflin, 1913 (originally published by R. Piper, Munich, 1911).

Elgar, Frank, *Van Gogh: A Study of His Life and Work*, translated by James Cleugh. New York, Praeger, and London, Thames and Hudson, 1958 (originally published as *Van Gogh*, Paris, F. Hazan, 1949).

Hammacher, A. M., *Van Gogh: A Documentary Biography*, translated by Mary Charles. London, Thames and Hudson, 1982.

Leymarie, Jean, *Who was Van Gogh?*, translated by James Emmons. Geneva, Albert Skira, 1968.

Lubin, A. J., *Stranger on the Earth: A Psychological Biography of Vincent Van Gogh*. New York, Holt, 1972.

Meier-Graefe, Julius, *Vincent van Gogh: A Biographical Study* (2 vols.), translated by John Holroyd Reece. London, Medici Society, 1922; Boston, Medici Society, 1926.

Nordenfalk, Carl, *The Life and Work of Van Gogh*, translated by Lawrence Wolfe. London, Elek, and New York, Philosophical Society, 1953 (originally published as *Vincent Van Gogh, en Livsvag*, Stockholm, P.A. Norstedt, 1943).

Piérard, Louis, *The Tragic Life of Vincent van Gogh*, translated by Herbert Garland. Boston, Houghton Mifflin, and London, J. Castle, 1925 (originally published by Éditions G. Gres, Paris, 1924).

Pollock, Griselda and Fred Orton, *Vincent van Gogh: Artist of His Time*. Oxford, Phaidon, and New York, Dutton, 1978.

Stone, Irving, *Lust for Life*. London and New York, Longman, 1934.

Tralbaut, Marc Edo, *Vincent Van Gogh*. London, Macmillan, and New York, Viking, 1969.

Wallace, Robert, *The World of Van Gogh 1853–90*. New York, Time-Life Books, 1969.

Zurcher, Bernard, *Vincent van Gogh: Art, Life, and Letters*, translated by Helga Harrison. New York, Rizzoli, 1985.

*

Anybody interested in the biography of Vincent van Gogh must turn in first instance to the artist's letters, an invaluable and eminently readable source of information about the artist's life from age 19 until the last days before his death. The complete three-volume French edition of the letters (edited by Georges Charensol, Paris, 1960) includes those to his brother Theo and his sister Willemien, as well as letters to his friends and fellow artists Emile Bernard, Paul Gauguin, and Anthon van Rappard. The letters to Theo, which make up the bulk of van Gogh's correspondence, were first published in 1914, in an edition that was prepared by Theo's wife, Johanna van Gogh-Bonger. It includes a biographical memoir which, excepting the *Recollections* of du Quesne, constitutes the first complete account of the artist's life. The essay is reprinted in the standard English edition of the letters with an addendum by Theo's son, the engineer Vincent Willem van Gogh (*Complete Letters*, Greenwich, Connecticut, 3 vols., 1958; based on the four-volume edition edited by J. van Gogh-Bonger, 1952–54).

Numerous selections of letters (by W. H. Auden, Irving Stone, Mark Roskill, and others) have been published in both hardcover and popular paperback editions. In addition, a number of recent books combine excerpts of letters with documentary photographs and reproductions of the artist's works to form what might be called "documentary biographies." The works by BERNARD and HAMMACHER fall into this category. Hammacher's book is particularly interesting for its illustrations, which include numerous reproductions of works by artists van Gogh admired. Related to these documentary biographies are books in the "art, life, and letters" genre, such as the work by ZURCHER, which is "guided by the artist's letters and even in its form . . . strives to follow the letters in their emotional twists and turns."

Nearly all biographies of van Gogh are based largely if not exclusively on the artist's correspondence, often at the expense of other sources. Thus in the first book-length biography of van Gogh, the two-volume work by the art critic and dealer Julius MEIER-GRAEFE, the author freely admits that the threads of his story are "the lines of the letters and what is written between them." Despite his dependence on the letters, however, Meier-Graefe manages to forge a powerful, if rather romantic, personal vision of van Gogh. Fascinated by the importance of contrast in the artist's career and personality, he tends to oppose, for example, the gloomy Dutch North and the sunny French South; the dark Nuenen palette and the vibrant colors of Arles; and the love of life and the tendency toward destruction. First published in Munich in 1921, at the height of the van Gogh revival in Germany, Meier-Graefe's book is still quite readable today.

Equally based on the letters are the biographies by NORDEN-FALK and CABANNE. Each work is laced with quotes, which tend, at times, to break up the narrative. Other biographies based on the letters, but which use quotes less extensively, are the works by BARRIELLE, ELGAR, and LEYMARIE. All five works are written by art historians or critics; their biographical narrative runs parallel to analyses of van Gogh's artistic development.

Few of the biographies listed above make use of the numerous memoirs that were written about van Gogh. Most of these were published as articles in newspapers and magazines and deal with short periods of the artist's career only. The memoir of Elizabeth DU QUESNE-VAN GOGH, a younger sister of the artist, exceptionally deals with the artist's entire career. As the first published account of the artist's life, it is interesting in particular because it makes clear how difficult it was for van Gogh's contemporaries, even his family members, to understand a man who was "indifferent to convention or form; a stranger to custom . . . ."

Though not exactly a memoir, PIÉRARD's volume is of interest as a work written by someone who was born in the Borinage, the mining district in Belgium where Vincent spent some time as a lay preacher. Writing in 1925, Piérard was able to interview a number of people in the Borinage who had known the artist and could provide him with some firsthand information about the time van Gogh had spent in Belgium, which in so many ways was a critical phase in the artist's life.

The first biographer of van Gogh who attempted to go beyond the letters was STONE. For his romanticized biography of van Gogh, Stone interviewed many of the descendants of the artist's relatives and friends in order to obtain background material for his work. Though unsatisfactory from a factual point of view, Stone nevertheless has captured the spirit of the man and his time in a work that has sold millions of copies and has contributed greatly to the current popularity of the artist.

Like Stone, TRALBAUT has done much documentary and oral history research to round out the "autobiography" provided by van Gogh's letters. Tralbaut's monumental "life" remains the most balanced and extensive biography of the artist to date. Its orientation is "psychobiographical," and the book is heavily indebted to the numerous psychological, psychoanalytical, and psychiatric studies of van Gogh published over the years by such behavioral scientists as Karl Jasper, G. Kraus, Charles Mauron, F. Minkowska, and Humberto Nagera.

The psychobiographical orientation is not unique to Tralbaut. In a sense it may be said that hardly any biographer, whether expert in psychology or not, has been able to withstand the temptation to analyze van Gogh, in a more or less expert fashion. No biography, however, is so exclusively written from the psychoanalytical point of view as LUBIN's, which for that very reason tends to become a bit "heavy."

A few words may be said about the biographies that have appeared in various series. BURRA's biography in the Great Lives series is undistinguished. WALLACE's *The World of van Gogh*, like most books in the Time-Life Books series, is eminently readable and firmly places the artist in the contemporary context. Outstanding is the brief biography by POLLOCK AND ORTON in Dutton's series of artists' biographies. The two authors are well aware of the pitfalls of overusing the letters and provide a concise but well-balanced account of the artist's life and artistic development.

—Petra ten-Doesschate Chu

VASCO DA GAMA. See **GAMA, Vasco da.**

VEGA CARPIO, Lope Félix de, 1562–1635; Spanish playwright and poet.

Hayes, Francis C., *Lope de Vega.* New York, Twayne, 1967.
Rennert, Hugo A., *The Life of Lope de Vega.* Glasgow, Gowans and Gray, and Philadelphia, Campion, 1904.

*

While English readers unable to read Spanish have few works available on Lope, they are fortunate to have RENNERT's biography (whose publication superseded the earlier work of Holland, *The Life of Lope de Vega*, London, 1807). The specialist will find it dated in some details, but the general reader will get from it an excellent picture of Lope and his age. In addition to his 400 pages of biography, Rennert has a 150-page bibliography whose purpose is to catalogue and quantify Lope's dramas. (His sober estimate is that Lope wrote 458 plays; other estimates have ranged as high as 1800.) In the biography proper, Rennert discusses the events of Lope's life together with the works he produced at each stage of his career; the life and the works are presented as an organic whole. He shows a good appreciation of where and how Lope innovated, and of which of his works contain lasting literary merit (not all of them do, he says). He presents a sympathetic picture of Lope without feeling the need either to praise everything he wrote or to create excuses for his shortcomings. Rennert catalogues the contradictions between Lope's life of debauchery and his vocation as a priest, and while he does not downplay Lope's faults, neither does he vilify him. He also carefully avoids using too much hindsight in analyzing Lope's work. Rennert shows that early in life Lope sought fame as an epic and lyric poet; writing plays was secondary, a way of earning money. As an older man, Lope realized that his lyric and epic works were destined to obscurity, while his drama would always bring him fame. Rennert skillfully analyzes Lope's *New Art of Playwrighting* as Lope's reassessment of the value of his own work. The conclusion of his biography contains a thoughtful appraisal of Lope's important role in Spanish literature.

HAYES shows a competent knowledge of Lope scholarship and provides a satisfactory short introduction to his work. Readers with more time will be better served by Rennert (whose work Hayes calls "authoritative"). Hayes lacks a sense of his audience; while his biography is too brief to be of interest to the specialist, he at times assumes a general knowledge of Spanish Golden Age literature that the non-specialist may not have. For example, he refers frequently to Gongorism in his survey of 16th-century Spanish drama, without ever explaining what it is; Gongora himself is mentioned later—only once and in passing. Much of his study is a dry catalogue of plays (those of Lope and of his contemporaries), accompanied by summaries of their plots; out of this one gets little sense of what made Lope's plays successful and what gives them enduring value. Too often, his main way to valorize one of Lope's works is to compare its plots or themes with those of a work by Shakespeare or Molière. There are several bright spots in Hayes' work: his discussion of the diversity of characters in Lope's drama and his analysis of the *New Art of Playwrighting* are examples. Some of his translation is flowery to the point of obscuring the original; he translates "puercos" (pigs) as "my lovely little porkers." His dismissal of the drama of Lope's predecessors as "childlike, artless, ingenuous" is too summary. He dates himself by calling Cosme Lotti "The Cecil De Mille of the 17th century," by referring to the 17th-century code of honor as "a sort of glottological Kingdom of Okeefenokee with Contradiction as its anointed tyrant," and by characterizing Lope's drama under the rubric of "The Four Esses: Suspense, Surprise, Sensation, Shock."

—John Tolan

VELÁZQUEZ, Diego, 1599–1660; Spanish painter.

Brown, Jonathan, *Velázquez, Painter and Courtier.* New Haven, Connecticut, Yale University Press, 1986.
Gudiol, José, *Velázquez,* translated by Kenneth Lyons. London, Secker and Warburg, and New York, Viking, 1974.
Harris, Enriqueta, *Velázquez.* Oxford, Phaidon, and Ithaca, New York, Cornell University Press, 1982.
Justi, Karl, *Diego Velázquez and His Times,* translated by A. H. Keane. London, Grevel, and Philadelphia, Lippincott, 1889 (originally published as *Diego Velázquez und sein Jahrhundert,* Bonn, Cohen, 1888).
Stevenson, Robert A. M., *Velázquez.* London, G. Bell, 1895; edited by Theodore Crombie, London, G. Bell, 1962.
Stirling-Maxwell, William, *Velázquez and His Works.* London, Parker, 1855.
Trapier, Elizabeth du Gué, *Velázquez.* New York, The Hispanic Society of America, 1948.

*

Justi observes, "the history of an artist is, above all, the history of his works," and the biographies of Velázquez are indeed essentially accounts of those works, given narrative shape by the events of his life. Information about that life is disappointingly sparse, and what there is does little to illuminate the sources of the artist's power. Although Keane, Justi's translator, claimed that he had curtailed nothing "by which the vivid picture of the great central figure, whether as a man of striking personality or as an artist of astounding originality, might in any way be impaired," his Velázquez, and the Velázquez presented by most subsequent biographers, remains an elusive and enigmatic figure.

All biographies, apart from the most recent, have leant heavily on Antonio Palomino (*El Parnaso Español Pintoresco Laureado*, Madrid, 1724). Writing at the end of his life, Palomino had access to a manuscript written by one of Velázquez's last pupils, and talked to people who had known the artist. For the years to 1638 he followed the memoir of Francisco Pacheco (*Arte de la Pintura*, Seville, 1649), Velázquez's master and father-in-law. These two texts are translated in Harris (see below). Later researchers have confirmed their historical reliability, and biographers have tended to accept the narrative structure established by Palomino: birth and apprenticeship in Seville; the immediate favour shown by Philip IV on Velázquez's move to the court at Madrid in 1622; the two visits to Italy, where Velázquez was exposed to the best models of art; the rise to a distinguished position in the king's household; the accolade of knighthood and death. They differ in the extent to which they adopt Palomino's reverential and (historically) uncritical attitude to their subject, in their styles of using the context of social and historical circumstances to reconstruct the significance of the life, in the insight with which they interpret the artistic traditions within which Velázquez worked, and in the skill with which they read the paintings.

Velázquez was little known outside Spain when STIRLING-MAXWELL wrote in 1855. He follows Pacheco and Palomino for the life, and draws on an enthusiast's detailed knowledge of Spain and of art to contextualize inventively, relating Spanish artistic traditions to those of other European countries. He has a fund of attractive anecdotal and antiquarian material to fill out episodes, supplying biographies of Velázquez's associates and rivals, and referring to a contemporary poem which claims to represent the artist's words preferring Titian to Raphael. The whole is detailed, lively and resourceful, given the shortage of real biographical material, and sound on the works. However, some aspects of the life tend to be romanticized, as when Stirling-Maxwell states, describing Velázquez's ancestry, "both his parents were of noble blood," or when he recounts Velázquez's wife, Juana Pacheco, "companion of his brilliant career, [who] closed his dying eyes."

JUSTI's substantial volume seeks to explain the artist, the art, and the times, emphasizing Velázquez's "intense and vivid realism." He contextualizes the early career by examining the economic and cultural importance of Seville. While following Palomino's narrative line and interpretation, Justi searches for the driving impulses of Velázquez's art; the early *bodegenes* are related to Dutch genre realism, and the religious paintings to the Marian controversy in the Seville of the 1610s. At all points he exemplifies the method of drawing on circumstantial material to fill the gaps: accounts of other court painters in Madrid, of the visits of Charles, Prince of Wales, and Rubens, of Philip IV's patronage of art, of the various individuals Velázquez met during his Italian visits; finally, he attempts to supply a succession for the master, a school of Velázquez. The works themselves are discussed throughout with shrewd critical insight.

STEVENSON writes primarily as an art critic and historian, providing reflective analysis of the sources of Velázquez's power, ranging over aesthetic theory and companion arts, analyzing technique (composition, colouring, modelling and brushwork), and assessing Velázquez's influence on more recent art, particularly his significance for Impressionism. TRAPIER's major volume follows Palomino's narrative structure, contextualizing with material on the economic and cultural character of Spain and enlarging on the complications of Velázquez's life as a court official. She writes with detail and insight about the works in terms of techniques and influences, and explores the question of Pacheco's influence as master. GUDIOL stays close to Palomino, but provides a full account of the works; this volume shares with those of Harris and Brown the significant advantage of full-colour reproduction.

HARRIS and BROWN each continues the tradition of close reading of the paintings; each uses the rapidly growing fund of modern information and scholarship in a historically disciplined manner, and each is cooler toward the romantic tendencies derived from Palomino's narrative, from which Brown in particular seeks to distance himself. Brown's approach is sophisticated: he recognizes that the evidence reveals little directly about "Velázquez as a person or as a thinker on art": "we lack the personal documents which would open his personal life to scrutiny." His contextualization re-examines the question of Pacheco's influence; Brown considers Pacheco a dull painter, though important for his leading role in a Sevillian circle of Renaissance humanists. In view of the restrictively unlettered, artisan status of the painter in Spain, Pacheco's more exalted vision, informing the *Art de la Pintura*, was therefore remarkable. Brown sees Velázquez's apprenticeship to Pacheco offering him an education in humanist ideals and critical thinking. His meeting with Rubens (diplomat, courtier, painter), and his reverence for Titian (knighted by Charles V) are thereby given significance. Brown's strength is in his independent historical analysis of the king's court at Madrid and of the pictorial displays furnishing the new palaces, which Brown sees as statements in the Renaissance vocabulary of power and prestige: Velázquez becomes "the complete master of political imagery." Brown is discriminating in his discussion of the contacts and influences of the journeys to Italy, and brings fuller information and interpretation to his account of Velázquez's career as court officer. The quality of Brown's relating of circumstantial material to the works is well exemplified in his sophisticated analysis of *Las Meninas;* at such moments Brown comes nearer than his predecessors to the reticent artist self-portrayed within that painting.

—Roger Lowman

VENERABLE BEDE. See BEDE.

VERDI, Giuseppe, 1813–1901; Italian composer.

Baldini, Gabrieli, *The Story of Giuseppe Verdi: Oberto to Un ballo in maschera*, translated and edited by Roger Parker. London and New York, Cambridge University Press, 1980 (originally published as *Abitare la battaglia: la storia di Giuseppe Verdi*, edited by Fedel d'Amico, Milan, Aldo Garzanti, 1970).

Bonavia, Ferruccio, *Verdi*. London, Oxford University Press, 1930.

Budden, Julian, *Verdi*. London, Dent, 1985; New York, Vintage, 1987.

Conati, Marcello, editor, *Encounters with Verdi*, translated by Richard Stokes. Ithaca, New York, Cornell University Press, 1984; as *Interviews and Encounters with Verdi*, London, Gollancz, 1984 (originally published as *Interviste e incontri con Verdi*, Milan, Edizioni il Formichieri, 1980).

Crowest, Frederick J., *Verdi: Man and Musician: His Biography with Especial Reference to His English Experiences*. New York, Scribner, and London, Milne, 1897.

Gatti, Carlo, *Verdi: The Man and His Music*, translated by Elisabeth Abbott. New York, Putnam, and London, Gollancz, 1955 (originally published by Edizioni "Alpes," Milan, 2 vols., 1931).

Hume, Paul, *Verdi: The Man and His Music*. New York, Dutton, 1977; London, Hutchinson, 1978.

Hussey, Dyneley, *Verdi*. New York, Dutton, and London, Dent, 1940.

Martin, George, *Verdi: His Music, Life and Times*. New York, Dodd Mead, 1963; London, Macmillan, 1965.

Osborne, Charles, *Verdi*. London, Macmillan, 1978.

Osborne, Charles, *Verdi: A Life in the Theatre*. London, Weidenfeld and Nicolson, and New York, Knopf, 1987.

Porter, Andrew, "Giuseppe Verdi," in *The New Grove Masters of Italian Opera*, edited by Stanley Sadie. New York and London, Norton, 1983.

Sheean, Vincent, *Orpheus at Eighty*. New York, Random House, 1958; London, Cassell, 1959.

Toye, Francis, *Giuseppe Verdi: His Life and Works*. New York, Knopf, and London, Heinemann, 1931.

Walker, Frank, *The Man Verdi*. New York, Knopf, and London, Dent, 1962.

Weaver, William, editor, *Verdi: A Documentary Study*. London, Thames and Hudson, and Palm Springs, California, Classic Publications, [n.d.].

Wechsberg, Josef, *Verdi*. New York, Putnam, and London, Weidenfeld and Nicolson, 1974.

Werfel, Franz and Paul Stefan, editors, *Verdi: The Man in His Letters*, translated by Edward Downes. New York, L. B. Fischer, 1942 (originally published as *Das Bildnis Giuseppe Verdi*, Berlin, 1926).

Ybarra, T. R., *Verdi: Miracle Man of Opera*. New York, Harcourt, 1955.

*

Verdi's autobiographical narrative for Giulio Ricordi, translated in the works by Weaver and Werfel/Stefan, certainly has some authority, but it is not reliable for facts. Though Verdi was a relatively young 65 when he wrote it, there are lapses in the recollection. For example, the dates of the deaths of his children are confused. The document tells as much about Verdi's state of mind at that particular time as it does about his entire life. In it are revealed his personal resentments and his perceptions of the major events of his life.

WEAVER's volume also includes excerpts from three contemporary sources: an unfinished biography by Melchiorre Delfico, an acquaintance of Verdi, which contains light-hearted observations and memories of the composer's youth; "Cenni biografici" ("biographical notes"), written down in the 1840s and 50s by a relative of Verdi, Giuseppe Demaldè (translated in the *Verdi Newsletter*, vols. 1–3); and Giovanni Fulcini's (a priest in Roncole) collection of local memories written shortly after Verdi's death. CROWEST, the first biography written in English, though lacking documentary evidence, gives a contemporary view of Verdi from across the Channel. None of these sources, however, should be read without the preparation of a more factual account found in some of the later biographies.

BONAVIA's work is overly romanticized and mostly anecdotal. It can not now be taken seriously because much of its factual material is out of date. But Hussey says of this volume that it is a "shorter monograph in which the sympathy of a compatriot and the knowledge of a practicing musician combine with a felicitous literary style to produce a general and radiant illumination of the whole man."

TOYE, on the other hand, offers an outstanding effort, divided into two parts. Part I, for the general reader, gives an overview of Verdi's life and activities, including a summary of important criticisms and general characteristics of his music. Part II goes into greater detail, mostly analyzing the operas, but also concerning the history of those works in Verdi's life. Though Toye's treatment is sometimes very in-depth, the general reader looking for information on these works should not feel intimidated. Toye leans heavily on his knowledge of the librettos and their sources. All of this is enriched by Toye's use of letters and other primary material. The work is well organized and makes for engaging reading.

HUSSEY's early work reappeared in 1963 with amendments following Frank Walker's achievements. This volume suffers from being out of date and undocumented, and some of the musical discussions may be beyond the technical limits of many readers. But Hussey integrates letters with text to good effect, and his book contains some helpful discussions of politics, the operas, and the history of their librettos.

WERFEL AND STEFAN's volume consists mostly of Verdi's autobiography, translations of numerous letters, and a lengthy biographical introduction by Franz Werfel. Since it is written by a man known for his writing ability, the introduction has a stylistic integrity. The essay is entirely subjective, but makes for interesting reading. A skeletal knowledge of Verdi's life might be helpful before reading this volume, especially since it is short on such facts as dates and names. It reads almost as a novel with a literary logic rather than the oddness one finds in people's lives.

The more substantial GATTI also tries to reduce Verdi's life to a flow of logic. This book, originally in two volumes, has been much reduced in the translation. The author never faults Verdi; in this portrayal, the composer is always in the right. Gatti assumes prior knowledge of the operas, discussing them quite freely without relating their stories. The book also includes some of the political background that was so important to Verdi's life. However, it gets sidetracked in its conjectures about possible intimate relations Verdi had with certain women, including Jenny Lind in London and Theresa Stolz in Italy.

SHEEAN's book sometimes reads like an investigative report. It begins with Verdi at the Milan performance of *Falstaff* and unfolds Verdi's life like a mystery, piecing together the events that led to this production. The book, however, is fairly reliable and when it gets onto the subjects of politics and history becomes quite engaging. Sheean, a journalist, also excels at proposing believable motivations for the mysterious junctures in the composer's life, such as his break with Merelli and his hesitation to marry Peppina (Giuseppina Strepponi).

The YBARRA volume deserves mention only because it exists. It portrays 19th-century Italy as a world run by people's desire for sex and money. Also, Ybarra tends to Americanize his subject: he calls the Italian currency "pennies" instead of *lira*. This fictionalized account of Verdi's life is only redeemed by the entertaining anecdotes it relates, few of which contain any verifiable truth.

WALKER's is certainly the most comprehensive of Verdi biographies up to 1962. Unlike most of the previous books, it includes no discussion of the operas, no musical commentary whatsoever. Walker admits being concerned only with the "intimate private life" of this very private man, and he includes long sections on Peppina. To obtain this goal, the author sought out every known and relevant source and questioned the veracity of all assumptions on the subject circulating at the time. His observations are fresh and well documented. Nor do they give way to hero worship, unlike many of the earlier accounts. For example, he portrays Verdi's aetheism and anti-German remarks unapologetically, but not as virtues. Overall his use of the letters is notable, particularly the manner in which they are introduced and commented upon.

MARTIN's book apparently wants to be the complete guide to Verdi. It includes pictures, maps, excerpts from librettos, and numerous appendices clarifying one complication or another. It even provides a portion of Pius IX's *Motu proprio* relating to musical settings of texts used in the liturgy. Since Verdi wrote nothing to be used for this purpose, the document's presence is superfluous. A large portion of this book covers political events surrounding and involving Verdi, sometimes in great detail. But though Martin brings various perspectives together, he relates nothing new in terms of biography. Concerning the details of Verdi's life, one would do better to read Walker. Martin's wide scope has some advantages, but his attempts at being interesting frequently falter. For example, his comparison of the "basic musical outlines" of *La Traviata* and *Rigoletto* is unconvincing.

In the mid-1970s a series of popular biographies appeared. Each of them is filled with illustrations that may enrich anyone's knowledge of the composer. WECHSBERG's volume does not wander from the truth so much as it subjects the composer to descriptions such as "with it" and calls his craft "a pretty commercial business." HUME's popular biography tends toward the sentimental and away from the factual: one must read it guardedly. OSBORNE's first volume on Verdi (1978), while well written, enters into hero worship. His discussion of the operas, especially his ability to draw together biography, history, and opera commentary, is superior to the treatment found in other popular works.

In BALDINI's unfinished work (it ends in mid-sentence), the "biographical sections rely heavily on four of the standard works of Verdi's life—Abbiati, Gatti, Toye and Walker," as Roger Parker tells us in the Preface. Baldini's volume is primarily a discussion of operas, but the writer also applies his sharp critical mind to the numerous mysteries of Verdi's life and comes up with explanations that are possible, reasonable, and fascinating to read. It may not serve well as a starting point for researching the life of Verdi, but it should be consulted for its insightfulness and for the enjoyment of reading it.

PORTER intersperses chapters of biography with commentary on the operas, including history of first performances and stylistic growth. The portions of the composer's life are reliable and succinct, providing one of the best starting points for Verdi research. One of the article's strongest attributes is Porter's references to the unresolved questions in Verdi biography, such as his date of birth.

CONATI's work is of interest for at least two reasons. First, it consists of 50 contemporary commentaries on the composer, each with an introduction. Though this book is not a chronological biography, it strives to develop the reader's understanding of Verdi's personality through the observations of his friends and acquaintances. Second, the Preface discusses other important biographies and comments on Verdi biographies in general. Because of its episodic quality, Conati's work requires of the reader some previous knowledge of the composer's life. One should also be wary of the sometimes awkward translation.

BUDDEN's well-researched tome attempts to summarize Verdi scholarship to date. As a practical matter, he divides the book into two sections, devoting the first half to Verdi's life and the second to his works. The text flows exceptionally well and includes many relevant details of the composer's life. The book also makes the reader aware of Verdi's idiosyncracies without portraying him in a negative light. In addition, Budden includes relevant and interesting stories of the people around Verdi, such as Boito's near death in a duel. Of all the biographies touched on, this one has the most to recommend it. It is both enjoyable to read and factually as close to the mark as can be found.

OSBORNE's 1987 work seems to be this writer's attempt to shift from the "popular" biographies of the 1970s to the more sophisticated biographies of the 1980s. His attempts to say something new about some of the Verdi mysteries sometimes end up confusing the reader and not shedding any light on the question. The birthdate issue, for example, in which he takes a controversial position, is only confused by his explanation. He fails to mention that Verdi not only remembered a different day, 9 October, but a different year as well, 1814. Also, the writing style is uneven. When using quotes from the letters, Osborne often does not explain exactly what the reader was to learn from them.

—Joseph T. Orchard

VERLAINE, Paul, 1844–1896; French poet.

Hanson, Lawrence and Elizabeth Hanson, *Verlaine, Prince of Poets.* London, Chatto and Windus, 1958.
Nicolson, Harold, *Paul Verlaine.* London, Constable, and Boston, Houghton Mifflin, 1921.
Richardson, Joanna, *Verlaine.* London, Weidenfeld and Nicholson, and New York, Viking, 1971.
Thorley, Wilfred E., *Paul Verlaine.* London, Constable, and Boston, Houghton Mifflin, 1914.

*

Toward the end of his troubled and rootless life, Verlaine produced several autobiographical sketches—on his early years, on his sojourns in prison and in hospital, on his lecture tour in Holland. But these memories—rambling, inconsequential, and totally unreliable—remain untranslated, except for his *Confessions*, recollections of his life before the fateful meeting with Rimbaud, first published in 1895, shortly before his death, and eventually, in 1950, translated into English as *Confessions of a Poet* by Joanna Richardson.

The first attempt to present Verlaine's life in English had come many years earlier in the shape of the little book by THORLEY. It consists of a rapid and superficial rehearsal of the salient facts as they were then known, with little more than a nod in the direction of the poetry and an overtly censorious attitude toward Verlaine's disreputable lifestyle (as witness this typically moralizing comment: "the closing years of Verlaine's life provide a spectacle which can only make the judicious grieve"). Rimbaud is firmly cast in the role of villain.

Much more sympathetic, though written only a short time later, is NICOLSON's elegantly written and more elaborate biography, though here condescension tends to replace condemnation: "Poor Verlaine" is almost a *leitmotiv*. Nicolson's comments on the poems are sensitive, and his portrait as a whole is soberly and effectively drawn, though details not relating directly to Verlaine sometimes go wrong (for instance, Xavier de Ricard becomes "le Ricard" throughout). But despite the greater amount of detail, Nicolson omits to supply even the summary bibliography provided by his predecessor, and, like him, gives neither notes nor references.

The next life of Verlaine, written by the HANSONs, is a much more abundantly documented work, as was very necessary given the amount of new material that had come to light in the meantime. However, the authors do not identify the sources of their quotations and are liable to wild inaccuracies over Verlaine's contemporaries (Huysmans was anything but a Catholic writer in the 1880s, Mallarmé, far from fastidiously shunning Verlaine, was always one of his warmest supporters, and the pages about Villiers de l'Isle-Adam are a tissue of confused nonsense). Despite these defects, the book is lively and readable, couched in a light and unpretentious tone, with perhaps something of an excess of imaginative reconstruction of what people's thoughts actually were at given moments. The view taken of Verlaine's always irresponsible and often outrageous behavior is cheerfully indulgent: "to condemn his life and praise his work is to ignore the reality that the one depends absolutely on the other." Hence an unexpectedly positive evaluation of his later years, exactly at the antipodes of Thorley's stern disapproval: "His life from 1885 onwards is not commonly put forward as an example of the good life, but it may well be that the general judgment is at fault."

Fortunately, the most recent life of Verlaine in English is also unmistakably the best. RICHARDSON is an expert biographer with a profound knowledge of the period, and her book on Verlaine, admirably full, detailed, and accurate, is based on extensive personal research and draws on many unpublished documents, including letters by Huysmans, Heredia, and Robert de Montesquiou. Her comments on the poetic collections are illuminating, especially on *Fêtes galantes*, where she is able to show, contrary to the assumption made by previous critics, that Verlaine could have seen the Watteau paintings in the Lacaze collection before composing the poems that so strongly recall the atmosphere they evoke. In addition, Richardson faces up to the question of Verlaine's homosexuality, largely eluded by earlier English biographers (Thorley briefly mentions it as a possibility, while Nicolson and the Hansons completely ignore it). The only slight criticism one could make of the book is that it might with advantage have been more fully on the literary milieu Verlaine was frequenting when he was producing his best work in the early 1870s. There would certainly have been interesting things to say about his connections with writers such as Charles Cros and, more particularly, Germain Nouveau, who at one time was one of Verlaine's most intimate friends, though he is scarcely mentioned here. On the other hand, Richardson has found many picturesque and entertaining anecdotes about his later years as an alcoholic celebrity-cum-reprobate in Paris' Latin Quarter. She is also much more effective than anyone else (notably his French biographers) on Verlaine's various periods in England. All in all, her work remains an excellent biography, unsurpassed by anything even in French.

—A. W. Raitt

VERMEER, Jan, 1632–1675; Dutch painter.

Blankert, Albert, *Vermeer of Delft.* Oxford, Phaidon, and New York, Dutton, 1978.

Blankert, Albert, John M. Montias, and Gilles Aillaud, *Vermeer.* New York, Rizzoli, 1988 (originally published by Hazan, Paris, 1986).

Goldscheider, Ludwig, *Jan Vermeer: the Paintings, Complete Edition.* London, Phaidon, and New York, Garden City Publishers, 1958.

Gowing, Lawrence, *Vermeer.* London, Faber, 1952; New York, Beechhurst Press, 1953; revised edition, London, Faber, and New York, Harper, 1970.

Koningsberger, Hans, *The World of Vermeer 1632–1675.* New York, Time-Life Books, 1967.

Montias, John M., *Vermeer and His Milieu: A Web of Social History.* Princeton, New Jersey, and London, Princeton University Press, 1989.

Slatkes, Leonard J., *Vermeer and His Contemporaries.* New York, Abbeville Press, 1981.

Snow, Edward A., *A Study of Vermeer.* Berkeley, University of California Press, 1979.

Swillens, P. T. A., *Johannes Vermeer, Painter of Delft 1632–1675*, translated by C. M. Breuning-Williamson. Utrecht, Spectrum, and New York, Studio Vista, 1950.

Thienen, Frithjof van, *Jan Vermeer of Delft.* New York, Harper, and London, Longman, 1949.

Vries, A. B. de, *Jan Vermeer Van Delft*, translated by Robert Allen. London and New York, B. T. Batsford, 1948 (originally published by J. M. Meulenhoff, Amsterdam, 1939).

*

The definitive work by MONTIAS surpasses any previous scholarly biography of Vermeer. The few existing documented sources that directly list the artist had been thoroughly examined by the late 1800s. Thus Montias searched the public documents referring to Vermeer's family and to his wife, Catharina Bolnes. From this information he painstakingly reconstructed the family histories and advanced cautious theories for the years where no mention of Vermeer appears in the Delft magistrate's records. Montias discovered new proof of Vermeer's artistic status in the region with the discovery of a document of 1653 linking Vermeer and Gerard ter Borch. This entry occurred during the time when the artist's public life was severely restricted by his status as a Catholic. Brought up in the Reformed Church, he converted to Catholicism shortly before his marriage. This act denied him any major public role in Delft politics, as the old religion was technically proscribed. However, it didn't prevent his election as a Dean of the Painter's Guild of St. Luke of Delft, an honor in the private business sector.

Montias found a connection between the Catholic Bolnes family and a small Jesuit group that illegally leased property near the Vermeer home in the old Catholic quarter. He used this information to clarify some of the mystifying symbolism found in several of Vermeer's works, symbolism that cannot be explained in terms of Protestant iconography.

Montias' work includes equivalency tables for currency along with detailed maps and genealogical charts. The end documents list reads like a novel and lends immediacy to the main text. The use of black-and-white photographs slightly mars the work, but given the wealth of new information and reorganized listings, this fine book will provide the serious scholar with the best source to date.

For the general reader, the 1988 volume by BLANKERT, MONTIAS, AND AILLAUD offers eight sections that cover Vermeer's life, work, and a detailed catalogue of the pictures. Information gathered by Montias for his scholarly edition is here abridged and incorporated into the narrative. One advantage of this work is that the large color illustrations are well positioned for textual comparison. This book offers the best synopsis of biographical material and critical analysis of the paintings.

SWILLENS devoted the largest part of his volume to thematic characteristics in the panels, tracing for instance Vermeer's use of table carpets and background illustrations. Along with the standard biographical information known in 1950, he also included a chapter on dubious works attributed to Vermeer, citing examples of signatures and lighting techniques to support his assertions. Swillens was the first to take serious note of Vermeer's Catholic faith but did not develop this information into a main theme. He did identify an interesting musical element in Vermeer's background based on the number of times instruments appear in the paintings. Black-and-white photographs with schematic diagrams and detailed analysis of the canvases still make this an important reference.

The book by de VRIES has proven to be one of the most interesting of all Vermeer references because of its various appendices, particularly one dealing with the forgeries by Van Meergeren. The volume itself was reorganised between the years 1939 and 1945, reflecting the startling reexamination of Vermeer's oeuvre in light of wartime thefts and forgeries. De Vries gave an honest account of how he reversed his critical pronouncement on the authenticity of "Supper at Emmaus" after the exposure of the Van Meergeren forgeries. For a scholar, de Vries' book offers a fascinating view of the scandalous war years that directly affected the evaluation of Vermeer's paintings by historians and artists alike.

SNOW's work attempts to interpret Vermeer's paintings in the Freudian context of art and sexuality, making references to Oedipal nostalgia and Vermeer's male-authorial self. His chapters offer thoughtful insights into the content of the works while presenting alternate ways of thinking about Vermeer's intent. Color reproductions and informative notes will make this a good scholarly addition to Vermeer criticism and shed light on the mysteries of the artist's life.

For the scholar, GOWING and SLATKES both present the basic details of Vermeer biography, but each focuses on the examination of the 35 paintings in light of the work of Vermeer's contemporaries. Slatkes' book has the best color plates while Gowing provides more detailed accounts of the individual iconographical elements. THIENEN repeats the available documented biographical information before turning his attention to the questions of style and artistic influence. His premise that Vermeer directly inspired Pieter de Hooch raises many possibilities for further research on references to Vermeer from records of contemporary painters.

BLANKERT (1978) made the direct connection with Pieter de Hooch by pinpointing the date 1658, when de Hooch's genre style of interior scenes was much copied by the Delft artists. With this chronological point, Blankert was able to establish the possible relationship in working styles of Vermeer and de Hooch. This small bit of information provides another course for examining Vermeer's working life. Blankert's volume also includes large color photographs, a catalog, and extensive references to aid in a text that can be appreciated by both the scholar and the general reader.

The two books by GOLDSCHEIDER and KONINGSBERGER were done specifically for the general public, not for the scholar. Goldscheider reviews the life briefly and moves straight to a discourse on the artworks. The volume contains mostly black-and-white pictures with several large, muddled color reproductions. However, Koningsberger's addition to the Time-Life series anchors Vermeer's life and works firmly in the historic panorama of the 17th century. With its limited biographical information, dearth of notes, and travelogue voice, it would appeal to few scholars. Fortunately, with the line drawings and comparative color plates illustrating contemporary artistic taste, it offers the general reader a rich background of information that will spark interest in further investigation of this "Sphinx of Delft."

—Linda K. Varkonda

VERONESE, Paolo [*born* **Paolo Caliari**], 1528–1588; Italian painter.

Cocke, Richard, *Veronese's Drawings: A Catalogue Raisonné*. Ithaca, New York, Cornell University Press, and London, Sotheby, 1984.
Rearick, W. R., *The Art of Paolo Veronese*. Cambridge, Cambridge University Press, and Washington, D.C., National Gallery of Art, 1988.

Stearns, Frank P., *Four Great Venetians: An Account of the Lives of Giorgione, Titian, Tintoretto, and Il Veronese.* New York and London, Putnam, 1901.

Vasari, Giorgio, *Lives of the Artists* (2 vols.), translated by George Bull. London and New York, Penguin, 1965 (originally published as *Le Vite de piu eccelenti architetti, pittori, et scultori italiani*, Florence, 1550, 1568).

*

In any study of Veronese's life, COCKE's volume must be one of the first to be examined. Cocke has contributed numerous articles to the body of scholarly writings on this artist. He focuses his attention primarily on Veronese's drawings, citing artistic themes inspired by Dürer and Michelangelo and building an argument for Veronese's superior compositional talents. He also enlarges on Vasari's comment in the 1568 edition of the *Lives* which relates the disapproval of Titian and other Venetian artists who approached painting without the benefit of pen and ink drawings. As a strong admirer of the Florentine tradition of drawing, Vasari praised this outsider for adhering to it. Cocke weaves the biographical information into his narrative description of the works. His writing style is direct, and his arguments are formed in a logical manner. Included in this volume is a complete catalogue of the artist's drawings, which is enhanced by excellent color and black-and-white plates. Although the book is written for the scholar, a general reader would find it easy to comprehend.

REARICK's recent work carefully includes the latest scholarship that asserts Veronese's status with his exceptional design elements. It details the artist's journeys through the Venetian territories, Rome, and finally Venice itself. Each of these locations provides a backdrop for the explanation of the themes found in individual works from that site. The meticulous scholarship and the illustrations make this a good choice for a serious Veronese scholar.

VASARI's 1568 edition of the *Lives* provides a contemporary account of Paolo's early career. It discusses his origins, his travels, his patrons, and glorifies the artist's adoption of the Florentine drawing tradition. However unreliable Vasari may be in relating facts about the lives of the early Renaissance artists, his section on Paolo Veronese provides a good starting point for reader investigation because Vasari and Veronese were contemporaries and moved in the same artistic circles.

By far the most enjoyable overview of Veronese's life can be found in STEARNS' *Four Great Venetians*. Stearns presents us with an example of 19th-century interpretation of "Lives and Works," which gives the modern reader a chance to see how much the concept of biographical study has changed. Stearns takes unbridled joy in proclaiming Veronese to be one of the incomparable artistic giants, attributing his talents to natural gifts of observation and diplomacy. Every description of Paolo's travels, relationships with patrons, artistic themes, and use of colors is lavishly praised. The resulting book takes an interested reader on a rewarding journey into the past, finding new scholarly considerations from Stearns' exuberant essay. Many scholars today frown on this non-objective biographical study, but many readers will find this book to be a refreshing look into the

past consideration of Veronese's talent. The only flaw in this delightful volume is that it lacks illustrations to bolster Stearns' arguments.

Unfortunately, a large number of books on Veronese have yet to be translated into English, so readers must either resort to the scattered articles in various languages or rely on the volumes in English that are listed above.

—Linda K. Varkonda

VICTORIA, 1819–1901; English monarch.

Benson, E. F., *Queen Victoria.* London and New York, Longman, 1935.

Bolitho, Hector, *Victoria, the Widow and Her Son.* London, Cobden-Sanderson, and New York, Appleton-Century, 1934.

Bolitho, Hector, *The Reign of Queen Victoria.* New York, Macmillan, 1948; London, Collins, 1949.

Cullen, Tom, *The Empress Brown: The Story of a Royal Friendship.* London, Bodley Head, 1969; with subtitle, *The True Story of a Victorian Scandal*, Boston, Houghton Mifflin, 1969.

Epton, Nina, *Victoria and Her Daughters.* London, Weidenfeld and Nicolson, and New York, Norton, 1971.

Longford, Elizabeth, *Victoria R.I.* London, Weidenfeld and Nicolson, 1964; as *Queen Victoria: Born to Succeed*, New York, Harper, 1965.

Rowell, George, *Queen Victoria Goes to the Theatre.* London, Elek, 1978.

Sitwell, Edith, *Victoria of England.* London, Faber, 1935; Boston, Houghton Mifflin, 1936.

Strachey, Lytton, *Queen Victoria.* New York, Harcourt, and London, Chatto and Windus, 1921.

Weintraub, Stanley, *Victoria, an Intimate Biography.* New York, Dutton, and London, Allen and Unwin, 1987.

Woodham-Smith, Cecil, *Queen Victoria: Her Life and Times* (volume one only). London, Hamilton, 1972.

*

The most startling fact concerning accounts of the life of Victoria of England is that so few full-length biographies of her have been written since her death. A number of factors contribute to this situation. First, as Elizabeth Longford suggests, the sheer longevity of Victoria's life and reign produced an "inevitable reaction against all things Victorian." Second, as readers and biographers alike became distanced from the Victorian era, there arose a greater need to understand the social and political context in which Victoria evolved. The complexity of such an endeavor, compounded by the longevity factor, proved discouraging to many would-be biographers. Finally, the gender of the subject almost certainly played a role in that, until recent years, women—even queens—have received disproportionately little attention from scholars.

STRACHEY's ground-breaking portrait of Victoria followed the pattern of his *Eminent Victorians* (1918) and set the tone that would characterize Victorian biography for several decades. By deliberately breaking the 19th-century tradition of dry, narrative biography, Strachey became the unwitting creator of psychobiography, or what has been termed the "modern" or "debunking" school of biography. Thus, Strachey was the first to portray Victoria and the Prince Consort as human and fallible, and the non-reverential attitude that he displayed toward his subject often translates into personal animus. Although Strachey was highly critical of Victoria (he scathingly criticizes her middle-class attitudes, for example), his attitude toward her softened over time. As Theodore Reik (*Listening with the Third Ear*, 1948) has written of Strachey, "He started with little affection for his subject, and ended practically in love with the old lady."

Strachey's portrait of Victoria is both concise and pithy. As the eminent biographer and critic Leon Edel has written (*Writing Lives: Principia Biographica*, 1984), the positive aspects of Strachey's work reside in "his genius for squeezing into a single phrase certain aspects of a person; his capacity for combing great masses of documents to find the substance of that phrase; the skill with which he captures incident and detail in order to light up a scene or to bring a personality into relief; above all the wit and liveliness of his prose by which he lifted biography from plodding narrative into literary expression." Negative aspects of Strachey's work include its blurring of distinction between fact and fiction, particularly through the use of quotation without footnote references, and its paucity of important contextual information. Despite these limitations, Strachey's work remains one of the most compelling examples of the genre.

BENSON appears more reliable than Strachey in that he discusses the process by which he draws certain conclusions; frequently, this involves a focus on sources. BOLITHO (1948) makes use of hitherto unknown correspondence between Victoria and the Princess Royal, and he presents a new account of the relationship between the Duke of Kent and his mistress Madame de St. Laurent. SITWELL acknowledges her debt to Strachey, Benson, and Bolitho's work on Prince Albert (*Albert, Prince Consort*, revised edition, 1970); though her style is novelistic, it lacks the force of Strachey's, and, in terms of content, she offers no fresh insights.

LONGFORD was hailed for providing the most important account of Victoria since Strachey. In her author's note, she claims—justifiably—that her approach eschews both the "early sentimental adulation" and "the impatience which succeeded it." Longford offers a corrective to many earlier accounts (for example, she dispels Bolitho's version of the life of Madame de St. Laurent). The unifying principle of the biography is psychological, even Freudian, analysis. However, despite frequent reference to terms such as "father figure," "mother figure," and "regression to childhood," the biographical subject does not suffer from facile reductionism because, at the same time, this is the first biography of Victoria to include the perspective of gender and to acknowledge the social construction of sexual difference. This is not to say that Longford portrays Victoria as a feminist. Rather, she places the queen within her socio-historical context as a woman and assesses her attitude on a number of gender-specific issues such as women's suffrage. Moreover, using gender as an analytical tool occasionally leads Longford to unconventional conclusions, such as her statement that "it may well be claimed that Queen Victoria's greatest gift to her people was a refusal to accept pain in childbirth as woman's divinely appointed destiny." Finally, this is also the first full-length biog-

raphy of Victoria that devotes an entire chapter to her relationship with John Brown. Despite her passing textual references to other biographers, Longford's notes only refer to primary sources and memoirs. The text is supplemented by numerous illustrations and a useful, if somewhat overwhelming, genealogy chart.

WOODHAM-SMITH deserves a special note in this chronological survey of full-length biographies. Though incomplete owing to the author's death (volume I ends in 1861 with the death of the Prince Consort; the work was subsequently published as a discrete work), the meticulous discussion of alternate accounts of a variety of subjects (such as Madame de St. Laurent's background and the legends surrounding the birth of Queen Victoria) provide insight into the biographer's interpretive methods.

WEINTRAUB is the first American to write a full-length biography of Victoria. This fact undoubtedly accounts, at least in part, for the multi-faceted approach he uses to great success. For example, this is the only biographer who discusses vital contextual information such as the history of British political parties or the shifting relationship between the Crown and Parliament. Weintraub also makes extensive use of press reports and political cartoons of the era and thus provides useful insight into public perceptions of the monarch. Unlike the other major accounts, this is the only one to begin with an event late in the life of Victoria: the Golden Jubilee of 1887. Such an introduction allows Weintraub to intertwine major themes of Victoria's life and reign with delightful details of the year-long, Empire-wide celebration. Other noteworthy aspects of this highly readable and scholarly biography include discussions of Victoria's religious beliefs, her artistic taste (in poetry, theatre, and painting), and her various medical problems. Scattered throughout the text are numerous illustrations and two well-designed genealogy charts ("The Race for the Throne" and "The Descendants of Victoria"). The bibliographic essay devoted to each chapter is particularly useful to scholars.

In addition to these full-length biographies, certain limited, specialized approaches warrant consideration. Though EPTON's work on the relationship between Victoria and her daughters is chatty and unscholarly, the premise on which it is based is interesting: given the prevalent image of Victoria as the mother of her people, Epton wonders what the monarch was like "as a mother in her own home"; her specific focus on the mother-daughter relationship relates to her interest in Victoriana. BOLITHO's account (1934) of the relationship between the widowed monarch and her eldest son offers a balanced—if scantily documented and badly dated—interpretation of the problems inherent in the interaction of a mother and son who were also monarch and heir to the throne. ROWELL's brief work will be of great interest to cultural/social historians. He not only examines Victoria's interest in all branches of theatre but, in so doing, he explores the ways in which she both reflected and shaped the artistic sensibilities of her people. This is a valuable contribution to Victorian biography because, though extremely limited in scope, it focuses on an aspect of Victoria's life that major biographers have overlooked. By far, the majority of partial biographies—too numerous to list—focus on the courtship and marriage of Victoria and Albert. Although some of these works include bibliographies, they bear more resemblance to novels than to biographies. CULLEN's narrow focus on the peculiar

friendship between the aging, widowed monarch and her Highland servant John Brown has the merit of relative novelty but is
plagued by the same fictional flavor as the other sentimental
studies.

—Amy B. Millstone

———————

VILLON, François, *ca.* 1430–1463 *or later*; French poet.

Anacker, Robert, *François Villon.* New York, Twayne, 1968.
Lewis, D. B. Wyndham, *François Villon: A Documented Sur-*
vey. New York, Coward McCann, and London, P. Davies,
1928.
Mackworth, Cecily, *François Villon.* London, Westhouse, 1947.
Stacpoole, H. de Vere, *François Villon: His Life and Times.*
London, Hutchinson, and New York, Putnam, 1916.

*

Villon's biographers face a difficult task. Comparatively little
is known for certain about the poet's life, and it is unlikely that
much more will be discovered. In addition, much of what is
known comes from official documents, especially those that
record Villon's troubles with the law, and some of the evidence
derived from these sources is inconclusive. This means that biographers must supplement the known facts with information
from Villon's poetry (a risky procedure), and that they must to
some degree follow a "life and times" model, since a great deal
must be conjectured from what is known about Villon's milieu.
Educated guesses and imaginative reconstruction are, therefore,
necessary and even desirable, though one might hope that biographers would distinguish what is actually known from what
they, or others, have construed. Ideally, they should cite sources
and refer the reader to discussions of other possibilities in questionable cases.

Unfortunately, all of the biographies in English fall somewhat
short in the matter of critical documentation. Perhaps the most
extreme case is Mackworth, whose "Bibliographical Note"
briefly mentions only the various English translations that had
appeared before 1947. Stacpoole is also limited in this regard,
although he does include a short chapter called "Modern Commentators, Writers, and Translators." Anacker's general introductory text, about one third of which is devoted to Villon's life
and times, is the most cautious with regard to biographical conjecture, but the author declares at the outset that he is not writing a scholarly work and so has chosen not to "burden [his]
sketch with notes and references." His selected bibliography is
more limited than one would like, as is that of Wyndham Lewis.
The latter, however, does include a substantial number of footnotes, and he quotes liberally from early documents, although
even he does not always state his sources of information. There
is, in fact, no English counterpart to Pierre Champion's landmark work, *François Villon: Sa vie et son temps* (1913), a
heavily documented, scholarly work that is, unfortunately, not
available in translation.

As far as the question of accuracy goes, and especially the
difference between what the author considers probable versus

what is actually known, there are some problems with all three
of the primarily biographical works. The reader has perhaps the
greatest difficulty in distinguishing the two in Mackworth's
book, since she seldom gives sources and makes many statements as if they were fact rather than reasonable supposition.
Mackworth's project was clearly to write a popular rather than
scholarly biography, so it is understandable that she chose not to
fill her text with uncertainties, and most of the statements she
makes are accurate or at least reasonable. Yet the sceptical
reader often wishes for more information or evidence. The same
problem can be seen to some extent in the works of Stacpoole
and Lewis, for both accounts contain much that is imaginative.
Only ANACKER is careful to state that certain points are only
conjectured rather than known for certain. As a result, however,
the biographical part of Anacker's book, while well rounded, is
much shorter and therefore less rich than that of any of the others. (All three primarily biographical texts will be discussed in
greater detail below.)

Because of Villon's colorful life, the compelling personality
that seems to shine through his writings, and the gaps in information about his life, he has evoked widely varying and often
very personal reactions, although certain generations have
tended to react to him in similar ways. For example, the studies
by Stacpoole and Lewis were written in the wake of the archival
studies begun in the late 19th century, which produced much
new information on Villon's life and troubles with the law and
which culminated in Champion's work. Many studies done
around this time tend to romanticize Villon's life and to focus on
his apparently contradictory, enigmatic character. More recent
scholarship, however, has tended to see him as less of an enigma
and more of a product of his time—albeit an extraordinary
one—and to recognize the literary function of many elements in
his work that appear biographical.

STACPOOLE's work is, as noted above, an imaginative and
highly vivid account of Villon's life. From the beginning, in
which the author invites the reader to "see" the changing faces
of Paris and then gives a bird's-eye view of the city in the 15th
century, the book is especially notable for its visual quality.
Stacpoole's descriptions of various characters and his narration
of events—such as the conversations between Pierre Marchant
and Guy Tabarie, which eventually led to Villon's arrest for rob-
bery—are especially colorful. The writer himself is a strong personal presence throughout the work, often addressing the reader
as "you" and seeming to invite a discussion of questionable
points; for example, when he claims—in part, it appears, in answer to Robert Louis Stevenson's excessively dark portrait—that
Villon was not really a hardened criminal, he says, "When you
have read all I have to say about him, you will perhaps agree
with me in this." It will be seen from this quotation that
Stacpoole's attitude toward his subject is one of strong sympathy, often one of justification, for he sees Villon as a victim who
drew inspiration—and much of his greatness—from misfortune.
It must be remembered, however, that Villon himself wished to
portray himself as a victim of circumstance in his poetry.
Stacpoole's appreciation of medieval culture and literature is
limited, and so he fails to place Villon properly in the context of
his time, seeing him as "the stock from which the bouillon of
French literature [was] made." This viewpoint is also seen in
Stacpoole's patronizing attitude toward Charles d'Orléans,
whom he dismisses as a mediocre rhymer. The textual discus-

sions at the end are often insightful, although the text and translations contain some errors. Despite some problems, the book remains both useful and highly readable.

Stacpoole's work might have remained the best English biography of Villon had it not been largely superseded by that of LEWIS. Though it shares some—not all—of the earlier work's faults, Lewis' book also demonstrates most of its virtues to a higher degree. Spiced with wit and *joie de vivre*, the book is replete with information on both the poet and his times, offering a wealth of lively background details and several appendices. Lewis' attitude toward his subject is, like that of Stacpoole, highly sympathetic despite the weaknesses he sees in the poet's character; as, for instance, when he describes Villon's unsavory companions as playing Mephistopheles to Villon's Faust. It must be noted, however, that the multifaceted character often projected in Villon's writings seems to be especially appealing to Lewis, and that he does not separate the persona from the man himself; he certainly shows a neo-Romantic tendency to see the works as completely "sincere," and therefore a reflection of the poet's "soul."

Lewis' writing is, like Stacpoole's, highly visual, frequently stimulating the other senses as well and often suggesting movement, as in the description of Villon's wild joy at being granted a reprieve from his sentence of death. The author's romanticized portrait of Villon, popular in company but prone to brood in the corner, is unforgettable, so much so that few readers will complain about the fact that much of the portrait is fanciful. Although Lewis still does not adequately place Villon in his literary context, his view of the Middle Ages is less narrow than Stacpoole's, and he can at least regard Charles d'Orléans as "a fine poet and a gentleman." Like Stacpoole's work, this one follows a "life and works" model; the biographical section is followed by an extended and often insightful discussion of Villon's principal works that contains some of the texts, with translations by such writers as Swinburne and Rossetti.

MACKWORTH's is the closest to a pure biography, the only one that does not contain a separate discussion of Villon's works. Like Lewis, she includes several poems with translations by Swinburne and others at the end. Mackworth's style is less subjective than that of the two earlier biographers, but, as indicated above, her apparently greater objectivity creates problems of its own. Mackworth's approach to her subject is less apologetic—perhaps because there was less need in 1947 to justify Villon on moral grounds—and more purely psychological, in that she seeks to find the "real Villon" behind his various masks and explain how his character developed. Her point of view, however, does not differ greatly from that of either Stacpoole or Lewis, for she sees Villon as being of a "double" nature, a contradictory personality who lived in contradictory times. Indeed, Mackworth seems to have relied heavily on the work of the earlier biographers, and her work, though less romanticized than theirs, does not contribute much that is new. Although the book is adequate for some purposes, there is probably no reason for a reader to prefer it to Lewis' more interesting work.

It is unlikely that anything like a "definitive" biography of Villon will ever be written, and different readers and generations will probably continue to react to him in widely varying and even eccentric ways. Yet it seems that the present moment would be an appropriate time for the appearance of a new scholarly biography in English, one that would take into account the work of recent scholarship on Villon. In the meantime, English-speaking readers who have no access to Champion will probably be most content with the work of Lewis, although they may wish to counter some of the fancifulness of this work with the more conservative sketch by Anacker.

—Colleen P. Donagher

VOLTAIRE [*born* **François-Marie Arouet**], 1694–1778; French writer.

Aldington, Richard, *Voltaire*. London, Routledge, and New York, Dutton, 1925.
Aldridge, A. Owen, *Voltaire and the Century of Light*. Princeton, New Jersey, Princeton University Press, 1975.
Besterman, Theodore, *Voltaire*. London, Longman, and New York, Harcourt, 1969.
Hearsey, John E. N., *Voltaire*. New York, Barnes and Noble, and London, Constable, 1976.
Lanson, Gustave, *Voltaire*, translated by Robert A. Wagoner, introduction by Peter Gay. New York, Wiley, 1966 (originally published by Hachette, Paris, 1906).
Morley, John, *Voltaire*. London, Macmillan, and New York, Appleton, 1872.
Noyes, Alfred, *Voltaire*. London and New York, Sheed and Ward, 1936.
Torrey, Norman L., *The Spirit of Voltaire*. New York, Columbia University Press, 1938.
Wade, Ira O., *The Intellectual Development of Voltaire*. Princeton, New Jersey, Princeton University Press, 1969.

*

To the principal modern full-length biographies of Voltaire available in English must be added a large number of specialized critical and biographical studies. Among these are Peter Gay, *Voltaire's Politics* (1959), René Pomeau, *La Religion de Voltaire* (1956), and the more than 100 volumes of *Studies on Voltaire and the 18th Century*. Much important information is also to be found in the notes to the definitive edition of Voltaire's *Correspondence and Related Documents*, edited by T. Besterman (107 vols., Geneva, 1953–65).

Voltaire's later biographers have usually started from the eight patient volumes in French by G. Desnoiresterres (1867–76), which disentangle the order of events but are marked by their period, with its preference for tastefulness over accuracy and its liking for gossip and anecdote. Desnoiresterres was more interested in the man than in his writings or his ideas, and so avoids ideological dating. He remains attractively readable, even if incomplete and unreliable.

Voltaire's stature had been carried to immense heights by Jules Michelet and Thomas Babington Macaulay, and MORLEY presents us with a rationalistic account of the life, asserting that "Voltairism . . . was one of the cardinal liberations of the growing race." At the same time Morley condemns what he wrongly took to be Voltaire's repudiation of any rational grounds for hope. LANSON added a preoccupation with Voltaire the thinker, whose "chaos of clear ideas," to quote Faguet's quip, was capable of slow evolution, abrupt change, and formulations in different genres and registers of expression. Lanson rightly saw that everything Voltaire wrote had to be interpreted with reference to the date at which it was written and the literary genre in which it was expressed, so explaining the unified and coherent, if changing, outlook on life that underlay Voltaire's huge variety of interests, attitudes, and literary forms. Lanson emphasises the cynicism of the free-thinking world that attracted the young Voltaire, and he explores the extent to which Voltaire in his historical writings adapted his sources in pursuit of his own ends without any serious betrayal of factual accuracy. Lanson gives us a generally theist image of Voltaire that held sway in the academic community for about half a century, buttressed no doubt by the strength of the Catholic hostility to Voltaire, whose *Candide* was kept on the Index of forbidden books until it was abolished. Lanson himself was a literary critic as well as a scholar and a biographer, and he gives particularly convincing accounts of Voltaire's poetry and drama without disguising what is now generally regarded as the inferior quality of both. On the other hand, by modern standards he underestimates the importance of the *contes*, a series of philosophical parables that show Voltaire's satirical wit at its sharpest and his style at its most pithy.

The trouble with ALDINGTON's biography is that, since the publication of Charles Doyle's biography of the angry and quarrelsome Aldington himself (*Richard Aldington: A Biography*, London, 1989), the Voltaire biography, which "continues to be widely and justly respected," has become much more important for what it tells us about Aldington than for what it says about Voltaire. Aldington referred to himself as "a professional whore of letters," but the *Voltaire*, coming early in his very long list of publications, focuses what was to become a lifelong relationship with Voltaire. In contrast to Aldington's later biographies, the *Voltaire* was well, although not rapturously received. Its achievement is compression, its weakness its prejudice and distorted vision. Aldington disliked so many people and things, including Roman Catholics, fascists, left-wing bigots and the British establishment—which he despised and blamed for the carnage of the war—that his view of Voltaire is too enflamed to be balanced and his admiration for *Candide* too uncritical to be properly based. This biography is one of Aldington's best books, and its portrayal of the view Aldington takes of his subject carries it along, but it antedates so much subsequent cultural change that it is now out of date in both its attitudes and its information. It remains of interest chiefly in the context of British literary life in the 1920s.

The NOYES *Voltaire* of 1936, issued by a Catholic publishing house, polemically defends Voltaire's Christianity, attacking not so much Lanson, whom Noyes respects, as Morley in a reassessment that regards Voltaire as "the Erasmus, not the Luther, of his age." The stories of Voltaire's death-bed deportment, about the truth of which we now have a fair idea, which had him repudiating his orthodox Catholic origins, "are unspeakably vile, and as false as they are filthy." For Noyes, Voltaire was above all the humane social reformer and pamphleteer dedicated to a justice that was both legal and social, as necessarily opposed to superstition and the excesses of the Inquisition as to the execution of his friend Admiral Byng "pour encourager les autres."

TORREY, treating of the all-important intellectual relationship between Voltaire and the English deists, writes of Voltaire's "political, anti-clerical, whiggish deism" and regards this deism as undoubtedly French in origin. Occasionally he understates the English influence. He emphasises Voltaire's repudiation of the traditional proofs of Christ's divinity from miracles and prophecies, and his book is in general both selective and scholarly in tracing the genesis of Voltaire's views.

WADE's approach is altogether more comprehensive, drawing on the whole vast literature on the Enlightenment while remaining thoroughly accessible to the general reader. Wade notably suggests a re-dating of the development of Voltaire's thinking and, although he can be criticised for presenting too unified a view of Voltaire's intellectual evolution, smoothing out some of the jolts and bumps that appear to have marked it, his overall account of Voltaire's intellectual positions represents a masterly synthesis and a highly intelligent penetration of Voltaire's intellectual development.

The most controversial biography is certainly BESTERMAN's. By the editor of the two editions of the 20,000 letters in Voltaire's correspondence, it is certainly the best informed. Perhaps Besterman knows too much and is too deeply immersed in his subject, but he does not avoid symbiosis. Few biographers can claim in regard to their subjects, "I live in his house, work in his library, sleep in his bedroom. . . . " The result is a confusion of the biographer's attitudes with those of his subject. Voltaire might have been irritated by Rousseau, but he would not even have thought in terms of "a mad letter from the great misanthrope." There is a passage about the influence of Voltaire on Sherlock Holmes that is gratingly out of place. Besterman may stick to the facts when he recounts them, but, as he explains, the life was too full and too long to be recounted as it took place. The over-confidence of Besterman's judgements, as well as of his personal identification with his subject, attracted unfavourable comment as soon as the biography appeared.

Besterman does not disguise his strong distaste for Catholicism and does not spare his readers his conjectures about what Voltaire's attitudes toward 20th-century circumstances and problems might have been, or about the relative qualities of the thought of Einstein, Newton, and Galileo. He speculates about the value of the opinions of Gibbon and Lecky and about the possibility of optimism in the 20th century. Whole pages that assume "few people now believe in God" discuss modern attitudes, Teilhard de Chardin, Tillich, and Wilde, clerical attitudes to mini-skirts, and "four-letter words." Particular modern British disasters seem out of place in a biography whose real excellence lies in its detailed accounts of Voltaire's economic circumstances and building activities rather than in such sweeping comments as "it is indeed obvious that Voltaire did not believe in religion."

ALDRIDGE writes of the Enlightenment that Voltaire has substantial claims to be considered "the greatest exponent of this philosophical and humanitarian movement of the 18th century." He emphasises Voltaire's humanity, his wit, and his ideology. Although Aldridge adds little new to Besterman and is pretentious in his claim to be "combining the methods of comparative literature and the history of ideas," his is a readable biography that aims to give a quick overall impression. Aldridge is, however, weak on those matters of interest to professional scholars and those concerned with the important material details of Voltaire's existence. Aldridge's judgements, too, are out of focus, even hurried and careless, like the writing. There are too many pretentious generalisations, great penumbras of imprecision with blurred edges, too meaningless to be misleading, but coupled with touches of preciousness and betraying a misplaced confidence that, together with a slovenly deficiency in literary craftsmanship, is discourteous to the reader. The account of *Candide* is badly integrated and does not decode the *conte* convincingly, while Aldridge misunderstands the place in Locke's thinking of the cursory reference to "thinking matter" in the fourth book of the *Essay Concerning Human Understanding* (1690). The erudition here is ostentatious but misplaced, unnecessary and in fact defective: Aldridge fails to note Voltaire's views on immortality as expressed in a manuscript kept in a locked drawer while Voltaire was holding significantly different ones in public.

HEARSEY's popular biography makes no pretentions either to scholarship or to style, and to that extent is less irritating than Aldridge's. But it is also badly overwritten ("His worn-out body wanted to return to dust, but his mind would not let it go") and less well informed. Hearsey gets the episode of the beating on the instructions of Beauregard about three quarters wrong. There is also a banality about the cliché-ridden style in which we are sententiously informed that "Death was in the air among the royal houses of Europe." When wasn't it? Hearsey writes gossip in innocent ignorance of the intellectual traditions he is traducing, but his views are not uninteresting. The saving grace is that in the end he understands the Voltaire of the public *persona*, and he avoids the major pitfall of glamourising his subject. He sees perfectly well just how mischievously provocative Voltaire so often was.

—A. H. T. Levi

WAGNER, (Wilhelm) Richard, 1813–1883; German composer.

Anderson, Robert, *Wagner, a Biography: With a Survey of Books, Editions, and Recordings.* London, C. Bingley, and Hamden, Connecticut, Linnet Books, 1980.

Barth, Herbert, Dietrich Mack, and Egon Voss, *Wagner: A Documentary Study.* London, Thames and Hudson, and New York, Oxford University Press, 1975.

Bekker, Paul, *Richard Wagner: His Life in His Work,* translated by M. M. Bozman. London, Dent, and New York, Norton, 1931 (originally published as *Wagner: Das Leben im Werke,* Stuttgart, Deutsche Verlags-Anstalt, 1924).

Burlingame, E. L., *Art, Life, and Theories of Richard Wagner Selected from His Writings.* New York, Holt, 1985.

Chamberlain, Houston Stewart, *Richard Wagner,* translated by G. Ainslie Hight. Philadelphia, Lippincott, and London, Dent, 1897 (originally published by Kunst und Wissenschaft, Munich, 1896).

Deathridge, John and Carl Dahlhaus, *The New Grove Wagner.* New York, Norton, and London, Macmillan, 1984.

Ellis, William Ashton, *Life of Richard Wagner* (6 vols.). London, K. Paul, 1900–08.

Finck, Henry T., *Wagner and His Works: The Story of His Life, with Critical Comments.* New York, Scribner, and London, H. Grevel, 1893.

Gal, Hans, *Richard Wagner,* translated by Hans-Hubert Schonzeler. New York, Stein and Day, and London, Gollancz, 1976 (originally published by Fischer, Frankfurt, 1963).

Gutman, R. W., *Richard Wagner: The Man, His Mind, and His Music.* New York, Harcourt, and London, Secker and Warburg, 1968.

Henderson, William James, *Richard Wagner: His Life and Dramas.* London and New York, Putnam, 1901.

Kapp, Julius, *The Women in Wagner's Life,* translated by Hannah Walker. New York, Knopf, 1931; London, Routledge, 1932; "authorized" translation published as *The Loves of Richard Wagner,* London, W. H. Allen, 1951 (originally published as *Richard Wagner und die Frauen,* Berlin, 1912).

Katz, Jacob, *The Darker Side of Genius: Richard Wagner's Anti-Semitism.* Hanover, New Hampshire, Brandeis University Press, 1986.

Kobbé Gustav, *Wagner's Life and Works.* New York, Schirmer, 1890.

Millington, Barry, *Wagner.* London, Dent, 1984.

Newman, Ernest, *Wagner as Man and Artist.* London, Dent, 1914; New York, Knopf, 1924.

Newman, Ernest, *The Life of Richard Wagner* (4 vols.). London, Cassell, and New York, Knopf, 1933–46.

Osborne, Charles, *Wagner and His World.* New York, Scribner, and London, Thames and Hudson, 1977.

Panofsky, Walter, *Wagner: A Pictorial Biography,* translated by Richard Rickett. New York, Viking, and London, Thames and Hudson, 1963 (originally published by Kindler, Munich, 1963).

Sabor, Rudolph, *The Real Wagner.* London, A. Deutsch, 1987.

Taylor, Ronald, *Richard Wagner: His Life, Art, and Thought.* New York, Taplinger, and London, Elek, 1979.

Westernhagen, Curt von, *Wagner: A Biography* (2 vols.), translated by Mary Whittall. Cambridge and New York, Cambridge University Press, 1978 (originally published by Atlantis, Zürich, 1968; revised and enlarged edition, 1978).

White, Chappell, *An Introduction to the Life and Works of Richard Wagner.* Englewood Cliffs, New Jersey, Prentice-Hall, 1967.

*

Wagner, a prolific writer as well as composer, supervised a collected edition of his writings in 1868, the first edition consisting of ten volumes (*Gesammelte Schriften und Dichtungen,* Leipzig, 1871–73). William Ashton Ellis' English translation excludes most of the poems (*Richard Wagner's Prose Works,* 8 vols., London, 1892–99). Alternative translations are available; see Robert Anderson's *Wagner* (discussed below) for a discussion of these.

Wagner was also an enthusiastic writer of letters; his correspondence totals about 5000 items. The *Sämtliche Briefe* (Leipzig, 1967–) contains seven volumes of a projected 15. While no English translation exists, a number of books in English do contain some of Wagner's letters, such as his correspondence with Nietzsche, Liszt, Mathilde Wesendonck, and others; all are discussed in Anderson.

One approach to Wagner's life might well begin with his diaries and autobiography. He first began collecting autobiographical notes in 1835 in the *Rote Brieftasche*, progressing to 1839. Using these notes, Wagner extended the story to his departure from Paris in 1842 in the "Autobiographical Sketch," first published in 1843. English translations appear in E. L. BURLINGAME's work, and in volume one of the Ellis translation of Wagner's prose works. An idiomatic modern translation appears in the Herbert Barth, Dietrich Mack, and Egon Voss study (see below).

The 1851 *A Communication to My Friends*, also published in Ellis' *Wagner's Prose Works*, contains Wagner's thoughts regarding the connection between his art and life, sketching his development since *Der fliegende Holländer*, and details his thoughts concerning the transition from opera to music drama with *Der Ring des Nibelungen* project.

The Diary of Richard Wagner 1865–1882: The Brown Book contains autobiographical jottings from 1846 to 1867 copied into the book in 1868, as well as a later continuation, taking the story to 1882. *The Brown Book* also contains intimate communications to Wagner's second wife, Cosima, as well as a number of prose works.

In 1865, Wagner began an autobiography at King Ludwig II's request, detailing his life from childhood to his financial rescue by the king in 1864. *Mein Leben* was completed in 1880, privately printed during Wagner's lifetime, and appeared in an abridged version under the family archive's auspices in 1911. Much controversy was created by the decision to expunge certain personal material, or to depict these in a less-than-accurate manner. The 1911 English translation was also harshly criticized for a number of errors and inaccuracies. An authentic edition of *Mein Leben* was not published until 1963, edited by M. Gregor-Dellin; this edition was translated by Andrew Gray and edited by Mary Whittall under the title *My Life* in 1983.

Of great value as commentaries on Wagner's life are a number of personal accounts by persons associated with the composer. Several of these accounts are available in English translations. *Cosima Wagner's Diaries* chronicle the composer's life from 1869 until the evening before he died. They provide firsthand commentary on Wagner's life, and are indicative of Cosima's devotion and adulation. They must, therefore, be utilized with some caution.

Of particular interest are Friedrich Nietzsche's dramatically-shifting perceptions of Wagner, which began with enchantment and later turned to revulsion. The philosopher's first book, *The Birth of Tragedy out of the Spirit of Music*, documents Wagner's profound influence on the 26-year-old Nietzsche. An evolving uneasiness concerning Wagner is first reflected in the 1878 *Human, All-too-Human*. The year 1888 brought a number of negative commentaries from Nietzsche on Wagner, including *The Case of Wagner*, *Nietzsche contra Wagner*, with tributes to the discoverer of "a music without a future," and his autobiographical sketches entitled *Ecce homo*, where Nietzsche expresses gratitude for his early stays with Wagner, admiration for Cosima, and loathing for Wagnerians. Other personal accounts are discussed in Robert Anderson's volume.

The biographies of Richard Wagner might best be divided into three groups: the first wave of accounts, begun during the composer's lifetime or shortly thereafter, including those biographies written under the sway of Bayreuth; a second group, beginning in the early part of the 20th century and culminating around the time of World War II, attempting to come to grips with Wagner in more critical terms and using some of the source materials withheld from or unavailable to the first group; and a third group, post-World War II to the present, working with almost all of the relevant source materials, influenced to a certain extent by the critical strides made by their predecessors, and rendering ever more critical judgments of both Wagner and his art.

The first major biography of Wagner was written in German by Carl Glasenapp, a member of Wagner's circle at the composer's villa ("Wahnfried") in Bayreuth. Glasenapp produced two editions during Wagner's lifetime, with a revised and enlarged version beginning publication in 1894. This edition formed the basis of the first major attempt at a biography in English, William Ashton Ellis' translation of Glasenapp (discussed below). Other biographies from this period include those by KOBBÉ, FINCK, CHAMBERLAIN, and HENDERSON. While such works have some merit, in general they represent the testimonials of the faithful, many with firsthand accounts of attendance at Bayreuth. For discussion of these, see Anderson.

A second wave of biographies begins with ELLIS' *Life of Richard Wagner*. Ellis intended his *Life* as a "free translation" of Glasenapp's *Das Leben Richard Wagner*; however, he considerably expanded Glasenapp's original. By volume three, 100 pages of Glasenapp became 500 pages of Ellis; volumes four-six are entirely his work. At the end of volume six Ellis had only reached 1859, and he abandoned the project. Ellis began his account at the very beginning of Wagner scholarship, before most of the important documents relating to the composer's career had been released for publication, so a degree of caution is necessary in the use of his account. Some scholars still feel, however, that certain sections continue to be the best presentation of facts in the extant literature. Ellis' influence upon subsequent biographers, especially Ernest Newman (who gave Ellis little credit), was quite strong.

The 1911 publication of *Mein Leben* stimulated a number of biographies. KAPP's 1912 study details Wagner's relationships with the women in his life. German critic Paul BEKKER strives to demonstrate, in the author's words, the "elemental unity in all Wagner's life and work," suggesting that Wagner's trials were all aspects of life for art's sake.

The culmination of the second wave of Wagnerian biography is reflected in the work of NEWMAN, who wrote a total of six books dealing with the composer over more than a 50-year period. Following three years after the publication of *Mein Leben*, Newman's 1914 *Wagner as Man and Artist* takes pains to depict the errors in the composer's autobiography and illustrates the author's conviction "of the dichotomy between genius and man with feet of clay," as Anderson notes.

NEWMAN's four-volume account, *The Life of Richard Wagner*, is the standard English biography to which almost all subsequent biographers defer. Although Newman's monumental account has been superseded by more recent research in a number of areas, the biography has not been surpassed; basic Wagner research begins with Newman's *Life*. While its length may deter some readers, Newman's lofty critical standards ensure ample rewards for the trouble.

Representative of the third wave of Wagnerian biography, following in the wake of World War II, is GAL's 1963 biography, translated into English in 1976. Anderson describes Gal as see-

ing Wagner as a "Narcissus with the innocence of a wild animal." Gal perceptively describes Wagner's flaws, and he is
dubious regarding the viability of a number of Wagner's creations. Gal offers stimulating justification for his criticisms.
WHITE's volume from the same period offers a succinct and
competent biography, with concise descriptions of the dramas
and some of the composer's writing.

Obsession with Wagner's anti-Semitism runs like a thread
through GUTMAN's work. The author's preface states that his
account is intended to meet "a need for a comprehensive, one-
volume biography . . . combined with critical discussions of his
works." Seeing "proto-Nazism" woven into Wagner's life and
work, Gutman assails the composer's motives at every turn. As
Gerald Abraham notes, the "nature of Mr. Gutman's book is
accurately reflected by its subtitle: Wagner's music takes third
place in the order of priorities."

First published in 1968, with a substantial revision ten years
later, WESTERNHAGEN's is the first major biography to have
dealt with Wagner's diaries (the *Rote Brieftasche*, *Das Braune
Buch*, and the Annals) as well as Cosima's diaries, which have
all become available since 1977. Scholars are divided as to the
fruit of Westernhagen's labor. Some feel that he has produced a
generally punctilious and balanced account. However, other
scholars have described Westernhagen's attitude as careless toward documentary evidence. In addition, Westernhagen apparently distorted and dramatically downplayed Wagner's virulent
anti-Semitism in an attempt to paint the composer in a more favorable light.

Westernhagen is also the author of the biographical portion of
the "Wagner" article in *The New Grove Dictionary of Music
and Musicians*. However, when *The New Grove Wagner* book (in
the series extracted from the *New Grove Dictionary*) was published in 1984, Westernhagen's portion was dropped, and a new,
more acerbic biography by John Deathridge (see below) was
substituted. While series editor Stanley Sadie noted Westernhagen's death, as well as the fast pace of Wagnerian research in
recent years, as precipitating the decision to invite Deathridge's
contribution, other scholars have described Westernhagen's
"Wagner" contribution to *The New Grove Dictionary* as a flagrant distortion of the composer's anti-Semitic feelings, thus ne-
cessitating the replacement of Westernhagen's account with
Deathridge's.

Citing the countless studies focusing either on Wagner the
man or Wagner the artist, TAYLOR's 1979 account attempts to
strike a middle ground between these two approaches. Concentrating on the principal sources, Taylor offers no detailed
analyses of the composer's works but investigates Wagner's literary and historical background, resulting in some interesting
conclusions.

The current Wagner biography in the Master Musicians series
edited by *The New Grove* editor Stanley Sadie is MILLING-
TON's account. Millington's purpose is to look critically at
some of the myths that have adorned most Wagner biographies,
beginning with *Mein Leben*. He succeeds with a well-rounded,
yet succinct, biography, with ample discussion of the issues and
controversies. Millington also directs the interested reader toward
studies that treat various aspects of Wagner's life and works in a
more detailed fashion.

ANDERSON's *Wagner* offers a brief biography followed by
succinct discussions of books in English about Wagner, editions

of music, and selected recordings. The biography is rather pedestrian, although entertaining; the concise descriptions of
nearly all the available Wagner literature in English, offered with
perceptive critical judgment, are quite helpful.

DEATHRIDGE AND DAHLHAUS offer one of the most impressive studies of Wagner to date. Informed by the latest research, its slim 225 pages offer an excellent, succinct biography,
concise explications of Wagner's theoretical writings, as well as
the letters, diaries, and autobiography. Particularly noteworthy
are Carl Dahlhaus' contributions in the sections on Wagner's
music, aesthetics, and critical, theoretical, and autobiographical
writings. Dahlhaus is regarded as one of the greatest scholars of
19th-century German music.

Leon Botstein has noted that one of the major unresolved biographical and historical issues plaguing Wagnerian research is
the composer's anti-Semitism, an issue addressed in KATZ's
1986 treatment. A distinguished historian and authority on German Jewry and anti-Semitism, Katz describes Wagner's anti-
Semitism as comparatively "naive" and "restrained," though
Wagner's "mentality and way of thinking are indeed an anticipation of future horrors."

The provocative title of SABOR's recent account, *The Real
Wagner*, reflects the author's attempt to illuminate the true character of the composer by juxtaposing the numerous relevant documents relating to a number of particular Wagnerian issues. As
he notes in his preface, Sabor's aim is not to provide yet another
life story; rather, the purpose is to underscore the numerous
contradictions inherent in the composer's personality, thus providing a more accurate view. Concluding his preface, Sabor
states that he "comments, sums up, and occasionally permits
himself the luxury of his own opinion, but he does not give a
final verdict. This he leaves to the reader." *The Real Wagner*
contains a fine selection of photographs, documents, drawings,
and score facsimiles.

The best of the Wagnerian documentary and pictorial biographies is the 1975 BARTH, MACK, AND VOSS compilation,
which contains a wonderfully produced selection of pictures and
documents. Other pictorial biographies, such as those by
PANOFSKY and by OSBORNE, while offering a pleasing selection of photographs and documents, suffer from rather pedestrian scholarship.

—Stephan D. Lindeman

WARHOL, Andy, 1927?–1987; American painter and filmmaker.

Bockris, Victor, *The Life and Death of Andy Warhol*. New
    York, Bantam Books, 1989.
Bourdon, David, *Warhol*. New York, Abrams, 1989.
Gidal, Peter, *Andy Warhol: Films and Paintings*. London, Stu-
    dio Vista, and New York, Dutton, 1971.
Koch, Stephen, *Stargazer: Andy Warhol's World and His Films*.
    New York, Praeger, and London, Calder and Boyers, 1973.
Rosenblum, Robert, *Andy Warhol: Portraits of the 70s*. New
    York, Random House/Whitney Museum of American Art,
    1979.

Smith, Patrick S., *Andy Warhol's Art and Films*. Ann Arbor, Michigan, UMI Research Press, 1986.

*

Both before and after his death in 1987, Andy Warhol was the subject of numerous books. *Books in Print* currently lists more than two dozen, several of which are forthcoming. Yet true biographies are rare, and only two cover his entire life.

A number of books deal with his films and the world around them, with his paintings or prints, and with Warhol as an artist in general. There are books on Pop and pre-Pop Warhol, a photographic memoir, a retrospective at the Museum of Modern Art, and even a book on his FBI file. All of these, though, treat only a particular facet of Warhol's many interests or cover only a specific period of his life.

In the true and complete biography category, only Bockris and Bourdon seem to fit. Two other oddities may serve—along with a selection of the "partial" works mentioned above—to round out the view of this unusual artist. They are Pat Hackett's edition of *The Andy Warhol Diaries* (New York, Warner Books, 1989) and the six-volume catalog of *The Andy Warhol Collection* (New York, Sotheby's, 1988) from the 1988 sale at Sotheby's.

The two major works on Warhol, by BOCKRIS and BOURDON, have some points in common. Both, for example, are extensively documented. Bockris includes a basic bibliography followed by "Source Notes" for each chapter. These list both the interviews and further published sources used. Bourdon uses conventional footnotes to document interviews or printed sources at the end of each chapter, and includes a substantial "Selected Bibliography" at the end of the book. Both authors worked with Warhol at various times, Bourdon primarily in the 1960s and early 70s, Bockris in the late 70s and early 80s. And both appear to have had the cooperation of members of the Warhol family and other longtime friends and associates in their interviews.

The two books tend to sort themselves out, however, in terms of their approach and the reader interests they focus on. Their respective treatments of the Pittsburgh years provide a good illustration. Bockris provides the conventional biography, with a selection of photographs bound in the middle. He does a particularly fine job of evoking something of the feeling of immigrant life in Pittsburgh at the time of Warhol's birth and childhood. In all he devotes more than 40 pages to the Pittsburgh years. Bourdon covers the same period in about ten. The reader of Bourdon is not short-changed, though, because his is a critical biography that devotes much more space to Warhol's art, including his films. He covers the Pittsburgh years concisely and includes artwork from the period as well.

The example of the handling of the early years in the two works characterizes their approaches throughout. Bockris, a freelance writer, proceeds chronologically through a detailed discussion of Warhol's film-making, the shooting, and all of the other elements of the many-faceted life, including quotations from interviews with Bourdon. Bockris also notes Warhol's gradual progress in the art world. But even though exhibitions and other indications of commercial success are suitably chronicled, no examples of his art are shown.

Bourdon, on the other hand, does what one might expect in a biography by an art critic: while following the outline of Warhol's life, he emphasizes Warhol's life in art and generously and judiciously illustrates that life. Anyone who equates Warhol with soup cans will be surprised, and perhaps impressed, by the range of his work, whether in commercial art, drawings, films, paintings, or prints. The work of each decade, from the 1940s to the 80s, is well represented. Bourdon presents examples, among many others, of Warhol's mid-80s collaborations with Basquiat and Clemente, and of Warhol's own work through 1986. The extent and the quality of illustrations in Bourdon makes his work essential for anyone interested in Warhol as artist as opposed to Warhol as mere celebrity.

In general, however, Bockris provides greater detail of the personal life, just as Bourdon does of the artistic side. Surprisingly, though, Bourdon offers the more substantial coverage of Warhol's final hospitalization and of the later controversy surrounding his death. He also includes a detailed commentary on the Sotheby's sale. Bockris offers more information on the will and the funeral. Ideally the serious reader should consult both, especially since both conclude with attempts to place his art in the context of the late 20th century.

Hackett's edition is of interest (although the *Diaries* begin only in 1976) because the entries take us almost to Warhol's deathbed. The last entry is 17 February 1987, five days before his death. While the comments are frequently mundane, that in itself is revealing, as is Warhol's obsession with recording costs of things, even cab fares. Also evident is the continuing fascination with celebrities.

The six volumes of the Sotheby sale mentioned by Bourdon also reveal something about the collector. Probably Warhol's obsession with acquisition is related to his obsession with costs. In any event the sheer range of the collection is astonishing: volume one contains Art Nouveau and Art Deco, volume two includes jewelry, furniture, decorations, and paintings, and the third volume continues with more jewelry and watches. The fourth volume, surprisingly to some, contains American Indian art. Volume five includes Americana and European and American paintings, drawings, and prints. According to Bourdon, the contemporary art of the final volume sold for $2.8 million, mostly generated by works of Cy Twombly, Jasper Johns, and Roy Lichtenstein. Warhol's famous collection of cookie jars sold for nearly a quarter of a million dollars.

A selection of the specialized or limited period works will provide an indication of the range of materials available. ROSENBLUM's text of a 1979 exhibition catalog, for example, offers a commentary on 112 portraits (two versions each of 56 people) from that particular facet of Warhol's art. GIDAL, although a dated little book, is perhaps more useful on Warhol's films than on his paintings. It includes illustrations from the films not seen in the more general works. The most detailed coverage of Warhol's films, however, is probably to be found in the extensive analytical and critical commentary of KOCH.

Koch is cited frequently and interviewed (as is Bourdon) in SMITH, one of the most comprehensive of the partial works. Smith, in fact, might have become the definitive study of Warhol's art and films if it had been done later and thus covered the entire life. Although published in 1986, it was written in 1981 as a Ph.D. dissertation at Northwestern University. The work is meticulously documented and contains an exhaustive bibliography that only fellow art historians would need. He makes an excellent use of both printed sources (as with Koch on Warhol's films) and interviews. Like Bourdon, Smith follows the outline of Warhol's life with an emphasis on the art, but the life is covered only through the late 1970s. And although Smith contains illustrations of the art, these are not in color, and the quality of reproduction does not compare with those in Bourdon. Minor problems are the occasional passages that read like an academic treatise and the fact that Smith passes on one of the supposedly inaccurate versions of the date and place of Warhol's birth. Still, Smith presents a thoughtful and thorough analysis of as much of Warhol's art and films as the timing of his study allowed.

The many facets of the life and art of Andy Warhol do not suffer from a lack of attention. Anyone seriously interested in Warhol should consult not only the major works, but a selection of the others available, including some of those not dealt with here. For the general reader, however, the choices are clear. Bockris is the standard biography, and Bourdon offers a comprehensive, well-illustrated life-and-art approach. Those interested primarily in Warhol as filmmaker may consult Koch and others. And the myriad of other books on Warhol, as varied in focus and approach as their subject, is available to shed some light on virtually any interest pertaining to the artist.

—Robert E. Burkhart

WASHINGTON, Booker T(aliaferro), 1856–1915; American educator and African-American leader.

Harlan, Louis R., *Booker T. Washington: The Making of a Black Leader 1856–1901.* New York and Oxford, Oxford University Press, 1972.

Harlan, Louis R., *Booker T. Washington: The Wizard of Tuskegee 1901–15.* New York and Oxford, Oxford University Press, 1983.

Mathews, Basil, *Booker T. Washington, Educator and Interracial Interpreter.* Cambridge, Massachusetts, Harvard University Press, 1948; London, SCM Press, 1949.

Scott, Emmett and Lyman Beecher Stowe, *Booker T. Washington: Builder of a Civilization.* New York, Doubleday, 1916.

Spencer, Samuel R., Jr., *Booker T. Washington and the Negro's Place in American Life.* Boston, Little Brown, 1955.

*

Biographies of Booker T. Washington fall into three categories: early biographies that attempt to defend his views on industrial education for the Negro and his compromise on political and social rights for the Negro; a later biography that tries to establish a balanced view of this controversial African-American as creator of a place for himself and his race in American life; and a third monumental biography that names Washington a wizard, a maneuverer against his white and black enemies, both those who defended white supremacy and those African-Americans who thought him too conservative.

Washington's autobiography, *Up From Slavery* (1901), stood until 1915 as the only full-length life of Washington. Its simple success-oriented narrative written in clear prose continues to draw readers in great numbers.

SCOTT AND STOWE (the former was Washington's most trusted adviser) make no claims to writing a biography in the ordinary sense. They omit, for example, any discussion of Wash-

ington's childhood and early education. The value of this book lies in its information about Washington's program of industrial education, especially its academic components. The reader will also appreciate discussions of the growth of Tuskegee Institute and of Washington's character as revealed in his treatment of students and supporters. The authors relied heavily on Washington's own works, on records kept at Tuskegee, and on interviews with several of Washington's associates. They also had the full cooperation of Tuskegee Institute. Although uncritical, this book contains valid and useful information. Other accounts of Washington's life that appeared at about the time of the Scott-Stowe biography, but which may now be ignored by the serious student of Washington, include Frederick S. Drinker's *Booker T. Washington: The Master Mind of A Child of Slavery* (1915); Benjamin F. Riley's *The Life and Times of Booker T. Washington* (1916); Sylvester Boone's *The Philosophy of Booker T. Washington: The Apostle of Progress, The Pioneer of the New Deal* (1939); and Shirley Graham's book for young readers, *Booker T. Washington* (1955).

Although MATHEWS was a supporter of Washington, his book is based on solid research. In addition to using Washington's published books along with unpublished documents and letters, Mathews also makes frequent use of interviews to support statements about Washington's gospel of industrial education and belief in a racially segregated South. Letters between Washington and W. E. B. DuBois inform Mathews' discussion of the controversy between DuBois, a champion of higher education for the Negro, and Washington, an advocate of industrial training for his people. Mathews expands on the Scott-Stowe information about Washington and DuBois, and his support of Washington remains as firm as that of his predecessors. His lengthy discussion of Washington's role in race relations includes some of Washington's secret maneuvers to secure civil rights for African Americans, but Mathews' conclusion that Washington's goal was equality and justice for all does little to mitigate the force of Washington's Atlanta compromise. The book is valuable for its insight into Washington as an administrator of Tuskegee, as a political adviser to presidents of the United States, and as a foreign traveler.

SPENCER's biography differs from the earlier life studies of Washington in that it attempts a balanced view of the controversial Washington as an educator and a leader of his race. Spencer consistently and forcefully describes Washington as having attitudes and ideas that enabled him to find a place for himself and his people in American life. His perception of Washington as an American of the same stature as Benjamin Franklin shapes his biography.

After discussing the phenomenal success of Tuskegee Institute, Spencer concludes with Washington that to read the history of Tuskegee Institute is to read Washington's biography. He adds that by 1895 Tuskegee Institute was judged the best product of African American enterprise in the country. Spencer has carefully selected and described experiences that prepared Washington for making the speech at the Cotton States and International Exposition in 1895. This speech in Atlanta catapulted Washington into national prominence and into a widening circle of influence. Spencer's careful choice of influences upon Washington makes it appear inevitable that Washington would compromise his political and social rights and those of his people.

Perhaps the most demanding topic for Spencer's stance as an objective writer is his discussion of DuBois' challenge to Washington's leadership. Spencer offers a cogent contrast of the complex personalities of these two men. Spencer illuminates Washington's personality and delineates his role in attempting to achieve a limited place in American life for himself and other African Americans, especially the Southern Negro. The book ends with a valuable critical discussion of Washington's belief in industrial education and his compromise of 1895. Yet Spencer's conclusion—that, considering the times, Washington did the best he could even though he failed to advocate unequivocally the Negro's full participation in American life—does not settle the controversy surrounding the quality of Washington's contribution to African Americans and to "the entire human family."

In accounting for Washington's program for African Americans, Spencer notes that in addition to methods of education he learned at Hampton, Washington carried to Tuskegee basic assumptions about his race. His economic, educational, social, and political program for African Americans evolved from these methods and beliefs. However, even while Washington developed his program, conditions for African Americans worsened. HARLAN, in his definitive two-volume biography of Washington, dramatizes this ironic fact. He depicts Washington as a man thirsty for power, while the people he supposedly led were often in conditions that defied promises of economic, social, and political progress. Harlan's thesis that Washington was a wizard, a secret maneuverer of people, is a daring one, and in his second volume Harlan tempers this notion by showing first that Washington's friends and associates often called him a wizard because at Tuskegee, he would solve problems that appeared to be unsolvable.

Harlan's views of Washington are likely to stand indefinitely. He devoted many years of solid, intensive research to the writing of this biography, and he views Washington from an African-American perspective markedly more than did earlier biographers of Washington. Harlan's knowledge gained as editor of the Washington papers, and his use of the methods of the historian, the political analyst, the social scientist, and the scientist, along with the assistance of many scholars, contribute to the excellence of this life of Washington. His occasional imaginative reconstruction of historical events, as in the chapter, "Night of Violence," is convincing. Harlan thoroughly researched and critically appraised most aspects of Washington's life, though he does not offer extended discussions of Washington's social philosophy or of his program of education (which Harlan believes is not unique). Harlan admits that he preferred to concentrate on "the sources, nature, uses, and consequences" of Washington's power. In examining Washington's life, Harlan interviewed people who knew him as a child and as an adolescent, thereby allowing him to compare Washington's statements about himself to those presented by his friends and associates. This method led Harlan to evaluate *Up From Slavery* as the first step in a process of self-creation that Washington continued throughout his life by means of anecdotes and illustrations. Through this self-made image Washington projected himself as one who possessed the virtues of Cotton Mather, Poor Richard, and Ralph Waldo Emerson, believing that these qualities made him a leader who could uplift his race.

Even though Harlan provides an excellent, extensive study of Washington, he admits to being unable to resolve several ambiguities, including the degree to which Washington believed in the optimism he preached about the progress of his race, his

views about higher education for African Americans, and his role in the Ulrich affair (in which he was accused of attempted rape). Obviously this biography supersedes earlier ones, but the first treatments can prepare the reader for a more thorough interpretation of this last biography.

—Doris B. Morton

WASHINGTON, George, 1732–1799; American political and military leader, first president of the United States.

Alden, John R., *George Washington: A Biography*. Baton Rouge, Louisiana State University Press, 1984.

Cunliffe, Marcus, *George Washington: Man and Monument*. Boston, Little Brown, 1958; London, Collins, 1959.

Emery, Noemie, *Washington: A Biography*. New York, Putnam, 1976; London, Cassell, 1977.

Ferling, John E., *The First of Men: A Life of George Washington*. Knoxville, The University of Tennessee Press, 1988.

Flexner, James Thomas, *George Washington* (4 vols.). Boston, Little Brown, 1965–72; condensed and published in one volume as *Washington: The Indispensable Man*, 1969.

Ford, Paul Leicester, *The True George Washington*. Philadelphia, Lippincott, 1896.

Freeman, Douglas Southall, *George Washington: A Biography* (7 vols.; vol. 7 completed by J. A. Carroll and M. W. Ashworth). New York, Scribner, 1948–57; condensed by Richard Harwell and published in one volume, 1968.

Hughes, Rupert, *George Washington* (3 vols.). New York, Morrow, 1926–30.

Irving, Washington, *The Life of George Washington* (5 vols.). New York, Putnam, 1855–59.

Lodge, Henry Cabot, *George Washington* (2 vols.) Boston, Houghton Mifflin, 1889.

Marshall, John, *Life of George Washington* (5 vols.). Philadelphia, C. P. Wayne, 1804.

Sparks, Jared, *The Life of George Washington*. Cincinnati, H. W. Derby, 1855.

Stephenson, Nathaniel Wright and Waldo Hilary Dunn, *George Washington* (2 vols.). New York, Oxford University Press, 1940.

Weems, Mason Locke, *The Life of Washington*. Philadelphia, Lippincott, 1800.

Wilson, Woodrow, *George Washington*. New York, Harper, 1896.

Wister, Owen, *The Seven Ages of Washington: A Biography*. New York, Macmillan, 1907.

Woodward, William E., *George Washington: The Image and the Man*. New York, Boni and Liveright, 1926; London, Cape, 1928.

*

Any student of Washington quickly faces a central issue: how does one untangle the man from the myth? Beginning with Weems' barely posthumous biography (see below), so many legends have flourished about "the father of his country" that most

Americans remember little more than the apocryphal story of the cherry tree, his leadership during the Revolution, and his service as the first president of the United States. Of course, legends about him were just as rife during his lifetime; stories about him and his actions during and after the Revolution became the property of popular culture. The man himself appeared in households in any number of guises: prints, transfer-printed creamware, textiles, books, flags, etc., all bore the features of arguably the most famous man in the country. Without a modern media to give cozy glimpses into his daily life at home with wife, stepchildren, pets, and relatives, many Americans assumed that he was that god-like man they saw over their fireplace, on their bookshelf, or at their table. Those who did not wholeheartedly participate in the secular worship of the man were often dismissed as cranks or viewed as traitors.

As a result, biographies of Washington have tended to fall into one of three roughly chronological categories: first came those works that sought to mythologize Washington, to consolidate the accomplishments of his life, and to celebrate his virtue. The grandfather of all these hagiographic volumes is WEEMS. Weems, a clergyman, used his account of Washington's upright and virtuous life to inspire America's youth to better behavior, as in the fabricated story of the cherry tree. Considering the veracity of many of his anecdotes, Weems obviously believed that the end justified the means. Fortuitously released two months after Washington's death, his book became a bestseller and may indeed have outsold any other biography of Washington.

The next biography to appear was the five-volume effort of MARSHALL, Chief Justice of the Supreme Court. Although Marshall's account was a great deal more realistic and factual, it still expressed so much respect and deference that one does not get a real picture of the man—or even the statesman—or of how he thought and acted at crucial times of his life. The next biography of notes was by SPARKS, who had the advantage of having had access to Washington's personal papers through the family and had already issued a 12-volume edition of his selected writings in the 1830s. Unfortunately, Sparks' penchant for deleting ''objectionable'' passages and altering Washington's wording when he found it unseemly makes both his edition and his biography suspect; his Washington is singularly sober and upright, and Sparks contributed to the legend of his humorlessness.

Soon after Sparks, the American writer IRVING weighed in with another multi-volume work. Far and away the best work of its time, it is remarkable for its attempt to understand and portray Washington as a human being, as well as for its pleasing prose. But, like its predecessors, it was occasionally laudatory at the expense of historical accuracy.

The path of 19th-century biographies of Washington continued in these hagiographic steps at the century's end and turn. LODGE, although a great statesman, was not a great biographer, and his two-volume effort is pedestrian with very little new to say. FORD's work was a praiseworthy interpretive attempt that shed a little more light on the man and his personality, but Ford still stood in awe of the man and his achievements. One would think that WILSON would have provided an interesting slant on Washington considering his training and political ambitions, but his biography is undistinguished although generally accurate. WISTER did not differ much in tone or substance from his predecessors.

The turn of the century also marked a shift to the second of the three categories of Washington biographies: the iconoclastic muckrakers. Disillusioned with their overly respectful predecessors and infused with populist enthusiasm, these men sought to show Washington as a member of the colonial elite who exploited his military and political opportunities to amass a fortune. WOODWARD's was the first and least dramatic of these works, paving the way for HUGHES' virulent three-volume attempt, left unfinished at his death. Reading these works helps one to appreciate the tenor of the time they were written as much as to understand their subject.

The third category is that of the much more satisfactory, three-dimensional portrayals of Washington. Beginning in 1940 with the collaboration of STEPHENSON AND DUNN, solid, well-researched biographies of Washington began to appear. Stephenson and Dunn were notable for their extensive use of the primary sources available and their evenhanded treatment of their subject. Historians began to rely on primary documents to explore Washington's world in more detail and to understand his motives and thinking. A more realistic but still admirable man began to emerge.

The next biography is undoubtedly the greatest of all works on Washington: FREEMAN's magisterial, seven-volume treatise. No scholar or student seriously interested in Washington can afford to ignore this comprehensive and sympathetic treatment that ranks among the best works of American biography. Freeman, a former newspaper man, turned his attention to Washington after working on another notable Virginian, Robert E. Lee. His careful and methodical search through manuscript collections throughout the world was rewarded, and he took full advantage of the resources to provide enlightening information on Washington's relationship with Sally Fairfax and, more pertinent, on the background of the life and fortune of his future wife, the wealthy widow Martha Dandridge Custis. Perhaps most interesting was Freeman's decision to focus on Washington's activities day by day. By this temporal approach, he hoped to show readers exactly how Washington's life unfolded without foreshadowing. He himself was amazed by what he learned about his subject and determined that the Revolution marked Washington's transformation from a self-centered, ambitious young man eager for fame and fortune to a mature, cautious leader who put the needs of those he led above his own. His enthusiasm for and admiration of his subject is not blind, however; Washington emerges as an impressive but human figure. For those unable or unwilling to wade through all seven volumes, HARWELL's condensation of Freeman should not be ignored.

CUNLIFFE's slim interpretive volume is an indispensable introduction to Washington and is still the bedrock of all subsequent discussion of the man and his life. FLEXNER's biography, the basis for the two television mini-series on Washington, is another literate and very well-researched biography, illuminating the character and motives of its subject. Flexner's Washington is perhaps more human and loveable than Freeman's, but Flexner may have fallen prey to interpreting an 18th-century man by 20th-century standards. There is also an excellent one-volume condensation available. For those laymen interested in an enjoyable, readable account of Washington's life and times, Flexner's is the biography to read. Cunliffe's and Flexner's works are probably the two best still in print.

The one exception to the quality of recent works on Washington is EMERY. Although she has written biographies on many of the figures of the day, this is a pedestrian, although adequate, effort. However, two recent one-volume biographies are very good, although they do not add much to our corpus of knowledge of Washington. ALDEN, a well-known historian of the period, produced a concise and admirable biography in 1984 that is widely available. Most recently, FERLING has produced another laudable biography. However, there is still no doubt that Freeman, Cunliffe, and Flexner are the most important and lively of the multitude of biographies.

—Jean V. Berlin

WAUGH, Evelyn (Arthur St. John), 1903–1966; English writer.

Sykes, Christopher, *Evelyn Waugh: A Biography*. London, Collins, and Boston, Little Brown, 1975.
Stannard, Martin, *Evelyn Waugh: The Early Years 1903–39*. London, Dent, 1986; New York, Norton, 1987.

*

SYKES' biography of his friend Evelyn Waugh was written at the request of Laura Waugh, the novelist's widow, and their son Auberon, himself a novelist. It is, therefore, an authorized, official biography written by a long-time friend. These facts notwithstanding, Sykes' portrait of Waugh is balanced and detached; he records alike his arrogance and conservative inflexibility, and his wit and intellectual grace.

Part memoir, part biography, Sykes' work is long on anecdote but short on scholarship. Moreover, it contains an excess of detail and trivia concerning some persons and events, and lengthy digressions on who provided the basis for which characters in the novels. But Sykes occasionally stints on, or literally skips, major biographical data on the theory that Waugh himself has done a better job either in his 1964 account of his early years, *A Little Learning*, or elsewhere. Although he does draw heavily on this volume of autobiography and makes copious use of interviews, documents, and his own recollections, Sykes includes little about Waugh's earlier days; this neglect, however, has its compensation in the wealth of wonderful anecdotes Sykes provides of Waugh's later years.

Sykes is sometimes reticent on such issues as Waugh's sexuality. He dismisses Waugh's "homosexual phase" at Oxford in a few unsatisfactory phrases, and he fails to discuss Waugh's politics and religion in any significant detail. These subjects do, however, elicit from Sykes the kind of extraordinarily opinionated and violent statements that one would expect from Waugh himself.

The product of ten years of research, STANNARD's work is the first volume of his projected two-volume life of Evelyn Waugh. Stannard provides a great deal of new information, much of it unavailable to Sykes. He corrects facts and dates in Sykes' earlier biography and can fairly claim to be "setting the record straight" in certain areas. Stannard also throws a great

deal of light on Waugh's methods of composition, revealing for the first time the full range of his intellect. He provides chapters dealing with the five pre-war novels in substantial detail, and a thorough bibliography of Waugh's works.

Stannard gives a far more complete and balanced portrait of Waugh than that found in Sykes' biography. He interviewed Evelyn Gardner (Waugh's first wife) and discusses their ill-fated marriage, suggesting that she was sexually unsatisfied by Waugh. Waugh's erotic life in general is also scrutinized; Stannard documents certain "strong, homosexual urges," apparently controlled at Lancing, and possibly given into at Oxford in the 1920s. His discussion of Waugh's conversion to Roman Catholicism successfully clears up various misconceptions about the aesthetic and mystical appeal Catholicism held for Waugh. On the other hand, Stannard tries too hard to explain away Waugh's infatuation with Italian Fascism—a flaw that stands out in an otherwise outstanding biography.

Stannard covers Waugh's career with a relentless roll of detail that at times threatens to crush the narrative flat. His accounts of Waugh's extensive travels in Africa, South America, the Arctic, and Mexico are so exhaustively detailed as to be a bit tiresome. Stannard has assembled a staggering amount of data from primary sources, interviews, and memoirs. He manages to maintain a healthy objectivity throughout and presents a composite portrait of Waugh as self-promoter, working man, reactionary snob tormented by demons and, above all, writer of brilliantly amusing novels and insightful essays.

—Lucilia M. C. Valério

WAYNE, John, 1907–1979; American film actor.

Barbour, Alan G., *John Wayne*. New York, Pyramid, 1974.
Bishop, George, *John Wayne: The Actor, the Man*. Ottowa, Illinois, Caroline House, 1979.
Carpozi, George, Jr., *The John Wayne Story*. New Rochelle, New York, Arlington House, 1972; London, R. Hale, 1974.
Eyles, Allen, *John Wayne and the Movies*. New York, A. S. Barnes, 1976.
Levy, Emanuel, *John Wayne: Prophet of the American Way of Life*. Metuchen, New Jersey, Scarecrow Press, 1988.
Ramer, Jean, *Duke: The Real John Wayne*. New York, Award Books, 1973.
Ricci, Mark and Boris and Steven Zmijewsky, *The Films of John Wayne*. Secaucus, New Jersey, Citadel, 1970; revised edition, 1983.
Tomkies, Mike, *Duke: The Story of John Wayne*. Chicago, H. Regnery, and London, Barker, 1971
Zolotow, Maurice, *Shooting Star: A Biography of John Wayne*. New York, Simon and Schuster, 1974.

*

TOMKIES provided the first of a line of anecdotal, film-by-film accounts of John Wayne while the star was still alive, just after he won his Oscar for *True Grit*. The resulting portrait is sincerely respectful. Wayne's controversial right-wing politics are ignored, while his presumed traits as a human being (honesty, integrity, and a sense of humor) are underscored. But like those of this biographical genre that would follow, Tomkie's book is not a true biography so much as a picture-filled portrait, with photographs of Wayne from his earliest days in *The Bib Trail* (1930) through his days as a "B" western star at the Republic Studios to his "break" in John Ford's *Stagecoach* (1939) and his great roles in *The Searchers* (1956), *Rio Bravo* (1959), and *The Man Who Shot Liberty Valance* (1962).

RAMER follows in the genre, offering another of the meager, fan-oriented bio-pics. Though he provides no footnotes, the author ascribes to know (and at times even quote) his subject's innermost thoughts. This book is an interesting example of shoehorning an actor's career into the well-known Horatio Alger myth.

CARPOZI offers yet another once-over-lightly version of the actor's life. This ex-newspaperman has made a career of penning star biographies in recent years, and so covers all the bases of the ascribed legend, from the failed marriages, to "how director John Ford rubbed young Wayne's face in the dirt—and taught him how to act!" to Wayne's unashamed patriotism, and, finally, to the beginnings of what would turn out to be his fatal lung cancer. There is a list of the actor's credits, but no source notes or bibliography. The pictures are routine at best.

ZOLOTOW provides the best of the fan biographies, indeed the source for Barbour, Bishop, and Tomkies. Still the drawbacks are many. The author, a longtime movie publicist, had the cooperation of Wayne in the days of his greatest glory (after the Oscar for *True Grit* and in the days of controversy over Wayne's positions and symbology regarding the Vietnam war). Here is Wayne's authorized version of his rise to stardom, multiple marriages, stormy relationships with John Ford, and battle with cancer. The center section contains a number of photographs, and the book includes an index.

BARBOUR is a cut above the preceding fan magazine biographies because at least the author is required to fit into the rigid structure imposed by the publisher, and so in a short amount of space provides all the basic film buff information. If you want to acquire the information in the previous biographies on the cheap, read Barbour. The work offers a bibliography, a filmography, and an index. Pyramid, however, never adequately reproduces its photographs.

EYLES is yet another fan-oriented biography, still aimed at the film buff, but with at least some analytical point of view: the story of the creation the John Wayne image. Eyles, a well-known writer based in London, always supplies complete filmographies, and detailed indexes. This volume even has well-reproduced photographs.

The RICCI AND ZMIJEWSKY volume is for the fan who wants lots and lots of photographs, and little else. After a short biography of Wayne (rehashing Zolotow), the authors go film by film, offering images, casts and credits, plot synopses, and a smattering of reviews. To accommodate the end of the actor's life the authors revised their book in 1983 to include all the films in Wayne's long career.

BISHOP is a gushy fan magazine tribute, published because its subject had just died. It is simply a rewrite of Eyles and Zolotow. To this is added opinion and conjecture of someone barely familiar with the workings of the American film industry. The actual text is less than 200 pages.

LEVY has written the lone serious study of John Wayne. This is not a standard chronological biography, but a study of the creation of the image of Wayne in the movies ("the war hero," "the western hero," and "Wayne's sex image"), an evaluation of Wayne's acting ability, and a study of Wayne as a political figure. This book contains a forward by noted critic Andrew Sarris, detailed footnotes, a bibliography, and an index. Levy rises above the usual mold of fan oriented John Wayne biographies, providing some understanding of his depth of ability and his importance to film history. Andrew Sarris is correct when he writes: "The great virtue of Levy's study of Wayne is its avoidance of the cant that has traditionally inundated the subject when treated by the politically and artistically censorious. Without embracing all the ideological implications of Wayne's career, Levy has stood off at enough of a disinterested distance to compute the pluses and minuses clearly and coherently. He has provided a multi-layered context in which John Wayne can be fully appreciated, warts and all, once and for all."

—Douglas Gomery

WEBER, Max, 1864–1920; German sociologist and economist.

Bendix, Rheinhardt, *Max Weber: An Intellectual Portrait*. New York, Doubleday, and London, Heinemann, 1960; revised edition, Berkeley, University of California Press, 1977.

Käsler, Dirk, *Max Weber: An Introduction to His Life and Work*, translated by Philippa Hurd. Cambridge, Polity Press, and Chicago, University of Chicago Press, 1988 (originally published as *Einführung in das Studium Max Webers*, Munich, Beck, 1979).

MacRae, Donald G., *Max Weber*. London, Fontana, and New York, Viking, 1974.

Mitzman, Arthur, *The Iron Cage: An Historical Interpretation of Max Weber*. New York, Knopf, 1970.

Parkin, Frank, *Max Weber*. Chichester, E. Horwood, and New York, Tavistock, 1982.

Weber, Marianne, *Max Weber: A Biography*, translated and edited by Harry Zohn. New York, Wiley, 1975 (originally published by Mohr, Tübingen, 1926).

*

The biography of a polymath is a big enough challenge: it becomes gigantic when the subject lived and worked in a culture that was intellectually complex and where language tended to be opaque. Yet Max Weber has inspired a stream of books about his life and work, especially since his centenary in 1964.

Their approaches differ, but all draw extensively on the biography written by MARIANNE WEBER, his widow, in the years following his death in 1920. First published in Germany in 1926, it has an immediacy and intimacy that only such a work could enjoy. Despite this debt to Marianne, time has provided new perspectives and later writers have been able to supply commentaries and interpretive glosses that eluded Marianne, or were not part of her intention.

Zohn's translation of her "Lebensbild" takes into account a second edition of the original text (Heidelberg, 1950), which incorporated some minor corrections. Zohn is therefore able to claim it as "the most complete, most accurate and perhaps even the clearest version of the work that has ever been published." The first of these claims remains valid 15 years on. Zohn also claims that his translation is "copiously annotated." Neither of the German editions has footnotes despite frequent references to "Professor X" or "Colleague B," and although Zohn clears up almost all of these enigmas, the notes remain brief and selective—though with a text running to over 700 pages, "copious" footnotes might be excessive!

Two problems confront Zohn—prose style and attribution. He properly sees the need to preserve the distinctive flavour of Marianne's writing, even though he judges it "metaphorical, soulful, highflown . . . even overblown." It belongs to a more leisurely and ornate age than ours. But how to differentiate Marianne's own words of 1926 from her earlier diaries and notes, not to mention the plethora of Weber's literary relics together with remembered (half-remembered?) conversations of yesteryear—there lies Zohn's problem and, though he strives admirably, he never fully solves it. The fullness and frankness of this biography is best illustrated by the detached and impersonal way Marianne includes what is tantamount to Max's letter proposing marriage—surely the most passionate yet lukewarm proposal offered a woman. It seems that their union was never consummated, and in a sense this biography is their offspring—given to the world entire, without debate or evaluation.

MACRAE's *Weber* is the opposite in every respect: 90 pages with no quotations or notes—all directed at explanation and commentary. It looks and reads like a lecture series, and none the worse for that. The first half deals with the man and his work, the second with interpreting his work in terms of the man himself—attitudes, values, methods.

The terrible tangle of family influence, public affairs, and academic work that served both to explain and to stimulate Weber's work is handled succinctly in terms readily accessible to a modern audience. MacRae's scholarship is outstanding, yet this is not a "scholarly" book. He tells what he has seen for himself, what he has been told, and then leaves the rest to the reader. He offers a route map to the maze that Weber left behind, but sees "no finality" in judging a man and mind so various. But he avoids hero-worship: Weber's blind spots are duly pointed out. The book is straightforward, the style direct, the translations (however complex or excessive the original German of Max or Marianne) never less than clear; a dry Scots humour is ever lurking just below the surface.

BENDIX stands preeminent in Weber studies. MacRae acknowledges that Bendix is also a cartographer: "the best map anywhere available" is how MacRae describes this "intellectual portrait." It cannot be classified as a true biography because it devotes so little space to personal events and their consequential impact upon the man's development: one short chapter is all we get, and that very selective of events. And yet the claim "portrait" is not an idle one. The man emerges from his writings rather than from events, for Bendix has cleverly shuffled the pack of Weber's voluminous work until the various suits are aligned in order. The Protestant Ethic, agrarian reform, stock exchange mechanisms, the religions of ancient India and China inform the reader of each other and also of Weber himself.

KÄSLER's is a more recent work in this vein, standing indebted to Philippa Hurd for an English translation of utmost clarity. The case for the unified biography/critique is clearly spelt out by Käsler: "More than is the case of most academic writers, we can only readily understand the evolution of Weber's work if we are aware of the events that shaped it." Käsler's biographical chapter is a great deal fuller than Bendix's, and there are valuable final chapters on both the impact Weber's work had during his lifetime and its current significance. Between these are the substantive sections, all well examined, and the inevitable chapter on methodology, which is as clear as anyone's.

A similar but shorter book, more on the lines of MacRae, is that by PARKIN—a book that enjoys a distinct whiff of the graduate seminar room at its most unbuttoned: "Weber and Freud never met but it is not hard to guess how Freud would have diagnosed Weber's malady." Parkin sums up MITZMAN's book as "beguiling and [presenting] only mildly outrageous views about the link between Weber's theories and his inner turmoil." *The Iron Cage*, with its deliberate ironic word association with Golden Age, is an interpretive biography, relating the man to his ideas and placing both within the context of cultural history and psychoanalysis. The chapter "Orestes and the Furies," dealing with events leading up to the death of Weber's father, his breakdown, and "indefinite leave" from Heidelberg, is a fine example of how speculation and deduction may fill in some of the blanks left by Marianne.

—David L. Howard

———————

WEBSTER, Daniel, 1782–1852; American statesman and orator.

Bartlett, Irving H., *Daniel Webster*. New York, Norton, 1978.

Baxter, Maurice G., *One and Inseparable: Daniel Webster and the Union*. Cambridge, Massachusetts, Harvard University Press, 1984.

Current, Richard N., *Daniel Webster and the Rise of National Conservatism*. Boston, Little Brown, 1955.

Curtis, George Tickner, *Life of Daniel Webster* (2 vols.). New York, Appleton, 1869.

Fuess, Claude M., *Daniel Webster* (2 vols). Boston, Little Brown, 1930.

Peterson, Merrill D., *The Great Triumvirate: Webster, Clay, and Calhoun*. New York and Oxford, Oxford University Press, 1987.

Shewmaker, Kenneth E., editor, *Daniel Webster, "The Completest Man:" Essays and Documents*. Hanover, New Hampshire, The University Press of New England, 1990.

*

CURTIS' two-volume work is the most important early biography of Daniel Webster. The author knew his subject well: he not only served as one of Webster's literary executors, but also drew up Webster's last will and testament and was present when the eminent statesman died. Curtis aptly characterizes his chronologically organized study as the life of a great man composed by a friend as a "labor of love." Despite his loyalty to Webster, Curtis is generally fair-minded in this clearly written and carefully documented account. "The purpose of biography," he states, "is, or should be, truth." In pursuing this goal, Curtis includes comments critical of Webster by such contemporaries as Senator Thomas Hart Benton and observes that while one might "lament that a great character is not in all things complete . . . we do not enhance its greatness by concealing its defects."

Although Curtis wrote his biography for the general reader, it is valuable today primarily to scholars. Prior to composing his account, Curtis interviewed numerous individuals who knew Webster, and he assiduously collected letters, recollections, and testimonials. Most of these documents are reprinted in the two volumes. Since many of these materials cannot be found elsewhere, some of the letters having been either lost or destroyed in a fire in 1881, Curtis's large biography remains an invaluable source for historians.

FUESS' admiring two-volume life of Webster was regarded as the standard account from 1930 until 1984, when it was superseded by Baxter's account. In a straightforward narrative, Fuess depicts Webster as an enormously talented statesman of power, majesty, and "glorious magnetism." Webster, he concludes, "was literally a superman." Fuess is less critical of his subject than was Curtis, excusing such faults as financial irresponsibility as "those of a large and liberal personality." Based primarily on the 18 volumes of James W. McIntyre's *National Edition of the Writings and Speeches of Daniel Webster* (Boston, Little Brown, 1903), Fuess' study remains useful for its scope and comprehensiveness. The general reader, however, would be better advised to draw upon Fuess' work for supplementary information rather than relying on it for an introduction to the life of Webster.

CURRENT's crisply written book, one of the volumes in the Library of American Biography series, is a good starting point for anyone interested in the life and times of Webster. Although only about 200 pages in length, the work is comprehensive in scope and contains a well rounded appraisal of Webster. Current understands Webster as a spokesman for a brand of national conservatism which assumed that property and power should go together, and as a politican who sought to promote that philosophy both in domestic and foreign policy. While critical of Webster for his involvement in conflict of interest situations, Current also depicts him as a talented statesman who advanced the interests of the dominant banking, business, and commercial groups of antebellum America. Current's interpretive study has no equal for its penetrating analysis of Webster's career in relation to the larger themes of American history.

Although they differ considerably in approach and methodology, the biographies by Bartlett and Peterson are also good choices for the general reader interested in Webster. Unlike other Webster scholars, BARTLETT emphasizes the private rather than the public side of his subject. He characterizes Webster as "a great man flawed" by his improvidence with money, opulent lifestyle, involvement in conflict of interest situations, and idiosyncratic politics. On the other side, he concludes that Webster "at his best represented the Establishment in America with an intelligence, dignity, and eloquence which have rarely been equaled in our history." Despite his focus on the inner man, Bartlett also provides outstanding appraisals of the content and impact of such major Webster orations as the Second Reply to

Hayne in 1830 and the Seventh of March Speech in 1850. He also offers the reader sensitive vignettes of the other members of Webster's family, such as Grace Fletcher, his first wife. Unfortunately, the book contains no bibliography and is inadequate in assessing Webster's record in foreign policy during two terms as secretary of state. Nevertheless, the reader can gain many insights into the character of Webster as a human being from Bartlett's elegantly written biography.

In his innovative, collective biography of what he calls "the great triumvirate," PETERSON is less interested in the private than in the public lives of Daniel Webster, Henry Clay, and John C. Calhoun. His emphasis is on national politics from the War of 1812 to the Compromise of 1850, and he characterizes the triumvirs as "the ornaments of American statesmanship in the era between the founding and the Civil War." He assesses Clay as the most gifted and constructive political leader of the three, Calhoun as a brilliant individual who "ruined all he touched," and Webster as a prodigiously talented tribune of national unity blemished by a weak moral sense and corrupted over time by money and power. In effect, Peterson offers readers an absorbing comparative political biography of three prominent antebellum Americans whose lives overlapped to a considerable degree. The book is based on diligent research in such primary sources as manuscripts, memoirs, and congressional documents, and it is enlivened by anecdotal material, some of which is of questionable validity.

The most valuable biography for scholars is BAXTER's cradle-to-grave study of Webster. Baxter's richly detailed work is anchored on impressive research in the primary sources. He makes effective use of the 41 reels of the Microfilm Edition of the *Papers of Daniel Webster* (Ann Arbor, Michigan, University Microfilms, 1971) and many of the 15 volumes of its companion letterpress publication (Hanover, New Hampshire, University Press of New England, 1974–89), both issued under the overall editorship of Charles M. Wiltse. Taken together, these collectios of primary sources constitute the definitive compilation of Webster documents, and Baxter has availed himself of these materials to author the best researched and most comprehensive biography of Webster in print.

In clear though not very lively prose, Baxter examines every aspect of Webster's versatile career as lawyer, diplomatist, politician, and orator. For example, in terms of legislative history, he provides a specific account of Webster's record for every session of Congress in which he participated. Although Baxter offers a full appraisal of Webster's life, he is particularly strong on law and politics and weakest on Webster's two terms as secretary of state from 1841-43 and 1850-52. He is sympathetic toward his subject but not uncritical, observing that on occasion Webster was "culpable of serious impropriety." Baxter concludes that Webster's nationalistic view of the Union as one and inseperable with liberty, which ultimately triumphed over Calhoun's philosophy of state sovereignty, is the statesman's greatest contribution to American history. With a keen eye for telling detail, Baxter has composed what is now the standard life of Webster. Unfortunately, the book contains no bibliography, only a sparse two-page "Bibliographical Note."

The volume edited by SHEWMAKER contains an introduction assessing Webster's importance in and impact on American history, and includes essays by four distinguished scholars that in their totality provide a concise but comprehensive account of the statesman's multifaceted career as politician, orator, lawyer, and diplomatist. Richard Current scrutinizes Webster's activities as a partisan politician; Irving Bartlett analyzes Webster's major speeches from 1800 until his death in 1852; Maurice Baxter examines Webster's extensive legal practice at all levels from the state and federal courts to the U.S. Supreme Court; and Howard Jones explores Webster's record as secretary of state. Appended to each essay is a set of documents selected from Webster's private correspondence and published writings, allowing readers to come to their own conclusions about historical issues. The book also features a foreword by Chief Justice William R. Rehnquist comparing the differing roles of public men and lawyers in the 19th and 20th centuries, and a bibliographical essay highlighting the most significant primary sources and secondary works on Webster's life and times. Although the work is intended especially for college students, it also offers the general reader a topically-oriented introduction to one of America's greatest statesmen.

—Kenneth E. Shewmaker

WEIL, Simone, 1909–1943; French philosopher, mystic, and political activist.

Cabaud, Jacques, *Simone Weil: A Fellowship in Love.* London, Harvill Press, 1964; New York, Channel Press, 1965.
Coles, Robert, *Simone Weil: A Modern Pilgrimage.* Reading, Massachusetts, Addison Wesley, 1987.
Fiori, Gabriella, *Simone Weil: An Intellectual Biography*, translated by J. R. Berrigan. Athens, University of Georgia Press, 1989 (originally published by Garzanti, Milan, 1981).
Little, J. P. , *Simone Weil, Waiting on Truth.* Oxford, Berg, and New York, St. Martin's, 1988.
McFarland, Dorothy Tuck, *Simone Weil.* New York, Ungar, 1983.
Pétrement, Simone, *Simone Weil: A Life.* New York, Pantheon, 1976; London, Mowbrays, 1977 (originally published as *La Vie de Simone Weil*, Paris, Fayard, 1973).

*

Simone Weil was extremely well versed in the history of religion as well as in philosophy. Her writings, composed mostly from notes and correspondence published after her death, reveal a profound duality. Although she was opposed to the Christian dogma, she developed an acute sense of mysticism in her search for God. Her statements regarding the Old Testament are ambiguous and at times have been interpreted as anti-Semitic. Simone Weil's Jewishness is therefore at the heart of the debate. Coles (see below) dedicates a whole chapter to the question of her Jewishness which, according to him, is the most problematic aspect of Simone Weil's life, as her letters indicate.

As McFarland (see below) writes: "understanding Simone Weil demands both an openness to difficult and sometimes disturbing ideas and a serious effort of attention. Without such attention, Weil believed, the transmission of truth between human beings was not possible. Therefore, it comes as no surprise that the biographies represented here discuss these multiple tenden-

cies inherent in Simone Weil's ideas. Simone Pétrement (see below) confirms this fact in her preface: Simone Weil's "picture is bound to be blurred and the story hampered and confused by the many subjective impressions." Part of this ambiguity is due to the fact that Simone Weil lived during very agitated times. In his chapter entitled "Introduction to Her Life," COLES situates Weil's birth "at the end of a decade during which France was virtually split in two by the Dreyfus case, by anti-Semitism and its strong roots in that nation's bourgeoisie." He emphasizes how she matured from the time of her fascination with Christianity to becoming a mystic in the same tradition of Juliana of Norwich and Saint-Thérèse of Lisieux. Coles' study focuses mainly on Weil's relationship to God and Christianity. He reports her travels to Assisi and to the benedictine Abbey at Solesnes, where she heard Gregorian chant.

Coles claims that Weil's reading of Saint John of the Cross led her to denounce material possessions and shows how ultimately "her anarchism influenced her view of Christianity." CABAUD, who is the first scholar to attempt to gather major biographical information on Simone Weil, discusses in detail her mystical experiences based on her letters to Joë Bousquet and to Father Perin. In particular, he raises the question of "affabulation": "Does she use," he asks, "fantasy in attempting to recreate her experience in words?"

McFARLAND on the other hand attributes Simone Weil's need for affliction to her experience of war. That is to say that McFarland's study is more historical in its approach and places Weil within the context of her times. McFarland's study is chronological and extremely well organized, and it avoids classifying Weil as only a spiritual thinker. All the while recognizing her "profoundly holistic vision of man and his relationship to the world," McFarland argues that in spite of Weil's fascination with Catharism, her "ultimate attitude toward the universe is not one of rejection but of profound all-embracing love." McFarland outlines step by step the development of Simone Weil's thought through her education to her commitment to social causes, which she manifested as early as 1929 when she became involved in manual work in order to better understand the needs of the proletariat. McFarland chooses Weil's lectures at Roanne (*Lectures on Philosophy*, 1978), where she was a teacher, to support her argument: "The text clearly shows the connections between Weil's epistemological and social/political thought and the relationship of both to her conception of what it is to be human." McFarland's study also analyzes important texts such as the *Journal d'usine*, a diary in which Simone Weil related her experiences in three different factories from 1934 to 1935.

FIORI's study is based on evidence provided by people who knew Weil and on an examination of her works. Although divided into clearly separated chapters, this study is poorly structured and is difficult to follow. It lacks synthesis and analysis.

PÉTREMENT's study on the other hand constitutes the most extensive and thoroughly researched biography of Simone Weil. Its biographical material sometimes duplicates that of Cabaud, to whose study Pétrement refers on several occasions. What distinguishes Pétrement's study is its use of several unpublished documents, manuscripts, letters, and articles. Pétrement became Weil's friend in 1925, and therefore her study is often written from her personal recollections. Full of anecdotes (relating for example Weil's preference for black coffee), and in spite of its general lack of focus and synthesis, this romanticized and personal study presents a solid overall picture of Simone Weil.

Pétrement discusses in detail Weil's participation in the Popular Front movement in France and in Spain, and she outlines her trips to Italy and Germany as well as her meeting with the *Nouveaux Cahiers* group, the *Cahiers du Sud*, and with such literary figures as André Malraux.

Pétrement dedicates a chapter to Weil's correspondence during her stay in New York, where her parents had escaped from anti-Semitisim in 1942. Her letters reveal how unhappy she was in New York after having left her country in distress. Pétrement recalls Weil telling her mother: "I can't go on living like this. If this must go on, I'll go to work in the South with the blacks, and there I am sure I will die because I can't stand this life.'' While this type of biographical information is valuable, the reader depends too often on Pétrement's selection of quotes and will find few bibliographical references to support these documents. Therefore, Pétrement's study will remain informative but not a good source of reference for the serious biographer or scholar.

LITTLE's study approaches Weil's works as a reflection of her life. He characterizes Weil first and foremost as a philosopher and offers an assessment of her contribution to our times. His analysis of *L'enracinement* emphasizes Weil's "determination to get to the origin of the malaise in French society." In Little's study, Weil stands as a social thinker and an historian who challenged the value of history throughout her life.

—Martine Natat Antle

WELLES, Orson, 1915–1985; American film and theatre director, writer, producer, and actor.

Bazin, André, *Orson Welles: A Critical View*, translated by Jonathan Rosenbaum. New York, Harper, and London, Elm Tree Books, 1978 (originally published by Chavane, Paris, 1950).

Brady, Frank, *Citizen Welles: A Biography of Orson Welles*. New York, Stein and Day, 1988; London, Hodder and Stoughton, 1990.

Carringer, Robert L., *The Making of Citizen Kane*. Berkeley, University of California Press, and London, J. Murray, 1985.

Higham, Charles, *Orson Welles: The Rise and Fall of an American Genius*. New York, St. Martin's, 1985; London, New English Library, 1986.

Leaming, Barbara, *Orson Welles: A Biography*. New York, Viking, and London, Weidenfeld and Nicolson, 1985.

Naremore, James, *The Magic World of Orson Welles*. New York, Oxford University Press, 1978.

Taylor, John Russell, *Orson Welles: A Celebration*. Boston, Little Brown, and London, Pavilion, 1986.

*

Shortly before Orson Welles died in 1985, a number of biographies and related works were published, which updated and, in some cases, advanced the scholarship on America's genius film director. Until then, most of the works on Welles had been written by cineastes who unraveled the films but not the man. Important among the latter is BAZIN's pioneering critical study of Welles' films, which was first published in 1950, then revised and expanded in 1958, republished with a foreword by François Truffaut in 1972, and finally translated into English by Rosenbaum in 1978. More typical is TAYLOR's illustrated career overview, which simply details the trials and tribulations of many of Welles' stage and film productions with little analysis or insight. NAREMORE's worthy but narrow account of Welles' career discusses only the films, emphasizing the historical and political context in which they were made. These works offer limited biographical information. Only near the end of his life did biographers—as opposed to film historians and cineastes—discover Welles to be a fascinating and profitable subject.

The task of deciphering Welles brings with it several built-in questions and problems, including the director's longstanding habit of embellishing his life story with gross exaggerations, misleading half-truths, and outright lies. Higham, Leaming, and Brady acknowledge this Wellesian idiosyncrasy, and the way each author approaches this problem points up the strengths and weaknesses of each biography.

HIGHAM uses this self-dramatizing aspect of Welles' character to justify his decision not to talk with Welles personally. In his introduction, Higham discusses several examples of Welles' exaggerations about his life and career, attributing this characteristic to an "impish sense of humor." He offers a veiled critique of his fellow biographers who have accepted Welles' statements "out of uncritical admiration," suggesting that access to Welles' interpretations of his life and career are more of a hindrance than a help. Perhaps because of this distanced stance, Higham chose to begin his biography with Welles' ancestry, reaching all the way back to 1750 to recount the genealogy of the Wells (later Welles) family. No other biography offers such a detailed account of Welles' background, though Higham almost ruins the impressive research by trying too hard to make the information relate to Welles' personal life and work.

Higham was aided by the famed Mormon libraries in Los Angeles and Salt Lake City in his search for Welles' ancestral background, which points out another strength of his work. Higham received assistance from several notable research centers and from many scholars—from the librarians at various universities to the noted film historian Anthony Slide. He also interviewed an amazing number of Welles' acquaintances—from the sister of the nursemaid who helped raise him to his contemporaries in the Hollywood industry, including Frank Capra.

Unfortunately, Higham chooses to use this impressive research to engage in pop psychology about his subject—not a particularly fair practice considering his lack of personal contact with Welles. For example, Higham theorizes that Welles suffered from a fear of completion, which supposedly accounts for the meager body of work after his auspicious film debut with *Citizen Kane*. Though this treatise was emphasized more in Higham's career overview of Welles (*The Films of Orson Welles*, 1970), it represents the author's penchant for simplistic cause-and-effect conclusions that the reader is supposed to accept at face value.

LEAMING obtained what many other writers have never had—Welles' complete cooperation. Leaming accounts for Welles' tendency to bend the facts by stating, " . . . sometimes there are inscrutable disparities between what Orson remembers and the data I unearth." Her explanation almost excuses his habit as the fault of a rusty memory rather than revealing it to be the deliberate act of a mischievous rebel as Higham has suggested. Leaming fails to make clear that Welles had manipulated interviewers with false information about his background since the beginning. Though a minor detail, it nonetheless reflects her partisan approach to her subject—as does her cloying habit of referring to Welles as "Orson."

Yet, instead of hurting her biography, Leaming's obvious affection for her subject results in a style that often allows the reader to arrive at his or her own conclusions. At the suggestion of Welles, Leaming peppers her biography with italicized vignettes that capture Welles' views at the time she was writing the book. A short anecdote about Welles' possible dalliance with *Citizen Kane* costar Ruth Warrick—which appears just before the chapter on the making of *Kane*—speaks volumes about Welles' personality. Whether the details about the affair are true or not becomes irrelevant; it is his musings about the dalliance, which he does not recall, that are revealing. Leaming was able to add Welles' voice to the telling of his life story, giving her biography an intimate touch that other books lack.

The third work released in 1985 was CARRINGER's well-documented production history on the making of *Citizen Kane*. Though not a biography, the book is a worthwhile addition to the scholarship on Welles because it is an extensive investigation on the director's masterwork, which proved to be the standard by which the rest of his career was judged.

BRADY's biography, published four years later, was begun before Welles died. In the foreword, Brady acknowledges several phone conversations with Welles but admits to having never met the great man personally. He seems to sincerely believe that Welles was interested in cooperating but hints in the same breath that his subject evaded him. Though Brady offers Welles' inaccessible lifestyle as a partial explanation, one suspects Welles' association with Leaming may have had some bearing on his aloofness as well. Eventually, Brady relied on extensive research to write the lengthy biography, which proves more exhaustive than Leaming's or Higham's.

Brady posits Welles' penchant for exaggeration as just another facet of his character—a way to drum up publicity or a reflection of his overactive imagination. Never seeming to regard it as a problem or hindrance, Brady uses his extensive research, including interviews with former Welles associates, to ferret out the facts. More detailed than Higham's or Leaming's biographies, Brady's work offers an in-depth description of such impressive Welles projects as his multivolumed guide understanding and producing Shakespeare (in association with mentor Roger Hill), his summer of stage productions at Todd School, his play *Bright Lucifer*, and other endeavors often mentioned but rarely examined.

Each of these authors emphasizes a different side to Welles, with Brady's biography keeping the largest distance between subject and writer. General readers searching for Welles the historical figure would do well to read Brady's book. Those film buffs who are curious about Welles the man should read, at the very least, all three major biographies. The deeds of a great man cannot be summed up in a single point of view, which is the lesson of *Citizen Kane*—an almost irresistible conclusion when considering the life and career of Orson Welles.

—Susan M. Doll

WELLINGTON, 1st Duke of [*born* Arthur Wellesley], 1769–1852; English general and statesman.

Aldington, Richard, *Wellington*. London, Heinemann, 1946.

Fortescue, Sir J. W., *Wellington*. London, Williams and Norgate, and New York, Dodd Mead, 1925.

Gleig, G. R., *Life of Arthur Duke of Wellington*. London, Longman, 1865; New York, Dutton, 1909.

Guedalla, Philip, *The Duke*. London, Hodder and Stoughton, and New York, Harper, 1931.

Longford, Elizabeth, *Wellington* (2 vols.). London, Weidenfeld and Nicolson, 1969–72; New York, Harper, 1970–73.

Maxwell, Sir Herbert, *The Life of Wellington*. London, Low Marston, and Boston, Little Brown, 1899.

*

The value of GLEIG's biography derives from the close personal contact Gleig maintained with his subject over a 40-year period. The work is characterized by a great deal of firsthand quotation as well as access to documents denied to or ignored by later biographers. There is also such an abundance of Wellingtonian anecdote that many subsequent writers appear to have used Gleig's work—not always in a very discriminating fashion—as a mine for this type of information.

Close attention is given to the Duke's military campaigns—Gleig had himself served in Wellington's highly efficient Peninsula Army—with the biographer taking a lofty and strategic view of events. Gleig undoubtedly felt himself greatly honoured by the Duke's friendship and obviously entertained no doubts as to the greatness of his subject. Hence the tone of the work is highly respectful: Gleig chooses to mitigate his subject's notoriously prickly character, for example, and to ignore those extra-marital liaisons that attracted scandalous comment at the time.

As a Tory of the Duke's own stamp, Gleig, in his analysis of the Duke's political career, inevitably lacks objectivity, and his work may strike the modern reader as burdensomely detailed. However, few other biographers bring out the straightforwardness and tough integrity of their subject so clearly as Gleig.

The first edition of MAXWELL's lengthy biography appeared nearly 50 years later and as a result gained an advantage over previous biographies "cramped by nearness in time to their subject . . . and the desire to avoid controversial matter." Although in no doubt as to the Duke's foremost position in the pantheon of British heroes, Maxwell is nevertheless prepared to allude to and censure events in his subject's life or aspects of his character that Gleig either leaves unmentioned or glosses over—for example the Duke's notoriously harsh criticism of the performance of his officers after the retreat from Burgos, or his unwarranted petulance at the rate of his promotion during his spell in India.

Maxwell's description of the Duke's military ventures is especially detailed, fleshed out with numerous battle-maps, illustrations, and statistics. The work as a whole is distinguished by a depth of research—evidenced in the extensive sources listed—perhaps unmatched until Elizabeth Longford's equally massive opus 70 years later. Maxwell's style is always clear and concise but lacking in the liveliness and humour that makes Longford's later biography such a pleasure to read.

FORTESCUE was a professional soldier and historian of the British Army, and his biography at all points reflects these two facts. Special emphasis and a good deal of specialized knowledge is brought to bear on the Duke's military life and on the state of the armies Wellington had to command. Fortescue's account of the strategies of the Napoleonic Wars is well written. His style, as one would expect, is efficient, brief and economical. As a professional soldier, Fortescue may be the closest in spirit to his subject of all Wellington's many biographers: he is able and willing to subject the campaigns to professional scrutiny, but his own soldierly dislike of politics and politicking tends to undermine his analysis of the Duke as politician. This is a soldierly assessment of a great soldier, and inevitably the Duke's personal life receives only cursory attention. Above all the reader of Fortescue's work will be left with an accurate impression of the Duke's highly developed sense of public patriotic duty.

Of entirely different stamp is GUEDALLA's biography of 1931. Guedalla brings to his subject and to his book a literary artifice quite foreign to the no-nonsense style of Fortescue, and, one suspects, to that of the Duke himself. Guedalla's style may well strike the contemporary reader as excessively mannered and intrusive—highly wrought, full of literary and classical allusion, the product of a highly educated mind writing for readers equally well versed in European literature and history. Lengthy, dramatic word-pictures preface narrative flows and supply the place of detailed historical context. Altogether Guedalla writes in a most Romantic vein; as a result the biography is weakest when analysing Wellington's military and civil campaigns, strongest when examining the society in which the Duke moved. As a work of art this biography is of considerable interest, but Guedalla loses sight of his subject's cardinal virtue: simplicity.

ALDINGTON's style in contrast is factual and restrained. What primarily recommends his biography is the amount of pertinent historical detail included to place his subject firmly in his era and to make sense of his motivations and subsequent actions both public and private. With a wide-ranging curiosity, Aldington delights in producing numerous interesting, sometimes quirky, asides, but he very rarely fails to see the wood for its trees. His account almost invariably maintains a correct focus on events and thereby a just estimate of their relative importance.

LONGFORD's is the most recent and most readable of the biographies reviewed in this essay. It is as long and as detailed as that of Maxwell but much more accessible to the modern reader. That the author is herself related by marriage to her subject's family is of more than passing interest and significance. First, it provides her with sources, especially relating to Kitty Packenham, the Duke's wife, that had been denied to earlier biographers. Second, it is important in determining her attitude toward her subject, for she is writing not only as a popular professional historian but also as a relative, albeit distant, of her subject. Consequently, her stance toward the Duke, although by no means hagiographic, is undoubtedly very favourable. She tends to explain away or downplay aspects of his character and beliefs that rightfully deserve censure. On the other hand, Longford's work is distinguished by a plenitude of historical detail gleaned from all manner of sources. Unusual and welcome, because all too rarely given, is an account of Kitty Packenham's relationship with her husband. Altogether the Longford biography is first-rate and will for some years continue to be regarded as the definitive work of its kind.

—D. H. O'Leary

WELLS, H(erbert) G(eorge), 1866–1946; English writer.

Dickson, Lovat, *H. G. Wells: His Turbulent Life and Times.* New York, Atheneum, and London, Macmillan, 1969.

Kagarlitski, J., *The Life and Thought of H. G. Wells*, translated by Moura Budberg. London, Sidgwick and Jackson, and New York, Barnes and Noble, 1966.

MacKenzie, Norman and Jeanne MacKenzie, *The Time Traveller: The Life of H. G. Wells.* London, Weidenfeld and Nicolson, 1973; as *H. G. Wells: A Biography*, New York, Simon and Schuster, 1973.

Parrinder, Patrick, *H. G. Wells.* Edinburgh, Oliver and Boyd, 1970; New York, Putnam, 1977.

Ray, Gordon N., *H. G. Wells and Rebecca West.* New Haven, Connecticut, Yale University Press, and London, Macmillan, 1974.

Smith, David C., *H. G. Wells, Desperately Mortal: A Biography.* New Haven, Connecticut, and London, Yale University Press, 1986.

West, Anthony, *H. G. Wells: Aspects of a Life.* London, Hutchinson, and New York, Random House, 1984.

*

Much of the biographical interest in Wells hinges on his relationship with Rebecca West, some biographers criticizing him, some defending him. RAY defends Rebecca West, with whom Wells had an affair from 1913 to 1924. West cooperated with Ray, and the main source of the book consists of a collection of letters written to her by Wells, enlivened with Wells' numerous line illustrations, with the couple represented as Jaguar and Panther. Ray, although biased toward Rebecca West, gives a good account of Wells' energy and drive. With great impetus, he chronicles the sequence of their affair, their parenthood, and their separation. Anthony WEST, the son of that union, defends Wells. He chronicles the love affair and describes Wells as father. He uses Rebecca West's "dossier" about the relationship, as does Ray, but his reading of it is an "allegory," a "private mythology" whose purpose was to control later views of Wells. He considers that Rebecca West was a self-dramatiser who used her son as a weapon against his father. He draws on "oral communication" with Wells' friends, on his own memories, as well as on Wells' papers and letters. Anthony also uses Rebecca West's correspondence with S. K. Radcliffe as an example of her "concoction and dissemination of evidence," claiming that "if her biographers were to portray her to her liking, she would have to provide them with suitable material to work on." Anthony West justifies Wells' sexual and political affiliations and describes in detail his friendships or antagonisms with such writers as Henry James, whose *The Spoils of Poynton* (1897) he parodied in *Boon* (1915); his concern for George Gissing and disturbance at his death is well described. West is in a particular position to describe domestic matters such as households and servants. He too considers Wells to be an "energiser."

SMITH's full and well-documented biography also emphasises Wells' energy, along with his influence. He aims to "provide a life in context—the whole life" and considers Wells' absorption of the doctrine of evolution as taught to him by T. H. Huxley, his feminism, and his demand for world education. The women in Wells' life (both wives, Odette Keun, Dorothy Richardson, Elizabeth von Arnim, Amber Reeves, as well as Rebecca West) are sympathetically treated, as are his male friends (Arnold Bennett, Joseph Conrad, Ford Madox Ford, George Gissing, George Bernard Shaw), as well as controversies with Henry James and Hilaire Belloc. Discussion of Wells' books is well integrated into that of the life. Smith's sources include Wells' own experiments in autobiography, such as *H. G. Wells in Love*; the Wells papers held at the University of Illinois and at the Mugar Memorial Library in Boston; the Fabian Society and T. H. Huxley papers; and B.B.C. archives. Smith inevitably drew as well on the earlier biography of Wells by Vincent Bromley (1951). PARRINDER also relates the work to the life, with more emphasis on the work. KAGARLITSKI too traces "the vital and unbreakable connection between man and writer." In this study, written for the Russian market, Kagarlitski places Wells' work in the 19th- and then the 20th-century context. He debates whether Wells was a writer, a journalist, or a populariser of the scientific outlook on the world.

DICKSON's study is mainly of Wells "in those years when he was turning away from the certain prospect of a successful career as a highly popular novelist to become a prophet and teacher, when in the wilder social world to which his growing fame was introducing him he was throwing off the constraints of his narrow upbringing and seeking satisfaction among a more interesting, better-educated and opulent class for another dominant instinct in his nature, sex." The MacKENZIE biography examines Wells as a student at the Normal School of Science in South Kensington under the influence of T. H. Huxley, his interest in the Fabian Society and the Labour Party, his involvement in and disillusion with the League of Nations, his disparagement of Marx, and his Science of Life. They stress the conflicts and uncertainties in Wells' personality and writing, using his autobiography, his mother's diary, and Geoffrey West's gleanings from Wells.

—Barbara Hayley

WESLEY, John, 1703–1791; English theologian and evangelist, founder of Methodism.

Ayling, Stanley, *John Wesley*. London, Collins, and Nashville, Tennessee, Abingdon, 1979.

Piette, Maximin, *John Wesley in the Evolution of Protestantism*, translated by J. B. Howard. London and New York, Sheed and Ward, 1937 (originally published as *La Réaction Wesléyenne dans l'évolution protestante*, Brussels, La Lecture au Foyer, 1925).

Rack, Henry D., *Reasonable Enthusiast: John Wesley and the Rise of Methodism*. London, Epworth Press, and Philadelphia, Trinity Press, 1989.

Southey, Robert, *Life of John Wesley*. Abridged version, with notes, New York, Stokes, and London, Hutchinson, 1903.

*

RACK's work, the most recent of these four biographies, must be regarded as the definitive. Running to more than 650 pages of close print (including bibliography, notes, and index), this latest life, though shorter than the multi-volume works of Luke Tyerman and J. S. Simon, is nevertheless equally magisterial in scope, if markedly less reverential in tone. Tyerman's three-volume work (*The Life and Times of Rev. John Wesley*, London, 1870–71) is notable for its wealth of documentation, which Simon, despite his five volumes, cannot match. But Simon's first volume (*John Wesley and the Religious Societies*, London, Epworth Press, 1921) is a particularly valuable study. The remaining volumes—all published by the Epworth Press—are: *John Wesley and the Methodist Societies* (1923), *John Wesley and the Advance of Methodism* (1925), *John Wesley, the Master Builder* (1927) and *John Wesley, the Last Phase* (1934).

It would be going too far to say that Rack is determined on reassessment at all costs, but he is at pains to call into play the latest scholarship on the period in order to re-define the context in which the Wesleys worked. Thus, in a "Prelude" of some 40 pages, Rack is notably kinder to 18th-century Anglicanism than most 19th- and early 20th-century historians have been. The Georgian Age was, he insists, a religious age, though "the old Reformation doctrine of justification by grace through faith had been eroded into a variable balance between grace and works."

The tension between grace and works is the central theme of Wesleyan theology. In examining the origins of Methodism in the Holy Club at Oxford, Rack describes the Wesley circle as more of a "shifting network" than a tightly-knit "club," and he stresses the gradual evolution of the group toward a code of ascetic practices. He reminds us how slowly John Wesley conquered his susceptibility to the charms of the Kirkham sisters, and how reluctantly Charles turned his back on the world of London actresses. "What!" Charles wrote to John, "would you have me be a saint at once?" Even by the time John Gambold became a member (probably in early 1732), Rack concludes that the club was "a group for social action rather than one cultivating its own devotional life," and he quotes Wesley's remark in October 1731 that "our hope is sincerity, not perfection, not to do well but to do our best."

Rack ends his first section with Wesley's Aldersgate Street "conversion," which (unlike most Methodist historians) he is inclined to play down. The two remaining sections are each preceded by an "interlude" devoted to the wider social context of Hanoverian England. The middle section of 150 pages is concerned with the rise of Methodism between 1738 and 1760. The emphasis is on theological issues—the author is Professor of Ecclesiastical History at Manchester—but matters of more human interest are treated under headings such as "Charles Wesley: sweet singer and uneasy colleague" and "John Wesley and Women." The final section of almost 300 pages contains less narrative and more analysis, and is even more concerned with theology—though there are a few pages on philanthropy and politics.

Rack's portrait of Wesley seems to dwell uncomfortably on the warts, and his final chapter ("Reckonings") does not altogether remove the negative impression he conveys of Wesley's character. He cites Wesley's obsessively fastidious neatness and tidiness that "extended from his person to his personality"; he reminds us that the Journal is "coloured by propaganda purposes"; he points to Wesley's strong sense of supernatural intervention but concedes that he saw providence "rather in events than voices"; he thinks Wesley's relationship with individuals was that of a tutor towards his pupil rather than a partnership; and he quotes approvingly Green's view of him as "granite in aspic." He also quotes—with one eye on the title of his biography—Alexander Knox's assessment that Wesley "would have been an enthusiast if he could," but that "there was a firmness in his intellectual texture which would not bend to illusions." This ambivalence is echoed in Rack's final judgment that Wesley brought together two halves of Georgian England—rationality, sense of order, and elegance on the one hand, and on the other the "sighs, and cries and convulsions" of the uneducated people who heard his preaching. It is hardly an heroic epitaph.

PIETTE, writing in the 1930s, sets Wesley's life in an even broader context: the evolution of Protestantism in England and on the continent between Luther and the Latitudinarian Anglicanism of Wesley's day. The first 94 pages embrace Luther, Zwingli, Calvin and the Anabaptists; the next hundred are concerned with Protestantism in Georgian England. Not until page 195 do we get to Wesley! Even then, we begin with a résumé of the principal biographies. Piette quotes Tyerman's assertion that Wesley is "best known by what he did; not by what philosophers may suspect he thought"—though Piette evidently thinks Tyerman's weight of detail overpowering.

Piette's own scholarly apparatus may deter the reader: there are 86 pages of notes compared with Rack's 82, though irritatingly no index. Even so, this is a humane and attractive treatment of Wesley. As a Roman Catholic, Piette can take a detached view of his subject, and his study is not without touches of gentle irony. He gives due weight to the influence of Wesley's mother, quoting freely from their letters—Elsie Harrison's *Son to Susanna: The Private Life of John Wesley* was published in the same year as the translation of Piette's biography—and he emphasizes the importance of Whitefield in the story of early Methodism. Piette, as befits a doctor of theology, disentangles the doctrinal differences between Whitefield and Wesley, and quotes Wesley's wise refusal to be over-explicit: "Although no man on earth can explain the particular manner wherein the Spirit of God works on the soul, yet whoever has these fruits cannot but know and feel that God has wrought them in his heart."

Piette is perhaps a little too inclined to take Wesley's own accounts of himself at face value, but his book can still be recommended after more than 50 years for its blend of sympathy and astringency. His suggested epitaph on Wesley is: "Organizer and Head of a Church in spite of Himself."

The two remaining lives are more popular in style. AYLING writes engagingly and centres on personalities rather than principles: the family home at Epworth, the friends at Oxford, Miss

Sophy Hopkey in Georgia, the influence of the Moravian Peter Bohler, the staff and boys at Kingswood School, the missed opportunity of marrying Grace Murray, the misfortune of marrying Molly Vazeille, quarrels between the brothers and with Whitefield. The emphasis on human interest is reinforced by the dozen or so excellent portraits, together with a photograph of one of Wesley's electrical machines.

Ayling does not neglect theological issues but presents them in personal terms—not inappropriately, since in Wesley's case the theology is highly individualistic. Ayling's account is descriptive rather than analytical, his approach that of a portraitist rather than a theologian (as we should expect of the biographer of George III and the elder Pitt). He nevertheless resists the temptation to over-emphasize the wars, or "load the debit account," as he puts it. He sees Wesley as "the single most influential Protestant leader of the English-speaking world since the Reformation," and thinks Wesley's single-minded determination to save souls has "defied alike the rebuffs of detractors and the passage of years."

SOUTHEY, who also had a best-selling life of Nelson to his credit, wrote in 1820 and was thus much closer to Wesley in date. His study accordingly lacks perspective and unfairly accuses Wesley of a passion for power. Piette dismissed Southey as worthless because of his inaccuracies. But Southey's remains arguably the most readable of all the lives of Wesley, and we can hardly quarrel with the author's oblique censure of his hero's capacity for self-deception: "Men are sometimes easily convinced of what they find it convenient or agreeable to believe." And Southey shows the particular perception of the near-contemporary in recording: "When Wesley began his years of itinerancy, there were no turnpikes in England, and no stage-coach which went farther than York." Wesley's sheer physical achievement remains prodigious.

—Stuart Andrews

———

WHARTON, Edith, 1862–1937; American writer.

Lawson, Richard, *Edith Wharton*. New York, Ungar, 1977.

Lewis, R. W. B., *Edith Wharton: A Biography*. New York, Harper, and London, Constable, 1975.

Lubbock, Percy, *Portrait of Edith Wharton*. New York, Appleton-Century, and London, Cape, 1947.

McDowell, Margaret B., *Edith Wharton*. Boston, Twayne, 1976.

Wolff, Cynthia Griffin, *A Feast of Words: The Triumph of Edith Wharton*. Oxford and New York, Oxford University Press, 1976.

*

Biographies of Edith Wharton, clustered in the mid-1970s, have brought renewed critical attention to a major American novelist. LEWIS' prize-winning volume was the first and most substantial. Lewis had used the immense collection of Wharton materials—manuscripts, correspondence, and memorabilia—at the Beinecke Library, Yale, as well as the biographer's usual sources of news files, personal contacts, and the author's writing. His book, nearly 600 pages long, impressed the reading world with its comprehensiveness, its new material, and its generally sympathetic tone. Lewis' descriptions of Wharton's life as an adolescent, her homes and travels, her life in the context of its place and time are impressive and moving.

For all the energy of his narrative, however, Lewis had some difficulty applying what he saw as the key events in Wharton's life to any new reading of her fiction, and when he moved into discussion of her work, his comments were strangely separate from the biographical narrative. It was as if Lewis had already written the "literary" discussion part of the biography before he had thoroughly assimilated Wharton's life experiences; and no matter how much he learned about those experiences, no matter how much he tried to sympathize with her often frustrating, and frustrated, life, he could not read her fiction with as much pertinent biographical understanding as might be expected.

The storehouse of new information that Lewis' biography provides is supplemented by a more sharply focused approach in WOLFF's 1977 treatment. *A Feast of Words* brings Wharton into consideration as feminist writer, which she is by virtue of her narrative strategies of disguise and irony as well as by gender. It also emphasizes the relevance of Wharton's life to her successive fictions, employing a clearly psychoanalytic method throughout. The differences in the biographers' readings of Wharton's fiction are apparent. Lewis, for example, insists that Wharton's *The Age of Innocence* is a nostalgic and mildly satiric account of the New York society the author knew as an adolescent, a championing of the stability of marriage. Wolff just as persuasively counters that that novel is a mature assessment of the value society might have, but that the novel is strongly informed with the horror of sexual power Wharton drew so convincingly in the fragment "Beatrice Palmato" (found by Wolff but given to Lewis for publication in his earlier biography).

Similarly, Wolff views *The Custom of the Country* as "a daring tour de force," most interesting for its narrative audacity; and Undine Spragg, its protagonist, as "both villain and victim." In Lewis' view, however, that novel is Wharton's "most powerful" (which in itself is not a derogation) but in his reading the characters are somewhat simplified: Undine is only "ruthlessly grasping." Rather than deal with basic problems about the novel—what Wharton's attitude toward Undine was, and what effects her characterization had on the reader's view of the novel—Lewis created a schema that identified Wharton with "each of the four main characters"—Undine, Raymond de Chelles, Ralph Marvell, and Elmer Moffatt. In Lewis' paradigm, Marvell rather than Undine embodies Edith Wharton's feminine side; Moffatt her masculine. The strictures of the biographer's drive to order are clear when the text itself is considered. The "best" biography of Wharton at this time would be a composite of these two studies.

Two shorter studies, not intended to be primarily biographical, are provided by McDowell and Lawson. McDOWELL considers nearly all of Wharton's long and short fiction, claiming for her the status of major novelist. She accurately summarizes Wharton's life, and connects her writing to her life events. McDowell's study makes good use of the Lewis biography, and goes on to read the fiction from a current, and sympathetic, perspective. LAWSON's study, in contrast, rehearses the Wharton-as-novelist-of-manners approach, choosing to discuss only a few

of her works. When Lawson does treat Wharton biographically, he goes against the most recent information and voices what appear to be summary judgments ("Despite Wharton's professions of happiness in *A Backward Glance*, she was an unhappy human being. One even feels she was unhappy as a woman"). Lawson's clipped pronouncements, bereft of much context, make his somewhat idiosyncratic judgments even less palatable.

One of the first "portraits" of Edith Wharton was the 1947 study by LUBBOCK, a man who had once been her good friend. As his book shows, however, Lubbock felt comparatively little sympathy with Wharton as writer. His opening image shows her "descending" on Henry James, invading, disturbing his serene writing life. Lubbock says explicitly, "how little she understood the life of the literary hermit. . . . "

Lubbock's denigrating portrait of Wharton as a serious and important novelist depends in part on testimony from other friends, most of them unliterary. He includes Charles Du Bos, Lady Aberconway, Elizabeth Norton, Daniel Updike, Judge Robert Grant, and others, with comments from Gaillard Lapsley woven throughout. He also insists on his own drawing of not only Wharton but Walter Berry, Anne Bahlmann, and Teddy Wharton. While he catches some elements of Wharton's personality (that she was an "intrepid teacher," for example), he does not mention others—the central role writing played in her existence (Updike notices that she writes every morning but once down for the day, never mentions her own work). Wharton's own admirable restraint becomes for Lubbock a way of allowing the woman as writer to disappear almost completely from his portrait. Wharton here is instead a warm, highly efficient hostess, aggressively finding interesting people to invite to her small parties. And instead of being the divorced woman who felt exiled from her America, Wharton's later life in France, England, and Italy appears to be the product of her preference for European living.

Any reader of Wharton's work might have wondered at the tenor, and content, of Lubbock's portrait. Unfortunately, academics took seriously what was in effect Lubbock's dismissal of Wharton as writer. It was all the more suitable, then, that the Lewis and Wolff biographies brought Wharton—and the immense quantity of her work—back into the literary mainstream.

—Linda Wagner-Martin

WHISTLER, James (Abbot) McNeill, 1834–1903; American painter.

Fleming, Gordon, *The Young Whistler 1834–66.* London, Allen and Unwin, 1978.

Gregory, Horace, *The World of James McNeill Whistler.* New York, T. Nelson, 1959; London, Hutchinson, 1961.

Laver, James, *Whistler.* New York, Cosmopolitan, 1930; revised edition, London, Faber, 1951.

McMullen, Roy, *Victorian Outsider: A Biography of J. A. M. Whistler.* New York, Dutton, 1973; London, Macmillan, 1974.

Pearson, Hesketh, *The Man Whistler.* London, Methuen, and New York, Harper, 1952.

Pennell, Elizabeth R. and Joseph Pennell, *The Life of James Mc-Neill Whistler*. Philadelphia, Lippincott, and London, Heinemann, 1908; 5th revised edition, 1911.

Pennell, Elizabeth R. and Joseph Pennell, *Whistler Journal*. Philadelphia, Lippincott, 1921.

Prideaux, Tom, *The World of Whistler 1834–1903*. New York, Time-Life, 1970.

Spalding, Frances, *Whistler*. Oxford, Phaidon, 1979.

Sutton, Denys, *Nocturne: The Art of James McNeill Whistler*. London, Country Life, 1963; Philadelphia, Lippincott, 1964.

Sutton, Denys, *James McNeill Whistler: Paintings, Etchings, Pastels, and Watercolors*. London, Phaidon, 1966.

Walker, John, *James McNeill Whistler*. New York, Abrams, 1987.

Weintraub, Stanley, *Whistler: A Biography*. New York, Weybright and Talley, and London, Collins, 1974.

*

James Whistler is not an easy subject for biographers. He preferred a good story to "facts," such as claiming in court that he was born in St. Petersburg when records show that he was born in Lowell, Massachusetts. Much of Whistler biography is a matter of sifting through stories, legends, and Whistler witticisms to determine what might have really happened. Careful biographers do not take Whistler's or his friends' or his enemies' or even their own versions as certainties; they also discuss how they can support their versions of the events.

Every biographer of Whistler agrees that one starts with the PENNELLs. In his old age, Whistler accepted the Philadelphian admirers, Joseph and Elizabeth Robins Pennell, as his official biographers. However, as they admit, he felt no great compunction to provide them with truthful accounts of his life, and, after his death, Whistler's sister-in-law denied them access to many of his papers. Their biography is anecdotal, with long quotations from interviews and letters of Whistler's friends, and is notably more complete on Whistler's later life, when the authors knew him. It is laudatory as one might expect, and they certainly ignore what they do not want to reveal, such as Whistler's various mistresses; despite their importance, both Joanna Heffernan and Maud Franklin are dismissed summarily in a paragraph. The first through fourth editions have more early drawings and include sketches for most of the more famous portraits; the fifth edition is a condensation of the two-volume set of the earlier editions. However, little text was cut and some supporting detail was added. More supplementary material appears in the Pennells' *Whistler Journal* (1921), which consists of their diary entries about meetings with Whistler, filled out with additional reminiscences and, again, interviews with and letters from other friends of Whistler. The *Journal* more than the *Life* shows their prejudice toward Beatrix Godwin, whom Whistler married. It is also arranged in the order of their recording of events, not as they happened. If Whistler recalled what he did in 1862 in a conversation in 1898, it is recorded in 1898, which makes the index indispensable for anyone not willing to read cover to cover. Their books and collection of Whistlerania donated to the Library of Congress designate them as the foremost authorities on Whistler, despite their partialities.

Of more recent biographers, the two that stand out are McMullen and Weintraub. McMULLEN indulges in some minor psychological probing and simplistic Freudian interpretation. He is more comfortable discussing the influences of Whistler's mother and his youth in Russia; the adult Whistler, irascible and witty, seems to elude him. McMullen uses few quotes and writes impressionistically and, at times, rather carelessly. WEINTRAUB consciously cites his sources much more carefully, although he summarizes his references in endnotes, chapter by chapter rather than directly footnoting. Victorian England is a time and place Weintraub knows well from the various biographies he has written, and he refers to prominent people Whistler knew with ease. He does not try to speculate much about Whistler's personality or his art, but paints an overall view of the life and times that is pleasurable reading. As Douglas Cooper claims in *The New York Review of Books* (8 August 1974), the book is a "racy, readable and authentic account of the life and a more realistic and acceptable interpretation of the character of James McNeill Whistler than can be found in any other book."

Since the publication of McMullen's and Weintraub's biographies, most earlier biographies have been outdated. LAVER harps on the "femininity" of Whistler's character, presenting him as a sort of hothouse flower out of place in Victorian England. He offers more on Whistler's art, especially on the influence of French etchers. GREGORY unduly emphasizes Russian influence on Whistler. He cites no sources, nor even gives a bibliography. The book seems like a novel written for adolescents and is inaccurate many times, although Gregory's versions are always presented without any questioning. FLEMING is much more skeptical, trying to determine where legend has obscured truth, and carefully reports his sources. However, inaccuracies have crept in, and Fleming's book ends with Whistler's trip to Valparaiso in 1866. PEARSON's book is adequate but like all but perhaps Fleming's, it has been superseded by Weintraub's careful research and readable style.

For an illustrated introduction to the art rather than a detailed discussion of the life, look at WALKER, PRIDEAUX, or SPALDING. Walker's and Prideaux's biographies are brief, undocumented and surprisingly slim on art criticism, but they provide large, colorful reproductions of Whistler's works. Prideaux also includes examples of Pre-Raphaelite paintings and examples of official Victorian taste for comparison. Spalding provides more text that focuses on artistic technique and influence so that she repeats few anecdotes and witticisms, omitting even the most famous. Also, the color in Spalding's reproductions seems a bit off. SUTTON's books unfortunately use primarily black-and-white reproductions. Both discuss Whistler's painting techniques, aesthetic theory, and artistic influences in interesting detail. The 1966 book includes the full texts of the "Ten O'Clock" and other of Whistler's writings.

For those who wish highly-colored description, there are several memoirs by associates of Whistler, such as Mortimore Menpes' *Whistler As I Knew Him* (London and New York, 1904), Thomas R. Way's *Memories of James McNeill Whistler: The Artist* (London and New York, 1912) and Theodore Duret's *Histoire de J. M. McN. Whistler: Et de son Oeuvre* (Paris, 1904; as *Whistler*, translated by Frank Rutter, Philadelphia and London, 1917). All these works added to the prejudices and confusion over Whistler's life, but also give firsthand (if unreliable) and technical information otherwise lost.

For additional help with finding one's way through Whistler material, a good source is Robert H. Getscher and Paul G.

Marks, *James McNeill Whistler and John Singer Sargent: Two Annotated Bibliographies* (New York, 1986.)

—Nan Hackett

WHITE, Stanford, 1853–1906; American architect.

Baker, Paul R., *Stanny: The Gilded Life of Stanford White.* New York, The Free Press, and London, Collier Macmillan, 1989.

Baldwin, Charles C., *Stanford White.* New York, Dodd Mead, 1931.

Langford, Gerald, *The Murder of Stanford White.* Indianapolis, Bobbs-Merrill, 1962; London, Gollancz, 1963.

White, Stanford, *Sketches and Designs by Stanford White, with an Outline of His Career by His Son, Lawrence G. White.* New York, Architectural Book Publishing, 1920.

Wodehouse, Lawrence, *White of McKim, Mead, and White.* New York and London, Garland, 1988.

*

White's unfortunate death at the hands of Harry K. Thaw, an eccentric millionaire, and the publicity that ensued, sullied his reputation and set him up as an immoral symbol of "The Gilded Age," overshadowing his solid contribution to the architecture and culture of America. It is only recently that books and articles have begun to re-evaluate his life and works and his true contributions to the period.

The first book to defend White and his professional career was by his son, Laurence G. WHITE, who at the time of writing was a member of his father's firm. While not an official biography, it contains an outline of White's career and an attempt to address the criticism that he sold out his talents to wealthy New Yorkers. Laurence offers interesting insight into his father, who was a strong influence in his early life. The main value of his book is its analysis of drawings, designs, architecture, and homes designed by White. Laurence also had the advantage of having access to the files of the firm of McKim, Mead and White, files which were later discarded or dispersed to various depositories.

Many of the firm's papers were gone by the time BALDWIN's book was issued. Baldwin takes a sympathetic, approach to White and explores his relationship with the American sculptor Augustus Saint Gaudens and other professional associates. Baldwin's strong point is his description of White's multiple talents; he includes photographs, drawings, and testimonials by associates and clients.

Because White was so closely identified with the firm of McKim, Meade and White, and was a close friend of Saint Gaudens, and because of their individual and corporate contributions to architecture and art, biographies and criticism of their works also contain much about White that should be consulted to get a fuller picture of him.

Nearly a dozen books, as well as several movies, have also appeared that retell the story of White's murder and the subsequent trials of the murderer. While most are sensational, the best

of these is LANGFORD's study. Its main concern, however, is with the excitement of the trials and the gullibility of the public at the time.

Recently, two books have appeared that offer a well-rounded portrait of White, his personality, and his work. WODEHOUSE attempts to evaluate White's work systematically. While Baldwin's evaluation of White's work is from the viewpoint of a classisist, Wodehouse is freer in his outlook and has benefited from the current re-evaluation and renewed interest in the Beaux Arts style after years of its being overshadowed by the Bauhaus and International styles.

BAKER's biography of White is the most recent, best balanced, and most complete to date. It is based on White's personal papers, which only became available in the 1970s, plus the remnants of the McKim, Mead and White papers in the Avery Library and the New York Historical Society. Baker also relies on data collected by the late Aileen Saarienen for her proposed biography. This book goes a long way to describe White's many activities and to explain his code of values and his unique life. Baker provides an excellent description of White's father, Richard Grant White, who was an unusual literary character in New York, and speculates on the effect of his lifestyle on the lifestyle of his son. Baker also discusses White's personal and professional friendships and the influence of frequent European trips on his collecting habits and design ideas.

Because White was a leading figure in the lifestyle of the "Gilded Age" and in death became a symbol of that complicated period, anyone serious in exploring his life should consult some of the numerous books about the period. Since architecture criticism is subjective, the White, Baldwin, and Wodehouse volumes should be read in an historical context. If one seeks a readable overall view of this unusual man and his period, Baker's treatment is best.

—Robert James Havlik

WHITMAN, Walt, 1819–1892; American poet.

Allen, Gay Wilson, *The Solitary Singer: A Critical Biography of Walt Whitman.* New York, Grove, 1959.

Allen, Gay Wilson, *The New Walt Whitman Handbook.* New York, New York University Press, 1975.

Binns, Henry Bryan, *A Life of Walt Whitman.* New York, Dutton, and London, Methuen, 1905.

Black, Stephen A., *Whitman's Journeys into Chaos: A Psychoanalytic Study of the Poetic Process.* Princeton, New Jersey, Princeton University Press, 1975.

Bucke, Richard Maurice, *Walt Whitman.* London, Trübner, and Philadelphia, D. McKay, 1883.

Burroughs, John, *Notes on Walt Whitman as Poet and Person.* New York, American News Co., 1867.

Carpenter, Edward, *Days with Walt Whitman: With Some Notes on His Life and Works.* New York, Macmillan, and London, G. Allen, 1906.

Cavitch, David, *My Soul and I: The Inner Life of Walt Whitman.* Boston, Beacon Press, 1985.

Holloway, Emory, *Whitman: An Interpretation in Narrative.*
New York and London, Knopf, 1926.

Kaplan, Justin, *Walt Whitman: A Life.* New York, Simon and
Schuster, 1980.

Killingsworth, M. Jimmie, *Whitman's Poetry of the Body: Sexuality, Politics, and the Text.* Chapel Hill, University of North
Carolina Press, 1989.

Miller, Edwin Haviland, *Walt Whitman's Poetry: A Psychological Journey.* Boston, Houghton Mifflin, 1968.

O'Connor, William Douglas, *The Good Gray Poet, a Vindication.* New York, Bunce and Huntington, 1866.

Perry, Bliss, *Walt Whitman, His Life and Work.* Boston,
Houghton Mifflin, and London, Constable, 1906.

Rubin, Joseph Jay, *The Historic Whitman.* University Park,
Pennsylvania State University Press, 1973.

Schyberg, Frederik, *Walt Whitman,* translated by Evie Allison
Allen. New York, Columbia University Press, 1951 (originally published by Gyldendal, Copenhagen, 1933).

Symonds, John Addington, *Walt Whitman, A Study.* London,
Routledge, and New York, Dutton, 1893.

Traubel, Horace, *With Walt Whitman in Camden* (6 vols.). Vol.
1, Boston, Small Maynard, 1906; vol. 2, New York, Appleton, 1908; vol. 3, New York, M. Kennerly, 1912; vol. 4, Philadelphia, University of Pennsylvania Press, 1953; vol. 5,
Carbondale, Southern Illinois University Press, 1959; vol. 6,
Carbondale, Southern Illinois University Press, 1982.

Zweig, Paul, *Walt Whitman: The Making of the Poet.* New
York, Basic Books, 1984; London, Viking, 1985.

*

The great number of Whitman biographies (less than a third of
those handy in a large university library are listed here) reflects
the difficulty of knowing the poet. Two great problems challenge
biographers of this century: how to account for Whitman's magnetic effect on many who knew him or read his poems; and how
one who seems so ordinary might suddenly, at age 35, have become, for five years, a great poet.

Neither puzzle was apparent to the biographers who knew
Whitman. To Bucke the poet seemed "an average man magnified to the dimensions of a god." One didn't ask how a god
created his works, or if they were good. O'CONNOR thought
Whitman a new incarnation of Christ, and *Leaves of Grass* a
new bible. Incisively denouncing an injustice to his friend
(Whitman was fired from a government job when it was learned
he was author of an immoral book), O'Connor earned a contemporary reputation as effective defender of an unworthy cause.
Later generations called Whitman worthy, and O'Connor a mystic and radical looking for a cause.

So in different ways seemed the other disciples. BUR-
ROUGHS, whose writing shows him far from credulous, nevertheless felt the power of Whitman's magnetism, first through the
poetry and later by knowing the man. He found Whitman god-
like in his affinity with elements and creatures. BUCKE, who
had read *Leaves of Grass* when he was going through vivid mystical experiences, hailed Whitman as a new Messiah when he
called on him, and wrote a biography that originally meant to
put the poet at the forefront of a new religion he called "Cosmic
Consciousness;" Lozynsky (*Richard Maurice Buck, Medical
Mystic,* Detroit, Wayne State University Press, 1977) shows that

Whitman, often a blatant self-publicist, excised most such extravagances. TRAUBEL made a verbatim account of daily conversations with Whitman during the last four years of Whitman's
life. Though exhausting to read, they give an unmatched account
of Whitman's relation with a disciple.

Mostly the disciples saw in Whitman what each most needed.
However, CARPENTER tried to get beneath the surface of the
looking-glass. Carpenter sensed something he called "tragic"
hidden in Whitman's affectional and sexual life that left the poet
unfulfilled. Whitman revealed himself more than usual to Carpenter in a remark quoted by almost all later biographers:
"There is something in my nature *furtive* like an old hen! . . . I
think there are truths which it is necessary to envelop or wrap
up." Carpenter's most important contribution is a subtle one, his
appreciation for the tricky, constantly shifting interaction of conscious and unconscious thought and feeling in the poems.

Appreciation for the complexity of Whitman's mind may have
been Carpenter's most important perception, but his most famous contribution was to print a letter Whitman wrote in 1890
to SYMONDS. There had been since the 1860s a considerable
following among British literati, including W. M. Rossetti,
Swinburne, Moncure Conway, Anne Gilchrist, and Symonds,
who corresponded with Whitman for more than 20 years. Symonds believed he had found in the "Calamus" poems a public
celebration of the love unnamed; his letters repeatedly asked
Whitman if such was intended. Though Whitman ignored the demands, he was irritated by them, as he revealed to Traubel; he
finally replied deviously by claiming he had fathered six children. By printing Whitman's letter to Symonds, Carpenter
spawned a whole sub-division of biographers who would search
for a sign of the children and their mother or mothers. In writing
his own book, Symonds withheld his speculation; he chiefly
pursued Whitman's mysticism, which seemed to match his own.

ALLEN in his 1975 *Handbook,* considers BINNS and PERRY
the first "critical" or academic biographers, especially praising
Binns' accurate and thorough research. Biographers as different
as Allen and Zweig regard Perry as still one of the most important interpreters of the relation between Whitman's poetry
and his life. HOLLOWAY, two decades later, published the results of laborious examination of documentary material on
which later biographers would base their interpretations. Fascinated by Whitman's sexuality, he catalogued the varieties of it
he found in the poems.

The emerging influence of psychoanalysis affected Whitman
biography very strongly. The pioneering Freudian study of Whitman, Jean Catel, *La Naissance du "poete"* (Paris, Rieder,
1929), still has not been translated into English (but is summarized in Allen's *Handbook*). Catel upset many by claiming that
Whitman's sexuality was primarily auto-erotic, a point pursued
by Black and Zweig. Another Freudian, SCHYBERG, soon followed, more palatable than Catel; Schyberg read the poems in a
context of European pantheism in which the "joy, confidence,
and optimism" of the first *Leaves of Grass* "need not, therefore,
have been the product of distinctly abnormal psychology." Schyberg found Whitman's crisis recorded in the third (1860) *Leaves
of Grass,* and assumed that Whitman had a bout of dissolute
saloon life which accounted for the pain and confusion apparent
in many of the best new poems. Other biographers have hypothesized an unhappy love affair, heterosexual or homosexual,

occurring in 1857–58, a relatively blank period in the Whitman annals.

For discussions of the many biographies written between Holloway's and Allen's (including those by Arvin, Asselineau, Bazalgette, Bertz, Canby, George Rice Carpenter, Chase, De Selincourt, D. H. Lawrence, Edgar Lee Masters, Molinoff, and Shephard), the reader should refer to the summaries in Allen's *Handbook*.

ALLEN's own biography, *The Solitary Singer*, is an outstanding example of mid-century academic biography: careful, thorough, judiciously detailed, open in its use of evidence and in the processes by which it reaches conclusions—skeptical but balanced. Allen declines to use the advantages of modern psychological knowledge which might have led him more deeply into the poetry or the life. After admiring all its virtues, the reader of *The Solitary Singer* may still wonder how so ordinary a man could have written those poems, or how he could have affected his friends and readers as he did.

Allen's biography has been called "definitive," and will always be a reliable source of information, but other biographies continue to appear. RUBIN gives a semi-novelized account of Whitman's early career as a journalist. KAPLAN's narrative, more lyrical than Allen's, artfully uses psychoanalytic studies by Miller and Black, and gives a better idea of what it might have been like to know Whitman. Kaplan only hints at the poetry's origins or meanings, however.

Increasing psychoanalytic sophistication among academics and biographers has brought about attempts to construe the poems from the life and vice versa. MILLER combines the knowledge of Whitman's life, gained by editing the six volumes of *Correspondence*, with psychological adeptness and a good ear. With art and subtlety he reads *Leaves of Grass* as an indirect account of Whitman's life and his homosexual sensibility. BLACK sees the poems themselves, and the writing of them, as the principle facts of Whitman's life and construes from them a biography of Whitman's imagination. He claims that writing the poems brought to consciousness incestuous longings and fantasies of death Whitman could not tolerate knowing, and made Whitman loath to attempt further ventures after 1859. (The view is opposite to that of Catel, Schyberg and others, who considered writing the poetry "therapeutic.")

CAVITCH builds on Miller and Black to address the two great puzzles of Whitman's personal magnetism, and the origin of the poems. Cavitch answers both riddles with a single ingenious and intriguing thesis: Whitman "is the only great poet who is surprised to discover that someone as ordinary as himself can represent everybody else." Cavitch convincingly establishes his thesis, that "Whitman gained his full power to write when he learned how to recreate his family relationships in the voice and structure of his poems, and then in being a poet he struggled against his poetry just as he spent his entire life in loving conflict with his family." The conflict manifests itself most conspicuously in the obscurity of the great poems, which were unintelligible to most of the readers Whitman meant to speak for.

Since the late 1970s, Whitman has been put at the forefront of the political sexual movement arguing for a new sense of sexual plurality. The strongest case so far has been made by KILLINGSWORTH: "As reactions to the "dead" literal language of friendship and love, Whitman's 'swerves in locution'—especially his celebration of homosexual themes—appear to

have been designed to create new linguistic paths to political consciousness." Whitman might have objected to this characterization as he objected to Symonds' nagging questions; but the point does not require Whitman's consent.

ZWEIG, in the biography for our time, possibly the best book yet about Whitman, firmly addresses the questions of Whitman's magnetism and the origin of the poems. Without presenting a particular theory or thesis, Zweig places Whitman in a richly detailed literary context. Seen among precisely chosen examples from the notebook experiments of Whitman's more orthodox contemporaries—experiments with language and poetic form, experiments that blended journalism with poetic and prose rhythms—it becomes by degrees ever less astonishing that the uneducated, ordinary Whitman might have written *Leaves of Grass*. Zweig shows us how much more bookish was the untutored bard than we have realized, and how much he learned from his reading. Although there is no explaining how, for a brief incandescence, a Rimbaud can suddenly become a poet, Zweig explains more plausibly than any previous biographer that Whitman might have been such a prodigy, albeit superannuated at 36. In his five creative years Whitman became "the ancestor . . . of all who have made of their writing an attack on the act of writing and on culture itself."

—Stephen A. Black

WHITTIER, John Greenleaf, 1807–1892; American poet.

Bennett, Whitman, *Whittier: Bard of Freedom*. Chapel Hill, University of North Carolina Press, 1941.

Burton, Richard, *John Greenleaf Whittier*. Boston, Small Maynard, 1901.

Byron, May, *A Day With Whittier*. London and New York, Hodder and Stoughton, 1911.

Carpenter, George Rice, *John Greenleaf Whittier*. Boston, Houghton Mifflin, 1903.

Claflin, Mary B., *Personal Recollections of John Greenleaf Whittier*. New York, T. Y. Crowell, 1893.

Cody, Sherwin, *Four American Poets: William Cullen Bryant, Henry Wadsworth Longfellow, John Greenleaf Whittier, Oliver Wendell Holmes*. New York, American Book Company, 1899.

Cooke, Frances E., *The Story of John Greenleaf Whittier*. London, The Sunday School Association, 1900.

Fields, Annie, *Whittier: Notes of His Life and Friendships*. New York, Harper, 1893.

Flower, Benjamin Orange, *Whittier, Prophet, Seer, and Man*. Boston, Arena, 1896.

Heath, Virginia, *The Story of Whittier*. Portland, Maine, L. H. Nelson, 1905.

Higginson, Thomas Wentworth, *John Greenleaf Whittier*. New York, Macmillan, 1902.

Hudson, William Henry, *Whittier and his Poetry*. London, Harrap, 1917.

Kennedy, William Sloane, *John Greenleaf Whittier: His Life, Genius, and Writings*. Boston, S. E. Cassino, 1882.

Leary, Lewis, *John Greenleaf Whittier*. New York, Twayne, 1961.

Lewis, Georgina King, *John Greenleaf Whittier: His Life and Works*. London, Headley Brothers, 1913.

Linton, William James, *Life of John Greenleaf Whittier*. London, W. Scott, 1893.

Mordell, Albert, *Quaker Militant: John Greenleaf Whittier*. Boston, Houghton Mifflin, 1933.

Perry, Bliss, *John Greenleaf Whittier: A Sketch of His Life*. Boston, Houghton Mifflin, 1907.

Pickard, John B., *John Greenleaf Whittier: An Introduction and Interpretation*. New York, Barnes and Noble, 1961.

Pickard, Samuel T., *Life and Letters of John Greenleaf Whittier* (2 vols.). Boston, Houghton Mifflin, 1894.

Pollard, John A., *John Greenleaf Whittier, Friend of Man*. Boston, Houghton Mifflin, 1949.

Rowntree, Arthur, *Whittier: Crusader and Prophet*. London, Headley Brothers, 1946.

Smith, Emily Binney, *Whittier*. Amesbury, Massachusetts, The Whittier Press, 1935.

Smith, Fredrika Shumway, *John Greenleaf Whittier, a Narrative Biography*. Boston, Christopher Publishing, 1948.

Sparhawk, Frances Campbell, *Whittier at Close Range*. Boston, Riverdale Press, 1925.

Underwood, Francis H., *John Greenleaf Whittier: A Biography*. Boston, J. R. Osgood, and London, Low Marston, 1884.

Vining, Elizabeth Gray, *The Taken Girl*. New York, Viking, 1972.

Vining, Elizabeth Gray, *Mr. Whittier*. New York, Viking, 1974.

Wagenknecht, Edward, *John Greenleaf Whittier: A Portrait in Paradox*. New York, Oxford University Press, 1967.

Whitten, Wilfred, *John G. Whittier: A Biographical Sketch*. London, E. Hicks, 1892.

Woodman, Aby J., *Reminiscences of John Greenleaf Whittier's Life at Oak Knoll*. Salem, Massachusetts, Essex Institute, 1908.

Woodwell, Roland H., *John Greenleaf Whittier: A Biography*. Haverhill, Massachusetts, Trustees of the John Greenleaf Whittier Homestead, 1985.

*

It is astonishing to find that the most recent biography of Whittier was written in 1967. A 1500-page typescript by WOODWELL, considered by some to be a definitive biography, has until recently been available only in typed manuscript in the Whittier collection of the Haverhill Public Library; it was published by the trustees of the Whittier homestead in 1985.

Aside from possible religious distortions, the primary controversy among biographers of Whittier has been the degree to which political reform affected Whittier's poetry. KENNEDY's book, the first biography of Whittier, emphasizes Whittier's patriotic as well as personal virtues. However, Whittier disliked the work because it tended to view Emerson's Transcendentalism as superior to Whittier's Quakerism. Kennedy was obliged to stretch the few facts available about Whittier's earlier life. In addition, Kennedy's own self-image as an advanced thinker is condescending enough to mar his discussion of Whittier's later life, which is further distorted by his concept of Whittier as a patriotic hero. This odd combination of attitudes seriously compromises his reading of the poems.

The "official" biographer of Whittier was S. T. PICKARD, husband of Whittier's niece. Whittier actively aided the work for several years until his death and tinkered somewhat with the contexts of a few of the documenting letters. Even so, this biography, written to express the relation between the poet and his politics, remains indispensable—broad, objective, well-balanced, and thorough. John B. Pickard's later edition of the letters (3 vols., 1975) serves to undo Whittier's meddling.

Some critics feel that POLLARD has written the most complete and dependable modern biography of Whittier, although some object to Pollard's emphasis on Whittier's politics. Well documented, judicious, and straightforward, this work corrects errors, incorporates new discoveries, and provides scholars with a necessary supplement to Pickard's book. HIGGINSON, relying on Pickard as well as Wasson and Stedman, furnishes authoritative chapters on Whittier's political and reform activities and his religious attitudes. UNDERWOOD wrote a "serious" authorized biography intended as a "friendly guide and interpreter" rather than a formal biography or scholarly study. It includes memoirs of Whittier and reminiscences by his friends. Underwood has special insights into Whittier's relations with *Atlantic* magazine. He's a sympathetic biographer who acceded to Whittier's admonition to be less adulatory, but admired the man who lived most austerely of all the great New England poets, having had "fewest advantages of culture and travel and has made the least show of scholarship." Underwood wrote to some extent in response to Whittier's disappointment with Kennedy's criticism of his poetry.

A second contention arose with MORDELL's psychological interpretation of Whittier, especially his assertion that Whittier was a "male coquet," a philanderer who paid for his celibacy with invalidism—conclusions that appear to be academically unsound. The biography reveals the author's Freudian and socialist bias. Nevertheless, Mordell's interest in Whittier's attitudes toward slavery, and the poet's activities as editor and propagandist, is supported by a great deal of new information, including uncollected poems and editorials. Mordell shows Whittier as a pioneer of New England regional literature, and as a militant, radical agitator who was charged on a number of occasions with blasphemy and sedition. WAGENKNECHT is a reputable scholar who presents Whittier as multi-faceted and paradoxical, the effect of which is to depict a more vibrant, complex personality than earlier biographers had portrayed.

In contrast, a number of general writers on Whittier have responded to his devoted membership in the Society of Friends by emphasizing evangelical issues, often at the expense of objectivity. However, one writer, Barrett Wendell, argues in his book entitled *Stelligeri and Other Essays* (New York, 1893) that in early 19th-century America, sectarian differences assert themselves in obvious differences of character, a view that could be prejudicial, but a possibility readers may wish to consider when choosing among religious biographies. BURTON, for instance, attends to Whittier's reputation as a devout Christian by taking at face value the poet's deprecation of his own poetry and literature in general. The book contains a few minor errors, but is the first to note Whittier's interest in Lucy Hooper and to identify 1857 as a crucial year in the poet's career. Burton's focus on "the man in his work" is to some extent maintained at the expense of the man in his associations.

Several other biographies stress Whittier's religious and social values. Unfortunately, there are too many errors in ROWN-TREE's pious effort for it to be helpful. COOKE's work, "intended to interest young people," is based on S. T. Pickard, yet it contains several inaccuracies. It avoids evangelical language, but over-stresses Whittier's virtues. By far the most sentimental treatment is the "inspirational biography" by FLOWER, who makes a point that his book is designed to confer "a peculiar value for aspiring youth." It is romantic and anecdotal, including passages such as: "Ah! thou little barefoot dreamer boy, who wanderest over hills and vales round thy native home, . . . thou child of pure and honest parents, had we more lives like thine, the curses of our day and generation would lose their power. . . . " FIELDS, a good friend of Whittier's and wife of his publisher, also epitomizes Victorian sentiment as she describes the poet's "keen wit," "burning eye," and "love and devotion . . . to the Quaker Church." The chief value of these reminiscences are their allusions to Whittier's reading.

CLAFLIN was the wife of Governor William Claflin, who often entertained Whittier. Her gossipy little book is the source of several colorful anecdotes about a man known for his sedate character. WOODMAN respectfully describes family life, local scenery, and the visits of friends during the final 16 years of Whittier's life, when he lived with the family of Col. Edmund Johnson at "Oak Knoll" in Danvers, Massachusetts. SPAR-HAWK's volume is a loose collection of sentimental anecdotes about the final 30 years of Whittier's life. Another tiny volume is E. B. SMITH's 38-page reminiscence. The last of that genre on Whittier, it contains a few "homely stories."

BENNETT's biography may be of interest to general readers, although it seems to have been inspired by sorrowful response to Mordell's book and is flawed by its adversarial position. A rare book dealer with a deep appreciation of Whittier's poetry, Bennett takes Mordell's facts and reinterprets them, reverting to previous ideas. He calls Whittier a "rabble rousing anti-slavery rhymster in the service of God Almighty against the demon of human physical bondage." The Canadian poet Bliss PERRY's eulogistic sketch was written for the centenary of Whittier's birth and is based on Carpenter's biography. It is followed by an anthology of the popular poems. WHITTEN wrote for an audience of English Quakers. His book's commentary is poor and contains misstatements, but it contains some useful source material on Whittier's anti-slavery work. LEWIS' authority is S. T. Pickard. Her volume, unoriginal but readable, is marred by awe and the last chapter's appeal to free the slaves of Zanzibar. LINTON compiled information from Underwood and Kennedy and quotes heavily from secondary sources; consequently his work adds nothing unique.

Useful for younger students, CARPENTER's volume is largely drawn from S. T. Pickard, though it contains some independent critical thought. A British biographer, HUDSON, also attempts to interest students by drawing on S. T. Pickard and Carpenter, in a "systematic attempt to link biography . . . with production." LEARY's volume for Twayne depends completely on previous biographies, as does J. B. PICKARD's *Introduction and Interpretation*. Each devotes about half of its space to biography and half to criticism. Leary's biographical section is uneven, claiming without proof that Whittier's illness of 1831 was a nervous breakdown. Leary makes several minor errors and exaggerates the impact of certain of Whittier's writings. Nevertheless, with its notes and annotated bibliography, it is a useful general overview for students. Pickard, who underscores Whittier's career as a poet, also serves the same purpose accurately.

Among children's biographies, HEATH's is a mere pamphlet, and CODY focuses on Whittier as journalist. F. S. SMITH's book is romanticized juvenile entertainment in novel form containing details presumed of interest to children, such as Whittier's own youth, the "barefoot boy with cheek of tan," his children's poems, and his disgust with cabbage. BYRON dramatizes a typical day in the poet's life. VINING's *The Taken Girl* is the story of a young girl's interest in Whittier, and her *Mr. Whittier*, though it has some factual errors, is an otherwise excellent children's book.

—Helen Killoran

WILDE, Oscar (Fingal O'Flahertie Wills), 1854–1900; Irish writer.

Douglas, Alfred, Lord, *Oscar Wilde and Myself.* London, J. Long, and New York, Duffield, 1914.

Douglas, Alfred, Lord, *Oscar Wilde: A Summing Up.* London, Richards Press, 1961.

Ellmann, Richard, *Oscar Wilde.* London, Hamilton, and New York, Viking, 1987.

Gide, André, *Oscar Wilde.* London, W. Kimber, 1951 (originally published, 1910).

Harris, Frank, *Oscar Wilde: His Life and Confessions.* New York, Garden City Publishing, 1930.

Housman, Laurence, *Écho de Paris: A Study from Life.* London, Cape, 1923; New York, Appleton, 1924.

Hyde, H. Montgomery, *Oscar Wilde: The Aftermath.* New York, Farrar Straus, and London, Methuen, 1963.

Jullian, Philippe, *Oscar Wilde,* translated by Violet Wyndham. New York, Viking, 1968; London, Constable, 1969.

O'Sullivan, Vincent, *Aspects of Wilde.* London, Constable, and New York, Holt, 1936.

Pearson, Hesketh, *The Life of Oscar Wilde.* London, Methuen, 1946.

Ransome, Arthur, *Oscar Wilde: A Critical Study.* London, Methuen, and New York, M. Kennerly, 1912.

Ricketts, Charles, *Oscar Wilde: Recollections.* London, Nonesuch Press, 1932.

Sherard, Robert H., *Oscar Wilde: The Story of an Unhappy Relationship.* Privately printed, London, 1902.

Sherard, Robert H., *Life of Oscar Wilde.* London, T. W. Laurie, and New York, Dodd Mead, 1906.

Sherard, Robert H., *The Real Oscar Wilde.* London, T. W. Laurie, 1916.

Winwar, Frances, *Oscar Wilde and the Yellow Nineties.* New York, Harper, 1940.

*

Oscar Wilde and the central tragedy of his life have attracted more books than most writers' careers, yet for many decades after his death the continuing atmosphere of sensation and controversy made it difficult for a truly objective biography of Wilde to appear. Thus we have many books that can be classed as biographical, but very few that pass muster as, in any complete sense, a biography.

Until his last years Wilde himself contributed very little that could be called autobiographical, except enough letters for two posthumous volumes that appeared more than half a century after his death: *The Letters of Oscar Wilde* (1962), and *More Letters of Oscar Wilde* (1985), both edited by Rupert Hart-Davis. But while he was imprisoned, Wilde wrote an extraordinary document of false repentance and accusation, *De Profundis* (1905), which might count partly as *apologia pro vita sua*—nearing self-hagiography—and partly as a fragment of somewhat veiled and slanted autobiography. It was aimed at thrusting the blame for his troubles on his former lover, Lord Alfred Douglas, who was indeed to an extent responsible. Another lover, Robert Ross, published the first version of *De Profundis*, heavily abridged to avoid giving offense to Douglas. But news of the existence of the work and of its full contents had already leaked out, and was to end in a whole spate of books that largely ignored the conventions of biographical objectivity as they sought to justify either Wilde or Douglas and to present others as gallant friends in time of need. As for *De Profundis*, a version that included some of the accusatory material was published in 1949 (edited by V. Holland), when the litigious Douglas was safely dead. A complete version finally appeared in Hart-Davis' edition of the *Letters* in 1962. By this time its relatively small value as biographical source material had become evident.

The first round was fired by SHERARD, a minor writer whom Wilde in his kindness had encouraged and endured, and who now took on himself the role of a heterosexual knight errant, and published an account of their relationship in 1902. He followed this up with an argumentative *Life of Oscar Wilde* (1906), which was in name at least the first biography, and in 1916 with yet another "revelatory" volume, *The Real Oscar Wilde*.

At this time Lord Alfred DOUGLAS entered the fray, largely because of his hatred for Robert Ross, who possessed the full script of *De Profundis* with its damning accusations against him. He began by suing Arthur RANSOME, who in 1912 published *Oscar Wilde: A Critical Study*, which was a portrait as well as a critique and might count for this reason as the first attempt at a really objective biography. Ross had shown Ransome the full manuscript of *De Profundis*, on the strength of which Ransome, without naming Douglas, made a reference to the young man who had helped bring about Wilde's downfall. Douglas sued for libel, and was defeated and thoroughly humiliated by the evidence brought against him in court. Douglas then entered the biographical melée in 1914 with his self-justificatory *Oscar Wilde and Myself*; he published a number of later books bearing in some way or another on the case, and then, long after his death, his shrill voice rang out again with *Oscar Wilde: A Summing Up* (1962). The gladiatorial period of Wilde biography was brought to an end with the mendacious and self-seeking Frank HARRIS' *Oscar Wilde, his Life and Confessions* (1930), in which Harris appears as the one solid friend who stood beside Wilde in all his troubles.

The stridency of these earlier quasi-biographies of Wilde was accentuated by the widespread prejudice against him as a homosexual, a prejudice that lingered through the first half of the present century. The best, most intimate, and most authentic books of this time were the modest memoirs by people who had known Wilde, particularly in the final expatriate years of his life. These included works by HOUSMAN, O'SULLIVAN, and RICKETTS. All these relatively small books stressed Wilde's good qualities, his likeability, his rash generosity, his marvelous kindness, and his ironic stoicism, but none of them added up to more than an impressionistic sketch of the aging Wilde. A somewhat more sinister portrait of Wilde as Mephistophelian tempter at the time of his greatest pride was given by GIDE in his recollection, *Oscar Wilde*. Despite their fragmented quality, these books helped move the image of Wilde out of the shadows of prejudice and the conflict of self-justifying egos, preparing the way for more objective biographies.

The first of these was by the American scholar WINWAR, whose well-researched book tends to take Wilde at his own valuation as a symbolic figure of the *fin de siècle*. Its background—the world of the Nineties decadents—is very well rendered, but Wilde's personality is not so clearly realized. Shortly afterwards, PEARSON, a popular biographer who had already written a life of Bernard Shaw, published his book on Wilde. Its broad acceptance showed that popular prejudice against Wilde as homosexual was declining, and, even if Pearson's commentary on Wilde's works is uncritical, he does offer the portrait of an extraordinary personality and a notable intelligence.

Two years later, a valuable addition to the available biographical material was offered when the lawyer H. Montgomery HYDE critically edited, and published under the title of *The Trials of Oscar Wilde* (1948), the transcripts of the proceedings against Wilde in 1895. Hyde later added his own contribution to actual biography with *Oscar Wilde: The Aftermath*, in 1963.

In 1968 appeared Violet Wyndham's translation of the French writer Philippe JULLIAN's *Oscar Wilde*, a somewhat romantic biography that flirts almost coyly with its subject and its readers; first names prevail. Still, Jullian had the advantage of seeing and using correspondence and other material not available to earlier biographers, and his book cannot be wholly neglected by the serious student of Wilde. During this post-World War II period a number of critical books on Wilde also appeared and, perhaps because of Wilde's preoccupations with the links between life and art, some of them have a degree of biographical content as they assess Wilde's works in the light of his life and personality, and *vice versa*. Notable among these are Edouard Roditi's *Oscar Wilde* (1947) and George Woodcock's *The Paradox of Oscar Wilde* (1949).

The book that must be regarded as the one truly definitive biography of Oscar Wilde did not appear until 1987, almost nine decades after his death. This is ELLMANN's *Oscar Wilde*. Ellmann had long been known as a leading authority on Irish writers of the late 19th and early 20th centuries; his books on Yeats and Joyce were justly famous by the time he started the Wilde biography. Ellmann had previously devoted much time to the study of Wilde, having edited collections of criticism by and about him. Most importantly, he respects Wilde as a writer and a thinker, seeing him as one of the great literary figures of his time. He has the essential biographer's gift of empathizing with his subject, and so his book, rigorous in its scholarship, more detailed in its information than any previous life of Wilde, is also written with such warmth and understanding that one feels Wilde has here not only his first true biographer but also his best advocate. Without any perceptible loss in objectivity, the reader finds himself involved, laughing with Wilde as well as learning from and about him, and in the end—so sensitive is Ellmann's treatment—moved by the account of Wilde's last days and his exile's death. It is almost a model of literary biography, largely owing to its subject, who had already challenged, by the sheer strangeness of his life, so many who sought to write about him. In Ellmann Wilde met his intellectual match.

—George Woodcock

WILDER, Laura Ingalls, 1867–1957; American writer.

Spaeth, Janet, *Laura Ingalls Wilder.* Boston, Twayne, 1987.
Zochert, Donald, *Laura: The Life of Laura Ingalls Wilder.* Chicago, H. Regnery, 1976.

*

Laura Ingalls Wilder entered the lives of many Americans through their television screens rather than through the pages of her books. The long-running television series, "Little House on the Prairie," was inspired by Wilder's stories of frontier life in the Midwest, and those programs transformed her life experiences into legend. In that process, the medium of television magnified an existing problem: events tend to acquire new form and color as they are told and retold. In the case of the television series, dramatic license was required to create a shooting script from a simple narrative. And in the case of the *Little House* books—well, Laura Ingalls Wilder wrote her *first* book nearly 60 years after the childhood experiences it describes.

Both Spaeth and Zochert address the problem of the transformation of truth as it makes its way from reality to literature. SPAETH notes that Wilder described her stories as "true," but suggests that metaphorical rather than literal truth was what Wilder meant—in other words, the "essence of experience" is captured in the *Little House* books, rather than precise correspondence with reality. Spaeth attempts to convey the distinction between the "Laura" of the books and Laura, the author, by referring to the latter as "Wilder."

This scholarly concern with accuracy distinguishes Spaeth's biography from Zochert's. Unfortunately, Spaeth's book is devoted only in part to the life of Laura Ingalls Wilder. As in other books in the Twayne series, a biographical chapter is followed by literary analysis of the subject's works. Spaeth devotes 88 pages to analysis—only 10 to biography. For this reason, if no other, her biography of Wilder cannot be regarded as satisfactory. But Spaeth does provide a useful annotated bibliography, and the book serves as a quick introduction to Wilder.

ZOCHERT's book, unlike Spaeth's, is a full-length biography. But there are no aids to further research—no bibliography, no footnotes. And the text itself fails to preserve the careful distinction made by Janet Spaeth. For example, Zochert blurs the distinction between Laura the child and Laura the author in this passage: "When Laura grew up and began writing the *Little House* books, people found it hard to believe that such a little girl could remember so much about her life in the Big Woods. But Laura remembered, no matter what grown-ups might say."

Zochert's prose is evocative and simple, descriptive and poetic—almost as if he were so mesmerized by Wilder's prose that he attempted to speak in her voice. This apparent desire to recreate the flavor of her writing in his own often makes his biography seem fanciful.

Zochert includes as an appendix an essay on the issue of truth in the *Little House* books. He concludes that the books "hold a treasurable truth that transcends fact," and that the truth of the books is the "truth of art."

Wilder called her books "historical novels" and claimed that each incident was true, although "not the whole truth." Rose Wilder Lane, Laura's daughter, insisted that nothing in her mother's books was fictionalized. Rose, an accomplished writer before her mother began writing in earnest, helped her mother with planning, writing, and marketing the *Little House* books.

Mother and daughter are co-authors of *A Little House Sampler* (Lincoln, University of Nebraska Press, 1988), a posthumous collection of their writings. The *Sampler* is neither autobiography nor biography, properly speaking, but it is replete with biographical detail supplied by the co-authors and by the editor of the collection, William T. Anderson. He has arranged the selections in order to "create a chronological account" of the lives of Laura, her husband, Almanzo, and their daughter, Rose. Anderson has written a brief introduction to each of the selections included in the *Sampler*, placing them in biographical context. And in some cases he provides annotation within the selections themselves, which he chose from "abandoned" manuscripts as well as from published articles. The result is a readable and cohesive account of the lives of a remarkable family.

—Whitney R. Mundt

WILDER, Thornton, 1897–1975; American writer.

Goldstone, Richard Henry, *Thornton Wilder, an Intimate Portrait.* New York, Saturday Review Press, 1975.
Harrison, Gilbert A., *The Enthusiast: A Life of Thornton Wilder.* New Haven, Connecticut, Ticknor and Fields, 1983.
Simon, Linda, *Thornton Wilder, His World.* New York, Doubleday, 1979.

*

GOLDSTONE wrote the first full-length biography of Wilder. Goldstone met Wilder during World War II, and their contact continued after the war. He eventually published "An Interview with Thornton Wilder" in the *Paris Review* of the winter of 1957.

Goldstone uses his acquaintance with Wilder and the Wilder family, and his own knowledge of the theater (he was for many years a professor of English at the City College of New York and is the author and editor of several books on drama), to offer a readable biography which in broad strokes captures the successes and failures of Wilder's career. Goldstone was fortunate in being able to interview in person or by letter a number of individuals important in Wilder's career, including Jed Harris, the director who first mounted *Our Town*, Tallulah Bankhead, who created the role of Lily Sabina in *The Skin of Our Teeth*, and Robert Maynard Hutchins, a friend of Wilder's since their college days who, when he became president of the University of Chicago, invited Wilder to teach there.

Goldstone opens, *in medias res*, as it were, with the enormous success that greeted *The Bridge of San Luis Rey* in 1927, before going back to cover Wilder's childhood, college years, and first teaching experience at the Lawrenceville School—a briskly efficient introduction to the forces that shaped Wilder's sensibility.

It is a pity, then, that in the area where Goldstone might be expected to demonstrate particular strength, theater history, he should be so surprsingly uninformed. Wilder's own earliest diaries and notebooks reveal a passionate and long-standing interest in theatre. He kept elaborate lists of productions in various European theaters as well as of the American productions he had seen, going back to his high school days in California. Years after seeing a production, he could recount casts and other details with professional acumen. To one correspondent, he recalled the specifics of every production he had seen of *Everyman*. Little of Wilder's enthusiasm or his sense of theater history is reflected in Goldstone's book.

For example, Goldstone credits a New York production (by Jacques Copeau) of Mérimée's *La Carrosse du Saint-Sacrement* with anticipating elements in Wilder's *The Bridge of San Luis Rey*. But he is wrong about the year Wilder might have seen it in New York, for the play was not offered in the 1918–19 New York season. Nor does he seem aware that Wilder saw the play more than once in the summer of 1921 in Paris (on one occasion accompanied by Edna St. Vincent Millay). Goldstone nowhere speaks about Copeau's production of Shakespeare's *Twelfth Night*, which had a profound effect on Wilder. He should also have known that the theater company founded by Copeau was the Théâtre du Vieux Colombier (1913–1924) and not La Compagnie des Quinze, which was founded in 1930 by Copeau's students. Goldstone on the importance to Wilder of Richard Boleslavsky and Max Reinhardt seems equally lacking in precision and depth.

SIMON's 1979 biography provides more detail on the early family life and on the background of Wilder's father, the rigid Amos P. Wilder, than does Goldstone. Simon lists and summarizes individual works and mentions honors Wilder received. She provides a wealth of facts, but, unfortunately, little focus. For all the biographical data gathered here, there is no interpretation, no imaginative understanding of how that information might be used to breathe life into the man responsible for the novels and plays which Simon thinks so important.

At the center of Simon's book is Wilder's relationship with Gertrude Stein. Wilder met Stein for the first time in November 1934. In the years that followed, through visits and correspondence, they formed a personal and intellectual bond that lasted beyond Stein's death in 1946. Stein remained in Wilder's thinking throughout his life, and while Simon illustrates their friendship with chatty anecdotes, she does not analyze what they offered each other, artistically or intellectually.

Simon is also skimpy with reliable information about Wilder's theatrical career. She accepts as gospel the statement by an ac-

quaintance of Wilder's that their walk one rainy night in Zurich, while Wilder was working on *Our Town*, resulted in the use of umbrellas in the play's last act (in fact the umbrellas were inspired by director Jed Harris). Her failure to give weight to Wilder's vast musical cultivation (a fault shared with Goldstone and Harrison) and her inability to explain his passionate interest, for example, in textual problems in Joyce or dating the plays of Lope de Vega also limits the biography's scope as a well rounded portrait of the man.

HARRISON's biography has the advantage of having been undertaken with full cooperation from the Wilder estate. Harrison was permitted access to the Wilder archives and was given permission to quote extensively, adding immensely to the shape of the biography. Wilder's letters and diary entries are filled with energy, and Harrison's journalistic style (he was for many years editor of *The New Republic*) evokes Wilder's criss-crossing of America on the lecture circuits of the 1920s and 1930s. Here the reader encounters the contagious enthusiasm and brilliant conversation of Wilder.

But Harrison is a chronicler and little more. His attempts at interpretation misrepresent Wilder as a tender and consoling philosopher of resignation. The grimly challenging Wilder who gave us *Our Town* and the sharply ironical Wilder of the underrated *Heaven's My Destination* is not to be found in Harrison's biography.

Harrison's work, though in readability a considerable improvement over its two predecessors, is shocking in its careless documentation and inaccuracy in quotations. Whereas both Goldstone and Simon supply ample, if occasionally erratic, apparatus for the scholar and student, Harrison gives us none at all. As a result, chronology is frequently lost, and one has the impression that quotations are being cobbled together out of entirely different contexts. A spot check of Harrison's quoted material against the original manuscript sources reveals errors in transcription so numerous and fundamental that one cannot simply atrribute them to poor proof-reading. The usefulness of Harrison's biography is thus seriously compromised.

Students of Thornton Wilder will find the outline of his life more or less adequately drawn in each of these biographies. But those who want to penetrate the enigma of this most gifted and unusual man, to understand what engrossed him, to see how his many interests are woven into the fabric of the plays and novels, are best advised to turn first to *The Journals of Thornton Wilder: 1939–1961*, selected and edited by Donald Gallup (New Haven, Connecticut, Yale University Press, 1985). Here is Wilder in the flesh: garrulous, sententious, a man of philosophic temper and literary curiosity. The definitive biography that Wilder deserves has yet to be written.

—Edward Burns

WILHELM II [Kaiser Wilhelm], 1859–1941; German emperor and king of Prussia.

Balfour, Michael, *The Kaiser and His Times*. Boston, Houghton Mifflin, and London, Cresset Press, 1964.

Cecil, Lamar, *Wilhelm II, Prince and Emperor 1859–1900*. Chapel Hill, University of North Carolina Press, 1989.

Cowles, Virginia, *The Kaiser*. New York, Harper, and London, Collins, 1963.

Davis, A. N., *The Kaiser I Knew: My 14 Years with the Kaiser*. London, Hodder and Stoughton, and New York, Harper, 1918.

Ludwig, Emil, *Kaiser Wilhelm II*, translated by E. C. Mayne. London and New York, Putnam, 1926.

Müller, George Alexander von, *The Kaiser and His Court*, translated by M. Savill, edited by Walter Görlitz. London, Macdonald, 1961; New York, Harcourt, 1964.

Nowak, Karl Friedrich, *Kaiser and Chancellor: The Opening Years of the Reign of Kaiser Wilhelm II*, translated by E. W. Dickes. New York, Macmillan, and London, Putnam, 1930.

Palmer, Alan, *The Kaiser: Warlord of the Second Reich*. New York, Scribner, and London, Weidenfeld and Nicolson, 1978.

Röhl, J. C. G., *Germany without Bismarck: The Crisis of Government in the Second Reich 1890–1900*. Berkeley, University of California Press, and London, Batsford, 1967.

Röhl, J. C. G. and N. Sombart, editors, *Kaiser Wilhelm II: New Interpretations*. Cambridge and New York, Cambridge University Press, 1982.

Whittle, Tyler, *The Last Kaiser: A Biography of Wilhelm II, German Emperor and King of Prussia*. London, Heinemann, 1977.

Wilson, Lawrence, *The Incredible Kaiser: A Portrait of William II*. London, R. Hale, 1963; New York, A. S. Barnes, 1965.

*

Although he was regarded by contemporaries as the most important leader in Europe, there is a lack of quality biographies in English of Kaiser Wilhelm II. The existing accounts fall into two types, the popular and the scholarly, with the latter primarily concerned with the extent to which the kaiser personally ruled Germany.

One of the first English works on the kaiser was the wartime sketch by DAVIS, his American dentist. As such, the book is infused with a patriotic tone, written to illuminate the kaiser's ambitions and plans. Although propagandistic, Davis gives a good sense of the popular mood and internal situation in Germany, as well as a feel for the contradictions of Wilhelm's personality. He describes him as intelligent and charming, but also arrogant, egotistical, and determined to have his own way on all matters.

Although intended as a portrait of the kaiser, LUDWIG's work traces the direct evolution of German foreign policy from the idiosyncrasies of Wilhelm. Drawing on memoirs and extensive documentary material, Ludwig pictures a mentally gifted, physically disabled man driven by an overly ambitious mother; a man who came to power too young, failed to mature, and who too easily succumbed to flatterers and his own overweening autocratic tendencies. Restless, ambitious, and unable to pursue a consistent policy, the young kaiser made irresponsible moves in foreign policy that led to disaster. Using the "new" insights of psychoanalysis, Ludwig provides a vivid image of a tragic figure, a man with the best intentions who came to ruin through the deficiencies of his character.

Less satisfactory is WILSON, whose portrait of the kaiser provides an occasional insight but is more often outrageous and annoying. His portrayal of the impact of Wilhelm's domineering mother is generally solid, while his depiction of German foreign policy is Anglophiliac, simplistic, strikingly one-sided, and often erroneous. Virtually useless is COWLES, whose superficial biography contains a host of factual errors, reduces complex leaders to caricature, and throws out a constant barrage of simplistic national stereotypes. She is totally out of her depth in trying to illuminate a complex man, as well as the intricacies of German foreign and domestic policy. Equally inconsequential is WHITTLE, an author more familiar with gardening books than history. His biography rambles, fails to capture the tensions in Wilhelm's character, and never provides a sense of the tragedy surrounding him and his nation. More annoying is the fact that this is as much a portrait of the English royal family as it is of Wilhelm.

PALMER aims at the more serious reader. In a balanced account based on documentary and unpublished private papers, Palmer captures Wilhelm's elusiveness. A man of considerable ability who remained an adolescent in temperament, energetic, restless, with a constant need to assert himself, Wilhelm covered his fear and insecurity with an arrogance that grew ever more autocratic. Remaining to a large extent a spectator while the crucial issue of war was being decided in July 1914, Wilhelm yearned for peace but was too indecisive and emotionally distraught to effect events.

The question of Wilhelm's personal rule dominates scholarly books on the kaiser. In a semi-official work, NOWAK portrays Wilhelm as domineering and inconsiderate but on a solid basis of right in his struggle for independence of Bismarck's control. A devastating portrait of a domineering mother who drove her son away emotionally, Nowak also depicts the impatience and restlessness of a young ruler who yearned for glory. Wilhelm emerges as a man who would have been fine as a private citizen but whose qualities were less suitable for a national leader.

The dispute with Bismarck also dominates RÖHL, who sees the Iron Chancellor's fall from power resulting in a period of quarreling and intrigue, culminating in Wilhelm's decision to impose his personal rule in order to restore unity to the government. Thus, by 1897 Wilhelm had emerged as the decisive figure within Germany. The collected scholarly accounts in RÖHL AND SOMBART also emphasize the personal rule of Wilhelm and his decisive influence in the areas of foreign and military policy. Utilizing a personalistic and psychological approach, which should be read with caution, the various authors present a collective portrait of a man whose turbulent behavior imparted a manic, erratic quality to German policy, not least because he appointed much of the high administration, intervened impetuously in foreign affairs, and controlled military policy. The authors, though, tend to overstate the extent of Wilhelm's personal rule. He admittedly exercised great influence up to 1900, but thereafter it declined steadily.

A sense of the kaiser's isolation and dwindling power comes through well in MÜLLER, whose diaries portray a complex, often brilliant man, who is nonetheless restless, undisciplined, arrogant, and irresponsible, whose bluster tries to hide his weakness and gnawing self-doubts. Wilhelm emerges as an ill-informed man who neither understood nor was fully aware of the momentous events swirling around him. Thus, unable to avert war in 1914, Wilhelm passively sank into isolation amid a de facto abdication of responsibility. Although the diaries were edited by both Müller and Görlitz to cast the kaiser in a more favorable light, Wilhelm still appears capricious and foolish.

CECIL's densely detailed and psychological account, the first volume of a projected larger work, also highlights Wilhelm's essential foolishness and superficiality. While not easily read, Cecil portrays well the narrowness and isolation of Wilhelm, a cold and callow man singularly ill-suited for the great role he was to play.

Although not a mere chronicle of the kaiser but an attempt to understand his character and influence in the light of his surroundings, BALFOUR nonetheless has written what remains the least subjective, most useful English biography of Wilhelm. He sprinkles a short historical sketch of Germany, a brief family background, and a mature psychological assessment of Wilhelm with flashes of insight, wit, and sardonic observations. Wilhelm emerges a complex and contradictory man, with a quick mind but lacking a sense of proportion. Wilhelm sought escape from the tensions underlying his character through retreat into a fantasy world of his own creation. Balfour notes that living in these illusions, believing what he chose to believe, Wilhelm played a smaller role in the formation of policy than is generally acknowledged.

—Stephen G. Fritz

WILLIAM I, ca. 1028–1087; Norman conqueror and king of England.

Barlow, Frank, *William I and the Norman Conquest.* London, English Universities Press, and Mystic, Connecticut, L. Verry, 1965.

Douglas, David, *William the Conqueror: The Norman Impact upon England.* Berkeley, University of California Press, and London, Eyre and Spottiswoode, 1964.

Freeman, Edward, *William the Conqueror.* New York, A. L. Burt, 1902; London, Macmillan, 1903.

*

FREEMAN's work paints the kind of heroic picture of William I that is extremely common in the "Whig" interpretation of history. In this view, greatness of all things English is left unquestioned. Freeman sees all the events in William's life as preparing him for the role he would eventually assume in England, and he devotes much space to the Norman (Germanic) background of William's family. This book reveals as much about the period in which it was written as it does about the subject. The idea of William's necessary role in the evolution of English greatness is shown by Freeman's attitude about the conquest: "The statesmanship of William had triumphed. The people of England had chosen their king, and a large part of the world had been won over by the arts of a foreign prince to believe that it was a righteous and holy work to set him on the throne to which the English had chosen the foremost man among themselves."

The early part of Freeman's book does an excellent job covering William's minority as Duke of Normandy, examining how his early difficulties helped to create "the Conqueror." Freeman is also strong in his coverage of the conquest itself, along with the results of the invasion of England. He effectively connects the Pope's blessing for the invasion with the future problems English kings had with Rome. Freeman raises interesting questions as to whether Harold actually took an oath to support William's claim to the English throne; and he describes the relationship between Archbishop Lanfranc and William, speculating on what might have happened if William had succeeded in taking control of Ireland before his death. The work is well written, but the period bias, while interesting, makes the work of less use to those doing serious research than later works.

BARLOW's work on William was written over 60 years later, and it serves a very different purpose. Designed as an overview of William's life, it devotes much space to discussing his conquest and reign in England. This work is poorly documented and will be of little assistance to the serious student of the period, but it can be enjoyable to general readers seeking background information, especially in the social history of both England and Normandy.

Revealing an occasional English bias, Barlow claims for example that "Norman sexual morals were loose even by the standards of the time. From a strictly ecclesiastical standpoint many members of the ruling family in Normandy were of doubtful legitimacy." On the pre-conquest English church: "The misunderstanding with Rome, common as such disagreements were in ecclesiastical history, was completely out of character of the Old-English church, for no church had periods of greater illumination, no church had been more loyal to St. Peter and the Threshold of the Apostles. The habit of the pilgrimage to Rome was engrained in the English people." The work does well in examining aspects of the period such as church-state relations and the development of the new Norman government of England. The section on the revolts during William's ducal minority make an interesting connection between the extension of royal justice into the shires and the beginnings of the revolt of 1075.

DOUGLAS does an excellent job of updating William's biography for academics, while giving enough background to help general readers understand William in his proper context. Over one half of the text covers William's early life and his preparation for the conquest. The work begins with coverage of the young duke's family going back to Rolf the Viking (who became ruler of Normandy in 911 A.D.). In dealing with the question of William's right to the English throne, Douglas provides three possible accounts of the oath of support Harold pledged to William. The second half of Douglas' work covers the period after the conquest, including the development of Norman England. While the questions of political and economic development during this period are better covered in more specialized works, Douglas does a good job of examining William's role in the transfer of the Norman feudal and administrative systems to England. In the appendices he deals with the facts of William's relationship with his mother and the questions concerning his marriage. Douglas surveys the possible reasons for the ban on William's marriage to Matilda, in the end giving his own explanation. He also gives a probable number of daughters in addition to William's sons. Douglas' objective coverage of individuals allows readers to draw their own conclusions about the people involved. He is broad and judicious in his use of sources, especially the Norman annals. His documentation, combined with his lively writing style, makes this the biography of preference for both scholars and general readers interested in William I of England and his period.

—Donald E. Heidenreich, Jr.

WILLIAMS, Tennessee [*born* Thomas Lanier Williams], 1911–1983; American playwright.

Maxwell, Gilbert, *Tennessee Williams and Friends: An Informal Biography.* Cleveland, World Publishing, 1965.

Rader, Dotson, *Tennessee, Cry of the Heart.* New York, Doubleday, 1985; as *Tennessee Williams: An Intimate Memoir,* London, Grafton, 1986.

Spoto, Donald, *The Kindness of Strangers: The Life of Tennessee Williams.* Boston, Little Brown, and London, Bodley Head, 1985.

Tischler, Nancy, *Tennessee Williams: Rebellious Puritan.* New York, Citadel Press, 1961.

Williams, Dakin, *Tennessee Williams: An Intimate Biography.* New York, Arbor House, 1983.

Williams, Edwina Dakin (as told to Lucy Freeman), *Remember Me to Tom.* New York, Putnam, 1963; London, Cassell, 1964.

*

Unfortunately there are, at present, no reliable, complete biographies of Tennessee Williams, for the playwright has been rather poorly served by most of those who have attempted to record his life. The best and most accurate work to date was published in 1961, when Williams was at the height of his career, and therefore does not cover the remaining 23 years of his life and work.

That book is, surprisingly, the first to be published, by TISCHLER. It covers the first 50 years of Williams' life and covers them well, providing facts that are generally accurate, and it contains as well the only in-depth study of the canon up to that time. Tischler seems to have been the first critic to take Williams seriously as a writer rather than dismissing him as a mere creator of popular entertainments. That there are blanks in her portrait is not surprising, given the time of its publication, for homosexuality was not openly discussed in 1961. Furthermore, Tischler did not have access to the abundance of letters, diaries, and other printed documents that have subsequently become available to would-be biographers. Despite these unavoidable weaknesses, however, the work has stood the test of time and is still the most honest and accurate study available.

Tischler was the first scholar to point out the major split in Williams' character, which he himself commented on in later works, between his Calvinistic background and his Romantic bent, a dichotomy acknowledged in Tischler's subtitle, "Rebellious Puritan." Combining a good history of the playwright's life with a solid critical evaluation of his works, Tischler made a significant contribution to Williams scholarship. It is unfortunate that she has never updated the work.

Two books by relatives of Williams offer considerable insight, though limited in scope, to his life. EDWINA DAKIN WILLIAMS' memoir of her son, written with the assistance of Lucy Freeman, is entertaining and touching as much because of the character of the author as because of its content. Page after page reveals the doting mother, proud of her famous son and his accomplishments as well as of her family's history, but naive concerning many of the details of his personal life and his work. There is considerable charm in the elderly southern lady's adamant denial that she is the model for Amanda Wingfield in *The Glass Menagerie* (1945) and in her explanations of her son's frustrated love affairs with several young women through the years. This readable and anecdotal book reveals, sometimes unintentionally, connections between people, settings, incidents, and traumas that were part of Williams' young life and the characters, events, and themes of his dramas. Even granting that the book was "told to" Lucy Freeman, Edwina Williams obviously possessed a way with words, a talent for brilliant turn of phrase, and a vivid memory that enabled her to recreate with credibility the scenes of the past, gifts that are reflected in the dialogue of her son's plays. The reader often comes upon passages that seem to echo the lines not just of Amanda but of numerous other Williams characters as well. Much of the material in her book, derived from letters and journals and from memory, would surely have been lost had she not recorded them. Thus subsequent biographers of Williams and their readers owe to her a considerable debt of gratitude.

When Williams died, his brother, DAKIN WILLIAMS, was at work on a biography that appeared shortly thereafter. Granting a rather large amount of sibling rivalry between the brothers, separated in age by a decade, and Dakin's need to justify his actions during the period of his brother's serious mental problems, the reader will find that this "intimate" biography nevertheless has value in that it offers yet another perspective on certain periods of the dramatist's life. Dakin Williams draws heavily on his mother's memoir and on other published sources, but there are facts to which he alone had access. If one reads his study in conjunction with *Remember Me to Tom,* a fairly well-rounded picture of the subject in relation to his family emerges. Where the books by both mother and brother are deficient, not surprisingly, is in their recounting and interpretation of those aspects of Tennessee Williams' personal life, including intimate relationships, sexual and otherwise, that occurred outside the family circle.

Because of Williams' extensive travels, he met and became friends with a great many people, despite a certain shy streak in his character. Several of these friends have recorded with varying degrees of success and candor their relationships with him. The first (and best) entry in this category is that by MAXWELL, who met Williams in 1940, at the very beginning of his phenomenal career. Though Maxwell's work covers the first 55 years of Williams' life, it is understandably the sections devoted to the 25 years when they were friends that contain the most valuable information. Maxwell provides another perspective, complementing those of family members, on a very complex personality. Like *Remember Me to Tom,* this work lacks candor in dealing with Williams' personal life, but here the mother's naieveté is replaced by Maxwell's reticence (certainly understandable in 1965) to discuss his friend's homosexuality and other aspects of his lifestyle that would have shocked many readers at the time. It was not until the 1975 publication of Williams' own *Memoirs*, indeed, that the subject was talked about openly.

Another entry in the "friends" category is the volume by RADER, a journalist who was for a few years acquainted with the dramatist. Rader pushes the facts into the mold of his predetermined notions about his subject. He is convinced, for example, that Williams was a political radical in the 1960s and that his life was essentially unhappy, even though the facts do not substantiate these evaluations. The portrait that emerges is of a sadly frustrated man unable to adjust to the world in which he lived, markedly at variance with the reality of a dramatist who produced more than 70 plays, many of them first rate. Rader draws heavily on previously published material, including the books by Edwina and Dakin Williams, and frequently introduces long quotes into his text without documentation. A further weakness of the book is what seems to be an attempt on the part of Rader to create for himself a much more significant role in the drama of Williams' life than he actually played. There is a depressing, even sleazy quality about the book, and since its biographical facts are derived from other available works, it contributes little to illuminate the life of its subject.

The closest thing to a biography that covers the entirety of Williams' life is *The Kindness of Strangers* by SPOTO. A lengthy study published two years after the playwright's death, Spoto's book can be useful in providing information essential to the scholar on events of the life and production data of the plays. Unfortunately, its benefits are limited to this single virtue, and even that virtue is not unmixed. Often facts are inaccurate or so carelessly assembled as to give false impressions of the sequence of events or the relationship between real incidents and those recorded in the plays. The reader seeking the dates of particular occurrences or performances will often be frustrated, since Spoto tends to be rather cavalier in identifying the times involved in his narrative. The text includes no chronology, something that is sorely needed to sort out the data of so prolific a writer as Williams. The overall impression is of a book assembled in haste to take timely advantage of the undeniable need for a biography and written by someone who seems almost to have a distaste for his subject and his dramas. For anyone seeking information on certain aspects of the subject, Spoto is, sadly, almost essential, but the reader should be aware of the faults and should seek to verify any facts before using them.

Currently there are at least four potential biographers engaged in various stages of research or writing. Lyle Leverich, the "authorized" biographer, was Williams' own choice to chronicle his life and worked with the playwright in the last years of his life. He has completed the first of his two-volume study, which covers the years up to the production of *The Glass Menagerie*. Another writer currently researching a life of Williams is Virginia Spencer Carr, author of a biography of Carson McCullers for which Williams wrote an introduction. Given that no reliable critical biography now exists, a serious need will be met when these studies become available to the public.

—W. Kenneth Holditch

WILLIAMS, William Carlos, 1883–1963; American poet.

Mariani, Paul, *William Carlos Williams: A New World Naked*. New York, McGraw Hill, 1981.

Whitaker, Thomas R., *William Carlos Williams*. New York, Twayne, 1968.

Whittemore, Reed, *William Carlos Williams: Poet from Jersey*. Boston, Houghton Mifflin, 1975.

*

Until the publication in 1975 of Reed Whittemore's *Poet from Jersey* (see below), the best accounts of Williams' life were his own. Though censured for some factual errors, his 1951 *Autobiography* is an effective if impressionistic account of the busy doctor-poet's life. His biographical comments in *I Wanted to Write a Poem* (edited by Edith Heal, 1958), in *Interviews with William Carlos Williams* (edited by Linda W. Wagner, 1976), and in *Yes, Mrs. Williams*, his disarming 1959 biography of his aged mother, are also helpful. Also of use is the 1968 Twayne volume by WHITAKER, the first substantial treatment of Williams to look at both the prose and the poetry. This comprehensive, accurate study is still valuable as an introduction to Williams and his work.

WHITTEMORE's focus is on Williams as difficult and ambitious American, caught in an impasse of his own making as he tried to practice medicine while simultaneously pursue a career as writer. Seeing Williams' writing as his real career, linking him throughout with that other unique poet from Jersey, Walt Whitman, Whittemore creates the life that his title emphasizes.

It is a neat paradigm, and ultimately unconvincing. Whittemore's anecdotal narrative leaves as much unexplained as it takes on. Considered aesthetically, Williams' work is far removed from Whitman's. His life, too, was consumed by concerns that Whitman chose to avoid: what practicing physician could have whimsically abandoned his day-to-day life? Williams is a much more complex person and writer than Whittemore's book suggests.

The biography is also dotted with passages that pertain more directly to Whittemore than to Williams—a long discussion of the generally unsatisfactory place of the artist in America, for example. Moreover, Whittemore tends to make ill-founded generalizations, as when he writes, "With his English-French-Spanish-Jewish blood and past [Williams] was a puritan on odd days, a libertine on even, but the puritanism was always strong enough in him to make him think he could not afford to be *too* happy." Much of the difficulty with this first biography is that it is comparatively short (358 pages of large-type text), devoting little space to the kind of proof that might have balanced the impressionistic interpretation of facts.

The obverse could be said about the MARIANI biography. Running to 770 pages of text, each page containing nearly 30% more print than the pages of the Whittemore biography, it draws on hundreds of unpublished letters and manuscript pages, as well as interviews: Mariani presents a view of Williams that echoes Williams' own self-portrait—a similarity convincing in its own right—but he buttresses that portrait with detail after detail that only the diligent scholar could have found. Diligence is, in fact, the hallmark of this book.

To illustrate the difference in tone between the Whittemore and Mariani biographies, one can compare their use of Williams' acquaintance with John Reed. Mariani notes briefly that Williams knew Reed, having met him at gatherings at Lola Ridge's. The entire discussion occurs in a section that describes Williams' period of depression after *Others* (1919) fails, before he begins to edit *Contact* (1920–23) with Robert McAlmon, while his own conception of himself as an American poet—not an expatriate—is being formed. Mariani's account of Williams' circle in the early 1920s shows this to be a difficult period for Williams. Whittemore, on the other hand, makes an issue of Williams' criticism of Reed as a radical but then goes on to criticize Williams for what Whittemore sees as his own do-nothing attitude toward social involvement. (Whittemore points out that Reed participated in the Paterson strike and went to jail because of his involvement, "while there is no record of WCW having picketed anything, signed any petitions, gone to the meeting at the Garden, or contributed a penny. What WCW did about the strike was steal a poem out of it.") The language Whittemore chooses here makes one question his motives. He then proceeds into a discussion of poetry vs. journalism, the remote poet vs. the involved, and winds his way eventually (in a digression that occupies more pages than the ostensible topic here) to a long discussion of the American dream à la Horatio Alger. In Whittemore's view, elite poets shared that dream along with would-be millionaires, and the reader thus finds Williams being attacked because he never joined the Community party, never participated in John Reed's manner, and chose instead to dream about fine art—though the comparison between Pound and Williams as effete artists who yet believed in the Horatio Alger myth is difficult to understand, especially in this context.

Mariani sticks closer to Williams' life, especially as that life is revealed through Williams' writing. Mariani sees *Paterson* as the center of all Williams' artistic efforts and spends much space on that major long poem. Because Williams lived in the service of his writing, Mariani's method is defensible. However, he documents in almost too much detail Williams' aesthetics and his relationships with other writers—from Pound, H. D., and Kreymborg to Creeley, Levertov, and Ginsberg. He also gives a great deal of attention to Williams' last years of ill health (both physical and mental), attention that may be disproportionate considering what Williams was writing during that last decade.

That sense of over-extension, of surfeit without an accompanying excitement, blunts the edge of this biography. If readers already know much of the factual material here—indeed, most of it is taken from Williams' autobiography, his novels about his wife Flossie's family, and his letters—then why was a biography of this length necessary? Mariani presents very little new material, very little new insight about this poet who worked as if possessed, aiming indefatigably toward a poetic accomplishment of the future, never reminiscent of the past. We know from Mariani only that Williams had problems with both his father and his mother, with his own sense of identity as he struggled against the influence of Ezra Pound, with the transfer of his affection from the beautiful Charlotte Herman to the loyal younger sister Flossie, his wife-to-be. Williams repeatedly gave us this information himself, and Mariani frequently uses Williams' accounts as the core of his own discussions.

One of Williams' most inexplicable personality traits, with both personal and artistic implications, was his continuous and

continual attraction to women. Out of deference to his wife and family, little has been published about the extent of Williams' extra-marital affairs, and Mrs. Williams' personal letters from her husband are closed for the standard 50 years after his death. Mariani's tactic is, unfortunately, insinuation: Williams wrote to this woman; perhaps they were also lovers. A more open stance on Mariani's part would have been helpful. Does he know more than Williams ever put into print? Williams has been dead more than 25 years, but surely people still available to interview could have given a sense of Williams as person, as physician, as neighbor, as lover. The only portrait of Williams emerging from the Mariani biography is a self-portrait. Other views, even that of Mariani himself, are missing. Rather than visit 75 libraries in search of material, Mariani might better have visited Rutherford and Paterson. Surely the child of the woman in "Four Bottles of Beer" is living there somewhere.

At issue here is the definition of "biographer": one who echoes and assembles a portrait from pieces already in place, or one who creates a believable portrait. Mariani took the former tack, and Whittemore tried to take the latter, though with comparatively little success. Useful as these books have been for students of Williams, the final, and definitive, biography of Williams remains to be written.

—Linda Wagner-Martin

WILSON, Woodrow, 1856–1924; American political leader, 28th president of the United States.

Baker, Ray Stannard, *Woodrow Wilson: Life and Letters* (8 vols.). New York, Doubleday, 1927–39.

Blum, John Morton, *Woodrow Wilson and the Politics of Morality.* Boston, Little Brown, 1956.

Bragdon, Henry Wilkinson, *Woodrow Wilson: The Academic Years.* Cambridge, Massachusetts, Belknap Press, 1967.

Cooper, John Milton, Jr., *The Warrior and the Priest: Woodrow Wilson and Theodore Roosevelt.* Cambridge, Massachusetts, Belknap Press, and London, Harvard University Press, 1983.

Garraty, John A., *Woodrow Wilson: A Great Life in Brief.* New York, Knopf, 1956.

George, Alexander L. and Juliette L. George, *Woodrow Wilson and Colonel House: A Personality Study.* New York, J. Day, 1956.

Link, Arthur S., *Wilson* (5 vols.). Princeton, New Jersey, Princeton University Press, 1947–65.

Osborn, George C., *Woodrow Wilson: The Early Years.* Baton Rouge, Louisiana State University Press, 1968.

Walworth, Arthur, *Woodrow Wilson* (2 vols.). New York, Longman, 1958.

Weinstein, Edwin A., *Woodrow Wilson: A Medical and Psychological Study.* Princeton, New Jersey, Princeton University Press, 1981.

*

LINK is the preeminent Wilson scholar, having devoted a long, distinguished career to the subject. He is editor of the Wilson papers and author of a one-volume biography as well as numerous studies of specific aspects of Wilson's career. All are of the highest quality. The multi-volume biography has become a basic source: it is comprehensive, well written, and rests on a rich assortment of manuscript materials as well as published sources.

Link's work shows great admiration for his subject, but his interpretations are still even-handed. He is, for instance, very critical of Wilson's policies toward Latin America. He is especially valuable in showing how Wilson's commitment as presidential candidate to "The New Freedom" (breaking up large corporations having monopolistic powers) became modified when he took office into something resembling Theodore Roosevelt's "The New Nationalism" (which endorsed regulating them). The emphasis in these volumes is on Wilson's mature years, with only one chapter devoted to his life before he became president of Princeton University in 1902.

Biographers of Wilson writing before Link have for the most part been rendered obsolete, since their authors did not have access to the primary sources that have since become available. BAKER's volumes are a partial exception. Baker, Wilson's Press Secretary at the Versailles Peace Conference, is uncritical in his treatment, but he does present a convenient sampling of Wilson's letters for those to whom the many published volumes of Wilson's papers are too daunting.

Two single-volume biographies nicely complement Link's study. OSBORN's work treats Wilson's youth, his education, and his development as a teacher and a scholar during his 12 years as a professor at Princeton University. BRAGDON covers some of the same ground, but nearly half his book is devoted to Wilson's tenure as president of Princeton. He analyzes in detail Wilson's unsuccessful struggle to reorganize the university's undergraduate system. Both are sound pieces of scholarship, both worth reading.

WALWORTH's study won the Pulitzer Prize. It covers Wilson's entire life, with the second volume devoted almost exclusively to World War I and the fight over the League of Nations. Walworth is highly sympathetic to his subject, as the subtitles of his books suggest. He compares Wilson's struggle at Princeton with his performance at the Versailles Peace Conference in 1919, and the later battle with the senate over the League of Nations. Walworth emphasizes the effect of Wilson's physical ailments on his behavior during all three encounters. The author belabors his subject's religious orientation throughout the volumes, and his frequent references to Wilson as "the prophet" wear thin.

BLUM's brief biography is extremely critical of Wilson. Stressing psychological factors, Blum underscores Wilson's narrowness of mind, his rigidity, and his habit of treating disagreement with impatient condescension. He also points out how easily Wilson adjusted his principles to his towering political ambition on his way to the Presidency. Blum attributes the American failure to join the League of Nations to the president's inability to tolerate disagreement or challenges to his authority. The book contains many judgments and sweeping generalizations for which no bases are offered. Blum closes with a tribute to Wilson unsupported by virtually anything found in the preceding pages. GARRATY also sets great store by psychological considerations, and arrives at many of the same conclusions as does Blum, but his book is less venomous toward its subject.

During the same year as Blum's and Garraty's books appeared, Alexander and Juliette GEORGE published a psychoanalytical study of Wilson (the title is misleading as House is treated only briefly), which explains its subject almost entirely on the basis of compensation for feelings of inferiority instilled in him by his father. the book was criticized as being based on scattered evidence insufficient to warrant such as all-embracing interpretation. In a more recent work, WEINSTEIN (a psychiatrist and neurologist) rebuts the Georges, and argues that Wilson's behavior is more properly explained by the consequences of physical ailments he suffered throughout his life—particularly a series of strokes in his later years. The authors and their respective allies carried on their battle for several years in the pages of various journals.

COOPER's dual biography devotes alternating chapters to his subjects. It is a masterly work of scholarship and interpretation. Cooper analyzes Wilson's aloof and restrained nature without indulging in facile psychological speculation, and he attributes Wilson's political outlook largely to the status of his family and to the region in which he was reared. With regard to the senate's rejection of the League of Nations, Cooper argues that Wilson's failure to prepare the American people for international involvement was more important than his personal conduct during the struggle. This is a well-written, persuasively argued study.

Wilson has continued to attract great attention over the years. There are numerous valuable monographs and articles about his involvement with progressivism, World War I, and the League of Nations, to name just a few subjects. Appropriate works should be consulted by those interested in learning more about various aspects of his career.

—Robert James Maddox

WITTGENSTEIN, Ludwig, 1889–1951; Austrian-born British philosopher.

Bartley, William W., III, *Wittgenstein*. Philadelphia, Lippincott, 1973; revised and enlarged edition, LaSalle, Illinois, Open Court, 1985; London, Cressett, 1986.

Malcolm, Norman, *Ludwig Wittgenstein: A Memoir, with a Biographical Sketch by G. H. von Wright*. London and New York, Oxford University Press, 1958; revised edition, with Wittgenstein's Letters to Malcolm, Oxford and New York, 1984.

McGuinness, Brian, *Wittgenstein, a Life: Young Ludwig 1889–1921*. Berkeley, University of California Press, and London, Duckworth, 1988.

Monk, Ray, *Ludwig Wittgenstein: The Duty of Genius*. London, Cape, and New York, Free Press/Maxwell Macmillan, 1990.

Rhees, Rush, editor, *Recollections of Wittgenstein*. Oxford and New York, Oxford University Press, 1984.

*

MALCOLM's brief memoir is widely read and accessible to all. He (as well as von Wright and Rhees, see below) was a student and friend of Wittgenstein's at Cambridge, and he writes poignantly and informatively of Wittgenstein's remarkable teaching and work habits, his dismissive attitude toward academic life, and his tastes and interests. Malcolm makes no attempt to introduce Wittgenstein's philosophy, although there are scattered allusions to what Wittgenstein was working on, and to some of his thoughts, in the late 1930s and 40s. The account is personal, contains many memorable anecdotes, and gives a vivid portrayal of how intense Wittgenstein was in all aspects of his life. The second edition contains all of Wittgenstein's letters to Malcolm. They provide a helpful backdrop to the spirit, and occasionally the content, of the memoir. G. H. von Wright's biographical sketch, published in the same volume, provides more details about Wittgenstein's life. It is brief, and now surpassed in depth by McGuinness' and Monk's biographies, but is a good companion piece to Malcolm's. Von Wright's speculations on the importance of Wittgenstein's style of writing (''It would be surprising if he were not one day ranked among the classic writers of German prose'') are helpful in drawing attention to this aspect of his work.

RHEES' collection of short memoirs by various of Wittgenstein's students and friends provides many insights into his character and thoughts that are not available elsewhere. Wittgenstein's Russian teacher, Fania Pascal, recounts the famous ''confession'' Wittgenstein once made to her and contributes helpful details behind his trips to Russia and Norway; Wittgenstein's sister, Hermine, writes (during his lifetime) of his character and his turning from engineering to philosophy; F. R. Leavis and John King contribute a series of interesting anecdotes about their meetings with Wittgenstein; M. O'C. Drury, writing from notes he took at the time, includes parts of conversations they had on topics ranging from religion to World War I to Drury's experiences working in psychiatry in a hospital. Rhees himself writes about Wittgenstein's ''confession'' as well as his plans to settle in Russia.

BARTLEY's monograph focuses on the ''mystery years'' in Wittgenstein's life from 1919–29, when he lived in Vienna and lower Austria and taught in elementary schools. Put forth as a corrective to all other biographies, since ''every portrait drawn of Wittgenstein is false,'' Bartley's work raises the issue of Wittgenstein's homosexuality. Believing that this is ''of central importance in understanding the man and his influence,'' Bartley engages in grand leaps of inference from scant evidence and in unabashed psychological speculation. The book is notable for its conjectural and sensationalistic tone, on matters ranging from Wittgenstein's philosophical influences and motivations to reasons behind various friendships. These slants render it useless as a reference work; many details in it have been questioned by scholars, and all of its claims must be checked against the work of others.

McGUINNESS' book, on the other hand, provides a great deal of documented detail about the first 30 years of Wittgenstein's life, leaving off roughly where Bartley's work begins. A sequel, covering the rest of Wittgenstein's life, is forthcoming. McGuinness' care in discovering and documenting various facts is beyond reproach, and the detail of his account is impressive. Here are to be found the dimensions of Wittgenstein's hut in Norway, as well as the results of the first heat of a sculls race at Cambridge on 9 November 1912. Diaries, notes, letters, newspapers, literary references, war archives, and obituary no-

tices are all checked in the interest of accuracy, and qualifiers such as ''possibly,'' ''presumably,'' and ''witnesses differ about . . . '' are used to indicate the quality of a source or a conjecture.

McGuinness' style of writing makes for slow reading, and although working through the text can be rewarding, one is often left wondering why references to others' writings have been included (Sextus Empiricus, Hugo von Hofmannsthal, Dante, Heraclitus, and Aristotle, for instance), and whether untranslated and unfootnoted references to Latin and Greek phrases are intended to help the reader. McGuinness justifies ''the apparent intrusions of [his] own opinions'' as being part of a literary device, but by including them he requires the reader to understand more of him—his attitudes, biases, and tastes—than one might think necessary.

Although he was given ''full access'' to Wittgenstein's manuscripts, diaries, and letters by his literary executors, McGuinness steers clear of mentioning the passages they contain of a highly personal nature. And while he emphasizes the depth of Wittgenstein's sense of his own sinful nature, it often remains a matter of conjecture as to what horrible deeds or thoughts form the basis of Wittgenstein's ruthless and unrelenting self-criticism.

MONK's biography, on the other hand, relies heavily on Wittgenstein's notebooks and letters to develop connections between his life and his work. For the first time there appear here translations of many of the coded passages from Wittgenstein's notebooks—passages referring to friends, students, colleagues, and lovers, many of which provide detailed reasons for the immense guilt he felt over his inability to live up to his high moral standards. What emerges is the picture of a man whose standards were those that no one could ever hope to achieve, and whose application of them was also extremely strict. Monk's research uncovers many new details of Wittgenstein's life that have not previously been revealed, such as a relationship he had with a Swiss woman he wished to marry, his thoughts about, and his family's dealings with, the Nazis. An appendix contains a very useful response to and corrective of many of Bartley's claims.

Monk's work also presents backgrounds for some of the kinds of philosophical issues Wittgenstein was dealing with in various periods of his life, and explanations of how he dealt with them. For the most part these discussions are philosophically uncontroversial, and as they require less expertise than McGuinness', they may help the reader who is not familiar with Wittgenstein's writings to understand some of his thought. The bridge Monk tries to build between his philosophical views and his life—what he refers to as the ''unity of [Wittgenstein's] philosophical concerns with his emotional and spiritual life''—is often weak, but the two sides of the bridge are well developed. Unlike McGuinness' presentations of much of the same material, Monk is eminently readable. And unlike Bartley's treatment of the more sensitive issues, the presentation here is neither sensationalistic nor hyperbolic. The author never intrudes on the subject, preferring to let Wittgenstein's own words and actions speak for themselves. Monk's study is a remarkable achievement that does justice to its subject.

—C. Grant Luckhardt

WOLFE, Thomas (Clayton), 1900-1938; American writer.

Donald, David Herbert, *Look Homeward Angel: A Life of Thomas Wolfe*. Boston, Little Brown, and London, Bloomsbury, 1987.

Evans, Elizabeth, *Thomas Wolfe*. New York, Ungar, 1984.

Nowell, Elizabeth, *Thomas Wolfe: A Biography*. New York, Doubleday, 1960; London, Heinemann, 1961.

Turnbull, Andrew, *Thomas Wolfe*. New York, Scribner, 1967; London, Bodley Head, 1968.

Walser, Richard G., *Thomas Wolfe, Undergraduate*. Durham, North Carolina, Duke University Press, 1977.

Wheaton, Mable Wolfe, *Thomas Wolfe and His Family*. New York, Doubleday, 1961.

*

Thomas Wolfe would seem to be the most unlikely candidate for the writer or reader of biography. He was, without question, the most autobiographical novelist in American literature and one of only two or three, including Marcel Proust, among the novelists of the world, who used their own lives almost to the exclusion of everything else as subject matter. Wolfe's careful chronicling of the facts of his own history and that of members of his family, along with his candor about his emotions and beliefs, would seem to leave nothing for the biographer to say. Elizabeth Nowell (see below) observed that when first asked to write his biography she felt that "if ever there was a writer who didn't need to be 'got right,' who had done it himself in hundreds of thousands of his own words, that writer was Thomas Wolfe."

It is, however, the very subjectivity of the novelist's approach to the writing of novels that provides the need for some outsider to take those facts, emotions, and beliefs, and turn the strong light of objectivity upon them. Furthermore, the acutely confessional nature of Wolfe's fiction seems to have sparked an intense interest in the very elements of his life he himself exposed. Consequently, there exist three major biographies of Wolfe, published over a 30-year period, each adding something significant to our understanding of this major American author.

NOWELL's biography was completed shortly before her death and published posthumously in 1960. Nowell had become Thomas Wolfe's literary agent in 1933, a position that gave her access to many details of the author's life, and she had already edited Wolfe's collected letters (1956) before undertaking to write his life. Counterbalancing the obvious advantage of such a position, however, is the fact that the biographer who knows his or her subject must struggle to achieve and retain objectivity, especially if the subject has been a close friend. Nowell achieves that better than most who have written biographies about relatives or associates. Determined that Wolfe would be the focus of all the attention of the reader and not her own part in his story, she describes her relationship to the novelist in a brief introduction, then refers to herself in the third person throughout the remainder of the work.

The result of her efforts is an effective recreation of a remarkable man who lived life to the fullest as revealed in his own words, with the added benefit of an interpretation from one who was there to hear and read those words when they were spoken and written, to witness his experiences, and to add her own view of the significance of it al. Nowell's work has many strengths other than those resulting from her closeness to the subject: honesty, sensitivity, and a command of language and style that produces a very readable narrative.

Seven years after Nowell's book appeared, TURNBULL published his biography of Wolfe. An historian who had previously edited F. Scott Fitzgerald's letters and written a life of Fitzgerald, Turnbull brought to his project the advantages of having Nowell's work to draw on, new information that had since come to light, and an objectivity that the previous biographer had, of course, lacked. Like his predecessor, Turnbull chose to write sparingly of the first 16 years of Wolfe's life. Nowell devoted to that period, which had been given a highly detailed recounting in Wolfe's *Look Homeward, Angel* (1929), only 11 pages, and Turnbull covered it in 15. Indeed, in that as in most other elements, Turnbull seems to have followed Nowell's lead, differing only in that he relies less on long quotations from Wolfe, his work, and his associates. While Turnbull's work lacks the overall value of Nowell's, it is a good, well-researched, and readable life of the man and a good critique of the quality and significance of his fiction that is well worth reading.

During the 1960s, the popularity of Wolfe's novels began to wane with the academic and general reading public, and it was not until 20 years after Turnbull's book was published that the third major biography of Wolfe appeared. In 1987, DONALD, who professed a lifelong devotion to Wolfe's fiction, particularly *Look Homeward, Angel*, which was something of a Bible for two generations of young Americans, published his study. As an historian and authority on the Civil War, Donald was here for the first time writing a book on a literary figure. He was drawn to depart from his previous works and undertake this biography, he wrote, because he found Wolfe's work to be "a remarkably full social history of the United States during the first four decades of the 20th century." Further, he argued that no one had written so well as Wolfe on family life, on small-town America, on higher education, or on New York's "harsh impersonality." This view of Wolfe as social historian adds a new dimension to Donald's work missing in those of his predecessors.

The advantages Donald brought to bear on this impressive biography also included familiarity with the work of his predecessors and access to a mass of additional material that had become available in the past two decades. Some discoveries he made shed new light on the author's famous relationships, one with his mistress, the stage designer Aline Bernstein, the other with noted Scribner editor Maxwell Perkins. Readers of Wolfe who imagine that the novelist put on paper everything there was to know about his relationship to his hometown, his family, his friends, and his lover will be surprised to discover completely new facets of his personality. Donald's masterful book combines the impressive narrative style of Nowell with the objectivity of Turnbull. The result is the best biography of Thomas Wolfe available, a comprehensive, literate, and sensitive examination of the man's life and a just and balanced critical evaluation of his fiction.

There are several smaller biographical studies, but none of much weight. EVANS' study of Wolfe, for example, an entry in the Literature and Life series from Ungar, is too brief to give any but the most surface reading of the man and his work. Only the reader totally unfamiliar with Wolfe—a high school student preparing a class assignment perhaps—would find such a work of any value. There are, however, a few specialized works with a biographical slant that deserve some attention. Mable Wolfe WHEATON, a sister of the novelist and prototype for the character of Helen in his fiction, supplies another view of the setting and many characters and events of the novels. Her somewhat naive view, combined with her genuine affection for her brother, produced a work that is a pleasure to read and valuable in that it provides considerable information on what the effect of the publication of *Look Homeward, Angel* had on the Wolfe family and on the community of Asheville, North Carolina. WALSER provides an in-depth examination of the author's student years at the University of North Carolina. Walser successfully sets out to prove that Wolfe's time at the school was of considerable importance in shaping his future literary career.

While the amount of biographical work on Thomas Wolfe is extensive, the reader interested in a detailed study of the man and his work will find any one of the three major biographies worthwhile. The best of the three, for several reasons, is that of David Herbert Donald.

—W. Kenneth Holditch

WOLLSTONECRAFT, Mary, 1759–1797; English writer and feminist.

Flexner, Eleanor, *Mary Wollstonecraft: A Biography*. New York, Coward McCann, 1972.

George, Margaret, *One Woman's "Situation": A Study of Mary Wollstonecraft*. Urbana, University of Illinois Press, 1970.

Pennell, Elizabeth Robins, *Life of Mary Wollstonecraft*. Boston, Roberts, 1884; as *Mary Wollstonecraft Godwin*, London, W. H. Allen, 1885.

Sunstein, Emily W., *A Different Face: The Life of Mary Wollstonecraft*. New York, Harper, 1975.

Tomalin, Claire, *The Life and Death of Mary Wollstonecraft*. London, Weidenfeld and Nicolson, 1974; New York, Harcourt, 1975.

Wardle, Ralph M., *Mary Wollstonecraft: A Critical Biography*. Lawrence, University of Kansas Press, 1951; revised edition, Lincoln, University of Nebraska Press, 1966.

*

As part of the Famous Women Series, PENNELL's was the first full-length biography of Wollstonecraft. It attempted to counter the earlier denunciations and charges that had nearly buried the memory of the pioneer of women's rights. Pennell relied chiefly on William Godwin's *Memoirs of the Author of a Vindication of the Rights of Woman* (1798) and on Kegan Paul's *Prefatory Memoir* to the *Letters to Imlay* (1879). From these Pennell presents her version of the life and works set in the historical context. Extremely sympathetic throughout, she emphasizes the purity of Wollstonecraft's principles despite being unconventional. The relationships with Fuseli and Imlay are put into the best light, even to the point of denying the infatuation with Fuseli and defending at great length Wollstonecraft's pretense of marriage to Imlay. The work is now obviously dated,

and many documents were not available at the time. Not even Wollstonecraft's novel *Mary, A Fiction* (1788) could be found. Though Pennell says that the faults of *A Vindication of the Rights of Woman* (1792) are many, she correctly assesses the book as an important forerunner of the women's movement. The biography gives a good perspective of Wollstonecraft by a late 19th-century feminist.

By the middle of this century, many new documents became available, resulting in the scholarly work of WARDLE, who drew on the material of Clark Durant in his supplement to his edition of Godwin's *Memoirs* and the letters in the Abinger collection. In this thoroughly researched critical biography, Wardle relates the details of Wollstonecraft's family, early life, and the main events of her 38 years. In the last chapter he carries the story beyond Wollstonecraft's death and deals with Godwin's second marriage, the fate of Fanny Imlay and the influence of the famous mother on her daughter Mary Shelley, all in greater detail than other biographers. He analyzes Wollstonecraft's works in depth but unsympathetically asserts that the unfinished novel *Maria* (1798) is "scarcely readable" and only has autobiographical interest, and that in *A Vindication of the Rights of Woman* Wollstonecraft's picture of the plight of women in her time was "overdrawn." Particularly in his assumptions about women and women's issues, Wardle is now dated, and too often he treats Wollstonecraft's works as antiques, unsuited for modern tastes. Nevertheless, his narrative is readable, thorough, and useful for the scholar.

Because of the development of the women's movement in the later part of this century, and because of Wardle's failure to emphasize Wollstonecraft's feminism, GEORGE's concise study reinterprets the facts of Wollstonecraft's life from a feminist perspective. George asserts that Wollstonecraft maintained her individuality and that her rebellion became "an active, creative force that pushed her to live in critical opposition to her society." Her feminism was the product of her life experience in "the driving spontaneity of her decisions, choices, and actions." Thus her record is an important feminist document. Although the study offers nothing new in sources or facts, it does present an incisive psychological interpretation, and it provides a good balance to Wardle, her main source.

Of the next three major biographies published in three years, FLEXNER's work is first. Based on previous biographies and original scholarship, it emphasizes Wollstonecraft's life rather than the intellectual trends of the times. Also, as indicated in the preface, it attempts to explain why Wollstonecraft was virtually alone among the women of her time in demanding basic rights for women. Although the *Christian Science Monitor* objected to Flexner's "tabloid psychologizing across the centuries" (13 September 1972), the biography is valuable for its modern explanations of Wollstonecraft's physical and emotional ills as the result of her repressed anger toward her family, especially her father. Flexner sharply disagrees with Wardle on some points, most notably Wollstonecraft's relationship to Waterhouse and the censored letters to George Blood of 1785–86. Overall, Flexner maintains a balanced view of her subject and keeps her narrative pace moving smoothly. The work contains a number of good, clear illustrations and portraits and six appendices. There are extensive notes to the text, but no bibliography.

Differing from the other recent biographies in many of her details as well as interpretations of some major events, TOMA-

LIN is more critical of her subject than Wardle, Flexner, or, a year later, Sunstein. For example, Tomalin faults Wollstonecraft for her role in breaking up the marriage of her sister Eliza, and she emphasizes the irritations and complaints that Wollstonecraft and Godwin had for each other. Tomalin says Wardle's case for "Neptune" being Waterhouse is convincing, but she leaves it at that. Some valuable additions include the corrected date of Wollstonecraft's mother's death, medical details about the birth of her daughter, which brought death to Wollstonecraft, and finally the answer to the question of what happened to Eliza's baby. An excellent final chapter summarizes the influence of Wollstonecraft on a number of women writers and their views of female education. Useful for the scholar are the extensive notes at the end and the annotated bibliography. There are also two appendices, a chronology, and a Wollstonecraft family tree. Janet Todd labels this work "the wittiest and most fluent of the recent biographies" (*Mary Wollstonecraft: An Annotated Bibliography*, New York, Garland, 1976).

In approaching SUNSTEIN's biography, the reader might be led to expect a totally different treatment on the basis of the title and the introductory portrait of Wollstonecraft by an unknown artist, one not seen in the other biographies. But such is not the case. Sunstein admits her debt to the other biographers and says she does not want anything to come between her study and the sources: the events of Wollstonecraft's life and everything she wrote. Other than her obvious sympathy for her subject, which surpasses that of more recent biographers, Sunstein has nothing new to offer. She does give a fairly full account of the life with psychological insights and, like the other biographers, she uses Wollstonecraft's novels for their autobiographical value while ignoring other possible approaches. Her summaries of the writings are generally sympathetic, but she dismisses *Maria* as "melodramatic," "wildly improbable," and "downright dull." There are few original thoughts about the events; Sunstein relies heavily on previous studies and quotes too generously from the letters. At the end of the work are bibliographical references and short notes on the chapters.

—Marlene A. Hess

WOLSEY, Thomas, *ca.* 1475–1530; English cardinal and statesman.

Cavendish, George, *The Memoirs of that Great Favourite, Cardinal Wolsey*. London, B. Bragg, 1706 (originally written in 1557).

Creighton, Mandell, *Cardinal Wolsey*. London and New York, Macmillan, 1891.

Ferguson, Charles W., *Naked to Mine Enemies: The Life of Cardinal Wolsey*. Boston, Little Brown, and London, Longman, 1958.

Fiddes, Richard, *The Life of Cardinal Wolsey*. London, J. Barber, 1724.

Guy, John Alexander, *The Cardinal's Court: The Impact of Thomas Wolsey in Star Chamber*. Hassocks, Harvester, and Totowa, New Jersey, Rowman and Littlefield, 1977.

Harvey, Nancy Lenz, *Thomas Cardinal Wolsey*. New York, Macmillan, and London, Collier Macmillan, 1980.

Howard, George, *Wolsey: The Cardinal and His Times*. London, 1824.

Pollard, A. F., *Wolsey*. London and New York, Longman, 1929.

Ridley, Jasper, *The Statesman and the Fanatic: Thomas Wolsey and Thomas More*. London, Constable, 1982; as *Statesman and Saint: Cardinal Wolsey, Sir Thomas More, and the Politics of Henry VIII*, New York, Viking, 1983.

Storer, Thomas, *The Life and Death of Thomas Wolsey, Cardinall, Divided into Three Parts: His Aspiring, Triumph, and Death*. London, T. Dawson, 1599.

Taunton, Ethereal Luke, *Thomas Wolsey, Legate and Reformer*. London, J. Lane, 1902.

Williams, Neville, *The Cardinal and the Secretary*. London, Weidenfeld and Nicolson, 1975; New York, Macmillan, 1976.

*

Among Wolsey's contemporaries, CAVENDISH produced the only significant biography of him. Cavendish was employed by Wolsey and produced a sympathetic interpretation. He structured his biography on Wolsey's character and advanced the classical dichotomy of the tragic fall from power of a great man. Wolsey emerges here as a strong and able leader who was industrious and loyal to Henry VIII and to the Church; his greatness was manifested in his consistency and in the strength of his convictions during the turbulence of the late 1520s. STORER was more critical (more Protestant) than Cavendish but nonetheless admired Wolsey for his ambition and for his early achievements. In the 18th century FIDDES sustained this interpretation in his scholarly though biased biography; Fiddes was condemned by his contemporaries for his sympathetic treatment of Wolsey and of the pre-Reformation Church in England.

While the impact of the Anglican Reformation on the interpretations of Wolsey can be detected through the mid-20th century, 19th-century historians such as HOWARD, CREIGHTON, and TAUNTON concluded that Wolsey was one of the great statesmen of his age. Taunton, a Catholic priest, contended that Wolsey was not only a highly effective political leader but also a great churchman. "Truth to say" writes Taunton, "the more Wolsey is studied in the setting of his own times, the greater every way does he appear. He stands head and shoulders above all his ecclesiastical contemporaries." Taunton, who relied almost exclusively on published State Papers and earlier biographies, argued that there was no real evidence to indicate that Wolsey had two illegitimate sons. Taunton suggests that Wolsey's greatness and contribution have not been recognized. On the title page of his biography, Taunton quotes Shakespeare: "That churchman bears a bounteous mind indeed, a hand as fruitful as the land that feeds us; his dews fall everywhere."

In the 20th century biographers of Wolsey have become more scholarly and imaginative. POLLARD's biography remains valuable for its comprehensiveness. Pollard points out that Wolsey the statesman and churchman made numerous errors but was an able and willing minister to Henry VIII. FERGUSON's study pursues the theme of Wolsey's life as tragedy; however, in this biography, Wolsey is more clearly the tragic hero—a victim of circumstances and of changing forces over which he had no control. Ferguson credits Wolsey with the diplomatic triumph that improved England's position *vis-à-vis* the Continental Powers; for 15 years Wolsey acted as an intelligent and responsible agent for Henry VIII, and the nation prospered. Ferguson relies heavily on J. S. Brewer's *Letters and Papers, Foreign and Domestic, of the Reign of Henry VIII* (1876), and he utilizes other printed primary sources including State Papers, the Spanish Calendar, and the Venetian Calendar.

Wolsey's life as tragedy is evident in HARVEY's recent biography, which is directed at a general audience. Of particular interest in Harvey's work is the description of Thomas More's role in Wolsey's fall; Wolsey was amazed and distressed by the vicious nature of More's attack. Harvey's sources include a range of printed primary sources acquired through the Folger Shakespeare Library, the British Library, and the National Portrait Gallery in London. GUY's biography goes beyond an analysis of Wolsey's career and treats the subject of Wolsey's court proceedings in detail. Guy's Wolsey is an efficient albeit not very farsighted administrator.

Perhaps the most significant biographies of Wolsey are to be found in the dual-biographies produced by Williams and Ridley. WILLIAMS' biographical study of Thomas Wolsey and Thomas Cromwell provides valuable insights into the practice of power and the administration during English government of the 1520s and 1530s. Williams, who relies on the archives in the British Museum and the Public Records Office, develops an interpretation of Wolsey as "the proud prelate, tenacious of clerical privilege and always looking over his shoulder towards Rome, who endeavoured through his mastery of diplomacy to make himself the 'arbiter of Europe.'" Williams concludes that Wolsey identified with the maintenance of the *status quo* and neglected domestic affairs, whereas his successor, Thomas Cromwell, directed his efforts toward changing accommodation to the new political realities of the period; Cromwell was comfortable with domestic developments but ill-equipped to handle the intricacies of increasingly complex foreign relationships. Williams argues that Wolsey and Cromwell served the interests of Henry VIII; both served as well-rewarded public servants who were political buffers and were expendable. While Williams notes Cromwell's expertise in manipulating the Reformation-Parliament and in extending monarchial power, Wolsey emerges as the more intriguing of the two ministers because of his clerical office and multiple ambitions. Williams appends an outstanding bibliography to his narrative.

As the title of his work suggests, RIDLEY presents a biographical analysis of Thomas Wolsey and Thomas More. Ridley concludes "that as a powerful first minister the pragmatic and much maligned Cardinal Wolsey was in fact far preferable to the idealist-turned-fanatic Thomas More." Unlike other comparative or dual biographies, Ridley's work is not structured in such a way as to separate Wolsey and More; rather, Ridley has succeeded in integrating their lives chronologically. Ridley, who uses a wide range of primary and secondary sources, concludes that "Wolsey, for all his faults—and he had many—was a great statesman, a man of natural dignity with a generous temperament, who preserved a relatively tolerant regime until he fell from power and was succeeded by More." The historiographical irony is that Cardinal Wolsey—long disparaged as a Catholic—would find favorable treatment by revisionist scholars who concluded that More was an "intellectual fanatic" who degenerated

into "a psychopathic courtier" and then to "a prosecuting bigot." While Ridley's biography constitutes the most provocative recent study of Wolsey, and Williams' and Pollard's books are exceptional for their scholarship, the definitive biography of Cardinal Thomas Wolsey is yet to be written.

—William T. Walker

WOOLF, Virginia, 1882–1941; English writer.

Bell, Quentin, *Virginia Woolf: A Biography* (2 vols.). London, Hogarth Press, and New York, Harcourt, 1972.
Bishop, Edward, *A Virginia Woolf Chronology*. London, Macmillan, and Boston, G. K. Hall, 1989.
Forster, E. M., *Virginia Woolf*. Cambridge, Cambridge University Press, and New York, Harcourt, 1942.
Pippett, Aileen, *The Moth and the Star: A Biography of Virginia Woolf*. Boston, Little Brown, 1955.
Rose, Phyllis, *Woman of Letters: A Life of Virginia Woolf*. London, Routledge, and New York, Oxford University Press, 1978.
Spater, George and Ian Parsons, *A Marriage of True Minds: An Intimate Portrait of Leonard and Virginia Woolf*. London, Cape, and New York, Harcourt, 1977.

*

The materials for the life of Virginia Woolf are so voluminous as to be overwhelming. The Bloomsbury group, of which she was a leading member, was composed of highly articulate people, much given to gossip about one another, which was recorded in their correspondence and diaries. They had easy access to publishers (Virginia and her husband Leonard were owners of the successful Hogarth Press) and the process of bringing all the material relevant to Virginia Woolf's life into print, which began during her lifetime, continues to the present day. She herself published two books, *A Room of One's Own* (1929) and *Three Guineas* (1938) that are largely autobiographical.

After her death several of Virginia Woolf's friends and associates put their impressions of her into print. Among the notable early works devoted to Woolf are FORSTER's 1942 Rede lecture and the essay by Duncan Grant ("Virginia Woolf" in *Horizon*, 1941). Most of these early portraits, however, which remain valuable materials for Woolf's biography, are either scattered throughout their writers' autobiographies (such as Stephen Spender's *World within World*, 1951, and John Lehmann's *Autobiography*, 2 vols., 1955–60) or find their place in works whose scope extends beyond the life of Virginia Woolf (such as Clive Bell's *Old Friends*, 1957, and John Maynard Keynes' *Two Memoirs*, 1949; other notable works of this kind include J. K. Johnstone, *The Bloomsbury Group*, 1954; Richard Kennedy, *A Boy at the Hogarth Press*, 1972; Leon Edel, *Bloomsbury: A House of Lions*, 1979; and Angelica Garnett [Virginia Woolf's niece], *Deceived with Kindness: A Bloomsbury Childhood*, 1984). Leonard Woolf published a selection of extracts from her diary (*A Writer's Diary*, 1953), which provided further material for a full-scale biography. A brief thesis-type biography by one outside this circle, PIPPETT, followed, based mainly on previously published materials.

Leonard Woolf began in 1960 publishing his autobiography (*Autobiographies*, 5 vols., 1960–70), which naturally included much further information about Virginia Woolf. Shortly before the latter's death, Leonard had commissioned her nephew, BELL, to write a full biography. This two-volume work is a masterly study. Bell had the advantage not only of being a member of the family and knowing his aunt but also of having access to the collection of documents both in public hands (notably in the New York Public Library) and in the possession of Leonard Woolf. Bell handled this mass of material expertly to produce a fine balance between accurate documentation and a well-written narrative. His is unquestionably the major biography of Virginia Woolf.

Since the publication of Bell's work in 1972, however, further biographical assessments and documentation have appeared in print. One important source is Nigel Nicolson, the son of Vita Sackville-West, who in his biography of his parents (*Portrait of a Marriage*, 1973) devotes two chapters to Virginia Woolf's relationship with Vita. Woolf's letters (*The Letters of Virginia Woolf*, edited by Nigel Nicolson and Joanne Trautmann, 6 vols., 1975–80) and diaries (*The Diary of Virginia Woolf*, edited by Anne Oliver Bell and A. McNeillie, 5 vols., 1977–84) together provide an unparalleled source for biographical material.

The complex nature of Virginia Woolf continues to attract writers of various types, from the purely factual chronological approach of BISHOP to the feminist approach of ROSE. The deposit after Leonard Woolf's death of his archive of over 60,000 documents in the University of Sussex has led to an interesting revaluation by two "outsiders": SPATER AND PARSONS' *Marriage of True Minds* must be read as a valuable addition to the major biography by Quentin Bell.

—Ian A. Gordon

WORDSWORTH, William, 1770–1850; English poet.

Davies, Hunter, *William Wordsworth: A Biography*. New York, Atheneum, and London, Weidenfeld and Nicolson, 1980.

Gill, Stephen, *William Wordsworth: A Life*. Oxford, Clarendon Press, and New York, Oxford University Press, 1989.

Harper, George McLean, *William Wordsworth: His Life, Works, and Influence* (2 vols.). New York, Scribner, and London, J. Murray, 1916.

Legouis, Émile, *The Early Life of William Wordsworth, 1770–98*, translated by J. W. Matthews. London, Dent, and New York, Scribner, 1897 (originally published by G. Masson, Paris, 1896).

Meyer, George Wilbur, *Wordsworth's Formative Years*. Ann Arbor, University of Michigan Press, 1943.

Moorman, Mary, *William Wordsworth: A Biography* (2 vols.). Oxford, Clarendon Press, 1957–65.

Reed, Mark L., *Wordsworth: The Chronology of the Early Years 1770–99*. Cambridge, Massachusetts, Harvard University Press, 1967.

Reed, Mark L., *Wordsworth: The Chronology of the Middle Years 1800–15*. Cambridge, Massachusetts, Harvard University Press, 1975.

Wordsworth, Christopher, *Memoirs of William Wordsworth* (2 vols.). London, Moxon, and Boston, Ticknor Reed, 1851.

*

Wordsworth made the story of his own life the foundation of his greatest poetry. But his most famous autobiographical poem, *The Prelude*, is not a memoir, as scholars know; it is an imaginative reconstruction of how his particular life made possible his art. The life as it appears in the work is only a beginning for any serious biographer. At the heart of that autobiographical work (and of the history of the Romantic period) is the French Revolution. Wordsworth began his career as a radical supporter of the Revolution and ended it as a Tory supporter of the Crown and the Established Church. Many have traced, parallel to this shift, a decline in his poetic powers. In one way or another, this shift in beliefs and apparent poetic decline has been the focus of everything written about his life.

CHRISTOPHER WORDSWORTH, the poet's nephew, defended his uncle by glossing over the early radical years. Bishop of Lincoln and a writer on religious topics, he wrote his book the year after the poet's death, emphasizing the relatively eminent social status achieved by the later Wordsworth (in many ways a Victorian), along with his religious orthodoxy. The result is a properly restrained, discreet, and—inevitably—only partial portrait. It claims only to be a kind of "biographical commentary on the Poet's works," drawing on letters and other records, not a complete biography. The *Memoirs* include the autobiographical memoranda dictated by the poet in 1847, but these are very general. On the crucial years in France, for example, Wordsworth offers only a few sentences, concluding: "But for these matters see also the Poem." In this insistence that the life be found in the works or not at all, the poet clearly influenced his nephew's reticent *Memoirs*.

During the 19th century numerous shorter biographical sketches appeared in magazines or personal memoirs, so that the general outlines of Wordsworth's life became widely known (see Walter Swayze, "Early Wordsworth Biography," *Bulletin of the New York Public Library*, 1960). Christopher Wordsworth's *Memoirs*, then, added little to the public's knowledge. Late in the century the French writer LEGOUIS published an important if limited study of the poet's childhood and youth, the first serious biographical study to focus on *The Prelude* as an aid for examining at least a portion of Wordsworth's life. In fact, Legouis presents his account as a commentary on the poem rather than as a biography proper.

In part as a response to Legouis and his methods, MEYER recounted Wordsworth's early years again in 1943, arguing that *The Prelude* is an unreliable source of biographical information. Though critics now assume that any imaginative work—even an autobiographical one—is never simply a mirror of life or reality, Meyer raised basic questions that have continued to be important in Wordsworth studies. The complex relationship between life and art in Wordsworth's poetry has been a crucial issue behind the two major scholarly biographies of this century, by Harper and Moorman (see below). It has become increasingly clear that the poet himself explored this issue and even made it the subject matter of much of his work.

HARPER's was the first serious, full-length biography, and it remained the standard scholarly account for many years. It is carefully researched and makes some new contributions to the record. For example, it first made publicly known the existence of Wordsworth's illegitimate French daughter. (Harper continued his research in later works, prompting even further detective work by Legouis and others.) More important, Harper fully appreciated the significance of his subject's life, focusing from the beginning on "artistic mastery" as Wordsworth's defining feature. He also judged Wordsworth "the most philosophical of all our great poets." However, in an understandable attempt to offset earlier antiseptic portraits, Harper sometimes overemphasizes Wordsworth's political shift, depicting his life as "broken in the middle," with "two halves" that remain "incongruous." This way of putting it is too black and white. Harper goes on to treat what he sees as the poet's "Retreat and Surrender," his "decline in moral vigour" after 1815, with undisguised opprobrium, in effect chastising his subject. Almost everyone agrees that such a political shift took place, but the most helpful criticism probes its motivations and causes in light of the larger context of England after Waterloo. Nonetheless, Harper deserves great credit for asserting so early on that Wordsworth's art had an essentially *political* basis, that questions of what has since come to be called "ideology" must be central to any serious study of his art or his life.

When it appeared, MOORMAN's biography largely superseded Harper as the standard scholarly work. It is a judicious, sympathetic, and historically detailed account of the whole of Wordsworth's life, scrupulously researched and fully documented. Moorman defends—or at least attempts to explain as understandable—many of Wordsworth's later political positions, and her two volumes (each with a convenient separate index) combine for a complete and balanced coverage of Wordsworth's earlier and later years. Moorman was able to take advantage of some new scholarship, particularly on the early drafts of *The Prelude*, but her readings of the poetry remain limited. She is more interested in using the poems as evidence to shed light on the life than in practicing literary criticism. In general, she presents no startling discoveries or major revisions in interpretation, but marshals what she sees as the available facts in a clear narrative that works at every turn to remain fair. This objective approach is what has made her work retain its importance to students of Wordsworth.

Since Moorman's volumes appeared, there have been several important developments in Wordsworth studies. First, that complex primary document, *The Prelude*, has been re-examined and re-edited in all its versions, 1799, 1805, and 1850, and the poet's revisions themselves have become an important topic for critics. Then, several scholarly editions of Wordsworth's works have been published, thus increasing the tools available to anyone writing on his life in context. These include the outstanding Cornell editions, which offer a wealth of textual information, and REED's minutely detailed *Chronology*, which simply plots the verifiable activities of the poet, day by day. Reed's impressive list of particular facts in their order makes for surprisingly fascinating reading, a kind of skeletal biography. As a research tool, it is unmatched. Finally, Beth Darlington published an important

edition of *The Love Letters of William and Mary Wordsworth* (1981), provoking reassessments of the personalities of both correspondents. Even popular books on the poet must now take into account at least some of this new work.

DAVIES' book is openly popular and very readable: it "is not meant for scholars." The author, a journalist (and the Beatles' biographer), set out to write the biography he wanted to read but could not find, one "which could be understood by the educated layman" (as stated in the endpaper blurb). Davies' aims here are modest. He has "tried to avoid expressing too many opinions" or shaping the life "in order to form a strong narrative." Still, his book illustrates how some degree of "scholarly research" is needed even by such intentionally popular treatments of historical figures. Davies makes limited use, with the acknowledged help of Beth Darlington, of the love letters of William and Mary Wordsworth, then recently discovered but still unpublished. And Davies has some difficulty dealing with one of the central issues—the place of *The Prelude*. He claims too easily (and illogically) that, because we are forced to rely on the poem as a source, "the facts of Wordsworth's early life can be simply stated."

GILL's much more serious work will be no less accessible to most "general" readers, but its excellent scholarship and historical sense make it a great deal more reliable and lasting. Gill is an editor and scholar of Wordsworth with an expert's knowledge of the primary sources and documents, especially the massive collection of Wordsworth's own manuscripts that have been so important to recent criticism. Gill intends, he says, to provide "the general reader" with a new biography that takes account of recent scholarship and that focuses in particular on "Wordsworth the writer." By this he means that the poet's profession, more than his domestic life, dominates the book's narrative. Textual criticism informs Gill's appreciation of the publication history of each individual volume of Wordsworth's poetry, the circumstances surrounding its printing, the arrangement of poems within it, and the contemporary reception of the work. Rather than more close reading of well-known individual texts, Gill often provides the history of Wordsworth's public role and artistic productivity.

New scholarship is generally well applied by Gill (though he devotes too little space to the newly available love letters). He begins with a sensitive introduction on the problem of *The Prelude*, and throughout shows an awareness of sophisticated readings of that work's complexities in recent decades. In many places, Gill's style reflects something of recent historical criticism's increased self-consciousness when writing about the past. Rather than fictionalize, Gill tends to make his own lack of information the subject for discussion, as in this passage on the reunion with Wordsworth's French lover and child: "Where one would most value Dorothy's perceptive observation and comment the journal fails. . . . How did she feel as she met the woman her brother had loved? What was Annette's reaction to the man who had caused her so much pain? And Caroline? . . ." This is both accessibly human in its curiosity and sympathy and scholarly in its recognition of the limits of historical knowledge.

Here, thankfully, the rigid division between "scholarly" (accurately documented but dry-as-dust) and "popular" (casual and often fictionalized) biography has broken down. Most educated general readers with an interest in Wordsworth will enjoy Gill's story, and scholars will profit from his marshalling of evidence. Overall, his meticulous research and clearly written narrative, which retains its respect for the unknowable, makes Gill's the best all-around biography now available on this most important of the Romantic poets.

—Steven E. Jones

WREN, Sir Christopher, 1632–1723; English architect, astronomer, and mathematician.

Beard, Geoffrey W., *The Work of Christopher Wren.* Edinburgh, J. Bartholomew, 1982; London, Bloomsbury Books, 1987.

Bennett, J. A., *The Mathematical Science of Christopher Wren.* Cambridge and New York, Cambridge University Press, 1982.

Briggs, Martin Shaw, *Christopher Wren.* London, Falcon Educational Books, 1951.

Briggs, Martin Shaw, *Wren, the Incomparable.* London, Allen and Unwin, 1953.

Downes, Kerry, *Christopher Wren.* London, A. Lane, 1971.

Downes, Kerry, *The Architecture of Wren.* London, Granada, and New York, Universe Books, 1982; 2nd revised edition, Reading, England, Redhedge, 1988.

Elmes, James, *Memoirs of the Life and Works of Sir Christopher Wren.* London, Priestly and Weale, 1823.

Fürst, Viktor, *The Architecture of Sir Christopher Wren.* London, Lund Humphries, 1956.

Hutchison, Harold F., *Sir Christopher Wren: A Biography.* New York, Stein and Day, and London, Gollancz, 1976.

Lindsay, John (John St. Clair Muriel), *Wren, His Work and Times.* London, Rich and Cowan, 1951; New York, Philosophical Library, 1952.

Little, Bryan D. G., *Sir Christopher Wren: A Historical Biography.* London, R. Hale, 1975.

Milman, Lena, *Sir Christopher Wren.* London, Duckworth, and New York, Scribner, 1908.

Pevsner, Nikolaus, *Christopher Wren 1632–1723.* New York, Universe Books, 1960.

Phillimore, Lucy, *Sir Christopher Wren, His Family and His Times.* London, K. Paul, and New York, Harper, 1881.

Sekler, Eduard F., *Wren and His Place in European Architecture.* London, Faber, and New York, Macmillan, 1956.

Stratton, Arthur James, *The Life, Work, and Influence of Sir Christopher Wren.* Liverpool, D. Marples, 1897.

Summerson, John, *Sir Christopher Wren.* London, Collins, and New York, Macmillan, 1953.

Weaver, Lawrence, *Sir Christopher Wren, Scientist, Scholar and Architect.* London, Country Life, and New York, Scribner, 1923.

Webb, Geoffrey, *Wren.* London, Duckworth, 1937.

Whinney, Margaret, *Wren.* London, Thames and Hudson, 1971; as *Christopher Wren,* New York, Praeger, 1971.

Whitaker-Wilson, Cecil, *Sir Christopher Wren: His Life and Times.* London, Methuen, and New York, R. M. McBride, 1932.

Wren, Christopher, Jr., editor, *Parentalia; or, Memoirs of the Family of Wrens.* London, T. Osborn and R. Dodsley, 1750; as *Life and Works of Sir Christopher Wren from the Parentalia, or Memoirs by His Son Christopher,* edited by Ernest J. Enthoven, London, E. Arnold, and New York, S. Buckley, 1903.

*

All biographies of Sir Christopher Wren depend in large part on *Parentalia,* published in 1750, which contains documents related to Wren, his father, and his uncle. This material was compiled by Wren's son, CHRISTOPHER WREN JR., beginning a few years before his father's death in 1723. Concerned with preserving his father's memory, Christopher Jr. attempted to transcribe original documents, some no longer extant, relating to his father's life and scientific and architectural work as accurately as possible. The accompanying biographical account of his father, however, cannot be relied on as an accurate record. It suffers from an uncritical use of material typical of the early 18th-century antiquarian, who in this case was further motivated to make certain modifications in order to memorialize his father.

The pioneering biographical work was by ELMES in 1823, the centenary of Wren's death. While it provides a chronological narrative of Wren's life and work as both a scientist and architect, it suffers from great inaccuracy and remains primarily a compilation of facts from *Parentalia* and a few other contemporary sources. The appearance of the work itself reflects the renewed appreciation in England for Wren's architecture after almost a century of neglect. In fact Elmes, an architect, was encouraged in his biographical endeavor by his friend C. R. Cockerell, the well-known Early Victorian architect whose enthusiasm for Wren's designs as a source of inspiration was reflected in his famous 1838 drawing of 60 of Wren's buildings, entitled "A Tribute to Sir Christopher Wren."

Although Elmes' biography helped to establish Wren's importance as a great English architect, it was followed by another period of neglect and disfavor, which ended near the close of the 19th century. The renewed appreciation is reflected in a series of biographies that appeared at almost ten year intervals from 1881. All are hampered by the plain fact that little information is available about the events of Wren's life and his personality. Those biographies by PHILLIMORE, STRATTON, MILMAN, and WHITAKER-WILSON are based for the most part on *Parentalia* and Elmes' book, sometimes enlivening the bare facts with passages from the diaries of Pepys and Evelyn or with imaginary conversations or scenes. Wren's significant accomplishments in science are given only a limited enumeration. More space is devoted to his enormous corpus of buildings, but without any critical examination. The biographies by WEAVER and WEBB should be noted for making use of previously untapped primary sources. Indeed, Webb's contribution to the "Great Lives" series stands out from this group, being highly informative and readable, although it has no illustrations. Using a wide range of primary sources, Webb was the first to provide a comprehensive view of Wren's life and work, both scientific and architectural, as well as a clear and succinct description and analysis of his significant buildings.

Webb's work indicates that a significant change was taking place in the focus and depth of biographies on Wren due to the publication by Oxford University Press of the 20 volumes of the Wren Society from 1923 to 1943, reproducing all documents, drawings, and engravings relating to his architectural work. Authors, primarily architectural historians, have used this extensive material to produce works that are less devoted to rehashing biographical details and more to a scholarly analysis of the nature of his architectural accomplishments. For the general reader there are the contributions by SUMMERSON to the "Brief Lives" series and by PEVSNER to the "Architecture Series," both only adequately illustrated. These works provide clear and readable accounts of Wren's life, but also treat certain issues that make them valuable to the specialized reader— Summerson's highly insightful discussion of the nature of Wren's scientific and architectural work and their relationship, and Pevsner's formal analysis of Wren's city churches followed by a perceptive explanation of his use of different styles. There are two other equally scholarly works that condense their treatments of Wren's life in order to allow extensive discussions of the formal influences on his architecture. SEKLER's clear, historically sound, and well-illustrated presentation is preferable to FÜRST's poorly organized, obtuse, and often controversial discussion, which nevertheless is valuable for its attempt to use the catalog of Wren's library as an indication of the range of his knowledge. These four publications merit study by the serious student of Wren's architecture.

For more recent introductions to this subject, which would also be of interest to specialists, there are the 1971 publications by WHINNEY and by DOWNES. Both equally well written and well illustrated, they are concerned with analyzing Wren's buildings in relationship to the contemporary architectural setting and continental influences. Downes goes further to consider Wren's intellectual orientation and its relationship to his architecture, a theme taken further in his 1982 publication. Scholarly and comprehensive in its approach, eloquently written, and illustrated with high quality photographs, this is the definitive large-scale monograph on Wren's architecture.

While these authors have focused on Wren as an architect, others have taken different viewpoints. LITTLE's meticulous chronological treatment of the life of Wren and his contemporaries is concerned with establishing the impact of social and political events on his architectural work. The first scholarly publication devoted to Wren's scientific activities and achievements is by BENNETT, who also attempts to link these philosophical attitudes to Wren's approach to building design. These works, along with Downes' 1982 monograph, are essential reading for the serious student of Wren, but may be more difficult for the beginner.

For the beginning reader, numerous popular accounts have been written since the Wren Society volumes appeared. These include the general treatments by BRIGGS and LINDSAY, now dated, and the more recent biography by HUTCHISON. The best of this type is now BEARD's publication in honor of the 350th anniversary of Wren's birth. Its short, readable biographical text provides a good introduction to Wren as an architect and scientist, enhanced by many high-quality illustrations, some in color, as well as an annotated list of the plates. Although geared toward a popular audience, Beard's use of the recent

scholarly publications, recorded in footnotes and a bibliography, makes this work a sound prelude to Downes' and Bennett's definitive investigations of the more intricate problems of Wren's life and work.

—Lydia M. Soo

WRIGHT, Orville, 1871–1948; **WRIGHT, Wilbur,** 1867–1912; American pioneers in aviation.

Combs, Harry, with Martin Caidin, *Kill Devil Hill: Discovering the Secret of the Wright Brothers.* Boston, Houghton Mifflin, 1979; as *Kill Devil Hill: The Epic of the Wright Brothers 1899–1909*, London, Secker and Warburg, 1980.

Crouch, Tom D., *The Bishop's Boys: A Life of Wilbur and Orville Wright.* New York, Norton, 1989.

Freudenthal, Elsbeth E., *Flight into History: The Wright Brothers and the Air Age.* Norman, University of Oklahoma Press, 1949.

Howard, Fred, *Wilbur and Orville: A Biography of the Wright Brothers.* New York, Knopf, 1987; London, Hale, 1988.

Kelly, Fred C., *The Wright Brothers: A Biography Authorized by Orville Wright.* New York, Harcourt, 1943; London, Harrap, 1944.

McMahon, John R., *The Wright Brothers: Fathers of Flight.* Boston, Little Brown, 1930.

Walsh, John Evangelist, *One Day at Kitty Hawk: The Untold Story of the Wright Brothers and the Airplane.* New York, Crowell, 1975; London, Allen and Unwin, 1976.

Young, Rosamond, *Twelve Seconds to the Moon: A Story of the Wright Brothers.* Dayton, Ohio, The Journal Herald, 1978.

*

The story of Wilbur and Orville Wright is unique since they are tied together so closely, not only by brotherhood, but by their collaborative invention of the first successful airplane. The relatively early death of Wilbur and the long life of Orville, with the many controversies over their attempts to protect their invention, has tended to muddy the stories of their lives and personalities and caused many biographers to take sides.

The bulk of correspondence, records, and photographs relating to the invention of the airplane is located in the Aeronautics Division of the Library of Congress. A guide to this material was made available by Marvin W. McFarland as *The Papers of Wilbur and Orville Wright, including the Chanute-Wright Letters and Other Papers of Octave Chanute* (2 vols., New York, McGraw-Hill, 1953). Since then guides to other manuscripts, such as those in the Wright State University Archives in Dayton, Ohio, have added much important family material that is necessary for the interpretation of the forces behind these two men. Early biographies not only suffered from the lack of organization of the complex material, but had to deal with Orville Wright himself, who was waging a long battle to establish his priority in the invention of the first airplane. At this writing there are eight significant one-volume biographies of the Wright brothers. Before 1975 there were only 3, those by McMahon, Kelly, and Freudenthal, none of which had the benefit of the full record available today.

McMAHON's is a popular work and contains "a mass of 'human interest' material, imaginary conversations, soliloquy and journalistic liveliness." Detested by Orville Wright, who at one point attempted to suppress its publication, McMahon's work touched, however, a theme in Orville's personality that would run throughout many of the later biographies. McMahon claims that Wilbur's early death "was a great shock to Orville, who has striven since then to write the chronicle of an epochal achievement, as much to obtain complete honor and justice for that beloved brother's memory as for his own vindication."

McMahon's book prompted the writing of an "authorized" biography by Orville's friend, Fred KELLY. Kelly's book naturally revolves around Orville, since the latter had complete control of the text. It does not delve into the technicalities of the invention of flight. It ends with the victorious return of the original "Wright Flyer" to the United States and recognition by the Smithsonian Institute. While Kelly's biography is still interesting reading today, the reader must be aware of what was omitted under the watchful eye of Orville.

FREUDENTHAL was a professional investment counselor who had an interest in the history of aviation. To help prove her thesis that the Wright brothers' primary motives were to make the science and theory of aeronautics into a paying business, she relies heavily on their relationship and correspondence with Octave Chanute, as well as other contemporaries who claimed the Wrights were not the first men to fly. The book fails in its interpretation of the personalities of the two brothers and is generally critical of them. Freudenthal unfortunately appears to have been under some influence of Albert Zahm, who as Chief of the Library of Congress Aeronautical Division carried on a 35 year campaign to discredit the Wright brothers.

WALSH, a professional writer, was the first to take advantage of the published Wright papers. Walsh takes their story through 1909, trying to differentiate the personalities and contributions of the two brothers. He concludes that Wilbur, who died many years before Orville, was the major contributor to the invention of flight. The book, written for the general reader, cannot be considered definitive, but the extensive notes and sources documenting the author's conclusions are very interesting and thought provoking.

YOUNG's book is probably the least known of the biographical works. Young, a columnist at a local Dayton, Ohio, newspaper, wrote his work as a commemorative of the 75th anniversary of the first flight. Though laudatory, the book contains numerous photographs of the Wright family and various early flights and exhibits of Wright equipment.

COMBS, an aeronautical engineer and admirer of the Wright brothers, issued his biography with the assistance of CAIDIN, an author of books on aviation. Combs used his technical knowledge as an engineer, accompanied by numerous drawings, to explain in a clear manner some of the basic principles of flight and how the Wrights' ingenuity solved the problems they faced. The work includes also a large collection of Wright or Wright-related photographs, demonstrating their early flights. While Combs' enthusiasm for flight frequently gets the better of him, the biography is still informative, and when it settles down is the best in describing the early technical problems of flight.

HOWARD was a member of the team that helped organize the Wright papers at the Library of Congress. As a science librarian with experience in the Air Force during World War II, he brings both substantial documentation and an understanding of flight to his biography. Howard sets out, first, to demonstrate that the Wright accomplishments were not made in a vacuum, and he includes discussion of other efforts to solve the problem of flight. Second, he carries the story beyond 1909 to demonstrate the effects that their invention, feuds, and patent wars had on the subsequent developments in aeronautics, which made flying simpler and more controlled. The battle over the priority of his own invention affected the life of Orville Wright and the attitudes of the man on the street toward the early history of flight, as Howard points out. This book is necessary reading for anyone interested in the trials of early aviation.

CROUCH, a curator at the Smithsonian Air and Space Museum, has written the biography to which readers should turn to get the best idea of what made these two brothers so unusual. The title of Crouch's book is the clue to the story he presents. Bishop Milton Wright, the father of Wilbur and Orville, was a controversial figure in the history of the Church of the United Brethren in Christ. Throughout the book the father's strong personality and the sons' deference to him prevails. Crouch puts to rest the myth of the superior inventiveness of Wilbur over Orville (as suggested by Walsh) pointing out that together they were a corporate entity. At the same time Crouch is careful to distinguish between their separate personalities. Crouch turns back the wheels of time and presents the story in a very readable manner. His background in history, aviation, and documentation makes this a very well-rounded, interesting, but long biography. More illustrations would be appreciated, including more technical illustrations of their approach to flight. But Crouch, who has written a considerable number of other publications on the Wrights and their technology, may have felt them unnecessary in this work.

—Robert James Havlik

WRIGHT, Frank Lloyd, 1867-1959; American architect.

Blake, Peter, *The Master Builders: Le Corbusier, Mies Van der Rohe, Frank Lloyd Wright.* New York, Norton, 1976.

Brooks, H. Allen, *Writings on Wright: Selected Comment on Frank Lloyd Wright.* Cambridge, Massachusetts, and London, MIT Press, 1981.

Brooks, H. Allen, *Frank Lloyd Wright and the Prairie School.* New York, G. Braziller, 1984.

Eaton, Leonard K., *Two Chicago Architects and Their Clients: Frank Lloyd Wright and Howard Van Doren Shaw.* Cambridge, Massachusetts, MIT Press, 1969.

Farr, Finis, *Frank Lloyd Wright: A Biography.* New York, Scribner, 1961; London, Cape, 1962.

Forsee, Aylesa, *Frank Lloyd Wright, Rebel in Concrete.* Philadelphia, MaCrea Smith, 1959.

Forsee, Aylesa, *Men of Modern Architecture.* Philadelphia, MaCrea Smith, 1966.

Gill, Brendan, *Many Masks: A Life of Frank Lloyd Wright*. New York, Putnam, 1987; London, Heinemann, 1988.

Jacobs, Herbert and Katherine Jacobs, *Building with Frank Lloyd Wright: An Illustrated Memoir*. San Francisco, Chronicle Books, 1978.

Jencks, Charles, *Kings of Infinite Space: Frank Lloyd Wright and Michael Graves*. London, Academy Editions, and New York, St. Martin's 1983.

Muschamp, Herbert, *Man about Town: Frank Lloyd Wright in New York City*. Cambridge, Massachusetts, and London, MIT Press, 1983.

Scully, Vincent J., *Frank Lloyd Wright*. New York, G. Braziller, and London, Mayflower, 1960.

Smith, Norris K., *Frank Lloyd Wright: A Study in Architectural Content*. Englewood Cliffs, New Jersey, Prentice-Hall, 1966.

Tafel, Edgar, *Apprentice to Genius: Years with Frank Lloyd Wright*. New York, McGraw-Hill, 1979.

Twombly, Robert C., *Frank Lloyd Wright: An Interpretive Biography*. New York, Harper, 1973.

Wright, John Lloyd, *My Father Who Is on Earth*. New York, Putnam, 1946.

Wright, Olgivanna Lloyd, *Shining Brow: Frank Lloyd Wright*. New York, Horizon, 1960.

Wright, Olgivanna Lloyd, *Frank Lloyd Wright: His Life, His Work, His Words*. New York, Horizon, 1966; London, Pitman, 1970.

*

Any attempt to study Wright is hampered by the sheer weight of material available stemming from a wide range of sources. Wright had his share of critics, admirers, and fanatics. At the same time, any attempt to separate a man from his work is bound to be a difficult undertaking. In Wright's case, this is a peculiarly acute situation, in that much of his work was inspired and driven by his own forceful ideas and convictions. There is a large number of purely architecture-oriented works featuring Wright, but most of these present no bibliographic material, or should be used with caution, as they concentrate on very narrow aspects of Wright's career and do not contribute to an understanding of Wright as a whole.

Wright seems to have been particularly negligent in family and personal relations while at the same time acting as the central influence in the lives of a number of his acquaintances. Some of those who knew him have recorded their own experiences. MUSCHAMP has written period biography that stands firmly behind Wright's own visions of self-importance and uniqueness. Unfortunately, the work is disorganized and sometimes confusing. Muschamp has selected a narrow and unique part of Wright's career as his focus, but erroneously implies that Wright was solely preoccupied with New York at this time and overlooks some of the major aspects of Wright's interests in that city.

TAFEL's work is an incomplete biography, concentrating mostly on the Arizona and Wisconsin years, with brief treatment of some other aspects of Wright's career. Major aspects of Wright's efforts during this period receive only peripheral treatment. Like many biographers, Tafel repeatedly switches tone from adoration for Wright's accomplishments to disdain for his personality. Though cited source material is scarce, the work is

recognized as one of the major authentic sources on Wright. Tafel has included a list of Wright buildings open to the public. His work is heavily illustrated, including some color plates, with a good balance between the architecture and depictions of Wright himself in various settings.

GILL's much reviewed and often criticized work attempts to serve as the definitive Wright biography. While the effort is well conceived, well documented, and perceptive, Gill falls into the familiar pattern of swaying between admiration and disdain for his subject. He portrays Wright as a genius/stinker, while at the same time treating the man's genius and ability with the respect that it deserves. Gill's work resembles the earlier work by JOHN LLOYD WRIGHT in many respects, though the younger Wright seems to have a particular axe to grind and utterly fails to give a complete picture of Frank Lloyd Wright as an individual.

OLGIVANNA LLOYD WRIGHT's *Shining Brow* (1960) is a somewhat gentler, but similarly written, account of the later part of Wright's career. Her 1966 work, *Frank Lloyd Wright*, takes a completely different tack in approaching their life together through a chronology of the architect's work. In this, the book is particularly valuable in getting at Wright's own feelings toward his work.

The JACOBS' work is a very interesting account of one family's encounter with Wright, detailing the painful process of dealing with the man as an architect and carrying through the execution of one of his designs. Chapter titles alone, such as "Just a Few Changes" and "Wright Disowns Us," give some insight into Wright's nature. JENCKS' gossipy, well-illustrated effort will serve as a good starting place to whet one's appetite for more in-depth study of Wright. The work is also of interest to those concerned with the methods of construction involved with a Wright house.

FARR's is one of the earliest full-length biographies of Wright. He gives Wright's life a complete chronological treatment, mixing the personal with the professional in a light, readable manner. The virtue of this account is that it is written from the perspective that Wright was a man, not some sort of demigod; Farr's work is free of the awe and reverence that typify most other efforts. Unfortunately, Farr failed to capture the essence of Wright's nature and helps little in understanding how that nature contributed to popular perception of the man and shaped his architecture.

BLAKE's work, contemporary with Farr's, is a good, solid, well-documented portrayal of the whole Wright. Blake does an excellent job of portraying the complexities of Wright's personality and life-style, while at the same time relating the character of the man to the eloquence of his architecture. Blake seems to have been able to take Wright at face value without becoming caught up in adoration or scorn. This has allowed him to present a frank, though cheerful, assessment of Wright and his work and its relation to modern architecture as a whole.

Probably the best all-around biography of Wright is the TWOMBLY book. The work is similar in scope and accomplishment to Farr's, in that the depiction of Wright is free of any unnatural attachment to or disdain for Wright. At the same time, the work resembles that of Blake, for Twombly has succeeded in exposing the difficult-to-define relationship between the psyche of the man and his architecture. A very readable effort, Twombly's book is especially interesting for its exposé into Wright's relationship with his parents.

FORSEE's *Rebel in Concrete* (1959) is an account of Wright's youth and early career, written with the younger audience in mind. Forsee barely succeeds at combining a chronological biography with insight into the many sides of Wright's personality and teachings. For adult readers this account will be very easy going and can serve as a general introduction to more serious study of Wright. The work is accurate and well supported with photographs. Forsee's later work, *Men of Modern Architecture* (1966), is a compilation of biographies on prominent architects, including Wright. This is a far less solid work than *Rebel*. Forsee treats Wright most sparingly, while at the same time providing much more extraneous material than an effort of this length needs.

In addition to providing a brief but profusely illustrated period biography of Wright's Prairie School years (1984), BROOKS has compiled a wide range of essays and reflections on Wright and his architecture in *Writings on Wright* (1981). Like many works, parts of this effort cannot help focusing on the architecture solely. However, the book features a number of individuals of various association presenting their feelings and experiences with Wright's life-style and personality, as well as personal accounts and memories from people who encountered Wright as his clients, fellows, and admirers. This in itself makes for interesting reading, presenting useful information as to how Wright is and was perceived outside his circle of friends and family.

SMITH's book is unusual in that it seeks, with some success, to show that Wright was not the mainstream modern-movement architect that most historians and critics consider him. SCULLY's biography, also outside the Wright mainstream, attempts to show that Wright could not have displayed his genius without contact with the art and architectural community as a whole. These two works present a "counter image" of the man without diminishing his abilities.

EATON's work contains brief errata on Wright's life and concentrates on his Chicago activities. It is interesting for the biographical material on some of Wright's clients and an in-depth essay on the nature of Wright's general clientele. The book has some use despite its irritating format of large voids on nearly every page.

Two recent books on Wright were unavailable for review at the time of this writing: Wendy B. Murphy, *Frank Lloyd Wright* (1990) and Donald L. Johnson, *Frank Lloyd Wright Versus America: the 1930s* (Cambridge, Massachusetts, MIT Press, 1990).

—Lawrence M. Enoch

WRIGHT, Richard, 1908–1960; American writer.

Bakish, David, *Richard Wright*. New York, Ungar, 1973.
Bone, Robert A., *Richard Wright*. Minneapolis, University of Minnesota Press, 1969.
Fabre, Michel, *The Unfinished Quest of Richard Wright*, translated by Isabel Barzum. New York, Morrow, 1973.
Felgar, Robert, *Richard Wright*. Boston, Twayne, 1980.
Gayle, Addison, *Richard Wright: Ordeal of a Native Son*. New York, Anchor Press/Doubleday, 1980.
Kinnamon, Keneth, *The Emergence of Richard Wright: A Study in Literature and Society*. Urbana, University of Illinois Press, 1972.
Walker, Margaret, *The Daemonic Genius of Richard Wright: A Portrait of the Man, a Critical Look at his Work*. Washington, D.C., Howard University Press, 1986.
Webb, Constance, *Richard Wright: A Biography*. New York, Putnam, 1968.
Williams, John A, *The Most Native of Sons: A Biography of Richard Wright*. New York, Doubleday, 1970.

*

WEBB's book, although it represents the first full-length biography of Wright, is an exercise in hero worship and not in scholarship. Of the 22 reviews of her book published in 1968 alone, 20 were unfavorable. Virtually every reviewer criticized Webb for being too closely involved with her subject to write an objective biography (her personal friendship with Wright was well known). More importantly, however, there is a surprising lack of specific dates to support her details, and she does not follow the life in chronological order. Webb also fails to account for Wright's involvement with the Communist party, or to consider Wright in relation to other African-American or American writers. Webb's study is more an examination of the personality of Wright than a critical biography of the author and his work. Of the 441 pages of this study, the most valuable portions today are the 34 illustrations and the bibliography of 173 primary items compiled by Michel Fabre and Edward Margolies, previously published in 1965 as "Richard Wright (1908–1960): A Bibliography" in *Bulletin of Bibliography and Magazine Notes*, 24 (January–April).

BONE offers the best short biographical treatment of Wright. In a study of 48 pages, Bone examines Wright's American and French periods and provides a detailed treatment of *Black Boy* (1945) and *Native Son* (1940). Pointing to elements of the picaresque, and to Wright's view of history, Bone de-emphasizes Wright's protest and his involvement with the Communist party. Although the study is brief, Bone examines both the life and the work, and as such it serves as an excellent introduction to the life and literary career of Richard Wright.

WILLIAMS' biography is written for juvenile readers. Consistent with the needs of his audience, Williams narrates the life, dividing it into three sections: "The Mississippi Mud," "Free at Last . . . Free at Last," and "European Sojourn." There is no new information included in 141 pages of text, with the exception of a few previously unpublished details concerning Wright's friendship with the novelist Chester Himes. For the most part, reviews were favorable, pointing to Williams' ability to praise Wright without falling into sentimentality.

KINNAMON provides a detailed examination of the life, literature, and social milieu of Richard Wright from his birth in 1908 until the publication of *Native Son* in 1940. Kinnamon includes a brief account of Wright's withdrawal from the Communist movement and of his expatriation.

BAKISH's 114-page monograph examines the life and literary career of Wright and includes a discussion of his unpublished sequel to *The Long Dream* (1958), entitled *Island of Hallucination*. Of interest in this brief study is Bakish's assessment of Wright's novels *The Outsider* (1953) and *Savage Holiday* (1954) as failures, and a brief discussion of James Baldwin's relation to Wright. This study is valuable too for its examination of Wright's short story, "Big Boy Leaves Home," and his novel, *Lawd Today* (1963).

FABRE's *Unfinished Quest* is a landmark study, not only in Richard Wright scholarship, but in the field of literary biography in general. Based on Fabre's doctoral thesis (1970), his work of 652 pages, divided into 21 chapters, examines the life and literary career of Richard Wright in exacting detail. Included here is an enlarged version of his previously published bibliography of Wright, and frequent use of heretofore unpublished letters, manuscripts, journals, and interviews. Fabre's treatment of Wright as both a writer and a humanist represents the first important challenge to discussions of Wright's life and literary career soley on the basis of his ethnic identity. Fabre's biography has yet to be superseded as the authoritative biography of Richard Wright.

FELGAR's *Richard Wright* contains no new information and is a bit superficial in its 189-page treatment of the life and literary contribution of Wright. For example, Felgar notes that Wright's "primary theme" is that oppression de-humanizes both the victim and the oppressor. Felgar provides a "selected bibliography," consisting of 34 primary sources and 49 annotated secondary sources. GAYLE, using documents he obtained under the Freedom of Information Acts, examines the harassment of Wright by the U.S. State Department. Gayle claims that all of Wright's later fiction should be examined in light of this harassment and of what Gayle refers to as Wright's alienation from progressive political forces. Reviews of this work were mixed at best: Gayle has been criticized on a number of fronts ranging from factual distortion to an overreliance on previous biographies.

WALKER's biography relies too heavily on her personal reminiscences of Richard Wright. The result is an unbalanced, subjective treatment of complex issues. For example, in mentioning the importance of Wright's beginnings as a poet, Walker writes: "it has something to do with his imagery, or visual perception." What this "something" might be is left up to the reader to determine. Her "Bibliographic Essay" is of little value to the scholar, and the citations to her biography demonstrate a lack of familiarity with research in the field published in the 15 years prior to the publication of her work. This biography is not without interest since it is by someone who knew Wright, but the reader is left with a sense that Walker confuses autobiography with biography, which should itself be a subject of concern to her since she claims "psychobiography" as her methodology. The major weakness is, however, her glossing over of virtually every significant issue raised by her narrative.

—Jeffrey D. Parker

WYCLIFFE, John, *ca.*1330–1384; English religious reformer and theologian.

Kenny, Anthony, *Wyclif.* Oxford and New York, Oxford University Press, 1985.

Lechler, G., *John Wycliffe and His English Precursors* (2 vols.). London, Kegan Paul, 1878 (originally published as *Johann von Wiclif und die Vorgeschichte der Reformation*, Leipzig, F. Fleischer, 1873).

McFarlane, Kenneth B., *John Wycliffe and the Beginnings of English Nonconformity.* London, English Universities Press, 1952; New York, Macmillan, 1953.

Workman, Herbert B., *John Wyclif, a Study of the English Medieval Church* (2 vols.). Oxford, Clarendon Press, 1926.

*

John Wycliffe—the "Morning Star of the Reformation"—is widely regarded as a precursor of both the European and English Reformations. This point is stressed by LECHLER, whose substantial biography may be regarded as laying the foundations of subsequent Wycliffe scholarship. Meticulously researched, with extensive quotation from primary sources, this biography exercised considerable influence over Wycliffe's interpreters for more than half a century and remained the most important and reliable life of Wycliffe available to the later Victorian period.

Lechler's study neatly illustrates two difficulties associated with biographies of Wycliffe. First, we know virtually nothing of Wycliffe's character or of what he intended to achieve through his writings and ministry. Second, what little is known of his character is often overlaid with "several layers of rich brown protestant varnish." Wycliffe has attracted the attention of biographers largely on account of his being the founder of a heretical sect (a rarity in medieval England) that believed itself capable of removing Henry V from his throne and defied all attempts to stamp Wycliffe out. Although we know much of Wycliffe's influence, we know little of the man, since he provides his readers with practically no autobiographical information. His biographers have thus been obliged to base interpretations of his actions and intentions on what is little more than informed guesswork—a tendency evident in both Lechler and the later work of WORKMAN. Like Lechler, Workman exhibits a strong biographical tendency, though he attempts to set Wycliffe more firmly in his historical context. Workman's 700 page study contains much useful information, based on primary source material, but lacks the critical acumen required to disentangle the complex interaction of Wycliffe with both the English state and church.

These shortcomings are remedied by McFARLANE's study, which is easily the most reliable biography of Wycliffe available. Although its 188 pages are unable to contain the mass of detail provided by Lechler and Workman, the material included is judiciously selected, and the assessments made are the most reliable currently available. While McFarlane—in his time the leading authority on English 15th-century history—may require supplementation at points, especially in relation to Wycliffe's philosophical and theological ideas, his narrative possesses both fluency and rigour. Wycliffe emerges as one who is "learned, subtle, ingenious, opinionated, tirelessly argumentative and rather humourless." If only one biography of Wycliffe is to be read, this is unquestionably the work to turn to.

For those who regard biography as embracing a detailed understanding of its subject's ideas, the study by KENNY, drawing on the best modern scholarship, provides an admirable introduction to the leading features of Wycliffe's thought. Our understanding of late medieval philosophy and theology has undergone something of a revolution since 1965, and Kenny is able to present a reliable account of Wycliffe's leading ideas, correcting the misunderstandings that abound in the earlier studies of Lechler and Workman.

—Alister E. McGrath

YEATS, William Butler, 1865–1939; Irish poet.

Ellmann, Richard, *Yeats: The Man and The Masks*. London and New York, Macmillan, 1948.

Hone, Joseph, *W. B. Yeats: 1865–1939*. London and New York, Macmillan, 1943; revised edition, 1962.

Jeffares, A. Norman, *W. B. Yeats: Man and Poet*. London, Routledge, and New Haven, Connecticut, Yale University Press, 1949.

Jeffares, A. Norman, *W. B. Yeats: A New Biography*. London, Hutchinson, 1988; New York, Farrar Straus, 1989.

Martin, Augustine, *W. B. Yeats*. Dublin, Gill and Macmillan, 1983.

Tuohy, Frank, *Yeats*. London and New York, Macmillan, 1976.

*

The major disadvantages faced by early biographers of Yeats are twofold. First, with the poet's wife and some of his contemporaries still alive, there is an inevitable reluctance to expose potentially hurtful details concerning personal relationships; so, for example, Hone, Jeffares, and Ellmann studiously avoid identifying "Diana Vernon," Yeats' mistress in the mid 1890s, as Olivia Shakespear. Second, while all three biographers had privileged access to manuscript material, they all pre-date the specialized scholarship that began to accrete significantly in the 1950s and that, for a contemporary biographer, presents massively informative documentation in letters, memoirs, and various accounts of particular events and people; in other biographies (including William Murphy's important study of John Butler Yeats, *Prodigal Father*, 1978); and in the publication of all of Yeats' prose (*Autobiographies*, 1955; *Mythologies*, 1959; *Essays and Introductions*, 1961; *Explorations*, 1962; *Uncollected Prose*, 1970; and *Memoirs*, 1972). Allan Wade's hitherto indispensable *Letters of W. B. Yeats* (1952) is in the process of being replaced by a greatly enlarged compilation, impeccably edited by John Kelly (*The Collected Letters of W. B. Yeats: Vol. 1, 1865–95*, Oxford, Clarendon Press, 1986; 12–14 vols. projected). Kelly's first volume presents new evidence of the nature and extent of Yeats' early preoccupations which, for example, helps to define more closely than was formerly possible Yeats' particular indebtedness to such figures as John O'Leary and Douglas Hyde; but the fact that only one of the projected 12- to 14-volume edition of the letters has as yet appeared in print must effectively defer publication of the official, definitive biography of the poet, assigned to the Oxford historian Roy Foster.

Partly because of his personal acquaintance with the poet and his milieu, HONE's pioneering study acts as a cornerstone to all subsequent biographies. However, Hone merely presents a very readable if not always reliable narrative of events and circumstances gleaned from a combination of private and public records, and with largely descriptive rather than analytic reference to the poetry. Fairly comprehensive at the surface level of life-story, it is strangely bland in failing to reveal its subject's complex personality.

JEFFARES' 1949 account provides a much more meticulously documented approach that incorporates a critical assessment of the poet's work in theme and technique and draws upon a wide range of previously unpublished sources. Characteristically, Jeffares writes in an unpretentious and lucid style but, while he quotes extensively from the poetry (and indeed directs most of his chapters in reference to its development), such quoting is more by way of illustration than explication, and for all the painstakingly accrued information there remains a gap between the poet as man and the poet as artist.

The durability of ELLMANN's study stems precisely from the fact that the way Yeats lived is seen principally in relation to the way his mind developed. As declared in his title, Ellmann's interpretive stance toward the different roles that may be assumed by the poetic personality gives an overall coherence to Yeats' various involvements, in literature and theatre, in mysticism and folklore, as well as to his changing attitudes toward the Ireland of his time. Ellmann fuses biography and criticism in his depiction of Yeats' unending struggle to achieve unity of being, to resolve antinomies of heart and mind, of subject and style—a view later commentators have been able in many ways to refine but not to supersede. Since it works more in terms of illuminating generalisation and synthesis rather than in particularized analysis, Ellmann's biography perhaps inevitably lacks detailed illustration from and explication of the poetry, an omission remedied by a fairly comprehensive though not in all cases definitive coverage in his next book, *The Identity of Yeats* (1954) which sets out to investigate the development of theme and technique in the poet's art.

The best early accounts of Yeats' Irish background are to be found in the opening chapters of two critical studies in the poet's evolution, Louis MacNeice's *The Poetry of W. B. Yeats* (1941) and T. R. Henn's *The Lonely Tower* (1950). TUOHY adopts a similar scheme throughout his biography in presenting Yeats' writings within a cultural, historical, and sociopolitical context, briefly outlining for example in his introductory pages the main elements in Daniel O'Connell's campaign for the repeal of the Act of Union (1801) that bound Ireland to England, the split between Catholic philistinism and the ideals of literary nationalism that continued into the 20th century, and various aspects of Yeats' native literary heritage. Subsequent chapters deal chronologically with Yeats' involvement with such major related issues as Irish theatre and Irish politics or the Easter Rebellion and the Irish Free State. Although Tuohy's deliberately lightweight, conversational approach precludes an exhaustive appraisal of the poetry, his text offers an attractive and gracefully written account for the general reader, amply illustrated with colour plates as well as reproductions of paintings and photographs (including a poignant juxtaposition of Yeats and Maud Gonne in their late years), of cartoons and drawings, and of playbills and scenes from Yeats' drama.

While it inevitably lacks the wider dimensions of Tuohy's study, MARTIN's brief but highly readable biography provides a good introduction for both student and layman since it deals fluently with the major events in the poet's life and illustrates both cultural and personal relationships by ample and pertinent quotation from the poetry, an emphasis clear in the order of the chapters, which follow the dates of Yeats' major publications. The 1983 text is in process of being reprinted, with numerous lines of emendation and with a diagrammatic analysis of Yeats' system of gyres adapted to a coherent reading of particular poems that appropriately illustrate each primary and antithetical phase in what the poet thought of as interdependent cycles of history.

As its author minutely acknowledges, JEFFARES' 1988 *New Biography* makes abundant use of the extensive resources in scholarship that have become available to him since his first book about the poet in 1949. Jeffares now lays more emphasis on Yeats' intense and continuing interest in the supernatural, on his occult studies and the part he played for over 30 years in the Order of the Golden Dawn. He pays more attention to the effects of Yeats' selective reading upon his work, shows how tenaciously the poet pursued his literary ambitions, assesses his influence on the creation of modern Ireland, and examines the nature of Yeats' diverse roles as a public figure, whether as senator, overseas lecturer, or defender of the freedom of the theatre. Illustrated with contemporary photographs, the narrative provides 18 chapters, each of which covers a period of from two to five years of the poet's lifetime. Marked at once by clarity of expression and density of treatment, it is the most authoritative and comprehensive study to date. Yet perhaps no single volume could hope to reveal all the complexities of that most eventful period of Irish history that occurred during Yeats' lifetime and at the same time present a unifying perception of the poet's many-sided personality and of his art.

—Colin Meir

ZOLA, Émile, 1840–1902; French writer.

Hemming, F. W. J., *The Life and Times of Émile Zola.* London, Elek, and New York, Scribner, 1977.

Lapp, John S., *Zola Before the "Rougon-Macquart".* Toronto, University of Toronto Press, 1964.

Nelson, Brian, *Zola and the Bourgeoisie.* London, Macmillan, and New York, Barnes and Noble, 1983.

Richardson, Joanna, *Zola.* London, Weidenfeld and Nicolson, and New York, St. Martin's, 1978.

Walker, Philip, *Émile Zola.* London, Routledge, and New York, Humanities Press, 1968.

Walker, Philip, *Zola.* London and Boston, Routledge, 1985.

Wilson, Angus, *Émile Zola: An Introductory Study of His Novels.* London, Secker and Warburg, and New York, Morrow, 1952; revised edition, Secker and Warburg, 1964.

*

An excellent and objective summary of Zola's life as the first author of a systematically constructed series of best sellers is WALKER's *Zola* (1985). This gives a good account of Zola's childhood in southern France, describes his early struggles, and

gives full details of his relationships with other writers and artists of his time. It dwells on his ill health and on the psychological hang-ups that impelled him to spend six hours a day writing without producing much good work after he had deserted his first wife (with whom he could not have children) for her fertile seamstress, Jeanne Rozerot. Walker describes Zola's part in the Dreyfus case in dramatic terms and emphasises how his popularity with the working people of Paris was reflected in the vast crowds that turned out for his funeral. He mentions the rumour that Zola was murdered by opponents of Dreyfus, but he is more austere in his approach than RICHARDSON, whose lively, well-illustrated account emphasises Zola's aggressivity, his success in using contemporary public-relations techniques to launch his novels, and provides a valuable set of links between Zola's inner tensions and his creativity as a writer.

Both books are heavily indebted, as is all writing on Zola, to the small book by WILSON. This was the first major biography to break away from the image Zola had tried to project of himself as a neutral and scientific observer of French 19th-century social and political life. It emphasises the dramatic effect of Zola's early development, of the early death of his father, and presents the 20-volume series *Les Rougon-Macquart* as an act of revenge on Zola's part for the early humiliations of his poverty-stricken childhood. The fullest and most scholarly account of Zola as a man nevertheless remains HEMMING's *Life and Times*. This provides a full account of Zola's finances, of his involvement in various publishing ventures, of his relationship with such impressionist painters of his time as Manet and Monet, and of the dramatic intervention of Zola in the Dreyfus case in 1898. Like other biographies in English, it comments on the immense difficulty Zola's novels faced in translation because of the prudery of late 19th-century English society. When Zola himself visited London as a refugee from the French authorities after having been sentenced to a year in prison for contempt of court at the Dreyfus case, he found London poverty relatively mild compared to what Paris could offer.

WALKER's short study, *Émile Zola* (1968), in the profiles in literature series, is probably the best beginning for a student. NELSON links Zola's life and works to the problems of 19th-century French life and presents Zola as one of the first and greatest French writers. The same author's *Émile Zola: A Selective Analytical Bibliography* (1982) is a very good guide to the enormous amount of critical writing on Zola in French and English. A detailed account of Zola's literary apprenticeship can be found in LAPP, and an entertaining account of Zola's links with other 19th-century writers in Ronald Pearsall's *The Worm in the Bud: The World of Victorian Sexuality* (1969).

—Philip Thody

ZWINGLI, Huldreich, 1484–1531; Swiss religious reformer and theologian.

Farner, Oskar, *Zwingli the Reformer: His Life and Work.* New York, Philosophical Library, and London, Lutterworth, 1952.

Gäbler, Ulrich, *Huldrych Zwingli: His Life and Work*, translated by Ruth C. L. Gritsch. Philadelphia, Fortress Press, 1986; Edinburgh, T. Clark, 1987 (originally published by Beck, Munich, 1983).

Potter, George R., *Zwingli*. Cambridge and New York, Cambridge University Press, 1976.

Rilliet, Jean, *Zwingli: Third Man of the Reformation*, translated by Harold Knight. Philadelphia, Westminster Press, and London, Lutterworth, 1964 (originally published by A. Fayard, Paris, 1959).

Stephens, W. P., *The Theology of Huldrych Zwingli*. Oxford, Clarendon Press, and New York, Oxford University Press, 1986.

*

Surprisingly few biographies of this major Swiss reformer are available in English. Widely regarded as the "third man of the Reformation," ranking after Martin Luther and John Calvin, Zwingli has suffered considerable neglect at the hands of biographers.

The most reliable and thorough biography to date is due to Oskar FARNER. His substantial work, published in German over the period 1943–60, is widely regarded as having set new standards for Zwingli biography. Drawing heavily on original sources, Farner builds up a reliable overview of the eventful career of his subject. The work is available in English, however, only in the form of a one-volume popular condensation, which is inadequate for the purposes of serious study. RILLIET provides a similarly popular introduction which, despite its ability to grasp the reader's attention, lacks weight and precision at crucial points of interpretation.

Happily, this deficiency is remedied by POTTER, who is generally considered to have written the definitive biography of Zwingli available in English. Potter—formerly professor of medieval history at Sheffield University, England—provides a meticulously reconstructed life of Zwingli, based largely on primary sources. One of the work's chief attractions is its careful attention to historical detail, a feature often conspicuously absent from biographies of major religious figures of the period. Rigorously eschewing both hagiography and character assassination, Potter provides his readers with as near to an objective, dispassionate, and scrupulously even-handed account of Zwingli's life as is likely to be possible. If one were going to read only one life of Zwingli, Potter's is unquestionably the work to select.

There are, however, some points—however infrequent—of genuine weakness in Potter. By his own admission, Potter is no theologian. Consequently, his sureness of touch falters at times, particularly when dealing with the specifically theological controversies in which Zwingli became embroiled. Thus his account of the sacramental controversy between Luther and Zwingli lacks the same sensitivity and insight so characteristic in Potter's more openly historical analysis.

This deficiency can easily be remedied with reference to STEPHENS, whose study of Zwingli's theology is prefaced by a helpful, if brief, biography of Zwingli, accompanied by an overview of trends in German-language Zwingli biography since the 1930s. The introduction is particularly helpful for understanding the radically divergent accounts of Zwingli one encounters in German-language works, where Zwingli is often portrayed in strongly reductionist terms, such as a "rationalist" or "humanist."

GÄBLER's collection of essays is not so much a biography as a series of historical and theological mineshafts sunk deep into aspects of Zwingli's life and thought. Gäbler, firmly established as one of the most important Zwingli scholars of the modern period, offers his readers invaluable insights into aspects of Zwingli's career. The collection may be regarded as an invaluable accompaniment to other biographies, in the stricter sense of the term, and a most useful guide to recent development in Zwingli research, upon which all such biographies ultimately depend.

—Alister E. McGrath

NOTES
ON
CONTRIBUTORS

ADAMS, Courtney S. Arthur and Katherine Shadek Humanities Professor of Music, Franklin and Marshall College, Lancaster, Pennsylvania. Author of *French Chansons for Three Voices*, 1982, and of articles in *Acta Musicologica* and *Journal of Musicology*. **Essays:** Sergey Prokofiev; Eric Satie.

AGORATUS, Steven A. Doctoral candidate, Carnegie-Mellon University, Pittsburgh, Pennsylvania. Co-author of *Christianity in China*, 1989. **Essays:** Humphrey Bogart; James Cagney; Andrew Carnegie.

AHO, Gary L. Professor of English, University of Massachusetts, Amherst; Chairman of the William Morris Society (U.S.) and Editor of *The William Morris Society Newsletter*, 1984–88. Author of *William Morris: A Sesquecentennial Exhibition 1834–1984*, 1984, and *William Morris: A Reference Guide*, 1985. **Essay:** William Morris.

AITKEN, Isabel. Freelance writer and translator, formerly with the BBC. **Essays:** Martin Buber; Saint Francis of Assisi; Johannes Gutenberg; Saint Joan of Arc; Pope John Paul II; Louis XI of France; Marie Antoinette.

ALEXANDER, John T. Professor of History and Soviet and East European Studies, University of Kansas, Lawrence. Author of *Autocratic Politics in a National Crisis: The Imperial Russian Government and Pugachev's Revolt 1773-75*, 1969, *Bubonic Plague in Early Modern Russia: Public Health and Urban Disaster*, 1980, *Catherine the Great: Life and Legend*, 1989, and numerous articles on Russian history in journals. Editor and translator of Russian works. **Essay:** Catherine II of Russia.

ALEXANDER, M. J. Berry Professor of English Literature, University of St. Andrews, Fife, Scotland. Author of *The Earliest English Poems*, 1966, *Beowulf*, 1973, *Twelve Poems*, 1978, *The Poetic Achievement of Ezra Pound*, 1979, *Old English Riddles from the Exeter Book*, 1980, and *History of Old English Literature*, 1983. General Editor, with A. Norman Jeffaries, of *Macmillan Anthologies of English Literature*, 1989. **Essay:** Ezra Pound.

ALMQUIST, Sharon G. Assistant Media Librarian, University of North Texas, Denton. Author of *Sound Recordings and the Library*, 1987. Video reviewer for ABC-CLIO, *Video Rating Guide for Libraries*, and CD reviewer for *ARSC Journal*. **Essays:** Giacomo Puccini; Jean Sibelius.

ANDREWS, Stuart. Freelance writer and independent scholar; Editor of *Conference*, 1971–82; Professor of History and Headmaster of Clifton College, Bristol, 1975–90. Author of *Eighteenth-Century Europe*, 1965, *Enlightened Despotism*, 1967, *Methodism and Society*, 1970, and numerous articles in *History Today*. **Essays:** Joseph II; Thomas Paine; Peter I of Russia; John Wesley.

ANGYAL, Andrew J. Professor of English, Elon College, Elon, North Carolina. Author of *Loren Eiseley*, 1983, and *Lewis Thomas*, 1989. **Essays:** Dante; Wallace Stevens.

ANTLE, Martine Natat. Assistant Professor of French Literature, University of North Carolina, Chapel Hill. Author of *Théâtre et Poésie Surréalistes: Vitrac et la Scène Virtuelle*, 1988, "Breton, Portrait and Anti-Portrait: From the Figural to the Spectral," in *André Breton Today*, 1989, and numerous articles on the avant-garde and 20th-century theater. **Essays:** André Breton; Simone de Beauvoir; André Gide; Paul Valéry; Simone Weil.

AUSTIN, William W. Given Foundation Professor of Musicology Emeritus, Cornell University, Ithaca, New York. Author of *Music in the 20th Century, from Debussy Through Stravinsky*, 1966, *Debussy, Prélude à L'Après-Midi d'un Faune: Critical Edition*, 1970, "Susanna," "Jeanie," and "The Old Folks at Home": *The Songs of Stephen Foster from His Time to Ours*, 1975 (2nd edition, 1987), and numerous articles in journals, congress reports, and volumes honoring various scholars. **Essays:** Louis Armstrong; Claude Debussy.

BABENER, Liahna. Associate Professor and Head of the Department of English, Montana State University, Bozeman; Assistant Editor of *Los Angeles in Fiction*; Contributing Editor to the Heath Reconstructing American Literature Project. Author of numerous articles on detective fiction. **Essays:** Louisa May Alcott; Dashiell Hammett.

BARNES, Christopher J. Professor and Head of the Department of Slavic Languages and Literatures, University of Toronto; Editor of *Research Bulletin* (Munich), 1974–75; Editorial Board of *Forum for Modern Language Studies*, 1970–89. Author of *Boris Pasternak: A Literary Biography, Vol. I*, 1989, and numerous articles and broadcasts on Russian literary and musical topics. Editor of *Studies in 20th-Century Russian Literature*, 1976. Translator of *Collected Short Prose of Boris Pasternak*, 1977, *The Voice of Prose*, by Boris Pasternak, 1986, and *People and Propositions*, by Boris Pasternak, 1990. **Essays:** Alexander Blok; Boris Pasternak; Sergei Rachmaninov; Alexander Scriabin.

BARRAL, Mary-Rose. Visiting Professor of Philosophy, Youngstown State University, Youngstown, Ohio. Author of *Merleau-Ponty: The Role of the Body-Subject in Interpersonal Relations*, 1965, *Progressive Neutralism: Philosophical Values in Education*, 1970, and numerous articles in journals. **Essay:** Henri Bergson.

BARRANGER, Milly S. Professor and Head of the Department of Dramatic Art, University of North Carolina, Chapel Hill; Past-President of the American Theatre Association, 1979, and of the National Theatre Conference, 1988–90; Editorial Boards of *Theatre Journal* and *The Tennessee Williams Literary Festival*; Executive Producer, PlayMakers Repertory Company, Chapel Hill, since 1982. Author of *Generations*, 1978, *Theatre: A Way of Seeing*, 1980, *Theatre: Past and Present*, 1984, *Understanding Plays*, 1990, and *Jessica Tandy: A Bio-Bibliography*, 1991. Co-editor of *Notable Women in the American Theatre: A Biographical Dictionary*, 1989. **Essays:** Lillian Hellman; Vivien Leigh.

BASSETT, Mark T. Adjunct Assistant Professor of English, Iowa State University, Ames. Author of *The Autobiography of Cornell Woolrich*, 1991, and *Conversations with Christopher*

Isherwood, forthcoming. **Essays:** Christopher Isherwood; Marilyn Monroe.

BATEMAN, B. W. Assistant Professor of Economics, Grinnell College, Grinnell, Iowa. Author of articles in *American Economic Review*, *Economics and Philosophy*, and *History of Political Economy*. Editor of *Keynes and Philosophy*, 1991. **Essay:** John Maynard Keynes.

BATTAGLIA, Rosemarie A. Assistant Professor in the Department of American Thought and Language, Michigan State University, East Lansing; Editorial Consultant, *Yeats Eliot Review*. Author of numerous articles and book chapters on modern literature, including in *J.M. Synge Literary Companion*, 1988, *New Alliances in Joyce Studies*, 1988, and *Novel: A Forum on Fiction*, 1989. **Essay:** Doris Lessing.

BECK, Roger B. Associate Professor of History, Eastern Illinois University, Charleston. Author of articles in *Journal of African History*. **Essays:** David Livingstone; Cecil Rhodes.

BECKWITH, Alice H. R. H. Associate Professor and Head of the Department of Art and Art History, Providence College, Providence, Rhode Island. Author of *Victorian Bibliomania: The Illuminated Book in 19th-Century Britain*, 1987, and of articles in *Great Lives from History: Renaissance to 1900*, 1989 and *Dictionary of Literary Biography: British Publishers*, 1991. **Essay:** Pierre-Auguste Renoir.

BELL, Robyn. Lecturer in Literature, College of Creative Studies, University of California, Santa Barbara. **Essay:** Emily Dickinson.

BERLIN, Jean V. Assistant Editor, The Correspondence of William T. Sherman; Research Assistant, The Papers of George Washington. Author of *Quiet but Unceasing Devotion: The Diary of Confederate Nurse Ada W. Bacot, 1860–63*, forthcoming. **Essay:** George Washington.

BINGHAM, Caroline. Freelance writer and independent scholar; Research Fellow, Royal Holloway and Bedford New College, University of London, 1984–87. Author of *The Making of a King: The Early Years of James VI and I*, 1968, *James V, King of Scots*, 1971, *The Life and Times of Edward II*, 1973, *The Stewart Kingdom of Scotland 1371–1603*, 1974, *James VI of Scotland*, 1979, *James I of Scotland*, 1981, and *The History of Royal Holloway College, 1886–1986*, 1987. **Essays:** Edward I of England; Edward II of England; Mary Queen of Scots.

BJORK, Daniel W. Associate Professor of History, Mercy College of Detroit. Author of *The Victorian Flight: Russell Conwell and the Crisis of American Individualism*, 1978, *The Compromised Scientist: William James in the Development of American Psychology*, 1983, and *William James: The Center of His Vision*, 1988. **Essay:** William James.

BLACK, Stephen A. Professor of English, Simon Fraser University, Burnaby, British Columbia; Associate Member, Seattle Institute for Psychoanalysis. Author of *James Thurber, His*

Masquerades, 1970, *Whitman's Journeys into Chaos: A Psychoanalytic Study of the Poetic Process*, 1975, and of essays in *PMLA, College English, American Literature*, and *Biography: An Interdisciplinary Quarterly*. **Essay:** Walt Whitman.

BLAKE, Robert G. William S. Long Professor of English, Elon College, Elon, North Carolina. Author of numerous articles and reference book entries, including "Algernon Charles Swinburne," in *Critical Survey of Poetry*, 1983. **Essay:** Algernon Charles Swinburne.

BLOOM, Lynn Z. Professor of English and Aetna Chair of Writing, University of Connecticut, Storrs. Author or co-author of *Doctor Spock: Biography of a Conservative Radical*, 1972, *American Autobiography 1945–80: A Bibliography*, 1982, *Strategic Writing*, 1983, *Fact and Artifact: Writing Nonfiction*, 1985, and articles, reviews, and poetry in journals. Editor of *Bear, Man, and God: Seven Approaches to William Faulkner's The Bear*, 1964 (revised, 1971), *Forbidden Diary: A Record of Wartime Internment 1941–45*, by Natalie Crouter, 1980, and *Forbidden Family: A Wartime Memoir of the Philippines 1941–45*, by Margaret Sams, 1989. **Essays:** Dorothy Parker; George Bernard Shaw.

BOCK, Catherine C. Professor of Art History, Theory, and Criticism, School of the Art Institute of Chicago. Author of *Henri Matisse and Neo-Impressionism 1898–1908*, 1981, and *Henri Matisse: An Annotated Bibliography*, forthcoming. **Essay:** Henri Matisse.

BOULARD, Garry. Freelance writer; Reporter for *The Los Angeles Times*, *The Christian Science Monitor*, and the New Orleans *Times-Picayune*. Author of *Just a Gigolo: The Life and Times of Louis Prima*, 1989, and of articles in *The Encyclopedia of American Political Parties and Elections*, 1990, *American Quarterly*, and *The Journal of Mississippi History*. **Essays:** Golda Meir; Eleanor Roosevelt.

BOWMAN, Larry G. Professor of History, University of North Texas, Denton. Author of *Captive Americans: Prisoners During the American Revolution*, 1976, and numerous articles and encyclopedia entries. Co-editor of *Our National Heritage*, 1989. **Essay:** George Armstrong Custer.

BRADFORD, James C. Associate Professor of History, Texas A and M University, College Station. Editor of *Command Under Sail: Makers of the American Naval Tradition 1775–1850*, 1985, *The Papers of John Paul Jones*, 1986, *Captains of the Old Steam Navy: Makers of the American Naval Tradition 1840–80*, 1986, and *Admirals of the New Steel Navy: Makers of the American Naval Tradition 1880–1930*, 1990. **Essay:** John Paul Jones.

BRAEMAN, John. Professor of History, University of Nebraska, Lincoln. Author of *Albert J. Beveridge: American Nationalist*, 1971, and *Before the Civil Rights Revolution: The Old Court and Individual Rights*, 1988. **Essays:** John Dewey; William O. Douglas; Henry Ford.

BRAND, Juliane. Associate Editor, *Journal of the Arnold*

Schoenberg Institute, University of Southern California, Los Angeles. Author of *Rudi Stephen*, 1983. Co-editor of *The Berg-Schoenberg Correspondence*, 1987. **Essay:** Arnold Schoenberg.

BRATTON, Mary Jo. Professor of History, East Carolina University, Greenville, North Carolina. Author of *East Carolina University: The Formative Years*, 1986. **Essay:** Patrick Henry.

BRAUCH, Patricia. Associate Librarian for Information Services, Brooklyn College Library, City University of New York. Author of numerous articles published in journals and reviewer for *Choice*. **Essays:** John Constable; Edvard Munch.

BROWN, Mary Elizabeth. Assistant Professor of History, Kutztown University, Kutztown, Pennsylvania. Author of essays in *The Encyclopedia of New York City*, forthcoming, and in numerous journals. **Essay:** Mother Francis Cabrini.

BRUNO, Maria F. Assistant Professor in the Department of American Thought and Language, Michigan State University, East Lansing. Author of short stories and essays in journals, and of a chapter in *Charlotte Perkins Gilman: The Woman and Her Work*, 1989. **Essay:** Margaret Fuller.

BRYANT, Hallman B. Professor of English and Director of Graduate Studies, Clemson University, Clemson, South Carolina; Editorial Board, *South Carolina Review*. Author of *Robert Graves*, 1986, and *A Separate Peace: The War Within*, 1990. **Essay:** Robert Browning.

BUCCO, Martin. Professor of English, Colorado State University, Fort Collins; President, Western Literature Association, 1981-82, and Executive Secretary, 1982–87; Editorial Board, *Western American Literature*, since 1974. Author of *The Voluntary Tongue* (poetry), 1957, *Frank Waters*, 1969, *Wilbur Daniel Steele*, 1972, *An American Tragedy Notes*, 1974, *E.W. Howe*, 1977, *René Wellek*, 1981, *Western American Literary Criticism*, 1984, and articles in *Dictionary of Literary Biography*, *American Literature*, and numerous other journals. Editor of *Critical Essays on Sinclair Lewis*, 1986. **Essay:** Sinclair Lewis.

BURKHART, Robert E. Professor of English, Eastern Kentucky University, Richmond. Author of *Shakespeare's Bad Quartos*, 1975, and numerous articles in journals. Co-editor of *Perspectives on Our Time*, 1970. **Essays:** Edith Piaf; Andy Warhol.

BURNS, Edward. Associate Professor of English, William Paterson College, Wayne, New Jersey. Editor of *Gertrude Stein on Picasso*, 1970, *Staying on Alone: Letters of Alice B. Toklas*, 1973, *Twentieth-Century Literature: Gertrude Stein Issue*, 1978, and *The Letters of Gertrude Stein and Carl Van Vechten 1913–46*, 2 vols., 1986. Co-editor of *The Letters of Thornton Wilder*, forthcoming. **Essay:** Thornton Wilder.

BURTON, David H. Professor of History, St. Joseph's University, Philadelphia. Author of *Theodore Roosevelt: Confident Imperialist*, 1968, *Theodore Roosevelt*, 1972, *Theodore Roosevelt and His English Correspondents*, 1973, *Oliver Wendell Holmes, Jr.*, 1980, *William Howard Taft in the Public Service*, 1986, *The Learned Presidency*, 1988, and *An Anglo-American Plutarch*, 1990. **Essay:** Theodore Roosevelt.

CAI, Camilla. Assistant Professor of Musicology, Kenyon College, Gambier, Ohio; Research Editor, *Harvard Dictionary of Music*, 1965–67. Author of numerous articles in journals and in *Encyclopedia of Keyboard Instruments*, forthcoming. **Essay:** Robert Schumann.

CARBON, John J. Assistant Professor of Music, Franklin and Marshall College, Lancaster, Pennsylvania. Author of numerous articles in journals and composer of musical works published by the California Philharmonic Association. **Essay:** Igor Stravinsky.

CARLTON, Paul. Member of the faculty of English, Converse College, Spartanburg, South Carolina. Author of articles in journals and reference works. **Essays:** Vladimir Nabokov; J.D. Salinger.

CARNALL, Geoffrey. Reader in English, University of Edinburgh. Author of *Robert Southey and His Age*, 1960, *Robert Southey*, 1964, and *The Mid-Eighteenth Century* (with John Butt), a volume in the Oxford History of English Literature, 1978. **Essays:** Edward Gibbon; William Hazlitt; Charles Lamb.

CASINES, Gisela. Associate Professor of English, Florida International University, Miami. Author of numerous essays in journals covering the Spanish Golden Age. **Essay:** Pedro Calderón de la Barca.

CAUSEY, Faya. Assistant Professor of Art, California State University, Long Beach. Author of articles in *The Impressionists and the Salon: California Collections*, 1974. **Essays:** Edgar Degas; Thomas Gainsborough.

CHU, Petra ten-Doesschate. Professor of Art, Seton Hall University, South Orange, New Jersey. Author of *French Realism and the Dutch Masters*, 1974, *Courbet in Perspective*, 1977, and *Im Lichte Hollands* (catalog), 1987. Editor of *Letters of Gustave Courbet*, 1991. **Essay:** Vincent van Gogh.

COCHRANE, Hamilton E. Assistant Professor of English, Canisius College, Buffalo, New York. Author of *Boswell's Literary Art: An Annotated Bibliography*, forthcoming, and numerous articles in journals. **Essay:** Bob Dylan.

COCKSHUT, A. O. J. G.M. Young Lecturer in 19th-Century Literature, Oxford University. Author of *Anthony Trollope: A Critical Study*, 1955, *Anglican Attitudes*, 1959, *The Imagination of Charles Dickens*, 1961, *The Unbelievers: English Agnostic Thought 1840–90*, 1964, *The Achievement of Walter Scott*, 1969, *Truth to Life*, 1974, *Man and Woman*, 1977, and *The Art of Autobiography*, 1984. **Essays:** Jane Austen; Lord Byron; Thomas Carlyle; G.K. Chesterton; Benjamin Disraeli; George Eliot; Gerard Manley Hopkins; John Ruskin.

COETZEE, Marilyn Shevin. Professor of History, Yale University, New Haven, Connecticut. Author of *The German*

Army League: Popular Nationalism in Wilhelmine Germany, 1990, and articles in *European History Quarterly* and *Contemporary History*. **Essay:** Otto von Bismarck.

COGSWELL, Michael. Jazz Specialist, Music Library, University of North Texas, Denton. Author of articles in *Annual Review of Jazz Studies*, 1991. **Essays:** Duke Ellington; George Gershwin.

COMPLIMENT, Anne. Graduate Teaching Fellow in American Literature, George Washington University, Washington, D.C. **Essay:** James Baldwin.

CONTOSTA, David R. Professor and Head of the Department of History, Chestnut Hill College, Philadelphia. Author of *Henry Adams and the American Experiment*, 1980, *A Philadelphia Family: The Houstons and Woodwards of Chestnut Hill*, 1988, and *America in the 20th Century: Coming of Age*, 1988. Editor of *Rise to World Power: Selected Letters of Whitelaw Reid*, 1986. **Essays:** Henry Adams; John Adams.

CORKIN, Stanley. Assistant Professor of English, University of Cincinnati. Author of numerous articles on film and 20th-century literature. **Essay:** Paul Robeson.

COTTER, Craig. Freelance writer and poet. Author of *The Aroma of Toast* (poetry), 1990. **Essay:** John Lennon.

CREGIER, Don M. Professor of History, University of Prince Edward Island, Charlottetown, P.E.I., Canada. Author of *Bounder from Wales: Lloyd George's Career Before the First World War*, 1976, *Novel Exposures: Victorian Studies Featuring Contemporary Novels*, 1979, *Chiefs Without Indians: Asquith, Lloyd George, and the Liberal Remnant 1916–35*, 1982, *The Decline of the Liberal Party: Why and How?*, 1985, and *Freedom and Order: The Growth of British Liberalism Before 1868*, 1988. **Essays:** Sir Richard Francis Burton; Elizabeth II of England; Sir Henry Morton Stanley.

CRIST, Lynda Lasswell. Editor of The Papers of Jefferson Davis, Rice University, Houston, Texas. **Essay:** Jefferson Davis.

CROUT, Robert Rhodes. Assistant Professor of History, Charleston University, Charleston, South Carolina. Co-editor of *Lafayette in the Age of the American Revolution: Selected Letters and Papers 1776–90*, 5 vols. to date, 1977– , *The Papers of Thomas Jefferson*, vol. 21, 1983, and *The Papers of James Madison*, 1 vol. to date, 1986– . **Essay:** Marquis de Lafayette.

CRUICKSHANK, John. Professor Emeritus of French Literature, University of Sussex. Author of *Albert Camus and the Literature of Revolt*, 1959, *French Literature and Its Background*, 6 vols., 1968–70, *Benjamin Constant*, 1974, *Variations on Catastrophe: Some French Responses to the Great War*, 1982, and *Pascal: Pensées*, 1983. **Essays:** Albert Camus; Blaise Pascal.

CURRAN, Judith M. Educational Administrator, Brooklyn and Staten Island High Schools; Adjunct Professor of Education,

College of Staten Island, City University of New York. **Essay:** Elizabeth Seton.

CURRAN, Thomas J. Member of the faculty of History, St. John's University, Jamaica, New York. **Essay:** Samuel Morse.

CURRENT-GARCIA, Eugene. Hargis Professor Emeritus of American Literature, Auburn University, Alabama; Editor of *Southern Humanities Review*, 1967–69. Author of *O. Henry (W.S. Porter): A Critical Study*, 1965, and *The American Short Story Before 1850*, 1985. Editor of *American Short Stories* (with Walton R. Patrick), 1952 (5th edition, 1990), *What is the Short Story?*, 1961, *Realism and Romanticism in Fiction*, 1962, *Short Stories of the Western World*, 1969, and *Shem, Ham, and Japteth: The Papers of W. O. Tuggle*, 1973. **Essay:** O. Henry.

DALBEY, Marcia A. Professor and Head of the Department of English, Eastern Michigan University, Ypsilanti. Author of numerous articles in journals. **Essay:** Kate Chopin.

DAY, John A. Dean of the College of Fine Arts, University of South Dakota, Vermillion; Art Editor, University of South Dakota Press, since 1988. Author of numerous articles in art journals and reviewer for *Choice*. **Essays:** Mary Cassatt; Auguste Rodin.

DEAN, Dennis R. Professor of English and Humanities, University of Wisconsin, Parkside. Author of numerous articles in literary and scientific journals. **Essays:** Confucius; Dwight D. Eisenhower; Ralph Waldo Emerson; Benjamin Franklin; Sir Charles Lyell; Douglas MacArthur; Sir Isaac Newton; Henry David Thoreau.

DENNARD, David C. Associate Professor of History, East Carolina University, Greenville, North Carolina. **Essay:** Malcolm X.

DEUTSCH, James I. Doctoral candidate in the Department of American Civilization, George Washington University, Washington, D.C. Author of articles on film in *Humboldt Journal of Social Relations*, *G.W. Forum*, and *Journal of Popular Culture*. **Essay:** Joan Crawford.

DEVINE, Michael J. Illinois State Historian and Director of the Illinois State Historical Society. Author of *John W. Foster*, 1981, and of articles in *Ohio History*, *Journal of Peace and Change*, and *Dictionary of American Biography*. **Essays:** Davy Crockett; W.E.B. DuBois.

DICKEY, Richard C. Assistant Reference Librarian, University of North Texas, Denton. Reviewer for *Choice*. **Essays:** Charlie Chaplin; Katharine Hepburn.

DITSKY, John. Professor of English, University of Windsor, Ontario. Author of numerous books of poetry, including *The Katherine Poems*, 1975, *Scar Tissue*, 1978, and *Friend and Lover*, 1981; and criticism, including *Essays on East of Eden*, 1977, *Onstage Christ: Studies in the Persistence of a Theme*, 1980, *John Steinbeck: Life, Works, and Criticism*, 1985, and *Critical Essays on Steinbeck's Grapes of Wrath*, 1989. **Essay:** John Steinbeck.

DOENECKE, Justus D. Professor of History, New College of the University of South Florida, Sarasota. Author of *Not to the Swift: The Old Isolationists in the Cold War Era*, 1979, *The Diplomacy of Frustration: The Manchurian Crisis of 1931–33 as Revealed in the Papers of Stanley K. Hornbeck*, 1981, *The Presidencies of James A. Garfield and Chester A. Arthur*, 1981, *When the Wicked Rise: American Opinion-Makers and the Manchurian Crisis 1931–33*, 1984, *Anti-Intervention: A Bibliographical Introduction to Isolationism and Pacifism from World War I to the Early Cold War*, 1987, *In Danger Undaunted: The Anti-Interventionist Movement of 1940–41 as Revealed in the Papers of the America First Committee*, 1990, and *From Isolation to War 1931–41*, 2nd edition, 1990. **Essays:** Ulysses S. Grant; William Randolph Hearst; Clare Boothe Luce; Mao Tse-Tung.

DOLL, Susan M. Editor, Publications International, Ltd., and Instructor, Oakton Community College, Des Plaines, Illinois; Assistant Editor, *St. James Press Dictionary of Films and Filmmakers*, 1982–84; Editor, *The Motion Picture Guide*, 1985–86; Managing Editor, *Video Times*, 1987. Author of *Elvis Presley: A Tribute to His Life*, 1989, and *Marilyn Monroe: Her Life and Legend*, 1990. **Essay:** Orson Welles.

DONAGHER, Colleen P. Doctoral candidate in the Department of Romance Languages, University of Chicago. **Essay:** François Villon.

DORNAN, Reade W. Adjunct Assistant Professor of English, University of Michigan, Flint. Author of *Arnold Wesker Revisited*, 1991, and of articles in *Masterplots II: Drama*, and *Victorian Britain*. Editor of *Preserving the Game: Gambling, Mining, Hunting, and Conservation in the Vanishing West: Western Stories and Yellowstone Essays*, 1989. **Essay:** Bertolt Brecht.

DOWNS, Linda. Head of Education, National Gallery of Art, Washington, D.C. Author of numerous articles in journals and introductions to exhibition catalogs. **Essay:** Diego Rivera.

DUBOVOJ, Sina. Freelance writer and independent scholar. **Essays:** Corazon Aquino; Indira Gandhi; Mahatma Gandhi.

DUNN, Richard J. Professor and Head of the Department of English, University of Washington, Seattle. Author of *David Copperfield: An Annotated Bibliography*, 1980, *Approaches to Teaching Dickens' David Copperfield*, 1984, and of numerous articles on 19th-century English writers. Editor of the Norton Critical Editions of *Jane Eyre*, 1987, and *Wuthering Heights*, 1989. **Essays:** The Brontës (Charlotte and Emily); Charles Dickens.

DWYER, John J. Graduate Student in the Department of History, University of Illinois, Urbana. **Essay:** Mikhail Gorbachev.

EDMONDS, Anthony O. Professor and Head of the Department of History, Ball State University, Muncie, Indiana; Editor, *Proceedings of the Indiana Academy of Social Sciences*, 1979–83; Editorial Board, *Forum*, since 1984. Author of *Joe Louis*, 1973. **Essays:** Lyndon Johnson; John F. Kennedy.

EISS, Harry Edwin. Assistant Professor of English, Eastern Michigan University, Ypsilanti. Author of *Dictionary of Language Games, Puzzles, and Amusements*, 1986, *Dictionary of Mathematical Games, Puzzles, and Amusements*, 1988, and *Literature for Youth on War and Peace*, 1989. **Essays:** Lewis Carroll; Stephen Crane; John Keats; Paul Klee; Edgar Allan Poe; Dante Gabriel Rossetti; Henri Rousseau.

ELLIS, Robert Richmond. Associate Professor of Spanish, Occidental College, Los Angeles. Author of *The Tragic Pursuit of Being: Unamuno and Sartre*, 1988, and of numerous articles on Spanish writers. **Essay:** Saint John of the Cross.

ENNIS, Martin. Director of Music, Christ's College, Cambridge University. **Essay:** Johannes Brahms.

ENOCH, Lawrence M. Coordinator for Online Services and Bibliographic Instruction; adjunct faculty, School of Library and Information Sciences, University of North Texas, Denton. **Essays:** Augustus Caesar; Hadrian; Julius Caesar; Ludwig Mies van der Rohe; Nero; Louis Sullivan; Frank Lloyd Wright.

FAHLMAN, Betsy. Associate Professor in the School of Art, Arizona State University, Tempe. Author of *Sculpture and Suffrage: Alice Morgan Wright*, 1978, *Guy Pene du Bois: Artist About Town*, 1980, and *Pennsylvania Modern: Charles Demuth of Lancaster*, 1983. **Essay:** Georgia O'Keeffe.

FLIBBERT, Joseph. Professor of English, Salem State College, Salem, Massachusetts. Author of *Melville and the Art of the Burlesque*, 1974, and of numerous articles on English and American literature. **Essay:** Herman Melville.

FLOYD, Phylis. Assistant Professor of Art History, Michigan State University, East Lansing. Author of numerous exhibition catalogs and articles in journals. **Essays:** Jacques-Louis David; Paul Gauguin; Wassily Kandinsky; Édouard Manet; Claude Monet; Berthe Morisot.

FORTIN, Maurice G. Assistant Director for Public Services, University of North Texas Libraries, Denton; Editor for *Texas Library Journal*, since 1987. **Essay:** Crazy Horse.

FOSTER, Mike F. Freelance writer and independent scholar; Assistant Professor of History, University of Illinois, Urbana, 1969–73. Author of *The Politics of Stability: A Portrait of the Rulers in Elizabethan London*, 1977, *Summits to Reach, an Annotated Edition of Franklin Rhoda's Report on the Topography of the San Juan Country*, 1984, and of numerous articles in journals. **Essays:** James Cook; Laurence Olivier.

FRANK, Mortimer H. Professor of English, Bronx Community College, City University of New York; Curator of the Toscanini Collection at Wave Hill; Contributing Editor for *Fanfare*, since 1978, and historical records critic for National Public Radio, since 1987. Author of *James Huneker on Music and Musicians*, 1974, and of numerous articles on music and literature. **Essay:** Arturo Toscanini.

FRITZ, Stephen G. Associate Professor of History, East Tennessee State University. Author of numerous articles on German history. **Essays:** Benito Mussolini; Wilhelm II of Prussia.

FRUS, Phyllis. Assistant Professor of English, Vanderbilt University, Nashville, Tennessee. Author of articles in *Biography: An Interdisciplinary Quarterly*, and in *Literary Nonfiction*, 1989. **Essays:** Saul Bellow; Robert Lowell; Mark Twain.

FURDELL, Elizabeth Lane. Associate Professor of History, University of North Florida, Jacksonville. Author of articles in *The Historian* and *Journal of the Royal Society of Medicine*. **Essays:** Anne Boleyn; Mary I of England.

GARGAN, William M. Professor, Library Department, Brooklyn College, City University of New York. Co-author of *Find That Tune: An Index to Rock, Folk Rock, Disco, and Soul in Collections*, 2 vols., 1988, and of numerous articles in journals and reference books. **Essay:** Henry Miller.

GATES, Robert A. Associate Professor of English, St. John's University, Jamaica, New York. Author of *The New York Vision: Interpretation of New York City in the American Novel*, 1987. **Essay:** Carl Sandburg.

GEORGE, Nadine F. Collection Management Librarian, Kenyon College, Gambier, Ohio. **Essay:** Niels Bohr.

GILLIAM, Brian. Assistant Professor of Music, Duke University, Durham, North Carolina. Author of *Richard Strauss' Elektra*, 1991, and of articles on Strauss in *Journal of the American Musicological Society*, *Nineteenth Century Music*, the *Richard Strauss Blätter*, and other journals. **Essay:** Richard Strauss.

GILLILAND, C. Herbert, Jr. Associate Professor of English, U.S. Naval Academy, Annapolis, Maryland. **Essay:** Sir Philip Sidney.

GLASS, Erlis. Associate Professor of German and Head of the Department of Modern Foreign Languages and Literature, Rosemont College, Rosemont, Pennsylvania. Author of numerous articles and reviews in journals. **Essay:** Gotthold Ephraim Lessing.

GLASSEY, Lionel K. J. Lecturer in Modern History, University of Glasgow; History Editor of *The Scriblerian*, since 1989. Author of *Politics and the Appointment of Justices of the Peace 1675–1720*, 1979. **Essay:** Anne of England.

GLIÈRE, Gerhard. Freelance writer and independent scholar. **Essay:** Henry Moore.

GODDARD, Charlotte. Research student in Latin Literature, Corpus Christi College, Cambridge University. **Essays:** Catullus; Horace.

GODDARD, Justin. Research student in Latin Literature, Corpus Christi College, Cambridge University. **Essay:** Cicero.

GOLDLEAF, Steven. Lecturer in English, State University of New York, Albany. Author of numerous short stories, poems, and essays in journals and anthologies, including *Signet's Contemporary American Short Stories*, 1985. **Essays:** F. Scott Fitzgerald; John O'Hara.

GOMERY, Douglas. Professor in the Department of Communication Arts and Theatre, University of Maryland, College Park; Senior Researcher, Media Studies Project, Woodrow Wilson Center for International Scholars, Washington, D.C. Author or co-author of *High Sierra: Screenplay and Analysis*, 1979, *Film History: Theory and Practice*, 1985, *The Hollywood Studio System*, 1986, *The Will Hays Papers*, 1987, and *American Media: The Wilson Quarterly Reader*, 1989. **Essays:** Bing Crosby; John Ford; John Wayne.

GOODSON, A. C. Professor of English, Michigan State University, East Lansing. Author of *Verbal Imagination: Coleridge and the Language of Modern Criticism*, 1988, and of the Coleridge biography in the *Dictionary of Literary Biography*, 1990. **Essay:** Samuel Taylor Coleridge.

GOOSSEN, Frederic. Professor of Music, University of Alabama, Tuscaloosa. Author of numerous articles in journals. Editor of *Landscape Remembered: Ross Lee Finney Collected*, 1991. Composer of the musical works *Equali*, 1972, *Death, Be Not Proud*, 1973, *American Meditations*, 1973, *Let Us Now Praise Famous Men*, 1975, *Temple Music*, 1980, *Clausulae*, 1980, and various orchestral and chamber works. **Essay:** Béla Bartók.

GORDON, Ian A. Dictionary editor and language consultant; Vice-Chancellor, University of New Zealand, 1947–52; Professor of English, University of Wellington, 1936–74; Editor, Collins English Dictionaries, since 1981. Author of *John Skelton*, 1943, *The Teaching of English*, 1947, *Katherine Mansfield*, 1954, *The Movement of English Prose*, 1966, *John Galt*, 1972, *Word Finder*, 1979, and *A Word in Your Ear*, 1980. Editor of *English Prose Technique*, 1948, and of works by William Shenstone, John Galt, and Katherine Mansfield. **Essays:** The Venerable Bede; A.E. Housman; Katherine Mansfield; Alexander Pope; Robert Louis Stevenson; Virginia Woolf.

GRAHAM, Susette Ryan. Professor of English, Nazareth College, Rochester, New York. Author of numerous articles in journals and reviewer for *Choice*. **Essays:** Nathaniel Hawthorne; William Dean Howells.

GRASSI, Patricia. Freelance writer. **Essay:** Mother Teresa.

GRAVE, Floyd K. Associate Professor of Music and Director of the Graduate Program in Music, Rutgers University, New Brunswick, New Jersey. Author of the Preface to *W.A. Mozart: Sa Vie Musicale et Son Oeuvre*, 1980, "Ignaz Holzbauer," in *The New Grove Dictionary of Music and Musicians*, 1980, *In Praise of Harmony: The Teachings of Abbé Vogler* (with Margaret Grupp Grave), 1988, *Franz Joseph Haydn: A Guide to Research*, 1990, and numerous articles in journals. Editor of musical works by Abbé Georg Joseph Vogler. **Essays:** Franz Joseph Haydn; Wolfgang Amadeus Mozart.

GRAY, Martin. Lecturer in English, University of Stirling, Scotland. Author of *A Dictionary of Literary Terms*, 1984, and *A Chronology of English Literature*, 1989. **Essays:** Thomas De Quincey; Robert Graves.

HACKETT, Nan. Assistant Professor, Concordia College, St. Paul, Minnesota. Author of *19th-Century British Working-Class Autobiographies: An Annotated Bibliography*, 1985, and of articles in *Biography: An Interdisciplinary Quarterly*. **Essay:** J.A.M. Whistler.

HAGEBAK, Mindy Friddle. Graduate Student in the Department of English, University of South Carolina, Columbia. **Essay:** Abigail Adams.

HAILEY, Christopher. Assistant Professor of Music, Occidental College, Los Angeles. Editor of *Alban Berg: Jugenlieder*, 2 vols., 1985–87, and co-editor of *The Berg-Schoenberg Correspondence*, 1987. **Essay:** Alban Berg.

HALL, Colin R. Graduate Student in the Department of Germanic Languages, University of California, Los Angeles. **Essays:** Friedrich Hölderlin; Rainer Maria Rilke.

HALLISEY, Charles. Assistant Professor of Theology, Loyola University, Chicago. **Essay:** Buddha.

HANSON, Craig L. Assistant Professor of Religion and Philosophy, Muskingum College, New Concord, Ohio. Author of numerous articles in journals. **Essays:** Constantine the Great; Saint Jerome; Justinian I; Mohammed.

HANSON, Robin Grollmus. Director of the Library, Muskingum College, New Concord, Ohio. Reviewer for *Choice*. **Essays:** Edward Fitzgerald; George Gissing.

HARDING, James. Senior Lecturer in French, Thames Polytechnic, London. Author of *Saint-Saëns and His Circle*, 1965, *Sacha Guitry, the Last Boulevardier*, 1968, *The Duke of Wellington*, 1968, *Massenet*, 1970, *Rossini*, 1971, *The Astonishing Adventure of General Boulanger*, 1971, *The Ox on the Roof*, 1972, *Gounod*, 1973, *Lost Illusions: Paul Léautaud and His World*, 1974, *Erik Satie*, 1975, *Folies de Paris: The Rise and Fall of French Operetta*, 1979, *Offenbach*, 1980, *Maurice Chevalier: His Life*, 1982, *Jacques Tati: Frame by Frame*, 1984, *Agate*, 1986, *Ivor Novello*, 1987, *The Rocky Horror Show Book*, 1987, *Cochran*, 1988, and *Gerald du Maurier: The Last Actor-Manager*, 1989. Editor of *Lord Chesterfield's Letters to His Son*, 1973. Translator of *Francis Poulenc: My Friends and Myself*, 1978. **Essays:** Hector Berlioz; Georges Bizet; Noël Coward; Somerset Maugham; Vaslav Nijinsky; Maurice Ravel.

HARMON, Maurice. Professor of Anglo-Irish Literature, University College, Dublin; Editor of the *Irish University Review, a Journal of Irish Studies*, 1970–86. Author of *Sean O'Faolain:*

A Critical Introduction, 1967 (revised, 1985), *Modern Irish Literature*, 1967, *The Poetry of Thomas Kinsella*, 1974, *Select Bibliography for the Study of Anglo-Irish Literature*, 1976, *Richard Murphy: Poet of Two Traditions*, 1977, *A Short History of Anglo-Irish Literature from Its Origins to the Present* (with Roger McHugh), 1982, and *Austin Clarke: A Critical Introduction*, 1989. Editor of numerous books and editions, including the works of William Shakespeare, *The Celtic Master*, 1969, *J.M. Synge Centenary Papers 1971*, 1972, *The Irish Novel in Our Times* (with Patrick Rafroidi), 1976, *Irish Poetry after Yeats: Seven Poets*, 1979, *Image and Illusion: Anglo-Irish Literature and Its Contexts*, 1979, and *The Irish Writer and the City*, 1985. **Essays:** Elizabeth Bowen; James Joyce; George Moore; Sean O'Casey; Frank O'Connor; John Millington Synge.

HARMOND, Richard P. Associate Professor of History, St. John's University, Jamaica, New York; Associate Editor of *Long Island Historical Journal*, since 1988. Co-author of *Long Island As America*, 1977, and author of numerous articles in journals. Co-editor of *Technology in the 20th Century*, 1983. **Essay:** John Pierpont Morgan.

HAVLIK, Robert James. Engineering/Architecture Librarian, University of Notre Dame, Indiana. Author of numerous articles in journals and reviewer for *Choice*. **Essays:** Alexander Graham Bell; Thomas Alva Edison; Abraham Lincoln; Mary Todd Lincoln; Stanford White; Wright Brothers.

HAWKSHAW, Paul. Associate Dean, Yale School of Music. Author of numerous articles in journals. **Essay:** Anton Bruckner.

HAYLEY, Barbara. Professor and Head of the Department of English, National University of Ireland, St. Patrick's College, Maynooth. Author of *Carleton's "Traits and Stories" and the 19th-Century Anglo-Irish Tradition*, 1985, and *A Bibliography of the Writings of William Carleton*, 1988. **Essays:** Arnold Bennett; John Galsworthy; Edith Sitwell; William Thackeray; H.G. Wells.

HEIDENREICH, Donald E., Jr. Instructor of History and Social Sciences, Kemper College, Boonville, Missouri. **Essays:** Charles Parnell; William I of England.

HEIDTMANN, Peter. Professor of English, Ohio University, Athens. Author of *Loren Eiseley: A Modern Ishmael*, 1990. **Essay:** Charles Lindbergh.

HERBERT, Michael. Member of the faculty of English, University of St. Andrews, Fife, Scotland. Editor of *Reflections on the Death of a Porcupine and Other Essays*, by D.H. Lawrence, 1988. **Essay:** D.H. Lawrence.

HESS, Marlene A. Member of the faculty, Davenport College, Grand Rapids, Michigan. **Essays:** John Bunyan; Harriet Beecher Stowe; Mary Wollstonecraft.

HEWETT, Roger S. Associate Professor of Economics, Drake University, Des Moines, Iowa. Author of numerous articles in journals covering the history of economic thought. **Essays:** John Stuart Mill; Adam Smith.

HICKS, Michael. Senior Lecturer in History, King Alfred's College, Winchester. Author of *False, Fleeting, Perjur'd Clarence: George Duke of Clarence 1449–78*, 1980, *Richard III as Duke of Gloucester: A Study in Character*, 1986, and *Profit, Piety, and Professions in Later Medieval England*, 1990. **Essays:** Henry IV of England; Henry V of England; Richard III of England.

HILFSTEIN, Erna. Affiliate of the Graduate Center of the City University of New York. Author of *Starowolski's Biographies of Copernicus*, 1980, and numerous articles in journals. Editor of *Nicholas Copernicus: Complete Works* (with Edward Rosen), 3 vols., 1972–85, and *Science and History*, 1978. **Essays:** Nicholas Copernicus; Johannes Kepler.

HILL, James L. Professor of English, Michigan State University, East Lansing. Author of articles on 19th-century English literature in *English Literary History*, *Studies in English Literature*, and *Journal of Aesthetics and Art Criticism*. **Essay:** Alfred, Lord Tennyson.

HOLDITCH, W. Kenneth. Research Professor of English, University of New Orleans, Louisiana; Editor and Publisher of the *Tennessee Williams Journal*, since 1988. Author of *In Old New Orleans*, 1983, and of numerous articles in journals. **Essays:** Carson McCullers; Tennessee Williams; Thomas Wolfe.

HOPPENSTAND, Gary. Assistant Professor in the Department of American Thought and Language, Michigan State University, East Lansing. Author of *In Search of the Paper Tiger: A Sociological Perspective of Myth, Formula, and the Mystery Genre in the Entertainment Print Mass Media*, 1987. **Essays:** Charles Brockden Brown; Cary Grant; Alfred Hitchcock.

HOPPER, Jeffrey. Associate Professor of History, Harding University, Searcy, Arkansas. **Essays:** Gustav Mahler; Franz Schubert.

HOWARD, David L. Associate Dean, North East Surrey College of Technology, England; Tutor in Management, The Open University, since 1977; Visiting Lecturer, Reading University, since 1979. Co-author of *Personal Management and the Supervisor*, 1990. **Essays:** Dorothy Sayers; Max Weber.

HOWARD, Patricia. Lecturer in Music, The Open University, England. Author of *Gluck and the Birth of Modern Opera*, 1963, *The Operas of Benjamin Britten: An Introduction*, 1969, *C.W. Gluck: "Orfeo"*, 1981, *Benjamin Britten: "The Turn of the Screw"*, 1985, *and Christoph Willibald Gluck: A Guide to Research*, 1987. **Essays:** Ludwig van Beethoven; Benjamin Britten; Henry Purcell.

HOWE, Kenneth A. Associate Professor in the Department of American Thought and Language, Michigan State University, East Lansing. Author of numerous articles in journals and reference books. **Essays:** Truman Capote; Theodore Dreiser.

HULICK, Diana Emery. Assistant Professor in the School of Art, Arizona State University, Tempe. Author of *Waldo Peirce: A New Assessment*, 1984, and of numerous catalog entries and articles in journals. **Essays:** Margaret Bourke-White; Alfred Stieglitz.

HUTCH, Richard A. Senior Lecturer of Religion and Psychological Studies, University of Queensland, Brisbane, Australia. Author of *Emerson's Optics: Biographical Process and the Dawn of Religious Leadership*, 1983, *Under the Shade of a Coolibah Tree: Australian Studies in Consciousness*, 1984, *Religious Leadership: Personality, History, and Sacred Authority*, 1990, and of numerous articles in journals, including *Biography: An Interdisciplinary Quarterly*. **Essay:** Carl Gustav Jung.

HUTCHISON, Jane Campbell. Professor of Art History, University of Wisconsin, Madison; Editorial Board, *The Illustrated Bartsch*, since 1977. Author of *The Master of the Housebook*, 1972, *Early German Artists* (vols. 8 and 9), 1981–82, *Graphic Art in the Age of Martin Luther* (exhibition catalogue), 1985, and *Albrecht Dürer: A Biography*, 1990. **Essay:** Albrecht Dürer.

INGUANZO, Anthony P. Research Associate, Bronx Institute, Lehman College, New York. Author of numerous entries in reference books. **Essays:** Marcus Aurelius; Aaron Burr.

IRVING, Donald C. Professor of English and American Studies, Grinnell College, Grinnell, Iowa. Author of numerous articles in journals. **Essays:** James Fenimore Cooper; Theodore Roethke.

JEANSONNE, Glen. Professor of History, University of Wisconsin, Milwaukee. Author of *Race, Religion, and Politics*, 1977, *Leander Perez: Boss of the Delta*, 1977, and *Gerald L.K. Smith: Minister of Hate*, 1988. Co-editor of *A Guide to the History of Louisiana*, 1982. **Essay:** Herbert Hoover.

JEFFERSON, Alan. Freelance writer; Editor of *Monthly Guide to Recorded Music* (London), 1980–82; Administrator of the London Symphony Orchestra, 1967–68; Orchestral Manager of the BBC, 1968–73. Author of *Lieder of Richard Strauss*, 1971, *Delius*, 1972, *Inside the Orchestra*, 1974, *The Glory of Opera*, 1976 (revised, 1983, 1991), *Sir Thomas Beecham*, 1979, *Complete Gilbert and Sullivan Opera Guide*, 1984 (revised, 1990), *Der Rosenkavalier*, 1986, *Lotte Lehmann*, 1988, and *The Musical Chronology*, 1990. **Essays:** George Balanchine; Maria Callas; Enrico Caruso; Sergei Diaghilev; Anna Pavlova.

JESSEPH, Douglas M. Assistant Professor of Philosophy, Illinois Institute of Technology, Chicago. **Essay:** George Berkeley.

JIMÉNEZ, Meri. Instructor in the Department of Spanish, Villanova University, Philadelphia. **Essays:** Miguel de Cervantes; Hernando Cortès.

JOHNSON, Douglas. Professor of French History, University College, London. Author of *Guizot: Aspects of French History 1787–1874*, 1964, *France and the Dreyfus Affair*, 1966, *A Concise History of France*, 1971, *Britain and France: Ten Centuries*, 1980, *The Idea of Europe*, 1987, and *The Age of Illusion: Art and*

Politics in France 1918–40, 1987. **Essays:** Charlemagne; Charles de Gaulle; Louis XIV of France; Maximilien Robespierre.

JONES, Marnie. Associate Professor of English, University of North Florida, Jacksonville. Author of numerous articles in journals. **Essays:** William Jennings Bryan; Eugene Debs; Elizabeth Gaskell.

JONES, Steven E. Assistant Professor of English, Loyola University, Chicago. Editor of Percy Bysshe Shelley's *Julian and Maddalo Draft Notebook: Bodleian Manuscript*, 1990. **Essays:** Mary Wollstonecraft Shelley; Percy Bysshe Shelley; William Wordsworth.

JUDD, Jacob. Professor and Head of the Department of History, Lehman College, City University of New York. Editor of *The Van Cortland Family Papers*, 4 vols., 1976–81. **Essay:** John D. Rockefeller.

KEARNS, William K. Professor of Music, University of Colorado, Boulder. Author of *Horatio Parker Parker 1863–1919: His Life, Music, and Ideas*, 1990, and of numerous articles in journals and in the *New Grove Dictionary of Music and Musicians*, 1980. Editor of *Musicology at the University of Colorado* (anthology), 1975. **Essays:** Count Basie; Jerome Kern.

KEY, Newton E. Assistant Professor of History, Eastern Illinois University, Charleston. Author of a chapter in *The Politics of Religion in Restoration England*, 1990. **Essay:** Samuel Pepys.

KILLORAN, Helen. Instructor in the Department of English, University of Washington, Seattle. **Essays:** Washington Irving; Henry Wadsworth Longfellow; John Greenleaf Whittier.

KIND, Joshua. Faculty Member of the School of Art, Northern Illinois University, DeKalb. **Essays:** Aubrey Beardsley; Marc Chagall; Salvador Dali; Eugène Delacroix; Francisco Goya; Pablo Picasso; Henri de Toulouse-Lautrec.

KINNAMON, Keneth. Ethel Pumphrey Stephens Professor of English and Head of the Department, University of Arkansas, Fayetteville. Author of *The Emergence of Richard Wright: A Study in Literature and Society*, 1972, and *A Richard Wright Bibliography: 50 Years of Criticism and Commentary 1933–82*, 1988. Editor of *Black Writers of America: A Comprehensive Anthology* (with Richard K. Barksdale), 1972, *James Baldwin: A Collection of Critical Essays*, 1974, and *New Essays on Native Son*, 1990. **Essays:** Ernest Hemingway; Langston Hughes.

KIRBY, David. McKenzie Professor of English, Florida State University, Tallahassee. Author of *Individual and Community* (with Kenneth Baldwin), 1975, *American Fiction to 1900*, 1975, *The Opera Lover* (poetry), 1977, *Grace King*, 1980, *America's Hive of Honey*, 1980, *The Sun Rises in the Evening*, 1982, *Sarah Bernhardt's Leg* (poetry), 1983, *The Plural World*, 1984, *Dictionary of Contemporary Thought*, 1984, *Diving for Poems*, 1985, *Saving the Young Men of Vienna* (poetry), 1987, *Writing Poetry*, 1989, *Mark Strand: The Poet as No One*, 1990, and *The Portrait of a Lady*, 1990. **Essay:** Henry James.

LAFORTE, Robert S. Professor and Head of the Department of History, University of North Texas, Denton. Author of *Leaders of Reform: Kansas Progressive Republicans 1900–16*, *Down the Corridor of Years: Centennial History of UNT*, 1989, and numerous articles in journals. Editor of *Our National Heritage*, 1989, and *Remembering Pearl Harbor*, 1991. **Essay:** Carrie Nation.

LAGO, Mary. Catherine Paine Middlebush Professor of English, University of Missouri, Columbia. Author of *Rabindranath Tagore*, 1971. Editor of *Imperfect Encounter: Letters of William Rothenstein and Rabindranath Tagore*, 1972, *Max and Will: Max Beerbohm and William Rothenstein, Their Correspondence and Friendship* (with K. Beckson), 1975, *Men and Memories: Recollections of William Rothenstein*, 1978, *Burne-Jones Talking: His Conversations Recorded by His Assistant Thomas Rooke*, 1981, and *Selected Letters of E.M. Forster* (with P.N. Furbank), 2 vols., 1983–85. Translator of Tagore's *The Broken Nest*, 1971, and *Selected Stories of Rabindranath Tagore*, 1991. **Essays:** E.M. Forster; Rabindranath Tagore.

LAUBY, Jacqueline. Instructor in the Department of English, Loyola University, Chicago. Author of numerous reviews and articles in journals. **Essay:** Flannery O'Connor.

LAWNICZAK, Donald A. Professor of English, Eastern Michigan University, Ypsilanti. **Essay:** John Coltrane.

LE BEAU, Bryan F. Associate Professor of History, Creighton University, Omaha, Nebraska. Author of *Frederic Henry Hedge: 19th-Century American Transcendentalist*, 1985, and of numerous articles in journals and encyclopedias. **Essays:** John Smith; Joseph Smith.

LEE, Judith. Assistant Professor of English, The American University, Washington, D.C. **Essays:** Isak Dinesen; Katherine Anne Porter.

LELAND, John L. Assistant Professor of English, Salem-Teikyo University, West Virginia. **Essays:** Edward III of England; Richard II of England.

LESLIE, Alison. Freelance writer and researcher. **Essays:** Leonardo da Vinci; Michelangelo; Raphael; Tintoretto.

LESLIE, Van Michael. Assistant Professor of History, University of Alabama, Huntsville. Author of numerous articles and reviews in journals and encyclopedias, including "British Wartime Government," in *The Encyclopedia of World War Two*, 1991. **Essays:** Arthur James Balfour; Neville Chamberlain.

LEVI, A. H. T. Freelance writer and independent scholar; Buchanan Professor of French Language and Literature, University of St. Andrews, Fife, Scotland, 1971–87; also Lecturer at Christ Church, Oxford, and Professor of French, University of Warwick, Coventry. Author of *French Moralists: The Theory of the Passions 1585–1649*, 1964, and *Religion in Practice*, 1966. Editor of *Erasmus: Satires*, 1986. **Essays:** Honoré de Balzac; Giovanni Boccaccio; Saint Catherine of Siena; Denis Diderot;

Alexandre Dumas (*père*); François I of France; Pope Gregory the Great; G.W.F. Hegel; Hermann Hesse; Saint Ignatius of Loyola; Immanuel Kant; Louis IX of France; Maimonides; Guy de Maupassant; Michel de Montaigne; Baron de Montesquieu; Sir Thomas More; Francesco Petrarch; François Rabelais; Jean Racine; Jean-Jacques Rousseau; Madame de Sévigné; Benedict de Spinoza; Stendhal; Voltaire.

LEVI, Honor. Freelance writer and independent scholar. **Essays:** Paul Cézanne; Armand (Cardinal) Richelieu.

LICHTMANN, Maria R. Visiting Assistant Professor, Georgetown University; Assistant Professor of Religion, Bowdoin College, Brunswick, Maine, 1988–90. Author of *Sylvia Plath: A Bibliography*, 1978, and *The Contemplative Poetry of Gerard Manley Hopkins*, 1989. **Essays:** Søren Kierkegaard; Thomas Merton.

LINDEMAN, Stephan D. Visiting Lecturer and Doctoral candidate in the Department of Music, Rutgers University, New Brunswick, New Jersey. **Essays:** Frédéric Chopin; Richard Wagner.

LINDSAY, Maurice. Honorary Secretary-General, Europa Nostra, since 1983; Director of the Scottish Civic Trust, Glasgow, 1967–83; Editor of *The Scottish Review*, 1972–81. Author of numerous books of poetry (*Collected Poems 1960–90*, 1990); plays; travel and historical works; an autobiography (*Thank You for Having Me*, 1983); and critical studies, including *Robert Burns: The Man, His Work, The Legend*, 1954 (revised, 1968, 1989), *The Burns Encyclopedia*, 1959 (revised, 1970, 1989), and *A History of Scottish Literature*, 1977. Editor of the Saltire Modern Poets series, several anthologies of Scottish writing, and works by Sir Alexander Gray, Sir David Lyndsay, Marion Angus, and John Davidson. **Essays:** Robert Burns; Sir Arthur Conan Doyle; John Dryden; Hugh MacDiarmid; Sir Walter Scott.

LLOYD-KIMBREL, Elizabeth Dominique. Lecturer in English, University of Hartford, Connecticut. Author of numerous articles in journals. **Essays:** Geoffrey Chaucer; Christina Rossetti.

LOONEY, Barbara A. Doctoral candidate in the Department of English, University of South Florida, Tampa. **Essay:** Willa Cather.

LOW, Alfred D. Professor Emeritus of History, Marquette University, Milwaukee. Author of *Lenin on the Question of Nationality*, 1958, *The Soviet Hungarian Republic and the Paris Peace Conference*, 1963, *The Anschluss Movement 1918-19 and the Paris Peace Conference*, 1974, *The Sino-Soviet Dispute: An Analysis of the Politics*, 1976, *Jews and Judaism in the Eyes of the Germans: From the Enlightenment to Imperial Germany*, 1979, *The Anschluss Movement 1918–38, Background and Aftermath: An Annotated Bibliography*, 1984, *The Anschluss Movement 1931–38 and the Great Powers*, 1985, *The Sino-Soviet Confrontation Since Mao Zedong*, 1987, and *Soviet Jewry and Soviet Policy*, 1990. **Essays:** David Ben-Gurion; Franz Joseph I of Austria; Frederick the Great of Prussia.

LOWMAN, Roger. Head of the Department of English, King Alfred's College, Winchester. **Essays:** George Frideric Handel; Diego Velázquez.

LUCKHARDT, C. Grant. Professor of Philosophy and Executive Director of the Honors Program, Georgia State University, Atlanta. Author of numerous articles on Ludwig Wittgenstein. Editor of *Wittgenstein: Sources and Perspectives*, 1979. Translator of Wittgenstein's *Remarks on the Philosophy of Psychology*, vol. II, 1980, and *Last Writings on the Philosophy of Psychology*, vol. I, 1982; vol. II, 1991. **Essay:** Ludwig Wittgenstein.

LURIE, Maxine N. Visiting Lecturer in History, Rutgers University, New Brunswick, New Jersey. Author of articles in journals. **Essays:** Christopher Columbus; Sir Francis Drake; James Madison.

MacGREGOR, Sally. Doctoral candidate in Music, Queen's College, Cambridge University. **Essay:** Sir Edward Elgar.

MacKENDRICK, Louis K. Professor of English, University of Windsor, Ontario. Editor of *Probable Fictions: Alice Munro's Narrative Acts*, 1983, *Robert Harlow and His Works*, 1989, and *Al Purdy and His Works*, 1990. **Essay:** W.C. Fields.

MADDOX, Robert James. Professor of History, Pennsylvania State University, University Park. Author of *William E. Borah and American Foreign Policy*, 1969, *The New Left and the Origins of the Cold War*, 1973, *The Unknown War with Russia: Wilson's Siberian Intervention*, 1977, and *From War to Cold War: The Education of Harry S. Truman*, 1988. **Essays:** Franklin D. Roosevelt; Woodrow Wilson.

MAGNER, Lois N. Associate Professor of History, Purdue University, West Lafayette, Indiana. Author of *A History of Life Sciences*, 1979. **Essays:** Marie Curie; Charles Darwin; Thomas Henry Huxley; Margaret Mead; Gregor Mendel; Florence Nightingale; Louis Pasteur; Margaret Sanger.

MALLER, Jane Nash. Associate Professor of Art, San Francisco State University, California. Author of *Veiled Images: Titian's Mythological Paintings for Philip II*, 1985. **Essay:** Titian.

MALLETT, Phillip. Lecturer in English, University of St. Andrews, Fife, Scotland. Author of *John Donne*, 1983, and *Kipling Considered*, 1989. **Essay:** Thomas Hardy.

MATTERN, David B. Assistant Editor, The Papers of James Madison, University of Virginia, Charlottesville. **Essay:** Benedict Arnold.

MAXWELL-STEWART, L. J. Freelance writer and researcher; Assistant Manager of The King's Consort. **Essays:** Gioacchino Rossini; Peter Ilyich Tchaikovsky.

McBRIDE, Robert. Professor of French, University of Ulster at Coleraine, Northern Ireland. Author of *The Sceptical Vision of Molière*, 1977, and *Aspects of 17th-Century Drama and Thought*,

1979. Co-editor of *Humanitas, Essays in Honor of Henri Godin*, 1984. **Essay:** Jean-Baptiste Molière.

McCARTHY, Joseph M. Professor of Education and Human Services, and Professor of History, Suffolk University, Boston, Massachusetts; Series General Editor, Garland Publishing, since 1979. Author of *Humanistic Emphases in the Educational Thought of Vincent of Beauvais*, 1976, *Guinea-Bissau and Cape Verde Islands*, 1977, and *Pierre Teilhard de Chardin: A Comprehensive Bibliography*, 1981. **Essays:** Francisco Franco; Martin Luther King, Jr.; Giuseppe Mazzini; Pierre Teilhard de Chardin.

McGOWAN, Ian. Director of the Centre for Publishing Studies, University of Stirling, Scotland; Chairman, Stirling University Press, 1987–90; Lecturer in English, Stirling University, since 1973. Author of *Charles Dickens: Little Dorrit*, 1984, and *The Restoration and the 18th Century*, 1989. **Essay:** Sir Allen Lane.

McGRATH, Alister E. Lecturer in Historical Theology, Oxford University. Author of *Luther's Theology of the Cross*, 1985, *The Intellectual Origins of the European Reformation*, 1987, *Reformation Thought*, 1988, *A Life of John Calvin*, 1990, and *The Genesis of Doctrine*, 1990. Editor of the *Blackwell Encyclopaedia of Modern Christian Thought*, forthcoming, and *Blackwell Encyclopaedia of Medieval, Renaissance, and Reformation Thought*, forthcoming. **Essays:** John Calvin; John Wycliffe; Huldreich Zwingli.

MEIR, Colin. Reader in English, University of Ulster at Jordanstown, Northern Ireland; Literary Editor of the *Linen Hall Review* (Belfast), since 1990. Author of *The Ballads and Songs of W.B. Yeats*, 1974, *Critical Analysis of Dylan Thomas' "Under Milk Wood,"* 1983, and numerous articles in journals. **Essay:** William Butler Yeats.

MERRILL, Thomas F. Professor of English, University of Delaware, Newark. Author of *Allen Ginsberg*, 1969 (revised, 1988), *Christian Criticism*, 1976, *The Poetry of Charles Olson*, 1982, and *Epic God-Talk*, 1986. **Essay:** Allen Ginsberg.

MEYERING, Sheryl L. Assistant Professor of English, Southern Illinois University, Edwardsville. Author of *Charlotte Perkins Gilman: The Woman and Her Work*, 1989, and *Sylvia Plath: A Reference Guide 1973–88*, 1990. **Essay:** Sylvia Plath.

MIKHAIL, E. H. Professor of English, University of Lethbridge, Alberta. Author of numerous critical bibliographies on writers, including Sean O'Casey, J.M. Synge, Oscar Wilde, Brendan Behan, and Lady Gregory, and of a series of interviews and recollections on O'Casey, W.B. Yeats, Synge, Lady Gregory, Wilde, Behan, James Joyce, Richard Brinsley Sheridan, and Oliver Goldsmith; other books include *The Social and Cultural Setting of the 1890s*, 1969, *John Galsworthy the Dramatist*, 1971, *Comedy and Tragedy: A Bibliography of Criticism*, 1972, *The Art of Brendan Behan*, 1979, *A Research Guide to Modern Irish Dramatists*, 1979, *An Annotated Bibliography of Modern Anglo-Irish Drama*, 1981, *Sean O'Casey and His Critics*, 1985,

and *The Abbey Theatre*, 1988. Editor of *The Letters of Brendan Behan*, 1991. **Essay:** Richard Brinsley Sheridan.

MILLER, Julia I. Assistant Professor of Art History, California State University, Long Beach; President of the Italian Art Society, since 1989. Author of articles in *Explorations in Renaissance Culture*, *Studies in Iconography*, and *Source*. **Essays:** Giovanni Bellini; Sandro Botticelli.

MILLER, Marcia J. Doctoral candidate in American Literature, University of South Carolina, Columbia. **Essay:** Jonathan Edwards.

MILLSTONE, Amy B. Associate Professor of French, University of South Carolina, Columbia. Author of book chapter in *The Image of the Prostitute in Modern Literature*, 1984, and articles in *Proceedings of the Annual Meeting of the Western Society for French History*, *Biography: An Interdisciplinary Quarterly*, and "The One and the Many: George Sand and Her Biographers," in *Nineteenth-Century French Studies*. **Essays:** George Sand; Victoria of England.

MOLLOY, F. C. Senior Lecturer in English, Charles Sturt University, New South Wales, Australia. Author of articles in *Biography: An Interdisciplinary Quarterly*, *Yeats Annual*, *Irish-Australian Studies*, *Irish University Review*, and *Critique*. **Essay:** Ford Madox Ford.

MORGAN, David. Reader in the History of the Middle East, University of London; Editor, *Journal of the Royal Asiatic Society*, since 1987. Author of *The Mongols*, 1986, and *Medieval Persia 1040–1797*, 1988. Editor of *Medieval Historical Writing in the Christian and Islamic Worlds*, 1982, and *The Mission of Friar William of Rubruck: His Journey to the Court of the Great Khan Möngke 1253–55* (with P. Jackson), 1990. **Essay:** Genghis Khan.

MORRILL, John. University Lecturer and Senior Tutor, Faculty of History, Cambridge University; Editor of *Historical Journal*, since 1987; General Editor of the Royal Historical British Bibliography Project, since 1988. Author of numerous books and articles, including *Cheshire 1630–60: Government and Society during the English Revolution*, 1974, *The Revolt of the Provinces: Conservatives and Radicals in the English Civil Wars 1630–60*, 1976 (revised, 1980), *Seventeenth-Century Britain*, 1980, *Reactions to the English Civil War*, 1982, *Charles I*, 1989, *Oliver Cromwell and the English Revolution*, 1990, and *The National Covenant in Its British Context*, 1990. Also Editor of three continuing multi-volume series: *Longman Studies in Modern History* (with David Cannadine), *Cambridge Studies in Early Modern British History* (with Anthony Fletcher and John Guy), and *Cambridge Topics in History* (with Christopher Daniels). **Essays:** Charles I of England; Charles II of England; Elizabeth I of England; Henry VIII of England; James I of England; James II of England.

MORTON, Doris B. Associate Professor of English, Auburn University, Alabama. **Essay:** Booker T. Washington.

MOSER, Charles A. Professor of Slavic Languages and

Literatures, George Washington University, Washington, D.C.; Editor of the Russian section for Twayne's World Author Series, since 1975. Author of *Antinihilism in the Russian Novel of the 1860s*, 1964, *Pisemsky: A Provincial Realist*, 1969, *A History of Bulgarian Literature 865–1944*, 1972, *Denis Fonvizin*, 1979, *Dimitrov of Bulgaria*, 1979, and *Esthetics as Nightmare: Russian Literary Theory 1855–70*, 1989. General Editor of *The Cambridge History of Russian Literature*, 1989. **Essays:** Nikolai Gogol; Alexander Solzhenitsyn; Ivan Turgenev.

MULLETT, Michael A. Senior Lecturer in History, University of Lancaster; Review Editor, *European History Quarterly*. Author of *Radical Religious Movements in Early Modern Europe*, 1980, *The Counter-Reformation and the Catholic Reformation in Early Modern Europe*, 1984, *Luther*, 1986, *Popular Culture and Popular Protest in Late Medieval and Early Modern Europe*, 1987, and *Calvin*, 1989. **Essays:** Lorenzo de' Medici; Girolamo Savonarola.

MUNDT, Whitney R. Associate Professor of Journalism, Louisiana State University, Baton Rouge; Editorial Board, *American Journalism*, and *Journalism History*. Author of numerous articles and entries in *World Press Encyclopedia*, *Encyclopedia Americana*, *Dictionary of Literary Biography*, *Biographical Dictionary of American Journalism*, and *Global Journalism*. **Essays:** James Agee; Sherwood Anderson; Ambrose Bierce; Edward R. Murrow; Laura Ingalls Wilder.

MURPHY, Alan. Freelance writer and media monitor for a news agency. **Essays:** Jorge Luis Borges; Lucrezia Borgia; Cleopatra; Georges Danton; Marcus Garvey; Billie Holliday; J. Robert Oppenheimer; Wilhelm Reich.

MURRAY, Bruce J. Associate Professor of Music, University of Alabama, Tuscaloosa. Author of an article in *Piano Literacy*. **Essay:** Franz Liszt.

NELSON, Nicolas H. Associate Professor of English, Indiana University, Kokomo. Author of articles in *Journal of the History of Ideas*, *Studies in English Literature*, and *Language and Style*. **Essay:** William Hogarth.

O'CONNOR, Robert E. Associate Professor of Political Science, Pennsylvania State University, University Park. Author of *Politics and Structure*, 1989, and articles in *American Political Science Review*, *Western Political Quarterly*, *British Journal of Political Science*, *Journal of Politics*, and other journals. **Essays:** Jimmy Carter; Fidel Castro; Joseph McCarthy; Richard Nixon; Ronald Reagan; Harry S. Truman.

O'LEARY, D. H. Law student, Polytechnic of Central London. **Essays:** Alexander the Great; Hannibal; Jawaharlal Nehru; Horatio Nelson; Sun Yat-sen; Margaret Thatcher; Duke of Wellington.

ORCHARD, Joseph T. Doctoral candidate in the Department of Music, Rutgers University, New Brunswick, New Jersey. **Essay:** Giuseppe Verdi.

OTTEN, Robert M. Professor of English and Head of the Department of Humanities, Indiana University, Kokomo. Author of *Joseph Addison*, 1982. **Essay:** Joseph Addison.

OVENDALE, Ritchie. Reader in International Politics, University College of Wales, Aberystwyth. Author of *"Appeasement" and the English-Speaking World*, 1975, *The Origins of the Arab-Israeli Wars*, 1984, *The English-Speaking Alliance: Britain, the United States, the Dominions of the Cold War 1945–51*, 1985, and *Britain, the United States, and the End of the Palestine Mandate 1942–48*, 1989. Editor of *The Foreign Policy of the British Labour Governments 1945–51*, 1984. **Essay:** Menachem Begin.

OVERMYER, Janet. Instructor in the Department of English, Ohio State University, Columbus. Author of numerous short stories, articles, poems, and reviews in journals. **Essays:** Richard Burton; Frank Sinatra; Elizabeth Taylor.

PAANANEN, Victor N. Professor and Head of the Department of English, Michigan State University, East Lansing. Author of *William Blake*, 1977, numerous articles in *Biographical Dictionary of Modern British Radicals*, and an article on Dylan Thomas. **Essay:** Dylan Thomas.

PARKER, Jacqueline K. Associate Professor of English, New Mexico State University, Las Cruces. Author of numerous articles in reference books and journals. **Essay:** Susan B. Anthony.

PARKER, Jeffrey D. Member of the faculty of English, University of North Carolina, A. and T. State University, Greensboro. Author of articles on Frank Yerby, Richard Wright, Henry Miller, and William Blake. **Essays:** William Blake; Richard Wright.

PATROUCH, Joseph F. Doctoral candidate in the Department of History, University of California, Berkeley. **Essay:** Klemens Metternich.

PAUL, Donna Price. Freelance writer and independent scholar. **Essay:** Bertrand Russell.

PELZ, William A. Assistant Professor of History, DePaul University, Chicago. Author of *Spartakusbund and the German Working-Class Movement 1914–19*, 1988, articles in *International Review of History and Political Science*, *German Studies*, *East European Quarterly*, and an essay on Garibaldi in *La Parola del Popolo*. **Essays:** Giuseppe Garibaldi; Vladimir Lenin; Rosa Luxemburg; Karl Marx; Joseph Stalin; Marshall Tito; Leon Trotsky.

PETERS, Jason R. Doctoral Candidate in the Department of English, Michigan State University, East Lansing. **Essay:** C.S. Lewis.

PETERSON, Barbara Bennett. Professor of History, University of Hawaii, Honolulu. Author of *Notable Women of Hawaii*, 1984, and *America in British Eyes*, 1988. Co-editor of *A Woman's Place Is in the History Books*, 1980. **Essay:** Pearl S. Buck.

PICKENS, Donald K. Professor of History, University of North Texas, Denton. Author of *Eugenics and the Progressives*, 1968, *American in Process* (co-author), 1973, and articles in *Journal of Thought*, *American Journal of Economics and Sociology*, *Contemporary Philosophy*, and an article on Franz Kafka and Max Weber in *Lamar Journal of the Humanities*. **Essay:** Franz Kafka.

PICKER, Martin. Professor of Music, Rutgers University, New Brunswick, New Jersey; former Editor in Chief and Chairman of the Publications Committee of the *Journal of the American Musicological Society*. Author of *The Chanson Albums of Marguerite of Austria*, 1965, *An Introduction to Music* (with Martin Bernstein), 1966 (revised, 1972), *The Motet Books of Andrea Antico*, 1987, and *Johannes Ockeghem and Jacob Obrecht*, 1988. **Essay:** Charles Ives.

PILCHER, Rebecca C. Freelance writer and researcher. **Essays:** Charles V, Holy Roman emperor; Philip II of Spain.

POLOS, Nicholas Christopher. Professor of History Emeritus, University of La Verne, California. Author of *John Swett: A California Frontier Schoolmaster*, 1978, *San Dimas: Preserving the Western Spirit*, 1990, and numerous articles in journals and reference books. **Essays:** Horatio Alger; Fred Astaire; George Washington Carver; Cole Porter.

POPE, Betty Frances. Assistant Catalog Librarian in Music, University of North Texas, Denton. Author of numerous book reviews in journals. **Essay:** Frederick Delius.

POTTER, George Thomas. Distinguished Professor of Economics and Human Development, Ramapo College, New Jersey; Founding President of Ramapo College, 1969–84. Author of *Conceptions of War: Visions of Peace*, 1988, and numerous articles in journals. **Essays:** Thomas Malthus; Richard I of England.

POWELL, Cecilia. Turner Scholar, Tate Gallery, London. Author of *Turner in the South: Rome, Naples, Florence*, 1987, and articles on Turner. **Essay:** J.M.W. Turner.

POWELL, John. Associate Professor of History and Director of the Honors Program, Hannibal-LaGrange College, Missouri; Consulting Editor, *Nineteenth-Century Prose*, since 1989. Author of *Liberal by Principle, Selections from the Papers of John Wodehouse, First Earl of Kimberley*, 1991, and articles on William Gladstone. **Essay:** William Gladstone.

PRATT, Alan. Member of the Faculty, Embry-Riddle Aeronautical University, Daytona Beach, Florida. **Essay:** Federico Fellini.

PRESTON, James J. Professor of Anthropology and Head of the Religious Studies Program, State University of New York, Oneconta. Author of *Mother Worship*, 1982, and *Cult of the Goddess*, 1985. **Essays:** Ruth Benedict; Francis Parkman; Saint Teresa of Avila.

PROUT, Ryan. Freelance writer and researcher. **Essays:** Federico García Lorca; Pablo Neruda.

RAGAN, Fred D. Professor of History, East Carolina University, Greenville, North Carolina. Author of an article on Oliver Wendell Holmes, Jr., in *Journal of American History*. Co-editor of *Politics, Bar, and Bench: A Memoir of U.S. District Court Judge John Davis Larkins, Jr.*, 1980. **Essay:** Oliver Wendell Holmes, Jr.

RAGEN, Brian Abel. Assistant Professor of English, University of Southern Illinois, Edwardsville. Author of *A Wreck on the Road to Damascus: Innocence, Guilt, and Conversion in Flannery O'Connor*, 1989. **Essays:** W.H. Auden; Rudyard Kipling.

RAITT, A. W. Reader in French Literature, Oxford University; General Editor, *French Studies*, since 1987. Author of *Villiers de l'Isle-Adam et le Mouvement Symboliste*, 1965, *Life and Letters in France: The 19th Century*, 1966, *Prosper Merimée*, 1970, and *The Life of Villiers de l'Isle-Adam*, 1981. Editor of *Villiers de l'Isle-Adam: Oeuvres Complètes* (with P.-G. Castex), 1986. **Essays:** Charles Baudelaire; Stéphane Mallarmé; Arthur Rimbaud; Paul Verlaine.

RAPHAEL WEINSTEIN, Honora. Music Librarian and Assistant Professor, Brooklyn College, City University of New York. Author of articles on D.W. Griffith and other musical topics. **Essays:** Samuel Goldwyn; Benny Goodman; Al Jolson.

REID, David. Lecturer in English Studies, University of Stirling, Scotland. Editor of *The Party-Coloured Mind: Prose Relating to the Conflict of Church and State in 17th-Century Scotland*, 1982, and *Rob Stene's Dream*, 1989. **Essays:** John Donne; John Milton.

RICHARDSON, Kelvin J. Instructor of History, California State University, Fullerton, and at the University of California, Riverside. **Essays:** Nikita Khrushchev; Dmitri Shostakovich.

RIDLAND, John. Professor of English, University of California, Santa Barbara. Author of numerous books of poetry, including *Fires of Home*, 1961, *Ode on Violence and Other Poems*, 1969, *In the Shadowless Light*, 1978, and *Elegy for My Aunt*, 1981. **Essay:** Robert Frost.

RIGGS, Paula R. Adjunct faculty, Marietta College, Marietta, Ohio. **Essay:** Catherine de' Medici.

RINTALA, Marvin. Professor of Political Science, Boston College. Author of *The Constitution of Silence: Essays on Generational Themes*, 1979. **Essays:** Herbert Henry Asquith; Winston Churchill; George V of England; David Lloyd George.

ROBERTS, Patricia. Assistant Professor of English, University of North Carolina, Greensboro. Author of a dissertation and numerous articles on John Muir. **Essay:** John Muir.

ROCKS, James E. Associate Professor of English, Loyola University, Chicago; Advisory Board, *University of Mississippi Studies in English*. Author of "William Cullen Bryant," in *Fifteen*

American Authors Before 1900, 1971 (revised, 1984), and of articles in journals. **Essay:** William Cullen Bryant.

RODRIGUEZ, Michael. Doctoral candidate in Creative Writing, University of Illinois, Chicago. **Essay:** Elvis Presley.

ROGERS, Kay. Instructor in the Department of History, Northern Arizona University, Flagstaff; Assistant Editor, *Proceedings of the Western Society for French History*, 1986–88. **Essays:** Eleanor of Aquitaine; Saint Thomas à Becket.

ROGERS, Pat. DeBartolo Professor in the Liberal Arts, University of South Florida, Tampa. Author of *Grub Street: Studies in a Subculture*, 1972, *The Augustan Vision*, 1974, *Henry Fielding: A Biography*, 1979, *Robinson Crusoe: A Critical Guide*, 1979, and of essays in *The Cambridge History of Literary Criticism*, *The New Cambridge Bibliography of English Literature*, *The New Penguin Guide to English Literature*, and *The Cambridge Guide to the Arts*. Editor of *A Tour Through Great Britain*, by Daniel Defoe, 1971 (revised, 1989), *Defoe: The Critical Heritage*, 1972, *The 18th Century: Contexts of English Literature*, 1978, *The Poems of Jonathan Swift*, 1983, *The Oxford Illustrated History of English Literature*, 1987, and *The Enduring Moment: Tercentenary Essays on Alexander Pope* (with G.S. Rousseau), 1988. **Essays:** James Boswell; Fanny Burney; Henry Fielding; Samuel Johnson.

ROLAND, Daniel Dean. Doctoral candidate, Claremont Graduate School, Claremont, California. Author of articles and encyclopedia entries in American history. **Essays:** James Monroe; Alexis de Tocqueville.

ROSENBERG, Daniel. Lecturer in American History, Adelphi University, Long Island, New York; Adjunct Professor of American Labor History, State University of New York, Center for Labor Studies. Author of *The Unbroken Record: Soviet Treaty Compliance*, 1985, and *New Orleans Dockworkers: Race, Labor, and Unionism 1892–1923*, 1988. **Essays:** John Brown; Frederick Douglass; Charlie Parker.

ROSENBLUM, Joseph. Lecturer in the Department of English, University of North Carolina, Greensboro. Author of articles in *Dickens Quarterly*, *Shakespeare Quarterly*, and *Studies in Short Fiction*. Editor of *The Plays of Thomas Holcroft*, 1980. **Essays:** Elizabeth Barrett Browning; Samuel Richardson; Sir Richard Steele; Laurence Sterne.

ROSSABI, Mary. Freelance writer and independent scholar. **Essay:** Ivan IV of Russia.

ROSSABI, Morris. Professor of East Asian Languages and Cultures, Columbia University, New York; Editor, *Central and Inner Asian Studies*. Author of *China and Inner Asia: From 1368 to the Present*, 1975, *The Jurchens in the Yüng and Ming*, 1982, *China Among Equals: The Middle Kingdom and its Neighbors, 10th-14th Centuries*, 1983, and *Khubilai Khan: His Life and Times*, 1988. **Essays:** Attila the Hun; Marco Polo.

ROWE, Matt. Freelance writer and researcher. **Essay:** Thomas Mann.

RUSSELL-WOOD, A. J. R. Professor and Head of the Department of History, Johns Hopkins University; Editorial Committee, *Latin American Studies: An International Journal* (Tokyo). Author of *Fidalgos and Philanthropists: The Santa Casa da Misericórdia of Bahia 1550–1755*, 1968, *From Colony to Nation: Essays on the Independence of Brazil* (co-author), 1968, and *The Black Man in Slavery and Freedom in Colonial Brazil*, 1982. **Essays:** Vasco da Gama; Ferdinand Magellan.

RYAN, Robert A. Professor of History, Ithaca College, Ithaca, New York. Author of articles in *The 18th Century: A Critical Bibliography*, and *The McGraw-Hill Encyclopedia of World Biography*. **Essays:** Oliver Cromwell; Alolf Hitler.

RYBA, Thomas W. Theologian in Residence, St. Thomas Aquinas Center, Purdue University, West Lafayette, Indiana. Author of articles in *Annals of Scholarship*, *Analecta Husserliana*, *Phenomenological Inquiry*, and *Method and Theory in the Study of Religion*. **Essays:** Saint Thomas Aquinas; Saint Augustine of Hippo; Saint Dominic; John Henry (Cardinal) Newman.

RYDEL, Christine A. Professor of Russian, Grand Valley State University, Grand Rapids, Michigan. Author of *A Nabakov Who's Who: A Complete Guide to Characters in His Fiction*, 1990. Editor of *The Ardis Anthology of Russian Romanticism*, 1984. **Essays:** Mikhail Bulgakov; Maxim Gorky.

SACHS, Mendel. Professor of Physics, State University of New York, Buffalo. Author of *Solid State Theory*, 1963, *The Search for Theory of Matter*, 1971, *The Field Concept in Contemporary Science*, 1973, *Ideas of the Theory of Relativity*, 1974, *Ideas of Matter*, 1981, *General Relativity and Matter*, 1982, *Quantum Mechanics from General Relativity*, 1986, and *Einstein Versus Bohr*, 1988. **Essay:** Albert Einstein.

SACHS, Murray. Professor of French and Comparative Literature, Brandeis University, Waltham, Massachusetts; Advisory Board, *Nineteenth-Century French Studies*, since 1974; Editorial Board, *Romance Quarterly*, since 1988. Author of *The Career of Alphonse Daudet: A Critical Study*, 1965, *The French Short Story in the 19th Century*, 1969, *Anatole France: The Short Stories*, 1974, and "The Legacy of Flaubert," in *L'Henaurme Siecle*, 1984. **Essays:** Gustave Flaubert; Anatole France; Victor Hugo; Madame de Staël.

SAMBROOK, James. Professor of English, University of Southampton. Author of *A Poet Hidden: The Life of Richard Watson Dixon*, 1962, *William Cobbett*, 1973, *English Pastoral Poetry*, 1983, and *The 18th Century: The Intellectual and Cultural Context of English Literature 1700–89*, 1986. Editor of *The Scribleriad*, 1967, *Pre-Raphaelitism: Patterns of Literary Criticism*, 1974, and of works by James Thomson. **Essays:** William Cobbett; Daniel Defoe; Oliver Goldsmith; Tobias Smollett.

SAMMONS, Todd H. Associate Professor of English, University of Hawaii, Manoa. Author of articles in *Paideuma* and *Milton Quarterly*. **Essay:** Andrew Marvell.

SCHAPSMEIER, Frederick H. Rosebush University Professor of History, University of Wisconsin, Oshkosh; Associate Editor, *Journal of the West*, 1970-87. Author of *Henry A. Wallace of Iowa: The Agrarian Years*, 1968, *Walter Lippmann: Philosopher-Journalist*, 1969, *Prophet in Politics: Henry A. Wallace and the War Years*, 1970, *Ezra Taft Benson and the Politics of Agriculture*, 1975, *Everett M. Dirkson of Illinois: Senatorial Statesman*, 1984, and *The Political Odyssey of Gerald R. Ford*, 1989. **Essay:** George Patton.

SCHRIBER, Carolyn Poling. Assistant Professor of History, Rhodes College, Memphis, Tennessee. Author of *The Dilemma of Arnulf of Lisieux: New Ideas, Old Ideas*, 1990, and an article in *Comitatus: A Journal of Medieval and Renaissance Studies*. **Essay:** Henri IV of France.

SEARS, Richard. Professor of English, Berea College, Berea, Kentucky; reviewer for *Choice*. Author of *The Day of Small Things*, 1985. **Essays:** James Dean; Marlene Dietrich; Judy Garland; James Stewart.

SHEWMAKER, Kenneth E. Professor of History, Dartmouth College, Hanover, New Hampshire. General Editor of *The Papers of Daniel Webster*, 2 vols., 1983–87. **Essay:** Daniel Webster.

SHOR, Francis. Associate Professor of Humanities, Wayne State University, Detroit. Author of articles in *Journal of American Culture*, *Biography: An Interdisciplinary Quarterly*, and *Film and History*. **Essay:** Jack London.

SIL, Narasingha P. Associate Professor of History, Western Oregon State College, Monmouth. Author of *William Lord Herbert of Pembroke: Politique and Patriot*, 1988, *Kautilya's Arthasastra: A Comparative Study*, 1989, *Ramakrishna Paramahamsa: Doctor Ecstaticus*, 1991, and articles in *Journal of Asian History*, *Modern Age*, *Africa Quarterly*, and *Midwest Quarterly*. **Essay:** Niccolò Machiavelli.

SIMPSON, Brooks D. Assistant Professor of History, Arizona State University, Tempe; Assistant Editor, The Papers of Andrew Johnson, 1984–87. Author of *Let Us Have Peace: Ulysses S. Grant and the Politics of War and Reconstruction 1861–68*, 1991, and articles in *The Journal of Southern History* and *Civil War History*. Co-editor of *Advice After Appomattox: Letters to Andrew Johnson 1865–66*, 1987. **Essays:** John Quincy Adams; Alexander Hamilton; Andrew Jackson; Thomas Jefferson.

SMITH, Clyde Curry. Professor of Ancient History and Religion, University of Wisconsin, River Falls. Author of numerous entries for reference books, including *The New International Dictionary of the Christian Church*, 1974, *The World's Religions*, 1982, *Great Lives from History: Ancient and Medieval Series*, 1988, and *Encyclopedia of Early Christianity*, 1990. **Essays:** Saint Patrick; Saint Paul; Saint Peter; Philip II of Macedon; Pompey.

SNAREY, John. Associate Professor of Ethics and Human Development, Emory University, Atlanta. Author of articles in *Comparative Education Review*, *Developmental Psychology*, *Journal of Applied Developmental Psychology*, *Psychology Today*, and many other journals. **Essay:** Erik Erikson.

SOLOMON, Julie Robin. Assistant Professor of English, American University, Washington, D.C. Author of a chapter on Francis Bacon in *Women and Reason*, 1991, and of articles in *Renaissance Quarterly*. **Essay:** Francis Bacon.

SOO, Lydia M. Assistant Professor in the Department of Architecture, Ohio State University, Columbus. Author of *Reconstructing Antiquity: Wren and His Circle and the Study of Natural History, Antiquarianism, and Architecture at the Royal Society* (dissertation), 1989. **Essay:** Christopher Wren.

STACY, Paul H. Professor of Cinema, Department of English, University of Hartford, Connecticut. **Essays:** Ingmar Bergman; Marlon Brando; Bette Davis.

STEARNS, S. J. Associate Professor of History, College of Staten Island, City University of New York. Author of articles in *Journal of British Studies* and *Military Affairs* and contributor to *Biographical Dictionary of British Radicals in the 17th Century* and *Biographical Dictionary of Modern Peace Leaders*. **Essays:** Sir Walter Raleigh; Lytton Strachey.

STRATTON, Suzanne. Curator of Exhibitions, The Spanish Institute, New York. Author of *La Immaculada en el arte espanol*, 1989, and of articles on El Greco, García Lorca, Goya, and Rembrandt. **Essay:** El Greco.

STUSSY, Susan A. Director of Library Services, Barton County Community College, Great Bend, Kansas. Author of numerous articles in historical and library journals, reviewer for *Library Journal*. **Essay:** Catherine of Aragon.

SUSSKIND, Jacob. Assistant Professor of Social Science and Education, Pennsylvania State University, Harrisburg; Editor, *The Social Studies Journal*, since 1986. Author of "William Penn," in *Research Guide to American History*, 1988. **Essay:** William Penn.

SUTHERLAND, Daniel E. Associate Professor of History, University of Arkansas, Fayetteville. Author of *Americans and Their Servants: Domestic Service in the United States 1800–1920*, 1981, *The Confederate Carpetbaggers*, 1988, and *The Expansion of Everyday Life 1860–76*, 1989. **Essays:** Stonewall Jackson; Robert E. Lee.

TAYLOR, Richard C. Assistant Professor of English, East Carolina University, Greenville, North Carolina. Author of articles on 18th-century literature in *Philological Quarterly*, *Review of English Studies*, *Modern Philology*, *English Language Notes*, and *Comparative Drama*. **Essays:** René Descartes; Thomas Hobbes; David Hume; John Locke; Friedrich Nietzsche; William Pitt (the younger); Arthur Schopenhauer.

TAYLOR, Thomas J. Freelance writer and independent scholar; formerly, Head of the Department of Theatre, Purdue University, West Lafayette, Indiana. Author of *Restoration Drama*, 1989, and *American Theatre History: An Annotated Bibliography*, 1991. **Essays:** Edward Albee; Samuel Beckett; Anton Chekhov; Henrik Ibsen; Arthur Miller; Nicholas II of Russia; Eugene O'Neill; Harold Pinter; Johann Friedrich von Schiller; August Strindberg.

THIES, Martin. Doctoral candidate in the Department of English, Duke University, Durham, North Carolina. **Essays:** Hart Crane; John Dos Passos; Sergei Eisenstein; Emma Goldman; Jack Kerouac.

THODY, Philip. Professor of French Literature, University of Leeds. Author of *Albert Camus*, 1957, *Jean-Paul Sartre*, 1960, *Jean Genet*, 1968, *Jean Anouilh*, 1968, *Aldous Huxley*, 1973, *Roland Barthes*, 1977, *Marcel Proust*, 1987, and *French Caesarism from Napoleon I to Charles de Gaulle*, 1989. **Essays:** Colette; Marcel Proust; Jean-Paul Sartre; Émile Zola.

TODD, R. Larry. Professor and Director of Graduate Studies in Music, Duke University, Durham, North Carolina; Editor, *American Musicological Society Newsletter*, 1982–84; Board of Directors, American Musicological Society, 1986–87. Author of *Mendelssohn's Musical Education*, 1983, *The Musical Art: An Introduction to Western Music*, 1989, and articles on Mendelssohn, Liszt, Webern, and other musical topics in *The Musical Quarterly*, *Music and Letters*, *Nineteenth Century Music*, and other journals. Editor of *Mendelssohn and Schumann Essays: Perspectives on Their Music and Its Context*, 1984, and *Nineteenth-Century Piano Music*, 1990. **Essay:** Felix Mendelssohn-Bartholdy.

TOLAN, John. Instructor in the Department of Classics, University of Wisconsin, Milwaukee. **Essays:** Galileo Galilei; Lope Félix de Vega Carpio.

TRUSSLER, Simon. Editor of *New Theatre Quarterly* (formerly *Theatre Quarterly*), since 1971; Reader in Drama, University of London; Founding Editor of the Royal Shakespeare Company's *Yearbook*, 1978–85. Author of over two dozen books on theatre and drama, including studies of John Osborne, Arnold Wesker, John Whiting, Harold Pinter, Edward Bond, and, most recently, *Shakespearean Concepts*, 1990, and *A Social History of the English Theatre*, forthcoming. **Essays:** Ben Jonson; Christopher Marlowe.

TUCKER, Bernard. Head of the Department of English, LSU College of Higher Education, Southampton. Author of *Jonathan Swift*, 1983. **Essay:** Jonathan Swift.

TURECK, Rosalyn. Founder and Director of the International Bach Society, 1966–72, and of the Tureck Bach Institute, New York, since 1981; Honorary Life Fellow, St. Hilda's College, Oxford University; Visiting Fellow, Wolfson College, Oxford University, since 1975. Author of *Introduction to the Performance of Bach*, 3 vols., 1959–60. Editor of the Tureck/Bach Urtext Series, as well as editor and transcriber of numerous individual works by J.S. Bach, Antonio Scarlatti, and Niccolò Paganini. Also performer with numerous recordings; specialist in the keyboard works of J.S. Bach. **Essays:** Johann Sebastian Bach; Leonard Bernstein; Glenn Gould.

TUTTLE, Howard N. Associate Professor of Philosophy, University of New Mexico, Albuquerque. **Essay:** Martin Heidegger.

UNGER, Nancy C. Lecturer in the Department of History, San Francisco State University, California; Member of the Biographer's Seminar, Stanford University, since 1989. Author of numerous articles on biographical topics. **Essay:** Clarence Darrow.

VALÉRIO, Lucilia M. C. Teaching Assistant in the Department of English, Tufts University, Medford, Massachusetts. **Essay:** Evelyn Waugh.

VAN MIEGROET, Hans J. Assistant Professor of Art History, Duke University, Durham, North Carolina. Author of *The Influence of Early Netherlandish Painting on Konrad Witz*, 1986, *Gerard David*, 1989, and numerous articles on Dutch painters. **Essays:** Rembrandt; Sir Anthony Van Dyck.

VARKONDA, Linda K. Assistant Professor of Visual Arts and History, Clemson University, Clemson, South Carolina. **Essays:** Piero della Francesca; Peter Paul Rubens; Jan Vermeer; Paolo Veronese.

VOELTZ, Richard A. Assistant Professor of History, Cameron University, Lawton, Oklahoma. Author of *German Colonialism and the South West Africa Company 1884–1914*, 1988, and numerous articles in journals and encyclopedias. **Essays:** Edward VII of England; George VI of England; Bernard Law Montgomery.

WACHTER, Phyllis E. Freelance writer and teacher of English; Bibliographer for *Biography: An Interdisciplinary Quarterly*. Author of "Current Bibliography of Life-Writing," *Biography*, 1985 through 1989, and of numerous articles on biographical topics. **Essay:** Matthew Arnold.

WAGNER-MARTIN, Linda. Haines Professor of English, University of North Carolina, Chapel Hill. Author of *The Poems of William Carlos Williams*, 1964, *Denise Levertov*, 1967, *The Prose of William Carlos Williams*, 1970, *Hemingway and Faulkner: Inventors/Masters*, 1975, *Introducing Poems*, 1976, *Hemingway: A Reference Guide*, 1977, *William Carlos Williams: A Reference Guide*, 1978, *John Dos Passos: Artist as American*, 1979, *Ellen Glasgow: Beyond Convention*, 1982, *Sylvia Plath: A Literary Biography*, 1987, *Anne Sexton: Critical Essays*, 1989, and *The Modern American Novel*, 1989. Editor of works by or about William Faulkner, T.S. Eliot, Ernest Hemingway, William Carlos Williams, Robert Frost, Denise Levertov, and Sylvia Plath. **Essays:** E.E. Cummings; Hilda Doolittle; Gertrude Stein; Edith Wharton; William Carlos Williams.

WALKER, William T. Associate Professor of History and Head of the Department of Humanities, Philadelphia College of Pharmacy and Science. Author of *Realism and Materialism,*

Europe 1848–1914, 1990, and numerous articles and reviews in journals. **Essay:** Thomas (Cardinal) Wolsey.

WASIOLEK, Edward. Distinguished Service Professor of English, Slavic, and Comparative Literature, University of Chicago; Editorial Boards of *Critical Inquiry*, *Studies in the Novel*, and *International Fiction*; Board of Consultants, Encyclopedia Britannica. Author of *Nine Soviet Portraits*, 1955, *Dostoevsky, the Major Fiction*, 1964, *Tolstoy's Major Fiction*, 1978, and over 100 shorter works and articles on English, French, and Russian literature. Editor and translator of five volumes of Dostoevsky's *Notebooks*, 1967–70. **Essays:** Fyodor Dostoevsky; Leo Tolstoy.

WATSON, Noelle A. Editor and freelance writer. **Essays:** Alexander I of Russia; Isadora Duncan; Louis Mountbatten; Napoleon III; Wilfred Owen; Eva and Juan Perón; Anwar Sadat.

WATTS, Harold H. Professor Emeritus of English, Purdue University, West Lafayette, Indiana. Author of *The Modern Reader's Guide to the Bible*, 1949, *Ezra Pound and the Cantos*, 1952, *Hound and Quarry*, 1953, *The Modern Reader's Guide to Religions*, 1964, and *Aldous Huxley*, 1969. **Essays:** Joseph Conrad; T.S. Eliot; William Faulkner; Aldous Huxley; Anthony Trollope.

WEILAND, Steven. Director of the Department of Professional Development, University of Minnesota, Minneapolis. Author of *Intellectual Craftsmen: Ways and Works in American Scholarship 1940-90*, 1990. **Essays:** Sigmund Freud; Martin Luther.

WHALEY, Leigh Ann. Assistant Professor of History, University of Toronto. Author of an article in *Modern and Contemporary France*. **Essays:** Edmund Burke; Honoré Mirabeau; Napoleon Bonaparte.

WHISTLER, Nick. Assistant Professor of English, University of Waterloo, Ontario. Author of the entry for John Galt in the *Dictionary of Canadian Biography*, 1988. **Essay:** John Galt.

WICKERSHAM, John. Professor and Head of the Department of Classical Studies, Ursinus College, Collegeville, Pennsylvania. Author of *Greek Historical Documents: The Fourth Century B.C.* (with G. Verbrugghe), 1973. Editor of *Myth and the Polis* (with D.C. Pozzi), 1991. **Essay:** Jesus Christ.

WILD, Peter. Professor of English, University of Arizona, Tucson; Contributing Editor for *The North Dakota Quarterly*, *Slant*, *Puerto del Sol*, and *U.S. Water News*. Author of *Pioneer Conservationists of Western America*, 1979, *Pioneer Conservationists of Eastern America*, 1986, *The Saguaro Forest*, 1986, and *John C. Van Dyke*, 1988. **Essays:** Walt Disney; Amelia Earhart.

WILLIAMS, John R. Senior Lecturer in German, St. Andrews University, Fife, Scotland. Author of *Goethe's Faust*, 1987, and of numerous articles and reviews on German literature in British and German journals. **Essay:** Johann Wolfgang von Goethe.

WILLSON, Robert F., Jr. Professor and Head of the Department of English, U̶ ̶ ̶ ̶ ̶ ̶ ̶Kansas City; Editor, Studies in Shakespeare ̶ ̶ ̶ ̶ ̶ ̶ ̶ ̶ ̶1988. Author of *Their Form Confounded: Studies in English Burlesque Drama*, 1975, *Shakespeare's Opening Scenes*, 1977, *Landmarks of Shakespeare Criticism*, 1978, *Shakespeare's Reflexive Endings*, forthcoming, and numerous articles on Shakespeare in journals. Editor of *The Macmillan Handbook of English*, 6th and 7th editions, 1975 and 1982. **Essays:** Francis Beaumont and John Fletcher; Desiderius Erasmus; William Shakespeare.

WOODCOCK, George. Freelance writer, lecturer, and editor. Author of over 100 books, including poetry (*Collected Poems*, 1983); plays; travel books; works of history and politics (*Social History of Canada*, 1988, and *The Marvelous Century*, 1988, are the two most recent); and biographies and critical studies, including *William Godwin*, 1946, *The Incomparable Aphra*, 1948, *The Paradox of Oscar Wilde*, 1949, *Pierre-Joseph Proudhon*, 1956, *Anarchism: A History of Libertarian Ideas and Movements*, 1962, *The Crystal Spirit: A Study of George Orwell*, 1966, *Hugh MacLennan*, 1969, *Odysseus Ever Returning: Canadian Writers and Writing*, 1970, *Mordecai Richler*, 1970, *Dawn and the Darkest Hour: A Study of Aldous Huxley*, 1972, *Herbert Read*, 1972, *Thomas Merton: Monk and Poet*, 1978, and *Orwell's Message*, 1984. Editor of anthologies, and of works by Charles Lamb, Malcolm Lowry, Wyndham Lewis, and many other writers. **Essays:** Aphra Behn; William Godwin; Graham Greene; George Orwell; Pierre-Joseph Proudhon; Oscar Wilde.

WOODRESS, James. Professor Emeritus of English, University of California, Davis; Founder and Editor of *American Literary Scholarship*, 1965–87. Author of *Howells and Italy*, 1952, *Booth Tarkington: Gentleman from Indiana*, 1955, *A Yankee's Odyssey: The Life of Joel Barlow*, 1958, *Willa Cather: Her Life and Art*, 1970, and *Willa Cather: A Literary Life*, 1987. Editor or co-editor of *Voices from America's Past*, 1961, *Eight American Authors*, 1971, *The Troll Garden*, by Willa Cather, 1983, and *Critical Essays on Whitman*, 1983. **Essays:** Robinson Jeffers; Amy Lowell; James Russell Lowell; Upton Sinclair.

WOODS, Leigh. Head of Theatre Studies, University of Michigan, Ann Arbor. Author of *Garrick Claims the Stage: Acting as a Social Emblem in 18th-Century England*, 1984, and of "Actors' Biography and Mythmaking: The Example of Edmund Kean," in *Interpreting the Theatrical Past*, edited by Postlewait and McConachie, 1989. **Essays:** Sarah Bernhardt; David Garrick; Edmund Kean.

WRIGHT, Esmond. Professor Emeritus of American History, University of London; Member of Parliament, 1967–70; Director of the Institute for United States Studies, 1971–83. Author of *Fabric of Freedom 1763–1800*, 1961 (revised, 1978), and *Franklin of Philadelphia*, 1986. Editor of *Benjamin Franklin: His Life as He Wrote It*, 1989. **Essay:** George III of England.

YALKUT, Carolyn. Director of Journalism, State University of New York, Albany. Author of *Egocentric and Genteel: Tradition and Innovation in American Journalism*, forthcoming. **Essays:** Norman Mailer; H.L. Mencken.

YOUNG, Bruce W. Associate Professor of English, Brigham Young University, Provo, Utah; Associate Editor, *Journal of the Rocky Mountain Medieval and Renaissance Association*, 1986. Author of articles on Shakespeare and 17th-century poetry. **Essay:** George Herbert.

ZOHN, Harry. Professor of German Literature, Brandeis University, Waltham, Massachusetts; Executive Director, Goethe Society of New England, 1963–68; Editor, Austrian Literature Series, P. Lang, since 1989; Editorial Board, *Modern Austrian Literature* and *Cross Currents*. Author of *Wiener Juden in der deutschen Literatur*, 1964, *Karl Kraus*, 1971, and *Jüdisches Erbe in der österreichischen Literatur*, 1986. Editor and translator of numerous editions, including works by Theodor Herzl, Karl Kraus, Kurt Tucholsky, Stefan Zweig, Sigmund Freud, Martin Buber, Gershom Scholem, Walter Benjamin, Alex Bein, André Kaminski, Arthur Schnitzler, Manès Sperber, and Nelly Sachs. **Essays:** Heinrich Heine; Theodor Herzl; Albert Schweitzer.